McGraw-Hill
networks™
A Social Studies Learning System

CHOOSE how you want to teach

- All print
- All digital
- Your own custom print and digital mix

MEETS YOU ANYWHERE —
TAKES YOU EVERYWHERE

McGraw-Hill
networks™

MEETS YOU ANYWHERE — TAKES YOU EVERYWHERE

MANAGE your classroom anytime

- Use prepared model lessons
- Clear pathway through critical content
- Quick, targeted instruction

From anywhere

- Plan instruction
- Create presentations
- Differentiate instruction

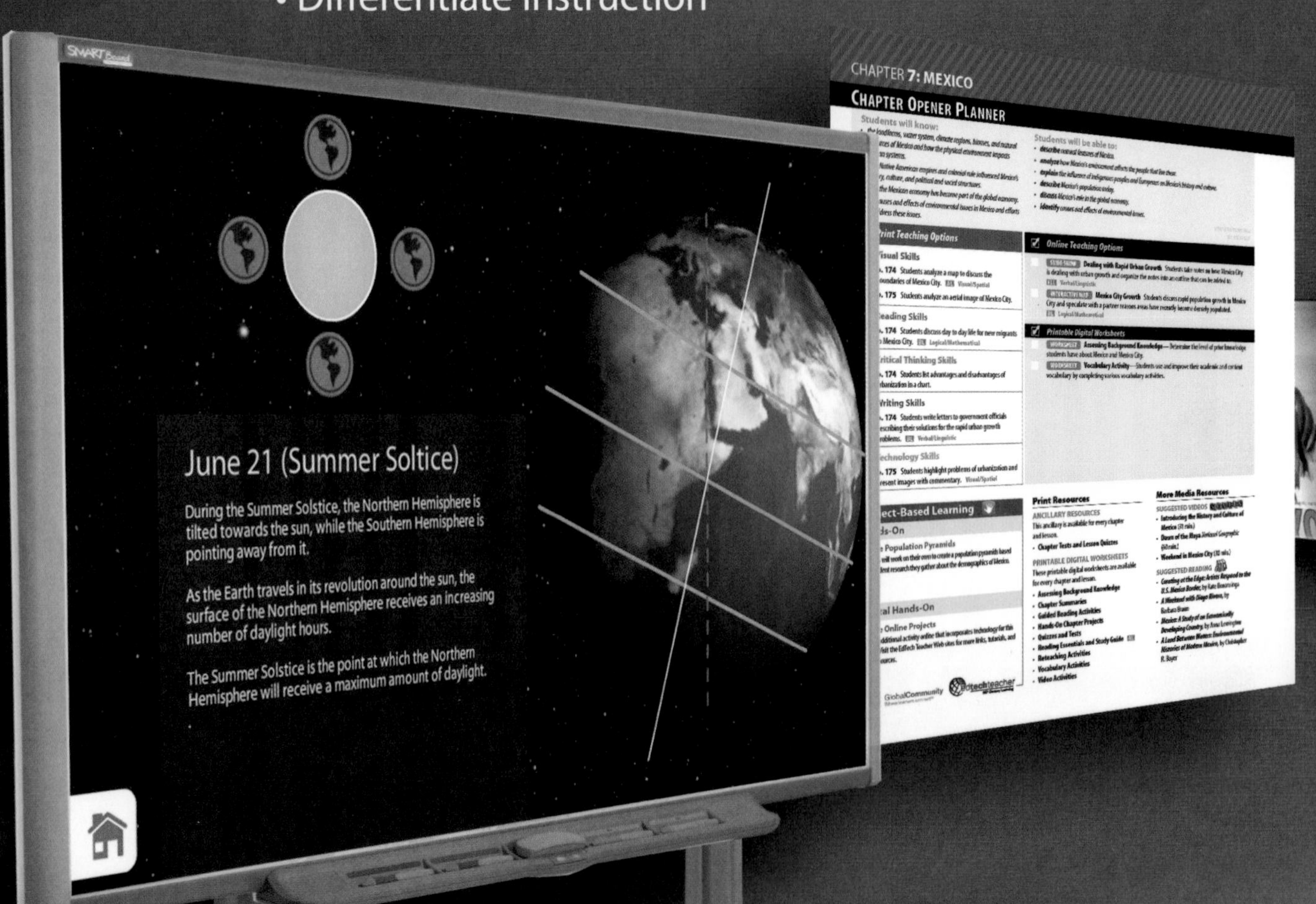

ORGANIZE with everything in one place

- Upload personal resources
- Search Resource Library
- Create class rosters
- File and Save

start networking

McGraw-Hill
networks™

MEETS YOU ANYWHERE — TAKES YOU EVERYWHERE

CUSTOMIZE everything for your students – easy, quick, and efficient

- Personalize lessons
- Create tests
- Modify assignments

DIFFERENTIATE instruction to meet the needs of all your students

- Assign different reading levels
- Access full audio
- Use PDFs or modify worksheets
- Print or assign online

start networking

McGraw-Hill
networks™

MEETS YOU ANYWHERE —
TAKES YOU EVERYWHERE

ENGAGE your students for the way they want to learn

- Hands-on projects
- interactive maps, presentations, and primary sources
- Streaming video and games

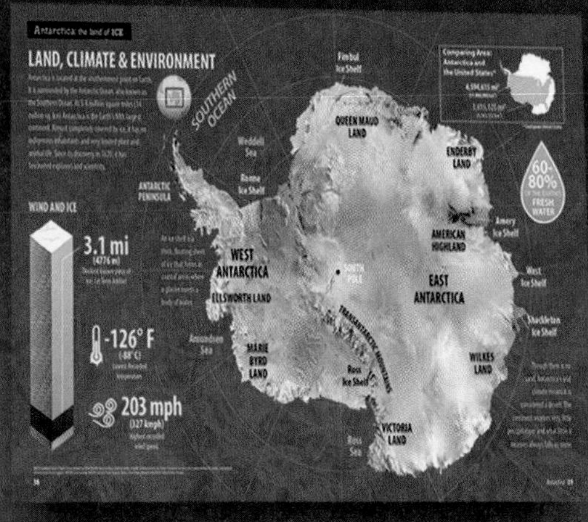

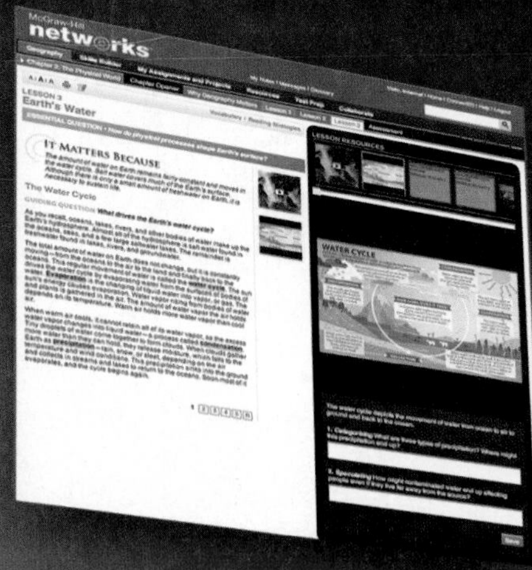
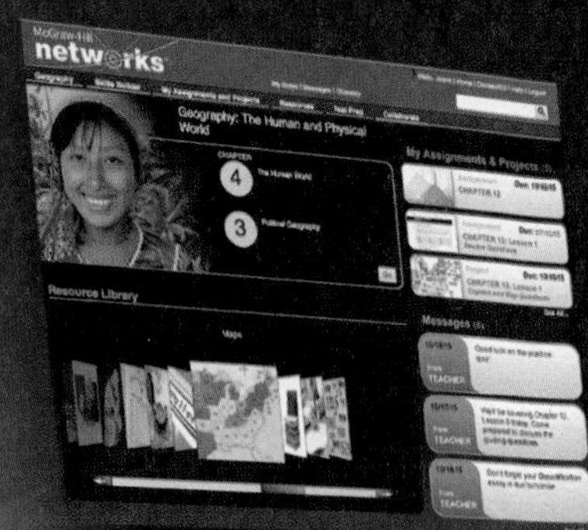

COMMUNICATE with your students

- Assign homework and tests
- Send messages
- Track and print student results

start networking

McGraw-Hill
networks™

MEETS YOU ANYWHERE — TAKES YOU EVERYWHERE

CONNECT with colleagues, students, experts, and content

1. Log on to the Internet and go to ***connected.mcgraw-hill.com***.
2. Enter User Name and Password.
3. Click on your **Networks** book.
4. Select your chapter and lesson.

Image Credits: Bruno Morandi/Robert Harding World Imagery/Getty Images; Apollo 15 commander David R. Scott/NASA; BananaStock/PictureQuest; C. Borland/PhotoLink/Getty Images; Historicus, Inc; Jack Star/PhotoLink/Getty Images; Library of Congress Prints and Photographs Division [LC-USZC4-7214]; Library of Congress, Prints and Photographs Division (LC-USZC4-2920); MedioImages/Getty Images; Radius Images/Corbis; ©Reed Kaestner/Corbis; D. Hurst/Alamy; Image Source/Getty Images; McGraw-Hill Education; Library of Congress Prints and Photographs Division [LC-USZC4-595]; Photographer's Choice RF/Getty Images; Shobido & Company/Library of Congress; U.S. Air Force; Eyewire/PunchStock; Library of Congress Prints & Photographs Divison [LC-USZ62-13016]; Library of Congress, Prints and Photographs Division [LC-USZC4-737]; ©Charles Smith/Corbis; Apollo 15 commander David R. Scott/NASA; NASA Kennedy Space Center (NASA-KSC); National Archives and Records Administration (NWDNS-208-FS-3200-5); Bartosz Hadyniak/the Agency Collection/Getty Images; Library of Congress Prints and Photographs Division [LC-USZC4-595]; ©Charles Smith/Corbis; ©Brand X Pictures/Punchstock; Wolfgang Poelzer/WaterFrame/Getty Images; ©Charles Smith/Corbis; Creatas Images/Jupiter Images; Apollo 15 commander David R. Scott/NASA.

start networking

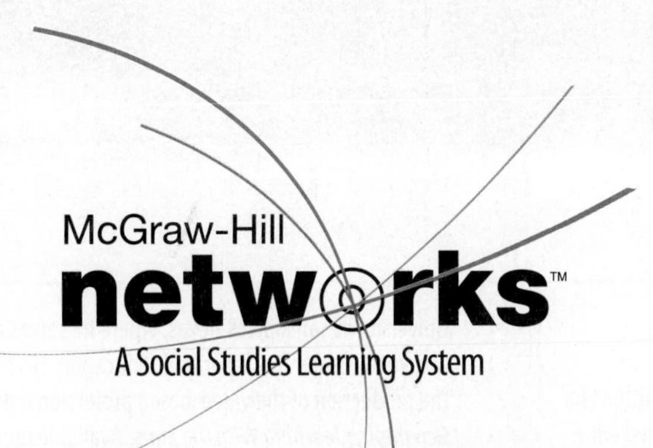

Teacher Edition

GEOGRAPHY

THE HUMAN AND PHYSICAL WORLD

Richard G. Boehm, Ph. D.

Bothell, WA • Chicago, IL • Columbus, OH • New York, NY

AUTHORS

Senior Author

Richard G. Boehm, Ph.D., was one of the original authors for *Geography for Life: National Geography Standards,* which outlined what students should know and be able to do in geography. He was also one of the authors of the *Guidelines for Geographic Education,* in which the Five Themes of Geography were first articulated. Dr. Boehm has received many honors, including "Distinguished Geography Educator" by the National Geographic Society (1990), the "George J. Miller Award" from the National Council for Geographic Education (NCGE) for distinguished service to geographic education (1991), "Gilbert Grosvenor Honors" in geographic education from the Association of American Geographers (2002), and the NCGE's "Distinguished Mentor Award" (2010). He served as president of NCGE, has twice won the *Journal of Geography* award for best article, and also received the NCGE's "Distinguished Teaching Achievement." Presently, Dr. Boehm holds the Jesse H. Jones Distinguished Chair in Geographic Education at Texas State University in San Marcos, Texas, where he serves as director of The Gilbert M. Grosvenor Center for Geographic Education. His most current project includes the production of the video-based professional development series, *Geography: Teaching With the Stars.* Available programs may be viewed at **www.geoteach.org**.

Contributing Author

Jay McTighe has published articles in a number of leading educational journals and has coauthored 10 books, including the best-selling *Understanding By Design* series with Grant Wiggins. McTighe also has an extensive background in professional development and is a featured speaker at national, state, and district conferences and workshops. He received his undergraduate degree from The College of William and Mary, earned a Masters degree from The University of Maryland and completed post-graduate studies at The Johns Hopkins University.

Cover Photo Credits: Main Image: Bruno Morandi/Robert Harding World Imagery/Getty Images; **Background:** Bruno Morandi/Robert Harding World Imagery/Getty Images; **Front Thumbnails:** (left to right) Kryssia Campos/Getty Images, ©Pete Atkinson/Getty Images, ©Ocean/Corbis, Matt Champlin/Getty Images. **Back Cover:** Bruno Morandi/Robert Harding World Imagery/Getty Images; **Back Thumbnails:** (left to right) Peter Zelei/Getty Images, Jack Goldfarb/Getty Images, Ingram Publishing, NASA/NOAA/SPL/Getty Images, D. Normark/PhotoLink/Getty Images.

The themes and learning expectations of the national social studies standards are excerpted from National Council for the Social Studies (NCSS), National Curriculum Standards for Social Studies (Silver Spring, MD: NCSS, 2010). See www.socialstudies.org.

Heffron, Susan Gallagher and Roger M. Downs, eds. (2012). Geography for Life: National Geography Standards, Second Edition. Washington, DC: National Council for Geographic Education.

www.mheonline.com/networks

Send all inquiries to:
McGraw-Hill Education
8787 Orion Place
Columbus, OH 43240

Teacher Edition:
ISBN: 978-0-07-664289-2
MHID: 0-07-664289-5

Student Edition:
ISBN: 978-0-07-664288-5
MHID: 0-07-664288-7

Printed in the United States of America.

2 3 4 5 6 7 8 9 DOW 17 16 15 14

REVIEWERS AND CONSULTANTS

ACADEMIC CONSULTANTS

Frederick L. Bein, Ph.D.
Professor of Geography
Indiana University-Purdue University
Indianapolis Adjunct Professor of Geography
Moi University
Indianapolis, Indiana

David Berger, Ph.D.
Ruth and I. Lewis Gordon Professor of Jewish History
Dean, Bernard Revel Graduate School
Yeshiva University
New York, New York

Randy Bertolas, Ph.D.
Professor of Geography
Wayne State College
Wayne, Nebraska

Lara Bryant, Ph.D.
Assistant Professor of Geography
Keene State College
Keene, New Hampshire

Tom Daccord
Educational Technology Specialist
Co-Director EdTechTeacher
Boston, Massachusetts

Charles Gritzner, Ph.D.
Professor of Geography, Retired
South Dakota State University
Brookings, South Dakota

P.P. Karan, Ph.D.
Professor of Geography
University of Kentucky
Lexington, Kentucky

Jeff Lash, Ph.D.
Associate Professor of Geography
University of Houston-Clear Lake
Houston, Texas

Elizabeth Leppman, Ph.D.
Writer
Map and Book Editor
Lexington, Kentucky

Joseph Manzo, Ph.D.
Professor of Geography
Concord University
Athens, West Virginia

Kent McGregor, Ph.D.
Associate Professor of Geography
University of North Texas
Denton, Texas

Olga Medvedkov, Ph.D.
Professor of Geography
Wittenberg University
Springfield, Ohio

Jerry Mitchell, Ph.D.
Research Associate Professor of Geography
University of South Carolina
Columbia, South Carolina

Shannon O'Lear, Ph.D.
Associate Professor of Geography
University of Kansas
Lawrence, Kansas

Justin Reich
Educational Technology Specialist
Co-Director EdTechTeacher
Boston, Massachusetts

David Rutherford, Ph.D.
Associate Professor of Geography & Public Policy
University of Mississippi
Oxford, Mississippi

Richard Sambrook, Ph.D.
Professor of Geography
Department Head
Eastern Michigan University
Ypsilanti, Michigan

Ginger Schmid, Ph.D.
Assistant Professor of Geography
Minnesota State University
Mankato, Minnesota

Joseph Stoltman, Ph.D.
Professor of Geography
Western Michigan University
Kalamazoo, Michigan

William Strong, Ph.D.
Professor Emeritus of Geography
University of North Alabama
Florence, Alabama

TEACHER REVIEWERS

Kimberly Coffelt
Social Studies Teacher
Southeast High School
Wichita, Kansas

Sara Heck
Social Studies Teacher
Teays Valley Local School District
Ashville, Ohio

Kenny Lee
Social Studies Curriculum Coordinator
Westerville City Schools
Westerville, Ohio

Barry Leonard
Social Studies Teacher
Graves County High School
Mayfield, Kentucky

Lorena McMenomy
Social Studies Educator
Hillcrest High School
Dallas, Texas

Jason Orendi
Social Studies Teacher
Boonsboro High School
Martinsburg, West Virginia

Jamie Reese
Social Studies Teacher
Buckhorn High School
New Market, Alabama

Adam Schwartz
Social Studies Teacher
Montgomery County Public Schools
Rockville, Maryland

Judi Shortt
Social Studies Teacher
Edmond Public Schools
Edmond, Oklahoma

Natalie Wojinski
Geography Teacher
Hercules High School
San Francisco, California

CONTENTS

Sue Flood/The Image Bank/Getty Images

©Tuul/Robert Harding World Imagery/Corbis

UNIT TWO

National Geographic Image Collection/Alamy

CONTENTS

Alexander Nicholson/Taxi/Getty Images

©Alison Wright/Corbis

Christian Aslund/Lonely Planet Images/Getty Images

Viviane Ponti/Lonely Planet Images/Getty Images

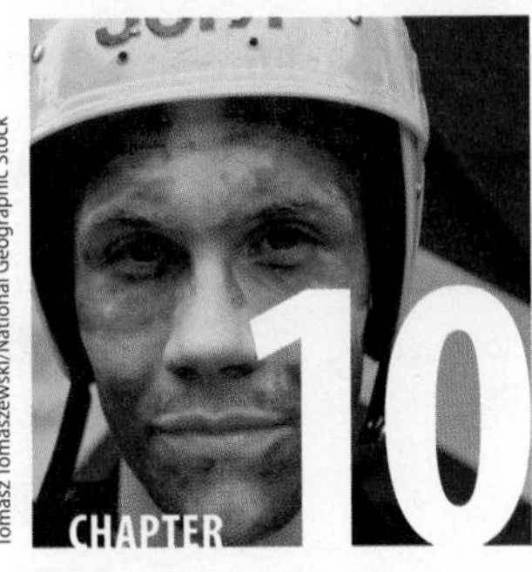

Tomasz Tomaszewski/National Geographic Stock

Vidler Steve/age fotostock

CONTENTS

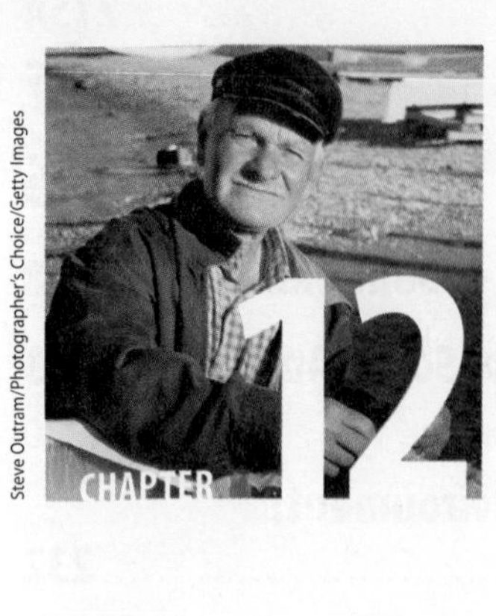

Steve Outram/Photographer's Choice/Getty Images

Matt Cardy/Alamy

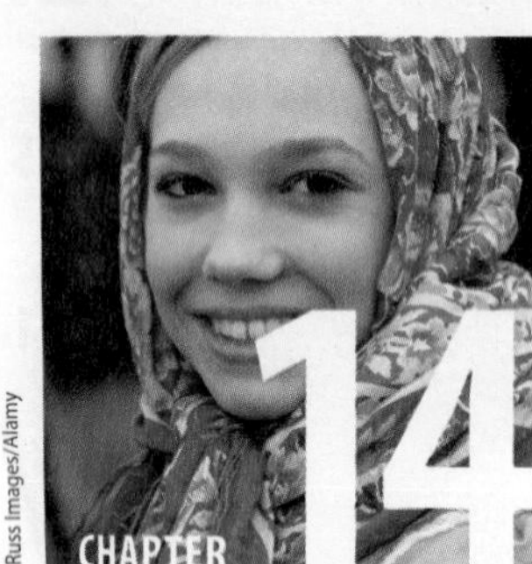

Russ Images/Alamy

Kimberley Coole/Lonely Planet Images/Getty Images

©Blaine Harrington III/Corbis

Rebecca Erol/Alamy

Morales/age fotostock

©Alison Wright/Corbis

UNIT SIX

Godong/age fotostock

Roy Toft/National Geographic Stock

Pius Utomi Ekpei/AFP/Getty Images

Thomas Imo/Photothek/Getty Images

Kelly Cestari/ASP/Getty Images

©Jens Kalaene/dpa/Corbis

CONTENTS

©Laurence Fordyce/Eye Ubiquitous/Corbis

©Lee Frost/Robert Harding World Imagery/Corbis

Jason Hosking/Taxi/Getty Images

Jeremy Sutton-Hibbert/Alamy

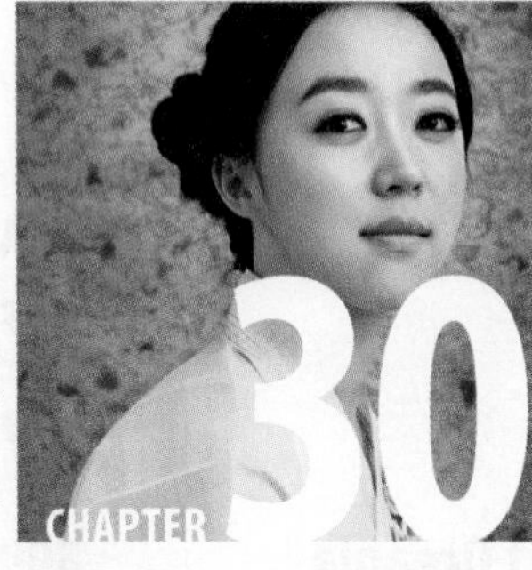

©Topic Photo Agency/Corbis

UNIT NINE

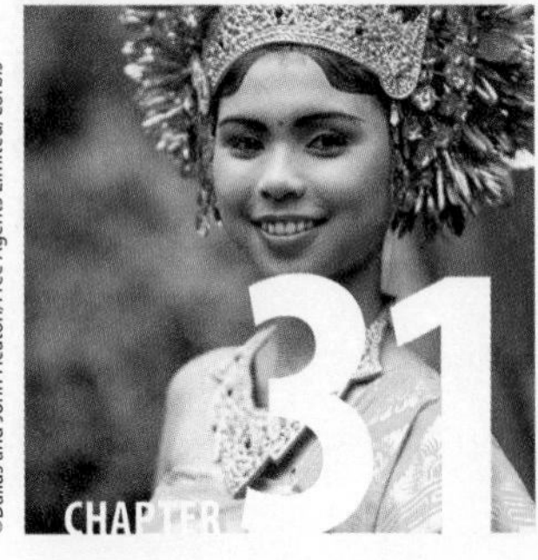

©Dallas and John Heaton/Free Agents Limited/Corbis

CONTENTS

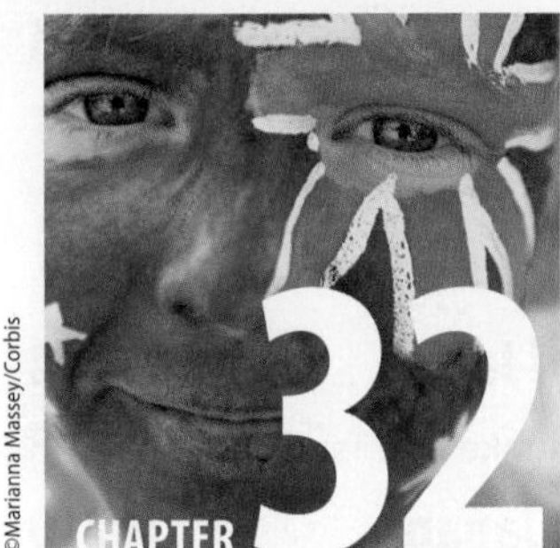

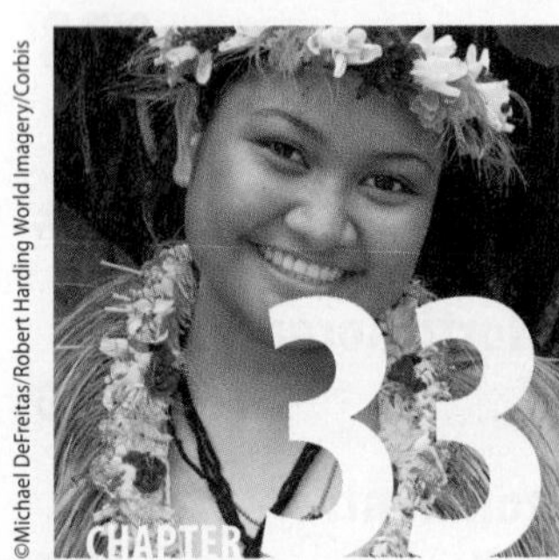

PRIMARY SOURCES

UNIT 1: THE WORLD

UNIT 2: THE UNITED STATES AND CANADA

UNIT 3: LATIN AMERICA

UNIT 4: EUROPE

UNIT 5: NORTH AFRICA, SOUTHWEST ASIA, AND CENTRAL ASIA

UNIT 6: AFRICA SOUTH OF THE SAHARA

UNIT 7: SOUTH ASIA

UNIT 8: EAST ASIA

UNIT 9: SOUTHEAST ASIA AND THE PACIFIC WORLD

FEATURES

Why Geography Matters

EXPLORE the REGION

Case Study

FEATURES

GLOBAL CONNECTIONS

Connecting Geography to ....

Analyzing PRIMARY SOURCES

Analyzing PRIMARY SOURCES

MAPS

UNIT 5: NORTH AFRICA, SOUTHWEST ASIA, AND CENTRAL ASIA

UNIT 6: AFRICA SOUTH OF THE SAHARA

UNIT 7: SOUTH ASIA

UNIT 8: EAST ASIA

UNIT 9: SOUTHEAST ASIA AND THE PACIFIC WORLD

GEO @ WORK

Explore specific examples of the principles and skills of geography applied to real-world challenges that impact people's lives. From agriculture to urban planning, to wiping out disease and managing changes in society—geography plays a key role in understanding relationships and generating solutions that make sense.

Videos

Every lesson has a video to help you learn more about your world!

Self-Check Quizzes

Every lesson has a self-check quiz to help you test your knowledge!

Games

Every lesson has games to help you review the material!

Vocabulary Flash Cards

Every chapter has vocabulary flash cards to help you remember important terms!

Infographics

Chapter 1
Lesson 1 GIS Layers

Chapter 2
Chapter Feature Salt vs. Freshwater
Desalination Through Distillation
Lesson 1 The Solar System
Water, Land, and Air
Inside the Earth
Underwater Landforms
Lesson 2 Forces of Change
Lesson 3 Water Cycle

Chapter 3
Lesson 1 The Earth's Seasons
The Greenhouse Effect
Earth's Tilt
Lesson 3 Latitude, Climate, and Vegetation

Chapter 5
Lesson 1 Western Topography
Hurricanes in the United States
Lesson 3 How Acid Rain is Created

Chapter 6
Chapter Feature A Closer Look: Alberta
Lesson 3 Canada's Boreal Forest

Chapter 7
Lesson 1 Plate Tectonics in Mexico
Vertical Climate Zones of Mexico

Chapter 8
Lesson 1 Biodiversity in Central America
Lesson 2 The Panama Canal

Chapter 9
Lesson 1 Impacts of El Niño in Latin America

Chapter 10
Chapter Feature Volcanic Eruption in Iceland
Lesson 1 Gulf Stream Effects in Northern Europe

Chapter 11
Lesson 1 Building Dikes and Polders

Chapter 12
Lesson 1 Rivers of Europe

Chapter 14
Chapter Feature Russia's Shrinking Population
Lesson 1 The Volga River Basin—Heart of Russia

Chapter 15
Lesson 1 North African Plates
Lesson 3 Egypt's Aswān High Dam

Chapter 16
Chapter Feature Israeli-Palestinian Conflict
Lesson 3 Managing Israel's Water Resources

Chapter 17
Lesson 3 Caspian Energy

Chapter 19
Lesson 3 Aral: A Sea Sacrificed

Chapter 20
Lesson 3 Great Green Wall of Africa

Chapter 21
Lesson 1 The Great Rift Valley

Chapter 22
Lesson 2 Today's Nigerian Family

Interactive Charts, Graphs, and Tables

Interactive Images and Slide Shows

Chapter 1
Lesson 2 Satellite Imagery

Chapter 4
Lesson 2 Times Square

Chapter 6
Lesson 1 Rock Formations
St. Lawrence Seaway
Lesson 3 Hydroelectric Power

Chapter 7
Lesson 1 Sonoran Desert
Lesson 3 Challenges of Urbanization

Chapter 8
Chapter Feature Columbian Exchange Trade

Chapter 9
Lesson 1 Landforms of Brazil
Lesson 3 South American Urbanization

Chapter 10
Lesson 1 Norwegian Landscape

Chapter 11
Chapter Feature Paris the Megacity
Lesson 1 Windmill and Polders
Lesson 3 Air Pollution

Chapter 12
Lesson 1 Mediterranean Climate
Lesson 3 Costa Concordia

Chapter 13
Chapter Feature Tito
Lesson 1 Karst Terrain
Lesson 3 Conservation in Eastern Europe

Chapter 14
Lesson 2 St. Basil's, the Kremlin, and Red Square

Chapter 15
Lesson 1 Mediterranean Climate and Agriculture

Chapter 16
Chapter Feature Rabin, Arafat, and Clinton
Lesson 1 360° View: A Beach in Tel Aviv, Israel
Lesson 3 Oases

Chapter 17
Chapter Feature The Kurds
Lesson 1 The Northeast's Physical Geography
Lesson 2 Foods of Ramadan
Arabic Fast Food
Lesson 3 Life Along the Tigris and Euphrates

Chapter 19
Chapter Feature Soviet Invasion of Afghanistan
Lesson 1 Ships Rest in what was the Aral Sea
Lesson 2 360° View: Samarkand, Uzbekistan
Lesson 3 The Aral Sea

Chapter 20
Lesson 1 Lake Chad

Chapter 21
Lesson 3 Animal Poaching in East Africa

Chapter 22
Lesson 1 West Africa's Variety of Land

Chapter 23
Lesson 1 The Congo River
Lesson 3 Harvest in Central Africa

Chapter 24
Lesson 1 360° View: Johannesburg, South Africa

Chapter 25
Lesson 3 Busy Street in Calcutta, India

Chapter 26
Lesson 3 Microloans in Bangladesh

Chapter 27
Lesson 1 Mount Everest

Chapter 28
Lesson 3 Floods in China

Chapter 29
Lesson 1 Mt. Fuji in Art
Lesson 2 Japan and the West

Chapter 31
Lesson 3 Teakwood

Chapter 32
Chapter Feature Aboriginal and Maori Protests
Lesson 1 360° View: Australian Outback

Chapter 33
Lesson 1 360° View: Bora Bora in the South Pacific
Lesson 2 Fiji Hotel

Interactive Maps

Primary Sources

Time Lines

Digital Worksheets

Environmental Case Studies

Asteroid Monitoring Programs	Unit 1
Regulating the Fracking Drilling Process	Unit 2
South American Rain Forests: Preserve, Harvest or Exploit?	Unit 3
The European Black Triangle and Global Rapid Industrialization	Unit 4
Invasive Marine Species	Unit 5
Agricultural Innovative Systems (AIS)	Unit 6
India's Ganges River and Pollution	Unit 7
Nuclear Power in East Asia	Unit 8
Tuna Fishing and the Pacific Islands	Unit 9

GeoLab Activities

Spreading the Sunlight	Unit 1
Evaporating Water	Unit 2
Dissolving Coral Reefs	Unit 3
Making Euros	Unit 4
Inheriting a Disease	Unit 5
Making a Diamond	Unit 6
Simulating a Nuclear Reaction	Unit 7
Examining a Tsunami	Unit 8
Examining Population Growth	Unit 9

GIS Simulations

Comparing Cities	Unit 1
Partners in Trade	Unit 2
Analyzing Land Use	Unit 3
Evaluating Biogeographical Regions	Unit 4
Preparing for Disaster	Unit 5
Africa South of the Sahara: Past and Present	Unit 6
Health Issues in India	Unit 7
Transportation in China and Japan	Unit 8
The Economies of Australia and New Zealand	Unit 9

Location Activities

The World	Unit 1
United States and Canada	Unit 2
Latin America	Unit 3
Europe	Unit 4
North Africa, Southwest Asia, and Central Asia	Unit 5
Africa South of the Sahara	Unit 6
South Asia	Unit 7
East Asia	Unit 8
Southeast Asia and the Pacific World	Unit 9

Reading Support

These activities are available for each chapter:

Assessing Background Knowledge

Hands-On Chapter Project

Vocabulary Activity

This activity is available for each lesson:

Guided Reading Activity

Differentiated Instruction, Intervention, and Remediation

These activities are available for each chapter:

Chapter Summaries

Approaching-Level Reader with ELL Support

Reading Essentials and Study Guide

Reteaching Activity

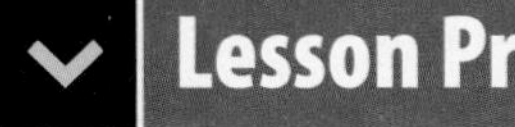

Lesson Presentation

Access pre-built lesson presentations or create customized presentations using resources you uploaded to fit your classroom.

McGraw-Hill eAssessment ™

Access pre-built lesson quizzes (1 per lesson) and chapter tests (2 per chapter) or create customized assessments for use in print or online and track results with robust reporting tools. Pre-built quizzes and tests are also available in the Chapter Tests and Lesson Quizzes blackline master.

Interactive Bellringers

Chapter 1 Interpreting a Thematic Map
Interpreting a Political Cartoon

Chapter 2 The Highest and Deepest Places on Earth
Interpreting a Map of Tectonic Plates
Desalination Capacity

Chapter 3 How Latitude Affects Sunlight
Elevation and Temperature
Acid Rain

Chapter 4 Top Ten Languages
Population Density
Types of Government
GDP Comparison
Top Ten Cities in Population

Chapter 5 Landforms of Southwestern United States
United States Population Density
Acid Rain in the United States

Chapter 6 Average Yearly Temperatures in Alberta
Indigenous Population in Canada
Canada's Boreal Forest

Chapter 7 Vertical Climate Zones of Mexico
Biography of Diego Rivera
Diminishing Frontier Forests in Mexico

Chapter 8 Physical Geography of Central America and the Caribbean
Maya Mother and Child
Mining and the Environment

Chapter 9 Effects of Altitude
Simón Bolívár's Message
The World's Rain Forests

Chapter 10 Navigation and Trade in Finland
Population Pyramid of Finland
Acid Rain in Northern Europe

Chapter 11 Building Dikes and Polders
Public Expenditures in Select European Countries
Commercial Fishing Stocks in Northwestern Europe

Chapter 12 Rivers of Europe
Leonardo Da Vinci and the Italian Renaissance
Haze in the Po River Valley

Chapter 13 Alpine Europe
The Road to a New Era
Nitrate Concentrations in Agricultural Runoff

Chapter 14 The Volga River Basin
GDP Per Capita in the Russian Core
Extent of Chernobyl Disaster

Chapter 15 Production of Phosphate Rock
Status of Women in North Africa
Egypt's Aswān High Dam

Chapter 16 Eastern Mediterranean Precipitation
Israeli-Palestinian Conflict
Desertification in Syria

Chapter 17 Water Systems of the Northeast
Ethnic Groups of the Northeast
Caspian Energy

Chapter 18 Physical Geography: The Arabian Peninsula
Arabian Peninsula Country Statistics
Smoke Plumes over Kuwait, 1991

Chapter 19 Central Asia's Water Tower
Economic Productivity in Central Asia
Aral: A Sea Sacrificed

Chapter 20 Average Rainfall in Transition Zone Cities
Kingdoms and Empires of the Transition Zone
Great Green Wall of Africa

Chapter 21 The Great Rift Valley
East Africa: European Colonization
Africa's Shrinking Elephant Population

Chapter 22 Shorelines of West African Countries
Today's Nigerian Family
West African Street Scene

Chapter 23 Anatomy of the Rain Forest
The Atlantic Slave Trade
Refugees and Internally Displaced Persons in the CAR

Chapter 24 Topography of Southern Africa
Gold Production
Loss or Gain of Natural Forests

Chapter 25 Brahmaputra River Valley, India
Population Growth in India
Water and Sanitation in India

Chapter 26 Landforms of Pakistan
Bangladesh: The Road to Independence
World's Worst Cities for Air Pollution

Chapter 27 Highest Mountain Peaks of Five Continents
Women in National Parliaments
Two Atolls in Maldives

Chapter 28 East Asia Monsoons
U.S. and China Trade Activities
Three Gorges Dam: Harnessing the Yangtze

Interactive Bellringers (continued)

Chapter 29 Physical Map of Japan
Japanese Balance of Trade with the U.S.
Japan's Nuclear Power Plants

Chapter 30 Waterways of the Korean Peninsula
Health Expenditures of Select Countries
Fog and Aerosol Plume over the Yellow Sea

Chapter 31 Eruption at Paluweh Volcano
Contribution to GDP by Economic Sector
Deforestation in Malaysian Borneo

Chapter 32 North Island and South Island, New Zealand
Patterns of European Settlement
Levels of Coral Bleaching in the Great Barrier Reef

Chapter 33 Society Islands, French Polynesia
Pacific Migrations and Settlement
Global Sea Level Trends

Hands-On-Chapter Projects and Digital Hands-On Chapter Projects

Developed in partnership with EdTechTeacher, these chapter projects can be used with or without the use of technology in an individual or collaborative setting.

ePals GlobalCommunity
Where learners connect™

Every project can be extended with ePals®, which allows your students to collaborate with schools around the world.

Chapter 1 Make a Recommendation: Community Issues
Chapter 2 Oral Presentation: Using Geography to Understand Earth
Chapter 3 Documenting: The Impact of Climate Change
Chapter 4 News Interview: The Human Impact
Chapter 5 Immigrant Journal: The United States
Chapter 6 Performing Skits: Canada's Geographic Systems
Chapter 7 Population Pyramid: Mexico
Chapter 8 Writing Magazine Articles: Environmental Impacts in Central America and the Caribbean
Chapter 9 Model Effects of Deforestation: Amazon Rain Forest
Chapter 10 Slide Presentations: Energy Resources of Northern Europe
Chapter 11 Debate: Geographical Issues of Northwestern Europe
Chapter 12 Podcasts: Foundations of Western Civilization in Southern Europe
Chapter 13 Mapping: Eastern Europe
Chapter 14 Poems: The Russian Core
Chapter 15 Current Affairs Newspaper: North Africa
Chapter 16 Time Line: The Eastern Mediterranean
Chapter 17 Disaster Preparedness Plans: The Northeast
Chapter 18 Tour Books: The Arabian Peninsula
Chapter 19 Mural: Time Line of Central Asia
Chapter 20 Documentary: Desertification in the Transition Zone
Chapter 21 Brochure: Education Issues for Females in East Africa
Chapter 22 Presentations: West African Art Form
Chapter 23 Nongovernmental Organization: Combat an Environmental Issue in Equatorial Africa
Chapter 24 Environmental Educational Materials: Southern Africa
Chapter 25 Graphic Novel: India's Colonialism Experiences and Quest for Independence
Chapter 26 Web Site: Issues Facing Modern Pakistan and Bangladesh
Chapter 27 Fictional Journal: A Family Member Living in the Maldives or Nepal
Chapter 28 Ideogram Report: Issues Facing China
Chapter 29 News Interviews: Current Issues in Japan
Chapter 30 Posters: Geographic Systems in North Korea and South Korea
Chapter 31 Conservation Plan: Environmental Issues in Southeast Asia
Chapter 32 Songs: Folk Songs about Australia or New Zealand
Chapter 33 Persuasive Essays: Geographic Systems in Oceania

Interactive Whiteboard Activities

Chapter 1 Purposes of Maps
Elements of Geography

Chapter 2 The Solar System
Forces of Change
Water Cycle

Chapter 3 Earth's Patterns
World Wind Patterns
Climate Zones

Chapter 4 Elements of Culture
Population Growth Rate
Systems of Government
Types of Economic Activities
Urban Land Use Models

Chapter 5 Climate and Vegetation in the United States
Physical and Human Factors
Limited Natural Resources

Chapter 6 The Land of Canada
British and French Roots
Cause and Effect in Canada's Environment

Chapter 7 Geography of Mexico
Indigenous Peoples of Mexico
Deforestation in Mexico

Chapter 8 Physical Features of Central America and the Caribbean
Central America and the Caribbean Time Line
Soil Erosion

Chapter 9 Waterways of South America
Population Patterns of South America
Environmental Problems and Solutions

Chapter 10 Northern Europe and Its Landforms
Population Patterns in Northern Europe
Managing the Resources of Northern Europe

Chapter 11 Climates of Northwestern Europe
Population Density in Northwestern Europe
Causes and Effects in the Environment of Northwestern Europe

Chapter 12 Peninsulas of Southern Europe
The Renaissance Period
Environmental Concerns in Southern Europe

Chapter 13 Waterways of Eastern Europe
Eastern Europe Members of EU
Acid Rain and Water Pollution

Chapter 14 Volga River Cities
Governmental Changes in the Russian Core
Environmental Issues in the Russian Core

Chapter 15 The Great Nile and Sahara
North Africa's Modern Economy
The Impact of the Aswān High Dam

Chapter 16 Waterways of the Eastern Mediterranean
Ethnic Groups in the Eastern Mediterranean
Managing Israel's Water Resources

Chapter 17 Landforms of the Northeast
From Mesopotamia to Modern Day
Human Impact on the Environment

Chapter 18 Landforms and Water Systems of the Arabian Peninsula
Impact of Islam on the Arabian Peninsula
Impact of the Petroleum Industry on the Environment

Chapter 19 Central Asia Water Systems
Historical Events That Shaped Central Asia
Addressing Environmental Issues in Central Asia

Chapter 20 The African Transition Zone
Empires of the Transition Zone
Environment Challenges of the Transition Zone

Chapter 21 Physical Geography of East Africa
Key Events in the History of East Africa
Human Impact of Environmental Challenges in East Africa

Chapter 22 Water Systems of West Africa
Internal Strife: Liberia
Challenges of West Africa

Chapter 23 Landforms of Equatorial Africa
Slavery and European Colonization in Equatorial Africa
Environmental Threats in Equatorial Africa

Chapter 24 Southern African Landforms
European Colonization of Southern Africa
Environment of Southern Africa

Chapter 25 Climates of India
Village and City Life
Pressures of Population Growth

Chapter 26 Landforms of Pakistan and Bangladesh
Comparing and Contrasting Pakistan and Bangladesh
Environment Dangers

Chapter 27 Landforms of Bhutan, Maldives, Nepal and Sri Lanka
Patterns of the Populace
Endangered Environment

Chapter 28 Mountains, Rivers, and Plains
Changes in the Farm Economy
Economic Growth and the Environment

Interactive Whiteboard Activities (continued)

Chapter 29 Major Climates and Forest Biomes
Modern Culture and Society
Resource Problems and Solutions

Chapter 30 Landforms, Biomes, and Resources
Shared History, Divided Growth
Human Actions and the Environment

Chapter 31 Southeast Asia and the Ring of Fire
Colonization and the Shatter Belt
Addressing Pollution and Deforestation

Chapter 32 Landforms, Biomes, and Resources
Effects of Migration and Colonization
Environmental Problems and Solutions

Chapter 33 The Low Islands and High Islands
Types and Systems of Government
Global Warming in Oceania

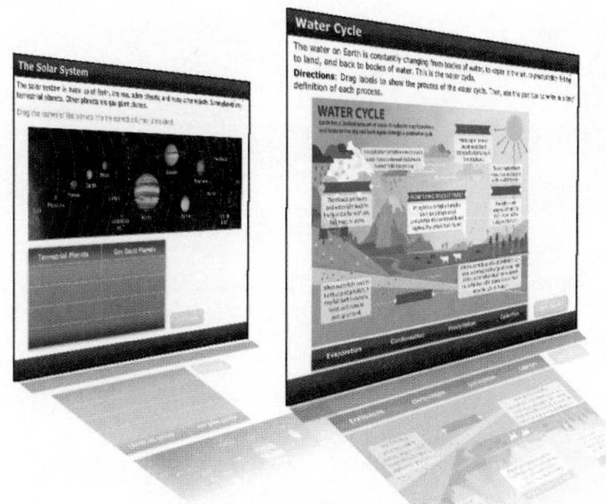

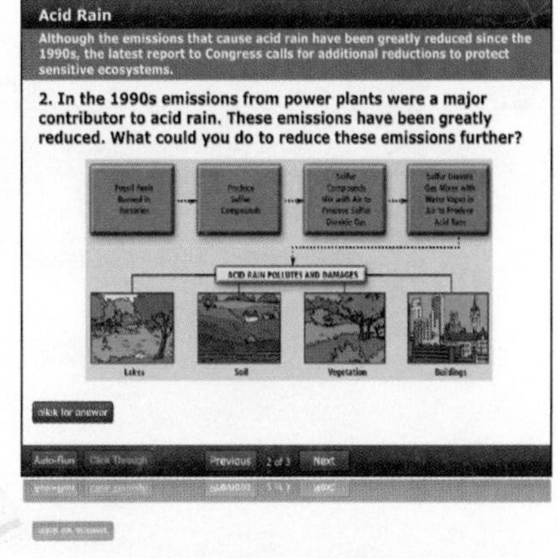

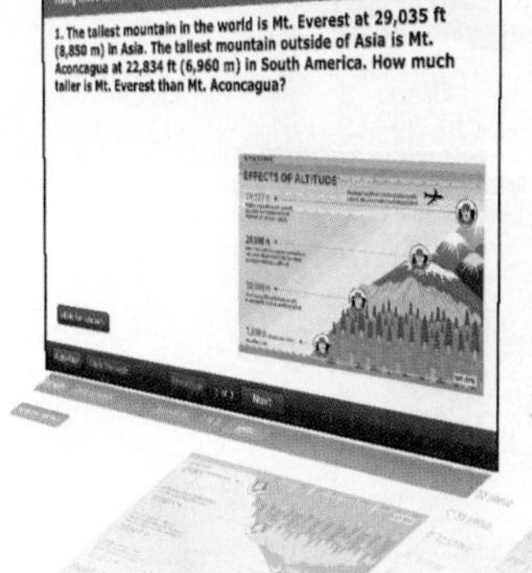

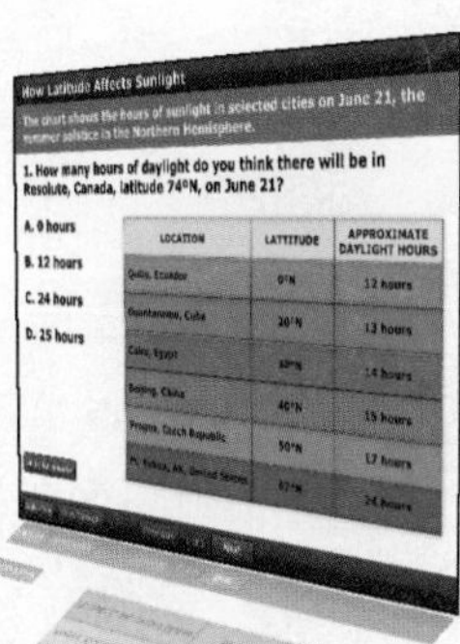

How Latitude Affects Sunlight
1. How many hours of daylight do you think there will be in Resolute, Canada, latitude 74°N, on June 21?
A. 0 hours
B. 12 hours
C. 24 hours
D. 25 hours

How do I study **Geography?**

Geographers have tried to understand the best way to teach and learn about geography. In order to do this, geographers created the Five Themes of Geography. The themes acted as a guide for teaching the basic ideas about geography to students like yourself.

People who teach and study geography, though, thought that the Five Themes were too broad. In 1994, geographers created 18 national geography standards, *Geography for Life*. These standards were more detailed about what should be taught and learned. The Six Essential Elements act as a bridge connecting the Five Themes with the standards.

These pages show you how the Five Themes are related to the Six Essential Elements and the 18 standards.

5 Themes of Geography

1 Location

Location describes where something is. Absolute location describes a place's exact position on the Earth's surface. Relative location expresses where a place is in relation to another place.

2 Place

Place describes the physical and human characteristics that make a location unique.

3 Regions

Regions are areas that share common characteristics.

4 Movement

Movement explains how and why people and things move and are connected.

5 Human-Environment Interaction

Human-Environment Interaction describes the relationship between people and their environment.

(t to b)Thorsten Henn/Cultura/Getty Images, David S. Boyer/Getty Images, John Lamb/Stone/Getty Images, Panoramic Images/Glow Images

6 Essential Elements	18 Geography Standards
I. The World in Spatial Terms Geographers look to see where a place is located. Location acts as a starting point to answer "Where Is It?" The location of a place helps you orient yourself as to where you are.	1 How to use maps and other tools 2 How to use mental maps to organize information 3 How to analyze the spatial organization of people, places, and environments
II. Places and Regions Place describes physical characteristics such as landforms, climate, and plant or animal life. It might also describe human characteristics, including language and way of life. Places can also be organized into regions. Regions are places united by one or more characteristics.	4 The physical and human characteristics of places 5 How people create regions to interpret Earth's complexity 6 How culture and experience influence people's perceptions of places and regions
III. Physical Systems Geographers study how physical systems, such as hurricanes, volcanoes, and glaciers, shape the surface of the Earth. They also look at how plants and animals depend upon one another and their surroundings for their survival.	7 The physical processes that shape Earth's surface 8 The distribution of ecosystems on Earth's surface
IV. Human Systems People shape the world in which they live. They settle in certain places but not in others. An ongoing theme in geography is the movement of people, ideas, and goods.	9 The characteristics, distribution, and migration of human populations 10 The complexity of Earth's cultural mosaics 11 The patterns and networks of economic interdependence 12 The patterns of human settlement 13 The forces of cooperation and conflict
V. Environment and Society How does the relationship between people and their natural surroundings influence the way people live? Geographers study how people use the environment and how their actions affect the environment.	14 How human actions modify the physical environment 15 How physical systems affect human systems 16 The meaning, use, and distribution of resources
VI. The Uses of Geography Knowledge of geography helps us understand the relationships among people, places, and environments over time. Applying geographic skills helps you understand the past and prepare for the future.	17 How to apply geography to interpret the past 18 How to apply geography to interpret the present and plan for the future

TO THE TEACHER Welcome to the McGraw-Hill Teacher Edition—a new approach to the Teacher Edition based on the principles of *Understanding By Design®*.

Planning the Unit

Understanding By Design®

All Networks programs have been created using the approach developed by Jay McTighe, coauthor of *Understanding By Design®*.

- The main goal is to focus on the desired results before planning each unit's instruction.
- The Unit Planner lists the Enduring Understandings and the Essential Questions that students will learn and use as they study the chapters in the unit.
- Identifying the Predictable Misunderstandings will help you anticipate misconceptions students might have as they read the chapters.
- Information in the Unit Planners is expanded upon in the Chapter Planners.

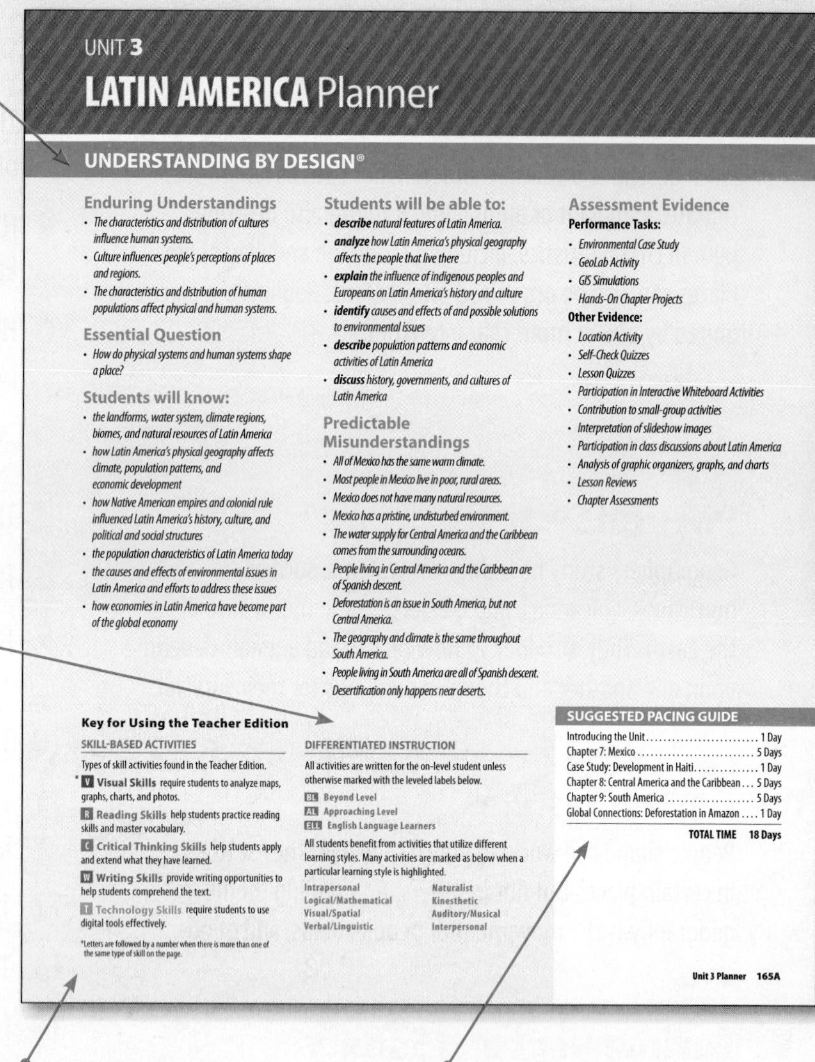

UNIT 3

LATIN AMERICA Planner

UNDERSTANDING BY DESIGN®

Enduring Understandings

- *The characteristics and distribution of cultures influence human systems.*
- *Culture influences people's perceptions of places and regions.*
- *The characteristics and distribution of human populations affect physical and human systems.*

Essential Question

- *How do physical systems and human systems shape a place?*

Students will know:

- *the landforms, water system, climate regions, biomes, and natural resources of Latin America*
- *how Latin America's physical geography affects climate, population patterns, and economic development*
- *how Native American empires and colonial rule influenced Latin America's history, culture, and political and social structures*
- *the population characteristics of Latin America today*
- *the causes and effects of environmental issues in Latin America and efforts to address these issues*
- *how economies in Latin America have become part of the global economy*

Students will be able to:

- ***describe*** *natural features of Latin America.*
- ***analyze*** *how Latin America's physical geography affects the people that live there*
- ***explain*** *the influence of indigenous peoples and Europeans on Latin America's history and culture*
- ***identify*** *causes and effects of and possible solutions to environmental issues*
- ***describe*** *population patterns and economic activities of Latin America*
- ***discuss*** *history, governments, and cultures of Latin America*

Predictable Misunderstandings

- *All of Mexico has the same warm climate.*
- *Most people in Mexico live in poor, rural areas.*
- *Mexico does not have many natural resources.*
- *Mexico has a pristine, undisturbed environment.*
- *The water supply for Central America and the Caribbean comes from the surrounding oceans.*
- *People living in Central America and the Caribbean are of Spanish descent.*
- *Deforestation is an issue in South America, but not Central America.*
- *The geography and climate is the same throughout South America.*
- *People living in South America are all of Spanish descent.*
- *Desertification only happens near deserts.*

Assessment Evidence

Performance Tasks:

- *Environmental Case Study*
- *GeoLab Activity*
- *GIS Simulations*
- *Hands-On Chapter Projects*

Other Evidence:

- *Location Activity*
- *Self-Check Quizzes*
- *Lesson Quizzes*
- *Participation in Interactive Whiteboard Activities*
- *Contribution to small-group activities*
- *Interpretation of slideshow images*
- *Participation in class discussions about Latin America*
- *Analysis of graphic organizers, graphs, and charts*
- *Lesson Reviews*
- *Chapter Assessments*

Key for Using the Teacher Edition

SKILL-BASED ACTIVITIES

Types of skill activities found in the Teacher Edition.

V Visual Skills require students to analyze maps, graphs, charts, and photos.

R Reading Skills help students practice reading skills and master vocabulary.

C Critical Thinking Skills help students apply and extend what they have learned.

W Writing Skills provide writing opportunities to help students comprehend the text.

T Technology Skills require students to use digital tools effectively.

*Letters are followed by a number when there is more than one of the same type of skill on the page.

DIFFERENTIATED INSTRUCTION

All activities are written for the on-level student unless otherwise marked with the leveled labels below.

BL Beyond Level

AL Approaching Level

ELL English Language Learners

All students benefit from activities that utilize different learning styles. Many activities are marked as below when a particular learning style is highlighted.

Intrapersonal	Naturalist
Logical/Mathematical	Kinesthetic
Visual/Spatial	Auditory/Musical
Verbal/Linguistic	Interpersonal

SUGGESTED PACING GUIDE

Introducing the Unit	1 Day
Chapter 7: Mexico	5 Days
Case Study: Development in Haiti	1 Day
Chapter 8: Central America and the Caribbean	5 Days
Chapter 9: South America	5 Days
Global Connections: Deforestation in Amazon	1 Day
TOTAL TIME	**18 Days**

Unit 3 Planner 165A

Differentiated Instruction

Activities are designed to meet the needs of:

BL Beyond Level

AL Approaching Level

ELL English Language Learners

In addition, activities are designed to address a range of *learning styles*.

Skill-Based Activities

Print-based and digital activities throughout the unit are designed to teach a range of skills, including:

C Critical Thinking Skills

V Visual Skills

R Reading Skills

T Technology Skills

W Writing Skills

Pacing Guide

Suggestions are provided on how to pace the unit's content based on your state's curriculum and number of school days.

networks

Don't forget! You can customize all your Lesson Plans online.

Unit Opener Planner

The Unit Opener Planner provides a menu of the print and digital resources available to teach the Unit Opener. These activities are organized by skill type, level, and learning style.

Introduce the Unit

Every unit has activities that introduce students to the region. The activities may include discussion questions or brief cooperative learning activities to help students make connections to the unit content.

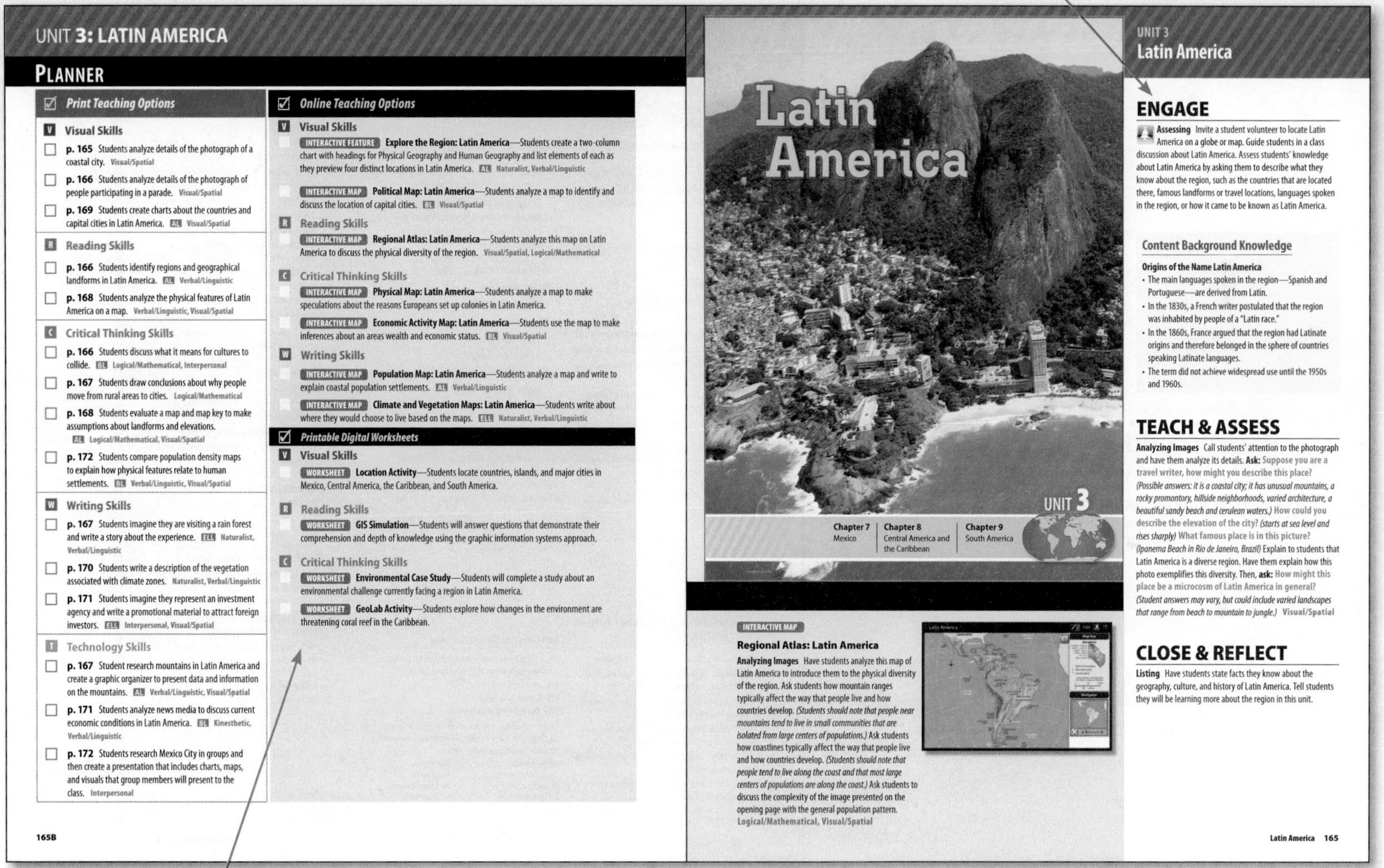

UNIT 3: LATIN AMERICA

PLANNER

Print Teaching Options

V Visual Skills
- p. 165 Students analyze details of the photograph of a coastal city. Visual/Spatial
- p. 166 Students analyze details of the photograph of people participating in a parade. Visual/Spatial
- p. 169 Students create charts about the countries and capital cities in Latin America. AL Visual/Spatial

R Reading Skills
- p. 166 Students identify regions and geographical landforms in Latin America. AL Verbal/Linguistic
- p. 168 Students analyze the physical features of Latin America on a map. Verbal/Linguistic, Visual/Spatial

C Critical Thinking Skills
- p. 166 Students discuss what it means for cultures to collide. BL Logical/Mathematical, Interpersonal
- p. 167 Students draw conclusions about why people move from rural areas to cities. Logical/Mathematical
- p. 168 Students evaluate a map and map key to make assumptions about landforms and elevations. AL Logical/Mathematical, Visual/Spatial
- p. 172 Students compare population density maps to explain how physical features relate to human settlements. BL Verbal/Linguistic, Visual/Spatial

W Writing Skills
- p. 167 Students imagine they are visiting a rain forest and write a story about the experience. ELL Naturalist, Verbal/Linguistic
- p. 170 Students write a description of the vegetation associated with climate zones. Naturalist, Verbal/Linguistic
- p. 171 Students imagine they represent an investment agency and write a promotional material to attract foreign investors. ELL Interpersonal, Visual/Spatial

T Technology Skills
- p. 167 Student research mountains in Latin America and create a graphic organizer to present data and information on the mountains. AL Verbal/Linguistic, Visual/Spatial
- p. 171 Students analyze news media to discuss current economic conditions in Latin America. BL Kinesthetic, Verbal/Linguistic
- p. 172 Students research Mexico City in groups and then create a presentation that includes charts, maps, and visuals that group members will present to the class. Interpersonal

Online Teaching Options

V Visual Skills
- INTERACTIVE FEATURE **Explore the Region: Latin America**—Students create a two-column chart with headings for Physical Geography and Human Geography and list elements of each as they preview four distinct locations in Latin America. ELL Naturalist, Verbal/Linguistic
- INTERACTIVE MAP **Political Map: Latin America**—Students analyze a map to identify and discuss the location of capital cities. BL Visual/Spatial

R Reading Skills
- INTERACTIVE MAP **Regional Atlas: Latin America**—Students analyze this map on Latin America to discuss the physical diversity of the region. Visual/Spatial, Logical/Mathematical

C Critical Thinking Skills
- INTERACTIVE MAP **Physical Map: Latin America**—Students analyze a map to make speculations about the reasons Europeans set up colonies in Latin America.
- INTERACTIVE MAP **Economic Activity Map: Latin America**—Students use the map to make inferences about an areas wealth and economic status. BL Visual/Spatial

W Writing Skills
- INTERACTIVE MAP **Population Map: Latin America**—Students analyze a map and write to explain coastal population settlements. AL Verbal/Linguistic
- INTERACTIVE MAP **Climate and Vegetation Maps: Latin America**—Students write about where they would choose to live based on the maps. ELL Naturalist, Verbal/Linguistic

Printable Digital Worksheets

V Visual Skills
- WORKSHEET **Location Activity**—Students locate countries, islands, and major cities in Mexico, Central America, the Caribbean, and South America.

R Reading Skills
- WORKSHEET **GIS Simulation**—Students will answer questions that demonstrate their comprehension and depth of knowledge using the graphic information systems approach.

C Critical Thinking Skills
- WORKSHEET **Environmental Case Study**—Students will complete a study about an environmental challenge currently facing a region in Latin America.
- WORKSHEET **GeoLab Activity**—Students explore how changes in the environment are threatening coral reef in the Caribbean.

165B

Latin America

UNIT 3

Chapter 7 Mexico | Chapter 8 Central America and the Caribbean | Chapter 9 South America

INTERACTIVE MAP

Regional Atlas: Latin America

Analyzing Images Have students analyze this map of Latin America to introduce them to the physical diversity of the region. Ask students how mountain ranges typically affect the way that people live and how countries develop. *(Students should note that people near mountains tend to live in small communities that are isolated from large centers of populations.)* Ask students how coastlines typically affect the way that people live and how countries develop. *(Students should note that people tend to live along the coast and that most large centers of populations are along the coast.)* Ask students to discuss the complexity of the image presented on the opening page with the general population pattern. Logical/Mathematical, Visual/Spatial

UNIT 3

Latin America

ENGAGE

Assessing Invite a student volunteer to locate Latin America on a globe or map. Guide students in a class discussion about Latin America. Assess students' knowledge about Latin America by asking them to describe what they know about the region, such as the countries that are located there, famous landforms or travel locations, languages spoken in the region, or how it came to be known as Latin America.

Content Background Knowledge

Origins of the Name Latin America
- The main languages spoken in the region—Spanish and Portuguese—are derived from Latin.
- In the 1830s, a French writer postulated that the region was inhabited by people of a "Latin race."
- In the 1860s, France argued that the region had Latinate origins and therefore belonged in the sphere of countries speaking Latinate languages.
- The term did not achieve widespread use until the 1950s and 1960s.

TEACH & ASSESS

Analyzing Images Call students' attention to the photograph and have them analyze its details. **Ask:** Suppose you are a travel writer, how might you describe this place? *(Possible answers: it is a coastal city; it has unusual mountains, a rocky promontory, hillside neighborhoods, varied architecture, a beautiful sandy beach and cerulean waters.)* How could you describe the elevation of the city? *(starts at sea level and rises sharply)* What famous place is in this picture? *(Ipanema Beach in Rio de Janeiro, Brazil)* Explain to students that Latin America is a diverse region. Have them explain how this photo exemplifies this diversity. Then, **ask:** How might this place be a microcosm of Latin America in general? *(Student answers may vary, but could include varied landscapes that range from beach to mountain to jungle.)* Visual/Spatial

CLOSE & REFLECT

Listing Have students state facts they know about the geography, culture, and history of Latin America. Tell students they will be learning more about the region in this unit.

Latin America 165

Online Teaching Activities

Digital assets and activities are cited here throughout the Teacher Edition to help you teach unit, chapter, and lesson content.

Teaching activities are provided for every digital asset in the Teacher Edition.

Digital assets include:

- interactive maps
- photos
- animations
- slide shows
- whiteboard activities
- lesson videos
- worksheets

Planning the Chapter

Understanding By Design®

Like the Unit Planner, the Chapter Planner focuses on *Understanding By Design®* principles, including learning expectations, student misconceptions, and assessment options.

Standards

Each Chapter Planner identifies the National Geography Standards that are covered in the chapter.

Pacing Guide

Time management suggestions for teaching the chapter are provided.

CHAPTER 9

South America Planner

UNDERSTANDING BY DESIGN®

Enduring Understandings

- *The characteristics and distribution of human populations affect physical and human systems.*

Essential Question

- *How do physical systems and human systems shape a place?*

Predictable Misunderstandings

Students may think:

- *The geography and climate is the same throughout South America. Explain that South America is a large continent with a variety of climates and geographical characteristics.*
- *People living in South America are all of Spanish descent. Explain that the cultures of South America are a mix of influences of Native Americans, many different types of Europeans, and Africans.*
- *Desertification only happens near deserts. Explain that desertification is the changing over of fertile land to unusable, dry land, and can happen anywhere.*

Assessment Evidence

Performance Tasks:

- *Hands-On Chapter Project*

Other Evidence:

- *Guided Reading Activities*
- *Vocabulary Activities*
- *Lesson Quizzes*
- *Chapter Tests, Forms A and B*

SUGGESTED PACING GUIDE

Introducing the Chapter	½ Day	Global Connections	1 Day
Lesson 1	1 Day	Lesson 3	1 Day
Lesson 2	2 Days	Chapter Wrap-Up and Assessment	½ Day
		TOTAL TIME	**6 Days**

Key for Using the Teacher Edition

SKILL-BASED ACTIVITIES

Types of skill activities found in the Teacher Edition.

V Visual Skills require students to analyze maps, graphs, charts, and photos.

R Reading Skills help students practice reading skills and master vocabulary.

C Critical Thinking Skills help students apply and extend what they have learned.

W Writing Skills provide writing opportunities to help students comprehend the text.

T Technology Skills require students to use digital tools effectively.

*Letters are followed by a number when there is more than one of the same type of skill on the page.

DIFFERENTIATED INSTRUCTION

All activities are written for the on-level student unless otherwise marked with the leveled labels below.

BL Beyond Level

AL Approaching Level

ELL English Language Learners

All students benefit from activities that utilize different learning styles. Many activities are marked as below when a particular learning style is highlighted.

Intrapersonal	Naturalist
Logical/Mathematical	Kinesthetic
Visual/Spatial	Auditory/Musical
Verbal/Linguistic	Interpersonal

National Geography Standards covered in "South America"

The student knows and understands:

(4) The physical and human characteristics of places

4.2 The interaction of physical and human systems result in the creation of and changes to places

(8) The characteristics and spatial distribution of ecosystems and biomes on Earth's surface

8.1 Ecosystems are dynamic and respond to changes in environmental conditions

(9) The characteristics, distribution, and migration of human populations on Earth's surface

9.2 Population distribution and density are a function of historical, environmental, economic, political, and technological factors

(15) How physical systems affect human systems

15.1 Depending on the choice of human activities, the characteristics of the physical environment can be viewed as both opportunities and constraints

15.3 Societies use a variety of strategies to adapt to changes in the physical environment

(16) The changes that occur in the meaning, use, distribution, and importance of resources

16.3 Policies and programs that promote the sustainable use and management of resources impact people and the environment

(17) How to apply geography and interpret the past

17.1 Geographic contexts (the human and physical characteristics of places and environments) can explain the connections between sequences of historical events

17.3 Historical events must be interpreted in the contexts of people's past perception of places, regions, and environments

(18) How to apply geography to interpret the present and plan for the future

18.1 Geographic contexts (the human and physical characteristics of places and environments) provide the bases for analyzing current events and making predictions about future issues

Chapter 9 Planner 215A

Skill-Based Activities

Each lesson includes a variety of print-based and digital activities designed to teach a range of skills, including:

- **C Critical Thinking Skills**
- **V Visual Skills**
- **R Reading Skills**
- **T Technology Skills**
- **W Writing Skills**

Differentiated Instruction

Activities are designed to meet the needs of:

- **BL Beyond Level**
- **AL Approaching Level**
- **ELL English Language Learners**

In addition, activities are designed to address a range of *learning styles*.

networks

Don't forget! You can customize all your Lesson Plans online.

Planners

The Chapter Opener and Lesson Planners provide a snapshot of the resources available to enhance and extend learning. The activities are organized by skill type, level, and learning style.

Student Objectives

Using *Understanding By Design*® as the framework, the planners outline the content and skills that students will be expected to know.

CHAPTER **9: SOUTH AMERICA**

Chapter Opener Planner

Students will know:

- *how South America's physical geography affects climate, population patterns, and economic development.*
- *that Native Americans, Europeans, and Africans have influenced the history, government, and cultures of South America.*
- *that South America faces many environmental issues related to urban growth, industrialization, and desertification.*

Students will be able to:

- ***discuss** the physical geography of South America and its effects.*
- ***discuss** history, governments, and cultures of South America.*
- ***describe** environmental issues and solutions.*

UNDERSTANDING BY DESIGN®

Print Teaching Options

V Visual Skills

- ☐ **p. 216** Students analyze the image to compare and contrast it to other images and to discuss how it relates to life in South America.
- ☐ **p. 217** Students create a flow chart to describe the principals of the core-periphery theory. **Visual/Spatial**

C Critical Thinking Skills

- ☐ **p. 216** Students discuss characteristics of developed and undeveloped nations. AL **Logical/Mathematical**
- ☐ **p. 217** Students problem-solve by answering a question of how a country can prevent brain drain. BL **Logical/Mathematical, Interpersonal**

W Writing Skills

- ☐ **p. 216** Students write a brief essay titled "My Day in the Food Line" about what it would be like to be one of the people in the food line. **Verbal/Linguistic**

Online Teaching Options

V Visual Skills

SLIDE SHOW **Skewed Economic Development of South America**—Students explore the instances of uneven development and choose one to further study and propose solutions to. BL **Verbal/Linguistic**

INTERACTIVE GRAPH **Brazil's Urban Population Growth**—Students analyze data in the graph about recent growth in urban areas. **Interpersonal, Visual/Spatial**

Printable Digital Worksheets

WORKSHEET **Assessing Background Knowledge**—Determine the level of prior knowledge students have about Mexico and Mexico City.

WORKSHEET **Vocabulary Activity**—Students use and improve their academic and content vocabulary by completing various vocabulary activities.

Project-Based Learning

Hands-On

Designing Deforestation Models

Students will design models that bring together information from all lessons about how deforestation affects the environment and people of Amazonia.

Digital Hands-On

Create Online Projects

Find an additional activity online that incorporates technology for this project. Visit the EdTech Teacher Web sites for more links, tutorials, and other resources.

ePals GlobalCommunity Where learners connect™ edtechteacher 21st Century Learning

Print Resources

ANCILLARY RESOURCES

This ancillary is available for every chapter and lesson.

- **Chapter Tests and Lesson Quizzes**

PRINTABLE DIGITAL WORKSHEETS

These printable digital worksheets are available for every chapter and lesson.

- **Assessing Background Knowledge**
- **Chapter Summaries**
- **Guided Reading Activities**
- **Hands-On Chapter Projects**
- **Quizzes and Tests**
- **Reading Essentials and Study Guide** AL
- **Reteaching Activities**
- **Video Activities**
- **Vocabulary Activity**

More Media Resources

SUGGESTED VIDEOS MOVIES

- **Mysterious World of the Inca** (53 min.)
- **Passport to Adventure: Buenos Aires and Bariloche** (26 min.)
- **Brazil** *New Dimension Media* (30 min.)

SUGGESTED READING

- ***Bolivar: American Liberator,*** by Marie Arana
- ***Brazil on the Rise: The Story of a Country Transformed,*** by Larry Rohter
- ***The Last Days of the Incas,*** by Kim MacQuarrie

215B

LESSON **1 PLANNER**

Physical Geography of South America

Students will know:

- *that South America's location on the Ring of Fire has impacted its physical geography.*
- *why the rugged landscape both attracts settlers and also isolates them.*
- *how South America's water systems are important to economic development.*
- *how elevation and location in the Tropics influences South America's climate.*
- *the ways in which climate influences human systems in South America.*

Students will be able to:

- ***explain** how South America's location affects its physical geography, which affects its population patterns.*
- ***describe** how water systems are important to the economy.*
- ***identify** how climate is influenced by elevation and location and influences human systems.*

UNDERSTANDING BY DESIGN®

Print Teaching Options

V Visual Skills

- ☐ **p. 218** Students create a chart of the major landforms of South America. ELL **Visual/Spatial**
- ☐ **p. 219** Students discuss the variety of landforms in South America. ELL **Visual/Spatial**
- ☐ **p. 219** Students study and describe the elevation profile and mountain image. **Visual/Spatial**
- ☐ **p. 221** Students create a vertical altitude-to-temperature diagram. BL **Visual/Spatial, Interpersonal**
- ☐ **p. 222** Students analyze a graph of resources in Latin America. BL **Visual/Spatial, Logical/Mathematical**

R Reading Skills

- ☐ **p. 220** Students compare the Paraguay-Paraná river system to the Amazon river system. **Verbal/Linguistic**

C Critical Thinking Skills

- ☐ **p. 218** Students discuss how mountain ranges can lead to a country's isolation. **Logical/Mathematical**
- ☐ **p. 219** Students hypothesize about how the Andes were formed. **Naturalist**
- ☐ **p. 221** Students identify and compare a biome in South America to the biome in North America where they live. BL **Naturalist, Logical/Mathematical**
- ☐ **p. 222** Students make a list of questions to help them understand the importance of mineral resources to local economies within South America. **Verbal/Linguistic**

W Writing Skills

- ☐ **p. 220** Students write a narrative describing everyday life during an El Nino year in a specific region in South America. **Verbal/Linguistic, Visual/Spatial**

T Technology Skills

- ☐ **p. 220** Students create a multimedia presentation about a major river system. BL **Technological**
- ☐ **p. 221** Students find a vegetation map and a rainfall map of South America and answer questions about them. **Visual/Spatial**

Online Teaching Options

V Visual Skills

INTERACTIVE MAP **South America: Elevation Profile**—Students discuss how landforms either facilitate the growth or decline of multiple different cultures. **Interpersonal, Verbal/Linguistic**

C Critical Thinking Skills

INTERACTIVE BELLRINGER **Effects of Altitude**—Students discuss how altitude affects life and activities at higher elevations. **Logical/Mathematical, Naturalist**

INFOGRAHIC **Impacts of El Nińo in Latin America**—Students compare and contrast El Nińo's effect in Latin America with South America in charts or graphs. AL **Visual/Spatial**

W Writing Skills

VIDEO **Around the World—Chile**—Students view the video and write a paragraph about Chile's varied terrain and how it affects population. BL **Verbal/Linguistic**

INTERACTIVE WHITEBOARD ACTIVITY **Waterways of South America**—Students will label the waterways on a map of South America and then will identify the correct descriptors to the proper locations on the map.

Printable Digital Worksheets

R Reading Skills

WORKSHEET **Guided Reading Activity**—Students use the Guided Reading Activity worksheets to review their comprehension of the content. **Verbal/Linguistic**

WORKSHEET **Chapter Summary**—Students review the main ideas of the chapter content. **Verbal/Linguistic**

C Critical Thinking Skills

WORKSHEET **Video Activity**—Students answer questions relating to the lesson content after they have viewed the video. **Visual/Spatial**

Chapter 9 Planner 215C

Project-Based Learning

Cumulative projects bring the subject to life for the student and help you assess your students' level of understanding. The program includes Hands-On Projects, as well as Digital Hands-On Projects.

Print Resources

Every chapter includes printable worksheets, including tests, quizzes, and materials to build vocabulary and improve reading comprehension.

Make It Relevant

Enrich and extend the content with videos and books.

Print and Digital Options

Each planner has two columns listing print-based activities and online digital options, including printable digital worksheets.

Using the Wraparound Resources and Activities

STUDENT EDITION PAGES AND WRAPAROUND ACTIVITIES

The entire Student Edition appears in the Teacher Edition. Activities and recommended resources appear in the side and bottom margins of the Teacher Edition, at point of use.

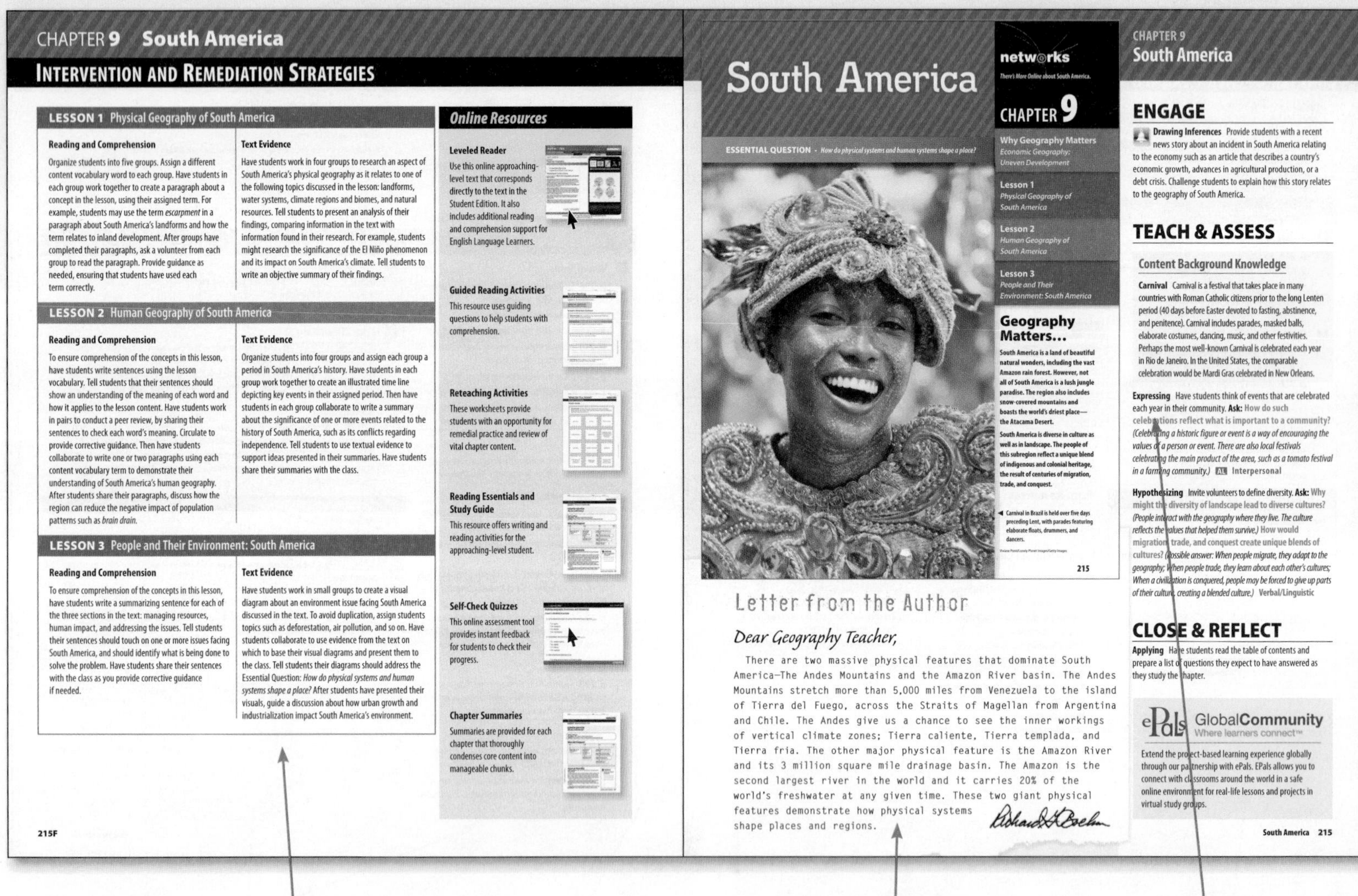

CHAPTER 9 South America

INTERVENTION AND REMEDIATION STRATEGIES

LESSON 1 Physical Geography of South America

Reading and Comprehension

Organize students into five groups. Assign a different content vocabulary word to each group. Have students in each group work together to create a paragraph about a concept in the lesson, using their assigned term. For example, students may use the term *escarpment* in a paragraph about South America's landforms and how the term relates to inland development. After groups have completed their paragraphs, ask a volunteer from each group to read the paragraph. Provide guidance as needed, ensuring that students have used each term correctly.

Text Evidence

Have students work in four groups to research an aspect of South America's physical geography as it relates to one of the following topics discussed in the lesson: landforms, water systems, climate regions and biomes, and natural resources. Tell students to present an analysis of their findings, comparing information in the text with information found in their research. For example, students might research the significance of the El Niño phenomenon and its impact on South America's climate. Tell students to write an objective summary of their findings.

LESSON 2 Human Geography of South America

Reading and Comprehension

To ensure comprehension of the concepts in this lesson, have students write sentences using the lesson vocabulary. Tell students that their sentences should show an understanding of the meaning of each word and how it applies to the lesson content. Have students work in pairs to conduct a peer review, by sharing their sentences to check each word's meaning. Circulate to provide corrective guidance. Then have students collaborate to write one or two paragraphs using each content vocabulary term to demonstrate their understanding of South America's human geography. After students share their paragraphs, discuss how the region can reduce the negative impact of population patterns such as *brain drain.*

Text Evidence

Organize students into four groups and assign each group a period in South America's history. Have students in each group work together to create an illustrated time line depicting key events in their assigned period. Then have students in each group collaborate to write a summary about the significance of one or more events related to the history of South America, such as its conflicts regarding independence. Tell students to use textual evidence to support ideas presented in their summaries. Have students share their summaries with the class.

LESSON 3 People and Their Environment: South America

Reading and Comprehension

To ensure comprehension of the concepts in this lesson, have students write a summarizing sentence for each of the three sections in the text: managing resources, human impact, and addressing the issues. Tell students their sentences should touch on one or more issues facing South America, and should identify what is being done to solve the problem. Have students share their sentences with the class as you provide corrective guidance if needed.

Text Evidence

Have students work in small groups to create a visual diagram about an environment issue facing South America discussed in the text. To avoid duplication, assign students topics such as deforestation, air pollution, and so on. Have students collaborate to use evidence from the text on which to base their visual diagrams and present them to the class. Tell students their diagrams should address the Essential Question: *How do physical systems and human systems shape a place?* After students have presented their visuals, guide a discussion about how urban growth and industrialization impact South America's environment.

Online Resources

Leveled Reader
Use this online approaching-level text that corresponds directly to the text in the Student Edition. It also includes additional reading and comprehension support for English Language Learners.

Guided Reading Activities
This resource uses guiding questions to help students with comprehension.

Reteaching Activities
These worksheets provide students with an opportunity for remedial practice and review of vital chapter content.

Reading Essentials and Study Guide
This resource offers writing and reading activities for the approaching-level student.

Self-Check Quizzes
This online assessment tool provides instant feedback for students to check their progress.

Chapter Summaries
Summaries are provided for each chapter that thoroughly condenses core content into manageable chunks.

215F

South America

networks
There's More Online about South America.

CHAPTER 9

ESSENTIAL QUESTION • *How do physical systems and human systems shape a place?*

Why Geography Matters
Economic Geography: Uneven Development

Lesson 1
Physical Geography of South America

Lesson 2
Human Geography of South America

Lesson 3
People and Their Environment: South America

Geography Matters...

South America is a land of beautiful natural wonders, including the vast Amazon rain forest. However, not all of South America is a lush jungle paradise. The region also includes snow-covered mountains and boasts the world's driest place—the Atacama Desert.

South America is diverse in culture as well as in landscape. The people of this subregion reflect a unique blend of indigenous and colonial heritage, the result of centuries of migration, trade, and conquest.

◀ Carnival in Brazil is held over five days preceding Lent, with parades featuring elaborate floats, drummers, and dancers.

215

Letter from the Author

Dear Geography Teacher,

There are two massive physical features that dominate South America—The Andes Mountains and the Amazon River basin. The Andes Mountains stretch more than 5,000 miles from Venezuela to the island of Tierra del Fuego, across the Straits of Magellan from Argentina and Chile. The Andes give us a chance to see the inner workings of vertical climate zones; Tierra caliente, Tierra templada, and Tierra fria. The other major physical feature is the Amazon River and its 3 million square mile drainage basin. The Amazon is the second largest river in the world and it carries 20% of the world's freshwater at any given time. These two giant physical features demonstrate how physical systems shape places and regions.

CHAPTER 9
South America

ENGAGE

Drawing Inferences Provide students with a recent news story about an incident in South America relating to the economy such as an article that describes a country's economic growth, advances in agricultural production, or a debt crisis. Challenge students to explain how this story relates to the geography of South America.

TEACH & ASSESS

Content Background Knowledge

Carnival Carnival is a festival that takes place in many countries with Roman Catholic citizens prior to the long Lenten period (40 days before Easter devoted to fasting, abstinence, and penitence). Carnival includes parades, masked balls, elaborate costumes, dancing, music, and other festivities. Perhaps the most well-known Carnival is celebrated each year in Rio de Janeiro. In the United States, the comparable celebration would be Mardi Gras celebrated in New Orleans.

Expressing Have students think of events that are celebrated each year in their community. **Ask:** How do such celebrations reflect what is important to a community? *(Celebrating a historic figure or event is a way of encouraging the values of a person or event. There are also local festivals celebrating the main product of the area, such as a tomato festival in a farming community.)* AL Interpersonal

Hypothesizing Invite volunteers to define diversity. **Ask:** Why might the diversity of landscape lead to diverse cultures? *(People interact with the geography where they live. The culture reflects the values that helped them survive.)* How would migration, trade, and conquest create unique blends of cultures? *(Possible answer: When people migrate, they adapt to the geography; When people trade, they learn about each other's cultures; When a civilization is conquered, people may be forced to give up parts of their culture, creating a blended culture.)* Verbal/Linguistic

CLOSE & REFLECT

Applying Have students read the table of contents and prepare a list of questions they expect to have answered as they study the chapter.

ePals GlobalCommunity
Where learners connect™

Extend the project-based learning experience globally through our partnership with ePals. EPals allows you to connect with classrooms around the world in a safe online environment for real-life lessons and projects in virtual study groups.

South America 215

Intervention and Remediation

Each Chapter Planner concludes with intervention and remediation strategies for every lesson, as well as Online Resources that can be used to help students understand the content.

Author Letter

Each chapter begins with the author's perspective about key concepts found in the chapter.

Introduce the Chapter

Each chapter begins with activities to engage students' interest in the chapter's content.

Don't forget! You can customize all your Lesson Plans online.

Why Geography Matters

These two pages of the Chapter Opener are designed to help students locate the region in the world that they will learn about, along with important issues that are taking place in that region.

The Teacher Edition contains activities and discussion questions for these features.

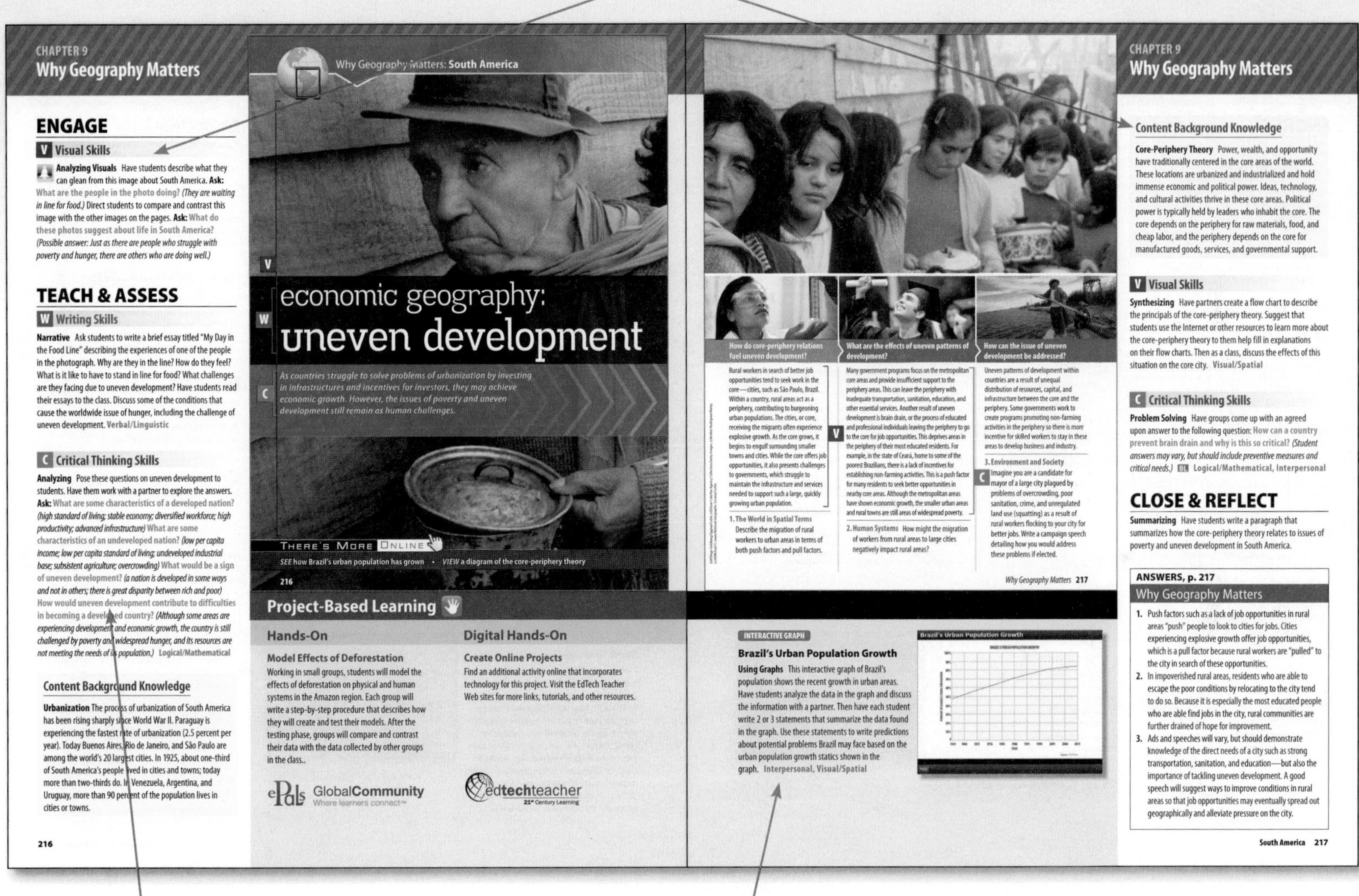

CHAPTER 9
Why Geography Matters

ENGAGE

V Visual Skills

Analyzing Visuals Have students describe what they can glean from this image about South America. **Ask:** What are the people in the photo doing? *(They are waiting in line for food.)* Direct students to compare and contrast this image with the other images on the pages. **Ask:** What do these photos suggest about life in South America? *(Possible answer: Just as there are people who struggle with poverty and hunger, there are others who are doing well.)*

TEACH & ASSESS

W Writing Skills

Narrative Ask students to write a brief essay titled "My Day in the Food Line" describing the experiences of one of the people in the photograph. Why are they in the line? How do they feel? What is it like to have to stand in line for food? What challenges are they facing due to uneven development? Have students read their essays to the class. Discuss some of the conditions that cause the worldwide issue of hunger, including the challenge of uneven development. Verbal/Linguistic

C Critical Thinking Skills

Analyzing Pose these questions on uneven development to students. Have them work with a partner to explore the answers. **Ask:** What are some characteristics of a developed nation? *(high standard of living; stable economy; diversified workforce; high productivity; advanced infrastructure)* What are some characteristics of an undeveloped nation? *(low per capita income; low per capita standard of living; undeveloped industrial base; subsistent agriculture; overcrowding)* What would be a sign of uneven development? *(a nation is developed in some ways and not in others; there is great disparity between rich and poor)* How would uneven development contribute to difficulties in becoming a developed country? *(Although some areas are experiencing development and economic growth, the country is still challenged by poverty and widespread hunger, and its resources are not meeting the needs of its population.)* Logical/Mathematical

Content Background Knowledge

Urbanization The process of urbanization of South America has been rising sharply since World War II. Paraguay is experiencing the fastest rate of urbanization (2.5 percent per year). Today Buenos Aires, Rio de Janeiro, and São Paulo are among the world's 20 largest cities. In 1925, about one-third of South America's people lived in cities and towns; today more than two-thirds do. In Venezuela, Argentina, and Uruguay, more than 90 percent of the population lives in cities or towns.

216

Why Geography Matters: South America

economic geography: uneven development

As countries struggle to solve problems of urbanization by investing in infrastructures and incentives for investors, they may achieve economic growth. However, the issues of poverty and uneven development still remain as human challenges.

THERE'S MORE ONLINE

SEE how Brazil's urban population has grown • *VIEW* a diagram of the core-periphery theory

216

Project-Based Learning

Hands-On

Model Effects of Deforestation

Working in small groups, students will model the effects of deforestation on physical and human systems in the Amazon region. Each group will write a step-by-step procedure that describes how they will create and test their models. After the testing phase, groups will compare and contrast their data with the data collected by other groups in the class..

ePals GlobalCommunity Where learners connect™

Digital Hands-On

Create Online Projects

Find an additional activity online that incorporates technology for this project. Visit the EdTech Teacher Web sites for more links, tutorials, and other resources.

edtechteacher 21st Century Learning

How do core-periphery relations fuel uneven development?

Rural workers in search of better job opportunities tend to seek work in the core—cities, such as São Paulo, Brazil. Within a country, rural areas act as a periphery, contributing to burgeoning urban populations. The cities, or core, receiving the migrants often experience explosive growth. As the core grows, it begins to engulf surrounding smaller towns and cities. While the core offers job opportunities, it also presents challenges to governments, which struggle to maintain the infrastructure and services needed to support such a large, quickly growing urban population.

1. The World in Spatial Terms Describe the migration of rural workers to urban areas in terms of both push factors and pull factors.

What are the effects of uneven patterns of development?

Many government programs focus on the metropolitan core areas and provide insufficient support to the periphery areas. This can leave the periphery with inadequate transportation, sanitation, education, and other essential services. Another result of uneven development is brain drain, or the process of educated and professional individuals leaving the periphery to go to the core for job opportunities. This deprives areas in the periphery of their most educated residents. For example, in the state of Ceará, home to some of the poorest Brazilians, there is a lack of incentives for establishing non-farming activities. This is a push factor for many residents to seek better opportunities in nearby core areas. Although the metropolitan areas have shown economic growth, the smaller urban areas and rural towns are still areas of widespread poverty.

2. Human Systems How might the migration of workers from rural areas to large cities negatively impact rural areas?

How can the issue of uneven development be addressed?

Uneven patterns of development within countries are a result of unequal distribution of resources, capital, and infrastructure between the core and the periphery. Some governments work to create programs promoting non-farming activities in the periphery so there is more incentive for skilled workers to stay in these areas to develop business and industry.

3. Environment and Society Imagine you are a candidate for mayor of a large city plagued by problems of overcrowding, poor sanitation, crime, and unregulated land use (squatting) as a result of rural workers flocking to your city for better jobs. Write a campaign speech detailing how you would address these problems if elected.

Why Geography Matters 217

INTERACTIVE GRAPH

Brazil's Urban Population Growth

Using Graphs This interactive graph of Brazil's population shows the recent growth in urban areas. Have students analyze the data in the graph and discuss the information with a partner. Then have each student write 2 or 3 statements that summarize the data found in the graph. Use these statements to write predictions about potential problems Brazil may face based on the urban population growth statics shown in the graph. Interpersonal, Visual/Spatial

Brazil's Urban Population Growth

CHAPTER 9
Why Geography Matters

Content Background Knowledge

Core-Periphery Theory Power, wealth, and opportunity have traditionally centered in the core areas of the world. These locations are urbanized and industrialized and hold immense economic and political power. Ideas, technology, and cultural activities thrive in these core areas. Political power is typically held by leaders who inhabit the core. The core depends on the periphery for raw materials, food, and cheap labor, and the periphery depends on the core for manufactured goods, services, and governmental support.

V Visual Skills

Synthesizing Have partners create a flow chart to describe the principals of the core-periphery theory. Suggest that students use the Internet or other resources to learn more about the core-periphery theory to them help fill in explanations on their flow charts. Then as a class, discuss the effects of this situation on the core city. Visual/Spatial

C Critical Thinking Skills

Problem Solving Have groups come up with an agreed upon answer to the following question: How can a country prevent brain drain and why is this so critical? *(Student answers may vary, but should include preventive measures and critical needs.)* BL Logical/Mathematical, Interpersonal

CLOSE & REFLECT

Summarizing Have students write a paragraph that summarizes how the core-periphery theory relates to issues of poverty and uneven development in South America.

ANSWERS, p. 217

Why Geography Matters

1. Push factors such as a lack of job opportunities in rural areas "push" people to look to cities for jobs. Cities experiencing explosive growth offer job opportunities, which is a pull factor because rural workers are "pulled" to the city in search of these opportunities.
2. In impoverished rural areas, residents who are able to escape the poor conditions by relocating to the city tend to do so. Because it is especially the most educated people who are able find jobs in the city, rural communities are further drained of hope for improvement.
3. Ads and speeches will vary, but should demonstrate knowledge of the direct needs of a city such as strong transportation, sanitation, and education—but also the importance of tackling uneven development. A good speech will suggest ways to improve conditions in rural areas so that job opportunities may eventually spread out geographically and alleviate pressure on the city.

South America 217

Print-Based Activities

Activities in the margins correspond to the text in the Student Edition. These activities are coded to indicate their level and the learning style they support.

Online Digital Activities

Online digital activities for the lesson appear at the bottom of each page. The gray icon indicates the type of activity available in the online Teacher Center. Activities include interactive whiteboard activities, animations, videos, interactive maps, images, and worksheets. Activities can be projected or used on your classroom whiteboard. Worksheets can be edited and printed, or assigned online, depending on student access to technology.

Using the Wraparound Resources and Activities *(continued)*

ENGAGE

Every lesson begins with an Engage activity designed to motivate students and focus their attention on the lesson topic.

Guiding Questions

Guiding Questions in the Student Edition point out key knowledge that students need to acquire to be able to answer the chapter's Essential Question.

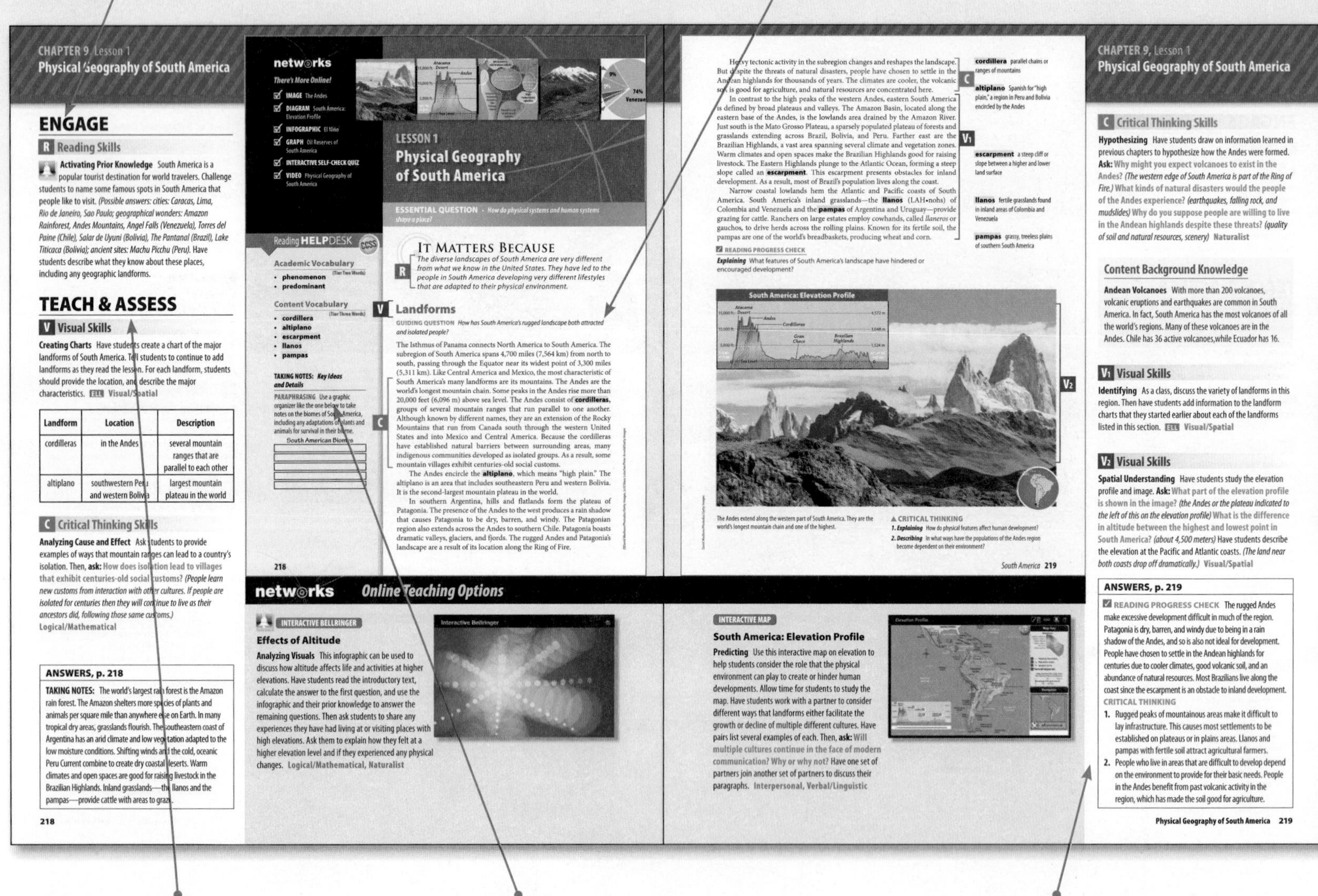

TEACH & ASSESS

Teach & Assess is the core of the lesson. It contains activities, lecture notes, background information, and discussion questions to teach the lesson.

Reading Help Desk

- Academic Vocabulary
- Content Vocabulary
- Note-Taking Activity and Graphic Organizer

Answers

Answers to questions and activities in the Student Edition appear in the bottom corner of the Teacher Edition pages.

Don't forget! You can customize all your Lesson Plans online.

Brackets

Brackets on the reduced Student Edition page correspond to teaching strategies and activities in the Teacher Edition. As you teach the lesson, the brackets show you where to use these activities and strategies.

Reading Progress Check

A Reading Progress Check appears at the end of each topic in the Student Edition to help gauge student reading comprehension.

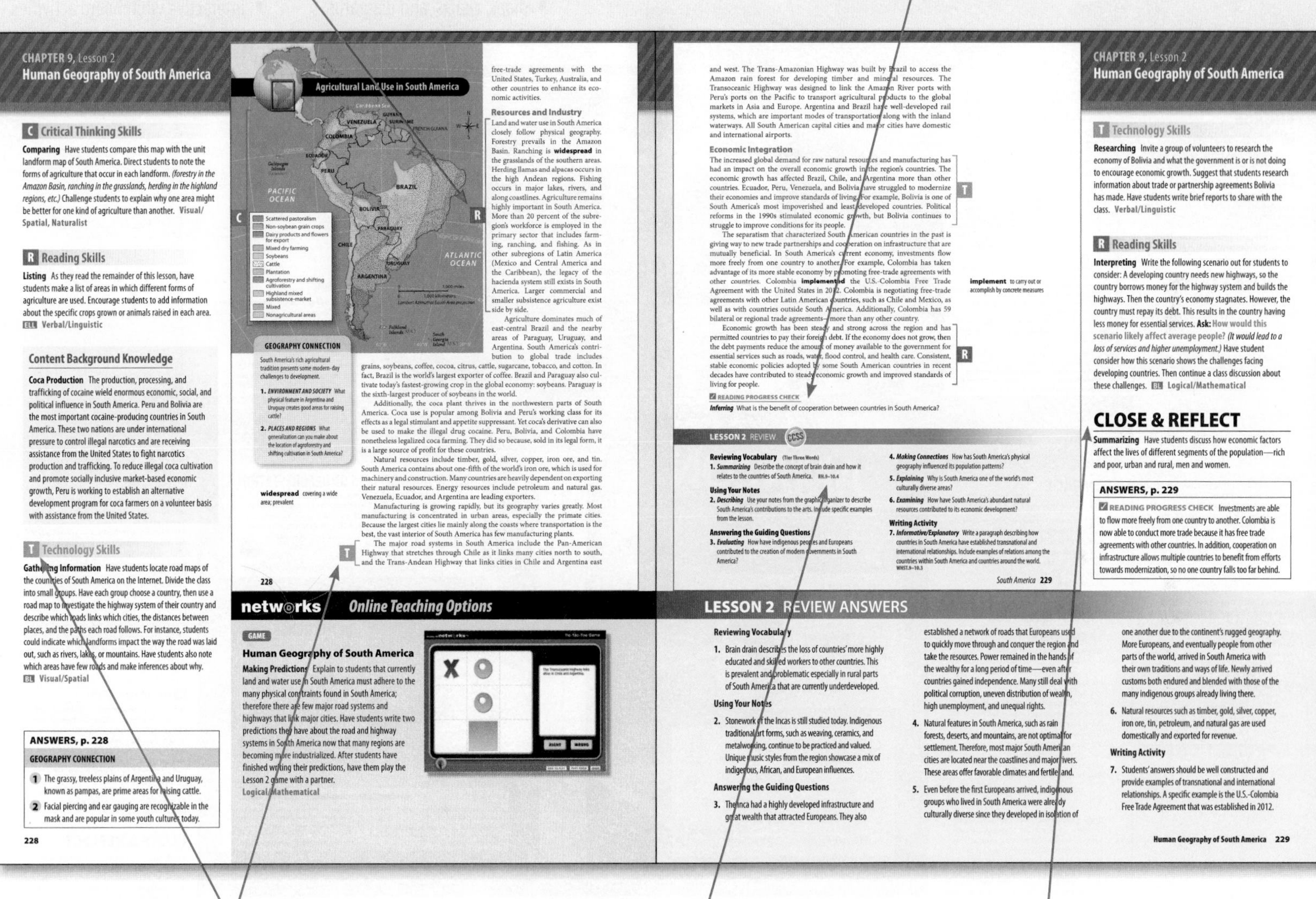

Letters

The letters on the reduced Student Edition page identify the type of activity. See the key on the first planning page of each chapter to learn about the different types of activities.

Common Core State Standards

Questions and activities throughout the Student Edition are correlated to the Reading Standards for Literacy in History/ Social Studies 9-10 (RH.9-10) and the Writing Standards for Literacy in History/ Social Studies 9-10 (WHST.9-10).

CLOSE & REFLECT

Each lesson ends with activities designed to help students link the content to the lesson's Guiding Questions and the chapter's Essential Question.

Special Features

Case Studies

Case Studies help students investigate a specific issue in a place or region by exploring two different sides or opposing viewpoints.

Dynamic photos enrich the study of the content.

Global Connections

Global Connections are provided for each unit. Each Global Connections feature focuses on an event or topic that affects the world community. The online Global Connections includes numerous interactive digital assets to enrich your teaching. Digital assets include:

- animations
- photos
- maps, charts, and diagrams
- videos
- worksheets
- interactive whiteboard activities

Fun and interesting statistics and facts are listed in a magazine-like format.

Maps, graphs, charts, and diagrams are engaging and student-friendly.

Questions assess students' understanding of the information in the feature.

Don't forget! You can customize all your Lesson Plans online.

Activities and Assessment

Chapter Assessment

Each chapter ends with a chapter assessment that includes the following:

- Applying Map Skills
- Lesson Review
- 21st Century Skills
- Exploring the Essential Question
- College and Career Readiness
- Critical Thinking Questions
- Document-Based Questions and Writing Activities

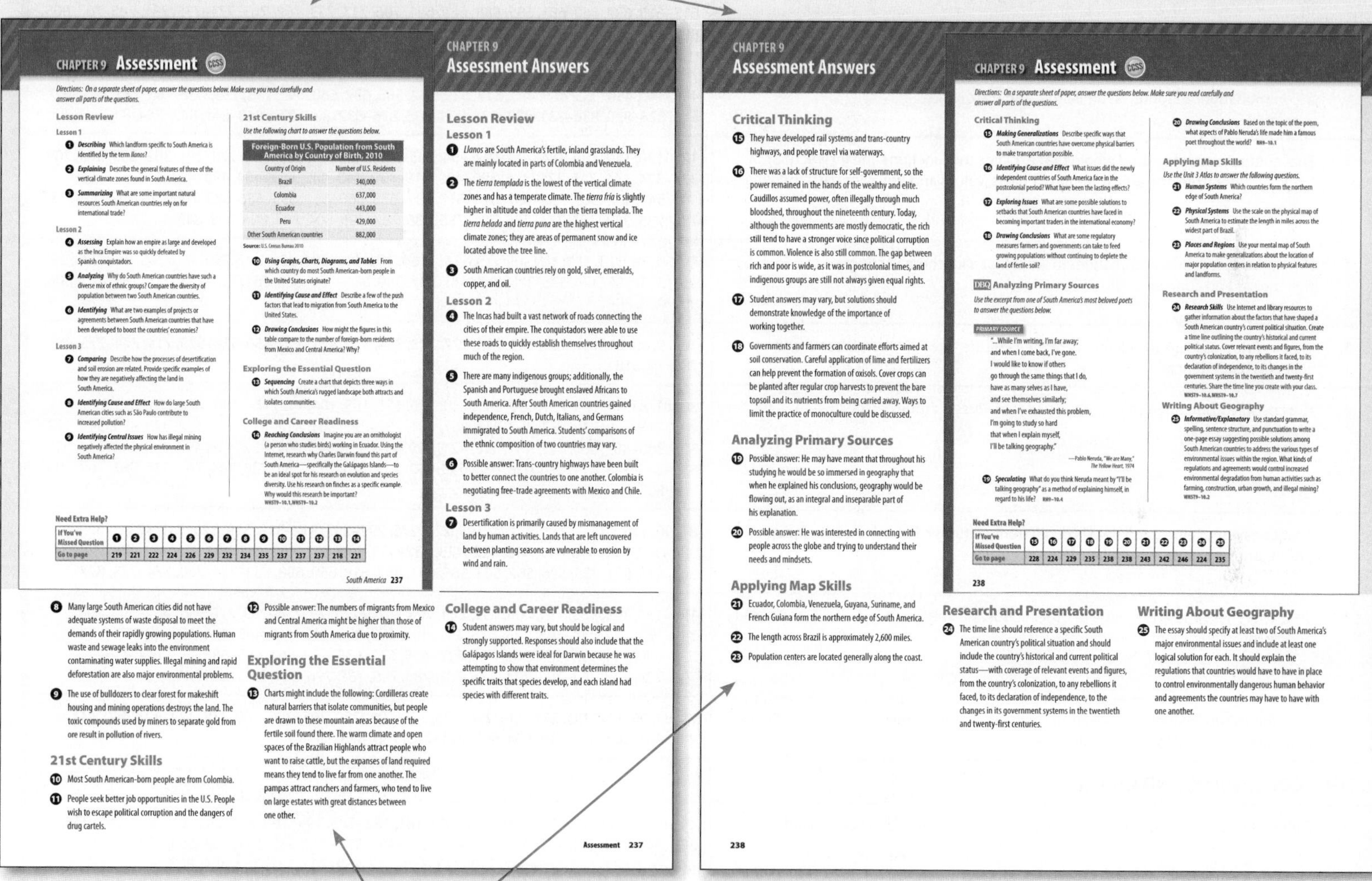

Answers

Answers to the chapter activities and assessment questions.

Online Assessment Options

Digital assessment opportunities are available for every chapter.

Correlation of *Geography: The Human and Physical World* to the Revised NCSS Thematic Strands

The revised National Council for the Social Studies Standards continue to be focused on ten themes, like the original standards. They represent a way of categorizing knowledge about the human experience, and they constitute the organizing strands that should thread through a social studies program.

NCSS Theme and Learning Expectation	Student Edition
1. CULTURE	
1. "Culture" refers to the socially transmitted behaviors, beliefs, values, traditions, institutions, and ways of living together of a group of people;	78–79, 81, 107, 119, 129, 149, 153, 166, 183, 191, 193, 203, 214, 240, 279, 281, 303, 304, 322, 374, 377, 395, 399, 407, 409, 410, 411, 416, 418, 440, 450, 463, 465, 493, 514, 539, 562, 586, 587, 607, 613–615, 637, 660, 681, 685, 688–689, 691, 706, 713, 733, 762–763, 774–775, 781, 785, 787, 805, 807, 808, 828–829, 830–831, 832–833, 834–835, 836–837, 838–839, 840–841, 842–844, 845
2. Concepts such as: beliefs, values, mores, institutions, cohesion, diversity, accommodation, adaption, assimilation, and dissonance;	78–79, 80–81, 83, 107, 119, 129, 149, 152, 182, 195, 203, 259, 279, 281, 303, 377, 395, 407, 411, 416, 440, 450, 463, 465, 493, 514, 539, 562, 586, 637, 660, 691, 713, 733, 762–763, 787, 805, 807, 808, 828–829, 830–831, 832–833, 834–835, 836–837, 838–839, 840–841, 842–844, 845
3. That culture is an integrated whole that explains the functions and interactions of language, literature, the arts, traditions, beliefs, values and behavior patterns;	129–130, 149, 180, 184, 203, 192, 204, 205, 213, 227, 229, 258–259, 279, 291, 302–303, 304, 309, 323–324, 344–345, 375–376, 399–400, 419–420, 440–442, 463–464, 493–494, 514–517, 539–540, 541, 562–563, 586–587, 613–615, 637–638, 660–661, 685–686, 689, 706, 713, 714, 716, 733, 734–735, 762–763, 774–775, 781, 785, 786, 787, 796, 804, 807, 808, 809, 845
4. How culture develops and changes in ways that allow human societies to address their needs and concerns;	79, 80–81, 119, 129, 149, 151, 153, 155, 164, 174, 191, 204, 226, 227, 256, 260, 265, 266, 276, 293, 320, 323, 355, 374, 376, 385, 394, 411, 537, 540, 586–587, 660, 661, 712–713, 714, 786, 805, 806, 807, 808, 809
5. That individuals learn the elements of their culture through interpersonal and collective experience;	78, 79, 80–81, 107, 153, 203, 214, 227, 303, 304, 322, 421, 440, 450, 528–529, 714, 774–775, 781, 783, 79, 818
6. How people from different cultures develop diverse cultural perspectives and frames of reference;	80–81, 83, 90, 129, 131, 139, 142, 149, 150, 151, 155, 164, 173, 174, 180, 181, 183, 186, 193, 195, 203, 215, 226, 229, 237, 257, 258, 267, 281, 292–293, 301, 312–313, 320, 322, 323, 325, 344, 373, 375, 388–389, 400, 401, 407, 418, 421, 429, 432–433, 440, 441, 452–453, 492, 493, 513, 514, 517, 542–543, 586, 611, 634, 636, 638, 657, 662, 723, 725, 733–734, 736, 744, 762, 736, 782, 768, 795, 804, 805
7. That behaviors, values, and beliefs of different cultures can lead to cooperation or pose barriers to cross-cultural understanding;	81, 90, 126, 142, 151, 152, 194–195, 226, 275, 292–293, 312–313, 319, 320, 321, 323, 373, 388–389, 396–398, 411, 418, 422–423, 432–433, 452–453, 462, 463, 483, 485, 491, 492, 495, 502, 513, 521, 525, 526, 562, 563, 565, 651, 657, 658, 659, 688, 733–734, 760, 774–775, 827
8. That awareness and knowledge of other cultures is important in a connected society and an interdependent world;	129–130, 149, 180, 184, 203, 192, 204, 205, 213, 227, 229, 258–259, 279, 291, 302–303, 304, 309, 323–324, 344–345, 375–376, 399–400, 419–420, 440–442, 463–464, 493–494, 514–517, 539–540, 541, 562–563, 586–587, 613–615, 637–638, 660–661, 685–686, 713, 714, 716, 733–734, 735, 762–763, 774–775, 781, 785, 786, 787, 796, 804, 807, 809, 845
9. That the cultural values and beliefs of societies influence their analysis of challenges, and their responses to these challenges.	78, 81, 90, 142, 205, 275, 276, 290, 323, 355, 388–389, 395–396, 409, 418, 422–423, 440, 441, 443, 461, 562–563, 614, 664, 691, 774–775, 786, 826
2. TIME, CONTINUITY, AND CHANGE	
1. Different interpretations of the history of societies, cultures, and humankind;	41, 45, 46, 125–127, 139, 149–151, 180–181, 182–183, 194–195, 200–201, 223–224, 255, 276, 300, 341–343, 411, 422–423, 438–439, 459–461, 511–513, 535–537, 552–553, 582–583, 611–612, 657–658, 685–687, 710–712, 730–732, 759–761, 781–782, 804–805
2. Concepts such as: era, chronology, causality, change, continuity, conflict, historiography, historical method, primary and secondary sources, cause and effect, and multiple perspectives;	119, 125–127, 149–151, 155, 164, 180–181, 182–183, 194–195, 200–201, 213, 214, 223–224, 238, 255–256, 275–277, 299–300, 341–343, 372–374, 377, 411, 416–418, 422–423, 438–439, 459–461, 489–491, 505, 511–513, 525, 535–537, 542–543, 552–553, 559–561, 571, 581–585, 587, 611–612, 634–635, 640–641, 657–658, 685–687, 710–712, 725, 730–732, 740, 759–761, 781–782, 804–805, 823
3. That knowledge of the past is influenced by the questions investigated, the sources used, and the perspective of the historian;	126, 149, 150, 181, 183, 184, 186, 191, 201, 275–276, 302, 304, 372, 395, 401, 416, 418, 440, 460, 541, 550, 583, 611, 625, 657, 685, 691, 725, 782
4. Different interpretations of key historical periods and patterns of change within and across nations, cultures, and time periods (e.g., the history of democratic principles and institutions, the development of political and economic philosophies; the rise of modern nation-states, and the establishment and breakdown of colonial systems);	118–119, 127, 139, 149–151, 180–181, 182–183, 200–201, 224, 275–276, 299–300, 319–321, 373, 395–398, 438–439, 453, 459–461, 511–513, 525, 535–537, 541, 552–553, 559–561, 581–585, 611–612, 634–635, 658, 685–687, 710–712, 730–732, 759–761, 781–782, 804–805
5. The impact across time and place of key historical forces, such as nationalism, imperialism, globalization, leadership, revolution, wars, concepts of rights and responsibilities, and religion;	90–91, 126–127, 150–151, 181, 182–183, 201, 202–203, 224–225, 249, 256–257, 276–277, 299, 300–301, 320–321, 335, 342–343, 347, 373, 374–375, 378–379, 396–397, 398, 411, 418–419, 422–423, 440–441, 453, 460–461, 492–493, 512–513, 536–537, 541, 559–561, 582–583, 584–585, 614–615, 625, 636–637, 658–659, 686–687, 712–713, 732–733, 760–761, 784–785, 805, 806–807, 823

NCSS Theme and Learning Expectation	Student Edition
6. Different interpretations of the influences of social, geographic, economic, and cultural factors on the history of local areas, states, nations, and the world;	139, 223–224, 226, 229, 256, 275, 276, 299, 341–342, 373, 378–379, 401, 411, 429, 512, 525, 536–537, 541, 552–553, 559, 582–583, 611–612, 618–619, 657–658, 685–687, 710–712, 730–732, 759–761, 781–782, 785, 804–805
7. The contributions of philosophies, ideologies, individuals, institutions, and key events and turning points in shaping history;	126, 150, 194–195, 214, 275, 276, 281, 289, 299, 300, 302, 304, 342, 343, 347, 373, 378–379, 387, 422–423, 441, 459, 461, 475, 489, 490–491, 512, 525, 536–537, 541, 582–583, 612, 625, 685–686, 710–712, 716, 722, 725, 730, 731, 760–761, 785, 805
8. The importance of knowledge of the past to an understanding of the present and to informed decision-making about the future.	12, 31, 33, 35, 59, 108, 119, 126, 131, 149, 150, 191, 193, 195, 200, 201, 202, 206–207, 213, 214, 223, 224, 227, 231, 237, 238, 255, 256, 260, 265, 275, 276, 299, 300, 302, 304, 308, 309, 311, 312–313, 319, 320, 321, 341, 342, 355, 372, 373, 374, 395, 396, 397, 401, 416, 417, 418, 419, 421, 429, 438, 439, 447, 450, 453, 459, 460, 489, 500, 501, 511, 521, 525, 526, 535, 536, 537, 550, 553, 559, 560, 571, 581–582, 583, 611, 613, 625, 626, 633, 634, 635, 636–637, 639, 657, 658, 685, 686, 687, 691, 694, 698, 702, 710, 711, 712, 720, 730, 731, 740, 741, 759, 760, 761, 771, 781, 782, 806–807, 823, 825
3. PEOPLE, PLACES, AND ENVIRONMENTS	
1. The theme of people, places, and environments involves the study of the relationships between human populations in different locations and regional and global geographic phenomena, such as landforms, soils, climate, vegetation, and natural resources;	7, 86, 102, 103, 104, 105, 106, 107, 127, 125, 128, 129, 132–133, 139, 142–143, 150, 151, 153, 163, 171, 172, 173, 174, 177, 179, 180, 181, 182, 188, 189, 196, 201, 202, 210, 211, 213, 216, 219, 222, 225, 234, 235, 237, 240, 245, 246, 249, 257, 258, 271, 272, 289, 297, 298, 302, 304, 309, 315, 316, 317, 322, 337, 355, 361, 364, 368, 369, 371, 385, 419, 439, 440, 442, 443, 457, 462, 464, 477, 480, 485, 488, 492, 497, 509, 510, 514, 534, 538, 539, 549, 550, 551, 555, 581, 585, 586, 599, 601, 613, 621, 633, 636, 651, 653, 659, 668, 670, 672, 681, 684, 688, 712, 718, 721, 727, 729, 732, 733, 741, 746, 750, 756, 757, 758, 780, 783, 784, 802, 802, 803, 804, 805, 806
2. Concepts such as: location, physical and human characteristics of national and global regions in the past and present, and the interactions of humans with the environment;	3, 5, 7, 9, 10, 31, 33, 34, 35, 66, 67, 72, 73, 105, 106, 107, 108, 124, 125, 129, 132–133, 135–137, 138, 139, 140, 142, 146, 148, 159, 160, 161, 163, 168, 171, 172, 173, 174, 177, 179, 180, 188, 189, 190, 192, 209, 210, 211, 230–231, 234, 236, 237, 240, 242, 263–264, 265, 266, 271, 272, 274, 285–286, 288, 289, 290, 296, 306, 307, 308, 309, 316, 318, 327–328, 330, 331, 349, 351–353, 355, 358, 364, 367, 369, 382–383, 384, 385, 404–405, 407, 425–427, 439, 446–447, 448, 456, 458, 462, 464, 467, 468–469, 474, 477, 485, 486, 488, 495, 497, 498, 500, 501, 522–523, 532, 533, 545–546, 550, 567–569, 571, 589–590, 596, 621–623, 626, 632, 644–645, 647, 648, 655, 656, 664–665, 666, 667, 670, 682, 684, 695, 697, 700, 718–719, 729, 738–739, 740, 744, 768, 769–770, 791–792, 801, 805, 813–814, 815, 816, 817
3. Consequences of changes in regional and global physical systems, such as seasons, climate, and weather, and the water cycle;	51, 52, 54, 55, 57, 58–59, 63, 66, 67, 69, 70, 71, 72, 73, 122–124, 135, 136, 146, 147, 148, 159, 161, 162, 163, 164, 178, 179, 187, 188, 189, 190, 209, 210, 221, 222, 230–231, 232, 233, 234, 235, 245, 253, 261, 262, 263, 264, 270, 273, 284, 285, 286, 297, 298, 305, 306, 307, 308, 317, 318, 326, 332, 339, 340, 355, 370, 371, 382, 383, 384, 393, 394, 402, 415, 424, 425, 426, 427, 428, 429, 436, 437, 445, 446, 468, 469, 471, 479, 488, 496, 497, 501, 509, 510, 522, 523, 524, 525, 532, 534, 538, 546, 549, 550, 567, 569, 578, 579, 580, 608, 610, 621, 624, 625, 633, 643, 644, 646, 655, 664, 665, 675, 682, 683, 696, 706, 707, 718, 728, 739, 758, 766, 767, 769, 770, 780, 790, 791, 792, 796, 803, 813, 814, 815, 816, 817
4. The causes and impact of resource management, as reflected in land use, settlement patterns, and ecosystem changes;	103, 132–133, 134–135, 136–137, 142, 148, 158–160, 164, 187–189, 208–210, 228, 230–231, 232–234, 236, 261–262, 284–285, 286–288, 305–306, 308, 309, 326–327, 350–351, 380–381, 402–403, 424–425, 444–446, 457, 466–467, 496, 520–521, 524, 544–545, 566–567, 570, 588–589, 620–621, 642–644, 663–664, 694, 717, 737–738, 766–768, 770, 790–791, 812–813
5. The cultural diffusion of customs and ideas:	81, 82, 107, 129, 130, 131, 184, 226, 299, 300, 375, 376, 396, 416, 441, 459, 482–483, 485, 514–515, 517, 535, 540, 562, 581, 586, 634, 657, 660, 671, 685, 686, 689, 691, 730, 807, 827
6. The social and economic effects of environmental changes and crises resulting from phenomena such as floods, storms, and drought;	38–39, 59, 66, 67, 122–123, 132–133, 137, 139, 187, 199, 206, 212, 220, 221, 248, 272, 273, 404, 445, 481, 486, 492–493, 499, 500, 501, 502, 513, 517, 522, 546, 589, 609, 628–629, 632, 633, 654, 662, 682, 684, 695–696, 698, 704, 706, 708–709, 755, 757, 814
7. Factors that contribute to cooperation and conflict among peoples of the nation and world, including language, religion, and political beliefs;	30, 33, 91, 151, 153, 163, 191, 203, 213, 226, 227, 258, 259, 260, 266, 276, 277, 279, 300, 302, 319, 320, 321, 322, 327, 344, 374, 377, 388, 395, 396, 397, 398, 399, 401, 411, 418, 419, 420, 421, 422–423, 430, 441, 453, 459, 462, 490–491, 494, 502, 528–529, 536–537, 553, 562, 563, 585, 586, 611, 613, 617, 635, 636, 637, 648, 660, 688, 691, 725, 732, 771, 826, 827, 828–829, 830–831, 832–833, 834–835, 836–837, 838–839, 840–841, 842–844, 845
8. The use of a variety of maps, globes, graphic representations, and geospatial technologies to help investigate spatial relations, resources, and population density and distribution, and changes in these phenomena over time.	2–3, 4–5, 6–7, 8–9, 10, 12, 13, 15, 16, 17, 19, 20, 21, 22, 23, 24, 25, 26, 27, 28, 29, 34, 35, 41, 46, 47, 53, 65, 67, 70, 76, 79, 80, 100–101, 112, 113, 114, 115, 116, 118, 122, 123, 128, 130, 135, 136, 140, 145, 146, 163, 168, 169, 170, 171, 172, 185, 188, 194, 197, 214, 226, 228, 238, 242, 243, 244, 245, 246, 263, 278, 280, 286, 290, 292, 306, 310, 312, 315, 316, 322, 332, 351, 352, 360, 361, 362, 363, 364, 370, 373, 386, 389, 393, 408, 410, 413, 417, 425, 430, 435, 450, 452, 462, 468, 472, 476, 477, 478, 479, 480, 485, 490, 497, 498, 502, 507, 526, 550, 552, 555, 560, 571, 574, 582, 598, 599, 600, 601, 602, 608, 626, 631, 640–641, 648, 650, 672, 673, 674, 675, 676, 681, 683, 705, 718, 722, 727, 746, 747, 748, 749, 750, 755, 772, 783, 788, 796, 798, 813, 818, 820–821, 826, 827

NCSS Theme and Learning Expectation	Student Edition
4. INDIVIDUAL DEVELOPMENT AND IDENTITY	
1. The theme of individual development and identity helps us know about different theories explaining individual development and identity;	78, 94, 129, 131, 183, 191, 276, 805
2. Concepts drawn from the behavioral sciences of psychology, sociology, and anthropology, such as: identity, development, personality, motivation, perception, and group membership;	33–34, 35, 92–93, 191, 422–423, 438, 515, 540, 689, 692–693, 706, 780, 805
3. Factors, both genetic and environmental, that contribute to individual development and identity;	94, 151, 153, 183, 191, 203, 226, 279, 420, 438, 523, 528–529, 660, 681
4. That complex and varied interactions among individuals, groups, cultures, and nations contribute to the dynamic nature of personal identity;	79, 151, 152, 157, 183, 203, 213, 224, 278, 293, 301, 376, 400, 420, 438, 463, 528–529, 615, 805
5. The variety of factors that contribute to and harm the mental health of individuals;	129, 151, 183, 201, 213, 224, 227, 259, 279, 293, 342, 376, 399, 400, 419, 433, 463, 493, 494, 515, 528–529, 567, 586, 637, 689, 713, 742, 763, 785
6. That each individual has personal connections to time and place.	91, 119, 127, 131, 152, 157, 180, 183, 191, 192, 203, 205, 226, 257, 258, 260, 266, 300, 313, 342, 373, 374, 388, 399, 408, 425, 430, 440, 441, 449, 450, 453, 459, 489, 607, 617, 626, 636, 660, 695, 716, 722, 725, 729, 762, 774, 775, 780, 785, 804
5. INDIVIDUALS, GROUPS, AND INSTITUTIONS	
1. This theme helps us use sociological and anthropological theories about how individuals are members of groups and institutions, and how they influence and shape those groups and institutions;	79, 92, 119, 129, 151, 152, 182, 184, 186, 194–195, 213, 259, 260, 287, 307, 344, 385, 450, 452–453, 465, 494, 495, 514, 540, 706, 780, 804, 807
2. Concepts such as: mores, norms, ritual, status, role, socialization, ethnocentrism, cultural diffusion, competition, cooperation, conflict, assimilation, race, ethnicity, and gender;	78, 81, 82, 92, 107, 119, 128, 129, 130, 131, 151, 152, 153, 154, 155, 184, 195, 213, 224, 226, 256, 259, 260, 279, 299, 300, 303, 320, 321, 323, 344, 374, 375, 376, 396–398, 399, 400, 407, 409, 416, 418, 420, 438, 442, 452–453, 459, 463, 471, 482–483, 485, 494, 514, 515, 516, 517, 521, 528–529, 535, 540, 562, 563, 581, 586, 634, 637, 657, 658–659, 660, 661, 671, 685, 688, 689, 690, 691, 712, 714, 730, 734, 763, 775, 804, 807, 808, 827
3. The influence of individuals, groups, and institutions on people and events in historical and contemporary settings;	90–91, 119, 125–126, 132–133, 137, 138, 139, 142, 143, 149, 150, 151, 180–181, 182, 183, 184, 185, 186, 194–195, 201, 224, 256, 260, 264, 265, 287, 292–293, 307, 308, 319, 320, 321, 322, 323, 325, 328, 329, 332, 342, 347, 372–373, 374, 395–398, 399, 405, 406, 407, 408, 416–417, 422–423, 428, 433, 441, 448, 460, 461, 465, 495, 513, 514, 521, 525, 526, 547, 548, 553, 559–561, 566–567, 572, 599, 611, 618–619, 640–641, 657, 659, 660, 661, 671, 685, 686, 690, 760–761, 774–775, 804, 806–807
4. How the various forms of groups and institutions change over time;	80–81, 92, 126, 149, 181, 182, 257, 265, 293, 320, 343, 460, 515, 516, 538, 540, 559, 611, 689, 690, 714, 774–775, 786, 804, 806, 808
5. The impact of tensions and examples of cooperation between individuals, groups, and institutions, with their different belief systems;	90, 119, 126, 127, 142, 149, 150, 151, 181, 201, 213, 287, 292–293, 308, 321, 328, 329, 343, 344, 350, 351, 373, 374, 385, 388–389, 396–398, 408, 417, 422–423, 433, 460–461, 482–483, 513, 553, 618–619, 658, 659, 660, 691, 760–761, 775, 782, 786
6. How the beliefs of dominant groups tend to become norms in a society;	119, 126, 180–181, 182, 185, 195, 201, 224, 320, 342, 344, 345, 373, 417, 419, 422–423, 442, 461, 482–483, 513, 521, 560, 635, 659, 688, 689, 692–693, 730, 742, 761, 775, 782, 786, 796
7. How in democratic societies, legal protections are designed to protect the rights and beliefs of minority groups;	86, 89, 142, 164, 260, 603, 614–615, 775, 786
8. How groups and institutions work to meet individual needs, and can promote the common good and address persistent social issues.	86, 265, 287, 308, 327, 345, 354, 378–379, 400, 405, 406, 407, 408, 420, 433, 470, 547, 548, 584, 612, 615, 690, 691, 775, 782, 785, 786
6. POWER, AUTHORITY, AND GOVERNANCE	
1. The need for respect for the rule of law, as well as a recognition of times when civil disobedience has been justified;	87, 286, 299, 378–379, 400, 612
2. Fundamental principles of American constitutional democracy (including those of the U.S. Constitution, popular sovereignty, the rule of law, separation of powers, checks and balances, minority rights, the separation of church and state, and Federalism);	13, 88, 89
3. Fundamental values of constitutional democracy (e.g., the common good, liberty, justice, equality, and individual dignity);	12–13, 86, 591, 623, 626, 661
4. The ideologies, political cultures, structures, institutions, and processes of political systems that differ from those of the United States, and compare these with the political system of the United States;	87, 88, 89, 91, 107, 150, 181, 201, 238, 256, 310, 342–343, 374, 398, 439, 443, 460, 465, 513, 521, 526, 553, 561, 584, 635, 658, 662, 686, 687, 711–712, 731, 735, 761, 782, 805, 809

NCSS Theme and Learning Expectation	Student Edition
5. Mechanisms by which governments meet the needs and wants of citizens, regulate territory, manage conflict, establish order and security, and balance competing conceptions of a just society;	12–13, 79, 80–81, 89, 90, 91, 138, 150, 151, 152, 153, 154, 162, 164, 174, 188, 211, 212, 235, 256, 259, 265, 279, 302, 307, 308, 334, 394, 463, 470, 516, 548, 575, 591, 603, 604, 623, 624, 625, 636, 646, 660, 661, 666, 688, 690, 697, 720, 770, 775
6. Ideas, theories, and modes of inquiry drawn from political science.	13, 91, 384, 618–619, 810–811
7. PRODUCTION, DISTRIBUTION, AND CONSUMPTION	
1. Scarcity and the uneven distribution of resources result in economic decisions, and foster consequences that may support cooperation or conflict;	38–39, 96, 98, 100–101, 107, 132–133, 142, 143, 148, 150, 154, 184, 205, 213, 216–217, 222, 224, 227, 237, 254, 260, 274, 298, 304, 340, 346, 371, 384, 394, 400, 401, 407, 415, 417, 436, 437, 443, 444, 448, 458, 465, 467, 488, 495, 510, 534, 541, 548, 580, 589, 593, 656, 662, 684, 707, 735–736, 753, 758, 780, 809
2. The causes and effects of inflation;	347
3. That regulations and laws (for example, on property rights and contract enforcement) affect incentives for people to produce and exchange goods and services;	130, 142, 143, 205, 227, 346, 735–736, 764, 770
4. Entrepreneurial decisions are influenced by factors such as supply and demand, government regulatory policy, and the economic climate;	185, 516, 529, 540, 549, 565, 587, 636, 763
5. The roles of institutions that are designed to support and regulate the economy (e.g., the Federal Reserve, and the World Bank);	91, 131, 280, 384, 467, 516, 521, 529, 645, 765
6. How factors such as changes in the market, levels of competition, and the rate of employment, cause changes in prices of goods and services;	191, 282, 346, 371, 377, 407, 421, 471, 505, 716
8. How markets fail, and the government response to these failures;	96, 131, 139, 282–283, 304, 322, 325
9. Various measures of national economic health (e.g., GNP, GDP, and the unemployment rate).	76–77, 97, 98, 99, 130, 131, 154, 155, 174, 185, 206, 249, 265, 277, 300, 304, 309, 346, 401, 439, 447, 494, 504, 564, 567, 617, 639, 662, 753, 771, 787
8. SCIENCE, TECHNOLOGY, AND SOCIETY	
1. Science is based upon the empirical study of the natural world and technology is the application of knowledge to accomplish tasks;	11, 21–25, 36, 39, 53–54, 72, 77, 81, 124, 127, 131, 148, 155, 163, 189, 205, 212, 268–269, 272, 276, 280, 330, 355, 380–381, 384, 394, 403, 406, 417, 436, 447, 448, 486, 487, 499, 500, 505, 517, 518–519, 532, 533, 547, 590, 617, 678, 679, 682, 717, 722, 736, 770, 814
2. Science and technology have had both positive and negative impacts upon individuals, societies, and the environment in the past and present;	39, 53, 54, 59, 72, 135, 136, 137, 138, 139, 140, 148, 160, 162, 163, 179, 189, 198, 208, 209, 211, 236, 252–253, 261, 262, 263, 264, 272, 286, 307, 327, 329, 330, 352, 353, 354, 381, 382, 386, 394, 403, 405, 424, 426, 427, 428, 445, 449, 456, 466–467, 470, 486, 487, 498, 501, 518–519, 532, 533, 546, 549, 550, 617, 620, 632, 645, 682, 694, 696, 697, 698, 699, 708, 717, 718, 721, 739, 742, 764, 766, 767, 814, 815, 816, 817
3. That the world is media saturated and technologically dependent;	76, 81, 92, 155, 281, 378–379, 400
4. Consequences of science and technology for individuals and societies;	22, 39, 53–54, 127, 130, 131, 136, 137–138, 142, 143, 148, 155, 163, 185, 189, 212, 228–229, 268–269, 272, 276, 281, 351, 352, 353, 355, 378–379, 380–381, 394, 400, 403, 405, 406, 417, 428, 436, 447, 448, 469, 472, 486, 487, 499, 501, 505, 516, 517, 518–519, 532, 533, 541, 547, 548, 549, 565, 590, 617, 625, 629, 640–641, 642, 678, 679, 682, 685, 687, 694, 696, 698, 699, 709, 715, 717, 721, 722, 736, 740, 741, 770, 785, 795, 808, 809, 814, 815, 816, 817
5. Decisions regarding the uses and consequences of science and technology are often complex because of the need to choose between or reconcile different viewpoints;	39, 53–54, 72, 132–133, 142, 143, 148, 162, 163, 207, 327, 352, 353, 380–381, 428, 430, 448, 469, 472, 486, 487, 500, 505, 518–519, 617, 640–641, 643, 694, 696, 698, 699, 700, 717, 722, 742, 814, 815
6. Prediction, modeling, and planning are used to focus advances in science and technology for positive ends;	25, 77, 106, 212, 272, 355, 403, 406, 518–519, 665–666, 678, 679, 696, 722, 740, 770
7. Findings in science and advances in technology sometimes create ethical issues that test our standards and values;	142, 143, 276, 505, 590, 617, 625, 719, 814
8. The importance of the cultural contexts in which media are created and received;	76, 92–93, 133, 155, 378–379, 400, 541, 549, 565, 709
9. Science, technology, and their consequences are unevenly available across the globe;	39, 53, 186, 330, 380–381, 384, 421, 463, 466, 539, 565, 639, 663, 735, 808
10. Science and technology have contributed to making the world increasingly interdependent;	21–25, 81, 92, 130, 148, 155, 228–229, 280, 281, 378–379, 400, 421, 541, 549, 565, 651, 678, 715, 814

NCSS Theme and Learning Expectation	Student Edition
11. That achievements in science and technology are increasing at a rapid pace and can have both planned and unanticipated consequences;	39, 53, 54, 59, 72, 135, 136, 137, 138, 139, 140, 148, 160, 162, 163, 179, 189, 198, 208, 209, 211, 236, 252–253, 261, 262, 263, 264, 272, 286, 307, 327, 329, 330, 352, 353, 354, 381, 382, 386, 394, 403, 405, 424, 426, 427, 428, 445, 449, 456, 466–467, 470, 486, 487, 498, 501, 518–519, 532, 533, 546, 549, 550, 617, 620, 632, 645, 682, 694, 696, 697, 698, 699, 708, 717, 718, 721, 739, 742, 764, 766, 767, 815, 816, 817
12. Developments in science and technology may help to address global issues.	23, 39, 210, 211, 230–231, 380–381, 400, 403, 428, 500, 501, 617, 625, 678–679, 720, 740, 793
9. GLOBAL CONNECTIONS	
1. Global connections are rapidly accelerating across cultures and nations, and can have both positive and negative effects on nations and individuals;	58–59, 87, 90–91, 92–93, 98–99, 108, 127, 129, 131, 149, 150, 151, 155, 157, 186, 194–195, 198, 205, 208, 286, 304, 325, 367, 371, 377, 378–379, 388–389, 405, 421, 467, 470, 483, 720, 764–765
2. The solutions to global issues may involve individual decisions and actions, but also require national and international approaches (e.g., agreements, negotiations, policies, or laws);	39, 55, 59, 90–91, 99, 138, 140, 151, 154, 156–157, 161, 186, 205, 228, 229, 236, 256, 277, 280, 281, 282–283, 287, 288, 307, 325, 330, 383, 384, 417, 418, 421, 443, 449, 470, 498, 499, 500, 501, 502, 505, 541, 553, 570, 591, 592, 666, 667, 691, 720, 739, 765, 778, 787, 810–811, 824, 825
3. Conflict and cooperation among the peoples of the earth influence the division and control of the earth's surface;	89, 90, 91, 107, 108, 126, 132–133, 149, 150, 181, 182, 200, 201, 203, 208, 222, 224, 275, 276, 277, 312–313, 319, 320, 321, 344, 373, 378–379, 388–389, 391, 396–397, 408, 417, 441, 444, 448, 449, 453, 460, 461, 462, 472, 483, 491, 502, 512, 513, 520, 521, 525, 534, 536, 546, 549, 552–553, 566, 567, 582, 583, 587, 589, 594, 599, 611, 612, 618–619, 635, 650–651, 658, 686, 711, 725, 731, 742, 756, 759, 760, 761, 782, 783, 810, 811, 824
4. The actions of people, communities, and nations have both short- and long-term effects on the biosphere and its ability to sustain life;	123, 135, 136, 148, 158, 159, 160, 161, 162, 187, 188, 189, 190, 209, 210, 230–231, 232, 233, 234, 235, 261, 262, 263, 264, 284, 285, 286, 290, 305, 306, 307, 308, 318, 326, 327, 328, 329, 331, 350, 351, 355, 382, 383, 384, 402, 424, 425, 426, 427, 428, 429, 445, 468, 469, 471, 486, 488, 496, 497, 500, 501, 522, 523, 524, 525, 546, 549, 567, 569, 592, 621, 622, 624, 625, 643, 644, 664, 675, 696, 707, 718–719, 739, 766, 767, 769, 770, 788–789, 790, 791, 792, 796, 813, 815, 816
5. The causes and consequences of various types of global connections;	100–101, 156–157, 230–231, 348–349, 378–379, 542–543, 740–741, 708–709, 788–789
6. Technological advances can both improve and detract from the quality of life;	39, 53, 54, 59, 72, 135, 136, 137, 138, 139, 140, 148, 160, 162, 163, 179, 189, 198, 208, 209, 211, 236, 252–253, 261, 262, 263, 264, 272, 286, 307, 327, 329, 330, 352, 353, 354, 381, 382, 386, 394, 403, 405, 424, 426, 427, 428, 445, 449, 456, 466–467, 470, 486, 487, 498, 501, 518–519, 532, 533, 546, 549, 550, 617, 620, 632, 645, 682, 694, 696, 697, 698, 699, 708, 717, 718, 721, 739, 742, 764, 766, 767, 814, 815, 816, 817
7. Individuals, organizations, nations, and international entities can work to increase the positive effects of global connections, and address the negative impacts of global issues.	59, 87, 90–91, 93, 99, 108, 119, 131, 137–138, 148, 151, 157, 161, 162, 208, 230–231, 236, 264, 282–283, 284–285, 287, 288, 289, 304, 321, 325, 330, 331, 354, 408, 421, 443, 470, 500, 666, 739, 814
10. CIVIC IDEALS AND PRACTICES	
1. The theme of civic ideals and practices helps us recognize where gaps between ideals and practices exist, and prepares us to work for social justice;	12–13, 142, 143, 151, 190, 201, 308, 321, 433, 442, 529, 584–585, 594, 603, 690, 691, 742, 761, 763, 775, 786
2. Concepts and ideals such as: human dignity, social justice, liberty, equality, inalienable rights, responsibilities, civil dissent, citizenship, majority and minority rights, the common good, and the rule of law;	12–13, 142, 152, 164, 190, 214, 287, 321, 442, 584–585, 590, 591, 594, 626, 691, 742, 775, 783
3. Key practices involving the rights and responsibilities of citizenship and the exercise of citizenship (e.g., respecting the rule of law and due process, voting, serving on a jury, researching issues, making informed judgments, expressing views on issues, and collaborating with others to take civic action);	13, 140, 190, 201, 783, 785
4. Scholarly interpretations of key documents that define and support democratic ideals and practices (e.g., the U.S. Declaration of Independence, the U.S. Constitution, the Declaration of Sentiments in Seneca Falls, New York, the Gettysburg Address, the Letter from Birmingham Jail; and international Documents such as the Declaration of the Rights of Man, and the Universal Declaration of the Rights of Children);	290, 408, 472, 515, 529
5. The origins, functions, evolution, and outcomes of major institutions and practices designed to sustain and more fully realize democratic ideals;	13, 276, 299, 300, 303
6. That seeking multiple perspectives is required in order effectively to grasp the complexity of issues involving civic ideals and practices;	142, 143, 190, 287, 354, 377, 584–585, 774–775, 786
7. The importance of becoming informed as the basis for thoughtful and positive contributions through civic action.	137, 138, 140, 190, 201, 214, 264, 265, 266, 287, 308, 321, 332, 354, 356, 469, 547, 585, 590, 591, 594, 626, 763, 775, 785, 786

Correlation of *Geography: The Human and Physical World* to the Common Core State Standards, Grades 6–12

Correlated to Common Core State Standards for Literacy in History/Social Studies, Science, and Technical Subjects, Grades 6–12

The grades 6–12 standards on the following pages define what students should understand and be able to do by the end of each grade span. They correspond to the College and Career Readiness (CCR) anchor standards below by number. The CCR and grade-specific standards are necessary complements—the former providing broad standards, the latter providing additional specificity—that together define the skills and understandings that all students must demonstrate.

College and Career Readiness Anchor Standards for Reading	
Key Ideas and Details	
1. Read closely to determine what the text says explicitly and to make logical inferences from it; cite specific textual evidence when writing or speaking to support conclusions drawn from the text.	**Student Edition:** *Reading HELPDESK: Taking Notes: Key Ideas and Details, Identifying* 14, 26, 44, 51, 69, 78, 120, 125, 149, 158, 187, 200, 208, 232, 261, 275, 299, 341, 372, 412, 416, 424, 434, 444, 454, 484, 489, 496, 506, 530, 535, 544, 554, 566, 576, 581, 588, 642, 652, 680, 710, 754, 759, 766, 776, 781, 790, 800, 812; *Describing* 40, 60, 64, 82, 87, 102; *Organizing* 94, 368, 438, 459, 611, 717; *Categorizing* 144, 314; *Listing* 250, 294, 606, 730; *Outlining* 255; *Exploring Issues* 466; *Formulating Questions* 620; *Identifying Cause and Effect* 630, 737; *Comparing and Contrasting* 634; *Evaluating* 663; *Describing* 685; *Comparing* 726 *Reading Progress Check: Explaining* 16, 21, 49, 51, 65, 72, 79, 81, 86, 121, 122, 127, 135, 154, 201, 219, 225, 253, 264, 271, 288, 315, 324, 330, 343, 377, 405, 414, 418, 425, 443, 455, 461, 470, 545, 556, 561, 586, 587, 589, 590, 607, 632, 633, 636, 639, 644, 646, 656, 732, 756, 757, 761, 762, 768, 778, 791, 792, 805, 808; *Identifying* 25, 54, 81, 84, 90, 124, 130, 138, 151, 197, 221, 222, 224, 252, 279, 295, 303, 308, 328, 338, 347, 369, 391, 392, 415, 419, 421, 442, 446, 447, 448, 467, 485, 507, 524, 531, 570, 607, 681, 698, 705, 714, 717, 728, 729, 736, 738, 763, 770, 777, 804, 806; *Identify* 32; *Drawing Conclusions* 41, 236, 258, 274, 439, 440, 463, 765; *Describing* 46, 67, 81, 131, 137, 161, 162, 178, 190, 198, 205, 254, 260, 297, 298, 323, 325, 400, 401, 406, 413, 427, 435, 465, 513, 555, 577, 587, 780, 801, 802, 815, 816; *Specifying* 148, 227, 234, 281, 371, 381, 727; *Interpreting* 177, 612; *Determining Importance* 202, 488, 509, 707; *Inferring* 229, 256, 517, 691, 716, 720; *Expressing* 321, 327; *Locating* 436; *Making Generalizations* 623; *Drawing Inferences* 654 *Explaining* 16, 21, 25, 35, 43, 49, 54, 55, 63, 68, 73, 86, 106, 107, 107, 121, 122, 124, 127, 131, 135, 138, 139, 150, 154, 163, 186, 191, 201, 212, 214, 219, 225, 229, 237, 253, 254, 260, 264, 265, 271, 274, 281, 288, 289, 298, 308, 309, 315, 318, 320, 323, 324, 330, 340, 342, 343, 347, 354, 355, 369, 377, 384, 385, 396, 400, 405, 406, 407, 414, 418, 421, 425, 443, 445, 448, 449, 457, 458, 461, 465, 467, 501, 510, 515, 532, 536, 545, 549, 556, 558, 561, 565, 571, 578, 580, 586, 587, 589, 590, 592, 593, 607, 632, 633, 636, 639, 644, 645, 647, 658, 662, 666, 667, 699, 721, 732, 740, 741, 756, 757, 761, 762, 765, 768, 769, 778, 780, 784, 787, 791, 792, 795, 803, 805, 806, 808, 809, 817 *Drawing Inferences* 20, 124, 164, 274, 295, 355, 408, 445, 586, 587, 617, 654, 770, 818 *Draw Conclusions* 22, 24, 36, 39, 213, 331 *Lesson Review: Answering the Guiding Questions* 25, 34, 43, 50, 54, 63, 68, 72, 81, 86, 91, 99, 106, 124, 131, 138, 148, 155, 158, 162, 179, 186, 190, 199, 205, 212, 222, 229, 236, 254, 260, 264, 274, 281, 288, 298, 304, 308, 318, 325, 330, 340, 347, 354, 371, 377, 384, 394, 401, 406, 415, 421, 428, 437, 443, 448, 458, 465, 470, 488, 495, 500, 510, 517, 524, 534, 541, 548, 558, 565, 570, 580, 587, 592, 610, 617, 624, 633, 639, 646, 656, 662, 666, 684, 691, 698, 707, 716, 720, 729, 736, 740, 758, 765, 770, 780, 787, 794, 803, 809, 816 *Identifying* 25, 34, 43, 50, 54, 72, 73, 81, 83, 84, 88, 89, 90, 91, 95, 99, 103, 104, 105, 124, 130, 131, 138, 148, 150, 151, 162, 190, 192, 197, 199, 213, 221, 222, 224, 237, 252, 253, 254, 256, 260, 264, 274, 279, 281, 288, 290, 295, 298, 300, 301, 303, 304, 308, 318, 325, 328, 339, 340, 347, 369, 374, 391, 392, 403, 415, 419, 420, 421, 442, 446, 447, 448, 449, 456, 458, 464, 467, 485, 507, 524, 531, 558, 570, 580, 587, 592, 607, 633, 639, 646, 656, 662, 666, 667, 681, 691, 698, 705, 714, 716, 728, 729, 736, 738, 757, 758, 763, 765, 770, 777, 780, 787, 795, 801, 802, 808 *Describing* 28, 35, 43, 46, 50, 55, 67, 68, 72, 73, 81, 95, 99, 103, 105, 106, 107, 124, 131, 137, 138, 139, 152, 161, 162, 163, 178, 179, 190, 191, 198, 199, 211, 212, 219, 222, 229, 236, 237, 254, 256, 260, 264, 274, 276, 281, 288, 289, 297, 298, 300, 304, 309, 323, 325, 330, 340, 342, 347, 354, 355, 371, 374, 377, 400, 401, 404, 406, 407, 415, 418, 421, 427, 428, 435, 437, 440, 449, 458, 460, 465, 471, 495, 510, 512, 513, 525, 534, 541, 549, 555, 558, 562, 577, 584, 587, 593, 633, 667, 686, 699, 707, 712, 721, 729, 741, 758, 760, 765, 771, 780, 784, 794, 795, 801, 802, 803, 806, 809, 814, 815, 816, 817 *DBQ Questions* 31, 66, 72, 86, 93, 108, 133, 138, 153, 160, 164, 186, 204, 212, 214, 235, 260, 266, 273, 297, 310, 325, 332, 345, 353, 371, 386, 394, 404, 415, 523, 526, 546, 563, 586, 594, 607, 612, 619, 626, 633, 648, 654, 668, 689, 693, 695, 700, 714, 732, 742, 765, 768, 796, 811, 815 *Naming* 34, 337, 375, 394, 406, 803 *Drawing Conclusions* 41, 42, 48, 49, 61, 72, 73, 81, 93, 101, 107, 121, 133, 139, 152, 177, 179, 186, 191, 198, 207, 214, 222, 236, 237, 238, 258, 265, 266, 272, 274, 289, 290, 297, 304, 325, 332, 407, 415, 423, 430, 439, 440, 443, 449, 463, 472, 495, 498, 499, 514, 515, 517, 521, 522, 524, 541, 549, 564, 610, 616, 619, 633, 638, 646, 656, 661, 667, 687, 690, 691, 693, 716, 720, 721, 728, 729, 736, 739, 741, 742, 762, 763, 765, 770, 771, 787, 811, 815, 817, 825 *Stating* 54, 86, 318, 330, 331, 401, 406 *Interpreting* 56, 62, 68, 74, 108, 123, 140, 177, 179, 199, 213, 310, 328, 332, 353, 356, 371, 450, 502, 524, 525, 550, 593, 607, 612, 648, 691, 700, 731, 742, 796 *Making Generalizations* 56, 73, 108, 190, 191, 238, 254, 266, 290, 298, 309, 331, 394, 407, 516, 623, 699 *Expressing* 91, 124, 131, 138, 274, 298, 304, 321, 327, 565, 570 *Inferring* 107, 155, 205, 256, 420, 443, 517, 556, 691, 716, 720 *Specifying* 148, 227, 234, 281, 371, 381, 394, 727, 771 *Determining Importance* 155, 192, 202, 212, 443, 500, 509, 707 *Making Inferences* 163, 164, 508, 533, 638, 731 *Depicting* 184 *Interpreting Significance* 204, 386, 414, 429, 430, 472, 626, 721, 722, 772, 818 *Reaching Conclusions* 237, 310, 386 *Locating* 377, 436 *Create and Analyze Arguments and Draw Conclusions* 647

College and Career Readiness Anchor Standards for Reading	
2. Determine central ideas or themes of a text and analyze their development; summarize the key supporting details and ideas.	**Student Edition:** *Reading HELPDESK: Taking Notes: Key Ideas and Details, Identifying* 14, 26, 44, 51, 69, 78, 120, 125, 149, 158, 187, 200, 208, 232, 261, 275, 299, 341, 372, 412, 416, 424, 434, 444, 454, 484, 489, 496, 506, 530, 535, 544, 554, 566, 576, 581, 588, 642, 652, 680, 710, 754, 759, 766, 776, 781, 790, 800, 812; *Describing* 40, 60, 64, 82, 87, 102; *Organizing* 94, 368, 438, 459, 611, 717; *Summarizing* 134, 176, 196, 223, 284, 326, 350, 380, 390, 395, 402, 511, 520, 704; *Categorizing* 144, 314; *Paraphrasing* 180, 218, 270, 305, 319, 336; *Listing* 250, 294, 606, 730; *Outlining* 255; *Exploring Issues* 466; *Formulating Questions* 620; *Comparing and Contrasting* 634; *Identifying Central Issues* 657; *Evaluating* 663; *Describing* 685; *Comparing* 726 *Analyzing* 24, 25, 27, 34, 45, 46, 48, 54, 55, 56, 72, 74, 83, 85, 89, 101, 107, 121, 140, 148, 155, 159, 182, 183, 184, 189, 191, 198, 202, 213, 224, 236, 237, 259, 262, 265, 266, 309, 310, 331, 344, 345, 354, 385, 396, 407, 418, 428, 429, 436, 437, 440, 442, 446, 447, 450, 460, 465, 471, 487, 492, 501, 512, 517, 521, 531, 533, 534, 536, 539, 540, 541, 545, 547, 556, 562, 584, 593, 614, 624, 633, 647, 658, 662, 665, 666, 668, 682, 684, 686, 690, 696, 697, 698, 699, 700, 712, 729, 732, 735, 740, 741, 742, 771, 780, 784, 787, 792, 793, 794, 795, 796, 817 *Lesson Review: Answering the Guiding Questions* 25, 34, 43, 50, 54, 63, 68, 72, 81, 86, 91, 99, 106, 124, 131, 138, 148, 155, 158, 162, 179, 186, 190, 199, 205, 212, 222, 229, 236, 254, 260, 264, 274, 281, 288, 298, 304, 308, 318, 325, 330, 340, 347, 354, 371, 377, 384, 394, 401, 406, 415, 421, 428, 437, 443, 448, 458, 465, 470, 488, 495, 500, 510, 517, 524, 534, 541, 548, 558, 565, 570, 580, 587, 592, 610, 617, 624, 633, 639, 646, 656, 662, 666, 684, 691, 698, 707, 716, 720, 729, 736, 740, 758, 765, 770, 780, 787, 794, 803, 809, 816 *Summarizing* 25, 35, 54, 55, 105, 107, 139, 148, 154, 163, 186, 191, 213, 229, 234, 237, 265, 289, 302, 304, 307, 309, 317, 318, 325, 355, 371, 377, 384, 394, 401, 421, 429, 448, 456, 458, 465, 470, 471, 487, 488, 498, 510, 517, 524, 525, 534, 546, 548, 549, 565, 587, 592, 593, 610, 617, 621, 625, 646, 647, 656, 662, 664, 666, 667, 682, 688, 691, 694, 699, 704, 707, 713, 733, 740, 741, 758, 765, 770, 771, 780, 794, 809, 813, 816 *Identifying the Central Issue* 27, 205 *Finding the Main Idea* 35, 163, 205, 283, 331, 407, 500, 610, 624, 716, 768 *Identifying Central Issues* 55, 93, 107, 133, 139, 146, 153, 160, 162, 207, 213, 235, 237, 260, 265, 266, 271, 277, 283, 286, 289, 290, 308, 309, 338, 355, 371, 385, 408, 488, 494, 500, 517, 524, 534, 565, 570, 571, 591, 593, 607, 612, 613, 619, 625, 668, 682, 689, 693, 697, 711, 721, 732, 811, 817 *Sequencing* 62, 126, 182, 220, 237, 331, 405, 571, 716, 722, 782 *Exploring Issues* 91, 164, 212, 236, 238, 262, 331, 385, 407, 429, 472, 495, 509, 525, 569, 625, 648, 667, 698, 721, 816 *Problem Solving* 98 *Reading Progress Check: Summarizing* 105, 234, 302, 304, 307, 317, 487, 498, 510, 534, 546, 621, 662, 664, 682, 688, 694, 704, 713, 733, 813; *Identifying Central Issues* 146, 277, 286, 494, 613; *Paraphrasing* 152; *Analyzing* 155, 183, 189, 259, 345, 354, 624, 658, 665, 666, 784; *Determining Importance* 202, 488, 509, 707; *Sequencing Information* 517, 712; *Synthesizing* 458, 787; *Sequencing* 782 *Paraphrasing* 152, 290, 371 *Determining Importance* 155, 192, 202, 212, 443, 500, 509, 707 *Sequencing Information* 155, 517, 712 *Synthesizing* 178, 272, 384, 394, 401, 458, 548, 580, 621, 668, 684, 695, 716, 787, 794, 803 *Exploring the Issues* 181, 189, 329, 355, 356 *Identifying Cause and Effect* 423 *Identifying Trends* 517 *Understanding Historical Interpretation* 517, 561, 626, 722, 772 *Analyzing Primary Sources* 550, 563, 714, 722 *Making Predictions* 633, 648 *Contrasting* 716 *Making Connections* 765 *Analyzing Information* 825
3. Analyze how and why individuals, events, or ideas develop and interact over the course of a text.	**Student Edition:** *Geography Matters* 11, 37, 57, 75, 109, 117, 141, 173, 193, 215, 247, 267, 291, 311, 333, 365, 387, 409, 431, 451, 481, 503, 527, 551, 573, 603, 627, 649, 677, 701, 723, 751, 773, 797 *Why Geography Matters* 12–13, 38–39, 58–59, 76–77, 110–111, 118–119, 142–143, 174–175, 194–195, 216–217, 248–249, 268–269, 292–293, 312–313, 334–335, 366–367, 388–389, 410–411, 432–433, 452–453, 482–483, 504–505, 528–529, 552–553, 574–575, 604–605, 628–629, 650–651, 678–679, 702–703, 724–725, 752–753, 774–775, 798–799 *There's More Online: Read* 13, 38, 195, 268, 335, 366, 411, 433, 453, 505, 575, 651, 703, 753; *Watch* 13, 58, 119, 143, 175, 249, 293, 335, 505, 529, 679, 775; *See* 38, 58, 216, 249, 268, 293, 313, 366, 575, 651, 679, 779, 799; *Compare* 77, 605, 725; *View* 77, 119, 175, 195, 216, 389, 411, 433, 453, 483, 628, 703, 753, 799; *Explore* 143, 313, 389, 483, 605, 628, 725; *Connect* 553; *Examine* 553 *Geography Connection* 15, 17, 19, 29, 46, 53, 65, 67, 70, 79, 80, 122, 128, 130, 135, 136, 145, 185, 188, 197, 226, 228, 263, 278, 280, 286, 306, 315, 316, 322, 351, 352, 373, 393, 413, 417, 425, 435, 462, 485, 490, 497, 555, 560, 582, 608, 631, 681, 683, 705, 718, 727, 755, 783, 813 *Making Connections* 34, 36, 68, 137, 145, 155, 164, 179, 190, 192, 199, 213, 222, 227, 229, 233, 279, 289, 300, 302, 306, 309, 327, 331, 344, 356, 376, 385, 399, 401, 407, 415, 421, 428, 429, 437, 448, 449, 455, 463, 468, 469, 471, 472, 486, 488, 494, 495, 500, 502, 521, 525, 541, 547, 549, 550, 567, 571, 577, 587, 593, 594, 609, 617, 626, 635, 643, 648, 661, 665, 667, 684, 690, 699, 707, 716, 719, 720, 736, 758, 764, 765, 771, 787, 795, 809, 816, 817 *Connecting Geography to Science: Astronomy* 41; *Climatology* 66, 199; *Soil Science* 124; *Biology* 148, 221; *Environmental Science* 189; *Geology* 254; *Cap–and–Trade Systems* 288; *Demography* 301; *Air–Conditioning* 436; *Saving the Aral Sea* 470; *Genetics* 660; *The DMZ* 729; *Tsunamis* 756; *Carbon Dating* 805 *Connecting Geography to Government: Geopolitics* 91, 384; *Environmental Politics* 330; *Soil Erosion in Iraq* 427; *Water Management* 448 *Case Study: Culture* 92–93, 422–423, 692–693; *The Environment* 132–133, 518–519; *Development* 206–207; *Economics* 282–283; *Geopolitics* 618–619, 810–811 *Global Connections: Patterns of Distribution* 100–101; *The United States and Canada* 156–157; *Latin America* 230–231; *Europe* 348–349; *North Africa, Southwest Asia, and Central Asia* 378–379; *Africa South of the Sahara* 542–543; *South Asia* 740–741; *Asia* 708–709; *Australia* 788–789 *Chapter Assessment: College and Career Readiness, Explaining Continuity and Change* 139, 265; *Change and Continuity in Economics* 191, 472, 647; *Change and Continuity of Groups* 356; *Identifying and Explaining Continuity and Change* 385 *Interact with Global Connections Online* 157, 231, 349, 379, 407, 543, 641, 709, 789 *Connecting Geography to History: Before Columbus* 201; *Naming Places* 510; *Slave Forts* 561; *Natural Disaster* 635 *Connecting Geography to Economics, Privatization* 347; *Development* 400 *Connecting Geography to Math: Geometry* 487; *Output of the Kariba Hydroelectric Dam* 579; *India's GDP* 617 *Connecting Geography to Sociology: Social Norms* 540; *Hanami: Viewing of Flowers* 706; *The Outback* 780 *Understanding Relationships Among Events* 571, 736

College and Career Readiness Anchor Standards for Reading

Craft and Structure	
4. Interpret words and phrases as they are used in a text, including determining technical, connotative, and figurative meanings, and analyze how specific word choices shape meaning or tone.	**Student Edition:** *Reading HELPDESK: Academic Vocabulary* 14, 26, 40, 44, 51, 60, 64, 69, 78, 82, 87, 94, 102, 120, 125, 134, 144, 149, 158, 176, 180, 187, 196, 200, 208, 218, 223, 232, 250, 255, 261, 270, 275, 284, 294, 299, 305, 314, 319, 326, 336, 341, 350, 368, 372, 380, 390, 395, 402, 412, 416, 424, 434, 438, 444, 454, 459, 466, 484, 489, 496, 506, 511, 520, 530, 535, 544, 554, 559, 566, 576, 581, 588, 606, 611, 620, 630, 634, 642, 652, 657, 663, 680, 685, 694, 704, 710, 717, 726, 730, 737, 754, 759, 766, 776, 781, 790, 800, 804, 812 *Reading HELPDESK: Content Vocabulary* 14, 26, 40, 44, 51, 60, 64, 69, 78, 82, 87, 94, 102, 120, 125, 134, 144, 149, 158, 176, 180, 187, 196, 200, 208, 218, 223, 232, 250, 255, 261, 270, 275, 284, 294, 299, 305, 314, 319, 326, 336, 341, 350, 368, 372, 380, 390, 395, 402, 412, 416, 424, 434, 438, 444, 454, 459, 466, 484, 489, 496, 506, 511, 520, 530, 535, 544, 554, 559, 566, 576, 581, 588, 606, 611, 620, 630, 634, 642, 652, 657, 663, 680, 685, 694, 704, 710, 717, 726, 730, 737, 754, 759, 766, 776, 781, 790, 800, 804, 812 *Lesson Review: Reviewing Vocabulary* 25, 34, 43, 50, 54, 63, 68, 72, 81, 86, 91, 99, 106, 124, 131, 138, 148, 155, 158, 162, 179, 186, 190, 199, 205, 212, 222, 229, 236, 254, 260, 264, 274, 281, 288, 298, 304, 308, 318, 325, 330, 340, 347, 354, 371, 377, 384, 394, 401, 406, 415, 421, 428, 437, 443, 448, 458, 465, 470, 488, 495, 500, 510, 517, 524, 534, 541, 548, 558, 565, 570, 580, 587, 592, 610, 617, 624, 633, 639, 646, 656, 662, 666, 684, 691, 698, 707, 716, 720, 729, 736, 740, 758, 765, 770, 780, 787, 794, 803, 809, 816 *Reading Progress Check: Defining* 33, 106; *Naming* 34, 337, 375, 394, 803 *Naming* 34, 337, 375, 394, 406, 803 *Finding the Main Idea* 35 *Defining* 50, 73, 90, 104, 106, 107, 131, 162, 259, 377, 384, 500, 647 *Interpreting* 140, 310, 648, 700, 796 *Speculating* 238 *Analyzing* 310, 700, 742 *Lesson Review: Reviewing Vocabulary, Applying* 421, 428 *Analyzing Primary Sources* 550, 563 *Chapter Assessment: DBQ Analyzing Primary Sources, Analyzing Arguments* 594 *Using Context Clues* 684 *Analyzing Text Structure* 698 *Labeling* 401 *Making Connections* 707, 720 *Understanding Relationships Among Events* 736 *Theorizing* 796 *Assessment: Reviewing Vocabulary* 845
5. Analyze the structure of texts, including how specific sentences, paragraphs, and larger portions of the text (e.g., a section, chapter, scene, or stanza) relate to each other and the whole.	**Student Edition:** *Identifying Cause and Effect* 36, 55, 56, 63, 68, 98, 108, 139, 164, 186, 190, 191, 205, 213, 237, 238, 265, 266, 287, 289, 295, 309, 347, 354, 355, 369, 370, 383, 384, 385, 408, 423, 427, 429, 449, 456, 464, 469, 471, 491, 492, 500, 501, 507, 508, 510, 545, 546, 549, 565, 567, 569, 570, 571, 578, 593, 612, 622, 624, 625, 643, 644, 647, 653, 659, 667, 695, 697, 698, 721, 739, 740, 741, 756, 764, 767, 770, 771, 801, 809, 817 *Case Study: Culture* 92–93, 422–423, 692–693; *The Environment* 132–133, 518–519; *Development* 206–207; *Economics* 282–283; *Geopolitics* 618–619, 810–811 *Cause and Effect* 139 *Evaluating Counter Arguments* 164 *Understanding Relationships* 309, 496, 514, 523, 533, 696, 719 *Considering Advantages and Disadvantages* 349, 385, 471, 565, 613, 655, 662, 699, 763, 771, 817 *Reading Progress Check: Identifying Cause and Effect* 383, 456, 464, 469, 491, 565, 567, 569, 659; *Understanding Relationships* 496, 514, 523, 533, 696, 719 *Analyzing Text Structure* 698
6. Assess how point of view or purpose shapes the content and style of a text.	**Student Edition:** *Hypothesizing* 20, 55, 93, 148, 161, 186, 210, 212, 235, 251, 252, 327, 381, 405, 437, 439, 449, 455, 457, 465, 469, 517, 522, 549, 557, 563, 569, 584, 593, 614, 619, 624, 647, 653, 655, 693, 698, 699, 707, 739, 741, 762, 767, 795, 811 *Cartoon* 35, 471, 571, 593, 699, 721, 817 *Case Study: Culture* 92–93, 422–423, 692–693; *The Environment* 132–133, 518–519; *Development* 206–207; *Economics* 282–283; *Geopolitics* 618–619, 810–811 *What do you think? DBQ* 93, 133, 207, 283, 423, 520, 619, 693, 811 *Problem Solving* 98, 221, 332, 386, 407, 426, 428, 450, 501, 502, 538, 549, 568, 594, 700, 741, 769, 793, 817 *Identifying Cause and Effect* 164 *Making Inferences* 164 *Determining Importance* 155, 192, 202, 212, 443, 500, 509, 707 *Identifying* 192 *Making Connections* 192 *Identifying Perspectives* 517, 583, 584, 594, 691, 695, 699 *Understanding Historical Interpretation* 517, 561, 626, 722, 772 *Interpreting* 550 *Chapter Assessment: DBQ Analyzing Primary Sources, Identifying Perspectives* 594 *Understanding Perspectives* 617 *Problem Solving* 700 *Identifying Perspectives and Differing Interpretations* 741 *Analyzing* 796

College and Career Readiness Anchor Standards for Reading

Standard	Correlation
Integration of Knowledge and Ideas	
7. Integrate and evaluate content presented in diverse formats and media, including visually and quantitatively, as well as in words.	**Student Edition:** *Maps* 2–3, 4–5, 6–7, 8–9, 10, 12, 15, 16, 17, 19, 20, 29, 46, 47, 53, 65, 67, 70, 76, 79, 80, 100–101, 112, 113, 114, 115, 116, 118, 122, 123, 128, 130, 135, 136, 145, 146, 168, 169, 170, 171, 172, 185, 188, 194, 197, 226, 228, 242, 243, 244, 245, 246, 263, 278, 280, 286, 292, 306, 312, 315, 316, 322, 351, 352, 360, 361, 362, 363, 364, 373, 389, 393, 410, 417, 425, 435, 452, 462, 468, 476, 477, 478, 479, 480, 485, 490, 497, 507, 552, 555, 560, 574, 582, 598, 599, 600, 601, 602, 608, 631, 640–641, 650, 672, 673, 674, 675, 676, 681, 683, 705, 718, 727, 746, 747, 748, 749, 750, 755, 783, 788, 798, 813, 820–821, 826, 827 *Use Graphic Organizer* 14, 25, 26, 40, 43, 44, 50, 51, 54, 60, 63, 64, 68, 69, 72, 78, 81, 82, 86, 87, 91, 94, 99, 102, 106, 120, 124, 125, 131, 134, 138, 144, 148, 149, 155, 162, 163, 176, 179, 180, 186, 187, 190, 196, 199, 200, 205, 208, 212, 218, 222, 223, 229, 232, 236, 254, 255, 260, 261, 264, 270, 274, 275, 281, 284, 288, 294, 298, 299, 304, 305, 308, 314, 318, 319, 325, 326, 330, 336, 340, 341, 347, 350, 354, 368, 371, 372, 377, 380, 384, 385, 390, 394, 395, 401, 402, 406, 412, 415, 416, 421, 424, 428, 434, 437, 438, 442, 443, 444, 448, 454, 458, 459, 465, 466, 470, 484, 488, 489, 495, 496, 500, 506, 510, 511, 517, 518, 530, 534, 535, 541, 544, 548, 554, 558, 559, 565, 566, 570, 576, 580, 581, 587, 588, 592, 606, 610, 611, 617, 620, 624, 625, 630, 633, 634, 639, 642, 646, 652, 656, 657, 662, 663, 666, 680, 684, 685, 691, 694, 698, 704, 707, 710, 716, 717, 720, 726, 729, 730, 736, 737, 740, 754, 758, 759, 765, 766, 770, 776, 780, 781, 787, 790, 794,800, 803, 804, 809, 810, 816 *Graph Skills* 23, 83, 84–85, 107, 139, 154, 163, 184, 191, 213, 222, 235, 258, 285, 289, 328, 331, 344, 346, 385, 398, 407, 429, 449, 564, 569, 587, 621, 647, 690, 715, 719, 741, 771, 792, 795, 827 *Chart Skills* 27, 73, 97, 237, 265, 309, 355, 439, 464, 501, 549, 662, 816 *Analyzing Visuals* 35, 123, 137, 147, 178, 179, 184, 190, 204, 209, 211, 252, 253, 274, 285, 298, 307, 324, 346, 376, 381, 391, 414, 420, 428, 442, 446, 455, 468, 494, 495, 498, 499, 500, 507, 531, 532, 564, 567, 568, 577, 589, 591, 609, 616, 621, 622, 645, 665, 706, 707, 715, 719, 758, 777, 786 *Chapter Assessment: Applying Map Skills* 35, 56, 74, 108, 140, 163, 192, 214, 238, 266, 290, 310, 332, 356, 386, 408, 430, 450, 472, 502, 526, 550, 571, 594, 626, 648, 667, 700, 722, 742, 772, 796, 818 *Cartoon* 35, 471, 571, 593, 699, 721, 817 *Diagram Skills* 41, 42, 45, 48, 55, 61, 68, 71, 103, 105, 121, 177, 525 *Infographic* 52, 62, 123, 159, 178, 198, 220, 253, 272, 296, 338, 382, 403, 426, 468, 499, 507, 538, 557, 616, 655, 696, 738, 767, 779, 801 *Chapter Assessment: 21st Century Skills: Using Graphs, Charts, Diagrams, and Tables* 55, 73, 107, 139, 163, 191, 237, 265, 429; *Creating and Using Graphs, Charts, Diagrams, and Tables* 385, 407, 549, 647, 741; *Using Graphs* 626, 771; *Creating Diagrams* 667, 771; *Satellite Image, Geography Skills* 667 *Time Line* 126–127, 150–151, 182–183, 202–203, 224–225, 249, 256–257, 276–277, 300–301, 320–321, 335, 342–343, 374–375, 396–397, 418–419, 440–441, 460–461, 492–493, 512–513, 536–537, 584–585, 614–615, 636–637, 658–659, 686–687, 712–713, 732–733, 760–761, 784–785, 806–807, 823 *Critical Thinking: Using Graphs* 587
8. Delineate and evaluate the argument and specific claims in a text, including the validity of the reasoning as well as the relevance and sufficiency of the evidence.	**Student Edition:** *Why Geography Matters* 12–13, 38–39, 58–59, 76–77, 110–111, 118–119, 142–143, 174–175, 194–195, 216–217, 248–249, 268–269, 292–293, 312–313, 334–335, 366–367, 388–389, 410–411, 432–433, 452–453, 482–483, 504–505, 528–529, 552–553, 574–575, 604–605, 628–629, 650–651, 678–679, 702–703, 724–725, 752–753, 774–775, 798–799 *Defending* 56, 623, 711 *Case Study: Culture* 92–93, 422–423, 692–693; *The Environment* 132–133, 518–519; *Development* 206–207; *Economics* 282–283; *Geopolitics* 618–619, 810–811 *What do you think? DBQ* 93, 133, 207, 283, 423, 520, 619, 693, 811 *Hypothesizing* 148 *Evaluating Counter Arguments* 164 *Lesson Review: Reviewing Vocabulary, Applying* 421, 428 *Chapter Assessment: DBQ Analyzing Primary Sources, Analyzing Arguments* 594 *Create and Analyze Arguments and Draw Conclusions* 647 *Constructing Arguments* 779
9. Analyze how two or more texts address similar themes or topics in order to build knowledge or to compare the approaches the authors take.	**Student Edition:** *Case Study: Culture* 92–93, 422–423, 692–693; *The Environment* 132–133, 518–519; *Development* 206–207; *Economics* 282–283; *Geopolitics* 618–619, 810–811 *What do you think? DBQ* 93, 133, 207, 283, 423, 520, 619, 693, 811 *Chapter Assessment: College and Career Readiness, Change and Continuity in Economics* 191 *Chapter Assessment: 21st Century Skills, Identifying Perspectives and Differing Interpretations* 741
Range of Reading and Level of Text Complexity	
10. Read and comprehend complex literary and informational texts independently and proficiently.	**Student Edition:** *Geography Matters* 11, 37, 57, 75, 109, 117, 141, 173, 193, 215, 247, 267, 291, 311, 333, 365, 387, 409, 431, 451, 481, 503, 527, 551, 573, 603, 627, 649, 677, 701, 723, 751, 773, 797 *Why Geography Matters* 12–13, 38–39, 58–59, 76–77, 110–111, 118–119, 142–143, 174–175, 194–195, 216–217, 248–249, 268–269, 292–293, 312–313, 334–335, 366–367, 388–389, 410–411, 432–433, 452–453, 482–483, 504–505, 528–529, 552–553, 574–575, 604–605, 628–629, 650–651, 678–679, 702–703, 724–725, 752–753, 774–775, 798–799 *There's More Online: Read* 13, 38, 195, 268, 335, 366, 411, 433, 453, 505, 575, 651, 703, 753 *Analyzing Primary Sources: The Island* 31; *Eyewitness: Icelandic Volcano* 48; *Why Tornadoes Take the Weekends Off in Summer* 72; *World Refugee Day* 2012 86; *Coffee Country* 98; *Can Natural Gas Help Tackle Global Warming?* 138; *Canada Slips in Gender Equality Rankings* 153; *Acid Rain: Sugar Maples at Risk* 160; *Maquiladoras and the Middle Class* 186; *The Mola: Colorful Kuna Culture* 204; *Indigenous Communities Protect Biodiversity* 212; *Urban Population Boom Threatens Lake Titicaca* 235; *The Nordic Model and Working Women* 260; *Documenting the Baltic Sea's Biodiversity* 262; *The Alps* 273; *Olive Oil Production in Italy* 297; *Improving the Business Climate in Poland* 325; *Poetry in Contemporary Russia* 345; *The Long Shadow of Chernobyl* 353; *Saving Mediterranean Habitats Worldwide* 371; *Lebanon's Forests: Going up in Smoke* 394; *Desertification in Syria* 404; *Iraq's Energy Resources* 415; *Threats to the Gulf* 446; *Ancient Geography Text* 455; *Secondary Education for Girls* 515; *Contrasting Views of Tanzania's Landscape* 523; *Local Fishermen Near Lake Chad* 546; *Crime in Kinshasa* 563; *Touring South Africa's Townships* 586; *Hindu Pilgrims* 607; *The Last Straw: Salt Satyagraha*, 1930 612; *Flooding in Bangladesh* 633; *Climbing Mount Everest* 654; *The Spread of Rap and Hip–Hop in China* 689; *Speaking Manchu* 695; *The History of Origami* 714; *The Invasion* 732; *Regional Cooperation* 765; *Mekong Giant Catfish* 768; *Rising Sea Levels Cause Plans for Relocation* 815 *Chapter Assessment: Primary Source* 36, 56, 74, 108, 140, 164, 192, 214, 238, 266, 290, 310, 332, 356, 386, 408, 430, 450, 472, 502, 526, 550, 572, 594, 626, 648, 668, 700, 722, 742, 772, 796, 818 *Connecting Geography to Science: Astronomy* 41; *Climatology* 66, 199; *Soil Science* 124; *Biology* 148, 221; *Environmental Science* 189; *Geology* 254; *Cap–and–Trade Systems* 288; *Demography* 301; *Air–Conditioning* 436; *Saving the Aral Sea* 470; *Genetics* 660; *The DMZ* 729; *Tsunamis* 756; *Carbon Dating* 805 *Connecting Geography to Government: Geopolitics* 91, 384; *Environmental Politics* 330; *Soil Erosion in Iraq* 427; *Water Management* 448 *Case Study: Culture* 92–93, 422–423, 692–693; *The Environment* 132–133, 518–519; *Development* 206–207; *Economics* 282–283; *Geopolitics* 618–619, 810–811 *Global Connections: Patterns of Distribution* 100–101; *The United States and Canada* 156–157; *Latin America* 230–231; *Europe* 348–349; *North Africa, Southwest Asia, and Central Asia* 378–379; *Africa South of the Sahara* 542–543; *South Asia* 740–741; *Asia* 708–709; *Australia* 788–789 *Interact with Global Connections Online* 157, 231, 349, 379, 407, 543, 641, 709, 789 *Connecting Geography to History: Before Columbus* 201; *Naming Places* 510; *Slave Forts* 561; *Natural Disaster* 635 *Connecting Geography to Economics, Privatization* 347; *Development* 400 *Connecting Geography to Math: Geometry* 487; *Output of the Kariba Hydroelectric Dam* 579; *India's GDP* 617 *Connecting Geography to Sociology: Social Norms* 540; *Hanami: Viewing of Flowers* 706; *The Outback* 780 *Special Feature: Antarctica* 819–825 *World Religions Handbook* 826–844

College and Career Readiness Anchor Standards for Writing

Standard	Correlation
Text Types and Purposes	
1. Write arguments to support claims in an analysis of substantive topics or texts using valid reasoning and relevant and sufficient evidence.	**Student Edition:** *Lesson Review: Writing Activity, Argument* 106, 190, 205, 288, 384, 428, 443, 448, 470, 500, 524, 570, 592, 639, 662, 666, 691, 720, 729, 816; *Persuasive* 465 *Chapter Assessment: Writing About Geography, Argument* 164, 192, 386, 450, 472, 594, 668, 796 *Chapter Assessment: College and Career Readiness, Change and Continuity in Economics* 191; *Reaching Conclusions* 310; *Decision Making* 818 *Chapter Assessment: Research and Presentation, Gathering Information* 626 *Making Connections: Human Systems* 789
2. Write informative/explanatory texts to examine and convey complex ideas and information clearly and accurately through the effective selection, organization, and analysis of content.	**Student Edition:** *Lesson Review: Writing Activity, Informative/Explanatory* 25, 34, 50, 54, 63, 68, 72, 91, 99, 131, 138, 148, 162, 179, 186, 199, 212, 222, 229, 236, 254, 260, 264, 274, 281, 298, 304, 308, 318, 330, 340, 347, 354, 371, 377, 394, 401, 406, 415, 421, 458, 488, 495, 510, 517, 534, 541, 548, 558, 565, 580, 587, 610, 617, 624, 633, 646, 656, 684, 707, 716, 736, 740, 758, 765, 770, 780, 787, 794, 809; *Explanatory* 81, 437 *Chapter Assessment: Research and Presentation, Research Skills* 36, 56, 74, 108, 140, 164, 192, 214, 238, 266, 290, 310, 332, 355, 450, 502, 550, 594, 648, 742, 796; *Explaining* 214; *Problem Solving* 386; *Evaluating* 408; *Gathering Information* 430, 472, 526, 572, 626, 668, 722, 772, 818; *Research and Presentation* 700 *Chapter Assessment: Writing About Geography: Informative/Explanatory* 36, 74, 108, 238, 266, 290, 310, 356, 408, 502, 550, 626, 648, 772; *Informative* 140 *Lesson Review: Reviewing Vocabulary, Summarizing* 54, 524, 610; *Displaying* 91; *Making Connections* 155, 720; *Discussing* 179; *Applying* 421, 580, 587; *Identifying Trends* 517; *Describing* 534, 541; *Identifying* 592, 633, 639, 646, 656, 662, 666, 765, 770; *Drawing Inferences* 617; *Hypothesizing* 624; *Understanding Relationships* 736; *Explaining* 740 *Chapter Assessment: Exploring the Essential Question, Making Connections* 56, 356, 472, 626, 700; *Drawing Conclusions* 332, 407; *Organizing* 386, 772, 817; *Analyzing* 550 *Chapter Assessment: College and Career Readiness, Economics* 107; *Reaching Conclusions* 237, 386, 626; *Explaining Continuity and Change* 265; *Comparing and Contrasting* 332; *Change and Continuity of Groups* 356; *Examining Information* 430, 722; *Multicultural Societies* 449; *Problem Solving* 502, 549, 594, 741; *Decision Making* 526, 699; *Change and Continuity in Economics* 647; *Clear Communication* 668, 771, 796 *Lesson Review: Using Your Notes, Identifying* 131; *Summarizing* 186, 448, 458, 465, 488, 517, 524, 534, 548, 587, 592, 617, 646, 656, 758, 765, 770, 794, 816; *Making Connections* 190; *Analyzing* 437, 541, 787; *Explaining* 470; *Describing* 495, 510, 558, 633; *Applying* 500; *Expressing* 570; *Synthesizing* 580; *Listing* 610; *Comparing and Contrasting* 639, 729; *Considering Advantages and Disadvantages* 662; *Interpreting* 691; *Sequencing* 716; *Transferring Information* 720; *Identifying Cause and Effect* 740 *Making Connections: The Uses of Geography* 157, 231; *Considering Advantages and Disadvantages* 349 *Human Systems* 174, 433, 702 *Environment and Society* 195, 217, 293, 483, 505 *Chapter Assessment: Critical Thinking, Evaluating* 266 *Places and Regions* 313 *Making Connections: The Uses of Geography* 379, 543 *Chapter Assessment: Critical Thinking, Exploring Issues* 429, 721 *Chapter Assessment: 21st Century Skills, Identifying Perspectives* 471 *Chapter Assessment: Critical Thinking, Exploring Issues* 525, 625; *Making Connections* 771, 817 *Thinking Geographically: Expository* 825 *Assessment: Problem-Solving Activity, Research Project* 845
3. Write narratives to develop real or imagined experiences or events using effective technique, well-chosen details and well-structured event sequences.	**Student Edition:** *Lesson Review: Writing Activity, Narrative* 43, 86, 124, 155, 325, 698, 803 *Chapter Assessment: Writing About Geography, Narrative* 56, 214, 332, 430, 525, 572, 700, 742, 772, 818 *Chapter Assessment: Exploring the Essential Question, Making Connections* 140 *Chapter Assessment: Research and Presentation, Research Skills* 164 *Human Systems* 248
Production and Distribution of Writing	
4. Produce clear and coherent writing in which the development, organization, and style are appropriate to task, purpose, and audience.	**Student Edition:** *Chapter Assessment: Writing About Geography, Informative/Explanatory* 74, 108, 238, 304, 406, 648; *Argument* 164, 192, 450, 668, 796; *Narrative* 332 *Lesson Review: Writing Activity, Narrative* 86, 124, 155, 698; *Informative/Explanatory* 131, 222, 229, 236, 260, 330, 347, 371, 377, 421, 646; *Argument* 288, 384, 443, 448, 470, 570, 666, 816 *Chapter Assessment: College and Career Readiness, Economics* 107; *Change and Continuity in Economics* 191; *Comparing and Contrasting* 332; *Reaching Conclusions* 310, 626; *Examining Information* 430; *Problem Solving* 502; *Change and Continuity in Economics* 647; *Clear Communication* 668, 771 *Making Connections: The Uses of Geography* 157, 231, 379, 543 *Chapter Assessment: Research and Presentation, Research Skills* 164; *Gathering Information* 722 *Chapter Assessment: Exploring the Essential Question, Making Connections* 430; *Synthesizing* 572; *Exploring Issues* 648 *Critical Thinking: Organizing* 571 *Making Connections: Human Systems* 789
5. Develop and strengthen writing as needed by planning, revising, editing, rewriting, or trying a new approach.	**Student Edition:** *Chapter Assessment: Exploring the Essential Question: Understanding Historical Interpretation* 35; *Making Connections* 56; *Informative* 140; *Organizing* 386, 817 *Chapter Assessment: Writing About Geography, Informative/Explanatory* 36, 74, 108, 238, 266, 290, 304, 310, 356, 406, 408, 502, 626, 648, 700, 772; *Informative* 140; *Argument* 164, 192, 386, 450, 472, 594, 668, 722, 796; *Narrative* 332, 430, 525, 572, 818 *Lesson Review: Writing Activity, Narrative* 86, 698; *Informative/Explanatory* 222, 229, 236, 260, 347, 371, 377, 421; *Argument* 384, 443, 470 *Chapter Assessment: Research and Presentation, Research Skills* 164 *Chapter Assessment: College and Career Readiness, Change and Continuity in Economics* 191; *Problem Solving* 502; *Reaching Conclusions* 626; *Clear Communication* 668
6. Use technology, including the Internet, to produce and publish writing and to interact and collaborate with others.	**Student Edition:** *There's More Online: Read* 13, 38, 195, 268, 335, 366, 411, 433, 453, 505, 575, 651, 703, 753; *Watch* 13, 58, 119, 143, 175, 249, 293, 335, 505, 529, 679, 775; *See* 38, 58, 216, 249, 268, 293, 313, 366, 575, 651, 679, 779, 799; *Compare* 77, 605, 725; *View* 77, 119, 175, 195, 216, 389, 411, 433, 453, 483, 628, 703, 753, 799; *Explore* 143, 313, 389, 483, 605, 628, 725; *Connect* 553; *Examine* 553 *Chapter Assessment: Research and Presentation, Research Skills* 36, 56, 74, 108, 164, 192, 238, 266, 290, 310, 355, 450, 648, 742, 796; *Problem Solving* 332, 386; *Evaluating* 408; *Gathering Information* 430, 472, 572, 626, 668, 722, 772, 818; *Research and Presentation* 700 *Chapter Assessment: College and Career Readiness, Clear Communication* 73; *Reaching Conclusions* 237; *Comparing and Contrasting* 332; *Examining Information* 356; *Problem Solving* 549, 594; *Change and Continuity in Economics* 647 *Interact with Global Connections Online* 157, 231, 349, 379, 407, 543, 641, 709, 789 *Chapter Assessment: Writing About Geography, Narrative* 214, 742; *Informative/Explanatory* 290 *Lesson Review: Writing Activity, Informative/Explanatory* 406, 740 *Chapter Assessment: Exploring the Essential Question, Analyzing* 550 *Assessment: Problem-Solving Activity, Research Project* 845

College and Career Readiness Anchor Standards for Writing

Research to Build and Present Knowledge	
7. Conduct short as well as more sustained research projects based on focused questions, demonstrating understanding of the subject under investigation.	**Student Edition:** *Chapter Assessment: Research and Presentation, Research Skills* 36, 56, 74, 108, 140, 164, 192, 214, 238, 266, 290, 310, 332, 355, 450, 550, 594, 648, 742, 796; *Problem Solving* 386; *Evaluating* 408; *Gathering Information* 430, 472, 526, 572, 626, 668, 722, 772, 818; *Research and Presentation* 700 *Chapter Assessment: College and Career Readiness, Clear Communication* 73; *Research Conclusions* 237; *Explaining Continuity and Change* 265; *Economics* 289; *Multicultural Societies* 449; *Decision Making* 526, 818; *Problem Solving* 594; *Change and Continuity in Economics* 647; *Decision Making* 699 *Chapter Assessment: Exploring the Essential Question, Making Connections* 74; *Researching* 108; *Analyzing* 550; *Sequencing* 722 *Lesson Review: Writing Activity, Explanatory* 81; *Informative/Explanatory* 401 *Chapter Assessment: Writing About Geography, Narrative* 214; *Informative/Explanatory* 290, 406, 626 *Assessment: Problem-Solving Activity, Research Project* 845
8. Gather relevant information from multiple print and digital sources, assess the credibility and accuracy of each source, and integrate the information while avoiding plagiarism.	**Student Edition:** *Chapter Assessment: Exploring the Essential Question, Understanding Historical Interpretation* 35; *Making Connections* 74; *Researching* 108; *Analyzing* 550; *Sequencing* 722 *Chapter Assessment: Research and Presentation, Research Skills* 36, 56, 74, 108, 140, 164, 192, 214, 238, 266, 290, 310, 332, 355, 450, 550, 594, 648, 742, 796; *Problem Solving* 386; *Evaluating* 408; *Gathering Information* 430, 472, 526, 572, 626, 668, 722, 772, 818; *Research and Presentation* 700 *Chapter Assessment: College and Career Readiness, Clear Communication* 73; *Research Conclusions* 237; *Explaining Continuity and Change* 265; *Economics* 289; *Comparing and Contrasting* 332; *Examining Information* 356; *Multicultural Societies* 449; *Decision Making* 526, 818; *Problem Solving* 549, 594; *Change and Continuity in Economics* 647; *Decision Making* 699 *Lesson Review: Writing Activity, Explanatory* 81; *Informative/Explanatory* 401, 406, 740 *DBQ Analyzing Primary Sources, Assessing* 214 *Chapter Assessment: Writing About Geography, Narrative* 214, 742; *Informative/Explanatory* 290, 406, 626 *Assessment: Problem-Solving Activity, Research Project* 845
9. Draw evidence from literary or informational texts to support analysis, reflection, and research.	**Student Edition:** *Lesson Review: Using Your Notes* 25, 34, 43, 50, 54, 63, 68, 72, 81, 86, 91, 99, 106, 124, 131, 138, 148, 155, 158, 162, 179, 186, 190, 199, 205, 212, 222, 229, 236, 254, 260, 264, 274, 281, 288, 298, 304, 308, 318, 325, 330, 340, 347, 354, 371, 377, 384, 394, 401, 406, 415, 421, 428, 437, 443, 448, 458, 465, 470, 488, 495, 500, 510, 517, 524, 534, 541, 548, 558, 565, 570, 580, 587, 592, 610, 617, 624, 633, 639, 646, 656, 662, 666, 684, 691, 698, 707, 716, 720, 729, 736, 740, 758, 765, 770, 780, 787, 794, 803, 809, 816 *Chapter Assessment: Research and Presentation, Research Skills* 36, 56, 74, 108, 140, 164, 192, 214, 238, 266, 290, 310, 332, 355, 450, 550, 594, 648, 742, 796; *Problem Solving* 386; *Evaluating* 408; *Gathering Information* 430, 472, 526, 572, 626, 668, 722, 772, 818; *Research and Presentation* 700 *Chapter Assessment: College and Career Readiness, Clear Communication* 73, 771; *Change and Continuity in Economics* 191, 647; *Research Conclusions* 237; *Explaining Continuity and Change* 265; *Economics* 289; *Multicultural Societies* 449; *Decision Making* 526, 818; *Problem Solving* 594; *Decision Making* 699, 818 *Chapter Assessment: Exploring the Essential Question, Making Connections* 74; *Researching* 108; *Sequencing* 237, 722; *Identifying Cause and Effect* 266; *Analyzing* 550 *Lesson Review: Writing Activity, Explanatory* 81; *Informative/Explanatory* 179, 401 *Chapter Assessment: Writing About Geography, Narrative* 214; *Informative/Explanatory* 290, 406, 626 *Chapter Assessment: Critical Thinking, Making Connections* 771 *Assessment: Problem-Solving Activity, Research Project* 845
Range of Writing	
10. Write routinely over extended time frames (time for research, reflection, and revision) and shorter time frames (a single sitting or a day or two) for a range of tasks, purposes, and audiences.	**Student Edition:** *Lesson Review: Using Your Notes* 25, 34, 43, 50, 54, 63, 68, 72, 81, 86, 91, 99, 106, 124, 131, 138, 148, 155, 158, 162, 179, 186, 190, 199, 205, 212, 222, 229, 236, 254, 260, 264, 274, 281, 288, 298, 304, 308, 318, 325, 330, 340, 347, 354, 371, 377, 384, 394, 401, 406, 415, 421, 428, 437, 443, 448, 458, 465, 470, 488, 495, 500, 510, 517, 524, 534, 541, 548, 558, 565, 570, 580, 587, 592, 610, 617, 624, 633, 639, 646, 656, 662, 666, 684, 691, 698, 707, 716, 720, 729, 736, 740, 758, 765, 770, 780, 787, 794, 803, 809, 816 *Lesson Review: Writing Activity, Informative/Explanatory* 25, 34, 50, 54, 63, 68, 72, 91, 99, 131, 138, 148, 162, 179, 186, 199, 212, 222, 229, 236, 254, 260, 264, 274, 281, 298, 304, 308, 318, 330, 340, 347, 354, 371, 377, 394, 401, 406, 415, 421, 458, 488, 495, 510, 517, 534, 541, 548, 558, 565, 580, 587, 610, 617, 624, 633, 646, 656, 684, 707, 716, 736, 740, 758, 765, 770, 780, 787, 794, 809; *Explanatory* 81, 437; *Narrative* 43, 86, 124, 155, 325, 698, 803; *Argument* 106, 190, 205, 288, 384, 428, 443, 448, 470, 500, 524, 570, 592, 639, 662, 666, 691, 720, 729, 816; *Persuasive* 465 *Chapter Assessment: Writing About Geography: Informative/Explanatory* 36, 74, 108, 238, 266, 290, 310, 356, 408, 502, 550, 626, 648, 772; *Narrative* 56, 214, 332, 430, 572, 700, 742, 772, 818; *Informative* 140; *Argument* 164, 192, 386, 450, 472, 594, 668, 796 *Research and Presentation: Research Skills* 36, 56, 74, 108, 140, 164, 192, 214, 238, 266, 290, 310, 332, 355, 450, 550, 594, 648, 742, 796; *Problem Solving* 386; *Evaluating* 408; *Gathering Information* 430, 472, 526, 572, 626, 668, 722, 772, 818; *Research and Presentation* 700 *Lesson Review: Reviewing Vocabulary, Summarizing* 54, 524, 610; *Displaying* 91; *Making Connections* 155, 720; *Discussing* 179; *Applying* 421, 580, 587; *Identifying Trends* 517; *Describing* 534, 541; *Identifying* 592, 633, 639, 646, 656, 662, 666, 765, 770; *Drawing Inferences* 617; *Hypothesizing* 624; *Understanding Relationships* 736; *Explaining* 740 *Chapter Assessment: Exploring the Essential Question, Making Connections* 56, 140, 356, 472, 626, 700; *Drawing Conclusions* 332, 407; *Organizing* 386, 772, 817; *Analyzing* 550 *Chapter Assessment: College and Career Readiness, Economics* 107; *Change and Continuity in Economics* 191, 647; *Reaching Conclusions* 237, 310, 386, 626; *Explaining Continuity and Change* 265; *Comparing and Contrasting* 332; *Change and Continuity of Groups* 356; *Examining Information* 430, 722; *Multicultural Societies* 449; *Problem Solving* 502, 549, 594, 741; *Decision Making* 526, 699, 818; *Clear Communication* 668, 771, 796 *Making Connections: The Uses of Geography* 157, 231, 379, 543; *Considering Advantages and Disadvantages* 349 *Human Systems* 174, 248, 433, 702, 789 *Environment and Society* 195, 217, 293, 483, 505 *Places and Regions* 313 *Chapter Assessment: Critical Thinking, Evaluating* 266; *Exploring Issues* 429, 525, 625, 721; *Making Connections* 771, 817 *Chapter Assessment: 21st Century Skills, Identifying Perspectives* 471 *Thinking Geographically: Expository* 825; *Human Systems* 789 *Assessment: Problem-Solving Activity, Research Project* 845

Reading Standards for Literacy in History/Social Studies Grades 9–10

Key Ideas and Details

Standard	Correlation
1. Cite specific textual evidence to support analysis of primary and secondary sources, attending to such features as the date and origin of the information.	**Student Edition:** *Analyzing Primary Sources: The Island* 31; *Eyewitness: Icelandic Volcano* 48; *Why Tornadoes Take the Weekends Off in Summer* 72; *World Refugee Day 2012* 86; *Coffee Country* 98; *Can Natural Gas Help Tackle Global Warming?* 138; *Canada Slips in Gender Equality Rankings* 153; *Acid Rain: Sugar Maples at Risk* 160; *Maquiladoras and the Middle Class* 186; *The Mola: Colorful Kuna Culture* 204; *Indigenous Communities Protect Biodiversity* 212; *Urban Population Boom Threatens Lake Titicaca* 235; *The Nordic Model and Working Women* 260; *Documenting the Baltic Sea's Biodiversity* 262; *The Alps* 273; *Olive Oil Production in Italy* 297; *Improving the Business Climate in Poland* 325; *Poetry in Contemporary Russia* 345; *The Long Shadow of Chernobyl* 353; *Saving Mediterranean Habitats Worldwide* 371; *Lebanon's Forests: Going up in Smoke* 394; *Desertification in Syria* 404; *Iraq's Energy Resources* 415; *Threats to the Gulf* 446; *Ancient Geography Text* 455; *Secondary Education for Girls* 515; *Contrasting Views of Tanzania's Landscape* 523; *Local Fishermen Near Lake Chad* 546; *Crime in Kinshasa* 563; *Touring South Africa's Townships* 586; *Hindu Pilgrims* 607; *The Last Straw: Salt Satyagraha, 1930* 612; *Flooding in Bangladesh* 633; *Climbing Mount Everest* 654; *The Spread of Rap and Hip-Hop in China* 689; *Speaking Manchu* 695; *The History of Origami* 714; *The Invasion* 732; *Regional Cooperation* 765; *Mekong Giant Catfish* 768; *Rising Sea Levels Cause Plans for Relocation* 815 *DBQ Questions* 31, 66, 72, 86, 93, 108, 133, 138, 153, 160, 164, 186, 204, 212, 214, 235, 260, 266, 273, 297, 310, 325, 332, 345, 353, 371, 386, 394, 404, 415, 523, 526, 546, 563, 586, 594, 607, 612, 619, 626, 633, 648, 654, 668, 689, 693, 695, 700, 714, 732, 742, 765, 768, 796, 811, 815 *Cartoon* 35, 471, 571, 593, 699, 721, 817 *Chapter Assessment: Primary Source* 36, 56, 74, 108, 140, 164, 192, 214, 238, 266, 290, 310, 332, 356, 386, 408, 430, 450, 472, 502, 526, 550, 572, 594, 626, 648, 668, 700, 722, 742, 772, 796, 818 *Primary Sources* 41, 53, 63, 67, 86, 93, 207, 353, 520, 560 *Case Study: Culture* 92–93, 422–423, 692–693; *The Environment* 132–133, 518–519; *Development* 206–207; *Economics* 282–283; *Geopolitics* 618–619, 810–811 *What do you think? DBQ* 93, 133, 207, 283, 423, 520, 619, 693, 811 *Using Primary Sources* 525, 817 *Analyzing Primary Sources* 550, 563, 714, 722
2. Determine the central ideas or information of a primary or secondary source; provide an accurate summary of how key events or ideas develop over the course of the text.	**Student Edition:** *Reading HELPDESK: Taking Notes: Key Ideas and Details, Identifying* 14, 26, 44, 51, 69, 78, 120, 125, 149, 158, 187, 200, 208, 232, 261, 275, 299, 341, 372, 412, 416, 424, 434, 444, 454, 484, 489, 496, 506, 530, 535, 544, 554, 566, 576, 581, 588, 642, 652, 680, 710, 754, 759, 766, 776, 781, 790, 800, 812; *Describing* 40, 60, 64, 82, 87, 102; *Organizing* 94, 368, 438, 459, 611, 717; *Summarizing* 134, 176, 196, 223, 284, 326, 350, 380, 390, 395, 402, 511, 520, 704; *Categorizing* 144, 314; *Paraphrasing* 180, 218, 270, 305, 319, 336; *Listing* 250, 294, 606, 730; *Outlining* 255; *Exploring Issues* 466; *Formulating Questions* 620; *Comparing and Contrasting* 634; *Identifying Central Issues* 657; *Evaluating* 663; *Describing* 685; *Comparing* 726 *Analyzing* 24, 25, 27, 34, 45, 46, 48, 54, 55, 56, 72, 74, 83, 85, 89, 101, 107, 121, 140, 148, 155, 159, 182, 183, 184, 189, 191, 198, 202, 213, 224, 236, 237, 259, 262, 265, 266, 309, 310, 331, 344, 345, 354, 385, 396, 407, 418, 428, 429, 436, 437, 440, 442, 446, 447, 450, 460, 465, 471, 487, 492, 501, 512, 517, 521, 531, 533, 534, 536, 539, 540, 541, 545, 547, 556, 562, 584, 593, 614, 624, 633, 647, 658, 662, 665, 666, 668, 682, 684, 686, 690, 696, 697, 698, 699, 700, 712, 729, 732, 735, 740, 741, 742, 771, 780, 784, 787, 792, 793, 794, 795, 796, 817 *Lesson Review: Answering the Guiding Questions* 25, 34, 43, 50, 54, 63, 68, 72, 81, 86, 91, 99, 106, 124, 131, 138, 148, 155, 158, 162, 179, 186, 190, 199, 205, 212, 222, 229, 236, 254, 260, 264, 274, 281, 288, 298, 304, 308, 318, 325, 330, 340, 347, 354, 371, 377, 384, 394, 401, 406, 415, 421, 428, 437, 443, 448, 458, 465, 470, 488, 495, 500, 510, 517, 524, 534, 541, 548, 558, 565, 570, 580, 587, 592, 610, 617, 624, 633, 639, 646, 656, 662, 666, 684, 691, 698, 707, 716, 720, 729, 736, 740, 758, 765, 770, 780, 787, 794, 803, 809, 816 *Summarizing* 25, 35, 54, 55, 105, 107, 139, 148, 154, 163, 186, 191, 213, 229, 234, 237, 265, 289, 302, 304, 307, 309, 317, 318, 325, 355, 371, 377, 384, 394, 401, 421, 429, 448, 456, 458, 465, 470, 471, 487, 488, 498, 510, 517, 524, 525, 534, 546, 548, 549, 565, 587, 592, 593, 610, 617, 621, 625, 646, 647, 656, 662, 664, 666, 667, 682, 688, 691, 694, 699, 704, 707, 713, 733, 740, 741, 758, 765, 770, 771, 780, 794, 809, 813, 816 *Identifying the Central Issue* 27, 205 *Finding the Main Idea* 35, 163, 205, 283, 331, 407, 500, 610, 624, 716, 768 *Identifying Central Issues* 55, 93, 107, 133, 139, 146, 153, 160, 162, 207, 213, 235, 237, 260, 265, 266, 271, 277, 283, 286, 289, 290, 308, 309, 338, 355, 371, 385, 408, 488, 494, 500, 517, 524, 534, 565, 570, 571, 591, 593, 607, 612, 613, 619, 625, 668, 682, 689, 693, 697, 711, 721, 732, 811, 817 *Sequencing* 62, 126, 182, 220, 237, 331, 405, 571, 716, 722, 782 *Exploring Issues* 91, 164, 212, 236, 238, 262, 331, 385, 407, 429, 472, 495, 509, 525, 569, 625, 648, 667, 698, 721, 816 *Problem Solving* 98 *Reading Progress Check: Summarizing* 105, 234, 302, 304, 307, 317, 487, 498, 510, 534, 546, 621, 662, 664, 682, 688, 694, 704, 713, 733, 813; *Identifying Central Issues* 146, 277, 286, 494, 613; *Paraphrasing* 152; *Analyzing* 155, 183, 189, 259, 345, 354, 624, 658, 665, 666, 784; *Determining Importance* 202, 488, 509, 707; *Sequencing Information* 517, 712; *Synthesizing* 458, 787; *Sequencing* 782 *Paraphrasing* 152, 290, 371 *Determining Importance* 155, 192, 202, 212, 443, 500, 509, 707 *Sequencing Information* 155, 517, 712 *Synthesizing* 178, 272, 384, 394, 401, 458, 548, 580, 621, 668, 684, 695, 716, 787, 794, 803 *Exploring the Issues* 181, 189, 329, 355, 356 *Identifying Cause and Effect* 423 *Identifying Trends* 517 *Understanding Historical Interpretation* 517, 561, 626, 722, 772 *Analyzing Primary Sources* 550, 563, 714, 722 *Making Predictions* 633, 648 *Contrasting* 716 *Making Connections* 765 *Analyzing Information* 825
3. Analyze in detail a series of events described in a text; determine whether earlier events caused later ones or simply preceded them.	**Student Edition:** *Making Connections* 34, 36, 68, 137, 145, 155, 164, 179, 190, 192, 199, 213, 222, 227, 229, 233, 279, 289, 300, 302, 306, 309, 327, 331, 344, 356, 376, 385, 399, 401, 407, 415, 421, 428, 429, 437, 448, 449, 455, 463, 468, 469, 471, 472, 486, 488, 494, 495, 500, 502, 521, 525, 541, 547, 549, 550, 567, 571, 577, 587, 593, 594, 609, 617, 626, 635, 643, 648, 661, 665, 667, 684, 690, 699, 707, 716, 719, 720, 736, 758, 764, 765, 771, 787, 795, 809, 816, 817 *Identifying Cause and Effect* 36, 55, 56, 63, 68, 98, 108, 139, 164, 186, 190, 191, 205, 213, 237, 238, 265, 266, 287, 289, 295, 309, 347, 354, 355, 369, 370, 383, 384, 385, 408, 423, 427, 429, 449, 456, 464, 469, 471, 491, 492, 500, 501, 507, 508, 510, 545, 546, 549, 565, 567, 569, 570, 571, 578, 593, 612, 622, 624, 625, 643, 644, 647, 653, 659, 667, 695, 697, 698, 721, 739, 740, 741, 756, 764, 767, 770, 771, 801, 809, 817 *Sequencing* 62, 126, 182, 220, 237, 331, 405, 571, 716, 722, 782 *Chapter Assessment: College and Career Readiness, Explaining Continuity and Change* 139, 265; *Change and Continuity in Economics* 191, 472, 647; *Change and Continuity of Groups* 356; *Identifying and Explaining Continuity and Change* 385 *Cause and Effect* 139 *Sequencing Information* 155, 517, 712 *Connecting Geography to History: Before Columbus* 201; *Naming Places* 510; *Slave Forts* 561; *Natural Disaster* 635 *Reading HELPDESK: Taking Notes: Key Ideas and Details, Outlining* 255; *Identifying Cause and Effect* 630, 737 *Reading Progress Check: Identifying Cause and Effect* 383, 456, 464, 469, 491, 565, 567, 569, 659; *Sequencing Information* 517, 712; *Sequencing* 782 *Understanding Relationships Among Events* 571, 736

Correlation of *Geography: The Human and Physical World* to the Common Core State Standards

Reading Standards for Literacy in History/Social Studies Grades 9–10

Craft and Structure	
4. Determine the meaning of words and phrases as they are used in a text, including vocabulary describing political, social, or economic aspects of history/social studies.	**Student Edition:** *Reading HELPDESK: Academic Vocabulary* 14, 26, 40, 44, 51, 60, 64, 69, 78, 82, 87, 94, 102, 120, 125, 134, 144, 149, 158, 176, 180, 187, 196, 200, 208, 218, 223, 232, 250, 255, 261, 270, 275, 284, 294, 299, 305, 314, 319, 326, 336, 341, 350, 368, 372, 380, 390, 395, 402, 412, 416, 424, 434, 438, 444, 454, 459, 466, 484, 489, 496, 506, 511, 520, 530, 535, 544, 554, 559, 566, 576, 581, 588, 606, 611, 620, 630, 634, 642, 652, 657, 663, 680, 685, 694, 704, 710, 717, 726, 730, 737, 754, 759, 766, 776, 781, 790, 800, 804, 812 *Reading HELPDESK: Content Vocabulary* 14, 26, 40, 44, 51, 60, 64, 69, 78, 82, 87, 94, 102, 120, 125, 134, 144, 149, 158, 176, 180, 187, 196, 200, 208, 218, 223, 232, 250, 255, 261, 270, 275, 284, 294, 299, 305, 314, 319, 326, 336, 341, 350, 368, 372, 380, 390, 395, 402, 412, 416, 424, 434, 438, 444, 454, 459, 466, 484, 489, 496, 506, 511, 520, 530, 535, 544, 554, 559, 566, 576, 581, 588, 606, 611, 620, 630, 634, 642, 652, 657, 663, 680, 685, 694, 704, 710, 717, 726, 730, 737, 754, 759, 766, 776, 781, 790, 800, 804, 812 *Lesson Review: Reviewing Vocabulary* 25, 34, 43, 50, 54, 63, 68, 72, 81, 86, 91, 99, 106, 124, 131, 138, 148, 155, 158, 162, 179, 186, 190, 199, 205, 212, 222, 229, 236, 254, 260, 264, 274, 281, 288, 298, 304, 308, 318, 325, 330, 340, 347, 354, 371, 377, 384, 394, 401, 406, 415, 421, 428, 437, 443, 448, 458, 465, 470, 488, 495, 500, 510, 517, 524, 534, 541, 548, 558, 565, 570, 580, 587, 592, 610, 617, 624, 633, 639, 646, 656, 662, 666, 684, 691, 698, 707, 716, 720, 729, 736, 740, 758, 765, 770, 780, 787, 794, 803, 809, 816 *Reading Progress Check: Defining* 33, 106; *Naming* 34, 337, 375, 394, 803 *Naming* 34, 337, 375, 394, 406, 803 *Finding the Main Idea* 35 *Defining* 50, 73, 90, 104, 106, 107, 131, 162, 259, 377, 384, 500, 647 *Interpreting* 140, 310, 648, 700, 796 *Speculating* 238 *Analyzing* 310, 700, 742 *Lesson Review: Reviewing Vocabulary, Applying* 421, 428 *Analyzing Primary Sources* 550, 563 *Chapter Assessment: DBQ Analyzing Primary Sources, Analyzing Arguments* 594 *Using Context Clues* 684 *Analyzing Text Structure* 698 *Labeling* 401 *Making Connections* 707, 720 *Understanding Relationships Among Events* 736 *Theorizing* 796 *Assessment: Reviewing Vocabulary* 845
5. Analyze how a text uses structure to emphasize key points or advance an explanation or analysis.	**Student Edition:** *Identifying Cause and Effect* 36, 55, 56, 63, 68, 98, 108, 139, 164, 186, 190, 191, 205, 213, 237, 238, 265, 266, 287, 289, 295, 309, 347, 354, 355, 369, 370, 383, 384, 385, 408, 423, 427, 429, 449, 456, 464, 469, 471, 491, 492, 500, 501, 507, 508, 510, 545, 546, 549, 565, 567, 569, 570, 571, 578, 593, 612, 622, 624, 625, 643, 644, 647, 653, 659, 667, 695, 697, 698, 721, 739, 740, 741, 756, 764, 767, 770, 771, 801, 809, 817 *Case Study: Culture* 92–93, 422–423, 692–693; *The Environment* 132–133, 518–519; *Development* 206–207; *Economics* 282–283; *Geopolitics* 618–619, 810–811 *Cause and Effect* 139 *Evaluating Counter Arguments* 164 *Understanding Relationships* 309, 496, 514, 523, 533, 696, 719 *Considering Advantages and Disadvantages* 349, 385, 471, 565, 613, 655, 662, 699, 763, 771, 817 *Reading Progress Check: Identifying Cause and Effect* 383, 456, 464, 469, 491, 565, 567, 569, 659; *Understanding Relationships* 496, 514, 523, 533, 696, 719 *Analyzing Text Structure* 698
6. Compare the point of view of two or more authors for how they treat the same or similar topics, including which details they include and emphasize in their respective accounts.	**Student Edition:** *Case Study: Culture* 92–93, 422–423, 692–693; *The Environment* 132–133, 518–519; *Development* 206–207; *Economics* 282–283; *Geopolitics* 618–619, 810–811 *What do you think? DBQ* 93, 133, 207, 283, 423, 520, 619, 693, 811 *Chapter Assessment: College and Career Readiness, Change and Continuity in Economics* 191 *Chapter Assessment: 21st Century Skills, Identifying Perspectives and Differing Interpretations* 741
Integration of Knowledge and Ideas	
7. Integrate quantitative or technical analysis (e.g., charts, research data) with qualitative analysis in print or digital text.	**Student Edition:** *Maps* 2–3, 4–5, 6–7, 8–9, 10, 12, 15, 16, 17, 19, 20, 29, 46, 47, 53, 65, 67, 70, 76, 79, 80, 100–101, 112, 113, 114, 115, 116, 118, 122, 123, 128, 130, 135, 136, 145, 146, 168, 169, 170, 171, 172, 185, 188, 194, 197, 226, 228, 242, 243, 244, 245, 246, 263, 278, 280, 286, 292, 306, 312, 315, 316, 322, 351, 352, 360, 361, 362, 363, 364, 373, 389, 393, 410, 417, 425, 435, 452, 462, 468, 476, 477, 478, 479, 480, 485, 490, 497, 507, 552, 555, 560, 574, 582, 598, 599, 600, 601, 602, 608, 631, 640–641, 650, 672, 673, 674, 675, 676, 681, 683, 705, 718, 727, 746, 747, 748, 749, 750, 755, 783, 788, 798, 813, 820–821, 826, 827 *Use Graphic Organizer* 14, 25, 26, 40, 43, 44, 50, 51, 54, 60, 63, 64, 68, 69, 72, 78, 81, 82, 86, 87, 91, 94, 99, 102, 106, 120, 124, 125, 131, 134, 138, 144, 148, 149, 155, 162, 163, 176, 179, 180, 186, 187, 190, 196, 199, 200, 205, 208, 212, 218, 222, 223, 229, 232, 236, 254, 255, 260, 261, 264, 270, 274, 275, 281, 284, 288, 294, 298, 299, 304, 305, 308, 314, 318, 319, 325, 326, 330, 336, 340, 341, 347, 350, 354, 368, 371, 372, 377, 380, 384, 385, 390, 394, 395, 401, 402, 406, 412, 415, 416, 421, 424, 428, 434, 437, 438, 442, 443, 444, 448, 454, 458, 459, 465, 466, 470, 484, 488, 489, 495, 496, 500, 506, 510, 511, 517, 518, 530, 534, 535, 541, 544, 548, 554, 558, 559, 565, 566, 570, 576, 580, 581, 587, 588, 592, 606, 610, 611, 617, 620, 624, 625, 630, 633, 634, 639, 642, 646, 652, 656, 657, 662, 663, 666, 680, 684, 685, 691, 694, 698, 704, 707, 710, 716, 717, 720, 726, 729, 730, 736, 737, 740, 754, 758, 759, 765, 766, 770, 776, 780, 781, 787, 790, 794,800, 803, 804, 809, 810, 816 *Graph Skills* 23, 83, 84–85, 107, 139, 154, 163, 184, 191, 213, 222, 235, 258, 285, 289, 328, 331, 344, 346, 385, 398, 407, 429, 449, 564, 569, 587, 621, 647, 690, 715, 719, 741, 771, 792, 795, 827 *Chart Skills* 27, 73, 97, 237, 265, 309, 355, 439, 464, 501, 549, 662, 816 *Analyzing Visuals* 35, 123, 137, 147, 178, 179, 184, 190, 204, 209, 211, 252, 253, 274, 285, 298, 307, 324, 346, 376, 381, 391, 414, 420, 428, 442, 446, 455, 468, 494, 495, 498, 499, 500, 507, 531, 532, 564, 567, 568, 577, 589, 591, 609, 616, 621, 622, 645, 665, 706, 707, 715, 719, 758, 777, 786 *Chapter Assessment: Applying Map Skills* 35, 56, 74, 108, 140, 163, 192, 214, 238, 266, 290, 310, 332, 356, 386, 408, 430, 450, 472, 502, 526, 550, 571, 594, 626, 648, 667, 700, 722, 742, 772, 796, 818 *Cartoon* 35, 471, 571, 593, 699, 721, 817 *Diagram Skills* 41, 42, 45, 48, 55, 61, 68, 71, 103, 105, 121, 177, 525 *Infographic* 52, 62, 123, 159, 178, 198, 220, 253, 272, 296, 338, 382, 403, 426, 468, 499, 507, 538, 557, 616, 655, 696, 738, 767, 779, 801 *Chapter Assessment: 21st Century Skills: Using Graphs, Charts, Diagrams, and Tables* 55, 73, 107, 139, 163, 191, 237, 265, 429; *Creating and Using Graphs, Charts, Diagrams, and Tables* 385, 407, 549, 647, 741; *Using Graphs* 626, 771; *Creating Diagrams* 667, 771; *Satellite Image, Geography Skills* 667 *Time Line* 126–127, 150–151, 182–183, 202–203, 224–225, 249, 256–257, 276–277, 300–301, 320–321, 335, 342–343, 374–375, 396–397, 418–419, 440–441, 460–461, 492–493, 512–513, 536–537, 584–585, 614–615, 636–637, 658–659, 686–687, 712–713, 732–733, 760–761, 784–785, 806–807, 823 *Critical Thinking: Using Graphs* 587

Reading Standards for Literacy in History/Social Studies Grades 9–10	
8. Assess the extent to which the reasoning and evidence in a text support the author's claims.	**Student Edition:** *Why Geography Matters* 12–13, 38–39, 58–59, 76–77, 110–111, 118–119, 142–143, 174–175, 194–195, 216–217, 248–249, 268–269, 292–293, 312–313, 334–335, 366–367, 388–389, 410–411, 432–433, 452–453, 482–483, 504–505, 528–529, 552–553, 574–575, 604–605, 628–629, 650–651, 678–679, 702–703, 724–725, 752–753, 774–775, 798–799 *Defending* 56, 623, 711 *Case Study: Culture* 92–93, 422–423, 692–693; *The Environment* 132–133, 518–519; *Development* 206–207; *Economics* 282–283; *Geopolitics* 618–619, 810–811 *What do you think? DBQ* 93, 133, 207, 283, 423, 520, 619, 693, 811 *Hypothesizing* 148 *Evaluating Counter Arguments* 164 *Lesson Review: Reviewing Vocabulary, Applying* 421, 428 *Chapter Assessment: DBQ Analyzing Primary Sources, Analyzing Arguments* 594 *Create and Analyze Arguments and Draw Conclusions* 647 *Constructing Arguments* 779
9. Compare and contrast treatments of the same topic in several primary and secondary sources.	**Student Edition:** *Case Study: Culture* 92–93, 422–423, 692–693; *The Environment* 132–133, 518–519; *Development* 206–207; *Economics* 282–283; *Geopolitics* 618–619, 810–811 *What do you think? DBQ* 93, 133, 207, 283, 423, 520, 619, 693, 811 *Chapter Assessment: College and Career Readiness, Change and Continuity in Economics* 191 *Chapter Assessment: 21st Century Skills, Identifying Perspectives and Differing Interpretations* 741
Range of Reading and Level of Text Complexity	
10. By the end of grade 10, read and comprehend history/social studies texts in the grades 9–10 text complexity band independently and proficiently.	**Student Edition:** *Geography Matters* 11, 37, 57, 75, 109, 117, 141, 173, 193, 215, 247, 267, 291, 311, 333, 365, 387, 409, 431, 451, 481, 503, 527, 551, 573, 603, 627, 649, 677, 701, 723, 751, 773, 797 *Why Geography Matters* 12–13, 38–39, 58–59, 76–77, 110–111, 118–119, 142–143, 174–175, 194–195, 216–217, 248–249, 268–269, 292–293, 312–313, 334–335, 366–367, 388–389, 410–411, 432–433, 452–453, 482–483, 504–505, 528–529, 552–553, 574–575, 604–605, 628–629, 650–651, 678–679, 702–703, 724–725, 752–753, 774–775, 798–799 *There's More Online: Read* 13, 38, 195, 268, 335, 366, 411, 433, 453, 505, 575, 651, 703, 753 *Analyzing Primary Sources: The Island* 31; *Eyewitness: Icelandic Volcano* 48; *Why Tornadoes Take the Weekends Off in Summer* 72; *World Refugee Day* 2012 86; *Coffee Country* 98; *Can Natural Gas Help Tackle Global Warming?* 138; *Canada Slips in Gender Equality Rankings* 153; *Acid Rain: Sugar Maples at Risk* 160; *Maquiladoras and the Middle Class* 186; *The Mola: Colorful Kuna Culture* 204; *Indigenous Communities Protect Biodiversity* 212; *Urban Population Boom Threatens Lake Titicaca* 235; *The Nordic Model and Working Women* 260; *Documenting the Baltic Sea's Biodiversity* 262; *The Alps* 273; *Olive Oil Production in Italy* 297; *Improving the Business Climate in Poland* 325; *Poetry in Contemporary Russia* 345; *The Long Shadow of Chernobyl* 353; *Saving Mediterranean Habitats Worldwide* 371; *Lebanon's Forests: Going up in Smoke* 394; *Desertification in Syria* 404; *Iraq's Energy Resources* 415; *Threats to the Gulf* 446; *Ancient Geography Text* 455; *Secondary Education for Girls* 515; *Contrasting Views of Tanzania's Landscape* 523; *Local Fishermen Near Lake Chad* 546; *Crime in Kinshasa* 563; *Touring South Africa's Townships* 586; *Hindu Pilgrims* 607; *The Last Straw: Salt Satyagraha*, 1930 612; *Flooding in Bangladesh* 633; *Climbing Mount Everest* 654; *The Spread of Rap and Hip-Hop in China* 689; *Speaking Manchu* 695; *The History of Origami* 714; *The Invasion* 732; *Regional Cooperation* 765; *Mekong Giant Catfish* 768; *Rising Sea Levels Cause Plans for Relocation* 815 *Chapter Assessment: Primary Source* 36, 56, 74, 108, 140, 164, 192, 214, 238, 266, 290, 310, 332, 356, 386, 408, 430, 450, 472, 502, 526, 550, 572, 594, 626, 648, 668, 700, 722, 742, 772, 796, 818 *Connecting Geography to Science: Astronomy* 41; *Climatology* 66, 199; *Soil Science* 124; *Biology* 148, 221; *Environmental Science* 189; *Geology* 254; *Cap-and-Trade Systems* 288; *Demography* 301; *Air-Conditioning* 436; *Saving the Aral Sea* 470; *Genetics* 660; *The DMZ* 729; *Tsunamis* 756; *Carbon Dating* 805 *Connecting Geography to Government: Geopolitics* 91, 384; *Environmental Politics* 330; *Soil Erosion in Iraq* 427; *Water Management* 448 *Case Study: Culture* 92–93, 422–423, 692–693; *The Environment* 132–133, 518–519; *Development* 206–207; *Economics* 282–283; *Geopolitics* 618–619, 810–811 *Global Connections: Patterns of Distribution* 100–101; *The United States and Canada* 156–157; *Latin America* 230–231; *Europe* 348–349; *North Africa, Southwest Asia, and Central Asia* 378–379; *Africa South of the Sahara* 542–543; *South Asia* 740–741; *Asia* 708–709; *Australia* 788–789 *Interact with Global Connections Online* 157, 231, 349, 379, 407, 543, 641, 709, 789 *Connecting Geography to History: Before Columbus* 201; *Naming Places* 510; *Slave Forts* 561; *Natural Disaster* 635 *Connecting Geography to Economics, Privatization* 347; *Development* 400 *Connecting Geography to Math: Geometry* 487; *Output of the Kariba Hydroelectric Dam* 579; *India's GDP* 617 *Connecting Geography to Sociology: Social Norms* 540; *Hanami: Viewing of Flowers* 706; *The Outback* 780 *Special Feature: Antarctica* 819–825 *World Religions Handbook* 826–844

Writing Standards for Literacy in History/Social Studies, Science, and Technical Subjects Grades 9–10

Text Types and Purposes	
1. Write arguments focused on *discipline-specific content.* **a.** Introduce precise claim(s), distinguish the claim(s) from alternate or opposing claims, and create an organization that establishes clear relationships among the claim(s), counterclaims, reasons, and evidence. **b.** Develop claim(s) and counterclaims fairly, supplying data and evidence for each while pointing out the strengths and limitations of both claim(s) and counterclaims in a discipline-appropriate form and in a manner that anticipates the audience's knowledge level and concerns. **c.** Use words, phrases, and clauses to link the major sections of the text, create cohesion, and clarify the relationships between claim(s) and reasons, between reasons and evidence, and between claim(s) and counterclaims. **d.** Establish and maintain a formal style and objective tone while attending to the norms and conventions of the discipline in which they are writing. **e.** Provide a concluding statement or section that follows from or supports the argument presented.	**Student Edition:** *Lesson Review: Writing Activity, Argument* 106, 190, 205, 288, 384, 428, 443, 448, 470, 500, 524, 570, 592, 639, 662, 666, 691, 720, 729, 816; *Persuasive* 465 *Chapter Assessment: Writing About Geography, Argument* 164, 192, 386, 450, 472, 594, 668, 796 *Chapter Assessment: College and Career Readiness, Change and Continuity in Economics* 191; *Reaching Conclusions* 310; *Decision Making* 818 *Chapter Assessment: Research and Presentation, Gathering Information* 626 *Making Connections: Human Systems* 789
2. Write informative/explanatory texts, including the narration of historical events, scientific procedures/ experiments, or technical processes. **a.** Introduce a topic and organize ideas, concepts, and information to make important connections and distinctions; include formatting (e.g., headings), graphics (e.g., figures, tables), and multimedia when useful to aiding comprehension. **b.** Develop the topic with well-chosen, relevant, and sufficient facts, extended definitions, concrete details, quotations, or other information and examples appropriate to the audience's knowledge of the topic. **c.** Use varied transitions and sentence structures to link the major sections of the text, create cohesion, and clarify the relationships among ideas and concepts. **d.** Use precise language and domain-specific vocabulary to manage the complexity of the topic and convey a style appropriate to the discipline and context as well as to the expertise of likely readers. **e.** Establish and maintain a formal style and objective tone while attending to the norms and conventions of the discipline in which they are writing. **f.** Provide a concluding statement or section that follows from and supports the information or explanation presented (e.g., articulating implications or the significance of the topic).	**Student Edition:** *Lesson Review: Writing Activity, Informative/Explanatory* 25, 34, 50, 54, 63, 68, 72, 91, 99, 131, 138, 148, 162, 179, 186, 199, 212, 222, 229, 236, 254, 260, 264, 274, 281, 298, 304, 308, 318, 330, 340, 347, 354, 371, 377, 394, 401, 406, 415, 421, 458, 488, 495, 510, 517, 534, 541, 548, 558, 565, 580, 587, 610, 617, 624, 633, 646, 656, 684, 707, 716, 736, 740, 758, 765, 770, 780, 787, 794, 809; *Explanatory* 81, 437 *Chapter Assessment: Research and Presentation, Research Skills* 36, 56, 74, 108, 140, 164, 192, 214, 238, 266, 290, 310, 332, 355, 450, 502, 550, 594, 648, 742, 796; *Explaining* 214; *Problem Solving* 386; *Evaluating* 408; *Gathering Information* 430, 472, 526, 572, 626, 668, 722, 772, 818; *Research and Presentation* 700 *Chapter Assessment: Writing About Geography: Informative/Explanatory* 36, 74, 108, 238, 266, 290, 310, 356, 408, 502, 550, 626, 648, 772; *Informative* 140 *Lesson Review: Reviewing Vocabulary, Summarizing* 54, 524, 610; *Displaying* 91; *Making Connections* 155, 720; *Discussing* 179; *Applying* 421, 580, 587; *Identifying Trends* 517; *Describing* 534, 541; *Identifying* 592, 633, 639, 646, 656, 662, 666, 765, 770; *Drawing Inferences* 617; *Hypothesizing* 624; *Understanding Relationships* 736; *Explaining* 740 *Chapter Assessment: Exploring the Essential Question, Making Connections* 56, 356, 472, 626, 700; *Drawing Conclusions* 332, 407; *Organizing* 386, 772, 817; *Analyzing* 550 *Chapter Assessment: College and Career Readiness, Economics* 107; *Reaching Conclusions* 237, 386, 626; *Explaining Continuity and Change* 265; *Comparing and Contrasting* 332; *Change and Continuity of Groups* 356; *Examining Information* 430, 722; *Multicultural Societies* 449; *Problem Solving* 502, 549, 594, 741; *Decision Making* 526, 699; *Change and Continuity in Economics* 647; *Clear Communication* 668, 771, 796 *Lesson Review: Using Your Notes, Identifying* 131; *Summarizing* 186, 448, 458, 465, 488, 517, 524, 534, 548, 587, 592, 617, 646, 656, 758, 765, 770, 794, 816; *Making Connections* 190; *Analyzing* 437, 541, 787; *Explaining* 470; *Describing* 495, 510, 558, 633; *Applying* 500; *Expressing* 570; *Synthesizing* 580; *Listing* 610; *Comparing and Contrasting* 639, 729; *Considering Advantages and Disadvantages* 662; *Interpreting* 691; *Sequencing* 716; *Transferring Information* 720; *Identifying Cause and Effect* 740 *Making Connections: The Uses of Geography* 157, 231; *Considering Advantages and Disadvantages* 349 *Human Systems* 174, 433, 702 *Environment and Society* 195, 217, 293, 483, 505 *Chapter Assessment: Critical Thinking, Evaluating* 266 *Places and Regions* 313 *Making Connections: The Uses of Geography* 379, 543 *Chapter Assessment: Critical Thinking, Exploring Issues* 429, 721 *Chapter Assessment: 21st Century Skills, Identifying Perspectives* 471 *Chapter Assessment: Critical Thinking, Exploring Issues* 525, 625; *Making Connections* 771, 817 *Thinking Geographically: Expository* 825 *Assessment: Problem-Solving Activity, Research Project* 845

Writing Standards for Literacy in History/Social Studies, Science, and Technical Subjects Grades 9–10	
3. (See note; not applicable as a separate requirement) Students' narrative skills continue to grow in these grades. The Standards require that students be able to incorporate narrative elements effectively into arguments and informative/explanatory texts. In history/social studies, students must be able to incorporate narrative accounts into their analyses of individuals or events of historical import. In science and technical subjects, students must be able to write precise enough descriptions of the step-by-step procedures they use in their investigations or technical work that others can replicate them and (possibly) reach the same results.	**Student Edition:** *Lesson Review: Writing Activity, Narrative* 43, 86, 124, 155, 325, 698, 803 *Chapter Assessment: Writing About Geography, Narrative* 56, 214, 332, 430, 525, 572, 700, 742, 772, 818 *Chapter Assessment: Exploring the Essential Question, Making Connections* 140 *Chapter Assessment: Research and Presentation, Research Skills* 164 *Human Systems* 248
Production and Distribution of Writing	
4. Produce clear and coherent writing in which the development, organization, and style are appropriate to task, purpose, and audience.	**Student Edition:** *Chapter Assessment: Writing About Geography, Informative/Explanatory* 74, 108, 238, 304, 406, 648; *Argument* 164, 192, 450, 668, 796; *Narrative* 332 *Lesson Review: Writing Activity, Narrative* 86, 124, 155, 698; *Informative/Explanatory* 131, 222, 229, 236, 260, 330, 347, 371, 377, 421, 646; *Argument* 288, 384, 443, 448, 470, 570, 666, 816 *Chapter Assessment: College and Career Readiness, Economics* 107; *Change and Continuity in Economics* 191; *Comparing and Contrasting* 332; *Reaching Conclusions* 310, 626; *Examining Information* 430; *Problem Solving* 502; *Change and Continuity in Economics* 647; *Clear Communication* 668, 771 *Making Connections: The Uses of Geography* 157, 231, 379, 543 *Chapter Assessment: Research and Presentation, Research Skills* 164; *Gathering Information* 722 *Chapter Assessment: Exploring the Essential Question, Making Connections* 430; *Synthesizing* 572; *Exploring Issues* 648 *Critical Thinking: Organizing* 571 *Making Connections: Human Systems* 789
5. Develop and strengthen writing as needed by planning, revising, editing, rewriting, or trying a new approach, focusing on addressing what is most significant for a specific purpose and audience.	**Student Edition:** *Chapter Assessment: Exploring the Essential Question: Understanding Historical Interpretation* 35; *Making Connections* 56; *Informative* 140; *Organizing* 386, 817 *Chapter Assessment: Writing About Geography, Informative/Explanatory* 36, 74, 108, 238, 266, 290, 304, 310, 356, 406, 408, 502, 626, 648, 700, 772; *Informative* 140; *Argument* 164, 192, 386, 450, 472, 594, 668, 722, 796; *Narrative* 332, 430, 525, 572, 818 *Lesson Review: Writing Activity, Narrative* 86, 698; *Informative/Explanatory* 222, 229, 236, 260, 347, 371, 377, 421; *Argument* 384, 443, 470 *Chapter Assessment: Research and Presentation, Research Skills* 164 *Chapter Assessment: College and Career Readiness, Change and Continuity in Economics* 191; *Problem Solving* 502; *Reaching Conclusions* 626; *Clear Communication* 668
6. Use technology, including the Internet, to produce, publish, and update individual or shared writing products, taking advantage of technology's capacity to link to other information and to display information flexibly and dynamically.	**Student Edition:** *There's More Online: Read* 13, 38, 195, 268, 335, 366, 411, 433, 453, 505, 575, 651, 703, 753; *Watch* 13, 58, 119, 143, 175, 249, 293, 335, 505, 529, 679, 775; *See* 38, 58, 216, 249, 268, 293, 313, 366, 575, 651, 679, 779, 799; *Compare* 77, 605, 725; *View* 77, 119, 175, 195, 216, 389, 411, 433, 453, 483, 628, 703, 753, 799; *Explore* 143, 313, 389, 483, 605, 628, 725; *Connect* 553; *Examine* 553 *Chapter Assessment: Research and Presentation, Research Skills* 36, 56, 74, 108, 164, 192, 238, 266, 290, 310, 355, 450, 648, 742, 796; *Problem Solving* 332, 386; *Evaluating* 408; *Gathering Information* 430, 472, 572, 626, 668, 722, 772, 818; *Research and Presentation* 700 *Chapter Assessment: College and Career Readiness, Clear Communication* 73; *Reaching Conclusions* 237; *Comparing and Contrasting* 332; *Examining Information* 356; *Problem Solving* 549, 594; *Change and Continuity in Economics* 647 *Interact with Global Connections Online* 157, 231, 349, 379, 407, 543, 641, 709, 789 *Chapter Assessment: Writing About Geography, Narrative* 214, 742; *Informative/Explanatory* 290 *Lesson Review: Writing Activity, Informative/Explanatory* 406, 740 *Chapter Assessment: Exploring the Essential Question, Analyzing* 550 *Assessment: Problem-Solving Activity, Research Project* 845
Research to Build and Present Knowledge	
7. Conduct short as well as more sustained research projects to answer a question (including a self-generated question) or solve a problem; narrow or broaden the inquiry when appropriate; synthesize multiple sources on the subject, demonstrating understanding of the subject under investigation.	**Student Edition:** *Chapter Assessment: Research and Presentation, Research Skills* 36, 56, 74, 108, 140, 164, 192, 214, 238, 266, 290, 310, 332, 355, 450, 550, 594, 648, 742, 796; *Problem Solving* 386; *Evaluating* 408; *Gathering Information* 430, 472, 526, 572, 626, 668, 722, 772, 818; *Research and Presentation* 700 *Chapter Assessment: College and Career Readiness, Clear Communication* 73; *Research Conclusions* 237; *Explaining Continuity and Change* 265; *Economics* 289; *Multicultural Societies* 449; *Decision Making* 526, 818; *Problem Solving* 594; *Change and Continuity in Economics* 647; *Decision Making* 699 *Chapter Assessment: Exploring the Essential Question, Making Connections* 74; *Researching* 108; *Analyzing* 550; *Sequencing* 722 *Lesson Review: Writing Activity, Explanatory* 81; *Informative/Explanatory* 401 *Chapter Assessment: Writing About Geography, Narrative* 214; *Informative/Explanatory* 290, 406, 626 *Assessment: Problem-Solving Activity, Research Project* 845

Writing Standards for Literacy in History/Social Studies, Science, and Technical Subjects Grades 9–10	
8. Gather relevant information from multiple authoritative print and digital sources, using advanced searches effectively; assess the usefulness of each source in answering the research question; integrate information into the text selectively to maintain the flow of ideas, avoiding plagiarism and following a standard format for citation.	**Student Edition:** *Chapter Assessment: Exploring the Essential Question, Understanding Historical Interpretation* 35; *Making Connections* 74; *Researching* 108; *Analyzing* 550; *Sequencing* 722 *Chapter Assessment: Research and Presentation, Research Skills* 36, 56, 74, 108, 140, 164, 192, 214, 238, 266, 290, 310, 332, 355, 450, 550, 594, 648, 742, 796; *Problem Solving* 386; *Evaluating* 408; *Gathering Information* 430, 472, 526, 572, 626, 668, 722, 772, 818; *Research and Presentation* 700 *Chapter Assessment: College and Career Readiness, Clear Communication* 73; *Research Conclusions* 237; *Explaining Continuity and Change* 265; *Economics* 289; *Comparing and Contrasting* 332; *Examining Information* 356; *Multicultural Societies* 449; *Decision Making* 526, 818; *Problem Solving* 549, 594; *Change and Continuity in Economics* 647; *Decision Making* 699 *Lesson Review: Writing Activity, Explanatory* 81; *Informative/Explanatory* 401, 406, 740 *DBQ Analyzing Primary Sources, Assessing* 214 *Chapter Assessment: Writing About Geography, Narrative* 214, 742; *Informative/Explanatory* 290, 406, 626 *Assessment: Problem-Solving Activity, Research Project* 845
9. Draw evidence from informational texts to support analysis, reflection, and research.	**Student Edition:** *Lesson Review: Using Your Notes* 25, 34, 43, 50, 54, 63, 68, 72, 81, 86, 91, 99, 106, 124, 131, 138, 148, 155, 158, 162, 179, 186, 190, 199, 205, 212, 222, 229, 236, 254, 260, 264, 274, 281, 288, 298, 304, 308, 318, 325, 330, 340, 347, 354, 371, 377, 384, 394, 401, 406, 415, 421, 428, 437, 443, 448, 458, 465, 470, 488, 495, 500, 510, 517, 524, 534, 541, 548, 558, 565, 570, 580, 587, 592, 610, 617, 624, 633, 639, 646, 656, 662, 666, 684, 691, 698, 707, 716, 720, 729, 736, 740, 758, 765, 770, 780, 787, 794, 803, 809, 816 *Chapter Assessment: Research and Presentation, Research Skills* 36, 56, 74, 108, 140, 164, 192, 214, 238, 266, 290, 310, 332, 355, 450, 550, 594, 648, 742, 796; *Problem Solving* 386; *Evaluating* 408; *Gathering Information* 430, 472, 526, 572, 626, 668, 722, 772, 818; *Research and Presentation* 700 *Chapter Assessment: College and Career Readiness, Clear Communication* 73, 771; *Change and Continuity in Economics* 191, 647; *Research Conclusions* 237; *Explaining Continuity and Change* 265; *Economics* 289; *Multicultural Societies* 449; *Decision Making* 526, 818; *Problem Solving* 594; *Decision Making* 699, 818 *Chapter Assessment: Exploring the Essential Question, Making Connections* 74; *Researching* 108; *Sequencing* 237, 722; *Identifying Cause and Effect* 266; *Analyzing* 550 *Lesson Review: Writing Activity, Explanatory* 81; *Informative/Explanatory* 179, 401 *Chapter Assessment: Writing About Geography, Narrative* 214; *Informative/Explanatory* 290, 406, 626 *Chapter Assessment: Critical Thinking, Making Connections* 771 *Assessment: Problem-Solving Activity, Research Project* 845
Range of Writing	
10. Write routinely over extended time frames (time for reflection and revision) and shorter time frames (a single sitting or a day or two) for a range of discipline-specific tasks, purposes, and audiences.	**Student Edition:** *Lesson Review: Using Your Notes* 25, 34, 43, 50, 54, 63, 68, 72, 81, 86, 91, 99, 106, 124, 131, 138, 148, 155, 158, 162, 179, 186, 190, 199, 205, 212, 222, 229, 236, 254, 260, 264, 274, 281, 288, 298, 304, 308, 318, 325, 330, 340, 347, 354, 371, 377, 384, 394, 401, 406, 415, 421, 428, 437, 443, 448, 458, 465, 470, 488, 495, 500, 510, 517, 524, 534, 541, 548, 558, 565, 570, 580, 587, 592, 610, 617, 624, 633, 639, 646, 656, 662, 666, 684, 691, 698, 707, 716, 720, 729, 736, 740, 758, 765, 770, 780, 787, 794, 803, 809, 816 *Lesson Review: Writing Activity, Informative/Explanatory* 25, 34, 50, 54, 63, 68, 72, 91, 99, 131, 138, 148, 162, 179, 186, 199, 212, 222, 229, 236, 254, 260, 264, 274, 281, 298, 304, 308, 318, 330, 340, 347, 354, 371, 377, 394, 401, 406, 415, 421, 458, 488, 495, 510, 517, 534, 541, 548, 558, 565, 580, 587, 610, 617, 624, 633, 646, 656, 684, 707, 716, 736, 740, 758, 765, 770, 780, 787, 794, 809; *Explanatory* 81, 437; *Narrative* 43, 86, 124, 155, 325, 698, 803; *Argument* 106, 190, 205, 288, 384, 428, 443, 448, 470, 500, 524, 570, 592, 639, 662, 666, 691, 720, 729, 816; *Persuasive* 465 *Chapter Assessment: Writing About Geography: Informative/Explanatory* 36, 74, 108, 238, 266, 290, 310, 356, 408, 502, 550, 626, 648, 772; *Narrative* 56, 214, 332, 430, 572, 700, 742, 772, 818; *Informative* 140; *Argument* 164, 192, 386, 450, 472, 594, 668, 796 *Research and Presentation: Research Skills* 36, 56, 74, 108, 140, 164, 192, 214, 238, 266, 290, 310, 332, 355, 450, 550, 594, 648, 742, 796; *Problem Solving* 386; *Evaluating* 408; *Gathering Information* 430, 472, 526, 572, 626, 668, 722, 772, 818; *Research and Presentation* 700 *Lesson Review: Reviewing Vocabulary, Summarizing* 54, 524, 610; *Displaying* 91; *Making Connections* 155, 720; *Discussing* 179; *Applying* 421, 580, 587; *Identifying Trends* 517; *Describing* 534, 541; *Identifying* 592, 633, 639, 646, 656, 662, 666, 765, 770; *Drawing Inferences* 617; *Hypothesizing* 624; *Understanding Relationships* 736; *Explaining* 740 *Chapter Assessment: Exploring the Essential Question, Making Connections* 56, 140, 356, 472, 626, 700; *Drawing Conclusions* 332, 407; *Organizing* 386, 772, 817; *Analyzing* 550 *Chapter Assessment: College and Career Readiness, Economics* 107; *Change and Continuity in Economics* 191, 647; *Reaching Conclusions* 237, 310, 386, 626; *Explaining Continuity and Change* 265; *Comparing and Contrasting* 332; *Change and Continuity of Groups* 356; *Examining Information* 430, 722; *Multicultural Societies* 449; *Problem Solving* 502, 549, 594, 741; *Decision Making* 526, 699, 818; *Clear Communication* 668, 771, 796 *Making Connections: The Uses of Geography* 157, 231, 379, 543; *Considering Advantages and Disadvantages* 349 *Human Systems* 174, 248, 433, 702, 789 *Environment and Society* 195, 217, 293, 483, 505 *Places and Regions* 313 *Chapter Assessment: Critical Thinking, Evaluating* 266; *Exploring Issues* 429, 525, 625, 721; *Making Connections* 771, 817 *Chapter Assessment: 21st Century Skills, Identifying Perspectives* 471 *Thinking Geographically: Expository* 825; *Human Systems* 789 *Assessment: Problem-Solving Activity, Research Project* 845

Correlation of *Geography: The Human and Physical World* to the National Geography Standards

The second edition of *Geography For Life,* as in the first edition, ensures that the National Geography Standards continue to challenge students and address the most important and enduring ideas in geography. The second edition of Geography For Life also incorporates new ideas about geography, the learning process, and additional skills that transcend disciplinary boundaries.

The goal of the *National Geography Standards* is to help students become geographically informed through knowledge and mastery of factual knowledge, mental maps and geographic tools, and ways of thinking.

Geography for Life: National Geography Standards	Student Edition
(1) How to use maps and other geographic representations, geospatial technologies, and spatial thinking to understand and communicate information	
The student knows and understands:	
1.1 The advantage of coordinating multiple geographic representations—such as maps, globes, diagrams, aerial and other photographs, remotely sensed images, and geographic visualizations to answer geographic questions	11, 14-15, 16, 17, 18, 19, 20, 22, 23, 24, 25, 26, 27, 28, 32, 33, 35, 46, 128, 140, 189, 212, 306, 370, 486, 560, 757
1.2 The technical properties and quality of geospatial data	14, 15, 16, 18, 19, 20, 21, 22, 23, 24, 25, 35, 36, 37, 74, 212
1.3 The appropriate and ethical uses of geospatial data and geospatial technologies in constructing geographic representations	12-13, 21, 23, 24, 25, 27, 74, 189, 212, 306, 332, 356
1.4 The uses of geographic representation and geospatial technologies to investigate and analyze geographic questions and to communicate geographic answers	3, 5, 7, 9, 10, 13, 15, 16, 17, 19, 21, 22, 23, 24, 25, 26, 27, 28, 34, 35, 41, 46, 113, 115, 116, 128, 130, 140, 145, 146, 163, 168, 171, 172, 185, 188, 197, 214, 226, 238, 242, 245, 263, 278, 280, 286, 290, 306, 310, 315, 316, 322, 332, 351, 352, 361, 363, 364, 370, 373, 386, 389, 393, 408, 413, 425, 430, 435, 450, 462, 472, 477, 479, 480, 485, 490, 497, 498, 502, 526, 550, 555, 560, 571, 582, 599, 601, 602, 608, 626, 631, 648, 672, 675, 676, 681, 683, 705, 718, 722, 727, 746, 748, 755, 772, 783, 796, 813, 818
Therefore, the student is able to:	
1.1.A. Explain the advantages of using multiple geographic representations to answer geographic questions	11, 14-15, 16, 17, 18, 19, 20, 22, 23, 24, 25, 26, 27, 28, 32, 33, 35, 46, 128, 140, 189, 212, 306, 370, 486, 560, 757
1.2.A. Identify and explain the metadata properties (e.g., resolution, date of creation, and method of collection) of geospatial data	21, 22, 23, 24, 25, 212
1.2.B. Evaluate the quality and quantity of geospatial data appropriate for a given purpose	15, 16, 18, 19, 23, 24, 25, 32, 34, 37, 212, 306, 560
1.3.A. Evaluate the appropriate and ethical uses of different geospatial technologies and methods for acquiring, producing, and displaying geospatial data	12-13, 21, 23, 24, 25, 27, 74, 189, 212, 306, 332, 356
1.4.A. Analyze geographic representations and suggest solutions to geographic questions at local to global scales using geographic representations and geospatial technologies	3, 5, 7, 9, 10, 13, 15, 16, 17, 19, 21, 22, 23, 24, 25, 26, 27, 28, 34, 35, 41, 46, 113, 115, 116, 128, 130, 140, 145, 146, 163, 168, 171, 172, 185, 188, 197, 214, 226, 238, 242, 245, 263, 278, 280, 286, 290, 306, 310, 315, 316, 322, 332, 351, 352, 361, 363, 364, 370, 373, 386, 389, 393, 408, 413, 425, 430, 435, 450, 462, 472, 477, 479, 480, 485, 490, 497, 498, 502, 526, 550, 555, 560, 571, 582, 599, 601, 602, 608, 626, 631, 648, 672, 675, 676, 681, 683, 705, 718, 722, 727, 746, 748, 755, 772, 783, 796, 813, 818
(2) How to use mental maps to organize information about people, places, and environments in a spatial context	
The student knows and understands:	
2.1 The locations, characteristics, patterns, and relationships of physical and human systems are the basis for mental maps at local to global scales	20, 21, 29, 31, 36, 140, 163, 192, 214, 238, 310, 332, 356, 386, 408, 430, 450, 472, 502, 526, 550, 571, 594, 626, 648, 667, 700, 742, 772, 796, 818
2.2 Mental maps can change through experience and iterative self-reflection	21
2.3 Mental maps are used to answer geographical questions about locations, characteristics, patterns, and relationships of places and regions	20, 21, 163, 192, 214, 238, 290, 310, 332, 356, 386, 408, 430, 450, 455, 472, 502, 526, 550, 571, 594, 626, 648, 700, 722, 742, 772, 796, 818
2.4 Changing perceptions reshape mental maps of people, places, regions, and environments	21

Geography for Life: National Geography Standards	Student Edition
Therefore, the student is able to:	
2.1.A. Identify from memory and explain the locations, characteristics, patterns, and relationships among physical and human systems	20, 56, 140, 163, 192, 214, 238, 290, 310, 332, 356, 386, 408, 430, 450, 472, 502, 526, 550, 571, 594, 626, 648, 667, 700, 722, 742, 772, 796, 818
2.2.A. Explain the development of completeness and accuracy in the student's mental maps of places and regions	20
2.3.A. Identify from memory and explain the locations, characteristics, patterns, and relationships of places and regions to answer geographic questions	56, 140, 163, 192, 214, 238, 310, 332, 356, 386, 408, 430, 450, 455, 472, 501, 526, 550, 571, 594, 626, 648, 700, 722, 742, 772, 796, 818
2.4.A. Compare an individual's mental maps before and after a geographic event or experience	21
(3) How to analyze the spatial organization of people, places, and environments on Earth's surface	
The student knows and understands:	
3.1 The meaning and use of complex spatial concepts, such as connectivity, networks, hierarchies, to analyze and explain the spatial organizations of human and physical phenomena	15, 16, 17, 23, 26, 27, 29, 34, 36, 47, 102, 103, 104, 105, 106, 108, 145, 146, 148, 214, 260, 299, 300, 302, 312-313, 316, 317, 318, 320, 321, 325, 331, 338, 340, 342, 356, 366-367, 374, 381, 391, 392, 401, 402, 406, 414, 415, 421, 426, 433, 443, 453, 454, 458, 459, 460, 466, 490, 505, 508, 512, 516, 517, 535, 542-543, 568, 571, 611, 626, 630, 631, 650-651, 658, 660, 720, 725, 748, 753, 754, 756, 764, 765, 772, 803, 804, 809
3.2 Complex processes change over time and shape patterns in the distribution of human and physical phenomena	13, 27, 47, 50, 59, 66-67, 102, 106, 119, 125, 145, 268-269, 273, 274, 293, 299, 300, 312-313, 319, 320, 321, 367, 373, 393, 415, 421, 425, 459, 485, 490, 505, 536, 611, 612, 621, 622, 635, 696, 709, 755, 776
3.3 Models are used to represent the structure and dynamics of spatial processes that shape human and physical systems	14, 23, 47, 68, 71, 83, 103, 104, 105, 106, 272
Therefore, the student is able to:	
3.1.A. Analyze and explain the spatial organization of people, places, and environments (where things are in relation to other things) using spatial concepts	3, 5, 17, 26, 28, 29, 35, 102, 103, 104, 141, 148, 179, 260, 290, 299, 316, 338, 340, 366-367, 485, 497, 508, 512, 535, 626, 630, 631, 650-651, 696, 722, 725, 753, 754, 764, 772, 803
3.2.A. Analyze and explain changes in spatial patterns as a result of the interactions among human and physical processes through time	26, 27, 33, 59, 102, 106, 143-144, 146, 148, 189, 209, 210, 268-269, 274, 293, 312-313, 316, 318, 321, 367, 425, 428, 696, 725, 813
3.3.A. Analyze and explain the spatial features, processes, and organization of people, places, and environments using models of human and/or physical systems (e.g., urban structure, sediment transport, and spatial interaction)	7, 15, 103, 104, 105, 208, 248, 268-269, 272, 825
(4) The physical and human characteristics of places	
The student knows and understands:	
4.1 The effects of place-based identities on personal, community, national, and world events	91, 119, 127, 131, 152, 157, 180, 183, 191, 192, 203, 205, 226, 257, 258, 260, 266, 300, 313, 342, 373, 374, 388, 399, 408, 425, 430, 440, 441, 449, 450, 453, 459, 489, 607, 617, 626, 636, 660, 695, 716, 722, 725, 729, 762, 774, 775, 780, 785, 804
4.2 The interaction of physical and human systems result in the creation of and changes to places	3, 5, 33, 36, 59, 72, 74, 122, 132-133, 135, 142-143, 148, 152, 173, 174, 180, 186, 188, 189, 191, 195, 199, 200, 208, 209, 210, 212, 217, 219, 223, 232, 233, 234, 261, 262, 263, 264, 269, 272, 275, 290, 293, 296-297, 306, 309, 319, 326, 327, 330, 336, 337, 354, 366-367, 386, 394, 422, 425, 428, 430, 446, 450, 456, 477, 484, 485, 486, 489, 490, 493, 497, 498, 502, 534, 548, 567, 568, 569, 570, 589-590, 617-618, 621-623, 624, 626, 633, 636, 660, 678, 680, 681, 682, 684, 706, 736, 737, 766, 767, 769, 770
Therefore, the student is able to:	
4.1.A. Explain how and why place-based identities can shape events at various scales	91, 119, 127, 131, 152, 157, 180, 183, 191, 192, 203, 205, 226, 257, 258, 260, 266, 300, 313, 342, 373, 374, 388, 399, 408, 425, 430, 440, 441, 449, 450, 453, 459, 489, 607, 617, 626, 636, 660, 695, 716, 722, 725, 729, 762, 774, 775, 780, 785, 804
4.2.A. Explain how physical or human characteristics interact to create a place by giving it meaning and significance	3, 74, 80, 91, 117, 125, 127, 131, 152, 173, 176, 180, 186, 192, 193, 199, 203, 214, 215, 218, 219, 223, 226, 251, 258, 261, 275, 300, 309, 336-337, 342, 388, 414, 450, 459, 477, 484, 489, 556, 607, 636, 660, 680, 681, 682, 684, 706, 729

Geography for Life: National Geography Standards	Student Edition
4.2.B. Explain how physical or human characteristics interact to change the meaning and significance of places	13, 33, 36, 173, 174, 195, 198, 208, 209, 210, 212, 217, 220, 232, 233, 234, 238, 261, 262, 263, 264, 269, 272, 275, 290, 293, 296-297, 306, 309, 313, 344, 354, 366-367, 388, 408, 422, 425, 430, 446, 450, 456, 485, 486, 490, 493, 497, 498, 502, 534, 548, 567, 568, 569, 570, 589-590, 621-623, 624, 626, 633, 678, 682, 737, 766, 767, 769, 770, 804
(5) That people create regions to interpret Earth's complexity	
The student knows and understands:	
5.1 Regions are defined by different sets of criteria and places can be included in multiple regions of different types	10, 29, 30, 32, 35, 70, 72, 79, 80, 115, 122-124, 130, 147, 171, 215, 222, 240, 250, 251, 253, 256, 302, 315, 317, 318, 358, 385, 443, 474, 596, 670, 695, 744, 751, 752, 753, 776
5.2 Regional change is caused by multiple interacting processes	13, 55, 80, 81, 136, 138, 146, 185, 194-195, 200, 201, 211, 212, 232, 240, 313, 678, 753, 765
Therefore, the student is able to:	
5.1.A. Identify and explain how a place can exist within multiple regional classifications	10, 29, 30, 32, 35, 70, 72, 79, 80, 115, 122-124, 130, 147, 171, 215, 222, 240, 250, 251, 253, 256, 302, 315, 317, 318, 358, 385, 443, 474, 596, 670, 695, 744, 751, 752, 753, 776
5.2.A. Describe and explain the processes that have resulted in regional change	13, 55, 80, 81, 136, 138, 146, 185, 194-195, 200, 201, 211, 212, 232, 240, 313, 678, 753, 765
(6) How culture and experience influence people's perceptions of places and regions	
The student knows and understands:	
6.1 People can view places and regions from multiple perspectives	26, 30, 33, 36, 77, 91, 151, 153, 163, 191, 226, 276, 279, 283, 287, 300, 319, 321, 327, 348-349, 354, 388-389, 395, 396, 397, 407, 411, 422-423, 429, 430, 441, 453, 459, 491, 494, 502, 518-519, 523, 528-529, 536, 553, 562, 563, 583, 585, 586, 611, 613, 617, 618-619, 635, 636, 637, 648, 660, 688, 691, 725, 771, 772
6.2 Changing perceptions of places and regions have significant economic, political and cultural consequences in an increasingly globalized and complex world	151, 153, 200, 201, 227, 283, 287, 300, 319, 320-321, 325, 327, 350, 354, 378-379, 386, 388-389, 422-423, 430, 441, 453, 463, 518-519, 536, 540, 541, 585, 618-619, 725, 772
Therefore, the student is able to:	
6.1.A. Explain how and why people view places and regions differently as a function of their ideology, race, ethnicity, language, gender, age, religion, politics, social class, and economic status	30, 33, 91, 151, 153, 163, 191, 203, 213, 226, 227, 258, 259, 260, 266, 276, 279, 300, 302, 319, 320, 321, 322, 327, 344, 374, 377, 388, 395, 396, 397, 398, 399, 401, 411, 418, 419, 420, 421, 422-423, 430, 441, 453, 459, 462, 491, 494, 502, 528-529, 536-537, 553, 562, 563, 585, 586, 611, 613, 617, 635, 636, 637, 648, 660, 688, 691, 725, 732, 771, 826, 827, 828-829, 830-831, 832-833, 834-835, 836-837, 838-839, 840-841, 842-844, 845
6.2.A. Explain the possible consequences of people's changing perceptions of places and regions in a globalized and fractured world	153, 201, 283, 287, 319, 320-321, 343, 422-423, 537, 618-619
(7) The physical processes that shape the patterns of Earth's surface	
The student knows and understands:	
7.1 The interaction of Earth's physical systems (the atmosphere, biosphere, hydrosphere, and lithosphere) vary across space and time	40, 42, 43, 48, 51, 55, 121, 123, 179, 189, 220, 263, 265, 273, 274, 436, 458, 488, 531, 579, 608, 610, 633, 655, 683, 684, 748, 757
7.2 Earth-Sun relationships are variable over long periods of time resulting in changes in physical processes and patterns on Earth	40, 43, 60, 61, 62, 63, 74, 179, 803, 817
7.3 Physical processes interact over time to shape particular places on Earth's surface	44, 45, 46, 47, 48, 49, 50, 55, 56, 120, 121, 122, 124, 139, 144, 145, 146, 163, 176, 177, 189, 197, 218, 248, 250, 251, 254, 265, 270, 294, 295, 298, 314-315, 318, 368, 369, 371, 385, 412, 413, 415, 434, 435, 449, 455, 502, 506, 507, 508, 510, 525, 530-531, 576, 580, 593, 599, 606, 607, 625, 630, 631, 647, 652, 653, 672, 705, 721, 727, 755, 756, 776, 777, 800, 801
Therefore, the student is able to:	
7.1.A. Explain how the effects of physical processes vary across regions of the world and over time	41, 43, 45, 46, 47, 48, 49, 50, 55, 56, 120, 121, 124, 146, 163, 176, 189, 197, 219, 250, 251, 254, 263, 265, 270, 368, 369, 412, 413, 434, 435, 449, 455, 506, 576, 577, 606, 625, 630, 631, 647, 652, 777, 779, 801

Geography for Life: National Geography Standards	Student Edition
7.1.B. Explain the ways in which Earth's physical processes are dynamic and interactive	44, 45, 46, 47, 48, 49, 50, 51, 52, 54, 55, 56, 59, 120, 121, 124, 139, 146, 163, 176, 177, 196, 197, 248, 250, 251, 253, 254, 265, 294, 295, 318, 368, 369, 385, 412, 413, 434, 435, 449, 455, 506, 507, 510, 525, 606, 625, 630, 631, 647, 652, 704, 707, 755, 777, 800, 801, 818
7.2.A. Explain how variability in Earth-Sun relationships affect Earth's physical processes over time	60, 61, 62, 63, 803
7.3.A. Analyze and explain the results of interactions of physical processes over time	43, 44, 45, 46, 47, 48, 49, 50, 55, 56, 120-121, 124, 139, 144, 145, 146, 163, 176, 177, 179, 219, 248, 250, 251, 252, 254, 265, 270, 294, 295, 318, 368, 369, 371, 385, 412, 413, 415, 434, 435, 449, 455, 506, 507, 508, 510, 525, 606, 625, 630, 631, 647, 652, 704, 705, 707, 753, 756, 776, 777, 801, 818
(8) The characteristics and spatial distribution of ecosystems and biomes on Earth's surface	
The student knows and understands:	
8.1 Ecosystems are dynamic and respond to changes in environmental conditions	135, 136, 159, 162, 187, 188, 189, 190, 209, 210, 230-231, 232, 233, 234, 235, 261, 262, 263, 264, 284, 285, 286, 305, 307, 308, 326, 355, 382, 383, 384, 402, 424, 425, 426, 427, 428, 429, 445, 468, 469, 471, 488, 496, 497, 501, 522, 523, 524, 525, 546, 549, 567, 569, 621, 624, 625, 643, 644, 664, 675, 696, 718, 739, 766, 767, 769, 770, 790, 791, 792, 796
8.2 The characteristics and geographic distribution of ecosystems	31, 122, 146, 147, 148, 158, 159, 163, 164, 171, 178, 187, 196, 197, 198, 199, 213, 214, 218, 220, 221, 230, 237, 253, 261, 271, 273, 274, 289, 297, 310, 318, 332, 339, 340, 350, 351, 355, 370, 371, 392-393, 407, 415, 424, 425, 426, 427, 429, 435, 484, 485, 487, 531, 532, 549, 554, 555, 557, 558, 572, 577, 578, 593, 631, 653, 656, 664, 780, 796, 822
8.3 The distribution and characteristics of biomes change over time	57, 69, 70, 71, 72, 122-124, 146, 147, 253, 263, 297, 305, 317, 318, 370, 436, 437, 479, 488, 497, 509, 510, 534, 549, 579, 580, 608, 610, 633, 682, 707, 728, 766, 767
Therefore, the student is able to:	
8.1.A. Explain how there are short-term and long-term changes in ecosystems	123, 135, 136, 148, 158, 159, 160, 161, 162, 187, 188, 189, 190, 209, 230-231, 232, 233, 235, 261, 262, 263, 264, 284, 285, 286, 290, 305, 306, 307, 308, 326, 327, 328, 329, 331, 350, 351, 382, 383, 384, 402, 424, 426, 427, 445, 468, 469, 471, 486, 488, 496, 497, 501, 522, 523, 524, 525, 546, 549, 567, 569, 592, 621, 622, 624, 625, 643, 644, 664, 696, 707, 718-719, 739, 766, 767, 769, 770, 788-789, 790, 791, 792
8.1.B. Explain how local and global changes influence ecosystems	135, 136, 148, 158, 159, 160, 161, 162, 187, 209, 210, 230-231, 232, 233, 261, 262, 285, 290, 305, 318, 326, 327, 328, 329, 331, 382, 383, 384, 402, 424, 425, 426, 427, 428, 445, 468, 469, 471, 488, 497, 500, 501, 522, 523, 546, 549, 621, 622, 644, 664, 696, 718, 719, 766, 767, 790, 791
8.2.A. Explain the geographic distribution of ecosystems	146, 147, 148, 158, 159, 163, 187, 196, 199, 218, 220, 221, 237, 261, 297, 298, 370, 371, 402, 415, 424, 425, 429, 435, 457, 484, 531, 532, 557, 558, 572, 631, 656, 778, 779
8.2.B. Evaluate ecosystems in terms of their biodiversity and productivity	147, 148, 158, 159, 162, 179, 198, 199, 209, 218, 221, 230, 237, 261, 262, 327, 338, 355, 371, 402, 424, 437, 488, 531, 557, 579, 633, 665, 682, 706, 728, 729, 758, 766, 771, 779, 780, 802, 822
8.3.A. Explain how climate can influence and change the characteristics and geographic distribution of biomes	57, 69, 70, 71, 72, 122-123, 124, 146, 147, 148, 161, 163, 164, 178, 179, 221, 222, 230, 245, 253, 263, 270, 273, 297, 298, 306, 317, 332, 339, 340, 370, 371, 393, 394, 415, 436, 437, 445, 468, 488, 496, 501, 509, 510, 532, 534, 549, 578, 579, 580, 608, 610, 646, 655, 665, 682, 683, 706, 707, 758, 780, 803, 813, 814, 816
(9) The characteristics, distribution, and migration of human populations on Earth's surface	
The student knows and understands:	
9.1 Culture, economics, and politics influence the changing demographic structure of different populations	82, 83, 84, 85, 86, 119, 127, 128, 129, 131, 139, 149, 150, 152, 153, 185, 186, 202, 223, 226, 237, 257, 258, 265, 277, 278, 281, 293, 301, 304, 309, 320, 325, 331, 344, 374, 377, 399, 407, 418, 429, 433, 449, 462, 465, 482-483, 501, 538, 549, 567, 604, 636, 699, 702, 721, 783, 784, 787, 795

Geography for Life: National Geography Standards	Student Edition
9.2 Population distribution and density are a function of historical, environmental, economic, political, and technological factors	84, 85, 86, 107, 108, 116, 118, 119, 127, 128, 129, 139, 149, 150, 151, 152, 153, 155, 163, 172, 176, 177, 181-182, 186, 201, 202, 210, 213, 214, 221, 223, 225, 229, 234, 237, 246, 257, 258, 260, 265, 268, 278, 289, 293, 301, 310, 322, 323, 325, 331, 343, 344, 355, 356, 364, 374, 385, 398, 399, 418, 439, 446, 449, 450, 461, 462, 480, 483, 492, 508, 514, 517, 538, 545, 549, 561, 572, 602, 604-605, 613, 621, 622, 626, 629, 636, 647, 648, 659, 662, 667, 676, 688, 700, 712, 716, 741, 742, 750, 757, 762, 765, 783, 795, 806, 818
9.3 Migration is one of the driving forces for shaping and reshaping the cultural and physical landscape of places and regions	31, 80, 81, 83, 86, 106, 109, 119, 127, 129, 131, 139, 153, 174, 182, 185, 186, 191, 202, 210, 213, 217, 225, 226, 234, 237, 257, 258, 278, 281, 290, 292-293, 301, 304, 319, 322, 323, 325, 344, 355, 372, 373, 375, 399, 418, 429, 432-433, 439, 492, 493, 511, 512, 517, 521, 562, 563, 581, 611, 613, 636, 637, 658, 660, 688, 691, 712, 762, 763, 775, 781, 782, 783, 784-785, 787, 795, 802, 804, 805, 807, 808, 817
Therefore, the student is able to:	
9.1.A. Explain the demographic history of countries using the demographic transition model	82, 83, 86, 107, 108, 361, 482-483, 484, 485, 492, 493, 494, 501, 604
9.1.B. Evaluate the effects of government policies on population characteristics	84, 119, 127, 151, 153, 217, 257, 258, 278, 293, 301, 334, 344, 399, 433, 483, 515, 516, 528-529, 538, 540, 548, 561, 567, 575, 604, 623, 624, 688, 690, 692-693, 702, 775, 783, 786
9.2.A. Identify and explain how historical, environmental, economic, political, and technological factors have influenced the current population distribution	84, 86, 106, 119, 128, 153, 174, 177, 202, 210, 213, 234, 257, 258, 278, 281, 293, 301, 322, 325, 334-335, 344, 399, 408, 436, 439, 461, 480, 483, 493, 538, 604-605, 613, 659, 688, 762, 765, 783, 787
9.2.B. Analyze demographic data and identify trends in the spatial distribution of population	82, 83, 84, 85, 86, 108, 116, 128, 172, 202, 213, 225, 257, 258, 266, 269, 279, 289, 301, 309, 325, 334-335, 377, 399, 401, 408, 418, 439, 495, 549, 613, 617, 647, 703, 733, 741
9.3.A. Compare and explain different examples of migrations in terms of the "laws of migration"	432-433, 439
9.3.B. Evaluate and explain the impact of international migration on physical and human systems	84, 86, 153, 185, 202, 213, 216, 225, 226, 257, 278, 292-293, 301, 433, 521, 783, 805, 806
9.3.C. Compare and explain the ways in which different groups and governments adjust to the departure and arrival of migrants	86, 174, 226, 257, 258, 278, 292-293, 301, 334-338, 375, 433, 521
(10) The characteristics, distribution, and complexity of Earth's cultural mosaics	
The student knows and understands:	
10.1 Cultural systems provide contexts for living in and viewing the world	29, 78, 107, 153, 180, 183, 191, 203, 204, 205, 213, 259, 323, 398, 462, 465, 471, 513, 514, 539, 710, 714, 733, 762, 763, 774, 775, 804
10.2 Cultural landscapes exist at multiple scales	78, 79, 80, 81, 107, 119, 129, 131, 153, 155, 163, 180, 183, 191, 203, 205, 213, 226, 229, 237, 259, 302, 312-313, 410-411, 420, 462, 471, 493, 513, 514, 515, 539, 613-614, 634, 660, 714, 715, 716, 730, 762, 763, 765, 774, 775, 805, 827
10.3 Cultures changes through convergence and/or divergence	80, 81, 92-93, 155, 181, 182, 194-195, 204, 205, 213, 218, 223, 256, 276, 324, 372, 373, 375, 376, 398, 482-483, 511, 516-517, 535, 689, 713, 730, 733, 734, 742, 775, 801, 805, 809
10.4 The rate of cultural changes has increased as a result of globalization	81, 92-93, 108, 205, 615, 695, 699, 808
Therefore, the student is able to:	
10.1.A. Describe and explain the characteristics that constitute any particular cultural system (e.g., Amish, Japanese, Maori, etc.)	129-130, 149, 180, 184, 203, 204, 205, 213, 258-259, 279, 302-303, 323-324, 344-345, 375-376, 399-400, 419-420, 440-442, 463-464, 493-494, 514-517, 539-540, 562-563, 586-587, 613-615, 637-638, 660-661, 685-686, 713, 714, 716, 733-734, 735, 762-763, 774-775, 781, 785, 786, 787, 796, 804, 807, 809, 845
10.1.B. Explain how different cultures provide contexts from which people may view the world differently	126, 180, 183, 204, 205, 255, 259, 276, 313, 420, 513, 716, 763, 775, 804
10.2.A. Identify and analyze the spatial patterns of cultural landscapes at multiple scales	79, 127, 129, 180, 181, 203, 313, 322, 374-375, 410-411, 482-483, 762, 763, 775

Geography for Life: National Geography Standards	Student Edition
10.2.B. Explain differences in the human imprints on the physical environment of different cultures	119, 126, 129, 195, 327, 328, 329, 373, 588, 655, 686
10.3.A. Identify and explain examples of cultures convergence	155, 182, 184, 204, 205, 213, 276, 372, 373, 375, 376, 398, 483, 511, 535, 689, 713, 775, 801, 805
10.3.B. Identify and explain examples of cultural divergence	194-195, 204, 205, 213, 218, 223, 255, 483, 516-517, 733, 734, 736, 775, 801, 805
10.4.A. Explain how and why globalizations has increased the rate of change in cultures	92-93, 185, 324, 689, 695, 714
(11) The patterns and networks of economic interdependence on Earth's surface	
The student knows and understands:	
11.1 The scale and organization of economic activities change over time	81, 98, 130, 131, 148, 154, 155, 163, 181, 182, 184, 185, 186, 191, 205, 227, 228, 245, 256, 260, 264, 276, 280, 281, 297, 303, 304, 309, 319, 324, 325, 331, 342, 343, 345, 346, 347, 355, 366-367, 376, 385, 401, 420, 442, 464, 466, 471, 490, 501, 505, 510, 516, 517, 521, 524, 541, 542-543, 549, 560, 564, 565, 587, 616, 617, 620, 632, 633, 639, 662, 678, 686, 687, 690, 691, 715, 720, 735, 736, 752-753, 764, 765, 771, 787, 794, 799, 808, 817
11.2 Patterns exist in the spatial organization of economic activities	9, 96, 97, 122, 124, 125, 130, 148, 154, 155, 156-157, 179, 181, 184, 185, 191, 205, 227, 228, 260, 280, 289, 304, 337, 340, 345, 401, 443, 464, 495, 504-505, 517, 564, 720, 735, 753, 764
11.3 Economic systems are dynamic organizations of interdependent economic activities for production, exchange, distribution, and consumption of goods and services	34, 35, 94, 95, 96, 98, 99, 107, 130, 131, 155, 185, 205, 228, 256, 260, 276, 304, 317, 324, 325, 342, 343, 345, 346, 347, 355, 450, 465, 565, 587, 611, 616, 617, 639, 647, 678, 686, 687, 690, 691, 715, 735, 752-753, 765, 771
11.4 Improvements in transportation and communication networks reduce the effects of distance and time on the movements of people, products, and ideas	34, 81, 92, 146, 155, 185, 186, 316, 337, 342, 347, 377, 400, 401, 421, 512, 541, 549, 565, 616, 632, 639, 713, 715, 722, 753, 764, 765, 809
Therefore, the student is able to:	
11.1.A. Explain how economic activities change over time	81, 98, 130, 131, 148, 154, 155, 163, 181, 182, 184, 185, 186, 191, 205, 227, 228, 245, 256, 260, 264, 276, 280, 281, 297, 303, 304, 309, 319, 324, 325, 331, 342, 343, 345, 346, 347, 355, 366-367, 376, 385, 401, 420, 442, 464, 466, 471, 490, 501, 505, 510, 516, 517, 521, 524, 541, 542-543, 549, 560, 564, 565, 587, 616, 617, 620, 632, 633, 639, 662, 678, 686, 687, 690, 691, 715, 720, 735, 736, 752-753, 764, 765, 771, 787, 794, 799, 808, 817
11.2.A. Identify and analyze the origins and development of and changes of patterns of economic activities	96, 97, 115, 124, 125, 130, 131, 148, 155, 160, 163, 179, 181, 182, 205, 227-228, 256, 260, 276, 280, 281, 303, 304, 324, 325, 343, 345, 346, 347, 385, 465, 505, 517, 521, 564, 587, 616, 735, 752-753, 764, 765
11.3.A. Explain how the economic systems of countries and regions consist of multiple coordinated economic activities	94, 95, 96, 99, 107, 130, 131, 155, 185, 186, 205, 228, 260, 276, 304, 324, 325, 342, 343, 347, 355, 450, 564, 587, 611, 617, 647, 687, 690, 691, 715, 735, 752-753, 764, 765
11.3.B. Explain why and how economic systems change	96, 186, 205, 276, 304, 319, 324, 325, 343, 346, 347, 355, 465, 521, 616, 678-679, 686, 687, 690, 736, 752-753, 764
11.4.A. Explain the effects of technological changes in communications and transportation systems on the speed and distances over which people, products, and ideas move	34, 81, 92, 127, 131, 146, 155, 185, 186, 228-229, 268-269, 281, 289, 325, 342, 347, 355, 377, 400, 401, 421, 512, 541, 549, 565, 616, 632, 639, 713, 715, 722, 753, 764, 765, 809
(12) The process, patterns, and functions of human settlement	
The student knows and understands:	
12.1 The numbers, types, and range of the functions of settlement change over space and time	86, 102, 103, 104, 105, 106, 107, 139, 150, 151, 153, 163, 172, 189, 201, 202, 210, 211, 213, 216, 234, 235, 237, 249, 257, 258, 289, 462, 492, 514, 538, 549, 621, 732, 783, 784
12.2 Settlements can grow and/or decline over time	86, 102, 104, 106, 107, 128, 129, 139, 150, 174, 182, 189, 196, 201, 202, 210, 211, 216, 234, 235, 249, 257, 258, 322, 419, 492, 538, 539, 549, 555, 581, 585, 688, 712, 721, 733, 756, 784
12.3 The spatial patterns of settlements change over time	102, 104, 106, 107, 127, 128, 129, 139, 150, 172, 174, 182, 234, 249, 257, 258, 289, 304, 322, 337, 538, 539, 585, 586, 653, 718, 727, 741, 746, 805, 806
12.4 Urban models are used to analyze the growth and form of urban regions	86, 103, 104, 105

Geography for Life: National Geography Standards	Student Edition
Therefore, the student is able to:	
12.1.A. Explain how and why the number and range of functions of settlements have changed and may change in the future	102, 103, 104, 106, 107, 127, 150, 174, 234, 257, 258, 322, 440, 492, 539, 549, 621
12.2.A. Explain and compare the factors that contribute to the growth or decline of settlements over time	86, 102, 103, 104, 105, 106, 107, 125, 150, 151, 172, 174, 181, 182, 196, 201, 234, 257, 258, 364, 440, 442, 443, 538, 539, 555, 585, 613, 688, 712, 756, 757, 783, 803, 804, 806
12.3 A. Compare and explain the changing functions, sizes, and spatial patterns of settlements	7, 102, 103, 104, 106, 107, 172, 234, 246, 613, 727
12.3.B. Analyze and explain the structure and development of megacities and megalopoli	7, 129, 175, 182-183, 186, 187, 189, 234, 268-269, 290, 613, 712
12.4.A. Explain and compare the growth and structure of cities using different urban models	102, 103, 104, 105
(13) How the forces of cooperation and conflict among people influence the division and control of Earth's surface	
The student knows and understands:	
13.1 The function and consequences of territorial divisions	89, 90, 91, 108, 126, 181, 200, 208, 277, 312-313, 320, 321, 373, 378-379, 388-389, 391, 396-397, 417, 449, 483, 512, 513, 520, 521, 536, 549, 552-553, 594, 599, 612, 618-619, 635, 650-651, 658, 711, 725, 731, 756, 759, 760, 810, 811, 824
13.2 Cooperation between countries and organizations may have lasting influences on past, present, and future global issues	90-91, 140, 150, 151, 154, 156-157, 161, 186, 190, 201, 205, 211, 227-228, 229, 236, 237, 256, 257, 264, 277, 281, 282-283, 287, 288, 303-304, 307, 308, 325, 330, 354, 383, 385, 418, 421, 443, 449, 500, 501, 524, 541, 547, 667, 668, 718-719, 720, 765, 770, 772, 787, 810, 815, 816, 824
13.3 Changes within, between, and among countries regarding division and control of Earth's surface may result in conflicts	90-91, 126, 149, 150, 181, 182, 200, 201, 203, 208, 224, 276, 277, 313, 319, 321, 344, 373, 379, 388-389, 396, 397, 408, 417, 444, 448, 449, 461, 462, 472, 502, 513, 521, 525, 546, 552-553, 612, 618-619, 635, 651, 658, 686, 711, 725, 731, 760, 761, 782
Therefore, the student is able to:	
13.1.A. Explain how territorial divisions are used to manage Earth's surface	89, 90, 91, 107, 150, 277, 312-313, 373, 388-389, 396, 397, 453, 460, 491, 520, 552-553, 582, 594, 599, 611, 612, 651, 731, 756, 759, 760, 810, 811, 824
13.1.B. Compare the reasons for and consequences of different systems for dividing and controlling space	91, 107, 132-133, 149, 150, 181, 182, 222, 275, 277, 313, 373, 388-389, 396-397, 460, 461, 491, 520, 521, 587, 589, 594, 650-651, 742, 759, 760, 810, 811
13.2.A. Evaluate how countries and organizations cooperate to address global issues	90, 91, 140, 151, 156-157, 161, 186, 190, 205, 211, 212, 229, 236, 237, 256, 264, 277, 281, 283, 287, 288, 307, 308, 325, 330, 418, 443, 449, 470, 487, 498, 499, 500, 501, 524, 541, 547, 667, 668, 718-719, 765, 770, 772, 810, 815, 824
13.3.A. Explain the ways conflict affects the cohesiveness and fragmentation of countries	91, 150, 181, 182, 277, 319, 321, 344, 373, 379, 396, 397, 408, 417, 441, 453, 460, 461, 462, 472, 483, 491, 502, 513, 521, 525, 534, 546, 552-553, 566, 567, 583, 589, 612, 618-619, 635, 658, 761, 783
13.3.B. Explain the causes and consequences of political and social revolutions resulting from issues of control of land and resources	150, 151, 181, 182, 183, 201, 202, 224, 276, 321, 342, 374, 377, 378-379, 398, 417, 453, 460, 512-513, 521, 552-553, 561, 584, 612, 760, 761, 771
(14) How human actions modify the physical environment	
The student knows and understands:	
14.1 Human modifications of the physical environment can have significant global impacts	31, 36, 39, 53, 59, 72, 134, 135, 136, 137, 138, 139, 159, 160, 161, 163, 190, 191, 198, 201, 209, 211, 213, 230-231, 232, 233, 234, 235, 236, 237, 262, 263, 264, 272, 284, 285, 286, 287, 288, 289, 305-306, 307, 327, 328, 329, 330, 331, 352, 353, 354, 366-367, 381, 382, 383, 402, 403, 404, 405, 424, 425, 426, 427, 428, 445, 449, 468, 469, 470, 471, 497, 500, 501, 518-519, 522, 523, 525, 546, 550, 567, 568, 569, 588, 589, 594, 620, 621, 623, 643, 646, 664, 665, 666, 694, 697, 718, 720, 737, 738-739, 740, 741, 766, 767, 768, 769, 770, 791, 792, 793, 795, 796, 814, 816

Geography for Life: National Geography Standards	Student Edition
14.2 The use of technology can have both intended and unintended impacts on the physical environment which may be positive or negative	39, 53, 54, 59, 72, 135, 136, 137, 138, 139, 140, 148, 160, 162, 163, 179, 189, 198, 208, 209, 211, 236, 252-253, 261, 262, 263, 264, 272, 286, 307, 327, 329, 330, 352, 353, 354, 381, 382, 386, 394, 403, 405, 424, 426, 427, 428, 445, 449, 456, 466-467, 470, 486, 487, 498, 501, 518-519, 532, 533, 546, 549, 550, 617, 620, 632, 645, 682, 694, 696, 697, 698, 699, 708, 717, 718, 721, 739, 742, 764, 766, 767, 815, 816, 817
14.3 People can either mitigate and/or adapt to the consequences of human modifications of the physical environment	132-133, 136, 140, 148, 163, 187, 190, 211, 213, 236, 327, 354, 425, 430, 486, 487, 498, 499, 500, 548, 550, 718, 720, 812
Therefore, the student is able to:	
14.1.A. Explain the global impacts of human changes in the physical environment	31, 36, 39, 53, 59, 72, 134, 135, 136, 137, 138, 139, 159, 160, 161, 163, 190, 191, 198, 201, 209, 211, 213, 230-231, 232, 233, 234, 235, 236, 237, 262, 263, 264, 272, 284, 285, 286, 287, 288, 289, 305-306, 307, 327, 328, 329, 330, 331, 352, 353, 354, 366-367, 381, 382, 383, 402, 403, 404, 405, 424, 425, 426, 427, 428, 445, 449, 468, 469, 470, 471, 497, 500, 501, 518-519, 522, 523, 525, 546, 550, 567, 568, 569, 588, 589, 594, 620, 621, 623, 643, 646, 664, 665, 666, 694, 697, 718, 720, 737, 738-739, 740, 741, 766, 767, 768, 769, 770, 791, 792, 793, 795, 796, 814, 816
14.2.A. Evaluate the intended and unintended impacts of using technology to modify the physical environment	39, 53, 54, 59, 72, 135, 136, 137, 138, 139, 140, 148, 160, 162, 163, 179, 189, 198, 208, 209, 211, 236, 252-253, 261, 262, 263, 264, 272, 286, 307, 327, 329, 330, 352, 353, 354, 381, 382, 386, 394, 403, 405, 424, 426, 427, 428, 445, 449, 456, 466-467, 470, 486, 487, 498, 501, 518-519, 532, 533, 546, 549, 550, 617, 620, 632, 645, 682, 694, 696, 697, 698, 699, 708, 717, 718, 721, 739, 742, 764, 766, 767, 815, 816, 817
14.3.A. Describe and evaluate scenarios for mitigating and/or adapting to environmental change caused by human modifications	132-133, 136, 140, 148, 163, 187, 190, 211, 213, 236, 327, 354, 425, 430, 486, 487, 498, 499, 500, 548, 550, 718, 720, 812
(15) How physical systems affect human systems	
The student knows and understands:	
15.1 Depending on the choice of human activities, the characteristics of the physical environment can be viewed as both opportunities and constraints	53, 55, 113, 132-133, 148, 177, 211, 213, 219, 222, 237, 238, 272, 289, 348-349, 394, 429, 457, 458, 479, 578, 593, 601, 609, 620, 621, 625, 632, 633, 656, 666, 682, 700, 717, 728, 750, 758, 790
15.2 Humans perceive and react to environmental hazards in different ways	160, 161, 189, 196, 211, 212, 285, 329, 330, 352, 382-383, 385, 428, 430, 445, 447, 448, 498, 499, 500, 607, 609, 629, 635, 665-666, 667, 684, 708-709, 735, 740, 816
15.3 Societies use a variety of strategies to adapt to changes in the physical environment	39, 53, 55, 132-133, 161, 177, 212, 218, 382-383, 385, 447, 448, 457, 492, 498, 535, 540, 601, 629, 735, 805, 816
Therefore, the student is able to:	
15.1.A. Explain how people may view the physical environment as both an opportunity or a constraint depending on their choice of activities	132-133, 148, 168, 177, 213, 219, 222, 238, 272, 289, 348-349, 394, 457, 458, 479, 578, 593, 601, 625, 632, 633, 656, 666, 682, 700, 728, 758, 790
15.2.A. Explain and compare how people in different environments think about and respond to environmental hazards	160, 179, 189, 206-207, 212, 285, 326, 369, 382-383, 385, 403, 404, 405, 428, 430, 447, 448, 492, 498, 500, 607, 621, 629, 635, 665-666, 667, 695, 696, 704, 708-709, 717, 735, 740, 816
15.2.B. Explain how environmental hazards affect human systems and why people may have different ways of reacting to them	59, 67, 123, 142, 189, 206-207, 211, 212, 285, 326, 385, 447, 448, 498, 499, 500, 607, 621, 629, 631, 654, 684, 695, 696, 708-709, 717, 740
15.3.A. Explain how societies adapt to reduced capacity in the physical environment	39, 53, 55, 160, 161, 189, 211, 326, 403, 448, 492, 498, 500, 524, 535
15.3.B. Analyze the concept of "limits to growth" to explain adaptation strategies in response to the restrictions imposed on human systems by physical systems	31, 168, 214

Geography for Life: National Geography Standards	Student Edition
(16) The changes that occur in the meaning, use, distribution, and importance of resources	
The student knows and understands:	
16.1 The meaning and use of resources change over time	124, 131, 134, 135, 137, 148, 154, 158, 160, 181, 187, 188, 208, 212, 228, 232, 254, 260, 274, 280, 304, 318, 326, 347, 367, 376, 394, 400, 414, 415, 421, 424, 436, 437, 444, 449, 458, 490, 508, 509, 510, 512, 521, 532, 533, 534, 536, 541, 542-543, 550, 558, 564, 571, 580, 585, 588, 610, 621, 625, 633, 645, 656, 682, 705, 719, 728, 729, 736, 758, 764, 766, 770, 780, 787, 803, 812
16.2 The spatial distribution of resources affects patterns of human settlement and trade	54, 98, 99, 100-101, 125, 150, 154, 179, 194-195, 221, 222, 257, 316, 317, 318, 322, 336, 338, 340, 347, 366-367, 369, 375, 377, 394, 401, 413, 414, 417, 421, 426, 436, 437, 443, 456, 510, 511, 532, 536, 541, 559, 560, 585, 587, 594, 606, 611, 656, 707, 715, 716, 717, 721, 727-728, 736, 753, 756, 764, 780, 802, 803, 804
16.3 Policies and programs that promote the sustainable use and management of resources impact people and the environment	38, 39, 52-53, 54, 124, 132-133, 134, 135, 137, 138, 142, 143, 148, 160, 161, 162, 163, 174, 188, 209, 211, 212, 236, 260, 264, 281, 286, 287, 288, 298, 307, 308, 309, 318, 325, 326, 354, 380-381, 385, 386, 394, 403, 405, 406, 407, 421, 428, 448, 467, 470, 472, 495, 498, 499, 500, 501, 502, 505, 522, 524, 532, 533, 543, 547, 548, 549, 570, 591, 592, 623, 624, 625, 642, 643, 645, 646, 647, 648, 663, 664, 665, 666, 678, 697, 698, 718, 720, 740, 741, 770, 791, 793, 794, 813, 815, 816
Therefore, the student is able to:	
16.1.A. Explain the relationship between the quest for resources and the exploration, colonization, and settlement of different regions of the world	142, 149-150, 158, 160, 180, 181, 182, 184, 194-195, 200, 221, 222, 224, 228, 234, 257, 300, 322, 348-349, 376, 394, 437, 490, 491, 512, 536, 559, 560, 564, 580, 582, 585, 587, 594, 611, 635, 782, 804
16.1.B. Explain how globalization and higher standards of living affect the meaning and use of resources	53, 96, 97, 185, 304, 373, 570, 624, 643, 694, 695, 698, 764, 769
16.2.A. Analyze and explain the relationships between the spatial patterns of settlement and resources	54, 98, 99, 100-101, 125, 150, 154, 179, 194-195, 221, 222, 257, 316, 317, 318, 322, 336, 338, 340, 347, 366-367, 369, 375, 377, 394, 401, 413, 414, 417, 421, 426, 436, 437, 443, 456, 510, 511, 532, 536, 541, 559, 560, 585, 587, 594, 606, 611, 656, 707, 715, 716, 717, 721, 727-728, 736, 753, 756, 764, 780, 802, 803, 804
16.2.B. Analyze and evaluate patterns of trade in resources	98, 99, 100-101, 179, 185, 186, 229, 237, 265, 318, 347, 458, 465, 490, 510, 511, 559, 560, 611, 656, 715, 716, 717, 721, 736, 753, 756, 764, 780, 781, 787, 802, 803, 809, 816
16.3.A. Explain and compare the costs and benefits of using various types of renewable, nonrenewable, and flow resources	39, 53, 54, 124, 132-133, 134, 135, 142, 143, 148, 160, 162, 179, 209, 212, 254, 264, 265, 326, 348-349, 381, 384, 403, 428, 437, 447, 448, 449, 488, 498, 517, 522, 547, 558, 569, 632, 642, 648, 666, 678, 694, 717, 718, 720, 766, 767, 770, 793, 794, 795, 815, 816
16.3.B. Evaluate policy decisions regarding the sustainable use of resources in different regions and at different spatial scales in the world	39, 132-133, 135, 148, 161, 162, 163, 179, 189, 190, 211, 212, 213, 214, 235, 236, 254, 264, 265, 286, 287, 288, 289, 307, 308, 327, 328, 329, 330, 331, 332, 348-349, 384, 385, 405, 406, 407, 421, 428, 448, 467, 470, 472, 498, 499, 500, 501, 502, 505, 522, 524, 532, 533, 543, 547, 548, 570, 591, 592, 623, 624, 625, 645, 646, 647, 648, 666, 678, 718, 720, 737, 740, 741, 767, 770, 793, 794, 813, 815, 816

Geography for Life: National Geography Standards	Student Edition
(17) How to apply geography and interpret the past	
The student knows and understands:	
17.1 Geographic contexts (the human and physical characteristics of places and environments) can explain the connections between sequences of historical events	33, 35, 108, 119, 126, 131, 149, 150, 191, 193, 195, 200, 201, 202, 213, 214, 223, 224, 227, 237, 238, 255, 256, 260, 265, 275, 276, 299, 300, 302, 304, 311, 312-313, 319, 320, 321, 341, 342, 355, 372, 373, 374, 395, 396, 397, 401, 416, 417, 418, 419, 421, 429, 438, 439, 450, 453, 459, 460, 489, 511, 521, 525, 526, 535, 536, 537, 550, 553, 559, 560, 571, 581-582, 583, 611, 625, 626, 634, 635, 636-637, 639, 657, 658, 685, 686, 687, 691, 710, 711, 712, 730, 731, 759, 760, 761, 771, 781, 782, 806-807, 823
17.2 The causes and processes of change in the geographic characteristics and spatial organizations of places, regions, and environments over time	33, 35, 72, 74, 80, 81, 108, 125, 149, 150, 164, 190, 191, 195, 200, 201, 213, 214, 224, 237, 255, 265, 275, 276, 300, 312-313, 320, 321, 341, 342, 372, 373, 374, 377, 401, 416, 417, 429, 459, 460, 465, 512, 521, 536-537, 550, 611, 685, 686, 731, 771
17.3 Historical events must be interpreted in the contexts of people's past perceptions of places, regions, and environments	126, 149, 150, 181, 183, 184, 186, 191, 201, 275-276, 302, 304, 372, 395, 401, 416, 418, 440, 460, 541, 550, 583, 611, 625, 657, 685, 691, 725, 782
Therefore, the student is able to:	
17.1.A. Analyze and explain the connections between sequences of historical events and the geographic contexts in which they occurred	33, 35, 108, 119, 126, 131, 149, 150, 191, 193, 195, 200, 201, 202, 213, 214, 223, 224, 227, 237, 238, 255, 256, 260, 265, 275, 276, 299, 300, 302, 304, 311, 312-313, 319, 320, 321, 341, 342, 355, 372, 373, 374, 395, 396, 397, 401, 416, 417, 418, 419, 421, 429, 438, 439, 450, 453, 459, 460, 489, 511, 521, 525, 526, 535, 536, 537, 550, 553, 559, 560, 571, 581-582, 583, 611, 625, 626, 634, 635, 636-637, 639, 657, 658, 685, 686, 687, 691, 710, 711, 712, 730, 731, 759, 760, 761, 771, 781, 782, 806-807, 823
17.2.A. Identify and explain the causes and processes of change in the geographic characteristics and spatial organization of places, regions, and environments over time	33, 35, 72, 74, 80, 81, 108, 125, 149, 150, 164, 190, 191, 195, 200, 201, 213, 214, 224, 237, 255, 265, 275, 276, 300, 312-313, 320, 321, 341, 342, 372, 373, 374, 377, 401, 416, 417, 429, 459, 460, 465, 512, 521, 536-537, 550, 611, 685, 686, 731, 771
17.3.A. Analyze and evaluate the role that people's past perceptions of places, regions, and environments played as historical events unfolded	126, 149, 150, 181, 183, 184, 186, 191, 201, 275-276, 302, 304, 372, 395, 401, 416, 418, 440, 460, 541, 550, 583, 611, 625, 657, 685, 691, 725, 782
(18) How to apply geography to interpret the present and plan for the future	
The student knows and understands:	
18.1 Geographic contexts (the human and physical characteristics of places and environments) provide the bases for analyzing current events and making predictions about future issues	12, 31, 59, 206-207, 231, 308, 309, 447, 453, 500, 501, 613, 633, 691, 694, 698, 702, 720, 740, 741, 771, 825
18.2 The current and possible future causes and processes of change in the geographic characteristics and spatial organization of places, regions, and environments	12, 59, 106, 107, 108, 151, 189, 261, 262, 308, 349, 350, 381, 430, 447, 500, 502, 698, 741, 765, 779
18.3 Multiple and diverse perceptions of the world must be taken into account to understand contemporary and future issues	53, 126, 142, 151, 157, 231, 266, 327, 348-349, 350, 693
Therefore, the student is able to:	
18.1.A. Explain and evaluate the influences of the geographic contexts on current events and issues in order to make informed decisions and predictions about the future	12, 31, 59, 206-207, 231, 308, 309, 447, 500, 501, 613, 633, 691, 694, 698, 702, 720, 740, 771, 825
18.1.B. Analyze and evaluate the connections between geographic contexts of current events and possible future issues	12-13, 59, 132-133, 206-207, 231, 648
18.2.A. Identify and explain the causes and processes of current and possible future changes in the geographic characteristics and spatial organizations of places, regions, and environments	12, 59, 151, 187, 189, 206-207, 230-231, 261, 262, 327, 348-349, 350, 502, 765
18.3.A. Evaluate how perceptions vary and affect people's views of contemporary issues and strategies for addressing them	53, 142, 151, 157, 207, 266, 327, 525, 693, 770

ePals GlobalCommunity

Where learners connect™

Stockbyte/Punchstock

ePals®, a global community of more than one million K-12 classrooms in 200 countries and territories, provides teachers with the opportunity to facilitate safe, authentic, and dynamic exchanges with other classrooms. McGraw-Hill Education, The Smithsonian Institution, International Baccalaureate, and leading educators around the globe have partnered with ePals® to help make learning dynamic for students, improve academic achievement, and meet multiple Common Core standards.

What Is Global Collaboration?

Global collaboration leverages the power of social media to connect classrooms around the world for real-life lessons and projects in virtual study groups, in and out of school. Students can safely work together on ePals® using familiar social media tools to collaborate on research, discussions, and multimedia projects. By connecting with peers in other parts of the world, students can discover people, places, and cultures far beyond the classroom.

Why Collaboration Is Crucial

Research shows that collaborative learning has a positive effect on student achievement. Collaborative, project-based experiences inspire students with real-world problems and bring lessons to life with dynamic, participatory learning. Students are more motivated and try harder because they're communicating with a real person, for a real purpose. ePals® collaboration benefits students and educators in a variety of ways:

- Facilitates classroom-led delivery of Common Core-aligned, project-based learning experiences, including Writing 6 and Writing 7
- Demonstrates student knowledge by publishing written projects to share ideas and receive feedback from an international audience
- Develops core academic, college and career skills such as critical thinking, problem solving, communication and global awareness

Connect Globally

On ePals®, teachers can browse hundreds of thousands of classroom profiles and projects by location, age range, language, and subject matter, to find collaboration partners. Classrooms then partner in virtual project workspaces for digital collaboration around tailored projects, activities, and content. Each project workspace enables roundtable classroom collaboration and includes a suite of safe social media tools (private to that workspace and controlled by the teacher), including blogs, wikis, forums, and media galleries. ePals® also provides safe student email accounts for one-on-one student exchanges.

ePals® is specifically designed for safe K-12 communication and collaboration, compliant with the Children's Online Privacy Protection Act (COPPA), Family Educational Rights and Privacy Act (FERPA) and Children's Internet Protection Act (CIPA). A team of ePals® educators moderates all classroom profiles and projects to maintain a robust education community safe for K-12 students.

Tips for Collaborating Globally on ePals®

Pair Students With Global Peers: Pair students within a project workspace with peers from other countries to accomplish specific goals, such as completing joint-inquiry projects.

Host Online Discussions: Host dynamic discussions between students by posting forum topics for students to build on one another's ideas and learn to express their own thoughts clearly and persuasively.

Share Student Work: Have students publish their work and ideas to the project group using media galleries and encourage peer review.

Create Collaborative Content: Use wikis to have student groups author joint content, such as digital presentations and multimedia research reports.

To get started, visit ePals® at http://www.epals.com/mhnetworks

UNDERSTANDING BY DESIGN®

by Jay McTighe

Understanding by Design® (UbD™) offers a planning framework to guide curriculum, assessment, and instruction. Its two key ideas are contained in the title: 1) focus on teaching and assessing for understanding and transfer, and 2) design curriculum "backward" from those ends.

UbD is based on seven key tenets:

1. UbD is a way of thinking purposefully about curricular planning, not a rigid program or prescriptive recipe.
2. A primary goal of UbD is developing and deepening student understanding: the ability to make meaning of learning via "big ideas" and transfer learning.
3. Understanding is revealed when students autonomously make sense of and transfer their learning through authentic performance. Six facets of understanding—the capacity to explain, interpret, apply, shift perspective, empathize, and self assess—serve as indicators of understanding.
4. Effective curriculum is planned "backward" from long-term desired results though a three-stage design process (Desired Results, Evidence, Learning Plan). This process helps to avoid the twin problems of "textbook coverage" and "activity-oriented" teaching in which no clear priorities and purposes are apparent.
5. Teachers are coaches of understanding, not mere purveyors of content or activity. They focus on ensuring learning, not just teaching (and assuming that what was taught was learned); they always aim and check for successful meaning making and transfer by the learner.
6. Regular reviews of units and curriculum against design standards enhance curricular quality and effectiveness.
7. UbD reflects a continuous improvement approach to achievement. The results of our designs —student performance—inform needed adjustments in curriculum as well as instruction.

Three Stages of Backward Design

In UbD, we propose a 3-stage "backward design" process for curriculum planning. The concept of planning "backward" from desired results is not new. In 1949 Ralph Tyler described this approach as an effective process for focusing instruction. More recently, Stephen Covey, in the best selling book, *Seven Habits of Highly Effective People*, reports that effective people in various fields are goal-oriented and plan with the end in mind. Although not a new idea, we have found that the deliberate use of backward design for planning curriculum units and courses results in more clearly defined goals, more appropriate assessments, more tightly aligned lessons, and more purposeful teaching.

Backward planning asks educators to consider the following three stages:

Stage 1 – Identify Desired Results

What should students know, understand, and be able to do? What content is worthy of understanding? What "enduring" understandings are desired? What essential questions will be explored?

In the first stage of backward design we consider our goals, examine established Content Standards (national, state, province, district), and review curriculum expectations. Since there is typically more "content" than can reasonably be addressed within the available time, teachers must make choices. This first stage in the design process calls for setting priorities.

More specifically, Stage 1 of UbD asks teachers to identify the "big ideas" that we want students to come to understand, and then to identify or craft companion essential questions. Big ideas reflect transferable concepts, principles and processes that are key to understanding the topic or subject. Essential questions present open-ended, thought-provoking inquiries that are explored over time.

More specific knowledge and skill objectives, linked to the targeted Content Standards and Understandings, are also identified in Stage 1. An important point in UbD is to recognize that factual knowledge and skills are not taught for their own sake, but as a means to larger ends. Ultimately, teaching should equip learners to be able to use or transfer their learning; i.e., meaningful performance with content. This is the "end" we always want to keep in mind.

Stage 2 – Determine Acceptable Evidence

How will we know if students have achieved the desired results? What will we accept as evidence of student understanding and proficiency? How will we evaluate student performance?

Backward design encourages teachers and curriculum planners to first "think like an assessor" before designing specific units and lessons. The assessment evidence we need reflects the desired results identified in Stage 1. Thus, we consider in advance the assessment evidence needed to document and validate that the targeted learning has been achieved. Doing so invariably sharpens and focuses teaching.

In Stage 2, we distinguish between two broad types of assessment—Performance Tasks and Other Evidence. The performance tasks ask students to apply their learning to a new and authentic situation as means of assessing their understanding. In UbD, we have identified six facets of understanding for assessment purposes[1]. When someone truly understands, they:

- Can explain concepts, principles and processes; i.e., put it in their own words, teach it to others, justify their answers, show their reasoning.
- Can interpret; i.e., make sense of data, text, and experience through images, analogies, stories, and models.
- Can apply; i.e., effectively use and adapt what they know in new and complex contexts.
- Demonstrate perspective; i.e., can see the big picture and recognize different points of view.
- Display empathy; i.e., perceive sensitively and "walk in someone else's shoes."
- Have self-knowledge; i.e., show metacognition, use productive habits of mind, and reflect on the meaning of their learning and experience.

These six facets do not present a theory of how people come to understand something. Instead, the facets are intended to serve as indicators of how understanding is revealed, and thus provide guidance as to the kinds of assessments we need to determine the extent of student understanding. Here are two notes regarding assessing understanding through the facets:

1) All six facets of understanding need not be used all of the time in assessment. In social studies, Empathy and Perspective may be added when appropriate.

2) Performance Tasks based on one or more facets are not intended for use in daily lessons. Rather, these tasks should be seen as culminating performances for a unit of study.

In addition to Performance Tasks, Stage 2 includes Other Evidence, such as traditional quizzes, tests, observations, and work samples to round out the assessment picture to

Examples of Essential Questions in Social Studies

Understandings or Big Ideas	Essential Questions
History involves interpretation, and different people may interpret the same events differently.	*Whose "story" is this? How do we know what really happened in the past?*
The geography, climate, and natural resources of a region influence the culture, economy, and lifestyle of its inhabitants.	*How does where we live influence how we live?*
History often repeats itself. Recognizing the patterns of the past can help us better understand the present and prepare for the future.	*Why study the past? What does the past have to do with today?*
Governments can change based on the changing needs of their people, the society, and the world.	*What makes an effective government? Why do/should governments change?*

[1] Wiggins, G. and McTighe, J. and (1998, 2005). *Understanding by Design.* Alexandria, VA: The Association for Supervision and Curriculum Development.

UNDERSTANDING BY DESIGN®

(continued)

determine what students know and can do. A key idea in backward design has to do with alignment. In other words, are we assessing everything that we are trying to achieve (in Stage 1) or only those things that are easiest to test and grade? Is anything important slipping through the cracks because it is not being assessed? Checking the alignment between Stages 1 and 2 helps insure that *all* important goals are appropriately assessed.

Stage 3 – Plan Learning Experiences and Instruction

How will we support learners in coming to an understanding of important ideas and processes? How will we prepare them to autonomously transfer their learning? What enabling knowledge and skills will students need in order to perform effectively and achieve desired results? What activities, sequence, and resources are best suited to accomplish our goals?

In Stage 3 of backward design, teachers now plan the most appropriate learning activities to help students acquire important knowledge and skills, come to understand important ideas and processes, and transfer their learning in meaningful ways. When developing a plan for learning, we propose that teachers consider a set of instructional principles, embedded in the acronym W.H.E.R.E.T.O. These design elements provide the armature or blueprint for instructional planning in Stage 3 in support of our goals of understanding and transfer.

Each of the W.H.E.R.E.T.O. elements is presented in the form of questions to consider.

W = *How will I help learners know – What they will be learning? Why this is worth learning? What evidence will show their learning? How their performance will be evaluated?*

Learners of all ages are more likely to put forth effort and meet with success when they understand the learning goals and see them as meaningful and personally relevant. The "W" in W.H.E.R.E.T.O. reminds teachers to clearly communicate the goals and help students see their relevance. In addition, learners need to know the concomitant performance expectations and assessments through which they will demonstrate their learning so that they have clear learning targets and the basis for monitoring their progress toward them.

H = *How will I hook and engage the learners?*

There is wisdom in the old adage: "Before you try to teach them, you've got to get their attention." The best teachers have always recognized the value of "hooking" learners through introductory activities that "itch" the mind and engage the heart in the learning process, and we encourage teachers to deliberately plan ways of hooking their learners to the topics they teach. Examples of effective hooks include provocative essential questions, counter-intuitive phenomena, controversial issues, authentic problems and challenges, emotional encounters, and humor. One must be mindful, of course, of not just coming up with interesting introductory activities that have no carry-over value. The intent is to match the hook with the content and

PHOTO: Banana Stock/Picture Quest

the experiences of the learners—by design—as a means of drawing them into a productive learning experience.

E = *How will I equip students to master identified standards and succeed with the transfer performances? What learning experiences will help develop and deepen understanding of important ideas?*

Understanding cannot be simply transferred like a load of freight from one mind to another. Coming to understand requires active intellectual engagement on the part of the learner. Therefore, instead of merely covering the content, effective educators "uncover" the most enduring ideas and processes in ways that engage students in constructing meaning for themselves. To this end, teachers select an appropriate balance of constructivist learning experiences, structured activities, and direct instruction for helping students acquire the desired knowledge, skill, and understanding. While there is certainly a place for direct instruction and modeling, teaching for understanding asks teachers to engage learners in making meaning through active inquiry.

R = *How will I encourage the learners to rethink previous learning? How will I encourage on-going revision and refinement?*

Few learners develop a complete understanding of abstract ideas on the first encounter. Indeed, the phrase "coming to understand" is suggestive of a process. Over time, learners develop and deepen their understanding by thinking and re-thinking, by examining ideas from a different point of view, from examining underlying assumptions, by receiving feedback and revising. Just as the quality of writing benefits from the iterative process of drafting and revising, so too do understandings become more mature. The "R" in W.H.E.R.E.T.O. encourages teachers to explicitly include such opportunities.

E = *How will I promote students' self-evaluation and reflection?*

Capable and independent learners are distinguished by their capacity to set goals, self-assess their progress, and adjust as needed. Yet, one of the most frequently overlooked aspects of the instructional process involves helping students to develop the meta-cognitive skills of self-evaluation, self-regulation, and reflection. The second "E" of W.H.E.R.E.T.O. reminds teachers to build in time and expectations for students to regularly self-assess, reflect on the meaning of their learning, and set goals for future performance.

T = *How will I tailor the learning experiences to the nature of the learners I serve? How might I differentiate instruction to respond to the varied needs of students?*

"One size fits all teaching" is rarely optimal. Learners differ significantly in terms of their prior knowledge and skill levels, their interests, talents, and preferred ways of learning. Accordingly, the most effective teachers get to know their students and tailor their teaching and learning experiences to connect to them. A variety of strategies may be employed to differentiate *content* (e.g., how subject matter is presented), *process* (e.g., how students work), and *product* (e.g., how learners demonstrate their learning). The logic of backward design offers a cautionary note here: the Content Standards and Understandings should *not* be differentiated (except for students with Individualized Education Plans —I.E.P.s). In other words, differentiate means keeping the end in mind for all.

O = *How will I organize the learning experiences for maximum engagement and effectiveness? What sequence will be optimal given the understanding and transfer goals?*

When the primary educational goals involve helping students acquire basic knowledge and skills, teachers may be comfortable "covering" the content by telling and modeling.

However, when we include understanding and transfer as desired results, educators are encouraged to give careful attention to how the content is organized and sequenced. Just as effective story tellers and filmmakers often don't begin in the "beginning," teachers can consider alternatives to sequential content coverage. For example, methods such as the Case Method, Problem or Project-Based Learning, and Socratic Seminars immerse students in challenging situations, even before they may have acquired all of the "basics." They actively engage students in trying to make meaning and apply their learning in demanding circumstances without single "correct" answers.

Conclusion

Many teachers who are introduced to the backward design process have observed that while the process makes sense in theory, it often feels awkward in use. This is to be expected since the principles and practices of UbD often challenge conventional planning and teaching habits. However, with some practice, educators find that backward design becomes not only more comfortable, but a way of thinking. The resources found in this program support teaching and assessing for understanding and transfer.

professional development

WHY TEACH WITH TECHNOLOGY?

by Tom Daccord and Justin Reich, EdTechTeacher

✔ **Technology is transforming the practice of historians and should transform history classrooms as well.** While printed documents, books, maps, and artwork constitute the bulk of the historical record before 1900, the history of the last century is also captured in sound and video recording and in Web sites and other Internet resources. Today's students need to learn how to analyze and build arguments using these multimedia records as well as traditional primary sources.

✔ **So many of the sources that helped historians and history teachers fall in love with the discipline are now available online.** In recent decades, universities, libraries, archives, and other institutions have scanned and uploaded many vast treasure troves of historical sources. The Internet-connected classroom increasingly has access to the world's historical record, giving students a chance to develop critical thinking skills as well as learning historical narratives.

✔ **Whoever is doing most of the talking or most of the typing is doing most of the learning, and the more people listening the better.** Technology allows us to transfer the responsibility for learning from teachers to students, and to put students in the driver's seat of their own learning. Students who are actively engaged in creating and presenting their understandings of history are learning more than students passively listening. Technology also allows students to publish their work to broader audiences of peers, parents, and even the entire Internet-connected world. Students find the opportunities challenging, exciting, and engaging.

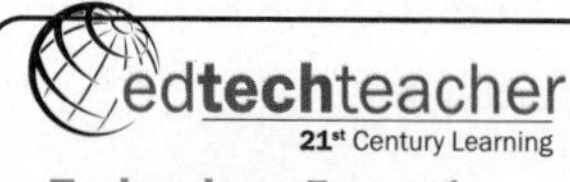

Technology Extension

- Find an additional activity online that incorporates technology for this project.
- Visit the EdTechTeacher Web sites (included in the Technology Extension for this chapter) for more links, tutorials, and other resources.

Teaching With Technology

In addition to the many other online resources embedded in this program, EdTechTeacher Technology Extensions are provided for every Hands-On Chapter Project. These detailed instructions and inspiration help history teachers creatively and effectively integrate technology in their classrooms. Each Technology Extension describes a technology project, explains the rationale for the suggested technology, and provides guidelines for classroom teachers to help conduct and facilitate the activity. Each Technology Extension also provides links to pages on Teaching History with Technology (www.thwt.org) with up-to-date tutorials, guides, links to examples, and exemplar projects.

✔ **The more ways students have to engage with content, the more likely they are to remember and understand that content.** The Internet can provide students and teachers with access to text documents, images, sounds and songs, video, simulations, and games. The more different ways students engage with historical content, the more likely they are to make meaning of that material.

✔ **Students live in a technology-rich world, and classrooms should prepare students for that world.** When students spend most of their waking hours connected to a worldwide, online network of people, resources, and opportunities, they experience dissonance and disappointment in entering a "powered-down" school. Many students will leave school to go on to workplaces completely transformed by technology, and teachers have a responsibility to prepare students for these environments.

Integrating Technology Effectively

Ben Shneiderman, in his book *Leonardo's Laptop,* lays out a four-part framework for teaching with technology: Collect-Relate-Create-Donate. This framework is a helpful blueprint for designing projects and learning experiences with technology.

Collect Students should begin a project by collecting the resources necessary to produce a meaningful presentation of their understanding. In some cases, students might collect these resources through textbook reading and teacher lecture, but students should also collect resources from online collections, school library Web sites, and online searches.

Relate Technology greatly facilitates the process of students working together socially. The ability to collaborate is essential to the workplace and civic sphere of the future. In creating technology projects, students should have the chance to work together, or at least comment on each other's work, using blogs, wikis, podcasts, and other collaborative publishing tools.

Create Using multimedia publishing tools, students should have the opportunity to design presentations and performances of their historical understanding. They should make historical arguments in linear text, as well as through images, audio and video recordings, and multimedia presentations.

Donate Finally, students should create work not just for their teachers, but for broader audiences. Students who have a chance to share their work with their peers, their families, their community, and the Internet-connected world find that opportunity rewarding. Today's students experience very few barriers to expression in their networked lives, and they crave these opportunities in schools.

Guidelines for Successful Technology Projects

1) **Plan for problems.** Things can go wrong when working with technology, and learning how to deal with these challenges is essential for students, and for their teachers. As you start using technology in the classroom, try to have an extra teacher, aide, student-teacher, or IT staff member in the room with you to help troubleshoot problems. When things do go wrong, stay calm, and ask your students to help you resolve challenges and make the most of class time. Always have a back up, "pencil and paper" activity prepared in case there are problems with computers or networks. Over time, teachers who practice teaching with technology experience fewer and fewer of these problems, but they can be very challenging the first time you experience them!

2) **Practice from multiple perspectives.** Whenever you develop a technology project, try to do everything that students will do from a student's perspective. If you create a blog or wiki with a teacher account, create a student account to test the technology.

3) **Adapt to your local technology resources, but don't let those resources keep you from using technology.** Some schools have excellent and ample technology resources—labs and laptop carts—that make completing technology projects straightforward. Other schools have fewer resources, but virtually every student can get access to a networked computer in school, at the library or at home, especially if you give them a few nights to do so. Many technology activities are described as if you could complete them in a few class periods, but if resources are limited, you might consider spreading the activity out over a few days or weeks to give students the chance to get online.

4) **Plan with a partner.** Going it alone can be scary. If possible, have another teacher in your department or on your team, design and pilot technology projects with you to help solve the challenges that crop up whenever trying out new pedagogies.

5) **It's harder, then it gets easier.** Learning new teaching strategies is always hard. With technology, however, once you get past the initial learning curve there are all sorts of ways technology can make teaching more efficient and simultaneously make learning more meaningful for students.

Learn More about Teaching History with Technology

EdTechTeacher has several Web sites designed to help social studies and history teachers learn more about teaching with technology. The Best of History Web Sites (www.besthistorysites.net) is the Internet's authoritative directory of history-related resources, Web sites, games, simulations, lesson plans, and activities. Teaching History with Technology (www.thwt.org) has a series of white papers, tutorials, and guides for enriching history teaching strategies (lecturing, discussion, presentations, assessments, and so forth) with educational technology. EdTechTeacher (www.edtechteacher.org) has additional teaching resources and information about learning opportunities such as free webinars and other professional development workshops.

Tom Daccord and Justin Reich are co-Directors of EdTechTeacher. Together they authored Best Ideas for Teaching With Technology: A Practical Guide for Teachers by Teachers.

professional development

MEETING THE DIVERSE NEEDS OF OUR STUDENTS

by Douglas Fisher, Ph.D.

Today's classroom contains students from a variety of backgrounds with a variety of learning styles, strengths, and challenges. As teachers we are facing the challenge of helping students reach their educational potential. With careful planning, you can address the needs of all students in the social studies classroom. The basis for this planning is universal access. When classrooms are planned with universal access in mind, fewer students require specific accommodations.

What Is a Universal Access Design for Learning?

Universal design was first conceived in architectural studies when business people, engineers, and architects began making considerations for physical access to buildings. The idea was to plan the environment in advance to ensure that everyone had access. As a result, the environment would not have to be changed later for people with physical disabilities, people pushing strollers, workers who had injuries, or others for whom the environment would be difficult to negotiate. The Center for Universal Design at www.design.ncsu.edu/cud defines Universal Design as:

The design of products and environments to be usable by all people, to the greatest extent possible, without the need for adaptation or specialized design.

Universal Design and Access in Education

Researchers, teachers, and parents in education have expanded the development of built-in adaptations and inclusive accommodations from architectural space to the educational experience, especially in the area of curriculum.

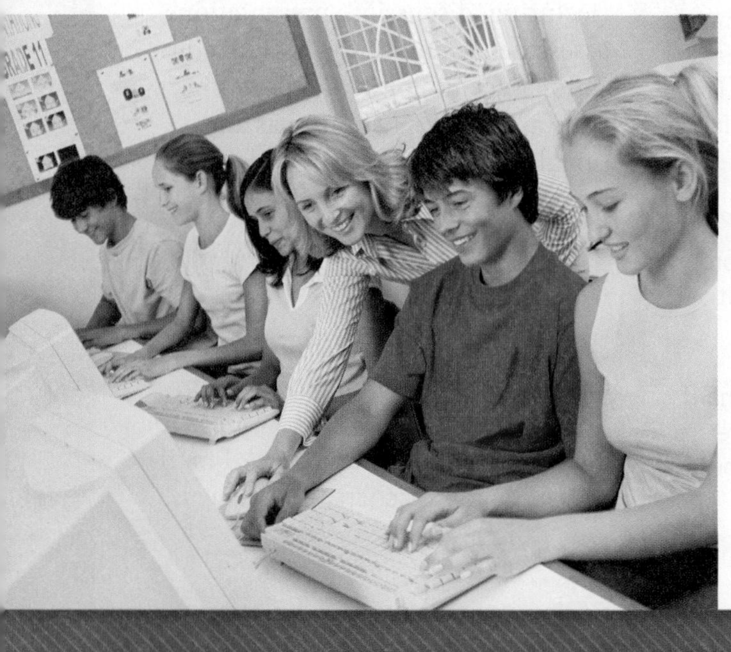

In 1998, the National Center to Improve the Tools of Educators (NCITE), with the partnership of the Center for Applied Special Technology (CAST), proposed an expanded definition of universal design focused on education:

In terms of learning, universal design means the design of instructional materials and activities that allows the learning goals to be achievable by individuals with wide differences in their abilities to see, hear, speak, move, read, write, understand English, attend, organize, engage, and remember.

How Does Universal Design Work in Education?

Universal design and access, as they apply to education and schooling, suggest the following:

- ✓ **Inclusive Classroom Participation**
  Curriculum should be designed with all students and their needs in mind. The McGraw-Hill social studies print and online texts and materials were designed with a wide range of students in mind. For example, understanding that English learners and students who struggle with reading would be using this text, vocabulary is specifically taught and reinforced. Similarly, the teacher-support materials provide multiple instructional points to be used depending on the needs of the students in the class. Further, the text is written such that essential questions and guiding questions are identified for all learners.

- ✓ **Maximum Text Readability**
  In universally designed classrooms that provide access for all students, texts use direct language, clear noun-verb agreements, and clear construct-based wording. In addition to these factors, the McGraw-Hill social

PHOTO: BananaStock/PictureQuest

studies texts use embedded definitions for difficult terms, provide for specific instruction in reading skills, use a number of visual representations, and include note-taking guides.

✔ **Adaptable and Accommodating**
The content in this textbook can be easily translated, read aloud, or otherwise changed to meet the needs of students in the classroom. The lesson and end-of-chapter activities and assessments provide students with multiple ways of demonstrating their content knowledge while also ensuring that they have practice with thinking in terms of multiple-choice questions. Critical thinking and analysis skills are also practiced.

How Is Differentiated Instruction the Key to Universal Access?

To differentiate instruction, teachers must acknowledge student differences in background knowledge and current reading, writing, and English language skills. They must also consider student learning styles and preferences, interests, and needs, and react accordingly. There are a number of general guidelines for differentiating instruction in the classroom to reach all students, including:

✔ **Link Assessment With Instruction**
Assessments should occur before, during, and after instruction to ensure that the curriculum is aligned with what students do and do not know. Using assessments in this way allows you to plan instruction for whole groups, small groups, and individual students. Backward planning, where you establish the assessment before you begin instruction, is also important.

✔ **Clarify Key Concepts and Generalizations**
Students need to know what is essential and how this information can be used in their future learning. In addition, students need to develop a sense of the big ideas—ideas that transcend time and place.

✔ **Emphasize Critical and Creative Thinking**
The content, process, and products used or assigned in the classroom should require that students think about what they are learning. While some students may require support, additional motivation, varied tasks, materials, or equipment, the overall focus on critical and creative thinking allows for all students to participate in the lesson.

✔ **Include Teacher- and Student-Selected Tasks**
A differentiated classroom includes both teacher- and student-selected activities and tasks. At some points in the lesson or day, the teacher must provide instruction and assign learning activities. In other parts of the lesson, students should be provided choices in how they engage with the content. This balance increases motivation, engagement, and learning.

How Do I Support Individual Students?

The vast majority of students will thrive in a classroom based on universal access and differentiated instruction. However, wise teachers recognize that no single option will work for all students and that there may be students who require unique systems of support to be successful.

Classroom Activity

Display a map of imperialism in Africa around 1914. Discuss with students the map's general information and have them list each country under the European power that controlled it.

To differentiate this activity:

- Have students imagine they are living in the early 1900s. Have them write a letter to a British newspaper about colonial rule in Africa.
- Have students record the number of African countries under European rule. Have them take the data and create a bar graph that shows which European powers were the most active colonizers at the time.
- Have students compose a song or poem about European rule in Africa, from an African's point of view.
- Have students choose a country of modern Africa to research. Have them write a three-page paper discussing how that country was affected by colonialism and how it has changed since the days of European rule.

MEETING THE DIVERSE NEEDS OF OUR STUDENTS

(continued)

Tips For Instruction

The following tips for instruction can support your efforts to help all students reach their maximum potential.

- ✔ Survey students to discover their individual differences. Use interest inventories of their unique talents so you can encourage contributions in the classroom.
- ✔ Be a model for respecting others. Adolescents crave social acceptance. The student with learning differences is especially sensitive to correction and criticism, particularly when it comes from a teacher. Your behavior will set the tone for how students treat one another.
- ✔ Expand opportunities for success. Provide a variety of instructional activities that reinforce skills and concepts.
- ✔ Establish measurable objectives and decide how you can best help students who meet them.
- ✔ Celebrate successes and make note of and praise "work in progress."
- ✔ Keep it simple. Point out problem areas if doing so can help a student effect change. Avoid overwhelming students with too many goals at one time.
- ✔ Assign cooperative group projects that challenge all students to contribute to solving a problem or creating a product.

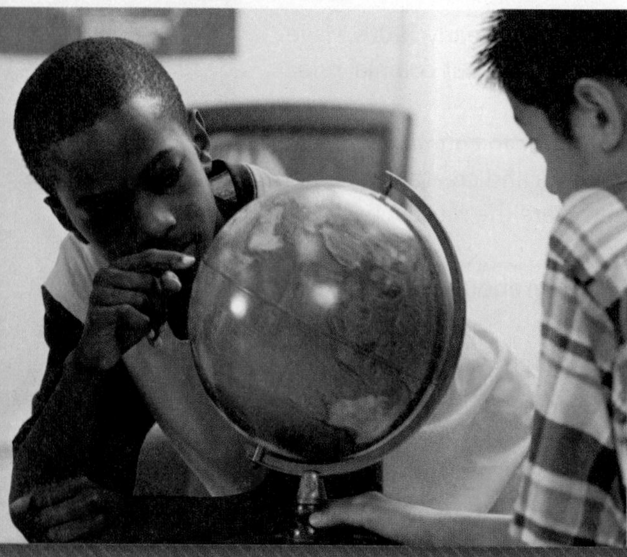

How Do I Reach Students With Learning Disabilities?

- ✔ Provide support and structure. Clearly specify rules, assignments, and responsibilities.
- ✔ Practice skills frequently. Use games and drills to help maintain student interest.
- ✔ Incorporate many modalities into the learning process. Provide opportunities to say, hear, write, read, and act out important concepts and information.
- ✔ Link new skills and concepts to those already mastered.
- ✔ If possible, allow students to record answers on audio.
- ✔ Allow extra time to complete assessments and assignments.
- ✔ Let students demonstrate proficiency with alternative presentations, including oral reports, role plays, art projects, and musical presentations.
- ✔ Provide outlines, notes, or recordings of lecture material.
- ✔ Pair students with peer helpers, and provide class time for pair interaction.

How Do I Reach Students With Behavioral Challenges?

- ✔ Provide a structured environment with clear-cut schedules, rules, seat assignments, and safety procedures.
- ✔ Reinforce appropriate behavior and model it for students.
- ✔ Cue distracted students back to the task through verbal signals and teacher proximity.
- ✔ Set goals that can be achieved in the short term. Work for long-term improvement in the big areas.

How Do I Reach Students With Physical Challenges?

- ✔ Openly discuss with the student any uncertainties you have about when to offer aid.
- ✔ Ask parents or therapists and students what special devices or procedures are needed and whether any special safety precautions need to be taken.
- ✔ Welcome students with physical challenges into all activities, including field trips, special events, and projects.
- ✔ Provide information to assist class members and adults in their understanding of support needed.

How Do I Reach Students With Visual Impairments?

- ✔ Facilitate independence. Modify assignments as needed.
- ✔ Teach classmates how and when to serve as visual guides.
- ✔ Limit unnecessary noise in the classroom if it distracts the student with visual impairments.
- ✔ Provide tactile models whenever possible.
- ✔ Foster a spirit of inclusion. Describe people and events as they occur in the classroom.

Remind classmates that the student with visual impairments cannot interpret gestures and other forms of nonverbal communication.

- ✔ Provide recorded lectures and reading assignments for use outside the classroom.
- ✔ Team the student with a sighted peer for written work.

How Do I Reach Students With Hearing Impairments?

- ✔ Seat students where they can see your lip movements easily and where they can avoid any visual distractions.
- ✔ Avoid standing with your back to the window or light source.
- ✔ Use an overhead projector so you can maintain eye contact while writing information for students.
- ✔ Seat students where they can see speakers.
- ✔ Write all assignments on the board, or hand out written instructions.
- ✔ If the student has a manual interpreter, allow both student and interpreter to select the most favorable seating arrangements.
- ✔ Teach students to look directly at each other when they speak.

How Do I Reach English Learners?

- ✔ Remember, students' ability to speak English does not reflect their academic abilities.
- ✔ Try to incorporate the students' cultural experience into your instruction. The help of a bilingual aide may be effective.
- ✔ Avoid any references in your instruction that could be construed as cultural stereotypes.
- ✔ Preteach important vocabulary and concepts.
- ✔ Encourage students to preview text before they begin reading, noting headings.
- ✔ Remind students not to ignore graphic organizers, photographs, and maps since there is much information in these visuals.
- ✔ Use memorabilia and photographs whenever possible to build background knowledge and understanding. An example of this would be coins in a foreign currency or a raw cotton ball to reinforce its importance in history.

How Do I Reach Gifted Students?

- ✔ Make arrangements for students to take selected subjects early and to work on independent projects.
- ✔ Ask "what if" questions to develop high-level thinking skills. Establish an environment safe for risk taking in your classroom.
- ✔ Emphasize concepts, theories, ideas, relationships, and generalizations about the content.
- ✔ Promote interest in the past by inviting students to make connections to the present.
- ✔ Let students express themselves in alternate ways such as creative writing, acting, debates, simulations, drawing, or music.
- ✔ Provide students with a catalog of helpful resources, listing such things as agencies that provide free and inexpensive materials, appropriate community services and programs, and community experts who might be called upon to speak to your students.
- ✔ Assign extension projects that allow students to solve real-life problems related to their communities.

Classroom Activity

Students respond eagerly to a subject when they can relate it to their own experiences. With the growing number of students who come from other world regions, explaining geography through a global theme (such as volcanoes) can give them a worldwide as well as a regional perspective. To develop this awareness, display a large world map. Have students use the library or the Internet to research the latitude and longitude of 15 major volcanoes around the world. Ask them to mark these locations on the map and answer the following questions:

- What patterns do you see in volcanic activity?
- What causes volcanic activity?
- Where in the world are volcanoes most active?

As a follow-up, suggest students go to http://volcano.und.nodak.edu/vwdocs/kids/legends.html to find legends about the origins of some of the world's volcanoes. Encourage students to share what they find with the class.

COLLEGE AND CAREER READINESS

Why Is College & Career Readiness Crucial?

- Only 70% of American students receive a high school diploma.
- Of that 70% of high school graduates, 53% of those who make it to college require remedial help.
- Over 90% of new jobs that will be available to students in the 21st century will require some postsecondary education.
- Most employers today cannot compete successfully without a workforce that has solid academic skills.
- The average difference in salary between someone with a high school degree and someone with postsecondary credentials can be $1 million over their lifetimes.

What Is College & Career Readiness?

Students are college and career ready when they have the level of preparation needed to academically, socially, and cognitively complete a postsecondary course of study without remediation. Students are prepared when they can enter the workforce at a level at which they are in line for promotion and career enhancement.

The ultimate goal of the college & career readiness initiative is to maintain America's competitive edge in the global economy of today. The workforce of the 21st century is an increasingly global, knowledge-based economy that demands the ability to:

- Think critically
- Solve problems
- Create and innovate
- Communicate
- Collaborate
- Learn new skills
- Use ICT (information and communications technology)

Explain College & Career Readiness to Students

One of the first steps you should take is to provide students with a framework that will help them see the relevancy of what they do in school. The three principal elements of College & Career Readiness (CCR) are:

- an understanding of core academic skills and the ability to apply them in educational and employment settings
- familiarity with skills valued by a broad range of employers such as communication, critical thinking, and responsibility
- mastery of the technologies and skill sets associated with a career pathway

Once students have been exposed to these elements, it is critical for them to see how they relate to their own plans for continuing education and career choice. Mention that CCR is more than just a personal issue, and it affects the country and our quality of life.

Most students—as well as many adults—consider work to be an obligation that they must perform in order to have money. Earning a salary is, of course, a central benefit of working, but so is the sense of satisfaction that comes from doing a job well. Moreover, every job contributes to the quality of life in our communities and our nation. Being prepared to pursue an education or get a job after high school is the hallmark of a good citizen.

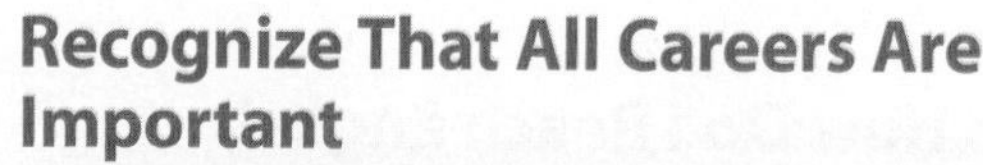

Recognize That All Careers Are Important

Without question, the greatest challenge faced by educators, parents, and the public is recognizing that all jobs are important. When you discuss careers, be generous with your reflections and encourage your students to do the same. Be sure to mention the enormous variety of opportunities available to them in diverse fields. The

PHOTO: Mark Scott/Photographer's Choice/Getty Images

more that students can recognize the rich possibilities of whatever career they pursue, the more likely they will be to enjoy success and personal satisfaction.

Students typically have a relatively narrow perspective on the careers and jobs available to them. As part of the discussion of careers, broaden this perspective by reviewing some opportunities that your students might not be aware of. An interesting place to start is in the high profile industries of sports and entertainment.

Many students dream of being celebrities and have no idea about how unlikely this is. What they don't realize is that for every professional athlete, singer, or movie star, there are a hundred or more fascinating careers including sports trainers, writers, administrative assistants, drivers, and a seemingly endless list of other jobs. Not surprisingly, students usually respond positively when they learn that just in case they are not the next superstar in sports or entertainment, there are other opportunities that will allow them to achieve their dream in a slightly different way.

Students can explore careers in many ways; one way is by reviewing the 16 career clusters. Career clusters are groups of similar occupations and industries. They were developed by the U.S. Department of Education as a way to organize career planning. Students can visit the Career Center at http://ccr.mcgraw-hill.com/ to begin their explorations.

Make It Clear That There Are Various Paths To Success

A surprisingly small percentage of adults reach their careers through a direct and well-planned strategy. Familiarizing students with the various paths to success provides them with a realistic view of what life is like after high school and college. It may also give them an anchor in their own lives in the future when they find that they are wandering, which most of them will inevitably do.

Divergence from a direct path to a career is almost inevitable, and in many cases, is a desirable and enriching experience. Helping students to recognize this will make their future challenges seem less intimidating.

Have students investigate and discuss the career paths of people they know personally and by reputation, including celebrities. This discussion will promote engagement while showing the twists and turns that usually lead to success. Be sure to include some common but less-known paths, like the college benefits associated with military service or the arrangements nurses might make with a hospital to exchange tuition payments for a commitment of several years.

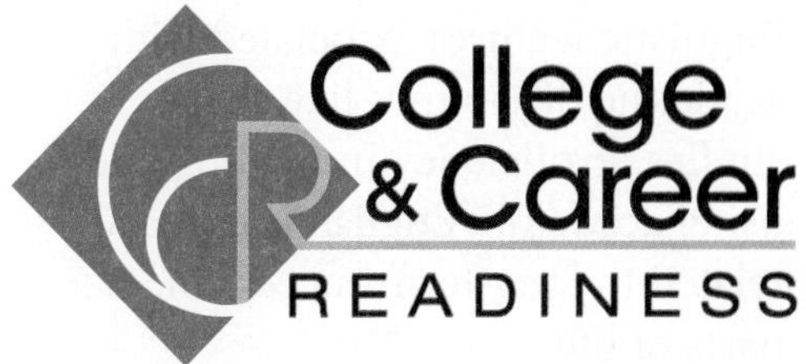

Make College & Career Readiness a regular part of interactive classroom discussions.

Unlike many other school subjects, a critical aspect of College & Career Readiness is its focus is on the future of each student, not the content of a course. Perhaps the best way to have students recognize this is to be sure that the time you spend discussing students' future pathways is truly interactive, with at least as much commentary from students as there is from you or other adult participants.

Because students are more willing to participate in discussions that have personal meaning to them, consider using these questions as starting points. These are "self-mentoring" questions that will help students clarify their thinking.

- What is something you really want to do in the next 10 years?
- How do you plan to get there?
- What is your back-up plan?
- What is something that you have done that made you proud?
- In which postsecondary courses do you think you would do best? Why do you think this?
- Imagine that you are going into the military. This choice involves activities that are hard physically and mentally. How would you handle these challenges?
- When you can't make up your mind about something important, what do you do?

Have students explore college & career readiness on their own at http://ccr.mcgraw-hill.com/ .

ACADEMIC VOCABULARY

How Can I Help My Students Learn Academic Vocabulary?

What Is Academic English?

Academic English is the language used in academics, business, and courts of law. It is the type of English used in textbooks, and contains linguistic features associated with academic disciplines like social studies. Proficiency in reading and using academic English is especially related to long-term success in all parts of life.

By reinforcing academic English, teachers can help learners to access authentic, academic texts—not simplified texts that dummy down the content. In this way, they can provide information that will help build their students' background knowledge rapidly.

What Is Academic Vocabulary?

Academic vocabulary is based on academic English. By the time children have completed elementary school, they must have acquired the knowledge needed to understand academic vocabulary. How many words should they acquire to be able to access their texts? A basic 2,000-word vocabulary of high-frequency words makes up 87% of the vocabulary of academic texts. Eight hundred other academic words comprise an additional 8% of the words. Three percent of the remaining words are technical words. The remaining 2% are low-frequency words. There may be as many as 123,000 low-frequency words in academic texts.

Why Should Students Learn Academic Vocabulary?

Knowledge of academic words and general words can significantly boost a student's comprehension level of academic texts. Students who learn and practice these words before they graduate from high school are more likely to master academic material with increased confidence and speed. They waste less time and effort in guessing words or consulting dictionaries than those who only know the basic 2,000 words that characterize general conversation.

How Do I Include Academic Vocabulary and Academic English in My Teaching?

Teachers can provide students with academic vocabulary and help students understand the academic English of their text.

To develop academic English, learners must have already acquired basic proficiency in everyday English.

Academic English should be taught within contexts that make sense. In terms of instruction, teaching academic English includes providing students with access to core curriculum—in this case social studies.

Academic English arises in part from social practices in which academic English is used. The acquisition of academic vocabulary and grammar is necessary to advance the development of academic English.

Tips for Teaching Academic Vocabulary

✔ **Expose Students to Academic Vocabulary** You do not need to call attention to words students are learning because they will acquire them subconsciously.

✔ **Do Not Correct Students' Mistakes When Using the Vocabulary Words** All vocabulary understanding and spelling errors will disappear once the student reads more.

✔ **Help Students Decode the Words Themselves** Once they learn the alphabet, they should be able to decode words. Decoding each word they don't recognize will help them more than trying to focus on sentence structure. Once they can recognize the words, they can read "authentic" texts.

✔ **Do Not Ignore the English Learner in This Process** They can learn academic vocabulary before they are completely fluent in oral English.

✔ **Helping Students Build Academic Vocabulary Leads to Broader Learning** Students who have mastered the basic academic vocabulary are ready to acquire words from the rest of the groups. To help determine which words are in the 2,000-word basic group, refer to *West's General Service List of English Words,* 1953. The list is designed to serve as a guide for teachers and as a checklist and goal list for students.

USING btw

McGraw-Hill's Current Events Web Site

The ***btw*** current events Web site was created specifically for students. It provides up-to-date coverage of important national and world news, along with contests, polls, and activities.

Each news story has activities and questions to extend the content and provide skills practice, including:

- Tips on how to use ***btw*** articles in your social studies classroom
- Ideas for using social media and other technology resources
- 21st Century Skill options

Use ***btw*** as a bellringer activity, to activate critical thinking, or to engage students in high-interest projects.

Engaging, student-friendly content guides readers through the major events that affect our nation and our world. ***Top Stories*** examine everything from unrest in Libya to the newest shows on television.

You Decide asks students to take a stand after they analyze different points of view on issues around the United States and the world.

Election Central takes a closer look at upcoming elections with information about party platforms, candidates, and important issues.

Real people ***Profiles*** provide first-person accounts of events, such as what it is like to be a soldier in Iraq or to testify in front of Congress.

Be an Active Citizen! helps students learn more about the government, courts, and economy to help them become informed citizens.

Visit the *btw* Current Events Web site at blog.glencoe.com.

SCAVENGER HUNT

NETWORKS contains a wealth of information. The trick is to know where to look to access all the information in the book. If you complete this scavenger hunt exercise with your teachers or parents, you will see how the textbook is organized and how to get the most out of your reading and studying time. Let's get started!

1 How many chapters are in Unit 1?
There are 4 chapters in unit 1.

2 What does Unit 3 cover?
Unit 3 covers Latin America.

3 Where can you find the Essential Question for each chapter?
The Essential Question is located at the beginning of each lesson, after the lesson title.

4 Where can you find primary sources in your textbook?
Primary sources can be found in the Analyzing Primary Sources and Case Study features, as well as in the narrative text and chapter assessments.

5 How can you identify content vocabulary and academic vocabulary in the narrative?
Content vocabulary terms are bold and highlighted yellow. Academic terms are bold.

6 Where do you find graphic organizers in your textbook?
Graphic organizers are at the beginning of each lesson in the Reading Helpdesk.

7 You want to quickly find a map in the book about climate in Europe. Where do you look?
The Reference Atlas is easy to find in the front of your book and contains world and regional maps.

8 Where would you find the latitude and longitude for Dublin, Ireland? You can find latitude and longitude as well as geographic features and capitals in the Gazetteer.

9 If you needed to know the Spanish term for *primate city*, where would you look?
The English-Spanish Glossary contains the Spanish terms and definitions for the content and academic vocabulary.

10 Where can you find a list of all the features in the book?
The Table of Contents in the front of your book, under the heading "FEATURES", lists the title and page number of the features.

Reference Atlas

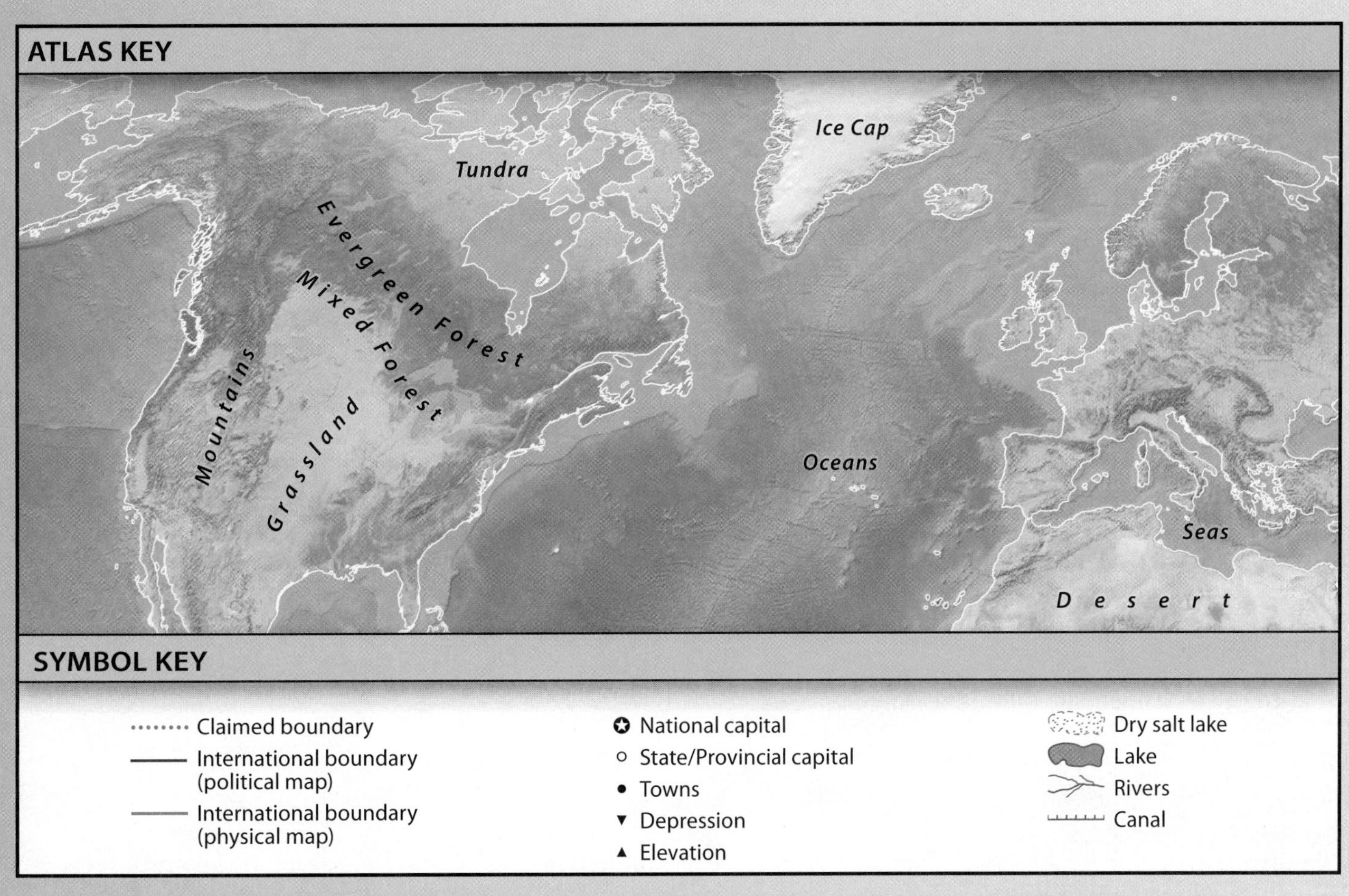

ATLAS KEY
Ice Cap
Tundra
Evergreen Forest
Mixed Forest
Mountains
Grassland
Oceans
Seas
Desert
SYMBOL KEY
Claimed boundary
International boundary (political map)
International boundary (physical map)
National capital
State/Provincial capital
Towns
Depression
Elevation
Dry salt lake
Lake
Rivers
Canal

GEOGRAPHIC DICTIONARY

archipelago a group of islands

basin area of land drained by a given river and its branches; area of land surrounded by lands of higher elevations

bay part of a large body of water that extends into a shoreline, generally smaller than a gulf

canyon deep and narrow valley with steep walls

cape point of land that extends into a river, lake, or ocean

channel wide strait or waterway between two landmasses that lie close to each other; deep part of a river or other waterway

cliff steep, high wall of rock, earth, or ice

continent one of the seven large landmasses on the Earth

delta flat, low-lying land built up from soil carried downstream by a river and deposited at its mouth

divide stretch of high land that separates river systems

downstream direction in which a river or stream flows from its source to its mouth

escarpment steep cliff or slope between a higher and lower land surface

glacier large, thick body of slowly moving ice

gulf part of a large body of water that extends into a shoreline, generally larger and more deeply indented than a bay

harbor a sheltered place along a shoreline where ships can anchor safely

highland elevated land area such as a hill, mountain, or plateau

hill elevated land with sloping sides and rounded summit; generally smaller than a mountain

island land area, smaller than a continent, completely surrounded by water

isthmus narrow stretch of land connecting two larger land areas

lake a sizable inland body of water

lowland land, usually level, at a low elevation

mesa broad, flat-topped landform with steep sides; smaller than a plateau

mountain land with steep sides that rises sharply (1,000 feet or more) from surrounding land; generally larger and more rugged than a hill

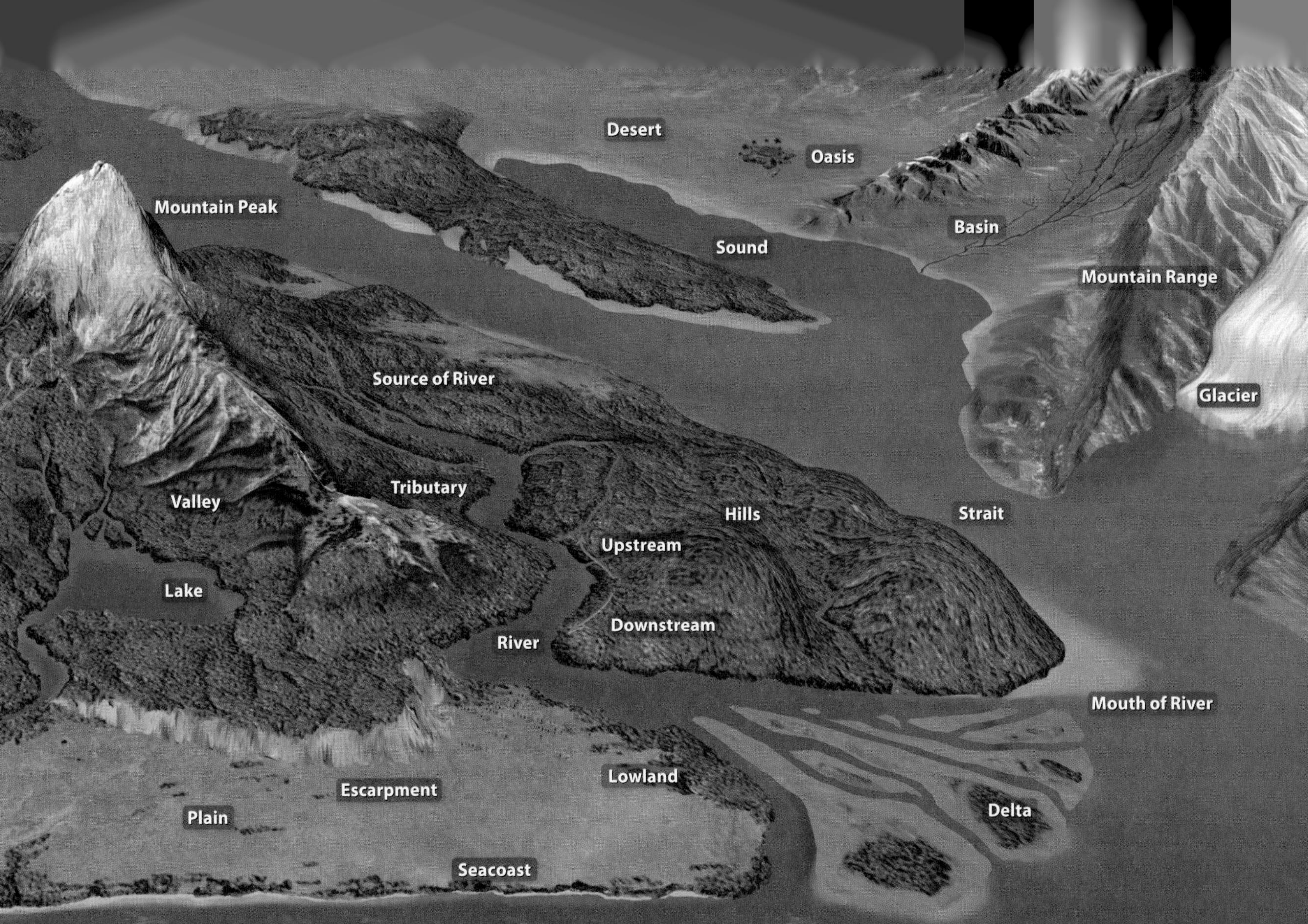

mountain peak pointed top of a mountain

mountain range a series of connected mountains

mouth (of a river) place where a stream or river flows into a larger body of water

oasis small area in a desert where water and vegetation are found

ocean one of the four major bodies of salt water that surround the continents

ocean current stream of either cold or warm water that moves in a definite direction through an ocean

peninsula body of land jutting into a lake or ocean, surrounded on three sides by water

physical feature characteristic of a place occurring naturally, such as a landform, body of water, climate pattern, or resource

plain area of level land, usually at low elevation and often covered with grasses

plateau area of flat or rolling land at a high elevation, about 300 to 3,000 feet (90 to 900 m) high

river large natural stream of water that runs through the land

sea large body of water completely or partly surrounded by land

seacoast land lying next to a sea or an ocean

sound broad inland body of water, often between a coastline and one or more islands off the coast

source (of a river) place where a river or stream begins, often in highlands

strait narrow stretch of water joining two larger bodies of water

tributary small river or stream that flows into a large river or stream; a branch of the river

upstream direction opposite the flow of a river; toward the source of a river or stream

valley area of low land usually between hills or mountains

volcano mountain or hill created as liquid rock and ash erupt from inside the Earth

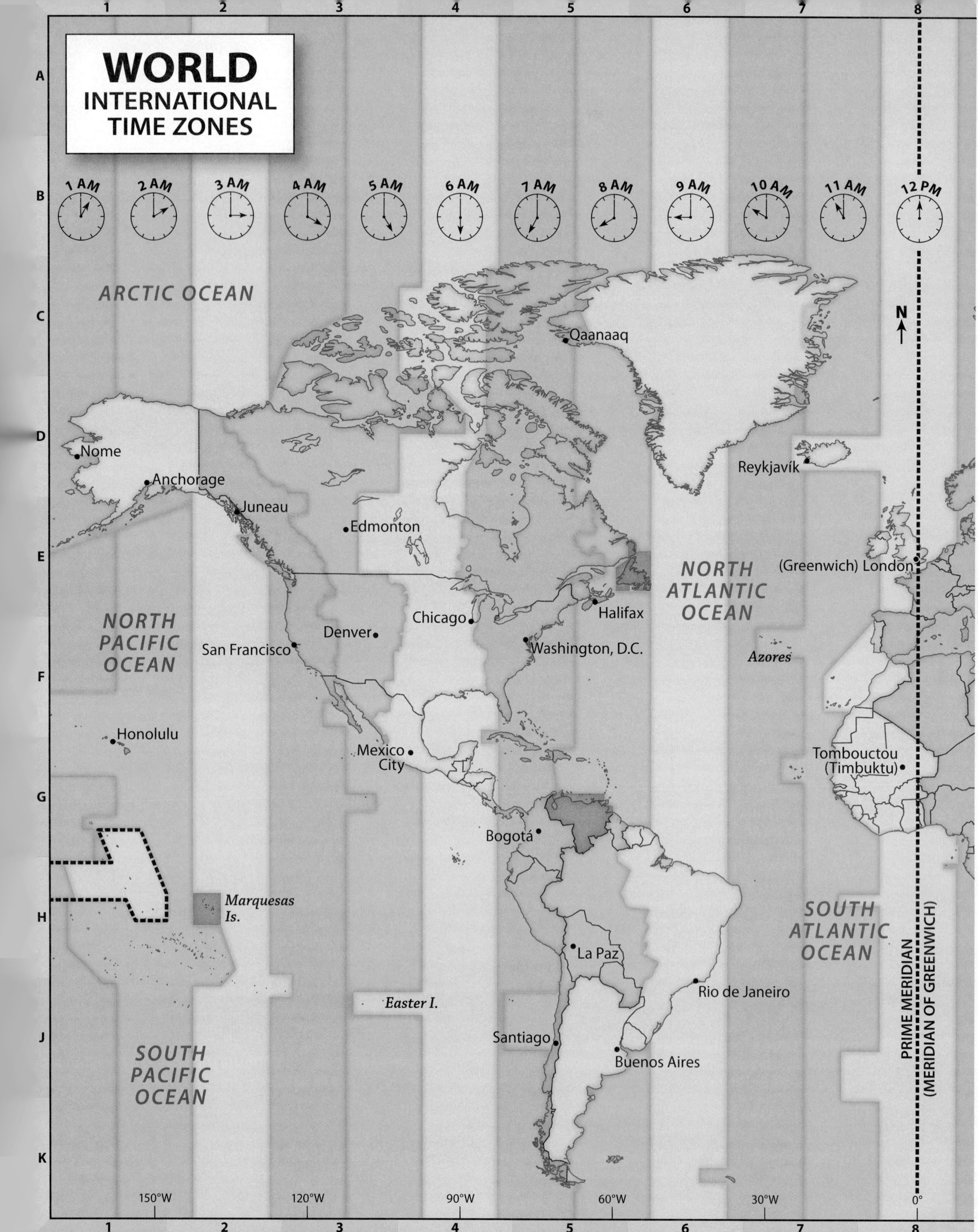
WORLD
INTERNATIONAL TIME ZONES
1 AM
2 AM
3 AM
4 AM
5 AM
6 AM
7 AM
8 AM
9 AM
10 AM
11 AM
12 PM
ARCTIC OCEAN
Qaanaaq
Nome
Anchorage
Juneau
Edmonton
Reykjavík
(Greenwich) London
NORTH ATLANTIC OCEAN
Halifax
Chicago
NORTH PACIFIC OCEAN
Denver
San Francisco
Washington, D.C.
Azores
Honolulu
Mexico City
Tombouctou (Timbuktu)
Bogotá
Marquesas Is.
SOUTH ATLANTIC OCEAN
La Paz
Rio de Janeiro
Easter I.
Santiago
Buenos Aires
SOUTH PACIFIC OCEAN
PRIME MERIDIAN (MERIDIAN OF GREENWICH)
N
150°W
120°W
90°W
60°W
30°W
0°

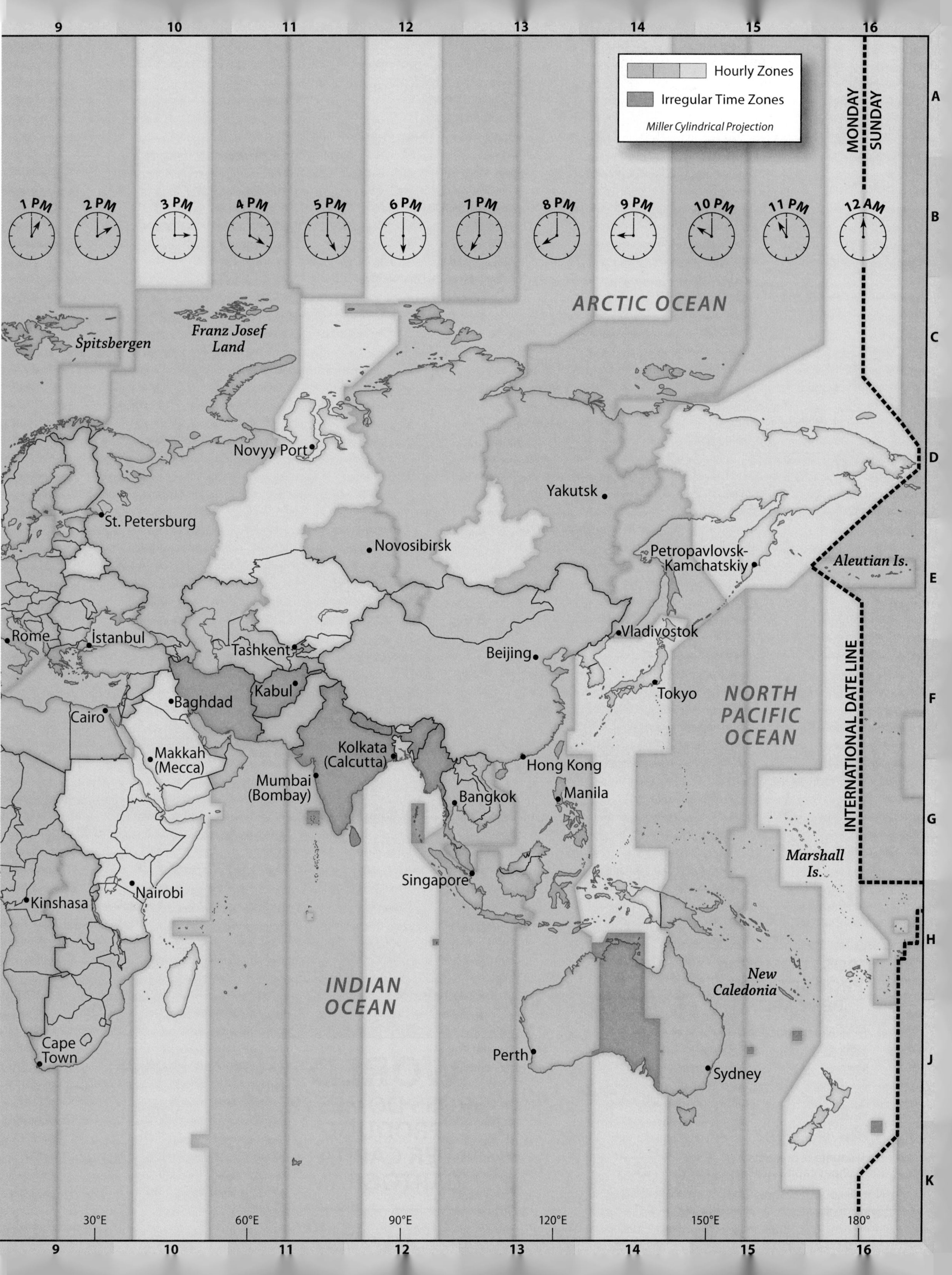

9
10
11
12
13
14
15
16
Hourly Zones
Irregular Time Zones
Miller Cylindrical Projection
MONDAY
SUNDAY
A
B
C
D
E
F
G
H
J
K
1 PM
2 PM
3 PM
4 PM
5 PM
6 PM
7 PM
8 PM
9 PM
10 PM
11 PM
12 AM
ARCTIC OCEAN
Spitsbergen
Franz Josef Land
Novyy Port
St. Petersburg
Novosibirsk
Yakutsk
Petropavlovsk-Kamchatskiy
Aleutian Is.
Rome
İstanbul
Tashkent
Vladivostok
Beijing
Tokyo
NORTH PACIFIC OCEAN
INTERNATIONAL DATE LINE
Baghdad
Kabul
Cairo
Makkah (Mecca)
Kolkata (Calcutta)
Mumbai (Bombay)
Hong Kong
Manila
Bangkok
Marshall Is.
Singapore
Nairobi
Kinshasa
INDIAN OCEAN
New Caledonia
Perth
Sydney
Cape Town
30°E
60°E
90°E
120°E
150°E
180°

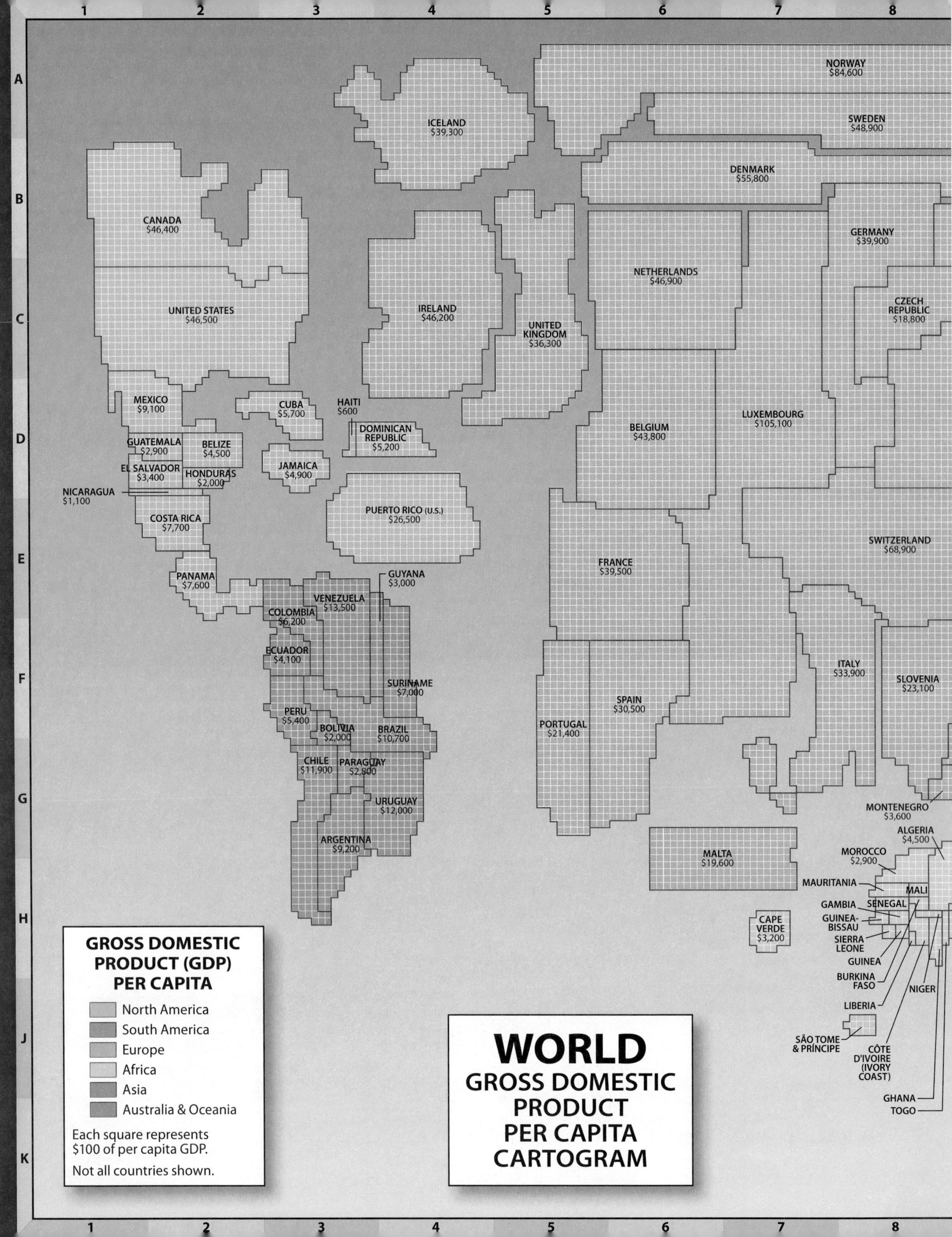

NORWAY $84,600
SWEDEN $48,900
ICELAND $39,300
DENMARK $55,800
CANADA $46,400
GERMANY $39,900
NETHERLANDS $46,900
UNITED STATES $46,500
IRELAND $46,200
UNITED KINGDOM $36,300
CZECH REPUBLIC $18,800
MEXICO $9,100
CUBA $5,700
HAITI $600
LUXEMBOURG $105,100
BELGIUM $43,800
DOMINICAN REPUBLIC $5,200
GUATEMALA $2,900
BELIZE $4,500
JAMAICA $4,900
EL SALVADOR $3,400
HONDURAS $2,000
NICARAGUA $1,100
PUERTO RICO (U.S.) $26,500
COSTA RICA $7,700
SWITZERLAND $68,900
FRANCE $39,500
PANAMA $7,600
GUYANA $3,000
VENEZUELA $13,500
COLOMBIA $6,200
ECUADOR $4,100
ITALY $33,900
SLOVENIA $23,100
SURINAME $7,000
SPAIN $30,500
PERU $5,400
PORTUGAL $21,400
BOLIVIA $2,000
BRAZIL $10,700
CHILE $11,900
PARAGUAY $2,800
URUGUAY $12,000
MONTENEGRO $3,600
ALGERIA $4,500
ARGENTINA $9,200
MALTA $19,600
MOROCCO $2,900
MAURITANIA
MALI
GAMBIA
SENEGAL
GUINEA-BISSAU
CAPE VERDE $3,200
SIERRA LEONE
GUINEA
BURKINA FASO
NIGER
LIBERIA
SÃO TOME & PRÍNCIPE
CÔTE D'IVOIRE (IVORY COAST)
GHANA
TOGO
GROSS DOMESTIC PRODUCT (GDP) PER CAPITA
North America
South America
Europe
Africa
Asia
Australia & Oceania
Each square represents $100 of per capita GDP.
Not all countries shown.
WORLD
GROSS DOMESTIC PRODUCT PER CAPITA CARTOGRAM

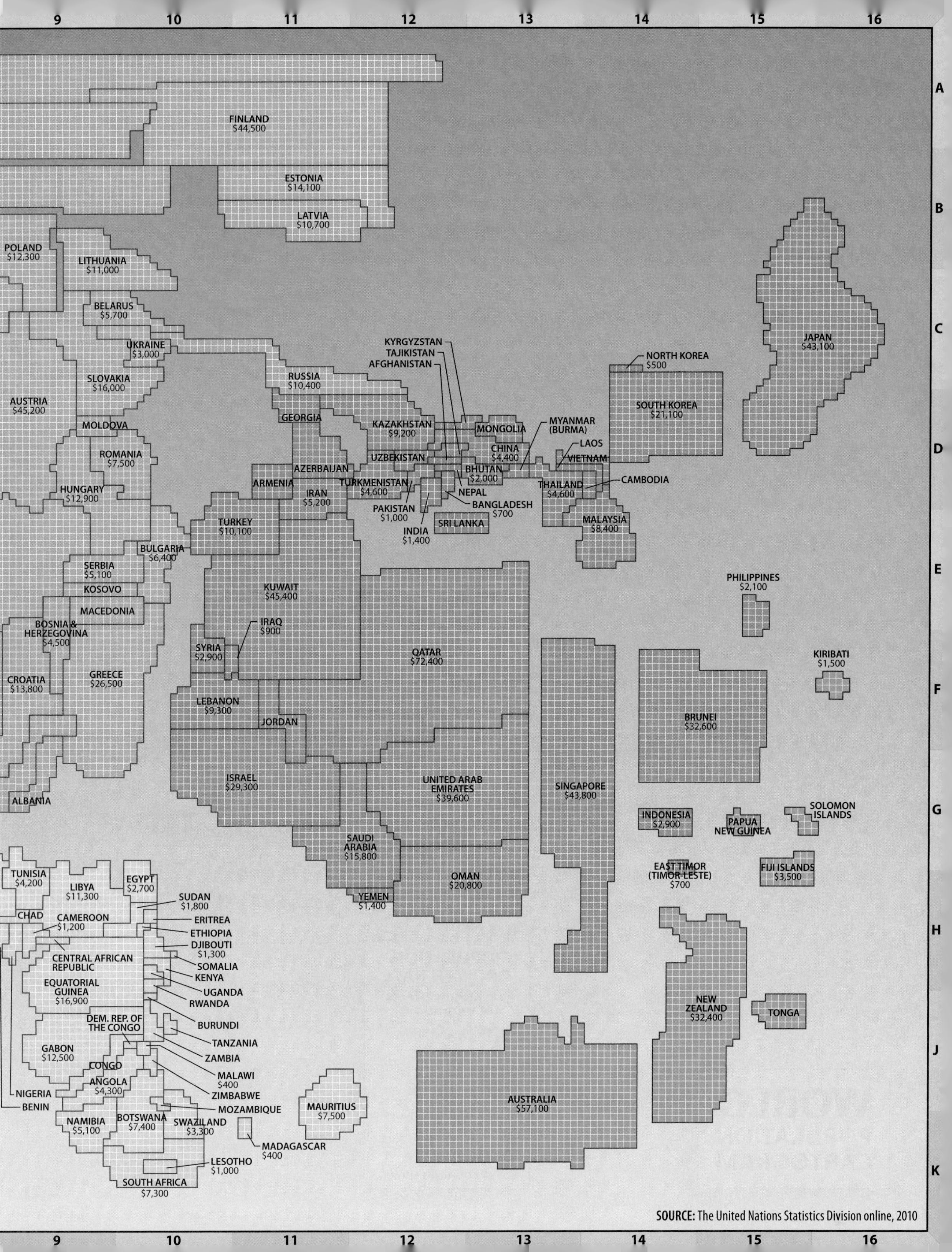

9
10
11
12
13
14
15
16
A
B
C
D
E
F
G
H
J
K
FINLAND
$44,500
ESTONIA
$14,100
LATVIA
$10,700
POLAND
$12,300
LITHUANIA
$11,000
BELARUS
$5,700
UKRAINE
$3,000
SLOVAKIA
$16,000
AUSTRIA
$45,200
MOLDOVA
ROMANIA
$7,500
HUNGARY
$12,900
RUSSIA
$10,400
GEORGIA
AZERBAIJAN
ARMENIA
TURKEY
$10,100
BULGARIA
$6,400
SERBIA
$5,100
KOSOVO
MACEDONIA
BOSNIA & HERZEGOVINA
$4,500
CROATIA
$13,800
GREECE
$26,500
ALBANIA
KYRGYZSTAN
TAJIKISTAN
AFGHANISTAN
KAZAKHSTAN
$9,200
MONGOLIA
UZBEKISTAN
CHINA
$4,400
BHUTAN
$2,000
TURKMENISTAN
$4,600
IRAN
$5,200
NEPAL
BANGLADESH
$700
PAKISTAN
$1,000
INDIA
$1,400
SRI LANKA
MYANMAR
(BURMA)
LAOS
VIETNAM
THAILAND
$4,600
CAMBODIA
MALAYSIA
$8,400
NORTH KOREA
$500
SOUTH KOREA
$21,100
JAPAN
$43,100
KUWAIT
$45,400
IRAQ
$900
SYRIA
$2,900
LEBANON
$9,300
JORDAN
QATAR
$72,400
ISRAEL
$29,300
UNITED ARAB EMIRATES
$39,600
SAUDI ARABIA
$15,800
OMAN
$20,800
YEMEN
$1,400
SINGAPORE
$43,800
PHILIPPINES
$2,100
BRUNEI
$32,600
KIRIBATI
$1,500
INDONESIA
$2,900
PAPUA NEW GUINEA
SOLOMON ISLANDS
EAST TIMOR
(TIMOR-LESTE)
$700
FIJI ISLANDS
$3,500
NEW ZEALAND
$32,400
TONGA
AUSTRALIA
$57,100
MAURITIUS
$7,500
TUNISIA
$4,200
LIBYA
$11,300
EGYPT
$2,700
SUDAN
$1,800
CHAD
CAMEROON
$1,200
ERITREA
ETHIOPIA
DJIBOUTI
$1,300
CENTRAL AFRICAN REPUBLIC
SOMALIA
KENYA
EQUATORIAL GUINEA
$16,900
UGANDA
RWANDA
DEM. REP. OF THE CONGO
BURUNDI
TANZANIA
GABON
$12,500
ZAMBIA
CONGO
MALAWI
$400
ANGOLA
$4,300
ZIMBABWE
NIGERIA
BENIN
MOZAMBIQUE
NAMIBIA
$5,100
BOTSWANA
$7,400
SWAZILAND
$3,300
MADAGASCAR
$400
LESOTHO
$1,000
SOUTH AFRICA
$7,300

SOURCE: The United Nations Statistics Division online, 2010

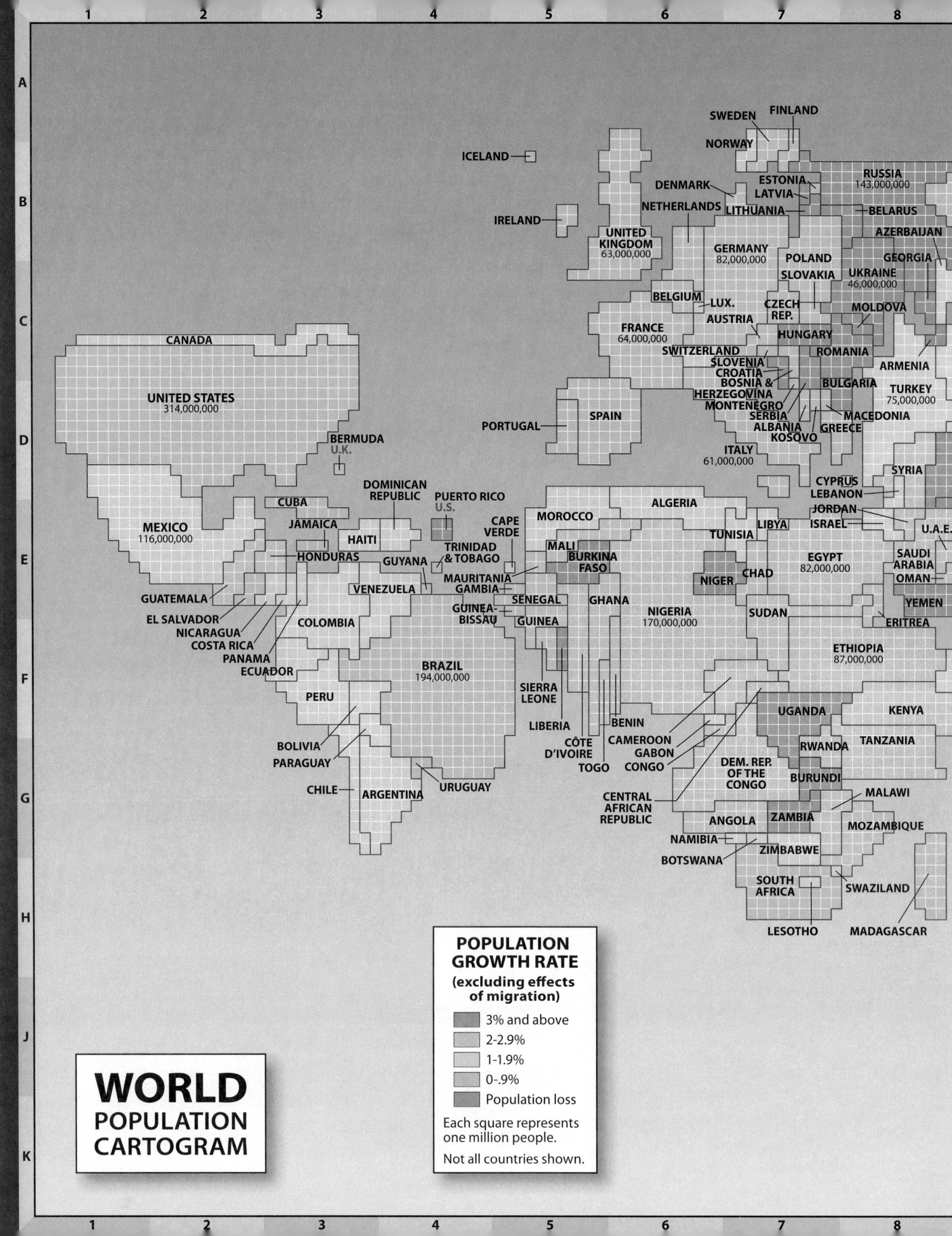

WORLD POPULATION CARTOGRAM
POPULATION GROWTH RATE (excluding effects of migration)
3% and above
2-2.9%
1-1.9%
0-.9%
Population loss
Each square represents one million people.
Not all countries shown.
CANADA
UNITED STATES 314,000,000
MEXICO 116,000,000
BERMUDA U.K.
CUBA
JAMAICA
HAITI
DOMINICAN REPUBLIC
PUERTO RICO U.S.
HONDURAS
GUATEMALA
EL SALVADOR
NICARAGUA
COSTA RICA
PANAMA
ECUADOR
COLOMBIA
VENEZUELA
GUYANA
TRINIDAD & TOBAGO
BRAZIL 194,000,000
PERU
BOLIVIA
PARAGUAY
CHILE
ARGENTINA
URUGUAY
ICELAND
IRELAND
UNITED KINGDOM 63,000,000
NORWAY
SWEDEN
FINLAND
DENMARK
NETHERLANDS
BELGIUM
LUX.
FRANCE 64,000,000
SWITZERLAND
GERMANY 82,000,000
AUSTRIA
CZECH REP.
POLAND
SLOVAKIA
HUNGARY
ESTONIA
LATVIA
LITHUANIA
RUSSIA 143,000,000
BELARUS
UKRAINE 46,000,000
MOLDOVA
ROMANIA
AZERBAIJAN
GEORGIA
ARMENIA
SLOVENIA
CROATIA
BOSNIA & HERZEGOVINA
MONTENEGRO
SERBIA
ALBANIA
KOSOVO
BULGARIA
MACEDONIA
GREECE
TURKEY 75,000,000
PORTUGAL
SPAIN
ITALY 61,000,000
CYPRUS
SYRIA
LEBANON
JORDAN
ISRAEL
U.A.E.
SAUDI ARABIA
OMAN
YEMEN
MOROCCO
ALGERIA
TUNISIA
LIBYA
EGYPT 82,000,000
CAPE VERDE
MAURITANIA
MALI
BURKINA FASO
NIGER
CHAD
GAMBIA
SENEGAL
GUINEA-BISSAU
GUINEA
SIERRA LEONE
LIBERIA
CÔTE D'IVOIRE
GHANA
TOGO
BENIN
NIGERIA 170,000,000
CAMEROON
GABON
CONGO
CENTRAL AFRICAN REPUBLIC
SUDAN
ERITREA
ETHIOPIA 87,000,000
UGANDA
KENYA
RWANDA
BURUNDI
TANZANIA
DEM. REP. OF THE CONGO
MALAWI
ANGOLA
ZAMBIA
MOZAMBIQUE
NAMIBIA
BOTSWANA
ZIMBABWE
SOUTH AFRICA
SWAZILAND
LESOTHO
MADAGASCAR

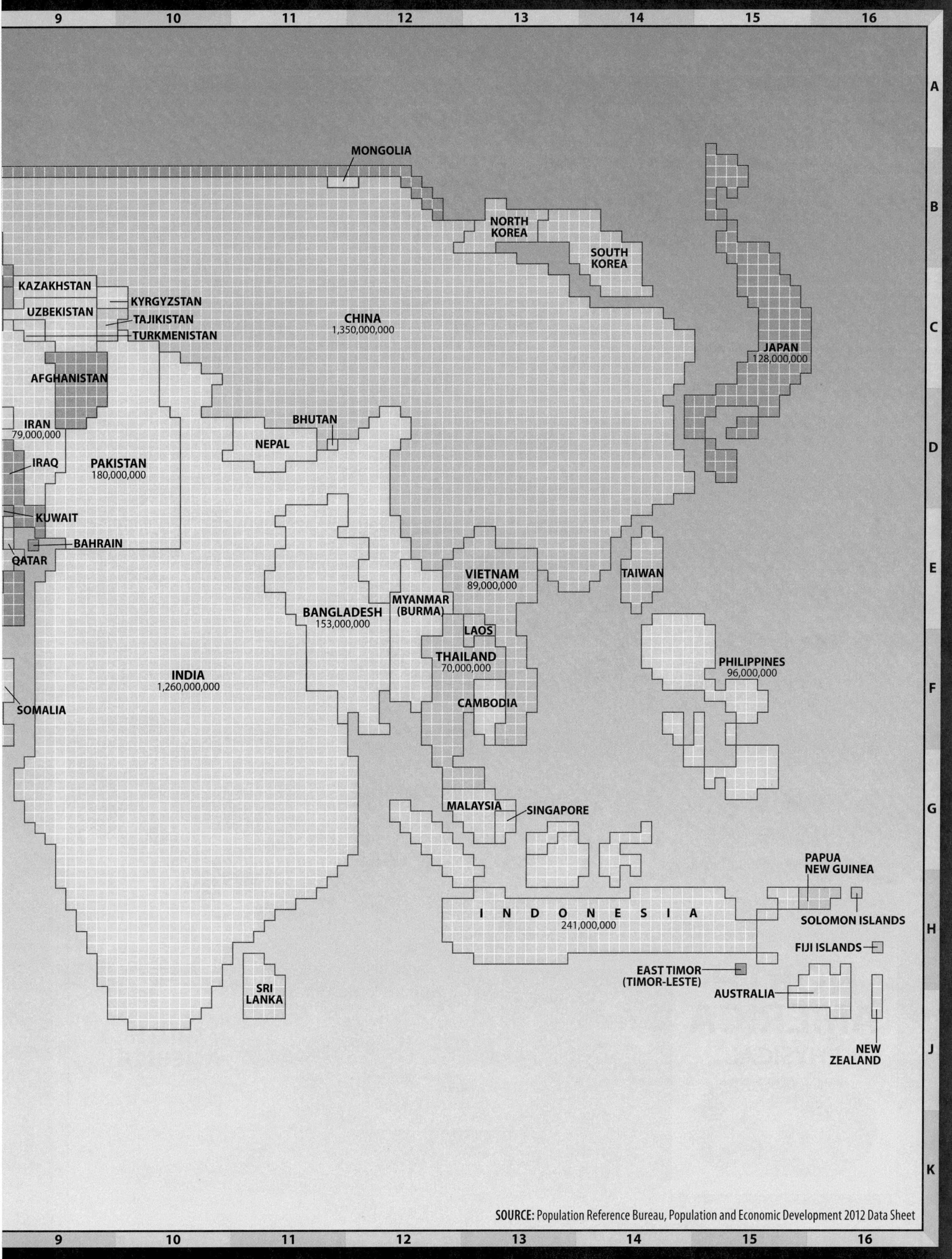

9
10
11
12
13
14
15
16
A
B
C
D
E
F
G
H
J
K
MONGOLIA
NORTH KOREA
SOUTH KOREA
KAZAKHSTAN
KYRGYZSTAN
UZBEKISTAN
TAJIKISTAN
TURKMENISTAN
CHINA
1,350,000,000
JAPAN
128,000,000
AFGHANISTAN
IRAN
79,000,000
BHUTAN
NEPAL
IRAQ
PAKISTAN
180,000,000
KUWAIT
BAHRAIN
QATAR
VIETNAM
89,000,000
TAIWAN
MYANMAR (BURMA)
BANGLADESH
153,000,000
LAOS
THAILAND
70,000,000
PHILIPPINES
96,000,000
INDIA
1,260,000,000
CAMBODIA
SOMALIA
MALAYSIA
SINGAPORE
PAPUA NEW GUINEA
I N D O N E S I A
241,000,000
SOLOMON ISLANDS
FIJI ISLANDS
EAST TIMOR (TIMOR-LESTE)
SRI LANKA
AUSTRALIA
NEW ZEALAND
SOURCE: Population Reference Bureau, Population and Economic Development 2012 Data Sheet

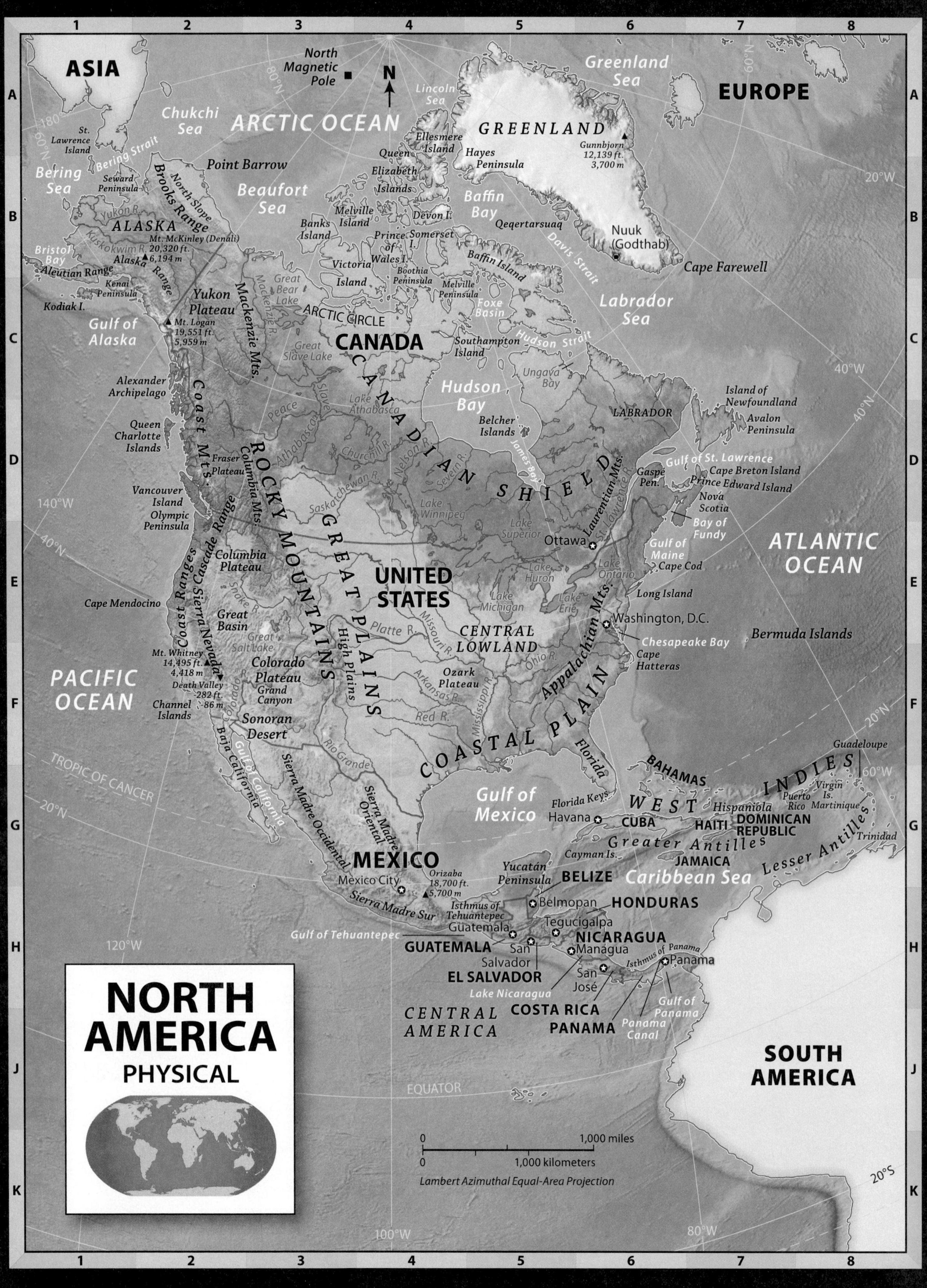
NORTH AMERICA
PHYSICAL
ASIA
EUROPE
ARCTIC OCEAN
North Magnetic Pole
Chukchi Sea
Lincoln Sea
Greenland Sea
GREENLAND
Gunnbjorn 12,139 ft. 3,700 m
Ellesmere Island
Queen Elizabeth Islands
Hayes Peninsula
St. Lawrence Island
Bering Strait
Bering Sea
Seward Peninsula
Point Barrow
Beaufort Sea
North Slope
Brooks Range
ALASKA
Yukon R.
Kuskokwim R.
Mt. McKinley (Denali) 20,320 ft. 6,194 m
Alaska Range
Bristol Bay
Aleutian Range
Kenai Peninsula
Kodiak I.
Melville Island
Banks Island
Devon I.
Prince of Wales I.
Somerset I.
Victoria Island
Boothia Peninsula
Melville Peninsula
Baffin Bay
Qeqertarsuaq
Nuuk (Godthab)
Davis Strait
Baffin Island
Cape Farewell
Labrador Sea
Foxe Basin
Hudson Strait
Yukon Plateau
Mt. Logan 19,551 ft. 5,959 m
Gulf of Alaska
Mackenzie Mts.
Mackenzie R.
Great Bear Lake
ARCTIC CIRCLE
CANADA
Great Slave Lake
Southampton Island
Ungava Bay
Hudson Bay
Island of Newfoundland
Avalon Peninsula
LABRADOR
Alexander Archipelago
Coast Mts.
Queen Charlotte Islands
Peace R.
Slave R.
Lake Athabasca
Athabasca R.
Churchill R.
Nelson R.
Severn R.
CANADIAN SHIELD
Belcher Islands
James Bay
Laurentian Mts.
Gulf of St. Lawrence
Cape Breton Island
Gaspé Pen.
Prince Edward Island
Nova Scotia
Bay of Fundy
Fraser Plateau
Columbia Mts.
ROCKY MOUNTAINS
GREAT PLAINS
Saskatchewan R.
Lake Winnipeg
Lake Superior
St. Lawrence R.
Ottawa
Vancouver Island
Olympic Peninsula
Cascade Range
Columbia Plateau
Gulf of Maine
Cape Cod
ATLANTIC OCEAN
UNITED STATES
Lake Huron
Lake Ontario
Lake Michigan
Lake Erie
Long Island
Cape Mendocino
Coast Ranges
Sierra Nevada
Snake R.
Great Basin
Great Salt Lake
Platte R.
Missouri R.
CENTRAL LOWLAND
Washington, D.C.
Chesapeake Bay
Cape Hatteras
Bermuda Islands
Mt. Whitney 14,495 ft. 4,418 m
Death Valley -282 ft. -86 m
Colorado Plateau
Colorado R.
Grand Canyon
High Plains
Ozark Plateau
Arkansas R.
Ohio R.
Mississippi R.
Appalachian Mts.
PACIFIC OCEAN
Channel Islands
Sonoran Desert
Red R.
COASTAL PLAIN
Florida
Baja California
Gulf of California
Rio Grande
TROPIC OF CANCER
Sierra Madre Occidental
Sierra Madre Oriental
Gulf of Mexico
Florida Keys
Havana
CUBA
BAHAMAS
WEST INDIES
Hispaniola
HAITI
DOMINICAN REPUBLIC
Puerto Rico
Virgin Is.
Guadeloupe
Martinique
Trinidad
Greater Antilles
Lesser Antilles
Cayman Is.
JAMAICA
MEXICO
Mexico City
Orizaba 18,700 ft. 5,700 m
Yucatán Peninsula
BELIZE
Caribbean Sea
Sierra Madre Sur
Isthmus of Tehuantepec
Belmopan
HONDURAS
Guatemala
Tegucigalpa
Gulf of Tehuantepec
GUATEMALA
San Salvador
NICARAGUA
Managua
Isthmus of Panama
Panama
EL SALVADOR
San José
Lake Nicaragua
Gulf of Panama
CENTRAL AMERICA
COSTA RICA
PANAMA
Panama Canal
SOUTH AMERICA
EQUATOR
0
1,000 miles
0
1,000 kilometers
Lambert Azimuthal Equal-Area Projection
180°
60°N
80°N
60°N
20°W
40°W
40°N
140°W
40°N
20°N
20°N
60°W
120°W
100°W
80°W
20°S
1 2 3 4 5 6 7 8
A B C D E F G H J K

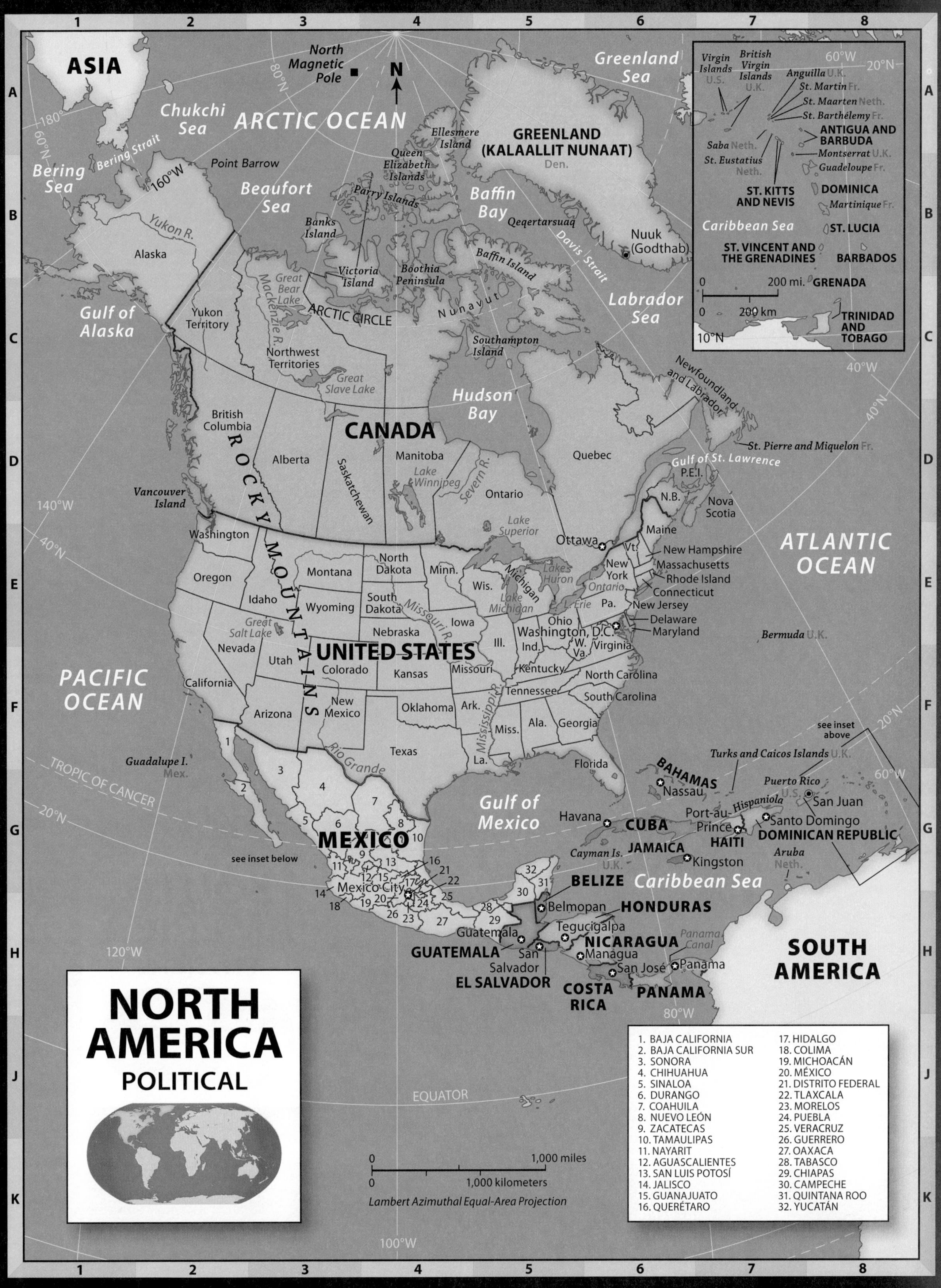

NORTH AMERICA
POLITICAL
ASIA
North Magnetic Pole
N
ARCTIC OCEAN
Chukchi Sea
Bering Strait
Bering Sea
Point Barrow
160°W
180°
60°N
80°N
Beaufort Sea
Queen Elizabeth Islands
Ellesmere Island
Parry Islands
Banks Island
Victoria Island
Boothia Peninsula
Greenland Sea
GREENLAND (KALAALLIT NUNAAT)
Den.
Baffin Bay
Qeqertarsuaq
Davis Strait
Nuuk (Godthab)
Baffin Island
Labrador Sea
Nunavut
ARCTIC CIRCLE
Southampton Island
Hudson Bay
Newfoundland and Labrador
St. Pierre and Miquelon Fr.
Gulf of St. Lawrence
P.E.I.
N.B.
Nova Scotia
Quebec
Ontario
Manitoba
Saskatchewan
Alberta
British Columbia
CANADA
Yukon Territory
Northwest Territories
Great Bear Lake
Great Slave Lake
Mackenzie R.
Yukon R.
Alaska
Gulf of Alaska
Lake Winnipeg
Severn R.
Lake Superior
Vancouver Island
Ottawa
ROCKY MOUNTAINS
140°W
40°N
40°W
ATLANTIC OCEAN
PACIFIC OCEAN
Washington
Oregon
Idaho
Montana
Wyoming
North Dakota
South Dakota
Minn.
Wis.
Michigan
Lake Michigan
Lake Huron
Lake Ontario
L. Erie
Maine
Vt.
New Hampshire
Massachusetts
Rhode Island
Connecticut
New York
New Jersey
Pa.
Delaware
Maryland
Washington, D.C.
Virginia
W. Va.
Ohio
Ind.
Ill.
Iowa
Nebraska
Missouri R.
Great Salt Lake
Nevada
Utah
California
Colorado
Kansas
Missouri
Kentucky
North Carolina
Tennessee
South Carolina
Arizona
New Mexico
Oklahoma
Ark.
Mississippi R.
Miss.
Ala.
Georgia
Texas
La.
Florida
Rio Grande
UNITED STATES
Bermuda U.K.
Guadalupe I. Mex.
TROPIC OF CANCER
20°N
Gulf of Mexico
MEXICO
Mexico City
see inset below
BAHAMAS
Nassau
Turks and Caicos Islands U.K.
see inset above
Havana
CUBA
Hispaniola
Port-au-Prince
HAITI
Santo Domingo
DOMINICAN REPUBLIC
Puerto Rico U.S.
San Juan
Cayman Is. U.K.
JAMAICA
Kingston
Aruba Neth.
Caribbean Sea
BELIZE
Belmopan
HONDURAS
Tegucigalpa
Guatemala
GUATEMALA
San Salvador
EL SALVADOR
NICARAGUA
Managua
San José
COSTA RICA
Panama Canal
Panama
PANAMA
SOUTH AMERICA
120°W
100°W
80°W
60°W
EQUATOR
Virgin Islands U.S.
British Virgin Islands U.K.
Anguilla U.K.
St. Martin Fr.
St. Maarten Neth.
St. Barthélemy Fr.
Saba Neth.
St. Eustatius Neth.
ANTIGUA AND BARBUDA
Montserrat U.K.
Guadeloupe Fr.
ST. KITTS AND NEVIS
DOMINICA
Martinique Fr.
ST. LUCIA
ST. VINCENT AND THE GRENADINES
BARBADOS
GRENADA
TRINIDAD AND TOBAGO
0 200 mi.
0 200 km
10°N
1. BAJA CALIFORNIA
2. BAJA CALIFORNIA SUR
3. SONORA
4. CHIHUAHUA
5. SINALOA
6. DURANGO
7. COAHUILA
8. NUEVO LEÓN
9. ZACATECAS
10. TAMAULIPAS
11. NAYARIT
12. AGUASCALIENTES
13. SAN LUIS POTOSÍ
14. JALISCO
15. GUANAJUATO
16. QUERÉTARO
17. HIDALGO
18. COLIMA
19. MICHOACÁN
20. MÉXICO
21. DISTRITO FEDERAL
22. TLAXCALA
23. MORELOS
24. PUEBLA
25. VERACRUZ
26. GUERRERO
27. OAXACA
28. TABASCO
29. CHIAPAS
30. CAMPECHE
31. QUINTANA ROO
32. YUCATÁN
0 1,000 miles
0 1,000 kilometers
Lambert Azimuthal Equal-Area Projection

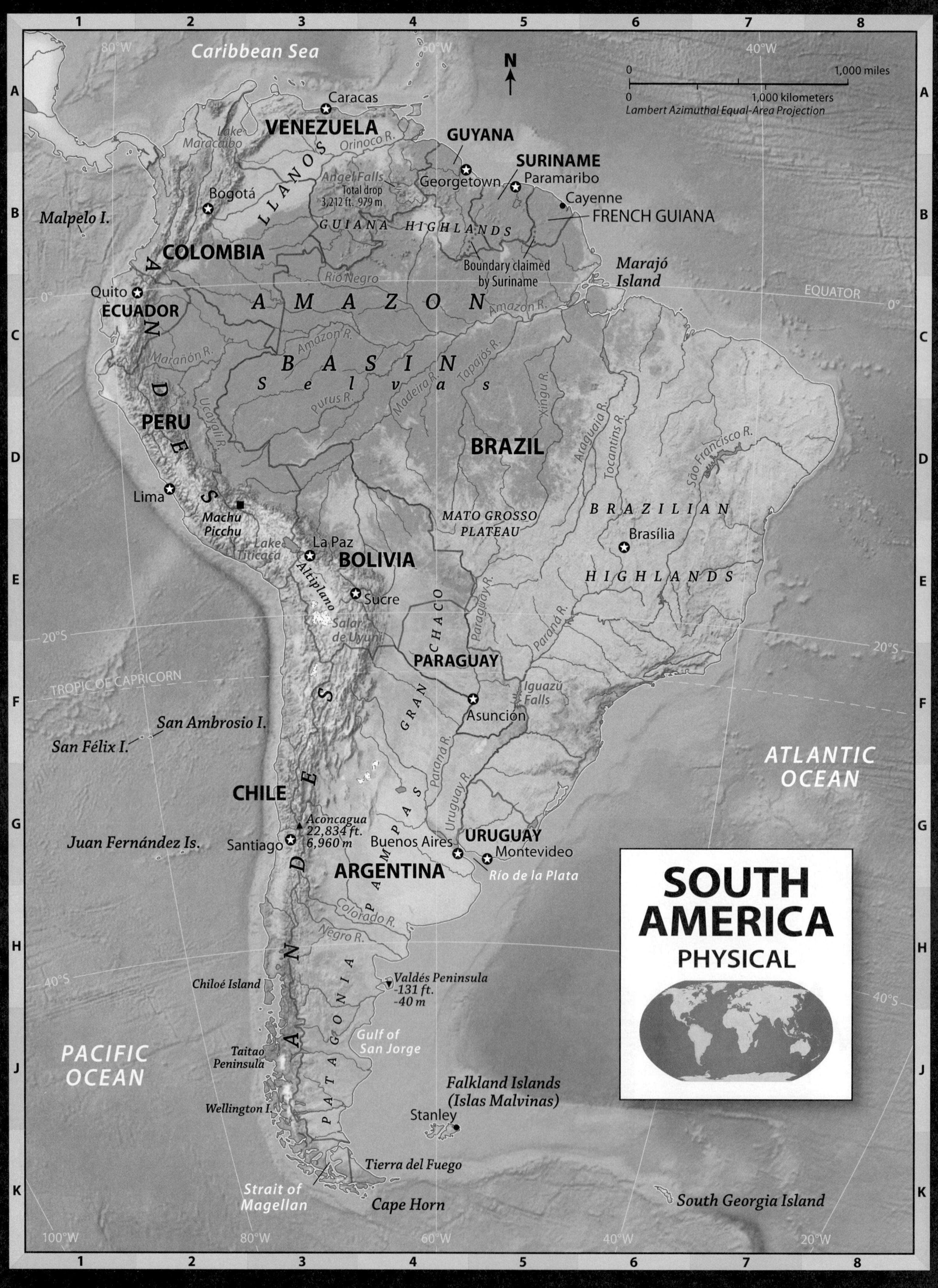

SOUTH AMERICA
PHYSICAL
Caribbean Sea
Lambert Azimuthal Equal-Area Projection
0 1,000 miles
0 1,000 kilometers
Caracas
VENEZUELA
Lake Maracaibo
Orinoco R.
GUYANA
SURINAME
Georgetown
Paramaribo
Cayenne
FRENCH GUIANA
LLANOS
Angel Falls
Total drop 3,212 ft. 979 m
Bogotá
Malpelo I.
GUIANA HIGHLANDS
Boundary claimed by Suriname
COLOMBIA
Marajó Island
Rio Negro
Quito
ECUADOR
EQUATOR
AMAZON BASIN
Selvas
Amazon R.
Marañón R.
Purus R.
Madeira R.
Tapajós R.
Xingu R.
Ucayali R.
Araguaia R.
Tocantins R.
São Francisco R.
PERU
BRAZIL
ANDES
Lima
Machu Picchu
MATO GROSSO PLATEAU
BRAZILIAN HIGHLANDS
Brasília
Lake Titicaca
La Paz
BOLIVIA
Altiplano
Sucre
Salar de Uyuni
CHACO
Paraguay R.
Paraná R.
PARAGUAY
TROPIC OF CAPRICORN
Iguazú Falls
Asunción
GRAN CHACO
San Ambrosio I.
San Félix I.
ATLANTIC OCEAN
CHILE
PAMPAS
Uruguay R.
Aconcagua 22,834 ft. 6,960 m
URUGUAY
Juan Fernández Is.
Santiago
Buenos Aires
Montevideo
ARGENTINA
Río de la Plata
Colorado R.
Negro R.
Chiloé Island
Valdés Peninsula -131 ft. -40 m
PATAGONIA
Gulf of San Jorge
PACIFIC OCEAN
Taitao Peninsula
Falkland Islands (Islas Malvinas)
Wellington I.
Stanley
Tierra del Fuego
Strait of Magellan
Cape Horn
South Georgia Island
100°W
80°W
60°W
40°W
20°W
0°
20°S
40°S

SOUTH AMERICA
POLITICAL
Lambert Azimuthal Equal-Area Projection
0 1,000 miles
0 1,000 kilometers
Caribbean Sea
PACIFIC OCEAN
ATLANTIC OCEAN
COLOMBIA
VENEZUELA
GUYANA
SURINAME
FRENCH GUIANA
ECUADOR
PERU
BRAZIL
BOLIVIA
PARAGUAY
CHILE
ARGENTINA
URUGUAY
AMAZON BASIN
ANDES
Santa Marta
Barranquilla
Cartagena
Maracaibo
Caracas
Valencia
Lake Maracaibo
Ciudad Guayana
Bucaramanga
San Cristóbal
Orinoco R.
Georgetown
Paramaribo
Cayenne
Medellín
Bogotá
Cali
Malpelo I.
Col.
Fr.
Boa Vista
Boundary claimed by Suriname
Marajó Island
Esmeraldas
Quito
Rio Negro
Amazon R.
Belém
São Luís
Guayaquil
Iquitos
Manaus
Santarém
Fortaleza
Marañón R.
Teresina
Natal
Purus R.
Madeira R.
Tapajós R.
Xingu R.
Araguaia R.
Tocantins R.
Campina Grande
Recife
Ucayali R.
Río Branco
Pôrto Velho
São Francisco R.
Callao
Lima
Machu Picchu
Cuzco
Ayacucho
Lake Titicaca
Trinidad
Salvador
Brasília
La Paz
Arequipa
Goiânia
Santa Cruz
Oruro
Sucre
Arica
Campo Grande
Paraguay R.
Uberlândia
Uberaba
Belo Horizonte
Paraná R.
Iquique
Tarija
20°S
Antofagasta
TROPIC OF CAPRICORN
Londrina
Campinas
Nova Iguaçu
São Paulo
Rio de Janeiro
Santos
Salta
Asunción
Curitiba
San Félix I.
San Ambrosio I.
Chile
San Miguel de Tucumán
Uruguaiana
La Serena
Coquimbo
Santa Maria
Pôrto Alegre
Córdoba
Uruguay R.
Rosario
Valparaíso
Mendoza
Juan Fernández Is.
Santiago
Buenos Aires
Montevideo
La Plata
Río de la Plata
Concepción
Mar del Plata
Colorado R.
Bahía Blanca
Negro R.
Puerto Montt
40°S
Comodoro Rivadavia
Falkland Islands (Islas Malvinas)
Stanley
Administered by United Kingdom
Claimed by Arg.
Río Gallegos
Punta Arenas
Ushuaia
Strait of Magellan
Cape Horn
South Georgia Island
U.K.
EQUATOR
0°
80°W
60°W
40°W
20°W
100°W

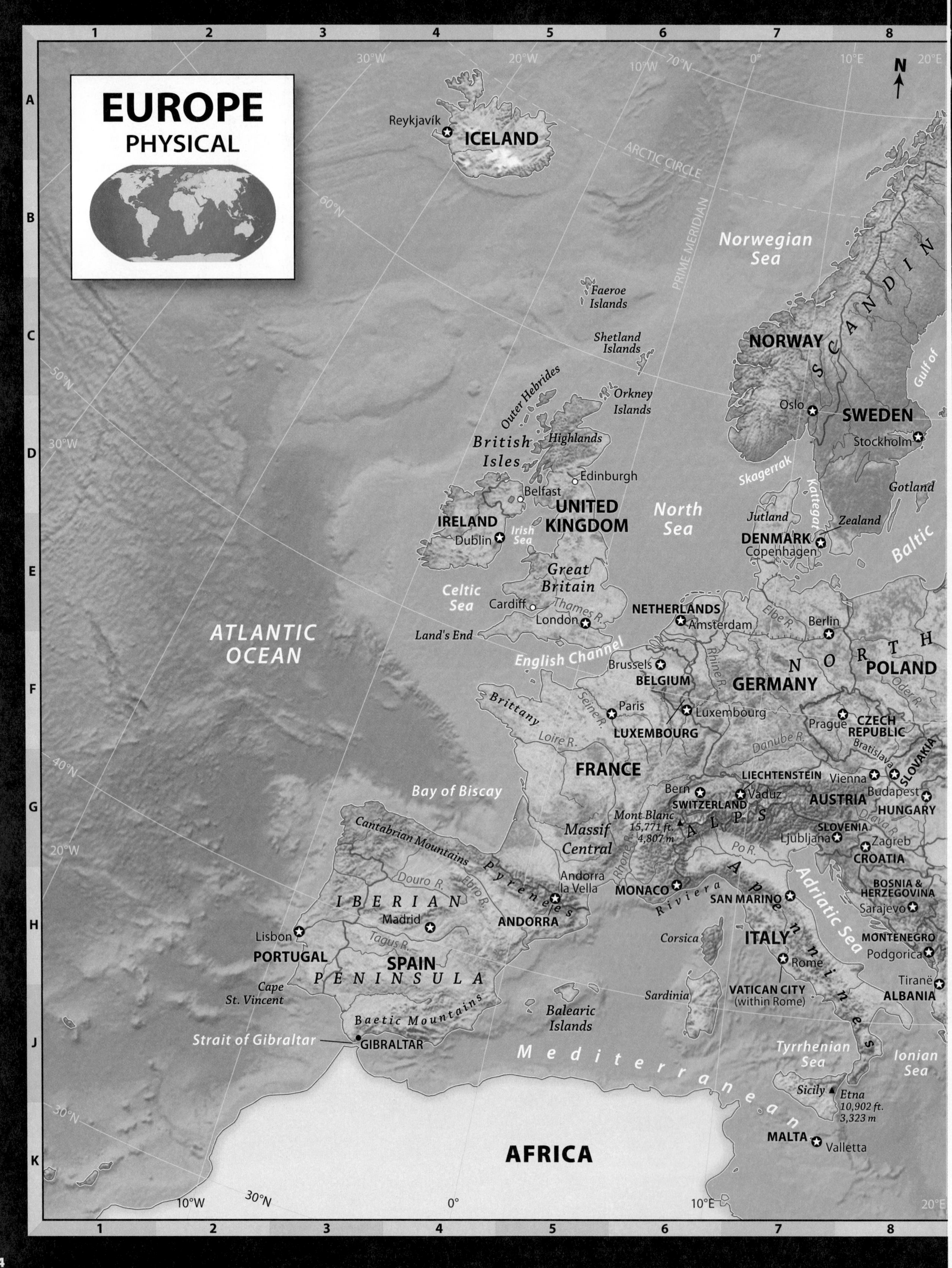
EUROPE
PHYSICAL
ICELAND
Reykjavík
ARCTIC CIRCLE
PRIME MERIDIAN
Norwegian Sea
Faeroe Islands
Shetland Islands
Orkney Islands
Outer Hebrides
Highlands
British Isles
Edinburgh
Belfast
UNITED KINGDOM
IRELAND
Dublin
Irish Sea
North Sea
Great Britain
Celtic Sea
Cardiff
Thames R.
London
Land's End
English Channel
ATLANTIC OCEAN
NORWAY
SWEDEN
Oslo
Stockholm
SCANDIN
Gulf of
Skagerrak
Kattegat
Gotland
Jutland
Zealand
DENMARK
Copenhagen
Baltic
NETHERLANDS
Amsterdam
Elbe R.
Berlin
NORTH
POLAND
Brussels
BELGIUM
Rhine R.
GERMANY
Oder R.
Brittany
Paris
Seine R.
Luxembourg
LUXEMBOURG
Prague
CZECH REPUBLIC
Loire R.
Danube R.
Bratislava
SLOVAKIA
FRANCE
LIECHTENSTEIN
Vienna
Bay of Biscay
Bern
Vaduz
Budapest
SWITZERLAND
AUSTRIA
HUNGARY
Mont Blanc
15,771 ft.
4,807 m
ALPS
Massif Central
SLOVENIA
Ljubljana
Zagreb
Drava R.
CROATIA
Po R.
Cantabrian Mountains
Pyrenees
Rhone R.
Andorra la Vella
MONACO
Riviera
Apennines
SAN MARINO
Adriatic Sea
BOSNIA & HERZEGOVINA
Sarajevo
Douro R.
Ebro R.
IBERIAN PENINSULA
Madrid
ANDORRA
Lisbon
Tagus R.
Corsica
ITALY
MONTENEGRO
Podgorica
PORTUGAL
SPAIN
Rome
Tiranë
ALBANIA
Cape St. Vincent
Sardinia
VATICAN CITY (within Rome)
Balearic Islands
Baetic Mountains
Strait of Gibraltar
GIBRALTAR
Mediterranean
Tyrrhenian Sea
Ionian Sea
Sicily
Etna
10,902 ft.
3,323 m
MALTA
Valletta
AFRICA
30°W
20°W
10°W
0°
10°E
20°E
70°N
60°N
50°N
40°N
30°N
N

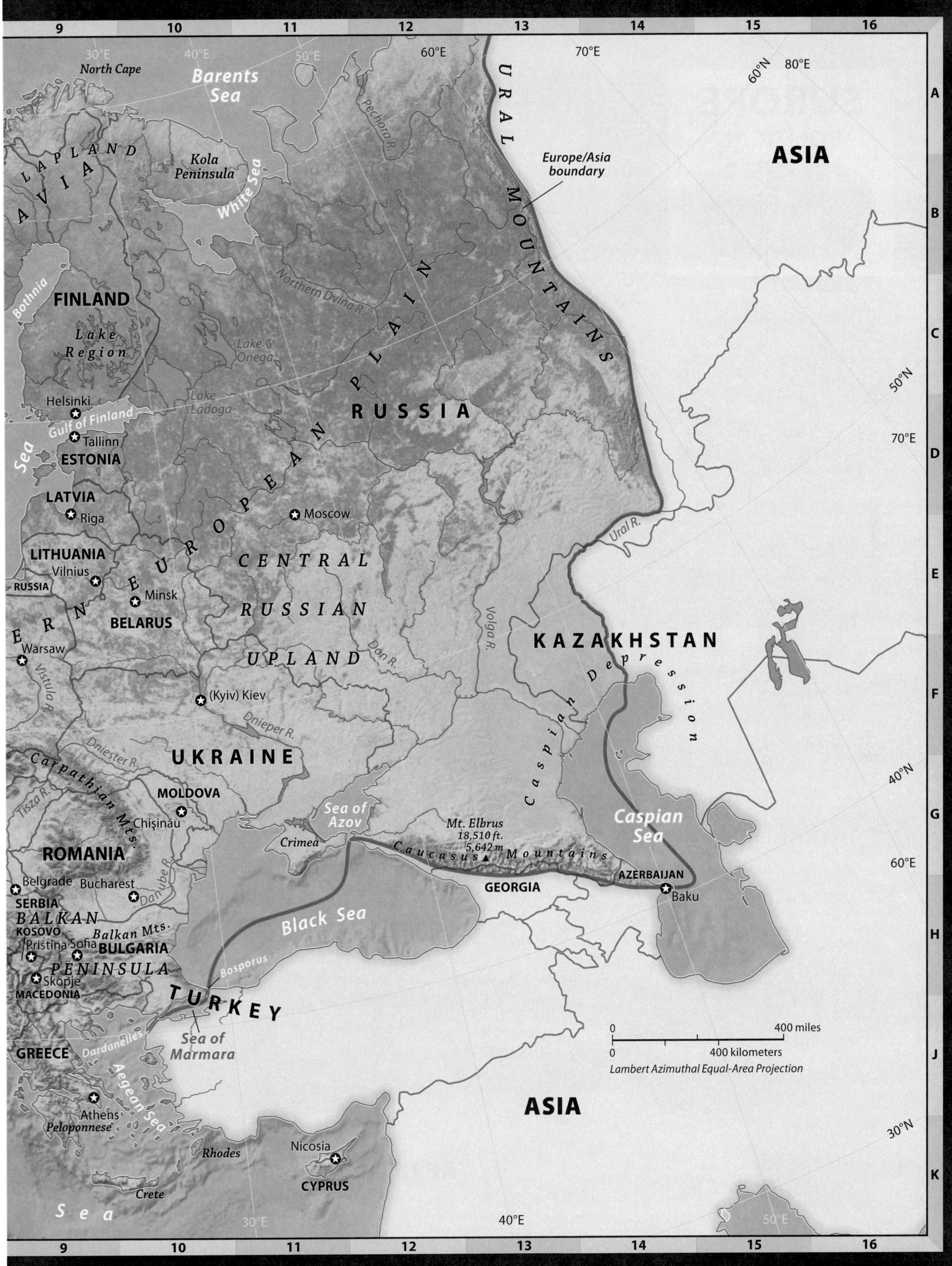

North Cape
Barents Sea
White Sea
Kola Peninsula
LAPLAND
FINLAND
Bothnia
Lake Region
Helsinki
Gulf of Finland
Tallinn
ESTONIA
Sea
LATVIA
Riga
LITHUANIA
Vilnius
RUSSIA
Minsk
BELARUS
Warsaw
Vistula R.
Lake Onega
Lake Ladoga
Northern Dvina R.
Pechora R.
URAL MOUNTAINS
Europe/Asia boundary
ASIA
RUSSIA
EUROPEAN PLAIN
Moscow
CENTRAL RUSSIAN UPLAND
Don R.
Volga R.
Ural R.
KAZAKHSTAN
Caspian Depression
(Kyiv) Kiev
Dnieper R.
Dniester R.
UKRAINE
Carpathian Mts.
Tisza R.
MOLDOVA
Chişinău
ROMANIA
Belgrade
Bucharest
Danube R.
SERBIA
BALKAN PENINSULA
KOSOVO
Priština
Sofia
Balkan Mts.
BULGARIA
Skopje
MACEDONIA
Sea of Azov
Crimea
Mt. Elbrus 18,510 ft. 5,642 m
Caucasus Mountains
GEORGIA
AZERBAIJAN
Baku
Caspian Sea
Black Sea
Bosporus
TURKEY
Sea of Marmara
Dardanelles
GREECE
Aegean Sea
Athens
Peloponnese
Rhodes
Crete
Sea
Nicosia
CYPRUS
ASIA
0 400 miles
0 400 kilometers
Lambert Azimuthal Equal-Area Projection
30°E
40°E
50°E
60°E
70°E
80°E
60°N
50°N
40°N
30°N

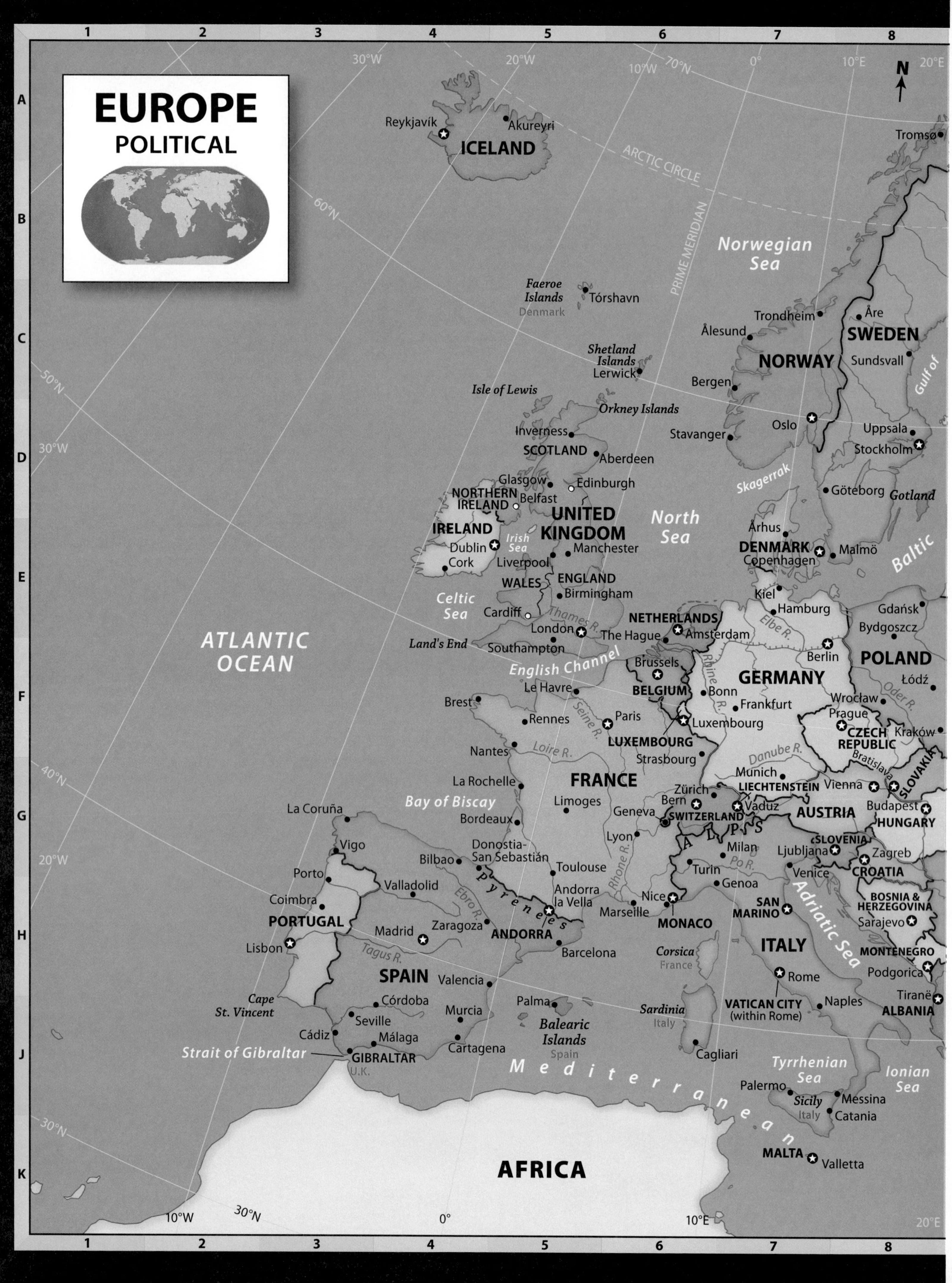
EUROPE
POLITICAL
ICELAND
Reykjavík
Akureyri
ARCTIC CIRCLE
PRIME MERIDIAN
Norwegian Sea
Faeroe Islands
Denmark
Tórshavn
Shetland Islands
Lerwick
Isle of Lewis
Orkney Islands
Inverness
SCOTLAND
Aberdeen
Glasgow
Edinburgh
NORTHERN IRELAND
Belfast
IRELAND
Dublin
Cork
Irish Sea
UNITED KINGDOM
Manchester
Liverpool
WALES
ENGLAND
Birmingham
Cardiff
Celtic Sea
London
Thames R.
Land's End
Southampton
English Channel
North Sea
Skagerrak
NORWAY
Trondheim
Ålesund
Bergen
Oslo
Stavanger
SWEDEN
Åre
Sundsvall
Gulf of
Uppsala
Stockholm
Göteborg
Gotland
Tromsø
DENMARK
Århus
Copenhagen
Malmö
Baltic
Kiel
Hamburg
Elbe R.
NETHERLANDS
Amsterdam
The Hague
Brussels
BELGIUM
GERMANY
Berlin
Bonn
Frankfurt
Rhine R.
Luxembourg
LUXEMBOURG
Strasbourg
Munich
Danube R.
POLAND
Gdańsk
Bydgoszcz
Łódź
Oder R.
Wrocław
Kraków
Prague
CZECH REPUBLIC
Bratislava
SLOVAKIA
Vienna
LIECHTENSTEIN
Vaduz
AUSTRIA
Budapest
HUNGARY
SLOVENIA
Ljubljana
Zagreb
CROATIA
BOSNIA & HERZEGOVINA
Sarajevo
MONTENEGRO
Podgorica
Tiranë
ALBANIA
ATLANTIC OCEAN
FRANCE
Le Havre
Paris
Seine R.
Brest
Rennes
Nantes
Loire R.
La Rochelle
Limoges
Bordeaux
Bay of Biscay
Lyon
Rhone R.
Toulouse
Marseille
Nice
MONACO
Geneva
Bern
Zürich
SWITZERLAND
ALPS
Milan
Turin
Po R.
Genoa
Venice
SAN MARINO
ITALY
Adriatic Sea
Rome
VATICAN CITY (within Rome)
Naples
Corsica
France
Sardinia
Italy
Cagliari
Tyrrhenian Sea
Palermo
Sicily
Italy
Messina
Catania
Ionian Sea
MALTA
Valletta
La Coruña
Vigo
Porto
Coimbra
PORTUGAL
Lisbon
Cape St. Vincent
SPAIN
Valladolid
Bilbao
Donostia-San Sebastián
Pyrenees
Ebro R.
Andorra la Vella
ANDORRA
Zaragoza
Madrid
Tagus R.
Barcelona
Valencia
Córdoba
Seville
Murcia
Cartagena
Málaga
Cádiz
Palma
Balearic Islands
Spain
Strait of Gibraltar
GIBRALTAR
U.K.
Mediterranean
AFRICA
N
30°W
20°W
10°W
0°
10°E
20°E
70°N
60°N
50°N
40°N
30°N
1 2 3 4 5 6 7 8
A B C D E F G H J K

A commonly accepted division between Asia and Europe—here marked by a gray line—is formed by the Ural Mountains, Ural River, Caspian Sea, Caucasus Mountains, and the Black Sea with its outlets, the Bosporus and the Dardanelles.
Europe/Asia boundary
ASIA
RUSSIA
URAL MOUNTAINS
Barents Sea
White Sea
Kola Peninsula
LAPLAND
FINLAND
ESTONIA
LATVIA
LITHUANIA
BELARUS
UKRAINE
MOLDOVA
ROMANIA
SERBIA
KOSOVO
BULGARIA
MACEDONIA
GREECE
TURKEY
KAZAKHSTAN
GEORGIA
AZERBAIJAN
CYPRUS
Caspian Sea
Black Sea
Sea of Azov
Sea of Marmara
Aegean Sea
Caucasus Mountains
Carpathian Mts.
Balkan Mts.
Bosporus
Dardanelles
Crimea
Peloponnese
Rhodes
Crete
Greece
Lake Onega
Lake Ladoga
Northern Dvina R.
Volga R.
Don R.
Dnieper R.
Dniester R.
Vistula R.
Ural R.
Bothnia
Tobseda
Murmansk
Pechora
Kirovsk
Ivalo
Kiruna
Umba
Kemi
Kem'
Arkhangel'sk
Severodvinsk
Luleå
Umeå
Oulu
Syktyvkar
Vaasa
Kuopio
Perm'
Pori
Tampere
Kirov
Turku
Helsinki
St. Petersburg
Ufa
Tallinn
Kazan'
Novgorod
Yaroslavl'
Nizhniy Novgorod
Tver'
Moscow
Orenburg
Samara
Riga
Daugavpils
Penza
Smolensk
Ryazan'
Vitsyebsk
Vilnius
Oral
Kaunas
Minsk
Saratov
Bryansk
Kaliningrad
Homyel'
Kursk
Chernihiv
Warsaw
Sumy
Kyiv (Kiev)
Kharkiv
Volgograd
Poltava
L'viv
Vinnytsya
Donets'k
Astrakhan
Dnipropetrovs'k
Rostov
Stavropol'
Chişinău
Odessa
Kerch
Grozny
Simferopol'
Belgrade
Bucharest
Sevastopol'
Yalta
Baku
Constanța
Varna
Priština
Sofia
Skopje
İstanbul
Thessaloníki
Athens
Nicosia
Iraklíon
Sea
0
400 miles
400 kilometers
Lambert Azimuthal Equal-Area Projection
30°E
40°E
50°E
60°E
70°E
80°E
60°N
50°N
40°N
30°N
9
10
11
12
13
14
15
16
A
B
C
D
E
F
G
H
J
K

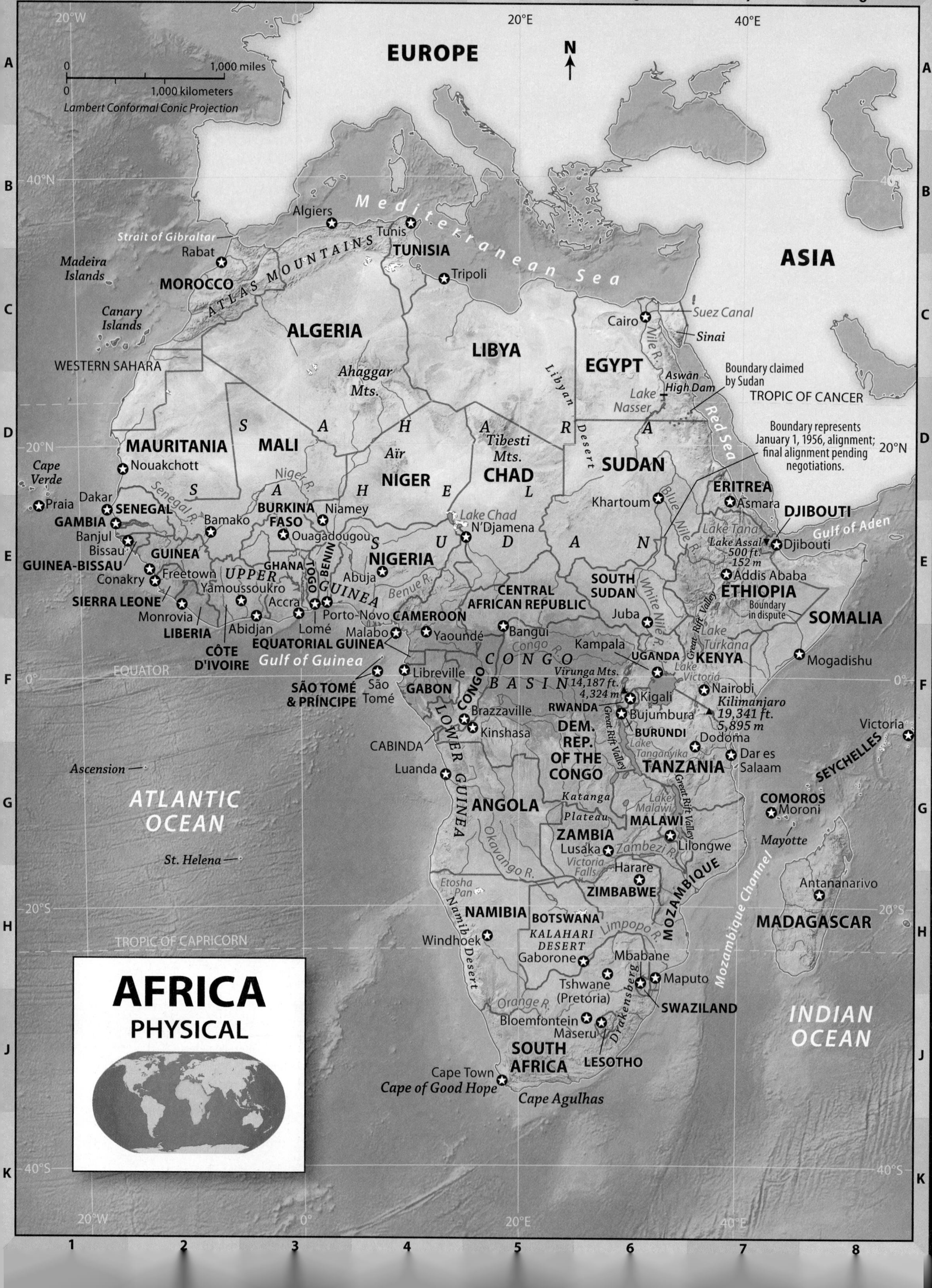

AFRICA
PHYSICAL
EUROPE
ASIA
ATLANTIC OCEAN
INDIAN OCEAN
Mediterranean Sea
Red Sea
Gulf of Aden
Gulf of Guinea
Mozambique Channel
1,000 miles
1,000 kilometers
Lambert Conformal Conic Projection
TROPIC OF CANCER
TROPIC OF CAPRICORN
EQUATOR
SAHARA
SAHEL
SUDAN
ATLAS MOUNTAINS
Ahaggar Mts.
Aïr
Tibesti Mts.
Libyan Desert
CONGO BASIN
UPPER GUINEA
LOWER GUINEA
Virunga Mts. 14,187 ft. 4,324 m
Kilimanjaro 19,341 ft. 5,895 m
Lake Assal -500 ft. -152 m
Katanga Plateau
KALAHARI DESERT
Namib Desert
Drakensberg
Great Rift Valley
Cape of Good Hope
Cape Agulhas
Strait of Gibraltar
Suez Canal
Sinai
Aswân High Dam
Lake Nasser
Boundary claimed by Sudan
Boundary represents January 1, 1956, alignment; final alignment pending negotiations.
Boundary in dispute
Madeira Islands
Canary Islands
Cape Verde
Ascension
St. Helena
MOROCCO
ALGERIA
TUNISIA
LIBYA
EGYPT
WESTERN SAHARA
MAURITANIA
MALI
NIGER
CHAD
SUDAN
SOUTH SUDAN
ERITREA
DJIBOUTI
ETHIOPIA
SOMALIA
SENEGAL
GAMBIA
GUINEA-BISSAU
GUINEA
SIERRA LEONE
LIBERIA
CÔTE D'IVOIRE
BURKINA FASO
GHANA
TOGO
BENIN
NIGERIA
CAMEROON
CENTRAL AFRICAN REPUBLIC
EQUATORIAL GUINEA
SÃO TOMÉ & PRÍNCIPE
GABON
CONGO
CABINDA
DEM. REP. OF THE CONGO
UGANDA
KENYA
RWANDA
BURUNDI
TANZANIA
ANGOLA
ZAMBIA
MALAWI
MOZAMBIQUE
ZIMBABWE
NAMIBIA
BOTSWANA
SOUTH AFRICA
SWAZILAND
LESOTHO
MADAGASCAR
COMOROS
SEYCHELLES
Mayotte
Algiers
Tunis
Rabat
Tripoli
Cairo
Nouakchott
Dakar
Praia
Banjul
Bissau
Conakry
Freetown
Monrovia
Bamako
Ouagadougou
Niamey
Yamoussoukro
Abidjan
Accra
Lomé
Porto-Novo
Abuja
N'Djamena
Khartoum
Asmara
Djibouti
Addis Ababa
Mogadishu
Juba
Bangui
Yaoundé
Malabo
São Tomé
Libreville
Brazzaville
Kinshasa
Luanda
Kampala
Nairobi
Kigali
Bujumbura
Dodoma
Dar es Salaam
Victoria
Moroni
Lilongwe
Lusaka
Harare
Antananarivo
Windhoek
Gaborone
Tshwane (Pretoria)
Mbabane
Maputo
Bloemfontein
Maseru
Cape Town
Lake Chad
Niger R.
Senegal R.
Benue R.
Congo R.
Nile R.
Blue Nile R.
White Nile R.
Lake Tana
Lake Turkana
Lake Victoria
Lake Tanganyika
Lake Malawi
Zambezi R.
Victoria Falls
Okavango R.
Etosha Pan
Limpopo R.
Orange R.
20°W
0°
20°E
40°E
40°N
20°N
20°S
40°S

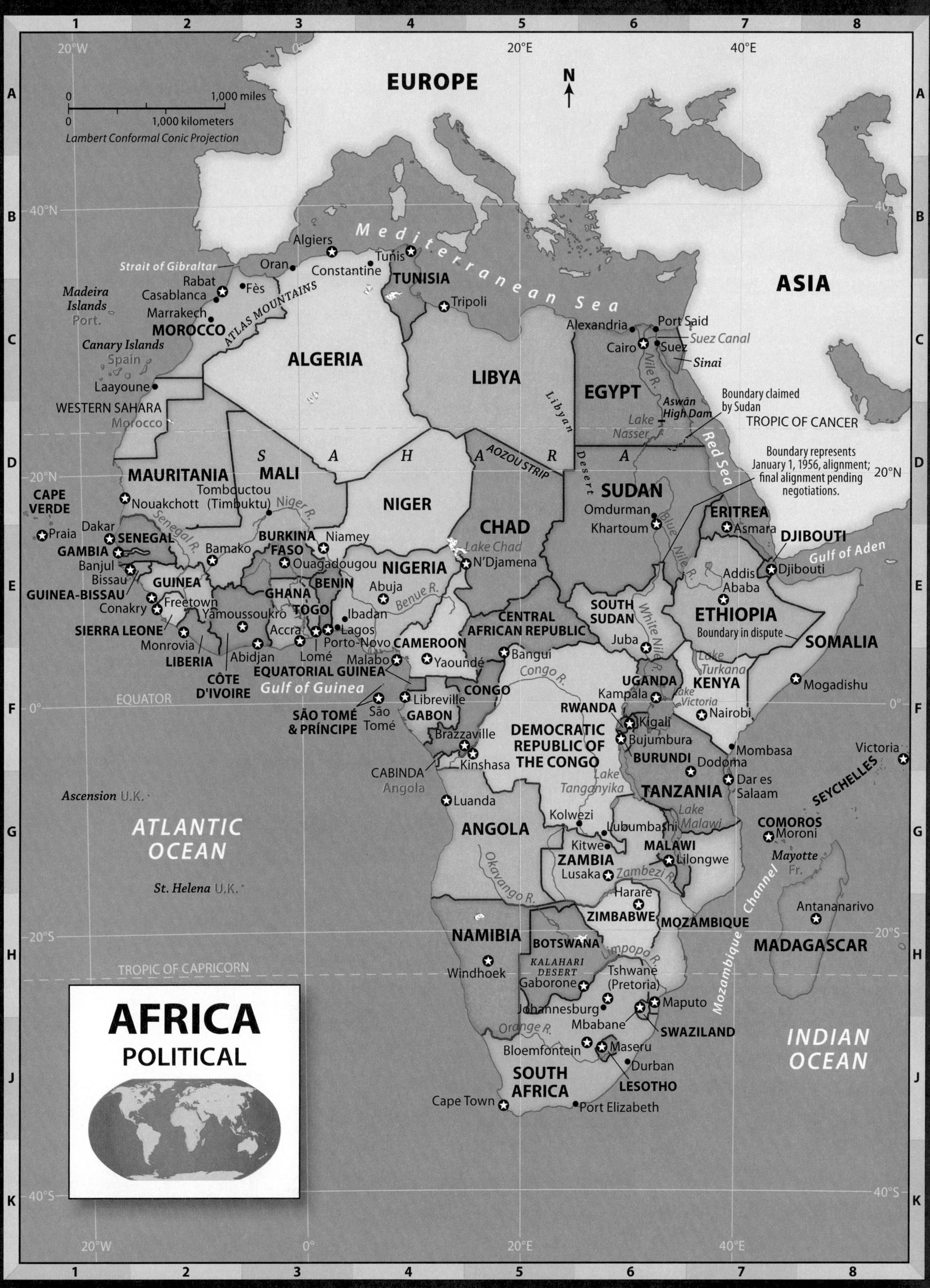
AFRICA
POLITICAL
EUROPE
ASIA
N
0 1,000 miles
0 1,000 kilometers
Lambert Conformal Conic Projection
Mediterranean Sea
Strait of Gibraltar
Madeira Islands Port.
Canary Islands Spain
ATLAS MOUNTAINS
MOROCCO
ALGERIA
TUNISIA
LIBYA
EGYPT
WESTERN SAHARA Morocco
MAURITANIA
MALI
NIGER
CHAD
SUDAN
SOUTH SUDAN
ERITREA
DJIBOUTI
ETHIOPIA
SOMALIA
CAPE VERDE
SENEGAL
GAMBIA
GUINEA-BISSAU
GUINEA
SIERRA LEONE
LIBERIA
CÔTE D'IVOIRE
BURKINA FASO
GHANA
TOGO
BENIN
NIGERIA
CAMEROON
CENTRAL AFRICAN REPUBLIC
EQUATORIAL GUINEA
SÃO TOMÉ & PRÍNCIPE
GABON
CONGO
DEMOCRATIC REPUBLIC OF THE CONGO
UGANDA
KENYA
RWANDA
BURUNDI
TANZANIA
CABINDA Angola
ANGOLA
ZAMBIA
MALAWI
MOZAMBIQUE
ZIMBABWE
NAMIBIA
BOTSWANA
SOUTH AFRICA
SWAZILAND
LESOTHO
MADAGASCAR
COMOROS
SEYCHELLES
Mayotte Fr.
Ascension U.K.
St. Helena U.K.
ATLANTIC OCEAN
INDIAN OCEAN
Gulf of Guinea
Gulf of Aden
Red Sea
Suez Canal
Sinai
Mozambique Channel
SAHARA
AOZOU STRIP
Libyan Desert
KALAHARI DESERT
Aswān High Dam
Lake Nasser
Lake Chad
Lake Turkana
Lake Victoria
Lake Tanganyika
Lake Malawi
Nile R.
Blue Nile R.
White Nile R.
Niger R.
Senegal R.
Benue R.
Congo R.
Zambezi R.
Okavango R.
Limpopo R.
Orange R.
Boundary claimed by Sudan
Boundary represents January 1, 1956, alignment; final alignment pending negotiations.
Boundary in dispute
TROPIC OF CANCER
EQUATOR
TROPIC OF CAPRICORN
Algiers
Oran
Tunis
Constantine
Rabat
Fès
Casablanca
Marrakech
Laayoune
Tripoli
Alexandria
Port Said
Cairo
Suez
Nouakchott
Tombouctou (Timbuktu)
Praia
Dakar
Banjul
Bissau
Bamako
Niamey
Ouagadougou
Conakry
Freetown
Monrovia
Yamoussoukro
Abidjan
Accra
Lomé
Porto-Novo
Lagos
Ibadan
Abuja
N'Djamena
Omdurman
Khartoum
Asmara
Djibouti
Addis Ababa
Juba
Bangui
Malabo
Yaoundé
São Tomé
Libreville
Brazzaville
Kinshasa
Kampala
Nairobi
Mogadishu
Kigali
Bujumbura
Mombasa
Dodoma
Dar es Salaam
Victoria
Moroni
Luanda
Kolwezi
Lubumbashi
Kitwe
Lusaka
Lilongwe
Harare
Antananarivo
Windhoek
Gaborone
Tshwane (Pretoria)
Johannesburg
Maputo
Mbabane
Bloemfontein
Maseru
Durban
Cape Town
Port Elizabeth
20°W
0°
20°E
40°E
40°N
20°N
0°
20°S
40°S
1 2 3 4 5 6 7 8
A B C D E F G H J K

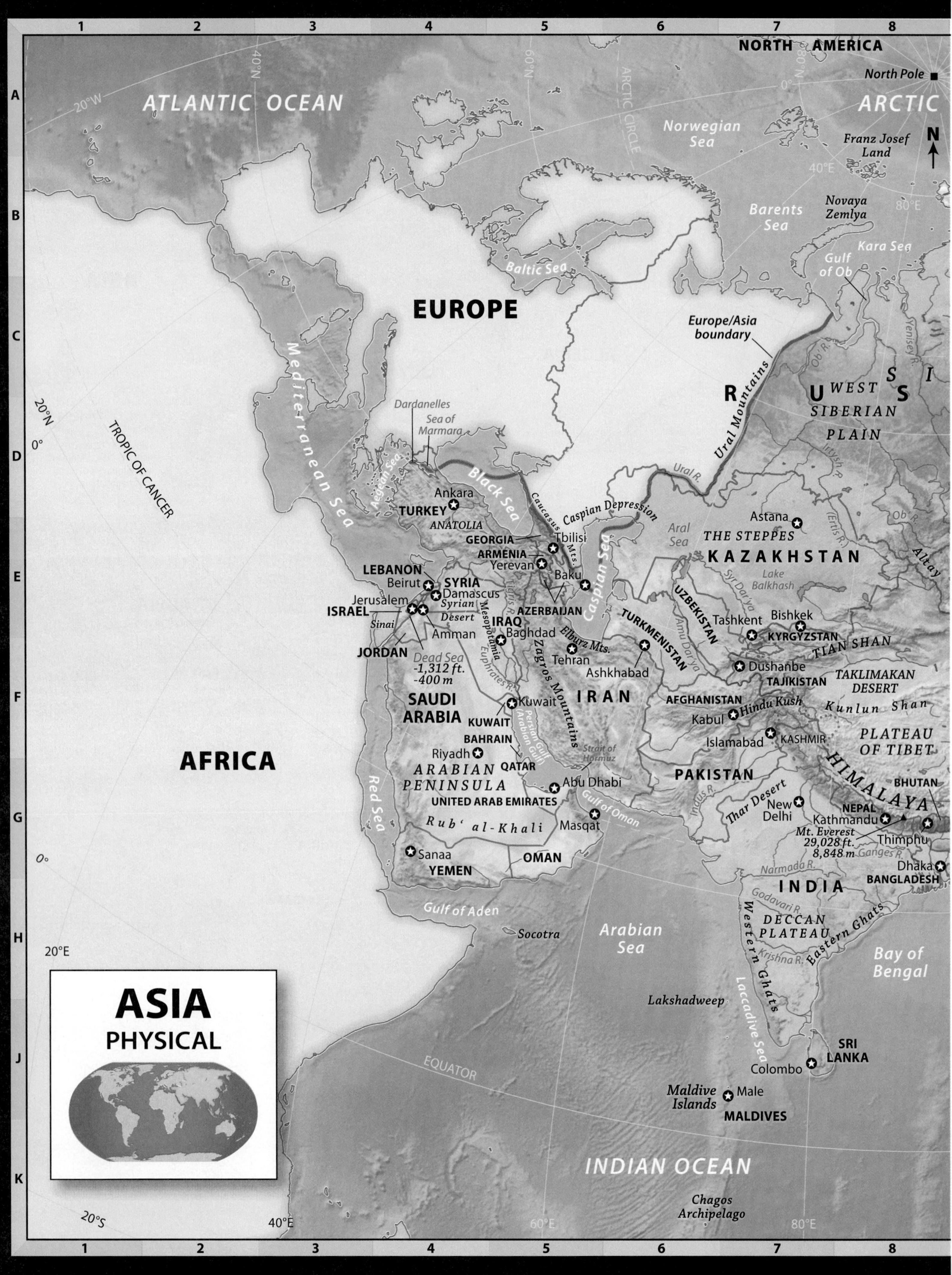
ASIA
PHYSICAL
ATLANTIC OCEAN
NORTH AMERICA
North Pole
ARCTIC
Norwegian Sea
Franz Josef Land
Barents Sea
Novaya Zemlya
Kara Sea
Gulf of Ob
Baltic Sea
EUROPE
Europe/Asia boundary
Ural Mountains
Ural R.
RUSSIA
WEST SIBERIAN PLAIN
Mediterranean Sea
Dardanelles
Sea of Marmara
Aegean Sea
Black Sea
Caucasus Mts.
Caspian Depression
Caspian Sea
Aral Sea
THE STEPPES
Astana
KAZAKHSTAN
Lake Balkhash
Altay
Ankara
TURKEY
ANATOLIA
GEORGIA
Tbilisi
ARMENIA
Yerevan
Baku
AZERBAIJAN
LEBANON
Beirut
SYRIA
Damascus
Jerusalem
ISRAEL
Syrian Desert
Sinai
Amman
JORDAN
Dead Sea -1,312 ft. -400 m
IRAQ
Baghdad
Mesopotamia
Tigris R.
Euphrates R.
Elburz Mts.
Tehran
Zagros Mountains
IRAN
TURKMENISTAN
Ashkhabad
UZBEKISTAN
Amu Darya
Syr Dar'ya
Tashkent
Bishkek
KYRGYZSTAN
TIAN SHAN
Dushanbe
TAJIKISTAN
TAKLIMAKAN DESERT
AFGHANISTAN
Kabul
Hindu Kush
Kunlun Shan
Islamabad
KASHMIR
PLATEAU OF TIBET
PAKISTAN
Indus R.
Thar Desert
New Delhi
HIMALAYA
NEPAL
Kathmandu
BHUTAN
Thimphu
Mt. Everest 29,028 ft. 8,848 m
Ganges R.
Dhaka
BANGLADESH
Narmada R.
INDIA
Godavari R.
DECCAN PLATEAU
Western Ghats
Eastern Ghats
Krishna R.
Bay of Bengal
SAUDI ARABIA
Kuwait
KUWAIT
Persian Gulf (Arabian Gulf)
BAHRAIN
Riyadh
QATAR
ARABIAN PENINSULA
Strait of Hormuz
Abu Dhabi
UNITED ARAB EMIRATES
Gulf of Oman
Masqat
Rub' al-Khali
Red Sea
Sanaa
YEMEN
OMAN
AFRICA
TROPIC OF CANCER
Gulf of Aden
Socotra
Arabian Sea
Lakshadweep
Laccadive Sea
SRI LANKA
Colombo
Maldive Islands
Male
MALDIVES
EQUATOR
INDIAN OCEAN
Chagos Archipelago
ARCTIC CIRCLE

NORTH AMERICA
Bering Strait
Chukchi Sea
Chukchi Peninsula
Gulf of Anadyr
Bering Sea
OCEAN
Wrangel I.
New Siberian Islands
East Siberian Sea
Aleutian Islands
Severnaya Zemlya
Laptev Sea
Taymyr Peninsula
Kolyma R.
Kolyma Mts.
Cherski Range
Verkhoyanski Mts.
Commander Is.
Kamchatka Peninsula
CENTRAL SIBERIAN PLATEAU
Lena R.
Sea of Okhotsk
Aldan R.
S I B E R I A
A S I A
Sakhalin
Kuril Islands
Angara R.
Lake Baikal
Yablonovyy Range
Amur R.
Greater Khingan Range
Manchurian Plain
Sikhote-Alin' Range
Hokkaidō
Honshū
Sea of Japan (East Sea)
JAPAN
Tokyo
Ulaanbaatar
MONGOLIA
GOBI
Shan
NORTH KOREA
P'yŏngyang
Seoul
SOUTH KOREA
Beijing
Nampo Shoto
Shikoku
Kyūshū
Yellow Sea
North China Plain
Huang He (Yellow R.)
Qilian Shan
Qaidam Basin
CHINA
East China Sea
Chang Jiang (Yangtze R.)
Mekong R.
Salween R.
Sichuan Basin
Gongga Shan 24,790 ft. 7,556 m
Okinawa
Ryukyu Islands
Taipei
TAIWAN
Mariana Islands
PACIFIC OCEAN
Philippine Sea
Caroline Islands
Xi R.
Brahmaputra
Irrawaddy R.
Hanoi
MYANMAR (BURMA)
LAOS
Hainan
Luzon
PHILIPPINE ISLANDS
Nay Pyi Taw
Vientiane
South China Sea
Manila
Samar
Mindoro
THAILAND
Bangkok
VIETNAM
PHILIPPINES
CAMBODIA
Phnom Penh
Palawan
Mindanao
Andaman Islands
Andaman Sea
Gulf of Thailand
Sulu Sea
Bandar Seri Begawan
BRUNEI
Celebes Sea
Nicobar Islands
Malay Peninsula
MALAYSIA
Moluccas
New Guinea
Kuala Lumpur
SINGAPORE
Borneo
Sulawesi (Celebes)
Buru
Ceram
Aru Is.
Dolak
Sumatra
INDONESIA
Tanimbar Is.
Arafura Sea
Mentawai Islands
Greater Sunda Islands
Java Sea
Dili
EAST TIMOR (TIMOR-LESTE)
Timor
Timor Sea
AUSTRALIA
Jakarta
Java
TROPIC OF CANCER
EQUATOR
0 1,000 miles
0 1,000 kilometers
Two-Point Equidistant Projection

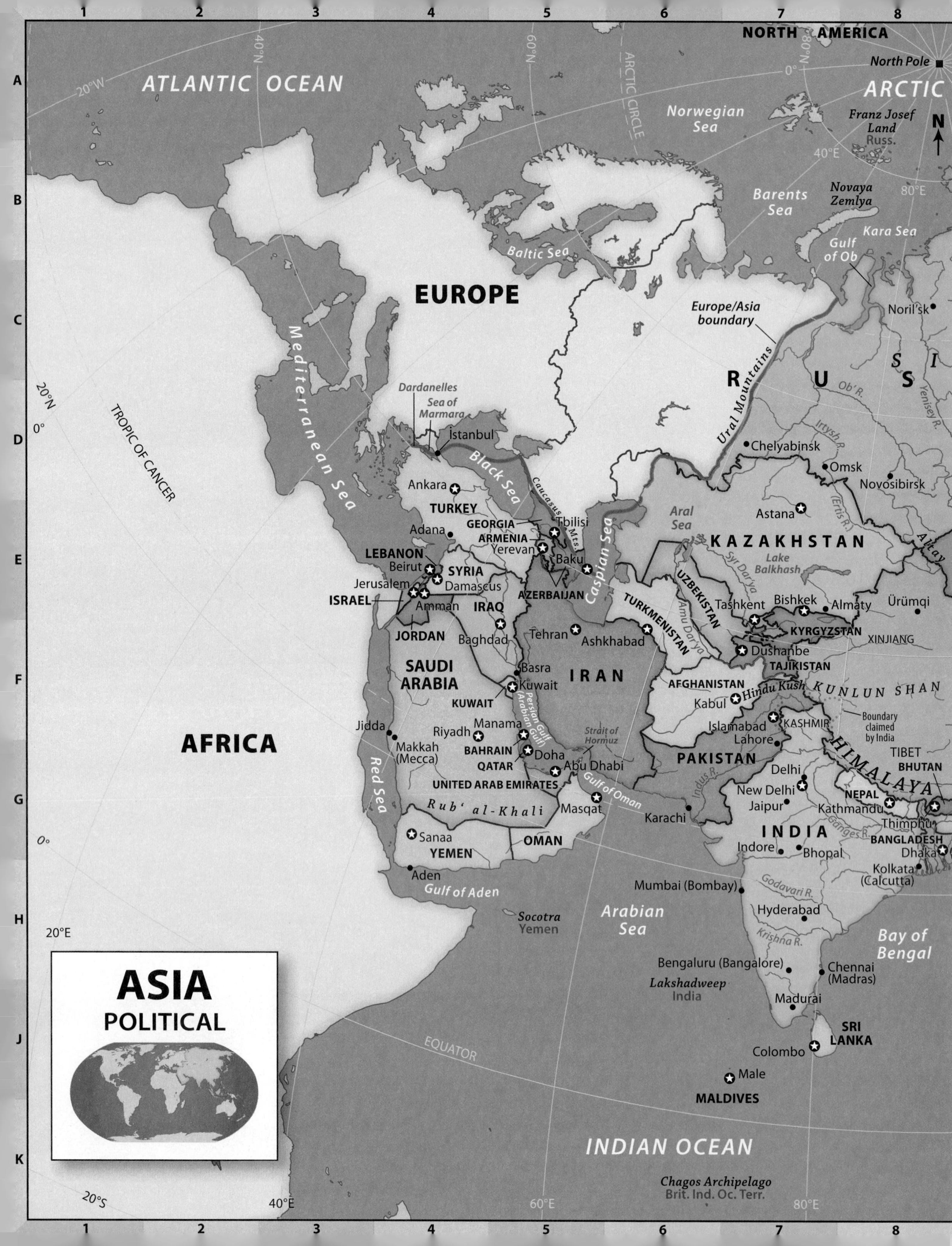

ASIA
POLITICAL
NORTH AMERICA
North Pole
ATLANTIC OCEAN
ARCTIC
Norwegian Sea
Franz Josef Land
Russ.
ARCTIC CIRCLE
Barents Sea
Novaya Zemlya
Kara Sea
Gulf of Ob
Baltic Sea
EUROPE
Europe/Asia boundary
Noril'sk
Mediterranean Sea
Ural Mountains
R U S S I
Ob' R.
Yenisey R.
Irtysh R.
Dardanelles
Sea of Marmara
Istanbul
Chelyabinsk
Omsk
Novosibirsk
TROPIC OF CANCER
Black Sea
Ankara
Caucasus Mts.
TURKEY
Aral Sea
Astana
(Ertis R.)
GEORGIA
Tbilisi
ARMENIA
Yerevan
Adana
Caspian Sea
KAZAKHSTAN
Altay
LEBANON
Beirut
Baku
SYRIA
Damascus
Lake Balkhash
Syr Darya
Jerusalem
AZERBAIJAN
ISRAEL
Amman
IRAQ
UZBEKISTAN
TURKMENISTAN
Tashkent
Bishkek
Almaty
Ürümqi
Amu Darya
KYRGYZSTAN
XINJIANG
JORDAN
Tehran
Ashkhabad
Baghdad
Dushanbe
TAJIKISTAN
SAUDI ARABIA
Basra
IRAN
Kuwait
AFGHANISTAN
Hindu Kush
KUNLUN SHAN
KUWAIT
Persian Gulf (Arabian Gulf)
Kabul
Boundary claimed by India
Jidda
Manama
Riyadh
Strait of Hormuz
Islamabad
KASHMIR
Makkah (Mecca)
Lahore
AFRICA
BAHRAIN
Doha
QATAR
Abu Dhabi
PAKISTAN
HIMALAYA
TIBET
BHUTAN
Red Sea
UNITED ARAB EMIRATES
Gulf of Oman
Indus R.
Delhi
New Delhi
NEPAL
Jaipur
Kathmandu
Rub' al-Khali
Masqat
Karachi
Thimphu
INDIA
Ganges R.
Sanaa
OMAN
BANGLADESH
Indore
Bhopal
Dhaka
YEMEN
Kolkata (Calcutta)
Aden
Mumbai (Bombay)
Godavari R.
Gulf of Aden
Socotra
Yemen
Arabian Sea
Hyderabad
Krishna R.
Bay of Bengal
Bengaluru (Bangalore)
Chennai (Madras)
Lakshadweep
India
Madurai
SRI LANKA
Colombo
EQUATOR
Male
MALDIVES
INDIAN OCEAN
Chagos Archipelago
Brit. Ind. Oc. Terr.
20°W
0°
40°N
60°N
80°N
40°E
80°E
20°N
20°E
20°S
60°E
N
1 2 3 4 5 6 7 8
A B C D E F G H J K

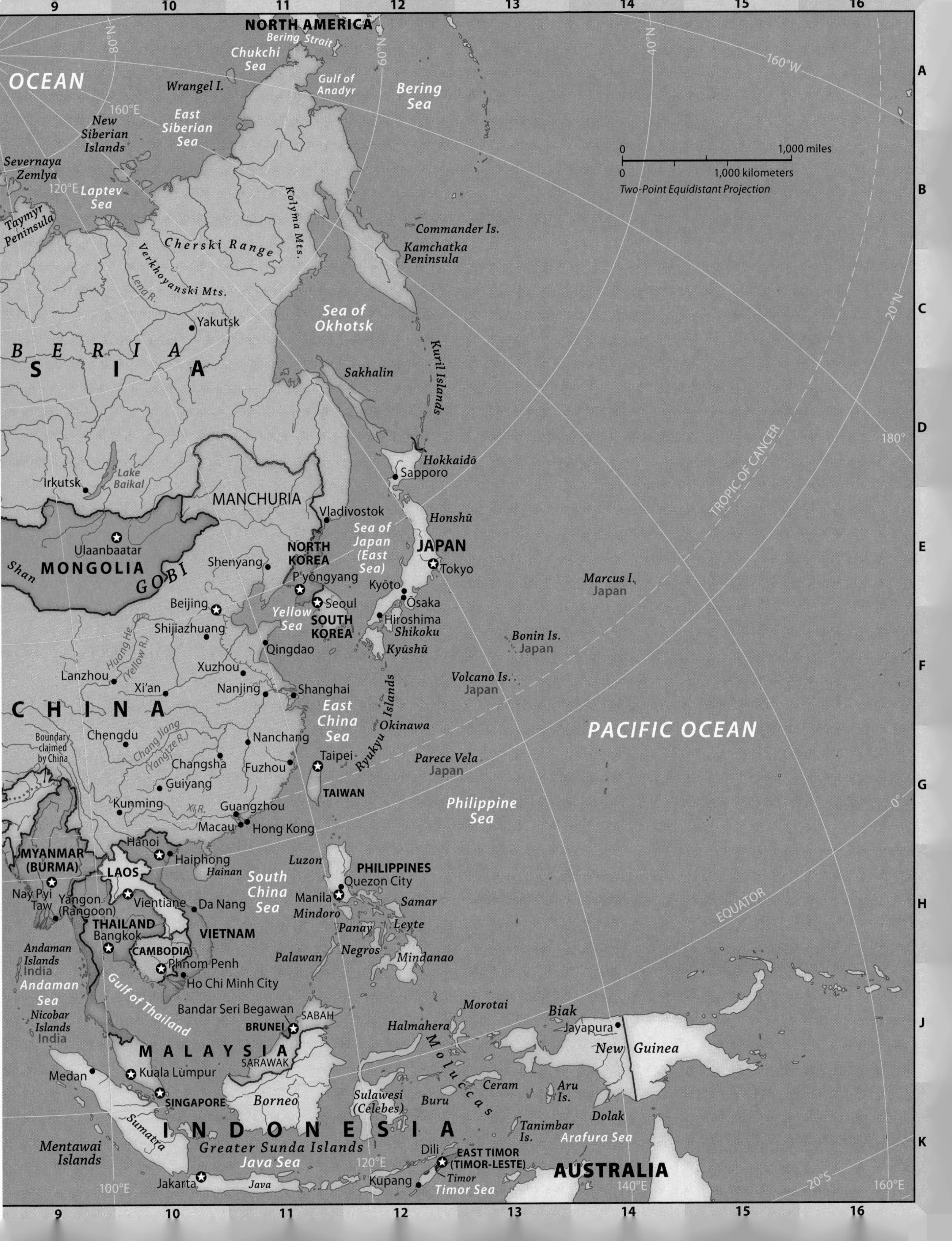

NORTH AMERICA
Bering Strait
Chukchi Sea
OCEAN
Wrangel I.
Gulf of Anadyr
Bering Sea
East Siberian Sea
New Siberian Islands
Severnaya Zemlya
Laptev Sea
Taymyr Peninsula
0 1,000 miles
0 1,000 kilometers
Two-Point Equidistant Projection
Kolyma Mts.
Commander Is.
Kamchatka Peninsula
Cherski Range
Verkhoyanski Mts.
Lena R.
Sea of Okhotsk
Yakutsk
SIBERIA
ASIA
Sakhalin
Kuril Islands
Hokkaidō
Sapporo
Irkutsk
Lake Baikal
MANCHURIA
Vladivostok
Honshū
TROPIC OF CANCER
Ulaanbaatar
MONGOLIA
Shan
GOBI
NORTH KOREA
Sea of Japan (East Sea)
JAPAN
Tokyo
Shenyang
P'yŏngyang
Kyōto
Osaka
Marcus I. Japan
Beijing
Seoul
Yellow Sea
SOUTH KOREA
Hiroshima
Shikoku
Shijiazhuang
Qingdao
Kyūshū
Bonin Is. Japan
Huang He (Yellow R.)
Lanzhou
Xuzhou
Volcano Is. Japan
Xi'an
Nanjing
Shanghai
CHINA
East China Sea
Ryukyu Islands
Okinawa
PACIFIC OCEAN
Boundary claimed by China
Chengdu
Chang Jiang (Yangtze R.)
Nanchang
Changsha
Fuzhou
Taipei
Parece Vela Japan
Guiyang
TAIWAN
Kunming
Xi R.
Guangzhou
Philippine Sea
Macau
Hong Kong
Hanoi
MYANMAR (BURMA)
Haiphong
Luzon
PHILIPPINES
LAOS
Hainan
South China Sea
Quezon City
Nay Pyi Taw
Yangon (Rangoon)
Vientiane
Da Nang
Manila
Mindoro
Samar
EQUATOR
THAILAND
Bangkok
VIETNAM
Panay
Leyte
Andaman Islands India
CAMBODIA
Phnom Penh
Negros
Palawan
Mindanao
Ho Chi Minh City
Andaman Sea
Gulf of Thailand
Bandar Seri Begawan
SABAH
Morotai
Biak
Nicobar Islands India
BRUNEI
Halmahera
Jayapura
MALAYSIA
SARAWAK
Moluccas
New Guinea
Medan
Kuala Lumpur
Ceram
Aru Is.
SINGAPORE
Borneo
Sulawesi (Celebes)
Buru
Dolak
Sumatra
INDONESIA
Tanimbar Is.
Arafura Sea
Mentawai Islands
Greater Sunda Islands
Java Sea
Dili
EAST TIMOR (TIMOR-LESTE)
Timor
AUSTRALIA
Jakarta
Java
Kupang
Timor Sea
80°N
60°N
40°N
20°N
160°W
160°E
120°E
100°E
140°E
180°
0°
20°S
A
B
C
D
E
F
G
H
J
K
9
10
11
12
13
14
15
16

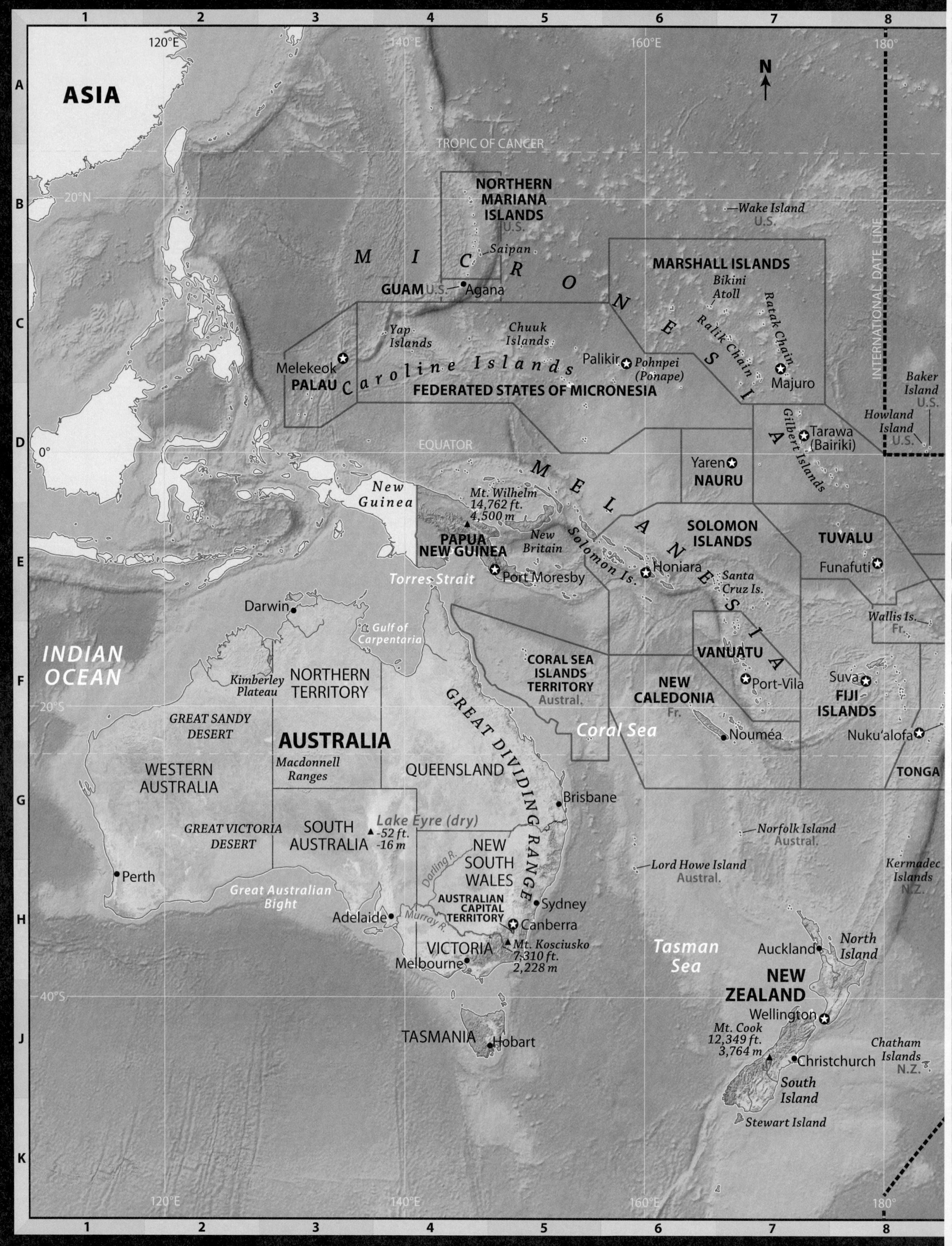
ASIA
INDIAN OCEAN
NORTHERN MARIANA ISLANDS
U.S.
Saipan
GUAM U.S.
Agana
MICRONESIA
Wake Island
U.S.
MARSHALL ISLANDS
Bikini Atoll
Ralik Chain
Ratak Chain
Majuro
Yap Islands
Chuuk Islands
Palikir
Pohnpei (Ponape)
Melekeok
PALAU
Caroline Islands
FEDERATED STATES OF MICRONESIA
TROPIC OF CANCER
EQUATOR
INTERNATIONAL DATE LINE
Baker Island
U.S.
Howland Island
U.S.
Tarawa (Bairiki)
Gilbert Islands
Yaren
NAURU
MELANESIA
New Guinea
Mt. Wilhelm
14,762 ft.
4,500 m
PAPUA NEW GUINEA
New Britain
Solomon Is.
Port Moresby
Torres Strait
SOLOMON ISLANDS
Honiara
Santa Cruz Is.
TUVALU
Funafuti
Wallis Is.
Fr.
VANUATU
Port-Vila
CORAL SEA ISLANDS TERRITORY
Austral.
NEW CALEDONIA
Fr.
Nouméa
Coral Sea
Suva
FIJI ISLANDS
Nuku'alofa
TONGA
Darwin
Gulf of Carpentaria
Kimberley Plateau
NORTHERN TERRITORY
GREAT SANDY DESERT
AUSTRALIA
Macdonnell Ranges
WESTERN AUSTRALIA
QUEENSLAND
GREAT DIVIDING RANGE
Brisbane
GREAT VICTORIA DESERT
SOUTH AUSTRALIA
Lake Eyre (dry)
-52 ft.
-16 m
NEW SOUTH WALES
Darling R.
Norfolk Island
Austral.
Lord Howe Island
Austral.
Kermadec Islands
N.Z.
Perth
Great Australian Bight
Adelaide
Murray R.
AUSTRALIAN CAPITAL TERRITORY
Sydney
Canberra
VICTORIA
Mt. Kosciusko
7,310 ft.
2,228 m
Melbourne
Tasman Sea
Auckland
North Island
NEW ZEALAND
Wellington
Mt. Cook
12,349 ft.
3,764 m
Christchurch
Chatham Islands
N.Z.
South Island
Stewart Island
TASMANIA
Hobart
120°E
140°E
160°E
180°
20°N
0°
20°S
40°S
N

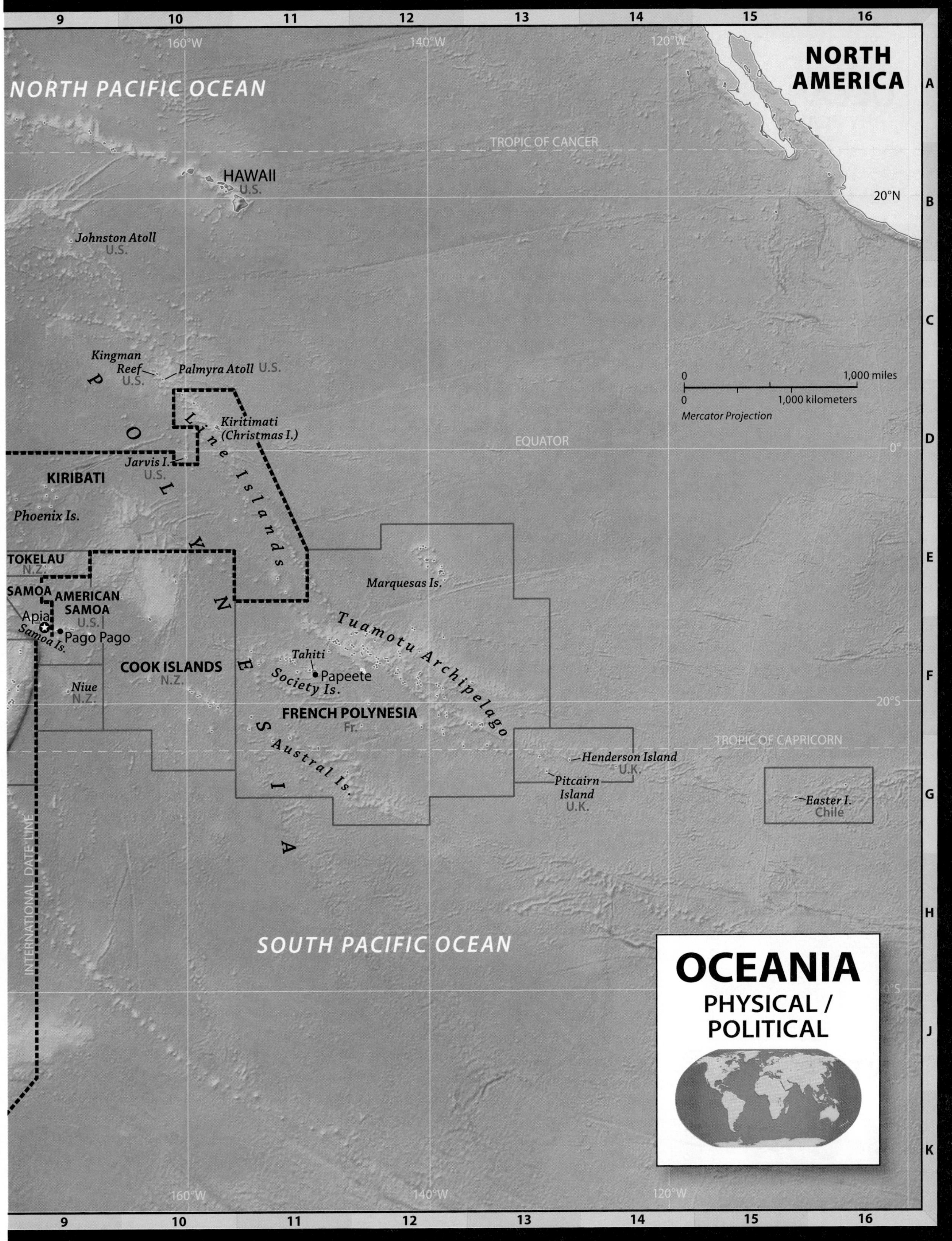

NORTH PACIFIC OCEAN
NORTH AMERICA
TROPIC OF CANCER
HAWAII
U.S.
Johnston Atoll
U.S.
Kingman Reef
U.S.
Palmyra Atoll U.S.
POLYNESIA
Line Islands
Kiritimati (Christmas I.)
Jarvis I.
U.S.
KIRIBATI
Phoenix Is.
EQUATOR
TOKELAU
N.Z.
SAMOA
AMERICAN SAMOA
U.S.
Apia
Samoa Is.
Pago Pago
COOK ISLANDS
N.Z.
Niue
N.Z.
Marquesas Is.
Tuamotu Archipelago
Tahiti
Papeete
Society Is.
FRENCH POLYNESIA
Fr.
Austral Is.
TROPIC OF CAPRICORN
Henderson Island
U.K.
Pitcairn Island
U.K.
Easter I.
Chile
INTERNATIONAL DATE LINE
SOUTH PACIFIC OCEAN
0 1,000 miles
0 1,000 kilometers
Mercator Projection
160°W
140°W
120°W
20°N
0°
20°S
OCEANIA
PHYSICAL / POLITICAL

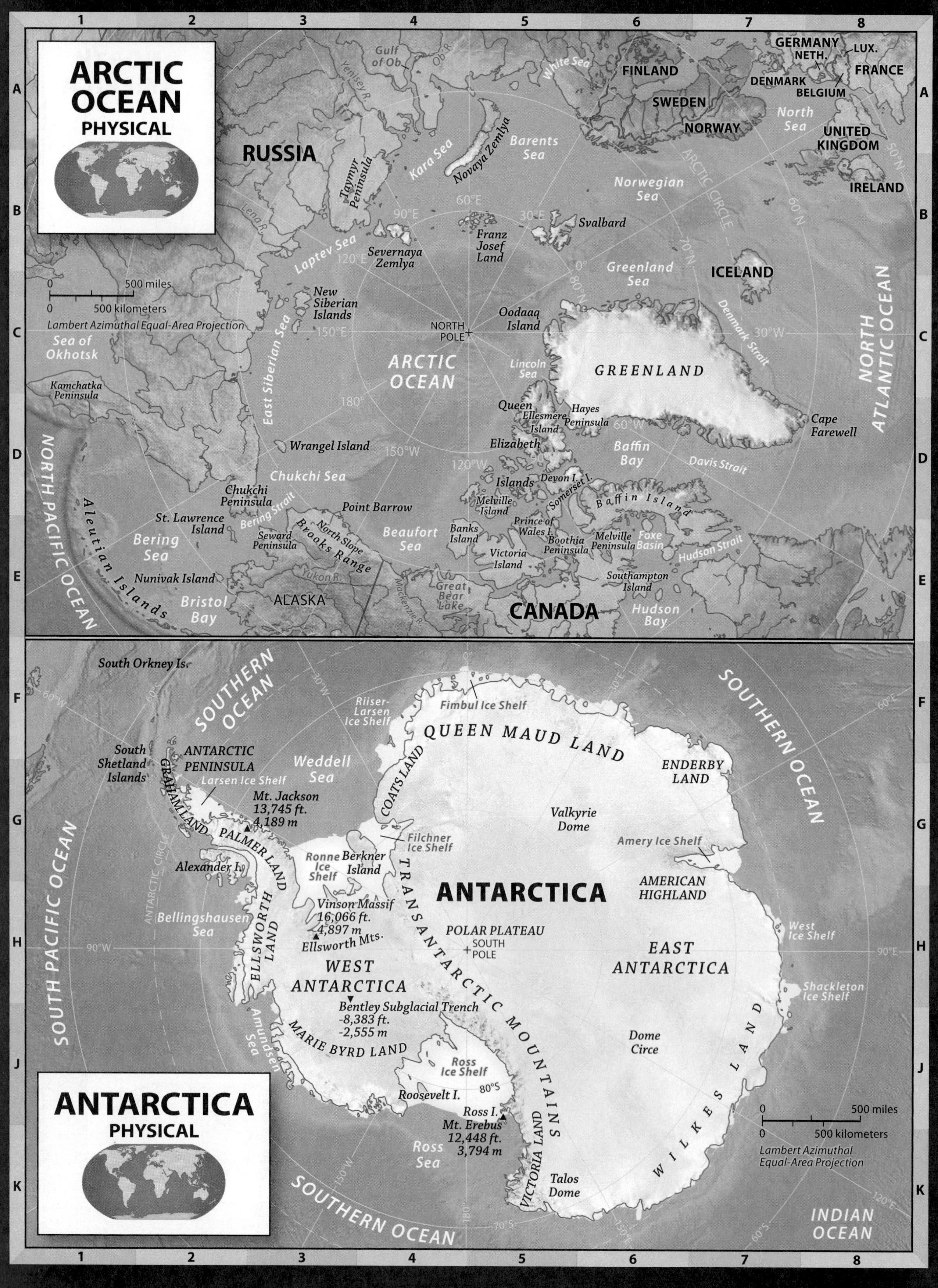
ARCTIC OCEAN
PHYSICAL
RUSSIA
FINLAND
SWEDEN
NORWAY
GERMANY
NETH.
LUX.
FRANCE
DENMARK
BELGIUM
UNITED KINGDOM
IRELAND
ICELAND
GREENLAND
CANADA
ALASKA
ARCTIC OCEAN
NORTH ATLANTIC OCEAN
NORTH PACIFIC OCEAN
North Sea
Norwegian Sea
Barents Sea
Kara Sea
White Sea
Greenland Sea
Laptev Sea
East Siberian Sea
Chukchi Sea
Beaufort Sea
Bering Sea
Bristol Bay
Sea of Okhotsk
Lincoln Sea
Baffin Bay
Davis Strait
Denmark Strait
Hudson Strait
Hudson Bay
Foxe Basin
Bering Strait
Gulf of Ob
Novaya Zemlya
Svalbard
Franz Josef Land
Severnaya Zemlya
New Siberian Islands
Taymyr Peninsula
Kamchatka Peninsula
Chukchi Peninsula
Seward Peninsula
Wrangel Island
St. Lawrence Island
Nunivak Island
Aleutian Islands
Point Barrow
North Slope
Brooks Range
Oodaaq Island
NORTH POLE
Queen Elizabeth Islands
Ellesmere Island
Hayes Peninsula
Devon I.
Somerset I.
Melville Island
Banks Island
Victoria Island
Prince of Wales I.
Boothia Peninsula
Melville Peninsula
Baffin Island
Southampton Island
Great Bear Lake
Cape Farewell
ARCTIC CIRCLE
0 500 miles
0 500 kilometers
Lambert Azimuthal Equal-Area Projection
ANTARCTICA
PHYSICAL
ANTARCTICA
SOUTHERN OCEAN
SOUTH PACIFIC OCEAN
INDIAN OCEAN
South Orkney Is.
South Shetland Islands
ANTARCTIC PENINSULA
GRAHAM LAND
PALMER LAND
Larsen Ice Shelf
Mt. Jackson 13,745 ft. 4,189 m
Weddell Sea
Riiser-Larsen Ice Shelf
Fimbul Ice Shelf
QUEEN MAUD LAND
COATS LAND
ENDERBY LAND
Valkyrie Dome
Amery Ice Shelf
Filchner Ice Shelf
Ronne Ice Shelf
Berkner Island
Alexander I.
Bellingshausen Sea
ELLSWORTH LAND
Vinson Massif 16,066 ft. 4,897 m
Ellsworth Mts.
TRANSANTARCTIC MOUNTAINS
POLAR PLATEAU
SOUTH POLE
AMERICAN HIGHLAND
EAST ANTARCTICA
WEST ANTARCTICA
West Ice Shelf
Shackleton Ice Shelf
Bentley Subglacial Trench -8,383 ft. -2,555 m
MARIE BYRD LAND
Amundsen Sea
Ross Ice Shelf
Roosevelt I.
Ross I.
Mt. Erebus 12,448 ft. 3,794 m
Ross Sea
VICTORIA LAND
Talos Dome
Dome Circe
WILKES LAND
ANTARCTIC CIRCLE
0 500 miles
0 500 kilometers
Lambert Azimuthal Equal-Area Projection

UNIT 1

THE WORLD Planner

UNDERSTANDING BY DESIGN®

Enduring Understandings

- *Geographers study how people, places, and environments are distributed on Earth's surface.*
- *Physical processes shape Earth's surface.*
- *The characteristics and distribution of cultures influence human systems.*

Essential Question

- *How does geography help us interpret the past, understand the present, and plan for the future?*
- *How do physical processes shape Earth's surface?*
- *Why is climate important to life on Earth?*
- *How do the characteristics and distribution of human populations affect human and physical systems?*

Students will know:

- *the characteristics and uses of globes, maps, and map projections.*
- *the six elements of geography and the methods used to gather geographic information.*
- *that Earth is part of a larger physical system that contains other planets, moons, and stars.*
- *the internal and external forces of change and how they shape Earth's surface .*
- *the elements of culture and how internal and external factors change culture over time.*
- *how wind, landforms, and bodies of water influence Earth's climate patterns.*
- *the factors that influence population movement, growth, and density.*

Students will be able to:

- ***explain** the physical processes that shape the patterns of Earth's surface, including weathering and erosion.*
- ***describe** the physical characteristics of places, including landforms and bodies of water.*
- ***analyze** a world map to identify physical features, political boundaries, population density, economic activities, climate zones, and vegetation.*
- ***identify** and apply geographer's tools, including globes, maps, the six elements of geography and geospatial technologies.*
- ***identify** factors that influence population movement, settlement, growth, and density.*
- ***explain** how landforms, bodies of water, and wind influence Earth's climate patterns.*

Predictable Misunderstandings

- *Geography entails studying only land, not people.*
- *Geography is static and unchanging, serving merely as a backdrop for people's activities.*
- *All maps are projected in the same way.*
- *Humans have very little effect on the environment and there is little people can do to alter geography.*
- *The ocean floor is flat.*
- *The continents are static.*
- *The amount of water on Earth varies depending on yearly rainfalls.*

Assessment Evidence

Performance Tasks:

- *Environmental Case Study*
- *GeoLab Activity*
- *GIS Simulations*
- *Hands-On Chapter Projects*

Other Evidence:

- *Location Activity*
- *Self-Check Quizzes*
- *Lesson Quizzes*
- *Participation in Interactive Whiteboard Activities*
- *Contribution to small-group activities*
- *Interpretation of slide show images*
- *Participation in class discussions about the World*
- *Analysis of graphic organizers, graphs, and charts*
- *Lesson Reviews*
- *Chapter Assessments*

Key for Using the Teacher Edition

SKILL-BASED ACTIVITIES

Types of skill activities found in the Teacher Edition.

* **V Visual Skills** require students to analyze maps, graphs, charts, and photos.

R Reading Skills help students practice reading skills and master vocabulary.

C Critical Thinking Skills help students apply and extend what they have learned.

W Writing Skills provide writing opportunities to help students comprehend the text.

T Technology Skills require students to use digital tools effectively.

*Letters are followed by a number when there is more than one of the same type of skill on the page.

DIFFERENTIATED INSTRUCTION

All activities are written for the on-level student unless otherwise marked with the leveled labels below.

BL Beyond Level
AL Approaching Level
ELL English Language Learners

All students benefit from activities that utilize different learning styles. Many activities are marked as below when a particular learning style is highlighted.

Intrapersonal	**Naturalist**
Logical/Mathematical	**Kinesthetic**
Visual/Spatial	**Auditory/Musical**
Verbal/Linguistic	**Interpersonal**

SUGGESTED PACING GUIDE

Introducing the Unit	1 Day
Chapter 1: How Geographers Look at the World	3 Days
Chapter 2: The Physical World	4 Days
Chapter 3: Climates of the Earth	4 Days
Chapter 4: The Human World	6 Days
Case Study: How Has Globalization Changed Modern Culture?	1 Day
Global Connections: Patterns of Resource Distribution	1 Day
TOTAL TIME	**20 Days**

PLANNER

☑ Print Teaching Options

V Visual Skills

- ☐ **p. 1** Students analyze and discuss a photo of Earth taken from space. ELL Visual/Spatial
- ☐ **p. 3** Students analyze a map scale to calculate distances. AL Visual/Spatial
- ☐ **p. 4** Students make flash cards of countries and their capital cities. AL Visual/Spatial, Verbal/Linguistic
- ☐ **p. 9** Students identify land uses on an economic map. ELL Verbal/Linguistic, Visual/Spatial

R Reading Skills

- ☐ **p. 2** Students read maps using the map key. AL Verbal/Linguistic, Visual/Spatial
- ☐ **p. 3** Students use a map compass to locate and identify landmasses and other map elements. Visual/Spatial, Verbal/Linguistic
- ☐ **p. 4** Students explain a political entity using a political map. Visual/Spatial, Logical/Mathematical
- ☐ **p. 7** Students read and discuss a population map. AL Visual/Spatial

C Critical Thinking Skills

- ☐ **p. 2** Students analyze a physical map to make comparisons in elevations between continents. ELL Logical/Mathematical, Visual/Spatial
- ☐ **p. 8** Students compare population density and economic activity maps. Logical/Mathematical, Visual/Spatial

W Writing Skills

- ☐ **p. 5** Students write a description of a country's physical characteristics based on map features. ELL Logical/Mathematical, Verbal/Linguistic
- ☐ **p. 8** Students write a description of a region's resources and where they are located. ELL Verbal/Linguistic, Visual/Spatial
- ☐ **p. 10** Students write a narrative travel blog. BL Naturalist, Intrapersonal

T Technology Skills

- ☐ **p. 4** Students research populations in a region and then rank countries by size. Visual/Spatial, Interpersonal
- ☐ **p. 6** Students make a presentation about how the population makeup of a large city impacts the life of its citizens. BL Logical/Mathematical, Visual/Spatial, Interpersonal

☑ Online Teaching Options

V Visual Skills

- INTERACTIVE MAP **Physical Map: World**—Students discuss and identify the features on a physical map. AL Visual/Spatial
- INTERACTIVE MAP **Economic Activity Map: World**—Students create charts listing the resources by country. ELL Visual/Spatial, Verbal/Linguistic
- INTERACTIVE MAP **Climate Map: World**—Students identify the world's major climate zones. ELL Visual/Spatial, Verbal/Linguistic

R Reading Skills

- INTERACTIVE IMAGE **Geographic Dictionary**—Students locate and name landforms and then start a glossary of terms that includes definitions. AL ELL Visual/Spatial, Verbal/Linguistic

C Critical Thinking Skills

- GEO @ WORK **Thinking Like a Geographer**—Students explore principles and skills of geography applied to real-world challenges.
- INTERACTIVE MAP **International Time Zones**—Students identify the current time in various locations and then write word problems about time zone calculations. Logical/Mathematical
- INTERACTIVE MAP **Population Density Map: World**—Students analyze a map to write three concluding statements about population density. AL Verbal/Linguistic
- CARTOGRAM **World Population**—Students compare the cartogram with a population map to determine the degree of distortion in the countries of Africa. BL Visual/Spatial, Interpersonal

W Writing Skills

- INTERACTIVE MAP **Political Map: World**—Students analyze a political map and then write about a physical feature that has had a political impact on history. BL Verbal/Linguistic, Visual/Spatial
- CARTOGRAM **Gross Domestic Product Per Capita**—Students write to explain why the size of Kuwait is enlarged on the cartogram. BL Verbal/Linguistic, Logical/Mathematical

☑ Printable Digital Worksheets

V Visual Skills

- WORKSHEET **Location Activity**—Students locate the continents, oceans, and physical features of the world.

C Critical Thinking Skills

- WORKSHEET **GeoLab Activity**—Students explore how the Earth-sun relationship determines world climate patterns.

T Technology Skills

- WORKSHEET **Environmental Case Study**—Students complete a study describing the organizations that track asteroids and the methodology that they use, and then determine whether there is an adequate system of asteroid monitoring.
- WORKSHEET **GIS Simulations**—Students develop an understanding of what GIS is and how people can use it to understand how different geographic variables interact with each other.

The World

UNIT 1

Chapter 1 How Geographers Look at the World | Chapter 2 The Physical World | Chapter 3 Climates of the Earth | Chapter 4 The Human World

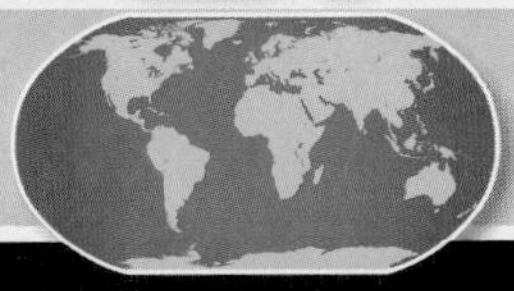

GEO @ WORK

Thinking Like a Geographer

Problem Solving Explore specific examples of the principles and skills of geography applied to real-world challenges that impact people's lives. From agriculture, to urban planning, to wiping out disease, and managing changes in society—geography plays a key role in understanding relationships and generating solutions that make sense.

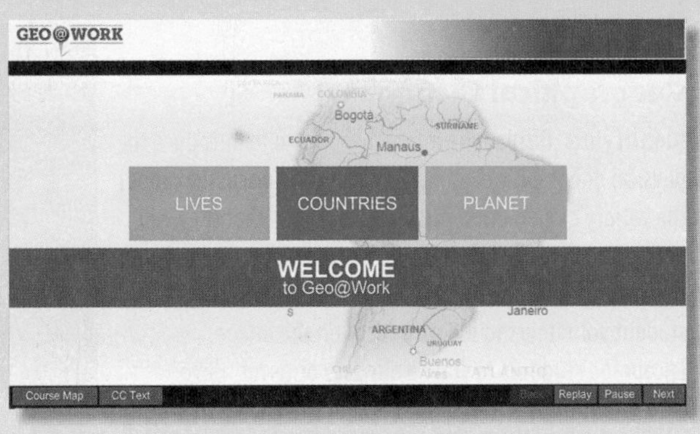

UNIT 1

The World

ENGAGE

Predicting Ask several student volunteers to state in a few words what geography is and what kinds of questions it answers. Encourage students to consider how geography differs from history and from other social sciences. As they study the unit, encourage students to think of ways that geography might be useful to them in their own lives.

TEACH & ASSESS

Analyzing Images Direct students to analyze the photograph of Earth from space. **Ask:** **How would you describe this photograph of Earth?** *(Possible answer: Earth is a blue, watery planet.)* **What is the burst of light?** *(the sun)* **What does this tell you about Earth and its location?** *(Earth is part of the solar system.)* Guide students in a discussion of how photographs like this are obtained. *(from cameras aboard satellites or spacecraft)* ELL **Visual/Spatial**

Assessing Call students' attention to the list of chapter titles at the bottom of the page. Note that the first chapter is titled "How Geographers Look at the World." Challenge students to predict some of those ways. *(Answers will vary, but students should understand that geographers look at the world from many perspectives and that they use a host of tools to ascertain information.)* Point out that one chapter in this unit deals with physical geography while another deals with human geography. Have students describe the difference. *(Possible answers: physical geography deals with physical systems: climate, land, water, plants, animals; human or cultural geography deals with human activities and how they relate to the physical environment.)* Encourage students to look for answers to these questions as they study the unit. **Logical/Mathematical, Visual/Spatial**

CLOSE & REFLECT

Questioning Working with a partner, have each pair write down three questions about world geography that they hope to have answered as they study this unit. Have students share their questions with the class.

ENGAGE

R1 Reading Skills

Previewing Explain that this opening section of the unit is an atlas. Ask students to define the term *atlas. (a collection of maps)* Have students leaf through the pages of the atlas and note what maps are included. *(physical, political, climate and vegetation, economic activity, and population density maps)* Explain that students will learn more about maps and map-making in Chapter 1. Encourage students to consult these world maps frequently as they continue their studies.

TEACH & ASSESS

R2 Reading Skills

Reading Maps Ask students to focus on the map key and to note what the different elements represent. **Ask:** How are differing elevations represented on this map? *(by colors)* Which color represents the highest elevations, those over 10,000 feet? *(dark orange)* The lowest elevations? *(blue)* What assumptions can you make about the landforms of the higher elevations? *(They are mountains.)* Of the lowest? *(They are mostly oceans.)* What does the upright-pointing triangle symbol indicate? *(mountain peak)* What is the symbol for a low point? *(downward-pointing triangle)* AL **Verbal/Linguistic, Visual/Spatial**

C Critical Thinking Skills

Analyzing Visuals Have students focus on the map and identify Earth's seven continents. *(North America, South America, Africa, Europe, Asia, Australia, and Antarctica)* Have students make comparisons about the elevations of each continent. **Ask:** Where in the world are Earth's highest elevations found? *(west coast of South America, Central Asia, Antarctica, and Greenland)* Is most of Europe lowlands or highlands? *(lowlands)* How about the United States? *(about half is under 2,000 ft. and half is over)* Which continent is mostly highlands? *(Antarctica)* How do elevations of South America and Africa compare? *(Possible answer: except for its coastal areas, elevations throughout most of South America tend to be lower than those in Africa.)* Have a volunteer locate the world's lowest points. *(Death Valley; Dead Sea; Lake Eyre)* ELL **Logical/Mathematical, Visual/Spatial**

R1 World
Physical

Elevations

10,000 ft. (3,000 m)
5,000 ft. (1,500 m)
2,000 ft. (600 m)
1,000 ft. (300 m)
0 ft. (0 m)
Below sea level

— National boundary
▲ Mountain peak
▼ Lowest point

networks ***Online Teaching Options***

INTERACTIVE IMAGE

Geographical Dictionary

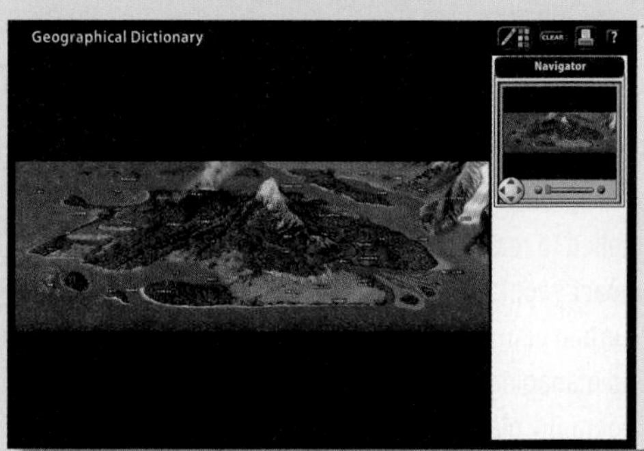

Identifying Display the interactive image to introduce the physical geographic elements. Lead a class discussion about the variety of elements. Explain to students that they will encounter all of the labeled landforms as they read through this text. Call out the names of the landforms and ask student volunteers to identify them on the image. Encourage students to start a glossary of terms. Have students start by entering these landforms and writing the definition of each term as it is presented. Then have students rewrite each definition in their own words to reinforce students' understanding. AL ELL **Visual/Spatial, Verbal/Linguistic**

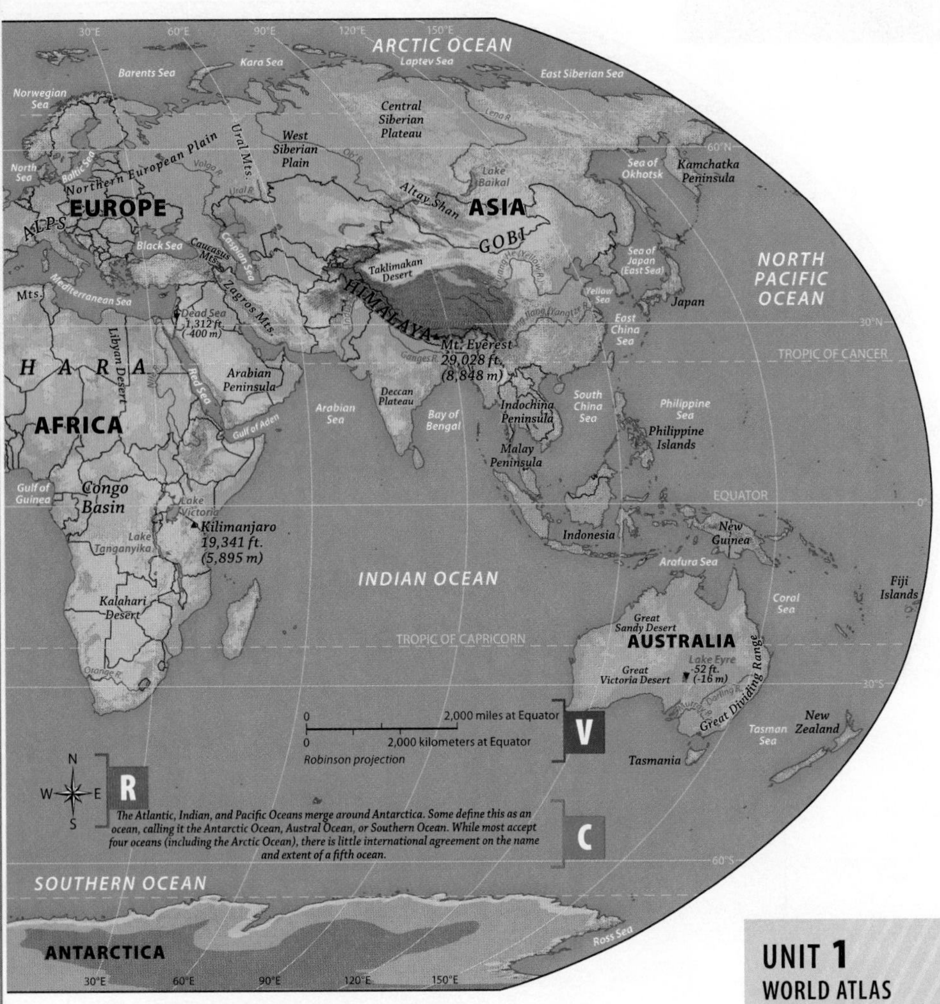

UNIT 1
WORLD ATLAS

MAP STUDY

1. ***Physical Systems*** Which part of North America has high elevations? Are they higher than the Andes of South America?
2. ***Environment and Society*** What types of physical features make Asia a crossroads for trade?

UNIT 1
The World

R Reading Skills

Identifying Have students focus on the map compass. Explain that on most maps north is located at the top of the map. Discuss the term *hemisphere*. Explain that the Equator divides Earth into two—a Northern Hemisphere and a Southern Hemisphere. **Ask: Which landmasses fall in the Northern Hemisphere?** *(North America, Europe, most of Asia, and much of Africa)* **The Southern Hemisphere?** *(Australia, Antarctica, most of South America, some of Africa, and parts of Asia,)* **What meridians divide the Earth into an eastern and western half?** *(0° longitude, or Prime Meridian, and 180° longitude)* **Which landmasses fall mainly in the Western Hemisphere or mainly in the Eastern Hemisphere?** *(Western: North and South America; Eastern: Europe, Africa, Asia, Australia; Antarctica straddles the hemispheres)* **Visual/Spatial, Verbal/Linguistic**

V Visual Skills

Calculating Have students explain how many miles an inch represents on the map. *(1 inch = 2,000 miles along the Equator)* Have volunteers use the scale to estimate distances between places along the Equator. Discuss why the map scale cannot be used to accurately estimate distances on other parts of the map. *(Most map projections are distorted in some way; distances between land masses are inaccurate on this map.)* **AL Visual/Spatial**

C Critical Thinking Skills

Evaluating Have students name the major oceans. *(Arctic, Pacific, Atlantic, Indian, Southern)* Point out that the Pacific and Atlantic are divided here into north and south. **Ask: Why might some geographers believe the Southern Ocean is a major ocean while others do not?** *(Possible answer: Some say it is merely a place on Earth where the Pacific, Atlantic, and Indian oceans merge.)* **Verbal/Linguistic**

INTERACTIVE MAP

Physical Map: World

Understanding Relationships Display the physical map of the world from the Unit 1 Atlas for students to analyze. Review that physical maps show the location and the topography or shape of Earth's physical features, which include water features, landforms, and elevation. **Ask: What additional items are included on this physical map?** *(Possible answers: names of oceans, continents, deserts, rivers, lakes, plains, plateaus, mountains, islands; lines of longitude and latitude; specific elevation heights)* Explain that often physical maps include political features such as boundary lines, countries, or landform names to provide content that adds further understanding to a map. **AL Visual/Spatial**

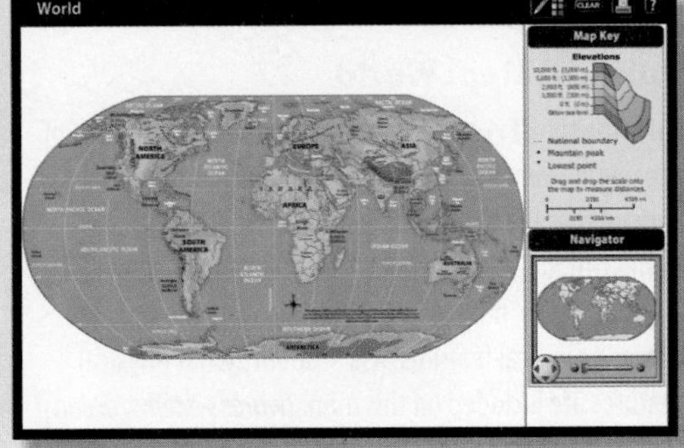

ANSWERS, p. 3

MAP STUDY

1. The Rocky Mountains in the west; no
2. Asia is surrounded by water—oceans, seas, straits—that make it easier for transportation and trade to occur.

R Reading Skills

Reading Maps Have students explain what is meant by a political entity. *(nations, states, towns, cities, and the like)* **Ask:** **What political entities are shown on this map?** *(countries of the world; capital cities)* **What important information can you gain from this map?** *(the location, boundaries, and relative sizes of countries; the location of capital cities; which countries border each other or are neighbors)* **Visual/Spatial, Logical/Mathematical**

V Visual Skills

Listing Begin by having students focus on the map key to identify the symbol for a capital city. *(small circle)* Organize students into small groups. Assign each group a region or group of countries to investigate. Direct students to make flash cards for each country. On one side of the card, students should write the name of a country and on the other side, its capital. Have students share the cards with each other and use them to learn the capital cities of the world's countries.
AL Visual/Spatial, Verbal/Linguistic

T Technology Skills

Analyzing Using the same small groups, assign each a region of the world to research online or in other library resources. Have students make a list of all of the countries in their region and rank them by size from largest to smallest, noting the area and population of each. Have students determine which are the world's ten largest countries and the ten smallest. Encourage them to explain to whom this information might be useful and how. **Visual/Spatial, Interpersonal**

World
Political

National capital

networks Online Teaching Options

INTERACTIVE MAP

Political Map: World

Informative/Explanatory Display the political map of the world from the Unit 1 Atlas for students to analyze. Explain that political maps contain elements that are human-made, such as country borders and locations of cities or towns, but that they may also include the names of some physical features. Ask students what physical features are included on this map. *(water systems, oceans)* Have students research and write an essay about a physical feature that has had a political impact on history, such as the construction of the Panama Canal or how a mountain range has served as protection. Invite students to share their findings with the class. **BL Verbal/Linguistic, Visual/Spatial**

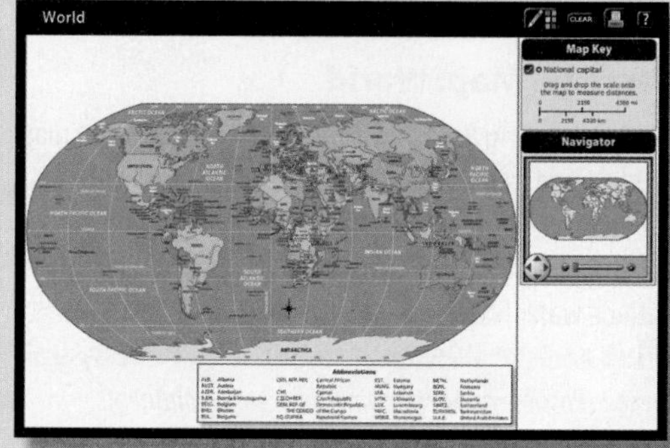

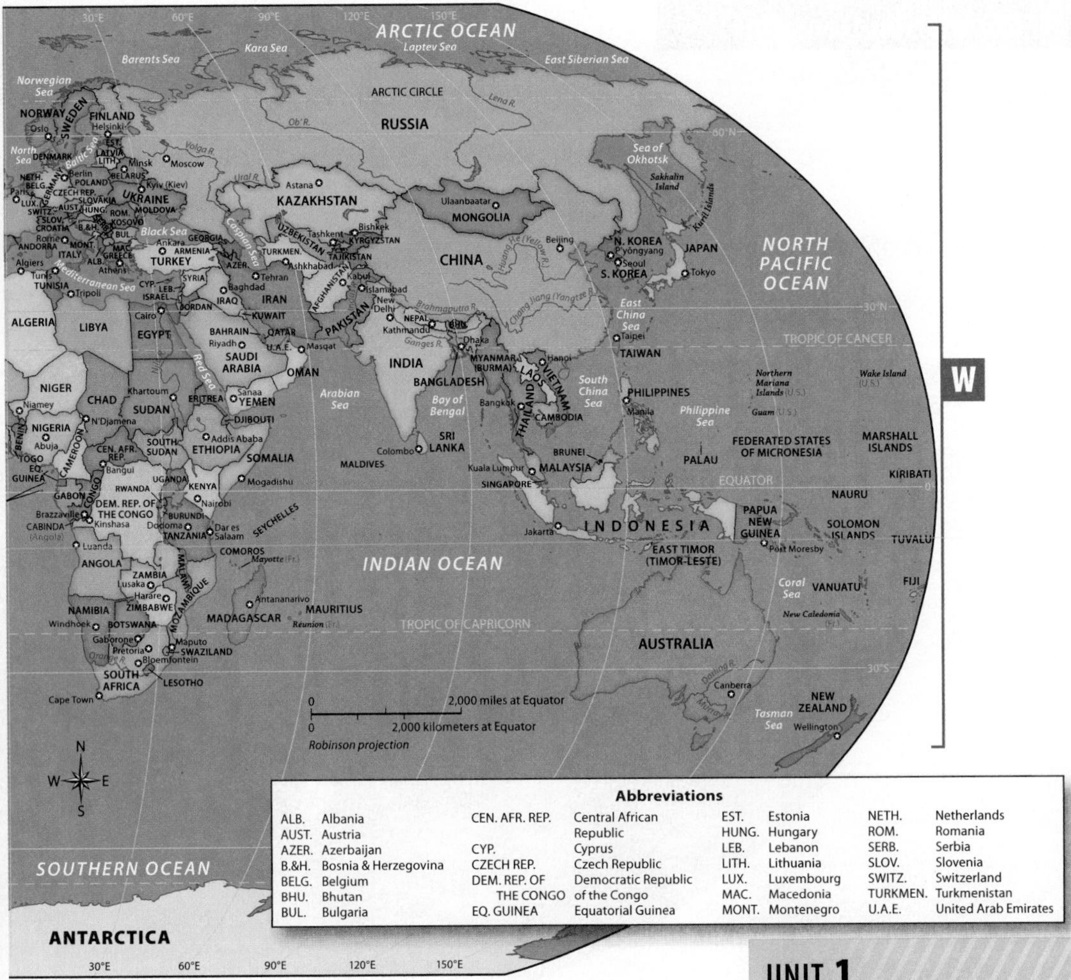

W

UNIT 1
WORLD ATLAS

MAP STUDY

1. ***Environment and Society*** How do Earth's physical features appear to have shaped the borders of countries in Southeast Asia?
2. ***Human Systems*** List three countries whose capital cities are located on the coast.

W Writing Skills

Informative/Explanatory Have students compare the world political map to the world physical map to determine important physical characteristics of selected countries. Each student might choose a country that interests him or her. Have students write a paragraph describing the location of that country and what they learn about its physical characteristics from studying the physical map. **ELL Logical/Mathematical, Verbal/ Linguistic**

Content Background Knowledge

Political Changes Over time political boundaries and political affiliations change. A few examples:

- 1990 East and West Germany reunite.
- 1990 North Yemen and South Yemen unite.
- 1991 The Soviet Union dissolves into 15 independent states.
- 1992 Bosnia and Herzegovina declares independence from Yugoslavia.
- 1993 Czechoslovakia dissolves into the Czech Republic and Slovakia.
- 1993 Eritrea breaks off from Ethiopia.
- 1997 Britain transfers Hong Kong to the People's Republic of China as a special administrative region.
- 1999 Portugal transfers Macau to the People's Republic of China as a special administrative region.
- 2002 East Timor attains independence from Indonesia.
- 2005 Israel hands over the Gaza Strip to the Palestinian Authority.
- 2006 Montenegro and Serbia become independent states.
- 2008 Kosovo declares independence from Serbia.
- 2011 South Sudan attains independence from The Republic of Sudan.

INTERACTIVE IMAGE

World Time Zones

Calculating Display the world time zones map for students. Explain that the world was divided into 24 time zones in 1884 and that the time zones were created for business and travel coordination. Have students identify the time, date, and the time zone in which they live. Then ask them to calculate the time and date in Cairo. *(Cairo's time is 7 to 10 hours ahead depending upon students' location.)* Then ask students to write three word problems based on the time zone image. Have students exchange their questions with a partner to calculate the answers. If some students are having difficulty, remind them that when they move to the west they should subtract and when they move to the east, add. **Logical/Mathematical**

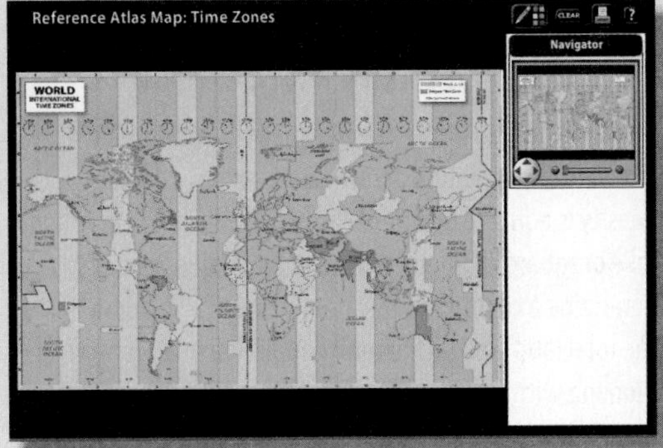

ANSWERS, p. 5

MAP STUDY

1. The natural boundaries of rivers and islands were used to delineate the political borders in Southeast Asia.
2. Possible answers include: Peru, Uruguay, Guyana, Morocco, Portugal, Algeria, Libya, South Africa, Somalia.

C Critical Thinking Skills

Assessing Have a student volunteer explain what population density means. *(how heavily or sparsely populated an area is; the number of people living in a set area)* **Ask: Why might a person, business, or government leader want to know how densely populated an area is?** *(Possible answers: it is often an indicator of quality of life; availability of services; kinds of economic activities)* **Logical/Mathematical, Visual/Spatial**

T Technology Skills

Presenting Have students focus on the cities map key. **Ask: What symbol is used to identify cities of over 5,000,000?** *(black square)* **What is the population range of cities shown as black dots?** *(1,000,000–2,000,000)* Have students identify which cities of the world have populations over 5,000,000. Then organize students into small groups and have each group research the population composition (which includes ethnic groups, age groups, etc.) of one of these cities and how it impacts life there. Encourage students to make a presentation to the class using charts, maps, and photographs. **BL Logical/Mathematical, Visual/Spatial, Interpersonal**

Making Connections

Have students think about the population density of their communities and how it impacts their lives. Have them consider such questions as: Is my community considered a rural, suburban, or urban community? How close are my neighbors? How much space do families have? How do people travel from one place to another? Does the community seem crowded, not crowded, or moderately crowded? Are there any problems caused by too many people or not enough people?

C World
Population Density

ARCTIC OCEAN
NORTH AMERICA
NORTH ATLANTIC OCEAN
NORTH PACIFIC OCEAN
SOUTH AMERICA
SOUTH PACIFIC OCEAN
SOUTH ATLANTIC OCEAN

T **Cities**
(Statistics reflect metropolitan areas.)
■ Over 5,000,000
□ 2,000,000–5,000,000
⊙ 1,000,000–2,000,000

networks Online Teaching Options

INTERACTIVE MAP

Population Density Map: World

Drawing Conclusions Use this map to introduce students to population density. Explain that population density is equal to the number of people living on a square mile or square kilometer of land and that geographers determine a country's population density by dividing the total land area by the total population of a country. Working with a partner, have student analyze the map and then write three concluding statements about population density. Have pairs share their statements with the class. **AL Verbal/Linguistic**

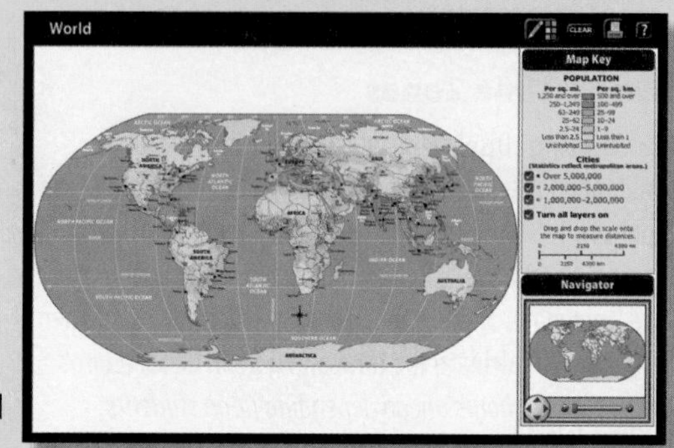

POPULATION		
Per sq. mi.		Per sq. km
1,250 and over		500 and over
250–1,249		100–499
63–249		25–99
25–62		10–24
2.5–24		1–9
Less than 2.5		Less than 1
Uninhabited		Uninhabited

0 2,000 miles at Equator
0 2,000 kilometers at Equator
Robinson projection

UNIT 1
WORLD ATLAS

MAP STUDY

1. ***Human Systems*** What cities in the United States have populations over five million people?

2. ***Environment and Society*** What generalizations can you make about the parts of the world that are least populated?

R Reading Skills

Reading Maps Have students focus on the population map key. **Ask:** **How are population densities distinguished on this map?** *(by color)* **What color represents the highest population density?** *(purple)* **No population?** *(gray)* **What is the population density of places colored in red?** *(250–1,240 people per square mile)* **Pink?** *(63–240 people per square mile)* **AL** **Visual/Spatial**

C Critical Thinking Skills

Comparing Have students compare the population densities of different parts of the world. **Ask:**

- **Which three areas in the Eastern Hemisphere have the largest concentrations of people?** *(Europe, India, South Asia)* **Which area in the Western Hemisphere has the largest concentration?** *(Northeastern United States)*
- **Describe the population pattern of North America?** *(Student answers may vary but should include that most of the densely populated areas of North America are along the coasts; the interior areas are less populated; parts of northern Canada are uninhabited.)*
- **What is the population density pattern in India?** *(most areas have more than 250 people per square mile; it is densest between the border with Nepal and the Ganges River.)*
- **How does the population density pattern in China compare?** *(Some areas are as densely populated as areas of India, but China also has large areas inland that are sparsely populated. The most densely populated areas of China are along the coast and in river valleys.)*
- **Are any areas of Europe as densely populated as India?** *(not really; while Western Europe has a large concentration of people, there are no large areas of 1,250 and over of people per sq. mi.)*
- **Why are some areas of the world uninhabited?** *(most areas covered by permanent ice, such as Antarctica and Greenland, are uninhabited)*

Have students compare the world population density map to the world physical map. Then lead a class discussion in which students explain how population density relates to elevation and bodies of water. Point out that while elevation can play a part in where people settle, a low elevation is not always desirable. **AL** **Logical/Mathematical, Visual/Spatial**

CARTOGRAM

World Population

Spatial Analysis This world population cartogram can be used to introduce world populations and to help students understand how maps can be used to show statistical information. Explain to students that some maps distort the size or shape of a country or location in order to show certain types of information. This cartogram shows population data. Working in groups, have students compare the cartogram with the population map to determine the degree of distortion in the countries of Africa. **BL** **Visual/Spatial, Interpersonal**

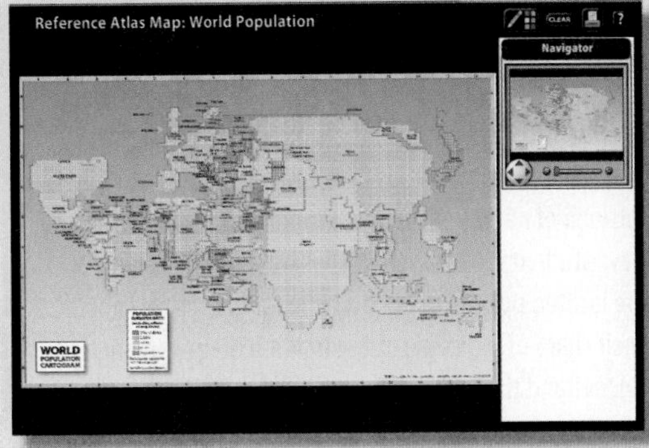

ANSWERS, p. 7

MAP STUDY

1. Los Angeles, Miami, Philadelphia, New York, Chicago
2. The least populated parts of the world tend to be in interior areas and not along the coasts.

C1 Critical Thinking Skills

Drawing Conclusions Direct students' attention to the map title. Explain that an economic activity map can indicate how the people of an area use the land and what they produce on that land to make a living. Point out that this map shows the location of important resources as well as land uses. **Ask: Why might geographers map the economic activities of a country?** *(Student answers may vary, but students should understand that geographers create economic activities maps to show how the location of resources affects the ways people make, transport, and use goods, and how and where services are provided.)* **Who might benefit from knowing this information?** *(Possible answer: This information can be valuable to individuals, political leaders, and businesses.)* **AL Logical/Mathematical, Visual/Spatial**

W Writing Skills

Informative/Explanatory Have students focus on the resources map key to identify the types of resources located on this map. **Ask: What symbol is used to designate coal deposits?** *(coal car)* **Petroleum deposits?** *(oil derrick)* **Natural gas?** *(flame)* Divide students into groups and assign each group a country or region to examine. Have students use the map and map key to identify the mineral resources found in that region. Then have students write a paragraph describing the region's important mineral resources and where they are located. **ELL Verbal/Linguistic, Visual/Spatial**

C2 Critical Thinking Skills

Comparing Have students compare the world economic activity map to the world population density map. **Ask: What generalizations can you make about the location of the world's important manufacturing and trade centers?** *(Student answers may vary, but could include that most manufacturing takes place in cities and areas of high population density.)* Have students brainstorm why this might be true. *(Possible answer: These are also centers of banking and finance with large labor forces and transportation available.)* **Logical/Mathematical, Visual/Spatial**

C1 World
Economic Activity

ARCTIC OCEAN
Beaufort Sea
Chukchi Sea
ARCTIC CIRCLE
Bering Sea
Greenland Sea
Labrador Sea
NORTH AMERICA
NORTH ATLANTIC OCEAN
TROPIC OF CANCER
Caribbean Sea
NORTH PACIFIC OCEAN
C2
EQUATOR
SOUTH AMERICA
TROPIC OF CAPRICORN
SOUTH ATLANTIC OCEAN
SOUTH PACIFIC OCEAN
ANTARCTIC CIRCLE
PRIME MERIDIAN
150°W 120°W 90°W 60°W 30°W 0°
30°N 0° 30°S 60°S

W

Resources

Coal	Nickel
Petroleum	Copper
Natural gas	Lead
Iron ore	Manganese
Tin	Gold
Zinc	Silver
Bauxite	Platinum
Cobalt	Gems
Uranium	

8 Unit 1

networks Online Teaching Options

INTERACTIVE MAP

Economic Activity Map: World

Creating Charts Display the world economic activity map from the Unit 1 Atlas to introduce students to the location of natural resources. Working in small groups, have students create a chart that lists where resources are located by country. Allow time for groups to complete their charts. Guide a class discussion to help students understand that natural resources are not evenly distributed on Earth and that uneven distribution affects the global economy. Ask students to explain which resources they feel are the most valuable and result in countries having a strong economy. *(Student answers may vary, but could include that oil often dictates a country's value in today's economic market.)* **ELL Visual/Spatial, Verbal/Linguistic**

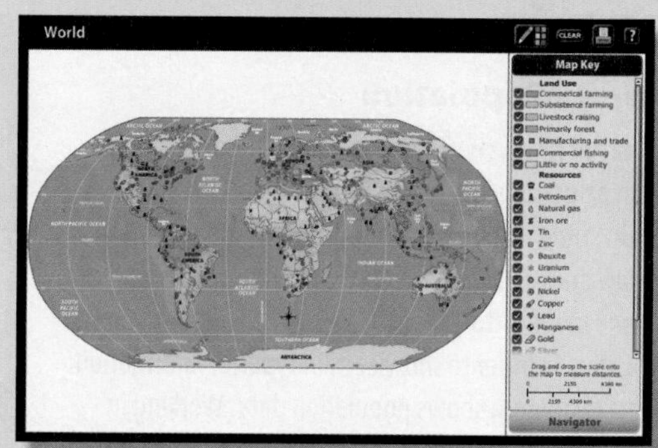

Land Use
Commercial farming
Subsistence farming
Livestock raising
Nomadic herding
Primarily forest
Manufacturing and trade
Commercial fishing
Little or no activity

0 2,000 miles at Equator
0 2,000 kilometers at Equator
Robinson projection

UNIT 1
WORLD ATLAS

MAP STUDY

1. ***Environment and Society*** What are the primary land use activities in high latitude climate regions?

2. ***Human Systems*** In which areas of the world is commercial fishing a dominant economic activity?

The World **9**

V Visual Skills

Identifying Have students focus on the land use map key. **Ask:** **How are different land uses designated on this map?** *(by colors)* **What color represents areas where commercial farming is the predominant land use?** *(bright green)* **Subsistence farming?** *(light green)* **What is the major land use in places colored in orange?** *(livestock raising)* **What does the square red box indicate?** *(manufacturing and trading centers)* **ELL** **Verbal/Linguistic, Visual/Spatial**

C Critical Thinking Skills

Analyzing Visuals Have students focus on the economic activity map to determine where different economic activities prevail. **Ask:**

- **In what part of North America is there a preponderance of manufacturing centers?** *(northeastern)* **What other important land use is prevalent there?** *(commercial farming)*
- **In what area of South America is forestry a major economic activity?** *(Amazon River Basin)*
- **What generalization can you make about land use in northern Africa, the Arabian Peninsula, and Central Asia?** *(Answers will vary, but students should understand that nomadic herding is practiced throughout these regions; however, in many desert areas there is little or no economic activity.)*
- **What are the primary land use activities in central and southern Africa?** *(subsistence farming; forestry)*
- **What is the predominant land use of Western Europe?** *(commercial farming; manufacturing)*
- **Name three areas where livestock raising is a significant land use.** *(Answers will vary; significant livestock raising areas occur in the American West, in eastern and southern South America, in southern Africa, and much of Australia)*

AL **Logical/Mathematical, Visual/Spatial**

CARTOGRAM

Gross Domestic Product Per Capita

Drawing Inferences Use this cartogram showing world gross domestic product breakdown by country to discuss economic activities with students. Display the cartogram and then have students compare it to land use as indicated on the world economic activity map. Ask students to consider how the relative size of Kuwait has been changed on the cartogram. Have them write a paragraph explaining what they can infer about why the size of Kuwait is enlarged on this cartogram.
BL **Verbal/Linguistic, Logical/Mathematical**

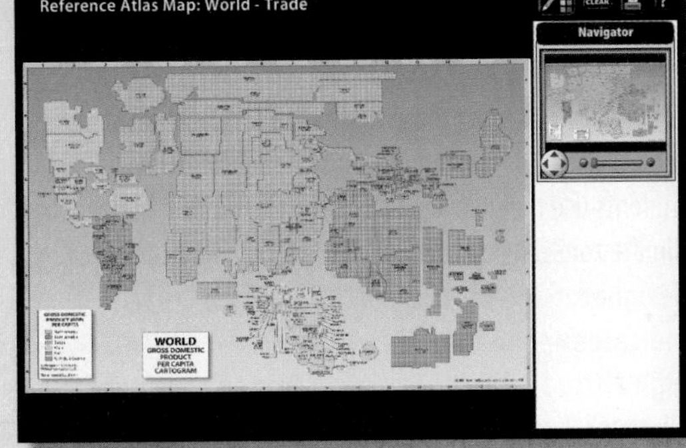

ANSWERS, p. 9

MAP STUDY

1. nomadic herding and forest
2. coastal areas

C Critical Thinking Skills

Evaluating Discuss what it means for an area to fall within a specific climate zone. **Ask:** **How would you describe the climate zone you live in?** *(Student answers may vary but should include the use of terms such as humid, semi-arid, and/or arid as well as tropical, continental, and/or subarctic in describing their climate.)* Discuss why geographers map the world's climates and how the knowledge of climates and climate zones is useful to people. **Logical/Mathematical, Visual/Spatial**

V Visual Skills

Creating Graphs Have students focus on the climate zones listed in the map key. Explain to students that geographers divide the world into climate regions based on these zones and that each of these can be broken down into smaller categories. Working with a partner, have students create a graph that shows the percentage of countries or regions that are in each climate zone. Students may conduct additional research to complete their graphs. **Visual/Spatial, Verbal/Linguistic**

W Writing Skills

Narrative Have students compare the climate of one of the world's regions to the physical map of the region. Ask them to imagine that they are traveling across their region as a writer for a travel blog. Have students write a blog noting the relationship between the area's climate to its elevation, latitude, and proximity to a major body of water. Ask students to include descriptive words and phrases in their blogs. Encourage them to draw illustrations or attach visuals to their writing.
BL **Naturalist, Intrapersonal**

CLOSE & REFLECT

Summarizing Have students review the Unit 1 Atlas maps and make a list of important facts about world geography that they gain from studying each map. Then lead a class discussion based on students' lists.

ANSWERS, p. 10
1. tropical rain forest, tropical wet/dry
2. subarctic, tundra and high altitude, ice cap

C World
Climate

ARCTIC OCEAN
ARCTIC CIRCLE
ASIA
EUROPE
NORTH AMERICA
NORTH ATLANTIC OCEAN
AFRICA
NORTH PACIFIC OCEAN
TROPIC OF CANCER
EQUATOR
SOUTH AMERICA
INDIAN OCEAN
SOUTH ATLANTIC OCEAN
PRIME MERIDIAN
TROPIC OF CAPRICORN
AUSTRALIA
SOUTH PACIFIC OCEAN
ANTARCTIC CIRCLE
SOUTHERN OCEAN
ANTARCTICA
0 2,000 miles at Equator
0 2,000 kilometers at Equator
Robinson projection

W V

- Tropical rain forest
- Tropical wet/dry
- Semi-arid (steppe)
- Arid (desert)
- Humid subtropical
- Marine west coast
- Mediterranean
- Humid continental
- Subarctic
- Tundra and high altitude
- Ice cap

UNIT 1
WORLD ATLAS

MAP STUDY

1. ***Physical Systems*** Which two climate regions occur on and around the Equator?
2. ***Physical Systems*** What types of climate occur in the high latitudes?

networks Online Teaching Options

INTERACTIVE MAP

Climate Map: World

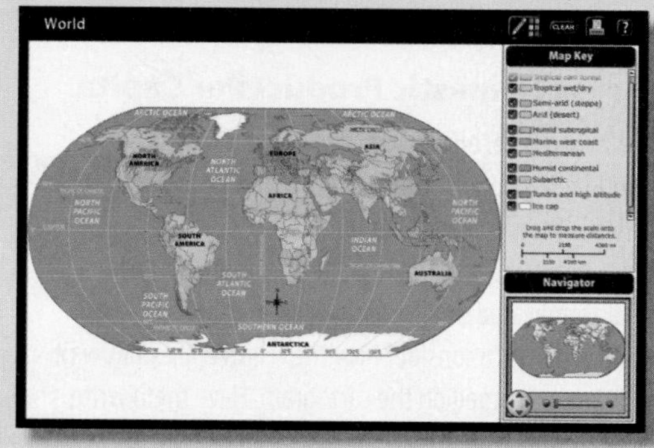

Identifying Display the climate map for students and ask them to focus on the climate map key. Have students use the map key to identify the world's major climate zones. **Ask:** **How are different climate zones designated on this map?** *(by colors)* **What color indicates a semi-arid climate?** *(yellow)* **A tundra/ high altitude climate?** *(purple)* **A humid continental climate?** *(bright green)* **What climate do areas colored in light green have?** *(humid subtropical)* **Lavender?** *(subarctic)* **Gold?** *(Mediterranean)* Continue to ask students questions until they become familiar with the various climate zones. ELL **Visual/Spatial, Verbal/ Linguistic**

CHAPTER 1

How Geographers Look at the World Planner

UNDERSTANDING BY DESIGN®

Enduring Understandings

- *Geographers study how people, places, and environments are distributed on Earth's surface.*
- *All maps are projected in the same way. Explain that there are several different types of map projections because it is not possible to place the information on a round globe or onto a flat surface. Each type of map projection has advantages and disadvantages.*

Essential Question

- *How does geography help us interpret the past, understand the present, and plan for the future?*

Predictable Misunderstandings

Students may think:

- *Geography entails studying only land, not people. Explain that geography also includes the study of how humans interact with their physical environment.*

Assessment Evidence

Performance Tasks:

- *Hands-On Chapter Project*

Other Evidence:

- *Guided Reading Activities*
- *Vocabulary Activity*
- *Lesson Quizzes*
- *Chapter Tests, Forms A and B*

SUGGESTED PACING GUIDE

Introducing the Chapter..............½ Day
Lesson 1........................... 1 Day
Lesson 2........................... 1 Day
Chapter Wrap-Up and Assessment......½ Day

TOTAL TIME 3 Days

National Geography Standards covered in "How Geographers Look at the World"

The student knows and understands:

(1) How to use maps and other geographic representations, geospatial technologies, and spatial thinking to understand and communicate information

1.1 The advantage of coordinating multiple geographic representations—such as maps, globes, diagrams, aerial and other photographs, remotely-sensed images, and geographic visualization to answer geographic questions

1.2 The technical properties and quality of geospatial data

1.4 The uses of geospatial technologies to investigate and analyze geographic questions and to communicate geographic answers

(2) How to use mental maps to organize information about people, places, and environments in a spatial context

2.1 The locations, characteristics, patterns, and relationships of physical and human systems are the basis for mental maps at local to global scales

2.2 Mental maps can change through experience and iterative self-reflection

2.4 Changing perceptions reshape mental maps of people, places, regions, and environments

(3) How to analyze the spatial organizations of people, places, and environments on Earth's surface

3.3 Models are used to represent the structure and dynamics of spatial processes which shape human and physical systems

(5) That people create regions to interpret Earth's complexity

5.1 Regions are defined by different sets of criteria and places can be included in multiple regions of different types

(6) How culture and experience influence people's perceptions of places and regions

6.1 People can view places and regions from multiple perspectives

(17) How to apply geography and interpret the past

17.1 Geographic contexts (the human and physical characteristics of places and environments) can explain the connections between sequences of historical events

(18) How to apply geography to interpret the present and plan for the future

18.1 Geographic contexts (the human and physical characteristics of places and environments) provide the bases for analyzing current events and making predictions about future issues

Key for Using the Teacher Edition

SKILL-BASED ACTIVITIES

Types of skill activities found in the Teacher Edition.

* **V Visual Skills** require students to analyze maps, graphs, charts, and photos.

R Reading Skills help students practice reading skills and master vocabulary.

C Critical Thinking Skills help students apply and extend what they have learned.

W Writing Skills provide writing opportunities to help students comprehend the text.

T Technology Skills require students to use digital tools effectively.

*Letters are followed by a number when there is more than one of the same type of skill on the page.

DIFFERENTIATED INSTRUCTION

All activities are written for the on-level student unless otherwise marked with the leveled labels below.

BL Beyond Level
AL Approaching Level
ELL English Language Learners

All students benefit from activities that utilize different learning styles. Many activities are marked as below when a particular learning style is highlighted.

Intrapersonal	Naturalist
Logical/Mathematical	Kinesthetic
Visual/Spatial	Auditory/Musical
Verbal/Linguistic	Interpersonal

CHAPTER OPENER PLANNER

Students will know:

- *the characteristics and uses of globes and various types of maps.*
- *how map projections are created and best used.*
- *how to determine absolute and relative location.*
- *how geospatial technologies are used and how geographers gather information.*
- *how the spatial perspective is unique to geography.*
- *the six elements of geography and geography's relationship to other disciplines.*

Students will be able to:

- ***describe** globes, maps, and the importance of scale.*
- ***analyze** various map projections and how they are created and used.*
- ***explain** how to determine absolute and relative location.*
- ***analyze** geospatial technologies and how geographers collect data.*
- ***describe** the spatial perspective.*
- ***identify** the six elements of geography and how geography is related to other disciplines.*

UNDERSTANDING BY DESIGN®

☑ Print Teaching Options

V Visual Skills

☐ **p. 11** Students discuss geographical features in their area and make inferences based on the image. **Verbal/Linguistic**

R Reading Skills

☐ **p. 13** Students summarize the section in gerrymandering.

C Critical Thinking Skills

☐ **p. 13** Students compare reasons for redistricting and supply reasons for decreases in population of a city.

W Writing Skills

☐ **p. 12** Students write about the ways geography affected elections prior to technological advances. **Verbal/Linguistic**

T Technology Skills

☐ **p. 13** Students research a state and its population over the last two to four censuses and create a display about their findings. **BL** **Visual/Spatial**

☑ Online Teaching Options

V Visual Skills

GAME **How Geographers Look at the World**—Students play a game to learn the definitions of vocabulary words. **ELL** **Verbal/Linguistic**

MAP **Interactive World Atlas**—Students use the interactive world atlas to identify the regions of the world and describe their terrain.

☑ Printable Digital Worksheets

WORKSHEET **Assessing Background Knowledge**—Students demonstrate their understanding and prior knowledge about how geographers study the world.

WORKSHEET **Chapter Summaries**—Summaries are provided for each chapter that thoroughly condense core content into manageable chunks.

WORKSHEET **Reteaching Activity**—These worksheets provide students with an opportunity for remedial practice and review of vital chapter content.

WORKSHEET **Vocabulary Activity**—Students apply their knowledge of content and academic vocabulary words.

Project-Based Learning 

Hands-On

Recommendation About a Community Issue
Students will develop a chapter project in which they make a recommendation about a community issue using geographical tools and skills.

Digital Hands-On

Create Online Projects
Find an additional activity online that incorporates technology for this project. Visit the EdTech Teacher Web sites for more links, tutorials, and other resources.

Print Resources

ANCILLARY RESOURCES
This ancillary is available for every chapter and lesson.

- **Chapter Tests and Lesson Quizzes**

PRINTABLE DIGITAL WORKSHEETS
These printable digital worksheets are available for every chapter and lesson.

- **Assessing Background Knowledge**
- **Chapter Summaries**
- **Guided Reading Activities**
- **Hands-On Chapter Projects**
- **Quizzes and Tests**
- **Reading Essentials and Study Guide** **AL**
- **Reteaching Activities**
- **Video Activities**
- **Vocabulary**

More Media Resources

SUGGESTED VIDEOS 

- **The Standard Deviants—Learn World Geography** (90 min.)
- **The World Atlas WORLD: HUMAN GEOGRAPHY** (45 min.)

SUGGESTED READING 

- **Why Geography Matters,** by Harm de Blij
- **Almanac of Geography,** National Geographic Almanacs
- **Maphead: Charting the Wide, Weird World of Geography Wonks,** by Ken Jennings

LESSON 1 PLANNER

THE GEOGRAPHER'S TOOLS

Students will know:
- *the characteristics and uses of globes and various types of maps.*
- *how map projections are created.*
- *the advantages and disadvantages of various map projections.*
- *how to determine absolute and relative location.*
- *the importance of scale when creating and using maps.*
- *how geospatial technologies are used.*

Students will be able to:
- ***describe** globes, maps, and the importance of scale.*
- ***analyze** various map projections and how they are created.*
- ***explain** how to determine absolute and relative location.*
- ***analyze** geospatial technologies.*

UNDERSTANDING BY DESIGN®

☑ Print Teaching Options

V Visual Skills

- ☐ **p. 15** Students make a chart describing different types of map projections. **Visual/Spatial**
- ☐ **p. 22** Students identify endangered animals within a region that are being tracked by GPS. **Visual/Spatial**
- ☐ **p. 24** Students compare and contrast early satellite images with modern satellite images. **Visual/Spatial**

R Reading Skills

- ☐ **p. 14** Students begin a vocabulary list in their notebooks with the word *geography*. **ELL** **Verbal/Linguistic**
- ☐ **p. 21** Students paraphrase a paragraph about mental maps. **AL** **Verbal/Linguistic**

C Critical Thinking Skills

- ☐ **p. 14** Students demonstrate the great circle route on a globe and discuss why a globe is the most accurate representation of the Earth. **Kinesthetic**
- ☐ **p. 16** Students analyze four types of common map projections. **AL** **Visual/Spatial**
- ☐ **p. 23** Students write a paragraph sequencing steps a geographer might take to use GIS to conduct a survey of recent weather patterns, use it to make a thematic map and later update the map. **BL** **Logical/Mathematical**
- ☐ **p. 24** Students think of ways different types of information might be useful to input into a GIS.

W Writing Skills

- ☐ **p. 20** Students write directions to a relative's house to practice mentally organizing special information.
- ☐ **p. 22** Students debate arguments for and against GPS apps for children's smart phones. **Interpersonal**

T Technology Skills

- ☐ **p. 15** Students present on how maps have changed by comparing historic and modern maps of a country. **BL** **Visual/Spatial, Interpersonal**
- ☐ **p. 17** Students use the Internet to identify some popular landmarks using absolute location with given coordinates. **Logical/Mathematical**

☑ Online Teaching Options

V Visual Skills

- ☐ INTERACTIVE BELLRINGER **Interpreting a Thematic Map**—Students interpret the map of Africa and discuss why so many countries in Africa have problems accessing safe drinking water. **AL** **Interpersonal**
- ☐ VIDEO **Mercator Map**—Students discuss why the Mercator map was necessary and how it changed the world. **Verbal/Linguistic**
- ☐ INTERACTIVE MAP **Latitude and Longitude**—Students learn about latitude and longitude and identify the lines within which an assigned continent is located. **Logical/Mathematical**
- ☐ INTERACTIVE MAP **Small-Scale and Large-Scale Maps**—Students calculate distances on small- and large-scale maps. **AL** **Logical/Mathematical**
- ☐ INFOGRAPHIC **GIS Layers**—Students study the graphic and write a paragraph explaining advantages of using multiple representations to answer geographic questions. **BL** **Verbal/Linguistic**
- ☐ INTERACTIVE IMAGE **Satellite Imagery**—Students write an essay describing the satellite image of a chosen location. **Verbal/Linguistic**
- ☐ INTERACTIVE WHITEBOARD ACTIVITY **Purposes of Maps**—Students complete an interactive whiteboard activity on the purposes of maps. **ELL** **Visual/Spatial, Kinesthetic**

C Critical Thinking Skills

- ☐ GAME **The Geographer's Tools**—Students play a concentration game to review concepts found in the lesson.
- ☐ INTERACTIVE MAP **Common Map Projections**—Students write a paragraph explaining which type of map they would choose to navigate to a chosen destination. **BL** **Visual/Spatial**
- ☐ INTERACTIVE GRAPHIC ORGANIZER **Geographer's Tools**—Students complete a graphic organizer to identify the tools geographers use to look at the world. **AL** **Visual/Spatial**

W Writing Skills

- ☐ INTERACTIVE WEB SITE **How Did We Get Here?**—Students outline the content in an article on mobile mapping technology advances. **ELL** **Verbal/Linguistic**

☑ Printable Digital Worksheets

V Visual Skills

- ☐ WORKSHEET **Video Activity**—Students will complete this worksheet about an aspect of the lesson content. **Visual/Spatial**

R Reading Skills

- ☐ WORKSHEET **Guided Reading Activity**—Students use Guided Reading Activity worksheets to review their comprehension of the content. **Verbal/Linguistic**
- ☐ WORKSHEET **Reading Essentials and Study Guide**—Students use this guide to help struggling and English language learners grasp key concepts and vocabulary. **AL** **Verbal/Linguistic**

LESSON 2 PLANNER

THE GEOGRAPHER'S CRAFT

Students will know:
- *how the spatial perspective is unique to geography.*
- *the six elements of geography.*
- *the methods geographers use to gather geographic information.*
- *the ways in which geography is related to other disciplines.*

Students will be able to:
- ***describe** the spatial perspective.*
- ***identify** the six elements of geography.*
- ***explain** geographic methods for gathering information.*
- ***analyze** how geography is related to other disciplines.*

UNDERSTANDING BY DESIGN®

☑ *Print Teaching Options*

V Visual Skills

- ☐ **p. 29** Students study the map of perceptual regions of the United States. AL Visual/Spatial
- ☐ **p. 32** Students sketch landscapes based on verbal descriptions and discuss why geographers need to see and experience a place. AL Auditory/Musical, Visual/Spatial
- ☐ **p. 33** Students use the data they collected to create a chart or diagram using the class results, and then look for patterns and trends. Logical/Mathematical, Visual/Spatial

R Reading Skills

- ☐ **p. 29** Students give a partner directions from a common point of knowledge to another using relative directions. Kinesthetic, Logical/Mathematical
- ☐ **p. 29** Students take turns providing a place they both know about and declaring its site and situation.
- ☐ **p. 33** Students discuss the things geographers can learn from the records that people have left behind.

C Critical Thinking Skills

- ☐ **p. 27** Students work in groups to consider geographical contributions the professions in the section bring to a real-life situation. BL Naturalist
- ☐ **p. 28** Students imagine they are moving to a new area and determine how to use each of the five geographic skills to find out about the new area. ELL Interpersonal
- ☐ **p. 34** Students consider how human geography can be used to analyze a photo.

W Writing Skills

- ☐ **p. 28** Students write an article on their city or neighborhood for a travel blog. Verbal/Linguistic

T Technology Skills

- ☐ **p. 27** Students research career options in geography and write a paragraph about what they find most interesting.
- ☐ **p. 34** Students research how the distribution of natural resources affects a country's economy and movement of money. BL Logical/Mathematical

☑ *Online Teaching Options*

V Visual Skills

- ☐ INTERACTIVE BELLRINGER **Interpreting a Political Cartoon**—Students study the political cartoon, ask questions, and discuss different perspectives of the world. Visual/Spatial
- ☐ INTERACTIVE IMAGE **Hiker Reading a Map**—Students jot down five physical features that help describe the location of the hiker in the image and consider what types of questions a geographer might ask to gather information about the location. AL Visual/Spatial, Interpersonal

W Writing Skills

- ☐ INTERACTIVE IMAGE **Scientist Studying a Glacier**—Students write a brief narrative of the observations they might need to study if they were studying the Russell Glacier. ELL Verbal/Linguistic

C Critical Thinking Skills

- ☐ INTERACTIVE WHITEBOARD ACTIVITY **Elements of Geography**—Students discuss the five geographer's skills and provide an example of a question or statement that could be used by a city planner to zone a piece of land. ELL Visual/Spatial
- ☐ INTERACTIVE MAP **Perceptual Regions of the United States**—Students learn how spatial relationships link people and places together based on their locations and discuss how regional perspectives may create bias. BL Visual/Spatial, Intrapersonal
- ☐ ONLINE LINK **Census Results Having Effects on State Representation**—Students discuss how geographic contexts provide the basis for analyzing the current population to make important political decisions in the future. BL Visual/Spatial
- ☐ GAME **The Geographer's Craft**—Students play an interactive True/False game to review concepts and terminology presented in the chapter.

☑ *Printable Digital Worksheets*

R Reading Skills

- ☐ WORKSHEET **Vocabulary Activity**—Students use the Vocabulary Activity worksheet to assess students' knowledge and understanding of the content and academic vocabulary in the chapter.
- ☐ WORKSHEET **Guided Reading Activity**—Students use Guided Reading Activity worksheets to review their comprehension of the content. Verbal/Linguistic
- ☐ WORKSHEET **Video Activity**—Students will complete this Video Activity worksheet after they watch the lesson video. Verbal/Spatial

INTERVENTION AND REMEDIATION STRATEGIES

LESSON 1 The Geographer's Tools

Reading and Comprehension

Tell students that previewing a text can be helpful when starting a course of study in which a wide range of concepts and terminology will be introduced. Go over the content vocabulary list with students, noting the use of the word *projection.* Ask volunteers to identify synonyms for the word. *(Sample answers: plan, prediction, representation)* To reinforce students' understanding, organize students into small groups, assigning three or four of the content vocabulary terms to each group. Have a student in each group read the definition of a word while the other students in the group try to guess the word and explain how it is used in the lesson. Have students take turns reading the definitions and guessing the words, and have students collaborate to create sentences that show their understanding of each of their assigned terms. Then have students skim the lesson to find new or unfamiliar words and use the textbook glossary or online dictionaries to define the terms. [RI.4]

Text Evidence

Tell students that as they read each chapter, identifying supporting evidence and examples from the text can help them better understand main ideas and concepts. Organize students into four groups, and assign one of the four main headings of the chapter to each group: *Globes and Map Projections, Determining Location, Using Maps,* and *Geospatial Technologies.* Have groups review their assigned segment of the text and collaborate to identify the main ideas or concepts. Encourage students to narrow down the main ideas to three or four, and to use subheadings as a guide. Then have students identify supporting evidence or examples to support each main idea or central concept. Challenge students to include real-life examples in addition to textual evidence. For example, students might refer to how they use a GPS or map application in their daily lives. [RI.1, RI.2]

LESSON 2 The Geographer's Craft

Reading and Comprehension

To aid students with their comprehension of the purposes and applications of skills for thinking like a geographer, have student pairs choose one of the five skills outlined in this lesson. Reinforce students' understanding by having them perform the tasks required for their chosen skill. For example, if partners choose the skill *Analyzing Geographic Information,* they should demonstrate the act of drawing conclusions based on maps and other visuals. Have student pairs take turns demonstrating their interpretation of the skill for the class. Allow time for a discussion about how these skills can be applied in different fields, such as health care, transportation, economic development, and so on. [RI.4]

Text Evidence

Organize students into six groups, and assign one of the six overall elements of geography to each group. Have students review the lesson and create a pictorial summary of their assigned element. Students may use images found online, magazine photographs, or create their own pictures to convey the meaning of their assigned element and examples. For example, students might create a map that identifies the world in spatial terms, or a map that shows places and regions, and so on. Tell students to review the text to identify the central idea about their topic and supporting details. Then have groups collaborate to write a short paragraph that summarizes their assigned topic to accompany their visuals. Have students present their pictorial and written summaries to the class. [RI.1, RI.2]

Online Resources

Leveled Reader

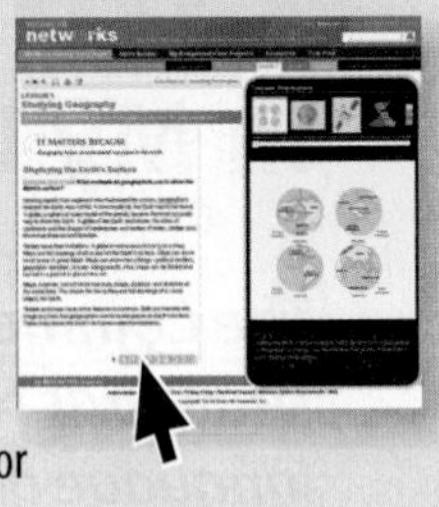

Use this online approaching-level text that corresponds directly to the text in the Student Edition. It also includes additional reading and comprehension support for English Language Learners.

Guided Reading Activities

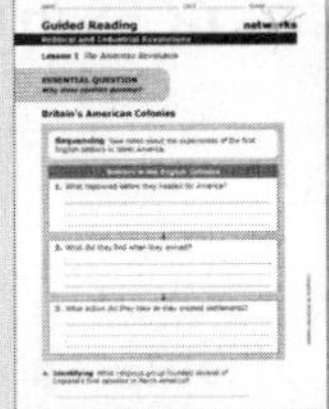

This resource uses guiding questions to help students with comprehension.

Reteaching Activities

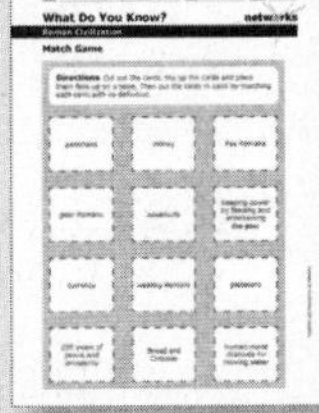

These worksheets provide students with an opportunity for remedial practice and review of vital chapter content.

Reading Essentials and Study Guide

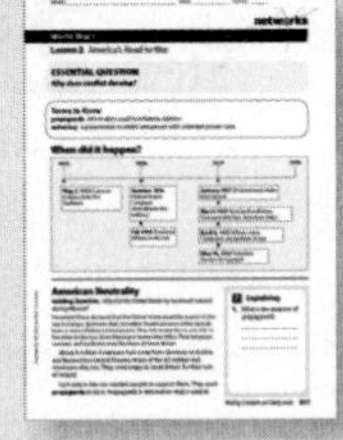

This resource offers writing and reading activities for the approaching-level student.

Self-Check Quizzes

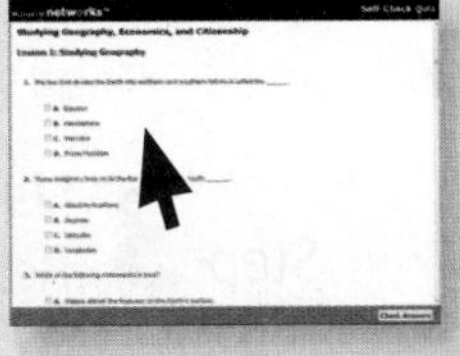

This online assessment tool provides instant feedback for students to check their progress.

Chapter Summaries

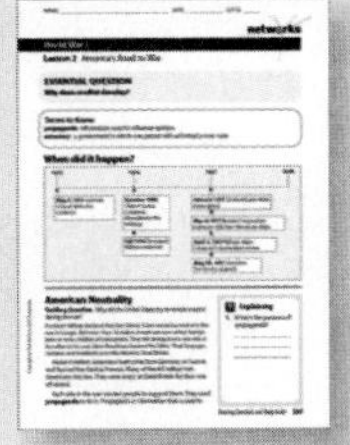

Summaries are provided for each chapter that thoroughly condense core content into manageable chunks.

How Do I Implement the Common Core State Standards in My Lessons?

The Common Core State Standards (CCSS) are national standards focused on ensuring that students master language arts skills by the time they complete high school. In grades 6 through 12, the standards require that some of this skill development and skill practice be part of other subjects, such as social studies. You can incorporate the CCSS in your lessons in a few simple steps.

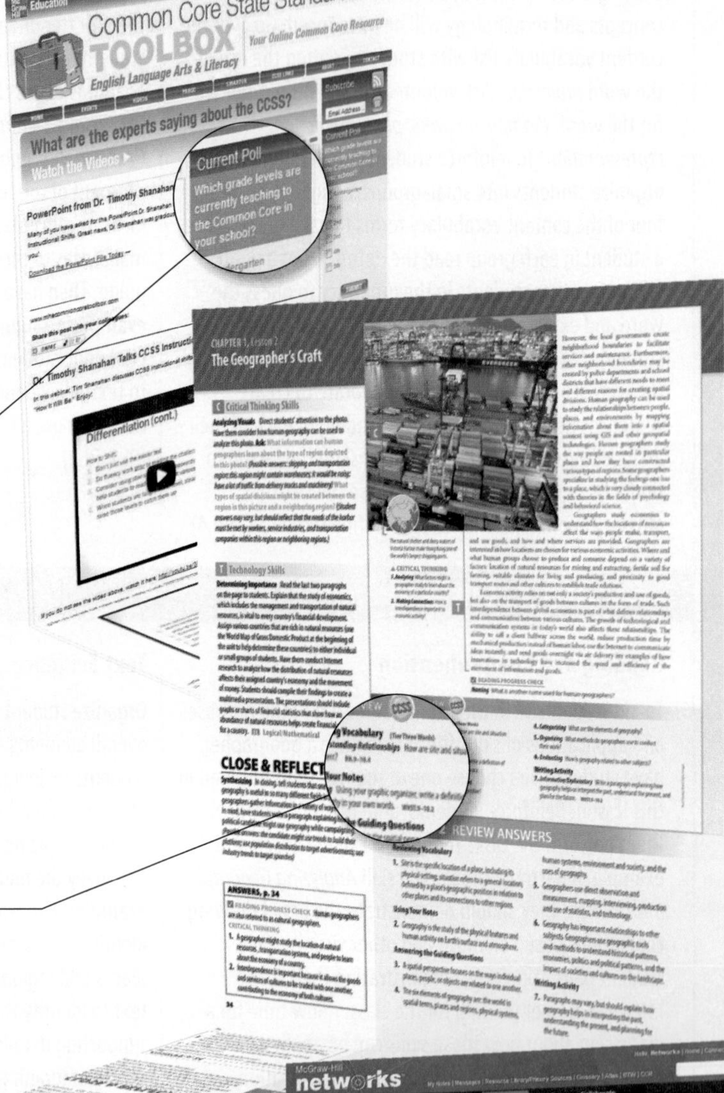

Step 1 Familiarize Yourself with the Standards.

- McGraw-Hill Education's Common Core State Standards Solutions Web site has several free training modules on the CCSS. These will help you quickly understand the standards.
- Another valuable resource, McGraw-Hill Education's Common Core State Standards Toolbox Web site, has articles and tips from other teachers and professionals that you can refer to throughout the year.

Step 2 Incorporate the Standards into Your Lessons.

- McGraw-Hill's print teacher edition and online teacher lesson plans provide practice and reinforcement of the Common Core State Standards.
- Student activities are coded to show their alignment to specific common core standards.

Step 3 Use the Additional Resources found in the Online Resource Library to Promote Student Skill Mastery.

Slide Shows that help students learn how to:

- Identify main ideas
- Understand cause and effect
- Compare and contrast
- Draw conclusions
- Analyze visuals, documents, videos

Writing and Analyzing Templates to help students:

- Write drafts
- Evaluate writing samples
- Write persuasive text
- Create expository text
- Compose narratives

How Geographers Look at the World

ESSENTIAL QUESTION • *How does geography help us interpret the past, understand the present, and plan for the future?*

networks

There's More Online about how geographers look at the world.

CHAPTER 1

Geography Matters...

Geographers are not the only ones who find value in geography skills. In fact, you use geography skills every day. The online maps you use to find the nearest grocery store, the GPS technology in your smartphone that tells your friends where you are, the weather reports that help you decide what to wear each day, the transportation systems that get you from place to place, and even your understanding of the people around you—their beliefs, values, and ways of life—are all examples of how geography is integrated into your daily life. Understanding the elements of geography in greater detail can help you become a better decision maker, planner, and citizen of the United States and the world.

◀ Philippe Cousteau, Jr., grandson of the famous marine explorer Jacques Cousteau, paddles in the waters of Blue Spring State Park in Florida while working on a documentary about Blue Spring and its manatees.

Orlando Sentinel/McClatchy-Tribune/Getty Images

11

Letter from the Author

Dear Geography Teacher,

Geographers are interested in people, places, and the environment. All is viewed from a spatial perspective that includes movement, organized territory, and how people live and interact on a daily basis. Geographers have an interest in the physical and human worlds and they have developed technology that helps them record and map the surface of Earth and everything that transpires there. Geographers have important roles in interpreting matters, such as climate change, globalization, homeland security, energy, and cultural diversity, to mention a few.

Richard G. Boehm

ENGAGE

Considering Ask a volunteer to read the *Essential Question*. Have students discuss geographical and environmental features in their area that affect the way people live in the present or plan to live in the future. Then discuss features they think are necessary or appealing. **Ask: What physical or human geographical features would be important to you in choosing a new place to live?** *(Student answers may vary, but should include specific physical features: hills, lakes, rivers; human features: cities, states; and human-made features: attractions, places of employment, stores.)*

TEACH & ASSESS

Making Connections Jacques Cousteau, a French marine conservationist and inventor, pioneered underwater exploration by bringing it alive to millions of people. For much of the late 20th century, he sailed around the world on his ship, *Calypso*, inspiring and educating the world about the ocean and its inhabitants. Cousteau's Oscar-winning documentaries brought a new world perspective to television viewers by exploring and filming parts of the ocean depths that had never been seen before. He pioneered scuba gear and underwater base camps, helped restrict commercial whaling, and fought to stop underwater dumping of nuclear waste. Today his family and supporters continue the fight against pollution, overfishing, and other threats to the world's oceans.

Inferring Direct students' attention to the image and caption of Philippe Cousteau, Jr. **Ask: How can we deduce that Philippe Cousteau, Jr., uses physical geography as well as a map for basic navigation?** *(Possible answers: He uses a population survey of manatees to know where to find them. He may use a map showing water depths to navigate his canoe.)* **How might he use human geography?** *(Possible answers: He may use maps to show boundaries of the park. He may read guides on laws governing the area.)* **Verbal/Linguistic**

CLOSE & REFLECT

Summarizing Have students write a paragraph to summarize what they learned about how geographers look at the world.

Extend the project-based learning experience globally through our partnership with ePals. EPals allows you to connect with classrooms around the world in a safe online environment for real-life lessons and projects in virtual study groups.

ENGAGE

C Critical Thinking Skills

Theorizing Encourage students to imagine themselves as geographers, seeing a new map of their city or state for the first time. Working with a partner, have them brainstorm reasons that maps might require changes after each decade and then, as a class, list these reasons on the board. Explain that geographers conduct studies about the physical aspects of Earth and that they also study changing economies, cultures, and politics that affect people and communities.

TEACH & ACCESS

W Writing Skills

Informative/Explanatory Read the section out loud to students. Explain that geography influences modern-day elections. Before the advances in modern maps, GPS systems, and transportation, and the use of modern technology, such as television, computers, the Internet, satellites, and other high-speed communications, presidential election campaigns and voting were very different from what they are today. Have students write a brief essay about the ways geography affected elections prior to these types of technological advances. **Verbal/Linguistic**

V Visual Skills

Interpreting Have students analyze the Ohio redistricting maps and the map key. **Ask:** **How many years passed between these two maps?** *(ten years)* **What do the colors on the maps indicate?** *(They represent each district.)* **What areas of the state have changed the most?** *(All of the big cities, except Columbus, have lost people.)* **What significant redistricting has taken place and how has this affected Ohio's political power?** *(Because there are fewer people in Ohio, the state lost two congressional seats, decreasing Ohio's political power.)* AL **Visual/Spatial**

Content Background Knowledge

U.S. Census Bureau The United States Census is a survey done by the government every ten years. Every household in the country must fill out a census survey. The goal is to count every person in the country, both adult and child. Besides the use of defining legislature districts, census information is used to allocate government money to plan future government services, such as where to build schools, bridges, and roads; and to facilitate research to improve neighborhoods, public health, and job training. Private citizens have the right to access most of the census information gathered.

Why Geography Matters: **How Geographers Look at the World**

C distribution *of* political power

W *Political geography deals with the ways in which political processes and spatial environments interact and affect one another. Political boundaries such as the borders of countries, states, cities, and electoral districts are all part of political geography. Even election outcomes can be affected by the interaction of politics and geography.*

Redistricting in Ohio

V

Ohio Districts, 2010

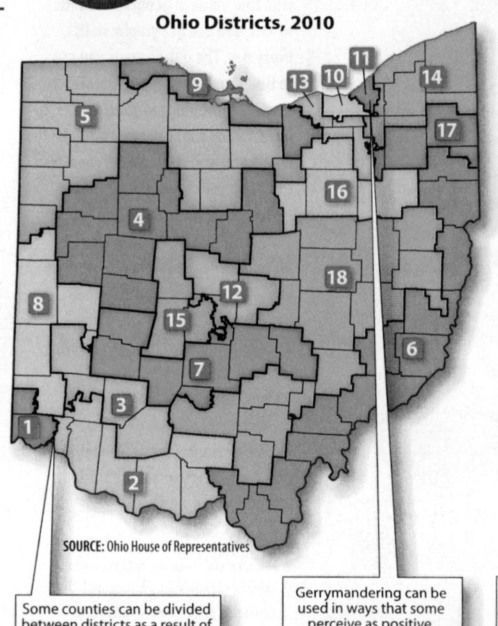

SOURCE: Ohio House of Representatives

Proposed Districts in Ohio

SOURCE: The Columbus Dispatch, September 14, 2011

Some counties can be divided between districts as a result of gerrymandering. For example, eastern Hamilton County is part of the Ohio 2nd district, while the rest of the county is part of the 1st district.

Gerrymandering can be used in ways that some perceive as positive. For example, districts are created in which a majority of the voters are a racial or ethnic minority, as in Ohio's 11th district.

During the process of reapportionment based on the 2010 Census, Ohio Republicans proposed a new congressional map that left them a good chance to hold many seats for the next decade.

The approved map of districts reflects some, but not all, of the Republicans' proposals.

The proposed 9th district, which would have snaked along Lake Erie from Toledo to Cleveland, packs concentrations of Democratic voters into one district.

The proposed 16th district moved a Democratic representative into a district that favored a Republican representative.

12

Project-Based Learning

Hands-On

Make a Recommendation About a Community Issue

Working in small groups, students will choose and evaluate an issue in their local community and prepare a plan of action that could be presented to local officials. As part of the presentation, students will create a three-column chart similar to The Skills for Thinking Like a Geographer in their textbooks. Groups will present their recommendations about a community issue to the class, explaining how they used the geographical tools and skills discussed in this chapter.

ePals GlobalCommunity
Where learners connect™

Digital Hands-On

Create Online Projects

Find an additional activity online that incorporates technology for this project. Visit the EdTech Teacher Web sites for more links, tutorials, and other resources.

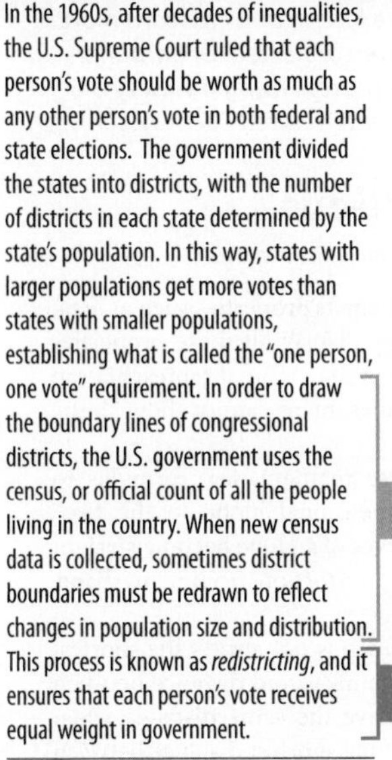

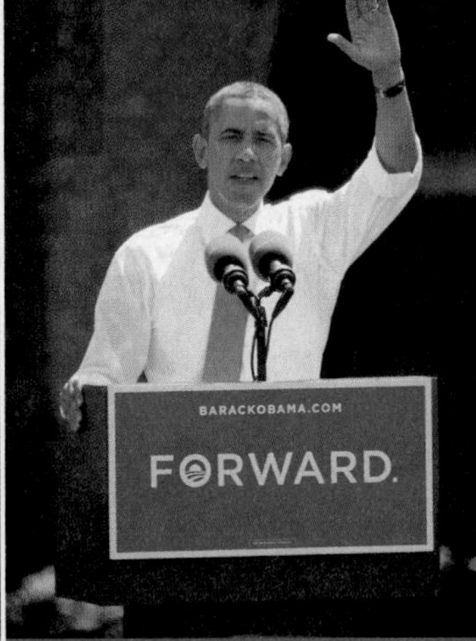

BARACKOBAMA.COM
FORWARD.

What is redistricting?

In the 1960s, after decades of inequalities, the U.S. Supreme Court ruled that each person's vote should be worth as much as any other person's vote in both federal and state elections. The government divided the states into districts, with the number of districts in each state determined by the state's population. In this way, states with larger populations get more votes than states with smaller populations, establishing what is called the "one person, one vote" requirement. In order to draw the boundary lines of congressional districts, the U.S. government uses the census, or official count of all the people living in the country. When new census data is collected, sometimes district boundaries must be redrawn to reflect changes in population size and distribution. This process is known as *redistricting*, and it ensures that each person's vote receives equal weight in government.

1. **Human Systems** What issues might have prompted the Supreme Court's ruling in the 1960s to establish the "one person, one vote" requirement?

How are electoral districts drawn?

Apportionment is the process used to decide how many representatives each state will have to represent it in the U.S. Congress. Census data is used to determine how many representatives each state will have. After the number of representatives for each state is determined, the state congressional districts are drawn so that there is one district for each representative. The government uses U.S. Census data along with geographic information systems (GIS) to create maps that draw district lines in such a way that each district in a state has a roughly equal population. For example, a district with people living fairly spread apart will cover a larger geographic area than a district that is densely populated, such as in urban areas. However, they both can be defined as districts with equal representation. In addition to population size, redistricting takes into account factors such as maintaining city boundaries, preserving boundaries from previous districts, and even avoiding contests between existing representatives.

T

C

2. **Human Systems** What term is used to describe the process the government uses in deciding how many representatives each state will have? What tools are used by the government to help make these decisions?

How does redistricting affect the distribution of political power?

Unfortunately, the process of redistricting is not perfect. This creates an opportunity for misuse by those who seek to manipulate the outcome of elections to favor particular candidates. *Gerrymandering* is a term used to describe the act of drawing political district boundary lines in such a way that one party or candidate has an advantage over another. *Packing* and *cracking* are methods of gerrymandering used to minimize the power of a particular group of voters. Packing concentrates members of a group in a single district, which helps the opposing party win other districts that are nearby. Cracking splits the voters among multiple districts, which dilutes their impact and prevents them from being a majority when they vote in the elections. Packing and cracking are commonly used together in such a way that they influence voting.

R

3. **Places and Regions** According to the maps, which districts would be significantly changed by the Ohio Republicans' plan? Which would remain the same?

THERE'S MORE ONLINE

READ about the effect of the census on redistricting • *WATCH* a video about the redistricting process

T Technology Skills

Change and Continuity of Groups Remind students that many things can affect population distribution in a community or region. Assign each small group of students to a state in the United States. Have them use the Internet to research a state's population numbers over the last two to four censuses. Students should identify where population numbers have remained the same and where they have changed within the state, as well as identify possible reasons for any changes in population that have affected a shift in political power. Have groups create a slide show to present their findings to the class. **BL Technological, Visual/Spatial**

C Critical Thinking Skills

Comparing Help students make comparisons between reasons for redistricting in Ohio with their own experiences. Explain that manufacturing jobs in Ohio are harder to get than they were in the past; therefore, many Ohio cities had a decrease in population because people moved to find employment. Have students supply examples of other United States cities throughout history that are less populated now than they were in the past, and supply the reasons for the decrease. *(Possible answers: Detroit: loss of automobile manufacturing; New Orleans: after Hurricane Katrina; Nevada City, CA: after the gold rush)* **AL Verbal/Linguistic**

R Reading Skills

Summarizing Allow time for students to reread the section. **Ask: How does gerrymandering provide an unfair advantage?** *(Political boundary lines are drawn in a way that a voting advantage goes to just one candidate or party.)* **Explain two possible methods of gerrymandering.** *(Packing and cracking; packing is placing voting members of a group into one district; cracking is splitting up members of a group into several districts)* **What would a fair redistricting map look like?** *(A fair redistricting map ensures that the people elected accurately represent the various groups in the area.)* **Verbal/Linguistic**

GAME

How Geographers Look at the World

Defining Tell students that understanding vocabulary is a key factor when reading textbooks. Divide the class into pairs of students. Provide each pair a set of vocabulary flashcards. Have one partner show and read the vocabulary word, as the other partner defines the word. Then have partners switch roles. Continue the activity until all students have successfully defined the vocabulary words. If pairs finish early, have them use a dictionary or a thesaurus to look up a synonym for each vocabulary word. **ELL Verbal/Linguistic**

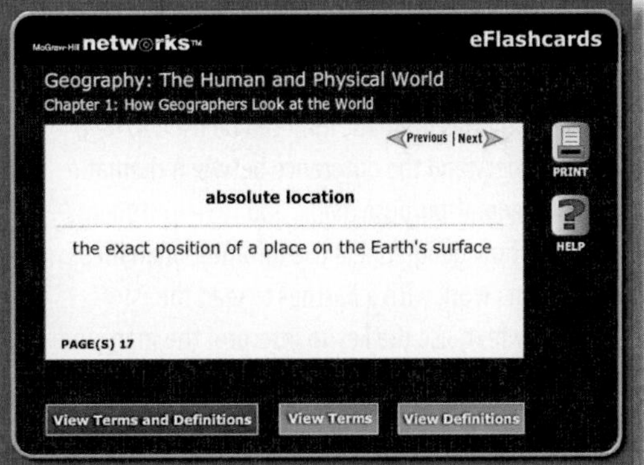

CLOSE & REFLECT

Inferring In a class discussion, have students review ways that maps can show political power.

ANSWERS, p. 13

Why Geography Matters

1. Redistricting issues might have prompted this ruling.
2. The term *apportionment* is used to decide how many representatives states will have. The tools to make these decisions are U.S. Census data and geographic information.
3. Districts 17 and 18 would be eliminated. Districts 3, 10, 13, and 15 would move locations and change in size. Districts 2, 8, and 14 would remain the same.

The Geographer's Tools

ENGAGE

V Visual Skills

Creating Visuals Have students use their mental map to sketch a map of the area around the school. Have students compare their maps with a partner. After determining the accuracy of their maps, have the student pairs evaluate how their maps might help or confuse a new student who has never been to the school. As a class, discuss the value of accuracy in cartography and explain that the world's first explorers often set out with maps that were incomplete or inaccurate.

TEACH & ASSESS

R Reading Skills

Determining Word Meanings Invite a student volunteer to read the *It Matters Because* section out loud. Tell students that many important academic and content vocabulary words will be included throughout each lesson. Content vocabulary words are boldfaced and highlighted, while the academic vocabulary words are only boldfaced. The meanings of these terms will be given in the narrative and the margin. Have students begin a vocabulary list in their notebooks by starting with the word *geography.* As a class, discuss what is included in the study of *geography.* Have students write their own definitions to explain the word. Remind students to add words to their lists as they encounter new or challenging vocabulary. ELL Verbal/Linguistic

C Critical Thinking Skills

Simulating Provide a student volunteer with a string and a globe. Have the volunteer stretch a piece of string around the globe from Mexico City to Cairo. Explain that the string forms an arc that is known as the *great circle route.* **Ask: Why does a globe present the most accurate scale model of the Earth?** *(The Earth is round; therefore a globe, which is also round, most accurately depicts geographical information of Earth, such as distance.)* Kinesthetic

ANSWERS, p. 14

TAKING NOTES: Graphic organizers should show knowledge of the tools geographers use: globes and map projections–conic, cylindrical, planar; determining location–absolute and relative location; using maps–thematic, political, and physical maps; geospatial technologies–GPS and GIS

networks

There's More Online!

- **IMAGE** Mental Map
- **IMAGE** Satellite Image of Earth
- **MAP** Common Map Projections
- **MAP** GIS Layers
- **MAP** Great Circle Routes
- **MAP** Latitude and Longitude
- **INTERACTIVE SELF-CHECK QUIZ**
- **VIDEO** The Geographer's Tools

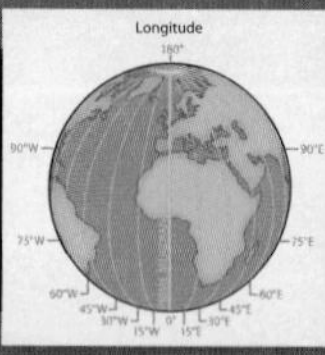

LESSON 1
V The Geographer's Tools

ESSENTIAL QUESTION • *How does geography help us interpret the past, understand the present, and plan for the future?*

Reading HELPDESK CCSS

Academic Vocabulary (Tier Two Words)
- **internal**
- **transmit**

Content Vocabulary (Tier Three Words)
- **great circle route**
- **map projection**
- **planar projection**
- **cylindrical projection**
- **conic projection**
- **absolute location**
- **relative location**
- **elevation**
- **relief**
- **thematic map**
- **global positioning system (GPS)**
- **geographic information systems (GIS)**
- **remote sensing**

TAKING NOTES: ***Key Ideas and Details***

IDENTIFYING As you read the lesson, use a graphic organizer like the one below to identify the tools geographers use to look at the world.

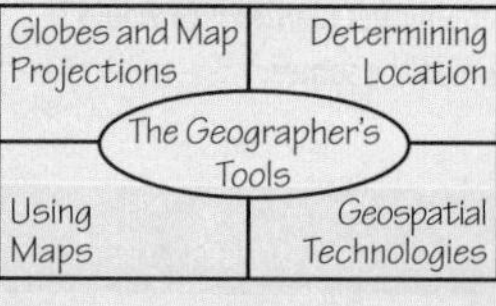

R IT MATTERS BECAUSE

The study of geography involves looking at every aspect of the Earth's systems. Aspects such as human economies, societies, and cultures, and plants, animals, climate, and the physical environment affect each other in many ways. Geography analyzes these diverse interactions to learn more about how Earth's systems are interconnected. Geographers gather information from various sources using a variety of tools to study these complex and interrelated Earth systems.

Globes and Map Projections

GUIDING QUESTION *How are globes and map projections related?*

A globe is a scale model of the Earth that depicts properties such as area, distance, and direction. Globes accurately display all these properties because they are round just like the Earth. A map is a flat representation of all or part of the planet. But, unlike globes, maps cannot show all the properties accurately.

Mapmakers, called cartographers, use mathematical formulas to transfer information from the three-dimensional globe to the two-dimensional map. However, when the curves of a globe become straight or only slightly curved lines on a map, distortion occurs in shape, distance, area, or direction.

C A straight line of true direction on a map is not always the shortest distance between two points on Earth. The measured distance between any two points on a flat map will not have the same distance when measured on a round globe. To find the actual shortest distance between any two places, stretch a piece of string around a globe from one point to the other. The string will form an arc that is part of a great circle, an imaginary line that follows the Earth's curvature. **Great circle routes** therefore mark the shortest distance that an object can travel between two points. They are useful because they indicate actual distances between two locations. Determining a great circle route is important for travel and transportation. Ship captains and airplane pilots use great circle routes to reduce travel time and conserve fuel.

14

networks ***Online Teaching Options***

INTERACTIVE BELLRINGER

Interpreting a Thematic Map

Interpreting This thematic map can be used to help students understand the difference between thematic maps and general-purpose maps, and to help students understand how geographers use information in maps. Have students work with a partner to read the introductory text, use the key to interpret the map, and answer the questions. Then ask pairs to discuss reasons why so many countries in Africa may have problems accessing safe drinking water. AL Interpersonal

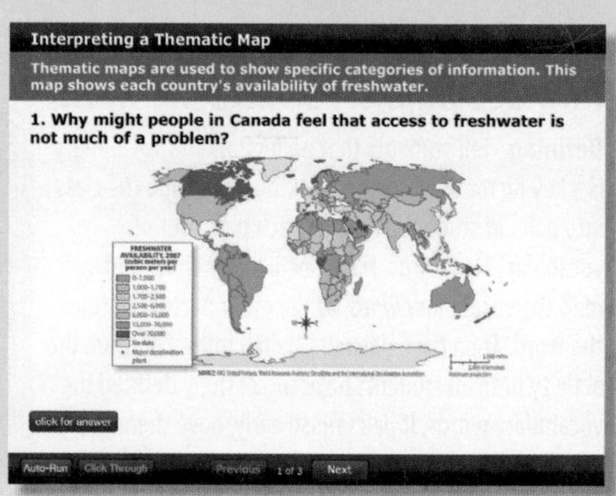

While globes are useful for portraying the entire Earth, their ability to display detailed features of a particular region are limited. Maps, however, are useful for showing more in-depth information. Cartographers convert the three-dimensional globe image onto a flat map by creating a **map projection**. But because map projections can distort one or more of the properties of size, shape, distance, area, or direction, the cartographer must choose the projection to use based on the purpose of the map. It is important to know which properties are distorted, and how much they are distorted, so you can use and interpret the map accurately.

There are many kinds of map projections, some with general names and some named after the cartographer who developed them. Three major categories of map projections are planar, cylindrical, and conic.

A **planar projection**, also known as an azimuthal projection, shows the Earth centered in such a way that a straight line coming from the center to any other point represents the shortest distance. Because a planar projection is most accurately represented from its center, it is often used for maps of the Poles.

A **cylindrical projection** is based on how a map would look if the globe was projected onto a cylinder. This type of projection is most accurate at the Equator because shapes and distances are increasingly distorted when moving away from the Equator and toward the Poles. A Mercator projection is a common example of a cylindrical projection. Because it displays true direction, a Mercator projection is useful for sea navigation.

A **conic projection** is the Earth's surface projected onto a map formed into a cone. Shape is relatively accurate on such projections, and straight lines drawn on them approximate great circle routes if distances are not great.

World maps used for general reference use the Winkel Tripel projection. This map projection cannot be used to determine precise distances, sizes, or shapes of specific global features. It does, however, provide a good balance between the overall size and shape of land areas shown.

A Robinson projection looks similar to a Winkel Tripel projection, although its east-west projections run in a straight line. The Robinson projection produces minor distortions, particularly in the polar areas that appear flattened on the map. The sizes and shapes near the eastern and western edges of the map are accurate, and outlines of the continents appear much as they do on the three-dimensional globe.

great circle route an imaginary line that follows the curve of the Earth and represents the shortest distance between two points

map projection a mathematical formula used to represent the curved surface of the Earth on the flat surface of a map

planar projection a map created by projecting an image of the Earth onto a geometric plane

cylindrical projection a map created by projecting Earth's image onto a cylinder

conic projection a map created by projecting an image of Earth onto a cone placed over part of an Earth model

V

T

Great Circle Routes

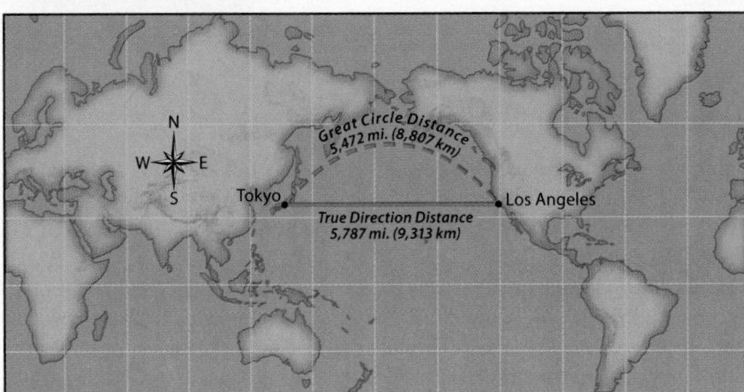

GEOGRAPHY CONNECTION

Great circle routes show the true distance between two places on Earth.

1. *THE USES OF GEOGRAPHY* Why do ship captains and airline pilots use great circle routes?
2. *THE WORLD IN SPATIAL TERMS* Why do distances appear longer on maps than on globes?

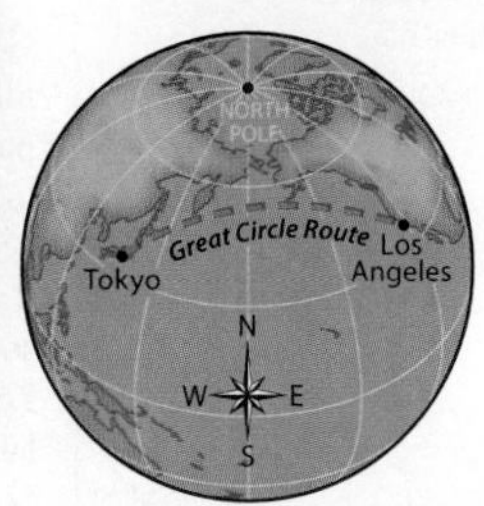

The Geographer's Tools

V Visual Skills

Creating Charts After reading about the different types of map projections, have students think about how each is like or different from a globe. Tell students that because Earth is a three-dimensional object, it is impossible to represent it in a two-dimensional format (called a projection) without some distortion. Yet geographers still find projections useful for various reasons. Have students make a chart listing the three main categories of projections along with their uses and distortions. **Visual/Spatial**

Projection	Uses	Distortions
Planar	greatest accuracy at its center	good for maps of the North and South Poles
Cylindrical	most accurate at the Equator and toward the Poles	useful for sea navigation
Conic	relatively accurate	straight lines approximate shorter great circle routes

T Technology Skills

Identifying Continuity and Change Explain to students that changes have occurred to the maps of the world over time. Divide students into small groups. Have groups use the Internet to find historic maps of a country of their choice. Have students print out or download the maps and prepare presentations to discuss how the maps of the countries have changed by comparing and contrasting the historic map to modern maps. Students may find that political events have altered country boundaries, small towns have become metropolitan areas, and technology has enabled more detailed or accurate representation of physical features. Have groups create a visual display that lists the map changes for the country they chose.
BL **Visual/Spatial, Interpersonal**

VIDEO

Mercator Map

Discussing Use this video about the Mercator map to introduce students to mapmaking. As they view the video, have students consider how the appearance of the Mercator map affected the way people thought about the world during the earlier time periods. Lead a class discussion on why the Mercator map was necessary and how the map changed the world. Further discuss how modern technologies used today in mapmaking have changed how we see the world.
Verbal/Linguistic

ANSWERS, p. 15

GEOGRAPHY CONNECTION

1. They are useful because they indicate actual distances between two locations.
2. A map is a flat representation. When the curves of a globe become straight or only slightly curved lines on a map, distortion occurs in distance.

C Critical Thinking Skills

Analyzing Have students work in pairs to analyze the four types of common map projections by creating three Venn Diagrams that identify the similarities and differences between the Winkel Tripel and Robinson projections, the Winkel Tripel and Mercator projections, and the Winkel Tripel and Goode's Interrupted Equal-Area projections. Allow time for partners to complete their diagrams. **Ask:** **Why do you think general reference world maps use the Winkel Tripel projection?** *(This map projection provides a good overall balance between the size and shape of the land areas shown.)* AL **Visual/Spatial**

Content Background Knowledge

Determining Location for Early Maritime Explorers

- The Chinese invented the compass around A.D. 1100. In the 1400s, a magnetic needle made measurements more accurate.
- A popular device used during the late fifteenth and early sixteenth centuries to determine latitude, longitude, and time of day by sailors was the astrolabe. It measured the altitude of the sun or the North Star above the horizon, and then sailors used related charts for calculations.
- Until the nineteenth century, mariners were also using hourglasses as timepieces to determine longitude.

T Technology Skills

Examining Have students work in small groups to use the Internet or library maps to locate the Grand Canyon, Niagara Falls, the Great Wall of China, Machu Picchu, Taj Mahal, and Stonehenge. Assign each group to one of the places. Have groups present multimedia presentations that include the exact location and show the map location, as well as satellite or other images to present to the class. **Visual/Spatial**

ANSWERS, p. 16

✓ **READING PROGRESS CHECK** The map is a flat representation and distorts distance. To travel the shortest distance, pilots and ship captains use great circle routes.

GEOGRAPHY CONNECTION

1. Conic projections form Earth's surface into a cone; shape is relatively accurate and straight lines drawn on them approximate great circle routes for short distances. The Robinson Projection produces minor distortions and outlines of continents appear much as they do on a globe. Goode's Interrupted Equal-Area projection resembles a globe cut apart and laid flat. It shows the true size and shape of Earth's landmasses, but distances are generally distorted. The Robinson Projection represents the best compromise.
2. Because it displays true direction, a Mercator projection is useful for sea navigation.

Common Map Projections

C

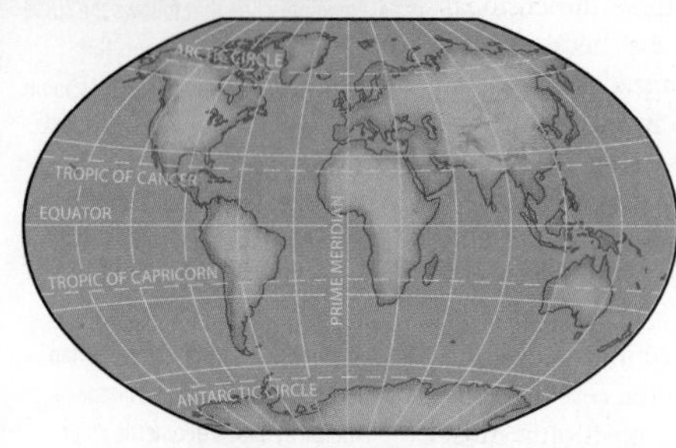

Winkel Tripel Projection

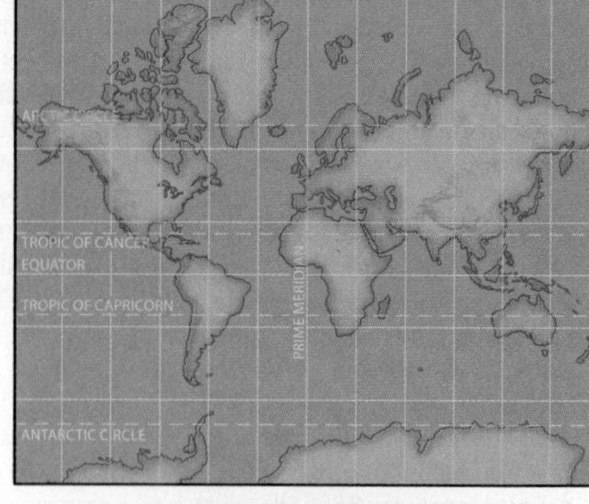

Mercator Projection

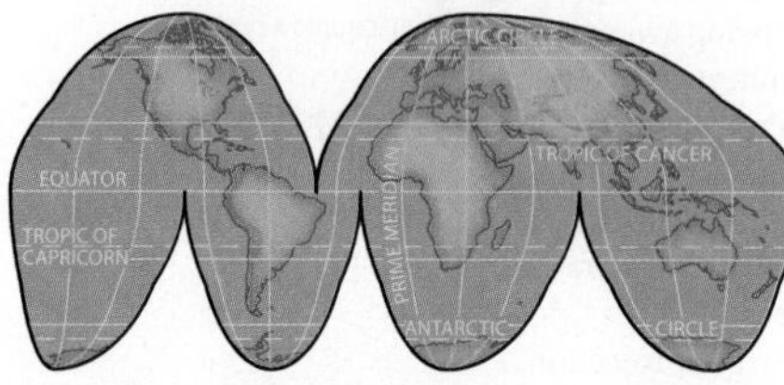

Goode's Interrupted Equal-Area Projection

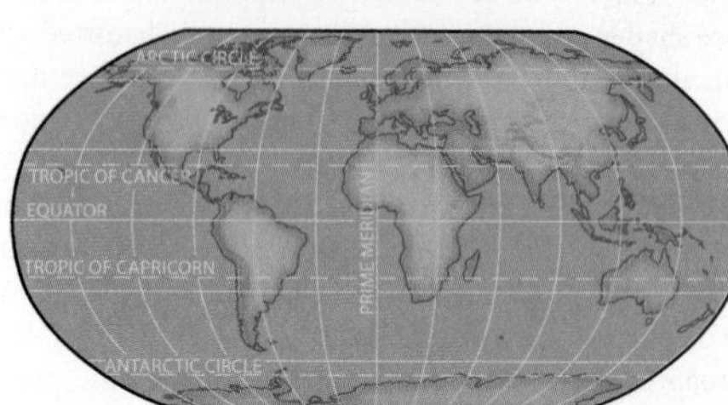

Robinson Projection

GEOGRAPHY CONNECTION

Each type of map projection has its advantages as well as some degree of inaccuracy. In addition to the major categories of map projections—planar, cylindrical, and conic—many other map projections can be used depending on the information the mapmaker wishes to show.

1. ***THE WORLD IN SPATIAL TERMS*** Which projection appears to have the least amount of distortion of distances and size of landmasses?
2. ***THE USES OF GEOGRAPHY*** Which projection is preferred for sea navigation? Why?

Goode's Interrupted Equal-Area projection resembles a globe that has been cut apart and laid flat. The process of creating this *interrupted projection* can be compared to slicing an orange peel in order to lay it flat on a page. Although this projection shows the true size and shape of Earth's landmasses, distances between land features are generally distorted.

✓ **READING PROGRESS CHECK**

Explaining Why is a trip from Tokyo to Los Angeles a longer distance than it appears to be on a map?

Determining Location

GUIDING QUESTION *How is location determined?*

Geography addresses the question of *where.* To answer this question, a geographer identifies a location. Both globes and maps use a grid system in order to form a pattern of lines that cross one another. These patterns are used to help find the location of places on the Earth's surface.

T

Lines of latitude, or parallels, circle the Earth parallel to the Equator. Although they run in an east-to-west direction, they measure distance to the north and south of the Equator. The measurements are in degrees. Parallels north of the Equator are called north latitude. Parallels south of the Equator are called south latitude. The Equator is defined as 0° latitude, the North Pole as 90° N, and the South Pole as 90° S.

networks Online Teaching Options

INTERACTIVE MAP

Common Map Projections

Considering Advantages and Disadvantages This interactive map shows several common map projections and how they are created by projecting a globe onto a flat surface. Review that each of these maps has its advantages as well as some disadvantages. Have students imagine that they are going to take a trip to a location of their choosing. Ask them to write a paragraph explaining which of these maps they will use to navigate to their chosen destination. Students should include the advantages of using this map on their journey. BL **Visual/Spatial**

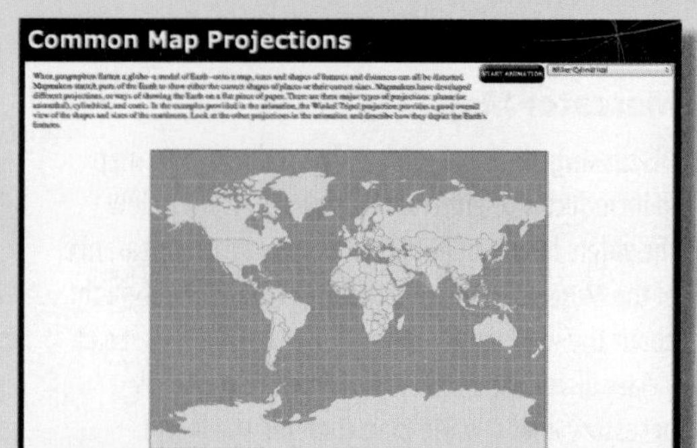

Longitude lines, also called meridians, are lines that connect the North and South Poles. They run in a north-to-south direction, but they measure distance east and west of the Prime Meridian, which is identified as 0° longitude. Meridians run perpendicular to the lines of latitude, and they also use the measurement of degrees. Meridian lines located east of the Prime Meridian are identified as east longitude, and lines located west are known as west longitude. The longitude line located 180° from the Prime Meridian, on the opposite side of the Earth, is called the International Date Line. R

The Equator divides the Earth in half, creating Northern and Southern Hemispheres. The Northern Hemisphere includes any location north of the Equator up to 90° N, while the Southern Hemisphere includes any location south of the Equator up to 90° S. Just as the Equator splits the Earth into Northern and Southern Hemispheres, the Prime Meridian and International Date Line split the globe into east and west halves. Locations east of the Prime Meridian are identified as part of the Eastern Hemisphere, and locations west of the Prime Meridian as part of the Western Hemisphere. All points on Earth are located in two of the four hemispheres: north or south and east or west.

An **absolute location** is an exact global address derived from the latitude and longitude lines that intersect at that place. For example, Tokyo, Japan, is located at approximately 36° N latitude and 140° E longitude. For a more precise reading of a location, a degree is divided into 60 minutes ('). Each minute is then divided into 60 seconds (") just as hours and minutes on a clock are divided to provide a more exact time. For example, the absolute location of the famous Tokyo Tower is 35°39′30.96″ N latitude and 139°44′43.59″ E longitude. T

absolute location the exact position of a place on the Earth's surface

While absolute location identifies exact points using latitude and longitude, **relative location** uses a reference point to identify one place in relation to another. To find relative location, find a reference point—a location you already know—on a map. Then look in the appropriate direction for the new location. For example, locate the city of Paris on the map of France and use this as your reference point. The relative location of the city of Lyon can be described as southeast of Paris.

relative location location in relation to other places

✓ READING PROGRESS CHECK

Listing List the four hemispheres of the Earth.

GEOGRAPHY CONNECTION

Lines of latitude and longitude create a grid system on Earth's surface.

1. ***THE WORLD IN SPATIAL TERMS*** Which lines of latitude and longitude divide the Earth into hemispheres?
2. ***THE USES OF GEOGRAPHY*** How are latitude and longitude used to determine absolute location?

Latitude and Longitude

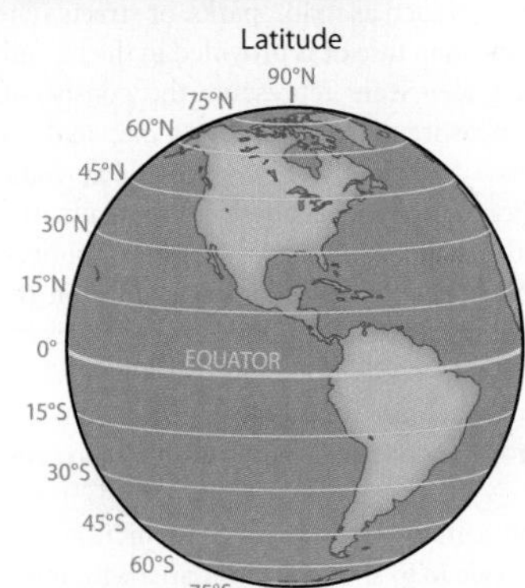

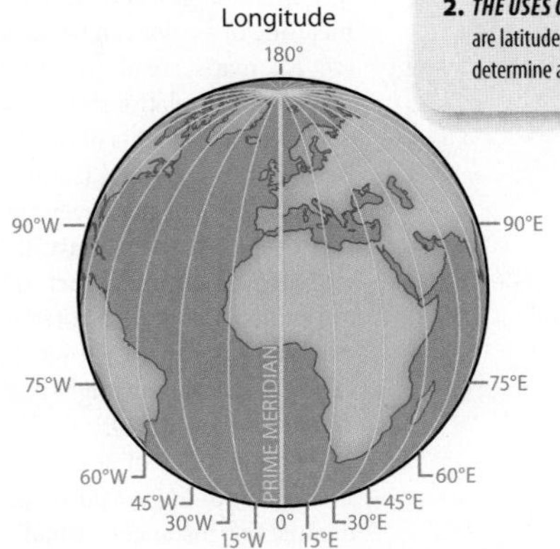

INTERACTIVE MAP

Latitude and Longitude

Locating Divide the class into small groups. Have groups click the entries showing the latitude, longitude, and global grids on these interactive maps. Allow time for groups to become familiar with the lines indicating the Prime Meridian, Equator, and the degree lines. Then have each group identify the latitude and longitude lines that an assigned continent is located within. **Logical/Mathematical**

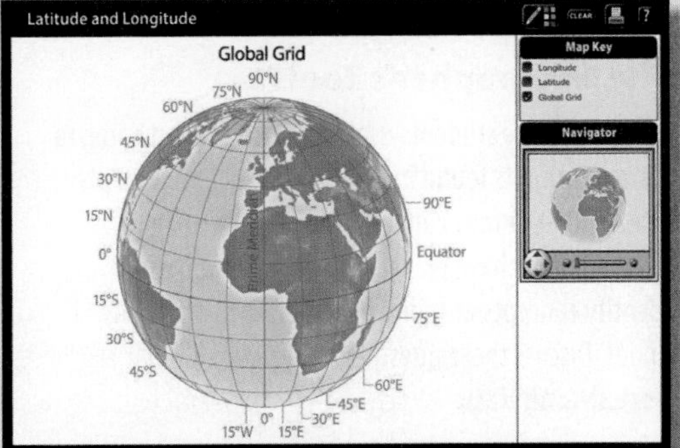

The Geographer's Tools

R Reading Skills

Using Context Clues Have students use context clues to find the meaning of words. **Ask:** **How does the definition of meridian help you understand what the Prime Meridian is?** *(Student answers may vary, but should include relevant details such as meridians are lines,* prime *means first or starting point, and the Prime Meridian is defined as 0° longitude.)*

ELL **Verbal/Linguistic**

Content Background Knowledge

Pinpointing the Prime Meridian Pedro Reinel, a Portuguese mapmaker, drew the first starting point of longitude, known as the Prime Meridian, on a nautical map in 1506. He used the Portuguese Madeira Islands as the reference point for his Prime Meridian. However, the Spanish then began to use the Canary Islands as the Prime Meridian on their maps. During the early 1800s, the English, who dominated most of the naval expeditions at the time, used the site of the Royal Observatory as the Prime Meridian. Finally in 1884, during a conference held in Washington, D.C., the placement of the Prime Meridian was determined to be in Greenwich, England. This line continues to serve as a reference point that measures internationally standardized time. However, even today, more than a dozen countries, including Austria, Norway, Switzerland, and Indonesia, do not recognize Greenwich, England, as 0° longitude, or the Prime Meridian of the world.

T Technology Skills

Applying Working alone or in pairs, have students use the Internet to identify some popular landmarks using absolute location with the following sets of coordinates.

- 40.6893° N, 74.0446° W *(Statue of Liberty, Liberty Island, New York)*
- 41.8902° N, 12.4923° E *(Roman Colosseum, Rome, Italy)*
- 51.5081° N, 0.0878° W *(London Bridge, London, England)*
- 29.9792° N, 31.1342° E *(Great Pyramid of Giza, Egypt)*

Logical/Mathematical

ANSWERS, p. 17

✓ READING PROGRESS CHECK The hemispheres are Northern, Southern, Eastern, and Western.

GEOGRAPHY CONNECTION

1. The Equator, Prime Meridian, and International Date Line divide Earth into hemispheres.
2. An absolute location is an exact global address derived from the latitude and longitude lines that intersect at that place.

The Geographer's Tools

R Reading Skills

Taking Notes After students have read about the various parts of a map—legend (key), compass rose, line symbols, colors, and scale—have them create a graphic organizer that includes a brief written explanation of each map part. *(Legend or key: explains the meaning of the map's symbols; Compass rose: indicates direction; Line symbols: features of human activity like boundaries, roads, and trade routes, and physical features like rivers, faults, shorelines; Colors: elements like elevation, water features, and land features; Scale: shows proportional relationships between map measurements and actual distance)* Have students share their graphic organizers with a partner to discuss the accuracy of each other's work. Answer any questions or concerns that students may have about map features. ELL Verbal/Linguistic

Making Connections

Explain to students that it is believed that the Chinese were the first culture to use compasses for sea navigation, around A.D. 1100. Prior to using it for navigational purposes, the Chinese used the magnetic properties of compasses for spiritual orienteering when practicing the design art of feng shui. This early invention has led to many modern-day location devices.

C Critical Thinking Skills

Gathering Information Students who have used hand-held compasses may also be familiar with the compass rose. Have a student explain what a compass is and how it works. Invite a small group of volunteers to use the Internet or library resources to determine when, by whom, and for what purposes others have used compasses since the Chinese in A.D. 1100. Have the group of student volunteers share their findings with the class.
BL Interpersonal

ANSWERS, p. 18

Connecting Geography Cartographers use mathematics to calculate the area of a landmass, volume of a body of water, and distance between locations.

Connecting Geography to MATH

Mapmaking

Mathematics plays an integral role in the study of geography, especially the process of projecting Earth's spherical features onto a flat map. Early cartographers hand-calculated their map projections using geometry, trigonometry, and even calculus. Today, computer programs take much of the mathematical legwork out of the process of mapmaking. However, geographers still use mathematics for many tasks, such as calculating the area of a landmass, determining the volume of a body of water, and computing distances between locations.

MAKING CONNECTIONS How does mathematics allow cartographers to create flat depictions of a spherical Earth?

elevation the height of a land surface above the level of the sea

Using Maps

GUIDING QUESTION *How do maps work?*

In addition to lines of latitude and longitude, maps include other important tools to help you understand the information they provide. Learning to use map tools will help you interpret the language of maps more easily.

Parts of a Map

The purpose of a map is identified by the map's title. For example, a map titled "Housing Developments in Washington, D.C." would show different details than a map titled "Topography of the Washington, D.C., area." The time period of a map is another important clue to understanding what the map shows. For example, a map titled "Europe Before World War I" would show country borders and national capitals of Europe that are quite different from Europe's current political borders. The map title is the first thing you should look at when reading a map because it provides context for the map's content.

An effective map will provide a legend, or key, to explain the meaning of various symbols used on the map. Geographic features represented on the map are identified by symbols, also called icons. Icons vary by map, depending on the details that are the focus of the map. Roads, highways, railroads, landmarks, parks, and buildings are all human-made features shown by icons. Dots are often used to represent cities. Sometimes the relative sizes of cities are shown using dots of different sizes. Capital cities can be identified by a star within a circle.

C The compass rose indicates direction or orientation of a map. North, east, south, and west are the four cardinal directions. The intermediate directions—northeast, northwest, southeast, and southwest—may also be shown. The compass rose looks like intersecting arrows or points of a star.

R Line symbols on a map emphasize various features of human activity, such as boundary lines, roads, streets, or routes of trade and transportation. On political maps, boundary lines highlight the borders between different countries and states. Line symbols can also represent physical features such as rivers, earthquake faults, and ocean shorelines.

Colors can be used to distinguish elements on a map. For example, a political map might make each country a different color. On a physical map, colors may indicate the various ranges of **elevation,** or the height above sea level. Colors are used for a variety of other purposes, including identifying water features such as oceans, lakes, or rivers; land features such as deserts, valleys, plains, or mountain ranges; and human-made features such as roads, parks, or streets. The meaning of a color can be identified by the map title or is provided in the legend.

All maps are drawn to a certain scale. Scale represents the consistent, proportional relationship between the measurements shown on a map and the actual measurements of the Earth's surface. Maps use scale to shrink what would be large distances and features of a region to a manageable size. When a map is scaled to fit on paper, every feature of the map is scaled by the same amount so that each feature will have the same proportion to every other feature on the map. However, not all parts of a map will be perfectly to scale because flat maps are subject to some distortion. A map's scale is identified by a scale bar, which compares distances shown by a map to actual distances on the Earth. For example, a scale bar might indicate that one inch (2.5 cm) on the map represents 100 miles (160.9 km).

The amount of scale portrayed on a map depends on its depiction as a *small-scale* or *large-scale* map. A small-scale map shows a larger area with fewer details. For instance, a small-scale map can focus on a specific country and its

networks Online Teaching Options

GAME

The Geographer's Tools

Naming Have students use this concentration game to review concepts found in this lesson. Students can play one another or they can form teams of two players. After students have played the game, have them identify concepts or topics that they have questions about. Discuss these questions as a class. AL Verbal/Linguistic

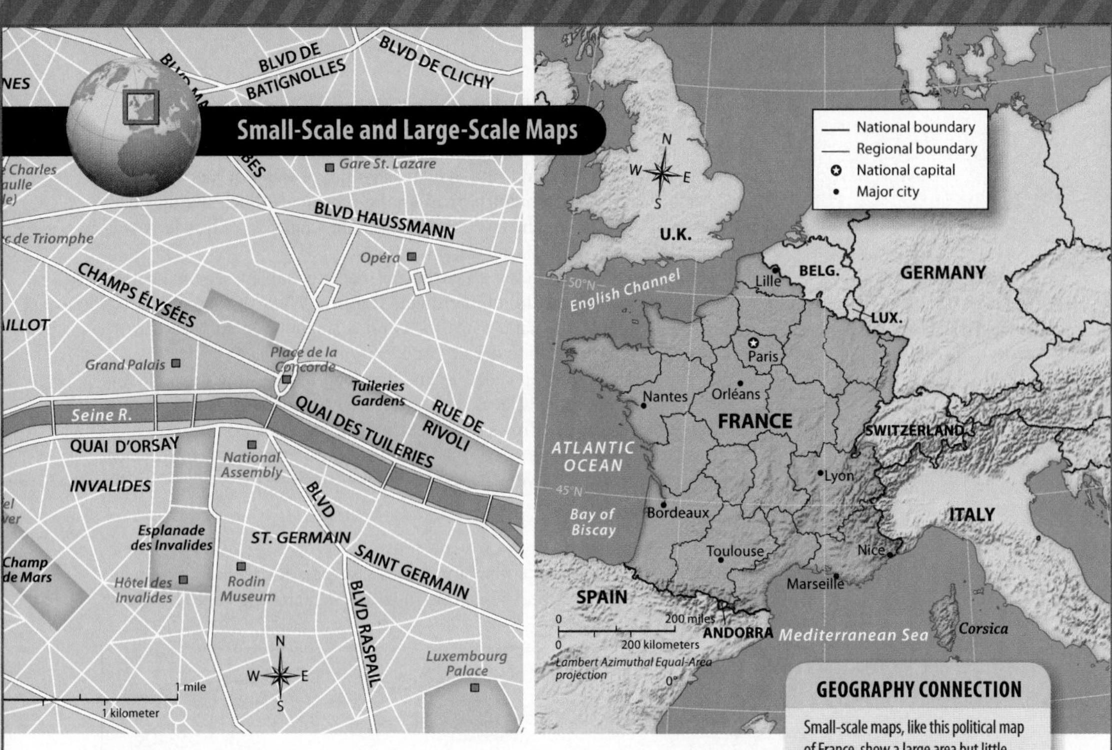

GEOGRAPHY CONNECTION

Small-scale maps, like this political map of France, show a large area but little detail. Large-scale maps, like the map of the city of Paris, can show a small area with a great amount of detail.

1. ***PLACES AND REGIONS*** Using the scale bar on the map of France, what is the distance from Paris to Nice in miles?
2. ***HUMAN SYSTEMS*** What types of human-made features does the map of Paris include that the map of France does not?

neighboring countries to show boundary lines, major cities and capitals, important land or water features, or regional topography. For example, the scale bar on a map of France and its bordering countries could show a relationship of one inch (2.5 cm) as equal to 200 miles (321.9 km) in actual distance. On the other hand, a large-scale map can show a small area with a great amount of detail. It narrows in on an identified region to show more specific details. The map measurements of a large-scale map use much smaller distances than on a map of France. For example, a large-scale map of the city of Paris shows the layout of streets, major roads, bridges, parks, and important landmarks such as museums, hotels, and churches. The scale bar of a map of Paris could show a relationship of one inch (2.5 cm) as equal to one mile (1.6 km) in actual distance. This measurement is much more specific than for a small-scale map of France. R1

Types of Maps

A cartographer can choose from several types of maps in order to convey geographic information. Physical maps, political maps, and thematic maps each serve a unique purpose and are suited to showing different types of information. A physical map shows location and topography, or shape, of the Earth's land features. A study of a country's land and other physical features can help to explain the historical development of the country. For example, mountains may be barriers to transportation, and rivers and streams can provide access to a country's interior. Physical maps show water features such as rivers, streams, and lakes. They also show landforms such as mountains, plains, plateaus, and valleys. V

Physical maps highlight general **relief** through shading and texture. Relief shows the differences in elevation between the various landforms of an area. An elevation key can use colors to indicate specific, measured differences in elevation above sea level. R2

relief the variation in elevation across an area of Earth's land

The Geographer's Tools

R1 Reading Skills

Defining Point out that some words have a specialized meaning that is different from their meaning in most other contexts. Have volunteers define *relationship* and *scale* in both geographic and nongeographic terms. Then have students turn to a partner and think of four other multiple-meaning words related to geography. *(Possible answers: feature, capital, projection, poles, direction)* **Verbal/Linguistic**

V Visual Skills

Depicting After reading about the features of physical maps, have students form small groups to draw a physical map of their city or town. Rivers, creeks, and ponds should be marked; if appropriate, encourage students to place symbols for hills, woods, parks, and other physical features on their maps. For larger cities, have students do a subsection or neighborhood of the city. Remind students to scale the map appropriately. Have groups compare their maps with those of other groups. **Visual/Spatial**

R2 Reading Skills

Explaining Have a volunteer read the last paragraph about *relief* to the class. Answer any student questions about the content vocabulary words. **Ask: Would a political map show *relief*? Why or why not?** *(Possible answer: No, maps usually show either human-made features or natural features of an area, but generally not both. Boundaries are human-made features and are shown on political maps. Elevation is a natural feature and is generally shown on physical maps. If maps included both features, it would be difficult to determine relief through shading and texture.)* **ELL Verbal/Linguistic**

INTERACTIVE MAP

Small-Scale and Large-Scale Maps

Calculating Have students work with a partner to analyze the small-scale map and a large-scale map. Have them use the scale bars on each map to calculate the following distances:

- Distance between Paris and Lyon *(about 250 miles)*
- Distance from the Eiffel Tower to Rodin Museum *(about 1 mile)*
- Distance from Blvd De Clichy to the Seine River *(1.75 miles)*
- Distance across France from Spain to Belgium *(about 675 miles)*

After students have finished the activity, discuss the best uses for each type of map. **AL Logical/Mathematical**

ANSWERS, p. 19

GEOGRAPHY CONNECTION

1. The distance from Paris to Nice is approximately 400 miles.
2. The map of Paris shows major roads, bridges, parks, and important landmarks.

The Geographer's Tools

C Critical Thinking Skills

Interpreting To check understanding, begin a discussion about thematic maps. **Ask:** **What types of professions might use a thematic map of an area's natural vegetation?** *(Possible answers: biologists, landscapers, farmers, park rangers)* Explain that most students have seen examples of flow-line maps, such as those used to show weather patterns or the movements of hot and cold fronts during news broadcasts on television. **Ask:** **Who might benefit from a flow-line map of the Arctic glaciers?** *(Possible answers: environmentalists that track the melting or movement of glaciers; shipping companies for navigating through the Arctic Ocean)* **Verbal/Linguistic**

W Writing Skills

Informative/Expository To ensure that students understand the importance of the concept *mentally organizing spatial information,* have students write out detailed directions to a relative's house that is at least ten miles away from their home. When they have finished writing, have students exchange directions with a partner. Have the other student draw a map using their partner's written directions. Do not allow students to communicate while they are drawing. After the maps have been completed, have both students compare and discuss their written directions with the drawn maps. **Ask:**

- **Which part of this activity was easier to complete, writing or drawing directions?** *(Student answers may vary, but should discuss solid reasoning for one direction type.)*
- **What types of difficulties arise when writing directions?** *(Student answers may vary, but should include specific difficulties of writing detailed directions that someone else can understand.)*
- **What types of difficulties arise when drawing directions on a map?** *(Student answers may vary, but should include specific difficulties of drawing a map which includes detailed directions that someone else can understand.)*
- **Why is it important to organize spatial information when creating a mental map?** *(Possible answer: spatial information must be organized in order to provide the correct directions, distances, and physical features often included on a mental map)* **AL** **Verbal/Linguistic, Interpersonal**

ANSWERS, p. 20

CRITICAL THINKING

1. The person who drew this mental map knows a little about the world. Sizes and perspectives are quite inaccurate, and there is a lack of detail.
2. Most students would believe that their maps would be more detailed since they are learning about world geography and the locations of places.

A political map provides the boundaries and locations of political units such as countries, states, counties, cities, and towns. It can show the networks and links that exist within and between political units. While some boundaries are distinguished by natural features such as bodies of water or landforms, the majority of features on a political map are human-made. Such human-made features can include boundary lines, cities and capitals, railroads, roads, highways, streets, buildings, and other landmarks.

thematic map a map that emphasizes a single idea or a particular kind of information about an area

C A **thematic map** emphasizes a particular theme or subject. Thematic maps can show various natural and human-made features. While a general map can cover various topics, thematic maps focus on a single topic such as climate, natural vegetation, population density, or economic activities.

A type of thematic map called a flow-line map displays the movement of people, animals, goods, and ideas. It also illustrates physical processes such as hurricanes and glaciers. Arrows illustrate the flow and direction of movement for the map subject. Arrows can be distinguished by different colors to represent the varied directions of movement, and the thickness of the arrows can show the amount that is moving.

Mental Maps

W While the diverse parts of a map are crucial elements for identifying a map's purpose, a map reader must also learn how to mentally organize the spatial

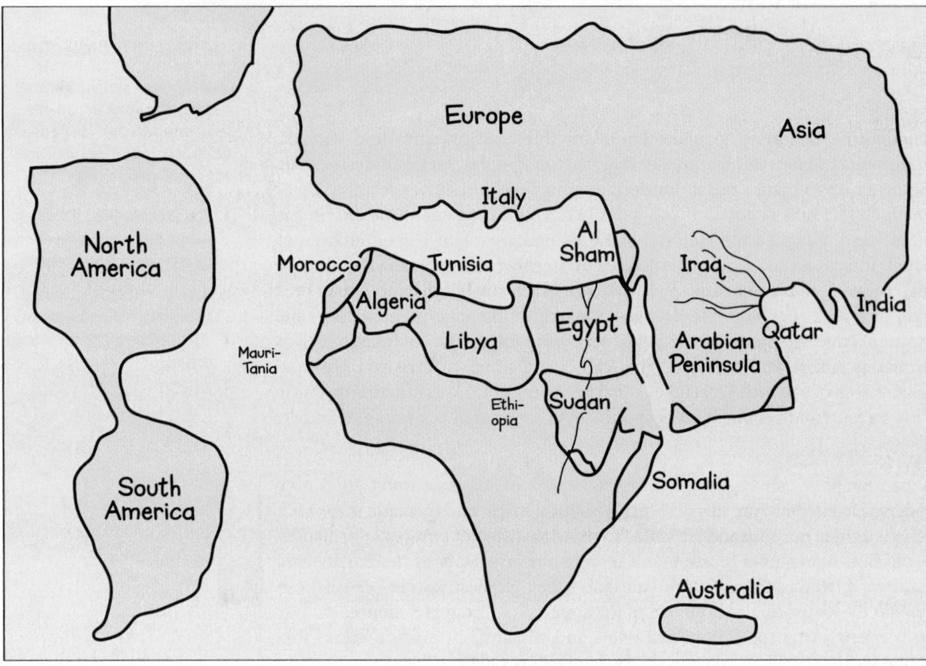

Mental maps reflect a person's personal point of view or perception about a place.

▲ **CRITICAL THINKING**

1. ***Drawing Inferences*** Based on this mental map, do you think the person who created it knows a lot or a little about the world? Explain.
2. ***Hypothesizing*** Do you think your mental map of the world would be more or less detailed than this one? Why?

20

networks Online Teaching Options

INTERACTIVE WHITEBOARD ACTIVITY

Purposes of Maps

Identifying Students may be exposed to concepts, ideas, and terminology that they have little familiarity with in this geography course. It is important to understand how well students can read the text and properly comprehend the content. As a class, complete this interactive whiteboard activity on the purposes of maps. Have students identify the different types of information that physical, political, and thematic maps contain. Discuss any incorrect answers or questions that arise during the activity. **ELL** **Visual/Spatial, Kinesthetic**

Purposes of Maps

Directions: Physical maps, political maps, and thematic maps each show different types of information. Drag each type of information listed below to the appropriate column of the chart.

Physical Map	Political Map	Thematic Map

climate · differences in elevation · roads and highways · human-made boundaries · population density · mountains, plains, valleys · shape of land features · cities and capitals · economic activities information emphasized by a map. Mental maps provide an effective method for answering and remembering important geographical questions about locations, characteristics, patterns, and relationships of places and regions. Mental maps describe an individual's **internal** map—his or her perception of features of the Earth's surface. Mental maps can be applied to local or global scales, from the orientation of an individual within a classroom or home, to the visualization one could see from an airplane on a transcontinental flight.

internal existing or lying within

A person's mental map helps geographers understand how individuals view their relationship to the space around them. Mental maps mix precise, objective data with an individual's subjective perception or existing knowledge of places. For example, a student may be asked to memorize locations and names of the original 13 colonies to contextualize his or her experience and understanding of those places today. A biologist's mental map of major climate regions could include his or her knowledge of the distribution of various types of animals and plants within each region. Using mental maps of the world's regions over time allows a geographer to analyze patterns of human settlement in the world and how settlements relate to land features and availability of resources. This information can be used to determine why particular routes of settlement, trade, and transportation developed. R1

Mental maps can change according to an individual's experience and perception of people, places, regions, and environments. Because mental mapping is based on the individual, one individual's memory of a place differs from another individual's memory. A new experience in an unfamiliar location would alter the accuracy and number of details recalled by a person's mental map of that place. For example, traveling through a country would help a person more easily recall city names and locations of that country than by memorizing such places by only looking at a map. The pictures of two students asked to sketch from memory their view of the Grand Canyon would vary depending on what features the individuals noticed at the time, as well as how much their memory of the place has changed since they saw the canyon. R2

Recalling a place related to emotion, such as a city that a student likes or dislikes, would also alter the details depicted in a mental map. An individual's personal connection to a place or event through personal experiences or exposure to written and visual accounts can influence what is part of a mental map. As a result, mental mapping is beneficial for geographers to understand the significance of information related to a specific place and how it is perceived by individuals.

✓ READING PROGRESS CHECK

Explaining What do relief maps show?

Geospatial Technologies

GUIDING QUESTION *How are geospatial technologies used to learn about the world?*

Geospatial technologies assist geographers and other professionals in answering geographic questions. Global positioning systems (GPS), geographic information systems (GIS), and remote sensing from satellites and aircraft incorporate multiple information sources to construct detailed geographic representations of specific aspects of the Earth's surface.

Global Positioning System

A **global positioning system (GPS)** is used to determine the exact, or absolute, location of something on Earth. Made up of a network of satellites and receiving instruments, GPS provides an accurate location with respect to latitude,

global positioning system (GPS) a navigational system that can determine absolute location by using satellites and receivers on Earth

The Geographer's Tools

R1 Reading Skills

Paraphrasing Have students reread the paragraph. Instruct them to paraphrase, as they explain how mental maps are useful to different people. Explain that paraphrasing content is a useful tool they can use to check their own reading comprehension. It also is an important part of the research process. Taking notes and paraphrasing sources is an important skill that will be used in projects and reports during the school year. **Ask:** **What is an internal map?** *(A person's perception, or mental map, of the features of the Earth's surface.)*

AL **Verbal/Linguistic**

R2 Reading Skills

Making Connections Have students test their skills in mental mapping. Place a large picture or poster that includes a lot of images on the board or wall before class begins. After students have arrived, remove the image and ask students to list all of the features or details that they can remember about the image. Explain that by recalling the features of the image, they have created their own mental maps. Replace the image and allow students time to read through their lists of details. Discuss how mental maps can change according to an individual's experiences and perceptions. **Ask:** **Why do mental maps vary between individuals?** *(Because each individual's memory varies.)* **What types of things affect individual's mental maps?** *(Possible answers: unfamiliar locations, types of features remembered, emotions, personal connections, personal experiences, exposure to written or visual accounts)* **Why is mental mapping helpful to geographers?** *(Mental mapping helps geographers understand the importance of information about a place and how individuals perceive it.)* **Intrapersonal, Logical/Mathematical**

Content Background Knowledge

Navigating with GPS Navigating by triangulating began with using stars, but this was of limited precision and required clear weather. In the twentieth century, radio-based navigation systems were pioneered. They worked the way GPS systems do, but their range was generally quite limited, and they were not nearly as precise. The first satellite system, Transit, became operational in 1964. It took a receiver 15 minutes to calculate its position using Transit. It wasn't until 1993 that the 24th GPS satellite was launched, though since then numerous additional types of satellites have been launched which are used for reporting, navigating, and transmitting data back to Earth. Remind students that technology is rapidly improving and changing.

INTERACTIVE WEB SITE

How Did We Get Here?

Outlining This article discusses mobile mapping technology advances found on smart phones and mobiles devices. Allow time for students to read the article content, either online or by reproducing the article content. Ask students to outline the content found in each section and to answer the questions in the *Dig Deeper* section. Then have students discuss their outlines and answers with another student.

ELL **Verbal/Linguistic**

ANSWERS, p. 21

✓ READING PROGRESS CHECK A relief map shows the variation in elevation across an area of Earth's land.

The Geographer's Tools

V Visual Skills

Creating Charts Point out the map and caption found below the photo. Explain that this photo was taken along the coast in Florida, as indicated on the map, and that various animals, such as this sea turtle, are tracked using GPS technology. Assign small groups various regions around the world. Ask each group to research and compile a list of endangered animals within their region that are currently being tracked using GPS technology. Have each group create a chart to display its findings. Then invite groups to explain and present the information in their charts to the class. **Visual/Spatial, Verbal/Linguistic**

W Writing Skills

Argument Many cell phone companies offer GPS apps that parents can install on their children's smart phones. The apps allow parents to track the location of their children's cell phones, and thereby the location of their children, as well. Civil rights advocates argue that this is an invasion of privacy, but those in public safety think this may help locate missing children. Knowing where children are at all times may also prevent them from getting into dangerous situations. Have students work in teams to develop debate arguments for and against these types of location apps. Teams may want to conduct research to develop their statements. Set up a mock debate forum, with teams alternating presentations of their arguments. Assign a panel of three students to judge the debate. **BL Interpersonal**

ANSWERS, p. 22

CRITICAL THINKING

1. The location information provided by GPS allows wildlife biologists to determine if there is food available and if it is an area where the possibility of human interaction could pose a threat to the elephants.
2. The military, shipping industries, emergency services, and seismologists all use GPS.

Biologists use GPS technology to track the movement and behavior of animals in the wild.

▲ CRITICAL THINKING

1. ***Drawing Conclusions*** How might wildlife biologists use GPS technology to protect endangered species such as the African elephant?
2. ***Classifying*** What other fields use GPS technology to gather information?

longitude, and even altitude. GPS technology in the United States relies on a system of 24 satellites that make 6 full orbits around the Earth every 12 hours. The European Union, as well as some individual countries such as Russia and China, have their own satellites that support GPS systems.

The satellites in all these systems send out radio signals that are picked up by GPS receivers on Earth. In a process called triangulation, a GPS receiver measures the precise time taken for radio signals from four or more satellites to travel to the receiver. The receiver then multiplies the time by the speed of a radio wave to calculate the distance between it and the satellite. When signals from the four or more satellites are processed in the same manner, the receiver's built-in computer determines the point at which at least four satellite signals intersect on the Earth. This intersection then identifies the receiver's latitude, longitude, and altitude. The more satellites that are used, the more accurate the location that is pinpointed.

GPS technology serves a commercial purpose for military machinery, space shuttles, aircraft, ships, submarines, trucks, trains, and ambulance fleets. Yet it can also aid in multiple forms of personal navigation. The GPS receiver in a car, for example, tracks the car's changing location on an electronic map to provide constantly updated directions based on where the car is located and where it is headed. Many current GPS receivers are battery-powered and are no larger than the palm of your hand, while GPS computer chips are smaller than your fingernail.

Many fields of science employ GPS technology. For example, seismologists, the scientists who study earthquakes, can use GPS to determine the size of earthquakes. Scientists first plant GPS receivers in the ground in regions vulnerable to tectonic, or earthquake-prone, activity. Once an earthquake hits,

networks Online Teaching Options

INTERACTIVE GRAPHIC ORGANIZER

Geographer's Tools

Monitoring This interactive graphic organizer allows students to review the vocabulary, key concepts, and learning objectives covered in the chapter. Students will fill out the graphic organizer as they read the lesson to identify the tools geographers use to look at the world. The organizer should include the headings: Globe and Map Projections, Determining Location, Using Maps, and Geospatial Technologies. Key ideas and details should be listed under each of the headings.

AL Visual/Spatial

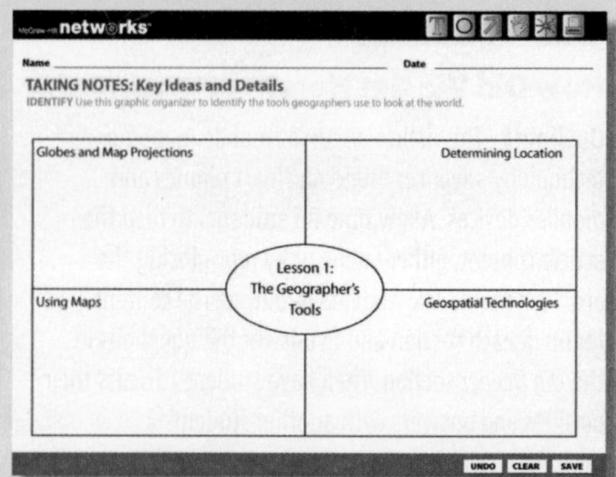

seismologists can quickly measure the strength of an earthquake by calculating how far the planted GPS receivers move. This measurement allows scientists to predict how likely the earthquake is to produce large ocean waves called tsunamis. Because tsunamis can cause devastating destruction to coastal communities, early warning would diminish loss of human life by advising people to flee as soon as possible.

T

Another function of GPS technology in the field of science is to track the migration of animals to determine any changing patterns within the animals' ecosystems. Biologists tag animals with GPS receivers so they can track their movement due to seasonal changes, changes of food or shelter, or threats to their habitat by human activity or by other animals.

Geographic Information Systems

Advances in technology have changed the way maps are made. An important tool in mapmaking today involves computers with software programs called **geographic information systems (GIS)**. But more than simply making maps, GIS can be used to perform advanced geographical analysis.

geographic information systems (GIS) computer programs that process and organize details about places on Earth and integrate those details with satellite images and other pieces of information

Many types of data can be entered into a GIS. These data come from a wide variety of sources such as maps, satellite images, printed text, and statistical databases. The primary and most important function of a GIS, however, is to link the location of a place with the characteristics, or attributes, found at that location. That function helps us not only identify and list the characteristics of places, but also analyze how places compare to one another and interact with one another. These patterns of interactions are known as spatial organization, and the study of them is called spatial analysis.

C

The locational data of places is stored in a GIS as latitude and longitude coordinates. These coordinates can be obtained from existing maps, GPS receivers, and satellite images. The attribute data come from a wide range of

GIS Layers

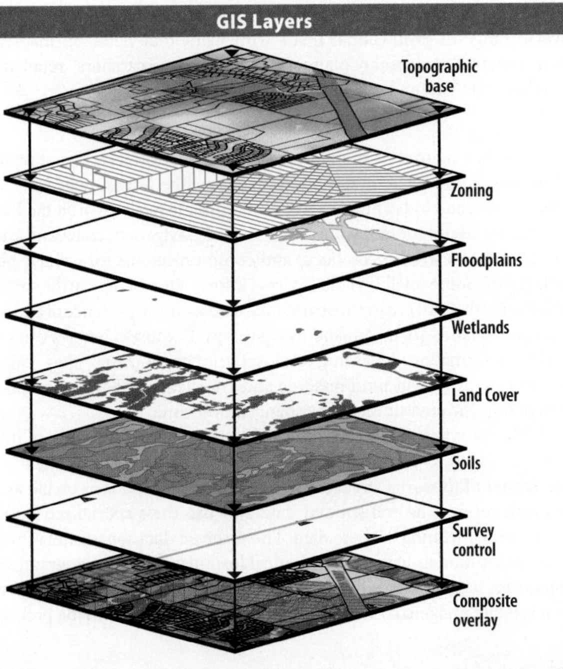

DIAGRAM SKILLS

Geographic information systems allow different kinds of information to be saved on separate layers.

CRITICAL THINKING

1. ***Formulating Questions*** What questions could a geographer answer using the layers of information in this sample GIS file?
2. ***Evaluating*** How does GIS allow cartographers to create maps and make changes quickly and easily?

T Technology Skills

Acquiring Information Invite interested students to use the Internet to research the characteristics and newest uses of GPS technology in mapping and how it affects human interaction. Topics may include predicting tsunamis or earthquakes, tracking animal migration or endangered animal species, or recent geographical impacts. Have students describe the uses and technological impacts of GPS by compiling their findings in a multimedia presentation for the class. BL **Technological**

C Critical Thinking Skills

Time, Chronology, and Sequencing Have students reread the entire "Geographic Information Systems" section. Have them write a paragraph sequencing the steps that a geographer might take to use GIS to conduct a survey of recent weather patterns in a certain location or region, which would then be used to make and later update a thematic map of that area. *(Student answers will vary, but should include the following steps: 1) Geographer makes a layer in GIS using weather pattern information 2) Geographer selects the new layer plus all other desired layers 3) GIS software produces finished map 4) Geographer updates map by compiling new weather information layer)* Have students share their paragraphs with a partner. Pairs should check each other's work for accuracy and check that all details are included in the steps. BL **Logical/Mathematical**

INFOGRAPHIC

GIS Layers

Spatial Understanding Display this infographic of a GIS file to illustrate the layers of geospatial data. Explain to students that geographical information systems allow different kinds of information to be saved on separate layers. As a class, click the graphic to reveal the text and layers. Have students write a paragraph explaining the advantages of using multiple geographic representations to answer geographic questions. BL **Verbal/Linguistic**

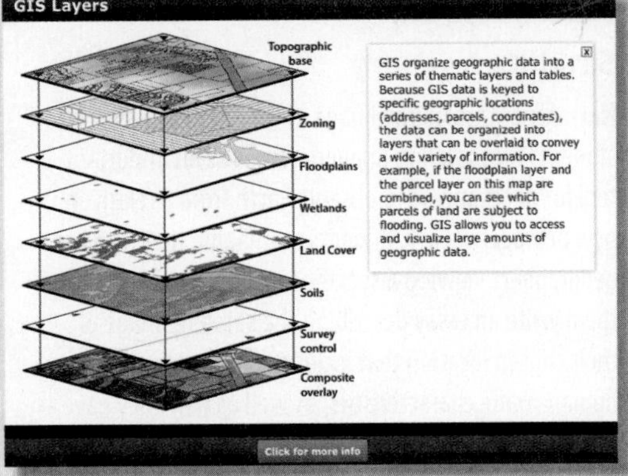

ANSWERS, p. 23

CRITICAL THINKING

1. Possible answers: What is the relationship between the location of wetlands and soils? How can I link the location of a place to its floodplains? How does land cover interact with soils?
2. GIS can show one layer of information or multiple layers at the same time. In this way, maps can be made and changed quickly and easily to display various complex types of information with a single map source.

C Critical Thinking Skills

Making Inferences GIS information helps to identify patterns over time by location. Tell students that there are different kinds of information that can be gathered and entered into GIS. Have students work in pairs to think of ways that the following information might be useful:

- **A map shows an Internet provider that one subdivision has twice as many outages as surrounding areas.** *(Student answers may vary, but may include that the Internet provider can send a technician to investigate the cables in the neighborhood.)*
- **A map shows a real estate developer recent changes in flooding patterns.** *(Student answers may vary, but may include that the developer will want to avoid building homes on land that is often flooding.)*
- **A map shows a public safety department an increase in robberies in a certain neighborhood of the city.** *(Possible answer: police could patrol that neighborhood more often)*
- **A map shows the city planner where the most bicycle accidents are occurring.** *(Possible answer: the city could install bike lanes on the most dangerous streets)* **Interpersonal, Logical/Mathematical**

V Visual Skills

Creating Visuals Have students work in small groups to look for images of satellites from the past and the present on the Internet. Have them analyze the images to compare and contrast early satellites with today's more modern satellites. Groups should take notes and print out various images to create a poster that they will present with their findings to the class. Encourage students to examine the changes in size, usage, and durability of the satellites. After the group presentations, display the posters in the classroom. **Visual/Spatial**

R Reading Skills

Context Clues Have a student read the section out loud. **Ask:** **What details, or context clues, help you to understand what *transmit* means?** *(The details about collecting data by satellite and then receiving the data by stations on Earth provide the reader with enough information to define the word.)* **What other words or synonyms of *transmit* could be used in this context?** *(Possible answers: send, convey, communicate, broadcast)* **ELL** **Verbal/Linguistic**

ANSWERS, p. 24

CRITICAL THINKING

1. Many more locations in North America than in Africa are lit at night. This would tend to indicate more activity at night and a better economy in North America.
2. Scientists can use the converted data from satellite imagery to study Earth's natural and human-made processes. For example, geographers might use this data to note and illustrate the shrinking ice shelf.

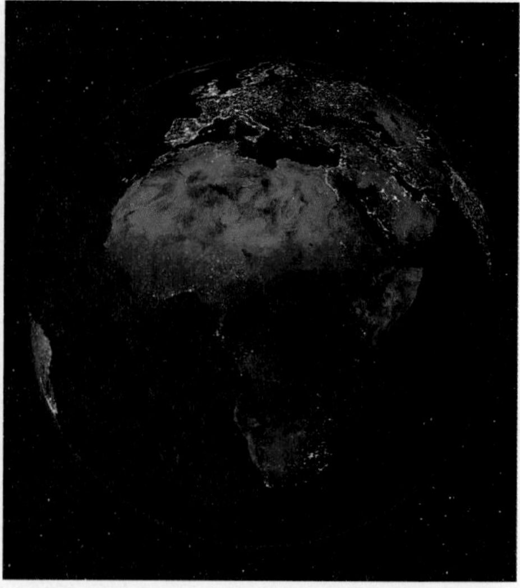

The stark differences between North America and Africa at night are clearly seen with satellite images.

▲ **CRITICAL THINKING**

1. ***Drawing Conclusions*** What do these images tell you about North America? About Africa?
2. ***Analyzing*** How might the information from these images be used by geographers?

sources. The GIS stores all these data in a digital database. Cartographers then select an appropriate map projection and program the GIS to produce thematic maps of the data. Each of the various types of attribute data in the database can be displayed on the map as a theme. The different themes can be saved as separate electronic layers that can be turned on or off. The GIS can show just one layer of information or multiple layers at the same time.

C In this way, maps can be made—and changed—quickly and easily to display various complex types of information with a single map source. GIS is used by a diverse range of professional fields with work that relies on maps, including environmental and urban planners, marketing researchers, retail developers, environmentalists, and other professionals.

Satellites

V A satellite is a natural or human-made object that orbits a planet or other large astronomical body. The first human-made satellite was launched in 1957 by the Soviet Union, and today hundreds of human-made satellites orbit the Earth. These satellites are useful for many purposes, such as navigation, collecting atmospheric data to make weather predictions, and communications for cellular phones and the Internet. Some satellites collect visual information of the Earth's surface as they orbit the Earth. Others carry instruments to observe the presence of and interaction between the land, ocean, air, and living things. Because scientists can gather very specific information regarding atmospheric phenomena, they can compare satellite images with ground research and knowledge of Earth's natural history to analyze how the environment has changed over time.

transmit to send from one place to another

R Different types of satellites are used to collect different types of information about the Earth. Once the data are collected, computers on a satellite store and then **transmit** those data by radio signals to receiving stations on Earth. Scientists on Earth receive the transmitted data and use their specialized knowledge to interpret the meaning of these data. The received data sometimes serve as inputs to computer models using mathematical formulas. Just as cartographers produce maps from data processed by GIS, so do scientists who use the converted data from satellite imagery to study Earth's natural and human-made processes.

networks Online Teaching Options

INTERACTIVE IMAGE

Satellite Imagery

Narrative Display the image of the satellite. Tell students that satellite imagery serves as an important tool for geographers to observe Earth from a relatively new perspective. Ask students to imagine that they are geographers viewing a specific location on Earth. Have them write an essay describing the satellite image of their chosen location that includes physical and/or human-made characteristics, as well as why they have chosen this location. Invite volunteers to share their essays. **Verbal/Linguistic**

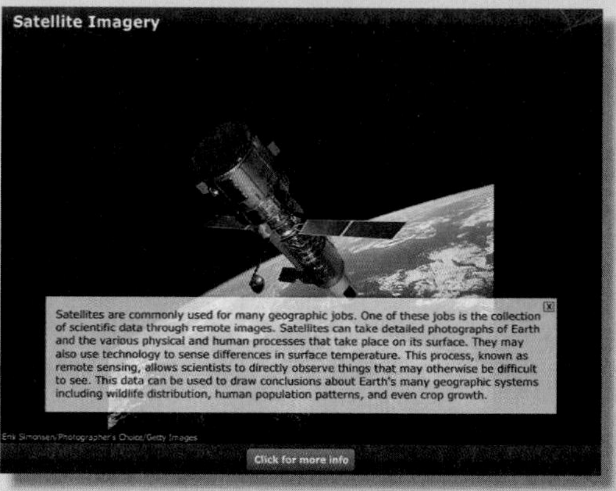

Satellite Imagery
Satellites are commonly used for many geographic jobs. One of these jobs is the collection of scientific data through remote images. Satellites can take detailed photographs of Earth and the various physical and human processes that take place on its surface. They may also use technology to sense differences in surface temperature. This process, known as remote sensing, allows scientists to directly observe things that may otherwise be difficult to see. This data can be used to draw conclusions about Earth's many geographic systems including wildlife distribution, human population patterns, and even crop growth.
Click for more info

Remote sensing is any technique used to measure, observe, or monitor a subject or process without physically touching the object under observation. For example, scientists use remote sensing when they analyze images from satellites, telescopes, and cameras in airplanes and spacecraft. Often, remote sensing collects images of things that could not be seen with the unaided human eye. It is also a useful process for obtaining information from locations that would otherwise be dangerous or difficult to reach, such as estimating precipitation rates in a desert region. The immediate and frequent flow of images from remote sensing allows cartographers to create detailed and relevant maps to estimate constant and changing environmental conditions, such as sediment buildup, air pollution, ocean surface roughness, surface temperatures, biomass volumes, mineral resources, and changes created by storms and floods.

remote sensing the science of obtaining information about an object or an area from a distance, typically from instruments in aircraft or satellites

W

Quality and Limitations of Geospatial Technologies

Geospatial technologies are excellent sources of information because they provide actual images and data related to a location and can provide a great amount of detail. While scientists can use observational and historical data to gather information about a place, geospatial technology acts as a primary source for compiling raw data. Because they are a relatively new innovation in comparison to traditional forms of mapmaking, the current uses of geospatial technologies can be limited. These informational technologies are constantly changing, and they will improve with the advancement of computer, aerospace, and Internet-based technology. Accelerated development in geospatial technology offers a number of possibilities for its use with government, private industry, scientists, and the general public. Because the economic, cultural, and political activities of the world's regions have become increasingly interconnected, information related to the world's physical and human systems needs to be readily available, consistent, and up-to-date. The combination of mental mapping with GPS, GIS, and aerial imagery can create a very detailed picture of places and regions.

C

Geospatial technologies allow access to a wealth of information about what sorts of features and objects are in the world and where those features and objects are located. This "geospatial information" can be very helpful for identifying and navigating, but by itself, does not help much in answering the "why" or the "why care" questions that lie at the heart of understanding and making decisions about the world in which we live. It is important to go beyond geospatial information to geographical understanding of peoples, places, and environments—and the connections among them—that are interesting as well as useful.

✓ READING PROGRESS CHECK

Identifying What type of data do geospatial technologies provide?

LESSON 1 REVIEW (CCSS)

Reviewing Vocabulary (Tier Three Words)

1. ***Identifying*** What is the difference between absolute location and relative location? RH.9–10.4

Using Your Notes

2. ***Describing*** Using your graphic organizer, list and describe the four common map projections.

Answering the Guiding Questions

3. ***Comparing*** How are globes and map projections related?
4. ***Explaining*** How is location determined?
5. ***Summarizing*** How do maps work?
6. ***Analyzing*** How are geospatial technologies used to learn about the world?

Writing Activity

7. ***Informative/Explanatory*** If you were planning to open a sporting goods store, in what ways could GIS technologies help you choose a good location? Discuss the types of layers that might be helpful to your decision. WHST.9–10.1

The Geographer's Tools

W Writing Skills

Narrative Have students write a short story as if they were a geologist who is traveling to a dangerous or difficult to reach location in order to obtain valuable information. Tell them to consider the obstacles that they might face and how they could overcome these obstacles using modern technological advances such as remote sensing. AL **Intrapersonal**

C Critical Thinking Skills

Drawing Conclusions Explain that there can be limitations and quality issues in the rapidly expanding technologies. **Ask:** **Why are geospatial technologies important to geographers?** *(They provide actual images and data related to a location.)* **What types of limitations or quality issues might new geospatial technologies have?** *(images may be blurry, new innovations may mean that not a lot of people know how to use or have access to the technology; expensive technology)* **What types of geospatial technologies might be helpful to you in the future?** *(Student answers may vary, but should demonstrate that the student understands uses of geospatial technology.)* **Logical/Mathematical, Verbal/Linguistic**

CLOSE & REFLECT

Explaining To close the lesson, write *globes, maps,* and *geospatial technologies* on the board. In a class discussion, have students review the many ways geographers use these tools, listing students' responses under each item.

ANSWERS, p. 25

✓ READING PROGRESS CHECK They provide data related to measurement, analyzing features of Earth, and viewing features of Earth.

LESSON 1 REVIEW ANSWERS

Reviewing Vocabulary

1. While absolute location identifies exact points using latitude and longitude, relative location uses a reference point to identify one place in relation to another.

Using Your Notes

2. A Mercator projection is a common example of a cylindrical projection. Because it displays true direction, it is useful for sea navigation. World maps used for general reference use the Winkel Tripel projection, which cannot be used to determine precise distances, sizes, or shapes of specific global features, but provides a good balance between the overall size and shape of land areas shown. A Robinson projection looks similar to a Winkel Tripel projection, although its east-west projections run in a straight line. Its projection produces minor distortions, particularly in the polar areas that appear flattened on the map. Goode's Interrupted Equal-Area projection resembles a globe that has been cut apart and laid flat. It shows the true size and shape of Earth's landmasses; however, distances between land features are generally distorted.

Answering the Guiding Questions

3. A globe is a scale model of the Earth that depicts properties such as area, distance, and direction. A map is a flat representation of all or part of the planet. Maps cannot show all the properties accurately; however, globes can.
4. Globes and maps use a grid system to form a pattern of lines that cross one another. Through lines of latitude and longitude, these patterns are used to help find the location of places on the Earth's surface.
5. Maps are drawn to a specific scale and provide information related to specific purposes; effective maps include a legend and a compass rose.
6. Geospatial technologies help answer geographic questions. Global positioning systems (GPS), geographic information systems (GIS), and remote sensing from satellites and aircraft incorporate multiple information sources to construct detailed geographic representations of the Earth's surface.

Writing Activity

7. Student answers will differ, but should be strongly supported. Students might state that zoning and floodplain layers would be beneficial to the decision.

The Geographer's Craft

ENGAGE

G1 Critical Thinking Skills

Considering Perspectives Tell students that understanding how geographers use perspective is an important concept. Ask a student to define perspective. *(Possible answers: how things appear visually and spatially or how our experience shapes our views)* Have students write a paragraph about how their perspective on something has changed over time, such as their perspective about middle or high school, a movie, a job, or a vacation destination. Invite students to share their paragraphs with the class.

TEACH & ACCESS

C2 Critical Thinking Skills

Demonstrating Explain to students that city planners often use geography skills in their policy and decision-making. Towns are generally divided into zones that allow certain kinds of development in order to organize how and where people live and work. Divide the class into three teams. The teams will represent a town zoning board, shopping mall developers, and developers of retirement housing project. The land in question is currently being used as a park. The two developer teams must prepare short presentations demonstrating how the park should be rezoned for their team's use. Based on the presentations, the zoning board will decide if the land will be rezoned or kept as a park.

After the presentations, lead a class discussion on how a variety of perspectives must be considered in geography. Relate the discussion to the zoning activity. **Ask:** **If you lived across the street from the park, how might your perspective about rezoning be influenced?** *(Student answers may vary, but should reflect that past experiences influence their feelings about the park, or that rezoning may affect them personally because of the location of their family home.)* Continue the discussion by pointing out that past experience and memories often play a vital role in a person's perspective. Explain that geographers strive for accuracy by combining spatial and experiential perspectives in their work. **Interpersonal, Verbal/Linguistic**

ANSWERS, p. 26

TAKING NOTES: These basic elements are: the world in spatial terms, places and regions, physical systems, human systems, environment and society, and the uses of geography.

networks

There's More Online!

- **CHART** Skills for Thinking Like a Geographer
- **IMAGE** Hiker Reading a Map
- **IMAGE** Rice Paddy in Southern China
- **IMAGE** Scientist Studying a Glacier
- **MAP** Perceptual Regions of the United States
- **INTERACTIVE SELF-CHECK QUIZ**
- **VIDEO** The Geographer's Craft

LESSON 2
The Geographer's Craft

ESSENTIAL QUESTION • *How does geography help us interpret the past, understand the present, and plan for the future?*

Reading HELPDESK (CCSS)

Academic Vocabulary (Tier Two Words)
- **primary**
- **obtain**
- **fluctuation**

Content Vocabulary (Tier Three Words)
- **spatial perspective**
- **site**
- **situation**
- **formal region**
- **functional region**
- **perceptual region**

TAKING NOTES: ***Key Ideas and Details***

IDENTIFYING As you read the lesson, use a graphic organizer like the one below to identify the basic elements of geography.

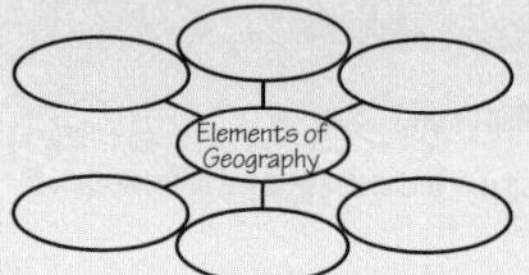

IT MATTERS BECAUSE

The root of the word geography is an ancient Greek word meaning "earth description." Geographers study the location and relationships of Earth's physical and living features. They look for links between places and people and identify patterns in order to learn why those patterns exist or occur.

G1 A Geographic Perspective

GUIDING QUESTION *What is the spatial perspective?*

Geographers focus on understanding the world and answering questions about it. An important part of the geographical perspective is the spatial perspective. A **spatial perspective** focuses on how individual places, people, or objects are related to one another across the surface of the Earth. Using a spatial perspective, geographers examine why things are located where they are. Geographers also use the spatial perspective to examine what makes regions distinct based on changes and movements of people over time and changes in the physical environment. This spatial perspective can also be viewed from a local perspective, such as where to select a new home, or the global perspective, such as the economic activities of countries in the form of trade. C2

Other aspects of the geographic perspective include the ecological perspective and the perspective of experience. The ecological perspective focuses on understanding Earth as a complex set of interacting living and nonliving components. It involves thinking about the connections and interactions that operate among ecosystems and human societies. The perspective of experience considers how people make meaning from the world in which we live. As people live in locations on Earth, they have experiences and build memories that give places on Earth unique characteristics. Awareness and sensitivity to these uniquenesses are an important part of the perspective of experience.

Not all people who study or incorporate geography into their profession are labeled geographers. Geography skills can be applied to a variety of fields, including government, business, and education.

networks ***Online Teaching Options***

INTERACTIVE BELLRINGER

Interpreting a Political Cartoon

Identifying Perspectives This political cartoon can be used to build on students' understanding of globes and maps and to help students understand how geographers use perspective to view different regions of the world. Have students work with a partner to read the introductory text, study the political cartoon, and answer the questions. Have pairs discuss different perspectives of the world. Then ask pairs to draw another political cartoon of a person or creature looking at a globe from its perspective. **Visual/Spatial**

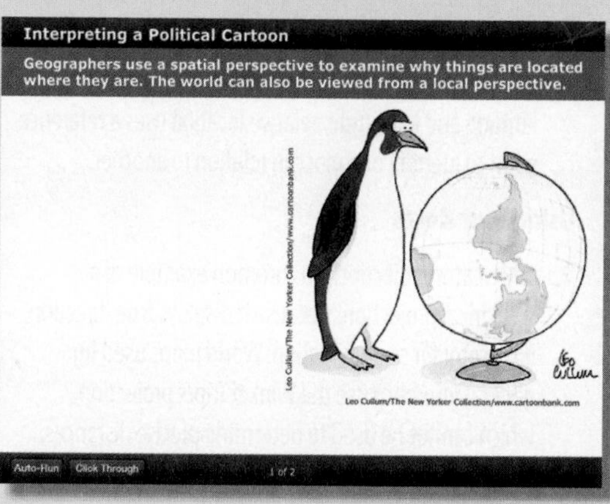

Interpreting a Political Cartoon
Geographers use a spatial perspective to examine why things are located where they are. The world can also be viewed from a local perspective.
Leo Cullum/The New Yorker Collection/www.cartoonbank.com
Auto-Run
Click Through
1 of 2

One broad cluster of career opportunities in geography is teaching and education. Teaching opportunities exist at all levels, from elementary to high school to university levels of education. Teachers with a background or training in geography topics are in demand in the United States for elementary and high schools. Students with formal geographic training from a university can find work in many diverse businesses, industries, and professional fields.

Because geography itself has many specialized fields, there are many ways that people use geography in their work. Those with a knowledge of physical geography can work as meteorologists who study the atmosphere and weather patterns; as emergency management officials dealing with natural hazards, such as earthquakes or hurricanes; as ecologists who study the interrelationships of organisms and their environment; as soil scientists; and as environmental managers. Work in the environmental field includes assessing the environmental impact of proposed development projects regarding air and water quality and wildlife. G1

spatial perspective a way of looking at the human and physical patterns on Earth and their relationships to one another

Skills for Thinking Like a Geographer C2

Skill	Examples	Tools and Technologies
Asking Geographic Questions helps you pose questions about your surroundings	• Why has traffic increased along this road? • What should be considered when building a new community sports facility?	• Maps • Globes • Internet • Remote sensing • News media
Acquiring Geographic Information helps you answer geographic questions	• Compare aerial photographs of a region over time. • Design a survey to determine who might use a community facility.	• Direct observation • Interviews • Reference books • Satellite images • Historical records
Organizing Geographic Information helps you analyze and interpret information you have collected	• Compile a map showing the spread of housing development over time. • Summarize information obtained from interviews.	• Field maps • Databases • Statistical tables • Graphs • Diagrams • Summaries
Analyzing Geographic Information helps you look for patterns, relationships, and connections	• Draw conclusions about the effects of road construction on traffic patterns. • Compare information from different maps that show available land and zoning districts.	• Maps • Charts • Graphs • GIS • Spreadsheets
Answering Geographic Questions helps you apply information to real-life situations and problem solving	• Present a report showing the results of a case study. • Suggest locations for a new facility based on geographic data gathered.	• Sketch maps • Reports • Research papers • Oral or multimedia presentations

One of the most important geographic tools is the ability to think geographically. The five skills identified above are key to geographic understanding.

▲ **CRITICAL THINKING**

1. ***Analyzing*** What types of patterns might you recognize by comparing aerial photographs of a region over a specific time period?
2. ***Identifying the Central Issue*** Provide a real-life example of how you might apply three of the skills described in the chart. Explain the issue, including which skills you chose, and how they would be used.

The Geographer's Craft

T Technology Skills

Researching Tell students that there are a variety of geography occupations. Have them research types of career choices that are available to someone with an undergraduate or graduate degree in geography. Then have students write a paragraph about a career in geography that they find most interesting. Remind them to make sure they use reliable online sites and to include their sources. AL **Intrapersonal**

G1 Critical Thinking Skills

Considering Perspectives Have students reread the section. Divide students into small groups. Assign one of the professions mentioned (meteorology, emergency management, ecology, soil science, and environmental management) to each group. Have the groups consider geographical contributions that each profession brings to a real-life situation within a community. Have groups share their findings with the class. BL **Naturalist**

C2 Critical Thinking Skills

Formulating Questions Allow time for students to study the chart. Using the information provided in the chart, have students write and answer three questions. Tell students to exchange their questions with a partner. Have pairs answer each other's questions, and then discuss any incorrect answers. To further discuss thinking geographically, **ask:** **How can thinking geographically help a community plan for the future?** *(Possible answers: city planning for future developments, such as number of schools or the best location for building a hospital; evacuation plans in case of an emergency; how many people will move to or move out of the city)* **Logical/Mathematical**

INTERACTIVE WHITEBOARD ACTIVITY

Thinking Like a Geographer Skills

Planning This interactive whiteboard activity about geographers' skills provides students with the understanding that one of the most important geographic tools is the ability to think geographically. As a class, complete the interactive whiteboard activity. Discuss the five skills that are identified. Then have students work with a partner to provide an example of a question or a statement of how each skill could be used by a city planner looking to zone an undeveloped section of land. Encourage students to be creative, yet come up with real-life examples. ELL **Visual/Spatial**

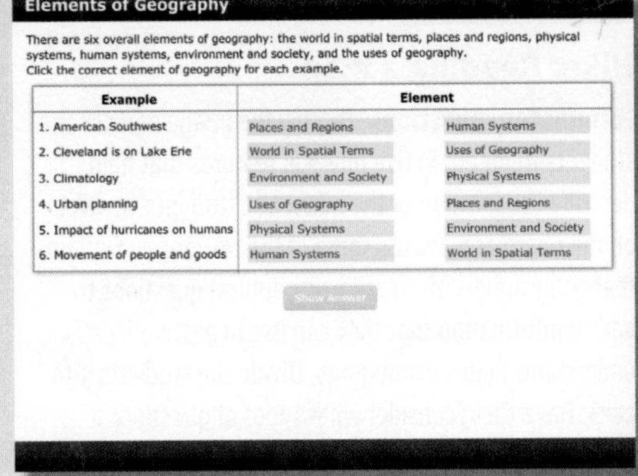

Elements of Geography
There are six overall elements of geography: the world in spatial terms, places and regions, physical systems, human systems, environment and society, and the uses of geography.
Click the correct element of geography for each example.
Example
Element
1. American Southwest
2. Cleveland is on Lake Erie
3. Climatology
4. Urban planning
5. Impact of hurricanes on humans
6. Movement of people and goods
Places and Regions
Human Systems
World in Spatial Terms
Uses of Geography
Environment and Society
Physical Systems
Uses of Geography
Places and Regions
Physical Systems
Environment and Society
Human Systems
World in Spatial Terms

ANSWERS, p. 27

CRITICAL THINKING

1. By comparing aerial photographs over time, geographers can determine the spread of urban development, the increase in traffic on roadways, the environmental impact of pollution or natural disasters, and many other patterns.
2. Examples and explanations will differ, but should be logical and strongly supported by information in the lesson and the table.

The Geographer's Craft

W Writing Skills

Informative/Explanatory Have students imagine they have been asked to write an article on their city or neighborhood for a travel blog. Their descriptions should discuss the people, the location within the region, types of jobs, food and entertainment, cultural heritage, historical facts, and any other element that is particularly interesting about their city or neighborhood. Remind students that they should consider that readers might not be familiar with the area, so their blogs must be detailed. **Verbal/Linguistic**

C1 Critical Thinking Skills

Gathering information Encourage students to consider that they are moving to a new house in a new city or new community. They will be living in a completely new neighborhood, and will know very little about the community ahead of time. Working in small groups, have students determine how they would use each of the five geographic skills *(asking, acquiring, organizing, analyzing, and answering geographic questions)* to find out about their new area. Have the groups consider how easy or difficult it would be to acquire the information they would need.
ELL Interpersonal

C2 Critical Thinking Skills

Comparing and Contrasting Tell students that each of the six overall elements mentioned can be used to describe or understand a place, but it often takes all six to get a full view. Have students divide up into pairs. Each student should separately write a description of their town or neighborhood using three of the six elements mentioned while their partner does the same using the other three elements. Then working together, have pairs compare and contrast the ways they individually described their town. How similarly or differently did they end up describing the same place? Invite a few pairs to share their results with the class. Explain that a variety of geographic perspectives are necessary to get a complete understanding of a region or area. **Verbal/Linguistic**

ANSWERS, p. 28

READING PROGRESS CHECK Three fields outside geography that utilize geography skills are government, business, and education.

CRITICAL THINKING

1. The map could tell the specific location, elevation, and vegetation of the area. It could also provide information regarding where the site is located in relationship to nearby locations.
2. A map can provide information regarding where the site is located in relationship to other locations.

Those with knowledge of human geography find work in many areas such as health care, transportation, population studies, economic development, public policy, and international economics. Human geographers with a background in urban planning are hired by local and state government agencies to focus on projects such as housing and community development and parks and recreation planning. An economic geographer examines human economic activities. He or she may work at such tasks as market analysis and site selection for stores, factories, and restaurants. A regional geographer studies the features of a particular region and may assist government and businesses in making decisions about land use. Geographers can also find employment as writers and editors for publishers of textbooks, maps, atlases, news and travel magazines, and Web sites. **W**

C1 One of the most important tools of a geographic perspective is the ability to think geographically about the world. Geographers use five basic skills that are key to geographic understanding: asking, acquiring, organizing, analyzing, and answering geographic questions. Asking geographic questions provides information that can be used to better understand one's surroundings. As knowledge is acquired, it can be applied to recognize patterns and relationships that will help in real-life situations.

READING PROGRESS CHECK

Listing List at least three fields outside of geography that use geography skills.

The Elements of Geography

GUIDING QUESTION *What are the elements of geography?*

C2 Geography uses the geographic perspective to study the peoples, places, environments, histories, and cultures of the world's regions. Geographers study the interactions between peoples, places, and environments to explain why and how patterns of interaction occur. There are six overall elements geographers consider in their work: the world in spatial terms, places and regions, physical systems, human systems, environment and society, and the uses of geography.

Maps can be used to determine site and situation.

▼ CRITICAL THINKING

1. ***Speculating*** What could this hiker's map tell her about the site and situation of the landscape she is viewing?
2. ***Describing*** Explain how a map, such as the one shown, could be used to identify spatial relationships.

Thorsten Henn/Cultura/Getty Images

28

networks Online Teaching Options

INTERACTIVE IMAGE

Hiker Reading a Map

Formulating Questions Display the image and ask the students to jot down five physical features that help describe the location of the hiker. List students' answers on the board and discuss some of the responses. Explain that geographers often ask geographical questions to gather information that they can use to better understand their surroundings. Divide the students into pairs. Have them consider what types of questions a geographer might ask to gather information about the location shown in this image. Ask each pair to write three questions. **AL Visual/Spatial, Interpersonal**

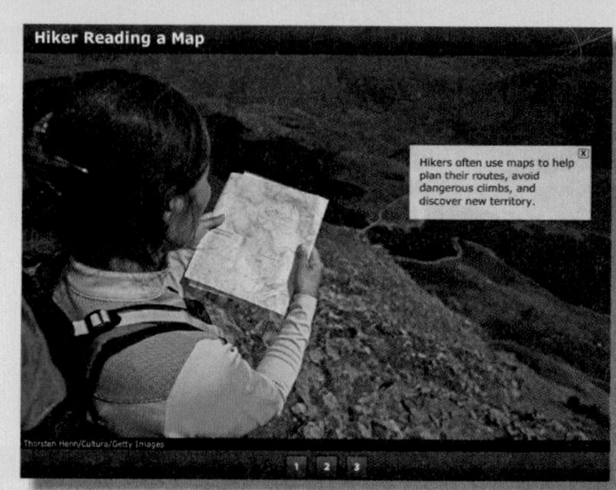

Hiker Reading a Map
Hikers often use maps to help plan their routes, avoid dangerous climbs, and discover new territory.
Thorsten Henn/Cultura/Getty Images
1 2 3

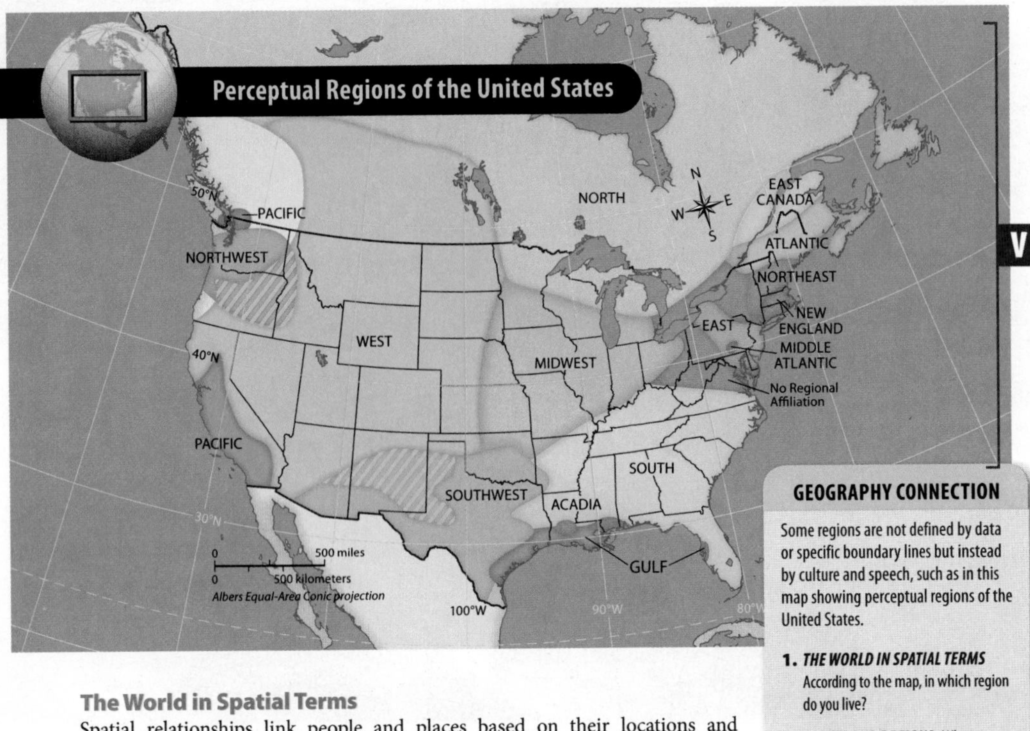

GEOGRAPHY CONNECTION

Some regions are not defined by data or specific boundary lines but instead by culture and speech, such as in this map showing perceptual regions of the United States.

1. ***THE WORLD IN SPATIAL TERMS*** According to the map, in which region do you live?
2. ***PLACES AND REGIONS*** What aspects of culture do you think define a perceptual region in the United States?

V

The World in Spatial Terms

Spatial relationships link people and places based on their locations and relationships to each other. Location is a reference point for geographers in the same way that dates serve as reference points for historians.

One way of locating a place is by describing its absolute location—the exact spot at which the place is found on the Earth. To determine absolute location, geographers use the system of latitude and longitude. On a day-to-day basis, humans tend to identify a place based on relative location—a place's location in relation to another place. For example, New Orleans is located near the mouth of the Mississippi River. Knowing the relative location of a place helps you to think spatially. By creating a mental map based on relative location, you can orient yourself in space and develop an awareness of the world around you. R1

The broad or specific definition of a geographic location based on relative or absolute location also takes into account a place's site and situation. **Site** is the specific location of a place, including its physical setting. For example, the site of San Francisco is its location at the end of a peninsula in northern California. **Situation** refers to a more general location, defined by a place's geographic position in relation to other places and its connections to other regions. San Francisco's situation is a port city on the Pacific coast, close to California's agricultural lands. R2

site the specific location of a place, including its physical setting

situation the geographic position of a place in relation to other places or features of a larger region

Places and Regions

A place has physical and human significance. It has distinguishing characteristics defined by its features and surroundings. Geographers study and assess the similarities and differences between places to express what features are unique to each place. To interpret the Earth's complexity, geographers group places with similar characteristics into regions. A region can be defined by physical traits

V Visual Skills

Analyzing Visuals Have students analyze the map. Explain that this map shows one way of dividing up the United States based on perceptions. **Ask:** What are other ways of dividing the country into perceptual regions? *(Student answers may vary, but should include actual perceptions. For instance, one could describe the country based on labels like Appalachia, Rust Belt, Sun Belt, etc.)* Looking at the map, do you agree with the location of the drawn regional lines? Why or why not? *(Student answers may vary, but should support their opinions, particularly if they disagree.)* AL Visual/Spatial

R1 Reading Skills

Spatial Analysis Tell students that it is very rare that people give directions without using relative locations. Explain that relative location is locating a place in relation to other places. Have students work with a partner. Each student should give the other directions from one point of common knowledge to another point without using relative directions. Suggest that students give directions from school to the movie theater, the public library, or to a local restaurant. After students have had time to give directions, discuss other ways that they supplied directions without using relative locations. Kinesthetic, Logical/Mathematical

R2 Reading Skills

Describing Students may find the difference between site and situation difficult to understand. Instruct students to work with a partner, having one of them name a place they both know about and declare its site or situation. The other student should then provide the other attribute. Then have partners switch roles using a different location. ELL Verbal/Linguistic

INTERACTIVE MAP

Perceptual Regions of the United States

Identifying Bias Use this interactive map to help students understand how spatial relationships link people and places together based on their locations. This map shows fifteen different perceptual regions in the United States and explains what makes each a region. As each slide is clicked, read the text and ask students to comment on it. Ask students to consider if the text is based on fact or if it is an opinion. Note that students' reactions to the text will vary with each slide. Explain that data or specific boundary lines do not define some regions. In some instances, regions may be defined by culture and speech. After all slides have been presented, guide a class discussion on how regional perspectives may create bias. BL Visual/Spatial, Intrapersonal

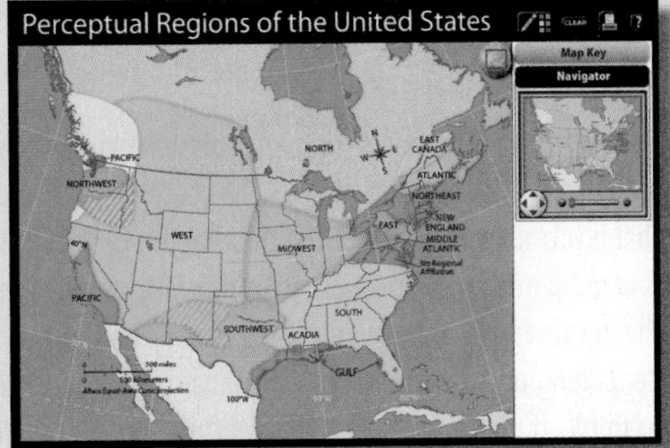

ANSWERS, p. 29

GEOGRAPHY CONNECTION

1. The response should accurately reflect the name of the region in which the student lives.
2. Terms referencing traditional values of family and hospitality, such as *heartland,* and spoken language, such as Creole, are aspects of culture that can define a perceptual region.

The Geographer's Craft

R1 Reading Skills

Understanding Relationships Have students define the word *primary* in their own terms, and explain what it means in this section. *(corn is the primary crop of the Corn Belt)* Ask them to provide possible types of secondary crops that might be grown here, and why these crops are not primary crops. *(Examples could include economic, ecological, or agricultural reasons, and need not be exact. Students should understand the term* primary *and how it relates to things that are of secondary importance or value. "Corn is more valuable than soybeans," for instance.)* ELL **Verbal/Linguistic**

C Critical Thinking Skills

Classifying Ask the students to begin naming regions of the world that they're familiar with. These could be local (neighborhoods within their town), intrastate, interstate, or international. The scale of the region doesn't matter. Make these into a list, and by show of hands find out whether the students classify each particular region as formal, functional, or perceptual. If there are disagreements, provide time for students to discuss or debate their opinions. *(Student answers may vary, but the descriptions should use the categories given in the text.)* **Verbal/Linguistic**

R2 Reading Skills

Defining Ask students to define the word *vernacular (native or spoken language of a group or in a region).* Explain that vernacular can also be a dialect of a specific population or culture. Have students write two or three sentences using the word. AL ELL **Verbal/Linguistic**

Content Background Knowledge

Understanding Perceptual Regions The concept of perceptual regions might be difficult for students to understand. One reason for that is that defining a perceptual region is subjective and not always agreed upon. A region might be designated out of a "quality" commonly associated with an area, not based on geographical boundaries or statistics. Perceptual regions are generalizations made out of one's "mental map," and sometimes they can be stereotypes. Additionally, perceptual regions can, and often do, vary over time as people move around or as tastes and habits change.

ANSWERS, p. 30

CRITICAL THINKING

1. Students may call it a formal region due to the significant production of rice.
2. An example of a student question is: "How has this land been used traditionally throughout the decades?"

Rice paddy fields in southern China reflect both human systems and physical systems at work.

▲ CRITICAL THINKING

1. ***Categorizing*** What type of region would you categorize the rice paddy fields as being? Explain your choice.
2. ***Formulating Questions*** Create one question you would ask the people living in the area that could help you determine whether the rice paddy is a formal or perceptual region.

formal region a region defined by a common characteristic, such as production of a product

primary of first rank, importance, or value

functional region a central place and the surrounding territory linked to it

such as climate, landforms, soils, vegetation, animal life, and natural resources. A region can also have human significance, as defined by characteristics such as language, religion, political or economic systems, and population distribution. Geographers identify three types of regions: formal, functional, and perceptual.

R1 A **formal region** features a unifying characteristic, such as a product produced in that region. For example, the Corn Belt is a band of farmland stretching from Ohio to Nebraska in the United States. It is a formal region because corn is its **primary** crop. A **functional region** incorporates a central node and a surrounding area that is connected to the node by some defined function. For example, a cell tower provides the central node for a surrounding area in which cell phone users can obtain phone reception. C A **perceptual region** uses a looser standard for characterization, defined more by commonly accepted tradition or value than by objective data. For example, the term "heartland" refers to a central area in the United States in which traditional values of family and hospitality are believed to predominate. R2 A perceptual region could also be labeled a vernacular region. This refers to patterns native to a particular region in spite of boundary lines. The Creole dialect that is spoken in southern Louisiana is an example of a vernacular region. It is defined more by the culture and speech of the region than by a designation of state and city boundaries.

Physical Systems and Human Systems

Because geography can cover a broad range of themes, geographers divide their focus into major branches: physical geography and human geography. Physical geography—climate, land, water, plants, and animal life—looks at these processes

networks Online Teaching Options

WORKSHEET

Vocabulary Activity

Defining Have students complete this worksheet to assess students' knowledge and understanding of the content and academic vocabulary that is introduced and taught in the chapter. Each chapter of the textbook is accompanied by a Vocabulary Activity worksheet. The classroom use of the Vocabulary Activity worksheet can vary from chapter to chapter, depending on the content and vocabulary needs of the chapter. For example, if most of the vocabulary terms exist in Lesson 2, then it is best to use the worksheet sometime during Lesson 2 rather than at the beginning or end of the chapter.

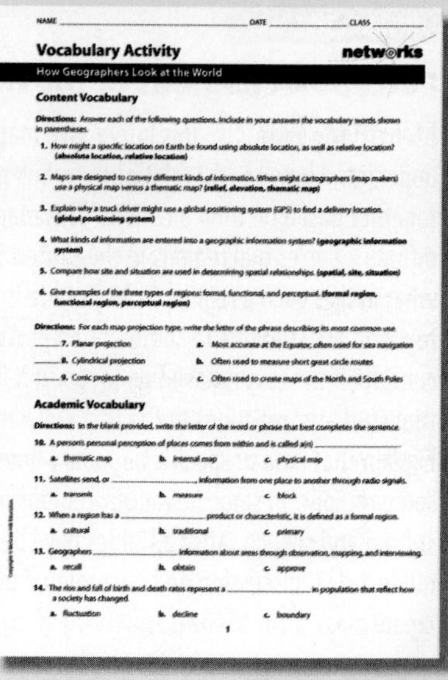

and their significance to humans. Human geography, or cultural geography, analyzes human activities and their relationship to the cultural and physical environments. Political, economic, social, and cultural factors can include themes such as urban development, economic production and consumption, and population change. Because physical and human geography are still very broad in their focus, they can be further divided into subject areas. For example, climatology is the study of climate and long-term atmospheric conditions and their impact on ecology and society. Historical geography is the study of places and human activities over time based on the geographic factors that have shaped them.

Geographers study how physical features and processes of land, water, and climate interact with plants and animals to create, support, or change ecosystems. An ecosystem is a community of plants and animals that depend upon one another and their surroundings for survival. Geographers also study the processes by which people operate across Earth's surface—how they settle the Earth, form societies, and create permanent features. A recurring theme in geography is the ongoing movement of people, goods, and ideas. Human migration and settlement, as well as the exchange of ideas and practices among cultures, can over time transform societies, traditions, and the landscape in which humans live. In studying human systems, geographers look at how people compete or cooperate to change or control aspects of the Earth to meet their needs.

Environment and Society

The relationship between people and their physical environment is a theme embodied by human-environment interaction. Ways in which people use their surroundings, ways in which they change it voluntarily and involuntarily, and the consequences that result from such human-environment interaction are very important themes for geographers. Pollution, construction, human population growth, conservation of parks, and reintroduction of species into the wild are just a few of the ways humans change the physical environment. Yet the physical environment can also have an effect on humans. For example, physical barriers such as rivers, mountains, and deserts limit human movement and growth. Natural phenomena such as hurricanes, earthquakes, and heavy storms or droughts force humans to adapt their activities and lifestyles to the changing environment. By understanding how the Earth's physical features and processes shape and are shaped by human activity, geographers help societies make informed decisions about their relationship with their surrounding physical environment.

The Uses of Geography

Geography provides insight into how physical features and living things developed in the past. It also takes into account current trends regarding the physical and human environment in order to plan for future needs. Planning and policy making must account for interactions between humans and the natural environment. Data regarding physical features and processes can highlight suitable sites for resource extraction or for human habitation. Urban planners analyze trends in human growth within a specified region to determine where and what systems, such as schools, roads, public services, and businesses, are necessary for supporting a growing population. Geographers analyze past data in order to determine effective future actions to sustain and support both the natural environment and human development. Although people trained in geography are in great demand in the workforce, many of them do not have geographer as a job title. Geography skills are useful in so many different situations that geographers have more than a hundred different job titles.

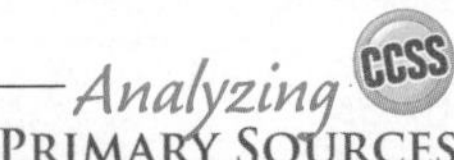

Analyzing PRIMARY SOURCES

The Island

"The island seems to have a tenacious hold on the human imagination. Unlike the tropical forest or the continental seashore it cannot claim ecological abundance, nor—as an environment—has it mattered greatly in man's evolutionary past. Its importance lies in the imaginative realm. Many of the world's cosmogonies, we have seen, begin with the watery chaos: land, when it appears, is necessarily an island.... In numerous legends the island appears as the abode of the dead or of immortals."

—Yi-fu Tuan, *Topophilia: a Study of Environmental Perception, Attitudes, and Values,* 1974

DBQ ***PLACES AND REGIONS*** What emotions do you feel when you think of an island? Explain whether it is based on your imagination or on real experiences. RH.9–10.10

perceptual region a region defined by popular feelings and images rather than by objective data

G1 Critical Thinking Skills

Explaining Continuity and Change Remind students that every place humans have lived is associated with historical geography and that over time these places may change. Invite interested students to form a group and research the historical geography of their area. When was their town founded? What sort of people founded it, and why? What were the earliest industries? Have there been significant events in the area? How has the city continued to develop and change? Have the group present their findings to the class. BL **Verbal/Linguistic**

G2 Critical Thinking Skills

Understanding Relationships In a class discussion brainstorm various ways that humans interact with their physical environment in both positive and negative ways. **Ask:** **How does our environment help us?** *(Possible answers: getting lumber for homes, providing water and food)* **How does our environment harm us?** *(Possible answers: natural disasters, unpredictable weather patterns, land formations that impede travel or development)* **How do we help our environment?** *(Possible answers: planting trees, designating conservation areas, maintaining parks)* **How do we harm our environment?** *(Possible answers: cutting down forests, destroying natural habitats, rerouting natural waterways with dams, polluting the air and water)*

Then divide the class into small groups. Assign each group one of the human/physical environment relationships. Have groups prepare an advertisement that will encourage the positive effects or discourage the negative effects. Advertisements should include music and audio. **Auditory/Musical, Naturalist**

W Writing Skills

Narrative Have students recall familiar plot lines from books or movies that take place on islands or where a secluded location is important to the story. Then have students write their own stories that take place on an island. The narrative should include specific details that explain the physical and human geography features of the island. **Verbal/Linguistic, Intrapersonal**

ONLINE LINK

Census Results Having Effects on State Representation

Understanding Relationships Have students view this online link about 2010 census numbers to explain how geography is connected to politics and government. While viewing the various state maps, lead a class discussion on how geographic contexts provide the basis for analyzing the current population so that important political decisions can be made in the future. Emphasize that population growth may mean more government representation, thus additional federal funding; loss in population may mean less government representation and less federal funding. This important relationship between population and government greatly affects citizens in the United States. BL **Visual/Spatial**

Census Results Having Effects on State Representation

ANSWERS, p. 31

DBQ Student answers may vary, but should clearly explain if their emotions are based on their imagination or previous experiences. Some students may express that they feel wonder and delight when thinking about an island, while others may express indifference.

V1 Visual Skills

Speculating Tell students that seeing a picture of a place can help them to speculate on the physical geography of an area. **Ask:** What clues indicate what it might be like to live on Greenland? *(Possible answers: there are glaciers, so it is cold most of the year; the land is rocky and barren so it might be difficult to farm)* How might the physical geography of an area like this affect its human residents? *(Student answers may vary, but may include that humans may stay indoors much of the year, and that cold climates limit the types of food that is naturally available so they probably import much of their food.)* How might Greenland's wildlife be affected by a warming of the climate? *(Possible answers: animals like penguins and polar bears that are used to cold climates may have trouble adjusting to warmer temperatures or may be forced to relocate.)* **Visual/Spatial**

Content Background Knowledge

Studying Glaciers Greenland is the world's largest island, which is slightly more than three times the size of Texas. It is located between the Arctic and the North Atlantic Oceans. Greenland is part of the kingdom of Denmark. None of the land is arable, meaning that it is not suitable for permanent crops. Nearly 90% of the population (just under 60,000) is native Inuit, who rely on an economy derived from exports of shrimp and fish, mining, tourism, and oil and gas exploration. Greenland is about 81 percent ice capped, but the island's glaciers have been steadily losing mass over the past decade. A heat wave in July of 2012 caused a great amount of glacial surface melting.

V2 Visual Skills

Describing Before class, gather a variety of landscape images. Partner students and provide one image to each pair. Have one student look at the picture of a landscape, but keep it hidden from their partner. While looking at it, the student should describe the landscape. Their partner should draw a quick sketch of the place, while listening to the description. Next provide a different image to each pair and have partners switch roles. When pairs have finished, they should compare the sketches to the original images. Discuss why geographers need to see and experience the places they study, either through direct observation or through remote sensing. **AL Auditory/Musical, Visual/Spatial**

ANSWERS, p. 32

READING PROGRESS CHECK Three types of regions are formal, functional, and perceptual.

CRITICAL THINKING

1. Three questions that the scientist might ask are: "What have I already learned about the glacier remotely? How does the size of the glacier compare to its size at specific times in the past? What is the appearance of the terrain surrounding the glacier?"
2. Students may describe the site as western coastal Greenland where the land is hilly, rocky, non-arable, and glacier-covered.

V1

Scientists study Russell Glacier in Greenland and the causes of its rapid melting.

Ashley Cooper/Alamy

▲ CRITICAL THINKING

1. ***Formulating Questions*** List three questions the scientist might be asking about the melting glacier.
2. ***Evaluating*** What words would you use to describe the site where the scientist is located?

Geographers work in a variety of jobs in government, business, and education. They often combine the study of geography with other areas of study. For example, an ecologist must know the geographic characteristics of a place or region in which he or she studies living organisms. Similarly, a travel agent must have knowledge of the physical and human geography of a place in order to plan trips for clients.

READING PROGRESS CHECK

Identifying What are the three types of regions?

Research Methods

GUIDING QUESTION *What methods do geographers use to conduct their work?*

To do their work, geographers use several research methods. Direct observation and measurement, mapping, interviewing, production and use of statistics, and the use of technology are all specialized research methods used by geographers.

V2

Direct observation and measurement involves analysis of patterns of human activity that take place on the Earth's surface. Geographers using this method will visit a place to gather information about it from what they observe of the place and its geographic features. Geographers also employ remote sensing from satellite images and aerial photographs to locate specific information without having to visit the site in person. For example, aerial photographs or satellite images can be used to locate mineral deposits, to determine the size of freshwater sources, or to see the extent of urban sprawl.

Mapping is essential to geographers. Many findings from geography research can be shown visually and spatially on maps better than they can be explained through statistical methods or written documents. Complex information can be collected and shown in more easily understood terms through using maps that highlight features, patterns, and relationships of people, places, and things. Maps

32

networks Online Teaching Options

INTERACTIVE IMAGE

Scientist Studying a Glacier

Narrative As a class, click through the images of Russell Glacier in Greenland and discuss some of the possible causes of its rapid melting. Ask students to imagine that they are geographers studying this glacier. Have them write a brief narrative of the observations that they might need to study, as well as the geography skills that they could use to help determine the possible causes for the rapid melting of Russell Glacier. **ELL Verbal/Linguistic**

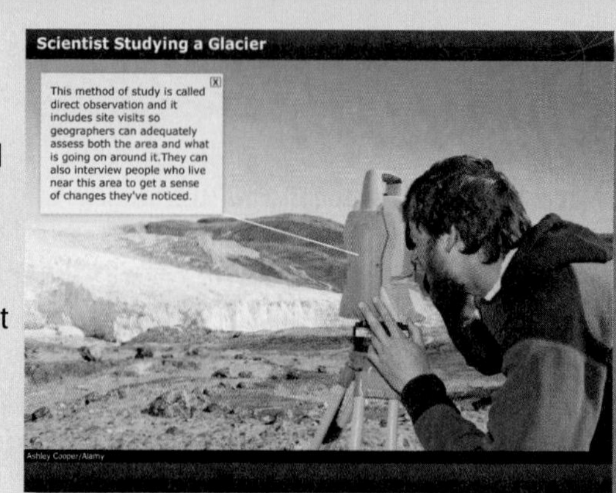

also are useful for making comparisons. For example, a geographer might compare population density maps or transportation networks maps of two counties in order to determine where to build new schools.

Interviewing requires a geographer to ask questions rather than just collect data, images, and on-site observations. Specifically, for human geographic studies, geographers may want to find out how people think or feel about certain places. They may also want to examine the ways in which people's beliefs and attitudes have affected the physical environment. To **obtain** such information, geographers interview their subjects. They can do this by selecting a particular group of people for study. Rather than contacting every individual in the group, however, geographers use a carefully selected sample of people whose answers represent the larger group.

C

obtain to gain or acquire, usually by planning or effort

Geographers also analyze *statistics*. Numerical data, such as temperature and snowfall, can provide insight into a region's climate trends. Geographers use computers to organize and present this information in an understandable manner, as well as to look in detail at the data for patterns and trends. For example, studies that identify age, ethnicity, and gender of specified regions can emphasize possible trends within a human population. After identifying such patterns and trends, geographers use statistical tests to see whether their ideas are valid.

V

READING PROGRESS CHECK

Defining What do geographers do?

Geography and Other Subjects

GUIDING QUESTION *How is geography related to other subjects?*

Geography has important relationships to other subjects. Geographers use geographic tools and methods to understand historical patterns, economies, politics and political patterns, and the impact of societies and cultures on the landscape.

To visualize what places could have looked like in the past, geographers take into account historical perspectives of the place. For example, to gather information about how a city has changed over time, geographers can collect information from historical sources regarding census data, economic output, birth and death rates, natural disasters, disease, and major **fluctuations** in population size. Such data can address questions concerning how human activities have changed the natural vegetation, or how waterways are different today than in the past. Such historical perspectives provide insight as to which institutions or development should be constructed to avoid repeating past complications between human growth and the physical environment.

R

fluctuation a shift from a previous condition

Additionally, analysis of historical and current political patterns emphasizes changing boundary lines and government systems. Geographers are also interested in how the natural environment has influenced political decisions and how governments change natural environments. For example, in the 1960s the Egyptian government built the massive Aswān High Dam on the Nile River to help irrigate the land. The dam altered the Nile River valley and significantly impacted the region's people.

Human geographers, also called cultural geographers, use the ideas of sociology and anthropology to study human tendencies and past cultures and their influence on current traditions and social norms. Because people come from diverse cultural backgrounds, their interpretations of information and experiences differ depending on their frame of reference. For example, residents of a particular neighborhood may define boundaries based on location of activities, such as stores they frequent and people with whom they have contact.

The Geographer's Craft

C Critical Thinking Skills

Gathering Information Tell students that interviewing can be a good way for geographers to gather information about a variety of things, such as perceptual regions. Have the class brainstorm five or six questions that geographers might ask to gain more knowledge about the statistics of students within the classroom. Questions may be about where they were born, how many siblings they have, how long they have lived in this community, or their family's heritage. Students should interview each other, and then share the results as a class. **ELL Interpersonal**

V Visual Skills

Identifying Trends Tell students that often the first stage of statistical analysis involves looking for trends. Have students look over the data they gathered via interviews conducted from the above activity and create a chart or diagram using the class results. Students should look for patterns and trends, as well as wide differences in answers. As a class, discuss the possible reasons why there could be similarities and differences even within a classroom located in the same city. **Logical/Mathematical, Visual/Spatial**

R Reading Skills

Inferring Encourage students to think about the types of things geographers can learn from the records that people have left behind. **Ask:** **What information can geographers learn about life in a particular place by studying the historical birth and death rates?** *(Possible answers: how hard or easy it was to survive, the population growth or fluctuation)* **What types of things might cause major fluctuations in a city's population?** *(Possible answers: disease, war, political changes, large migration into or out of the area, natural disaster)* **What types of things might a human geographer study to learn the details about an outbreak of a disease?** *(Possible answers: census data, diaries or written accounts from people alive at the time, burial records)* **Verbal/Linguistic**

GAME

The Geographer's Craft

Applying Use this interactive True/False Game to review concepts and terminology presented in this chapter. Divide the class up into pairs or small teams. Allow time for teams to discuss and answer each of the questions. Once students have provided answers for all of the questions, they can check their answers and a score will appear. The incorrect answers will return to another column and students will be asked to retry any incorrect answers. The option to *Play Again* is given at the end of the game.

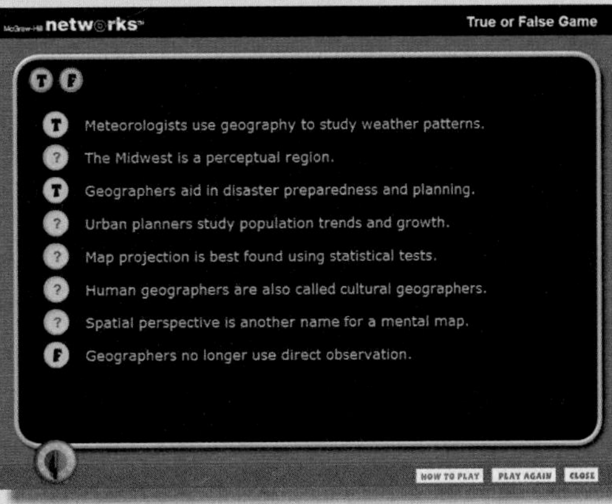

networks
True or False Game
T F
Meteorologists use geography to study weather patterns.
The Midwest is a perceptual region.
Geographers aid in disaster preparedness and planning.
Urban planners study population trends and growth.
Map projection is best found using statistical tests.
Human geographers are also called cultural geographers.
Spatial perspective is another name for a mental map.
Geographers no longer use direct observation.
HOW TO PLAY
PLAY AGAIN
CLOSE

ANSWERS, p. 33

READING PROGRESS CHECK A cartographer develops maps.

The Geographer's Craft

C Critical Thinking Skills

Analyzing Visuals Direct students' attention to the photo. Have them consider how human geography can be used to analyze this photo. **Ask:** **What information can human geographers learn about the type of region depicted in this photo?** *(Possible answers: shipping and transportation region; this region might contain warehouses; it would be noisy; have a lot of traffic from delivery trucks and machinery)* **What types of spatial divisions might be created between the region in this picture and a neighboring region?** *(Student answers may vary, but should reflect that the needs of the harbor must be met by workers, service industries, and transportation companies within this region or neighboring regions.)*

T Technology Skills

Determining Importance Read the last two paragraphs on the page to students. Explain that the study of economics, which includes the management and transportation of natural resources, is vital to every country's financial development. Assign various countries that are rich in natural resources (use the World Map of Gross Domestic Product at the beginning of the unit to help determine these countries) to either individual or small groups of students. Have them conduct Internet research to analyze how the distribution of natural resources affects their assigned country's economy and the movement of money. Students should compile their findings to create a multimedia presentation. The presentations should include graphs or charts of financial statistics that show how an abundance of natural resources helps create financial stability for a country. BL Logical/Mathematical

CLOSE & REFLECT

Synthesizing In closing, tell students that one reason geography is useful in so many different fields is because geographers gather information in a variety of ways. With this in mind, have students write a paragraph explaining how a political candidate might use geography while campaigning. *(Possible answers: the candidate might use trends to build their platform; use population distribution to target advertisements; use industry trends to target speeches)*

ANSWERS, p. 34

READING PROGRESS CHECK Human geographers are also referred to as cultural geographers.

CRITICAL THINKING

1. A geographer might study the location of natural resources, transportation systems, and people to learn about the economy of a country.
2. Interdependence is important because it allows the goods and services of cultures to be traded with one another, contributing to the economy of both cultures.

C

The natural shelter and deep waters of Victoria Harbor make Hong Kong one of the world's largest shipping ports.

▲ **CRITICAL THINKING**

1. ***Analyzing*** What factors might a geographer study to learn about the economy of a particular country?
2. ***Making Connections*** How is interdependence important to economic activity?

However, the local governments create neighborhood boundaries to facilitate services and maintenance. Furthermore, other neighborhood boundaries may be created by police departments and school districts that have different needs to meet and different reasons for creating spatial divisions. Human geography can be used to study the relationships between people, places, and environments by mapping information about them into a spatial context using GIS and other geospatial technologies. Human geographers study the way people are rooted in particular places and how they have constructed various types of regions. Some geographers specialize in studying the feelings one has about a place, which is very closely connected with theories in the fields of psychology and behavioral science.

Geographers study economies to understand how the locations of resources affect the ways people make, transport, and use goods, and how and where services are provided. Geographers are interested in how locations are chosen for various economic activities. Where and what human groups choose to produce and consume depend on a variety of factors: location of natural resources for mining and extracting, fertile soil for farming, suitable climates for living and producing, and proximity to good transport routes and other cultures to establish trade relations.

Economic activity relies on not only a society's production and use of goods, but also on the transport of goods between cultures in the form of trade. Such interdependence between global economies is part of what defines relationships and communication between various cultures. The growth of technological and communication systems in today's world also affects these relationships. The ability to call a client halfway across the world, reduce production time by mechanical production instead of human labor, use the Internet to communicate ideas instantly, and send goods overnight via air delivery are examples of how innovations in technology have increased the speed and efficiency of the movement of information and goods.

READING PROGRESS CHECK

Naming What is another name used for human geographers?

LESSON 2 REVIEW (CCSS)

Reviewing Vocabulary (Tier Three Words)

1. ***Understanding Relationships*** How are site and situation different? RH.9–10.4

Using Your Notes

2. ***Listing*** Using your graphic organizer, write a definition of *geography* in your own words. WHST.9–10.2

Answering the Guiding Questions

3. ***Identifying*** What is the spatial perspective?
4. ***Categorizing*** What are the elements of geography?
5. ***Organizing*** What methods do geographers use to conduct their work?
6. ***Evaluating*** How is geography related to other subjects?

Writing Activity

7. ***Informative/Explanatory*** Write a paragraph explaining how geography helps us interpret the past, understand the present, and plan for the future. WHST.9–10.2

34

LESSON 2 REVIEW ANSWERS

Reviewing Vocabulary

1. *Site* is the specific location of a place, including its physical setting; *situation* refers to a general location, defined by a place's geographic position in relation to other places and its connections to other regions.

Using Your Notes

2. Geography is the study of the physical features and human activity on Earth's surface and atmosphere.

Answering the Guiding Questions

3. A spatial perspective focuses on the ways individual places, people, or objects are related to one another.
4. The six elements of geography are: the world in spatial terms, places and regions, physical systems, human systems, environment and society, and the uses of geography.
5. Geographers use direct observation and measurement, mapping, interviewing, production and use of statistics, and technology.
6. Geography has important relationships to other subjects. Geographers use geographic tools and methods to understand historical patterns, economies, politics and political patterns, and the impact of societies and cultures on the landscape.

Writing Activity

7. Paragraphs may vary, but should explain how geography helps in interpreting the past, understanding the present, and planning for the future.

CHAPTER 1 Assessment (CCSS)

Directions: On a separate sheet of paper, answer the questions below. Make sure you read carefully and answer all parts of the questions.

Lesson Review

Lesson 1

1. ***Describing*** Describe the problems that arise when the curves of a globe become straight lines on a map.
2. ***Comparing and Contrasting*** Explain the similarities and differences between the Winkel Tripel projection and the Mercator projection.
3. ***Describing*** What is the importance of scale in reading maps?
4. ***Listing*** List three examples of things a map can show.

Lesson 2

5. ***Explaining*** Why is the U.S. Corn Belt considered a formal region?
6. ***Discussing*** What are two research methods used by geographers?
7. ***Differentiating*** What is the difference between physical geography and human geography?
8. ***Summarizing*** Why is human-environment interaction an important theme for geographers?

Applying Map Skills

Refer to the Unit 1 Atlas to answer the following questions.

9. ***Places and Regions*** Which continent has the most countries with the highest population densities?
10. ***Environment and Society*** Look at the map of world economic activities. Name three forms of land use for the continent of Africa. 1.1.I.1
11. ***Physical Systems*** What physical features in Africa might explain areas with little or no economic activity? 6.3.I.1
12. ***The World in Spatial Terms*** Look at the political map. What is the absolute location of Houston, Texas? What is the relative location of Houston?

DBQ Analyzing Primary Sources

Use the cartoon to answer the following questions.

PRIMARY SOURCE

Leo Cullum/The New Yorker Collection/www.cartoonbank.com

13. ***Analyzing Visuals*** Why do we see the globe as being upside down? How is the penguin's point of view different? Why? RH.9–10.6
14. ***Finding the Main Idea*** What does this cartoon say about the broad definition of geography? RH.9–10.2, RH.9–10.4

Exploring the Essential Question

15. ***Understanding Historical Interpretation*** Imagine you are studying an archaeological site to determine why a civilization came to end. What kind of geographic information might you want to gather in order to determine what happened to the civilization? Consider the skills for thinking geographically. Write a paragraph containing your response. WHST.9–10.8

Need Extra Help?

If You've Missed Question	1	2	3	4	5	6	7	8	9	10	11	12	13	14	15
Go to page	14	15	18	18	30	32	30	30	2	2	2	2	35	35	32

CHAPTER 1 Assessment Answers

Lesson Review

Lesson 1

1. When the curves of a globe become straight lines on a map, the distance, size, shapes, and directions become distorted.
2. Both the Winkel Tripel projection and the Mercator projection distort distances. However, the Winkel Tripel projection better shows the overall size and shape of land areas in relation to each other, while the Mercator projection is better for sea navigation as it shows true direction.
3. Knowing the scale allows you to determine the distance between places on a map.
4. Examples will vary, but can include items such as roads, airports, buildings, countries, cities, mountains, and bodies of water.

Lesson 2

5. The Corn Belt is a formal region because it is identified by a single characteristic, which is its primary crop of corn.
6. Direct observation and measurement as well as mapping are research methods used by geographers.
7. Physical geography looks at the processes of climate, land, water, plants, and animal life in relation to human activity. Human geography looks at human activities in relation to physical and cultural environments.
8. By studying human-environment interaction, geographers can help societies make decisions about the future that benefit both people and the environment.

Applying Map Skills

9. Europe is the continent with the highest population density.
10. Possible answers: commercial farming, subsistence farming, livestock raising, nomadic herding, forest
11. Very little economic activity occurs in the desert areas of Africa.
12. The absolute location of Houston is approximately 30° N latitude and 95° W longitude. The relative location of Houston is southeastern Texas.

Analyzing Primary Sources

13. The globe appears upside down because we live in the Northern Hemisphere, so our perspective is opposite of the penguin's point of view. The penguin's point of view is different because he lives in Antarctica. He views the world from the perspective of living in the Southern Hemisphere.
14. The way that we use geography and its tools is influenced by our place and perspective in the world.

Exploring the Essential Question

15. Paragraphs may vary, but should show how using geography skills such as observation and measurement, as well as mapping of land features, can help offer explanations of why the civilization came to an end.

Assessment Answers

Critical Thinking

16. The different types of geospatial technologies are global positioning systems (GPS), geographic information systems (GIS), and remote sensing systems. This technology allows for more highly accurate information to be used to quickly create and change maps.

17. GIS information about the areas surrounding a road could offer explanations such as urban growth to explain traffic increases.

18. Student answers may vary, but should include information about how spatial relationships (particularly location) influence geography.

19. By analyzing data on Earth's physical features and processes, geographers can help societies make decisions about future plans for economic and urban growth.

20. Mental maps describe students' internal maps. A mental map might be of a small area such as their house or neighborhood, or where they are in relation to the rest of the world.

College and Career Readiness

21. Student answers may vary, but could include how geographic knowledge or tools help people understand patterns in professions such as economics, politics, history, sociology, or anthropology.

Research and Presentation

22. Paragraphs may vary, but could include how geography can be used to determine locations for filming, writing scripts, and researching facts used in films.

Writing About Geography

23. Paragraphs will differ but should include information about using observation and measurement, mapping, and interviewing to determine things such as location and size of the new community center.

21st Century Skills

24. Possible answers: environmental problems, pollution, health epidemics, natural disasters, climate change, political issues

25. According to George Demko, the main objective of geography is to discover the processes that move over space and connect places and continually transform the location and character of everything.

CHAPTER 1 Assessment 

Directions: On a separate sheet of paper, answer the questions below. Make sure you read carefully and answer all parts of the questions.

Critical Thinking

16. ***Assessing*** What are the different types of geospatial technologies? How has this advanced technology improved the way maps are created?

17. ***Making Connections*** What type of information would help you determine why traffic has increased on a certain road?

18. ***Evaluating*** How could geography be interpreted differently based on changing human perspectives?

19. ***Drawing Conclusions*** How can we use geography to make decisions for the future?

20. ***Compare and Contrast*** What differentiates mental mapping from other forms of visual mapping?

College and Career Readiness

21. ***Examining Information*** Describe three ways geographic knowledge or tools are used in professions other than geography.

Research and Presentation

22. ***Research Skills*** Using the Internet, conduct research to learn about how geography is used in the film industry. Write one paragraph describing a specific example of this use. WHST.9–10.8

Writing About Geography

23. ***Informative/Explanatory*** Imagine you are a geographer working on a plan for a new community center. Using the different types of research methods as your guide, what factors would you use to develop the plan? Explain your choices in a paragraph. WHST.9–10.7

21st Century Skills

Use the excerpt below to answer the questions that follow.

PRIMARY SOURCE

"Geography—real-world geography—is the art and science of location, or place. It is about spatial patterns and spatial processes. It is about which way the wind blows from Chernobyl, the Pacific 'ring of fire,' AIDS, terrorists, and refugees. It is about acid rain, El Niño, ocean dumping, cultural censorship, droughts and famines. . . .

Real-world geography also explores things in locations: why something is where it is and what processes change its distribution. Geography is the why of where of an ever-changing universe. Its surpassing objective is to discover the processes that move over space and connect places and continually transform the location and character of everything."

—George J. Demko, *Why in the World: Adventures in Geography*, 1992

24. ***Geography Skills*** What are some of the world issues that George Demko lists as concerns of geography? RH.9–10.1

25. ***Primary and Secondary Sources*** According to the excerpt, what is the main objective of geography? RH.9–10.2

26. ***Identifying Cause & Effect*** Identify how the physical environment affects human activity, and likewise how human activity affects the physical environment.

27. ***Economics*** How might the economic activities of a region affect its physical and human geography?

Need Extra Help?

If You've Missed Question	16	17	18	19	20	21	22	23	24	25	26	27
Go to page	21	22	28	31	20	33	36	32	36	36	36	36

26. Student answers may vary, but should include the positive and negative impacts of humans on the environment and vice versa. Examples could include limited human activity in very harsh regions of the world such as deserts and arctic regions, as well as industries using natural resources and polluting the environment.

27. Student answers may vary, but may include examples of how increasing/decreasing economic activities in a region cause more/less people to inhabit that area and what the consequences are of an increasing/decreasing population.

CHAPTER 2

The Physical World Planner

UNDERSTANDING BY DESIGN®

Enduring Understandings

- *Physical processes shape Earth's surface.*

Essential Question

- *How do physical processes shape Earth's surface?*

Predictable Misunderstandings

Students may think:

- *Earth's biosphere is the same as Earth's atmosphere. Explain that Earth's atmosphere is only the layer of gases above Earth's surface while the biosphere is the part of Earth that supports life and includes the hydrosphere, lithosphere, and atmosphere.*
- *Changes in Earth's surface are caused only by tectonic plate movement.*
- *Water is produced in the water cycle.*
- *Desalination provides an easy and inexpensive method of producing freshwater.*

Assessment Evidence

Performance Tasks:

- *Hands-On Chapter Project*

Other Evidence:

- *Guided Reading Activities*
- *Vocabulary Activity*
- *Lesson Quizzes*
- *Chapter Tests, Forms A and B*

SUGGESTED PACING GUIDE

Introducing the Chapter	½ Day	Lesson 3	1 Day
Lesson 1	1 Day	Chapter Wrap-Up and Assessment	1 Day
Lesson 2	1 Day		

TOTAL TIME 4½ Days

Key for Using the Teacher Edition

SKILL-BASED ACTIVITIES

Types of skill activities found in the Teacher Edition.

* **V Visual Skills** require students to analyze maps, graphs, charts, and photos.

R Reading Skills help students practice reading skills and master vocabulary.

C Critical Thinking Skills help students apply and extend what they have learned.

W Writing Skills provide writing opportunities to help students comprehend the text.

T Technology Skills require students to use digital tools effectively.

*Letters are followed by a number when there is more than one of the same type of skill on the page.

DIFFERENTIATED INSTRUCTION

All activities are written for the on-level student unless otherwise marked with the leveled labels below.

BL Beyond Level
AL Approaching Level
ELL English Language Learners

All students benefit from activities that utilize different learning styles. Many activities are marked as below when a particular learning style is highlighted.

Intrapersonal	Naturalist
Logical/Mathematical	Kinesthetic
Visual/Spatial	Auditory/Musical
Verbal/Linguistic	Interpersonal

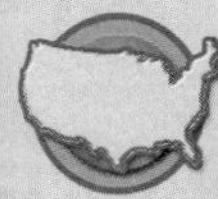

National Geography Standards covered in "The Physical World"

The student knows and understands:

(3) How to analyze the spatial organizations of people, places, and environments on Earth's surface

3.1 The meaning and use of complex spatial concepts, such as connectivity, networks, hierarchies, to analyze and explain the spatial organization of human and physical phenomena

3.2 Complex processes change over time and shape patterns in the distribution of human and physical phenomena

3.3 Models are used to represent the structure and dynamics of spatial processes which shape human and physical systems

(4) The physical and human characteristics of places

4.2 The interaction of physical and human systems result in the creation of and changes to places

(7) The physical processes that shape the patterns of Earth's surface

7.1 The interaction of Earth's physical systems (the atmosphere, biosphere, hydrosphere, and lithosphere) vary across space and time

7.3 Physical processes interact over time to shape particular places on Earth's surface

(14) How human actions modify the physical environment

14.2 The use of technology can have both intended and unintended impacts on the physical environment

14.3 People can either mitigate and/or adapt to the consequences of human modifications of the physical environment

(16) The changes that occur in the meaning, use, distribution, and importance of resources

16.3 Policies and programs that promote the sustainable use and management of resources impact people and the environment

CHAPTER OPENER PLANNER

Students will know:
- *that Earth is part of a larger physical system that contains other planets, moons, and stars that revolve around the sun.*
- *that Earth's biosphere is made up of the hydrosphere, lithosphere, and atmosphere.*
- *how internal and external forces shape Earth's surface.*
- *how the water cycle works, sources of freshwater, and how desalination can provide freshwater.*

Students will be able to:
- ***describe*** *Earth and the solar system.*
- ***analyze*** *how plate tectonics and continental drift affect Earth's surface.*
- ***describe*** *how the water cycle works and explain desalination.*

UNDERSTANDING BY DESIGN®

☑ *Print Teaching Options*

R Reading Skills

☐ **p. 37** Students hypothesize how geographers interpret the physical world. BL Logical/Mathematical

V Visual Skills

☐ **p. 38** Students use the image of villagers to discuss the basic need for freshwater. Visual/Spatial

☐ **p. 39** Students draw a flowchart of the desalination process.

C Critical Thinking Skills

☐ **p. 39** Students discuss the advantages and disadvantages of desalination. Intrapersonal

W Writing Skills

☐ **p. 38** Students write a narrative about what it would be like to live for a week without water.

T Technology Skills

☐ **p. 39** Students research countries with low amounts of annual rainfall and describe how their climates affect their economies.

☑ *Online Teaching Options*

V Visual Skills

SLIDE SHOW **Water Scarcity and Economic Impact**—Students learn about water scarcity and its economic impact. Visual/Spatial

INFOGRAPHIC **Salt Water vs. Freshwater**—Students create visuals identifying where people lack freshwater worldwide or which lakes in the United States are too polluted for aquatic life. Interpersonal, Visual/Spatial

MAP **Interactive World Atlas**—Students use the interactive world atlas to identify the regions of the world and describe their terrain.

☑ *Printable Digital Worksheets*

WORKSHEET **Assessing Background Knowledge**—Students demonstrate their understanding and prior knowledge about the physical world.

WORKSHEET **Chapter Summaries**—Summaries are provided for each chapter that thoroughly condense core content into manageable chunks.

WORKSHEET **Reteaching Activity**—These worksheets provide students with an opportunity for remedial practice and review of vital chapter content.

WORKSHEET **Vocabulary Activity**—Students apply their knowledge of content and academic vocabulary words.

Project-Based Learning

Hands-On

Oral Presentation

Students will work in small groups to prepare an oral presentation about Earth's place in the solar system, the forces of change on Earth, and bodies of water on Earth.

Digital Hands-On

Create Online Projects

Find an additional activity online that incorporates technology for this project. Visit the EdTech Teacher Web sites for more links, tutorials, and other resources.

Print Resources

ANCILLARY RESOURCES

This ancillary is available for every chapter and lesson.

- **Chapter Tests and Lesson Quizzes**

PRINTABLE DIGITAL WORKSHEETS

These printable digital worksheets are available for every chapter and lesson.

- **Assessing Background Knowledge**
- **Chapter Summaries**
- **Guided Reading Activities**
- **Hands-On Chapter Projects**
- **Quizzes and Tests**
- **Reading Essentials and Study Guide** AL
- **Reteaching Activities**
- **Video Activities**
- **Vocabulary Activities**

More Media Resources

SUGGESTED VIDEOS 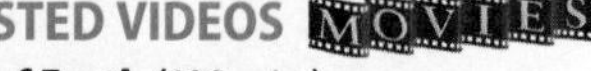

- **Faces of Earth** (180 min.)
- **Violent Earth** (52 min.)

SUGGESTED READING 

- ***Undersea Frontiers: An Introduction to Oceanography***, by C.B. Colby
- ***Rain of Troubles: The Science and Politics of Acid Rain,*** by Laurence Pringle

PLANET EARTH

Students will know:

- *that Earth is part of a larger physical system that contains other planets, moons, and stars.*
- *that the planets, moons, stars, asteroids, comets, and meteorites revolve around the sun.*
- *that Earth's surface is a complex mix of landforms and water systems.*
- *how the hydrosphere, lithosphere, and atmosphere work together to form the biosphere.*

Students will be able to:

- ***describe** the planets and other bodies in the solar system.*
- ***analyze** the biosphere.*
- ***describe** landforms.*

UNDERSTANDING BY DESIGN®

☑ Print Teaching Options

V Visual Skills

- ☐ **p. 41** Students compare and contrast the planets. AL Visual/Spatial
- ☐ **p. 42** Students interpret a diagram of the atmosphere. AL Visual/Spatial
- ☐ **p. 43** Students name and locate the continents on a world map. AL Visual/Spatial

R Reading Skills

- ☐ **p. 40** Students discuss the meaning of the term *solar system*. ELL Verbal/Linguistic
- ☐ **p. 41** Students determine how the terrestrial planets are alike and how the gas giant planets are alike. ELL Naturalist
- ☐ **p. 42** Students identify characteristics of the hydrosphere, lithosphere, and atmosphere and explain the relationship between them. ELL Interpersonal

C Critical Thinking Skills

- ☐ **p. 40** Students discuss the role of gravity and keeping Earth and other objects revolving in orbit around the sun. BL Logical/Mathematical
- ☐ **p. 42** Students analyze the biosphere and how it supports life. Verbal/Linguistic

W Writing Skills

- ☐ **p. 41** Students write a narrative imagining a meteor strike in their region. Verbal/Linguistic

T Technology Skills

- ☐ **p. 40** Students conduct online research about Pluto's changing status from a planet to a dwarf planet. Interpersonal
- ☐ **p. 43** Students use Internet and library resources to compare and contrast dry landforms and underwater landforms and create a diagram showing the landforms of the ocean floor. BL Naturalist

☑ Online Teaching Options

V Visual Skills

- INTERACTIVE BELLRINGER **The Highest and Deepest Places on Earth**—Students discuss a diagram and use it to calculate the answers to the bellringer questions. AL Logical/Mathematical, Naturalist
- VIDEO **Changing Landscapes**—Students explore the relationship between climate and landscape shown in the video. AL Visual/Spatial, Verbal/Linguistic

R Reading Skills

- INTERACTIVE INFOGRAPHIC **The Solar System**—Students learn about each of the planets, the Earth-sun relationship, and explore why Earth's position in the solar system makes it ideal to sustain human life. AL Verbal/Linguistic
- INTERACTIVE WHITEBOARD ACTIVITY **Solar System**—Students identify the planets of the solar system to help them understand that Earth is part of a larger physical system that contains other planets.

☑ Printable Digital Worksheets

R Reading Skills

- WORKSHEET **Guided Reading Activity**—Students use Guided Reading Activity worksheets to review their comprehension of the content. Verbal/Linguistic
- WORKSHEET **Chapter Summary Worksheet**—Students review the main ideas of the chapter content. Verbal/Linguistic

C Critical Thinking Skills

- WORKSHEET **Video Activity**—Students answer questions after they have viewed a lesson video about the relationship to the chapter content. Visual/Spatial

FORCES OF CHANGE

Students will know:
- *the three layers of Earth.*
- *the theory of continental drift and the process of plate tectonics.*
- *the internal forces of change and how they shape Earth's surface.*
- *the external forces of change and how they shape Earth's surface.*

Students will be able to:
- ***describe** Earth's layers.*
- ***explain** plate tectonics and continental drift.*

UNDERSTANDING BY DESIGN®

☑ Print Teaching Options

V Visual Skills

- ☐ **p. 44** Students compare and contrast Earth's layers. AL Visual/Spatial
- ☐ **p. 46** Students work in small groups to visually demonstrate the processes of plate tectonics and continental drift. ELL Visual/Spatial

R Reading Skills

- ☐ **p. 45** Students cite evidence for how Earth's landmasses changed over the last 500 million years. Verbal/Linguistic
- ☐ **p. 47** Students explain how *accretion, convergence,* and *spreading* differ. Interpersonal
- ☐ **p. 48** Students describe earthquakes and the Ring of Fire. Logical/Mathematical

C Critical Thinking Skills

- ☐ **p. 45** Students study a diagram of Earth's layers and note temperature changes from the core to the crust. BL Logical/Mathematical
- ☐ **p. 45** Students discuss the causes and effects of tectonic plates on Earth's surface. AL Naturalist
- ☐ **p. 47** Students explain the difference between a fold and a fault and explain the process that causes each. Logical/Mathematical
- ☐ **p. 49** Students distinguish between internal and external forces that shape Earth's surface. BL Logical/Mathematical
- ☐ **p. 50** Students review the destructive power of glaciers. AL Logical/Mathematical

W Writing Skills

- ☐ **p. 44** Students report on one of Earth's destructive events. Verbal/Linguistic
- ☐ **p. 47** Students write a paragraph explaining what the map shows about plate movement. AL Verbal/Linguistic
- ☐ **p. 48** Students use the diagram of Forces of Change to write a step-by-step process paper. Verbal/Linguistic

T Technology Skills

- ☐ **p. 46** Students evaluate the helpfulness of Web sites on continental drift and plate tectonics. Logical/Mathematical
- ☐ **p. 49** Students research natural formations found in National Parks. Interpersonal, Verbal/Linguistic

☑ Online Teaching Options

V Visual Skills

- ☐ INTERACTIVE BELLRINGER **Interpreting a Map of Tectonic Plates**—Students interpret and discuss a map showing Earth's tectonic plates to answer questions.
- ☐ INTERACTIVE MAP **Continental Drift**—Students explore how the continents drifted apart and continue to move and make a step-by-step process chart that explains the scientific beliefs of Pangaea. Visual/Spatial, Naturalist
- ☐ INFOGRAPHIC **Forces of Change**—Students explore geological processes that shape Earth's surface. BL Naturalist

W Writing Skills

- ☐ VIDEO **Death Valley is Sinking**—Students watch the video and write a paragraph predicting what will happen to Death Valley over time. Verbal/Linguistic
- ☐ INTERACTIVE MAP **Tectonic Plate Boundaries**—Students explore the Ring of Fire and write a paragraph speculating how people in Japan have adapted to their physical environment. AL Verbal/Linguistic, Naturalist

C Critical Thinking Skills

- ☐ VIDEO **Water Eroding Mountains**—Students learn how water shapes Earth's surface and write three questions. ELL Verbal/Linguistic
- ☐ INTERACTIVE WHITEBOARD ACTIVITY **Forces of Change**—Students categorize forces of change on the Earth's surface as internal or external and then place the definition for the change in a chart.

☑ Printable Digital Worksheets

R Reading Skills

- ☐ WORKSHEET **Guided Reading Activity**—Students use Guided Reading Activity worksheets to review their comprehension of the lesson content. Verbal/Linguistic
- ☐ WORKSHEET **Reading Essentials and Study Guide**—Students complete the study guide and answer Reading Progress Check and vocabulary questions. AL

C Critical Thinking Skills

- ☐ WORKSHEET **Video Activity**—Students will complete this worksheet by answering the questions about this lesson video content. Visual/Spatial

EARTH'S WATER

Students will know:
- *how the water cycle works.*
- *Earth's bodies of saltwater.*
- *sources of freshwater on Earth.*
- *how desalination can address the need for freshwater.*

Students will be able to:
- ***describe*** *the stages of the water cycle.*
- ***identify*** *Earth's saltwater bodies and freshwater sources.*
- ***explain*** *how desalination works.*

UNDERSTANDING BY DESIGN®

☑ *Print Teaching Options*

V Visual Skills

- ☐ **p. 51** Students explain the difference between *evaporation* and *condensation.* AL Visual/Spatial
- ☐ **p. 52** Students locate smaller bodies of water and discuss the differences between a gulf, sea, and bay. ELL Intrapersonal, Visual/Spatial
- ☐ **p. 54** Students locate Earth's freshwater sources on a world map. Visual/Spatial

R Reading Skills

- ☐ **p. 51** Students discuss the water cycle and the sun's role. ELL Verbal/Linguistic
- ☐ **p. 52** Students name and discuss the five oceans. Verbal/Linguistic, Visual/Spatial
- ☐ **p. 54** A volunteer creates a pie graph showing Earth's freshwater supply and students discuss conservation of freshwater. ELL Visual/Spatial

C Critical Thinking Skills

- ☐ **p. 51** Students explain how the total volume of water in the water cycle is constant. Logical/Mathematical
- ☐ **p. 53** Students explore how to solve a growing water problem in a community. Logical/Mathematical
- ☐ **p. 54** Students list major environmental concerns surrounding desalination. Intrapersonal

W Writing Skills

- ☐ **p. 52** Students write a short essay explaining how they would move through the water cycle if they were a drop of water. BL Naturalist

T Technology Skills

- ☐ **p. 53** Students gather statistics about worldwide freshwater supplies and create a bulletin board to show how economics affects desalination processes. BL Visual/Spatial

☑ *Online Teaching Options*

V Visual Skills

- ☐ INTERACTIVE BELLRINGER **Desalination Capacity**—Students read a graph to discuss and answer questions about the different amounts of freshwater and salt water available in the world.
- ☐ INTERACTIVE MAP **Global Desalination**—Students use a map to answer questions about desalination plants. AL Visual/Spatial
- ☐ VIDEO **Water Eroding Mountains**— Students write three questions they have about the Earth's water cycle after watching the video. ELL Verbal/Linguistic

C Critical Thinking Skills

- ☐ MAP **Roads and Accessible Resources in New Guinea**—Students use the interactive map to discuss the roads of New Guinea and challenges in constructing roads to accessible areas of the country. Visual/Spatial, Verbal/Linguistic
- ☐ INTERACTIVE WHITEBOARD ACTIVITY **Water Cycle**—Students define and identify the key steps in the water cycle process.

☑ *Printable Digital Worksheets*

R Reading Skills

- ☐ WORKSHEET **Guided Reading Activity**—Students use Guided Reading Activity worksheets to review their comprehension of the content.
- ☐ WORKSHEET **Reading Essentials and Study Guide**—Students complete the study guide and answer Reading Progress Check and vocabulary questions. AL

C Critical Thinking Skills

- ☐ WORKSHEET **Reteaching Activity**—Students use this activity worksheet to review and reteach chapter content and vocabulary. This worksheet can be used with struggling students who need additional help with difficult concepts.

INTERVENTION AND REMEDIATION STRATEGIES

LESSON 1 Planet Earth

Reading and Comprehension

To ensure comprehension of the concept that Earth is part of a larger physical system known as the solar system, have students take turns acting as the teacher of this lesson. You may wish to have students work in small groups, or you can assign a key concept, place, or content vocabulary term from the lesson for individual students to explain to the rest of the class. Have students make a brief presentation to "teach" the topic or term to the rest of the class, encouraging the use of visuals. Tell students they may use the board to draw diagrams or charts to better explain their assigned concept. Encourage student "teachers" to conduct a question-and-answer session to ensure that their "students" comprehend lesson concepts.

Text Evidence

Have students review the lesson and write four paragraphs, each describing one of the "sphere" terms used in the text. Students should use each term correctly, and explain its meaning as it relates to Earth and the support of life on the planet. Tell students to use textual evidence to support ideas presented in their paragraphs, using the lesson narrative and graphics for ideas. Ask volunteers to read their paragraphs to the class. Then, have students quiz a partner, using the terms as described in their paragraphs.

LESSON 2 Forces of Change

Reading and Comprehension

Organize students into four groups. Assign four different content vocabulary terms to each group. Have students in each group work together to write a paragraph, using the terms they have been assigned. After groups have completed their paragraphs, ask a volunteer from each group to read the paragraph. Challenge groups to incorporate the academic vocabulary terms in their paragraphs. Provide guidance as needed, ensuring that students have used each content and academic vocabulary term correctly.

Text Evidence

Tell students they will work in teams to conduct research about a real-life event that relates to one of the following categories: Earth's structure, internal forces of change, or external forces of change. Either assign or have students choose the event, ensuring that each group has a different event to research. Have groups present a summary of their findings to the class, citing textual evidence that supports their research. Encourage students to provide visuals to accompany their presentations, such as a model that shows continental drift as it relates to internal forces of change.

LESSON 3 Earth's Water

Reading and Comprehension

Organize students into small groups. Have groups outline key facts and processes related to one of the following topics: the water cycle, desalination, and the importance of freshwater to life on Earth. To ensure comprehension of the topics, have groups create a slide show using presentation software that explains the topic or process. After each group presents its slide show to the class, allow time for groups to conduct a question-and-answer session in which students from each group answer questions about their topic.

Text Evidence

Have students brainstorm different activities that involve bodies of water in your community. Then write the headings *Recreational, Commercial,* and *Industrial* on the board. As students come up with each activity, ask them to write it in the correct column on the board. Have students consider how human activity affects the water cycle. Then have students use information in the text to write a short essay addressing the Essential Question: *How do physical processes shape Earth's surface?* Circulate to provide guidance if students struggle to make connections. Ask volunteers to read their essays to the class.

Online Resources

Leveled Reader

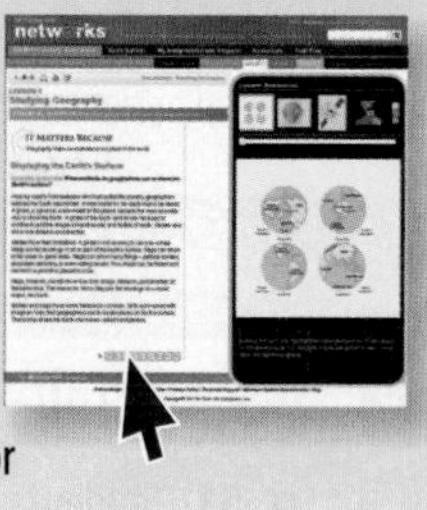

Use this online approaching-level text that corresponds directly to the text in the Student Edition. It also includes additional reading and comprehension support for English Language Learners.

Guided Reading Activities

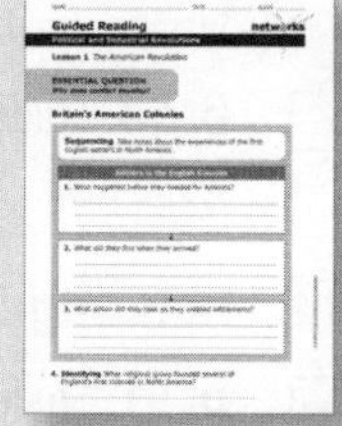

This resource uses guiding questions to help students with comprehension.

Reteaching Activities

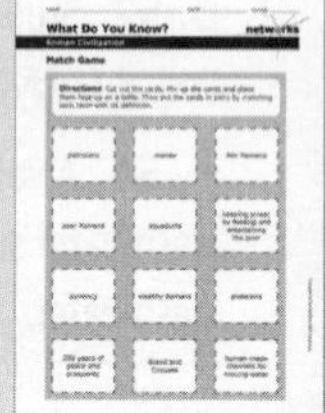

These worksheets provide students with an opportunity for remedial practice and review of vital chapter content.

Reading Essentials and Study Guide

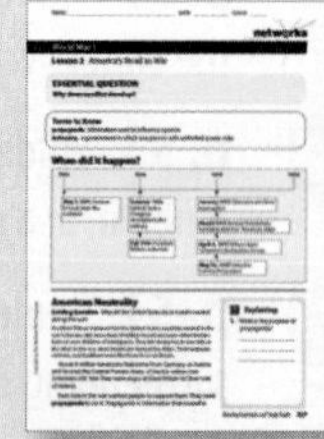

This resource offers writing and reading activities for the approaching-level student.

Self-Check Quizzes

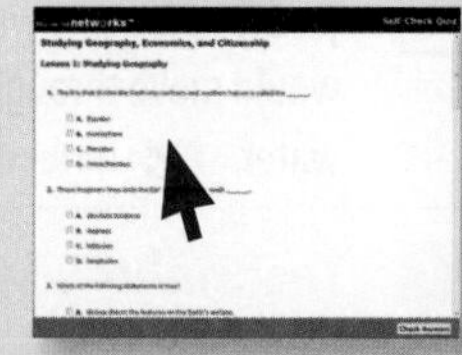

This online assessment tool provides instant feedback for students to check their progress.

Chapter Summaries

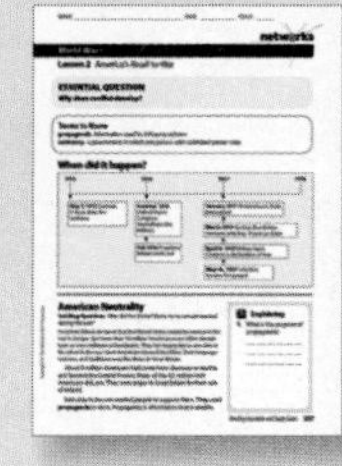

Summaries are provided for each chapter that thoroughly condense core content into manageable chunks.

The Physical World

ESSENTIAL QUESTION • *How do physical processes shape Earth's surface?*

networks

There's More Online about the physical world.

CHAPTER 2

Geography Matters...

Because much of our world had not been explored before 1800, geography prior to that time focused on discovery, basic data collection, and observation. Geographers were busy determining the elevation of land surfaces, describing landforms, identifying weather and climate patterns, and classifying soils and ecosystems. The geographers of today use sophisticated tools and research methods to monitor the processes that shape Earth's surface, the natural resources essential to our survival, and the ways in which humans affect and are affected by the physical environment. Understanding the planet we call home helps us make better decisions about how to utilize, preserve, and protect the Earth and adapt to its changing environments.

◄ A climber rests alone on Mount Everest.

37

Letter from the Author

Dear Geography Teacher,

The physical environment of Earth is the stage on which humans play out their lives. To look at the world physical maps in the atlas tells only part of the story. Students can learn where the mountains, oceans, seas, plains, plateaus, and river valleys are located but there is a deeper story to be told. The physical environment is dynamic, changing because of variations in heat or cold, wind systems, plate tectonics, ocean currents, changing climates, and, in some cases, the ravages of human activities. Air, water, and land pollution can challenge the physical environment and make us wonder what will be there for future generations.

Richard G. Boehm

ENGAGE

Activating Prior Knowledge Invite students to list the features that make up the physical world around them. Then have them look at the photographs and diagrams in the chapter to add features to their lists. Review their lists in a class discussion. Help them distinguish between what was made by natural forces and what is human-made.

TEACH & ASSESS

Making Connections Call students' attention to the image of the climber on Mt. Everest, while reading:

- Mount Everest is the most prominent mountain in the world, with an elevation of 29,028 feet (8,848 m).
- In 1999, an American expedition implanted a GPS device on the highest rock on Mt. Everest to assess the current elevation. The device shows that Mt. Everest is actually rising. It rises about 1/3 of an inch each year (from 3 to 6 mm) and moves to the northeast about 3 inches each year.
- The first successful ascent of Mt. Everest took place in 1953 by the team of Sir Edmund Hillary of New Zealand and Tenzing Norgay of Nepal.

Hypothesizing Ask: What tools might a geographer take along to study processes that shape Earth's surface? *(maps, globes, telescope, binoculars, measuring tools, compass, scales, surveying tools, magnifying glass, GPS, navigational tools, computer, pick, coring apparatus)* Have volunteers research some of the tools today's geographers use, such as seismographs, GIS software, electromagnetic geophysical instruments, geological compasses, paramagnetic susceptibility analyzers, soil core sampling apparatus, sonars, and remote sensing devices. **BL Logical/Mathematical**

CLOSE & REFLECT

Applying Have students describe how knowledge of the physical world is helpful to them in their day-to-day lives or has helped them or their families make an important decision. Discuss how understanding the physical world helps community, state, and federal leaders plan for the future.

ePals GlobalCommunity
Where learners connect™

Extend the project-based learning experience globally through our partnership with ePals. EPals allows you to connect with classrooms around the world in a safe online environment for real-life lessons and projects in virtual study groups.

ENGAGE

W Writing Skills

Narrative Ask students to write a paragraph titled "My Week Without Water" describing the difficulties they might experience if they were without water for a week.

TEACH & ASSESS

V Visual Skills

Analyzing Visuals Direct students to study the main image and text about the villagers and the basic need for freshwater. **Ask: What can you tell about these women's environment?** *(Possible answers: dry, rocky, no vegetation, drought prone, scarcity of water)* **What do you suppose these women are carrying and why?** *(Possible answers: water; because there is a lack of water, these women must travel to get freshwater for drinking, bathing, and other human uses)* Have students explain how these women's lives might change if they had running water in their homes. **Visual/Spatial**

C Critical Thinking Skills

Interpreting Significance Have students discuss the importance of freshwater resources in their community. **Ask:**

- **Where does the water you drink come from?** *(Possible answers: well, reservoir, lake, spring, rainwater, desalination plant)*
- **Is this the same place that supplies water to farmers and industry in your area?** *(In many areas, water for agriculture and industry comes from rivers, lakes, or reservoirs; in some areas, the source is a desalination plant.)*
- **What economic activities depend on water?** *(Possible answers: farming, fishing, hydroelectricity, sewage, nurseries, and other industries that use water for manufacturing or cooling)*
- **How would a scarcity of freshwater impact the economy in your community?** *(Student answers will vary, but should reflect that their community would probably have very limited agricultural and industrial resources resulting in a poor economy.)* BL **Logical/Mathematical**

Content Background Knowledge

Water usage in the United States:

- Thermoelectric 49%
- Irrigation 31%
- Public Supply 11%
- Other (mining, industrial, aquaculture, livestock) 8%
- Domestic (indoor/outdoor residential use) 1%

Why Geography Matters: **The Physical World**

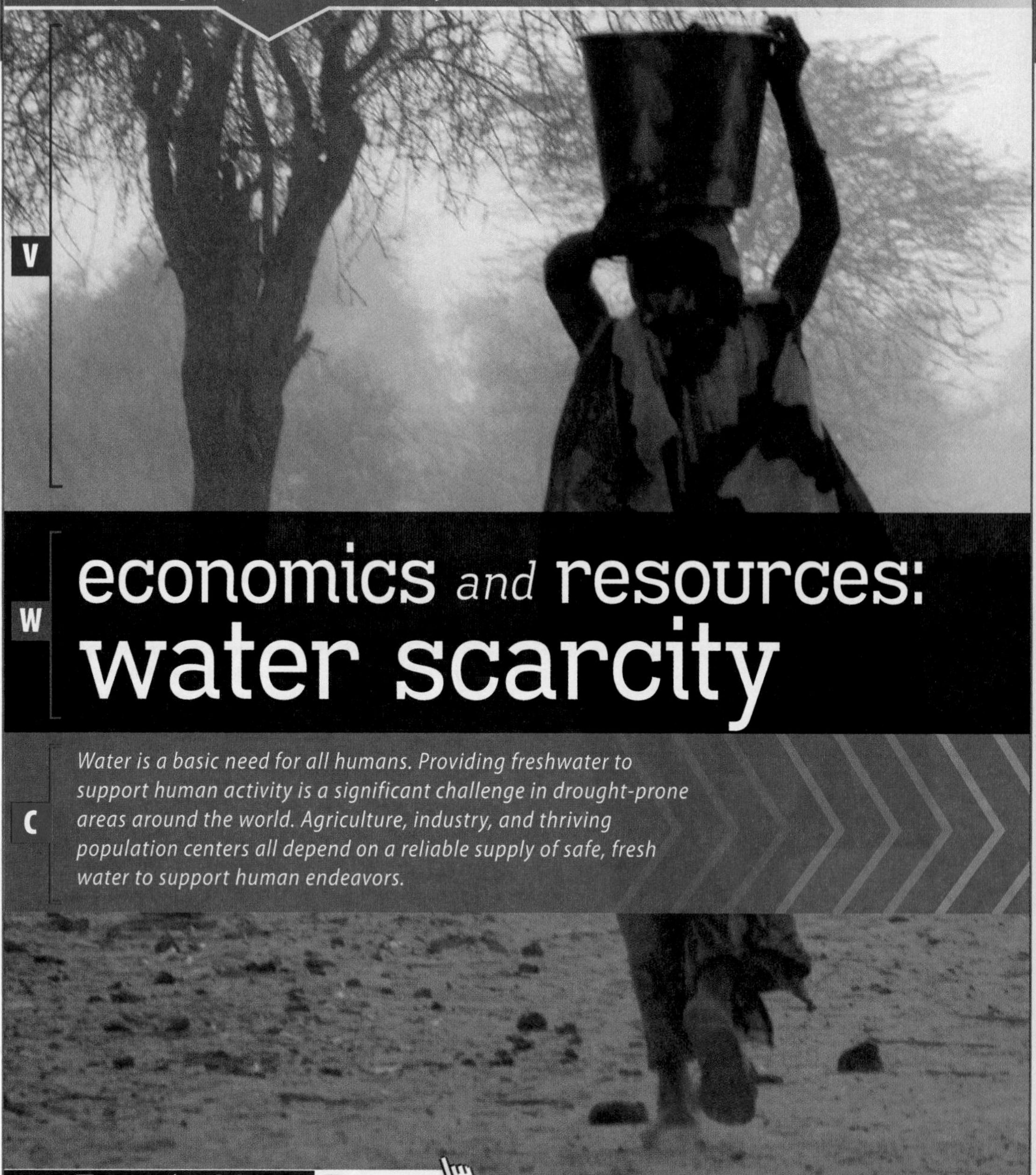

V

W

economics and resources: water scarcity

C

Water is a basic need for all humans. Providing freshwater to support human activity is a significant challenge in drought-prone areas around the world. Agriculture, industry, and thriving population centers all depend on a reliable supply of safe, fresh water to support human endeavors.

THERE'S MORE ONLINE

SEE **a diagram of the desalination process** • ***READ*** **an infographic about freshwater resources**

38

Project-Based Learning

Hands-On

Oral Presentation

Students will work in small groups to create a chapter project about how geography helps us to better understand Earth. Groups will use information from the chapter lessons, along with library or online research, to explore how the science of geography has been used to help us further understand Earth's past, its present, or its future. Then each group will prepare an oral presentation about Earth's place in the solar system, the forces of change on Earth, and bodies of water on Earth.

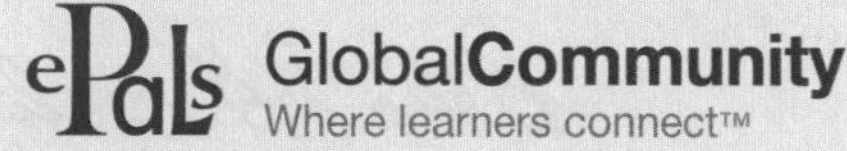

Digital Hands-On

Create Online Projects

Find an additional activity online that incorporates technology for this project. Visit the EdTech Teacher Web sites for more links, tutorials, and other resources.

How does water scarcity impact economic activity?

North Africa and Southwest Asia are two areas of the world where there is a scarcity—lack of an adequate supply—of freshwater for agriculture, industry, drinking, bathing, and other human uses of water due to limited resources. A scarcity of freshwater limits the ability of a city, region, or country to engage in many economic pursuits that allow people to live comfortably and thrive. Without water, agricultural fields cannot be irrigated, industrial production cannot occur, and hospitals cannot provide the necessary quality of care.

1. **Environment and Society** Why is water scarcity a problem? Explain what the term *water scarcity* means and discuss how it affects human activities.

How is technology being used to solve the problem of water scarcity?

The town of Ashqelon is located on Israel's Mediterranean coast with an abundant supply of salt water lapping at its shore. Desalination (salt removal) technology is being used to turn the sea water into freshwater for Israeli citizens and industries that have faced recent droughts and population growth. Ashqelon, 40 miles (64.4 km) south of Tel Aviv, has the largest desalination plant of its kind in the region and one of the largest in the world. Seawater is pumped through a series of filters and reverse-osmosis membranes which allow the smaller water molecules to pass through while excluding the larger molecules of salt and other impurities. The plant provides approximately five percent of Israel's freshwater and is predicted to soon make Israel an exporter of water.

2. **Human Systems** How has desalination technology affected Israel's economy? What countries may import freshwater from Israel?

What are the environmental effects of desalination?

The freshwater provided by the Ashqelon desalination plant supports Israel's thriving agricultural and high-tech industries, both heavily dependent on a steady supply of freshwater. However, this water comes with several costs to the environment. Fossil fuels are used to power the pumps that circulate the water through the filter plant, contributing to pollution. The brine, or leftover material that the filters remove, is pumped back into the sea, resulting in a salty desert on the sea floor around the outflow pipes. The plant also occupies a coastal area that might otherwise harbor wildlife and offer recreation options.

3. **Environment and Society** Explain the costs and benefits of providing freshwater using reverse-osmosis desalination.

T Technology Skills

Assessing Have students research which nations or regions have the least annual rainfall. Then assign each student one of these nations or regions to assess how climate affects the economic activities of that nation or region. Students will present their findings to the class. BL **Verbal/Linguistic**

V Visual Skills

Diagramming Have students draw a flowchart of the desalination process. **Ask: What other parts of the world would benefit from desalination technology?** *(Possible answers: dry areas near oceans; any country or region where water is a scarcity)* AL **Visual/Spatial**

Content Background Knowledge

Desalinating Water Saudi Arabia is the world's largest producer of desalinated water. Other nations with significant desalination facilities include: Algeria, Aruba, Australia, China, Israel, Spain, the United Arab Emirates, and the United States. Nations that obtain water from desalination need access to a coastline, significant financial resources, and sufficient power-generating resources.

C Critical Thinking Skills

Considering Advantages and Disadvantages As a class, discuss both the advantages and disadvantages of desalination. **Ask: Are the environmental costs of desalination worth the benefits?** *(Student answers should consider the benefits and/or costs to people and the environment.)* **Intrapersonal**

CLOSE & REFLECT

Summarizing Review how a scarcity of freshwater affects people's everyday lives. Discuss the impact limited water resources have on a nation's industry and economy. Brainstorm ways that countries could increase their freshwater supplies.

INFOGRAPHIC

Salt Water vs. Freshwater

Creating Visuals Guide students to interpret and analyze the visuals, focusing on each of the key elements. Divide the class into groups. Assign half of the groups to create a visual illustrating regions of the world where people lack access to clean drinking water and assign the other half of the groups to create a visual illustrating lakes in the United States that are too polluted for fishing or aquatic life. Have each group present and explain their visuals to the class. **Interpersonal, Visual/Spatial**

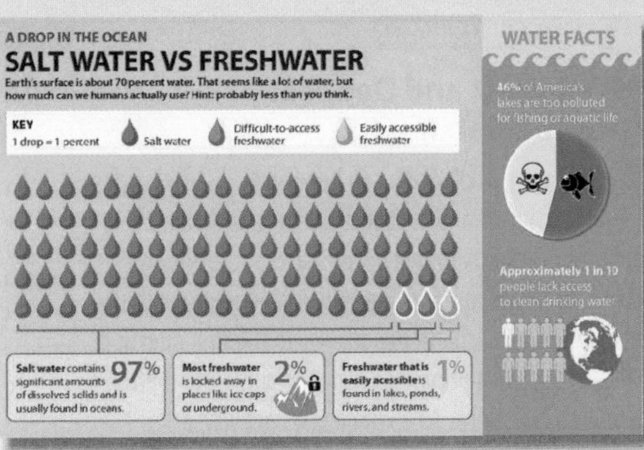

A DROP IN THE OCEAN
SALT WATER VS FRESHWATER
Earth's surface is about 70 percent water. That seems like a lot of water, but how much can we humans actually use? Hint: probably less than you think.
KEY
1 drop = 1 percent
Salt water
Difficult-to-access freshwater
Easily accessible freshwater
Salt water contains significant amounts of dissolved solids and is usually found in oceans. 97%
Most freshwater is locked away in places like ice caps or underground. 2%
Freshwater that is easily acessible is found in lakes, ponds, rivers, and streams. 1%
WATER FACTS
46% of America's lakes are too polluted for fishing or aquatic life
Approximately 1 in 10 people lack access to clean drinking water

ANSWERS, p. 39

Why Geography Matters

1. Water scarcity is a lack of adequate water supply. Without water, agricultural and industrial production cannot occur; people lack freshwater for drinking, bathing, and other human needs; and hospitals cannot provide quality care.
2. Student answers may vary, but should be logical, based on location and on current geopolitical issues.
3. The freshwater provided supports Israel's agricultural and high-tech industries; however, the fossil fuels used contribute to pollution. The brine pumped back into the ocean results in a salty desert on the ocean floor. The area occupied by the plant might otherwise harbor wildlife.

CHAPTER 2, Lesson 1
Planet Earth

ENGAGE

C1 Critical Thinking Skills

Activating Prior Knowledge Have students brainstorm what they already know about Earth and its place in space with another student. Then have partners share their knowledge of Earth in a class discussion. Show students a picture of Earth taken from space. Ask students to use this image to describe Earth's physical features. Guide students to reason that because Earth has clouds means it has an atmosphere, and that it is mainly blue because it is a watery planet. Discuss why these physical features are important to life on Earth.

TEACH & ASSESS

R Reading Skills

Defining Discuss the meaning of the term *solar system*. **Ask: Why might the planetary system that contains Earth be called the solar system?** *(The word* solar *refers to sun and the sun is the main, driving body in the system.)* **What is a system and how does this term apply to the solar system?** *(Possible answer: A system is a group of bodies that interact under the influence of related forces. In the case of the solar system, all the bodies in the system are under the sun's influence.)* If students need help defining these terms, allow them to consult a dictionary. **ELL Verbal/Linguistic**

C2 Critical Thinking Skills

Explaining Discuss the role of gravity in keeping Earth and other objects revolving in orbit around the sun. **Ask: What physical force keeps Earth and the other objects revolving around the sun?** *(the sun's gravitational pull)* **What would happen if the sun lost its gravitational pull?** *(Possible answer: The planets might go hurling off into space.)* Have volunteers explain the law of gravitation in general terms and how gravity works to keep Earth and other objects in orbit around the sun. **BL Logical/Mathematical**

T Technology Skills

Researching Combine students into groups to conduct online research about Pluto's changing status from a planet to a dwarf planet in 2003. Have the group present their findings to the class. **Interpersonal**

ANSWERS, p. 40

TAKING NOTES: **hydrosphere**—the watery areas of the Earth, including oceans, lakes, rivers, and other bodies of water; **lithosphere**—uppermost layer of the Earth that includes the crust, continents, and ocean basins; **atmosphere**—a thin layer of gases that surrounds the Earth; **biosphere**—the part of the Earth where life exists

networks

There's More Online!

- **DIAGRAM** The Solar System
- **DIAGRAM** Underwater Landforms
- **DIAGRAM** Water, Land, and Air
- **INTERACTIVE SELF-CHECK QUIZ**
- **VIDEO** Planet Earth

LESSON 1
Planet Earth

ESSENTIAL QUESTION • *How do physical processes shape Earth's surface?*

Reading **HELPDESK** 

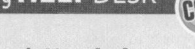

Academic Vocabulary (Tier Two Words)
- sphere
- theory

Content Vocabulary (Tier Three Words)
- hydrosphere
- lithosphere
- atmosphere
- biosphere
- continental shelf

TAKING NOTES: ***Key Ideas and Details***

DESCRIBING Use a graphic organizer like the one below to list descriptions for the components that make life on Earth possible: the hydrosphere, lithosphere, atmosphere, and biosphere.

Component	Description
hydrosphere	
lithosphere	
atmosphere	
biosphere	

It Matters Because

Physical processes shape Earth's surface. Understanding that Earth is part of a larger physical system called the solar system helps us see how it is possible for life on our planet to survive and thrive. Earth's physical systems are affected by natural forces such as earthquakes and volcanoes that can influence human activity on the planet.

Our Solar System

GUIDING QUESTION *In what physical system does Earth exist?*

Earth is part of our solar system, which is made up of the sun and all of the countless objects that revolve around it. At our solar system's center is the sun—a star, or ball of burning gases. About 109 times wider than Earth, the sun's enormous mass—the amount of matter it contains—creates a strong pull of gravity. This basic physical force keeps the Earth and the other objects revolving in orbit around the sun.

Except for the sun, **spheres** called planets are the largest objects in the solar system. At least eight planets are known to exist, and each is in its own orbit around the sun. Mercury, Venus, Earth, and Mars are the inner planets, or those nearest the sun. Earth, the third planet from the sun, is about 93 million miles (150 million km) away from the sun. Farthest from the sun are the outer planets—Jupiter, Saturn, Uranus, and Neptune.

The planets vary in size with Jupiter being the largest. Earth ranks fifth in size, and Mercury is the smallest. All of the planets except Mercury and Venus have moons—smaller spheres or satellites that orbit them. Earth has 1 moon, and Saturn has at least 18 moons. At least five other objects are dwarf planets. Pluto was known as the smallest planet in the solar system until 2003 when astronomers changed its status. Today Pluto is called a *dwarf planet*. Dwarf planets are small round bodies that orbit the sun, but do not have enough gravity to have cleared the area around their orbits of other orbiting bodies, thus making them too small to be considered planets.

networks ***Online Teaching Options***

INTERACTIVE BELLRINGER

The Highest and Deepest Places on Earth

Calculating This diagram can be used to discuss Earth's various landforms and to help students understand how geographers use diagrams to compare landforms and other data. Have students read the introductory text, use the diagram to calculate the answer to the first question, and then use their prior knowledge to complete the remaining questions. As a whole class activity, ask students to share their sketches of familiar landforms. **AL Logical/Mathematical, Naturalist**

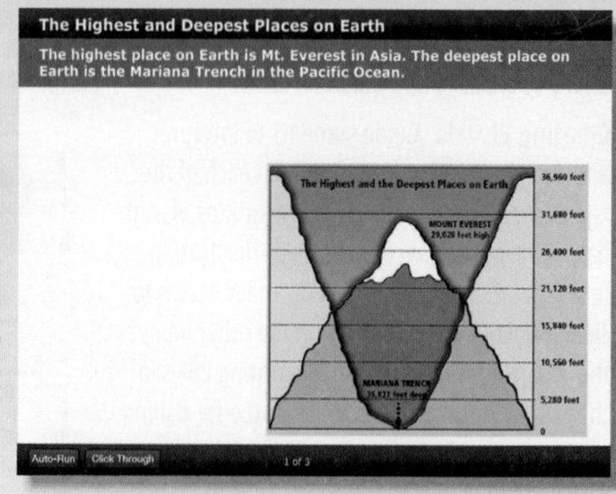

The four inner planets are called *terrestrial planets* because they have solid, rocky crusts. Mercury and Venus are scalding hot, and Mars is a cold, barren desert. Only Earth has temperatures that are moderate enough to allow liquid water at the surface and to support a variety of life. **V**

The four outer planets are called the *gas giant planets*. They are more gaseous and less dense than the terrestrial planets, although they are larger in diameter. Each gas giant is like a miniature solar system, with orbiting moons and encircling rings. Only Saturn's rings, however, are easily seen from Earth by telescope. **R**

Thousands of smaller objects—including asteroids, comets, and meteoroids—revolve around the sun. Asteroids are small, irregularly shaped, planet-like objects. They are found mainly between Mars and Jupiter in the asteroid belt. A few asteroids follow paths that cross Earth's orbit. Others, like the recently discovered asteroid 2010 TK7, are held in a balance between the gravitational pull from the sun and an equal force from the Earth.

Comets, made of icy dust particles and frozen gases, look like bright balls with long, feathery tails. Their orbits are inclined at every possible angle to Earth's orbit. They may approach from any direction.

Meteoroids are pieces of space debris—chunks of rock and iron. When they occasionally enter Earth's atmosphere, friction usually burns them up before they reach the Earth's surface. Those that collide with Earth are called meteorites. Meteorite strikes, although rare, can significantly affect the landscape, leaving craters and causing other devastation. In 1908 a huge area of forest in the remote Russian region of Siberia was flattened and burned by a mysterious fireball. Scientific **theory**—a plausible general principle offered to explain observed facts—speculates that it was a meteorite or comet. A writer describes the effects:

PRIMARY SOURCE

> "The heat incinerated herds of reindeer and charred tens of thousands of evergreens across hundreds of square miles. For days, and for thousands of miles around, the sky remained bright with an eerie orange glow—as far away as western Europe people were able to read newspapers at night without a lamp." **W**
>
> —Richard Stone, "The Last Great Impact on Earth," *Discover*, September 1996

Connecting Geography to SCIENCE

Astronomy

Like geographers, astronomers use maps to organize information. Geographers focus on mapping the Earth's surface, while astronomers map the sky. Astronomers have divided the sky into 88 sectors, or boxes, made up of patterns of stars. These sectors are a way to spatially organize the landscape of the sky, called the skyscape. Astronomy has also become part of everyday geography here on Earth. Many towns have been given astronomical names. Some of these towns are Neptune, Tennessee; Earth, Texas; Jupiter, Florida; Moon Township, Pennsylvania; and Orion, Alabama, named after the well-known constellation.

COMPARING In what way is the job of the astronomer similar to that of a geographer?

✓ **READING PROGRESS CHECK**

Drawing Conclusions What prevents most asteroids, comets, and meteoroids from colliding with Earth?

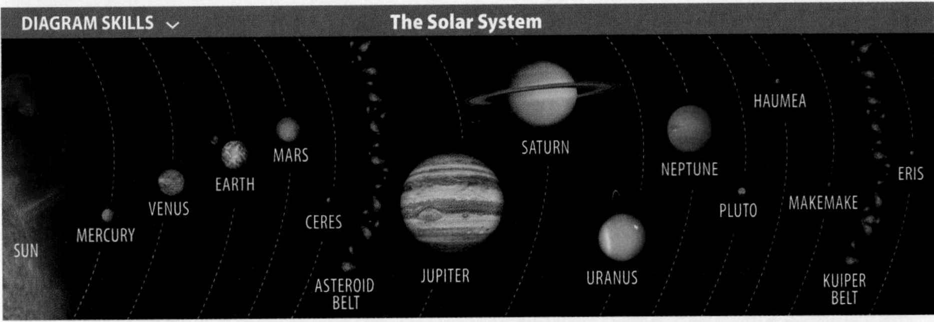

Planet Earth is part of a solar system centered on the sun. Earth is one of at least eight planets orbiting the sun.

▲ **CRITICAL THINKING**

1. ***Classifying*** Which four planets are closest to the sun?
2. ***Drawing Conclusions*** Why might it be impossible for life to exist on Neptune? Think about where it is located.

(sun)NASA/SDO, (Mercury, Earth, Mars, Uranus)Caltech/JPL/USGS/NASA, (Venus, Jupiter, Saturn, Neptune, Pluto)JPL/Caltech/NASA, (star maps)Caltech/JPL/NASA

INTERACTIVE INFOGRAPHIC

The Solar System

Discussing This interactive graphic provides information about each of the planets and illustrates that Earth is a part of a larger physical system called the solar system. As a class, discuss the importance of the Earth-Sun relationship. Ask students to explain why Earth's position in the solar system makes it ideal to sustain human life *(Earth is not too close and not too far from the sun, so the planet has moderate/livable temperatures)*. Continue to ask students questions about the facts and characteristics presented in the infographic. **AL** **Verbal/Linguistic**

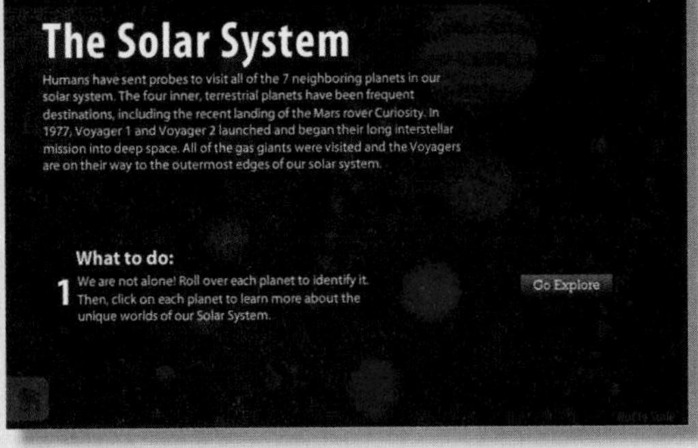

The Solar System
Humans have sent probes to visit all of the 7 neighboring planets in our solar system. The four inner, terrestrial planets have been frequent destinations, including the recent landing of the Mars rover Curiosity. In 1977, Voyager 1 and Voyager 2 launched and began their long interstellar mission into deep space. All of the gas giants were visited and the Voyagers are on their way to the outermost edges of our solar system.
What to do:
1 We are not alone! Roll over each planet to identify it. Then, click on each planet to learn more about the unique worlds of our Solar System.
Go Explore

Planet Earth

V Visual Skills

Comparing and Contrasting Have students create a chart to compare and contrast the planets. Use the following headings: *Name, Size, Type, Moons (number of), and Other Features.*

Name	Size	Type	Moons	Other Features
Earth	5th largest	terrestrial	1	moderate temperatures

Encourage students to add more information to their charts as they continue the lesson. **AL** **Visual/Spatial**

R Reading Skills

Interpreting Have students read about the different types of planets: terrestrial and the gas giants. **Ask: How are the four terrestrial planets alike?** *(They all have solid, rocky crusts like Earth.)* **How are they different from each other?** *(Mercury and Venus are scalding hot, Earth has moderate temperatures that allow liquid water, and Mars is cold and barren)* **How are the four outer gas giant planets alike?** *(They are large planets that are more gaseous and less dense than the terrestrial planets. They all have orbiting moons and encircling rings.)* **ELL** **Naturalist**

Content Background Knowledge

Mission to Mars Our knowledge of the solar system is constantly expanding. In November 2011, NASA sent an exploration rover, *Curiosity,* to Mars. The trip took more than eight months. Equipped with cameras and other devices, *Curiosity* sent back information about Mars' climate, atmosphere, and surface. Its main mission is to analyze rocks and soil to determine if the Red Planet's environment was once suitable for life.

W Writing Skills

Narrative Have students write a narrative imagining a meteor strike in their region. Have them use descriptive words and phrases and encourage them to include illustrations of their stories. **Verbal/Linguistic**

ANSWERS, p. 41

✓ **READING PROGRESS CHECK** Most are held in a balance between the gravitational pull from the sun and an equal force from the Earth.

Connecting Geography Both use maps to organize information.

CRITICAL THINKING

1. Mercury, Venus, Earth, and Mars are closest to the sun.
2. Possible response: Extremely cold temperatures might make it impossible.

CHAPTER 2, Lesson 1
Planet Earth

R Reading Skills

Understanding Relationships Write these terms on the board: *Hydrosphere, Lithosphere, Atmosphere.* Working with a partner, have students list important facts or characteristics of each. Then have them write a brief statement explaining the relationship between the three terms. **ELL Interpersonal**

C Critical Thinking Skills

Analyzing Remind students that Earth is the only habitable planet as far as the scientific community is concerned and that humans, animals, and plants exist because of the unique layers found in and above Earth. **Ask:** **Why are the parts of Earth that support life called the biosphere?** *(Bio refers to life. Sphere refers to the spherical outer parts of the Earth that support life: the atmosphere, hydrosphere, and lithosphere. Together, these are called the biosphere.)* **What are the key resources provided by each layer that makes life on Earth possible?** *(Possible answers: atmosphere: air to breathe; hydrosphere: water to drink, water for plants, a home for fish and other creatures; lithosphere: food to eat, resources for shelter. The atmosphere and hydrosphere interact to create our climate.)* **If Earth were closer (or farther) from the sun would it still be a good place to live? Why or why not?** *(Possible answer: No. If Earth were closer to the sun, it would be too hot to support life. If it were farther away, it would be too cold.)* **Verbal/ Linguistic**

V Visual Skills

Interpreting a Diagram Have students interpret the diagram in a class discussion. **Ask:** **What are the four layers of the atmosphere called?** *(troposphere, stratosphere, mesosphere, thermosphere)* **Which region is closest to Earth?** *(troposphere)* **In what layer is oxygen present?** *(troposphere)* Have students answer the *Critical Thinking* questions on their own. **AL Visual/Spatial**

ANSWERS, p. 42

CRITICAL THINKING

1. Earth's water systems are part of the hydrosphere which contains oceans, lakes, rivers, underground water, and other bodies of water.
2. Possible answer: Human activity can pollute the biosphere and cause damage to many species.

---

sphere a globe-shaped body

theory a plausible general principle offered to explain observed facts

hydrosphere the water areas of the Earth, including oceans, lakes, rivers, and other bodies of water

lithosphere uppermost layer of the Earth that includes the crust, continents, and ocean basins

atmosphere a thin layer of gases that surrounds the Earth

biosphere the part of the Earth where life exists

Getting to Know Earth

GUIDING QUESTION *How does the biosphere support life on Earth?*

The Earth is a rounded object that is slightly wider around the center than from top to bottom. Earth has a larger diameter at the Equator—about 7,930 miles (12,760 km)—than from Pole to Pole, but the difference is less than 1 percent. With a circumference of about 24,900 miles (40,060 km), Earth is the largest of the inner planets in the solar system.

R The surface of the Earth is made up of water and land. About 70 percent of our planet's surface is water. Oceans, lakes, rivers, underground water, and other bodies of water make up a part of the Earth called the **hydrosphere**.

About 30 percent of the Earth's surface is land, including continents and islands. Land makes up a part of the Earth called the **lithosphere**, the Earth's crust. The lithosphere also includes the ocean basins, or the land beneath the oceans.

The air we breathe is part of Earth's **atmosphere**, a thin layer of gases extending above the planet's surface. The atmosphere is composed of 78 percent nitrogen, 21 percent oxygen, and small amounts of argon and other gases.

C All people, animals, and plants live on or close to the Earth's surface or in the atmosphere. The part of the Earth that supports life is the **biosphere**. Life outside the biosphere, such as on a space station orbiting Earth, exists only with the assistance of mechanical life-support systems.

DIAGRAM SKILLS — Water, Land, and Air

V

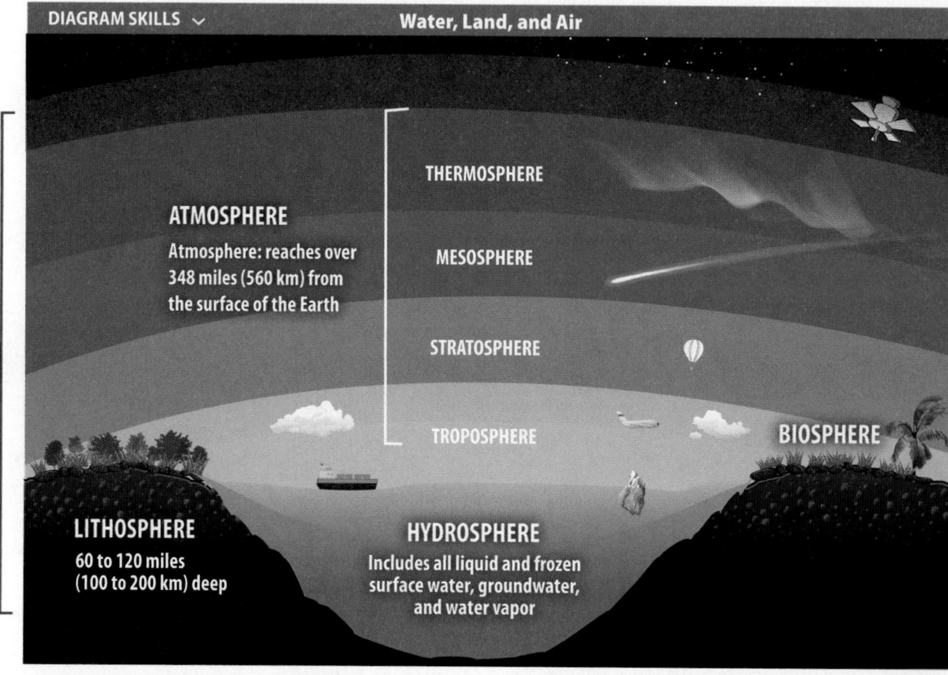

The atmosphere, hydrosphere, and lithosphere form the biosphere, the part of Earth where life exists.

©Chad Baker/Photodisc/Getty Images

▲ **CRITICAL THINKING**

1. ***Classifying*** What are Earth's water systems called?
2. ***Drawing Conclusions*** How does human activity impact the biosphere?

networks Online Teaching Options

VIDEO

Changing Landscapes

Understanding Relationships Have students watch this video about Earth's changing landscapes. After the video, explain to students that there is a relationship between climate and landscape and that a change in Earth's climate also means a change in the Earth's landscape. Have students provide examples from the video of this relationship. **AL Visual/Spatial, Verbal/Linguistic**

Landforms are natural features at the surface of the Earth's lithosphere. Many of the Earth's landforms have a particular shape or elevation. Landforms often contain rivers, lakes, and streams.

Underwater landforms are as diverse as those found on dry land. In some places the ocean floor is a flat plain. Other parts feature mountain ranges, cliffs, valleys, and deep trenches. Seen from space, Earth's most visible landforms are the seven large landmasses called continents. Australia and Antarctica stand alone, while the others are joined in some way. Europe and Asia are parts of one landmass called Eurasia. A narrow strip of land called the Isthmus of Panama links North America and South America. At the Sinai Peninsula, the human-made Suez Canal separates Africa and Asia. **V**

The **continental shelf** is an underwater extension of the coastal plain. Continental shelves slope out from land for as far as 800 miles (1,287 km). They descend gradually to a depth of about 660 feet (200 m), where a sharp drop marks the beginning of the continental slope. This area drops sharply to the ocean floor.

Great contrasts exist in the heights and depths of the Earth's surface. The highest point on Earth is in South Asia at the top of Mount Everest, which is 29,028 feet (8,848 m) above sea level. The lowest dry land point at 1,312 feet (400 m) below sea level is the shore of the Dead Sea in Southwest Asia. Earth's deepest known depression lies under the Pacific Ocean, southwest of Guam in the Mariana Trench, a narrow, underwater canyon about 36,198 feet (11,033 m) deep. **T**

Mt. Everest has such low oxygen levels and atmospheric pressure that hikers must prepare their bodies well in advance to adjust to altitude changes in order to avoid illness or death.

▲ CRITICAL THINKING

1. ***Categorizing*** In which part of the Earth's biosphere is Mt. Everest located?
2. ***Predicting*** Mt. Everest has such high altitudes that it is almost outside of which part of the biosphere?

continental shelf part of a continent that extends out underneath the ocean

✓ READING PROGRESS CHECK

Categorizing What organisms might live in the hydrosphere?

LESSON 1 REVIEW

Reviewing Vocabulary (Tier Three Words)

1. ***Explaining*** Define *continental shelf* and explain where it is located. RH.9–10.4

Using Your Notes

2. ***Describing*** Use your graphic organizer to describe the three parts of the Earth's biosphere.

Answering the Guiding Questions

3. ***Identifying*** In what physical system does Earth exist?
4. ***Discussing*** How does the biosphere support life on Earth?

Writing Activity

5. ***Narrative*** Consider the ratio of water and land on Earth. How might life on Earth be different if the proportions were reversed? WHST.9–10.2

V Visual Skills

Locating Display a world map that includes the names of the continents. Have students name and locate the continents. **Ask: Which continent is the largest?** *(Asia)* Explain that Asia is the largest continent in size and population. Have a student locate the islands of Oceania. Tell students that more than 15 million people in the world do not live on a continent. Almost all of these people live in the island countries of Oceania, which is a world region. Have volunteers locate two waterway divisions between continents. Explain that these are two human-made canals built to divide the continents to expedite shipping and trade. **Ask: Which continents are divided by a human-made canal?** *(North and South America—Panama Canal; Africa and Asia—Suez Canal)* **AL** **Visual/Spatial**

Content Background Knowledge

Continental Shelf The continental shelf regions of the world are economically important. Not only are they a source of seafood (most of the world's major fisheries are located on them); they also hold vast mineral and energy reserves, including oil and natural gas.

T Technology Skills

Comparing and Contrasting Have students work in small groups to compare and contrast dry landforms to underwater landforms by using the Internet or library resources. Also have groups create a diagram showing the landforms of the ocean floor: coastal plain, continental shelf, continental slope, mountains, deep trenches, etc. Suggest that they superimpose outlines of the highest land mountains to compare to the highest mountains on the ocean floor. Diagrams should include a key and scale. Have groups report their findings and explain their diagrams in a multimedia class presentation. **BL** **Naturalist**

LESSON 1 REVIEW ANSWERS

Reviewing Vocabulary

1. The continental shelf is an underwater extension of the coastal plain. Continental shelves slope out from land for as far as 800 miles (1,287 km). They descend gradually to a depth of about 660 feet (200 m), where a sharp drop marks the beginning of the continental slope. This area drops sharply to the ocean floor.

Using Your Notes

2. The three parts are the hydrosphere, lithosphere, and atmosphere. The hydrosphere is made up of the watery areas of the Earth, including oceans, lakes, rivers, and other bodies of water. The lithosphere is the uppermost layer of the Earth; it includes the crust, continents, and ocean basins. The atmosphere is a thin layer of gases that surrounds Earth.

Answering the Guiding Questions

3. Earth is part of the solar system.
4. The biosphere provides oxygen, water, and nutrients.

Writing Activity

5. Possible answer: There would be fewer ocean plants and animals. Industry would have developed differently, as the quantity of water available for running textile mills and the like would not have been available. Additionally, modes of transportation would likely have developed differently, as there would have been a narrower focus on transportation across waterways.

CLOSE & REFLECT

Summarizing Have students summarize the physical makeup of Earth and why it is a suitable environment for life. Review how the biosphere is a complex system spanning parts of the lithosphere, atmosphere, and hydrosphere.

ANSWERS, p. 43

✓ READING PROGRESS CHECK Fish and whales live in the hydrosphere.

CRITICAL THINKING

1. Mt. Everest is part of the atmosphere.
2. Mt. Everest is almost outside the troposphere.

ENGAGE

C Critical Thinking Skills

Analyzing Cause and Effect Ask students to think about any destructive natural occurrences they or someone they know has experienced, such as earthquakes, violent storms, tornadoes, or floods. Encourage students to note the *who, what, when, where,* and *how* of the experience. Have students share their notes with the class, and then **ask:** Was this change permanent or temporary? *(Student answers will vary, but should include relevant details about how natural occurrences changed the environment around them.)* Point out that such occurrences have been going on for millions of years and many have had lasting effects on Earth's structure and surface.

TEACH & ASSESS

W Writing Skills

Narrative Have students imagine they are eyewitness reporters assigned to report on one of Earth's sudden and destructive events—an earthquake, tsunami, or major storm. Students should write a news report that provides specific details about the event. Students could report an event they actually experienced or one they have read about in the news. **Verbal/Linguistic**

V Visual Skills

Comparing and Contrasting Have students create a three-column chart that will help them compare and contrast Earth's layers. Use the following headings: *Crust, Mantle, Core.* Have students list important facts about each layer under the headings, such as composition, location, temperature, etc. Then discuss the role pressure plays in the makeup of Earth's layers. **Ask:** Since Earth's inner core is hotter than the outer core, why isn't it liquid as well? *(It is under crushing pressure caused by gravity. As the pressure on a solid material increases, so does its melting temperature.)* AL **Visual/Spatial**

ANSWERS, p. 44

TAKING NOTES: Possible answer: **Force of Change**–subduction; **How It Works**–oceanic plates dive beneath continental plates, causing mountains to form on land; **Example**–Andes Mountains

networks

There's More Online!

- ☑ **DIAGRAM** Forces of Change
- ☑ **DIAGRAM** Inside the Earth
- ☑ **MAP** Continental Drift
- ☑ **MAP** Tectonic Plate Boundaries
- ☑ **INTERACTIVE SELF-CHECK QUIZ**
- ☑ **VIDEO** Forces of Change

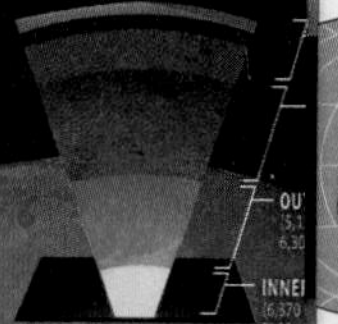

LAURASIA
GONDWANA

SPREADING

LESSON 2
Forces of Change

ESSENTIAL QUESTION • *How do physical processes shape Earth's surface?*

Reading HELPDESK CCSS

Academic Vocabulary (Tier Two Words)
- create
- external

Content Vocabulary (Tier Three Words)
- core
- mantle
- crust
- continental drift
- plate tectonics
- magma
- subduction
- accretion
- spreading
- fold
- fault
- faulting
- weathering
- erosion
- glacier
- moraine

TAKING NOTES: ***Key Ideas and Details***

IDENTIFYING Use a graphic organizer like the one below to decribe the processes of plate tectonics.

Force of Change	How it Works	Example

It Matters Because

Plate tectonics acts upon the Earth's internal and external structures to help create the continents, ocean basins, and mountain ranges. Plate tectonics operates by folding, lifting, bending, and breaking parts of the Earth's surface. Other forces such as weathering and erosion also help shape the Earth's surface.

Earth's Structure

GUIDING QUESTION *How is Earth's structure related to the creation of continents, oceans, and mountain ranges?*

For hundreds of millions of years, the surface of the Earth has been in motion. Pressures generally build up slowly inside the Earth and are then released in sudden events such as volcanic eruptions and earthquakes. Other forces that change the Earth, such as wind and water, occur on the surface.

The Earth is composed of three main layers—the core, the mantle, and the crust. At the very center of the planet is a super-hot but solid inner **core**. Scientists believe that the inner core is made up of iron and nickel that is under enormous pressure. Surrounding the inner core is another band also composed of iron and nickel called the liquid outer core. Even though the liquid outer core is composed of the same elements as the inner core, it is liquid because the pressure is not as great as it is in the inner core.

Next to the outer core is a thick layer of hot, dense rock called the **mantle**. The mantle consists of silicon, aluminum, iron, magnesium, oxygen, and other elements. This dense mixture is soft enough to slowly but continually rise, cool, sink, warm up, and rise again, releasing 80 percent of the heat generated from the Earth's interior.

The outer layer is the **crust**, a hard rocky shell forming the Earth's surface. This relatively thin layer of rock ranges from about 2 miles (3.2 km) thick under oceans to about 75 miles (120.7 km) thick under mountains. The crust is broken into more than a dozen great slabs of

Jim Kruger/Getty Images

44

networks *Online Teaching Options*

INTERACTIVE BELLRINGER

Interpreting a Map of Tectonic Plates

Analyzing Visuals Have students use this map to discuss Earth's tectonic plates and how the movement of these plates can cause earthquakes and volcanoes. Remind students that underwater earthquakes often cause tsunamis, as well. Have pairs of students read the introductory text, study the map, and answer the questions. Then ask students to discuss and write a paragraph on how volcanoes can be constructive as well as destructive. **Visual/Spatial, Verbal/Linguistic**

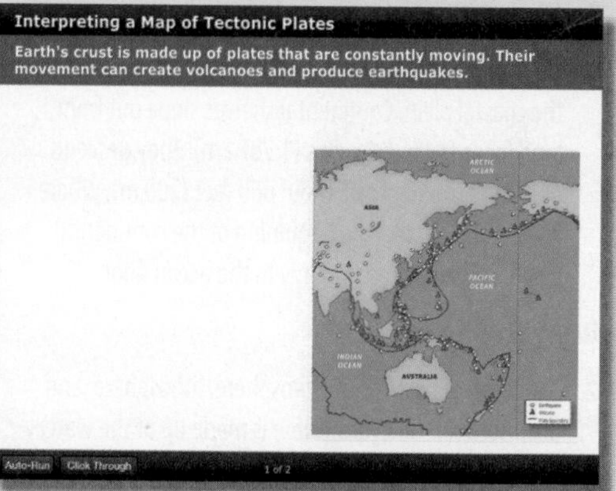
Interpreting a Map of Tectonic Plates
Earth's crust is made up of plates that are constantly moving. Their movement can create volcanoes and produce earthquakes.
AUSTRALIA
Auto-Run
Click Through
1 of 2

rock called plates that rest—or more accurately, float—on a partially melted layer in the upper portion of the mantle. The plates carry the Earth's oceans and continents.

R If you had seen the Earth from space 500 million years ago, the planet probably would not have looked at all like it does today. Many scientists believe that most of the landmasses forming our present-day continents were once part of one gigantic supercontinent called Pangaea (pan•JEE•uh). The maps on the next page show that over millions of years, this supercontinent has broken apart into smaller continents. These continents in turn have drifted and, in some places, recombined. The theory that the continents were once joined and then slowly drifted apart is called **continental drift**.

C2 The term **plate tectonics** refers to all of the physical processes that create many of the Earth's physical features. Many scientists theorize that plates moving around the globe have produced Earth's largest features—not only continents, but also oceans and mountain ranges. Most of the time, plate movement is so gradual—only about 1 inch (2 to 3 cm) a year—that it cannot be felt unless there is an earthquake strong enough to detect the movement. As they move, the plates may crash into each other, pull apart, or grind and slide past each other. Whatever their actions, plates are constantly changing the face of the planet. They push up mountains, **create** volcanoes, and produce earthquakes. Plates spread apart because **magma**, or molten rock, is pushed up from the mantle and ridges are formed. When plates bump together, one may slide under another, forming a trench.

Many scientists estimate that plate tectonics has been shaping the Earth's surface for 2.5 to 4 billion years. According to some scientists, plate tectonics will have sculpted a whole new look for the planet millions of years from now that could make it difficult for us to recognize.

Scientists, however, have not yet determined exactly what causes plate tectonics. They theorize that heat rising from the Earth's core may create slow-moving currents within the mantle. Over millions of years, these currents of molten rock may shift the plates around, but the movements in the mantle are extremely slow and difficult to detect.

core innermost layer of the Earth made up of a super-hot but solid inner core and a super-hot liquid outer core

mantle thick middle layer of the Earth's interior structure consisting of hot rock that is dense but flexible

crust outer layer of the Earth, a hard rocky shell forming Earth's surface

continental drift the theory that the continents were once joined and then slowly drifted apart

plate tectonics the term scientists use to describe the activities of continental drift and magma flow, which create many of Earth's physical features

create to bring into being or cause to exist

magma molten rock that is located below Earth's surface

Inside the Earth

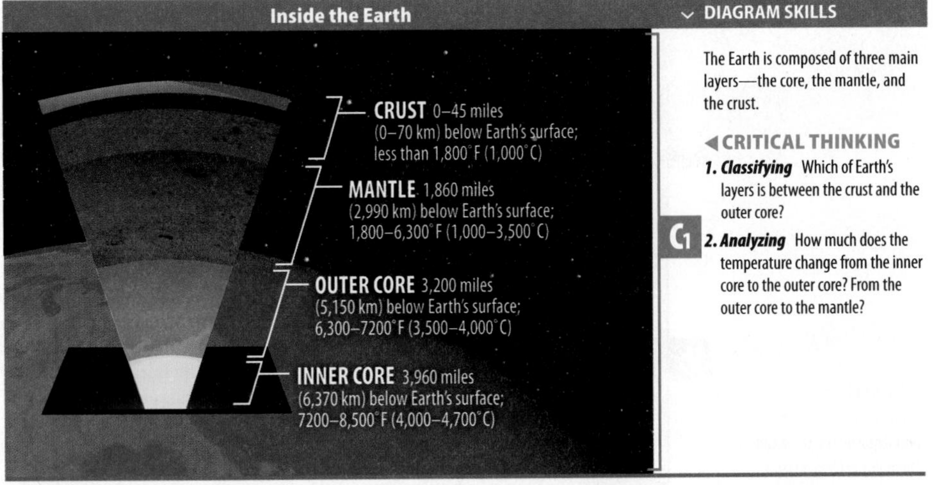

DIAGRAM SKILLS

The Earth is composed of three main layers—the core, the mantle, and the crust.

CRITICAL THINKING

C1
1. ***Classifying*** Which of Earth's layers is between the crust and the outer core?
2. ***Analyzing*** How much does the temperature change from the inner core to the outer core? From the outer core to the mantle?

C1 Critical Thinking Skills

Hypothesizing Have students study the diagram of Earth's layers and note how the temperature changes from the core to the crust. As a class, discuss and answer the *Critical Thinking* questions. Then **ask: Why do you suppose the layers get cooler towards the Earth's surface?** *(Possible answer: Heat from inside Earth filters up through the mantle and eventually escapes into the atmosphere. Plate tectonics and volcanic activity allow heat to escape from the mantle.)* **BL Logical/Mathematical**

R Reading Skills

Citing Text Evidence Remind students that when they answer questions, they should strive to cite text evidence to support their answers. **Ask: How did Earth's landmasses change over the last 500 million years? What text evidence supports this?** *(Present-day continents emerged out of one gigantic supercontinent called Pangaea. The text describes how over millions of years this supercontinent broke into smaller continents, which drifted apart and in some places recombined.)* **What does the word *drift* mean in this context?** *(to move slowly, as on a current)* **Verbal/Linguistic**

C2 Critical Thinking Skills

Determining Cause and Effect Have students read the section on plate tectonics. Then discuss the causes and effects that the plates have had on Earth's surface. **Ask: What is the relationship between a plate and a continent?** *(There are two kinds of plates, continental and oceanic. The continental plates support the continents.)* **What are some of the ways that the movement of plates changes Earth's surface?** *(They move continents, create mountains and volcanoes.)* **What actions cause ridges to form?** *(magma pushes up from Earth's mantle, forming ridges)* **What actions cause trenches to form?** *(plates sliding under each other form trenches)* **What is the engine that might cause the movement of the plates?** *(currents of molten rock)* **AL Naturalist**

VIDEO

Death Valley is Sinking

Predicting Use this video to show how plate tectonics change Earth's surface. Remind students that for many years, it was believed that continental drifting was described as the building up of mountains, but in this video, scientists can prove that plate tectonics spread out and also break down. As students consider these building up and breaking down forces found in Death Valley, have them write a paragraph predicting what they think will happen to this region over time. Ask them to explain if they believe the entire region will sink into the mantle based on the information provided in the video. **Verbal/Linguistic**

Content Background Knowledge

Continental Drift and Plate Tectonics The theory of continental drift and plate tectonics was proposed by German scientist Alfred Wegener in the 1920s, but was not accepted until the 1960s. Now geographers could use Wegener's theory to explain some of Earth's anomalies.

ANSWERS, p. 45

CRITICAL THINKING

1. The mantle is between the crust and the outer core.
2. The temperature range can decrease 900°F to 2,200°F from the inner core to the outer core. The temperature range can decrease 900°F to 5,400°F from the outer core to the mantle.

V1 Visual Skills

Analyzing Visuals The rough outlines of the continents as they are today can be discerned at various periods over time. Have students compare the supercontinent as it was millions of years ago to a map of the world today. Have students analyze from what part of the supercontinent each continent emerged. **Ask:** **How might the shape of the continents have led scientists to theorize that they were once joined?** *(The shapes of the continents seem to fit together.)* **If the drifting of continents continues over time, what other changes might occur?** *(Possible answers: North America and South America might separate; Africa might drift farther away from Eurasia.)* Point out that some scientists believe that in another hundred million years, the continents may rejoin, creating another supercontinent. **Visual/Spatial**

T Technology Skills

Evaluating There are many online resources dealing with plate tectonics and continental drift. Have students work with a partner to discover which sites are the most helpful in explaining these processes. Before beginning their research, have students create a list of the criteria they will use to judge the sites. For example: *Which site explains the movement processes the most thoroughly? Which site is the easiest to understand? Which has the best graphics/images? Does the site have animation? Which sites are the most reliable? Which sites have credible sources or exports?* Have students share their findings with the class. **Logical/Mathematical**

V2 Visual Skills

Spatial Understanding In small groups, have students find ways to visually demonstrate the processes of plate tectonics and continent drift. Groups might create a multimedia presentation, draw a series of illustrations, or create a clay model of the supercontinent showing how it evolved into several continents. Have students use the same sources they evaluated on plate tectonics and continental drift from the earlier activity to create their visuals. ELL **Visual/Spatial**

ANSWERS, p. 46

READING PROGRESS CHECK Iron and nickel make up the inner core.

GEOGRAPHY CONNECTION

1. The first map of Pangaea shows all the continents pushed together. The map of Earth 65 million years ago shows the continents moving apart.
2. The first map of Pangaea shows all the continents pushed together, but the plate movement map shows all the plates and continents separated and the direction of their movement.

Continental Drift

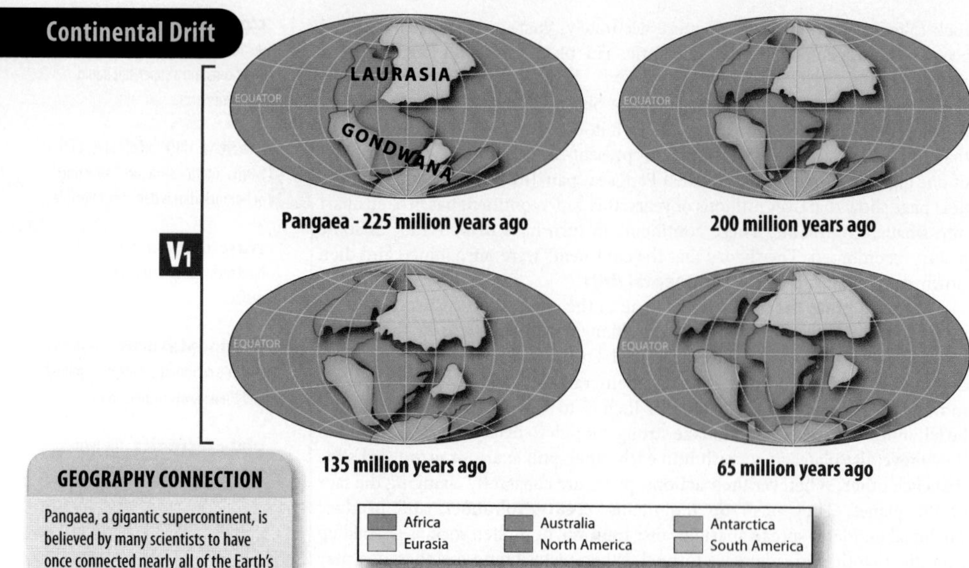

V1

GEOGRAPHY CONNECTION

Pangaea, a gigantic supercontinent, is believed by many scientists to have once connected nearly all of the Earth's landmasses.

1. ***THE WORLD IN SPATIAL TERMS*** How does the first map of Pangaea compare to the map of the Earth 65 million years ago?
2. ***PHYSICAL SYSTEMS*** How does the first map of Pangaea compare with the map of plate movement?

PRIMARY SOURCE

"[W]e have a highly successful theory, called plate tectonics, that explains . . . why continents drift, mountains rise, and volcanoes line the Pacific Rim. Plate tectonics may be one of the signature triumphs of the human mind. . . ."

—Joel Achenbach, "The Next Big One," *National Geographic*, April 2006

READING PROGRESS CHECK

Describing What elements make up the inner core?

Internal Forces of Change

GUIDING QUESTION: *How does plate tectonics affect Earth's surface?*

T

Earth's surface has changed greatly over time. Scientists believe that some of these changes come from forces associated with plate tectonics. One of these forces relates to the movement of magma within the Earth. Others involve movements that can fold, lift, bend, or break the solid rock at the Earth's crust.

Colliding and Spreading Plates

V2

Mountains are formed in areas where the giant plates collide. In some places, *continental plates* collide with each other. For example, the Himalaya mountain ranges in South Asia were thrust upward when the Indian landmass drifted against Eurasia. Himalayan peaks are getting higher as the Indian Plate continues to move northward and collide with the Eurasian Plate.

Mountains are also created when an *oceanic plate* collides with a continental plate. The heavier oceanic plate dives beneath the lighter continental plate in a process called **subduction** (suhb•DUHK•shuhn). The oceanic plate plunges steeply into the Earth's interior, becoming molten material. Then, as magma, it

subduction process by which oceanic plates dive beneath continental plates, often causing mountains to form on land

46

networks Online Teaching Options

INTERACTIVE MAP

Continental Drift

Reaching Conclusions Have students use this interactive map that illustrates the shifting of the continents over millions of years to understand how the continents have drifted apart and continue to move. Review with students that Pangaea, a gigantic supercontinent, is believed by many scientists to have once connected nearly all of Earth's landmasses. Working with a partner, have students create a step-by-step process chart that explains the theory of Pangaea. **Visual/Spatial, Naturalist**

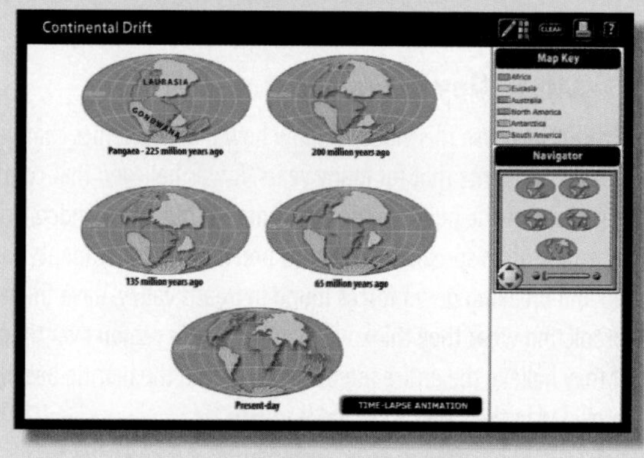

rises and bursts through the crust to form volcanic mountains. The Andes, a mountain system in South America, was formed over millions of years as a result of subduction as the Nazca Plate slides beneath the South American Plate.

In other cases where continental and oceanic plates meet, a different process, known as accretion, occurs. During **accretion** (uh•KREE•shuhn), pieces of the Earth's crust come together slowly as the oceanic plate slides under the continental plate at a shallow angle. This movement levels off seamounts—underwater mountains with steep sides and sharp peaks—and piles up the resulting debris in trenches. This buildup can cause continents to grow outward. Most scientists believe that much of western North America expanded outward into the Pacific Ocean over 200 million years as a result of accretion.

New land can also form when two oceanic plates converge. In this process, one plate moves under the other, often forming an island chain at the boundary. Oceanic plates can also be pushed apart in a process known as **spreading**. The resulting rift, or deep crack, allows magma from within the Earth to well up between the plates. The magma hardens to build undersea volcanic mountains or ridges and some islands. This spreading activity occurs down the middle of the Atlantic Ocean's floor, forming the Mid-Atlantic Ridge, pushing Europe and North America away from each other.

Folds and Faults

Moving plates sometimes squeeze the Earth's surface until it buckles. This activity forms **folds**, or bends, in layers of rock. In other cases, plates may grind or slide past each other, creating cracks in the Earth's crust called **faults**. One famous fault is the highly visible San Andreas Fault in California.

The process of **faulting** occurs when the folded land cannot be bent any further. The Earth's crust cracks and breaks into huge blocks. The blocks move along the faults in different directions, grinding against each other. The resulting tension builds up and is then released by shaking of the Earth's crust.

accretion slow process in which an oceanic plate slides under a continental plate, creating debris that can cause continents to grow outward

spreading process by which magma wells up between oceanic plates and pushes the plates apart

fold a bend in layers of rock, sometimes caused by plate movement

fault a crack or break in Earth's crust

faulting process of cracking that occurs when the folded land cannot be bent any further

GEOGRAPHY CONNECTION

Tectonic plates make up Earth's crust.

1. ***PHYSICAL SYSTEMS*** Identify and describe physical features that are the result of plate movement.
2. ***THE WORLD IN SPATIAL TERMS*** Which plates are moving toward each other? Away from each other?

Plates and Plate Movement

EURASIAN PLATE
NORTH AMERICAN PLATE
EURASIAN PLATE
JUAN DE FUCA PLATE
CARIBBEAN PLATE
ARABIAN PLATE
PHILIPPINE PLATE
COCOS PLATE
AFRICAN PLATE
INDIAN PLATE
PACIFIC PLATE
SOMALI PLATE
NAZCA PLATE
SOUTH AMERICAN PLATE
AUSTRALIAN PLATE
ANTARCTIC PLATE
SCOTIA PLATE
N, S, E, W
Plate boundary
Direction of plate movement

CHAPTER 2, Lesson 2
Forces of Change

R Reading Skills

Contrasting Have students read about *accretion, convergence,* and *spreading* and then work with a partner to explain how each process differs. Then, **ask: How does the angle at which a plate slides under another plate affect the outcome?** *(In subduction, the oceanic plate plunges into Earth's interior. It becomes molten and bubbles up through the crust, forming volcanic mountains. In accretion, the oceanic plate slides under the continental plate at an angle. It does not go deep enough into Earth's interior to become molten and creates a pile of debris at the edge of the plates instead, causing the plate to grow.)* **Interpersonal**

C Critical Thinking Skills

Analyzing Have students explain the difference between a *fold* and a *fault.* Then have them explain the process that causes each and leads to *faulting.* **Ask: Which process are you most likely to feel, faulting or folding? Why?** *(Faulting; tension builds up along plates that are grinding against each other. When this tension is released, the Earth's crust shakes. The process of folding is very slow and is not felt.)* **BL Logical/Mathematical**

W Writing Skills

Informative/Explanatory Have students write a paragraph describing the plate movement of one of the continents. They should identify the tectonic plates associated with the continent and whether or not the continent is moving away from or toward another continent. They should also predict what might happen to the continent as it continues to move. **AL Verbal/Linguistic**

INTERACTIVE MAP

Tectonic Plate Boundaries

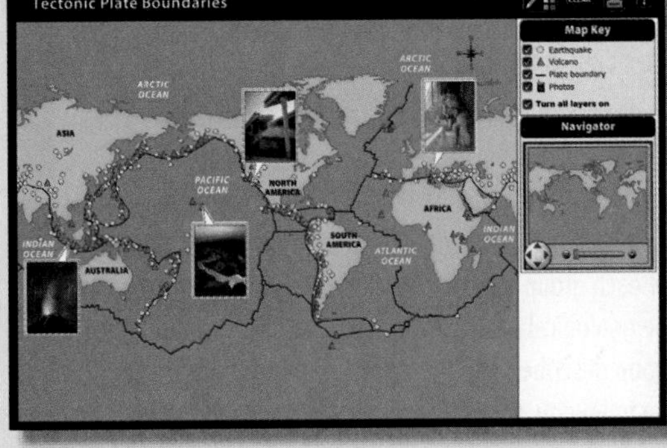

Speculating As students view this interactive map showing Earth's tectonic plate boundaries, have them note the numerous volcanoes and earthquakes in the area termed the Ring of Fire. Ask them to identify the countries located in and around the Ring of Fire. Then explain that Mount Fuji, Japan's tallest mountain, is a volcano that has not erupted in nearly 300 years, though scientists feel it could erupt again, and that more than 1,000 small earthquakes shake Japan every year. Ask students to write a paragraph speculating about ways in which the people in Japan have adapted to their physical environment.
AL Verbal/Linguistic, Naturalist

Content Knowledge Background

San Andreas Fault The fault is not a single, continuous fault; it is actually a fault zone made up of many segments, over 800 miles long. It is part of the boundary between the North American and Pacific Plates. It is a transform fault, meaning the two plates move horizontally past each other. The plates may not move for years. Then when stress builds up, they move suddenly, causing an earthquake.

ANSWERS, p. 47

GEOGRAPHY CONNECTION

1. Mountains, volcanic mountains, and islands result when continental plates, oceanic plates, or continental and oceanic plates collide. Continents grow from the buildup of debris created by oceanic plates sliding under continental plates. Other physical features are underwater mountains and ridges and cracks called faults.
2. Plates moving toward each other are: Nazca, South American, Eurasian, Philippine, Cocos, and Caribbean Plates. Plates moving away from each other are: South American, African, Nazca, Antarctic, North American, and Eurasian Plates.

Forces of Change

R1 Reading Skills

Specifying Invite a volunteer to write a definition for *earthquake* on the board. Have other volunteers list some of the causes of earthquakes. *(Possible answers: sudden moving apart of tectonic plates, volcanic eruption, tension builds where plates meet, etc.)* **Ask:** Where have devastating earthquakes occurred in recent years? *(Japan, Indonesia, Mexico, the United States)* What part of the United States is most subject to violent earthquakes? *(the West Coast, especially California and Alaska)*

R2 Reading Skills

Defining Have students define the term *Ring of Fire*. **Ask:** Why do you suppose the most earthquake-prone area on Earth is termed *Ring of Fire*? *(Possible answer: It is a descriptive term expressing the fact that this area of earthquake and volcanic activities forms a ring around the Pacific Ocean and that volcanoes can be fiery and hot.)* ELL Verbal/Linguistic

Making Connections

Many people believe that earthquakes in the United States occur only on the west coast, but earthquakes can and have occurred in the central, eastern, and southern United States as well. In 1811 and 1812 some very powerful earthquakes occurred along a major fault in the Mississippi Valley, causing much destruction and loss of life. More recently earthquakes have occurred in Pennsylvania, Kentucky, Arkansas, Louisiana, Indiana, Ohio, Illinois, and New York. Florida and North Dakota have the smallest number of recorded earthquakes in the United States.

W Writing Skills

Informative/Explanatory Allow time for students to analyze and ask questions about the diagram. Have them use the diagram to write a step-by-step process paper that explains the processes of subduction, accretion, spreading, and faulting; the movement of the plates; and the result of each process. Encourage students to be as detailed and as specific as possible. *(Subduction results in the formation of volcanic mountains; accretion results in the growth of continents; spreading results in the growth of oceans and creates undersea volcanic mountains; faulting creates cracks and breaks in the Earth's crust and causes earthquakes.)* Verbal/Linguistic

ANSWERS, p. 48

DBQ There was a cloud of volcanic ash near Gina Christie's house.

CRITICAL THINKING

1. During accretion, pieces of the Earth's crust come together slowly as the oceanic plate slides under the continental plate at a shallow angle. This movement levels off seamounts—underwater mountains with steep sides and sharp peaks—and piles up the resulting debris in trenches. This buildup can cause continents to grow outward.
2. You might see tears in the land or land jutting upward.

Analyzing PRIMARY SOURCES

Eyewitness: Icelandic Volcano

"I woke up on Friday with a weird feeling that something just wasn't right. It wasn't light as it normally is—we don't really have night-time at this time of year.

I looked outside and there was a thick, black cloud of ash directly above us. It was exactly like the middle of winter. What is even more surreal was the absolute bright daylight on either side of our village."

—Gina Christie, BBC News, May 17, 2010

DBQ ***DRAWING CONCLUSIONS*** Why do you think it could have been dark at Gina Christie's house, yet bright across town? RH.9–10.1

Many of these events occur as a series of small jumps, felt as minor tremors on the Earth's surface. A few, however, occur as sudden and violent movements of Earth's surface.

Earthquakes and Volcanoes

R1 Sudden, violent movements of the lithosphere along fault lines are known as earthquakes. These shaking activities dramatically change the surface of the land and the floor of the ocean. During a severe earthquake in Alaska in 1964, a portion of the ground lurched upward 38 feet (11.6 m).

Earthquakes often occur where plates meet. Tension builds up along fault lines as the plates stick. The strain eventually becomes so intense that the rocks suddenly snap and shift. This movement releases stored-up energy along the fault. The ground then trembles and shakes as shock waves surge through it, moving away from the area where the rocks first snapped apart.

R2 Disastrous earthquakes have occurred in Kōbe, Japan; in the U.S. cities of Los Angeles and San Francisco; near the Indonesian island of Sumatra; and in Oaxaca, Mexico. These places are located along the *Ring of Fire*, one of the most earthquake-prone areas on the planet. It is a zone of earthquake and volcanic activity around the perimeter of the Pacific Ocean. Here the plates that cradle the Pacific meet the plates that hold the continents surrounding the Pacific. North America, South America, Asia, and Australia are affected by their location on the Ring of Fire.

Volcanoes are mountains formed by lava or by magma that breaks through the Earth's crust. Volcanoes often rise along plate boundaries where one plate plunges beneath another, as along the Ring of Fire. In such a process, the rocky plate melts as it dives downward into the hot mantle. If the molten rock is too thick, its flow is blocked and pressure builds. A cloud of ash and gas may then spew forth, creating a funnel through which the red-hot magma rushes to the surface. There the lava flow may eventually form a large volcanic cone topped by a crater—a bowl-shaped depression at a volcano's mouth.

DIAGRAM SKILLS

Forces of Change

W

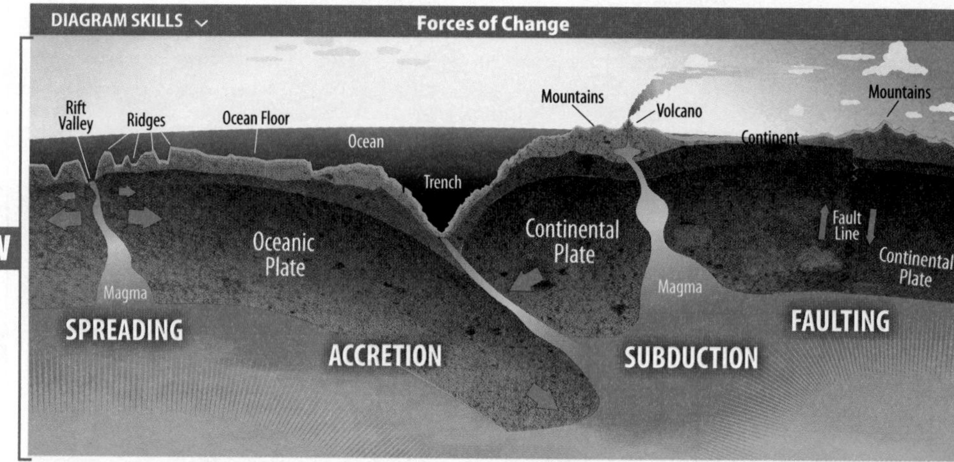

The forces of subduction, accretion, spreading, and faulting shape our planet, creating the landforms we see today.

▲ **CRITICAL THINKING**

1. ***Analyzing*** How does the process of accretion create deep trenches on the Earth's surface?
2. ***Speculating*** What observable evidence might you see after movement along a fault line?

networks Online Teaching Options

INFOGRAPHIC

Forces of Change

Understanding Relationships Among Events This infographic demonstrates the action of the four major forces of change: subduction, accretion, spreading, and faulting. Divide students into small groups. Allow time for each group to click infographic to understand how the geological processes shape Earth's surface. Have each group describe the physical processes that affect one of the following: weather, earthquakes, erosion, soil-building processes, volcanic eruptions, and landforms, such as mountains or islands. BL Naturalist

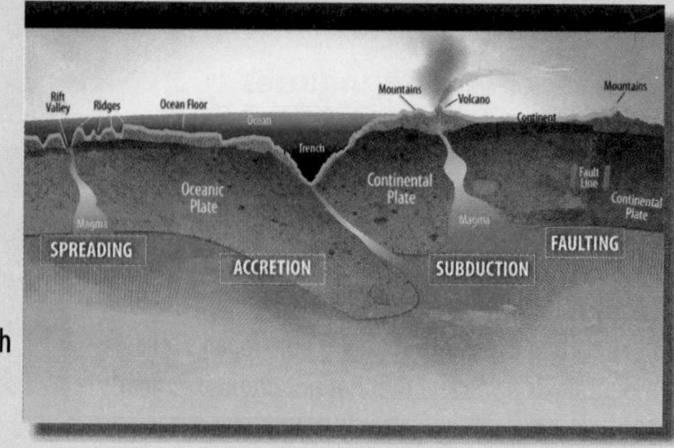

The Colorado River has been shaping the main gorge of the Grand Canyon for thousands of years.

Volcanoes also arise in areas away from plate boundaries. Some areas deep in the Earth are hotter than others, and magma often blasts through the crust and creates volcanoes at the surface. As a moving plate passes over these hot spots, molten rock flowing out of the Earth may create volcanic island chains, such as the Hawaiian Islands. At some hot spots, molten rock may also heat underground water, resulting in hot springs or geysers like Old Faithful in Yellowstone National Park.

▲ CRITICAL THINKING

1. ***Comparing and Contrasting*** How does weathering differ from erosion?
2. ***Classifying*** What are the three different types of erosion?

☑ READING PROGRESS CHECK

Explaining How are volcanoes formed and where are they typically located?

External Forces of Change

GUIDING QUESTION *What external forces shape Earth's surface?*

External forces, such as wind and water, also change the Earth's surface. Wind and water movements involve two processes. **Weathering** breaks down rocks, and **erosion** wears away the Earth's surface by wind, glaciers, and moving water.

external arising outside of

weathering chemical or physical processes that break down rocks into smaller pieces

erosion the movement of weathered rock and material by wind, glaciers, and moving water

Weathering and Erosion

The Earth is changed by two basic kinds of weathering. Physical weathering occurs when large masses of rock are physically broken down into smaller pieces. For example, water seeps into the cracks in a rock and freezes, expanding and causing the rock to split. Chemical weathering changes the chemical makeup of rocks. For example, rainwater that contains carbon dioxide from the air easily dissolves certain rocks such as limestone. Many of the world's caves have been and continue to be formed by this process.

Wind erosion carries small particles of dust, sand, and soil from one place to another. Plants help protect the land from wind erosion. However, in dry places where people have cut down trees and plants, winds pick up large amounts of soil and blow it away. Wind erosion can provide some benefits; the dust carried by wind often forms large deposits of mineral-rich soil. Another cause of erosion is **glaciers**, large bodies of ice that move across the Earth's surface. Glaciers form

glacier a large body of ice that moves across the surface of the Earth

VIDEO

Water Eroding Mountains

Formulating Questions Use this video about the power of water to introduce one of Earth's most powerful forces—water. Ask students to write three questions they have after watching the video. Collect the questions and have the class answer them after reading the lesson. Discuss with students how the physical landforms on Earth are moving and changing all of the time, and that change is fairly constant.
ELL **Verbal/Linguistic**

Forces of Change

G1 Critical Thinking Skills

Hypothesizing Before students read about external forces of change, have them study the photograph at the top of the page of the Grand Canyon. **Ask: What forces led to the formation of this physical feature?** *(Water erosion from the Colorado River has shaped the canyon.)* **Visual/Spatial**

T Technology Skills

Informative/Explanatory Ask a volunteer to define "geyser." *(A hot spring that intermittently spews hot water into the air.)* Tell students that Old Faithful, in Yellowstone National Park, is the most famous geyser in the United States. Working in pairs, have students research other natural formations found in National Parks around the United States. They should pick one formation and prepare a travel brochure touting the wonder of its display. Encourage students to give details about the processes that cause the natural phenomenon. Partners should share their brochures with the class. **Interpersonal, Verbal/Linguistic**

G2 Critical Thinking Skills

Contrasting Have students distinguish between the external forces of change that shape the Earth's surface and those that are internal. Explain that external forces occur on the Earth's surface and that internal forces occur below the Earth's surface. **Ask: What external forces occur on the surface of Earth?** *(wind, water, physical and chemical weathering, and erosion)* **What internal forces occur below the surface of Earth?** *(continental drift, earthquakes, and volcanoes)* **Which forces do you think have the most effect in shaping Earth's surface?** *(Possible answers: Internal forces are responsible for the most obvious, large-scale changes: creating mountains and volcanoes, separating continents, etc. Often, changes brought about by external forces are less monumental; however, there are exceptions. Water can be a powerful force. The eroding power of water created canyons like the Grand Canyon, and glaciers have worn down mountaintops and carved out valleys.)*
BL **Logical/Mathematical**

ANSWERS, p. 49

☑ READING PROGRESS CHECK Volcanoes are mountains formed by lava or by magma that breaks through the Earth's crust. Volcanoes often rise along plate boundaries where one plate plunges beneath another, as along the Ring of Fire.

CRITICAL THINKING

1. Weathering breaks down rocks, and erosion wears away the Earth's surface by wind, glaciers, and moving water.
2. The types of erosion are wind, glaciers, and moving water.

Forces of Change

C Critical Thinking Skills

Comparing and Contrasting Review with students the destructive power of glaciers. **Ask:** **How are sheet and mountain glaciers similar?** *(They are both large, heavy bodies of ice that can move across Earth, changing the landscape.)* **What is the difference between a sheet glacier and a mountain glacier?** *(Sheet glaciers are flat, broad sheets of ice, covering huge areas of land. They advance a few feet each winter and recede in summer. Mountain glaciers are found in high mountain valleys and can only be formed in very cold climates. As they move, they gouge out rounded, U-shaped valleys. As they melt, rocks and soil are deposited.)* Explain that sheet (continental) glaciers can be more than a mile thick. Mountain (alpine) glaciers can be more than 2700 feet (900 m) thick. **Ask:** **How is it that glaciers can so greatly change the landscape?** *(They are huge and weigh a lot. When they're on the move, nothing can stop them.)* **How is a glacier like a river of ice?** *(it flows downhill, across land like a river, just much slower.)* Have students draw a Venn diagram to compare and contrast sheet and mountain glaciers. AL Logical/Mathematical

Content Background Knowledge

Wind Barriers Plants retard wind erosion in two ways. First, they form a cover for the land and reduce the wind's ability to blow soil away. Second, their roots form a network that grips the soil and keeps it in place. Because of its dense cover, grass is a soil stabilizer. Farmers plant lines of trees, as wind barriers, to shield land from wind and erosion.

R Reading Skills

Describing Have students describe the soil-building process. **Ask:** **How do worms and other organisms help in changing organic matter into nutrients that enrich and produce soil?** *(Earthworms consume organic matter that is deposited on the soil. As it passes through their digestive system, this matter is broken down into chemical nutrients and excreted into the soil.)* Have students think of places where they have seen soil erosion. Discuss why protecting soil is important to everyone. Logical/Mathematical

CLOSE & REFLECT

Analyzing Have students consider the ways that Earth is a work in progress. Have them analyze the forces of change, such as continents and oceans forming and changing, and mountains building up and tearing down. Explain that Earth is constantly changing.

ANSWERS, p. 50

✓ **READING PROGRESS CHECK** The five factors are: climate, topography, geology, biology, and length of time the other four factors have been interacting.

---

moraine piles of rocky debris left by melting glaciers

C over time as layers of snow press together and turn to ice. Their great weight causes them to move slowly downhill and spread outward. As they move, glaciers pick up rocks and soil in their paths, changing the landscape. They can remove forests, carve out valleys, alter the courses of rivers, and wear down mountaintops.

When glaciers melt and recede in some places, they leave behind large piles of rocks and debris called **moraines**. Some moraines form long ridges of land, while others form dams that hold water back and create glacial lakes.

There are two types of glaciers. Ice sheets are flat, broad sheets of ice. Today, ice sheet glaciers cover most of Greenland and all of Antarctica. They advance a few feet each winter and recede in the summer. Large blocks of ice often break off from the coastal edges of sheet glaciers to become icebergs floating in the ocean. Mountain glaciers, which are a more common type of glacier today, are located in high mountain valleys where the climate is cold. They scar the Earth's surface, gouging out rounded, U-shaped valleys as they move downhill. As they melt, rocks and soil are deposited in new locations.

Water erosion begins when springwater and rainwater flow downhill in streams, cutting into the land and wearing away the soil and rock. The resulting sediment grinds away the surface of rocks along the stream's path. Over time, the eroding action of water forms first a gully and then a V-shaped valley. Sometimes, valleys are eroded even further to form canyons. The Grand Canyon is an example of the eroding power of water. Oceans also play an important role in water erosion. Pounding waves continually erode coastal cliffs, wear rocks into sandy beaches, and move sand away to other coastal areas.

Soil Building

Soil is the product of thousands of years of weathering, erosion, and biological activity. Soil development begins when weathering breaks down solid rock into smaller pieces. Worms and other organisms help break down organic matter—dead plant and animal material—that comes to rest on these particles. Living organisms also add nutrients to the soil and create passages for air and water.

R Five factors influence soil formation, with *climate* being the most significant. Wind, temperature, and rainfall determine the type of soil that can develop. *Topography*—the shape and position of Earth's physical features—affects surface runoff of water, drainage, and the rate of erosion. *Geology* determines the parent material (original rock), which influences depth, texture, drainage, and nutrient content of soil. *Biology*, living and dead plants and animals, adds organic matter to the soil. The length of *time* the other four factors have been interacting also affects soil formation. These factors combine to produce different types of soils.

✓ **READING PROGRESS CHECK**

Listing List the five factors that influence soil formation.

LESSON 2 REVIEW 

Reviewing Vocabulary (Tier Three Words)

1. ***Explaining*** Explain the difference between subduction and accretion and the significance of each. RH.9–10.4

Using Your Notes

2. ***Describing*** Use your graphic organizer to explain how plate tectonics folds, lifts, bends, and breaks parts of the Earth's surface.

Answering the Guiding Questions

3. ***Discussing*** How is Earth's structure related to the creation of continents, oceans, and mountain ranges?
4. ***Defining*** How does plate tectonics affect Earth's surface?
5. ***Identifying*** What external forces shape Earth's surface?

Writing Activity

6. ***Informative/Explanatory*** Describe three kinds of erosion that shape Earth's surface. How does erosion help create soil? WHST.9–10.2

50

LESSON 2 REVIEW ANSWERS

Reviewing Vocabulary

1. Subduction is when an oceanic plate dives beneath a continental plate to form a mountain on land. Accretion is when an oceanic plate slides under a continental plate to form a continent.

Using Your Notes

2. Possible answer: Subduction causes oceanic plates to dive beneath continental plates. It often causes mountains, such as the Andes, to form on land.

Answering the Guiding Questions

3. Earth's crust carries the oceans and continents. Movement of the tectonic plates creates mountains, land, volcanoes, oceans, and earthquakes.
4. Plate tectonics act upon the Earth's internal and external structures to help create the continents, ocean basins, and mountain ranges. Plate tectonics operates by folding, lifting, bending, and breaking parts of the Earth's surface.
5. Wind and water shape Earth's surface.

Writing Activity

6. Wind erosion carries dust, sand, and soil from one place to another. Glaciers pick up rocks and soil in their paths, changing the landscape. Water erosion wears away the soil and rock. Erosion helps create soil by moving large amounts of mineral-rich dust, increasing the nutrients and soil deposits in an area.

There's More Online!

- INFOGRAPHIC The Water Cycle
- MAP Global Desalination
- INTERACTIVE SELF-CHECK QUIZ
- VIDEO Earth's Water

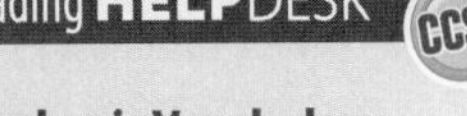

LESSON 3
Earth's Water

ESSENTIAL QUESTION • *How do physical processes shape Earth's surface?*

Reading HELPDESK

Academic Vocabulary (Tier Two Words)

- **constant**
- **enormous**

Content Vocabulary (Tier Three Words)

- **water cycle**
- **evaporation**
- **condensation**
- **precipitation**
- **desalination**
- **groundwater**
- **aquifer**

TAKING NOTES: *Key Ideas and Details*

IDENTIFYING As you read the lesson, use a concept map like the one below to write descriptions of the freshwater sources on Earth, including how they are used by humans.

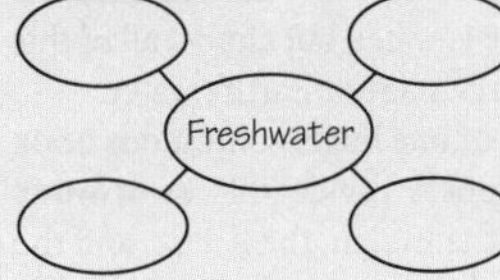

IT MATTERS BECAUSE

The amount of water on Earth remains fairly constant and moves in the water cycle. Salt water covers much of the Earth's surface. Although there is only a small amount of freshwater on Earth, it is necessary to sustain life. R1

The Water Cycle

GUIDING QUESTION *What drives the Earth's water cycle?*

As you recall, oceans, lakes, rivers, and other bodies of water make up the Earth's hydrosphere. Almost all of the hydrosphere is salt water found in the oceans, seas, and a few large saltwater lakes. The remainder is freshwater found in lakes, rivers, glaciers, and groundwater.

The total amount of water on Earth does not change, but it is constantly moving—from the oceans to the air to the land and finally back to the oceans. This regular movement of water is called the **water cycle**. The sun drives the water cycle by evaporating water from the surfaces of bodies of water. **Evaporation** is the changing of liquid water into vapor, or gas. The sun's energy causes evaporation. Water vapor rising from bodies of water and plants is gathered in the air. The amount of water vapor the air holds depends on its temperature. Warm air holds more water vapor than cool air. R2 V

When warm air cools, it cannot retain all of its water vapor, so the excess water vapor changes into liquid water—a process called **condensation**. Tiny droplets of water come together to form clouds. When clouds gather more water than they can hold, they release moisture, which falls to the Earth as **precipitation**—rain, snow, or sleet, depending on the air temperature and wind conditions. This precipitation sinks into the ground and collects in streams and lakes to return to the oceans. Soon most of it evaporates, and the cycle begins again.

The amount of water that evaporates is approximately the same amount that falls back to Earth. This amount varies little from year to year. Thus, the total volume of water in the water cycle is fairly **constant**. C

READING PROGRESS CHECK

Explaining What causes evaporation?

ENGAGE

R1 Reading Skills

Setting a Purpose Before beginning the lesson, write a few headlines on the board to dramatize freshwater shortages, e.g. *Water Shortages Driving Conflicts in Kenya, Water Crisis Will Make Gaza Strip "Unlivable," Nile Countries Continue Fight Over Water, Drought Threatens World Food Prices, California Faces Water Rationing.* Have students write a paragraph about their knowledge of how freshwater shortages affect peoples' lives around the world. Then discuss ways people use water and how water shortages impact lives.

TEACH & ASSESS

R2 Reading Skills

Identifying Have a volunteer describe the hydrosphere and its relation to Earth's biosphere. Point out that the water cycle takes place between the atmosphere and the hydrosphere. Discuss the role the sun plays in the water cycle. **Ask:** **How is the sun the engine that drives the water cycle?** *(It evaporates water from the surfaces of bodies of water, transferring it into the atmosphere.)* ELL **Verbal/Linguistic**

V Visual Skills

Contrasting Have students explain the difference between *evaporation* and *condensation*. **Ask:** **What causes water to evaporate into the atmosphere?** *(heat from the sun changes liquid into vapor)* **What causes water to condense?** *(warm air cools, water vapor changes into liquid)* Have students draw a diagram of the two processes. AL **Visual/Spatial**

C Critical Thinking Skills

Drawing Conclusions Have students explain how the total volume of water in the water cycle is constant. **Ask:** **If total volume of the Earth's water is constant, how can it be that some regions experience droughts and other regions are flooding?** *(Stating that the water cycle is constant refers to the total volume of water on Earth. Some areas may be dry, some wet, but the amount of water in the hydrosphere and atmosphere remain the same.)* **Logical/Mathematical**

networks Online Teaching Options

INTERACTIVE BELLRINGER

Desalination Capacity

Reading Graphs Have students use this graph to discuss the different amounts of freshwater and salt water in the world and the need for desalination plants in some countries that are primarily desert. Have pairs of students read the introductory text, study the graph, and answer the first question. Encourage students to use their background knowledge to answer questions 2 and 3, but allow them to use a world map if necessary. Then ask students to name other countries that might benefit from having desalination plants. **Visual/Spatial, Logical/Mathematical**

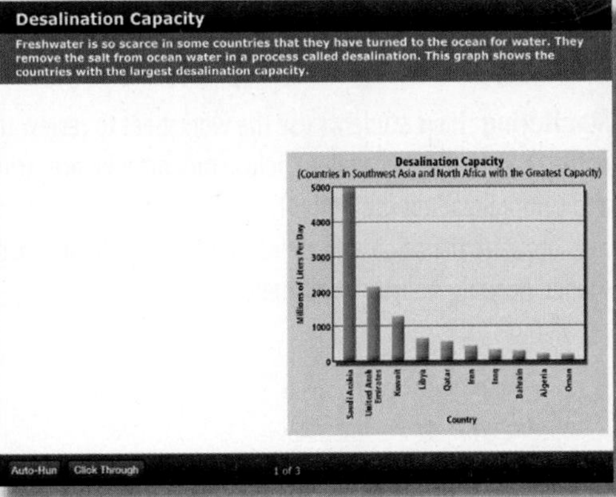

ANSWERS, p. 51

READING PROGRESS CHECK Evaporation is caused by water changing into vapor, or gas, upon heating.

TAKING NOTES: Freshwater sources on Earth include lakes, rivers, and groundwater. Humans use freshwater for drinking, bathing, and cooking.

Earth's Water

W Writing Skills

Narrative Draw students' attention to the water cycle diagram at the top of the page. Have students imagine that they are a droplet of water. Have them write a short essay explaining how they move through the water cycle starting in the ocean, then to air, down to ground, and back to the ocean again. **BL** **Naturalist**

R Reading Skills

Analyzing Maps Point to the connecting oceans on a globe or world map. Have students name the five oceans. **Ask:** **Why do some geographers say that there is really just one big super ocean?** *(All of the oceans are connected.)* **How does the Southern Ocean differ from the other oceans?** *(It does not lie in a large basin between the continents as the others do.)* **What is unique about the Pacific Ocean?** *(It is the largest ocean and the deepest.)* **Verbal/Linguistic, Visual/Spatial**

Content Background Knowledge

Smaller Bodies of Salt Water Besides oceans, there are other types of saltwater bodies.

- Sea: a smaller division of the world's oceans that is more or less surrounded by land; a sea can also be a landlocked body of salt water not related to the world's oceans (for example, the Salton Sea and the Caspian Sea)
- Gulf: a large, usually deep, part of an ocean extending into land
- Bay: a part of an ocean or sea extending into land, but usually significantly smaller than a gulf

V Visual Skills

Locating Have students locate the Mediterranean Sea, the Gulf of Mexico, and the Chesapeake Bay on a world map. Ask students to identify other seas, gulfs, and bays on the map. Discuss the differences between a gulf, a sea, and a bay. Then have students locate the map key and estimate how far away they are from an ocean, a gulf, or a sea. Have volunteers relate experiences they have had at both ocean shores and lake shores. Then have them describe important ways that an ocean is different from a lake. **ELL** **Intrapersonal, Visual/Spatial**

ANSWERS, p. 52

CRITICAL THINKING

1. Rain, snow, sleet or hail are types of precipitation. They might end up as groundwater or in lakes, oceans, and streams.
2. Water could evaporate and be carried to another location as vapor and then fall as rain; water could flow to another location.

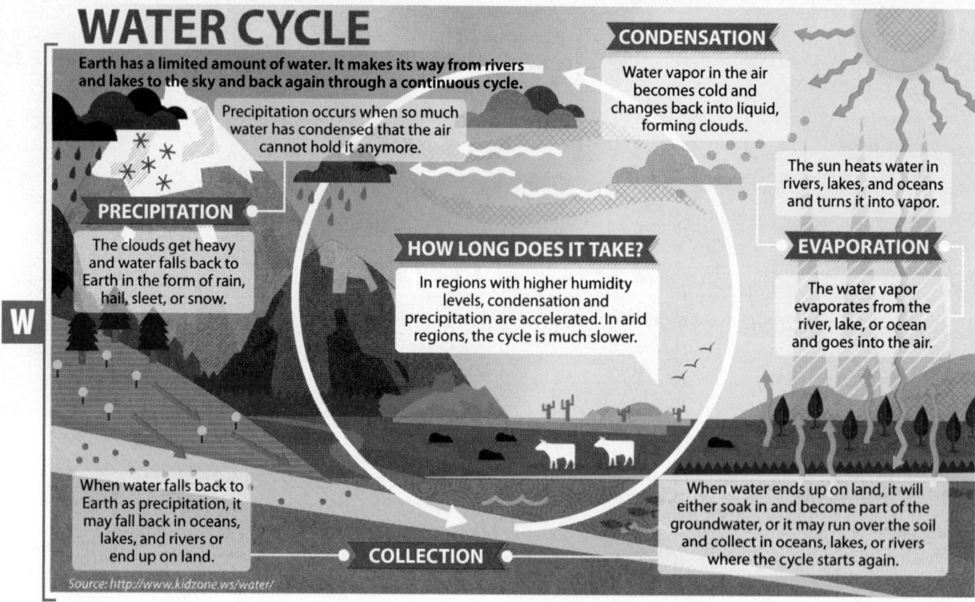

WATER CYCLE
Earth has a limited amount of water. It makes its way from rivers and lakes to the sky and back again through a continuous cycle.
Precipitation occurs when so much water has condensed that the air cannot hold it anymore.
CONDENSATION
Water vapor in the air becomes cold and changes back into liquid, forming clouds.
The sun heats water in rivers, lakes, and oceans and turns it into vapor.
PRECIPITATION
The clouds get heavy and water falls back to Earth in the form of rain, hail, sleet, or snow.
HOW LONG DOES IT TAKE?
In regions with higher humidity levels, condensation and precipitation are accelerated. In arid regions, the cycle is much slower.
EVAPORATION
The water vapor evaporates from the river, lake, or ocean and goes into the air.
When water falls back to Earth as precipitation, it may fall back in oceans, lakes, and rivers or end up on land.
COLLECTION
When water ends up on land, it will either soak in and become part of the groundwater, or it may run over the soil and collect in oceans, lakes, or rivers where the cycle starts again.
Source: http://www.kidzone.ws/water/

The water cycle depicts the movement of water from ocean to air to ground and back to the ocean.

▲ CRITICAL THINKING

1. ***Categorizing*** What are three types of precipitation? Where might this precipitation end up?
2. ***Speculating*** How might contaminated water end up affecting people even if they live far away from the source?

water cycle regular movement of Earth's water from ocean to air to ground and back to the ocean

evaporation the process of converting liquid into vapor, or gas

condensation the process of excess water vapor changing into liquid water when warm air cools

precipitation moisture that falls to the Earth as rain, sleet, hail, or snow

constant unchanging

enormous gigantic; exceedingly large

Bodies of Salt Water

GUIDING QUESTION *What is salt water?*

Seen from space, the Earth's oceans and seas are more prominent than its landmasses. About 70 percent of the Earth's surface is water, but almost all of this is salt water. Freshwater makes up only a small percentage of Earth's water.

About 97 percent of the Earth's water consists of one huge, continuous body of water that circles all the continents. Geographers divide this **enormous** expanse into five oceans: the Pacific, the Atlantic, the Indian, the Arctic, and the Southern. The first four lie in large basins between the continents, while the Southern Ocean extends from the coast of Antarctica north to 60° S latitude. The Pacific, the largest of the oceans, covers more area than all the Earth's land combined. The Pacific Ocean is also deep enough in some places to cover Mount Everest, the world's highest mountain, with more than 1 mile (1.6 km) to spare.

Seas, gulfs, and bays are bodies of salt water smaller than oceans. These bodies of water are often partially enclosed by land. As one of the world's largest seas, the Mediterranean Sea is almost entirely encircled by southern Europe, northern Africa, and southwestern Asia. The Gulf of Mexico is nearly encircled by the coasts of the United States and Mexico.

Although 97 percent of the world's water is found in oceans, the water is too salty for drinking, farming, or manufacturing. The world's growing population and increasing urbanization require freshwater for such activities. Governments,

networks Online Teaching Options

WORKSHEET

Guided Reading Activity

Monitoring Have students use the worksheet to review their comprehension of the content. This worksheet helps students who are struggling with reading and comprehending the content. It is also valuable for on-level students to help organize their notes. Each lesson of the textbook is accompanied by a Guided Reading Activity worksheet.

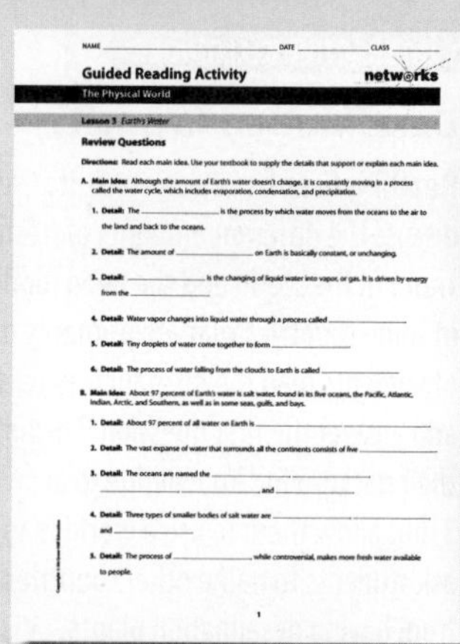
Guided Reading Activity

The Physical World

Review Questions

planners, and scientists continue to look for ways to meet the world's growing need for freshwater. Today, some of these efforts focus on ways to remove the salt from ocean water or groundwater in a process known as **desalination**.

desalination the removal of salt from seawater to make it usable for drinking and farming

Desalination is a controversial topic, however. Supporters point out that it is one of the most promising solutions to the problem of freshwater shortages.

PRIMARY SOURCE

> "Desalination is a promise fulfilled. Today, hundreds of million people around the world have access to clean water thanks to desalination. Just as importantly, desalination is also a promise for the future, with its unique ability to deliver a reliable, sustainable and new source of water to our thirsty planet."
>
> —Corrado Sommariva, invitation to the International Desalination Association 2013 World Congress

Critics of the process argue that it does not come without economic and environmental costs. Desalinated ocean water is one of the most expensive forms of freshwater available because of the costs associated with collecting the ocean water, removing the salt, and distributing the new freshwater. For example, desalinated water in the United States can cost up to five times more than other sources of freshwater. Such high costs make desalination an impossible option for many less developed countries, where limited funds are already stretched too thin.

Some countries, such as Saudi Arabia and the United Arab Emirates, use desalination because other freshwater sources are scarce and because they have the financial and energy resources to support such ventures. In fact, about three-fourths of the world's desalinated water is produced in North Africa and Southwest Asia. Desalination plants in the United States—mostly in California, Florida, and Texas—also produce a small amount of freshwater.

The environmental concerns surrounding desalination are related to ocean and marine biodiversity. When ocean water is collected, marine life is drawn up in the intake pipe and eventually destroyed during the desalination process.

GEOGRAPHY CONNECTION

Desalination is an option for some countries to meet freshwater needs.

1. ***PLACES AND REGIONS*** In which general region of the world are many of the desalination plants located?
2. ***ENVIRONMENT AND SOCIETY*** Which energy resource allows North Africa and Southwest Asia to be the world leader in freshwater production?

Global Desalination

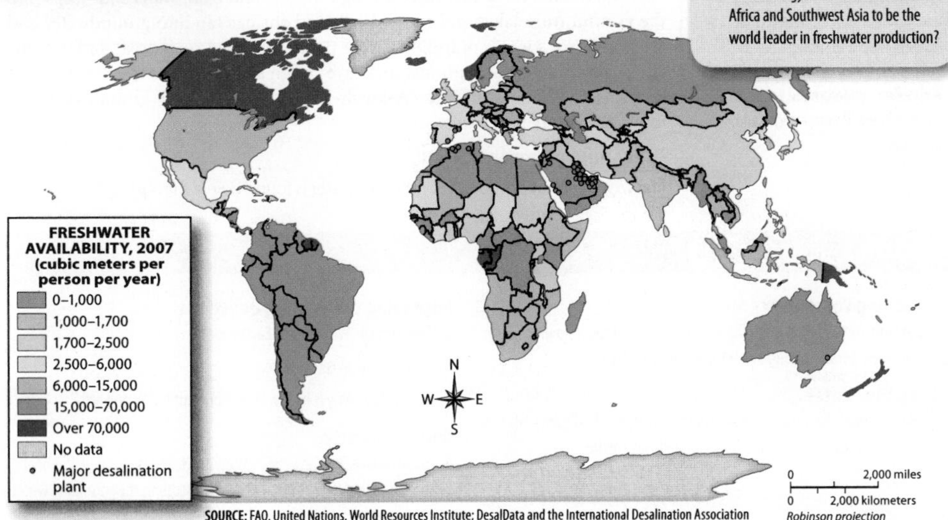

SOURCE: FAO, United Nations, World Resources Institute; DesalData and the International Desalination Association

Making Connections

Explain the difference between salt water and freshwater.

- Humans and animals need freshwater to survive. If either drinks salt water, the body tries to eliminate the excess sodium by producing higher levels of urine. So the body is actually depleting itself of more fluids than it has.
- Ingestion of salt water in humans and animals can lead to increased heart rates, nausea, weakness, and even delirium because the body becomes dehydrated. Eventually, drinking salt water will lead to coma, organ failure, and death.
- Plants and crops also need freshwater; if they receive saltwater, they too become dehydrated. Plants receive water via their root systems. Sodium draws water out of plants, inhibiting their growth, and causes them to wither.

T Technology Skills

Assessing Discuss how a growing population and increasing urbanization infrastructure impact the demand on freshwater resources. Explain to students that the geography or location of a country can affect its economic activities. Countries that are rich in natural resources, such as Saudi Arabia, are economically able to afford desalination plants to produce freshwater. Many countries may not be able to afford this expensive process.

Challenge students to gather statistics, using the Internet or online sources, about worldwide water supplies and assess how water shortages impact drought-prone countries and regions. Suggest that students create a bulletin board display to show how economics affects the development of freshwater technology in countries where water is a scarcity. **BL** **Visual/Spatial**

C Critical Thinking Skills

Problem Solving Have students imagine that they are officials in a community with a growing water problem. Have students work in small groups to answer important questions. **Ask:** **Would building a desalination facility be possible or desirable? Why or why not? What other ways might there be to solve the water problem?** *(building a new reservoir; catching rain water; channeling water from a river; new wells; starting a major conservation initiative)* Students should research their ideas. Then hold a "town meeting" or class discussion to analyze the problem and to look for long- and short-term solutions. List the pros and cons of each group's ideas. **Logical/Mathematical**

INTERACTIVE MAP

Global Desalination

Reading Maps This world map shows available freshwater in each country, as well as locations of major desalination plants. Ask the following questions to the class to gauge their map reading skills.

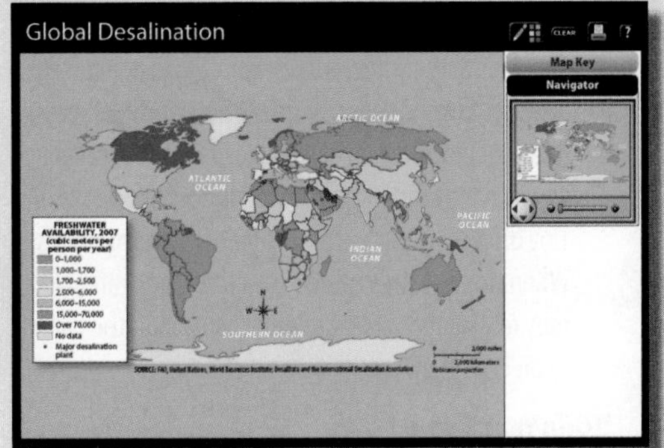

- **What does the legend on the map indicate?**
- **Which countries have desalination plants?**
- **Which states in the United States have desalination plants?**
- **Across which lines of latitude are most desalination plants located? Why do you think so many desalination plants are located across this area?** *(Student answers may vary somewhat, however they should be able to identify specific details of the map.)* **AL** **Visual/Spatial**

ANSWERS, p. 53

GEOGRAPHY CONNECTION

1. North Africa and Southwest Asia
2. North Africa and Southwest Asia have oil reserves which generate enough money to make desalination possible.

C Critical Thinking Skills

Defending Have students list the major environmental concerns surrounding desalination on the board. **Ask:** **Which environmental hazard disturbs you the most? Why?** *(Student answers may vary, but should defend their answers by demonstrating an understanding of desalination.)* **Intrapersonal**

R Reading Skills

Visualizing To help students visualize the importance of protecting surface water resources, have a volunteer create a pie graph showing how Earth's freshwater supply is divided between glaciers and ice caps (68.6%), surface water—lakes, ponds, streams, rivers (1.3%), and underground water (30.1%). **Ask:** **How important is it for communities to protect their lakes, ponds, streams, and rivers?** *(Very; they hold 1.3% of Earth's fresh water supply.)* **Why is it that much of the world's freshwater supply is not available for consumption?** *(most of the world's freshwater, 68.6%, is locked up in glaciers)* **ELL** **Visual/Spatial**

V Visual Skills

Analyzing Visuals Have students work in pairs to locate Earth's freshwater sources on a world map. Tell students to locate frozen glaciers and ice caps around the world, as well as major lakes and rivers found on each continent. Then have students locate the major lakes, rivers, and tributaries in the United States. Next have partners analyze a community map to determine where the main water source is in their community. Explain that water generally flows from a main source, such as a lake or mountain, then into streams, and finally to a larger body of water or reservoir from which communities draw water supplies. **Visual/Spatial**

CLOSE & REFLECT

Explaining To close this lesson, have students write a brief essay to answer the questions: **What are Earth's water resources, where can you find them, and why is protecting them important?**

ANSWERS, p. 54

✓ READING PROGRESS CHECK The process that removes salt from ocean water is called desalination.

✓ READING PROGRESS CHECK One-sixth of Earth's total water is found beneath the surface.

CRITICAL THINKING

1. North America has many glacial lakes.
2. Freshwater sources include glaciers, ice caps, groundwater, lakes, rivers, and streams.

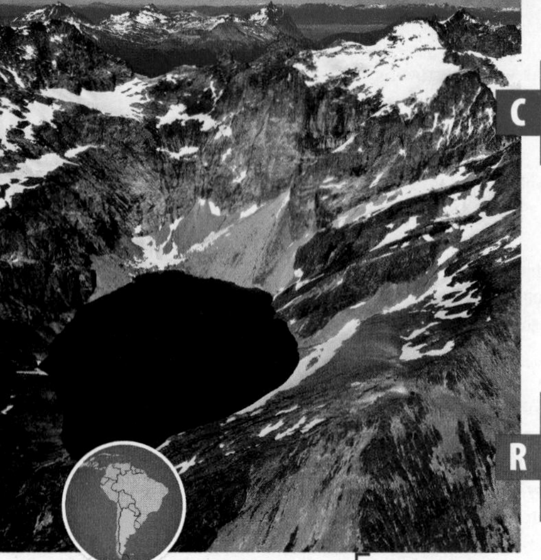

Glacial lakes, like this one in Argentina, are most abundant in high-altitude areas that were once occupied by glaciers.

▲ CRITICAL THINKING

1. ***Identifying*** Other than Argentina, where else could you find glacial lakes?
2. ***Classifying*** What are the different sources of freshwater?

C In addition, wastewater from the process affects coastal water quality. Besides being very salty, this brine may be warmer in temperature and contain chemicals, which have detrimental effects on water and marine organisms.

✓ READING PROGRESS CHECK

Identifying What is the name of the process that removes salt from ocean water?

Bodies of Freshwater

GUIDING QUESTION *Why is freshwater important to life on Earth?*

R Only about 3 percent of Earth's total water supply is freshwater, and most is not available for human consumption. More than two-thirds of Earth's freshwater is frozen as glaciers and ice caps. Another sixth is found beneath the surface. Lakes, streams, and rivers contain less than one-third of 1 percent of Earth's freshwater.

A lake is a body of water completely surrounded by land. Most lakes contain freshwater, although some, such as Southwest Asia's Dead Sea, are saltwater remnants of ancient seas. Many lakes are found where glacial movement has cut deep valleys and built up dams of soil and rock that held back melting ice water. North America has thousands of glacial lakes.

V Flowing water forms streams and rivers. Meltwater, an overflowing lake, or a spring may be the source, or the beginning, of a stream. Streams may combine to form a river, a larger stream of higher volume that follows a channel along a particular course. When rivers join, the major river systems that result may flow for thousands of miles. The smaller streams or rivers that flow into larger rivers are called *tributaries*. Rain, runoff, and water from these tributaries swell rivers as they flow toward a lake, gulf, sea, or ocean. The place where the river empties into another body of water is its mouth.

Groundwater, freshwater that lies beneath the Earth's surface, comes from rain and melted snow that filter through the soil and from water that seeps into the ground from lakes and rivers. Wells and springs tap into groundwater and are important sources of freshwater for people in many rural areas and in some cities. An underground porous rock layer often saturated by very slow flows of water is called an **aquifer** (A•kwuh•fuhr). Aquifers and groundwater are important sources of freshwater.

groundwater water located underground within the Earth that supplies wells and springs

aquifer underground water-bearing layers of porous rock, sand, or gravel

✓ READING PROGRESS CHECK

Identifying What portion of Earth's freshwater is found below the surface?

LESSON 3 REVIEW (CCSS)

Reviewing Vocabulary (Tier Three Words)

1. ***Summarizing*** Summarize the water cycle using the following terms: evaporation, condensation, and precipitation. WHST.9–10.2, WHST.9–10.4

Using Your Notes

2. ***Identifying*** Use your web diagram to identify the bodies of freshwater that are necessary to sustain life on Earth.

Answering the Guiding Questions

3. ***Explaining*** What drives Earth's water cycle?
4. ***Stating*** What is salt water?
5. ***Analyzing*** Why is freshwater important to life on Earth?

Writing Activity

6. ***Informative/Explanatory*** Many cities and towns develop near sources of water. Write a paragraph describing the sources of water used by your community. WHST.9–10.2

LESSON 3 REVIEW ANSWERS

Reviewing Vocabulary

1. The sun drives the water cycle through evaporation, as water turns to vapor, or gas. When warm air cools, it cannot hold onto all of its water vapor; the excess vapor changes into liquid water during condensation. Tiny droplets of water come together to form clouds. When clouds gather more water than they can hold, they release moisture. The moisture falls to the Earth as precipitation.

Using Your Notes

2. Bodies of freshwater necessary to sustain life on Earth include oceans, lakes, and rivers.

Answering the Guiding Questions

3. The sun drives Earth's water cycle.
4. Salt water is water that contains salt, such as the Pacific and Atlantic Oceans.
5. Freshwater is necessary for drinking, bathing, and cooking, as well as for supporting many plants and animals.

Writing Activity

6. Paragraphs may vary, but should describe the sources of water used by the student's community.

CHAPTER 2 Assessment 

Directions: On a separate sheet of paper, answer the questions below. Make sure you read carefully and answer all parts of the questions.

Lesson Review

Lesson 1

1. ***Describing*** Describe the larger physical system of which Earth is a part.
2. ***Explaining*** How do the hydrosphere, lithosphere, and atmosphere work together to form the biosphere?
3. ***Hypothesizing*** What conditions would have to exist in order for a space station to support life?

Lesson 2

4. ***Evaluating*** How have earthquakes and volcanoes influenced the size and location of Earth's physical features?
5. ***Analyzing*** How has erosion been beneficial and harmful to agricultural communities?
6. ***Summarizing*** How do physical processes such as tectonic forces, erosion, and soil building affect different regions? Give examples.

Lesson 3

7. ***Identifying Central Issues*** Explain how the statement "The total amount of water on Earth does not change" relates to the water cycle. RH.9–10.4
8. ***Explaining*** How have technological innovations like desalination allowed people living in areas without adequate freshwater sources to adapt to their environment?
9. ***Identifying Cause and Effect*** How can pollution in streams affect the oceans?

21st Century Skills

Review the diagram. Then answer the questions that follow.

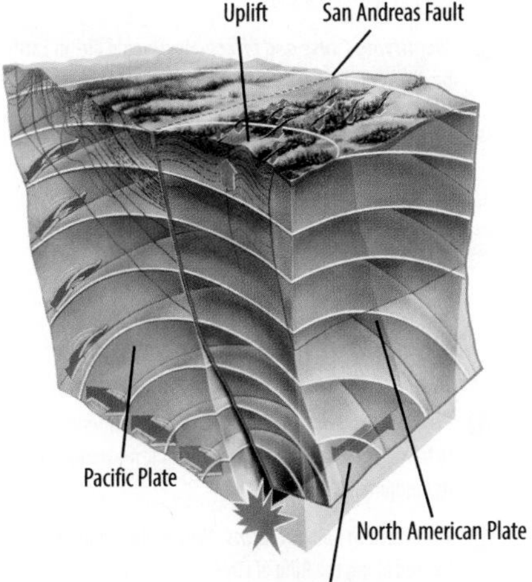

10. ***Using Graphs, Charts, Diagrams, and Tables*** Describe the movement of the San Andreas Fault.
11. ***Compare and Contrast*** How does accretion differ from subduction? What are the effects of each?

College and Career Readiness

12. ***Global Analysis*** Discuss the ways in which the United States could help less developed countries prepare for natural disasters, such as earthquakes and volcanic eruptions.

Richard Leech/National Geographic Stock

Need Extra Help?

If You've Missed Question	1	2	3	4	5	6	7	8	9	10	11	12
Go to page	40	42	42	48	49	45	51	53	54	55	47	48

networks Online Teaching Options

WORKSHEET

Chapter Test and Lesson Quizzes

Assessing Have students complete the Chapter Test and Lesson Quizzes to assess student understanding throughout the chapter. These assessment tools offer chapter and lesson evaluation through a variety of question formats including document-based questions.

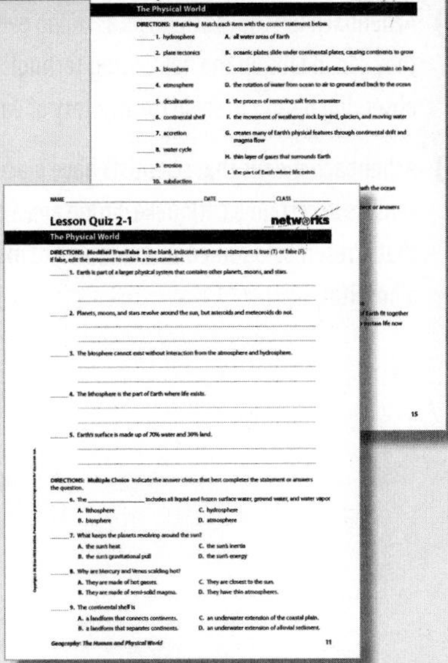

CHAPTER 2 Assessment Answers

LESSON REVIEW

Lesson 1

1. Earth is part of the solar system which contains 8 planets orbiting the sun.
2. The hydrosphere contains all the bodies of water on Earth, the lithosphere contains all the land, and the atmosphere contains a layer of gases that includes the air we breathe. Together they form the biosphere, but without any one of them life could not be supported on Earth.
3. There would need to be an atmosphere and water to support life. Currently, the space station operates with life support systems and supplies that must be replenished from Earth.

Lesson 2

4. Islands and island chains are formed by earthquakes and volcanoes and are common in areas like the Ring of Fire.
5. Erosion removes soil, which is harmful to agricultural communities, but also deposits mineral-rich soil in some areas, which is helpful.
6. Student answers may vary, but could include: tectonic forces and the Ring of Fire, water erosion and the Grand Canyon, and soil building and fertile or desert regions.

Lesson 3

7. The amount of water in the water cycle does not change, only the form that the water is in at different points in the cycle.
8. Desalination allows people to live, grow food, and mine natural resources in areas without many freshwater sources.
9. Streams flow into rivers which eventually empty into the ocean, causing any pollution that was originally in the stream to also pollute the ocean.

21st Century Skills

10. The San Andreas Fault moves back and forth in a horizontal direction.
11. Accretion is when an oceanic plate slides under a continental plate at a shallow angle, instead of a deep angle as in subduction. Accretion causes continents to grow outward. Subduction causes plates to dive so deep into the earth that magma rises and volcanic mountains form.

College and Career Readiness

12. Student answers may vary, but could include helping set up monitoring systems, sharing information from U.S. systems, and helping design disaster and evacuation plans.

Assessment Answers

Critical Thinking

⑬ Weathering begins the soil creation process by breaking down rocks into smaller pieces. Climate, topography, geology, and biologic processes of a place impact how much and what kind of erosion can occur, which determines the content and amounts of soil created.

⑭ Without precipitation, the water cycle would not be able to function. No water would fall back to Earth after it evaporates, eventually causing all freshwater on Earth to be used and not replenished. Life would cease to exist without freshwater.

⑮ Groundwater comes from precipitation and water from lakes and rivers that seep into the ground. Aquifers are an underground porous rock layer saturated by very slow flows of groundwater. While both are important sources of freshwater, aquifers would not have any water to hold if they were not supplied by groundwater.

⑯ Wind erosion can deposit mineral-rich dust, making the soil rich and fertile in areas.

Applying Map Skills

⑰ The west coast of South America has higher elevations due to the formation of mountains, indicating more tectonic plate movement.

⑱ North America, South America, Asia, and Australia are all located along the Ring of Fire.

⑲ The map must be representative of shape and location of the continents and have labels for the Indian, Pacific, Atlantic, Arctic, and Southern Oceans.

Exploring the Essential Question

⑳ Student essays will vary, but must include two examples. Possible examples include knowledge of where earthquakes and volcanic eruptions are most likely to occur, ability to plan and publish evacuation routes, and the capacity to plan development away from areas prone to natural disasters.

Writing About Geography

㉑ Student answers will vary, but must include landforms in the area where the student lives, and also describe the process that created the landform. Landforms could include mountains, canyons, caves, rivers, and lakes. Processes could include water erosion, glacial erosion, and tectonic plate movement.

CHAPTER 2 Assessment 

Directions: On a separate sheet of paper, answer the questions below. Make sure you read carefully and answer all parts of the questions.

Critical Thinking

⑬ ***Making Generalizations*** Explain how weathering and erosion help create soil.

⑭ ***Identifying Cause and Effect*** How would life on Earth be different if there were no precipitation?

⑮ ***Comparing and Contrasting*** What is the difference between groundwater and aquifers, and why is the distinction important?

⑯ ***Defending*** How can wind erosion actually be helpful in some areas?

Applying Map Skills

Refer to the Unit 1 Atlas to answer the following questions.

⑰ ***Physical Systems*** Which coast of South America appears to have the most signs of plate tectonic movement due to its landforms?

⑱ ***The World in Spatial Terms*** Which continents are located along the Ring of Fire?

⑲ ***Places and Regions*** Use what you know of the world's oceans to draw a mental map showing the continents and oceans. Be sure to label the five oceans.

Exploring the Essential Question

⑳ ***Making Connections*** Write a one-page essay explaining how knowledge of plate tectonics can help governments prepare for natural disasters. Provide at least two specific examples. WHST.9–10.2

Writing About Geography

㉑ ***Informative/Explanatory*** Describe at least three landforms found in the region of the world where you live. Include the name of each landform and the processes that created it.

DBQ Analyzing Primary Sources

Use the document to answer the following questions.

The center of the Earth is filled with intense heat and pressure. These natural forces drive numerous changes such as volcanoes and earthquakes that renew and enrich Earth's surface. The physical processes can also disrupt, and often destroy, human life. As a result, scientists are working to learn how to predict them.

PRIMARY SOURCE

"Scientists are doing everything they can to solve the mysteries of earthquakes. They break rocks in laboratories, studying how stone behaves under stress. They hike through ghost forests where dead trees tell of long-ago tsunamis. They make maps of precarious, balanced rocks to see where the ground has shaken in the past, and how hard. They dig trenches across faults, searching for the active trace. They have wired up fault zones with so many sensors it's as though the Earth is a patient in intensive care."

—Joel Achenbach, "The Next Big One," *National Geographic*, April 2006

㉒ ***Analyzing*** How does Achenbach describe the work done to solve earthquake mysteries? RH.9–10.1

㉓ ***Interpreting*** What did Achenbach mean by "wired up fault zones. . .as though the Earth is a patient in intensive care"? RH.9–10.4

Research and Presentation

㉔ ***Research Skills*** Using the Internet, research the U.S. Geological Survey and the specific role it plays in contributing to our knowledge of earthquakes. Create a multimedia presentation to share your findings. RH.9–10.6, RH.9–10.8

Need Extra Help?

If You've Missed Question	13	14	15	16	17	18	19	20	21	22	23	24
Go to page	50	51	54	49	4	4	4	45	43	56	56	48

56

Analyzing Primary Sources

㉒ Achenbach describes scientists as doing everything they can in labs, in the field, using technology, and also observing nature to solve the mystery of earthquakes.

㉓ Achenbach means that scientists have placed so many sensors in certain earthquake-prone areas of the Earth that it resembles someone connected to machines in a hospital.

Research and Presentation

㉔ Student presentations will vary, but could include information on research, education programs, and mapping that the U.S. Geological Survey does to provide information on earthquakes.

CHAPTER **3**

Climates of the Earth Planner

UNDERSTANDING BY DESIGN®

Enduring Understandings

- *Physical processes shape Earth's surface.*

Essential Questions

- *Why is climate important to life on Earth?*

Predictable Misunderstandings

- *The location of the sun and the Earth in the solar system play small roles in climate.*
- *Climate patterns are unchanging and unaffected by human actions.*
- *The oceans do not influence climate.*
- *Climate and the distribution of biomes is influenced only by how close to or far from the equator a place is.*

Assessment Evidence

Performance Tasks:

- *Hands-On Chapter Project*

Other Evidence:

- *Guided Reading Activities*
- *Reteaching Activity*
- *Vocabulary Activity*
- *Lesson Quizzes*
- *Chapter Tests, Form A and B*

SUGGESTED PACING GUIDE

Introducing the Chapter	½ Day	Lesson 3	1 Day
Lesson 1	1 Day	Chapter Wrap-Up and Assessment	1 Day
Lesson 2	1 Day		

TOTAL TIME 4½ Days

Key for Using the Teacher Edition

SKILL-BASED ACTIVITIES

Types of skill activities found in the Teacher Edition.

V **Visual Skills** require students to analyze maps, graphs, charts, and photos.*

R **Reading Skills** help students practice reading skills and master vocabulary.

C **Critical Thinking Skills** help students apply and extend what they have learned.

W **Writing Skills** provide writing opportunities to help students comprehend the text.

T **Technology Skills** require students to use digital tools effectively.

*Letters are followed by a number when there is more than one of the same type of skill on the page.

DIFFERENTIATED INSTRUCTION

All activities are written for the on-level student unless otherwise marked with the leveled labels below.

BL **Beyond Level**

AL **Approaching Level**

ELL **English Language Learners**

All students benefit from activities that utilize different learning styles. Many activities are marked as below when a particular learning style is highlighted.

Intrapersonal	Naturalist
Logical/Mathematical	Kinesthetic
Visual/Spatial	Auditory/Musical
Verbal/Linguistic	Interpersonal

National Geography Standards covered in "Climates of the Earth"

The student knows and understands:

(3) How to analyze the spatial organizations of people, places, and environments on Earth's surface

3.2 Complex processes change over time and shape patterns in the distribution of human and physical phenomena

3.3 Models are used to represent the structure and dynamics of spatial processes which shape human and physical systems

(5) That people create regions to interpret Earth's complexity

5.1 Regions are defined by different sets of criteria and places can be included in multiple regions of different types

(7) The physical processes that shape the patterns of Earth's surface

7.2 Earth-Sun relationships are variable over time resulting in changes in physical processes and patterns on Earth

7.3 Physical processes interact over time to shape particular places on Earth's surface

(8) The characteristics and spatial distribution of ecosystems and biomes on Earth's surface

8.3 The distribution and characteristics of biomes change over time

(14) How human actions modify the physical environment

14.1 Human modifications of the physical environment can have significant global impacts

CHAPTER OPENER PLANNER

Students will know:

- *how Earth's position in relation to the sun affects temperatures, night and day, and seasons.*
- *the natural process of the greenhouse effect and issues over global warming.*
- *how latitude and elevation, wind and water, and landforms and bodies of water influence Earth's weather and climate.*
- *the world's climate and vegetation regions and influence of climate on the distribution of biomes.*
- *that recurring climate phenomena influence climate patterns.*

Students will be able to:

- ***analyze** how the Earth-Sun relationship affects life on Earth.*
- ***describe** factors that affect climate.*
- ***explain** world climate patterns.*

UNDERSTANDING BY DESIGN®

☑ Print Teaching Options

V Visual Skills

☐ **p. 59** Students create a visual montage showing signs and examples of climate change. ELL Visual/Spatial

R Reading Skills

☐ **p. 57** Students define *biome.* ELL Verbal/Linguistic

☐ **p. 59** Students define *climate change.* AL Verbal/Linguistic

C Critical Thinking Skills

☐ **p. 58** Students describe the climate where they live and compare it to Greenland's climate.

W Writing Skills

☐ **p. 57** Students write a paragraph analyzing how climate influences everyday activities. Verbal/Linguistic

T Technology Skills

☐ **p. 59** Students list and research potential impacts of climate change. BL Verbal/Linguistic, Logical/Mathematical

☑ Online Teaching Options

V Visual Skills

VIDEO **Warming Global Climate**—Students will identify the continents, countries, waterways, and the equator on a map and then discuss information and facts presented on the map. ELL Visual/Spatial

MAP **Interactive World Atlas**—Students use the interactive world atlas to identify the regions of the world and describe their terrain.

☑ Printable Digital Worksheets

WORKSHEET **Assessing Background Knowledge**—Students demonstrate their understanding and prior knowledge about the climates of the Earth.

WORKSHEET **Chapter Summaries**—Summaries are provided for each chapter that thoroughly condense core content into manageable chunks.

WORKSHEET **Reteaching Activity**—These worksheets provide students with an opportunity for remedial practice and review of vital chapter content.

WORKSHEET **Vocabulary Activity**—Students apply their knowledge of content and academic vocabulary words.

Project-Based Learning 

Hands-On

Documenting the Impact of Climate Change

Students will create a multimedia presentation about Earth-sun relationships, factors that affect climate, and world climate patterns.

Digital Hands-On

Create Online Projects

Find an additional activity online that incorporates technology for this project. Visit the EdTech Teacher Web sites for more links, tutorials, and other resources.

Print Resources

ANCILLARY RESOURCES

Ths ancillary is available for every chapter and lesson.

- **Chapter Tests and Lesson Quizzes**

PRINTABLE DIGITAL WORKSHEETS

These printable digital worksheets are available for every chapter and lesson.

- **Assessing Background Knowledge**
- **Chapter Summaries**
- **Guided Reading Activities**
- **Hands-On Chapter Projects**
- **Quizzes and Tests**
- **Reading Essentials and Study Guide** AL
- **Reteaching Activities**
- **Video Activities**
- **Vocabulary Activities**

More Media Resources

SUGGESTED VIDEOS 

- **History of the World in Two Hours** (120 min.)
- **Human Planet** (3 discs–480 min.)
- **Earth Keepers** (83 min.)

SUGGESTED READING 

- ***Global Warming,*** by Jenny Tesar
- ***The World of Whales,*** by Stanley M. Minasian, et al.

EARTH-SUN RELATIONSHIPS

Students will know:
- *how Earth's position in relation to the sun affects temperatures and night and day.*
- *how Earth's position in relation to the sun affects seasons.*
- *the natural process of the greenhouse effect.*
- *the issues in the debate over global warming.*

Students will be able to:
- ***explain** how Earth's position affects temperatures, night and day, and the seasons.*
- ***explain** the greenhouse effect.*
- ***analyze** issues surrounding global warming.*

UNDERSTANDING BY DESIGN®

☑ Print Teaching Options

V Visual Skills
- ☐ **p. 62** Students label the continents, oceans, and latitude lines on a world map. AL Visual/Spatial
- ☐ **p. 62** Students analyze the graphic of the greenhouse effect. Visual/Spatial

R Reading Skills
- ☐ **p. 60** Students discuss the difference between *climate* and *weather.* AL Verbal/Linguistic
- ☐ **p. 60** Students model Earth revolving around the sun and discuss Earth's tilt. ELL Kinesthetic
- ☐ **p. 61** Students define *revolution.* ELL Verbal/Linguistic
- ☐ **p. 63** Students define *greenhouse effect* and then students discuss this effect on Earth. ELL Verbal/Linguistic

C Critical Thinking Skills
- ☐ **p. 61** Students explain *equinox* in their own words and use *revolution* and *equinox* to describe the Earth-sun relationship. ELL Verbal/Linguistic

T Technology Skills
- ☐ **p. 62** Students research and present about the concept of *midnight sun.* Logical/Mathematical
- ☐ **p. 63** Students collect and analyze data about the changes in climate that have occurred over the last thirty years. BL Logical/Mathematical

☑ Online Teaching Options

V Visual Skills
- INTERACTIVE BELLRINGER **How Latitude Affects Sunlight**—Students use the chart to discuss how latitude affects sunlight in different areas. AL Naturalist, Logical/Mathematical
- INFOGRAPHIC **Earth's Seasons**—Students learn about Earth's revolution and create a diagram highlighting one country during a revolution of Earth around the Sun. AL Verbal/Linguistic

C Critical Thinking Skills
- INTERACTIVE WHITEBOARD ACTIVITY **Earth's Patterns**—Students drag descriptive facts about the terms *equinox, solstice,* or *midnight sun* beneath each heading in the three-column chart.

W Writing Skills
- VIDEO **Greenhouse Gases**—Students watch the video and write a paragraph about how the sun, greenhouse gases, and climate are related. Naturalist, Verbal/Linguistic

☑ Printable Digital Worksheets

R Reading Skills
- WORKSHEET **Guided Reading Activity**—Students use the Guided Reading Activity worksheets to review their comprehension of the content.
- WORKSHEET **Chapter Summary**—Students review the main ideas of the chapter content.

C Critical Thinking Skills
- WORKSHEET **Video Activity**—Students answer questions related to a topic in the chapter content after they have viewed a lesson video.

FACTORS AFFECTING CLIMATE

Students will know:

- *that latitude and elevation affect the angle of the sun's rays and temperatures on Earth.*
- *how wind and water combine with the effects of the sun to influence Earth's weather and climate.*
- *how landforms and bodies of water influence Earth's climate patterns.*

Students will be able to:

- ***describe** the effect of latitude and elevation on climate.*
- ***explain** how wind, water, and the sun influence weather and climate.*
- ***identify** how landforms and water affect climate.*

UNDERSTANDING BY DESIGN®

☑ Print Teaching Options

V Visual Skills

- ☐ **p. 64** Students identify how latitude, climate, and elevation relate to each other. Visual/Spatial
- ☐ **p. 65** Students create a diagram that describes how wind occurs and how it affects the weather. Visual/Spatial
- ☐ **p. 65** Students discuss how winds are named for the directions from which they blow. ELL Visual/Spatial
- ☐ **p. 67** Students analyze a world map with ocean currents. AL Visual/Spatial
- ☐ **p. 67** Students summarize how wind and water work together to affect climate. Interpersonal
- ☐ **p. 68** Students analyze the Rain Shadow Effect diagram. ELL Visual/Spatial

R Reading Skills

- ☐ **p. 66** Students define and then use a globe to model prevailing winds and the *Coriolis Effect.* AL ELL Kinesthetic

C Critical Thinking Skills

- ☐ **p. 65** Students discuss why climbers on Mount Everest have to wear oxygen masks. Logical/Mathematical
- ☐ **p. 67** Students discuss the effects of El Niño. Verbal/Linguistic

W Writing Skills

- ☐ **p. 65** Students write an essay about which climate zone they would like to live in and why. Verbal/Linguistic

T Technology Skills

- ☐ **p. 66** Students research the ocean currents that affect climates and create a multimedia presentation showing their research. BL Auditory/Musical, Visual/Spatial

☑ Online Teaching Options

V Visual Skills

- INTERACTIVE BELLRINGER **Elevation and Temperature**—Students use the map to answer questions on how latitude and elevation affect temperatures. Verbal/Linguistic
- VIDEO **Ocean Currents and Sea Level**—Students watch the video to learn how wind and water work together to affect climate and explain examples of this relationship. AL Verbal/Linguistic

C Critical Thinking Skills

- INTERACTIVE WHITEBOARD ACTIVITY **World Wind Patterns**—Students identify wind patterns on a map and then discuss how ocean currents affect wind patterns. Verbal/Linguistic, Interpersonal

W Writing Skills

- INTERACTIVE MAP **World Zones of Latitude and Wind Patterns**—Each member of a group writes a summary explaining a wind pattern in the zone the group was assigned. Verbal/Linguistic, Interpersonal

☑ Printable Digital Worksheets

R Reading Skills

- WORKSHEET **Guided Reading Activity**—Students use Guided Reading Activity worksheets to review their comprehension of the content.
- WORKSHEET **Reading Essentials and Study Guide**—Students complete the study guide and answer Reading Progress Check and vocabulary questions. AL

C Critical Thinking Skills

- WORKSHEET **Video Activity**—Students answer questions related to a topic in the chapter content after they have viewed a lesson video.

LESSON 3 PLANNER

World Climate Patterns

Students will know:
- *the world's climate and vegetation regions.*
- *the influence of climate on the distribution of biomes.*
- *that recurring climate phenomena influence climate patterns.*

Students will be able to:
- ***identify** climate and vegetation regions.*
- ***explain** how climates affect biomes.*
- ***describe** climate phenomena that influence climate patterns.*

UNDERSTANDING BY DESIGN®

☑ Print Teaching Options

V Visual Skills

☐ **p. 69** Students create a chart to describe the climate zones. AL ELL Visual/Spatial

☐ **p. 71** Students add information about the four regions under the midlatitude climate zone to their charts. Visual/Spatial

R Reading Skills

☐ **p. 70** Students discuss dry climates. ELL Verbal/Linguistic

C Critical Thinking Skills

☐ **p. 69** Students discuss biomes and how climate influences biomes and their vegetation. Verbal/Linguistic, Logical/Mathematical

☐ **p. 71** Students discuss the diagram about latitude, climate, and vegetation. Logical/Mathematical

☐ **p. 72** Students list similarities and differences in the four major climate zones. Verbal/Linguistic

W Writing Skills

☐ **p. 69** Students write a paragraph describing a tropical wet climate's influence on soil building in rain forests. BL Logical/Mathematical

☐ **p. 70** Students define *savanna* and include it in a short essay about tropical dry climates. Verbal/Linguistic

T Technology Skills

☐ **p. 71** Students research types of trees in their assigned country and create a visual to classify the types. BL Visual/Spatial

☐ **p. 72** Students discuss indicators of climate change. BL Kinesthetic

☑ Online Teaching Options

V Visual Skills

☐ INTERACTIVE BELLRINGER **Causes of Acid Rain**—Students use the flow chart to analyze causes of acid rain and answer questions. BL Visual/Spatial, Verbal/Linguistic

☐ VIDEO **Sahara Desert**—Students use the video to discuss one of the dry climate biomes and make a chart that contrasts the desert extremes. ELL Visual/Spatial

R Reading Skills

☐ INFOGRAPHIC **Latitude, Climate, and Vegetation**—Students use the infographic to take notes on biomes in the four types of climate zones. Visual/Spatial, Logical/Mathematical

C Critical Thinking Skills

☐ INTERACTIVE WHITEBOARD ACTIVITY **Climate Zones**—Students identify climate zones and the characteristics that describe the climates.

☑ Printable Digital Worksheets

R Reading Skills

☐ WORKSHEET **Guided Reading Activity**—Students use Guided Reading Activity worksheets to review their comprehension of the content.

☐ WORKSHEET **Reading Essentials and Study Guide**—Students complete the study guide and answer Reading Progress Check and vocabulary questions. AL

☐ WORKSHEET **Vocabulary Activity**—Students review the chapter content and academic vocabulary words.

☐ WORKSHEET **Chapter Summary**—Students review the main ideas of the chapter content.

C Critical Thinking Skills

☐ WORKSHEET **Video Activity**—Students answer questions based on a lesson video.

☐ WORKSHEET **Reteaching Activity**—Students use this activity worksheet to review and reteach chapter content and vocabulary. This worksheet can be used with struggling students who need additional help with difficult content concepts.

INTERVENTION AND REMEDIATION STRATEGIES

LESSON 1 Earth-Sun Relationships

Reading and Comprehension

Have students work with a partner to scan the lesson and use context clues to define the meaning of each content vocabulary term. Have partners write sentences using each term to demonstrate their understanding of the word's meaning. Ask volunteers to clarify terms that may be confusing, such as the difference between the terms *weather* and *climate.* Then have partners collaborate to create sentences that show their understanding of the two academic vocabulary terms. Challenge students to identify other meanings of the content vocabulary term *revolution* in addition to the word's technical meaning presented in the text.

Text Evidence

Organize students into four groups and assign each group one of the following terms: *equinox, solstice, midnight sun, greenhouse effect.* Have students in each group work together to determine the central idea in the text about their assigned term. Then have each group write a summary about the significance of the term as it relates to Earth's climate. Tell students to use textual evidence to support ideas presented in their summaries. After students share their summaries with the class, direct their attention to the primary source about the greenhouse effect. Have groups identify reasoning in the text to support the statement *The greenhouse effect is one of the fundamental facts of atmospheric science.*

LESSON 2 Factors Affecting Climate

Reading and Comprehension

Have students work in pairs to identify cause-and-effect relationships as they read. Remind students to look for signal words that indicate cause or effect, such as *because, since, as a result, due to, therefore, thus, consequently, so, resulted in, cause,* or *effect.* Then have partners choose a statement from the text, such as "elevation influences climate," or "as elevation increases, temperatures decrease." Have pairs create a diagram or flowchart that illustrates the cause-and-effect relationship in their chosen statement. Have student pairs share their diagrams or charts with the class.

Text Evidence

Organize students into six groups and assign one of the following topics to each group: latitude, climate, elevation, winds, ocean currents, and landforms and climate. Have each group create and complete a three-column chart with the headings *Central Idea, Supporting Details,* and *Summary.* Tell students to review the text to identify the central idea about their topic and supporting details, writing the information into the correct column. Then have groups collaborate to complete the chart by writing a short paragraph that summarizes their assigned topic.

LESSON 3 World Climate Patterns

Reading and Comprehension

Ensure students' understanding of the meaning of unfamiliar or confusing content vocabulary words, such as the difference between *deciduous* and *coniferous.* Have student groups play a "Pictionary" style guessing game in which a member of the group draws clues to describe a content vocabulary term for the group to guess. Instruct students to take turns giving clues so each group member has a turn. After students have finished guessing each of the terms, have groups compete against other groups to see who can guess the most terms correctly in a certain amount of time. As a "bonus" or tiebreaker question, have each team try to give clues and guess one of the academic vocabulary terms.

Text Evidence

Tell students they will act as weather forecasters who predict and report on the weather and for a region discussed in the text. In preparing their forecast, students should use content vocabulary terms correctly, and should consider the type of climate found in their chosen region. Allow students time to prepare their forecasts before they present them to the class. Encourage students to use visuals, such as maps, diagrams, and illustrations, to indicate temperatures and vegetation in the region.

Online Resources

Leveled Reader

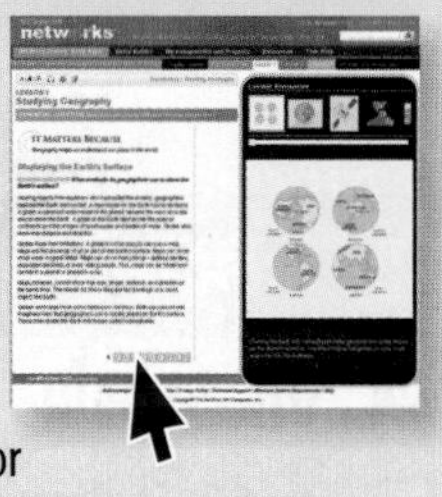

Use this online approaching-level text that corresponds directly to the text in the Student Edition. It also includes additional reading and comprehension support for English Language Learners.

Guided Reading Activities

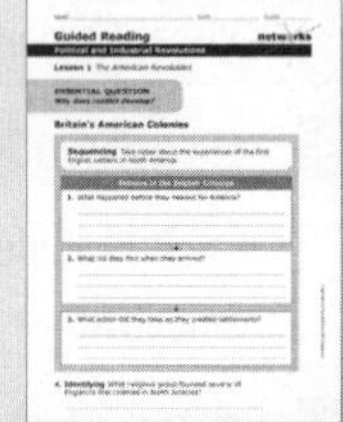

This resource uses guiding questions to help students with comprehension.

Reteaching Activities

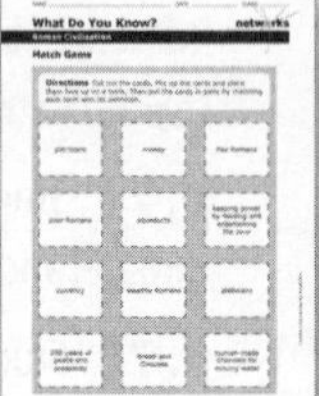

These worksheets provide students with an opportunity for remedial practice and review of vital chapter content.

Reading Essentials and Study Guide

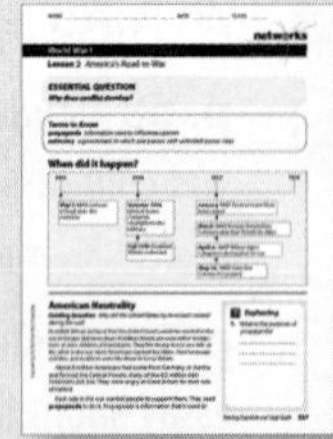

This resource offers writing and reading activities for the approaching-level student.

Self-Check Quizzes

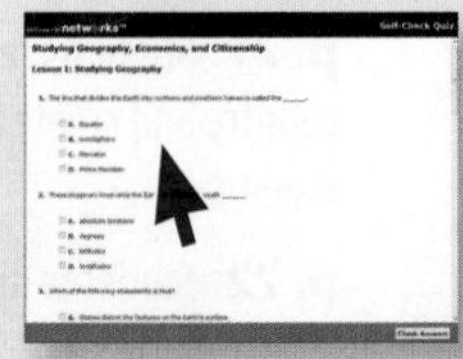

This online assessment tool provides instant feedback for students to check their progress.

Chapter Summaries

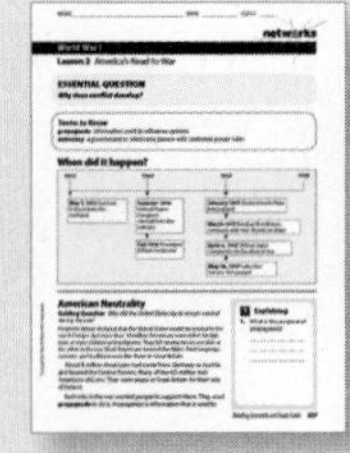

Summaries are provided for each chapter that thoroughly condense core content into manageable chunks.

Climates of the Earth

ESSENTIAL QUESTION • *Why is climate important to life on Earth?*

networks

There's More Online about climates of the Earth.

CHAPTER 3

Geography Matters...

The relationships between the Earth and the sun influence climate and weather patterns all over the Earth. The various climates on Earth support different communities of plants and animals that are called biomes. Human activity is also affected by Earth's climates, such as knowing that only certain vegetables can grow in our backyard gardens. Fortunately, our planet is just the right distance from our sun to make life on Earth possible.

◀ A young Inuit boy on Canada's Baffin Island wears warm clothing to protect against the cold Arctic conditions.

Sue Flood/The Image Bank/Getty Images

57

Letter from the Author

Dear Geography Teacher,

It is essential that your students have a firm grasp of basic Earth-sun relationships. It will give them an important platform of knowledge about why we have seasons, why the seasons are opposite in the Northern and Southern Hemispheres, why the lengths of day and night vary, and the influence of insolation. From here geography students need to realize that there are climatic regions and that those regions are likely to be changing. The great debate seems to center on climate changes as a natural phenomenon as opposed to climate change related to human activities, or both. A good geography student should be able to debate the 'climate change' issue.

Richard G. Boehm

ENGAGE

Inferring Direct students' attention to the image of the young Inuit boy. **Ask:** **What can you infer about the climate this boy lives in?** *(He lives somewhere that is very cold because he is wearing a fur hood that surrounds his face.)* Discuss ways that we can make generalizations about climate or seasons from the clothes that people wear.

TEACH & ACCESS

Defining Emphasize that the relationship between Earth and the sun determines climates. Climates support many different ecological communities of plants and animals that live all over Earth, called a *biome.* Write *biome* on the board. Invite students to define the term and to use it in a sentence. Explain that biomes are a major type of ecological community and that a desert or a forest is a biome. ELL **Verbal/Linguistic**

Making Connections

Biomes Major biomes on Earth include the rain forests, temperate deciduous forests, boreal (or taiga forests), deserts, chaparrals, savannas, grasslands, oceans, and tundra. The importance of biomes to the environment on Earth cannot be overestimated. During the history of life on Earth, biomes have changed and moved many times. Most recently, human activities have drastically altered these ecological communities. Many governments around the world are working together to conserve and preserve biomes.

Analyzing Tell students that climate affects many everyday activities, such as how and what foods are grown or the types of houses built in a community. Have students write a paragraph analyzing how climate influences everyday activities in their community or state. **Verbal/Linguistic**

CLOSE & REFLECT

Discussing Have students share what they know about climate, including how the sun affects the climate and the current changes happening in Earth's climate. Explain that they will be learning about the climates of Earth in this chapter, including Earth-Sun relationships, factors that affect climate, and world climate patterns.

ePals GlobalCommunity
Where learners connect™

Extend the project-based learning experience globally through our partnership with ePals. EPals allows you to connect with classrooms around the world in a safe online environment for real-life lessons and projects in virtual study groups.

ENGAGE

C Critical Thinking Skills

Identifying Issues Before class, display a map of North America that includes Greenland. Show its location in proximity to that of the students. Explain that about 80 percent of Greenland is covered by ice. Have students work in pairs to answer the following questions: **What kind of climate do you live in? How does your climate change based on seasons or time of year? How do you think the climate where you live compares with the climate in Greenland?**

Allow partners time to share their answers. Then tell students that many believe the world's climate is changing and cite the melting of the ice caps in Greenland as scientific evidence. **Ask: Do you think our climate is changing?** *(Student answers will vary, but should include relevant details supporting each answer.)*

TEACH & ASSESS

R Reading Skills

Calculating Invite a student to read the paragraph to the class. Then write a math problem showing the current year subtracted by 1980 on the board. Emphasize that during this time frame the temperature of Earth has increased by about 1.4°F. Have students calculate how much more Earth's temperature could increase by 2100, if the current rise remains the same. *(approximate temperature increase of another 3.4–3.5°F by 2100)* **Logical/Mathematical**

Making Connections

Controversial Issues Although climate change and global warming have been controversial issues in the past, causing disagreement in the scientific community, in the twenty-first century most major scientific agencies in the United States agree that climate change is happening. Many scientific agencies, including NASA, think it is very likely that some increased aspects of climate change are caused by human activities. Not every scientist agrees. Some feel that climate change is a natural occurrence in Earth's climate cycle where there are both warming and cooling time periods. There is, however, a broad agreement that climate change is happening and that human activity can increase or decrease these changes.

Why Geography Matters: **Climates of the Earth**

C

climate change: *the* impacts *on* humans

R

Climate scientists have amassed data on weather patterns and climate since the 1980s. Most agree that the average surface air temperature across the globe has increased about 1.4°F (0.8°C) since then. Predictions show that warming of the planet, or global warming, will accelerate through the end of the twenty-first century.

AFP/Getty Images

THERE'S MORE ONLINE

WATCH a video of a melting glacier • *SEE* a map of rising global temperatures

58

Project-Based Learning

Hands-On

Documenting Biome Climate Change

Working in small groups, students will choose a specific biome, gather information about the climate zone the biome is located within, and compile visual models of the climate effects based on researched qualitative and quantitative data. Students will then use this information to create a group multimedia presentation on a major climate zone that includes the effects of biome climate changes to present to the class.

ePals GlobalCommunity
Where learners connect™

Digital Hands-On

Create Online Projects

Find an additional activity online that incorporates technology for this project. Visit the EdTech Teacher Web sites for more links, tutorials, and other resources.

Why Geography Matters

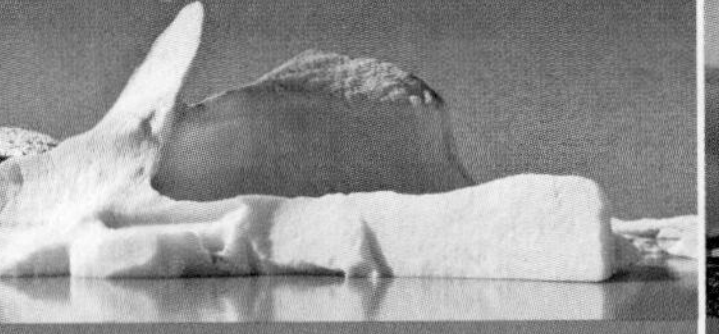

What is climate change and global warming?

Climate change is a significant change in temperature, precipitation, and wind patterns that lasts for at least several decades. These changes may be difficult to notice, but there are several signs of climate change that are observable, such as heat waves, flooding, droughts, melting glaciers, and extreme weather events. Global warming refers to warming of Earth's average temperature that has occurred since the mid-1800s. It represents only one aspect of climate change. Global warming does not simply mean that the climate everywhere on Earth will become warmer. An important part of what it means is that some weather patterns will become more extreme. R

1. **Physical Systems** How is global warming different from climate change?

What are the causes of climate change?

Although average global surface temperature does fluctuate due to natural causes, most climate scientists agree that human activity is a major contributing factor to recent warming of the planet. As global population and industrialization increase, a variety of human activities increase the presence of so-called "greenhouse gases" in Earth's atmosphere. In contrast, the greenhouse effect is a naturally occurring process in which these gases act as a blanket, trapping the sun's heat within the atmosphere. The human-produced greenhouse gases amplify the effect and increase the warming of Earth. These gases—primarily carbon dioxide and methane—are released into the atmosphere through the burning of fossil fuels and wood, along with some industrial processes. Agricultural practices and the decay of organic waste in landfills also contribute to greenhouse gases.

2. **Physical Systems** Describe two factors contributing to climate change.

V

What are the potential impacts of climate change on people?

As Earth's surface temperature warms and its climate becomes less stable, people will be affected in several ways. Melting glaciers will cause sea levels to rise, likely rendering some coastal regions and islands uninhabitable. Increased droughts, heat waves, and wildfires will affect some regions, while other areas will be impacted by severe flooding. Storms and other extreme weather events may increase in their frequency and intensity as well. As a result, people may face increased health and safety risks along with threats to their homes, cities, and critical infrastructure systems. T

3. **Environment and Society** How will climate change affect humans? Consider water supplies, agriculture, power and transportation systems, the environment, and human health.

V Visual Skills

Creating Visuals Ask students to discuss what they see in the three images. Explain that scientists do know that there are changes in rainfall, that ice caps are melting, and extreme weather events are occurring. Have students create a visual montage depicting signs and examples of climate change. These could be photos, drawings, illustrations, or news clippings. Then have them present their montages of climate change to the class. ELL **Visual/Spatial**

R Reading Skills

Defining Direct students' attention to the explanation of climate change and global warming. **Ask:** **What happens when there is climate change?** *(A significant change in temperature, rain, and wind patterns lasting for several decades.)* Have students write a sentence using *climate change* and a sentence using *global warming.* AL **Verbal/Linguistic**

T Technology Skills

Examining Information Have students explain the potential impacts of climate change and list them on the board. Discuss any questions they have on any of the terms. Then have students research the potential impacts of climate change online. Tell them to identify three reliable Internet sources that either confirm or refute the potential impacts of climate change. Review acceptable Internet sources with students as needed. BL **Verbal/Linguistic, Logical/Mathematical**

CLOSE & REFLECT

Making Predictions Based on the preliminary information of climate change and global warming that has been presented, have students write three questions that they predict will be answered in this chapter. Have students check the questions occasionally to see if they can fill in the answers using information provided in the chapter lessons.

VIDEO

Warming Global Climate

Analyzing Maps As a class, view this video to discuss some of the regions affected by climate change. Have students identify the continents, as well as various countries, oceans, identifiable seas and large rivers, the North and South Poles, and the equator. As a class, discuss the information and facts presented. Guide the focus of the discussion to answer any questions or explain any vocabulary words that students are unfamiliar with. ELL **Visual/Spatial**

ANSWERS, p. 59

Why Geography Matters

1. Global warming refers to the warming of Earth's average temperature and represents only one aspect of climate change.
2. Greenhouse gases are released into the atmosphere through the burning of fossil fuels, wood, and other industrial processes. Agricultural practices and the decay of organic waste also contribute to greenhouse gases.
3. Melting glaciers will cause sea levels to rise, rendering some coastal regions and islands uninhabitable. Increased droughts, heat waves, and wildfires will affect some regions, while other areas may suffer severe flooding. Extreme weather events may increase in frequency and intensity, so people may face health and safety risks.

ENGAGE

C Critical Thinking Skills

Discussing Show students an image of our solar system and have them point out Earth and the sun. Have students think about what they know about Earth's relationship with the sun. In a class discussion, encourage students to share and explain how Earth's position to the sun influences how we live on Earth.

TEACH & ASSESS

R1 Reading Skills

Defining Write the words *climate* and *weather* on the board. Discuss with students what they think the difference is between the two. Have a student read the paragraph to the class. **Ask:** **What are the average weather conditions outside our school building that are measured over years called?** *(climate)* **What is the condition of the atmosphere outside our school building today called?** *(weather)* Have students write two sentences using each word. Encourage students to share their sentences in a class discussion. Have students add the words, definitions, and sentences to their chapter glossary started at the beginning of the chapter. **AL Verbal/Linguistic**

R2 Reading Skills

Visualizing Review that Earth's relationship with the sun affects climate. Tell students that Earth's axis is an imaginary line that runs through the center of Earth from the North Pole to the South Pole. Earth's axis is tilted, or Earth is on a slant, as it revolves around the sun. Have a volunteer hold a tennis ball (Earth) at a tilt and another volunteer hold a slightly larger ball (sun). Have the student holding Earth revolve around the student holding the sun. **Ask:** **What is the current tilt of Earth?** *(23.5°)* **How does the tilt affect the amount of direct sunlight that places on Earth receive?** *(Not all places receive the same amount of sunlight at the same time.)* **What affects the temperature of places on Earth?** *(the tilt of Earth, which determines the amount of direct sunlight the location receives)* **ELL Kinesthetic**

ANSWERS, p. 60

TAKING NOTES: Earth's tilted axis—Because of Earth's tilted axis, not all places on Earth receive the same amount of direct sunlight at the same time. For this reason, Earth's tilt affects the temperature of a particular place. **Earth's revolution**—Earth makes one rotation every 24 hours, ensuring every part of the world receives sunlight in a predictable pattern. The side facing the sun is warmer than the opposite side. **Earth's revolution and tilt**—affects the amount of sunlight reaching different locations on Earth at different times of the year.

networks

There's More Online!

- **DIAGRAM** The Earth's Seasons
- **INFOGRAPHIC** The Greenhouse Effect
- **INTERACTIVE SELF-CHECK QUIZ**
- **VIDEO** Earth-Sun Relationships

Sun

LESSON 1
Earth-Sun Relationships

ESSENTIAL QUESTION • *Why is climate important to life on Earth?*

Reading HELPDESK CCSS

Academic Vocabulary

- **predictable**
- **eventually**

Content Vocabulary

- **weather**
- **climate**
- **axis**
- **revolution**
- **equinox**
- **solstice**
- **midnight sun**
- **greenhouse effect**

TAKING NOTES: ***Key Ideas and Details***

DESCRIBING As you read the lesson, use a chart like the one below to list the characteristics of Earth-sun relationships and describe their effects on climate.

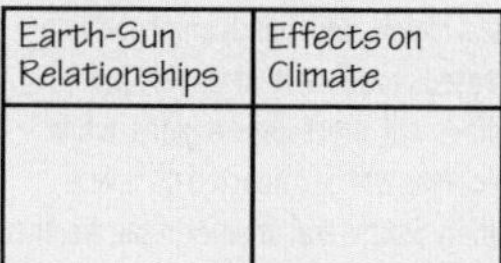

Earth-Sun Relationships	Effects on Climate

IT MATTERS BECAUSE

C *Daily life on Earth is influenced by the dynamic relationship between the Earth and the sun. The amount of direct sunlight reaching Earth's surface plays an important role in affecting the temperature of different places. The Earth's rotation determines when we receive sunlight, giving us day or night. The Earth's tilt and its revolution around the sun result in the four seasons we experience.*

Climate and Weather

GUIDING QUESTION *How do the relationships between the Earth and the sun affect climate?*

R1 There is an important difference between climate and weather. **Weather** is the condition of the atmosphere in one place over a short period of time, such as hours or days. For example, when you look outside the window in the morning to decide what to wear that day, you are checking the weather. **Climate**, on the other hand, refers to the average weather conditions as measured over many years. Climate is the reason why you decide to buy certain types of clothing to wear based on where you live.

Earth's Tilt and Rotation

R2 The relationship between the Earth and the sun directly affects climate. An important aspect of the Earth-sun relationship is that the Earth's **axis** is tilted. The axis runs from the North Pole to the South Pole through the center of the planet. Currently, the Earth is tilted at about 23½°.

Because of the Earth's tilted axis, not all places on Earth receive the same amount of direct sunlight at the same time. For this reason, Earth's tilt affects the temperature of a particular place. Temperature is the measure of how hot or cold a place is. Temperature is measured in degrees on a set scale. The most common scales for measuring temperature are Fahrenheit (°F) and Celsius (°C).

Why is it usually warmer during the day than it is during the night? This depends on which side of the planet is facing the sun. The Earth rotates on its axis, making one complete rotation every 24 hours, or one day. The Earth's rotation from west to east ensures that every part of the

networks Online Teaching Options

INTERACTIVE BELLRINGER

How Latitude Affects Sunlight

Activating Prior Knowledge Use this chart to introduce a class discussion about how latitude affects the amount of sunlight regions and cities receive. Continue the discussion by analyzing how geographers use charts to compare such data. Have students read the introductory text, use the chart to answer the first question, and use their prior knowledge to answer the remaining questions. Then ask students to share what they know about the tilt of Earth's axis and how that tilt affects the seasons in the Northern and Southern Hemispheres. **AL Naturalist, Logical/Mathematical**

How Latitude Affects Sunlight

The chart shows the hours of sunlight in selected cities on June 21, the summer solstice in the Northern Hemisphere.

1. How many hours of daylight do you think there will be in Resolute, Canada, latitude 74°N, on June 21?

A. 0 hours
B. 12 hours
C. 24 hours
D. 25 hours

LOCATION	LATTITUDE	APPROXIMATE DAYLIGHT HOURS
Quito, Ecuador	0°N	12 hours
Guantanamo, Cuba	20°N	13 hours
Cairo, Egypt	30°N	14 hours
Beijing, China	40°N	15 hours
Prague, Czech Republic	50°N	17 hours
Ft. Yukon, AK, United States	67°N	24 hours

click for answer

Auto-Run Click Through Previous 1 of 3 Next

world receives sunlight in a **predictable** pattern during those 24 hours. The side of the planet not facing the sun is colder, and the side of the planet facing the sun is warmer.

Earth's Revolution

While the Earth rotates on its axis, it also revolves around the closest star to us, the sun. It takes the Earth one year, approximately 365 days, to complete one **revolution** around the sun. The Earth's revolution, combined with its tilted axis, affects the amount of sunlight that reaches different locations on the Earth at different times of the year. People who live in the Northern Hemisphere experience summer when the Northern Hemisphere is tilted toward the sun and is receiving the most direct sunlight. The seasons are reversed north and south of the Equator. When it is summer in the Northern Hemisphere, it is winter in the Southern Hemisphere because the Southern Hemisphere is tilted away from the sun and receives less direct sunlight. Likewise, when it is fall in the Northern Hemisphere, it is spring in the Southern Hemisphere.

Twice a year (around March 21 and September 23), the direct sunlight falls on the Equator. This day is called an **equinox**, meaning "equal night," because daytime and nighttime hours are equal. On the equinox, equal amounts of light reach the Northern and Southern Hemispheres. The two equinoxes mark the shift in seasons between winter and spring and between summer and fall.

In addition to the Equator, there are two other lines of latitude that run parallel to the Equator and mark important changes in the Earth's seasons. As the Earth proceeds in its revolution around the sun, the direct rays of the sun

weather condition of the atmosphere in one place during a short period of time

climate weather patterns typical for an area over a long period of time

axis an imaginary line that runs through the center of the Earth between the North and South Poles

predictable expected or able to be foreseen

revolution in astronomy, the Earth's yearly trip around the sun, taking 365¼ days

equinox one of two days (about March 21 and September 23) on which the sun is directly above the Equator, making day and night equal in length

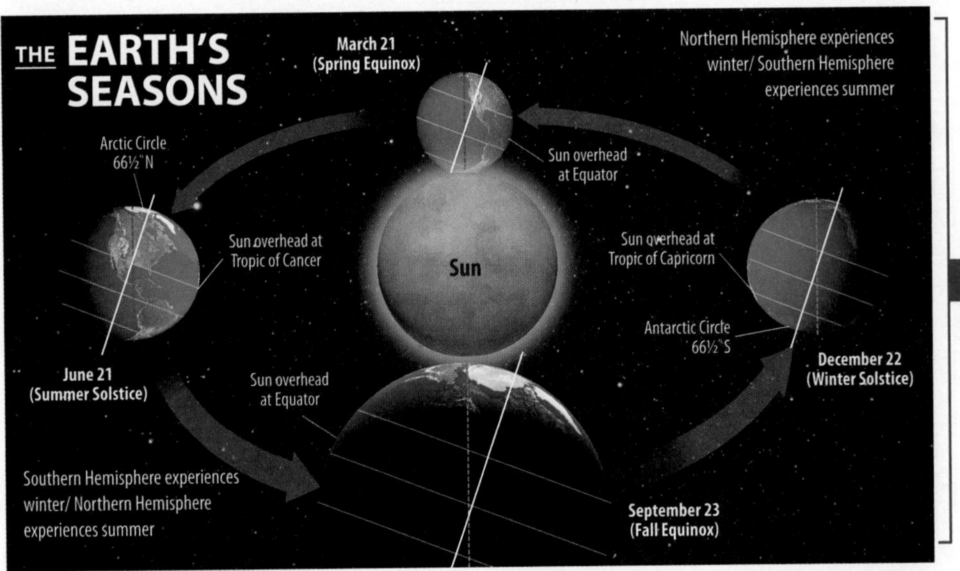

The angle of the sun's rays as they strike the Earth affects the Northern and Southern Hemispheres differently.

▲ **CRITICAL THINKING**

1. ***Contrasting*** Explain the difference between solstices and equinoxes.
2. ***Drawing Conclusions*** In what months do the sun's rays directly strike the Equator? The Tropics of Cancer and Capricorn?

Earth-Sun Relationships

R Reading Skills

Defining Have students read this section. Write the word *revolution* on the board. Point out that the word *revolution* has many meanings, but here it means that Earth moves around the sun in a path. **Ask:** **How many days does it take Earth to make one revolution around the sun?** *(about 365 days)* **ELL Verbal/Linguistic**

C Critical Thinking Skills

Understanding Relationships Discuss how Earth's revolution around the sun determines the seasons and the weather. Have students explain the term *equinox* in their own words. Emphasize that twice each year, direct sunlight falls on the Equator and daytime and nighttime hours are equal in both the Northern and Southern Hemispheres. **Ask:** **What is this day called?** *(the equinox)* Have students write sentences using the words *revolution* and *equinox* describing the Earth-sun relationship. Then write the words and meanings into their chapter glossaries. **ELL Verbal/Linguistic**

V Visual Skills

Analyzing Illustrations Direct students' attention to the illustration. Tell students that it shows the path and tilt of Earth during Earth's seasons. **Ask:** **What season do people in the Southern Hemisphere mark on September 23?** *(spring)* Have students analyze the illustration with a partner and then list three additional facts shown in the illustration. **AL Visual/Spatial**

Content Background Knowledge

Keeping Track of Time The Sumerians of Babylonia were probably the first to make a calendar. It was lunar, or based on the phases of the moon. The Maya and the Aztec also developed calendars. Today most of the world uses the Gregorian calendar, developed in 1582. It is a solar calendar based on the rotation of Earth around the sun. Several old calendar systems are still used such as the Jewish and Chinese calendars (which are lunisolar, meaning the years are marked according to the sun, but the months according to the moon) and the Muslim lunar calendar..

INFOGRAPHIC

Earth's Seasons

Creating Diagrams Use this infographic to help struggling students understand the process of Earth's revolution around the sun. Assign each student a country located in various regions around the world. Have students create a diagram, similar to the graphic, showing or highlighting their assigned country during a rotation of Earth around the sun. Students' diagrams should include the same dates listed on The Earth's Seasons diagram shown in the text. **AL Verbal/Linguistic**

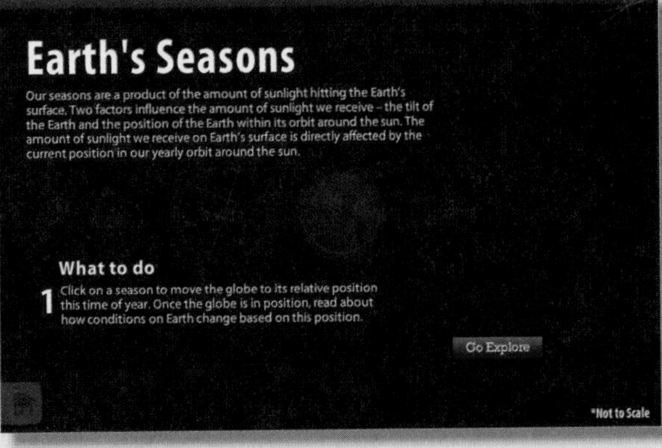

Earth's Seasons
Our seasons are a product of the amount of sunlight hitting the Earth's surface. Two factors influence the amount of sunlight we receive - the tilt of the Earth and the position of the Earth within its orbit around the sun. The amount of sunlight we receive on Earth's surface is directly affected by the current position in our yearly orbit around the sun.
What to do
1 Click on a season to move the globe to its relative position this time of year. Once the globe is in position, read about how conditions on Earth change based on this position.
Go Explore
*Not to Scale

ANSWERS, p. 61

CRITICAL THINKING

1. An equinox is one of two days (about March 21 and September 23) on which the sun is directly above the Equator, making day and night equal in length, while a solstice is one of two days (about June 21 and December 22) on which the sun's rays strike directly on the Tropic of Cancer or Tropic of Capricorn, marking the beginning of summer or winter.
2. The sun's rays directly strike the Equator in March and September. They directly strike the Tropics of Cancer and Capricorn in June and December.

C Critical Thinking Skills

Locating Explain that in addition to the Equator, there are two other latitude lines that mark changes in Earth's seasons: the Tropic of Cancer and Tropic of Capricorn. **Ask:** What happens when the sun hits the Tropic of Cancer on June 21? *(It brings the longest day of sunlight to the Northern Hemisphere, signaling the beginning of summer, or the summer solstice. In the Southern Hemisphere, it brings the shortest day of sunlight signaling the start of winter, or the winter solstice.)* Have students define and add *solstice* to their glossaries.

T Technology Skills

Researching on the Internet **Ask:** Where do you think the greatest amount of variation in sunlight occurs? *(near the Poles)* Tell students there is continuous daylight or twilight for six months of the year in Polar Regions. The phenomenon is called *midnight sun.* Invite a small group of students to research the concept of *midnight sun* on the Internet. Have them create a visual presentation about the midnight sun and present it to the class. BL Logical/Mathematical

V1 Visual Skills

Synthesizing Provide a copy of a world map without labels to pairs of students (available online at the Teacher Resource Center). Have pairs label the continents, oceans, and latitude lines including the Equator, Tropics of Cancer and Capricorn, and the Poles. Then have students summarize the ways in which the seasons change or do not change across the lines of latitude. AL Visual/Spatial

V2 Visual Skills

Analyzing Graphics Explain that Earth is surrounded by an atmosphere and the sun's rays, or radiation, penetrate it. **Ask:** What happens to the sun's rays that shine on Earth through the atmosphere? *(Earth absorbs the rays.)* How do solar rays, or radiation, help life on Earth? *(They help plants grow, keep the planet warm, and determine weather and climate.)* Have students add *atmosphere* and its definition to their glossaries. Visual/Spatial

ANSWERS, p. 62

✓ READING PROGRESS CHECK Time distinguishes weather from climate. Weather is the condition of the atmosphere in one place over a short period of time while climate refers to the average weather conditions as measured throughout many years.

CRITICAL THINKING

1. Solar radiation passes through the atmosphere and is absorbed by Earth warming the surface and radiating heat energy, in the form of greenhouse gas molecules, back into the atmosphere.
2. Radiation not absorbed by Earth is reflected back into space.

solstice one of two days (about June 21 and December 22) on which the sun's rays strike directly on the Tropic of Cancer or Tropic of Capricorn, marking the beginning of summer or winter

C eventually strike the Tropic of Cancer, the latitude line at 23½° N that passes through Mexico, North Africa, and India. The sun usually hits the Tropic of Cancer around June 21, bringing the longest day of sunlight to the Northern Hemisphere. This date is known as the summer **solstice** and marks the beginning of the summer season in the Northern Hemisphere. By about September 23, the Earth has revolved so that the direct rays of the sun hit the Equator again. This equinox marks the end of summer and the beginning of the fall season in the Northern Hemisphere.

V1 As the Earth continues in its revolution, the direct rays of the sun eventually strike the Tropic of Capricorn—the latitude line at 23½° S running through South America, the southern tip of Africa, and Australia—around December 22. This marks the winter solstice, bringing the shortest day of sunlight to the Northern Hemisphere and signaling the beginning of the winter season.

midnight sun continuous daylight, a time when the sun is visible at midnight during the summer in either the Arctic or Antarctic Circle

T The most dramatic variation in the amount of sunlight occurs near the Poles. For six months of the year, one Pole gets continuous sunlight while the other Pole receives none. From about March 20 to about September 23, the polar area north of the Arctic Circle (66½° N) experiences continuous daylight or twilight. The polar area south of the Antarctic Circle (66½° S) experiences continuous daylight or twilight for the other six months of the year. Continuous daylight, a phenomenon also known as **midnight sun**, is caused by the tilt of the Earth's axis as it revolves around the sun. The Poles are very sparsely populated, so many people remain unaffected by midnight sun. However, parts of northern North America and northern Europe—such as Alaska, Sweden, Denmark, Norway, Finland, and others—have become popular tourist destinations particularly because of midnight sun.

✓ READING PROGRESS CHECK

Contrasting What factor distinguishes weather from climate?

V2

THE GREENHOUSE EFFECT
Infrared radiation is emitted from the Earth's surface.
ATMOSPHERE
EARTH'S SURFACE
Some of the infrared radiation passes through the atmosphere, and some is absorbed and reemitted in all directions by greenhouse gas molecules. The effect is to warm the Earth's surface.
Solar radiation passes through the clear atmosphere.
Most radiation is absorbed by the Earth's surface and warms it.
Some solar radiation is reflected by the Earth and the atmosphere.

Solar radiation, when combined with greenhouse gases like carbon dioxide and methane, results in the warming of the Earth's surface. Without this greenhouse effect, Earth would be too cold for most living things.

▲ CRITICAL THINKING

1. ***Interpreting*** What processes of the greenhouse effect contribute to the warming of the Earth's surface?
2. ***Sequencing*** What happens to the solar radiation that is not absorbed by the Earth?

networks Online Teaching Options

VIDEO

Greenhouse Gases

Understanding Relationships Use this video to introduce the greenhouse effect and its influence on climate. Have students write a paragraph explaining the relationship between the sun, greenhouse gases, and climate. Invite volunteers to read their paragraphs aloud. Work with students to address any misunderstandings or to answer any questions. Tell them that in this lesson they will learn more about the importance of the Earth-Sun relationship between weather and climate. Naturalist, Verbal/Linguistic

The Greenhouse Effect

GUIDING QUESTION *What is the greenhouse effect?*

Even on the warmest days, only some of the sun's rays pass through the Earth's atmosphere. The atmosphere reflects some of the radiation back into space. Enough radiation reaches Earth's surface, however, to warm the air, land, and water. Once Earth's surface absorbs the radiation from the sun and is warmed, it radiates this heat energy back again into the atmosphere.

Normally, the atmosphere provides just the right amount of insulation to promote life on the planet. The 50 percent of the sun's radiation that reaches the Earth is converted into infrared radiation, or heat. As shown in the infographic, clouds and greenhouse gases—atmospheric gases such as water vapor, methane, and carbon dioxide (CO_2)—absorb the reradiated heat energy and trap it so that most of it cannot escape back into space. The atmosphere is therefore like a greenhouse. It traps enough radiation to warm the land, water, and air and help plants grow while reflecting some radiation to ensure that the Earth does not overheat. R

This **greenhouse effect** is the warming of the Earth that occurs when the sun's radiation passes through the atmosphere, is absorbed by the Earth, and is radiated as heat energy back into the atmosphere where it cannot escape into space. Without the greenhouse effect, Earth's average temperature would be below 0°F (-17°C) and life as we know it could not exist.

greenhouse effect the capacity of certain gases in the atmosphere to trap heat, thereby warming the Earth

To understand the planet's natural greenhouse effect, consider that according to the laws of physics the radiation Earth receives from the sun must be equally balanced by the heat Earth radiates back out to space. If Earth gave back less energy than it received, the planet would **eventually** become too warm to support life. Likewise, if Earth gave back more energy than it received, the planet would be too cold for life.

eventually taking place later; in the end

PRIMARY SOURCE

> "The greenhouse effect is one of the fundamental facts of atmospheric science. It is real; that fact is beyond dispute. Without it, the entire surface of the ocean would be frozen solid. Life—at least the kind that depends on liquid water and warmth—could not survive. We owe our existence to the greenhouse effect. So why are we worried about it? . . . The answer is that some of the heat radiation leaks out through the atmosphere, because there is not enough water vapor, carbon dioxide, and other gases to absorb all of the IR [infrared heat radiation]. Think of the atmosphere as a leaky blanket."
>
> —Richard A. Muller, from the Columbia Forum, "Physics for Future Presidents," January/February 2009

T

READING PROGRESS CHECK

Assessing How does the greenhouse effect influence Earth's surface temperature?

LESSON 1 REVIEW (CCSS)

Reviewing Vocabulary (Tier Three Words)

1. ***Making Connections*** What is the relationship between weather, climate, axis, temperature, revolution, equinox, and solstice? RH.9–10.4

Using Your Notes

2. ***Discussing*** Using your graphic organizer, discuss how temperature is affected by the tilt of the Earth.

Answering the Guiding Questions

3. ***Identifying Cause and Effect*** How do the relationships between the Earth and the sun affect climate?
4. ***Explaining*** What is the greenhouse effect?

Writing Activity

5. ***Informative/Explanatory*** Write a paragraph explaining the differences in weather you would expect in Alaska and Florida. WHST.9–10.2

R Reading Skills

Defining Have the class write a definition for the *greenhouse effect.* Prompt students to explain that the atmosphere provides the right amount of insulation from the sun's rays to promote life on Earth. It also traps enough radiation to warm Earth while reflecting some radiation back into space to make sure Earth does not overheat. Help students understand that this warming is called the *greenhouse effect.* **Ask:** What do you think would happen if Earth did not have the *greenhouse effect?* *(Earth's temperature would be too cold for humans to live.)* **ELL** Verbal/Linguistic

T Technology Skills

Analyzing Data Tell students that the *greenhouse effect* is a term used in the media and it is often cited in discussions about global warming. Working with a partner, have students collect and analyze data about the changes in climate that have occurred over the last thirty years regarding the *greenhouse effect.* Make sure they are citing data from credible Web sites. Have pairs present their data to the class. **BL** Logical/Mathematical

CLOSE & REFLECT

Explaining Have students explain how Earth's tilt and rotation, Earth's revolution, and the greenhouse effect influence climate and weather patterns. Point out that all of these effects show the importance of the relationship between the Earth and the sun.

ANSWERS, p. 63

READING PROGRESS CHECK It warms Earth's surface. Without the greenhouse effect, Earth's average temperature would be below 0°F (–17°C), and life as we know it could not exist.

LESSON 1 REVIEW ANSWERS

Reviewing Vocabulary

1. The relationship between the Earth and the sun directly affects climate. Due to Earth's tilted axis, not all places on Earth receive the same amount of direct sunlight at the same time. For this reason, Earth's tilt affects the temperature of a particular place. Earth's revolution and its tilted axis affect the amount of sunlight reaching different locations on Earth at different times of the year. An equinox is one of two days on which the sun is directly above the Equator, making day and night equal in length, while a solstice is one of two days on which the sun's rays strike directly on the Tropic of Cancer or Tropic of Capricorn, marking the beginning of summer or winter.

Using Your Notes

2. Due to Earth's tilted axis, not all places on Earth receive the same amount of direct sunlight at the same time. Places that receive more direct sunlight have a higher temperature.

Answering the Guiding Questions

3. The tilt of Earth's axis results in different places on Earth receiving different amounts of direct sunlight at the same time, resulting in different climates. The revolution and tilt result in different amounts of sunlight reaching different locations on Earth at different times of the year, which results in a climate experiencing seasonal changes.
4. The greenhouse effect is the warming of the Earth that occurs when the sun's radiation passes through the atmosphere, is absorbed by the Earth, and is radiated as heat energy back into the atmosphere where it cannot escape into space.

Writing Activity

5. Because of Florida's location, the state receives more direct sunlight than Alaska year-round, so it would have warmer weather.

Factors Affecting Climate

ENGAGE

C Critical Thinking Skills

Interpreting Working with a partner, have students consider other factors that affect the climate on Earth besides Earth revolving around the sun. Allow time for pairs to brainstorm what those other factors might be and compile a list. Then lead class discussion to help students list factors such as wind and ocean currents, elevations and altitude, landforms like valleys and mountains, and latitude.

TEACH & ASSESS

V Visual Skills

Identifying Have students identify how latitude, climate, and elevation relate to each other. **Ask:** What does Earth's revolution around the sun create? *(seasons and predictable weather patterns)* Explain to students that these predictable weather patterns occur within three zones of latitude: low latitude, high latitude, and midlatitude zones. Have students identify the three zones on a map. Explain that the low latitude zone receives direct rays from the sun year-round and has warm to hot climates. **Ask:** What latitude zone falls between 60° N to 90° N and from 60° S to 90° S? *(the high latitude zone)* What areas of Earth does it cover? *(Earth's polar areas)* Then explain that the midlatitude zone has the most variable weather on Earth. Have students identify and name the location of the midlatitude zone on a map, as well as which continents are located within this zone. Visual/Spatial

R Reading Skills

Defining Tell students the midlatitude zone has a temperate climate. **Ask:** What is a temperate climate? *(It is not an extreme climate, either hot or cold. It is a mild climate with seasonal weather changes.)* Have students add *temperate* and its meaning to their glossaries. Then, **ask:** How is the high latitude zone different in temperature and sunlight from the low latitude zone? *(It has cold weather, and depending on the tilt of the sun, the North Pole and the South Pole areas receive almost continuous but indirect sunlight or no sunlight at all.)* ELL Verbal/Linguistic

ANSWERS, p. 64

TAKING NOTES: Wind Currents—Sunlight heats Earth's atmosphere and surface unevenly, causing wind to move across Earth's surface. Warm air rises, then cool air flows in to replace it. This movement of warm and cool air creates wind and distributes the sun's energy. **Ocean Currents**—Ocean currents happen when cold water from polar areas flows toward the Equator while warm water moves away from the Equator.

networks

There's More Online!

- **DIAGRAM** The Rain Shadow Effect
- **MAP** World Zones of Latitude and Wind Patterns
- **MAP** World Ocean Currents
- **INTERACTIVE SELF-CHECK QUIZ**
- **VIDEO** Factors Affecting Climate

Westerlies
NORTH AMERICA
Cool moist air drops moisture
NORTH AMERICA
ATLANTIC OCEAN
EQUATOR
SOUTH AMERICA

LESSON 2
Factors Affecting Climate

ESSENTIAL QUESTION • *Why is climate important to life on Earth?*

Reading HELPDESK (CCSS)

Academic Vocabulary (Tier Two Words)
- **crucial**
- **derive**

Content Vocabulary (Tier Three Words)
- **current**
- **prevailing wind**
- **Coriolis effect**
- **doldrums**
- **El Niño**
- **windward**
- **leeward**
- **rain shadow**

TAKING NOTES: ***Key Ideas and Details***

DESCRIBING As you read the lesson, use a web diagram like the one below to list the factors that cause both wind and ocean currents.

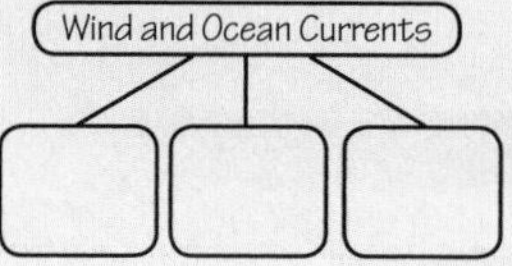
Wind and Ocean Currents

IT MATTERS BECAUSE

The climate of a particular place may have extreme weather and temperature ranges that are caused by several geographic features. Both the latitude and the elevation of a place, along with wind and ocean currents, influence its climate. Two sides of a mountain range may also have two different climates. While one side receives more precipitation as air rises, the opposite side has drier, warmer air as air descends.

Latitude, Climate, and Elevation

GUIDING QUESTION *How are climate patterns related to each zone of latitude?*

The Earth's annual revolution around the sun creates predictable climate patterns. These patterns correspond with bands, or zones, of latitude.

The low latitude zone is between 30° S and 30° N. This zone includes the Tropic of Capricorn, the Equator, and the Tropic of Cancer. Portions of the low latitude zone receive direct rays from the sun year-round and therefore have warm to hot climates.

The high latitude zone includes the Earth's polar areas, which stretch from 60° N to 90° N and from 60° S to 90° S. When either the Northern or the Southern Hemisphere is tilted toward the sun, its polar area receives nearly continuous, but indirect, sunlight.

The midlatitude zone, between 30° N and 60° N in the Northern Hemisphere and between 30° S and 60° S in the Southern Hemisphere, is home to climates that have the most variable weather on Earth. The midlatitudes generally have a temperate climate, or one that varies from fairly hot to fairly cold, with dramatic seasonal weather changes. Warm/hot and cool/cold air masses move across the midlatitudes. These movements and the interactions between the different air masses affect weather in this latitude zone throughout the year.

At all latitudes, elevation influences climate because of the relationship between the elevation of a place and its temperature. The Earth's atmosphere thins as altitude increases. Less dense air retains less heat. As elevation increases, temperatures decrease by about 3.5°F (1.9°C) for each 1,000 feet (305 m). This effect occurs at all latitudes.

networks Online Teaching Options

INTERACTIVE BELLRINGER

Elevation and Temperature

Analyzing Maps Have students use this map to discuss how elevation affects the average temperature of four places at the same latitude. Then have students read the introductory text and use the map to answer the questions on how latitude and elevation affect temperatures on Earth. Allow time for students to write their paragraphs. Then have them exchange their paragraphs with a partner to review and discuss the information. Verbal/Linguistic

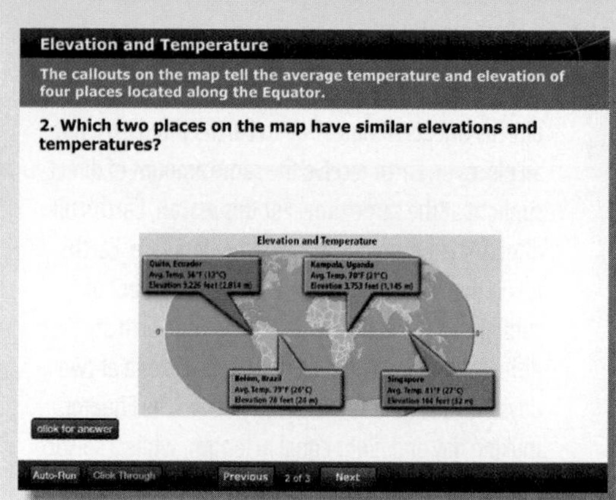
Elevation and Temperature
The callouts on the map tell the average temperature and elevation of four places located along the Equator.
2. Which two places on the map have similar elevations and temperatures?
Elevation and Temperature
click for answer
Auto-Run
Click Through
Previous
2 of 3
Next

For example, in Ecuador, the city of Quito (KEE•toh) is nearly on the Equator. However, Quito is located in the Andes at an elevation of more than 9,000 feet (2,743 m), so average temperatures there are more than 20 degrees cooler than in the coastal lowlands. Sunlight is bright in places with high elevation because the thinner atmosphere filters fewer rays of the sun. But even in bright sunlight, the world's highest mountains, such as the Andes, are cold and snowy. **W** **C**

✓ READING PROGRESS CHECK

Explaining What happens to temperature as elevation increases?

Winds and Ocean Currents

GUIDING QUESTION *How do winds and ocean currents affect climate?*

How do wind and water work together to affect weather? Air moving across the surface of the Earth is called wind. Winds occur because sunlight heats the Earth's atmosphere and surface unevenly. Warm temperatures cause air to rise and create areas of low pressure. Cool temperatures cause air to sink, which creates areas of high pressure. Air moves along the pressure gradient from areas of high pressure to low pressure, so the cool air then flows in to replace the warm rising air. These movements cause winds to distribute the sun's energy around the planet. For this reason, wind patterns are **crucial** to a region's climate. **V1**

Ocean **currents** also help distribute energy around the planet. As they circulate, cold water from the polar areas moves slowly toward the Equator. These are cold ocean currents because they consist of cooler water flowing into warmer water. The opposite is also true: warm water moves away from the Equator and these are warm currents because they consist of warmer water flowing into cooler water.

crucial vitally important

current cold or warm stream of seawater that flows in the oceans, generally in a circular pattern

GEOGRAPHY CONNECTION

Global wind patterns are affected by latitude.

1. ***PHYSICAL SYSTEMS*** In what direction are winds deflected in the Northern Hemisphere?
2. ***PLACES AND REGIONS*** In what latitude zone are the warm winds deflected toward the west?

World Zones of Latitude and Wind Patterns **V2**

Cold wind
Warm wind
Polar front
High latitudes
Midlatitudes
Low latitudes

0 2,000 miles
0 2,000 kilometers
Robinson projection

Factors Affecting Climate

W Writing Skills

Narrative Have students think about what climate zone they would like to live in and then have them write an essay describing why they picked that climate region. Encourage artistic students to include drawings with their essays. **AL** **Verbal/Linguistic**

C Critical Thinking Skills

Drawing Conclusions Tell students that in all three of the latitude zones, the elevation of the land influences the climate. **Ask:** Why do climbers on Mount Everest, the highest mountain on Earth, have to wear oxygen masks when they approach the summit? *(Earth's atmosphere thins as elevation increases, so as climbers get close to the top of Mount Everest, they need oxygen masks to help them breathe.)* **Logical/Mathematical**

V1 Visual Skills

Creating Diagrams Write the following questions on the board and have student pairs create a diagram that describes how wind occurs and how it affects the weather.

- Why do winds occur?
- What happens to warm air?
- What happens to cool air?
- How is the sun's energy distributed?

(Diagram content should include: sunlight warms Earth's air > warm air rises > cool air flows in to replace warm air > the movement of warm and cool air creates what we call wind > these movements cause winds to distribute sun's energy) **Visual/Spatial**

V2 Visual Skills

Analyzing Maps Tell students that winds are named for the directions from which they blow. **Ask:** In what latitude zone do the most winds flow to the East? *(midlatitudes)* In what latitude zone are there primarily cold wind currents? *(high latitudes)* What do we call the winds that flow near the Tropic of Cancer over the continent of Africa? *(North Easterly)* Have students answer the *Geography Connection* questions. Correct any misconceptions students might have about the direction of Earth's winds. **ELL** **Visual/Spatial**

INTERACTIVE MAP

World Zones of Latitude and Wind Patterns

Informative/Explanatory Divide the class into groups of four. Assign each member in the group one of the wind patterns (Westerlies, Polar Easterlies, North Easterly, or South Easterly). Have each group member write a summary explaining a wind pattern that includes the zone(s) and where it is located. Then have group members combine their summaries together into an informative essay on wind patterns. **Verbal/Linguistic, Interpersonal**

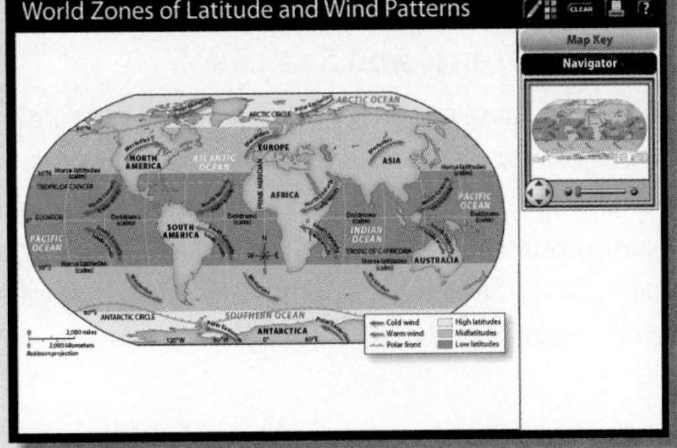

ANSWERS, p. 65

✓ READING PROGRESS CHECK Temperatures drop as elevation increases.

GEOGRAPHY CONNECTION

1. They are deflected clockwise, to the east.
2. In low latitude zones, they are deflected toward the west.

T Technology Skills

Presenting Remind students that ocean currents help distribute energy on Earth, which in turn affects the climate. Have students work in small groups to research the ocean currents that affect climate in various countries around the world. Have groups create a multimedia presentation showing their research to present to the class. Presentations may include visuals, music, or other auditory enhancements. BL Auditory/Musical, Visual/Spatial

Content Background Knowledge

Tropical Cyclones Hurricanes, cyclones, and typhoons are all tropical cyclones. Tropical cyclones are comprised of intense circular (rotating) winds with thunderstorms. These weather systems form in the low latitude zone usually between 10° and 25° from the Equator. They form in the Atlantic Ocean, Caribbean Sea, Gulf of Mexico, and the eastern Pacific Ocean. Depending on their location, these storms are called by different names. The term "hurricane" is used in the Atlantic and Northeast Pacific. In the Northwest Pacific, these storms are called "typhoons" and in the South Pacific and Indian Ocean they are called "cyclones." Hurricanes form when ocean temperatures exceed 80°F (27°C) and have sustained winds of 74 mph. In the first 12 years of the twenty-first century, the United States experienced 13 hurricanes.

R Reading Skills

Defining Write the terms *prevailing winds* and *Coriolis effect* on the board. Tell students that these words describe the winds that blow across Earth's surface. Have a student hold a globe in front of the class. As you explain the movement of the prevailing winds, have a second student show that movement on the globe. *(In the Northern Hemisphere, prevailing winds are deflected to the right; in the Southern Hemisphere, these winds are deflected to the left.)* Review that latitude and the speed of Earth's rotation determine the direction of the *prevailing winds*. It means, since the winds are "displaced" or deflected, the winds blow diagonally over Earth rather than along strict north, south, east, or west directions—the *Coriolis effect*. Now have the second student show the *Coriolis effect* by using his or her hands to indicate the diagonal path the prevailing winds take. Have students write and define *prevailing winds* and *Coriolis effect* in their chapter glossaries. AL ELL Kinesthetic

ANSWERS, p. 66

Connecting Geography Questions asked by climatologists are framed in the same way a geographer explains phenomena through cause-and-effect relationships. The geographer and the climatologist both interpret information and predict future patterns.

Connecting Geography to SCIENCE

Climatology

We know that climate is influenced by location or geography. Climatology, the study of atmospheric changes that define average climates and their change over time, is closely connected to the work of the geographer. Changes in climate can be due to natural processes and human activities. Questions climatologists ask are framed in the same way a geographer explains phenomena using cause-and-effect relationships. Both the geographer and the climatologist interpret information and predict future patterns.

COMPARING What similarities does the work of the geographer have with that of the climatologist?

prevailing wind wind in a region that blows in a fairly constant directional pattern

Coriolis effect the resulting deflection of prevailing winds caused by the Earth's rotation

doldrums a frequently windless area near the Equator

derive to acquire

Patterns of Wind and Ocean Currents

T As winds blow because of pressure differences on Earth's surface, warm tropical air moves toward the Poles and cool polar air moves toward the Equator. This movement of air creates the global winds that blow in fairly constant patterns called **prevailing winds**. The direction of prevailing winds is determined by latitude and is also affected by the Earth's movement. R As the Earth rotates from west to east, the paths of the global winds are deflected to the right in the Northern Hemisphere and to the left in the Southern Hemisphere. This phenomenon is called the **Coriolis effect** and causes prevailing winds to blow diagonally rather than along strict north, south, east, or west directions. The strength of the Coriolis effect is proportional to the speed of Earth's rotation at different latitudes.

Winds are generally named for the direction from which they blow, but they sometimes were given names from the early days of sailing. Named for their ability to move trading ships through the region, the prevailing winds of the low latitudes are called trade winds. They blow from the northeast toward the Equator from about latitude 30° N and from the southeast toward the Equator from about latitude 30° S. Westerlies are the prevailing winds in the midlatitudes, blowing diagonally from west to east between about 30° N and 60° N and between about 30° S and 60° S. In the high latitudes, the polar easterlies blow diagonally east to west, pushing cold air toward the midlatitudes.

Near the Equator, the horizontal movement of the trade winds subsides as the warm air rises. This rising air leaves a narrow, generally windless band called the **doldrums**. Two other narrow bands of calm air encircle the globe just north of the Tropic of Cancer and just south of the Tropic of Capricorn. These bands result from descending, high pressure air. In the days of wind-powered sailing ships, crews feared being stranded in these windless areas. With no moving air to lift the sails, ships were stranded for weeks in the hot, still weather. Food supplies dwindled, and perishable cargoes spoiled as the ships sat, helpless and windless. To lighten the load so the ships could take advantage of the slightest breeze, sailors would toss excess cargo and supplies overboard, including livestock being carried to colonial settlements. The *horse latitudes,* the calm areas at the edges of the Tropics, **derived** their name from this practice.

Just as winds move in patterns, the cold and warm ocean currents move through the ocean in patterns. Ocean currents are caused by many of the same factors that cause winds, including the Earth's rotation, changes in air pressure, and differences in water temperature. The Coriolis effect is also observed in ocean currents. Ocean currents affect climate in the coastal lands along which they flow. Cold ocean currents cool the lands they pass, while warm ocean currents bring warmer temperatures. For example, the warmer North Atlantic Current flows near western Europe. This current gives western Europe a relatively mild climate in spite of its northern latitude.

Influences on Weather

Wind and water work together to affect weather in an important way. Driven by temperature, condensation creates precipitation, or water falling to the Earth in the form of rain, sleet, hail, or snow. The sudden cloudburst that cools a steamy summer day is an example of how precipitation both affects and is affected by temperature. Water vapor forms in the atmosphere from evaporated surface water. The high temperature causes the air to rise. As the air rises, however, it cools and this results in condensation of the water vapor into liquid droplets, forming clouds. Further cooling causes rain to fall, which can help lower the temperature on warm days.

66

networks Online Teaching Options

VIDEO

Ocean Currents and Sea Level

Identifying Cause and Effect Use this video to introduce how wind and water work together to affect climate. As students watch the video, have them write down examples of the effect of ocean currents on Earth's weather and climate. Have students discuss their examples with a partner. Then in a class discussion, ask students to explain how a slight rise in water temperature will affect landmasses all over the world. AL Verbal/Linguistic

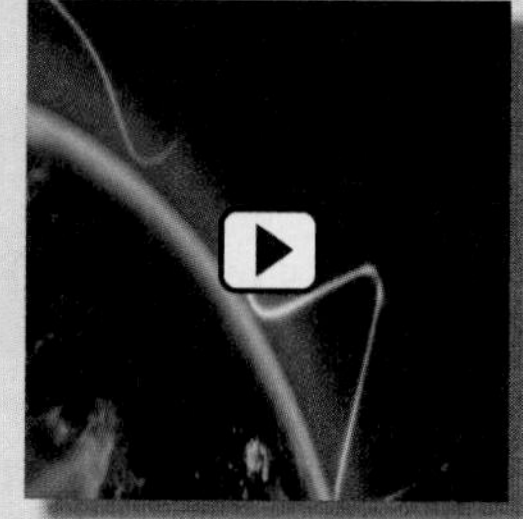

World Ocean Currents

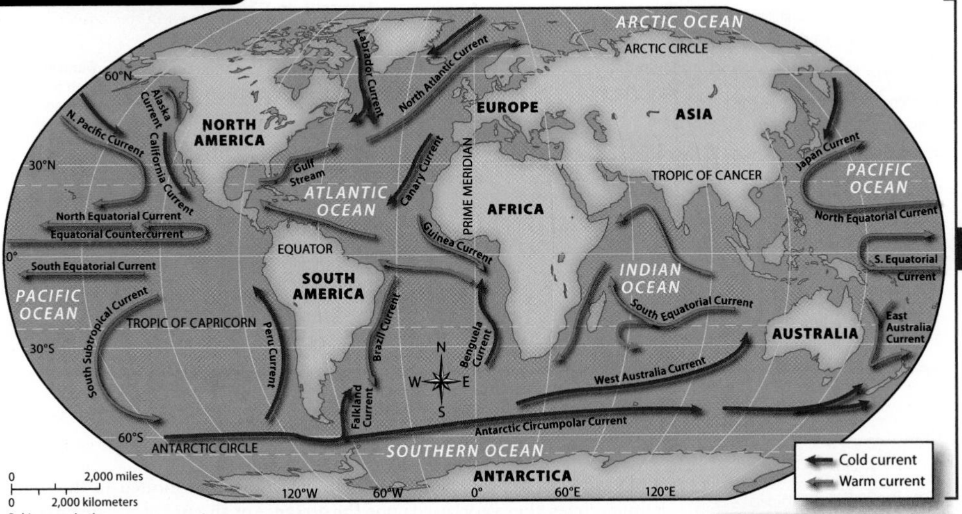

V1

GEOGRAPHY CONNECTION

Ocean currents, when combined with wind patterns and the effects of the sun, influence Earth's weather and climate.

1. ***PHYSICAL SYSTEMS*** Which type of current is located near the Equator?
2. ***PLACES AND REGIONS*** Why would the ocean temperatures along the western coast of southern Africa be colder than the ocean temperatures along the eastern coast?

One example of the way climate is affected by recurring events that alter weather patterns is the **El Niño** (ehl NEE•nyoh) phenomenon. El Niño is a periodic change in the pattern of ocean currents, water temperatures, and weather in the mid-Pacific region. El Niño does not occur every year, but its frequency has increased since the 1970s. In an El Niño year, the normally low atmospheric pressure over the western Pacific is replaced by higher pressure, and the normally high pressure over the eastern Pacific drops. This reversal causes the trade winds to diminish or even to reverse direction. The change in wind pattern reverses the equatorial ocean currents, drawing warm water from near Indonesia east to Ecuador, where it spreads along the coasts of Peru and Chile. V2

These changes in the Pacific influence climates around the world. Precipitation increases along the coasts of North and South America, making the winters warmer and increasing the risk of floods. In Southeast Asia and Australia, drought and occasional massive forest fires occur. Climates in the midlatitudes are affected as well; for example, winter rains are heavier along the west coast of the United States during El Niño years. The costs in human and economic terms, such as damaged homes and flooded crops, make learning about and preparing for an El Niño year vitally important. C

El Niño a periodic reversal of the pattern of ocean currents and water temperatures in the mid-Pacific region

PRIMARY SOURCE

"It rose out of the tropical Pacific in late 1997, bearing more energy than a million Hiroshima bombs. By the time it had run its course eight months later, the giant El Niño of 1997–98 had . . . killed an estimated 2,100 people, and caused at least 33 billion [U.S.] dollars in property damage."

—Curt Suplee, "El Niño/La Niña," *National Geographic Magazine*, March 1999

✓ READING PROGRESS CHECK

Describing What happens to global winds at the Equator?

INTERACTIVE WHITEBOARD ACTIVITY

World Wind Patterns

Analyzing Visuals Have students use this interactive whiteboard activity to identify global wind patterns. As a class, allow time for students to analyze the map. Then have student volunteers drag the global wind pattern to the correct place on the world map. After all of the wind patterns have been placed, guide a class discussion on how wind patterns and ocean currents influence temperature, precipitation, and distribution of climate regions. **Verbal/Linguistic, Interpersonal**

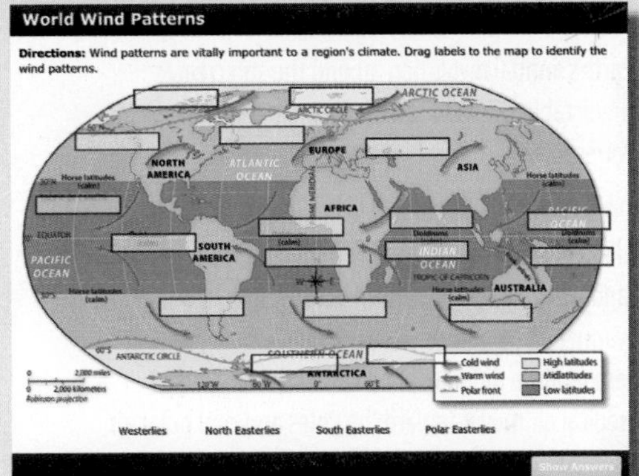

World Wind Patterns
Directions: Wind patterns are vitally important to a region's climate. Drag labels to the map to identify the wind patterns.
Westerlies
North Easterlies
South Easterlies
Polar Easterlies

Factors Affecting Climate

V1 Visual Skills

Analyzing Maps Explain that this map shows cold and warm ocean currents. **Ask:** **What currents affect the western coast of North America?** *(the California and Alaska currents)* **What type of weather does eastern South America generally have?** *(warm weather)* **From the currents affecting Greenland, not its latitudes, what type of weather does it generally have?** *(cold or frigid weather)* In a class discussion lead students to realize that there are more warm currents in Earth's oceans than cold currents. AL **Visual/Spatial**

V2 Visual Skills

Summarizing Remind students that both wind and water work together to affect weather on Earth. **Ask:** **What are the three factors that cause wind patterns and ocean currents?** *(water temperature, Earth's rotation, and changes in air pressure)* With a partner, have students create a graphic organizer that summarizes the wind and water patterns on Earth. **Interpersonal**

C Critical Thinking Skills

Analyzing Cause and Effect Point out that warm and cold ocean currents move in patterns and that the temperature of ocean currents near land affects the climate of that landmass. **Ask:** **What areas of Earth does El Niño affect?** *(It affects climates around the world.)* **How does the phenomenon of El Niño affect the climate worldwide?** *(El Niño causes changes in the water temperatures, ocean currents, and weather patterns in the Pacific, which spreads along the coasts of Peru and Chile.)* **How does El Niño cause an increased risk of floods in North and South America?** *(Precipitation increases along the coastlines of these areas, making the winters warmer, which causes an increased risk of flooding along these areas.)* **How might economic costs rise during El Niño years in the United States?** *(Because winter rains are heavier along the west coast of the United States, crops can flood, causing higher food prices, and homes might be damaged, causing rebuilding costs.)* Continue the discussion by having students identify other causes and effects that El Niño has on the weather patterns around the world. **Verbal/Linguistic**

ANSWERS, p. 67

✓ **READING PROGRESS CHECK** Near the Equator, the trade winds subside when warm air rises, leaving a windless band called the doldrums.

GEOGRAPHY CONNECTION

1. Warm currents are located near the Equator.
2. Ocean temperatures are colder because the currents flow north from the colder waters of the Southern Ocean to the western coast of southern Africa. Warm ocean currents flow south along the eastern coast.

Factors Affecting Climate

V Visual Skills

Analyzing Diagrams Draw students' attention to the diagram about the rain shadow effect. Tell them that landforms, such as mountain ranges, can affect climate. Point out to students there is a rain shadow area on the leeward side of the mountain. **Ask:** What is the rain shadow area? *(It is an area of warm, dry air.)* How is the rain shadow area formed? *(After it rains on the windward side of the mountain, the winds become warmer and drier as they descend on the leeward side of the mountain. There is little moisture in the hot, dry air, which creates the effect known as the rain shadow.)* Write the definition of *rain shadow* that the class arrives at on the board. Then **ask:** Where do deserts form? *(usually on the leeward side of the mountain range where there is warm, dry air)* ELL Visual/Spatial

CLOSE & REFLECT

Summarizing Have students identify the five factors that affect climate on Earth *(latitude, elevation, winds, ocean currents, landforms)*. Ask them to write a brief summary on how each affects climate. Discuss students' summaries as a review of the factors and their effects on climate.

ANSWERS, p. 68

READING PROGRESS CHECK After rising air cools and releases participation, winds become warmer and drier.

CRITICAL THINKING

1. Mountain ranges push wind upward, which cools the rising air and releases moisture in the form of precipitation.
2. The western side would be greener and have more trees.

GRAPH SKILLS

The Rain Shadow Effect

The rain shadow effect is influenced by landforms and climate.

▶ CRITICAL THINKING

1. ***Interpreting*** Why does air lose moisture as it rises over mountains?
2. ***Speculating*** Winds are blowing from the west toward the east of a mountain range running from north to south. Which side of the mountain range is greener and has more trees, the western side or the eastern side?

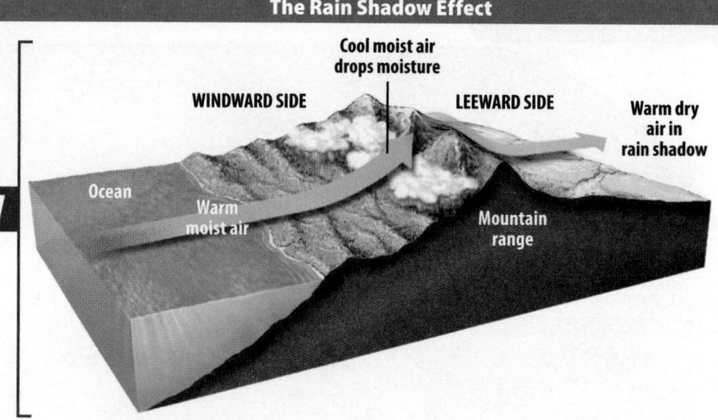

Landforms and Climate

GUIDING QUESTION *How can landforms and bodies of water affect climate?*

While one can generalize about the climates of places located in the same latitude zones, they vary based upon the presence or absence of certain physical features. Large bodies of water, for example, are slower to heat and cool, so they tend to keep temperatures in surrounding lands moderate. Coastal lands receive the benefit of this influence and experience less changeable weather. Conversely, the interiors of the continents tend to experience extremes in seasonal temperatures.

Yet another physical feature that affects the climates in the latitude zones are the mountain ranges. As the diagram shows, mountain ranges push wind upward and, as a result, the rising air cools and releases moisture in the form of precipitation. Most of the precipitation falls on the **windward** side of the mountain, or the side of the mountain range facing the wind. After the precipitation is released, winds become warmer and drier as they descend on the opposite, or **leeward**, side of the mountains. The hot, dry air produces little precipitation in an effect known as a **rain shadow**. The rain shadow effect often causes dry areas—and even deserts—to develop on the leeward sides of mountain ranges.

windward being in or facing the direction from which the wind is blowing

leeward being in or facing the direction toward which the wind is blowing

rain shadow result of a process by which dry areas develop on the leeward sides of mountain ranges

READING PROGRESS CHECK

Discussing What happens to winds after they release precipitation?

LESSON 2 REVIEW

Reviewing Vocabulary

1. ***Describing*** How are prevailing winds influenced by the Coriolis effect?

Using Your Notes

2. ***Making Connections*** Which of the factors from your graphic organizer do you think have the strongest effect on the climate where you live?

Answering the Guiding Questions

3. ***Explaining*** How are climate patterns related to each zone of latitude?
4. ***Identifying Cause and Effect*** How do wind currents and ocean currents affect climate?
5. ***Evaluating*** How can landforms and bodies of water affect climate?

Writing Activity

6. ***Informative/Explanatory*** Suppose you are on a ship sailing in the low latitudes. Write a paragraph explaining what might happen as you drift near the Equator.

68

LESSON 2 REVIEW ANSWERS

Reviewing Vocabulary

1. The direction of prevailing winds is determined by latitude and is also affected by Earth's movement. Because the Earth rotates from west to east, the paths of the global winds are displaced clockwise in the Northern Hemisphere and counterclockwise in the Southern Hemisphere. This phenomenon, the Coriolis effect, causes prevailing winds to blow diagonally, rather than along strict north, south, east, or west directions.

Using Your Notes

2. Student answers may vary, but should be based on the location where the student lives and should be strongly supported by information from the lesson.

Answering the Guiding Questions

3. Earth's annual revolution around the sun creates predictable climate patterns. These patterns correspond with bands, or zones, of latitude.
4. Ocean currents affect climate in the coastal lands along which they flow. Cold ocean currents cool the lands they pass, while warm ocean currents bring warmer temperatures. As winds blow because of temperature differences on Earth's surface, warm tropical air moves toward the Poles and cool polar air moves toward the Equator.
5. Large bodies of water are slower to heat and cool, so they tend to keep temperatures in surrounding lands moderate. Coastal lands receive the benefit of this influence and experience less changeable weather, while the interiors of the continents tend to experience extremes in seasonal temperatures. Mountain ranges push wind upward and, as a result, the rising air cools and releases moisture in the form of precipitation. Most of the precipitation falls on the windward side of the mountain. After the precipitation is released, winds become warmer and drier as they descend on the leeward side. The hot, dry air produces little precipitation due to rain shadow effect, which often causes dry areas.

Writing Activity

6. Paragraphs will vary but should clearly explain doldrums and the impact of no wind on a ship sailing in low latitudes, drifting near the Equator.

networks

There's More Online!

 **MAP** World Biomes

 **PRIMARY SOURCE** Controversy Over Climate Change

 **INTERACTIVE SELF-CHECK QUIZ**

 **VIDEO** World Climate Patterns

LESSON 3
World Climate Patterns

ESSENTIAL QUESTION • *Why is climate important to life on Earth?*

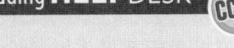

Reading HELPDESK (CCSS)

Academic Vocabulary
(Tier Two Words)
- **overlap**
- **distinct**

Content Vocabulary
(Tier Three Words)
- **biome**
- **natural vegetation**
- **average daily temperature**
- **oasis**
- **prairie**
- **coniferous**
- **deciduous**
- **mixed forest**
- **permafrost**

TAKING NOTES: ***Key Ideas and Details***

IDENTIFYING Use a web diagram like the one below to take notes about the Earth's four climate zones.

IT MATTERS BECAUSE

Climate patterns vary from region to region. However, factors such as wind and air pressure can create zones where a climate becomes quite dramatic. For example, most of Australia has a dry climate, but when trade winds meet during the summer months, Australia's northern coast sees intense thunderstorms. C1

Climate Regions and Biomes

GUIDING QUESTION *How are world climates and biomes organized?*

Climates in the world are organized into four climate zones: tropical, dry, midlatitude, and high-latitude climates. These climates support different kinds of biomes. A **biome** is a major type of ecological community defined primarily by distinctive **natural vegetation** and animal groups. The characteristics of biomes may **overlap** with one another. V C2

Tropical Climates

Tropical climates are found in or near low latitudes in areas otherwise referred to as the Tropics. The two most widespread kinds of tropical climate regions are wet climates and dry climates.

Tropical rain forest climates have an **average daily temperature** of 80°F (27°C), and since the warm air is humid, or saturated with moisture, it rains almost daily. Annual rainfall averages from 50 to 260 inches (125 to 660 cm). This continual rain tends to strip the soil of nutrients. The biome in these climates are the tropical rain forests, characterized by thick vegetation that grows in layers. Tall trees form a canopy over shorter trees and bushes, and shade-loving plants grow on the completely shaded forest floor. The world's largest tropical rain forest is in the Amazon River basin. Similar climate and vegetation exist in other parts of South America, the Caribbean, Asia, and Africa. Due to the vast amount of plant food, wildlife is also abundant, and scientists estimate that more than half of all of the plant and animal species exist in the tropical rain forests. As with all biomes, plants and animals vary within a given rain forest, with differentiation often occurring. For example, trees that grow in the mountains of the Amazon rain forest do not grow in the lowlands of the same rain forest. W

ENGAGE

C1 Critical Thinking Skills

Discussing Discuss with students the type of climate they live in. Have them identify different ways climate affects how people live and what activities people do. Introduce students to the concept that factors, such as wind and air pressure, influence climate to create climate zones.

TEACH & ASSESS

V Visual Skills

Creating Charts Tell students that climate zones are associated with latitudes. On the board, write the names of the four major climate zones: *tropical, dry, midlatitude,* and *high latitude.* Have students create a chart listing the climate zones as column heads. Explain that students will complete their charts using the information provided in this lesson. AL ELL **Visual/Spatial**

C2 Critical Thinking Skills

Explaining Tell students that *bio* means "life" and *ecological community* means "a community that sustains life or living things." Have students explain *natural vegetation* refers to the plants that grow in a certain area or biome and how climate influences biomes. **Ask:** **What is a biome?** *(It is an ecological community with specific animal and plant groups.)* **What factors influence the types of natural vegetation that grow in an area?** *(Possible answers: soil conditions, amount of sunlight, annual rainfall, length of growing season)* **How does climate influence biomes?** *(Because climate patterns vary by region, different climates support different biomes.)* **If the climate is hot with little rain, what type of biome might it support?** *(The biome would support little vegetation and only animals that survive on small amounts of water and plants.)* Have students add the definitions for *biome* and *natural vegetation* in their glossary. **Verbal/Linguistic, Logical/Mathematical**

W Writing Skills

Informative/Explanatory Remind students that climate is the most significant factor influencing soil formation. Have them write a paragraph describing how the environment of the tropical wet climate zone affects the soil-building process in rain forests. If needed, review the soil-building process provided in the previous chapter. BL **Logical/Mathematical**

ANSWERS, p. 69

TAKING NOTES: Earth's four climate zones are: tropical, dry, midlatitude, and high-latitude. These climate zones are further classified into climate regions.

networks *Online Teaching Options*

 **INTERACTIVE BELLRINGER**

Causes of Acid Rain

Analyzing Cause and Effect The series of steps that cause acid rain are displayed in this flowchart, along with some of the environmental resources that are affected by acid rain. Ask students to read the introductory text and then analyze the flowchart to answer the questions. Have students write their paragraphs for question three and exchange them with a partner to review and discuss their answers. BL **Visual/Spatial, Verbal/Linguistic**

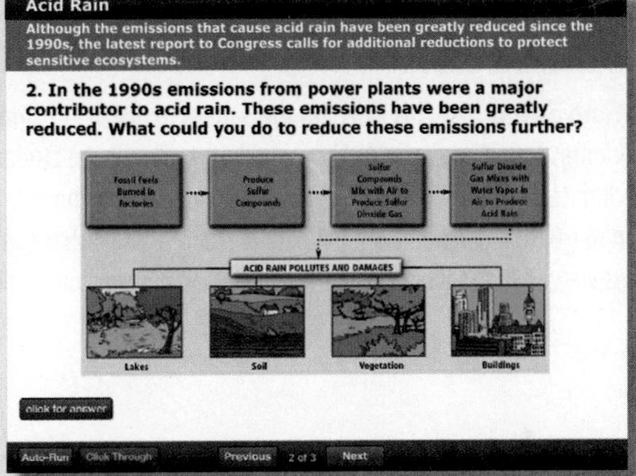

World Climate Patterns

W Writing Skills

Informative/Explanatory Have students define a savanna *(a region of tropical grassland that contains scattered trees with both wet and dry seasons).* Have students include the word *savanna* as they write a short essay summarizing the information about tropical dry climates. Encourage them to share their essays with another student to check for accuracy. **Verbal/Linguistic**

R Reading Skills

Defining Discuss as a class dry climates. Explain to students that there are two majors types of dry climates—semi-arid (or steppe) and arid (or desert). **Ask:** **In which latitude zones are dry climates located?** *(low and midlatitude zones)* **What does the term *semi-arid* mean and what type of climate is experienced in the region?** *(Semi-arid means the region is only partially dry, with an average of 10–30 inches of rain or snow each year. It is also known as the steppe climate, where the summers are warm and winters are cold.)* **Are semi-arid areas classified as deserts? Why or why not?** *(No, deserts are classified as arid because they are dry and receive less than 10 inches of rain a year.)* **What areas in the United States have arid climates?** *(There are arid areas located in the western United States, including parts of Arizona, California, Idaho, Nevada, and Utah.)* Have them add *steppes and desert* in their glossaries. **ELL** **Verbal/Linguistic**

Making Connections

Dry conditions, evolving into drought conditions, have occurred frequently in the twenty-first century in the United States. A drought is defined as a long period of dry weather with no rain. The area west of the Mississippi River to the Rocky Mountains, a heavy agricultural area, has been hit with various degrees of drought ranging from mild to extreme. The impact that droughts have on agriculture and eventually the economy is enormous. The U.S. Drought Monitor, available online, records and tracks droughts across the country.

ANSWERS, p. 70

GEOGRAPHY CONNECTION

1. Desert biomes would have the smallest populations because they lack adequate water sources for large numbers of humans to survive.
2. Student answers may vary, but must reflect the biome in which the student resides.

biome major type of ecological community defined primarily by distinctive plant and animal groups

natural vegetation plant life that grows in a certain area if people have not changed the natural environment

overlap to partly cover

average daily temperature the average of the daily high temperature and the overnight low; often used for comparison across climate regions

distinct recognizably different

oasis small area in a desert where water and vegetation are found

W *Tropical wet/dry* climates have pronounced dry and wet seasons, with high year-round temperatures. These regions, also called savannas, have fewer plants and animals than the tropical rain forest climates. One distinguishing characteristic of a tropical wet/dry climate is that sunlight is not blocked by trees and is able to reach much of the ground surface. This makes for more highly specialized plant and animal species. Tropical savannas are found in Africa, Central and South America, Asia, and Australia. Each maintains **distinct** types of plant and animal life. A key factor determining the types of plants and animals is the length and severity of the dry season.

Dry Climates

R The two main types of dry climates are semi-arid (or steppe) and arid (or desert), both of which occur in low latitudes and midlatitudes. Geographers distinguish these dry climates based on the amount of rainfall and the vegetation in each.

Steppes are usually located away from oceans or large bodies of water and therefore are less humid. However, they do receive an average of 10 to 30 inches (25 to 76 cm) of rainfall per year. Steppes experience warm summers and harshly cold winters. Some steppes have heavy snowfall, while others are susceptible to droughts and violent winds. Steppes are found on almost every continent and are home to a diverse variety of grasses.

Deserts are extremely dry areas that receive about 10 inches (25 cm) of rainfall or less per year and support a very small amount of plant and animal life. Only plants that can live without much water and tolerate unreliable precipitation and extreme temperatures live in the desert. Deserts are usually hot and dry, although some deserts experience snowfall in the winter. In some desert areas, underground springs support an **oasis**, an area of lush vegetation. Temperatures tend to vary widely from day to night, as well as from season to season.

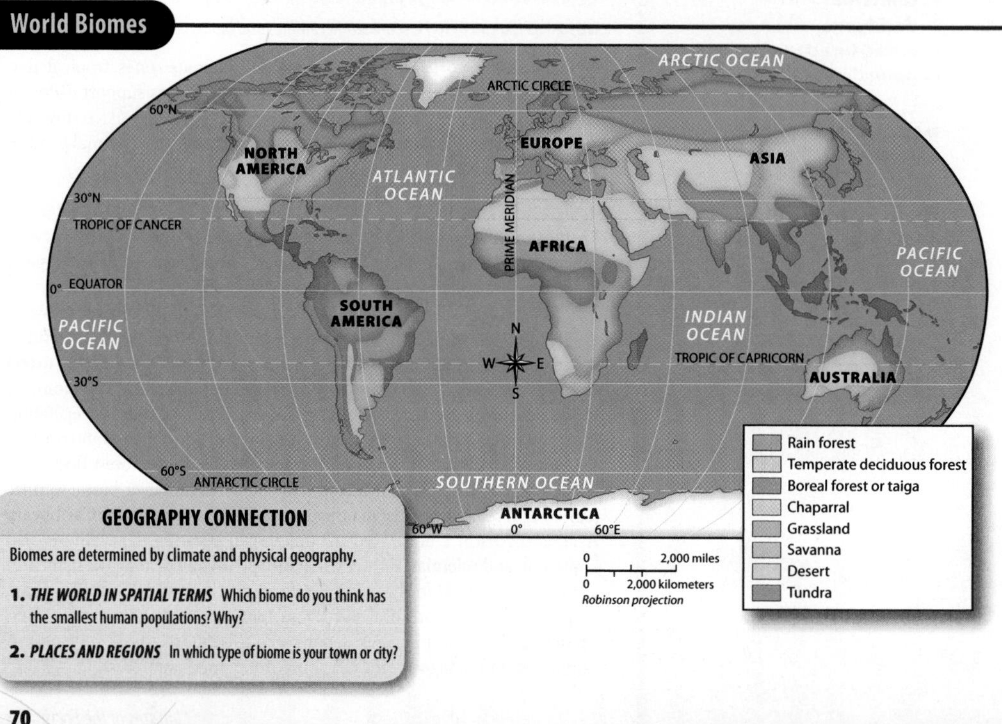

GEOGRAPHY CONNECTION

Biomes are determined by climate and physical geography.

1. ***THE WORLD IN SPATIAL TERMS*** Which biome do you think has the smallest human populations? Why?
2. ***PLACES AND REGIONS*** In which type of biome is your town or city?

70

networks Online Teaching Options

VIDEO

Sahara Desert

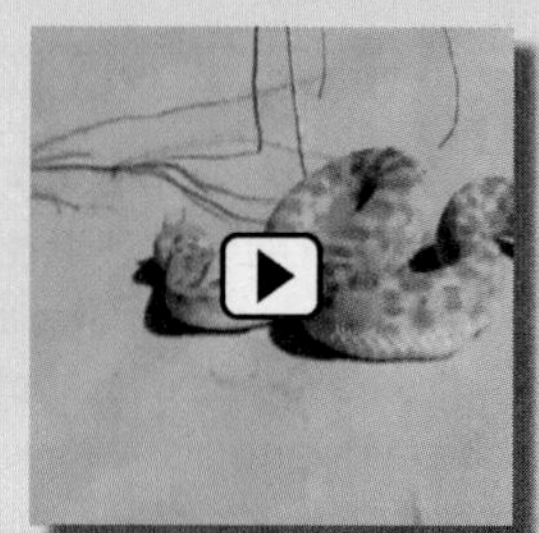

Contrasting Use this video on the Sahara to discuss just one of the dry climate biomes found on Earth. As they watch the video, have students take notes about the climate and wildlife as described in the video. After the video, have students share their notes with a partner. Then have pairs create a chart that contrasts the desert extremes as viewed in the video: the sandy areas and a desert oasis. **ELL** **Visual/Spatial**

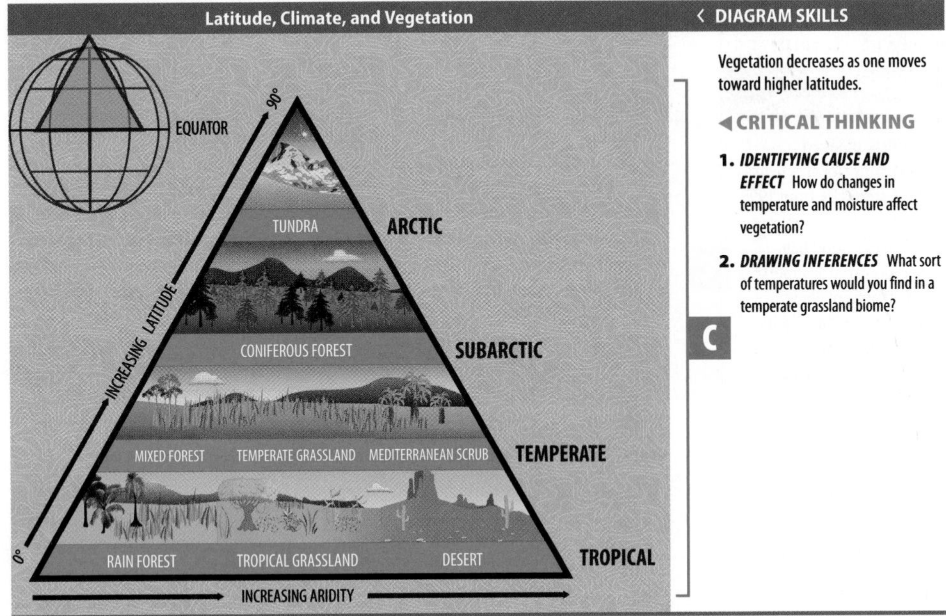

DIAGRAM SKILLS

Vegetation decreases as one moves toward higher latitudes.

CRITICAL THINKING

1. ***IDENTIFYING CAUSE AND EFFECT*** How do changes in temperature and moisture affect vegetation?
2. ***DRAWING INFERENCES*** What sort of temperatures would you find in a temperate grassland biome?

C

Midlatitude and High-Latitude Climates

The midlatitude climates include four temperate climate regions: humid subtropical, marine west coast, Mediterranean, and humid continental. Midlatitude climates experience variable weather patterns due to two conflicting air masses. Tropical air masses move from the Equator to the Poles, and polar air masses move in the opposite direction from the Poles to the Equator.

Humid subtropical climates, which include the southeastern United States as well as parts of Brazil, China, Japan, Australia, and India, are characterized by short, mild winters and nearly year-round rain. The wind patterns and high pressure from nearby oceans keep humidity levels high. Vegetation consists of **prairies** and evergreen and deciduous forests. **Coniferous** trees, most of which are evergreens, have cones. **Deciduous** trees, most of which have broad leaves, change color and drop their leaves in autumn.

Marine west coast climates, including the southern coast of Chile, parts of Australia, the British Isles, and the Pacific coast of North America, are mainly between the latitudes of about 30° N and 60° N and about 30° S and 60° S. Ocean winds bring cool summers and cool, damp winters. Abundant rainfall supports both coniferous and deciduous trees, often resulting in **mixed forests**.

Lands surrounding the Mediterranean Sea, in addition to the southwestern coast of Australia and central California, have mild, rainy winters and hot, dry summers. The natural vegetation includes thickets of woody bushes and short trees known as Mediterranean shrubs. Geographers classify as *Mediterranean* any coastal midlatitude area with similar climate and vegetation.

In some midlatitude regions of the Northern Hemisphere, landforms influence climate more than winds, precipitation, or ocean temperatures do. *Humid continental* climate regions do not experience the moderating effect of ocean winds because of their northerly continental, or inland, locations. The farther north one travels, the longer and more severe are the snowy winters, and the shorter and

V

T

prairie an inland grassland area

coniferous referring to vegetation having cones and needle-shaped leaves, including many evergreens, that keep their foliage throughout the winter

deciduous falling off or shed seasonally or periodically; trees such as oak and maple, which lose their leaves in autumn

mixed forest forest with both coniferous and deciduous trees

permafrost permanently frozen layer of soil beneath the surface of the ground

World Climate Patterns

C Critical Thinking Skills

Applying Discuss each section of the diagram about latitude, climate, and vegetation. Point out that geographers divide the Earth into regions that have similar climates. Direct students' attention to the Temperate climate section of the diagram. **Ask:** What are the approximate latitude lines of the temperate climate? *(about 30° N to 60° N and 30° S to 60° S)* Explain that most of the world's human population lives in the midlatitude climate zone, which includes four temperate climate regions. **Ask:** Why do you think so many people live in the temperate climate region? *(Possible answers: the temperate climate region has the most vegetation; it has average temperatures, which are not too hot or too cold; the climate is good for growing crops; it has moderate elevations)* **Logical/Mathematical**

V Visual Skills

Gathering Information Have students read about the four temperate climate regions. **Ask:** What are the four types of regions in the midlatitude climate zone? *(humid subtropical, marine west coast, Mediterranean, and humid continental)* What type of climate do midlatitude zones have? *(variable climates)* Tell students to add the four regions under the midlatitude climate zone in their charts. Have them supply climate information about each of these regions. **Visual/Spatial**

T Technology Skills

Classifying Divide students into small groups and assign each group a country from the midlatitudes. Have students use the Internet or library resources to research the types of trees found in their assigned country. Groups should create a visual that classifies the types (coniferous, deciduous, mixed) and names of trees that grow in that country and in which temperate climate region the trees grow. Have groups present their visuals to the class. Use the presentations to further class discussion about the midlatitude climate regions. BL **Visual/Spatial**

INFOGRAPHIC

Latitude, Climate, and Vegetation

Summarizing Display this infographic that shows the four types of climate zones of the world, including the biomes existing in each. As a class, click on the graph to explore the 360° panoramic views of the biomes found in each zone of latitude. Guide students to understand that biomes are controlled by climate and that climate is affected by latitude. Have students take notes on each biome and then write a one-sentence summarization about the graphic. *(Students' statements should reflect that vegetation decreases as latitude increases.)* **Visual/Spatial, Logical/Mathematical**

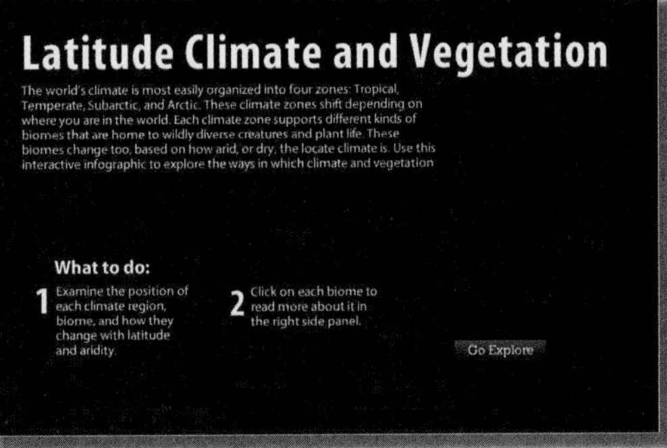

Latitude Climate and Vegetation
What to do:
1 Examine the position of each climate region, biome, and how they change with latitude and aridity.
2 Click on each biome to read more about it in the right side panel.
Go Explore

ANSWERS, p. 71

CRITICAL THINKING

1. As the temperature and moisture increases, so does vegetation. However, if temperature increases but moisture does not, there is limited vegetation. If temperatures are very cold, vegetation is also limited.
2. Moderate temperatures with hot summers and mild winters.

World Climate Patterns

C Critical Thinking Skills

Comparing and Contrasting Have student pairs list the similarities and differences of the four major climate zones. Encourage students to add the information to their individual charts. **Ask:** What similarities are there between dry and high-latitude climates? *(Possible answers: both have little precipitation; both sustain small amounts of vegetation)* How do midlatitude and high-latitude climates differ? *(Possible answers: the midlatitude zone experiences variable temperatures by region, abundant vegetation, sunny summers, fertile soil, and mild to severe winters; the high-latitude zone experiences freezing temperatures, limited vegetation, thin layers of soil, and long, cold, severe winters)* Continue to ask questions that compare and contrast the climate zones. Verbal/Linguistic

T Technology Skills

Constructing Arguments Direct students to the text. **Ask:** What are some indicators of climate change? *(rising global temperatures, changes in precipitation, rising sea levels, increases in severe weather events such as tornadoes, hurricanes, and tsunamis)* Direct student groups to structure a debate about climate change. Allow class time for groups to research the differing points of view and to construct their arguments. Then have the groups present their views in classroom debates.
BL Kinesthetic

CLOSE & REFLECT

Summarizing Identify climate zones and regions. Divide the class into two teams. Each team gets ten points for correctly answering each question. 1. Name the four climate zones. *(tropical, dry, midlatitude, high-latitude)* 2. Name two types of tropical climates. *(tropical wet: rain forests and tropical dry: savannas)* 3. Name two types of dry climates. *(semi-arid, or steppe, and desert, or arid)* 4. Name the four types of midlatitude climates. *(humid subtropical, marine west coast, Mediterranean, humid continental)* 5. Name the three types of high-latitude climate. *(subarctic, tundra, and ice cap regions)* Total up the team scores and discuss any student questions.

ANSWERS, p. 72

READING PROGRESS CHECK These climates have winter darkness and bitter cold with limited warming, so the layer of thawed soil is thin. Trees cannot establish roots, so vegetation is limited to low bushes, very short grasses, mosses, and lichens.

READING PROGRESS CHECK Exhaust released from burning fossil fuels is heated in the atmosphere by the sun's ultraviolet rays, which creates smog.

DBQ Yes, there appears to be a connection. The fact that tornadoes occurred at a rate of about 20 percent above average during the middle of the week and 20 percent below average on the weekend would seem to indicate a tie to the number of vehicles on the road.

Why Tornadoes Take the Weekends Off in Summer

"Scientists analyzed summertime storm activity in the eastern U.S. from 1995 to 2009.... They discovered that tornadoes and hailstorms occurred at a rate of about 20 percent above average during the middle of the week. In contrast, the phenomena occurred at a rate of roughly 20 percent below average on the weekend....The team then investigated Environmental Protection Agency air-quality monitoring data and noted that human-made, summertime air pollution over the eastern U.S. peaks midweek. The cycle is linked to more human-made pollution created during the five-day workweek, such as commuters driving to and from work."

—Charles Q. Choi, *National Geographic News*, December 29, 2011

DBQ ***ANALYZING*** Do you think there is a cause-and-effect relationship between increased air pollution and increased tornado activity? Explain. RH.9–10.3, RH.9–10.8

cooler are the summers. Vegetation is similar to that found in marine west coast areas, with evergreens outnumbering deciduous trees in the northernmost areas.

In high-latitude climates, freezing temperatures are common all year because of the lack of direct sunlight. As a result, the amount and variety of vegetation is limited here. Just south of the Arctic Circle are the *subarctic* climate regions. Winters here are bitterly cold, and summers are short and cool. Subarctic regions have the world's widest temperature ranges. In parts of the subarctic, only a thin layer of surface soil thaws each summer. Below is permanently frozen subsoil, or **permafrost**. Brief summer growing seasons may support needled evergreens.

C Closer to the Poles are *tundra* climate regions. Winter darkness and bitter cold last for months, while summer has only limited warming. The layer of thawed soil is even thinner than in the subarctic. Trees cannot establish roots, so vegetation is limited to low bushes, very short grasses, mosses, and lichens (LY• kuhns).

Snow and ice, often more than 2 miles (3 km) thick, constantly cover the surfaces of *ice cap* regions. Lichens are the only form of vegetation that can survive in these areas where monthly temperatures average below freezing.

READING PROGRESS CHECK

Making Connections Why do high-latitude climates have limited vegetation?

Climate Change

GUIDING QUESTION *What causes climates to change over time?*

Climate change refers to major changes in the factors used to measure climate over an extended period of time. For example, scientists have concluded that the average global temperature has increased by 1.4°F (0.8°C) over the last century. Some indicators of climate change include rising global temperatures, severe weather changes such as intense heat waves and changes in precipitation, an increase in severe weather events, and rising sea levels. Scientists search for answers by studying the interrelationships among ocean temperatures, greenhouse gases, wind patterns, and cloud cover. While scientists continue to disagree about the causes of climate T change, we do know that the Earth undergoes natural and predictable cycles of cooling and warming caused by factors such as solar flares and volcanic activity.

However, increased global temperatures can also be attributed to greenhouse gas emissions. Burning fossil fuels releases gases that mix with water in the air, forming acids that fall in rain and snow. Acid rain can destroy forests. Fewer forests may result in climate change. The exhaust released from burning fossil fuels in automobile engines and factories is heated in the atmosphere by the sun's ultraviolet rays, forming smog, a visible chemical haze in the atmosphere.

READING PROGRESS CHECK

Explaining How does the burning of fossil fuels create smog?

LESSON 3 REVIEW

Reviewing Vocabulary (Tier Three Words)

1. ***Identifying*** Use the following three terms in one sentence that describes humid subtropical climate regions: prairie, coniferous, deciduous. RH.9–10.4, WHST.9–10.4

Using Your Notes

2. ***Describing*** Use your graphic organizer to describe the Earth's four climate zones.

Answering the Guiding Questions

3. ***Categorizing*** How are world climates organized?
4. ***Drawing Conclusions*** What causes climates to change over time?

Writing Activity

5. ***Informative/Explanatory*** Write a paragraph detailing how the four major climate regions are related to the three zones of latitude. WHST.9–10.2

72

LESSON 3 REVIEW ANSWERS

Reviewing Vocabulary

1. Humid subtropical climates experience short, mild winters and nearly year-round rain, with vegetation that is comprised of prairies and evergreen, deciduous, and coniferous forests.

Using Your Notes

2. Tropical—located in or near low latitudes and includes tropical rain forests and tropical wet/dry regions; Dry—occurs at low and midlatitudes and includes semi-arid and arid regions; Midlatitude—variable weather patterns and includes four temperate regions: humid subtropical, marine west coast, Mediterranean, and humid continental; High-Latitude—freezing temperatures are common and regions include subarctic, tundra, and ice cap.

Answering the Guiding Questions

3. The world climates are organized into four climate zones: tropical, dry, midlatitude, and high-latitude climates.
4. Scientists study ocean temperatures, greenhouse gases, wind patterns, and cloud cover to determine causes of climate change. While they disagree about the causes, it is clear that Earth undergoes natural and predictable cycles of cooling and warming such as by solar flares and volcanic activity. However, increased global temperatures can also be attributed to greenhouse gas emissions in the atmosphere.

Writing Activity

5. Paragraphs will differ, but should be supported through information from the chapter.

CHAPTER 3 Assessment 

Directions: On a separate sheet of paper, answer the questions below. Make sure you read carefully and answer all parts of the questions.

Lesson Review

Lesson 1

1. ***Listing*** What are the two types of solstices?
2. ***Explaining*** Why are the seasons different in the Northern and Southern Hemispheres?
3. ***Describing*** Describe what is meant by "midnight sun."

Lesson 2

4. ***Defining*** How are winds named?
5. ***Describing*** Describe the Coriolis effect. How does it differ based on latitude?
6. ***Discussing*** What effects do mountain ranges have on climates in a region?

Lesson 3

7. ***Identifying*** What are the four temperate climate regions into which midlatitude climates are classified?
8. ***Explaining*** How do geographers distinguish between the types of dry climate?
9. ***Listing*** What are three indicators of climate change?

Critical Thinking

10. ***Making Generalizations*** Has human activity had a positive or negative effect on the global climate? Explain.
11. ***Comparing and Contrasting*** How are tropical rain forest and tropical wet/dry climates alike? How are they different?
12. ***Drawing Conclusions*** How might human activities negatively affect plants and animals?

21st Century Skills

13. ***Creating and Using Graphs, Charts, Diagrams, and Tables*** All of the cities in the table are located in the Tropics except for Telluride. Why does Quito have a lower average temperature than the other tropical cities? RH.9–10.7
14. ***Compare and Contrast*** Use the information in the table to compare and contrast how elevation and latitude affect temperatures on Earth. Provide two examples. RH.9–10.7

The Influence of Elevation on Temperature

	Elevation	Latitude & Longitude	Average Temperature
Quito, Ecuador	9,233 ft. (2,811 m)	0°09′ S 78°29′ W	58°F (14°C)
Nairobi, Kenya	5,327 ft. (1,623 m)	1°19′ S 36°55′ E	67°F (19°C)
Bjumbura, Burundi	2,568 ft. (782 m)	3°19′ S 29°19′ E	77°F (25°C)
Manaus, Brazil	276 ft. (84 m)	3°09′ S 59°59′ W	81°F (27°C)
Telluride, Colorado	8,760 ft. (2,670 m)	37°57′ N 107°49′ W	39°F (3°C)

Source: www.weatherbase.com

College and Career Readiness

X 15. ***Clear Communication*** Use the Internet to research careers in climatology and meteorology. Then write a job posting for one of the careers you learned about. Be sure that the job posting describes the required skills and experience necessary for the position. WHST.9–10.7

Need Extra Help?

If You've Missed Question	1	2	3	4	5	6	7	8	9	10	11	12	13	14	15
Go to page	62	61	62	65	66	68	71	70	72	72	69	72	73	73	66

CHAPTER 3 Assessment Answers

Lesson Review

Lesson 1

1. The two types of solstices are the summer solstice, which occurs around June 21, and the winter solstice, which occurs around December 22.
2. The seasons are different in the Northern and Southern Hemisphere because of the differing amounts of sun each hemisphere receives due to the tilt of Earth's axis and the revolution of Earth around the sun.
3. The term "midnight sun" is used to describe the continuous daylight or twilight that the Poles experience for 6 months each year.

Lesson 2

4. Winds are normally named for the direction from which they blow, but sometimes they have names that were given in the early days of sailing.
5. Global winds are deflected to the right in the Northern Hemisphere and to the left in the Southern Hemisphere, which is known as the Coriolis effect. This causes prevailing winds to blow diagonally. The strength of the Coriolis effect is proportional to the speed of Earth's rotation at different latitudes.
6. Mountain ranges push wind up, causing the air to cool and release precipitation. The precipitation falls mostly on the windward side of the mountain, making it cooler and wetter. After the precipitation falls, the wind becomes warmer and drier on the opposite or leeward side of the mountain. This causes a rain shadow effect where the area on this side of the mountain range has little rain and may even be desert.

Lesson 3

7. The four temperate climate regions for the midlatitude climates are the humid subtropical, marine west coast, Mediterranean, and humid continental.
8. Geographers identify two types of dry climates, the semi-arid (or steppe) and arid (or desert). Each is distinguished by the amount of rainfall and the types of vegetation that exist in the climate.
9. Student answers will vary, but should include three of the following indicators of climate change: rising global temperatures, severe weather changes including heat waves and changes in precipitation, increase in severe weather events, and rising sea levels.

Critical Thinking

10. Human activity has had a negative effect. Explanations may vary, but could include the burning of fossil fuels in automobiles and factories contributing to smog and acid rain.
11. Topical wet and dry climates both have warm temperatures. Tropical wet climates have more rain and tall, thick vegetation. Tropical dry climates have a wet and a dry season. The vegetation is not as tall or thick, which allows sunlight to reach the ground.
12. Student answers will vary, but could include human activities such as the burning of fossil fuels contributing to acid rain, increasing temperatures, and severe weather, which can destroy forests and water sources that plants and animals need to survive.

21st Century Skills

13. Quito has a higher elevation than the other tropical cities in the chart, resulting in a cooler climate.
14. As the elevation increases, the temperature decreases. Quito and Telluride are at higher elevations, so they have lower temperatures. As the latitudes approach the Equator, as with Manaus and Bjumbura, the temperature increases.

College and Career Readiness

15. Student answers will vary, but could include skills/experience in forecasting, knowledge of climate and precipitation, and use of specialized equipment.

Assessment Answers

Applying Map Skills

16 Student answers will vary, but should be supported by climate region, population density, and land use maps in the atlas. Answers could include heavy populations with commercial farming activities in humid continental regions to little or no activity in desert and tundra regions.

17 Climate regions that have adequate rainfall such as humid continental, humid subtropical, marine west coast, and tropical wet/dry are more densely populated.

Exploring the Essential Question

18 Posters will vary, but should contain information on plants, animals, temperatures, and precipitation in the selected biome. Content should be visual, including pictures, photos, graphs, and charts.

Research and Presentation

19 Student presentations will vary, but should include information such as where leatherback sea turtles are found (the Atlantic, Pacific, and Indian Oceans; Mediterranean Sea) and the migration patterns from one of these locations, which can be up to 3,700 miles. Supply a purpose for migration, such as breeding and nesting on particular beaches. Presentations should also indicate the endangered status as well as current and historical numbers of leatherback sea turtles. Issues revolving around climate change and human activities, such as the ingestion of plastic waste by turtles and changing ocean temperatures, should be identified.

Analyzing Primary Sources

20 Scientists learned of past climate changes by studying environmental data such as tree rings, pollen assemblages, lake sediment, and ice cores.

21 The example that a narrow tree ring could mean a dry spell and/or a cold spring is used to show that climate change data is difficult to interpret.

Writing About Geography

22 Student essays will vary, but should include information on how Earth's annual revolution around the sun creates predictable climate patterns. These patterns correspond with bands, or zones, of latitude. The latitude determines how much sun a region receives, influencing the overall temperatures in specific regions. Essays should also include that the midlatitudes have temperate climates, high latitudes have cold climates, and low latitudes have hot climates, as well as examples of climate types in each zone.

CHAPTER 3 Assessment

Directions: On a separate sheet of paper, answer the questions below. Make sure you read carefully and answer all parts of the questions.

Applying Map Skills

Refer to the Unit 1 Atlas to answer the following questions.

16 ***Environment and Society*** How is human activity affected by specific climate regions? Using the maps in the unit atlas, choose a climate region and provide an example of how it influences human activity.

17 ***Human Systems*** Using the maps in the unit atlas, what connections can you make between densely populated areas and climate regions?

Exploring the Essential Question

X 18 ***Making Connections*** Choose one of the biomes discussed in this chapter: tropical rain forest, tropical wet/dry, semi-arid (steppe), arid (desert), humid subtropical, marine west coast, Mediterranean, humid continental, subarctic, tundra, and ice cap. Use what you have learned about the biome to create a poster illustrating the plants and animals in the biome. Conduct additional research to include statistics on average rainfall and amount of direct sunlight. Posters should also illustrate the interactions of human systems within this biome. Posters should be highly visual and can include photos of typical vegetation, graphs/charts, and maps. WHST.9–10.9

Research and Presentation

X 19 ***Research Skills*** Use Internet and library resources to gather information about the leatherback sea turtle. Create a multimedia presentation outlining the leatherback sea turtle's migration and mating patterns in map and graph/chart forms. Compare and contrast historical and current data regarding how many leatherback sea turtles existed in the past and exist today. Be sure to (1) explain why the turtle follows these migratory and mating patterns and (2) how climate change and human activity have impacted these patterns. WHST.9–10.6, WHST.9–10.8

DBQ Analyzing Primary Sources

Use the document to answer the following questions.

PRIMARY SOURCE

"*It has been demonstrated that climate changes at millennial, centennial, and even decadal scales, as many studies in the twentieth century have revealed. Such studies were largely done by examining environmental data such as tree rings, pollen assemblages, lake sediment, and ice cores. These data are objective and usually continuous, but they are often difficult to interpret. For example, a narrow tree ring could mean either a dry spell or cold spring, or both. Consequently, conclusions obtained this way are often associated with considerable uncertainties or ambiguities.*"

—Pao K. Wang, "Chinese historical documents and climate change", www.accessscience.com

20 ***Analyzing*** According to the excerpt, how did scientists learn that climates have changed in the past? RH.9–10.1

21 ***Interpreting*** What example is provided to explain why climate change data is often difficult to interpret? RH.9–10.1

Writing About Geography

Y 22 ***Informative/Explanatory*** Use standard grammar, spelling, sentence structure, and punctuation to write a one-page essay explaining how the Earth's rotation on its axis and its revolution around the sun creates certain types of climate conditions in low, mid-, and high latitude regions. Be sure to cite specific examples in your essay. WHST.9–10.2, WHST.9–10.4

Need Extra Help?

If You've Missed Question	16	17	18	19	20	21	22
Go to page	4	4	69	72	74	74	60

74

networks Online Teaching Options

WORKSHEET

Chapter Test and Lesson Quizzes

Assessing Have students complete the Chapter Test and Lesson Quizzes to assess student understanding throughout the chapter. These assessment tools offer chapter and lesson evaluation through a variety of question formats, including document-based questions.

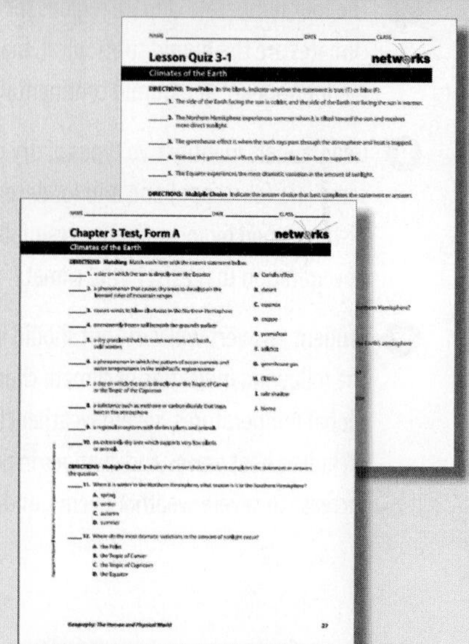

CHAPTER 4

The Human World Planner

UNDERSTANDING BY DESIGN®

Enduring Understandings

- *The characteristics and distribution of cultures influence human systems.*

Essential Question

- *How do the characteristics and distribution of human populations affect human and physical systems?*

Predictable Misunderstandings

Students may think:

- *Geography involves land, but not people. Explain that there are many concepts in geography including population geography, political geography, human geography, and economic geography.*
- *Cultures remain the same over time. Explain that although most cultures maintain traditions, cultures are also always changing, particularly in the modern era when it is so simple to share ideas.*
- *Population distribution is relatively even throughout the world. Explain that population distribution is uneven throughout the world due to many factors, including geography.*

Assessment Evidence

Performance Tasks:

- *Hands-On Chapter Project*

Other Evidence:

- *Guided Reading Activities*
- *Vocabulary Activities*
- *Lesson Quizzes*
- *Chapter Tests, Forms A and B*

SUGGESTED PACING GUIDE

Introducing the Chapter	½ Day
Lesson 1	1 Day
Lesson 2	1 Day
Lesson 3	1 Day
Case Study	1 Day
Lesson 4	1 Day
Global Connections	1 Day
Lesson 5	1 Day
Chapter Wrap-Up and Assessment	½ Day
TOTAL TIME	**8 Days**

Key for Using the Teacher Edition

SKILL-BASED ACTIVITIES

Types of skill activities found in the Teacher Edition.

*V **Visual Skills** require students to analyze maps, graphs, charts, and photos.

R **Reading Skills** help students practice reading skills and master vocabulary.

C **Critical Thinking Skills** help students apply and extend what they have learned.

W **Writing Skills** provide writing opportunities to help students comprehend the text.

T **Technology Skills** require students to use digital tools effectively.

*Letters are followed by a number when there is more than one of the same type of skill on the page.

DIFFERENTIATED INSTRUCTION

All activities are written for the on-level student unless otherwise marked with the leveled labels below.

BL **Beyond Level**

AL **Approaching Level**

ELL **English Language Learners**

All students benefit from activities that utilize different learning styles. Many activities are marked as below when a particular learning style is highlighted.

Intrapersonal · **Logical/Mathematical** · **Visual/Spatial** · **Verbal/Linguistic** · **Naturalist** · **Kinesthetic** · **Auditory/Musical** · **Interpersonal**

National Geography Standards covered in "The Human World"

The student knows and understands:

(3) How to analyze the spatial organizations of people, places, and environments on Earth's surface

3.2 Complex processes change over time and shape patterns in the distribution of human and physical phenomena

(4) The physical and human characteristics of places

4.1 The effects of place-based identities on personal, community, national, and world events

(5) That people create regions to interpret Earth's complexity

5.1 Regions are defined by different sets of criteria and places can be included in multiple regions of different types

(6) How culture and experience influence people's perceptions of places and regions

6.2 Changing perceptions of places and regions have significant economic, political and cultural consequences in an increasingly globalized and complex world

(9) The characteristics, distribution, and migration of human populations on Earth's surface

9.2 Population distribution and density are a function of historical, environmental, economic, political, and technological factors

(10) The characteristics, distribution, and complexity of Earth's cultural mosaics

10.3 Culture changes through convergence and/or divergence

10.4 The rate of cultural changes has increased as a result of globalization

(11) The patterns and networks of economic interdependence on Earth's surface

11.3 Economic systems are dynamic organizations of interdependent economic activities for production, exchange, distribution, and consumption of goods and services

(12) The process, patterns, and functions of human settlement

12.4 Urban models are used to analyze the growth and form of urban regions

(13) How the forces of cooperation and conflict among people influence the division and control of Earth's surface

13.2 Cooperation between countries and organizations may have lasting influences on past, present, and future global issues

CHAPTER OPENER PLANNER

Students will know:

- *the elements of culture, the factors that change culture over time, and how cultural diffusion works.*
- *the factors that influence population growth, causes of population movement, and why population distribution is uneven.*
- *different government structures and how they are connected to geography.*
- *the characteristics of economic systems, types of economic activities, and reasons for world trade.*
- *the functions and structures of cities, how they grow, and problems they may have.*

Students will be able to:

- ***identify** the elements of culture and describe how culture changes over time.*
- ***describe** population growth and movement.*
- ***describe** different types of governments.*
- ***identify** features of economic systems.*
- ***explain** world trade.*
- ***analyze** cities and their structures and functions.*

UNDERSTANDING BY DESIGN®

☑ Print Teaching Options

V Visual Skills

- ☐ **p. 77** Students describe and explain the cause-and-effect relationship between technological progress and the way people live their daily lives. ELL Visual/Spatial

R Reading Skills

- ☐ **p. 76** Students discuss the map key showing the Human Development Index. AL Visual/Spatial

C Critical Thinking Skills

- ☐ **p. 76** Students discuss the world map of the Human Development Index.
- ☐ **p. 76** Students compare and contrast the level of development and the standard of living of various countries by creating a chart. BL Visual/Spatial

W Writing Skills

- ☐ **p. 77** Students write a paragraph that explains how governments might make policy decisions and choose to spend money. Intrapersonal, Verbal/Linguistic

☑ Online Teaching Options

V Visual Skills

- GRAPHS **Population Indicators and Change in HDI Rank**—Students analyze and discuss the information on the graphs and write a summary identifying trends in population. AL Visual/Spatial, Logical/Mathematical
- HANDBOOK **Interactive World Religions**—Students use the interactive world religions handbooks to learn more about world religions.

☑ Printable Digital Worksheets

- WORKSHEET **Assessing Background Knowledge**—Determine the level of prior knowledge students have about the human world.
- WORKSHEET **Chapter Summaries**—Students review the main idea of each lesson of the chapter content.
- WORKSHEET **Reteaching Activity**—These worksheets provide students with an opportunity for remedial practice and review of vital chapter content.
- WORKSHEET **Vocabulary Activity**—Students apply their knowledge of content and academic vocabulary words.

Project-Based Learning 

Hands-On

News Interview

Students will research and produce a news interview that brings together information about how human populations affect human and physical systems through the influences of cultural, demographic, political, economic, and urban elements of a region.

Digital Hands-On

Create Online Projects

Find an additional activity online that incorporates technology for this project. Visit the EdTech Teacher Web sites for more links, tutorials, and other resources.

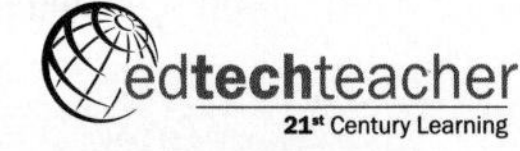

Print Resources

ANCILLARY RESOURCES

This ancillary is available for every chapter and lesson.

- **Chapter Tests and Lesson Quizzes**

PRINTABLE DIGITAL WORKSHEETS

These printable digital worksheets are available for every chapter and lesson.

- **Assessing Background Knowledge**
- **Chapter Summaries**
- **Guided Reading Activities**
- **Hands-On Chapter Projects**
- **Quizzes and Tests**
- **Reading Essentials and Study Guide** AL
- **Reteaching Activities**
- **Video Activities**
- **Vocabulary Activities**

More Media Resources

SUGGESTED VIDEOS 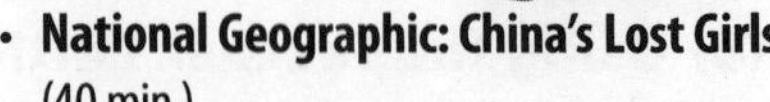

- **National Geographic: China's Lost Girls** (40 min.)
- **The Ultimate Resource: Pennies a Day** (13 min.)
- **The World Atlas WORLD: HUMAN GEOGRAPHY** (45 min.)

SUGGESTED READING 

- ***The World Today: Concepts and Regions in Geography,*** by Harm de Blij, Peter O. Muller, Jan Nijman, and Antoinette M.G.A. WinklerPrins
- ***Economic Geography: Places, Networks, and Flows,*** by Andrew Wood and Susan Roberts
- ***Urban Geography: A Global Perspective,*** by Michael Pacione

GLOBAL CULTURES

Students will know:

- *the elements of culture and how they can shape a particular culture.*
- *how internal and external factors change culture over time.*
- *the process of cultural diffusion.*
- *why culture hearths are important in the study of geography and history.*

Students will be able to:

- ***describe** the elements of culture and how factors change culture over time.*
- ***describe** the process of cultural diffusion.*
- ***analyze** why culture hearths are important.*

UNDERSTANDING BY DESIGN®

☑ Print Teaching Options

V Visual Skills

- ☐ **p. 79** Students discuss regions of the United States. AL Logical/Mathematical
- ☐ **p. 80** Students review the common features of the five culture hearths on the map. Visual/Spatial
- ☐ **p. 81** Students summarize the factors that affect why people migrate. ELL Visual/Spatial

R Reading Skills

- ☐ **p. 78** Students cite text evidence while answering questions about culture. ELL Verbal/Linguistic
- ☐ **p. 79** Students create outlines that map out the main idea and details about social systems that might make up a culture. Logical/Mathematical

C Critical Thinking Skills

- ☐ **p. 80** Students discuss why cities are developing at a greater rate over the past few centuries. AL Verbal/Linguistic
- ☐ **p. 81** Students consider why cultural diffusion occurred at a greater rate over the past few centuries. AL Logical/Mathematical

W Writing Skills

- ☐ **p. 79** Students analyze information about the structure of different governments and the services they provide. BL Verbal/Linguistic

T Technology Skills

- ☐ **p. 81** Students research concrete ways ideas have been spread by means such as email, cell phone apps, and social networking sites. Verbal/Linguistic, Interpersonal

☑ Online Teaching Options

V Visual Skills

- INTERACTIVE MAP **World Language Families**—Students explore the 12 language families and how they may have spread or traveled to other regions. Verbal/Linguistic
- VIDEO **World's Best Ancient Sites–North America**—Students use information from the video and text to create a list of the similarities and differences in cultural features between two Native American tribes. AL Verbal/Linguistic

C Critical Thinking Skills

- INTERACTIVE BELLRINGER **Top Ten Languages**—Students use the chart to discuss the languages spoken in various countries of the world. Visual/Spatial, Verbal/Linguistic
- INTERACTIVE WHITEBOARD ACTIVITY **Elements of Culture**—Students identify elements of culture by dragging and dropping various cultural characteristics.

☑ Printable Digital Worksheets

R Reading Skills

- WORKSHEET **Guided Reading Activity**—Students use Guided Reading Activity worksheets to review their comprehension of the content.

C Critical Thinking Skills

- WORKSHEET **Video Activity**—Students answer questions related to a topic in the chapter content after they have viewed a lesson video.

POPULATION GEOGRAPHY

Students will know:
- *that population growth varies from country to country.*
- *how the demographic transition model is used to trace the population history of a country.*
- *the factors that influence population growth and density.*
- *why world population distribution is uneven.*
- *the causes of population movement.*

Students will be able to:
- ***describe** how population growth varies and how models are used to trace population history.*
- ***identify** factors that influence population growth and density.*
- ***explain** why population distribution is uneven and the causes of population movement.*

UNDERSTANDING BY DESIGN®

☑ Print Teaching Options

V Visual Skills

- ☐ **p. 83** Students work in pairs to summarize what the Demographic Transition Model is showing and why this information is valuable. AL Visual/Spatial, Verbal/Linguistic
- ☐ **p. 84** Students analyze population pyramid graphs. AL Visual/Spatial
- ☐ **p. 85** Students consider where they live to answer a series of questions about population distribution. Logical/Mathematical

R Reading Skills

- ☐ **p. 83** Students discuss reasons why death rates decline more rapidly than birthrates. ELL Verbal/Linguistic
- ☐ **p. 84** Students use context clues to understand the word *host*. ELL Verbal/Linguistic

C Critical Thinking Skills

- ☐ **p. 82** Students work together to create lists of places they can think of that have high and low populations.
- ☐ **p. 82** Students work in pairs to review cause-and-effect relationships between how people live and the decline in death rates. AL Logical/Mathematical
- ☐ **p. 83** Students compare and contrast birthrates in less industrialized countries to birthrates in more technologically developed countries. BL Verbal/Linguistic
- ☐ **p. 86** Students evaluate a statement released by Hillary Rodham Clinton when she was Secretary of State. BL Verbal/Linguistic
- ☐ **p. 86** Students review a primary source quote and answer questions about it. AL Interpersonal, Verbal/Linguistic

W Writing Skills

- ☐ **p. 84** Students write essays supporting a particular view on problems of population growth. BL Verbal/Linguistic

T Technology Skills

- ☐ **p. 85** Students work in groups to research the population density of a state and how it compares to other states, write a summary, and create charts or graphs to support their findings. BL Verbal/Linguistic, Logical/Mathematical

☑ Online Teaching Options

V Visual Skills

- ☐ INTERACTIVE BELLRINGER **Population Density**—Students discuss how to read a population density map and consider how geography impacts where people live. Logical/Mathematical, Visual/Spatial
- ☐ VIDEO **Population**—Students create lists of ways to address rapid population growth in Zambia. Interpersonal

C Critical Thinking Skills

- ☐ INTERACTIVE CHARTS **Population Pyramids**—Students analyze population pyramids for a more developed country and a less developed country. Logical/Mathematical
- ☐ INTERACTIVE MAP **Egypt: Population Density**—Students analyze the population map and consider why certain areas are very densely populated. AL Verbal/Linguistic
- ☐ INTERACTIVE WHITEBOARD ACTIVITY **Population Growth Rate**—Students analyze a table of population growth rates.

☑ Printable Digital Worksheets

R Reading Skills

- ☐ WORKSHEET **Guided Reading Activity**—Students use Guided Reading Activity worksheets to review their comprehension of the content.

C Critical Thinking Skills

- ☐ WORKSHEET **Video Activity**—Students answer questions related to a topic in the chapter content after they have viewed a lesson video.

LESSON 3 PLANNER

POLITICAL GEOGRAPHY

Students will know:
- *the levels and types of government.*
- *how geography and government are connected.*
- *how the world is organized into political units.*
- *how cooperation and conflict affect international relationships.*

Students will be able to:
- ***explain** how different types of government are structured.*
- ***analyze** how humans geography affects government.*
- ***analyze** the effects of cooperation and conflict on international relationships.*

UNDERSTANDING BY DESIGN®

☑ Print Teaching Options

V Visual Skills

- ☐ **p. 89** Students analyze images to describe types of boundaries. Visual/Spatial, Logical/Mathematical

R Reading Skills

- ☐ **p. 87** Students discuss the current governments in England and France. ELL Verbal/Linguistic
- ☐ **p. 87** Students sequence the different forms of government in the United States from the time of independence. AL Logical/Mathematical
- ☐ **p. 88** Students use context clues to define *divine power.* ELL Verbal/Linguistic

C Critical Thinking Skills

- ☐ **p. 87** Students compare the United States government to others around the world.
- ☐ **p. 88** Students compare oligarchies and totalitarian dictatorships. BL Logical/Mathematical
- ☐ **p. 89** Students review how a democracy works. ELL Logical/Mathematical
- ☐ **p. 90** Students discuss how the United States acquired land in the Southwest. AL Logical/Mathematical
- ☐ **p. 91** Students define and answer questions about the terms *terrorism* and *globalization.* ELL Logical/Mathematical

W Writing Skills

- ☐ **p. 90** Students write an essay describing formal, functional, and vernacular cultural regions. Kinesthetic, Verbal/Linguistic
- ☐ **p. 91** Students write a paragraph defending a position about whether a country benefits by joining an international organization. BL Verbal/Linguistic

T Technology Skills

- ☐ **p. 88** Students research a type of government and give a short presentation describing how it works and giving real-world examples. AL Verbal/Linguistic
- ☐ **p. 90** Students research a country formed by a shared spirit of nationalism and prepare a short presentation that analyzes issues related to geographic borders. BL Visual/Spatial, Verbal/Linguistic

☑ Online Teaching Options

V Visual Skills

- ☐ SLIDE SHOW **Types of Boundaries**—Students learn about types of boundaries and then create their own visuals depicting boundaries. Visual/Spatial, Kinesthetic

C Critical Thinking Skills

- ☐ INTERACTIVE BELLRINGER **Types of Government**—Students discuss the different types of governments around the world. AL Verbal/Linguistic, Logical/Mathematical
- ☐ INTERACTIVE WHITEBOARD ACTIVITY **Types and Systems of Governments**—Students match the names of the types and systems of governments with their definitions and create a chart to categorize countries based on type of government. Visual/Spatial
- ☐ VIDEO **Hong Kong: Perfect Blend of East and West**—Students discuss how Hong Kong was governed before and after Chinese rule and write a paragraph explaining how natural boundaries affect culture and lifestyle in Hong Kong. Visual/Spatial, Verbal/Linguistic

☑ Printable Digital Worksheets

R Reading Skills

- ☐ WORKSHEET **Guided Reading Activity**—Students use Guided Reading Activity worksheets to review their comprehension of the content.
- ☐ WORKSHEET **Reading Essentials and Study Guide**—Students complete the study guide and answer Reading Progress Check and vocabulary questions. AL

C Critical Thinking Skills

- ☐ WORKSHEET **Video Activity**—Students answer questions based on the content in the lesson video.

ECONOMIC GEOGRAPHY

Students will know:
- *the characteristics of the three major economic systems.*
- *the four types of economic activities classified by geographers and economists.*
- *how economic activities, including industrialization, help influence a country's level of development.*
- *the components of and reasons for world trade.*

Students will be able to:
- ***identify** characteristics of economic systems and economic activities.*
- ***analyze** how economics affects development.*
- ***explain** how and why world trade exists.*

UNDERSTANDING BY DESIGN®

☑ Print Teaching Options

V Visual Skills
- ☐ **p. 97** Students interpret the table about economic activities and economic development. AL Visual/Spatial, Logical/Mathematical

R Reading Skills
- ☐ **p. 94** Students discuss the author's purpose in repeating the phrase *increasingly interdependent.* Verbal/Linguistic
- ☐ **p. 94** Students paraphrase the text and write a definition of a traditional economy in their own words. ELL Verbal/Linguistic
- ☐ **p. 95** Students practice citing text evidence while answering questions about economies. Verbal/Linguistic
- ☐ **p. 98** Students determine the meaning of *multinational.* ELL Verbal/Linguistic

C Critical Thinking Skills
- ☐ **p. 95** Students contrast a market economy and a command economy. AL Logical/Mathematical
- ☐ **p. 96** Students classify where various countries fall along the economic spectrum between the points of free enterprise and communism. AL Visual/Spatial
- ☐ **p. 96** Students describe primary and secondary economic activities and identify how they are alike and different. BL Logical/Mathematical
- ☐ **p. 98** Students discuss factors that affect world trade. AL Intrapersonal, Logical/Mathematical
- ☐ **p. 99** Students discuss how capital and labor are used to produce goods and services. Verbal/Linguistic

W Writing Skills
- ☐ **p. 96** Students work in small groups to form a theory about which form of economic system is best and write an argument defending their chosen economic system.

T Technology Skills
- ☐ **p. 97** Students research agriculture in a country and prepare a list of factors that affect agricultural activities in that country. Verbal/Linguistic
- ☐ **p. 99** Students research nations with emerging markets and present their findings. BL Verbal/Linguistic

☑ Online Teaching Options

C Critical Thinking Skills
- ☐ INTERACTIVE BELLRINGER **GDP Comparison**—Students use a graph depicting GDP to discuss the economies of eight different countries. BL Logical/Mathematical
- ☐ GAME **Economic Geography**—Students play Tic-Tac-Toe by answering questions that define and describe economic activities and systems. Visual/Spatial
- ☐ TABLE **Economic Activities and Economic Development**—Students discuss the level of economic development in various countries and write a summarizing statement about each of the three levels of economic development. Verbal/Linguistic, Visual/Spatial
- ☐ VIDEO **China and the US Fight to Lead World in Green Energy**—Students discuss how new technology affects both China and the United States in relationship to the video content. BL Verbal/Linguistic
- ☐ INTERACTIVE IMAGE **Oil Trade and Transportation**—Students discuss how oil is a major commodity of trade in world markets. ELL Verbal/Linguistic
- ☐ INTERACTIVE WHITEBOARD ACTIVITY **Types of Economic Activities**—Students categorize a list of business activities to a matching economic activity.

☑ Printable Digital Worksheets

R Reading Skills
- ☐ WORKSHEET **Guided Reading Activity**—Students use Guided Reading Activity worksheets to review their comprehension of the content.
- ☐ WORKSHEET **Reading Essentials and Study Guide**—Students complete the study guide and answer Reading Progress Check and vocabulary questions. AL

C Critical Thinking Skills
- ☐ WORKSHEET **Video Activity**—Students answer critical thinking questions based on the video content.

LESSON **5 PLANNER**

URBAN GEOGRAPHY

Students will know:

- *the functions of cities.*
- *the structure of cities.*
- *the factors involved in the growth of cities.*
- *patterns in the distribution and size of cities.*
- *the problems associated with urban areas.*

Students will be able to:

- ***describe*** *structure and functions of cities.*
- ***analyze*** *how and why cities grow.*
- ***identify*** *issues common in urban areas.*

UNDERSTANDING BY DESIGN®

☑ *Print Teaching Options*

V Visual Skills

- ☐ **p. 106** Students work in small groups to draw a plan for their own city. Visual/Spatial

R Reading Skills

- ☐ **p. 102** Students discuss what they know about how their city or community has changed over time.
- ☐ **p. 102** Students express key points in the section *The Function of Cities.* Logical/Mathematical
- ☐ **p. 104** Students determine the meaning of *depleted* using context clues. ELL Verbal/Linguistic
- ☐ **p. 105** Students discuss the central place theory diagram. AL Visual/Spatial, Verbal/Linguistic

C Critical Thinking Skills

- ☐ **p. 102** Students discuss cause-and-effect relationships related to population movement. AL Verbal/Linguistic
- ☐ **p. 103** Students describe what each urban land use model shows and compare and contrast the models. ELL Visual/Spatial, Verbal/Linguistic
- ☐ **p. 104** Students discuss reasons why various activities are located near to or far from one another. Intrapersonal, Logical/Mathematical
- ☐ **p. 106** Students compare and contrast paths to industrialization in a Venn diagram. BL Visual/Spatial

W Writing Skills

- ☐ **p. 105** Students write an essay to identify where their community fits in to the local urban system. Verbal/Linguistic

T Technology Skills

- ☐ **p. 103** Students design, draw, and describe a new land use model that accurately charts the growth patterns of their community. BL Visual/Spatial
- ☐ **p. 105** Students research economic aspects of a world city online. BL Visual/Spatial

☑ *Online Teaching Options*

V Visual Skills

- ☐ VIDEO **New Urbanists**—Students watch the video and list factors that isolate people and factors that bring people closer together. AL Interpersonal, Verbal/Linguistic
- ☐ INTERACTIVE WHITEBOARD ACTIVITY **Urban Land Use Models**—Students label geographic models and then drag and drop the explanations to the models.

C Critical Thinking Skills

- ☐ INTERACTIVE BELLRINGER **Top Ten Cities in Population**—Students discuss the largest cities of the world. Logical/Mathematical, Visual/Spatial
- ☐ INFOGRAPHIC **Urban Land Use Models**—Students use urban land use models to understand the patterns of human settlement. Verbal/Linguistic
- ☐ INTERACTIVE GRAPH **Population Indicators in 2011**—Students make comparisons and contrasts using data in the graphs. Visual/Spatial, Naturalist

☑ *Printable Digital Worksheets*

R Reading Skills

- ☐ WORKSHEET **Guided Reading Activity**—Students use Guided Reading Activity worksheets to review their comprehension of the content.
- ☐ WORKSHEET **Reading Essentials and Study Guide**—Students complete the study guide and answer Reading Progress Check and vocabulary questions. AL
- ☐ WORKSHEET **Vocabulary Activity**—Students review the chapter content and academic vocabulary words.
- ☐ WORKSHEET **Chapter Summary**—Students review the main ideas of the chapter content.

C Critical Thinking Skills

- ☐ WORKSHEET **Video Activity**—Students answer questions based on a lesson video.
- ☐ WORKSHEET **Reteaching Activity**—Students use this activity worksheet to review and reteach chapter content and vocabulary. This worksheet can be used with struggling students who need additional help with difficult content concepts.

INTERVENTION AND REMEDIATION STRATEGIES

LESSON 1 Global Cultures

Reading and Comprehension

Have students work with a partner to scan the lesson and write sentences using each content vocabulary term to demonstrate its meaning. Then have partners collaborate to create sentences that show their understanding of the two academic vocabulary terms. Challenge students to brainstorm synonyms for the term *diffusion* in addition to the word's meaning as it relates to cultural development.

Text Evidence

Have students review the text to identify examples of how and why cultures can change. Tell students to write at least one example of cultural change in history and in the contemporary world. Ask volunteers to share their examples with the class, and guide a discussion about how cultural contact among different groups can promote change and spread ideas.

LESSON 2 Population Geography

Reading and Comprehension

Have students skim the lesson to look for unfamiliar or confusing words. Tell students to write down what they think the word might mean based on context clues in the text. Then have students look up each word in the dictionary to find its definition. Then have students review the content vocabulary terms and take turns quizzing a partner on each term's definition.

Text Evidence

Have students choose one of the following concepts to define and explain: *the demographic transition model, population distribution,* or *population density.* Students may wish to relate the meaning of the concept using a visual display, such as those shown in the text, or in a written summary. Remind students to explain how geographers use the concept.

LESSON 3 Political Geography

Reading and Comprehension

Have students work in pairs to compare and contrast two or three of the content vocabulary terms. You may wish to assign words to each pair in order to avoid duplication. Have partners write a compare-contrast paragraph in which they use each term and explain how the terms are similar to or different from each other.

Text Evidence

Students may have trouble differentiating between the various forms of government. Have students work in the same pairs to provide an example of each type of government system. Have partners summarize how each form of government works. Encourage students to use academic vocabulary terms in their summaries.

LESSON 4 Economic Geography

Reading and Comprehension

Have students work in pairs to identify cause-and-effect relationships as they read. Have partners choose a concept to illustrate, such as the impact of industrialization on economic development. Have pairs create a diagram or flowchart that illustrates the cause-and-effect relationship of their chosen concept. Have student pairs share their diagrams or charts with the class.

Text Evidence

Organize students into six groups and assign one of the first six content vocabulary terms to each group. Have each group create and complete a two-column chart with the headings *Main Idea* and *Supporting Details.* Tell students to review the text to identify the central idea about their term and supporting details, writing the information into the correct column.

LESSON 5 Urban Geography

Reading and Comprehension

Assign one of the content vocabulary terms to each of five groups. Have students collaborate to create a visual that relates the meaning of their assigned term. Encourage students to get creative in their efforts to convey the term's meaning. For example, students might form a line in which they each hold hands one at a time to demonstrate the term *connectivity.*

Text Evidence

Have students work in small groups to research urbanization patterns in different parts of the world. Tell students to present an analysis of their findings, including charts or graphs to show the impact of the change. After groups have presented their reports, discuss some of the causes and effects of urbanization patterns.

Online Resources

Leveled Reader

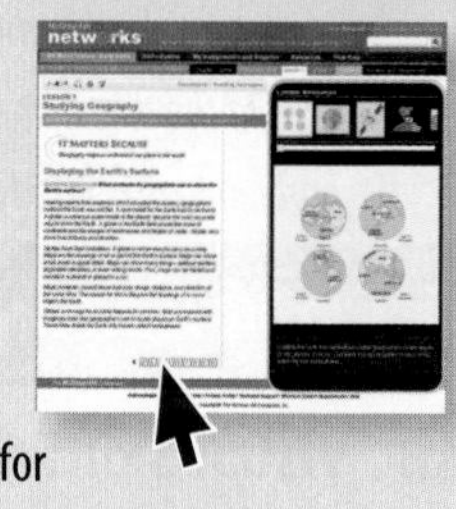

Use this online approaching-level text that corresponds directly to the text in the Student Edition. It also includes additional reading and comprehension support for English Language Learners.

Guided Reading Activities

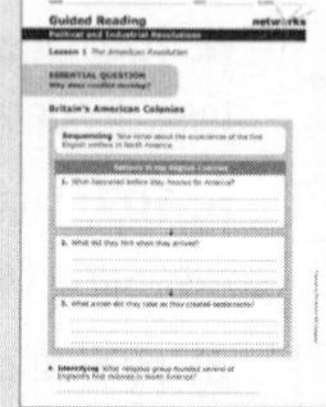

This resource uses guiding questions to help students with comprehension.

Reteaching Activities

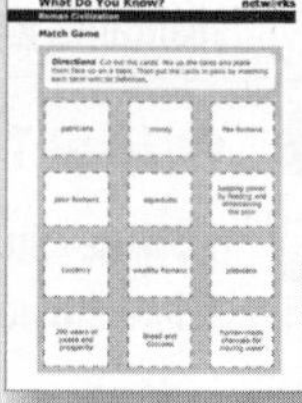

These worksheets provide students with an opportunity for remedial practice and review of vital chapter content.

Reading Essentials and Study Guide

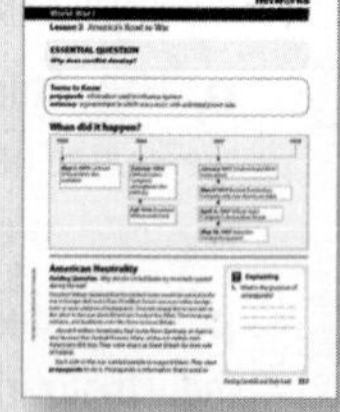

This resource offers writing and reading activities for the approaching-level student.

Self-Check Quizzes

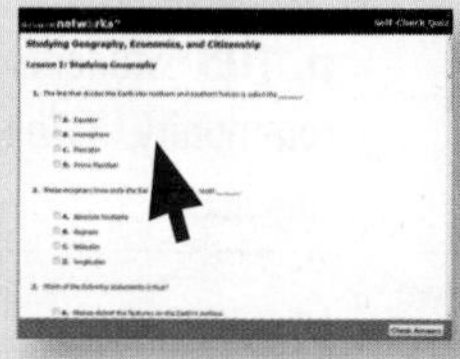

This online assessment tool provides instant feedback for students to check their progress.

Chapter Summaries

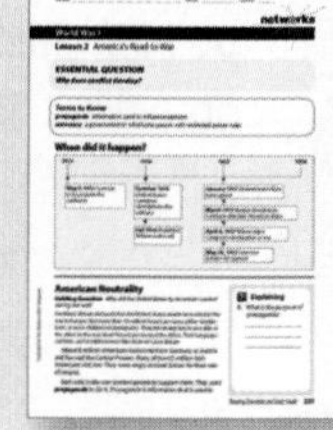

Summaries are provided for each chapter that thoroughly condense core content into manageable chunks.

The Human World

ESSENTIAL QUESTION • *How do the characteristics and distribution of human populations affect human and physical systems?*

networks

There's More Online about the human world.

CHAPTER 4

Geography Matters...

Have you ever traveled far from home and had new experiences of sight, sound, and taste? Examining these varieties in the human experience is the work of the human geographer. Human geographers study relationships between humans and their natural environment and analyze geographic patterns. They look at present-day events with an eye for trends, knowing that human actions and decisions can have major impacts on people near and far.

◀ A woman works on a tea plantation in Kerala, India.

75

Letter from the Author

Dear Geography Teacher,

We are inching up on 7.5 billion people on planet Earth. Projections tell us to be prepared for 9 billion by the year 2050. This rather astounding population growth has been uneven over time and very uneven from one geographical region to another. Clarity in these matters can begin when your students master the concept of demographic transition. To help students understand why population has grown so rapidly and to allow them to see that population growth is very uneven, have them use the Internet and go to the Population Reference Bureau's website. The PRB publishes a world population data sheet and a raft of articles explaining birthrates, death rates, and doubling time for virtually every country.

Richard G. Boehm

ENGAGE

Activating Prior Knowledge Explain to students that they will be exploring the relationship between the people that live in a place and the geographical features of this place, particularly how one affects the other. Have students work in pairs to identify some potential ways that the environment of a place might affect the way of life for the people that live there. *(Student answers may vary, but could mention farmland that can grow different kinds of crops, physical features that could protect a settlement from enemies, or rivers and lakes that could provide people with a source of freshwater and a way to transport goods.)*

TEACH & ASSESS

Making Connections

Explain to students that geographers examine where people live, why they settle there, and how they use natural resources. Hudson Bay, the first European settlement in Canada, is an example of how people adapt to their natural surroundings. The climate was described by early settlers as nine months of ice followed by three months of mosquitoes. Hudson Bay is rich in wildlife and has continued to sustain a trading and fur industry for hundreds of years.

Drawing Inferences Have students examine the photograph and read the caption. **Ask:** **How does the work that this woman does relate to where she lives?** *(Possible answer: She works the land where she lives to grow tea. The climate and type of soil found in her area must be good for growing this type of crop.)* **How might this tea plantation help the woman and her community meet their needs?** *(Possible answers: The community might grow tea to meet their own need for food or drink to live. They might also sell the tea to meet other needs.)*

CLOSE & REFLECT

Identifying Have students think about the relationship between the geography of their community and the people living there. Have students identify key aspects that they could use to compare life in their community with the lives of people in other communities, such as types of jobs available, the size of the population, and what kinds of natural resources are found there.

ENGAGE

C1 Critical Thinking Skills

Analyzing Explain that the world map of the Human Development Index depicts each country's level of development by examining the health, education, and living standards of the population. Have students work with a partner to discuss the benefits of this map. *(Possible answers: The map makes it easier to see how developed different areas of the world are when compared to each other. Researchers can identify areas of the world that are most developed and easily see if there are any physical features located in these regions that might explain why some places are more developed than others.)*

TEACH & ASSESS

R Reading Skills

Reading Maps Have students focus on the map key showing the Human Development Index. **Ask:** According to the map, what color indicates that a region has a high HDI? *(red)* Low HDI? *(yellow)* What are some of the most developed countries on this map? *(Possible answers: the United States, Canada, Australia, Japan, Norway)* Which is more developed, Mexico or India? *(Mexico is more developed.)* Continue asking questions to gauge students' understanding. AL Visual/Spatial

C2 Critical Thinking Skills

Comparing and Contrasting Discuss whether all of the countries in the world are measured by the human development index. Point out that there is no data submitted for a few of the countries. Working with a partner, have students use the map to compare and contrast the level of development and the standard of living of various pairs of countries by creating a chart that lists the pairings. Also have partners use the HDI to determine newly industrialized and less developed countries and to add this information to their charts. BL Visual/Spatial

Content Background Knowledge

Human Development Index The Human Development Index (HDI) includes a country only if it has reliable data on all three dimensions of development. In some cases, the HDI includes countries if the compilers of the report were able to make a good estimate about a missing component. Sometimes researchers examine the data from the HDI for a country by disaggregating it, or breaking it into parts. By treating groups inside a country or region as if they were their own countries, researchers can study inequalities between people of different income levels, genders, ethnicity, or regions. Identifying such inequalities can give policy makers the information needed to encourage better human development by channeling resources to the areas that need them most.

Why Geography Matters: **The Human World**

the human development index

The relative social and economic status of countries is often described in the media and among academics as either "less developed," "newly industrialized," or "more developed." What precisely is meant by the term development*? And how is development measured?*

Human Development

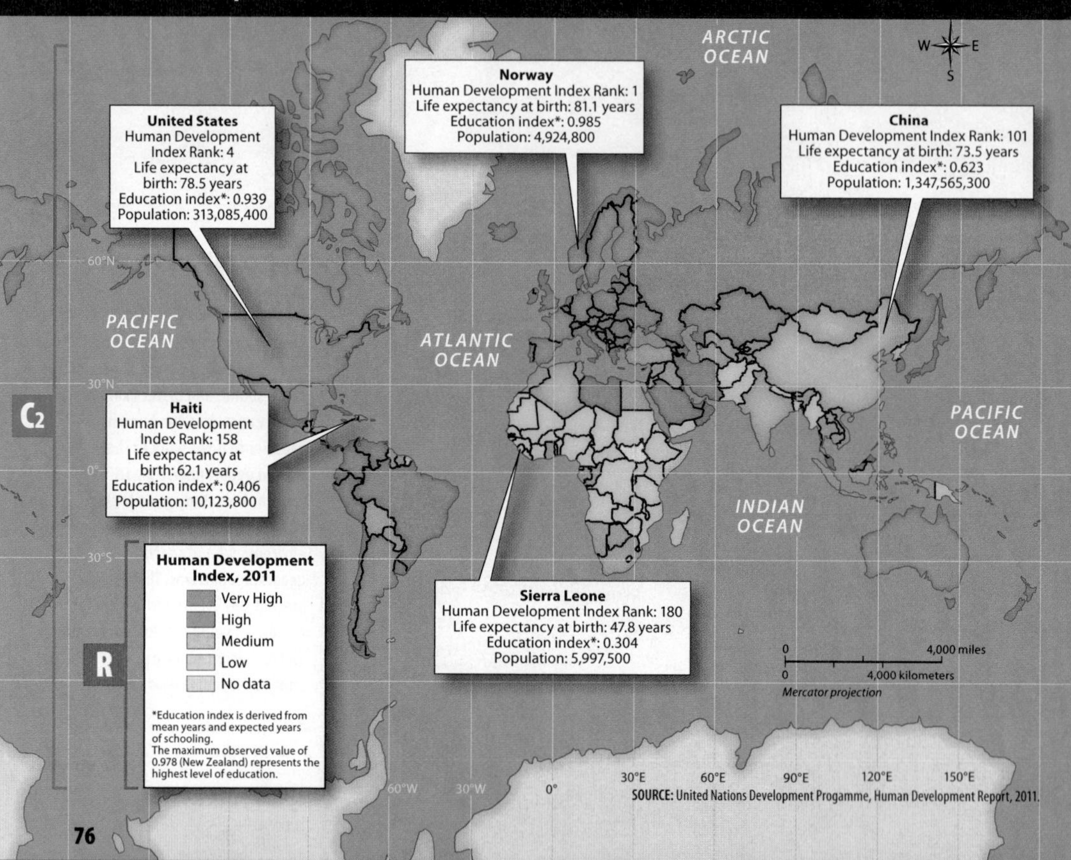

Project-Based Learning

Hands-On

News Interview

Working in small groups, students will research and produce a news interview that brings together information about how human populations affect human and physical systems through the influences of cultural, demographic, political, economic, and urban elements of a region. Each group will present its news interview in front of the class. Afterwards, students will discuss the information in the news interviews in a whole-class discussion.

ePals GlobalCommunity
Where learners connect™

Digital Hands-On

Create Online Projects

Find an additional activity online that incorporates technology for this project. Visit the EdTech Teacher Web sites for more links, tutorials, and other resources.

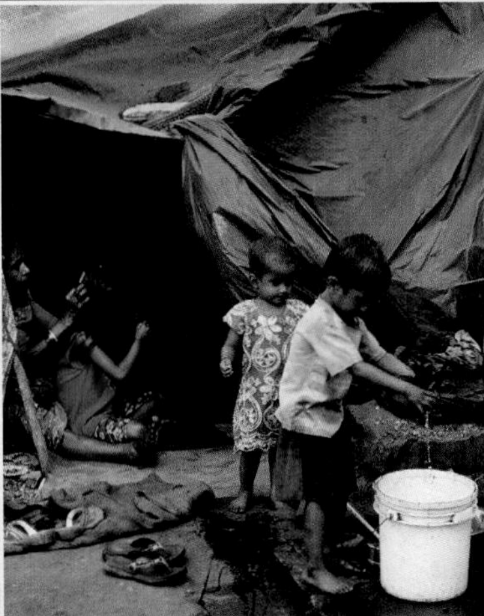

What is development?

Although different societies and cultures have their own perspectives and values that shape the types of human development that occur, most agree that development includes technological progress that leads to a better standard of living for people. The modern notion of development as a means of improving people's lives gained favor during the Industrial Revolution. Advances in science and technology led to increased agricultural and industrial production, which in turn provided a greater food supply and more manufactured products that people needed. Such new inventions and products led to easing some people's workloads, providing comfort and convenience, and allowing many to begin acquiring wealth. Broadly speaking, development is improvement in people's living situations and economic prospects.

1. **Human Systems** Why is human development an important topic? Define the term *human development* and describe the role of technology as a component of it.

Why do we measure development?

Governments rely on measures of development when making important policy decisions and addressing the specific needs of both their own citizens and those of other countries. For example, local governments use measures of development as a way to bring the needs of people to the attention of the central government in the hopes of having funds and resources allocated appropriately. Geographers and other social scientists are also interested in measures of development because they study the spatial patterns of human need and well-being, looking for cause-and-effect relationships. Identifying these types of relationships helps governments, aid agencies, and others make changes to improve the economic, social, or environmental conditions in which people live. Although there are many ways to measure development, many governments today use the Human Development Index (HDI), a statistic used to rank countries by their level of human development. The index, devised by Pakistani economist Magbub-ul-Haq in 1990, was designed to include measurements of improvement in people's well-being, rather than focusing solely on national economic indicators.

2. **Places and Regions** How is measuring development useful? Explain how measures of development are used.

How does the Human Development Index (HDI) measure development?

The HDI ranks countries' level of human development by measuring three dimensions of development: health, education, and living standards. The measure of health is determined by life expectancy at birth. Access to education is measured by examining mean, or average, years of schooling and expected years of schooling. Living standards are measured by gross national income per capita. The Human Development Index uses the data from these three dimensions of development to calculate one composite statistic for each country. The HDI is published annually by the United Nations Development Programme, and it is used to measure how economic policy decisions affect people's quality of life.

3. **The Uses of Geography** Why do you think the HDI incorporates more than one dimension of development? What do these dimensions indicate about the level of development in a country? Provide examples to support your answer.

THERE'S MORE ONLINE 

VIEW a graph of changes in HDI ranking over time • *COMPARE* population indicators of several countries

V Visual Skills

Identifying Cause and Effect Have students describe and explain the cause-and-effect relationship between technological progress and the way people live their daily lives. Draw students' attention to the city in the photograph and have them identify a few examples of how technology might be used to improve the lives of people living in a large city, such as constructing highways for easier transportation of people and goods. **ELL Visual/Spatial**

W Writing Skills

Informative/Explanatory Have students write a paragraph that explains how governments might make policy decisions and choose to spend money differently if they measured levels of development based on economic indicators instead of on people's well-being. **Intrapersonal, Verbal/Linguistic**

CLOSE & REFLECT

Expressing Have students review how and why human development is measured. Then have them write a paragraph outline, including a topic sentence that expresses how life can be improved by having scientists study the development level of different countries. Students should create a chart that shows how development changes over time. They should list at least three specific details from the lesson to support their view.

GRAPHS

Population Indicators and Change in HDI Rank

Identifying Trends Display both the Population Indicators map and the Change in HDI Rank graph for students. Have students work in small groups to analyze and discuss the information on both assets. Each group should write a brief summary that identifies the trends in population shown on the projected 2050 map and explain how this may change a country's HDI rank. Ask each group to present its summary to the class. **AL Visual/Spatial, Logical/Mathematical**

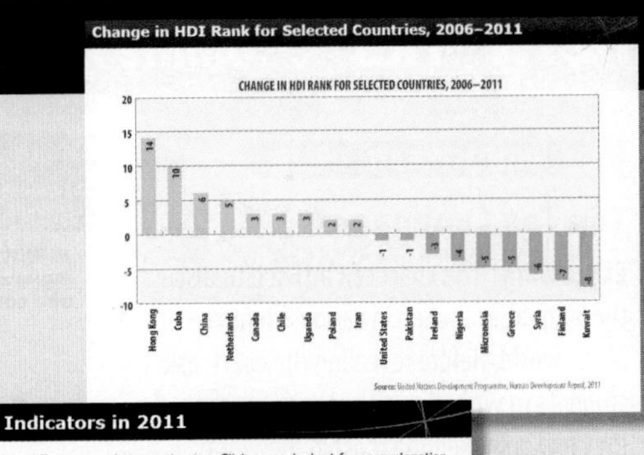

Population Indicators in 2011

This chart shows four different population estimates. Click on each chart for an explanation.

This chart shows the 2011 birthrates in these seven countries. The number for each country is the number of babies born per 1000 people. Why might some countries have a much higher birthrate?

ANSWERS, p. 77

Why Geography Matters

1. Human development, the improvement in living situations and economic prospects, is important because it relates to stability and contentment for humans. Development includes technological progress that leads to a better standard of living by providing a greater food supply and manufactured products that ease workloads, provide convenience, and allow many to acquire wealth.
2. Governments rely on measures of development such as the HDI when making policy decisions and addressing the needs of their citizens.
3. The HDI ranks countries by measuring three dimensions of development: health is determined by life expectancy at birth; education by examining average and expected years of schooling; and living standards by gross national income per capita.

ENGAGE

V Visual Skills

Creating Visuals Before students begin the lesson, have small groups work together to create web diagrams that record information about the culture of their community and/or state. Provide groups with a variety of elements to list in the ovals attached to the center *Culture* oval of their graphic organizer, such as Language, Religion, Government, and Art. Then have students identify, in ovals branching off from each of these elements, details about their local culture such as what languages are commonly spoken, what religions are most popular, what type of government is used, and what are some well-known local art forms. Invite groups to present their completed webs to the class.

TEACH & ASSESS

R Reading Skills

Citing Text Evidence Remind students that their answers to a question will be stronger if they include specific details from the text that supports their ideas. Have them practice this skill with the following questions. **Ask:** **What are some differences you might find within the language used in a culture?** *(People might speak using a dialect, pronounce the same words differently, or assign different meanings to the same words.)* **What is a linguist?** *(a scientist who studies languages)* **What are some effects religions have had on cultures around the world?** *(Religions shape people's identities, affect how people behave, lead to the development of special holidays and traditions, and inspire works of art.)* ELL **Verbal/Linguistic**

ANSWERS, p. 78

TAKING NOTES: Elements of Culture—Language is a key element in a culture's development. Religious beliefs vary significantly around the world. For many people, religion provides an important sense of identity. A social system develops to help the members of a culture work together to meet basic needs. In all cultures, the family forms an important group. Governments of the world share certain features, such as maintaining order within the country, providing protection from outside dangers, and supplying other services to the people; **Cultural Change**—Internal factors, such as new ideas, lifestyles, and inventions, create change within cultures. Change can also come through spatial interaction such as trade, migration, and war. Computers now make it possible to store huge amounts of information and instantly send it all over the world, thus allowing more rapid spread of ideas and traditions among the cultures of the world.

networks

There's More Online!

- **CHART** Cultural Universals
- **MAP** World Language Families
- **MAP** World Culture Hearths
- **INTERACTIVE SELF-CHECK QUIZ**
- **VIDEO** Global Cultures

LESSON 1
Global Cultures

ESSENTIAL QUESTION • *How do the characteristics and distribution of human populations affect human and physical systems?*

Reading HELPDESK CCSS

Academic Vocabulary (Tier Two Words)
- **similar**
- **major**

Content Vocabulary (Tier Three Words)
- **culture**
- **language family**
- **ethnic group**
- **culture region**
- **cultural diffusion**
- **culture hearth**

TAKING NOTES: ***Key Ideas and Details***

IDENTIFYING Use a graphic organizer like the one below to take notes as you read about global cultures in this lesson.

Elements of Culture	Cultural Change

It Matters Because

V *The world's people organize communities, develop ways of life, and adjust to the differences and similarities they experience. As the world becomes increasingly interconnected, cultures spread and are shared. To help understand this cultural diversity, geographers divide the Earth into culture regions, which are defined by the presence of common cultural elements such as language and religion.*

Elements of Culture

GUIDING QUESTION *What are the elements of culture?*

Geographers study **culture**, the way of life of a group of people who share **similar** ways of thinking, believing, and living, expressed in common elements or features. For example, a particular culture can be understood by looking at language, religion, daily life, history, art, government, technology, and economy.

R Language is a key element in a culture's development. Through language, people communicate information and experiences and pass on cultural values and traditions. Even within a culture, however, there are language differences. Some people may speak a dialect, or a local form of a language, that differs from the main language. These differences may include variations in the pronunciation and meaning of words.

Linguists, scientists who study languages, organize the world's languages into **language families**—large groups of languages having similar roots. Seemingly diverse languages may belong to the same language family. For example, English, Spanish, and Russian are all members of the Indo-European language family.

Religion is another important element of a culture. Religious beliefs vary significantly around the world. For many people, religion provides an important sense of identity. It also influences many aspects of daily life, from the practice of moral values to the celebration of holidays and festivals. Throughout history, religious symbols and stories have shaped cultural expressions such as literature, painting and sculpture, architecture, and music.

SuperStock/age fotostock

78

networks *Online Teaching Options*

INTERACTIVE BELLRINGER

Top Ten Languages

Expressing This chart can be used to discuss the languages spoken in various countries of the world. Before revealing the chart, ask students to write down the language that they feel is spoken the most in the world. Reveal the chart and allow students to analyze it to see if they guessed correctly. Have students use the chart to answer the questions and write their paragraphs. Then have students exchange their paragraphs with a partner to review and discuss. **Visual/Spatial, Verbal/Linguistic**

Top Ten Languages

Language is a key element in a culture's development. Understanding one another through language is key to people binding together in a culture.

1. Why do you think some of these languages are spoken in so many different parts of the world, while others are spoken in just one country?

Language	Speakers (in millions)	Main Areas Where Spoken
English	1,000	British Isles, Anglo-America, Australia, New Zealand, south Africa, former British colonies in tropical Africa, Philippines
Mandarin	1,000	China, Taiwan, Singapore
Hindi	900	Northern India
Spanish	450	Spain, Latin America, southwestern United States
Russian	320	Russia, Kazakhstan, parts of Ukraine and other former Soviet republics
Bengali	250	Bangladesh, eastern India
Arabic	250	Southwest Asia, North Africa
Portuguese	200	Portugal, Brazil, southern Africa
Malaysian	200	Brunei, Indonesia, Malaysia, Singapore, Philippines
Japanese	130	Japan

click for answer

Auto-Run Click Through Previous 1 of 2 Next

A social system develops to help the members of a culture work together to meet basic needs. In all cultures, the family forms an important group. Most cultures are also made up of social classes, groups of people ranked according to ancestry, wealth, education, or other criteria. Moreover, cultures may include people who belong to different ethnic groups. An **ethnic group** is made up of people who share a common language, history, or place of origin.

Geographers also analyze governments to help understand a culture. Governments of the world share certain features, such as maintaining order within the country, providing protection from outside dangers, and supplying other services to the people. Governments can be categorized by levels of power—national, regional, and local—and by type of authority—a single ruler, a small group of leaders, or a body of citizens and their representatives.

Economic activities also influence and shape a culture. People must make a living, whether in farming, industry, or by providing services. Geographers study how a culture utilizes its natural resources to meet such needs as food and shelter. They also analyze the ways in which people produce, obtain, use, and sell goods and services.

To organize their understanding of cultural development, geographers divide the Earth into culture regions. Each **culture region** includes areas that have certain traits in common. They may share similar economic systems, forms of government, or social groups. Their histories, religions, and art forms may share similar influences.

READING PROGRESS CHECK

Explaining Why are social groups important to the development of a culture?

culture way of life of a group of people who share similar culture traits, including beliefs, customs, technology, and material items

similar comparable

language family group of related languages that have all developed from one earlier language

ethnic group group of people who share common ancestry, language, religion, customs, or place of origin

GEOGRAPHY CONNECTION

Most languages spoken throughout the world belong to one of 12 language families. Languages within a family have a common origin.

1. ***PLACES AND REGIONS*** Where are the Dravidian languages spoken?
2. ***HUMAN SYSTEMS*** Do people within the same language family necessarily speak the same language? Explain your response.

World Language Families

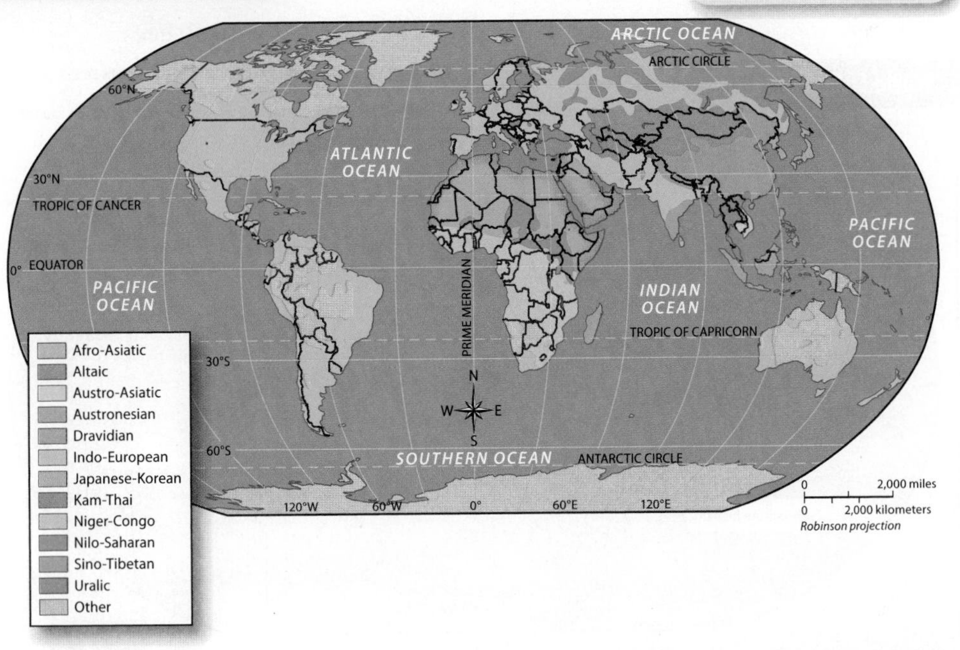

Global Cultures

R Reading Skills

Outlining Have students work in pairs to create outlines that map out the main idea and details that the author presents about the social systems that might make up a culture. Encourage pairs to share their completed outlines with another pair and compare their understanding of the material. **Logical/Mathematical**

W Writing Skills

Argument Governments of the world share certain features because people's needs are similar, regardless of their place of origin. Have students consider this statement while analyzing the information provided in the text about the structure of different governments and the services they provide. Then have students use facts and details to write an argument that agrees or disagrees with this statement. Remind students to state their point of view clearly and address any counter-arguments. Point out additional text or online sources students might use to gather more support for their views. Then pair students who have argued opposing views and have them hold a short debate with each other. **BL** **Verbal/Linguistic**

V Visual Skills

Making Connections Explain that the boundaries of the cultural regions of the United States are not set in stone or even agreed upon universally and that a common way to group the states of our country is into the West, the Midwest, the Northeast, the Southeast, and the Southwest. Have students study a regional map of the United States. **Ask:** **In which region is our state found?** *(Student answers should identify the cultural region.)* **What are some cultural similarities between our state and the neighboring states in our region? Do you agree that we belong in the same cultural region?** *(Student answers may vary, but should cite specific examples of similarities including economic resources, geographic features, or other cultural elements, and use facts or details to support their opinions.)* **AL** **Logical/Mathematical**

INTERACTIVE MAP

World Language Families

Discussing This world map shows the 12 language families and provides examples of languages found in each family. Review with students how languages within a family have a common origin. Click each language in the legend to activate the pop-up box that shows the other languages in that language family. Then invite a volunteer to explain how the language families may have spread or traveled to another region or continent. Continue this activity until all of the languages have been discussed. **Verbal/Linguistic**

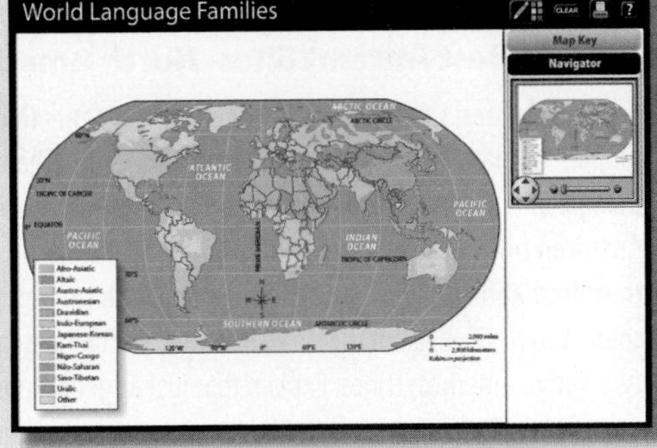

ANSWERS, p. 79

READING PROGRESS CHECK They share similar traits and characteristics, and they interact to give a culture meaning.

GEOGRAPHY CONNECTION

1. The Dravidian languages are mainly spoken in southeastern India.
2. No, they do not necessarily speak the same language. Some people within the same region or culture may speak another dialect of a language that differs from the main language.

Global Cultures

Content Background Knowledge

The Nile River The presence of a river helps a culture hearth by supplying a community with freshwater for irrigating crops. The Nile River provides Egypt with water for irrigation and other uses. For example, the Nile River serves as a protective barrier on one side of Egypt (while the Sahara Desert made it hard for enemies to attack from the other side). The Egyptians also use the Nile River for transportation of people and goods.

C Critical Thinking Skills

Determining Cause and Effect Have students think about why cities are developing at a greater rate over the past few centuries. **Ask: What effect did the ability to produce a surplus of crops have on cultures?** *(Once people could trade or sell extra food, they were left with profits they could use to build cities. The rise in trade created a necessity for new writing systems to record information and for the establishment of government to organize what crops were grown and defend the newly established cities.)* **AL Verbal/Linguistic**

V Visual Skills

Integrating Visual Information Have students locate each culture hearth on the map. Then have students study the map key and review the information from the text about the common features of these five culture hearths. **Ask: What features do these culture hearths have in common?** *(Possible answer: They are all located along a similar line of latitude and share similar climates and temperatures. These culture hearths are also located near bodies of water.)* **Visual/Spatial**

ANSWERS, p. 80

GEOGRAPHY CONNECTION

1. The first major settlements in Asia were located in Huang He Valley, Indus Valley, and Mesopotamia.
2. They are located near rivers.

culture region division of the Earth in which people share a similar way of life, including language, religion, economic systems, and values

cultural diffusion the spread of culture traits, material and non-material, from one culture to another

major greater in importance or interest

culture hearth a center where cultures developed and from which ideas and traditions spread outward

Cultural Change

GUIDING QUESTION *What are two major ways in which cultures change over time?*

Cultures are dynamic and continually changing. Internal factors—new ideas, lifestyles, and inventions—create change within cultures. Change can also come through spatial interaction such as trade, migration, and war. The spread of new knowledge from one culture to another is called **cultural diffusion**. Cultural diffusion has been a **major** factor in cultural development since the dawn of human history, and the pace of cultural change has accelerated in contemporary times. The earliest humans were small groups of hunters and gatherers, who moved from place to place in search of animals to hunt, plants to gather, water, and useful materials. As they migrated, they helped spread culture traits from one group and place to another.

Cultural Change in History

The world's first civilizations arose in **culture hearths**—early centers of civilization whose ideas and practices spread to surrounding areas. The map shows that some of the most influential culture hearths developed in areas that make up the modern countries of Egypt, Iraq, Pakistan, China, and Mexico.

C These five culture hearths had certain geographic features in common. They all emerged from farming settlements in areas with a mild climate and fertile land. In addition, all five culture hearths were located near a major river or source of water. Making use of favorable environments, the people dug canals and ditches to irrigate the land. All of these factors contributed to what is known as the agricultural revolution, a major shift from food gathering to food production that enabled people to grow surplus crops.

Surplus food set the stage for the rise of cities and civilizations and the development of long-distance trade. The increased wealth from trade led to the rise of cities and complex social systems. These new cities needed a well-organized

GEOGRAPHY CONNECTION

Culture hearths are centers where the world's first civilizations arose.

1. ***PLACES AND REGIONS*** Where in Asia were the first major settlements located?
2. ***HUMAN SYSTEMS*** What water feature do most of the culture hearths have in common?

V **World Culture Hearths**

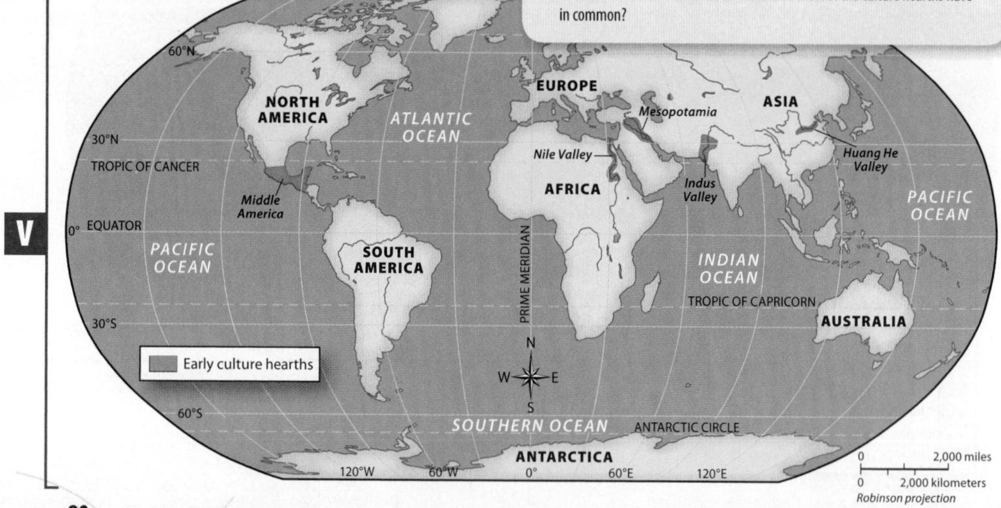

networks Online Teaching Options

VIDEO

World's Best Ancient Sites–North America

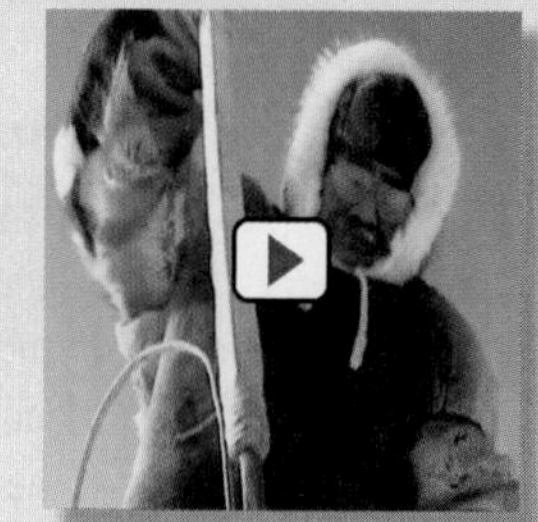

Comparing and Contrasting Review with students that many years ago the first migrant humans crossed the Bering land bridge, and that they traveled more or less as a single unit and culture to North America. Today there are about five hundred Native American tribes scattered across North America. Working in pairs, have students use the information provided in the video along with content from the library or online sources to create a list of the similarities and differences in cultural features between two Native American tribes. Explain that just as geographers study culture, students should also consider the cultural features of language, religion, daily life, history, art, or government to write their lists. **AL Verbal/Linguistic**

government to coordinate harvests, plan building projects, and manage an army for defense. Officials and merchants created writing systems to record and transmit government and trade information.

Cultural diffusion has increased rapidly during the last 250 years. In the 1700s and 1800s, some countries began to industrialize, using power-driven machines and factories to mass-produce goods. This period is known as the Industrial Revolution. With new production methods, these countries produced goods quickly and cheaply, and their economies changed dramatically. These developments also led to social changes. As people left farms for jobs in factories and mills, cities grew larger.

Contact between different cultures usually leads to change in both systems.

▲ **CRITICAL THINKING**

1. ***Describing*** In what way is this picture an example of cultural contact?
2. ***Speculating*** What types of ideas and practices might be exchanged due to this example of cultural contact?

Cultural Change in the Contemporary World

At the end of the twentieth century, the world experienced a new turning point—the information revolution. Computers now make it possible to store huge amounts of information and instantly send it all over the world, thus allowing more rapid spread of ideas and traditions among the cultures of the world. The Internet has been responsible for communication and socialization around the world via social networking sites and other sites that allow users to share many types of information and stay connected with others. Consequently, the world feels much smaller than it might have previously.

Cultural contact among different peoples promotes cultural change as ideas and practices spread. Computer technology certainly accelerates the spread of cultural change, but other connections among people do as well. Trade and travel are important avenues by which cultural change occurs. Migration has also fostered cultural diffusion. People migrate for many reasons. Positive factors—better social and economic conditions and religious or political freedoms—may draw people from one place to another. Most people move from one place to another in search of better economic opportunity. Negative factors—wars, persecution, and famines—also motivate people to migrate. In some instances, as in the case of enslaved Africans brought to the Americas, mass migrations have been forced. Regardless of the reasons, migrants carry their cultures with them, and their ideas and practices often blend with those of the people already living in the migrants' adopted countries.

☑ **READING PROGRESS CHECK**

Identifying Where were the five earliest culture hearths located?

LESSON 1 REVIEW 

Reviewing Vocabulary (Tier Three Words)

1. ***Explaining*** Explain the relationships between culture, ethnic group, culture region, cultural diffusion, and culture hearth. RH.9–10.4

Using Your Notes

2. ***Describing*** Use your graphic organizer to describe the external factors that change cultures.

Answering the Guiding Questions

3. ***Identifying*** What are the elements of culture?
4. ***Drawing Conclusions*** What are two major ways in which cultures change over time?

Writing Activity

5. ***Explanatory*** Research to find three different definitions of culture. Write a paragraph comparing the definitions. WHST.9–10.9

C Critical Thinking Skills

Determining Cause and Effect Have students consider why cultural diffusion occurred at a greater rate over the past few centuries. **Ask:** What caused cultural diffusion to occur more rapidly over the last 250 years? *(Possible answer: New technologies allowed people to produce goods to trade more quickly. Industry and new factories created more jobs in the city, which encouraged people to move from rural areas to urban ones.)* **AL** Logical/Mathematical

T Technology Skills

Researching on the Internet Have students consider how computers and the Internet have made it easier to spread information and ideas around the world. Organize students into groups and assign each group a different way new computer technologies spread information, such as through email, cell phone apps, or various social networking sites. Then have groups conduct online research to find facts and examples of concrete ways ideas have been spread by each of these means. Tell groups to share their findings with the class by preparing a short multimedia presentation. Verbal/Linguistic, Interpersonal

V Visual Skills

Creating Visuals After students read the text about the positive and negative factors pertaining to the reasons why people migrate, ask volunteers to summarize these factors. Then have students work in pairs to relate the information visually by creating a Venn diagram or two-column chart. Have pairs present their completed graphic organizers to the class. **ELL** Visual/Spatial

CLOSE & REFLECT

Summarizing Tell students to review what they have learned about the way cultures change and spread. Have individual students pick one aspect of culture and use specific examples from this lesson to describe ways this element might spread and affect people's ways of life.

LESSON 1 REVIEW ANSWERS

Reviewing Vocabulary

1. All terms relate to relationships among people. A culture is the way of life of a group of people who share similar culture traits, including beliefs, customs, technology, and material items. An ethnic group is a group of people who share common ancestry, language, religion, customs, or place of origin. A culture region includes areas that have certain traits in common. They may share similar economic systems, forms of government, or social groups, and their histories, religions, and art forms may share similar influences. Cultural diffusion is the spread of culture traits, material and non-material, from one culture to another. A culture hearth is a center where cultures developed and from which ideas and traditions spread outward.

Using Your Notes

2. External factors that change cultures are those such as trade, migration, and war, which create change based on spatial interaction.

Answering the Guiding Questions

3. Elements of culture include language, religion, social system, government, and economic activities.
4. Internal factors and spatial interaction are two major ways cultures change over time.

Writing Activity

5. Definitions and paragraphs may vary, but should provide three different definitions of *culture* compared in a compelling way.

ANSWERS, p. 81

☑ **READING PROGRESS CHECK** They were located in areas that now make up the countries of Egypt, Iraq, Pakistan, China, and Mexico.

CRITICAL THINKING

1. Ideas are being spread, possibly globally, through use of computers and the Internet.
2. People might be exchanging ideas regarding culture, cooking, or ways to build or cultivate crops.

Population Geography

ENGAGE

C1 Critical Thinking Skills

Activating Prior Knowledge Have small groups work together to create lists of places they can think of that have high and low populations. Have groups speculate what might cause these places to have as many or as few people living there as they do. Then read the *Essential Question* aloud and discuss reasons why the population of an area might rise or decline. **Ask:** How might the physical features of a place affect its population? *(Student answers may vary, but should include relevant details about the ways the physical features of a place can help people meet their needs or make a place too difficult to settle.)* How might economic factors affect the population of a place? *(Possible answer: People might move from one area to another to find better work or because they are transferred from one job to another.)* Tell students they will learn more about populations and how they grow or fall in this lesson.

TEACH & ASSESS

C2 Critical Thinking Skills

Analyzing Cause and Effect Have students work in pairs to review cause-and-effect relationships between how people live and the decline in death rates. **Ask:** How does the demographic transition model trace the population history of a country? *(The model uses birthrates and death rates to show how populations can change over time.)* What are some factors that can cause the death rate of a country to fall? *(Possible answer: an improved food supply, better health care and living conditions, more access to medicine and technology)* Why would these factors help people to live longer, causing death rates to decline? *(Possible answer: If people have good nutrition and have access to medicine and doctors to keep from getting sick, they will stay healthy longer.)*

AL Logical/Mathematical

ANSWERS, p. 82

TAKING NOTES: Demographic Transition Model—A demographic transition model uses birthrates and death rates to show how populations in countries or regions change over time. They include statistics gathered by scientists; **Challenges of Growth**—Rapid population growth presents many challenges that affect individual countries and the global community. As the number of people increases, so does the difficulty of producing enough food to feed them. Populations that grow rapidly use resources more quickly.

networks *There's More Online!*

- DIAGRAM Demographic Transition Model
- GRAPH Projected Populations
- INTERACTIVE SELF-CHECK QUIZ
- VIDEO Population Geography

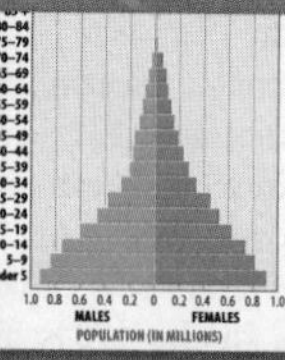

LESSON 2

Population Geography

Reading HELPDESK 

Academic Vocabulary (Tier Two Words)

- community
- trend

Content Vocabulary (Tier Three Words)

- birthrate
- death rate
- natural increase
- migration
- demographic transition
- doubling time
- population pyramid
- population distribution
- population density

TAKING NOTES: ***Key Ideas and Details***

DESCRIBING As you read, use a graphic organizer like the one below to take notes on the demographic transition model and challenges of growth.

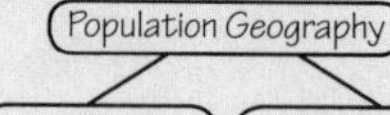
Population Geography
The Demographic Transition Model
Challenges of Growth

C1 **ESSENTIAL QUESTION** • *How do the characteristics and distribution of human populations affect human and physical systems?*

IT MATTERS BECAUSE

Earth's human population increased dramatically during the nineteenth century and much of the twentieth century. Although that growth has begun to slow in recent decades, there are far more people on Earth today than ever before. The result is that issues of population growth or decline are crucial to all countries. Geographers play an important role in examining ways to plan for the future and solve problems of tomorrow.

Population Growth

GUIDING QUESTION *What factors influence population growth?*

More than 7 billion people now live on Earth, and most of the population inhabits about 30 percent of the planet's land area. Global population continues to grow and is expected to level off at 9 billion by the year 2050. Such rapid growth was not always the case. From the year 1000 until 1800, the world's population increased slowly. Then the number of people on Earth more than doubled between 1800 and 1950. It doubled again between 1950 and about 2000.

The Demographic Transition Model

Scientists in the field of *demography,* the study of populations, use statistics to learn about population growth. The **birthrate** is the number of births per year for every 1,000 people. The **death rate** is the number of deaths per year for every 1,000 people. **Natural increase**, or the growth rate of a population, is the difference between an area's birthrate and its death rate. **Migration**, or the movement of people from place to place, must also be considered when examining population changes.

C2 The **demographic transition** model uses birthrates and death rates to show how populations in countries or regions can change over time. The model was first used to show the relationship of declining birthrates and death rates to industrialization in Western Europe. Death rates can fall quickly as a result of more abundant and reliable food supplies, improved health care, access to medicine and technology, and better living conditions. Birthrates decline more slowly because the declines result from changes in cultural traditions that can often take longer.

networks *Online Teaching Options*

 INTERACTIVE BELLRINGER

Population Density

Contrasting Use this population density map of North America to discuss with students how to read a population density map and consider how geography impacts where people live. Have students work with a partner. Pairs should read the introductory text and study the map to answer the questions. If there is time, have pairs locate the largest city that is closest to where they live on the map.

Logical/Mathematical, Visual/Spatial

Population Density
Population density is the number of people living on a square mile or square kilometer of land. Population density can be shown on a thematic map.
1. Which area of Canada is the least-densely populated? Why do you think this is so?
click for answer
Auto-Run
Click Through
Previous
1 of 3
Next

Today, most of the world's industrialized and technologically developed countries have experienced the transition from high birthrates and death rates to low birthrates and death rates. These countries have reached what is known as *zero population growth,* in which the birthrate and death rate are equal. When this balance occurs, a country's population does not grow as a result of natural increase, although it can still grow as a result of migration.

Although birthrates have fallen significantly in many countries in Asia, Africa, and Latin America over the past 40 years, they are still higher than in the industrialized world. Families in these regions traditionally are large because of cultural beliefs about marriage, family, and the value of children. For example, a husband and wife in a rural agricultural area may choose to have several children who will help farm the land. The high number of births often continues after death rates decrease as a result of improved living conditions. This causes the population to greatly increase. As a result, the **doubling time**, or the number of years it takes a population to double in size, has been reduced to below 50 years in some parts of Asia, Africa, and Latin America. In contrast, the average doubling time of a more developed country can be more than 300 years.

C

R

birthrate number of births per year for every 1,000 people

death rate number of deaths per year for every 1,000 people

natural increase the growth rate of a population; the difference between birthrate and death rate

migration the movement of people from place to place

demographic transition the model that uses birthrates and death rates to show how populations in countries or regions change over time

doubling time the number of years it takes for a population to double in size

Challenges of Growth

Rapid population growth presents many challenges that affect individual countries and the global **community**. As the number of people increases, so does the difficulty of producing enough food to feed them. In Africa, for example, food shortages in

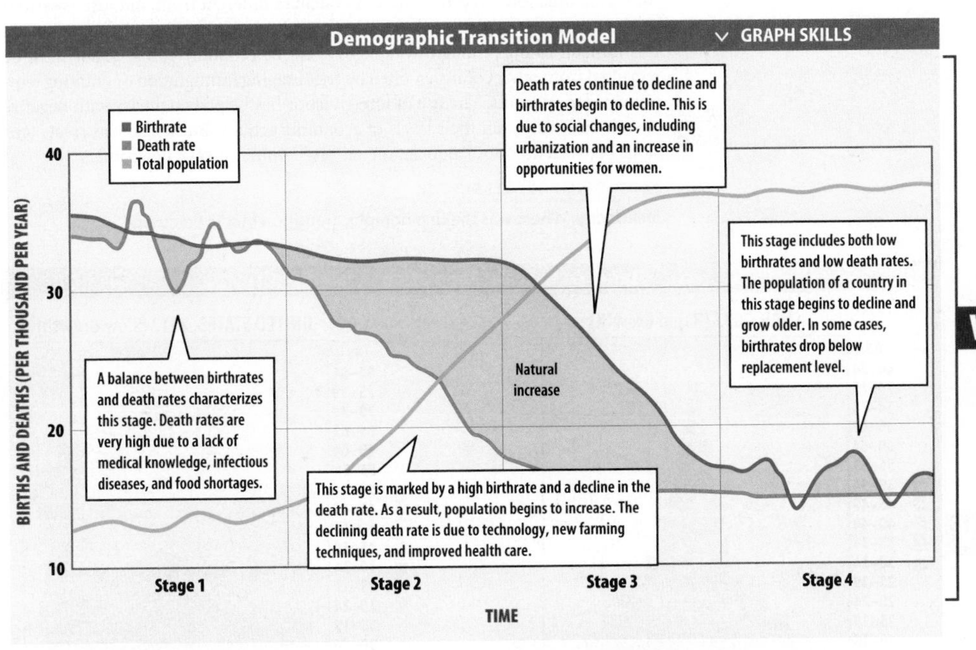

Demographic Transition Model
GRAPH SKILLS
Birthrate
Death rate
Total population
Death rates continue to decline and birthrates begin to decline. This is due to social changes, including urbanization and an increase in opportunities for women.
This stage includes both low birthrates and low death rates. The population of a country in this stage begins to decline and grow older. In some cases, birthrates drop below replacement level.
Natural increase
A balance between birthrates and death rates characterizes this stage. Death rates are very high due to a lack of medical knowledge, infectious diseases, and food shortages.
This stage is marked by a high birthrate and a decline in the death rate. As a result, population begins to increase. The declining death rate is due to technology, new farming techniques, and improved health care.
BIRTHS AND DEATHS (PER THOUSAND PER YEAR)
40
30
20
10
Stage 1
Stage 2
Stage 3
Stage 4
TIME

V

Changes in population trends can be identified by examining the relationships between birthrates and death rates.

▲ **CRITICAL THINKING**

1. ***Analyzing*** What characteristics of Stage 2 create an increase in population?
2. ***Identifying*** What effect does an increase in opportunities for women have on populations? Of what stage is it a characteristic?

Content Background Knowledge

Declining Birthrate Although the birthrate in the United States hit an all-time high in 2007, following the Great Recession, it declined by 2012 to a point not seen since 1920. People studying this drop in the birthrate speculate that the effects of the recession are causing families to wait longer to have children, and that immigrants, who often help buoy the birthrate by having many children, are also holding off. The falling birthrate may cause problems for the country and its economy down the line if the United States does not have enough workers available in the future.

C Critical Thinking Skills

Comparing and Contrasting Divide students into small groups. Have groups review the information about the birthrate in less industrialized areas in Asia, Africa, and Latin America, and compare and contrast it with the information given about the birthrate in more technologically developed countries by answering the following questions: **How and why might the birthrate be different in these two types of areas?** *(It might be higher in the less industrialized areas because families place a cultural value on having children and often need many offspring to help work on farmland in rural areas.)* **What about the birthrate is similar in these two types of areas?** *(Possible answer: Overall, the birthrate has fallen in both types of places.)* BL **Verbal/Linguistic**

R Reading Skills

Defining As a class, review and discuss some of the reasons why death rates decline more rapidly than birthrates. Ask a student to read the sentence containing *doubling time* and then have another student explain the sentence in his or her own words without using the word "double." *(Doubling time refers to the number of years it takes a population to double in size, usually as a result of high birthrates and low death rates.)* ELL **Verbal/Linguistic**

V Visual Skills

Analyzing Visuals Allow time for students to analyze the diagram of the Demographic Transition Model. Have volunteers identify what each line is charting and describe what is happening at various points throughout time. Then have pairs work together to write summaries that explain what the model as a whole is showing and why this information is valuable for geographers to chart and analyze. AL **Visual/Spatial, Verbal/Linguistic**

VIDEO

Population

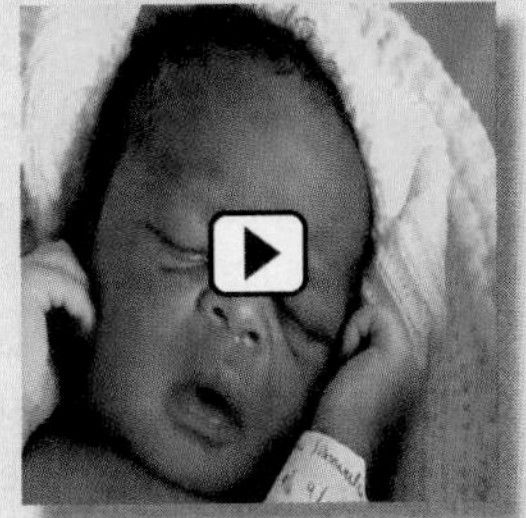

Problem-Solving Write this quote from the video on the board, "As nations becomes richer, population growth stabilizes . . ." Working in small groups, ask students to use this quote to help them problem solve by creating a list of ways to address the overpopulation issue in Zambia. Ask half of the groups to create a list of solutions as if they were Zambian citizens, and the other half of the groups to create a list of solutions as if they were policy makers in Zambia. Allow time for students to work together. Then have groups share their lists with the class. **Interpersonal**

ANSWERS, p. 83

CRITICAL THINKING

1. There is a high birthrate and a decline in the death rate, which causes the population to increase.
2. During Stage 3, death rates continue to decline and birthrates begin to decline.

W Writing Skills

Argument Have students do additional research to learn more about problems related to rapid population growth and potential solutions. Divide the students into two groups: one representing the view that rapid population growth is a serious problem; the other representing the view that new technologies will mitigate any bad effects from rapid population growth. Have students write essays explaining their viewpoints, using facts and details to support their opinion. Then have groups with similar opinions meet to discuss their essays.
BL **Verbal/Linguistic**

R Reading Skills

Using Context Clues Ask students to reread the last two sentences on the page. **Ask:** **What are some context clues that help you understand the meaning of *host*?** *(foreign labor, communities of newcomers)* **What does *host population* mean?** *(Possible answer: the people born or raised in the country)* **Why might *newcomers* create tension?** *(Possible answers: the foreign labors might bring in new beliefs; cultures may conflict with the culture already established)*
ELL **Verbal/Linguistic**

V Visual Skills

Comparing and Contrasting Graphs Point out that these population pyramid graphs are from three countries in different stages of population growth. **Ask:** **Which age group is the largest in Chad? In the United States? In Italy?** *(Chad: under 5 years old; U.S.: ages 50–54; Italy: ages 40–44)* **Which age and gender group is the smallest in Chad? In the United States? In Italy?** *(Chad: males ages 70–74; United States: males ages 85 and over; Italy: males ages 85 and over)* **What would it tell you about the country if the bars at the bottom of the graph were shorter than the ones at the top of the graph?** *(It would show that the birthrate is falling because fewer children are being born now than were being born in the past.)*

Have students analyze the population pyramid of Italy. **Ask:** **What does this graph illustrate about the population pattern in Italy?** *(Because there are a higher number of people in the age groups of 35–54, it shows that the birthrate is falling because fewer children are being born now than were being born in the past.)* **AL** **Visual/Spatial**

ANSWERS, p. 84

READING PROGRESS CHECK The demographic transition model was first used to show the relationship of declining birthrates and death rates to industrialization in Western Europe.

---

community people with common interests living in a particular area

population pyramid a diagram that shows the distribution of a population by age and gender

trend a general movement

production and availability continue to be an issue. In better circumstances, Africa's agricultural sector would respond to rising prices by increasing food supply. In Africa, however, lack of government investment and other support of agriculture—along with warfare, poor access to rural areas, and weather and pests that can ruin crops—have combined to bring hunger to the region.

In addition, populations that grow rapidly use resources more quickly. Some countries face shortages of water, housing, and clothing, for instance. Rapid population growth strains these limited resources. Another concern is that the world's population is unevenly distributed by age, with the majority of some countries' populations being infants and young children who cannot contribute to food production. This population structure can be seen with a **population pyramid**.

While some experts are pessimistic about the long-term effects of rapid population growth, others are optimistic that, as the number of humans increases, the levels of technology and creativity will also rise. For example, scientists continue to study and develop ways to boost agricultural productivity. Fertilizers can improve crop yields. Irrigation systems can help increase the amount of land available for farming. New varieties of crops have been created to withstand severe conditions and yield more food.

In the late 1900s some countries in Europe began to experience a **trend** called *negative population growth,* in which the annual death rate exceeds the annual birthrate. Hungary and Germany, for example, both show change rates of about -0.2. This situation has economic consequences different from, but just as serious as, those caused by high growth rates. In countries with negative population growth, it is difficult to find enough workers to keep the economy going. Labor must be recruited from other countries, often by encouraging immigration or granting temporary work permits. The use of foreign labor has helped countries with negative change rates maintain their levels of economic activity. But it also can create tensions between the "host" population and the communities of newcomers.

READING PROGRESS CHECK

Identifying Where was the demographic transition model first used?

Stages Of Growth: Population Pyramids

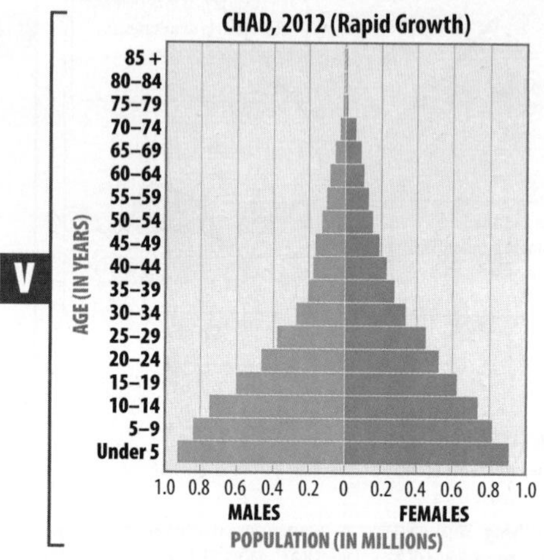

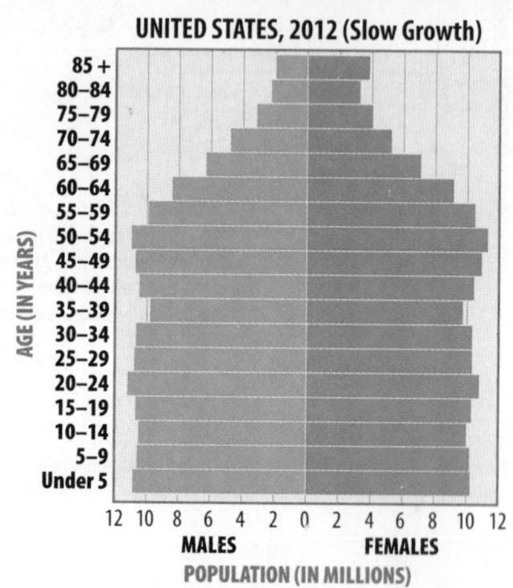

84

networks Online Teaching Options

INTERACTIVE GRAPHS

Population Pyramids

Formulating Questions These interactive graphs show the population structure of a more developed nation and a less developed nation in population pyramids. Allow time for the students to analyze the graphs. Have them write three questions about the graphs. Then the partners should exchange questions and answer them. Have partners discuss any discrepancies. **Logical/Mathematical**

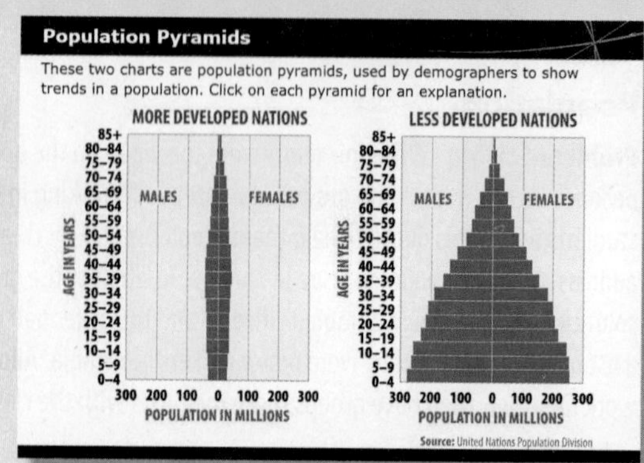

Population Distribution

GUIDING QUESTION *What influences population distribution?*

Not only do population growth rates vary among Earth's regions, but the pattern of human settlement, or **population distribution**, is uneven as well. Population distribution is related to the Earth's physical geography. Only about 30 percent of Earth's surface is made up of land, and much of that land is inhospitable. High mountain peaks, barren deserts, and frozen tundra make human activity difficult in many places. Almost everyone on Earth lives on a relatively small portion of the planet's land—a little less than one-third. Most people live where fertile soil, available water, and a climate without harsh extremes make human life possible.

population distribution the variations in population that occur across a country, a continent, or the world

Of all the continents, Europe and Asia are the most densely populated. Asia alone contains more than 60 percent of the world's people. Many people throughout the world live in metropolitan areas—cities and their surrounding urbanized areas—where populations are highly concentrated. Today, most people in Europe, North America, South America, and Australia live in or around urban areas. **V**

Geographers determine how crowded a country or region is by measuring **population density**—the number of people living on a square mile or square kilometer of land. To determine population density in a country, geographers divide the total population of the country by its total land area. **T**

population density the average number of people living on a square mile or square kilometer of land

Population density varies widely from country to country. Canada, with a low population density of about 8 people per square mile (3 people per sq. km), offers wide-open spaces and the choice of living in thriving cities or quiet rural areas. In contrast, Bangladesh has one of the highest population densities in the world—about 2,721 people per square mile (1,046 people per sq. km).

Countries with populations of about the same size do not necessarily have similar population densities. For example, both Tunisia and the Czech Republic have about 10.5 million people. Tunisia, with a larger land area, has only 169 people per square mile (65 people per sq. km). However, the Czech Republic has 349 people per square mile (134 people per sq. km).

GRAPH SKILLS

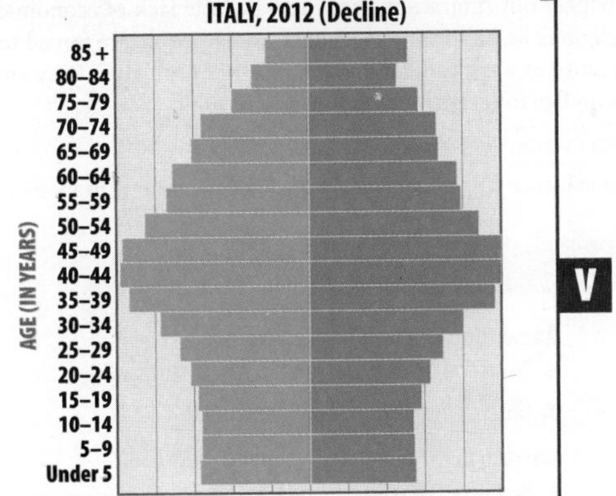

V

Source: U.S. Census Bureau, Statistical Abstract of the United States: 2012

Population pyramids include information about the age and gender distribution of a country's population. The population structure of a country provides insight into population growth trends and the country's stage in the demographic transition.

CRITICAL THINKING

1. ***Comparing and Contrasting*** How does the shape of the population pyramid for a country undergoing rapid growth differ from that of a country experiencing population decline?
2. ***Analyzing*** What does the shape of the U.S. population pyramid tell you about the country's population structure?

V Visual Skills

Making Connections Review that Earth's population is not evenly distributed, or spread, across the land. Explain that in the United States, much of the population is clustered in cities along the east and west coasts, while large areas of land across the western states are sparsely populated. Share with students a visual reference of a population density map. Have students go to the population density map of the United States found in their texts on page 116. Then have students consider where they live to answer this series of questions. **Ask:** **In our community, where is most of the population distributed? Are there any parts of the land where it is harder for people to live? Are there any parts where it was easier for people to settle? What geological or human-made features affect the ways our community has organized places for people to live and work?** *(Student answers may vary, but should mention factors affecting population distribution such as the locations of major roads, sources of water, and geologic features such as forests or mountains.)* **Logical/Mathematical**

T Technology Skills

Researching on the Internet Have small groups of students conduct online research to find out more about the population density of a state in the United States and how it compares to other states in our country. Have them write a summary of their findings, including information about the density rank of the state and their theory (supported with facts and details from their research) for why its population is more or less dense than that of other states. Groups should provide charts or graphs to illustrate their findings along with their written summary.
BL **Verbal/Linguistic, Logical/Mathematical**

INTERACTIVE MAP

Egypt: Population Density

Analyzing Maps Use this interactive map of Egypt as an illustrative example of population density. As students analyze the map, ask them to consider why certain areas are very densely populated. Students should note that the Nile River has drawn people to this region for thousands of years. Write these headings on the board: *Environmental, Historical,* and *Economical.* In small groups, have students identify and explain how these factors influence population distribution. Then in a class discussion, have groups read their explanations. **AL** **Verbal/Linguistic**

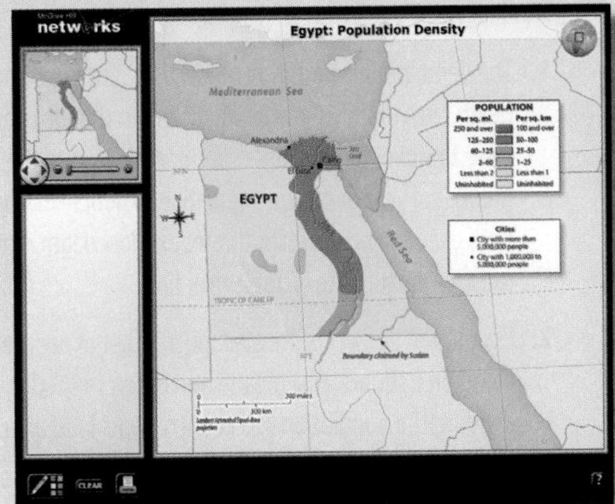

ANSWERS, p. 85

CRITICAL THINKING

1. For rapid growth, the pyramid is wide at the bottom and progressively narrows toward the top. For decline, it is widest in the middle, with the top and the bottom narrower than the middle.
2. It is experiencing slow growth.

Population Geography

C1 Critical Thinking Skills

Evaluating Primary Sources Explain that this press statement was released by Hillary Rodham Clinton as part of her work as Secretary of State. **Ask:** **For what occasion was this statement released?** *(as part of World Refugee Day 2012)* **How do you think Secretary Hillary Rodham Clinton feels about the effects of letting refugees enter the United States?** *(She thinks the country will benefit from allowing refugees to seek shelter in the United States. She supports her argument by noting that refugees have a positive effect on areas such as business, academia, science, the arts, and technology.)* **BL** **Verbal/Linguistic**

C2 Critical Thinking Skills

Examining Primary Sources Have students review the primary source quote from Doug Saunders. Have students work in pairs to answer the following questions. **Ask:** **From where does this quote originate?** *(a newspaper article)* **What does it tell you about the causes of the growth of population in cities?** *(It says that both migration and births can cause the population of a city to increase.)* **Why do you think the author included this quote here?** *(Possible answer: It supports the information in the main text about urbanization and provides more specific details and facts about the topic of the growth of cities in Africa and Asia.)* **AL** **Interpersonal, Verbal/Linguistic**

CLOSE & REFLECT

Understanding Relationships Among Events Tell students to review the main headings and vocabulary terms covered in this lesson and think about the physical and cultural causes of both positive and negative population changes. Have students write a few paragraphs explaining some reasons why the rate of population growth sped up during much of the twentieth century and identify problems caused by population growth. Invite volunteers to share their paragraphs with the class.

ANSWERS, p. 86

✓ **READING PROGRESS CHECK** Economic factors often attract people to a place; these factors are pull factors. Religious and political freedoms are also examples of pull factors that attract a person to another country. Push factors cause out-migration. Push factors include a lack of economic opportunities and religious or political persecution. Some people are forced to leave their countries due to wars, food shortages, or other problems.

DBQ The United States offers resettlement to more refugees each year than all other countries in the world combined. There are opportunities that exist in the United States that do not exist in other countries. Refugees might face challenges such as language barriers and discrimination.

Analyzing PRIMARY SOURCES (CCSS)

World Refugee Day 2012

C1 "The United States is strongly committed to protecting and assisting refugees and we offer resettlement to more refugees each year than all other countries in the world combined. Since 1975, more than three million refugees have made new homes in the United States, and nearly half of them have become U.S. citizens.

Refugees are contributing in ways large and small to business, academia, the arts, science and technology. Today we celebrate the success of refugees who have built new lives here and in other resettlement countries, but we also recognize the millions of refugees who remain displaced in camps, cities, and rural settlements around the world."

—Hillary Rodham Clinton, press statement, June 20, 2012

DBQ ***SPECULATING*** Why might refugees choose to migrate to the United States? What difficulties might refugees face? RH.9–10.2

Because the measure of population density includes all the land area of a country, it does not account for uneven population distribution within a country. In Egypt, for example, overall population density is 216 people per square mile (83 people per sq. km). In reality, over 90 percent of Egypt's people live along the Nile River. The rest of Egypt is desert. Thus, some geographers describe a country's population density in terms of land that can be used to support the population rather than total land area. When Egypt's population density is measured this way, it is about 6,993 people per square mile (2,688 people per sq. km)!

The Earth's population is moving in great numbers. People are moving from city to city or from rural villages to cities. The resulting growth of city populations brought about by such migration and the changes that come with this increase are called *urbanization.* The primary cause of urbanization is the desire of rural people to find jobs and a better life in more prosperous urban areas. Rural populations have certainly grown in some countries, but the amount of farmland has not increased to meet the growing number of people. As a result, many rural migrants find urban jobs in manufacturing and service industries.

About half of the world's people live in cities. Between 1960 and 2012, the population of metropolitan Mexico City rose from about 5 million to more than 19 million. Other cities in Latin America, as well as in Asia and Africa, have seen similar growth. Some cities contain a large part of their country's entire population. For example, about one-third of Argentina's population lives in Buenos Aires.

PRIMARY SOURCE

C2 "Never in human history have so many people changed their locations and lifestyles so quickly. Each month, there are 5 million new city dwellers created through migration or birth in Africa, Asia, and the Middle East. . . ."

—Doug Saunders, "The great shift from farm to city," *Los Angeles Times*, June 19, 2011

Population movement also occurs between countries. Some people emigrate from the country of their birth and move to another. They are known as emigrants in their homeland and immigrants in their new country. In the past 40 years, millions of people have left Africa and Asia to find jobs in the wealthier countries of Europe. These types of economic factors that attract people to a place are called *pull factors.* Religious and political freedoms are also examples of pull factors that attract people to another country. Other factors of migration, called *push factors*, trigger out-migration; these also include lack of economic opportunities and religious or political persecution. Some people are forced to flee their country because of wars, food shortages, or other problems. They are refugees, or people who flee to escape persecution or disaster.

✓ **READING PROGRESS CHECK**

Explaining What factors influence the migration of people from one country to another?

LESSON 2 REVIEW (CCSS)

Reviewing Vocabulary (Tier Three Words)

1. ***Explaining*** Define demographic transition model and doubling time. How are they related to each other? RH.9–10.4
2. ***Calculating*** Define population density and how it is calculated. RH.9–10.4

Using Your Notes

3. ***Describing*** Use your graphic organizer to explain why population growth varies from place to place. WHST.9–10.2

Answering the Guiding Questions

4. ***Discussing*** What factors influence population growth?
5. ***Stating*** What influences population distribution?

Writing Activity

6. ***Narrative*** What human-made structures might be present in countries that have large numbers of people concentrated in relatively small areas? Write a paragraph with supporting details to explain your answer. WHST.9–10.1

86

LESSON 2 REVIEW ANSWERS

Reviewing Vocabulary

1. The demographic transition model uses birthrates and death rates to show how populations can change over time. Doubling time is more specific and refers to the number of years it takes a population to double in size. Both examine how high birthrates and low death rates cause populations to increase over time.
2. Population density is the average number of people living on a square mile of land and is determined by dividing the population of a country by its land area.

Using Your Notes

3. Population growth varies based on birth and death rates in a given area.

Answering the Guiding Questions

4. Death rates may fall quickly due to reliable food supplies, improved health care, and better living conditions. Birthrates generally decline slowly because changes in cultural traditions take longer.
5. Most people live where fertile soil, available water, and a climate without harsh extremes make human life possible. Most people live in urban areas.

Writing Activity

6. Paragraphs will vary, but should be logical and strongly supported by identifying human-made structures that might be present in countries with large numbers of people concentrated in small areas.

networks
There's More Online!

- ☑ **CHART** WTO Members
- ☑ **IMAGE** Rhine River Valley
- ☑ **IMAGE** Four Corners
- ☑ **IMAGE** Pakistan-India Border
- ☑ **IMAGE** Terrorist Attack on Mumbai
- ☑ **INTERACTIVE SELF-CHECK QUIZ**
- ☑ **VIDEO** Political Geography

LESSON 3
Political Geography

ESSENTIAL QUESTION • *How do the characteristics and distribution of human populations affect human and physical systems?*

Reading HELPDESK

Academic Vocabulary
(Tier Two Words)
- **unique**
- **authority**

Content Vocabulary
(Tier Three Words)
- **unitary system**
- **federal system**
- **autocracy**
- **monarchy**
- **oligarchy**
- **theocracy**
- **democracy**
- **natural boundary**
- **cultural boundary**
- **geometric boundary**

TAKING NOTES: ***Key Ideas and Details***

DESCRIBING As you read, use a graphic organizer like the one below to take notes on the features of government.

Features of Government	
Levels of Government	Types of Government
Geography and Government	Conflict and Cooperation

It Matters Because
Governments and economies of countries around the world are becoming increasingly interconnected. Some countries or groups of countries, such as the European Union, have strong economies that allow them to help improve standards of living in other countries.

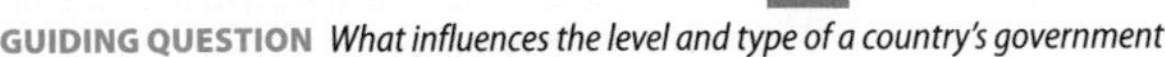

Features of Government **C**

GUIDING QUESTION *What influences the level and type of a country's government?*

Today the world includes nearly 200 independent countries that vary in size, military might, natural resources, and world influence. Each country is defined by characteristics such as territory, population, and sovereignty, or freedom from outside control. These elements are brought together under a government. A government must make and enforce policies and laws that are binding upon all people living within its territory.

Levels of Government

The government of each country has **unique** characteristics that relate to that country's historical development. To carry out their functions, governments are organized in a variety of ways. Most large countries have several different levels of government. These usually include a national or central government, as well as the governments of smaller internal divisions such as provinces, states, counties, cities, towns, and villages.

R1 A **unitary system** of government gives all key powers to the national or central government. This structure does not mean that only one level of government exists. Rather, it means that the central government creates state, provincial, or other local governments and gives them limited sovereignty. The United Kingdom and France both developed unitary governments as they emerged from smaller territories during the late Middle Ages and early modern times.

R2 A **federal system** of government divides the powers of government between the national government and state or provincial governments. Each level of government has sovereignty in some areas. The United States developed a federal system after the thirteen colonies became independent from Great Britain.

ENGAGE

C Critical Thinking Skills

Formulating Questions Have students consider how the United States government compares to other governments around the world. Have them write down three facts they already know about this topic and three questions to which they would like to find the answers. Tell students to look for the answers as they work their way through the lesson.

TEACH & ASSESS

R1 Reading Skills

Activating Prior Knowledge Explain that England and France were the most powerful countries during the Middle Ages and ruled by kings or queens who inherited the positions. **Ask:** What type of a government do both England and France currently have? *(unitary system of government)* Who has the power? *(the national or central government)* How is that power divided? *(the central government creates state, provincial, and local governments and gives them limited ruling rights)* What is sovereignty? *(quality of having independent authority over a region)* Explain that England still has a monarch that shares governmental powers. **ELL** **Verbal/Linguistic**

R2 Reading Skills

Sequencing Information Working in pairs, have students review the formation and evolution of the U.S. government. Then have partners work together to put in sequence the different forms of government our country has had starting when it first won independence from Great Britain to our current federal system. **AL** **Logical/Mathematical**

networks Online Teaching Options

INTERACTIVE BELLRINGER

Types of Government

Making Inferences This chart can be used to discuss the types of governments established in various countries around the world. Have students read the introductory text. Tell students to use their background knowledge along with the chart to make inferences to answer the questions and to write their paragraphs. Invite volunteers to read their paragraphs aloud to the class. **ELL** **Verbal/Linguistic, Logical/Mathematical**

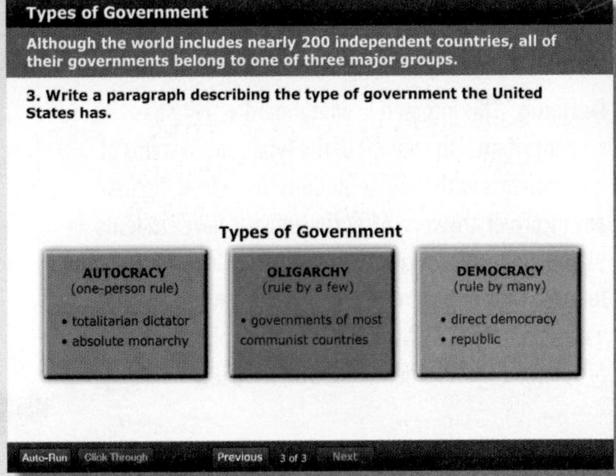

ANSWERS, p. 87

TAKING NOTES: Levels of Government—Most large countries have national or central governments, as well as smaller, internal divisions such as provinces, states, counties, cities, and villages; **Types of Government:** autocracy—rule by one person, oligarchy—rule by a few people, and democracy—rule by many people; **Geography and Government**—Geography influences governments as they develop policy to provide people with goods and services. Governments must know where and why their citizens are moving, and how this affects their relationship with the environment. Infrastructures, such as roads, bridges, and power plants, must be built based on this geographic distribution; **Conflict and Cooperation**—contribute to and result from political geographic divisions of the world, global cooperation is frustrated by border disputes, tensions over larger territories, multiple ethnic groups within one state, competition over resources, and control of strategic sites.

Political Geography

T Technology Skills

Making Presentations As a class, review the first two types of government discussed in this section—autocracy and oligarchy. Organize students into small groups, assigning each group one of these types of government. Have them conduct online research to find additional examples (past or present) of this type of government. Tell groups to classify and compare these examples and the ones discussed in the text. For example, compare totalitarian dictatorships in one group and countries headed by monarchies in another. Groups should then prepare a short presentation that explains how their type of government works in general and can manifest itself in the real world in several different ways, illustrating their points with specific facts and details about different countries. **AL** **Verbal/Linguistic**

R Reading Skills

Using Context Clues Remind students that if they are puzzled by an unfamiliar word, they can examine the words and phrases around it for clues to its meaning. **Ask:** **What does the phrase *divine power* mean?** *(It describes something as coming from a higher power beyond humans.)* **What context clues help you figure out this meaning?** *(The first sentence of the paragraph states: "Sometimes religion is the source of power in an oligarchy.")* **How might you use an understanding of the phrase *divine power* to describe how a theocracy compares to a monarchy?** *(Possible answer: The leaders in a theocracy claim that a divine power is the leader of their government. They say their power and the decisions they make come from this divine power. The leaders of a monarchy inherit their positions.)* **ELL** **Verbal/Linguistic**

C Critical Thinking Skills

Comparing Have students compare oligarchies and totalitarian dictatorships. Review that sometimes both systems try to make it seem as if the people are in charge. **Ask:** **Why do you think these types of governments try to give the appearance that the people are in control?** *(Possible answer: If the people think they are the ones with power, they are less likely to try to rise up and take power from the person (dictator) or group truly in charge.)* **BL** **Logical/Mathematical**

ANSWERS, p. 88

CRITICAL THINKING

1. The president of the United States presides over a democracy.
2. A unitary system is a form of government in which all key powers are given to the national or central government, while a democracy is a system of government in which leaders rule with consent of the citizens.

President Barack Obama is the leader in the United States federal system.

▲ **CRITICAL THINKING**

1. ***Identifying*** Over what type of government does the president of the United States preside?
2. ***Contrasting*** How is this form of government different from an oligarchy?

unique being the only one; without a like or an equal

unitary system form of government in which all key powers are given to the national or central government

federal system form of government in which powers are divided between the national government and state or provincial governments

autocracy system of government in which one person rules with unlimited power and authority

authority power to influence or command thought, opinion, or behavior

monarchy a form of autocracy with a hereditary king or queen exercising supreme power

oligarchy system of government in which a small group holds power

Another similar type of government structure is a confederation, or a loose union of independent territories. The United States at first formed a confederation, but this type of political arrangement failed to provide an effective national government for the new nation. As a result, the U.S. Constitution established a strong national government while preserving some state government powers. Today, other countries with federal or confederate systems include Canada, Switzerland, Mexico, Brazil, Australia, and India.

Types of Governments

T Governments can be classified by asking the question: Who governs the state? Under this classification system, all governments belong to one of the three major groups: (1) autocracy, or rule by one person; (2) oligarchy, or rule by a few people; or (3) democracy, or rule by many people.

Any system of government in which the power and authority to rule belongs to a single individual is an **autocracy** (aw•TAH•kruh•see). Autocracies are the oldest and one of the most common forms of government. Most autocrats achieve and maintain their position of **authority** through inheritance or by the ruthless use of military or police power.

Several forms of autocracy exist. One is an absolute or totalitarian dictatorship in which the decisions of a single leader determine government policies. The government under such a system can come to power through a revolution or an election. The totalitarian dictator seeks to control all aspects of social and economic life. Examples of totalitarian dictatorships include Adolf Hitler in Nazi Germany, Saddam Hussein in Iraq, Raul Castro of Cuba, and Kim Jong Un of North Korea.

Monarchy (MAH•nuhr•kee) is another form of autocratic government. In a monarchy, a king or queen exercises the supreme powers of government. Monarchs usually inherit their positions. Absolute monarchs have complete and unlimited power to rule. The king of Saudi Arabia, for example, is an absolute monarch. Absolute monarchs are rare today, but from the 1400s to the 1700s, kings or queens with absolute power ruled most of Western Europe.

Today, some countries, such as the United Kingdom, Sweden, Japan, Jordan, and Thailand, have constitutional monarchies. Their monarchs share governmental powers with elected legislatures or serve as ceremonial leaders.

An **oligarchy** (AH•luh•GAHR•kee) is any system of government in which a small group holds power. The group derives its power from wealth, military power, social position, or a combination of these elements. Today the governments of communist countries, such as China, are mostly oligarchies. Leaders in the Communist Party and the military control the government.

R Sometimes religion is the source of power in an oligarchy. A **theocracy**, for example, is a government of officials believed to be divinely inspired. In a theocracy, a divine power is thought to be the head of the government. Government officials receive their inspiration, guidance, and authority to rule from this divine power. For example, Islamic sharia law is imposed in parts of North Africa and Southwest Asia today.

C Both dictatorships and oligarchies sometimes claim they rule for the people. Such governments may try to give the appearance of control by the people. For example, they might hold elections but offer only one candidate. Such governments may also have some type of legislature or national assembly elected by or representing the people. These legislatures, however, only approve policies and decisions already made by the leaders. As in a dictatorship, oligarchies usually suppress all political opposition.

networks Online Teaching Options

INTERACTIVE WHITEBOARD ACTIVITY

Types and Systems of Governments

Defining This interactive whiteboard activity has students match the names of the types and systems of governments with their definitions. As a class, discuss any incorrect answers. After the activity, have students use online resources to create a simple chart with a head for each type of government, and then have them list various countries below each head that follow each form or system of government. **Visual/Spatial**

Systems of Government

Directions: Governments can be classified by asking the question: Who governs the state? Drag each type of government to its appropriate description in the table.

Types and Systems of Government	
	system of government in which the power and authority to rule belongs to a single individual
	a hereditary king or queen exercises the supreme powers of government
	system of government in which a small group holds power
	system of government officials that are believed to be divinely inspired
	form of government in which all key powers are given to the national or central government
	system of government in which leaders rule with the consent of the citizens
	form of government in which powers are divided between national government and state or provincial governments

autocracy	federal system	oligarchy	unitary system
democracy	monarchy	theocracy	

A **democracy** is any system of government in which leaders rule with the consent of the citizens. The term *democracy* comes from the Greek *demos* (meaning "the people") and *kratia* (meaning "rule"). The ancient Greeks used the word *democracy* to mean government by the many in contrast to government by the few. The key idea of democracy is that people hold sovereign power.

Direct democracy, in which citizens themselves decide on issues, exists in some places at local levels of government. No country today has a national government based on direct democracy. Instead, democratic countries have representative democracies, in which the people elect representatives with the responsibility and power to make laws and conduct government. An assembly of the people's representatives may be called a council, a legislature, a congress, or a parliament.

C

theocracy system of government in which those who rule are regarded as divinely inspired

democracy system of government in which leaders rule with consent of the citizens

Many democratic countries, such as the United States and France, are republics. In a republic, voters elect all major officials, who are responsible to the people. The head of state—or head of government—is usually a president elected for a specific term. Not every democracy is a republic. The United Kingdom, for example, is a democracy with a monarch as head of state. This monarch's role is ceremonial, however, and elected officials hold the actual power to rule.

☑ READING PROGRESS CHECK

Contrasting How does an autocracy differ from an oligarchy?

Geography and Government

GUIDING QUESTION *How does geography influence a country's government?*

Governments can be greatly influenced by geography. Geographic areas can actually determine how political and administrative units are drawn up and how they will be governed. Democratic countries have entities based on location, which are divided into local bodies that might have different laws.

A government must consider the cultural and religious beliefs of its citizens in order to govern effectively. In autocracies, governments frequently suppress

Types of Boundaries

Natural Boundary: The Rhine River Valley near Ruggell forms the border between Switzerland (left bank) and Liechtenstein (right bank).

Geometric Boundary: The Four Corners site in the United States occurs where the states of Utah, New Mexico, Arizona, and Colorado all meet.

Cultural Boundary The Wagah border post that separates northern India from eastern Pakistan is an example of a cultural boundary.

V

▲ CRITICAL THINKING

1. ***Identifying*** Which of the boundary types might change slowly over time without the consent of the governments involved? Explain your choice.
2. ***Analyzing*** Describe the Four Corners site and explain why it is considered a geometric boundary.

C Critical Thinking Skills

Making Inferences Help students review how a democracy works. **Ask:** **Why might it be difficult for a country to have a national government based on direct democracy?** *(Possible answer: In a direct democracy, each person votes directly on every single issue. It would take too long to have every person vote on every issue facing that country. It is more efficient for nations to set up a representative government.)*
ELL **Logical/Mathematical**

Content Background Knowledge

The Commonwealth of Nations This is a group of 54 countries that have experienced direct or indirect rule by the United Kingdom or were linked to a commonwealth country. These countries continue to work together even after becoming independent to promote such objectives as democracy, peace, and free trade. The monarch, who is the sovereign of the United Kingdom, is also the Head of State of 15 other countries from the Commonwealth, such as Canada, Australia, and New Zealand. The monarch plays a separate role in each Commonwealth and consults with a different parliament in each country. Other countries in the Commonwealth have various governments, including sultanates, their own monarchies, and republics led by elected presidents.

V Visual Skills

Analyzing Images Have students examine the images, maps, and captions to describe the types of boundaries. **Ask:** **How are these boundaries alike and different?** *(Possible answer: They are alike because all three were chosen by people or governments, even the natural boundary of a river. They are different because the shape of a natural boundary is determined by the path of a formation found in nature (a river), while the shape of geometric and cultural boundaries are determined by decisions and actions taken by people.)* **Visual/Spatial, Logical/Mathematical**

VIDEO

Hong Kong: Perfect Blend of East and West

Identifying Cause and Effect Use this video about Hong Kong to discuss natural boundaries. As a class discuss how Hong Kong was governed before and after Chinese rule. On a world map, have a volunteer locate Hong Kong. Ask students to explain Hong Kong's natural boundaries. Then have students write a paragraph explaining possible ways that Hong Kong's natural boundaries affect the cultural boundaries and lifestyles of Hong Kong citizens.
Visual/Spatial, Verbal/Linguistic

ANSWERS, p. 89

☑ **READING PROGRESS CHECK** An autocracy is a system of government in which one person rules with unlimited power and authority, while an oligarchy is a system of government in which a small group holds power.

CRITICAL THINKING

1. The natural boundary might change slowly over time without the consent of the governments involved, as it would change as a function of physical forces.
2. The Four Corners site in the United States occurs where the states of Utah, New Mexico, Arizona, and Colorado all meet. It is a geometric boundary because it is a boundary that follows a geometric pattern.

Political Geography

W Writing Skills

Informative/Explanatory Review with students that geographers often identify three types of regions: formal (common characteristic(s)), functional (central or organized place), and vernacular (perceived, rather than objective area). Explain that cultural boundaries are often created using these three region types. Have students research and collect data about the cultural boundaries in large cities or regions. Then have them use the gathered data to write an essay defining and describing formal, functional, and vernacular cultural regions. Essays should include specific details and boundary locations describing each type of cultural region. Encourage students to add illustrations or images to accompany their essays. **Kinesthetic, Verbal/Linguistic**

C Critical Thinking Skills

Identifying Cause and Effect Have students reread the information about how the United States acquired land in the Southwest, including present-day California. **Ask: How do you think the discovery of gold affected the settlement of California?** *(Possible answer: People migrated to this area to mine and sell gold.)* **Why do you think the gold rush affected how quickly California became a state?** *(Possible answer: The discovery of a valuable resource and the rapidly growing population made California an important economic addition to the United States.)* AL **Logical/Mathematical**

T Technology Skills

Researching on the Internet Have students consider how nationalism can affect the borders of a country. Organize students into small groups and have each group research a country formed by a shared spirit of nationalism—for example, they could chart the stages of German unification or learn how the kingdom of Italy was formed by uniting independent states located on the Italian peninsula. Have students research issues relating to geographical borders, such as the conflicts Germany and France had over Alsace-Lorraine. Students should prepare a short presentation that includes visuals such as time lines and maps. Allow time for students to share their findings with the class. BL **Visual/Spatial, Verbal/Linguistic**

ANSWERS, p. 90

READING PROGRESS CHECK Border disputes often arise from unsettled territorial claims or as a result of one state desiring the resources of a neighboring state.

CRITICAL THINKING

1. Terrorism is any violent and destructive act designed to intimidate people or a government. The photo depicts a terrorist attack that has incited fear in and around the Taj Palace Hotel in Mumbai, India.
2. They might experience psychological trauma, such as Post-Traumatic Stress Disorder.

Firefighters extinguish the flames coming out from the Taj Palace Hotel in Mumbai, India, during a terrorist attack in the city in November 2008.

Bhaskar Paul/The India Today Group/Getty Images

▲ CRITICAL THINKING

1. ***Defining*** What elements of the definition of terrorism are shown in the photo?
2. ***Speculating*** What are some of the long-term effects that people might have who survived but witnessed the bombing?

natural boundary a fixed limit or extent defined along physical geographic features such as mountains and rivers

cultural boundary a geographical boundary between two different cultures

geometric boundary a boundary that follows a geometric pattern

cultural and religious groups in order to maintain order and power. In democracies, governments usually take account of cultural and religious beliefs in order to protect their people's freedoms and ensure their well-being.

Geography influences governments as they develop policy to provide people with goods and services. Governments must also know where their citizens are moving, why they are moving there, and how that affects their relationship with the environment. Infrastructures, such as roads, bridges, and power plants, must be built based on the geographic distribution of people using both current demographic data and future projections.

Several geographic factors influence the development of political boundaries. A **natural boundary** follows physical geographic features such as mountains and rivers. For example, the Mississippi River forms the borders between several U.S. states. Natural boundaries are often more defensible and easy to identify.

W Other boundaries develop to separate areas with cultural differences, such as places with different religions or languages. These **cultural boundaries** geographically divide two identifiable cultures. For example, when Britain partitioned India and created Pakistan, it created a religious cultural boundary. Muslims were reorganized into Pakistan and Hindus into India.

At other times, cultural and natural landforms are not considered when boundaries are drawn. In these cases, treaties might create **geometric boundaries** to separate countries or nations. Geometric boundaries—which often follow straight lines and do not account for natural and cultural features—exist between Libya, Egypt, and Algeria.

C Political boundaries, referred to as borders, are not always permanent. Many areas of the world have seen changing borders as the result of wars and territorial disputes. Border disputes arise from unsettled territorial claims or as a result of one state desiring the resources of a neighboring state. In February 1848, Mexico and the United States signed a treaty which ended the war between them and gave large portions of the Southwest, including present-day California, to the United States. Several days earlier, gold had been discovered near the present-day capital of Sacramento. This started the gold rush and sped up California's statehood.

READING PROGRESS CHECK

Identifying What is the cause of many boundary disputes?

Conflict and Cooperation

GUIDING QUESTION *How do cooperation and conflict shape the division of Earth's surface?*

Cooperation and conflict have contributed to and resulted from the political geographic divisions of the world. Global cooperation is frustrated by many factors, including border disputes, tensions over larger territories, multiple ethnic groups within one state, competition for fewer resources, and control of strategic sites.

T Nationalism often contributes to political conflicts. Nationalism is a belief that the individual's loyalty and devotion to the nation or state surpasses other individual or group interests. After passing through the new countries of Latin America, nationalism spread in the early nineteenth century to central Europe and from there, toward the middle of the century, to eastern and southeastern Europe. This period is considered the age of nationalism in Europe. Asia and Africa saw a rise in nationalism at the beginning of the twentieth century as powerful movements took place. Nationalism can breed conflict if it reaches fanatical levels. This can and often does lead to war.

Terrorism is also a type of political conflict. Terrorism inspires fear and is any violent and destructive act committed to intimidate a people or a government.

networks Online Teaching Options

SLIDE SHOW

Types of Boundaries

Creating Visuals This slide show represents examples of the three types of boundaries that separate countries, states, and cultures. They are natural, geometric, and cultural boundaries. Have students create their own visuals depicting boundaries. Allow students time to research and print images, cut out photos from magazines, or draw illustrations to create a collage that depicts one of the types of boundaries. Have students present their collages to the class and then display the visuals in the classroom. **Visual/Spatial, Kinesthetic**

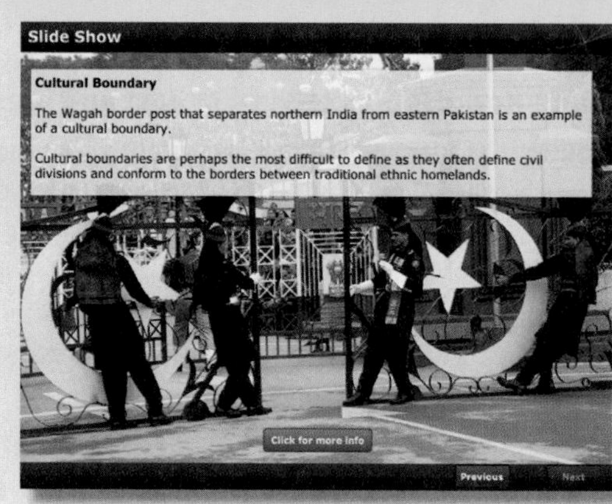

Slide Show
Cultural Boundary
The Wagah border post that separates northern India from eastern Pakistan is an example of a cultural boundary.
Cultural boundaries are perhaps the most difficult to define as they often define civil divisions and conform to the borders between traditional ethnic homelands.
Click for more info
Previous
Next

Terrorist attacks are usually carried out in such a way as to maximize the severity and length of the psychological impact. Not usually government supported, each act of terrorism is devised to have an impact on many large audiences. Terrorists also attack national symbols to show power and to attempt to shake the foundation of the country or society they are opposed to. For example, there was a series of terrorist attacks on September 11, 2001, at the World Trade Center in New York City, the Pentagon near Washington, D.C., and in the sky over western Pennsylvania. In 2012 there was an attack on the U.S. embassy in Libya. Terrorist acts frequently have a political purpose. They desire change so badly that failure to achieve change is seen as a worse outcome than the deaths of civilians.

Terrorism can be influenced by geographic factors, as in the Israeli-Palestinian conflict in which many innocent lives were lost. In 1947 Palestine was divided to establish the nation of Israel, resulting in two separate homelands for the Palestinian and Jewish peoples. This division of the land has polarized Israelis and Palestinians for over 60 years, resulting in ongoing violent conflicts in the region.

Alliances and cooperation can also be explored from a geographic perspective. Treaties and international organizations are examples of how countries work together to resolve conflicts and establish ways to share resources. For example, much of the acid rain in Canada comes from pollution in the United States. As a result, in the early 1990s the two countries signed a cooperative agreement that would reduce acid rain.

The United Nations (UN) is an international organization whose stated aims are facilitating cooperation in international law, international security, economic development, social progress, human rights, and aspirations to achieve world peace. The UN was founded in 1945 after World War II to stop wars between countries and to provide a platform for international dialogue. The North Atlantic Treaty Organization (NATO) is an alliance of 16 sovereign Euro-Atlantic countries dedicated to maintaining democratic freedom by means of collective defense. The World Trade Organization (WTO) is an international body that oversees trade agreements and settles trade disputes among countries. A country's membership in the WTO is an important step in its development, and less developed countries strive to become members. In 2000, hoping that trade might open China to democratic change, the United States granted full trading privileges to China and supported its entrance into the WTO. The following year China was admitted to the WTO. W

✓ READING PROGRESS CHECK

Discussing What is the function of the United Nations?

Connecting Geography to GOVERNMENT

Geopolitics

The *how* and *why* of the creation of political divisions—such as zones, countries, states within countries, and territories—are examples of the connection between geography and politics. *Geopolitics* examines how political units are influenced by geographic factors, such as a country's size, location, and resources. Geopolitical issues influence government and foreign policies, and guide political and economic decisions. It is crucial in a world with terrorism, globalization, and technological advances that governments understand how people and places are interconnected. C

EXPLORING ISSUES Discuss a specific example of how geography and politics are related.

LESSON 3 REVIEW

Reviewing Vocabulary (Tier Three Words)

1. ***Contrasting*** Describe the difference between a unitary system and a federal system. RH.9–10.4

Using Your Notes

2. ***Displaying*** Use your graphic organizer to summarize features of government. Include both the levels of government and types of governments. WHST.9–10.2

Answering the Guiding Questions

3. ***Identifying*** What influences the level and type of a country's government?
4. ***Discussing*** How does geography influence a country's government?
5. ***Expressing*** How do cooperation and conflict shape the division of Earth's surface?

Writing Activity

6. ***Informative/Explanatory*** Write a one-page essay explaining the human and physical geographic characteristics that can influence a country's foreign policy. WHST.9–10.2

Political Geography

W Writing Skills

Argument Discuss the pros and cons of a country joining an international organization such as the UN, NATO, or WTO. Have students write a paragraph defending a position about whether a country benefits by becoming a member of these organizations. BL **Verbal/Linguistic**

C Critical Thinking Skills

Speculating Guide students to discuss and define the terms *terrorism* and *globalization.* **Ask: Why might terrorism, globalization, and technological advances make it crucial for governments to understand how people and places are interconnected?** *(Technological advances allow countries to communicate and trade over distances and include the invention of weapons that cause mass destruction. For these reasons, it is more important than ever that nations understand and communicate positively.)* ELL **Logical/Mathematical**

CLOSE & REFLECT

Outlining Have students look through the headings and subheadings used in each section. Tell them to use these as a guide to outline the main ideas and important details. Then have students share their outlines with a partner to discuss what details could be included or left out.

ANSWERS, p. 91

✓ **READING PROGRESS CHECK** The United Nations is an international organization whose stated aims are facilitating cooperation in international law, international security, economic development, social progress, human rights, and aspirations to achieve world peace.

Connecting Geography Geopolitical issues influence government and foreign policies, and guide political and economic decisions.

LESSON 3 REVIEW ANSWERS

Reviewing Vocabulary

1. In a unitary system, all key powers are with the national or central government. The central government creates state or other local governments and gives them limited sovereignty. In a federal system, governmental powers are divided between national and state governments.

Using Your Notes

2. Types of government include autocracy–rule by on person, oligarchy–rule by a few people, and democracy–rule by many people. Governments have various levels such as national, state, city, or town.

Answering the Guiding Questions

3. The level and types of a country's government is influenced by the size and geographical features of the territory, the total population and ethnicities of its residents, and other unique characteristics that relate to its historical development.
4. Geographic areas can determine how political and administrative units are drawn up and how they will be governed. Geography influences governments as they develop policy to provide people with goods and services. Governments must know where their citizens are moving, why they are moving there, and how that affects their relationship with the environment. Infrastructures, such as roads, bridges, and power plants, must be built based on the geographic distribution of people, using both current demographic data and future projections.
5. Cooperation and conflict have contributed to and resulted from the political geographic divisions of the world. Global cooperation is frustrated by many factors, including border disputes, tensions over large territories, competition over natural resources, and multiple ethnic groups residing in a single political unit.

Writing Activity

6. Essays will differ, but should be logical and strongly supported through information from the lesson. Essays should explain the human and physical geographic characteristics that can influence a country's foreign policy.

ENGAGE

V Visual Skills

Analyzing Visuals Direct students' attention to the image of the girl holding a soft drink can. Define globalization as the widening exchange of commodities, ideas, and culture. Briefly discuss the elements in the photo that are most likely part of the girl's unique culture *(head piece, neck band, clothes)* and the items that are mostly likely the result of globalization *(soft drink, plastic straw, fingernail polish).* Divide the class into groups. Have each group generate three factors that facilitate globalization, such as a willing government, an active international trade, and religious acceptance. Have groups share their ideas with the class.

TEACH & ASSESS

Content Background Knowledge

UNESCO UNESCO began in 1945, when 37 countries agreed to work toward reconstructing educational systems in response to the destruction caused by World War II. UNESCO's current focus is to create a "culture of peace." It recognizes that international relations often lack peaceful resolution, but that creative and collective responses can foster nonviolent solutions to difficult problems. It works to build peace, eliminate poverty, create sustainable development, and promote intercultural dialogue.

R Reading Skills

Stating Have a student volunteer read the first paragraph aloud. **Ask:** What two factors have had the greatest impact on globalization? *(communication and transportation)* How long has globalization affected world cultures? *(for as long as trade has existed)* AL **Verbal/Linguistic**

C Critical Thinking Skills

Considering Advantages and Disadvantages Lead a class discussion on globalization. **Ask:** What are the advantages of globalization? *(increased economic efficiency, improved standard of living, goods specialization, cultural awareness)* What disadvantages are associated with globalization? *(dilution of traditional cultural heritages, loss of native languages, loss of unique cultural traditions and apparel)* Have students discuss possible ways to protect traditional cultures as globalization continues. **Interpersonal**

Case Study: **Culture** 

HOW HAS GLOBALIZATION CHANGED MODERN CULTURE?

R Globalization—the widening exchange of culture traits such as trade, technology, and ideas—is a process that has been taking place for as long as trade has existed. As the world becomes increasingly interconnected economically and socially, largely thanks to advances in communication and transportation, the process of globalization has reached every corner of the Earth.

There are many benefits to globalization. For example, technology developed in one country and shared with others helps to increase economic efficiency and standards of living. International trade has also allowed countries to specialize in the goods they produce well and trade for the goods they do not, enabling economies to grow more rapidly and giving people access to products and resources they may not otherwise have. Globalization has helped us become more aware of the cultures and lifestyles of others around the world, giving us new and unique perspectives on the diversity of life. V

C While globalization has many benefits, it also has drawbacks. As ideas, products, and even lifestyles are shared between cultures, traditional cultural heritage can become diluted by outside influences. Language, artistic traditions, clothing styles, and even behaviors can all be altered through interactions with other cultures. Language, for example, is one way in which globalization can lead to the permanent loss of some of the world's rare languages, such as Xyzyl, a language spoken in northwest Mongolia. Experts predict that there may be more than 500 languages that are spoken by fewer than 10 people. Many groups, including the United Nations Educational, Scientific and Cultural Organization (UNESCO), urge the protection of traditional culture in the face of increasing globalization.

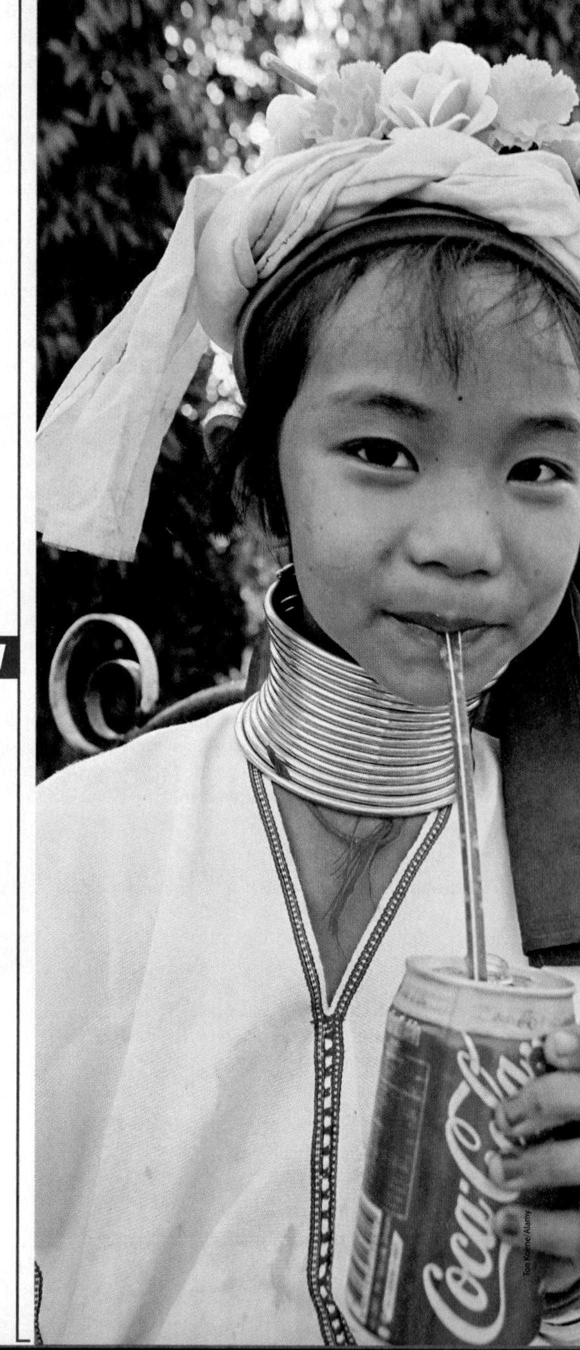

92

networks Online Teaching Options

IMAGE

Protect Cultural Heritage

Analyzing Visuals Project the image depicting the band proudly playing music representing their cultural heritage and ask the following questions to the class to encourage students' ability to improve visual analysis.

- What do you see? What action is taking place?
- What choices has the photographer made in taking the picture—such as the scene or placement of the camera—that conveys a point of view?
- What is the subjects' point of view? Do they know that they are being photographed?

(Student answers may vary, but should identify significant details of the image and properly understand the goal of the photographer.)
Visual/Spatial

Protect Cultural Heritage

T

PRIMARY SOURCE

"Today, with the rapid advance of globalization, the loss of intangible cultural heritage . . . can now be observed throughout the world. The threat of extinction to intangible cultural heritage is particularly noticeable in developing countries in Asia, Africa and the Middle East, today. Therefore, while modernization and industrialization remain urgent issues, it is at the same time essential to preserve and transmit these traditional cultures.

Taking into consideration the fact that every culture has been more or less influenced by others, and has forged a cultural identity within history, it goes without saying that the openness of one culture to others is very significant. However, the rapid flow of people, products and information—or rapid cultural interpenetration caused by globalization—menaces minority cultures, especially their intangible cultural heritage, which should be handed down from generation to generation. It is therefore most necessary that measures be taken to prevent this loss."

—Shogo Arai, Parliamentary Secretary for Foreign Affairs, "Japan and the Preservation of Intangible Cultural Heritage," 2004

Increase Cultural Awareness

PRIMARY SOURCE

"Paradoxically, it is precisely in the context of increasing globalization that more and more peoples and communities of the world have begun to recognize the importance of their cultural heritage—whether tangible or intangible—as a contribution to the world's cultural diversity. Communities in every land have come to realize that their cultural heritage, which is by nature fragile, plays a crucial role in their identity and that their engagement in safeguarding activities contributes to a sense of continuity. As a result, while globalization has undeniably contributed to the dissemination of cultures, its effects on cultural diversity can, if we are not careful, be negative. . . .

But more is needed in order to respond to peoples' growing awareness of the importance of their culture . . ."

C

—Koïchiro Matsuura, Director-General of UNESCO, "Globalization, Intangible Cultural Heritage and the Role of UNESCO," 2004

What do you think?

1. ***Drawing Conclusions*** Arai states that the loss of cultural heritage is most noticeable in developing countries. Why might the culture of more developed countries have such a strong impact on less developed countries? RH.9–10.8
2. ***Identifying Central Issues*** According to Matsuura, how has globalization increased cultural awareness? RH.9–10.1
3. ***Hypothesizing*** What steps do you think can be taken to ensure that cultural heritage is not diminished as a result of globalization? How might international organizations like UNESCO play a role? WHST.9–10.9

IMAGE

Increase Cultural Awareness

Analyzing Visuals Project the image showing a photographer filming a group of children and discuss how this image increases cultural awareness. **Ask:** **Why did the photographer choose to include another photographer in this photograph? What statement might this make?** *(Student answers may vary, but should identify significant details of the image and properly understand the goal of the photographer.)* Then have students explain whether or not they feel this image exemplifies the title, "Increase Cultural Awareness."
AL **Intrapersonal, Visual/Spatial**

T Technology Skills

Making Presentations Divide the class into small groups. Have each group research an assigned country to create a "You Are There" documentary. Each group member should assume a different aspect of the country's cultural heritage. For example, one individual could address fashion, another performing arts, religious traditions, food, etc. The presentation should strive for creativity and go beyond simple explanations.
ELL **Interpersonal**

C Critical Thinking Skills

Analyzing Primary Resources Have students reread both positions on cultural heritage. **Ask:** **Are Shogo Arai's concerns about the impact of globalization on traditional cultures justified? Why or why not?** *(Student answers may vary, but should include relevant details and explanations.)* **Do you agree with Matsuura that cultural heritage is "fragile"? Why or why not?** *(Student answers may vary, but should discuss their reasoning.)* **In what ways might globalization contribute to cultural diversity?** *(Possible answer: globalization creates an appreciation of cultural heritage)*

Explain to students that intangible cultural heritage can be passed on between generations through a variety of ways. Working with a partner, have students imagine two worlds: one in which globalization has merged the entire world into one culture and a world in which unique cultural distinctions are still clear. Have pairs write a list of pros and cons for each scenario. As a class, discuss these lists. **BL** **Verbal/Linguistic**

CLOSE & REFLECT

Narrative Have students write a paragraph describing how an intangible cultural heritage has been passed down in their own families or lost through the generations. Students should reflect on the importance of cultural heritage: whether these traditions help establish an identity within their community, or whether their families have had to eliminate traditions over the years in order to become a part of the community.

ANSWERS, p. 93

What do you think?

1. The culture of more developed countries provides comforts and advances that have been absent in the less developed countries.
2. More peoples and communities of the world have begun to recognize the importance of their cultural heritage—whether tangible or intangible—as a contribution to the world's cultural diversity.
3. Organizations can be set up to address specific programs to preserve cultural heritage. UNESCO could be the organization to set up special programs.

Economic Geography

ENGAGE

C Critical Thinking Skills

Previewing Have students quickly flip through the lesson to preview the visuals and headings as they consider what they already know about different economic systems and how different countries interact through the production and trade of various goods and services. Then have students write down three predictions on what they will read and learn about in this lesson.

TEACH & ASSESS

R1 Reading Skills

Setting a Purpose Invite a volunteer to read this paragraph. **Ask:** What key phrase is repeated in both the first and last line of this section? *(increasingly interdependent)* Based on this reading, what purpose might the author of this text have for repeating this phrase? *(Possible answer: the author might use this phrase to stress that in order for global economies to grow, people need to realize that they must depend on one another.)* Explain that this section is setting a purpose for the lesson content. **Verbal/Linguistic**

R2 Reading Skills

Paraphrasing Have students work with a partner taking turns paraphrasing each line of the paragraph. Then have each student write the definition of a traditional economy that includes the advantages and disadvantages, in their own words. **ELL Verbal/Linguistic**

networks

There's More Online!

- ☑ **IMAGE** New York Stock Exchange
- ☑ **IMAGE** Alaska Oil Marine Terminal
- ☑ **MAP** World GDP
- ☑ **TABLE** Economic Activities and Economic Development
- ☑ **INTERACTIVE SELF-CHECK QUIZ**
- ☑ **VIDEO** Economic Geography

Reading **HELP**DESK

Academic Vocabulary (Tier Two Words)

- **regulate**
- **incentive**

Content Vocabulary (Tier Three Words)

- **traditional economy**
- **market economy**
- **free enterprise**
- **capitalism**
- **mixed economy**
- **command economy**
- **more developed country**
- **newly industrialized country**
- **less developed country**

TAKING NOTES: *Key Ideas and Details*

ORGANIZING As you read about economic geography, complete a web diagram like the one below to list the major concepts of economic systems, development, and world trade.

Economic Geography → Economic Systems; Economies and World Trade; Economic Development

LESSON 4

C Economic Geography

ESSENTIAL QUESTION • *How do the characteristics and distribution of human populations affect human and physical systems?*

IT MATTERS BECAUSE

R1 *The growth of the global economy continues to make the world's peoples increasingly interdependent, or reliant on each other. Natural resources are extracted and traded around the world. Other trade items could be goods, services, and even labor. Countries with varying levels of economic development have become increasingly interdependent through this world trade.*

Economic Systems

GUIDING QUESTION *What are the three main types of economic systems?*

All economic systems must make three basic economic decisions: (1) what and how many goods and services should be produced, (2) how they should be produced, and (3) who gets the goods and services that are produced. These decisions are made differently in the three major economic systems—traditional, market, and command.

R2 In a **traditional economy**, habit and custom determine the rules for all economic activity. Individuals are not free to make decisions based on what they would like to have. Instead, their behavior is defined by the customs of their elders and ancestors. For example, it was a tradition in the Inuit society of northern Canada that a hunter would share the food from the hunt with the other families in the village. Today, traditional economies exist in very limited parts of the world. One of the few advantages in a traditional economy is that the roles of individuals are clearly defined. There are also many disadvantages to this type of society. These societies are often very slow to change. When new technologies are introduced, these ideas and techniques are discouraged.

In a **market economy**, individuals and private groups make decisions about what things to produce. People, as shoppers, choose what products they will or will not buy, and businesses produce more of what they believe consumers want. A market economy is based on the concept of **free enterprise**, the idea that private individuals or groups have the right to own property or businesses and make a profit with only limited government interference. In a free enterprise system,

networks ***Online Teaching Options***

ANSWERS, p. 94

TAKING NOTES: Economic Systems—All economic systems must make three basic economic decisions: what and how many goods and services should be produced, how they should be produced, and who gets the goods and services that are produced. These decisions are made differently in the three major economic systems, which are: traditional, market, and command; **Economies and World Trade**—World trade is the exchange of capital, labor, goods, and services across international borders or territories, involving the import and export of goods. In most countries, such trade represents a significant share of gross domestic product (GDP); **Economic Development**—Most natural resources are not evenly distributed throughout the Earth. This uneven distribution affects the global economy. As a result, countries specialize in the economic activities best suited to their resources.

INTERACTIVE BELLRINGER

GDP Comparison

Calculating This graph can be used to discuss the economies of eight different countries. Explain that these are not the top eight countries in the world, but that the top two on the graph are the top two in the world. Have students read the introductory text and use the chart to answer the questions. Then have students write their own question and answer based on the graph and exchange questions with a partner to answer and discuss.

BL Logical/Mathematical

GDP Comparison

Gross domestic product (GDP) represents the total dollar value of all goods and services produced over a specific period of time.

1. The graph compares the GDP of eight countries over one year's time. How do the top two countries' GDP compare?

The United States' GDP is about twice as large as China's.

COUNTRY	U.S. DOLLARS (IN TRILLIONS)
Mexico	1.15
Australia	1.48
India	1.67
United Kingdom	2.41
Brazil	2.49
Japan	5.86
China	7.29
United States	15.09

Source: CIA World Factbook, 2011

Auto-Run Click Through Previous 1 of 3 Next

All economic systems must make decisions about the types and quantity of goods and services, including how they are going to be produced and sold.

◀ **CRITICAL THINKING**

1. ***Identifying*** Which type of system does the image on the left represent?
2. ***Describing*** What features in the image on the right represent characteristics of a traditional economy?

people are free to choose what jobs they will have and for whom they will work. People have the ability to make as much money as they can and do what is in their best interest. Another positive aspect of market economies is that the government tries to stay out of the way of businesses and there is a great variety of goods and services for consumers. An economic system organized in this way is referred to as **capitalism**.

One major problem with this type of economy is that it does not always provide the basic needs to everyone in the society. The weak, sick, disabled, and old sometimes have trouble providing for themselves and often slip into poverty.

No country in the world, however, has a pure market economy system. Today, the U.S. economy and others like it are described as mixed economies. A **mixed economy** is one in which the government supports and **regulates** free enterprise through decisions that affect the marketplace. In this arrangement, the government's main economic task is to preserve the free market by keeping competition free and fair and by supporting public interests. Governments in modern mixed economies also influence their economies by spending tax revenues to support social services.

C In a **command economy**, the government owns or directs the means of production—land, labor, capital (machinery, factories), and business managers—and controls the distribution of goods. Believing that such economic decision making benefits all of society and not just a few people, countries with command economies try to distribute goods and services equally among all citizens. Public taxes, for example, are used to support social services, such as housing and health care, for all citizens. However, citizens have no voice in how this tax money is spent.

R1 Socialism and communism are examples of command economies because they involve heavy government control. However, in practice these two economic systems are mixed economies. In a socialist economy, the government owns some, but not all, of the basic productive resources. The government also provides for some of the basic needs of the people, such as education and health care. Communism is an extreme form of socialism in which all property is collectively, not privately, owned. Under communism, the government decides how much to produce, what to produce, and how to distribute the goods and services produced. R2 One political party—the Communist Party—makes decisions and may even use various forms of coercion to ensure that the decisions are carried out at lower political and economic levels.

traditional economy a system in which tradition and custom control all economic activity; exists in only a few parts of the world today

market economy an economic system based on free enterprise, in which businesses are privately owned and production and prices are determined by supply and demand

free enterprise a system in which private individuals or groups have the right to own property or businesses and make a profit with limited government interference

capitalism a system in which factors of production are privately owned

mixed economy a system of resource management in which the government supports and regulates enterprise through decisions that affect the marketplace

regulate to govern or direct according to rule

command economy a system of resource management in which decisions about production and distribution of goods and services are made by a central authority

(tl)Stan Honda/AFP/Getty Images, (tr)Bernd Rohrschnei/age fotostock

The Human World **95**

C Critical Thinking Skills

Contrasting Review with students the aspects of a market economy and a command economy. **Ask:** **How are market and command economies different?** *(Possible answers: In a market economy, individuals and groups make decisions about what things to produce and buy, while in a command economy, the government controls the production and distribution of these goods. A pure market economy may not meet the basic needs of all people, while in a pure command economy, the government will try to make sure that everyone's needs are met.)* **AL** **Logical/Mathematical**

R1 Reading Skills

Citing Text Evidence Remind students to cite the wording from the text when answering a question to provide a more explicit response. Present the following questions and have students practice using the skill. **Ask:** **How is socialism in practice an example of a mixed economy?** *(Possible answer: In a socialist economy, the government owns some, but not all, of the basic productive resources. In a true command economy, the government would own or direct all of these resources.)* **How is property dealt with in a communist system?** *(Possible answer: In a communist system, all property is collectively owned, or owned by everyone all together, instead of privately owned.)* **Verbal/Linguistic**

R2 Reading Skills

Using Context Clues Review with students that if they come across an unfamiliar word, they can use other words or phrases in the sentence to figure out its meaning. **Ask:** **What does the word *coercion* mean?** *(Possible answer: forcing someone to do something)* **What context clues help you figure out this meaning?** *(Possible answer: The communist government in the example is making decisions that people may not want to go along with, so sometimes it may need to force them to obey.)* **AL** **Logical/Mathematical**

GAME

Economic Geography

Describing This interactive Tic-Tac-Toe game has students answer questions that define and describe economic activities and systems. Before beginning the game, have each student review the lesson, paying particular attention to the content vocabulary and definitions. Then ask students to find a partner to play the game. After students have had a chance to complete the game, discuss any definitions, terms, or answers that caused concerns. **Visual/Spatial**

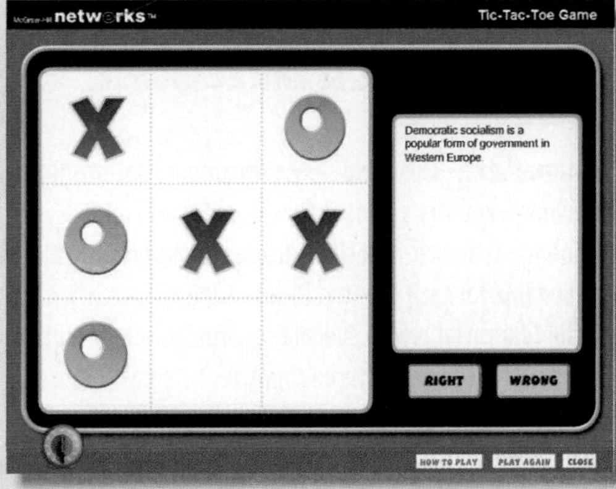

ANSWERS, p. 95

CRITICAL THINKING

1. It represents a market economy.
2. It appears that habit and custom have established the rules for the economy.

C1 Critical Thinking Skills

Classifying Have students reread the *Economic Systems* section. Discuss with students the differences between the economic systems and how countries use them. Then have students classify where various countries fall along the economic spectrum between the points of free enterprise and communism, including both countries mentioned in the text (such as the United States, the old Soviet Union, modern Russia, and Vietnam) and ones they research on their own. Invite students to share their results and discuss why they placed each country where they did and how some countries (Soviet Union and the modern countries into which it split) have changed over time. **AL** **Visual/Spatial**

W Writing Skills

Argument Have students consider the positive and negative aspects of the different kinds of economic systems. Discuss real-life examples of how these governments work in practice, either from the text or from students' prior knowledge. Organize students into small groups. Ask each group to form a theory about which form of economic system is best by using the text, their own knowledge, or by conducting online research. Have groups use their research to write an argument defending their chosen economic system. Remind them to support their ideas with specific facts and examples and to address any possible counter arguments. Have groups share their finished writing with the class and discuss their ideas with other groups who chose and defended the same economic system.
BL **Verbal/Linguistic**

C2 Critical Thinking Skills

Making Inferences Have students briefly describe primary and secondary economic activities and identify how they are alike *(both use raw resources)* and different *(primary economic activities take and use the resources as is, while secondary ones turn the original raw material into something else)*. Then **ask:** **Why might both of these types of economic activities take place near the source of the natural resource or the market for a finished good?** *(Possible answer: The people taking part in these primary and secondary economic activities can save money on transportation costs by locating their efforts near where the resource or its market is found.)* **BL** **Logical/Mathematical**

ANSWERS, p. 96

READING PROGRESS CHECK A market economy is an economic system based on free enterprise, in which businesses are privately owned, and production and prices are determined by supply and demand.

incentive something that motivates one to act

Recent history has demonstrated, however, that communist economies lack the free decision making and **incentives** that foster business innovation and generation of products that people need and want. Customers can be limited in their choices, and economies can stagnate. As a result of these problems, command economies often decline. The Soviet Union, as described below by a Russian observer, provided an example of this situation:

C1

PRIMARY SOURCE

"In 1961, the [Communist] party predicted . . . that the Soviet Union would have the world's highest living standard by 1980. . . . But when that year came and went, the Soviet Union still limped along, burdened by . . . a stagnant economy."

—Dusko Doder, "The Bolshevik Revolution," *National Geographic*, October 1992

W

By 2000, Russia and the other countries that were once part of the Soviet Union were developing market economies. Communist China and Vietnam have also allowed some free enterprise to promote economic growth, although their governments tightly control political affairs.

Socialism allows a wider range of free enterprise. It has three main goals: (1) an equitable distribution of wealth and economic opportunity; (2) society's control, through its government, of decisions about public goods; and (3) public ownership of services and factories that are essential. Some socialist countries, like those in Western Europe, are democracies. Under democratic socialism people have basic human rights and elect their political leaders.

READING PROGRESS CHECK

Assessing On what idea is a market economy based?

Economic Development

GUIDING QUESTION *What influences economic development?*

C2

Most natural resources are not evenly distributed throughout the Earth. This uneven distribution affects the global economy. As a result, countries specialize in the economic activities best suited to their resources.

Geographers and economists classify all of the world's economic activities into four types. Primary economic activities—such as farming, grazing, fishing, forestry, and mining—involve taking or using natural resources directly from the Earth. Such activities take place near the natural resources that are being gathered or used. For example, coal mining occurs at the site of a coal deposit.

Secondary economic activities use raw materials to make a tangible product that is new and more valuable than the original raw material. Such activities include manufacturing automobiles, assembling electronic goods, producing electric power, or making pottery. These activities occur close to the resource or to the market for the finished good.

Tertiary economic activities do not involve directly acquiring and remaking natural resources. Instead, these activities provide services to people and businesses. Doctors, teachers, lawyers, bakers, truck drivers, and store clerks all provide professional, wholesale, or retail services.

Quaternary economic activities are concerned with the processing, management, and distribution of information. They are vitally important to modern economies that have been transformed in recent years by the information revolution. Just as with tertiary economic activities, people performing these activities include "white collar" professionals working in education, government, business, information processing, and research.

96

networks Online Teaching Options

TABLE

Economic Activities and Economic Development

Summarizing This table shows the direct relationship between a country's level of development and its economic activities. As a class, discuss the information in the table for each country. Direct students' attention to the column labeled "Level of Economic Development." Point out that there are three countries listed as "More Developed," three as "Newly Industrialized," and three as "Less Developed." Have students write a summarizing statement about each of the three levels of economic development based on the information of the three countries within that level as presented in the table. **Verbal/Linguistic, Visual/Spatial**

Economic Activities and Economic Development

Country	Level of Economic Development	Major Economic Activities	GDP per Capita (purchasing power parity)
United States	More Developed	service industries, commercial agriculture, industrial supplies	$49,000
Sweden	More Developed	service industries, iron and steel, precision machinery	$40,900
South Korea	More Developed	electronics, telecommunications, automobiles	$32,100
Mexico	Newly Industrialized	service industries, food and beverages, consumer goods manufacturing	$14,800
South Africa	Newly Industrialized	service industries, mining, automobile assembly	$11,100
China	Newly Industrialized	mining and ore processing, textiles, petroleum	$8,500
Palau	Less Developed	tourism, subsistence agriculture, fishing	$8,100
Pakistan	Less Developed	agriculture, textiles, crude oil production	$2,800
Zimbabwe	Less Developed	mining, steel production, wood products	$500

Help

Economic Activities and Economic Development			CHART SKILLS
Country	**Level of Economic Development**	**Major Economic Activities**	**GDP per Capita (purchasing power parity)**
United States	More Developed	service industries, commercial agriculture, industrial supplies	$49,000
Sweden	More Developed	service industries, iron and steel, precision machinery	$40,900
South Korea	More Developed	electronics, telecommunications, automobiles	$32,100
Mexico	Newly Industrialized	service industries, food and beverages, consumer goods manufacturing	$14,800
South Africa	Newly Industrialized	service industries, mining, automobile assembly	$11,100
China	Newly Industrialized	mining and ore processing, textiles, petroleum	$8,500
Palau	Less Developed	tourism, subsistence agriculture, fishing	$8,100
Pakistan	Less Developed	agriculture, textiles, crude oil production	$2,800
Zimbabwe	Less Developed	mining, steel production, wood products	$500

Source: *CIA World Factbook*, 2012

V

The major economic activities of a country have a direct relationship to the country's level of development. The level of development also has a relationship to standard of living, as shown in this table with GDP per capita (gross domestic product per person).

▲ **CRITICAL THINKING**

1. ***Classifying*** Which countries in the table have a major economic activity that is considered a primary economic activity?
2. ***Evaluating*** What information in the table illustrates the standard of living in each country? What is the relationship between economic development and standard of living?

Economic activities, including *industrialization*, or the spread of industry, help influence a country's level of economic development. Those countries having more technology and manufacturing, such as the United States and Canada, are called **more developed countries**. Most people work in service or information industries and enjoy a high standard of living. Because of modern techniques, only a small percentage of workers in more developed countries is needed to grow enough food to feed entire populations. For similar reasons, relatively small percentages of the people are employed in manufacturing industries in more developed countries.

T

Newly industrialized countries have moved from primarily agricultural activities to primarily manufacturing and industrial activities. This transition to manufacturing and industry often brings improvements in socioeconomic development. Examples of newly industrialized countries are Mexico, Malaysia, and Turkey.

Those countries that, according to the United Nations, exhibit the lowest indicators of socioeconomic development are **less developed countries**. In many less developed countries, which are primarily in Africa, Asia, and Latin America, agriculture remains dominant. Even though some commercial farming occurs, most farmers in these countries engage in subsistence farming, growing only enough food for family needs. Some countries' involvement in light industry grows out of a history of cottage industries, businesses that employ workers in their homes. As a result, most people in less developed countries remain poor, as economic development typically reduces poverty.

more developed country a country that has a highly developed economy and advanced technological infrastructure relative to other less developed nations

newly industrialized country a country that has begun transitioning from primarily agricultural to primarily manufacturing and industrial activity

less developed country a country that, according to the United Nations, exhibits the lowest indicators of socioeconomic development

✓ **READING PROGRESS CHECK**

Listing List the four types of economic activities and explain how these economic activities relate to a country's level of development.

VIDEO

China and the US Fight to Lead World in Green Energy

Identifying Invite volunteers to identify types of products that they have purchased with the label *Made in China* and products they have purchased with the label *Made in USA*. Lead a class discussion on how new technology affects the economy of both China and the United States in relationship to the video content. Then have students identify ways that the trade of goods, services, and even labor impacts the economy of the United States, China, and the rest of the world. BL **Verbal/Linguistic**

Content Background Knowledge

Palau The country of Palau is geographically suited to grow crops. Even though freshwater can be a limited resource, making certain plants difficult to grow, most of the land is covered in rich soil. Farming is not a thriving industry, however, and barely rises to the subsistence level because of economic reasons; thus it is less expensive for the country to import food than it is to grow it.

V Visual Skills

Reading Tables Have students interpret the table. Provide students with resources to research the economic activities of each country. **Ask:** **What are some of the major economic activities in more developed countries?** *(service industries, commercial agriculture, electronics, telecommunications)* **What are some of the economic activities in countries with low GDP per capita?** *(farming, agriculture, fishing, mining)* Direct students' attention to the three countries listed as "Newly Industrialized." **Ask:** **What commonalities do the economic activities in these countries have?** *(Most of the economic activities are manufacturing or industry based.)* Continue to ask questions about information provided in the chart. AL **Visual/Spatial, Logical/Mathematical**

T Technology Skills

Identifying Factors Assign student partners to research agriculture in a more developed, newly industrialized, or less developed country. Have pairs conduct online research to prepare a short list of factors (supported by detailed examples) that affect the economic agriculture activities that are ongoing in that country. Invite pairs to present their results to the class. **Verbal/Linguistic**

ANSWERS, p. 97

✓ **READING PROGRESS CHECK** Primary economic activities, such as farming, fishing, and mining, involve taking or using natural resources directly from Earth. Secondary economic activities use raw materials to make a tangible product that is new and more valuable than the original raw material. Tertiary economic activities provide services to people and businesses. Quaternary economic activities are the processing, management, and distribution of information.

CRITICAL THINKING

1. Countries that have a major economic activity considered a primary economic activity are: South Africa, China, Palau, Pakistan, Zimbabwe, Sweden, and the United States.
2. The *Level of Economic Development* column indicates the standard of living in each country. Countries with a more developed level of economic development tend to have the highest standard of living.

R Reading Skills

Determining Word Meanings Ask students what the word *national* means. Then point out the word *multinational* in the text. Ask students what the prefix *multi- (many)* means. **Ask:** Based on your understanding of the prefix *multi-*, what does the word *multinational* mean? *(something that operates in more than one nation or country, such as a business)* ELL Verbal/Linguistic

C1 Critical Thinking Skills

Making Inferences Discuss factors that affect world trade in a class discussion. **Ask:** What do you think education has to do with the labor costs in a country? *(Possible answer: People in less developed countries may find it harder to attain a higher level of education and may only be qualified to work manufacturing jobs that do not pay as well, thus saving businesses from high labor costs.)* Why do you think less developed countries have allowed multinationals to build factories and form partnerships with local companies? *(Possible answer: They may think that the new job opportunities brought to the country by these multinationals will improve their economies, help them become more developed, and enjoy a higher standard of living.)* AL Intrapersonal, Logical/Mathematical

C2 Critical Thinking Skills

Analyzing Primary Sources Working with a partner, have students discuss the international coffee crisis. Have pairs write a paragraph analyzing how the management of the natural resource of coffee plants affects the location and patterns of movement of people, money, and the coffee products. Then share their findings with the class. *(Students should discuss how the management affects both the location and the patterns of movement of people, money, and products, including analysis of factors such as how competition from large companies who manage differently than family farms can cause people (families) to change location, how coffee producers can use different strategies such as massive agribusiness techniques or focusing on quality to make money, and how consumers may reject the management techniques of some coffee producers and import the coffee produced by other farmers instead.)* BL Logical/Mathematical

ANSWERS, p. 98

DBQ Document-Based Questions

1. It could have an impact on the economy by providing revenue when coffee is purchased.
2. Through fair trade, farmers can sell their coffee directly to buyers. This means they can cut out the person in the middle and not lose so much of the profit.

Economies and World Trade

GUIDING QUESTION *What stimulates and supports world trade?*

World trade is the exchange of capital, labor, goods, and services across international borders or territories, involving the import and export of goods. In most countries, such trade represents a significant share of gross domestic product (GDP). Trade among countries has been present throughout history, but its economic, social, and political importance has increased in recent centuries.

The unequal distribution of natural resources is one factor that promotes a complex network of trade among countries. Countries export their specialized products, trading them to other countries that cannot produce those goods. When countries cannot produce as much as they need of a certain good, they import it, or buy it from another country. That country, in turn, may buy the first country's products, making the two countries trading partners.

R C1 Other factors affecting world trade are differences in labor costs and education. Multinationals often base their business decisions on these factors. They locate their headquarters in a more developed country and locate their manufacturing or assembly operations in less developed or newly industrialized countries with low labor costs. In recent decades, many less developed countries have allowed multinationals to build factories or form partnerships with local companies.

ANALYZING PRIMARY SOURCES 

Coffee Country

Coffee has a long tradition as an important export crop for both Guatemala and Mexico, employing thousands of workers and bringing income to the region. However, a coffee crisis is causing families that have grown coffee for generations to leave their fields and head for the city or for the border, leaving entire coffee estates abandoned.

"The problem is what is known as the international coffee crisis. Simply put, there's too much cheap coffee flooding the market these days. It comes from countries such as Brazil, and more recently Vietnam, which have been using massive agribusiness techniques. However, some small family farmers have found a way to prosper by following the environmental guidelines for what is known as fair trade. They sell their coffee directly to buyers, thereby cutting out the middleman. The difficulty is that the success depends upon the taste of the coffee.

C2 And so the tasting process becomes a critical make-or-break step for many farmers, and failure of the taste test can mean taking a loss on an entire season.

'In the current crisis,' [reporter Sam] Quinones observes, 'peasant coffee growers have to learn the Starbucks lesson and focus on quality. Consumers, meanwhile, have to be willing to pay extra for the best coffee, searching out regional coffees the way they do with wine.'

Even those consumers who like good coffee don't know where it comes from. And many haven't even heard of the fair trade concept. Until all that changes, the international coffee crisis may not be going away anytime soon."

—PBS Frontline/World, "Guatemala/Mexico- Coffee Country," May 2003

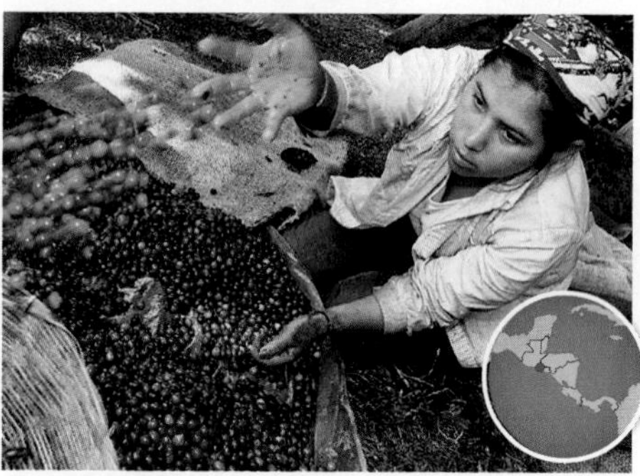

A woman working on a large coffee estate separates the green coffee seeds from the ripe ones.

Roberto Escobar/AFP/Getty Images

DBQ ▲ CRITICAL THINKING

1. ***Identifying Cause and Effect*** In what ways could coffee purchased in countries far from Guatemala or Mexico affect people living there? RH.9–10.2
2. ***Problem Solving*** How does fair trade help the coffee farmers in this region? RH.9–10.2

98

networks Online Teaching Options

INTERACTIVE IMAGE

Oil Trade and Transportation

Finding the Main Idea Use this interactive image of oil trade and transportation to provide an understanding of trade in world markets. As a class, read aloud each text box script. Then display each of the text boxes again and allow time for students to write down the main idea of each script in their own words. Afterwards, guide a class discussion on how oil is a major commodity of trade in world markets. Be sure to include the terms *domestic trade, international trade, imports,* and *exports* in the discussion. ELL Verbal/Linguistic

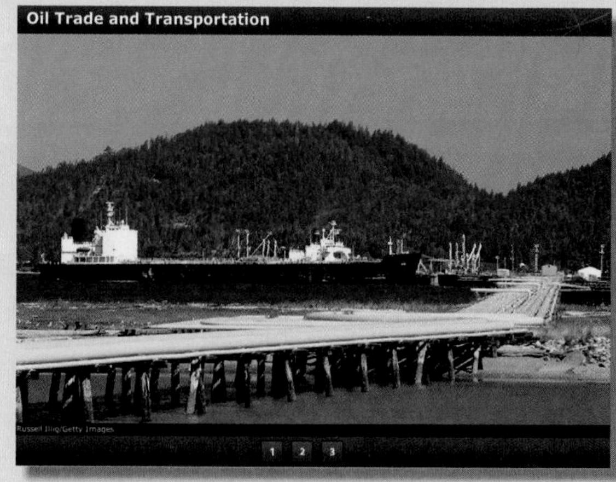

Russell Illig/Getty Images

Oil is a major commodity of trade in the world markets.

◀ **CRITICAL THINKING**

1. ***Contrasting*** How is an import different from an export?
2. ***Evaluating*** Explain why a country would need to import oil.

International trade is, in principle, not different from domestic trade. The main difference is that international trade is typically more costly due to additional costs such as tariffs, time costs due to border delays, and costs associated with country differences such as language, the legal system, or other cultural barriers.

Another difference between domestic and international trade is that factors of production such as capital and labor are typically more mobile within a country than across countries. Thus, international trade is mostly restricted to trade in goods and services, and only to a lesser extent to trade in capital, labor, or other factors of production. Trade in goods and services can serve as a substitute for trade in factors of production. **C**

Sometimes, a country can import goods that make extensive use of that factor of production and thus embody it. An example is the import of labor-intensive goods by the United States from China. Instead of importing Chinese labor, the United States imports goods that were produced with Chinese labor.

Emerging markets are nations with social or business activity in the process of rapid growth and industrialization. The economies of China and India are considered to be the largest. The seven largest emerging and developing economies by either nominal GDP or GDP (PPP) are China, Brazil, Russia, India, Mexico, Indonesia, and Turkey. The ASEAN–China Free Trade Area, launched on January 1, 2010, is the largest regional emerging market in the world. **T**

✓ **READING PROGRESS CHECK**

Contrasting Explain the differences between international trade and domestic trade.

LESSON 4 REVIEW (CCSS)

Reviewing Vocabulary (Tier Three Words)

1. ***Identifying*** What are the advantages and disadvantages to a command economy? RH.9–10.4

Using Your Notes

2. ***Describing*** Use your graphic organizer to describe the three basic economic decisions that are made by economic systems. WHST.9–10.2

Answering the Guiding Questions

3. ***Listing*** What are the three main types of economic systems?
4. ***Describing*** What influences economic development?
5. ***Discussing*** What stimulates and supports world trade?

Writing Activity

6. ***Informative/Explanatory*** Write an essay explaining the advantages and disadvantages a less developed country might experience by joining a free trade agreement. WHST.9–10.2

C Critical Thinking Skills

Predicting Consequences Discuss with students how capital and labor are used to produce goods and services. **Ask:** **Why are these factors more mobile within a country than across countries?** *(It is easier to ship a product to another country than to relocate workers.)* **How would the cost of goods from China change if wages in China rose?** *(The cost of the goods would rise, too.)* **How might the way the United States acquires goods change if the cost of importing goods from China rose?** *(If labor costs in China rise, the United States might use its own domestic labor.)* **Verbal/Linguistic**

T Technology Skills

Examining Information The concept of emerging markets may be difficult for students to understand. Invite a group of students to research nations with emerging markets and present their findings to the class. BL **Verbal/Linguistic**

CLOSE & REFLECT

Summarizing Tell students to review this lesson and write a summary of how and why the countries of today are becoming more interdependent.

ANSWERS, p. 99

✓ **READING PROGRESS CHECK** The difference is that international trade is more costly due to additional costs such as tariffs, border delays, and country differences such as language, legal systems, or cultural barriers.

CRITICAL THINKING

1. An import is an item brought into a country, while an export is an item sent to another country.
2. Some countries have little or no oil reserves. In these cases, they need to import oil to meet their needs.

LESSON 4 REVIEW ANSWERS

Reviewing Vocabulary

1. In a command economy, the government owns or directs the means of production and controls the distribution of goods. Countries with command economies try to distribute goods and services equally among all citizens; however, citizens have no voice in how money taken in through taxes is being spent.

Using Your Notes

2. A traditional economy is a system in which tradition and custom control all economic activity; it exists in only a few parts of the world today. A market economy is an economic system based on free enterprise, in which businesses are privately owned and production and prices are determined by supply and demand. In a command economy the government owns or directs the means of production—land, labor, capital (machinery, factories)—and controls the distribution of goods.

Answering the Guiding Questions

3. The three main economic systems are traditional, market, and command economies.
4. Most natural resources are not evenly distributed throughout the Earth. This uneven distribution affects the global economy. As a result, countries specialize in the economic activities best suited to their resources.
5. Countries' needs and their availability—or lack of availability—of natural resources and labor can stimulate and support world trade.

Writing Activity

6. Essays will differ, but should be logical and strongly supported by information from the chapter. Essays should explain the advantages and disadvantages a less developed country might experience by joining a free trade agreement.

ENGAGE

C1 Critical Thinking Skills

Synthesizing Read the title aloud and then have students identify each of the continents and as many countries as they can. Direct their attention to the content legend, explaining that oil, water, timber, and grains are all important natural resources. Divide the class into teams. Have each team determine which of the featured countries is the richest in resources. Have teams explain their resource assessments. Come to a class consensus and list the countries in order of economic strength based on the four resources shown, with 1 being the country that potentially has the greatest economic strength.

TEACH & ASSESS

R Reading Skills

Explaining Ask a volunteer to read about the patterns of resource distribution. Discuss the content. **Ask:** **According to the text, why do some countries have a limited supply of resources?** *(because resources are distributed unevenly around the world)* **Saudi Arabia has a low amount of timber. Which countries might be willing to export timber to Saudi Arabia?** *(United States, Canada, Brazil, or China)* **What conflicts do you know of that may have resulted over natural resources?** *(Possible answers: conflicts in the Middle East over oil, the Persian Gulf War over oil, Congo, Liberia, and Angola conflicts over diamonds)* **Verbal/Linguistic**

Content Background Knowledge

The Amazon The Amazon forest, also called *Amazonia,* covers more than half of the country of Brazil. The Amazon River cuts through the Amazon forest, beginning in the Peruvian Andes, flowing east until it meets the Atlantic Ocean. About 1,100 tributaries drain into the Amazon forest and then into the Amazon River. The Amazon forest provides nearly 20 percent of Earth's oxygen and may contain approximately half of the world's animal and plant species. Over 20 percent of the Amazon rain forest has disappeared because of excessive mining, logging, and agriculture. Over 50 percent of the rain forests throughout the world have been destroyed in the last 50 years.

C2 Critical Thinking Skills

Making Inferences Based on the information provided in the Content Background Knowledge and in the Brazil Resource Distribution Chart, have students explain the importance of the Amazon rain forest and the Amazon River to the country of Brazil. *(Student answers may vary, but should include relevant connections between the Amazon forest and river to Brazil's wealth of natural resources.)* **Interpersonal**

C1 PATTERNS OF RESOURCE DISTRIBUTION

R *Earth's natural resources are unevenly distributed across the globe. As a result, a country might have abundant access to one resource but may have a limited supply of another resource. Saudi Arabia, for example, is a country rich in petroleum, but it has very limited access to freshwater. This uneven distribution of resources is a major reason countries trade with one another, exchanging the resources they have for the ones they need. Access to natural resources can also be a cause of conflict in some parts of the world.*

LEGEND

- Proven Oil Reserves
- Renewable Water Resources
- Forest Area (timber)
- Cereal Yield (grains)

GLOBAL SCALE
Relative amount compared to total world resources.

VERY LOW LOW MED HIGH VERY HIGH

networks Online Teaching Options

GAME

Population Geography

Setting a Purpose This fill-in-the-blank game on population geography can be played at any time during Unit 1. Play as a whole-class activity or have students play each other on teams or in pairs. After students have completed the game, have them find one recent news article about a positive or negative effect of population and bring the articles into the classroom to exchange with another student. Each student should read an article and then write a paragraph on what he or she found interesting or surprising about the information in the article. **Verbal/Linguistic, Intrapersonal**

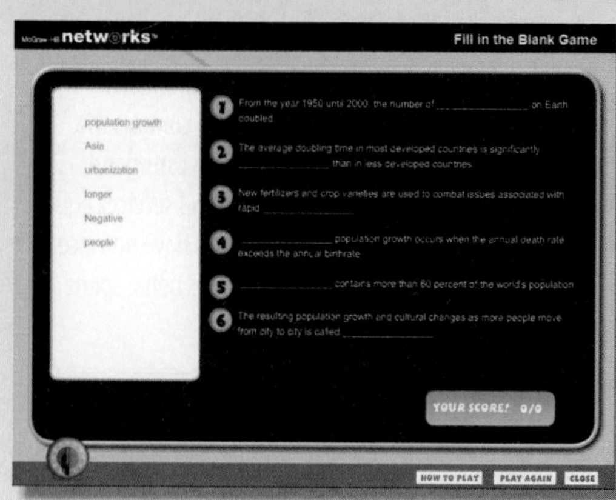

GERMANY
276,000,000 BBL
110,760 sq km
188 cu km
6,716 kg per hectare

SAUDI ARABIA
262,600,000,000 BBL
9,770 sq km
2.4 cu km
5,621 kg per hectare

CHINA
14,800,000,000 BBL
2,068,610 sq km
2,829.6 cu km
5,521 kg per hectare

INDIA
5,682,000,000 BBL
684,340 sq km
1,907.8 cu km
2,537 kg per hectare

SOUTH AFRICA
15,000,000 BBL
56,660 sq km
50 cu km
4,162 kg per hectare

Making Connections

1. ***Analyzing*** Which of the four resources on this map do you think Canada supplements with imports? From which country might Canada import this resource?
2. ***Drawing Conclusions*** Using one of the countries featured on this map as an example, explain how a country's physical geography, including climate, location, and landforms, influences its access to natural resources.

C Critical Thinking Skills

Understanding Relationships Review with students the relationship between world trade, natural resources, and the global economy. Remind students that international trade is increasingly important to a country's economic, social, and political position in the world. **Ask:** **As you analyze the natural resources in Saudi Arabia, what economic impact does Saudi Arabia have to global trading?** *(Student answers may vary, but should focus on the impact of Saudi Arabia's rich oil reserves and their economic and political importance to trading in world markets.)* **How might the imbalance of resources impact economic decisions made by the government of Saudi Arabia?** *(Student answers should focus on how resources impact patterns of economic growth and affect the country's need to import and export goods and services.)* **Verbal/Linguistic**

T Technology Skills

Making Presentations Divide the class into small groups. Assign each group a featured country from this activity: the United States, Brazil, Canada, Germany, Saudi Arabia, South Africa, India, or China. Using available technology, have students create multimedia presentations about that country's resources. Each presentation should include a resource page providing information about the four resources, as well as a hyperlink with a page of images they have gathered from online research. These images will illustrate information about the resource and provide a visual account of the economic impact of each resource as it relates to the assigned country. Each presentation will also include a similar resource graphic to those illustrated in this lesson, emphasizing each resource. Groups may also wish to add an audio element to each page or hyperlink image. For example, students could include a voice-over description and/or musical background. Have groups share their presentations with the class. **BL** **Visual/Spatial, Auditory/Musical**

TABLE

Economic Development Table

Comparing and Contrasting This interactive table will provide information on the economic development of various countries throughout the world. Have students choose two countries in the table and analyze the data of both countries. Then have them write a paragraph that explains the economic development similarities and the differences between the two countries. Lead a class discussion in which students provide a list of valuable natural resources such as precious metals, diamonds, oil, or petroleum. **BL** **Visual/Spatial**

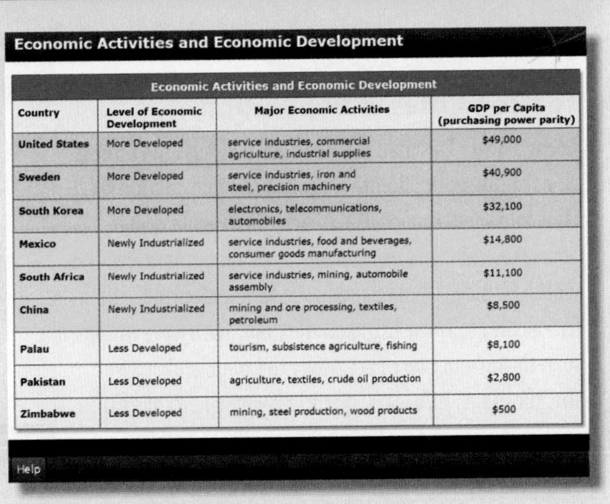

Economic Activities and Economic Development

Country	Level of Economic Development	Major Economic Activities	GDP per Capita (purchasing power parity)
United States	More Developed	service industries, commercial agriculture, industrial supplies	$49,000
Sweden	More Developed	service industries, iron and steel, precision machinery	$40,900
South Korea	More Developed	electronics, telecommunications, automobiles	$32,100
Mexico	Newly Industrialized	service industries, food and beverages, consumer goods manufacturing	$14,800
South Africa	Newly Industrialized	service industries, mining, automobile assembly	$11,100
China	Newly Industrialized	mining and ore processing, textiles, petroleum	$8,500
Palau	Less Developed	tourism, subsistence agriculture, fishing	$8,100
Pakistan	Less Developed	agriculture, textiles, crude oil production	$2,800
Zimbabwe	Less Developed	mining, steel production, wood products	$500

Help

CLOSE & REFLECT

Discussing As a class, review the uneven distribution pattern of natural resources. Have students describe the relationship between natural resources and trade to each featured country's economic status.

ANSWERS, p. 101

Making Connections

1. Canada would import grain from either the United States or Germany.
2. Student answers will vary depending on the country selected. Every answer should clearly describe how the physical geography improves or hinders its access to natural resources.

Urban Geography

ENGAGE

R1 Reading Skills

Activating Prior Knowledge Have students work in pairs to describe what they know about their community or city and how it has changed over time. Have partners discuss why the area was first settled, when and why the population began to change, and how different areas of the community have developed over the years. For example, are certain sections industrialized, filled with new housing structures or new retail complexes? Have students share their knowledge with the class.

TEACH & ASSESS

C Critical Thinking Skills

Analyzing Cause and Effect Have students discuss cause-and-effect relationships relating to population movement. **Ask:** What caused people to move to cities after the Industrial Revolution? *(The creation of new industries and factories created new jobs in the city.)* What effect did this higher population have on cities? *(Possible answer: The physical size of the cities increased and urban areas spread onto undeveloped land near the cities.)* AL Verbal/Linguistic

R2 Reading Skills

Calculating Have students express the key points in this section. **Ask:** What three things have contributed to the growth of cities? *(industrialization, economic growth, and global population growth)* Currently, what percentage of the world's population lives in cities? *(50%)* It is estimated that there will be approximately 8 billion people in the world by 2025. How many will live in urban areas? *(about 5.3 billion people, or two-thirds of the world population, will live in urban areas)* Logical/Mathematical

ANSWERS, p. 102

TAKING NOTES: Nature of Cities—The world's urban population is growing; more than half of the world's people live in cities and is highest in the developed regions of the world. Cities can support various functions because they have a large number of workers and consumers, infrastructure to support the production of goods and services, and social services for residents; **Patterns of Urbanization**—People settle where there are navigable water sources, available food sources, and geographical features that provide protection;, new trends include the development of suburbia, which has office centers, retail complexes, and is near highways and transportation centers; **Challenges of Urban Growth**—strained ability to provide energy, education, health care, transportation, sanitation, and physical security services; large number of workers may create a surplus in the labor force, keeping wages low. Other challenges include overcrowding, poverty, pollution, crime and violence, and urban sprawl.

networks *There's More Online!*

- IMAGE Urban Landfill
- DIAGRAM Central Place Theory
- INFOGRAPHIC Urban Land Use Models
- GRAPH Ten Largest Cities
- INTERACTIVE SELF-CHECK QUIZ
- VIDEO Urban Geography

City
Town
Market To
Village

LESSON 5
Urban Geography

ESSENTIAL QUESTION • *How do the characteristics and distribution of human populations affect human and physical systems?*

Reading HELPDESK CCSS

Academic Vocabulary (Tier Two Words)
- **function**
- **structure**

Content Vocabulary (Tier Three Words)
- **urban sprawl**
- **connectivity**
- **metropolitan area**
- **central place theory**
- **world cities**

TAKING NOTES: ***Key Ideas and Details***

DESCRIBING Complete a graphic organizer similar to the one below describing the nature of cities, patterns of urbanization, and challenges of urban growth.

Urban Geography		
The Nature of Cities	Patterns of Urbanization	Challenges of Urban Growth

It Matters Because

R1 *Urban geography is a branch of human geography concerned with cities and the people who live in them. An urban geographer analyzes patterns of settlement and growth in urban areas and evaluates the impact of cities on people and the environment.*

The Nature of Cities

GUIDING QUESTION *How does a city's function influence its structure?*

C The Industrial Revolution ushered in a new age of urbanization in the world's history. As the focus shifted from agricultural production to industrial production, people began moving to cities in large numbers. As more people moved to cities, the physical size of cities also began to grow. This spreading of urban areas onto undeveloped land near cities is called **urban sprawl**. Currently, the world's urban population is growing at a much faster rate than that of the rural population. Over half of the world's people now live in cities, and this proportion is highest in the developed regions of the world. Eighty-two percent of Americans now live in urban areas, and more than two-thirds of the people of Europe, Russia, Japan, and Australia do as well. This growth is due to **connectivity**, the directness of routes and communication linking pairs of places.

The Function of Cities

R2 Only recently have people gathered in the densely populated and highly structured settlements we call cities. The first cities were established about 5,000 years ago, but it has only been in the last 200 years—with the expansion of industrialization, economic growth, and global population at exponential rates—that cities have grown significantly in size and number. At the start of the twentieth century, only about one person in ten lived in a city. Today, the proportion of urban and rural dwellers is approximately equal. By 2025, it is expected that nearly two-thirds of the world's population will live in urban areas.

All cities serve a variety of **functions**. For example, manufacturing, retail, and service centers are often located in urban areas. These functions are the economic base of a city, generating employment and wealth. The

networks *Online Teaching Options*

INTERACTIVE BELLRINGER

Top Ten Cities in Population

Comparing This map can be used to discuss the largest cities of the world. Before revealing the map, divide the class into small groups. Have each group write down what they think are the top ten cities in population in the world. Display the map and have students compare their list of cities to those listed on the map. Then have groups read the introductory text, study the map, and answer the questions. As a class, discuss how each group's list of cities compared to the top ten cities listed on the map. Logical/Mathematical, Visual/Spatial

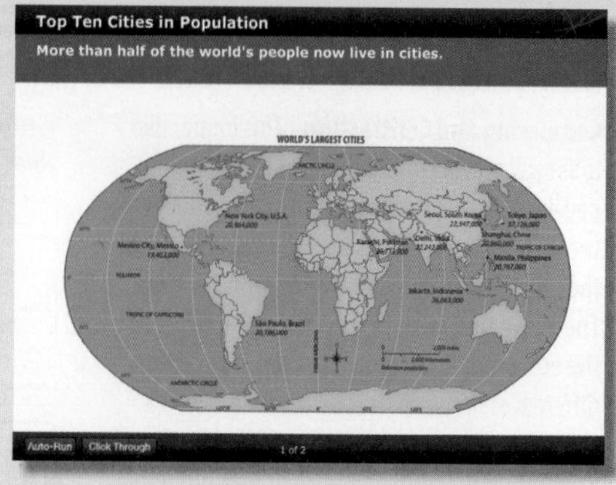

larger a city is, the more numerous and highly specialized its functions are likely to be. Smaller cities and towns have fewer functions, which tend to be of a more general nature. In the field of health care, for example, clinics are found in a wide range of places, but specialized teaching hospitals tend to be located only in larger cities.

Cities also tend to be centers of culture and creativity. Artists, musicians, architects, philosophers, scientists, and writers gravitate toward cities where there are patrons, communities of other artists, universities, clients, and a skilled workforce. Today's urban centers of culture have changed over time, mostly based on their economic or political strength with the outside world.

There are several reasons cities can support a variety of functions. The large population of a city means there are plenty of workers available to support a variety of industries. The large population also means there is a large market of consumers to sustain the demand for specialized functions. From a functional perspective, infrastructure facilitates the production of goods and services, and also the distribution of finished products to markets. In addition, it provides basic social services such as schools and hospitals. Roads provide adequate transportation, and safe buildings provide secure housing.

G1

Urban areas have both advantages and challenges. The diversity of peoples and activities encourages innovation and creativity, but overcrowding, crime, poverty, social conflict, and pollution can become challenges. An urban area differs from country to country, but each is considered a **metropolitan area**—a region that includes a central city and its surrounding suburbs.

urban sprawl spreading of urban developments on land near a city

connectivity the directness of routes linking pairs of places

function a special purpose

metropolitan area region that includes a central city and its surrounding suburbs

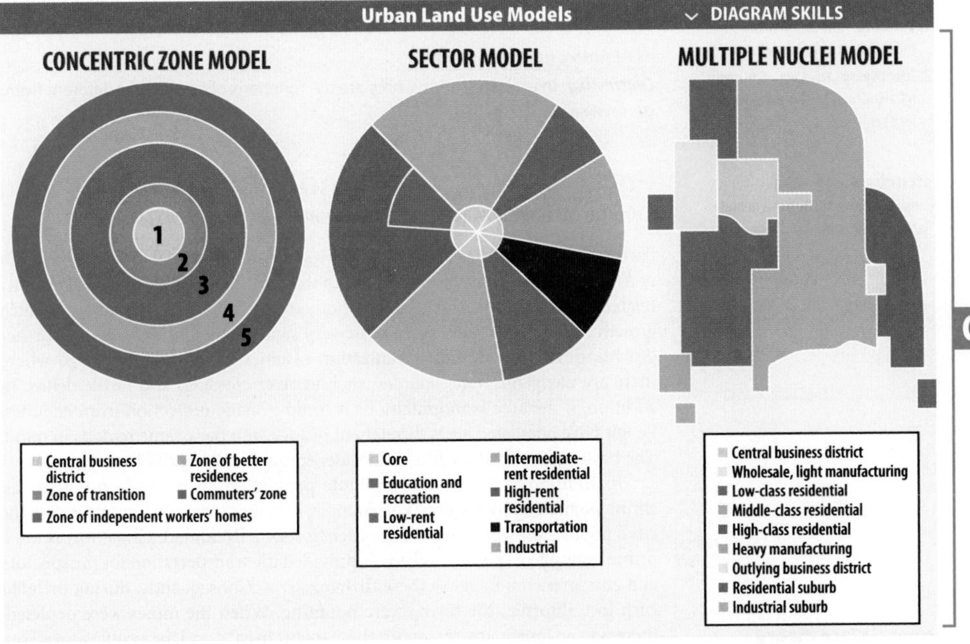

C2

T

Urban geographers use urban land use models like these to describe the internal structure of cities. They examine location patterns of people and businesses within the urban setting.

▲ CRITICAL THINKING

1. ***Identifying*** What district is typically largest in the multiple nuclei model?
2. ***Describing*** What zone is located between the commuters' zone and the zone of independent workers' homes in the concentric zone model?

G1 Critical Thinking Skills

Making Generalizations Have students think about the characteristics and functions of a large city. **Ask:** **What main point about large cities and their functions is the author making?** *(Possible answer: Because some cities are so large, they contain a great number and variety of people, which encourages the development of industries, social services, and other amenities that attract even more people to move to the cities.)*
AL **Logical/Mathematical**

C2 Critical Thinking Skills

Comparing and Contrasting Divide the class into pairs of students and have them work together to describe what each model shows, ensuring that students understand how the individual models are organized. Then have each set of partners compare and contrast the models, noticing things such as where similar areas are located in each one or which areas are unique to a model. If necessary, allow class time for students to ask questions. **ELL** **Visual/Spatial, Verbal/Linguistic**

T Technology Skills

Spatial Analysis Have students form small groups. Have groups use online resources to investigate the makeup of their community or the nearest large city. Ask students to consider which of the three urban land use models their community most resembles. Then have groups design, draw, and describe a new model that more accurately charts the growth pattern and various areas of their community or city. Have groups present their model and discuss their ideas in a class presentation.
BL **Visual/Spatial**

VIDEO

New Urbanists

Comparing Explain that this video clip is from a few years ago, but is still relevant to an ongoing concern. As they watch the video, have students think about various ways of living, be it in the city, suburbs, or rural areas, and how where they live relates to community and community building. Working with a partner, have students list factors that isolate people and factors that bring people closer together. Then have students compare the communities in the video with their own. In a class discussion, ask pairs to explain if they feel their community isolates or tends to bring people closer together.
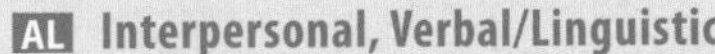
AL **Interpersonal, Verbal/Linguistic**

ANSWERS, p. 103

CRITICAL THINKING

1. The middle-class residential district is typically largest in the multiple nuclei model.
2. The zone of better residences is located between them.

Urban Geography

Content Background Knowledge

Structure of Cities Sociologists Robert E. Park and Ernest W. Burgess theorized that, as creatures in nature do, people and businesses in cities compete for a limited number of resources, and that this competition leads to different groups organizing themselves into separate areas. Park and Burgess believed that as people and businesses became more successful, they would move from the inner rings to the outer ones. They used the models they made to study issues such as unemployment and crime.

C Critical Thinking Skills

Making Inferences Discuss with students possible reasons why various activities are located near to or far from one another. For example, **ask:** **Why do you think heavy industry and high-income housing are not often located near each other?** *(Possible answer: Heavy industry can be loud and dirty. People with enough money to choose where they can live would most likely prefer to live somewhere more peaceful and clean.)* **Intrapersonal, Logical/Mathematical**

R Reading Skills

Using Context Clues Ask students to reread the information about ghost towns. Point out the word *depleted*. Explain that if students have concerns and need help understanding the meaning of a word they can use other words in the sentence, or context clues. **Ask:** **What are some context clues that help you understand the meaning of *depleted*?** *(shrink population, no longer needed, were booming, people moved on)* **What does *depleted* mean?** *(used up or emptied)* **How do you know?** *(Possible answer: As long as the mines were full of gold, many people lived in the towns. People left after the mines were "depleted," so that must mean there was no gold left to keep the people in the cities.)* **ELL Verbal/Linguistic**

Landfills are examples of the type of infrastructures a city must have in order to support large populations.

▲ **CRITICAL THINKING**

1. ***Defining*** How does a landfill fit the definition of an infrastructure?
2. ***Identifying*** What are a few other infrastructures a city must maintain for its citizens?

structure something constructed or arranged in a definite pattern of organization

The Structure of Cities

Urban **structure** is the arrangement of land use in urban areas. Sociologists, economists, and geographers have developed several models explaining where different types of people and businesses tend to exist within the urban setting. Urban structure can also refer to the urban spatial structure, which concerns the arrangement of public and private space in cities and the degree of connectivity and accessibility.

The *concentric zone model* was the first to explain distribution of social groups within urban areas. Based on a single city, Chicago, it was created by sociologist Ernest Burgess in 1924. According to this model, a city grows outward from a central point in a series of rings. A second theory of urban structure was proposed in 1939 by economist Homer Hoyt. The *sector model* proposed that a city develops in sectors instead of rings. Certain areas of a city are more attractive for various activities, whether by chance or geographic and environmental reasons. As the city grows and these activities flourish and expand outward, they do so in a wedge shape and become a sector of the city.

C Geographers C. D. Harris and E. L. Ullman developed the *multiple nuclei model* in 1945. According to this model, a city contains more than one center around which activities revolve. Some activities are attracted to particular nodes while others try to avoid them. For example, a university node may attract well-educated residents, pizzerias, and bookstores, whereas an airport may attract hotels and warehouses. Other businesses may also form clusters for automobile repair, tire stores, or arts districts. Incompatible activities will avoid clustering in the same area, thus explaining why heavy industry and high-income housing rarely exist together in the same neighborhood.

☑ **READING PROGRESS CHECK**

Contrasting In economic terms, how are the functions of larger cities different from those of smaller cities?

Patterns of Urbanization

GUIDING QUESTION *What influences the location and growth of cities?*

Factors that led to the early growth of cities are still influential today. The growth of American cities, for example, began in the late 1700s. This growth was directly related to certain influential factors. Some of the same factors that led to such growth hundreds of years ago are the very same factors influencing the further growth, development, and urbanization of cities today. People will go where there are navigable water sources, such as river crossings and fertile deltas. In addition, if the area is mountainous it could provide protection from enemies. People have populated areas throughout history with these same reasons in mind. The basics of survival are food and water sources and security from enemies.

R In addition to factors that promote population, there are factors that can shrink population in a region. For example, if an industry is no longer needed, the city's population will move on in order to seek a livelihood. Ghost towns are a prime example of this. The railroads provided the transportation for prospectors and entrepreneurs to get to these thriving areas. Consequently, during the gold rush in California, the towns were booming. When the mines were depleted, there was no longer any reason for these towns to exist and the people moved on.

central place theory geographical theory that seeks to explain the number, size, and location of human settlements in an urban system

The **central place theory** is a spatial theory in urban geography that attempts to explain the reasons behind the distribution patterns, size, and number of cities and towns around the world. It attempts to illustrate how settlements locate in relation to one another, the amount of market area a central

networks Online Teaching Options

INFOGRAPHIC

Urban Land Use Models

Interpreting This infographic shows three urban land use models. Click through the text boxes that explain the three urban land use models to help students understand the patterns of human settlement. Allow time for them to interpret the urban land use data in each model. Then have students write a few sentences explaining their own interpretation of each of the models, including information about the primary use, information in the key/legend, and any similarities or differences between the models. **Verbal/Linguistic**

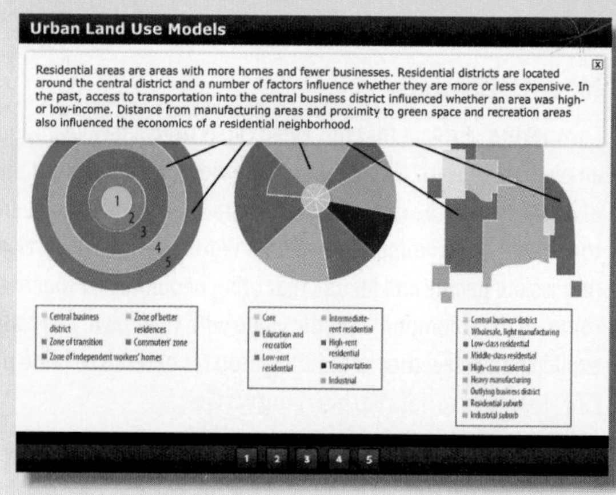

Urban Land Use Models
Residential areas are areas with more homes and fewer businesses. Residential districts are located around the central district and a number of factors influence whether they are more or less expensive. In the past, access to transportation into the central business district influenced whether an area was high- or low-income. Distance from manufacturing areas and proximity to green space and recreation areas also influenced the economics of a residential neighborhood.
1
2
3
4
5
1 2 3 4 5

ANSWERS, p. 104

CRITICAL THINKING

1. Infrastructure provides basic needs and services. Landfills provide the necessary service of waste disposal to meet basic sanitation needs.
2. Cities should maintain basic social services such as schools and hospitals, as well as roads that provide adequate transportation.

☑ **READING PROGRESS CHECK** Larger cities have more numerous and highly specialized functions than smaller cities and towns. Smaller cities tend to have generalized functions. Larger cities have more workers and consumers that sustain the demand for specialized functions.

place can control, and why some central places function as hamlets, villages, towns, or cities. It also attempts to provide a framework by which those areas can be studied both for historical reasons and for the locational patterns of areas today.

A **world city** is a city generally considered to play an important role in the global economic system. World cities possess such features as having international diverse cultures, an active influence on and interaction in world affairs, a large population, a major international airport, and an advanced transportation system. The world city concept comes from geography and urban studies. It can be seen as a type of "point of entry" for studying the changes that come from globalization.

world cities cities generally considered to play an important role in the global economic system

T

One important world city that has resulted from the geography of its location is İstanbul. It straddles a strait, thus placing it on vital land and sea trade routes. In addition, it can easily defend itself against enemy factions because of its water location. Farming is good because of its fertile soil, and consequently İstanbul has been under attack and conquered many times. Its desirable location is the very thing that has made it vulnerable.

New trends in cities have emerged, including the development of suburban business districts and major diversified centers, to name just two. Typically, suburbia refers to an outlying community around a city. These communities are business districts in their own right. The name that is now most commonly used to describe these terms is "edge cities."

W

These new suburban cities have sprung up all over and are home to glistening office towers and huge retail complexes. They are always located close to major highways. "Boomers" are the most common type of edge cities, having developed around a shopping mall or highway interchange such as Pasadena, California. On the suburban fringe of Phoenix, Arizona, Sun City is a "greenfield"—a new, master-planned city built on undeveloped land. In contrast, "uptown" edge cities are historic activity centers built over an older city or town, such as the Rosslyn-Ballston Corridor in Virginia.

✓ READING PROGRESS CHECK

Summarizing What does the central place theory attempt to explain?

Central Place Theory

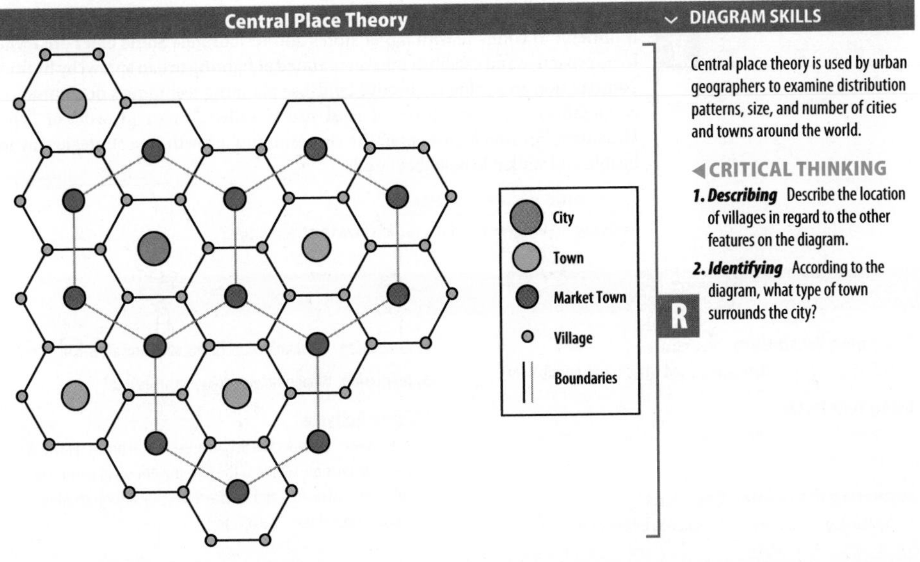

DIAGRAM SKILLS

Central place theory is used by urban geographers to examine distribution patterns, size, and number of cities and towns around the world.

◀ CRITICAL THINKING

1. ***Describing*** Describe the location of villages in regard to the other features on the diagram.
2. ***Identifying*** According to the diagram, what type of town surrounds the city?

R

Urban Geography

T Technology Skills

Supporting Perspectives Using the information in the text as a starting point, have students conduct online research about the economic aspects of a world city. Then have students compile their research to create a visual that describes and illustrates how this city matches the characteristics of a typical world city. **BL** **Visual/Spatial**

W Writing Skills

Informative/Explanatory Provide students with a map of your community. Review some of the types of communities discussed in this section, from world cities to edge cities. Have students write an essay to identify where their community fits into the local urban system. They should consider if they live in a major city or if they live in a suburban business district. Have students cite evidence from the real world to support their ideas. Then have them use concepts from the lesson to describe areas around their community, such as if their community is surrounded by edge cities or located near a world city. **Verbal/Linguistic**

R Reading Skills

Understanding Relationships Allow time for students to study the diagram. **Ask:** **What is the relationship between the type of settlement and the icon used for it in the diagram?** *(The larger the population of the community, the larger the size of the circle that represents it.)* **Why might the designer of this diagram have labeled both towns and market towns?** *(Market towns provide a different function than a regular town because they are full of places where people can buy the goods and services they need to live.)* **AL** **Visual/Spatial, Verbal/Linguistic**

INTERACTIVE GRAPH

Population Indicators in 2011

Reading Graphs Display the four graphs depicting the population data of seven countries in 2011. Review with students how HDI measures development through health, education, and living standards. Ask students to explain how birthrate and infant mortality rates affect the overall population totals. Direct students' attention to Nigeria and ask them to speculate as to why they think infant mortality rates are so high in this country. Continue to discuss various countries, asking students to make comparisons and contrasts using the data in the graphs. Be sure to make connections between low infant mortality rates and high global economic systems. **Visual/Spatial, Naturalist**

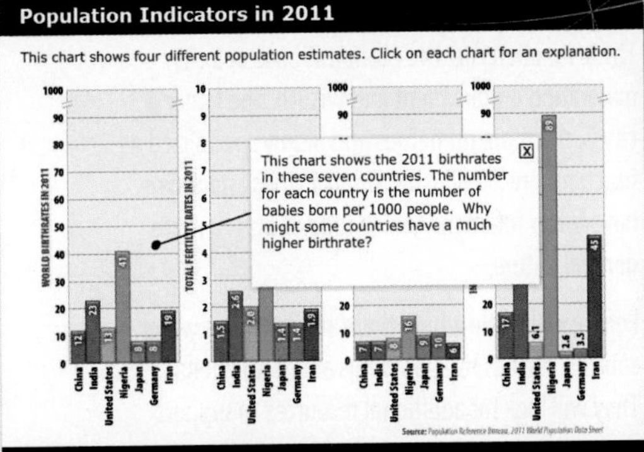

Population Indicators in 2011
This chart shows four different population estimates. Click on each chart for an explanation.
This chart shows the 2011 birthrates in these seven countries. The number for each country is the number of babies born per 1000 people. Why might some countries have a much higher birthrate?

ANSWERS, p. 105

✓ **READING PROGRESS CHECK** The central place theory is a geographical theory that seeks to explain the number, size, and location of human settlements in an urban system.

CRITICAL THINKING

1. Villages form circles around the City, Towns, and Market Towns.
2. Market towns surround the city.

Urban Geography

C Critical Thinking Skills

Comparing and Contrasting Have students create a Venn diagram identifying the similarities and differences experienced by more developed countries as they underwent industrialization and the experiences facing less developed countries today. **Ask:** How are the situations more developed countries faced in the past, and less developed countries face now, different? *(Student answers may vary, but should identify any similarities and differences faced by these countries.)*

BL Visual/Spatial

V Visual Skills

Designing Organize students into small groups and have them demonstrate the use of spatial organization by keeping "smart growth" techniques in mind as they draw a plan for their own city. Suggest that students recall population growth patterns, urban land use models, and how city activities should be situated next to one another. Encourage groups to do further research. Have groups present their finished plans to the class and monitor as other groups support and critique each plan. Visual/Spatial

CLOSE & REFLECT

Expressing Review the key concepts of urban geography by asking students to consider the positive and negative consequences of urbanization. Have them write a topic sentence that expresses the effects of these consequences and then list three relevant details that describe specific examples from the text.

ANSWERS, p. 106

☑ READING PROGRESS CHECK The rapid growth of cities strains their capacity to provide services such as energy, education, health care, transportation, and physical security.

Challenges of Urban Growth

GUIDING QUESTION *What problems do urban areas face?*

The urbanization process refers to much more than simple population growth. It involves changes in the economic, social, and political structures of a region. Rapid urban growth is responsible for many environmental and social changes, and its effects are strongly related to issues of pollution and economics. These changes are not always positive. The rapid growth of cities strains their capacity to provide services such as energy, education, health care, transportation, sanitation, and physical security.

C The more developed countries experienced urbanization during the nineteenth and twentieth centuries along with the Industrial Revolution. During this time, urbanization resulted from and contributed to industrialization. New job opportunities in the cities motivated people to migrate from rural areas to cities. At the same time, migrants provided cheap, plentiful labor for the emerging factories. Today, the circumstances are rather different in less developed countries. People are forced out of rural areas because of insufficient land on which to grow subsistence crops. Meanwhile, there are not enough jobs to accommodate the many migrants looking for employment, creating a large surplus labor force. This influx keeps wages low and can lead to poverty in many urban areas. Foreign investment companies from more developed countries see such situations as attractive. By employing these workers they can produce goods for far less.

Modern cities all over the world face many of the same problems: poor housing, homelessness, pollution, and social problems such as addiction, crime, and gang violence. People often live in old houses or other structures without electricity or sanitation. Some live on the streets with little access to adequate food or shelter. In addition, cars and industries pollute city air and water. Unemployment continues to grow. Larger multiethnic cities continue to face conflicts between different cultural groups.

V One of the major effects of rapid urban growth is urban sprawl—scattered development that increases traffic, saps local resources, and destroys open space. Urban sprawl is responsible for changes in the physical environment and can also diminish the local character of the community. Small local businesses find it difficult to compete with larger stores and restaurants. Some cities are trying to be proactive and establish measures aimed at fighting urban sprawl by limiting construction and using innovative land-use planning techniques or community cooperation. One new form of land use is called "smart growth" or "New Urbanism," in which cities plan the communities' growth in a strategic way for livable and walkable neighborhoods.

☑ READING PROGRESS CHECK

Defining In what ways does rapid growth strain cities?

LESSON 5 REVIEW

Reviewing Vocabulary (Tier Three Words)

1. ***Defining*** What is urban sprawl, and what is it responsible for? RH.9–10.4

Using Your Notes

2. ***Listing*** Use your graphic organizer to list the three models of urban structures.

Answering the Guiding Questions

3. ***Explaining*** How does a city's function influence its structure?
4. ***Describing*** What influences the location and growth of cities?
5. ***Discussing*** What problems do urban areas face?

Writing Activity

6. ***Argument*** Consider the negative aspects of urban sprawl. What are some possible solutions the government could provide to bolster infrastructure and services? Develop an argument to support your ideas. WHST.9–10.2

106

LESSON 5 REVIEW ANSWERS

Reviewing Vocabulary

1. Urban sprawl happens when urban areas spread onto undeveloped lands. This development increases traffic, saps local resources, and destroys open space. It is responsible for changes in the physical environment and can also diminish the local character of the community.

Using Your Notes

2. The three models of urban structures are the concentric zone model, sector model, and multiple nuclei model.

Answering the Guiding Questions

3. These functions are the economic base of a city, generating employment and wealth. The larger a city is, the more numerous and highly specialized its functions are likely to be. Smaller cities and towns have fewer functions, which tend to be of a more general nature.
4. People will settle where there are navigable water sources, such as river crossings and fertile deltas. They will look for additional resources to support their needs; these resources include employment opportunities. Cities will grow when they can continue to provide resources.
5. Urban areas can face problems such as pollution and a need to provide services such as energy, education, health care, transportation, sanitation, and physical security.

Writing Activity

6. Arguments will differ, but should be logical and strongly supported through information from the lesson. Arguments should provide possible solutions the government could provide to bolster infrastructure and services as related to urban sprawl.

CHAPTER 4 Assessment 

Directions: On a separate sheet of paper, answer the questions below. Make sure you read carefully and answer all parts of the questions.

Lesson Review

Lesson 1

1. ***Describing*** Describe how culture affects the daily lives of people.
2. ***Explaining*** Explain the elements of culture geographers use to organize the world into culture regions.
3. ***Drawing Conclusions*** How did the agricultural revolution influence cultural diffusion?

Lesson 2

4. ***Evaluating*** What factors contribute to the uneven distribution of the world's population?
5. ***Analyzing*** How is the demographic transition model used to explain a country's population growth?
6. ***Summarizing*** How do the effects of zero population growth and negative population growth differ? How are they similar?

Lesson 3

7. ***Comparing and Contrasting*** What different roles might local citizens have in government decision making under a unitary system, a federal system, and a confederation?
8. ***Explaining*** Explain the different ways in which an autocracy, an oligarchy, and a democracy exercise authority.
9. ***Defining*** List and describe the three types of political boundaries.

Lesson 4

10. ***Listing*** What are the characteristics of a mixed economy?
11. ***Contrasting*** Contrast a more developed country with a less developed country. What are the primary differences?
12. ***Analyzing*** What are the advantages and disadvantages of a capitalist economy?

Lesson 5

13. ***Explaining*** Explain two functions of urban areas.
14. ***Inferring*** What are some issues associated with urban sprawl? Discuss some solutions to address these issues.
15. ***Identifying Central Issues*** What factors have influenced the site and growth of cities? Give examples.

21st Century Skills

RECENT TRENDS IN DEVELOPMENT

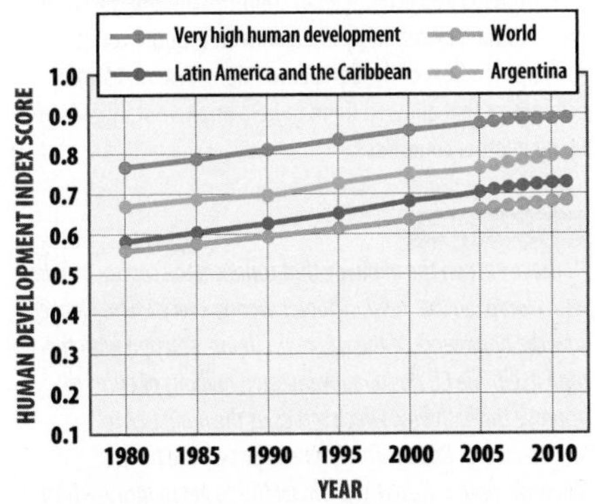

Source: United Nations Development Programme

16. ***Using Graphs, Charts, Diagrams, and Tables*** According to the graph, how does the Human Development Index score of Argentina compare to that of the world?

College and Career Readiness

17. ***Economics*** Imagine that you are interviewing people for a position studying economic geography. Write a series of interview questions (with sample answers) that assesses the interviewees' understanding of economic activities and economic development. WHST.9–10.4

Need Extra Help?

If You've Missed Question	1	2	3	4	5	6	7	8	9	10	11	12	13	14	15	16	17
Go to page	78	78	80	85	82	83	87	88	90	95	97	95	102	106	104	107	94

CHAPTER 4 Assessment Answers

Lesson Review

Lesson 1

1. Culture affects the way people think, believe, and live their daily lives.
2. Geographers organize the world into culture regions based on forms of government, economic systems, and social groups, as well as common histories, religions, and art forms.
3. The agricultural revolution created a surplus food supply that allowed cities and civilizations to rise. This resulted in many changes including trade with other civilizations, which led to cultural diffusion.

Lesson 2

4. People live where there is access to water, fertile soil, and a comfortable climate. Cities are also more highly populated due to the access to goods, services, and employment.
5. The demographic transition model uses birthrates and death rates to show how populations in countries or regions can change over time.
6. Zero population growth is when the birthrate and death rates are equal. A negative growth rate is when the death rates exceed the birthrates.

Lesson 3

7. Local citizens have little or no role in government decisions in a unitary system, while in a federal system citizens have more input into decisions. In a confederation citizens have a great deal of input into government.
8. In an autocracy, the authority to rule rests with a single person. In an oligarchy, a small group of people hold the authority to rule. In a democracy, the government rules with the consent of the people.
9. A natural boundary is a boundary based on physical geography features such as rivers and mountains. A geometric boundary is a boundary that follows lines such as where some states or countries meet. A cultural boundary follows the boundaries made by people of different cultures grouping together in geographic areas.

Lesson 4

10. In a mixed economy, the government regulates and supports free enterprise. Private individuals and groups own businesses and make profits.
11. In more developed countries, most people work in service and information industries. The standard of living is high and few people work in agriculture. In less developed countries, most people work in agriculture. There is light industry, but people still largely work out of their homes in cottage industries.
12. The advantage of a capitalist economy is that people have the right to own businesses and make profits, as well as choose what kind of job they will have and where they will work. The disadvantage is that a capitalist economy does not always provide the basic needs to everyone in a society.

Lesson 5

13. Student answers may vary, but should include two of the following: manufacturing, retail, service centers, social centers, culture and creative centers.
14. Student answers may vary, but should include the identification and discussion of solutions to some of the following issues: pollution, homelessness, crime, drug addiction, violence, lack of sanitation, unemployment, and urban sprawl.
15. Cities need water, food, and security to thrive. Factors that influence the location include nearby water sources such as rivers for trade and travel, fertile soil where crops can grow, and geographic features such as mountains that offer protection.

21st Century Skills

16. The Human Development Index score for Argentina is higher than the score for the world as a whole.

College and Career Readiness

17. Student answers may vary, but could include questions and answers for capitalism, market economy, command economy, and free enterprise, as well as the basic economic decisions of what/how goods and services should be produced and who receives goods and services.

Assessment Answers

Writing About Geography

18 Student essays will vary, but should include the identification and discussion of solutions to some of the following issues: pollution, homelessness, crime, drug addiction, violence, lack of sanitation, unemployment, and urban sprawl.

Analyzing Primary Sources

19 Possible answers could include supporting infrastructure such as roads that are mutually beneficial to trade and to prevent pollution that could ultimately impact other countries within the EU.

20 Belt means that it was evident that the EU was behind the improvements that he was seeing all around him, starting with basic infrastructure such as the road.

Applying Map Skills

21 The Ural Mountains serves as a natural border between Asia and Europe.

22 The overall population density of Australia is very low with slightly higher concentrations in the coastal areas.

23 Venezuela, Colombia, Peru, Argentina, Brazil

Exploring the Essential Question

24 Countries in Stage 2 of the demographic transition model are involved in farming and ways to increase crop yields as their population is growing.

25 Student answers will vary based on the two countries the student chooses, but should identify the major exports for both countries and explain how the natural resources available in the chosen countries support the economy.

Critical Thinking

26 The physical geography of a country and the cultural and religious beliefs of the citizens influence a country's ability to control territory. These can be used to determine how political and administrative areas will be structured and governed and also if the government is promoting or suppressing cultural and religious beliefs.

27 The information revolution has resulted in the Internet and the ability to send information instantly around the world, which makes socializing between groups of people much easier and increases the spread of ideas and traditions to many cultures.

28 Cultures first developed in and then spread from culture hearths. A culture region is a division of Earth where people share similar ways of life, languages, religions, values, and economic systems.

CHAPTER 4 Assessment 

Directions: On a separate sheet of paper, answer the questions below. Make sure you read carefully and answer all parts of the questions.

Writing About Geography

18 ***Informative/Explanatory*** Use standard grammar, spelling, sentence structure, and punctuation to write a one-page essay discussing problems in today's urban areas. Include examples suggesting solutions and their feasibility. WHST.9–10.4

DBQ Analyzing Primary Sources

Use the document to answer the following questions.

Governments and economies of countries around the world are becoming increasingly interconnected. Some countries, such as members of the European Union, have had strong economies that allowed them to help improve standards of living in other countries.

PRIMARY SOURCE

"I drove east on the highway that connects the capital of Talinn with Narva, on the Russian border. Nearly everywhere I looked I saw the handiwork of the European Union, starting with the road itself. The EU has already invested millions of euros to improve the highway, which serves as the main link to St. Petersburg, Russia. This highway passes the town of Sillamäe, once a 'closed' city run by the Soviet military, which enriched uranium for weapons programs in a huge factory overlooking the sea. The EU is here, too, kicking in more than a million dollars to help prevent the radioactive waste from leaching into the Baltic Sea."

—Don Belt, "Europe's Big Gamble," *National Geographic,* May 2004

19 ***Speculating*** Why would the EU want to invest in the improvement of other countries? RH.9–10.2

20 ***Interpreting*** What did Belt mean by "I saw the handiwork. . .starting with the road itself"? RH.9–10.4

Applying Map Skills

Use the Unit 1 Atlas to answer the following questions.

21 ***Places and Regions*** The Ural Mountains are a natural border that divides Asia from what other continent?

22 ***Human Systems*** How would you describe the population density pattern of Australia?

23 ***The Environment and Society*** Which of the countries in South America have petroleum resources?

Exploring the Essential Question

24 ***Making Connections*** Recall what you have learned about the demographic transition model. In which types of economic activities would a country in Stage 2 most likely be involved?

25 ***Researching*** Research and compare two countries in the ways they depend on the environment for the products they export. WHST.9–10.7

Critical Thinking

26 ***Making Generalizations*** Explain the factors that influence a country's ability to control territory.

27 ***Identifying Cause and Effect*** What cultural changes have resulted from the information revolution?

28 ***Comparing and Contrasting*** What is the difference between a culture region and a culture hearth?

Research and Presentation

29 ***Research Skills*** Use Internet and library resources to gather information about a city plagued by urban sprawl. Your research should focus on the past, present, and future of this city. Create a multimedia presentation outlining that city's experiences along the road to urbanization. Be sure to (1) describe the human systems that affected the city's growth and (2) explain how other cities in the region might learn from its experience. WHST.9–10.6, WHST.9–10.8

Need Extra Help?

If You've Missed Question	18	19	20	21	22	23	24	25	26	27	28	29
Go to page	106	108	108	2	6	8	82	97	89	81	79	102

108

Research and Presentation

29 Student presentations will vary based on the city chosen by the student, but should include reasons why the city grew, such as employment and social services. Presentations should also include what lessons another nearby city could learn based on the success or problems of the chosen city.

UNIT **2**

THE UNITED STATES AND CANADA Planner

UNDERSTANDING BY DESIGN®

Enduring Understandings

- *Certain patterns, processes, and functions help determine where people settle.*
- *The physical environment affects people and their activities.*

Essential Question

- *How do physical systems and human systems shape a place?*

Students will know:

- *how the landscape, waterways, and natural resources of the United States and Canada contribute to their economies.*
- *the factors affecting population, population distribution, and cultural diversity in the United States and Canada.*
- *the importance of the United States economy to the global economy.*
- *the environmental issues that affect the environment and natural resources in the United States and Canada.*
- *how French and English roots and immigration have shaped Canada's history.*
- *the relationships between economic activities and resource management in a postindustrial market economy.*

Students will be able to:

- ***explain** the importance of water systems and natural resources to the economies in this region.*
- ***describe** how physical geography, immigration, and urbanization affect population distribution and cultural diversity in this region.*
- ***analyze** the role of the United States in the global economy.*
- ***analyze** efforts to address environmental issues.*
- ***describe** the influence of the English and French on Canada.*
- ***analyze** how resources and economic activities are connected in the United States and Canada.*

Predictable Misunderstandings

- *The geography of the United States does not change greatly from coast to coast.*
- *The United States economy is large enough to stand on its own.*
- *The United States has a wealth of natural resources that will last indefinitely.*
- *The physical and human geography of Canada is similar to the United States.*
- *Canada's climate is harsh and cold.*
- *Canada has few resources.*

Assessment Evidence

Performance Tasks:

- *Environmental Case Study*
- *GeoLab Activity*
- *GIS Simulation*
- *Hands-On Chapter Projects*

Other Evidence:

- *Location Activity*
- *Self-Check Quizzes*
- *Lesson Quizzes*
- *Participation in Interactive Whiteboard Activities*
- *Contribution to small-group activities*
- *Interpretation of slide show images*
- *Participation in class discussions about the United States and Canada*
- *Analysis of graphic organizers, graphs, and charts*
- *Lesson Reviews*
- *Chapter Assessments*

Key for Using the Teacher Edition

SKILL-BASED ACTIVITIES

Types of skill activities found in the Teacher Edition.

* **V** **Visual Skills** require students to analyze maps, graphs, charts, and photos.

R **Reading Skills** help students practice reading skills and master vocabulary.

C **Critical Thinking Skills** help students apply and extend what they have learned.

W **Writing Skills** provide writing opportunities to help students comprehend the text.

T **Technology Skills** require students to use digital tools effectively.

*Letters are followed by a number when there is more than one of the same type of skill on the page.

DIFFERENTIATED INSTRUCTION

All activities are written for the on-level student unless otherwise marked with the leveled labels below.

BL Beyond Level
AL Approaching Level
ELL English Language Learners

All students benefit from activities that utilize different learning styles. Many activities are marked as below when a particular learning style is highlighted.

Intrapersonal	Naturalist
Logical/Mathematical	Kinesthetic
Visual/Spatial	Auditory/Musical
Verbal/Linguistic	Interpersonal

SUGGESTED PACING GUIDE

Introducing the Unit	1 Day
Chapter 5: The United States	5 Days
Case Study: How Can Drought Lead to Conflict in the United States?	1 Day
Chapter 6: Canada	5 Days
Global Connections: Two Decades of NAFTA	1 Day
TOTAL TIME	**13 Days**

PLANNER

Print Teaching Options

V Visual Skills

- [ ] **p. 109** Students analyze an image to discuss physical map characteristics. **Visual/Spatial, Naturalist**
- [ ] **p. 111** Students sketch a map of the U.S. and Canada showing the Rocky Mountains. **ELL Visual/Spatial**
- [ ] **p. 115** Students create charts that show land usage. **Logical/Mathematical, Visual/Spatial**

R Reading Skills

- [ ] **p. 110** Students define and discuss the word *exile.* **ELL Verbal/Linguistic**
- [ ] **p. 114** Students discuss inset maps. **ELL Interpersonal, Visual/Spatial**
- [ ] **p. 116** Students discuss advantages and disadvantages to living in urban and rural areas. **AL Visual/Spatial, Intrapersonal, Logical/Mathematical**

C Critical Thinking Skills

- [ ] **p. 110** Students discuss the advantages and disadvantages of immigrants to the U.S. and Canada. **BL Intrapersonal, Logical/Mathematical**
- [ ] **p. 112** Students discuss, sketch, and identify types of map projections. **BL Visual/Spatial**
- [ ] **p. 113** Students compare and contrast physical and political maps. **ELL Visual/Spatial**
- [ ] **p. 116** Students make generalizations about population density. **ELL Logical/Mathematical, Visual/Spatial**

W Writing Skills

- [ ] **p. 113** Students research the dispute over Machias Seal Island and North Rock and write an argument on which country should claim the land. **BL Verbal/Linguistic, Kinesthetic**
- [ ] **p. 114** Students write a paragraph describing dominant vegetation in each climate zone of the region. **AL Naturalist, Verbal/Linguistic**
- [ ] **p. 115** Students write a letter to a potential business owner from the viewpoint of an economic development recruiter. **BL Intrapersonal, Verbal/Linguistic**

T Technology Skills

- [ ] **p. 111** Students research and create a visual story about an economically important river. **BL Visual/Spatial**
- [ ] **p. 114** Students create a multimedia presentation on climate zones. **Visual/Spatial**
- [ ] **p. 115** Students analyze news articles on economic data and make generalizations. **AL Verbal/Linguistic**

Online Teaching Options

V Visual Skills

- [ ] **INTERACTIVE MAP** **Climate and Vegetation Maps: United States and Canada**—Students write predictions about how climate affects population density. **Verbal/Linguistic, Visual/Spatial**

R Reading Skills

- [ ] **INTERACTIVE FEATURE** **Explore the Region: The United States and Canada**—Students create a list of similarities between where they live and the region. **Verbal/Linguistic**

C Critical Thinking Skills

- [ ] **GEO @ WORK** **Thinking Like a Geographer**—Students explore principles and skills of geography applied to real-world challenges.
- [ ] **INTERACTIVE MAP** **Political Map: United States and Canada**—Students locate states and provinces in the U.S. and Canada and then calculate distances. **BL Visual/Spatial, Logical/Mathematical**
- [ ] **INTERACTIVE MAP** **Economic Activity Map: United States and Canada**—Students discuss the resources and land uses of the U.S. and Canada and then use this information to draw conclusions about their economies. **BL Visual/Spatial, Logical/Mathematical**

W Writing Skills

- [ ] **INTERACTIVE MAP** **Population Density Map: United States and Canada**—Students write a travel journal about what it might be like to visit an uninhabited island. **Verbal/Linguistic**
- [ ] **INTERACTIVE MAP** **Physical Map: United States and Canada**—Students write to explain what it might be like to live near a mountain. **AL Visual/Spatial, Verbal/Linguistic**

Printable Digital Worksheets

V Visual Skills

- [ ] **WORKSHEET** **Location Activity**—Students locate countries, water systems, and physical features in the United States and Canada.

C Critical Thinking Skills

- [ ] **WORKSHEET** **Environmental Case Study**—Students complete a study about whether fracking has a positive or negative effect on the environment and to the economy in the region.
- [ ] **WORKSHEET** **GeoLab Activity**—Students explore how water can be made to evaporate so quickly that a drought can result.

T Technology Skills

- [ ] **WORKSHEET** **GIS Simulation**—Students research and evaluate the trade relationship between the United States and Canada.

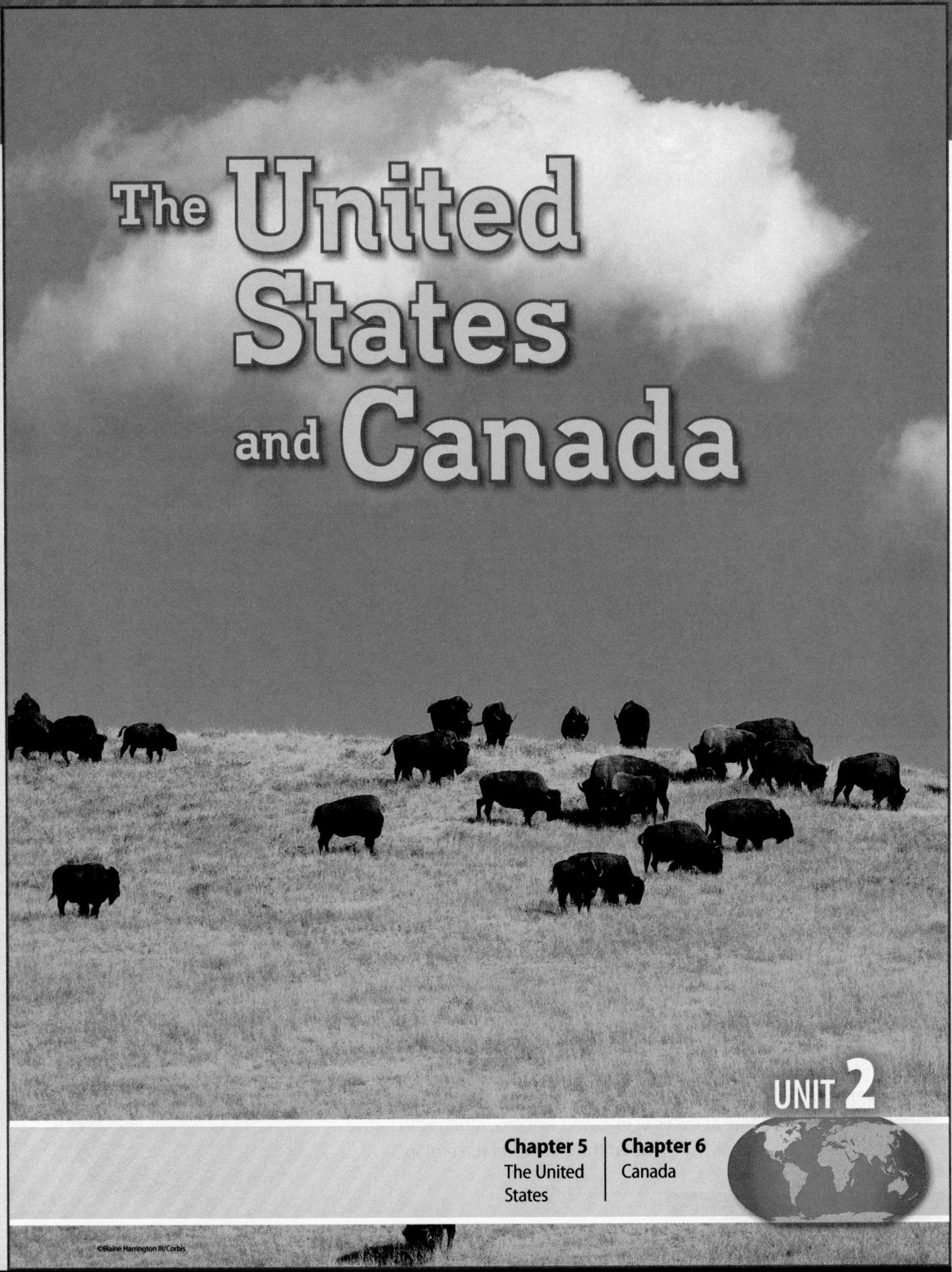

The United States and Canada

UNIT 2

Chapter 5 The United States | Chapter 6 Canada

©Blaine Harrington III/Corbis

GEO @ WORK

Thinking Like a Geographer

Problem Solving Explore specific examples of the principles and skills of geography applied to real-world challenges that impact people's lives. From agriculture, to urban planning, to wiping out disease, and managing changes in society—geography plays a key role in understanding relationships and generating solutions that make sense.

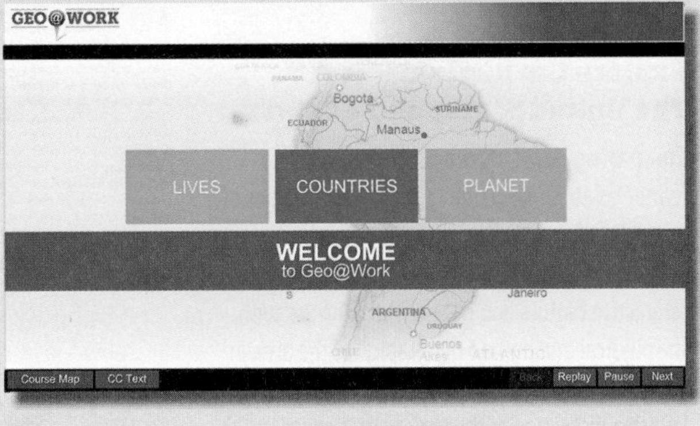

ENGAGE

Activating Background Knowledge Invite volunteers to identify the dominant or important physical features of the United States and Canada that make each country unique. Ask students to list examples of how the physical and human geography of the two countries are similar and different. Instruct students to write three questions about the United States and three questions about Canada to pose to a partner to assess his or her knowledge of the region.

TEACH & ASSESS

Making Connections

Explain to students how the land and climate of the United States and Canada are diverse. However, some characteristics are similar in both countries. Have students use their current location in the United States, including its nearby landforms, bodies of water, and climate, to compare to a similar location in Canada. Have students indicate the absolute location of both places and the geographic elements that they have in common.

Analyzing Images Ask students to examine the unit opener image. Discuss the physical characteristics, including the land, vegetation, and American bison. **Ask:** **What area of the United States and Canada does this image represent?** *(Possible answer: Great Plains)* Discuss with students how the American bison was unique to the United States and Canada, including its historic and cultural importance. Ask students to name or describe other physical features, vegetation, or animals that are unique to North America. **Visual/Spatial, Naturalist**

CLOSE & REFLECT

Labeling Have students label landforms, bodies of water, and other physical features on an outline map of the United States and Canada. Tell students that they will be learning more about these features in this unit.

ENGAGE

V Visual Skills

Analyzing Images Explain to students that just as the land and climate of the United States and Canada are diverse, so are their cultures. Have students describe how this image is representative of the diverse cultures in this region. **Ask:** What culture or celebration is being expressed in the photograph? *(Chinese New Year)* Where might this celebration be taking place? *(in a large urban area with a significant Chinese population, such as San Francisco or New York City)* How has immigration affected the cultures of the region? *(Possible answer: It has contributed to its diversity and made it a rich culture.)*

TEACH & ASSESS

R Reading Skills

Defining Ask students what the word *exile* means. *(someone who is forced to leave his or her homeland for political or religious reasons)* Point out that in the text, the word is used as a noun but it can also be used as a verb. **Ask:** What words are synonyms to the verb *exile*? *(Possible answers:* banish, cast out, displace, expel*)* What are antonyms of *exile*? *(Possible answers:* welcome, take in*)* Have students write the definition of the noun *exile* in their own words. Then ask them to rewrite the sentence from the text using the verb form of the word *exile*. ELL Verbal/Linguistic

C Critical Thinking Skills

Considering Advantages and Disadvantages Invite volunteers to share with the class stories of immigration to the United States or Canada, including personal stories. Discuss with them examples of push and pull factors, both past and present. **Ask:** What advantages did immigrants have when they came to the region? *(Possible answers: new job opportunities, education, political, or religious freedom)* What disadvantages did they face? *(Possible answers: discrimination, language issues, homesickness)* Have students work in small groups to consider whether the advantages outweighed the disadvantages for immigrants or vice versa. Ask them to identify specific details to support their responses and to present them to the class. BL Intrapersonal, Logical/Mathematical

1 Culture Immigration to the United States and Canada from other areas of the world has had a dramatic effect on the cultures of the two countries. Parades celebrating these cultural roots are common throughout the region.

EXPLORE the REGION

The region of the **UNITED STATES** and **CANADA** stretches from the Pacific Ocean in the west to the Atlantic Ocean in the east. The two countries share many physical features—mountains frame their eastern and western edges, cradling a central area of vast plains. The region is a land of immigrants. Many made this land their home by choice. Others were forced to come as exiles or enslaved workers. Along with native peoples, these groups have shaped the cultures of the region.

THERE'S MORE ONLINE

110

networks Online Teaching Options

INTERACTIVE FEATURE

Explore the Region: The United States and Canada

Comparing Students can use this interactive feature as an introduction to the culture, bodies of water, landforms, and economies of the United States and Canada. Have student pairs view the interactive feature and note any similarities with the physical and human geography of the area in which they live. Have students share their lists to launch a discussion of the variety that exists in these two countries. Verbal/Linguistic

The United States and Canada

INTRODUCTION

The region of the United States and Canada stretches from the Pacific Ocean in the west to the Atlantic Ocean in the east. The two countries share many physical features—mountains frame their eastern and western edges, cradling a central area of vast plains. The region is a land of immigrants. Many made this land their home by choice. Others were forced to come as exiles or enslaved workers. Along with native peoples, these groups have shaped the cultures of the region.

3 Lakes and Rivers Long rivers, such as the Mississippi River, have played an important role in trade and industry in both the United States and Canada.

2 Mountains The Rocky Mountains are the longest mountain range in North America, stretching from British Columbia in Canada to New Mexico in the United States.

4 Economy Today the service industry employs most of the workers in the United States and Canada. Many of these jobs are located in urban centers such as Toronto, Canada's largest city.

UNIT 2

The United States and Canada

V Visual Skills

Spatial Understanding Ask students to read the caption and then to make a mental map of the extent of the Rocky Mountains. **Ask:** Does this mountain chain form any country borders or boundaries? Explain. *(No, it does not. It runs north to south, and Canada and the United States are north and south of each other, respectively.)* How do you think the Rocky Mountains affected settlement to the west? *(Possible answer: The mountains were difficult to cross, which slowed settlement to the west of them.)* Have students sketch a map of the United States and Canada showing the location of the Rocky Mountains. Ask them to add labels to surrounding states, landforms, lakes, and rivers. ELL Visual/Spatial

T Technology Skills

Researching Have students work together in small groups to research the history of one river in the United States or Canada that is important to the economy. Then ask them to use computer software to create a visual story of the river's role in that country's economy and population growth. Provide an opportunity for students to present their visual stories to the class. BL Visual/Spatial

W Writing Skills

Informative/Explanatory Ask students to research the service industries in the United States and Canada to find out how they are similar and different, as well as their importance to both countries' economies. Then have them write a research report to share their findings. Remind students that they should use recent economic data and cite their sources in their papers. Verbal/Linguistic

CLOSE & REFLECT

Comparing and Contrasting Discuss with students the similarities and differences in the geography, history, and culture of the United States and Canada. Ask students to write a thesis statement based on what they know now about these similarities and differences. When students have finished the unit, ask them to revise their thesis statements or modify as needed.

DIGITAL WORKSHEETS

United States and Canada

Demonstrating Use these online digital unit worksheets to have students demonstrate their depth of knowledge and comprehension and to provide them with extended unit content through project-based activities.

- **Environmental Case Study**
- **GIS Simulation**
- **Location Activity**
- **GeoLab Activity**

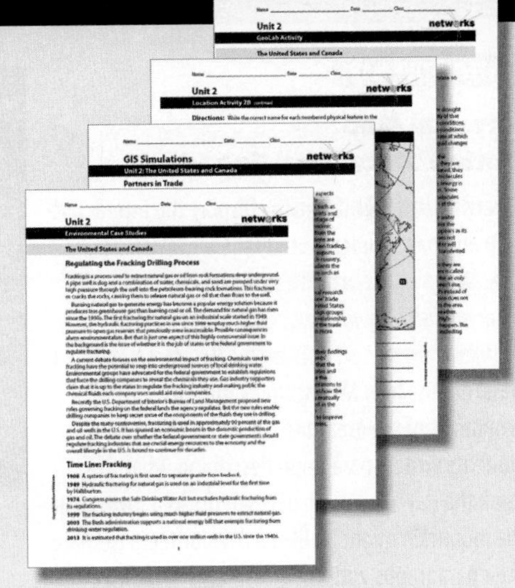

ENGAGE

R Reading Skills

Reading Maps Invite volunteers to take turns identifying different physical features and places on the map by using the map key, scale, and lines of latitude and longitude. Then ask students to compare and contrast elevations of different landforms and regions of the United States and Canada. Point out to students that they will be learning more about these and other physical features as they study this unit.

TEACH & ASSESS

V Visual Skills

Calculating Ask students to study the map scales, noting the distances the scales represent on the map. **Ask:** About how many miles is the Great Salt Lake from Lake Michigan? *(about 1,400 miles)* Is the distance greater between the Rocky Mountains and Canadian Shield or the Rocky Mountains and the Appalachian Mountains? *(The distance between the Rocky Mountains and Appalachian Mountains is greater.)* Which map scale would you use to calculate the distance between the islands of Hawaii and Maui? *(the scale that shows a maximum of 100 miles)* AL Logical/Mathematical

C Critical Thinking Skills

Identifying Perspectives Discuss with students the various kinds of map projections (Equal Area, Mercator, Robinson, and so forth). Show examples of different map projections as a reference. Explain that different projections can distort features on the map. Tell students that the purpose of the map can often drive what map projection is used by a mapmaker. **Ask:**

- Which projection does this map use? *(Lambert Azimuthal Equal-Area)*
- What is the purpose of this map? *(to show the physical features of the United States and Canada)*
- Does this map appear to show any distortions? Explain. *(Yes, it shows areas equally but does not include an accurate projection for angles.)*
- What map projection might you use to show direction angles accurately but may distort the sizes of areas? *(Mercator)*

Challenge students to sketch a Mercator or Robinson projection of the United States and Canada or show them different projections and ask students to identify them. BL Visual/Spatial

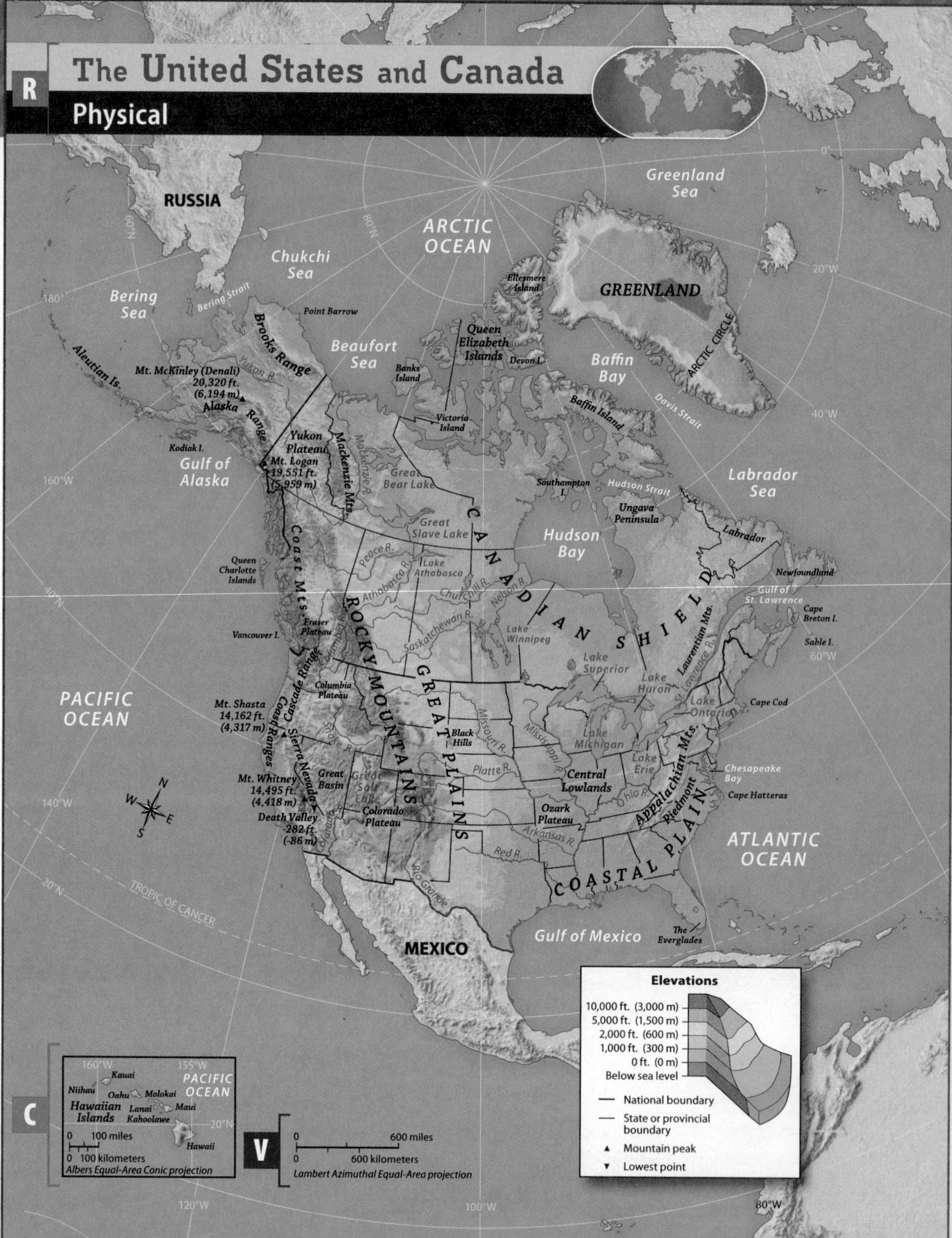

R The United States and Canada
Physical

Elevations
10,000 ft. (3,000 m)
5,000 ft. (1,500 m)
2,000 ft. (600 m)
1,000 ft. (300 m)
0 ft. (0 m)
Below sea level

National boundary
State or provincial boundary
▲ Mountain peak
▼ Lowest point

C Hawaiian Islands: 0–100 miles; 0–100 kilometers; Albers Equal-Area Conic projection

V 0–600 miles; 0–600 kilometers; Lambert Azimuthal Equal-Area projection

112 Unit 2

networks Online Teaching Options

INTERACTIVE MAP

Physical Map: United States and Canada

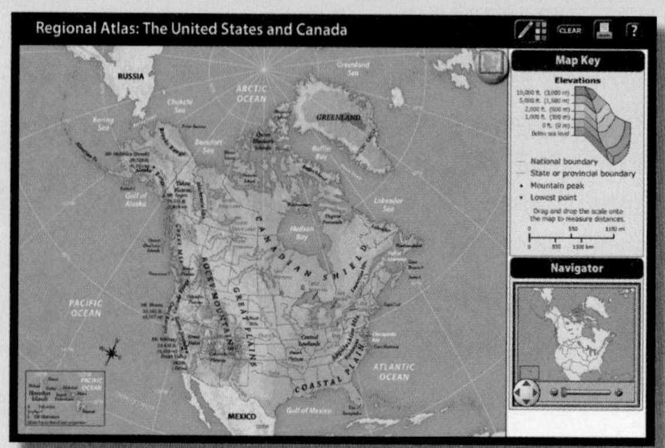

Interpreting Significance Display the interactive map and have students study the elevation key. **Ask:** What color are the highest elevations? *(dark reddish brown)* What is the highest mountain peak on this map? *(Mt. McKinley)* As a class, discuss how Mt. McKinley may affect the economics of the area surrounding it. Then have students write a paragraph describing what they think the day-to-day life of residents in a town near the mountain might be like. Ask volunteers to share their paragraphs with the class. AL Visual/Spatial, Verbal/Linguistic

The United States and Canada

Political

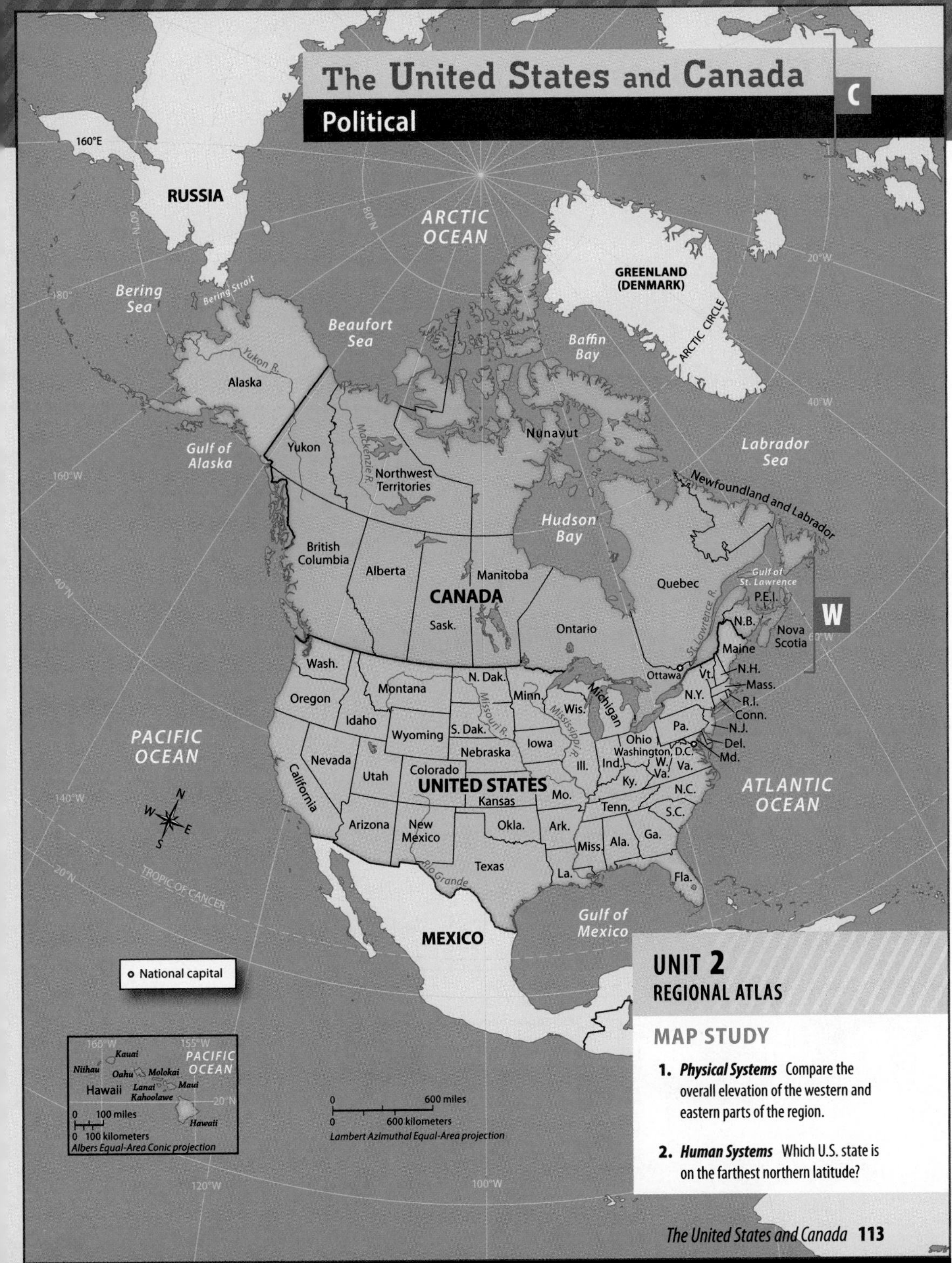

○ National capital

0 600 miles
0 600 kilometers
Lambert Azimuthal Equal-Area projection

0 100 miles
0 100 kilometers
Albers Equal-Area Conic projection

UNIT 2
REGIONAL ATLAS

MAP STUDY

1. ***Physical Systems*** Compare the overall elevation of the western and eastern parts of the region.
2. ***Human Systems*** Which U.S. state is on the farthest northern latitude?

C Critical Thinking Skills

Comparing and Contrasting Discuss with students the difference between physical and political maps. Explain how political maps show boundaries between states, provinces, territories, countries, and continents. Invite students to identify some of the boundaries. Then ask them to examine the physical map of the United States and Canada. **Ask: What physical features form or nearly form political boundaries that are visible on the political map?** *(Possible answer: The St. Lawrence River forms a boundary between the United States and Canada. The Rio Grande forms a boundary between Mexico and the United States. Some of the Great Lakes form a boundary between the United States and Canada.)* Have students work with a partner to compare and contrast other boundaries that are shown on the physical and political maps of the United States and Canada. ELL **Visual/Spatial**

Making Connections

Have students identify which states were admitted last to the United States. *(Hawaii and Alaska)* Ask them to consider why these two territories provided strategic opportunities for the United States. Have them conduct research to find out whether the admission of their state to the United States had any strategic or political importance.

W Writing Skills

Argument Explain to students that governments of countries and states have argued over political boundaries and borders. Invite volunteers to identify any recent events in the world about border disputes (i.e., the Sudan and South Sudan; Pakistan and India). Organize the class into two groups—one representing the United States and the other Canada. Explain that only two areas of land are disputed by the United States and Canada, Machias Seal Island and North Rock. Ask students to research the dispute and history of these tracts of land and then write an argument from their assigned perspective on which country should be able to claim the land. Consider having students present their papers to the class in the form of a debate. BL **Verbal/Linguistic, Kinesthetic**

INTERACTIVE MAP

Political Map: United States and Canada

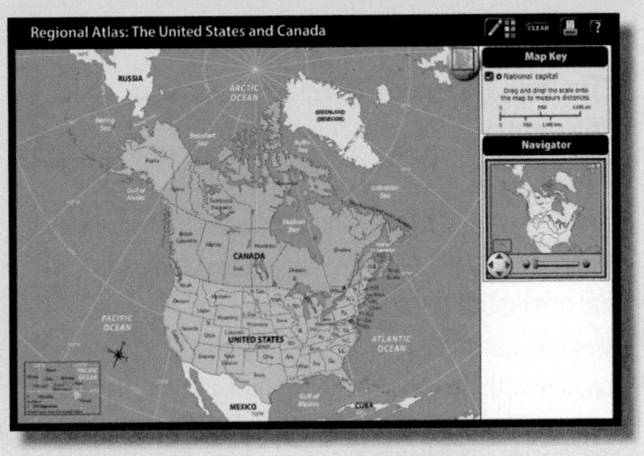

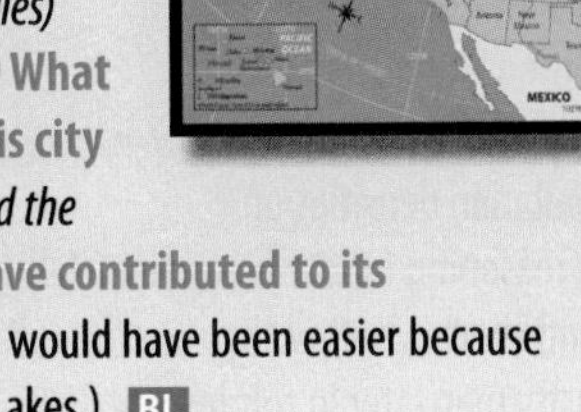

Spatial Analysis Tell students that they can use this political map to identify and locate the states of the United States and the provinces and territories of Canada. Point out the map scale and ask how far past the Arctic Circle Canada extends. *(about 1,200 miles)* **Ask: What is the capital of Canada?** *(Ottawa)* **What features on the map might explain how this city became the capital?** *(the St. Lawrence River and the Great Lakes)* **How might Ottawa's location have contributed to its becoming the capital?** (Early travel to the city would have been easier because of its location near both the river and the Great Lakes.) BL **Visual/Spatial, Logical/Mathematical**

ANSWERS, p. 113

MAP STUDY

1. The western part of the region sits at a higher elevation overall than the eastern part of the region.
2. Alaska

T Technology Skills

Researching Have students use the map key to identify a climate zone in the United States or Canada that they will research online. Point out that they should use the map key as a guide to help focus their research on a specific area. For example, if they have chosen semi-arid (steppe), they may want to use keyword searches that include Denver. Ask students to collect the following data on their climate zone: location, weather, precipitation, and vegetation.

Challenge students to also determine whether the area has high or low population density. Have students create multimedia presentations to illustrate the data. Then provide an opportunity for students to share the information about their climate zone with the class. **Visual/Spatial**

Content Background Knowledge

Gulf Stream The Gulf Stream is a warm ocean current that starts in the Gulf of Mexico and flows northward to the Atlantic Ocean. This warm current keeps the water surface and land along the east coast warm or mild, depending on latitude. The climates of Florida, Georgia, Alabama, Texas, and Louisiana are all affected by this ocean current.

R Reading Skills

Describing Ask students what information the inset map displays that the larger map cannot show. Then ask students to describe how inset maps are best used. Have students explain the climate(s) pattern indicated in this inset map. **ELL** **Interpersonal, Visual/Spatial**

W Writing Skills

Informative/Explanatory Have students compare the climate map to the vegetation map of the United States and Canada. Ask them to write a paragraph describing the vegetation that is dominant within each climate zone. Instruct students to draw conclusions in their writing about the effects of climate on types of vegetation. **AL** **Naturalist, Verbal/Linguistic**

The United States and Canada
Climate and Vegetation

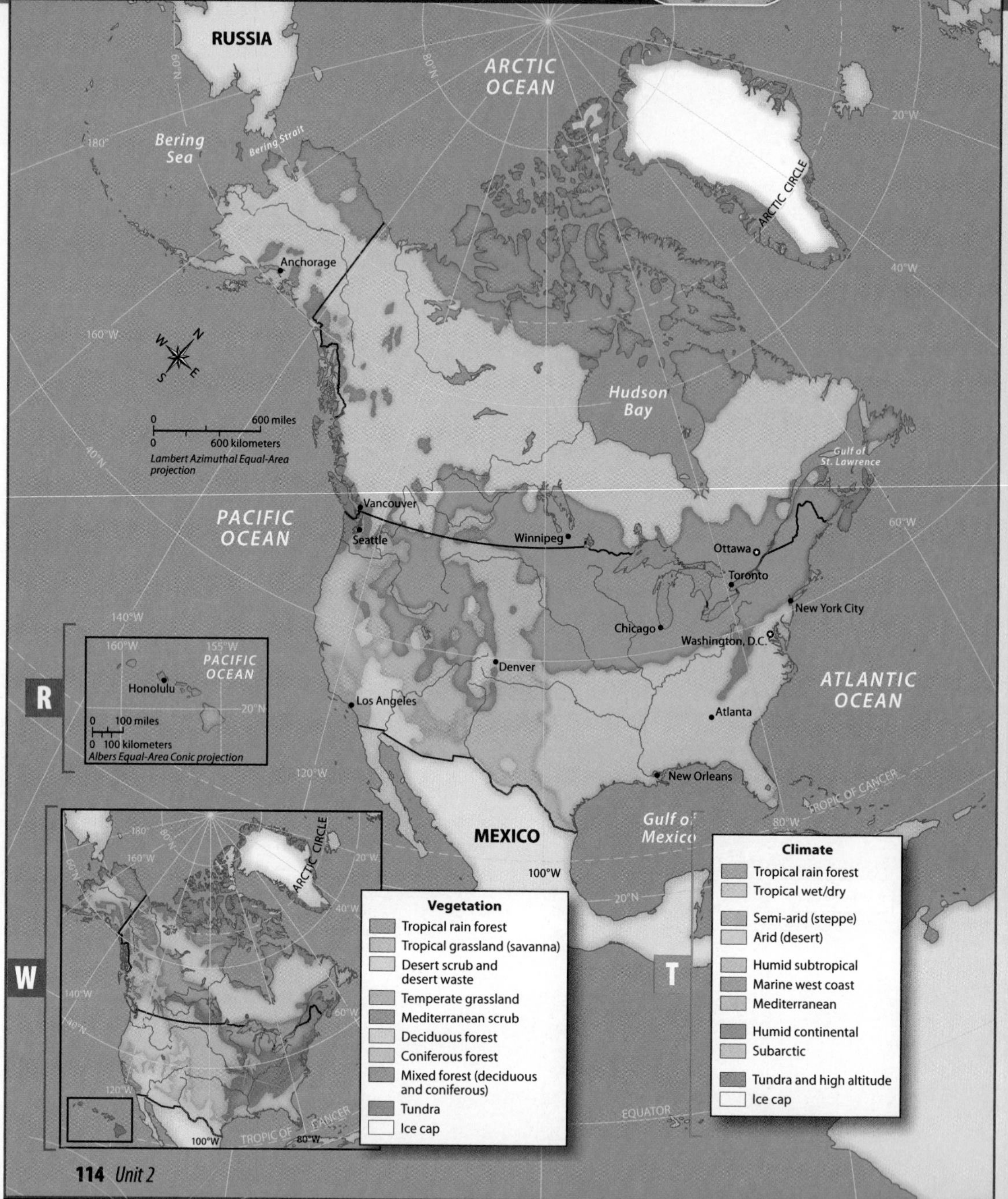

RUSSIA
ARCTIC OCEAN
Bering Sea
Bering Strait
ARCTIC CIRCLE
Anchorage
Hudson Bay
Gulf of St. Lawrence
0 600 miles
0 600 kilometers
Lambert Azimuthal Equal-Area projection
PACIFIC OCEAN
Vancouver
Seattle
Winnipeg
Ottawa
Toronto
New York City
Chicago
Washington, D.C.
Denver
Los Angeles
Atlanta
ATLANTIC OCEAN
New Orleans
MEXICO
Gulf of Mexico
TROPIC OF CANCER
EQUATOR

Honolulu
PACIFIC OCEAN
0 100 miles
0 100 kilometers
Albers Equal-Area Conic projection

Climate
- Tropical rain forest
- Tropical wet/dry
- Semi-arid (steppe)
- Arid (desert)
- Humid subtropical
- Marine west coast
- Mediterranean
- Humid continental
- Subarctic
- Tundra and high altitude
- Ice cap

Vegetation
- Tropical rain forest
- Tropical grassland (savanna)
- Desert scrub and desert waste
- Temperate grassland
- Mediterranean scrub
- Deciduous forest
- Coniferous forest
- Mixed forest (deciduous and coniferous)
- Tundra
- Ice cap

114 *Unit 2*

networks *Online Teaching Options*

INTERACTIVE MAP

Climate Map: United States and Canada

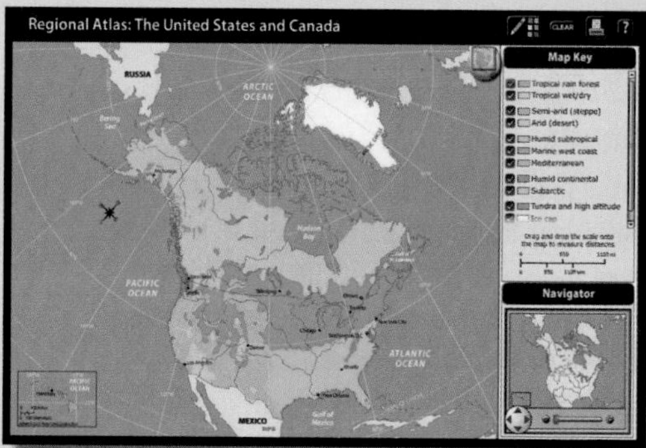

Making Predictions Display the map, allowing time for students to study the climate map key. Discuss with students the characteristics of two types of climate that cover much of Canada: the tundra and the subarctic. Ask students how the climates of Canada compare with the climates of the United States. Have students write a prediction about how these differences in climate affect the population densities of these two countries, including their reasoning for the prediction. Tell students to keep their predictions and check whether they are correct when they view the Population Density map later in this lesson. **Verbal/Linguistic, Visual/Spatial**

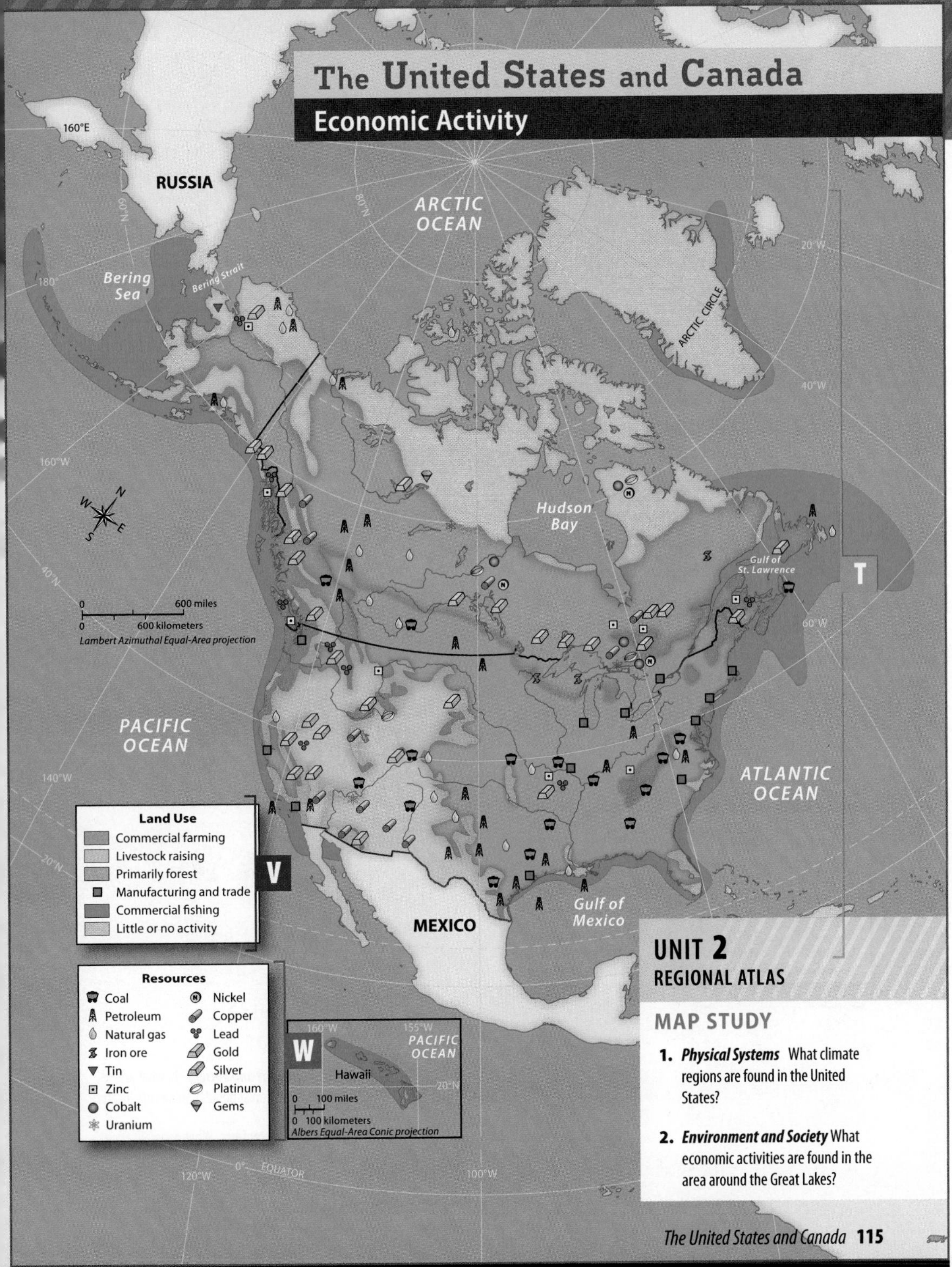

The United States and Canada

Economic Activity

160°E
RUSSIA
ARCTIC OCEAN
Bering Sea
Bering Strait
ARCTIC CIRCLE
Hudson Bay
Gulf of St. Lawrence
PACIFIC OCEAN
ATLANTIC OCEAN
Gulf of Mexico
MEXICO
EQUATOR

0 — 600 miles
0 — 600 kilometers
Lambert Azimuthal Equal-Area projection

Land Use
Commercial farming
Livestock raising
Primarily forest
Manufacturing and trade
Commercial fishing
Little or no activity

Resources	
Coal	Nickel
Petroleum	Copper
Natural gas	Lead
Iron ore	Gold
Tin	Silver
Zinc	Platinum
Cobalt	Gems
Uranium	

Hawaii
PACIFIC OCEAN
0 — 100 miles
0 — 100 kilometers
Albers Equal-Area Conic projection

UNIT 2 REGIONAL ATLAS

MAP STUDY

1. ***Physical Systems*** What climate regions are found in the United States?

2. ***Environment and Society*** What economic activities are found in the area around the Great Lakes?

The United States and Canada **115**

T Technology Skills

Examining Information Ask students to work in small groups to research online to find recent news articles or Web sites that include articles on the economies of different states in the United States or provinces and territories of Canada. Assign groups different searches that include manufacturing, agriculture, industry, GDP, unemployment, trade, exports, and imports. Have students present the economic data they gathered and any interesting recent facts or news about their selected economy. Then in a class discussion, ask students to analyze the data and make generalizations about the state and provincial economies of both countries. AL **Verbal/Linguistic**

V Visual Skills

Creating Charts Have students study the map of land use and resources. Ask students to identify climate zones on the map from memory and call on volunteers to make comparisons between climate zones and land use. Then have student pairs create a chart that estimates the percentage of land use for each particular activity in the United States and Canada. After they create their charts, ask each student to write a summary to explain what the most prominent kind of land use is. Challenge them to relate climate factors in their summaries. **Logical/Mathematical, Visual/Spatial**

W Writing Skills

Narrative Ask students to take the role of an economic development recruiter for a region of the United States or Canada. Explain that an economic development recruiter attempts to attract new businesses to an area. Assign students a region and have them study the Resources map key to identify what resources are found and developed in that area. Tell them to write a letter to a business owner who is considering opening a company in their assigned area. As the economic development recruiter, students should include information about existing resources and how a new business would be an ideal addition to the local economy. BL **Intrapersonal, Verbal/Linguistic**

INTERACTIVE MAP

Economic Activity Map: United States and Canada

Drawing Conclusions Use this map to discuss the different land uses and resources of the United States and Canada. Tell students to look carefully at the map and the keys. Then have students use the information in the map to write a paragraph that explains which country they think is more commercially developed than the other. Tell them to make sure they include why they think this is so and what evidence they have to support their conclusions. Ask volunteers to read their paragraphs to the class, and then discuss how various geography factors contribute the economies of the two countries. BL **Visual/Spatial, Logical/Mathematical**

ANSWERS, p. 115

MAP STUDY

1. The United States has the following climate regions: tropical rain forest, tropical wet/dry, semi-arid, arid, humid subtropical, marine west coast, Mediterranean, humid continental, subarctic, tundra and high altitude. The only climate region not present in the United States is ice cap.
2. Mining, manufacturing and trade, petroleum and natural gas industries, and commercial farming are economic activities located around the Great Lakes.

C Critical Thinking Skills

Making Generalizations Point out the map key that shows population per square mile and per square kilometer. Invite a volunteer to explain how population density is illustrated on the map. **Ask:** **Which color/population density is most represented on the map?** *(light yellow, which indicates the population density is at less than 2.5 persons per sq. mi. or less than 1 person per sq. km)* **The least?** *(purple, which indicates the population density is at 1,250 and over persons per sq. mi. or 500 and over persons per sq. km)* **What generalizations can you make about the least and most populated areas of the United States and Canada?** *(In Canada, the lowest population density is in the north, while the highest is in the south and southeast; in the United States, the lowest population density is in the western half and the highest is in the eastern half.)* Have students work with a partner to make generalizations about the population density of the United States and Canada and factors that might affect it. ELL Logical/Mathematical, Visual/Spatial

R Reading Skills

Locating Have students locate the most populous cities in the United States and Canada. Then ask them to locate on the map the closest city to the west of their school and the one to the east of their school. **Ask:** **How would you measure the distance between the two most populous cities on either side of your school?** *(use the map scale)* Ask students to measure the distance. Then have students measure the distance between their school and a low population density area. Discuss with students the advantages and disadvantages of living in or near urban and rural areas. Have students write a one-page paper explaining which area they would prefer living in or near and why. AL Visual/Spatial, Intrapersonal, Logical/Mathematical

CLOSE & REFLECT

Categorizing Have students work with a partner to review the unit maps and categorize important information from each map in a chart. Allow students to choose their own headings, but point out that all topics covered on the maps should be included in the chart. Then ask students to exchange their charts with another pair to evaluate.

ANSWERS, p. 116

MAP STUDY

1. In Canada, the highest population density is located along the southern border with the United States near the St. Lawrence River and the Great Lakes.
2. The largest population centers in both the United States and Canada are located in the eastern portion of the countries. These population centers are usually located near water and are valuable locations for trade.

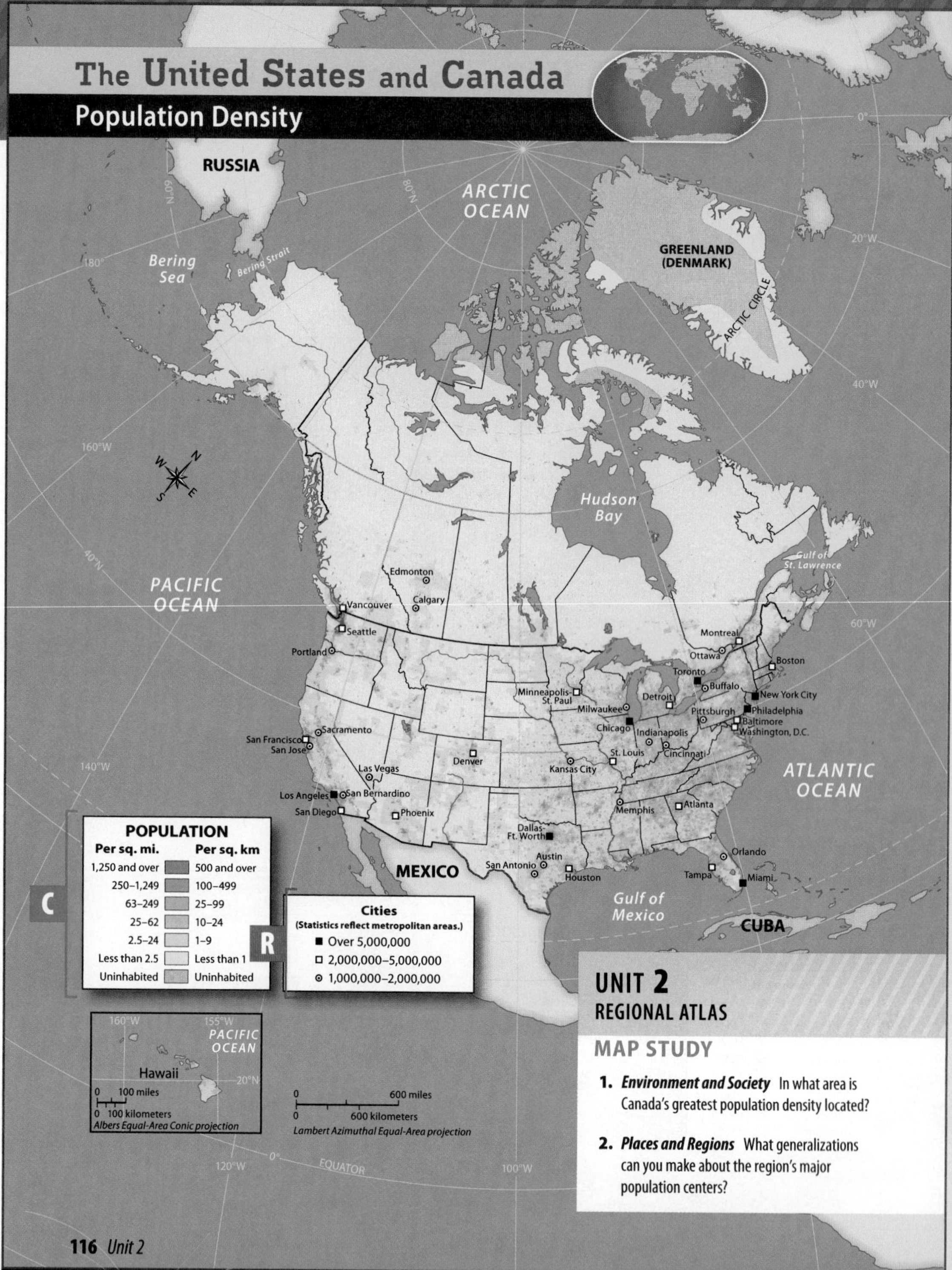

The United States and Canada
Population Density

POPULATION

Per sq. mi.	Per sq. km
1,250 and over	500 and over
250–1,249	100–499
63–249	25–99
25–62	10–24
2.5–24	1–9
Less than 2.5	Less than 1
Uninhabited	Uninhabited

Cities
(Statistics reflect metropolitan areas.)
■ Over 5,000,000
□ 2,000,000–5,000,000
⊙ 1,000,000–2,000,000

Lambert Azimuthal Equal-Area projection

Albers Equal-Area Conic projection

UNIT 2
REGIONAL ATLAS

MAP STUDY

1. ***Environment and Society*** In what area is Canada's greatest population density located?
2. ***Places and Regions*** What generalizations can you make about the region's major population centers?

networks Online Teaching Options

INTERACTIVE MAP

Population Density Map: United States and Canada

Narrative Display the map and point out the major cities and their populations. Have students check the predictions they made when viewing the climate map. Then point out that several islands in the northern latitudes are uninhabited or partially uninhabited. Ask students to consider what it might be like to visit one of the uninhabited islands. Have them write an entry for a travel journal about their visit, including a description of the weather, what animals and plants they see, and any other descriptive observations they might make while they are there. Verbal/Linguistic

CHAPTER 5

The United States Planner

UNDERSTANDING BY DESIGN®

Enduring Understandings

- *Certain patterns, processes, and functions help determine where people settle.*

Essential Question

- *How do physical systems and human systems shape a place?*

Predictable Misunderstandings

Students may think:

- *The geography does not change drastically across the United States. Explain that the United States covers a vast area and the landscape is extremely varied.*
- *The United States economy is large enough to stand on its own. Explain that the economy of the United States is closely linked to the global economy and that many billions of dollars are involved in the global exchange of goods and materials.*
- *The United States has a wealth of natural resources that will last indefinitely. Explain that although the United States does have numerous natural resources, these resources will not last indefinitely and need to be managed responsibly to ensure they continue to be available.*

Assessment Evidence

Performance Tasks:

- *Hands-On Chapter Project*

Other Evidence:

- *Guided Reading Activities*
- *Vocabulary Activities*
- *Lesson Quizzes*
- *Chapter Tests, Forms A and B*

SUGGESTED PACING GUIDE

Introducing the Chapter. . . . . .½ Day
Lesson 1 . . . . 1 Day
Lesson 2 . . . . .2 Days
Case Study . . . . 1 Day
Lesson 3 . . . . 1 Day
Chapter Wrap-Up and Assessment. . . . . .½ Day

TOTAL TIME 6 Days

Key for Using the Teacher Edition

SKILL-BASED ACTIVITIES

Types of skill activities found in the Teacher Edition.

* **V Visual Skills** require students to analyze maps, graphs, charts, and photos.

R Reading Skills help students practice reading skills and master vocabulary.

C Critical Thinking Skills help students apply and extend what they have learned.

W Writing Skills provide writing opportunities to help students comprehend the text.

T Technology Skills require students to use digital tools effectively.

*Letters are followed by a number when there is more than one of the same type of skill on the page.

DIFFERENTIATED INSTRUCTION

All activities are written for the on-level student unless otherwise marked with the leveled labels below.

BL Beyond Level
AL Approaching Level
ELL English Language Learners

All students benefit from activities that utilize different learning styles. Many activities are marked as below when a particular learning style is highlighted.

Intrapersonal	**Naturalist**
Logical/Mathematical	**Kinesthetic**
Visual/Spatial	**Auditory/Musical**
Verbal/Linguistic	**Interpersonal**

National Geography Standards covered in "The United States"

The student knows and understands:

(7) The physical processes that shape the patterns of Earth's surface

7.3 Physical processes interact over time to shape particular places on Earth's surface

(9) The characteristics, distribution, and migration of human populations on Earth's surface

9.2 Population distribution and density are a function of historical, environmental, economic, political, and technological factors

9.3 Migration is one of the driving forces for shaping and reshaping the cultural and physical landscape of places and regions

(10) The characteristics, distribution, and complexity of Earth's cultural mosaics

10.3 Cultures change through convergence and/or divergence

(11) The patterns and networks of economic interdependence on Earth's surface

11.2 Patterns exist in the spatial organization of economic activities

11.3 Economic systems are dynamic organizations of interdependent economic activities for production, exchange, distribution, and consumption of goods and services

(14) How human actions modify the physical environment

14.2 The use of technology can have both intended and unintended impacts on the physical environment

14.3 People can either mitigate and/or adapt to the consequences of human modifications of the physical environment

(15) How physical systems affect human systems

15.1 Depending on the choice of human activities, the characteristics of the physical environment can be viewed as both opportunities and constraints

(16) The changes that occur in the meaning, use, distribution, and importance of resources

16.3 Policies and programs that promote the sustainable use and management of resources impact people and the environment

(18) How to apply geography to interpret the present and plan for the future

18.1 Geographic contexts (the human and physical characteristics of places and environments) provide the bases for analyzing current events and making predictions about future issues

CHAPTER OPENER PLANNER

Students will know:

- how the landscape, waterways and natural resources of the United States contribute to its economy.
- understand factors affecting population, population distribution, and cultural diversity.
- the importance of the U.S. economy to the global economy.
- the environmental issues that affect natural resources in the United States.

Students will be able to:

- **explain** the importance of water systems and natural resources to the economy.
- **describe** how physical geography, immigration, and urbanization affect population distribution and cultural diversity.
- **analyze** the role of the U.S. in the global economy.
- **analyze** efforts to address environmental issues.

UNDERSTANDING BY DESIGN®

☑ Print Teaching Options

C Critical Thinking Skills

- ☐ **p. 118** Students use a map to identify the various ancestries of people in their state.

V Visual Skills

- ☐ **p. 119** Students create montages depicting Americans in the twenty-first century. ELL Visual/Spatial

W Writing Skills

- ☐ **p. 119** Students write a paragraph identifying one period of immigration and the push and pull factors that led to that immigration. AL Verbal/Linguistic

T Technology Skills

- ☐ **p. 118** Students list the percentages of different populations as they read the introductory paragraph. Logical/Mathematical
- ☐ **p. 119** Students summarize the cultural influences of twenty-first century immigration on their region and research these influences online. BL Verbal/Linguistic

☑ Online Teaching Options

V Visual Skills

- INTERACTIVE MAP **Largest Ancestry Reported by County**—Students discuss varying ancestry populations in the United States and create a document that categorizes the ancestries by location or regions. AL Visual/Spatial
- MAP **Interactive Regional Atlas**—Students use the interactive regional atlas to understand the physical and human geography of the United States.

☑ Printable Digital Worksheets

- WORKSHEET **Assessing Background Knowledge**—Determine the level of prior knowledge students have about the United States.
- WORKSHEET **Chapter Summaries**—Students review the main idea of each lesson of the chapter content.
- WORKSHEET **Reteaching Activity**—These worksheets provide students with an opportunity for remedial practice and review of vital chapter content.
- WORKSHEET **Vocabulary Activity**—Students apply their knowledge of content and academic vocabulary words.

Project-Based Learning 

Hands-On

Immigrant Journal

Students will write a fictional journal as if they were immigrants traveling to and arriving in the United States.

Digital Hands-On

Create Online Projects

Find an additional activity online that incorporates technology for this project. Visit the EdTech Teacher Web sites for more links, tutorials, and other resources.

Print Resources

ANCILLARY RESOURCES

This ancillary is available for every chapter and lesson.

- **Chapter Tests and Lesson Quizzes**

PRINTABLE DIGITAL WORKSHEETS

These printable digital worksheets are available for every chapter and lesson.

- **Assessing Background Knowledge**
- **Chapter Summaries**
- **Guided Reading Activities**
- **Hands-On Chapter Projects**
- **Quizzes and Tests**
- **Reading Essentials and Study Guide** AL
- **Reteaching Activities**
- **Video Activities**
- **Vocabulary Activities**

More Media Resources

SUGGESTED VIDEOS 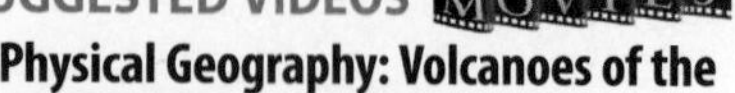

- **Physical Geography: Volcanoes of the United States** (24 min.)
- **Point of Entry: An Intimate Look at Modern Immigration** (27 min.)
- **Great American Landmarks** (23 min.)

SUGGESTED READING 

- ***The Real State of America Atlas: Mapping the Myths and Truths of the United States,*** by Cynthia Enloe and Joni Seager
- ***The Making of Modern Immigration: An Encyclopedia of People and Ideas,*** by Patrick J. Hayes
- ***Implementing Innovation: Fostering Enduring Change in Environmental and Natural Resource Governance,*** by Toddi A. Steelman

LESSON 1 PLANNER

PHYSICAL GEOGRAPHY OF THE UNITED STATES

Students will know:

- *how physical processes have shaped landscapes in the United States.*
- *why lakes and rivers in the United States have been important to economic development.*
- *the abundant natural resources that have made the United States wealthy.*
- *which natural resources are in need of protection.*

Students will be able to:

- ***explain** how the landscapes of the United States were formed.*
- ***describe** how water systems are important to the economy.*
- ***identify** natural resources in the United States.*

UNDERSTANDING BY DESIGN®

☑ Print Teaching Options

V Visual Skills

- ☐ **p. 121** Students create a diagram explaining how either the Appalachian Mountains and Piedmont or Hawaiian Islands were formed. Visual/Spatial, Naturalist
- ☐ **p. 123** Students create a chart to identify and list the different regions and climates of the United States. AL Visual/Spatial

R Reading Skills

- ☐ **p. 120** Students discuss the meanings of the terms *shifted* and *altered.* ELL Verbal/Linguistic
- ☐ **p. 121** Students read about tributaries and headwaters. ELL Verbal/Linguistic
- ☐ **p. 123** Students discuss the term *Coriolis.* ELL Verbal/Linguistic

C Critical Thinking Skills

- ☐ **p. 120** Students identify aspects of the physical geography of the United States.
- ☐ **p. 122** Students discuss the Great Lakes and its role in the U.S. economy. AL Logical/Mathematical
- ☐ **p. 124** Students discuss how natural resources are related to the economy. AL Logical/Mathematical

W Writing Skills

- ☐ **p. 121** Students write a paragraph explaining the divide in the western United States and the fall line in the eastern United States. AL Verbal/Linguistic
- ☐ **p. 122** Students write a one-page essay describing climates in the United States. Verbal/Linguistic

T Technology Skills

- ☐ **p. 120** Students work in groups to research either current tectonic movement or current lava flow incidences in the United States. Interpersonal, Naturalist
- ☐ **p. 124** Students work in small groups to research one of Earth's soil types or one of the careers of pedologists and present their research to the class. BL Verbal/Linguistic

☑ Online Teaching Options

V Visual Skills

VIDEO **Southwest in Need of Water**—Students explore one of the major waterways in the southwestern United States and how it makes it possible to live in Las Vegas. Verbal/Linguistic

C Critical Thinking Skills

INTERACTIVE BELLRINGER **Landforms of the Southwestern United States**—Students discuss and answer questions about the landforms in the southwestern United States. AL Visual/Spatial

INFOGRAPHIC **Hurricanes in the United States**—Students use the infographic to extrapolate on the effects of hurricanes on the rest of the country and answer questions about these effects. BL Logical/Mathematical

INTERACTIVE WHITEBOARD ACTIVITY **Climate and Vegetation in the United States**—Students match statements about climate in the United States with the factors that cause variations in climate and vegetation in the United States.

W Writing Skills

INTERACTIVE MAP **The Continental Divide and the Fall Line**—Students view the map and imagine how life east and west of the fall line is different, recording their thoughts in a paragraph. Verbal/Linguistic, Visual/Spatial

☑ Printable Digital Worksheets

R Reading Skills

WORKSHEET **Guided Reading Activity**—Students use Guided Reading Activity worksheets to review their comprehension of the content.

C Critical Thinking Skills

WORKSHEET **Video Activity**—Students answer questions related to a topic in the chapter content after they have viewed a lesson video.

HUMAN GEOGRAPHY OF THE UNITED STATES

Students will know:

- *how physical geography and ideas of independence influenced U.S. development.*
- *the effect of immigration on the population of the United States.*
- *how urbanization has affected population distribution.*
- *the factors affecting cultural diversity in the United States.*
- *the importance of the U.S. economy to the global economy.*

Students will be able to:

- ***discuss** influences on U.S. development, including geography, independence, and immigration.*
- ***explain** how urbanization affects population distribution.*
- ***describe** the role of the United States in the global economy.*

UNDERSTANDING BY DESIGN®

☑ Print Teaching Options

V Visual Skills

- ☐ **p. 125** Students analyze physical and political maps of their region. ELL Visual/Spatial, Naturalist
- ☐ **p. 128** Students discuss the cartograms and the ethnic populations represented in each. Visual/Spatial

R Reading Skills

- ☐ **p. 127** Students discuss the terms *dry farming* and *Manufacturing Belt.* ELL Verbal/Linguistic
- ☐ **p. 129** Students write the term *megalopolis,* its definition, and a sentence using it. ELL Verbal/Linguistic
- ☐ **p. 131** Students discuss the terms *service* and *technology industries* and write a paragraph discussing the effects the postindustrial economy has had on their region. ELL Verbal/Linguistic

C Critical Thinking Skills

- ☐ **p. 130** Students discuss the economy of the United States. Verbal/Linguistic
- ☐ **p. 131** Students discuss the recent economic downturn and its effects. Logical/Mathematical

W Writing Skills

- ☐ **p. 125** Students create a three-column chart comparing and contrasting the strengths and weaknesses of the three European colonial areas. Verbal/Linguistic
- ☐ **p. 127** Students write a one-page essay on social and economic changes in the United States after World Wars I and II. AL Verbal/Linguistic
- ☐ **p. 128** Students write a one-page essay describing how geography, industry, and populations are interconnected.
- ☐ **p. 129** Students describe a place or event that expresses cultural diversity. AL Verbal/Linguistic

T Technology Skills

- ☐ **p. 126** Students research conflicts in the United States in the 1700s and 1800s. BL Interpersonal
- ☐ **p. 127** Students research immigration data and display their findings in bar graphs. BL Logical/Mathematical
- ☐ **p. 129** Students research a type of music and give a multimedia presentation on its history. BL Auditory/Musical

☑ Online Teaching Options

V Visual Skills

- INTERACTIVE BELLRINGER **Population Density for States**—Students discuss population density and compare the population density in their state to other states. Verbal/Linguistic, Interpersonal
- INTERACTIVE MAP **U.S. Expansion**—Students speculate about the pros and cons early settlers faced based on the natural resources in various destinations of the United States. AL Visual/Spatial

C Critical Thinking Skills

- TIME LINE **Terrorism and the United States**—Students discuss how the War on Terror has affected Americans' attitude and policies toward immigrants. AL Verbal/Linguistic
- INTERACTIVE MAP **Ethnic Populations in the United States**—Students analyze the uneven spread of diversity in the United States. AL Visual/Spatial
- INTERACTIVE MAP **Foreign-Born Population as Percent of State Population, 2010**—Students create a graph that compares the foreign-born population of one nationality across five or six states, summarize their information, and present their graphs. AL Verbal/Linguistic, Visual/Spatial
- INTERACTIVE MAP **Homes in Negative Equity in 2010**—Students discuss how negative equity affects the free market of the United States. ELL Interpersonal
- INTERACTIVE WHITEBOARD ACTIVITY **Physical and Human Factors**—Students will drag and drop human and physical factors into a graphic organizer to help them describe the relationship between the factors that influenced U.S. development.

W Writing Skills

- INTERACTIVE MAP **U.S. Expansion**—Students speculate about pros and cons early settlers faced and write a paragraph about where they would have chosen to settle and why. AL Visual/Spatial

☑ Printable Digital Worksheets

R Reading Skills

- WORKSHEET **Guided Reading Activity**—Students use Guided Reading Activity worksheets to review their comprehension of the content.

C Critical Thinking Skills

- WORKSHEET **Video Activity**—Students answer questions related to a topic in the chapter content after they have viewed a lesson video.

PEOPLE AND THEIR ENVIRONMENT: THE UNITED STATES

Students will know:
- *the issues that require the responsible management of water and timber resources in the United States.*
- *the ways in which human activities have created air and water pollution.*
- *examples of the efforts to address environmental issues in the United States.*

Students will be able to:
- ***identify** resource management issues in the United States.*
- ***describe** how humans are responsible for pollution.*
- ***analyze** efforts to address environmental issues.*

UNDERSTANDING BY DESIGN®

Print Teaching Options

V Visual Skills
- ☐ **p. 135** Students discuss the consumption of freshwater in the United States. AL Visual/Spatial
- ☐ **p. 136** Students analyze the level of acid rain in the state where they live. Verbal/Linguistic
- ☐ **p. 137** Students create diagrams of the different stages of the process of eutrophication. ELL Visual/Spatial

R Reading Skills
- ☐ **p. 134** Students define *clear-cutting.* ELL Verbal/Linguistic
- ☐ **p. 135** Students identify causes and effects of acid rain.
- ☐ **p. 136** Students define *smog.* ELL Verbal/Linguistic
- ☐ **p. 138** Students discuss how aqueducts are part of the solution in handling water shortages.

C Critical Thinking Skills
- ☐ **p. 134** Students list areas in their state that have been developed with housing or industry in the last eight years.
- ☐ **p. 134** Students identify and answer questions about pollution threats to areas in their state or region. AL Verbal/Linguistic

W Writing Skills
- ☐ **p. 134** Students write a narrative describing how they use water each day. Intrapersonal
- ☐ **p. 135** Students write about how humans have damaged water resources in the United States. Verbal/Linguistic
- ☐ **p. 137** Students write a short story about a natural resource they feel needs protection and what the characters do to protect it. AL Verbal/Linguistic

T Technology Skills
- ☐ **p. 136** Students research the levels of acid rain in a large city in the United States, create a multimedia presentation, and present their research. Auditory/Musical, Naturalist
- ☐ **p. 137** Students research U.S. drought conditions and create a chart comparing the first ten of the last twenty years to the last ten. BL Visual/Spatial
- ☐ **p. 138** Students research efforts in their community to curb air and water pollution. Verbal/Linguistic

Online Teaching Options

C Critical Thinking Skills
- INTERACTIVE BELLRINGER **Acid Rain in the United States**—Students identify how acid rain is formed and why it is a problem and discuss effects of acid rain they have witnessed. AL Visual/Spatial
- INTERACTIVE MAP **U.S. Water Withdrawals**—Students research the main water use or uses in a specific state and share their findings. BL Verbal/Linguistic
- INTERACTIVE MAP **Acid Rain in the United States**—Students discuss how acid rain is formed and work with a partner to rewrite the definition of acid rain. ELL Verbal/Linguistic
- INTERACTIVE IMAGE **Wind as Renewable Energy**—Student groups discuss and list the pros and cons of harnessing wind power. Interpersonal, Naturalist
- INTERACTIVE WHITEBOARD ACTIVITY **Limited Natural Resources**—Students identify causes, effects, and solutions to environmental problems in the United States.

Printable Digital Worksheets

R Reading Skills
- WORKSHEET **Guided Reading Activity**—Students use Guided Reading Activity worksheets to review their comprehension of the content.
- WORKSHEET **Reading Essentials and Study Guide**—Students complete the study guide and answer Reading Progress Check and vocabulary questions. AL
- WORKSHEET **Vocabulary Activity**—Students review the chapter content and academic vocabulary words.

C Critical Thinking Skills
- WORKSHEET **Video Activity**—Students answer questions based on a lesson video.
- WORKSHEET **Reteaching Activity**—Students use this activity worksheet to review and reteach chapter content and vocabulary. This worksheet can be used with struggling students who need additional help with difficult content concepts.

INTERVENTION AND REMEDIATION STRATEGIES

LESSON 1 Physical Geography of the United States

Reading and Comprehension

Have students work with a partner to scan the lesson and use context clues to define the meaning of each content vocabulary term. Have partners write sentences using each term to demonstrate their understanding of the word's meaning. Then have partners collaborate to create sentences that show their understanding of the two academic vocabulary terms. Challenge students to use two vocabulary terms in the same sentence.

Text Evidence

Have students select an area in the United States that they have lived in, visited, or know about. Have students write an outline about the physical geography of the area, using the lesson headings and subheadings. Tell students to fill in facts that they know about the area under the appropriate headings. Then have students complete the outline using textual evidence to support ideas presented in their outlines. Tell students to evaluate whether information in the text is sufficient to support the facts they first listed, revising their outlines as needed. Then have students share their outlines, relating any new information they learned about the area.

LESSON 2 Human Geography of the United States

Reading and Comprehension

Have students scan the lesson and use context clues to define the meaning of each content vocabulary word. Ask volunteers to choose one of the words and use it in a sentence that shows an understanding of the word's meaning. Clarify terms that English language learners may find confusing, such as *Manufacturing Belt* and *Sunbelt.* Explain that here the word *belt* is used to describe a specific area with a common characteristic. For example, the term *Snowbelt* refers to a region that receives heavy snowfall.

Text Evidence

Organize students into small groups and have them use information from the text to create, rehearse, and perform a skit that depicts a "living history" of the United States. Students may choose a topic or vocabulary term on which to focus their skit, but remind students that the skit should be realistic and use textual evidence to support the dialogue and action. Have groups present their skits for the class, allowing students in the audience to provide constructive feedback.

LESSON 3 People and Their Environment: The United States

Reading and Comprehension

Have students work in pairs to identify cause-and-effect relationships as they read about environmental issues in the United States. Remind students to look for signal words and phrases such as *cause, effect, as a result,* and *consequently.* Then have partners choose a statement from the text, such as *"Acid rain. . .affects a large area of the eastern United States,"* or *"The accidental or deliberate introduction of nonnative plant and animal species. . . also causes environmental problems."* Have pairs create a diagram or flowchart that illustrates the cause-and-effect relationship in their chosen statement. Have student pairs share their diagrams or charts with the class.

Text Evidence

Assign student groups one of the challenges discussed in this lesson such as acid rain, smog, eutrophication, water pollution, and water shortages. Have students in each group work together to summarize the problems related to their topic and how or if the problems are being solved. Encourage students to use content vocabulary terms in their summaries.

Online Resources

Leveled Reader

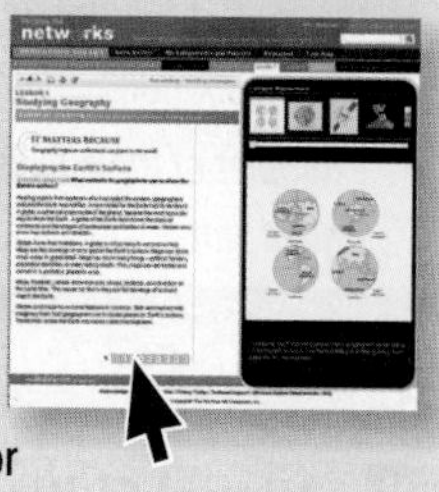

Use this online approaching-level text that corresponds directly to the text in the Student Edition. It also includes additional reading and comprehension support for English Language Learners.

Guided Reading Activities

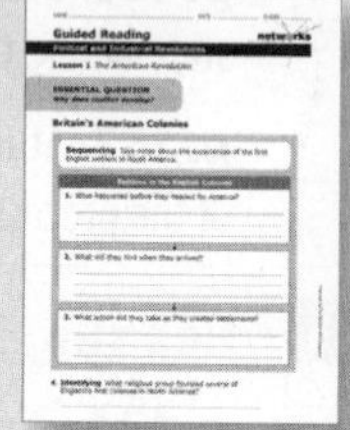

This resource uses guiding questions to help students with comprehension.

Reteaching Activities

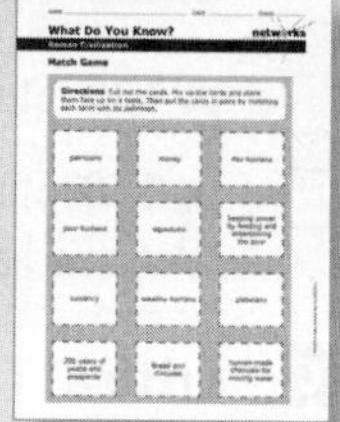

These worksheets provide students with an opportunity for remedial practice and review of vital chapter content.

Reading Essentials and Study Guide

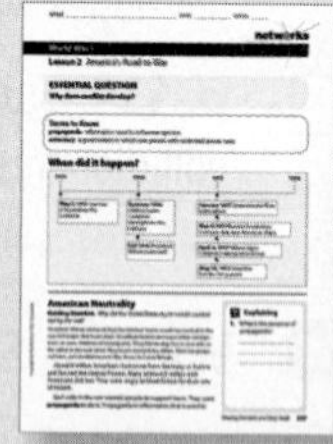

This resource offers writing and reading activities for the approaching-level student.

Self-Check Quizzes

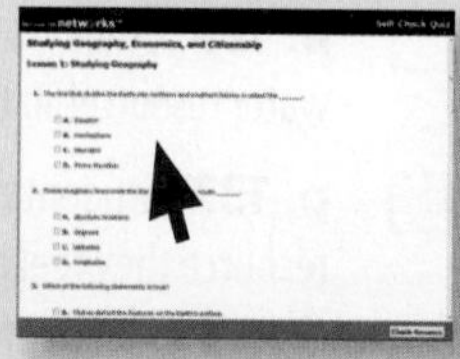

This online assessment tool provides instant feedback for students to check their progress.

Chapter Summaries

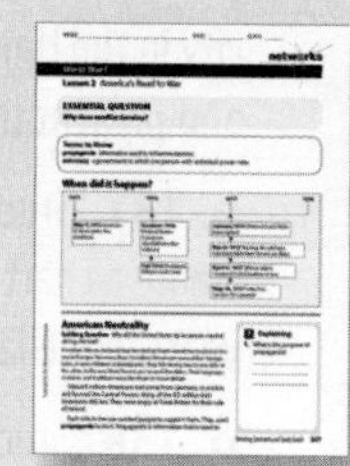

Summaries are provided for each chapter that thoroughly condense core content into manageable chunks.

The United States

ESSENTIAL QUESTION • *How do physical systems and human systems shape a place?*

networks

There's More Online about the United States.

CHAPTER 5

Geography Matters...

What do the words *the United States* bring to mind? The images are endless for a land that offers so many opportunities. Some people hope to travel across its four million miles of highways, while others seek the "American Dream" of economic opportunity or religious and cultural freedom. It is not easy to characterize the American experience because the United States is a land of many cultures and peoples. The country is also known for its varied landscape of big cities, rugged mountains, wide plains, and forests that cover vast stretches of land.

◀ Native Americans such as this Navajo girl keep their traditions alive through dance, dress, and spiritual practices.

National Geographic Image Collection/Alamy

117

Letter from the Author

Dear Geography Teacher,

The United States is a mix of bustling urban areas and rural agriculture. The French geographer Jean Gottman coined the term *megalopolis* when he described the eastern coast of the United States. Gottman was describing the almost continuous urban development stretching from Washington, D.C., to Boston. Characterized by tall skyscrapers and snakelike transportation routes, this area accounts for a very large proportion of the U.S.'s population and economy. A rural view of the U.S. may be accessed by visiting www.geotech.org. Program 3 deals with water and agriculture, and it includes a 16 minute case study of the Villrock farm in Indiana.

ENGAGE

Describing Tell students this chapter is about the cultural and physical landscape of the United States. Emphasize that it is not easy to characterize the cultural landscape because the United States offers so many opportunities. Have students describe the opportunities they have. List them on the board and review in a class discussion.

TEACH & ASSESS

Identifying Invite a student to read the caption accompanying the photo of a Native American girl. Remind students that in the United States different cultural groups are able to keep their traditions. Working in small groups, have students identify cultural communities and their locations in their state. In a class discussion have student groups share their answers. **AL** **Verbal/Linguistic**

Making Connections

Read aloud the major aspects of a culture's tradition:

- Traditional songs
- Stories, fairy tales, ghost stories
- Riddles, proverbs, jokes
- Handed-down recipes for special foods
- Childhood games and rhymes

Analyzing Emphasize that in continuing a particular cultural tradition, different ethnic groups have contributed and continue to contribute to the larger American culture. Ask students to identify songs, stories, and/or foods from their own traditions that have become part of the larger American culture. **Verbal/Linguistic**

CLOSE & REFLECT

Discussing Have students share what they know about various cultures that contribute to the larger American culture. Then ask them to describe which culture they believe has had the most influence on the United States. Explain that they will be learning about the varied cultural and physical landscapes that contribute to the American experience.

ePals GlobalCommunity
Where learners connect™

Extend the project-based learning experience globally through our partnership with ePals. EPals allows you to connect with classrooms around the world in a safe online environment for real-life lessons and projects in virtual study groups.

ENGAGE

C Critical Thinking Skills

Identifying Trends Direct students' attention to the map showing the ancestry of people reported in the United States. Have students identify the various ancestries of people in their state. Discuss whether this list corresponds to the list they made during a previous chapter about various cultural communities in their state. **Ask:** **Does one ancestry dominate the region in which our state is located? If so, which ancestry and how do these people treat others of a different ancestry? If not, how do the people of a mix of ancestries in the region get along?** *(Student answers will vary, but should include relevant details supporting each answer.)*

TEACH & ASSESS

T Technology Skills

Calculating Invite a student to read the introductory paragraph aloud and list the percentages of different populations as they read. **Ask:** **What percentage of the U.S. population is descended from immigrants?** *(85 percent)* Have students find the current U.S. population number. *(According to U.S. Census Bureau, approximately 314,000,000 people live in the United States.)* Remind students that 85 percent of the population is descended from immigrants. **Ask:** **What is the total number of people in the United States descended from immigrants?** *(Students figure 85 percent of 314,000,000; approximately 266,900,000 people are descended from immigrants.)* **Logical/Mathematical**

patterns of immigration

One of the defining attributes of the United States is that it is largely a country of immigrants and their descendants. About 13 percent of people in the United States are foreign born, while Native Americans, Alaska Natives, and Native Hawaiians make up about 2 percent of the population. The remaining population is descended from immigrants.

Largest Ancestry Reported by County 2000

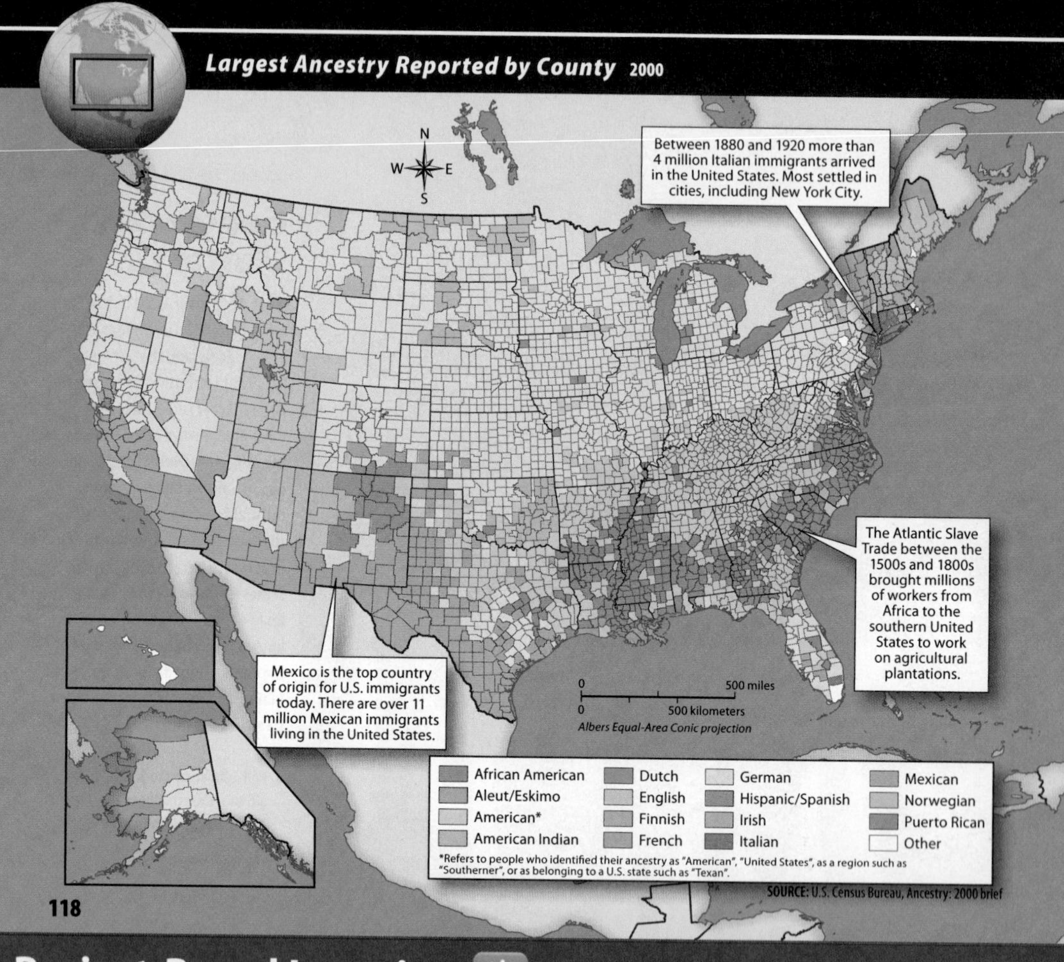
N
W
E
S
Between 1880 and 1920 more than 4 million Italian immigrants arrived in the United States. Most settled in cities, including New York City.
The Atlantic Slave Trade between the 1500s and 1800s brought millions of workers from Africa to the southern United States to work on agricultural plantations.
Mexico is the top country of origin for U.S. immigrants today. There are over 11 million Mexican immigrants living in the United States.
0 500 miles
0 500 kilometers
Albers Equal-Area Conic projection
African American
Aleut/Eskimo
American*
American Indian
Dutch
English
Finnish
French
German
Hispanic/Spanish
Irish
Italian
Mexican
Norwegian
Puerto Rican
Other
*Refers to people who identified their ancestry as "American", "United States", as a region such as "Southerner", or as belonging to a U.S. state such as "Texan".
SOURCE: U.S. Census Bureau, Ancestry: 2000 brief

118

Project-Based Learning

Hands-On

Immigrant Journal

Students will write a fictional journal that brings together information from all lessons about the physical geography and human geography of the United States as well as interactions between people and the environment.

Digital Hands-On

Create Online Projects

Find an additional activity online that incorporates technology for this project. Visit the EdTech Teacher Web sites for more links, tutorials, and other resources.

ePals GlobalCommunity
Where learners connect™

edtechteacher
21st Century Learning

Where have immigrants to the United States come from?

The history of immigration to the United States can be divided into four distinct periods. The earliest period, the colonial period, was characterized by an influx of English and other European peoples, many of whom came as indentured servants to work for little or no pay. During the mid-nineteenth century, the majority of immigrants originated from the countries of northern and western Europe. The third major period of immigration was primarily from southern and eastern Europe. The start of the fourth wave of immigrants is marked by the abolishment in 1965 of the quotas that limited immigration from the Eastern Hemisphere based on country of origin. This opened the doors to a wave of immigrants from Asia and Africa. At the same time, worsening economic conditions in many Latin American countries led to a rise in the number of Latino immigrants to the United States. Today, Mexicans are the largest single immigrant group in the United States.

1. **Places and Regions** Describe the four periods into which immigration to the United States can be divided.

Why did they immigrate to the United States?

Two sets of factors influence immigration patterns: push factors and pull factors. Push factors motivate people to leave their countries of origin. They can be quite varied, including religious and ethnic persecution, lack of economic prospects or personal security, civil strife, and war. Environmental conditions such as drought, famine, and flooding and events such as earthquakes and volcanic eruptions can also push people to migrate to a new country. In the nineteenth century, for example, many Irish immigrants came to the United States to escape the Irish potato famine of 1845 to 1852. **W** Similarly, many Chinese began migrating to the United States during this same time because of the population explosion and food shortages in China. Pull factors are those which draw people to a new country, such as employment opportunities, political and religious freedom, and better living conditions, including access to education and health care. Pull factors drew people to the United States during all four major periods of immigration, as people came seeking work, freedom, and a better way of life.

2. **Human Systems** What are the reasons for immigration to the United States? Define push factors and pull factors and list at least three examples of each.

How has immigration shaped human geography in the United States?

Successive waves of immigrants have absorbed, challenged, and ultimately reshaped American culture. As people move, their cultural traits and ideas move with them, creating and modifying the cultural landscape in their new home. These imprints on the United States include spoken languages, religious beliefs and institutions, family and ethnic traditions, architectural styles, art, music, and food. These cultural modifications can be seen in the ethnic neighborhoods of both small and large cities where grocery stores, churches and other places of worship, schools, restaurants, and other businesses reflect the immigrant culture of each community. Examples of ethnic neighborhoods include Little Tokyo in Los Angeles, California; Little Havana in Miami, Florida; Polish Hill in Pittsburgh, Pennsylvania; and Arabian Village in Detroit, Michigan. **T**

3. **Human Systems** Write a paragraph describing three examples of how immigrants have left their imprint on the cultural landscape of your community or a place you have visited.

THERE'S MORE ONLINE

VIEW a graph of the ethnic makeup of the United States • *WATCH* a video about U.S. ethnic diversity

V Visual Skills

Creating Visuals Ask students to discuss the diversity they see in the three images. Using drawings and photos from news clippings and online sources, have students create montages depicting Americans in the twenty-first century.
ELL Visual/Spatial

W Writing Skills

Informative Direct students' attention to the explanation of the four periods of immigration to the United States. Have students write a paragraph identifying one period of immigration and the push and pull factors that led to that immigration. Encourage students to share their paragraphs with the class. AL Verbal/Linguistic

T Technology Skills

Reaching Conclusions Have students summarize the cultural imprints twenty-first century immigration has had in their region and then research these cultural influences online. Tell them to identify a reliable Internet source that discusses the cultural landscape of their region. Review acceptable Internet sources with students as needed. BL Verbal/Linguistic

CLOSE & REFLECT

Summarizing Based on the information about the cultural landscape of the United States, have students write three statements predicting what they think will be the key concepts in this chapter. They should keep their statements in a notebook. Have students check their statements occasionally to see if their predictions follow the concepts in the chapter.

INTERACTIVE MAP

Largest Ancestry Reported by County, 2000

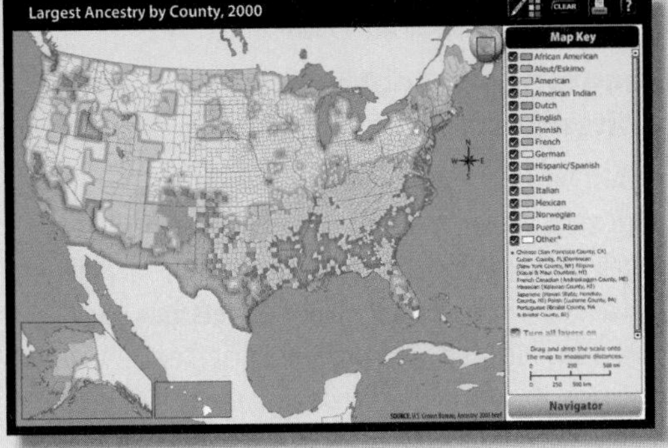

Categorizing Use this interactive map to discuss with students the varying ancestry populations in the United States. Click through the interactive captions that explain how and when groups of immigrants arrived in America. Have students form small groups. Ask them to use the map to create a document that categorizes the ancestries by location or regions and write an statement explaining each category. Then in class discussion, have groups share their information. AL Visual/Spatial

ANSWERS, p. 119

Why Geography Matters

1. The first period was characterized by an influx of English and other European peoples. The second was characterized by immigrants originating from the countries of northern and western Europe during the mid-nineteenth century. The third period of immigration was primarily from southern and eastern Europe. The start of the fourth wave of immigrants is marked by the abolishment of the quotas that limited immigration based on national origin.
2. Push factors motivate people to leave their countries of origin, such as escaping religious and ethnic persecution, lack of economic prospects or personal security, civil strife, and war. Pull factors draw people to a new country, such as employment opportunities, political and religious freedom, better living conditions, and access to education and health care.
3. Paragraphs will vary, but students should include at least three specific examples of cultural imprints by immigrants.

ENGAGE

C Critical Thinking Skills

Activating Prior Knowledge Have students brainstorm and identify aspects of the physical geography of the United States. *(List should include mountains, plateaus, rivers, lakes, divides, and the fall line.)* Tell students in this lesson they will learn how the physical geography of the United States has made it a wealthy country.

TEACH & ASSESS

R Reading Skills

Defining Discuss the meaning of the terms *shifted* and *altered*. **Ask:** **How does the term *shifted* connect to the tectonic plates underneath Earth's crust?** *(When the tectonic plates shifted, or moved, they forced giant rock slabs upward that formed mountains.)* **How does the term *altered* relate to volcanic lava and forming plateaus?** *(Lava flows seeped upward through cracks in Earth's crust and altered or changed the land and formed plateaus.)* Have students start a Chapter 5 glossary using these two words. ELL **Verbal/Linguistic**

T Technology Skills

Researching Organize students into groups to conduct online research. Half of the groups should research current tectonic movement in the United States and how it affects landforms and people. The other half of the groups should research current lava flow incidences in the United States and how they affect landforms and people. Have each group present their findings to the class. **Interpersonal, Naturalist**

networks

There's More Online!

- **DIAGRAM** Western Topography
- **INFOGRAPHIC** Hurricanes in the United States
- **MAP** The Continental Divide and the Fall Line
- **INTERACTIVE SELF-CHECK QUIZ**
- **VIDEO** Physical Geography of the United States

Cool, moist air
Hot, dry winds
Pacific Ranges

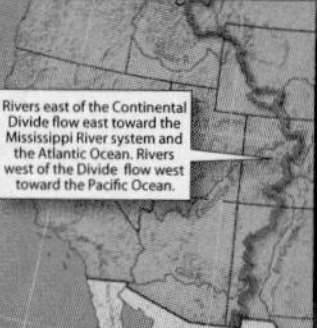
Rivers east of the Continental Divide flow east toward the Mississippi River system and the Atlantic Ocean. Rivers west of the Divide flow west toward the Pacific Ocean.

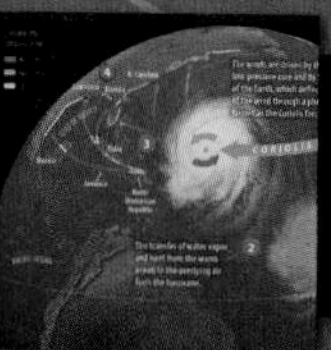

LESSON 1
Physical Geography of the United States

ESSENTIAL QUESTION • *How do physical systems and human systems shape a place?*

Reading HELPDESK 

Academic Vocabulary (Tier Two Words)
- **shift**
- **alter**

Content Vocabulary (Tier Three Words)
- **tributary**
- **headwaters**
- **divide**
- **fall line**
- **hurricane**
- **fossil fuel**

TAKING NOTES: ***Key Ideas and Details***

IDENTIFYING Use a graphic organizer like the one below to take notes on the physical geography of the United States as you read.

Physical Geography of the United States		
Landforms	Water Systems	Climate, Biomes, and Resources

IT MATTERS BECAUSE

C *With over 3.5 million square miles (9 million sq. km) of land, the United States is the third-largest country in the world. Its natural environment is diverse and makes the country one of the world's most productive regions.*

Landforms

GUIDING QUESTION *How has tectonic activity helped create so many of the landforms in the United States?*

Many of the landforms of the United States can be traced back to glacial activity and the tectonic plate movement of the Earth's crust. The Pacific and Rocky Mountain ranges in the west and the Appalachian Mountains in the east are the result of powerful tectonic plate activity. The tectonic forces **shifted** giant rock slabs upward.

R Considered young in geologic terms, the Pacific Ranges of the United States consist of the Sierra Nevada, the Cascade Range, the Coast Range, and the Alaska Range. Mount McKinley in the Alaska Range, at 20,320 feet (6,194 m), is the highest point in the United States. The Rocky Mountains begin in New Mexico and stretch northward over 3,000 miles (4,828 km). Between the Pacific Ranges and the Rocky Mountains is an area of plateaus and dry basins that was formed by volcanic lava seeping upward through cracks in the Earth's crust. These lava flows **altered**, or changed, the land forming the Columbia Plateau. Farther south are the flat-topped mesas of the Colorado Plateau and the spectacular gorge of the Grand Canyon, which plunges more than a mile into the Earth at its deepest points.

T Extending eastward from the Rockies, the landscape flattens considerably to form the Great Plains, which stretch from 300 miles (483 km) to over 700 miles (1,126 km) wide. The land of the plains is higher in the west and slopes downward until it reaches the Central Lowlands. The plains continue eastward to the base of the Appalachian Mountains, the oldest mountain range on the North American continent. This range extends 1,500 miles (2,414 km), from Canada into the state of Alabama. As

120

networks ***Online Teaching Options***

 **INTERACTIVE BELLRINGER**

Landforms of Southwestern United States

Identifying Use the introductory text and the image to discuss the landforms found in the southwestern United States. Ask students to study the image and answer the first question independently. Have students form small groups and further discuss landforms that they are familiar with, such as the Grand Canyon and the Rocky Mountains. Then have them discuss their answers for the first question with their group and answer the remaining questions. Ask each group to write agreed-upon answers to all of the questions. AL **Visual/Spatial**

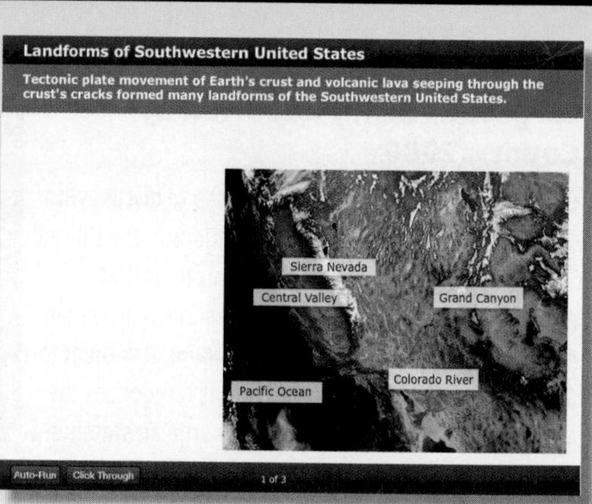
Landforms of Southwestern United States
Tectonic plate movement of Earth's crust and volcanic lava seeping through the crust's cracks formed many landforms of the Southwestern United States.
Sierra Nevada
Central Valley
Grand Canyon
Colorado River
Pacific Ocean
Auto-Run
Click Through
1 of 3

ANSWERS, p. 120

TAKING NOTES: Landforms—the Pacific Ranges, the Rocky Mountains, the Great Plains, plateaus, dry basins, and mesas; **Water Systems**—the Mississippi River system, the Gulf of Mexico, and the Pacific and Atlantic Oceans; **Climates**—a humid subtropical, continental, humid continental, semiarid, arid Mediterranean, high-altitude, marine west coast, and subarctic; **Biomes**—Temperate Deciduous Forest, Boreal or Taiga Forest, Desert, Chaparral, Grassland; **Resources**—water, fossil fuels, timber, fish, and minerals.

tectonic plates within the Earth's crust collided and pushed upward, they formed the Appalachians. The resulting peaks were shaped further by ice and water. Between the Appalachian Mountains and the Atlantic Coastal Plain lies the Piedmont, a low-rolling, fertile plateau cut by many rivers.

The Hawaiian Islands, located about 2,400 miles (3,862 km) off the western coast of the mainland United States, were formed when magma erupted from a spot on the seafloor, called a hot spot. This hot spot created a string of 8 major and 124 smaller islands that make up the Hawaiian Island chain.

shift to change the place, position, or direction of

alter to change partly

V

✓ READING PROGRESS CHECK

Explaining How were the Pacific Ranges formed?

Water Systems

GUIDING QUESTION *How have rivers and lakes been important to the economic development of the United States?*

Many lakes, rivers, and **tributaries** play a crucial role in many aspects of life. The Mississippi River is one of the longest rivers in North America. It flows 2,350 miles (3,782 km) from its **headwaters**, or source, in Minnesota and reaches a width of 1.5 miles (2.4 km) at its mouth, where it empties into the Gulf of Mexico. The Colorado River and the Rio Grande both have their headwaters in the Rocky Mountains where many tributaries merge to form these two major waterways.

R

A physical feature called a **divide** determines the direction of river flow. The Continental Divide is a high ridge in the Rocky Mountains. Waterways to the west of the divide flow into the Pacific Ocean. Waterways to the east of the divide flow toward the Arctic Ocean, Hudson Bay, Atlantic Ocean, and Mississippi River system.

In the eastern United States, the **fall line** marks the place where the higher land of the Piedmont drops to the lower Atlantic Coastal Plain. Along the fall line, eastern rivers break into rapids and waterfalls, preventing ships from the Atlantic Ocean from traveling farther inland. Many cities, such as Philadelphia, Baltimore, and Washington, D.C., were established along the fall line.

W

tributary a smaller river or stream that feeds into a larger river

headwaters the source of a stream or river

divide a high point or ridge that determines the direction rivers flow

fall line a boundary in the eastern United States where the higher land of the Piedmont drops to the lower Atlantic Coastal Plain

Western Topography ⌄ DIAGRAM SKILLS

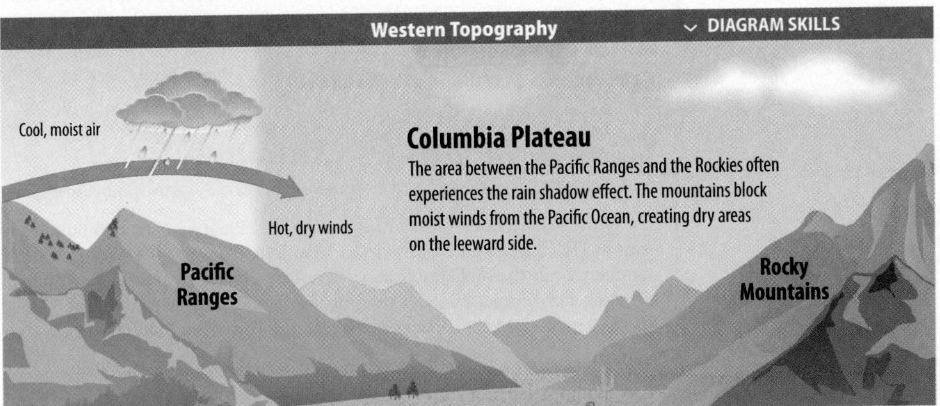
Cool, moist air
Hot, dry winds
Columbia Plateau
The area between the Pacific Ranges and the Rockies often experiences the rain shadow effect. The mountains block moist winds from the Pacific Ocean, creating dry areas on the leeward side.
Pacific Ranges
Rocky Mountains

The shape and location of the Cascade Range affect conditions on the Columbia Plateau.

▲ CRITICAL THINKING

1. ***Drawing Conclusions*** What type of vegetation would you expect to find in the flat plateau areas between mountain ranges?
2. ***Analyzing*** How does the rain shadow effect impact the Columbia Plateau?

V Visual Skills

Creating Diagrams Emphasize that movement, either of tectonic plates, lava, or glaciers, formed much of the U.S. landscape. Organize the class into pairs and have half of the pairs create a diagram explaining how the Appalachian Mountains and the Piedmont were created. Have the other pairs create diagrams explaining how the Hawaiian Islands were formed. Have pairs share their diagrams in a class discussion. **Visual/Spatial, Naturalist**

R Reading Skills

Explaining Have students read about tributaries and headwaters. **Ask: What are tributaries and what is their relationship to large rivers?** *(Tributaries are smaller rivers and streams that feed into larger rivers.)* **What are headwaters?** *(Headwaters are the source of a stream or river.)* **Where are the headwaters of the Mississippi River and the Colorado River?** *(The headwaters of the Mississippi River are in Minnesota and the headwaters of the Colorado River are in the Rocky Mountains.)* **ELL Verbal/Linguistic**

W Writing Skills

Informative/Explanatory After students read the text, have them write a paragraph explaining the divide in the western United States and a paragraph explaining the fall line in the eastern United States. Have students share their paragraphs in class discussion. **AL Verbal/Linguistic**

VIDEO

Southwest In Need of Water

Analyzing Ethical Issues Use this video to introduce the class to one of the major waterways in the American southwest. Have students explain how this waterway makes life possible for people living in Las Vegas and how the lives of the people there have permanently changed the waterway. **Ask: Should humans radically change their lifestyles to make life in Las Vegas sustainable? What lifestyle changes are needed?** *(Students should explain how residents and visitors can make life sustainable in Las Vegas.)* **Verbal/Linguistic**

ANSWERS, p. 121

✓ **READING PROGRESS CHECK** The Pacific Ranges were formed through powerful tectonic plate activity shifting giant rock slabs upward.

CRITICAL THINKING

1. Winds become warmer and drier as they descend the leeward side of the mountain, creating little precipitation. Therefore, vegetation that grows between mountain ranges needs to survive with little water.
2. The rain shadow effect creates a dry, semi-arid climate on the Columbia Plateau.

C Critical Thinking Skills

Analyzing Have students read the first paragraph. **Ask:** **What did glaciers uncover in the region of the Great Lakes?** *(The glaciers uncovered deposits of iron ore, coal, and other natural resources.)* **Ask:** **What is the role of the Great Lakes to the U.S. economy?** *(With the region's natural resources and the Great Lakes-St. Lawrence Seaway System, the lakes are a significant factor in the U.S. economy.)*
AL **Logical/Mathematical**

W Writing Skills

Informative/Explanatory Have students write a one-page essay describing the variety of climates the United States has and why it has such different climates. Have students identify the climate of the local area. **Verbal/Linguistic**

Making Connections

Have students make connections to forest and aquatic biomes and consider how their lives might change if one of these biomes was lost to industrial development.

- We share the world with many other species of plants and animals. It is important to preserve all types of biomes as each houses many unique forms of life. The continued heavy exploitation of forest and aquatic biomes may have severe implications.
- Forests are home to the most diverse biotic communities in the world. Also forests have a global climate-buffering capacity, so their destruction may cause large-scale changes in global climate.
- Aquatic biomes are probably the most important of all the biomes as water is a major natural resource. Water is the basis of life, and it supports life. Freshwater biomes supply drinking water and water for crop irrigation. The world's oceans have high capacity for heat, and because Earth is mostly covered with water, the temperature of the atmosphere is kept fairly constant and able to support life.

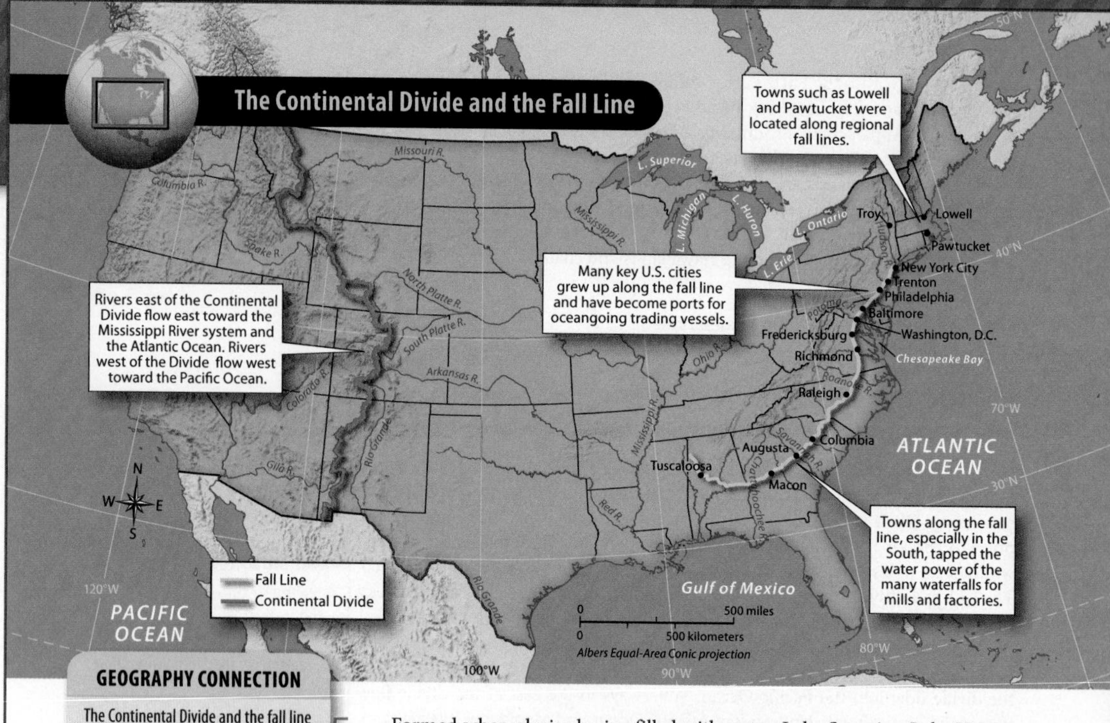
The Continental Divide and the Fall Line
Towns such as Lowell and Pawtucket were located along regional fall lines.
Many key U.S. cities grew up along the fall line and have become ports for oceangoing trading vessels.
Rivers east of the Continental Divide flow east toward the Mississippi River system and the Atlantic Ocean. Rivers west of the Divide flow west toward the Pacific Ocean.
Towns along the fall line, especially in the South, tapped the water power of the many waterfalls for mills and factories.
Fall Line
Continental Divide
Missouri R.
Columbia R.
Snake R.
North Platte R.
South Platte R.
Arkansas R.
Colorado R.
Rio Grande
Gila R.
Red R.
Mississippi R.
Ohio R.
L. Superior
L. Michigan
L. Huron
L. Erie
L. Ontario
Troy
Lowell
Pawtucket
New York City
Trenton
Philadelphia
Baltimore
Washington, D.C.
Fredericksburg
Richmond
Raleigh
Columbia
Augusta
Macon
Tuscaloosa
Chesapeake Bay
ATLANTIC OCEAN
PACIFIC OCEAN
Gulf of Mexico
500 miles
500 kilometers
Albers Equal-Area Conic projection
120°W
100°W
90°W
80°W
70°W
40°N
30°N
50°N

GEOGRAPHY CONNECTION

The Continental Divide and the fall line are important to the flow of rivers and river traffic in the United States.

1. ***PHYSICAL SYSTEMS*** How does the Continental Divide affect the flow of rivers in the western United States?
2. ***PLACES AND REGIONS*** Describe how the fall line influenced economic development in the eastern United States.

C

Formed when glacier basins filled with water, Lake Superior, Lake Huron, Lake Erie, Lake Ontario, and Lake Michigan make up the Great Lakes. The glaciers uncovered major deposits of natural resources, including iron ore and coal, that later spurred explosive economic growth. The Great Lakes serve many economic and recreational purposes, but none more valuable than the Great Lakes–St. Lawrence Seaway System, a series of canals, rivers, and waterways linking the Great Lakes with the Atlantic Ocean. The seaway helped make cities along the Great Lakes, such as Chicago, powerful trade and industrial centers.

☑ **READING PROGRESS CHECK**

Explaining How were the Great Lakes formed?

Climate, Biomes, and Resources

GUIDING QUESTION *What factors cause variations in climate and vegetation in the United States?*

W

The United States has a variety of climates. The climates differ for a number of reasons. The high latitudes of Alaska have long, cold winters and brief, mild summers while the midlatitude areas have temperate climates. Places with high elevation have cooler climates than do those with low elevation. The United States even has tropical climates in the states of Hawaii and Florida.

Climate Regions and Biomes

The Southeast has a humid subtropical climate that is rainy with long, muggy summers and mild winters. Since it borders large bodies of water—the Atlantic Ocean and Gulf of Mexico—there is no dry season. Maple, oak, and pine trees are plentiful, and many types of mammals, reptiles, and amphibians are common.

Wetlands and swamps such as Florida's Everglades shelter a great variety of vegetation and wildlife. In late summer and early autumn, **hurricanes**—ocean

hurricane a large, powerful windstorm that forms over warm ocean waters

122

networks Online Teaching Options

INTERACTIVE MAP

The Continental Divide and the Fall Line

Hypothesizing This map of the United States shows the Continental Divide and the fall line. Have the students focus on the fall line along the eastern seaboard. Ask students to imagine how life might be different for someone who lived east of the fall line in an urban center such as Baltimore, Maryland, versus someone who lived west of the Appalachian Mountains. Have students hypothesize by writing a paragraph about how their lives would be different. **Visual/Spatial, Verbal/Linguistic**

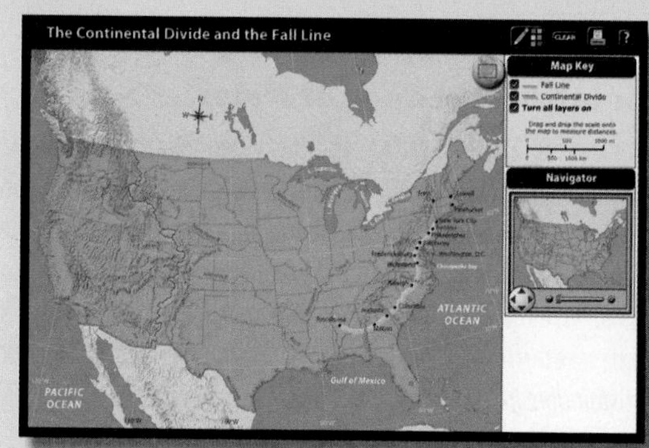
The Continental Divide and the Fall Line
Map Key
Navigator
ATLANTIC OCEAN
PACIFIC OCEAN
Gulf of Mexico

ANSWERS, p. 122

☑ **READING PROGRESS CHECK** The Great Lakes were formed when glacier basins filled with water.

GEOGRAPHY CONNECTION

1. West of the Continental Divide, waterways flow west into the Pacific Ocean. East of the divide, waterways flow east towards the Mississippi River system, the Atlantic Ocean, Hudson Bay, and the Arctic Ocean.
2. In the eastern United States, mills and factories used the waterfalls for power. The fall line also influenced economic development by preventing oceangoing ships from traveling further inland; many eastern cities became ports for these trading vessels.

storms hundreds of miles wide with sustained winds of about 74 miles per hour (119 km per hour) or more—can pound the region's coastlines.

The climate of the Great Plains reflects its location in the center of the continent. Because this area is far from the moderating influences of the ocean waters, it experiences very cold winters and hot summers. This is known as a continental climate. Moreover, parts of this area have a humid continental climate because they receive significant precipitation. This interior climate also extends into the hills and plateaus between the Mississippi River and the Appalachian Mountains. In the Great Plains and the eastern United States, violent spring and summer thunderstorms called supercells often spawn tornadoes with winds that can reach 200 miles (339 km) per hour. **V**

Some areas west of the Great Plains have a semiarid climate with a mixture of vegetation, depending on latitude and elevation. These are transitional climates that occur between the humid continental climates and the arid climates of the Colorado Plateau. Animals in semiarid regions include deer, bison, coyotes, and wolves.

To the west of the semiarid regions, dry air moves down the leeward side of the mountains, creating an arid climate. This is called the rain shadow effect. Plants in arid climates, such as scrub bushes and cacti, have developed long root systems and other adaptations that allow them to survive with little water.

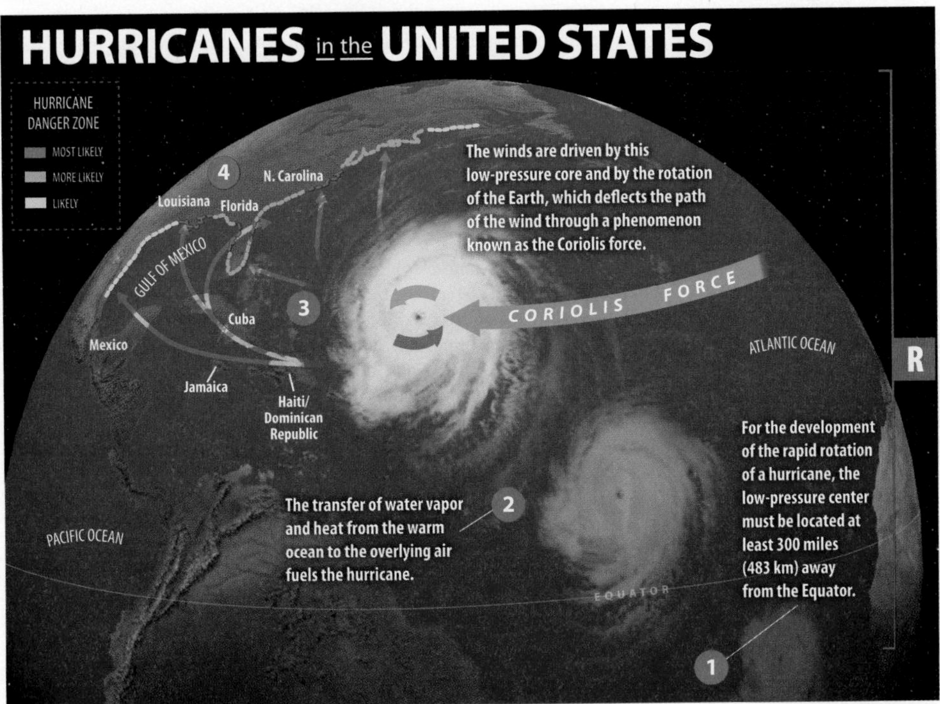

R

Tropical storms that are known as hurricanes in the United States are called typhoons in the western North Pacific Ocean and cyclones in the South Pacific and Indian Oceans.

▲ **CRITICAL THINKING**

1. ***Interpreting*** Describe the air pressure inside the core of a hurricane and how proximity to the Equator affects the development of this type of storm.
2. ***Analyzing Visuals*** Which parts of the United States are most vulnerable to damage from hurricanes?

INFOGRAPHIC

Hurricanes in the United States

Comparing and Contrasting Based on the infographic about hurricanes in the United States, have students extrapolate about the effects to the rest of the country such as how the hurricane danger zone changes as one travels westward. Then ask students to work with a partner to answer the following questions: **What effects might the Midwest region experience after a hurricane along the Gulf of Mexico? How might the fall line affect this?** *(Student answers will vary, but should include information that relates to weather events in the Midwest.)* **BL** **Logical/Mathematical**

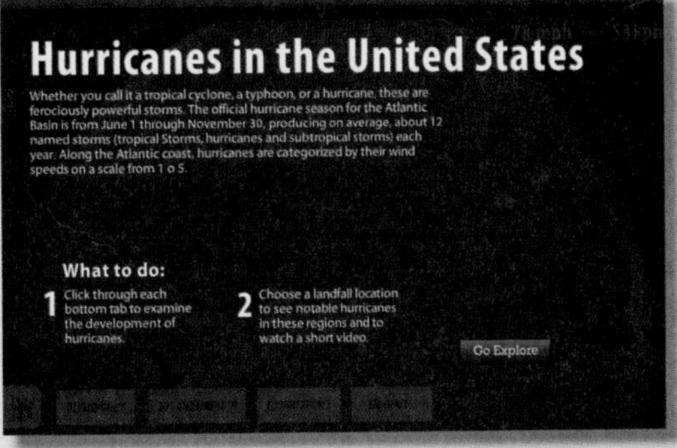

Hurricanes in the United States
Whether you call it a tropical cyclone, a typhoon, or a hurricane, these are ferociously powerful storms. The official hurricane season for the Atlantic Basin is from June 1 through November 30, producing on average, about 12 named storms (tropical Storms, hurricanes and subtropical storms) each year. Along the Atlantic coast, hurricanes are categorized by their wind speeds on a scale from 1 o 5.
What to do:
1 Click through each bottom tab to examine the development of hurricanes.
2 Choose a landfall location to see notable hurricanes in these regions and to watch a short video.
Go Explore

V Visual Skills

Creating Charts Have students create a chart to identify and list the different regions and climates of the United States. Title the first column *Regions of the United States* and the second column *Type of Climates*. Have students complete the chart as they read the text. **AL** **Visual/Spatial**

Content Background Knowledge

Hurricanes A hurricane is a severe tropical storm with sustained winds over 74 miles per hour. These storms form in the southern Atlantic Ocean, Caribbean Sea, Gulf of Mexico, and the eastern Pacific Ocean.

- All Atlantic and Gulf of Mexico coastal areas are subject to hurricanes. Parts of the southwest United States and the Pacific Coast also experience heavy rains and floods each year from hurricanes spawned off Mexico.
- Hurricanes can cause catastrophic damage to coastlines and to areas several hundred miles inland. They can produce winds exceeding 155 miles per hour as well as tornadoes and microbursts. They can create storm surges along the coast and cause extensive damage from heavy rainfall.
- Floods and flying debris from excessive winds are often the deadly and destructive results of hurricanes. Slow-moving hurricanes tend to produce especially heavy rain that can trigger mudslides, landslides, and flash flooding.

R Reading Skills

Expressing Direct the students' attention to the term *Coriolis Force* on the infographic. Point out that this is another way to describe the Coriolis effect that they learned about in Chapter 3. Write the term on the board and invite a student to define it. *(The Coriolis force is a result of the rotation of Earth that deflects the path of the wind.)* Have students write a sentence that expresses their understanding of the term. They may want to use a dictionary for further clarification. Have students add their sentences and the term into their chapter glossaries. **ELL** **Verbal/Linguistic**

ANSWERS, p. 123

CRITICAL THINKING

1. Air pressure inside the core is very low. Because the low-pressure center of a hurricane's proximity to the Equator must be located at least 300 miles from the Equator, locations extremely close to the Equator are not likely to see hurricanes.
2. The areas along the Gulf of Mexico and Atlantic Ocean in the southern United States are the most vulnerable to damage.

Physical Geography of the United States

C Critical Thinking Skills

Analyzing After students read the text under Natural Resources, write the terms *Natural Resources* and *Economy* on the board and draw an arrow from Natural Resources pointing to Economy. **Ask:** **What are some natural resources the United States has?** *(Possible answers: soil, water, fossil fuels, timber, fish, and minerals including copper, iron, gold, and silver.)* Write the resources on the board as students list them. **Ask:** **Of all natural resources listed, which ones are economically valuable?** *(Students might answer those natural resources directly related to industries—fossil fuels, timber, fish, and minerals, and probably leave out soil and water.)* Tell students that all of the natural resources listed, including water, are economically valuable. In class discussion examine why soil and water are just as important as fossil fuels and the other resources listed. *(Discussion should point out that soil and water are extremely important for agriculture and that water is also important for generating power.)* AL Logical/Mathematical

T Technology Skills

Acquiring Information Organize students into small groups. Have each group research one of Earth's soil types or one of the careers of pedologists. Have the groups researching soil types report on the physical and chemical characteristics of their assigned soil type and what kinds of plants grow best in it. Have the groups researching careers of pedologists report on the type of job, what is involved, where the job would be, and how much money that type of job pays. Have groups present their research to the class. BL Verbal/Linguistic

CLOSE & REFLECT

Summarizing Have students consider the role the physical landscape of the United States plays in the economy. Have students write a summary of how the landscape and natural resources of the country are important to the U.S. economy. Encourage students to share their summaries with the class.

ANSWERS, p. 124

READING PROGRESS CHECK The interplay of ocean currents and westerly winds with the Pacific Ranges contributes to the marine west coast climate.

Connecting Geography Agriculture and food-production industries are likely to benefit from this advice, as they could more effectively grow and market crops.

Connecting Geography to SCIENCE

Soil Science

T Soil, the thin outer layer of Earth's crust, is necessary for human survival. We get most of our food directly or indirectly from plants growing in soil. Our water supply is filtered by the soil, and soil products supply many engineering materials needed for buildings and infrastructure. Pedologists (soil scientists) study Earth's soil types, their physical and chemical characteristics, and how they can be used to meet human needs without degrading or depleting this resource. Many pedologists work for government agencies, universities, and private industry.

DRAWING INFERENCES Which industries are likely to benefit from the advice of soil scientists? Why?

fossil fuel a resource formed in the Earth by plant and animal remains

A Mediterranean climate is found in central and southern California. Such a climate is confined to coastal areas and is characterized by mild, wet winters and summers that are warm to hot and dry. The vegetation consists of twisted, drought-resistant broad-leafed trees, known as chaparral (SHA•puh•RAL).

The Rockies and the Pacific Ranges have a high altitude climate characterized by cold, snowy winters and warm, dry summers. Coniferous forests cover the middle elevations, and lichens and mosses grow in higher elevations. In early spring, a warm, dry wind called the chinook (shuh•NUK) blows down the eastern slopes of the Rockies. Mountain goats and mountain lions are common. The interplay of ocean currents and westerly winds with the Pacific Ranges gives the Pacific coast from northern California to southern Alaska a marine west coast climate. Parts of this region receive more than 100 inches (254 cm) of rain each year. Ferns, mosses, grasses, and coniferous forests grow here.

Large parts of Alaska have a subarctic climate with frigid winter temperatures of −70°F (−57°C) in some places. Conifers such as pine and spruce are able to survive the cold. Many animals thrive in the harsh climate of the subarctic, including grizzly bears, bald eagles, wolves, and bobcats.

Natural Resources

C The United States is rich with natural resources including water, **fossil fuels**, timber, fish, and more. Fossil fuels were formed over hundreds of millions of years from the fossilized remains of plants and animals. This makes them nonrenewable. Also, because they must be retrieved from the ground, there can be damage to the environment when they are extracted from the Earth. Fossil fuels include coal, petroleum, and natural gas. They can be found in great supply in Texas and Alaska, which rank first and second respectively in U.S. petroleum reserves. The United States has the largest known coal reserves in the world and soon may be the largest producer of oil.

The United States has plentiful mineral resources as well. The Rocky Mountains yield gold and silver. Other minerals include copper, lead, phosphates, uranium, bauxite, iron, mercury, nickel, silver, tungsten, and zinc. Free and abundant access to this natural wealth helped to speed the industrialization of the United States and has helped to create one of the most prosperous countries in the world.

Fish are also an important natural resource. Commercial fishing in the Atlantic and Pacific Oceans and the Gulf of Mexico is important to the U.S. economy. The large commercial fishing companies and small family businesses provide employment for many people, as well as food for domestic consumption and for export.

READING PROGRESS CHECK

Identifying What factors contribute to the marine west coast climate?

LESSON 1 REVIEW

Reviewing Vocabulary (Tier Three Words)

1. ***Explaining*** Explain how fossil fuels are formed. RH.9–10.4

Using Your Notes

2. ***Describing*** Use your graphic organizer to list three major water systems in the United States.

Answering the Guiding Questions

3. ***Discussing*** How has tectonic activity helped create so many of the landforms in the United States?
4. ***Expressing*** How have rivers and lakes been important to the economic development of the United States?
5. ***Identifying*** What factors cause variations in climate and vegetation in the United States?

Writing Activity

6. ***Narrative*** Write a paragraph that describes the path of the Mississippi River as if you were writing for a travel magazine. Describe the climate, landforms, and biomes along its path. WHST.9–10.2

124

LESSON 1 REVIEW ANSWERS

Reviewing Vocabulary

1. Fossil fuels were formed during hundreds of millions of years from the fossil remains of plants and animals.

Using Your Notes

2. Major waterways in the United States are: Mississippi River, the Great Lakes, and the St. Lawrence River.

Answering the Guiding Questions

3. Tectonic plate activity shifts giant rock slabs.
4. They allow for transportation of goods and people. Cities form along them and offer port facilities for trade.
5. Latitude and elevation are two major factors that cause variations in climate and vegetation.

Writing Activity

6. Paragraphs will vary, but should be engaging, with a description of climate, landforms, and biomes along the Mississippi River.

networks

There's More Online!

- **MAP** Ethnic Populations in the United States
- **MAP** Homes in Negative Equity, 2010
- **MAP** U.S. Expansion
- **TIME LINE** Terrorism and the United States
- **INTERACTIVE SELF-CHECK QUIZ**
- **VIDEO** Human Geography of the United States

LESSON 2

Human Geography of the United States

ESSENTIAL QUESTION • *How do physical systems and human systems shape a place?*

Reading **HELP**DESK (CCSS)

Academic Vocabulary (Tier Two Words)

- **conflict**
- **immigrate**

Content Vocabulary (Tier Three Words)

- **Underground Railroad**
- **dry farming**
- **Manufacturing Belt**
- **Sunbelt**
- **megalopolis**
- **jazz**
- **postindustrial**
- **foreclosure**

TAKING NOTES: ***Key Ideas and Details***

IDENTIFYING Use a graphic organizer like the one below to take notes about the major economic activities of the United States.

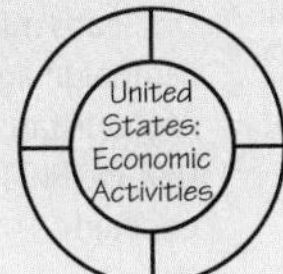

It Matters Because

Urban lifestyles predominate in the United States, but traditional and rural values are still respected. The country has also been enriched by the tens of millions of immigrants who have come to America hoping to improve their lives. **C**

History and Geography

GUIDING QUESTION *How did physical geography and a spirit of independence influence the development of the United States?*

The physical environment has played a significant role in the patterns of settlement in the United States. The largest city, New York City, is located on one of the world's finest harbors as a result of physical geography. Similarly, many people today choose to live in California for its favorable climate and beautiful landscapes. **V**

Growth, Division, and Unity

Scientific studies suggest that there were at least three migrations of people from Asia to Alaska. They began about 15,000 years ago and occurred by land and by boat. The lives of Native Americans, the descendants of these early peoples, were shaped by location and climate.

Native Americans occupied North America undisturbed until the mid-1500s when European immigration began. The Spanish explored the southern region, setting up farms, ranches, military posts, and missions. The French settled in the northeast and were involved in the fur trade. **W**

After 1670, Britain controlled much of the land along the Atlantic coast, divided into three colonial regions. The New England Colonies had rocky soil and a short growing season, but the area's harbors and an abundant supply of timber and fish made shipbuilding and fishing important industries. The Middle Colonies had the fertile soil, mild winters, and warm summers needed for growing cash crops for export. The mild climate, rich soils, and open land of the coastal plain of the Southern Colonies were a favorable environment for plantation agriculture.

ENGAGE

C Critical Thinking Skills

Categorizing Have pairs write a paragraph describing whether their state is more urban or rural. Paragraphs should identify specific areas of their state, such as urban centers or small towns, that fall into either category. Then in class discussion, list on the board the specific areas students describe and lead the class to conclude whether their state is more urban or rural.

TEACH & ASSESS

V Visual Skills

Analyzing Show students a physical map of the region they live in. During a class discussion, have students identify the physical features such as rivers, lakes, mountain ranges, plateaus, and/or coastline on the map. Then display a political map of the region and have student volunteers identify the location of population centers in the state. **Ask:** **What physical features are located near those population centers?** *(Student answers will vary, but should include answers such as a river, a valley, a lake, a harbor, or a plateau.)* **Ask:** **Do you think physical features had more effect on the development of population centers in the 1700s and 1800s than it does in the twenty-first century?** *(Student answers will vary, but should include that geography, such as rivers and lakes and coastlines, affected development of an area more in the 1700s and 1800s because waterways were a major means of transportation.)* ELL **Visual/Spatial, Naturalist**

W Writing Skills

Informative/Explanatory Have a student volunteer read aloud the text under the heading *Growth, Division, and Unity.* Have students create a three-column chart identifying the European colonial areas and comparing and contrasting the geographic strengths and weaknesses each of the three regions had. In a class discussion encourage students to share their charts. **Verbal/Linguistic**

networks ***Online Teaching Options***

INTERACTIVE BELLRINGER

United States Population Density

Interpreting Maps Use this map to discuss population density in the United States. Ask students to describe the population density of their own state. Have students form small groups and compare the population density in their own states to other states with which they are familiar. Have groups write agreed-upon answers to each question. Then in a class discussion, have each group share its answers. **Verbal/Linguistic, Interpersonal**

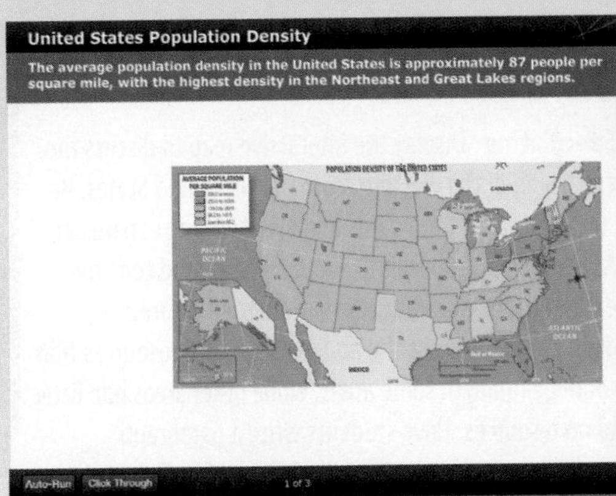

United States Population Density
The average population density in the United States is approximately 87 people per square mile, with the highest density in the Northeast and Great Lakes regions.
Auto-Run
Click Through
1 of 3

ANSWERS, p. 125

TAKING NOTES: Based on free market economy; manufacturing allows people to profit from own company's wealth; U.S. has abundant natural resources, high agricultural output and highly developed industries; U.S. has strong trade partnerships and is a leading producer and consumer of energy.

T Technology Skills

Researching After students have read the text, organize the class into small groups. Tell students they will use the Internet to research conflicts in the United States in the 1700s and 1800s. They will make a list of those conflicts and identify the region involved in those conflicts. Have half of the small groups research the 1700s and the other half research the 1800s. In a class discussion have groups share the results of their research. Lead students to see that many of the conflicts involved disputes over land or waterways. BL Interpersonal

C Critical Thinking Skills

Drawing Conclusions Review with students their previous knowledge of enslaved African Americans and the term *Underground Railroad.* **Ask:** What was the connection between enslaved African Americans and the economic growth of the South? *(Enslaved African Americans were the labor force that grew cotton, a major cash crop of the South.)* **Ask:** What does the creation of the Underground Railroad represent? *(It represents the people who wanted to abolish slavery.)* Logical/Mathematical

Content Background Knowledge

Slavery and the Americas From the sixteenth through the nineteenth centuries, the Americas were dependent on enslaved African labor. According to European colonial officials, the abundant land they had "discovered" in the Americas was useless without sufficient labor to exploit it.

- The trans-Saharan slave trade had long supplied enslaved African labor to work on sugar plantations in the Mediterranean alongside white slaves from Russia and the Balkans. This same trade also sent as many as 10,000 slaves a year to serve owners in North Africa, the Middle East, and the Iberian Peninsula. Having proved themselves competent workers, enslaved Africans became the labor force of choice in the Western Hemisphere.
- Of the 6.5 million immigrants who survived the crossing of the Atlantic and settled in the Western Hemisphere between 1492 and 1776, only 1 million were Europeans. The remaining 5.5 million were African. An average of 80 percent of these enslaved Africans—men, women, and children—were field-workers on plantations.

conflict a competition or struggle

In 1763 France was forced to give up much of its North American empire to Great Britain. **Conflicts** soon arose between Native Americans and colonial settlers. Settlers arriving in the British colonies took the land of Native Americans. Loss of hunting and farming lands, combined with European diseases, reduced Native American populations and severely disrupted their cultures.

In the 1760s, the British government angered the colonists by imposing new taxes and limiting their freedoms. The thirteen colonies eventually fought for independence from Britain in the American Revolution (1775–1783). The outcome was an independent federal republic called the United States of America.

During the 1800s, the United States more than doubled its territory. The country gained valuable land and natural resources. For Native Americans, however, expansion led to the steady loss of lands and restrictions on traditional ways of life.

T Industrialization transformed the United States during this time. The first factories harnessed the power of waterfalls along the fall line in the Northeast. Later, large supplies of coal in the Midwest were used to fuel cheap steam power, thus making manufacturing profitable. As a result, the Midwest became a leading center of industry, using the Great Lakes and rivers for transportation.

C In the South, cotton became a major cash crop as the textile industry grew in the Northeast. Land was cleared for more plantations, and the labor of enslaved African Americans became critical to the Southern economy. By the 1800s, however, some people were working to end slavery, and many African Americans made their way north to freedom along the **Underground Railroad**—a network of safe houses.

Underground Railroad a network of safe houses in the United States that helped thousands of enslaved people escape to freedom

Tensions between the industrialized North and the agricultural South mounted steadily until they erupted in the American Civil War in 1861. After four bloody years, the North triumphed. Slavery was abolished after the war and the country began rebuilding.

TIME LINE

TERRORISM and the United States

President George W. Bush was the first U.S. president to use the term "War on Terror."

▶ CRITICAL THINKING
1. ***Sequencing*** What events led to the passage of the USA PATRIOT Act?
2. ***Assessing*** Why do you think Congress renewed the USA PATRIOT Act in March 2006?

1990

1991 U.S. forces play dominant role in war against Iraq after invasion of Kuwait

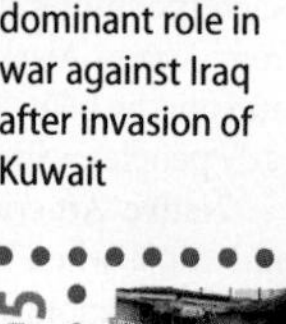

1995 Domestic terrorist bombs federal building in Oklahoma City, killing 168 people.

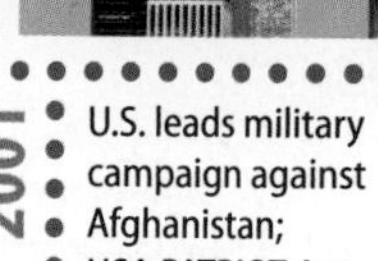

2001 Coordinated suicide attacks by al-Qaeda on multiple high-profile U.S. targets

2001 U.S. leads military campaign against Afghanistan; USA PATRIOT Act enacted

(tr)Spencer Platt/Getty Images News/Getty Images, (bl)Roberto Schmidt/AFP/Getty Images

126

networks Online Teaching Options

INTERACTIVE MAP

U.S. Expansion

Speculating Display the interactive map to discuss the expansion of the western states in the United States. Be sure to highlight the dates and events of the expansion. Ask students to speculate about the pros and cons the early settlers faced as they reached their desired destinations. Discuss the abundant natural resources that could be found in some areas, while other areas had little to no resources. Have students write a paragraph explaining which area they would have chosen to settle in, if they were part of the U. S. expansion during the 1800s. AL Visual/Spatial

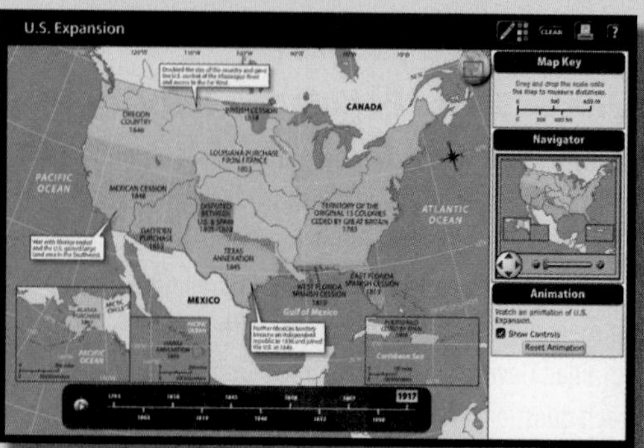

ANSWERS, p. 126

CRITICAL THINKING
1. The events that led to the creation of the USA PATRIOT Act included the war against Iraq, the military campaign against Afghanistan, and suicide terrorist attacks on multiple high-profile U.S. targets.
2. Student answers will vary, but should be supported with information from the time line.

Changes and Challenges

In the late 1800s, the government encouraged the movement of people to the Great Plains to speed up the settlement of the United States. New immigrants wanted land, and there was an increasing need for food in the growing cities. Due to the dry conditions on the Great Plains, settlers developed **dry farming**. Steel plows and steam tractors made farming easier, and fewer people were needed for farm work. At the same time, the Industrial Revolution brought people to cities in the Northeast and Great Lakes regions, or the **Manufacturing Belt.** R

dry farming a farming method used in dry regions in which crops are grown that rely only on the natural precipitation

Europeans, Chinese, Mexicans, and others **immigrated** to the United States. Many helped build the railroads. Joining the Central Pacific and Union Pacific railroads created a transcontinental railroad. A network of railways moved manufactured goods from east to west and food products from west to east. T

Manufacturing Belt a concentrated region of manufacturing industries in the northeastern and midwestern United States

Two world wars spurred economic growth. Assembly lines increased efficiency and improved the standard of living. The population became more mobile and urbanized. By the 1990s, many manufacturing activities were less important than the rising high-tech industries.

Social changes also took place. Immigration from Latin America and Asia increased. Minority groups began to participate in business and politics. Native Americans negotiated with the government over land claims. W

immigrate to change residence from a country to begin living permanently in another country

Terrorism became a major concern of many Americans after September 11, 2001, when terrorists hijacked four passenger planes, crashing them into the World Trade Center, the Pentagon, and a Pennsylvania field. After such devastation, the United States launched a war on terrorism focused on Afghanistan and Iraq.

✓ READING PROGRESS CHECK

Explaining Why did the Midwest become a center of industry?

2002

2002 President Bush signs into law a bill creating a Department of Homeland Security, aimed at protecting the country against terrorist attacks.

2003 Missile attacks on Baghdad mark the start of a U.S.-led campaign to topple Iraqi leader Saddam Hussein. U.S. forces advance into Baghdad in early April.

2004 Senate report says U.S. and its allies went to war in Iraq on flawed information. Report on 9/11 attacks highlights deep institutional failings in U.S. intelligence services.

2006 U.S. Congress renews USA PATRIOT Act. The government agrees to curbs on information gathering.

2011 May—U.S. forces kill terrorist leader Osama bin Laden in Pakistan

2012

2012 September—U.S. ambassador to Libya and three others are killed in attack on U.S. consulate in Benghazi

TIME LINE

Terrorism and the United States

Inferring This time line shows a sequence of events that occurred in the United States concerning the U.S. foreign and domestic policy. Have students think about how the events on this time line relate to the process of immigration and if they think that people still immigrating into the United States are faced with similar events. As a class, discuss how the War on Terror has affected Americans' attitude and policies toward immigrants. **AL Verbal/Linguistic**

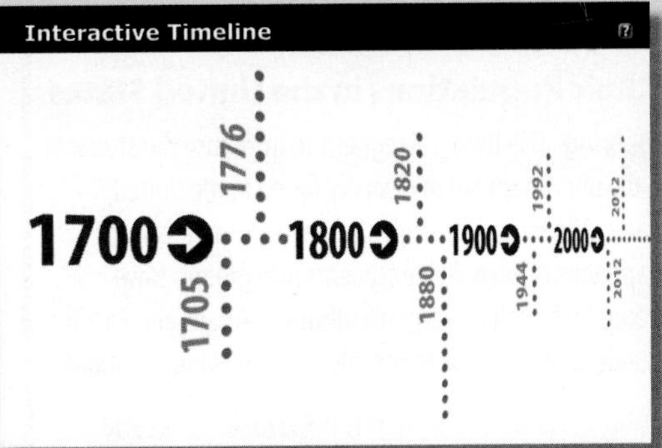

R Reading Skills

Applying Emphasize that the terms *dry farming* and *Manufacturing Belt* are related to the U.S. economy. **Ask:** **Do you think the technique of dry farming was good economically for farmers?** *(Yes. It meant farmers did not have to have costly irrigation systems.)* **Why is the development of the Manufacturing Belt an important part of the economic success of the United States?** *(The Manufacturing Belt was an area of concentrated manufacturing industries that created goods to be sold and created many jobs.)* Have students write sentences using the terms and share their sentences with the class. Have students put both terms in their chapter glossaries. **ELL Verbal/Linguistic**

T Technology Skills

Creating Graphs Organize students into four groups to research immigration data using the Internet and to create bar graphs to display their findings. Emphasize that the immigration of Europeans, Asians, and Mexicans has been an important factor in the economic success of the United States. Assign each group one of the time periods listed below and have them research national immigration numbers for their assigned time period. Have them make a bar graph depicting the data. The years are: 1860–1900; 1900–1940; 1940–1980; 1980–2012. **BL Logical/Mathematical**

W Writing Skills

Informative/Explanatory Have students write a one-page essay explaining the social and economic changes that occurred in the United States after World Wars I and II. Encourage students to share their essays with the class. **AL Verbal/Linguistic**

Content Background Knowledge

Responding to Terrorism In October 2001, Congress passed the USA PATRIOT Act in response to the 9/11 attack on the World Trade Center and the Pentagon, giving the Federal Bureau of Investigation (FBI) wide powers of search and surveillance in pursuing suspected terrorists, including great leeway in eavesdropping and detaining suspects. The act continues to draw criticism from civil liberties advocates.

ANSWERS, p. 127

✓ READING PROGRESS CHECK The Industrial Revolution brought manufacturing industries to the Midwest.

V Visual Skills

Analyzing Maps Have students identify the ethnic population represented in each of the four cartograms. Ask students to describe why the ethnic group most likely lives in the areas shown in each of the cartograms. Have students discuss the visual effectiveness of using the cartograms as well as the color keys to convey the selected information. **Ask:** **What additional types of information would be well-represented by a cartogram? What types of information would be inaccurately conveyed by using cartograms?** *(Student answers will vary, but should provide evidence to support their response.)* **Visual/Spatial**

W Writing Skills

Informative/Explanatory Have students read about the population patterns in the United States. Tell students to think about why urban population centers developed where they did and consider whether it was geography or industry that created urban centers. Have them write a one-page essay describing the interconnection of geography, industry, and populations. In a class discussion have students share their essays. **BL Verbal/Linguistic**

Content Background Knowledge

Immigration and American Culture Cultural diversity in the United States is often described by three different metaphors. People say: *The United States is a* ______.

- melting pot: implies that immigrants change to fit the society of their new home
- salad bowl: implies that immigrants retain their cultural identity in their new home
- kaleidoscope: implies that both the immigrants and society adapt and change

All three metaphors highlight the important role immigration has played in U.S. identity and culture. These metaphors will probably continue to change as cultural diversity in the United States continues to change.

ANSWERS, p. 128

GEOGRAPHY CONNECTION

1. The Central Plains has the greatest percentage of Native Americans.
2. The distribution of Asian Americans is concentrated along the east and west coast with higher percentages along the Pacific Coast.

V

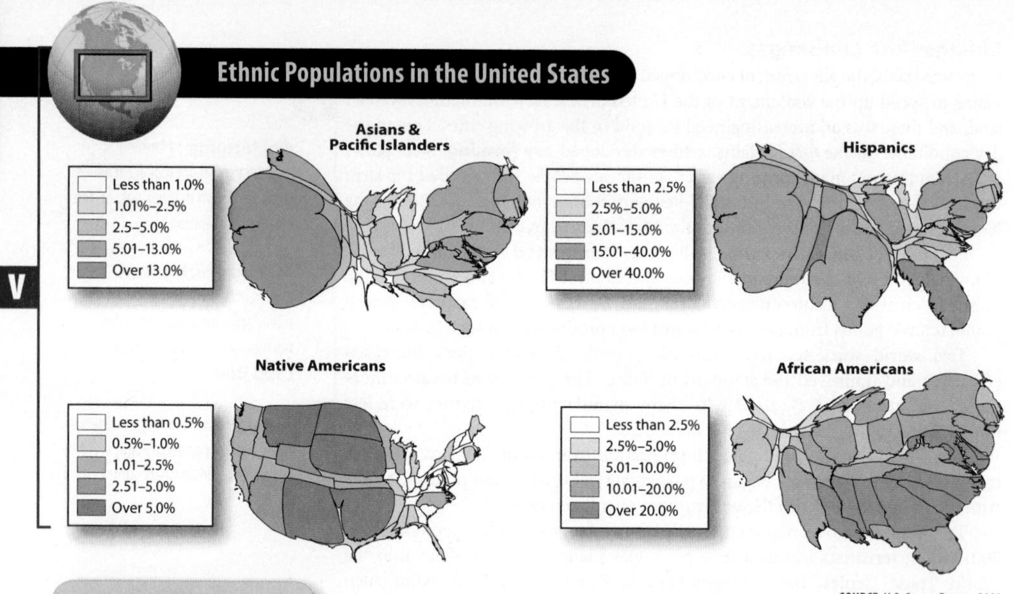

SOURCE: U.S. Census Bureau, 2009

GEOGRAPHY CONNECTION

The United States Census captures the country's ethnic diversity.

1. ***PLACES AND REGIONS*** Which region of the United States has the greatest percentage of Native Americans, the Central Plains or the East?
2. ***PLACES AND REGIONS*** How would you characterize the distribution of the Asian American population in the United States?

Population Patterns

GUIDING QUESTION *What factors influence population patterns in the United States?*

More than 315 million people live in the United States today. While about 2.5 million are Native Americans, a majority are immigrants or the descendants of immigrants from Europe, Asia, Africa, and Latin America. Some arrived only recently, while others belong to families whose ancestors came to the region centuries ago.

The average population density of the United States is about 87 people per square mile (33 people per sq. km). Outside of large urban areas, however, the population is widely distributed. The Northeast and Great Lakes regions are densely populated because they are the historic centers of industry and commerce. The Pacific coast attracts people looking for a mild climate and economic opportunities, resulting in a population cluster there. The least densely populated areas of the country include the subarctic region of Alaska, the dry Great Basin, and parts of the arid and semiarid Great Plains.

W

The population structure of the United States is changing. The U.S. Census Bureau projects that the population aged 65 and older will likely grow from some 40.2 million in 2010 to about 88.5 million by the year 2050. This increase presents challenges to the federal government as costs for Social Security and Medicare rise. The health care sector, the business sector, and families will also be affected.

Since the 1960s, the Manufacturing Belt has suffered a decline in population and economic strength as manufacturers relocated. Many businesses moved to **Sunbelt** states in the South and Southwest. Over the years, as mechanized agriculture has required fewer workers, the United States also has experienced urbanization, the movement of people from rural areas to cities. Today, most people in the United States live in the country's 366 metropolitan areas. A metropolitan area is a city with a population of at least 50,000 people including outlying communities, called suburbs.

Sunbelt a mild climate region in the southern and southwestern portions of the United States

networks Online Teaching Options

INTERACTIVE MAP

Ethnic Populations in the United States

Applying Use these cartograms to introduce the students to the uneven spread of diversity found in the United States. Allow time for students to analyze and read the map content. Then divide students into groups. Have groups look at the cartogram subtitled "Asians and Pacific Islanders." Ask groups to consider the following questions:

- **Why is New York so big, if it's closer to Europe than East Asia?**
- **Is New York State's population of Asians equally distributed across the entire state?**
- **If one were to make a map like this of New York, where do you anticipate the largest area would be?**

AL Visual/Spatial

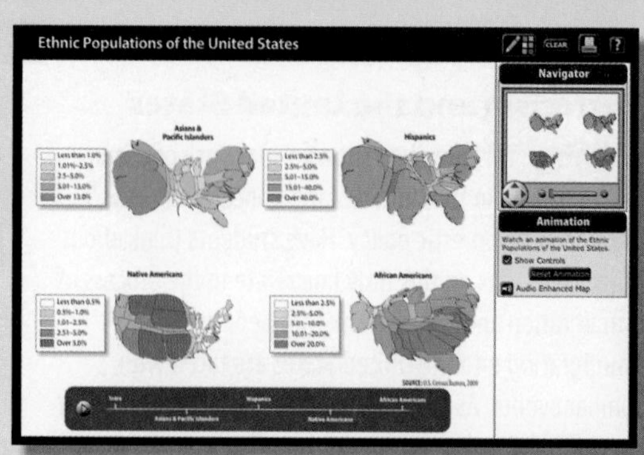

Many U.S. population clusters lie in coastal areas with strong economies linked to world trade. Pacific coast cities provide important links to the rest of the world, especially to the growing Asian economies. The **megalopolis** that stretches from Santa Barbara, California, to Mexico is also an important corridor for world trade. Along the Atlantic coast, a chain of closely linked metropolitan areas from Boston, Massachusetts, to Washington, D.C., form the Boswash megalopolis. The Great Lakes region has three megalopolises: one centered in Chicago, Illinois, another in Buffalo, New York, and a third in Detroit, Michigan.

R

megalopolis a large population concentration made up of several large and many smaller cities, such as the area between Boston and Washington, D.C.

✓ READING PROGRESS CHECK

Speculating Provide a specific example of how the aging of the population might affect Americans.

Society and Culture Today

GUIDING QUESTION *How has immigration influenced the culture of the United States?*

Today, the United States has one of the most diverse populations in the world. Some immigrants have come to the United States to seek political and religious freedom or to find economic opportunities. Others are fleeing wars or natural disasters. Rich natural resources, industry, and economic wealth make the United States an attractive destination.

Throughout history, immigrants have often faced discrimination, but they have invariably enriched their new country through their hard work and talents and by bringing greater cultural diversity to the country. In 2012 the Census Bureau reported that 13 percent of the total U.S. population was foreign born and that more than half of the foreign-born population came from Latin America.

Immigrants have contributed to the country's diverse religious beliefs. Since the country's founding, religious freedom has been a core value in the United States. Today, most Americans who are members of an organized religion are Christian, with the majority being Protestant. Judaism, Islam, and Buddhism are among the other religions practiced in the United States. About 16 percent of the U.S. population today is not affiliated with any organized religion.

Family and Status of Women

Although population patterns in the United States continue to change, the family remains a vital institution. About half of adults are married, but some are single people living alone, or single mothers or fathers living with their children. More and more women work outside the home. Women have also continued to make gains in college completion rates, exceeding the graduation rate of men for the people between the ages of 25 and 34.

The Arts

The history of music in the United States can be traced back to Native American traditions. Europeans later brought their own folk and religious music. At the start of the 1900s, a distinct form of music known as **jazz** developed in African American communities throughout the United States. Jazz blended African rhythms with European harmonies. By the second half of the century, country music and rock-and-roll had become popular, not only in North America but around the world. Blues, punk rock, and hip-hop all have their origins in the United States, though hip-hop also traces its roots to the dance hall musicians of Jamaica.

jazz musical form that developed in the United States in the early 1900s, blending African rhythms and European harmonies

Many styles of art can also be found in the United States. In the early 1900s, a group of American artists known as the Ashcan School painted the grim realities of urban America. In the mid-1900s, many artists adopted European abstract styles, which express artists' emotions and attitudes without depicting recognizable images.

R Reading Skills

Expressing Invite a student to read the definition of the term *megalopolis*. **Ask:** Is there a megalopolis in your state? If so, why do you think it is located where it is? If not, why do you think there isn't one? *(Student answers will vary, but if there is a megalopolis in the region, have students identify it and the physical geography around it—whether, for example, it is on a river, or lake, or the coast.)* Have students write the term, its definition, and a sentence using the term in their chapter glossaries. **ELL Verbal/Linguistic**

W Writing Skills

Narrative Have students consider the cultural diversity in their region of the United States. In a class discussion have them identify a specific place or event that expresses cultural diversity. Then have them write a one-page description of another place or event that expresses cultural diversity. Discuss descriptive adjectives and adverbs and figurative language as needed. Encourage students to include these in their descriptions. **AL Verbal/Linguistic**

T Technology Skills

Gathering Information Organize the class into six small groups. Invite a student to read aloud the last two paragraphs about the arts. Write each type of music mentioned in the paragraphs on the board: jazz, country music, rock and roll, blues, punk rock, and hip-hop. Assign each group one of the types of music and have them use the Internet to research and make a multimedia presentation of the history of their music type. Each group will present their music histories to the class. **BL Auditory/Musical**

INTERACTIVE MAP

Foreign-Born Population as Percent of State Population, 2010

Creating Graphs Display the interactive map to students. Engage students in a class discussion highlighting the highest and lowest percentages of foreign born populations in various states on the map. Have students work with a partner to create a graph that compares the foreign born population of one nationality across five or six states. Then have pairs write a paragraph that summarizes the information in their graph. Provide class time for each set of students to present and explain their graphs. **AL Verbal/Linguistic, Visual/Spatial**

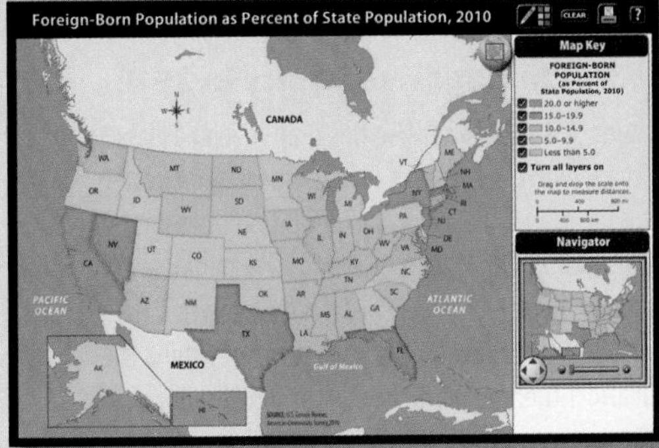

ANSWERS, p. 129

✓ READING PROGRESS CHECK Possible answers: Costs of Social Security and Medicare will rise and the health care sector will have to provide care for more people who are aging.

V Visual Skills

Designing Display various photos of graffiti designs. Tell students that they are going to create graffiti designs that they would like to see on the side of their school. Have student partners create a graffiti design. Have pairs display their work to the class, explaining the concept and intent of their graffiti. **Visual/Spatial, Interpersonal**

C Critical Thinking Skills

Analyzing Have students read the text under the heading *Economic Activities*. Emphasize to students that the United States is a relatively wealthy country. **Ask:** **What kind of economy is the U.S. economy?** *(It is a free market economy.)* **Ask:** **What does the U.S. economy enable people who own businesses to do?** *(It allows them to profit from owning their own businesses.)* **Ask:** **What are three reasons the United States has a wealthy economy?** *(Possible answers: universal education, technology and innovation, natural resources, high agricultural output, developed industries.)* **Verbal/Linguistic**

Making Connections

After reading the following to students, have them analyze their spending and where the products they buy are made.

- The U.S. dollar is used in most international transactions, thus anything that happens with the U.S. economy will affect international finances in a substantial way. If the United States Federal Reserve raises interest rates, for example, the foreign exchange value of the dollar usually goes up as well.
- One of the biggest ways the United States affects the world's economy is through its buying power. If Americans are buying less, many countries that export goods to the United States will have a reduction in demand for their products. Nations with less than stable economies could suffer dramatically, which would cause them to be less capable of buying American exports, furthering the downward spiral. The U.S. government often tries to combat this vicious cycle by promoting free trade with foreign countries and economic stimulus packages.

ANSWERS, p. 130

READING PROGRESS CHECK Most Americans who are members of an organized religion are Christian, with the majority being Protestant.

GEOGRAPHY CONNECTION

1. Montana, North Dakota, Nebraska, Iowa, Oklahoma, Alabama, Kentucky, Pennsylvania, New York, and Hawaii
2. Arizona and Nevada have a greater than 50% negative equity statistic.

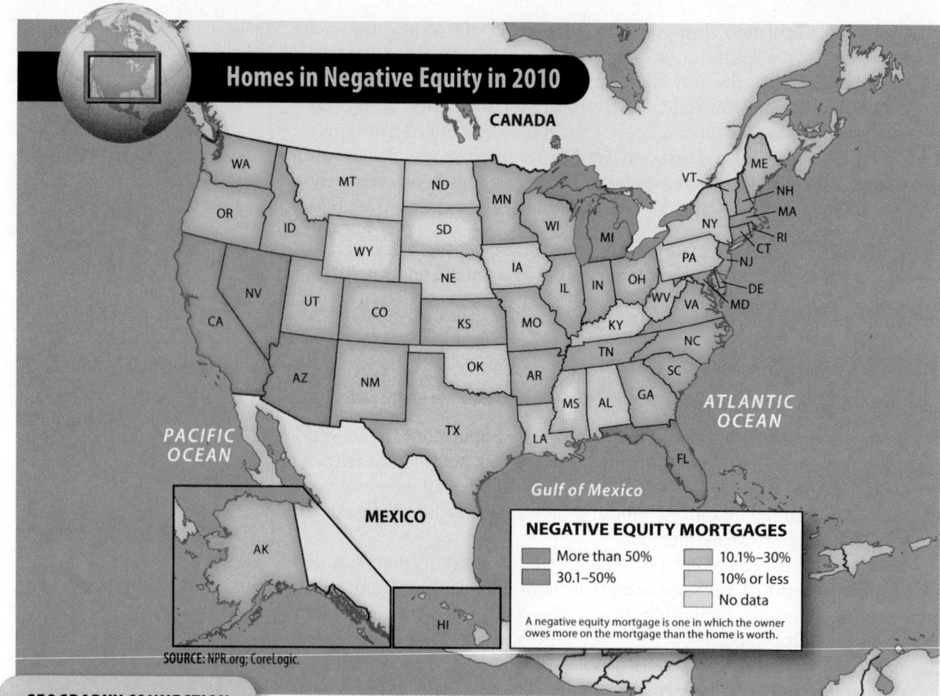

GEOGRAPHY CONNECTION

During the foreclosure crisis, millions of Americans were unable to pay their home mortgages.

1. ***PLACES AND REGIONS*** Which states were least affected by negative equity mortgages?
2. ***HUMAN SYSTEMS*** Which states are shown with a more than 50% negative equity statistic?

V The American-born graffiti art movement, begun by disenfranchised urban youth, has grown into a worldwide phenomenon. Graffiti is now created by artists who are commissioned by governments and private citizens to create enormous and intricate works of art.

READING PROGRESS CHECK

Identifying What is the most common religion practiced in America today?

Economic Activities

GUIDING QUESTION *How is the U.S. economy an important part of the global economy?*

C The United States has always been based on a free market economy and experiences ups and downs. Between the two world wars in the twentieth century, a long and devastating depression affected tens of millions of Americans. As the 1950s began, the manufacturing sector became a driving force of the economy. Manufacturers helped the economy by turning from wartime production to the manufacturing of cars, televisions, and appliances.

Today, the U.S. economy is a free market economy that allows people to profit from owning their own businesses. This freedom—coupled with laws that protect private property rights, employment opportunities, and the health and safety of workers—has created a great economic power. The country's wealth, measured in terms of gross national product (GNP), is due to universal education, technology and innovation, abundant natural resources, high agricultural output, and highly developed industries. The country has important reserves of natural gas and petroleum and is also a world leader in coal exports.

130

networks Online Teaching Options

INTERACTIVE MAP

Homes In Negative Equity in 2010

Making Connections Use this map to lead a class discussion on other aspects of the free market system. Have the students look up the definition of "equity." Ask them what it means for a house to have negative equity, and how this affects the life of the homeowner. Have them get into groups and discuss how they think this will affect the free market of the United States.
ELL Interpersonal

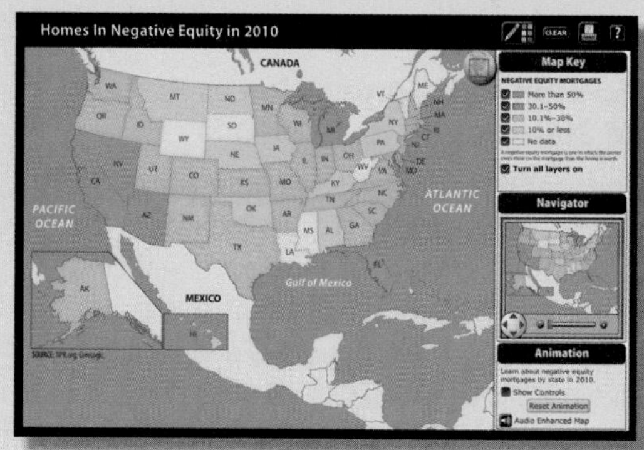

Resources, Power, and Industry

Agriculture in the United States has undergone many changes since the 1950s. The average size of farms has grown and continues to grow. Manufacturing has also evolved. The number of manufacturing jobs has declined while time efficiency and productivity have increased for most U.S. factories.

While agriculture and manufacturing are still important, the **postindustrial** economy is dominated by high-tech, biotechnology, and service industries. The service sector has grown more than any other part of the economy in recent decades. In the high-tech industry, California's Silicon Valley and cities such as Seattle, Washington, and Austin and Dallas, both in Texas, are leaders in software development. The North Carolina cities of Raleigh, Durham, and Chapel Hill form the Research Triangle region, known for attracting biotechnology companies.

postindustrial economy that emphasizes services and technology rather than industry and manufacturing

In recent years, businesses in the United States have turned to offshoring, the practice of setting up plants abroad to produce parts or products for domestic use and international sale. While offshoring decreases the costs of goods, some people argue that it takes jobs away from American workers.

Good transportation and reliable communications are crucial to the economy of the United States. The automobile is still the most commonly used personal transportation method in the country. Its use has resulted in large investments in the building and maintenance of highways, roads, and bridges. The country also relies on air travel as a major method of transportation. A large percentage of the freight in the United States is transported by truck. The country's long-distance communications are carried via wireless, microwave, and satellite relays. Cellular and digital services have made mobile communication the norm, with fewer and fewer households using traditional landline telephones.

The Economic Downturn

In 2008 the United States entered a serious economic downturn caused by an excessive number of ill-advised home mortgage loans. This resulted in a record number of homes going into **foreclosure**. The downturn was called the subprime mortgage crisis. At the same time, the stock market became unstable and unemployment rose. The bad loans led to the failure of some large banks and required large government investments to save many other banks. Because the U.S. economy and financial system are so important to the global economy, many other countries also spiraled into an economic downturn. The U.S. and global economies are improving but still growing less than is needed for robust health.

foreclosure legal proceeding in which a borrower's rights to a property are relinquished due to his or her inability to make payments on the loan

☑ READING PROGRESS CHECK

Describing What are the characteristics of the U.S. free market economy?

LESSON 2 REVIEW 

Reviewing Vocabulary (Tier Three Words)

1. ***Defining*** Define Sunbelt and megalopolis, and describe the locations of each. RH.9–10.4

Using Your Notes

2. ***Identifying*** Use the notes from your graphic organizer to write a paragraph describing the economic activities of the United States.

Answering the Guiding Questions

3. ***Describing*** How did physical geography and a spirit of independence influence the development of the United States?
4. ***Explaining*** What factors influence population patterns in the United States?
5. ***Discussing*** How has immigration influenced the culture of the United States?
6. ***Expressing*** How is the U.S. economy an important part of the global economy?

Writing Activity

7. ***Informative/Explanatory*** Write an essay describing the postindustrial economy of the United States. WHST.9–10.2, WHST.9–10.4

R Reading Skills

Identifying Trends Discuss with the class whether there are more service and technology industries in their region than manufacturing industries. Have students write a paragraph using the terms and discuss what effect the postindustrial economy has on job opportunities in their region. Students should put the term in their chapter glossaries. ELL **Verbal/Linguistic**

C Critical Thinking Skills

Summarize Emphasize to students that the recent U.S. economic downturn affected many people. **Ask: What three factors caused the downturn?** *(Bad or ill-advised home mortgage loans, an unstable stock market, and high unemployment caused the economic downturn.)* **Ask: What did bad mortgage loans lead to?** *(failure of some large banks)* **Ask: How did the U.S. economic downturn affect the global economy?** *(Many countries around the world also spiraled into an economic downturn.)* **Logical/Mathematical**

CLOSE & REFLECT

Summarize Review with students how physical and human geography has created many population centers in the United States. Then have students summarize how immigration has affected the growth, creating a diverse culture, and how this diverse culture is expressed throughout the United States.

ANSWERS, p. 131

☑ **READING PROGRESS CHECK** A free market economy allows people to profit from owning their own businesses. They can manage their businesses as they see fit, as long as they operate within the parameters of the law.

LESSON 2 REVIEW ANSWERS

Reviewing Vocabulary

1. The Sunbelt is made up of states in the South and Southwest, so named for their mild climate. A megalopolis is a "great city" that is made up of several large and small cities; an example of a megalopolis is the area between Boston and Washington, D.C.

Using Your Notes

2. Paragraphs will vary, but should describe economic activities of the U.S. based on the student's graphic organizer.

Answering the Guiding Questions

3. Climate and proximity to waterways influenced the development, as some areas were conducive to growth of specific products and some were in ideal locations for transportation and shipping goods. People wanted their independence from Great Britain, which led them to establish an independent presence in America.
4. The Northeast and Great Lakes regions, the historic centers of American commerce and industry, are densely populated. The Pacific coast attracts people looking for a mild climate and economic opportunities. The least densely populated areas include the subarctic region of Alaska, the parched Great Basin, and parts of the arid and semi-arid Great Plains. Urbanization has also played a great role in population patterns.
5. Due to immigration, the United States has one of the most diverse populations in the world. The immigrant population has also helped contribute to the country's diverse religious beliefs.
6. U.S. exports and imports represent major percentages of the world total. Consumers from the United States have tremendous global buying power. The United States participates in outsourcing, which involves setting up plants abroad to produce parts or products for domestic use or sale. The importance of the U.S. financial system to the global economy was made clear during the financial crisis, as other countries spiraled into recession.

Writing Activity

7. Essays will vary, but should accurately describe the postindustrial economy of the U.S., noting that the postindustrial economy is dominated by high-tech, biotechnology, and service industries.

ENGAGE

C Critical Thinking Skills

Making Connections Ask students if they or their families purchase bottled water. Have students estimate approximately how many bottles their families buy weekly, monthly, and annually. Tell students to consider the number of different brands of bottled water and where that water comes from. Explain that this Case Study provides information about water demand, economic importance, and what can happen when the water runs out. **Verbal/Linguistic**

TEACH & ASSESS

V Visual Skills

Identifying Inferences Have students view a map of the United States showing the different climate zones, which is available online at the Teacher Resource Center. Organize students into five groups, and assign each group one of the following climate zones or regions: arid, humid continental, humid subtropical, tropical wet and dry, and subarctic. Have groups identify the water resources in their assigned region and then answer and explain the following question: **Based on the water sources and type of climate shown on the map, does this region face any water or drought issues? Visual/Spatial**

T Technology Skills

Researching Point out the phrase "region-specific problems" in the text and explain that other regions in the United States may face similar water shortage issues. Have students return to their original groups and direct them to conduct research to identify drought-related conflicts that have occurred in other regions of the United States. Have groups prepare a slide show using presentation software that outlines the issue or conflict and how, or if, it was resolved. Then have students present their findings to the class. **BL Interpersonal, Visual/Spatial**

Case Study: **The Environment** 

HOW CAN DROUGHT LEAD TO CONFLICT IN THE UNITED STATES?

Chris Rank/Bloomberg/Getty Images

The southeastern United States has a humid subtropical climate characterized by high year-round precipitation. This part of the country is considered *water rich*—having large amounts of water available as a natural resource. Surface streams account for the majority of water resources. Despite the abundant water resources in the region, however, many large cities are located far from surface streams. As a result, they experience periodic drought.

Much of this region also has a population growth rate calculated to exceed the U.S. average. Consequently, the demand for water is rapidly increasing. Water quality in this region is a concern because water resources are affected by industrial discharges, surface mining, and contamination by salt water. With a growing urban population, an increasing demand for water, and region-specific problems that affect water quality, cities and states often disagree over where and how water should be diverted and distributed. Moreover, after an almost three-year rainfall deficit from 2005 to 2008, Georgia, South Carolina, and Tennessee experienced drought conditions resulting in damages to crops, potentially dangerous drops in reservoir levels, and increased risk of fire. This sudden and unexpected lack of water threw the region into drought-related conflict.

To address the drought, the state of Georgia requested that the U.S. Army Corps of Engineers limit the flow of water from the Lake Lanier reservoir to the Chattahoochee River and the Apalachicola River. These rivers provide water for Georgia, Florida, and Alabama. While this step would fill Lake Lanier and provide much-needed drinking water for the city of Atlanta, it would also limit the water supply to Alabama and Florida.

132

networks Online Teaching Options

INTERACTIVE IMAGE

Drought and Conflict

Using Case Studies Use this interactive image to introduce students to the Unit 2 Case Study topic of drought and conflict. Before viewing the image, ask students to share what they have read or heard about the drought crisis in the United States and to list the states that they discuss on the board. Click through the interactive components to discuss the content. Have students write a paragraph about one aspect of the image that was interesting or surprising to them. Then compare the list of states written before viewing the image and discuss states not listed. **AL Visual/Spatial, Verbal/Linguistic**

Chris Rank/Bloomberg/Getty Images

Foster Economic Development

PRIMARY SOURCE

"The U.S. Supreme Court on Monday secured metro Atlanta's claim to water from Lake Lanier, handing Georgia an enormous legal victory in the tri-state water dispute. . .

'We can legally drink the water of Lake Lanier,' Williams said to booming applause throughout the banquet hall.

The much-anticipated decision could have monumental ramifications for economic development across the state and growth of the metro region.

Some companies have been hesitant to move to or expand in Atlanta, given the uncertainty of water supply, Williams said.

'That danger is gone now,' Williams said. 'It's time to sit down with our friends in Alabama and Florida. . . . We can go sit down and resolve this."

—Greg Bluestein, Bill Rankin, and Scott Trubey, "High court grants Georgia water-wars victory," *Atlanta Journal Constitution*, June 25, 2012

C1

Preserve Local Economies

PRIMARY SOURCE

"This drought and possible further flow reductions have threatened the very existence for some 1,300 families of 3rd and 4th generation oystermen and a way of life that is an integral part of the community. Florida's Apalachicola River and Bay is the most productive contained commercial fishery in Florida. The local economy depends on the entire ecosystem, which has annual seafood landings reaching millions of dollars dockside."

—Florida governor Charlie Crist, letter to the United States Department of the Interior, May 28, 2009

C2

What do you think? DBQ

1. ***Drawing Conclusions*** According to the *Atlanta Journal Constitution* article, how might Atlanta's economy benefit from an increased water supply?
2. ***Identifying Central Issues*** Provide an example of the importance of water to the local economy in Florida.
3. ***Evaluating*** Who do you think provides the stronger argument, the writers of the *Atlanta Journal Constitution* article or Governor Crist? Explain your answer.

C1 Critical Thinking Skills

Understanding Perspectives Have students reread the position about fostering economic development as reported in the *Atlanta Journal Constitution* article. **Ask:** What might be some of the "monumental ramifications" of the court's decision? Cite textual evidence to support your answer. *(Possible answer: The court's decision to secure a water supply for Atlanta will likely prevent businesses and companies from being "hesitant" about moving to the area. By providing much-needed drinking water for the city of Atlanta, the court's decision allows for economic development in the city.)* Logical/Mathematical

C2 Critical Thinking Skills

Evaluating Counter Arguments Have students reread the quote by Florida governor Charlie Crist. **Ask:** Do you think Governor Crist's concerns about the impact of possible flow reductions are valid? Why or why not? *(Student answers may vary, but should explain if they think Crist's concerns are valid. Possible answer: Crist's concerns are valid because the commercial fishing industry depends on the ecosystem in the Apalachicola River and Bay.)* Do you think Crist exaggerates to make a point? Why or why not? *(Student answers may vary, but should explain if they think Crist exaggerates. Possible answer: Governor Crist exaggerates because he states that "the very existence of some 1,300 families" is in danger because of the court's ruling. Families might struggle, and their "way of life" might change dramatically, but families would probably not cease to exist.)*

CLOSE & REFLECT

Describing Have students write a paragraph describing how water- or drought-related issues could present a conflict in their own communities. Using what they have learned from analyzing this Case Study, students should state potential water issues, possible conflicts, and plausible solutions to potential problems.

WORKSHEET

Evaporating Water

Applying In this unit and through out this geography program students will learn about the value of drinkable water. Use this printable unit worksheet to reinforce that even here in the United States water shortages are a crucial environmental issue.

Divide the class into small groups or teams. Assign this worksheet to the groups, reminding students to follow each step of the instructions in the lab activity. In this GeoLab Activity, students will explore how water can be made to evaporate so quickly that a drought can result. Each group will be responsible for completing the lab activity report and the critical thinking question. Kinesthetic, Naturalist

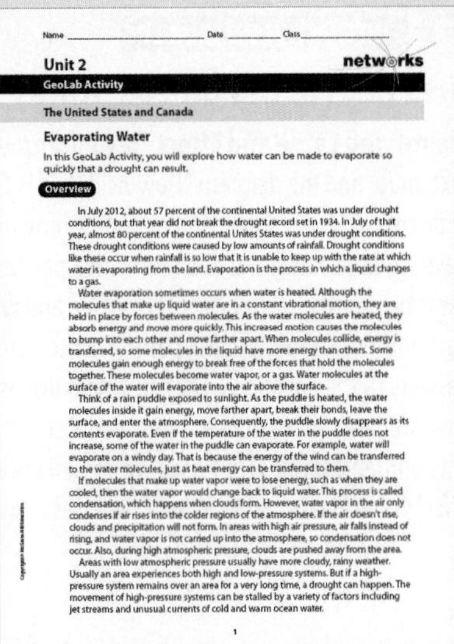

ANSWERS, p. 133

DBQ What do you think?

1. Because there is certainty of water supply in Atlanta, existing Atlanta companies will be more comfortable expanding, and new companies will be more comfortable moving to Atlanta.
2. The local economy depends on the entire ecosystem, which has annual seafood landings reaching millions of dollars dockside.
3. Responses will differ, but should be strongly supported with information from the arguments.

ENGAGE

G1 Critical Thinking Skills

Activating Prior Knowledge Tell students this lesson is about how people affect their environment. Display a map of the students' state showing cities and towns. Working in pairs, have them list areas that they are aware of that have been developed with housing or industry within the past eight years in their state. Have pairs share their lists in a class discussion about how these developments may affect the state's environment.

TEACH & ACCESS

R Reading Skills

Defining Write the word *clear-cutting* on the board. Ask for several students to define the term using their own words. **Ask:** Do you know of any areas where clear-cutting has been done or is scheduled to be done in the state? *(Student answers will vary, but should include specific locations.)* Have students write three sentences that include the word and then add it to their chapter glossaries. ELL Verbal/Linguistic

W Writing Skills

Narrative Ask students to consider how they use water each day and whether they take the availability of freshwater for granted. Have students write a narrative describing various ways that they use water each day. Intrapersonal

C2 Critical Thinking Skills

Identifying Have students identify pollution threats to wetland areas, marshes, ponds, and swamps in their state or region. **Ask:** Why are wetland areas important to the environment? *(Possible answers: They are valuable water supplies and fisheries; they buffer coastal areas from storms and floods.)* **Ask:** How do wetlands disappear? *(Possible answers: pollution destroys wetlands; many wetlands are drained for agricultural purposes; urban development takes over wetlands)* AL Verbal/Linguistic

ANSWERS, p. 134

TAKING NOTES: Forests must be managed. Acid rain, smog, and other problems caused by humans must be addressed. Laws are important to addressing the issues.

networks

There's More Online!

- **INFOGRAPHIC** Formation of Acid Rain
- **IMAGE** Wind as Renewable Energy
- **MAP** U.S. Water Withdrawals
- **MAP** Acid Rain in the United States
- **INTERACTIVE SELF-CHECK QUIZ**
- **VIDEO** People and Their Environment: The United States

LESSON 3
People and Their Environment: The United States

ESSENTIAL QUESTION • *How do physical systems and human systems shape a place?*

Reading HELPDESK CCSS

Academic Vocabulary (Tier Two Words)
- contribute
- abandon

Content Vocabulary (Tier Three Words)
- clear-cutting
- acid rain
- smog
- eutrophication
- aqueduct

TAKING NOTES: ***Key Ideas and Details***

SUMMARIZING Use a web diagram like the one below to take notes as you read about people and their environment in the United States.

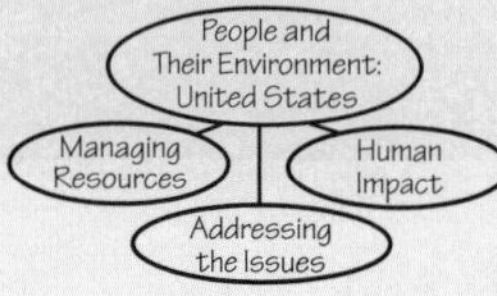
People and Their Environment: United States
Managing Resources
Human Impact
Addressing the Issues

IT MATTERS BECAUSE

G1 *Although the United States is a land of unparalleled opportunity, its natural resources are not limitless, and its environment is not immune to potential harm. In many ways, modern life—with its ravenous use of natural resources, destruction of habitats, and contamination of the environment—poses a threat to American society. Efforts have occurred among concerned citizens and their federal, state, and local governments to ensure that U.S. resources will continue to exist in the future.*

Managing Resources

GUIDING QUESTION *Why are water and timber resources in the United States in need of responsible management?*

R Forests are one of the United States's major natural resources. However, **clear-cutting**, or the removal of whole forests when harvesting timber, occurs in many areas today. Clear-cutting has destroyed much of the country's old-growth forests. As a result, forest ecosystems are less diverse. In addition, wildlife is endangered and the land is subject to erosion and flooding.

W In addition to threats posed by the destruction of the forests, people in some areas of the country also face water shortages and groundwater depletion. This is due partly to the fact that people in the United States consume much more freshwater than people in any other country. People use water in all aspects of daily life—at home and in manufacturing, energy production, and agriculture. The Environmental Protection Agency (EPA) calculates that each U.S. home uses an average of 400 gallons (1515 l) of water daily. The EPA also estimates that industry accounts for 46 percent of water usage overall.

C2 Pollution threatens many wetland areas, which include marshes, ponds, and swamps. Wetlands also disappear when they are converted to agricultural or urban land uses. Wetlands are important because they hold valuable water supplies and fisheries and in many cases buffer

Media Bakery

134

networks Online Teaching Options

INTERACTIVE BELLRINGER

Acid Rain in the United States

Identifying Cause and Effect Use the introductory text, map, and the diagram "How Acid Rain is Created" to discuss acid rain and its impact on the environment. Have students study the diagram with a partner and then use it to identify how acid rain is formed and why it is an environmental problem. Ask pairs to write agreed-upon answers to the questions. Then in a class discussion, have students share their answers and discuss any environmental issues they have witnessed because of the effects of acid rain. AL Visual/Spatial

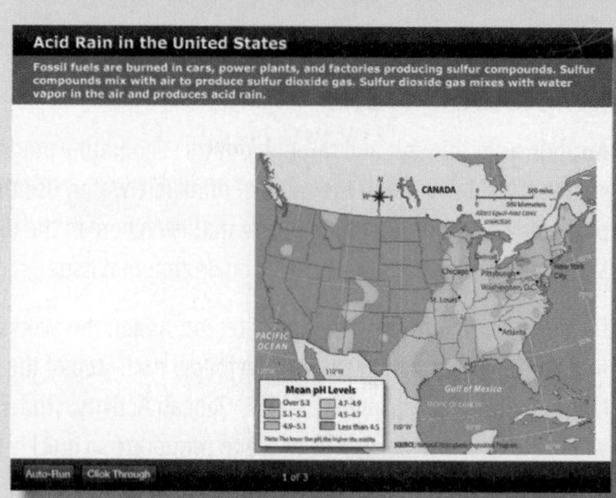
Acid Rain in the United States
Fossil fuels are burned in cars, power plants, and factories producing sulfur compounds. Sulfur compounds mix with air to produce sulfur dioxide gas. Sulfur dioxide gas mixes with water vapor in the air and produces acid rain.
CANADA
PACIFIC OCEAN
Gulf of Mexico
Mean pH Levels
Auto-Run
Click Through
1 of 3

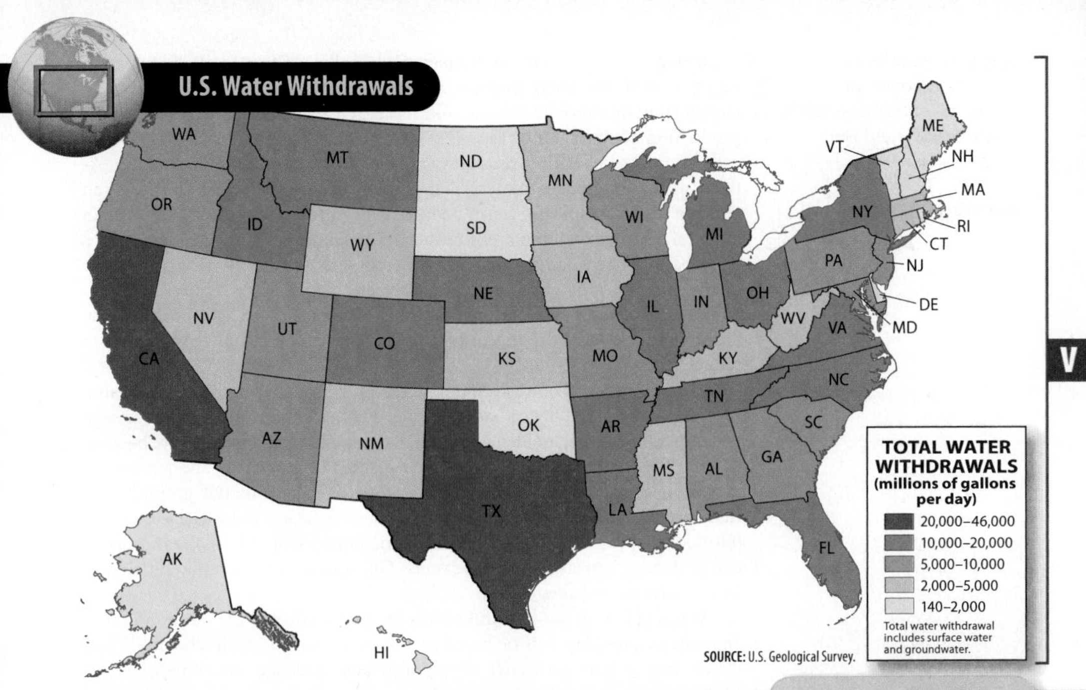

GEOGRAPHY CONNECTION

Every five years, the United States Geological Survey (USGS) compiles and estimates water-use data documenting how water resources in the United States are used.

1. ***HUMAN SYSTEMS*** What economic sector would you predict accounts for the majority of water used in California?
2. ***PLACES AND REGIONS*** List two states that have daily withdrawals between 140–2,000 gallons per day.

coastal areas from storms and floods. In New Orleans, Louisiana, for example, the building of levees, or raised embankments, around the city has destroyed wetlands that once protected the area from flooding.

Successful resource management must include understanding and respecting the balances that exist in natural ecosystems. Overfishing, which occurs when the number of fish that are caught exceeds the number that can be resupplied by natural reproduction, has depleted many of the region's fisheries. The accidental or deliberate introduction of non-native plant and animal species, on the rise because of increased global travel and trade, also causes environmental problems. These include blocked waterways, crop destruction, and displacement of crucial native species. Efforts to reverse the damage to the environment have begun, but the country has a long way to go toward achieving the sustainable use of its natural resources.

✓ **READING PROGRESS CHECK**

Explaining What are two causes of wetland habitat destruction in the United States?

Human Impact

GUIDING QUESTION *How can human activity lead to air and water pollution?*

While economic growth and industrial development have dramatically improved the standard of living in the United States, an unfortunate consequence has been the polluting of the air and water. **Acid rain**, precipitation carrying high amounts of acidic material, affects a large area of the eastern United States. Acid rain corrodes stone and metal buildings, damages crops, and pollutes the soil. It is especially damaging to the region's waters, as plant life and fish cannot survive in highly acidic waters. Over time, lakes can become biologically dead, or unable to support most organisms.

clear-cutting the removal of all trees in a stand of timber

acid rain precipitation carrying large amounts of dissolved acids, which kills wildlife and damages buildings, forests, and crops

People and Their Environment: The United States

V Visual Skills

Analyzing Visuals Remind students that people in the United States are the number one consumers of freshwater in the world. **Ask:** How many gallons of water are used per day in our state? *(Student responses will vary depending on location.)* Is more water used in the eastern or western United States? *(western United States)* What are three states that use the least amount of water? *(Possible answers: South Dakota, North Dakota, Oklahoma, Alaska, and Hawaii)* Why do you think these states use the least amount of water? *(Student answers will vary, but may include that farmers do not use crop irrigation; the states have a low population; the states have little industry.)* AL **Visual/Spatial**

W Writing Skills

Informative/Explanatory In an essay have students explain how humans have damaged water resources in the United States. Students should include examples of damage to water resources that they have personally seen or witnessed, as well as examples that they have read or heard about in the news or online. Encourage students to share their essays with the class. **Verbal/Linguistic**

Content Background Knowledge

Turning Seawater into Freshwater As the competition for water resources becomes more intense, increasing attention is being given to desalination, a process by which freshwater can be made from seawater. The first land-based seawater-desalting plant was built in Kuwait in 1949. Since then, the cost of desalting has been substantially lowered because of larger plant construction and use of improved materials and processes by individual plants. There are now more than 1,500 land-based desalting plants in the world..

R Reading Skills

Defining Have students reread the paragraph about acid rain. **Ask:** What are some of the causes of acid rain? *(Industrial development and population centers burning fossil fuels)* How does acid rain affect the ecosystem of a region's waters? *(Acid rain affects plant life and fish that cannot survive in acidic waters.)* Have students write the term and definition in their chapter glossaries. ELL **Verbal/Linguistic**

ANSWERS, p. 135

✓ **READING PROGRESS CHECK** Pollution and urban land use are two causes of wetland habitat destruction.

GEOGRAPHY CONNECTION

1. Agriculture
2. Possible answers: North Dakota, South Dakota, Oklahoma, Alaska, and Hawaii

INTERACTIVE MAP

U.S. Water Withdrawals

Informative/Explanatory This map shows the water withdrawals in the United States and can be used to discuss the variations of state water usages with students. Explain that they should consider the population size of the state with the usage amount. Have students choose a state to research the main water use or uses in that state. Then have them write a paragraph about water use in that state. Paragraphs should include the source(s) of the information. If time allows, have students share their findings with the class. BL **Verbal/Linguistic**

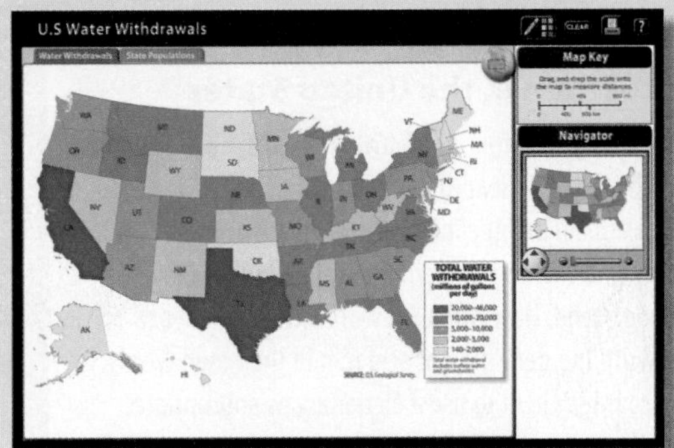

People and Their Environment: The United States

R Reading Skills

Defining Invite a student to read the definition for the term *smog* and then give the definition in his or her own words. **Ask:** Who and what creates smog? *(Humans create smog—chemicals from automobile exhaust and industrial emissions interact with the sun's rays to create smog.)* Students should write the term and the definition in their chapter glossaries.
ELL **Verbal/Linguistic**

T Technology Skills

Researching Divide the class into groups. Tell students each group will research the levels of acid rain in a large city in the United States. Allow groups to decide on a city to research. Review acceptable and credible online Web sites that students should use such as government environmental Web sites. Have students create a multimedia presentation that includes speaking parts for each member of the group, visuals that support research findings, and a question-and-answer session at the end of the presentation. Encourage students to add music or sound effects to their presentations. **Auditory/Musical, Naturalist**

V Visual Skills

Analyzing Direct students' attention to the map on the page. Emphasize that the lower the pH levels, the higher the acid rain amount. Have students determine whether the level of acid rain in the state they live in is high or low. **Ask:** Why do you think the acid rain levels are high near Pittsburgh? *(Industries are located in the region and the region is highly populated with many automobiles on the roads.)* Point to the area of the map where the Rocky Mountains are located. **Ask:** Why do you think the acid rain levels are lower in this region? *(This region is not as densely populated and there are not as many industries. This area is mountainous.)* **Verbal/Linguistic**

ANSWERS, p. 136

GEOGRAPHY CONNECTION

1. Ohio, Pennsylvania, and parts of New York are most affected by acid rain.
2. The eastern United States has more industry and a larger population than the western United States; as a result it experiences more acid rain.

smog haze caused by the interaction of ultraviolet solar radiation with chemical fumes from automobile exhausts and other pollution sources

contribute to give or add to

Smog is a second type of human-made pollution that has had long-term negative environmental impacts in the United States. Various chemicals, largely from automobile exhaust and industrial emissions, **contribute** to the production of smog. Smog is a mixture of atmospheric pollutants, including carbon monoxide, sulfur, nitrogen oxide, hydrocarbons, and particulates. As the sun's rays interact with these chemicals, a visible haze forms. This haze can damage or kill plants and harm people's eyes, throats, and lungs. Officials in many of the metropolitan areas in the United States measure air quality on a daily basis. When dangerous levels of smog are detected, officials issue air quality alerts urging children, the elderly, and people with respiratory problems to limit their physical activity and to stay indoors. Authorities may prohibit nonessential driving and the use of other gasoline-powered engines to reduce smog.

Massive amounts of waste and pollutants are produced in the United States. Although the United States has extensive facilities to control and treat sewage and industrial wastes, problems still arise. As a result, water systems have become tainted. Industrial wastes may be illegally dumped into rivers and streams or may find their way through small, unnoticed leaks into the groundwater. Industries also cause thermal pollution by releasing heated industrial wastewater into cooler lakes and rivers. Runoff from agricultural chemicals, such as fertilizers and pesticides, can also pollute the water. One area with serious water pollution issues is the Great Lakes region.

Water pollution has harmful effects on marine life and the birds and other animals that feed on fish or breed in the wetlands. The toxic chemicals and wastes that pollute the water supply also pose a danger to humans. Water

Acid Rain in the United States

CANADA
0 500 miles
0 500 kilometers
Albers Equal-Area Conic projection
ATLANTIC OCEAN
PACIFIC OCEAN
Gulf of Mexico
TROPIC OF CANCER
Detroit
Chicago
Pittsburgh
New York City
Washington, D.C.
St. Louis
Atlanta
120°W
110°W
100°W
90°W
80°W
40°N

Mean pH Levels

- Over 5.3
- 5.1–5.3
- 4.9–5.1
- 4.7–4.9
- 4.5–4.7
- Less than 4.5

Note: The lower the pH, the higher the acidity.

SOURCE: National Atmospheric Deposition Program.

GEOGRAPHY CONNECTION

Acid rain forms when cars, power plants, and factories release sulfur dioxide and nitrogen oxide that react with water vapor in the air.

1. ***PLACES AND REGIONS*** Which two states are most affected by acid rain?
2. ***HUMAN SYSTEMS*** Why might the eastern United States experience higher levels of acid rain than the western areas?

networks Online Teaching Options

INTERACTIVE MAP

Acid Rain in the United States

Defining Use this interactive map to discuss acid rain with students. Read the text and allow time for students to read and ask questions about the map. Some students may find the definition of acid rain a bit hard to understand. Have students work with a partner to rewrite the definition of acid rain in their own words. Encourage them to use a dictionary as appropriate. Students who finish quickly may be encouraged to do research to learn more about the chemistry of acid rain and include it in their definitions.
ELL **Verbal/Linguistic**

Wind turbines provide a source of renewable energy.

◀ **CRITICAL THINKING**

1. ***Analyzing Visuals*** Describe the landscape shown including why it might have been chosen as the location for wind turbines.
2. ***Making Connections*** Why is wind considered a renewable energy source?

pollution speeds **eutrophication** (yu•TROH•fuh•KAY•shuhn), the process by which a body of water becomes rich in dissolved nutrients, encouraging the overgrowth of small plants, especially algae. The algae growth can deplete the water's oxygen, suffocating fish. Algae overgrowth can also turn a lake into a marsh and then, over many years, into dry land. One wetland area that has been severely damaged in this way is the Florida Everglades.

eutrophication process by which a body of water becomes too rich in dissolved nutrients, leading to plant growth that depletes oxygen in the water

Another problem is the growing water shortage crisis across the country. Of major concern is the projection that 36 states will face water shortages in the next several years. In 2012 alone, water shortages turned into full-on droughts across much of the United States, causing billions of dollars in crop and livestock losses. By September 2012, it was estimated that more than two-thirds of the continental United States had been caught in the worst drought the country had experienced in more than half a century.

☑ **READING PROGRESS CHECK**

Describing Describe how industries contribute to water pollution in the United States.

Addressing the Issues

GUIDING QUESTION *How are environmental issues in the United States being addressed?*

The United States has made major strides toward protecting the environment. Clean-air practices have substantially reduced air pollution in some major cities. Renewable sources of energy for power—including hydroelectric, solar, and wind—are growing in popularity. Automobile manufacturers are producing more fuel-efficient vehicles, including hybrid vehicles that have both an electric motor and a gasoline engine. Engineers are working to develop other alternatives, including fuel cell vehicles, which produce electricity using hydrogen fuel and oxygen; biofuel vehicles, which use fuel from organic sources such as plant oils; and solar-powered cars. Legislation sets limits on the amount of sulfur and other pollutants that can be present in fuels. In addition, many individuals try to do their part to reduce smog by **abandoning** automobiles in favor of other modes of transportation, such as walking, bicycling, subways, and buses.

abandon to give up; to let sit empty or unused

Media Bakery

V Visual Skills

Creating Diagrams In a class discussion, review that water pollution can damage bodies of freshwater, turning them into marshes. Explain the term *eutrophication*, providing information to students who need further explanations. Then have student create a diagram of the different stages of the process of *eutrophication*. Diagrams should provide text that helps explain the process of *eutrophication*. **ELL** **Visual/Spatial**

T Technology Skills

Comparing and Contrasting Emphasize to students that there is a growing water shortage in the United States. Have students work with a partner to conduct online research on drought conditions in the U.S. over the last twenty years. Have pairs create a T-chart with each column representing ten years. Have them list the information they found for the first ten years in column one. Then list the information for the second ten years (most recent years) in column two. Have pairs make a class presentation comparing and contrasting drought conditions. **BL** **Visual/Spatial**

Making Connections

Today nonpoint source (NPS) pollution remains the largest source of water quality problems in the U.S. Approximately 40 percent of our surveyed rivers, lakes, and estuaries are not clean enough to meet basic uses for fishing or swimming. NPS pollution occurs when rainfall or irrigation runs over land or through the ground, picks up pollutants, and deposits them into rivers, lakes, and coastal waters, or into groundwater. During the last 10 years, significant federal level NPS control programs have been established.

W Writing Skills

Narrative Emphasize to students that many natural resources need protection. Have student write a short story about one natural resource that they feel needs protection and what the characters in their story do to protect the resource. **AL** **Verbal/Linguistic**

INTERACTIVE IMAGE

Wind as Renewable Energy

Assessing Tell students that giant wind farms are developing all over the country. Each windmill is generally the size of a multiple-story building. The blades themselves are often 100 feet long each. Divide the class into groups. Have groups discuss and list the pros and cons of harnessing wind power. Then encourage each group to come to a consensus about the use of wind farms in their community; would they support it? If their community already has wind farms, have groups come to a consensus if they should remain or be removed. **Interpersonal, Naturalist**

ANSWERS, p. 137

☑ **READING PROGRESS CHECK** Industrial wastes may be illegally dumped into rivers and streams or may find their way through unnoticed leaks into the groundwater. Runoff from fertilizers and pesticides can also pollute the water.

CRITICAL THINKING

1. Student answers may vary, but should include a description of the landscape as flat and without obstructions and an explanation as to why this landscape would be appropriate for wind turbines.
2. Student answer may vary, but should explain how wind in not a finite resource and while it may be harnessed, it does not deplete the amount that is available for use to generate power.

People and Their Environment: The United States

T Technology Skills

Examining Information Have student groups conduct research about efforts in their community or state to curb air and water pollution. Students can start with their community or government websites, by searching for *department of natural resources* or *environmental protection agency.* They can also look to private conservation agencies. Have each group provide a list explaining both local and regional efforts. In a class discussion, have groups share and discuss their findings.
Verbal/Linguistic

R Reading Skills

Defining Discuss with students how aqueducts are part of the solution in handling water shortages. Emphasize that aqueducts have been used throughout history to provide water supplies to populations of people in various regions all over the world. Have students provide examples of past civilizations they know of that have used aqueducts. Have students write the term and its definition in their chapter glossaries.
ELL **Verbal/Linguistic**

CLOSE & REFLECT

Summarizing Review with students the effect human populations have had on the environment. Discuss various environmental concerns that the United States faces in the twenty-first century. Lead students to arrive at some actions they can personally take to address these environmental issues.

ANSWERS, p. 138

DBQ Possible response: details that could provide the exact decrease in greenhouse gas, as well as additional methods to decrease greenhouse gas

✓ **READING PROGRESS CHECK** Solar panels, wind power, and biofuels are three renewable energy sources.

Analyzing Primary Sources (CCSS)

Can Natural Gas Help Tackle Global Warming?

"As David McCabe, an atmospheric scientist with the Clean Air Task Force explains, many of the half-dozen recent studies that have tried to compare coal with natural gas are plagued by questionable assumptions and flaws. 'From the best of the collective work,' McCabe notes, 'we believe that burning natural gas for electricity produces about 30–50% less greenhouse gas than burning coal.' But that's not a definitive number, and more research needs to be done here."

—Brad Plumer, "Can natural gas help tackle global warming? A primer," *Washington Post,* August 20, 2012

DBQ ***SPECULATING*** What additional information would be helpful to the studies? RH.9-10.1

aqueduct a channel or pipeline for carrying a large quantity of flowing water

Reducing waste and recycling help limit pollution. Many cities and towns practice recycling to help reduce the amount of garbage in the country's landfills. Scientists in the United States are also working to further this goal by developing plastics that will degrade naturally.

Since about the 1970s, many private and governmental organizations have championed the cause of environmental conservation. For example, numerous federal agencies have stepped up their efforts not only to conserve and protect the forests, but also to promote passage of legislation that ensures the timber industry will behave responsibly in their use of this resource. Replanting and conservation have also had a favorable impact on the country's forests.

Another form of federal legislation is the Clean Water Act, passed by the federal government in 1972. It has done much to restore the quality of water throughout the United States. The Great Lakes Water Quality Agreement, signed by the United States and Canada in 1972, led to the end of asbestos dumping in the Nashua River and spurred the construction of wastewater treatment plants. These facilities protected the river from paper pulp, chemical dyes, and other industrial wastes. Like many of the country's waterways, the Nashua River slowly regained its health. Today it is once again safe for wildlife and people.

The passage of the North American Free Trade Agreement (NAFTA), however, has shifted some environmental concerns south to the U.S.-Mexico border. Along the Rio Grande, rapid industrial growth threatens the environment. Various agencies are monitoring the environmental effects of NAFTA and suggesting ways to reduce pollution.

An example of human-environment interaction is the California State Water Project, the country's largest state-built water and power development project. It was designed to meet the needs of California's ever-growing population. **Aqueducts**, or systems of channels and pipelines, are used to carry water for hundreds of miles to more than 25 million Californians and to 750,000 acres (303,515 ha) of irrigated farmland. County and state water commissions have implemented plans to manage demand during times of limited supply. Similar policies have been put into action in counties and states across the country.

In response to global warming and greenhouse gases, the United States is working to diversify energy sources to lessen its dependence on fossil fuels. Governments offer subsidies to utility companies to limit emissions and to include renewable energy sources in their future plans. Solar panels and biofuels made from corn and other organic sources are among the potential renewable energy sources.

✓ **READING PROGRESS CHECK**

Identifying What are three types of renewable energy sources?

LESSON 3 REVIEW

Reviewing Vocabulary (Tier Three Words)

1. ***Explaining*** Explain the significance of clear-cutting, acid rain, smog, and eutrophication. RH.9–10.4

Using Your Notes

2. ***Identifying*** Use your graphic organizer to list the types of resources that need to be protected in the United States.

Answering the Guiding Questions

3. ***Expressing*** Why are water and timber resources in the United States in need of responsible management?
4. ***Describing*** How can human activity lead to air and water pollution?
5. ***Discussing*** How are environmental issues in the United States being addressed?

Writing Activity

6. ***Informative/Explanatory*** Pollution and the overuse of resources affect different areas in different ways. Write a descriptive paragraph about one region within the United States, explaining the environmental problems the region faces. WHST.9–10.2

LESSON 3 REVIEW ANSWERS

Reviewing Vocabulary

1. These are all issues that can be addressed to help decrease the negative impact of humans on the environment. Clear-cutting is the removal of whole forests when harvesting timber; acid rain is precipitation carrying large amounts of dissolved acids; smog kills wildlife and damages buildings, forests, and crops; eutrophication is a process by which a body of water becomes too rich in dissolved nutrients, leading to plant growth that depletes oxygen.

Using Your Notes

2. Lists will vary, but should include types of resources that need to be protected in the U.S. based on the student's graphic organizer.

Answering the Guiding Questions

3. Clear-cutting and other activities are depleting timber resources; water resources are being polluted by industries and individuals.
4. Vehicles and industry waste produce air pollution. Industrial wastes may be illegally dumped into rivers and streams or may find their way into groundwater. Industries also cause thermal pollution by releasing heated industrial wastewater into cooler lakes and rivers. Runoff from agricultural chemicals, such as fertilizers and pesticides, can also pollute the water.
5. Legislation has helped to resolve these issues. Vehicles that produce little or no pollution have been developed. Scientists continue to work to find ways to alleviate pollution.

Writing Activity

6. Paragraphs will differ, but should address one U.S. region and be strongly supported with information from the lesson.

CHAPTER 5 Assessment 

Directions: On a separate sheet of paper, answer the questions below. Make sure you read carefully and answer all parts of the questions.

Lesson Review

Lesson 1

1. ***Describing*** Explain how tectonic forces created the Appalachian Mountains and describe how they have been shaped.
2. ***Explaining*** Where are the Continental Divide and the fall line located in the United States? Explain their significance.
3. ***Contrasting*** How are the Mediterranean climate and the humid continental climate of the United States different?

Lesson 2

4. ***Evaluating*** How do most archaeologists believe the first inhabitants came to the area that is now Alaska, and from where did they come?
5. ***Explaining*** What were two reasons the United States encouraged settlement of the Great Plains during the late 1800s? Identify and explain the method of farming developed by settlers in the Great Plains during this time.
6. ***Summarizing*** Summarize the relationships among urbanization, metropolitan area, and suburb. Within your discussion, define each of these terms.

Lesson 3

7. ***Identifying Central Issues*** Write a paragraph describing the negative impacts humans have had on the natural environment in the United States.
8. ***Identifying Cause and Effect*** Explain the process of eutrophication, and discuss its impact on wetlands. Identify at least two ways human activity can lead to eutrophication.
9. ***Discussing*** How do water shortages impact the economy in areas affected by drought?

21st Century Skills

U.S. Mortgage Crisis

	Foreclosure Rate	Total Mortgage Debt
Florida	3.11%	$6.75 billion
Nevada	2.70%	$1.04 billion
Arizona	2.69%	$2.20 billion
Illinois	2.58%	$3.66 billion
Georgia	2.58%	$2.46 billion

Source: Realty Trac 2012 Year-end Foreclosure Market Report

10. ***Compare and Contrast*** How does Florida's total mortgage debt compare to that of Illinois?
11. ***Understanding Relationships Among Events*** Why do you think Nevada's total mortgage debt is lower but its foreclosure rate is higher than that of Georgia?

College and Career Readiness

12. ***Explaining Continuity and Change*** As a geographer conducting research, you have been hired to list and describe the reasons why the United States is one of the most ethnically diverse countries in the world. Create a report that summarizes your findings. WHST.9–10.2

Critical Thinking

13. ***Identifying Cause and Effect*** Describe how tectonic activity created the Hawaiian Islands.
14. ***Drawing Conclusions*** How might the water-shortage crisis in the United States affect economic activities in the country?
15. ***Making Decisions*** What choices can you make as a consumer to help protect the environment?

Need Extra Help?

If You've Missed Question	1	2	3	4	5	6	7	8	9	10	11	12	13	14	15
Go to page	121	121	124	125	127	128	134	136	137	139	139	119	121	137	137

CHAPTER 5 Assessment Answers

Lesson Review

Lesson 1

1. Tectonic plates collided and pushed upward to form the Appalachian Mountains. Over time, ice and water shaped the mountains.
2. The Continental Divide is a high ridge in the Rocky Mountains. Waterways to the west of the divide flow into the Pacific Ocean. Waterways to the east of the divide flow toward the Arctic Ocean, Hudson Bay, Atlantic Ocean, and Mississippi River system. The fall line is in the eastern United States and marks the place where the higher land of the Piedmont drops to the Atlantic Coastal Plain. The rivers along the fall line break into waterfalls and rapids, preventing ships from traveling farther inland.
3. A Mediterranean climate has mild and wet winters while a humid continental climate has very cold winters.

Lesson 2

4. Most archaeologists believe the first inhabitants in what is now Alaska arrived by boat and by land from Asia.
5. People were encouraged to settle in the Great Plains to speed development and to grow food for the expanding population in cities. Settlers developed dry farming to grow crops using only the natural precipitation that falls in the Great Plains.
6. Urbanization, the moving of people from rural areas to cities, creates metropolitan areas. A metropolitan area is a city with at least 50,000 people including suburbs, which are outlying areas. Urban sprawl is the spreading of cities onto the natural landscape.

Lesson 3

7. Paragraphs will vary, but could include clear-cutting of forests, overfishing, water shortages, pollution of water and air, and introduction of nonnative plants and animals.
8. Eutrophication is when water becomes too rich in nutrients, resulting in an overgrowth of plants that depletes the nitrogen in the water. It can cause a lake to first turn into a marsh and eventually to dry land. Human activities that cause eutrophication include the dumping of industrial waste and the runoff of fertilizers from agriculture into water systems.
9. Drought causes billions of dollars in crop and livestock losses.

21st Century Skills

10. Florida has approximately $3.09 billion more in total mortgage debt than Illinois.
11. Students may say that since Georgia has a higher population the overall foreclosure rate in Georgia is less than Nevada, which has fewer people. The mortgage debt rate is lower in Nevada since the overall foreclosure number, not the rate, is most likely less than in Georgia.

College and Career Readiness

12. Reports and lists will vary, but could include push and pull factors. Push factors motivate people to leave their countries of origin. They can be quite varied, including religious and ethnic persecution, lack of economic prospects or personal security, civil strife, and war. Pull factors are those which draw people to a new country, such as employment opportunities, political and religious freedom, and better living conditions, including access to education and health care.

Critical Thinking

13. Tectonic activity created hot spots on the ocean floor that allowed magma to erupt forming the Hawaiian Islands.
14. Water shortages can decrease the amount of crops we can grow and sell as well as livestock that are able to be raised.
15. Student answer will vary, but could include taking the bus, cycling, walking, or purchasing a hybrid vehicle.

Applying Map Skills

16 The elevation decreases from over 10,000 feet to sea level as you travel east from California to Oklahoma.

17 The Gulf of Mexico and the Atlantic Ocean surround Florida.

18 The most central part of the United States is temperate grasslands.

Exploring the Essential Question

19 Plot summaries will vary, but should include two of the following: acid rain, smog, water pollution, and/or eutrophication.

Research and Presentation

20 Presentations will vary, but could include impacts to the Rio Grande area in the water quality/pollution, wildlife depletion, and water shortages. Presentations should explain that NAFTA requires cooperation on pollution controls of the member countries.

Writing About Geography

21 Essays will vary, but must include an example of pollution in the students' town or state along with steps that are being taken to eliminate the problem.

Analyzing Primary Sources

22 The author is installing solar panels that will be used to generate electricity by using the power of the sun.

23 Parfit means that he is happy to not be dependent upon any of the traditional means of generating energy that have been a constant source of debates, controversy, and crises for the last few decades.

CHAPTER 5 Assessment 

Directions: On a separate sheet of paper, answer the questions below. Make sure you read carefully and answer all parts of the questions.

Applying Map Skills

Use the Unit 2 Atlas to answer the following questions.

16 ***Physical Systems*** Describe the general differences in elevation you encounter as you travel from California east to Oklahoma.

17 ***Places and Regions*** Using your mental map of the United States, list the bodies of water that surround Florida.

18 ***Human Systems*** What vegetation type is found in the most central part of the United States?

Exploring the Essential Question

19 ***Making Connections*** Imagine you are writing a science fiction novel about a person who has the power to change history by going back in time to sources that contributed substantially to two types of major pollution in the United States. Write a summary of the plot in your novel to explain the changes you would make to humans' actions—and the impact of these changes.

Research and Presentation

20 ***Research Skills*** Use the Internet and other resources to gather information about the effects of NAFTA on the physical environment of member countries. What cooperation issues other than trade does NAFTA cover? Create a multimedia presentation to share your findings.

Writing About Geography

21 ***Informative*** Use standard grammar, spelling, sentence structure, and punctuation to write a one-page essay that explains the effects of a specific type of pollution on your town or state. Discuss steps your town or state is taking to alleviate the problems.

DBQ Analyzing Primary Sources

Use the document to answer the following questions.

In the United States today, years of industrial emissions, automobile exhaust gases, and the extraction of natural resources have taken their toll on the environment. Curbing dependency on nonrenewable energy sources is an important issue. More and more people are exploring alternative energy sources that are both clean and renewable.

PRIMARY SOURCE

"Freedom! I stand in a cluttered room surrounded by the debris of electrical enthusiasm: wire peelings, snippets of copper, yellow connectors, insulated pliers. For me these are the tools of freedom. I have just installed a dozen solar panels on my roof, and they work. A meter shows that 1,285 watts of power are blasting straight from the sun into my system, charging my batteries, cooling my refrigerator, humming through my computer, liberating my life.

The euphoria of energy freedom is addictive. . . . Maybe that's because for me, as for most Americans, one energy crisis or another has shadowed most of the past three decades."

—Michael Parfit, "Powering the Future," *National Geographic*, August 2005

22 ***Analyzing*** What is the author installing and what will they be used for? RH.9–10.1

23 ***Interpreting*** What did Parfit mean by "the euphoria of energy freedom"? RH.9–10.4

Need Extra Help?

If You've Missed Question	16	17	18	19	20	21	22	23
Go to page	112	112	114	136	138	135	140	140

140

networks Online Teaching Options

WORKSHEET

Chapter Test and Lesson Quizzes

Assessing Have students complete the Chapter Test and Lesson Quizzes to assess student understanding throughout the chapter. These assessment tools offer chapter and lesson evaluation through a variety of question formats, including document-based questions.

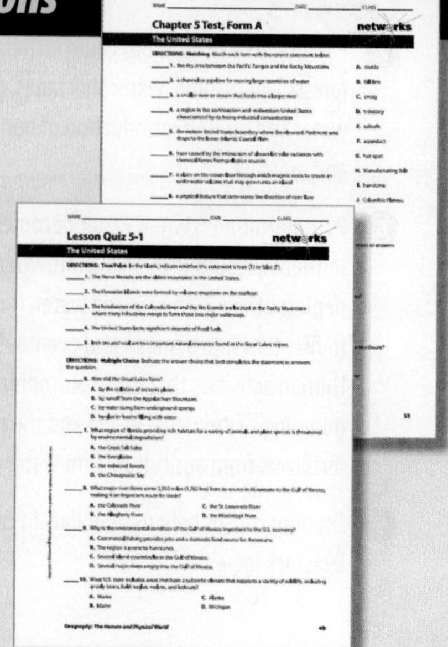

CHAPTER 6

Canada Planner

UNDERSTANDING BY DESIGN®

Enduring Understandings

- *The physical environment affects people and their activities.*

Essential Question

- *How do physical systems and human systems shape a place?*

Predictable Misunderstandings

Students may think:

- *The physical and human geography of Canada is similar to the United States. Explain that Canada's higher latitude leads to colder climates and different physical geography than the U.S. and that although Canada was also historically influenced by England, there is a much greater French influence in Canada than in the United States.*
- *Canada has few resources. Explain that although Canada has colder climates than the U.S., it has many natural resources, including timber and oil.*

Assessment Evidence

Performance Tasks:

- *Hands-On Chapter Project*

Other Evidence:

- *Guided Reading Activities*
- *Vocabulary Activities*
- *Lesson Quizzes*
- *Chapter Tests, Forms A and B*

SUGGESTED PACING GUIDE

Introducing the Chapter	½ Day	Global Connections	1 Day
Lesson 1	1 Day	Lesson 3	1 Day
Lesson 2	2 Days	Chapter Wrap-Up and Assessment	½ Day

TOTAL TIME 6 Days

Key for Using the Teacher Edition

SKILL-BASED ACTIVITIES

Types of skill activities found in the Teacher Edition.

* **V Visual Skills** require students to analyze maps, graphs, charts, and photos.

R Reading Skills help students practice reading skills and master vocabulary.

C Critical Thinking Skills help students apply and extend what they have learned.

W Writing Skills provide writing opportunities to help students comprehend the text.

T Technology Skills require students to use digital tools effectively.

*Letters are followed by a number when there is more than one of the same type of skill on the page.

DIFFERENTIATED INSTRUCTION

All activities are written for the on-level student unless otherwise marked with the leveled labels below.

BL Beyond Level

AL Approaching Level

ELL English Language Learners

All students benefit from activities that utilize different learning styles. Many activities are marked as below when a particular learning style is highlighted.

Intrapersonal	**Naturalist**
Logical/Mathematical	**Kinesthetic**
Visual/Spatial	**Auditory/Musical**
Verbal/Linguistic	**Interpersonal**

National Geography Standards covered in "Canada"

The student knows and understands:

(3) How to analyze the spatial organizations of people, places, and environments on Earth's surface

3.2 Complex processes change over time and shape patterns in the distribution of human and physical phenomena

(4) The physical and human characteristics of places

4.2 The interaction of physical and human systems result in the creation of and changes to places

(7) The physical processes that shape the patterns of Earth's surface

7.3 Physical processes interact over time to shape particular places on Earth's surface

(8) The characteristics and spatial distribution of ecosystems and biomes on Earth's surface

8.3 The distribution and characteristics of biomes change over time

(9) The characteristics, distribution, and migration of human populations on Earth's surface

9.2 Population distribution and density are a function of historical, environmental, economic, political, and technological factors

9.3 Migration is one of the driving forces for shaping and reshaping the cultural and physical landscape of places and regions

(10) The characteristics, distribution, and complexity of Earth's cultural mosaics

10.3 Cultures change through convergence and/or divergence

(11) The patterns and networks of economic interdependence on Earth's surface

11.1 The scale and organization of economic activities change over time

11.2 Patterns exist in the spatial organization of economic activities

(15) How physical systems affect human systems

15.1 Depending on the choice of human activities, the characteristics of the physical environment can be viewed as both opportunities and constraints

(16) The changes that occur in the meaning, use, distribution, and importance of resources

16.2 The spatial distribution of resources affects patterns of human settlement and trade

(17) How to apply geography and interpret the past

17.1 Geographic contexts (the human and physical characteristics of places and environments) can explain the connections between sequences of historical events

CHAPTER OPENER PLANNER

Students will know:

- *how physical processes shaped the physical geography of Canada.*
- *how climate and water systems affect settlement and economic activities in Canada.*
- *how French and English roots and immigration have shaped Canada's history.*
- *the characteristics of Canada's diverse population.*
- *the relationships between economic activities and resource management in a postindustrial market economy.*
- *the activities causing environmental issues in Canada and how they are being addressed.*

Students will be able to:

- ***describe** the physical geography of Canada and the processes that shaped it.*
- ***analyze** how climate and water systems affect the economy.*
- ***describe** the influence of the English and French on Canada.*
- ***understand** the diverse populations and cultures of Canada.*
- ***analyze** how resources and economic activities are connected.*
- ***describe** environmental issues in Canada.*

UNDERSTANDING BY DESIGN®

☑ Print Teaching Options

V Visual Skills

- ☐ **p. 142** Students write captions for photos that summarize the text and capture the emotion in the images. AL Visual/Spatial, Interpersonal

R Reading Skills

- ☐ **p. 141** Students formulate questions they have about the chapter content. Verbal/Linguistic
- ☐ **p. 142** Students make predictions about negative impacts of resource development. Logical/Mathematical
- ☐ **p. 143** Students interpret the map of natural resources. Visual/Spatial

C Critical Thinking Skills

- ☐ **p. 141** Students compare and contrast Canada's geography to the geography in the United States.
- ☐ **p. 143** Students consider positive and negative impacts of developing resources. Verbal/Linguistic

☑ Online Teaching Options

V Visual Skills

- INTERACTIVE MAP **Canada Oil and Natural Gas Pipelines**—Students discuss the influences of oil and gas pipelines between the U.S. and Canada on the countries' economies. AL Verbal/Linguistic
- MAP **Interactive Regional Atlas**—Students use the interactive regional atlas to understand the physical and human geography of Canada.

☑ Printable Digital Worksheets

- WORKSHEET **Assessing Background Knowledge**—Determine the level of prior knowledge students have about Canada.
- WORKSHEET **Chapter Summaries**—Students review the main idea of each lesson of the chapter content.
- WORKSHEET **Reteaching Activity**—These worksheets provide students with an opportunity for remedial practice and review of vital chapter content.
- WORKSHEET **Vocabulary Activity**—Students apply their knowledge of content and academic vocabulary words.

Project-Based Learning 

Hands-On

Skits about Canada's Geographic Systems

Students will write and conduct a skit presenting the geographic systems issue from the Stakeholders perspective.

Digital Hands-On

Create Online Projects

Find an additional activity online that incorporates technology for this project. Visit the EdTech Teacher Web sites for more links, tutorials, and other resources.

Print Resources

ANCILLARY RESOURCES

This ancillary is available for every chapter and lesson.

- **Chapter Tests and Lesson Quizzes**

PRINTABLE DIGITAL WORKSHEETS

These printable digital worksheets are available for every chapter and lesson.

- **Assessing Background Knowledge**
- **Chapter Summaries**
- **Guided Reading Activities**
- **Hands-On Chapter Projects**
- **Quizzes and Tests**
- **Reading Essentials and Study Guide** AL
- **Reteaching Activities**
- **Video Activities**
- **Vocabulary Activities**

More Media Resources

SUGGESTED VIDEOS MOVIES

- **Destination Canada** (52 min.)
- **Standard Deviants: World Geography Module 3—The US and Canada** (26 min.)
- **Canada** *New Dimension Media* (30 min.)

SUGGESTED READING 

- ***The Geographies of Canada,*** by Rémy Tremblay and Hugues Chicoine
- ***Regional Geography of the United States and Canada (4th Edition),*** by Tom L. McKnight
- ***Canada's Diverse Peoples: A Reference Sourcebook (Ethnic Diversity Within Nations),*** by John M. Bumsted

LESSON 1 PLANNER

PHYSICAL GEOGRAPHY OF CANADA

Students will know:

- *the main lines of Canadian landforms and their relationship to the geography of the United States.*
- *how physical processes shaped the physical geography of Canada.*
- *the importance of water and water systems to Canada's economy.*
- *how climate affects settlement and economic activities in Canada.*

Students will be able to:

- ***identify*** *major landforms and how they were formed.*
- ***describe*** *Canada's climate and its effects.*
- ***identify*** *important water systems and how they affect the economy.*

UNDERSTANDING BY DESIGN®

☑ Print Teaching Options

V Visual Skills

- ☐ **p. 144** Students complete a Venn diagram to compare and contrast features of the western United States and western region of Canada. **Visual/Spatial**
- ☐ **p. 145** Students discuss the effect of glaciers of the last age on Canada's land. **Visual/Spatial**
- ☐ **p. 146** Students label maps with bodies of water connected by the St. Lawrence Seaway system and summarize how the system contributes to the economy. **Visual/Spatial, Interpersonal**
- ☐ **p. 147** Students work in groups to demonstrate the way ocean currents impact Canada's climate. **Kinesthetic**

R Reading Skills

- ☐ **p. 144** Students review what is meant by the phrase *tectonic activity.*
- ☐ **p. 144** Students discuss what they know about the Rocky and Appalachian Mountains. **AL** **Logical/Mathematical**
- ☐ **p. 145** Students discuss the definition of *shield* in relation to *Canadian Shield.* **AL** **ELL** **Verbal/Linguistic**
- ☐ **p. 147** Students use context clues to figure out the meanings of *coniferous* and *timberline.* **AL** **ELL** **Verbal/Linguistic**

C Critical Thinking Skills

- ☐ **p. 145** Students discuss how lakes and rivers contribute to Canada's economy. **Interpersonal, Naturalist**

W Writing Skills

- ☐ **p. 147** Students write a travel blog for the Canadian government's tourism Web site. **AL** **Verbal/Linguistic**
- ☐ **p. 148** Students write an argumentative essay in which they defend a position about the extraction or development of natural resources in Canada. **BL** **Verbal/Linguistic**

T Technology Skills

- ☐ **p. 146** Students identify differences and similarities between the St. Lawrence River and Mississippi River and present summaries. **Logical/Mathematical, Visual/Spatial**
- ☐ **p. 148** Students research and create a slide show about the impact of development of timber and fishing resources. **Logical/Mathematical, Visual/Spatial**

☑ Online Teaching Options

V Visual Skills

- **INTERACTIVE MAP** **St. Lawrence Seaway System**—Students discuss the importance of waterway transportation and compare the St. Lawrence Seaway to the Mississippi River. **BL** **Naturalist**
- **VIDEO** **British Columbia**—Students list geography features they see in the video and write a paragraph on how these features make tourism an important economic activity in Canada. **BL** **Logical/Mathematical**

C Critical Thinking Skills

- **INTERACTIVE BELLRINGER** **Average Yearly Temperatures in Four Towns in Alberta, Canada**—Students discuss and answer questions about the landforms in the southwestern United States. **AL** **Visual/Spatial**
- **INTERACTIVE MAP** **Glaciers of the Last Ice Age**—Students discuss current climate conditions on Earth and write a paragraph considering whether glaciers are likely to return to widespread areas in Canada. **ELL** **Verbal/Linguistic**
- **INTERACTIVE WHITEBOARD ACTIVITY** **The Land of Canada**—Students match the names of Canada's physical features with the correct definition or description that applies to it.

☑ Printable Digital Worksheets

R Reading Skills

- **WORKSHEET** **Guided Reading Activity**—Students use Guided Reading Activity worksheets to review their comprehension of the content.

C Critical Thinking Skills

- **WORKSHEET** **Video Activity**—Students answer questions related to a topic in the chapter content after they have viewed a lesson video.

HUMAN GEOGRAPHY OF CANADA

Students will know:

- *how French and English roots influenced Canada's history.*
- *the ways in which immigration has shaped Canada's population and culture.*
- *the characteristics of Canada's diverse population.*
- *the factors involved in making the Canadian economy a postindustrial market economy.*

Students will be able to:

- ***describe** French and English influences in Canada's history.*
- ***analyze** how immigration affected culture and population in Canada.*
- ***identify** how Canada developed a postindustrial market economy.*

UNDERSTANDING BY DESIGN®

☑ Print Teaching Options

V Visual Skills

- ☐ **p. 151** Students quiz each other on Canada's history between 1982 and 2012. Visual/Spatial, Interpersonal
- ☐ **p. 152** Students create a circle graph showing the breakdown of Canada's ethnic groups. Logical/Mathematical
- ☐ **p. 152** Students depict the information about Canada's population density and percentages visually in a map.
- ☐ **p. 155** Students create a display to show information about Canada's imports and exports. BL Visual/Spatial

R Reading Skills

- ☐ **p. 150** Students create a time line noting important events and dates as they read. AL Verbal/Linguistic
- ☐ **p. 153** Students distinguish between *emigrate* and *immigrate.* ELL Verbal/Linguistic
- ☐ **p. 154** Students use word parts to define *postindustrial.* ELL Verbal/Linguistic

C Critical Thinking Skills

- ☐ **p. 150** Students consider the French influence on Canada. Verbal/Linguistic
- ☐ **p. 151** Students discuss the advantages and disadvantages of NAFTA. AL Logical/Mathematical
- ☐ **p. 155** Students discuss the impact of the 2008 global recession on Canada and the U.S. Logical/Mathematical

W Writing Skills

- ☐ **p. 151** Students compare the plight of Native Americans in U.S. history with First Nations peoples in Canada.
- ☐ **p. 153** Students write and perform a short skit about daily life of a Canadian family. Kinesthetic, Musical/Auditory

T Technology Skills

- ☐ **p. 149** Students research one of the three main indigenous groups in Canada. BL Verbal/Linguistic
- ☐ **p. 151** Students read about French-speaking Canadians' separatist viewpoints and prepare arguments to either defend or refute separatism. BL Verbal/Linguistic
- ☐ **p. 153** Students compare and contrast women's rights in the United States and Canada. BL Verbal/Linguistic

☑ Online Teaching Options

V Visual Skills

- VIDEO **War of Words**—Students discuss the history and culture of language in Canada. Verbal/Linguistic
- IMAGE **First Nations and the Inuit Peoples**—Students discuss ethnic politics and divisions within Canada. BL Verbal/Linguistic

C Critical Thinking Skills

- INTERACTIVE BELLRINGER **Aboriginal Population by Province/Territory, 2006**—Students explore population statistics about the Aboriginal population in Canadian provinces. Logical/Mathematical, Verbal/Linguistic
- INTERACTIVE MAP **Canadian Explorations**—Students discuss Canadian expansion and diversity. Logical/Mathematical, Interpersonal
- GAME **Human Geography of Canada**—Students play a game to foster discussion of Canada's ethnic diversity. AL Verbal/Linguistic
- GRAPH **Annual Growth Rate of Canadian Industries**—Students interact with the graph and write a paragraph summarizing Canada's economic status in 2011. BL Verbal/Linguistic
- INTERACTIVE WHITEBOARD ACTIVITY **British and French Roots**—Students place events from Canada's history in correct chronological sequence into the appropriate boxes on a chart.

☑ Printable Digital Worksheets

R Reading Skills

- WORKSHEET **Guided Reading Activity**—Students use Guided Reading Activity worksheets to review their comprehension of the content.
- WORKSHEET **Reading Essentials and Study Guide**—Students complete the study guide and answer Reading Progress Check and vocabulary questions. AL

C Critical Thinking Skills

- WORKSHEET **Video Activity**—Students answer questions related to a topic in the chapter content after they have viewed a lesson video.

PEOPLE AND THEIR ENVIRONMENT: CANADA

Students will know:

- *the relationships between economic activities and the need for resource management and conservation in Canada.*
- *the activities causing growing concern over climate change in Canada.*
- *how human activities cause air and water pollution in Canada.*
- *the ways in which the government and others in Canada are addressing environmental issues.*

Students will be able to:

- ***understand** how resource management and the economy are connected.*
- ***identify** ways in which activities cause pollution and climate change.*
- ***analyze** efforts to address environmental issues.*

UNDERSTANDING BY DESIGN®

☑ Print Teaching Options

V Visual Skills

- ☐ **p. 158** Students create a visual to show the logging extraction process. ELL Visual/Spatial, Interpersonal
- ☐ **p. 160** Students create a visual that shows how electricity is generated from flowing water. AL Visual/Spatial, Interpersonal
- ☐ **p. 160** Students create a display to show the process of extracting, developing, manufacturing, or transporting an assigned natural resource. Visual/Spatial, Intrapersonal

R Reading Skills

- ☐ **p. 161** Students make a list of environmental impacts that human activities have had in Canada. AL Verbal/Linguistic
- ☐ **p. 162** Students summarize information about how individual provinces have taken actions to address climate change. AL Verbal/Linguistic

C Critical Thinking Skills

- ☐ **p. 158** Students discuss the economic and environmental impacts of logging on Canada's boreal forest.
- ☐ **p. 161** Students discuss how environmental issues affect political and international relations. Logical/Mathematical
- ☐ **p. 162** Students discuss the Kyoto Protocol.

W Writing Skills

- ☐ **p. 158** Students write slogans and banners stating their opinions about logging, mining, or oil and gas extraction. Kinesthetic, Verbal/Linguistic
- ☐ **p. 159** Students explain the term "bank account" as it relates to the global boreal forest. Verbal/Linguistic

T Technology Skills

- ☐ **p. 160** Students research the status of the Keystone XL pipeline and create a slide show presentation that explains both sides of the issue. BL Visual/Spatial, Interpersonal
- ☐ **p. 162** Students research efforts to protect Canada's renewable resources and write a song or poem to emphasize the need to protect these resources. Interpersonal, Auditory/Musical

☑ Online Teaching Options

C Critical Thinking Skills

- ☐ INTERACTIVE BELLRINGER **Canada's Boreal Forest**—Students discuss how Canada's boreal forest affects life on Earth. ELL Interpersonal, Verbal/Linguistic
- ☐ INFOGRAPHIC **Canada's Boreal Forest**—Students use the infographic to discuss the value of lumber as a resource. BL Naturalist
- ☐ INTERACTIVE WHITEBOARD ACTIVITY **Cause and Effect in Canada's Environment**—Students complete a cause-and-effect chart showing the impact humans have had on the environment in Canada.
- ☐ VIDEO **The Wolves of Northern Canada**—Students discuss their views on protecting wolves, research environmental resource management for saving endangered wolves, and conduct a short debate. BL Interpersonal

☑ Printable Digital Worksheets

R Reading Skills

- ☐ WORKSHEET **Guided Reading Activity**—Students use Guided Reading Activity worksheets to review their comprehension of the content.
- ☐ WORKSHEET **Reading Essentials and Study Guide**—Students complete the study guide and answer Reading Progress Check and vocabulary questions. AL
- ☐ WORKSHEET **Vocabulary Activity**—Students review the chapter content and academic vocabulary words.

C Critical Thinking Skills

- ☐ WORKSHEET **Video Activity**—Students answer questions based on a lesson video.
- ☐ WORKSHEET **Reteaching Activity**—Students use this activity worksheet to review and reteach chapter content and vocabulary. This worksheet can be used with struggling students who need additional help with difficult content concepts.

Intervention and Remediation Strategies

LESSON 1 Physical Geography of Canada

Reading and Comprehension

Have students work with a partner to scan the lesson and use context clues to define the meaning of each content vocabulary term. Have partners write sentences using each term to demonstrate their understanding of the word's meaning. Ask volunteers to clarify words or concepts in the text that may be confusing, such as the terms *boreal forest* and *taiga.* Then have partners collaborate to create sentences that show their understanding of the two academic vocabulary terms.

Text Evidence

Have students work in four groups to research an aspect of Canada's physical geography as it relates to one of the following topics discussed in the lesson: landforms, water systems, climate regions and biomes, and natural resources. Tell students to present an analysis of their findings, comparing information in the text with information found in their research. For example, students might research the importance of the St. Lawrence Seaway System. Tell students to write an objective summary of their findings.

LESSON 2 Human Geography of Canada

Reading and Comprehension

Have students work in pairs to quiz each other on the meanings of the content vocabulary terms in this lesson. Tell students to review the text in order to understand the difference between the Inuit, the Métis, and the First Nations peoples. Have students use the content vocabulary terms in sentences that show their understanding of each word's meaning. Ask students to turn to a partner and discuss reasons people might *emigrate* to another country.

Text Evidence

Organize students into four groups and assign each group one of the following terms: *Dominion of Canada, Quebecois, separatism, Loyalists.* Have students in each group work together to determine the central idea in the text about their assigned term. Then have each group write a summary about the significance of the term as it relates to the history of Canada. Tell students to use textual evidence to support ideas presented in their summaries. Have students share their summaries with the class.

LESSON 3 People and Their Environment: Canada

Reading and Comprehension

To ensure comprehension of the concepts in this lesson, have students write a summarizing sentence for each of the three sections in the text: managing resources, human impact, and addressing the issues. Tell students their sentences should touch on one or more issues facing Canada, and should identify what is being done to solve the problem. Have students share their sentences with the class, providing corrective guidance if needed.

Text Evidence

Have students work in small groups to create a visual diagram about an issue discussed in the text related to Canada's environment. You may wish to assign students topics to avoid duplication, such as overfishing, Canada's boreal forest, hydroelectricity, acid rain, and so on. Have students collaborate to use evidence from the text on which to base their visual diagrams and present them to the class. After students have presented their visuals, guide a discussion about how the Canadian government is working to address environmental issues.

Online Resources

Leveled Reader

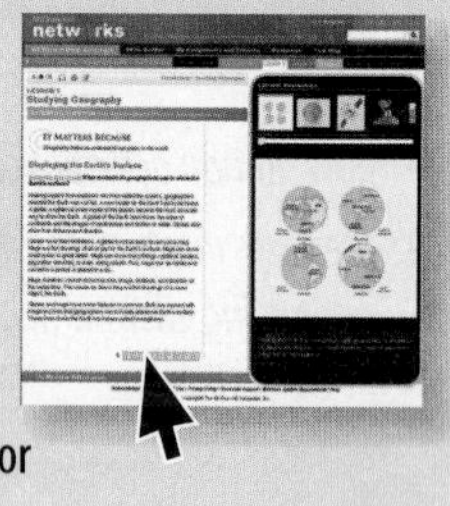

Use this online approaching-level text that corresponds directly to the text in the Student Edition. It also includes additional reading and comprehension support for English Language Learners.

Guided Reading Activities

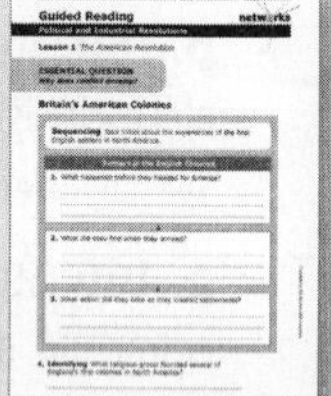

This resource uses guiding questions to help students with comprehension.

Reteaching Activities

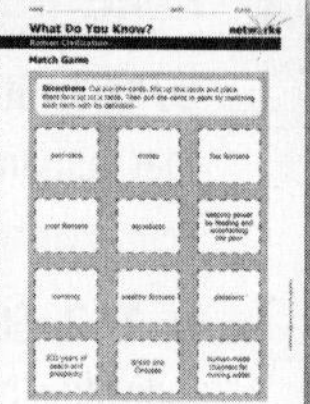

These worksheets provide students with an opportunity for remedial practice and review of vital chapter content.

Reading Essentials and Study Guide

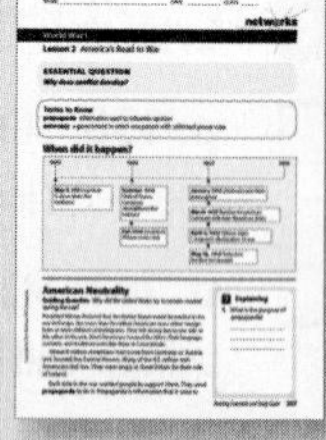

This resource offers writing and reading activities for the approaching-level student.

Self-Check Quizzes

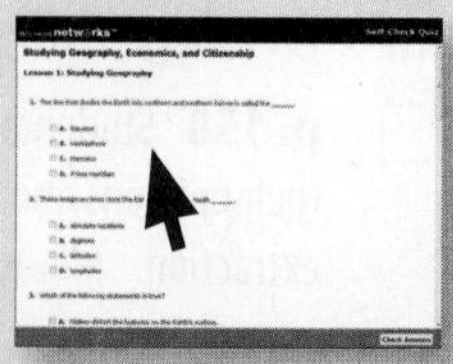

This online assessment tool provides instant feedback for students to check their progress.

Chapter Summaries

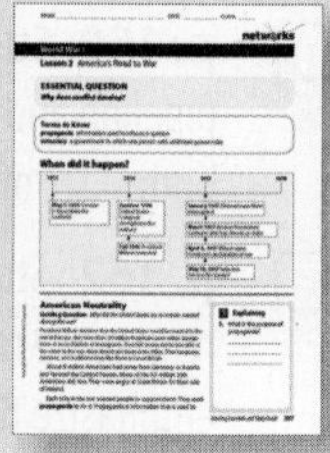

Summaries are provided for each chapter that thoroughly condense core content into manageable chunks.

Canada

ESSENTIAL QUESTION • *How do physical systems and human systems shape a place?*

networks
There's More Online about Canada.

CHAPTER 6

Geography Matters...

Although Canada borders the United States, many Americans do not know much about our neighbor. The world's second-largest country in land area, Canada stretches across the northern half of North America. The vast land is rich in resources, especially energy resources. It has many climate regions, each with different landscapes and peoples. Most Canadians, however, live in the southern part of the country, near the border with the United States.

◀ A Canadian woman plays ice hockey on a pond. Hockey is a popular sport in Canada.

Alexander Nicholson/Taxi/Getty Images

141

Letter from the Author

Dear Geography Teacher,

The story of Canada is a lot like that of the United States—westward movement with an outpost on the Pacific Ocean. A vast interior plain shadowed by majestic mountains in the west. Democracy and capitalism, fueled by individual initiative, has made modern Canada great. Another story in Canada is diversity. French culture and language are so strong in the province of Quebec that many people believe they should seek independence from the rest of the country. For now, unity has been preserved, but the issue lingers. In Toronto, Ontario, you will find every possible ethnic, racial, social, and religious minority represented. It conjures up the long-held notion of a "melting pot."

Richard G. Boehm

ENGAGE

Comparing and Contrasting Ask volunteers to state what they know about Canada's geography based on reading about, or visiting the country, or what they have seen on television or in movies. **Ask:** **Based on what you know about Canada, how does its geography compare to the geography of the United States?** *(Possible answer: Canada shares landforms such as the Great Plains in the midwest and the Rocky Mountains in the west. It also shares the water systems of Niagara Falls and four of the Great Lakes.)*

TEACH & ASSESS

Formulating Questions Direct students' attention to the image of the Canadian woman wearing ice hockey gear. Have students jot down questions that come to mind as they look at the image. Have students exchange their list of questions with a partner and work to answer each other's questions. Tell students to keep their list of questions and to make revisions to their answers based on the text. **Verbal/Linguistic**

Making Connections

Even though Canada is the world's second largest country in land area (next to Russia), it is sparsely populated and has vast forests. More than 400 million hectares of forests cover Canada. To help students grasp the vast expanse of forestland that covers Canada, have them visualize one acre, offering examples with which they are familiar (the school's property is approximately X amount of acres, and so on). Then have students calculate the number of acres that make up one hectare *(2.47 acres)* and the number of acres in 400 hectares. *(approximately 988,421,526 acres)*

CLOSE & REFLECT

Describing Have students read the *Geography Matters* section. Have students write a paragraph describing how they think daily life in Canada differs from daily life in the United States. Ask students to review their paragraphs after reading the chapter to check for any misconceptions they had.

Extend the project-based learning experience globally through our partnership with ePals. EPals allows you to connect with classrooms around the world in a safe online environment for real-life lessons and projects in virtual study groups.

ENGAGE

C Critical Thinking Skills

Exploring Issues Before discussing the issue involving resource development and its impact on indigenous populations, ensure that students understand key concepts by sharing what they know about the indigenous peoples of Canada and the need for countries to export their resources to increase their economic wealth. Have students discuss whether it would be better politically and economically for the United States to import oil from Canada or from the Middle East.

TEACH & ASSESS

V Visual Skills

Analyzing Visuals Remind students that photos are chosen for very distinct purposes to correspond with text. Divide students up into small groups. Have groups analyze the photos and read the text together. Then have each group write a one or two sentence caption for each of the photos. Tell students that the captions should help capture both the feelings and emotions in the photo and summarize the text. Encourage groups to share their captions with the class. AL **Visual/Spatial, Interpersonal**

R Reading Skills

Predicting Have students consider the negative impact of developing resources. **Ask:** **What are the negative effects of oil sands extraction?** *(The cost of extraction generally exceeds the benefits, land usually cannot be used for agriculture after extraction, and extraction can be harmful to wildlife.)* Before reading the third column of text on this page, have students predict how the causes of conflict between resource extraction companies and indigenous peoples might be resolved. **Logical/Mathematical**

ANSWERS, p. 142

Why Geography Matters

1. Paragraphs should show an understanding of how extraction impacts Canada's economy.
2. Indigenous peoples' food sources are harmed, and indigenous peoples have been forced to leave their land to make way for resource extraction.
3. Indian Oil and Gas Canada manages and regulates energy resources on indigenous peoples' lands. The Canadian government also works with indigenous peoples to address concerns over land rights.

Why Geography Matters: **Canada**

energy resources and indigenous rights

*As an energy-rich country, **Canada** has massive coal reserves and enough petroleum and natural gas to supply its population. Extracting these resources, however, affects local populations. In Canada's northern frontier, this often pits the rights of the indigenous peoples who live there against those involved in the extraction.*

What are the economic benefits of extracting energy resources?

Canada has the third-largest proven oil reserves in the world after Saudi Arabia and Venezuela. Canada's economy depends on the United States as an export market. Pipelines connect Canadian oil production regions with refining and export centers in the United States. Canada also has a surplus of natural gas and electricity available to export.

Energy reserves fuel economic growth. Besides profiting from exports, the Canadian economy benefits from the jobs created by the extraction of fossil fuels. Canadian households and businesses also enjoy access to an abundant supply of affordable energy. All of these factors boost the country's economic growth.

1. **Environment and Society** Write a paragraph making the case for the extraction of an energy resource.

What are the human and environmental impacts of extracting energy resources?

The three main sources of oil production in Canada are the oil sands of Alberta, the conventional resources in western Canada, and the offshore oil fields in the Atlantic. The oil sands currently produce the majority of Canadian oil. These "tar sands" require traditional pit mining for surface deposits, but extracting deeper reserves involves the injection of steam underground. Oil sands extraction is very energy intensive and poses environmental risks, such as oil spills from pipelines.

The cost of extraction to indigenous communities has generally exceeded any benefit they receive. Land usually cannot be used for agriculture after extraction. The wildlife upon which many indigenous peoples rely for food may also be harmed by extraction. Indigenous peoples have even been forced to leave their land so companies could use the land for resource extraction.

2. **Human Systems** Describe the causes of conflict between resource extraction companies and indigenous peoples.

How have groups worked together to address this issue?

The Canadian government has addressed land rights of some indigenous communities for years. Currently, the government has ownership of their reserves. Indian Oil and Gas Canada is a government organization that manages and regulates oil and gas resources on indigenous peoples' lands.

The government has also cooperated with indigenous peoples to address conflicts and concerns over land rights. In 2012 it held hearings over a challenge by the Athabasca Chipewyan to a tar sands project proposed by Shell Oil Canada. The hearings provided an opportunity for the Athabasca Chipewyan to voice their concerns about the environmental damage the project might cause to their lands.

3. **Human Systems** How can groups work together to ease the negative impacts of resource extraction?

(tl)Norm Betts/Bloomberg/Getty Images, (tc)Jeff Malet Photography/Newscom, (tr)Rick Madonik/Newscom

142

Project-Based Learning

Hands-On

Skits About Canada's Geographic Systems

Students will perform skits that bring together information from all lessons about the physical and human systems of Canada, as well as interactions between Canadians and the environment.

Digital Hands-On

Create Online Projects

Find an additional activity online that incorporates technology for this project. Visit the EdTech Teacher Web sites for more links, tutorials, and other resources.

THERE'S MORE ONLINE

EXPLORE a map of Canada's natural resources • *WATCH* a video about oil production in Canada

A CLOSER LOOK: ALBERTA

The Canadian province of Alberta is the source of most of Canada's mineral wealth. In addition to oil sands, it leads the nation in production of coal, natural gas, and crude oil. Alongside its resources, Alberta also has one of the largest indigenous populations in Canada. Nearly 200,000 indigenous people call Alberta home.

CRUDE OIL & TAR SANDS
COAL
NATURAL GAS
INDIGENOUS SETTLEMENTS

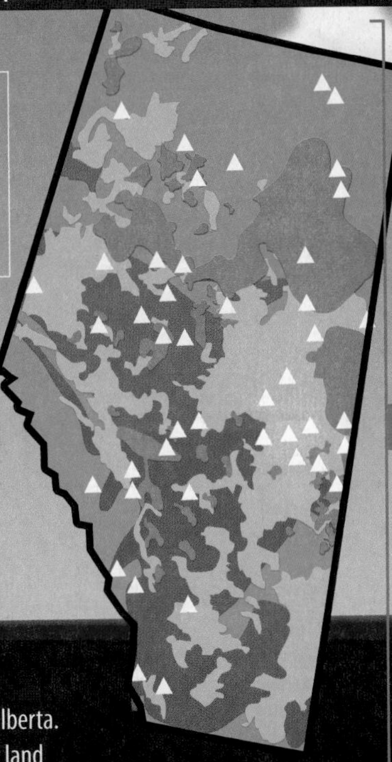

THE INDIGENOUS POPULATION

BLOOD TRIBE	SADDLE LAKE FIRST NATION	SAMSON CREE NATION	SIKSIKA NATION	LITTLE RED RIVER CREE NATION
7,555	5,883	5,550	3,634	3,341

Energy and Indigenous Rights in Alberta

There are over 5,000 square miles of indigenous reserves and settlements in Alberta. This, along with Alberta's vast mineral reserves, has led to some disputes over land rights and resource ownership. To attempt to resolve these disputes fairly, Alberta developed Canada's first mineral rights consultation policy in 2005.

CANADA'S ENERGY PRODUCTION

VERY LOW LOW MED HIGH VERY HIGH

TAR SANDS	1.5 MILLION BARRELS PER DAY	#1 RANK IN THE WORLD
OIL	1.2 MILLION BARRELS PER DAY	#20 RANK IN THE WORLD
COAL	68.2 MILLION METRIC TONNES PER YEAR	#14 RANK IN THE WORLD
NATURAL GAS	14.7 BILLION CUBIC FEET PER DAY	#3 RANK IN THE WORLD

INTERACTIVE MAP

Canada Oil and Natural Gas Pipelines

Determining Cause and Effect Use the interactive map of the oil and gas pipelines that travel between Canada and the United States to discuss the influences on the two countries' economies. Remind students that many project that Canada may have some of the richest natural energy resources in the world. Have students determine the negative and positive effects of the pipelines for both countries. AL **Verbal/Linguistic**

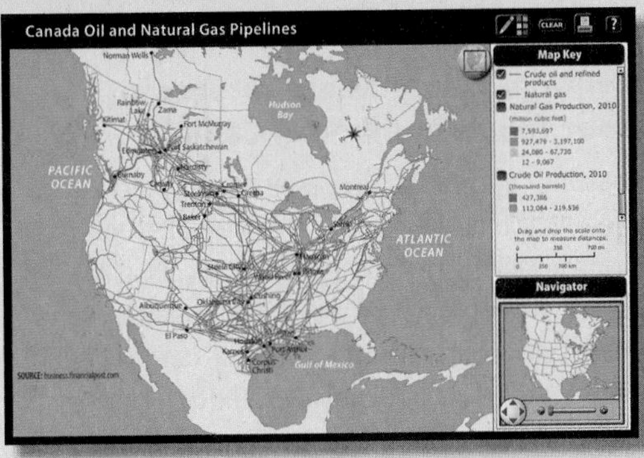

C Critical Thinking Skills

Considering Advantages and Disadvantages Have students consider both the positive and negative impacts of developing resources. **Ask:** **What has the Canadian government done to address the issue of resource extraction on indigenous peoples' lands?** *(The government has regulated oil and gas resources on indigenous peoples' lands and it has held hearings with indigenous peoples to address their concerns about the potential environmental damage a proposed tar sands project could cause.)* **Do you think the advantages of oil extraction outweigh the disadvantages? Why or why not?** *(Student answers will vary, but should cite examples from the text to support their responses. Sample answer: The advantages of oil extraction outweigh the disadvantages because of the economic importance of the resources to the region.)* Invite a small group of volunteers to research Canada's first indigenous mineral rights consultation policy in 2005. Then share their findings with the class. **Verbal/Linguistic**

R Reading Skills

Interpreting Have students work in pairs to discuss and interpret the bar graphs. Then have them consider which for of energy production resources might be the easiest and least expensive to extract and transport. Have pairs write a brief paragraph explaining their agreed-upon choice.
BL **Visual/Spatial, Interpersonal**

CLOSE & REFLECT

Paraphrasing To conclude the lesson, have students paraphrase the key concepts surrounding the issues of extracting Canada's energy resources and indigenous rights in a class discussion.

ENGAGE

R1 Reading Skills

Discussing After students read the *It Matters Because* text, have a volunteer review what is meant by the phrase *tectonic activity. (movement of Earth's plates and the impact of that movement on landforms over time)* Guide a discussion about the "natural wealth" that these landforms might provide. Have students consider how a country can gain wealth from its natural resources in a variety of industries. For example, forestland can provide lumber as well as benefit tourism due to people who visit a country for its natural beauty.

TEACH & ASSESS

R2 Reading Skills

Activating Prior Knowledge Ask students what they know about the Appalachian Mountains and the Rocky Mountains in the United States. *(Possible answer: The Appalachian Mountains run along the eastern part of the country from Maine to Alabama and are more rounded; the Rocky Mountains, or "the Rockies," stretch along the western part of the country, are taller; both are popular tourist destinations for outdoor activities such as hiking, camping and skiing.)* **Ask:** **In what part of Canada are the Appalachian Mountains located?** *(to the east of a central region of plains)* **Why are the Rocky Mountains described as "younger"?** *(They were formed later than the Appalachian Mountains, which are much older.)* **AL** **Logical/Mathematical**

V Visual Skills

Comparing and Contrasting Display a map of North America and have volunteers identify the Pacific Ranges and the Rocky Mountains in the United States and the Canadian Rockies. Discuss similarities and differences between the western part of the United States and the western region of Canada. Have students read the paragraph and work in pairs to complete a Venn diagram showing unique features of each region and features that are shared in both countries. **Ask:** **What do the Pacific Ranges and the Rocky Mountains have in common?** *(Both mountain ranges were formed by geologic forces that heaved slabs of rock upward.)* **Visual/Spatial**

ANSWERS, p. 144

TAKING NOTES: Landforms—mountains, plains, lowlands; **Water Systems**—freshwater lakes and rivers; **Climates, Biomes, and Resources**—continental, marine west coast, steppe, subarctic, tundra, ice cap, taiga climates; energy, minerals, timber, fish.

networks

There's More Online!

- **IMAGE** Grazing Bull Moose
- **MAP** Glaciers of the Last Ice Age
- **MAP** St. Lawrence Seaway System
- **INTERACTIVE SELF-CHECK QUIZ**
- **VIDEO** Physical Geography of Canada

LESSON 1
Physical Geography of Canada

ESSENTIAL QUESTION • *How do physical systems and human systems shape a place?*

Reading **HELP**DESK 

Academic Vocabulary (Tier Two Words)
- **series**
- **controversy**

Content Vocabulary (Tier Three Words)
- **timberline**
- **chinook**
- **tar sands**
- **fishery**
- **overfishing**
- **aquaculture**

TAKING NOTES: ***Key Ideas and Details***

CATEGORIZING As you read the lesson, use a graphic organizer like the one below to take notes on the physical geography of Canada.

Physical Geography of Canada		
Landforms	Water Systems	Climate, Biomes, and Resources

IT MATTERS BECAUSE

R1 *Canada is a country of great physical variety and natural wealth. This wealth includes breathtaking landforms shaped by water, wind, ice, and tectonic activity over millions of years. It also includes abundant water and energy resources as well as a variety of wildlife.*

Landforms

GUIDING QUESTION *How do landforms link the geography of Canada and the United States?*

Canada covers approximately the northern third of North America, stretching from the Pacific to the Atlantic. It is made up of 3 territories and 10 provinces. A province is a political unit similar to a state.

R2 Mountains on Canada's eastern and western edges cradle a central region of plains. When people first arrived on the plains, they found a sea of grass and dark, fertile soil that later became some of the world's most productive farmland. To the east of the plains stand the rocks of the Laurentian Highlands, the Canadian Shield, and the ancient, rounded Appalachian Mountains. To the west are the younger Rocky Mountains. A variety of climates are found in Canada, from the frozen tundra and cold, subarctic climates in the north to the steppe and humid continental climates along the border with the United States.

The western third of Canada is mountainous. Collisions between tectonic plates millions of years ago thrust up a **series** of sharp-peaked mountains called the Pacific Ranges. These ranges include the Cascade Range and the Coast Range. Mount Fairweather, on the border of Alaska and western British Columbia, at 15,300 feet (4,663 m) is one of the tallest coastal mountains in the world.

V Like the Pacific Ranges, the Rocky Mountains farther east grew as geologic forces heaved slabs of rock upward. The Rocky Mountains link the United States and Canada, stretching more than 3,000 miles (4,828 km) from New Mexico to Alaska. The Canadian Rockies extend northward from the Rockies in the United States.

East of the Rockies, the land falls in elevation and flattens into the Great Plains and Interior Lowlands, which extend across the center of

networks ***Online Teaching Options***

INTERACTIVE BELLRINGER

Average Yearly Temperatures in Four Towns in Alberta, Canada

Drawing Conclusions Use the introductory text to present the concept of climate and connect it to the map and table. Have students form small groups. Ask them to create a table that will help them draw conclusions about the climate in Alberta, Canada, similar to the table in the bellringer. The table should have three columns with the labels *Towns, Latitude,* and *Average Temperature.* Then have students use the information in the map and table to complete their tables and to answer the questions. Review the answers in a class discussion. **AL** **Interpersonal, Visual/Spatial**

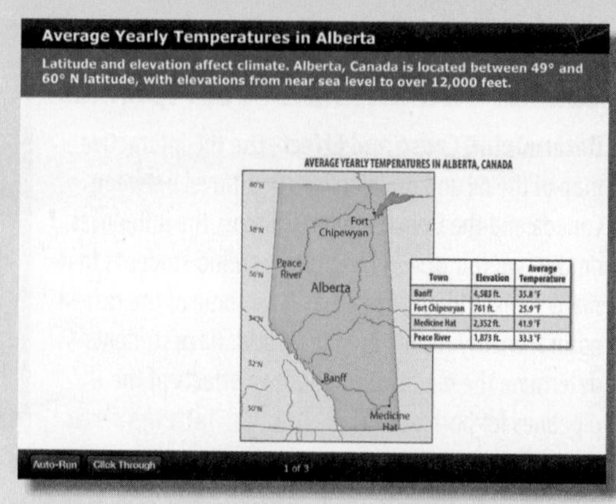

the region and south into the United States. These plains and lowlands are generally flat, but diverse in terms of landscape types. They can include hills, escarpments, low mountains, forests, and river valleys. Water from these lowlands drains into the Atlantic Ocean through the St. Lawrence River. The region was shaped by glacial activity during the last ice age. It therefore has deep arable soil that makes it important for agriculture.

series a number of things of the same type following one after the other in space or time

At the eastern edge of the Interior Lowlands lies the Canadian Shield. The Canadian Shield is a giant core of rock anchoring the continent and centered on Hudson Bay and James Bay. This stony land makes up the eastern half of Canada and parts of the northeastern United States. Erosion and glacial ice from the last ice age have smoothed the surface and created lakes, rivers, and streams. **R**

The heavily eroded Appalachian Mountains are North America's oldest mountains. They extend from Canada's Maritime Provinces south through the eastern United States to the state of Alabama. The Appalachians were formed by tectonic plate movements. Over time they were shaped by ice and running water. Coastal lowlands lie to the east of the Appalachians.

READING PROGRESS CHECK

Making Connections Why are landforms an important part of Canada's geography?

Water Systems

GUIDING QUESTION *How are water systems important to the Canadian economy?*

Freshwater lakes and rivers have helped make Canada prosperous. Abundant water satisfies the needs of cities and rural areas. It also provides power for homes and industries and moves resources across the country. The Mackenzie River, which flows from the Great Slave Lake to the Arctic Ocean, drains much of Canada's northern interior. The Fraser River flows southwest and drains into the Pacific Ocean just south of Vancouver. **C**

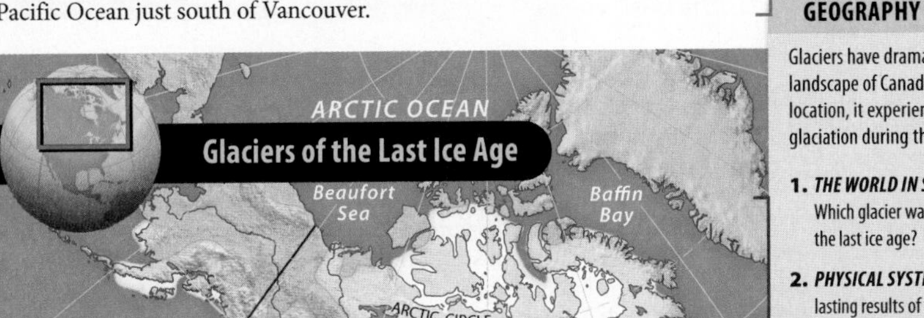

V

GEOGRAPHY CONNECTION

Glaciers have dramatically changed the landscape of Canada. Due to Canada's location, it experienced widespread glaciation during the last ice age.

1. ***THE WORLD IN SPATIAL TERMS*** Which glacier was the largest during the last ice age?
2. ***PHYSICAL SYSTEMS*** What are the lasting results of the glaciers, as seen in the landscape today?

R Reading Skills

Defining Before students read this page, write the word *shield* on the board and have students define it in their own words. Explain that the word *shield* can be used as a verb, as in "to protect from something," or as a noun meaning "something that acts as a protective cover or barrier." Then have students read the second paragraph, noting the definition of *Canadian Shield.* **Ask: How does the Canadian Shield relate to the definition of the word *shield*?** *(The Canadian Shield could be described as a shield made of rock.)* **AL ELL Verbal/Linguistic**

C Critical Thinking Skills

Understanding Relationships Discuss how Canada's lakes and rivers contribute to the country's economy. Guide students to understand the relationship between Canada's waterways and its economic wealth. **Ask: What are some ways that Canada's rivers and lakes have a positive impact on its economy?** *(transportation of goods along rivers, energy provided by hydroelectric power, tourism helped by recreational activities, provides drinking water supply)* **Interpersonal, Naturalist**

V Visual Skills

Analyzing Visuals Tell students that this map shows the extent of glaciation across Canada during the last ice age. **Ask: How did the glaciers of the last ice age affect Canada's land?** *(Glacial activity helped shape the land and ground rocks and other materials into soil. For example, land across the region near the St. Lawrence River has deep arable soil that is good for farming.)* Have students create a flowchart or diagram that shows the cause-and-effect relationship between glaciation and agriculture. **Visual/Spatial**

Content Background Knowledge

Canadian Glaciers Canada has a number of national parks, including the Glacier National Park of Canada, which is part of the Columbia Mountains Natural Region in British Columbia. It contains steep mountains with a variety of wildlife. The park offers a number of recreational activities such as cross-country skiing, hiking, camping, and fishing.

INTERACTIVE MAP

Glaciers of the Last Ice Age

Defining Use this map showing glacier coverage in Canada during the last Ice Age to discuss landscape changes. Explain past climate conditions and then lead students into a discussion of the current climate conditions on Earth. Based on this discussion, have students write a paragraph considering whether glaciers are likely to return to widespread areas in Canada. Tell students to support their answers using information in earlier chapters in the text.
ELL Verbal/Linguistic

ANSWERS, p. 145

READING PROGRESS CHECK Landforms determined where people could find productive farmland.

GEOGRAPHY CONNECTION

1. The Laurentide Ice Sheet was the largest glacier in Canada.
2. Glacial activity from the last ice age has smoothed the surface of the land and created lakes, rivers, and streams such as the Great Lakes.

V1 Visual Skills

Synthesizing Have students work with a partner to reinforce their understanding of the importance and impact of the St. Lawrence Seaway System. Provide each set of students a copy of the North America Outline Map, which is available online at the Teacher Resource Center. Have partners use the maps in their texts to label and name the key bodies of water that are connected by the St. Lawrence Seaway System. As students label their maps, have them summarize the ways in which the system contributes to the economy of the region. Have pairs collaborate with other pairs to compare their maps, checking for accuracy. **Visual/Spatial, Interpersonal**

T Technology Skills

Comparing and Contrasting Have students refer to a map of North America and compare the length of the St. Lawrence River to that of the Mississippi River in the United States. *(The St. Lawrence River is about 760 miles long; the Mississippi River is more than 2,000 miles long.)* Then have students conduct research to identify similarities and differences between the two rivers. Have students present the information in a short summary. Students may wish to present their findings in a visual display, such as a compare-and-contrast chart or Venn diagram. After students have presented their summaries, guide a brief discussion about the importance of the two rivers. **Logical/Mathematical, Visual/Spatial**

V2 Visual Skills

Describing Have students describe the process by which dams and lakes were formed in northern Canada. Working with a partner, have students create a flowchart or model to show the process by which one of the lakes mentioned in the text was formed. **Ask: How does the process differ between the way Great Bear Lake and Great Slave Lake were formed and the way the Great Lakes were formed?** *(Great Bear Lake and Great Slave Lake were formed by dams that were created by glacial ice. The Great Lakes were formed by moving glaciers that tore at the earth, leaving behind basins.)* **AL Visual/Spatial, Naturalist**

ANSWERS, p. 146

READING PROGRESS CHECK Homes and industries use hydroelectric power, and resources are moved on waterways.

GEOGRAPHY CONNECTION

1. The Gulf of St. Lawrence, the St. Lawrence River, Lake Ontario, Lake Erie, Lake Huron, Lake Michigan, and Lake Superior are connected by a series of canals and locks.
2. The St. Lawrence Seaway System carries over 45 million tons of cargo each year and reaches the interior of the nation to provide goods.

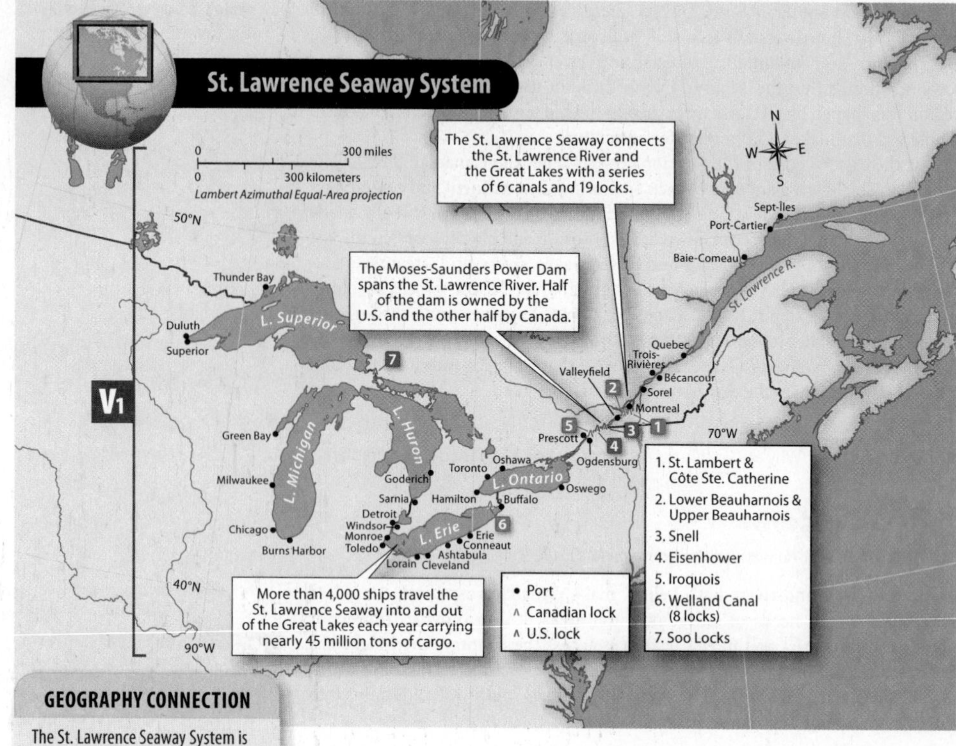

GEOGRAPHY CONNECTION

The St. Lawrence Seaway System is an important link in Canada's transportation network.

1. ***PLACES AND REGIONS*** List the bodies of water that are connected by the St. Lawrence Seaway System.
2. ***HUMAN SYSTEMS*** How does the system contribute to the economy of the region?

The St. Lawrence River flows about 760 miles (1,223 km) from Lake Ontario to the Gulf of St. Lawrence in the Atlantic. It forms part of Canada's border with the United States. The cities of Quebec, Montreal, and Ottawa grew up along the St. Lawrence and its tributaries. Niagara Falls, on the Niagara River, forms another part of the Canada-U.S. border. The falls are a key source of hydroelectric power.

In northern Canada, naturally occurring dams created by glacial ice formed Great Bear Lake and Great Slave Lake. Elsewhere, moving glaciers tore at the earth, leaving behind basins that became the Great Lakes. Deposits of coal, iron ore, and other minerals nearby favored industrial development and urban growth here.

READING PROGRESS CHECK

Identifying Central Issues How does water help the Canadian economy?

Climate, Biomes, and Resources

GUIDING QUESTION *What factors cause variations in climate and vegetation in Canada?*

Due to its great expanse of latitude, Canada experiences a large variation in climate and vegetation types. It varies from the bitter cold of the high-latitude areas to the radically changing seasons of the interior regions. Canada is characterized by biomes common to the midlatitude and high latitude.

Canada is rarely affected by natural weather hazards. The waters off the Pacific and Atlantic coasts are too cold to support hurricanes. Also, the extreme temperatures needed for thunderstorms, tornadoes, and hail are less common.

Russ Heinl/age fotostock

146

networks Online Teaching Options

INTERACTIVE MAP

St. Lawrence Seaway System

Comparing Use this map of the St. Lawrence Seaway System to discuss with students the connection between geography and local economics. Have students view the interactive map and answer the Geography Connection questions. Then lead a class discussion on the importance of waterway transportation. Ask students to explain how the St. Lawrence Seaway compares economically to the Mississippi River in the United States. *(Student answers will vary, but should include explanations that compare the transportation and economic advantages of both of these waterways.)* **BL Naturalist**

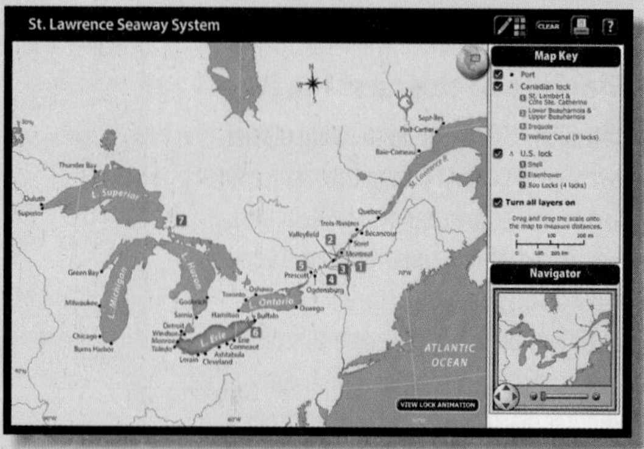

Climate Regions and Biomes

Ocean currents play a key role in Canada's climates. The Gulf Stream, for example, is a warm, northward-flowing ocean current off the southeastern coast of Canada. It moderates coastal temperatures and carries nutrients as far north as Newfoundland. Merging with the colder air and water of the southward-flowing Labrador Current off eastern Canada, the potential for fog-bound coastal conditions is always present. Off the Pacific coast, the cold Alaska Current flows southward and parallel to British Columbia. It churns up nutrients from the ocean floor, inviting whales to follow a moving feast during their migrations. **V**

Climate and vegetation are variable in the southern third of Canada—from about 40° N to 50° N latitude. The area's humid continental climate ranges from hot and humid to cool and wet. The farther north one travels, the more severe and snowy the winters become, with shorter and cooler summers. Coniferous evergreen trees tend to outnumber deciduous trees in the northernmost areas.

Canada's Pacific coast has a marine west coast climate. The Pacific Ranges force moist ocean air upward, where it cools and releases moisture, causing heavy rainfall. Winters are overcast and rainy. Summers are cloudless and cool, appealing to many varieties of warblers and other small birds that go north to nest. Ferns, mosses, and coniferous forests grow here. The soils in Canada's forests are quite acidic. This is due to the leaching (removal) of minerals out of the topsoil during rainfall. With fewer minerals, the soils are unfit for agriculture. The exceptions are the soils in the mixed and deciduous forests.

Areas between the Pacific Ranges and Rocky Mountains have a drier climate due to the rain shadow effect. This area has a semi-arid (steppe) climate, with grasslands and coniferous forests. Spruce and fir trees cover the middle elevations of the ranges. Beyond the **timberline**, the elevation above which trees cannot grow, lichens (LY• kuhns) and mosses are found. These higher elevations of the Canadian Rockies and Pacific Ranges are high-latitude climate regions. Rocky Mountain sheep, mountain goats, elk, mule deer, and black bears are common in the southern latitudes of these mountains. The semi-arid (steppe) climate predominates east of the Rocky Mountains, again because of the rain shadow effect. In addition, in spring, a warm, dry wind called the **chinook** (shuh•NUK) blows down the eastern slopes of the Rockies and melts the snow. **R**

In the north, there are subarctic, tundra, and ice cap climates. In these high-latitude climates, freezing temperatures are common all year because of a lack of direct sunlight. The amount and variety of vegetation is limited.

Boreal forest, also known as taiga, occupies the bulk of Canada's northern areas. It is the world's second-largest area of uninterrupted forest. The boreal forest has long winters and moderate to high precipitation each year. Covered mostly with coniferous evergreen trees, the region is an important source of pulpwood and lumber. The forest is also home to moose, black bears, beavers, Canada lynx, wolves, snowshoe hares, Canada jays, blue jays, crows, and ravens. **W**

Just south of the Arctic Circle lie the subarctic climate regions. These regions have Earth's widest temperature ranges, varying by as much as 120°F (49°C) from their bitterly cold winters to cool, short summers. In parts, only a thin layer of surface soil thaws each summer. Below is permanently frozen subsoil, or permafrost.

timberline elevation above which it is too cold for trees to grow

chinook a seasonal warm wind that blows down the Rockies in late winter and early spring

tar sands sand or sandstone naturally impregnated with petroleum

fishery an area in which fish or sea animals are caught

Chris Harris/age fotostock

A bull moose grazes in Bowron Lake Park in British Columbia.

▼ CRITICAL THINKING

1. ***Analyzing Visuals*** What features of the moose make it suited for its biome?
2. ***Speculating*** How might large populations of moose be a threat to the forests in some parts of Canada?

VIDEO

British Columbia

Supporting Perspectives Use this video to analyze the visual aspects of the landscape found in British Columbia, Canada. As students view the video, have them list the physical geography features they see in the video and provide any facts or statistics mentioned. After the video, have students use their lists to write a paragraph, from their perspective, on how these features make tourism an important economic activity in Canada. BL **Logical/Mathematical**

V Visual Skills

Demonstrating Organize students into small groups. Have students in each group work together to demonstrate the way ocean currents impact Canada's climates. Tell students to use the information presented in the text to show how currents move and their resulting impact on climates. Instruct students to use their bodies and sound effects, not words. For example, students may form two lines and then merge to show the Labrador Current, make the sound of a fog horn to demonstrate a fog-bound coast, or shiver and mime putting on a jacket to demonstrate a colder climate, and so on. Allow time for groups to prepare their current-climate skits before presenting them to the class. **Kinesthetic**

R Reading Skills

Using Context Clues Have students read the fourth paragraph, working with a partner to clarify pronunciation of unfamiliar words. Then have students use context clues to determine the meaning of words that they may find confusing. **Ask:** **What context clues help you understand the meaning of the word *coniferous*?** *("forests," "spruce and fir trees")* **What context clues tell you the meaning of the word *timberline*?** *("the elevation above which trees cannot grow")* Encourage students to look for context clues to help them identify word meanings as they read through the lesson. AL ELL **Verbal/Linguistic**

W Writing Skills

Informative/Explanatory Tell students they have been hired by the Canadian government to write a travel blog for its tourism Web site. Have students use the text to identify information that would be important for tourists visiting the boreal forest in Canada's northern region to know. Students may wish to conduct online research to embellish their travel blogs with information about safety and travel tips. For example, students may advise tourists about the best camping locations, or provide warnings about black bears such as the need to keep food in tightly sealed containers, and so on. Ask volunteers to share their travel blogs with the class and guide students to discuss the importance of Canada's boreal forest. AL **Verbal/Linguistic**

ANSWERS, p. 147

CRITICAL THINKING

1. The moose's coat keeps it warm during the long winters and its antlers help protect it from wolves.
2. The moose might consume large quantities of resources.

W Writing Skills

Argument Have students write an argumentative essay in which they defend a position about the extraction or development of natural resources in Canada. Students may wish to conduct additional research to provide supporting evidence for their arguments, but should cite any sources used in their research. Remind students about the importance of avoiding plagiarism by paraphrasing information and using quotation marks when directly citing sources. **Ask:** **How can extraction of crude oil have both a negative and positive impact?** *(Possible answer: Extraction of crude oil can have a positive impact by providing energy and economic value to the region, but it can also harm the environment and wildlife in the region.)*
BL **Verbal/Linguistic**

T Technology Skills

Gathering and Presenting Information After students read about Canada's timber and fishing resources, have them work in small groups to research the development of these resources and its impact. Have students present their findings in a slide show using presentation software. Tell students their presentations should answer the following questions: **How has development of the timber and fishing industries impacted Canada's economy? How has extraction of these natural resources impacted the surrounding environment? What efforts are being made to reduce damage caused to the ecosystems that have been negatively impacted?**

Remind students to use credible Web sites to gather the information. After students have presented their slide shows, guide a brief discussion about the impact of developing natural resources. **Logical/Mathematical, Visual/Spatial**

CLOSE & REFLECT

Assessing Have students work in pairs to ask and answer questions about Canada's physical geography based on what they have learned in this lesson. Suggest that partners divide lesson content according to each heading to quiz each other about Canada's landforms, water systems, climates, biomes, and resources.

ANSWERS, p. 148

READING PROGRESS CHECK Some of Canada's natural energy resources are coal, petroleum, including crude oil found in the Athabasca Tar Sands, and natural gas.

Connecting Geography Countries could export seafood, providing a new source of income for their citizens.

Connecting Geography to SCIENCE

Biology

Using aquaculture, fish can be raised in concrete or earthen ponds, coastal pools, or floating cages in the open ocean, where they are protected from predators and environmental hazards. Aquaculture is an important industry in Canada. People raise Atlantic salmon, cod, tilapia, rainbow trout, and more. The industry provides income and jobs and can help meet the increasing global demand for seafood and restore threatened wild populations of species.

HYPOTHESIZING How might aquaculture provide economic benefits for countries lacking land-based resources for international trade? RH.9–10.8

A few needled evergreens survive here, along with herds of woodland caribou that are endangered in some areas.

Closer to the North Pole is the tundra climate region. Winter darkness and bitter cold last for months, and the brief summer period brings only limited warming effects. The layer of thawed soil is even thinner here than in the subarctic, with vegetation limited to low bushes, short grasses, mosses, and lichens. Winter temperatures can fall to –70°F (–57°C).

Natural Resources

W Abundant natural resources such as energy, minerals, timber, and fish have made Canada wealthy. Their extraction, however, has led to depletion and environmental problems. Energy resources include coal, petroleum, and natural gas. Canada's petroleum and natural gas reserves lie largely in or near Alberta. The Athabasca **Tar Sands** contain large deposits of extremely heavy crude oil, much of which is in semisolid form. Large inputs of energy and water are required to transform these substances into synthetic crude oil for use by humans.

Mineral resources are also plentiful in Canada. The Rocky Mountains yield gold, silver, and copper. Parts of the Canadian Shield are rich in iron ore and nickel. Canada's mineral inventory includes 33 percent of the world's production of potash (a mineral salt used in fertilizers), 4 percent of its copper and gold, and 5 percent of its silver. Because mining involves heavy equipment, uses large quantities of water, and moves a great deal of rock and other natural materials, it can damage land, water, and air systems.

T Timber is a vital resource in Canada. Trees once covered much of Canada. Today, forests cover only about 34 percent of the country. Trees are a renewable resource, but only if people take steps to protect forests and their ecosystems. Cutting down trees can have a negative effect on the other plants and animals. Many species have been lost. Positive efforts to preserve forests include replanting trees, cooperating to protect the many species of native forest animals facing extinction, and preserving old-growth forests.

The coastal Atlantic and Pacific waters have long been important **fisheries**, or places for catching fish and other sea animals. The Grand Banks, once one of the world's richest fishing grounds, covers about 139,000 square miles (360,000 sq. km) of Canada's southeast coast. In recent years, **overfishing** has caused fish stocks to drop dangerously. Canada is now working to protect key species. **Aquaculture**, or fish farming, is a growing economic activity. This has caused some **controversy**, as crowded conditions can lead to disease among farmed species. The industry is working to minimize risks to consumers.

overfishing harvesting fish to the point that species are depleted and the value of the fishery reduced

aquaculture the cultivation of seafood

controversy the presence of opposing views

READING PROGRESS CHECK

Specifying What are Canada's natural energy resources?

LESSON 1 REVIEW

Reviewing Vocabulary (Tier Three Words)

1. ***Summarizing*** Explain the significance of timberline, chinook, fishery, overfishing, aquaculture, and tar sands. RH.9–10.4

Using Your Notes

2. ***Listing*** Using your notes from the graphic organizer, describe the major Canadian landforms.

Answering the Guiding Questions

3. ***Applying*** How do landforms link the geography of Canada and the United States?

4. ***Analyzing*** How are water systems important to the Canadian economy?

5. ***Identifying*** What factors cause variations in climate and vegetation in Canada?

Writing Activity

6. ***Informative/Explanatory*** Write a short paragraph explaining how tectonic forces have influenced landscapes in Canada. WHST.9–10.2

148

LESSON 1 REVIEW ANSWERS

Reviewing Vocabulary

1. The timberline is the elevation above which trees cannot grow. The chinook is a seasonal warm, dry wind that melts snow. Fisheries are coastal waters where fish are caught. Overfishing causes fish stocks to drop. Aquaculture is when fish are raised on fish farms. Tar sands are areas of sand containing petroleum.

Using Your Notes

2. Landforms include the Pacific Ranges and the Rocky Mountains in the west and the Canadian Shield and Appalachian Mountains in the east.

Answering the Guiding Questions

3. Canada and the United States are linked by the Rocky Mountains in the west, the Great Plains and Interior Lowlands in the center, and the Canadian Shield and Appalachian Mountains in the east.

4. Water provides hydroelectric power to homes and industries, resources are moved on waterways, and cities grew up along the St. Lawrence River and its tributaries.

5. One factor is Canada's great expanse of latitude encompasses many climate zones. Ocean currents are also a factor.

Writing Activity

6. Collisions between tectonic plates millions of years ago created the Pacific Ranges and the Rocky Mountains. The Appalachians were formed by tectonic plate movements.

networks

There's More Online!

- **GRAPH** Annual Growth Rate of Canadian Industries
- **IMAGE** Inuit People
- **TIME LINE** Canada: Expansion and Diversity
- **INTERACTIVE SELF-CHECK QUIZ**
- **VIDEO** Human Geography of Canada

LESSON 2

Human Geography of Canada

ESSENTIAL QUESTION • *How do physical systems and human systems shape a place?*

Reading **HELP**DESK 

Academic Vocabulary (Tier Two Words)

- **trace**
- **advocate**

Content Vocabulary (Tier Three Words)

- **Inuit**
- **First Nations**
- **dominion**
- **Quebecois**
- **separatism**
- **Loyalist**
- **emigrate**

TAKING NOTES: ***Key Ideas and Details***

IDENTIFYING As you read the lesson, use a graphic organizer like the one below to take notes on the human geography of Canada.

Human Geography of Canada

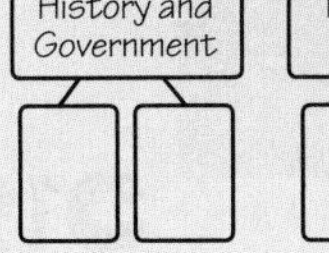

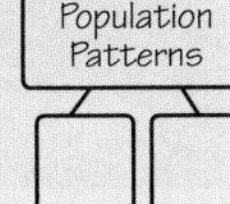

It Matters Because

Diversity has been important in shaping Canada. The indigenous peoples who have lived on the land for centuries, the French and British colonists who settled the area later, and the waves of immigrants from Europe, Asia, Africa, and Latin America have all influenced the human geography of this country. C2

History and Government

GUIDING QUESTION *How did British and French cultures influence Canada's history?*

Many Canadians can **trace** their roots back to countries from around the world. Some are descendants of the country's native peoples. Their earliest ancestors arrived in North America thousands of years ago. R

Unity, Expansion, and Diversity

About 200,000 native peoples were living in what is now Canada when Europeans arrived off the coast of Newfoundland in 1497. In the next 200 years the native populations declined, as Europeans claimed their lands and diseases from Europe spread. After 1950 high birthrates and access to improved medical care contributed to population growth.

The main indigenous groups that exist in Canada today are the **Inuit**, the Métis, and **First Nations** peoples. The Inuit are the indigenous people of the Canadian Arctic. Métis are persons who have both indigenous and French Canadian ancestry. *First Nations* is a term that refers to indigenous peoples of Canada who are neither Inuit nor Métis. The current population of First Nations peoples is about 700,000 of the 1.25 million indigenous people in Canada today. T

French explorers helped establish claims to land in the region in the early 1600s. This land was named New France, and part of it became the province of Quebec. Territorial rivalry between Great Britain and France began in 1670, when the British chartered the Hudson's Bay Company to seek a northwest passage to the Pacific Ocean. A clash of French and British interests along the Atlantic coast led to wars.

Britain and France were first drawn to the North American continent to gain riches from precious metals and beaver pelts that came mainly from the Atlantic coast. Exploration inland soon followed, however.

networks ***Online Teaching Options***

 **INTERACTIVE BELLRINGER**

Indigenous Population in Canada

Reading Graphs and Calculating Use the bar graph to explore population statistics about the indigenous population in Canadian provinces and territories. One purpose of this activity is to help students understand the difference between the percentage of a population and the total number in a population. Have students work with a partner. Each pair will need to use a calculator. Have students discuss each question and identify how to solve it. Then in a class discussion, have pairs share their answers. **Logical/Mathematical, Verbal/Linguistic**

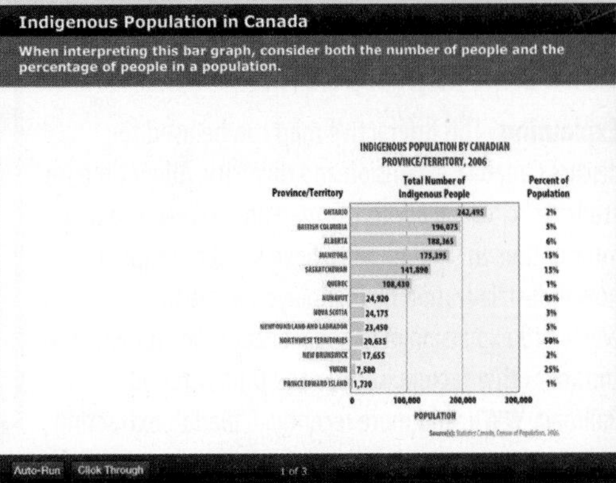

ENGAGE

C1 Critical Thinking Skills

Making Generalizations Direct students to examine the images at the top of the page. **Ask: What is a general statement you could make about Canada's human geography based on these images?** *(Possible answer: Canada has a diverse population with a rich cultural history.)* Lead a class discussion about the similarities and differences between the human geography of Canada and the United States. Ask students to use the images to consider historical, cultural, and economic features of each country.

TEACH & ASSESS

C2 Critical Thinking Skills

Formulating Questions Have students write a list of questions they have about the human geography of Canada. Guide students with topics to consider such as attending school in Canada, government and politics, entertainment, culture, languages, and the arts. Encourage students to write answers to their questions as they read through the lesson. **Intrapersonal**

R Reading Skills

Using Correct Terminology and Grammar Have a volunteer define the words *descendants* and *ancestors*. Explain that *descendants* is used in the text as a noun, meaning "people who come from a common stock or family" and that *ancestor* is a noun derived from the Latin word *praedecessor,* meaning "one that goes before." In the text, the word *ancestor* is used to mean "from whom a person or group is descended." **ELL Verbal/Linguistic**

T Technology Skills

Researching Organize students into three groups and assign each group one of the three main indigenous groups now in Canada to research: Inuit, the Métis, and First Nations peoples. Have them organize the information they find into a short presentation that they can share with the rest of the class. **BL Verbal/Linguistic**

ANSWERS, p. 149

TAKING NOTES: Possible answers: **History and Government**—Quebec Act passed by the British in 1774; **Population Patterns**—1400s: About 200,000 native peoples were living in Canada when Europeans arrived, native populations decline in next 200 years.

R Reading Skills

Analyzing Text Structure Have students reread the information in the paragraphs. **Ask:** What type of text structure is used in these paragraphs? *(chronological)* Why do you think the author organizes the information this way? *(The text deals with many important dates and events, so placing them in chronological order helps readers better comprehend the series of events that took place in Canada's history.)* Suggest that students create a time line—either horizontal as shown on the bottom of the page, or vertical—noting important dates and events as they read. Tell students to use their time lines as a study tool when reviewing the lesson.
AL Verbal/Linguistic

C Critical Thinking Skills

Identifying Cause and Effect Have students consider the French influence on Canada's history and culture. **Ask:** What caused Canada's population to change in the 1800s? *(After Canada acquired lands, the British government encouraged immigration and more than a million people arrived from Great Britain.)* What was a result of these population changes? *(The French-speaking citizens became a minority, which in turn strengthened French nationalism among Quebecois.)* **Verbal/Linguistic**

V Visual Skills

Time, Chronology, and Sequencing Have students work with a partner to develop questions based on the dates and events on the first half of the time line. Tell students to take turns quizzing each other on facts related to Canada's history of expansion and diversity between 1776 and 1900. Their questions could include: What group settled in Canada in 1776? *(loyalist refugees from the American War of Independence)* What happened to Canada's population in the 1800s? *(It grew due to the arrival of thousands of immigrants as well as the gold rush.)* **Visual/Spatial, Interpersonal**

trace to follow or study in detail or step by step

Inuit a member of the Arctic native peoples of North America; once known as Eskimo

First Nation one of the indigenous peoples of Canada who are neither Inuit nor Métis

dominion a partially self-governing country with close ties to another country

Quebecois Quebec's French-speaking inhabitants

Both European powers sought to claim more resources and more colonies. The British eventually drove the French from the Hudson Bay area, capturing Quebec in 1759 and winning control of New France in 1763. The Quebec Act, passed by the British in 1774, gave French settlers the right to keep their language, religion, and laws. The act also extended Canadian territory south to the Ohio River. This angered American colonists and brought them closer to war with the British.

R During the early 1800s, English- and French-speaking communities feuded over colonial government policies. Fears of a takeover by the United States, however, forced both to work together. In 1867 the colonies of Quebec, Ontario, Nova Scotia, and New Brunswick united as provinces of the **Dominion** of Canada, a new country within the British Empire. Manitoba, British Columbia, Alberta, Saskatchewan, Prince Edward Island, and Newfoundland became provinces over the next 100 years.

Canada was created as a dominion, a partially self-governing country with close ties to Great Britain. It gained full independence in 1931, but the British government kept the right to approve changes to Canada's constitution. This legislative link to Great Britain finally ended in 1982 with passage of the Constitution Act. Today, Canada is a constitutional monarchy.

C The executive part of Canada's federal government includes the governor-general, the prime minister, and the cabinet. The British monarch serves as the head of state and appoints a governor-general to act in his or her place. The national legislature, or Parliament, includes the Senate and the House of Commons. Canada's prime minister is the actual head of government. Nine judges sit on the Supreme Court of Canada, the country's highest court.

In the 1800s, Canada acquired lands stretching from the Atlantic to the Pacific and from the Arctic to the U.S. border. The British government encouraged immigration to Canada. Between 1815 and 1855, a million people arrived from Great Britain. This made the French-speaking citizens a minority and fueled French nationalism among **Quebecois** (kay•beh•KWAH), Quebec's French-speaking inhabitants. This nationalism has been present throughout Canada's history.

Widespread immigration from other parts of the world began in Canada in the late 1800s. Some came for the Klondike Gold Rush, but many more were attracted by the fertile soil of the prairies of Alberta, Saskatchewan, and Manitoba.

TIME LINE

CANADA Expansion and Diversity

Canada's history features steady expansion and multiculturalism.

▶ **CRITICAL THINKING**
1. ***Identifying*** What are two events that show how or why Canada's settlement expanded?
2. ***Explaining*** How has Canada attempted to address past mistreatment of native peoples?

V 1776 → 1900

1776 Loyalist refugees from the American War of Independence settle in Canada.

1800s Thousands of immigrants from England, Scotland, and Ireland arrive each year.

1885 Canadian Pacific Railroad is completed.

1898 Gold rush along upper Yukon River; Yukon Territory is given separate status.

150

networks Online Teaching Options

INTERACTIVE MAP

Canadian Explorations

Explaining This interactive map can be used to discuss Canada's expansion and diversity. Allow time for students to interact with the map and to read the text information. In small groups, have students explain how industrialization further played a role in the westward expansion of Canada. Encourage students to consider other factors, such as the Underground Railroad, WWII, and more recently, Canada's extracting of natural resources. Ask groups to create an agreed-upon explanation that predicts where, when, and why areas of Canada will continue to expand.
BL Logical/Mathematical, Interpersonal

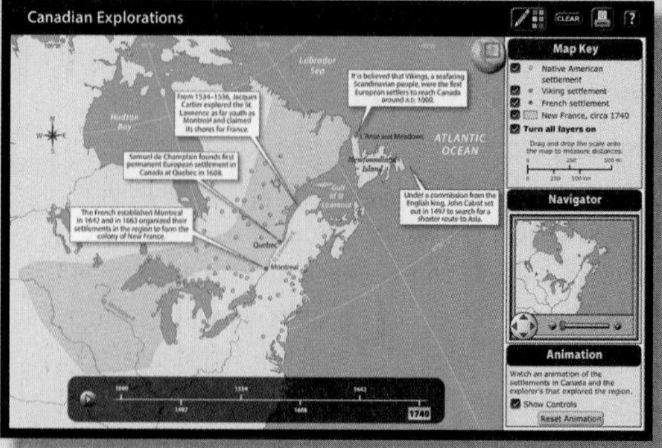

ANSWERS, p. 150

CRITICAL THINKING
1. Two events are the gold rush and completion of the Canadian Pacific Railroad.
2. The Truth and Reconciliation Commission began hearings about past policies harmful to indigenous peoples and their cultural identities.

Immigrants from Germany, Scandinavia, Ukraine, Japan, and China arrived to settle the land. In the 1800s Canada also sheltered African Americans who had escaped slavery in the United States. Canada never practiced slavery. These refugees, many of whom escaped via the Underground Railroad, were safely beyond the reach of American laws once they arrived in Canada.

Westward expansion in Canada came at a price, however, as immigrants pushed First Nations peoples off their lands. The injustice was formally recognized in 1998, when the Canadian government apologized to native peoples for their mistreatment. The government established a "healing fund" to make reparations. **W**

In the 1900s Canada became an industrialized, urban country. Mineral resources were utilized, and hydroelectric projects and transportation systems were developed. World War II stimulated the economy, making it a crucial military and industrial power. After the war, Canada sought to improve federal assistance to its citizens through pensions, unemployment insurance, and medical care.

Modern Challenges

The United States has more trade with Canada than any other country. Being neighbors and sharing a border has permitted international trade that is beneficial to the economies of both countries. In 1994 the North American Free Trade Agreement (NAFTA) eliminated tariffs and other trade barriers between Canada, Mexico, and the United States. Although the open border and a history of cooperation have benefited both countries, some Canadians continue to dislike the effect free trade has had on their culture. Canadians struggle to maintain a separate identity while being bombarded by U.S. popular culture. **C**

Conflicts continue as French-speaking Canadians seek greater protection for their language and culture. Many desire Quebec's independence and strongly support **separatism**—the breaking away of one part of a country to create a separate, independent country. In 2012 members from the Parti Québécois, a political party in Quebec that **advocates**—or publicly supports—separatism, were elected to political office in Quebec. **T**

separatism the breaking away of one part of a country to create a separate, independent country

advocate to publicly recommend or support

☑ READING PROGRESS CHECK

Identifying What factors led to the decline of the native populations of Canada?

1982 Great Britain transfers final legal powers to Canada. A new constitution is adopted.

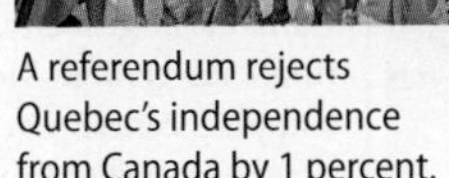

1998 A referendum rejects Quebec's independence from Canada by 1 percent.

2010 Truth and Reconciliation Commission begins hearings about past policies harmful to indigenous peoples and their cultural identities.

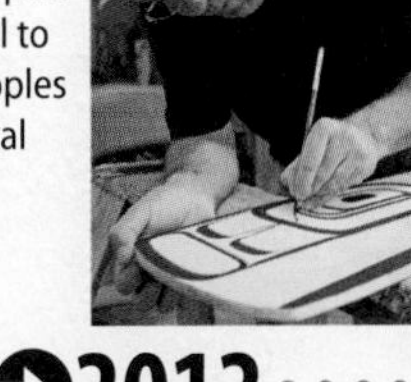

1992 North American Free Trade Agreement (NAFTA) enacted

1999 Nunavut is formed, becoming the first Canadian territory with a majority indigenous population.

➔2012

2012 Prime Minister Harper calls for fresh start in government relations with First Nations peoples. **V**

VIDEO

War of Words

Making Connections Use this video about French and English language laws to discuss the culture and history of language in Canada. Tell students this video was filmed before 2012, when the Official Language Act was passed in Canada, and that businesses now have the right to use either English or French. Have students form groups to discuss the Canadian language issue and how Canada's issue is similar to or different from the language issue in the United States, where the two most commonly spoken languages are English and Spanish. Ask groups to decide if "language police" might be used in the United States in the future. **Verbal/Linguistic**

W Writing Skills

Informative/Explanatory Have students consider the long-term impact immigration has had on indigenous peoples in Canada. Then have them write a short essay that draws comparisons between the way Native Americans have been treated throughout U.S. history and the plight of First Nations peoples in Canada. Review the information about western expansion in the United States during the 1800s provided in the previous chapter. Encourage students to conduct online research to provide supporting evidence for their essays. **Verbal/Linguistic**

C Critical Thinking Skills

Considering Advantages and Disadvantages Guide a class discussion about the advantages and disadvantages of NAFTA. **Ask:** **What are the benefits of NAFTA gained by Canada, Mexico, and the United States?** *(NAFTA eliminated tariffs and other trade barriers, so the agreement provides economic advantages for companies and industries involved in trade.)* **Do you agree with criticism of NAFTA by some Canadians seeking to maintain its national identity?** *(Student answers may vary, but should include either the economic and cultural advantages or disadvantages.)* **AL** **Logical/Mathematical**

T Technology Skills

Creating and Analyzing Arguments Discuss the ongoing conflicts involving French-speaking Canadians and their separatist viewpoints. Have students choose a position either for or against separatism. Tell students to read online articles about the issue and gather information to prepare arguments for a debate in which they defend or refute separatism and provide evidence to support their reasoning. Moderate a classroom debate in which students present each side of the issue. Then have students evaluate each other's arguments. **BL** **Verbal/Linguistic**

V Visual Skills

Time, Chronology, and Sequencing Have students work with the same partner they performed the time line activity on the previous page to formulate questions based on the dates and events on the second half of the time line. Tell students to take turns quizzing each other on facts related to Canada's history between 1982 and 2012. **Visual/Spatial, Interpersonal**

ANSWERS, p. 151

☑ READING PROGRESS CHECK Europeans claimed the lands of native populations and brought diseases from Europe.

W Writing Skills

Narrative Tell students they have been selected by the Canadian tourism bureau to compete in a song-writing contest in which the winning song will be used in a series of advertisements to promote tourism. Encourage musically inclined students to perform their songs for the class with vocal or instrumental accompaniment. **Auditory/Musical**

V1 Visual Skills

Creating Charts Have students read the information about the diverse ethnic origins of Canadians. Have students work with a partner to create a circle graph that shows the breakdown of Canada's different ethnic groups. Students may conduct online research by visiting Web sites such as the CIA World Factbook. Examples of circle graphs are available online at the Teacher Lesson Center. **Visual/Spatial, Logical/Mathematical**

V2 Visual Skills

Spatial Analysis Have students read the information about Canada's population density and percentages. Then have students work in pairs or small groups to depict the information visually in a map. Students' maps should show the spatial relationship between climate, resources, and population. Ask volunteers to present their maps to the class. **ELL Visual/Spatial, Logical/Mathematical**

C Critical Thinking Skills

Analyzing Cause and Effect Discuss with students the reasons that a large percentage of Canada's population lives in urban areas. **Ask: Why is Canada's population higher in the Great Lakes region and areas near the St. Lawrence lowlands?** *(These regions support agriculture, fishing, and trade, especially along the St. Lawrence River, which offers transportation of goods via cargo ships.)* **Verbal/Linguistic**

ANSWERS, p. 152

READING PROGRESS CHECK Rugged terrain and an Arctic climate make much of Canada difficult to settle; about 90 percent of the population lives along the U.S.-Canada border. More densely populated areas are clustered near waterways and in places that support agriculture, fishing, and trade.

CRITICAL THINKING

1. Many Inuit live in settlements of 25 to 500 people, with a few larger towns.
2. It was important for the Inuit people because it gave them land of their own from which they could not be forced.

Population Patterns

GUIDING QUESTION *What explains Canada's diverse mix of people and settlement patterns?*

Canada is a highly developed country with bustling cities. It also has sparsely populated areas of beautiful, pristine wilderness. These rugged natural areas sometimes have difficulty supporting communities. But they are as much a part of the country's cultural identity as are the busy metropolitan areas.

Nunavut is the cultural and economic homeland for the Inuit people. Today, about 25,000 Inuit from the Arctic live mostly in settlements of 25 to 500 people, with just a few larger towns. In recent decades, mining, oil exploration, and pipeline construction, along with a decline in the demand for fur, have increased their reliance on government services.

Immigrants to Canada came in search of political and religious freedom, economic and educational opportunities, and refuge from wars. For example, **Loyalists**, or American colonists who remained loyal to the British government, fled to Canada after the American Revolution. They settled in the Maritime Provinces of Nova Scotia, New Brunswick, and Prince Edward Island. Some immigrant groups settled in areas that let them keep their familiar ways of life.

Loyalist an American colonist who remained loyal to the British government

The ethnic origins of Canadians vary from province to province. Today, more than one-fourth of Canadians identify themselves as being of mixed ethnic origins. In addition, more than 1 million or 4 percent of all Canadians identify themselves as of North American Indian, Inuit, or Métis ancestry.

Rugged terrain and a cold arctic climate with a short growing season make much of Canada difficult for human settlement. About 90 percent of the population lives within 100 miles (160 km) of the U.S.-Canada border. Average population density is about 9 people per square mile (3 people per sq. km). More densely populated areas are clustered near the coasts, the Great Lakes, and in places that support agriculture, fishing, and trade. Over the past 100 years, most internal migration has been westward to the Prairie Provinces of Manitoba, Saskatchewan, and Alberta. This move was due in part to the discovery of oil and natural gas since the 1960s.

According to 2012 estimates, 70 percent of the country's population is between the ages of 15 and 64. Since Canadians enjoy a long life expectancy and low infant mortality rates, Canada has an aging population. This presents economic challenges, as a larger share of the population reaches retirement and requires more government-funded health care.

Approximately 81 percent of Canada's 34 million inhabitants live in urban areas. These urban areas developed in places with intensive commercial agriculture in the Great Lakes and St. Lawrence lowlands areas. Smaller settlements were merged into larger metropolitan areas. Today, these cities are important centers for commerce, education, and transportation. As Canada's largest city, Toronto is an industrial and financial center. Montreal is an industrial and shipping center. On the Pacific coast, Vancouver handles nearly all of the trade between Canada and Asia. Edmonton grew with the development of the petroleum industry.

Nunavut, home to many Inuit people, was established as a separate territory in 1999.

Eric Baccega/age fotostock

CRITICAL THINKING

1. ***Describing*** What kinds of settlements do many Inuit people live in?
2. ***Drawing Conclusions*** Why do you think it was important for the Inuit people to have Nunavut declared a separate territory?

READING PROGRESS CHECK

Paraphrasing How has Canada's physical geography influenced its settlement patterns?

networks Online Teaching Options

IMAGE

First Nations and the Inuit Peoples

Hypothesizing Use this image to discuss ethnic politics and divisions within the nation of Canada. Remind students that for years the Quebecois have had their own province, and have agitated for nationhood. However, the Inuit people have not had an equivalent push for Inuit independence, at least on the same scale. Have the students write down three possible explanations for this situation. Invite volunteers to share their explanations with the class. **BL Verbal/Linguistic**

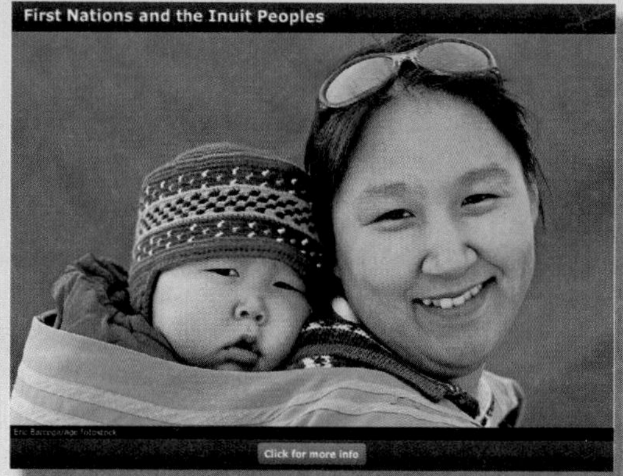

Society and Culture Today

GUIDING QUESTION *Why is Canada often called a multicultural society?*

Canada has a truly multicultural society, largely due to immigration. There are many reasons people decide to **emigrate**, or leave their countries to settle in another. Canada's high standard of living and government policies protecting multiculturalism are appealing to people of diverse ethnic origins. Historically these immigrants have arrived primarily from Europe. Recent migration patterns, however, feature large increases in immigration from Asia and Central and South America, and an overall decrease in immigration from Europe.

Language and religion reflect Canada's diverse immigrant population. There are two official languages—English and French. The British introduced English to most of Canada. In the province of Quebec, however, French was established as the dominant language. Languages spoken also include German, Italian, and Chinese. Native languages include Cree and Inuktitut, the language of the Inuit. Christians make up the largest religious group in Canada. Other religions practiced in Canada by small minorities include Islam, Buddhism, Hinduism, Judaism, and Sikhism.

Education and health care are supported by the government. The literacy rate in Canada is 99 percent, and there is an extensive network of public and private schools. Attending school is required for children ages 6 to 16. Each province is responsible for organizing and administering public education. The federal government sets standards, with each province responsible for financing and managing its own system. In some cases, rising costs resulting in part from an aging population have created a need to limit benefits or raise taxes.

Family and Status of Women

Today, the average Canadian family contains three members. Two parents live in 67 percent of Canadian families, but the percentage is decreasing just as in the United States. The overall composition of the Canadian family is changing and families have fewer children. Since women are increasingly joining the Canadian workforce, there are a growing number of dual-income households.

The government of Canada has passed several laws protecting the rights of women. The Status of Women in Canada (SWC) was created in 1971 to increase women's participation and equality in all aspects of life. In 1982 the Canadian Charter of Rights and Freedom ensured gender equality in employment, public life, and education. Canadian women have the same literacy rate as men and outnumber men in getting secondary and university-level educations. They still, however, face barriers to equality in the labor market.

The Arts

The arts in Canada have been influenced primarily by native and European cultures. For example, First Nations artists combine old and modern techniques with traditional color schemes and motifs that often relate to the natural world. In the twentieth century, museums and scholars began to focus on art created by native peoples. Immigration has also added distinctive features to Canadian art.

French explorers, missionaries, and settlers wrote the earliest Canadian literature. Their writings had strong historical and religious themes. Popular modern Canadian fiction writers include Margaret Atwood, author of *The Handmaid's Tale*, and Yann Martel, author of *Life of Pi*.

Toronto is highly regarded in the realms of theater and music. It is the third-largest production center in the English-speaking world, after London and New York City. The world-renowned Toronto Symphony Orchestra and the top-ranked National Ballet of Canada call Toronto home.

Canada Slips in Gender Equality Rankings

"Canada is losing ground in a key global measure of gender equality, sliding out of the world's top 20 chiefly due to a lack of female representation in politics.

'In the future, talent will be more important than capital or anything else,' said Klaus Schwab, the forum's [World Economic Forum] founder and executive chairman. 'To develop the gender dimension is not just a question of equality; it is the entry card to succeed and prosper in an ever more competitive world.'"

—Tavia Grant, *The Globe and Mail*, October 24, 2012

DBQ ***IDENTIFYING CENTRAL ISSUES*** What is the chief cause of Canada's slide from the world's top 20 in gender equality? RH.9–10.1

emigrate to leave one's own country to settle permanently in another

CHAPTER 6, Lesson 2
Human Geography of Canada

R Reading Skills

Applying Direct students' attention to the term *emigrate.* Clarify the terms *emigrate* and *immigrate.* Explain that a person who emigrates leaves his or her own country to settle in a different country. The word *immigrate* means "to come into a country, usually to become established." Tell students that one way to distinguish between the two words is to think of the word *into* for immigrate and *exit* for emigrate. Have students write three sentences using each word. Challenge students to use both words in one sentence. **ELL** **Verbal/Linguistic**

W Writing Skills

Narrative Organize students into groups of varying sizes. Tell each group to use information about family life in Canada to write, rehearse, and perform a short skit that portrays daily life of a Canadian family. Tell students to consider the overall composition of today's Canadian family, how it is changing, and the impact of those changes. Allow time for students to prepare their skits before presenting them to the class. **Kinesthetic, Musical/Auditory**

T Technology Skills

Explaining Continuity and Change Review the information about women's rights in Canada with students and then have them consider women's rights issues in the United States. As homework, have students conduct additional research to identify how, or if, the United States government has made steps to ensure gender equality. Tell students their research should identify whether bias exists for women in the workplace, public life, and education. Then have students write a short essay that compares and contrasts women's rights in the United States and Canada. Essays should also describe changes made in an effort to ensure gender equality. **BL** **Verbal/Linguistic**

GAME

Human Geography of Canada

Monitoring Use this game to discuss Canada's ethnic diversity. Allow students to work in pairs to complete the crossword puzzle. Then lead a class discussion about the diversity of the immigrants that came to Canada during the 1800 and 1900s and how indigenous people struggle to keep their culture and traditions alive. Encourage students to consider other factors, such as the recent immigration from Asia and Central and South America, education and health care systems that are government funded, and more advanced transportation systems that has lead Canada to become a diverse multicultural society. **AL** **Verbal/Linguistic**

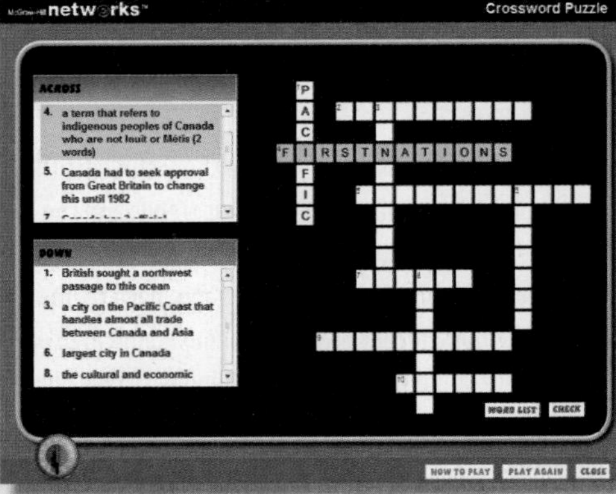

ANSWERS, p. 153

DBQ The chief cause for Canada's slide is a lack of female representation in politics.

V Visual Skills

Using Graphs Draw students' attention to the graph that shows annual growth rate of Canadian industries. Have students study the graph and answer the questions. Then have pairs create fill-in-the-blank and multiple-choice quiz questions based on information in the graph. Provide students with examples.

After partners have had time to formulate their quiz questions, have pairs switch quiz questions with other pairs. The team that answers the most quiz questions correctly wins. **Logical/Mathematical, Interpersonal**

R1 Reading Skills

Using Word Parts Ask a volunteer to read the Guiding Question aloud. Draw students' attention to the word *postindustrial.* Tell students that using prefixes and suffixes can help them determine the meaning of unfamiliar or confusing words. **Ask: What word parts help you identify the meaning of the term *postindustrial*?** *(Possible answer: The prefix* post- *means "after or behind," so* postindustrial *means "after or behind industry.")* To reinforce understanding, have students call out other words with the prefix *post-* as you write them on the board. *(postelection, postseason, post-show, post-trial, etc.)* Then ask volunteers to restate the Guiding Question in their own words. Discuss the meaning of a "postindustrial market economy," stressing that because Canada has a strong service sector today, it is mainly a postindustrial society. **ELL Verbal/Linguistic**

R2 Reading Skills

Defining Review with students the meaning of the term *GDP.* Remind students that a country's Gross Domestic Product, or GDP, is the total value of goods and services it produces during a year, excluding any income earned in foreign countries. **Ask: What percentage of Canada's GDP is produced from economic activity involving its natural resources and agriculture?** *(4 percent)* **AL Verbal/Linguistic**

ANSWERS, p. 154

READING PROGRESS CHECK The government has passed laws protecting the rights of women. It created Status of Women in Canada, and gender equality was ensured by the Canadian Charter of Rights and Freedom.

CRITICAL THINKING

1. Agriculture, Forestry, Fishing, and Hunting show a sharp increase in growth from 2007 to 2008 and a sharp decrease from 2008 to 2009; other industries show a gradual decrease from 2007 to 2009.
2. Since 2009, Canadian industry has seen an increase in growth to pre-recession levels.

GRAPH SKILLS — **Annual Growth Rate of Canadian Industries**

Canadian industries generally faced some difficult times as a result of the 2008 global recession, but have since shown signs of bouncing back.

CRITICAL THINKING

1. ***Contrasting*** Which industry's performance is most unlike the others?
2. ***Summarizing*** What has been the general trend in Canadian industry in recent years?

V

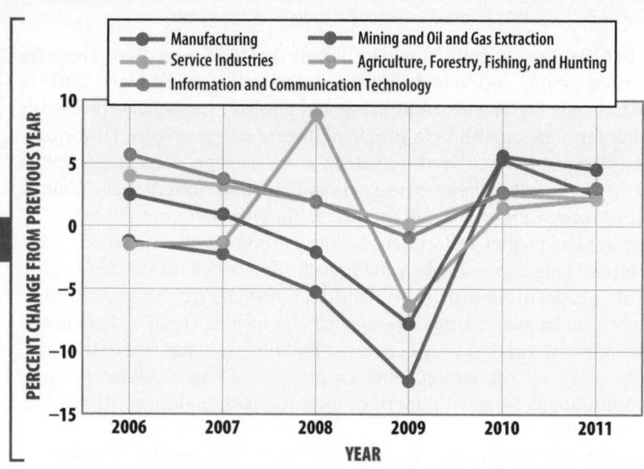

Source: Statistics Canada, 2012

Canada is also at the forefront of contemporary art. The "Vancouver School" artists focus on photoconceptualism, and the Nova Scotia College of Art and Design is known for innovation in photography and graphic design.

READING PROGRESS CHECK

Explaining How has the government worked to improve the status of women?

Economic Activities

GUIDING QUESTION *What factors define Canada as a postindustrial market economy?*

R1 Like the United States, Canada maintains a market economy. In 2009, 58 percent of Canada's exports were made up of agricultural, energy, forestry, and mining products. Thus, natural resources are essential to the Canadian economy. Canada also has the second-largest oil reserves in the world and makes a substantial amount of money from exporting oil and natural gas.

Resources, Power, and Industry

Canada is a leader in the production of uranium, iron ore, coal, petroleum, copper, and silver. Canada is the world's third-largest producer of hydroelectricity, relies heavily on coal-fueled power, and can meet its own petroleum needs while still having a surplus of oil and natural gas. These surpluses are exported worldwide. The tar sands in Alberta are a major source of crude oil.

R2 Natural resources and agriculture make up over 60 percent of Canada's exports. Despite this, those economic activities provide Canada with only about 4 percent of its GDP. Services such as transportation and communication, retail, health care, and others provide about 70 percent of GDP. The Canadian economy produces goods and services at home as well as being linked to the global economy through imports, exports, and trade agreements such as NAFTA.

Canada continues to be one of the world's important suppliers of agricultural products, specifically wheat, corn, and other grain crops. Canada's Prairie Provinces are major grain producers. They are also home to many cattle ranches.

networks Online Teaching Options

GRAPH

Annual Growth Rate of Canadian Industries

Analyzing Graphs Use the graph to show students the connection between national economic trends and the lives of people within these countries. As students interact with the information in the graph, have them consider the more recent economic trends found in Canada. Have students identify which industry was hit the hardest by the downturn and discuss how this may have affected people's lives (loss of jobs, decreased sales, etc.). Then have students write a brief paragraph that summarizes Canada's economic status in 2011 based on this graph. **BL Verbal/Linguistic**

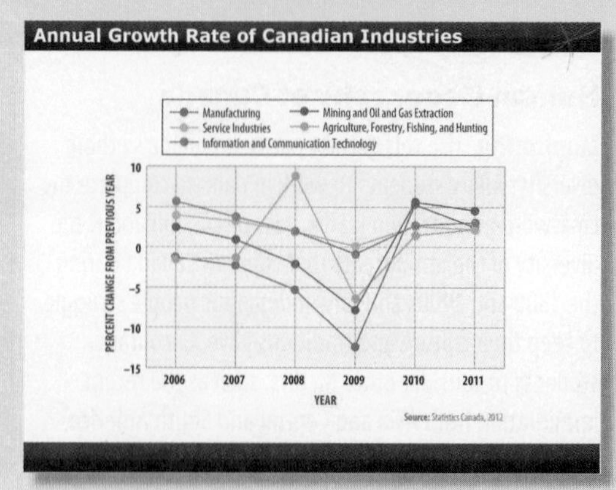

The fishing industry used to heavily support the economy of the Atlantic coast. In the past few decades, however, overfishing has reduced this industry's impact. Forestry is important for certain provinces, such as British Columbia.

The last few decades have seen a rapid growth of high-tech and electronics industries. Canada has 28 million Internet users—82 percent of its population. Another high-tech industry in Canada is its space and aircraft industry.

The development of reliable transportation systems has been essential to the economic growth of Canada due to its large land area. The majority of Canada's transportation systems are located in the southern part of the country. The Trans-Canada Highway runs 4,860 miles (7,821 km) from Victoria, British Columbia, to St. John's, Newfoundland. Communication networks have also promoted development of the economy. Cellular and digital services using satellites have made telephone communication more accessible in distant places. Business transactions and personal communications can be completed instantaneously using e-mail and the Internet. V1

The Economy Today

Since Canada's economy is linked to the global market, it suffered some losses in the 2008 global recession. However, it was not as seriously affected as the United States. This was largely because Canadian banks were more conservative in extending credit. The housing market stayed healthy as a result. Also, Canada's federal deficit is one of the smallest in the Western world. Unemployment rates have been generally lower than those in the United States and much of Europe. C

Trade is still central to the Canadian economy. In addition to forestry products, leading exports are automobiles, auto parts, crude petroleum, natural gas, electricity, aluminum, machinery, and equipment. Canada tends to import manufactured goods, such as chemical products, textiles, and foods. Exports to the United States amount to over half of all Canadian trade. Canada exports more to the United States than it imports from it, resulting in a trade surplus. V2

While natural resources and trade are important to Canada's economy, the service sector employs more people than all other sectors combined, with 70 percent of the over 18 million Canadians in the labor force. For this reason, Canada is considered a postindustrial society. The service industry includes retail jobs in the increasingly common large chain stores such as Walmart and Best Buy. Tourism is also a fast-growing service industry because Canada offers natural and cultural diversity in addition to national parks and historic sites.

☑ READING PROGRESS CHECK

Analyzing Why was Canada less affected than the United States by the 2008 global recession?

LESSON 2 REVIEW 

Reviewing Vocabulary (Tier Three Words)

1. ***Making Connections*** Use the following vocabulary terms in a paragraph about the early history of Canada: First Nation, Inuit, Loyalist, and dominion. RH.9–10.4

Using Your Notes

2. ***Describing*** Use your graphic organizer to describe the ethnic makeup of Canada today.

Answering the Guiding Questions

3. ***Sequencing Information*** How did British and French cultures influence Canada's history?
4. ***Outlining*** What explains Canada's diverse mix of people and settlement patterns?
5. ***Inferring*** Why is Canada often called a multicultural society?
6. ***Determining Importance*** What factors define Canada as a postindustrial market economy?

Writing Activity

7. ***Narrative*** Suppose you are an immigrant writing a letter to relatives about your new home in Canada. Explain your reasons for settling where you live. WHST.9–10.2

V1 Visual Skills

Synthesizing Have students work with a partner to create a map displaying information in the text about Canada's transportation systems. Provide each set of students a copy of the North America Outline Map, which is available online at the Teacher Resource Center. Students may wish to use an online mapping program to view features discussed in the text, such as the Trans-Canada Highway. Tell students to create a key and legend, assigning symbols to show and label key features that are integral to the country's transportation systems. After students complete their maps, have them summarize the importance of Canada's transportation systems. **Visual/Spatial, Interpersonal**

C Critical Thinking Skills

Analyzing Cause and Effect Guide a class discussion about the impact of the 2008 global recession on Canada and the United States. **Ask:** **What lessons might the United States learn from Canada's economic behavior?** *(Possible answer: U.S. banks could learn to take fewer risks and not to overextend credit.)* **Logical/Mathematical**

V2 Visual Skills

Creating Charts Have students work in small groups to transfer information from the text about Canada's imports and exports into a visual display, such as a flowchart. Encourage students to conduct additional research to identify which countries import Canada's manufactured products, and from which countries Canada imports products. Consider recommending that students view information about Canada's trade activity at the CIA World Fact Book Web site. Have groups share their charts with the class. BL **Visual/Spatial**

LESSON 2 REVIEW ANSWERS

Reviewing Vocabulary

1. Paragraphs should show knowledge of the meaning of these terms: First Nation, Inuit, Loyalist, and dominion.

Using Your Notes

2. More than one-fourth of Canadians state that they are of mixed ethnic origins. More than 4 percent of all Canadians state that they are Native American, Inuit, or of mixed European and Native American ancestry.

Answering the Guiding Questions

3. Rivalry between Great Britain and France in Canada began in 1670, but in 1867, the English- and French-speaking communities worked together to create the Dominion of Canada.
4. Immigrants to Canada came in search of political and religious freedom, economic and educational opportunities, and refuge from wars.
5. People come from all over the world to take advantage of Canada's high standard of living and its government policies protecting multiculturalism.
6. Natural resources and trade are important to Canada's economy; however, the service sector employs more people than all other sectors combined.

Writing Activity

7. Letters should show knowledge of Canada's population patterns and economic activities.

CLOSE & REFLECT

Summarizing Have students write a journal entry describing a recent fictional visit to Canada. Tell students to use information from this lesson to describe where they visited, reasons for choosing each location, and what they saw. Encourage students to include information about the "sights and sounds" of the country, including languages spoken and foods they ate.

ANSWERS, p. 155

☑ READING PROGRESS CHECK Canada was less affected because its banks did not extend as much credit. As a result, its housing market remained healthy.

ENGAGE

C1 Critical Thinking Skills

Formulating Questions Have students recall what they previously learned about NAFTA. Remind them that NAFTA eliminated tariffs and other trade barriers, providing economic advantages for companies and industries involved in trade. Then have students work with a partner to brainstorm and write a list of questions they have about NAFTA. Have students fill in the answers to their questions as they complete this lesson.

TEACH & ASSESS

C2 Critical Thinking Skills

Calculating Invite a volunteer to explain what the color-coding on the map means, clarifying as needed. Have students find a partner to play a game of "Higher or Lower." Explain that they will calculate answers to questions they create based on calculations. Provide a sample question for students to give them an idea of how to phrase their questions. **Ask:** **Which is higher: revenue from trade between Canada and the United States, or between Canada and Mexico?** *(from trade between Canada and the United States)* **How much higher?** *(by more than 309 billion dollars)*

After partners have had a chance to ask and answer two to three questions, guide a class discussion about the economic impact of NAFTA on Canada, the United States, and Mexico.
AL **Logical/Mathematical**

V Visual Skills

Comparing and Contrasting Have students draw a three-column chart, labeling the columns with the names of each country shown on the map. Then organize students into three groups, assigning each group a country. Have groups complete their column of the chart by listing advantages or disadvantages of NAFTA for each country. **Visual/Spatial**

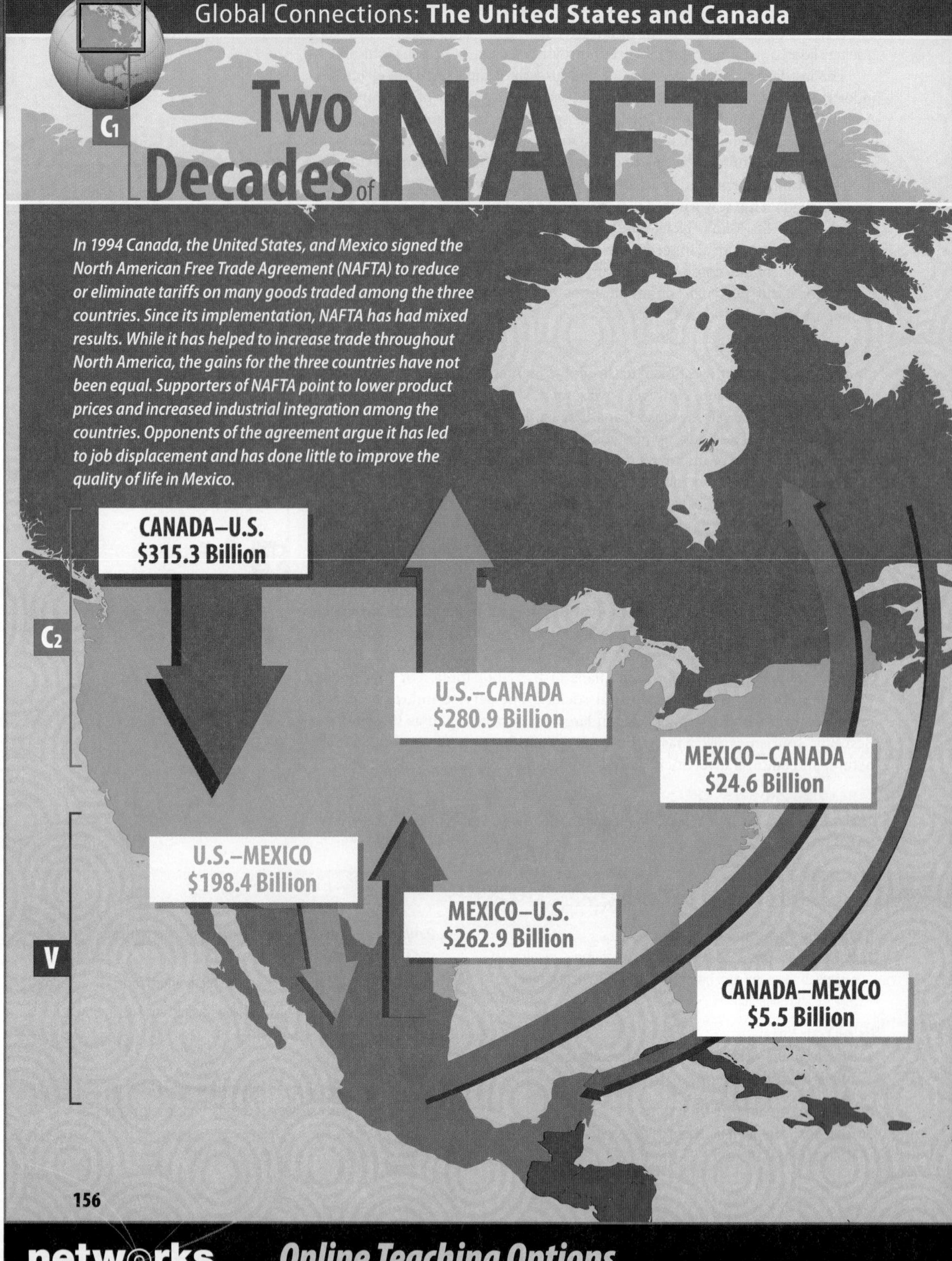
Global Connections: The United States and Canada
C1
Two Decades of NAFTA
In 1994 Canada, the United States, and Mexico signed the North American Free Trade Agreement (NAFTA) to reduce or eliminate tariffs on many goods traded among the three countries. Since its implementation, NAFTA has had mixed results. While it has helped to increase trade throughout North America, the gains for the three countries have not been equal. Supporters of NAFTA point to lower product prices and increased industrial integration among the countries. Opponents of the agreement argue it has led to job displacement and has done little to improve the quality of life in Mexico.
CANADA–U.S. $315.3 Billion
C2
U.S.–CANADA $280.9 Billion
MEXICO–CANADA $24.6 Billion
U.S.–MEXICO $198.4 Billion
MEXICO–U.S. $262.9 Billion
V
CANADA–MEXICO $5.5 Billion
156

networks Online Teaching Options

INFOGRAPHIC

Pros and Cons of NAFTA

Summarizing Use this infographic to discuss with students the NAFTA trading profits between Mexico, Canada, and the United States. As a class, discuss the details as they are displayed. Answer any questions or misconceptions that students may have about the information. Then have students write two or three sentences summarizing the information in the graphic.
ELL **Visual/Spatial**

Pros and Cons of NAFTA

Place each statement from the Answer Bank in the chart. Place Pros of NAFTA in Column A. Place Cons of NAFTA in Column B.

Pros	Cons

Answer Bank
Some industries lost jobs
Factories pay low wages to workers
Decreased tariffs
Easier to purchase goods
Increased trade in goods and services
Reduced cost of trade
Companies move production to other countries
Regulations are barriers to trade

CANADA

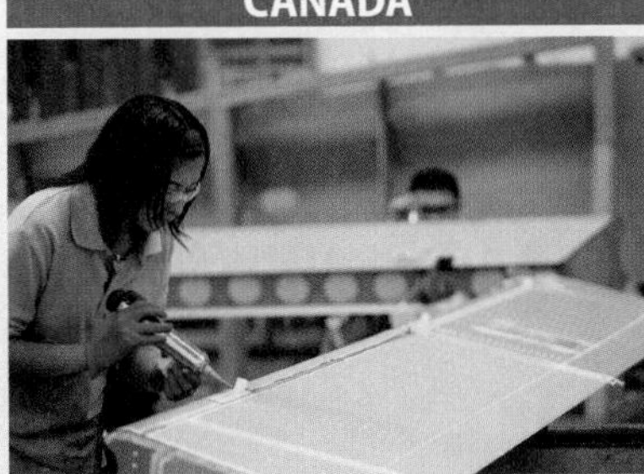

"Few Canadians speak up for enhancing ties with Mexico. But before leaving Ottawa this month, Emilio Goicoechea, Mexico's ambassador, wrote a rebuttal urging Canada to stay the trilateral course. Trade between the two has grown fivefold since 1994. . . . Some Canadian companies have invested in Mexico: Bombardier has factories making aircraft parts and trains, while Scotiabank is Mexico's seventh-biggest bank."

–The Economist
"No mariachis, please," February 12, 2009

UNITED STATES

"[A] worker . . . whose 16.6% tariff was eliminated by Nafta, saw wage growth rate about 11 percentage points less than a worker in a business that didn't depend on high tariffs. So . . . Nafta did hurt workers at the lower end of education spectrum. Blue-collar workers in vulnerable industries suffered large absolute declines in real wages as a result of the agreement. . . ."

–Bob Davis
"The Battle Over NAFTA Continues,"
Wall Street Journal, *November 22, 2010*

MEXICO

". . . NAFTA has made it easier to buy American products in Mexico. I can shop at H-E-B and other stores in Mexico and buy Procter & Gamble and other American-made products that we could not buy in Mexico before NAFTA. When I lived in Mexico and wanted American products before NAFTA, the taxes imposed on American products made them unaffordable."

–Eduardo Bravo
"NAFTA Has Fueled Job Growth,"
SanAntonio Express-News, *November 19, 2012*

Making Connections

1. ***Places and Regions*** Which NAFTA member country exports the largest volume of goods to the other two member countries?
2. ***Human Systems*** How might a person's role in the economy, such as an industrial worker, a business owner, or a policy maker, impact his or her views on NAFTA?
3. ***The Uses of Geography*** Using what you know about NAFTA, write a one-page letter to the editor of a local newspaper explaining why you think the overall effect of NAFTA has been positive or negative.

*Interact with **Global Connections** Online*

C Critical Thinking Skills

Analyzing Primary Sources Have students read the excerpt from the article in *The Economist.* **Ask:** **Why did Mexico's ambassador write a rebuttal urging Canada to "stay the trilateral course"?** *(Trade between the two countries has grown and benefited Mexico.)* **Verbal/Linguistic**

R Reading Skills

Drawing Inferences Draw students' attention to the title of the article and ask a Spanish-speaking student to explain the meaning of the term *mariachis. (Mexican street bands)* **Ask:** **What does the title of the article indicate about how some Canadians feel about NAFTA?** *(The title presents a sentiment expressed by some Canadians who want to preserve their own culture, fearing that increased trade with Mexico may threaten their cultural heritage.)* **ELL** **Verbal/Linguistic**

T Technology Skills

Making Presentations Divide the class into small groups. Assign each group one of the three countries participating in NAFTA. Have students identify a company, business, or industry in their assigned country. Have groups conduct online research to identify the profits and losses or growth of the company since NAFTA went into effect. Have each group present their findings to the class in a short verbal report. **BL** **Logical/Mathematical, Verbal/Linguistic**

CLOSE & REFLECT

Paraphrasing Have students review each excerpt and choose one to paraphrase in their own words. Then ask volunteers to share what they wrote with the class. Guide a discussion about the advantages and disadvantages of NAFTA for each country.

ONLINE QUIZ

Self-Check Quiz

Assessing The Interactive Self-Check Quiz is a type of review that the student may use to check their understanding of lesson content. This review asset allows students to check their answers, identifies if students have incorrectly answered a question, and provides a hint to help students select the correct answer. There is one self-check quiz for each lesson in this program. Each self-check quiz consists of 10 multiple-choice questions. **AL**

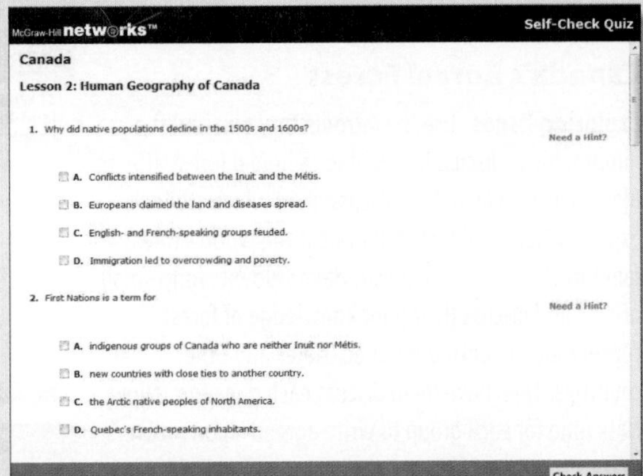

ANSWERS, p. 157

Making Connections

1. The United States exports the largest value of goods to the other two countries. The United States exports 479.3 billion dollars worth of goods to Canada and Mexico.
2. Possible answers: A person's role in the economy might impact his or her views on NAFTA. For example, an industrial worker in the United States may view NAFTA negatively if their job was moved to Mexico or Canada. A government policy maker might approve of NAFTA because it improves political relations with other countries. Business owners may approve of NAFTA because it cuts their labor costs and eliminates tariffs on goods so they can sell their goods to more consumers.
3. Student letters to the editors will vary, but should clearly explain their opinions on the overall effect of NAFTA.

People and Their Environment: Canada

ENGAGE

C1 Critical Thinking Skills

Predicting Have students consider the type of products and resources they or their families use every day. Discuss how these products and resources were made, extracted, developed, or manufactured. Then ask students to write three predictions about the human activities that pose threats to Canada's natural resources, wildlife, and natural landscapes.

TEACH & ASSESS

V Visual Skills

Creating Charts As students read about the logging industry, have them create a flowchart or draw a sketch that shows the logging extraction process. Then have them create another chart or sketch that shows the impact on the environment. Invite volunteers to present their charts and sketches. **ELL Visual/Spatial, Interpersonal**

C2 Critical Thinking Skills

Identifying Cause and Effect Discuss the impacts of the logging industry on Canada's boreal forest. **Ask:** **What are the economic effects of increased productivity in the logging industry?** *(The more trees a logger can cut down, the more products can be manufactured, sold, and shipped.)* **What are the environmental effects of increased productivity in the logging industry?** *(Trees can be removed quickly, but grow back very slowly, so the environmental effects are devastating and can lead to the depletion of the animals and plants.)* **Verbal/Linguistic**

W Writing Skills

Argument Tell students to write slogans and banners stating their opinions about logging, mining, or oil and gas extraction. Have students brainstorm who might attend a protest to express their vested interest, such as presidents of logging, mining, and oil companies; owners of a paper company; natural gas utilities company representatives; and nature and conservancy groups. Have students display their slogans and banners in a staged mock protest. Discuss the use and value of public protests as a method of influencing government agencies, politicians, and companies. **Verbal/Linguistic, Kinesthetic**

ANSWERS, p. 158

TAKING NOTES: Issues that arise include overfishing, logging, and mining. These activities can have a serious impact on the environment.

networks

There's More Online!

- **IMAGE** Human Impact on Wildlife
- **INFOGRAPHIC** Canada's Boreal Forest
- **INTERACTIVE SELF-CHECK QUIZ**
- **VIDEO** People and Their Environment: Canada

LESSON 3
People and Their Environment: Canada

ESSENTIAL QUESTION • *How do physical systems and human systems shape a place?*

Reading **HELP**DESK 

Academic Vocabulary (Tier Two Words)
- **extract**
- **diminish**

Content Vocabulary (Tier Three Words)
- **old-growth forest**

TAKING NOTES: ***Key Ideas and Details***

IDENTIFYING As you read, use a web diagram like the one below to outline issues that arise as a result of interactions between the Canadian people and their environment.

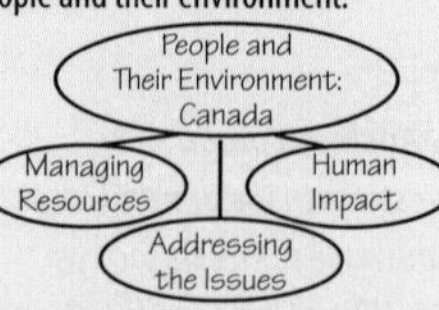

158

It Matters Because

While Canada once had an abundance of wildlife and natural resources, human activity has caused many of these resources to decline and some to even disappear. Human activities also cause pollution and contribute to climate change.

Managing Resources

GUIDING QUESTION *How do economic activities in Canada put the country's natural resources at risk?*

Canada engages in numerous economic activities that involve **extracting**, or removing, natural resources. Logging, which involves cutting down trees for human use, has resulted in more trees being cut down in a given amount of time than can grow. For example, a logger can cut down 100 trees in one day. However, it will take decades for the same number of trees to grow back. Logging, when left unchecked, can lead to the complete destruction of forests and the animals that live in those forests.

Canada's boreal forest is one of the largest forest and wetland ecosystems remaining on Earth. It is home to some of the biggest populations of wolves, grizzly bears, and caribou. It also has lakes that support many types of fish and trees that shelter billions of birds.

The boreal forest has been shrinking because of logging, mining, and oil and gas extraction. As of 2011, only 10 percent of it was federally protected. Many nature advocates and conservation groups are calling on the Canadian government to protect more of the boreal forest from these devastating activities, which can deplete the animal and plant populations. Parts of the boreal at high risk are old-growth forests.

Old-growth forests are complex forests that have developed over a long period of time and are relatively untouched by human activity. They are increasingly rare and also need to be protected.

The same is true for wetlands. Home to large numbers of plant and animal species, wetlands are considered one of the most productive ecosystems in the world. Wetlands cover about 14 percent of Canada,

networks ***Online Teaching Options***

INTERACTIVE BELLRINGER

Canada's Boreal Forest

Exploring Issues Use the introductory text and the infographic to discuss how Canada's boreal forest affects life on Earth. Lead a class discussion in which students explain what the effects might be if the world's forests/rain forests were to disappear. Have students form small groups and discuss their prior knowledge of forest conservation in both the United States and other countries. Then have them discuss each question. Allow class time for each group to write agreed-upon answers to the questions. **ELL Interpersonal, Verbal/Linguistic**

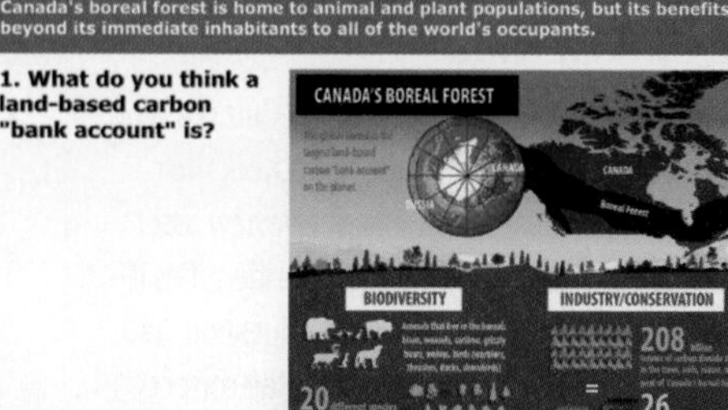

mainly in Ontario, Manitoba, and the Northwest Territories. Just like old-growth forests, Canadian wetlands are at risk. Wetlands have been drained so the land can be used for industrial, commercial, and agricultural purposes. If wetlands are not protected, even more will be destroyed.

Overfishing is caused by catching more fish than an ecosystem can replenish naturally. As with logging, if the fish cannot multiply at the same rate as they are caught, then the fish supply will seriously **diminish**, or become less. Overfishing can lead to the extinction of fish species if it is not stopped or regulated. This could have happened with Pacific salmon, which migrate in a route that takes them through waters in both Canada and the United States. Overfishing by both countries seriously depleted the salmon stock, and fishing industries in both countries suffered. In 1999 Canada and the United States signed an agreement to promote salmon conservation and harvest-sharing principles. While conservation efforts and fishery regulation have been implemented, some species of Pacific salmon are still endangered.

R1

extract to remove

old-growth forest complex forest that has developed over a long period of time and is relatively untouched by human activity

diminish to make less or cause to appear less

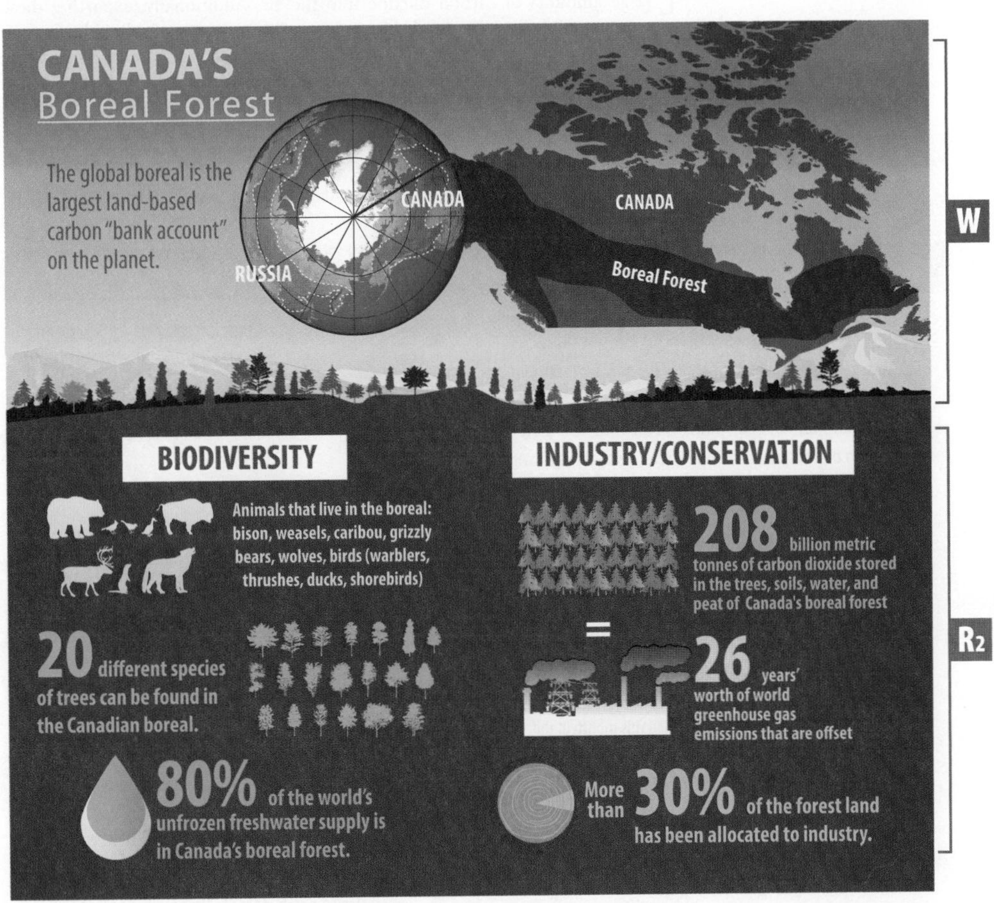

CANADA'S
Boreal Forest
The global boreal is the largest land-based carbon "bank account" on the planet.
CANADA
RUSSIA
CANADA
Boreal Forest
BIODIVERSITY
Animals that live in the boreal: bison, weasels, caribou, grizzly bears, wolves, birds (warblers, thrushes, ducks, shorebirds)
20 different species of trees can be found in the Canadian boreal.
80% of the world's unfrozen freshwater supply is in Canada's boreal forest.
INDUSTRY/CONSERVATION
208 billion metric tonnes of carbon dioxide stored in the trees, soils, water, and peat of Canada's boreal forest
=
26 years' worth of world greenhouse gas emissions that are offset
More than 30% of the forest land has been allocated to industry.

W

R2

Canada's boreal forest in the far north latitudes is situated just south of the treeless tundra of the polar region.

▲ **CRITICAL THINKING**

1. ***Analyzing*** Explain how Canada's boreal forest affects all life on Earth.
2. ***Assessing*** What are some threats facing Canada's boreal forest today?

INFOGRAPHIC

Canada's Boreal Forest

Analyzing Ethical Issues Use this infographic about Canada's boreal forest to discuss with students the value of lumber as a resource. Have students consider the many reasons that forests are cut down either for expansion or for the use of the lumber. Ask students to explain if they feel these uses add value to human life as they consider the value of the forest as a whole. Then have students list possible ways to maximize the use of lumber without reducing the forest. BL **Naturalist**

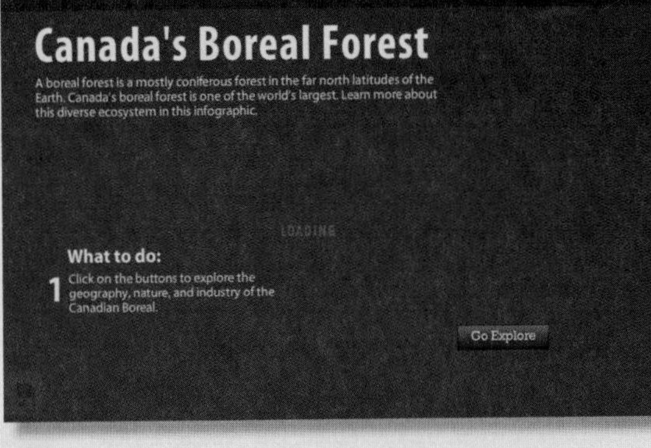

Canada's Boreal Forest
A boreal forest is a mostly coniferous forest in the far north latitudes of the Earth. Canada's boreal forest is one of the world's largest. Learn more about this diverse ecosystem in this infographic.
What to do:
1 Click on the buttons to explore the geography, nature, and industry of the Canadian Boreal.
Go Explore

R1 Reading Skills

Defining/Using Context Clues Direct students to locate the term *replenish* in the text. Ask volunteers to offer what they think the term means based on context clues in the text. *(Possible answers: refill, restock, replace)* Have students use the term *replenish* in a sentence that shows their understanding of the word's meaning, but in a different way than it is used in the text. Then discuss the meaning of the word *diminish* as it relates to the issue of overfishing. **Ask:** **How can overfishing impact the environment?** *(It can lead to the extinction of fish species.)* **What can be done to help replenish the fish supply?** *(Overfishing needs to be stopped or regulated.)* AL **Verbal/Linguistic**

W Writing Skills

Informative/Explanatory Tell students to analyze the information in the diagram that shows facts and figures about Canada's boreal forest. Have them write a paragraph that explains what is meant by the term "bank account" as it relates to the global boreal forest. Allow students to share their paragraphs with the class as you discuss the diagram. **Verbal/Linguistic**

R2 Reading Skills

Defining Direct students to locate the term *tonnes* in the diagram. Explain that the word *tonne* is pronounced the same as the word *ton,* which is also a form of measurement. Though the two words are spelled differently, they have similar meanings. A tonne is a metric ton, or unit of weight equal to 1,000 kilograms, or about 2204.6 pounds. Ask students to describe what objects weigh in tons, conducting online research if needed. *(Possible answers: A car weighs about 1 to 3 tons; an elephant weighs about 6 tons.)* ELL **Verbal/Linguistic**

ANSWERS, p. 159

CRITICAL THINKING

1. The boreal forest keeps 208 billion tonnes of carbon dioxide from entering the atmosphere.
2. Some threats are logging, mining, and oil and gas extraction. 30 percent of the forest land has been allocated for industrial uses.

People and Their Environment: Canada

V1 Visual Skills

Creating Diagrams Have students work with a partner to create a visual, such as a poster, drawing, or diagram that shows the process in which electricity is generated from flowing or falling water. After students present their visual displays, guide a discussion about the impact of dam building. **Ask:** **Do the benefits of producing hydroelectricity outweigh the negative impacts? Why or why not?** *(Student answer will vary, but should support a logical explanation.)* AL **Visual/Spatial, Interpersonal**

T Technology Skills

Identifying Perspectives Have small groups conduct online research about the current status of the Keystone XL pipeline. Explain that the pipeline construction is a controversial project that involves extracting and burning oil from Alberta's tar sands. Assign the activity as homework. Tell students to gather information for a slide show that describes the pipeline, which will transport oil from Canada to the Gulf of Mexico. Have groups use presentation software to create their slide shows, assigning members different tasks such as researching, fact-checking, writing, creating slides, and presenting. Groups should discuss both sides of the issue and provide a concluding statement about the impact of the pipeline on the environment and the economy. Have groups present their slide shows to the class. BL **Visual/Spatial, Interpersonal**

V2 Visual Skills

Global Analysis Tell students they have been asked to present a demonstration at a global conference titled "Natural Resources: Friends or Foes." Assign each student a natural resource. Have them demonstrate the process of extracting, developing, manufacturing, or transporting their assigned resource. For example, students assigned to crude oil might show how synthetic crude oil is converted into usable substances, such as gasoline and kerosene. Encourage creativity by suggesting the use of recycled materials in their displays or by writing a speech or poem to accompany their visual display. Have students present their visual displays to the class. **Visual/Spatial, Intrapersonal**

ANSWERS, p. 160

READING PROGRESS CHECK Trees, wetlands, fish, and waterways are most at risk.

DBQ Document-Based Questions

1. It prevents dead maple leaves from decaying on the forest floor, which creates a barrier that hampers growth of new trees.
2. It could greatly decrease the amount of syrup exported, which would result in decreased income.

V1 Canada is the world's third-largest producer of hydroelectricity—electricity generated from flowing or falling water. While the cost of hydroelectricity is low, making it a great source of renewable energy, it often requires damming. Many environmental groups and indigenous communities protest dam building because damming interrupts the flow of rivers and impacts local ecosystems. In some cases, these protests have succeeded in persuading companies to change their plans and work toward projects that do less harm to local ecosystems.

T The continued extraction of natural resources—particularly coal, oil, and natural gas from the tar sands in Alberta—fuels a growing concern among many people over climate change. It requires a large amount of energy to convert the heavy crude oil found in the tar sands into the more useful synthetic crude oil. V2 Furthermore, the process of converting synthetic crude oil into usable substances, such as gasoline and kerosene, is also energy intensive and releases large amounts of carbon dioxide into the air. Additionally, exporting these substances via airplanes and ships releases still more carbon dioxide. Carbon dioxide is believed to contribute directly to climate change and the rising of the Earth's temperatures. Like people around the world, many Canadians are looking for ways to develop renewable sources of energy that do not contribute to climate change.

READING PROGRESS CHECK

Assessing What natural resources are most at risk in Canada?

ANALYZING PRIMARY SOURCES CCSS

Acid Rain: Sugar Maples at Risk

As acid rain and other effects of air and water pollution escalate, the risk to plant life is increasing. In addition to damaging existing plants, acid rain can slow the growth of new plant life or, as scientists are learning by studying sugar maple trees in Canada, stop new growth altogether. Over time, entire forests can be obliterated as a result of acid rain destruction.

"Sugar maple abundance already has dropped in parts of the northeastern U.S. and southeastern Canada over the past 40 years, primarily because of high acid levels in soils.

The upper Great Lakes region has mostly escaped the damage because its soils are rich in calcium, which provides a buffer against acid. But in an article published this month in the *Journal of Applied Ecology*, scientists say they've discovered another way that acid rain harms sugar maple seedlings in upper Great Lakes forests.

Donald Zak of the University of Michigan says acid rain prevents dead maple leaves from decaying on the forest floor, creating a barrier that hampers growth of new trees."

—"Acid Rain Could Kill Maples Near Great Lakes," Associated Press, December 16, 2011

Industrial smokestacks emit pollutants, including sulfur and nitrogen oxides, that rise into the upper atmosphere, leading to acid rain.

DBQ CRITICAL THINKING

1. ***Identifying Central Issues*** According to Donald Zak, how does acid rain interfere with seedling development? RH.9–10.1
2. ***Speculating*** Maple syrup from sugar maple trees is an important export product in parts of Canada. How might acid rain affect the economy in areas where maple syrup is harvested?

networks Online Teaching Options

INTERACTIVE WHITEBOARD ACTIVITY

Causes and Effects in Canada's Environment

Understanding Relationships This interactive whiteboard activity has students complete a cause-and-effect chart showing the impact humans have had on the environment in Canada. After students have completed the activity, discuss the advantages and disadvantages of extracting and developing natural resources. Ask students to explain how these changes influence the ecosystems in Canada and whether they feel there is a need for stricter resource management and conservation measures in the region. **Intrapersonal, Verbal/Linguistic**

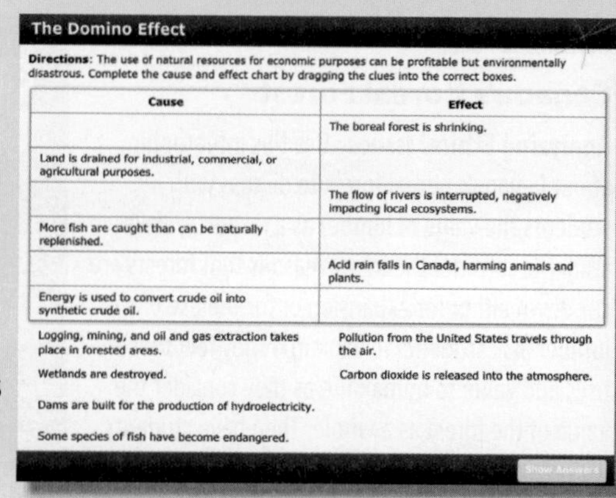

The Domino Effect
Directions: The use of natural resources for economic purposes can be profitable but environmentally disastrous. Complete the cause and effect chart by dragging the clues into the correct boxes.
Cause
Effect
The boreal forest is shrinking.
Land is drained for industrial, commercial, or agricultural purposes.
The flow of rivers is interrupted, negatively impacting local ecosystems.
More fish are caught than can be naturally replenished.
Acid rain falls in Canada, harming animals and plants.
Energy is used to convert crude oil into synthetic crude oil.
Logging, mining, and oil and gas extraction takes place in forested areas.
Pollution from the United States travels through the air.
Wetlands are destroyed.
Carbon dioxide is released into the atmosphere.
Dams are built for the production of hydroelectricity.
Some species of fish have become endangered.

Canadian Wildlife Service scientists evaluate the condition of a tranquilized mother polar bear and her young triplet cubs near western Hudson Bay. This is part of an effort to help protect animals living in Canada's boreal forest.

▲ CRITICAL THINKING

1. ***Speculating*** What data do you think the scientists are checking to assess the health of the polar bear and her cubs?
2. ***Hypothesizing*** How might the bears' health be an indicator of the health of their habitat?

Human Impact

GUIDING QUESTION *How do human activities impact the environment in Canada?*

Human activities, such as overfishing, logging, and mining, can seriously impact the environment in Canada. Agricultural, industrial, mining, and forestry activities have also contributed to pollution of the ocean waters. Acid rain is another serious threat that can even contaminate lakes, streams, and rivers far from the source of the pollution. These acids can come from natural sources, such as volcanoes, but human activities such as burning fossil fuels also release such acids into the air. Acid rain causes lakes, streams, and rivers to be contaminated. Since Canada is connected to the United States through a number of wind and water systems, pollution in the United States is negatively affecting the environment in Canada. For example, emissions in the United States can result in acid rain in Canada, threatening timber and water resources. C

Acid rain contributes to water pollution, but it is not the only threat to water supplies. Many companies and factories put their waste, such as heavy metals and pesticides, into water sources. Water pollution affects plants, animals, and small organisms living in the water. Contaminated water can kill trees, plants, and animals. It can also be harmful to humans. The United States and Canadian governments worked together to produce the Great Lakes Water Quality Agreement and the Clean Water Act in the 1970s to address the serious issue of water pollution that threatens the Great Lakes. The result has been greatly improved water quality and the resurgence of some fish populations. R

☑ READING PROGRESS CHECK

Describing How have human activities affected water systems in Canada?

Addressing the Issues

GUIDING QUESTION *How is the Canadian government working to address environmental issues?*

In Canada, climate change is an issue that the provinces, not the federal government, address. In 2009 Canada was ranked seventh in total greenhouse gas emissions, behind China, the United States, India, Russia, Japan, and Germany.

VIDEO

The Wolves of Northern Canada

Defending Before watching the video, ask the students to discuss what they know about wolves and whether they consider wolves and other wildlife species important to a country's environment. After viewing the video, ask students if their views on the endangered wolf species have changed. Have them consider whether they think wolves are a resource worth protecting. Divide the class into teams to research the pros and cons of environmental resource management for saving endangered wolves and then have teams conduct a short debate defending their views on the topic. BL **Interpersonal**

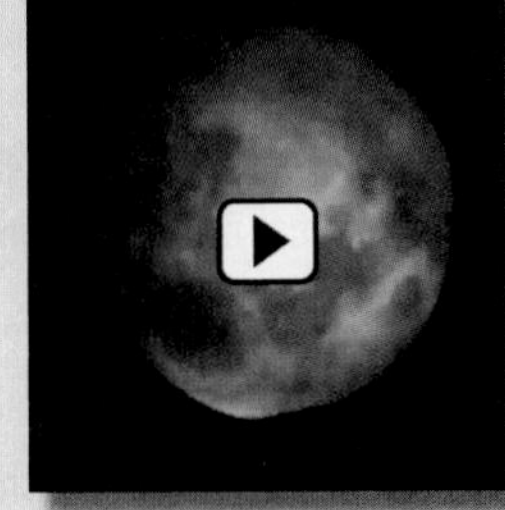

C Critical Thinking Skills

Understanding Relationships Have students read the information about wind and water systems that connect Canada and the United States. **Ask:** **How can environmental issues affect political or international relations?** *(If a country that shares a border with another country impacts the environment of the neighboring country, it could weaken political relationships.)* **What is an example of how environmental issues can affect relations between the United States and Canada?** *(Emissions in the United States can cause acid rain in Canada, which threatens Canada's timber and water resources.)* Have students research the Canada-United States Air Quality Agreement signed in 1991 that addresses these issues. **Logical/Mathematical**

R Reading Skills

Listing Ask students to reread the section as they create a list of all the environmental impacts that human activities have had in Canada and compare these to the predictions that they made at the beginning of this lesson. Then have students discuss their lists with a partner. AL **Verbal/Linguistic**

Making Connections

Have students consider what they might do to help solve issues that impact their environment. Read the following information to students:

The Canadian Arctic Resources Committee (CARC) is a citizens' group that is funded by donations. CARC conducts scientific research to study environmental and societal impacts on the land and people. Issues that the group studies include "sustainable development," the impact and management of Canada's natural resources, and climate change.

In 2009, CARC hosted "2030 North," a conference held to discuss and evaluate how Canada's arctic region will look in the year 2030. Participants determined that climate change remains a major issue facing northern Canada and stressed the importance of reducing greenhouse gas emissions.

ANSWERS, p. 161

☑ READING PROGRESS CHECK Acid rain is a serious threat that can contaminate lakes, streams, and rivers far from the source of the pollution.

CRITICAL THINKING

1. They are checking the polar bear's heart rate and other vital signs.
2. If polar bears' vital signs are not as generally expected, a problem in the environment could be the cause.

C Critical Thinking Skills

Speculating As a class, discuss the Kyoto Protocol. **Ask:** What was the intent of participating countries when they signed the Kyoto Protocol? *(The countries wanted to reduce their greenhouse gas emissions.)* Do you think Canada's failure to meet its goals and subsequent removal from the agreement impacted its relations with the other countries that signed the agreement? Why or why not? *(Student answers will vary, but should include support for their explanations.)* **BL** **Logical/Mathematical**

R Reading Skills

Summarizing Have students work in pairs and reread the paragraph about how individual provinces have taken actions to address climate change. Have students take notes about the key points. Tell partners to summarize the information into two or three sentences. Remind students that a summary should only include main ideas and key details. **Ask:** What is the purpose of the Green Energy and Green Economy Act? *(to promote energy conservation and the development of renewable and efficient "green" energy projects)* **AL** **Verbal/Linguistic**

T Technology Skills

Gathering Information Organize students into small groups and have each group use the Internet to research efforts being made to protect Canada's renewable resources. Remind students to use reliable Web sites as they gather information. Have students in each group collaborate to write a song or poem that emphasizes the need for preserving and protecting natural resources. Ask groups to present their songs and poems to the class. **Interpersonal, Auditory/Musical**

CLOSE & REFLECT

Critical Listening Tell students they will play a game show in which they will ask questions of the "studio audience," their classmates, about the lesson. Students should write one question for each of the three headings in the lesson: *Managing Resources, Human Impact,* and *Addressing Issues.* Tell students their questions may be fill-in-the-blank, true or false, or multiple choice. Have students take turns asking their questions, calling on members of the class who raise their hand to indicate they know the answer.

ANSWERS, p. 162

READING PROGRESS CHECK The Canadian government is exploring wind and solar power options to produce energy in the southern provinces.

C The main sources of greenhouse gas emissions are transportation, electricity generation, and producing and refining fossil fuels and petroleum. In 2011 Canada pulled out of the Kyoto Protocol. The Kyoto Protocol is an international agreement signed by 37 industrialized countries that agreed to reduce their greenhouse gas emissions. The Canadian government failed to meet its goals and chose to remove itself from the agreement.

R Individual provinces have taken actions to address the climate change issue. In 2009 Ontario passed sweeping legislation to support renewable energy and promote conservation. The new law—the Green Energy and Green Economy Act (GEGEA)—promotes the development of renewable "green" energy projects within the province. The act also advocates for efficient energy and energy conservation efforts in homes, schools, and offices. GEGEA offers all of Ontario's residents—including home owners and large companies—financial incentives to develop small- and large-scale renewable energy sources. As an added benefit, it was projected to produce some 50,000 jobs, both directly and indirectly, in its first three years. Ontario is also the leader in Canadian wind and solar energy projects. So far, Nova Scotia is the only province besides Ontario to set formal goals for wind power projects. Such projects can attract billions of dollars in international investments and also help create jobs.

Hydroelectricity is the most efficient source of renewable energy in Canada and accounts for more than half of all the electricity produced. It is far from a perfect solution, however. The places suitable for the installation of hydroelectric facilities are limited. In addition, the damming of rivers can seriously disrupt the surrounding ecosystems.

T The Canadian government has begun to explore wind and solar power options for energy production in the southern provinces. Organizations outside the government are also working hard to address environmental issues in Canada—and to put pressure on the Canadian government to address them more effectively.

There are positive efforts to report. Canada is taking steps to protect its renewable resources. Protection of Pacific salmon is one example, although it remains to be seen whether those efforts will enjoy ultimate success. Still, the effort illustrates how the government and others can take aggressive action to protect and preserve precious natural resources.

READING PROGRESS CHECK

Describing What kinds of renewable energy sources is the Canadian government exploring?

LESSON 3 REVIEW

Reviewing Vocabulary (Tier Three Words)

1. ***Defining*** Provide a definition and example for the following term: old-growth forest. RH.9–10.4

Using Your Notes

2. ***Listing*** Using your web diagram, identify a way in which Canadians are impacting their environment and one way in which they are trying to manage that impact.

Answering the Guiding Questions

3. ***Identifying*** How do economic activities in Canada put natural resources at risk?
4. ***Evaluating*** How do human activities impact the environment in Canada?
5. ***Identifying Central Issues*** How is the Canadian government working to address environmental issues?

Writing Activity

6. ***Informative/Explanatory*** With a partner, select one natural resource from the following list: water, oil, natural gas, and coal. Write a paragraph describing why this resource is valuable. How has human activity affected this resource, and what are the ways the Canadian government can do more to address the conservation of this resource? WHST.9–10.2

LESSON 3 REVIEW ANSWERS

Reviewing Vocabulary

1. Old-growth forest is forest that has become extremely old and is relatively untouched by human activity. Old-growth forests are threatened by logging.

Using Your Notes

2. Ecosystems can be disrupted when dams are built for hydroelectric power. The Canadian government is exploring wind and solar power options for energy production in some provinces.

Answering the Guiding Questions

3. Extracting natural resources through activities such as logging depletes natural resources. Overfishing takes more fish out of an ecosystem than it can replace.
4. They can deplete availability of resources, and can have a negative impact on existing resources.
5. Provinces are addressing environmental issues through legislation. The government has begun to explore wind and solar power, and is taking steps to protect natural resources.

Writing Activity

6. Paragraphs will vary, but should be logical and strongly supported with content from the lesson.

CHAPTER 6 Assessment

Directions: On a separate sheet of paper, answer the questions below. Make sure you read carefully and answer all parts of the questions.

Lesson Review

Lesson 1

1. ***Describing*** Describe how tectonic forces have played a role in shaping Canada's physical geography.
2. ***Discussing*** Provide two examples of Canadian lakes that were formed by glacier activity and describe the process.
3. ***Explaining*** How does Canada's climate change as one travels farther north?

Lesson 2

4. ***Assessing*** Describe the ways in which physical geography and natural resources have influenced Canadian culture and economy.
5. ***Finding the Main Idea*** How have the cultures of various indigenous groups influenced Canada's cultural diversity?
6. ***Describing*** Describe some ways that the Canadian family has changed in recent years.

Lesson 3

7. ***Summarizing*** What efforts have been made to promote renewable "green" energy by the Canadian government?
8. ***Making Inferences*** Why is it in the best interest of industries to use natural resources responsibly?
9. ***Evaluating*** Why do many environmental groups and indigenous communities feel that hydroelectricity does more harm than good?

Exploring the Essential Question

10. ***Diagramming*** Create a cause-and-effect chart that shows how physical features and climate have influenced the human settlement of Canada. How have these relationships shaped Canada today? WHST.9–10.1

21st Century Skills

Review the circle graph. Then answer the questions that follow.

CHINESE IMPORTS FROM CANADA BY SECTOR, 2011 (as a share of total imports from Canada)*

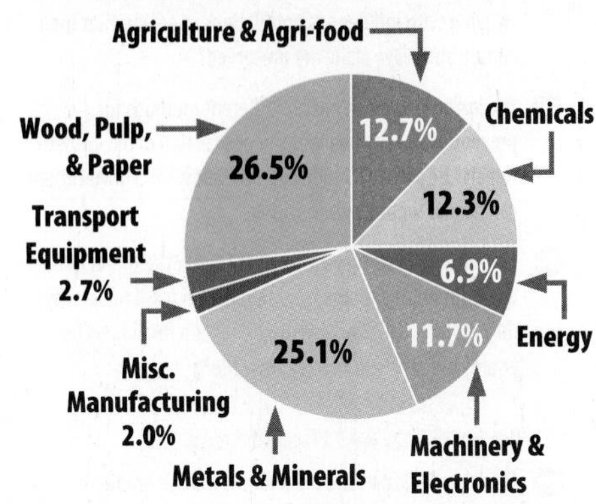

Source: Global Trade Atlas (Chinese statistics)
*May not add up to 100% due to rounding.

11. ***Using Graphs, Charts, Diagrams, and Tables*** China imports the most products from Canada in which two categories?
12. ***Geography Skills*** What does the high percentage of exports of wood imply about Canada's physical geography?

Applying Map Skills

Use the Unit 2 Atlas maps to answer the following questions.

13. ***Physical Systems*** List all the climate regions found in Canada and describe their location in relation to latitude.
14. ***The World in Spatial Terms*** Which parts of Canada are the most densely populated and which are the least densely populated? Why do you think this is the case?
15. ***Human Systems*** Use your mental map of Canada to describe the relative location of Ottawa.

Need Extra Help?

If You've Missed Question	1	2	3	4	5	6	7	8	9	10	11	12	13	14	15
Go to page	144	146	146	149	153	153	162	158	162	147	163	163	116	112	147

CHAPTER 6 Assessment Answers

Lesson Review

Lesson 1

1. The collisions between tectonic plates that occurred millions of years ago resulted in the Pacific Ranges. Geologic forces forced slabs of rock upward, which resulted in formation of the Rocky Mountains.
2. Two examples are Great Bear Lake and Great Slave Lake, which occurred as a result of dams created by glacial ice.
3. The climate becomes less humid and colder. Winters are longer; freezing temperatures and snow are more common.

Lesson 2

4. Canada's economy is bolstered by its oil reserves; it derives greater income from export of oil and natural gas. Tourism is a fast-growing service industry because of Canada's natural and cultural diversity.
5. There has been great influence on the arts by indigenous groups. For example, First Nations artists combine old and new techniques with traditional color schemes and motifs, generally related to the natural world.
6. There are fewer two-parent families, and families consist of fewer members. More women have entered the workforce, so there are more dual-income households.

Lesson 3

7. The Green Energy and Green Economy Act promotes development of renewable energy projects, and advocates for efficient energy and energy conservation. Ontario residents are offered financial incentives to develop renewable energy sources.
8. If industries use natural resources more responsibly, the industries will be around for a longer time. It can also help create goodwill in the community.
9. Hydroelectricity often requires damming. Dam building interrupts the flow of rivers and can disrupt local ecosystems.

Exploring the Essential Question

10. Chart should show populations grew up around waterways, which provide transportation and boost the economy. Charts should also show subarctic climate regions and subarctic regions are not conducive to large human populations, while the Pacific Coast and southern third of Canada are.

21st Century Skills

11. China imports the most products from the Wood, Pulp, & Paper and the Metals & Minerals categories.
12. It implies that Canada is rich in timber resources.

Applying Map Skills

13. The following climate regions can be found in Canada: ice cap, tundra and high altitude, subarctic, humid continental, marine west coast, and semi-arid. The further north in latitude one goes, the cooler the climate becomes—humid continental gives way to subarctic, tundra, and ice cap.
14. The most densely populated areas in Canada are along the St. Lawrence River and the U.S.-Canadian border on both coasts. These areas are along waterways which provide transportation and trade opportunities. The least populated areas are in the high latitude areas where the climate is less hospitable.
15. Students' answers will vary, but may include: Ottawa is located northeast of Lake Ontario. Ottawa is located east of Lake Superior.

Assessment Answers

Critical Thinking

16 Areas between the Pacific Ranges and Rocky Mountains have a drier climate; this is a result of the rain shadow effect. The area experiences a semiarid (steppe) climate, with grasslands and coniferous forests.

17 The government values the roots of the country and wants to preserve and promote them.

18 To prevent overfishing, the Canadian government has been working to protect key species. In 1999, Canada and the United States signed an agreement to promote salmon conservation and harvest-sharing principles. Many groups are cooperating to protect old-growth forests. Additional efforts to help old-growth forests include replanting trees and cooperating to protect the species of native forest animals facing extinction.

19 Developing alterative energy resources can be expensive, so perhaps they are being developed slowly in Canada. Canada might be continuing to rely on fossil fuels as a commodity for trade due to the substantial income generated.

College and Career Readiness

20 Student answers will vary, but should include chapter details to explain the area of Canada where the student would like to live based on landforms, climates, and cultural features.

Writing About Geography

21 Essays will vary, but should address overfishing, loss of old-growth forests, acid rain, or climate change and should detail one of the problems, while explaining why it is the most significant.

Analyzing Primary Sources

22 Smaller sockeye populations have collapsed after a century of overfishing.

23 The salmon are sockeye salmon, and the term *fever* references the fact that people should not let their excitement regarding the bounty of sockeye salmon blind them to the reality of problems posed to the salmon.

Research and Presentation

24 Notes should reference major immigrant groups that came to Canada during a variety of periods of history.

CHAPTER 6 Assessment 

Directions: On a separate sheet of paper, answer the questions below. Make sure you read carefully and answer all parts of the questions.

Critical Thinking

16 ***Making Connections*** What is the connection between the semi-arid (steppe) climate region and the Pacific Ranges?

17 ***Drawing Inferences*** What can you infer from the fact that the Canadian government has recently begun working with indigenous populations to ensure that their culture and ways of life are preserved?

18 ***Exploring Issues*** What are different methods for preventing overfishing and the destruction of old-growth forests? Be sure to include examples of what a government can do and what a citizen can do.

19 ***Evaluating Counter Arguments*** Given the threat of environmental damage from reliance on fossil fuels, why do you think Canada continues to rely on fossil fuels for energy and as a commodity for trade?

College and Career Readiness

20 ***Decision Making*** You are a recent college graduate seeking a teaching job in Canada. Based on your knowledge of the landforms, climates, and cultural features of Canada, in which area of the country would you choose to live and why? Explain your answer using details from the chapter. WHST.9–10.1.b

Writing About Geography

21 ***Argument*** Environmentalists working on resource management in Canada face many challenges, such as overfishing, loss of old-growth forests, acid rain, and climate change. Which challenge do you feel is the most significant? Write a one-page essay explaining your position. Be sure to describe the problem and to explain why you feel it is the most significant.
WHST.9–10.7, WHST.9–10.8, WHST.9–10.9

DBQ Analyzing Primary Sources

Use the document to answer the following questions.

PRIMARY SOURCE

"A conservation group is warning against allowing too much fishing of sockeye salmon on the Fraser River despite expectations that this year's run will be one of the biggest in 100 years.

Society director Craig Orr said in a release headlined 'Don't succumb to sockeye fever' that most of this year's sockeye are from one place—the Adams River—while stocks from many other sources are severely depleted.

'We should all rejoice in this year's bounty, but remember that returns of Fraser River sockeye in this decade have been extremely low for reasons not yet understood,' said Orr.

Environmentalist Vicky Husband, an advisor to Watershed Watch, said the future of the whole fishery ecosystem has to be taken into account.

'We've endured a century of over-fishing and collapse of smaller sockeye populations,' said Husband."

—"Salmon Overfishing Warning Issued," CBC News, September 1, 2010

22 ***Identifying Cause and Effect*** Why does Husband feel that overfishing threatens the entire fishery ecosystem? RH.9–10.6

23 ***Making Inferences*** Why does Orr use the phrase "sockeye fever" to warn against overfishing of salmon on the Fraser River? RH.9–10.6

Research and Presentation

24 ***Research Skills*** Use the Internet to research the major immigrant groups who came to Canada during different periods of its history. As you read, take notes. Use your notes to share what you learned with a classmate.
WHST.9–10.3, WHST.9–10.4, WHST.9–10.5, WHST.9–10.7

Need Extra Help?

If You've Missed Question	16	17	18	19	20	21	22	23	24
Go to page	147	151	158	142	146	149	164	164	152

networks Online Teaching Options

WORKSHEET

Chapter Test and Lesson Quizzes

Assessing Have students complete the Chapter Test and Lesson Quizzes to assess student understanding throughout the chapter. These assessment tools offer chapter and lesson evaluation through a variety of question formats, including document-based questions.

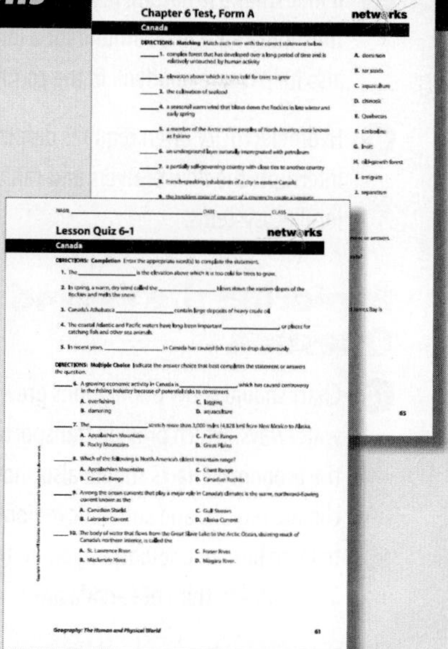

UNIT 3

LATIN AMERICA Planner

UNDERSTANDING BY DESIGN®

Enduring Understandings

- *The characteristics and distribution of cultures influence human systems.*
- *Culture influences people's perceptions of places and regions.*
- *The characteristics and distribution of human populations affect physical and human systems.*

Essential Question

- *How do physical systems and human systems shape a place?*

Students will know:

- *the landforms, water system, climate regions, biomes, and natural resources of Latin America.*
- *how Latin America's physical geography affects climate, population patterns, and economic development.*
- *how Native American empires and colonial rule influenced Latin America's history, culture, and political and social structures.*
- *the population characteristics of Latin America today.*
- *the causes and effects of environmental issues in Latin America and efforts to address these issues.*
- *how economies in Latin America have become part of the global economy.*

Students will be able to:

- ***describe** natural features of Latin America.*
- ***analyze** how Latin America's physical geography affects the people that live there.*
- ***explain** the influence of indigenous peoples and Europeans on Latin America's history and culture.*
- ***identify** causes and effects of and possible solutions to environmental issues.*
- ***describe** population patterns and economic activities of Latin America.*
- ***discuss** history, governments, and cultures of Latin America.*

Predictable Misunderstandings

- *All of Mexico has the same warm climate.*
- *Most people in Mexico live in poor, rural areas.*
- *Mexico does not have many natural resources.*
- *Mexico has a pristine, undisturbed environment.*
- *The water supply for Central America and the Caribbean comes from the surrounding oceans.*
- *People living in Central America and the Caribbean are of Spanish descent.*
- *Deforestation is an issue in South America, but not Central America.*
- *The geography and climate is the same throughout South America.*
- *People living in South America are all of Spanish descent.*
- *Desertification only happens near deserts.*

Assessment Evidence

Performance Tasks:

- *Environmental Case Study*
- *GeoLab Activity*
- *GIS Simulation*
- *Hands-On Chapter Projects*

Other Evidence:

- *Location Activity*
- *Self-Check Quizzes*
- *Lesson Quizzes*
- *Participation in Interactive Whiteboard Activities*
- *Contribution to small-group activities*
- *Interpretation of slide show images*
- *Participation in class discussions about Latin America*
- *Analysis of graphic organizers, graphs, and charts*
- *Lesson Reviews*
- *Chapter Assessments*

Key for Using the Teacher Edition

SKILL-BASED ACTIVITIES

Types of skill activities found in the Teacher Edition.

* **V Visual Skills** require students to analyze maps, graphs, charts, and photos.

R Reading Skills help students practice reading skills and master vocabulary.

C Critical Thinking Skills help students apply and extend what they have learned.

W Writing Skills provide writing opportunities to help students comprehend the text.

T Technology Skills require students to use digital tools effectively.

*Letters are followed by a number when there is more than one of the same type of skill on the page.

DIFFERENTIATED INSTRUCTION

All activities are written for the on-level student unless otherwise marked with the leveled labels below.

BL Beyond Level
AL Approaching Level
ELL English Language Learners

All students benefit from activities that utilize different learning styles. Many activities are marked as below when a particular learning style is highlighted.

Intrapersonal	**Naturalist**
Logical/Mathematical	**Kinesthetic**
Visual/Spatial	**Auditory/Musical**
Verbal/Linguistic	**Interpersonal**

SUGGESTED PACING GUIDE

Introducing the Unit	1 Day
Chapter 7: Mexico	5 Days
Case Study: What Kind of Development Is Best for Haiti?	1 Day
Chapter 8: Central America and the Caribbean	5 Days
Chapter 9: South America	5 Days
Global Connections: Amazon in the Balance	1 Day
TOTAL TIME	**18 Days**

PLANNER

☑ Print Teaching Options

V Visual Skills

- ☐ **p. 165** Students analyze details of the photograph of a coastal city. Visual/Spatial
- ☐ **p. 166** Students analyze details of the photograph of people participating in a parade. Visual/Spatial
- ☐ **p. 169** Students create charts about the countries and capital cities in Latin America. AL Visual/Spatial

R Reading Skills

- ☐ **p. 166** Students identify regions and geographical landforms in Latin America. AL Verbal/Linguistic
- ☐ **p. 168** Students analyze the physical features of Latin America on a map. Verbal/Linguistic, Visual/Spatial

C Critical Thinking Skills

- ☐ **p. 166** Students discuss what it means for cultures to collide. BL Logical/Mathematical, Interpersonal
- ☐ **p. 167** Students draw conclusions about why people move from rural areas to cities. Logical/Mathematical
- ☐ **p. 168** Students evaluate a map and map key to make assumptions about landforms and elevations. AL Logical/Mathematical, Visual/Spatial
- ☐ **p. 172** Students compare population density maps to explain how physical features relate to human settlements. BL Verbal/Linguistic, Visual/Spatial

W Writing Skills

- ☐ **p. 167** Students imagine they are visiting a rain forest and write a story about the experience. ELL Naturalist, Verbal/Linguistic
- ☐ **p. 170** Students write a description of the vegetation associated with climate zones. Naturalist, Verbal/Linguistic
- ☐ **p. 171** Students imagine they represent an investment agency and write promotional material to attract foreign investors. ELL Interpersonal, Verbal/Linguistic

T Technology Skills

- ☐ **p. 167** Student research mountains in Latin America and create a graphic organizer to present data and information on the mountains. AL Verbal/Linguistic, Visual/Spatial
- ☐ **p. 171** Students analyze news media to discuss current economic conditions in Latin America. BL Kinesthetic, Verbal/Linguistic
- ☐ **p. 172** Students research Mexico City in groups and then create a presentation that includes charts, maps, and visuals that group members will present to the class. Interpersonal

☑ Online Teaching Options

V Visual Skills

- ☐ INTERACTIVE FEATURE **Explore the Region: Latin America**—Students create a two-column chart with headings for Physical Geography and Human Geography and list elements of each as they preview four distinct locations in Latin America. AL Naturalist, Verbal/Linguistic
- ☐ INTERACTIVE MAP **Political Map: Latin America**—Students analyze a map to identify and discuss the location of capital cities. BL Visual/Spatial

R Reading Skills

- ☐ INTERACTIVE MAP **Regional Atlas: Latin America**—Students analyze this map on Latin America to discuss the physical diversity of the region. Visual/Spatial, Logical/Mathematical

C Critical Thinking Skills

- ☐ INTERACTIVE MAP **Physical Map: Latin America**—Students analyze a map to make speculations about the reasons Europeans set up colonies in Latin America.
- ☐ INTERACTIVE MAP **Economic Activity Map: Latin America**—Students use the map to make inferences about an area's wealth and economic status. BL Visual/Spatial

W Writing Skills

- ☐ INTERACTIVE MAP **Population Map: Latin America**—Students analyze a map and write to explain coastal population settlements. AL Verbal/Linguistic
- ☐ INTERACTIVE MAP **Climate and Vegetation Maps: Latin America**—Students write about where they would choose to live based on the maps. ELL Naturalist, Verbal/Linguistic

☑ Printable Digital Worksheets

V Visual Skills

- ☐ WORKSHEET **Location Activity**—Students locate countries, islands, and major cities in Mexico, Central America, the Caribbean, and South America.

R Reading Skills

- ☐ WORKSHEET **GIS Simulation**—Students will answer questions that demonstrate their comprehension and depth of knowledge using the graphic information systems approach.

C Critical Thinking Skills

- ☐ WORKSHEET **Environmental Case Study**—Students will complete a study about an environmental challenge currently facing a region in Latin America.
- ☐ WORKSHEET **GeoLab Activity**—Students explore how changes in the environment are threatening coral reef in the Caribbean.

Latin America

UNIT 3

Chapter 7
Mexico

Chapter 8
Central America and the Caribbean

Chapter 9
South America

©Imageplus/Corbis

ENGAGE

Assessing Invite a student volunteer to locate Latin America on a globe or map. Guide students in a class discussion about Latin America. Assess students' knowledge about Latin America by asking them to describe what they know about the region, such as the countries that are located there, famous landforms or travel locations, languages spoken in the region, or how it came to be known as Latin America.

Content Background Knowledge

Origins of the Name Latin America

- The main languages spoken in the region—Spanish and Portuguese—are derived from Latin.
- In the 1830s, a French writer postulated that the region was inhabited by people of a "Latin race."
- In the 1860s, France argued that the region had Latinate origins and therefore belonged in the sphere of countries speaking Latinate languages.
- The term did not achieve widespread use until the 1950s and 1960s.

TEACH & ASSESS

Analyzing Images Call students' attention to the photograph and have them analyze its details. **Ask:** **Suppose you are a travel writer. How might you describe this place?** *(Possible answers: it is a coastal city; it has unusual mountains, a rocky promontory, hillside neighborhoods, varied architecture, a beautiful sandy beach and cerulean waters.)* **How could you describe the elevation of the city?** *(starts at sea level and rises sharply)* **What famous place is in this picture?** *(Ipanema Beach in Rio de Janeiro, Brazil)* Explain to students that Latin America is a diverse region. Have them explain how this photo exemplifies this diversity. Then, **ask:** **How might this place be a microcosm of Latin America in general?** *(Student answers may vary, but could include varied landscapes that range from beach to mountain to jungle.)* **Visual/Spatial**

CLOSE & REFLECT

Listing Have students state facts they know about the geography, culture, and history of Latin America. Tell students they will be learning more about the region in this unit.

GEO @ WORK

Thinking Like a Geographer

Problem Solving Explore specific examples of the principles and skills of geography applied to real-world challenges that impact people's lives. From agriculture to urban planning, to wiping out disease and managing changes in society—geography plays a key role in understanding relationships and generating solutions that make sense.

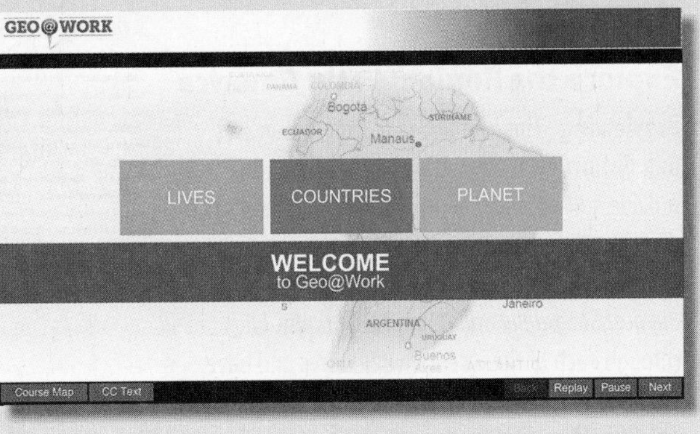

ENGAGE

V Visual Skills

Analyzing Images Encourage students to analyze the image by asking the following series of questions, **ask:** What is happening in the photo? *(people holding a parade)* Where might this be? Explain. *(Possible answer: It might be in the old part of a city because there are old looking buildings and churches in the photo.)* What can you tell about the people? *(dressed in traditional garb or costumes; native ethnicity)* What does this tell you about the culture of Latin America? *(Possible answers: people are religious; people value old traditions; a mix of old and new; celebrating an event or marching in a traditional parade)* Visual/Spatial

TEACH & ASSESS

C Critical Thinking Skills

Interpreting Discuss what it means for cultures to collide. **Ask:** Does the phrase "cultures have collided" mean the cultures are at odds or at war? *(Possible answer: In some cases, yes, but in other cases it means they have melded or blended. The people of the region have held to old customs, but have taken on new ones.)* In the case of Latin America, what cultures have collided or blended? *(the native or indigenous with Europeans)* Brainstorm which Europeans first settled in Latin America. *(Spanish and Portuguese, followed by French)* Have students discuss what they know about the colonial history of the region and how it compares to the history of North America. BL Interpersonal, Logical/Mathematical

R Reading Skills

Identifying Have a student volunteer read aloud the section "Explore the Region." **Ask:** What regions make up Latin America? *(Mexico, Central America, the Caribbean, and South America)* Which of these is a continent? *(South America)* What are some important geographical landforms in Latin America? *(Andes Mountains, rain forests, Amazon River)* Have students name as many countries as they can in Central and South America, as well as some of the countries that make up the Caribbean Islands. AL Verbal/Linguistic

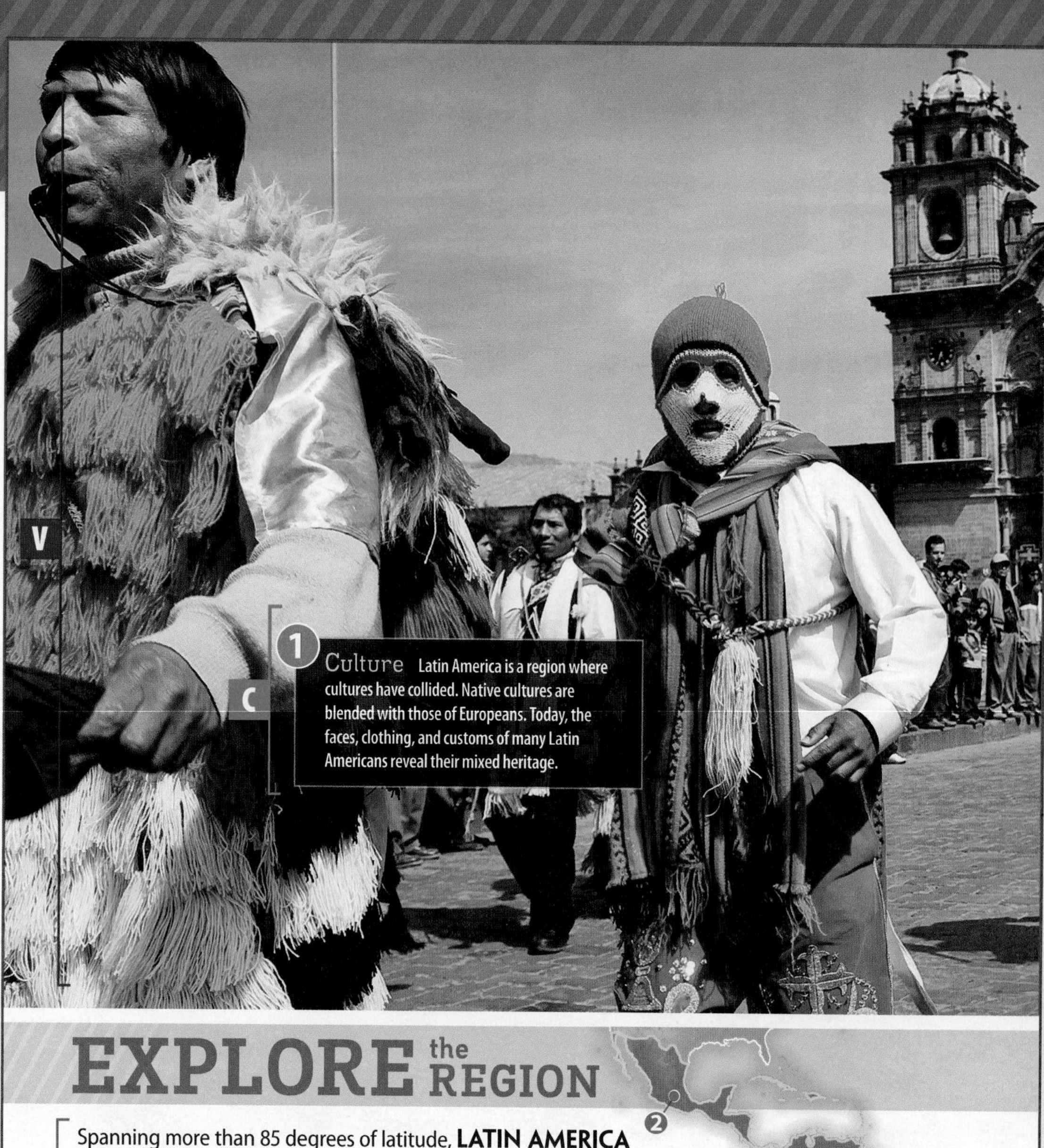

V

C

1 Culture Latin America is a region where cultures have collided. Native cultures are blended with those of Europeans. Today, the faces, clothing, and customs of many Latin Americans reveal their mixed heritage.

EXPLORE the REGION

R

Spanning more than 85 degrees of latitude, **LATIN AMERICA** encompasses Mexico, Central America, the Caribbean, and South America. It is a region of startling physical contrasts, from the high peaks of the Andes to the lush rain forests of the Amazon. Latin America's human geography reflects a shared colonial legacy, but does present some contrasts between urban and rural, rich and poor, more developed and less developed.

HUGHES HervÃ©/hemis.fr/Getty Images

THERE'S MORE ONLINE

166

networks Online Teaching Options

INTERACTIVE FEATURE

Explore the Region: Latin America

Previewing This interactive feature showcases four distinct locations within Latin America to provide students with a preview of the region's rich diversity. Before starting the activity, have students create a two-column chart with the headings *Physical Geography* and *Human Geography.* Click through each of the interactive features and have students list diverse elements presented under each heading. Then guide a class discussion as students share their lists to contrast the physical and human geography of Latin America. AL Naturalist, Verbal/Linguistic

LATIN AMERICA

INTRODUCTION

Spanning more than 85 degrees of latitude, Latin America encompasses Mexico, Central America and the Caribbean, and South America. It is a region of startling physical contrasts, from the high peaks of the Andes to the lush rain forests of the Amazon. Latin America's human geography reflects a shared colonial legacy but does present some contrasts between urban and rural, rich and poor, more developed and less developed.

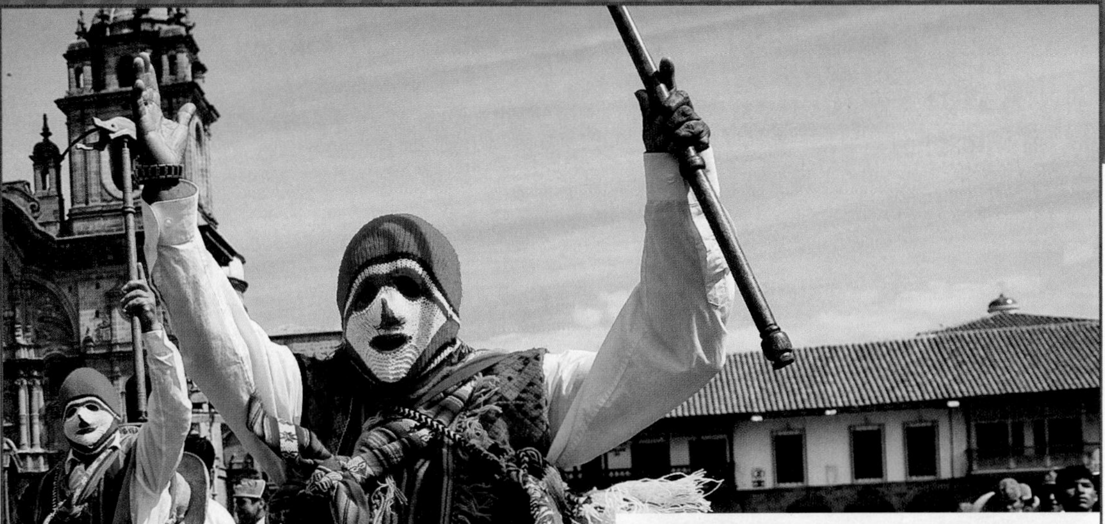

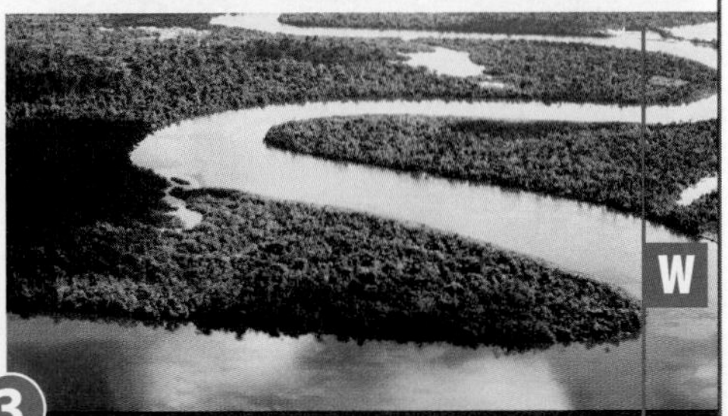

③ Rain Forests Like a snake slithering through the grass, the Nanay River meanders through the Peruvian rain forest.

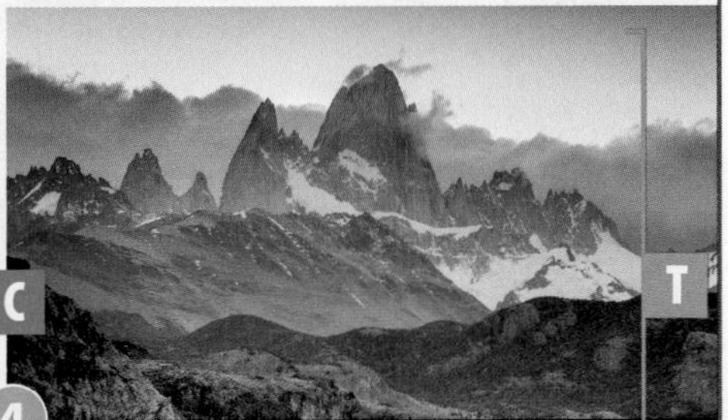

④ Mountains The jagged peaks of Chile's Torres del Paine are part of the Andes, the world's longest mountain chain.

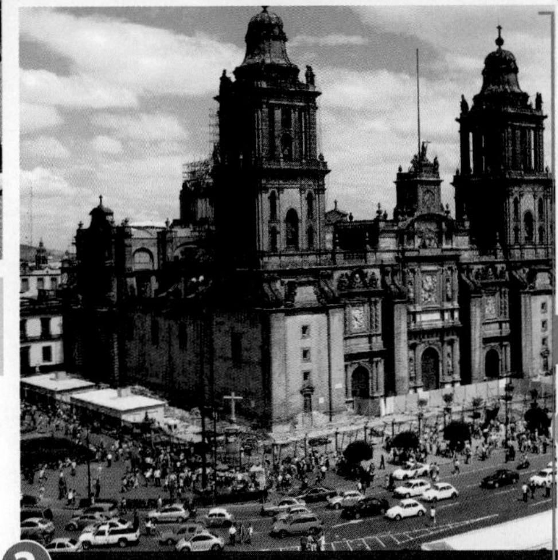

② Cities Many people migrate to urban centers such as Mexico City where work offers the possibility of economic advancement. This rapid growth forces cities to look for ways to provide their growing populations with necessary resources.

(t)Paul Harris/AWL Images/Getty Images, (bl)Luiz Felipe Castro/Flickr/Getty Images, (br)Ken Hornbrook/Flickr/Getty Images

C Critical Thinking Skills

Drawing Conclusions Point out to students that this photograph shows a famous cathedral in one of the world's largest cities, Mexico City. **Ask:** **Why do you suppose many people in Latin America are moving from rural areas to cities?** *(mainly for work or economic advancement)* **Why would opportunities be better in a city than in a rural area?** *(more businesses; need for service providers)* **What are the pros and cons of living and working in a city?** *(Possible answers: cities offer work opportunities, cultural advantages, and many services, but are crowded and sometimes unhealthy; rural areas offer a quieter life, close-knit communities but fewer opportunities and services)* **What effect does rapid population growth have on cities?** *(Possible answers: strains on city services, housing, and infrastructure)* **Logical/Mathematical**

W Writing Skills

Narrative Review what students know about rain forests and their importance. Have students imagine that they are visiting a rain forest in one of the regions in Latin America. Have them write a story about their experience, making sure they describe the flora, fauna, and important features of the region. ELL **Naturalist, Verbal/Linguistic**

T Technology Skills

Researching Have students research some of the world's major mountain chains, such as the Andes, Sierras, Alps, Rockies, and Himalaya. Have students create a graphic organizer that ranks these mountains in terms of length, height, most volcanoes, or other unique features. Then have students present their findings to the class. AL **Verbal/Linguistic, Visual/Spatial**

CLOSE & REFLECT

Reaching Conclusions Review the various factors that have been introduced to students in this unit feature. Ask students to consider all of these factors and write a concluding statement about Latin America.

WORKSHEETS

Latin America

Demonstrating Use these unit digital worksheets to have students demonstrate their depth of knowledge and comprehension, and to provide them with extended unit content through project-based and case studies activities.

- **Environmental Case Study**
- **GIS Simulation**
- **Location Activity**
- **GeoLab Activity**

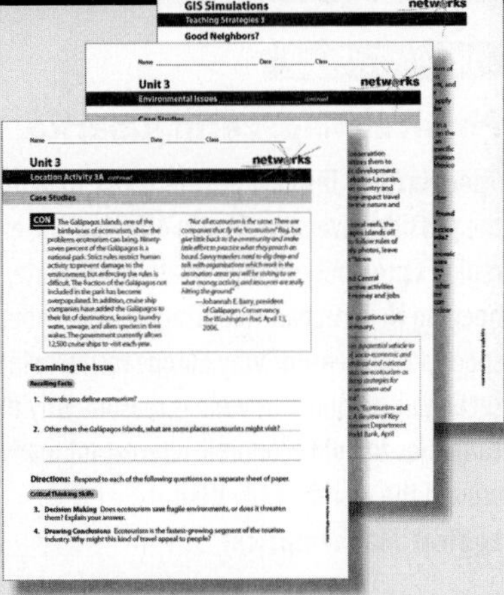

ENGAGE

R1 Reading Skills

Activating Prior Knowledge Before class, write out the names of the five or six most iconic physical features of Latin America, such as the Andes, the Sierra Madre, the Amazon, the Isthmus of Panama, Tierra de Fuego, and Cape Horn. Challenge students to name the country in which each is located. Tell students that they will be learning more about these and other geographical features of Latin America as they study the maps in this unit.

TEACH & ASSESS

C Critical Thinking Skills

Evaluating Ask students to focus on the map key and to note what the different colors represent. **Ask:** **Which color represents the highest elevations?** *(dark orange)* **What assumptions can you make about the landforms that represent the areas at the highest elevations?** *(mostly mountains)* **Where would you expect to find the lowest elevations?** *(beaches, river deltas)* Have students examine the map to see if their hypotheses are accurate. AL **Logical/Mathematical, Visual/Spatial**

R2 Reading Skills

Analyzing Visuals Have students analyze the physical features of Latin America. **Ask:**

- **Where are the highest elevations found in South America?** *(along the western rim)*
- **Would you say most of South America is lowlands or highlands?** *(lowlands)*
- **What about Mexico, Central America, and the Caribbean Islands?** *(Mexico: mostly highlands; Central America and the Caribbean: mostly lowlands)*
- **Which mountain range is highest?** *(Andes)*
- **What do you notice about the flow of the major river systems in South America?** *(drain into the Atlantic Ocean)*

Have students locate and discuss the land barriers in Latin America that may have slowed human travel and development. **Verbal/Linguistic, Visual/Spatial**

ANSWERS, p. 168

MAP STUDY

1. Mountains, rivers, and the rain forest present physical barriers to the development of Latin America.
2. France, the Netherlands, and the United Kingdom still control territory in Latin America.

R1 Latin America
Physical

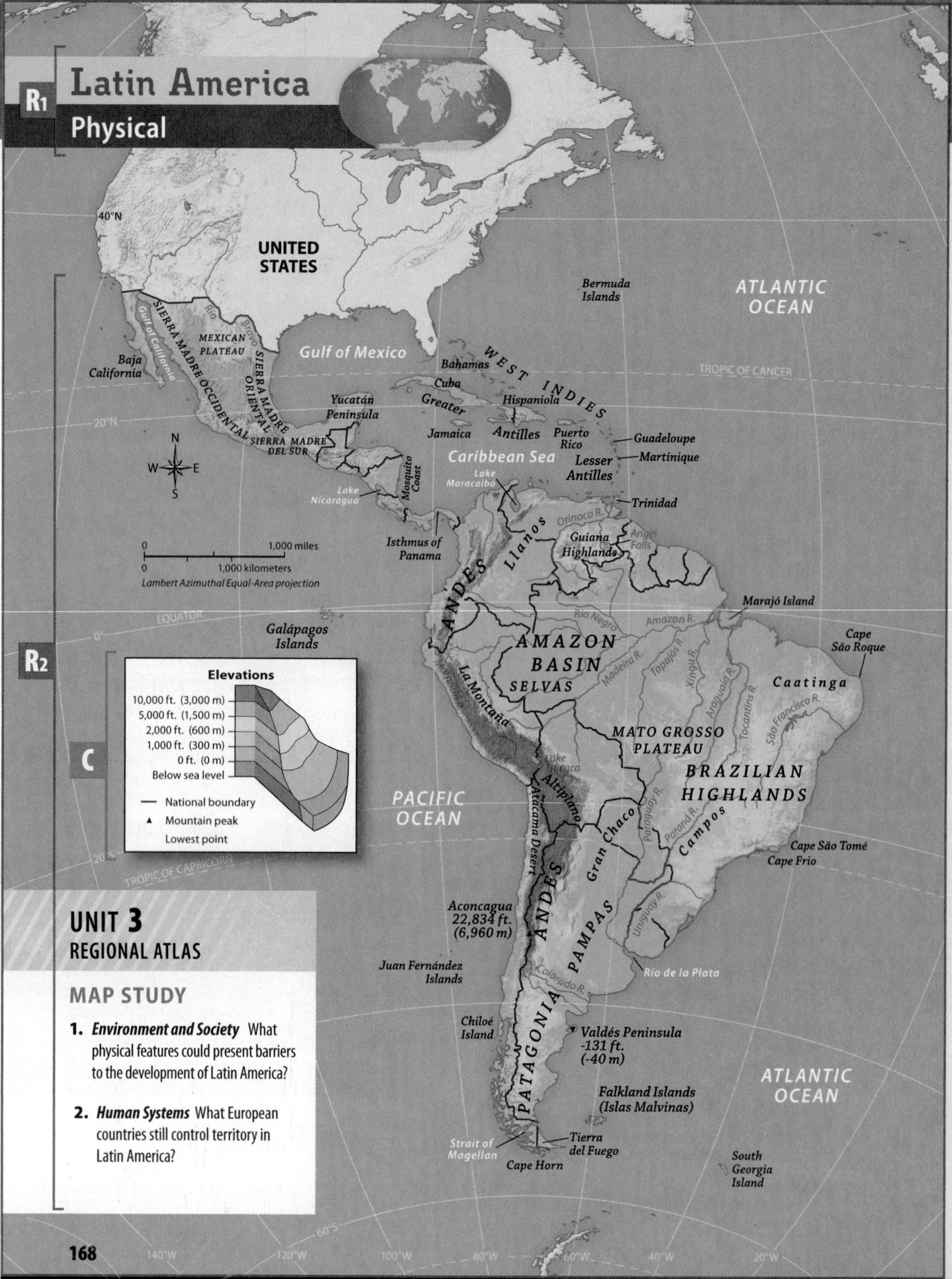

Elevations: 10,000 ft. (3,000 m); 5,000 ft. (1,500 m); 2,000 ft. (600 m); 1,000 ft. (300 m); 0 ft. (0 m); Below sea level

National boundary; Mountain peak; Lowest point

0 — 1,000 miles; 0 — 1,000 kilometers; Lambert Azimuthal Equal-Area projection

UNIT 3
REGIONAL ATLAS

MAP STUDY

1. ***Environment and Society*** What physical features could present barriers to the development of Latin America?
2. ***Human Systems*** What European countries still control territory in Latin America?

168

networks Online Teaching Options

INTERACTIVE MAP

Physical Map: Latin America

Speculating Display the interactive map to discuss the physical diversity of Latin America, the effect of the region's proximity to the equator on climate, and its opening to European colonization. Ask students to speculate on reasons why Europeans were interested in setting up colonies, as well as reasons why this region continues to hold economic interest for many countries around the world. BL **Visual/Spatial, Logical/Mathematical**

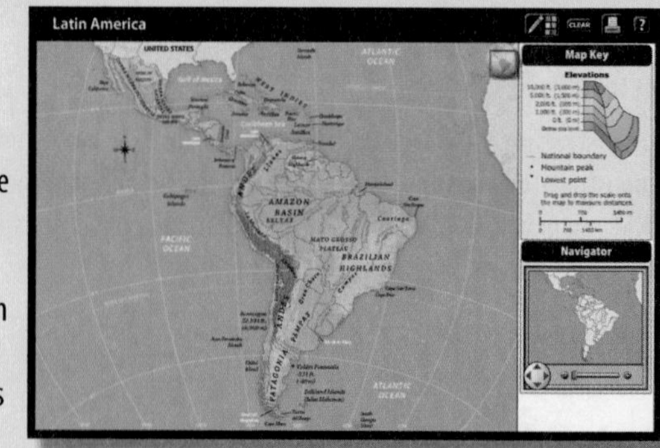

Latin America

Political V

0 — 1,000 miles
0 — 1,000 kilometers
Lambert Azimuthal Equal-Area projection

- National capital
- Department capital
- Major city

Latin America 169

UNIT 3

Latin America

V Visual Skills

Creating Charts Discuss the purpose of political maps and the kinds of information that can be gained from them. *(locations of countries, national boundaries, capital and other cities, major bodies of water and waterways)* Have students use the map to make a chart of the countries of Latin America and their capitals. Challenge students to makes comparisons about the countries and add these to the chart, noting such things as biggest, smallest, coastal, landlocked, and other facts. AL Visual/Spatial

R Reading Skills

Reading Maps Ask students to explain the purpose of the inset on the map. Ask a student volunteer to explain the difference between an independent nation and a dependent territory. Have students name the major Caribbean Islands and identify which islands are dependent territories and to what country each belongs. Verbal/Linguistic, Visual/Spatial

Making Connections

The United States has a large population of people from Puerto Rico, Cuba, and other Caribbean Islands. These islands are also popular vacation destinations. Invite students who have visited any of these islands or have other connections to them to describe their experiences.

W Writing Skills

Informative/Explanatory Ask students to find recent news articles about countries located in Latin America. Topics could include presidential elections, political uprisings, economic forecasts, land or resource disputes, climate-related problems, or natural disasters. Have students write headlines for each of these stories. Use these headlines to lead a class discussion on current events in Latin America. Have students locate each country on the political map of Latin America. ELL Verbal/Linguistic

INTERACTIVE MAP

Political Map: Latin America

Spatial Analysis Use this map to discuss the location of capital cities. Have students locate and identify several capital cities of countries in Latin America, specifically pointing out Guatemala, San Salvador, Managua, San Jose, and Panama. Have students form small groups. Ask groups to discuss what they have learned about centers of population and how this might relate to the location of these capital cities. Then have them locate other capital cities that have similar spatial locations. Students should note that many capital cities are located along the coastlines, which are often the centers of population. BL Visual/Spatial

C Critical Thinking Skills

Drawing Conclusions Ask: Have students use the map key to identify the major climate zones in Latin America.

- **What can be said about the climate of Mexico?** *(diverse; ranges from arid to tropical rain forest)* **And of South America?** *(even more diverse)*
- **Where is the climate coldest in Latin America?** *(in western South America in the Andes and at the very tip of the continent in the high latitudes where it is closest to Antarctica)*
- **What is the relationship, if any, between the climate zones and their proximity to the Equator?** *(Generally climates are warmest near the Equator.)*
- **How does elevation affect this overall pattern?** *(Mountainous areas on the Equator have cooler temperatures than lowland areas due to elevation.)*

Logical/Mathematical, Visual/Spatial, Verbal/Linguistic

W Writing Skills

Informative/Explanatory Have students compare the climate map to the vegetation map of Latin America. Have students write a paragraph describing the vegetation associated with each climate zone. **ELL Naturalist, Verbal/Linguistic**

Latin America
Climate and Vegetation
Climate
Tropical rain forest
Tropical wet/dry
Semi-arid (steppe)
Arid (desert)
Humid subtropical
Marine west coast
Mediterranean
Tundra and high altitude
C
Vegetation
Tropical rain forest
Tropical grassland (savanna)
Desert scrub and desert waste
Temperate grassland
Mediterranean scrub
Deciduous forest
Coniferous forest
Mixed forest (deciduous and coniferous)
Highland (vegetation varies with elevation)
W
UNITED STATES
Tijuana
Gulf of Mexico
Nassau
TROPIC OF CANCER
Mexico City
Caribbean Sea
San Salvador
Panama
Caracas
Bogotá
Paramaribo
ATLANTIC OCEAN
PACIFIC OCEAN
EQUATOR
Manaus
Belém
Lima
La Paz
Brasília
Asunción
Rio de Janeiro
Santiago
Buenos Aires
ATLANTIC OCEAN
40°N
20°N
0°
20°S
40°S
60°S
140°W
120°W
100°W
80°W
60°W
40°W
20°W
TROPIC OF CAPRICORN
0 1,000 miles
0 1,000 kilometers
Lambert Azimuthal Equal-Area projection
170

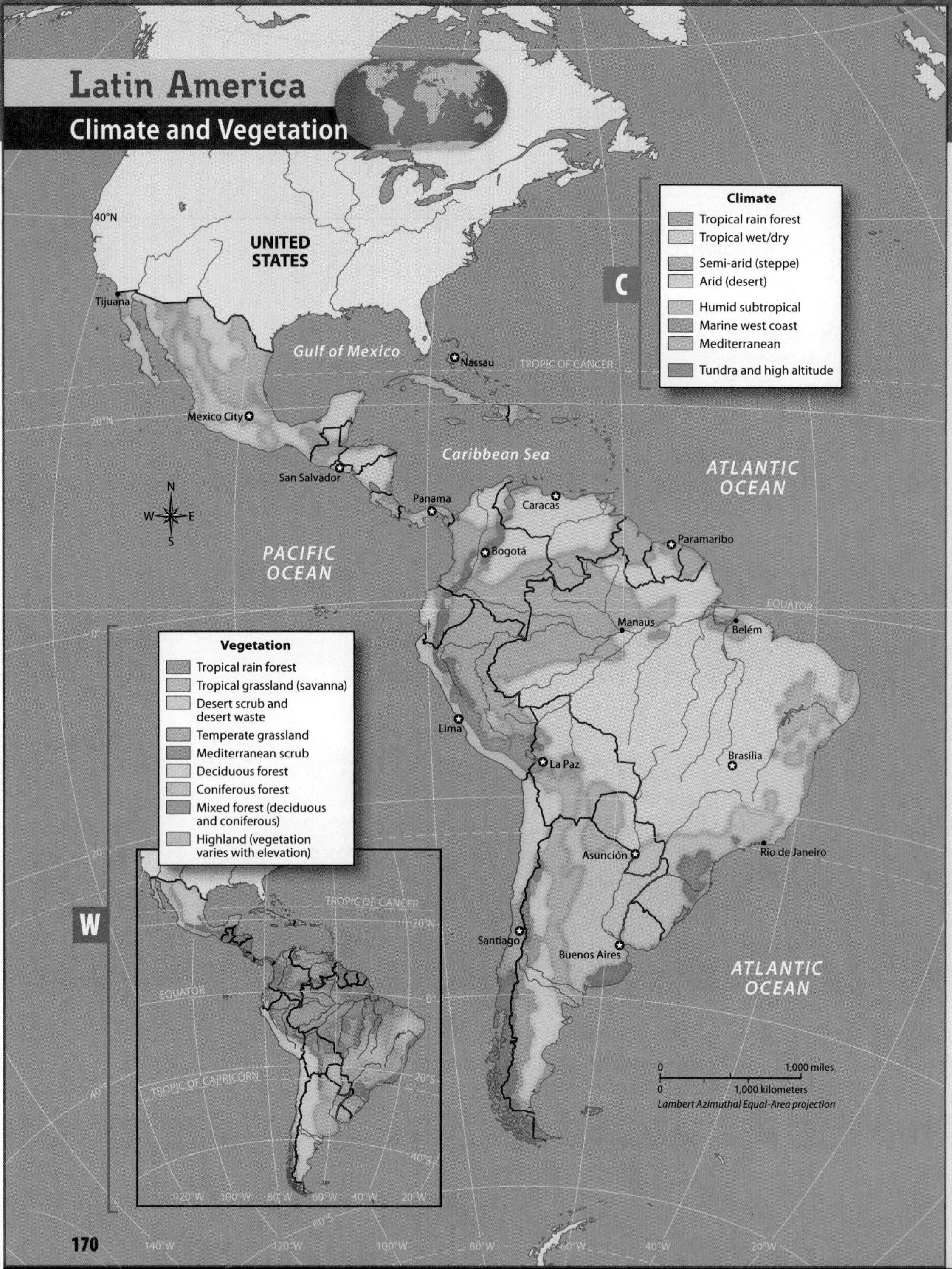

networks Online Teaching Options

INTERACTIVE MAP

Climate and Vegetation Maps: Latin America

Narrative Display the interactive maps, allowing time for students to analyze and discuss the climate patterns and vegetation in the various regions. Then ask students to write a brief essay explaining where they would choose to live in Latin America based on data they analyzed from the climate and vegetation maps. Invite several volunteers to share their essays with the class. **ELL Naturalist, Verbal/Linguistic**

Latin America
Map Key
Climate
Tropical rain forest
Tropical wet/dry
Semi-arid (steppe)
Arid (desert)
Humid subtropical
Marine west coast
Mediterranean
Tundra and high altitude
Cold current
Warm current
Navigator

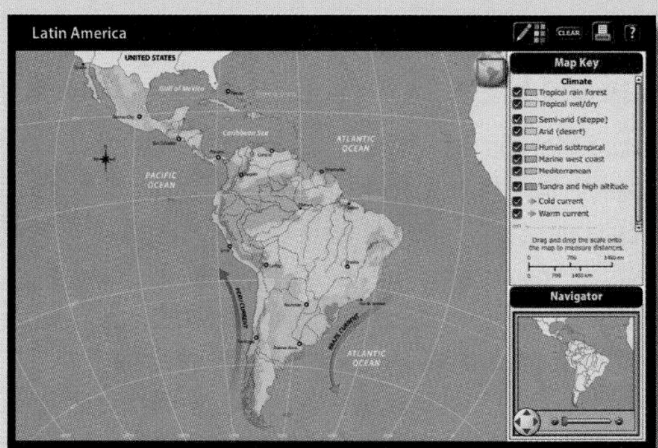

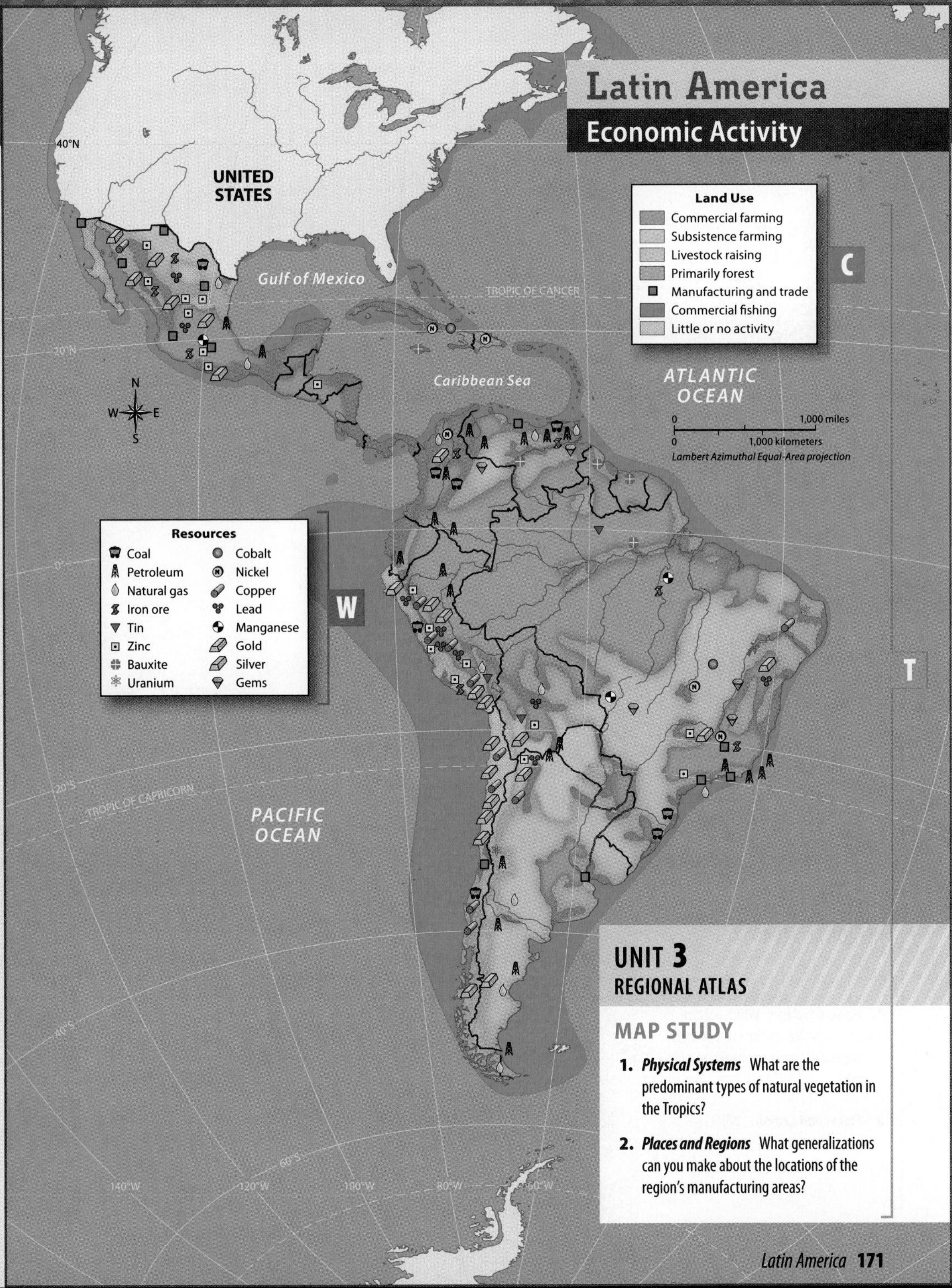

Latin America
Economic Activity

Land Use
- Commercial farming
- Subsistence farming
- Livestock raising
- Primarily forest
- Manufacturing and trade
- Commercial fishing
- Little or no activity

Resources
- Coal
- Petroleum
- Natural gas
- Iron ore
- Tin
- Zinc
- Bauxite
- Uranium
- Cobalt
- Nickel
- Copper
- Lead
- Manganese
- Gold
- Silver
- Gems

UNITED STATES
Gulf of Mexico
Caribbean Sea
ATLANTIC OCEAN
PACIFIC OCEAN
TROPIC OF CANCER
TROPIC OF CAPRICORN
0 1,000 miles
0 1,000 kilometers
Lambert Azimuthal Equal-Area projection

UNIT 3
REGIONAL ATLAS

MAP STUDY

1. ***Physical Systems*** What are the predominant types of natural vegetation in the Tropics?
2. ***Places and Regions*** What generalizations can you make about the locations of the region's manufacturing areas?

C Critical Thinking Skills

Analyzing Visuals Have students focus on the map key to identify the areas of Latin America that support commercial farming, commercial forestry, livestock raising, and manufacturing. Have students brainstorm geographic conditions that provide a country with economic advantages. *(Possible answers: size, favorable climate, good farmland, river systems, coastline, and mineral wealth)* Then ask students to study the map and identify which countries have these advantages. **Logical/Mathematical, Visual/Spatial**

T Technology Skills

Analyzing News Media Divide students into pairs or small groups. Ask students to conduct online research to find recent news articles about the economies of different countries of Latin America. Topics could include manufacturing and/or agricultural news, stock indexes, inflation, unemployment, commodity prices, GDP data, foreign or domestic investment, and trade agreements and/or statistics. Have students use these articles to lead a class discussion on current economic conditions in Latin America. Students should tag each story to their location on a map of the region. **BL Kinesthetic, Verbal/Linguistic**

W Writing Skills

Informative/Explanatory As a class, discuss how the presence of natural resources can benefit a country and attract outside investors. Divide students into groups and assign each group a country of Latin America to explore. Have students use the map to identify the mineral resources of that country. Have students imagine that they represent an investment promotion agency. Have them write a promotional piece designed to attract foreign investors to their country. **ELL Interpersonal, Verbal/Linguistic**

INTERACTIVE MAP

Economic Activity Map: Latin America

Inferring This map can be used with students to discuss the economy and financial status of various areas within Latin America. Click through the interactive layers of this map. Guide a class discussion about which countries students can infer are the wealthiest or poorest countries based on their land uses and resources. Then have students choose one location to research further to see if their hypothesis about that country's financial status is correct. Have students report their findings to the class. **BL Visual/Spatial**

ANSWERS, p. 171

MAP STUDY

1. The predominant types of natural vegetation are tropical rain forest, tropical grassland, and desert scrub and waste.
2. Mexico has manufacturing and trade in various locations along the coast and in the interior where large cities are located. In South America, manufacturing and trade locations are primarily located along the coasts.

G1 Critical Thinking Skills

Evaluating Discuss the meaning of population density. *(average number of people living in a square mile area)* Have students focus on the map key. **Ask:** Which color represents the highest population density? *(purple)* The lowest? *(light yellow)* Without looking at the map, where would you expect to find the highest population densities in Latin America? *(around big cities; coastal areas)* The lowest? *(mountain or desert areas)* Have students examine the map to see if their hypotheses are accurate. AL Logical/Mathematical, Visual/Spatial

G2 Critical Thinking Skills

Comparing Have students describe the population density of Mexico. **Ask:** Where are population densities the greatest in Mexico? *(in the southern half of the country, particularly around cities)* How do the population densities of the countries of Central America compare? *(They have a similar range of densities, but none of the cities are as densely populated as Mexico City.)* The Caribbean Islands? *(lots of high density areas; no cities over 5,000,000; few low density areas)* South America? *(similar population density range but a greater percentage of low density areas)* Have students compare the population density map to the physical map of Latin America. Ask them to explain how population density relates to landform regions, such as which physical features discourage dense settlements and which attract them. BL Verbal/Linguistic, Visual/Spatial

T Technology Skills

Presenting Have students explain what the map tells them about the population of Mexico City. *(over 5,000,000 people)* Tell students that Mexico City is one of the most populated cities in the world. Divide students into small groups and have them research Mexico City and its population makeup. Encourage students to make a presentation to the class using charts, maps, and photographs. Interpersonal

CLOSE & REFLECT

Summarizing Divide students into pairs. Have partners review the unit maps and use them to make a list of important information about the geography of Latin America.

ANSWERS, p. 172

MAP STUDY

1. In Central and South America, people live along the coast due to the rough terrain—mountains and tropical rain forests—in the interior of the continent.
2. Large cities are usually located along the coast.

Latin America
Population Density

POPULATION	
Per sq. mi.	Per sq. km
1,250 and over	500 and over
250–1,249	100–499
63–249	25–99
25–62	10–24
2.5–24	1–9
Less than 2.5	Less than 1
Uninhabited	Uninhabited

Cities
(Statistics reflect metropolitan areas.)
- ■ Over 5,000,000
- □ 2,000,000–5,000,000
- ⊙ 1,000,000–2,000,000
- • 500,000–1,000,000
- ○ Under 500,000

0 — 1,000 miles
0 — 1,000 kilometers
Lambert Azimuthal Equal-Area projection

UNIT 3
REGIONAL ATLAS

MAP STUDY

1. ***Human Systems*** Which parts of Latin America are the most densely populated? What might account for this?
2. ***Places and Regions*** What generalizations can you make about the locations of South America's cities?

172

networks *Online Teaching Options*

INTERACTIVE MAP

Population Map: Latin America

Analyzing Visuals Use this map to provide students with a visual of settlement patterns in Latin America. Have students read the interactive text layers in the map. Students should work with a partner to discuss living patterns in Latin America. Then ask pairs to consider how and why population patterns have developed in these areas by writing a short paragraph that explains their answers. AL Verbal/Linguistic

CHAPTER 7

Mexico Planner

UNDERSTANDING BY DESIGN®

Enduring Understandings

- *The characteristics and distribution of cultures influence human systems.*

Essential Question

- *How do physical systems and human systems shape a place?*

Predictable Misunderstandings

Students may think:

- *All of Mexico has the same warm climate. Explain that Mexico has vertical climate zones. Even though it is located closer to the equator than the United States, its climates vary based on elevation.*
- *Most people in Mexico live in poor, rural areas. Explain that Mexico City, the nation's capital, is a megacity, and home to millions of people.*
- *Mexico does not have many natural resources. Explain that Mexico has many natural resources such as petroleum, silver, gold, and timber, but accessing them presents environmental issues.*
- *Mexico has a pristine, undisturbed environment. Explain that Mexico grapples with the same environmental issues as any other growing economy such as deforestation, pollution, and waste disposal.*

Assessment Evidence

Performance Tasks:

- *Hands-On Chapter Project*

Other Evidence:

- *Guided Reading Activities*
- *Vocabulary Activities*
- *Lesson Quizzes*
- *Chapter Tests, Forms A and B*

SUGGESTED PACING GUIDE

Introducing the Chapter	½ Day
Lesson 1	1 Day
Lesson 2	2 Days
Lesson 3	1 Day
Chapter Wrap-Up and Assessment	½ Day
TOTAL TIME	**5 Days**

Key for Using the Teacher Edition

SKILL-BASED ACTIVITIES

Types of skill activities found in the Teacher Edition.

* **V Visual Skills** require students to analyze maps, graphs, charts, and photos.

R Reading Skills help students practice reading skills and master vocabulary.

C Critical Thinking Skills help students apply and extend what they have learned.

W Writing Skills provide writing opportunities to help students comprehend the text.

T Technology Skills require students to use digital tools effectively.

*Letters are followed by a number when there is more than one of the same type of skill on the page.

DIFFERENTIATED INSTRUCTION

All activities are written for the on-level student unless otherwise marked with the leveled labels below.

BL Beyond Level
AL Approaching Level
ELL English Language Learners

All students benefit from activities that utilize different learning styles. Many activities are marked as below when a particular learning style is highlighted.

Intrapersonal	Naturalist
Logical/Mathematical	Kinesthetic
Visual/Spatial	Auditory/Musical
Verbal/Linguistic	Interpersonal

National Geography Standards covered in "Mexico"

The student knows and understands:

(3) How to analyze the spatial organizations of people, places, and environments on Earth's surface

3.1 The meaning and use of complex spatial concepts, such as connectivity, networks, hierarchies, to analyze and explain the spatial organization of human and physical phenomena

(4) The physical and human characteristics of places

4.2 The interaction of physical and human systems result in the creation of and changes to places

(7) The physical processes that shape the patterns of Earth's surface

7.3 Physical processes interact over time to shape particular places on Earth's surface

(8) The characteristics and spatial distribution of ecosystems and biomes on Earth's surface

8.1 Ecosystems are dynamic and respond to changes in environmental conditions

(9) The characteristics, distribution, and migration of human populations on Earth's surface

9.2 Population distribution and density are a function of historical, environmental, economic, political, and technological factors

(12) The processes, patterns, and functions of human settlement

12.2 Settlements can grow and/or decline over time

(14) How human actions modify the physical environment

14.1 Human modifications of the physical environment can have significant global impacts

14.1.A Explain the global impacts of human changes in the physical environment

14.2 The use of technology can have both intended and unintended impacts on the physical environment

(15) How physical systems affect human systems

15.1 Depending on the choice of human activities, the characteristics of the physical environment can be viewed as both opportunities and constraints

(18) How to apply geography to interpret the present and plan for the future

18.1 Geographic contexts (the human and physical characteristics of places and environments) provide the bases for analyzing current events and making predictions about future issues

CHAPTER OPENER PLANNER

Students will know:

- *the landforms, water system, climate regions, biomes, and natural resources of Mexico and how the physical environment impacts human systems.*
- *how Native American empires and colonial rule influenced Mexico's history, culture, and political and social structures.*
- *how the Mexican economy has become part of the global economy.*
- *the causes and effects of environmental issues in Mexico and efforts to address these issues.*

Students will be able to:

- ***describe** natural features of Mexico.*
- ***analyze** how Mexico's environment affects the people that live there.*
- ***explain** the influence of indigenous peoples and Europeans on Mexico's history and culture.*
- ***describe** Mexico's population today.*
- ***discuss** Mexico's role in the global economy.*
- ***identify** causes and effects of environmental issues.*

UNDERSTANDING BY DESIGN®

☑ *Print Teaching Options*

V Visual Skills

- ☐ **p. 174** Students analyze a map to discuss the boundaries of Mexico City. AL Visual/Spatial
- ☐ **p. 175** Students analyze an aerial image of Mexico City.

R Reading Skills

- ☐ **p. 174** Students discuss day-to-day life for new migrants to Mexico City. BL Logical/Mathematical

C Critical Thinking Skills

- ☐ **p. 174** Students list advantages and disadvantages of urbanization in a chart.

W Writing Skills

- ☐ **p. 174** Students write letters to government officials describing their solutions for the rapid urban growth problems. BL Verbal/Linguistic

T Technology Skills

- ☐ **p. 175** Students highlight problems of urbanization and present images with commentary. Verbal/Linguistic

☑ *Online Teaching Options*

- SLIDE SHOW **Dealing with Rapid Urban Growth**—Students take notes on how Mexico City is dealing with urban growth and organize the notes into an outline that can be added to. ELL Verbal/Linguistic
- INTERACTIVE MAP **Mexico City Growth**—Students discuss rapid population growth in Mexico City and speculate with a partner reasons areas have recently become densely populated. BL Logical/Mathematical

☑ *Printable Digital Worksheets*

- WORKSHEET **Assessing Background Knowledge**—Determine the level of prior knowledge students have about Mexico and Mexico City.
- WORKSHEET **Vocabulary Activity**—Students use and improve their academic and content vocabulary by completing various vocabulary activities.

Project-Based Learning 

Hands-On

Create Population Pyramids

Students will work on their own to create a population pyramid based on independent research they gather about the demographics of Mexico.

Digital Hands-On

Create Online Projects

Find an additional activity online that incorporates technology for this project. Visit the EdTech Teacher Web sites for more links, tutorials, and other resources.

Print Resources

ANCILLARY RESOURCES

This ancillary is available for every chapter and lesson.

- **Chapter Tests and Lesson Quizzes**

PRINTABLE DIGITAL WORKSHEETS

These printable digital worksheets are available for every chapter and lesson.

- **Assessing Background Knowledge**
- **Chapter Summaries**
- **Guided Reading Activities**
- **Hands-On Chapter Projects**
- **Quizzes and Tests**
- **Reading Essentials and Study Guide** AL
- **Reteaching Activities**
- **Vocabulary Activities**
- **Video Activities**

More Media Resources

SUGGESTED VIDEOS 

- **Introducing the History and Culture of Mexico** (31 min.)
- **Dawn of the Maya** *National Geographic* (60 min.)
- **Weekend in Mexico City** (30 min.)

SUGGESTED READING 

- ***Curating at the Edge: Artists Respond to the U.S. Mexico Border,*** by Kate Bonansinga
- ***A Weekend with Diego Rivera,*** by Barbara Braun
- ***Mexico: A Study of an Economically Developing Country,*** by Anna Lewington
- ***A Land Between Waters: Environmental Histories of Modern Mexico,*** by Christopher R. Boyer

PHYSICAL GEOGRAPHY OF MEXICO

Students will know:

- *the landforms and water systems of Mexico.*
- *the climate regions of Mexico and their impact on the physical environment.*
- *the characteristics of Mexico's biomes.*
- *how Mexico's physical environment impacts human systems.*
- *the characteristics, location, and uses of natural resources in Mexico.*

Students will be able to:

- ***describe** the landforms, water systems, climate regions, and biomes of Mexico.*
- ***explain** the impact of Mexico's physical environment on people.*
- ***identify** natural resources in Mexico.*

UNDERSTANDING BY DESIGN®

☑ Print Teaching Options

V Visual Skills

- ☐ **p. 176** Students make a mental map of Mexico in relation to the United States and Central America, then draw their map and compare it to an actual map. ELL Visual/Spatial
- ☐ **p. 177** Students study the information on a plate tectonics diagram. AL Visual/Spatial
- ☐ **p. 178** Students discuss the diagram on vertical climate zones. AL Visual/Spatial

R Reading Skills

- ☐ **p. 176** Students brainstorm what they already know about the physical geography of Mexico.
- ☐ **p. 178** Students work together to translate the names of each climate zone into English. ELL Verbal/Linguistic
- ☐ **p. 179** Students identify factors that affect Mexico's climates and explain the relationship between factors and effects they can produce. Verbal/Linguistic, Naturalist

C Critical Thinking Skills

- ☐ **p. 176** Students classify landforms in Mexico in a graphic organizer. AL Interpersonal, Naturalist
- ☐ **p. 177** Students consider how Mexico's landforms affect the population settlements. Logical/Mathematical

W Writing Skills

- ☐ **p. 178** Students write a poem about one of the water systems in Mexico. BL Auditory/Musical, Naturalist

T Technology Skills

- ☐ **p. 179** Students create a presentation on the biomes in northern or southern Mexico and then compare and contrast northern and southern biomes as a class. BL Visual/Spatial, Interpersonal

☑ Online Teaching Options

V Visual Skills

INTERACTIVE BELLRINGER **Vertical Climate Zones of Mexico**—Students use a diagram to discuss the relationship between increasing elevation and different climate zones. Visual/Spatial, Logical/Mathematical

C Critical Thinking Skills

INFOGRAPHIC **Climate Zones in Mexico**—Students use the infographic to consider the profitability of crops based on climate, growing season, and rainfall and decide on a crop to grow, considering local implications of processing, selling, and collecting a profit. Naturalist

INTERACTIVE WHITEBOARD ACTIVITY **Geography of Mexico**—Students will identify landforms and major water systems in Mexico on a map. Visual/Spatial

W Writing Skills

INFOGRAPHIC **Ring of Fire/Tectonic Plates**—Students discuss plate tectonics and write an argument to defend whether they believe the plate tectonics around Mexico will build up or break apart the land bridge between North and South America. BL Logical/Mathematical, Verbal/Linguistic

☑ Printable Digital Worksheets

R Reading Skills

WORKSHEET **Guided Reading Activity**—Students use the Guided Reading Activity worksheets to review their comprehension of the content. Verbal/Linguistic

WORKSHEET **Chapter Summary**—Students review the main ideas of the chapter content. Verbal/Linguistic

C Critical Thinking Skills

WORKSHEET **Video Activity**—Students answer questions related to the chapter content after they have viewed the lesson video. Visual/Spatial

LESSON **2 PLANNER**

Human Geography of Mexico

Students will know:

- *how Native American empires influenced Mexico's history and culture.*
- *the ways in which European colonial rule shaped Mexico's political and social structures.*
- *the population characteristics—the people, density and distribution, and urban areas—of Mexico today.*
- *that Mexican society today reflects a blending of indigenous and European cultures and beliefs.*
- *how the Mexican economy has become part of the global economy.*

Students will be able to:

- ***discuss** the influence of Native American empires and colonial rule on Mexico's history, culture, and political and social structures.*
- ***describe** population characteristics of Mexico and how Mexican society is a blend of indigenous and European cultures.*
- ***explain** Mexico's role in the global economy.*

UNDERSTANDING BY DESIGN®

☑ Print Teaching Options

V Visual Skills

- ☐ **p. 180** Students view a map to write about how physical geography affects life in Mexico. Verbal/Linguistic
- ☐ **p. 184** Students analyze and interpret a graph about the female employees in Mexico. AL Visual/Spatial
- ☐ **p. 185** Students create a two-column chart to track Mexico's actions to globalize its economy and the challenges it has faced. Interpersonal, Visual/Spatial
- ☐ **p. 185** Students identify features on a migration map. AL Visual/Spatial, Logical/Mathematical

R Reading Skills

- ☐ **p. 180** Students write predictions about the lesson.
- ☐ **p. 182** Students define the prefix *mega-* and the root word *primate.* ELL Verbal/Linguistic
- ☐ **p. 185** Students discuss the word *privatize* and the suffix *-ize.* ELL Verbal/Linguistic

C Critical Thinking Skills

- ☐ **p. 180** Students compare and contrast information on indigenous peoples of Mexico. AL Logical/Mathematical
- ☐ **p. 181** Students discuss the changing systems of Mexico's government. AL Logical/Mathematical
- ☐ **p. 183** Students discuss changing attitudes in Mexican society and the future effects. BL Verbal/Linguistic
- ☐ **p. 184** Students consider how Mexican cultures have met, clashed, and blended. BL Logical/Mathematical

W Writing Skills

- ☐ **p. 186** Students write essays to propose solutions to improve United States and Mexican economies. BL Verbal/Linguistic

T Technology Skills

- ☐ **p. 183** Students create multimedia presentations about life in Mexico City. BL Verbal/Linguistic, Visual/Spatial
- ☐ **p. 184** Students create a poster interpreting one of Diego Rivera's works. Visual/Spatial, Verbal/Linguistic

☑ Online Teaching Options

V Visual Skills

- VIDEO **Mexico City**—Students learn about how Mexico City has diversified and changed and create a chart to list traditional influences and modern influences. ELL Visual/Spatial
- INTERACTIVE IMAGE **Women in the Workforce**—Students discuss the issue of gender and society in Mexico. AL Verbal/Linguistic
- INTERACTIVE MAP **Migration to U.S.**—Students write three questions about the map of Mexican migration to the United States. AL Verbal/Linguistic

R Reading Skills

- INTERACTIVE BELLRINGER **Biography of Diego Rivera**—Students read a passage about Diego Rivera and draw conclusions about what life might have been like for workers and peasants in Mexico during Diego Rivera's time. Interpersonal, Verbal/Linguistic

W Writing Skills

- INTERACTIVE MAP **Civilizations of Mesoamerica**—Students write a short paragraph explaining why they feel Mexico City has become such a large city based on its physical location in Mexico. Visual/Spatial

C Critical Thinking Skills

- TIME LINE **Mexican Independence and Change**—Students discuss the various ancient civilizations and tragic conquests that lead to Mexico's independence. BL Verbal/Linguistic
- INTERACTIVE WHITEBOARD ACTIVITY **Indigenous Peoples of Mexico**—Students identify characteristics about the three major indigenous groups in Mexico, the Aztec, the Maya, and the Nomadic and Semi-Nomadic People.

☑ Printable Digital Worksheets

R Reading Skills

- WORKSHEET **Guided Reading Activity**—Students use the Guided Reading Activity worksheets to review their comprehension of the lesson content. Verbal/Linguistic
- WORKSHEET **Reading Essentials and Study Guide**—Students complete the study guide and answer Reading Progress Check and vocabulary questions. AL ELL

C Critical Thinking Skills

- WORKSHEET **Video Activity**—Students will complete this worksheet by answering the questions after they have viewed the lesson video. Visual/Spatial

LESSON 3 PLANNER

PEOPLE AND THEIR ENVIRONMENT: MEXICO

Students will know:

- *the causes and effects of deforestation in Mexico.*
- *why water scarcity is a growing issue in Mexico.*
- *the causes and effects of desertification in Mexico.*
- *how population growth and economic development contribute to environmental issues.*
- *the efforts of different groups to address environmental issues.*

Students will be able to:

- ***describe** the causes and effects of deforestation and desertification.*
- ***explain** water scarcity.*
- ***analyze** environmental issues and efforts to address them.*

UNDERSTANDING BY DESIGN®

☑ Print Teaching Options

V Visual Skills

- ☐ **p. 188** Students analyze the map showing environmental deterioration in Mexico. AL Visual/Spatial, Logical/Mathematical

R Reading Skills

- ☐ **p. 187** Students brainstorm the ways people extract and use natural resources and their environmental effects.
- ☐ **p. 187** Students discuss the words *diverse* and *biodiversity,* the prefix *bio-* and the suffix *-ity.* ELL Verbal/Linguistic
- ☐ **p. 189** Students discuss the urban water crisis in Mexico City and why it threatens the poor the most. Logical/Mathematical

C Critical Thinking Skills

- ☐ **p. 187** Students create a graphic organizer to list cause-and-effect relationships in the lesson. AL Visual/Spatial
- ☐ **p. 190** Students make generalizations based on the text. AL Logical/Mathematical

W Writing Skills

- ☐ **p. 188** Students write a paragraph describing the importance of water to life in Mexico. Logical/Mathematical

T Technology Skills

- ☐ **p. 189** Students create a visual to present information about the work an environmental scientist does. BL Verbal/Linguistic, Visual/Spatial
- ☐ **p. 190** Students work in small groups to create a presentation on an assigned program and its success in combatting the problem it was designed to solve. BL Verbal/Linguistic

☑ Online Teaching Options

R Reading Skills

- VIDEO **U.S. Mexico Border**—Students learn about environmental and economic changes in Mexico, choose a particular change, and write a list of potential solutions. BL Verbal/Linguistic

C Critical Thinking Skills

- INTERACTIVE WHITEBOARD ACTIVITY **Deforestation in Mexico**—Students will identify the causes and effects of deforestation in Mexico.

W Writing Skills

- INTERACTIVE BELLRINGER **Diminishing Frontier Forests in Mexico**—Students study the map about deforestation and discuss and write a paragraph about how this map might look in the future and why. Visual/Spatial, Verbal/Linguistic
- INTERACTIVE MAP **Environmental Deterioration in Mexico**—Students study the map and then write a paragraph predicting what they think will happen to this region over time. Verbal/Linguistic

☑ Printable Digital Worksheets

R Reading Skills

- WORKSHEET **Guided Reading Activity**—Students use the Guided Reading Activity worksheets to review their comprehension of the content.
- WORKSHEET **Reading Essentials and Study Guide**— Students complete the study guide and answer Reading Progress Check and vocabulary questions. AL ELL
- WORKSHEET **Vocabulary Activity**—Students review the chapter content and academic vocabulary words. Verbal/Linguistic
- WORKSHEET **Chapter Summary**—Students review the main ideas of the chapter content.

C Critical Thinking Skills

- WORKSHEET **Video Activity**—Students will answer questions about the lesson video. Logical/Mathematical
- WORKSHEET **Reteaching Activity**—Students use this activity to review and revisit chapter content and vocabulary. This worksheet can be used with struggling students who need additional help with difficult content concept.
- WORKSHEET **Hands-On Chapter Project**—Students conduct research about the demography of Mexico. They will study Mexico's population, global population rank, age structure, birthrate, death rate, and other significant population data. Then use this information to create population pyramids. BL Visual/Spatial, Logical/Mathematical

Intervention and Remediation Strategies

LESSON 1 Physical Geography of Mexico

Reading and Comprehension

Have students work with a partner to create an outline of the lesson that highlights key facts related to Mexico's landforms, water systems, climate, biomes, and resources. To ensure comprehension of the topics, have partners create a slide show using presentation software that explains a topic or process, such as how plate tectonics impacted Mexico's formation. Encourage students to incorporate content vocabulary terms in their presentations. Have students present their slide shows to the class, allowing time for groups to conduct a question-and-answer session in which students from each group answer questions about their topic.

Text Evidence

Organize students into four groups and give each group one of the following terms written on a piece of paper: *land bridge, seismic, plate tectonics, vertical climate zone.* Have students in each group work together to act out their assigned term without using words as the student audience tries to guess the term. If students have trouble acting out their assigned term, whisper suggestions for clues. After each group has acted out its term and presented its summary, discuss as a class how the term applies to Mexico's physical geography.

LESSON 2 Human Geography of Mexico

Reading and Comprehension

Have student pairs choose two of the lesson's content vocabulary words. Tell students to work with their partner to write each word in a sentence using both words correctly. Then have pairs play a "Pictionary" style guessing game in which their partner draws clues to describe a content vocabulary term for their partner to guess. After students have finished guessing each of the terms, have partners compete against other pairs to see who can guess the most terms correctly in a certain amount of time. As a "bonus" or tiebreaker question, have each team try to give clues and guess one of the academic vocabulary terms.

Text Evidence

Have students review the lesson to identify key concepts and events. Encourage them to identify time-order relationships as they read. Remind students that looking for sequence signal words can help them organize and remember historical events. Have students jot down time-order words and phrases, such as *before, after, in the late 1700s, in 1992,* and so on. Then have partners create a time line of key historical events. Have student pairs share their time lines with the class. Then have student pairs collaborate to write a short paragraph that summarizes the events depicted on their time lines.

LESSON 3 People and Their Environment: Mexico

Reading and Comprehension

Ensure students' understanding of unfamiliar or confusing content vocabulary words, such as the meaning of the term *sustainable development.* Review with students the map in this lesson. Then discuss Mexico's deteriorating environment and the National Biodiversity Strategy and Action Plan. Guide them to paraphrase the following statement from the text, "*The plan has four major objectives: to conserve and protect the biodiversity components, to value the different components of biodiversity, to promote knowledge of biodiversity, and to encourage sustainable and diversified use of biodiversity components.*"

Text Evidence

Tell students to choose one of the following statements from the *It Matters Because* paragraph to identify supporting evidence: *Mexico has been so focused on increasing economic development that conservation of resources has not been as high a priority. However, concerned Mexican citizens are working hard to find ways to preserve the land and all that it provides.* In addition to identifying evidence from the text, students may conduct online research to identify facts to support their chosen statement.

Online Resources

Leveled Reader

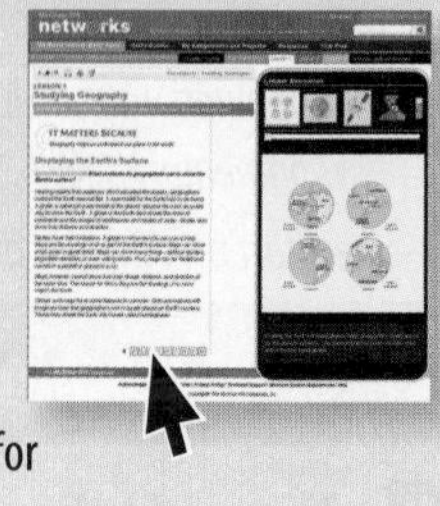

Use this online approaching-level text that corresponds directly to the text in the Student Edition. It also includes additional reading and comprehension support for English Language Learners.

Guided Reading Activities

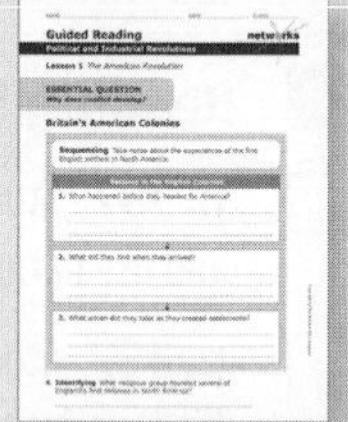

This resource uses guiding questions to help students with comprehension.

Reteaching Activities

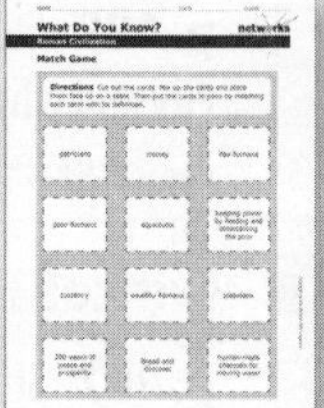

These worksheets provide students with an opportunity for remedial practice and review of vital chapter content.

Reading Essentials and Study Guide

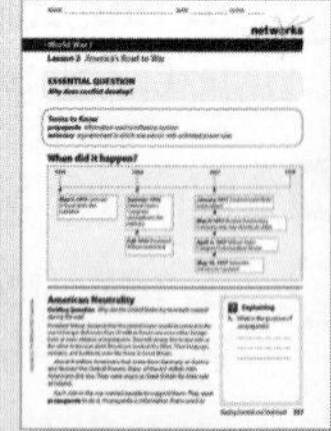

This resource offers writing and reading activities for the approaching-level student.

Self-Check Quizzes

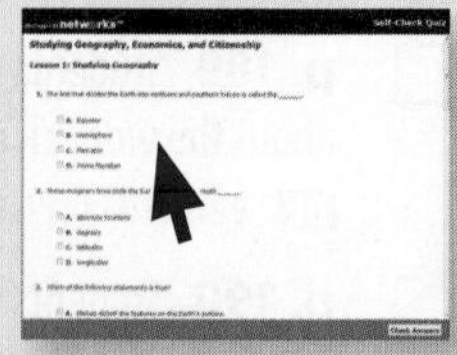

This online assessment tool provides instant feedback for students to check their progress.

Chapter Summaries

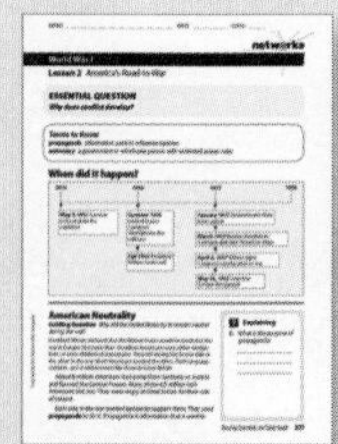

Summaries are provided for each chapter that thoroughly condense core content into manageable chunks.

Mexico

networks

There's More Online about Mexico.

CHAPTER 7

ESSENTIAL QUESTION • *How do physical systems and human systems shape a place?*

Geography Matters...

Places reflect their relationship between humans and their environment. Mexico today is a result of history, geography, and increased globalization. Cultures have collided in Mexico for centuries. Indigenous civilizations flourished, followed by Europeans who brought new laws, languages, and religions. Today, the faces and customs of many Mexican people reflect their mixed heritage. Economic forces have pulled Mexico into the global economy with a promise of prosperity dependent on natural resources and industrial growth.

◀ Traditional Mexican dress is colorful and reflects the style of the region.

173

ENGAGE

Activating Prior Knowledge Explain to students that they will be exploring the ways that the physical environment and the pattern of human settlement have affected Mexico. Have students work in pairs to brainstorm what they already know about Mexico and how colonists and other migrants settling the land may have changed it over time. Have pairs share their ideas with the class.

TEACH & ASSESS

Analyzing Have students read the "Geography Matters..." introduction. **Ask:** **On what is Mexico basing its potential future prosperity?** *(Mexico is entering the global economy, but the effectiveness of this long term strategy will rely on how well Mexico can use and maintain its natural resources and keep its industries growing.)* Have students examine the photograph and read the caption. **Ask:** **What might have affected the development of the style of this girl's traditional way of dressing?** *(The style may be the result of combining indigenous cultures with those of later settlers.)*

Making Connections

Explain to students that Mexico, like the United States, was shaped by the arrival of European colonists who settled in places already populated by indigenous peoples. For the most part, British settlers remained separated from the indigenous people in the United States. However, the Spanish settlers in Mexico used the indigenous people as a source of labor to mine precious metals and grow crops; therefore the original Spanish settlements were established based on where the native people were already living.

CLOSE & REFLECT

Questioning Have students think about the systems of living that different cultures follow and what might happen when two or more cultures mix or clash in one place. Ask students to identify questions they have about how the various cultures might have affected the settlement of Mexico over time. Tell students to consider these questions as they read the chapter.

Letter from the Author

Dear Geography Teacher,

The one shadow that hovers over Mexico is the danger posed by continuous wars between drug cartels that fight viciously to control pathways into the United States for illegal drugs that originate in South and Central America. Fighting drug related crime is high on the agendas of the Mexican and U.S. governments. Despite these difficulties, Mexico's economy is booming, partly fueled by the tourist industry. The Yucatan Peninsula offers a look at the old and the new. Mayan ruins dot the lowlands at sites like Chichen Itza and Tulum. A short distance away, tourists frolic in the surf at resorts in Cancun and Cozumel. Ancient temples and modern resort hotels. Quite a contrast!

Richard G. Boehm

Extend the project-based learning experience globally through our partnership with ePals. EPals allows you to connect with classrooms around the world in a safe online environment for real-life lessons and projects in virtual study groups.

ENGAGE

C Critical Thinking Skills

Drawing Conclusions Note that urbanization brings both benefits and unfortunate outcomes. Have partners create a two-column chart to record potential advantages and disadvantages to rapid urbanization. They can use their prior knowledge to brainstorm a list of advantages and use the information from the text to populate the disadvantages column. In class discussion, ask students to share their ideas.

TEACH & ASSESS

V Visual Skills

Analyzing Maps Have students examine the map key. **Ask:** According to the map, what color indicates the oldest boundaries of Mexico City? *(red)* Most recent boundaries? *(purple)* How has the size of Mexico City changed over time? *(It has grown larger over the past 100 years.)* What can you tell about the rate of growth over the past century? *(The rate of growth has accelerated.)* Continue asking questions to gauge students' understanding. AL Visual/Spatial

R Reading Skills

Inferring Have students review what life may be like for new migrants to Mexico City and what resources are available to them. **Ask:** How might the scarcity of potential resources affect the lives of new migrants? *(Possible answers: Without proper health care, people may become ill and unable to work. Without education, children may not learn the skills they need, even if jobs are available.)* BL Logical/Mathematical

W Writing Skills

Argument Have students write a letter to the government of Mexico City suggesting solutions to the city's problems of rapid urban growth. Ask students to research innovative ideas for these problems and then convince the government that these ideas would be the best to use. BL Verbal/Linguistic

ANSWERS, p. 174

Why Geography Matters

1. The pull forces are related to industrial jobs; the push forces are related to rural land policies.
2. People do not always have access to health care and education. Lack of infrastructure leads to the development of shantytowns, which are built in environmentally sensitive areas.
3. Paragraphs should show an understanding of the environmental problems facing Mexico City and of efforts being made to solve them.

Why Geography Matters: **Mexico**

challenges of urbanization

C *Rapid urban growth brings challenges to city governments around the world as they struggle to provide housing, services, infrastructure, and jobs, as well as curb pollution. Governments have limited funds to spend on basic upkeep and services. As a result, cities like* ***Mexico City*** *experience challenges such as environmental problems and poverty.*

V

Growth of Mexico City
1910
1960
2000

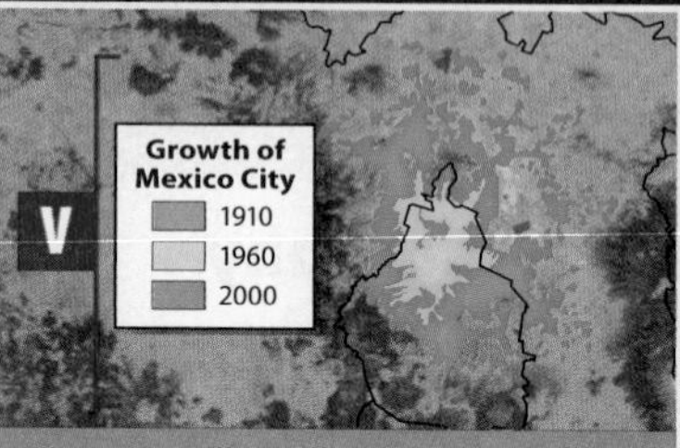

Why has Mexico City grown so fast?

Today's Mexico City is the result of years of rural-to-urban migration by people looking for better economic opportunities. The first influx of these economic migrants coincided with rapid industrialization in the late nineteenth century. The pull forces of industrial jobs and the push forces of rural land policies drew people to Mexico City. The rural poor moved to the city as land was purchased around them by wealthy landowners. Similar factors continue to bring economic migrants to Mexico City seeking a better life for themselves and their families.

1. **Human Systems** What are the pull factors influencing migration to Mexico City? How are these different from the push factors that bring people to the city?

What is the social impact of rapid growth?

Economic migrants move to the city expecting to find jobs. Unfortunately, unemployment is common. Some migrants find temporary jobs or work in the informal sector—"underground economies" that are not taxed or regulated by the government. R People often do not have access to health care and education. Lack of infrastructure—housing, electrical grids, sewer facilities, and roads—to support the growing population leads to the development of shantytowns. The influx of people to Mexico City puts enormous pressures on the natural environment. Underground water aquifers are being depleted, causing the city to sink. Inadequate sewer facilities lead to polluted land and water. Full of rubbish, landfills have been closed. Unregulated by the government, shantytowns are built in environmentally sensitive areas such as hill slopes.

2. **Environment and Society** What challenges has rural-to-urban migration created for the government of Mexico City?

What can be done?

W Government agencies and other groups continue to establish initiatives and special projects to address these challenges. The government of Mexico and public-private partnerships are investing in sustainable and environmentally friendly housing development. Plan Verde (Green Plan) includes a range of programs to promote environmental sustainability by easing traffic congestion, reducing greenhouse gas emissions, and encouraging public transportation, cycling, and walking options. The Mexico City Climate Action Program provides funding for sustainable housing as well as renewable energy programs.

3. **Human Systems** Write a paragraph explaining how environmentally friendly policies could improve life in Mexico City.

174

Project-Based Learning

Hands-On

Population Pyramids

Students will individually create a population chart based on their research of the demographics of Mexico. After they finish their charts, students will make population pyramids using the information they gathered. Students will then work in pairs to compare and contrast their population pyramids and researched data.

Digital Hands-On

Create Online Projects

Find an additional activity online that incorporates technology for this project. Visit the EdTech Teacher Web sites for more links, tutorials, and other resources.

Why Geography Matters

Sprawling Mexico City TODAY

THERE'S MORE ONLINE

VIEW a map of the world's megacities • *WATCH* a video of Mexico's urban sprawl

V Visual Skills

Examining Have students examine the aerial photograph of Mexico City. **Ask:** **How does this photograph help you better understand settlement patterns and problems of residents in their daily lives?** *(Student answers may vary, but should mention aspects of the photo such as the crowded masses of houses, the presence of clusters of trees and some small waterways in the heart of the city, the large roads that help organize the city, and the taller buildings indicating the centers of business being far from the residential areas.)* **Visual/Spatial**

T Technology Skills

Researching Have students work in small groups to locate recent photos and images of Mexico City. Ask them to compare and contrast the information they have seen and read in the text with what they can see in the images they find online. In particular, have them point out examples of problems such as congestion, visible pollution, or lack of adequate housing. Invite groups to present the images they have found to the class, along with a commentary about how these additional visuals might help the class better understand the challenges of urbanization facing Mexico City today. **Verbal/Linguistic**

Content Background Knowledge

Tenochtitlán Previous civilizations found the current site of Mexico City a good place to build their own large cities. Before Spanish conquistadors first set foot in the Americas, Aztec kings built their capital city of Tenochtitlán in the 1470s on swampy lands reclaimed from Lake Texcoco. Wanting to establish Spanish supremacy over the newly conquered Aztecs, Hernán Cortes had this city razed to the ground in 1521–1522 so that the settlement that would become present-day Mexico City could be erected in its place.

INTERACTIVE MAP

Mexico City Growth

Speculating Use this interactive map of Mexico City to discuss rapid population growth with students. Have students work with a partner to identify areas of the map that have recently become densely populated. Allow time for pairs to list possible reasons why these areas are more populated than others. Then guide a class discussion in which pairs share their lists and the other students evaluate the list as plausible reasons. *(Student answers may vary, but should reflect thought-out explanations for densely populated locations, such as: locations are near to public transportation, locations are further from the city center so housing is less expensive, locations are near industry.)*

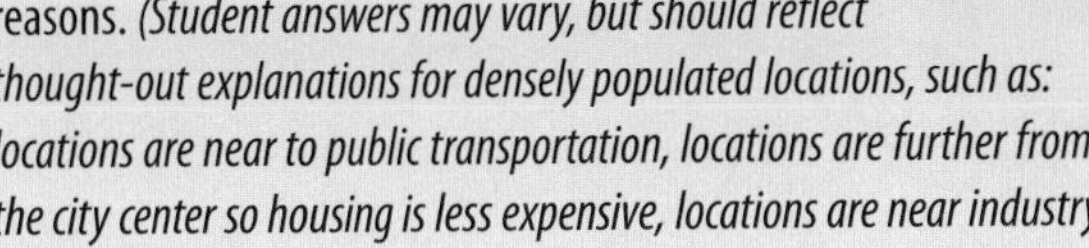

BL **Logical/Mathematical**

CLOSE & REFLECT

Evaluating Tell students to review the images, headings, and information in this section, and then to write a summary of the major problems facing Mexico City due to urbanization. They should describe the factors that have created the problems and the ways the government is proposing to solve them. Invite students to share their summaries, and then challenge students to evaluate the adequacy of the government's plans.

ENGAGE

R Reading Skills

Activating Prior Knowledge Before students begin the lesson, have pairs work together to brainstorm what they already know about the physical geography of Mexico. Display a physical map or satellite photograph of Mexico and have students write a description of this country's physical features, organizing them by whether they are landforms or water systems. Then have students describe what they know about Mexico's climate. Discuss any relationship students already know about or can deduce between the landforms and climate of Mexico.

TEACH & ASSESS

V Visual Skills

Spatial Understanding Have students read the first paragraph and use the text along with their prior knowledge to make a mental map of Mexico and its relationship to the United States and Central America. Then have them draw their mental map. Finally, display a physical map of North and Central America, and have them compare their drawings to the actual map. Have them make corrections and notes on their drawings as needed. **ELL Visual/Spatial**

C Critical Thinking Skills

Classifying After students read about the different kinds of landforms found in Mexico—including mountains, plateaus, and plains—ask volunteers to identify and write them down in a list. Then have students work in pairs to classify the information by creating a chart with columns that records information about the types of landforms and biomes in each place. Have pairs present their completed graphic organizers to the class. **AL Interpersonal, Naturalist**

ANSWERS, p. 176

TAKING NOTES: Landforms—land bridge connecting North and South America, Sierra Madre Occidental and Oriental, Barranca del Cobre, Northern and Central Plateau; **Water Systems**—Rio Grande, Lerma River, Lake Chapala, Gulf of Mexico; **Climate, Biomes, and Resources**—vertical climate zones, chaparral biome in the north, variety of biomes in the south including a hot climate along coasts and heavy daily rain and high humidity on the east coast; minerals including silver, lead, gold, mercury, cadmium, antimony, manganese, and copper; natural resources of oil and natural gas.

networks
There's More Online!

- ☑ **IMAGE** Land Stripped by Copper Mine in Chihuahua, Mexico
- ☑ **DIAGRAM** Mexico's Location on the Tectonic Plates
- ☑ **INFOGRAPHIC** Vertical Climate Zones of Mexico
- ☑ **INTERACTIVE SELF-CHECK QUIZ**
- ☑ **VIDEO** Physical Geography of Mexico

LESSON 1
Physical Geography of Mexico

ESSENTIAL QUESTION • *How do physical systems and human systems shape a place?*

Reading **HELP**DESK 

Academic Vocabulary (Tier Two Words)
- **feature**
- **inevitable**

Content Vocabulary (Tier Three Words)
- **land bridge**
- **seismic**
- **vertical climate zone**

TAKING NOTES: ***Key Ideas and Details***

SUMMARIZING As you read the lesson, use a graphic organizer like the one below to take notes on the physical geography of Mexico.

Physical Geography of Mexico		
Landforms	Water Systems	Climates, Biomes, and Resources

IT MATTERS BECAUSE

R *Mexico has rich farmland, abundant access to the ocean, and freshwater resources. With diverse climates and biomes it supports a variety of food crops. The country also has substantial mineral resources and has developed strong manufacturing and service sectors.*

Landforms

GUIDING QUESTION *Why is the Mexican Plateau considered the heartland of Mexico?*

V Mexico is the southernmost country in North America. It shares its entire northern border with the United States. Mexico, along with Central America, joins the continents of North America and South America. This physical feature is called a **land bridge** because it connects two geographic landforms.

The western side of Mexico is part of the Ring of Fire. The Ring of Fire is the area where the Pacific tectonic plate collides with other tectonic plates, creating areas of **seismic** activity with earthquakes. This activity helps shape the landforms of Mexico. Seismic activity opens parts of the Earth's crust and triggers the formation of volcanoes.

The mountains that stretch along the northwestern edge of Mexico are called the Sierra Madre Occidental. These mountains have been deeply cut by westward-flowing rivers and streams, which have formed deep gorges. The largest is *Barranca del Cobre* (Copper Canyon), a beautiful natural wonder in the state of Chihuahua, Mexico.

C The Sierra Madre Oriental is considered the southern extension of the Rocky Mountains of Canada and the United States. The average mountain height is between 8,000 and 9,000 feet (2,438 and 2,743 m). A few exceptions include mountains that reach heights of 12,000 feet (3,657 m).

Between these two mountain ranges is the inland Mexican Plateau. Moderate, consistent temperatures make this area an attractive place to live. It is the largest and most densely populated region of

networks *Online Teaching Options*

INTERACTIVE BELLRINGER

Vertical Climate Zones of Mexico

Interpreting Have students use this diagram to discuss the relationship between increasing elevation and different climate zones. Have pairs of students read the introductory text, study the colors and symbols used to designate different parts of the diagram, and answer the questions. Then ask students to predict which of the five levels would most likely be the hardest place to make a living through agriculture and why. Invite pairs to share their responses with the whole class. **Visual/Spatial, Logical/Mathematical**

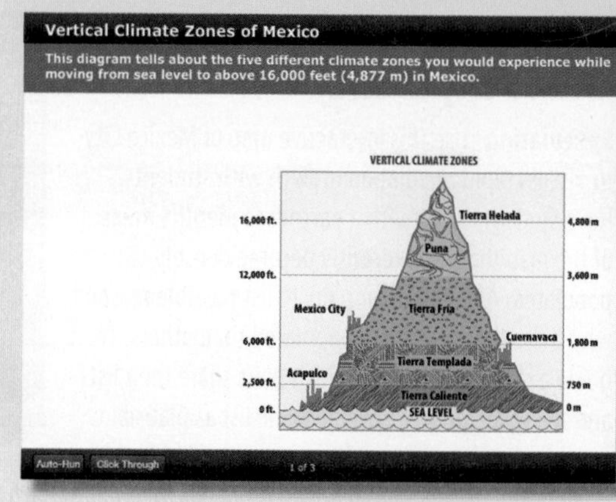

Mexico. The Mexican Plateau is broken into two parts, the huge *Mesa del Norte* (Northern Plateau) and the smaller but heavily populated *Mesa Central* (Central Plateau).The dry Northern Plateau is home to several large cities. The Central Plateau is considered the breadbasket—or major grain-producing region—of Mexico. It is less arid than the Northern Plateau and **features** several smaller valleys. Most of the food grown in Mexico comes from this area.

The Gulf Coastal Plain is a wide stretch of land east of the Sierra Madre Oriental. These mountains extend from the Texas-Mexico border along the Gulf of Mexico to the Yucatán Peninsula. In the south, a series of mountain ranges and plateaus called the Southern Highlands reach from just south of Mexico City to the southwest edge of Mexico's border with Guatemala.

The variety of landforms in Mexico—from large plateaus and valleys to long mountain ranges and highlands—has made it possible to support large communities of people. There are ample grazing and farmlands on the North and Central Plateaus, in the Southern Highlands, and along the coastlines. The population density in Mexico is greater near parts that have the most agriculture, especially on the Central Plateau and in the Southern Highlands.

✓ READING PROGRESS CHECK

Interpreting How has the geography of Mexico affected the way people use the land?

land bridge a strip of land that connects two larger landmasses, enabling migration of plants and animals to new areas

seismic relating to or caused by an earthquake

feature to have as a characteristic or as a prominent attribute

Plate Tectonics in Mexico — DIAGRAM SKILLS

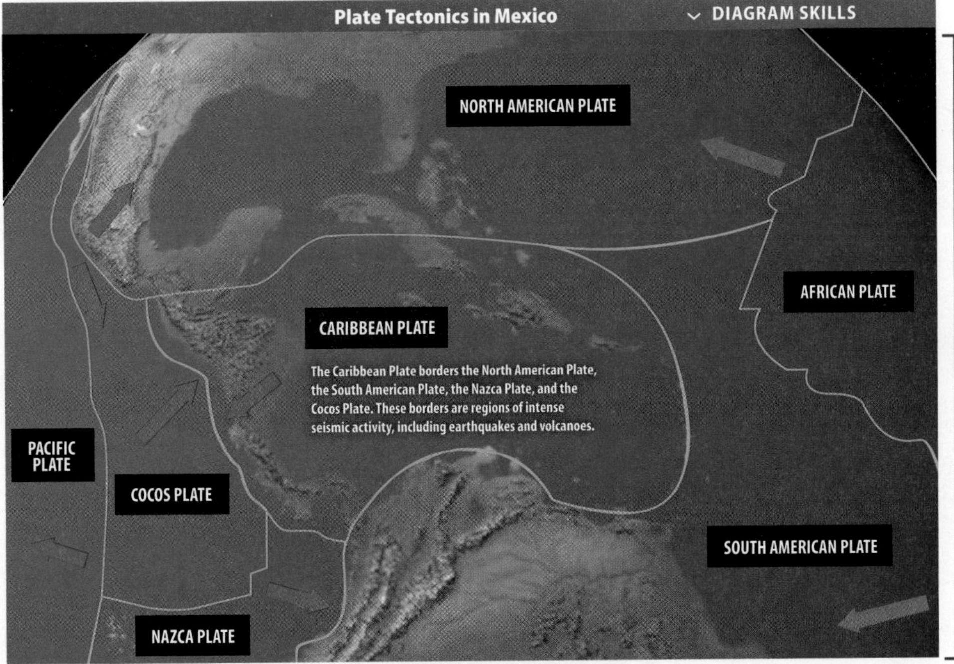

Mexico's location near the edges of tectonic plates makes it a hot spot for volcanoes and earthquakes.

▲ CRITICAL THINKING

1. ***Classifying*** On which tectonic plates is Mexico located?
2. ***Drawing Conclusions*** Why do you think this area of tectonic activity is called the Ring of Fire?

C Critical Thinking Skills

Identifying Cause and Effect Have students review the information about Mexico's landforms and population and consider how landforms affect the population. **Ask:** **What is the relationship between landforms and the distribution of population?** *(More people live in the parts that sustain the most agriculture and have consistent temperatures.)* **How would you explain this relationship?** *(People live in places where their needs can be met, so more people will tend to live in places where it is easier to grow the crops they need.)* **Logical/Mathematical**

V Visual Skills

Analyzing Visuals Have students study the diagram and consider its parts and what information it is conveying. **Ask:** **What do the orange lines indicate?** *(the boundaries of each of the tectonic plates)* **What do the red arrows indicate?** *(the direction in which each plate is moving)* **Using information from the diagram, explain the type of seismic activity experienced by Mexico.** *(The diagram shows the red arrow of the Caribbean plate and the red arrow of the Cocos plate pointing toward one another. The force of these two plates meeting must cause the earthquakes and volcanoes.)* AL **Visual/Spatial**

Making Connections

Ring of Fire Formed by the movement of different tectonic plates, the Ring of Fire is a belt of volcanic and seismic activity that stretches all around the Pacific Ocean. Its effects are felt not only by Mexico, where the subduction of the Cocos plate under the Caribbean plate causes earthquakes, but by other countries that border the Ring of Fire as well. In North America, the movement of two plates scraping against each other as one moves north and the other slides south causes earthquakes to shake the coast of California. Further north, the movement of one plate sinking under another causes magma to bubble to the surface and form volcanoes such as Mount St. Helens in Washington and the Aleutian islands of Alaska.

INFOGRAPHIC

Plate Tectonics in Mexico

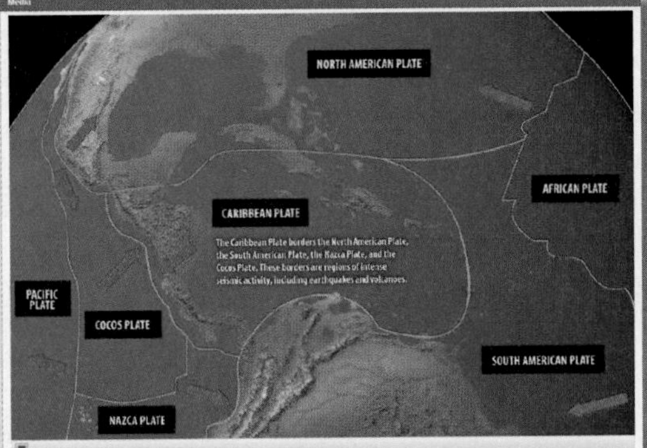

Defending This diagram shows plate tectonics around Mexico and Central America. Review with students that some forces of plate tectonics affect Earth's surface through the movement of magma within Earth; other forces involve movements that can fold, lift, bend, or break Earth's crust; and that Pangaea, a gigantic supercontinent, is believed by many scientists to have once connected nearly all of Earth's landmasses. Have students work with a partner to write an argument to defend whether they believe the plate tectonics around Mexico will build up or break apart the land bridge between North and South America. Allow students to conduct library or online research to defend their arguments. BL **Logical/Mathematical, Verbal/Linguistic**

ANSWERS, p. 177

✓ **READING PROGRESS CHECK** The variety of landforms means large communities of people can be supported. Ample grazing and farmlands exist on the North and Central Plateaus, in the Southern Highlands, and along the coastlines.

CRITICAL THINKING

1. Mexico is located on the Pacific, Cocos, and North American plates.
2. Volcanic eruptions and other tectonic activity are common here.

R Reading Skills

Determining Word Meanings Write these terms on the board: *Tierra Helada, Tierra Fria, Tierra Templada,* and *Tierra Caliente*. Explain that these are the names of Mexico's vertical climate zones. If possible, pair Spanish speakers with non-Spanish speakers. Then have pairs work together to translate the name of each vertical climate zone: freezing land, cold land, temperate land, and warm or hot land. Invite pairs to share their definitions and then discuss as a class why each vertical climate zone might have this name. **ELL Verbal/Linguistic**

W Writing Skills

Narrative Have students discuss the importance of water to life in Mexico and identify some ways its presence or absence affects the way that people have settled and used the land. Then have students write a poem about one of the water systems in Mexico. Encourage students to think about the sights and sounds of water and how these sights and sounds and the vital importance of water could be expressed in poetry. **BL Auditory/Musical, Naturalist**

V Visual Skills

Using Diagrams Have students interpret the diagram in a class discussion. **Ask: What are the four vertical climate zones of Mexico called?** *(Tierra Helada, Tierra Fria, Tierra Templada,* and *Tierra Caliente)* **Where are the majority of the crops shown grown?** *(in the bottom three climate zones)* **What information does the diagram provide about each climate zone?** *(its altitude and the range of temperatures found there)* **How might you describe the relationship between climate zone and altitude?** *(Temperatures drop as you move to higher climate zones.)* Have students answer the *Critical Thinking* questions on their own. **AL Visual/Spatial**

ANSWERS, p. 178

READING PROGRESS CHECK The Rio Bravo del Norte, or the Rio Grande, forms part of the border between Mexico and the United States. It is also one of the few rivers that is not in the central part of the country.

CRITICAL THINKING

1. Tierra Fría and Tierra Helada are found above 6,000 feet.
2. As the elevation increases, it gets colder, so crops that like a colder climate do better in higher elevations.

Water Systems

GUIDING QUESTION *Why does Mexico have few major rivers and natural lakes?*

vertical climate zone a climate zone that occurs as elevation increases, with its own natural vegetation and crops

R Northern Mexico is generally characterized by a dry climate. This makes permanent waterways rare. The high mountain ranges and plateaus create temperate **vertical climate zones** that do not collect the volume of water that is more common in tropical regions. The few rivers and natural lakes that exist are found in the central part of the country and are generally small. One important exception is the Rio Grande. Known as the Río Bravo del Norte in Mexico, it forms part of the border between Mexico and the United States.

W The Lerma River is one of Mexico's most important rivers. It begins in the Toluca Basin, on the Central Plateau west of Mexico City. The Lerma River feeds into Lake Chapala, the largest natural lake in Mexico.

The Gulf of Mexico is the large body of water that forms Mexico's east coast. It supports diverse sea life including an ancient sea creature known as the manatee. The Gulf of Mexico is famous for shrimp and supplies the fishing industry in both the United States and Mexico. The waters in the Gulf of Mexico are relatively sheltered from ocean currents, so the beaches are calm and the waters are warm.

On the western side of Mexico, the Gulf of California divides the Baja Peninsula from the northern coast of Mexico. This body of water supports a remarkable diversity of aquatic animals. These include several types of whales, the giant Pacific manta ray, endangered leatherback sea turtles, and great white sharks.

READING PROGRESS CHECK

Describing What is the importance of the Río Bravo del Norte to Mexico?

Climate, Biomes, and Resources

GUIDING QUESTION *How does climate affect human activities in Mexico?*

inevitable incapable of being avoided or evaded

The climate of a particular region **inevitably** affects the way of life that people have in each place. For example, people who graze cattle on the Northern Plateau anxiously await rain each year. The farmers in the valleys of the Central Plateau

Vertical CLIMATE ZONES of Mexico

Tierra Helada
20°F–55°F
(-7°C–13°C)
– 10,000 feet (3,048 m)
Tierra Fría
55°F–65°F
(13°C–18°C)
– 6,000 feet (1,829 m)
Tierra Templada
65°F–75°F
(18°C–24°C)
– 2,500 feet (762 m)
Tierra Caliente
75°F–80°F
(24°C–27°C)
– Sea Level

Differences in elevation create distinct climate zones in Mexico and other high-altitude areas in Latin America.

V **CRITICAL THINKING**

1. ***Analyzing Visuals*** Which climate zones are found above 6,000 feet (1,829 m)?
2. ***Synthesizing*** How might increasing elevation affect the type of resources found in each vertical climate zone?

networks Online Teaching Options

INFOGRAPHIC

Vertical Climate Zones of Mexico

Making Connections Use this infographic on the vertical climate zones of Mexico to help students understand how environments affect human activities. Have students work in small groups to discuss and compare the climate zones. Ask each group which of the products shown in the graph they consume. Then have each group consider which crops, if grown for trade, would be the most profitable based on the climate, growing season, and rainfall in Mexico. Have each group decide on one crop to grow and consider the local implications of processing, selling, and collecting a profit for this crop. Have groups share their reasoning in a class discussion. **Naturalist**

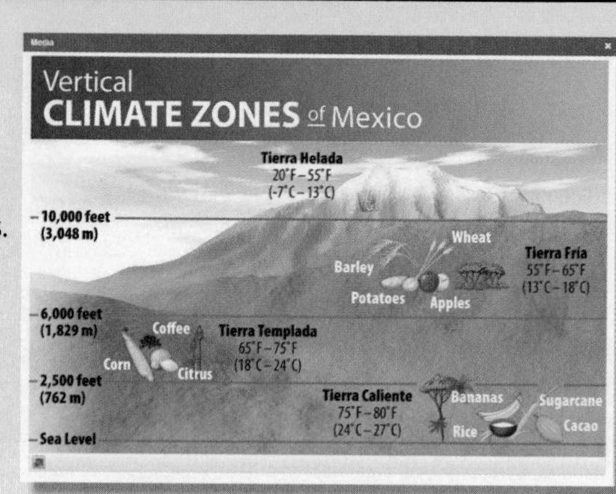

depend on their climate to help them get enough water for their crops. The three factors that influence Mexico's climates are the regional high-pressure systems, the northeast trade winds, and the vertical climate zones.

Regional high-pressure systems keep the north and central parts of Mexico dry and cause occasional droughts. The northeast trade winds are responsible for the pattern of tropical storms. Vertical climate zones create the temperate or mild climates found throughout the southern part of Mexico. The elevation of the highlands keeps them at a comfortable temperature that is also helpful for growing certain crops. **R**

Northern Mexico is defined as a chaparral biome. It has mild, rainy winters and hot, dry summers. The plant life consists of cacti, shrubs, and shrub oak. High winds and low-growing plants make the soil in this region good for grasslands. The soil is also thin and rocky, however, so it is not good for crops.

Southern Mexico has a variety of biomes. In the lower altitudes along the coasts, the climate is hot. On the east coast, daily rainfall and high humidity occur. This biome supports very diverse plant and animal life and is essentially a rain forest.

Minerals are an important part of Mexico's economy, especially silver. Mexico is the world's leading producer of silver. In the area called the "Silver Belt" on the Mexican Plateau, both industrial and precious minerals are mined. Zinc, bauxite (the ore of aluminum), lead, gold, mercury, cadmium, and such trace minerals as antimony, manganese, and copper are also important. Timber, fish, and agricultural products are also a significant part of Mexico's economy. **T**

Mexico is a leading petroleum-producing country. Petroleum exports account for a large share of foreign-exchange earnings. Mexico ranks thirteenth in the world for crude oil exports. About three-fourths of Mexico's electricity is generated by thermal power plants that are fired mainly by oil and natural gas. Another one-tenth of Mexico's electric power is created by nuclear power and renewable resources of wind, solar energy, and biomass (plant materials and animal waste used as a source of fuel).

Copper mining takes place in the Mexican copper belt in the west part of the country.

Beth Wald/Aurora/Getty Images

▲ **CRITICAL THINKING**

1. ***Analyzing Visuals*** Describe the negative impacts of strip mining as depicted in this photo.
2. ***Comparing*** Where is Mexico's copper belt located in comparison to the "Silver Belt"?

✓ **READING PROGRESS CHECK**

Assessing How do vertical climate zones affect the economic activity of the Southern Highlands?

LESSON 1 REVIEW (CCSS)

Reviewing Vocabulary (Tier Three Words)

1. ***Discussing*** Write a paragraph that discusses the geography of vertical climate zones. RH.9–10.4

Using Your Notes

2. ***Describing*** Use your graphic organizer from the lesson to describe three of Mexico's water systems.

Answering the Guiding Questions

3. ***Drawing Conclusions*** Why is the Mexican Plateau considered the heartland of Mexico?
4. ***Interpreting*** Why does Mexico have few major rivers and natural lakes?
5. ***Making Connections*** How does climate affect human activities in Mexico?

Writing Activity

6. ***Informative/Explanatory*** Write a paragraph describing Mexico's location along the Ring of Fire and how that creates natural hazards. WHST.9–10.9

R Reading Skills

Understanding Relationships Review how different natural factors can influence the climate of an area. Ask students to identify the three factors that influence Mexico's climates—regional high pressure systems, northeast trade winds, and the vertical climate zones. Direct students to write brief statements explaining the relationship between each factor and the type of effect it can produce. **Verbal/Linguistic, Naturalist**

Content Background Knowledge

Mexican Oil Production Mexico possesses several areas of oil reserves. Most Mexican oil—about three-fourths—is collected from reserves located offshore in the Campeche Basin in the Gulf of Mexico. Other basins of oil are located in the northern part of the country. Unfortunately, some studies indicate that Mexico has reached peak oil, or the point in time when the production of oil will continue to decline, rather than rise or stay steady.

T Technology Skills

Comparing and Contrasting Divide students into two groups and assign one group northern Mexico and one group southern Mexico. Have each group use the Internet or library resources to research the biomes for each area and the crops and natural resources found in each biome. Groups should create visuals that illustrate the different biomes, describing the climate, fauna, and flora. Have groups present their visuals to the class. Then use the presentations to hold a class discussion comparing and contrasting the different biomes found in northern and southern Mexico. BL **Visual/Spatial, Interpersonal**

CLOSE & REFLECT

Summarizing Tell students to review how the physical environment of Mexico has affected where people have established settlements and how they make a living. Have students pick one area of Mexico to explain why people do or do not live there using specific information from the lesson.

LESSON 1 REVIEW ANSWERS

Reviewing Vocabulary

1. Paragraphs should show an understanding of vertical climate zones and their relation to Mexico's geography.

Using Your Notes

2. Answers should include three of the following: The Lerma River is one of Mexico's most important rivers and feeds into Lake Chapala, Mexico's largest natural lake. The Balsas River is a steep, swift river that is the major source of hydroelectric power. The Gulf of Mexico forms Mexico's east coast and supplies the fishing industry. The Rio Grande forms part of the border between Mexico and the United States and is the largest river outside of the central regions of the country.

Answering the Guiding Questions

3. The Mexican Plateau is the largest and most densely populated region of Mexico, and most of the food grown in Mexico comes from its Central Plateau.
4. In general, Northern Mexico is characterized by a dry climate, which makes permanent waterways rare.
5. The farmers in the valleys of the Central Plateau depend on the climate to help them get enough water for their crops.

Writing Activity

6. Paragraphs should show an understanding of the Ring of Fire, plate tectonics, and how seismic activity shapes landforms, including volcanoes.

ANSWERS, p. 179

✓ **READING PROGRESS CHECK** The climate is mild, so agriculture is abundant and supports the economy.

CRITICAL THINKING

1. Some negative impacts of strip mining are deforestation, soil erosion, and air pollution.
2. The "Silver Belt" is on the Mexican Plateau in the center of the country while the copper belt is located in the western part of the country.

Human Geography of Mexico

ENGAGE

R Reading Skills

Previewing Have students quickly flip through the lesson to preview the images and headings as they consider what they already know about Mexican history and how the interaction of various cultures and groups of people can affect the human geography of a place. Then have students write down three predictions for what they will read and learn about in this lesson.

TEACH & ASSESS

V Visual Skills

Identifying Perspectives Have students refer to a physical map of Mexico as they read about the diverse cultures of Mexico. Have them find the areas on the map referred to in the text and identify the landforms that would impact life in that region. Have students write a short paragraph from the perspective of a person in each group about how the physical geography of the area must have affected his or her life. **Verbal/Linguistic**

C Critical Thinking Skills

Comparing and Contrasting Have students work in pairs to make a three-circle Venn diagram to help them compare and contrast information about the indigenous peoples found in the northern and southern parts of Mexico. Students should consider issues such as where the people lived, how their environment affected the sort of civilization they created, and what sort of presence they have in modern-day Mexico. Invite pairs to share their completed diagrams with the class. Hold a discussion during which students articulate how these indigenous cultures were alike and different in the ways they influenced Mexico's history and culture. AL **Logical/Mathematical**

ANSWERS, p. 180

TAKING NOTES: History and Government—indigenous peoples included the Maya and the Aztec, the Aztec Empire arose in central Mexico and was ruling when the Spanish arrived in 1519, Mexico was a colony of Spain until 1821, a political system that was controlled by wealthy landowners, clergy, or military dictators called caudillos fought for power until 1917, when Mexico became a federal republic; the PRI controlled the government until 2000 when the PAN party gained power; **Population Patterns**—indigenous peoples developed cultures to suit the environments they lived in; the Maya civilization was one of the earliest, and the Aztec ruled over central Mexico; Spanish settlements grew into large cities; today, rural-to-urban migration has led to 78 percent of people living in urban settings

networks

There's More Online!

- **GRAPH** Female Labor in Mexico
- **IMAGE** Maquiladora Along the U.S.-Mexico Border
- **IMAGE** Women in Mexican Labor Force
- **MAP** Mexican Migration to the United States
- **INTERACTIVE SELF-CHECK QUIZ**
- **TIME LINE** Mexican Independence and Change
- **VIDEO** Human Geography of Mexico

LESSON 2
Human Geography of Mexico

ESSENTIAL QUESTION • *How do physical systems and human systems shape a place?*

Reading HELPDESK CCSS

Academic Vocabulary (Tier Two Words)
- **culture**
- **diverse**

Content Vocabulary (Tier Three Words)
- **mestizo**
- **conquistador**
- **cash crop**
- **syncretism**
- **megacity**
- **primate city**
- **extended family**
- **gross domestic product**
- **maquiladora**
- **free trade zone**

TAKING NOTES: ***Key Ideas and Details***

PARAPHRASING Use a graphic organizer like the one below to describe the human geography of Mexico.

Human Geography of Mexico	
History and Government	Population Patterns

IT MATTERS BECAUSE

R *Mexico's human geography reflects influences from the Maya and Aztec civilizations, the introduction of Spanish culture during the colonial era, and cultural and social elements shared from recent interaction with the United States and other countries.*

History and Government

GUIDING QUESTION *What influenced Mexico's political and social structures?*

V Variations in the physical geography of Mexico led to the development of diverse **cultures,** languages, and civilizations among the indigenous peoples of Mexico. These differing peoples developed cultures to suit the environments in which they lived. These cultures can be seen in the regional distinctions of Mexico today.

C The northern half of Mexico, on the inland plateau and in the mountains, originally had a small population of mostly independent groups of nomadic people. Agriculture was used to supplement hunting, herding, and gathering of food. Some of these seminomadic groups still live in their traditional homelands, separated from most outside influences. The Tarahumara people in the Sierra Madre Occidental are one example of an indigenous group who still live in northern Mexico.

The southern half of Mexico was geographically more **diverse.** It could support large-scale agriculture and produce the variety and abundance of foods necessary to maintain empires and cities. Centered in the Yucatán Peninsula, the Maya civilization was one of the earliest and largest civilizations in Mexico. The Maya built huge stone cities, which were abandoned a few hundred years before the arrival of the first Spanish explorers. The Maya ruled a vast territory and engaged in long-distance trade with other cultures, including Teotihuacán and the Zapotec. Their descendants still live in and around the areas of their former empire. Many of these Mayan people maintain their culture, speak their ancestral languages, and practice the same cultural traditions.

The Aztec Empire arose in central Mexico. The Aztec ruled from their capital, Tenochtitlán (tay•NAWCH•teet•LAHN), the site of present-day Mexico City. They had conquered other peoples in the area when the

(tl)Courtesy Everett Collection/Alamy, (tc)Jack Kurtz/ZUMA/Corbis, (tr)David Maung/Bloomberg/Getty Images

180

networks Online Teaching Options

INTERACTIVE BELLRINGER

Biography of Diego Rivera

Drawing Conclusions This biographical passage can be used to introduce students to the life of Diego Rivera and his use of the European art form of the mural to communicate his political beliefs. Have students work with a partner to read the passage and answer the questions. Then ask them to use what they already know about the Mexican revolution and the purpose of unions to draw some conclusions about what life might have been like for workers and peasants in Mexico at this time. As a class, have pairs present their conclusions. **Interpersonal, Verbal/Linguistic**

Biography of Diego Rivera

Diego Rivera was born in Guanajuato in 1886. His father was a municipal councilor, and from an early age Diego was interested in politics as well as art. He was particularly fascinated by the Russian revolution and the conflict between the Tsar and Marxist revolutionaries. During this time, he began painting more murals and became more involved in workers' movements. In 1922 he helped found the Revolutionary Union of Technical Workers, Painters, and Sculptors. His murals often showed Mexican workers and peasants in their struggle for independence and civil rights.

1. What might have inspired Diego Rivera to pursue the interests that he did?

click for answer

Auto-Run Click Through Previous 1 of 2 Next

Spanish arrived in 1519. Although **mestizos**, people of mixed Spanish and indigenous heritage, now densely populate the region, there are groups that trace their ancestry to the Aztec.

After the conquest of the Aztec by Spanish **conquistador** Hernán Cortés and his men, the Spanish took the wealth of Mexico's gold and silver resources. They also found value in the variety of food available to the local people, quickly taking corn, tomatoes, chocolate, and other native crops on the return trips to Spain. Large tracts of land in Mexico were given to the Spanish settlers of Mexico. These landowners began growing **cash crops** such as cacao (chocolate) and maize (corn) in large quantities, which they exported to Spain. This further enriched the Spanish. Mexico remained a part of the Spanish Empire for nearly three centuries. It was governed by Spain under a highly structured political system ruled by officials called viceroys who were appointed by the Spanish monarch.

In the late 1700s, throughout Mexico and the rest of Latin America, people started to protest European rule. In 1821 Mexico became the first Spanish territory to win its independence. Mexico was free from Spain, but the political system was ruled by a small group of wealthy landowners, army officers, and Catholic clergy who remained in power. Power struggles, public dissatisfaction, and civic revolts made the new republic fragile and chaotic. During this time a new type of leader emerged, the caudillo (kow•DEE•yoh), or military dictator. For brief periods in the 1800s, the government moved toward democratic principles. However, the caudillos found ways to return to power.

The long and bloody Mexican Revolution overthrew the caudillos and established a new constitution in 1917. This brought reforms and established the current Mexican government as a federal republic. Power was divided into three branches of government—legislative, executive, and judicial—and a president could only be elected for one six-year term. However, the rule of law did not last for long. In 1929 one political party, the *Partido Revolucionario Institucional* (PRI), was elected and established a corrupt monopoly on the political system of Mexico. The PRI went on to control the political establishment for nearly 70 years. Not until 2000 was the opposition party, *Partido Acción Nacional* (PAN), able to win the presidency. In 2012, however, the PRI was reelected.

Over the past few decades, drug cartels have come to control different regions of Mexico. New cartels have been forming or breaking away from older and larger cartels. These new cartels compete with old cartels for power and control of drug-producing territories. The result is internal warfare in Mexico. The cartels have increasingly incited street gun battles, massacres in the mountains, and other acts of violence and terror.

Struggles for additional reforms in the government continue. Indigenous communities, small farmers, and groups of underpaid laborers are continuing to pressure the government for greater inclusion in the political system. Corruption remains a common reality in the government. A small group of very wealthy landowners still controls most of Mexico's wealth.

☑ READING PROGRESS CHECK

Exploring the Issues Why do drug cartels have such a powerful influence in Mexico?

Population Patterns

GUIDING QUESTION *What factors have shaped Mexico's population patterns?*

For unknown reasons, the Maya had abandoned their cities in the Yucatán and southern Mexico by the time the Spanish conquistadors arrived. They were mainly living as subsistence farmers in small communities, where many still live today.

culture the customary beliefs, social forms, and material traits of a racial, religious, or social group

diverse differing from one another

mestizo refers to people of mixed indigenous and European descent

conquistador Spanish for "conqueror"; Spanish soldier who participated in conquest of indigenous peoples of Latin America

cash crop farm product grown to be sold or traded rather than used by the farm family

Human Geography of Mexico

C1 Critical Thinking Skills

Evaluating Have students recall the reasons why conquistadors first journeyed from Spain to the Americas. **Ask:** How would you evaluate the way Spanish rulers felt about the discoveries Cortés made in Mexico? *(Possible answer: Mexico had valuable resources such as precious minerals like gold and silver, native crops such as corn, tomatoes, and chocolate, and large areas of land that could be farmed to produce even more crops that could be exported for profit. Therefore, the Spanish rulers must have valued his discoveries, which is shown by the fact that they settled Mexico and made it part of the Spanish Empire.)* Verbal/Linguistic

C2 Critical Thinking Skills

Making Generalizations Discuss the changing systems of government that have ruled Mexico. **Ask:** Who governed Mexico while it was part of the Spanish Empire? *(viceroys appointed by the Spanish monarch)* Who ruled Mexico after it won its independence? *(a small group of wealthy landowners, army officers, and Catholic clergy)* Who contested with the new republic for power? *(caudillos, or military dictators)* Who controlled the current form of Mexican government for most of the twentieth century? *(one political party—the Partido Revolucionario Institucional or PRI—who established a corrupt monopoly)* What generalization can you make about the pattern of government in Mexico over the centuries? *(Possible answer: Time after time, a select group of rich and powerful people has risen to take over the rule of Mexico and dictated what will happen to the poorer majority.)*

AL Logical/Mathematical

Content Background Knowledge

Mestizos Mexicans today hold some ambivalence about using the label *mestizo.* The term began as an insult, meant to draw distinctions between Spanish settlers with a single heritage and people from new families created by the mingling of several cultures. The Spanish even set up a caste system that organized people based on the "purity" of their ethnic background. Over time the term *mestizo* has been redefined by some to stand for a proud cultural identity. Categorizing themselves as *mestizo* allowed groups that had been treated as second-class citizens to draw strength and a sense of unity from their indigenous roots. At the same time, other groups would rather avoid using the label to escape its past offensive connotations.

INTERACTIVE MAP

Civilizations of Mesoamerica

Interpreting Use this interactive map of the early civilizations in Mexico and Mesoamerica to illustrate to students where various populations where first established. Have students identify possible reasons for the locations, such as proximity to a major waterway, fertile soil, etc. Then have a volunteer point to the location of Mexico City on the map. Explain that Mexico City is one of the largest cities in the world. Have students write a short paragraph explaining why they feel Mexico City has become such a large city based on its physical location in Mexico. Visual/Spatial

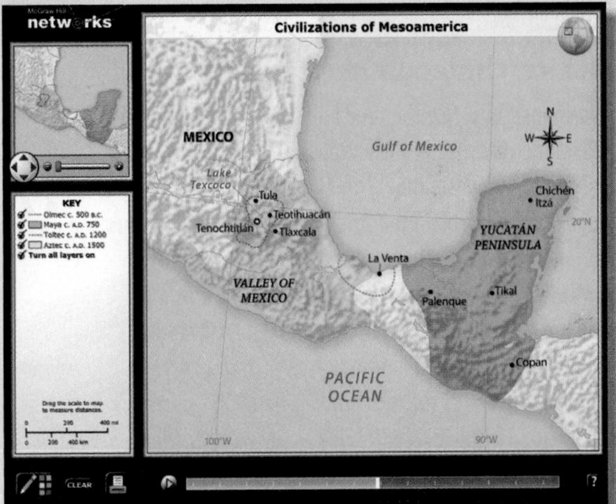

ANSWERS, p. 181

☑ READING PROGRESS CHECK Drug cartels control different regions of Mexico. New cartels compete with old cartels for power, resulting in street gun battles, massacres in the mountains, and other acts of violence or abuse.

Human Geography of Mexico

Making Connections

Because the Spanish settled large areas of land in the western United States, people today can visit presidios and missions not just in Mexico, but in U.S. states such as California, Texas, New Mexico, and Arizona. These settlements were meant to firmly establish Spain's claim to these lands and protect them from the encroachments of other colonizing countries such as France and Britain.

R Reading Skills

Using Word Parts Ask students to reread the last paragraph on the page. Remind students that if they are unsure of the meaning of a word, they can break it apart and consider the meaning of any prefixes or root words. Have students define the prefix *mega-*, using resources to look it up if necessary. **Ask:** What can breaking the word *megacity* apart help you understand about its meaning? *(Possible answer: The prefix* mega- *means "big," so a megacity is a settlement that is very large, possibly a city made up of many cities put together.)* What root word can you identify in the word *primate*? (prime, *meaning "first"*) What can this root word help you understand about the meaning of the term *primate city*? *(Possible answer: A primate city is the "first" city in a country because it has the most economic activity, is the biggest center of culture, and has the largest population.)* ELL Verbal/Linguistic

V Visual Skills

Analyzing Visuals Review the parts of the time line with students. Then have pairs work together to read each entry and consider what type of information it provides to them about Mexico. Have pairs finish by writing summaries that describe in their own words what the time line is explaining about Mexico. *(Possible answer: The events on the time line chart changes in government and leadership over time. The time line illustrates the volatility of systems of government in Mexico and how the leadership has seesawed back and forth between corrupt dictators and a spirit of reform.)* AL Visual/Spatial, Verbal/Linguistic

The Aztec were the growing military and governing power in central Mexico, conquering their neighbors and establishing a powerful central urban region in the Valley of Mexico.

The indigenous peoples of Mexico were a mixture of different groups and empires, having multiple languages and belief systems. Intermarriage between these indigenous peoples and the Spanish resulted in the mestizo population. The Spanish arrival brought other changes to Mexico. It resulted in war and disease outbreaks. The Spanish also established the Catholic Church in Mexico. A unique melding of traditional indigenous beliefs and the newly introduced Catholic culture occurred in a process called **syncretism**.

syncretism a blending of beliefs and practices from different religions into one faith

The Spanish established a solid footing in Mexico by using Catholic missions as religious outposts to help spread Christian ideas. They centralized power around presidios, or military outposts, to protect Spanish towns and missions. Communities expanded near the missions, and Spanish estate farming and ranching were introduced. Some Spanish settlements grew into large cities, using a variety of local resources. For example, Oaxaca de Juárez grew rich on the cochineal (KAH•chuh•NEEL) insect used to make a permanent red dye.

Spanish landowners took advantage of Mexico's large and impoverished indigenous communities. Workers on large landowners' estates, known as haciendas, harvested cash crops but were paid very little for their labor. It was, and in many places still is, very difficult for poor workers to earn enough to become independent of their landlord. After independence from Spain, members of poor rural communities sought independence from the landowners.

megacity a great city that is made up of several large and small cities

primate city a city that dominates a country's economy, culture, and government and in which population is concentrated; usually the capital

R Rural-to-urban migration has greatly altered the population's distribution. Today, more than 78 percent of Mexican citizens live in urban areas. Mexico City is a **megacity** that has absorbed surrounding towns and smaller cities into the urban sprawl of the dominant city. It has received millions of migrants as well. The poor seek work in urban areas, migrating to regional capitals or to Mexico City. Mexico City is important because it is the **primate city**. It is more than just

TIME LINE

MEXICAN Independence and Change

The story of Mexico's history is a fascinating one. Starting with ancient civilizations and tragic conquest, it is followed by independence and revolution, resulting in the Mexico of today.

▶ CRITICAL THINKING

1. ***Analyzing*** Why do you think Benito Juárez is considered a hero to Mexicans?
2. ***Sequencing*** What political party did Vicente Fox oppose and when did it regain power?

V 1800

1810 Father Miguel Hidalgo sparks the decade-long struggle for independence from Spain.

1821 Treaty recognizes Mexican independence from Spain.

1824 Mexico becomes a republic and adopts a federal constitution.

1833 Caudillo Antonio López de Santa Anna becomes president and halts reforms.

1846–1848 Mexico engages in war with the United States over Texas territory. Treaty of Guadalupe Hidalgo ends war in 1848.

networks Online Teaching Options

TIME LINE

Mexican Independence and Change

Hypothesizing Use the time line on Mexico's history to help students consider the various ancient civilizations and tragic conquests that ultimately lead to the country's independence. Explain that the Spanish set up numerous Catholic missions in Mexico to establish a strong presence in Mexico. Point to the year 1810 on the time line and read the text about Father Miguel Hidalgo. Ask students the following questions: What does it mean that he is titled a "father"? *(he is a Catholic priest)* Do you think he is most likely a Spaniard or a Native Mexican? *(He was born in Pénjamo, Guanajuato, so he is a Native Mexican.)* How might this revolution have been different if the opposite group led it? *(Student answers may vary, but they should reflect logical reasoning.)* BL Verbal/Linguistic

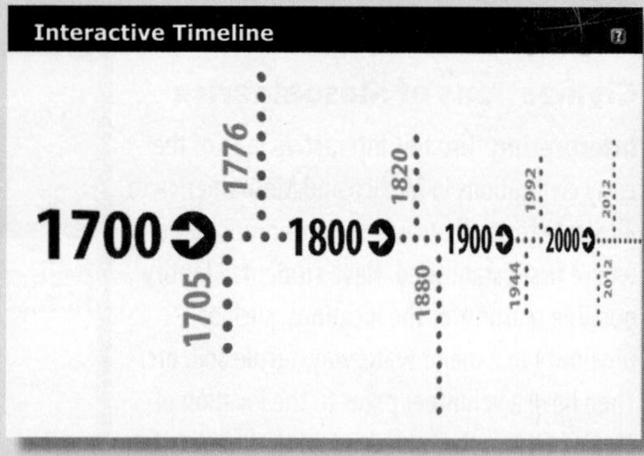

ANSWERS, p. 182

CRITICAL THINKING

1. Benito Juárez brought great changes to Mexico during La Reforma.
2. Vicente Fox opposed PRI. It regained power in 2012.

the political capital and largest city. It is also the cultural and economic center of Mexico. Mexico City has the best schools, hospitals, and housing in the country. It also has serious overcrowding, the most impoverished neighborhoods, and high levels of air pollution and water pollution. **T**

✓ READING PROGRESS CHECK

Analyzing How did Spanish landowners take advantage of the indigenous people?

Society and Culture Today

GUIDING QUESTION *How does Mexican society and culture reflect the country's colonial past?*

Colonial rule lasted for nearly 300 years in Mexico and gave the country's different cultures an important point of unifying identity. The majority of Mexicans identify themselves as Catholic. The rituals practiced in churches, however, are a blend of the diverse internal influences that drive Mexican culture.

Family and the Status of Women

Mexican culture highly values family. Today, many upper-class families are moving into more nuclear living arrangements, with only two generations in one house. The majority of Mexican homes, however, still hold three or four generations. The **extended family**, including cousins and grandparents, acts as a social support network with older generations raising younger ones. This is especially common in rural areas and in poorer communities.

extended family household made up of several generations of family members

Spanish culture established the tradition of machismo, or male dominance, in Mexico. As in other Latin American countries, women in Mexico have traditionally been limited to culture-specific roles in society. Their first obligation is to the family. However, women have made huge strides toward equality in the last few decades. More women are entering the workforce and are involved in traditionally male professions, as well as in the political arena.

1858–1872 *La Reforma* ("The Reform") President Benito Juárez brings great changes to Mexico.

1900

1910–1920 Corrupt dictatorial rule of General Porfirio Díaz leads to Mexican Revolution.

1917 New constitution brings additional reforms and establishes Mexico as a federal republic.

1929 One political party, the *Partido Revolucionario Institucional* (PRI), begins its domination of Mexican politics.

2000 PRI's control ends when Vicente Fox Quesada of the opposition party *Partido Acción Nacional* (PAN) is elected president.

2012

2012 PRI regains control with Enrique Peña Nieto winning the presidency.

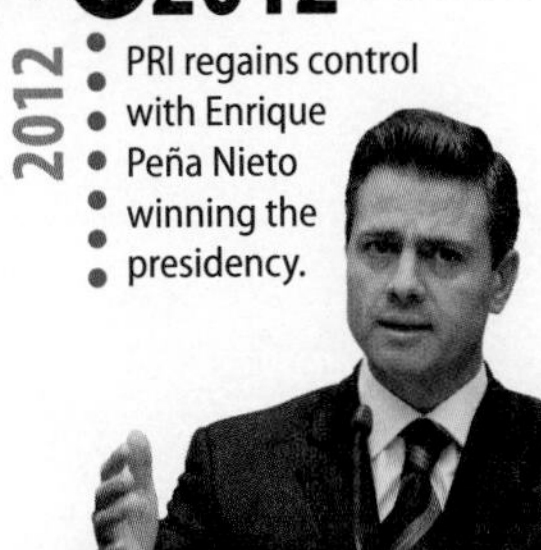

(bl)©Jack Kurtz/ZUMA/Corbis, (br)Odd Andersen/AFP/Getty Images

T Technology Skills

Acquiring Information Have small groups of students use online resources to collect more in-depth information about life in the megacity of Mexico City. Assign each group a specific area to research, such as cultural institutions, systems of housing, industries and businesses, school systems, and transportation. Once groups have completed their research, have them create multimedia presentations using photographs, video clips, and charts or graphs to organize their data. Invite groups to present their findings to the class. Finish with a class discussion about the advantages and drawbacks of living in this city.
BL Verbal/Linguistic, Visual/Spatial

C Critical Thinking Skills

Exploring Issues Have students think about how attitudes in Mexican society are changing and what positive and negative effects these shifting beliefs might have on society in the future. **Ask:** How is family life changing over time? *(Possible answer: Although most Mexican homes, particularly in poor or rural areas, still house extended families, many upper-class families are using their prosperity to live in homes with only one or two generations present.)* How might this change affect how people live? *(Possible answer: Previously, Mexican families could rely on the support network of family to share work such as child-rearing or looking after older family members who could no longer take care of themselves. If more and more people live apart from each other, families will have to find other ways to compensate for the lack of this support network, such as paying for outside help to provide child or elder care.)* What limited the kinds of work that women could do the in past? *(Possible answer: A tradition of male dominance inherited from the Spanish settlers trapped women in certain roles.)* What problems might women face as they work to gain equality? *(Possible answer: They will have to overcome and replace the ingrained tradition of machismo with one that accepts women as equals.)*
BL Verbal/Linguistic, Logical/Mathematical

VIDEO

Mexico City

Creating Charts Use this video about Mexico City to show how the city has diversified and changed over time. Explain that over the years Mexico City has gone from an Aztec society to a thriving metropolis that blends indigenous, European, and modern architectures and cultures into one city. Working with a partner, have students create a two-column chart. Have them list *traditional influences* in one column and *modern influences* in the other. Have pairs share their charts in a class discussion. **ELL** Visual/Spatial

ANSWERS, p. 183

✓ READING PROGRESS CHECK Workers on Spanish landowners' estates were paid very little for the labor they provided, making it difficult for poor workers to earn enough to become independent.

V Visual Skills

Using Graphs Provide time for students to analyze and interpret the graph. Then in a class discussion, **ask:** What are the three labor sectors represented on the graph? *(industry, agriculture, and services)* What do the colored slices on the graph tell you? *(the percentage of all working women employed in each area)* Which sector employs the smallest percentage of women? *(agriculture)* Have students answer the questions on their own. AL Visual/Spatial

C Critical Thinking Skills

Analyzing Have students consider what they have read so far about the composition of the population of Mexico and how different cultures have met, clashed, and blended over time. **Ask:** How would you summarize the point this paragraph is making about the relationship between Mexican culture and traditional folk culture? *(Although formed by a collection of different influences, Mexican culture is trying to establish a kind of unity by treating parts of folk culture as universally Mexican.)* What are some examples of pieces of folk culture that are now recognized as "Mexican"? *(Maya pyramids, Aztec temples, the mural form)* Why might the Mexican people find it useful to unite their culture in this way? *(Sharing a common cultural identity that joins and preserves, rather than ignores, past accomplishments might unite the people politically and socially.)* BL Logical/Mathematical

T Technology Skills

Identifying Perspectives Have students explore the work of Diego Rivera in greater depth. Organize students into pairs. Have each pair conduct online research to locate an example of Rivera's wall paintings and frescos. Pairs should present to the class a poster displaying their chosen artwork, along with their interpretation of Rivera's perspective on his subject and an explanation of how they feel this piece of art uses images to reflect Mexico's cultural heritage. Visual/Spatial, Verbal/Linguistic

ANSWERS, p. 184

☑ READING PROGRESS CHECK Rivera's work is culturally and politically themed. In his fresco *From Conquest to 1930,* the images of peasants and workers show foreign influence and Mexico's struggle for independence.

CRITICAL THINKING

1. The service sector employs the most women in Mexico.
2. This photo depicts the industry sector.

V

GRAPH SKILLS — Female Labor in Mexico

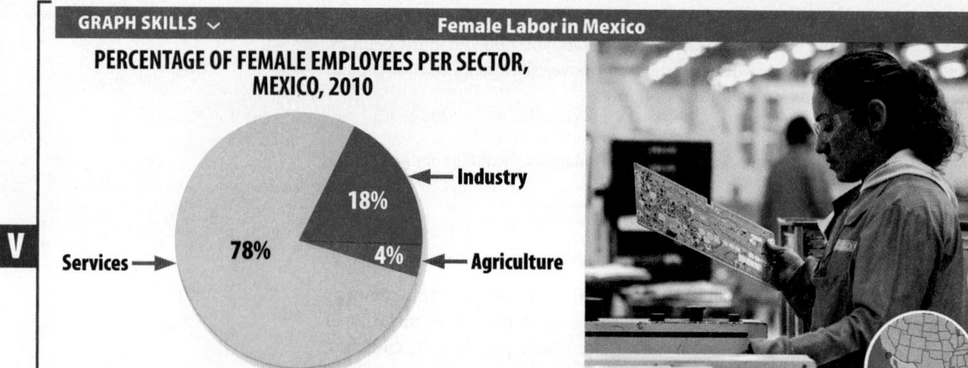

Source: http://data.worldbank.org/, World Bank, *World Development Indicators*

Women in Mexico have been entering the labor force in increasing numbers in recent years.

▲ CRITICAL THINKING

1. Analyzing What economic sector employs the most women in Mexico?

2. Analyzing Visuals Which sector is the photo depicting?

The Arts

C Mexico's arts have been greatly influenced by its indigenous cultures and Spanish heritage. Since the 1930s, Mexican culture has been seeking a unified image through the promotion of traditional folk culture. Art forms that were once region-specific or limited to a particular cultural group are now universally recognized as Mexican. Early indigenous architecture includes Maya pyramids and Aztec temples and palaces. Many of these buildings were decorated with murals (wall paintings) and mosaics (wall pictures made with stones or tiles). Murals were also popular in the European tradition, and the Spanish encouraged this art form.

T Murals continue to be an important art form in Mexico. The most famous Mexican muralist was Diego Rivera. He became known for his elaborate and often culturally and politically themed wall paintings and frescoes (paintings done in wet plaster). His art is displayed in museums and government and civic buildings in Mexico City and in the United States. In the central arch detail of his fresco *From Conquest to 1930,* Rivera used images of peasants and workers to show foreign influence and Mexico's struggle for independence.

☑ READING PROGRESS CHECK

Depicting How does the art of Diego Rivera reflect Mexico's cultural heritage?

Economic Activities

GUIDING QUESTION *How has Mexico's place in the global economy changed over time?*

In the 1500s Mexico became the center of the Spanish Empire in the Americas. It was a rich colony because of its many natural resources. Because it was the first Spanish colony to win independence, Mexico became a cultural leader and example for other colonies ruled by Spain and Portugal. Mexico is still trying to create an economy that benefits all Mexicans, not just the wealthy upper class. In fact, Mexico is still struggling to be a completely free and equal republic. Colonialism still influences Mexico's economy.

David Maung/Bloomberg/Getty Images

184

networks Online Teaching Options

INTERACTIVE IMAGE

Women in the Workforce

Analyzing Use this interactive image and graph to discuss the issue of gender and society in Mexico. Divide students into small groups to discuss the following questions based on what they have learned:

- Why is the largest percentage of women employed in the service industry?
- How might family values influence this employment choice?
- How might equality and political changes influence this employment choice?
- What events or actions might change the shape of this chart?

AL Verbal/Linguistic

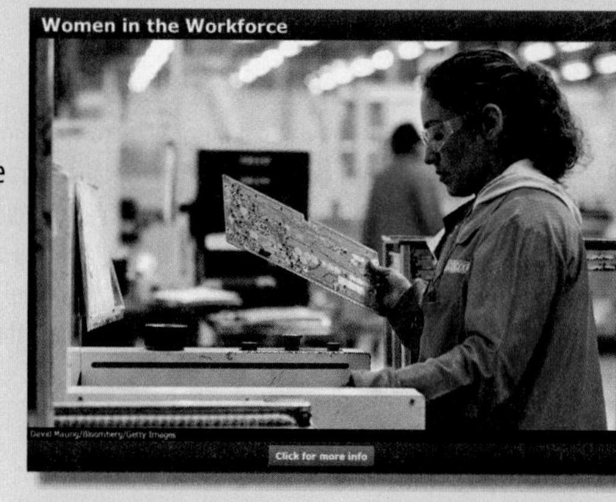

Resources, Power, and Industry

Mexico has a higher standard of living than many countries in Latin America. Mexico's **gross domestic product** (GDP) is the twelfth highest globally. The per capita GDP, or average income, is above $15,000 per year. However, this does not account for the huge gap between the rich and the poor. One reason for Mexico's economic prosperity is its high level of economic diversity.

gross domestic product (GDP) the value of goods and services produced within a country in a year

V1

Mexico's many natural resources are controlled by the rich and by the government. The wealthy upper class controls the land that provides access to resources and enterprise holdings. Mexico has globalized its economy and invested in high-tech industries. Industries in Mexico face competition from countries in other regions, especially Asia and Central America. Wages, transportation costs, government supports, and political considerations are all important in deciding the best location for a manufacturing or production facility.

Mexico's diverse landscape has always presented a challenge to building a national transportation system. This is especially true for east-to-west travel in the northern region. Mexico City remains the major hub for all rail travel. Buses and trucks also carry passengers and freight in Mexico via the highway systems, including trucks that carry manufactured goods to the United States. In the 1990s the Mexican government began to privatize the airline industry. Today, there are domestic and international airports across the country, making air travel common for upper- and middle-class Mexicans and tourists.

R

More than one million people cross the U.S.-Mexico border every day in both directions. Goods are imported and exported between the countries, and tourists travel in both directions. Cross-border shopping in the border towns is a major part of the lives of many citizens in both Mexico and the United States.

GEOGRAPHY CONNECTION

Mexicans in the U.S. workforce play a significant role in the economies of both countries. They provide valuable labor in the United States and add to the cash flow in Mexico through money that is sent home to their families.

1. ***PLACES AND REGIONS*** What are the pull factors drawing Mexican citizens to the United States?
2. ***HUMAN SYSTEMS*** How would U.S. economic downturns affect the pull of workers to the United States?

V2

INTERACTIVE MAP

Migration to U.S.

Formulating Questions Display this interactive map about Mexican migration to the United States. Ask students to write three questions they have about the map and how it relates to Mexico's immigration and foreign relations policy with the United States. Collect the questions and have the class answer them after reading the lesson. If there are some questions that are not answered, encourage students to research the answers as homework and then report their findings to the class. AL Verbal/Linguistic

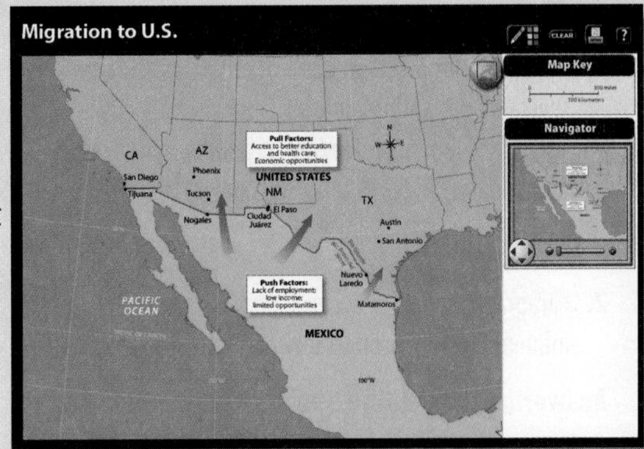

V1 Visual Skills

Creating Charts Have students work in pairs to create a two-column chart to keep track of the actions Mexico has taken to globalize its economy and the challenges it has faced in doing so. Suggest that students enhance their charts by doing additional research to learn more about issues such as competition between industries in Mexico and other countries or the construction of Mexico's transportation system. Invite volunteers to share their completed charts with the class. **Interpersonal, Visual/Spatial**

R Reading Skills

Defining Ask students what the word *private* means. Then point out the word *privatize* in the text. Ask students what the suffix *-ize* means. *(It changes a noun or adjective into a verb.)* **Ask:** **Based on your understanding of the suffix *-ize*, what does the word *privatize* mean?** *(to make private, or in this case, to put in the hands of private businesses the work of running different airlines)* ELL **Verbal/Linguistic**

V2 Visual Skills

Analyzing Visuals Have students examine the map and identify its parts and features. **Ask:** **According to this map, which country offers the greater prospect for good employment and why?** *(The United States offers the greater prospect because it contains better markets and more jobs.)* **If nothing changes, what will be the long-term effect on the labor force in Mexico?** *(Possible answer: If Mexico is not able to establish better markets and stronger sources of employment, so much of its labor force will move north that its economic fortunes will be inextricably linked with those of the United States and its own industries may begin to collapse with nothing to replace them.)* AL **Visual/Spatial, Logical/Mathematical**

ANSWERS, p. 185

GEOGRAPHY CONNECTION

1. Markets and jobs are the pull factors drawing Mexican citizens to the United States.
2. Because there would be fewer jobs in the U.S., it is possible the pull would decrease.

W Writing Skills

Informative/Explanatory Have students do additional research to learn more about the economic relationship between the United States and Mexico and how each country benefits and suffers by the current state of affairs. Have students write essays using facts and details to explain the situation and propose solutions that might improve the economies of both countries. BL Verbal/Linguistic

C Critical Thinking Skills

Identifying Central Issues Have students review the information about drug cartels. **Ask:** What makes drug cartels influential to the economy? *(By pumping money into local economies in the form of bribes and loans, they support these economies and allow the people to make a living.)* Guide a class discussion on the types of things that might need to happen to end the reign of drug cartels. Logical/Mathematical

CLOSE & REFLECT

Understanding Relationships Among Events Have students write a few paragraphs explaining some ways life in Mexico has improved over time, some recurring problems Mexico has faced, and the challenges that this country faces today. Invite volunteers to share their paragraphs with the class.

Maquiladoras and the Middle Class

"Without deep political and social reforms, experts say, the thousands of maquiladora plants that cluster at the U.S. border and around cities in the interior will remain a fixture for decades to come, and Mexico won't build a middle class that's big enough to fuel faster economic growth."

—Tim Johnson, "Mexico's 'maquiladora' labor system keeps workers in poverty," *The Miami Herald*, June 18, 2012

DBQ ***IDENTIFYING CAUSE AND EFFECT*** Why does the author believe that Mexico cannot build a middle class? RH.9–10.1, RH.9–10.2

maquiladora in Mexico, a manufacturing plant owned by a foreign company

free trade zone an area of a country in which trade restrictions do not apply

Communications are also essential to the Mexican economy. The use of cell phones has increased rapidly since the mid-1990s. The infrastructure and availability of high-speed Internet exists, although not in all areas. People in Mexico City, in some areas along the border with Texas, and in business centers like Monterrey and Guadalajara have the most access. The vast majority of Mexicans, however, are left out of the digital age. According to the Mexican Internet Association, about 82 million people—70 percent of Mexicans—had no access to a computer or the Internet in 2012.

NAFTA, Trade, and Maquiladoras

In 1992 Mexico, the United States, and Canada signed the North American Free Trade Agreement (NAFTA). NAFTA is a comprehensive agreement that eliminated most trade restrictions. As a result, trade among the three countries grew by 10 to 15 percent annually. Mexico's economy has been transformed by these increases in trade and the flow of investment.

W NAFTA has also been a source of controversy and concern. Mexico is more dependent on the economy of its northern neighbor than the United States is on the Mexican economy. Mexico has protested the harmful effects of subsidized agricultural exports from the United States that may be forcing Mexican small landholders off their farms and into service-based or industrial jobs. Meanwhile, many U.S. workers are concerned about the loss of their jobs to workers in Mexico.

During the past 50 years, American and Japanese firms have built manufacturing plants in Mexico. Many of these factories, known as **maquiladoras**, are located close to the U.S.-Mexico border. Maquiladoras are located in **free trade zones**. Such areas benefit foreign corporations by allowing them to hire low-cost labor and produce duty-free exports. They also offer the host country employment opportunities and investment income. Critics of maquiladoras charge that the system often ignores labor laws, thus encouraging low-paying or dangerous jobs.

C The illegal drug trade is both an influential and dangerous part of the Mexican economy. Drug cartels often reinvest the money they make into their communities—both through private loans to small businesses and in the form of bribes to police and politicians. This makes them a powerful social and economic force. Many rural mountain communities have relied for generations on the poppy and marijuana fields, controlled by cartels, that support their families. The government has not been able to discourage the growing of these crops because no legal crop can match their cash value for these isolated farmers.

READING PROGRESS CHECK

Assessing What factors contribute to Mexico's higher standard of living compared to other Latin American countries?

LESSON 2 REVIEW CCSS

Reviewing Vocabulary (Tier Three Words)

1. ***Classifying*** In what ways is Mexico City both a megacity and a primate city? RH.9–10.4

Using Your Notes

2. ***Summarizing*** Use your graphic organizer on the human geography of Mexico to write a paragraph summarizing society and culture in Mexico today.

Answering the Guiding Questions

3. ***Drawing Conclusions*** What influenced Mexico's political and social structures?
4. ***Hypothesizing*** What factors have shaped Mexico's population patterns?
5. ***Evaluating*** How does Mexican society and culture reflect the country's colonial past?
6. ***Explaining*** How has Mexico's place in the global economy changed over time?

Writing Activity

7. ***Informative/Explanatory*** Write a paragraph discussing how maquiladoras involve Mexico in world trade. WHST.9–10.2

186

ANSWERS, p. 186

READING PROGRESS CHECK One reason for Mexico's economic prosperity is its high level of economic diversity. Mexico globalized its economy and invested in high-tech industries, resulting in the twelfth highest GDP globally.

DBQ There are thousands of maquiladoras that cluster at the U.S. border and around cities in the interior. Without political and social reforms, Mexico cannot build a middle class large enough to fuel economic growth.

LESSON 2 REVIEW ANSWERS

Reviewing Vocabulary

1. It is a megacity because it is a city that has absorbed several towns and small cities. It is a primate city because it dominates Mexico's economy, culture, and government, and population is concentrated there.

Using Your Notes

2. Paragraphs should show understanding of the influences on Mexican society and culture today.

Answering the Guiding Questions

3. Indigenous peoples and the Spanish influenced Mexico's political and social structures. Protests against European rulers and the 1917 constitution were of great influence.
4. The Spanish established missions that grew into large cities. Internal migration to cities has greatly altered the population's current distribution. Today, more than 78 percent of Mexican citizens live in urban areas.
5. Mexico's arts have been influenced by both its indigenous cultures and Spanish heritage.
6. Mexico was the center of the Spanish empire in the West because of its natural resources. Today, it still has many natural resources, but Mexico has diversified its economy and invested in high-tech industries.

Writing Activity

7. U.S. and Japanese firms have built maquiladoras in Mexico. They are located in free trade zones, which benefit foreign corporations by allowing them to hire low-cost labor and produce duty-free exports.

networks

There's More Online!

- **IMAGE** Mexican Surfers Make a Statement for Protecting Nature
- **MAP** Environmental Deterioration in Mexico
- **INTERACTIVE SELF-CHECK QUIZ**
- **VIDEO** People and Their Environment: Mexico

Reading **HELP**DESK 

Academic Vocabulary (Tier Two Words)
- **corporate**
- **ignorance**

Content Vocabulary (Tier Three Words)
- **deforestation**
- **sustainable development**
- **land subsidence**

TAKING NOTES: ***Key Ideas and Details***

IDENTIFYING Use a web diagram similar to the one below to take notes as you read about the issues that relate to people and their environment in Mexico.

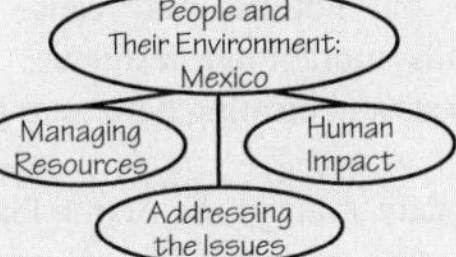

(t)Yuri Cortez/AFP/Getty Images, (tcl)Jorge Uzon/AFP/Getty Images, (tcr)Eco Images/Universal Images Group/Getty Images, (tr)Stephen Alvarez/National Geographic/Getty Images

LESSON 3
People and Their Environment: Mexico

ESSENTIAL QUESTION • *How do physical systems and human systems shape a place?*

IT MATTERS BECAUSE

The ways that people extract and use resources today can have substantial impacts on their well-being in the future. Resource management and sustainable development are important so that future generations can continue to benefit from an area's natural resources. Mexico has been so focused on increasing economic development that conservation of resources has not been as high a priority. However, concerned Mexican citizens are working hard to find ways to preserve the land and all that it provides. R1

Managing Resources

GUIDING QUESTION *Why are Mexico's resources in jeopardy?*

Mexico has many natural resources. These include petroleum, silver, copper, gold, lead, zinc, natural gas, and timber. Industrial access to these resources enriches the economy and creates jobs and new investment opportunities. Obtaining and using these resources, however, often results in significant problems that threaten Mexico's environmental health. C

Mexico's many ecosystems are experiencing the effects of global climate change and environmental destruction. For example, semi-arid regions are seeing longer droughts and more desertification, or the development of desertlike conditions. Forested areas throughout Mexico are experiencing new patterns in rainfall. Many changes in the environment are a result of increasing migration to urban centers. This puts pressure on the surrounding environment. As cities grow, the surrounding land is cleared and developed.

At the same time, environmental degradation itself is increasing urbanization. The destruction of rural resources forces migration to urban areas. People move to the cities to seek employment away from the hardship of living in regions destroyed by poor environmental management.

About one-third of Mexico is covered in large forests ranging from deciduous and coniferous forests to tropical rain forests. Forest destruction and the loss of biodiversity, however, is occurring at an alarming rate. As Mexico's economy grows, so does the demand for timber R2

networks *Online Teaching Options*

 **INTERACTIVE BELLRINGER**

Diminishing Frontier Forests in Mexico

Interpreting Visuals This map can be used to introduce the concept of deforestation in Mexico. Explain that there are many causes for deforestation, or the loss or destruction of forests. For example, people might harvest the trees for wood or clear them to make space for farming or cattle raising. Have pairs of students read the introductory text, study the map, and answer the questions. Then ask students to write a paragraph discussing how and why this map might look different in future years. **Visual/Spatial, Verbal/Linguistic**

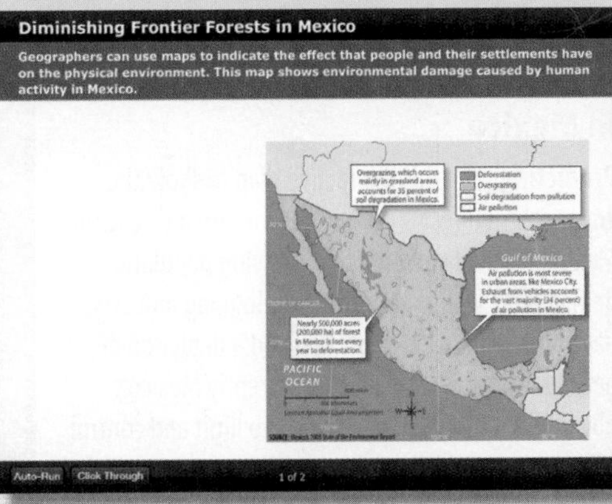

Diminishing Frontier Forests in Mexico
Geographers can use maps to indicate the effect that people and their settlements have on the physical environment. This map shows environmental damage caused by human activity in Mexico.
Gulf of Mexico
PACIFIC OCEAN
Auto-Run
Click Through
1 of 2

ENGAGE

R1 Reading Skills

Activating Prior Knowledge Have pairs work together to brainstorm the ways people extract and use natural resources and how these methods may hurt the planet and deplete the resources. Then have partners discuss things people and countries can do to conserve resources. Invite students to share their knowledge with the class.

TEACH & ASSESS

C Critical Thinking Skills

Identifying Cause and Effect Have students create a graphic organizer that will help them record information about the many cause-and-effect relationships described in this lesson that explain current issues in Mexico such as deforestation, water scarcity, and desertification.

Issue	Cause	Effect
Deforestation	land around cities is cleared	loss of biodiversity

Point out that some issues may have many different relevant causes and effects to record. Students should continue to add more information to their charts as they read on in the lesson.
AL Visual/Spatial

R2 Reading Skills

Defining Ask students what the word *diverse* means *(showing a lot of variety)*. Then point out the word *biodiversity* in the text. Ask students what the prefix *bio-* means *(life)*. Ask students what the suffix *-ity* means *(state or quality of being)*. **Ask: How might you use these word parts to define *biodiversity*?** *(Possible answer: the state of containing a great variety of life.)*
ELL Verbal/Linguistic

ANSWERS, p. 187

TAKING NOTES: Managing Resources—Mexico's ecosystems are experiencing the effects of global climate change and environmental destruction; increasing migration to urban centers is contributing to deforestation and pollution; **Human Impact**—increased access to manufactured goods results in waste accumulation; increased carbon emissions results in air pollution, causing chronic health conditions; **Addressing the Issues**—government investment in education and health services leads to a better educated and more literate population that demands more from government and from society

V Visual Skills

Analyzing Visuals Have students study the map key, labels, and other parts of this map. **Ask:** **What do the different colors of land indicate?** *(the environmental threat that puts each area in danger)* **What threatens brown land?** *(deforestation)* **What threat is most prevalent in the northern plateau area of Mexico?** *(overgrazing)* **How could looking at this map help the government and businesses of Mexico plan a better strategy for reducing environmental deterioration?** *(Possible answer: They could see how types of environmental degradation correspond to the geography of Mexico and make connections to the cause-and-effect relationships between pollution and geography. Once they understand these relationships, they can adjust the collection and use of natural resources to create new effects and outcomes.)* AL **Visual/Spatial, Logical/Mathematical**

Content Background Knowledge

Controlling Deforestation To help control the spread of deforestation, the Mexican government pays landowners not to cut down the forests in some areas. The government tries to limit the amount of these incentive payments so that the landowners do not pursue other ways of making money, which would hurt the economy, but they do hope to reduce poverty with this money. Concerned that some people may resort to cutting down trees on unprotected lands, they are monitoring the areas bordering the protected land to see if they detect any sudden reduction in trees there.

W Writing Skills

Informative/Explanatory Have students recall what they have read about the limited water resources in Mexico. Have them write a paragraph describing the importance of water to life in Mexico and what factors affect people's use of this natural resource. **Logical/Mathematical**

ANSWERS, p. 188

GEOGRAPHY CONNECTION

1 The west coast of Mexico has the most industrial contamination.

2 Overgrazing affects the largest area of land in Mexico.

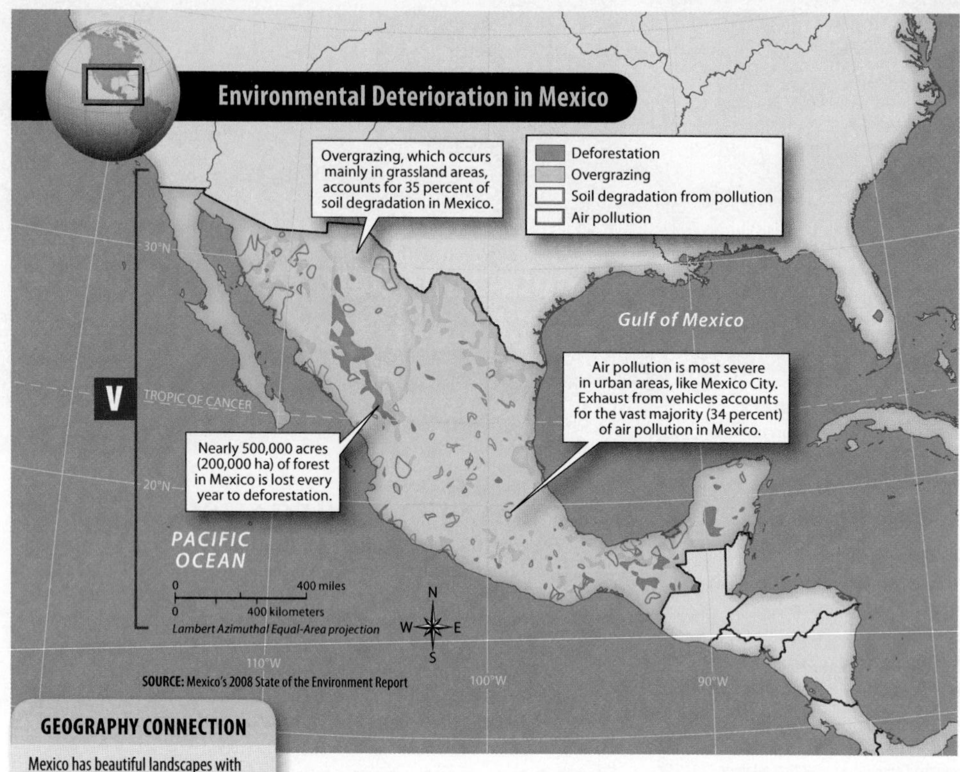
Environmental Deterioration in Mexico
Overgrazing, which occurs mainly in grassland areas, accounts for 35 percent of soil degradation in Mexico.
Deforestation
Overgrazing
Soil degradation from pollution
Air pollution
Gulf of Mexico
Air pollution is most severe in urban areas, like Mexico City. Exhaust from vehicles accounts for the vast majority (34 percent) of air pollution in Mexico.
30°N
TROPIC OF CANCER
Nearly 500,000 acres (200,000 ha) of forest in Mexico is lost every year to deforestation.
20°N
PACIFIC OCEAN
0 400 miles
0 400 kilometers
Lambert Azimuthal Equal-Area projection
N
W
E
S
110°W
100°W
90°W
SOURCE: Mexico's 2008 State of the Environment Report

GEOGRAPHY CONNECTION

Mexico has beautiful landscapes with abundant resources, but environmental deterioration threatens its lands.

1. ***THE WORLD IN SPATIAL TERMS*** Which coast of Mexico experiences the most industrial contamination?
2. ***ENVIRONMENT AND SOCIETY*** Which threat affects the largest area of land in Mexico?

resources, which are an important part of Mexico's export economy. The **corporate** logging industry is one source of the problem, but not the only cause of **deforestation**. The growing population demands more food resources. In response, ranchers and farmers are clearing the forests and creating new areas for growing food and grazing cattle.

In 2000 Mexico developed the National Biodiversity Strategy and Action Plan. The plan has four major objectives: to conserve and protect the biodiversity components, to value the different components of biodiversity, to promote knowledge of biodiversity, and to encourage sustainable and diversified use of biodiversity components. Reducing public **ignorance** of the consequences of environmental mismanagement should reduce the loss of Mexican forest resources. **Sustainable development** projects that utilize natural resources responsibly are the only solution to the demands of a growing population.

Mexico has numerous mountain ranges, dry northern plains, vast southern jungles, and many large cities. Consequently, only 12.7 percent of Mexico's land is arable, or suitable for farming. Producing enough agricultural products is difficult in Mexico. With only a few major rivers and lakes, water resources are precious.

The demand for water resources in the northern part of the country is so high that desertification is a growing problem. Climate change has meant that recent years have seen an increase in drought throughout northern Mexico. Both ranchers and farmers have suffered from the water shortages.

More than 50 percent of Mexico's population lives below the poverty line, many in substandard conditions in large urban centers. Both rural and urban

corporate formed into an association and endowed by law with the rights and liabilities of an individual

deforestation the loss or destruction of forests, mainly for logging or farming

ignorance lack of knowledge, education, or awareness

networks *Online Teaching Options*

INTERACTIVE MAP

Environmental Deterioration in Mexico

Predicting Use this interactive map to show the environmental resources and deterioration threats in Mexico. Remind students that growing population demands, as well as the corporate logging industry, have both lead to deforestation and a depletion of natural resources. Explain that currently Mexico's government has stepped in to try to limit and control environmental mismanagement. Have students write a paragraph predicting what they think will happen to this region over time. Ask them to explain if they believe the rain forests and other natural resources in Mexico can be preserved for future generations to enjoy. **Verbal/Linguistic**

areas struggle to provide basic resources like clean water, electricity, and garbage removal. Human needs are putting heavy demands on land, water, and timber resources. Pollution of water, air, and land is a growing concern for Mexico.

Mexico City in particular is facing serious problems with its water supply. Providing water to more than 20 million residents is a challenge for the city's struggling infrastructure. The natural underground reserves of water have been pumped dry. Once water is removed, the clay soil compacts in the empty space and the water cannot be replaced. Over the years, these empty water reservoirs in and around Mexico City have been collapsing. This creates sinkholes, or depressions in the land, and relevels the surface. Buildings in Mexico City are tilting because the land underneath them has been emptied of water. This process is called **land subsidence**.

R The poor are the greatest victims of the urban water crisis. Municipal water supplies often do not reach their settlements on the outskirts of the city. Citizen groups have been working to improve the water supply through advocacy and education, and by encouraging the government to privatize water management.

✓ READING PROGRESS CHECK

Exploring the Issues Describe how large-scale urbanization has affected Mexico City.

Human Impact

GUIDING QUESTION *How do human activities impact Mexico's environment?*

Rapid urban growth in the last century and high rates of poverty have made social development a constant challenge in Mexico. As portions of the economy grow, access to consumer goods and the number of consumers increase. As a result, waste accumulation is a growing challenge. Without infrastructure to support proper waste disposal, pollution is an enormous problem in urban areas.

Mexico's economy is still growing. When people achieve a new economic status, they invest in material goods such as electronics and cars. Cars are a major contributing factor to air pollution problems. Mexico City is located in a valley. Carbon emissions from cars are often trapped in the valley. This creates a toxic haze over the city. As a result, the sky around Mexico City is often a dull gray or brown. The government has been making emission regulations a priority to try to reduce the level of pollution in the air. Until these regulations take effect, citizens will continue to suffer from health problems related to air pollution, such as an increased risk of asthma and chronic lung infections.

✓ READING PROGRESS CHECK

Analyzing What are the causes and consequences of air pollution in an urban environment?

Addressing the Issues

GUIDING QUESTION *How are governments in Mexico addressing environmental issues?*

The last 20 years have seen a rise in political action and activity by many Mexican citizens. As a result of government investment in health and education, a better educated and more literate population has begun to demand more from their government and from society. These citizens want better living conditions and have also shown a concern for protecting the environment.

Mexico has enacted new regulations to try to curb the destruction of natural resources. The government is also working to support farms and businesses that contribute to the economy and are interested in protecting those resources.

Connecting Geography to SCIENCE

Environmental Science

T Investigating how human societies affect the natural world and how the environment, in turn, affects human life is the work of environmental scientists. They also examine how to preserve and repair these relationships in order to create a sustainable society. Environmental science crosses the boundaries of several subjects, including geography. Environmental scientists use many geographic tools, such as geographic information systems (GIS) and remote sensing. They determine the condition of and changes in environments to examine the causes of destruction and to create plans for remediation and development.

COMPARING What tools are commonly used in both the fields of environmental science and geography?

sustainable development technological and economic growth that does not deplete the human and natural resources of a given area

land subsidence the sinking or settling of land to a lower level in response to various natural and human-caused factors

R Reading Skills

Inferring Discuss with students the reasons behind the urban water crisis in Mexico City and why it threatens the poor more than anyone else. **Ask: Why are the poor residents more affected than other people living in Mexico City?** *(The poor cannot afford the more expensive housing inside the city, so they live in the cheaper surrounding areas where clean water may not be piped.)* **Why might privatizing the water supply solve this problem?** *(Possible answer: The government is overextended and does not have the resources needed. Private businesses with their own sources of funding might be more successful in building the pipes and infrastructure needed to transport clean water to all areas.)* **Logical/Mathematical**

Making Connections

Geography of Air Pollution Mexico City is not the only metropolitan area with air pollution problems. Many cities in the United States struggle with issues of pollution, too. The geography of certain cities works to trap the pollution, causing poor air quality. Los Angeles, California, is located in a basin with mountains to the east that trap and hold polluted air over the city. Chattanooga, Tennessee, is located in a valley where air flows over neighboring mountains and is trapped, holding air pollution in place. At one time it was the most polluted city in the country for poor air quality.

T Technology Skills

Acquiring Information Have students form groups and use online resources to collect more in-depth information about the work an environmental scientist does. Have groups create a visual that presents information about representative jobs an environmental scientist performs, places where they work around the world, and images of the types of equipment they use. Invite groups to present their visuals to the class.

BL **Verbal/Linguistic, Visual/Spatial**

VIDEO

U.S.–Mexico Border

Problem-Solving Use this video about Tijuana and the Mexican border to show some of the environmental and economic changes occurring in Mexico. Allow students to take turns citing examples from the video of the changes. Have students choose one of the changes that they think is critical to the population or economy of Mexico. Group students by their critical change selection, and then have each group write a list of potential solutions.

BL **Verbal/Linguistic**

ANSWERS, p. 189

✓ READING PROGRESS CHECK More than 50 percent of Mexico's population lives below the poverty line, in substandard conditions in large urban centers. There is a struggle to provide basic resources like clean water, electricity, and garbage removal. The removal of water from underground reserves to meet the needs of a growing population has resulted in sinkholes, causing buildings to tilt.

✓ READING PROGRESS CHECK As portions of the economy grow, access to manufactured goods, such as cars, increases. Carbon emissions from cars can be trapped above a city, making a toxic haze. This air pollution can be carried into waterways.

Connecting Geography Environmental scientists use many geographic tools, including geographic information systems and remote sensing.

C Critical Thinking Skills

Making Generalizations Review the first two paragraphs with students. **Ask:** **What is significant about those involved in decision making as part of the Border 2020 Program?** *(It is designed to empower local citizens and businesses in affected communities to make the decisions.)* **What risk of the REDD+ program do some groups worry about?** *(They fear companies will buy carbon credits to avoid having to reduce pollution, which would affect indigenous people and forest communities because their lands would be taken.)* Have students recall the relationship between the governing groups in Mexico and the people who have been governed. **AL Logical/Mathematical**

T Technology Skills

Exploring Issues Divide students into small groups and assign each group one of the programs mentioned in this section—the Border 2020 Program, the REDD+, and *Muévete en Bici*. Have each group use the Internet or library resources to research more details about the history and outcomes of their assigned program. Groups should use their research to evaluate how effective their assigned program has been so far at combatting the problem it was designed to solve. Have groups present their findings to the class. Then lead a class discussion about the serious issues facing Mexico today. **BL Verbal/Linguistic**

CLOSE & REFLECT

Expressing Have students think about the reasons Mexican people rely on their natural resources and the negative outcomes that are sometimes produced when they harvest and use them. Ask each student to pick one way that Mexico's resources are in jeopardy, write a description of the impact of human activity on this resource, and then explain how Mexico is responding to try to fix this situation.

ANSWERS, p. 190

READING PROGRESS CHECK The Border 2020 Program addresses the environmental and public health problems in the border region. The Reducing Emissions from Deforestation and Forest Degradation program uses incentives to reduce the emission of greenhouse gases.

CRITICAL THINKING

1. They are promoting taking care of beaches and oceans.
2. They can provide education and information on issues that encourage people to participate in protecting their environment. They can organize large groups of people and generate great enthusiasm.

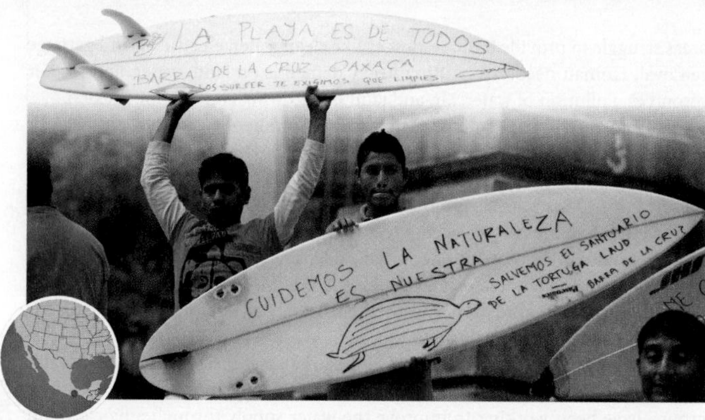

Private citizens of Mexico and nongovernmental organizations are making efforts to fill the needs of protecting the environment.

▶ **CRITICAL THINKING**

1. ***Analyzing Visuals*** What cause do you think the surfers may be promoting?
2. ***Identifying Cause and Effect*** Explain how efforts by grassroots organizations can lead to positive change in environmental issues.

Yuri Cortez/AFP/Getty Images

For example, the Border 2020 Program is an environmental program that emphasizes regional and local approaches for decision making, priority setting, and project implementation. It also addresses the environmental and public health problems in the U.S.-Mexico border region. The program empowers citizens by encouraging meaningful participation from communities and local business owners.

The Reducing Emissions from Deforestation and Forest Degradation (REDD+) program is a program designed to use market and financial incentives to reduce the emission of greenhouse gases. Yet some groups worry that for indigenous peoples and other forest communities, REDD+ poses significant risks. That is because it enables companies to buy carbon credits rather than reduce pollution at home. This could lead to indigenous lands being taken in exchange for permits that allow industries to continue to pollute.

Another program aimed at protecting the environment and reducing pollution is *Muévete en Bici*. Launched in 2007 by Mexico City mayor Marcelo Ebrard, the program closes major thruways to auto traffic on Sundays and gives the right of way to tens of thousands of cyclists in a 14-mile (22.5-km) loop. The mayor followed the Sunday rides with the city's *Ecobici* program in 2010. This gives subscribers unlimited access to bicycles at stations for $25 a year. In 2012 the program had 4,000 bicycles at 275 stations for 73,000 bicyclists. Encouraging the use of bicycles contributes to the reduction of air pollution in Mexico City by reducing the number of cars on the roads.

READING PROGRESS CHECK

Describing Describe two specific steps taken by the Mexican government to address pollution and resource management.

LESSON 3 REVIEW 

Reviewing Vocabulary (Tier Three Words)

1. ***Describing*** Define sustainable development and provide at least one example of how it pertains to Mexico. RH.9–10.4

Using Your Notes

2. ***Making Connections*** Using your graphic organizer, write a paragraph discussing how Mexico manages its resources.

Answering the Guiding Questions

3. ***Making Generalizations*** Why are Mexico's resources in jeopardy?
4. ***Speculating*** How do human activities impact Mexico's environment?
5. ***Identifying*** How are governments in Mexico addressing environmental issues?

Writing Activity

6. ***Argument*** Write a letter designed to persuade the government of Mexico to address an environmental problem discussed in this lesson. WHST.9–10.1

LESSON 3 REVIEW ANSWERS

Reviewing Vocabulary

1. Sustainable development is technological and economic growth that does not deplete the human and natural resources of an area. The National Biodiversity Strategy and Action Plan was developed to encourage sustainable and diversified use of biodiversity components.

Using Your Notes

2. Mexico's ecosystems are experiencing the effects of global climate change and environmental destruction. As natural resources are destroyed, humans migrate to urban areas, which stresses the surrounding environment. The government has taken steps to promote sustainable development, including the National Biodiversity Strategy and Action Plan.

Answering the Guiding Questions

3. Mexico's resources are in jeopardy due to global climate change and a growing economy, which leads to environmental destruction.
4. Manufactured goods are being produced at greater rates; without infrastructure to support proper waste disposal, pollution is a problem. Carbon emissions from cars become trapped in the air, creating a toxic haze.
5. Governments have created a variety of programs to address environmental issues.

Writing Activity

6. Letters should show an understanding of how the environmental problem impacts Mexico and how solving the problem would help Mexico.

CHAPTER 7 Assessment 

Directions: On a separate sheet of paper, answer the questions below. Make sure you read carefully and answer all parts of the questions.

Lesson Review

Lesson 1

1. ***Explaining*** Describe how Mexico's location on the "Ring of Fire" has helped to shape its landscape.
2. ***Describing*** Describe the Mexican Plateau and its importance to Mexico in terms of agriculture.
3. ***Drawing Conclusions*** What industries would be most affected when an oil spill occurs in the Gulf of Mexico?

Lesson 2

4. ***Evaluating*** How has colonialism and indigenous culture shaped the human geography of Mexico?
5. ***Analyzing*** How has the Catholic Church influenced Mexican culture?
6. ***Summarizing*** How does family shape Mexican society?

Lesson 3

7. ***Analyzing*** Describe how the growth of Mexico's urban middle class has affected the economy of Mexico.
8. ***Explaining*** What are two results of rural-to-urban migration in Mexico?
9. ***Identifying Cause and Effect*** What are the causes and effects of deforestation in Mexico?

Critical Thinking

10. ***Making Generalizations*** Has the maquiladora system had a positive or negative effect on Mexico's people? Explain.
11. ***Identifying Cause and Effect*** Explain how the growth of the middle class in Mexico has contributed to an increase in awareness and political action in regard to environmental issues.
12. ***Drawing Conclusions*** How might wars between drug cartels affect the economy of Mexico?

21st Century Skills

Review the graph, then answer the questions that follow.

MEXICAN MANUFACTURING AND AGRICULTURE

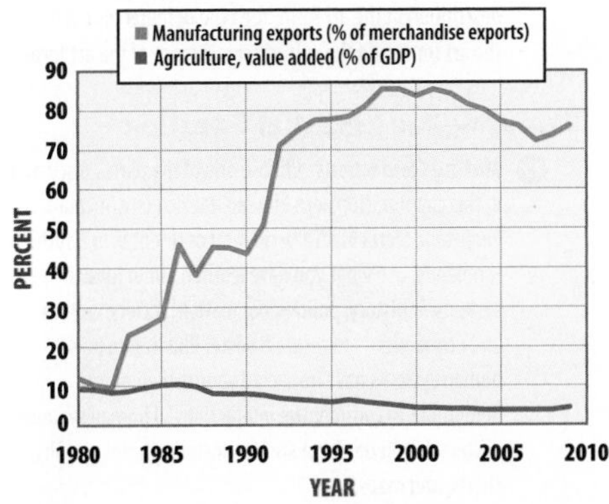

Source: World Bank

13. ***Using Graphs, Charts, Diagrams, and Tables*** Describe the change in Mexico's agricultural exports from 1980 to 2010.
14. ***Comparing and Contrasting*** How does Mexico's manufacturing growth rate compare to its agricultural growth rate?

College and Career Readiness

15. ***Change and Continuity in Economics*** As an economic geographer working for the Inter-American Development Bank, you have been asked to help the Mexican government diversify agricultural output. Write a proposal explaining why dependence on a single cash crop can be risky. Then describe how the government could use subsidies, improved technology, and cash payments to help diversify agriculture. Cite an example from primary and secondary sources.

Need Extra Help?

If You've Missed Question	1	2	3	4	5	6	7	8	9	10	11	12	13	14	15
Go to page	176	177	178	181	182	183	189	187	187	186	189	186	191	191	179

CHAPTER 7 Assessment Answers

Lesson Review

Lesson 1

1. The Pacific Plate has collided with other tectonic plates, and the seismic activity has helped shape Mexico's landforms.
2. It has moderate consistent temperatures, which give rise to crops such as grain. Most of the food grown in Mexico comes from the Mexican Plateau.
3. Fishing industries would be most affected.

Lesson 2

4. Colonialism provided the many cultures of Mexico a unifying identity. It also created the large gap between the wealthy and the poor that still exists today. Indigenous cultures brought many languages and belief systems, and have had a strong influence on the arts.
5. The Spanish used Catholic missions to get a foothold in Mexico. Mission churches were used as military outposts and market towns. The traditional indigenous beliefs melded with Catholic culture in a process called syncretism.
6. Family is important in Mexican society. Many Mexican families are extended families, with several generations in the same home. This is particularly true in rural areas and poorer communities. Extended families provide social support.

Lesson 3

7. People are able to purchase material goods, such as electronics and cars. This places money into the economy, causing it to grow.
8. As more people move to the cities, the surrounding land is cleared and developed. Cities do not have the infrastructure to support a growing urban population, leading to pollution and limited water supplies.
9. Corporate logging and ranchers and farmers clearing the forests to create new areas for growing food and grazing cattle cause deforestation. Effects include loss of habitat, issues with greenhouse gases, and rural-to-urban migration.

Critical Thinking

10. Student answers may vary, but must be supported by the lesson. Answers could include the negative effects of companies ignoring labor laws, which encourages dangerous and low-paying jobs.
11. The population is becoming more literate and better educated, and has begun to demand better living conditions and to focus on protecting the environment.
12. Cartels often reinvest in communities, which supports the local economy. Farmers are also unable to make as much growing legal crops as they can from growing illegal drugs for the cartel. The loss of income for these farmers and communities would hurt the economy.

21st Century Skills

13. Mexico's agricultural exports decreased by about five percent from 1980 to 2010.
14. The growth rate of Mexico's manufacturing exports is much higher.

College and Career Readiness

15. Each proposal should include: an explanation as to why dependence on a single cash crop creates risk to the economy and environment; a discussion of ways the Mexican government could utilize subsidies, improved technology, and cash payments to aid in diversification; and examples from a primary and a secondary source.

CHAPTER 7
Assessment Answers

Research and Presentation

16 Student answer may vary, but should identify a specific art form such as murals, weaving, mosaics, and/or ceramics. They should describe the art form, explain the type of materials used in it, and explain the cultural significance of the art form.

Exploring the Essential Question

17 Poster should illustrate how human systems have had an impact on Northern Plateau, Mexico City, Yucatán Peninsula, Sierra Madre Occidental or Oriental, or Southern Highlands; posters should include photos, graphs, charts, and maps.

Applying Map Skills

18 Mining locations are scattered in the interior and on the northwest coast. Mining contributes to the deforestation of these areas.

19 The semi-arid climate dominates Mexico along the Tropic of Cancer causing the vegetation to be limited to shrubs, grassland, and cacti.

20 Student answers may vary, but should identify the Rio Grande and explain how it appears as a border between Mexico and Texas.

Analyzing Primary Sources

21 It marked the end of a 26,000 year galactic cycle and began a new one.

22 Each Baktun represents 144,000 days, almost 400 years.

23 Student answers may vary, but should be represented by historical evidence from the chapter such as gaining independence from Spain.

Writing About Geography

24 The essay should suggest suitable locations for constructing new cities to relieve Mexico's population pressures. It should also detail the types of resources required to sustain large populations.

CHAPTER 7 Assessment 

Directions: On a separate sheet of paper, answer the questions below. Make sure you read carefully and answer all parts of the questions.

Research and Presentation

16 ***Research Skills*** Use Internet and library resources to gather information about a particular art form popular in Mexico. Specifically, your research should focus on a description of the art form, the type of materials used in the art form, and the cultural significance of the art form.

Exploring the Essential Question

17 ***Making Connections*** Choose one of the places discussed in this chapter: Northern Plateau, Mexico City, Yucatán Peninsula, Sierra Madre Occidental or Oriental, or Southern Highlands. Use what you have learned about human systems—history, politics, population, society, culture, and economics—to create a poster illustrating how human systems have impacted your chosen place. Remember to consider the interactions of human systems. Posters should be visual and can include photos, graphs, charts, and maps.

Applying Map Skills

Refer to the Unit 3 Atlas to answer the following questions.

18 ***Environment and Society*** What generalizations can you make about the location of Mexico's mining areas?

19 ***Physical Systems*** What is the predominant type of vegetation along the Tropic of Cancer in Mexico?

20 ***Human Systems*** Using your mental map, imagine you are traveling with your family from the southern tip of Texas to the Mexican Plateau. What major river would you see during your travels? Explain how you visualize this body of water as you read a map, and then explain how this body of water would appear if you were to fly over it during your trip.

DBQ Analyzing Primary Sources

Use the document to answer the following questions.

PRIMARY SOURCE

"In the most of simple terms, this time is solstice. December 21, 2012, marks the end of the 13th Baktun[each Baktun is 144,000 days—or nearly 400 years on the Maya calendar], and it marks the beginning of the 14th Baktun. The significance of 21 December, 2012, this calendar's end, and this particular 13/14 Baktun transition, is that it marks the end of a 26,000 year galactic cycle, and begins the calendar of the next 26,000 years galactic cycle. By the very detailed prophecies of the Mayas, this means leaving the calendar of Night and beginning the calendar of Day."

—Jon Waterhouse, "How the Maya of Today Are Marking December 21," *National Geographic Explorers Journal*, December 19, 2012

21 ***Determining Importance*** What was the significance of December 21, 2012, on the Mayan calendar? RH.9–10.6

22 ***Identifying*** How many days and years does each Baktun represent on the Mayan calendar?

23 ***Making Connections*** What events in Mexico's history might be symbolic of the transition of "leaving the calendar of Night and beginning the calendar of Day"?

Writing About Geography

24 ***Argument*** Use standard grammar, spelling, sentence structure, and punctuation to write a one-page essay suggesting suitable locations for constructing new cities to relieve the population pressures that exist in Mexico City. Be sure to describe the types of resources required to sustain large populations. WHST.9–10.1

Need Extra Help?

If You've Missed Question	16	17	18	19	20	21	22	23	24
Go to page	184	176	171	170	168	192	192	192	176

networks Online Teaching Options

WORKSHEET

Chapter Test and Lesson Quizzes

Assessing Have students complete the Chapter Test and Lesson Quizzes to assess student understanding throughout the chapter. These assessment tools offer chapter and lesson evaluation through a variety of question formats including document-based questions.

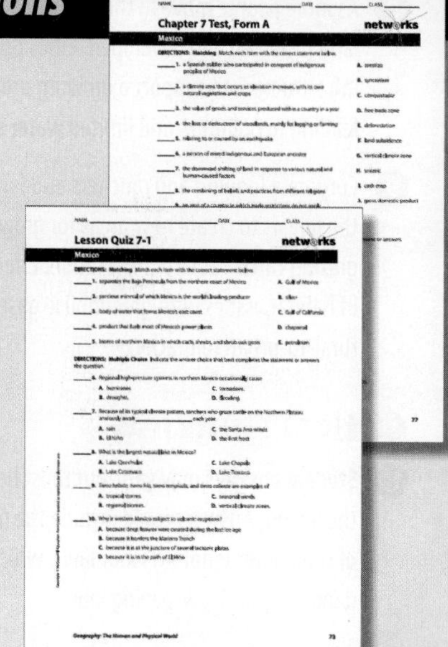

CHAPTER 8

Central America and the Caribbean Planner

UNDERSTANDING BY DESIGN®

Enduring Understandings

- *Culture influences people's perceptions of places and regions.*

Essential Question

- *How do physical systems and human systems shape a place?*

Predictable Misunderstandings

Students may think:

- *The water supply for Central America and the Caribbean comes from the surrounding oceans. Explain that there are many freshwater lakes and rivers located throughout the region.*
- *People living in Central America and the Caribbean are of Spanish descent. Explain that although much of this area was colonized by Spain, some areas were colonized by France, and there was great influence from indigenous peoples on the population today. As a result, the population of Central America and the Caribbean is a mix of ethnic groups.*
- *Deforestation is an issue in South America, but not Central America. Explain that deforestation is also a major issue in Central America and governments are working together toward sustainable development.*

Assessment Evidence

Performance Tasks:

- *Hands-On Chapter Project*

Other Evidence:

- *Guided Reading Activities*
- *Vocabulary Activities*
- *Lesson Quizzes*
- *Chapter Tests, Forms A and B*

SUGGESTED PACING GUIDE

Introducing the Chapter	½ Day	Case Study	1 Day
Lesson 1	1 Day	Lesson 3	1 Day
Lesson 2	2 Days	Chapter Wrap-Up and Assessment	½ Day

TOTAL TIME 6 Days

Key for Using the Teacher Edition

SKILL-BASED ACTIVITIES

Types of skill activities found in the Teacher Edition.

* **V Visual Skills** require students to analyze maps, graphs, charts, and photos.

R Reading Skills help students practice reading skills and master vocabulary.

C Critical Thinking Skills help students apply and extend what they have learned.

W Writing Skills provide writing opportunities to help students comprehend the text.

T Technology Skills require students to use digital tools effectively.

*Letters are followed by a number when there is more than one of the same type of skill on the page.

DIFFERENTIATED INSTRUCTION

All activities are written for the on-level student unless otherwise marked with the leveled labels below.

BL Beyond Level
AL Approaching Level
ELL English Language Learners

All students benefit from activities that utilize different learning styles. Many activities are marked as below when a particular learning style is highlighted.

Intrapersonal	**Naturalist**
Logical/Mathematical	**Kinesthetic**
Visual/Spatial	**Auditory/Musical**
Verbal/Linguistic	**Interpersonal**

National Geography Standards covered in "Central America and the Caribbean"

The student knows and understands:

(3) How to analyze the spatial organizations of people, places, and environments on Earth's surface

3.1 The meaning and use of complex spatial concepts, such as connectivity, networks, hierarchies, to analyze and explain the spatial organization of human and physical phenomena

(4) The physical and human characteristics of places

4.2 The interaction of physical and human systems result in the creation of and changes to places

(8) The characteristics and spatial distribution of ecosystems and biomes on Earth's surface

8.1 Ecosystems are dynamic and respond to changes in environmental conditions

8.3 The distribution and characteristics of biomes change over time

(9) The characteristics, distribution, and migration of human populations on Earth's surface

9.2 Population distribution and density are a function of historical, environmental, economic, political, and technological factors

(11) The patterns and networks of economic interdependence on Earth's surface

11.3 Economic systems are dynamic organizations of interdependent economic activities for production, exchange, distribution, and consumption of goods and services

(14) How human actions modify the physical environment

14.1 Human modifications of the physical environment can have significant global impacts

14.3 People can either mitigate and/or adapt to the consequences of human modifications of the physical environment

(15) How physical systems affect human systems

15.3 Societies use a variety of strategies to adapt to changes in the physical environment

(16) The changes that occur in the meaning, use, distribution, and importance of resources

16.3 Policies and programs that promote the sustainable use and management of resources impact people and the environment

(17) How to apply geography and interpret the past

17.2 The causes and processes of change in the geographic characteristics and spatial organizations of places, regions, and environments in the past

17.3 Historical events must be interpreted in the contexts of people's past perception of places, regions, and environments

CHAPTER OPENER PLANNER

Students will know:
- *the landforms, water systems, and climates of Central America and the Caribbean and how tectonic activity shaped the landscape.*
- *the impact of colonialism, migration and urban growth on the population patterns of Central America and the Caribbean.*
- *how physical geography impacts the economic activities of the region.*
- *the causes and effects of environmental issues and how the government addresses them in Central America and the Caribbean.*

Students will be able to:
- ***describe** natural features of Central America and the Caribbean.*
- ***explain** how tectonic activity shaped the landscape of the region.*
- ***describe** population patterns and economic activities of the region.*
- ***explain** causes, effects, and possible solutions of environmental issues.*

UNDERSTANDING BY DESIGN®

☑ Print Teaching Options

V Visual Skills
- ☐ **p. 195** Students analyze an image and speculate how it supports the text. Intrapersonal

R Reading Skills
- ☐ **p. 194** Students view a map to identify foods introduced through the Columbian Exchange. Visual/Spatial

C Critical Thinking Skills
- ☐ **p. 194** Students discuss the effects of the Columbian Exchange on North America. AL Logical/Mathematical

W Writing Skills
- ☐ **p. 194** Students write about a time when they were sick and discuss how the human immune system works.

T Technology Skills
- ☐ **p. 195** Students research statistics for agricultural crops that were part of the Columbian Exchange and their importance to United States and European economies. BL Verbal/Linguistic

☑ Online Teaching Options

V Visual Skills
- ☐ SLIDE SHOW **The Columbian Exchange**—Pairs of students choose one item that was traded in the Columbian Exchange to research further, particularly the costs of exporting and importing that item in the 1400s compared to today. Verbal/Linguistic

W Writing Skills
- ☐ INTERACTIVE MAP **The Columbian Exchange**—Students study the Columbian Exchange map and write a paragraph explaining whether they feel the negative effects of the diseases were worth the positive effects of the exchange. BL Intrapersonal

☑ Printable Digital Worksheets

- ☐ WORKSHEET **Assessing Background Knowledge**—Determine the level of prior knowledge students have about Central America and the Caribbean.
- ☐ WORKSHEET **Chapter Summaries**—Students review the main ideas of each lesson of the chapter content.

Project-Based Learning 

Hands-On

Writing Magazine Articles
Students will write magazine articles that bring together information from all lessons about the region's physical and human geography.

Digital Hands-On

Create Online Projects
Find an additional activity online that incorporates technology for this project. Visit the EdTech Teacher Web sites for more links, tutorials, and other resources.

Print Resources

ANCILLARY RESOURCES
This ancillary is available for every chapter and lesson.
- **Chapter Tests and Lesson Quizzes**

PRINTABLE DIGITAL WORKSHEETS
These printable digital worksheets are available for every chapter and lesson.
- **Assessing Background Knowledge**
- **Chapter Summaries**
- **Guided Reading Activities**
- **Hands-On Chapter Projects**
- **Quizzes and Tests**
- **Reading Essentials and Study Guide** AL
- **Reteaching Activities**
- **Video Activities**
- **Vocabulary Activities**

More Media Resources

SUGGESTED VIDEOS 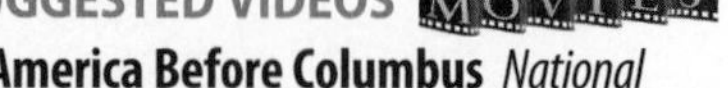

- **America Before Columbus** *National Geographic* (90 min.)
- **My Village, My Lobster** (61 min.)
- **A Man, A Plan, A Canal—Panama** (60 min.)

SUGGESTED READING 
- ***The History of Central America,*** by Thomas L. Pearcy
- ***Panama Fever: The Epic Story of the Building of the Panama Canal,*** by Matthew Parker
- ***The Caribbean: A History of the Region and Its Peoples,*** by Stephan Palmie

PHYSICAL GEOGRAPHY OF CENTRAL AMERICA AND THE CARIBBEAN

Students will know:

- *the landforms and water systems of Central America and the Caribbean.*
- *how tectonic activity shaped the landscape of Central America and the Caribbean.*
- *the influence of a tropical location on the climate of Central America and the Caribbean.*
- *how elevation and latitude can affect climate in Central America and the Caribbean.*

Students will be able to:

- ***describe** the landforms and water systems of the region.*
- ***explain** how tectonic activity affected the landscape of the region.*
- ***identify** how elevation, latitude, and a tropical location affect the climate of the region.*

UNDERSTANDING BY DESIGN®

☑ *Print Teaching Options*

V Visual Skills

- ☐ **p. 197** Students compare the lakes and waterways of Central America in a graphic organizer. AL Visual/Spatial
- ☐ **p. 198** Students interpret a diagram about biodiversity. AL Visual/Spatial

R Reading Skills

- ☐ **p. 196** Students brainstorm what they know about the physical geography of Central America and the Caribbean.
- ☐ **p. 196** Students read about the physical geography of the region and sketch a physical map of the region. ELL Visual/Spatial
- ☐ **p. 197** Students define and discuss the terms *isthmus* and *archipelago*. ELL Kinesthetic

C Critical Thinking Skills

- ☐ **p. 196** Students discuss the location of the region and its proximity to the Ring of Fire. AL Logical/Mathematical
- ☐ **p. 198** Students sketch and label a diagram of how hydroelectricity is generated. ELL Interpersonal
- ☐ **p. 199** Students discuss climate and create diagrams to compare the climates of two regions. AL Visual/Spatial
- ☐ **p. 199** Students create a diagram showing the differences in elevation in Central America and the animals and plants that live in each climate zone. BL Naturalist

W Writing Skills

- ☐ **p. 197** Students write a news report about the earthquake that struck Haiti in 2010 or the volcano that erupted in Montserrat in 1996 or 2009–2010. BL Verbal/Linguistic

T Technology Skills

- ☐ **p. 196** Students create presentations about a landform in Central America or the Caribbean. Interpersonal, Visual/Spatial
- ☐ **p. 198** Students gather data about how the building of the Panama Canal affected commerce in the Western Hemisphere. Mathematical/Logical

☑ *Online Teaching Options*

V Visual Skills

- ☐ INTERACTIVE WHITEBOARD ACTIVITY **Landform Characteristics in Central America and the Caribbean**—Students will locate and then identify characteristics about various landforms in the region. Visual/Spatial

R Reading Skills

- ☐ INTERACTIVE BELLRINGER **Physical Geography of Central America and the Caribbean**—Students discuss the Panama Canal, why it was built, and obstacles that hindered its construction. Visual/Spatial, Interpersonal

C Critical Thinking Skills

- ☐ INTERACTIVE MAP **Physical Geography of Central America**—Students discuss the differences in living and disaster recovery for various countries. AL Interpersonal
- ☐ INFOGRAPHIC **Biodiversity in Central America**—Students analyze an infographic to discuss biodiversity and the term *endemic,* and the issue of preserving plant and animal life. ELL Verbal/Linguistic

☑ *Printable Digital Worksheets*

R Reading Skills

- ☐ WORKSHEET **Guided Reading Activity**—Students use the Guided Reading Activity worksheets to review their comprehension of the content. Verbal/Linguistic
- ☐ WORKSHEET **Chapter Summary**—Students review the main ideas of the chapter content. Verbal/Linguistic

C Critical Thinking Skills

- ☐ WORKSHEET **Video Activity**—Students answer questions related to a topic in the chapter content after they have viewed a lesson video. Visual/Spatial

Human Geography of Central America and the Caribbean

Students will know:

- *how colonialism influenced the human geography of Central America and the Caribbean.*
- *the impact of migration and urban growth on the population patterns of Central America and Caribbean.*
- *how physical geography impacts the economic activities of Central America and the Caribbean.*

Students will be able to:

- ***discuss** colonialism's influence on human geography.*
- ***describe** population patterns in the region.*
- ***explain** how physical geography affects the economy.*

UNDERSTANDING BY DESIGN®

☑ Print Teaching Options

V Visual Skills

- ☐ **p. 200** Students create a time line based on information about the conquests of European explorers. Visual/Spatial
- ☐ **p. 204** Students study and discuss the designs on the mola artwork in the photograph. AL Naturalist

R Reading Skills

- ☐ **p. 202** Students discuss and create word webs for factors that affect population pressure. ELL Kinesthetic
- ☐ **p. 203** Students discuss how culture is a product of this region's history. AL Verbal/Linguistic
- ☐ **p. 204** Students discuss how the Kuna culture blends yet maintains its identity. ELL Visual/Spatial
- ☐ **p. 205** Students discuss the meanings of *latifundia* and *minifundia*. ELL Kinesthetic

C Critical Thinking Skills

- ☐ **p. 200** Students brainstorm a list of advantages and disadvantages of European interaction with the Americas.
- ☐ **p. 200** Students compare the purpose of Columbus's voyages to later explorers' voyages. ELL Verbal/Linguistic
- ☐ **p. 203** Students identify problems and propose solutions to education and health care issues. Interpersonal
- ☐ **p. 204** Students discuss factors that have affected the decrease in births in the region. Verbal/Linguistic
- ☐ **p. 205** Students discuss and evaluate ecotourism as a growing industry in the region. AL Verbal/Linguistic

W Writing Skills

- ☐ **p. 201** Students write a narrative as an African or Native American who had been enslaved during the European conquest. AL Verbal/Linguistic
- ☐ **p. 203** Students write about whether the United States should have gone to war with Spain. BL Verbal/Linguistic

T Technology Skills

- ☐ **p. 202** Students research population and migration of two countries in the region and create graphs or charts to present their data. BL Auditory/Musical, Visual/Spatial

☑ Online Teaching Options

V Visual Skills

- ☐ INTERACTIVE BELLRINGER **Maya Mother and Child**—Students draw inferences about the family and the role of women in rural areas of Central America. AL Interpersonal, Visual/Spatial
- ☐ VIDEO **The Panama Canal**—Students fill in a two-column chart on physical geography and human aspects of the Panama Canal as they view the video. Logical/Mathematical
- ☐ INTERACTIVE WHITEBOARD ACTIVITY **Voyages of Christopher Columbus**—Students will place events on the correct dates of a time line. Visual/Spatial

C Critical Thinking Skills

- ☐ IMAGE **The Panama Canal**—Students discuss how physical geography and politics were important in the building of the Panama Canal. AL Intrapersonal
- ☐ TIME LINE **Central America and the Caribbean: Paths to Independence**—Students discuss diverse ethnic groups found in the region and speculate from where François Toussaint-Louverture's ancestors may have originated. ELL Verbal/Spatial
- ☐ GAME **Human Geography of Central America and the Caribbean**—Before playing, students discuss issues of authenticity regarding molas. Interpersonal

☑ Printable Digital Worksheets

R Reading Skills

- ☐ WORKSHEET **Guided Reading Activity**—Students use the Guided Reading Activity worksheets to review their comprehension of the lesson content. Verbal/Linguistic
- ☐ WORKSHEET **Reading Essentials and Study Guide**—Students complete the study guide and answer Reading Progress Check and vocabulary questions. AL ELL

C Critical Thinking Skills

- ☐ WORKSHEET **Video Activity**—Students will complete this worksheet by answering questions about this lesson video content. Visual/Spatial

PEOPLE AND THEIR ENVIRONMENT: CENTRAL AMERICA AND THE CARIBBEAN

Students will know:

- *the causes and effects of deforestation in Central America and the Caribbean.*
- *how urban growth contributes to environmental issues in Central America and the Caribbean.*
- *the causes and effects of soil erosion and decline in Central America and the Caribbean.*
- *the efforts being made at various levels of local and government to address certain environmental issues.*

Students will be able to:

- ***describe** the causes and effects of deforestation and soil erosion in the region.*
- ***explain** urban growth's effect on environmental issues.*
- ***analyze** efforts to address environmental issues.*

UNDERSTANDING BY DESIGN®

☑ Print Teaching Options

V Visual Skills

- ☐ **p. 208** Students research and graph water usage data in the region over the last five to ten years and the projected future use. BL Naturalist, Visual/Spatial

R Reading Skills

- ☐ **p. 210** Students list causes and effects of slash-and-burn cultivation and commercial logging and create a word web for *deforestation.* ELL Interpersonal
- ☐ **p. 211** Students use context clues to define unfamiliar words and then perform demonstrations on how sedimentation occurs. ELL Kinesthetic
- ☐ **p. 212** Students discuss the difference between deforestation and reforestation. ELL Verbal/Linguistic

C Critical Thinking Skills

- ☐ **p. 208** Students discuss the role of the UN in the conflict between Costa Rica and Nicaragua. Verbal/Linguistic
- ☐ **p. 210** Students compare the urban problems associated with growth in the U.S. to concerns in the region. Interpersonal, Verbal/Linguistic
- ☐ **p. 211** Students create an ad campaign against dumping garbage and other wastes. BL Visual/Spatial
- ☐ **p. 211** Students discuss the challenges of managing resources, and then write a proposal to the government explaining their solution. Verbal/Linguistic

W Writing Skills

- ☐ **p. 209** Students write to support or refute an environmental practice regarding the clearing of rain forests for agriculture. AL Verbal/Linguistic

T Technology Skills

- ☐ **p. 209** Students explore how a hydroelectric dam works and create a sketch or 3-D model of the process. ELL Logical/Mathematical
- ☐ **p. 212** Students research recent issues in the region and write a potential resolution. AL Logical/Mathematical

☑ Online Teaching Options

V Visual Skills

- IMAGE **Water Pollution in Central America**—Students analyze an image about patterns and consequences of erosion to write predictions. BL Verbal/Linguistic
- VIDEO **The Caribbean**—Students discuss how the aquatic environment of the Caribbean is vulnerable to damage from human activities. Logical/Mathematical, Naturalist

C Critical Thinking Skills

- INTERACTIVE BELLRINGER **Mining and the Environment**—Students discuss the impact of mining on the environment and consider how communities feel when a local mine is owned by a foreign company. BL Interpersonal, Verbal/Linguistic
- INTERACTIVE WHITEBOARD ACTIVITY **Soil Erosion in the Caribbean**—Students will categorize the causes and the effects of soil erosion on the Caribbean Islands.

W Writing Skills

- INTERACTIVE MAP **Haiti Earthquake** Students explore causes and effects of earthquakes and write a paragraph considering if soil erosion could have caused the earthquake in Haiti. Verbal/Linguistic

☑ Printable Digital Worksheets

R Reading Skills

- WORKSHEET **Guided Reading Activity**—Students use Guided Reading Activity worksheets to review their comprehension of the content.
- WORKSHEET **Reading Essentials and Study Guide**—Students complete the study guide and answer Reading Progress Check and vocabulary questions. AL
- WORKSHEET **Vocabulary Activity**—Students review the chapter content and academic vocabulary words. Verbal/Linguistic
- WORKSHEET **Chapter Summary**—Students review the main ideas of the chapter content.

C Critical Thinking Skills

- WORKSHEET **Video Activity**—Students answer questions based on a lesson video. Logical/Mathematical
- WORKSHEET **Reteaching Activity**—Students use this activity worksheet to review and reteach chapter content and vocabulary. This worksheet can be used with struggling students who need additional help with difficult content concept. Verbal/Linguistic
- WORKSHEET **Hands-On Chapter Project**—Students each write a magazine article about a topic that concerns a specific area of Central America and the Caribbean. The topic can be historical or current. Each article must explain how the topic impacts physical systems and human systems, including any environmental impacts. Logical/Mathematical

INTERVENTION AND REMEDIATION STRATEGIES

LESSON 1 Physical Geography of Central America and the Caribbean

Reading and Comprehension

To help students organize and comprehend the concepts discussed in this lesson, have them work in pairs to create an outline using the lesson's main headings. As partners gather information, have them note key ideas and details under each heading as well as content vocabulary terms. Encourage students to illustrate their outlines to develop a coherent understanding of each concept. For example, students may wish to use a graphic organizer like the one on the Lesson Opener to organize their ideas about natural resources. Ask volunteers to present their outlines to the class.

Text Evidence

Assign student groups a region, island, or group of islands in Central America and the Caribbean discussed in this lesson. Tell students they will create a travel brochure about their region that answers the Essential Question: *How do physical systems and human systems shape a place?* Brochures should use simple sketches and phrases to describe the region's physical features and a list of reasons tourists might want to visit. Students may wish to conduct additional research about their region to give them ideas for their brochures. After students present their brochures, guide a class discussion about what makes the physical geography of this region unique.

LESSON 2 Human Geography of Central America and the Caribbean

Reading and Comprehension

Have students work in pairs to look up the definitions of each of the content vocabulary terms in a print or online dictionary. If some terms are not listed, such as *latifundia* and *minifundia,* have students use context clues in the text to determine the term's meaning. Have students write sentences using each word, showing a clear understanding of each word's meaning as it is used in the lesson. Then have students work with their partner to brainstorm other ways to use each word in a sentence. Encourage students to use the academic vocabulary word in one of their sentences. Circulate to provide corrective guidance.

Text Evidence

To ensure that students have a firm grasp of lesson content, have them write a summary of a topic or issue discussed in the lesson. You may wish to assign topics to students to avoid duplication. For example, students might describe various aspects of the Kuna culture or the various ecotourism opportunities throughout the region. Remind students to support claims in their summaries with evidence from the text. Encourage students to use content vocabulary words in their summaries.

LESSON 3 People and Their Environment: Central America and the Caribbean

Reading and Comprehension

Have student pairs identify cause-and-effect relationships as they read about the tenuous balance between economic development and the natural environment of Central America and the Caribbean. Tell one student in each pair to choose a statement from the text that highlights a positive element of a specific issue, such as *"Costa Rica benefits from the power generated by hydroelectric plants."* Then have partners identify a statement that reveals a negative aspect of the same issue such as, *"However, hydroelectric systems threaten the natural environment of the areas from which they extract energy."* Remind students that identifying signal words such as *however, as a result,* and *consequently* can help them find negative facets of an issue. Have pairs share their statements with the class.

Text Evidence

Assign student groups one of the challenges discussed in this lesson such as conflicts over depleting natural resources, the impact caused by and aid needed from natural disasters, or the struggle to protect biodiversity in the region. Have students in each group work together to summarize the problems related to their topic and how or if the problems are being addressed or solved. Students may wish to conduct online research to provide sufficient evidence in support of claims made in their summaries. Encourage students to use content vocabulary terms in their summaries.

Online Resources

Leveled Reader

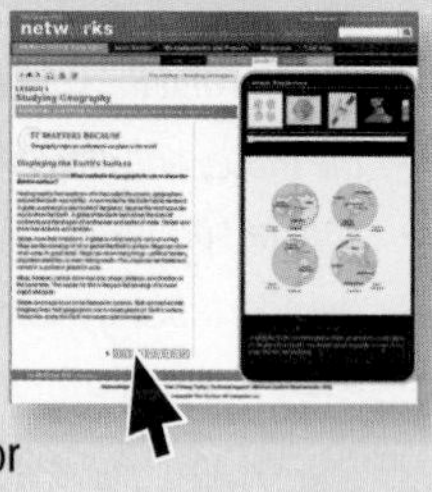

Use this online approaching-level text that corresponds directly to the text in the Student Edition. It also includes additional reading and comprehension support for English Language Learners.

Guided Reading Activities

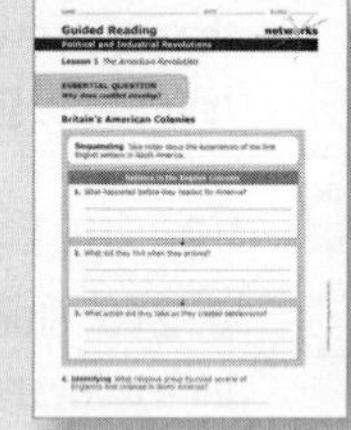

This resource uses guiding questions to help students with comprehension.

Reteaching Activities

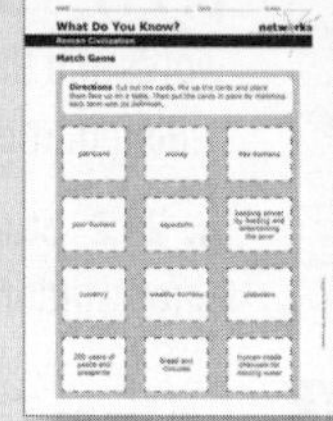

These worksheets provide students with an opportunity for remedial practice and review of vital chapter content.

Reading Essentials and Study Guide

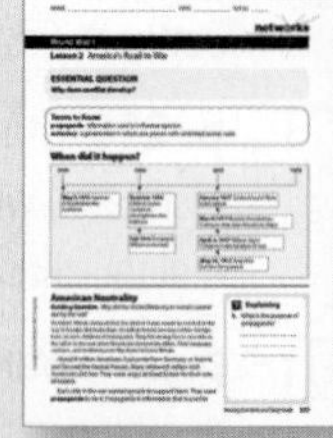

This resource offers writing and reading activities for the approaching-level student.

Self-Check Quizzes

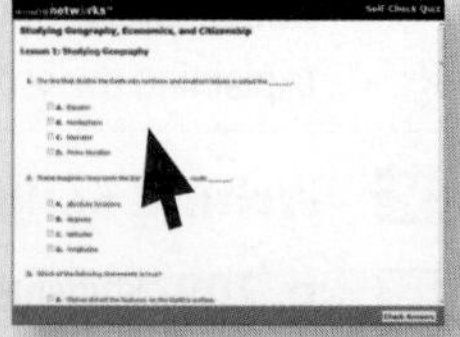

This online assessment tool provides instant feedback for students to check their progress.

Chapter Summaries

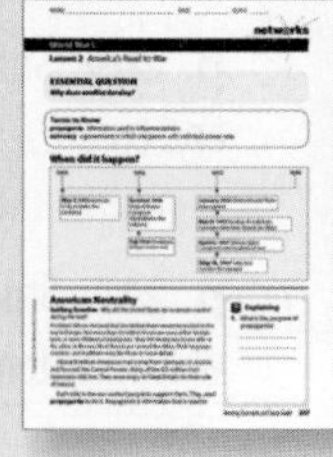

Summaries are provided for each chapter that thoroughly condense core content into manageable chunks.

Central America and the Caribbean

ESSENTIAL QUESTION • *How do physical systems and human systems shape a place?*

networks

There's More Online about Central America and the Caribbean.

CHAPTER 8

Geography Matters...

Central America and the Caribbean is one of the most biologically diverse regions in the world. Many types of landforms and climates support abundant plant and animal species. Cultures here have been influenced by ancient civilizations, colonial pasts, political upheavals, and by a modern mix of peoples migrating in and out of the region. No single influence, culture, or history can characterize this region of diversity and biological and cultural wealth.

◀ Caribbean music is a diverse blend of African, European, and indigenous influences.

193

Letter from the Author

Dear Geography Teacher,

The only openly communist country in Latin America, Cuba sits 90 miles off the coast of Florida. Long ruled by Fidel and now Raul Castro, Cuba enjoyed a long, friendly relationship with the Soviet Union. After the fall of the USSR in 1991 that friendship faltered and foreign aid to Cuba was halted. New friendships had to be developed and Cuba now receives foreign aid from Venezuela. Health care and education are bright spots but the consumer economy and availability of industrial resources are not. In the meantime, Cuban communist philosophy has been picked up in Bolivia, Peru, Venezuela, and Nicaragua. While these countries do not follow a rigid form of social and economic communism, they reflect the legacy of Fidel.

Richard G. Boehm

ENGAGE

Activating Prior Knowledge Before beginning the chapter, invite students to list what they already know about the physical geography, history, culture, and economy of Central America and the Caribbean. Then have them look at the photograph. **Ask:** **What does this photograph reveal about the culture of the region?** *(Possible answer: Music is important to the people and culture in this region.)* Discuss ways to analyze images in order to learn information about a topic.

TEACH & ASSESS

Hypothesizing Have students consider how physical and human systems have shaped the region. Discuss the difference between both systems and invite volunteers to give examples of each. **Ask:** **Based on the location of Central America and the Caribbean Islands, how has this region been impacted by both physical and human systems?** *(Possible answers: The region is susceptible to violent weather and natural disasters. The Caribbean Islands have little protection from the weather or from humans. People from other countries can easily access the unprotected islands.)* **BL** **Logical/Mathematical**

Making Connections

Explain that this region is culturally and biologically diverse. The Caribbean Islands are made up of twelve independent nations, in addition to British and French jurisdictions.

- About 13,000 different plant species have been identified; more than 6,500 are endemic to a single island.
- More than 600 bird species live in the Caribbean.
- Nearly 100 different kinds of mammals make their homes here, with 40 species being endemic to the islands.
- There are 500 types of reptiles, nearly 470 are endemic.
- About 13 percent of Caribbean's land area is designated as protected to manage the plethora of biological diversity.

CLOSE & REFLECT

Applying Have students describe how knowledge of physical and human systems is helpful in learning about the world around them and the communities in which they live. Discuss how understanding the impacts of physical and human systems on places helps people prepare and plan for the future.

Extend the project-based learning experience globally through our partnership with ePals. EPals allows you to connect with classrooms around the world in a safe online environment for real-life lessons and projects in virtual study groups.

ENGAGE

W Writing Skills

Narrative Introduce this section by asking students to write a paragraph about a time when they were sick. Ask them to describe the symptoms they suffered and the healing process. Invite students to share their paragraphs. Then discuss with students how the human immune system works. Discuss the discovery and use of vaccines as well.

TEACH & ASSESS

C Critical Thinking Skills

Evaluating Have students discuss the positive and negative effects of the Columbian Exchange on the people of North America. **Ask:** **What were the positive effects?** *(Possible answers: new crops that became important to sustaining populations and for economic development; it brought new ideas that helped cultures advance and adopt aspects of other cultures)* **What were the negative effects?** *(Possible answer: communicable diseases that made many people ill)* **Do you think the benefits outweighed the costs? Explain.** *(Possible answer: Yes, because the exchange of ideas, cultures, and foods was important to advancing civilization in the Americas.)* AL **Logical/Mathematical**

R Reading Skills

Reading Maps Direct students to study the map of the Columbian Exchange. **Ask:** **What foods were introduced to North America?** *(Possible answers: sugarcane, bananas, coffee)* **What foods were introduced to Europe?** *(Possible answers: corn, sweet potatoes, pumpkins)* Have students explain how the exchange of foods and crops might have affected agriculture and the economies in the Americas and in Europe. **Visual/Spatial**

Content Background Knowledge

European Explorers Exchanges Explain that the diaries of famous explorers who traveled during the 1400s between the "Old" and "New" Worlds (Europe and North America, respectively) listed some of the popular Columbian Exchange products:

- Christopher Columbus: balls of cotton, parrots, javelins in North America
- Bartolomé de Las Casas: maize, potatoes, yams, cassava from North America and rice, wheat, barley, and oats from Europe

Why Geography Matters: **Central America and the Caribbean**

spatial diffusion: *the* columbian exchange

W C *Christopher Columbus's voyage to the Americas began a dramatic process of interchange of peoples, animals, plants, cultures, ideas, and diseases between the Eastern and Western Hemispheres. This exchange had both positive and negative consequences. The Columbian Exchange, also known as the Grand Exchange, profoundly altered the course of human development across the globe.*

R

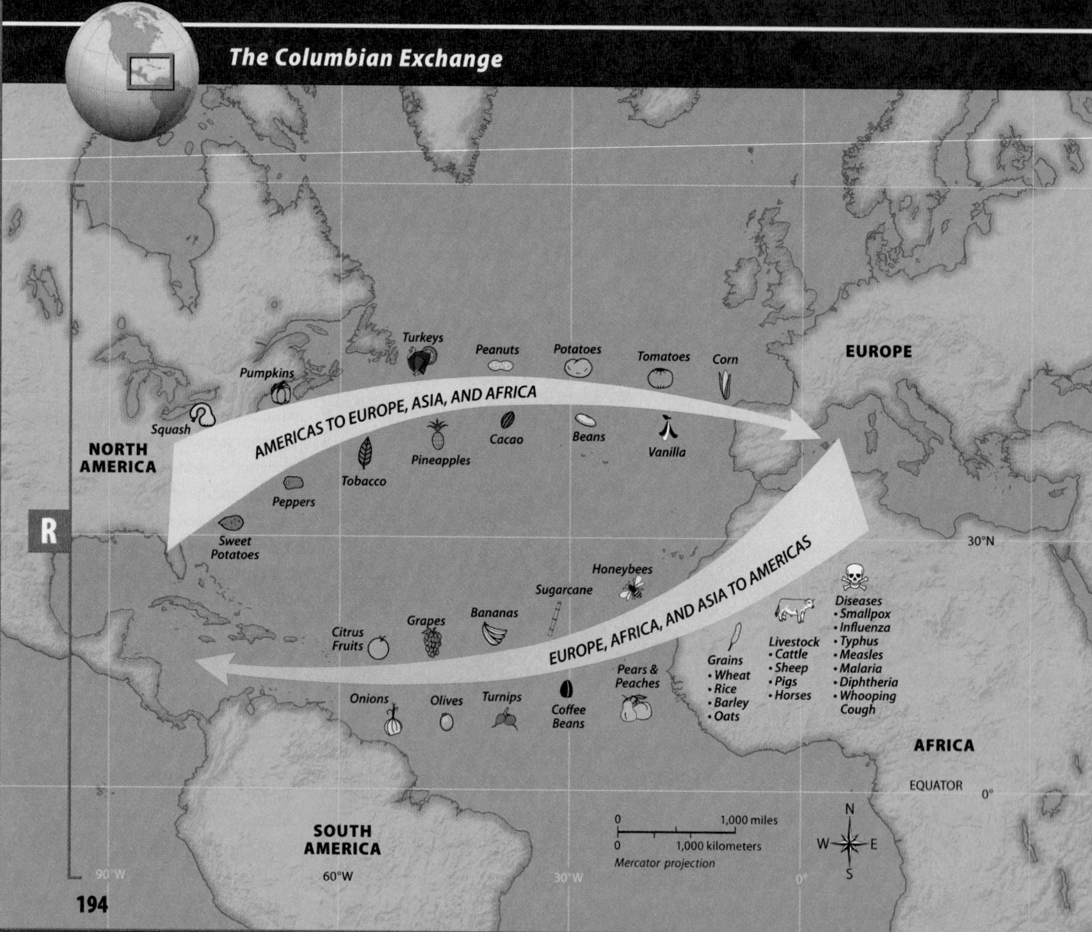

194

Project-Based Learning

Hands-On

Magazine Articles

Students will each write a magazine article about a topic that concerns a specific area of Central America and the Caribbean. The topic can be historical or current and will focus on how physical and human systems impact areas, including any environmental impacts. After writing their articles, students will pair up to compare and contrast their data.

Digital Hands-On

Create Online Projects

Find an additional activity online that incorporates technology for this project. Visit the EdTech Teacher Web sites for more links, tutorials, and other resources.

Why Geography Matters

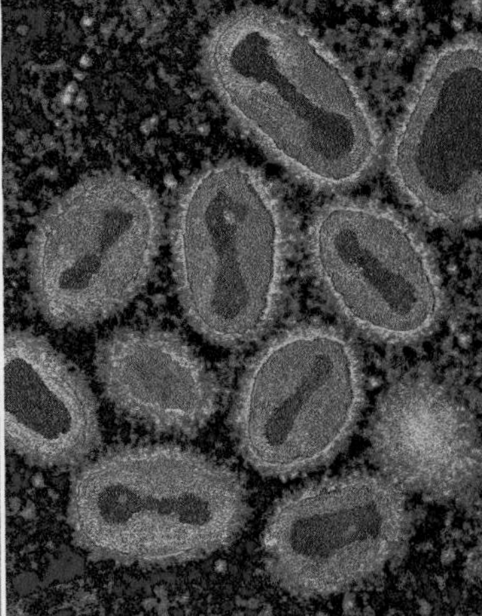

How did the Columbian Exchange affect agriculture?

New foods were exchanged between Europe and the Americas as a major part of the Columbian Exchange. Europeans introduced new food plants and domesticated animals to the Americas in an attempt to "Europeanize" the region. The plants involved in the exchange altered the economies of peoples in the Americas, Europe, and other continents, leaving a lasting imprint on all. Europeans introduced livestock such as cattle, pigs, and sheep as well as grains such as wheat. Sugarcane, coffee, and citrus fruits from Asia were also brought by the Europeans. Yams, bananas, and rice were brought from Africa to the Americas. Europeans also took food crops native to the Americas back across the Atlantic Ocean. Europeans discovered a variety of valuable Native American crops, including beans, squash, chili peppers, sunflowers, tomatoes, sweet potatoes, avocados, and cacao; but potatoes and corn were most important.

1. **Human Systems** Describe how the exchange of food left a lasting imprint in the Americas and Europe.

What was an unintended consequence of the Columbian Exchange?

T

The unintentional transmission of infectious diseases had serious and long-lasting effects on the peoples and cultures on both sides of the Atlantic Ocean. Human populations that develop in isolation from one another are often highly vulnerable to new infectious diseases introduced by outsiders. Lack of antibodies to the new diseases and lack of access to medicine can result in widespread illness and death. Smallpox, malaria, typhus, cholera, and a host of other diseases were introduced to the Americas by the Europeans. The native populations had no experience with these diseases and therefore had no resistance to them. As a result, native populations were decimated. Although it is difficult to determine the full extent of the population loss, estimates suggest that 80–95 percent of the indigenous peoples may have died in the first 100 to 150 years following the arrival of the Europeans in 1492. Other unintentional consequences included transmission of diseases from the Americas to Europe, although much fewer in number.

2. **Environment and Society** Write a summary of how the culture and history of Central America and the Caribbean might have been different if diseases had not been transmitted during the Columbian Exchange.

How were the lifestyles of indigenous peoples altered?

V

Contact with Europeans not only wiped out most of the native population of the Americas through disease, but also permanently altered the culture of those who survived. For example, because the Americas lacked large animal species, indigenous peoples had no beasts of burden. Asians and Europeans had long since domesticated several large animals for use in agriculture, trade, and warfare. Horses, long extinct from the Americas, were reintroduced by the Spanish, whose horse-mounted soldiers quickly overran and dominated indigenous forces. The horse transformed the Americas through warfare, hunting, and culture. Of even greater significance was that people themselves crossed the Atlantic. The presence of new peoples and their impact on the indigenous peoples of the Americas, due to the Columbian Exchange, initiated one of the largest cultural transformations in human history.

3. **Human Systems** What advantages did horses give Spanish invaders in the Americas?

THERE'S MORE ONLINE

VIEW a slide show of goods that were exchanged • *READ* a quote about the effects of the Columbian Exchange

T Technology Skills

Researching Have students work in small groups to identify which crops were part of the Columbian Exchange and became important to the U.S. and European economies. Suggest to students that they research statistics for agricultural output. Challenge students to investigate whether these crops eventually became export crops, dietary staples, or both. Have groups present their findings to the class. **BL** **Verbal/Linguistic**

Content Background Knowledge

The Diseases An unintended consequence of the Columbian Exchange was the transmission of infectious diseases. Some diseases that were transmitted:

- smallpox—a virus that may have originated in cattle or monkeys; causes disfigurement and blindness
- malaria—caused by a parasite that is carried by infected mosquitoes; causes flu-like symptoms
- typhus (typhoid fever)—caused by bacterial infection that humans carry; causes high fever and stomachaches
- cholera—caused by bacterial infection; often contracted by drinking contaminated water
- measles—a virus that may have originated in cattle; causes a red body rash and white spots in the mouth

V Visual Skills

Analyzing Visuals Ask students to speculate why this image of horses was chosen to support the text before they read the section. Discuss how horses may have given Europeans an advantage over the indigenous population. **Intrapersonal**

CLOSE & REFLECT

Summarizing Review how the Columbian Exchange impacted the indigenous population as well as their ways of life. Brainstorm ways that European explorers could have prevented the introduction of communicable diseases.

INTERACTIVE MAP

The Columbian Exchange

Drawing Conclusions This interactive map of the Columbian Exchange shows the cultural trading of food, livestock, and diseases between Europe, Africa, Asia, and the Americas. Ask students to provide any information that they know about the diseases listed and discuss some of the effects of the various diseases. Then have students write a paragraph explaining whether they feel the negative effects of the diseases were worth the positive effects of the food and livestock exchange. **BL** **Intrapersonal**

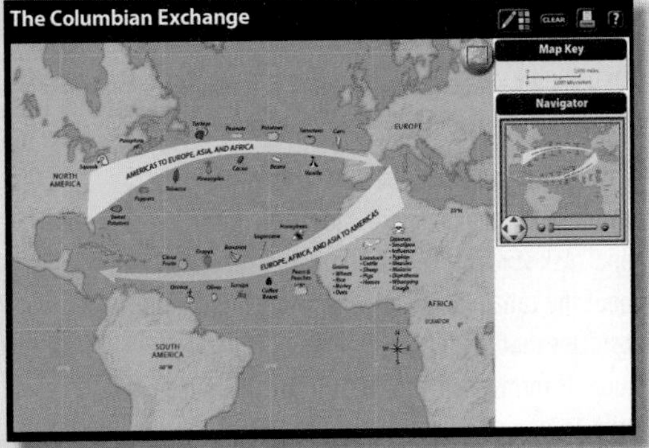

ANSWERS, p. 195

Why Geography Matters

1. Europeans introduced new food plants to the Americas, which altered the economies of peoples in the Americas, Europe, and other continents.
2. Paragraphs should show knowledge that populations of native peoples would not have been decimated, so their continued influence would have been apparent.
3. Spanish soldiers were able to overtake indigenous forces and were able to transport needed items.

ENGAGE

R1 Reading Skills

Activating Prior Knowledge Have students brainstorm what they already know about the physical geography of Central America and the Caribbean. Display the chapter opener map, and invite volunteers to describe different landforms and bodies of water in the region. Guide students to an understanding that its location makes it susceptible to earthquakes and volcanic eruptions. Discuss how these factors affect the way people live and where they settle in the region.

TEACH & ASSESS

R2 Reading Skills

Visualizing Direct students to visualize each sentence as you read it aloud to the class. Then ask students to sketch a physical map of the region, adding labels to the major landforms that are described in the text. **Ask:** **Based on the physical geography of the region, where do you think the majority of the population lives, in the lowlands or the highlands? Explain.** *(Possible answers: They live in the highlands for protection. They live in the lowlands near the coast, where they have access to the ocean.)* ELL **Visual/Spatial**

C Critical Thinking Skills

Identifying Cause and Effect Discuss the location of Central America and the Caribbean and its proximity to the Ring of Fire. **Ask:** **What effect have volcanic eruptions had on the region's human and physical geography?** *(The lava from the eruptions has made the soil fertile and rich. People have settled in these areas because of the good agricultural production.)* Have students work in pairs to make a T-chart in response to the following questions: **What are the benefits and the risks for people who live in areas where agricultural production is strong? What are the risks?** Invite students to share their charts with the class.
AL **Logical/Mathematical**

T Technology Skills

Presenting Working in small groups, have students choose one landform or landform belt in Central America or the Caribbean to research. Have them gather facts, details, and visuals, and then use presentation software to create displays to post on a class bulletin board. **Interpersonal Visual/Spatial**

ANSWERS, p. 196

TAKING NOTES: Graphic organizers should show knowledge of natural resources of Central America: water, fish, volcanic soil, timber, minerals (nickel, iron ore), and crude oil or petroleum.

networks
There's More Online!
- ☑ **MAP** Physical Geography: Central America and the Caribbean
- ☑ **INFOGRAPHIC** Biodiversity in Central America
- ☑ **INTERACTIVE SELF-CHECK QUIZ**
- ☑ **VIDEO** Physical Geography of Central America and the Caribbean

Reading **HELP**DESK 

Academic Vocabulary (Tier Two Words)
- **energy**
- **exhibit**

Content Vocabulary (Tier Three Words)
- **isthmus**
- **archipelago**
- **biodiversity**

TAKING NOTES: ***Key Ideas and Details***

SUMMARIZING Use a graphic organizer like the one below to take notes on the natural resources of Central America and the Caribbean.

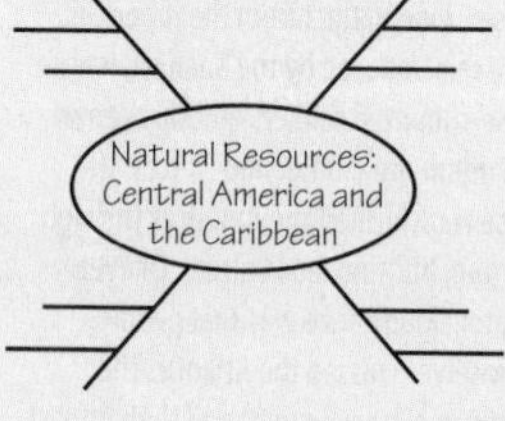

LESSON 1

Physical Geography of Central America and the Caribbean

ESSENTIAL QUESTION • *How do physical systems and human systems shape a place?*

IT MATTERS BECAUSE

R1 *Central America acts as a land bridge connecting North and South America. The region boasts dense rain forests, coastal plains, and high mountains, and is one of the world's great biodiversity hotspots. The more than 7,000 islands of the Caribbean exhibit their own unique landforms and living things. Shaped in part by the Ring of Fire, this region is a volatile zone of earthquakes and volcanic eruptions.*

Landforms

GUIDING QUESTION *Why are the majority of Central America's people concentrated in the Central Highlands?*

Much of Central America is hilly or mountainous, although swamps and lowlands extend along both coasts. These landforms create three distinct belts: the Pacific Lowlands, the Caribbean Lowlands, and the Central Highlands. The narrow plains of the Pacific Lowlands extend from Guatemala to Panama. The Caribbean Lowlands are also narrow, except in Nicaragua and Honduras. Central America's most distinctive landforms—mountains—form the Central Highlands. The region climbs steadily higher west of the Caribbean Lowlands. It rises up to the western plateau highlands where mountains and some 40 volcanic cones attain elevations of more than 12,000 feet (3,700 m). These are the volcanic highlands, or the Volcanic Axis. These mountains are an extension of the Sierra Madre of Mexico. Volcanic eruptions and earthquakes are not uncommon. The weathered lava produces fertile soil, making these highlands rich agricultural zones and areas of dense population.

Its location on the Ring of Fire brings potential hazards to living there. Yet humans have thrived in the mountains, valleys, and plateaus of the Central Highlands for thousands of years. The region's cooler climates, adequate rainfall, and rich natural resources—water, volcanic soil, timber, and minerals—attracted the area's earliest peoples and is where the majority of the people live today.

196

networks ***Online Teaching Options***

 **INTERACTIVE BELLRINGER**

Physical Geography of Central America and the Caribbean

Activating Prior Knowledge Use this map to introduce the region and the location of the Panama Canal. Ask students to discuss their prior knowledge about the canal, including why it was built and the obstacles that hindered its creation. Then have students form small groups to study the map and write agreed-upon answers to each of the questions. After groups have finished, ask them share to their answers. **Visual/Spatial, Interpersonal**

Physical Geography of Central America and the Caribbean

Construction on the Panama Canal began in 1880 and was completed in 1914.

1. Based on the map, what physical features of the region do you think influence its climate?

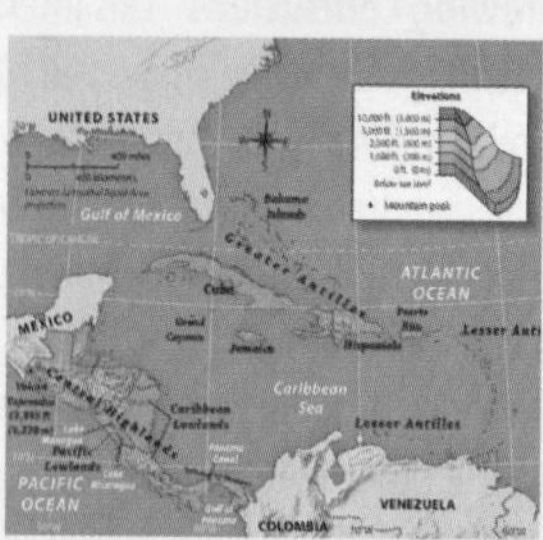

Another distinctive feature is the **Isthmus** of Panama. It extends west to east, connecting North and South America and separating the Caribbean Sea from the Gulf of Panama. The mountains, swampy coastal lands, and dense rain forests make contact between people difficult in this area.

R

In the Caribbean, many of the more than 7,000 islands are the tops of mountains that are part of the mainland's Central Highlands. The islands of the Greater and Lesser Antilles, however, are part of an **archipelago**. This archipelago is composed of the crests and peaks of a mountain range formed from collisions between the Caribbean plate and other tectonic plates. Tectonic activity continues to change the landscape. In 2010, for example, an earthquake struck Haiti's capital, Port-au-Prince, collapsing buildings and killing large numbers of people.

W

isthmus a narrow strip of land connecting two larger land areas

archipelago a group or chain of islands

✓ READING PROGRESS CHECK

Identifying What factors attracted people to settle in the highlands?

Water Systems

GUIDING QUESTION *How are Central American rivers and lakes important to the human systems of the area?*

Inland lakes and waterways play a vital role in Central America, aiding growth and development. The water systems also provide transportation, drinking water, drainage, irrigation, and a source of hydroelectric power. Lake Nicaragua is Central America's largest freshwater lake. It is the only one in the world to contain oceanic animal life such as sharks, swordfish, and tarpon. Nearby Lake Managua has commercially viable fish and alligators. It is drained by a river that flows into Lake Nicaragua and fed by streams from the highlands. Nicaragua's capital city, Managua, is located on the southern shore of Lake Managua.

V

GEOGRAPHY CONNECTION

A wide array of landforms and varied elevations give Central America and the Caribbean a diverse physical landscape.

1. ***PHYSICAL SYSTEMS*** What is the name of the most dominant mountain range in Central America that runs from north to south?
2. ***PLACES AND REGIONS*** Name the bodies of water that border the islands of the Caribbean.

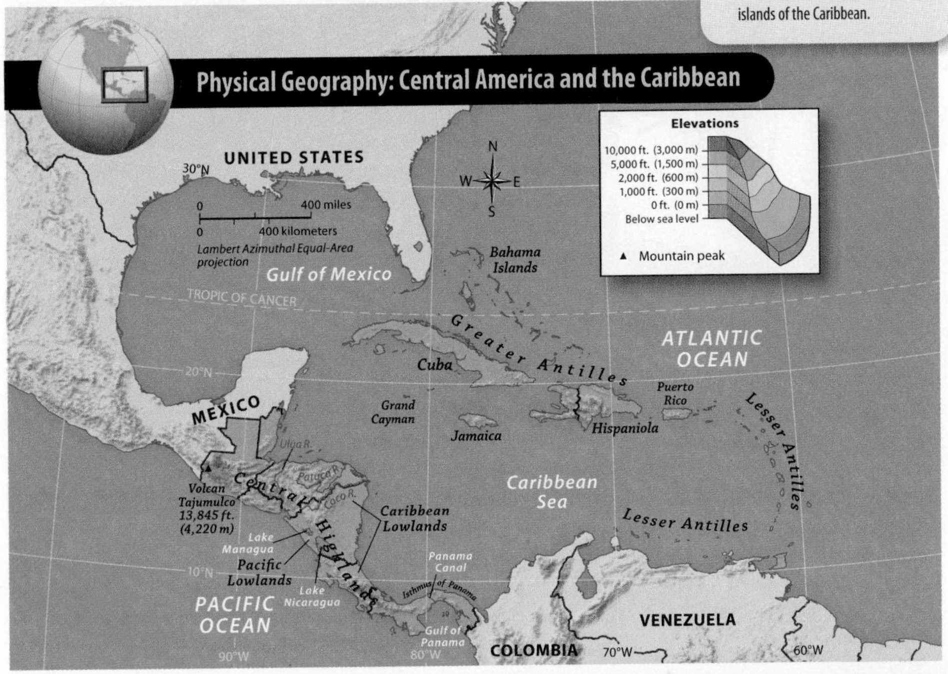

Physical Geography of Central America and the Caribbean

R Reading Skills

Defining Have students read about the distinctive features of the region: isthmus and archipelago. Invite volunteers to define both words and to point out where they are located on the map in their text. **Ask:** **Do these physical features affect interaction among people in the region? If so, how?** *(Yes, they may limit interaction and make communication and contact more challenging because water separates land and the Caribbean Islands are spread out.)* Divide the class into two groups, asking one group to stand up in the classroom in the formation of an isthmus, and the other group to model an archipelago. Ask students the same question to see if they would modify their answer. Challenge them to consider how factors such as isolation affect the culture and economy of the region.

ELL Kinesthetic

W Writing Skills

Informative/Explanatory Have students write a news report about the earthquake that struck Haiti in 2010 or the volcano that erupted in Montserrat, Lesser Antilles, in 1996 or 2009–2010. Suggest that students use print and electronic sources to gather information about the event. Instruct students to use excerpts of primary source accounts from eyewitnesses to the event, as well as statistics on the effects of the disaster. Invite students to present their news reports orally to the class.

BL Verbal/Linguistic

V Visual Skills

Creating Charts Have students create a graphic organizer like the one shown that will help them compare the lakes and waterways of Central America. Supply students with the following headings and sample.

Name	Freshwater	Salt Water	Animal Life	Other Features
Lake Nicaragua	X		sharks, swordfish, tarpon	largest freshwater lake
Lake Managua				

Encourage students to add more information to their charts as they continue the lesson. **AL Visual/Spatial**

INTERACTIVE MAP

Physical Geography of Central America

Contrasting Lead a class discussion with students on the differences in living and disaster recovery for various countries highlighted on the map. Remind them that generally hurricanes approach the eastern seaboard from the south. Have students form small groups to discuss the different experiences people would have during a hurricane in Central America compared to the United States, considering the physical geography. Then discuss the different experiences people on a Caribbean Island would have compared to the United States. **AL Interpersonal**

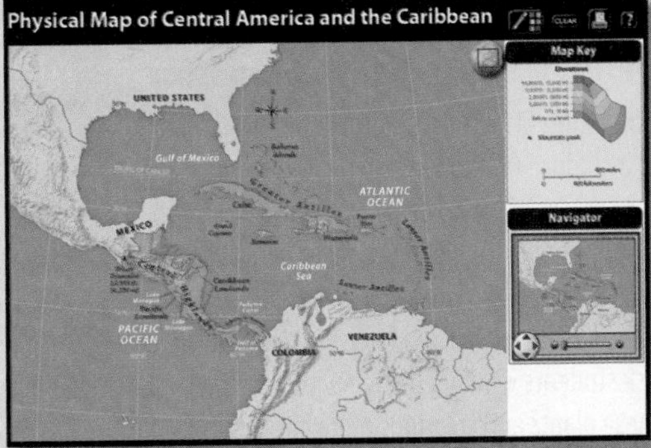

ANSWERS, p. 197

✓ **READING PROGRESS CHECK** People were attracted by the region's cooler climates, rainfall, and wealth of natural resources.

GEOGRAPHY CONNECTION

1. Central Highlands
2. Gulf of Mexico, Atlantic Ocean, and the Caribbean Sea

Physical Geography of Central America and the Caribbean

T Technology Skills

Researching Invite a volunteer to point out the location of the Panama Canal on a map. Discuss how building the Panama Canal shortened travel between the Atlantic and Pacific Oceans. Ask students to determine the distance before and after the Panama Canal was completed from New York to San Francisco *(before: just over 13,000 miles, or 21,000 km; after: about 5,000 miles, or 8,000 km)*. **Ask: How did the building of the Panama Canal affect commerce in the Western Hemisphere?** *(It increased commerce and made the transport of goods much faster and easier.)* Have students work in pairs to gather data on the impact of the Panama Canal on commerce. Ask them to find statistics prior to 1914 when it was completed, and then after 1930 when the use of the canal flourished. Have students compile the data in a chart or graph. **Mathematical/Logical**

C Critical Thinking Skills

Speculating In pairs, have one student explain the process of how hydroelectricity is generated, while the other student sketches it out. Then have both students work together to label the diagram. Ask student pairs to compare their sketches with another group and modify as needed. **Ask: Is hydroelectricity an example of using a renewable or nonrenewable resource? Explain.** *(Possible answer: It is an example of a renewable resource because water is a resource that can be replaced.)* **Will water ever become an exhaustible resource in the region? Explain.** *(Possible answer: Probably not, because water is a plentiful resource in the region, but conservation also needs to be practiced by the people of the region to protect this vital resource.)* Remind students to add the information about the San Juan River and the Lempa River to the charts that they created earlier in the lesson. **ELL Interpersonal**

V Visual Skills

Analyzing Visuals Have students interpret the diagram in a class discussion. **Ask: Why is biodiversity so rich in this region?** *(because of its location between North America and South America)* **What human activities might negatively affect the biodiversity of the region?** *(fishing, logging, agriculture)* Have students list ways in which human activities can positively affect the biodiversity of the region. Invite students to share their ideas in a class discussion. **AL Visual/Spatial**

ANSWERS, p. 198

✓ READING PROGRESS CHECK The Panama Canal is one of the world's most important human-made waterways. It allows ships to travel between the Atlantic and Pacific Oceans without the long trip around South America's Cape Horn.

CRITICAL THINKING

1. A variety of animal and plant life might be transported from one to the other, so nonindigenous species could exist on each.
2. It could result in fewer revenue-providing resources.

T The Panama Canal bisects the Isthmus of Panama. It is one of the world's most important human-made waterways. The canal allows ships to travel between the Atlantic and Pacific Oceans without making the long trip around South America's Cape Horn. International traffic through the Canal Zone is dominated by ships traveling between East Asia and the eastern United States. Approximately two-thirds of trading ships are sailing to or from U.S. ports.

Many of Central America's rivers provide commercial water routes because they are short and steep. The San Juan River, an outlet for Lake Nicaragua, drains **C** into the Caribbean Sea. El Salvador's only navigable river, the Lempa River, generates hydroelectricity from the **energy** of moving water.

energy usable power

exhibit to demonstrate or show openly

The warm, clear waters of the Antillean regions of the Caribbean Sea contain coral reefs. These reefs **exhibit** a wide variety of reef fish. Other common types of characteristic marine life include manatees, manta rays, spiny lobsters, dolphins, and numerous species of sea turtles. Commercial fishing of sardines and tuna and the utilization of other marine resources have increased international trade.

✓ READING PROGRESS CHECK

Describing Describe the importance of the Panama Canal to international trade.

V

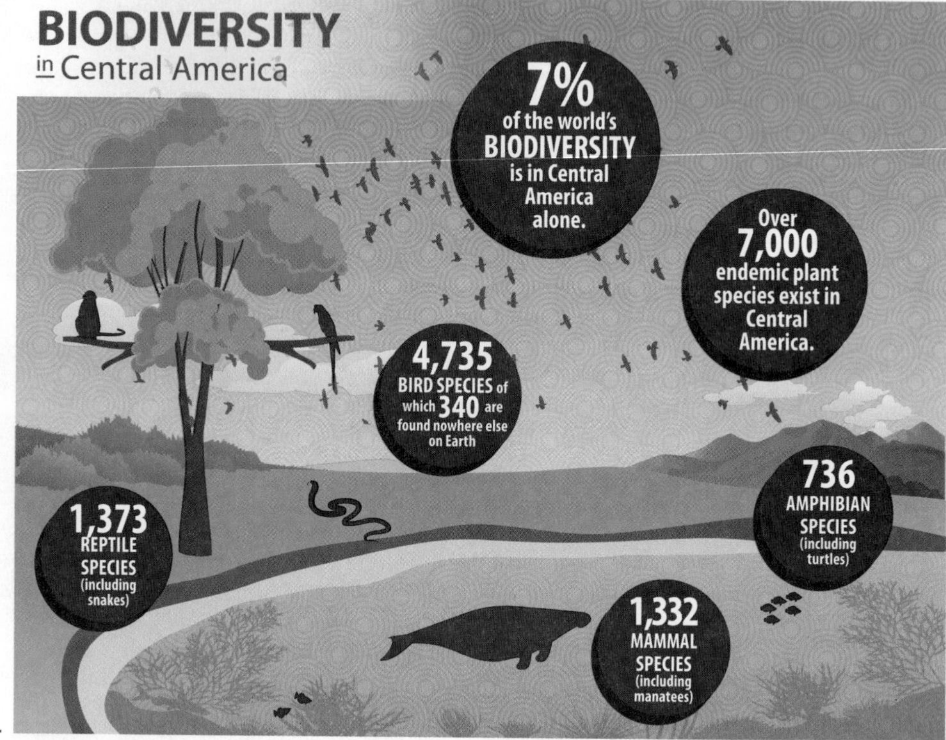

The natural richness of Central America is evident in its diverse animal and plant life.

▲ CRITICAL THINKING

1. ***Analyzing*** In what way might Central America's position as a land bridge linking two continents affect its biodiversity?
2. ***Drawing Conclusions*** What might be one effect of the loss of biodiversity in Central America?

networks Online Teaching Options

INFOGRAPHIC

Biodiversity in Central America

Analyzing Ethical Issues Use this infographic to introduce the students to the term *endemic* in the context of biology. Have students work with a partner to discuss what *endemic* means as it is used on the chart *(prevalent in or found in a specific region and nowhere else in the world)*. Ask students whether being endemic makes these plants and creatures more important or deserving of protection than plant and animal species that are spread out around the world. Have each pair join another pair to discuss this issue. **ELL Verbal/Linguistic**

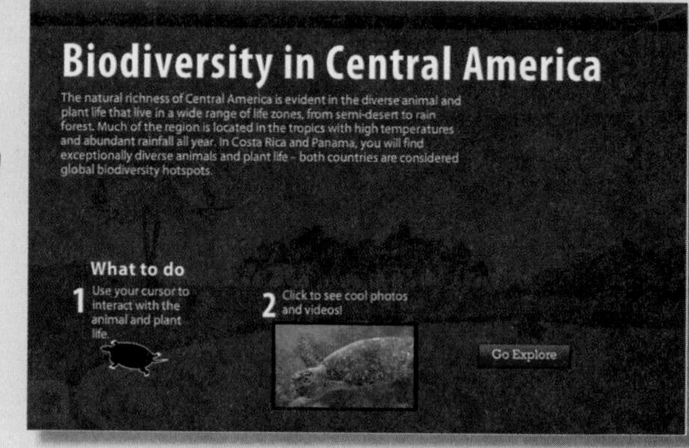

Biodiversity in Central America
The natural richness of Central America is evident in the diverse animal and plant life that live in a wide range of life zones, from semi-desert to rain forest. Much of the region is located in the tropics with high temperatures and abundant rainfall all year. In Costa Rica and Panama, you will find exceptionally diverse animals and plant life - both countries are considered global biodiversity hotspots.
What to do
1 Use your cursor to interact with the animal and plant life.
2 Click to see cool photos and videos!
Go Explore

Climate, Biomes, and Resources

GUIDING QUESTION *How does its location in the Tropics affect the climate of Central America and the Caribbean?*

C1 Climates in the region are dependent on many factors, such as proximity to the sea, elevation, latitude, and local topography. For much of the region, its location in the Tropics and the prevailing winds that carry warm, moist air from the Atlantic Ocean result in high temperatures and abundant rainfall year-round. A tropical rain forest climate and rain forests dominate much of Central America. The tropical forest biome has a continuous canopy of trees and diversity of species. These species include tall trees, ferns, and mosses, as well as birds, bats, small mammals, and insects. Costa Rica and Panama are global **biodiversity** hotspots, rich in natural resources that may one day provide medicines and other products.

A tropical wet/dry climate is typical of Caribbean islands. Moist winds sweep in from the east. This leaves leeward island areas—those not exposed to wind—dry. Thus some islands may have high temperatures and rainfall but also an extended dry season. Grasslands flourish, although soils may not be very fertile or suitable for large-scale agriculture. On mountainous islands, windward slopes facing moist winds help cool the warm, humid air and increase precipitation. Intense hurricanes strike each year from June to November in the northern Caribbean and the Gulf of Mexico.

C2 Elevation affects the climate and ecosystems of some parts of Central America more than distance from the Equator. Such areas have vertical climate zones in which animals, plants, and climates change as altitude increases. The *tierra caliente*, or "hot land," lies at elevations below 2,500 feet (762 m). Bananas and sugarcane are grown here. The *tierra templada*, or "temperate land," lies between 2,500 to 6,000 feet (762 to 1,829 m) and is the most densely populated. Ecosystems with broadleaf evergreens at lower altitudes give way to evergreens at upper elevations. Land at 6,000 to 10,000 feet (1,829 to 3,048 m) is known as the *tierra fria*, or "cold land." Winter frosts are common here, and potatoes and barley are grown. Above the tree line is the *tierra helada*, or "frozen land." This is an area of permanent ice and snow.

Natural resources extracted or used throughout Central America include nickel, iron ore, fish, timber, and petroleum. Guatemala and certain islands refine petroleum, while Belize extracts crude oil. Much commercial fishing also takes place around the Caribbean islands.

✓ **READING PROGRESS CHECK**

Categorizing How is the climate of Central America different from that of the Caribbean islands?

Connecting Geography to SCIENCE

Climatology

Predicting when hurricanes will form and where they will land is often difficult. In recent years, climatologists have used El Niño to help predict hurricanes. El Niño is a climatic change that affects the equatorial Pacific. It includes uncommonly warm waters off the western coast of Peru and Ecuador. Often the increased wind levels during El Niño prevent hurricanes from forming, so there tend to be fewer Atlantic hurricanes during El Niño. Knowing when El Niño winds will develop can help predict when hurricanes are a threat and when they are not.

IDENTIFYING How do climatologists use El Niño to help them predict the behavior of hurricanes?

biodiversity biological diversity in an environment as indicated by numbers of different species of plants and animals

LESSON 1 REVIEW 

Reviewing Vocabulary (Tier Three Words)

1. ***Making Connections*** Write a sentence to describe the difference between an isthmus and an archipelago.

Using Your Notes

2. ***Listing*** Use your graphic organizer to list the natural resources of Central America and the Caribbean and their importance to the region.

Answering the Guiding Questions

3. ***Describing*** Why are the majority of Central America's people concentrated in the Central Highlands?
4. ***Examining*** How are Central American rivers and lakes important to the human systems of the area?
5. ***Interpreting*** How does its location in the Tropics affect the climate in Central America and the Caribbean?

Writing Activity

6. ***Informative/Explanatory*** Write a paragraph describing how altitude affects the climates and biodiversity of Central America and the Caribbean. WHST.9–10.2

LESSON 1 REVIEW ANSWERS

Reviewing Vocabulary

1. An isthmus is a narrow strip of land that connects two larger land areas and an archipelago is a group or chain of islands.

Using Your Notes

2. Natural resources contribute to the region's economy: waterways aid growth and development; volcanic soil is good for growing crops; timber is needed for lumber; petroleum is refined; and marine resources increase international trade.

Answering the Guiding Questions

3. This part of Central America has cooler climates, rainfall, and many resources.
4. They aid growth and development, and provide transportation, drinking water, drainage, irrigation, and a source of hydroelectric power.
5. Prevailing winds carry warm, moist air from the Atlantic Ocean and result in high temperatures and abundant rainfall year-round.

Writing Activity

6. Paragraphs should show knowledge that altitude affects ecosystems and the climate.

C1 Critical Thinking Skills

Comparing and Contrasting Discuss with students the factors that affect climate. **Ask:** **What factors cause the high temperatures and plentiful rainfall in Central America?** *(its location in the Tropics and the prevailing winds that carry warm, moist air from the Atlantic)* **Why do rain forests dominate much of the region?** *(its location and climate)* Have students identify another region that lies in the Tropics but experiences a different climate than that of Central America. Then have them complete a Venn diagram to compare and contrast the climate, flora, and fauna of both regions. Invite students to share their diagrams. Ask students to draw conclusions about the different factors that affect climate. **AL Visual/Spatial**

Content Background Knowledge

Rain Forest The climate of the rain forest produces poor soil for agriculture, but the rain forest feeds the fauna of the biome. Plants of the rain forest are a food source for rain forest animals and provide an abundance of oxygen.

C2 Critical Thinking Skills

Diagramming Discuss with students how elevation affects climate and the flora and fauna of ecosystems. Have students work together to create a diagram showing the differences in elevation in Central America and the animals and plants that thrive in each particular climate zone. Provide an opportunity for students to display their diagrams. **BL Naturalist**

CLOSE & REFLECT

Summarizing Review with students the physical geography of Central America and the Caribbean. Have students summarize the key landforms, waterways, climate, biomes, and resources of the region. Review the hotspots of biodiversity that may hold important resources and resources that may be threatened by human activities. Discuss the importance of protecting these resources, as well as mineral resources, to the region's economy.

ANSWERS, p. 199

✓ **READING PROGRESS CHECK** Central America is predominantly a tropical wet climate. Caribbean islands are typically a tropical dry climate.

Connecting Geography Climatologists know that increased wind levels during El Niño can help prevent hurricanes from forming.

ENGAGE

C1 Critical Thinking Skills

Considering Advantages and Disadvantages Ask partners to brainstorm a list of advantages and disadvantages of European interaction with the Americas. Point out that students should consider social, cultural, and economic aspects. Then in a class discussion, invite students to share their ideas.

TEACH & ASSESS

C2 Critical Thinking Skills

Comparing and Contrasting Have students identify the central idea. **Ask:** **What event led to the exploration of Central America?** *(the voyages of Christopher Columbus to the Americas)* Discuss with students the purposes of Columbus's voyages. Then **ask:** **How were the purposes of the voyages by Columbus and those of later explorers who arrived in Central America similar and different? What were the potential long-term profits?** *(Like Columbus, Spanish conquistadors were searching for riches in Central America, but they also wanted to plant colonies for Spain. By establishing colonies, the conquistadors profited, and Spain used the resources of the region to expand its economy.)* ELL **Verbal/Linguistic**

V Visual Skills

Creating Time Lines Have students read about the conquests of European explorers in Central America. **Ask:** **What motives brought European explorers to the region?** *(riches, profit, power)* Ask students to create a time line based on the information. When they have finished, **ask:** **Which event on the time line illustrates the attitudes of the native people toward European conquest and colonization?** *(The resistance by the native population to the Spanish conquest of Costa Rica)* **Do you think that resistance was widespread or isolated? What factors affected native resistance?** *(Possible answer: It was probably widespread. Weapons and the will of the native people, as well as the strength, weapons, and manpower of the Spanish might have been factors in successful conquests and resistance.)* Have students add to their time lines as they read the lesson. **Visual/Spatial**

ANSWERS, p. 200

TAKING NOTES: Key Ideas—colonialism influenced the history and government of Central America and the Caribbean; migration and rapid growth resulted in a large population; traditions and beliefs of indigenous peoples, Africans, and Europeans shaped society and culture.

networks
There's More Online!

- **IMAGE** Kuna Molas
- **IMAGE** The Panama Canal
- **INTERACTIVE SELF-CHECK QUIZ**
- **TIME LINE** Central America and the Caribbean: Paths to Independence
- **VIDEO** Human Geography of Central America and the Caribbean

LESSON 2

Human Geography of Central America and the Caribbean

ESSENTIAL QUESTION • *How do physical systems and human systems shape a place?*

Reading **HELPDESK** CCSS

Academic Vocabulary (Tier Two Words)
- attribute
- obvious

Content Vocabulary (Tier Three Words)
- population pressure
- dialect
- patois
- matriarchal
- *latifundia*
- *minifundia*
- cottage industry
- ecotourism

TAKING NOTES: *Key Ideas and Details*

IDENTIFYING Use a graphic organizer like the one below to take notes as you read the lesson.

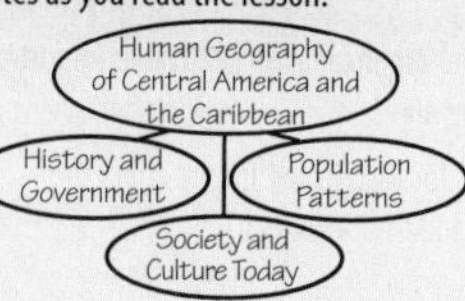
Human Geography of Central America and the Caribbean
History and Government
Population Patterns
Society and Culture Today

It Matters Because

C1 *A study of the human geography of Central America and the Caribbean highlights how history, geography, and the blending of native and outside cultures have shaped the region. The region's mixing of languages, religions, economic practices, and social customs combine traditional and modern. Such diversity provides both benefits and challenges as the region works toward increased economic and social development.*

History and Government

GUIDING QUESTION *How did colonialism influence the history and government of Central America and the Caribbean?*

C2 The voyages of Christopher Columbus to the Americas from 1492 to 1504 triggered a period of conquest and colonization in Central America and the Caribbean. Spain founded the region's first permanent European settlement on the island of Hispaniola in 1493. Rodrigo de Bastidas made Spain's first claim to Central America in March 1501. Other Spanish conquistadors followed. They attempted to subdue the local people and establish permanent colonies. Vasco Nuñez de Balboa explored extensively, crossing the isthmus, claiming land for Spain, and finding enough gold and pearls to establish the first profitable colony in the Americas, called Castilla del Oro.

V The king of Spain replaced Balboa with Pedro Arias Dávila, known as Pedrarias. Pedrarias expanded the colony, but was notorious for enslaving and murdering indigenous people. In 1519, as governor of Panama, he established Panama City on the Pacific coast and later moved the capital there. In 1524 Pedrarias sent Francisco Hernández de Córdoba to Nicaragua to conquer the region. Córdoba established Granada on Lake Nicaragua. He also founded León not far from Lake Managua and attempted to rule Nicaragua himself. Pedrarias had Córdoba executed and named himself governor of Nicaragua. While Pedrarias and Córdoba fought to conquer southern Central America, Cristóbal de Olid set sail

networks *Online Teaching Options*

 INTERACTIVE BELLRINGER

Maya Mother and Child

Drawing Inferences Use this image of a Maya mother and child to draw inferences about the family and the role of women in rural areas of Central America. In small groups, have students answer the first question independently by listing as many ideas as possible. Then have students share their lists with their group members and discuss how they drew their inferences. Have students discuss and answer the second question as a group. Ask each group to write an agreed-upon one or two sentence answer to the second question.

AL **Interpersonal, Visual/Spatial**

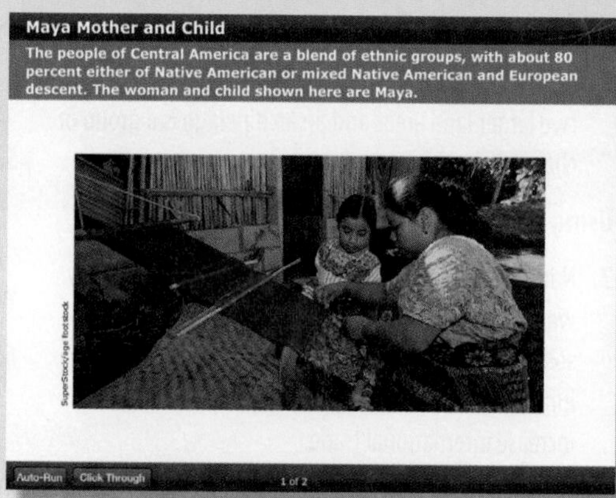
Maya Mother and Child
The people of Central America are a blend of ethnic groups, with about 80 percent either of Native American or mixed Native American and European descent. The woman and child shown here are Maya.
Auto-Run
Click Through
1 of 2

to Honduras. Pedro de Alvarado, who had served with Cortés in the conquest of Mexico, set out overland to conquer Guatemala and El Salvador. When gold was discovered in Honduras, various Spanish forces fought each other for control of the region. In Costa Rica, the native population strenuously resisted Spanish efforts at conquest. Spain did not establish a permanent colony there until 1561.

C The physical geography influenced colonization of the region. Remote areas of Central America remained outside of Spanish control. This allowed Great Britain to colonize Belize and the Mosquito Coast of Nicaragua. British Honduras (Belize) was the only non-Spanish colony in Central America. In time, however, France, the Netherlands, and Portugal also established colonies in the Caribbean and other parts of the Americas.

W By the mid-1600s, forced labor, starvation, and European diseases had nearly killed the entire indigenous population. For the Europeans, the drastically reduced numbers of indigenous people meant a labor shortage. They began bringing Africans, who had been forcibly captured, enslaved, and transported by ship, to the Caribbean to meet the demand for workers.

R In the late 1700s, Africans and indigenous people began to take organized action to free themselves from slavery and European control. François Toussaint-Louverture, a soldier born to enslaved parents, led a revolt of enslaved Africans in Haiti. By 1804, Haiti had won its independence from France. Haitian independence inspired downtrodden people throughout Latin America, but frightened many of the elite who had much to lose. Most Caribbean colonies did not gain independence until the 1900s. Cuba gained self-rule in 1898 as a result of the Spanish-American War, but remained under the protection of the United States until 1902. Some islands remain under foreign control or continue to have foreign ties today.

During the 1800s, several Central American colonies struggled for independence from Spain. In 1823 the federation of the United Provinces of Central America was formed. Eventually it divided into five separate countries: Costa Rica, El Salvador, Guatemala, Honduras, and Nicaragua. In 1903 Panama declared its independence from Colombia and signed a treaty with the United States creating the Panama Canal Zone. The Panama Canal opened in 1914 and was controlled by the United States. Today, under Panamanian control, the canal is being upgraded to reduce traffic congestion and to allow larger ships to pass.

In the 1900s, many Central American and Caribbean countries faced political, social, and economic upheaval. In Panama, the Canal Zone and related industries brought new wealth to the upper classes. Most Panamanians benefited little from the canal, however. In Cuba, a revolution in 1959 produced a communist state. Fidel Castro ruled until 2008 when he handed power to his brother Raúl, who initiated some economic reforms. Armed conflict, civil wars, unstable economies, and poor social conditions were all problems in the region. By the end of the twentieth century, however, Central American governments sought ways to increase international trade and diversify their economies. In the twenty-first century, many Central Americans have exercised their right to vote, demanding positive change. For example, Guatemala ended its history of rule by military regime and continues its political and economic recovery, including regular elections since 1996.

The Panama Canal provides a passage through the isthmus by means of a system of canal locks.

▼ CRITICAL THINKING

1. ***Speculating*** What major challenges would builders of the Panama Canal have faced?
2. ***Identifying*** Which bodies of water does the Panama Canal link?

Kip Ross/National Geographic/Getty Images

✓ READING PROGRESS CHECK

Explaining What role did Haiti play in the movement for independence from European control in the region?

C Critical Thinking Skills

Analyzing Discuss with students the physical geography of Central America and the Caribbean, using the chapter opener map as a point of reference. Have students explain how the physical geography of the region influenced where European countries colonized. Then **ask:** **Did the physical geography of the region hinder or encourage European colonization?** *(Possible answer: It most likely encouraged it. European explorers were able to access islands in the Caribbean and coastal areas; highlands and mountainous areas posed bigger challenges to colonization.)* **Logical/Mathematical**

W Writing Skills

Narrative Have students write a personal narrative from the point of view of an African or Native American who has suffered and been enslaved during the time of the European conquest and joined others to fight against this oppression. Invite students to read their personal narratives to the class. **AL Verbal/Linguistic**

R Reading Skills

Skimming Explain to students that when they have a large amount of text to read, they can often skim the text quickly to gain a brief understanding of the topic. Have students skim the first paragraph of this section. **Ask:** **What is the topic of this paragraph?** *(how African and Native Americans took action to free themselves)* **How were you able to identify the topic?** *(By finding the main idea, which is often near the beginning of a paragraph.)* **What other information or facts did you learn by skimming?** *(Possible answer: Cuba gained self-rule in 1898.)* Now have students read the last two paragraphs and discuss the content with a partner. Tell pairs to compare and contrast skimming and reading, and then brainstorm ways that skimming can be effective and useful. **ELL Interpersonal**

INTERACTIVE IMAGE

The Panama Canal

Considering Perspectives Use this image to discuss with students how physical geography and politics were important factors in the building of the Panama Canal. As students are observing the image, ask them to consider the following statement, "The Panama Canal is a continuation of the white colonization of Central America." Considering what they learned about the canal so far, have students write a paragraph explaining whether they agree or disagree with this statement. **AL Intrapersonal**

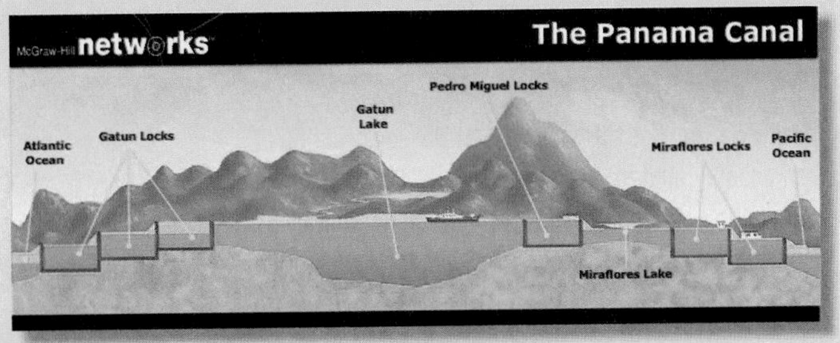

ANSWERS, p. 201

✓ READING PROGRESS CHECK François Toussaint-Louverture led a revolt of enslaved Africans in Haiti and by 1804, Haiti had won its independence from France. Haitian independence inspired people throughout Latin America.

CRITICAL THINKING

1. The terrain, the necessary equipment, and the size would have been major challenges.
2. It links the Atlantic Ocean to the Pacific Ocean.

T Technology Skills

Presenting Review with students the effects of migration on the populations and cities of Central America and the Caribbean. Then allow students to form small groups and select two countries to research in the region. Ask them to find data for in-migration and out-migration, as well as the urban/rural population for both countries and the major cities. Have students present their findings orally to the class using presentation software. Point out that they should use graphs and charts to present the data and also include a summary and an analysis. BL **Auditory/Musical, Visual/Spatial**

R Reading Skills

Defining Write the term *population pressure* on the board. Then invite students to call out factors that affect population pressure, using examples from the text and their own ideas. Discuss with students how each factor affects population pressure. Consider having students work in pairs to create a word web for each factor, identifying how each affects population pressure. Then ask student pairs to work within a small group and choose one of the factors to demonstrate to the class. Point out that students should model how this factor affects population pressure. Challenge them to be creative and to use props if needed. After student groups have modeled all of the factors, discuss the long-term effects of population pressure in Central America and the Caribbean. ELL **Kinesthetic**

C Critical Thinking Skills

Identifying Cause and Effect As a class, discuss the time line entries for 1823 and 1804 and the possible reasons why the Central American provinces formed the United Provinces of Central America. **Ask:** **Why do you think the provinces separated in 1840?** *(Possible answer: They were too distinct and diverse and realized after some time as a united entity that they wanted to be independent of one another.)* **What influence did colonization of this region have on the provinces' decision to separate from each other?** *(Possible answer: Under colonial rule, Spain probably ignored cultural and social aspects in these provinces, which, after they united, posed challenges and prompted the need for independent countries.)* Have students identify other causes and effects of both events independently in a brief essay. **Verbal/Linguistic**

ANSWERS, p. 202

READING PROGRESS CHECK People migrate within the region seeking economic opportunities or escape from civil wars and instability, mostly moving to cities.

Connecting Geography Answers should recognize that cultural influences today are a mixture of influences from Europe, the United States, Latin America, native populations, and Africa.

CRITICAL THINKING

1. Spain lost control of Cuba, Guam, and Puerto Rico to the United States.
2. Oppression by the French colonizers was a major factor.

Connecting Geography to **HISTORY**

Before Columbus

Settlement of Central America and the Caribbean did not begin with the arrival of Christopher Columbus. Before 1492, indigenous groups such as the Arawaks and Caribs called the Caribbean home. In Central America, the Maya civilization flourished between A.D. 300 and 900. It began to weaken around A.D. 800, and the native population of the Caribbean began a swift decline with the arrival of Europeans. However, rather than disappearing, indigenous cultures blended with European cultures and influence the region today.

SPECULATING What cultural influences may be active in Central America and the Caribbean today?

Population Patterns

GUIDING QUESTION *How have migration and rapid growth affected the population?*

The populations of Central America and the Caribbean reflect, to varying degrees, a blending of ethnic groups. In Central America, about 60 percent are mestizos and 20 percent indigenous, with other groups of mixed ancestry making up the rest. For example, in Guatemala about half the population is Maya; in the Bahamas, the majority is of African descent.

T Until about 1900, more people immigrated to Central America and the Caribbean than left. Since then outmigration has increased as people sought economic opportunities or escaped civil wars and instability. Many people also migrate within the region for similar reasons, mostly moving to cities.

R Population density varies throughout Central America and the Caribbean. About 79 percent of Central Americans live in highland cities and towns, however. Most countries have a single primate city, usually the capital. El Salvador is Central America's most densely populated country. The population density of the Caribbean is among the highest in Latin America and greatest near cities and ports. Caribbean countries combine small land areas with large populations that tend to grow at a rapid rate, causing **population pressure**.

The population growth rate of Central America is one of the highest in the world. In 2007 Central America had more than 40 million people, quadruple its population in the 1950s. Fertility rates have decreased overall but are high relative to more developed countries, particularly given high infant mortality rates and low life expectancy. Projected rapid population growth may strain the environment and the ability of the region to accommodate the number of people.

READING PROGRESS CHECK

Determining Importance Why have countries in Central America and the Caribbean experienced a dramatic increase in migration to cities?

TIME LINE

CENTRAL AMERICA and the CARIBBEAN Paths to Independence

Central America and the Caribbean have been influenced by struggles for independence and modern challenges.

CRITICAL THINKING

1. ***Analyzing*** What territories did Spain lose after the Treaty of Paris of 1898?
2. ***Predicting*** What conditions might have led to the Haitian revolt against France?

C

1800

1804 Following revolt led by François Toussaint-Louverture, Haiti declares independence.

1823 Central American provinces declare independence from Mexico; establish the United Provinces of Central America

1838–1841 United Provinces of Central America separates into five independent countries: Costa Rica, El Salvador, Honduras, Guatemala, and Nicaragua.

202

networks Online Teaching Options

VIDEO

The Panama Canal

Categorizing Use this video about the construction of the Panama Canal to categorize the environmental connection between physical and human geography of this region. As students view the video, have them fill in a two-column chart, one listing the physical geography aspects of the canal, and the other listing the human aspects. Then lead a class discussion on the physical and human geography effects to this region before, during, and after the building of the Panama Canal. **Logical/Mathematical**

Society and Culture Today

GUIDING QUESTION *How have the traditions and beliefs of indigenous peoples, Africans, and Europeans shaped society and culture in Central America and the Caribbean?*

The merging of indigenous, European, African, and Asian cultures has created a distinct Latin American identity. This is expressed through unique blendings of language, traditions, and art. In Central America, the primary language of most countries is Spanish. In the Caribbean, primary languages include Dutch, English, French, and Spanish. Each country has its own **dialects**, or local languages, and millions of people speak indigenous languages and are bilingual. Some speak a form of **patois** (PA•TWAH), dialects that blend languages. Haitian Creole, for example, blends French vocabulary with African and Spanish words. **R**

Many types of religions are practiced in the region. In Central America, 80 percent of people are Roman Catholic while in the Caribbean, similarly high populations of Roman Catholics occur mainly where French or Spanish is spoken. Protestant religions are common where English is spoken. Other faiths include Hinduism, Islam, and indigenous and African religions, often mixed with Christianity and other faiths. Santería in Cuba and voodoo in Haiti are examples.

The quality of education and health care varies greatly from country to country, as well as within rural and urban areas. Generally, children are required to complete elementary school, but many do not, lacking money for clothing and supplies or the means to travel long distances to school. Countries with less-developed economies and a lower standard of living tend to have more disease and malnutrition and a low life expectancy. **C**

population pressure the sum of factors within a population that reduce the ability of an environment to support the population, therefore resulting in migration or population decline

dialect local form of a language used in a particular place or by a certain group

patois a dialect used in everyday speech that blends elements of several languages

Family and Status of Women

In the Caribbean, family structure is often **matriarchal**, or headed by a woman. This type of family is characteristic of West Africa, from where many local people trace their roots. This is not the case in Central America, where families are mostly male dominated. Current trends show alterations in the

matriarchal family ruled by a woman such as a mother, grandmother, or aunt

(c)Sven Creutzmann/Mambo Photography/Getty Images News/Getty Images, (b)©Corbis

1914 The Panama Canal opens for use across the Isthmus of Panama.

1959 Fidel Castro becomes the dictator of Cuba as a newly established communist state.

2008 Fidel Castro hands over power to his brother Raúl.

1900 — 2008

1898 The United States engages in a war with Spain to liberate Cuba from Spanish rule. The Treaty of Paris of 1898 ends the war. Spain loses control over Cuba and cedes Guam and Puerto Rico to the United States.

W

TIME LINE

Central America and the Caribbean: Paths to Independence

Classifying Use this time line showing the history of independence for Central America and the Caribbean to discuss the diverse ethnic groups found in this region. Focus on the 1804 text and photo of François Toussaint-Louverture. Review the definition of the word *mestizo (a person of combined ancestry)*. Explain to students that many people in this region were of mixed descent. Considering his name, ask students where his ancestors may have originated. *(Possible answer: Haiti and France)* Tell students that he was a self-educated slave, adopted his name and pledged his allegiance to France, but devoted his life to the Haitian people. Continue to discuss other aspects of the time line. **ELL** **Verbal/Spatial**

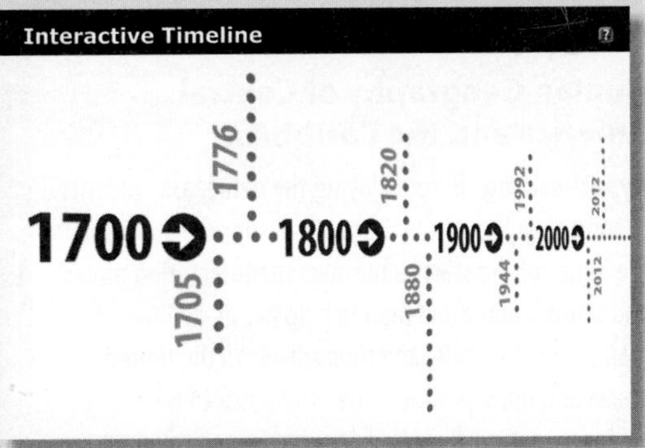

R Reading Skills

Inferring Discuss with students how the cultures of Central America and the Caribbean are a product of the region's history. **Ask:** **Why do you think each country has its own dialect?** *(Because there are so many different languages spoken in the region, resulting from native speakers mixing with European settlers.)* **How does speaking dialects help countries maintain an identity?** *(Possible answers: Having a dialect spoken in one country may provide the people with a special identity or feeling of pride for their country.)* **Why have some religions also blended to form new faiths?** *(Possible answer: Like languages, the blending of religions has enabled the people to have their own unique religion.)* In a class discussion, talk about why Roman Catholicism is still the major religion in the region, even though the people of the region have let go of other aspects of European culture. **AL** **Verbal/Linguistic**

Content Background Knowledge

Endangered Language Some languages have such few speakers that the language is deemed endangered. One such language is Garifuna. This Central American language is mainly spoken by people who live in Honduras and Belize, as well as Nicaragua and Guatemala. The ancestors of the native speakers originated in West Africa, were enslaved, and escaped en route to South America when the ship that was carrying them sunk. Eventually they mixed with the Arawakan and Carib tribes.

C Critical Thinking Skills

Problem Solving Have students reread the paragraph about education and health care. Then ask them to work together in pairs or small groups to identify the problems that people and countries face in this region with regard to education and health care and to propose solutions. Explain to students that they may want to brainstorm ideas for solutions and then refine their list through a discussion. After students identify their strongest solution, have them write a proposal that outlines specific steps that should be taken to resolve these problems. Invite groups to share their solutions with the class. **Interpersonal**

W Writing Skills

Argument Review the causes and effects of the Spanish-American War on the region. Then pose this writing prompt to students: **Should the United States have gone to war with Spain? How did the effects of the war change the region?** Provide an opportunity for students to plan their response and writing. Remind them that they need to support their claims with supporting reasons and evidence and that they should address any counterclaims. Consider having students share their responses in small groups. **BL** **Verbal/Linguistic**

Human Geography of Central America and the Caribbean

R Reading Skills

Examining Primary Sources After students read the feature on the Kuna culture, ask them to compare it to the primary source excerpt. **Ask:** **How does this primary source connect to the idea that the region is a blending of cultures but also that its cultures maintain their own identities?** *(Paolo Fortis explains that the Kuna believe people have their own independent lives and that the categories to which people belong can be expressed through art.)* Have students think about another culture that expresses their beliefs and traditions through brightly colored cloth. *(Possible answer: kente cloth of the Asante people in Africa)* Ask them to compare and contrast the art forms. **ELL Visual/Spatial**

V Visual Skills

Interpreting Ask students to study the designs on the mola in the photograph and to take note of the artwork. **Ask:** **Why do you think this Kuna woman has created a mola with these designs?** *(The birds and animals can be found in her surrounding environment.)* **What drives the use of color, and what colors make up the palette for this particular mola?** *(Possible answer: The mola may represent colors that are seen in nature)* Have students find out more about the flora and fauna of Panama to determine if the designs shown in this mola are representative of its environment. Invite volunteers to share their findings with the class. **AL Naturalist**

C Critical Thinking Skills

Making Predictions Discuss with students the factors that have affected the decrease in births per family in the region. **Ask:** **Based on what you have learned about women and education, what will the average household size, number of women in the workforce, and poverty level be like in the next decade? In 2050? Explain.** *(Possible answer: The family size may decrease slightly, women in the workforce will increase, and poverty levels may remain the same or improve slightly. Even though more opportunities have allowed women to delay childbearing, the social and economic challenges people face in this region are massive and will take many decades to eradicate.)* Have students consider ways countries can help women lead large families on their own. **Verbal/Linguistic**

ANSWERS, p. 204

✓ **READING PROGRESS CHECK** Rumba, salsa, Merengue, and Latin jazz are dance and music styles found in Central America and the Caribbean.

DBQ Document-Based Questions

1. Designs and images are not abstract concepts; they are part of the Kuna people's everyday social customs.
2. There are many designs of colorful birds. The clues include the display and the English writing.

ANALYZING PRIMARY SOURCES 

The Mola: Colorful Kuna Culture

Created by Kuna women in Panama, molas are made from layers of cloth that are cut and stitched into brightly colored, intricate designs. Molas are worn by Kuna women as part of their everyday garments and are inspired by ancient and contemporary sources.

R "... [T]he relation between designs and images lies at the core of the Kuna theory of personhood. Kuna people consider persons as formed by elements that have their own independent life in the universe, which are then transformed and molded into human bodies by adult people. The Kuna theory of visual art is therefore identical to their ontology [nature of their existence]; it provides people with categories to know the world. Concepts such as image and design are embedded in social praxis [customs] and not just abstract ones. Images and designs are not categories of the aesthetic; they are category of praxis [customs]."

—Paolo Fortis, *Kuna Art and Shamanism: An Ethnographic Approach*, 2012

V 

Molas are an important cultural art form and serve as a source of livelihood for those who sell them in markets to tourists.

DBQ ▲ CRITICAL THINKING

1. ***Interpreting Significance*** Describe the importance of designs and images to the Kuna people. RH.9–10.2
2. ***Analyzing Visuals*** Describe some of the motif-designs seen in the photo. What are the clues that suggest the molas pictured are intended to be sold to tourists?

attribute to explain by indicating a cause

traditional size and structure of families in Central America and the Caribbean. Fertility rates have decreased. Women are delaying childbearing as well as increasing their participation in the labor force. Increases in the number of working women are **attributed** to advancing levels of education, as well as to social movements promoting gender equality. Still, households living below the poverty line tend to be larger and headed by single women, or to contain at least one elderly person living alone or in charge of the household.

The Arts

Indigenous artisans living before the arrival of Columbus in the pre-Columbian era produced the earliest art forms in the region. These included stonework, woodcarving, pottery, metalwork, and weaving. For example, the stone Hieroglyphic Stairway in Copán, Honduras, an ancient Maya city, was carved with over a thousand symbols. The work of contemporary artisans often reflects this ancient heritage. In Guatemala today, hand-woven textiles display ancient Maya symbols and weaving techniques as well as modern influences.

Cross-cultural influences also combine to produce musical styles and dances unique to particular regions of Central America and the Caribbean. Styles evolved from multiple musical traditions. These include indigenous wind and percussion instruments, European string instruments, and African drums, rhythms, and dances. Many countries have their own distinct dance or music styles. Rumba and salsa originated in Cuba, while merengue began in the Dominican Republic and Haiti. Latin jazz permeates the cultures of Cuba and the Spanish Caribbean.

✓ **READING PROGRESS CHECK**

Evaluating What dance and music styles are found in Central America and the Caribbean?

204

networks Online Teaching Options

GAME

Human Geography of Central America and the Caribbean

Hypothesizing Before playing the game, ask students to consider a hypothetical situation: suppose a woman in the Kuna culture starts a business manufacturing molas and trains a non-Kuna man to help her make them. The man learns the trade, and then travels to the United States and mass-produces the products for his own business venture. Does he have the right to call them molas? As a class, discuss the students' responses. Then have students break into teams to play the game. **Interpersonal**

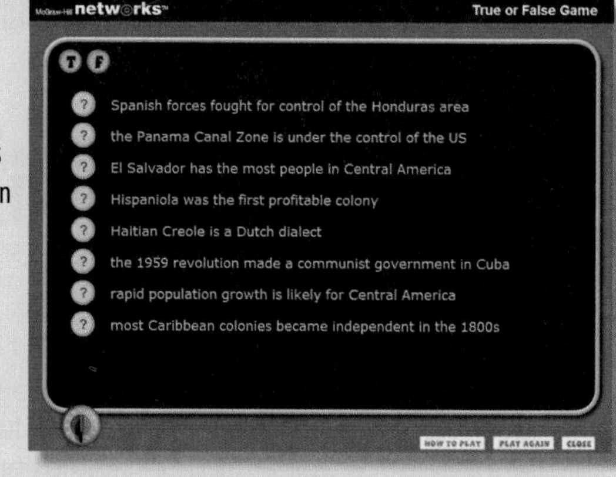

Economic Activities

GUIDING QUESTION *What economic factors have helped maintain an unequal distribution of wealth in Central America and the Caribbean?*

Countries in Central America and the Caribbean face the challenge of developing and diversifying economies in which wealth is unevenly distributed. In most Central American countries, agriculture employs more workers than other sectors. The legacy of the hacienda system hampers reform. Traditionally, these large farms were owned by wealthy families and worked by the poor. Such estates were known as ***latifundia***, and the relationships between landowners and workers persist even today, with corporations owning the land and the poor providing the labor. These highly mechanized operations yield high returns for low investment in labor. As mechanization increases, rural farmers and workers, or campesinos (kam•puh•SEE•nohs), leave and look for work in cities. Some campesinos still farm ***minifundia***, or small plots of land, to feed their families. However, workers rarely own the land and may be forced to work to pay off debts to landowners.

R

Some governments are passing laws to distribute farmland more fairly, and many campesinos have combined *minifundia* into large cooperative farms. But the legacy of economic inequality is difficult to overcome, and campesinos remain very poor. Large-scale growers farm cash crops, such as bananas, sugarcane, and coffee. Countries run **obvious** risks, however, if they depend on just one or two export products.

Many countries in the region are still considered less developed countries. In Central America, most industrial employment is in **cottage industries**, those which employ workers in their homes. Other industries include food, beverage, and tobacco processing and the production of textiles, clothing, shoes, furniture, and leather. In the Caribbean, manufacturing of textiles, electronics and clothing, oil refining, and offshore banking are important.

Service and technology industries have grown rapidly in recent years. In the Caribbean new types of tourism, such as **ecotourism**, provide new opportunities. The Dominican Republic, once dependent on sugar production, has capitalized on the telecommunications sector. Other new industries are offshore education, health services, and information technology. In 2005 the United States and six countries signed into law the Dominican Republic-Central American Free Trade Agreement (DR-CAFTA) to lower trade barriers.

latifundia in Latin America, large agricultural estates owned by families or corporations

minifundia in Latin America, small farms that produce food chiefly for family use

obvious easily discovered, seen, or understood

cottage industry a business that employs workers in their homes

ecotourism the practice and business of recreational travel based on concern for the environment

✓ **READING PROGRESS CHECK**

Describing What new industries are contributing to the Caribbean economy?

LESSON 2 REVIEW (CCSS)

Reviewing Vocabulary (Tier Three Words)

1. ***Inferring*** Describe the relationship between *latifundia* and *minifundia.* RH.9–10.4

Using Your Notes

2. ***Listing*** Use your graphic organizer to list the major religions practiced in Central America.

Answering the Guiding Questions

3. ***Evaluating*** How did colonialism influence the history and government of Central America and the Caribbean?
4. ***Finding the Main Idea*** How have migration and rapid growth affected the population of Central America and the Caribbean?
5. ***Identifying Cause and Effect*** How have the traditions and beliefs of indigenous peoples, Africans, and Europeans shaped society and culture in Central America and the Caribbean?
6. ***Identifying Central Issues*** What economic factors have helped maintain an unequal distribution of wealth in Central America and the Caribbean?

Writing Activity

7. ***Argument*** Write a paragraph describing why the hacienda system was not beneficial to the people of Central America and Caribbean and how it is still practiced in a form today. WHST.9–10.1

Human Geography of Central America and the Caribbean

R Reading Skills

Defining Ask a volunteer to read and define the italicized words. **Ask: What is the difference between a latifundia and a minifundia?** *(Both produce crops, but a latifundia produces crops for corporations, while minifundias are small farms that are used by families to grow their own food.)* **What smaller Spanish words in these two terms help you understand their meanings?** *(Lati [large] and mini [small])* **Are cottage industries similar or different? Explain.** *(They are different because they employ workers in their homes.)* Divide the class into three groups, assigning each one of the three terms. Have groups become experts on their assigned topic by gathering additional information. Then have groups share their topics and model the economic activities. **ELL Kinesthetic**

C Critical Thinking Skills

Evaluating Activate prior knowledge by asking students if they have or know someone who has participated as an ecotourist. Ask them to explain ecotourism, how it works, as well as how it has expanded in recent years. **Ask: Why is ecotourism a growing industry in this region?** *(Possible answer: Because the physical geography is rich and diverse, it attracts people to the area. Many tourists want to continue to travel, but they also care for the environment. This type of economic activity combines the two.)* **Will ecotourism become a more important industry than service and technology industries? Why or why not?** *(Possible answer: Service and technology industries will become important because the region cannot rely on tourism to support its economy. Tourism may fluctuate, affecting the service industry. However, the technology industry may not be as volatile.)* Have students write a paragraph explaining if they feel the region should further develop the ecotourism industry or further diversify their economy.
AL Verbal/Linguistic

CLOSE & REFLECT

Summarizing Have students describe the aspects of the various cultures of Central America and the Caribbean and the influence of the region's history on that diversity. Ask them to write a poem that expresses the unique blend of cultures in this region. Invite students to share their poems orally with the class.

LESSON 2 REVIEW ANSWERS

Reviewing Vocabulary

1. *Latifundia* are highly mechanized estates owned by corporations; *minifundia* are small plots of land farmed by, but rarely owned by, farmers to feed their families.

Using Your Notes

2. Catholicism is practiced by the most people in Central America, with Protestant religions common where English is spoken. Other faiths include Hinduism, Islam, and Native American and African religions.

Answering the Guiding Questions

3. Forced labor, starvation, and European diseases destroyed a great deal of the population. Revolutions followed.
4. Many people migrate within the region, mainly to cities, to seek economic opportunities or to escape civil war and instability. When small land areas experience a rapid growth in population, population pressure occurs.
5. The blending of indigenous, European, African, and Asian cultures has created a distinct Latin American identity expressed through language, religion, traditions, and art.
6. The legacy of the *hacienda* system makes reform difficult. *Campesinos* who want to find work in cities are often prevented from leaving their *minifundia* by landowners, so *campesinos* remain very poor.

Writing Activity

7. Paragraphs should show knowledge of the *hacienda* system, *latifundia, minifundia,* and their economic and social impacts.

ANSWERS, p. 205

✓ **READING PROGRESS CHECK** New industries include: service and technology industries, new types of tourism, telecommunications, offshore education, health services, and information technology.

ENGAGE

C1 Critical Thinking Skills

Analyzing Visuals Direct students' attention to the image. **Ask:** **Based on the photograph, what do you think the standard of living is in Haiti? Explain why.** *(Student answers may vary, but should infer from the damaged building and rubble that Haiti has a poor standard of living.)* Then ask a volunteer to read aloud the first sentence. Review Human Development Index (HDI) with students. *(measures life expectancy, levels of education, income, health care, and living standards in a region)* Tell students to consider these factors as they read about development in Haiti.

TEACH & ASSESS

C2 Critical Thinking Skills

Drawing Inferences Ask a volunteer to read aloud the last sentence of the first paragraph. **Ask:** **What do you think are the short-term effects of low school attendance for Haitian children?** *(Student answers may vary, but should include relevant effects of low school attendance.)* **What might be some of the long-term effects of a poorly educated population?** *(Student answers may vary, but should mention long-term impacts such as a lack of job opportunities.)* **Verbal/Linguistic**

Content Background Knowledge

Haiti's Political History Even before the 2010 earthquake devastated Haiti, the country had been mired in political turmoil and violence. Though the country declared its independence in 1804, political tensions prevailed. A series of uprisings and revolts followed the Great Depression. Then Haiti endured 28 years of tyranny and violence under the dictator Francois Duvalier, known as Papa Doc, and his son, Jean-Claude, "Baby Doc." After the Duvaliers were driven from power, President Jean-Bertrand became Haiti's president, working as an advocate for the poor and underprivileged until 2004. Despite ongoing violence throughout governments, Haiti has managed to hold democratic elections. Michel Martelly, a Haitian musician, became president in 2011.

T Technology Skills

Identifying Central Issues Lead a class discussion about development in Haiti, explaining that foreign aid can be crucial to a struggling country, especially after a natural disaster. Have students work in small groups to identify and research the countries and organizations that provided foreign aid to Haiti after the 2010 earthquake. Have students present a short report about the countries that provided aid, the type and amount of aid, and if the countries faced obstacles in getting aid to Haiti.
BL Interpersonal, Verbal/Linguistic

WHAT KIND OF DEVELOPMENT IS BEST FOR HAITI?

The Human Development Index ranks Haiti as the poorest country in the Western Hemisphere. Most of the population lives in absolute poverty, while a large percentage is unemployed or underemployed. Health care resources, including basic sanitation systems, are lacking. Although education is required for children between the ages of six and twelve, only a small percentage of children actually attend school because of a lack of facilities and staff.

In geography, the term *development* refers to improvements in the social and economic welfare of people as well as improvements in production and technology. The ways in which a country experiences development vary greatly—from NGO (nongovernmental organization) programs to government initiatives to foreign business arrangements. Funding in the form of foreign aid, investments, and loans makes development possible, but such support often includes special requirements or limits.

A devastating magnitude 7.0 earthquake on January 12, 2010, reduced much of Port-au-Prince, Haiti, to rubble. Southern areas of the country were also affected. Buildings of all kinds—from shantytowns to hospitals to national landmarks—were damaged or completely collapsed. Telephone service and electricity were knocked out. According to reports, more than 300,000 people lost their lives and over 600,000 were displaced. Estimates show the total cost of the disaster to be between $8 billion and $14 billion. In October 2010, after the earthquake, one of history's worst cholera outbreaks hit Haiti. Cholera is a waterborne disease that is spread through contaminated water. The outbreak was made worse by the earthquake's destruction and lack of public sewage systems. Such loss has only served to magnify Haiti's need for economic and social development.

206

networks Online Teaching Options

INTERACTIVE IMAGE

Redevelopment of Haiti

Analyzing Images Display the interactive image of the devastation from the 2010 earthquake in Haiti and ask the following questions to the class to encourage their ability to improve visual analysis.

What do you see? What action is taking place? What outside influences do you notice in the image? What is the subjects' point of view? Do they know that they are being photographed? *(Student answers may vary slightly, but they should be able to identify significant details and supply reasonable explanations about the image.)*
AL Visual/Spatial, Verbal/Linguistic

Create Market Opportunities

PRIMARY SOURCE

“Haiti has duty-free, quota-free access to the American market guaranteed for the next nine years, with generous rules of origin well-suited to the garment industry. . . .

Of course, market access is not enough: costs of production must be globally competitive. . . . In garments the largest single component of costs is labour. Due to its poverty and relatively unregulated labour market, Haiti has labour costs that are fully competitive with China, which is the global benchmark.

Market access and costs of production are not the only factors of importance: transport to market is also a fundamental consideration. . . . Haiti is on the doorstep of its market. Since it is the only low-wage economy in the region, it has a transport advantage over competing low-wage economies of several thousand miles. . . .”

—Paul Collier, *Haiti: From Natural Catastrophe to Economic Security*, A Report for the Secretary General of the United Nations, January 2009

Develop Local Agriculture

PRIMARY SOURCE

“Municipal governments should construct properly equipped marketplaces for the women who sell rural produce. The Haitian state should develop trade policies aimed at protecting the agricultural sector, and take the lead in fixing roads and ports, confronting deforestation and improving systems of water management. . . .

The return on the investment in the rural economy would be self-reliance, the alleviation of dangerous overcrowding in cities and, most important, a path toward ending Haiti's now chronic problems of malnutrition and food insecurity. . . .”

—Laurent Dubois and Deborah Jenson, “Haiti can be rich again,” *New York Times*, January 8, 2012

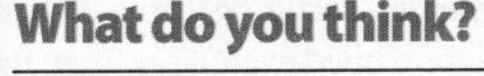

What do you think? DBQ

1. ***Drawing Conclusions*** According to Collier, why is the garment industry an ideal market opportunity for Haiti?
2. ***Identifying Central Issues*** Why do Dubois and Jenson argue that protecting the agricultural sector is best for Haitian development?
3. ***Evaluating*** Who do you think makes the stronger argument, Collier or Dubois and Jenson? Explain.

WORKSHEET

Location Activity

Locating This Location Activity worksheet allows students to comprehend the spatial relationship between countries and major cities located in Latin America. Before students complete this worksheet, display a map of Central America and the Caribbean and ask a volunteer to point to the county to Haiti. Then guide a class discussion by asking students to review what they know about the Ring of Fire and the physical geographical threats that Haiti faces because of its location. **Visual/Spatial, Interpersonal**

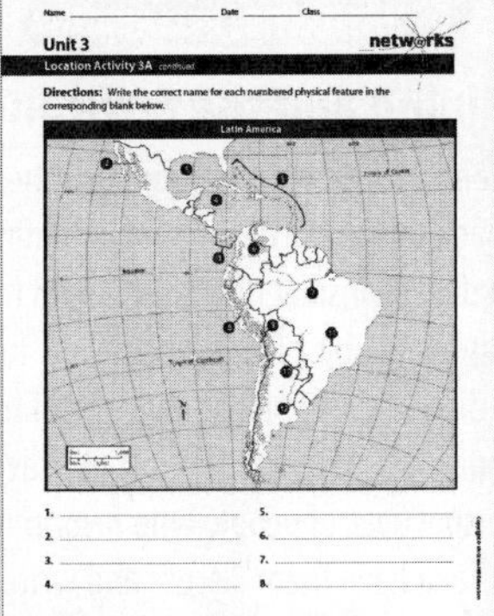

R Reading Skills

Paraphrasing Have a student volunteer read the first two paragraphs aloud. Then have students work in pairs to paraphrase them, looking up unfamiliar words in the dictionary. Call on teams to read their paraphrases to the class, offering corrective guidance if needed. **Ask:** **What does the phrase *unregulated labour market* mean?** *(Possible answer: If the labor market is unregulated, there is no government oversight, so companies can pay and charge what they want.)* **What does Collier mean by stating that China is the “global benchmark” regarding the cost of labor?** *(Possible answer: He means that in economies around the world, China is the most competitive because it has the lowest cost of labor.)*

AL Verbal/Linguistic

V Visual Skills

Spatial Understanding/Transferring Information Have students reread the third paragraph. **Ask:** **What does Collier mean in the statement “Haiti is on the doorstep of its market”?** *(Possible answer: He means that Haiti has a geographical advantage in the market.)* **What context clues help you to determine the phrase's meaning?** *(“it is the only low-wage economy in the region” and “transport advantage”)* Have students create a visual display that depicts the position Haiti has in the global market and in the garment industry. Encourage students to create a flow chart or illustration that interprets how Haiti is “on the doorstep” of its market. **Visual/Spatial**

CLOSE & REFLECT

Narrative Have students write a short narrative describing what it must be like to live in Haiti. Students may wish to write their narratives in the form of a journal entry told from a Haitian child's point of view, a short skit depicting daily struggles for a family in the country, or a song or poem about the hardships endured by people who live there. Invite students to share their narratives with the class.

ANSWERS, p. 207

DBQ What do you think?

1. Duty-free, quota-free access to the American market, labor costs that are competitive with China, and a transport advantage make the garment industry an ideal market opportunity for Haiti.
2. The results of investing in the rural economy would be self-reliance, the alleviation of dangerous overcrowding in cities, and a way to end malnutrition and food insecurity.
3. Responses should express a clear opinion regarding the stronger argument and should be strongly supported by content from the text.

ENGAGE

C1 Critical Thinking Skills

Interpreting Direct students to work in pairs and brainstorm factors that affect the development of the economies of countries in Central America and the Caribbean, as well as the preservation of the region's resources. Then in a class discussion, provide an opportunity for students to share the factors, as well as ideas on how the region can work to balance human needs with practices to sustain the environment.

TEACH & ASSESS

V Visual Skills

Creating Graphs Have students reread the section. **Ask:** Based on what you have already read in the chapter, what can you infer about the beginning of water disputes in Central America? *(Two hundred years ago much of Central America was controlled by Europeans who had colonized the area. The conflict would most likely have erupted during or shortly after the colonization period.)* Combine students into groups to research water usage in Central America and the Caribbean over the last 5 to 10 years and, if possible, projected use for the next 5 or 10 years. Ask students to select three countries in the region to research and to plot the data on a graph. Have groups present their graphs to the class, and then use the graphs for students to draw conclusions about the region's current and future use of freshwater.
BL Visual/Spatial, Naturalist

C2 Critical Thinking Skills

Analyzing Invite a volunteer to identify the swamp island on the Chapter Opener map. Discuss with students the conflict between Costa Rica and Nicaragua. **Ask:** Why did Costa Rica ask the United Nations for help? *(Costa Rica's government was not making any progress dealing with Nicaragua.)* Based on Costa Rica's actions after the Nicaraguan forces withdrew, do you think that Costa Rica is invested in protecting the environment? Explain. *(Possible answer: Yes, Costa Rica's actions illustrate that Costa Rica is encouraging sustainable environmental practices.)* Invite volunteers to provide an update on this issue by conducting online research.
Verbal/Linguistic

ANSWERS, p. 208

TAKING NOTES: Managing Resources—Issues related to waterways are a concern for the region; **Human Impact**—High pollution rates endanger people; **Addressing the Issues**—Cooperation in addressing issues reaching beyond national borders will help the region move forward.

networks

There's More Online!

- **IMAGE** Deforestation in Central America
- **IMAGE** Urban Pollution in Central America
- **IMAGE** Pollution of Freshwater Sources
- **INTERACTIVE SELF-CHECK QUIZ**
- **VIDEO** People and Their Environment: Central America and the Caribbean

LESSON 3

People and Their Environment: Central America and the Caribbean

ESSENTIAL QUESTION • *How do physical systems and human systems shape a place?*

Reading **HELP**DESK

Academic Vocabulary (Tier Two Words)
- **cooperation**
- **sustainable**

Content Vocabulary (Tier Three Words)
- **sedimentation**
- **reforestation**

TAKING NOTES: ***Key Ideas and Details***

IDENTIFYING Use a graphic organizer like the one below to take notes as you read about the issues relating to people and their environment in Central America and the Caribbean.

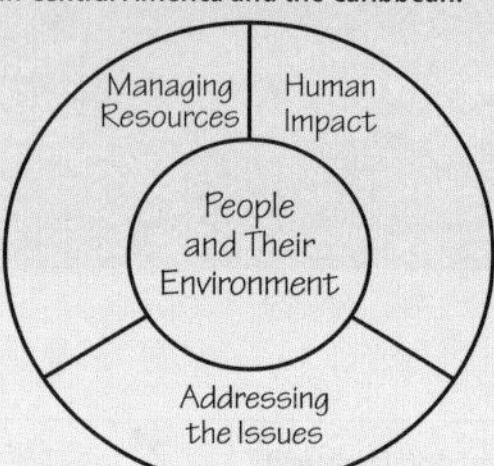

IT MATTERS BECAUSE

C1 *People and governments in Central America and the islands of the Caribbean struggle to develop modern economies without destroying the natural environment and the invaluable resources and biodiversity it provides. Balancing the needs of humans with sustainable environmental practices is both an important goal and a major challenge for countries of the subregion.*

Managing Resources

GUIDING QUESTION *How do growing human needs affect resources and the environment in Central America and the Caribbean?*

Countries in Central America and the Caribbean face a daunting challenge: How can they preserve and manage their resources while developing their economies and meeting the increasing needs of a growing population? Water shortages, access to freshwater, and legal issues related to waterways are a big concern for several countries in the subregion. Urban populations in Central America and the Caribbean increase at a rate that strains their cities' ability to provide freshwater for personal and industrial use. V

Water has been at the center of border disputes throughout Central America's history. The latest dispute is part of a conflict that is two centuries old. It involves a wetlands area that is part of a nature reserve owned by Costa Rica. The conflict erupted in October 2010 when Nicaragua began a controversial dredging project to redirect the San Juan River—a Nicaraguan-controlled waterway that forms part of the border—and posted Nicaraguan troops at the site. Costa Rica and other neighboring countries asked to have the troops withdrawn. The Nicaraguan government refused, saying it was reclaiming a natural resource. Costa Rica took the dispute to the United Nations. The United Nations ordered all troops to withdraw. This allowed Costa Rica to monitor potential damage to the wetlands environment, but did not stop Nicaragua from clearing sand from the river's channel. C2

networks Online Teaching Options

INTERACTIVE BELLRINGER

Mining and the Environment

Identifying Perspectives Use the introductory text and the image to discuss the impact of mining on the environment. Have students consider how they would feel if they knew a local mine was owned by a foreign company. In small groups, ask students to discuss their prior knowledge of mining in the United States and in less developed countries. Have students identify the perspectives of people who favor mining and people who oppose it. Then have them discuss and write agreed-upon answers to the questions. BL Interpersonal, Verbal/Linguistic

Mining and the Environment

In Guatemala, almost 400 mining concessions have been granted to transnational gold, silver, nickel, and zinc companies.

Auto-Run Click Through

To increase the power supply necessary for industry, some countries in Central America and the Caribbean turn to the construction of hydroelectric power plants. Such plants are located within human-made dams that raise the level of water so that when intake channels are opened, water flows rapidly through the dams, turning water turbines. The water turbines capture the energy of fast-falling or flowing water and produce electricity from generators.

Costa Rica benefits from the power generated by hydroelectric plants. The plants supply energy to Costa Rica's industries, allowing them to increase production capabilities and become more competitive in international trade. In the early twenty-first century, about four-fifths of Costa Rica's electricity was produced from hydroelectric plants. Hydroelectric dams promote clean energy use by harnessing the power of water, a renewable resource. **T**

However, hydroelectric systems threaten the natural environment of the areas from which they extract energy. The interaction of plant and animal species within an ecosystem is very sensitive and complex. Fish habitats, for example, are affected by factors such as water level, water velocity, and the availability of food and shelter from predators. The flooding created by hydroelectric dams dramatically alters the habitats and devastates native fish populations. Hydroelectric projects on El Salvador's Lempa River provide most of the country's power needs. These dams harm the natural environment, however, because of changing water levels and the construction of roads through otherwise unaffected landscapes. Similarly, the hydroelectric project on the Patuca River in Honduras blocks fish migrations, alters habitats, and threatens the survival of the region's indigenous population who depend on the environment.

Central America boasts a biodiversity hotspot with naturally fertile soil. Yet much of the subregion's timberland has been cleared by slash-and-burn farmers. In this process of cultivation, all plants are cut down and any trees are stripped of bark. After the plants and trees have dried out, they are set on fire. The ash from the fire adds nutrients to the soil, making agriculture more productive. Unfortunately, frequent rains leach away the beneficial nutrients and within a year or two the soil loses its fertility. Crop yields decline due to poor soils, and farmers move on to clear new parts of the forest. The spent land supports little growth of vegetation. Within just a few years, huge swaths of centuries-old rain forests have disappeared. **W**

Deforestation is a major threat to biodiversity as shown here in Panama and throughout Central America and the Caribbean.

◀ **CRITICAL THINKING**

1. ***Analyzing Visuals*** What features of the land shown in the forest signify that deforestation has taken place?
2. ***Predicting*** How does the destruction of rain forests affect biodiversity?

INTERACTIVE MAP

2010 Earthquake in Haiti

Identifying Cause and Effect This map shows the destructive path of an earthquake in Haiti that can be used to help students understand the relationship between human activity and natural disasters. Discuss ways in which deforestation affects the soil. Then review possible causes for earthquakes as discussed in earlier chapters. Have students consider if soil erosion could have caused this massive earthquake. Ask them to write a brief paragraph explaining their answer. **Verbal/Linguistic**

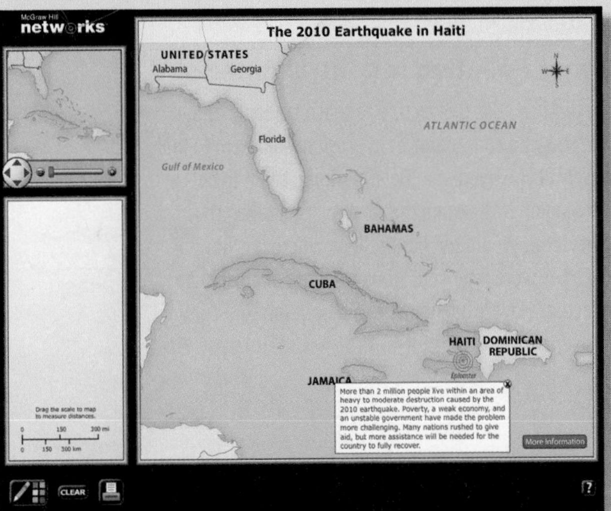

People and Their Environment: Central America and the Caribbean

T Technology Skills

Diagramming Review the definition of *hydroelectricity* with students and then have them work together to find out how a hydroelectric dam works. Ask them to create a sketch or 3-D model and to label it so that each step of the process is clear. Point out that students may make their models digitally and even add interactive elements. Provide an opportunity for students to share their models with the class. Then discuss whether students think the benefits outweigh the costs of building more dams and hydroelectric plants in the subregion. **ELL Logical/Mathematical**

Content Background Knowledge

Hydroelectric Power About half of Central America's renewable energy comes from hydroelectricity. In Costa Rica in particular, nearly 90 percent of the country's energy is produced by hydroelectricity. One project in Costa Rica, El Diquí, has been proposed but has undergone much criticism. The building of this project would not only displace more than 1,000 people but would also threaten the ecosystem, including the area's mangroves. Debate and resistance to the project continues.

W Writing Skills

Argument Assign students the following prompt with half of the class writing in support of current environmental practices in Central America and the other half writing in support of a change in environmental practices in the subregion: **Should the government set restrictions on the clearing of rain forests for agricultural purposes?** Remind students to introduce their claim in the form of a thesis statement and to support their claim with reasons and evidence. Point out that they will make their argument stronger and more appealing to their audience if they use formal language and address counterclaims. Have students present their arguments to the class in the form of a debate. **AL Verbal/Linguistic**

ANSWERS, p. 209

CRITICAL THINKING

1. The deforested area is brown and covered with tree trunks; very little is growing there.
2. Biodiversity is severely threatened. Habitats are destroyed as the forest dwindles, leading to a loss of plant and animal life.

R Reading Skills

Understanding Relationships Write these terms on the board: *slash-and-burn cultivation* and *commercial logging.* Working with a partner, have students list important causes and effects of each. Then have students create a word web with *deforestation* in the center oval, adding the details they listed. Then have them write a brief statement explaining the relationship between the two terms and deforestation, as well as the challenges they pose to the people and environment of this region. **ELL Interpersonal**

Content Background Knowledge

Exploring for Oil Deforestation and slash and burn are not the only causes for the loss of forests in the region; they are also being cleared for oil exploration. In Belize, a U.S. company received government approval to engage in exploratory drilling in Sarstoon Temash National Park. The park is home to a protected wetland, endemic species, and the only known comfra palm forest in the country.

C Critical Thinking Skills

Analyzing Cause and Effect Discuss with students the urban problems that are associated with the growth of cities in the United States and then compare these to the concerns found in this region. **Ask:** **How does the expansion of slums affect biodiversity in the region?** *(Possible answer: As more people move to the cities, the inner city becomes crowded, so they move outward, encroaching on areas important to the subregion's biodiversity.)* **What is the impact of overpopulation in the cities on humans?** *(Unsanitary conditions can lead to illnesses and the spread of diseases.)* Have students write a journal entry or blog from the perspective of a person who has moved to a large city in Central America in search of employment, which describes the conditions and challenges that they face. **Verbal/Linguistic, Intrapersonal**

R Slash-and-burn cultivation is not the only activity that contributes to deforestation, or the clearing or destruction of forests. Commercial logging operations are key components of the region's economies. The logging companies harvest trees for timber and other products, which are sold as exports.

As Central American forests are depleted, habitats are lost, resources are threatened, and Earth's biodiversity dwindles. Deforestation severely alters biologically rich ecosystems of tropical rain forests and threatens various species of plants and organisms from which key medicines are derived. Scientists are trying to save species from extinction by creating corridors of vegetation that connect remaining areas of the forest to provide animals with access to habitats. Deforestation may also mean that less carbon dioxide is captured in plants. This would cause higher levels of carbon dioxide to remain in the atmosphere.

✓ READING PROGRESS CHECK

Gathering Information What are the effects of slash-and-burn farming?

Human Impact

GUIDING QUESTION *Why is soil erosion and soil decline such an issue in Central America and the Caribbean?*

C As cities in Central America and the Caribbean experience rapid urbanization, population growth exceeds available resources like housing, running water, sewage systems, and electricity. Rural workers migrating to cities often cannot find jobs or adequate housing. Thousands are forced to live in slums or shantytowns on the edges of cities. Such communities often rest on dangerous slopes and near delicate wetlands. Mud slides, floods, and other natural disasters can wipe out entire communities. Because they lack running water and underground sewage systems, these areas are unsanitary. As a result, disease can spread rapidly. Cities that expand rapidly may also encroach on natural landscapes that have previously been untouched by human impact.

Runoff from chemical fertilizers and pesticides used on commercial farms pollutes freshwater sources in Central America and the Caribbean.

CRITICAL THINKING ▼

1. ***Assessing*** Explain how water pollution can affect areas far from the source of the pollution.
2. ***Hypothesizing*** How could pollution in waters cause sickness in humans even if it is not used for drinking?

210

networks ***Online Teaching Options***

INTERACTIVE IMAGE

Water Pollution in Central America

Predicting Use this picture to teach students about patterns and consequences of erosion. Ask them to look closely at the riverbank. Does anything seem to be growing on it? Imagine the same picture taken ten years later. Would the bank still be where it is now? If the trees were removed, would the rate of erosion be affected? Have students write a paragraph to answering these questions. **BL Verbal/Linguistic**

ANSWERS, p. 210

✓ **READING PROGRESS CHECK** It destroys forests and causes soil to erode and lose fertility over time.

CRITICAL THINKING

1. Currents can carry pollutants far away from the source.
2. Contaminants in the water can be absorbed by crops or remain on the outside of the crop. If fruits and vegetables aren't washed or cooked thoroughly, a person can get sick.

The rapid growth of cities creates high pollution rates from overloaded sewage, electric, and water systems. Air pollution affects people in cities without adequate clean-air laws. Vehicles clog city streets and release massive amounts of exhaust (greenhouse gases) into the air. Industrial pollutants from factory smokestacks built by multinational firms under free-trade agreements also foul the air. Similarly, runoff from chemical fertilizers and pesticides used on commercial farms damages oceans and freshwater areas, including the Caribbean's coral reefs.

City sewage is a major contributor to water pollution in Central America.

▲ CRITICAL THINKING

1. ***Analyzing Visuals*** What items in the photograph could pose a threat to sea animals?
2. ***Describing*** In what way could the pollution shown be an effect of rapid urbanization? Explain.

As cities in Central America and the Caribbean grow, the demand for food also increases. The effect of expanding agriculture on the natural environment can be devastating. To increase food supplies, Central American farmers and ranchers clear forested regions, which not only destroys forests but also causes the soil to erode and lose fertility over time. In the Caribbean, small islands colonized for intensive plantation agriculture became prone to soil erosion because of the elimination of natural vegetation. Furthermore, after more than 300 years of commercial agriculture, soil fertility has decreased to the point where large applications of fertilizer are necessary for plant production.

Another factor affecting vegetation loss and soil erosion is the construction of hotels and other structures to support the tourism industry. As rain falls, it washes soil eroded by construction and farming down hills and into the sea, resulting in the **sedimentation** of the reef system. Ultimately, sedimentation may kill coral beds in the water. When fertilizers also become part of the runoff into the sea, they damage coral further and threaten the hundreds of fish species, marine turtles, and sharks that live in the reefs. Communities that depend on the reefs for their livelihoods and food security are also affected.

sedimentation the action or process of forming or depositing sediment

☑ READING PROGRESS CHECK

Assessing How has human activity influenced soil erosion and its threat to coral reefs?

Addressing the Issues

GUIDING QUESTION *Why is biodiversity protection so important in Central America?*

Central America and the Caribbean face many international challenges, including conflicts over natural resources and the need to prepare for wide-scale natural disasters. Regional **cooperation** in addressing issues that reach beyond national borders will help the subregion move forward. Government, private industries and grassroots efforts all contribute to protecting the environment.

If the issue of deforestation is not addressed, the rain forests of this subregion will be greatly reduced within 40 years. Although the threats to the world's rain forests are well known, the proposed strategies for preserving them are hotly debated. For instance, Costa Rica and other countries with rain forests listen to the advice of scientists and environmentalists, but they still face pressing social and economic realities. If Costa Rica were to ban the use of rain forest lands, for example, how would it provide for the people who would no longer have a way to support themselves? How would the country handle

cooperation a common effort

sustainable a method of harvesting or using a resource so that the resource is not depleted or permanently damaged

reforestation planting young trees or seeds on lands where trees have been cut or destroyed

VIDEO

The Caribbean

Speculating Use this video to discuss how the aquatic environment of the Caribbean is vulnerable to damage from human activities. Ask students to discuss how the ocean enriches the lives of the people who live in the Caribbean. With a partner, have students write a list of possible ways that urban growth and the development of tourism in the area might contribute to the environmental issues in the Caribbean. Have volunteers share their lists with the class.
Logical/Mathematical, Naturalist

People and Their Environment: Central America and the Caribbean

G1 Critical Thinking Skills

Creating and Analyzing Arguments Have students work in pairs to create an ad campaign against dumping garbage and other wastes. They may create a digital ad campaign or a static one. Have students show their ads to the class. Then, allow students to evaluate the campaigns, noting which ones were most effective and why. BL **Visual/Spatial**

R Reading Skills

Using Context Clues Have students identify context clues that help them understand the meaning of *sedimentation. (runoff; eroded)* With students, demonstrate how sedimentation occurs. Place a board inside a plastic tray. Pour sand on the tray, and then pour a small amount of water on the sand, angling the board so the sand and water run off, leaving sediment. Allow students to try the experiment on their own and to record the results. Have them repeat the experiment several times, measuring the amount of sediment that is eroded each time.
Ask: How did this experiment help you understand what sedimentation is and how if affects coral beds? *(Student answers may vary, but should be supported.)* ELL **Kinesthetic**

Content Background Knowledge

Coral Reef In 2013, the Environmental Protection Agency (EPA) launched the Caribbean Coral Reef Protection Group to work with the Caribbean governments to save and protect the coral reef ecosystem. Coral reefs serve vital purposes, including providing a habitat for many fish, protecting land from storm surges, and incubating organisms used in pharmaceutical manufacturing.

G2 Critical Thinking Skills

Evaluating Discuss with students the different challenges that the subregion faces with regard to managing its resources.
Ask: What obstacles do some countries face when dealing with protection issues? *(Possible answers: issues relating to lack of funds; lack of political or corporate support.)* Ask students to write a proposal to the government of Costa Rica on how to best address the social, economic, and environmental challenges the country faces. Invite students to share their proposals with the class. **Verbal/Linguistic**

ANSWERS, p. 211

☑ READING PROGRESS CHECK Runoff from chemical fertilizers and pesticides damages coral reefs. Soil eroded by construction and farming is washed into the sea, resulting in the sedimentation of the reef system, which may kill coral beds.

CRITICAL THINKING

1. Plastic chairs and bags could pose this threat.
2. The rapid growth of cities creates high pollution rates, including a lack of proper waste disposal.

People and Their Environment: Central America and the Caribbean

R Reading Skills

Differentiating After students read the paragraph about sustainable development, discuss the difference between deforestation and reforestation. Point out how the prefix *re-* means "again" and the prefix *de-* means "to take away" or is the opposite of the noun or verb to which it is attached. Have them look for other words in the paragraph with prefixes such as *bio-* in *biodiversity* and suffixes such as *-tion* in *conservation*. Discuss how understanding the meaning of prefixes and suffixes can help to break down words into smaller parts. **Ask:** **In the next paragraph, what do you think *renewable* means?** *(something that can be new again)* **What word is the opposite of *renewable*?** *(nonrenewable)* Have students write three or four sentences using each word from this activity to demonstrate their understanding. ELL **Verbal/Linguistic**

T Technology Skills

Exploring Issues Discuss with students how different groups are working corroboratively to address the region's challenges and needs. **Ask:** **Why are laws and programs not enough to combat these challenges?** *(Possible answer: Because some factors are out of the control of humans, such as weather.)* Ask students to find out more about recent issues in the region and how groups and governments are tackling them. Have students gather information from print and electronic sources, examine the issue, and then write about whether they see potential for the issue to be resolved. Ask them to cite evidence to support their point of view. Have students present their findings to the class. AL **Logical/Mathematical**

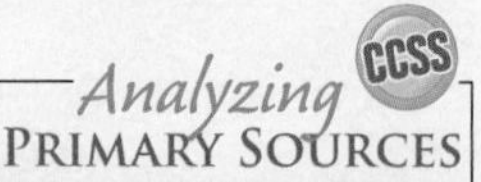

Analyzing PRIMARY SOURCES

Indigenous Communities Protect Biodiversity

"José López Hernández, a member of the Oxlajuj No'j tribe, would chop down trees in Santa Maria de Jesus, Guatemala, before IDB (Inter-American Development Bank) started a project to restore local traditions and culture as a way to prevent further land degradation and to preserve the region's biodiversity.

Now Hernández is a leader of his indigenous community and is working, together with another 600 families, to plant 60,000 new trees by the end of the year using traditional organic methods."

—Silvia Lambiase, "Indigenous communities in Central America use traditions to protect biodiversity," Platform for Agrobiodiversity Research, May 2011

DBQ ***HYPOTHESIZING*** Based on the passage above, what can be inferred about the traditional organic methods in regard to biodiversity? RH.9–10.2

R population growth in coastal areas if vast parts of the interior were not open to settlement? Some of these answers lie in **sustainable** development—technological and economic growth that does not deplete the human and natural resources of a given area. Given time, of course, rain forests would regenerate on their own, but with a considerable loss of biodiversity. Laws requiring **reforestation**—the planting of young trees or the seeds of trees on the land that has been stripped—can help. Developing new methods of farming, mining, and logging and combining conservation with responsible tourism protect the forests and boost local economies.

Initiatives are also underway across Central America to develop "green businesses." The businesses include environmentally-friendly organic food production, renewable energy, and sustainable tourism. Large industries are looking at ways to increase energy efficiency and improve production practices in an effort to be more environmentally friendly.

T Governments, international agencies, and grassroots groups are beginning to address the needs of the subregion's urban areas. Work is being done to create programs that limit rural-to-urban migration and to improve the infrastructure of cities. Programs that encourage cooperation with other countries to establish incentives for industries to reduce pollution have also been implemented. A United Nation's initiative in Central America called Reducing Emissions from Deforestation and Forest Degradation, or REDD+, is a program of environmental credits. PRODESEC (Economic Development Program for the Dry Region of Nicaragua) is a Nicaraguan plan aimed at providing new opportunities for rural families. Environmental laws and programs, however, have not reduced the risks of increased pollution associated with industrial growth.

Human activity is not the only source of potential problems for Central America and the Caribbean. The physical geography of the region leaves the area vulnerable to extreme weather-related disasters, such as hurricanes and floods, as well as devastating earthquakes. In order to increase the region's emergency preparedness, governments are cooperating in the use of sophisticated technology, such as satellite imaging and computer modeling, to forecast the direction and severity of natural disasters such as hurricanes.

Scientists are also gathering detailed information about volcanic eruptions in the Caribbean. Since a 1997 major volcanic eruption in Montserrat, scientists are closely monitoring the volcano, which continues to be active. Montserrat's volcano is similar to those on other continents, so the information and lessons learned will help produce more detailed forecasts and predictions around the world.

✓ READING PROGRESS CHECK

Exploring Issues Why is reforestation so important?

LESSON 3 REVIEW

Reviewing Vocabulary (Tier Three Words)

1. ***Determining Importance*** What is the significance of sedimentation and reforestation? RH.9–10.4

Using Your Notes

2. ***Describing*** Use your graphic organizer to describe the threats to coral reefs from development and pollution.

Answering the Guiding Questions

3. ***Assessing*** How do growing human needs affect resources and the environment in Central America and the Caribbean?

4. ***Explaining*** Why is soil erosion and decline such an issue in Central America and the Caribbean?

5. ***Applying*** Why is biodiversity protection so important in Central America?

Writing Activity

6. ***Informative/Explanatory*** Think about the physical environment of the state in which you live. In two paragraphs, compare the ways urban populations in Central America and those in your state have modified their physical environments. WHST.9–10.2

212

CLOSE & REFLECT

Summarizing Review with students the many challenges that Central America and the Caribbean face, both human and physical. Discuss the solutions and actions that have recently been taken. Then ask students to determine what they think is the biggest concern of the region and the steps needed to resolve it.

ANSWERS, p. 212

✓ **READING PROGRESS CHECK** Planting young trees or the seeds of trees on the land that has been stripped is faster than letting rain forests regenerate on their own and maintains biodiversity.

DBQ Traditional methods are more effective in maintaining biodiversity.

LESSON 3 REVIEW ANSWERS

Reviewing Vocabulary

1. Eroded soil is washed down hills and into the sea, resulting in the sedimentation of the reef system, which may kill coral beds. Reforestation replaces forest that has been removed much more quickly and helps preserve biodiversity.

Using Your Notes

2. Runoff from chemical fertilizers and pesticides damages oceans and freshwater areas, including coral reefs. Rain washes eroded soil into the sea, which results in sedimentation and may kill coral beds.

Answering the Guiding Questions

3. Population growth strains and damages the environment, and it depletes resources.

4. Soil erosion can damage coral reefs; it can also result in fewer crops. Farmers try to boost productivity by using slash-and-burn techniques to fertilize the soil, leading to deforestation and soil erosion.

5. Without biodiversity, plant and animal species are depleted or disappear completely. People will not be able to utilize these resources for survival and support.

Writing Activity

6. Responses should address specifics of the physical environment of the student's state and should compare modification of physical environment in the student's state to that of Central America. Responses should be supported by content from the text.

Directions: On a separate sheet of paper, answer the questions below. Make sure you read carefully and answer all parts of the questions.

Lesson Review

Lesson 1

1. ***Evaluating*** Which Central American waterways provide an important link among the region's countries? Give examples.
2. ***Identifying*** List some natural resources of the Central America and Caribbean subregion that are important to the global economy.

Lesson 2

3. ***Summarizing*** Describe the ways in which each of the following factors have influenced history and government in Central America and the Caribbean: indigenous cultures, colonialism, slavery, and struggles for freedom.
4. ***Identifying Cause and Effect*** What urban challenges have been caused by the migration of many people in Central America and the Caribbean to capital cities and major ports?

Lesson 3

5. ***Interpreting*** What does the phrase "sustainable development" mean? What is one example of sustainable development?
6. ***Identifying Central Issues*** Why is deforestation a major problem in Central America? Include reasons why many people cut down forests and reasons many others want to restore them.

Exploring the Essential Question

7. ***Speculating*** How do physical systems and human systems shape a place? Give specific examples showing why the highland regions have attracted human settlement and migration throughout Central America.

21st Century Skills

8. ***Analyzing*** Why is regional cooperation particularly important to address international challenges in Central America?
9. ***Compare and Contrast*** Create a chart of the countries in Central America, ranking them in order of population. Use the Internet to research the latest statistics.
10. ***Making Connections*** What circumstances might make environmental protection a low priority for some Central American people? List one government program aimed at meeting the needs of the people and protecting the environment.

College and Career Readiness

ETHNIC GROUPS IN THE CARIBBEAN

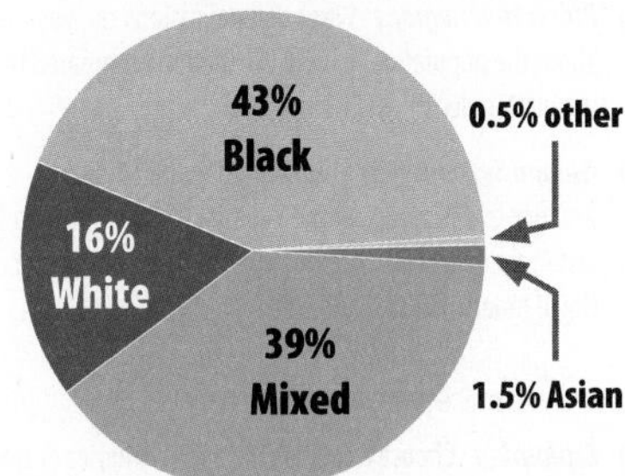

Source: Encyclopedia Britannica Almanac 2009

Use the circle graph to answer the questions below.

11. ***Draw Conclusions*** Based on what the circle graph shows about ethnic groups in the Caribbean, how do you think these ethnic groups are reflected in the culture of the subregion? RH.9–10.2
12. ***Compare and Contrast*** How does the percentage of White compare to the percentage of Mixed in the Caribbean? WHST.9–10.6

Need Extra Help?

If You've Missed Question	1	2	3	4	5	6	7	8	9	10	11	12
Go to page	197	199	200	202	212	210	199	211	202	211	213	213

CHAPTER 8 Assessment Answers

Lesson Review

Lesson 1

1. The Panama Canal allows ships to travel between the Atlantic and Pacific Oceans. Rivers are also commercial water routes. The San Juan River flows from Lake Nicaragua to the Caribbean Sea.
2. Natural resources include nickel, iron ore, fish, timber, and petroleum.

Lesson 2

3. By the mid-1600s, Europeans had almost wiped out indigenous people, leading to a labor shortage, so enslaved Africans were brought to Central America. By the late 1700s, Africans and Native Americans organized to gain their freedom. By 1804, Haiti won independence from France, giving rise to other struggles for independence.
4. Population pressure has resulted, which is the sum of factors within a population that reduce the ability of an environment to support the population.

Lesson 3

5. Sustainable development refers to a method of using resources so that they are not depleted. An example is new logging practices, which includes reforestation practices.
6. Farmers often remove trees using slash-and-burn techniques to add nutrient rich ash to the soil. The nutrients are washed away over time and deforestation of more land is necessary to grow crops. Commercial logging also results in deforestation. Many work to stop deforestation and restore forests, as they recognize the threats to biologically rich ecosystems; the loss of some species which provide key medicines; and the reduced ability to capture carbon dioxide in plants, resulting in higher levels in the atmosphere.

Exploring the Essential Question

7. The volcanic action from the Ring of Fire in the region has given rise to fertile soil. This results in rich agricultural zones. The mountains this volcanic activity created provide a cooler climate and natural resources. These factors attracted substantial settlement and migration.

21st Century Skills

8. The complex ecosystems, biodiversity, and regional resources of Central America cross national borders. This is particularly the case in the Central American subregion, where countries all inhabit a relatively narrow strip of land.
9. Charts should reflect the most recent statistics relative to the populations of countries in Central America.
10. The environment provides the means for people to earn an income, farm for food, and expand development to support increasing populations, which makes environmental protection a low priority in many countries. One government program is PRODESEC (Economic Development Program for the Dry Region of Nicaragua), a Nicaraguan plan aimed at providing new opportunities for 23,000 rural families.

College and Career Readiness

11. Black and Mixed ethnic groups are the predominant culture in the subregion.
12. The percentage of Mixed ethnic groups in the Caribbean is almost double the percentage of White ethnic groups in the region.

CHAPTER 8
Assessment Answers

Critical Thinking

13 There are three distinct belts: the Pacific Lowlands, the Caribbean Lowlands, and the Central Highlands. Mountains define many of the borders of these belts, which can result in isolation.

14 Students' paragraphs should include knowledge of the following: Spanish conquistadors' arrival; France, the Netherlands, and Portugal establishing colonies; Native American population succumbing to forced labor, starvation, and European diseases; enslaved Africans being brought to the region to work.

15 As altitude increases, the climate cools and there are distinct vertical climate zones. In the *tierra caliente* (hot land), bananas and sugarcane are grown; the *tierra templada* (temperate land) is densely populated; in the *tierra fria* (cold land), potatoes and barley are grown; in the *tierra helada,* (frozen land), there is permanent ice and snow.

Applying Map Skills

16 Central America is predominantly a tropical wet climate which supports tropical rain forests that have dense vegetation.

17 El Salvador is more densely populated than Honduras. Honduras has a greater land area while El Salvador is largely coastal.

18 Ships are able to travel the Pacific Ocean along the west coast of North America, Mexico, and Central America to Panama Canal, which allows them to cut across to the Atlantic Ocean into the Caribbean without traveling all the way along Cape Horn at the tip of South America.

Research and Presentation

19 The paragraph should reference a specific country in Central America, describe the landforms, and explain how the landforms affect trade within the country and with other countries.

Writing About Geography

20 The account should detail a cultural event important to people living in Central America or the Caribbean.

Analyzing Primary Sources

21 The parks benefit the economy by attracting ecotourism and related services, providing clean drinking water, and generating hydroelectricity.

22 Costa Rica's parks continue to face many threats, such as poaching; reliable funding is necessary to counter these threats in a prolonged, sustainable manner.

CHAPTER 8 Assessment 

Directions: On a separate sheet of paper, answer the questions below. Make sure you read carefully and answer all parts of the questions.

Critical Thinking

13 ***Exploring*** Describe how physical features have kept some of Central America's people isolated.

14 ***Drawing Conclusions*** Write a paragraph describing the series of events that led to the exploration, conquest, and colonization of Central America and the Caribbean.

15 ***Explaining*** Describe how elevation can affect the climate and ecosystems more than distance from the Equator in some parts of tropical Central America. Provide specific examples.

Applying Map Skills

Use your Unit 3 Atlas to answer the following questions.

16 ***Physical Systems*** What is the predominant type of natural vegetation found in Central America?

17 ***Places and Regions*** What generalizations can you make about the population density in Honduras compared to the population density of El Salvador?

18 ***Human Systems*** Use your mental map of Central America to describe how the Panama Canal saves travel distance and time for ocean travel from the west coast of North America to the Caribbean.

Research and Presentation

19 ***Explaining*** Choose a country in Central America or the Caribbean. Write a paragraph describing the landforms within that country. Explain how those landforms affect trade both within the country and with other countries.

Writing About Geography

20 ***Narrative*** Use the Internet to research and write a three-paragraph account of a cultural event, such as a festival, holiday, or music or dance concert, important to people living in Central America or the Caribbean. WHST.9–10.9

DBQ Analyzing Primary Sources

Read the excerpt and use it to answer the following questions.

At a summit on biodiversity in Japan, the World Future Council announced that Costa Rica had won the 2010 Future Policy award.

PRIMARY SOURCE

"Costa Rica channels funds from a fuel tax, car stamp duty and energy fees to pay for nature reserve management and environmental services like clean air, fresh water and biodiversity protection.

Landowners are paid to preserve old-growth forests and to plant new trees. As a result, forest cover has risen from 24% in 1985 to close to 46% today.

It has also established a national commission on biodiversity, comprising scientists, civil servants and indigenous representatives, which proposes policies to the government and promotes green education among the public.

'We are declaring peace with nature,' said Mario Fernández Silva, the ambassador of Costa Rica, referring also to his country's abolition of its army in 1958. 'We feel a strong sense of responsibility about looking after our wealth of biodiversity. Our attitude is not progressive; it is conservative. Our view is that until we know what we have, it is our duty to protect it.'"

—Jonathan Watts, "Costa Rica Recognized for Biodiversity Protection," The Guardian, October 2010

21 ***Assessing*** Why do you think Costa Rica decided to tax fuel, cars, and energy rather than other goods and services? WHST.9–10.8

22 ***Making Decisions*** What choices do you think individuals can make to help prevent the loss of rain forests and what incentives can governments provide?

Need Extra Help?

If You've Missed Question	13	14	15	16	17	18	19	20	21	22
Go to page	196	200	199	170	172	168	199	204	214	214

214

networks Online Teaching Options

WORKSHEET

Chapter Test and Lesson Quizzes

Assessing Have students complete the Chapter Test and Lesson Quizzes to assess student understanding throughout the chapter. These assessment tools offer chapter and lesson evaluation through a variety of question formats including document-based questions.

CHAPTER 9

South America Planner

UNDERSTANDING BY DESIGN®

Enduring Understandings

- *The characteristics and distribution of human populations affect physical and human systems.*

Essential Question

- *How do physical systems and human systems shape a place?*

Predictable Misunderstandings

Students may think:

- *The geography and climate is the same throughout South America. Explain that South America is a large continent with a variety of climates and geographical characteristics.*
- *People living in South America are all of Spanish descent. Explain that the cultures of South America are a mix of influences of Native Americans, many different types of Europeans, and Africans.*
- *Desertification only happens near deserts. Explain that desertification is the changing over of fertile land to unusable, dry land, and can happen anywhere.*

Assessment Evidence

Performance Tasks:

- *Hands-On Chapter Project*

Other Evidence:

- *Guided Reading Activities*
- *Vocabulary Activities*
- *Lesson Quizzes*
- *Chapter Tests, Forms A and B*

SUGGESTED PACING GUIDE

Introducing the Chapter	½ Day	Global Connections	1 Day
Lesson 1	1 Day	Lesson 3	1 Day
Lesson 2	2 Days	Chapter Wrap-Up and Assessment	½ Day
		TOTAL TIME	**6 Days**

National Geography Standards covered in "South America"

The student knows and understands:

(4) The physical and human characteristics of places

4.2 The interaction of physical and human systems result in the creation of and changes to places

(8) The characteristics and spatial distribution of ecosystems and biomes on Earth's surface

8.1 Ecosystems are dynamic and respond to changes in environmental conditions

(9) The characteristics, distribution, and migration of human populations on Earth's surface

9.2 Population distribution and density are a function of historical, environmental, economic, political, and technological factors

(15) How physical systems affect human systems

15.1 Depending on the choice of human activities, the characteristics of the physical environment can be viewed as both opportunities and constraints

15.3 Societies use a variety of strategies to adapt to changes in the physical environment

(16) The changes that occur in the meaning, use, distribution, and importance of resources

16.3 Policies and programs that promote the sustainable use and management of resources impact people and the environment

(17) How to apply geography and interpret the past

17.1 Geographic contexts (the human and physical characteristics of places and environments) can explain the connections between sequences of historical events

17.3 Historical events must be interpreted in the contexts of people's past perception of places, regions, and environments

(18) How to apply geography to interpret the present and plan for the future

18.1 Geographic contexts (the human and physical characteristics of places and environments) provide the bases for analyzing current events and making predictions about future issues

Key for Using the Teacher Edition

SKILL-BASED ACTIVITIES

Types of skill activities found in the Teacher Edition.

* **V Visual Skills** require students to analyze maps, graphs, charts, and photos.

R Reading Skills help students practice reading skills and master vocabulary.

C Critical Thinking Skills help students apply and extend what they have learned.

W Writing Skills provide writing opportunities to help students comprehend the text.

T Technology Skills require students to use digital tools effectively.

*Letters are followed by a number when there is more than one of the same type of skill on the page.

DIFFERENTIATED INSTRUCTION

All activities are written for the on-level student unless otherwise marked with the leveled labels below.

BL Beyond Level
AL Approaching Level
ELL English Language Learners

All students benefit from activities that utilize different learning styles. Many activities are marked as below when a particular learning style is highlighted.

Intrapersonal	Naturalist
Logical/Mathematical	Kinesthetic
Visual/Spatial	Auditory/Musical
Verbal/Linguistic	Interpersonal

CHAPTER OPENER PLANNER

Students will know:

- *how South America's physical geography affects climate, population patterns, and economic development.*
- *that Native Americans, Europeans, and Africans have influenced the history, government, and cultures of South America.*
- *that South America faces many environmental issues related to urban growth, industrialization, and desertification.*

Students will be able to:

- ***discuss** the physical geography of South America and its effects.*
- ***discuss** history, governments, and cultures of South America.*
- ***describe** environmental issues and solutions.*

UNDERSTANDING BY DESIGN®

Print Teaching Options

V Visual Skills

- p. 216 Students analyze the image to compare and contrast it to other images and to discuss how it relates to life in South America.
- p. 217 Students create a flowchart to describe the principles of the core-periphery theory. Visual/Spatial

C Critical Thinking Skills

- p. 216 Students discuss characteristics of developed and undeveloped nations. Logical/Mathematical
- p. 217 Students problem-solve by answering a question of how a country can prevent brain drain. BL Logical/Mathematical, Interpersonal

W Writing Skills

- p. 216 Students write a brief essay titled "My Day in the Food Line" about what it would be like to be one of the people in the food line. Verbal/Linguistic

Online Teaching Options

V Visual Skills

- SLIDE SHOW **Skewed Economic Development of South America**—Students explore the instances of uneven development and choose one to further study and propose solutions to. BL Verbal/Linguistic
- INTERACTIVE GRAPH **Brazil's Urban Population Growth**—Students analyze data in the graph about recent growth in urban areas. Interpersonal, Visual/Spatial

Printable Digital Worksheets

- WORKSHEET **Assessing Background Knowledge**—Determine the level of prior knowledge students have about South America.
- WORKSHEET **Vocabulary Activity**—Students use and improve their academic and content vocabulary by completing various vocabulary activities.

Project-Based Learning 

Hands-On

Designing Deforestation Models

Students will design models that bring together information from all lessons about how deforestation affects the environment and people of Amazonia.

Digital Hands-On

Create Online Projects

Find an additional activity online that incorporates technology for this project. Visit the EdTech Teacher Web sites for more links, tutorials, and other resources.

Print Resources

ANCILLARY RESOURCES

This ancillary is available for every chapter and lesson.

- **Chapter Tests and Lesson Quizzes**

PRINTABLE DIGITAL WORKSHEETS

These printable digital worksheets are available for every chapter and lesson.

- **Assessing Background Knowledge**
- **Chapter Summaries**
- **Guided Reading Activities**
- **Hands-On Chapter Projects**
- **Quizzes and Tests**
- **Reading Essentials and Study Guide** AL
- **Reteaching Activities**
- **Video Activities**
- **Vocabulary Activity**

More Media Resources

SUGGESTED VIDEOS MOVIES

- **Mysterious World of the Inca** (53 min.)
- **Passport to Adventure: Buenos Aires and Bariloche** (26 min.)
- **Brazil** *New Dimension Media* (30 min.)

SUGGESTED READING 

- ***Bolivar: American Liberator,*** by Marie Arana
- ***Brazil on the Rise: The Story of a Country Transformed,*** by Larry Rohter
- ***The Last Days of the Incas,*** by Kim MacQuarrie

LESSON 1 PLANNER

PHYSICAL GEOGRAPHY OF SOUTH AMERICA

Students will know:

- *that South America's location on the Ring of Fire has impacted its physical geography.*
- *why the rugged landscape both attracts settlers and also isolates them.*
- *how South America's water systems are important to economic development.*
- *how elevation and location in the Tropics influence South America's climate.*
- *the ways in which climate influences human systems in South America.*

Students will be able to:

- ***explain*** *how South America's location affects its physical geography, which affects its population patterns.*
- ***describe*** *how water systems are important to the economy.*
- ***identify*** *how climate is influenced by elevation and location and influences human systems.*

UNDERSTANDING BY DESIGN®

☑ Print Teaching Options

V Visual Skills

- ☐ **p. 218** Students create a chart of the major landforms of South America. ELL Visual/Spatial
- ☐ **p. 219** Students discuss the variety of landforms in South America. ELL Visual/Spatial
- ☐ **p. 219** Students study and describe the elevation profile and mountain image. Visual/Spatial
- ☐ **p. 221** Students create a vertical altitude-to-temperature diagram. BL Visual/Spatial, Interpersonal
- ☐ **p. 222** Students analyze a graph of resources in Latin America. BL Visual/Spatial, Logical/Mathematical

R Reading Skills

- ☐ **p. 220** Students compare the Paraguay-Paraná river system to the Amazon river system. Verbal/Linguistic

C Critical Thinking Skills

- ☐ **p. 218** Students discuss how mountain ranges can lead to a country's isolation. Logical/Mathematical
- ☐ **p. 219** Students hypothesize about how the Andes were formed. Naturalist
- ☐ **p. 221** Students identify and compare a biome in South America to the biome in North America where they live. BL Naturalist, Logical/Mathematical
- ☐ **p. 222** Students make a list of questions to help them understand the importance of mineral resources to local economies within South America. Verbal/Linguistic

W Writing Skills

- ☐ **p. 220** Students write a narrative describing everyday life during an El Niño year in a specific region in South America. Verbal/Linguistic, Visual/Spatial

T Technology Skills

- ☐ **p. 220** Students create a multimedia presentation about a major river system. BL Visual/Spatial
- ☐ **p. 221** Students find a vegetation map and a rainfall map of South America and answer questions about them. Visual/Spatial

☑ Online Teaching Options

V Visual Skills

- INTERACTIVE MAP **South America: Elevation Profile**—Students discuss how landforms facilitate either the growth or decline of multiple different cultures. Interpersonal, Verbal/Linguistic

C Critical Thinking Skills

- INTERACTIVE BELLRINGER **Effects of Altitude**—Students discuss how altitude affects life and activities at higher elevations. Logical/Mathematical, Naturalist
- INFOGRAPHIC **Impacts of El Niño in Latin America**—Students compare and contrast El Niño's effect in Latin America with South America in charts or graphs. AL Visual/Spatial

W Writing Skills

- VIDEO **Around the World—Chile**—Students view the video and write a paragraph about Chile's varied terrain and how it affects population. BL Verbal/Linguistic
- INTERACTIVE WHITEBOARD ACTIVITY **Waterways of South America**—Students will label the waterways on a map of South America and then will identify the correct descriptors to the proper locations on the map.

☑ Printable Digital Worksheets

R Reading Skills

- WORKSHEET **Guided Reading Activity**—Students use the Guided Reading Activity worksheets to review their comprehension of the content. Verbal/Linguistic
- WORKSHEET **Chapter Summary**—Students review the main ideas of the chapter content. Verbal/Linguistic

C Critical Thinking Skills

- WORKSHEET **Video Activity**—Students answer questions relating to the lesson content after they have viewed the video. Visual/Spatial

LESSON 2 PLANNER

HUMAN GEOGRAPHY OF SOUTH AMERICA

Students will know:

- *that Native Americans and Europeans shaped the history and government of South America.*
- *how population patterns in South America have been affected by physical geography, migration, and urban growth.*
- *the ways in which Native Americans, Europeans, and Africans influenced the culture of South America.*
- *that the modern economic geography of South America is dominated by agriculture and natural resources.*

Students will be able to:

- ***discuss** how Native Americans, Europeans, and Africans shaped the history, government, and culture of South America.*
- ***describe** population patterns influenced by geography, migration, and urban growth.*
- ***identify** agricultural and natural resources and their effect on the economy.*

UNDERSTANDING BY DESIGN®

Print Teaching Options

V Visual Skills

- ☐ **p. 225** Students compare population and physical maps of South America. BL Visual/Spatial, Logical/Mathematical
- ☐ **p. 226** Students use a map to create a table listing ethnic populations by countries. Visual/Spatial

R Reading Skills

- ☐ **p. 223** Students discuss the terrain and its challenges in the area where the Inca lived. Verbal/Linguistic, Visual/Spatial
- ☐ **p. 226** Students discuss ethnic groups and languages in South America. AL Verbal/Linguistic
- ☐ **p. 228** Students make a list of areas in which different forms of agriculture are grown. ELL Verbal/Linguistic
- ☐ **p. 229** Students discuss challenges facing developing countries. BL Logical/Mathematical

C Critical Thinking Skills

- ☐ **p. 223** Students discuss the process of blending among indigenous and other groups and why some remote people have kept their cultures. AL Logical/Mathematical
- ☐ **p. 226** Students identify cause-and-effect relations between religions in South America. Logical/Mathematical
- ☐ **p. 227** Students discuss the standard of living and causes of poverty in South America. AL Verbal/Linguistic
- ☐ **p. 227** Students develop a list of criteria to measure the status of women in society. BL Verbal/Linguistic

W Writing Skills

- ☐ **p. 225** Students write a narrative that discusses what life might be like in poor rural areas and why people often migrate to a city. AL Verbal/Linguistic

T Technology Skills

- ☐ **p. 224** Students research important dates in South America's colonial period to create a time line. Verbal/Linguistic
- ☐ **p. 228** Students investigate the road and highway system of a country in South America. BL Visual/Spatial
- ☐ **p. 229** Students research and write a brief report on the economy of Bolivia. Verbal/Linguistic

Online Teaching Options

V Visual Skills

- INTERACTIVE MAP **Cultures of South America, A.D. 700–1530**—Students study how settlement patterns have changed as human society has changed and write a short paragraph explaining how and why population patterns have changed. AL Verbal/Linguistic
- INTERACTIVE MAP **Dominant Ethnic Groups of South America**—Students consider travel and migration routes and answer questions about how geography contributes to ethnic groups remaining in certain regions. AL Logical/Mathematical

R Reading Skills

- VIDEO **Machu Picchu**—Students make a list of Inca contributions still observed today and then classify their lists in a large chart as cultural, religious, or technical. Verbal/Linguistic, Interpersonal
- GAME **South America**—Students make predictions about roads and highways in South America now that regions are becoming more industrialized, then play the game. Logical/Mathematical

C Critical Thinking Skills

- INTERACTIVE MAP **European Colonies in Latin America, 1800**—Students compare ancient cultures to the map locations of European colonies to decide whether an artifact can be dated pre-or post-European based on its style. AL Verbal/Linguistic
- INTERACTIVE WHITEBOARD ACTIVITY **Population Patterns of South America**—Students will identify physical factors that encourage or discourage human settlement in areas of South America.

W Writing Skills

- INTERACTIVE BELLRINGER **Analyzing Simón Bolívar's Message**—Students discuss how colonists of South America felt during their fight for independence, and then write a paraphrase of Bolívar's message. Verbal/Linguistic, Interpersonal

Printable Digital Worksheets

R Reading Skills

- WORKSHEET **Guided Reading Activity**—Students use the Guided Reading Activity worksheets to review their comprehension of the content. Verbal/Linguistic
- WORKSHEET **Reading Essentials and Study Guide**—Students complete the study guide and answer Reading Progress Check and vocabulary questions. AL

C Critical Thinking Skills

- WORKSHEET **Video Activity**—Students answer questions relating to the lesson content after they have viewed the lesson video. Visual/Spatial

PEOPLE AND THEIR ENVIRONMENT: SOUTH AMERICA

Students will know:
- *how the mismanagement of forest resources results in the deterioration of biodiversity.*
- *the causes and effects of the degradation of farmland in South America.*
- *the ways in which urban growth and industrialization impact the environment in South America.*
- *examples of the efforts made to address environmental issues in South America.*

Students will be able to:
- ***describe** loss of biodiversity and degradation of farmland in South America.*
- ***identify** environmental issues due to urban growth and industrialization.*
- ***analyze** efforts to address environmental issues.*

UNDERSTANDING BY DESIGN®

☑ Print Teaching Options

V Visual Skills
- ☐ **p. 233** Students develop a flowchart describing the soil-making process. ELL Visual/Spatial

R Reading Skills
- ☐ **p. 232** Students explain how South American countries are taking advantage of their natural resources. Verbal/Linguistic
- ☐ **p. 232** Students discuss deforestation and loss of biodiversity. Naturalist, Verbal/Linguistic
- ☐ **p. 234** Students list and discuss positive and negative effects of gold mining. AL Verbal/Linguistic
- ☐ **p. 235** Students summarize the steps farmers can take to restore damaged soil. AL Verbal/Linguistic
- ☐ **p. 236** Students describe some specific factors relating to urbanization. Verbal/Linguistic, Naturalist

C Critical Thinking Skills
- ☐ **p. 232** Students describe what they know and list questions they expect to have answered about environmental issues as they read.
- ☐ **p. 233** Students discuss what it means for soil to be vulnerable to erosion. Naturalist, Logical/Mathematical
- ☐ **p. 234** Students discuss pollution associated with cities. Verbal/Linguistic
- ☐ **p. 235** Students discuss how environmental degradation affects people. Logical/Mathematical

W Writing Skills
- ☐ **p. 235** Students write an informative essay on soil management practices after interviewing a local farmer or representative from a state agriculture agency. Naturalist, Verbal/Linguistic
- ☐ **p. 236** Students write newspaper editorials on protecting the environment and developing a sustainable economy. Verbal/Linguistic

T Technology Skills
- ☐ **p. 233** Students discuss desertification and collect before and after images of areas that have been affected by desertification. AL Visual/Spatial

☑ Online Teaching Options

V Visual Skills
- INTERACTIVE BELLRINGER **The World's Rain Forests**—Students discuss environmental issues facing rain forests and efforts to protect these ecosystems. Visual/Spatial, Naturalist
- VIDEO **Amazon Crude**—Students discuss the disagreement between Texaco and PetroEcuador and identify how points of view influence public policies on international levels. BL Logical/Mathematical

C Critical Thinking Skills
- INTERACTIVE IMAGE **South American Urbanization**—Students imagine they are government leaders that must come to an agreed-upon decision on how to deal with *favelas*, settlements on the outskirts of a large city. Interpersonal, Verbal/Linguistic
- INTERACTIVE GRAPH **Per Capita CO_2 Emissions**—Students write three analytical statements based on information about carbon dioxide emissions and discuss regulations to reduce greenhouse gas emissions. ELL Visual/Spatial
- INTERACTIVE WHITEBOARD ACTIVITY **Environmental Problems and Solutions**—Students will identify the cause-and-effect elements of an environmental issue to lead to a solution.

☑ Printable Digital Worksheets

R Reading Skills
- WORKSHEET **Guided Reading Activity**—Students use Guided Reading Activity worksheets to review their comprehension of the content.
- WORKSHEET **Reading Essentials and Study Guide**—Students complete the study guide and answer Reading Progress Check and vocabulary questions. AL ELL
- WORKSHEET **Vocabulary Activity**—Students review the chapter content and academic vocabulary words. Verbal/Linguistic
- WORKSHEET **Chapter Summary**—Students review the main ideas of the chapter content.

C Critical Thinking Skills
- WORKSHEET **Video Activity**—Students will answer questions about the lesson video in order to make connections with the chapter content. Logical/Mathematical
- WORKSHEET **Reteaching Activity**—Students use this activity worksheet to review and reteach chapter content and vocabulary. This worksheet can be used with struggling students who need additional help with difficult content concept.
- WORKSHEET **Hands-On Chapter Project: Model Effects of Deforestation**—Working in small groups, students will use the chapter lessons along with library or online research to create a chapter project about deforestation of the Amazon rain forest. Students will design models that bring together information about how deforestation affects the environment and people of Amazonia. BL Interpersonal, Naturalist

INTERVENTION AND REMEDIATION STRATEGIES

LESSON 1 Physical Geography of South America

Reading and Comprehension

Organize students into five groups. Assign a different content vocabulary word to each group. Have students in each group work together to create a paragraph about a concept in the lesson, using their assigned term. For example, students may use the term *escarpment* in a paragraph about South America's landforms and how the term relates to inland development. After groups have completed their paragraphs, ask a volunteer from each group to read the paragraph. Provide guidance as needed, ensuring that students have used each term correctly.

Text Evidence

Have students work in four groups to research an aspect of South America's physical geography as it relates to one of the following topics discussed in the lesson: landforms, water systems, climate regions and biomes, and natural resources. Tell students to present an analysis of their findings, comparing information in the text with information found in their research. For example, students might research the significance of the El Niño phenomenon and its impact on South America's climate. Tell students to write an objective summary of their findings.

LESSON 2 Human Geography of South America

Reading and Comprehension

To ensure comprehension of the concepts in this lesson, have students write sentences using the lesson vocabulary. Tell students that their sentences should show an understanding of the meaning of each word and how it applies to the lesson content. Have students work in pairs to conduct a peer review, by sharing their sentences to check each word's meaning. Circulate to provide corrective guidance. Then have students collaborate to write one or two paragraphs using each content vocabulary term to demonstrate their understanding of South America's human geography. After students share their paragraphs, discuss how the region can reduce the negative impact of population patterns such as *brain drain.*

Text Evidence

Organize students into four groups and assign each group a period in South America's history. Have students in each group work together to create an illustrated time line depicting key events in their assigned period. Then have students in each group collaborate to write a summary about the significance of one or more events related to the history of South America, such as its conflicts regarding independence. Tell students to use textual evidence to support ideas presented in their summaries. Have students share their summaries with the class.

LESSON 3 People and Their Environment: South America

Reading and Comprehension

To ensure comprehension of the concepts in this lesson, have students write a summarizing sentence for each of the three sections in the text: managing resources, human impact, and addressing the issues. Tell students their sentences should touch on one or more issues facing South America and should identify what is being done to solve the problem. Have students share their sentences with the class as you provide corrective guidance if needed.

Text Evidence

Have students work in small groups to create a visual diagram about an environment issue facing South America discussed in the text. To avoid duplication, assign students topics such as deforestation, air pollution, and so on. Have students collaborate to use evidence from the text on which to base their visual diagrams and present them to the class. Tell students their diagrams should address the Essential Question: *How do physical systems and human systems shape a place?* After students have presented their visuals, guide a discussion about how urban growth and industrialization impact South America's environment.

Online Resources

Leveled Reader

Use this online approaching-level text that corresponds directly to the text in the Student Edition. It also includes additional reading and comprehension support for English Language Learners.

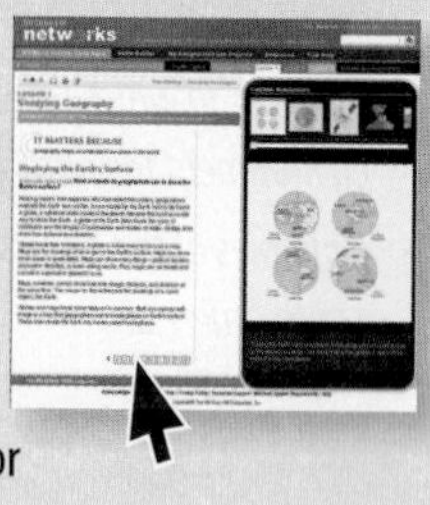

Guided Reading Activities

This resource uses guiding questions to help students with comprehension.

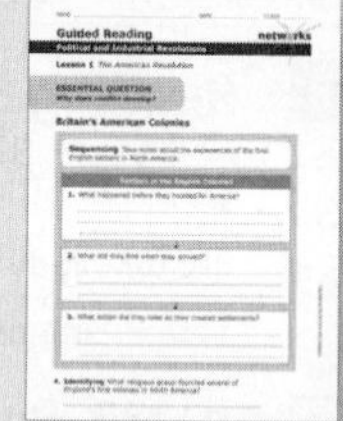

Reteaching Activities

These worksheets provide students with an opportunity for remedial practice and review of vital chapter content.

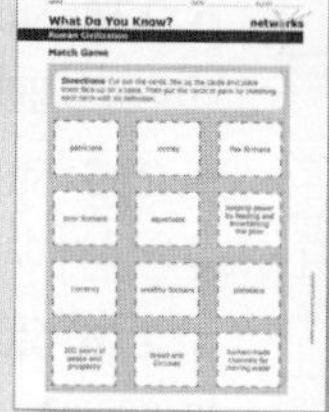

Reading Essentials and Study Guide

This resource offers writing and reading activities for the approaching-level student.

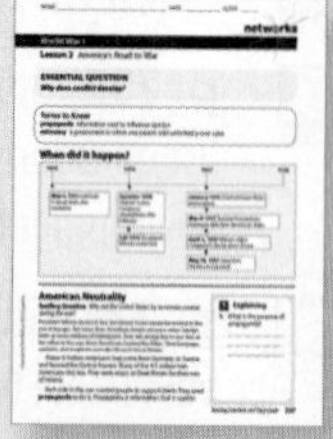

Self-Check Quizzes

This online assessment tool provides instant feedback for students to check their progress.

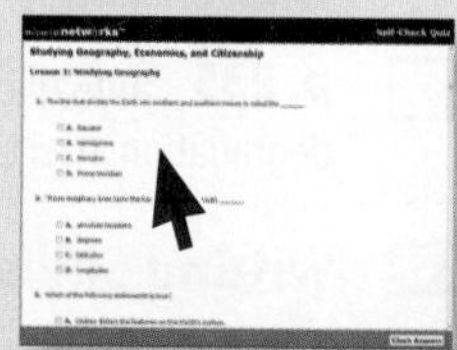

Chapter Summaries

Summaries are provided for each chapter that thoroughly condense core content into manageable chunks.

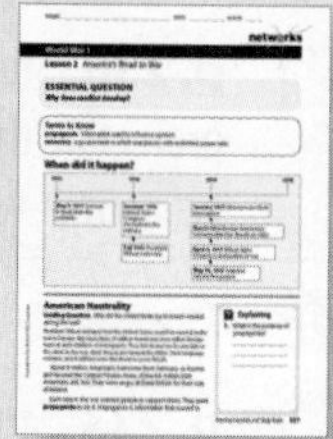

South America

networks

There's More Online about South America.

CHAPTER 9

ESSENTIAL QUESTION • *How do physical systems and human systems shape a place?*

Geography Matters...

South America is a land of beautiful natural wonders, including the vast Amazon rain forest. However, not all of South America is a lush jungle paradise. The region also includes snow-covered mountains and boasts the world's driest place—the Atacama Desert.

South America is diverse in culture as well as in landscape. The people of this subregion reflect a unique blend of indigenous and colonial heritage, the result of centuries of migration, trade, and conquest.

◀ Carnival in Brazil is held over five days preceding Lent, with parades featuring elaborate floats, drummers, and dancers.

Viviane Ponti/Lonely Planet Images/Getty Images

215

Letter from the Author

Dear Geography Teacher,

There are two massive physical features that dominate South America—the Andes Mountains and the Amazon River basin. The Andes Mountains stretch more than 5,000 miles from Venezuela to the island of Tierra del Fuego, across the Straits of Magellan from Argentina and Chile. The Andes give us a chance to see the inner workings of vertical climate zones; Tierra caliente, Tierra templada, and Tierra fria. The other major physical feature is the Amazon River and its 3 million square mile drainage basin. The Amazon is the second largest river in the world and it carries 20% of the world's freshwater at any given time. These two giant physical features demonstrate how physical systems shape places and regions.

Richard G. Boehm

ENGAGE

Drawing Inferences Provide students with a recent news story about an incident in South America relating to the economy, such as an article that describes a country's economic growth, advances in agricultural production, or a debt crisis. Challenge students to explain how this story relates to the geography of South America.

TEACH & ASSESS

Content Background Knowledge

Carnival Carnival is a festival that takes place in many countries with Roman Catholic citizens prior to the long Lenten period (40 days before Easter devoted to fasting, abstinence, and penitence). Carnival includes parades, masked balls, elaborate costumes, dancing, music, and other festivities. Perhaps the most well-known Carnival is celebrated each year in Rio de Janeiro. In the United States, the comparable celebration would be Mardi Gras celebrated in New Orleans.

Expressing Have students think of events that are celebrated each year in their community. **Ask:** **How do such celebrations reflect what is important to a community?** *(Celebrating a historic figure or event is a way of encouraging the values of a person or event. There are also local festivals celebrating the main product of the area, such as a tomato festival in a farming community.)* **AL** **Interpersonal**

Hypothesizing Invite volunteers to define *diversity*. **Ask:** **Why might the diversity of landscape lead to diverse cultures?** *(People interact with the geography where they live. The culture reflects the values that helped them survive.)* **How would migration, trade, and conquest create unique blends of cultures?** *(Possible answer: When people migrate, they adapt to the geography; when people trade, they learn about each other's cultures; when a civilization is conquered, people may be forced to give up parts of their culture, creating a blended culture.)* **Verbal/Linguistic**

CLOSE & REFLECT

Applying Have students read the table of contents and prepare a list of questions they expect to have answered as they study the chapter.

Extend the project-based learning experience globally through our partnership with ePals. EPals allows you to connect with classrooms around the world in a safe online environment for real-life lessons and projects in virtual study groups.

ENGAGE

V Visual Skills

Analyzing Visuals Have students describe what they can glean from this image about South America. **Ask:** What are the people in the photo doing? *(They are waiting in line for food.)* Direct students to compare and contrast this image with the other images on the pages. **Ask:** What do these photos suggest about life in South America? *(Possible answer: Just as there are people who struggle with poverty and hunger, there are others who are doing well.)*

TEACH & ASSESS

W Writing Skills

Narrative Ask students to write a brief essay titled "My Day in the Food Line" describing the experiences of one of the people in the photograph. Why are they in the line? How do they feel? What is it like to have to stand in line for food? What challenges are they facing due to uneven development? Have students read their essays to the class. Discuss some of the conditions that cause the worldwide issue of hunger, including the challenge of uneven development. Verbal/Linguistic

C Critical Thinking Skills

Analyzing Pose these questions on uneven development to students. Have them work with a partner to explore the answers. **Ask:** What are some characteristics of a developed nation? *(high standard of living; stable economy; diversified workforce; high productivity; advanced infrastructure)* What are some characteristics of an undeveloped nation? *(low per capita income; low per capita standard of living; undeveloped industrial base; subsistent agriculture; overcrowding)* What would be a sign of uneven development? *(a nation is developed in some ways and not in others; there is great disparity between rich and poor)* How would uneven development contribute to difficulties in becoming a developed country? *(Although some areas are experiencing development and economic growth, the country is still challenged by poverty and widespread hunger, and its resources are not meeting the needs of its population.)* Logical/Mathematical

Content Background Knowledge

Urbanization The process of urbanization of South America has been rising sharply since World War II. Paraguay is experiencing the fastest rate of urbanization (2.5 percent per year). Today Buenos Aires, Rio de Janeiro, and São Paulo are among the world's 20 largest cities. In 1925, about one-third of South America's people lived in cities and towns; today more than two-thirds do. In Venezuela, Argentina, and Uruguay, more than 90 percent of the population lives in cities or towns.

Why Geography Matters: **South America**

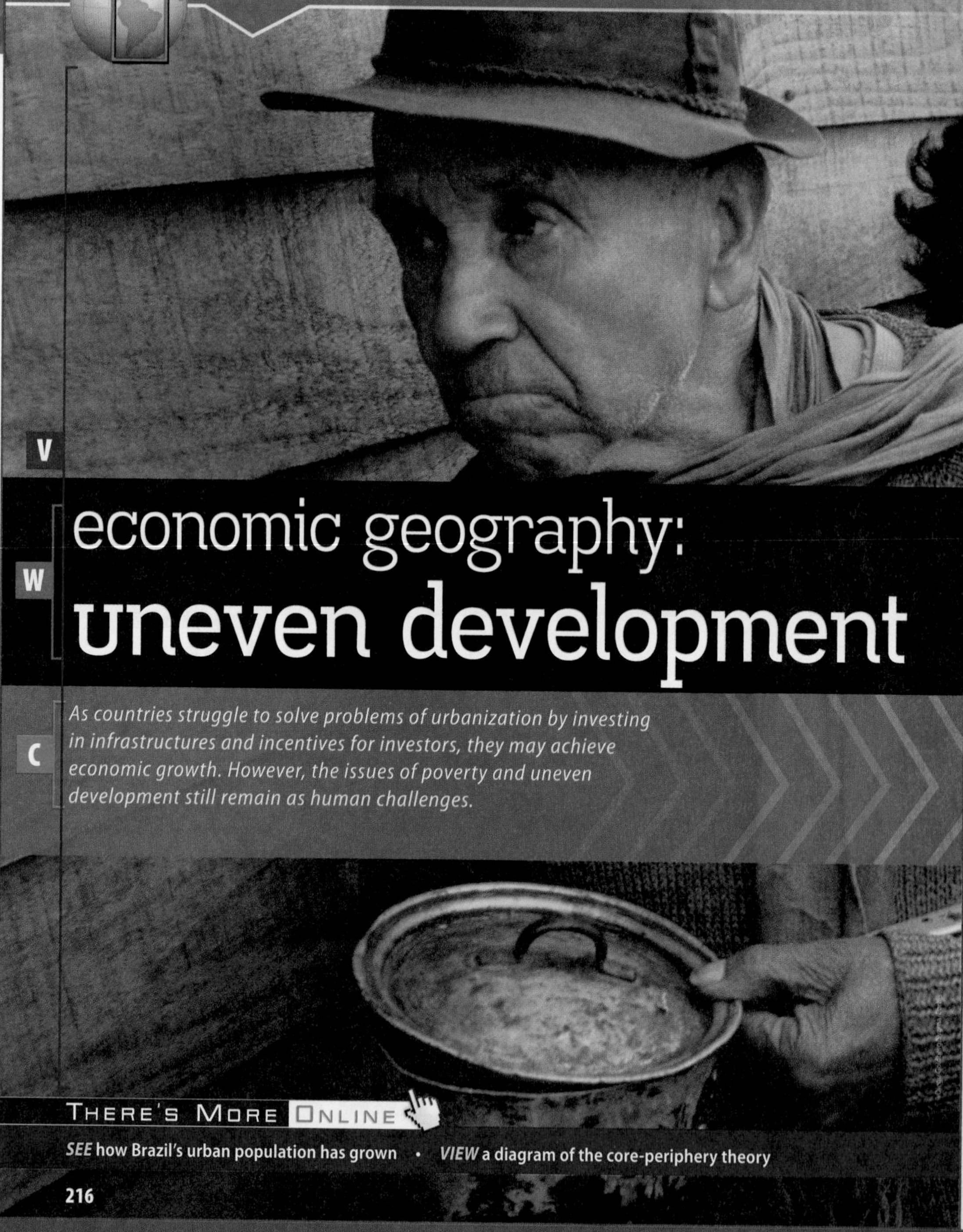

V

W

economic geography: uneven development

C

As countries struggle to solve problems of urbanization by investing in infrastructures and incentives for investors, they may achieve economic growth. However, the issues of poverty and uneven development still remain as human challenges.

THERE'S MORE ONLINE

SEE **how Brazil's urban population has grown** • ***VIEW*** **a diagram of the core-periphery theory**

216

Project-Based Learning

Hands-On

Model Effects of Deforestation

Working in small groups, students will model the effects of deforestation on physical and human systems in the Amazon region. Each group will write a step-by-step procedure that describes how they will create and test their models. After the testing phase, groups will compare and contrast their data with the data collected by other groups in the class..

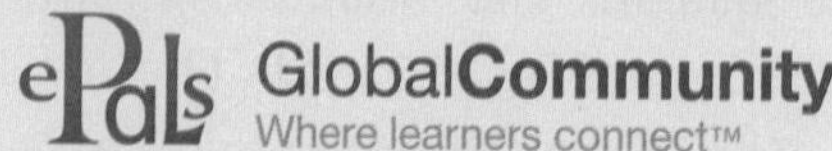

Digital Hands-On

Create Online Projects

Find an additional activity online that incorporates technology for this project. Visit the EdTech Teacher Web sites for more links, tutorials, and other resources.

Why Geography Matters

How do core-periphery relations fuel uneven development?

Rural workers in search of better job opportunities tend to seek work in the core—cities, such as São Paulo, Brazil. Within a country, rural areas act as a periphery, contributing to burgeoning urban populations. The cities, or core, receiving the migrants often experience explosive growth. As the core grows, it begins to engulf surrounding smaller towns and cities. While the core offers job opportunities, it also presents challenges to governments, which struggle to maintain the infrastructure and services needed to support such a large, quickly growing urban population.

1. **The World in Spatial Terms** Describe the migration of rural workers to urban areas in terms of both push factors and pull factors.

What are the effects of uneven patterns of development?

Many government programs focus on the metropolitan core areas and provide insufficient support to the periphery areas. This can leave the periphery with inadequate transportation, sanitation, education, and other essential services. Another result of uneven development is brain drain, or the process of educated and professional individuals leaving the periphery to go to the core for job opportunities. This deprives areas in the periphery of their most educated residents. For example, in the state of Ceará, home to some of the poorest Brazilians, there is a lack of incentives for establishing non-farming activities. This is a push factor for many residents to seek better opportunities in nearby core areas. Although the metropolitan areas have shown economic growth, the smaller urban areas and rural towns are still areas of widespread poverty.

2. **Human Systems** How might the migration of workers from rural areas to large cities negatively impact rural areas?

How can the issue of uneven development be addressed?

Uneven patterns of development within countries are a result of unequal distribution of resources, capital, and infrastructure between the core and the periphery. Some governments work to create programs promoting non-farming activities in the periphery so there is more incentive for skilled workers to stay in these areas to develop business and industry.

3. **Environment and Society** Imagine you are a candidate for mayor of a large city plagued by problems of overcrowding, poor sanitation, crime, and unregulated land use (squatting) as a result of rural workers flocking to your city for better jobs. Write a campaign speech detailing how you would address these problems if elected.

Content Background Knowledge

Core-Periphery Theory Power, wealth, and opportunity have traditionally centered in the core areas of the world. These locations are urbanized and industrialized and hold immense economic and political power. Ideas, technology, and cultural activities thrive in these core areas. Political power is typically held by leaders who inhabit the core. The core depends on the periphery for raw materials, food, and cheap labor, and the periphery depends on the core for manufactured goods, services, and governmental support.

V Visual Skills

Synthesizing Have partners create a flowchart to describe the principles of the core-periphery theory. Suggest that students use the Internet or other resources to learn more about the core-periphery theory to them help fill in explanations on their flowcharts. Then as a class, discuss the effects of this situation on the core city. **Visual/Spatial**

C Critical Thinking Skills

Problem Solving Have groups come up with an agreed-upon answer to the following question: **How can a country prevent brain drain and why is this so critical?** *(Student answers may vary, but should include preventive measures and critical needs.)* **BL** **Logical/Mathematical, Interpersonal**

CLOSE & REFLECT

Summarizing Have students write a paragraph that summarizes how the core-periphery theory relates to issues of poverty and uneven development in South America.

INTERACTIVE GRAPH

Brazil's Urban Population Growth

Using Graphs This interactive graph of Brazil's population shows the recent growth in urban areas. Have students analyze the data in the graph and discuss the information with a partner. Then have each student write 2 or 3 statements that summarize the data found in the graph. Use these statements to write predictions about potential problems Brazil may face based on the urban population growth statistics shown in the graph. **Interpersonal, Visual/Spatial**

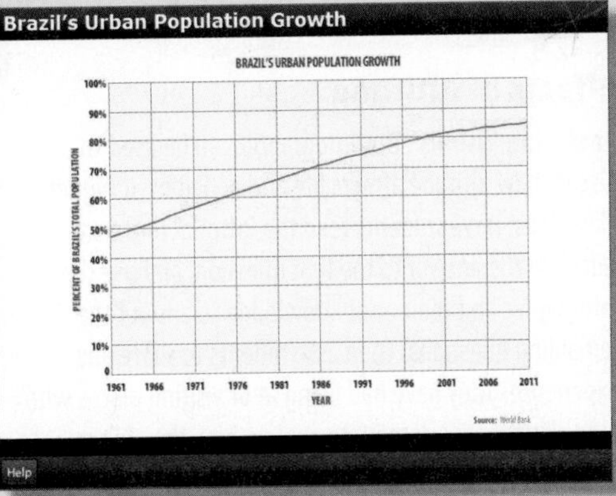

ANSWERS, p. 217

Why Geography Matters

1. Push factors such as a lack of job opportunities in rural areas "push" people to look to cities for jobs. Cities experiencing explosive growth offer job opportunities, which is a pull factor because rural workers are "pulled" to the city in search of these opportunities.
2. In impoverished rural areas, residents who are able to escape the poor conditions by relocating to the city tend to do so. Because it is especially the most educated people who are able find jobs in the city, rural communities are further drained of hope for improvement.
3. Ads and speeches will vary, but should demonstrate knowledge of the direct needs of a city such as strong transportation, sanitation, and education—but also the importance of tackling uneven development. A good speech will suggest ways to improve conditions in rural areas so that job opportunities may eventually spread out geographically and alleviate pressure on the city.

ENGAGE

R Reading Skills

Activating Prior Knowledge South America is a popular tourist destination for world travelers. Challenge students to name some famous spots in South America that people like to visit. *(Possible answers: cities: Caracas, Lima, Rio de Janeiro, São Paulo; geographical wonders: Amazon rain forest, Andes Mountains, Angel Falls (Venezuela), Torres del Paine (Chile), Salar de Uyuni (Bolivia), The Pantanal (Brazil), Lake Titicaca (Bolivia); ancient sites: Machu Picchu (Peru).* Have students describe what they know about these places, including any geographic landforms.

TEACH & ASSESS

V Visual Skills

Creating Charts Have students create a chart of the major landforms of South America. Tell students to continue to add landforms as they read the lesson. For each landform, students should provide the location and describe the major characteristics. ELL Visual/Spatial

Landform	Location	Description
cordilleras	in the Andes	several mountain ranges that are parallel to each other
altiplano	southwestern Peru and western Bolivia	largest mountain plateau in the world

C Critical Thinking Skills

Analyzing Cause and Effect Ask students to provide examples of ways that mountain ranges can lead to a country's isolation. Then, **ask:** How does isolation lead to villages that exhibit centuries-old social customs? *(People learn new customs from interaction with other cultures. If people are isolated for centuries then they will continue to live as their ancestors did, following those same customs.)* Logical/Mathematical

ANSWERS, p. 218

TAKING NOTES: The world's largest rain forest is the Amazon rain forest. The Amazon shelters more species of plants and animals per square mile than anywhere else on Earth. In many tropical dry areas, grasslands flourish. The southeastern coast of Argentina has an arid climate and low vegetation adapted to the low moisture conditions. Shifting winds and the cold, oceanic Peru Current combine to create dry coastal deserts. Warm climates and open spaces are good for raising livestock in the Brazilian Highlands. Inland grasslands—the llanos and the pampas—provide cattle with areas to graze.

networks *There's More Online!*

- IMAGE The Andes
- DIAGRAM South America: Elevation Profile
- INFOGRAPHIC El Niño
- GRAPH Oil Reserves of South America
- INTERACTIVE SELF-CHECK QUIZ
- VIDEO Physical Geography of South America

LESSON 1
Physical Geography of South America

ESSENTIAL QUESTION • *How do physical systems and human systems shape a place?*

Reading HELPDESK CCSS

Academic Vocabulary (Tier Two Words)
- **phenomenon**
- **predominant**

Content Vocabulary (Tier Three Words)
- **cordillera**
- **altiplano**
- **escarpment**
- **llanos**
- **pampas**

TAKING NOTES: ***Key Ideas and Details***

PARAPHRASING Use a graphic organizer like the one below to take notes on the biomes of South America, including any adaptations of plants and animals for survival in their biome.

South American Biomes

IT MATTERS BECAUSE

R *The diverse landscapes of South America are very different from what we know in the United States. They have led to the people in South America developing very different lifestyles that are adapted to their physical environment.*

V Landforms

GUIDING QUESTION *How has South America's rugged landscape both attracted and isolated people?*

The Isthmus of Panama connects North America to South America. The subregion of South America spans 4,700 miles (7,564 km) from north to south, passing through the Equator near its widest point of 3,300 miles (5,311 km). Like Central America and Mexico, the most characteristic of South America's many landforms are its mountains. The Andes are the world's longest mountain chain. Some peaks in the Andes rise more than 20,000 feet (6,096 m) above sea level. The Andes consist of **cordilleras,** groups of several mountain ranges that run parallel to one another. C Although known by different names, they are an extension of the Rocky Mountains that run from Canada south through the western United States and into Mexico and Central America. Because the cordilleras have established natural barriers between surrounding areas, many indigenous communities developed as isolated groups. As a result, some mountain villages exhibit centuries-old social customs.

The Andes encircle the **altiplano**, which means "high plain." The altiplano is an area that includes southeastern Peru and western Bolivia. It is the second-largest mountain plateau in the world.

In southern Argentina, hills and flatlands form the plateau of Patagonia. The presence of the Andes to the west produces a rain shadow that causes Patagonia to be dry, barren, and windy. The Patagonian region also extends across the Andes to southern Chile. Patagonia boasts dramatic valleys, glaciers, and fjords. The rugged Andes and Patagonia's landscape are a result of its location along the Ring of Fire.

218

(t)David Madison/Photodisc/Getty Images, (c)Chlaus Lotscher/Peter Arnold/Getty Images

networks *Online Teaching Options*

INTERACTIVE BELLRINGER

Effects of Altitude

Analyzing Visuals This infographic can be used to discuss how altitude affects life and activities at higher elevations. Have students read the introductory text, calculate the answer to the first question, and use the infographic and their prior knowledge to answer the remaining questions. Then ask students to share any experiences they have had living at or visiting places with high elevations. Ask them to explain how they felt at a higher elevation level and if they experienced any physical changes. Logical/Mathematical, Naturalist

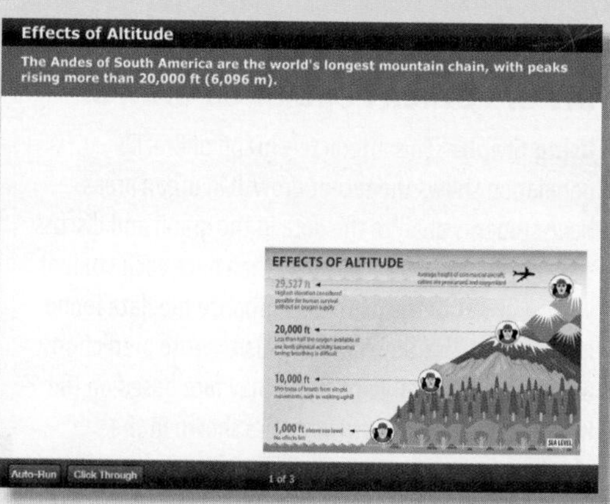

Heavy tectonic activity in the subregion changes and reshapes the landscape. But despite the threats of natural disasters, people have chosen to settle in the Andean highlands for thousands of years. The climates are cooler, the volcanic soil is good for agriculture, and natural resources are concentrated here. C

In contrast to the high peaks of the western Andes, eastern South America is defined by broad plateaus and valleys. The Amazon Basin, located along the eastern base of the Andes, is the lowlands area drained by the Amazon River. Just south is the Mato Grosso Plateau, a sparsely populated plateau of forests and grasslands extending across Brazil, Bolivia, and Peru. Farther east are the Brazilian Highlands, a vast area spanning several climate and vegetation zones. Warm climates and open spaces make the Brazilian Highlands good for raising livestock. The Eastern Highlands plunge to the Atlantic Ocean, forming a steep slope called an **escarpment**. This escarpment presents obstacles for inland development. As a result, most of Brazil's population lives along the coast. V1

Narrow coastal lowlands hem the Atlantic and Pacific coasts of South America. South America's inland grasslands—the **llanos** (LAH•nohs) of Colombia and Venezuela and the **pampas** of Argentina and Uruguay—provide grazing for cattle. Ranchers on large estates employ cowhands, called *llaneros* or gauchos, to drive herds across the rolling plains. Known for its fertile soil, the pampas are one of the world's breadbaskets, producing wheat and corn.

cordillera parallel chains or ranges of mountains

altiplano Spanish for "high plain," a region in Peru and Bolivia encircled by the Andes

escarpment a steep cliff or slope between a higher and lower land surface

llanos fertile grasslands found in inland areas of Colombia and Venezuela

pampas grassy, treeless plains of southern South America

✓ READING PROGRESS CHECK

Explaining What features of South America's landscape have hindered or encouraged development?

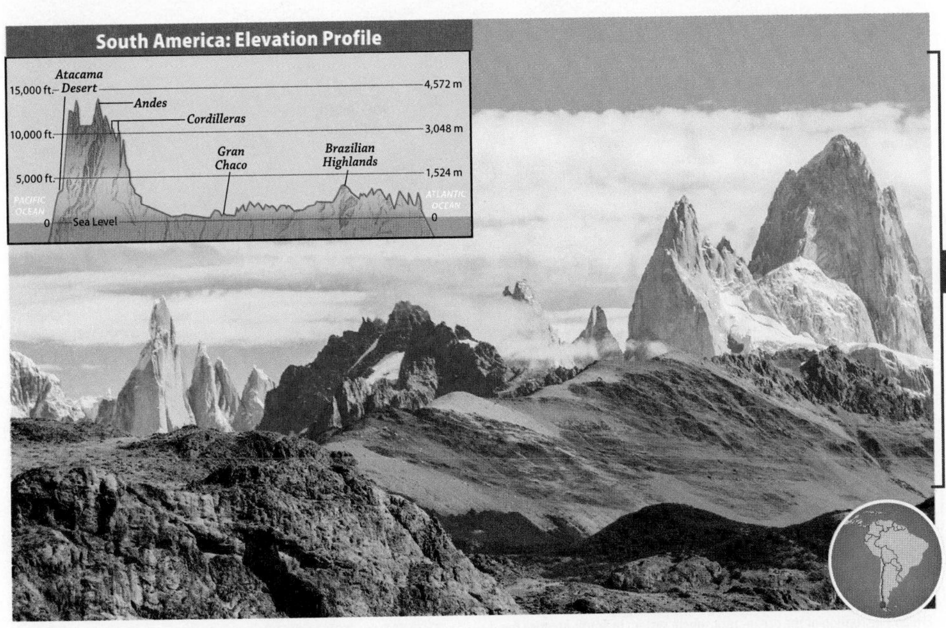

V2

The Andes extend along the western part of South America. They are the world's longest mountain chain and one of the highest.

▲ CRITICAL THINKING

1. ***Explaining*** How do physical features affect human development?
2. ***Describing*** In what ways have the populations of the Andes region become dependent on their environment?

David Madison/Photodisc/Getty Images

INTERACTIVE MAP

South America: Elevation Profile

Predicting Use this interactive map on elevation to help students consider the role that the physical environment can play to create or hinder human developments. Allow time for students to study the map. Have students work with a partner to consider different ways that landforms facilitate either the growth or decline of multiple different cultures. Have pairs list several examples of each. Then, **ask:** **Will multiple cultures continue in the face of modern communication? Why or why not?** Have one set of partners join another set of partners to discuss their paragraphs. **Interpersonal, Verbal/Linguistic**

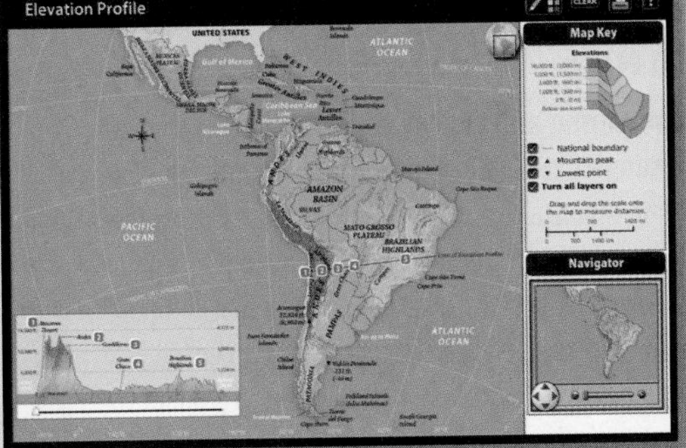

C Critical Thinking Skills

Hypothesizing Have students draw on information learned in previous chapters to hypothesize how the Andes were formed. **Ask:** **Why might you expect volcanoes to exist in the Andes?** *(The western edge of South America is part of the Ring of Fire.)* **What kinds of natural disasters would the people of the Andes experience?** *(earthquakes, falling rock, and mudslides)* **Why do you suppose people are willing to live in the Andean highlands despite these threats?** *(quality of soil and natural resources, scenery)* **Naturalist**

Content Background Knowledge

Andean Volcanoes With more than 200 volcanoes, volcanic eruptions and earthquakes are common in South America. In fact, South America has the most volcanoes of all the world's regions. Many of these volcanoes are in the Andes. Chile has 36 active volcanoes,while Ecuador has 16.

V1 Visual Skills

Identifying As a class, discuss the variety of landforms in this region. Then have students add information to the landform charts that they started earlier about each of the landforms listed in this section. ELL **Visual/Spatial**

V2 Visual Skills

Spatial Understanding Have students study the elevation profile and image. **Ask:** **What part of the elevation profile is shown in the image?** *(the Andes or the plateau indicated to the left of this on the elevation profile)* **What is the difference in altitude between the highest and lowest point in South America?** *(about 4,500 meters)* Have students describe the elevation at the Pacific and Atlantic coasts. *(The land near both coasts drops off dramatically.)* **Visual/Spatial**

ANSWERS, p. 219

✓ READING PROGRESS CHECK The rugged Andes make excessive development difficult in much of the region. Patagonia is dry, barren, and windy due to being in a rain shadow of the Andes, and so is also not ideal for development. People have chosen to settle in the Andean highlands for centuries due to cooler climates, good volcanic soil, and an abundance of natural resources. Most Brazilians live along the coast since the escarpment is an obstacle to inland development.

CRITICAL THINKING

1. Rugged peaks of mountainous areas make it difficult to lay infrastructure. This causes most settlements to be established on plateaus or in plains areas. Llanos and pampas with fertile soil attract agricultural farmers.
2. People who live in areas that are difficult to develop depend on the environment to provide for their basic needs. People in the Andes benefit from past volcanic activity in the region, which has made the soil good for agriculture.

T Technology Skills

Presenting Have students work in small groups to gather additional facts about either the Amazon or Paraguay-Paraná river systems. Have groups create a multimedia presentation for the class showing their research. Presentations should include visuals, including a schematic showing the intricate nature of the river systems and how they drain the basins they pass through. BL Visual/Spatial

R Reading Skills

Comparing and Contrasting Have students compare the Paraguay-Paraná river system to the Amazon river system. **Ask:** In what important ways are the two systems alike? *(both are large systems; both drain large areas; both eventually empty into the Atlantic Ocean; both are used to transport goods and people)* In what important ways do they differ? *(They drain different basins; the Paraguay-Paraná drains into an estuary before it flows into the Atlantic; the Paraguay-Paraná system provides hydroelectric power.)* Why do you think that the Amazon River system is not used for hydroelectric power? *(Possible answer: The Amazon does not have as much elevation drop.)* Verbal/Linguistic

W Writing Skills

Narrative Assign a different region of the map to different students. Have students write a narrative describing everyday life during an El Niño year, based on the information about the region provided on the map. Then have students read their narratives to the class. Once all narratives have been read, have students discuss the range of effects that El Niño creates throughout South America. Verbal/Linguistic, Visual/Spatial

Water Systems

GUIDING QUESTION *How are South America's rivers important for economic development?*

Waterways are important for the subregion's economic development because they provide ways to transport goods and people within and between the countries of South America. As the Western Hemisphere's longest river and the world's second longest, the Amazon River flows about 4,000 miles (6,400 km) through the heart of South America. It begins in the headwaters of the Peruvian Andes, flows across the lowlands of the Amazon Basin in the interior of Brazil, and drains into the Atlantic Ocean. Hundreds of smaller rivers join the Amazon as it flows from the Andes to the Atlantic Ocean. Together these rivers form the Amazon Basin. The basin drains an area of more than 2 million square miles (5.2 million sq. km).

The Paraná, Paraguay, and Uruguay Rivers form the second-largest river system in Latin America, draining the rainy eastern half of South America. These rivers flow through the Pantanal, one of the world's largest tropical wetlands. After coursing through inland areas, the rivers flow into a broad estuary where the ocean tide meets a river current. This estuary, the Río de la Plata, or "River of Silver," flows into the Atlantic Ocean.

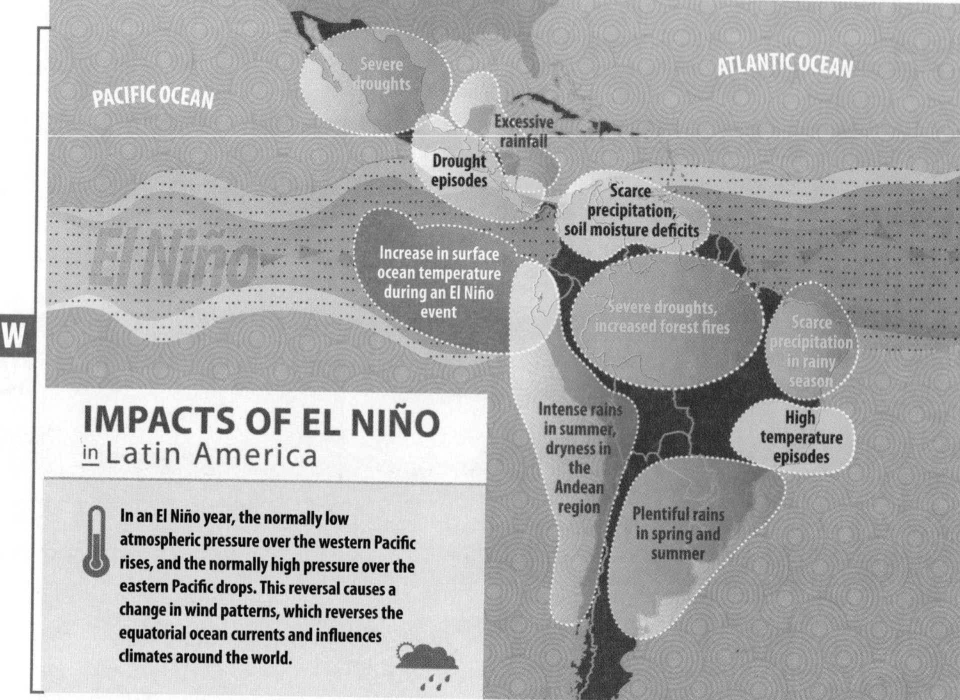
PACIFIC OCEAN
ATLANTIC OCEAN
Severe droughts
Excessive rainfall
Drought episodes
Scarce precipitation, soil moisture deficits
El Niño
Increase in surface ocean temperature during an El Niño event
Severe droughts, increased forest fires
Scarce precipitation in rainy season
Intense rains in summer, dryness in the Andean region
High temperature episodes
Plentiful rains in spring and summer
IMPACTS OF EL NIÑO in Latin America
In an El Niño year, the normally low atmospheric pressure over the western Pacific rises, and the normally high pressure over the eastern Pacific drops. This reversal causes a change in wind patterns, which reverses the equatorial ocean currents and influences climates around the world.

El Niño's disruption of the ocean-atmosphere system in South America has a great impact on climate and economies in the region.

▲ **CRITICAL THINKING**

1. ***Sequencing*** Describe the order of events beginning with changes in the atmospheric pressure systems that lead to the impacts caused by El Niño.
2. ***Speculating*** Explain how the environmental impacts of El Niño could have negative economic effects on countries.

220

networks Online Teaching Options

INFOGRAPHIC

El Niño

Comparing and Contrasting This infographic can be used to explain El Niño's effect on human life in Latin America to students. Have students study the image detailing the consequences of El Niño. Then have students create charts or graphs that compare and contrast El Niño's effects in Mexico, Central America, and South America. Suggest to students that their charts and graphs could be organized to show similarities or differences between regions. Display students' completed charts and graphs in the classroom. AL Visual/Spatial

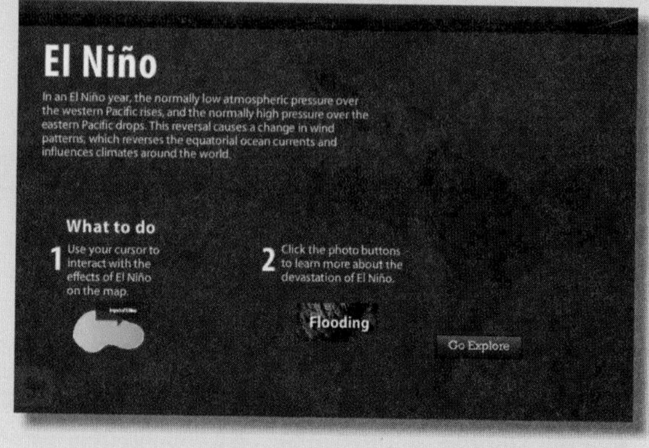
El Niño
In an El Niño year, the normally low atmospheric pressure over the western Pacific rises, and the normally high pressure over the eastern Pacific drops. This reversal causes a change in wind patterns, which reverses the equatorial ocean currents and influences climates around the world.
What to do
1 Use your cursor to interact with the effects of El Niño on the map.
2 Click the photo buttons to learn more about the devastation of El Niño.
Flooding
Go Explore

ANSWERS, p. 220

CRITICAL THINKING

1. When the atmospheric pressure rises over the western Pacific Ocean but drops over the eastern Pacific, wind patterns are reversed. Because wind patterns determine ocean currents, the equatorial ocean currents also become reversed. As cool surface temperatures become warm with the arrival of new currents, so does the air above them.
2. El Niño can cause droughts in areas that depend on rain for crops. It can also disrupt the food chain by killing plankton, which leads to lower fish populations for countries that rely on fishing. Low crop yields and low fish harvest make for fewer exports and less income for the country.

Though Latin America has few large lakes, some of its largest lakes are located in South America. Lake Maracaibo (MAH•rah•KY•boh) in Venezuela and Lake Titicaca (TEE•tee•KAH•kah), which run through Bolivia and Peru, are South America's largest lakes. Lake Titicaca is also the world's highest large lake.

READING PROGRESS CHECK

Identifying Which rivers drain the eastern part of South America?

Climate, Biomes, and Resources

GUIDING QUESTION *How does climate affect human activities in South America?*

Diverse climates make South America a region of astonishing contrasts. Steamy rain forests, arid deserts, grassy plains, and sandy beaches can all be found in the subregion. The dense, nearly impenetrable vegetation of South America's tropical rain forests represents a tremendous resource and supports many communities.

Climate Regions and Biomes

The vertical climate zones found in the highland areas of Central America and Mexico also exist in the highlands of South America. The Andes are distinct not only because of their dramatic height, but also because they have such cold climates despite their proximity to the otherwise tropical equatorial zone. The range in elevation has produced a wide variety of climate and ecological zones.

V

The temperate climate of the *tierra templada* is found in areas of Peru, Brazil, and Colombia. Many Andean communities are located in the *tierra fría*. People in the highlands subsist on potato, barley, and quinoa crops that grow well in this colder climate. South America's colonial cities in Peru, Bolivia, and Colombia were developed over historical indigenous cities at high altitudes to extract valuable mineral resources found in the Andes. Consequently, several South American capitals are located in the *tierra fría* zone. The *tierra helada* and the *puna,* the highest vertical climate zones located above the tree line, are zones of permanent snow and ice on the peaks of the Andes.

The El Niño **phenomenon** also affects climate in South America. El Niño creates unusually warm ocean conditions on the west coast that extend as far north as Ecuador and as far south as Chile. As in Central America and the Caribbean, El Niño can have negative effects on coastal weather, fishing, and agriculture.

C

Tropical wet (rain forest) and tropical wet/dry (savanna) are the **predominant** climates of eastern South America, which is home to the Amazon rain forest, the world's largest rain forest. It is located primarily in Brazil but also extends into Peru, Colombia, Venezuela, Ecuador, Bolivia, Guyana, Suriname, and French Guiana. The Amazon shelters more species of plants and animals per square mile than anywhere else on Earth. It covers one-third of South America and is the world's wettest tropical plain. Heavy rains drench the densely forested lowlands.

A tropical wet/dry climate is typical of north-central South America. These areas have high temperatures and abundant rainfall, but also experience an extended dry season. In many tropical wet/dry areas, grasslands flourish. Some of these grasslands, such as the llanos of Colombia and Venezuela, are covered with scattered trees and are considered transition zones between grasslands and forests. A humid subtropical climate exists in much of southeastern South America. Winters here are short with cool to mild temperatures. Summers are long, hot, and humid. Rainfall is generally uniform throughout the year, but it can be heavier during the summer.

T

Much of the inland parts of Peru, Bolivia, and Chile experience an arid climate. In these areas, cold air and high elevations result in very little precipitation. Shifting winds and the rain shadow effect of the Andes produce

Connecting Geography to SCIENCE

Biology

The Galápagos Islands are located about 600 miles (965 km) off Ecuador's Pacific coast. They are home to the northernmost species of penguin, the Galapagos penguin. These small penguins feed on fish and marine crustaceans, but their population is vulnerable to disruptions in their food supply. Episodes of El Niño can trigger such shortages. El Niño causes the ocean surface to warm, which reduces the number of plankton. Plankton form the base of the food chain on which the penguins rely. Fish and crustacean populations that feed on plankton dwindle as a result. This, in turn, limits the food supply of the penguins.

PROBLEM SOLVING What can humans do to ensure the survival of Galapagos penguins when El Niño events occur? Is this a desirable goal? Explain your answer.

phenomenon a fact or event of scientific interest that can be scientifically explained or described

predominant main or most common

V Visual Skills

Creating Diagrams Have students work with a partner to create a vertical altitude-to-temperature diagram showing how climate zones in South America vary according to altitude. The diagram should include these climate zones: Tierra Caliente, Tierra Templada, Tierra Fria, Tierra Helada, and Puna. Have students note the altitude ranges and the predominant vegetation and climates of each zone. Encourage students to use their textbook, atlases, and online resources to complete their diagrams. **BL** **Visual/Spatial, Interpersonal**

T Technology Skills

Researching To augment the climate zone information presented in the text, have students use the Internet to find a vegetation map and a rainfall map of South America. In pairs, have students study the maps to answer the following questions:

- **What areas of South America have the heaviest rainfall?** *(the northeast coast (the Guianas and parts of Brazil and Venezuela), the northwest coast (Colombia), the southwest coast (Chile), and the western part of the Amazon Basin)*
- **What is the predominant vegetation in these areas?** *(tropical rain or other forests)*
- **What areas of South America have the least rainfall?** *(west-central coast (Peru and parts of Chile), southeastern coast (Argentina))*
- **What is the predominant vegetation in these areas?** *(little or no vegetation or desert shrub)*
- **What is the annual rainfall in the tall grassland areas?** *(predominantly subtropical climate; rainfall varies from 100–200 centimeters annually)* **Visual/Spatial**

C Critical Thinking Skills

Comparing In small groups, have students think about the geography and climate zone of the region where they live. Have students identify a comparable biome in South America, if possible. Have students identify the similarities and differences between the biome in South America and their own home biome. If there are no comparable biomes in South America, have students describe what makes their biome so different from those found in South America. **BL** **Naturalist, Logical/Mathematical**

VIDEO

Around the World – Chile

Describing Use the video to give the students a visual impression of South America's varied geography. Ask them to describe all of the different kinds of terrain that are displayed in the video. Have them write a paragraph about how Chile's wildly varied terrain is representative of the land in South America, and how this has affected the way that population is dispersed through the continent. **ELL** **Verbal/Linguistic**

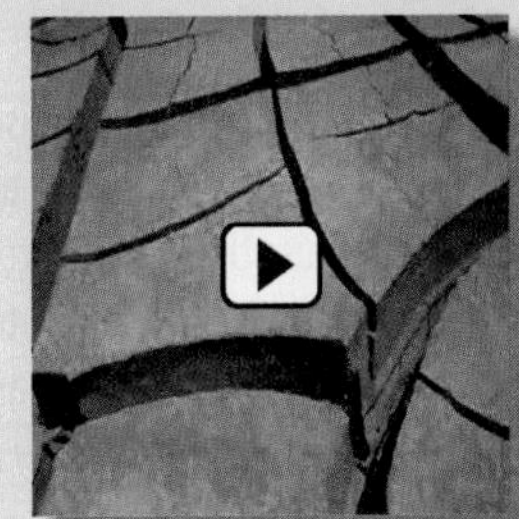

ANSWERS, p. 221

READING PROGRESS CHECK The Paraná, Paraguay, and Uruguay Rivers form a system that drains the eastern half of South America.

Connecting Geography Possible answer: Humans might add plankton to the ocean after an El Niño event in order to replenish the supply. Yes, this is a desirable goal, as it helps to stem the possibility of a species becoming extinct.

V Visual Skills

Analyzing Visuals Draw students' attention to the graph. **Ask:** What can you infer about Venezuela's economy? *(Venezuela has a stronger economy because of its extremely large share of the oil reserves.)* Does this graph tell the whole story about the different economies in Latin America? *(Possible answer: No, there are other important resources that may be prevalent in some of the countries that do not have large oil reserves)* BL **Visual/Spatial, Logical/Mathematical**

C Critical Thinking Skills

Posing Questions Have students think about the importance of mineral resources to the local economies. Explain that the best way to understand the full economic impact is to learn about the way such resources are produced, used, and sold. Have students make a list of questions that would help them to better understand this impact. **Verbal/Linguistic**

CLOSE & REFLECT

Summarizing Have students use the landform charts they created to write a brief visitor's guide to South America. Use the guides to review the lesson.

ANSWERS, p. 222

READING PROGRESS CHECK The three predominant climates of South America are tropical wet, found in the Amazon rain forest, which covers one-third of South America, primarily Brazil; tropical wet/dry, typical of north-central South America; and humid subtropical, which exists in much of southeastern South America.

CRITICAL THINKING

1. Venezuela has almost 25 times more oil reserves than Ecuador.
2. The areas with the most oil reserves are likely the most economically prosperous, while those with the least must rely on resources other than oil for income.

V

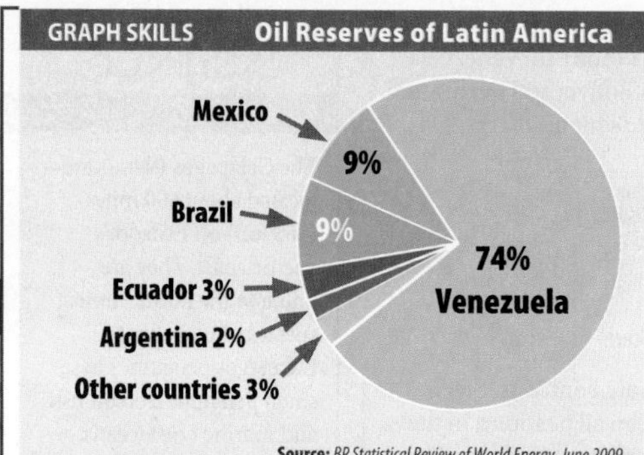

Oil reserves in Latin America are not evenly distributed, as shown in the circle graph.

▲ CRITICAL THINKING

1. ***Contrasting*** How do the oil reserves in Venezuela compare to those of Ecuador?
2. ***Making Connections*** How might the uneven balance of oil reserves be reflected in the region's economic development?

aridity in the southeastern part of Argentina. The low vegetation here is adapted to the low moisture conditions. The cold, oceanic Peru Current creates dry coastal deserts along the Pacific coast of Chile and Peru. These desert areas are called the Atacama. It is so arid that in some places no rainfall has ever been recorded. A dense fog known as *camanchaca* is the only appreciable source of precipitation.

Natural Resources

South American countries are among the world's leading producers of energy resources. Energy resources have supported major growth in economies such as that of Venezuela, which holds most of the subregion's oil reserves. Because of South America's substantial natural resources and active tectonic plates that allow for oil extraction, countries continue to search for additional, yet untapped oil reserves.

C

South America also has an abundance of mineral resources. For example, the foothills along Venezuela's Orinoco River contain large amounts of gold, and Peru is known for silver. Mines in Colombia have been producing the world's finest emeralds for more than 1,000 years. South America's non-precious minerals also have significant economic value. Chile is the world's largest exporter of copper. Peru and Chile together hold almost one-fourth of the world's known copper reserves.

Countries in South America do not have equal access to the continent's natural resources. The size of Venezuela's oil reserves in comparison to the rest of the subregion's countries is a clear example of this unbalanced distribution of energy resources. The physical geography within and surrounding each country largely dictates its access to natural resources. Alongside political borders dictated by physical geography, distribution of natural resources within South America was a decisive factor in defining countries' political borders. Extraction of resources also relates to a country's infrastructure, level of economic development, and relationships between people and their government. Countries with low capital, social and political divisions, and lack of advanced technology for extracting resources have been at a disadvantage in comparison to countries that can cope with such factors.

READING PROGRESS CHECK

Identifying Name three predominant climates in South America and describe their locations.

LESSON 1 REVIEW (CCSS)

Reviewing Vocabulary (Tier Three Words)

1. ***Identifying*** Name and describe the two inland grasslands areas of South America. RH.9–10.4

Using Your Notes

2. ***Listing*** Using your graphic organizer, describe the llanos and the Atacama. Include the climates of the regions and any adaptations that plants and animals must have to survive.

Answering the Guiding Questions

3. ***Assessing*** How has South America's rugged landscape both attracted and isolated people?
4. ***Describing*** How are South America's rivers important for economic development?
5. ***Drawing Conclusions*** How does climate affect human activities in South America?

Writing Activity

6. ***Informative/Explanatory*** How has varied access to natural resources in South America promoted different rates of development among countries? Identify specific examples of natural resources in South American countries. WHST.9–10.2

222

LESSON 1 REVIEW ANSWERS

Reviewing Vocabulary

1. Two grasslands are the llanos, located in Colombia and Venezuela, and the pampas, in Argentina and Uruguay. These areas provide grazing for cattle. Also, the pampas is considered a breadbasket, producing wheat and corn.

Using Your Notes

2. Llanos are part of South America's inland grasslands and have a tropical wet/dry climate with high temperatures and abundant rainfall, but also have an extended dry season. Animals and plants must adapt to be able to survive during the dry season without great quantities of water. The Atacama is a coastal desert in Chile and Peru. The climate is so arid that in some places no rainfall has ever been recorded. A dense fog is the only source of precipitation. Plants and animals must adapt to survive on small amounts of water.

Answering the Guiding Questions

3. Despite the threats of natural disasters, for thousands of years people have been attracted to the South American highlands because the climate is cooler, the volcanic soil is good for agriculture, and natural resources are concentrated in the high altitude areas. The cordilleras have isolated people because they act as natural barriers.
4. Waterways are important for economic development because they provide ways to transport goods and people within and between countries of South America.
5. Many Andean communities live in the *tierra fría* and subsist off potato, barley, and quinoa crops that grow well in the colder climate zone. Colonial cities in Peru, Bolivia, and Colombia were developed over indigenous cities to extract mineral resources found at high altitudes in the Andes.

Writing Activity

6. Venezuela has long been profiting from a large number of oil reserves. Borders established in favor of one country's ability to extract resources limit the potential of neighboring countries to tap into that wealth. More highly developed countries with solid infrastructure and economies are able to develop better technology for extracting oil and mineral resources, which pushes them further ahead while others continue to struggle.

networks

There's More Online!

- **IMAGE** Moche Funeral Mask
- **MAP** Dominant Ethnic Groups of South America
- **MAP** Agricultural Land Use in South America
- **TIME LINE** South America: Movements of Change
- **INTERACTIVE SELF-CHECK QUIZ**
- **VIDEO** Human Geography of South America

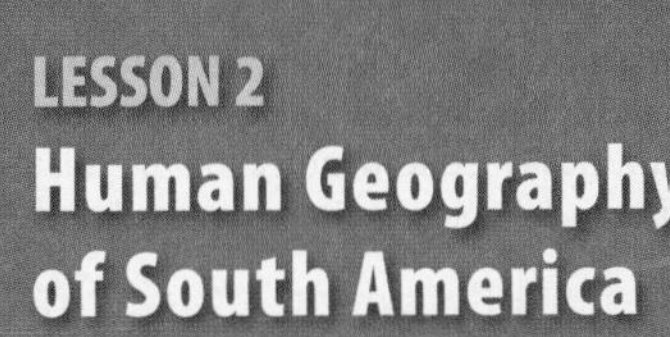

LESSON 2
Human Geography of South America

ESSENTIAL QUESTION • *How do physical systems and human systems shape a place?*

Reading **HELP**DESK 

Academic Vocabulary (Tier Two Words)
- **widespread**
- **implement**

Content Vocabulary (Tier Three Words)
- **quipu**
- **brain drain**
- **uneven development**

TAKING NOTES: ***Key Ideas and Details***

SUMMARIZING Use a graphic organizer like the one below to take notes on the human geography of South America as you read.

Human Geography of South America
- History and Government →
- Population Patterns →
- Society and Culture Today →

It Matters Because

The society and governments of South America have been shaped by the subregion's rich history of indigenous peoples and their interactions with Europeans, Africans, and Asians. The modern economic geography—based on agricultural practices, the continent's natural resources, and industrial development—has resulted in an imbalance in overall wealth and development. R1

History and Government

GUIDING QUESTION *How have indigenous peoples and Europeans contributed to the creation of modern governments in South America?*

South America's diverse population is the result of centuries of blending among hundreds of indigenous groups, Europeans, Africans, and Asians. Some areas in South America are a microcosm of these diverse cultures. In other areas—many of them remote and isolated—indigenous peoples live much as their ancestors did hundreds of years ago, virtually untouched by the influence of other cultures or modern technology. C

Early Cultures and European Conquest

Before the Inca established their empire in the Andes, other early indigenous groups—such as the Moche, Mapuche, and Aymara—developed societies that were based primarily on agriculture. The Inca later established a highly developed civilization in the area. At its height, the Inca Empire stretched from present-day Ecuador to central Chile. R2

The Inca were skilled engineers. They built temples and fortresses and laid out a network of roads that crossed mountain passes and penetrated forests. Inca farmers cut terraces into the slopes of the Andes and built irrigation systems. Machu Picchu, Peru's most well-known archaeological site, is a grand display of Inca engineering that is remarkably preserved. With no Inca written language, knowledge was passed on to each generation through storytelling. The Inca used **quipus** (KEE•poos) to account for financial and historical records.

ENGAGE

R1 Reading Skills

Interpreting Have the class brainstorm what they know about the history of South America. Record students' information on the board, organizing it into categories such as Culture, Religion, or Historical Events. Then discuss the content in the *It Matters Because* section.

TEACH & ASSESS

C Critical Thinking Skills

Drawing Inferences After students have reread the section, **ask:** **How would you describe the process of blending among indigenous and other groups?** *(As people from different cultures live and work together for long periods of time, they share ideas and traditions and intermarry. Eventually a new population develops with characteristics from the different original cultures.)* **Why would indigenous people in remote areas keep their old ways?** *(They are less likely to be exposed to newcomers, to exchange ideas, and to intermarry.)*
AL **Logical/Mathematical**

R2 Reading Skills

Applying Display the online chapter map of South America. Ask a student to point out how far the Inca Empire extended at its height. *(Students should trace a line from Ecuador and Chile.)* **Ask:** **What challenges does the terrain in this area present to settlers?** *(Steep, rocky terrain makes transportation, building, and farming difficult.)* **How did the Inca meet these challenges?** *(They used their engineering skills to carve roads out of rock, to build into hillsides, and to create terraces for farming.)* Invite a small group of students to research Machu Picchu and then present their findings to the class. **Verbal/Linguistic, Visual/Spatial**

INTERACTIVE BELLRINGER

Simón Bolívar's Message

Analyzing This passage can be used to discuss how the colonists of South America felt during their fight for independence from Spain. Have students read the passage and use their prior knowledge to answer the questions. Then ask students to write a paraphrase of Bolívar's message showing that they understand his meaning. **Verbal/Linguistic, Interpersonal**

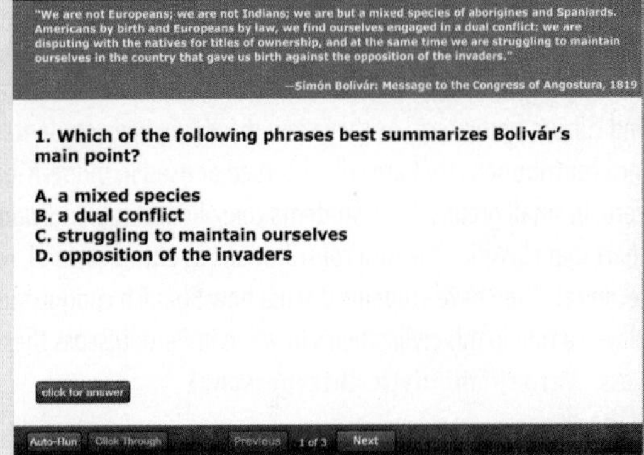

Simón Bolivár's Message
"We are not Europeans; we are not Indians; we are but a mixed species of aborigines and Spaniards. Americans by birth and Europeans by law, we find ourselves engaged in a dual conflict: we are disputing with the natives for titles of ownership, and at the same time we are struggling to maintain ourselves in the country that gave us birth against the opposition of the invaders."
—Simón Bolivár: Message to the Congress of Angostura, 1819
1. Which of the following phrases best summarizes Bolivár's main point?
A. a mixed species
B. a dual conflict
C. struggling to maintain ourselves
D. opposition of the invaders
click for answer
Auto-Run
Click Through
Previous
1 of 3
Next

ANSWERS, p. 223

TAKING NOTES: History and Government—Hundreds of indigenous groups existed on the continent before the arrival of Europeans, Asians, and Africans. A history of colonialism and periods of harsh rule by the wealthy elite are still affecting the government of some South American countries today. **Population Patterns**—South America is home to almost 400 million people. Population numbers are rapidly increasing. Population density is highest in urban regions. The high rate of population growth magnifies the challenges to settlement already presented by physical geography. **Society and Culture Today**—South America has an ethnically diverse population. European, Asian, African, and indigenous cultural influences can be found. In parts of the subregion, especially in rural or more remote areas, many indigenous cultures still live much as their ancestors did.

T Technology Skills

Researching Have students work in groups to research important dates in the region's colonial period and develop a time line beginning with the Spanish conquest of the Inca in 1532 through the independence revolutions of 1800s. Direct students to assign each group member a specific country to research. Time lines might include the dates when key Indian groups were conquered, countries and cities that were settled, important wars and rebellions, or other significant events. Have groups present their time lines to the class. **Verbal/Linguistic**

R Reading Skills

Summarizing Guide students in a discussion about how South America's postcolonial period differed from that of the United States. **Ask:** **What hindered the newly independent countries of South America in forming stable democratic governments?** *(Possible answers: They lacked the tradition of self-government; power remained in the hands of a wealthy elite; dictators in many nations were able to seize power with military backing.)* **How was the situation in the United States different?** *(Colonists had some experience with self-government and were dedicated to the principles of democracy as spelled out in the Constitution and the Bill of Rights.)* **How has governance in South American nations changed?** *(In many nations, dictatorships have given way to democratically elected governments. However, corruption, violence, poverty, inequality, and other problems threaten many of these democracies.)*
AL Verbal/Linguistic

V Visual Skills

Reading Charts Have students study the time line and give it other titles. **Ask:** **How does the first event on the time line help to explain the second event?** *(The first event describes how Bolivia ended up as a landlocked country, showing that Bolivia was not always landlocked and explaining why Bolivia would want to regain access to the Atlantic coast.)* **What can you infer about what happened in Argentina between 1952 and 1973?** *(There was some type of war that led to the overthrow of the government. During that time, Perón left the country.)* Encourage students to do online research to add recent political events to the time line.
Verbal/Linguistic, Visual/Spatial

ANSWERS, p. 224

✓ READING PROGRESS CHECK The Inca dominated much of western South America.

CRITICAL THINKING

1. Bolivia lost the Atacama Desert and territory along the southern Pacific coast.
2. Perón and Chávez both followed the ideology of nationalism and initiated populist policies.

quipu knotted cords of various lengths and colors used by the Inca to keep financial records

Silver and gold were important resources in the Inca culture. The precious metals and the wealth of farmers of the Inca Empire attracted Spanish conquistadors to Peru. After defeating the Inca army and its rulers, they looted the empire's capital and network of cities. The Inca connected their vast empire with a network of roads that extended throughout the empire. This allowed the Spanish conquerors to move quickly through the region. Spanish conquistadors expanded into Colombia, Argentina, and Chile. The Portuguese settled on the coast of Brazil, and the British, French, and Dutch later settled in parts of northern South America. The effects of epidemics caused by diseases introduced by the Europeans and the hardships of intensive labor on colonial plantations drastically reduced indigenous populations. To meet the resulting labor shortage, European colonists imported enslaved Africans.

Independence and Movements for Change

In the 1800s, independence movements arose in South America. These were inspired by the French and American Revolutions, as well as by the struggles for independence in Mexico and the Caribbean. By the mid-1800s, led by revolutionaries such as Simón Bolívar of Venezuela and José de San Martín of Argentina, most South American countries had won independence.

The postcolonial period was politically and economically unstable for most of the newly independent countries. They lacked a tradition of self-government. Power remained in the hands of the wealthy and elite classes of residents, despite written constitutions. With military backing, caudillos, or dictators, throughout South America seized power in the nineteenth century. Caudillos often gained power illegally and with much bloodshed among civilians.

Dictatorships have given way to democratically elected governments across South America. Today, however, these countries are struggling with many issues. These include political corruption and violence, wide gaps between the rich and poor, unemployment, and protecting the rights of indigenous groups.

✓ READING PROGRESS CHECK

Identifying What early indigenous civilization dominated much of western South America?

TIME LINE

SOUTH AMERICA
Movements of Change

The history of South America traces the rise of ancient empires that were nearly destroyed by colonialism, followed by wars of independence. Today, contemporary protests are fueled by social inequalities.

▶ CRITICAL THINKING

1. ***Analyzing*** What did Bolivia lose as a result of the War of the Pacific?
2. ***Comparing*** How were the policies of Perón similar to those of Chávez?

1850

1879–1883 Chile fights Bolivia and Peru in the War of the Pacific. Dispute arises over Bolivian-held Atacama Desert along the Pacific coast. Peru and Bolivia lose the war, ceding land to Chile. Bolivia is left landlocked.

1932–1935 Bolivia tries to gain access to the Atlantic coast by taking land from Paraguay, resulting in the Chaco War. A peace treaty grants Paraguay most of the disputed region.

networks Online Teaching Options

VIDEO

Machu Picchu

Classifying Use this video about Machu Picchu to discuss the history, society, and culture of the Inca. As they view the video, have students list the different Inca contributions that are still observed or used in modern-day societies in Peru. In small groups, have students consolidate their individual lists into a chart that classifies the Inca contributions as either cultural, religious, or technical. Then have students discuss how Spanish conquistadors may have played a role in this civilization's location in Peru. Discuss these answers as a class. **Verbal/Linguistic, Interpersonal**

Population Patterns

GUIDING QUESTION *How has South America's physical geography influenced its population patterns?*

South America is the world's fourth-largest continent. The continent's 12 countries are home to nearly 400 million people. Like much of the rest of the developing world, population growth is steady, and so is the migration of people into large, urban areas.

South America's once high rate of population growth is beginning to slow. Urban populations now include fewer children as well as women and men with increased levels of education. Most people live on or near the coasts and along major rivers of the continent. These coastal regions offer favorable climates, fertile land, and access to transportation. The rain forests, deserts, and mountainous areas of South America's interior have discouraged human settlement.

South American countries tend to have low population densities. Ecuador, the most densely populated country in South America, has an average of 132 people per square mile (51 people per sq. km). Brazil has a population of nearly 200 million. However, because Brazil has about 3.2 million square miles (8.4 million sq. km), its average population density is about 60 people per square mile (23 people per sq. km). Despite population densities that are lower overall than other world regions, much of the economic and structural development is concentrated in major cities. Today about 80 percent of the subregion's population lives in urban areas.

In highly populated urban areas such as São Paulo, Buenos Aires, and Bogotá, finding employment and suitable living conditions is difficult for migrants arriving in the city. Rural-to-urban migrants seek higher wages, better living conditions, and sometimes an escape from the violence of drug cartels or criminal groups. Countries across the region are experiencing **brain drain** to North America and Europe as people search for a better life.

brain drain the loss of highly educated and skilled workers to other countries

READING PROGRESS CHECK

Explaining Why do most South Americans live along the continent's coasts?

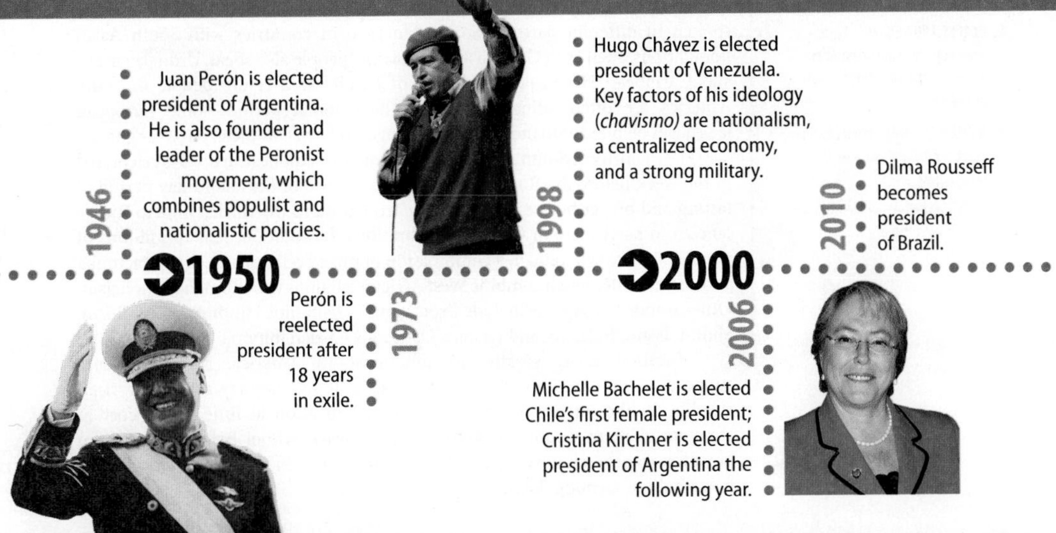

1946
Juan Perón is elected president of Argentina. He is also founder and leader of the Peronist movement, which combines populist and nationalistic policies.
1950
1973
Perón is reelected president after 18 years in exile.
1998
Hugo Chávez is elected president of Venezuela. Key factors of his ideology (chavismo) are nationalism, a centralized economy, and a strong military.
2000
2006
Michelle Bachelet is elected Chile's first female president; Cristina Kirchner is elected president of Argentina the following year.
2010
Dilma Rousseff becomes president of Brazil.

INTERACTIVE MAP

Cultures of South America, A.D. 700–1530

Analyzing Visuals Use this map to provide students with a visual of how settlement patterns have changed as human society has changed in South America. Have students read the interactive text layers in the map. Point out that South Americans have settled primarily in coastal areas. Have students work with a partner to discuss living patterns in South America. Then ask pairs to consider how and why population patterns have changed by writing a short paragraph that explains their answers. **AL** **Verbal/Linguistic**

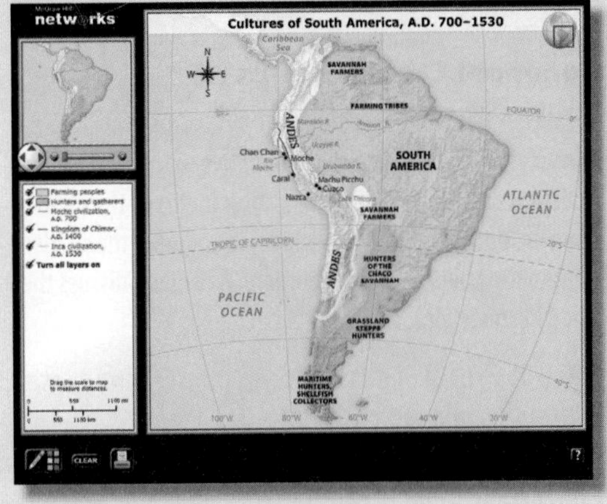

V Visual Skills

Understanding Relationships Divide students into small groups. Have groups compare the population density map to the physical map of South America. Then in a class discussion, **ask:** **Why might the relatively low population density of South American countries be misleading?** *(There may be large areas of a country where there are very few people. In this case, the population density would be much higher where most of the people live.)* Next, have groups research the population and population density of several large cities in the United States, as well as the following South American cities: São Paulo, Brazil; Buenos Aires, Argentina; Lima, Peru; Rio de Janeiro, Brazil; Bogotá, Colombia; and Salvador, Brazil. Have groups create a chart or diagram that compares the population densities of the South American cities to one another, as well as to the cities in the United States that they researched. **BL** **Visual/Spatial, Logical/Mathematical**

Content Background Knowledge

Population Densities Rio de Janeiro's area is 485 square miles (1,255 sq. km). Its population in 2010 was 6,320,446. Therefore, its population density is 13,032 people per square mile. In contrast, the greater Rio area is 2,079 square miles (5,384 sq. km) with a population of 11,875,063 in 2010. The population density is 5,712 people per square mile.

W Writing Skills

Narrative Discuss what life might be like in poor rural areas of South America and why people often migrate to a city. Challenge students to imagine that they are poor peasants living in one of those rural villages. Have them write a brief account describing life in a village, the decision to move to a city, and experiences in the city after they make the move. Encourage students to do additional research for their project. **AL** **Verbal/Linguistic**

ANSWERS, p. 225

READING PROGRESS CHECK Most South Americans live along the coasts because coastal areas were easier to develop than the continent's interior, which is covered by humid rain forests, dry deserts, and rugged mountains. The coastal areas also offer residents more favorable climates, fertile land, and access to transportation.

V Visual Skills

Analyzing Maps Explain that the map indicates where various ethnic groups are concentrated in South America. **Ask:** **Where are Europeans largely concentrated?** *(Argentina and southeast Brazil)* **Where are Andean indigenous groups located?** *(Andes from northern Chile and western Bolivia north into Peru and Ecuador)* **Which ethnic groups live along the west coast of South America?** *(Mestizo, European, and Indigenous)* Have students create a two-column table listing the ethnic population by countries using the map and information from the text as a resource. **Visual/Spatial**

R Reading Skills

Discussing Lead a class discussion about the diverse ethnic groups in South America, as well as the variety of languages they speak. **Ask: Where do most of the indigenous groups live?** *(in the rural and less populated areas; in the Andes region of Ecuador, Peru, and Bolivia and in southern Chile)* **What are the main European languages that are probably spoken in South America?** *(French, Dutch, Italian, German, Spanish, Portuguese)* **How does the population of Argentina contrast with that of the population of Venezuela?** *(Argentina's population is mainly of European descent, while Venezuela's population is of Mestizo and African descent.)* **AL Verbal/Linguistic**

C Critical Thinking Skills

Identifying Cause and Effect Point out that many religions are practiced in South America today. **Ask: Why is Catholicism the predominant religion in South America?** *(When the Spanish and Portuguese arrived in the 1500s and 1600s, they imposed their religious beliefs on the indigenous people.)* **Why do you suppose tens of millions of people practice syncretism in this region?** *(Possible answer: The indigenous people and immigrants such as West Africans did not want to give up their native religions. Over time they adopted some Catholic practices and melded them to their own religions.)* **Logical/Mathematical**

ANSWERS, p. 226

GEOGRAPHY CONNECTION

1. The majority of indigenous people live in the rain forests and mountainous areas that are rural and isolated from the dominant ethnic groups.
2. The countries along the northern, northeastern, and eastern coasts of South America—Colombia, Venezuela, Guyana, Suriname, French Guiana, and Brazil—have large African populations.

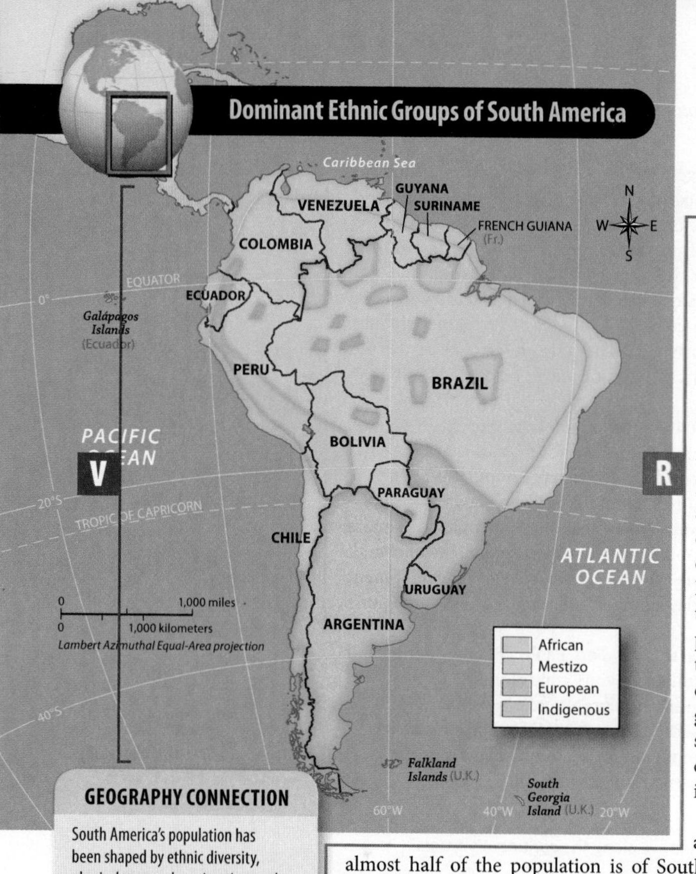

GEOGRAPHY CONNECTION

South America's population has been shaped by ethnic diversity, physical geography, migration, and urban growth.

1. ***PLACES AND REGIONS*** What landforms are found in the areas where the majority of indigenous people live?
2. ***HUMAN SYSTEMS*** What countries in South America have large African populations?

Society and Culture Today

GUIDING QUESTION *Why is South America one of the world's most culturally diverse areas?*

South America is home to an ethnically diverse population. Today many indigenous cultural groups inhabit the subregion, especially in rural or less populated areas. Most indigenous groups—of which there are more than 350—live in the Andes region of Ecuador, Peru, and Bolivia.

The Spanish and Portuguese were the first Europeans in South America. Enslaved Africans were later brought as laborers. After South American countries gained their independence, other European groups—French, Dutch, Italians, and Germans—moved to South America. In fact, Argentina's population is 97 percent European, as the majority of Argentines are descendants of Spanish and Italian immigrants. Towns in the lakes region of southern Chile exhibit architecture, cuisine, and traditions influenced by its German population.

Immigrants from Asia also arrived in South America. In Guyana, almost half of the population is of South Asian descent. People of Chinese descent have immigrated to Peru. Many people of Japanese descent live in Brazil, Argentina, and Peru. Spanish, Portuguese, Dutch, French, and English are each spoken in different parts of South America. In countries with South Asian populations, such as in Guyana and Suriname, people also speak Urdu, Javanese, and Caribbean Hindustani, a dialect of Hindi. As a result, people in South America are often bilingual. During the colonial period, some European languages blended with indigenous languages to form completely new languages.

The majority of South Americans are Roman Catholic. Carnival is celebrated in the week before the Roman Catholic observance of Lent, a 40-day period of fasting and prayer before Easter. People from around the world come to Rio de Janeiro to participate in Carnival celebrations. In addition, tens of millions of people practice syncretism, a combination of mixed religions, such as Macumba and Candomblé, which combine West African religions with Roman Catholicism. Other minority religions include Protestant Christianity, Hinduism, Buddhism, Shinto, Islam, Judaism, and Eastern Orthodox Christianity.

Education varies greatly throughout South America. Many countries support public education through high school, and literacy rates have risen steadily. Public universities provide higher education at little or no cost to students in many countries. Many children leave school before completion, however, to help support the family by selling goods in markets or engaging in household or farming duties.

226

networks Online Teaching Options

INTERACTIVE MAP

Dominant Ethnic Groups of South America

Identifying Trends Use this interactive map to help students consider travel and migration routes of the people living in South America. Have students compare the shaded areas to the political country borders. As a class, discuss the following questions. **Ask:**

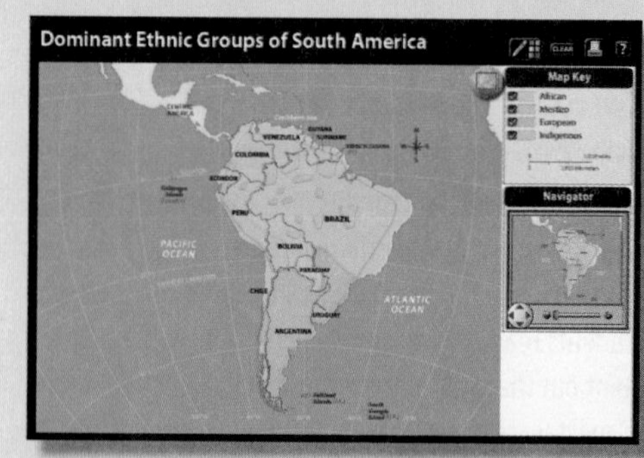

- **Why do you think certain ethnic groups tend to stay within certain regions?**
- **What physical landforms generally prevent the spread of ethnic growth?**
- **Do certain ethnic groups seem to remain in certain countries? Why do you think this is?** *(Student answers may vary, but should consider landscape and borders and show logical reasoning.)* **AL Logical/Mathematical**

In countries with stable economies and high standards of living, people have access to better health care and live longer, healthier lives. This results in a situation of **uneven development** among countries. The health of a country's people is linked to poverty, lack of sanitation, infectious diseases, and malnutrition. These conditions persist in rural areas and especially in the slums on the outskirts of cities where millions of people live in overcrowded conditions.

uneven development condition in which some places do not benefit as much as others from social and economic advancement

Family and the Status of Women

In urban upper and middle classes, the family unit is likely to consist of a nuclear household—father, mother, and dependent children—rather than an extended family. Loyalty and responsibility toward the extended family, however, remain very strong. The *compadre* relationship, in which parents and godparents share in the upbringing of a child, is valued in parts of Latin America. However, changes brought about by urban society have diminished its overall importance.

The elevation of women's rights has grown as countries have established more stable governments and economies in the past few decades. The result is an increasing proportion of women entering the workforce. Work codes in Chile and Colombia provide benefits for pregnant employees, and women's earnings are increasing in comparison to men's wages. Although women can still face discrimination and mistreatment, there are signs of change. Some countries now provide shelters for abused women and enforce stricter penalties for offenders.

The Arts

Indigenous arts survive in many different forms. The massive buildings of the ancient Inca at Cuzco and Machu Picchu reveal a mastery of stone and engineering that are still studied today for their ingenuity. Traditional arts and crafts dating from before the arrival of the Europeans—such as weaving, ceramics, and metalworking—have been passed from generation to generation.

Music also has ancient ties. Panpipes are one of the most common pre-Columbian musical instruments from the Andean region. Musical traditions later mixed Native American, African, and European influences to create unique styles. The Brazilian samba, Chilean cumbia, and the Argentine tango complement the Cuban salsa and Dominican merengue to exemplify the diversity of music developed from a mixture of cultural and geographical roots.

READING PROGRESS CHECK

Specifying How has South America's role as a cultural melting pot contributed to its unique cultural elements?

This funeral mask from the Moche culture of South America is pre-Columbian, meaning it dates from before the arrival of Europeans.

▼ CRITICAL THINKING

1. ***Theorizing*** Why might geographers use the term *pre-Columbian* when studying cultures? Think about the significance of the arrival of Europeans.
2. ***Making Connections*** What features do you recognize in the mask as being similar to a popular fad in youth cultures today?

Economic Activities

GUIDING QUESTION *How have South America's abundant natural resources contributed to its economic development?*

Several countries in the region have combined their abundance of natural resources with current changes in government and improved economic conditions. Argentina is not only rich in natural resources, but also has a highly literate population and a diversified economic base that have helped to fuel a strong expansion in its economy. Brazil, the largest country in South America, has been undergoing continuous growth and development since 1970. Taking advantage of its natural resources, Brazil has become a powerful country in economic terms. Chile has established

G1 Critical Thinking Skills

Interpreting Guide students in a discussion on the standard of living in South America. **Ask:** What are some of the indicators of a high standard of living? *(high rates of literacy, employment, health care, and income, long life expectancy)* What is the connection between the health of a country's people and its wealth or poverty? *(Countries that have high rates of poverty also generally have limited access to doctors, as well as poor nutrition, sanitation, and living conditions.)* Which parts of South America's population are most likely to have a low standard of living and poor health care? *(people in rural areas and in urban slums)* What are some of the causes of poverty in South America? *(unemployment or lack of opportunity; illiteracy; no land and overcrowding; limited resources)* What are some of the causes of uneven development among nations? *(unequal distribution of resources, capital, and infrastructure; lack of economic opportunity; an agricultural-based economy)* AL Verbal/Linguistic

C2 Critical Thinking Skills

Identifying Central Issues Explain that while women in South America have the right to vote (Chile granted suffrage in 1931; Peru in 1955), women traditionally have not shared equal status with men. While that may be changing, there are still inequalities. Challenge sets of students to develop a list of criteria by which to measure the status of women in a society. Suggest that they use criteria used by notable world organizations. BL Verbal/Linguistic

T Technology Skills

Presenting Have students work in small groups to research South America's architectural, arts and crafts, or musical traditions. Groups should prepare audiovisual presentations with illustrations and accompanying music for the class, describing the art/music/architecture as well as the region known for that art. **Auditory/Musical, Interpersonal**

INTERACTIVE MAP

European Colonies in Latin America, 1800

Hypothesizing Use this interactive map to explore the relationship between culture and art by analyzing the placement of European colonies in Latin America during the 1800s. Have students compare the ancient cultures to the map locations of European colonies. Have students write a hypothesis on whether or not it is possible to look at the style of an indigenous artifact to decide whether it was pre- or post-European. Students' hypotheses should reflect consideration of professional geologists and archaeologists. AL Verbal/Linguistic

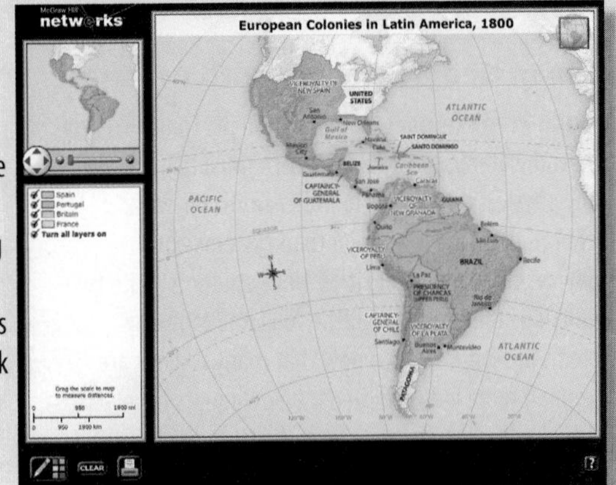

ANSWERS, p. 227

READING PROGRESS CHECK Evidence of many different cultures can be found in South America. Some are from past indigenous civilizations, such as Incan buildings at Cuzco and Machu Picchu. Cultural traditions of weaving, ceramics, and metalworking are still alive today. European culture is evident in architecture and cuisine. Some religious practices and languages come from Asia. Influences from different cultures are especially evident in the music, which mixes indigenous, African, and European elements.

CRITICAL THINKING

1. The term *pre-Columbian* is used to distinguish indigenous cultural elements that arose before the arrival of Europeans from cultural elements that appeared after the introduction and possible influence of European culture.
2. Facial piercing and ear gauging are recognizable in the mask and are popular in some youth cultures today.

C Critical Thinking Skills

Comparing Have students compare this map with the unit landform map of South America. Direct students to note the forms of agriculture that occur in each landform. *(forestry in the Amazon Basin, ranching in the grasslands, herding in the highland regions, etc.)* Challenge students to explain why one area might be better for one kind of agriculture than another. **Visual/Spatial, Naturalist**

R Reading Skills

Listing As they read the remainder of this lesson, have students make a list of areas in which different forms of agriculture are used. Encourage students to add information about the specific crops grown or animals raised in each area. **ELL Verbal/Linguistic**

Content Background Knowledge

Coca Production The production, processing, and trafficking of cocaine wield enormous economic, social, and political influence in South America. Peru and Bolivia are the most important cocaine-producing countries in South America. These two nations are under international pressure to control illegal narcotics and are receiving assistance from the United States to fight narcotics production and trafficking. To reduce illegal coca cultivation and promote socially inclusive market-based economic growth, Peru is working to establish an alternative development program for coca farmers on a volunteer basis with assistance from the United States.

T Technology Skills

Gathering Information Have students locate road maps of the countries of South America on the Internet. Divide the class into small groups. Have each group choose a country, then use a road map to investigate the highway system of their country and describe which roads link which cities, the distances between places, and the paths each road follows. For instance, students could indicate which landforms impact the way the road was laid out, such as rivers, lakes, or mountains. Have students also note which areas have few roads and make inferences about why. **BL Visual/Spatial**

ANSWERS, p. 228

GEOGRAPHY CONNECTION

1. The grassy, treeless plains of Argentina and Uruguay, known as pampas, are prime areas for raising cattle.
2. Agroforestry and shifting cultivation take place in the Amazon Basin.

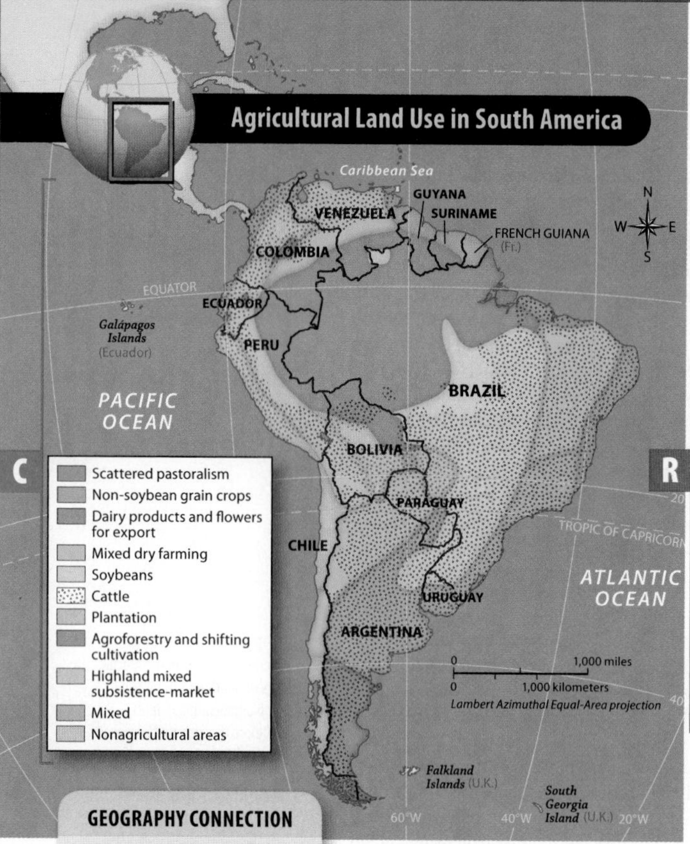

GEOGRAPHY CONNECTION

South America's rich agricultural tradition presents some modern-day challenges to development.

1. ***ENVIRONMENT AND SOCIETY*** What physical feature in Argentina and Uruguay creates good areas for raising cattle?
2. ***PLACES AND REGIONS*** What generalization can you make about the location of agroforestry and shifting cultivation in South America?

free-trade agreements with the United States, Turkey, Australia, and other countries to enhance its economic activities.

Resources and Industry

Land and water use in South America closely follow physical geography. Forestry prevails in the Amazon Basin. Ranching is **widespread** in the grasslands of the south. Herding llamas and alpacas occurs in the high Andean regions. Fishing occurs in major lakes, rivers, and along coastlines. Agriculture remains highly important in South America. More than 20 percent of the subregion's workforce is employed in the primary sector that includes farming, ranching, and fishing. As in other subregions of Latin America (Mexico and Central America and the Caribbean), the legacy of the hacienda system still exists in South America. Larger commercial and smaller subsistence agriculture exist side by side.

Agriculture dominates much of east-central Brazil and the nearby areas of Paraguay, Uruguay, and Argentina. South America's contribution to agricultural global trade includes grains, soybeans, coffee, cocoa, citrus, cattle, sugarcane, tobacco, and cotton. In fact, Brazil is the world's largest exporter of coffee. Brazil and Paraguay also cultivate today's fastest-growing crop in the global economy: soybeans. Paraguay is the sixth-largest producer of soybeans in the world.

Additionally, the coca plant thrives in the northwestern parts of South America. Coca use is popular among Bolivia and Peru's working class for its effects as a legal stimulant and appetite suppressant. Yet coca's derivative can also be used to make the illegal drug cocaine. Peru, Bolivia, and Colombia have nonetheless legalized coca farming. They did so because, sold in its legal form, it is a large source of profit for these countries.

Natural resources include timber, gold, silver, copper, iron ore, and tin. South America contains about one-fifth of the world's iron ore, which is used for steel making and machine building. Many countries are heavily dependent on exporting their natural resources. Energy resources include petroleum and natural gas. Venezuela, Ecuador, and Argentina are leading exporters.

Manufacturing is growing rapidly, but the region's geography varies greatly. Most manufacturing is concentrated in urban areas, especially the primate cities. Because the largest cities lie mainly along the coasts where transportation is the best, the vast interior of South America has few manufacturing plants.

The major road systems in South America include the Pan-American Highway that stretches through Chile as it links many cities north to south, and the Trans-Andean Highway that links cities in Chile and Argentina east

widespread covering a wide area; prevalent

228

networks Online Teaching Options

GAME

Human Geography of South America

Making Predictions Explain to students that currently land and water use in South America must adhere to the many physical constraints found in South America; therefore there are few major road systems and highways that link major cities. Have students write two predictions they have about the road and highway systems in South America now that many regions are becoming more industrialized. After students have finished writing their predictions, have them play the Lesson 2 game with a partner. **Logical/Mathematical**

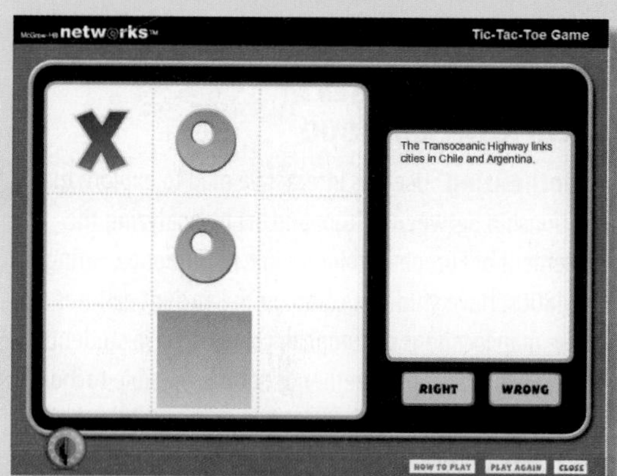

and west. The Trans-Amazonian Highway was built by Brazil to access the Amazon rain forest for developing timber and mineral resources. The Transoceanic Highway was designed to link the Amazon River ports with Peru's ports on the Pacific to transport agricultural products to the global markets in Asia and Europe. Argentina and Brazil have well-developed rail systems, which are important modes of transportation along with the inland waterways. All South American capital cities and major cities have domestic and international airports.

Economic Integration

The increased global demand for raw natural resources and manufacturing has had an impact on the overall economic growth in the region's countries. The economic growth has affected Brazil, Chile, and Argentina more than other countries. Ecuador, Peru, Venezuela, and Bolivia have struggled to modernize their economies and improve standards of living. For example, Bolivia is one of South America's most impoverished and least developed countries. Political reforms in the 1990s stimulated economic growth, but Bolivia continues to struggle to improve conditions for its people.

The separatism that characterized South American countries in the past is giving way to new trade partnerships and cooperation on infrastructure that are mutually beneficial. In South America's current economy, investments flow more freely from one country to another. For example, Colombia has taken advantage of its more stable economy by promoting free-trade agreements with other countries. Colombia **implemented** the U.S.-Colombia Free Trade Agreement with the United States in 2012. Colombia is negotiating free-trade agreements with other Latin American countries, such as Chile and Mexico, as well as with countries outside South America. Additionally, Colombia has 59 bilateral or regional trade agreements—more than any other country.

implement to carry out or accomplish by concrete measures

Economic growth has been steady and strong across the region and has permitted countries to pay their foreign debt. If the economy does not grow, then the debt payments reduce the amount of money available to the government for essential services such as roads, water, flood control, and health care. Consistent, stable economic policies adopted by some South American countries in recent decades have contributed to steady economic growth and improved standards of living for people.

✓ **READING PROGRESS CHECK**

Inferring What is the benefit of cooperation between countries in South America?

LESSON 2 REVIEW 

Reviewing Vocabulary (Tier Three Words)

1. ***Summarizing*** Describe the concept of brain drain and how it relates to the countries of South America. RH.9–10.4

Using Your Notes

2. ***Describing*** Use your notes from the graphic organizer to describe South America's contributions to the arts. Include specific examples from the lesson.

Answering the Guiding Questions

3. ***Evaluating*** How have indigenous peoples and Europeans contributed to the creation of modern governments in South America?
4. ***Making Connections*** How has South America's physical geography influenced its population patterns?
5. ***Explaining*** Why is South America one of the world's most culturally diverse areas?
6. ***Examining*** How have South America's abundant natural resources contributed to its economic development?

Writing Activity

7. ***Informative/Explanatory*** Write a paragraph describing how countries in South America have established transnational and international relationships. Include examples of relations among the countries within South America and countries around the world. WHST.9–10.3

T Technology Skills

Researching Invite a group of volunteers to research the economy of Bolivia and what the government is or is not doing to encourage economic growth. Suggest that students research information about trade or partnership agreements Bolivia has made. Have students write brief reports to share with the class. **Verbal/Linguistic**

R Reading Skills

Interpreting Write the following scenario out for students to consider: A developing country needs new highways, so the country borrows money for the highway system and builds the highways. Then the country's economy stagnates. However, the country must repay its debt. This results in the country having less money for essential services. **Ask:** **How would this scenario likely affect average people?** *(It would lead to a loss of services and higher unemployment.)* Have students consider how this scenario shows the challenges facing developing countries. Then continue a class discussion about these challenges. **BL** **Logical/Mathematical**

CLOSE & REFLECT

Summarizing Have students discuss how economic factors affect the lives of different segments of the population—rich and poor, urban and rural, men and women.

ANSWERS, p. 229

✓ **READING PROGRESS CHECK** Investments are able to flow more freely from one country to another. Colombia is now able to conduct more trade because it has free trade agreements with other countries. In addition, cooperation on infrastructure allows multiple countries to benefit from efforts towards modernization, so no one country falls too far behind.

LESSON 2 REVIEW ANSWERS

Reviewing Vocabulary

1. Brain drain describes the loss of countries' more highly educated and skilled workers to other countries. This is prevalent and problematic especially in rural parts of South America that are currently underdeveloped.

Using Your Notes

2. Stonework of the Inca is still studied today. Indigenous traditional art forms, such as weaving, ceramics, and metalworking, continue to be practiced and valued. Unique music styles from the region showcase a mix of indigenous, African, and European influences.

Answering the Guiding Questions

3. The Inca had a highly developed infrastructure and great wealth that attracted Europeans. They also established a network of roads that Europeans used to quickly move through and conquer the region and take the resources. Power remained in the hands of the wealthy for a long period of time—even after countries gained independence. Many still deal with political corruption, uneven distribution of wealth, high unemployment, and unequal rights.
4. Natural features in South America, such as rain forests, deserts, and mountains, are not optimal for settlement. Therefore, most major South American cities are located near the coastlines and major rivers. These areas offer favorable climates and fertile land.
5. Even before the first Europeans arrived, indigenous groups who lived in South America were already culturally diverse since they developed in isolation of one another due to the continent's rugged geography. More Europeans, and eventually people from other parts of the world, arrived in South America with their own traditions and ways of life. Newly arrived customs both endured and blended with those of the many indigenous groups already living there.
6. Natural resources such as timber, gold, silver, copper, iron ore, tin, petroleum, and natural gas are used domestically and exported for revenue.

Writing Activity

7. Students' answers should be well constructed and provide examples of transnational and international relationships. A specific example is the U.S.-Colombia Free Trade Agreement that was established in 2012.

ENGAGE

C Critical Thinking Skills

Formulating Questions Display the Unit 3 Physical map of the region found in the online Teacher Lesson Center and ask a volunteer to identify where the Amazon rain forest is located and which countries the Amazon rain forest extends into. Then have students work with a partner to brainstorm and write a list of questions they have about the Amazon rain forest.

TEACH & ASSESS

R Reading Skills

Using Word Parts and Context Clues Point to the word *deforestation* in this section and guide students to understand its word parts. Explain that the prefix *de-* means "reverse, against, or to do the opposite"; the suffix *-ation* means "action, or resulting state."

Pair English language learners with proficient students and have them read the paragraph together. **Ask:** **What context clues in the paragraph give clues to the meaning of *deforestation*?** *(The context clues "depletion and extinction of plants and animals that call it home" and "threatens us all" confirm this meaning.)* Have partners brainstorm other words with the root word *-de. (decompose, decline, deplete, etc.)*

AL **ELL** **Interpersonal, Verbal/Linguistic**

T Technology Skills

Changing Continuity of Groups Help students visualize the size of four square miles by offering examples in your community. Organize students into small groups and have students research the different types of plant and animal life that live in the Amazon rain forest. Tell groups to identify the number of endangered or protected species in the Amazon rain forest and present their findings in a short report. Group reports should show "before and after" deforestation figures to identify how the populations of various species have changed over time. Encourage groups to elaborate on why these species have become endangered. **AL** **Logical/Mathematical**

Global Connections: **Latin America**

C AMAZON IN THE BALANCE

R *The Amazon rain forest is the largest and most diverse rain forest on Earth, holding an abundance of plant and animal life. This rain forest and the life in it is under constant threat. Deforestation caused by logging, farming, and ranching threatens its depletion and the extinction of the plants and animals that call it home. In some ways the loss of the Amazon rain forest threatens us all.*

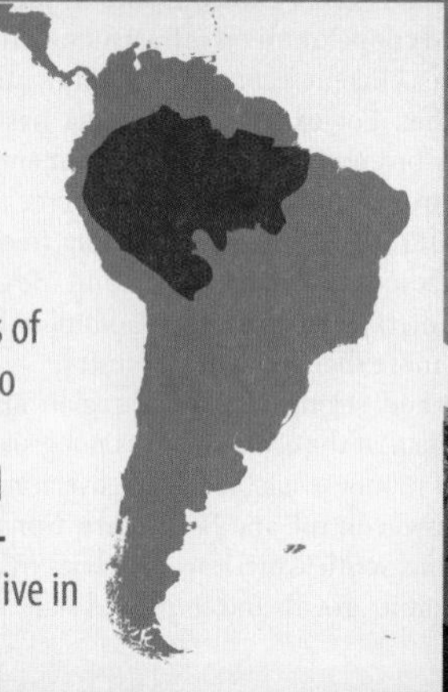

FULL OF LIFE

T In every 4 square miles of the Amazon rain forest, there are **1,500** flowering plant species, **750** tree species, and **900** tons of living plants. The Amazon is also home to **30 million** insect species, **175** lizard species, and **500** mammalian species. **One-third** of the world's birds also live in the Amazon.

CARBON CONTROL

The Amazon rain forest holds nearly **half** of the 247 billion tons of carbon contained in the world's tropical rain forests. Carbon is stored in the woods and roots, but when trees are **cut, burned, or decompose**, carbon is released into the atmosphere. This has **consequences** for the Earth's climate. According to NASA "...the average global temperature on Earth has **increased** by about 0.8°Celsius (1.4°Fahrenheit) since 1880. Two-thirds of the warming has occurred since 1975, at a rate of roughly 0.15-0.20°C per decade."

230

networks Online Teaching Options

WORKSHEET

Dissolving Coral Reefs

Understanding Relationships This Unit 3 GeoLab Activity about the dissolving coral reefs in the Caribbean can be used to further explain the environmental need to control the release of carbon into the atmosphere. This worksheet will explain the relationship between the release of carbon due to deforestation in the Amazon and acid rain, which causes coral reefs in the Caribbean to dissolve.

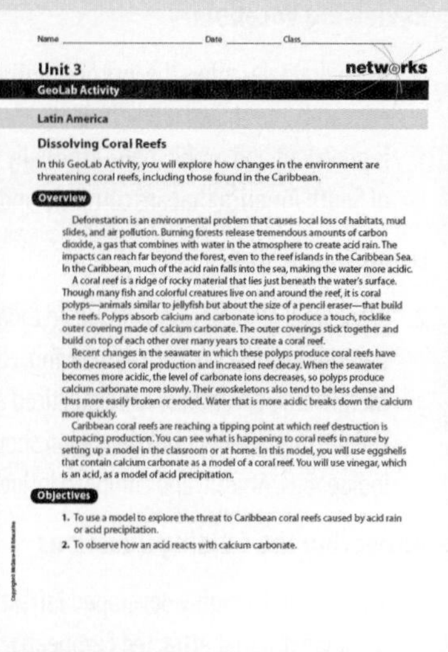

Name ______ Date ______ Class ______

Unit 3 networks

GeoLab Activity

Latin America

Dissolving Coral Reefs

In this GeoLab Activity, you will explore how changes in the environment are threatening coral reefs, including those found in the Caribbean.

Overview

Deforestation is an environmental problem that causes local loss of habitats, mud slides, and air pollution. Burning forests release tremendous amounts of carbon dioxide, a gas that combines with water in the atmosphere to create acid rain. The impacts can reach far beyond the forest, even to the reef islands in the Caribbean Sea. In the Caribbean, much of the acid rain falls into the sea, making the water more acidic.

A coral reef is a ridge of rocky material that lies just beneath the water's surface. Though many fish and colorful creatures live on and around the reef, it is coral polyps—animals similar to jellyfish but about the size of a pencil eraser—that build the reefs. Polyps absorb calcium and carbonate ions to produce a touch, rocklike outer covering made of calcium carbonate. The outer coverings stick together and build on top of each other over many years to create a coral reef.

Recent changes in the seawater in which these polyps produce coral reefs have both decreased coral production and increased reef decay. When the seawater becomes more acidic, the level of carbonate ions decreases, so polyps produce calcium carbonate more slowly. Their exoskeletons also tend to be less dense and thus more easily broken or eroded. Water that is more acidic breaks down the calcium more quickly.

Caribbean coral reefs are reaching a tipping point at which reef destruction is outpacing production. You can see what is happening to coral reefs in nature by setting up a model in the classroom or at home. In this model, you will use eggshells that contain calcium carbonate as a model of a coral reef. You will use vinegar, which is an acid, as a model of acid precipitation.

Objectives

1. To use a model to explore the threat to Caribbean coral reefs caused by acid rain or acid precipitation.
2. To observe how an acid reacts with calcium carbonate.

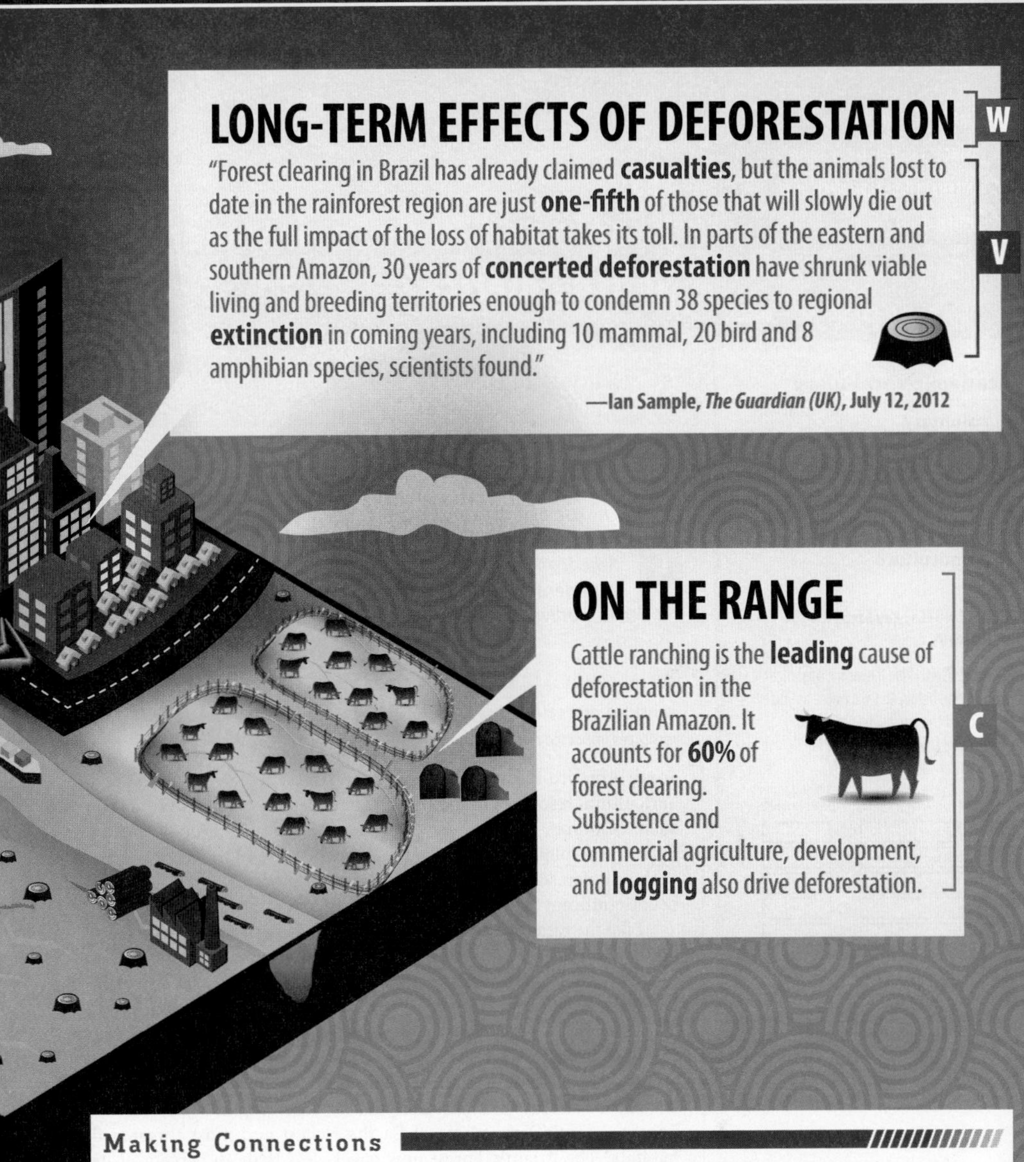

LONG-TERM EFFECTS OF DEFORESTATION
"Forest clearing in Brazil has already claimed **casualties**, but the animals lost to date in the rainforest region are just **one-fifth** of those that will slowly die out as the full impact of the loss of habitat takes its toll. In parts of the eastern and southern Amazon, 30 years of **concerted deforestation** have shrunk viable living and breeding territories enough to condemn 38 species to regional **extinction** in coming years, including 10 mammal, 20 bird and 8 amphibian species, scientists found."
—Ian Sample, *The Guardian (UK)*, July 12, 2012
W
V
ON THE RANGE
Cattle ranching is the **leading** cause of deforestation in the Brazilian Amazon. It accounts for **60%** of forest clearing. Subsistence and commercial agriculture, development, and **logging** also drive deforestation.
C

Making Connections

1. ***Making Predictions*** What may happen to the rain forest if land clearing continues unchecked?
2. ***Drawing Conclusions*** How might the continued deforestation and clearing of the Amazon rain forest have a direct effect on your life?
3. ***Environment and Society*** What circumstances might make environmental protection of the Amazon rain forest a low priority for some Latin American countries?

Interact with ***Global Connections*** Online

INFOGRAPHIC

Amazon in the Balance

Hypothesizing Display the infographic about the effects of deforestation in the Amazon rain forest. Have students form small groups. Ask each group to choose one of the elements and research it using the Internet. Then have groups create a more detailed infograph that hypothesizes what the Amazon rain forest will be like in the year 2065. Encourage groups to include visuals in their infographics.
BL Logical/Mathematical, Naturalist

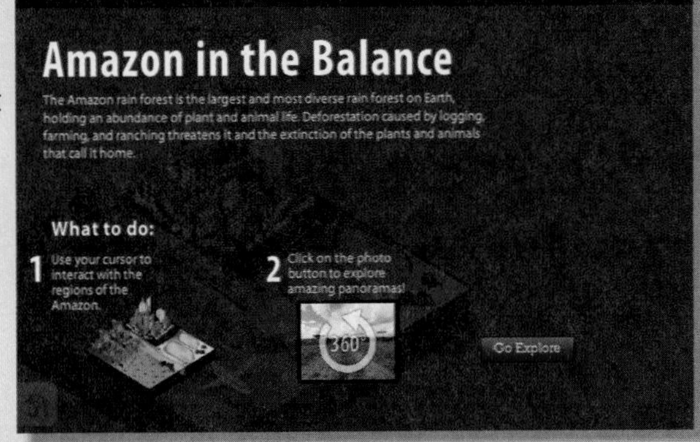

W Writing Skills

Informative/Explanatory Have students write a summarizing paragraph that answers the chapter's Essential Question: *How do physical systems and human systems shape a place?* Tell students to use information in this feature to support their summaries. **Verbal/Linguistic**

V Visual Skills

Calculating Help students comprehend the facts and figures used in this excerpt, guiding them to restate fractions as percentages. Ask a student to read the section as you write out the key figures *one-fifth, 30 years, 38 species, 10 mammals, 20 birds, eight amphibian species.* Have students work in pairs to calculate the percentage of animals in the Amazon rain forest that are "casualties," and the number projected to die out over time. Tell students to depict the information in a chart and present it to the class. ELL **Interpersonal, Logical/Mathematical**

C Critical Thinking Skills

Recognizing Counter Arguments Tell students they will participate in a debate in which they will express a viewpoint related to issues involving deforestation of the Amazon rain forest. For example, students may role-play a scientist concerned about the environment, a cattle rancher/farmer who relies on cleared land, or a lumber company worker whose livelihood depends on the rain forest. When students prepare their arguments, have them consider the positive or negative impacts for that person by deforestation. Moderate a class debate in which students present their arguments and counter arguments. BL **Verbal/Linguistic**

CLOSE & REFLECT

Identifying Cause and Effect Have students review each excerpt in this feature and create a cause-and-effect diagram showing the impact of deforestation on the Amazon rain forest. Then guide a discussion about possible solutions to remedy the issues discussed in this feature.

ANSWERS, p. 231

Making Connections

1. The rain forest will disappear at a much faster rate. Additionally, the vast number of animal and plant species will rapidly decrease. As deforestation continues, the land itself may become unable to support farming, ranching, or the rain forest itself.
2. It will have an impact on the global temperature, slightly changing the climate of the area.
3. Some Latin American countries may feel internal and external pressures to develop industrially. These countries will need to clear land for industrial development and make use of the rain forest's natural resources.

ENGAGE

C Critical Thinking Skills

Speculating Write these terms on the board: *deforestation, desertification, dust storms, pollution, loss of biodiversity, salinization, soil degradation, soil erosion, urban sprawl, unrestricted growth.* Have students describe what they know about these terms and their relationships to the environmental issues facing South America. Then have them list questions they expect to have answered as they read through this lesson.

TEACH & ASSESS

R1 Reading Skills

Explaining Have students explain how South American countries are taking advantage of their forest and agricultural resources to improve their economies and overall wealth. **Ask:** What resources can be obtained from the Amazon rain forest? *(timber, coffee, foods, pharmaceuticals)* What agricultural resources are available from the grasslands? *(crops, livestock, related products)* How are people able to use these resources to improve their economies and overall wealth? *(income gained from working in these sectors adds to the economy; the sale of products adds to the wealth of the economy)* **Verbal/Linguistic**

R2 Reading Skills

Interpreting Invite a volunteer to locate the affected deforestation areas on a map of South America. **Ask:** How does deforestation threaten biodiversity? *(Deforestation destroys habitats by reducing the diversity of plants and animals, which can lead to extinction.)* Why is the loss of biodiversity a problem? *(Possible answers: It inhibits nature's ability to function properly because it changes the natural balance within a food web in a habitat. It allows less desirable invasive species to flourish.)* **Naturalist, Verbal/Linguistic**

ANSWERS, p. 232

TAKING NOTES: **Deforestation**—occurring at a rapid rate in the Amazon rain forest, reduces the diversity of plants and animals living in a forested region; **Large-scale agriculture**—worsens the progression of soil erosion; **Grazing livestock**—consume plants to the point at which plants surface above ground, therefore weakening the plant's ability to grow; **Urban growth**—has created multiple forms of environmental pollution; **Mining**—has damaged natural land and water features

networks

There's More Online!

- **GRAPH** Per Capita CO_2 Emissions
- **IMAGE** EcoTaxi
- **IMAGE** Large-Scale Monoculture
- **INTERACTIVE SELF-CHECK QUIZ**
- **VIDEO** People and Their Environment: South America

Reading **HELP**DESK

Academic Vocabulary (Tier Two Words)
- **voluntary**
- **alternative**

Content Vocabulary (Tier Three Words)
- **oxisol**
- **monoculture**

TAKING NOTES: ***Key Ideas and Details***

IDENTIFYING Use a graphic organizer like the one below to take notes as you read about the issues that relate to people and their environment in South America.

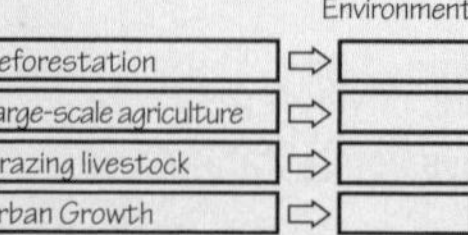

	Impact on Environment
Deforestation	
Large-scale agriculture	
Grazing livestock	
Urban Growth	
Mining	

LESSON 3
People and Their Environment: South America

ESSENTIAL QUESTION • *How do physical systems and human systems shape a place?*

IT MATTERS BECAUSE

C *The use of natural resources for economic advancement has benefited the livelihood and stability of many South American countries. It has also caused damage to the continent's natural environment and dramatic changes to its biodiversity.*

Managing Resources

GUIDING QUESTION *How has the management of forest and agricultural resources impacted the environment in South America?*

R1 South America is home to some of the largest reserves of forest and agricultural resources in the world. Countries are taking advantage of such resources to improve their economies and overall wealth. Extensive exploitation of resources comes at a cost, however. Issues such as deforestation, soil erosion, desertification, and pollution have been significant problems for all countries in South America.

R2 Like the rain forests of Costa Rica and Panama, the rain forests of South America are threatened by intensive human activity. Rain forests harbor at least half of all animal and plant species on Earth. Deforestation is occurring at a rapid rate in the Amazon rain forest. This has reduced the diversity of plants and animals there. Brazil has the world's largest remaining expanses of tropical rain forest, but almost 20 percent of the Amazon rain forest has already been destroyed. The loss of biodiversity is also occurring in Brazil's lesser-known Atlantic Forest, one of Earth's richest and most threatened habitats. The Atlantic Forest now covers less than 10 percent of its original area.

Soil erosion in South America has diminished the ability of soils to produce food and vegetation. Intensive farming, construction, logging, fires, and overgrazing all increase the rate of soil erosion. Certain soil types in South America—such as the volcanic soils and

networks ***Online Teaching Options***

INTERACTIVE BELLRINGER

The World's Rain Forests

Locating This map can be used to discuss the locations of the world's rain forests and their various climates. Have students read the introductory text and use the map along with their prior knowledge to answer the questions. Then ask students to share any background knowledge they have about the world's rain forests. Ask students to discuss current environment issues facing all rain forests and what efforts are being done to protect these ecosystems. **Visual/Spatial, Naturalist**

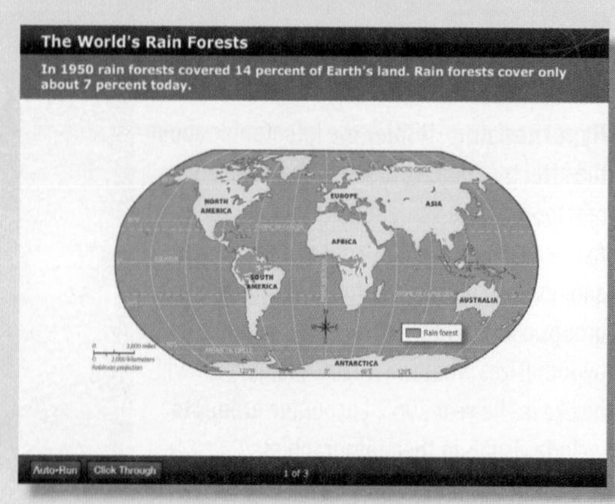

oxisols found in the humid tropical lowlands—are especially vulnerable to erosion. The oxisols, sometimes known as laterites, can degrade into a baked clay-like form when too much of the natural vegetation cover is removed. The removal of topsoil occurs as a result of intensive agriculture, especially on landscapes that have been cultivated for long periods of time. C

Large-scale agriculture also worsens the progression of soil erosion. **Monoculture**, the growth of a single type of crop on agricultural or forested land, depletes the soil of its nutrients. It disrupts the natural cycle of growth and breakdown of plants, animals, and bacteria. Without these natural processes, soil cannot rebuild its nutrients. Vast monoculture soybean crops in Brazil, for example, are quickly depleting soil fertility. V

The general process of soil erosion summarizes the progression and effects of desertification. Because ecosystems are dynamic and respond to changes in environmental conditions, processes such as soil erosion and desertification are drastically changing the landscapes and ecology of South America's extensive croplands and grazing lands. The primary cause of desertification is not drought, but rather mismanagement of land by human activities such as overgrazing of livestock and deforestation. Rain-fed crops in drylands, such as wheat and corn, can lead to desertification. After wheat and corn are harvested, the lands left uncovered between planting seasons become vulnerable to erosion by climatic forces such as wind and rain. Wind can create heavy dust storms by sweeping up uncovered topsoil. This deprives extensive land areas of the nutrients from organic matter contained by topsoil. Though rainfall in drylands is uncommon, heavy downpours do occur. This results in otherwise fertile and nutrient-rich topsoil being washed away. For large-scale irrigation on drylands, salinization is also a significant issue. Once fields are irrigated, water dries quickly and leaves behind salt. These salts collect and reduce the ability of plant roots to absorb water and grow. T

Desertification also occurs in rangelands, which support a large population of grazing animals such as cattle and sheep. Grazing livestock consume plants almost to ground level. This weakens plants' ability to grow.

oxisol a thick, weathered soil of the humid tropics that is largely depleted of fertility and nutrients

monoculture the cultivation or growth of a single crop over a wide area for a consecutive number of years

Large-scale monoculture, like this soybean farm in Brazil, depletes soil fertility.

▼ CRITICAL THINKING

1. ***Making Connections*** What factors contribute to the decline of soil fertility with the practice of monoculture?
2. ***Speculating*** Why is monoculture still practiced even though its negative impacts are known?

South America 233

C Critical Thinking Skills

Interpreting Significance Discuss what it means for soil to be vulnerable to erosion. **Ask:** What happens when vegetation is removed from fragile oxisols? *(Exposed to the atmosphere, oxisols degrade into a baked clay-like form.)* How does this affect the soil's ability to support plant life? *(Since the soil has very little nutrients, it has little ability to support plant life.)* How might this lead to a cycle of further destruction of soil? *(As that soil does not support plant life, there will be fewer trees and flora. The land will not recover and can become a desert or wasteland.)*
Naturalist, Logical/Mathematical

V Visual Skills

Creating Diagrams Have students develop a flowchart describing the soil-making process. Diagrams may include drawn illustrations, cut-outs from magazines, online images, or other pieces of information that depict the process. Have students explain their diagrams to the class. ELL **Visual/Spatial**

T Technology Skills

Global Analysis Invite a volunteer to define the term *desertification*. *(Desertification occurs when an area that was once fertile becomes a desert.)* Discuss the relationship between soil erosion and desertification. **Ask:** What practices lead to desertification? *(mainly land use mismanagement—overgrazing and deforestation)* What kinds of landscapes are particularly prone to desertification? *(rain forests; croplands and rangelands in dry areas)* To help students better understand the devastating nature of desertification, have volunteers collect before and after photographs or images online or from library sources showing landscapes that have been affected by desertification. AL **Visual/Spatial**

VIDEO

Amazon Crude

Analyzing Ethical Issues Have students briefly summarize the disagreement between Texaco and PetroEcuador. Tell them that one-half of all plant and animal species on Earth live in tropical rain forests and that almost 20 percent of the Amazon rain forest has already been destroyed and that soil has been polluted; however, environmental laws have not reduced the risks of increased pollution, increased multinational industrial growth, or the need for oil and natural resources. Have small groups identify possible ways that different points of view influence public policies on international levels. BL **Logical/Mathematical**

ANSWERS, p. 233

CRITICAL THINKING

1. Growing a single crop on a plot of land for an extended period of time disrupts the natural cycle of nutrient production from the breakdown of plants, animals, and bacteria.
2. It is still an easy and cheap way to grow massive quantities of high-demand crops needed to satisfy the demands of rapidly growing populations.

C Critical Thinking Skills

Analyzing Cause and Effect Have students brainstorm forms of environmental pollution associated with cities. **Ask:** **What are some of the serious problems cities like São Paulo are experiencing because of an influx of millions of poor migrants?** *(The expansion of slums leads to large amounts of sewage entering the soil and water supply. The cities grow very quickly but do not have the means to build the infrastructure needed to handle the waste created by the large population.)* **Why might migrants choose to move to the slums despite these conditions?** *(Possible answer: Most of the people are looking for work. There may be no work opportunities in the rural areas. People may not know what the conditions are really like until they get there and it may be very difficult to go back.)* **Verbal/Linguistic**

R Reading Skills

Taking Notes After students read about illegal mining, have them list the positive and negative effects of gold mining. As a class, discuss their lists. **Ask:** **How does illegal mining exacerbate the problems caused by mining?** *(Possible answers: leads to lawlessness; creates chaos; guerrilla groups use ill-gotten money for illicit operations; creates slums—tens of thousands of people move into the mining areas and set up makeshift housing)* **What steps are countries taking to deal with the problems?** *(passing laws; employing police and/or military personnel to enforce regulations and stop illegal activities)* **AL** **Verbal/Linguistic**

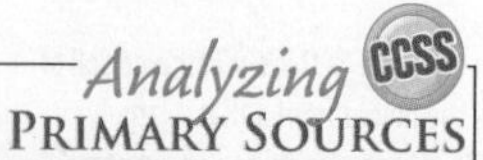

Urban Population Boom Threatens Lake Titicaca

"Because of its size and history, El Alto [Bolivian city connected to Lake Titicaca via the Pallina River] is a political powerhouse, yet the chronic poverty and lack of access to services widely faced by Bolivia's indigenous peoples persist there, and tackling pollution is a struggle. Changing the waste disposal habits of the sparsely populated countryside is one obstacle. But at the heart of the matter is weak enforcement of environmental laws and inadequate infrastructure."

—Sara Shahriari, "Urban Population Boom Threatens Lake Titicaca," *The Guardian*, January 12, 2012

DBQ ***IDENTIFYING CENTRAL ISSUES*** What two issues are central to the inadequate treatment of wastewater?
RH.9–10.2

The movement of herds of livestock also destroys plant roots that bind the soil. When rain comes, water often washes away unprotected topsoil. This process of desertification in rangelands is a serious issue in places with a strong livestock industry: Argentina, Uruguay, Brazil, and Paraguay.

READING PROGRESS CHECK

Summarizing How does overgrazing worsen processes of desertification?

Human Impact

GUIDING QUESTION *Why does urban growth and industrialization create environmental problems in South America?*

Large-scale economic production and urban growth have created multiple forms of environmental pollution. São Paulo, Brazil, is an example of the significant amount and effect of multiple sources of urban pollution. With a population of some 19 million, São Paulo is the largest city in the Southern Hemisphere. São Paulo has attracted millions of poor migrants. Many have settled in favelas, or slums on the outskirts of the city consisting of crudely built shacks. These favelas are disconnected from the services of the established city. They are thus particularly problematic as sources of sewage and unrestricted residential growth.

C

Rapid urban growth also requires cities to find methods for disposing of human waste and sewage. Many urban regions, particularly those in less developed countries, lack the funding and organization to build extensive networks of piped water, drains, and sewage treatment plants. One example is the Bolivian city of El Alto, which is located along the Pallina River that flows into Lake Titicaca. El Alto has seen rapid growth resulting in increased pollution from human waste and sewage. The polluted Pallina River had once been a source of clean water for the people who lived on its banks, but now the waters that flow into Lake Titicaca are contaminated.

Illegal mining has further damaged the natural land and water features of South America. Since 2007, the price of gold has doubled in value. For gold-producing countries such as Peru, the sixth-largest producer in the world, this has presented a potential for immense wealth and economic development. Yet the rise in the value of gold has also encouraged illegal mining activity, especially in countries with an impoverished majority population and ineffective regulatory procedures in government. In Peru, for example, tens of thousands of people have set up camp in the Amazon rain forest in search of vast gold reserves. Alongside individual prospecting, large-scale mining by use of bulldozers and barges has also increased. Rapid deforestation has resulted from rapid migration, makeshift housing, and industrial-scale mining operations. Also, because miners use mercury and other toxic compounds to separate gold from ore, high levels of mercury and cyanide pollution in rivers have been reported.

R

Though clashes between security forces and miners have created hostility and further chaos, countries affected by illegal mining have made efforts to regulate the vulnerable regions. Colombia is cracking down on illegal mining because anti-government guerrilla groups have been using profits from illegal mining to finance their efforts. Meanwhile, Brazil has employed 8,700 military personnel to fight illegal gold mining along its northern borders.

READING PROGRESS CHECK

Specifying What are three sources of pollution in South America?

234

ANSWERS, p. 234

DBQ Weak enforcement of environmental laws and inadequate infrastructure are two issues central to the inadequate treatment of wastewater in El Alto.

READING PROGRESS CHECK Livestock eat plants almost to ground level which makes the plants weak and they take longer to grow back. Hooves also destroy plant roots as herds move across the land. Destroyed roots are no longer able to hold the soil together, and rain washes it away.

READING PROGRESS CHECK Favelas are disconnected from services of the city, so the sewage produced by them directly contaminates the environment around them. Rapidly growing populations in areas such as El Alto, Bolivia, also create waste and sewage in quantities that exceed the limits, so pollutants enter river water. Mining relies on bulldozers and barges, which pollute and destroy the land and rivers. Mining also pollutes rivers when mercury and cyanide used to separate gold from ore enters the water systems.

networks Online Teaching Options

INTERACTIVE IMAGE

South American Urbanization

Simulating Use this interactive image to discuss the environmental pollution impacts of urban growth with students. Have students form small groups. In groups, have them imagine that they are the goverment leaders of a large city and must deal with the favela settlements on the outskirts of their city. Have groups consider what should be done to the settlement. Each group must come to an agreed-upon decision. Then have each group present its decision and explanation for its decision to the class. **Interpersonal, Verbal/Linguistic**

Addressing the Issues

GUIDING QUESTION *How are people and governments addressing environmental issues in South America?*

Addressing issues related to human impact on the natural environment is important not only for protecting regional biodiversity, but also for preserving the livelihood of human populations. Many South American countries, such as Uruguay, Paraguay, and Guyana, depend on crops and agriculture as their economic base. These countries are very vulnerable to changing weather patterns and infertile lands.

South American countries that recognize the impact of deforestation are passing laws to protect their lands. For example, in response to the high rate of deforestation in Paraguay, the country's government passed the Zero Deforestation Law in 2004. This law prohibits forested areas from being converted to landscapes for other uses in the eastern region of Paraguay. The law's enforcement has dramatically reduced Paraguay's deforestation rate.

At a local level, farmers can implement management strategies to slow the process of soil erosion. Specifically, soil erosion due to the formation of oxisols can be prevented with careful application and management of lime and fertilizers. Cover crops, which are plants that cover topsoil after crops have been harvested, prevent potential soil erosion from wind and water. At large scales, plant cover can contribute to more regular rainfall patterns, reducing the occurrence of drought and further soil erosion.

Soil conservation efforts will slow land degradation, but restoring soil fertility is much more difficult. On average, a millimeter of soil is generated in about 100 years. Therefore, soil erosion is a more rapid process than soil generation. Once soil has begun to erode, the amount by which it can be restored to fertility depends on how much it has degraded. Lightly degraded soils can be improved by using farm practices. Severely eroded land is generally abandoned because required resources to restore the soil are often too costly. Furthermore, without coordinated prevention efforts among farmers and government, areas of infertile soil will continue to reduce the region's biodiversity. Land available for food production will also be reduced.

Countries across South America are taking steps to reduce air pollution at the local level by establishing regulations. The results of the regulations can be seen in the reduction of greenhouse gas emissions in the continent's

Per Capita CO_2 Emissions

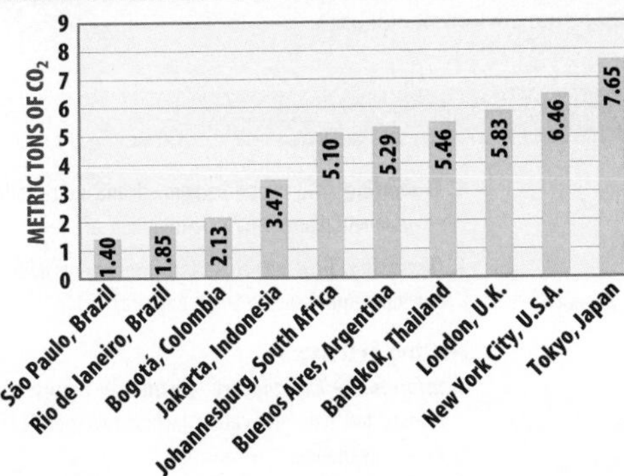

GRAPH SKILLS

Many South American countries have established regulations in an effort to reduce greenhouse gas emissions.

CRITICAL THINKING

1. ***Comparing*** How do the carbon dioxide emissions from the South American cities shown on the graph compare to other cities on the graph?
2. ***Hypothesizing*** What factors other than population do you think contribute to the emission levels of greenhouse gases such as carbon dioxide?

C Critical Thinking Skills

Analyzing Cause and Effect As a class, discuss how environmental degradation affects people. **Ask:** How are people's livelihoods affected by changing weather patterns or poor agriculture practices? *(Possible answers: farmers make less money; people lose jobs; the local economy suffers)* What is one step Paraguay has taken to deal with deforestation? *(passed the Zero Deforestation Law in 2004 that protects the forested areas in the eastern region of the country)* Do you think this was a good measure? Why? *(Student answers may vary, but should reflect specific reasoning based on the information provided in the text.)* **Logical/Mathematical**

W Writing Skills

Informative/Explanatory Have students interview a local farmer or a representative from a state agricultural agency to learn about some of the soil management practices followed in the United States. Direct students to write an informative essay describing the soil management practices. **Naturalist, Verbal/Linguistic**

R Reading Skills

Summarizing Have students summarize the steps farmers can take to restore damaged soil. **Ask:** What are the beneficial effects of each procedure? *(Applying lime and fertilizers can help prevent soil erosion of oxisols because it adds nutrients back into the soil. Cover crops can help prevent soil erosion from wind and water. Large-scale plant cover can help create more regular rainfall patterns and prevent droughts that would lead to erosion.)*
AL **Verbal/Linguistic**

INTERACTIVE GRAPH

Per Capita CO_2 Emissions

Analyzing Graphs This graph illustrates the carbon dioxide emissions of several cities around the world and can be used with students to discuss established regulations to reduce greenhouse gas emissions. Ask students to compare and contrast the CO_2 emissions of several of the cities shown on the graph. Then have students write three analytical statements based on information provided in the graph. Have students share their statements with a partner. Have partners check each other's statements for accuracy.
ELL **Visual/Spatial**

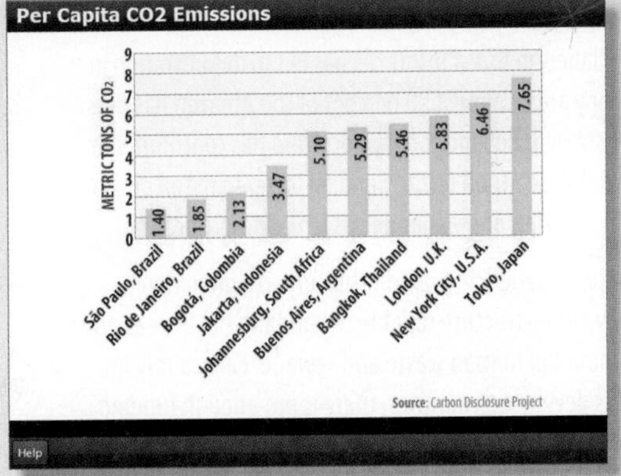

ANSWERS, p. 235

CRITICAL THINKING

1. With the exception of Buenos Aires, Argentina, all South American cities have lower carbon dioxide emissions.
2. Other factors that can determine a city's greenhouse gas emission levels are the type and size of its transportation system and whether or not it has air-quality management programs.

CHAPTER 9, Lesson 3

People and Their Environment: South America

R Reading Skills

Discussing Have students describe some specific factors related to urbanization. Then, **ask:** **What does it mean to have voluntary greenhouse emissions targets?** *(that each country determines its own emissions target and that the country is not required to meet a specific goal)* **Why would Argentina and Uruguay want to monitor pollution along the Uruguay River?** *(The Uruguay River is important to both countries; they need to monitor it to see if things are improving or getting worse.)* **Verbal/Linguistic, Naturalist**

W Writing Skills

Argument Have students write editorials for a South American newspaper on the subject of protecting the environment and developing a sustainable economy. Editorials should describe what should be done, who should pay for the effort, and why it should be done. **Verbal/Linguistic**

CLOSE & REFLECT

Evaluating Have students make a list of the environmental problems covered in this lesson and the short- and long-term effects of these problems. Then have students identify the most dire problems that require immediate solutions.

ANSWERS, p. 236

READING PROGRESS CHECK Human modifications of the physical environment can have significant global impacts. Finding solutions to environmental challenges should be a task for the entire international community.

CRITICAL THINKING

1. The main sources of air pollution, such as automobiles and manufacturing, are mostly in large cities. This is an effective approach because a greater amount of pollution can be decreased in this way.
2. EcoTaxis can decrease pollution by reducing emissions of greenhouse gases.

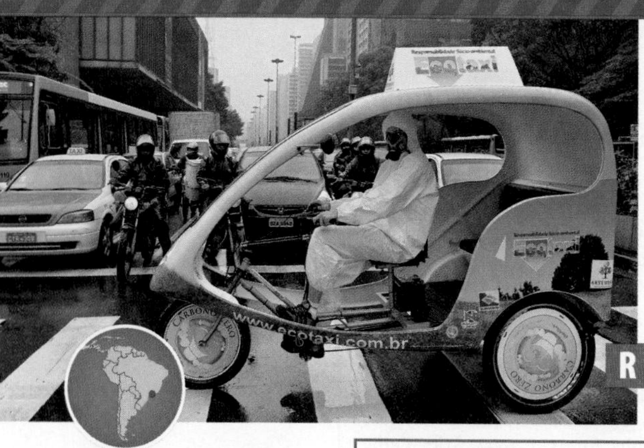

Countries throughout South America are developing programs for air quality management. They tend to be focused on primary metropolitan areas such as São Paulo. EcoTaxis, like the one shown here, are part of World Car-Free Day and help to reduce emissions in the city.

Mauricio Lima/AFP/Getty Images

▲ CRITICAL THINKING

1. ***Analyzing*** Why do governments focus air-quality management efforts on large cities? Do you think that is an effective approach?
2. ***Drawing Conclusions*** How would an EcoTaxi help combat air pollution?

voluntary of one's own choice or consent

alternative different from the usual or regular

largest cities. For example, although São Paulo is one of the world's largest cities, it has much lower levels of carbon dioxide emissions than other large cities. Other large cities in South America also have lower greenhouse gas emissions than might be expected given their high populations.

In order to fix current problems and reduce future ones, South American countries must address the specific factors related to urbanization. The problems include urban sprawl, longer distances that residents travel within cities, increased use of cars, and inefficient public transport systems. Argentina is a global role model for setting **voluntary** greenhouse gas emissions targets. Furthermore, in 2010 Argentina and Uruguay formed a joint effort to monitor pollution along the Uruguay River, which defines the Argentina-Uruguay border.

Another issue for establishing effective policies is that regulations established by governments or international agreements could restrict countries' access to natural resources for export production. South American countries that lack the money to invest in **alternative** export resources are reluctant to establish environmental restrictions. Therefore, to promote the growth of sustainable economies, more developed countries must work closely with less developed countries in South America. Assistance in the area of enforcing and creating policies is of great importance.

Human modifications of the physical environment can have significant global impacts. Therefore, the international community is motivated to work together to find solutions to increasing environmental changes. Despite measures taken to produce effective policies, however, there is a weak foundation of air and water quality management among South America countries. Efforts are focused more on primary metropolitan areas rather than smaller urban regions, which are now among the urban areas of South America with the most rapid growth rates. Environmental awareness and policy making is relatively recent and therefore will require time, resources, and cooperation among the world's institutions in order to ensure an improved quality of life for South Americans.

READING PROGRESS CHECK

Drawing Conclusions Why is it important for countries to work together to create regulations for future environmental use?

LESSON 3 REVIEW 

Reviewing Vocabulary (Tier Three Words)

1. ***Describing*** How are oxisols formed in soil? RH.9–10.4

Using Your Notes

2. ***Describing*** Use your graphic organizer to describe how mining has affected the environments of South America.

Answering the Guiding Questions

3. ***Exploring Issues*** How has the management of forest and agricultural resources impacted the environment in South America?
4. ***Evaluating*** Why does urban growth and industrialization create environmental problems in South America?
5. ***Discussing*** How are people and governments addressing environmental issues in South America?

Writing Activity

6. ***Informative/Explanatory*** Describe the process of physical change due to desertification. Include two specific factors that cause this change. WHST.9–10.2

LESSON 3 REVIEW ANSWERS

Reviewing Vocabulary

1. When too much natural vegetation cover is removed, the soil degrades and becomes clay-like. This thick, clay-like soil is called oxisol.

Using Your Notes

2. Mining has damaged land and water features of South America. Rapid deforestation has resulted from industrial-scale mining operations and from clearing for makeshift housing as tens of thousands of people have moved nearer to mining areas. Mercury used in mining processes leaks into rivers and has become a major pollutant.

Answering the Guiding Questions

3. Reliance on forest resources has led to deforestation in many areas; almost 20 percent of the Amazon has been destroyed. Reliance on monoculture has contributed to a decrease in soil fertility and an increase in soil erosion. Overgrazing of grasslands has led to desertification.
4. Cities experiencing rapid urban growth often don't have infrastructure capable of handling the increasing amount of human waste and sewage. Particularly in less developed countries, there is not enough funding to build the extensive networks of piped water, drains, and sewage treatment plants required. Industrialization results in pollutants being emitted into the water and air supply.
5. Many governments are passing legislation, such as the Zero Deforestation Law, to protect forests. Locally, farmers have been trying different management strategies aimed at slowing the process of soil erosion. Argentina has set its own greenhouse gas emissions targets. Perhaps most importantly, though, South American countries have begun working together to find policies that will promote sustainable growth while protecting the environment.

Writing Activity

6. The main two causes of desertification are deforestation and overgrazing. Lands that are left uncovered due to either of these factors become vulnerable to erosion. Wind and water carry away nutrient-rich topsoil, which is very difficult to restore.

CHAPTER 9 Assessment 

Directions: On a separate sheet of paper, answer the questions below. Make sure you read carefully and answer all parts of the questions.

Lesson Review

Lesson 1

1. ***Describing*** Which landform specific to South America is identified by the term *llanos*?
2. ***Explaining*** Describe the general features of three of the vertical climate zones found in South America.
3. ***Summarizing*** What are some important natural resources South American countries rely on for international trade?

Lesson 2

4. ***Assessing*** Explain how an empire as large and developed as the Inca Empire was so quickly defeated by Spanish conquistadors.
5. ***Analyzing*** Why do South American countries have such a diverse mix of ethnic groups? Compare the diversity of population between two South American countries.
6. ***Identifying*** What are two examples of projects or agreements between South American countries that have been developed to boost the countries' economies?

Lesson 3

7. ***Comparing*** Describe how the processes of desertification and soil erosion are related. Provide specific examples of how they are negatively affecting the land in South America.
8. ***Identifying Cause and Effect*** How do large South American cities such as São Paulo contribute to increased pollution?
9. ***Identifying Central Issues*** How has illegal mining negatively affected the physical environment in South America?

21st Century Skills

Use the following chart to answer the questions below.

Foreign-Born U.S. Population from South America by Country of Birth, 2010

Country of Origin	Number of U.S. Residents
Brazil	340,000
Colombia	637,000
Ecuador	443,000
Peru	429,000
Other South American countries	882,000

Source: U.S. Census Bureau 2010

10. ***Using Graphs, Charts, Diagrams, and Tables*** From which country do most South American-born people in the United States originate?
11. ***Identifying Cause and Effect*** Describe a few of the push factors that lead to migration from South America to the United States.
12. ***Drawing Conclusions*** How might the figures in this table compare to the number of foreign-born residents from Mexico and Central America? Why?

Exploring the Essential Question

13. ***Sequencing*** Create a chart that depicts three ways in which South America's rugged landscape both attracts and isolates communities.

College and Career Readiness

14. ***Reaching Conclusions*** Imagine you are an ornithologist (a person who studies birds) working in Ecuador. Using the Internet, research why Charles Darwin found this part of South America—specifically the Galápagos Islands—to be an ideal spot for his research on evolution and species diversity. Use his research on finches as a specific example. Why would this research be important?
WHST9–10.1, WHST9–10.2

Need Extra Help?

If You've Missed Question	1	2	3	4	5	6	7	8	9	10	11	12	13	14
Go to page	219	221	222	224	226	229	232	234	234	237	237	237	218	221

CHAPTER 9 Assessment Answers

Lesson Review

Lesson 1

1. *Llanos* are South America's fertile, inland grasslands. They are mainly located in parts of Colombia and Venezuela.
2. The *tierra templada* is the lowest of the vertical climate zones and has a temperate climate. The *tierra fría* is slightly higher in altitude and colder than the tierra templada. The *tierra helada* and *puna* are the highest vertical climate zones; they are areas of permanent snow and ice located above the tree line.
3. South American countries rely on gold, silver, emeralds, copper, and oil.

Lesson 2

4. The Inca had built a vast network of roads connecting the cities of their empire. The conquistadors were able to use these roads to quickly establish themselves throughout much of the region.
5. There are many indigenous groups; additionally, the Spanish and Portuguese brought enslaved Africans to South America. After South American countries gained independence, French, Dutch, Italians, and Germans immigrated to South America. Students' comparisons of the ethnic composition of two countries may vary.
6. Possible answer: Trans-country highways have been built to better connect the countries to one another. Colombia is negotiating free-trade agreements with Mexico and Chile.

Lesson 3

7. Desertification is primarily caused by mismanagement of land by human activities. Lands that are left uncovered between planting seasons are vulnerable to erosion by wind and rain.
8. Many large South American cities did not have adequate systems of waste disposal to meet the demands of their rapidly growing populations. Human waste and sewage leaks into the environment, contaminating water supplies. Illegal mining and rapid deforestation are also major environmental problems.
9. The use of bulldozers to clear forest for makeshift housing and mining operations destroys the land. The toxic compounds used by miners to separate gold from ore result in pollution of rivers.

21st Century Skills

10. Most South American-born people are from Colombia.
11. People seek better job opportunities in the U.S. People wish to escape political corruption and the dangers of drug cartels.
12. Possible answer: The numbers of migrants from Mexico and Central America might be higher than those of migrants from South America due to proximity.

Exploring the Essential Question

13. Charts might include the following: Cordilleras create natural barriers that isolate communities, but people are drawn to these mountain areas because of the fertile soil found there. The warm climate and open spaces of the Brazilian Highlands attract people who want to raise cattle, but the expanses of land required means they tend to live far from one another. The pampas attract ranchers and farmers, who tend to live on large estates with great distances between one other.

College and Career Readiness

14. Student answers may vary, but should be logical and strongly supported. Responses should also include that the Galápagos Islands were ideal for Darwin because he was attempting to show that environment determines the specific traits that species develop, and each island had species with different traits.

Assessment Answers

Critical Thinking

15. They have developed rail systems and trans-country highways, and people travel via waterways.

16. There was a lack of structure for self-government, so the power remained in the hands of the wealthy and elite. Caudillos assumed power, often illegally through much bloodshed, throughout the nineteenth century. Today, although the governments are mostly democratic, the rich still tend to have a stronger voice since political corruption is common. Violence is also still common. The gap between rich and poor is wide, as it was in postcolonial times, and indigenous groups are still not always given equal rights.

17. Student answers may vary, but solutions should demonstrate knowledge of the importance of working together.

18. Governments and farmers can coordinate efforts aimed at soil conservation. Careful application of lime and fertilizers can help prevent the formation of oxisols. Cover crops can be planted after regular crop harvests to prevent the bare topsoil and its nutrients from being carried away. Ways to limit the practice of monoculture could be discussed.

Analyzing Primary Sources

19. Possible answer: He may have meant that throughout his studying he would be so immersed in geography that when he explained his conclusions, geography would be flowing out, as an integral and inseparable part of his explanation.

20. Possible answer: He was interested in connecting with people across the globe and trying to understand their needs and mindsets.

Applying Map Skills

21. Ecuador, Colombia, Venezuela, Guyana, Suriname, and French Guiana form the northern edge of South America.

22. The length across Brazil is approximately 2,600 miles.

23. Population centers are located generally along the coast.

CHAPTER 9 Assessment 

Directions: On a separate sheet of paper, answer the questions below. Make sure you read carefully and answer all parts of the questions.

Critical Thinking

15. ***Making Generalizations*** Describe specific ways that South American countries have overcome physical barriers to make transportation possible.

16. ***Identifying Cause and Effect*** What issues did the newly independent countries of South America face in the postcolonial period? What have been the lasting effects?

17. ***Exploring Issues*** What are some possible solutions to setbacks that South American countries have faced in becoming important traders in the international economy?

18. ***Drawing Conclusions*** What are some regulatory measures farmers and governments can take to feed growing populations without continuing to deplete the land of fertile soil?

DBQ Analyzing Primary Sources

Use the excerpt from one of South America's most beloved poets to answer the questions below.

PRIMARY SOURCE

"...While I'm writing, I'm far away;
and when I come back, I've gone.
I would like to know if others
go through the same things that I do,
have as many selves as I have,
and see themselves similarly;
and when I've exhausted this problem,
I'm going to study so hard
that when I explain myself,
I'll be talking geography."

—Pablo Neruda, "We are Many," *The Yellow Heart*, 1974

19. ***Speculating*** What do you think Neruda meant by "I'll be talking geography" as a method of explaining himself, in regard to his life? RH9–10.4

20. ***Drawing Conclusions*** Based on the topic of the poem, what aspects of Pablo Neruda's life made him a famous poet throughout the world? RH9–10.1

Applying Map Skills

Use the Unit 3 Atlas to answer the following questions.

21. ***Human Systems*** Which countries form the northern edge of South America?

22. ***Physical Systems*** Use the scale on the physical map of South America to estimate the length in miles across the widest part of Brazil.

23. ***Places and Regions*** Use your mental map of South America to make generalizations about the location of major population centers in relation to physical features and landforms.

Research and Presentation

24. ***Research Skills*** Use Internet and library resources to gather information about the factors that have shaped a South American country's current political situation. Create a time line outlining the country's historical and current political status. Cover relevant events and figures, from the country's colonization, to any rebellions it faced, to its declaration of independence, to its changes in the government systems in the twentieth and twenty-first centuries. Share the time line you create with your class. WHST9–10.6,WHST9–10.7

Writing About Geography

25. ***Informative/Explanatory*** Use standard grammar, spelling, sentence structure, and punctuation to write a one-page essay suggesting possible solutions among South American countries to address the various types of environmental issues within the region. What kinds of regulations and agreements would control increased environmental degradation from human activities such as farming, construction, urban growth, and illegal mining? WHST9–10.2

Need Extra Help?

If You've Missed Question	15	16	17	18	19	20	21	22	23	24	25
Go to page	228	224	229	235	238	238	169	168	172	224	235

238

Research and Presentation

24. The time line should reference a specific South American country's political situation and should include the country's historical and current political status—with coverage of relevant events and figures, from the country's colonization, to any rebellions it faced, to its declaration of independence, to the changes in its government systems in the twentieth and twenty-first centuries.

Writing About Geography

25. The essay should specify at least two of South America's major environmental issues and include at least one logical solution for each. It should explain the regulations that countries would have to have in place to control environmentally dangerous human behavior and agreements the countries may have to have with one another.

UNIT **4**

EUROPE Planner

UNDERSTANDING BY DESIGN®

Enduring Understandings

- *Geographers organize Earth into regions that share common characteristics.*
- *Cooperation and conflict among people influence the division and control of Earth's surface.*
- *Culture influences people's perceptions of places and regions.*

Essential Question

- *How do physical systems and human systems shape a place?*

Students will know:

- *how the history of Europe was shaped by migrations, trade, and invasions.*
- *the characteristics of Europe's modern economies and modern governments.*
- *the importance of various landforms and water sources to Europe.*
- *the factors that affect climate and vegetation in the region.*
- *how urbanization and industrialization have shaped population patterns.*
- *the reasons for and the effects of the creation of the European Union.*
- *the threats posed by pollution, acid rain, and human activities and how they are being addressed.*
- *that Eastern European countries transitioned to democratic governments and market economies after the fall of communism.*

Students will be able to:

- ***analyze** the influence of migrations, trade, and invasions on Europe's history.*
- ***describe** Europe's modern economies and governments.*
- ***identify** factors that affect climate, vegetation, and population patterns in this region.*
- ***explain** why the European Union was created and its effects.*
- ***describe** environmental issues and how they are being addressed.*
- ***analyze** the transition from command to market economies and the impacts of the Soviet era.*

Predictable Misunderstandings

- *The climate of Europe is consistent throughout the region.*
- *The countries of Europe have been in existence for hundreds of years with stable borders.*
- *Most Northwestern European countries are landlocked.*
- *Most countries in Europe have similar cultures.*
- *The physical geography of Southern Europe is similar to that of Northwestern Europe.*
- *Russia is largely barren and cold with few natural resources.*
- *Russia is still a communist country.*

Assessment Evidence

Performance Tasks:

- *Environmental Case Study*
- *GeoLab Activity*
- *GIS Simulation*
- *Hands-On Chapter Projects*

Other Evidence:

- *Location Activity*
- *Self-Check Quizzes*
- *Lesson Quizzes*
- *Participation in Interactive Whiteboard Activities*
- *Contribution to small-group activities*
- *Interpretation of slide show images*
- *Participation in class discussions about Europe*
- *Analysis of graphic organizers, graphs, and charts*
- *Lesson Reviews*
- *Chapter Assessments*

Key for Using the Teacher Edition

SKILL-BASED ACTIVITIES

Types of skill activities found in the Teacher Edition.

* **V Visual Skills** require students to analyze maps, graphs, charts, and photos.

R Reading Skills help students practice reading skills and master vocabulary.

C Critical Thinking Skills help students apply and extend what they have learned.

W Writing Skills provide writing opportunities to help students comprehend the text.

T Technology Skills require students to use digital tools effectively.

*Letters are followed by a number when there is more than one of the same type of skill on the page.

DIFFERENTIATED INSTRUCTION

All activities are written for the on-level student unless otherwise marked with the leveled labels below.

BL Beyond Level
AL Approaching Level
ELL English Language Learners

All students benefit from activities that utilize different learning styles. Many activities are marked as below when a particular learning style is highlighted.

Intrapersonal	**Naturalist**
Logical/Mathematical	**Kinesthetic**
Visual/Spatial	**Auditory/Musical**
Verbal/Linguistic	**Interpersonal**

SUGGESTED PACING GUIDE

Introducing the Unit	1 Day
Chapter 10: Northern Europe	5 Days
Chapter 11: Northwestern Europe	5 Days
Case Study: How Beneficial is the European Union?	1 Day
Chapter 12: Southern Europe	5 Days
Chapter 13: Eastern Europe	5 Days
Chapter 14: The Russian Core	5 Days
Global Connections: Arctic Oil Frontiers	1 Day
TOTAL TIME	**28 Days**

PLANNER

☑ Print Teaching Options

V Visual Skills

- ☐ **p. 239** Students analyze a photograph of Venice. **Visual/Spatial**
- ☐ **p. 242** Students analyze the physical features of Europe. **Verbal/Linguistic, Visual/Spatial**
- ☐ **p. 243** Students make a chart of the countries of Europe and their capitals. **AL** **Visual/Spatial**

R Reading Skills

- ☐ **p. 240** Students discuss how Europe is a peninsula of peninsulas. **Verbal/Linguistic**
- ☐ **p. 244** Students use the map key to identify major climate zones. **AL** **Interpersonal, Visual/Spatial**
- ☐ **p. 245** Students identify the predominant uses of land in Europe. **AL** **Logical/Mathematical, Visual/Spatial**

C Critical Thinking Skills

- ☐ **p. 240** Students interpret the concept of a region's history being intertwined with its modern-day culture. **BL** **Logical/Mathematical, Interpersonal**
- ☐ **p. 241** Students discuss what attracts tourists to Venice. **Intrapersonal**
- ☐ **p. 245** Students analyze the economic activity map. **Logical/Mathematical, Visual/Spatial**
- ☐ **p. 246** Students compare and contrast population densities of different parts of Europe. **Verbal/Linguistic, Visual/Spatial**

W Writing Skills

- ☐ **p. 241** Students write a description of Europe's major mountain ranges. **ELL** **Verbal/Linguistic, Visual/Spatial**
- ☐ **p. 243** Students write headlines for news articles about an assigned European country. **BL** **Verbal/Linguistic**
- ☐ **p. 244** Students write an essay describing the vegetation associated with each climate zone in Europe. **BL** **Naturalist, Verbal/Linguistic**
- ☐ **p. 245** Students write a paragraph describing the important mineral resources of a particular country or subregion. **ELL** **Interpersonal, Verbal/Linguistic**

T Technology Skills

- ☐ **p. 241** Students research a major river and present their findings as if they were a riverboat captain or tour guide. **BL** **Naturalist, Visual/Spatial**
- ☐ **p. 246** Students research and give a multimedia presentation about the ethnic makeup of one of Europe's larger cities. **BL** **Visual/Spatial, Interpersonal**

☑ Online Teaching Options

V Visual Skills

- **GEO @ WORK** **Thinking Like a Geographer**—Students explore principles and skills of geography applied to real-world challenges.
- **INTERACTIVE FEATURE** **Explore the Region: Europe**—Students create a chart listing the geography, people, and environments of Europe. **ELL** **Verbal/Linguistic**

R Reading Skills

- **INTERACTIVE MAP** **Population Density Map: Europe**—Students compare maps to write generalizations about the relationship between land use/resources and population density. **Visual/Spatial, Logical/Mathematical**

C Critical Thinking Skills

- **INTERACTIVE MAP** **Political Map: Europe**—Students discuss how location contributed to the growth of capital cities within countries of Europe. **AL** **Visual/Spatial**
- **INTERACTIVE MAP** **Physical Map: Europe**—Students discuss how waterways influenced Europe's history and economic development. **AL** **Visual/Spatial, Logical/Mathematical**

W Writing Skills

- **INTERACTIVE MAP** **Climate and Vegetation Maps: Europe**—Students write correlations between climate and vegetation in the region. **BL** **Visual/Spatial**

T Technology Skills

- **INTERACTIVE MAP** **Economic Activity Map: Europe**—Students make multimedia presentations on an economic activity and its effects on the resources of Europe. **Visual/Spatial, Auditory/Musical**

☑ Printable Digital Worksheets

V Visual Skills

- **WORKSHEET** **Location Activity**—Students locate countries, water systems, and physical features of Europe.
- **WORKSHEET** **GeoLab Activity**—Students explore how to change a penny so that it looks more like a euro coin, which is used throughout much of Europe.

C Critical Thinking Skills

- **WORKSHEET** **Environmental Case Study**—Students complete a study about the European Black Triangle and the effects of global rapid industrialization.

T Technology Skills

- **WORKSHEET** **GIS Simulation**—Students learn about a biogeographical region in the European Union and evaluate and present information about how member states with land that falls within the boundaries of this region are working to preserve their natural ecosystems.

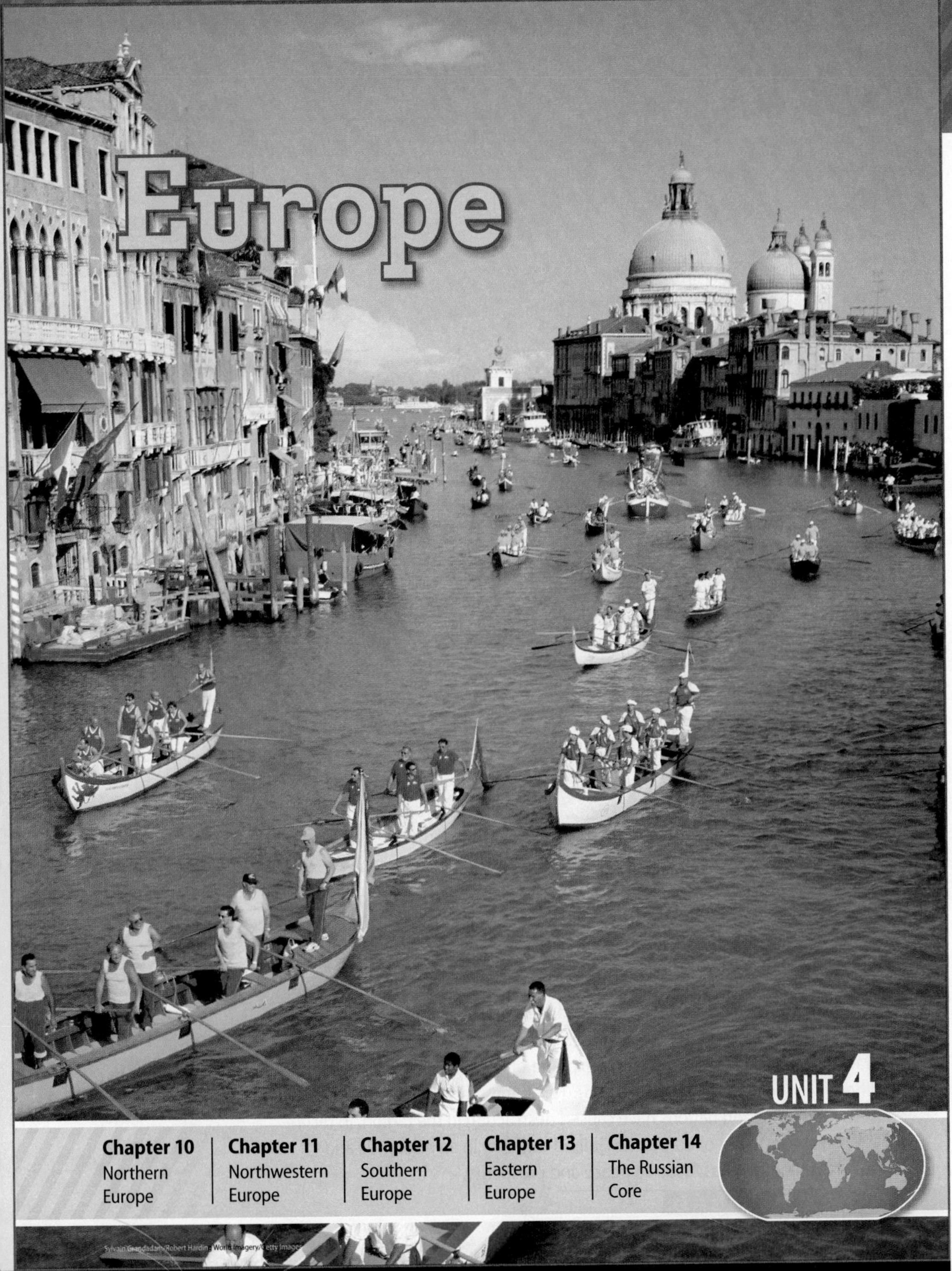

Europe

UNIT 4

Chapter 10	Chapter 11	Chapter 12	Chapter 13	Chapter 14
Northern Europe	Northwestern Europe	Southern Europe	Eastern Europe	The Russian Core

Sylvain Grandadam/Robert Harding World Imagery/Getty Images

networks Online Teaching Options

GEO @ WORK

Thinking Like a Geographer

Problem Solving Explore specific examples of the principles and skills of geography applied to real-world challenges that impact people's lives. From agriculture to urban planning, to wiping out disease and managing changes in society—geography plays a key role in understanding relationships and generating solutions that make sense.

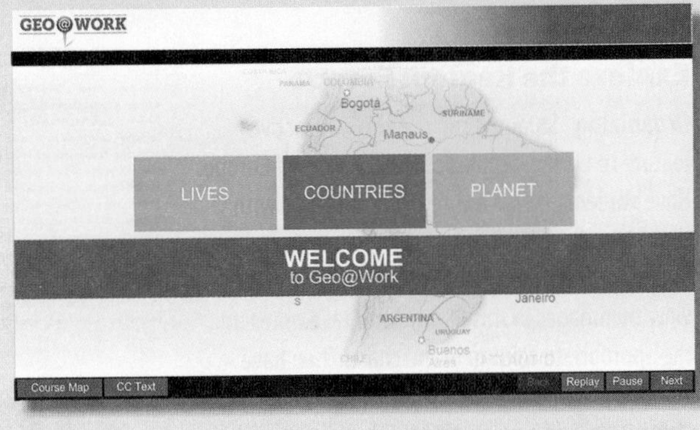

UNIT 4
Europe

ENGAGE

Assessing Call students' attention to the chapter titles at the bottom of the page. Challenge students to name a country or major city in each of the named subregions of Europe: Northern Europe, Northwestern Europe, Southern Europe, Eastern Europe, and the Russian Core. Invite volunteers to locate each of the countries or cities on a map. Assess students' knowledge about Europe by asking them to describe what they know about its countries and great cities, famous landforms and landmarks, languages, and history.

TEACH & ASSESS

Analyzing Images Have students study the photograph. **Ask:** How might you describe this place? *(Possible answers: It is an old city on a major waterway, possibly a river or a canal; the water comes right up to the first floor of the buildings; each building has a dock; people move around the city on boats)* Where is this place? Hint: Think of a famous city in Europe that is known for its canals. *(Grand Canal in Venice, Italy)* Who are these people and what are they doing? *(Possible answers: They seem to be teams of rowers; they are traveling down the waterway. Possibly they have taken part in or will take part in a competition.)* Explain to students that Europe has a long and diverse history. Have students explain how this photo exemplifies this fact. **Visual/Spatial**

Content Background Knowledge

Venice's Grand Canal The Canal Grande is an ancient waterway that snakes through the city of Venice, Italy. It is lined by buildings, most built by wealthy Venetians hundreds of years ago. All kinds of boats are used on the canal, but the iconic water taxis, or gondolas, are favored by tourists. Each year Venice holds a series of boat races on the canal as part of its Regata Storica.

CLOSE & REFLECT

Listing In a class discussion, invite several students to state a fact they have learned about the geography, culture, and/or history of Europe. Tell students they will add to their knowledge of the region as they study this unit.

ENGAGE

V Visual Skills

Analyzing Images Help students analyze the photograph by asking the following questions. **Ask:** What is happening in the photo? *(young men running with bulls)* Where might this be? *(Possible answers: in an old city; in Pamplona, Spain; someplace where bullfighting is practiced)* What can you tell about the event? *(Possible answers: It is a joyous, celebratory event; young men like to run with the bulls; this may be a test of their courage.)* What does this tell you about the culture of Europe? *(Possible answer: People value old traditions; bullfighting is enjoyed in some places.)*

TEACH & ASSESS

C Critical Thinking Skills

Interpreting Discuss what it means for a region's history to be "intertwined with its modern-day culture." **Ask:** As exemplified by the photograph, how are Spain's history and modern-day culture intertwined? *(Possible answer: The event is taking place today, but bullfighting is an old tradition. The running of the bulls is part of that bullfighting tradition; the bulls are escorted by people to a bullfighting facility.)* Point out that the running of the bulls is part of a religious festival to honor St. Fermin, the patron saint of Pamplona. BL Logical/Mathematical, Interpersonal

R Reading Skills

Identifying Have a student volunteer locate Europe on a globe or wall map and outline its boundaries. **Ask:** Into what bodies of water does Europe extend? *(Atlantic Ocean, Mediterranean Sea, and Arctic Ocean)* How is Europe a peninsula of peninsulas? *(It is a ragged peninsula composed of many pieces of land that extend into the sea.)* What are the main peninsulas of Europe? *(Balkan, Apennine or Italian, Iberian, Scandinavian, Jutland or Denmark)* How might a peninsula be an advantage to a country? *(oceans a source of food; avenues for trade and exploration)* How might it be a disadvantage? *(Possible answers: There could be disputes over resources and ownership.)* Verbal/Linguistic

V

C

1 Culture Europe's cultural heritage is as varied as its landscape. Centuries-old traditions, such as the running of the bulls in Pamplona, Spain, illustrate how the region's history is intertwined with its modern-day culture.

EXPLORE the REGION

R

EUROPE is a peninsula of peninsulas, with many pieces of land extending into the Atlantic Ocean and the Mediterranean Sea. Over the centuries, Europeans have taken advantage of their location, using the seas as a source of food and an avenue for trade and exploration. Europe is home to many different languages and culture groups. Throughout history, conflicts between competing nations have caused destruction in the region. In recent years, however, most of Europe has joined together in an economic and political union that has fostered peace and prosperity.

THERE'S MORE ONLINE

networks Online Teaching Options

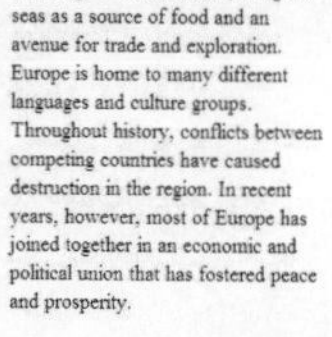

INTERACTIVE FEATURE

Explore the Region: Europe

Organizing Students can use this interactive feature to view examples of the diversity of Europe. Have students create a three-column chart with these labels: *Physical Geography, Human Geography,* and *People and Their Environment*. Have students view the images in this feature and take notes in the appropriate column of the chart. Then have volunteers share the information in their charts. Tell students to add any important information to their charts as they listen to the information others share. They can also use this chart format to take notes throughout the unit.

ELL Verbal/Linguistic

Europe

INTRODUCTION

Europe is a peninsula of peninsulas, with many pieces of land extending into the Atlantic Ocean and the Mediterranean Sea. Over the centuries, Europeans have taken advantage of their location, using the seas as a source of food and an avenue for trade and exploration. Europe is home to many different languages and culture groups. Throughout history, conflicts between competing countries have caused destruction in the region. In recent years, however, most of Europe has joined together in an economic and political union that has fostered peace and prosperity.

rtve.es

3
Rivers The Danube River flows from southern Germany to the Black Sea. Like many European rivers, it is an important commercial route as well as a scenic highlight.

4
Mountains The Alps stretch 750 miles (1,200 km) through eight countries, separating Southern Europe from the north. The mountain range's imposing peaks are the source of many of the region's rivers.

2
Economy Tourism is an important sector of the European economy. It comprises a wide variety of destinations and employs a large percentage of the European workforce. Venice, with its beautiful canals, is a top choice among travelers.

DIGITAL WORKSHEETS

Europe

Demonstrating Use these online digital unit worksheets to have students demonstrate their depth of knowledge and comprehension and to provide them with extended unit content through project-based activities.

- **Environmental Case Study**
- **GIS Simulation**
- **Location Activity**
- **GeoLab Activity**

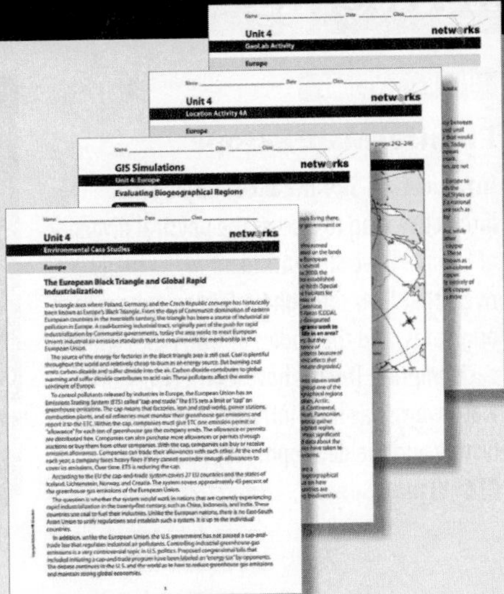

C Critical Thinking Skills

Drawing Conclusions Point out to students that the photograph shows a famous European tourist destination—Venice. **Ask:** What do you know about Venice? *(Possible answers: an old Italian city; many canals; people use gondolas for transportation; the scene of many movies)* What features of Venice attract tourists? *(Possible answers: old and beautiful; many historic and cultural sites; beautiful canals; romantic)* What other famous destinations attract tourists to Europe and why? *(Answers will vary; students might note that Europe has many historic cities, museums, architectural wonders, cultural spots, beaches, resorts, and the like.)* **Intrapersonal**

Making Connections

Many European tourists travel to the United States each year. Have students name some of the sites in their communities that might be of interest to Europeans and explain why.

T Technology Skills

Presenting Organize students into pairs or small groups and assign each group one of Europe's major rivers. Have groups research the river's commercial and scenic importance and then present their findings to the class using maps, photographs, and other visuals. Suggest that students make their presentations as if they were river boat captains or tour guides taking people on a journey down the river. BL **Naturalist, Visual/Spatial**

W Writing Skills

Informative/Explanatory Have students locate Europe's major mountain ranges on a physical map. Then have them write a description of the mountain ranges, noting their locations, extent, relative heights, proximity to cities, rivers that originate in them, or other unique characteristics. ELL **Verbal/Linguistic, Visual/Spatial**

CLOSE & REFLECT

Reaching Conclusions Review the various factors that have been introduced to students in this unit feature. Ask students to consider all of these factors and write a concluding statement about the geography of Europe.

ENGAGE

R Reading Skills

Activating Prior Knowledge Invite volunteers to name several of Europe's smaller seas such as Norwegian, Barents, Kara, Celtic, North, Baltic, Black, Caspian, Adriatic, Tyrrhenian, Ionian, Adriatic, and Aegean. Challenge students to locate these seas on a map and to identify the country or countries each borders. Tell students that they will be learning more about these seas and other geographical features of Europe as they study the maps in this unit.

TEACH & ASSESS

C Critical Thinking Skills

Evaluating Ask students to focus on the map key and to note what the different colors represent. **Ask: Which color represents the highest elevations?** *(dark orange)* **What assumptions can you make about the landforms of the higher elevations?** *(mostly mountains)* **What does the upright-pointing triangle symbol indicate?** *(mountain peak)* **What is the symbol for the lowest point?** *(downward-pointing triangle)* Have students identify low points on the map or inset. *(Possible answer: Caspian Sea shoreline)*
AL Logical/Mathematical, Visual/Spatial

V Visual Skills

Analyzing Visuals Have students analyze the physical features of Europe. **Ask:**

- **Where are the highest elevations in Europe?** *(Western Europe)*
- **Which of Europe's mountain ranges is highest?** *(Alps)*
- **Would you say most of Europe is lowlands or highlands?** *(lowlands)*
- **What is the huge lowland area of Northern Europe called?** *(Northern European Plain)*
- **What do you notice about the origin and flow of the major river systems in Europe?** *(Possible answer: Many form in the Alps and drain into the sea.)*

Have students locate land features in Europe that may have formed barriers between regions and slowed human travel and development. **Verbal/Linguistic, Visual/Spatial**

ANSWERS, p. 242

MAP STUDY

1. Balkan, Apennine or Italian, Iberian, Scandinavian, Jutland or Denmark
2. Austria, Belarus, Czech Republic, Hungary, Kosovo, Liechtenstein, Luxembourg, Macedonia, Moldova, Serbia, Slovakia, Switzerland, and Vatican City

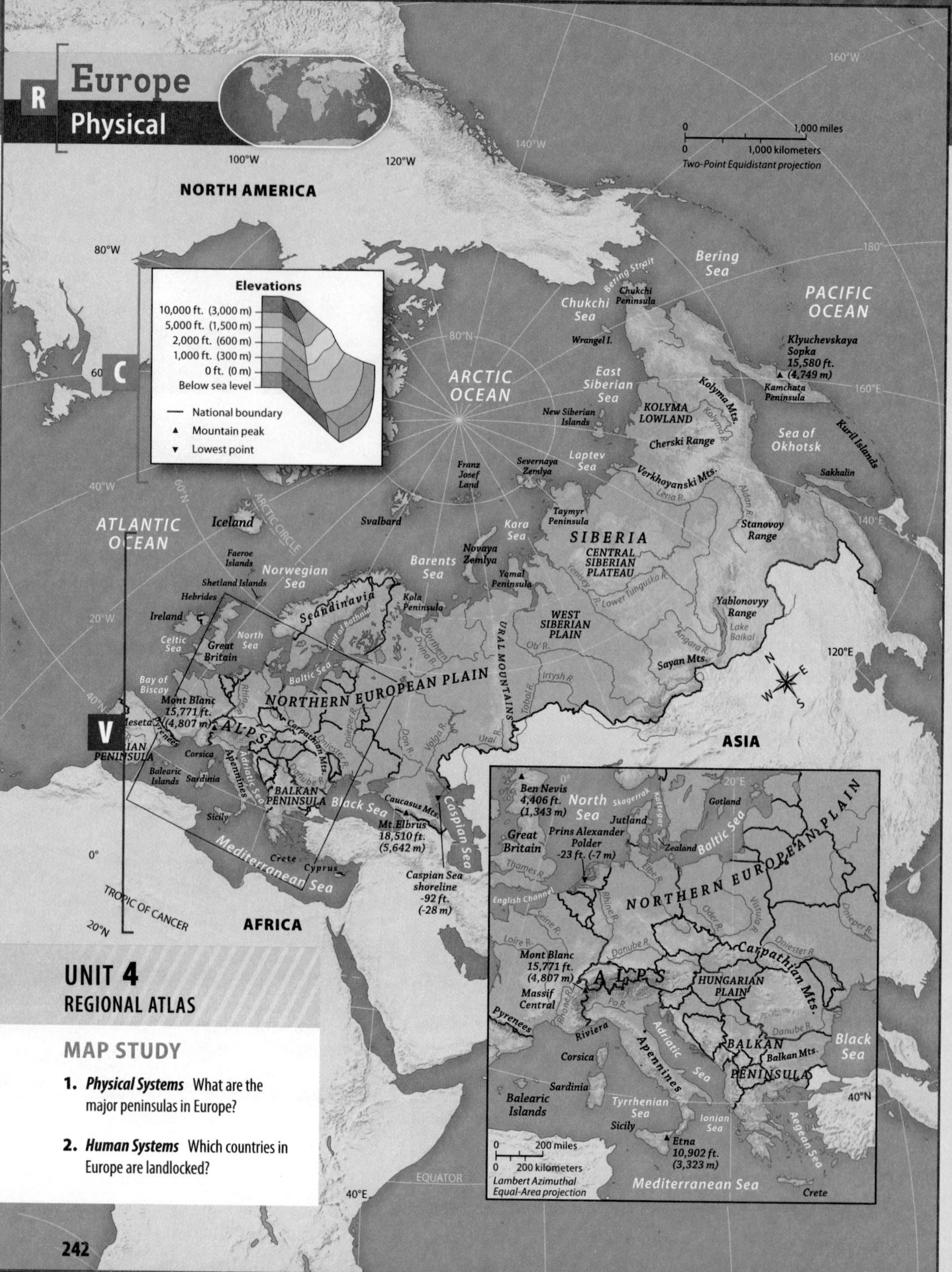

R Europe Physical

Elevations
10,000 ft. (3,000 m)
5,000 ft. (1,500 m)
2,000 ft. (600 m)
1,000 ft. (300 m)
0 ft. (0 m)
Below sea level
National boundary
▲ Mountain peak
▼ Lowest point

0 1,000 miles
0 1,000 kilometers
Two-Point Equidistant projection

0 200 miles
0 200 kilometers
Lambert Azimuthal Equal-Area projection

UNIT 4
REGIONAL ATLAS

MAP STUDY

1. ***Physical Systems*** What are the major peninsulas in Europe?
2. ***Human Systems*** Which countries in Europe are landlocked?

242

networks Online Teaching Options

INTERACTIVE MAP

Physical Map: Europe

Interpreting Significance Display the interactive map to discuss the physical diversity of Europe. Have students identify the many rivers that flow throughout Europe, where each originates, and the bodies of water into which each empties. Discuss how this network of waterways may have influenced Europe's history and the development of its economy.
AL Visual/Spatial, Logical/Mathematical

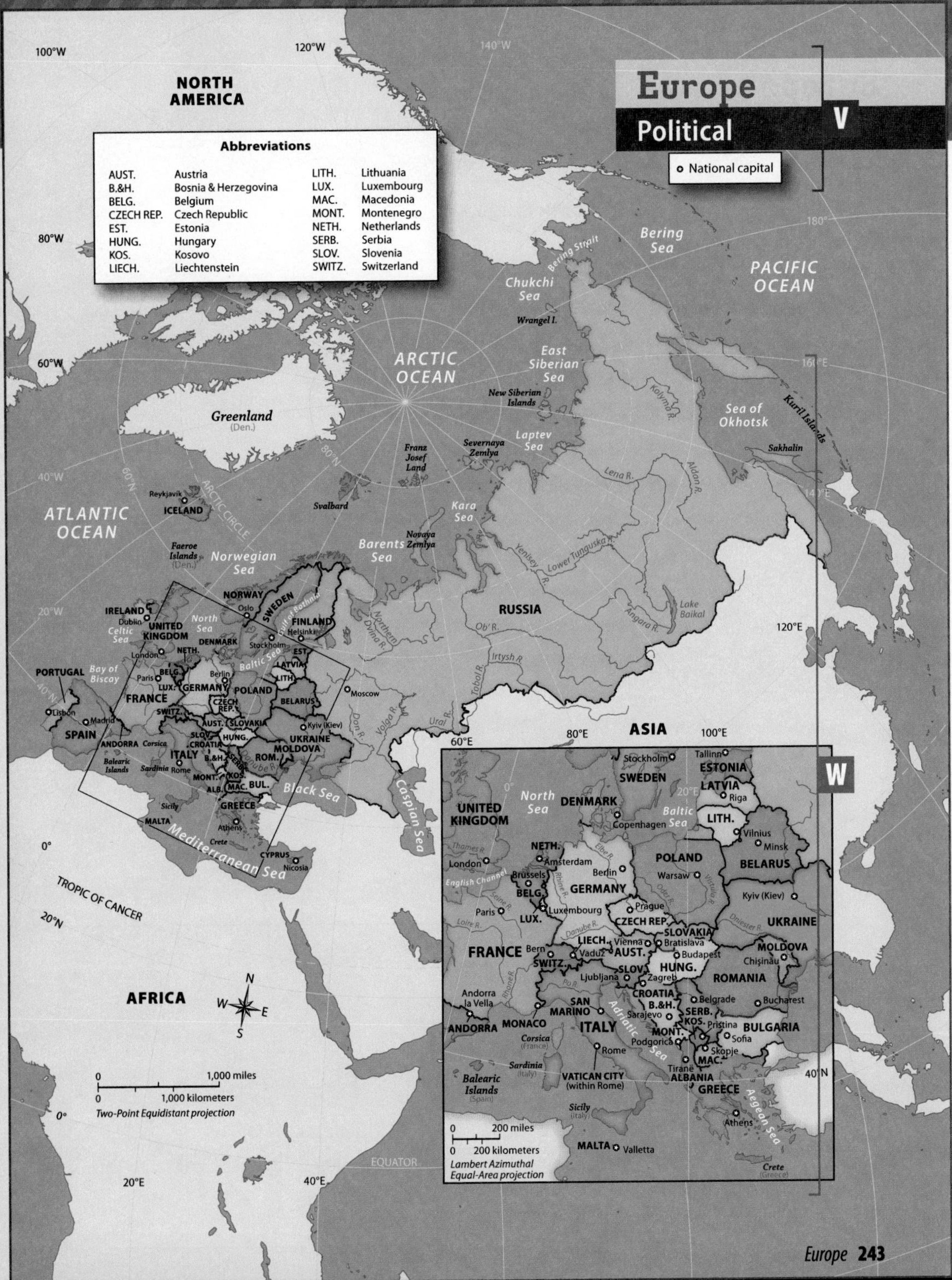
Europe
Political
V
National capital
Abbreviations
AUST. Austria
B.&H. Bosnia & Herzegovina
BELG. Belgium
CZECH REP. Czech Republic
EST. Estonia
HUNG. Hungary
KOS. Kosovo
LIECH. Liechtenstein
LITH. Lithuania
LUX. Luxembourg
MAC. Macedonia
MONT. Montenegro
NETH. Netherlands
SERB. Serbia
SLOV. Slovenia
SWITZ. Switzerland
NORTH AMERICA
ARCTIC OCEAN
ATLANTIC OCEAN
PACIFIC OCEAN
Greenland (Den.)
ICELAND
RUSSIA
ASIA
AFRICA
Mediterranean Sea
Black Sea
Caspian Sea
Barents Sea
Norwegian Sea
North Sea
Baltic Sea
W
0 1,000 miles
0 1,000 kilometers
Two-Point Equidistant projection
0 200 miles
0 200 kilometers
Lambert Azimuthal Equal-Area projection
Europe 243

V Visual Skills

Creating Charts Have students use the political map to make a chart of the countries of Europe and their capitals. Challenge students to make comparisons about the countries and add these to the chart, noting characteristics such as largest, smallest, coastal, landlocked, and other facts. AL
Visual/Spatial

Making Connections

Europeans have been immigrating to the United States since colonial times. Today, people of European descent make up the majority of the population, although this is changing. In some parts of the country certain European groups live in large enclaves, for instance, Russians in New York City, Poles in Chicago, and Czechs in Wilber, Nebraska. Have students describe any European enclaves in their communities.

W Writing Skills

Informative/Explanatory Assign students or pairs of students European countries to explore. Ask students to find recent news articles about their country and write headlines for each of these stories. Use these headlines to lead a class discussion on current events in Europe. As you discuss each country, have students locate it on the political map of Europe.
BL **Verbal/Linguistic**

INTERACTIVE MAP

Political Map: Europe

Spatial Analysis Use this map to help students identify the countries of Europe and their capital cities. Tell students to look closely at the location of capital cities to see whether they can find a common factor among many of them. *(Many are located either adjacent to or near a body of water.)* Ask groups of students to discuss how this location may have contributed to the growth of the capital cities. Discuss other factors that may have had an influence, such as landforms, resources, or climate.
AL **Visual/Spatial**

Regional Atlas: Europe
Map Themes
Physical map
Political map
Population Density map
Economic Activity map
Climate map
Vegetation map
Map Key
National capital
Navigator

R Reading Skills

Reading Maps Have students focus on the map key and use it to identify the major climate zones in Europe. **Ask:** **What color indicates a humid continental climate?** *(bright green)* **What climate do areas colored in light green have?** *(humid subtropical)* Have students explain how these two climates differ. Organize students into pairs and have them analyze and identify the various climate zones and locate the countries in each zone. Then, **ask:** **What can be generalized about the climate of Europe?** *(Possible answers: diverse; ranges from semi-arid to subarctic and tundra; part covered by ice cap)* **AL Interpersonal, Visual/Spatial**

C Critical Thinking Skills

Analyzing Have students analyze the climate map. **Ask:** **What is the relationship between the climate zones and their proximity to the Atlantic Ocean?** *(Most lands close to the Atlantic enjoy a marine west coast climate; exceptions are Norway, Iceland, Spain, and Portugal.)* **Proximity to the Arctic Ocean?** *(These regions are cold and either subarctic, tundra, or ice cap climate zones.)* **Characterize the climate of Russia.** *(The climate ranges from ice cap and tundra to subarctic and further south to humid continental.)* **The climate of Northwestern Europe?** *(marine west coast)* **Logical/Mathematical, Verbal/Linguistic**

W Writing Skills

Informative/Explanatory Have students identify the major vegetation zones, noting how much of Europe is mainly forested. Have students compare the climate map to the vegetation map of Europe. Ask students to write an essay describing the vegetation associated with each climate zone. **BL Naturalist, Verbal/Linguistic**

Content Background Knowledge

Changing Biomes At one time, Europe was covered with deciduous forests, but little of this biome is left. Huge expanses of old forests were cut down for agriculture and urbanization. Much was cut for lumber and fuel. The forests and grasslands of Northwestern and Eastern Europe have been almost completely domesticated with crops and livestock. Today the only old-growth forests that survive are in preserves such as the Białowieza Forest, located on the border of Poland and Belarus.

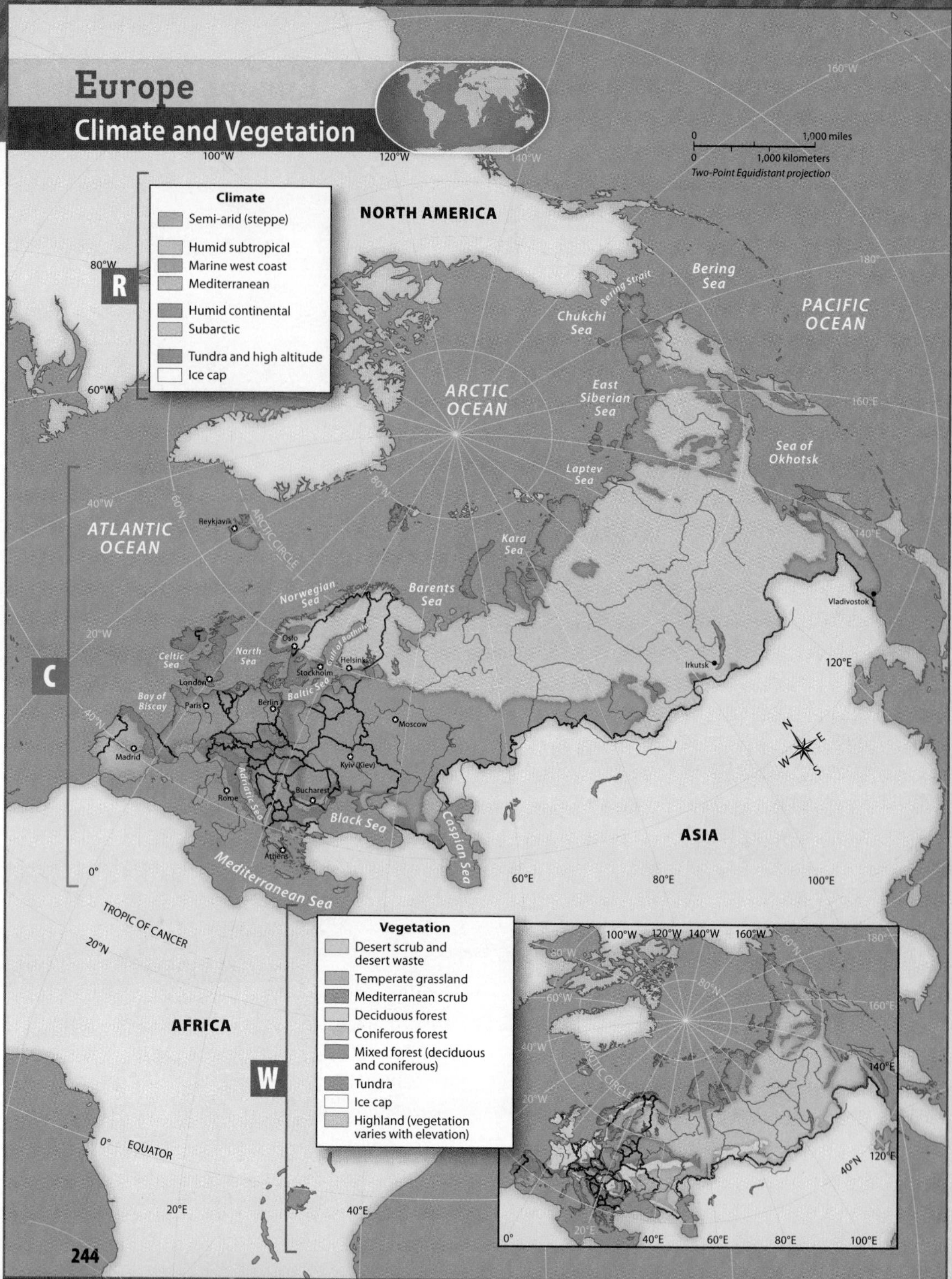

Europe
Climate and Vegetation

Climate
- Semi-arid (steppe)
- Humid subtropical
- Marine west coast
- Mediterranean
- Humid continental
- Subarctic
- Tundra and high altitude
- Ice cap

Vegetation
- Desert scrub and desert waste
- Temperate grassland
- Mediterranean scrub
- Deciduous forest
- Coniferous forest
- Mixed forest (deciduous and coniferous)
- Tundra
- Ice cap
- Highland (vegetation varies with elevation)

0 — 1,000 miles
0 — 1,000 kilometers
Two-Point Equidistant projection

NORTH AMERICA
Bering Sea
PACIFIC OCEAN
Chukchi Sea
East Siberian Sea
ARCTIC OCEAN
Sea of Okhotsk
Laptev Sea
ATLANTIC OCEAN
Reykjavik
Kara Sea
Barents Sea
Norwegian Sea
Vladivostok
Celtic Sea
North Sea
Oslo
Helsinki
Stockholm
Irkutsk
London
Bay of Biscay
Paris
Berlin
Baltic Sea
Moscow
Madrid
Kyiv (Kiev)
Rome
Bucharest
Black Sea
Caspian Sea
Athens
Mediterranean Sea
ASIA
AFRICA
TROPIC OF CANCER
EQUATOR

networks Online Teaching Options

INTERACTIVE MAP

Climate and Vegetation Maps: Europe

Comparing Display the interactive map and have students identify the types of climate found throughout Europe. **Ask:** **Which kinds of climate are most common in Europe?** *(humid subtropical, humid continental, and subarctic)* Then direct attention to the vegetation map. Have small groups compare the vegetation map to the climate map. Tell them to write a paragraph that describes any correlation they find between climate and the type of vegetation. Have groups share their paragraphs with the class, and then discuss any differences.
BL Visual/Spatial

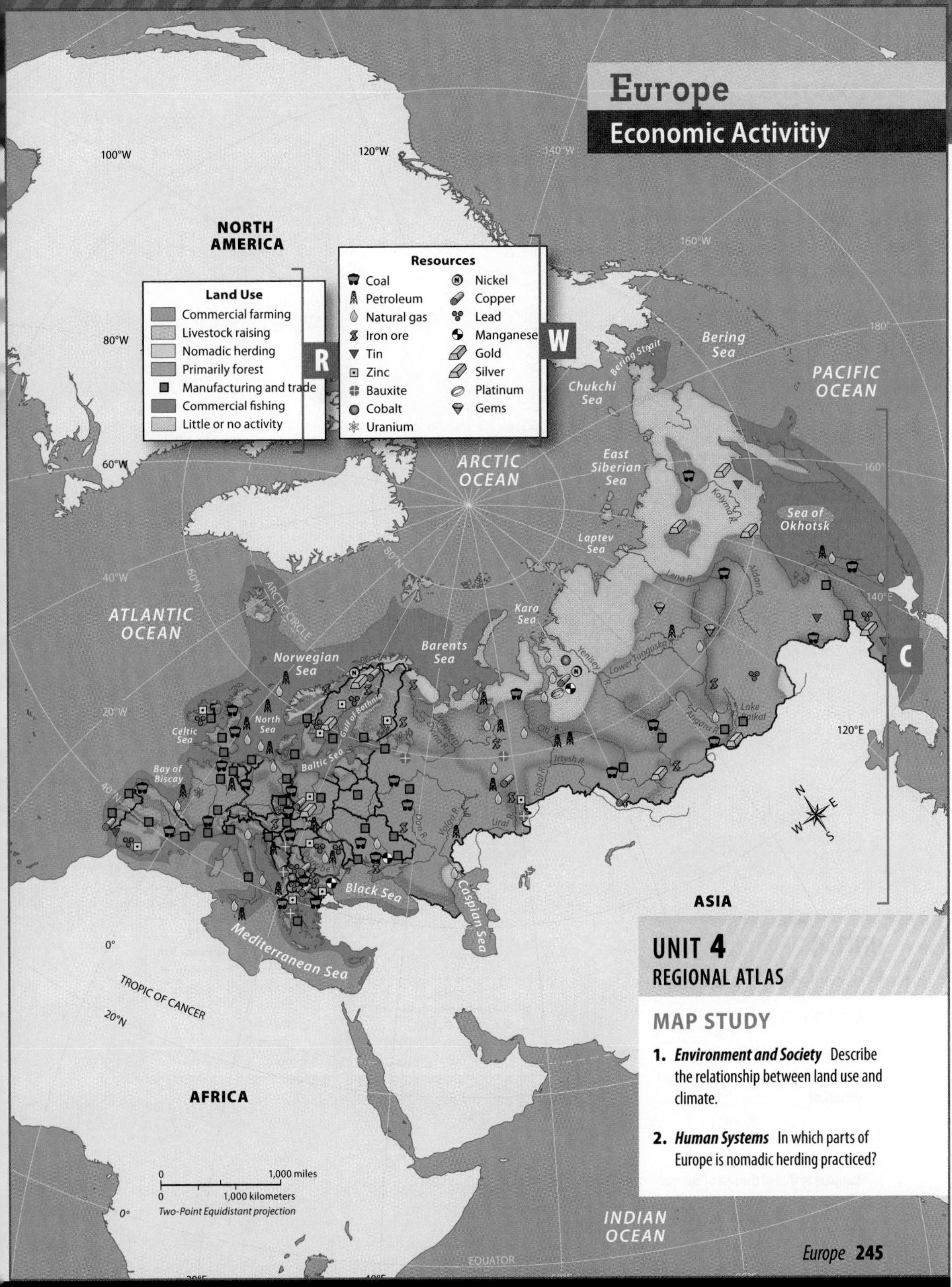

Europe
Economic Activitiy

Land Use
- Commercial farming
- Livestock raising
- Nomadic herding
- Primarily forest
- Manufacturing and trade
- Commercial fishing
- Little or no activity

Resources
- Coal
- Petroleum
- Natural gas
- Iron ore
- Tin
- Zinc
- Bauxite
- Cobalt
- Uranium
- Nickel
- Copper
- Lead
- Manganese
- Gold
- Silver
- Platinum
- Gems

NORTH AMERICA
ARCTIC OCEAN
PACIFIC OCEAN
ATLANTIC OCEAN
INDIAN OCEAN
ASIA
AFRICA

0 — 1,000 miles
0 — 1,000 kilometers
Two-Point Equidistant projection

UNIT 4
REGIONAL ATLAS

MAP STUDY

1. ***Environment and Society*** Describe the relationship between land use and climate.
2. ***Human Systems*** In which parts of Europe is nomadic herding practiced?

INTERACTIVE MAP

Economic Activity Map: Europe

Gathering Information Display the map and point out the land use key. Have students find the areas on the map that are used for commercial fishing, commercial farming, and manufacturing and trade. Have small groups of students choose and research one of these economic activites. Tell groups to prepare a multimedia presentation with interesting facts and figures about how their activity affects the economy, land and water, and people of Europe. Encourage groups to use visuals, audio clips, voice-overs, music, and other media to make their presentations interesting and relevant. **Visual/Spatial, Auditory/Musical**

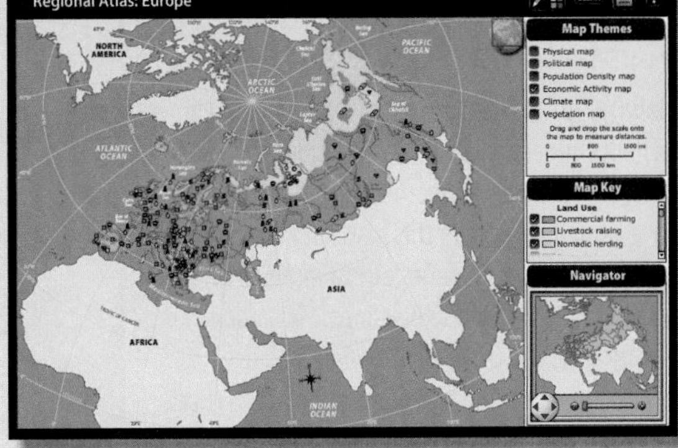

R Reading Skills

Analyzing Visuals Have students focus on the land use map key to identify the types of land use activities predominant in Europe. **Ask: What color is used to designate commercial farming?** *(bright green)* **What color is used to designate livestock raising?** *(orange)* **Forestry?** *(olive green)* **Based on the map, what land land use seems to predominate in Europe?** *(Possible answers: Commercial farming and forests predominate the region, as do many sectors of manufacturing and trade.)* **AL Logical/Mathematical, Visual/Spatial**

W Writing Skills

Informative/Explanatory Have students focus on the resources map key to identify the types of resources found in Europe. Organize students into groups and assign each group a country or region to explore. Have students use the map to identify the mineral resources of that area. Then have them write a paragraph describing the country or region's important mineral resources. **ELL Interpersonal, Verbal/Linguistic**

C Critical Thinking Skills

Evaluating Have students analyze the economic activity map. **Ask: In what parts of Europe is forestry a major economic activity?** *(northern, particularly in Russia and Scandinavia)* **What is the predominant land use of Western Europe?** *(commercial farming; manufacturing)* **Identify three countries where livestock raising is a significant activity.** *(Student answers may vary but should include that pockets are scattered throughout Western Europe)* **In what parts of Scandinavia are major manufacturing centers located?** *(southern)* **Logical/Mathematical, Visual/Spatial**

ANSWERS, p. 245

MAP STUDY

1. The majority of commercial farming, manufacturing and trade, and livestock raising are located south of the subarctic and tundra into the humid continental, marine west coast, and Mediterranean climate regions. Pockets of economic activity, such as mining and petroleum and natural gas industries, also appear in the subartic regions.
2. The majority of nomadic herding is north of the Arctic Circle. However, a few patches of nomadic herding are in Norway on the Scandinavian Peninsula and in Russia east of Lake Baikal where the vegetation is desert scrub.

C Critical Thinking Skills

Comparing and Contrasting Have students compare and contrast the population densities of different parts of Europe. **Ask:** **What color represents the highest population density?** *(purple)* **In what countries are population densities 1,250 and over per square mile (500 and over per sq. km)?** *(Answers will vary, but students should note that much of Northwestern Europe has these population densities.)* **How do the population densities of the Russian Core and Northwestern Europe compare?** *(Possible answer: Overall, the Russian Core has a much lower population density.)* **Which part of Northern Europe is more heavily populated?** *(southern)* Have students compare the population density map to the climate zones map of Europe. Then lead a class discussion in which students explain how population density relates to climate. **Verbal/Linguistic, Visual/Spatial**

T Technology Skills

Presenting Have students focus on the cities map key. **Ask:** **What symbol is used to identify cities of over 5,000,000?** *(black square)* **What is the population range of cities shown as black dots?** *(1,000,000–2,000,000)* Have students identify which European cities have populations over 5,000,000. Then divide students into small groups and have each group research the ethnic composition of one of Europe's larger cities. Have groups present a multimedia presentation that includes charts, maps, and visuals. **BL** **Visual/Spatial, Interpersonal**

CLOSE & REFLECT

Summarizing Organize students into pairs. Have partners review the unit maps and make a list of important information about the geography of Europe they gain from each map.

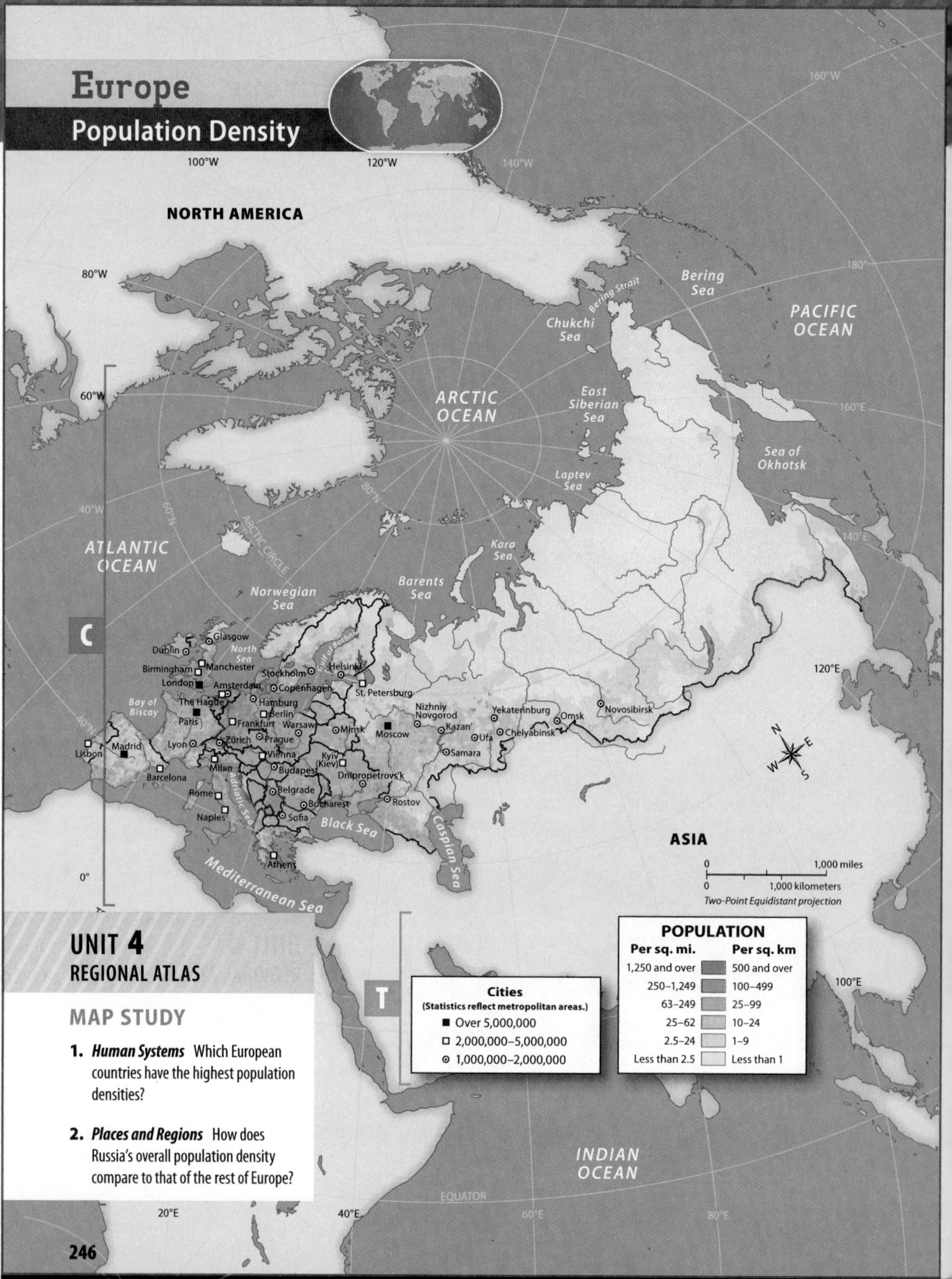

ANSWERS, p. 246

MAP STUDY

1. Monaco, Vatican City, United Kingdom, Belgium, Germany, and the Netherlands have the highest population densities in Europe.
2. Russia's overall population density is much lower than that of the rest of Europe. Russia has a large population, but it has a large amount of area; therefore, the population density is lower than for other countries in Europe.

Europe
Population Density

NORTH AMERICA · ASIA · ATLANTIC OCEAN · ARCTIC OCEAN · PACIFIC OCEAN · INDIAN OCEAN

0 — 1,000 miles
0 — 1,000 kilometers
Two-Point Equidistant projection

Cities
(Statistics reflect metropolitan areas.)
- ■ Over 5,000,000
- □ 2,000,000–5,000,000
- ⊙ 1,000,000–2,000,000

POPULATION

Per sq. mi.	Per sq. km
1,250 and over	500 and over
250–1,249	100–499
63–249	25–99
25–62	10–24
2.5–24	1–9
Less than 2.5	Less than 1

UNIT 4
REGIONAL ATLAS

MAP STUDY

1. ***Human Systems*** Which European countries have the highest population densities?
2. ***Places and Regions*** How does Russia's overall population density compare to that of the rest of Europe?

networks *Online Teaching Options*

INTERACTIVE MAP

Population Density Map: Europe

Making Generalizations Use this map to help students understand the relationship between population density and resources and land use. Have students compare this map with the economic activity map. Ask student pairs to make a two-column chart with these headings: *Population Density* and *Land Use/Resources* and then use information from the two maps to fill in the chart. Tell pairs to use their charts to write a sentence that generalizes the relationship between resources and land use, and population density. **Visual/Spatial, Logical/Mathematical**

CHAPTER 10

Northern Europe Planner

UNDERSTANDING BY DESIGN®

Enduring Understandings

- *Geographers organize Earth into regions that share common characteristics.*

Essential Question

- *How do physical systems and human systems shape a place?*

Predictable Misunderstandings

Students may think:

- *The climate of Northern Europe is similar to the climate of the northern United States. Explain that Northern Europe is actually found at higher latitudes than the northern United States, which affects its climate. Additionally, large bodies of water affect Northern Europe's climate.*
- *The countries in Northern Europe have existed for hundreds of years. Explain that Denmark, Norway, Sweden, Finland, and Iceland were all united under the Kalmar Union, which was dominated by Denmark until 1523. Norway and Sweden did not become independent countries until the early 1900s and Finland was part of Russia until 1917.*

Assessment Evidence

Performance Tasks:

- *Hands-On Chapter Project*

Other Evidence:

- *Guided Reading Activities*
- *Vocabulary Activities*
- *Lesson Quizzes*
- *Chapter Tests, Forms A and B*

SUGGESTED PACING GUIDE

Introducing the Chapter ½ Day	Lesson 3 1 Day
Lesson 1 1 Day	Chapter Wrap-Up and Assessment ½ Day
Lesson 2 2 Days	

TOTAL TIME 5 Days

Key for Using the Teacher Edition

SKILL-BASED ACTIVITIES

Types of skill activities found in the Teacher Edition.

* **V Visual Skills** require students to analyze maps, graphs, charts, and photos.

R Reading Skills help students practice reading skills and master vocabulary.

C Critical Thinking Skills help students apply and extend what they have learned.

W Writing Skills provide writing opportunities to help students comprehend the text.

T Technology Skills require students to use digital tools effectively.

*Letters are followed by a number when there is more than one of the same type of skill on the page.

DIFFERENTIATED INSTRUCTION

All activities are written for the on-level student unless otherwise marked with the leveled labels below.

BL Beyond Level
AL Approaching Level
ELL English Language Learners

All students benefit from activities that utilize different learning styles. Many activities are marked as below when a particular learning style is highlighted.

Intrapersonal	**Naturalist**
Logical/Mathematical	**Kinesthetic**
Visual/Spatial	**Auditory/Musical**
Verbal/Linguistic	**Interpersonal**

National Geography Standards covered in "Northern Europe"

The student knows and understands:

(3) How to analyze the spatial organizations of people, places, and environments on Earth's surface

3.2 Complex processes change over time and shape patterns in the distribution of human and physical phenomena

(4) The physical and human characteristics of places

4.2 The interaction of physical and human systems result in the creation of and changes to places

(7) The physical processes that shape the patterns of Earth's surface

7.3 Physical processes interact over time to shape particular places on Earth's surface

(8) The characteristics and spatial distribution of ecosystems and biomes on Earth's surface

8.3 The distribution and characteristics of biomes change over time

(9) The characteristics, distribution, and migration of human populations on Earth's surface

9.2 Population distribution and density are a function of historical, environmental, economic, political, and technological factors

(10) The characteristics, distribution, and complexity of Earth's cultural mosaics

10.3 Cultures change through convergence and/or divergence

(14) How human actions modify the physical environment

14.1 Human modifications of the physical environment can have significant global impacts.

14.2 The use of technology can have unintended impacts on the physical environment which may be positive or negative.

14.3 People can either mitigate and/or adapt to the consequences of human modifications of the physical environment.

(15) How physical systems affect human systems

15.1 Depending on the choice of human activities, the characteristics of the physical environment can be viewed as both opportunities and constraints

15.3 Societies use a variety of strategies to adapt to changes in the physical environment.

(16) The changes that occur in the meaning, use, distribution, and importance of resources

16.3 Policies and programs that promote the sustainable use and management of resources impact people and the environment.

CHAPTER OPENER PLANNER

Students will know:

- *how the last ice age shaped the physical geography of Northern Europe.*
- *the relationships between glaciation and hydroelectric power and tectonic activity and geothermal energy.*
- *how the history of Northern Europe was shaped by migrations, trade, and invasions.*
- *the characteristics of Northern Europe's modern economies and modern governments.*
- *how human activities and invasive species have affected the natural environment of Northern Europe.*
- *how people are trying to improve environmental quality.*

Students will be able to:

- ***describe*** *the physical geography of Northern Europe.*
- ***identify*** *factors that have shaped Northern Europe and its population.*
- ***analyze*** *the importance of the welfare state to modern governments of Northern Europe.*
- ***identify*** *threats to the natural environment of Northern Europe.*
- ***analyze*** *the effects of climate change on Northern Europe.*

UNDERSTANDING BY DESIGN®

☑ *Print Teaching Options*

R Reading Skills

☐ **p. 248** Students sequence events in 2010 that led to pollution of Northern Europe's environment.

C Critical Thinking Skills

☐ **p. 249** Students review the meaning of GDP and discuss why the volcanic eruption led to a high GDP loss.

W Writing Skills

☐ **p. 249** Students write and perform a "live television newscast" based on an event in the time line.

T Technology Skills

☐ **p. 249** Students research the current economic status of an airline impacted by the volcanic eruption and present their findings. **BL Verbal/Linguistic, Logical/Mathematical**

☑ *Online Teaching Options*

C Critical Thinking Skills

☐ **VIDEO Eruption of Eyjafjallajökull Volcano, Effects of Eyjafjallajökull's Eruption**—Students view two videos to understand the eruption of the volcano and its effects and write a three-paragraph essay explaining how they are related. **AL Logical/Mathematical**

☐ **MAP Interactive Regional Atlas**—Students use the interactive regional atlas to understand the physical and human geography of Northern Europe.

☑ *Printable Digital Worksheets*

☐ **WORKSHEET Assessing Background Knowledge**—Determine the level of prior knowledge students have about Northern Europe.

☐ **WORKSHEET Chapter Summaries**—Students review the main idea of each lesson of the chapter content.

☐ **WORKSHEET Reteaching Activity**—These worksheets provide students with an opportunity for remedial practice and review of vital chapter content.

☐ **WORKSHEET Vocabulary Activity**—Students apply their knowledge of content and academic vocabulary words.

Project-Based Learning 

Hands-On

Slide Presentations of Energy Resources

Students will research and develop a slide presentation on the impacts of physical and human geography of Northern Europe's resources and how energy resources are managed in the region.

Digital Hands-On

Create Online Projects

Find an additional activity online that incorporates technology for this project. Visit the EdTech Teacher Web sites for more links, tutorials, and other resources.

Print Resources

ANCILLARY RESOURCES

This ancillary is available for every chapter and lesson.

- **Chapter Tests and Lesson Quizzes**

PRINTABLE DIGITAL WORKSHEETS

These printable digital worksheets are available for every chapter and lesson.

- **Assessing Background Knowledge**
- **Chapter Summaries**
- **Guided Reading Activities**
- **Hands-On Chapter Projects**
- **Quizzes and Tests**
- **Reading Essentials and Study Guide** **AL**
- **Reteaching Activities**
- **Video Activities**
- **Vocabulary**

More Media Resources

SUGGESTED VIDEOS MOVIES

- **Waterfalls of Northern Iceland** *Nature Wonders* (11 min.)
- **Passport to Adventure Enchanting, Natural Norway** (26 min.)
- **SUOMI Land Of A Thousand Lakes** *Cosmos Global Documentaries* (53 min.)

SUGGESTED READING 

- ***Northern Europe: An Environmental History (Nature and Human Societies),*** by Tamara L. Whited
- ***Woden's Warriors: Warriors and Warfare in 6th–7th Century Northern Europe,*** by Paul Mortimer
- ***The Conversion of Scandinavia: Vikings, Merchants, and Missionaries in the Remaking of Northern Europe,*** by Andres Winroth

LESSON 1 PLANNER

PHYSICAL GEOGRAPHY OF NORTHERN EUROPE

Students will know:

- *the landforms created by glaciation during the last ice age in Northern Europe.*
- *how tectonic activity affects the islands of Northern Europe.*
- *how its location in the higher latitudes affects Northern Europe's climate and vegetation patterns.*
- *the relationship between glaciation and hydroelectric power in Northern Europe.*
- *the relationship between tectonic activity and geothermal energy in Northern Europe.*

Students will be able to:

- ***identify** landforms from the last ice age and describe the relationship between glaciation and hydroelectric power.*
- ***describe** how location affects climate and vegetation in Northern Europe.*
- ***explain** how tectonic activity affects islands and how it is related to geothermal energy.*

UNDERSTANDING BY DESIGN®

☑ Print Teaching Options

V Visual Skills

- ☐ **p. 250** Students create a visual display to describe *continental rebound.* **Visual/Spatial, Kinesthetic**
- ☐ **p. 252** Students label key bodies of water in Northern Europe. **AL** **Visual/Spatial, Interpersonal**
- ☐ **p. 253** Students visually depict factors that impact Northern Europe's climate patterns. **AL** **Visual/Spatial**

R Reading Skills

- ☐ **p. 251** Students use context clues to understand *archipelago* and *constitution.* **ELL** **Verbal/Linguistic**
- ☐ **p. 253** Students identify factors that cause vegetation to be limited in Northern Europe's arctic tundra.
- ☐ **p. 254** Students discuss the importance of natural resources to Finland. **Verbal/Linguistic**

C Critical Thinking Skills

- ☐ **p. 250** Students discuss how landforms were created in parts of Northern Europe. **Logical/Mathematical**
- ☐ **p. 252** Students compose questions for a quiz comparing the size of a river nearby to one of the water systems in the lesson. **Visual/Spatial, Interpersonal**

W Writing Skills

- ☐ **p. 251** Students write a narrative describing a day in the life of teenager living in Iceland. **Verbal/Linguistic**
- ☐ **p. 252** Students discuss the meaning of "geographically young" and write a paragraph about a country in Northern Europe describing its landscape and water systems without revealing its name. **BL** **Verbal/Linguistic**

T Technology Skills

- ☐ **p. 253** Students research other parts of the world where the Gulf Stream impacts a region's climate. **AL**
- ☐ **p. 254** Students research and present information about natural resources in one of the Northern European countries and present their information in a Resource Fair. **BL** **Visual/Spatial, Interpersonal**

☑ Online Teaching Options

V Visual Skills

- **INTERACTIVE BELLRINGER** **Navigation and Trade in Finland**—Students discuss landforms created by glaciers in the last ice age and consider how they affect human activity. **Visual/Spatial, Interpersonal**
- **INTERACTIVE IMAGE** **Geyser in Iceland**—Students discuss geysers in Iceland and a group of volunteers researches to find out more information about geysers to present to the class. **BL** **Verbal/Linguistic**
- **INTERACTIVE WHITEBOARD ACTIVITY** **Northern Europe and Its Landforms**—Students complete a chart to describe cause-and-effect relationships. **AL** **Logical/Mathematical**

W Writing Skills

- **INTERACTIVE IMAGE** **Norwegian Landscape**—Students write a two to three paragraph journal entry as if they were tourists visiting the Norwegian landscape in the image. **ELL** **Verbal/Linguistic, Visual/Spatial**

☑ Printable Digital Worksheets

R Reading Skills

- **WORKSHEET** **Guided Reading Activity**—Students use the Guided Reading Activity worksheets to review their comprehension of the content.

C Critical Thinking Skills

- **WORKSHEET** **Video Activity**—Students answer questions related to a topic in the chapter content after they have viewed a lesson video.

HUMAN GEOGRAPHY OF NORTHERN EUROPE

Students will know:

- *how the history of Northern Europe was shaped by migrations, trade, and invasions.*
- *why the welfare state is important to the modern governments of Northern Europe.*
- *the factors that influence the population patterns of Northern Europe.*
- *how Northern Europe's culture has been affected by its history.*
- *the characteristics of Northern Europe's modern economies.*

Students will be able to:

- ***identify** factors that have shaped Northern Europe and its population.*
- ***analyze** the importance of the welfare state to modern governments of Northern Europe.*
- ***describe** the modern economies of Northern Europe.*

☑ Print Teaching Options

V Visual Skills

- ☐ **p. 256** Students create a chart that depicts information about the time period in the text. AL Visual/Spatial
- ☐ **p. 258** Students examine and discuss a graph of Finland's population structure. AL Visual/Spatial

R Reading Skills

- ☐ **p. 255** Students share what they think the word *Nordic* means. ELL Verbal/Linguistic

C Critical Thinking Skills

- ☐ **p. 255** Students consider how geography can play a role in the development of societies. BL Logical/Mathematical
- ☐ **p. 256** Students discuss the Kalmar Union, its formation, and eventual dissolution. BL Logical/Mathematical
- ☐ **p. 258** Students discuss Finland's population distribution. Logical/Mathematical
- ☐ **p. 259** Students compare and contrast welfare systems in the U.S. with welfare states in Northern Europe. BL
- ☐ **p. 260** Students discuss factors that have contributed to Northern Europe's economies. Logical/Mathematical

W Writing Skills

- ☐ **p. 256** Students discuss how social classes played a role in nineteenth-century Europe. Verbal/Linguistic
- ☐ **p. 257** Students discuss why Norway has not joined the European Union and write an essay arguing for or against membership for Norway. Verbal/Linguistic
- ☐ **p. 259** Students write a short essay to either defend or refute the idea that opportunities for women in Norway exceed those that exist in the U.S. BL Verbal/Linguistic

T Technology Skills

- ☐ **p. 257** Students research a region to identify what shaped migration and the formation of ethnic groups. BL Interpersonal, Visual/Spatial
- ☐ **p. 259** Students research cultural facts about a chosen Northern European country and present their findings in a "Nordic Culture Fair." Auditory/Musical, Kinesthetic

☑ Online Teaching Options

V Visual Skills

- INTERACTIVE BELLRINGER **Population Pyramid of Finland**—Students discuss how population statistics reveal trends. AL Verbal/Linguistic

C Critical Thinking Skills

- VIDEO **A Viking**—Students discuss how the many years of Viking invasions have helped Norway to become a country of peaceful democracy. ELL Visual/Spatial
- GAME **Human Geography of Northern Europe**—Students play a game to match a human or physical geography term about Northern Europe with its description. ELL Verbal/Linguistic
- PRIMARY SOURCE **Working Women**—Students discuss the Nordic model and how it relates to working women and discuss the important of working women to Norway. Verbal/Linguistic, Logical/Mathematical
- INTERACTIVE WHITEBOARD ACTIVITY **Population Patterns in Northern Europe**—Students discuss the factors that influenced population structure in Northern Europe. Interpersonal, Logical/Mathematical

☑ Printable Digital Worksheets

R Reading Skills

- WORKSHEET **Guided Reading Activity**—Students use Guided Reading Activity worksheets to review their comprehension of the content.
- WORKSHEET **Reading Essentials and Study Guide**—Students complete the study guide and answer Reading Progress Check and vocabulary questions. AL

C Critical Thinking Skills

- WORKSHEET **Video Activity**—Students answer questions related to a topic in the chapter content after they have viewed a lesson video.

PEOPLE AND THEIR ENVIRONMENT: NORTHERN EUROPE

Students will know:

- *how invasive species are affecting the natural environment of Northern Europe.*
- *the threats to the boreal forest.*
- *how human activities create water and air pollution in Northern Europe.*
- *how climate change will impact Northern Europe.*
- *the various efforts made to improve environmental quality in Northern Europe.*

Students will be able to:

- ***identify*** *threats to the natural environment of Northern Europe.*
- ***analyze*** *the effects of climate change on Northern Europe.*
- ***describe*** *efforts to improve environmental quality in Northern Europe.*

UNDERSTANDING BY DESIGN®

☑ Print Teaching Options

V Visual Skills

- ☐ **p. 262** Students create an illustrated diagram to show how various threats can damage freshwater habitats. **Visual/Spatial**

R Reading Skills

- ☐ **p. 261** Students rewrite the *It Matters Because* text with a partner.
- ☐ **p. 261** Students use context clues to understand the term *invasive species.* **AL** **ELL** **Verbal/Linguistic**
- ☐ **p. 262** Students paraphrase an excerpt about the Baltic Sea's biodiversity. **ELL** **Verbal/Linguistic**
- ☐ **p. 263** Students discuss the effects of Northern Europe's rapidly changing climate. **Logical/Mathematical**

C Critical Thinking Skills

- ☐ **p. 261** Students create a graphic organizer to record information about negative impacts on the environment and resources of Northern Europe. **AL** **Visual/Spatial**
- ☐ **p. 262** Students identify problems facing Northern Europe's original forests and Scandinavia's and Russia's boreal forests. **AL** **Logical/Mathematical**
- ☐ **p. 263** Students discuss why Northern Europe is impacted by air pollution. **BL** **Logical/Mathematical**

W Writing Skills

- ☐ **p. 263** Students write a paragraph explaining how acid rain has impacted Northern Europe. **AL** **Verbal/Linguistic**

T Technology Skills

- ☐ **p. 264** Students research the work of the LIFE + Environmental Policy and Governance, identify current projects being implemented in their assigned country, and present their findings. **BL** **Verbal/Linguistic**

☑ Online Teaching Options

C Critical Thinking Skills

- **INTERACTIVE BELLRINGER** **Acid Rain in Northern Europe**—Students use a map to discuss acid rain in Northern Europe. **Interpersonal, Verbal/Linguistic**
- **PRIMARY SOURCE** **Invasive Species in the Baltic**—Students discuss the primary source and research a water source near them where an invasive species has affected the ecosystem. **Visual/Spatial, Verbal/Linguistic**
- **VIDEO** **Frozen Forests**—Students discuss the effects of temperature changes on animals and plants. **AL** **Naturalist, Interpersonal**
- **INTERACTIVE WHITEBOARD ACTIVITY** **Managing the Resources of Northern Europe**—Students drag answer statements that reflect the cause-effect hierarchy of environmental problems affecting the seas of Northern Europe to the correct box on the graphic organizer.

☑ Printable Digital Worksheets

R Reading Skills

- **WORKSHEET** **Guided Reading Activity**—Students use Guided Reading Activity worksheets to review their comprehension of the content.
- **WORKSHEET** **Reading Essentials and Study Guide**—Students complete the study guide and answer Reading Progress Check and vocabulary questions. **AL**
- **WORKSHEET** **Vocabulary Activity**—Students review the chapter content and academic vocabulary words.

C Critical Thinking Skills

- **WORKSHEET** **Video Activity**—Students answer questions based on a lesson video.
- **WORKSHEET** **Reteaching Activity**—Students use this activity worksheet to review and reteach chapter content and vocabulary. This worksheet can be used with struggling students who need additional help with difficult content concepts.

INTERVENTION AND REMEDIATION STRATEGIES

LESSON 1 Physical Geography of Northern Europe

Reading and Comprehension

Have students work with a partner to scan the lesson and write sentences using each content vocabulary term to demonstrate their understanding of each word's meaning. Have partners collaborate to create sentences that show their understanding of the two academic vocabulary terms. Challenge students to brainstorm synonyms for the term *emerge* in addition to the word's meaning as it relates to glaciation and the formation of Northern Europe's landforms. Then have students write a sentence using the term *emerge* in a different context. Circulate to provide corrective guidance as needed.

Text Evidence

Have students review the text to identify examples of how and why landforms and the geography of a place can change. Tell students to write at least one example of Northern Europe's changing geography using evidence from the lesson. Encourage students to conduct an online search to identify the appearance of Northern Europe thousands of years ago to compare it to a current physical map of the region today. Ask volunteers to share their examples with the class. Guide a discussion about the reasons why Northern Europe's landscape is dotted with lakes.

LESSON 2 Human Geography of Northern Europe

Reading and Comprehension

Organize students into five groups and assign each team one of the following lesson headings: *The Rise of Northern Europe, Industrialization, Democracy, and Independence; Population Patterns; Society and Culture Today;* and *Economic Activities.* Have teams collaborate to develop three quiz questions based on the text in their assigned section. After students have had time to develop and write down their quiz questions, have teams exchange papers. Allow time for each team to answer the quiz questions.

Text Evidence

Have students choose one of the following concepts from the lesson to define and explain: *continental, industrialization,* or *welfare state.* Tell students to use their chosen term in a sentence or paragraph that demonstrates their understanding of the term's meaning. Encourage students to relate the meaning of the concept using a visual display. Challenge students to use two or all of the terms in a paragraph.

LESSON 3 People and Their Environment: Northern Europe

Reading and Comprehension

Have students work in pairs to identify cause-and-effect relationships as they read this lesson. Have partners choose a concept from the text to illustrate, such as the impact of invasive species on the Baltic Sea, how deforestation is impacting the boreal forest, or the effect of climate change on Northern Europe's ecosystems. Have pairs create a diagram or flowchart that illustrates the cause-and-effect relationship of their chosen concept. Have student pairs share their diagrams or charts with the class.

Text Evidence

Organize students into five groups and assign one of the Northern European countries to each group. Have groups collaborate to research the status of the environmental protection and conservation efforts in their assigned country. Tell students to present an analysis of their findings, including charts or graphs to show the impact of the efforts being made over time. Encourage students to make predictions about the long-term impacts of environmental management efforts in their assigned country.

Online Resources

Leveled Reader

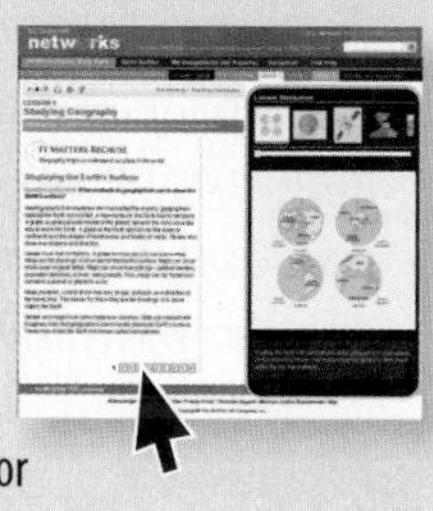

Use this online approaching-level text that corresponds directly to the text in the Student Edition. It also includes additional reading and comprehension support for English Language Learners.

Guided Reading Activities

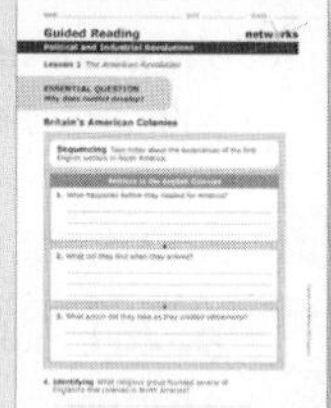

This resource uses guiding questions to help students with comprehension.

Reteaching Activities

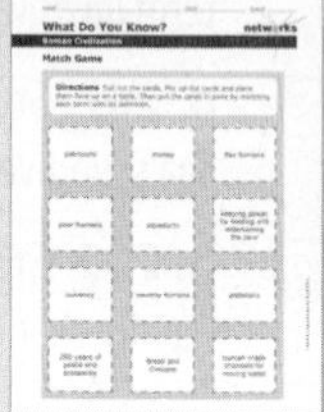

These worksheets provide students with an opportunity for remedial practice and review of vital chapter content.

Reading Essentials and Study Guide

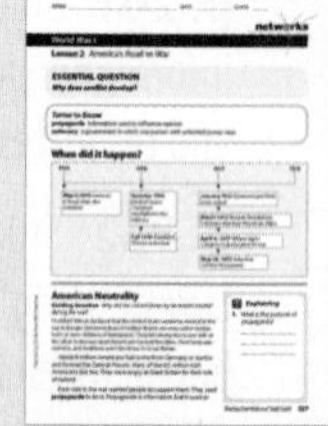

This resource offers writing and reading activities for the approaching-level student.

Self-Check Quizzes

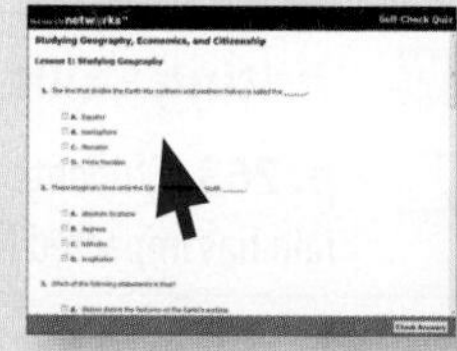

This online assessment tool provides instant feedback for students to check their progress.

Chapter Summaries

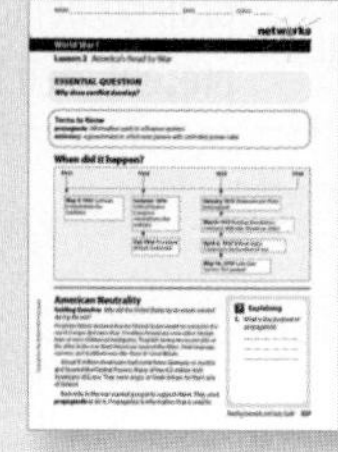

Summaries are provided for each chapter that thoroughly condense core content into manageable chunks.

Northern Europe

ESSENTIAL QUESTION • *How do physical systems and human systems shape a place?*

networks

There's More Online about Northern Europe.

CHAPTER 10

Geography Matters...

The countries of Northern Europe rank among the highest in the world in happiness surveys. Maybe it is the beautiful landscapes, high standard of living, cutting-edge cities, and eco-friendly planning that lead their citizens to this contentment. The region is also a destination for visitors to view the amazing phenomenon of the northern lights—a spectacular array of colorful lights appearing in the sky that can be seen in the northern reaches of Europe, attracting people from all over the world.

◀ This hockey player proudly wears Sweden's flag painted on his face.

Tomasz Tomaszewski/National Geographic Stock

247

Letter from the Author

Dear Geography Teacher,

Generally, Northern European countries are among the most prosperous in the world, with high per capita incomes and a generous social system that guarantees universal education and health care. How can this be in countries with limited physical resources? Beyond that while these countries have a similar northern location, they are vastly different geographically. Denmark has been built through the process of deposition, while Norway, Sweden, and Finland have been scoured by vast ice sheets. Iceland sits in splendid isolation in the North Atlantic Ocean. Perhaps the answer to some of their questions can be found in the world of human systems.

Richard G. Boehm

ENGAGE

Analyzing Visuals Have students examine the image. **Ask:** **What clues does this photograph relate about the culture and people of Northern Europe?** *(Possible answer: Sporting events such as hockey are important to the people and cultures of Northern Europe. The image also gives a clue about national pride, as the man has a flag of Sweden painted on his face.)* Discuss other ways that people might display pride in their country or national heritage.

TEACH & ASSESS

Analyzing Cause and Effect Have students consider where they might like to live someday. Have them share their reasons. **Ask:** **Do you think people are happiest in a cold or warm climate?** *(Student answers may vary, but might suggest that people would be happiest in a warm, sunny climate.)* Discuss the *Geography Matters* section. **Ask:** **What reasons are listed in the text that may cause people who live in Northern Europe to be happy?** *(beautiful landscapes, high standard of living, modern cities, and eco-friendly planning)* Point to the region of Northern Europe on a world map that can be found on the Teacher Lesson Center. Have students discuss examples of how Northern European countries are affected by the physical systems that surround them and the human systems that affect them. **AL** **Visual/Spatial**

Content Background Knowledge

The Northern Lights Also known as Aurora Borealis, the northern lights are a phenomenon caused by a convergence of electrons and protons from the sun with atoms of Earth's upper atmosphere. The result is a spectacular light show, usually occurring in regions of higher latitudes, such as Northern Europe and some parts of North America.

CLOSE & REFLECT

Applying Have students describe how learning about the human and physical geography of other regions can help us better understand our own. Ask volunteers to suggest ways that the United States might learn from countries in Northern Europe.

ePals GlobalCommunity
Where learners connect™

Extend the project-based learning experience globally through our partnership with ePals. EPals allows you to connect with classrooms around the world in a safe online environment for real-life lessons and projects in virtual study groups.

ENGAGE

V Visual Skills

Analyzing Visuals Ask students to read the title and examine each photograph. Before reading the text, have students create a flowchart that predicts the cause-and-effect relationship shown in the series of images. Then discuss how a natural event can impact human activity. Have students add or revise information in their charts after they read this feature.

TEACH & ASSESS

R Reading Skills

Sequencing Information Call on volunteers to explain the sequence of events that happened in 2010, suggesting they use sequence signal words such as *first, next, last,* and *finally.* Encourage students to sequence the information visually, using poster board or by using a drawing or painting computer program. Tell students to identify each step of the process, creating a diagram and labeling as needed. Have students answer these questions. **Ask:**

- What started the physical process that led to the chain of events? *(A dormant volcano became active.)*
- What event happened first on March 21, 2010? *(Lava erupted from a vent, sending fountains of lava up into the air.)*
- How was the atmosphere impacted? *(Huge plumes of smoke and ash were sent nearly seven miles into the atmosphere, where they were carried by wind toward Europe.)*
- How do you think human activity was affected? *(It was probably devastating to people who lived nearby.)*
- What do you think were some of the long-term effects of the event? *(Possible answer: It had an impact on the environment, such as air pollution and damage to the surrounding land.)* AL Logical/Mathematical

C Critical Thinking Skills

Analyzing Cause and Effect Have students read about the resulting economic impact caused by the volcanic eruption. **Ask:** What was a positive outcome that eventually occurred? *(Iceland experienced an increase in tourism.)*

ANSWERS, p. 248

Why Geography Matters

1. The lava melted the glacier above it, producing mud and ice that flowed down into the rivers and caused them to overflow.
2. Student answers will vary, but should show knowledge that flights were grounded due to the threat posed to jet engines by the thick volcanic ash in the air. Students might include a decision to use a different method of transportation.
3. They could devise back-up plans for transporting goods when the primary means of transportation are disrupted.

Why Geography Matters: **Northern Europe**

volcanic eruption in Iceland

The island of Iceland is a geologically young country located within the Mid-Atlantic Ridge, a 10,000-mile- (16,093-km-) long undersea mountain range. This ridge sits at the juncture of two tectonic plates, resulting in frequent seismic activity, including earthquakes, volcanic eruptions, and geothermal venting. Iceland experiences all of these as a result of its location along the Mid-Atlantic Ridge.

What was the physical process that occurred?

In 2010 the long-dormant Eyjafjallajökull, one of Iceland's largest volcanoes, became increasingly active. The world watched as several small earthquakes were followed by intense and frequent quakes. On March 21, lava erupted from a 0.3-mile- (500-m-) long vent in the Fimmvörduháls Pass. The volcano, often called Eyja (EYE-yah) for short, spewed fountains of lava up to 328 feet (100 m) high and released lava flows up to 66 feet (20 m) thick. The glacier above the lava melted, sending mud and ice into the rivers. This caused flooding that damaged roads and farmland. Huge plumes of smoke and ash were sent nearly seven miles (11 km) into the atmosphere, where they were carried by wind toward continental Europe.

1. **Physical Systems** How did the eruption of the volcano lead to massive flooding?

How did this affect transportation systems in Europe?

The airborne ash posed a dangerous threat to jet engines. Volcanic ash consists of tiny pieces of glass. When those pieces get sucked into a jet engine, they melt and cause the engine to seize up. Within two days of the 2010 eruption, air travel authorities across northern and central Europe were forced to cancel thousands of commercial flights in the largest disruption of peacetime air travel in history. Millions of passengers were stranded or delayed as the ripple effects of the eruption spread across air travel systems worldwide. Many Europeans were stranded abroad. Other transportation systems, such as trains and ferry boat operations, benefited as passengers who could not travel by air made other arrangements.

2. **Human Systems** Imagine you were a traveler stranded in Northern Europe by the eruption of Eyja. How would you cope with the situation? Write a paragraph detailing your experience.

What were the resulting economic effects?

Airlines lost hundreds of millions of dollars because of canceled flights, and Europe's ability to respond effectively to a crisis was called into question. Tourism in Europe was also affected. Many tourists ended up spending their money elsewhere. Countries that relied heavily on air travelers to sustain their tourist sectors were negatively affected by the sudden disruption. Exports and imports were impeded as well. Countries with perishable exports that depend on air travel suffered extra losses. Iceland eventually experienced an increase in tourism, however, as visitors sought out views of the now-famous volcano.

3. **Environment and Society** How could individual governments across a region cooperate to minimize the economic disruption caused by events like the eruption of Eyja?

Project-Based Learning

Hands-On

Slide Presentations on Energy Resources

Students will create slide presentations that bring together information from all lessons about how energy resources impact the physical and human geography of Northern Europe.

Digital Hands-On

Create Online Projects

Find an additional activity online that incorporates technology for this project. Visit the EdTech Teacher Web sites for more links, tutorials, and other resources.

THERE'S MORE ONLINE

WATCH a video of Eyjafjallajökull's eruption • *HEAR* a news story about the volcano's effect on tourism

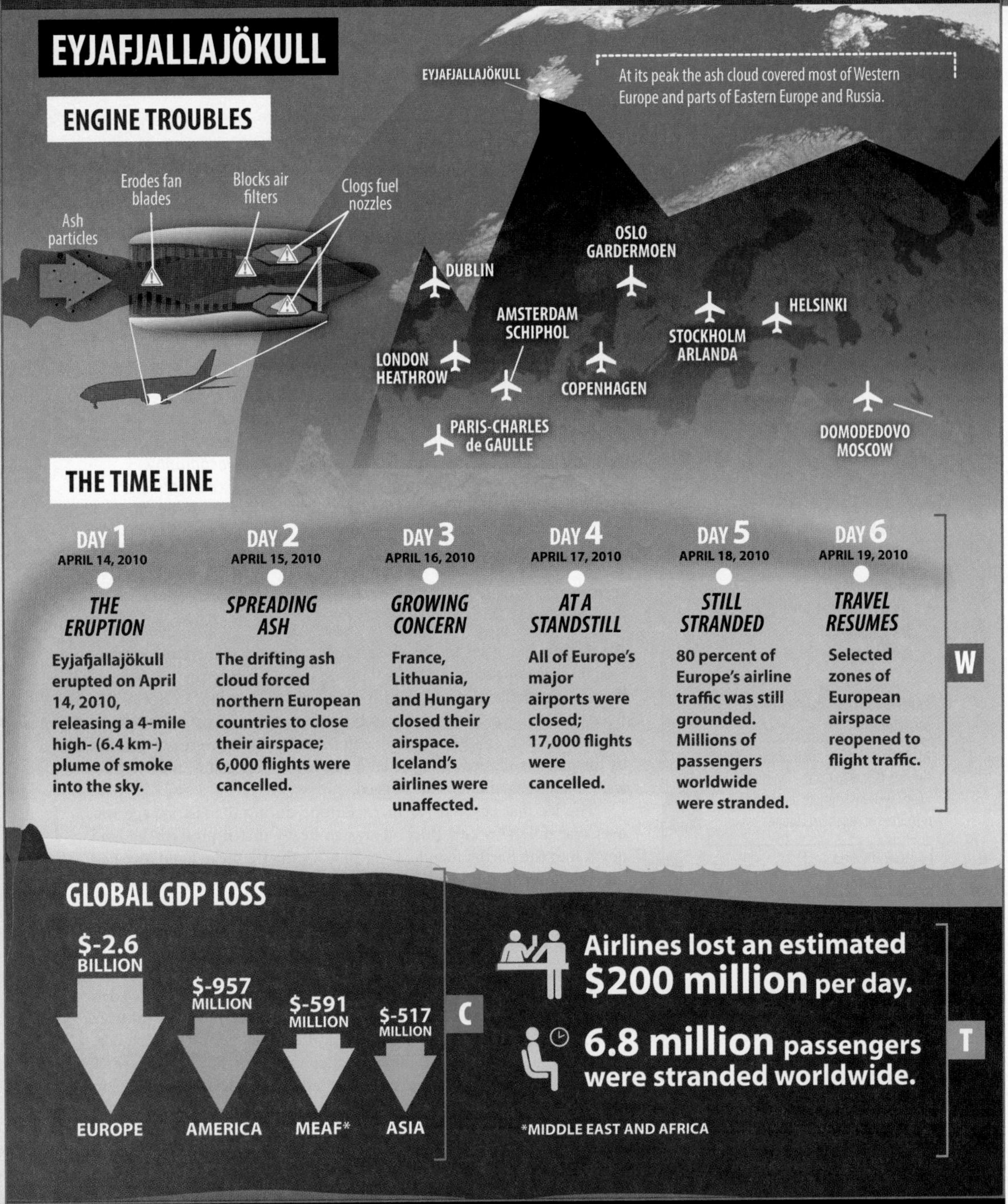

EYJAFJALLAJÖKULL

ENGINE TROUBLES

Ash particles

Erodes fan blades

Blocks air filters

Clogs fuel nozzles

EYJAFJALLAJÖKULL

At its peak the ash cloud covered most of Western Europe and parts of Eastern Europe and Russia.

DUBLIN

OSLO GARDERMOEN

AMSTERDAM SCHIPHOL

STOCKHOLM ARLANDA

HELSINKI

LONDON HEATHROW

COPENHAGEN

PARIS-CHARLES de GAULLE

DOMODEDOVO MOSCOW

THE TIME LINE

DAY 1 — APRIL 14, 2010
THE ERUPTION
Eyjafjallajökull erupted on April 14, 2010, releasing a 4-mile high- (6.4 km-) plume of smoke into the sky.

DAY 2 — APRIL 15, 2010
SPREADING ASH
The drifting ash cloud forced northern European countries to close their airspace; 6,000 flights were cancelled.

DAY 3 — APRIL 16, 2010
GROWING CONCERN
France, Lithuania, and Hungary closed their airspace. Iceland's airlines were unaffected.

DAY 4 — APRIL 17, 2010
AT A STANDSTILL
All of Europe's major airports were closed; 17,000 flights were cancelled.

DAY 5 — APRIL 18, 2010
STILL STRANDED
80 percent of Europe's airline traffic was still grounded. Millions of passengers worldwide were stranded.

DAY 6 — APRIL 19, 2010
TRAVEL RESUMES
Selected zones of European airspace reopened to flight traffic.

W

GLOBAL GDP LOSS

EUROPE	AMERICA	MEAF*	ASIA
$-2.6 BILLION	$-957 MILLION	$-591 MILLION	$-517 MILLION

C

Airlines lost an estimated $200 million per day.

6.8 million passengers were stranded worldwide.

*MIDDLE EAST AND AFRICA

T

VIDEO

Eruption of Eyjafjallajökull Volcano

Effects of Eyjafjallajökull's Eruption

Understanding Relationships Among Events Have students view both of these videos to help them understand the relationship among events. The first video highlights the volcanic eruption that occurred in Iceland. The second video is a new story that explains how tourism has increased in Iceland since the volcanic eruption. Have students write a three-paragraph report explaining the relationship among events. **AL** **Logical/Mathematical**

CHAPTER 10

Why Geography Matters

W Writing Skills

Informative/Explanatory Organize students into six groups, assigning each group a day shown on the time line. Have students collaborate to write and perform a "live television newscast" based on the events described on the time line. Tell groups to assign roles to each member of their group, including reporter, people interviewed (pilots, politicians, tourists, etc.), and anchors on the "news desk." Allow time for students to prepare interview questions and to rehearse their skits before presenting them to the class in sequential order.
BL **Verbal/Linguistic, Kinesthetic, Interpersonal**

C Critical Thinking Skills

Analyzing Review with students the meaning of GDP, or gross domestic product. *(the total value of goods and services produced by a country in one year, excluding income earned in foreign countries)* **Ask:** **Why do you think the volcanic eruption caused Europe to have such a high GDP loss?** *(Possible answer: The eruption not only caused an inconvenience to travelers, but it delayed the transportation of goods by air. This meant not only were products delayed, but members of the workforce could not reach their destinations either.)*
Logical/Mathematical

T Technology Skills

Researching Have students conduct research on the Internet to identify the current economic status of the airlines affected by the volcanic eruption and subsequent ash cloud. Challenge students to investigate how the airlines handled the event from a public relations perspective as well as a logistical one. Provide an opportunity for students to present their findings to the class, inviting them to enhance their presentations with visual displays. **BL** **Verbal/Linguistic, Logical/Mathematical**

CLOSE & REFLECT

Understanding Relationships Review with students the immediate and the long-term effects of the volcanic eruption in Iceland. Have students consider reasons people fly to various destinations such as business, vacation, or special family event trips. Guide students to brainstorm the long-term economic impact of the volcanic event, such as the loss of productivity due to people stranded at airports.

ENGAGE

R Reading Skills

Determining Importance Before beginning the lesson, invite volunteers to share what they already know about the physical geography of countries in Northern Europe. Display a physical map or satellite photograph of the region found online in the Teacher Resource Center. Ask students to identify the peninsulas shown on the map and then describe how these landforms might be important to the region.

TEACH & ASSESS

C Critical Thinking Skills

Analyzing Cause and Effect Assess students' comprehension of how landforms were created in different parts of Northern Europe. **Ask:** **What caused the formation of landforms in Northern Europe?** *(a process called glaciation)* **How did this process cause valleys to form?** *(During the last ice age, glaciers formed and spread. Ice filled valleys in the region and carved out long, narrow, steep-sided fjords, which are now filled with seawater.)* **How were plains created?** *(As glaciers covered the land, it was scraped flat, creating plains.)* **What did the ice sheet that covered Northern Europe leave in its wake?** *(many islands, rivers, streams, and lakes)*
AL ELL Visual/Spatial, Logical/Mathematical

V Visual Skills

Demonstrating Have students create a visual display that describes the term *continental rebound.* Challenge students to be creative in how they demonstrate the process. For example, students may call on a volunteer to help them convey the process, using their bodies to create a "living model."
Visual/Spatial, Kinesthetic

ANSWERS, p. 250

TAKING NOTES: Landforms—many mountains, plains, some sloping lowlands in southern Sweden, many deep fjords; **Water systems**—Glaciers left behind many lakes, rivers, and streams. Iceland has hot springs, waterfalls, and geysers. The region is bordered by the Baltic Sea, the North Sea, the Norwegian Sea, and the Atlantic Ocean; **Climate regions**—tundra, subarctic, marine west coast, and humid continental; **Resources**—peat deposits, hydroelectric and geothermal power, wind energy, iron ore, nickel, zinc, cobalt, copper, chromium, trees, oil, natural gas

networks
There's More Online!

- **DIAGRAM** Gulf Stream Effects on Northern Europe
- **IMAGE** Fjords of Northern Europe
- **IMAGE** Geyser in Northern Europe
- **INTERACTIVE SELF-CHECK QUIZ**
- **VIDEO** Physical Geography of Northern Europe

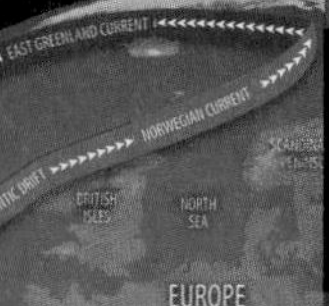

LESSON 1
Physical Geography of Northern Europe

R **ESSENTIAL QUESTION** • *How do physical systems and human systems shape a place?*

Reading HELPDESK (CCSS)

Academic Vocabulary (Tier Two Words)
- **emerge**
- **migrate**

Content Vocabulary (Tier Three Words)
- **glaciation**
- **fjord**
- **geothermal energy**
- **hot spring**
- **geyser**

TAKING NOTES: ***Key Ideas and Details***

LISTING Use a graphic organizer like the one below to list the landforms, water systems, climate regions, and resources of Northern Europe.

Landforms	
Water Systems	
Climate Regions	
Resources	

IT MATTERS BECAUSE

Europe is a large peninsula made up of numerous peninsulas, such as the Scandinavian Peninsula and the Jutland Peninsula found in Northern Europe. The unique physical geography, shaped by glaciers and plate tectonics, and the cold northern climate have influenced the lives of people in this subregion.

Landforms

GUIDING QUESTION *How did the last ice age impact the landforms of Northern Europe?*

Glaciation has been the primary process by which the landforms of Northern Europe came to be as they are today. During the last ice age, the process of glaciation scoured the land and shaped the landforms. Ice filled the valleys and carved out long, narrow, steep-sided **fjords** (fee•AWRDS) that are now filled with seawater. Plains were scraped flat by the glaciers that covered the land, while the mountains in the region were made steeper and more rugged. **C**

The ice that covered Northern Europe during the last ice age was over one mile (1.6 km) thick. It was so heavy that it pressed the land down into the Earth's mantle. Over time, as the ice melted and lessened the weight on the land beneath, the land began to rise in a process called continental rebound. The entire land surface continues to rise today. **V** When the ice sheet melted about 10,000 years ago, it also gouged the surface of the land and left in its wake innumerable islands, rivers, and streams as well as countless lakes.

Northern Europe is made up of five countries. Norway and Sweden are found on the scenic Scandinavian Peninsula. The Jutland Peninsula forms the mainland part of Denmark and extends into the North Sea. Although not situated on the Scandinavian Peninsula, Denmark is considered part of the cultural region called Scandinavia. Finland lies in the eastern part of the region, and the island country of Iceland is located in the North Atlantic Ocean.

250

networks ***Online Teaching Options***

INTERACTIVE BELLRINGER

Navigation and Trade in Finland

Identifying Have students read the introductory text and study the image of Oulu, Finland and the Gulf of Bothnia. Working in small groups, have discuss their knowledge of glaciation and the last ice age. Then have students identify the landforms created by an ice sheet during the last ice age using the bellringer image. Encourage groups to consider how those landforms affect human activity. Then have them discuss each question and write agreed-upon answers to the questions. Allow groups time to complete the activity, then in a class discussion, have groups share their answers.
Visual/Spatial, Interpersonal

Navigation and Trade in Finland
During the last Ice Age, a huge ice sheet covered Northern Europe. It was thickest over the Gulf of Bothnia and moved eastward across Finland.
1. What landforms shaped by the ice sheet are evident in the image?

Most of Norway and northern Sweden are mountainous, but in southern Sweden lowlands slope gently to the Baltic Sea. Glaciers from the last ice age left behind thousands of sparkling lakes in these two countries as well as in Finland. Many deep fjords lie on the Atlantic coastline of the Scandinavian Peninsula.

Svalbard is an archipelago in the Arctic Ocean that constitutes the northernmost part of Norway. This group of islands is located about 400 miles (644 km) north of the mainland, midway between mainland Norway and the North Pole. Today glaciers and snowfields cover more than 50 percent of the islands' land. Glaciers cut the former plateau into fjords and valleys, and the geological processes of folding and faulting cause the mountainous landscape to **emerge**. The landforms of Svalbard were created through repeated ice ages and the folding and faulting associated with continental drift and plate tectonics. Norway's strongest earthquake, measuring 6.5 on the Richter scale, occurred in Svalbard on March 6, 2009. **R**

Finland is mostly flat with a few hills and mountains. Over 10 percent of its area is covered with inland waters such as lakes and rivers. Its rugged coastline is deeply indented with bays and inlets, and the offshore region is dotted with thousands of islands.

Formerly a possession of Denmark, Iceland is an island country in the North Atlantic. Iceland is located 186 miles (300 km) east of Greenland and 621 miles (1,000 km) west of Norway. It is situated on a geological hot spot along the Mid-Atlantic Ridge. The island is very geologically active. With about 200 volcanoes, volcanic activity is frequent. Earthquakes are also frequent but rarely result in serious damage. **W**

Although considered to be a European country, Iceland sits partly on ocean crust shared with the North American continent, as it straddles the Mid-Atlantic Ridge that marks the boundary between the Eurasian and North American tectonic plates. The tectonic activity caused by these plates' separating is the source of the abundant **geothermal energy** in the region. Iceland's many rivers and waterfalls are also harnessed to produce hydropower. These two natural resources provide Iceland with sustainable and inexpensive sources of energy.

Additional physical features include Iceland's numerous mountains, countless **hot springs**, rivers, small lakes, waterfalls, glaciers, and **geysers**. Glaciers cover roughly 11 percent of the island. The largest, Vatnajökull, is nearly 1,300 feet (400 m) thick and covers about 8 percent of the island. It is by far the largest glacier in Europe. The word *geyser* is derived from a geyser in Iceland named Geysir.

During the last ice age, glaciers deposited sand and gravel on the Jutland Peninsula's flat western side and carved fjords on the coastline of the east. Flat plains make up most of the Jutland Peninsula's interior in Denmark. The Kingdom of Denmark also includes the Faeroe Islands and Greenland in the North Atlantic.

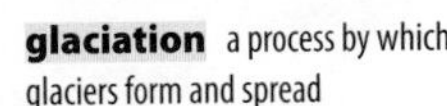

glaciation a process by which glaciers form and spread

fjord a long, steep-sided glacial valley now filled by seawater

emerge to rise from an obscure position or condition; to become visible

geothermal energy a form of energy conversion that captures heat energy from within Earth

hot spring a spring whose water issues at a temperature higher than that of its surroundings

geyser a spring that throws forth intermittent jets of heated water and steam

Fjords and geysers are both signature features of the Northern European landscape.

▼ CRITICAL THINKING

1. ***Comparing*** How are geysers similar to volcanoes?
2. ***Hypothesizing*** How might fjords have influenced the history of Northern Europe?

251

R Reading Skills

Using Context Clues Have students locate the term *archipelago* in the second paragraph. **Ask: What context clues help you understand the meaning of the word *archipelago*?** *("group of islands")* Have students locate the term *constitutes* and reinforce their understanding of the word. **Ask: What word or words could be used in this sentence to replace the word *constitutes*?** *(creates, makes up)* **What word can you think of that is related to the word *constitutes*?** *(constitution)* Tell students that the term *constitution* is a noun that means "an established law" as well as "the physical makeup of a person's health or strength." Have students clarify their understanding of the nuances in meaning by using the word in two different sentences. **ELL Verbal/Linguistic**

W Writing Skills

Narrative Have students use their imaginations to write a narrative describing a day in the life of a teenager living in Iceland. Suggest that students write a first-person narrative, as they would in a journal or diary entry. Tell students to use the information in the text about Iceland's history and geography to serve as a backdrop for their journals. Invite students to share their narratives with the class. Challenge students to use the vocabulary terms listed on this page in their narratives. **Verbal/Linguistic**

Making Connections

Iceland vs. Greenland There have been some misconceptions over the years about how Iceland and Greenland were named. The fact that Iceland is green for part of the year and many parts of Greenland are covered in ice has been the source of debate over their names. Some historians once believed that the Viking explorer, Erik the Red, who founded the first settlement on Greenland, may have given it the name to make it sound appealing to settlers. This has not been verified, but it certainly makes for a good story. The naming of Iceland is actually much simpler. In the Norse language, the word for *ice* is *íss,* and the word "Iceland" actually means "island."

INTERACTIVE IMAGE

Geyser in Iceland

Researching Use this interactive image and video to discuss how geysers have become signature landform features in Iceland. Ask a small group of volunteers to research various geysers that are located in Iceland. Then use the group's research along with the information provided in the interactive image and video to guide a class discussion about geysers. Have volunteers who may have visited or seen an actual geyser describe what they witnessed. **BL Verbal/Linguistic**

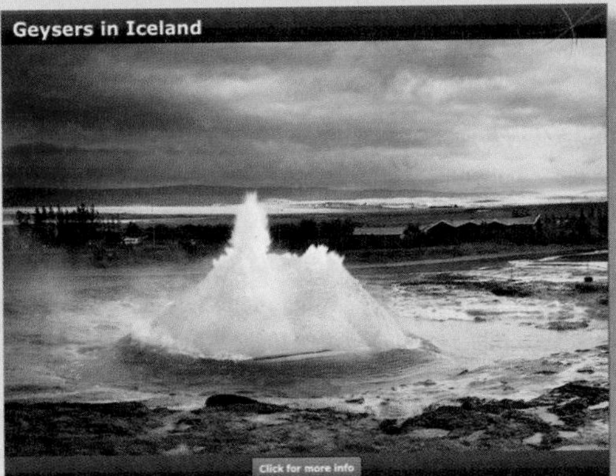

ANSWERS, p. 251

CRITICAL THINKING

1. Both geysers and volcanoes are expulsions of heated material from far beneath Earth's surface. Geysers expel water and steam and volcanoes expel lava.
2. They may have formed natural boundaries between peoples. They may have allowed more parts of the region to be reached more quickly by boat.

W Writing Skills

Informative/Explanatory Discuss with students the significance of the term "geographically young." Organize students into small groups, assigning each group one of the countries in Northern Europe. Display a political map of Northern Europe. Have students in each group create a short paragraph that relates the geographic age of their assigned country and describes its landscape and water systems, without revealing its name. Students may wish to conduct additional research to identify facts about their country. Have groups present their paragraphs to the class, allowing classmates to guess the country being described. **BL Verbal/Linguistic**

C Critical Thinking Skills

Formulating Questions Ask students to think of a river or body of water nearby or in your state. Have students consider how the size of that river compares to one of the water systems discussed in the text. Tell students to compose "less than/greater than" questions (and variations) for a quiz to exchange with a partner. For example, "[name of your local waterway] is longer than/shorter than the Klar-Göta River." Have students exchange their questions with a partner. **Ask: In what Scandinavian country is the Klar-Göta River?** *(Norway)* **In what direction does the Glåma River flow?** *(north to south, running almost the entire length of Norway)* **Visual/Spatial, Interpersonal**

V Visual Skills

Labeling Have students work with a partner to reinforce their understanding of water systems in Northern Europe. Display a political map of Northern Europe and provide each set of students with a copy of the Europe Outline Map, which is available online at the Teacher Resource Center. Have partners use information in the text to label and name the key bodies of water in Northern Europe. Have pairs collaborate with other pairs to compare their maps, checking for accuracy. Encourage students to continue labeling their maps as they complete the lesson. **AL Visual/Spatial, Interpersonal**

During the last ice age, glaciers scraped across the land, making the mountains steeper and more rugged.

▲ **CRITICAL THINKING**

1. ***Analyzing Visuals*** Describe the landforms shown in the picture.
2. ***Hypothesizing*** How might the same landscape have looked during the last ice age?

At 839,399 square miles (2.1 million sq. km), Greenland is the world's largest island. The Faeroe Islands, an island group and archipelago, are located about halfway between Iceland and Norway. They are made up of volcanic rocks with high and rugged cliffs.

READING PROGRESS CHECK

Identifying What landforms were created by glaciation during the last ice age in Northern Europe?

Water Systems

GUIDING QUESTION *Why is the landscape of Northern Europe dotted with so many lakes?*

Continental glaciers covered much of Northern Europe during the last ice age. The scouring action of these glaciers created a landscape dotted with hundreds of thousands of lakes. After the glaciers melted, the debris left behind on a flat landscape blocked rivers and trapped water like dams.

W The landscape of Iceland is geologically young. It is characterized by impressive waterfalls and an abundance of small lakes and numerous, swift-moving rivers that are filled by glacier meltwater and heavy rainfall. The majority of rivers in Iceland consist of meltwater from glaciers. Thus, they contain large amounts of glacial debris that makes the water cloudy. The longest river is called Thjórsá. Located in the southern region of Iceland, it extends for 143 miles (230 km). **V**

C Many of the rivers of the Scandinavian Peninsula are short and do not provide easy connections between cities. Norway's chief rivers stem from the mountains of Norrland. These rivers mostly flow toward the southeast with many falls and rapids, eventually emptying into the Gulf of Bothnia or the Baltic Sea. The country's longest river is the Klar-Göta. It flows 447 miles (719 km) until it reaches Lake Vänern. The Glåma River drains an area of 16,236 square miles (42,051 sq. km), running almost the entire length of Norway from north to south.

The Kemi River in Finland is harnessed for hydroelectric power. It rises near the Russian border and flows generally southwest for about 300 miles (483 km)

Guy Edwardes/age fotostock

252

networks ***Online Teaching Options***

INTERACTIVE IMAGE

Norwegian Landscape

Analyzing Images Have students view this interactive image of Norwegian landscape to help them understand the landscape formations and the beauty that draws tourists to this region. Discuss the 360° views of the cities with students and answer any questions they may have. Then ask students to write a two to three paragraph journal entry as if they were a tourist visiting the scene in this image. Students should include descriptive phrases explaining the visual. **ELL Verbal/Linguistic, Visual/Spatial**

Ola Heloe/360 Cities

ANSWERS, p. 252

READING PROGRESS CHECK Glaciation carved valleys, formed fjords, and flattened parts of the land into plains.

CRITICAL THINKING

1. There are glaciers, cold lakes, and rugged mountains.
2. There would likely have been extensive glaciers, rather than lakes. If the land was exposed, it was likely less steep and less rugged than after glacial carving.

to the Gulf of Bothnia in the town of Kemi. The Muonio and Torne Rivers flow along the border of Finland and Sweden. Sweden has many small hydroelectric power plants that harness the power of the country's rivers.

✓ READING PROGRESS CHECK

Explaining From what landforms do most rivers originate?

Climate, Biomes, and Resources

GUIDING QUESTION *How does Northern Europe's location affect its climate and vegetation?*

Latitude, mountain barriers, wind patterns, and distance from large bodies of water influence Northern Europe's climate patterns. Climate regions include marine west coast, humid continental, subarctic, and tundra. Location influences vegetation patterns. Natural vegetation varies from forests and grasslands to tundra plants. In Iceland, the Gulf Stream creates a mild climate even though the country is located in higher latitudes.

Climate Regions and Biomes

Strong interrelationships exist between climate and plant and animal life in Northern Europe. The arctic tundra regions lie in the extreme northern parts of Scandinavia and Iceland. Due to dry conditions, poor soil quality, extremely cold temperatures, and frozen ground, vegetation in this climate is limited. Arctic tundra plants must adapt to the short, cold growing seasons. The frozen ground prevents plants with deep roots, like trees, from growing. Animals in the alpine zone **migrate** to lower elevations in the winter to escape the cold and find food. South of the tundra biome is the subarctic climate region. This covers most of the northern half of Scandinavia. It has long, very cold winters and short, cold to mild summers. The vegetation is limited to only the few species that can tolerate the cold conditions. Along the Atlantic coast and in southern Sweden, the climate is the marine west coast type that has milder

migrate to move from one place to another

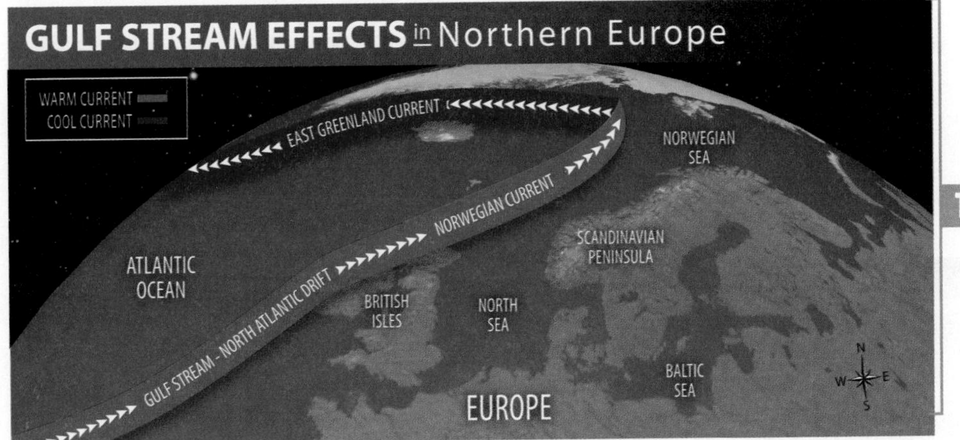

The Gulf Stream is a warm ocean current that originates in the Gulf of Mexico. As it crosses the Atlantic Ocean, the Gulf Stream splits into two currents, the North Atlantic Drift and the Canary Current. The North Atlantic Drift warms the climates of Northern Europe.

▲ **CRITICAL THINKING**

1. ***Analyzing Visuals*** In what direction is the Gulf Stream's North Atlantic Drift moving as it approaches Europe?
2. ***Identifying*** Over what other part of Europe does the Gulf Stream flow before it reaches Scandinavia?

V Visual Skills

Transferring Information Discuss the various factors that impact Northern Europe's climate patterns. Then have students visually depict the information using a word web or flowchart. Assess their comprehension of varying climate regions in different parts of Northern Europe. **Ask: What factors influence Northern Europe's climate patterns?** *(latitude, mountain barriers, wind patterns, distance from large bodies of water)* **What are the different climate regions in Northern Europe?** *(marine west coast, humid continental, subarctic, and tundra)* **What type of climate does Iceland have? Why?** *(Iceland has a milder climate created by the Gulf Stream.)* **AL Visual/Spatial**

R Reading Skills

Understanding Relationships Review how the climate and plant and animal life of a region are interrelated. Have students work with a partner to identify the factors that cause vegetation to be limited in Northern Europe's arctic tundra—dry conditions, poor soil quality, extremely cold temperatures, and frozen ground. Have students take turns asking and answering questions about the cause-and-effect relationship between the climate and plant and animal life in Scandinavia, Finland, and Iceland. **Verbal/Linguistic**

T Technology Skills

Spatial Analysis Have students analyze the diagram to discuss the effects of the Gulf Stream on Northern Europe. Then have students conduct online research to identify other parts of the world where the Gulf Stream impacts a region's climate. Have students present their findings to the class in a short oral report. Encourage students to use visuals to enhance their reports. **AL Visual/Spatial**

INTERACTIVE WHITEBOARD ACTIVITY

Physical Features of Northern Europe

Determining Cause and Effect This interactive whiteboard activity has a chart that describes the cause-and-effect relationships. Students will drag causes into the boxes of a chart that describes common physical landform features in Northern Europe. When completed, the chart will describe cause-and-effect relationships between landforms and the processes that create them. This activity can be completed as a whole class or small group activity. **AL Logical/Mathematical**

Physical Features of Northern Europe

Directions: Landforms are created by geographic processes. Complete the chart by dragging the correct cause into appropriate box. When correctly completed, each row of the chart will describe a cause-and-effect relationship between a landform and the process by which it was created.

CAUSE	EFFECT
	Ice-filled valleys
	Land began to rise
	Carved out fjords
	Scraped the plains flat
	Gouged the land
	Made islands, rivers, streams, and lakes
	Made mountains steeper and more rugged

Glaciations

Continental Rebound

ANSWERS, p. 253

✓ **READING PROGRESS CHECK** Most rivers in Northern Europe originate from glaciers.

CRITICAL THINKING

1. The Gulf Stream's North Atlantic Drift is moving northeast towards Europe.
2. British Isles

R Reading Skills

Summarizing Discuss the importance of peat and other natural resources to the economy of Finland. **Ask:** **What are Finland's most important natural resource?** *(trees)* Have students write a short summary about Finland's natural resources and how they play a role in the country's economy and way of life. **Verbal/Linguistic**

T Technology Skills

Interpreting Significance Organize students into five groups and assign them a Northern European country. Have each group use information in the text, as well as research using reliable online sources, to identify key issues regarding natural resources, their development, and economic impact in their country. **BL** **Visual/Spatial, Interpersonal**

CLOSE & REFLECT

Theorizing Tell students to review what they have learned about the landforms, water systems, climate patterns, biomes, and resources of Northern Europe. Have students formulate a theory about how one or more of these aspects of Northern Europe's physical geography impacts the way of life there.

ANSWERS, p. 254

READING PROGRESS CHECK Animals migrate to lower elevations in the winter to escape the cold and find food.

Connecting Geography Geothermal electricity plants use steam from underground hot spots to power electricity-generating turbines. Iceland has zones of recent volcanic activity and areas where tectonic plates meet, both of which make it a prime location for harnessing geothermal energy.

Connecting Geography to SCIENCE

Geology

Exploiting the energy stored under Earth's surface has a long human history. There is evidence that ancient Romans, Chinese, and Native American cultures used hot mineral springs for bathing, cooking, and eating. Geothermal power plants today use steam from underground hot spots to power electricity-generating turbines. They are usually located in zones of recent volcanic activity or where tectonic plates meet. Iceland has both of these criteria and is the location of many state-of-the-art geothermal power plants.

IDENTIFYING How is Iceland's location favorable for generating energy from geothermal plants?

winters. This area supports a vast coniferous forest. The rest of the Scandinavian Peninsula and Finland has a humid continental climate with cold, wet winters. The temperatures of most of the region are warmer than most other regions of similar latitudes due to the influence of the Baltic Sea, inland waters, and airflows from the Atlantic that are warmed by the Gulf Stream.

Natural Resources

R Finland's peat deposits cover nearly one-third of the country. Peat is vegetable matter found in swamps. It is dug up, chopped into blocks, and dried so it can be burned. Hydroelectric power and geothermal energy are significant renewable resources in Finland. The diversity of minerals in the country includes modest amounts of iron ore, nickel, zinc, cobalt, copper, and chromium. Trees, however, are Finland's most important natural resource. In 2012 Finland exported over 10 percent of the paper and paperboard traded on the global market.

Deposits of iron ore lie in Sweden near Kiruna. Other natural resources in the area include gold, copper, lead, and zinc. Forest products are a major source of revenue. In 2010 Sweden exported 10 percent of the world's sawnwood, a wood used to make lumber. Hydroelectric power is a renewable resource in Sweden as it is in most Northern European countries.

T Norway is one of the world's leading producers of hydroelectric power. One important use of this hydroelectric power is the production of aluminum, a process that requires large amounts of electricity. Although Norway lacks the mineral bauxite from which aluminum is made, it imports bauxite and utilizes its hydroelectric power to produce aluminum. Magnesium is an important natural resource in Norway. Norway is also Europe's largest oil producer and the world's second-largest natural gas exporter. Other European countries rely on Norway as an important supplier of both sources of fuel. In 2009 Norway exported 2.184 million barrels per day on the world market.

Denmark also has oil and natural gas, but renewable wind energy is its most important energy source. Denmark ranks number one in the world for electricity generated from renewable sources. This makes it a model that other countries can follow to transition to renewable energy.

Iceland has vast energy resources. Only a small fraction of the hydroelectric power of the country's rivers has been tapped, however. Geothermal energy provides heat for the entire capital city of Reykjavík and several other communities. It also provides steam for industrial energy and is used in commercial vegetable farming in greenhouses.

READING PROGRESS CHECK

Describing How have animals in the arctic and alpine tundra biomes adapted to survive in the harsh climate?

LESSON 1 REVIEW 

Reviewing Vocabulary (Tier Three Words)

1. ***Explaining*** Explain the significance of glaciation, fjords, and geysers to the landscape of Northern Europe. RH.9–10.4

Using Your Notes

2. ***Listing*** List the natural resources found in Northern Europe by using your graphic organizer.

Answering the Guiding Questions

3. ***Assessing*** How did the last ice age impact the landforms of Northern Europe?
4. ***Explaining*** Why is the landscape of Northern Europe dotted with so many lakes?
5. ***Making Generalizations*** How does Northern Europe's location affect its climate and vegetation?

Writing Activity

6. ***Informative/Explanatory*** Write an essay that describes the geographic factors that contribute to the water systems of Iceland. WHST.9–10.2

254

LESSON 1 REVIEW ANSWERS

Reviewing Vocabulary

1. Glaciation is the main process that shaped the land of Northern Europe into what it is today. Glaciers cut the land into fjords, steep valleys that have become filled with seawater. The geological processes of folding and faulting formed many mountains. Geysers are a signature feature of Iceland.

Using Your Notes

2. Natural resources include peat deposits, hydroelectric and geothermal power, iron ore, nickel, zinc, cobalt, copper, chromium, lead, and trees. Norway and Denmark also produce oil and natural gas. One of Denmark's most important resources is wind energy.

Answering the Guiding Questions

3. Glaciation during the last ice age is responsible for giving the land the shape it has today. Ice cut steep fjords that are now filled with seawater. In other areas, glaciers flattened land that was beneath them, creating plains. As heavy ice that covered most of the land melted away, the land rose, and it continues to rise today.
4. As glacial ice melted, its waters settled in the form of rivers and lakes in the crevices that had been carved out underneath its huge mass.
5. Northern Europe's location creates four main climate regions: tundra, subarctic, marine west coast, and humid continental. The arctic tundra regions have cold, dry conditions which support only vegetation with short roots—no trees. Farther south, the subarctic climate zone also has limited vegetation, but does have mild summers. Farther south still is the slightly warmer west coast climate, where coniferous forests are able to grow. Lastly, a humid continental climate is found in the rest of the Scandinavian Peninsula and in Finland. The region's proximity to the warm Gulf Stream provides a milder climate than might be expected at such a high latitude.

Writing Activity

6. Essays will vary, but should describe geographic factors such as glaciers, fjords, hot springs, rivers, small lakes, waterfalls, and geysers.

There's More Online!

- **DIAGRAM** Population Pyramid of Finland
- **IMAGE** Community Art in Norway
- **TIME LINE** Northern Europe: Democracy and Independence
- **INTERACTIVE SELF-CHECK QUIZ**
- **VIDEO** Human Geography of Northern Europe

LESSON 2

Human Geography of Northern Europe

ESSENTIAL QUESTION • *How do physical systems and human systems shape a place?* V

Reading HELPDESK 

Academic Vocabulary (Tier Two Words)
- integrate
- achieve

Content Vocabulary (Tier Three Words)
- continental
- entrepôt
- break-of-bulk
- welfare state

TAKING NOTES: *Key Ideas and Details*

OUTLINING Use a graphic organizer like the one below to take notes about society and culture in Northern Europe.

Elements of Culture	
Family and the Status of Women	
The Arts	

(tl)INTERFOTO/Personalities/Alamy, (tcl)JK Salminen/age fotostock, (tc)Arctic-Images/The Image Bank/Getty Images, (tcr)Sean Gallup/Getty Images News/Getty Images, (tr)John Borthwick/Lonely Planet Images/Getty Images

It Matters Because

The countries of Northern Europe, also called the Nordic countries, have fascinating histories and cultures. Scandinavia (Denmark, Norway, and Sweden) and Finland are lands of castles, Viking museums, and progressive contemporary cities. Iceland is the least densely populated country in Europe and has blended strong cultural traditions with a modern capital city. R

History and Government

GUIDING QUESTION *What influenced the creation of new social classes and peaceful democracies in Northern Europe?*

Geographically, the Scandinavian Peninsula includes mainland Sweden, mainland Norway, and part of Finland. The Jutland Peninsula includes mainland Denmark and a small part of Germany. The history of Northern Europe has been shaped by thousands of years of migrations, invasions, and trade. The Nordic countries have similar structures of societies and cultural traits, which collectively differentiate them from mainland Europe. From about A.D. 793 to 1050—a period of European history known as the Viking Age—Scandinavian Viking raiding parties in powerful warships roamed the coastal waters of Europe. Their territories expanded over time, and the numerous Viking kingdoms emerged as Denmark, Sweden, and Norway.

The Rise of Northern Europe

In Norway the coasts, mountainous terrain, and fjords formed strong natural boundaries. Communities there remained independent of each other. By A.D. 800, some 30 small kingdoms existed in Norway. The sea was the easiest way of communication between the Norwegian kingdoms and the outside world. During the Viking Age, Norsemen—also known as Vikings—built ships of war and sent them on raiding expeditions into western and eastern Europe. Their language, Old Norse, became the basis for present-day Nordic languages. C

networks Online Teaching Options

 INTERACTIVE BELLRINGER

Population Pyramid of Finland

Identifying Trends Use the bar graph and introductory text to discuss how population statistics reveal trends such as population booms and declines. Ask students to identify a time period that they may know of in the United States when a population boom occurred. *(Possible answer: baby boomers; a time period after WWII when soldiers came home from the war and started families, causing the population to boom)* Have students write out answers to each question. Then in a class discussion, invite students to share their answers. **AL Verbal/Linguistic**

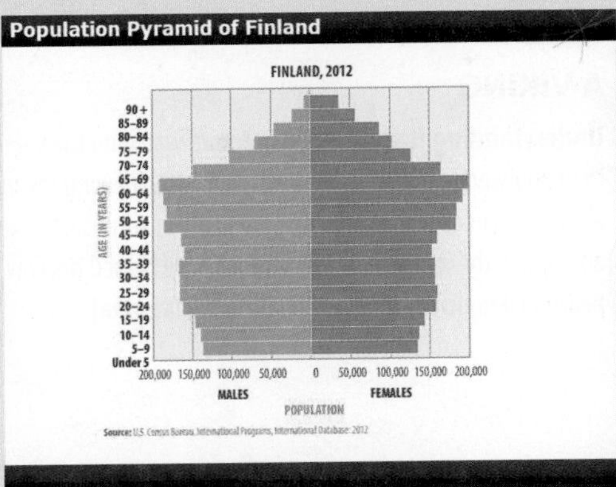

ENGAGE

V Visual Skills

Analyzing Visuals Ask a volunteer to read aloud the *Essential Question*. Then direct students' attention to the images at the top of the page. Have students analyze each image and write one or two sentences about how they think each image relates to the human geography of Northern Europe. Then in a class discussion, invite students to share their ideas. Have students consider these ideas as they work through the lesson.

TEACH & ASSESS

R Reading Skills

Defining Ask students if they have heard the word *Nordic* and to share what they think it means based on context clues. *(Students may say they have heard the word* Nordic *as it relates to competitive skiing events, such as those held during the Winter Olympics. They may conclude that the word relates to the north, or Northern Europe.)* Explain that *Nordic* is a Germanic term that relates to the people of Northern Europe, Scandinavia in particular. Discuss other words that share the root *nord,* which means "north". *(north, Norse, Norway)* **ELL Verbal/Linguistic**

C Critical Thinking Skills

Identifying Cause and Effect Have students read the paragraph and consider how geography can play a role in the development of societies. **Ask:** **How did the geography of Norway impact its early communities?** *(Due to the coasts, mountainous terrain, and fjords, communities in Norway remained independent of each other.)* Then have students reread and consider the Guiding Question. **Ask:** **How do you think the geography of Norway affected the people in these early communities?** *(Possible answer: Due to the isolating impact of mountains and coastline, people in Norway's early communities probably had little interaction with other communities.)* **BL Logical/Mathematical**

ANSWER, p. 255

TAKING NOTES: Religious freedom is valued. This region's populations are some of the most educated. The government provides many social services and encourages an equal balance between family and work life. There are equal opportunities for women. Northern Europe has a diverse cultural history. Museums, symphony halls, and opera houses provide citizens access to art, literature, music, and dance. Fairy tales by Danish writer Hans Christian Andersen are known throughout the world. Danes have also made valuable contributions in the way of design.

V Visual Skills

Creating Charts Have students work in pairs to read the information in the paragraph, taking notes about key dates and events. Help reinforce students' understanding of the material by having them create a flowchart that visually depicts the information. Students' charts should show the series of events that occurred during the time period discussed in the text. Ask partners to share their charts or diagrams with the class. Then reinforce the academic and content vocabulary terms discussed in the paragraph. **Ask:** What led to Nordic countries becoming integrated? *(increased trade)* What was the result of this integration? *(Nordic society became increasingly continental.)* AL **Visual/Spatial**

W Writing Skills

Narrative Discuss how social classes played a role in nineteenth-century Europe. Have students imagine what it was like to live in Northern Europe at that time. Have students research the different social classes and select one class to write a personal narrative from the point of view of a person who was a member of that class and lived in the Nordic region during the nineteenth century. Students' narratives should convey the proper lifestyle to which the person belonged and what life was like for him or her at that time. Invite students to read their personal narratives to the class. **Verbal/Linguistic**

C Critical Thinking Skills

Identifying Cause and Effect Discuss with students the Kalmar Union, its formation, and eventual dissolution. **Ask:** Why do you think the Kalmar Union was formed? *(Possible answer: Due to their geographic location, it may have been easier to rule the countries by forming a union.)* What do you think caused the Kalmar Union's dissolution? *(Possible answer: Nordic countries likely wanted to become independent.).* BL **Logical/Mathematical**

ANSWERS, p. 256

READING PROGRESS CHECK The Nordic countries share a history of wars, kingdoms, independence, and cooperation. Additionally, Denmark, Sweden, Finland, Norway, and Iceland were all united for over 100 years in the Kalmar Union under the control of Denmark. In the nineteenth century, all the countries experienced a similar industrial and population boom, which led to new social classes and new ideas.

CRITICAL THINKING

1. The Kalmar Union was dissolved when Sweden's successful rebellion enabled them to no longer be under Denmark's control. Norway lost its status and became a province owned by Denmark.
2. As of 1995, Denmark, Sweden, and Finland were all members of the European Union.

integrate to blend into a functioning whole

continental relating to or characteristic of a continent

V Norway, Sweden, Denmark, and Iceland shared similar cultures, languages, and religions. A Christian mission was established in Denmark in the 800s, but conversion to Christianity progressed slowly in Northern Europe. From the 1100s, what is now Finland began sharing common developments as it became economically **integrated** with Sweden. In the 1300s, Denmark, Norway (with Iceland), and Sweden (with Finland) were united under one regent in the Kalmar Union, which Denmark dominated. The increased trade during this time connected the countries to mainland Europe, and Nordic society became increasingly **continental**. In 1523 Sweden became a separate kingdom. Denmark's domination over Norway lasted until 1814, when the king was forced to cede Norway to the king of Sweden. Iceland, Greenland, and the Faeroe Islands remained under the control of Denmark.

Industrialization, Democracy, and Independence

The nineteenth century brought many changes to Europe and the Nordic region. Industrialization required a larger population as more people were needed for jobs. W This influx brought new social classes as well as different socioeconomic levels. The political culture changed as these new classes of people brought new ideas and, ultimately, democracy and independence to the countries of Northern Europe.

In the period following World War II, the Nordic countries developed democracies. Norway, Sweden, Denmark, Finland, and Iceland are now governed by democratically elected parliaments, although Norway, Sweden, and Denmark are constitutional monarchies. They also share similar traits in the policies implemented during the postwar period. For example, all Nordic countries have large, tax-funded public welfare sectors and extensive social-democratic legislation. These programs support health care, education for elementary through college students, and retirement income for senior citizens.

READING PROGRESS CHECK

Inferring Why do the Nordic countries share so many similar characteristics today?

TIME LINE

DEMOCRACY and Independence

The countries of Northern Europe have a shared history of wars, kingdoms, independence, and cooperation.

CRITICAL THINKING

1. ***Describing*** Discuss the results of the disintegration of the Kalmar Union, including the subsequent status of the countries.
2. ***Identifying*** As of 1995, which Northern European countries were members of the European Union?

C

1300s

1389 Denmark, Norway, and Sweden are united under the rule of Margaret of Denmark, forming the Kalmar Union.

1523 The Kalmar Union is dissolved when Sweden rebels and becomes independent under King Gustav I Vasa. Norway loses its status and becomes a Danish province (1536).

1814 Denmark's King Frederick VI cedes Norway to Sweden.

INTERFOTO/Personalities/Alamy

networks Online Teaching Options

VIDEO

A VIKING

Understanding Relationships Before watching the video, ask students to discuss their knowledge of the Viking invasions. After viewing the video, have students write about an aspect of the video that was new or surprising to them. Guide a class discussion about how the many years of invasions have helped Norway to become a country of peaceful democracy today. ELL **Visual/Spatial**

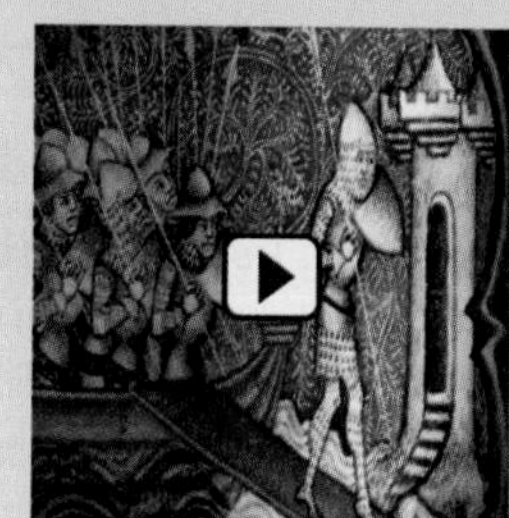

Population Patterns

GUIDING QUESTION *What factors influence the population structure of Northern Europe?*

Population patterns in Northern Europe have been shaped by the influences of migration and the distinct ethnic groups of each country. Sweden, for example, is home to Finnish-speaking indigenous inhabitants in the northeast on the border with Finland as well as the Sami, the native people of northern Norway, Sweden, and Finland. The Sami are the descendants of nomadic peoples who lived in northern Scandinavia for thousands of years. Most other residents of Sweden—some 80 percent—live in and around Stockholm, the capital. **T**

From the 1970s to the present, many people from other regions of Europe have migrated to Northern Europe for work. Others have arrived in large numbers from war-torn regions of Africa, especially Somalia. These migrants are seeking political asylum to escape conflicts in their home countries. They have increased the cultural diversity of much of Northern Europe. 

Norway is not a member of the European Union, but has attracted numerous international workers to petroleum exploration and processing. It is Europe's largest oil producer and second-largest producer of natural gas. Those industries create jobs. Norway's immigration policies have allowed guest workers and students to enter. Most have come from other European countries, such as Poland, Germany, Sweden, and Lithuania. The majority of Norwegians reside in Oslo, the capital, and along the coastlines of the warmer southern portion of the country. 

The Kingdom of Denmark includes its continental areas as well as the largely self-governing Faeroe Islands and Greenland. Denmark allows guest workers to obtain a work permit for a limited time, and it permits international students the opportunity to study. A low birthrate among Danish women, who are among the best educated and highest paid in Europe, has resulted in slowing population growth. Current aging trends show there are more people in Denmark over the age of 60 than under the age of 15.

(c)Arctic-Images/The Image Bank/Getty Images, (cr)Sean Gallup/Getty Images News/Getty Images, (b)JK Salminen/age fotostock

1900s

1905 Norway becomes an independent country.

1917 Finland gains independence from Russia.

1944 Iceland gains independence from Denmark and becomes a republic.

1973 Denmark joins the expanding European Economic Community (now known as the European Union).

1995 Sweden and Finland join the European Union.

2000

T Technology Skills

Presenting Organize the class into small groups, assigning each group a region of Northern Europe. Have groups research their assigned region to identify factors that shaped migration and the formation of ethnic groups. Have students prepare and present their findings to the class, using electronic presentation software. Point out that they should use graphs and charts to present the data and also include a summary and an analysis. **BL** **Interpersonal, Visual/Spatial**

R Reading Skills

Defining Write the term *political asylum* on the board. Ask volunteers to describe what they think the term means. Then invite students to call out factors that might lead to people seeking political asylum, using examples from the text and their own ideas. Discuss with students how each factor affects population pressure. **Ask:** **How can people seeking political asylum affect the population of a region?** *(By migrating to a region to seek political asylum, people of different ethnic groups and backgrounds can change the cultural landscape of a region over time.)* **ELL** **Verbal/Linguistic**

W Writing Skills

Argument Read aloud the statement to students, and discuss with students possible reasons why the country of Norway is not a member of the European Union. Explain that Norway voted on whether or not to join the European Union in 1972 and again in 1994. Each time, Norway's citizens voted to reject EU membership. Have students conduct online research to identify reasons that Norway has chosen to remain separate from the European Union in a brief essay. Challenge students to choose one side or the other in their essay, arguing for either membership in the EU or continued separation. **Verbal/Linguistic**

INTERACTIVE WHITEBOARD ACTIVITY

Population Patterns in Northern Europe

Identifying This interactive whiteboard activity has students identify countries and characteristics about locations on a map. Lead a class discussion about the variety of factors that influenced the population structure of Northern Europe. Have student provide examples of population density that relate to historical, environmental, economic, political, and technological factors. Complete the activity as a class, inviting several volunteers to drag and drop the answers.
Interpersonal, Logical/Mathematical

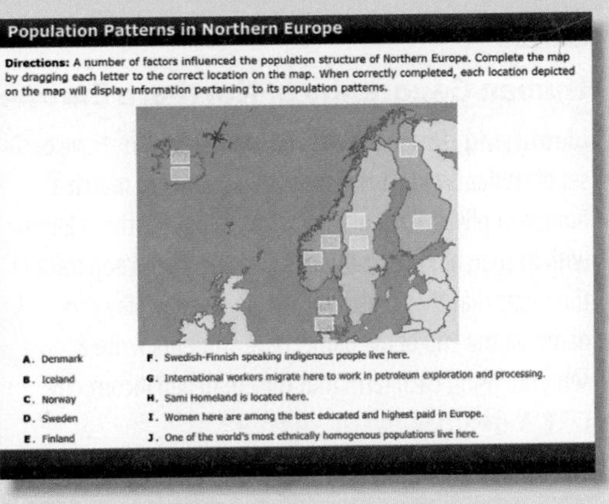

Population Patterns in Northern Europe
Directions: A number of factors influenced the population structure of Northern Europe. Complete the map by dragging each letter to the correct location on the map. When correctly completed, each location depicted on the map will display information pertaining to its population patterns.
A. Denmark
B. Iceland
C. Norway
D. Sweden
E. Finland
F. Swedish-Finnish speaking indigenous people live here.
G. International workers migrate here to work in petroleum exploration and processing.
H. Sami Homeland is located here.
I. Women here are among the best educated and highest paid in Europe.
J. One of the world's most ethnically homogenous populations live here.

V Visual Skills

Using Graphs Have students examine the graph of Finland's population and read the caption. **Ask:** **What factors displayed in the graph of Finland's population structure make it "typical" of other Northern European countries?** *(The graph indicates that Finland has a high number of people ages 45–64, which is a recurring trend among many other Northern European countries.)* Guide a class discussion about the makeup of Northern European's population. Then direct students to answer the Critical Thinking questions. **AL** **Visual/Spatial**

C Critical Thinking Skills

Identifying Continuity and Change Have students read the information about Finland, noting the change in its population over the years and how it is distributed. **Ask:** **Why do you think such a large percentage of Finland's population lives in urban areas?** *(Possible answer: People may live in or near cities because they have more employment opportunities.)* **Why has the trend of people moving out of Finland reversed in the twenty-first century?** *(Immigrants are arriving in Finland due to relaxed immigration policies and improved economic conditions there.)* Guide a class discussion about the makeup of Northern Europe's population as well as factors that influence how its population is distributed. **Logical/Mathematical**

Content Background Knowledge

The Sami Despite Finland's harsh northern climate, the Sami have learned to adapt to their surrounding environment, even in the face of climate change. Due to elevated temperatures over time, the amount of ice levels have dropped in the Arctic Circle, increasing the risk of flooding. To adapt, a group of Sami in northern Finland constructed "nilis," or raised huts to store food. The huts are raised aboveground to prevent animals from taking the food and to keep it dry in case of flooding. According to some scientists, the Arctic region is growing warmer at twice the rate as the rest of the world.

ANSWERS, p. 258

READING PROGRESS CHECK Many people have immigrated to Northern Europe because of the high number of job opportunities that can be found there. Many refugees have sought asylum there, which has increased the cultural diversity a great deal.

CRITICAL THINKING

1. In the population aged 0 to 59, the ratio of females to males is almost one to one. Women over age 65 begin to significantly outnumber men of the same age, and the trend continues with each additional year, indicating that women tend to live longer. There are almost six times more females over the age of 90 than males.
2. Employment opportunities, levels of education, economic stability, and social welfare programs are some of the factors that have an effect on birthrate.

GRAPH SKILLS **Population Pyramid of Finland**

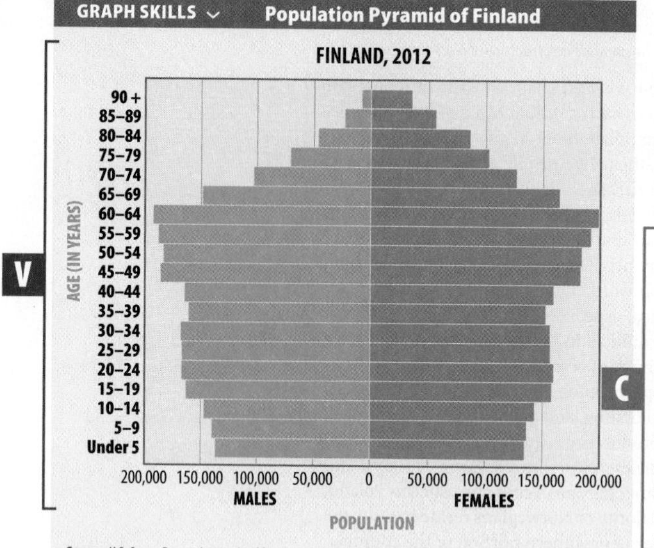

Source: U.S. Census Bureau, International Programs, International Database: 2012

Finland's population structure is typical of many Northern European countries.

▲ **CRITICAL THINKING**

1. ***Assessing*** Write a brief description of Finland's population based on the pyramid.
2. ***Speculating*** What factors do you think contribute to the birthrate in Finland?

Finland became an independent country in 1917 and has achieved a reputation as one of the world's leading proponents of humanitarian causes. The second-largest ethnic group, the Sami, resides in the northernmost part of the country called the Sami Homeland. Swedish-speaking ethnic communities live along the southwestern Baltic coast. Approximately 80 percent of Finland's population lives in urban areas. The major cities are in the southern part of the country near coastal harbors. Helsinki is the largest city and the capital. Finland was the source of many migrants to the United States and other countries. In the twenty-first century, the trend has reversed due to relaxed immigration policies and improved economic conditions in Finland. Immigrants today are arriving from Somalia, Russia, Sweden, and Estonia.

Iceland's population grew from about 50,000 in the early 1700s to about 315,000 in 2013. Iceland is one of the world's most ethnically homogenous populations since few people have immigrated to the island. Reykjavík is the country's capital and largest city. The population lives near the coastlines, where the residents rely on the sea for commercial fishing and surrounding farmland for growing basic foods.

Overall, Northern European countries have lower population densities than most other countries in Europe. This is due to a number of factors, including the northern climate that limits agriculture and the mountainous terrain. Northern Europe's populations concentrate in areas near the sea, where fishing and shipping industries are prominent. Northern Europe's metropolitan areas, such as Stockholm, are also its economic centers. Copenhagen, Denmark, for example, has been called the Singapore of the Baltic. Copenhagen has always been a major port for collecting, storing, and shipping goods across the globe. This makes it an **entrepôt** (AHN•truh•POH), or a port where goods are received and then reshipped. Here, the **break-of-bulk** practices result in large shipments being divided into smaller amounts for distribution to other places.

entrepôt commercial center where goods are received and reshipped

break-of-bulk act of unloading, transferring, or distributing part or all of a shipment

READING PROGRESS CHECK

Drawing Conclusions How have immigrants influenced the population patterns of Northern Europe?

Society and Culture Today

GUIDING QUESTION *How do society and culture in Northern Europe reflect the subregion's history?*

Although a Protestant religion is dominant in every country of the subregion (in most cases, Evangelical Lutheran), these countries value religious freedom and minority religions are practiced. Finland is the only Northern European country without an official religion. As in much of the rest of Europe, this subregion also has a high percentage of people who do not practice a religion.

258

networks Online Teaching Options

GAME

Human Geography of Northern Europe

Identifying Divide the class into student pairs. Have each set of students play this identification game to match a human or physical geography terms about Northern Europe with its matching description. Ask students to keep track of the terms that they match incorrectly as they play the game. At the end of the game, have students write a sentence using each term that they matched incorrectly. **ELL** **Verbal/Linguistic**

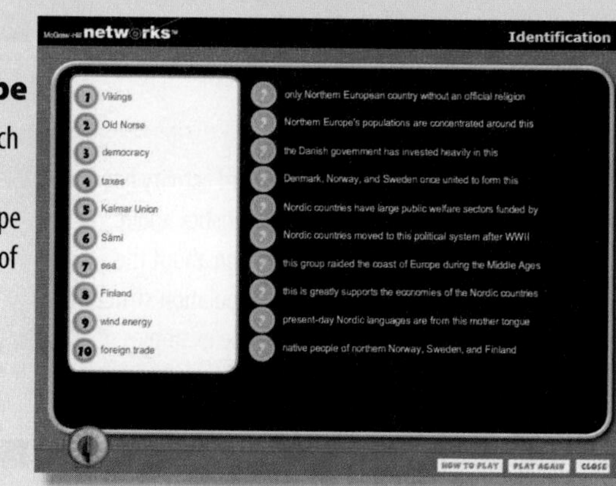

Northern Europe has some of the world's most educated populations. School is mandatory for children for at least 10 years, and literacy rates are nearly 100 percent in all of Scandinavia, Finland, and Iceland. All children are required to know at least one language other than their own, and in most cases they learn several, including English.

Northern European countries are known as **welfare states.** They have programs for the well-being of all residents that are funded by their governments. Countries such as Sweden offer complete social welfare programs to their citizens. In general, residents of Scandinavia, Finland, and Iceland pay high taxes. In return, however, they benefit from a wide array of social services that include health care, child care, and assisted senior living.

welfare state a state that assumes primary responsibility for the social welfare of its citizens

C

Family and Status of Women

The Nordic countries are known as places where changes in attitudes toward unconventional living arrangements are accepted along with traditional views of the family. The family structure today is composed of both single and married-couple households. Compared to many Western countries, the Nordic countries have relatively high birthrates. This has been attributed to family-friendly social welfare policies that provide generous maternity and paternity leave and state-supported day care.

W

Overall, Northern Europe favors equal work opportunities for women. These countries have placed importance on **achieving** a more equitable balance between family and employment than many other places. They have been able to reconcile family life and employment and attain a balance between employment and other activities for both men and women.

achieve to carry out successfully; to accomplish

Iceland, Norway, Finland, Sweden, and Denmark are front-runners in the area of achieving equal status for women. These countries have made great strides in the area of political empowerment. There has been an increase of women in business and high-level government jobs. Nearly as many women as men are elected to serve in the parliaments of Northern Europe.

The Arts

Northern Europe has a well-developed appreciation of the cultural achievements among the countries. Museums, exhibits, symphony halls, and opera houses provide the opportunity to enjoy art, literature, music, and dance. In 2007 in Oslo, Norway, a new cultural center was dedicated. Named the Oslo Opera House, it is home to the Norwegian National Opera and Ballet.

T

Denmark has a rich literary tradition. The fairy tales of Hans Christian Andersen are known throughout the world. Danish designers are sought after globally as highly trained curators of museums, designers of modern furniture, and architects. A keen focus on landscape, architectural, and interior design can be seen in all aspects of Danish culture.

READING PROGRESS CHECK

Analyzing Why have Northern European welfare states placed such high value on social services to all their citizens?

Public art, such as this monumental sculpture of Finnish composer Jean Sibelius by Eila Hiltunen, is enjoyed in Northern European countries.

▼ CRITICAL THINKING

1. ***Defining*** What do you think is meant by public art?
2. ***Contrasting*** How is this art different from art found in a museum?

C Critical Thinking Skills

Comparing and Contrasting Discuss the term *welfare* and ask students what they think the word means as it relates to the United States. Explain that the United States welfare system was implemented during the Great Depression in response to a large number of poverty-stricken families that needed assistance. Then discuss similarities and differences between the United States and Northern Europe's welfare systems. **Ask:** **Based on what you have learned about welfare states in Northern Europe and what you understand about the welfare system in the United States, which system do you think is the most effective? Explain.** *(Students may include that Northern Europe's welfare states cost taxpayers more money, but serve the population more effectively by offering health care, child care, and assisted senior living; whereas the welfare system in the United States is less inclusive.)* Moderate a class debate in which students voice their opinions, supported by information in the text, about the responsibility of a government to provide for its citizens. **BL** **Intrapersonal**

W Writing Skills

Argument Review the information about Nordic countries' social welfare policies and opportunities for women. Then have students write a short essay to either defend or refute the following statement: **Policies and opportunities for women in Nordic countries exceed those that exist in the United States.** Remind students that they need to support their claims with evidence and that they should address any counterclaims through additional research. **BL** **Verbal/Linguistic**

T Technology Skills

Researching Allow students to choose one of the countries in Northern Europe. Have them conduct research to identify cultural facts for a presentation about that country's art, music, literature, museums, theaters, or concert halls. Have students present their findings in a "Nordic Culture Fair," encouraging them to create costumes, make food, or play music representative of the country. Invite musically and theatrically inclined students to play and perform music and dance pieces as part of their presentations. **Auditory/Musical, Kinesthetic**

PRIMARY SOURCE

Working Women

Summarizing Display this primary source quote to discuss the Nordic Model and how it relates to working women. Allow time for students to study they text and to ask questions. Have students write three summarizing statements about the information. Then use the students' statements to lead a class discussion about the importance of working women to Norway's prosperity. **Verbal/Linguistic, Logical/Mathematical**

Analyzing Primary Sources

The Nordic Model and Working Women

"Sweden, Finland and Denmark can't rely on fossil fuel reserves—but lucrative human resources: The region combines the world's highest female employment rates with some of the most impressive fertility rates in developed countries—one reason why it has weathered the crisis with solid public finances and respectable growth (Iceland being the notable exception).

'One Norwegian lesson,' Prime Minister Jens Stoltenberg said from his modestly sized office one afternoon, 'is that if you can raise female participation, it helps the economy, birthrates and the budget.'"

—Katrin Bennhold,
"Working Women Are the Key to Norway's Prosperity,"
New York Times, June 28, 2011.

ANSWERS, p. 259

READING PROGRESS CHECK By providing residents with social services, governments are able to increase the quality of life of their citizens and achieve better participation rates in their labor force.

CRITICAL THINKING

1. This sculpture is community art because it is outside and free to the public.
2. Possible answer: Its setting makes it seem as though the sculpture may not have been commissioned, like many public works are in the U.S., but created spontaneously as a contribution by an artist to his community.

C Critical Thinking Skills

Evaluating After students read the section Resources, Power, and Industry, discuss with the class the factors that have contributed to the success of Northern Europe's economies. **Ask:** **Why is commercial fishing an important industry to Iceland?** (*Fish and fish products from Iceland make up more than 70 percent of its exports, so it is a major factor in contributing to Iceland's economy.*) Have students brainstorm products that come from Northern European countries, such as the Sweden-based furniture store Ikea. **What industry is perhaps the most vital to Norway, Sweden, and Finland? Why?** (*Possible answer: Forestry is a vital industry because it provides resources for furniture.*) **Logical/Mathematical**

CLOSE & REFLECT

Determining Importance Assign student pairs one of the subheads from the lesson. Tell partners to review the text and write a sentence that describes the importance of the topic to Northern Europe. In determining the importance of their topic, remind students to consider the Essential Question: *How do physical systems and human systems shape a place?*

ANSWERS, p. 260

✓ **READING PROGRESS CHECK** Nordic countries are socially responsible, as evidenced by their welfare policies. They are also environmentally aware, as evidenced by their reliance on renewable, sustainable energy sources.

DBQ Human resources, and in particular, women, are critical to the Nordic model. High female employment and high fertility rates are a big reason that the Nordic nations have remained stable in times of crisis.

Analyzing PRIMARY SOURCES (CCSS)

The Nordic Model and Working Women

"Sweden, Finland and Denmark can't rely on fossil fuel reserves—but lucrative human resources: The region combines the world's highest female employment rates with some of the most impressive fertility rates in developed countries—one reason why it has weathered the crisis with solid public finances and respectable growth (Iceland being the notable exception). 'One Norwegian lesson,' Prime Minister Jens Stoltenberg said from his modestly sized office one afternoon, 'is that if you can raise female participation, it helps the economy, birthrates and the budget.'"

—Katrin Bennhold, "Working Women Are the Key to Norway's Prosperity," *New York Times*, June 28, 2011

DBQ ***IDENTIFYING CENTRAL ISSUES*** What lucrative resource is critical to the Nordic model, according to this excerpt? Why? RH.9–10.2

Economic Activities

GUIDING QUESTION *What factors have contributed to the success of the economies of Northern Europe?*

Economically, the Nordic countries have much in common. They are all small, open economies in which foreign trade has great economic significance. They also rapidly evolved from agrarian-based economies into modern, industrialized economies. The Nordic model of industrialization and social responsibility is of interest to policy makers in other countries.

Resources, Power, and Industry

Northern Europe relies on a variety of energy sources. Most of Iceland's energy comes from hydroelectric power and geothermal energy. Sweden and Norway also rely heavily on hydroelectric power. Finland relies on peat as a source of energy. Denmark has limited amounts of nonrenewable energy such as oil and natural gas. However, the Danish government has invested heavily in wind energy.

C Commercial fishing is important to Iceland and Norway. In Iceland, fish and fish products constitute more than 70 percent of exports. The seas near Iceland and the warm Gulf Stream provide favorable conditions for various kinds of fish. Fisheries are also a central component of the Norwegian economy. In addition to the rich fishing waters of the North Atlantic, Norway has deep fjords and a very long coastline that provide both wild and farmed Norwegian salmon.

Other major industries in the subregion include forestry, manufacturing, agriculture, and service industries. Forestry is important in Norway, Sweden, and Finland. Denmark's economy is based on service industries, trade, manufacturing, and agriculture. Denmark was also the first of the Northern European countries to join what would eventually become the European Union.

The Nordic Model

The Nordic model refers to the economic and social models of the Northern European countries. This particular brand of mixed economy is characterized by welfare policies in which governments play important roles in protecting the social and economic health of their citizens. The Nordic model emphasizes labor force participation and promotes gender equality and fiscal expansion. Additionally, the Nordic model offers low barriers to trade and supports union membership, both of which are intended to offset the risks associated with participation in an open economy.

✓ **READING PROGRESS CHECK**

Describing What are two cultural characteristics that fit the Nordic countries?

LESSON 2 REVIEW

Reviewing Vocabulary (Tier Three Words)

1. ***Explaining*** Explain the break-of-bulk concept. RH.9–10.4

Using Your Notes

2. ***Listing*** Use your graphic organizer to identify the contributions Northern Europe has made to the arts.

Answering the Guiding Questions

3. ***Identifying*** What influenced the creation of new social classes and peaceful democracies in Northern Europe?
4. ***Describing*** What factors influence the population structure of Northern Europe?
5. ***Explaining*** How do society and culture in Northern Europe reflect the subregion's history?
6. ***Listing*** What factors have contributed to the success of the economies of Northern Europe?

Writing Activity

7. ***Informative/Explanatory*** Write a paragraph describing the Sami, the indigenous people of Finland, including their history and spatial patterns of settlement in the region. WHST.9–10.2

260

LESSON 2 REVIEW ANSWERS

Reviewing Vocabulary

1. Break-of-bulk describes what happens at major ports such as Copenhagen when goods arrive in bulk. Large shipments of bulk goods are unloaded and divided into smaller amounts to be redistributed elsewhere.

Using Your Notes

2. Museums, symphony halls, and opera houses provide citizens access to art, literature, music, and dance. Northern Europeans have also contributed design elements to architecture, furniture, landscapes, and interior design.

Answering the Guiding Questions

3. Industrialization boosted the population as more people were needed for jobs. This increase led to the development of new social classes and socioeconomic levels. The convergence of many different perspectives fostered new ideas and ultimately led to democracy and independence.
4. The population structure of Northern Europe has been shaped by the influences of migration and the distinct ethnic groups of each country. Migration is determined by the amount of work available in the countries as well as their policies on immigration and social welfare.
5. Northern European governments were influenced by many different voices from new classes of migrant workers. A single religion is dominant in most Northern European countries, but religious freedom is also strongly valued, and many minority religions exist. Northern Europe has some of the world's most educated populations and highest levels of equality among citizens. All citizens benefit from social services provided by the state.
6. The countries of Northern Europe have small, open economies, which allow them to participate heavily in foreign trade. They successfully kept up with the times by transforming from poor, agrarian countries into modern, competitive, industrialized countries.

Writing Activity

7. Paragraphs will vary, but should show knowledge of the following: the Sami are the descendants of nomadic peoples who lived in northern Scandinavia for thousands of years. They now live in northern Norway, Sweden, and Finland.

networks

There's More Online!

- **IMAGE** Sea Life from the Baltic Sea
- **IMAGE** Renewable Energy Sources
- **MAP** Acid Rain in Northern Europe
- **INTERACTIVE SELF-CHECK QUIZ**
- **VIDEO** People and Their Environment: Northern Europe

LESSON 3

People and Their Environment: Northern Europe

ESSENTIAL QUESTION • *How do physical systems and human systems shape a place?*

Reading **HELP**DESK 

Academic Vocabulary (Tier Two Words)

- **undergo**
- **occur**

Content Vocabulary (Tier Three Words)

- **invasive species**
- **ecotourism**

TAKING NOTES: ***Key Ideas and Details***

IDENTIFYING Use a graphic organizer like the one below to take notes on the damage humans have caused to the Baltic Sea, boreal forest, and the wetlands of Northern Europe.

Northern Europe: Managing Resources and the Human Impact	
Feature	Damage
Baltic Sea	
Boreal Forest	
Wetlands	

IT MATTERS BECAUSE

The natural environment is one of the assets of Northern Europe, with its abundant energy, forests, and maritime resources. However, the region is vulnerable and under threat from pollution, exploitation, and climate change. There is also an urgent need to preserve the unique species that have adapted for life in some of the harshest climates. R1

Managing Resources

GUIDING QUESTION *Why are Northern Europe's waters and forests in need of protection?*

The North Sea is home to about 230 species of fish, including cod, haddock, mackerel, and herring. These are all common species and are a target of commercial fishing. Due to overfishing, however, many key commercial species are close to collapse. Bottom trawling, or towing a net along the seafloor, as a form of commercial fishing also threatens the seabed habitats.

The Baltic Sea possesses a unique ecology. Its connection to the open ocean is restricted, so it is only semi-salty. In addition, this isolation from the open ocean makes it particularly vulnerable to various ecological problems. The Baltic Sea **undergoes** water stratification, a situation in which the water layers do not mix. These factors contribute to eutrophication, a serious problem in which there is an increase in plant production. Eutrophication limits the amount of plankton produced—a major source of food for many species in the sea. C

Additionally, the Baltic Sea ecosystem is susceptible to pollution from runoff from both coastal and river areas, which are in close proximity to population centers and industrial and agricultural development. An increase in ship traffic since the 1950s has also introduced a number of **invasive species** which travel on ships' water tanks or hulls. Given the relatively low number of species in the Baltic Sea, invasive species can have an especially detrimental effect on the sea. R2

ENGAGE

R1 Reading Skills

Paraphrasing Have pairs work together to read the *It Matters Because* text, clarifying confusing or unknown words by looking them up in a print or online dictionary. Then have partners rewrite the paragraph in their own words. Invite students to share their paraphrases, launching into a class discussion about the various factors that pose a threat to regions in Northern Europe.

TEACH & ASSESS

C Critical Thinking Skills

Identifying Cause and Effect Have students create a graphic organizer to record information about the cause-and-effect relationships involving negative impacts on the environment and resources of Northern Europe. Tell students to draw a two-column Cause and Effect chart. Have students use information from the paragraph to fill in each column. Encourage students to add more information to their charts as they continue to read the lesson. AL **Visual/Spatial**

R2 Reading Skills

Using Context Clues Direct students' attention to the term *invasive species*. Tell students that understanding a word's origin and using context clues can help them to better understand a word's meaning. **Ask: What is the root word of *invasive*, and what does it mean?** *(invade, to attack or take over)* Then have students use context clues to define the term. **Ask: What context clues in the paragraph help you understand the term *invasive species*?** *(Possible answers: "introduced a number of," "travel on ships' water tanks or hulls," "detrimental effect on the sea")* **What is an example of how invasive species affect the environment of Northern Europe?** *(Possible answer: Invasive species that travel on ships' water tanks or hulls have had a detrimental effect on the Baltic Sea.)* ELL AL **Verbal/Linguistic**

networks ***Online Teaching Options***

 INTERACTIVE BELLRINGER

Acid Rain in Northern Europe

Interpreting Maps Have students interpret this map to discuss the impact of air pollution in the United Kingdom and other industrialized countries in Northern Europe. Have students form small groups and discuss their prior knowledge of acid rain. Have students answer each bellringer question. Ask each group to write agreed-upon answers to the questions. Then in a class discussion, have groups share and explain their answers. **Interpersonal, Verbal/Linguistic**

ANSWERS, p. 261

TAKING NOTES: Baltic Sea—overfishing, trawling, polluted chemical runoff from coastal and river areas near industries, high ship traffic bringing invasive species; **Boreal Forest**—ecosystems destroyed by deforestation; increased levels of carbon dioxide in atmosphere because of deforestation; **Wetlands**—cleared to make way for industry and homes; disrupted by dams built for hydroelectric power; polluted by industrial drainage and the process of peat production.

People and Their Environment: Northern Europe

C Critical Thinking Skills

Identifying Central Issues Have students identify the problems facing Northern Europe's original forests as well as the boreal forests of Scandinavia and Russia. **Ask:** **What human activity poses a threat to the boreal forest?** *(deforestation)* **What has been an effect of this activity?** *(It has caused major disruptions to animal and plant ecosystems.)* **What might happen over time if this activity continues?** *(Excess carbon from stored organic matter might decompose more rapidly and release carbon dioxide into the atmosphere.)* AL Logical/Mathematical

V Visual Skills

Creating Diagrams Have partners create an illustrated diagram that shows how various threats can damage the freshwater habitats of birds and animals. Tell students to clearly label their diagrams to show the various threats to these freshwater habitats. **Ask:** **Why are freshwater tidal marshes important?** *(They provide freshwater to surrounding communities and habitats for many birds and other animals.)* **What has caused damage to these habitats?** *(industrialization; human populations encroaching on and draining wetlands to create dry land for homes, agriculture, and other uses; and changed river flows and dam construction for hydroelectric developments)* Visual/Spatial

R Reading Skills

Examining Primary Sources Ask students to read the excerpt about documenting the Baltic Sea's biodiversity. Clarify any confusing words, such as *precedent* (*example, instance*), and have students work with a partner to paraphrase the excerpt. **Ask:** **What was the mission of the expedition?** *(to improve the network of Marine Protected Areas and their management)* **Why was the expedition valuable?** *(It proved that there are still areas that are "rich in biodiversity" that serve as an example of how the Baltic Sea can look "if adequately protected.")* ELL Verbal/Linguistic

ANSWERS, p. 262

READING PROGRESS CHECK There are many ships that travel through the area, and invasive species travel on the ships' water tanks or hulls.

DBQ Document-Based Questions

1. The study proves that some areas of the devastated sea are still rich in biodiversity. These areas show what could be if the Baltic Sea is protected.
2. It covered all the Baltic countries and filmed depths ranging from 3 to 450 meters.

undergo to go through, experience

invasive species a non-indigenous or non-native species that threatens ecosystems, habitats, or other species

C In addition to its waters, Northern Europe's forests are also in need of careful management. Logging and agriculture led to the deforestation of much of Europe's original forests. Much of the remaining forest is the boreal forest, or taiga, of Scandinavia and Russia. However, even here deforestation has caused major disruptions to animal and plant ecosystems. Also, trees and soils of the boreal forest store a large amount of carbon as decomposed or partly decomposed material. If deforestation continues, the stored organic matter will decompose more rapidly and the stored carbon will be released into the atmosphere as carbon dioxide.

V Northern Europe's freshwater tidal marshes are important for many reasons. They are a source of freshwater to surrounding communities and also provide habitats for many birds and other animals. Industrialization has damaged or destroyed those habitats. Many plant and animal species have become endangered as a result of human populations encroaching on and draining wetlands to create dry land for homes, agriculture, and other uses. Additionally, hydroelectric developments, although a good alternative to fossil fuels, cause damage by changing river flows and by the construction of dams that flood some areas and drain others.

Another threat to wetlands is the industrial drainage of large areas of Northern Europe for peat production. In countries such as Finland, peat is an important source of biomass fuel. While burning peat produces valuable energy, it also releases a considerable amount of carbon dioxide into the atmosphere. Even more carbon dioxide is released by peat bogs drained for agriculture and forestry.

READING PROGRESS CHECK

Speculating Why is the Baltic Sea susceptible to invasive species?

ANALYZING PRIMARY SOURCES CCSS

Documenting the Baltic Sea's Biodiversity

To improve the network of Marine Protected Areas and their management, a scientific expedition covering 7,000 nautical miles (12,964 km) collected data on the state of conservation of the Baltic Sea.

R "'There is no precedent of any other international expedition that has covered all the Baltic countries and filmed depths ranging from 3 to 450 meters (the deepest area being Landsort Deep, Sweden),' explains Xavier Pastor, Executive Director of Oceana Europe and the leader of the expedition. 'Oceana's expedition is valuable because it proves that there are areas still rich in biodiversity in this devastated sea; areas that show how the Baltic Sea can look like if adequately protected. We've also seen areas that have been completely destroyed or are heavily polluted, proof of the lack of adequate conservation measures.'"

—Marta Madina, "Oceana Concludes Expedition to Document Biodiversity and Fisheries in the Baltic," Oceana.org, June 7, 2011

The unique ecology of the Baltic Sea makes it particularly vulnerable to various ecological problems.

Wolfgang Poelzer/WaterFrame/Getty Images

DBQ CRITICAL THINKING

1. ***Analyzing*** What hope for the Baltic Sea is offered by this study? RH.9–10.1
2. ***Exploring Issues*** What elements of this expedition made it unique when compared to previous research projects? RH.9–10.1

networks Online Teaching Options

PRIMARY SOURCE

Invasive Species in the Baltic

Using Primary Sources Display this primary source for students and ask them to read and discuss the content with a partner. Then have partners research a lake, river, or waterway within their own region where an invasive species has affected the ecosystem. Tell student pairs to compile their research in an oral report and suggest that they include a visual display or diagram to share with the class. Visual/Spatial, Verbal/Linguistic

Analyzing Primary Sources

Invasive Species in the Baltic

"Alien species may have very strong negative impacts on their new environment. But a new study published in the latest issue of Global Change Biology shows that an alien species can also have beneficial effects by counteracting the lack of oxygen near the bottom. . . .

'We have seen an improvement in some areas and it has coincided with the spread of the American polychaete worm *Marenzelleria*, which is now one of the most common benthic [bottom-dwelling] species in the northern Baltic Sea. It made us wonder what effects the worms have on the ecosystem, and if they could have contributed to the improved oxygen conditions,' says Daniel Reed, one of the main authors behind the new study.

The modeling study shows that the invasive worms can contribute to the binding of phosphorus in the sediments, reducing the eutrophication [excess build-up of nutrients] of the Baltic Sea and the risk of algal blooms. 'According to our alculations, the positive effect of the worms can be twice as great as the enhanced wastewater treatment, for example in the Stockholm area. This way,

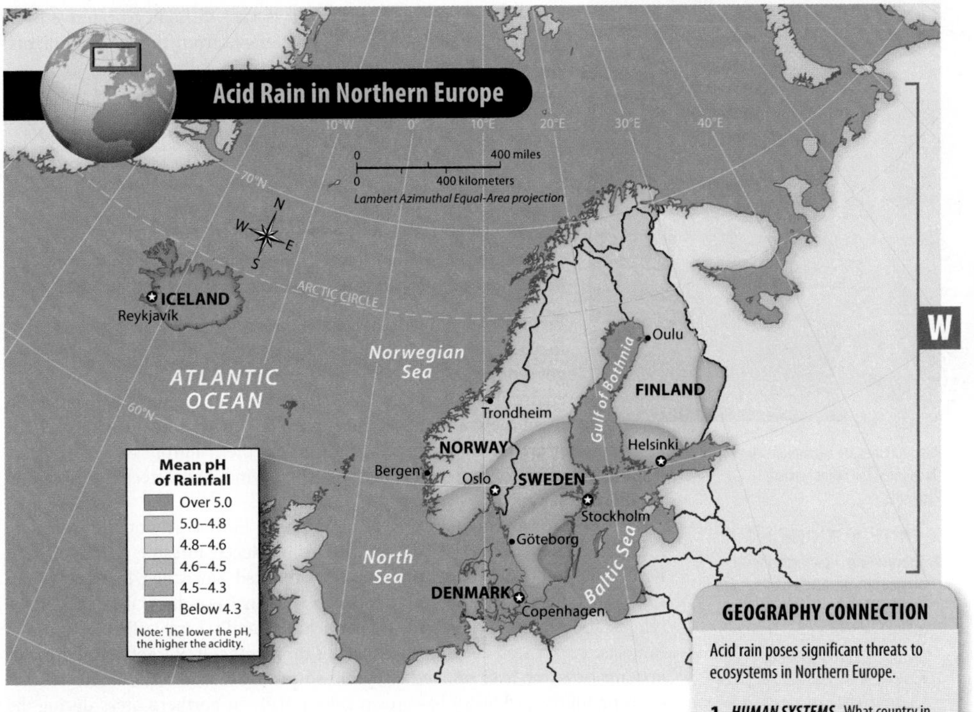

GEOGRAPHY CONNECTION

Acid rain poses significant threats to ecosystems in Northern Europe.

1. ***HUMAN SYSTEMS*** What country in Northern Europe is most affected by acid rain, showing a low pH?
2. ***ENVIRONMENT AND SOCIETY*** Why might Iceland have less acid rain than other countries in the subregion?

Human Impact

GUIDING QUESTION *How have human activities affected the natural environment in Northern Europe?*

Because of its location in the high latitudes, the climate is changing more rapidly in Northern Europe than in most other places in the world. These changes are especially detrimental to the subregion's ecosystems. Warmer temperatures are causing ice to melt, which endangers land used for traditional herding and farming practices. The rising temperatures also affect the distribution of animals. Many species are moving closer to the North Pole as temperatures rise. Birds are migrating and arriving at their nesting grounds earlier. In some countries, the birds have stopped leaving, as the climate is suitable all year round.

Scandinavian scientists in the 1950s were some of the first to understand the effects of acid rain as they discovered acidic damage to lakes and streams. Although Northern Europe is less industrialized than many other parts of Europe, air pollution from the United Kingdom and other more industrialized areas of Europe is carried by winds to the northern regions of Europe. In the atmosphere these pollutants form sulfuric and nitric acid, which are released in rain or snow. Acid rain is contributing to wetland destruction, with many lakes in Norway and a significant proportion of lakes in Sweden and Finland showing serious acidification.

The runoff of chemicals and waste from industrialized areas nearby adds to the pollution of coastal areas, wetlands, and rivers in Northern Europe. This pollution threatens plant and animal life. Occasional oil spills from ships also

People and Their Environment: Northern Europe

W Writing Skills

Informative/Explanatory Have students review the map, noting the color-coded key. Instruct students to write a paragraph explaining how acid rain has impacted Northern Europe based on the information provided in the map. AL **Verbal/Linguistic**

R Reading Skills

Explaining Continuity and Change Have students discuss the effects of Northern Europe's rapidly changing climate. **Ask:** **Why is Northern Europe's climate changing more rapidly than most other places in the world?** *(because of its location in the high latitudes)* **What is the impact of these changes on the region?** *(Warmer temperatures cause ice to melt, which endangers land used for traditional herding and farming practices as well as impacting how animals are distributed.)* **How have animals in the subregion's ecosystems reacted to these changes?** *(Many species move closer to the North Pole as temperatures rise, birds migrate and arrive in their nests earlier, and sometimes the birds stop migrating altogether.)* **Logical/Mathematical**

C Critical Thinking Skills

Problem Solving Review the second paragraph with students. **Ask:** **Why is Northern Europe impacted by air pollution even though it is less industrialized than many other parts of Europe?** *(Air pollution from the United Kingdom and other more industrialized areas of Europe is carried by winds to regions in Northern Europe.)* **What could be a possible solution to prevent this problem from perpetuating?** *(Possible answer: Governments of Northern European countries could impose fines on companies that contribute to air pollution or could raise tariffs on products made by these companies that are imported to Northern European countries.)* BL **Logical/Mathematical**

VIDEO

Frozen Forests

Identifying Cause and Effect Use this video about the importance of trees and forest areas to animals to discuss the effects of temperature changes with students. Have them consider how much effort it has taken the animals and plants in this region to adapt to their environment and how a warmer climate will affect this ecosystem if, as scientists suspect, Earth's temperature is rising. In small groups, have students discuss possible environmental effects to the region, and then have groups present their responses to the class. AL **Naturalist, Interpersonal**

ANSWERS, p. 263

GEOGRAPHY CONNECTION

1. Sweden appears to be the Northern European country most affected by acid rain.
2. Iceland is farther away from highly industrialized countries, which are a main source of acid rain.

People and Their Environment: Northern Europe

T Technology Skills

Acquiring Information Organize the class into small groups, assigning each group a region of Northern Europe. Using reliable online sources, students should acquire more in-depth information about the work of the LIFE+ Environment Policy and Governance. Have students identify specific projects currently being implemented by the program in their assigned country. Invite groups to present their findings to the class. Then hold a class discussion about how the work of this program can improve environmental issues. BL Verbal/Linguistic

CLOSE & REFLECT

Problem Solving Have students review the various environmental issues discussed in this lesson. Tell them to choose one issue and brainstorm a possible solution. Encourage students to write a letter to a local politician expressing their concern about a local environmental issue and suggesting a possible solution.

ANSWERS, p. 264

✓ **READING PROGRESS CHECK** Emissions coming from the more industrialized areas are carried by winds to the northern regions of Europe.

✓ **READING PROGRESS CHECK** harsh climate and the importance of sheep farming to the country's economy

CRITICAL THINKING

1. Wind energy is a clean source of power. Using it as an alternative energy source allows countries to not rely as heavily on burning fossil fuels to provide their power.
2. The turbines are located near the water, and air moving over large bodies of water generates a lot of wind energy that the turbines are able to capture.

Wind turbines are a common sight throughout the Scandinavian Peninsula.

▲ **CRITICAL THINKING**

1. ***Speculating*** How might the use of wind turbines help a country burn less fossil fuels?
2. ***Assessing*** What physical feature that appears in the photo indicates this would be a good location for the turbines to capture the most wind?

occur to come into existence, happen

ecotourism the practice and business of recreational travel based on concern for the environment

wreak havoc on marine life. Oil is very difficult to remove from water and nearly impossible to remove from the wildlife, plants, and mosses found in wetland areas after spills **occur**.

✓ **READING PROGRESS CHECK**

Explaining How does industrial development in other parts of Europe contribute to acid rain in Northern Europe?

Addressing the Issues

GUIDING QUESTION *What actions are governments and other groups in Northern Europe taking to address environmental issues?*

Environmental planning and management in Northern Europe has focused on sustainability and long-term planning. All levels of government and grassroots organizations work together to address environmental issues. Recycling programs, reducing reliance on fossil fuels, and regulations for higher environmental standards for air and water are making a positive impact. Northern European countries are leaders in the use of renewable energy, such as wind, hydroelectric power, and geothermal power.

Conservation is not a new issue in Northern Europe. About 100 years ago, Finland, Norway, Sweden, and Denmark introduced forestry legislation that limited the amount of timber that could be harvested. Since then, forest resources in these countries have increased substantially. In Iceland, on the other hand, reforestation has not advanced as much. Iceland's harsh climate and the importance of sheep farming have made it more difficult. Recent restrictions on grazing, however, have resulted in a promising move toward restoring forest land.

The tourism industry has grown substantially in northern areas during the last few years, especially in arctic destinations. Although tourism helps the region's economies, there are also potential threats to the fragile environment. The Sustainable Model for Arctic Regional Tourism was a program aimed at teaching how the arctic tourism sector could be developed in such a way that limits damage to the unique lands of Northern Europe. This form of tourism is called **ecotourism**.

Sweden and Finland are part of the LIFE+ Environment Policy and Governance established by the European Union. The program creates projects that offer environmental benefits to the region, including programs that encourage innovation in environmental protection and conservation.

✓ **READING PROGRESS CHECK**

Identifying What factors have limited reforestation in Iceland?

LESSON 3 REVIEW CCSS

Reviewing Vocabulary (Tier Three Words)

1. ***Explaining*** Why are invasive species a problem in the Baltic Sea? RH.9–10.4

Using Your Notes

2. ***Listing*** Use your graphic organizer to describe the impact of human activities on the Baltic Sea, the boreal forest, and the wetlands of Northern Europe.

Answering the Guiding Questions

3. ***Identifying*** Why are Northern Europe's waters and forests in need of protection?
4. ***Describing*** How have human activities affected the natural environment in Northern Europe?
5. ***Explaining*** What actions are governments and other groups in Northern Europe taking to address environmental issues?

Writing Activity

6. ***Informative/Explanatory*** Write a paragraph describing how human activity has affected the environment in Northern Europe. Discuss some solutions that are being implemented. Are they working? WHST.9–10.2

264

LESSON 3 REVIEW ANSWERS

Reviewing Vocabulary

1. The ecosystems of the Baltic Sea already face threats, such as eutrophication, which limits the food supply, and there is already a low number of native species. Competition from non-native, invasive species further alters the delicate balance of the environment and endangers the original inhabitants.

Using Your Notes

2. The Baltic Sea is damaged by overfishing; trawling, which disrupts seafloor habitats; polluted runoff from industrial development; and by increased shipping traffic, which has brought invasive species to the area. The boreal forest suffers from deforestation, which disrupts animal and plant ecosystems and increases amounts of carbon dioxide entering the atmosphere. Wetlands have been damaged by damming for hydroelectric power, clearing for housing and industry, and by industrial pollution related to peat production.

Answering the Guiding Questions

3. There is a relatively low number of species adapted to the unique conditions of Northern Europe's environment, which makes them more susceptible to the effects of human changes.
4. The environmental threats imposed by humans include the introduction of invasive species, polluted runoff, deforestation, and effects of peat production and industrialization. The effects of climate change are more rapid in Northern Europe due to its high latitudes. Warmer temperatures cause ice to melt and flood the area.
5. Government and grassroots organizations work together by creating recycling programs, reducing reliance on fossil fuels, and regulating standards for air and water. The region is also a leader in the use of renewable energy, which helps reduce its environmental impact. Forestry legislation protects forests by limiting the amount of timber that can be harvested and the amount of grazing that can occur.

Writing Activity

6. Paragraphs will vary, but should address human activities such as ship travel, deforestation, dam building, peat burning, and reliance on industry. Solutions may include recycling programs, reduced reliance on fossil fuels, standards for air and water quality, and forestry legislation.

CHAPTER 10 Assessment 

Directions: On a separate sheet of paper, answer the questions below. Make sure you read carefully and answer all parts of the questions.

Lesson Review

Lesson 1

1. ***Identifying Cause and Effect*** Describe the role of glaciation in the formation of the fjords of Northern Europe.
2. ***Explaining*** Explain the location of the Faeroe Islands. Why are they not considered part of Scandinavia?
3. ***Drawing Conclusions*** What factors influence the climate in Northern Europe? Give examples.

Lesson 2

4. ***Evaluating*** Describe how the welfare states benefit the people of Northern Europe. How are they funded?
5. ***Analyzing*** How has the history of Northern Europe been shaped by migrations, invasions, and trade?
6. ***Summarizing*** Explain how industrialization affected the societies of Northern Europe in the nineteenth century.

Lesson 3

7. ***Identifying Central Issues*** Describe how human activities have created water and air pollution in Northern Europe.
8. ***Explaining*** Explain why Northern Europe's waters and forests are in need of protection.
9. ***Comparing and Contrasting*** How are private and public groups in Northern Europe addressing environmental issues?

21st Century Skills

Use the following chart to answer the questions below.

Norway's Gross Domestic Product by Economic Sector	
Agriculture	2.6%
Industry	39.7%
Services	57.7%

Source: CIA World Factbook, 2011

10. ***Using Graphs, Charts, Diagrams, and Tables*** What sector of Norway's economy in the chart constitutes the smallest percentage of the country's total GDP?
11. ***Decision Making*** What types of imports do you think Norway must rely on due to the percentages shown in the chart? Explain your answer.
12. ***Economics*** Describe the types of jobs that may be part of Norway's service industry.

College and Career Readiness

13. ***Explaining Continuity and Change*** As a sociologist, you have been hired by the United Nations Population Fund to list and describe the new family structure in Northern Europe and explain why the change has occurred. Conduct the necessary research, and then write a one-page report evaluating the causes of the change. WHST.9–10.7

Need Extra Help?

If You've Missed Question	1	2	3	4	5	6	7	8	9	10	11	12	13
Go to page	250	251	253	259	255	256	261	262	264	265	265	265	259

CHAPTER 10 Assessment Answers

Lesson Review

Lesson 1

1. As glaciers moved through Northern Europe, they carved valleys and steep-sided fjords into the land that was in their path. The fjords are now partially filled with seawater.

2. The Faeroe Islands are located about halfway between Iceland and Norway. The cultural region of Scandinavia includes Denmark even though Denmark is not on the Scandinavian Peninsula. Although the Faeroe Islands are a part of Denmark, they are far away from the Scandinavian Peninsula and outside the limits of the Scandinavian cultural region.

3. Factors that influence climate include latitude, elevation, wind patterns, and distance from large bodies of water. The extreme northern latitude makes for a cold, dry climate. The high elevation of the alpine zone is also extremely cold. The farther south or closer to sea level one travels, the warmer the climate. The proximity of the region to the Baltic Sea and the Gulf Stream cause it to be warmed by airflows over these waters.

Lesson 2

4. Welfare states have programs for the well-being of all residents. The programs are funded by the governments, which is possible due to the generally higher taxes their citizens pay in order to receive these benefits.

5. During the Viking Age (A.D. 793 to 1050), Scandinavian Vikings sailed the coastal European waters and would raid the inland areas. Over time, they claimed territories, which expanded, and the many Viking kingdoms emerged as Denmark, Sweden, and Norway. Under the Kalmar Union, the countries became more integrated with one another and engaged in increased trade with Europe, which made their societies more continental.

6. In the nineteenth century, industrialization resulted in an abundance of jobs and an influx of migrant workers who sought them. This population boom led to new social classes and various socioeconomic levels.

Lesson 3

7. Air pollution from industrialized areas of Europe harms Northern Europe in the form of acid rain and snow. The burning of peat for energy releases carbon dioxide into the atmosphere. Runoff of chemicals and waste from industrialized areas contaminate rivers and coastal areas. Oil spills endanger marine life.

8. Overfishing has resulted in many species being close to collapse. Commercial fishing threatens seabed habitats. Waterways also experience runoff from chemicals. Invasive species have come into the waterways through an increase in ship traffic. Logging and agriculture have resulted in deforestation of a great deal of original forests, and habitats have been damaged.

9. Government and grassroots organizations work together through such efforts as recycling programs and reduction of reliance on fossil fuels. The government has passed regulations for higher environmental standards for air and water. Renewable energy is used extensively. Finland and Sweden are part of the LIFE+ Environmental Policy and Governance established by the European Union, a program that creates projects to offer environmental benefits to the region.

21st Century Skills

10. Agriculture constitutes the smallest percentage.

11. Possible answer: Norway must rely on imports of crops, such as fruits and vegetables, since their agriculture sector is small.

12. Possible answer: Norway's service industry most likely includes jobs in social services, particularly in health care, child care, and assisted senior living since the government provides such services for all of its citizens.

College and Career Readiness

13. Responses should include a list of characteristics of the new family structure in Northern Europe. Analysis should include discussion of at least two factors that led to the change.

CHAPTER 10

Assessment Answers

CHAPTER 10 Assessment 

Directions: On a separate sheet of paper, answer the questions below. Make sure you read carefully and answer all parts of the questions.

Critical Thinking

14 ***Making Generalizations*** How does tectonic activity affect the islands of Northern Europe?

15 ***Identifying Central Issues*** What is the relationship between glaciation and hydroelectric power in Northern Europe?

16 ***Evaluating*** Write a paragraph discussing the economic characteristics of the Nordic model and why it has been considered successful.

17 ***Drawing Conclusions*** How has Northern Europe's culture been affected by its physical environment?

Applying Map Skills

Use the Unit 4 Atlas to answer the following questions.

18 ***Place and Regions*** Using the political map of Europe, which Northern European countries lie partially within the Arctic Circle?

19 ***Physical Systems*** Describe the elevation of Finland compared to that of Norway as shown on the physical map of Europe.

20 ***Environment and Society*** Use your mental map to list the seas that border the countries of Northern Europe.

Exploring the Essential Question

21 ***Identifying Cause and Effect*** Create a flow chart that shows the geologic events that led to the eruption of the Eyjafjallajökull volcano in Iceland. How did it affect the economy and transportation? How is this event an example of how physical systems and human systems shape a place?

DBQ Analyzing Primary Sources

Use the document to answer the following questions.

In Denmark, some families have decided to generate their own electricity as a way of protecting the environment.

PRIMARY SOURCE

"We like using computers, and watching the television. And we like taking hot showers like everybody else. By having a windmill we can do that with a good conscience, because we know that the power we consume doesn't expose the environment. Now we produce electricity without producing carbon dioxide. It feels right to take our little part of the responsibility of getting a better environment."

—Hans Chresten Jeppesen, *National Geographic News*, November 4, 2009

22 ***Analyzing*** Describe what the Jeppesen family is doing to help limit their impact on global warming. RH9–10.1

23 ***Speculating*** How could the governments of countries in Northern Europe and elsewhere encourage more people to take action like the Jeppesen family?

Research and Presentation

24 ***Research Skills*** Use the Internet and other resources to gather information about religions in Northern Europe and how they have changed throughout the centuries. Create a multimedia presentation to share your findings. WHST9–10.6, WHST9–10.7

Writing About Geography

25 ***Informative/Explanatory*** Use standard grammar, spelling, sentence structure, and punctuation to write a one-page essay discussing current population trends in Northern Europe, including birthrates, life expectancy, and international migration. WHST9–10.2

Need Extra Help?

If You've Missed Question	14	15	16	17	18	19	20	21	22	23	24	25
Go to page	251	251	260	255	243	242	242	248	266	266	258	259

266

Critical Thinking

14 Folding and faulting caused by plate tectonics formed the landforms of Svalbard and caused Norway's strongest earthquake to occur there in 2009. Tectonic activity caused by the separation of the Eurasian and North American tectonic plates provides a great deal of geothermal energy to Iceland, which is situated on these two plates. This also causes Iceland to have about 200 volcanoes as well as many hot springs and geysers.

15 As glaciers melted, they left behind many bodies of water. The energy of these bodies of water can be harnessed for hydroelectric power.

16 Paragraphs should demonstrate knowledge that the Nordic model references a mixed economy in which the government establishes welfare policies to protect the social and economic health of its citizens. Labor force participation and fiscal expansion are encouraged. Low barriers to trade and support of union membership lower the risk of participating in an open economy.

17 In some areas, fjords, coasts, and mountainous terrain formed natural boundaries, which resulted in isolated independent communities.

Applying Map Skills

18 The following countries of Northern Europe lie within the Arctic Circle: Iceland, Norway, Sweden, and Finland.

19 Norway has a higher elevation than Finland, which is mostly at sea level.

20 The countries of Northern Europe are bordered by the Baltic Sea, the North Sea, the Norwegian Sea, the Greenland Sea, and the Barents Sea.

Exploring the Essential Question

21 The flowchart should show that the process started with small earthquakes followed by more intense earthquakes, which became more frequent before eventually culminating in the eruption of Eyjafjallajökull. The explanation should show knowledge that the ash from the eruption impeded air traffic and resulted in many stranded passengers. This event demonstrated the effects that physical systems of a place can have on human systems even when they are far away from one another.

Analyzing Primary Sources

22 The Jeppesens are using a windmill to generate electricity without producing carbon dioxide.

23 Possible answer: The government could offer financial incentives, such as reimbursements, for use of clean, alternative energy sources.

Research and Presentation

24 The multimedia presentation should include major religions from Northern Europe's past up to present-day religions. A presentation would not be complete without mentioning Christianity, specifically the Protestant sect, as this is the dominant religion in every country of the subregion. The historical or social reasons for any change in each religion's popularity should also be conveyed.

Writing About Geography

25 The essay should provide an overview of current population trends in Northern Europe. There should be mention of current birthrates, average life expectancy, and international migration.

CHAPTER **11**

Northwestern Europe Planner

National Geography Standards covered in "Northwestern Europe"

The student knows and understands:

(3) How to analyze the spatial organizations of people, places, and environments on Earth's surface

(4) The physical and human characteristics of places

4.2 The interaction of physical and human systems result in the creation of and changes to places

(7) The physical processes that shape the patterns of Earth's surface

7.3 Physical processes interact over time to shape particular places on Earth's surface

(8) The characteristics and spatial distribution of ecosystems and biomes on Earth's surface

(9) The characteristics, distribution, and migration of human populations on Earth's surface

9.2 Population distribution and density are a function of historical, environmental, economic, political, and technological factors

9.3 Migration is one of the driving forces for shaping and reshaping the cultural and physical landscape of places and regions

(10) The characteristics, distribution, and complexity of Earth's cultural mosaics

10.3 Cultures change through convergence and/or divergence

(11) The patterns and networks of economic interdependence on Earth's surface

11.2 Patterns exist in the spatial organization of economic activities

11.3 Economic systems are dynamic organizations of interdependent economic activities for production, exchange, distribution, and consumption of goods and services

(14) How human actions modify the physical environment

14.1 Human modifications of the physical environment can have significant global impacts.

14.2 The use of technology can have unintended impacts on the physical environment which may be positive or negative.

(15) How physical systems affect human systems

15.3 Societies use a variety of strategies to adapt to changes in the physical environment.

(16) The changes that occur in the meaning, use, distribution, and importance of resources

16.3 Policies and programs that promote the sustainable use and management of resources impact people and the environment.

UNDERSTANDING BY DESIGN®

Enduring Understandings

- *Cooperation and conflict among people influence the division and control of Earth's surface.*

Essential Question

- *How do physical systems and human systems shape a place?*

Predictable Misunderstandings

Students may think:

- *Most Northwestern European countries are landlocked. Explain that many Northwestern European countries have port cities and most of Europe lies within 300 miles (483 km) of a seacoast.*
- *Only French people live in France, only German people live in Germany, and so on. Explain that migration and immigration have affected all countries in Northwestern Europe. Many of these countries have large populations of residents that are not originally from the country.*

Assessment Evidence

Performance Tasks:

- *Hands-On Chapter Project*

Other Evidence:

- *Guided Reading Activities*
- *Vocabulary Activities*
- *Lesson Quizzes*
- *Chapter Tests, Forms A and B*

SUGGESTED PACING GUIDE

Introducing the Chapter .... ½ Day	Case Study .... 1 Day
Lesson 1 .... 1 Day	Lesson 3 .... 1 Day
Lesson 2 .... 2 Days	Chapter Wrap-Up and Assessment ...... ½ Day

TOTAL TIME 6 Days

Key for Using the Teacher Edition

SKILL-BASED ACTIVITIES

Types of skill activities found in the Teacher Edition.

* **V Visual Skills** require students to analyze maps, graphs, charts, and photos.

R Reading Skills help students practice reading skills and master vocabulary.

C Critical Thinking Skills help students apply and extend what they have learned.

W Writing Skills provide writing opportunities to help students comprehend the text.

T Technology Skills require students to use digital tools effectively.

*Letters are followed by a number when there is more than one of the same type of skill on the page.

DIFFERENTIATED INSTRUCTION

All activities are written for the on-level student unless otherwise marked with the leveled labels below.

BL Beyond Level

AL Approaching Level

ELL English Language Learners

All students benefit from activities that utilize different learning styles. Many activities are marked as below when a particular learning style is highlighted.

Intrapersonal	**Naturalist**
Logical/Mathematical	**Kinesthetic**
Visual/Spatial	**Auditory/Musical**
Verbal/Linguistic	**Interpersonal**

CHAPTER OPENER PLANNER

Students will know:
- *the importance of various landforms, including water sources, to Northwestern Europe.*
- *how urbanization and industrialization have shaped population patterns.*
- *the basis of economic activities in the region.*
- *the reasons for and the effects of the creation of the European Union.*
- *the threats posed by pollution, acid rain, and human activities and how they are being addressed.*

Students will be able to:
- ***describe*** *the physical geography of Northwestern Europe.*
- ***explain*** *the importance of water in Northwestern Europe.*
- ***describe*** *economic activities in Northwestern Europe.*
- ***explain*** *why the European Union was created and the results.*
- ***describe*** *environmental problems and possible solutions.*

UNDERSTANDING BY DESIGN®

☑ Print Teaching Options

V Visual Skills
- ☐ **p. 268** Students discuss what it might be like to live in a city or country with an extensive train system.

R Reading Skills
- ☐ **p. 268** Students plan a route from one end of Paris to another using a map of the Paris Metro subway system.

C Critical Thinking Skills
- ☐ **p. 268** Students discuss transportation in a megacity.
- ☐ **p. 269** Students make a flowchart to show the relationship between gentrification, deindustrialization, and population density.  **Logical/Mathematical**

W Writing Skills
- ☐ **p. 269** Students write a few paragraphs explaining what they think would be a good solution to the problems caused by the Metro's outdated design. **Verbal/Linguistic**

☑ Online Teaching Options

C Critical Thinking Skills
- **INTERACTIVE IMAGE** **Paris the Megacity**—Students compare challenges of growth in Paris with growth in a U.S. megacity. **Visual/Spatial, Verbal/Linguistic**
- **MAP** **Interactive Regional Atlas**—Students use the interactive regional atlas to understand the physical and human geography of Northwestern Europe.
- **TIME LINE** **The Rise of Northwestern Europe**—Students use the interactive time line to learn more about the region's human geography.

☑ Printable Digital Worksheets
- **WORKSHEET** **Assessing Background Knowledge**—Determine the level of prior knowledge students have about Northwestern Europe.
- **WORKSHEET** **Chapter Summaries**—Students review the main idea of each lesson of the chapter content.
- **WORKSHEET** **Vocabulary Activity**—Students apply their knowledge of content and academic vocabulary words.

Project-Based Learning

Hands-On

Debate Issues of Northwestern Europe
Students will debate a chosen topic that affects the region as a whole, by providing the pros and cons of the topic.

Digital Hands-On

Create Online Projects
Find an additional activity online that incorporates technology for this project. Visit the EdTech Teacher Web sites for more links, tutorials, and other resources.

Print Resources

ANCILLARY RESOURCES
This ancillary is available for every chapter and lesson.
- **Chapter Tests and Lesson Quizzes**

PRINTABLE DIGITAL WORKSHEETS
These printable digital worksheets are available for every chapter and lesson.
- **Assessing Background Knowledge**
- **Chapter Summaries**
- **Guided Reading Activities**
- **Hands-On Chapter Projects**
- **Quizzes and Tests**
- **Reading Essentials and Study Guide** AL
- **Reteaching Activities**
- **Video Activities**
- **Vocabulary**

More Media Resources

SUGGESTED VIDEOS 

- **Best of Europe Guide** (1 h. 56 min.)
- **The World Atlas: Europe Orients and Baltic** (1 h. 11 min.)
- **Europe's Most Beautiful Places** *World's Nature* (54 min.)

SUGGESTED READING 
- ***Rural Economy and Society in North-Western Europe, 500–2000: Making a Living. Family, Income and Labour,*** by Yannick Devos, Thijs Lambrecht, and E. Vanhaute
- ***The Birth of the West: Rome, Germany, France, and the Creation of Europe in the Tenth Century,*** by Paul Collins
- ***Europe's Immigration Challenge: Reconciling Work, Welfare and Mobility (Policy Network),*** by Grete Brochmann

LESSON 1 PLANNER

PHYSICAL GEOGRAPHY OF NORTHWESTERN EUROPE

Students will know:

- *the importance of the Northern European Plain to Northwestern Europe.*
- *the location and characteristics of the Alps, the Central Uplands, and the Western Uplands.*
- *how water plays a significant role in the lives of the people of Northwestern Europe.*
- *the factors that affect climate in Northwestern Europe.*

Students will be able to:

- ***identify** major landforms and their importance.*
- ***describe** the role water plays in the lives of people of Northwestern Europe.*
- ***identify** factors that affect climate in the region.*

UNDERSTANDING BY DESIGN®

Print Teaching Options

V Visual Skills

- [ ] **p. 272** Students discuss the role of dikes, polders, canals, and water pumps in reclaiming water from the sea.
- [ ] **p. 274** Students infer the dangers of coal mining.

R Reading Skills

- [ ] **p. 270** Students discuss the meaning of *loess.*
- [ ] **p. 272** Students infer how windmills changed life in the Netherlands. **ELL** **Visual/Spatial**
- [ ] **p. 273** Students make a list of questions to clarify the historical and economic importance of rivers in the region.

C Critical Thinking Skills

- [ ] **p. 270** Students locate and discuss what they know about iconic landforms in the region.
- [ ] **p. 270** Students discuss the climate in the Alps.
- [ ] **p. 271** Students research major European shipping ports and record their statistics in a chart. **AL** **Visual/Spatial**
- [ ] **p. 273** Students contrast the advantages of transporting by ship or by truck throughout Europe. **AL** **Visual/Spatial**

W Writing Skills

- [ ] **p. 273** Students write a one-page narrative that takes place in one of the climates described in the text. **Naturalist**
- [ ] **p. 274** Students write a persuasive essay in support of building new wind turbines. **Naturalist**

T Technology Skills

- [ ] **p. 270** Students create a virtual tour of Northwestern Europe's most noteworthy landforms. **Interpersonal**
- [ ] **p. 272** Students research major floods in the Netherlands in the last 100 years and brainstorm ways to prevent future flooding. **AL** **Interpersonal**
- [ ] **p. 273** Students compare photographs of the Alps to Salter's description. **Visual/Spatial, Interpersonal**
- [ ] **p. 274** Students research one of the main producers of hydroelectric power in Northwestern Europe and create presentations about a hydroelectric plant. **BL** **Verbal/Linguistic**

Online Teaching Options

V Visual Skills

- [ ] **INFOGRAPHIC** **Building Dikes and Polders**—Students create their own infographic about Amsterdam as a port in Europe. **BL** **Visual/Spatial, Interpersonal**

C Critical Thinking Skills

- [ ] **INTERACTIVE BELLRINGER** **Building Dikes and Polders**—Students analyze an infographic on dikes and polders to answer questions about the water systems of Northwestern Europe.
- [ ] **VIDEO** **Landmarks: Rhine River**—Students create a table to compare and contrast the geography along the Rhine with their own region. **ELL** **Naturalist, Visual/Spatial**
- [ ] **INTERACTIVE WHITEBOARD ACTIVITY** **Climates of Northwestern Europe** Students identify regions and climates in Northwestern Europe, and then drag the correct characteristics into a chart about each biome.

W Writing Skills

- [ ] **INTERACTIVE IMAGE** **The Alps and Northwestern Europe**—Students explore the physical features of Northwestern Europe and write a poem or song based on the emotions the image of the Matterhorn evokes in them. **Intrapersonal, Naturalist**

Printable Digital Worksheets

R Reading Skills

- [ ] **WORKSHEET** **Guided Reading Activity**—Students use the Guided Reading Activity worksheets to review their comprehension of the content.

C Critical Thinking Skills

- [ ] **WORKSHEET** **Video Activity**—Students answer questions related to a topic in the chapter content after they have viewed a lesson video.

HUMAN GEOGRAPHY OF NORTHWESTERN EUROPE

Students will know:

- *how the Industrial Revolution changed the human geography of Northwestern Europe.*
- *the causes and effects of the creation of the European Union.*
- *how urbanization and immigration have shaped the population patterns of Northwestern Europe.*
- *that economic activities in Northwestern Europe are based on a combination of manufacturing, service and technology, and agriculture.*

Students will be able to:

- ***analyze*** *changes in human geography due to the Industrial Revolution.*
- ***explain*** *the creation of the European Union and its effects.*
- ***identify*** *factors that have affected population patterns.*
- ***describe*** *the basis for economic activities in the region.*

UNDERSTANDING BY DESIGN®

☑ Print Teaching Options

V Visual Skills

- ☐ **p. 276** Students identify and draw possible trade routes from Europe to the Eastern Mediterranean on a political map. AL Visual/Spatial
- ☐ **p. 278** Students create a graphic that shows increasing and then declining population. BL Visual/Spatial
- ☐ **p. 279** Students find an example of Realism in the visual arts and write an essay describing the image. Visual/Spatial

R Reading Skills

- ☐ **p. 276** Students use word parts to understand *Enlightenment.* ELL Verbal/Linguistic
- ☐ **p. 278** Students summarize how urbanization has affected population patterns. AL Verbal/Linguistic
- ☐ **p. 279** Students discuss the importance of female leaders.

C Critical Thinking Skills

- ☐ **p. 275** Students hold roundtable discussions on the historical and current influence of religion on society. BL Logical/Mathematical
- ☐ **p. 276** Students work in pairs to create a short skit about how the Industrial Revolution created industrial capitalism and gave rise to communism. Kinesthetic, Interpersonal
- ☐ **p. 278** Students discuss the advantages and disadvantages of inviting guest workers to a country. Logical/Mathematical, Interpersonal
- ☐ **p. 279** Students compare and contrast samples of related and unrelated languages. Auditory/Musical
- ☐ **p. 281** Students discuss how the size of Northwestern Europe plays a role in its transportation and communications infrastructure. AL Visual/Spatial

W Writing Skills

- ☐ **p. 277** Students write an argument either in favor or against joining the EU. BL Logical/Mathematical

T Technology Skills

- ☐ **p. 280** Students research and present on a tourist destination in Northwestern Europe. BL Visual/Spatial

☑ Online Teaching Options

V Visual Skills

- INTERACTIVE BELLRINGER **Public Expenditures in Select European Countries**—Students explore how much Northwestern European countries spend on education and health care and compare it to the United States. Verbal/Linguistic, Visual/Spatial
- TIME LINE **The Rise of Northwestern Europe**—Students discuss how the events on the time line relate to conflict, war, and religious beliefs. AL Verbal/Linguistic
- INTERACTIVE GRAPH **Jewish Population in Europe Before and After World War II**—Students discuss the graph and how the Jewish population changed. AL Logical/Mathematical, Visual/Spatial
- VIDEO **France Public Veil Ban**—Students discuss the veil ban and ethnic issues that arise through the process of immigration and population patterns. BL Verbal/Linguistic

C Critical Thinking Skills

- GAME **Human Geography of Northwestern Europe**—Students play an identification game and discuss the role of women in society in Northwestern Europe. ELL Interpersonal
- INTERACTIVE MAP **European Union Member Countries**—Students use the map to compare and contrast economies of Northwestern Europe to economies of Northern Europe and explore the role geography has made in economic development. BL Visual/Spatial, Verbal/Linguistic
- INTERACTIVE WHITEBOARD ACTIVITY **Population Density in Northwestern Europe**—Students identify the population density of cities in Northwestern Europe.

☑ Printable Digital Worksheets

R Reading Skills

- WORKSHEET **Guided Reading Activity**—Students use Guided Reading Activity worksheets to review their comprehension of the content.
- WORKSHEET **Reading Essentials and Study Guide**—Students complete the study guide and answer Reading Progress Check and vocabulary questions. AL

C Critical Thinking Skills

- WORKSHEET **Video Activity**—Students answer questions related to a topic in the chapter content after they have viewed a lesson video.

PEOPLE AND THEIR ENVIRONMENT: NORTHWESTERN EUROPE

UNDERSTANDING BY DESIGN®

Students will know:
- *the threats posed to wildlife and wildlife habitats in Northwestern Europe.*
- *the causes of water pollution in Northwestern Europe.*
- *the causes of air pollution in Northwestern Europe.*
- *how acid rain has affected areas of Northwestern Europe.*
- *the ways in which human activities have affected marine and coastal ecosystems in Northwestern Europe.*

Students will be able to:
- ***identify** threats to wildlife and their habitats in the region.*
- ***identify** causes of water and air pollution in Northwestern Europe*
- ***analyze** the effects of acid rain on Northwestern Europe.*
- ***describe** effects of human activities on marine and coastal ecosystems in the region.*

☑ Print Teaching Options

V Visual Skills

- ☐ **p. 285** Students discuss overfishing. AL Visual/Spatial

R Reading Skills

- ☐ **p. 286** Students discuss acid deposition. ELL Verbal/Linguistic
- ☐ **p. 288** Students design a cap-and-trade game in which players represent countries. Visual/Spatial

C Critical Thinking Skills

- ☐ **p. 284** Students make a list of environmental issues facing Northwestern Europe. AL Visual/Spatial
- ☐ **p. 285** Students categorize examples of pollution and overuse of land or water. Logical/Mathematical
- ☐ **p. 286** Students discuss how the geography of Northwestern Europe contributes to acid deposition. AL Naturalist
- ☐ **p. 287** Students discuss their feelings on the cap-and-trade system. Verbal/Linguistic
- ☐ **p. 288** Students evaluate the World Wide Fund for Nature as a source. Logical/Mathematical
- ☐ **p. 288** Students discuss why some may disagree with local governments in the United Kingdom forwarding fines imposed by the EU on to local offenders. AL Interpersonal

W Writing Skills

- ☐ **p. 285** Students write a letter to a town council arguing against building a new road to connect two existing freeways due to its environmental impact. BL Verbal/Linguistic

T Technology Skills

- ☐ **p. 284** Students research the issue of invasive species. Naturalist
- ☐ **p. 286** Students research a specific EU environmental protection law and find a U.S. or local state law to compare it to. Visual/Spatial, Verbal/Linguistic
- ☐ **p. 287** Students research an alternative form of energy and create a short visual presentation about it. BL Visual/Spatial

☑ Online Teaching Options

V Visual Skills

- ☐ INTERACTIVE IMAGE **Addressing Environmental Issues**—Students design a poster for an upcoming environmental protest as if they were an exchange student from one of the Northwestern European countries that has a severe environmental pollution problem. ELL Intrapersonal

C Critical Thinking Skills

- ☐ INTERACTIVE BELLRINGER **Commercial Fishing Stocks**—Students discuss overfishing and safe limits of commercial fishing stocks in Northwestern Europe. AL Naturalist, Interpersonal
- ☐ VIDEO **Water Pollution**—Students discuss the global impact of water pollution, listing causes, concerns, and solutions. BL Logical/Mathematical
- ☐ INTERACTIVE MAP **Oxygen Depletion in Coastal Marine Ecosystems**—Students work in groups to research a Northwestern European country's efforts to lower its oxygen depletion. Logical/Mathematical, Visual/Spatial
- ☐ INTERACTIVE WHITEBOARD ACTIVITY **Causes and Effects in the Environment**—Students complete a cause-and-effect chart showing the impact humans have had on the environment in Northwestern Europe.

☑ Printable Digital Worksheets

R Reading Skills

- ☐ WORKSHEET **Guided Reading Activity**—Students use Guided Reading Activity worksheets to review their comprehension of the content.
- ☐ WORKSHEET **Reading Essentials and Study Guide**—Students complete the study guide and answer Reading Progress Check and vocabulary questions. AL

C Critical Thinking Skills

- ☐ WORKSHEET **Video Activity**—Students answer questions based on a lesson video.
- ☐ WORKSHEET **Reteaching Activity**—Students use this activity worksheet to review and reteach chapter content and vocabulary. This worksheet can be used with struggling students who need additional help with difficult content concepts.

INTERVENTION AND REMEDIATION STRATEGIES

LESSON 1 Physical Geography of Northwestern Europe

Reading and Comprehension

Have students work in pairs to create an outline using the lesson's headings and subheadings. As partners gather information from each section, have them note key ideas and details under each heading. Encourage students to illustrate their outlines to illustrate each content vocabulary term. For example, students may wish to draw a picture of an avalanche under their outline subheading *Climate Regions and Biomes*. Or they may choose to use a graphic organizer like the one on the Lesson Opener to organize information about the influences on climate in Northwestern Europe. Ask volunteers to present their outlines to the class.

Text Evidence

Assign student groups a region or country in Northwestern Europe discussed in this lesson. Tell groups they will create a travel brochure about their region that answers one of the Guiding Questions in the lesson. For example, students may include information about interesting landforms such as the Alps in a brochure that answers the first Guiding Question: *How did the Northern European Plain affect the development of Europe?* Students should use simple sketches and phrases to describe the region's physical features and a list of reasons tourists might want to visit. Students may wish to conduct additional research about their region to give them ideas for their brochures. After students present their brochures, guide a class discussion about what makes the physical geography of the region unique.

LESSON 2 Human Geography of Northwestern Europe

Reading and Comprehension

To help students comprehend the complex history of countries in Northwestern Europe, assign student pairs one of the content vocabulary terms from the lesson. Have partners work together to identify the term's meaning. Then have students conduct research using print or online sources to find out more about their topic. Tell students to write a short summary of the information and present it to the class. Ask students if they have any questions about their topic that was not answered in their research. Guide a class discussion to provide clarification if necessary.

Text Evidence

To ensure that students have a firm grasp of lesson content, have them create a "living" time line of the lesson. Assign small groups a heading or subheading from the lesson. Have students work as a group to gather key facts about their topic, suggesting that each student in the group write one summarizing sentence. After students have had time to prepare their sentences, organize groups in sequential order, according to the order of the headings and subheadings. Then have students in each group recite their sentences.

LESSON 3 People and Their Environment: Northwestern Europe

Reading and Comprehension

Assign student groups one of the challenges discussed in this lesson such as management of natural resources, pollution, overfishing, and the struggle to maintain economic independence in the region. Have students in each group work together to summarize the problems related to their topic and how or if the problems are being addressed or solved. Students may wish to conduct online research to provide sufficient evidence in support of claims made in their summaries. Encourage students to use content vocabulary terms in their summaries.

Text Evidence

Have students write a paragraph that answers the Guiding Question: *How has modern development resulted in challenges to the management of resources in Northwestern Europe?* Call on volunteers to share their paragraphs. Then guide a class discussion to reinforce students' understanding. Discuss the fragile balance between managing development and resources and preserving the natural environment of Northwestern Europe's land and water. Have students identify a statement in the text that supports economic development and one that supports environmental protection. Remind students that identifying signal words such as *however, the result of,* and *consequences* can help them find opposing facets of an issue. Have students share their statements with the class.

Online Resources

Leveled Reader

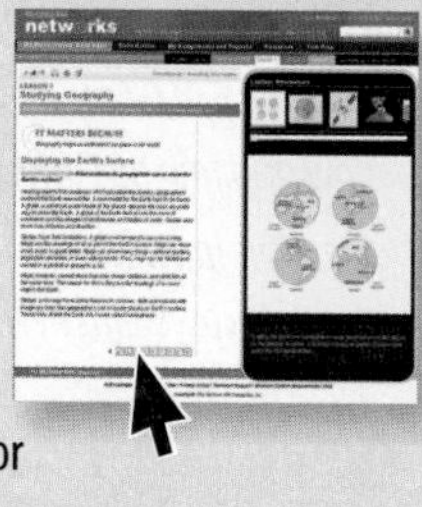

Use this online approaching-level text that corresponds directly to the text in the Student Edition. It also includes additional reading and comprehension support for English Language Learners.

Guided Reading Activities

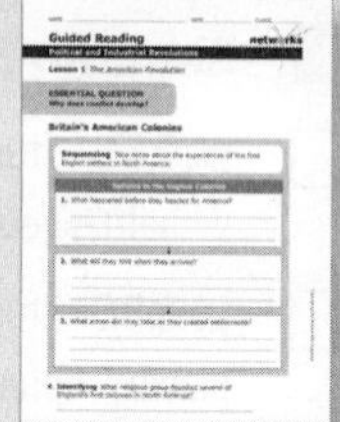

This resource uses guiding questions to help students with comprehension.

Reteaching Activities

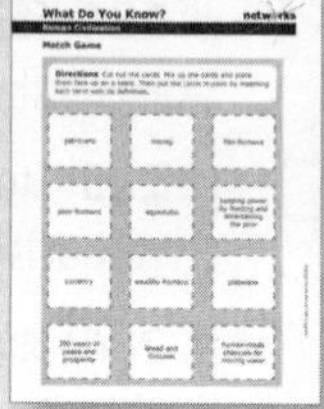

These worksheets provide students with an opportunity for remedial practice and review of vital chapter content.

Reading Essentials and Study Guide

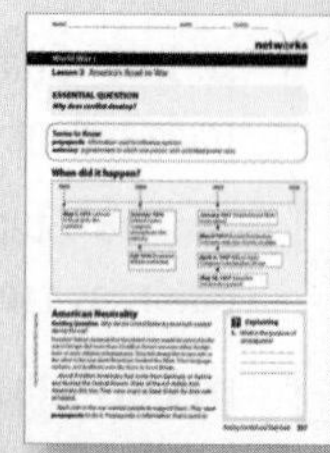

This resource offers writing and reading activities for the approaching-level student.

Self-Check Quizzes

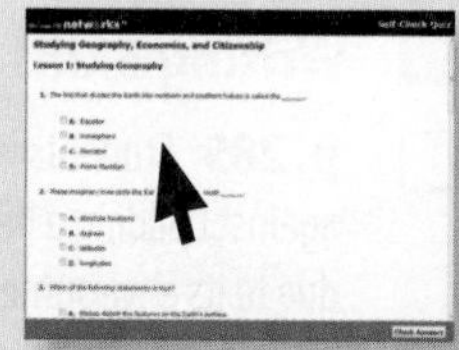

This online assessment tool provides instant feedback for students to check their progress.

Chapter Summaries

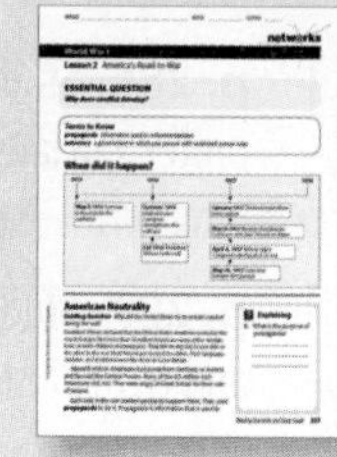

Summaries are provided for each chapter that thoroughly condense core content into manageable chunks.

Northwestern Europe

ESSENTIAL QUESTION • *How do physical systems and human systems shape a place?*

networks

There's More Online about Northwestern Europe.

CHAPTER 11

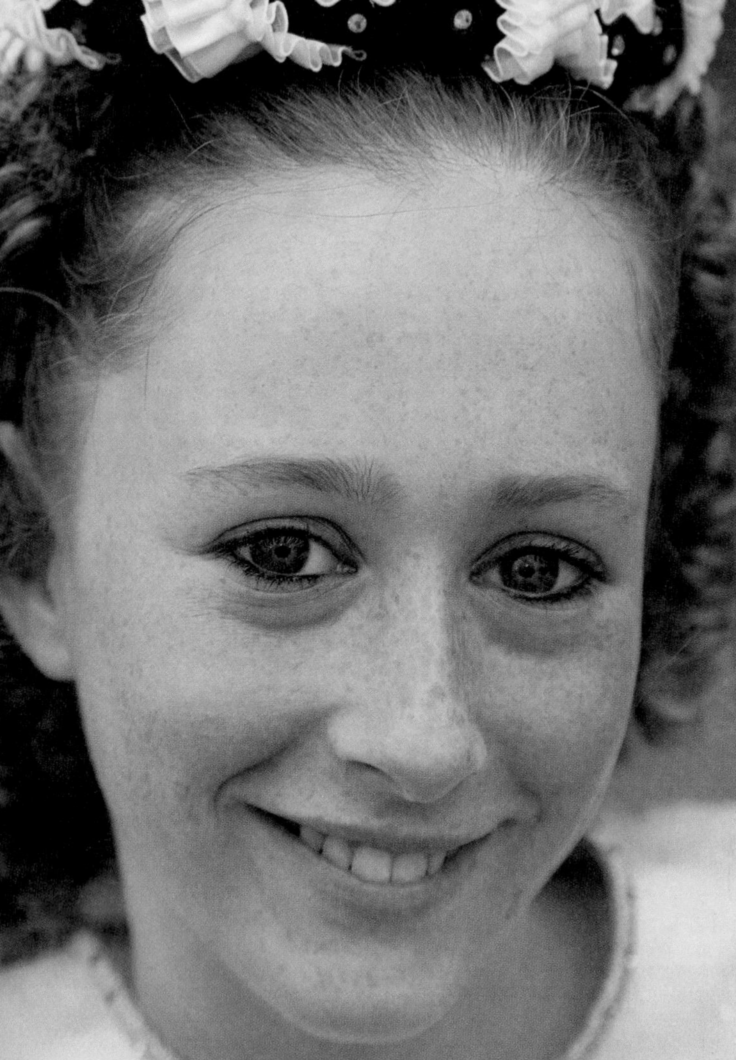

Geography Matters...

The countries of Northwestern Europe have long been at the crossroads of many cultures. There you will see a colorful mix of the old and the new. People in the subregion enjoy a higher standard of living than many other subregions. This is reflected in high levels of education, long life expectancies, and industrialized economies. The people of Northwestern Europe include an ethnic mix. Some countries are made up of two or more ethnicities that have blended over the centuries. Switzerland, for example, has three official languages.

◀ A young girl from Ireland is dressed for traditional folk dancing.

Vidler Steve/age fotostock

267

Letter from the Author

Dear Geography Teacher,

An interesting juxtaposition in Northwestern Europe is the North Sea and the countries surrounding it. The British and Norwegians might see the North Sea as a resource bonanza with substantial oil and natural gas reserves. Several countries see the North Sea as a source of fish, a potential problem with pollution, and a focus of attempts to limit further degradation of marine life and coastal ecosystems. Because of the ravages of monster storms combined with Dutch land below sea level protected by man-made dikes, the people of the Netherlands view it as a threat to everyday life. Therefore, here we have a geographical feature that means different things to different people.

Richard G. Boehm

ENGAGE

Activating Prior Knowledge Before beginning the chapter, invite students to list what they know about Northwestern Europe. Then have them scan the photographs and maps throughout the chapter to add to their lists. Have students share their lists to create a class list. Discuss the items that were common to many of the students' lists and why they are well known.

TEACH & ASSESS

Making Connections

Call students' attention to the information about Paris, France:

- France is the most visited tourist destination in the world with upwards of 70 million visitors a year.
- Three-quarters of the visitors to France each year come from other European countries. The largest number come from Britain, followed by Germany.
- Destinations such as the Louvre and the Eiffel Tower in Paris continually attract more visitors than any other area in France.

Inferring Have students consider what draws visitors to France. **Ask:** **What would you be most interested in visiting in France?** *(Possible answers: art museums, restaurants and street cafes, shops, watching the Tour de France bike race)* Have volunteers research other tourist attractions in France. Have small groups put together a visual tour of France to share with the class. **BL** **Intrapersonal**

CLOSE & REFLECT

Predicting Have students predict what topics the chapter will explore. Discuss the different countries that are included in Northwestern Europe, their different cultures, and how geography and people can shape a place. For example, discuss how people have migrated to Paris for centuries and have shaped the city and its culture.

ePals GlobalCommunity
Where learners connect™

Extend the project-based learning experience globally through our partnership with ePals. EPals allows you to connect with classrooms around the world in a safe online environment for real-life lessons and projects in virtual study groups.

ENGAGE

R Reading Skills

Describing Have students use a map of the Paris Metro subway system to determine how to travel from one end of Paris to another via the subway. Tell them they must choose a start point and an end point and use at least three different metro lines to arrive at their destination. Have them map out their route.

TEACH & ASSESS

V Visual Skills

Analyzing Visuals Direct students to study the photograph of the trains. **Ask:** **What can you tell about transportation in Paris and France based on the photograph?** *(Possible answer: The trains are a major component of mass transit in Paris and in France.)* **What can you infer about the trains in the photograph based on their appearance?** *(Possible answer: They look very modern and fast.)* Have students discuss what it might be like to live in a city or country with an extensive train system. **Ask:** **How would your life be different if you lived in a city of 11 million people with a large train system?** *(Students may comment about how they would be able to do more things and go more places because they could get to places on their own by taking the train.)* **Visual/Spatial**

C Critical Thinking Skills

Identifying Central Issues Have students discuss transportation in a megacity. **Ask:** **What may be some of the challenges, in addition to transportation, that a megacity like Paris faces?** *(Possible answers: having enough housing, jobs, and providing basic services to its residents)* **How does a transit system, like the Paris Metro system, help to alleviate the transportation problem in a megacity?** *(Possible answers: Trains can move large numbers of people quickly. Public transportation such as trains and subways reduces congestion and the need for larger numbers of cars and trucks that pollute the environment.)* **Verbal/Linguistic**

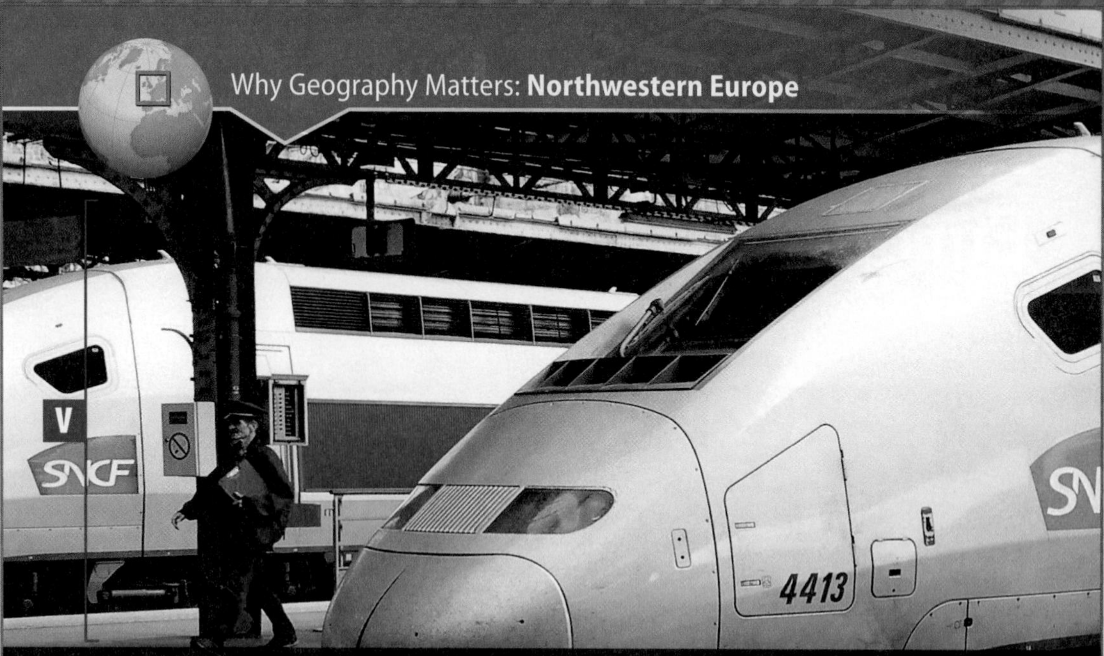

Why Geography Matters: **Northwestern Europe**

SNCF

4413

suburban growth and transportation

With a population approaching 11 million, Paris is a megacity. Since 1921 its growth has been primarily in the suburbs, while the urban core's population has dropped. Providing effective transportation for surburban populations is an ongoing challenge. Important to meeting this challenge is understanding the city's geography.

THERE'S MORE ONLINE

READ a news article about suburbanization in Paris • *SEE* a map of Paris's population density

268

Project-Based Learning

Hands-On

Debate Issues of Northwestern Europe

Students will engage in debates that bring together information from all lessons about how current affairs impact the physical, environmental, and human geography of Northwestern Europe.

Digital Hands-On

Create Online Projects

Find an additional activity online that incorporates technology for this project. Visit the EdTech Teacher Web sites for more links, tutorials, and other resources.

What is fueling suburban growth in Paris?

Various factors contribute to suburban growth in Paris. Housing prices have risen dramatically in the urban core. This is largely a result of gentrification, a process in which older areas of a city are revived by wealthier residents. This has caused many people to look for more affordable housing in locations outside the city. Deindustrialization has also occurred in the urban core, a process in which older manufacturing industries shut down. Also, many housing units have been converted into office space. These two processes have led residents to migrate to suburbs to find new jobs and places to live. G1

1. **Human Systems** What trends have contributed to the population growth in the Paris suburbs while the urban core population has declined?

How does this affect transportation needs in Paris?

The Paris Metro subway system has served the city since 1900 and is considered one of the world's finest. The Metro trains are both fast and frequent. However, as population growth has shifted from the urban core to the suburbs, the geographic pattern of the Metro has presented problems. Rail lines have been built to connect the city to the suburbs in a "hub and spoke" arrangement. This makes travel between suburbs and city easier, but rail travel across the region typically requires a trip into the urban core to change trains. This takes extra time, and residents increasingly use automobiles to commute, causing significant congestion. Official campaigns to discourage daily automobile use have not had much success because, even with reduced traffic congestion, it can still be more efficient to drive than to take the train. W

2. **Places and Regions** How has this population shift affected the transportation needs of Paris's residents?

How is Paris responding to these needs?

The Paris Metro system is slated for a significant upgrade aimed at serving the growing suburban population and alleviating traffic problems mainly caused by commuters. A highlight of the planned system expansion (the Metro Grand Paris Plan) is a 96-mile (154.5-km) automated rail line linking suburban areas and connecting to existing Metro lines. Transportation planners think that the suburb-to-suburb expansion of the Metro system will eliminate needless trips to the city center. They also predict that the fast travel times on the new lines will encourage travelers to use the Metro system rather than automobiles. G2

3. **Physical Systems** How are transportation planners responding to regional travelers' needs?

(l)Egon Bömsch/Alamy, (cl)Bernard Rouffignac/Photononstop/Getty Images, (c)Grant Faint/Photographer's Choice/Getty Images, (cr)©William Ryall 2007

G1 Critical Thinking Skills

Identify Cause and Effect Have students make a flowchart to show how gentrification and deindustrialization are related to population density in the suburbs of Paris. Ask them to identify each cause and its effect in the flowchart.
BL Logical/Mathematical

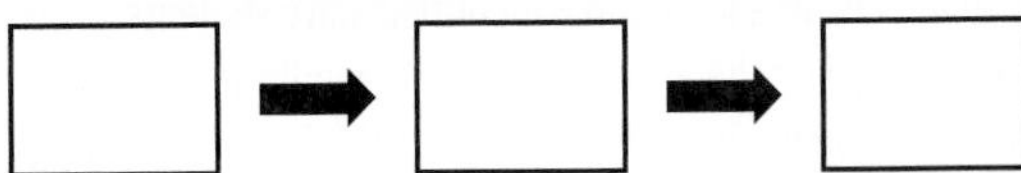

W Writing Skills

Informative/Explanatory After students have read about the problems caused by the Metro's outdated design, ask them to research solutions to the problem other than building all new rail lines to connect the suburbs. Have students write two or three paragraphs explaining what they think would be a better solution to the problem. Verbal/Linguistic

G2 Critical Thinking Skills

Decision Making Have students think about how decisions are made concerning the placement of the new metro line.
Ask: What factors might be considered when building a new train line? *(Possible answers: how many people will use it, where people live, where they are coming from, and where they are going)* Logical/Mathematical

CLOSE & REFLECT

Summarizing Review how suburban growth has affected the city of Paris. Discuss how the changing demographics require a changing infrastructure. Review ways in which people's daily lives are affected by the lack of mass transportation to the cities in the suburbs and the effects changes to the train system could have.

INTERACTIVE IMAGE

Paris the Megacity

Comparing Use this image of Paris to ask students to consider what possible challenges rapid growth in the city of Paris may cause its inhabitants. Have them compare these challenges with growth in a United States megacity, such as New York or Chicago. Then have students write three possible challenges that people living in Paris may face and how these challenges compare with those in a United States megacity. Challenges should include transportation, cultural identity, and employment opportunities. Later in the chapter have students review what they wrote to see if there are other challenges they could include. Visual/Spatial, Verbal/Linguistic

ANSWERS, p. 269

Why Geography Matters

1. Rising housing prices, a result of gentrification, have pushed people to look for more affordable housing in the suburbs. Deindustrialization of the urban core has also forced people to follow jobs to the suburbs.
2. Residents of Parisian suburbs who don't consistently need to travel to the city are no longer satisfied by the original rail system's design that served to connect the suburbs only to the city center. There is now a need to save time by avoiding the city when traveling to a different part of town or to a different region.
3. They are planning an upgrade to the Paris Metro system to include fast lines between suburbs, which will eliminate needless trips to the city center.

ENGAGE

G1 Critical Thinking Skills

Categorizing Have students reference a physical map of Northwestern Europe. Ask them to locate the Seine River and the Alps. Then have them look for other iconic landforms in this subregion. As a landform is identified, have students discuss what they already know about the landform and how and why it stands out for them. Continue this activity, allowing several students to participate.

TEACH & ASSESS

R Reading Skills

Defining Discuss the meaning of the term *loess*. **Ask: Why would the deposits of sediment left behind by glaciers be rich and fertile?** *(As glaciers moved across the land, they collected sediment and other debris that was then deposited along the sides or the front of the glacier as the ice melted. These deposits contained top soil and were rich in nutrients and minerals.)* Have students consult a dictionary to explore the origin of the word *loess*. **ELL Verbal/Linguistic**

C2 Critical Thinking Skills

Making Predictions Discuss the expected climate in the Alps. **Ask: What type of climate is most common in a mountain system?** *(The climate changes as elevation increases. The higher elevations will have snow in the mountains.)* **What can you predict about how the Alps affect the economies of Switzerland, Austria, and France?** *(Possible answer: The Alps contribute greatly to the economy because of tourism from skiers, hikers, and other visitors that want to see the scenery of the area.)* **BL Verbal/Linguistic**

T Technology Skills

Presenting Have students work in small groups to create a virtual tour of some of Northwestern Europe's most noteworthy landforms using presentation software. Ask them to include brief descriptions of each type of landform and to caption photos of actual landforms in their visual tours. Have groups present their visual tours to the class. **Interpersonal**

ANSWERS, p. 270

TAKING NOTES: Climate: Most of the subregion has a marine west coast climate. This means mild winters, cool summers, and a lot of rain; **Influences on Climate:** Air from above the warm North Atlantic Current warms the region. **Climate:** Snow covers the Alps; **Influences on Climate:** Moist Atlantic winds become cooled when they reach the high altitudes of the Alps.

networks
There's More Online!

- ☑ **IMAGE** The Alps of Northwestern Europe
- ☑ **INFOGRAPHIC** Netherlands' Reclaimed Lands: Polders
- ☑ **MAP** Gulf Stream Effects on Climates in High-Latitude Northern Europe
- ☑ **INTERACTIVE SELF-CHECK QUIZ**
- ☑ **VIDEO** Physical Geography of Northwestern Europe

LESSON 1
Physical Geography of Northwestern Europe

ESSENTIAL QUESTION • *How do physical systems and human systems shape a place?*

Reading HELPDESK

Academic Vocabulary (Tier Two Words)
- consist
- significant

Content Vocabulary (Tier Three Words)
- loess
- dike
- polder
- mistral
- foehn
- avalanche

TAKING NOTES: ***Key Ideas and Details***

PARAPHRASING Use a graphic organizer like the one below to take notes on the climate regions of Northwestern Europe.

Climate	Influences on Climate

IT MATTERS BECAUSE

Together, the United Kingdom, Ireland, France, the Netherlands, Belgium, Switzerland, Germany, Austria, Liechtenstein, Monaco, and Luxembourg make up the subregion known as Northwestern Europe. Within these countries lie some of Europe's most iconic landscapes, from the banks of the Seine River that runs through Paris to the jagged, awe-inspiring Alps.

Landforms

GUIDING QUESTION *How did the Northern European Plain affect the development of Europe?*

Northwestern Europe's landscape **consists** of plains interrupted by mountains. Scoured by Ice-Age glaciers, the Northern European Plain, or Great European Plain, is an area of relatively flat and low-lying land. It stretches from southeastern England and western France to central France and across Germany. The plain's fertile soil and wealth of rivers originally drew farmers to the area. The southern edge is especially fertile because it is covered by deposits of **loess**, a fine, rich, wind-borne sediment left by glaciers.

In contrast, the Alps are a high and jagged mountain range that lies to the south of the Northern European Plain. Created by the folding of the Earth's crust and shaped by glaciation, the Alps mountain system forms a crescent that runs from southern France through Switzerland and Austria to the Balkan Peninsula. Mont Blanc, the highest peak in the Alps, stands in France on the border with Italy at a height of 15,771 feet (4,807 m).

The Central Uplands lie between the Alps and the Northern European Plain—in parts of eastern France, southern Belgium, and southern Germany. This landform is made up of low rounded mountains, hills, and high plateaus with scattered forests. The Central Uplands are rich in natural resources.

The British Isles lie northwest of the mainland. They consist of the two large islands—Great Britain and Ireland—and thousands of smaller islands. The rugged coastline of the British Isles features rocky cliffs that

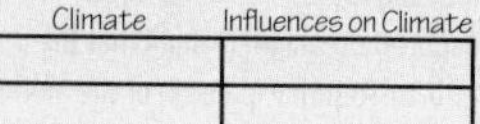

networks Online Teaching Options

INTERACTIVE BELLRINGER

Building Dikes and Polders

Interpreting Use the graphic and introductory text to discuss polders and how they protect the Netherlands from flooding from seawater. Ask students to discuss their prior knowledge of the Netherlands and its use of dikes to prevent flooding. Have students work with a partner to answer each question. Ask each pairs to write agreed-upon answers to the questions. Then in a class discussion, have students share their answers.
ELL Interpersonal, Verbal/Linguistic

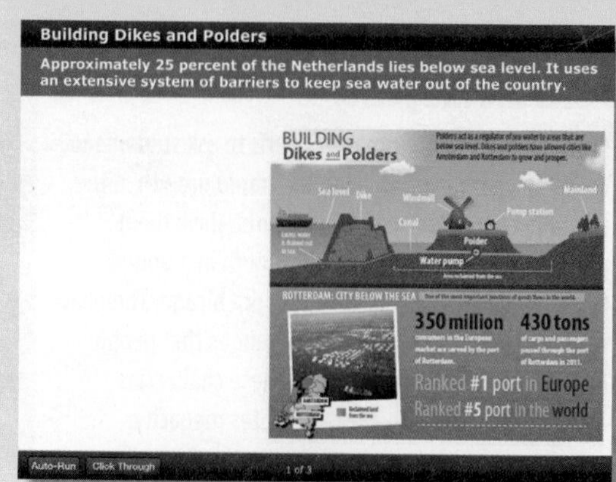

drop to deep bays. Mountains, plateaus, and valleys make up most of northern and western Great Britain. Low hills and rolling plains dominate in the south and in Ireland.

✓ READING PROGRESS CHECK

Explaining What makes the Northern European Plain good land for agriculture?

consist to be composed of or made up of

loess fine, yellowish, brownish topsoil made up of particles of silt and clay, carried and deposited by the wind

Water Systems

GUIDING QUESTION *How have the rivers in Europe's heartland contributed to the region's development?*

Water plays a crucial role in the lives and economic activities of many people who live in Northwestern Europe. Most of Northwestern Europe lies within 300 miles (483 km) of a sea or ocean coast, so ocean transportation is important. In addition, people here depend on the many rivers that flow across the subregion for transportation, trade, and recreational activities. **C**

The Alps are the location of major water sources. Eleven **significant** European lakes surround the Alps. Most are in valleys that were formed during the geological uplift of the Alps. They are long, narrow, deep lakes and have provided good places for people to settle because of water power for industry and convenient water routes for transportation. The spectacular scenery also makes the lake areas popular as tourist attractions.

significant important

In the Netherlands, water can be friend or foe. Approximately 25 percent of the country lies below sea level. There are extensive coastal dunes, but they have not always been helpful in keeping out the North Sea waters.

Mark Harris/Photodisc/Getty Images

V

The Alps are considered relatively young mountains in geologic terms.

◀ CRITICAL THINKING

1. ***Identifying Central Issues*** How do the Alps benefit the people of Northwestern Europe?
2. ***Speculating*** What features show that the Alps are relatively young?

INTERACTIVE IMAGE

The Alps and Northwestern Europe

Narrative Use this image of the Alps to discuss the physical features of Northwestern Europe. Have students identify any of the iconic features that they know in the interactive image. Then focus students' attention on the image of the Matterhorn. Explain that the Matterhorn has evoked inspirational emotions of strength and power to some, while others have seen majestic beauty. Ask students to write a poem, verse, song, or rap based on the emotions the image of the Matterhorn evokes in them. **Intrapersonal, Naturalist**

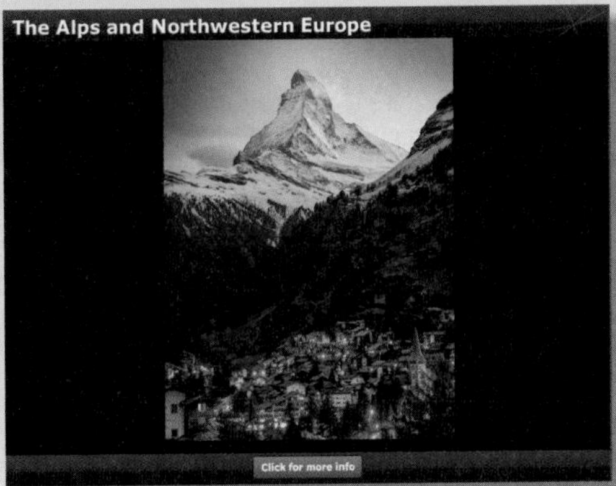

C Critical Thinking Skills

Acquiring Information Have students research major shipping ports in Europe. For each of the five major ports in this part of Europe, ask them to find basic statistics such as number of passengers or amount of cargo freight that passes through a port each year. Then have students record their statistics in a chart similar to the one below.

Country	Port	Statistics
Germany	Hamburg	131 million tons of cargo in 2012

AL Visual/Spatial

V Visual Skills

Analyzing Visuals The text refers to the long, narrow, deep lakes of the Alps as good places for people to settle because of water power and convenient transportation routes. Based on the photograph, discuss some of the disadvantages of living in this region. **Ask:** **What might be some of the practical challenges of living in the community shown in the photograph?** *(Possible answers: There is likely only one or two ways in or out of the community. There is little room for farming, so food must be shipped in from elsewhere. It is somewhat isolated.)* **What industry do you think many people that live in this community are likely involved in? What might their daily jobs be?** *(Possible answer: Many of them are likely involved in tourism or hydroelectric power. They may run hotels, resorts, restaurants, or work in hydroelectric power plants.)*

Content Background Knowledge

The Matterhorn The mountain in the photograph is the Matterhorn, located in Zermatt, Switzerland. It is one of the most recognizable mountains in the world. Zermatt itself is a car-free community. Only electric cars are allowed in the village. There are several car parks for visitors 5 kilometers away in the village of Täsch, from which one can travel to Zermatt by train. Nearly one-third of all the 4,000-meter-high peaks in the Alps are grouped around Zermatt—38 peaks. More than 3,000 people climb the Matterhorn every year.

ANSWERS, p. 271

✓ **READING PROGRESS CHECK** The plain's many rivers and fertile soil makes it good for agriculture. Loess deposits along the southern edge make it even more fertile.

CRITICAL THINKING

1. The Alps provide the region with major water sources. Lakes provide transportation and water power for industry. The Alps are also a major tourist attraction.
2. The jagged peaks show that the Alps are young because they haven't eroded or been smoothed by wind.

R Reading Skills

Inferring Point out that the Netherlands is well known for its tulips and dikes, as well as a third iconic object. Have students infer, based on the information about how polders were drained, what the third object is and discuss how this iconic image has likely affected the Netherlands. *(Power provided by windmills allowed the Dutch to reclaim land by draining the seawater. Even though they use other power sources now to run pumps to remove the water, the windmill is still associated with these polders and has contributed to the tourism industry in the country.)* **ELL** **Visual/Spatial**

V Visual Skills

Interpreting Direct students to the "Building Dikes and Polders" infographic. Have students work with a partner to discuss the role of the dikes, canals, polders, and water pumps in reclaiming land from the sea. Have them look at the map that shows the amount of land that has been reclaimed. **Ask: About what fraction of the Netherlands is land that was reclaimed from the sea?** *(about one-quarter)* **What risks are involved in living or working on a polder? Would you choose to live or work there considering the risks? Why or why not?** *(Possible answers: There is still a risk of flooding, which could devastate the area. Students may respond that they would choose to live or work there because the risk is small or that they would not choose to live or work there because the devastation would be too great.)* **Verbal/Linguistic**

T Technology Skills

Researching Have students work with a partner to research major floods in the Netherlands during the last 100 years. Ask them to find the causes of the floods and explore what changes were made to help prevent similar floods from happening again. Have them brainstorm in small groups other ways to enhance the dike system and prevent flooding.
AL **Interpersonal**

ANSWERS, p. 272

CRITICAL THINKING

1. Stone and earth were used to build the dikes that allowed the polders to form. Wood and stone were likely used to build the windmills that originally drained and kept dry the polders. Today pumps that have replaced the windmills are probably made from various types of metal and powered by fossil fuels.
2. The need to be able to benefit from the fertile soil that was being lost to the sea likely pushed the Dutch to seek a way to get it back.

---

dike large bank of earth and stone that holds back water

polder low-lying area from which seawater has been drained to create new land

R Since the Middle Ages, the Dutch have built **dikes**, or large banks of earth and stone, to hold back the water. With the dikes as protection, they have reclaimed land from the sea. These reclaimed lands, called **polders**, once were drained and kept dry by the use of windmills. Today, other power sources run pumps to remove water. Polders provide hundreds of thousands of acres of land for farming and settlement. Still, stormy seas have breached the dikes, creating devastating floods.

The rivers of Northwestern Europe have differing characteristics. Although relatively short, England's Thames River allows oceangoing ships to reach the port of London. On the European mainland, however, the relatively long rivers provide links between inland areas as well as to the sea. The Rhine River, the most important river in Northwestern Europe, flows from the Swiss Alps through France and Germany and into the Netherlands. It connects many industrial cities of the interior to the port of Rotterdam on the North Sea.

V

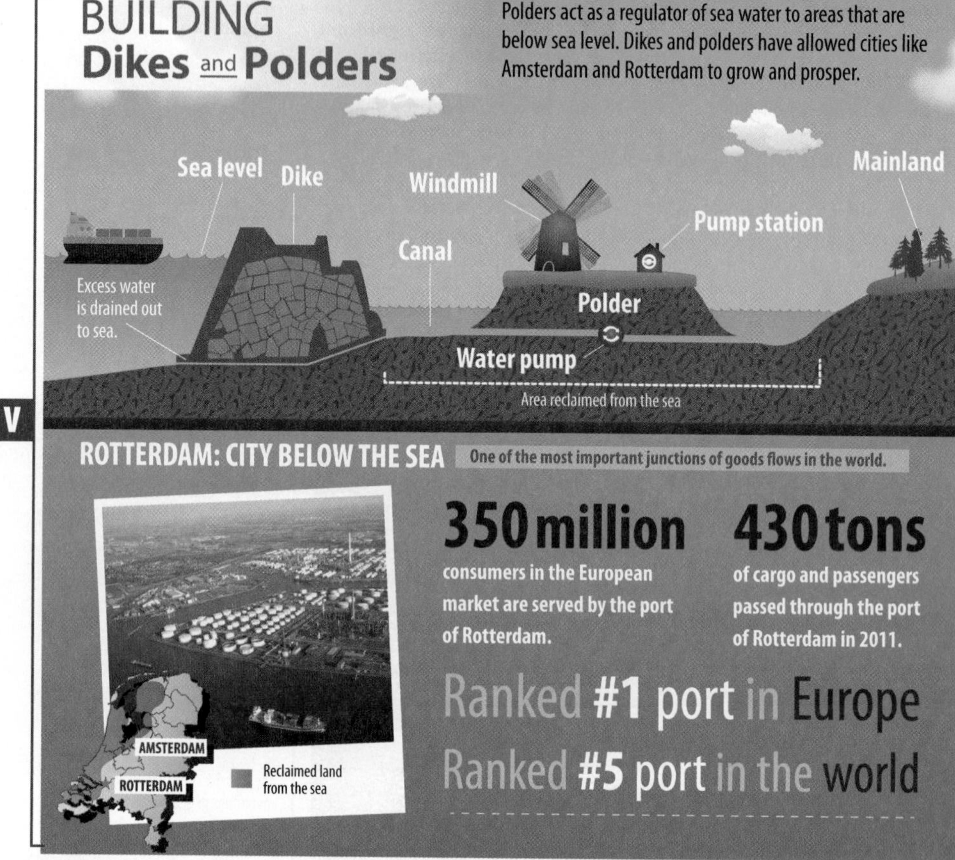

T Polders provide hundreds of thousands of acres for farming and settlement in the Netherlands, but the dikes built to protect them are no guarantee against flooding.

▲ **CRITICAL THINKING**

1. ***Synthesizing*** What natural resources were needed to create polders?
2. ***Drawing Conclusions*** What geographic factors pushed the Dutch—and enabled them—to reclaim so much land from the sea?

networks Online Teaching Options

INFOGRAPHIC

Polders and Dikes

Creating an Infographic Have students work with a partner to conduct online or library research about Amsterdam, another major port in Europe that is below sea level. Have them create an infographic of their own on Amsterdam's ranking as a port in Europe, its ranking as a port in the world, and the number of consumers in the European market that are served by the port of Amsterdam, including the number of tons of cargo and passengers that have passed through the port of Amsterdam in a recent year. Also have them include a photo of the port of Amsterdam. **BL** **Visual/Spatial, Interpersonal**

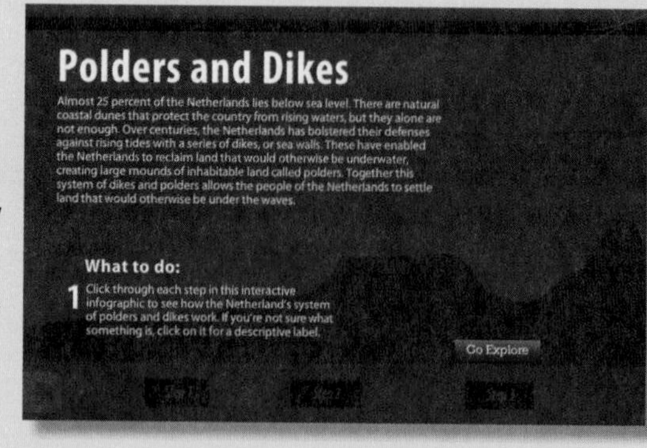

Polders and Dikes
Almost 25 percent of the Netherlands lies below sea level. There are natural coastal dunes that protect the country from rising waters, but they alone are not enough. Over centuries, the Netherlands has bolstered their defenses against rising tides with a series of dikes, or sea walls. These have enabled the Netherlands to reclaim land that would otherwise be underwater, creating large mounds of inhabitable land called polders. Together this system of dikes and polders allows the people of the Netherlands to settle land that would otherwise be under the waves.
What to do:
1 Click through each step in this interactive infographic to see how the Netherland's system of polders and dikes work. If you're not sure what something is, click on it for a descriptive label.
Go Explore

The Seine River, whose source is in central France, flows northwest through Paris and empties into the English Channel. It carries most of France's inland waterway traffic. The Loire River is the longest river in France. From its source in southern France, it flows north and then west before emptying into the Atlantic Ocean. Silting, shallowness, and fluctuations in volume throughout its course limit the use of the Loire for navigation. Canals connect the river with both the Seine and Rhône river systems. Important to conservationists and the environment, these systems form unique habitats for migratory birds.

The Rhône River begins in the Swiss Alps and flows through Switzerland and France. It is the only major river in the subregion that flows directly to the Mediterranean Sea. Important for hydroelectric power, the Rhône is 505 miles (813 km) long and has a drainage basin of 37,750 square miles (97,775 sq. km).

Another important European river that runs through the subregion is the Danube River. Both historically and economically important, the Danube River runs from southern Germany's Black Forest through Austria and into Eastern Europe. After flowing some 1,770 miles (2,850 km), it empties into the Black Sea.

✓ READING PROGRESS CHECK

Listing For what activities are Europe's waterways used?

Climate, Biomes, and Resources

GUIDING QUESTION *Why does most of Northwestern Europe have a generally mild climate?*

Several factors affect climate in Northwestern Europe. These factors include the presence of the Alps and the location of the subregion near or along large bodies of water. The winter storms that originate over the North Atlantic Ocean also affect Northwestern Europe's climate.

Climate Regions and Biomes

Northwestern Europe generally has a mild climate compared with other regions located at the same latitude. This results from the North Atlantic Current, a powerful warm-ocean current. It is warm because it is a continuation of the Gulf Stream that emerges from the tropical waters of the Caribbean. This warm water flows along the coast of Northwestern Europe and carries warm, maritime air that bathes the coasts and also blows far inland across the Northern European Plain.

When the moist Atlantic winds reach the Alps, the winds rise up the slopes and the temperature of the air cools. This cooling air produces snow that covers the mountains in winter. Local winds in a region sometimes cause changes in the normal weather pattern. For example, the **mistral**, a strong north wind from the Alps, can send gusts of bitterly cold air into southern France. At other times, dry winter winds called **foehns** (FUHRNS) blow down from the mountains into valleys and plains. Foehns can trigger **avalanches**, which are destructive masses of ice, snow, and rock sliding down mountainsides. Avalanches represent a serious natural hazard in the Alps. They destroy everything in their paths, threatening skiers, hikers, and villages.

As is the case anywhere, climate influences the distribution of biomes in Northwestern Europe. Most of the subregion has a marine west coast climate with mild winters, cool summers, and abundant rainfall. This type of climate produces soils that are often rich in humus—a material formed from decaying leaves and other organic matter that makes soil extremely fertile. A mild Mediterranean climate is found in Monaco, which enjoys an average annual temperature of 61°F (16°C) and receives about 60 days a year of rain.

Natural vegetation in Northwestern Europe includes varieties of deciduous and coniferous trees. Deciduous trees, or those that lose their leaves seasonally,

Analyzing CCSS
PRIMARY SOURCES

The Alps

"... I learned to ski in ... [t]he Alps, the great upper story of Europe. From the mountains, in all directions, flow mighty rivers, the Rhine, Rhône, Po, and Danube; a necklace of immortal cities lies in the surrounding foothills and plains. ... You are simultaneously in the center of civilization and the most majestic, thrilling wilderness. ... The timberline is relatively low; above the trees typically are meadows that for centuries have been used for summer grazing. There are few wild animals. ... These are [t]he Alps. High up, near the sky."

—James Salter, "The Alps," *National Geographic Traveler,* October 1999

DBQ ***ANALYZING PRIMARY SOURCES*** Why does Salter describe the Alps as being in the center of civilization and yet a wilderness? RH.9–10.1

mistral a strong northerly wind from the Alps that can bring cold air to southern France

foehn a dry wind that blows from the leeward sides of mountains, sometimes melting snow and causing avalanches; term used mainly in Europe

avalanche a large mass of ice, snow, and rock that slides down a mountainside

Physical Geography of Northwestern Europe

C Critical Thinking Skills

Contrasting Have students locate some of the rivers referred to in the text on a map. Point out that many of these rivers are used to transport cargo throughout Europe. Have them complete a Venn diagram to contrast the advantages of transporting by ship to the advantages of transporting by truck throughout Europe. Remind them to take into account the geography of many of the countries. AL **Visual/Spatial**

R Reading Skills

Questioning Rivers in Northwestern Europe are both historically and economically important. Have students make a list of specific questions that will help clarify the historical and economic importance of these rivers. AL **Verbal/Linguistic**

W Writing Skills

Narrative Have students imagine they or a character in a narrative are in one of the climates described. Have them write a one-page narrative that takes place in this climate. Although the narrative should follow a storyline, the main focus of the writing should include descriptive language about factors that affect and describe the climate in this setting. **Naturalist**

T Technology Skills

Examining Primary Sources Have students examine visual primary sources of the Alps in the form of online photographs. Have them discuss how Salter's description matches the visual images they have seen of the Alps. Have them look at a physical map of the Alps that includes cities and towns. **Ask:** **What does Salter mean by a "necklace of immortal cities"?** *(He is referring to how the cities and towns seem to form a ring, like a necklace, around the mountain peaks.)* Have students write their own personal reflection of the Alps based on some of the images they found. **Visual/Spatial, Intrapersonal**

VIDEO

Landmarks: Rhine River

Comparing and Contrasting Use this video about the Rhine River to discuss with students the physical landscape of Northwestern Europe. Provide a map that illustrates the course of the Rhine River and that lists the countries along its borders. Explain to students that water plays an important role in the lives of many Europeans. Working with a partner, ask students to create a table that compares and contrasts the geography along the Rhine River with their own region. ELL **Naturalist, Visual/Spatial**

ANSWERS, p. 273

✓ READING PROGRESS CHECK They are used for transportation, trade, recreation, and hydroelectric power.

DBQ There are major cities in the foothills surrounding the Alps; however, as people travel to higher elevations, they feel that they are more isolated from civilization.

V Visual Skills

Analyzing Visuals Have students analyze the photograph of the underground coal mine. Ask them to infer what the dangers of coal mining and extraction may be based on the photograph. Discuss the concept that because coal is easy to ship and burn, it is less expensive than other sources of energy and how economics and environmental concerns are locked in a battle as far as energy resources are concerned. **Visual/Spatial**

T Technology Skills

Presenting Divide students into small groups. Each group will research one of the main producers of hydroelectric power in Northwestern Europe. Ask students to create a 2–4 minute presentation to provide information about each hydroelectric plant in Northwestern Europe. Tell them to include data that would be helpful for a city debating whether to use hydroelectric power as one of their main sources of energy. Groups should present to the class. **BL Verbal/Linguistic**

W Writing Skills

Argument Germany has installed more wind turbines than any other European country. Have students write a persuasive letter to a local government in support of building new wind turbines to provide energy to a community. Have them cite specific data on environmental impact, cost, and energy output based on German and current United States informational statistics. **Naturalist**

CLOSE & REFLECT

Summarizing Have students make a four-column chart with the heads: *Landforms, Water Systems, Climate Zones,* and *Natural Resources*. Their charts should reiterate the importance of the Northern European Plain and the Central and Western Uplands, the significance of water systems, factors that affect climate in Northwestern Europe, and characteristics of the Alps.

Although coal creates pollution, it still has the advantages of being abundant and easy to ship and burn.

▲ CRITICAL THINKING

1. ***Drawing Inferences*** Why do you think Europeans are using less coal, even if it is relatively plentiful?
2. ***Analyzing Visuals*** Based on this photograph and prior knowledge, what effects might coal mining have on the environment?

Monty Rakusen/Cultura/Getty Images

such as ash, beech, and oak, thrive in the subregion's marine west coast climate. Coniferous trees—cone-bearing fir, pine, and spruce—are found in cooler, alpine mountain areas up to the timberline, the elevation above which trees cannot grow. The wildlife in this region includes deer, brown bears, badgers, squirrels, and numerous songbirds.

Natural Resources

Northwestern Europe's abundant supply of coal and iron ore fueled the development of modern industry in the 1700s. Today, people in the subregion still rely on coal, but it is being replaced by oil, natural gas, nuclear, and hydroelectric energy sources. Vast oil and natural gas deposits under the North Sea contribute greatly to Europe's energy needs. France, which lacks large oil and gas reserves, has invested heavily in nuclear power. People in the Netherlands rely on natural gas for a majority of their energy needs, but continue to use some wind power. Mountainous Switzerland and Austria get most of their electricity  from renewable sources, such as hydroelectric plants. They also have substantial timber resources. The peat bogs of Ireland serve as a source of fuel, especially in the rural countryside where it is used to heat homes. In contrast to much of the subregion, Germany has relatively few natural resources and imports more than half of its energy needs.

☑ READING PROGRESS CHECK

Drawing Conclusions Why does Northwestern Europe have a generally mild climate compared with other places at the same latitude?

LESSON 1 REVIEW CCSS

Reviewing Vocabulary (Tier Three Words)

1. ***Explaining*** Explain the relationship between foehns and avalanches. RH.9–10.4

Using Your Notes

2. ***Expressing*** Use your notes to describe the factors that influence the climate regions of Northwestern Europe.

Answering the Guiding Questions

3. ***Identifying*** How did the Northern European Plain affect the development of Europe?
4. ***Describing*** How have the rivers in Europe's heartland contributed to the region's development?
5. ***Explaining*** Why does most of Northwestern Europe have a generally mild climate?

Writing Activity

6. ***Informative/Explanatory*** Write an essay explaining which geographic factors contribute to climate differences between the highlands area of the Alps and the Northern European Plain. WHST.9–10.2

274

ANSWERS, p. 274

☑ READING PROGRESS CHECK The mild climate is a result of the region's proximity to the North Atlantic Current. The warm-ocean current creates warm air that blows over the coast and across the Northern European Plain.

CRITICAL THINKING

1. Extracting coal requires a difficult, dangerous, and time-consuming process. It also causes a great deal of air pollution.
2. It releases toxins into the air; it results in the land above being unstable, due to the many caves carved out for its mining.

LESSON 1 REVIEW ANSWERS

Reviewing Vocabulary

1. Foehns are dry, winter winds that blow down mountainsides and cause avalanches, which are falling masses of ice, snow, and rock.

Using Your Notes

2. The warm North Atlantic Current influences the climate of the region and allows for a mild marine west coast climate. Proximity to the Mediterranean Sea creates an even warmer Mediterranean climate in Monaco. Due to their high elevation, the Alps are covered by snow in the winter.

Answering the Guiding Questions

3. Because the plain offered fertile soil and many rivers, farming became popular in the region.
4. The abundance of rivers originally drew farmers to the area. Today rivers serve as important pathways for transporting goods from inland regions to other regions and to the sea. The Thames provides access to the port of London; the Rhine connects cities to the port of Rotterdam.
5. The mild climate is owed to the North Atlantic Current. The current carries water that was warmed in the Tropics and warms the air that is above it. This warm air blows over the coast and across the Northern European Plain.

Writing Activity

6. Essays will vary, but should include geographic factors such as elevation and proximity to large bodies of water.

networks
There's More Online!

- MAP Population Density of Northwestern Europe
- IMAGE Paris World of Fashion
- MAP The European Union
- INTERACTIVE SELF-CHECK QUIZ
- TIME LINE The Rise of Northwestern Europe
- VIDEO Human Geography of Northwestern Europe

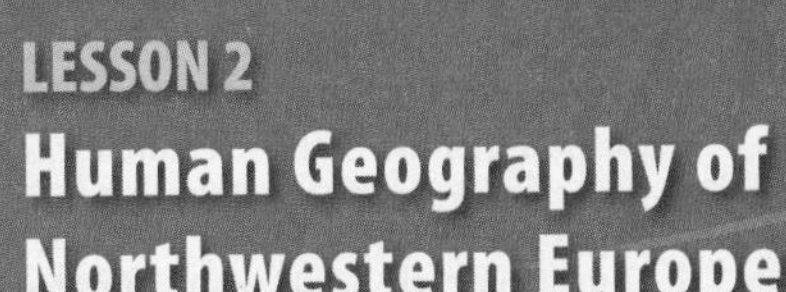

LESSON 2

Human Geography of Northwestern Europe

ESSENTIAL QUESTION • *How do physical systems and human systems shape a place?*

Reading **HELP**DESK 

Academic Vocabulary (Tier Two Words)
- comprehensive
- focus

Content Vocabulary (Tier Three Words)
- Industrial Revolution
- industrial capitalism
- communism
- Holocaust
- Cold War
- devolution
- guest worker
- agribusiness

TAKING NOTES: ***Key Ideas and Details***

IDENTIFYING Use a graphic organizer like the one below to take notes on the population, society, and culture of Northwestern Europe.

Human Geography of Northwestern Europe → Population Patterns; Society and Culture Today

It Matters Because

The countries of Northwestern Europe have a long and complex history shaped by migration, ethnic differences, wars and revolutions, and efforts at peaceful integration. From the Industrial Revolution to the establishment of the European Union, this subregion has had an enormous impact on world events past and present. **R**

History and Government

GUIDING QUESTION *How have new ideas influenced the development of governments and economies in Northwestern Europe?*

Northwestern Europe was shaped by thousands of years of migrations and invasions. Over the centuries, a variety of ethnic groups came into contact in this subregion. Additionally, Northwestern Europe was profoundly influenced by Christianity, beginning with the arrival of the Romans and its inclusion in their empire. **T**

The Rise of Northwestern Europe

Most of Northwestern Europe was once part of the Roman Empire, one of the largest empires in history. The Romans built towns, roads, and cities throughout Europe and brought stability and general prosperity to the subregion. However, the collapse of the Roman Empire during the A.D. 400s left the subregion vulnerable to invading Germanic groups for the next several hundred years.

During Roman times, Christianity was established as the official religion of the empire, and this had long-lasting effects on the peoples and cultures of this subregion. Beginning in the A.D. 1000s, armies that consisted primarily of Northwestern Europeans fought the Crusades. **G1** The Crusades were a series of religious wars against Islamic states of the eastern Mediterranean. The goal of the Crusades was to regain the Holy Land, the birthplace of Christianity, from Muslim rule. European forces did not win permanent control of the region. **G2**

ENGAGE

R Reading Skills

Activating Prior Knowledge Have students brainstorm with a partner what they already know about Northwestern Europe and its history, society, population, and economy. Then have students share their knowledge in a class discussion. Relate the migration and ethnic differences in Northwestern Europe to the United States and explore how the issues may be similar and different. **Verbal/Linguistic**

TEACH & ASSESS

T Technology Skills

Gathering Information Inform students that the Roman Empire was technologically advanced for its time, which enabled it to grow quite large. Have students explore the inventions, innovations, and achievements that allowed the Roman Empire to prosper. Have them choose one major invention or innovation and give a brief oral report to the class about how it affected Roman society. **BL Verbal/Linguistic**

G1 Critical Thinking Skills

Identifying Perspectives and Differing Interpretations Discuss the Crusades and the reasons for their occurrence. **Ask:** **What was the perspective of Christians in Northwestern Europe on the Muslim faith at the time of the Crusades?** *(They thought that Islam was a threat to Christianity and they wanted to free Jerusalem and the Holy Land from the Muslims.)* **How did this perspective enable them to justify the Crusades?** *(Possible answer: They likely believed the Crusades were necessary because they felt that Christians should reclaim the Holy Land.)* **AL Interpersonal**

G2 Critical Thinking Skills

Exploring Issues Have students convene in small groups to hold roundtable discussions on religion and its historical and current influence on society. If possible, mix students from different religious backgrounds. Have students focus on the questions: **Is it right, fair, or just for one group to wage war on another group based on their religious beliefs? What responsibility do other groups or nations have in intervening in these types of conflicts?** **BL Logical/Mathematical**

ANSWERS, p. 275

TAKING NOTES: Population—densely populated overall, but low density in rural areas, high density in urban areas, especially near rivers; **Society and Culture Today**—Indo-European languages, Christianity is primary religion, education and health care provided by government, equality for women, leading force in literature, architecture, music, visual arts.

networks *Online Teaching Options*

 **INTERACTIVE BELLRINGER**

Public Expenditures in Select European Countries, 2009

Interpreting Graphs Display this bar graph and introductory text to discuss how much select countries in Northwestern Europe spend on education and comprehensive health care with students. Ask them to discuss what they know about federal spending in the United States by asking them what the government spends money on for the public benefit. Then continue the class discussion, by asking volunteers to answers the bellringer questions. **Verbal/Linguistic, Visual/Spatial**

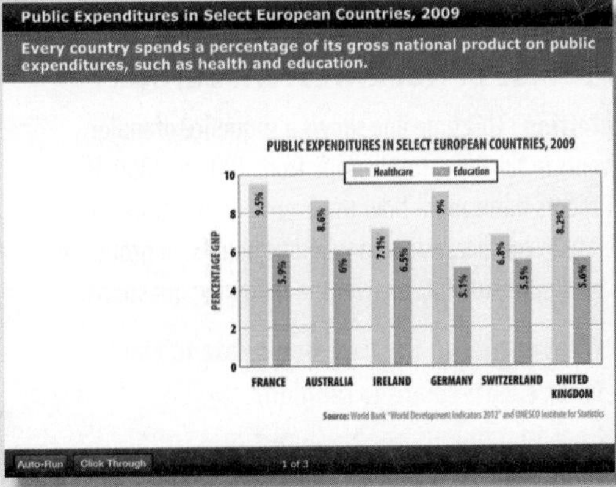

V Visual Skills

Labeling Provide students with copies of the political unit map. In small groups, have students identify and draw possible trade routes from Europe to the Eastern Mediterranean on the maps. Have them label Palestine, Judaea, Rome, and other major settlements at the time, as well as major bodies of water. When they are finished, have them compare their maps to maps showing the actual trade routes used at the time and discuss how they are alike and different. AL Visual/Spatial

R Reading Skills

Using Word Parts Have students break the word *Enlightenment* into parts—a prefix, base word, and suffix. Ask them to define each part. **Ask:** **Which definition of the base word *lighten* best relates to the concept of Enlightenment?** *(Possible answer: Lighten means "to make lighter or clearer," which makes sense in that the Enlightenment was a rejection of currently accepted ideas, replaced with new understanding and ways of thinking.)* ELL Verbal/Linguistic

C Critical Thinking Skills

Understanding Relationships Among Events Ask students to think about how the Industrial Revolution, industrial capitalism, and communism are related. Have them work in pairs to create a short skit to portray how the Industrial Revolution created industrial capitalism, which in turn gave rise to communism. Have students perform their skits for the class. After all of the skits have been performed, lead a class discussion on how the relationships between the Industrial Revolution and communism were portrayed in the skits. Invite students to critique which skits best exemplified the relationship. Kinesthetic, Interpersonal

ANSWERS, p. 276

CRITICAL THINKING

1. Students' answers will vary, but they should thoroughly describe the event and why they believe it left a lasting impact on Europe.
2. Possible answer: The countries of Northwestern Europe were involved in many conflicts and wars as they rose to become world powers. Some conflicts were over religious beliefs while others were about expanding territories.

V However, the Crusades did open trade routes to the eastern Mediterranean. These trade routes later resulted in the exchange of cultural ideas about economics and politics between Europe and Southwest Asia.

In the late 1400s, educated Europeans developed a new interest in the cultures of ancient Greece and Rome. The ideas of the Renaissance spread throughout Europe. They inspired major changes in art, politics, culture, and religion.

In the 1500s the Protestant Reformation, a religious reform movement, began in Germany. Launched by the monk Martin Luther, the Reformation decreased the power of the Roman Catholic Church and introduced Protestantism to Europe. This had a major impact on some parts of Northern Europe, where the power of the Catholic Church was often unwelcome.

Winds of Change Bring a New Era

R During the early 1700s, many educated Europeans embraced the Enlightenment, a movement to value reason and question tradition. Among the many significant philosophical ideas that emerged at this time was belief in the idea of progress. Prior to this, people expected life to remain much the same for their children as it was for them. During the Enlightenment, people began to think that society and government could improve.

The Enlightenment was a time of dramatic change. Many Europeans fought for a voice in government. For example, the French Revolution resulted in the overthrow of the French monarchy in 1792. The ideas of the Enlightenment helped encourage democracy and social change in Northwestern Europe.

C In the mid-1700s, the **Industrial Revolution** transformed manufacturing in Europe with the change from human labor to machines. At that time, Great Britain had the labor, capital, technology, natural resources, and access to waterways for transporting goods. It became the epicenter of the Industrial Revolution, which spread to Belgium, France, Germany, and ultimately the United States.

Widespread industrial and social change created **industrial capitalism**, an economic system in which owners use profits to expand their companies. A negative impact was that many factory workers were poorly paid and lived in crowded, unhealthy conditions. These conditions led to the rise of **communism**—a theory that calls for economic equality and ownership of resources and factories

Industrial Revolution beginning in the 1700s, the rapid, major change in the economy with the introduction of power-driven machinery

industrial capitalism an economic system in which business leaders use profits to expand their companies

communism the idea that society should be based on public ownership and communal control of property

TIME LINE

THE RISE of Northwestern Europe

Countries of Northwestern Europe rose through the centuries to become dominant world powers.

CRITICAL THINKING

1. ***Evaluating*** Which event on the time line do you think had the most lasting impact on Europe? Explain your response.
2. ***Describing*** Based on the events of the time line, how would you characterize the history of Northwestern Europe in respect to conflict and war?

1000

1400s In England, the Plantagenets and the Tudors strengthen the power of the monarchy.

1100s Europeans fight the Crusades to win the Holy Land from Muslim rule.

networks Online Teaching Options

TIME LINE

The Rise of Northwestern Europe

Inferring This time line shows a sequence of major events in Northwestern Europe from 1000 to 1800. Have students think about how the events on this time line relate to conflict, war, and religious beliefs. In groups of 3 or 4, have students answer the following questions:

- **What events on the time line relate to war?**
- **What events relate to religion?**
- **How do religious beliefs sometimes trigger conflict and war?**

AL Verbal/Linguistic

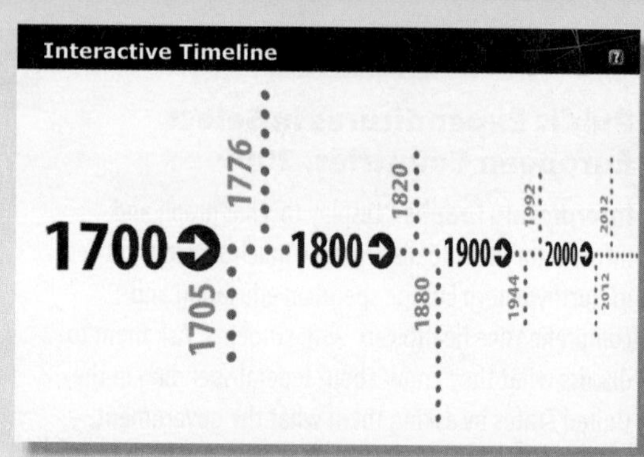

by the state. The jobs and urban lifestyle that accompanied industrialization reduced the need for children to help with agricultural work. Family size began to decrease, resulting in a demographic transition that continues today.

Rivalries and alliances among the Central Powers (Germany, Austria-Hungary, the Ottoman Empire, and Bulgaria) and the Allied Powers (Britain, France, and Russia) led Europe into World War I (1914–1918). The Treaty of Versailles, signed at the end of the war, blamed Germany for starting the conflict and demanded that it make reparations, or payment for damages. German resentment contributed to the start of World War II (1939–1945). German leader Adolf Hitler and his Nazi Party planned and carried out the **Holocaust**, the mass murder of more than 6 million European Jews, as well as other groups.

Holocaust the mass murder of 6 million Jews by Germany's Nazi regime during World War II

After World War II, the division of Europe led to the **Cold War**, a power struggle between the communist world, led by the Soviet Union, and the non-communist world, led by the United States. Germany was divided into communist East Germany and democratic West Germany. Germany reunited in 1990 and the Soviet Union collapsed the following year. Since then, many of the formerly state-owned industries in East Germany have closed. The result has been high unemployment and the migration of its youngest and most skilled citizens to other countries.

Cold War the power struggle between the Soviet Union and the United States after World War II

In the 1950s, several European countries formed trade agreements. By the twenty-first century it was called the European Union (EU), with 27 member countries seeking economic unity. Seventeen EU members have replaced their national currencies with a common currency—the euro.

Several countries in the subregion, including France, Wales, Scotland, and Northern Ireland, have experienced **devolution**, or the granting of powers of self-rule to local and regional authorities. In 1997 the powers of the United Kingdom Parliament were transferred back to Wales, Scotland, and Northern Ireland. In France, beginning in the 1980s, power was transferred to regional authorities. Those authorities are able then to run their own internal affairs. However, in every case there are reserved powers that the larger country continues to exercise.

devolution the granting of self-rule to local and regional authorities

✓ READING PROGRESS CHECK

Identifying Central Issues In what ways did the Roman Empire influence the development of Northwestern Europe?

1500

1500s Martin Luther leads the Protestant Reformation, becoming the founder of Lutheranism.

1600s The Thirty Years' War (1618–1648), rooted in territorial and religious conflicts, ravages Western Europe. France emerges as a major power.

1700s Industrial Revolution begins in Britain

late 1700s The French Revolution brings social, political, and economic change to France. King Louis XVI is executed by the guillotine, ending absolute monarchy.

1800

INTERACTIVE GRAPH

Jewish Population in Europe Before and After World War II

Locating Information on a Graph Explain to students how to interpret the information on this graph by first identifying the x-axis (countries) and the y-axis (millions of people). Then explain that the color key shows the differences in population from 1933 to 1945. As a class, discuss the graph and answer the following questions: Which country had the highest Jewish population in 1933? How did the Jewish population in Germany compare to the Jewish population in Poland in 1945? How many Jewish people died in Europe during World War II? How did you figure this out?
AL Logical/Mathematical, Visual/Spatial

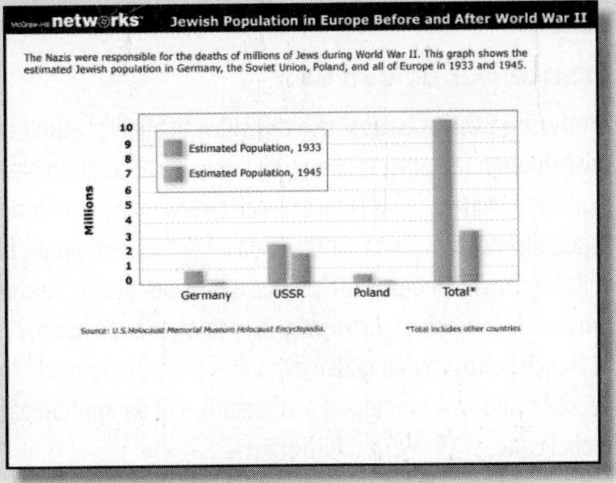
networks
Jewish Population in Europe Before and After World War II
The Nazis were responsible for the deaths of millions of Jews during World War II. This graph shows the estimated Jewish population in Germany, the Soviet Union, Poland, and all of Europe in 1933 and 1945.
Millions
10
9
8
7
6
5
4
3
2
1
0
Estimated Population, 1933
Estimated Population, 1945
Germany
USSR
Poland
Total*
Source: U.S. Holocaust Memorial Museum Holocaust Encyclopedia.
*Total includes other countries

C Critical Thinking Skills

Contrasting Discuss how the population demographics in Northwestern Europe were different before the Industrial Revolution and after the Industrial Revolution. Have students research these demographic variations and then complete a graphic organizer to illustrate the differences in where people lived, what people did, and how large their families were. Verbal/Linguistic

V Visual Skills

Analyzing Primary Sources Have students use the Internet and library reference materials to locate primary and secondary sources related to the Holocaust. Have them pull together photographs and quotes about the Holocaust to create a collage of images and thoughts about the Holocaust. Have them share their works with the class.
BL Verbal/Linguistic, Visual/Spatial

W Writing Skills

Argument Point out that not all European countries have joined the EU. Have students work in small groups to brainstorm and speculate why these countries have opted not to join. Have half of the groups write an argument against joining the EU from the perspective of a wealthier nation that is not part of the EU, such as Norway. Have the other half write in favor of joining, again from the perspective of a wealthier nation, such as Germany. Students should include specific reasons for joining or not joining the EU. BL Logical/Mathematical

Content Background Knowledge

Germany and the Treaty of Versailles Many Germans were angered with the conditions of the Treaty of Versailles, which ended World War I and called for Germany to give up lands on the eastern front and pay reparations to the allied nations. They felt that although they may have been fairly defeated on the western front, they were indeed victorious on the eastern front. This anger, as well as the inability of France, Britain, and the United States to work together to contain German power, was a contributing factor to World War II.

ANSWERS, p. 277

✓ READING PROGRESS CHECK Towns, roads, and cities established by the Romans set the region up for stability and prosperity. Christianity, the official religion of the Roman Empire, was the motivating force behind the Crusades. Although the Crusades did not result in permanent control of the Holy Land, they did open trade routes which eventually allowed for a great exchange of cultural ideas.

R Reading Skills

Summarizing Have students summarize how urbanization has affected population patterns in Northwestern Europe. Ask them to relate urbanization to the changes in demographics during the Industrial Revolution. **AL** **Verbal/Linguistic**

C Critical Thinking Skills

Drawing Conclusions Discuss with students the advantages and disadvantages of inviting guest workers to a country. **Ask:** **How can the economic climate in a country be described at a time when they are inviting guest workers to come?** *(Possible answer: The economy is likely doing well and unemployment is low. This is why they need guest workers—to fill the jobs that are open.)* **How might a downturn in a country's economy affect guest workers?** *(Possible answer: They may lose their jobs. They may be asked to leave the country.)* **How might a downturn in a country's economy lead people in that country to feel about guest workers?** *(Possible answer: They may get frustrated that guest workers are taking jobs previously meant for permanent residents.)* **Does the United States have a similar situation?** *(Possible answer: Yes, many immigrants come to the United States to work, and when the economy is doing poorly, people may blame them for taking jobs.)* Point out that the issue of guest workers and immigration are very important issues in many European countries. **Logical/Mathematical, Interpersonal**

V Visual Skills

Creating Graphs Have students create a graph that depicts an increasing and then declining population. Have them label the y-axis "Population" and the x-axis "Time." They do not need to use actual numbers, but to draw the line that shows a population in decline. Have students identify the point at which population ceases to increase and begins to decrease. Ask them to explain what change is happening in the birthrate and death rate at this point. **BL** **Visual/Spatial**

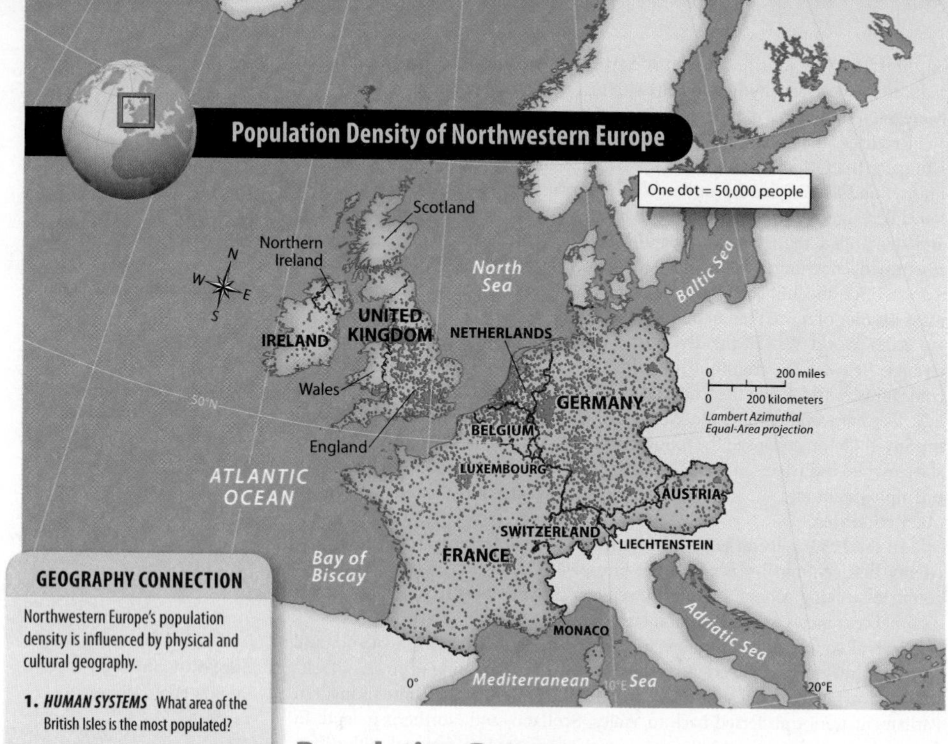

GEOGRAPHY CONNECTION

Northwestern Europe's population density is influenced by physical and cultural geography.

1. ***HUMAN SYSTEMS*** What area of the British Isles is the most populated?
2. ***PLACES AND REGIONS*** What areas of Northwestern Europe have the lowest population density?

Population Patterns

GUIDING QUESTION *How have physical geography, migration, and world events shaped the population of Northwestern Europe?*

R Most of Northwestern Europe is densely populated. Temperate climates, fertile soil, manufacturing, and trade have historically supported large populations. The Netherlands and Belgium have the highest population densities, followed by the United Kingdom. Rural population densities are much lower than those of cities. City population densities may exceed 14,000 per square mile (36,260 per sq. km), compared to less than 50 per square mile (129 per sq. km) in rural areas.

guest worker a foreign laborer living and working temporarily in another country

C Both internal and external migration have shaped this subregion of Europe. In 1945, at the end of World War II, Great Britain welcomed a large number of immigrants from South Asia and the West Indies. Beginning in the 1950s, Germany began inviting **guest workers** to encourage economic growth. Guest workers are foreign laborers working temporarily in an industrialized, usually European, country. France has also attracted many immigrants as workers, especially from its former colonies Algeria and Morocco.

V Aging is starting to have a significant effect on the demographics of Northwestern Europe. Low birthrates and higher life expectancies have led to an older population. Consequently, the number of working-age people is shrinking while the number of retired people is expanding. Young women have developed careers and delayed having children until a later age. This has resulted in fewer children being born than elderly people reaching the end of their lives. The result is a decreasing total population in some countries.

Internal migration is driven by poverty. People leave poor places. Migration also occurs when people move to urban areas to find jobs. Suburbanization occurs

278

networks Online Teaching Options

VIDEO

France Public Veil Ban

Analyzing Ethical Issues Use this video to analyze ethnic issues that arise through the process of immigration and population patterns. Explain to students that France has attracted many immigrants, especially Muslims, and that the French law banning public full-faced veils was passed in April 2011. Guide a class discussion. Ask students to provide their opinions about why they think the veil has become an issue in French politics; what global dynamics, if any, have made this ban possible; and why immigrant settlements and emigration patterns are a global issue. **BL** **Verbal/Linguistic**

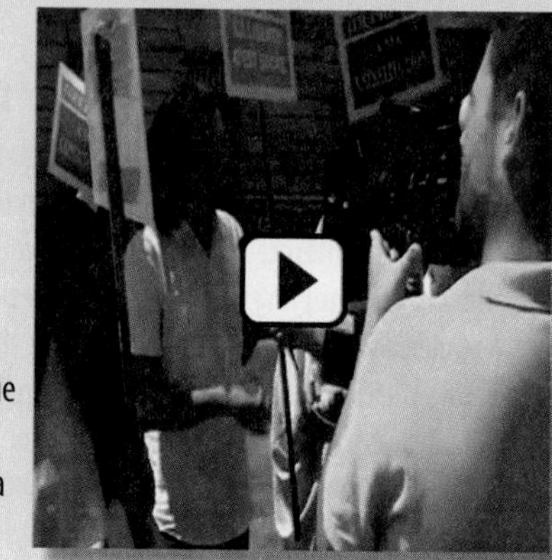

ANSWERS, p. 278

GEOGRAPHY CONNECTION

1. Central and southeast England are the most densely populated.
2. Northern Scotland and western Ireland have the lowest population density.

when people settle in places near cities. Middle-class and working-class populations may find more affordable housing in suburbs.

Many cities emerged as key trading centers along navigable rivers, such as the Thames and the Seine. As populations in these areas increased, people moved to these growing urban centers. Today this part of Europe is home to some of the world's most famous cities: Paris, London, Brussels, and Amsterdam.

✓ READING PROGRESS CHECK

Making Connections How has migration shaped the population of Northwestern Europe?

Society and Culture Today

GUIDING QUESTION *How has its location as a crossroads of Europe influenced society and culture in Northwestern Europe?*

Many countries in Northwestern Europe have one or more official languages. Most people in the region speak languages that are part of the Indo-European language family, including German and French. A small number of Basque people speak Euskera, one of few languages that are unrelated to any other.

Christianity is the primary religion in the subregion, consisting mainly of Roman Catholics and members of various Protestant sects. Nevertheless, most people in the subregion today are only nominally members of a religion. They may state that they have a religion but do not attend church or regularly practice their faith.

Compulsory education for children and **comprehensive** health care and social services are valued in Northwestern Europe. The population is 98 to 100 percent literate, and laws in each country provide for the education of children through secondary school. Europeans have been innovators in education and developing programs to improve quality of life. This subregion values caring for their people through education, health care, and other social programs.

comprehensive covering completely or broadly; inclusive

focus to concentrate attention or effort

The Status of Women

Northwestern Europe has made great strides regarding equality and political empowerment for women. Countries support equal work opportunities for women and promote public policies to balance work and family life. Roughly an equal number of women and men receive degrees in higher education. Women also find opportunities in political participation. They were generally granted suffrage (the right to vote) before women in the United States and other areas of the world. Margaret Thatcher became the first female prime minister of Great Britain in 1979, Gro Harlem Brundtland became prime minister of Norway in 1981, and Angela Merkel became the chancellor of Germany in 2005.

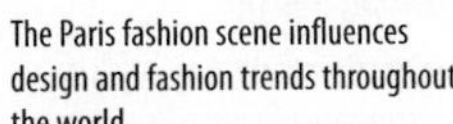

The Paris fashion scene influences design and fashion trends throughout the world.

▼ CRITICAL THINKING

1. ***Analyzing Visuals*** Describe what you think is about to take place in the picture.
2. ***Classifying*** How is fashion a part of culture? Explain your answer.

The Arts

Northwestern Europe has long been a leading force in literature, architecture, music, and the visual arts. Influential artistic movements began here. In the early 1800s, Romanticism was embodied in the works of Lord Byron and Ludwig van Beethoven. Realism, which **focused** on the realistic depiction of everyday life, became prominent in the mid-1800s. This was a change from the emotional style of Romanticism. Later in the century, another group of French painters, the impressionists, moved outdoors to capture immediate experiences, or impressions, of the natural world.

Martin Bureau/AFP/Getty Images

✓ READING PROGRESS CHECK

Identifying How have countries of Northwestern Europe worked for equality for women?

G1 Critical Thinking Skills

Transferring Information Have students recall information about rivers and waterways in Northwestern Europe and how they are used. **Ask:** **How has geography influenced where people live and how has that influenced the growth of cities?** *(Cities grow in areas where there is good transportation and easy access to trade. This is why cities often grow along navigable rivers and waterways.)* **ELL Logical/Mathematical**

C2 Critical Thinking Skills

Critical Listening Have students listen to samples of different but related Northwestern European languages, such as German and French, and then to samples of other regional languages that are not related, such as Euskera. Ask them to compare and contrast the related languages with each other, and then the related languages with an unrelated language to discuss the differences and similarities. **Auditory/Musical**

R Reading Skills

Naming Have students recall the names, countries, and dates they came to power of the women leaders mentioned. Have them discuss the importance of female leaders. **Ask:** **What unique perspectives might women bring to leadership roles?** *(Possible answers: They have knowledge of issues that affect women's health. They may be experienced in issues that are important to children and families.)* **AL Interpersonal**

V Visual Skills

Describing Have students find an example of Realism in the visual arts. Then have them write a brief essay that describes the image and the meaning behind it by considering the following questions: **Why do you think there was a move at this time away from Romanticism? What might this have to do with the Industrial Revolution and urbanism? Visual/Spatial**

GAME

Human Geography of Northwestern Europe

Monitoring Have student play this identification game with a partner. After they play the game, ask students to consider how society, culture, and economics have changed over time. Have students discuss changes in the educational systems, health care systems, and other social programs of the countries in Northwestern Europe. **ELL Interpersonal**

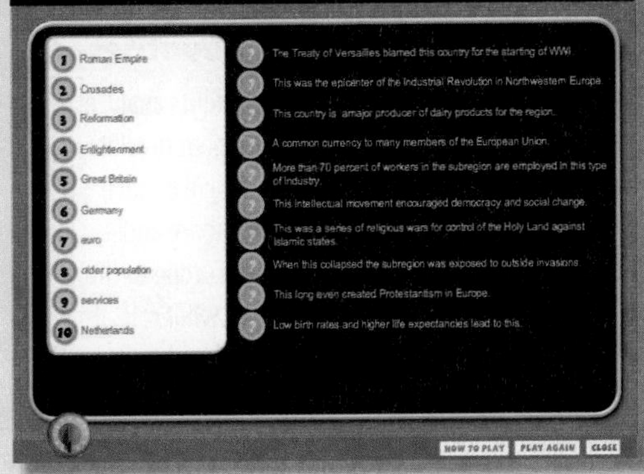

ANSWERS, p. 279

✓ READING PROGRESS CHECK After World War II, Great Britain welcomed immigrants from South Asia and the West Indies. France also became home to many immigrants, especially from Algeria and Morocco. Internal migration of people from rural areas to urban and suburban areas has made cities more populated.

✓ READING PROGRESS CHECK Public policies have been enacted to promote a balance of work and family life so that women do not have to choose between a career and a family. Women in Northwestern Europe received the right to vote before women in the United States. They have also achieved prominent roles in politics.

CRITICAL THINKING

1. The model will walk down a runway in a fashion show.
2. Fashion is considered an art form and an expression of the culture.

C Critical Thinking Skills

Organizing As students read the information in *Economic Activities*, have them complete a three-column chart with the headings *Resource*, *Location*, and *Industry*. Have them list important economic resources, where they are located, and the industries they support. AL **Visual/Spatial**

T Technology Skills

Presenting Have students research a tourist destination in Northwestern Europe. Have them create a presentation about this destination in one of the following formats: a tourism brochure highlighting the main tourist attraction or attractions in the area, a home page for a website for a tourist attraction or tourist area, or a slide show with audio displaying the main attractions in an area. BL **Visual/Spatial**

Making Connections

Service Industries Point out to students that service industries include any industry that provides a service to customers. Some are easily identified, such as those in the tourism industry like hotels and restaurants. Others are not as easily identified, such as the banking and insurance industries. Have students look at their own community and categorize and classify the main industries as service and nonservice industries.

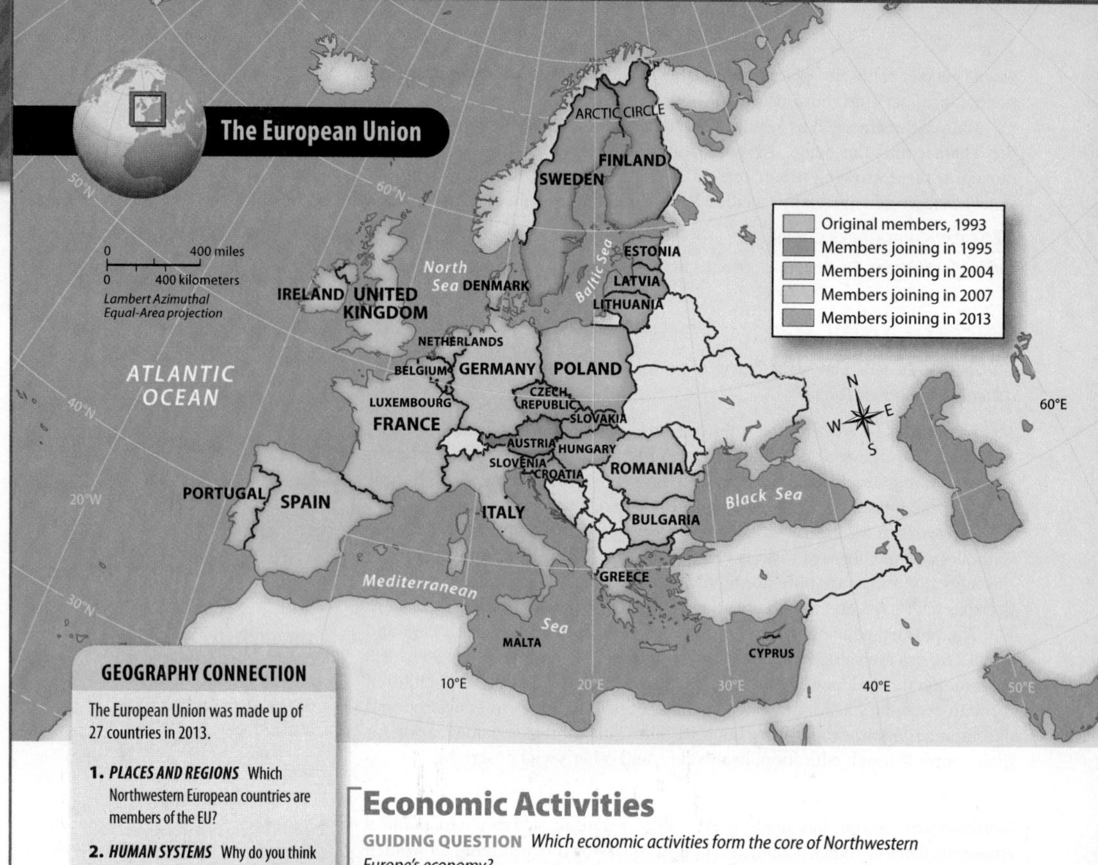

GEOGRAPHY CONNECTION

The European Union was made up of 27 countries in 2013.

1. ***PLACES AND REGIONS*** Which Northwestern European countries are members of the EU?
2. ***HUMAN SYSTEMS*** Why do you think original members of the EU were from Northwestern Europe?

Economic Activities

GUIDING QUESTION *Which economic activities form the core of Northwestern Europe's economy?*

Northwestern European economies have developed various combinations of agriculture, manufacturing, services, and technology (which includes banking, tourism, and high-tech industries). As in all parts of the world, economic activities in Northwestern Europe are related to the natural resources, the people, and the culture of the area.

Resources, Power, and Industry

The Industrial Revolution made Europe the birthplace of modern industry. The development of industry is often linked to the availability of raw materials. In the 1800s, Europe's large deposits of coal and iron ore, especially in the Ruhr and the Middle Rhine districts in Germany and the Lorraine-Saar district in France, sparked the growth of heavy industry—the manufacture of machinery and industrial equipment. Northwestern Europe's leading industrial centers remain in these areas. Today, the region produces everything from computers to transportation equipment. However, service industries provide a large percentage of countries' GDPs.

More than 70 percent of workers in Northwestern Europe are employed in service industries. Among the top industries are international banking and insurance. Switzerland and the United Kingdom are the leaders in these fields. Tourism is another large service industry, especially in Great Britain, the Netherlands, and France.

280

ANSWERS, p. 280

GEOGRAPHY CONNECTION

1. The United Kingdom, Ireland, Germany, Italy, France, Spain, Portugal, Greece, Cyprus, Malta, Belgium, Luxembourg, the Netherlands, Denmark, Sweden, Finland, Austria, Estonia, Latvia, Lithuania, Poland, Czech Republic, Slovakia, Hungary, Slovenia, Romania, Bulgaria, and Croatia
2. Northwestern Europe was the birthplace of the Industrial Revolution. This part of Europe was more economically developed than other subregions.

networks Online Teaching Options

INTERACTIVE MAP

European Union Member Countries

Comparing and Contrasting Have students analyze the map of the European Union and ask them to relate it to news media reports of countries that have or have had economic difficulties. Have them compare and contrast the economies of Northwestern Europe to the economies of Northern Europe. Ask them what role, if any, they think that geography has played in the economic development of these countries. Ask them what they think are the advantages and disadvantages of many different countries using the same currency.
BL **Visual/Spatial, Verbal/Linguistic**

The economies of the subregion are supported by transportation and communication systems that are of a high quality everywhere and state-of-the art in many places. Transportation infrastructure in Northwestern Europe includes highways, high-speed railroads, waterways, and airline routes. Modern communications systems also link most parts of Europe to one another and to the rest of the world. C1

Although largely industrialized, Northwestern Europe also has fertile farmland. Agricultural crops vary with the geography of the region. Olives, citrus fruits, and grapes grow in warm Mediterranean areas of southern France. Farther north, in the cooler plains region, farmers grow wheat, rye, and other grains as well as raise livestock. Northern countries, such as the Netherlands, are major producers of dairy products. Farmers use advanced technology to make the best use of limited agricultural space and climate differences.

In the twentieth century, people began flocking to cities. This left a shrinking population of farmers who struggled to meet the demand for food. Eventually, agricultural companies arose and created **agribusiness**, an industry engaged in large-scale, corporate farming operations.

agribusiness an industry engaged in agriculture on a large scale, sometimes including the manufacture and distribution of farm supplies

Many Northwestern European countries have made the switch from coal to natural gas, wind, and solar collections for energy production. The subregion is a global leader in the development and use of wind energy. The European Union has developed long-term plans that focus on biofuels, solar, wind, and other renewable energy resources. This is part of an effort to preserve the environment and to decrease reliance on imported fuels, such as oil.

The European Union

Trade, both within Europe and between Europe and the rest of the world, is changing as the result of the European Union (EU). The EU, which unites much of Europe into one trading community, or bloc, enjoys one of the largest volumes of trade in the world. The EU accounts for about one-sixth of the world's trade in goods.

The EU has achieved its large trade activity by eliminating tariffs and other trade barriers among member nations. The EU has also formed favorable trade relationships with other countries, including the United States and China. Its educated and technologically advanced workforce, its locations with access to water transportation, and its adaptability to changes in global trade give the EU trade advantages over other regions of the world. C2

✓ READING PROGRESS CHECK

Specifying What service industries rank among the most important in Northwestern Europe?

LESSON 2 REVIEW  

Reviewing Vocabulary (Tier Three Words)

1. ***Explaining*** Describe what is meant by the *Cold War,* and explain how it affected Germany's geography. RH.9–10.4

Using Your Notes

2. ***Describing*** Use your graphic organizer to describe society and culture of today in Northwestern Europe.

Answering the Guiding Questions

3. ***Identifying*** How have new ideas influenced the development of governments and economies in Northwestern Europe?

4. ***Describing*** How have physical geography, migration, and world events shaped the population of Northwestern Europe?

5. ***Explaining*** How has its location as a crossroads of Europe influenced society and culture in Northwestern Europe?

6. ***Identifying*** Which economic activities form the core of Northwestern Europe's economy?

Writing Activity

7. ***Informative/Explanatory*** Write an essay about the development of current population patterns of Northwestern Europe. WHST.9–10.2

Human Geography of Northwestern Europe

C1 Critical Thinking Skills

Interpreting Significance Explain that Europe is much smaller than the continental United States. For example, France is close in size to the state of Texas. Many other countries, such as Germany, are not much longer from north to south than the state of Illinois. Discuss how the size of Northwestern Europe plays a significant role in its transportation infrastructure and communications systems. **Ask: What transportation and communications issues does the United States face that Northwestern Europe does not?** *(Possible answer: The United States is larger in area so the transportation and communication systems have to cover more miles than Europe. Since these systems are much larger, they take more time and money to maintain.)* AL **Visual/Spatial**

C2 Critical Thinking Skills

Making Generalizations Have students make a generalization about being a member of the European Union based on the information. For example, *Membership in the European Union is advantageous.* Have students share their generalizations and cite the details that support the generalization. **Verbal/Linguistic**

CLOSE & REFLECT

Summarizing Review with students the history of Northwestern Europe. Have them summarize society and culture today and current primary economic activities in the region. Discuss the role of the European Union in government and society in Northwestern Europe.

ANSWERS, p. 281

✓ READING PROGRESS CHECK International banking and insurance, as well as tourism, are the top service industries in the region.

LESSON 2 REVIEW ANSWERS

Reviewing Vocabulary

1. Europe was divided after World War II in a power struggle between the communist world, led by the Soviet Union, and the noncommunist world, led by the United States. This power struggle was known as the Cold War. Germany was divided into communist East Germany and democratic West Germany.

Using Your Notes

2. Most people in Northwestern Europe speak Indo-European languages. The primary religion is Christianity, though many are not practicing members. Education, health care, and other social services are provided by the government. Countries are working towards full equality for women. The region is a leader in literature, architecture, music, and visual arts.

Answering the Guiding Questions

3. In the late 1400s, the ideas of the Renaissance brought major changes in art, politics, and culture. In the 1700s, the Enlightenment brought a value of reason and a questioning of tradition, empowering people to demand a voice in government. This led to democracy and social change.

4. Northwestern Europe's temperate climates, fertile soil, manufacturing, and trade opportunities have attracted many people, causing the region to become densely populated. After World War II, many immigrants began arriving in the region, adding to the diversity. Internal migration to urban and suburban areas has resulted in even more highly populated cities.

5. Possible answer: Being the crossroads of Europe meant that many ideas intersected here, helping the region to become a leader in literature, architecture, music, and the visual arts. Another result of the crossroads location is that several countries in Northwestern Europe have more than one official language.

6. Over 70 percent of workers in Northwestern Europe work in service industries. However, the economy is also fueled by agriculture and manufacturing.

Writing Activity

7. Essays will vary, but should include internal and external migration factors, aging population concerns, and rural versus urban population densities.

ENGAGE

V Visual Skills

Identifying Perspectives Direct attention to the image of the flags. Point out that the flags represent the different countries that are members of the EU. Point to the blue flag with gold stars, explaining that this flag represents the EU. Ask a volunteer to read aloud the first paragraph. **Ask:** **Why do you think the European Union was awarded the Nobel Peace Prize?** *(Possible answer: The EU may have received the prize to recognize its attempt to work as a united body to improve the conditions in Europe.)* **Why was the reaction "mixed"?** *(At the time the EU received the award, the group of countries were in an economic crisis.)* As students read about the EU in this Case Study, have them consider the perspective of the people who voted to give the Nobel Peace Prize to the EU and the perspective of people who disagreed with the decision.

TEACH & ASSESS

C Critical Thinking Skills

Identifying Perspectives and Different Interpretations Ask a volunteer to read aloud the second paragraph. **Ask:** **Why was the EU created?** *(so that European countries would be more unified and economically and politically stable)* **What do EU supporters cite as its advantage for European businesses?** *(They say that a single business market strengthens the business community and increases competition, innovation, and productivity.)* AL **Verbal/Linguistic**

R Reading Skills

Analyzing Text Structure Direct students' attention to the word *however.* Tell students that identifying signal words in a text can help them better understand the meaning of a text. Explain that some words show a cause-and-effect relationship, others help compare or contrast, some indicate that a description or example will follow, and others indicate chronological order. **Ask:** **What does *however* indicate?** *(a contrast or another side to an argument)* Have students work with a partner to identify signal words and their meanings in the paragraph. ELL **Verbal/Linguistic**

T Technology Skills

Identifying Central Issues Direct students' attention to the image of the sculpture. **Ask:** **What do you think the sculpture represents?** *(Possible answer: the union of different countries working together to achieve common goals)* Have small groups research the European headquarters and artwork created to symbolize the EU, including the controversial piece "Entropa" in the European Council building. Then have groups design a sculpture to represent the European Union. Have students present their designs to the class, explaining the purpose and intent of their designs. BL **Interpersonal, Visual/Spatial**

Case Study: **Economics** 

How beneficial is THE EUROPEAN UNION?

V

In November 2012, the European Union (EU) was awarded the Nobel Peace Prize. The world's reaction was decidedly mixed. The prize was awarded, not to an individual or an organization, but to this entire group of 27 countries that, at the time, was in the midst of an economic crisis. A nagging question was raised once again: Just how beneficial is the European Union?

C The EU was officially created in November 1993, with the goal of establishing a more unified and economically and politically stable Europe. EU supporters argue that its single market has provided companies a strong business arena. Businesses do not have to worry about currency exchanges and complex international tax laws. Competition, innovation, and productivity have increased, leading to lower costs and a wider variety of consumer products. Moreover, students can study abroad in any of the EU member countries. Most importantly, after two major wars in the last century, Europe has enjoyed a long era of peace.

R However, EU detractors point out that the single market has always been inherently unstable. As evidence, they point to the financial crisis Europe experienced beginning in 2010. The EU became entangled in a multibillion euro crisis, and EU members hotly debated the merits and ramifications of bailouts. Since 2008, the EU has scrambled to support failing economies in Greece, Italy, and Spain. In 2010 and 2011, for example, the EU made loans to Greece to rescue its faltering economy. The loans were conditional on the adoption of strict austerity measures by the government of Greece, which led to a worsening recession and increased social unrest. Such social unrest in countries suffering from failing economies has pitted the poorer southern European countries against the generally more affluent northern European countries. EU bureaucracy also slowed down solutions. Some worry that the EU has gone beyond the goal of economic unity, and that larger countries dominate at the expense of smaller ones.

T

networks Online Teaching Options

INTERACTIVE SLIDE SHOW

How to Analyze Primary Sources

Evaluating Primary and Secondary Sources Before students read the primary source quotes in this feature, have them complete the interactive slide show, found in the online Teachers Resource Center, to learn how to analyze the viewpoint and perspective in each primary source. After students analyze the primary sources in the slide show lesson, have them read and analyze the two primary source quotes in this feature. Tell students to look for bias in the arguments and to be aware of the persuasive tools the speakers might use to appeal to their readers. Then have students copy the title for each primary source and list the support that each person provides for his statements. **Verbal/Linguistic, Logical/Mathematical**

The EU Is a Stabilizing Force

PRIMARY SOURCE

"The union and its forerunners have for over six decades contributed to the advancement of peace and reconciliation, democracy and human rights in Europe. . . . The dreadful suffering in World War II demonstrated the need for a new Europe. Over a seventy-year period, Germany and France had fought three wars. Today war between Germany and France is unthinkable. This shows how, through well-aimed efforts and by building up mutual confidence, historical enemies can become close partners. . . . The stabilizing part played by the EU has helped to transform most of Europe from a continent of war to a continent of peace."

—Thorbjorn Jagland, the chairman of the Norwegian Nobel Committee, October 2012

The EU Is Driving Europe into Recession

PRIMARY SOURCE

"You only have to open your eyes to see the increasing violence and division within the EU which is caused by the Euro project. Spain is on the verge of a bail-out, with senior military figures warning that the Army may have to intervene in Catalonia. In Greece people are starving and abandoning their children through desperate poverty and never a week goes by that we don't see riots and protests in capital cities against the troika [a committee composed of the European Commission, the European Central Bank, and the International Monetary Fund that organized loans to rescue the economies of faltering EU countries] and the economic prison they have imposed. . . . The last attempt in Europe to impose a new flag, currency and nationality on separate states was called Yugoslavia. The EU is repeating the same tragic mistake. . . . Rather than bring peace and harmony, the EU will cause insurgency and violence."

—Nigel Farage, UK Independence Party leader, October 2012

R

C

What do you think? DBQ

1. ***Finding the Main Idea*** According to Jagland, how has the EU benefited Europe?
2. ***Identifying Central Issues*** What arguments does Farage give to support his opinion that the EU has failed?
3. ***Evaluating*** Who do you think makes the stronger argument, Jagland or Farage? Explain.

R Reading Skills

Using Case Studies Some terms in this paragraph may be confusing for English language learners. Pair English language learners with proficient students and have them read the quote together, pausing to clarify the meaning of confusing or unfamiliar terms such as *verge, bail-out, intervene, faltering,* and *insurgency.* After students review the paragraph to reinforce their understanding, have partners use the case study to write a sentence stating whether they think the EU should have received the Nobel Peace Prize. Encourage students to use evidence from each primary source to support their statements. **ELL Intrapersonal, Verbal/Linguistic**

C Critical Thinking Skills

Evaluating Counter Arguments Have students reread Farage's quote, taking notes about how it differs from Jagland's argument. Call on students to read their notes to the class, ensuring that they fully comprehend the position of each side. **Ask: What examples does Farage list to support his argument that the EU is causing Europe to fall into recession?** *(He lists the economic struggles of Spain and Greece and the protests in capital cities against the troika.)* **What does Farage mean by stating that the EU "will cause insurgency and violence"?** *(Possible answer: He uses Yugoslavia as an example of the EU "repeating the same tragic mistake" and believes that riots and protests will continue in countries like Spain and Greece.)*

CLOSE & REFLECT

Argument Have students write an argument defending one of the primary sources in this Case Study. Students may wish to conduct additional research to provide supporting evidence for their arguments, but remind them to use reliable online sources. Invite students to share their arguments with the class.

INTERACTIVE WHITEBOARD ACTIVITY

Drag and Drop: Is the European Union an Effective Economic Union?

Analyzing Use this activity to help students analyze information and identify supporting statements regarding the effectiveness of the European Union. Have volunteers drag and drop each item to its correct location. Have each volunteer give a reason for his or her placement. **Logical/Mathematical**

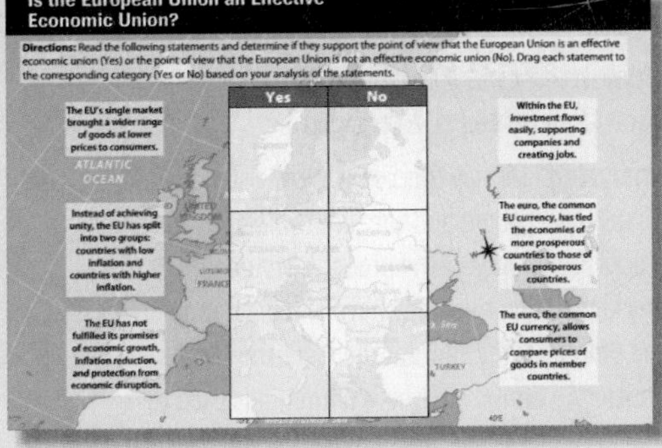

ANSWERS, p. 283

DBQ What do you think?

1. The EU has brought a much-needed era of peace to Europe.
2. Greece received a bailout, and its people are now facing extreme poverty and starvation. Spain is also on the verge of a bailout. Riots and protests are breaking out in capital cities to fight the economic prison imposed by the EU's troika.
3. Students' answers may vary but should be logical and strongly supported by the text and the quotes.

ENGAGE

R Reading Skills

Predicting Have students predict topics that will be covered in this lesson. Have them highlight supporting details in *It Matters Because* that lead them to make their predictions. Ask them to make connections to their own environment and environmental issues facing their area. Naturalist

TEACH & ASSESS

C1 Critical Thinking Skills

Identifying Central Issues As students read this lesson, have them make a running list of environmental issues facing Northwestern Europe. Have them begin by listing the issue and its source. As they continue through the lesson, have them add ways in which Northwestern Europe is trying to minimize or reverse environmental damage. AL Visual/Spatial

C2 Critical Thinking Skills

Posing Questions Remind students that there is typically not one magical solution to environmental issues. Have students work with a partner to compile a list of questions that need to be asked in order to examine the issue of pollution in the ocean before moving toward possible solutions. Have them share their questions with the class to compile a class list. Then together prioritize the questions in order of critical need for a viable solution. AL Verbal/Linguistic, Logical/Mathematical

T Technology Skills

Researching Have students research the issue of foreign, or invasive, species and how they are affecting waterways in Northwestern Europe. Have them answer the following questions pertaining to a foreign species of their choice: What is the species? How long has it been in the waterways of Northwestern Europe? Which native species does it compete with? How does this affect the native ecosystem? AL Naturalist

ANSWERS, p. 284

TAKING NOTES: Human Impact—Natural resource harvesting alters ecosystems and generates pollution; waste disposal from growing populations pollutes coastal waters; overfishing is leading to unsustainable fish populations; traffic exhaust and industrial fumes create air pollution and acid deposition; Addressing the Issues—There are now environmental protection laws; buildings are protected with acid-resistant coatings; older vehicles are banned; many power plants now burn natural gas instead of coal; the Kyoto Protocol addresses issues around the world.

networks
There's More Online!

- **IMAGE** Fishing Vessel in Northwestern Europe
- **IMAGE** Environmental Activism
- **GRAPH** Overfishing in Northwestern Europe
- **MAP** Oxygen Depletion in Coastal Marine Ecosystems
- **INTERACTIVE SELF-CHECK QUIZ**
- **VIDEO** People and Their Environment: Northwestern Europe

LESSON 3
People and Their Environment: Northwestern Europe

ESSENTIAL QUESTION • *How do physical systems and human systems shape a place?*

Reading HELPDESK CCSS

Academic Vocabulary (Tier Two Words)
- **isolate**
- **ensure**

Content Vocabulary (Tier Three Words)
- **acid deposition**
- **Kyoto Protocol**
- **cap-and-trade**

TAKING NOTES: *Key Ideas and Details*

SUMMARIZING Use a graphic organizer like the one below to take notes about the human impact on the environment in Northwestern Europe and how people are addressing the issues.

Humans and Their Environment

Human Impact	Addressing the Issues

It Matters Because

R *Humans have been changing the environment of Northwestern Europe for thousands of years. Today, very little of the region has escaped substantial alteration from its natural condition. Nevertheless, a healthy and beautiful environment is important to the region's people. They have been successful in finding ways to reverse the environmental damage. But water quality and pollution are still major issues facing Northwestern Europe.*

Managing Resources

GUIDING QUESTION *How has modern development resulted in challenges to the management of resources in Northwestern Europe?*

C1 With its highly developed and industrialized economy, Northwestern Europe consumes large amounts of natural resources and generates considerable waste products. While many natural resources are imported from other parts of the world, some of them are extracted from mines, quarries, forests, and other operations within the subregion. Such activities cause pollution and land-use changes that require careful management.

C2 Pollution contaminates marine and animal life and creates health hazards for humans. France and other countries that border the Mediterranean Sea use the sea for waste disposal. In the past, bacteria broke down most of the waste. However, growing populations and tourism along the coasts have increased the environmental problems. Small tides and weak currents tend to keep pollution where it is discharged.

T Overfishing has been a problem in the subregion as well. Global fishing levels are estimated to be four times greater than the amount of fish left to catch. Adding to the problem, native species of seaweed and shellfish often compete with foreign species carried into local waterways by ships. Unsustainable fishing remains a major issue for the European Union (EU), where 75 percent of stocks are overfished and catches are only a fraction of what they were 15 to 20 years ago. However, in many fishing grounds that

networks *Online Teaching Options*

INTERACTIVE BELLRINGER

Commercial Fishing Stocks in Northwestern Europe

Analyzing Display this commercial fishing stock map to discuss overfishing and safe limits of commercial fishing stocks in Northwestern Europe. Ask students to share any knowledge they may have of fishing regulations in the United States and/or other countries that have been enacted to limit overfishing or methods used to maintain safe levels of fish. Have students answer each question individually. Then in a class discussion, have students share their answers. AL Naturalist, Interpersonal

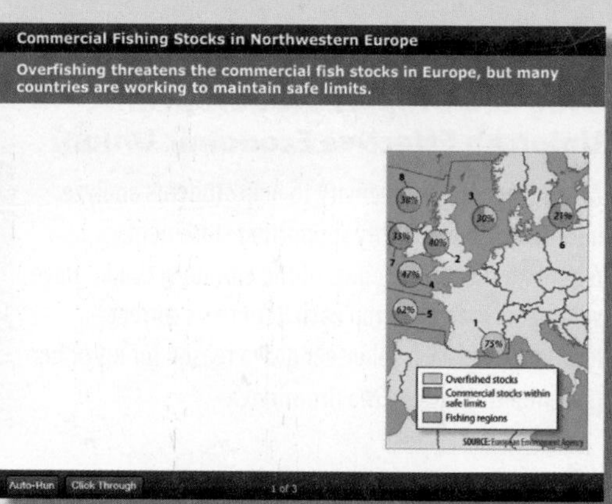

affect Great Britain and Germany, progress has been made. Reports show that overfishing in the northeast Atlantic, the North Sea, and the Baltic Sea declined from 72 percent in 2010 to 47 percent in 2012.

As new roads and railways intersect Northwestern Europe, the fragmentation of the landscape limits the migration of wildlife and causes some animal populations to become **isolated**. The highest levels of fragmentation in the subregion are found in the Benelux countries (Belgium, the Netherlands, and Luxembourg), followed by Germany and France. Fragmentation also reduces the development of healthy ecosystems upon which human and animal life rely.

isolate to place or keep by itself

READING PROGRESS CHECK

Evaluating How has industry affected Northwestern Europe's environment?

Human Impact

GUIDING QUESTION *In what ways have human activities impacted the environment in Northwestern Europe?*

The degradation of marine and coastal ecosystems is occurring in Northwestern Europe. This trend has intensified due largely to overfishing, agriculture, pollution, tourism, industrial chemicals, and coastal development.

Air pollution is a problem throughout Europe due to manufacturing industries and the heavy use of vehicles. Industrial fumes and vehicle exhaust cause eye irritation, asthma, and respiratory infections in people who live in industrial areas of Northwestern Europe. Factories built during the Communist era in East Germany, for example, still give off soot, sulfur, and carbon dioxide into the air. Some former Communist countries are closing polluting factories. Yet they are putting more cars on the road, emitting sulfur, nitrogen oxides, and carbon.

Overfishing in Northwestern Europe

GRAPH SKILLS

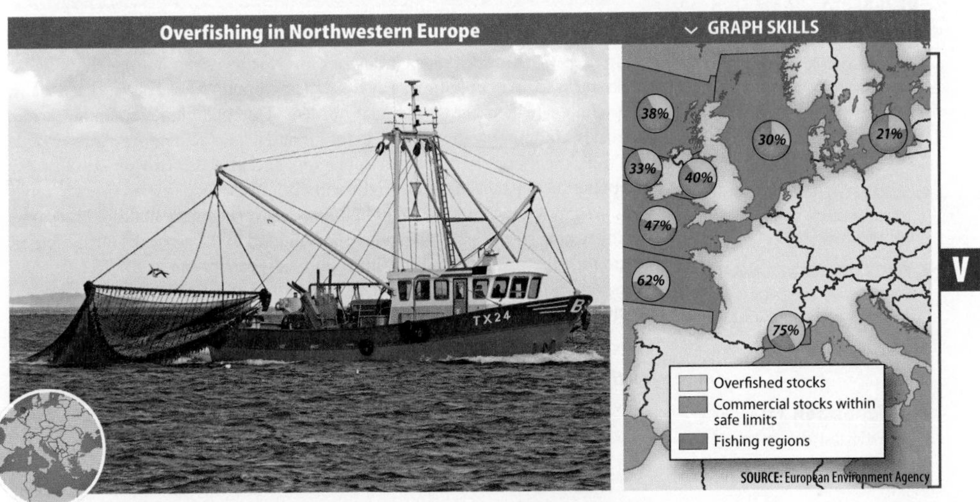

Overfishing in the coastal waters of Northwestern Europe has led to reduced catches for fishers of the subregion.

Voorspoels Kurt/Alamy

▲ CRITICAL THINKING

1. ***Analyzing Visuals*** What body of water suffers the most from overfishing?
2. ***Making Predictions*** What might be the consequences if overfishing in this subregion continues?

W Writing Skills

Argument Have students research further information about landscape fragmentation and its effect on wildlife and humans. Ask them to write a letter to a town council arguing against the building of a new road to connect two existing freeways on the outside of a nearby city or town. Have them cite specific reasons in their letter and explain the environmental impact, as well as the impact on humans and wildlife. BL **Verbal/Linguistic**

C Critical Thinking Skills

Categorizing Ask a volunteer to read the two paragraphs under the heading *Human Impact*. Point out that there are different ways that humans impact the environment—they may pollute by putting waste into the environment, or they may overuse the resources. **Ask:** What are some examples of pollution? *(industrial fumes, vehicle exhaust, industrial chemicals)* Which are examples of overuse of land or water? *(agriculture, tourism, coastal development, overfishing)* Which are examples of both? *(agriculture, tourism, coastal development, industry)* **Logical/Mathematical**

V Visual Skills

Locating Direct students to the graph showing overfishing. **Ask:** Which country borders the most overfished waters in Northwestern Europe? *(France)* What is a logical reason for this? *(Possible answer: France is a major market for seafood.)* AL **Visual/Spatial**

VIDEO

Water Pollution

Problem Solving Use this video about water pollution around the British Isles to discuss the global impact of this issue. As they view the video, have students list the causes and the concerns of water pollution in Northwestern Europe and the rest of the world. In small groups, have students compare their individual lists and then discuss ways that human activities continue to pollute the world's oceans. Have each group come up with a list of solutions to help control global water pollution. As each group presents their solutions to the class, have other groups consider if the solutions are globally possible. BL **Logical/Mathematical**

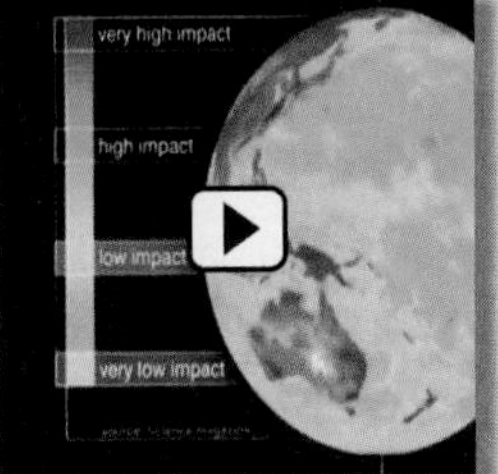

ANSWERS, p. 285

READING PROGRESS CHECK Industry relies on natural resources, which are taken from the environment. Extraction of resources also pollutes the environment and creates health hazards for humans. Industry also generates a lot of waste that contaminates surrounding areas.

CRITICAL THINKING

1. the Mediterranean Sea
2. Fish populations may be reduced to a point from which they can no longer rebound, and some species may become extinct.

R Reading Skills

Defining As a class, discuss acid deposition. **Ask:** **How is acid deposition different than localized pollution?** *(It moves with the clouds, so it is hard to know where it will affect the environment until it falls.)* **What does the term *deposition* mean?** *(Deposition refers to the act of depositing or something that has been deposited.)* **How does this definition relate to acid deposition?** *(Acid deposition is the wet or dry acid pollution that falls to the ground.)* **How can acid deposition be reduced?** *(by reducing the amount of pollutants that are put into the air)* **ELL Verbal/Linguistic**

C Critical Thinking Skills

Understanding Relationships Among Events Discuss with students how the geography of Northwestern Europe makes it easier for acid deposition to pollute more areas. **Ask:** **In what geographical area of Northwestern Europe will you find melting snow and ice?** *(in the Alps and other mountain regions)* Discuss how melting snow and ice from the Alps is carried into many other geographic areas, spreading the acidic deposition further into various regions. **AL Naturalist**

T Technology Skills

Examining Information Have students research EU environmental protection laws. Ask them to choose a specific law and find a U.S. law or local state law that pertains to the same topic. Have them write two paragraphs explaining how the laws are similar and how they are different. **Ask:** **Which law do you consider to be stricter? Why?** *(Student answers will vary based on the law they selected, but should include supporting information for their viewpoint on which law is stricter.)* **Visual/Spatial, Verbal/Linguistic**

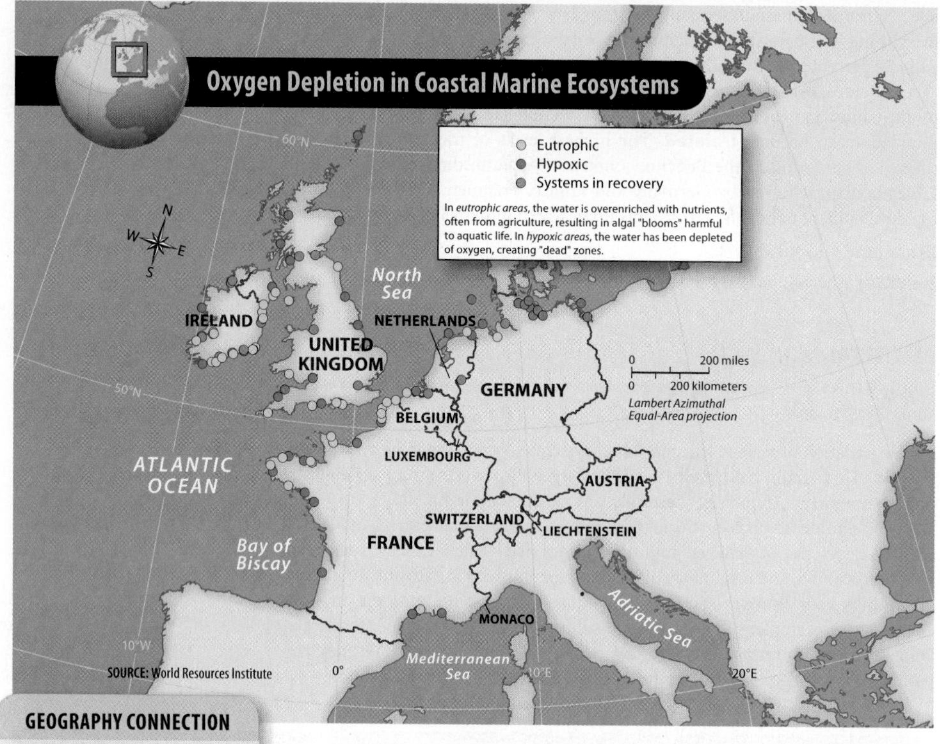

GEOGRAPHY CONNECTION

Marine coastal ecosystems in Northwestern Europe have been polluted, resulting in areas of over-enriched nutrients that are dangerous to aquatic life and areas where aquatic life cannot survive.

1. ***HUMAN SYSTEM*** Which type of oxygen depletion is the result of the agricultural pollutants?
2. ***PLACES AND REGIONS*** How does France compare to the United Kingdom in terms of areas in recovery?

R In the 1970s and 1980s, industries in Northwestern Europe built taller smokestacks to carry pollution away from their communities. This worked locally, but pollution drifted across national borders. This pollution, containing acidic chemicals, combines with moisture in the air and falls as acid rain. Polluted clouds drift from the industrial belt of the subregion, and **acid deposition**—wet or dry acid pollution that falls to the ground—withers forests and damages rivers in other areas. Acid pollution even damages buildings, especially those made of limestone. C During winter, snow carries the industrial pollution to the ground. During spring, meltwater—the result of melting snow and ice—carries the acid into lakes and rivers. As acid concentrations build, fish and other aquatic life die. Many lakes in Northwestern Europe have a declining fish population or even no fish at all.

acid deposition wet or dry airborne acids that fall to the ground

READING PROGRESS CHECK

Identifying Central Issues What human activities have led to withered forests and damaged rivers and buildings?

Addressing the Issues

GUIDING QUESTION *What actions have been taken to address environmental issues in Northwestern Europe?*

T In recent decades, Europeans have made concerted efforts to clean up the environment. Countries in the EU can face legal action if they do not respect environmental protection laws. Individual countries are also addressing the

286

networks Online Teaching Options

INTERACTIVE MAP

Oxygen Depletion in Coastal Marine Ecosystems

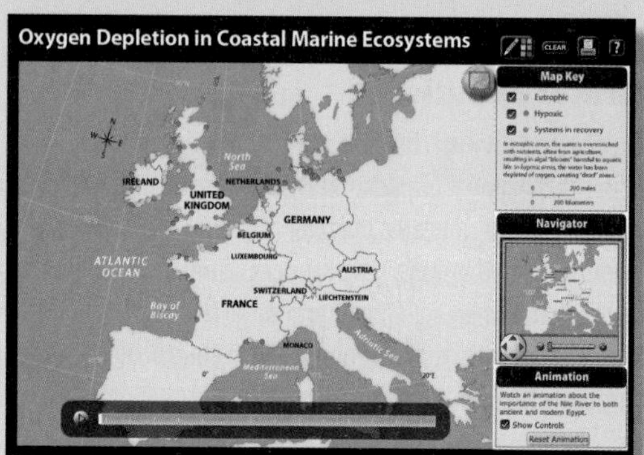

Predicting Divide the class into groups and assign each group one of the Northwestern European countries. Have them research online or in the library the efforts being made by that country to lower their oxygen depletion. Then have them draw a rough sketch of their country and label it by revising the number of symbols to match what they think the oxygen depletion situation in that country will be by the year 2030. Have them compare their predictions with the map in the textbook to see by how much the symbols have increased or decreased. **Logical/Mathematical, Visual/Spatial**

ANSWERS, p. 286

READING PROGRESS CHECK Industries emit smoke that carries chemicals which combine with moisture in the atmosphere to form acid rain. Acid pollution is harmful to forests, rivers and buildings.

GEOGRAPHY CONNECTION

1. eutrophic
2. France does not have any systems in recovery while the United Kingdom has four systems in recovery.

consequences of pollution. For example, cities in Northwestern Europe now protect buildings and statues with acid-resistant coatings. In 2012 the mayor of Paris proposed a ban on older vehicles that produce higher emissions from the city and surrounding suburbs.

The EU and others continue to develop ways to protect the environment. Many power plants now burn natural gas instead of lignite coal. Natural gas burns cleaner and results in less pollution. Some countries are also developing alternative fuel sources, such as solar and wind.

Global climate change is another process that has implications for Northwestern Europe. Scientists have not identified the exact cause of climate change, but it appears clear that emissions of greenhouse gases from human activities are partly responsible for it.

In response, all the countries in the Northwestern Europe have ratified the **Kyoto Protocol**—an amendment to the international treaty on climate change designed to reduce the amount of greenhouse gases emitted by specific countries. The Kyoto Protocol sets emissions targets for participating countries and establishes a system of **cap-and-trade**.

Under a cap-and-trade system, a limit is set on the amount of air pollution that can be emitted. Businesses that produce amounts lower than the cap receive credits for the difference between their actual emissions and the cap.

Kyoto Protocol an amendment to the international treaty on climate change designed to reduce the amount of greenhouse gases emitted by specific countries

cap-and-trade a method for managing pollution in which a limit is placed on emissions and businesses or countries can buy and sell emissions allowances

Boris Horvat/AFP/Getty Images

Many Northwestern Europeans, such as these protesters, are deeply concerned about damage to the environment in their subregion.

▲ **CRITICAL THINKING**

1. ***Speculating*** What are some environmental issues that concern citizens in Northwestern Europe that may be the cause of this protest?
2. ***Identifying Cause and Effect*** Describe how protests like the one pictured can lead to change in government policies.

INTERACTIVE IMAGE

Addressing Environmental Issues

Creating Posters Ask students to imagine that they are exchange students visiting the United States from one of the Northwestern European countries that is experiencing a severe environmental pollution problem. Ask them to design a poster for an upcoming protest about the pollution issue. Tell them that since they will be protesting with many others, they must keep their message very clear and succinct. Ask them to decide on the issue, what they want to say about it, and the simplest way to convey the message. Encourage students to include graphics on their posters. ELL **Intrapersonal**

T Technology Skills

Presenting Have students research an alternative form of energy used in one of the countries in Northwestern Europe. Have them gather facts and statistics about the usage of that form of energy, including information about what percentage of energy comes from the alternative source. Ask students to create a short visual presentation to present their findings to the class. BL **Visual/Spatial**

C Critical Thinking Skills

Communicating Discuss with students their feelings on the cap-and-trade system. **Ask:** **Do you think businesses or countries should be able to buy and sell emission allowances? Why or why not?** *(Student answers may vary, but should be well supported with details.)* **Verbal/Linguistic**

V Visual Skills

Differing Interpretations Discuss with students why the protestors in the photograph want exportation stopped. Review what exportation means and that often exporting implies economic advantages for a country. Speculate with students on what goods or resources these protestors could be protesting. **Ask:** **Why might these protestors not want these things or resources to be exported?** *(Possible answer: They feel that selling the resource from their country is too damaging to the environment.)* Discuss the two pulls involved in environmental issues—damage to the environment versus monetary gain. AL **Verbal/Linguistic**

Content Background Knowledge

The Kyoto Protocol The Kyoto Protocol was originally adopted in 1997 in Kyoto, Japan, but was not enforced until 2005. In December 2012, the Doha Amendment to the Kyoto Protocol was adopted. This amendment included a new commitment period from January 2013 to December 2020, which included a revised list of greenhouse gases. Under the protocol, countries need to meet three emissions targets: International Emissions Trading, or cap-and-trade, Clean Development Mechanism, and Joint Implementation. Some of these targets allow countries to aid developing country in order to receive credit toward emissions reduction.

ANSWERS, p. 287

CRITICAL THINKING

1. They might be referencing exporting hazardous waste.
2. Protests serve to spread awareness of issues. Legislators can also see what issues are of the most concern to constituents.

People and Their Environment: Northwestern Europe

R Reading Skills

Applying Challenge students to design a cap-and-trade game in which people in the game represent countries. Each country should be given the same number of emission allowances. However, countries should randomly be assigned a number of emissions that they already produce. Have students work in small groups to design and play the game. **Visual/Spatial**

C1 Critical Thinking Skills

Evaluating Primary and Secondary Sources Have students evaluate the World Wide Fund for Nature as a source. **Ask:** **What should you look for when evaluating a source?** *(Possible answer: Find out if it is credible. Find out if it is biased in any way. Find out what its goals are.)* **Is the World Wide Fund for Nature a credible source? Why or why not?** *(World Wide Fund for Nature is known as the World Wildlife Fund, or WWF, in the United States. It has been around since 1961 and has invested in conservation initiatives. It is active in many countries around the world and is a credible source because of its strong history.)* **Logical/Mathematical**

C2 Critical Thinking Skills

Defending Discuss why some local businesses and industries, as well as citizens in the United Kingdom, may disagree with the ability of local governments to forward fines imposed by the European Union on to local offenders or to remove the most polluting vehicles from the roads. Have students work in small groups to actively debate this issue. One side should defend the local governments and the other side should defend the offenders. AL **Interpersonal**

CLOSE & REFLECT

Outlining Have students look back through the headings and subheadings used in each section and use them to outline the main ideas and details of the lesson. Have them compare their outlines with a partner's outline to see what details they may have missed or which details should be included.

ANSWERS, p. 288

READING PROGRESS CHECK The EU can take legal action against countries that do not respect environmental protection laws. The EU Water Framework Directive established new regulations that will require several rivers in Europe to undergo major restoration.

Connecting Geography Pros may include reduction of pollutants and clear maximum limits. Cons may include that greenhouse gas producers monitor their own emissions and that the nature of some industries necessitates that they emit more than others. Factories built during the Communist era in East Germany might not be able to afford to pay for their extra emissions. This could be countered by the argument that they should be incentivized to reform their procedures to not be contributing so much to the pollution problem.

Connecting Geography to SCIENCE

Cap-and-Trade Systems

In 2005 the European Union began a cap-and-trade system aimed at reducing the impact of pollutants that are linked to the burning of fossil fuels. The program sets a maximum overall limit (cap) on greenhouse gas emissions. Sources of the emissions receive permits to emit (emissions allowances), which can be traded. Greenhouse gas producers in the program are responsible for monitoring emissions and using permits to pay for emission privileges. The program is designed to provide both flexibility and an incentive to reduce emissions. Between 2005 and 2010, greenhouse-gas emissions dropped 13 percent.

CONSIDERING ADVANTAGES AND DISADVANTAGES What are some potential pros and cons of a cap-and-trade system? Discuss which industries may have objections to a strict cap-and-trade program and provide effective counter-arguments.

Then the businesses can "trade" their pollution credits, so that a business that produces pollution at levels higher than the cap may purchase credits from businesses who earned credits. This creates an economic incentive to reduce the emissions, and the cap can be lowered over time, so that emissions continue to decline.

Protecting water resources in the subregion has also become a high priority. By the end of 2015, as required by the EU Water Framework Directive, several rivers in Europe will be required to have major restoration to meet the new regulations. Progress has been made, but the rivers in the region still suffer from floodplain drainage, industrial discharge, and the heavy use of fertilizers.

PRIMARY SOURCE

> "It will require a substantial investment but the costs of reviving Europe's rivers will be more than repaid by long-term savings in flood damage, water treatment and public health. WWF will be keeping a close eye on EU countries to make sure they live up to these commitments."
>
> —Julian Scola, "Europe's Rivers Ready for Revival," World Wide Fund for Nature, April 20, 2001.

In 1992 the Convention on Biological Diversity (CBC) was signed by 159 governments at the United Nation's Earth Summit in Rio de Janeiro, Brazil, creating the first treaty to provide a legal framework for biodiversity conservation. Following the convention, the United Kingdom created the UK BAP (Biodiversity Action Plan) a national strategy to conserve, protect and enhance biological diversity. It describes the United Kingdom's biological resources, including species and habitats, with a detailed plan for protecting their resources.

To address air pollution and improve air quality, the government of the United Kingdom allows community governments to forward fines imposed by the European Union to the local offenders. Local authorities can remove the most polluting vehicles from the roads. Governments of the countries in Northwestern Europe are not only working on solutions to environmental problems together, but with nongovernmental organizations (NGOs) as well. For example, the European Union's common fisheries policy is designed to **ensure** fisheries are more sustainably managed to prevent overfishing.

Three NGOs that are working to protect, restore, and improve the marine and coastal ecosystems are Greenpeace, Oceana, and Seas At Risk. The mission of all three of these international organizations is to limit further degradation of marine areas and loss of species, and to provide awareness, education, and concrete steps to arrest further damage. Seas At Risk, in particular, focuses its efforts on the North Atlantic and the Irish and North Seas.

ensure to make sure or certain

READING PROGRESS CHECK

Explaining How is the EU encouraging countries to develop new ways to protect the environment?

LESSON 3 REVIEW

Reviewing Vocabulary (Tier Three Words)

1. ***Explaining*** Explain the Kyoto Protocol. RH.9–10.4

Using Your Notes

2. ***Describing*** Use your graphic organizer to describe how Northwestern Europe is addressing the issues of pollution in the region.

Answering the Guiding Questions

3. ***Identifying*** How has modern development resulted in challenges to the management of resources in Northwestern Europe?

4. ***Describing*** In what ways have human activities impacted the environment in Northwestern Europe?

5. ***Explaining*** What actions have been taken to address environmental issues in Northwestern Europe?

Writing Activity

6. ***Argument*** Imagine that you live in a polluted area of Northwestern Europe. Write a letter to the editor of a local newspaper advocating steps to halt environmental damage. WHST.9–10.2

288

LESSON 3 REVIEW ANSWERS

Reviewing Vocabulary

1. The Kyoto Protocol is an amendment to the international treaty on climate change designed to reduce the amount of greenhouse gases by setting emissions targets for specific countries and establishing a system of cap-and-trade.

Using Your Notes

2. A variety of environmental protection laws targeting each particular threat are now being enacted.

Answering the Guiding Questions

3. More people living in and visiting coastal areas has led to more waste near the sea. Overfishing and invasive species threaten fish populations. New roads and railways fragment the land and limit the migration of wildlife, isolating some animal populations.

4. Traffic exhaust and industrial fumes cause air pollution. Acid deposition, a result of industrial emissions, is a serious problem. Overfishing, agriculture, pollution, tourism, industrial chemicals, and coastal development all contribute to the degradation of marine and coastal ecosystems.

5. All countries in the subregion ratified the Kyoto Protocol, agreeing to meet emissions targets and participate in cap-and-trade.

Writing Activity

6. Letters will differ but should be logical and strongly supported with evidence.

CHAPTER 11 Assessment 

Directions: On a separate sheet of paper, answer the questions below. Make sure you read carefully and answer all parts of the questions.

Lesson Review

Lesson 1

1. ***Describing*** Describe the geography of the Northern European Plain and its appeal to early farmers.
2. ***Explaining*** Explain how water plays an important role in the lives of Northwestern Europeans.
3. ***Drawing Conclusions*** What are some factors affecting climate in Northwestern Europe? Why are they significant?

Lesson 2

4. ***Evaluating*** How did the Industrial Revolution change the human geography of Northwestern Europe?
5. ***Discussing*** Describe the impact of the aging population on population patterns in Northwestern Europe.
6. ***Summarizing*** What are the main service industries that fuel Northwestern Europe's economy?

Lesson 3

7. ***Identifying Central Issues*** Describe the problem of overfishing in Northwestern Europe and provide some viable solutions to reduce its impact.
8. ***Explaining*** What is the main reason for poor air quality and air pollution in parts of Northwestern Europe?
9. ***Comparing and Contrasting*** Explain cap-and-trade and the Kyoto Protocol. How are they related?

Exploring the Essential Question

10. ***Making Connections*** Write a paragraph that explains the effect of the Seine River on the location of cities in France.

21st Century Skills

Use the following graph to answer the questions below.

ELECTRICITY GENERATED FROM NUCLEAR FUEL

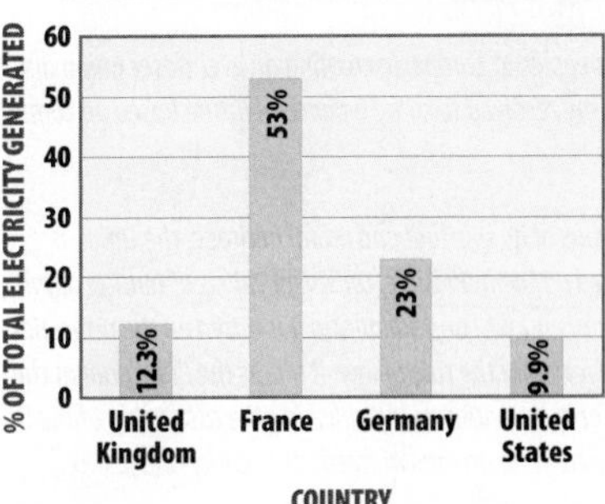

Source: CIA World Factbook

11. ***Compare and Contrast*** How does France compare to Germany and United Kingdom in regard to nuclear fuels generated?
12. ***Identifying Cause and Effect*** What factors may contribute to the higher percentage of nuclear fuels generated in Northwestern Europe, as compared to the amount generated in the United States?

College and Career Readiness

13. ***Economics*** As a consultant for a global conglomerate, you have been hired to research the importance of transportation and communications systems to the economy of Northwestern Europe. What are the strengths and weaknesses of the current systems, and how can they be improved?

Need Extra Help?

If You've Missed Question	1	2	3	4	5	6	7	8	9	10	11	12	13
Go to page	270	271	273	276	278	280	284	286	287	273	289	289	280

CHAPTER 11 Assessment Answers

Lesson Review

Lesson 1

1. It is a span of flat, low-lying land that stretches from the Pyrenees Mountains on the French-Spanish border across Europe to the Ural Mountains in Russia. Its fertile soil and many rivers were appealing to early farmers.
2. Water is relied on for transportation, trade, and recreational activities.
3. Factors include the presence of the Alps and being located near and along large bodies of water. Being bordered by the North Atlantic Ocean to the west makes the region warmer than it would be otherwise since warm winds blow inland as a result of the North Atlantic current. The high altitude of the Alps cools these winds, producing snow.

Lesson 2

4. Great Britain was the hub of the Industrial Revolution, so many job seekers became concentrated near industrial centers there and eventually in Belgium, France, Germany, and the U.S., too, as the revolution spread.
5. Aging populations result in increasingly lower total populations.
6. The main service industries are international banking and insurance.

Lesson 3

7. Overfishing depletes fish populations to a point from which they cannot regenerate quickly enough, making the current level of fishing unsustainable. It further threatens fish populations and ecosystems by introducing invasive species. One solution is to limit the amount of fishing that can occur in particular areas. Another is to manage fisheries in a more sustainable way.
8. Manufacturing industry practices and heavy use of vehicles result in industrial fumes and vehicle exhaust.
9. The Kyoto Protocol was designed to reduce the amount of greenhouse gases emitted by specific countries, and establishing a cap-and-trade system is one way it does this. Cap-and-trade limits the total amount of emissions allowed, and businesses or countries can buy and sell emissions allowances.

Exploring the Essential Question

10. Paragraphs should reflect knowledge that many cities emerged as key trading centers along navigable rivers, such as the Seine.

21st Century Skills

11. In France, over 50 percent of generated electricity comes from nuclear fuel. Germany and the United Kingdom generate less electricity using nuclear fuel than France.
12. Students' answers will vary. Possible answers may include that Northwestern Europe has fewer natural resources, such as coal and natural gas, to generate electricity.

College and Career Readiness

13. Responses should explain the importance of, as well as the strengths and weaknesses of, current transportation and communications systems in Northwestern Europe.

Assessment Answers

Analyzing Primary Sources

14 human dignity, freedom, equality and solidarity

15 Students' answers will vary but they should thoroughly summarize the charter's meaning in their own words.

Research and Presentation

16 The presentation should include the name of the city and some basic facts, at least one major thing the city is known for, and similarities to and differences from other cities in the region.

Applying Map Skills

17 The Alps, which extend through parts of France, Switzerland, Italy, and Austria, are located southwest of the Northern European Plain.

18 Great Britain is bordered by the Celtic Sea, the English Channel, the North Sea, and the North Atlantic Ocean.

19 Ireland and Great Britain are northwest of continental Europe.

Critical Thinking

20 After World War II, immigration diversified and enlarged the populations of Northwestern Europe. Immigrants from South Asia and the West Indies arrived in Great Britain, guest workers from different countries went to Germany, and many immigrants from Algeria and Morocco arrived in France. Urbanization resulted in more heavily populated cities as more people moved there for jobs.

21 Internal migration occurs as people move between rural and urban areas. Populations shifted from rural to urban when people moved away from the poverty in rural areas to find better jobs in cities. Cities become so large that they spill into surrounding areas, creating suburbs. Suburbanization occurs when people move away from the city centers and follow jobs into the suburbs, where many middle-class and working-class populations can now find more affordable housing.

22 Overfishing, agriculture, pollution, tourism, industrial chemicals, and coastal development all contribute to the deterioration of marine and coastal ecosystems.

Writing About Geography

23 The one-page essay should detail the main reasons that Paris became a megacity. It should include factors that led to a decline in out-migration and a rise in population rate.

CHAPTER 11 Assessment 

Directions: On a separate sheet of paper, answer the questions below. Make sure you read carefully and answer all parts of the questions.

DBQ Analyzing Primary Sources

Use the document to answer the questions that follow.

PRIMARY SOURCE

"The peoples of Europe, in creating an ever closer union among them, are resolved to share a peaceful future based on common values.

Conscious of its spiritual and moral heritage, the Union is founded on the indivisible, universal values of human dignity, freedom, equality and solidarity; it is based on the principles of democracy and the rule of law. It places the individual at the heart of its activities, by establishing the citizenship of the Union and by creating an area of freedom, security and justice."

—Charter of Fundamental Rights of the European Union, 2000

14 ***Identifying*** According to the excerpt, what core values are held by the European Union? RH.9–10.2

15 ***Paraphrasing*** In your own words, summarize the meaning of the Charter of Fundamental Rights of the European Union. RH.9–10.2

Research and Presentation

16 ***Research Skills*** Use the Internet and other resources to gather information about one of Northwestern Europe's most famous cities, such as Paris, London, Brussels, or Amsterdam. What is the city most known for? How is it alike and different from other cities in the subregion? Create a multimedia presentation to share your findings.

Applying Map Skills

Use your Unit 4 Atlas to answer the following questions.

17 ***Places and Regions*** Describe the location and extent of the Alps in relation to the Northern European Plain.

18 ***Physical Systems*** Use the physical map of Europe from the unit atlas to list the bodies of water that border Great Britain.

19 ***The World in Spatial Terms*** Use your mental map of Europe to describe the location of Ireland and Great Britain in relation to continental Europe.

Critical Thinking

20 ***Identifying Central Issues*** How have urbanization and immigration shaped the population patterns of Northwestern Europe?

21 ***Making Generalizations*** What are the characteristics of internal migration and suburbanization, and how did they affect population patterns?

22 ***Drawing Conclusions*** Discuss the ways in which human activities have affected marine and coastal ecosystems in Northwestern Europe.

Writing About Geography

23 ***Informative/Explanatory*** Use standard grammar, spelling, sentence structure, and punctuation to write a one-page essay about Paris's rise to megacity status. Use library and Internet resources to gather information to discuss the city's population and how it has changed over the decades. Describe the factors regarding the decline in out-migration and a higher natural population rate increase. WHST.9–10.2

Need Extra Help?

If You've Missed Question	14	15	16	17	18	19	20	21	22	23
Go to page	290	290	278	242	242	242	278	278	286	269

290

networks Online Teaching Options

WORKSHEET

Chapter Test and Lesson Quizzes

Assessing Have students complete the Chapter Test and Lesson Quizzes to assess student understanding throughout the chapter. These assessment tools offer chapter and lesson evaluation through a variety of question formats, including document-based questions.

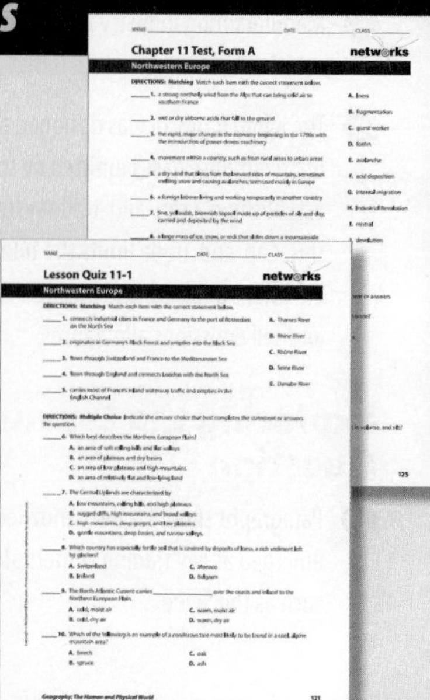

CHAPTER 12

Southern Europe Planner

UNDERSTANDING BY DESIGN®

Enduring Understandings

- *Culture influences people's perceptions of places and regions.*

Essential Question

- *How do physical systems and human systems shape a place?*

Predictable Misunderstandings

Students may think:

- *Crops similar to those grown throughout the rest of Europe are grown in Southern Europe. Explain that the climate of Southern Europe is warmer than the rest of Europe so that many crops that cannot be grown in the rest of Europe, such as olives, grapes, citrus fruits, and figs, can be grown in Southern Europe.*
- *The physical geography of Southern Europe is similar to that of Northwestern Europe. Explain that countries in Southern Europe, like Portugal and Spain, were only partially affected by glaciers during the last Ice Age and therefore have fewer lakes than other areas of Europe that experienced more glaciation.*

Assessment Evidence

Performance Tasks:

- *Hands-On Chapter Project*

Other Evidence:

- *Guided Reading Activities*
- *Vocabulary Activities*
- *Lesson Quizzes*
- *Chapter Tests, Forms A and B*

SUGGESTED PACING GUIDE

Introducing the Chapter ½ Day	Lesson 3 1 Day
Lesson 1 1 Day	Chapter Wrap-Up and Assessment ½ Day
Lesson 2 2 Days	

TOTAL TIME 5 Days

Key for Using the Teacher Edition

SKILL-BASED ACTIVITIES

Types of skill activities found in the Teacher Edition.

*V **Visual Skills** require students to analyze maps, graphs, charts, and photos.

R **Reading Skills** help students practice reading skills and master vocabulary.

C **Critical Thinking Skills** help students apply and extend what they have learned.

W **Writing Skills** provide writing opportunities to help students comprehend the text.

T **Technology Skills** require students to use digital tools effectively.

*Letters are followed by a number when there is more than one of the same type of skill on the page.

DIFFERENTIATED INSTRUCTION

All activities are written for the on-level student unless otherwise marked with the leveled labels below.

BL Beyond Level
AL Approaching Level
ELL English Language Learners

All students benefit from activities that utilize different learning styles. Many activities are marked as below when a particular learning style is highlighted.

Intrapersonal	**Naturalist**
Logical/Mathematical	**Kinesthetic**
Visual/Spatial	**Auditory/Musical**
Verbal/Linguistic	**Interpersonal**

National Geography Standards covered in "Southern Europe"

The student knows and understands:

(3) How to analyze the spatial organizations of people, places, and environments on Earth's surface

3.1 The meaning and use of complex spatial concepts, such as connectivity, networks, hierarchies, to analyze and explain the spatial organizations of human and physical phenomena

3.2 Complex processes change over time and shape patterns in the distribution of human and physical phenomena

(4) The physical and human characteristics of places

4.2 The interaction of physical and human systems result in the creation of and changes to places

(7) The physical processes that shape the patterns of Earth's surface

7.3 Physical processes interact over time to shape particular places on Earth's surface

(8) The characteristics and spatial distribution of ecosystems and biomes on Earth's surface

8.1 Ecosystems are dynamic and respond to changes in environmental conditions.

8.3 The distribution and characteristics of biomes change over time

(9) The characteristics, distribution, and migration of human populations on Earth's surface

9.2 Population distribution and density are a function of historical, environmental, economic, political, and technological factors

9.3 Migration is one of the driving forces for shaping and reshaping the cultural and physical landscape of places and regions

(10) The characteristics, distribution, and complexity of Earth's cultural mosaics

10.3 Cultures change through convergence and/or divergence

(11) The patterns and networks of economic interdependence on Earth's surface

11.2 Patterns exist in the spatial organization of economic activities

(14) How human actions modify the physical environment

14.3 People can either mitigate and/or adapt to the consequences of human modifications of the physical environment.

(15) How physical systems affect human systems

15.3 Societies use a variety of strategies to adapt to changes in the physical environment.

CHAPTER OPENER PLANNER

Students will know:

- *the characteristics and influence of Southern Europe's mountains, rivers, climate, and vegetation.*
- *how early civilizations and other factors influenced the development of Southern Europe.*
- *that services and agriculture are important to Southern Europe's economy.*
- *the causes and consequences of soil erosion and deforestation in Southern Europe.*
- *the threats to the environment and how people are working to protect the environment.*

Students will be able to:

- ***identify*** *how the physical geography of Southern Europe has influenced the region.*
- ***analyze*** *influences on the development of Southern Europe and its cultures.*
- ***describe*** *economic activities in Southern Europe.*
- ***identify*** *causes and consequences of soil erosion and deforestation in the region.*
- ***describe*** *environmental issues and possible solutions.*

UNDERSTANDING BY DESIGN®

☑ Print Teaching Options

V Visual Skills

☐ **p. 292** Students collect data about recent migrations and the current political status of a selected country and create a graph to show their data. BL Visual/Spatial

W Writing Skills

☐ **p. 292** Students write an essay summarizing information about labor migration from North Africa.

C Critical Thinking Skills

☐ **p. 293** Students explain that political or economic upheaval in one country affects adjacent countries and other continents. AL Verbal/Linguistic

T Technology Skills

☐ **p. 293** Students research which nations in North Africa have been affected by the Arab Spring and create a multimedia presentation to show how the country was affected. BL Verbal/Linguistic

☑ Online Teaching Options

C Critical Thinking Skills

☐ SLIDE SHOW **North African Migration to Southern Europe**—Students choose a migration pattern from the slide show, research the distances of the travel routes, and discuss the shortest and longest distances traveled. ELL Logical/Mathematical

☐ MAP **Interactive Regional Atlas**—Students use the interactive regional atlas to understand the physical and human geography of Southern Europe.

☐ TIME LINE **Interactive Time Line**—Students use the interactive time line to learn more about the region's human geography.

☑ Printable Digital Worksheets

☐ WORKSHEET **Assessing Background Knowledge**—Determine the level of prior knowledge students have about Southern Europe.

☐ WORKSHEET **Chapter Summaries**—Students review the main idea of each lesson of the chapter content.

Project-Based Learning 

Hands-On

Podcasts about the Foundations of Western Civilization

Students will use the chapter lesson content along with library and online research to create podcasts about Southern Europe's impact on Western civilization.

Digital Hands-On

Create Online Projects

Find an additional activity online that incorporates technology for this project. Visit the EdTech Teacher Web sites for more links, tutorials, and other resources.

Print Resources

ANCILLARY RESOURCES

This ancillary is available for every chapter and lesson.

- **Chapter Tests and Lesson Quizzes**

PRINTABLE DIGITAL WORKSHEETS

These printable digital worksheets are available for every chapter and lesson.

- **Assessing Background Knowledge**
- **Chapter Summaries**
- **Guided Reading Activities**
- **Hands-On Chapter Projects**
- **Quizzes and Tests**
- **Reading Essentials and Study Guide** AL
- **Reteaching Activities**
- **Video Activities**
- **Vocabulary**

More Media Resources

SUGGESTED VIDEOS 

- **Italy Venice** *World Odysseys Series* (25 min.)
- **Sintra Portugal** *Global Treasures* (11 min.)
- **Vista Point Athens Greece** (27 min.)

SUGGESTED READING 

- ***Urban Governance in Southern Europe (Urban and Regional Planning and Development Series),*** by Joao Seixas and Abel Albet
- ***Southern Europe and the Making of the European Union, 1945–1980s,*** by Antonio Costa Pinto and Nuno S. Teixeira
- ***Constructing Democracy in Southern Europe: A comparative analysis of Italy, Spain and Turkey (Democratization Studies),*** by Lauren M. McClaren

PHYSICAL GEOGRAPHY OF SOUTHERN EUROPE

Students will know:
- *how the mountains of Southern Europe have affected the subregion's connection to the rest of Europe.*
- *the limits of Southern Europe's rivers to trade and transportation.*
- *the characteristics of Southern Europe's climate and vegetation.*

Students will be able to:
- ***explain*** *how Southern Europe is affected by its mountains.*
- ***describe*** *the limits of Southern Europe's rivers.*
- ***identify*** *characteristics of climate and vegetation in the region.*

UNDERSTANDING BY DESIGN®

☑ Print Teaching Options

V Visual Skills
- ☐ **p. 295** Students describe what they see in an image of massifs. ELL Visual/Spatial
- ☐ **p. 296** Students identify information in the Rivers of Europe infographic. AL Visual/Spatial
- ☐ **p. 297** Students create a diagram, including photos or illustrations, which depicts Southern Europe's climate zones. BL Visual/Spatial

R Reading Skills
- ☐ **p. 294** Students define *massifs.* ELL Verbal/Linguistic
- ☐ **p. 298** Students discuss the natural resources found in some Southern European countries. BL Naturalist

C Critical Thinking Skills
- ☐ **p. 294** Students brainstorm ways landforms may have affected the history and development of Southern Europe.
- ☐ **p. 294** Students use a physical map to discuss the Iberian Peninsula and its geography. AL Visual/Spatial
- ☐ **p. 295** Students write a few paragraphs analyzing the influence of the Pyrenees and the Alps. AL Verbal/Linguistic
- ☐ **p. 297** Students discuss the rivers in Italy and Greece. AL Verbal/Linguistic

W Writing Skills
- ☐ **p. 295** Students write an essay explaining why the islands in the Mediterranean were geographically more important to Southern European countries. Verbal/Linguistic

T Technology Skills
- ☐ **p. 296** Students use the Internet to research and design a graphic organizer to diagram the strengths and weaknesses that each river of Europe contributes to trade and transportation industries. Visual/Spatial, Interpersonal
- ☐ **p. 297** Students discuss olive oil production in Italy and research olive growing throughout the world. Verbal/Linguistic

☑ Online Teaching Options

V Visual Skills
- ☐ INFOGRAPHIC **Rivers of Europe**—Students discuss their prior knowledge of rivers and answer questions about rivers of Europe. BL Verbal/Linguistic
- ☐ VIDEO **First Map of the Alps**—Students locate countries that border the Alps and discuss how the size and location of the Alps have affected human and cultural development in the surrounding areas. Interpersonal, Naturalist

C Critical Thinking Skills
- ☐ INTERACTIVE BELLRINGER **Rivers of Europe**—Students discuss the rivers of Europe and summarize what economic value they believe each river brings to the economy of the region. BL Interpersonal, Logical/Mathematical
- ☐ INTERACTIVE IMAGE **Natural Resources of Southern Europe**—Students discuss the negative and positive effects of mining. Logical/Mathematical, Interpersonal
- ☐ INTERACTIVE WHITEBOARD ACTIVITY **Peninsulas of Southern Europe**—Students label landforms and countries of Southern Europe on the map.

☑ Printable Digital Worksheets

R Reading Skills
- ☐ WORKSHEET **Guided Reading Activity**—Students use the Guided Reading Activity worksheets to review their comprehension of the content.

C Critical Thinking Skills
- ☐ WORKSHEET **Video Activity**—Students answer questions related to a topic in the chapter content after they have viewed a lesson video.

HUMAN GEOGRAPHY OF SOUTHERN EUROPE

Students will know:

- *the ways in which the early civilizations of Greece and Rome influenced the development of Southern Europe.*
- *why the road to political and economic stability was difficult for the countries of Southern Europe.*
- *the general population patterns in Southern Europe today.*
- *the factors that have influenced society and culture in Southern Europe today.*
- *that services and agriculture are two of the most important sectors of the economy of Southern Europe.*

Students will be able to:

- ***analyze*** *the influence of early civilizations on Southern Europe.*
- ***explain*** *why political and economic stability is difficult for some countries.*
- ***identify*** *population patterns in the region.*
- ***identify*** *factors that influence society and culture in the region.*
- ***explain*** *why services and agriculture are important to Southern Europe's economy.*

UNDERSTANDING BY DESIGN®

☑ Print Teaching Options

V Visual Skills

- ☐ **p. 300** Students discuss the enormity of changes that occurred during the Renaissance period. AL Verbal/Linguistic
- ☐ **p. 301** Students discuss political and economic stability in Southern Europe. ELL Verbal/Linguistic

R Reading Skills

- ☐ **p. 303** Students discuss family and the status of women in the region in small groups. AL Interpersonal

C Critical Thinking Skills

- ☐ **p. 300** Students discuss the stability of governments in Spain, Italy, and Greece. BL Logical/Mathematical
- ☐ **p. 302** Students discuss the culture and society found today in Southern Europe. AL Logical/Mathematical
- ☐ **p. 304** Students discuss the current relationship between the European Union and the countries of Southern Europe. Verbal/Linguistic

W Writing Skills

- ☐ **p. 301** Students write a blog explaining the population trends in Southern Europe. BL Verbal/Linguistic
- ☐ **p. 302** Students write an essay about whether Italy, Spain, and Greece share common cultures.
- ☐ **p. 304** Students write an essay comparing and contrasting the sectors of the economy most challenged in Spain, Italy, and Greece. AL Verbal/Linguistic

T Technology Skills

- ☐ **p. 299** Students work in groups to give a multimedia presentation on the cultural and political contribution of either Athens or Sparta. BL Auditory/Musical, Visual/Spatial
- ☐ **p. 301** Students research and create a graph showing the current population and projected population for Spain, Italy, Portugal, or Greece in five-year increments. AL Visual/Spatial, Logical/Mathematical
- ☐ **p. 303** Students develop multimedia presentations on two artists from either the Renaissance or modern art periods.

☑ Online Teaching Options

V Visual Skills

- VIDEO **Islam in Spain and the Alhambra**—Students analyze how religious interaction has shaped the development of society and culture in this region. ELL Visual/Spatial, Kinesthetic

C Critical Thinking Skills

- INTERACTIVE BELLRINGER **Leonardo da Vinci and the Italian Renaissance**—Students work in groups to create a list of Renaissance traits and compare their lists to those in the text. ELL Verbal/Linguistic
- INTERACTIVE MAP **Greek City-States, c. 500 B.C.**—Students compare and contrast the locations of ancient city-states to the locations of the cities and countries today. Visual/Spatial
- TIME LINE **Foundations of Western Civilization**—Students rank the eight historic events on the time line in order of importance students feel they have played in the human geography of Southern Europe. Visual/Spatial, Logical/Mathematical
- CHART **The Effects of Geography on the Rise of Rome**—Students use the chart and map to describe how geography affected the rise of Rome. BL Verbal/Linguistic
- INTERACTIVE WHITEBOARD ACTIVITY **The Renaissance Period**—Students answer statements that reflect the cause-effect hierarchy of factors pertaining to the Renaissance in Southern Europe.

☑ Printable Digital Worksheets

R Reading Skills

- WORKSHEET **Guided Reading Activity**—Students use Guided Reading Activity worksheets to review their comprehension of the content.
- WORKSHEET **Reading Essentials and Study Guide**—Students complete the study guide and answer Reading Progress Check and vocabulary questions. AL

C Critical Thinking Skills

- WORKSHEET **Video Activity**—Students answer questions related to a topic in the chapter content after they view a lesson video.

PEOPLE AND THEIR ENVIRONMENT: SOUTHERN EUROPE

Students will know:

- *the causes and consequences of soil erosion in Southern Europe.*
- *the causes and consequences of deforestation in Southern Europe.*
- *how tourism, industrialization, and trade have contributed to the pollution of the Mediterranean Sea.*
- *examples of the efforts of people in Southern Europe to protect the environment.*

Students will be able to:

- ***identify** causes and consequences of soil erosion and deforestation in Southern Europe.*
- ***identify** contributing factors to pollution of the Mediterranean Sea.*
- ***analyze** how people in Southern Europe are working to protect the environment.*

UNDERSTANDING BY DESIGN®

Print Teaching Options

V Visual Skills

- [ ] **p. 306** Students discuss the risk of soil erosion in different countries. AL Visual/Spatial

R Reading Skills

- [ ] **p. 305** Students discuss the available resources in Southern Europe. AL Verbal/Linguistic
- [ ] **p. 306** Students list the steps that lead to soil erosion and write two paragraphs explaining why loss of topsoil creates other ecological issues in an environment. ELL Verbal/Linguistic
- [ ] **p. 307** Students define the term *pollution hot spots.* ELL Verbal/Linguistic

C Critical Thinking Skills

- [ ] **p. 305** Students consider ecological challenges facing Southern Europe.
- [ ] **p. 307** Students analyze how industrial pollution and tourism can cause environmental damage. Verbal/Linguistic

W Writing Skills

- [ ] **p. 306** Students write a short essay on the process of deforestation and its link to soil erosion. BL Verbal/Linguistic
- [ ] **p. 307** Students write an essay discussing whether they think legislative efforts are enough to stop pollution or if other solutions are needed. BL Intrapersonal

T Technology Skills

- [ ] **p. 305** Students research algae blooms throughout the world. Interpersonal, Visual/Spatial
- [ ] **p. 308** Students work in groups to research a particular environmental protection need in one of the four areas of Southern Europe. BL Visual/Spatial, Auditory/Musical

Online Teaching Options

V Visual Skills

- [ ] VIDEO **Grand Canal of Venice**—Students discuss the history of Venice, whether they'd like to live there, and what could be done for the city if sea levels rose. Verbal/Linguistic

C Critical Thinking Skills

- [ ] INTERACTIVE BELLRINGER **Haze in the Po River Valley, Italy**—Students discuss the causes of smog, contributing factors to smog, and ozone alerts. Interpersonal, Verbal/Linguistic
- [ ] INTERACTIVE IMAGE **The Impact of Industrialization**—Students list sources of air, water, or earth pollution shown in the image and for each one suggest a less polluting alternative. BL Visual/Spatial
- [ ] INTERACTIVE WHITEBOARD ACTIVITY **Environmental Concerns in Southern Europe**—Students drag answer statements that reflect the causes and consequences of soil erosion pertaining to environmental concerns in Southern Europe.

Printable Digital Worksheets

R Reading Skills

- [ ] WORKSHEET **Guided Reading Activity**—Students use Guided Reading Activity worksheets to review their comprehension of the content.
- [ ] WORKSHEET **Reading Essentials and Study Guide**—Students complete the study guide and answer Reading Progress Check and vocabulary questions. AL
- [ ] WORKSHEET **Vocabulary Activity**—Students review the chapter content and academic vocabulary words.

C Critical Thinking Skills

- [ ] WORKSHEET **Video Activity**—Students answer questions based on a lesson video.
- [ ] WORKSHEET **Reteaching Activity**—Students use this activity worksheet to review and reteach chapter content and vocabulary. This worksheet can be used with struggling students who need additional help with difficult content concepts.

INTERVENTION AND REMEDIATION STRATEGIES

LESSON 1 Physical Geography of Southern Europe

Reading and Comprehension

Organize students into small groups and tell them they will play a "Pictionary" style game. Have students in each group choose a term or concept from the lesson and take turns drawing a picture of it on the board for the other members of the group to guess. For example, students might draw a crack in the earth to represent fault-line activity that creates a massif. Or they might draw a mountain range to show the Pyrenees. After students have had a turn to draw their chosen term, discuss as a class how the term plays a role in the physical geography of Southern Europe.

Text Evidence

Have students work in four groups to research an aspect of Southern Europe's physical geography as it relates to one of the following topics discussed in the lesson: landforms, water systems, climate regions and biomes, and natural resources. Tell students to present an analysis of their findings, comparing information in the text with information found in their research. For example, students might research the importance of Southern Europe's climate to tourism and agriculture. Tell students to write an objective summary of their findings. Have students present their slide shows to the class, allowing time for groups to conduct a question-and-answer session in which students from each group answer questions about their topic.

LESSON 2 Human Geography of Northwestern Europe

Reading and Comprehension

Have students work in pairs to review the time line in this lesson. Tell students to conduct online research to identify other important dates and events to add to the time line. Students may wish to research events that occurred during the time span shown on the time line, before 1900, or after 2012. Have students present their additional dates and events to the class, encouraging them to include visuals in their presentations.

Text Evidence

Have student groups review the lesson to identify cultural attributes of a country in Southern Europe. Tell students in each group to collaborate on a script for a short skit about life in the country today or in the past. Encourage students to write a realistic scene that depicts a family living in their chosen country. Tell students to conduct additional research to identify how people dressed in the time period during which the skit takes place. Allow time for groups to rehearse their skits before performing them for the class. Guide students in a discussion to answer the Guiding Question: *How have religion, the arts, and Southern Europe's rich intellectual traditions shaped society and culture today?*

LESSON 3 People and Their Environment: Southern Europe

Reading and Comprehension

To ensure comprehension of the concepts in this lesson, have students write a summarizing sentence for each of the three sections in the text: *Managing Resources, Human Impact,* and *Addressing the Issues.* Tell students their sentences should touch on one or more issues facing Southern Europe and should identify what is being done to solve the problem or problems. Have students share their sentences with the class, providing corrective guidance if needed.

Text Evidence

Tell students to choose one of the following statements from the *It Matters Because* paragraph to identify supporting evidence: 1. *The Mediterranean Sea is essential to the culture and economy of Southern Europe.* 2. *The human population growth of the region is slowing after 100 years of expansion.* 3. *Maintaining the balance between human needs and the environment is often challenging with such a large population.* In addition to identifying evidence from the text, students may conduct online research to identify facts to support their chosen statement.

Online Resources

Leveled Reader

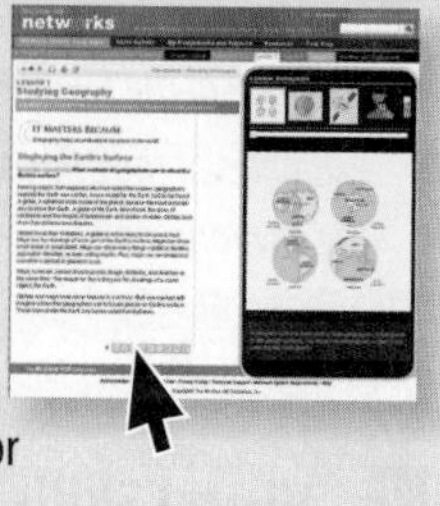

Use this online approaching-level text that corresponds directly to the text in the Student Edition. It also includes additional reading and comprehension support for English Language Learners.

Guided Reading Activities

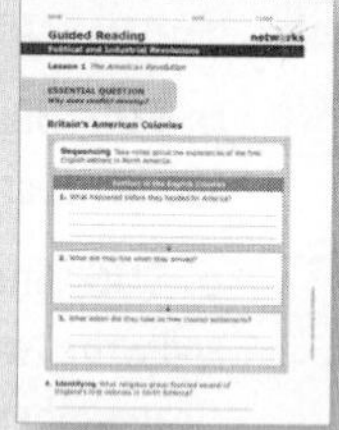

This resource uses guiding questions to help students with comprehension.

Reteaching Activities

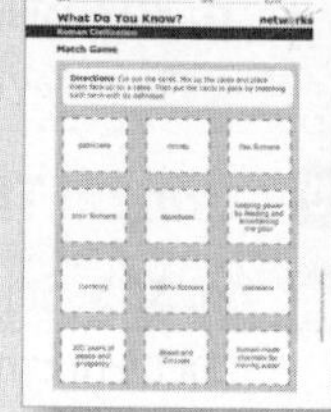

These worksheets provide students with an opportunity for remedial practice and review of vital chapter content.

Reading Essentials and Study Guide

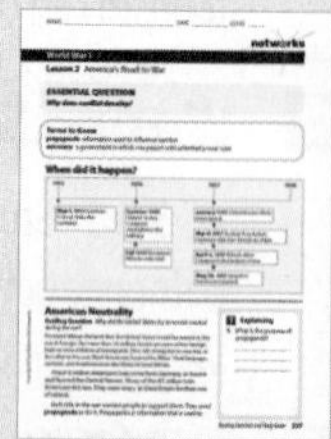

This resource offers writing and reading activities for the approaching-level student.

Self-Check Quizzes

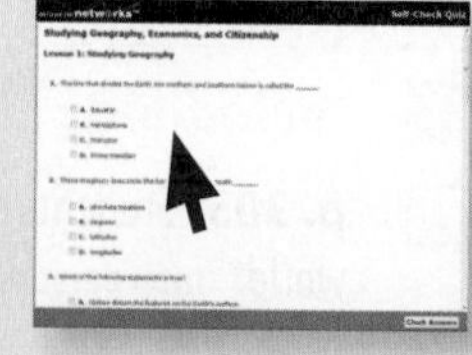

This online assessment tool provides instant feedback for students to check their progress.

Chapter Summaries

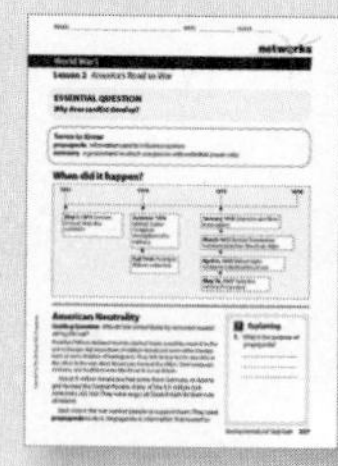

Summaries are provided for each chapter that thoroughly condense core content into manageable chunks.

Southern Europe

ESSENTIAL QUESTION • *How do physical systems and human systems shape a place?*

networks

There's More Online about Southern Europe.

CHAPTER 12

Geography Matters...

Have you ever heard of the Seven Wonders of the World? Europe is the continent where that idea was born. There have been many lists, so no one knows for certain what all of the Seven Wonders were. The cultures of Southern Europe have created architectural wonders. Among them are the Roman Colosseum, the Parthenon of ancient Greece, and the elaborate Spanish palace called the Alhambra. The natural wonders of Southern Europe are also abundant, from the Mediterranean Sea to Basque Country—home of the largest cavern in Europe.

◀ Greece's many islands and long coastlines have always supported a strong tradition of fishing.

Steve Outram/Photographer's Choice/Getty Images

291

Letter from the Author

Dear Geography Teacher,

Two very unique political units exist within Italy and both need to be investigated by your students. I have been in Venice when much of the city has been flooded, and it is difficult for car crazy Americans to imagine a city with no streets, only canals. Also, it is hard to imagine beautifully designed buildings that are slowly sinking into the sea. The Italian government has built giant barriers to keep out the sea and protect Venice, an international treasure. The other geographically unusual piece of land in Italy is the Vatican, an independent city-state within Rome. It is the smallest independent state in the world, at 0.2 square miles, with a population of 800.

Richard G. Boehm

ENGAGE

Creating Charts Before beginning the chapter, have students make a two-column chart listing the physical and human-made features of Southern Europe. Have students list features of Southern Europe that they may already know. Then have them look at the photographs, headings, and diagrams in the chapter to list additional features to their charts.

TEACH & ASSESS

Making Connections Call students' attention to the image of the Greek fisherman while reading the following information.

- The Mediterranean Sea intricately links humans and nature. The rocky sea bottom anchors algae and invertebrates like corals, mollusks, and crustaceans. They act as refuge feeding and spawning grounds for fish. These fish are sources of food as well as livelihood for many residents along the coast.
- In an effort to stop overfishing in the Mediterranean Sea, over fifty countries have agreed on protection measures at a recent United Nations conference. They include a common set of benchmarks for measuring the capacity of fishing fleets and assessing their impacts on shared fish stocks in the region.
- The nearly landlocked waters of the Mediterranean have a very low renewal rate (80 to 90 years) and are extremely sensitive to pollution. The 150 million people living along the coast produce over 31 billion barrels of wastewater each year. Over 20 million barrels are produced by the 220 million tourists visiting the Mediterranean region every year. With tourism increasing, this will be an ongoing issue.

Hypothesizing Emphasize to students that physical systems such as the Mediterranean Sea have influenced cultural development throughout history in Southern Europe and are currently being challenged by human and industrial pollution. **Ask:** **What are some ways humans can reverse environmental challenges to the region?** *(Possible answers: Educate people on the dangers of pollution to the environment; regulate industrial outputs; create wildlife refuges.)*

CLOSE & REFLECT

Summarizing Have students summarize the environmental, social, and economic challenges facing Southern Europe in the twenty-first century. Have a student volunteer write the key concepts on the board as the discussion evolves.

Extend the project-based learning experience globally through our partnership with ePals. EPals allows you to connect with classrooms around the world in a safe online environment for real-life lessons and projects in virtual study groups.

ENGAGE

R Reading Skills

Activating Prior Knowledge As students read the text and study the map, ask them to brainstorm what they have learned about other world population migrations that have resulted when seeking employment. Have student pairs make a list of migrations that they know about and then share these lists in a class discussion.

TEACH & ASSESS

W Writing Skills

Informative/Explanatory Have students write an essay summarizing the information from the text and in the map about labor migration from North Africa. Ask them to answer the following questions to guide them in their essay writing: **Where do the majority of migrants come from within Africa? To which Southern European countries do most Africans migrate? What are some of the possible reasons for the migration?** AL **Verbal/Linguistic**

V Visual Skills

Creating Graphs Have students form small groups. Using the map, have groups select a North African country from which people have migrated to Southern Europe. To correlate migrations with the political status of that country, have students conduct online research to collect data of the most recent migrations of populations and the current political status of their selected country. Have groups create a graph showing their data. Students should then share their graphs in class presentations. BL **Visual/Spatial**

Content Background Knowledge

Africans on the Move Many Africans have also moved to the United States in the twenty-first century.

- Between 1960 and 2007, the number of African immigrants in the United States grew tremendously from 35,355 to 1.4 million. Most of this growth has taken place since 1990.
- Nigeria, Egypt, and Ethiopia are the top individual countries of origin of these immigrants.
- About two of every five African foreign-born adults had a bachelor's or higher degree.
- About one-third of all refugees admitted to the United States in 2007 were from Africa.

Why Geography Matters: **Southern Europe**

R labor migration *from* North Africa

W *The migration of people from place to place is an important theme in the study of geography. Throughout history people have migrated in search of better opportunities. One modern example is the migration of North African workers to the countries of Southern Europe. This has had important consequences both for the North African migrants and the countries of Southern Europe.*

V **Migration: North Africa to Southern Europe**

Direction of migration
Sahara (desert)

0 500 miles
0 500 kilometers
Lambert Azimuthal Equal-Area projection

292

Project-Based Learning

Hands-On

Creating Podcasts

Students will create podcasts that bring together information from all lessons about how Southern European civilization has affected both its own geographic systems and the geographic systems of other places.

Digital Hands-On

Create Online Projects

Find an additional activity online that incorporates technology for this project. Visit the EdTech Teacher Web sites for more links, tutorials, and other resources.

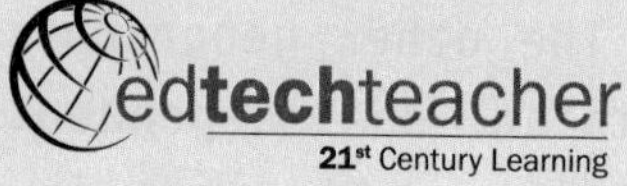

(l)©David Turnley/Corbis, (c)Directphoto/age fotostock/SuperStock, (r)Andrew Woodley/Alamy

Why do people from North Africa migrate to Southern Europe?

Several factors cause North African workers to migrate to Southern Europe in search of employment. The economic opportunities in Southern Europe represent major pull factors. Migrants are drawn to the Southern European countries in search of employment. Demographic changes have made this trend greater. The population of Southern Europe has aged. Young workers are needed to fill the spaces left as older people retire and stop working, thus increasing the demand for migrants. Other factors push people out of North Africa. As countries in North Africa face increasingly high unemployment and wages decline for workers, many choose to leave their home countries—a push factor. In addition, political instability and conflict arising from the "Arab Spring" uprisings and the Libyan civil war have forced many to flee to Southern Europe.

1. **Human Systems** Describe the causes of North African migration to Southern Europe. Include both push and pull factors.

How is Southern Europe affected by this migration?

An economic boom has resulted in increased demand for low-skilled labor in several Southern European countries. Italy and Spain, with their long Mediterranean coastlines, have become popular entry points for undocumented migrants as they fill the need for service industry jobs. During the prosperous economic times, the labor of these migrants helped fuel the engine of economic development by providing sources of cheap labor. However, besides providing labor, North African migrants (whether documented or not) have influenced the cultural development of the receiving countries of Southern Europe. The migrants have enriched the cultural landscape of their new countries. They have brought their religious beliefs, social customs, arts, cuisine, and dress to Southern Europe. In some places in Southern Europe the change has come at the expense of the migrants. The arrival of migrants from North Africa has led to racism and to a backlash against them as they try to establish their new lives in Southern Europe.

2. **Human Systems** How does North African migration to Southern European countries benefit the receiving countries?

How is North Africa affected by this migration?

North Africa is affected both negatively and positively by the migration to Southern Europe. Many North African migrants send some of their pay home to help support their families. The money sent by a migrant to his or her home country is called a remittance. These remittances have reduced poverty in their countries of origin. The remittances also help the country even when the money goes to families that are relatively wealthy since it contributes to the economy of the North African home country. Other positive effects include more funds being available for North Africans to invest in children's health and education and a reduction in child labor. Not all of the effects are positive, as the migrations can cause labor shortages in the home country.

3. **Environment and Society** What are some of the potential long-term effects of the remittances by North African migrants? Write a paragraph discussing the possible impacts on North African society and on the economies of the home countries.

THERE'S MORE ONLINE

SEE a graph of remittances from Southern European countries • *WATCH* a video about migrants

SLIDE SHOW

North African Migration to Southern Europe

Drawing Conclusions This slide show provides images and text about the North African labor migrants that have traveled to Southern Europe. Working with a partner, have students choose one of migrant patterns. Have partners research the distances of the travel routes. Each pair should try to research a different route. Have pairs share their findings by creating a list on the board. Discuss the shortest and longest distances traveled. Then have students draw conclusions about some of the reasons why labor migration is an element in the history of so many regions around the world. ELL **Logical/Mathematical**

T Technology Skills

Assessing Divide the class into small groups. Have students conduct online research to discover which nations in North Africa have been affected by the Arab Spring. Then choose one of these countries to prepare multimedia presentations reporting how the Arab Spring has affected that country, migration to Southern Europe, and what if anything has changed since the Arab Spring. Groups should conclude their presentations by explaining current policies that are in place to help the people in North Africa. BL **Verbal/Linguistic**

C Critical Thinking Skills

Considering Advantages and Disadvantages Have students explain that political or economic upheaval in one country often affects adjacent countries and other continents. **Ask:** **How are the areas that migrants leave in North Africa being affected?** *(Possible answers: North Africa is being affected negatively by losing workers and positively because the migrants send money back to their families.)* **What negative consequences have occurred in Southern Europe since the arrival of North African migrants?** *(In some areas of Southern Europe the arrival of migrants has led to racism and prejudice against the migrants.)* AL **Verbal/Linguistic**

CLOSE & REFLECT

Summarizing Discuss how push and pull factors cause migration, which in turn cause rippling effects on regions, countries, and the world. Have students write a paragraph summarizing migration effects.

ANSWERS, p. 293

Why Geography Matters

1. Southern Europe's economic opportunities are a major pull factor for migrants. An aging population in Southern Europe has led to a surplus of jobs that can be filled by immigrants. Push factors responsible for migration include high unemployment and declining wages in North Africa, as well as political instability and conflict.
2. Economically, the cheap labor of migrants allowed the region to prosper. Culturally, religious beliefs, social customs, arts, cuisine, and dress brought by migrants have enriched the region.
3. Possible answers: Remittances help North African countries meet basic needs of their people, but too heavy reliance on these funds could be detrimental. If countries don't improve their own employment conditions, an economic downturn in Southern Europe could have devastating consequences in North Africa. It is also not a sustainable system for either region since it causes an uncharted deficit from Southern Europe's economy and the illusion of a healthy economy in North Africa.

ENGAGE

C1 Critical Thinking Skills

Making Inferences Display the unit physical map of Southern Europe. Have students identify various features, such as mountains, rivers, and plains. In a class discussion, have students brainstorm ways in which the landforms may have affected the history and development of Southern Europe.

TEACH & ASSESS

C2 Critical Thinking Skills

Interpreting Show students a physical map that focuses on the Iberian Peninsula as found in the Reference Atlas or in the Teacher Lesson Center. **Ask:** **What makes up most of the interior of the peninsula?** *(the Meseta, a large plateau)* **What effect has the location of the Pyrenees had on the peninsula?** *(The Pyrenees have always isolated the peninsula from the rest of Europe.)* **What effect do you think the proximity of the tip of southern Spain to North Africa had on life in the peninsula?** *(There has been a long history of trade and interaction with North Africa.)* **AL Visual/Spatial**

R Reading Skills

Defining Write the word *massifs* on the board. Through a class discussion arrive at a definition of the word. **Ask:** **What is responsible for the rise of the massifs?** *(The forces of plate tectonics)* **What occurs as the mountains build up?** *(earthquakes)* Have students write a sentence using the word *massifs* and then have several volunteers share their sentences. **ELL Verbal/Linguistic**

Content Background Knowledge

Tunnels To improve travel, tunnels were built through the Pyrenees and Alps between Southern and Northern Europe.

- The Somport Tunnel is a cross-border tunnel for vehicle traffic through the Pyrenees between Spain and France. It is 5.3 miles (8.608 m) long and is the longest tunnel through the Pyrenees. It opened in 2003 and took twelve years to build.
- The Gotthard will be the world's longest tunnel. It will be 35.4 miles long (57 km) and provide a rail link through the Alps connecting Northern Europe with Zurich, Switzerland, in Northwestern Europe. The Gotthard has been under construction since 1999 and is scheduled to open in 2016.

ANSWERS, p. 294

TAKING NOTES: Landforms—Iberian Peninsula, Italian Peninsula, Balkan Peninsula, Pyrenees Mountains, Alps, Mount Etna, Apennine Mountains, massifs, coastal plains, the Meseta, the plain of Lombardy, numerous islands, Mount Etna; **Rivers**—Po, Tagus, Ebro, Tiber, Maritsa, Vardar, Aliákmon

networks
There's More Online!

- **IMAGE** Mining in Spain
- **INFOGRAPHIC** Rivers of Europe
- **IMAGE** Massifs in Southern Europe
- **INTERACTIVE SELF-CHECK QUIZ**
- **VIDEO** Physical Geography of Southern Europe

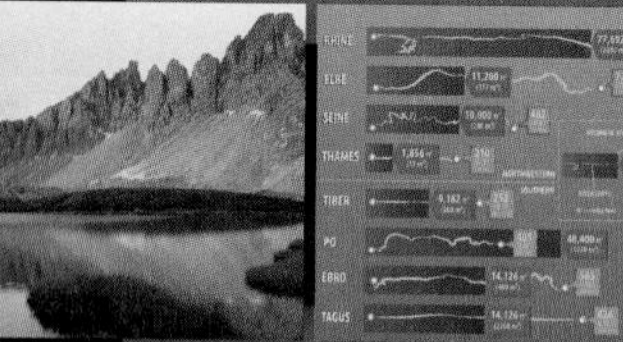

LESSON 1
Physical Geography of Southern Europe

ESSENTIAL QUESTION • *How do physical systems and human systems shape a place?*

Reading HELPDESK

Academic Vocabulary (Tier Two Words)
- **access**
- **resource**

Content Vocabulary (Tier Three Words)
- **massif**
- **tungsten**

TAKING NOTES: ***Key Ideas and Details***

LISTING Use a fishbone graphic organizer like the one below to list the landforms and rivers of Southern Europe.

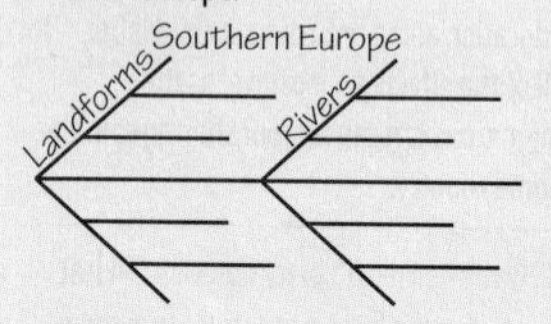
Southern Europe
Landforms
Rivers

It Matters Because

C1 *The seaports of the Iberian Peninsula, the mountains and rivers of the Italian Peninsula, and the rocky islands of Greece have played important roles in the history of Southern Europe. Its geographic location has made this subregion—which includes the countries of Italy, Spain, Andorra, Greece, Portugal, Vatican City, Malta, Cyprus, and San Marino—important for trade and agriculture stretching back more than 3,000 years.*

Landforms

GUIDING QUESTION *What two types of physical features dominate Southern Europe's physical geography?*

Geographically, Europe is a continent made up of peninsulas. The southern part of the region includes three major peninsulas: the Iberian Peninsula, the Italian Peninsula, and the Balkan Peninsula.

C2 Extending off southwestern Europe, the Iberian Peninsula is the location of Spain and Portugal. This landmass separates the Atlantic Ocean from the Mediterranean Sea, leaving only the 20-mile-(32-km-) wide Strait of Gibraltar to connect them. Coastal plains give way to the Meseta, a large plateau that makes up most of the interior of the peninsula. To the north, the Iberian Peninsula is separated from the rest of Europe by the Pyrenees, mountains that have isolated the peninsula's residents for centuries. The independent principality of Andorra is located high in the Pyrenees between modern-day Spain and France. Andorra owes its political autonomy to its isolated location in the mountains.

R The most southwestern of Europe's mountain ranges, the Pyrenees stretch from the Bay of Biscay on the Atlantic side of Spain to the Mediterranean Sea. At its widest the Pyrenees range is a daunting 80 miles (128 km) across. The Pyrenees are characterized by flat-topped **massifs**—a body of mountain ranges formed by fault-line activity. The forces of plate tectonics are responsible for the rise of these massifs, and earthquakes occur as the mountains are built up.

294

networks Online Teaching Options

INTERACTIVE BELLRINGER

Rivers of Europe

Sequencing This graphic introduces students to the major river systems in Europe by sequencing the rivers using their lengths and the volumes of river water per second. Have students form small groups. Ask groups to discuss their prior knowledge of rivers based on rivers that are fast moving, such as those that have whitewater rapids, and ones that are slow moving. Have students answer each question individually and then discuss their answers as a group. Ask each group to write agreed-upon answers to the questions. Then in a class discussion, have groups share their answers. **BL Interpersonal, Logical/Mathematical**

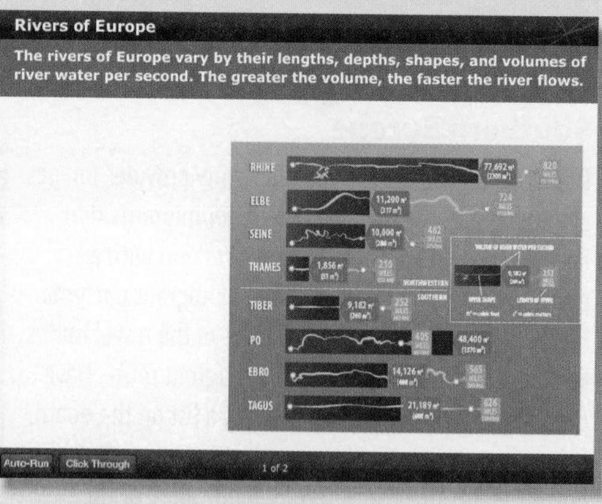
Rivers of Europe
The rivers of Europe vary by their lengths, depths, shapes, and volumes of river water per second. The greater the volume, the faster the river flows.
RHINE
ELBE
SEINE
THAMES
TIBER
PO
EBRO
TAGUS
Auto-Run
Click Through
1 of 2

Italy occupies the Italian Peninsula, which extends from the south of Europe into the heart of the Mediterranean Sea. Plains cover only about one-third of the Italian Peninsula. The largest is the plain of Lombardy along the Po River in the north. The coastline of Italy varies from high, rocky cliffs to long, sandy beaches, and has several well-sheltered ports to support trade. The Apennine Mountains run down the spine of the peninsula all the way through the center of the large island of Sicily off the southwestern tip of Italy. The range is about 1,245 miles (2,000 km) long.

massif a body of mountain ranges formed by fault-line activity

To the north of the Italian Peninsula lie the majestic Alps, the most recognizable range of mountains on the European continent. They loom over Southern Europe and form a natural barrier between the Italian Peninsula and Northern Europe. Because the Alps are the highest mountain range in Europe, they are also the source of Europe's largest and most important rivers. These rivers flow north into France and Germany or south where they empty into the Mediterranean, Adriatic, and Black Seas.

C

In southeastern Europe, the Balkan Peninsula is bounded by the Adriatic and Ionian Seas to the west and the Aegean and Black Seas to the east. Greece is the southernmost country on the Balkan Peninsula. The numerous mountains on this peninsula have limited the area's potential for communication and development. However, this has been offset by the region's easy **access** to the sea. Greece is known for the large numbers of islands—nearly 2,000—that spread out from its coastline in the Aegean Sea.

access a way to approach or enter

The islands that lie south of the mainland of the Iberian, Italian, and Balkan Peninsulas are geographically and politically important to Spain, Italy, and Greece. They serve as trading posts in the Mediterranean. Rugged mountains form the larger islands of Sicily, Sardinia, Corsica, Crete, and Cyprus. Tectonic activity is characteristic of this region. Sicily, the largest of these islands, is dominated by Mount Etna. At 10,700 feet (3,261 m), Mount Etna is Europe's tallest active volcano. Smaller island groups include Spain's Balearic Islands in the Mediterranean, Italy's Lipari Islands in the Tyrrhenian Sea, and the three islands of Malta in the Mediterranean.

W

READING PROGRESS CHECK

Identifying What seas surround the Balkan Peninsula?

Massifs, such as these in the Dolomite range of the Alps in northeast Italy, developed as a result of tectonic activity.

▼ CRITICAL THINKING

1. ***Identifying Cause and Effect*** Why do massifs form?
2. ***Drawing Inferences*** Other than the Alps, where else can massifs be found in Southern Europe?

V

VIDEO

First Map of the Alps

Locating Ask students to identify the location and name of the mountain range where this video was filmed. *(the Alps in Val Camonica, Italy)* Provide student pairs with a map of Southern Europe. Have partners locate the countries that border this mountain range and list major civilizations they know of that existed there long ago. Then have pairs discuss how the size and location of these mountains affected human and cultural development in the surrounding regions. **Interpersonal, Naturalist**

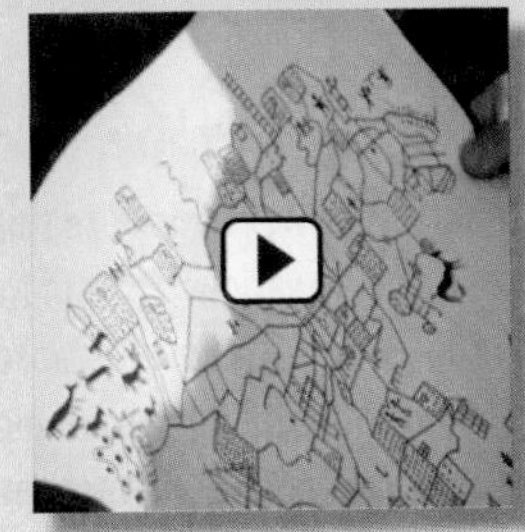

C Critical Thinking Skills

Understanding Relationships Display the physical map of Europe. **Ask: What landforms separate Southern and Northern Europe?** *(Pyrenees mountains in Spain; the Alps mountain range in Italy; the many mountain ranges of Greece)* **How do you think geography influences the trade and cultural interaction of Southern Europe with Northern Europe?** Have students write one or two paragraphs analyzing the influence of these geographic landforms. Have students share their paragraphs. *(Student paragraphs will vary, but may include that since Southern Europe is located along the Mediterranean Sea, it has great influence over trade and culture.)* **AL Verbal/Linguistic**

W Writing Skills

Informative/Explanatory Have students conduct research using reliable online sources to write an essay that explains why the islands in the Mediterranean were geographically important to Southern European countries. *(Essays will vary, but should conclude that mountains made access difficult to Northern Europe, whereas the Mediterranean Sea provided easy access to the islands in the Mediterranean for trade and political alliances.)* **Verbal/Linguistic**

V Visual Skills

Describing As students look at the image of massifs, ask them to describe what they see. **Ask: What do you think residents in the area do for a living?** *(Student answers will vary, but should note that there are no trees for forestry jobs, and there is not much arable land for crops. Some may suggest fishing or tourism-related jobs.)* Continue the class discussion on how physical features affect a region. **ELL Visual/Spatial**

ANSWERS, p. 295

READING PROGRESS CHECK The Adriatic and Ionian Seas to the west, and the Aegean and Black Seas to the east

CRITICAL THINKING

1. Massifs form as a result of fault-line activity; the forces of plate tectonics cause them to rise.
2. Massifs are also found in the Pyrenees and in the Apennines.

T Technology Skills

Comparing and Contrasting Read aloud the text about the Tagus and the Ebro Rivers on the Iberian Peninsula. Divide the class into small groups and have each group use the Internet to research and design a graphic organizer that diagrams the strengths and weaknesses that each river contributes to the region's trade and transportation industry. Explain to groups that their graphic organizers should include the source of each river, where it flows, its length, geographic strengths and weaknesses, and the economic activities that occur on each river. Have groups present their graphic organizers in a class presentation. **Visual/Spatial, Interpersonal**

Making Connections

Hydroelectric power is energy created and captured when water moves downhill.

- Water at higher elevations has more potential energy due to gravity. Falling water is used to turn a turbine and generator, which creates electrical energy.
- Often the process is facilitated by damming a river to ensure a constant supply of water, which moves through the turbines, making the hydroelectric energy output fairly consistent.
- Hydroelectricity reduces carbon dioxide emissions since it does not require fossil fuels to operate, making it environmentally friendly.
- Hydroelectricity is economically favorable because it is not affected by rising oil prices.

V Visual Skills

Interpreting Visuals Direct students' attention to the "Rivers of Europe" infographic. **Ask:** **What is the slowest river in Europe?** *(Thames)* **What is Italy's shortest river?** *(Tiber)* **Why do the rivers play a different economic role in Southern Europe than they do in Northern Europe?** *(Rivers in Southern Europe are generally too shallow for large ships.)* **AL Visual/Spatial**

ANSWERS, p. 296

CRITICAL THINKING

1. The rivers of Southern Europe are generally shorter than those of Northwestern Europe.
2. No, there is no direct correlation between the length of rivers and the volume of water flow. For example, the Tagus and Ebro Rivers release the same volume of water at 14,126 cubic feet per second but the lengths of the rivers vary by 576 miles.

Water Systems

GUIDING QUESTION *How do Southern Europe's rivers compare to those of Northwestern Europe?*

T The two major rivers on the Iberian Peninsula are the Tagus and the Ebro. Both rivers play crucial roles in the economy and ecology of the region. However, their roles are limited because they, like all rivers on the Iberian Peninsula, are generally too shallow for large ships.

The Tagus River begins near the eastern edge of Spain and travels westward for 626 miles (1,007 km) through Portugal to the Atlantic Ocean. In northern Spain, nearly 200 tributaries, mostly from the rainy Pyrenees, feed the Ebro River, Spain's longest river. The steep gorges and rocky terrain that this river flows through make it inaccessible to boats. However, the Ebro has been dammed to provide a significant portion of Spain's hydroelectric power. In addition, the

V

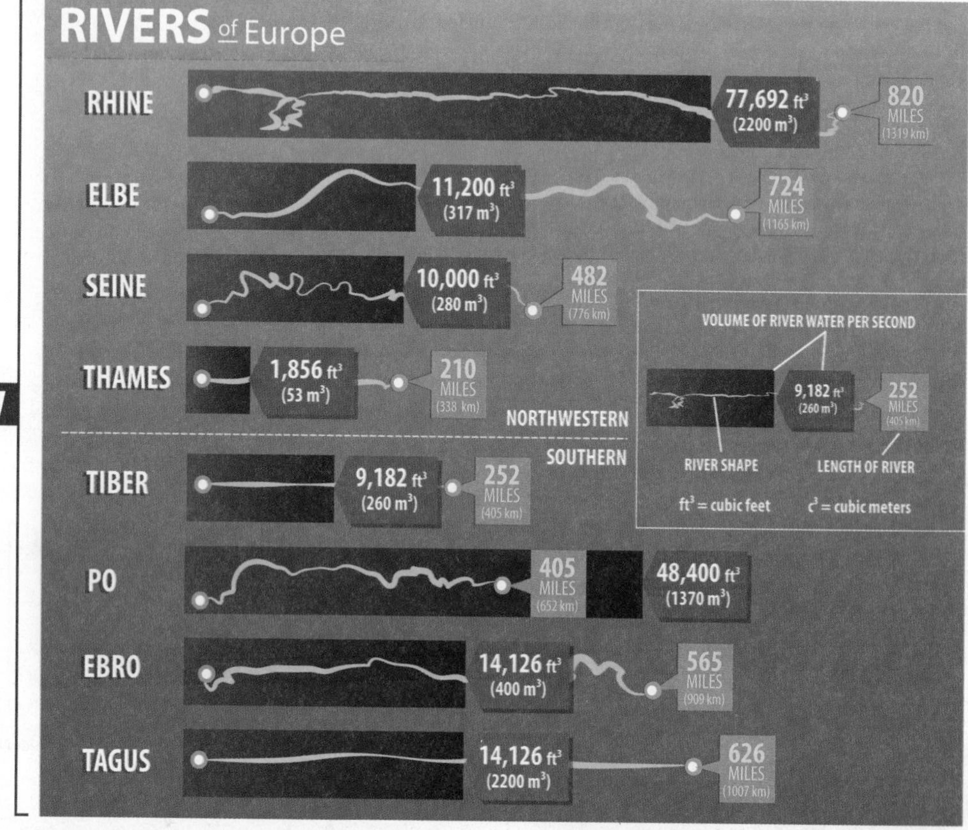

Although critically important to the ecology of the region, the rivers of Southern Europe have less importance as transportation and trade routes than the rivers of Northwestern Europe.

▲ **CRITICAL THINKING**

1. ***Contrasting*** How are the rivers of Southern Europe different from the rivers of Northwestern Europe in regard to length?
2. ***Evaluating*** Is there a correlation between length of rivers in Europe and the volume of water flow? Provide an example to support your answer.

networks Online Teaching Options

INFOGRAPHIC

Rivers of Europe

Making Connections Use this infographic to discuss with students the various rivers in Northwestern and Southern Europe. Guide students to make connections between the various rivers and the economic values of the rivers within each region. As students interact with the information in the graph, have them consider the lengths and differences between the rivers. Ask them to consider which rivers might be best suited for transportation and trade routes. Then have students write a brief statement about the four Southern Europe rivers that summarizes what economic value they believe each river brings to the economy of the region. **BL Verbal/Linguistic**

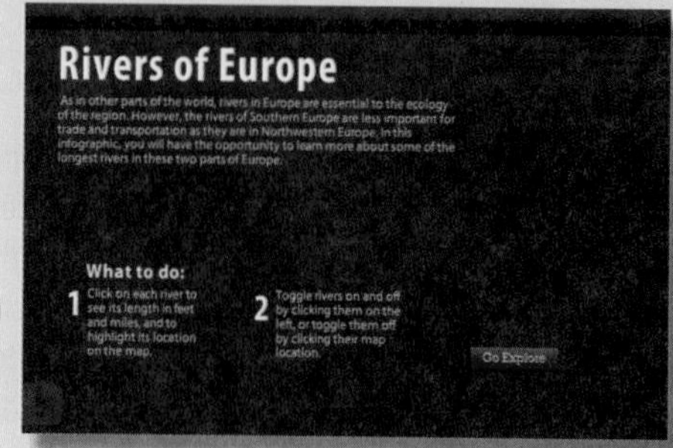

resulting reservoirs provide water to an impressive network of irrigation canals that support the agriculture of Spain.

The Apennines form a mountain range that runs down the center of the long and narrow Italian Peninsula. This has created rivers that are steep, short, and relatively narrow and shallow, and not suitable for transportation by boat. In the north, however, the Po River runs through the plain of Lombardy. Although it is Italy's longest and most significant river, it is still only 405 miles (652 km) long.

Venice is located at the mouth of the Po on the Adriatic Sea. The city has built a complicated system of dikes and canals to help control the river's outflow. Efforts to claim marshy areas of the Po Delta for small farms failed due to floods, especially in the 1950s and 1960s. Nevertheless, the drainage basin of the Po River forms Italy's largest and most fertile agricultural plain, covering 27,062 square miles (70,091 sq. km).

The Tiber River is Italy's second-longest river and has great historical significance. A mere 252 miles (405 km) long, this short river is nevertheless very important to Italy's economic history. It is the primary water source for the capital, Rome. Civitavecchia, on the lower part of the river, is a significant port and naval harbor for Rome. The Tiber River empties into the Tyrrhenian Sea.

Greece, on the southern tip of the Balkan Peninsula, has a mountainous terrain. Its rivers are short, unsuitable for navigation, and unusable for irrigation. In their upper courses, near their sources, the rivers flow in broad, gently sloping valleys. However, in their middle courses they plunge through basins into narrow gorges. In their lower courses, as they near their mouths, they meander across coastal plains into marshy deltas. Northeastern Greece is home to the Maritsa River, located in a low valley full of marshes. The Maritsa marks Greece's border with Turkey. In northeastern Greece, the two main rivers are the Vardar and the Aliákmon.

Glacial movement in the last ice age did not reach Southern Europe's peninsulas. As a result, the landforms of these countries lack the natural lakes or reservoirs found in Northern Europe and Northwestern Europe. The climate of Southern Europe is also much drier than farther north, another reason why there are fewer rivers and lakes in this subregion.

C

READING PROGRESS CHECK

Describing Describe the importance of the Po River.

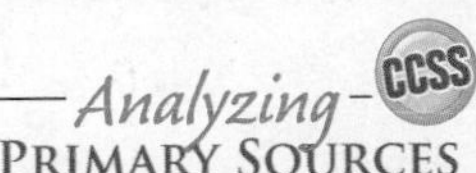

Analyzing Primary Sources

Olive Oil Production in Italy

"From a geographical point of view, the prime area of Italian olive production is located between 30 and 45 °N, which in general is the geographical distribution of suitable areas for olive-tree production in the northern hemisphere. In the Mediterranean area, Italy represents the central point of olive production because of its history and environmental conditions. . . . In terms of olive-oil production, Italy ranks second in the world (after Spain), producing an average oil quantity over the last four years of 550,000 tonnes."

—G. Fontanazza, "Importance of olive-oil production in Italy," *Integrated Soil and Water Management for Orchard Development*, 2005

T

DBQ ***DRAWING CONCLUSIONS*** What aspect of Italy's geography makes the country a suitable location for growing olives? RH.9–10.2

Climate, Biomes, and Resources

GUIDING QUESTION *Why does Southern Europe's climate make it popular with tourists and ideal for agricultural activities?*

Southern Europe's location on the Mediterranean Sea influences the climate and biomes of the subregion. The climate also makes the subregion a popular vacation destination. The subregion is particularly suited for growing grapes, olives, and shrub herbs and raising goats and other livestock.

Climate Regions and Biomes

The Alps separate two major climate zones: the marine west coast climate to the north and the warm Mediterranean climate of Italy and the Balkans to the south. The Alps block most Atlantic winds from the north, causing less precipitation to fall in Southern Europe. Generally, Southern Europe experiences the warm, dry summers and the mild, rainy winters characteristic of the Mediterranean climate.

The Mediterranean climate of Southern Europe results, in part, from the warm waters of this sea. Average yearly rainfall across Southern Europe is less than 30 inches (76 cm), and most of the yearly rainfall occurs in the winter months.

V

C Critical Thinking Skills

Analyzing Have students discuss the rivers in Italy and Greece. **Ask:** What is the Po River's main effect in Italy? *(The basin of the river forms a large and fertile agricultural plain.)* How does Greece's mountainous terrain affect rivers in Greece? *(The mountainous terrain causes the rivers to be short and not suitable for navigation or irrigation.)* Why does Southern Europe lack natural lakes? *(The glacial movement of the last ice age did not reach Southern European peninsulas.)* **AL** **Verbal/Linguistic**

T Technology Skills

Researching In pairs, have students read and answer the *Analyzing Primary Sources* feature. Then **ask:** What is the claim of the primary source? *(that growing olives is generally suitable between 30 and 45 °N)* Partners should continue to research olive growing throughout the world using online resources to determine if this claim is valid. Additionally, have pairs search for other areas in the world where olives are typically grown. Have them prepare a brief list of their findings. **Verbal/Linguistic**

V Visual Skills

Creating Diagrams Have students read the two paragraphs under *Climate, Biomes, and Resources*. Have students create a diagram that depicts Southern Europe's climate zones. Diagrams should include photos, images, or illustrations. Students should provide an explanation of how the mountains in this region affect the climate. **BL** **Visual/Spatial**

INTERACTIVE IMAGE

Natural Resources of Southern Europe

Considering Advantages and Disadvantages This interactive image can be used with students to discuss the negative and positive effects of mining. Allow time for the students to discuss and ask questions about the image and then divide them into pairs. Have partners make two lists, one of the benefits of this mining operation, and another of the negative drawbacks to mining. When students have completed their lists, have them then assign a value to each of the items, indicating a positive value for the good and a negative value for the drawbacks. Then ask each pair to decide whether the coal mining operation is an advantage or disadvantage for Spain. **Logical/Mathematical, Interpersonal**

ANSWERS, p. 297

READING PROGRESS CHECK The Po River's drainage basin forms Italy's largest and most fertile agricultural plain.

DBQ Italy's latitudinal location is within the prime geographical area for olive production, between 30 and 45 °N.

Physical Geography of Southern Europe

R Reading Skills

Determining Importance Discuss the natural resources found in some of the Southern European countries. **Ask: Why are Spain's mining operations unlikely to be reduced?** *(Because tungsten has been found in Spain and is a rare and valuable natural resource.)* **Notice that Italy is mentioned twice in this section. What importance can the reader determine about Italy to this region?** *(Student answers will vary, but should include that Italy is an important economic and political country within this region.)* **What importance can the reader determine about Greece's use of its resources?** *(Possible answer: That Greece has natural resources, such as its rivers, that it is not fully utilizing.)* **BL Naturalist**

CLOSE & REFLECT

Creating Charts To summarize the geographic features of each peninsula, write the questions below on the board. Have students create charts with a row for each of the three peninsulas in Southern Europe and four columns titled *Mountains, Rivers, Plains, Climate Zones.* Have students answer the questions, filling out each column with their answers. If they cannot find the answers in the text, encourage them to consult the unit maps or Reference Atlas.

- **What are the mountain ranges of each peninsula?**
- **What are the main rivers of each peninsula?**
- **What are the plains of each peninsula?**
- **What climate zone does each peninsula fall in?**

Emphasize to students that all three peninsulas have all three geographic features, and although it is not mentioned in the text, Greece's plain, Marathon, was the site of a historical battle in ancient times between the Greeks and the Persians.

Spain has more mineral resources than Italy due to their different geological histories.

Luis Castaneda/age fotostock

▲ **CRITICAL THINKING**

1. ***Making Generalizations*** Why does Italy have fewer mineral resources than Spain?
2. ***Analyzing Visuals*** Based on the photo, what might be a drawback to plentiful mineral resources?

The plants and animals native to the subregion are well-suited for less water and the long summer dry period. The coastal areas are covered in chaparral, or shrubs and shrub trees that are drought resistant. Most agriculture in Southern Europe takes place on coastal plains that receive more rainfall and develop a thicker topsoil as a result of runoff and sediment left by rivers.

The ecosystems in the Mediterranean are diverse and ecologically sensitive to climate change. Gorges channel water away from the land, leaving much of the region warm, dry, and covered in scrub plants. The coastal plains have rich sedimentary soil and a high diversity of plant life, and support most of the regional agriculture. However, they are prone to flooding.

Natural Resources

Italy has few mineral resources. Portugal, however, has large deposits of copper. Northern Spain, along the Pyrenees and the Atlantic Ocean, is rich in coal, tin, and **tungsten.** Tungsten is an extremely rare heavy-metal element which is essential in high-tech industries. Spain's mining operations in search of this valuable natural element are unlikely to be reduced.

Both Italy and Spain have benefited from the production of hydroelectricity. Greece has many rivers suitable for producing hydroelectricity. However, Greece has not fully developed these **resources.**

tungsten an extremely rare heavy-metal element essential in high-tech industry

resource a usable stock or supply

☑ **READING PROGRESS CHECK**

Describing Describe the ecosystem of the Mediterranean climate.

LESSON 1 REVIEW (CCSS)

Reviewing Vocabulary (Tier Three Words)

1. ***Explaining*** Explain what massifs are and how they are formed. RH.9–10.4

Using Your Notes

2. ***Listing*** Use your graphic organizer to list the major landforms in Southern Europe.

Answering the Guiding Questions

3. ***Identifying*** What two types of physical features dominate Southern Europe's physical geography?
4. ***Comparing*** How do Southern Europe's rivers compare to those of Northwestern Europe?
5. ***Expressing*** Why does Southern Europe's climate make it popular with tourists and ideal for agricultural activities?

Writing Activity

6. ***Informative/Explanatory*** Write a paragraph describing how the rivers of Southern Europe can be an asset for the countries in the subregion. WHST.9–10.2

298

ANSWERS, p. 298

☑ **READING PROGRESS CHECK** The plants and animals found in Mediterranean climate areas are those that have adapted to survive long, hot, dry summers. Coastal areas are covered in chaparral.

CRITICAL THINKING

1. Over the course of history, the two countries underwent different geological formation.
2. The extraction of these resources could result in serious damage to the land and destruction of habitat for a variety of animal and plant species.

LESSON 1 REVIEW ANSWERS

Reviewing Vocabulary

1. Massifs are bodies of mountain ranges formed by fault-line activity.

Using Your Notes

2. The major landforms in Southern Europe are the Iberian Peninsula, Italian Peninsula, Balkan Peninsula, the Pyrenees Mountains, the Alps, the Apennine Mountains, and Mount Etna.

Answering the Guiding Questions

3. the mountains and peninsulas
4. Most rivers in Southern Europe are short and shallow, a contrast to the longer, deeper rivers of Northwestern Europe. The dry climate of Southern Europe also makes for fewer rivers than the wetter climate of Northwestern Europe.
5. The warm, dry, sunny summers of the Mediterranean climate are attractive to vacationers. The coastal plains receive more rainfall and have rich soil which, combined with the warm, dry climate, makes them well suited for growing grapes, olives, and shrub herbs.

Writing Activity

6. Paragraphs will vary, but may include benefits such as hydroelectric power, irrigation networks, and freshwater sources. Paragraphs should be supported by information from the chapter.

networks

There's More Online!

- ☑ **IMAGE** Classic Greek Architecture
- ☑ **IMAGE** Classic Roman Architecture
- ☑ **TIME LINE** Foundations of Western Civilization
- ☑ **INTERACTIVE SELF-CHECK QUIZ**
- ☑ **VIDEO** Human Geography of Southern Europe

LESSON 2

Human Geography of Southern Europe

ESSENTIAL QUESTION • *How do physical systems and human systems shape a place?*

Reading **HELP**DESK

Academic Vocabulary (Tier Two Words)

- **issue**
- **accurate**

Content Vocabulary (Tier Three Words)

- **city-state**
- **Renaissance**
- **complementarity**

TAKING NOTES: ***Key Ideas and Details***

IDENTIFYING Use a graphic organizer like the one below to take notes about the human geography of Southern Europe.

Southern Europe
- History and Government →
- Population Patterns →
- Society and Culture Today →

It Matters Because

The European countries in the region of the Mediterranean Sea have a rich cultural heritage. Greece was the birthplace of classical civilization, the Roman Empire was born in Italy, and Spain and Portugal became leaders in the Age of Exploration. Today the region is highly developed and plays an important role in geopolitics and the world economy and as a cultural center. **C**

History and Government

GUIDING QUESTION *What characteristics of early civilizations are evident in Southern Europe today?*

Evidence of the cultural inheritance of Southern Europe is visible in the ruins of ancient civic architecture, such as the Parthenon. Those majestic ruins are a reminder of the lasting impact that past civilizations have had on this region and around the world. The civilizations of ancient Greece and Rome laid the foundations for European—and Western—civilization.

Early History

Ancient Greece was a collection of **city-states,** each independent with its own form of government and society. They were linked only by their common language and shared cultural identity. The classical period of Greek history reached its height in the 400s B.C. The city-state of Athens introduced the concept of democracy to the world. The city-state of Sparta was built on the glory of war. Sparta's generals created battle strategies that are still studied and used today. The mythology of the Greeks and Romans has influenced and inspired the art and culture of Western civilization for over 2,000 years. **R** **T**

The Roman Republic, founded in Italy, was established on the rule of law and the balance of power. It was the foundation of the largest empire of the ancient world. The empire reached the height of its power in 27 B.C. and experienced a resurgence around 200 years later, in A.D. 180.

ENGAGE

C Critical Thinking Skills

Exploring Issues Have students brainstorm ways that Southern Europe plays a role in today's world economy. Tell them to consider what worldwide economic events have affected countries in Southern Europe. Have students make a list of products, events, or other ways that Southern Europe plays a part in world economy.

TEACH & ASSESS

R Reading Skills

Defining Have students read the first three lines of text under *Early History.* Write the term *city-state* on the board. **Ask: What was a city-state?** *(an independent city that had its own type of government and society)* Then **ask: If each city-state was independent, how were they linked to each other to form ancient Greece?** *(City-states were linked by a common language and a shared cultural identity.)* Have students write sentences using the term *city-state* and share their sentences. Students should add the term to their chapter glossaries.

ELL **Verbal/Linguistic**

T Technology Skills

Understanding Historical Interpretation Divide the class into four groups, assigning two groups to research the ancient Greek city-state of Athens and the other two groups to research Sparta. Direct one of each of the groups to research the cultural contributions made by their city-state, such as art, literature, architecture, philosophy, or sports events. The other two groups should research political contributions made by their city-state, either through democratic philosophy or wars. Groups should include their own comments or opinions as to why they think historians have found these contributions to be important. Have students prepare a multimedia presentation of their findings to present to the class. Presentations should include visuals, as well as music or other auditory enhancements.

BL **Auditory/Musical, Visual/Spatial**

networks ***Online Teaching Options***

INTERACTIVE BELLRINGER

Leonardo da Vinci and the Italian Renaissance

Identifying Perspectives Before revealing the bellringer content, have students form small groups and discuss what they think it means to be a Renaissance person. Ask each group to write a list of Renaissance traits. In a class discussion, have groups share their lists. Reveal the introductory bellringer text and the text in the text box to identify the characteristics that define a Renaissance person. Compare and contrast these answers with group lists. Then have students complete the interactive bellringer questions either as a group or individually. **ELL** **Verbal/Linguistic**

Leonardo da Vinci and the Italian Renaissance

The Renaissance was a period that marked the shift from the medieval world to the modern world. It began in Italy in the early 1300s.

The word *renaissance* means "rebirth." During the fifteenth century, Italy experienced a rediscovery of ancient philosophy, literature, art, and science. Leonardo da Vinci (1412-1519) was an Italian painter, architect, sculptor, inventor, and engineer. He is considered to be one of the greatest painters of all time and is sometimes referred to as the quintessential "renaissance man."

Auto-Run | Click Through | 1 of 2

ANSWERS, p. 299

TAKING NOTES: History and Government—Ancient Greece was comprised of independent city-states; The Roman Republic was established on the rule of law and the balance power; Today, governments are democratically elected; Four countries are members of the EU. **Population Patterns**—very densely populated and very diverse; aging populations. **Society and Culture Today**—mostly Roman Catholic, high literacy, government-supported health care and education, approaching gender equality, highly supportive of the arts.

W Writing Skills

Informational/Explanatory Have students select an area of renewed interest from the Renaissance that interests them (art, architecture, politics, science, philosophy). After researching their selection, have students write two or three paragraphs describing their cultural revival choice. **AL** **Verbal/Linguistic**

C Critical Thinking Skills

Drawing Conclusions Have a student volunteer read the last paragraph on the page. **Ask:** **What events hindered the development of stable democracies in Southern Europe?** *(Possible answers: invasions from Northern Europe, North Africa, and Asia, two world wars in the twentieth century)* **Do you think the current governments are stable in Spain, Italy, and Greece, given their current unstable economies?** *(Student answers will vary, but should supply reasons for their thinking that include economic turmoil as a major factor contributing to a stable or unstable government.)* **BL** **Logical/Mathematical**

V Visual Skills

Analyzing Visuals Direct students' to the time line at the bottom of the page. **Ask:** **About how long was the Roman Republic a force in the Western world?** *(almost 500 years)* **What was the importance of the Renaissance?** *(It sparked the renewal of Western civilization.)* Then, in a class discussion, lead students to understand the enormity of the changes that occurred during the Renaissance period. **AL** **Verbal/Linguistic**

ANSWERS, p. 300

READING PROGRESS CHECK Nationalism played a large part in forming the Southern European countries of today, as the smaller entities that were culturally and linguistically similar became unified.

CRITICAL THINKING

1. The Allied victory in North Africa over the Axis forces led to the invasion of Italy.
2. The Hellenic Period is significant because it is when democracy was born.

city-state an independently governed community consisting of a city and the surrounding lands, notably present in ancient Greece

Renaissance rebirth; the period in European civilization characterized by a surge of interest in classical learning and values

issue a vital or unsettled matter

The Path to Today

W The period that followed the fall of the Roman Empire in the West is known as the Middle Ages. Beginning in Italy in the 1300s, a new era called the **Renaissance** (from the French word for "rebirth") signaled a major cultural revival. Much of Europe experienced a renewed interest in the arts, politics, science, and philosophy.

This blossoming was possible because of the level of wealth and stability that the Italian city-states achieved. Wealth and stability made it possible for people to devote themselves to study and innovative thought. They could also afford to be patrons for artists, writers, and thinkers. This cultural revival eventually spread across Europe and was later carried by explorers to other regions of the world.

At the beginning of the Renaissance, Europe was lagging behind the Chinese and Islamic empires in innovation and enterprise. However, by the 1400s Southern Europe, led by Portugal and Spain, was exploring new opportunities beyond the Mediterranean. By the early 1500s, both countries had established footholds in the Americas where they would build empires. Portugal also established colonies in India. New trade routes and colonization created enormous wealth.

The 1800s and 1900s brought dramatic changes to all of Europe. In the Mediterranean, small kingdoms, principalities, and city-states that shared a linguistic and cultural identity began to unify under the concept known as nationalism. Others pushed for independence from older multiethnic regimes. As a result, the modern countries of Southern Europe emerged.

C The road to political stability in Southern Europe was not easy due to the history of invasions from North Africa, Asia, and other parts of Europe. Today, Southern European countries have democratically elected governments. Portugal, Spain, Italy, and Greece are members of the European Union (EU). The subregion was mainly agricultural until the 1980s when industrialization arrived. Economic **issues** have been a problem in recent decades, however. Spain, Italy, and Greece have experienced high unemployment rates, face credit problems, and are undergoing the transition to an industrial and, more recently, a service economy.

READING PROGRESS CHECK

Making Connections What was the impact of nationalism on the development of modern Southern Europe?

TIME LINE

FOUNDATIONS of Western Civilization

The origin of modern democratic principles can be traced to the ancient civilizations of Greece and Rome.

V ▶ **CRITICAL THINKING**

1. ***Identifying*** What Allied victory during World War II led to the invasion of Italy?
2. ***Describing*** What is the significance of the Hellenic Period?

509–27 B.C. The Early Roman Republic flourishes.

479–323 B.C. The Hellenic Period marks the high point of Athenian culture and the birth of democracy.

1000

1300–1600 The Renaissance, which begins in Italy, sparks a renewal of Western civilization.

1400–1700 The Age of Exploration spawns the foundation of the Spanish Empire.

networks Online Teaching Options

INTERACTIVE MAP

Greek City-States, c. 500 B.C.

Comparing and Contrasting This map showing the locations of the Greek city-states of Ancient Greece in 500 B.C. can be used to discuss the early history of Southern Europe with students. After students have read through and studied the interactive map levels, display a current map of Southern Europe. Working alone or in pairs, have students compare and contrast the locations of ancient city-states to the locations of the cities and countries today. Ask students to write a few statements explaining the similarities and differences between the maps. **Visual/Spatial**

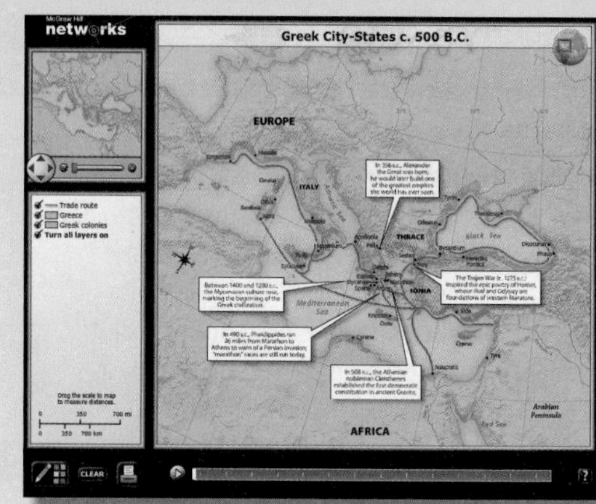

Population Patterns

GUIDING QUESTION *How have migration and aging populations affected Southern Europe's population patterns?*

Europe is one of the most densely populated regions of the world. It is a relatively small region with a large population, which is mostly urbanized. Opportunities for education, employment, and social services during the past 50 years have been greater in urban areas. Vatican City, just 0.17 square miles (0.44 sq. km) in area, is the most densely populated state in Southern Europe. In contrast, Greece has about 222 people per square mile (86 people per sq. km). It is still the most agrarian (based on farming) and rural of all Southern European countries.

As in most European countries, the populations of Italy, Spain, and Greece are aging. The birthrates are not high enough to replace the current generation. In the coming decades there will be a greater number of older people than young people. As older people die, the population will decline.

General political and economic stability in the last 50 years has meant an increase in the quality of life and the alternatives open to individuals. One result is an increase in income. A consequence of the increase is smaller families. Many people are choosing not to have children since the economic cost of raising a child is great. Another reason is the full inclusion of women into society. Women are postponing having children to pursue careers and, as a consequence, are having fewer children.

The care of the aging is another issue in Southern Europe. Traditionally, younger generations cared for older family members. This practice is declining in Europe where older people do not have adult children to care for them. The aging population is beginning to strain the social welfare systems of countries, and governments must often provide the costs of caring for an older society.

Demands for necessary labor are being met by migrants within the European Union. Newly admitted EU countries in Eastern Europe have larger proportions of their populations living in rural areas. They are attracted to work in urban centers throughout the EU for wages. Often they are unskilled, but have a strong work ethic and make good employees. Economic migration throughout the EU has resulted in a growing diversity of cultures and ethnic groups.

Connecting Geography to SCIENCE

Demography

Demography, the statistical study of human populations, tracks changes in populations and seeks to identify trends, their causes, and possible consequences. Tracking fertility (birth) and mortality (death) rates is an important part of the work of a demographer, but patterns of immigration, civil or regional armed conflict, and the effects of health care and disease on populations are also important factors. The work of demographers can influence government decisions, including immigration policy, economic planning, and decisions about the distribution of services within the country.

IDENTIFYING Describe the work of a demographer and provide an example of how it might affect government policy.

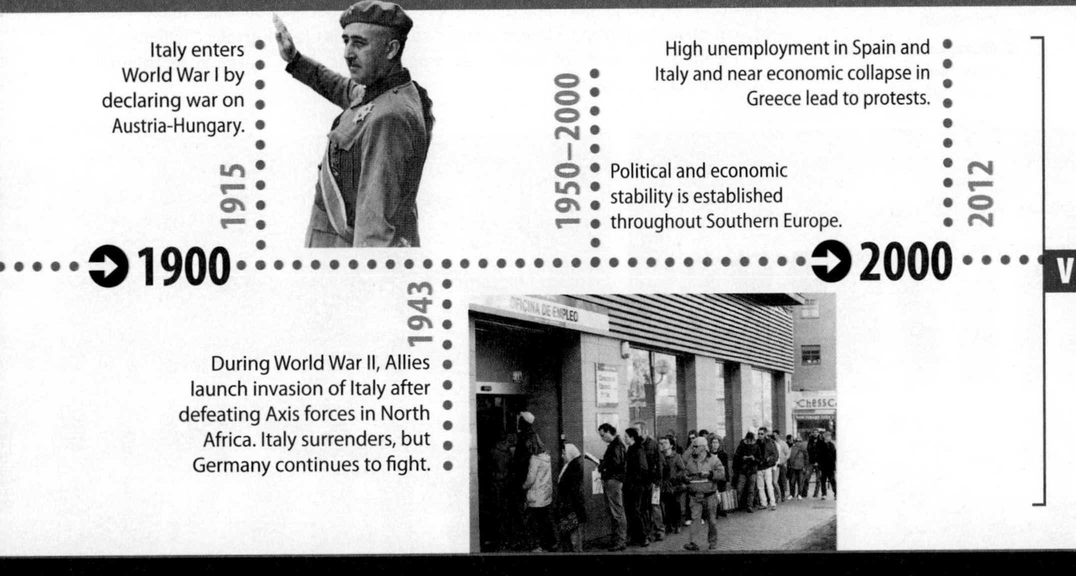

(bl)©Bettmann/Corbis, (br)Angel Navarrete/Bloomberg/Getty Images

CHAPTER 12, Lesson 2
Human Geography of Southern Europe

T Technology Skills

Creating Graphs Divide students into small groups and assign each group to research either Spain, Italy, Portugal, or Greece. Have groups conduct online research to find statistics of current population numbers and projected population numbers from now through 2050. Each group should then create a graph showing the population numbers in five-year increments. Display the graphs in the classroom. **AL** **Visual/Spatial, Logical/Mathematical**

W Writing Skills

Narrative In a class discussion, have students identify some of the changes in population patterns in Southern European countries. Tell students to write a blog explaining the population trends in Southern Europe. In their blog they can present information in bulleted lists and include links to reliable Internet sources. Have students share their blogs in a class discussion. **BL** **Verbal/Linguistic**

V Visual Skills

Summarizing Direct students' attention to the time line at the bottom of the page. **Ask:** **What hindered political and economic stability in Southern Europe until 1950?** *(Countries in Southern Europe were involved in two world wars.)* **Is there political and economic stability in Southern Europe in the twenty-first century?** *(No. Greece and Cyprus have been near economic collapse, and high unemployment in Spain and Italy has led to public protests.)* **ELL** **Visual/Spatial, Verbal/Linguistic**

Content Background Knowledge

The History of Demography The science of demography can be traced back to Englishman John Graunt, who documented the deaths of people living in London and rural communities using weekly records of deaths and baptisms dating back to the end of the 1500s. He published his results in 1662 and is known for constructing the first mortality table and for predicting life expectancy. Until the mid-1800s, demography studied only mortality rates. Demographers began studying fertility and reproduction rates when, in the mid-1800s, a decline of births in industrialized countries was noticed.

TIME LINE

Foundations of Western Civilization

Organizing This time line allows students to interact with eight important historic dates and events from the early Roman Republic to the current economic collapse in Greece. Have students work with a partner to rank and organize the eight historic events featured on the time line in the order of importance students feel they have played in the human geography of Southern Europe. The events should be organized by listing the event that they feel is most important first and listing the event that they feel is least important last. Pairs will need to produce an agreed-upon list. Then have pairs share their lists in a class discussion. **Visual/Spatial, Logical/Mathematical**

Interactive Timeline

1700 · 1705 · 1776 · 1800 · 1820 · 1880 · 1900 · 1944 · 1992 · 2000 · 2012

ANSWERS, p. 301

Connecting Geography Possible answer: A demographer tracks changes in human populations and tries to identify trends, causes, and consequences. A demographer's work might lead to changes in immigration policy.

C Critical Thinking Skills

Analyzing Have students discuss the culture and society found today in Southern Europe. **Ask:** What are some factors that have influenced culture in Southern Europe? *(Southern Europe's location on the Mediterranean made it prime for being influenced by travelers and traders from Africa, Asia, and Northern European countries; politically, the region's civil societies first formed representative government.)* What cultural aspects do countries in Southern Europe share? *(Most of the countries speak a language derived from Latin, and have been influenced by the Roman Catholic Church.)* AL Logical/Mathematical

W Writing Skills

Argument Have students write an essay answering: **Do Italy, Spain, and Greece share common cultures?** Emphasize that there are good arguments for either a *yes* or *no* answer. Have students write an essay presenting their opinion with a minimum of two supporting details for their argument. In a class discussion of student essays, make a two-column chart on the board listing the *Yes* and *No* reasons students discuss in their essays. BL Intrapersonal, Verbal/Linguistic

Content Background Knowledge

Restoring the Greek Monuments The ancient Athenians built the Parthenon in just eight or nine years, but repairing it is taking much longer. The restoration project is now in its thirty-fourth year as archaeologists, architects, civil engineers, and craftsmen strive not simply to imitate the workmanship of the ancient Greeks but to re-create it. There are more questions than answers: How did the Athenians construct the temple apparently without building plans? How were the builders able to achieve faultless proportions and balance without modern tools? The Parthenon remains a mysterious miracle.

Plans to restore the Roman Colosseum are more controversial. Members of the Restorers Association of Italy claim that their group has been sidelined in favor of nonspecialist restorers who run the risk of causing damage to the monument. Another concern about preserving the Colosseum is that the car traffic surrounding the site causes the exterior to be tarnished with pollution.

ANSWERS, p. 302

READING PROGRESS CHECK Low birthrates are leading to a population decline. Low birthrates are largely attributed to more people avoiding the economic cost of raising a child and a greater number of women pursuing careers and having fewer children.

CRITICAL THINKING

1. Their perfect dimensions are a testament to the intelligence of ancient cultures. Their continued relevance to modern architecture makes it seem that the ancient cultures have been kept alive.
2. The White House, the Lincoln Memorial, and the U.S. Capitol all feature Greek and Roman architecture.

complementarity relationship between two places in which one produces something the other needs, resulting in an exchange

The largest cities in Southern Europe are economic and cultural hubs founded on ancient trade routes. Within the city of Rome, the modern capital of Italy, is Vatican City. It is an independent country that is home to the Roman Catholic Church. Vatican City was formally established as an independent city-state in 1929. This country is unique in its purpose because it relies on a **complementarity,** or an interdependence, with Rome for its goods and services. Greece has its modern capital in the ancient city of Athens. Spain's major cities, such as Madrid and Barcelona, were once the capitals of kingdoms. Today regions of Spain maintain separate cultural, and even linguistic, identities. Andalusia and the Basque regions have greater autonomy since their ethnic backgrounds are different from the rest of Spain. The importance of trade is apparent with Portugal, since its capital, Lisbon, is also its largest port.

READING PROGRESS CHECK

Summarizing What factors are resulting in a decreasing population in the region?

Society and Culture Today

GUIDING QUESTION *How have religion, the arts, and Southern Europe's rich intellectual traditions shaped society and culture today?*

C Southern Europe is culturally dominated by two legacies. The first is its location as a geographic crossroad for the cultures surrounding the Mediterranean Sea. The second is the historic events that occurred as a place where civil societies first formed representative governments elected by the people. As a result of empires and territorial control, the countries share roots in language, religion, and the arts. The people of Italy, Spain, and Portugal all speak Romance languages that evolved from Latin, the language of the Romans. Many inhabitants of these countries are also heavily influenced by the Roman Catholic Church.

W Throughout the region, literacy is very high (about 95 percent). The high literacy rate reflects the strong government support of education. Education is compulsory for all children, and university education is increasingly common.

Southern European governments have developed as providers of health care and other social welfare services that are funded by taxes. Spain and Italy have well-established universal health care systems that cover the basic health care needs of the people. Spain has more doctors per person than many other countries in Europe. Greece is more rural and has faced greater challenges in meeting the needs of health care among a less dense, more geographically distributed population.

The Greek Parthenon (left) and the Roman Colosseum (right) are two of the greatest architectural achievements of ancient Southern Europe. Both have provided inspiration for later builders and architects up to the present day.

CRITICAL THINKING

1. ***Speculating*** Why do you think that these structures have been so inspirational?
2. ***Making Connections*** Name two modern buildings that have features like the Parthenon or Colosseum.

networks Online Teaching Options

VIDEO

Islam in Spain and the Alhambra

Creating Visuals Use this video to analyze how religious interaction has shaped the development of society and culture in this region. Ask students to identify the regions of the world they think Islam comes from. Lead them to think about how Muslims traveled from the Middle East all the way to Europe. Have them draw rough maps describing the route that Muslims may have traveled over the centuries. Then discuss how historical and religious events influenced population patterns and the culture in this region. ELL Visual/Spatial, Kinesthetic

Family and Status of Women

Italian women have achieved a high level of gender equality. They enjoy access to higher education and success in business. However, integration of women into Italian politics suffers from a long period of male dominance and poor attitudes toward the contributions of qualified women.

Like Italy, Greece and Spain have a family-centered culture. In Greece, the family is the primary social support. Despite the rise of a large middle class since World War II, it is still common for members of extended families to live together. In the 1980s, laws were enacted that changed traditional family life but also created more freedoms. Spain enjoys similar social structures to Italy and Greece with smaller families and gender equality in higher education and business. R

The Arts

The ancient Greeks and Romans developed many important and basic elements of architecture, including columns, arches, and domes. The classical architectural style of these two cultures remains popular to this day, especially in civic buildings. The ancient Greeks valued a type of idealized realism in sculpture; the human figure is portrayed **accurately,** or perfectly, in Greek art. The Romans embraced Greek realism and carried it further, depicting people much as they really were.

accurate free from error

The Renaissance saw a revival of the classical style and its subjects in the arts. Artwork during the Renaissance also reflected a trend towards realism through new techniques such as perspective. Italian Renaissance artists, such as Leonardo da Vinci (1452–1519) and Michelangelo (1475–1564), created many of the era's masterpieces.

Spain has given the world some of the best examples of modern art. Artists in this genre include Pablo Picasso (1881–1973) and architect Antoni Gaudí (1852–1926). Salvador Dalí (1904–1989) led the surrealist movement. Surrealist works and ideas changed the definition of art in the twentieth century. T

✓ READING PROGRESS CHECK

Identifying Describe the major contributions of the Romans and Greeks to the arts.

Economic Activities

GUIDING QUESTION *What are the characteristics of Southern Europe's economy today?*

The global economic downturn at the beginning of the twenty-first century had a major impact on the subregion. Greece's fragile economy, based on small, family-owned businesses and agriculture, collapsed under a real-estate crash caused largely by a lack of regulation. In 2012 the general unemployment rate topped 25 percent, but youth unemployment was over 50 percent. Recovery was supported by other EU countries.

Resources, Power, and Industry

For all Southern European countries, access to the Mediterranean Sea and the Atlantic Ocean has been essential to economic development and stability. Like many developed countries, Southern European countries have seen steady decreases in their manufacturing sectors in the last 30 years. Instead, the service sectors have become more important, with an increase in industries such as banking, retail and wholesale sales, tourism, health care, and telecommunications. The countries in this subregion have relied on their warm, attractive climate, proximity to the sea, and rich food culture to attract tourists. Tourism is a major part of the service sector of the economy. C

Since the 1990s, Spain's economy has grown as a result of lower costs of operating factories and a large supply of workers. Membership in the EU provided

R Reading Skills

Explaining Continuity and Change Emphasize to students that the role of women has changed particularly since the beginning of the twentieth century. Have students read the two paragraphs under *Family and Status of Women*, and then form small groups to discuss family and the status of women in this region. Have them write three details that explain how status has changed or remained the same. Invite volunteers to conduct research to find additional information about the role of women in the last thirty years. **AL Interpersonal**

T Technology Skills

Presenting Discuss with students what they know about artwork during the Renaissance and modern art periods. Emphasize to students that Southern Europe is known throughout the world for its artists. Assign small groups of students to research two artists from either period. Each group should gather visual examples of its artists' creations and present these examples in a multimedia presentation to the class. Encourage groups to include an audio accompaniment to their presentations. **BL Auditory/Musical, Visual/Spatial**

C Critical Thinking Skills

Interpreting Have students read about the economic activities in Southern Europe. **Ask:** **How has the economy of Southern European changed?** *(Once a manufacturing economy, the service sectors and tourism have become major parts of the economy of most Southern European countries.)* **Is this change similar to or different from other Western countries, such as the United States?** *(Students' answers will vary, but should include reasons such as: it is similar to other Western countries including the United States as both regions transition from a declining manufacturing economy to one of services industries like banking, health care, telecommunications, and retail and wholesale marketing.)* **Verbal/Linguistic**

CHART

The Effects of Geography on the Rise of Rome

Making Connections Use this chart and map to help students visualize and understand how the relationship between physical and human geography has changed over time. Have them read the information in the chart and study the map. Invite a few volunteers to describe how geography affected the rise of Rome. Ask students to consider if these effects are still relevant to modern Europe. Have them write a paragraph answering this question. **BL Verbal/Linguistic**

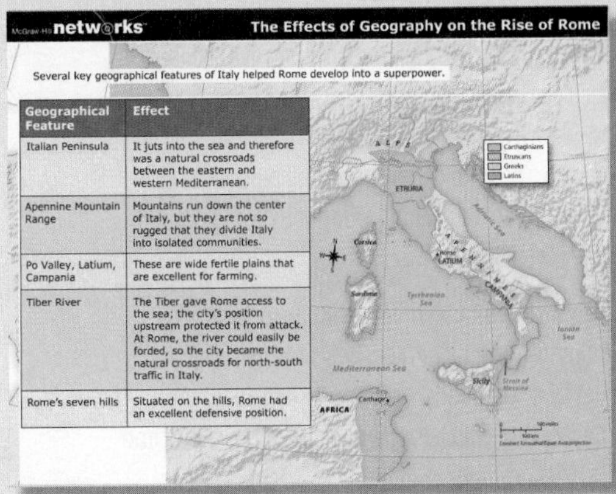
McGraw-Hill networks — The Effects of Geography on the Rise of Rome

Several key geographical features of Italy helped Rome develop into a superpower.

Geographical Feature	Effect
Italian Peninsula	It juts into the sea and therefore was a natural crossroads between the eastern and western Mediterranean.
Apennine Mountain Range	Mountains run down the center of Italy, but they are not so rugged that they divide Italy into isolated communities.
Po Valley, Latium, Campania	These are wide fertile plains that are excellent for farming.
Tiber River	The Tiber gave Rome access to the sea; the city's position upstream protected it from attack. At Rome, the river could easily be forded, so the city became the natural crossroads for north-south traffic in Italy.
Rome's seven hills	Situated on the hills, Rome had an excellent defensive position.

ANSWERS, p. 303

✓ **READING PROGRESS CHECK** Major architectural contributions of both include columns, arches, and domes. Ancient Greeks, through idealized realism, portrayed the human figure in sculpture. Roman sculpture took realism further and depicted humans in a less idealized way.

W Writing Skills

Informative/Explanatory Tell students to write an essay comparing and contrasting the main sectors of the economic challenges faced by Spain, Italy, and Greece. Have students share their essays with the class. AL **Verbal/Linguistic**

C Critical Thinking Skills

Hypothesizing Discuss with students the current relationship between the European Union and the countries of Southern Europe. **Ask: Given the current economic challenges and the tense relationship within the European Union, what do you predict the relationship will be in the future between the EU and countries in Southern Europe?** *(Student answers will vary, but should give reasons for their predictions.)* In a class discussion, have students summarize their predictions. **Verbal/Linguistic**

CLOSE & REFLECT

Analyzing Have students write an analysis of the role Southern Europe has played in Western civilization and its current status on the world stage. In a class discussion, have students share their analyses.

ANSWERS, p. 304

✓ READING PROGRESS CHECK Because Greece does not have a wealth of natural resources, the country did not quickly embrace industrialization. It instead relied on income from more unstable sources such as small, family-owned business and agriculture.

a market for Spanish products. Although it was severely affected by the global recession, Spain has continued its important economic role in the region.

Italy went through an industrial reconstruction after World War II. Areas along the Po River valley became the leading industrial region of the country. The EU opened other countries for the import of Italian Fiat cars and trucks, clothing, and home furnishings. Today Italy continues to thrive on high-tech engineering and metallurgical manufacturing. Certain portions of Italy's agricultural market play an important part in the export market, namely olive oil and wine.

W

Greece's economy is one of the least developed in Southern Europe. Natural resources are limited and industrialization has been slow to develop. A large sector of the economy is tourism. EU membership has been beneficial to agriculture and industrialization, since EU investments and subsidies compensate for low productivity. Today Greece faces major challenges to reduce its public spending. Generous social programs, tax evasion, and persistently high unemployment continue to be issues facing Greece.

Southern Europe faces many challenges in meeting its energy needs. The EU in general is the world's largest energy importer and is focusing more on natural gas due to its plans to reduce carbon dioxide emissions. While regional resources are limited, just south across the Mediterranean are rich oil- and natural gas-producing countries in North Africa. Pipelines on the seafloor deliver important energy supplies.

Future Prospects

Prior to 2009, membership in the EU was good for countries' economies. Member countries were doing well, and trade among them was growing annually. Easier migration within the EU across the borders between countries was filling the labor shortage. Living standards increased steadily.

C

In the twenty-first century the EU faces its first great test of economic stability within the subregion. The Southern European members are dealing with economic issues such as too much national debt, too high unemployment, and too much governmental spending. Those problems have stretched resources and goodwill very thin across all of Europe. Tensions have grown as the EU has provided special assistance to the Southern European members through loans and subsidies.

✓ READING PROGRESS CHECK

Summarizing Why is the Greek economy one of the least developed in Southern Europe?

LESSON 2 REVIEW

Reviewing Vocabulary (Tier Three Words)

1. ***Drawing Conclusions*** How did city-states influence the political history of Italy and Greece? RH.9–10.4

Using Your Notes

2. ***Summarizing*** Use your lesson graphic organizer to describe society and culture today in Southern Europe.

Answering the Guiding Questions

3. ***Identifying*** What characteristics of early civilizations are evident in Southern Europe today?
4. ***Expressing*** How have migration and aging populations affected Southern Europe's population patterns?
5. ***Discussing*** How have religion, the arts, and Southern Europe's rich intellectual traditions shaped society and culture today?
6. ***Describing*** What are the characteristics of Southern Europe's economy today?

Writing Activity

7. ***Informative/Explanatory*** Write a paragraph describing the contributions Southern Europe has made to the arts, both classical and modern art. Include specific time periods and forms of art and architecture. WHST.9–10.2

LESSON 2 REVIEW ANSWERS

Reviewing Vocabulary

1. The concept of democracy was born in the city-state of Athens and endured through the establishment of modern Greece. Rule of law and balance of power began under the Roman Republic and were preserved when the Italian city-states merged into modern Italy.

Using Your Notes

2. Countries share ancient Roman roots in language, religion, and the arts. Most people are Roman Catholic and benefit from government-provided social services such as quality education and health care.

Answering the Guiding Questions

3. Civic engineering capabilities and architectural intelligences of early civilizations are evidenced by the ruins of ancient structures found throughout Southern Europe. In addition to impressive architecture, Athenian democracy, Spartan war strategies, Roman and Greek mythology, and the idea of Roman rule of law with a balance of power have all passed the test of time and are still valued today both in and beyond Southern Europe.
4. An aging population means that the population is declining. Migrant workers help Southern Europe meet labor demands. Migrants also increase the population of Southern Europe and at the same time add to its diversity.
5. The Roman Catholic Church remains a strong influence in Italy, Spain, and Portugal. Appreciation and encouragement of the arts dating back to Roman times enabled the subregion to form many great artists. A rich history of intellectual traditions is evidenced by the subregion's high literacy rates achieved through government-supported education.
6. Southern Europe's economy is heavily reliant on the service sectors: banking, retail and wholesale sales, entertainment, health care, telecommunications, and tourism. Serious issues in the subregion, such as high national debt and high unemployment, are testing the economic stability of the EU.

Writing Activity

7. Paragraphs will differ, but may include contributions from Renaissance artists, such as da Vinci and Michelangelo, and modern artists, such as Picasso, Gaudí, and Dalí.

networks

There's More Online!

- **IMAGE** Southern Europe Addressing the Issues
- **IMAGE** Pollution Around the Mediterranean Sea
- **MAP** Soil Erosion in Southern Europe
- **INTERACTIVE SELF-CHECK QUIZ**
- **VIDEO** People and Their Environment: Southern Europe

LESSON 3
People and Their Environment: Southern Europe

ESSENTIAL QUESTION • *How do physical systems and human systems shape a place?*

Reading HELPDESK (CCSS)

Academic Vocabulary
(Tier Two Words)
- **promote**
- **factor**

Content Vocabulary
(Tier Three Words)
- **pollution hot spot**

TAKING NOTES: ***Key Ideas and Details***

PARAPHRASING Use a web diagram like the one below to take notes about the human impact on the environment of Southern Europe.

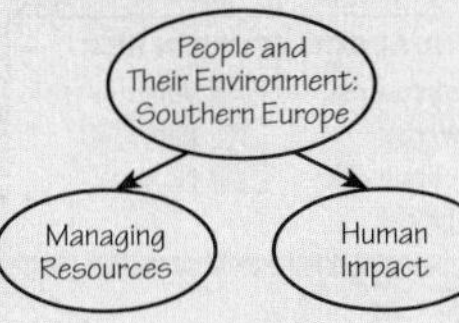

People and Their Environment: Southern Europe
Managing Resources
Human Impact

(b)SuperStock/age fotostock, (tc)Marco Secchi/Getty Images News/Getty Images, (tr)Cyril Bana/Author's Image/PunchStock

IT MATTERS BECAUSE

The Mediterranean Sea is essential to the culture and economy of Southern Europe. The human population growth of the region is slowing after 100 years of rapid expansion. Maintaining the balance between human needs and the environment is often challenging with such a large population. **C**

Managing Resources

GUIDING QUESTION *What are the threats that require closer management of resources in Southern Europe?*

Southern Europe's landscape is full of natural wonders—beautiful rivers, seas, and forests. Across most of the region, the climate is suitable for outdoor activity year-round, encouraging tourists and residents to spend a good deal of time exploring the outdoors. Human settlement has greatly increased over the last few decades, which has resulted in a number of concerns for the area's resources and environment. **R**

One major environmental concern in the region is the presence of large algae blooms in the Adriatic Sea. This sea forms a smaller part of the Mediterranean Sea between Italy and Greece. The algae blooms are evidence of the effects of human activity on delicate marine biomes. These visible clusters of organisms appear when there is an imbalance in the ecological structure. Warmer water, chemical fertilizer runoff from agriculture, and human settlements are all possible causes for an algae bloom. The bloom is potentially harmful because it can use up the dissolved oxygen in the water, killing fish and other marine life. Toxins produced by particularly harmful algae blooms can kill marine life and humans who consume affected marine life. **T**

The Mediterranean climate is known for its long, dry summers and wet, mild winters. However, changes in the global climate have made summers unpredictable. Some summers turn into droughts and others produce unseasonable rain. Both scenarios can result in excessive soil

networks Online Teaching Options

INTERACTIVE BELLRINGER

Haze in the Po River Valley

Identifying Cause and Effect Use the introductory text and the image to discuss the causes of smog and the effect of landforms, such as mountains or valleys, on smog. Ask students if they have ever heard of an ozone alert, or a weather condition when the level of air pollutants is so high it creates an unhealthy concentration of ozone. Have students form small groups and discuss their prior knowledge of ozone alerts, the causes of smog, and contributing factors to smog, such as heat and wind direction. Have students discuss each question. Ask each group to write agreed-upon answers to the questions. Then in a class discussion, have each group share its answers. **Interpersonal, Verbal/Linguistic**

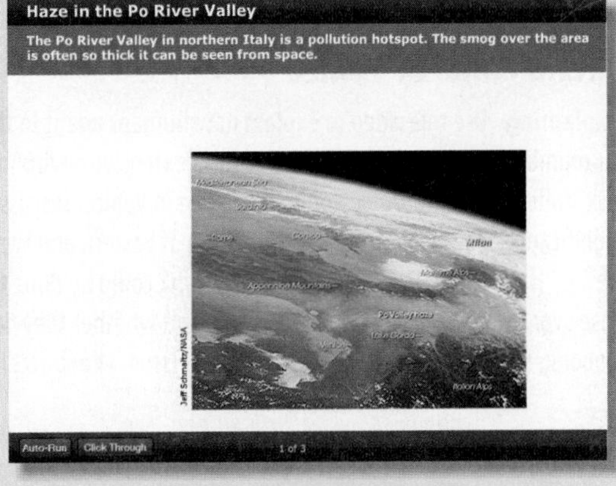

Haze in the Po River Valley
The Po River Valley in northern Italy is a pollution hotspot. The smog over the area is often so thick it can be seen from space.
Auto-Play
Click Through
1 of 3

ENGAGE

C Critical Thinking Skills

Examining Information To introduce the lesson, have students consider the question: **What ecological challenges do you think Southern Europe faces in the twenty-first century?** Have students browse through the lesson pages, making a list of the ecological challenges discussed in the text. Then have students share their lists with a partner.

TEACH & ASSESS

R Reading Skills

Interpreting Have students discuss the available resources in Southern Europe. **Ask: What are two reasons tourists and residents find the outdoor environment of Southern Europe attractive?** *(Possible answers: There are beautiful rivers and forests, and the climate is warm enough year-round for outdoor activities.)* **How is this attractiveness causing ecological challenges to Southern Europe's environment?** *(The human population in the area has increased, taxing the region's natural resources.)*

AL Verbal/Linguistic

T Technology Skills

Researching Explain to students that algae blooms are a worldwide concern. Invite student volunteers to conduct online research to find more information about algae blooms in different bodies of water throughout the world, including images or photos. Have the volunteers share their findings with the class. **Interpersonal, Visual/Spatial**

ANSWERS, p. 305

TAKING NOTES: Managing Resources—dangerous algae blooms in the Adriatic Sea need attention; important to know impacts of global warming such as drought, soil erosion, fires, deforestation; **Human Impact**—overfishing has depleted fish; industrial manufacturing pollutes; tourism creates extra waste and leads to land development, which destroys ecosystems; pollutants in water systems have led to pollution hot spots.

R Reading Skills

Identifying After students have read about soil erosion, have them list the steps that lead to soil erosion. Then have students write two paragraphs explaining why the loss of topsoil creates other ecological issues in an environment. Have students share their paragraphs with a partner, checking for accuracy and that all steps have been listed and explained. ELL Verbal/Linguistic

W Writing Skills

Informative/Explanatory Have students conduct online or library research on the process of deforestation and its link to soil erosion. Students should write a short essay on their findings and offer possible solutions to these problems in Southern Europe, focusing in on one particular region or forest area. BL Verbal/Linguistic

V Visual Skills

Interpreting Visuals Direct students' attention to the map of *Soil Erosion in Southern Europe.* **Ask:** What countries have an overall low risk of soil erosion? *(Spain and Portugal)* At what longitude is the country with the highest risk located? *(Between 10° and 20° E)* What country should be the most concerned about soil erosion? *(Italy)* Continue to lead a class discussion by asking students other questions about the soil erosion map. AL Visual/Spatial

promote to help something grow or develop

factor something that actively contributes to the production of a result

erosion. Loss of topsoil and soil erosion can threaten the natural balance of an ecosystem by removing potential footholds for vegetation. When bare rock is exposed, the land becomes vulnerable to other environmental threats, such as fire or desertification. When there is no plant life to hold dry soil to steep hillsides, rain can wash away already thin topsoil on the rocky terrain of much of the subregion. Too much rain can also **promote** the growth of vegetation that can become fuel for a fire.

Dry season fires are a natural part of Mediterranean climate ecosystems. They are necessary to maintain the native vegetation. However, fire is a contributing **factor** in the deforestation of human-modified areas. Climate change is also a significant contributing factor to deforestation. The Mediterranean region is experiencing longer and hotter summers with less humidity and more wind. Both low humidity and more wind provide conditions that increase the incidence of forest fires.

Higher altitude areas are also affected by climate change. Parts of the Pyrenees and the Alps that normally experience sufficient snowfall and cold temperatures to maintain glaciers and forests of coniferous trees are changing. The glaciers are shrinking, while the forests are being attacked by beetles and other insects that flourish in the warmer temperatures. Awareness of these effects of climate change is needed to protect the environments that support life in the Mediterranean areas.

✓ READING PROGRESS CHECK

Making Connections How is climate change related to soil erosion in Southern Europe?

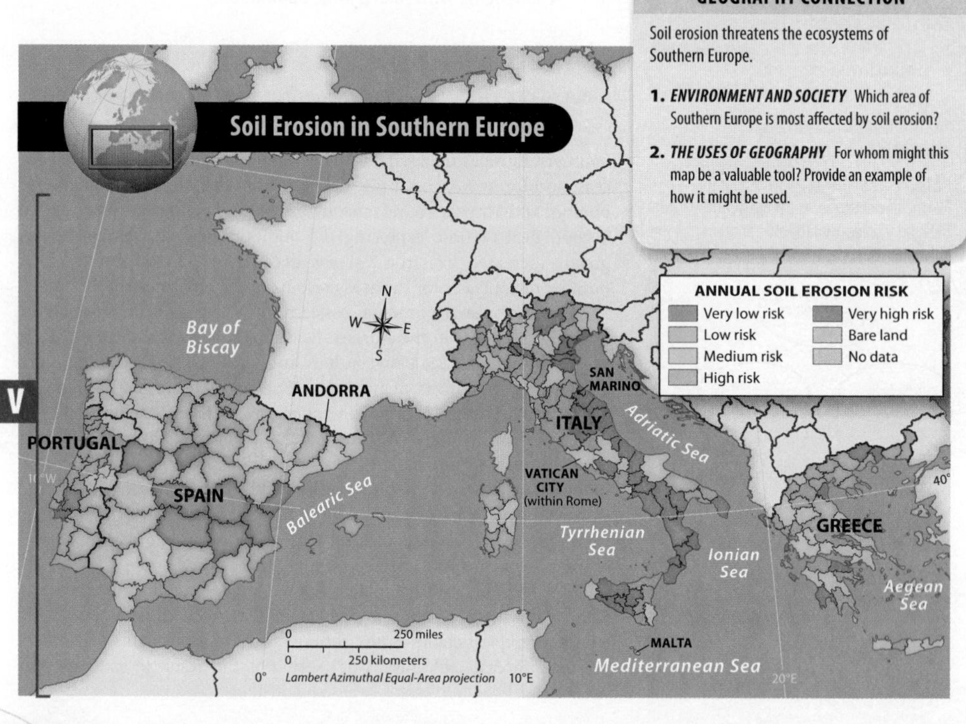

GEOGRAPHY CONNECTION

Soil erosion threatens the ecosystems of Southern Europe.

1. ***ENVIRONMENT AND SOCIETY*** Which area of Southern Europe is most affected by soil erosion?
2. ***THE USES OF GEOGRAPHY*** For whom might this map be a valuable tool? Provide an example of how it might be used.

306

networks Online Teaching Options

VIDEO

Grand Canal of Venice

Explaining Use this video to explain how humans adapt to their physical surroundings and how these places require extensive environmental management. Ask students whether they would like to live in Venice. Discuss Venice's historical significance, especially the artistic blending of Eastern and Western culture and design. Have students explain what they think could be done for Venice if sea levels rose over the course of the next 100 years and whether they believe the possibility of flooding in Venice is a global environmental issue. Verbal/Linguistic

ANSWERS, p. 306

✓ **READING PROGRESS CHECK** A changing climate has made summers unpredictable, bringing either drought or too much rain. Drought kills plants, allows wind to carry away topsoil, and increases risk of extensive forest fires. Excessive rain produces extra vegetation which can become extra fuel for forest fires.

GEOGRAPHY CONNECTION

1. Italy is most affected.
2. This map would be valuable to the Forest Stewardship Council, the NGO working on reforestation. They would use it to concentrate their replanting efforts in the areas most at risk.

Human Impact

GUIDING QUESTION *What are the environmental concerns regarding tourism in Southern Europe?*

Southern Europe is well known for its food culture. In the coastal areas, this means fish and other seafood are common in the local diets. As a result, overfishing has occurred. Fish stocks are not being replenished as quickly as they are being depleted. As the fish stocks have declined, the overall health of the marine biome has declined as well.

C

Two sectors of the economy in Southern Europe that have seen tremendous growth in the last 50 years are industrial manufacturing and tourism. Industrial pollution is a major threat to the surrounding seas and to the quality of water and agricultural resources. Development associated with tourism causes major damage to coastal ecosystems, loss of natural habitat, overuse of freshwater resources, as well as pollution and waste.

Tourism inundates regions that are normally sparsely populated with huge numbers of people. More people make a greater impact on the local environment. Waste management issues are the primary concern. One popular form of vacationing is via cruise ship. Oil spills and oil pollutants from ships of all kinds are a growing concern in the subregion.

R

Pollutants and other human impacts in the water systems have given rise to **pollution hot spots** in the Mediterranean Sea. These hot spots are locations where such impacts have led to the degradation, and even the death, of the local ecosystem. These spots do not support marine life. The water is warmer and more vulnerable to the development of algae and other microorganisms, some of which are harmful to humans.

Industrialization and development along coastal Southern Europe has led to numerous problems in the marine biomes of the region.

▲ CRITICAL THINKING

1. ***Analyzing Visuals*** How might the human activity in this photo affect the nearby waterway?
2. ***Formulating Questions*** If you were an ecologist, what are two questions you would ask to evaluate the health of this waterway?

pollution hot spot a location where pollution and other human activities have led to the degradation, or even death, of an ecosystem

☑ READING PROGRESS CHECK

Summarizing How are manufacturing and tourism affecting the environment?

Addressing the Issues

GUIDING QUESTION *How are groups, governments, and others addressing environmental issues in Southern Europe?*

As early as 1975, European countries in the Mediterranean region recognized that rapid population expansion, industrialization, and a general increase in human activity were threatening the region's natural beauty and resources. The Mediterranean Action Plan was created at that time to help plan a way to curb damage to the environment. Each participating country set goals for reducing its environmental impact on the region, and governments in the region have been diligent in addressing the issues. Legislation has been enacted in all participating countries to try to regulate the effects of industrialization and population growth.

W

In 1990 the European Union (EU) created the European Environmental Agency. Its purpose is to help evaluate threats to the region and create plans to effectively deal with environmental issues. This agency makes independent reports to the European Union, which can then work with member countries to enact action plans to address environmental concerns.

SuperStock/age fotostock

C Critical Thinking Skills

Analyzing Cause and Effect Have students read the first and second paragraphs. **Ask:** **What are the two fastest-growing sectors of the economy in Southern Europe?** *(industrial manufacturing and its subsequent trade and tourism)* **How does industrial pollution threaten the region?** *(Industrialization threatens the region's seas, agricultural resources, and the quality of water.)* **How does an increase in tourism cause damage to the coastal region?** *(Tourism development damages coastal ecosystems, affects natural habitats and freshwater systems, and creates excessive waste.)* **Verbal/Linguistic**

Content Background Knowledge

Tourism in Southern Europe According to the United Nations World Tourism Organization, Europe is the most frequently visited region in the world. In 2009, five of the top ten regions for visitors in the world were EU member states: Spain, Italy, Greece, and Cyprus; the Canary Islands had the most overnight hotel stays by foreign tourists.

R Reading Skills

Defining Write out the term *pollution hot spots* and through a class discussion arrive at the definition. Have students write a paragraph using the term and explaining its relevance to Southern European countries. ELL **Verbal/Linguistic**

W Writing Skills

Argument Ask students to think about the pollution problems of Southern Europe and the efforts made to address the problems. Then, have students write an essay discussing whether they think legislative efforts are enough to stop the pollution or if other solutions are needed. They should argue in favor of or against one of those solutions. Have students cite two or three reasons for their choice. Students should share their essays with the class. BL **Intrapersonal**

INTERACTIVE IMAGE

The Impact of Industrialization

Analyzing Visuals This interactive image showing the impact of industrialization can be used to help students consider the effects of pollution. Have them study the image and list every individual source of air, water, or earth pollution shown in the picture. Then, for each of the sources of pollution on their lists, have students identify the part and suggest a less polluting alternative. Allow time for students to complete the activity. Afterwards, ask students how these alternative options can be explored. BL **Visual/Spatial**

ANSWERS, p. 307

☑ READING PROGRESS CHECK Industrial pollution from manufacturing threatens the seas, the quality of water supplies, and agricultural resources. Tourism creates excessive waste that current systems struggle to manage. Land development for tourism disrupts coastal ecosystems and strains freshwater resources.

CRITICAL THINKING

1. Industrial pollution can be emitted into the waterway through runoff or as acid rain after its chemicals combine with the atmosphere.
2. Possible answers: How much and what kind(s) of algae are present? What is the current quantity of species that previously lived here in abundance?

CHAPTER 12, Lesson 3

People and Their Environment: Southern Europe

T Technology Skills

Presenting Divide the class into four small groups and assign each group to research a particular environmental protection need in the four areas of Southern Europe: the Mediterranean Sea region, the Alps, the Po River in Piedmont, Italy and the Ebro River Delta in Spain. Have each group create a multimedia presentation to share with the class. BL **Visual/Spatial, Auditory/Musical**

Content Background Knowledge

European Environmental Agency As an EU agency, it provides information on the environment. It is also a source for those involved in developing, adopting, implementing, and evaluating environmental policy, such as members of the business community, academia, nongovernmental organizations, and other parts of civil society.

CLOSE & REFLECT

Summarizing Have students summarize the environmental problems facing Southern Europe and the recent efforts to resolve these issues.

ANSWERS, p. 308

READING PROGRESS CHECK The agency evaluates threats to the region's environment and creates plans to deal with the issues it finds. It submits reports to the EU, which helps member countries enact the plans.

CRITICAL THINKING

1. They might spill oil into a waterway. They might dump waste into a waterway. They unload tourists who add extra waste.
2. The cruise ships bring revenue to the area.

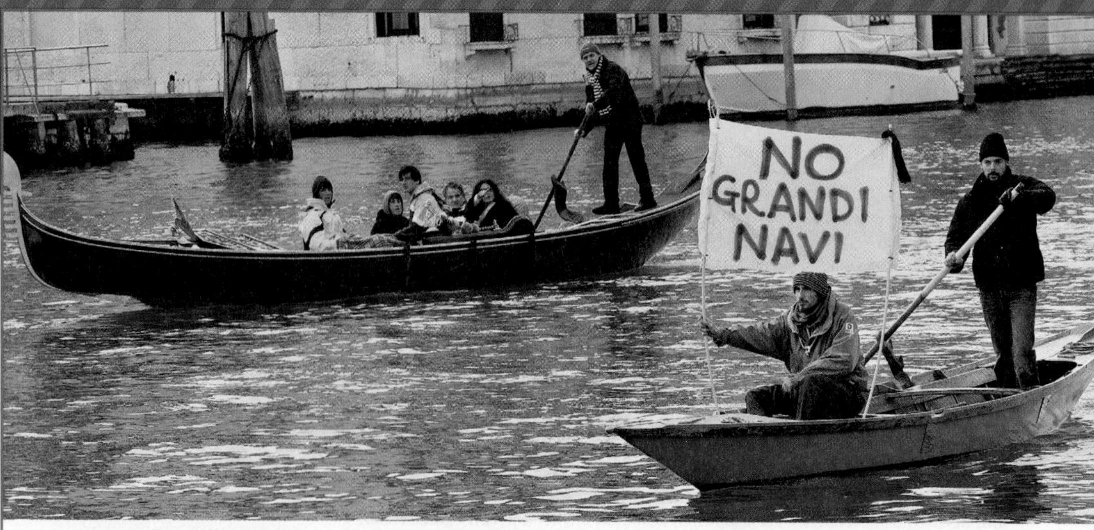

Marco Secchi/Getty Images News/Getty Images

In Venice, Italy, demonstrators protest against the docking of huge cruise ships—*grandi navi*—in the city's bay, or lagoon.

▲ **CRITICAL THINKING**

1. ***Identifying Central Issues*** What types of damage might very large cruise ships cause?
2. ***Speculating*** Why might some people in Venice want cruise ships to keep docking in the lagoon, even if they cause problems?

Many nongovernmental organizations (NGOs) are dedicated to addressing issues that affect the region and that may have a lasting impact on the welfare of the global environment. These include the World Wildlife Fund (WWF), Earthwatch, and the Nature Conservancy. These organizations work to solve the problems, including industrial pollution, algae blooms, and soil erosion, which are prominent in Southern Europe. There are many ways for individuals to get involved with organizations that protect the regions of the world that are essential to a region's cultural and natural heritage.

Deforestation is also a growing concern in Europe. The Forest Stewardship Council (FSC), an international NGO, is leading a grassroots campaign in Europe to reforest or protect forest biomes. Specifically, they are working to reduce soil erosion and the risk of forest fires and fighting causes of global warming. Certification is one way to ensure that forest resources are being used responsibly. When resource extractors obtain certification, consumers can be assured that they support products and services that avoid exploiting forest resources. A public awareness campaign has helped to some extent, although it is hard to measure by how much. Teaching the public about these issues helps people make decisions that support responsible stewardship of the environment.

READING PROGRESS CHECK

Identifying What is the role of the European Environmental Agency?

LESSON 3 REVIEW (CCSS)

Reviewing Vocabulary (Tier Three Words)

1. ***Making Predictions*** How might pollution hot spots in the waters of Southern Europe affect future economic activity in the region? RH.9–10.4

Using Your Notes

2. ***Explaining*** Use your web diagram to describe the major impacts humans are having on the environment in Southern Europe.

Answering the Guiding Questions

3. ***Evaluating*** What are the threats that require closer management of resources in Southern Europe?
4. ***Explaining*** What are the environmental concerns regarding tourism in Southern Europe?
5. ***Discussing*** How are groups, governments, and others addressing environmental issues in Southern Europe?

Writing Activity

6. ***Informative/Explanatory*** In a paragraph, explain how soil erosion poses a threat to the ecosystems of the subregion. What can be done to lessen the negative effects of climate change and the problem of soil erosion in Southern Europe? WHST.9–10.2

308

LESSON 3 REVIEW ANSWERS

Reviewing Vocabulary

1. If hot spots continue to increase, more of the Mediterranean will become not only useless to humans, but harmful as it is taken over by microorganisms. Resources from this important sea could disappear along with the revenue they once brought to the economies.

Using Your Notes

2. Overfishing has depleted fish populations. Industrial manufacturing pollutes ecosystems and causes health problems to humans. Waste management, especially with additional tourists, is a problem, as untreated waste is often dumped into waterways. Pollutants in water systems have created pollution hot spots in the Mediterranean Sea where natural ecosystems are now dead.

Answering the Guiding Questions

3. Threats include algae blooms in the Adriatic Sea and effects of climate change such as drought, soil erosion, forest fires, and glacial melting.
4. The main concern is waste management since the areas overwhelmed by tourists were mostly built to meet modest needs of a small population of residents. Tourism necessitates land development, which damages coastal ecosystems by causing loss of natural habitat and overuse of freshwater resources. Cruise ships are prone to oil spills, which kill marine life.
5. They are creating action plans, forming agencies, and enacting pro-environment legislation. NGOs are trying to solve problems of industrial pollution, algae blooms, and soil erosion. Certification is now given to items produced in forest-friendly ways and consumers can choose these products.

Writing Activity

6. Paragraphs will vary, but should be strongly supported by information from the chapter showing the progression of the effects of climate change, for example, how drought or extra rainfall contributes to various types of erosion, which lead to fires, deforestation, and desertification. Lastly, there should be a list of steps Southern Europe can take to decrease the negative effects of climate change and soil erosion.

CHAPTER 12 Assessment 

Directions: On a separate sheet of paper, answer the questions below. Make sure you read carefully and answer all parts of the questions.

Lesson Review

Lesson 1

1. ***Analyzing*** Several of the rivers of Southern Europe are not navigable because they are not wide or deep enough for large ships to travel on. Why are rivers still important to the region?
2. ***Explaining*** What factors of the Mediterranean climate of Southern Europe make it ideal for growing grapes and olives?
3. ***Describing*** Describe the geographic locations of the three major Southern European peninsulas.

Lesson 2

4. ***Evaluating*** How has Southern Europe contributed to the arts? Provide specific examples.
5. ***Identifying Central Issues*** How have changes in population growth affected demographics in Italy? **RH.9–10.2**
6. ***Understanding Relationships*** What effect does tourism have on the economies of Southern Europe?

Lesson 3

7. ***Identifying Cause and Effect*** What are the causes and consequences of deforestation in the region?
8. ***Summarizing*** What key factors have contributed to pollution in the Mediterranean Sea?
9. ***Analyzing*** In what ways have the governments of Southern Europe taken steps to reduce pollution?

Exploring the Essential Question

10. ***Making Connections*** Create a poster illustrating one of the three peninsulas of Southern Europe. Show how the peninsula has been influenced by human systems, including history, art, politics, and economics. Use photos, graphs, charts, and maps.

21st Century Skills

Use the chart to answer the questions below.

The Labor Force in Southern Europe

	% of Labor Force in Agriculture	% of Labor Force in Industry	% of Labor Force in Services
Greece	12.4	22.4	65.1
Italy	3.9	28.3	67.8
Portugal	11.7	28.5	59.8
Spain	4.3	24	71.7

Source: CIA World Factbook

11. ***Economics*** In which two countries is agriculture still a relatively significant contributor to the economy?
12. ***Compare & Contrast*** What generalization can you make about Spain and its level of economic development compared to the other countries listed?

Critical Thinking

13. ***Making Generalizations*** What long-term effects will Italy's aging population have on the country?
14. ***Comparing and Contrasting*** Compare the levels of development and industrialization in northern Italy to those in Greece. What factors help explain the differences?
15. ***Predicting*** Why should Southern European countries be concerned about high rates of unemployment among educated youth?

Need Extra Help?

If You've Missed Question	1	2	3	4	5	6	7	8	9	10	11	12	13	14	15
Go to page	296	297	294	303	301	304	306	307	307	294	309	309	301	303	303

CHAPTER 12 Assessment Answers

Lesson Review

Lesson 1

1. Many of the region's rivers are able to be dammed for hydroelectric power and to create irrigation networks and freshwater reserves. Additionally, river basins, such as that of the Po River, provide areas with fertile soil.
2. The long, warm, dry Mediterranean summers are ideal for grapes and olives.
3. The Iberian Peninsula is in the westernmost part of the region, the Italian Peninsula is in the center but angled towards the southeast, and the Balkan Peninsula is in the easternmost part of the region.

Lesson 2

4. Renaissance artists such as Leonardo da Vinci and Michelangelo are respected around the world. Modern artists such as Pablo Picasso and Antonin Gaudí contributed new ways of depicting the modern world. Salvador Dalí ushered in the surrealist movement.
5. Low birthrates cause an aging population and a deficit of working-age people. Immigrants come to fill jobs and increase the diversity of the region's population.
6. Tourism is a major part of the region's economy, as it brings a lot of revenue to the region.

Lesson 3

7. Climate change has led to longer dry seasons with low humidity and high wind, both of which fuel forest fires, causing deforestation. Excessive deforestation can lead to desertification, a condition that is almost irreversible.
8. Industrial pollutants enter the sea through runoff. Excess waste produced by tourism is often dumped into the sea. Oil spills and oil pollutants from large ships also damage the Mediterranean.
9. Governments of countries participating in the Mediterranean Action Plan have enacted legislation to regulate industrialization and population growth. Governments work with the European Environmental Agency on plans for environmental restoration.

Exploring the Essential Question

10. Posters should show one of the following: the Iberian Peninsula, the Italian Peninsula, or the Balkan Peninsula. There should be photos, graphs, charts, and maps that demonstrate the influences of history, art, politics, and economics on the peninsula.

21st Century Skills

11. Greece and Portugal
12. Spain is more economically developed than the other countries because it has a larger number of laborers in the Services and Industry fields compared to the number of workers in Agriculture.

Critical Thinking

13. It will lead to an imbalance in the population contributing to the tax pool and taking from the tax pool since there will be fewer people of working age and more people of retiring age.
14. Italy experienced industrial reconstruction after World War II, but Greece did not. Greece lacks the natural resources needed for industry and doesn't have navigable rivers to assist in trade, whereas Italy is able to take advantage of the Po River.
15. If solid career opportunities are not created in the region, educated people will leave to find them elsewhere, incurring a brain drain.

Assessment Answers

Analyzing Primary Sources

16 The two regions are very close geographically, and many North African immigrants to South America brought their art forms with them.

17 Vast expanses of dry, windy plains

Applying Map Skills

18 Climate: Mediterranean, marine west coast, and humid subtropical; Vegetation: Mediterranean scrub and mixed forest (deciduous and coniferous)

19 The more densely populated areas of Spain include the coastal areas and along the border with Portugal. Madrid is the exception to this generalization since it is in the center of the country.

20 The Apennine Mountains run northwest to southeast through the center of the country. The Alps cover the northernmost portion of the country.

College and Career Readiness

21 Recommendations will vary, but should include at least two benefits of investing in locally produced power and two examples of natural resources Greece could use.

Research and Presentation

22 Presentations will vary, but should include an explanation of Andorra's government structure, including how it developed, how it became a dual principality, and how it is still able to function today.

Writing About Geography

23 The one-page essay should detail at least three possible solutions to the Mediterranean Sea's pollution problems. Each solution should stipulate what is required of governments, outside groups, or individuals for the solution to be effective.

CHAPTER 12 Assessment 

Directions: On a separate sheet of paper, answer the questions below. Make sure you read carefully and answer all parts of the questions.

DBQ Analyzing Primary Sources

Use the document to answer the following questions.

Federico García Lorca (1898–1936) was a Spanish poet and playwright who was part of a group of avant-garde Spanish artists that also included Salvador Dalí.

PRIMARY SOURCE

Rider's Song

Córdoba
Far away and alone.

Black pony, big moon,
and olives in my saddle-bag.
Although I know the roads
I'll never reach Córdoba.

Through the plain, through the wind,
black pony, red moon.
Death is looking at me
from the towers of Córdoba.

Ay! How long the road!
Ay! My valiant pony!
Ay! That death should wait me
before I reach Córdoba.

Córdoba.
Far away and alone.

—Federico García Lorca, *The Selected Poems of Federico García Lorca*, 2006

16 ***Analyzing*** The North African poets of the Middle Ages used literary forms of allusion and repetition similar to those used by the author of this poem. Why would there be similarities between Spanish and North African poetry? RH.9–10.1, RH.9–10.4

17 ***Interpreting*** What aspects of Spain's physical geography can be identified in this poem? RH.9–10.1, RH.9–10.4

Applying Map Skills

Use your Unit 4 Atlas to answer the following questions.

18 ***Places and Regions*** What climate and vegetation types are found in Greece?

19 ***Human Systems*** What generalizations can you make about the population density of Spain in regard to its physical geography? What city is the exception?

20 ***Physical Systems*** Use your mental map of Southern Europe to describe the location of the major mountain ranges in Italy.

College and Career Readiness

21 ***Reaching Conclusions*** Imagine you are an economic geographer working for a nongovernmental organization (NGO). Write a recommendation for the Greek government explaining the benefits of investing in locally produced power. What natural resources can the Greek government use? WHST.9–10.1, WHST.9–10.4

Research and Presentation

22 ***Research Skills*** Use Internet and library resources to gather information about the country of Andorra. Focus specifically on the unique government structure of this small country. Create a presentation explaining the history of this country's government. How did it become a dual principality and how does it maintain the system today? WHST.9–10.6, WHST.9–10.7

Writing About Geography

23 ***Informative/Explanatory*** Use standard grammar, spelling, sentence structure, and punctuation to write a one-page essay suggesting possible solutions to the problem of pollution in the Mediterranean Sea. Who will need to participate for the solution to be successfully implemented? WHST.9–10.2, WHST.9–10.4

Need Extra Help?

If You've Missed Question	16	17	18	19	20	21	22	23
Go to page	310	310	244	246	242	298	294	307

networks Online Teaching Options

WORKSHEET

Chapter Test and Lesson Quizzes

Assessing Have students complete the Chapter Test and Lesson Quizzes to assess student understanding throughout the chapter. These assessment tools offer chapter and lesson evaluation through a variety of question formats, including document-based questions.

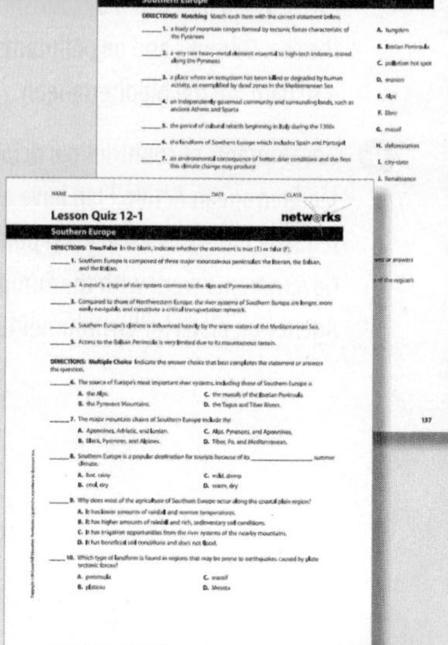
Chapter 12 Test, Form A
Southern Europe

Lesson Quiz 12-1
Southern Europe

CHAPTER **13**

Eastern Europe Planner

UNDERSTANDING BY DESIGN®

Enduring Understandings

- *Cooperation and conflict among people influence the division and control of Earth's surface.*

Essential Question

- *How do physical systems and human systems shape a place?*

Predictable Misunderstandings

Students may think:

- *The borders of Eastern European countries have been stable for centuries. Explain that many Eastern European countries are very new having resulted from the breakup of Yugoslavia into several smaller countries in the 1990s.*
- *Many countries in Eastern Europe still have communist governments. Explain that the countries of Eastern Europe broke free of the Soviet Union in 1989 and many went on to form democratic governments.*

Assessment Evidence

Performance Tasks:

- *Hands-On Chapter Project*

Other Evidence:

- *Guided Reading Activities*
- *Vocabulary Activities*
- *Lesson Quizzes*
- *Chapter Tests, Forms A and B*

SUGGESTED PACING GUIDE

Introducing the Chapter .... ½ Day
Lesson 1 .... 1 Day
Lesson 2 .... 2 Days
Lesson 3 .... 1 Day
Chapter Wrap-Up and Assessment ...... ½ Day

TOTAL TIME 5 Days

Key for Using the Teacher Edition

SKILL-BASED ACTIVITIES

Types of skill activities found in the Teacher Edition.

* **V Visual Skills** require students to analyze maps, graphs, charts, and photos.

R Reading Skills help students practice reading skills and master vocabulary.

C Critical Thinking Skills help students apply and extend what they have learned.

W Writing Skills provide writing opportunities to help students comprehend the text.

T Technology Skills require students to use digital tools effectively.

*Letters are followed by a number when there is more than one of the same type of skill on the page.

DIFFERENTIATED INSTRUCTION

All activities are written for the on-level student unless otherwise marked with the leveled labels below.

BL Beyond Level
AL Approaching Level
ELL English Language Learners

All students benefit from activities that utilize different learning styles. Many activities are marked as below when a particular learning style is highlighted.

Intrapersonal **Naturalist**
Logical/Mathematical **Kinesthetic**
Visual/Spatial **Auditory/Musical**
Verbal/Linguistic **Interpersonal**

National Geography Standards covered in "Eastern Europe"

The student knows and understands:

(3) How to analyze the spatial organizations of people, places, and environments on Earth's surface

(4) The physical and human characteristics of places

4.2 The interaction of physical and human systems result in the creation of and changes to places

(7) The physical processes that shape the patterns of Earth's surface

7.3 Physical processes interact over time to shape particular places on Earth's surface

(8) The characteristics and spatial distribution of ecosystems and biomes on Earth's surface

(9) The characteristics, distribution, and migration of human populations on Earth's surface

9.2 Population distribution and density are a function of historical, environmental, economic, political, and technological factors

(10) The characteristics, distribution, and complexity of Earth's cultural mosaics

(11) The patterns and networks of economic interdependence on Earth's surface

11.3 Economic systems are dynamic organizations of interdependent economic activities for production, exchange, distribution, and consumption of goods and services

(14) How human actions modify the physical environment

(15) How physical systems affect human systems

15.1 Depending on the choice of human activities, the characteristics of the physical environment can be viewed as both opportunities and constraints

(16) The changes that occur in the meaning, use, distribution, and importance of resources

16.3 Policies and programs that promote the sustainable use and management of resources impact people and the environment

(17) How to apply geography to interpret the past

17.1 Geographic contexts (the human and physical characteristics of places and environments) can explain the connections between sequences of historical events

(18) How to apply geography to interpret the present and plan for the future

18.1 Geographic contexts (the human and physical characteristics of places and environments) provide the bases for analyzing current events and making predictions about future issues

CHAPTER OPENER PLANNER

Students will know:

- *the influence of the Alpine mountain system, the Northern European Plain, the Hungarian Plain, and the rivers and seas on human activities in Eastern Europe.*
- *the factors that affect climate and vegetation in the region.*
- *the early peoples, empires, conflicts, and divisions that have shaped Eastern Europe.*
- *that Eastern European countries transitioned to democratic governments and market economies after the fall of communism and how the communist era affects the environment today.*
- *the causes and consequences of deforestation, acid rain, and pollution in Eastern Europe and how governments address these issues.*

Students will be able to:

- ***identify** how the physical geography of Eastern Europe has influenced the region.*
- ***identify** factors that affect climate and vegetation in the region.*
- ***describe** people, empires, and conflicts that have shaped Eastern Europe.*
- ***identify** causes and consequences of deforestation and pollution in the region.*
- ***describe** environmental issues and possible solutions.*

UNDERSTANDING BY DESIGN®

☑ Print Teaching Options

R Reading Skills

- ☐ **p. 313** Students list three conditions that contributed to the conflict in Yugoslavia. AL Verbal/Linguistic

W Writing Skills

- ☐ **p. 312** Students write a paragraph explaining the conditions that contributed to the breakup of Yugoslavia.

C Critical Thinking Skills

- ☐ **p. 312** Students explore the term "powder keg."

T Technology Skills

- ☐ **p. 313** Students research why some military leaders were charged with war crimes for the wars in Yugoslavia in the 1990s. BL Verbal/Linguistic

☑ Online Teaching Options

C Critical Thinking Skills

- ☐ INTERACTIVE MAP **The Former Yugoslavia**—Student groups consider how the map shows the spatial changes to this region and write a brief essay analyzing how the area has become an ethnically diverse nation of cultural change. BL Verbal/Linguistic

V Visual Skills

- ☐ TIME LINE **The Breakup of Yugoslavia**—Students discuss the events on the time line, then choose a date and sketch a map of Yugoslavia's boundaries at that exact date. Visual/Spatial, Kinesthetic

☑ Printable Digital Worksheets

- ☐ WORKSHEET **Assessing Background Knowledge**—Determine the level of prior knowledge students have about Eastern Europe.
- ☐ WORKSHEET **Chapter Summaries**—Students review the main idea of each lesson of the chapter content.

Project-Based Learning 

Hands-On

Mapping Eastern Europe

Students create detailed maps of an assigned country in Eastern Europe. The maps will label important places and the physical and human geography of their country, such as its climate, main ethnic groups, and languages. Explain that students will include this information in captions, labels, and talking boxes on their maps. Maps will also include a map key, scale, and legend.

Digital Hands-On

Create Online Projects

Find an additional activity online that incorporates technology for this project. Visit the EdTech Teacher Web sites for more links, tutorials, and other resources.

Print Resources

ANCILLARY RESOURCES

This ancillary is available for every chapter and lesson.

- **Chapter Tests and Lesson Quizzes**

PRINTABLE DIGITAL WORKSHEETS

These printable digital worksheets are available for every chapter and lesson.

- **Assessing Background Knowledge**
- **Chapter Summaries**
- **Guided Reading Activities**
- **Hands-On Chapter Projects**
- **Quizzes and Tests**
- **Reading Essentials and Study Guide** AL
- **Reteaching Activities**
- **Video Activities**
- **Vocabulary Activities**

More Media Resources

SUGGESTED VIDEOS 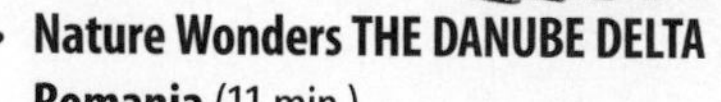

- **Nature Wonders THE DANUBE DELTA Romania** (11 min.)
- **Rick Steves' Eastern Europe DVD** (4 hr.)
- **Broadcast Diversity in Eastern Europe, 1990** (58 min.)

SUGGESTED READING 

- ***The Post-Socialist City: Urban Form and Space Transformations in Central and Eastern Europe after Socialism),*** by Kiril Stanilov
- ***Landscapes and Societies in Medieval Europe East of the Elbe: Interactions between Environmental Settings and Cultural Transformations,*** by Sunhild Kleingartner (Editor), Timothy P. Newfield (Editor), Sebastien Rossignol (Editor), Donat Wehner (Editor)
- ***Eastern European Capitalism in the Making,*** by Elena A. Iankova

PHYSICAL GEOGRAPHY OF EASTERN EUROPE

Students will know:

- *how the Alpine mountain system connects Eastern Europe with other subregions.*
- *why the Northern European Plain and the Hungarian Plain are important to human activities in Eastern Europe.*
- *the role rivers and seas had in the settlement and development of Eastern Europe.*
- *the factors affecting climate and vegetation in Eastern Europe.*

Students will be able to:

- ***explain** how physical geography of Eastern Europe affects its connection to other subregions and human activities.*
- ***describe** how rivers and seas impacted settlement and development.*
- ***identify** factors that affect climate and vegetation in the region.*

UNDERSTANDING BY DESIGN®

☑ Print Teaching Options

V Visual Skills

- ☐ **p. 314** Students create a chart to group Eastern European countries by location and land features.
- ☐ **p. 314** Students use various colors to represent landform features on an outline map of Eastern Europe. **Visual/Spatial**
- ☐ **p. 317** Students make a 3-column chart to compare the climate regions and biomes of Eastern Europe. **ELL** **Visual/Spatial, Naturalist**
- ☐ **p. 318** Students add a column for Agriculture to their 3-column climate regions and biomes charts. **Visual/Spatial**

R Reading Skills

- ☐ **p. 316** Students explain why the Main-Danube Canal is economically important. **AL** **Logical/Mathematical**
- ☐ **p. 317** Students compare a transportation map of Eastern Europe to a physical or political map of the region.

C Critical Thinking Skills

- ☐ **p. 315** Students compare the Carpathian Mountains to the Swiss Alps. **AL** **Verbal/Linguistic**
- ☐ **p. 317** Students discuss the importance of the various waterways to the economies of the Eastern European countries. **AL** **Verbal/Linguistic**

W Writing Skills

- ☐ **p. 315** Students write a narrative describing an imaginary trip across the region. **BL** **Verbal/Linguistic**
- ☐ **p. 316** Students write an imaginary travel blog describing a trip down the Danube River. **Verbal/Linguistic**

T Technology Skills

- ☐ **p. 315** Students research karst topography and find images, diagrams, and flowcharts to show how features are formed. **Verbal/Linguistic, Visual/Spatial**
- ☐ **p. 316** Students research a river in Eastern Europe and create a slide show presentation, including music, about the river. **BL** **Auditory/Musical, Visual/Spatial**
- ☐ **p. 318** Students research data about the level of economic development in an Eastern European country.

☑ Online Teaching Options

V Visual Skills

- ☐ **INTERACTIVE IMAGE** **Karst Terrain**—Students list features that are characteristic of karst terrain, choose one of the characteristics to research, and write a few paragraphs to describe the feature and its location. **AL** **Verbal/Linguistic, Visual/Spatial**

R Reading Skills

- ☐ **INTERACTIVE WHITEBOARD ACTIVITY** **Waterways of Eastern Europe**—Students use a map to match the name of the correct major waterway of Eastern Europe to its proper description in the chart.

C Critical Thinking Skills

- ☐ **INTERACTIVE BELLRINGER** **Alpine Europe**—Students analyze how the Alpine mountain system connects Eastern Europe with other regions and discuss their prior knowledge of mountains in Europe. **AL** **Interpersonal, Visual/Spatial**
- ☐ **INTERACTIVE MAP** **Alpine Europe**—Student pairs focus on an assigned region to draw new and more logical maps to show where they think national borders should be, based on the locations of rivers and mountains. **Visual/Spatial**
- ☐ **VIDEO** **European Alps**—Students use this video about Alpine mountain animals to discuss the types of climate biomes found in Eastern Europe and how people have adapted to living there. **ELL** **Interpersonal, Verbal/Linguistic**

☑ Printable Digital Worksheets

R Reading Skills

- ☐ **WORKSHEET** **Guided Reading Activity**—Students use the Guided Reading Activity worksheets to review their comprehension of the content.
- ☐ **WORKSHEET** **Chapter Summary**—Students review the main ideas of the chapter content.

C Critical Thinking Skills

- ☐ **WORKSHEET** **Video Activity**—Students answer questions related to a topic in the chapter content after they have viewed a lesson video.

HUMAN GEOGRAPHY OF EASTERN EUROPE

Students will know:
- *the early peoples and empires of Eastern Europe.*
- *how conflict and ethnic divisions have shaped Eastern Europe's history and culture.*
- *that Eastern European countries transitioned to democratic governments and market economies after the fall of communism.*
- *the population patterns in Eastern Europe today.*

Students will be able to:
- ***identify** the first residents of Eastern Europe.*
- ***describe** the influence of conflict and ethnic divisions on the history and culture of the region.*
- ***analyze** the effects of the fall of communism in the region.*
- ***describe** current population patterns.*

UNDERSTANDING BY DESIGN®

☑ Print Teaching Options

R Reading Skills
- ☐ **p. 319** Students define the term *shatter belt.* ELL Verbal/Linguistic
- ☐ **p. 320** Students discuss the events that led up to World War I. AL Verbal/Linguistic
- ☐ **p. 322** Students study the map of ethnic groups in Europe. AL Verbal/Linguistic
- ☐ **p. 323** Students discuss the differences between a nuclear and an extended family. AL Verbal/Linguistic

C Critical Thinking Skills
- ☐ **p. 319** Students explain the difference between a communist-based economy and a market economy. Logical/Mathematical
- ☐ **p. 322** Students use maps to compare the population density and physical landforms of Eastern Europe.
- ☐ **p. 324** Students discuss why transitioning from a command economy to a market economy may be difficult. Verbal/Linguistic
- ☐ **p. 325** Students discuss factors that are essential to economic development. AL Verbal/Linguistic

W Writing Skills
- ☐ **p. 321** Students use the time line to write a brief essay about the history of Eastern Europe from 1945 to the present.
- ☐ **p. 323** Students groups research how factors on the HDI compare among the Eastern European countries and write a report about one of the countries.

T Technology Skills
- ☐ **p. 320** Students work in groups to research how the borders of an Eastern European country changed before and after World War I and after World War II. Logical/Mathematical, Naturalist
- ☐ **p. 321** Students research the ethnic-based conflicts in Eastern Europe during the 1990s and early 2000s and write an editorial essay on one of the conflicts as if they were eyewitness reporters. BL Verbal/Linguistic
- ☐ **p. 323** Students research a particular art form or music that originated in Eastern Europe to create a multimedia presentation. BL Auditory/Musical, Visual/Spatial

☑ Online Teaching Options

V Visual Skills
- VIDEO **Hungarian Pigs**—Students use the video to discuss the traditions of society and culture in Hungary. Logical/Mathematical
- GRAPHIC ORGANIZER **Human Geography of Eastern Europe**—Students use a graphic organizer to provide details about the history and government of Eastern European countries. BL Visual/Spatial, Logical/Mathematical
- INTERACTIVE WHITEBOARD ACTIVITY **Eastern Europe Members of EU**—Students reference a map to identify the names of the EU member countries of Eastern Europe.

C Critical Thinking Skills
- INTERACTIVE BELLRINGER **The Road to a New Era**—Students discuss the fall of communism in Europe and the formation of new countries. Interpersonal, Verbal/Linguistic
- INTERACTIVE MAP **Major Nazi Death Camps**—Students discuss political, economic and ethnic struggles and their influence on the history and culture of Eastern Europe and discuss how the attempted genocide of the Jews is similar to more recent incidents of ethnic cleansing. BL Intrapersonal
- INTERACTIVE MAP **Ethnic Groups in Eastern Europe**—Students use the map to discuss ethnic groups and language families and create a chart to organize information about languages. BL Visual/Spatial

☑ Printable Digital Worksheets

R Reading Skills
- WORKSHEET **Guided Reading Activity**—Students use Guided Reading Activity worksheets to review their comprehension of the content.
- WORKSHEET **Reading Essentials and Study Guide**—Students complete the study guide and answer Reading Progress Check and vocabulary questions. AL

C Critical Thinking Skills
- WORKSHEET **Video Activity**—Students answer questions related to a topic in the chapter content after they have viewed a lesson video.

LESSON 3 PLANNER

People and Their Environment: Eastern Europe

Students will know:
- *the causes and consequences of forest destruction in Eastern Europe.*
- *how the legacy of the communist era affects the environment in Eastern Europe today.*
- *how acid rain and pollution affect the environment in Eastern Europe.*
- *the efforts of people and governments in Eastern Europe to address environmental issues.*

Students will be able to:
- ***analyze** causes and effects of deforestation in Eastern Europe.*
- ***identify** environmental effects of the communist era.*
- ***identify** causes of pollution and ways people and governments are addressing these issues.*

UNDERSTANDING BY DESIGN®

☑ Print Teaching Options

V Visual Skills

- ☐ **p. 327** Students create a map showing the boundaries and cities in Eastern Europe's black triangle. AL Visual/Spatial

R Reading Skills

- ☐ **p. 326** Students discuss environmental issues facing their community today. Interpersonal
- ☐ **p. 328** Students discuss nitrate concentrations from agricultural runoff. AL Verbal/Linguistic
- ☐ **p. 329** Students discuss the importance of the Baltic and Black Seas to Eastern Europe. AL Verbal/Linguistic

C Critical Thinking Skills

- ☐ **p. 326** Students create flowcharts to show the effects of illegal and uncontrolled logging. Visual/Spatial, Logical/Mathematical
- ☐ **p. 326** Students discuss ways Eastern Europeans are dealing with deforestation. AL Verbal/Linguistic, Interpersonal
- ☐ **p. 327** Students research the impact of acid rain in Eastern Europe. BL Logical/Mathematical
- ☐ **p. 328** Students discuss whether it is worth the economic benefits for Eastern European countries to comply with EU pollution controls in order to join the EU. BL Logical/Mathematical, Interpersonal
- ☐ **p. 329** Students identify challenges involved in addressing environmental issues. Logical/Mathematical
- ☐ **p. 330** Students discuss why the U.S. is interested in helping Eastern Europe. AL Logical/Mathematical

W Writing Skills

- ☐ **p. 330** Students research and write about a bird that is threatened in Eastern Europe. Verbal/Linguistic

T Technology Skills

- ☐ **p. 327** Students hold an imaginary environmental hearing to consider the future of the Białowieza Forest. BL Logical/Mathematical

☑ Online Teaching Options

V Visual Skills

- ☐ GRAPH **Water Pollution in Eastern Europe**—Students discuss the environmental effects of acid rain and write three statements that interpret the content in the graph. AL Visual/Spatial

R Reading Skills

- ☐ INTERACTIVE WHITEBOARD ACTIVITY **Acid Rain and Water Pollution**—Students identify the cause-and-effect hierarchy of factors pertaining to acid rain and water pollution in Eastern Europe. Verbal/Linguistic

C Critical Thinking Skills

- ☐ INTERACTIVE BELLRINGER **Nitrate Concentrations from Agricultural Runoff**—Students discuss agricultural pollution in the United States compared to countries they know about in Eastern Europe. AL Interpersonal, Visual/Spatial
- ☐ VIDEO **Karkonosze Forest-Monoculture Forest**—Students discuss environmental impacts on the forest and write about what they think the best use for such a forest is. AL Intrapersonal

☑ Printable Digital Worksheets

R Reading Skills

- ☐ WORKSHEET **Guided Reading Activity**—Students use Guided Reading Activity worksheets to review their comprehension of the content.
- ☐ WORKSHEET **Reading Essentials and Study Guide**—Students complete the study guide and answer Reading Progress Check and vocabulary questions. AL
- ☐ WORKSHEET **Vocabulary Activity**—Students review the chapter content and academic vocabulary words.

C Critical Thinking Skills

- ☐ WORKSHEET **Video Activity**—Students answer questions based on a lesson video.
- ☐ WORKSHEET **Reteaching Activity**—Students use this activity worksheet to review and reteach chapter content and vocabulary. This worksheet can be used with struggling students who need additional help with difficult content concepts.

INTERVENTION AND REMEDIATION STRATEGIES

LESSON 1 Physical Geography of Eastern Europe

Reading and Comprehension

Have students work with a partner to read the *It Matters Because* text. Tell students to take turns paraphrasing each sentence, replacing difficult terms with simpler words. Then have partners use the text to create an outline of the lesson, using each sentence in the paragraph to guide them. Encourage students to use the name of each country in the region as a heading in their outlines. As students work on their outlines, circulate to provide guidance with challenging vocabulary, such as *encountered, facilitated* and *inhibited,* guiding students to identify synonyms for each term *(met, helped, hindered/ held back).*

Text Evidence

Organize students into three groups and assign each group one of the three Guiding Questions (or, for smaller groups, divide the class into six groups and assign the same question to two groups). Have students in each group use the text to compile a summary that answers the Guiding Question. Tell students to conduct additional research to learn more about an aspect of Eastern Europe's physical geography as it relates to their assigned question. For example, students might research the importance of the Danube River to the region's economy. Have each group present a summary of their findings, comparing information in the text with information found in their research.

LESSON 2 Human Geography of Eastern Europe

Reading and Comprehension

Have students work in pairs to quiz each other on the meanings of the content vocabulary terms in this lesson. To ensure that students fully understand the meaning of the term *shatter belt,* tell students to review the text and take turns explaining to their partner the meaning of "splintering" and "fracturing" as they pertain to a piece of wood, and then to the political and ethnic struggles in Eastern Europe. Have partners collaborate to write a summarizing paragraph that answers the Guiding Question: *How have political and ethnic struggles shaped the Eastern Europe of today?* Ask volunteers to present their summaries to the class.

Text Evidence

Organize students into small groups and assign each group one or two of the events shown on the time line in this lesson, *The Road to a New Era.* Have students in each group work together to determine the central idea in the text about their assigned event. Then have each group write a summary about the significance of the event as it relates to the history of Eastern Europe. Tell students to use textual evidence to support ideas presented in their summaries. Have students share their summaries with the class.

LESSON 3 People and Their Environment: Eastern Europe

Reading and Comprehension

To ensure comprehension of the concepts in this lesson, have students write a summarizing sentence for each of the three sections in the text: Managing Resources, Human Impact, and Addressing the Issues. Tell students their sentences should touch on one or more issues facing a region of Eastern Europe and should identify what is being done to solve the problem. Have students share their sentences with the class, providing corrective guidance if needed.

Text Evidence

Have students work in small groups to create a visual diagram about an issue discussed in the text related to Eastern Europe's environment. You may wish to assign students topics to avoid duplication, such as the impact of rapid industrialization, water and agricultural pollution, acid rain, and so on. Have students collaborate to use evidence from the text on which to base their visual diagrams and present them to the class. After students have presented their visuals, guide a discussion about how governments and NGOs in Eastern Europe are working to address environmental issues.

Online Resources

Leveled Reader

Use this online approaching-level text that corresponds directly to the text in the Student Edition. It also includes additional reading and comprehension support for English Language Learners.

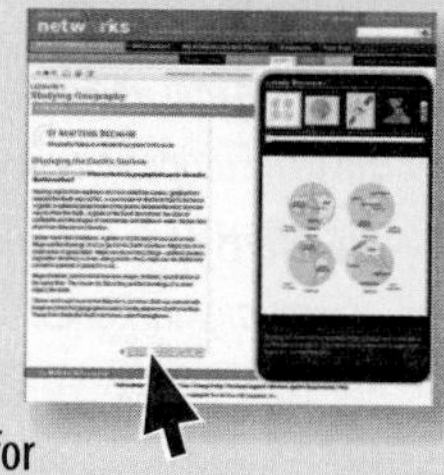

Guided Reading Activities

This resource uses guiding questions to help students with comprehension.

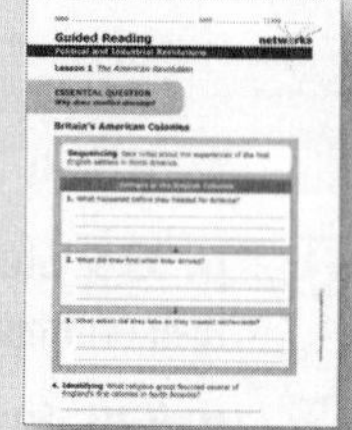

Reteaching Activities

These worksheets provide students with an opportunity for remedial practice and review of vital chapter content.

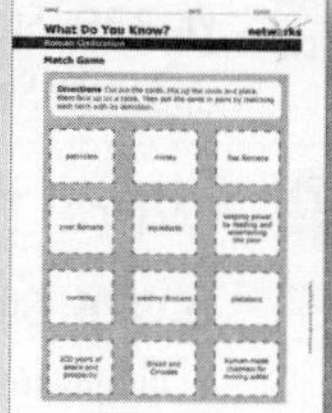

Reading Essentials and Study Guide

This resource offers writing and reading activities for the approaching-level student.

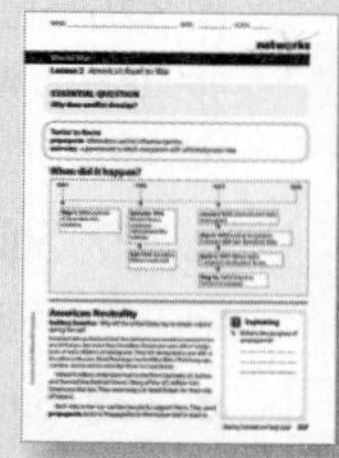

Self-Check Quizzes

This online assessment tool provides instant feedback for students to check their progress.

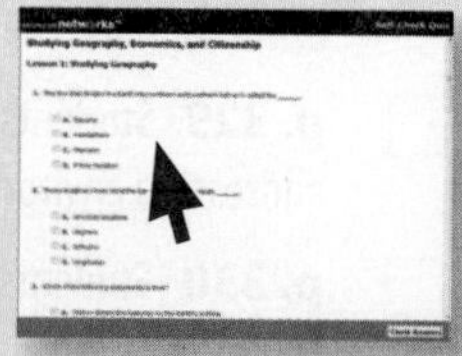

Chapter Summaries

Summaries are provided for each chapter that thoroughly condense core content into manageable chunks.

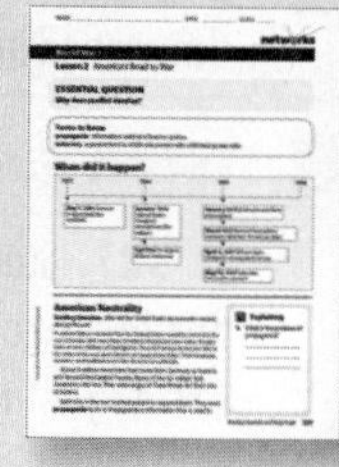

Eastern Europe

networks

There's More Online about Eastern Europe.

CHAPTER 13

ESSENTIAL QUESTION • *How do physical systems and human systems shape a place?*

Geography Matters...

Borders in Eastern Europe have quite a history. Political changes have made the subregion's borders a source of division and conflict. Physical features also play a role. The Danube River divides countries physically, but it also helps connect Eastern and Western Europe economically. The Eastern European countries of today were once part of large powerful empires. Most modern countries of the subregion did not gain independence until after World War I. The subregion today is a unique land with a turbulent past, but with richness in literature, art, and culture.

◀ A young Roma woman in Slovakia holds her child.

Matt Cardy/Alamy

311

Letter from the Author

Dear Geography Teacher,

The Main-Danube Canal offers an interesting teaching opportunity. It serves a unique purpose by linking between Black and North Seas. I have taken a steamboat ride on both the Danube and the Rhine (the river into which the Main flows). The scenery is stunning with castles and forts bristling along the high ground—what a view of history and culture. This canal opens up the potential for trade and transport. Corn from Romania? Wheat and oats from Germany? Iron ore from Austria? Using the Internet and studying the text, students can try to determine what other types of cargo move on these rivers.

Richard G. Boehm

ENGAGE

Identifying Before students open their texts, ask them to identify as many Eastern European countries as they can. Then encourage students to think of famous people from Eastern Europe. *(Possible answers: Josip Tito (Yugoslavia), Lech Walesa (Poland), Nichita Stănescu (Romania), Călin Alupi (Romania),* Ana Ivanovic (Serbia), *Nicolae Ceaușescu (Romania), Pope John Paul II (Poland), Slobodan Milosevic (Serbia), Václav Havel, (Czech Republic).*

TEACH & ASSESS

Hypothesizing Have students read the *Geography Matters* section. **Ask:** **In what ways can a river both divide and connect a country?** *(A river can divide countries physically and be a source of conflict over who has the rights to use the river. But a river can connect countries as a way to transport people and goods and serve as a means for trade, communication, and exchange of ideas.)* **AL** **Logical/Mathematical**

Content Background Knowledge

History of Yugoslavia At the beginning of World War I, Slovenia, Croatia, Bosnia-Herzegovina, Hungary, the Czech Republic, Slovakia, and Romania were under control of the Austro-Hungarian Empire. Serbia, Kosovo, Montenegro, Macedonia, Bulgaria, and Albania were under control of the Ottoman Empire. The Paris Peace Conference of 1918 created the Kingdom of Serbs, Croats and Slovenes from the Austrian and Ottoman empires, namely Slovenia, Croatia, Bosnia-Herzegovina, Serbia, Montenegro, Kosovo, and Macedonia. The Kingdom of Serbs, Croats and Slovenes was renamed Yugoslavia in 1929. During World War II, Yugoslavia began to unravel as different factions began to fight. In 1945, Josip Tito reunited Yugoslavia and established strict control; however in 1980 when Tito died, the ties that held Yugoslavia began to unravel again.

CLOSE & REFLECT

Previewing Have students read the table of contents at the top of the page and ask them to prepare a list of questions they expect to have answered as they study the chapter.

Extend the project-based learning experience globally through our partnership with ePals. EPals allows you to connect with classrooms around the world in a safe online environment for real-life lessons and projects in virtual study groups.

ENGAGE

C Critical Thinking Skills

Analyzing Have students read about and explore the term *powder keg*. **Ask:** What visual image comes to mind when you hear the term *powder keg*? *(Possible answer: a barrel of gunpowder that must be handled carefully because a spark could ignite it)* How might the term apply to conflicts between countries? *(Possible answer: Disputes and animosities build up until some incident causes one side to attack the other.)* What events in the United States's history might have led to a powder keg moment? *(Possible answers: buildup to the Civil War; buildup to the Revolutionary War)*

TEACH & ASSESS

V Visual Skills

Drawing Inferences Allow time for students to study the map to make inferences about the countries. **Ask:** What significant natural resource did Croatia have that it shared with Slovenia and Montenegro? Explain how this resource may be important. *(Student answers may vary, but should include references to Croatia's coastline, which may be valuable for reasons such as transportation, trade, and fishing.)* **Visual/Spatial**

W Writing Skills

Informative/Explanatory Ask students to read the call outs on the map. Have them write a paragraph explaining the conditions that contributed to the breakup of Yugoslavia. Invite a volunteer to define the term *nationalism*. Discuss circumstances in which nationalism can have negative and positive effects. **BL Verbal/Linguistic, Intrapersonal**

Content Background Knowledge

Powder Keg of Europe Because of its long history of conflict, the Balkans have often been characterized as the "powder keg of Europe." Events leading up to the breakup of Yugoslavia were powder keg moments, as were events leading up to World War I. The assassination of the heir to the Austro-Hungarian throne was the spark that ignited the Great War.

Why Geography Matters: **Eastern Europe**

the breakup *of* Yugoslavia

C *The former Yugoslavia was historically a crossroads. Because the countries of Eastern Europe have a long history of belonging to different empires at different times, they have a complex mix of ethnic and religious influences. Conflict was common, and the region became known as the "powder keg" of Europe.*

The Former Yugoslavia

312

Project-Based Learning

Hands-On

Mapping Eastern Europe

Students will create maps that bring together information from all lessons about how geographic features and resources impact physical and human systems in Eastern Europe.

Digital Hands-On

Create Online Projects

Find an additional activity online that incorporates technology for this project. Visit the EdTech Teacher Web sites for more links, tutorials, and other resources.

Why Geography Matters

(tl)Gavin Hellier/AWL Images/Getty Images, (tc)David Brauchli/Getty Images News/Getty Images, (tr)©Howard Davies/Corbis

Why was Yugoslavia considered an ethnic melting pot?

Yugoslavia (a combination of the Slavic words meaning "south" and "Slavs") was, for a time, a true ethnic mix. The country did not exist until 1918 with the dissolution of the Austro-Hungarian and Ottoman Empires. Originally created as the Kingdom of Serbs, Croats, and Slovenes, it united several distinct Slavic ethnic groups in its population: Bosnians, Bulgarians, Croats, Macedonians, Montenegrins, Serbs, and Slovenes. It also included non-Slavic peoples such as Albanians. Yugoslavia was religiously diverse as well. Eastern Orthodox Christians, Muslims, Catholics, Protestants, and Jews composed the population. Animosities between some of the ethnic groups stretched back hundreds of years. After World War II, under the firm Communist rule of Josip Broz Tito, the country enjoyed internal peace. Despite the country's wide ethnic and cultural differences, Tito managed to prevent several nationalist movements from instigating rebellions that threatened his rule, at times arresting or executing protest leaders.

1. **Human Systems** What were the conditions that helped set the stage for ethnic conflict in Yugoslavia?

How did this contribute to the breakup of Yugoslavia?

The 1970s brought an economic crisis to Yugoslavia. The crisis was triggered by government borrowing to support export growth. A general recession, however, made Western economies unable to purchase those exports. In 1974 a new constitution decreased the federal government's power, giving more powers to the country's six republics and two autonomous provinces. Nonetheless, Tito's authority kept the country together until his death in 1980, after which ethnic and nationalistic tensions quickly escalated. The republics of Croatia and Slovenia demanded looser ties to central authority. In March and April of 1981, riots broke out in Kosovo, an autonomous province with a majority Albanian-speaking Muslim population that was located within the republic of Serbia. Serbia had a majority Serbo-Croatian-speaking Eastern Orthodox population. Kosovo demanded outright secession from Yugoslavia or republican status within the federation. In 1989 Serbian politician Slobodan Milošević became president of Serbia and responded to new demonstrations by taking away what remained of Kosovo's autonomy and incorporating it into Serbia.

2. **Human Systems** How did Yugoslavia's ethnic makeup contribute to the conflicts that caused the breakup of the country?

How did the breakup change the political geography of Europe?

Political maneuvering failed to pacify the competing groups. During the 1990s, a series of wars culminated in Europe's bloodiest period since World War II. Genocide, mass murder, and ethnic cleansing—a policy aimed at removing an ethnic or religious rival from a region through violence and terror—characterized the conflicts. Many of the political and military leaders, including Slobodan Milošević, were subsequently charged with war crimes. By 1995, Yugoslavia ceased to exist. In its place were five Yugoslav successor countries: Bosnia-Herzegovina, Croatia, Macedonia, Slovenia, and the Federal Republic of Yugoslavia, which later became the countries of Serbia and Montenegro. In 2008 the republic of Kosovo declared its independence. International recognition of Kosovo is still disputed by some countries, including Russia.

3. **Places and Regions** Write a paragraph describing how the political map of Europe was transformed by the breakup of Yugoslavia.

THERE'S MORE ONLINE

SEE a photo of Josip Broz Tito • *EXPLORE* a time line of the breakup of Yugoslavia

R Reading Skills

Listing Have students work with a partner to list three conditions that contributed to the conflict in Yugoslavia. *(Possible answers: It was a melting pot of different ethnic or national groups; The people practiced diverse religions; There were old, unresolved animosities between some of the groups.)* Then have pairs brainstorm how differences in ethnicity or religion might lead to conflict. AL Verbal/Linguistic

C Critical Thinking Skills

Explaining Continuity and Change Have students think about the kinds of strains people suffer during recessions. Discuss how these conditions might lead to further conflicts between groups who are already hostile toward one another. Discuss how a strong leader might be able to hold a country of disparate people together, and what can happen when such a leader dies or loses power. Logical/Mathematical

T Technology Skills

Examining Information Ask students to share what they know about the wars that took place in Yugoslavia during the 1990s. Then have students do online or library research into the "war crimes" that occurred at that time. Have students write 2 to 3 paragraphs about why some of the military leaders were charged with war crimes, paying special attention to the trials of Slobodan Milosevic, one of the leaders. Students should present their findings to the class. BL Verbal/Linguistic

CLOSE & REFLECT

Summarizing Have students reread the three columns of text. Then have them write a summary of each column to explain how and why Yugoslavia broke up into many countries.

TIME LINE

The Breakup of Yugoslavia

Visualizing This time line shows the breakup of Yugoslavia and provides details about the conflicts and changes that occurred throughout the country's history. Click each time period in the legend to show and discuss the content with the class. Continue this activity until all of the events have been discussed. Then invite students to choose a time period on the time line and sketch a map of Yugoslavia's boundaries at that exact date. Encourage students to include a map key or legend with their illustration. Visual/Spatial, Kinesthetic

ANSWERS, p. 313

Why Geography Matters

1. The population of Yugoslavia included several distinct ethnic groups and distinct religious sects. Animosities between some ethnic groups originated hundreds of years ago.
2. The republics and autonomous regions that made up Yugoslavia were ethnically distinct from one another. Ethnic tensions caused nationalism to grow within each republic or province and eventually led some to demand separation from federal authority.
3. Yugoslavia once occupied a large area on the map, but after it was dissolved in 1995, five much smaller countries filled its previous borders: Bosnia-Herzegovina, Croatia, Macedonia, Slovenia, and the Federal Republic of Yugoslavia. Not much later, the Federal Republic of Yugoslavia became three separate countries: Serbia, Montenegro, and Kosovo.

ENGAGE

V1 Visual Skills

Categorizing Explain that the countries of Eastern Europe can be grouped together in different ways depending on their geography and locations, such as Balkan, Baltic, and Alpine countries. Using the unit maps in their textbooks, have students create a chart like the one below that groups the countries of Eastern Europe by location and land features. Discuss other categories by which to group the countries of Eastern Europe, such as former Yugoslavian countries once part of the Ottoman Empire or the Austro-Hungarian Empire. Have students continue filling out their charts as they study the lesson.

Country	Baltic Country	Balkan Country	Alpine Country
Albania		x	x

TEACH & ASSESS

V2 Visual Skills

Creating Maps Provide students with outline maps of Eastern Europe available online in the Teacher Lesson Center. Student maps should indicate the location of the major landforms including mountains, lowlands, small plains, and deltas of Eastern Europe described in the text. Have them use various colors to represent each feature. Encourage students to also use a detailed physical map of Europe as a source. **Visual/Spatial**

R Reading Skills

Identifying Have students describe the karst terrain. **Ask: Can you identify regions in the United States that have karst topography?** *(Karst topography occurs in many regions of the United States. Nearly all of Florida exhibits karst topography, as well as the Mammoth Cave system of Kentucky, which is the world's longest cave system.)* Discuss with students the areas in Eastern Europe that have the karst terrain. **AL Verbal/Linguistic**

ANSWERS, p. 314

TAKING NOTES: Landforms—In the south are the Carpathian Mountains, the Balkan Mountains, and the Dinaric Alps—all an eastern extension of the Swiss Alps, karst topography exists in the Dinaric Alps region, the Northern European Plain runs through the northern part of Eastern Europe; **Rivers**—The Danube River is the second longest river in Europe and an international highway for trade, the Vistula River is the largest river in Poland and empties into the Baltic Sea, the Oder River leads to the Baltic Sea.

networks
There's More Online!
- **IMAGE** European Bison
- **MAP** Alpine Europe
- **MAP** Main-Danube Canal
- **INTERACTIVE SELF-CHECK QUIZ**
- **VIDEO** Physical Geography of Eastern Europe

LESSON 1
Physical Geography of Eastern Europe

ESSENTIAL QUESTION • *How do physical systems and human systems shape a place?*

Reading HELPDESK (CCSS)

Academic Vocabulary (Tier Two Words)
- economy
- comprise

Content Vocabulary (Tier Three Words)
- karst

TAKING NOTES: *Key Ideas and Details*

CATEGORIZING Use a graphic organizer like the one below to take notes about the landforms and waterways of Eastern Europe.

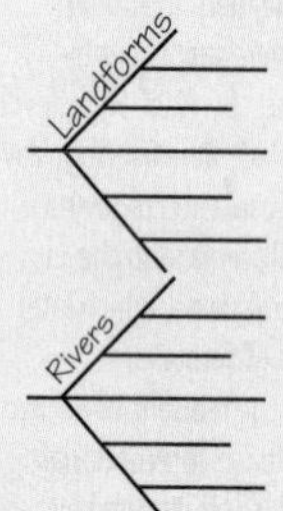

IT MATTERS BECAUSE

V1 *Eastern Europe is made up of a diverse group of countries. They range from the Baltic countries in the north to the Balkan countries in the south. The entire subregion includes Estonia, Latvia, Lithuania, the Czech Republic, Slovakia, Poland, Hungary, Bulgaria, Moldova, Albania, Romania, Serbia, Montenegro, Bosnia and Herzegovina, Croatia, Slovenia, Macedonia, and Kosovo. These many countries are united by a shared history as a crossroads where different cultures from Asia and Europe have encountered one another. Such encounters have been both facilitated and inhibited by Eastern Europe's diverse physical geography.*

Landforms

GUIDING QUESTION *How do mountains and plains define Eastern Europe?*

The physical geography of Eastern Europe is characterized by mountains and plains, which influence the human geography of the subregion's countries. Mountains dominate in the south, part of Europe's Alpine system, with the curve of the Carpathian Mountains in Slovakia and northern Romania, along with the Balkan Mountains of Bulgaria and the coastal ranges of the Dinaric Alps. All of these are the eastern extension of the Swiss Alps. While not as high as the Swiss Alps, these ranges create mountainous and hilly landscapes.

V2 Lowlands within these mountainous areas are restricted to relatively small plains and deltas formed by deposits of rock fragments and particles carried down by rivers that erode the mountains. The Dinaric Alps span the countries of Slovenia, Croatia, Bosnia and Herzegovina, Macedonia, Albania, and Montenegro. They run parallel to the Adriatic coast (sometimes referred to as the Dalmatian coast). This region exhibits R **karst** topography, which refers to limestone bedrock sculpted into steep-sided cliffs and rocky columns. Karst terrain is characterized by caves, sinkholes, underground rivers, and the absence of surface rivers, streams,

©Raymond Gehman/Corbis

314

networks ***Online Teaching Options***

INTERACTIVE BELLRINGER

Alpine Europe

Analyzing Maps This introductory text and map of Alpine Europe can be used to introduce students to the landforms in Eastern Europe. Have students analyze the map to understand how the Alpine mountain system connects Eastern Europe with other regions. Have students form small groups and discuss their prior knowledge of mountains in Eastern Europe, as well as other European locations they know about. Ask groups to discuss and write agreed-upon answers to the bellringer questions. Then in a class discussion, have groups share their answers. **AL Interpersonal, Visual/Spatial**

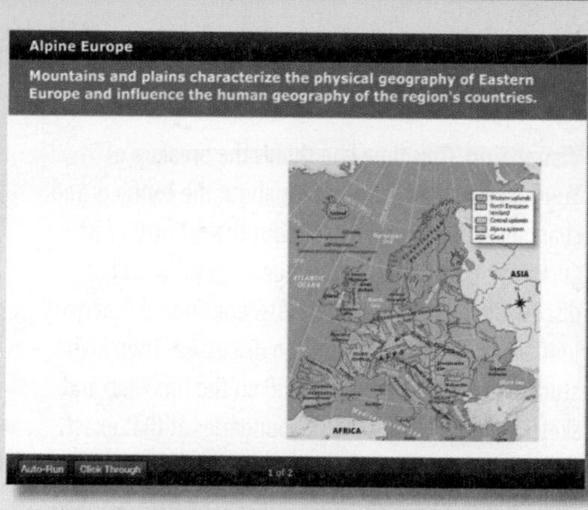

and lakes. These features are due to the soluble limestone rock that underlies the region. The limestone is dissolved by organically produced acids in groundwater, creating depressions and holes in the earth. Forestry and mining are the primary economic activities for people living in the Dinaric Alps.

karst terrain dominated by limestone bedrock and characterized by rocky ground, caves, sinkholes, underground rivers, and the absence of surface streams and lakes

The geologically young Carpathian Mountains run from Slovakia to Romania. These mountains are less compact than the Swiss Alps to the west and are distinguished by mountains separated by large basins. The water from the Carpathians generally flows into the Black Sea. This region is sparsely populated. Its inhabitants depend on agriculture and forestry, especially on the Transylvanian Plateau, for income.

The Balkan Peninsula is the easternmost of Europe's three great southern peninsulas. It is dominated by the Balkan Mountains, an extension of the Alpine-Carpathian ranges to the north. Due to its rugged landscape and deep snow during winter, traveling over land in the Balkan Peninsula is difficult. The mountains form a major land divide between two points of human transit, the Danube River to the north and the Maritsa River to the south. While the mountains can be crossed through several passes, people have historically tended to move by way of rivers and seas in order to avoid the mountains. The Balkan Mountains are also a climate barrier between the continental climate of the Danube River valley and the transitional climate south of the mountains.

North of the Carpathians, the landscape displays broad, extensive plains, such as the lowland areas that dominate Poland and the Baltic countries. These lowlands are part of the Northern European Plain. They are home to a number of navigable rivers in Eastern Europe, mainly the Elbe, Oder, and Vistula Rivers. Another prominent lowland, the Hungarian Plain, extends from southeastern Hungary into eastern Croatia, northern Serbia, and western Romania. In these lowlands, farmers cultivate grains, fruit, and vegetables. They also raise livestock along the banks of the Danube River.

✓ READING PROGRESS CHECK

Explaining How have the Balkan Mountains defined the region?

Alpine Europe

Western uplands
North European lowland
Central uplands
Alpine system
Canal

500 miles
500 kilometers
Lambert Azimuthal Equal-Area projection

GEOGRAPHY CONNECTION

Much of Eastern Europe is part of Europe's Alpine system with numerous mountain ranges, most of which are extensions of the Swiss Alps.

1. ***PLACES AND REGIONS*** Which mountain ranges are part of the Alpine system in Eastern Europe?
2. ***PHYSICAL SYSTEMS*** Describe how the Alpine system differs from the central uplands in regard to landforms.

Physical Geography of Eastern Europe

T Technology Skills

Researching Working in small groups, have students research karst topography by conducting library or online research. Point out that karst topography can occur in the highlands, lowlands, or anywhere that soluble limestone rock underlies the region. Have students find images, diagrams, and flowcharts to show how these features are formed. Have groups present their findings in a multimedia presentation. **Visual/Spatial, Verbal/Linguistic**

C Critical Thinking Skills

Comparing and Contrasting Have students compare the Carpathian Mountains to the Swiss Alps. As a class, invite volunteers to describe where each is located and then discuss the similarities and differences in the topography of the mountains. Students might need to reference the unit physical map to compare the elevations of each mountain range. Review population density in these regions. **AL Verbal/Linguistic**

Content Background Knowledge

Mountain Ranges of Eastern Europe Numerous mountains ranges are found in the Balkans, including the namesake Balkan Mountains, the Rhodope Mountains, and others. These ranges are extensions of the Alpine-Carpathian folds. The highest, Mt. Olympus, is actually in Greece. The Balkan Mountains are crossed by about 20 passes and by the Iskŭr River, but the Dinaric Alps have no natural passes. The average elevation of the Carpathians is much lower than the Swiss Alps: Gerlachovsky Stit, the highest of the Carpathians, is 8,711 feet tall, which is considerably lower than the Alps' Mont Blanc (15,771 feet).

W Writing Skills

Narrative Have students use the information in the text and on the map at the bottom of the page to write a narrative describing an imaginary trip across the region. Their stories should integrate geographic details from the textbook. Have students share their stories with the class. **BL Verbal/Linguistic**

INTERACTIVE IMAGE

Karst Terrain

Informative/Explanatory This online image can be used with students to show them karst topography. Have students list features that are characteristic of karst terrain *(rocky ground, caves, sinkholes, underground rivers, and the absence of surface streams and lakes)*. Tell students to choose one of these characteristics to research. Have them write a few paragraphs describing the feature and its location in Eastern Europe. Then have students share their findings with the class. **AL Verbal/Linguistic, Visual/Spatial**

ANSWERS, p. 315

✓ **READING PROGRESS CHECK** The Balkan Mountains make the peninsula rugged and cause a lot of snow during the winter. They are a land barrier between the Danube and the Maritsa Rivers and a climate barrier between the continental climate of the Danube River Valley and the transitional climate to the south.

GEOGRAPHY CONNECTION

1. The Carpathian Mountains, Balkan Mountains, and Dinaric Alps are part of the Alpine system.
2. There are several mountain ranges in the Alpine system, but not in the central uplands.

T Technology Skills

Presenting Have students work in small groups to gather additional facts about the rivers of Eastern Europe. Assign each group to research a river and to create a slide show presentation for the class. Presentations should include visuals showing the origins and outlets of each river, the cities located along the river, and the basins they pass through and drain. Encourage students to include music in their presentations. **BL Auditory/Musical, Visual/Spatial**

R Reading Skills

Calculating Have students explain why the Main-Danube Canal is economically important. Have them locate the canal on the map and describe by how many miles it increased the reach of the 1,777-mile-long Danube. *(Danube 1,777 miles (2860 km) + canal 106 miles (171 km) + Main 327 miles (527 km); total distance 2,210 miles (3,500 km))* **AL Logical/Mathematical**

W Writing Skills

Informative/Explanatory Have students imagine they are writers for a travel magazine taking an imaginary trip down the Danube River. Ask students to write a travel blog that describes specific details about the landscape, cities, towns, and other features they pass while on their boat tour. Allow time for students to use the Internet to conduct research or to locate travel brochures or articles. **Verbal/Linguistic**

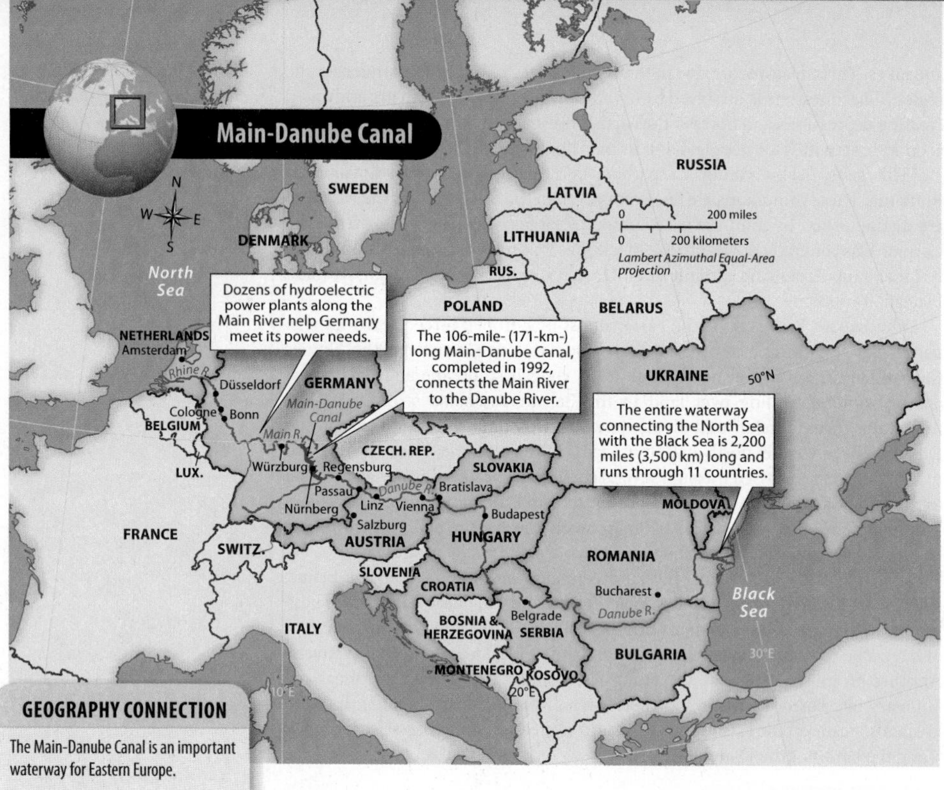

GEOGRAPHY CONNECTION

The Main-Danube Canal is an important waterway for Eastern Europe.

1. ***HUMAN SYSTEMS*** What bodies of water are linked by the canal?
2. ***PLACES AND REGIONS*** Which Eastern European countries are situated along the Main-Danube waterway?

Water Systems

GUIDING QUESTION *Why are the Danube and Vistula Rivers important to economic activity in Eastern Europe?*

A number of large rivers flow through the northern part of Eastern Europe and are extremely important to economic activities in the region. The Danube River is the second-longest river in Europe. It starts in the Black Forest of western Germany and empties into the Black Sea, passing through nine countries. The Danube has played a vital role in the settlement and development of Europe. Historically, its banks have formed the boundaries between great empires and were most famously the frontier of the Roman Empire.

Today, the Danube River maintains its geographical and political importance. For example, it divides Budapest—the capital of Hungary—into its two main parts: Buda and Pest. The Danube is officially an international waterway and has served as a commercial highway for many countries, contributing to their economic development.

The Danube is connected to the Main River, a tributary of the Rhine River, by the Main-Danube Canal. The waterway was completed in 1992 after over 30 years of construction. Many of the waterway's locks on the Main River also have hydroelectric power stations. The Main-Danube Canal provides an important connection that links the North Sea and Northwestern Europe with Eastern Europe and the Black Sea. The canal allows for goods—such as food and animal feed, ores, iron and other metals, and fertilizers—to be transferred in both directions. Tourism along the canal also contributes to its economic importance.

316

networks Online Teaching Options

INTERACTIVE MAP

Alpine Europe

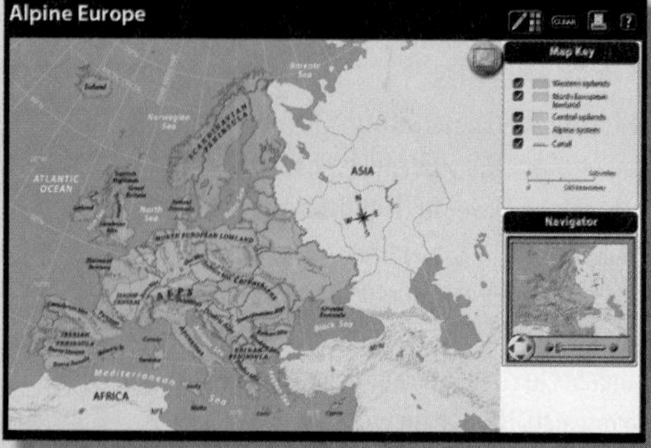

Exploring Issues Use this interactive map showing the Alpine regions of Europe to discuss how Eastern Europe's mountains and rivers have had a significant impact on the region's social, economic and political systems. To deepen students' understanding of this, assign pairs of students to a specific region on the map. Explain that sometimes on maps rivers are like "roads" and mountains like "walls." Have each pair focus on their assigned region to draw new and more logical maps showing where they think national borders should be, based on the location of the rivers and surrounding mountains. Have students share their maps indicating the new borders and discuss their reasoning with the class. **Visual/Spatial**

ANSWERS, p. 316

GEOGRAPHY CONNECTION

1. the North Sea and the Black Sea
2. Slovakia, Hungary, Croatia, Serbia, Romania, Bulgaria

The Vistula River, the largest river in Poland, flows from south to north and empties into the Baltic Sea. A number of major cities and industrial centers—such as Warsaw, the capital of Poland—lie on the banks of the Vistula River.

The Vistula is connected by canal to the Oder River, which originates in the Czech Republic. The Oder also empties into the Baltic Sea by way of western Poland via a heavily industrialized canal. The river forms part of the border between Poland and Germany. In supplementing the overburdened railway and highway systems that link the industrialized areas of the south with ports on the Baltic Sea, the Oder is crucial to the Polish **economy**.

economy an ordered system for the production, distribution, and consumption of goods and services

Several major seas surround Eastern Europe and serve as vital channels of trade and economic development. The Black Sea is an inland sea that hugs the eastern coast of the Balkan Peninsula and has served to link Europe to Asia for centuries. A narrow channel connects the Black Sea to the Mediterranean Sea that borders the region to the south. The Mediterranean connects to the Atlantic Ocean, creating an important link for trade between Eastern Europe and the rest of the world. The Baltic Sea in the north, between mainland Europe and the Scandinavian Peninsula, has historically been used as a trade route for importing oil and coal and exporting minerals, timber, and wood products. The Adriatic Sea between the Balkan Peninsula and the Italian Peninsula is a primary mode of importing and exporting goods and provides fish to the surrounding countries.

C

✓ READING PROGRESS CHECK

Summarizing Explain how waterways facilitate trade between Eastern Europe and other regions of the world.

Climate, Biomes, and Resources

GUIDING QUESTION *What are the general climate conditions in much of Eastern Europe?*

Eastern Europe is located within the midlatitudes. Much of the region has a humid continental climate characterized by cold, snowy winters and hot summers. Eastern Europe does not benefit from the warm ocean currents that moderate the climates in Western Europe. Summer and winter temperatures inland vary more widely than they do on the coasts.

Climate Regions and Biomes

The Baltic Sea region and the Northern European Plain are marked by long, cold winters with temperatures reaching an average low of 14°F (−10°C) in midwinter. The summers are relatively short in this area of continental climate. In the forests of the Baltic Sea region, evergreens outnumber deciduous trees, while an equal mix of evergreens and deciduous trees are found across the Northern European Plain.

The region south of the Northern European Plain is sometimes referred to as the Danube region and **comprises** the Carpathian and Balkan Mountains together with the Hungarian Plain. The Danube region also has a continental climate. Winters and summers, however, are about equally long, and the region enjoys moderate average temperatures. Some of the coastal regions of the landlocked Black Sea have micro-biomes that are a combination of humid continental and humid subtropical climates. These regions are characterized by mild winters and a great deal of precipitation during the warm summers. The basin northeast of the Black Sea is typified by a steppe climate, with cold winters and hot, dry summers, and a grassland biome. Subtropical air flowing across the Mediterranean and Black Seas ensures warm, moist summers on the southwestern shores.

V

comprise to contain; to consist of

VIDEO

European Alps

Applying Use this video about Alpine mountain animals to discuss the types of climate biomes found in Eastern Europe. As they watch the video, have students list details about the climate and wildlife as provided in the video. Then have students share and discuss their lists with a partner. Ask pairs to discuss ways in which they think people have adapted to live in this Alpine environment. ELL **Interpersonal, Verbal/Linguistic**

Physical Geography of Eastern Europe

R Reading Skills

Reading Maps Supply students with a transportation map of Eastern Europe. Have student compare the transportation map to a physical or political map of the region. Have students trace the route of the Oder River. **Ask:** **How does this river supplement the overburdened railway and highway systems?** *(It links the industrialized areas in the south with ports on the Baltic Sea.)* Discuss why this is important to Poland's economy. **Visual/Spatial, Logical/Mathematical**

C Critical Thinking Skills

Drawing Conclusions After students have read this paragraph, lead a class discussion on the importance of the various waterways to the economies of the Eastern European countries. Have students list the countries linked by each body of water and locate the channel linking the Black Sea to the Mediterranean. Discuss which European countries do not border a sea and how they might transport their merchandise out of Europe. AL **Verbal/Linguistic**

Making Connections

Comparing Climates Have students think about the geography of the United States and weather reports they have recently seen or heard in the past. Have students explain which parts of the United States have a humid continental climate similar to that of parts of Eastern Europe. *(northeastern and north central United States)* Students may need to consult a world climate zones map.

V Visual Skills

Creating Charts Have students make a 3-column chart with the heads ***Region, Climate,*** and ***Biome*** that compares the climate regions and biomes of Eastern Europe. ELL **Visual/Spatial, Naturalist**

ANSWERS, p. 317

✓ READING PROGRESS CHECK The Danube River acts as a commercial highway, facilitating trade for many countries. The Main-Danube Canal connects Eastern Europe to the North Sea, allowing goods to flow in and out. The Vistula and Oder Rivers provide trade routes from Eastern Europe to ports on the Baltic Sea. Surrounding major bodies of water serve as channels that allow Eastern Europe to trade with almost all parts of the world.

Physical Geography of Eastern Europe

V Visual Skills

Creating Charts Have students insert a column with the head ***Agriculture*** to their climate regions and biomes chart of Eastern Europe, by adding information about the Adriatic regions. Also have students add information about agricultural products using the economic activity map. **Visual/Spatial**

T Technology Skills

Gathering Information Have students work in small groups to make a list of the natural resources of each country in this region. Tell groups to choose a country to conduct online research to collect data about the level of economic development to compile in a chart. Ask the class to brainstorm what indicators they will use to compare economies. Ask groups to discuss the economic impact of these facts for each country. **Verbal/Linguistic**

CLOSE & REFLECT

Questioning Have students write questions on one side of index cards relating to facts and concepts in this lesson and then write answers to those questions on the other side. Ask students to use their cards with a partner to review the lesson.

ANSWERS, p. 318

READING PROGRESS CHECK The Hungarian Plain and Carpathian and Balkan Mountains are in the Danube region.

CRITICAL THINKING

1. Their population could decrease substantially or die out entirely, as they depend on a forested habitat.
2. Hunters could make a profit from bison meat.

Large land mammals such as these European bison can be found in the forests of Eastern Europe.

▲ **CRITICAL THINKING**

1. ***Explaining*** How would deforestation affect the European bison in Eastern Europe?
2. ***Speculating*** Why might the European bison be a target for hunters in Eastern Europe?

Areas around most of the Adriatic Sea have a Mediterranean climate characterized by mild, rainy winters and hot, dry, and sunny summers. The natural vegetation here is predominantly shrubland interspersed with woodlands and some forests. The Mediterranean climate supports crops such as olives and grapes.

V The northern Adriatic has a humid subtropical climate, which means it has short, mild winters and year-round rain. The vegetation in this climate consists of prairies, inland grasslands, and evergreen and deciduous forests. The Adriatic Sea has many fish species that are endemic, or restricted to a particular region, especially in the northern part of the sea. Many are endangered due to overfishing. To the east of the Adriatic Sea, the Dinaric Alps experience cold and dry continental air, cooling Croatia's coastal cities such as Split and Dubrovnik.

Natural Resources

Eastern Europe has large quantities of natural resources. The Carpathian Mountains, for example, contain reserves of natural gas, oil, and coal. The Baltic Mountains do not have as many natural resources. However, some countries, such as Latvia, have begun to take advantage of water as a potential source of hydroelectric power. Hydroelectricity accounts for about 71 percent of Latvia's total electric capacity. Similarly, Romania, which has diminishing petroleum reserves, uses the Danube River to generate hydroelectric power. Romania T obtains over one-third of its electricity from hydroelectric plants.

Poland has vast coal, natural gas, iron, zinc, lead, and copper reserves, as well as smaller amounts of silver. Poland is famous for its amber, often called "Baltic gold." The raw amber was transported for centuries along the ancient Amber Route from the Baltic Sea to the Adriatic coast.

Many Eastern European countries have bauxite reserves. Bauxite is the main ore used to make aluminum. Although the region is not the world's leading source of bauxite, the demand for aluminum is rising, making bauxite an important resource for Eastern European countries.

READING PROGRESS CHECK

Listing What landforms are found in the Danube region?

LESSON 1 REVIEW (CCSS)

Reviewing Vocabulary (Tier Three Words)

1. ***Summarizing*** What is karst terrain and what causes it to form? RH.9–10.4

Using Your Notes

2. ***Listing*** Use your graphic organizer from the lesson to list the important waterways in Eastern Europe.

Answering the Guiding Questions

3. ***Applying*** How do mountains and plains define Eastern Europe?
4. ***Stating*** Why are the Danube and Vistula Rivers important to economic activity in Eastern Europe?
5. ***Identifying*** What are the general climate conditions in much of Eastern Europe?

Writing Activity

6. ***Informative/Explanatory*** Write a short paragraph explaining how the geography of the Baltic and Adriatic Seas is important for trade. WHST.9–10.2

318

LESSON 1 REVIEW ANSWERS

Reviewing Vocabulary

1. Karst is a type of barren, rocky terrain with caves, sinkholes, and underground rivers, but no surface streams or lakes. This type of terrain forms as the limestone that lies beneath the region is dissolved by acids in groundwater.

Using Your Notes

2. The Danube River, the Main-Danube Canal, the Vistula River, the Oder River, the Black Sea, the Mediterranean Sea, and the Adriatic Sea

Answering the Guiding Questions

3. Three major mountain ranges are found in the south of the region, which give it a very rugged landscape, interrupted only briefly by small plains and deltas. These mountains influence human geography by acting as land and climate barriers. As the Northern European Plain runs through the north part of the region, this part is characterized by broad expanses of plains that have many rivers and good land for agriculture.
4. The Danube benefits many countries by serving as a major international highway for trade. Many industrial centers developed along the banks of the Vistula River because it empties into the Baltic Sea and can be used to transport goods to ports there.
5. Most of the region has a humid continental climate, which means cold, snowy winters and hot summers, with temperature variations between the two seasons being greater inland than on the coasts.

Writing Activity

6. Possible answer: The location of the Baltic Sea makes it an important trade route between the Scandinavian Peninsula and Eastern Europe. Oil and coal are imported into Eastern Europe, and minerals, timber, and wood products are exported. The location of the Adriatic Sea makes it an important trade route between the Balkan Peninsula and the Italian Peninsula.

networks

There's More Online!

- **IMAGE** Agriculture in Eastern Europe
- **IMAGE** Religious Conflict in Eastern Europe
- **MAP** Eastern European Migration
- **INTERACTIVE SELF-CHECK QUIZ**
- **TIME LINE** The Road to a New Era
- **VIDEO** Human Geography of Eastern Europe

LESSON 2

Human Geography of Eastern Europe

ESSENTIAL QUESTION • *How do physical systems and human systems shape a place?*

Reading HELPDESK

Academic Vocabulary (Tier Two Words)
- **persistent**
- **ethnic**

Content Vocabulary (Tier Three Words)
- **shatter belt**
- **Balkanization**
- **ethnic cleansing**

TAKING NOTES: ***Key Ideas and Details***

PARAPHRASING Use a graphic organizer like the one below to take notes about the population patterns of Eastern Europe.

Population Patterns: Historical: The Slavs; Geographic Factors: Location; Industrialization; Migration/Immigration

It Matters Because

Eastern Europe has undergone many changes in the past few decades. The political geography of the subregion has changed drastically as the result of the dissolution of the Soviet Union in 1991. Eastern European economies are being integrated into the European Union and world markets. They have made variable progress in the difficult transition from communist-based command economies to market economies.

History and Government

GUIDING QUESTION *How have political and ethnic struggles shaped the Eastern Europe of today?*

Eastern Europe is known as a **shatter belt** region because it has **persistently**, or constantly, experienced political and territorial splintering and fracturing along cultural and **ethnic** lines. Shatter belt regions are more likely to engage in interstate wars and undergo internal conflicts such as civil wars. During the Cold War period (1945–1991), Eastern Europe was dominated by the Soviet Union. After 1991 the countries had to determine their own futures. The change resulted in old animosities recurring between and within some countries. For others, it began a period of unprecedented political cooperation.

Early Peoples, Empires, and Conflict

The earliest Slavs migrated from Asia thousands of years ago and settled in Eastern Europe alongside Celtic and Germanic tribes. By the A.D. 400s and 500s, they had spread across the region. The Slavic peoples living on the Balkan Peninsula established independent states. The mountainous terrain allowed them to resist invading armies. The Slavic peoples to the east of the Balkan Peninsula, however, experienced invasions from peoples coming from Asia, particularly the Mongols in the 1200s. They ultimately settled in sparsely populated and widely separated communities in the forests and plains north of the Caucasus Mountains.

ENGAGE

G1 Critical Thinking Skills

Understanding Relationships Among Events Write the term *Balkanization* on the board. Challenge students to define the word and to speculate how the term applies to Eastern Europe. Have students use a dictionary to research the origins of the term.

TEACH & ASSESS

G2 Critical Thinking Skills

Comparing and Contrasting Have volunteers explain the difference between a communist-based command economy and a market economy. **Ask:** What type of economy does the United States and the countries of Western Europe have? *(market economy)* What type did the Soviet Union have? *(command economy)* **Logical/Mathematical**

R1 Reading Skills

Defining Have students reread the section. Have students define the term *shatter belt* in their own words. **Ask:** What kinds of events are likely to create shatter belt conditions in a region? *(Possible answers: political rivalries, territorial disputes, cultural and ethnic differences)* **ELL Verbal/Linguistic**

R2 Reading Skills

Analyzing Discuss the meaning of the term *Slav. (a person whose native tongue is a Slavic language)* Point out that the majority of the people living in Eastern Europe are Slavs and speak Slavic languages. Review with students that there are 12 language families. Explain how languages often have a common origin and that language families have spread or traveled to various regions, countries, and continents throughout the world. **ELL Verbal/Linguistic**

networks ***Online Teaching Options***

INTERACTIVE BELLRINGER

The Road to a New Era

Interpreting Information on a Time Line This introductory text and time line can be used to help students recognize that Eastern European countries transitioned to democratic governments and market economies after the fall of communism. Guide a class discussion about the fall of communism in Europe and the formation of new countries, in which students provide their prior knowledge of the subject. Then continue the class discussion by inviting volunteers to answer the bellringer questions and explain their answers. **Interpersonal, Verbal/Linguistic**

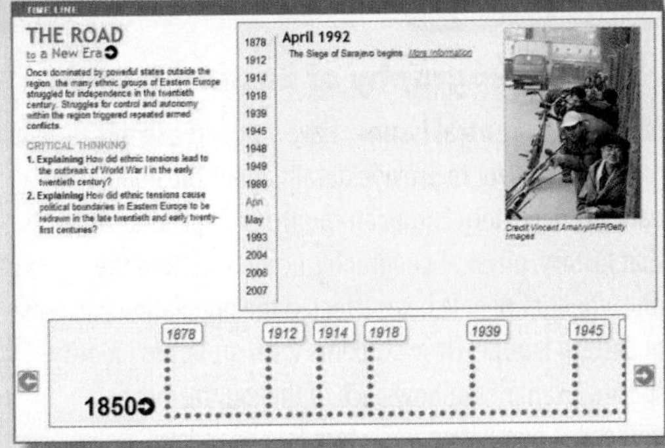

ANSWERS, p. 319

TAKING NOTES: History—The Slavs descended from Indo-European peoples who migrated from Asia thousands of years ago; there are west Slavs (Poles, Czechs, Slovaks) and south Slavs (Serbs, Croats, Slovenes, Macedonians); languages share Indo-European roots. **Industrialization**—led to urbanization as people moved to cities that rose up near waterways used for trading industrial products; **Location**—Poland is most highly populated because of fertile soil and abundant water; after industrialization, population shifted to urban centers near navigable waterways; **Migration/Immigration**—difficult economic and political circumstances resulting from war caused internal migration and emigration, causing the population to decline.

R Reading Skills

Monitoring Discuss the events that led up to World War I. **Ask:** What was the political climate in Eastern Europe prior to the war? *(Possible answers: political and military alliances between countries and hostilities between ethnic groups)* What event in 1914 set the war off? *(the assassination of Archduke Francis Ferdinand)* How did the demise of the Ottoman and Austro-Hungarian Empires lead to the Balkanization of the region? *(The region was divided into new countries based on ethnicity, population, politics, and economics.)* Discuss how Balkanization affected the region. **Ask:** How did the creation of Yugoslavia reverse the pattern? *(It joined hostile ethnic groups into one nation.)* **AL** **Verbal/Linguistic**

T Technology Skills

Changing Continuity of Groups Divide the class into small groups. Have each group choose an Eastern European country to study. Have groups research and describe how the borders of each country changed before and after World War I and again after World War II. Students should use online sources as well as consult historical maps and almanacs in their research. Have students present their findings to the class. **Logical/Mathematical, Naturalist**

V Visual Skills

Determining Importance Have students study and interpret the information in the time line. **Ask:** What events are outlined in this time line? *(important political events in the history of Eastern Europe)* How does the time line augment the text? *(Possible answer: It highlights some facts from the text and includes new information about the Balkan Wars and the rise of Adolf Hitler that are not in the text.)* **ELL** **Verbal/Linguistic**

ANSWERS, p. 320

CRITICAL THINKING

1. Ethnic groups had long been struggling for independence, but the war officially began after a Serbian nationalist assassinated the heir to the Austro-Hungarian throne.
2. The newly established ethnic-based countries within Yugoslavia battled with each other for control; eventually individual countries began seceding and Yugoslavia was divided into eight independent countries.

shatter belt a region where political alliances are constantly splintering and fracturing based on ethnicity

persistent continuing, existing, or acting for a long time

ethnic of or relating to large groups of people classed according to common traits and customs

Balkanization division of a region into smaller regions

Around A.D. 106 the Romans conquered the lands between the Carpathian Mountains and the Danube River and named the area Romania. As part of the eastern half of the Roman Empire, the area became part of the Byzantine Empire that emerged after the fall of Rome. The Byzantine Empire lasted for a thousand years before falling to the Ottoman Turks in 1453. The Ottoman Empire then ruled much of southern Eastern Europe until the end of World War I.

Conflict, Union, and Division

The Balkan Peninsula, like much of Eastern Europe, has long been a region of instability. The ethnic conflict in the region contributed to the start of World War I when a Serbian nationalist assassinated Archduke Francis Ferdinand, heir to the Austro-Hungarian throne, in 1914.

R The breakup of the Ottoman and Austro-Hungarian Empires after World War I left regions of peoples without formally recognized countries. A new map of Europe was drawn based on ethnicity, population, politics, and economic strengths. One new country, Yugoslavia, combined many ethnic groups in lands that had been contested between the Austro-Hungarian and Ottoman Empires for hundreds of years.

As a shatter belt, the Balkan Peninsula had seen the division of the larger regions or countries into smaller regions or countries for many centuries, often as a result of war. Because of this long history, this process of division has become known as **Balkanization**. Yugoslavia attempted to reverse that pattern, since it took many smaller regions based on ethnicity and combined them into one country.

T After World War II, Eastern Europe fell under the control of the communist Soviet Union. The control of communist Eastern Europe in contrast to democratic Western Europe brought about the Cold War, an ideological, political, and geographical war. Based on the devastation of Russia and other Soviet lands in both world wars, the Soviets used Eastern Europe as a "buffer zone." The eastern countries of Europe separated the Soviet Union from Western Europe's democracies. This buffer zone provided military protection and led to very different types of social, economic, and political developments between Eastern and Western Europe.

TIME LINE

THE ROAD to a New Era

Once dominated by powerful states outside the region, the many ethnic groups of Eastern Europe struggled for independence in the twentieth century. Struggles for control and autonomy within the region triggered repeated armed conflicts.

CRITICAL THINKING

1. ***Explaining*** How did ethnic tensions lead to the outbreak of World War I in the early twentieth century?
2. ***Explaining*** How did ethnic tensions cause political boundaries in Eastern Europe to be redrawn in the late twentieth and early twenty-first centuries?

V

1900

1912 — The first of two brief wars in the Balkans is started by an alliance between Bulgaria, Greece, Serbia, and Montenegro.

1914 — Archduke Francis Ferdinand is assassinated by a Serbian nationalist, triggering World War I.

1918 — World War I ends, signaling the end of the Ottoman and the Austro-Hungarian Empires.

1939 — World War II begins and Nazi Germany rapidly takes over Eastern Europe.

DEA/A. DAGLI ORTI/De Agostini Picture Library/Getty Images

320

networks Online Teaching Options

GRAPHIC ORGANIZER

Human Geography of Eastern Europe

Identifying Central Issues Have students use this graphic organizer to provide details about the population patterns of Eastern European countries. Explain to students that history, physical geography, economics, and the movement of people have affected the population patterns of Eastern Europe. Have students form groups to identify specific examples of how each of the four factors has influenced population in Eastern Europe today.
BL **Visual/Spatial, Logical/Mathematical**

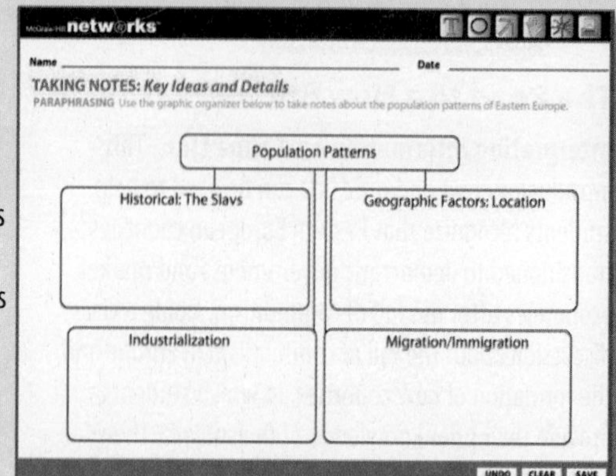

The Road to a New Era

From the 1950s to the 1980s, revolts against communist rule periodically swept Eastern Europe. In 1989 large-scale public demonstrations contributed to the fall of the communist governments in the east. By 1991 the nationalist protests and financial crisis led to new, ethnic-based countries within Yugoslavia. Slovenia, Croatia, Bosnia-Herzegovina, and Macedonia all seceded from Yugoslavia, leaving just Serbia and Montenegro. Power struggles by ethnic and political groups resulted in civil war. What followed was a horrific practice called **ethnic cleansing**. Ethnic cleansing was used mainly by military units, but civilians did participate. The "cleansing" resulted in certain ethnic groups being killed or expelled from the disputed territories where they lived. Ethnic cleansing affected all groups, but Bosnian Croats and Bosnian Muslims were affected the most. Military aircraft from NATO countries bombed Serbian military and civilian targets to stop Serbia's support of the ethnic cleansing. Eventually international peacekeeping efforts were able to dislodge Serb leaders and end the conflict. Balkanization continued, and Montenegro declared independence from Serbia in 2006, with Kosovo declaring independence in 2008. In less than 20 years, the country of Yugoslavia was divided into eight smaller independent countries.

T

ethnic cleansing the expelling from a country or genocide of an ethnic group

READING PROGRESS CHECK

Expressing What did the public demonstrations of 1989 in Yugoslavia lead to?

Population Patterns

GUIDING QUESTION *How have wars, migrations, and changing political borders influenced the population patterns of Eastern Europe?*

Most Eastern Europeans are ethnically Slavic. Slavs are descended from Indo-European peoples who migrated from Asia and settled in the region. Eastern Europe contains west Slavs, including Poles, Czechs, and Slovaks, and south

1945 World War II ends and the Cold War begins.

1949 The United States and its allies in Western Europe form the North Atlantic Treaty Organization (NATO).

1950

1989 Public demonstrations lead to the fall of the communist governments in Eastern Europe. Yugoslavia descends into civil war.

1992 The UN recognizes independent Slovenia, Croatia, and Bosnia as member states.

1993 Macedonia is admitted to the UN. Czechoslovakia splits into the Czech Republic and Slovakia. The European Union is created.

2000

2004 The EU admits the Czech Republic, Hungary, Latvia, Lithuania, Poland, Slovakia, and Slovenia.

2006 Montenegro declares itself independent from Serbia.

2007 Bulgaria and Romania join the European Union.

2008 Kosovo declares independence from Serbia.

W

INTERACTIVE MAP

Major Nazi Death Camps

Comparing and Contrasting Have students examine this map of Nazi death camps in Europe. As a class, discuss how political, economic, and ethnic struggles have shaped the history and culture of Eastern Europe. Invite students to explain the various genocides of modern history that they know about. Have students consider how the attempted genocide of Jews by the Germans before and during World War II is similar to more recent incidents of ethnic cleansing in some of the regions of the world. Ask them if it is different and if they feel that these religious and ethnic events are inevitable. Lead a discussion on this topic. BL Intrapersonal

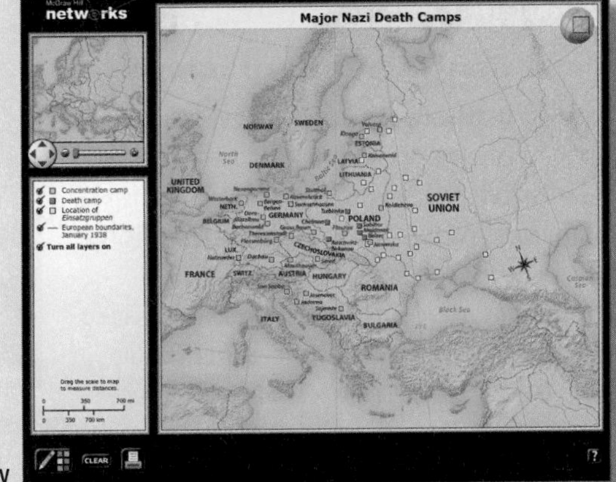

T Technology Skills

Reaching Conclusions Have students research the ethnic-based conflicts that broke out in Bosnia, Kosovo, Serbia, and elsewhere in Eastern Europe during the 1990s and early 2000s. Have them write an editorial essay on one of the conflicts as if they were eyewitness reporters. The essays should include when and why NATO eventually stepped in to end the conflict. Each editorial should conclude with an explanation on whether the conflict benefited the political, social, or economical agenda of anyone or any group. BL Verbal/Linguistic

Making Connections

Eastern European Connections Have students find out if anyone in their own families or their neighborhoods came from an Eastern European country. Have them find out the original country of origin, the language(s) spoken, religious practices, level of education, or other customs and traditions. Also ask students to discover how long their family members or neighbors have lived in the United States. Have students report their findings to the class.

W Writing Skills

Informative/Explanatory Have students use the time line to write a brief essay about the history of Eastern Europe from 1945 to the present. Students should include additional information provided in the text. Invite students to research topics of interest online or by using reference materials to add to their essays. Verbal/Linguistic

ANSWERS, p. 321

READING PROGRESS CHECK The demonstrations led to the fall of communist governments in Eastern Europe and eventually the creation of ethnic-based countries.

R Reading Skills

Reading Maps Have students study the map and map key. **Ask:** According to the key, which countries are largely Slavic? *(Poland, Czech Republic, Slovakia, Slovenia, Croatia, Bulgaria, Macedonia, Serbia, and Montenegro)* Which countries are populated mainly by non-Slavic groups? *(Hungary, Albania, Romania, Latvia, Lithuania, and Estonia)* Direct students to study the callouts on the map. Have them explain where some of the major minority groups of Eastern Europe live, such as the Roma or the Pomaks, and why these groups have settled in these areas. **AL** **Verbal/Linguistic**

C Critical Thinking Skills

Comparing Have students compare the population density and physical landforms of Eastern Europe by referring to the unit maps found in their text. Have students note where the greatest (and least) population densities occur. **Ask:** What geographic factors favor large populations? *(Possible answers: ample water resources, good farmland, transportation routes, and natural resources)* Which factors appear to discourage large populations? *(Possible answer: rugged terrain)* Where are many large urban centers developed? Why do you think they are located in these areas? *(Possible answers: regions near navigable water, plains, and other lowland regions that favor trade routes, ease of transportation, and access resources)* **AL** **Verbal/Linguistic**

Ethnic Groups in Eastern Europe
The Roma are the largest minority group in Europe. Thought to have migrated west from India into Europe, many live today in Bulgaria, Romania, Hungary, Slovakia, and the Czech Republic. The Roma continue to live nomadic lives, clashing with European governments as they move farther west.
Some of the earliest Slavs migrated from Asia thousands of years ago to settle in Poland.
The central portion of Eastern Europe includes countries that once formed the country of Yugoslavia. Ethnic and cultural groups living here include southern Slavic peoples such as Eastern Orthodox Serbs, Roman Catholic Croats, and Bosnian Muslims.
The Pomaks are thought to be descendants of native Bulgarians who converted to Islam during the period of Ottoman rule. Today they live in parts of Turkey, Macedonia, Kosovo, Greece, and Albania as well as Bulgaria.
Slavic
Poles
Czechs
Slovaks
Slovenes
Croats
Muslims
Bulgars
Russians
Macedonians
Serbs
Montenegrins
Non-Slavic
Magyars
Albanians
Romanians
Turks
Pomaks
Latvians
Lithuanians
No group over 50%
ESTONIA
LATVIA
LITHUANIA
POLAND
CZECH REPUBLIC
SLOVAKIA
HUNGARY
MOLDOVA
ROMANIA
SLOVENIA
CROATIA
BOSNIA AND HERZ.
SERBIA
MONT.
KOS.
MAC.
BULGARIA
ALBANIA
Baltic Sea
Adriatic Sea
Black Sea
Sea of Azov
50°N
40°N
10°E
20°E
30°E
40°E
0 400 miles
0 400 kilometers
Lambert Azimuthal Equal-Area projection

GEOGRAPHY CONNECTION

Historical migrations to Eastern Europe resulted in a subregion that is very ethnically diverse.

1. ***PLACES AND REGIONS*** Which Eastern European countries have the largest populations of Roma today?
2. ***HUMAN SYSTEMS*** What major religions do the southern Slavic people practice?

Slavs, including Serbs, Croats, Slovenes, and Macedonians. Slavs are an ethnic group defined mainly by their language. They speak languages today that have words and grammar that vary by country, but are traced to the same Indo-European root languages.

Another ethnic group, the Roma, traces its language to Indo-European origins. Roma are thought to have migrated from northern India to Europe centuries ago. Today there are several million Roma who live in Europe. They generally have less education, poorer health care, and shorter life expectancies than other groups.

Population density and distribution in Eastern Europe are influenced by geographic factors. For example, Poland has fertile soil and ample water resources that support large populations. Montenegro, by contrast, is the least populous country in Eastern Europe. It is located along the Dalmatian coast with a jagged coastline of narrow coastal plains backed by rugged limestone mountains and plateaus. The capital, Podgorica, has the main population concentration. Located along the Adriatic Sea, it provides access to the Mediterranean and therefore global transportation routes.

Industrialization throughout the 1900s led to urbanization in Eastern Europe. The majority of Eastern Europe's population today lives in and around large towns and cities. However, during much of the twentieth century, about half the population lived in rural areas. The cities that developed in the subregion were located near navigable water, such as the Danube and Vistula Rivers. Water

322

networks Online Teaching Options

INTERACTIVE MAP

Ethnic Groups in Eastern Europe

Creating Charts Display this interactive map to analyze ethnic groups and discuss language families of Eastern Europe. Have students compare this map to an online language map of Europe. Have students create a chart indicating which language predominates in each country and to what language group it belongs. Student charts should include the heads *Country, Dominant Ethnic Group,* and *Language Family. (Most of the languages spoken in Eastern Europe belong to the Slavic language family; Albanese (Albanian)—Illyrian family; Latvian and Lithuanian—Baltic family; Romanian— Romanic family; Estonian—Finnic family; Hungarian—Ugrian family; Finnic and Ugrian are not Indo-European languages)* **BL** **Visual/Spatial**

ANSWERS, p. 322

GEOGRAPHY CONNECTION

1. Bulgaria, Romania, Hungary, Slovakia, and the Czech Republic.
2. Christianity and Islam

transportation is not as expensive as other forms of transport and provided the cities with advantages as industrial and trade centers. During the Cold War, Eastern Europe was the major trading partner for the Soviet Union. New trade connections were necessary after 1991, and cities have new economic objectives based on tourism and services. Joining the European Union (EU) has been a major advantage to those Eastern European countries that met the requirements for membership.

Eastern European countries faced many difficult economic and political circumstances during and following World War II. Following the war there were large-scale internal and external migrations. Eastern European populations experienced heavy declines. Many Jewish people emigrated to Israel and to countries on other continents. People left in great numbers to escape communism. With the fall of communism, Eastern European countries underwent additional changes in economics, politics, and social conditions that continue to affect them today.

READING PROGRESS CHECK

Describing How did industrialization affect population distribution in Eastern Europe?

Society and Culture Today

GUIDING QUESTION *How has conflict affected society and culture in Eastern Europe?*

Since almost all of Eastern Europe was a part of the Soviet bloc, the region has a recent history of free education for the population. As a result, literacy rates are improving throughout the region. However, in the transition to democratic governments, some countries have faced economic challenges. A lack of funds has affected the education systems in some countries. The health care system, known as "cradle to grave," was affected by the change to the market economy and by the lower birthrates and higher numbers of senior citizens. Despite this, most Eastern Europeans continue to have access to quality health care provided by national governments. The European outlook on health care makes it a basic human right.

Religious and ethnic differences were at the heart of conflict in the Balkan Peninsula in the 1990s. Tensions between Serbs and other ethnic groups such as Croats and Bosnians erupted into armed violence. Layered on top of such tensions were also religious divisions between people practicing Eastern Orthodox Christianity and Islam. Roman Catholicism and Judaism are also practiced in the region.

Family and Status of Women

In traditional Eastern European culture, the family is the basic social unit and serves to reinforce social values. However, twentieth-century industrialization, World War I, and new political movements introduced greater mobility and attracted rural populations to urban areas to find work. Since the beginning of industrialization and urbanization in Europe, families have tended to live in small houses or apartments. Eastern European families today have fewer children, and extended family members often live in other places. Women have made gains in education and, as a result, are employed in professional jobs.

The Arts

Many traditional forms of art and music exist throughout Eastern Europe. Folk and classical music are particularly important among Czech, Hungarian, Slovak, and Slovene peoples. In larger cities,

A crucifix stands against a bullet-riddled wall in the former Yugoslavia.

▼ CRITICAL THINKING

1. ***Describing*** In what ways has war shaped Eastern European culture and politics?
2. ***Explaining*** How has religion played a role in the conflicts of Eastern Europe?

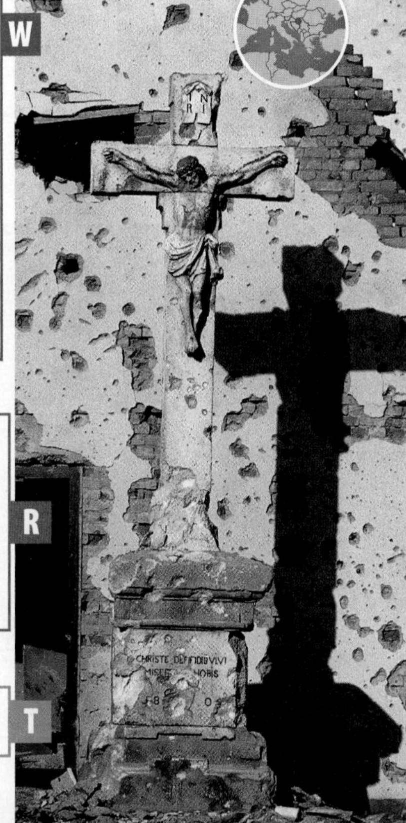

W Writing Skills

Informative/Explanatory Discuss with students the criteria they would use to judge a person's quality of life and how education, access to health care, and religious freedom fit in with the Human Development Index (HDI). Assign each group a different Eastern European country, and have students groups research how these factors compare among the Eastern European countries. Have students write reports about their country based on their research and share them with the class. **Interpersonal, Verbal/Linguistic**

R Reading Skills

Applying Guide a class discussion on the differences between a nuclear and an extended family. **Ask:** **What conditions caused many Eastern Europeans from rural areas to move to cities in the twentieth century?** *(industrialization, World War I, and new political movements)* Ask students to speculate how and why these changes affected the size of families in Eastern Europe. **AL Verbal/Linguistic**

T Technology Skills

Presenting Assign students to conduct online research about forms of art or music that originated in Eastern Europe. Encourage students to research a particular art form or music that is unique or of interest to them. They could also consider noted artists or musicians from this region. Have students make multimedia presentations to the class. Presentations should include music, images, and videos clips. **BL Auditory/Musical, Visual/Spatial**

WORKSHEETS

Guided Reading Activities

Monitoring Use these Guided Reading Activity worksheets to reinforce the lesson content for students who are struggling with the reading and comprehension of the lesson content. These worksheets ask students to think critically about the lesson material and to summarize the main points in their own words. These worksheets may also serve as a lesson review for students who need additional skills practice. **AL ELL Verbal/Linguistic**

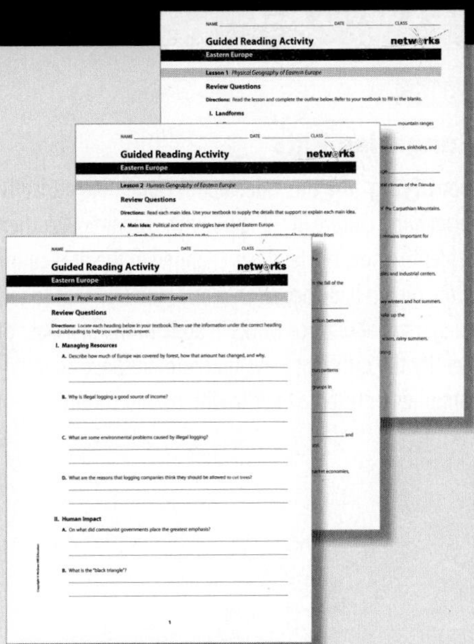

ANSWERS, p. 323

READING PROGRESS CHECK Industrialization led to the urbanization of Eastern European populations. Today, most people in the region live in and around large industrial towns and cities located near waterways.

CRITICAL THINKING

1. Recovery from war set the region back economically and caused worry over lack of funds for education and health care, but the governments have still been able to provide these important components. War also caused populations to both decline and became more urban. Works of art from the region often reflect the tragedy of war.
2. Religious differences, particularly between those practicing Eastern Orthodox Christianity and those practicing Islam, added to the already strong ethnic tensions between groups in the region.

C Critical Thinking Skills

Comparing and Contrasting Review how a market economy differs from a command economy. Discuss why transitioning from one to the other might be difficult. **Ask:** **What kinds of production problems might arise?** *(dealing with new forms of ownership and management; establishing new relationships with labor; finding new markets)* **What types of consumption problems might arise?** *(finding products to manufacture that people want to buy)* **How might having a close relationship with a Western European nation benefit a country?** *(access to new ideas about doing business in a market economy; access to investors; ease of developing trade arrangements)* **Verbal/Linguistic**

Content Background Knowledge

Eastern Europe: GDP Composition by Sector (2012)

Nation	GDP (Billion $)	Agricultural	Industrial	Services (est.)
Albania	12.96	20.4%	19.1%	60.5%
Bosnia-Herzegovina	4.75	8.2%	26.2%	65.6%
Bulgaria	53.51	5.6%	31.2%	63.2%
Croatia	63.85	4.7%	33.1%	62.2%
Czech Republic	215.22	1.8%	39.6%	58.6%
Estonia	22.19	3.7%	30.2%	66.1%
Hungary	140.33	4.5%	27.2%	68.3%
Kosovo	6.45	12.9%	22.6%	64.5%
Latvia	28.25	4.4%	26.3%	69.3%
Lithuania	42.73	3.3%	28.4%	68.4%
Macedonia	10.17	9.6%	27.35	63.1%
Montenegro	4.55	0.8%	11.3%	87.9%
Poland	514.50	3.5%	34.2%	62.3%
Romania	179.79	7.5%	33%	59.9%
Serbia	45.04	10.6%	18.6%	70.8%
Slovakia	95.99	2.7%	36.4%	59.8%
Slovenia	49.54	2.7%	27.6%	69.7%

ANSWERS, p. 324

READING PROGRESS CHECK Themes in the region's literature reflect its history of war, ethnic conflict, and economic depressions.

CRITICAL THINKING

1. subsistence farming
2. Although Eastern Europe experienced industrialization during the communist era, many parts of the region retained their agricultural roots.

contemporary music from Western Europe and the United States is also popular. Some areas have thriving nightclub scenes. Some of the large countries also have a long musical history and continue to perform the works of famous composers in historic concert halls and opera houses.

Literature is a valued art form in Eastern Europe. The region has produced world-famous writers, such as Czech-born Franz Kafka (1883–1924), known for his novel *The Metamorphosis*. The most common themes in Eastern European literature reflect the region's history. Many authors wrote about the despair and darkness that fell over the region due to war, ethnic conflict, and economic depressions.

READING PROGRESS CHECK

Explaining What are the common themes in Eastern European literature?

Economic Activities

GUIDING QUESTION *How have Eastern European economies developed since the fall of communism?*

Eastern European countries have made the transition to market economic systems over the past 20 years. The change to a market economy has presented both problems of production and consumption—of providing items that others want to buy and managing the changes in ownership from government to private corporations. The countries located nearest to Western Europe benefited early from the market system and received investments from countries such as Germany, Sweden, and the United Kingdom. Slovenia, for example, prospered after the fall of communism because it developed economic relationships with Germany. Political instability in the 1990s resulted in countries such as Macedonia having less success attracting investment than countries neighboring on Western Europe.

Agriculture and Industry

While Eastern Europe was largely industrialized under communist rule, many parts maintained their agricultural roots. The countries with Mediterranean climates such as Bulgaria, Serbia, Croatia, Macedonia, Bosnia and Herzegovina,

Growing crops such as these potatoes in Romania reflects the agricultural roots of Eastern Europe.

CRITICAL THINKING

1. ***Analyzing Visuals*** How would you describe the type of farming you see in the picture?
2. ***Contrasting*** How was Eastern European society changed in terms of industrialization during the era of communist rule?

Diana Mayfield/Lonely Planet Images/Getty Images

networks Online Teaching Options

VIDEO

Hungarian Pigs

Identifying Use this video about Hungarian agriculture to discuss the traditions of society and culture in Hungary with students. Ask them to use references in the video to identify how the land has changed in the past couple of centuries. Explain that much of the region had once been marshland and that today almost 50 percent of the Hungarian labor force works in agriculture. In a class discussion, ask students to identify the different ways that humans have adapted to their environment and continue to preserve their traditions and culture. **Logical/Mathematical**

and Montenegro produce olives, citrus fruits, dates, and grapes. The types of agricultural products explain why the geography of the Balkans is a transition zone between Southern Europe and the northern regions of Eastern Europe. Farther north in Eastern Europe the climate is continental and farmers grow wheat, rye, and other grains. They also raise livestock.

Fishing is an industry in Eastern Europe that has depended largely on rivers and lakes. While large rivers like the Danube provide fish such as carp and perch, many rivers have been seriously overfished. The EU has introduced limits on fish catches and species protection rules in order to restore this important resource.

C While Eastern Europe continues to produce small quantities of natural resources such as coal, it has become a global center for low-cost manufacturing of electronics products. International investors are attracted by high educational levels among the population and low labor costs. Automobile production has also been one of the region's main successes. Tourism is yet another success story, and many countries have been able to rebuild their economies and attract foreign investment through hotel and hospitality tourist services.

Communication systems throughout Northwestern and Eastern Europe have become increasingly linked. Railway, airway, and highway systems link major cities, which facilitates trade and tourism. Seas and rivers also connect Eastern Europe with international shipping by water at a low cost. Most countries have world-class Internet services in urban centers and in many rural regions.

The European Union

R The Czech Republic, Hungary, Latvia, Lithuania, Estonia, Poland, Slovakia, Slovenia, Bulgaria, and Romania all were members of the European Union (EU) by 2012. The global economic crisis that began in 2008 had a major effect on the EU and the rest of Eastern Europe. The economic downturn was most serious in Greece, Portugal, Ireland, Italy, and Spain. While the consequences of a harsh economy were most serious in those countries, the EU functioned as a unit to help all member countries through the economic crisis. More prosperous countries, such as Germany, helped weaker countries after much debate and negotiations among the EU members. It was the first major crisis for the EU, and the leaders of member countries demonstrated the belief that the EU was strong enough to survive. Their success will be judged sometime in the future if the EU continues as a strong regional organization in Europe.

READING PROGRESS CHECK

Describing How did the European Union help all member countries through the economic crisis that began in 2008?

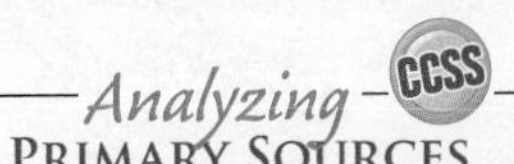

Analyzing PRIMARY SOURCES

Improving the Business Climate in Poland

"Poland . . . made it easier to register property, pay taxes, enforce contracts and resolve business insolvency, making it the most improved country out of the 185 tracked in the report.

. . . The desire to catch up with more established European Union members continues to drive improvements in business regulations in Eastern Europe. . . . Poland is now the 55th best place to do business, up from 62nd place last year. The country has been a rare bright spot in Europe over the past few years, managing to sustain robust growth even while its neighbors slumped."

—Anna Yukhananov, "Poland makes greatest strides in business reforms—World Bank," Reuters, October 22, 2012

DBQ ***DRAWING CONCLUSIONS*** How is Poland working to make the country a more attractive place for businesses to locate? RH.9–10.2

LESSON 2 REVIEW (CCSS)

Reviewing Vocabulary (Tier Three Words)

1. ***Explaining*** Explain the significance of Balkanization and ethnic cleansing. RH.9–10.4

Using Your Notes

2. ***Summarizing*** Use your graphic organizer to summarize the population patterns of Eastern Europe.

Answering the Guiding Questions

3. ***Identifying*** How have political and ethnic struggles shaped the Eastern Europe of today?
4. ***Assessing*** How have wars, migrations, and changing political borders influenced the population patterns of Eastern Europe?
5. ***Evaluating*** How has conflict affected society and culture in Eastern Europe?
6. ***Discussing*** How have Eastern European economies developed since the fall of communism?

Writing Activity

7. ***Narrative*** Suppose you are a farmer in Eastern Europe. Write one paragraph describing how your life has changed since the fall of communism. WHST.9–10.2

Human Geography of Eastern Europe

C Critical Thinking Skills

Analyzing Have students discuss factors that are essential to economic development. **Ask:** **Why would high education levels among a population attract international investors?** *(Possible answer: educated people bring the necessary tools to do a job and are easier to train)* **Why would low labor costs attract investors?** *(They reduce overall business costs and usually lead to bigger profits for a company.)* **Why are good communication systems important to a nation's economy?** *(Possible answer: ready access to information; speed up communication and transactions between businesses, their partners, suppliers, and customers)* **AL** **Verbal/Linguistic**

R Reading Skills

Interpreting Discuss the goals and benefits EU members. Have students list which Eastern European nations became part of the EU by 2012. Ask volunteers to determine if any other nations have joined since 2012. Discuss how wealthier EU members are able to help floundering ones. Ask students to collect news stories about the EU. **Verbal/Linguistic**

CLOSE & REFLECT

Summarizing Review the many changes that Eastern Europe has experienced in the past few decades. Then have students write a brief essay titled *Eastern Europe: Past and Present*.

ANSWERS, p. 325

READING PROGRESS CHECK More prosperous countries in the EU came to the aid of struggling countries.

DBQ Poland has been improving business regulations by making it easier to register property, pay taxes, enforce contracts, and resolve business insolvency.

LESSON 2 REVIEW ANSWERS

Reviewing Vocabulary

1. Balkanization refers to the breaking down of a large region into smaller regions. The term originated from the Balkan Peninsula. Ethnic tension can sometimes become so strong that one or more groups attempt to eradicate others by killing or driving them away.

Using Your Notes

2. Slavs migrated from Asia to Eastern Europe and by the A.D. 500s, they had spread across the region. Most Eastern Europeans lived in rural areas until the 1900s, when industrialization attracted people to cities. Possession of navigable waterways helped Poland become the most populated country in the region. After World War II, the population declined as people migrated for economic and political reasons.

Answering the Guiding Questions

3. Eastern Europe has been known as a shatter belt region because political borders have constantly changed due to ethnic conflict. Many countries that occupy the region today are relatively small.
4. Many internal and external migrations took place after World War II as a result of communist rule. This caused a major decline in the regional population.
5. After World War II, Eastern Europe transitioned to democracy. This was an economically difficult period as countries struggled to preserve education and health care. There are still a lot of cultural and religious differences in the region, but there is hope for a better future. Conflict is a common artistic theme.
6. Eastern European countries have been transitioning to market economies. Countries closest to Western Europe benefited from investments from Germany, Sweden, and the U.K. Many countries are still strongly dependent on agriculture. Manufacturing of electronics and cars has been a success. Tourism is also steadily increasing thanks to greater political stability and improvements to communication systems.

Writing Activity

7. Essays will vary, but should be logical and strongly supported by information from the chapter. Narratives should present changes that might result from the switch from a communist economic system to a market economic system.

ENGAGE

R Reading Skills

Activating Prior Knowledge Have students name some environmental issues facing their communities today. Have students make a list of these problems, their origins, and possible solutions. Tell students that many of the Eastern European countries are dealing with environmental problems our country has faced now and in the past. Have students look for comparisons as they study the lesson. **Interpersonal**

TEACH & ASSESS

C1 Critical Thinking Skills

Analyzing Cause and Effect Have students create flowcharts showing how illegal and uncontrolled logging in Eastern Europe has lead to air pollution and losses in the biodiversity in many forested areas. Discuss why illegal logging continues in some countries despite these growing problems. **Visual/ Spatial, Logical/Mathematical**

C2 Critical Thinking Skills

Assessing Discuss two ways Eastern Europeans are dealing with the problem of deforestation. *(reforestation and forest preservation)* If students have experience with reforestation projects in their own communities, encourage them to describe them. **Ask:** **Why is the loss of biodiversity a concern?** *(Possible answers: inhibits nature's ability to function properly; changes the natural checks and balances of a habitat; allows less desirable, invasive species to flourish)* **What are some possible solutions to dealing with the problem of illegal logging?** *(Possible answers: stricter laws, better enforcement; conservation initiatives; lower the cost of electricity; provide other ways for people to heat their homes)* **AL** **Verbal/Linguistic, Interpersonal**

ANSWERS, p. 326

TAKING NOTES: Deforestation is occurring as a result of illegal logging and other activities. Industries emit a lot of air pollution from burning coal. This pollution is carried to many areas in a number of ways, including acid rain and meltwater. Agricultural pollution from chemical fertilizers and pesticides is also having a strong impact.

networks
There's More Online!

- GRAPH Water Pollution in Europe
- IMAGE Białowieza Forest
- IMAGE Communist-Era Pollution
- INTERACTIVE SELF-CHECK QUIZ
- VIDEO People and Their Environment: Eastern Europe

LESSON 3

People and Their Environment: Eastern Europe

Reading **HELP**DESK 

Academic Vocabulary (Tier Two Words)
- **emphasis**

Content Vocabulary (Tier Three Words)
- **reforestation**
- **meltwater**

TAKING NOTES: *Key Ideas and Details*

SUMMARIZING Use a graphic organizer like the one below to identify ways humans are affecting the environment in Eastern Europe.

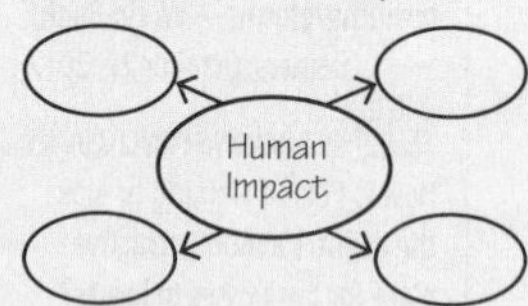
Human Impact

ESSENTIAL QUESTION • *How do physical systems and human systems shape a place?*

IT MATTERS BECAUSE

R *Natural resources, people, and culture combine to influence the nature of human impact on the environment in a given region. For example, some countries in Eastern Europe have followed plans of rapid and intense industrialization without regard to the effects on the environment. In addition, dams, dikes, and other types of development have damaged water quality, posing a threat to wetlands, fish, and bird populations.*

Managing Resources

GUIDING QUESTION *Why do forest resources in Eastern Europe need to be managed effectively?*

C1 It is believed that about 80 percent of Europe was once covered by forest, two-thirds of which has been removed over time. Historically, people cut down trees to create space for cities and farms. Today some countries in Eastern Europe, such as Bulgaria and Albania, have a problem with illegal logging, or the unlicensed cutting and selling of wood. Selling illegally logged wood can be a lucrative business, especially in countries with stagnating economies. Individuals and groups who engage in illegal logging seldom get caught. This is because many wood-processing companies, formerly in charge of responsible logging and forest maintenance, went out of business in the 1990s. One reason for the popularity of illegal logging is the high cost of electricity, which leads many people to burn wood for heat. This generates air pollution, especially in urban areas. Romania and Bulgaria rank at the top of the United Nations Development Programme's list of countries where citizens have died from urban air pollution. Illegal logging has also led to huge losses in the biodiversity of many areas.

C2 As communist rule declined, Eastern European countries rushed to take part in the global economy. Individuals left rural farmlands to work in cities, and government interest in **reforestation**, or replanting trees, grew. People in Eastern Europe also began to focus on preserving what little

326

networks ***Online Teaching Options***

INTERACTIVE BELLRINGER

Nitrate Concentrations in Agricultural Runoff

Reading Graphs Use the introductory text and the graph to identify how agricultural pollution affects the environment in Eastern Europe. Have students form small groups and discuss their prior knowledge of agricultural pollution in the United States and then compare them to countries they know about in Eastern Europe. Have students discuss each question based on the information in the graph. Ask each group to write agreed-upon answers to the questions. Then in a class discussion, have groups share their answers. **AL** **Interpersonal, Visual/Spatial**

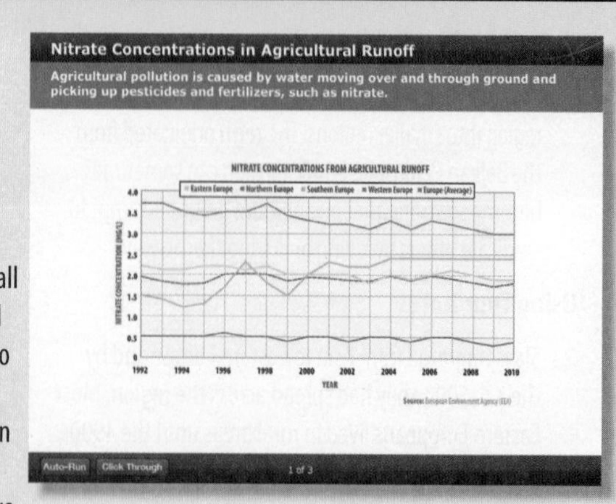
Nitrate Concentrations in Agricultural Runoff
Agricultural pollution is caused by water moving over and through ground and picking up pesticides and fertilizers, such as nitrate.
Auto-Run
Click Through
1 of 3

forest remains. For example, the Białowieza Forest, located in eastern Belarus and western Poland, is the site of debate between the Polish government and environmental activists. Most of the forest is home to some of the tallest trees in Europe, which are over 100 years old. It is also home to wolves, lynx, and the European bison. The forest is nationally protected and has been for centuries. However, in nonprotected forestry-managed areas, logging is ruining the habitats of many birds and animals and destroying trees that have stood longer than Poland has been a country. While environmental activists are fighting to save the trees, the logging industry provides jobs to many otherwise unemployed Polish workers. The workers argue that the wood would likely be stolen if they did not legally log in the area. The debate continues over whether forests should be preserved in order to protect endangered wildlife and preserve biodiversity or be used to create jobs.

T

The Białowieza Forest is one of the last forests left preserved in its ancient state in Europe.

▲ CRITICAL THINKING

1. ***Hypothesizing*** What characteristics of the trees in the Białowieza Forest make them sought after for logging?
2. ***Making Connections*** Why is it important to preserve the Białowieza Forest?

✓ READING PROGRESS CHECK

Expressing What is the debate over forest preservation in Eastern Europe?

Human Impact

GUIDING QUESTION *What human activities result in acid rain and water pollution in Eastern Europe?*

The communist governments in Eastern Europe placed an **emphasis** on rapid industrialization and heavy manufacturing. Eastern Europe's high concentration of industry has had a devastating impact on the environment. For example, the black triangle is a heavily industrialized area of Poland, eastern Germany, and the Czech Republic that relies primarily on burning coal as a power source. Soot covers the ground, and the air smells of sulfur from smokestacks. Although efforts are now under way to clean up the environment, the black triangle still bears the scars of poorly planned development from the Communist years.

V

Excessive reliance on coal burning in this small geographic region led to air, soil, and water pollution and caused people to develop respiratory diseases and cancer. In the 1970s and 1980s, Eastern European industries built smokestacks to carry pollution away from industrial sites. Air pollution then began to drift across national borders and made the problem more widespread. This coal pollution, which contains acid-producing chemicals, combines with moisture in the air and falls to the ground as acid rain. Polluted clouds drift away from the black triangle and other industrial areas and spread the pollution to forests in Northwestern Europe, degrading those environments as well.

Acid rain not only affects forests but lakes and rivers as well. In the cold Eastern European winters, snow carries industrial pollution to the ground. When this snow melts in the spring, **meltwater**, the result of melting snow and ice, carries the acid into lakes and rivers. As acid rain and meltwater pollution increased, fish and other aquatic life became endangered and even extinct. Some rivers and forests in the Czech Republic, for example, can no longer sustain life.

C

reforestation the action of renewing forest cover (as by natural seeding or by the artificial planting of seeds or young trees)

emphasis importance

meltwater water formed by melting snow and ice

GRAPH

Water Pollution in Eastern Europe

Interpreting Graphs This graph can be used with students to visualize the statistics on acid rain. Lead a class discussion about the environmental effects of acid rain. Explain that acid rain affects lakes, rivers, and forests. Have students study the graph and write three statements that interpret the content in the graph. Then have students exchange statements with a partner, checking each other's statements for accuracy.

AL Visual/Spatial

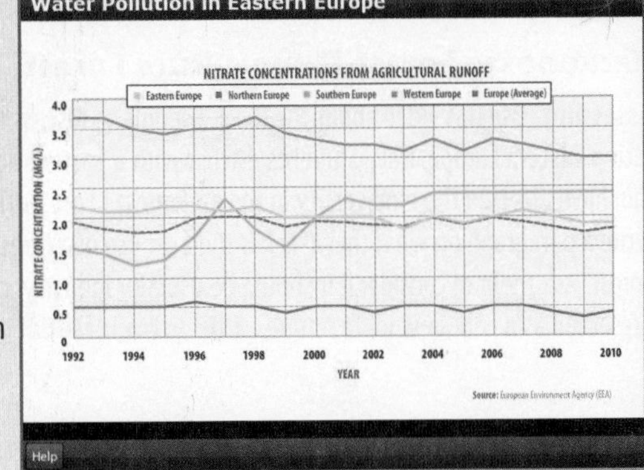

People and Their Environment: Eastern Europe

T Technology Skills

Constructing Arguments Have students hold an imaginary environmental hearing to consider the future of the Białowieza Forest. Divide the students into three groups. Designate one group of students as environmental activists, another group as unemployed workers, and the third group to represent logging company executives. Have each group present its side of the argument in front of a panel of mock judges on this issue. Allow each side to rebut the others' positions. BL Logical/Mathematical

Content Background Knowledge

Endangered Wildlife of Eastern Europe Many species of wildlife have already become extinct in Europe and Eastern Europe.

- Currently extinction threatens 15 percent of Europe's 228 species of mammals.
- Out of the 524 bird species found in Europe, 13 percent are threatened.
- Europe's most endangered bird is the slender-billed curlew.
- Many amphibians, reptiles, fish, and other animals are also threatened.

V Visual Skills

Creating Maps Have students create a map showing the boundaries and cities in Eastern Europe's black triangle. Have students write 3 or 4 detailed callout captions for their maps explaining the major industries responsible for the pollution, affected areas, or other environmental concerns in the black triangle. Students may need time to conduct further research. AL Visual/Spatial

C Critical Thinking Skills

Exploring Issues Invite a small group of students to research how acid rain impacts forests, lakes, and rivers in this region. Encourage students to use images and charts to present their findings to the class. Then lead a class discussion on the global impact of acid rain. BL Logical/Mathematical

ANSWERS, p. 327

✓ READING PROGRESS CHECK Ancient forests and their habitats are at risk of being destroyed, but protecting them from logging is controversial because logging provides much needed jobs.

CRITICAL THINKING

1. Possible answer: They are very tall and offer wood that is good for burning.
2. Possible answer: The ancient forest is the last remnant of the original forest that covered most of Europe. As such, its ecosystems are complex and destruction would severely decrease wildlife and biodiversity in the region.

R Reading Skills

Reading Graphs Ask a volunteer to explain what a nitrate is. Have students study the graph at the top of the page. **Ask:** What does this graph show? *(how nitrate concentrations from agricultural runoff changed in Europe from 1992 to 2010)* Which region produces the greatest concentrations of nitrates? *(Western Europe)* Why might this be so? *(Possible answer: Western Europe is a major agricultural producer. Nitrate concentrations reflect the relative proportion and intensity of agricultural activities.)* How did the situation change from 1992 to 2010? *(decreased)* Which region is responsible for the least amount of nitrate runoff? *(Northern Europe)* How would you describe the situation in Eastern Europe? *(Nitrate concentrations in runoff were barely reduced from 1992 to 2010.)* Students might research how the problems of agricultural runoff in the United States compare to Europe's runoff. **AL** **Verbal/Linguistic**

C Critical Thinking Skills

Drawing Conclusions Have students brainstorm why the EU requires member nations to adhere to certain environmental protection standards and to establish emissions regulations. *(Pollution travels across national boundaries affecting the health and well-being of people outside the offending region. Pollution is costly and a drain on both health and economies.)* Then have students form groups to discuss whether it is worth the economic benefits for Eastern European countries to comply with EU pollution controls in order to join. **BL** **Logical/Mathematical, Interpersonal**

GRAPH SKILLS — **Water Pollution in Europe**

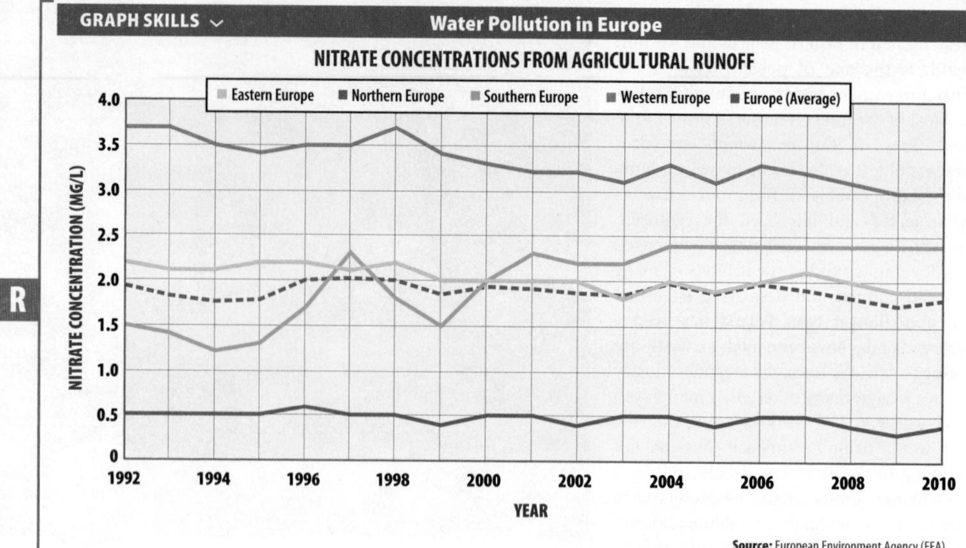

Nitrates from agricultural fertilizer contribute to water pollution in Eastern Europe.

▲ **CRITICAL THINKING**

1. ***Comparing and Contrasting*** How does the level of nitrate concentration in Eastern Europe compare to the European average?
2. ***Interpreting*** Based on what you know of Northern Europe, why do you think it has the lowest nitrate concentration?

Agricultural pollution in Eastern Europe is also a huge problem. As water moves over and through the ground, it picks up chemical fertilizers and pesticides. This agricultural runoff deposits pollutants into water sources and has severely polluted both the Danube and Vistula Rivers. Outdated mining methods have also released different kinds of polluted mine drainage into rivers and lakes.

Before 1989, Eastern European countries had virtually no laws to protect the environment against pollution, which increased until it affected public health. Poor air quality in Eastern Europe also has global consequences, and climate change has been accelerated by the industrialization of the twentieth century. But as Eastern European countries joined the European Union (EU), they have come under the environmental protection standards and cleanup required of member countries. The EU has also set strict emissions regulations for industries and vehicles. This often involves equipping smokestacks and vehicle exhaust systems with devices that remove sulfur and nitrogen compounds from their emissions.

✓ **READING PROGRESS CHECK**

Identifying What is the black triangle?

Addressing the Issues

GUIDING QUESTION *How are Eastern Europeans working to address the environmental issues related to resource management and human activity?*

In the past few decades, Eastern Europeans have made serious efforts to clean up the environment. Potential EU member countries have to meet certain

328

networks Online Teaching Options

VIDEO

Karkonosze Forest-Monoculture Forest

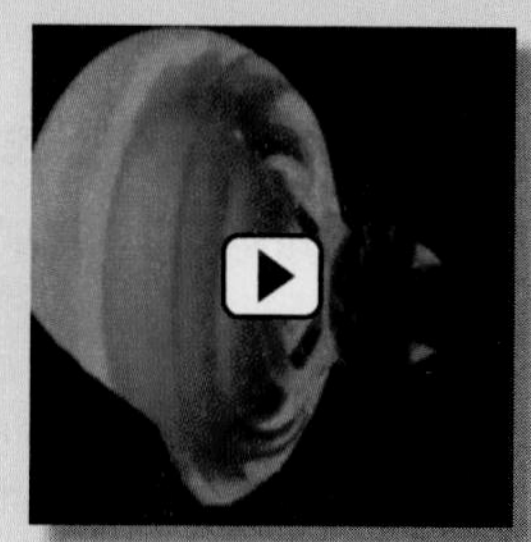

Assessing Use this video about the Black Triangle to discuss the environmental issues facing Eastern Europe. Have students discuss with a partner how forestation and acid rain have affected the biodiversity in the Karkonosze Forest. Then have each student write a paragraph on what they think is the best use of a forest, like the Karkonosze Forest. Ask them to consider if it should be used for industry, cleared for agriculture, or preserved as a park or wildlife refuge. **AL** **Intrapersonal**

ANSWERS, p. 328

✓ **READING PROGRESS CHECK** It refers to a heavily industrialized area partially in Poland, eastern Germany, and the Czech Republic, where coal burning is the primary power source, and the surrounding environment is greatly polluted as a result.

CRITICAL THINKING

1. The level in Eastern Europe is very close to the European average.
2. Northern Europe does not rely heavily on agriculture and, therefore, does not use a lot of fertilizers.

environmental standards to be admitted into the EU. Furthermore, member states can face legal action if they do not respect international environmental laws. The EU also created a system of low-emission zones, which are areas where vehicles whose pollutant emissions are too high cannot enter. This emission system is currently in place in the Czech Republic and in Hungary. Since cleanup costs amount to billions of dollars, Eastern European countries are now seeking advanced technology and investment from EU countries in Western Europe. **C**

Pollution that crosses national borders presents a complex situation. For example, pollution in the Danube River threatens wildlife in its outlet, the Black Sea. Many Eastern European governments recognize that improving water quality is necessary. Directing and financing cleanup, however, is difficult when the process involves many countries. Furthermore, the involvement of such a wide area makes tracking down one main source of contamination extremely challenging for regulators.

Non-EU Eastern European countries are also contributing to global efforts to protect the environment. The Baltic countries signed the Helsinki Convention for the Protection of the Marine Environment of the Baltic Sea Area. The Convention marked the first time the international community had regulated land-based sources of pollution, such as agricultural runoff, in a shared marine environment. The International Maritime Organization (IMO) has listed the Baltic and Black Seas as areas that need a high level of regulation and protection in order to prevent sea pollution. **R** Since fish are the most important resource in the Black Sea, conservation efforts by the surrounding countries include banning dolphin fishing and preventing industrial waste from entering the sea. In 1994 Bulgaria, Georgia, Romania, Russia, Turkey, and Ukraine signed the Convention for the Protection of the Black Sea Against Pollution. The Convention addressed programs to control pollution, sustain fisheries, and protect marine life.

The World Wildlife Fund (WWF), an international nongovernmental organization (NGO), has opened up offices in Bulgaria, Hungary, Latvia, Poland, and Romania. It supports conservation work such as cleaning up the Danube

Johann Brandstatter/Alamy

In the 1970s and 1980s, smokestacks were built to carry pollution away from industrial sites in Eastern Europe. Air pollution began to drift across the borders and made the problem more widespread.

◀ **CRITICAL THINKING**

1. ***Assessing*** Why is air pollution a major concern in Eastern Europe?
2. ***Exploring the Issues*** What steps are countries taking to resolve the growing environmental crisis?

C Critical Thinking Skills

Analyzing Cause and Effect Review the main sources of air and water pollution in Eastern Europe. Have students identify the challenges involved in addressing these problems. **Ask: What is one way the EU is dealing with vehicular pollution?** *(The EU created a system of low-emission zones.)* **Do you think this was a good measure? Why?** *(Student answers will vary, but might conclude that the regulation has reduced air pollution in the Czech Republic and Hungary.)* **Why is dealing with Eastern Europe's environmental problems difficult?** *(Possible answers: high costs, pollution issues cross borders, cleanup often involves many countries, difficulty identifying sources of pollution)* **Logical/Mathematical**

R Reading Skills

Listing Discuss the importance of the Baltic and Black Seas to this region and why the IMO has listed them as areas needing a high level of regulation and protection. Have students make a list describing measures taken by different countries to protect the seas. *(Baltic countries—signed the Helsinki Convention to protect Marine Environment; Bulgaria and Romania—signed the Convention for the Preservation of the Black Sea with Georgia, Russia, Turkey, and the Ukraine)* **AL** **Verbal/Linguistic**

Making Connections

Have students identify the areas of the United States where fishing is a major industry. Have students think of different measures taken by local, state, and federal governments to protect these marine environments. Ask students to think of instances that they are aware of when important United States fisheries were threatened. *(Possible answers: deepwater oil spill along the Gulf Coast in 2010; various oil spills in Alaskan waters)*

INTERACTIVE WHITEBOARD ACTIVITY

Causes of Acid Rain and Water Pollution in Eastern Europe

Identifying Cause and Effect This interactive whiteboard activity has students identify the cause-and-effect hierarchy of factors pertaining to acid rain and water pollution in Eastern Europe. Allow time for students to complete the activity. Then lead a class discussion about how industrialization has brought about changes in environmental conditions. Ask students to explain how industrialization has effected local and global changes that have influenced ecosystems in this region. **Verbal/Linguistic**

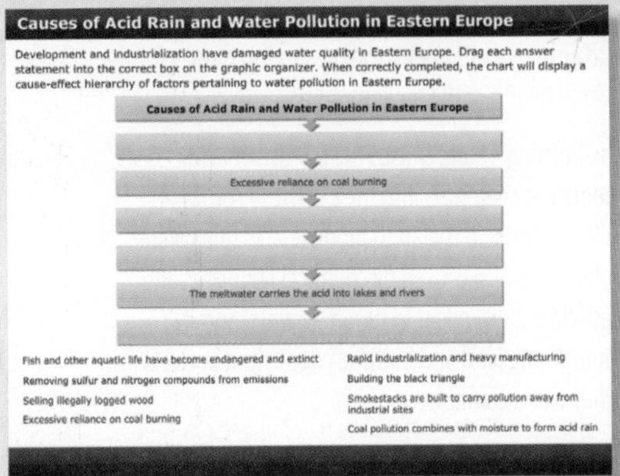

ANSWERS, p. 329

CRITICAL THINKING

1. Industrial air pollution contains chemicals that combine with moisture in the air to form acid rain, which falls not only in the region but in surrounding areas as well, making the effects of the pollution far-reaching.
2. Eastern European countries have been requesting investments from EU countries in Western Europe for environmental cleanup and to get advanced technology. Low-emission zones have been established in countries to cut down on air pollution from vehicles. Overall, countries are realizing the importance of working together to meet environmental goals.

People and Their Environment: Eastern Europe

C Critical Thinking Skills

Evaluating Perspectives Discuss why the U.S. is interested in helping the nations of Eastern Europe. **Ask:** **How is the United States helping European countries solve environmental problems?** *(financial assistance)* **How does helping these countries benefit the United States?** *(Possible answers: Many environmental problems reach across borders; cooperation helps world harmony.)* **AL** **Logical/Mathematical**

W Writing Skills

Informative/Explanatory Have students research one of the birds in a particular country or region of Eastern Europe. Students should write an essay that identifies the region, the current threatened status, as well as why they are threatened and what is being done to protect the birds. **Verbal/Linguistic**

CLOSE & REFLECT

Finding the Main Idea To close the lesson, have students reduce the information covered in each section to a main idea or topic sentence.

ANSWERS, p. 330

READING PROGRESS CHECK Political instability in the Balkans was a setback to environmental preservation. Working across political borders is a challenge, but it must be overcome if they are to effectively protect their resources. Other factors that have set them back are a lack of modern technological methods and low environmental awareness.

Connecting Geography The U.S. might provide educational information and advice on how to respond to specific concerns.

Connecting Geography to GOVERNMENT

Environmental Politics

Earth's natural resources are not confined within country borders, so it is important for governments to cooperate internationally. The Regional Environmental Center (REC) for Central and Eastern Europe was created in 1990 as a collaboration between the United States, Hungary, and the European Commission. The program provides financial assistance to help solve environmental problems in Central and Eastern Europe, with over $12 million in funding thus far given by the United States. Cooperation among the governments of all countries is promoted with a free exchange of information and the establishment of public participation in environmental decision-making.

SPECULATING How might the United States be able to provide help beyond financial assistance to the countries of Eastern Europe through the REC?

and Vistula Rivers, stopping illegal logging, preventing overfishing, and creating protected areas so plants and animals can no longer be harmed directly by human activity. It is particularly devoted to preserving the Danube-Carpathian region and protecting biodiversity in the region. These efforts have been supported by various governments and are largely successful. The Bulgarian government established the Srebarna Nature Reserve. It protects a lake that feeds into the Danube and is also a bird sanctuary. The reserve was made a UNESCO World Heritage Site in 1983. Another park in Bulgaria is the Rila National Park that protects abundant varieties of animals, particularly birds.

The Balkan countries lag behind larger Eastern European countries such as the Czech Republic and Hungary in terms of addressing environmental issues. This is largely due to political instability in the Balkans throughout the 1990s and early 2000s. However, Albania, Bosnia and Herzegovina, Macedonia, Montenegro, and Serbia are all looking to join the EU. The desire for EU membership provides an incentive to more wisely manage their resources and to minimize their environmental impacts. The major challenge that the Balkan countries face is working across political borders. For example, after the breakup of Yugoslavia produced six new Balkan states, the countries now share 13 river basins. Other ecologically important areas are located in the mountains and cross international borders. The remoteness of these mountainous border areas has helped to protect them in the past. The sharing of such important resources requires cooperation because an entire ecosystem needs to be protected in order for the efforts to be successful.

To ensure effective resource management and to meet EU standards, the Balkan countries will need to cooperate. They first need to regulate their outdated mining methods and to adopt modern technologies. The Balkan countries have a wealth of precious minerals at their disposal and need to ensure that their mining techniques are environmentally friendly.

In addition to technological improvement, education about environmental sustainability is also needed. Overall, environmental awareness among people in the Balkans is very low. Efforts to show how environmental protection can develop local economies can help. For example, the Durmitor National Park in Montenegro includes the Tara River canyon. The Tara River flows through Europe's deepest gorges and is one of the last wild rivers in Europe. It is an attractive destination for hikers and nature tourists and helps to support the local tourism industry.

READING PROGRESS CHECK

Explaining Why do the Balkan countries lag behind other Eastern European countries in terms of addressing environmental issues?

LESSON 3 REVIEW 

Reviewing Vocabulary (Tier Three Words)

1. ***Describing*** Explain what meltwater is and describe how it can carry pollution to new locations. RH.9-10.4

Using Your Notes

2. ***Explaining*** What are some ways humans have affected their environment negatively in Eastern Europe?

Answering the Guiding Questions

3. ***Evaluating*** Why do forest resources in Eastern Europe need to be managed effectively?

4. ***Stating*** What human activities result in acid rain and water pollution in Eastern Europe?

5. ***Explaining*** How are Eastern Europeans working to address the environmental issues related to resource management and human activity?

Writing Activity

6. ***Informative/Explanatory*** Imagine that you live in a polluted area in Eastern Europe. Write a letter to the editor of a newspaper there and suggest ways to halt environmental damage. WHST.9-10.2

330

LESSON 3 REVIEW ANSWERS

Reviewing Vocabulary

1. Meltwater is a combination of melted snow and ice that eventually flows into rivers and lakes. Acid that was in the snow and ice is carried with the meltwater to rivers and lakes, where it poisons aquatic life.

Using Your Notes

2. Possible response: They have participated in illegal logging, burning coal, chemical fertilizing, and pesticide use.

Answering the Guiding Questions

3. Illegal logging is destroying forests at an extremely rapid rate. Effective management is necessary to strike a balance between using wood to meet energy and employment needs and preserving forests for the overall health of the environment.

4. The burning of coal causes the release of acid-producing chemicals into the air. These combine with moisture in the air to produce acid rain. Water pollution is also caused by chemical fertilizers and pesticides that collect in runoff as water moves through the land and becomes deposited in rivers and other water sources.

5. Some countries have begun requesting investment from wealthier countries in order to make technological advances that will be environmentally beneficial. Low-emission zones are enforced to decrease air pollution. Countries have collaborated by establishing conventions and organizations to protect the environments of the Baltic Sea and the Black Sea, particularly from overfishing and waste disposal. Declaring certain areas as parks and nature reserves has helped other countries protect wildlife and their habitats from human destruction.

Writing Activity

6. Letters will vary, but should be logical and strongly supported by information from the lesson. At least one specific pollution concern should be included along with a possible solution.

CHAPTER 13 Assessment CCSS

Directions: On a separate sheet of paper, answer the questions below. Make sure you read carefully and answer all parts of the questions.

Lesson Review

Lesson 1

1. ***Stating*** Which rivers have historically served as a link for the people in Eastern Europe, and what has been created to supplement the passages?
2. ***Contrasting*** How do the mineral resources of the Carpathian Mountains differ from those of the Baltic Mountains?

Lesson 2

3. ***Making Connections*** Why are the Balkans considered a shatter belt region? Be sure to use the term *Balkanization* in your response.
4. ***Finding the Main Idea*** How have political activities affected settlement and population patterns in Eastern Europe?

Lesson 3

5. ***Making Generalizations*** What efforts have been made to preserve forests in Eastern Europe?
6. ***Exploring Issues*** How has industrialization resulted in acid rain and water pollution in Eastern Europe?

Critical Thinking

7. ***Assessing*** Describe the term *ethnic cleansing* and how it was used in Eastern Europe.
8. ***Classifying*** What were many of the new borders based upon after World War I?
9. ***Analyzing*** What impact has EU membership had on the environment in member countries? Give examples from the chapter to support your answer.
10. ***Contrasting*** Write a paragraph describing how the role of tourism in the economy of Eastern European countries today is different from how it was during the Soviet era. Include factors you think may draw tourists to the countries of Eastern Europe today.
11. ***Sequencing*** Prepare an itinerary for a 10-day trip to Eastern Europe, including the countries you plan to visit and the natural features you plan to see in each country. Make sure your itinerary reflects a logical sequence of travel given the location of the countries.

21st Century Skills

Use the circle graph to answer the following questions.

POLAND'S EXPORTS, 2011

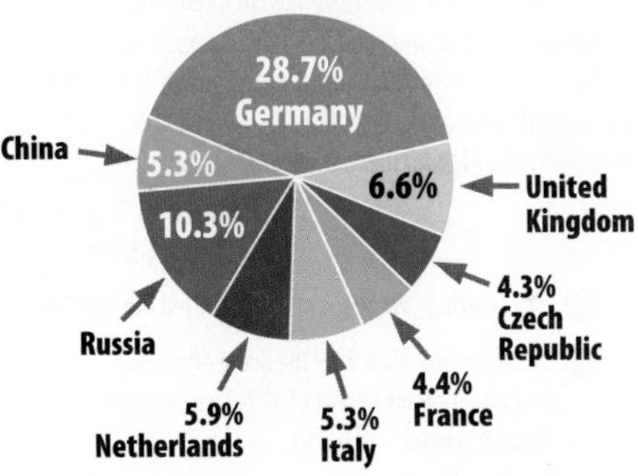

Source: CIA World Factbook

12. ***Economics*** Where does Poland send the greatest percentage of its exports?
13. ***Draw Conclusions*** Refer to your response to question 12 above. Explain the significance of its location to the comparative size of the percentage. Based on this significance, why do you think the percentage is not higher for the Czech Republic?

Need Extra Help?

If You've Missed Question	1	2	3	4	5	6	7	8	9	10	11	12	13
Go to page	316	318	319	319	327	327	321	320	328	325	314	331	331

CHAPTER 13 Assessment Answers

Lesson Review

Lesson 1

1. The Danube has served as a link to the Black Sea. The Vistula has served as a link to the Baltic Sea. Canals have been created to connect the Danube to the Main River and the Vistula to the Oder River.
2. The Carpathian Mountains have many natural resources, such as natural gas, oil, and coal, whereas the Baltic Mountains do not.

Lesson 2

3. The Balkans have a history of conflict that has continually caused political borders to be redrawn in the region. The term *Balkanization* has come to be applied to any region that divides into smaller, autonomous units.
4. When the region's economies were heavily dependent on agriculture, most people lived in rural areas. When the communist era brought industry to the region, urbanization increased as more people sought jobs in the industrial cities. The region's entire population declined after ethnic and religious conflict led to wars for political control, prompting many to emigrate in an effort to escape the difficulties.

Lesson 3

5. Countries have attempted reforestation to offset damage done by logging and established national protection for some forests, such as the Białowieza Forest.
6. Industries in the region burn coal for energy and the smoke produced by this process contains chemicals that pollute the air. They react with moisture to form acid rain, which can be carried great distances. Acid precipitation damages not only the areas it directly falls on but also rivers and lakes into which it eventually drains.

Critical Thinking

7. Ethnic cleansing is a result of extreme conflict among ethnicities in which one seeks to advance its own interests by either killing or driving out people of other ethnicities. In the 1990s NATO intervened to stop ethnic cleansing that was being performed by Serbian military and civilians who did not want Bosnian Croats, Bosnian Muslims, and others to be in their country.
8. Ethnicity, population, politics, and economic strengths
9. Because the EU requires members to follow strict environmental laws, countries wishing to join have been incentivized to make progress towards environmental health. The Czech Republic and Hungary now have low-emission zones where extremely polluting vehicles cannot enter. Some Eastern European countries have been able to get investments from Western European countries for technology that will make less of an environmental impact.
10. Paragraphs will vary, but should include that during the Soviet era Southern European economies relied on trade with the Soviet Union, but after they separated a major focus of the region's economy became tourism. Draw factors may include unique scenery and terrain, specifically karst topography, and many national parks.
11. Itineraries will vary, but should include a logical order of destinations with features to be seen at each.

21st Century Skills

12. Germany
13. Germany and Poland share a long border, making trade convenient. Poland also shares a border with the Czech Republic, but the Czech Republic does not have as strong of an economy as Germany does.

Assessment Answers

DBQ Analyzing Primary Sources

14 Exceptionally hot temperatures and dry conditions led to wildfires.

15 It provides real and extreme examples of the effects of exceptional heat and goes on to warn that it will likely only become worse.

Research and Presentation

16 Presentations will vary, but should include at least two issues the plan seeks to resolve, challenges it faces in doing so, and one proposed solution. Maps and images should be used for support. At least one chart, diagram, or graph should also be incorporated.

Applying Map Skills

17 mixed forest (deciduous and coniferous)

18 The Mediterranean connects the region to the Atlantic Ocean. The Main-Danube Canal connects the region to the North Sea.

19 Coal, silver, copper, and zinc are found in Poland. Zinc is located near Warsaw.

College and Career Readiness

20 Summaries will vary, but should include the fund's mission and specific projects it is working on, particularly from its offices in Bulgaria, Hungary, Latvia, Poland, and Romania. Activities may include river cleanup, illegal logging restriction efforts, overfishing control, and habitat preservation.

Exploring the Essential Question

21 Maps will vary, but should depict and label the chosen country's major physical features. Paragraphs should explain the relationship between the country's physical features and human systems in place there.

Writing About Geography

22 Narratives will vary, but should be logical and strongly supported by information from the chapter. Descriptions should convey difficulties to travel presented by the rugged, mountainous landscape.

CHAPTER 13 Assessment 

Directions: On a separate sheet of paper, answer the questions below. Make sure you read carefully and answer all parts of the questions.

DBQ Analyzing Primary Sources

Use the document to answer the following questions.

In 2007 Europe experienced exceptionally hot temperatures during the summer.

PRIMARY SOURCE

"Up to 500 people are estimated to have died across Hungary last week, partly due to a heat wave gripping central and southeast Europe. . . .

Record-breaking high temperatures also killed 12 Romanians, one man in Macedonia and another man on the island of Corfu . . . while firefighters, soldiers and volunteers battled wildfires across a tinderbox southeastern Europe. . . .

'Extreme events such as we have seen in recent weeks herald the specter of climate change and it would be irresponsible to imagine that they won't become more frequent,' Nick Reeves, executive director of The Chartered Institution of Water and Environmental Management, a scientific group, said."

—"Deadly Heat Wave Grips Europe," CNN.com: Reuters (Budapest), July 25, 2007

14 ***Speculating*** What do you think spurred the wildfires?

15 ***Interpreting*** How does the quote effectively communicate the impact of global warming on Eastern Europe? RH.9–10.1

Research and Presentation

16 ***Problem Solving*** Based on information you have gathered, create a multimedia presentation to inform others of the main issues covered by the Baltic Sea Action Plan and the specific challenges it faces. Within your presentation, provide at least one solution to help address at least one of the challenges. For the presentation, include maps and images of places, as well as charts, diagrams, or graphs. WHST.9–10.6; WHST.9–10.7

Applying Map Skills

Use your Unit 4 Atlas to answer the following questions.

17 ***Physical Systems*** What type of vegetation is most dominant in Eastern Europe?

18 ***The World in Spatial Terms*** Use your mental map of the region to list the bodies of water that connect Eastern Europe to the Atlantic Ocean and the North Sea.

19 ***Environment and Society*** Which types of natural resources can be found in Poland? Which type is most abundant near Warsaw?

College and Career Readiness

20 ***Comparing and Contrasting*** You are working for the World Wildlife Fund and have been asked to create a two-page summary of its mission and its activity in Eastern Europe. The purpose of the summary is to inspire college students in Eastern Europe to support the fund's efforts. Use Internet sources to gather information and write this summary, making the summary engaging and exciting for the college students who make up its intended audience. WHST.9–10.2; WHST.9–10.4

Exploring the Essential Question

21 ***Drawing Conclusions*** Draw a map of one country that has been discussed in this chapter. Using the map from the book, label the physical features that exist in the country, such as lakes, mountains, and rivers. Then, using the information you have drawn, write a paragraph describing how geographic features and human systems are related. WHST.9–10.3

Writing About Geography

22 ***Narrative*** Based on details in the chapter, write a one-page narrative to describe the landscape and your experience as you take an imaginary hike across the Balkan Peninsula. Make certain the descriptive details within your narrative make sense within the context of the geography of the Balkan Peninsula. WHST.9–10.3

Need Extra Help?

If You've Missed Question	14	15	16	17	18	19	20	21	22
Go to page	332	332	329	244	242	245	329	314	314

332

networks Online Teaching Options

WORKSHEET

Chapter Test and Lesson Quizzes

Assessing Have students complete the Chapter Test and Lesson Quizzes to assess student understanding throughout the chapter. These assessment tools offer chapter and lesson evaluation through a variety of question formats, including document-based questions.

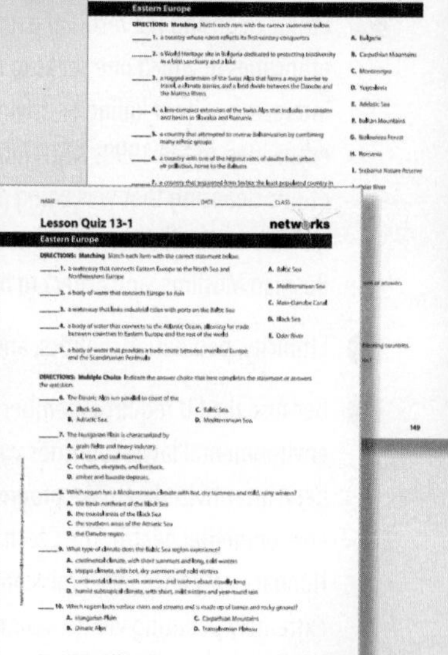

CHAPTER 14

The Russian Core Planner

UNDERSTANDING BY DESIGN®

Enduring Understandings

- *Geographers organize Earth into regions that share common characteristics.*

Essential Question

- *How do physical systems and human systems shape a place?*

Predictable Misunderstandings

Students may think:

- *Russia is largely barren and cold with few natural resources. Explain that Russia covers more area than any other country in the world. It is rich in natural resources and is a large-scale exporter of fuels such as oil and natural gas.*
- *Russia is still a communist country. Explain that Russia is no longer a communist state, but a federal legal state with a republican form of government. It has legislative, executive, and judicial powers as well as a president and prime minister and has converted from a command to a market economy.*

Assessment Evidence

Performance Tasks:

- *Hands-On Chapter Project*

Other Evidence:

- *Guided Reading Activities*
- *Vocabulary Activities*
- *Lesson Quizzes*
- *Chapter Tests, Forms A and B*

SUGGESTED PACING GUIDE

Introducing the Chapter	½ Day	Global Connections	1 Day
Lesson 1	1 Day	Lesson 3	1 Day
Lesson 2	2 Days	Chapter Wrap-Up and Assessment	½ Day
		TOTAL TIME	**6 Days**

Key for Using the Teacher Edition

SKILL-BASED ACTIVITIES

Types of skill activities found in the Teacher Edition.

* **V Visual Skills** require students to analyze maps, graphs, charts, and photos.

R Reading Skills help students practice reading skills and master vocabulary.

C Critical Thinking Skills help students apply and extend what they have learned.

W Writing Skills provide writing opportunities to help students comprehend the text.

T Technology Skills require students to use digital tools effectively.

*Letters are followed by a number when there is more than one of the same type of skill on the page.

DIFFERENTIATED INSTRUCTION

All activities are written for the on-level student unless otherwise marked with the leveled labels below.

BL Beyond Level
AL Approaching Level
ELL English Language Learners

All students benefit from activities that utilize different learning styles. Many activities are marked as below when a particular learning style is highlighted.

Intrapersonal	**Naturalist**
Logical/Mathematical	**Kinesthetic**
Visual/Spatial	**Auditory/Musical**
Verbal/Linguistic	**Interpersonal**

National Geography Standards covered in "The Russian Core"

The student knows and understands:

(3) How to analyze the spatial organizations of people, places, and environments on Earth's surface

(4) The physical and human characteristics of places

(7) The physical processes that shape the patterns of Earth's surface

7.3 Physical processes interact over time to shape particular places on Earth's surface

(8) The characteristics and spatial distribution of ecosystems and biomes on Earth's surface

8.3 The distribution and characteristics of biomes change over time.

(9) The characteristics, distribution, and migration of human populations on Earth's surface

9.2 Population distribution and density are a function of historical, environmental, economic, political, and technological factors

(10) The characteristics, distribution, and complexity of Earth's cultural mosaics

10.3 Cultures change through convergence and/or divergence

(11) The patterns and networks of economic interdependence on Earth's surface

11.3 Economic systems are dynamic organizations of interdependent economic activities for production, exchange, distribution, and consumption of goods and services

(14) How human actions modify the physical environment

(15) How physical systems affect human systems

(16) The changes that occur in the meaning, use, distribution, and importance of resources

16.3 Policies and programs that promote the sustainable use and management of resources impact people and the environment

(17) How to apply geography to interpret the past

17.1 Geographic contexts (the human and physical characteristics of places and environments) can explain the connections between sequences of historical events

(18) How to apply geography to interpret the present and plan for the future

18.1 Geographic contexts (the human and physical characteristics of places and environments) provide the bases for analyzing current events and making predictions about future issues

CHAPTER OPENER PLANNER

Students will know:

- *the traditional boundary between European Russia and Asian Russia.*
- *the characteristics of the Caucasus, plains areas, and rivers of the Russian Core.*
- *the causes and effects of the Russian Revolution and the impacts of the Soviet era.*
- *the ethnic influences on population and culture in the Russian Core.*
- *how human activities in the past continue to affect the environment.*
- *the ways in which environmental issues are being addressed.*

Students will be able to:

- ***identify*** *the boundary between European Russia and Asian Russia.*
- ***describe*** *characteristics of the Caucasus region, plains areas, and rivers.*
- ***discuss*** *the causes and effects of the Russian Revolution and effects of the Soviet era.*
- ***describe*** *influences on population and culture.*
- ***analyze*** *the residual effects of human activities on the environment.*
- ***describe*** *conflict between environmental interests and economic interests.*

UNDERSTANDING BY DESIGN®

☑ Print Teaching Options

V Visual Skills

☐ **p. 334** Students interpret how an image represents Russia's population problems. BL Logical/Mathematical

R Reading Skills

☐ **p. 335** Students discuss the population graph.

W Writing Skills

☐ **p. 335** Students summarize the causes of the declining Russian population and efforts to solve the crisis.

C Critical Thinking Skills

☐ **p. 334** Students discuss advantages of a growing population and disadvantages of a shrinking population.

T Technology Skills

☐ **p. 334** Students research population patterns in countries other than Russia and make a chart to compare changes in Russia to another country. Visual/Spatial

☑ Online Teaching Options

V Visual Skills

MAP **Interactive Regional Atlas**—Students use the interactive regional atlas to understand the physical and human geography of the Russian Core.

TIME LINE **Soviet Era of the Russian Core**—Students use the interactive time line to learn more about the region's human geography.

☑ Printable Digital Worksheets

WORKSHEET **Assessing Background Knowledge**—Determine the level of prior knowledge students have about the Russian Core.

WORKSHEET **Chapter Summaries**—Students review the main idea of each lesson of the chapter content.

Project-Based Learning 

Hands-On

Poetry Writing

Students will write two poems that bring together information from all lessons about physical and human geography in the Russian Core but reflect different viewpoints or eras in the history of the region. Their poems may focus on the religion, culture, cities, or historical event of Russia, Ukraine, or Belarus. Students will share their poems with the class, and then all of the poems will be combined into a poetry booklet or binder.

Digital Hands-On

Create Online Projects

Find an additional activity online that incorporates technology for this project. Visit the EdTech Teacher Web sites for more links, tutorials, and other resources.

Print Resources

ANCILLARY RESOURCES

This ancillary is available for every chapter and lesson.

- **Chapter Tests and Lesson Quizzes**

PRINTABLE DIGITAL WORKSHEETS

These printable digital worksheets are available for every chapter and lesson.

- **Assessing Background Knowledge**
- **Chapter Summaries**
- **Guided Reading Activities**
- **Hands-On Chapter Projects**
- **Quizzes and Tests**
- **Reading Essentials and Study Guide** AL
- **Reteaching Activities**
- **Video Activities**
- **Vocabulary**

More Media Resources

SUGGESTED VIDEOS 

- **Russia** *New Dimension Media* (30 min.)
- **The World Atlas Russia and Asia Center** (40 min.)
- **The Russian People—Revolution and Evolution 1988** (41 min.)

SUGGESTED READING 

- ***Geology of Russia,*** by Andrei K Khudoley and Anatoly M. Nikishin
- ***Cows, Kin, and Globalization: An Ethnography of Sustainability,*** by Susan Alexandra Crate
- ***A Geography of Russia and Its Neighbors,*** by Mikhail S. Blinnikov, PhD

LESSON **1** PLANNER

PHYSICAL GEOGRAPHY OF THE RUSSIAN CORE

Students will know:

- *what marks the traditional boundary between European Russia and Asian Russia.*
- *why the Caucasus region is attractive to human settlement.*
- *the characteristics of the plains areas of the Russian Core.*
- *the importance of the rivers of the Russian Core.*
- *how the Russian Core's climate and vegetation are affected by the physical environment.*

Students will be able to:

- ***identify*** *the boundary between European Russia and Asian Russia.*
- ***describe*** *characteristics of the Caucasus region and the plains areas.*
- ***analyze*** *the importance of rivers in the region.*
- ***describe*** *how the physical environment affects climate and vegetation in the region.*

UNDERSTANDING BY DESIGN®

☑ Print Teaching Options

V Visual Skills

- ☐ **p. 337** Students identify and observe the expanse of the Ural Mountains compared to the Caucasus Mountains. AL Visual/Spatial
- ☐ **p. 338** Students study the visual about the Volga River Basin. BL Visual/Spatial

R Reading Skills

- ☐ **p. 338** Students consider associations that go with the term *mother*. Verbal/Linguistic, Logical/Mathematical
- ☐ **p. 338** Students review the information about how the waterways of Siberia change form over the course of a year. ELL Interpersonal
- ☐ **p. 339** Students examine the word *permafrost*. ELL Verbal/Linguistic
- ☐ **p. 340** Students review the information in the section "Natural Resources." AL Verbal/Linguistic

C Critical Thinking Skills

- ☐ **p. 336** Students identify features on a map of Russia and discuss advantages and disadvantages regarding trade over such a large area.
- ☐ **p. 336** Students create a graphic organizer to compare and contrast the Ural and Caucasus Mountains. BL Verbal/Linguistic

W Writing Skills

- ☐ **p. 337** Students write a narrative imagining they are traveling along one of the major waterways in Russia, Ukraine, or Belarus. ELL Verbal/Linguistic

T Technology Skills

- ☐ **p. 339** Students create a map that depicts the climate regions of the Russian Core. Visual/Spatial
- ☐ **p. 340** Student groups conduct research on a specific country's natural resources and create a thematic map to show the locations of the natural resources. BL Visual/Spatial

☑ Online Teaching Options

R Reading Skills

- GAME **Physical Geography of the Russian Core**—Students play a True/False game to review physical geography of the Russian Core. ELL Verbal/Linguistic
- INTERACTIVE WHITEBOARD ACTIVITY **Volga River Cities**—Students connect the information about the cities that lie on the Volga River to their corresponding locations, and then organize the information about the cities in a chart.

C Critical Thinking Skills

- INTERACTIVE BELLRINGER **The Volga River Basin**—Students discuss Russia's social and economic development. AL Interpersonal, Verbal/Linguistic
- INTERACTIVE GRAPH **Russia's Oil Reserves: A World Comparison**—Students discuss Russia's oil reserves and how they affect Russia's political influence. BL Logical/Mathematical
- VIDEO **Lake Baikal**—Students use the video to discuss the importance of protecting ecosystems and freshwater supplies. BL Naturalist, Verbal/Linguistic

☑ Printable Digital Worksheets

R Reading Skills

- WORKSHEET **Guided Reading Activity**—Students use the Guided Reading Activity worksheets to review their comprehension of the content.

C Critical Thinking Skills

- WORKSHEET **Video Activity**—Students answer questions related to a topic in the chapter content after they have viewed a lesson video.

HUMAN GEOGRAPHY OF THE RUSSIAN CORE

Students will know:
- *the causes and effects of the Russian Revolution.*
- *the impact of the Soviet era.*
- *how new ideas about political and economic systems led to changes in the Russian Core.*
- *the ethnic influences on population and culture in the Russian Core.*

Students will be able to:
- ***discuss** the causes and effects of the Russian Revolution.*
- ***analyze** how the Soviet era has impacted life in the region.*
- ***analyze** changes in political and economic systems in the Russian Core.*
- ***describe** influences on population and culture.*

UNDERSTANDING BY DESIGN®

☑ Print Teaching Options

V Visual Skills
- ☐ **p. 342** Students review the time line and write summaries. Visual/Spatial, Interpersonal
- ☐ **p. 344** Students examine the graphs about ethnic composition of the Russian Core. AL Visual/Spatial

R Reading Skills
- ☐ **p. 345** Students review information about the status of women and discuss how it can be explained as a combination of the past and present.
- ☐ **p. 346** Students discuss the graph about GDP per capita in the Russian Core. AL Visual/Spatial
- ☐ **p. 347** Students discuss the interdependent relationship between Russia and Ukraine. AL Logical/Mathematical

C Critical Thinking Skills
- ☐ **p. 342** Students review how and why Russian rulers expanded their territories. AL Logical/Mathematical
- ☐ **p. 342** Students review information about the social and economic problems facing the people of Russia before the Russian Revolution. BL Verbal/Linguistic
- ☐ **p. 344** Students discuss why different ethnic groups are demanding independence or self-rule now. BL Logical/Mathematical
- ☐ **p. 346** Students compare and contrast the Russian economy under Gorbachev, Yeltsin, and today.

W Writing Skills
- ☐ **p. 346** Students write essays explaining their viewpoints on which changes in policy were most helpful and most harmful. BL Intrapersonal, Verbal/Linguistic
- ☐ **p. 347** Students write a paragraph describing the importance of transportation in the Russian Core.

T Technology Skills
- ☐ **p. 341** Students create time lines to sequence important events in Russia's history. Interpersonal, Visual/Spatial
- ☐ **p. 343** Students research the policy of perestroika.
- ☐ **p. 345** Students research a Russian artist and his or her perspective on Russian life and create a multimedia presentation. BL Visual/Spatial, Auditory/Musical

☑ Online Teaching Options

R Reading Skills
- INTERACTIVE WHITEBOARD ACTIVITY **Governmental Changes in the Russian Core**—Students order historical events and government changes that impacted the Russian Core from the 1920s to the 1990s on a time line.
- VIDEO **The Beginning of Communist Russia**—Students use information presented in the video to understand the rise and fall of Communist Russia. Verbal/Linguistic

C Critical Thinking Skills
- INTERACTIVE BELLRINGER **GDP Per Capita in the Russian Core**—Students analyze data in the graph about how the economy of the Russian Core has changed since 1991. AL Interpersonal, Visual/Spatial
- INTERACTIVE MAP **Russian Revolution and Civil War, 1917–1922**—Students use the map to explore the dynamics of the Russian Revolution. ELL Visual/Spatial, Interpersonal
- INTERACTIVE MAP **Breakup of the Soviet Union, 1991**—Students use the map to examine the statement "Belarusian history is a study of regional conflicts and territorial claims by neighbors to the east and west." AL Verbal/Linguistic
- INTERACTIVE GRAPHS **Ethnic Composition of the Russian Core**—Students discuss the diversity of people in Russia and the advantages and disadvantages of diversity. BL Interpersonal, Logical/Mathematical

☑ Printable Digital Worksheets

R Reading Skills
- WORKSHEET **Guided Reading Activity**—Students use Guided Reading Activity worksheets to review their comprehension of the content.
- WORKSHEET **Reading Essentials and Study Guide**—Students complete the study guide and answer Reading Progress Check and vocabulary questions. AL

C Critical Thinking Skills
- WORKSHEET **Video Activity**—Students answer questions related to a topic in the chapter content after they have viewed a lesson video.

LESSON 3 PLANNER

PEOPLE AND THEIR ENVIRONMENT: THE RUSSIAN CORE

Students will know:

- *how human activities in the past continue to affect the environment in the Russian Core today.*
- *examples of conflict over economic development and environmental protection.*
- *the ways in which environmental issues are being addressed in the Russian Core.*

Students will be able to:

- ***analyze** the residual effects of human activities on the environment in the Russian Core..*
- ***describe** conflict between environmental interests and economic interests.*
- ***identify** ways people and governments are addressing environmental issues.*

UNDERSTANDING BY DESIGN®

☑ Print Teaching Options

V Visual Skills

- ☐ **p. 351** Students create a graphic organizer to record cause-and-effect relationships that explain how Russia's environment has become damaged. AL Visual/Spatial
- ☐ **p. 352** Students discuss the map of the Chernobyl disaster. BL Visual/Spatial

R Reading Skills

- ☐ **p. 350** Students discuss environmental issues and solutions.
- ☐ **p. 350** Students discuss the word *irreversible.* ELL Verbal/Linguistic
- ☐ **p. 353** Students use context clues to define *boreal.* ELL Verbal/Linguistic
- ☐ **p. 354** Students review the proposed mining operation in Kamchatka. Logical/Mathematical

C Critical Thinking Skills

- ☐ **p. 350** Students summarize the main points in the conflict of interest between those for and against Arctic drilling. AL Logical/Mathematical
- ☐ **p. 351** Students study the map of where industrial pollution is found in the Russian Core. AL Visual/Spatial, Logical/Mathematical

W Writing Skills

- ☐ **p. 352** Students research and write an informative essay describing the benefits and risks of relying on nuclear technology. AL Verbal/Linguistic
- ☐ **p. 353** Students research and write an essay about an endangered resource, using facts and details to describe the environmental situation. BL Intrapersonal, Verbal/Linguistic
- ☐ **p. 354** Students write a few paragraphs about an environmental issue in the Russian Core. BL Verbal/Linguistic

T Technology Skills

- ☐ **p. 353** Students create a presentation about the new business prospects raised by the melting of Arctic ice and the potential pollution that could be caused by these businesses. BL Auditory/Musical, Visual/Spatial

☑ Online Teaching Options

V Visual Skills

- INTERACTIVE MAP **Environmental Issues in the Russian Core**—Students explore the effects of human impact to the environment during the Soviet-era industrialization. Verbal/Linguistic, Visual/Spatial

R Reading Skills

- VIDEO **Russian Forest Under Threat**—Students use the video about boreal forests to discuss environmental issues in Russia. AL Interpersonal, Verbal/Linguistic
- INTERACTIVE WHITEBOARD ACTIVITY **Acid Rain and Water Pollution**—Students identify the cause-and-effect hierarchy of factors pertaining to acid rain and water pollution in the Russian Core. Verbal/Linguistic

C Critical Thinking Skills

- INTERACTIVE BELLRINGER **Extent/Reach of Chernobyl Disaster**—Students discuss the impact of nuclear reactor accidents on the environment. Verbal/Linguistic, Visual/Spatial
- GRAPH **The Nuclear Arms Race**—Students use the graph to discuss the nuclear arms race and the dynamics and ethics of the Cold War. BL Interpersonal

☑ Printable Digital Worksheets

R Reading Skills

- WORKSHEET **Guided Reading Activity**—Students use Guided Reading Activity worksheets to review their comprehension of the content.
- WORKSHEET **Reading Essentials and Study Guide**—Students complete the study guide and answer Reading Progress Check and vocabulary questions. AL
- WORKSHEET **Vocabulary Activity**—Students review the chapter content and academic vocabulary words.
- WORKSHEET **Chapter Summary**—Students review the main ideas of the chapter content.

C Critical Thinking Skills

- WORKSHEET **Video Activity**—Students answer questions based on a lesson video.
- WORKSHEET **Reteaching Activity**—Students use this activity worksheet to review and reteach chapter content and vocabulary. This worksheet can be used with struggling students who need additional help with difficult content concepts.

INTERVENTION AND REMEDIATION STRATEGIES

LESSON 1 Physical Geography of the Russian Core

Reading and Comprehension

Have students work with a partner to create an outline of the lesson that highlights key facts related to landforms, water systems, climates, biomes, and resources of the Russian Core. To ensure comprehension of the topics, have partners create a slide show using presentation software that explains a topic or process. For example, students might explain how lowlands, plains, and plateaus are related to human activities such as transportation and agriculture. Encourage students to incorporate content vocabulary terms in their presentations. Have students present their slide shows to the class, allowing time for groups to conduct a question-and-answer session in which students from each group answer questions about their topic.

Text Evidence

Organize students into small groups and assign each group one of the countries in the Russian Core. Have each group create a graphic organizer, like the chart on the first page of the lesson, to organize information about the country. Encourage students to include content vocabulary in their charts. Then have groups present their graphic organizers to the class, describing key facts about the physical geography of their assigned country. After each group has presented its visual to the class, guide a class discussion about how the Russian Core benefits from natural resources despite harsh winters.

LESSON 2 Human Geography of the Russian Core

Reading and Comprehension

Have student pairs choose two of the lesson's content vocabulary words. Tell students to work with their partner to write each word in a sentence using both words correctly. Then have pairs play a "Pictionary" style guessing game in which their partner draws clues to describe a content vocabulary term for their partner to guess. For example, students might draw a throne or a crown to represent the term *czar.* After students have finished guessing each of the terms, have partners compete against other pairs to see who can guess the most terms correctly in a certain amount of time. As a "bonus" or tiebreaker question, have each team try to give clues and guess one of the academic vocabulary terms.

Text Evidence

Have students review the lesson to identify key concepts and events. Encourage them to identify cause-and-effect relationships as they read. Remind students that looking for signal words can help them organize and remember historical events. Have students jot down cause-and-effect signal words and phrases they find in the lesson, such as *because of, due to, as a result,* and so on. Then have partners identify a key historical event that occurred either before or after the events shown on the time line in this lesson. Have student pairs share their event with the class, explaining how it helped to shape the history of the Russian Core.

LESSON 3 People and Their Environment: The Russian Core

Reading and Comprehension

Have students work in pairs to review one of the two maps in this lesson. Then discuss as a class the environmental issues facing various regions in the Russian Core, including the extent of the Chernobyl disaster. Tell partners to conduct research about one of the issues discussed in the text to identify the status of the problem and what, if anything, is being done to fix it. Have students present their findings to the class. Encourage students to include visuals, such as graphs and diagrams, with their presentations.

Text Evidence

Tell students to choose one of the following statements from the *It Matters Because* paragraph to identify supporting evidence from the text: 1. *Industrialization and economic progress in the Russian Core have had both positive and negative impacts on the region.* 2. *Russia has to deal with considerable past damage to the environment.* 3. *At the same time, it is working to manage natural resources and encourage economic growth while minimizing further harm.* In addition to identifying evidence from the text, students may conduct online research to identify facts to support their chosen statement.

Online Resources

Leveled Reader

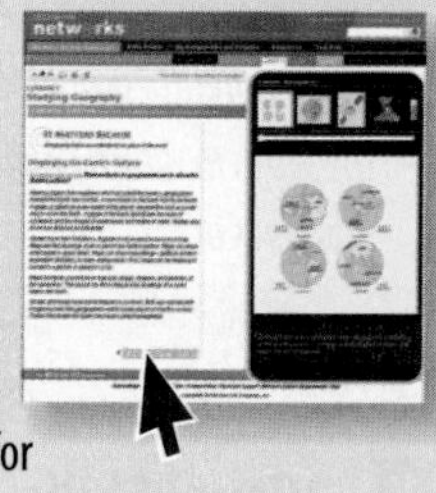

Use this online approaching-level text that corresponds directly to the text in the Student Edition. It also includes additional reading and comprehension support for English Language Learners.

Guided Reading Activities

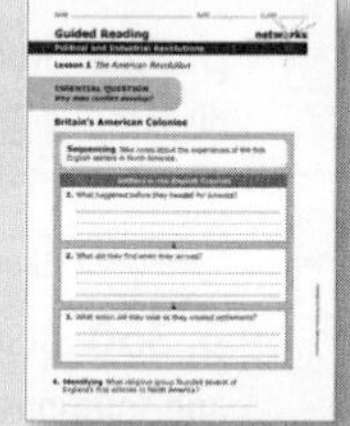

This resource uses guiding questions to help students with comprehension.

Reteaching Activities

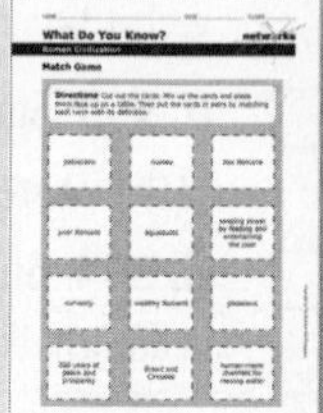

These worksheets provide students with an opportunity for remedial practice and review of vital chapter content.

Reading Essentials and Study Guide

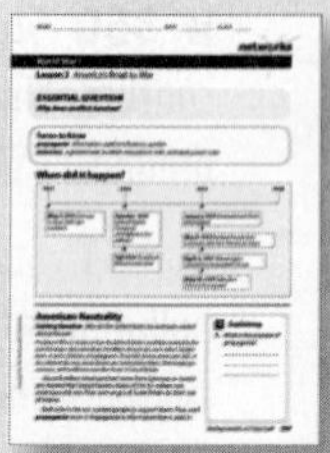

This resource offers writing and reading activities for the approaching-level student.

Self-Check Quizzes

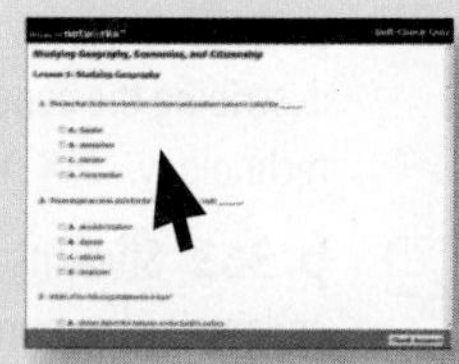

This online assessment tool provides instant feedback for students to check their progress.

Chapter Summaries

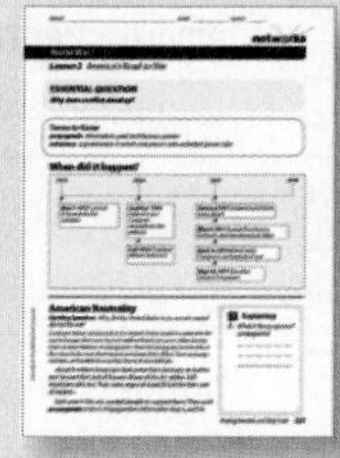

Summaries are provided for each chapter that thoroughly condense core content into manageable chunks.

The Russian Core

ESSENTIAL QUESTION • *How do physical systems and human systems shape a place?*

networks

There's More Online about the Russian Core.

CHAPTER 14

Geography Matters...

People rely on natural resources to provide for their everyday needs. The harsh geography of the Russian Core has stimulated empire building. For centuries, the people of the subregion have sought out waterways that connect to other lands and resources. This subregion has a violent political history, as well as a rich cultural heritage. After the fall of the Communist regime, the Russian Core today is claiming a new identity in the global economy.

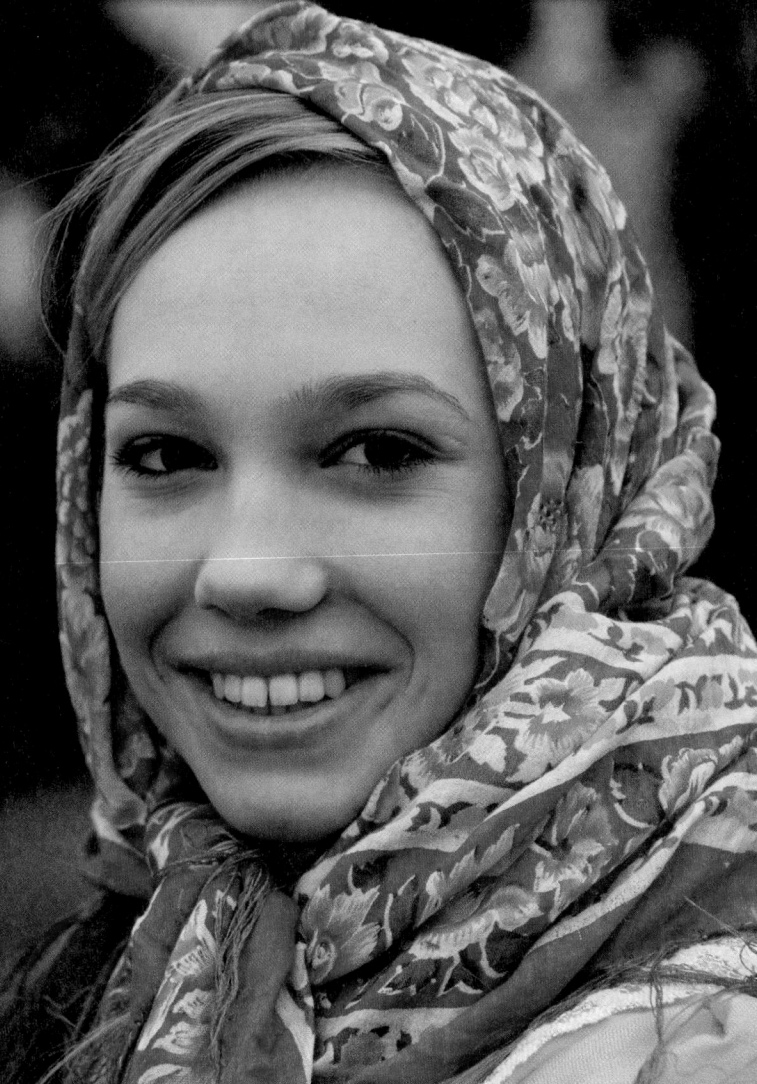

◀ Russian girl wearing a colorful head scarf during a traditional religious festival

Russ Images/Alamy

333

Letter from the Author

Dear Geography Teacher,

The Volga River has been central to Russia's history, economy, and the arts. This grand river cuts through western Russia and touches the lives of millions of people. Water from the Volga River basin is used for municipal, industrial, and agricultural purposes, and dams generate huge amounts of hydroelectric power. Russians flock to the shores of these mammoth lakes for all types of recreational activities. The only downside to a fully developed river basin is that with so much Volga water being used, less and less reaches the Caspian Sea. Astrakhan, formerly a Caspian seaport at the mouth of the Volga River, is now located 52 miles from the edge of a shrinking sea.

Richard G. Boehm

ENGAGE

Activating Prior Knowledge Explain that students will examine how the large size and unique geography of the Russian Core influenced the subregion's settlement. Have groups discuss what they already know about the ways people in the Russian Core have worked to meet their needs and how the physical geography has helped or hindered this effort.

TEACH & ASSESS

Applying Discuss the geography of the Russian Core. **Ask:** **What does it mean to build an empire?** *(Countries build empires when they join different geographic areas together to form one nation.)* **What characteristic of the location of the Russian Core encouraged the people living there to build an empire?** *(Possible answer: Because the geography was so harsh, the people spread out to secure all the resources they needed, such as waterways for transporting people and goods.)*

Making Connections

During the late 1600s, the United States had many seaports. The Russian Empire, ruled by Czar Peter I (Peter the Great), however, lacked good access to trade with Europe. For centuries before Peter's reign, Russia and Sweden had fought over Russian access to the Baltic Sea. In May 1703, Peter's army captured a Swedish fortification built at the point where the Neva River meets Lake Ladoga. Wanting to reform his country and improve its economy by establishing sea trade with Europe, Peter built a new city, St. Petersburg, on this spot and made it the new capital of Russia.

CLOSE & REFLECT

Evaluating Have students think about what can happen when two groups clash over limited resources. Have students discuss how one group of people spreading out to take the land and resources they need can affect the lives of other groups of people living in the surrounding areas.

ePals GlobalCommunity
Where learners connect™

Extend the project-based learning experience globally through our partnership with ePals. EPals allows you to connect with classrooms around the world in a safe online environment for real-life lessons and projects in virtual study groups.

ENGAGE

C Critical Thinking Skills

Making Predictions Have students work with a partner to consider the relationship between a country's population and its economy. Have pairs brainstorm a list of advantages to be gained from a growing population and the negative effects of a decreasing population. Have partners write a few predictions about what problems Russia might be facing because of its shrinking population.

TEACH & ASSESS

T Technology Skills

Researching Have students work in small groups to research the population growth or decline in countries other than Russia during the last two decades. Assign each group a nation to research, such as France, China, Japan, or India. Then have groups work together to make a chart that draws comparisons between the changes in population and the male and female life expectancies in each country. **Visual/Spatial**

V Visual Skills

Interpreting Have students consider the picture at the top of the right column. **Ask:** **How does this picture represent Russia's population problems?** *(The person appears to be a foreign-born worker at an industrial job, indicating that immigrants are needed in the workforce.)* **For what reason is the government offering subsidies and financial initiatives?** *(The government is providing incentives for women to have more children to halt the drop in population.)* **Why is the government battling alcoholism?** *(to improve people's health to reduce the death rate)* **How would you assess the effectiveness of these proposed solutions?** *(Student answers will vary but should address topics such as the economic effects of providing subsidies for women to have more children, the inclusion of foreign workers coming to Russia, and encouraging Russians living abroad to return.)* BL **Logical/Mathematical**

ANSWERS, p. 334

Why Geography Matters

1. Population decline can cause a country to have difficulty maintaining its army, industry, and agricultural production.
2. A decline in birthrate, an increase in mortality rate, and a drop in life expectancy all contributed to a negative population growth rate. Poor nutrition and health care were largely responsible for the drop in life expectancy.
3. They thought that allowing foreigners to enter would lead to a loss of national identity.

Why Geography Matters: **The Russian Core**

Russia's shrinking population

The breakup of the Union of Soviet Socialist Republics (USSR) in 1991 signaled the beginning of a decline in Russia's population. Government officials and demographers (scientists who study population data) expressed deep concern over reduced population size and its threat to the country's society and economy. Leaders hope that improvements in the economic circumstances will help reverse the decline.

What happened to Russia's population after 1991?

When Vladimir Putin became Russia's president and prime minister in 1999, he inherited a demographic crisis with potentially dire outcomes for the country. Population declined by five million between 1992 and 2002 and has continued to decline, dropping from 145.2 million in 2002 to 142.9 million in 2011. Life expectancy plummeted to its lowest peacetime level ever from a high of 70.1 years in 1986–1987 to only 59 years for men and 72 years for women in 1992. Demographers voiced concerns about the country's ability to maintain its army, industry, and agricultural production.

1. **Human Systems** What problems can a steep population decline cause for a country? Explain the effects on labor, government services, prosperity, and the environment.

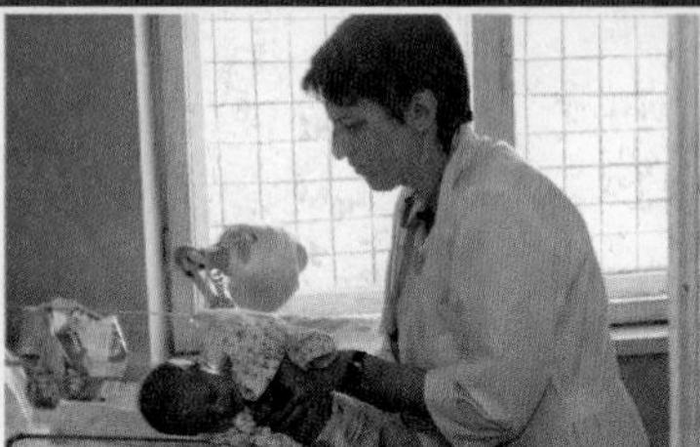

Why did Russia's population decline?

An important factor contributing to Russia's negative population growth rate during the 1990s was a steep decline in the birth (fertility) rate. At the same time, there was an increase in the death (mortality) rate and a sharp drop in life expectancy. In 1991, for the first time in the postwar history of Russia, the number of deaths exceeded that of births. The total population decreased by 30,900 in 1992 and by 307,600 in 1993. The life expectancy decreased largely due to poor nutrition and health care. Poverty, stress, alcoholism, heavy smoking, suicide, diseases such as HIV/AIDS, strict immigration policies, and homicide all made the trend more severe. The trend was especially strong among working-age men.

2. **Human Systems** Why did Russia's population begin to decline after the collapse of the Soviet Union? Summarize the factors contributing to the decline.

What is being done to address the issue?

Russian president Putin directed his government to halt the drop in population, offering subsidies and financial incentives for women to have more children. He has also proposed new initiatives to battle alcoholism and to provide better education and housing opportunities for all Russians. Another proposal is an attempt to use the immigration policy to lure Russians living abroad to return and to attract skilled foreign workers. This last component of Putin's proposal is one that Russian leaders have historically avoided. They feared a loss of national identity if foreigners were allowed to enter Russian society.

3. **Places and Regions** Why have Russian immigration officials historically resisted allowing non-Russians to immigrate?

(l)Vladimir Godnik/Getty Images, (c)Maxim Marmur/AFP/Getty Images, (r)Alexander Petrov/Epsilon/Getty Images News/Getty Images

334

Project-Based Learning

Hands-On

Poetry Writing

Students will write poems that bring together information from all lessons about physical and human geography in the Russian Core, as well as researched topic-specific information. The two poems will reflect different viewpoints or eras in the history of the region. The poems will focus on the countries of Russia, Ukraine, or Belarus. The poems will then be compiled into a booklet or binder titled "Poems about the Russian Core" to be displayed in the classroom or school library.

Digital Hands-On

Create Online Projects

Find an additional activity online that incorporates technology for this project. Visit the EdTech Teacher Web sites for more links, tutorials, and other resources.

CHAPTER 14
Why Geography Matters

THERE'S MORE ONLINE

WATCH a video about Russia's shrinking population • *READ* a quote about Russian population trends

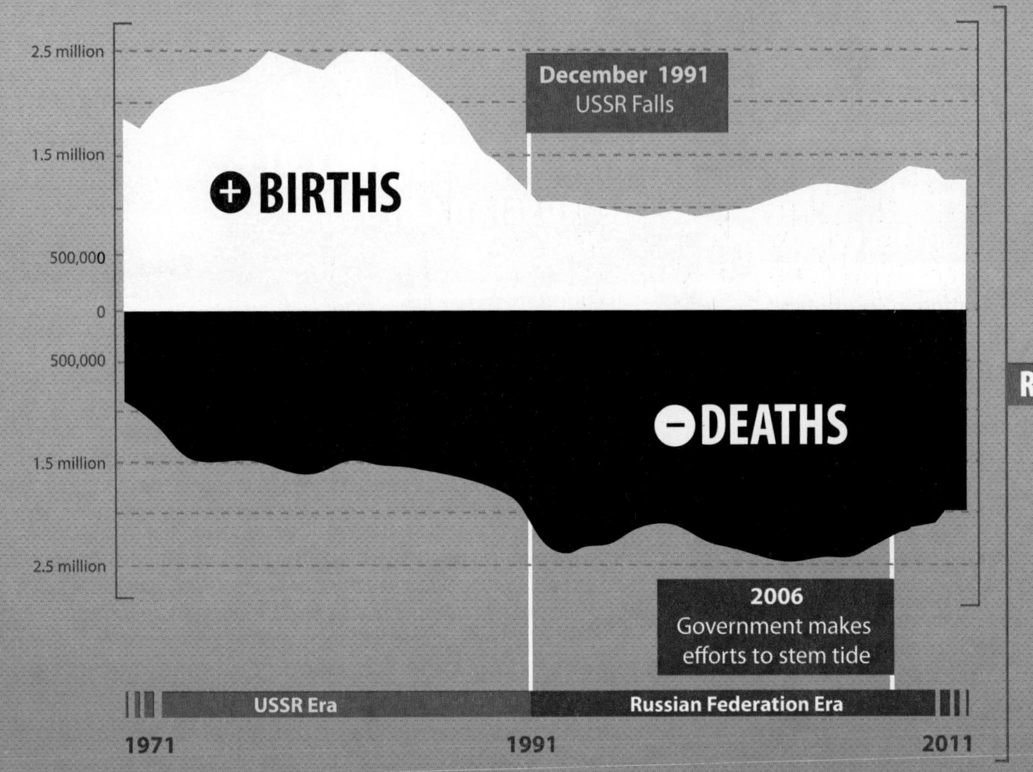

CAUSES OF THE DECLINE

AGING POPULATION
Russians overall are getting older. By 2015 20% will be over age 60.

MOSCOW CALLING
Despite an increase in incentives, Russia has difficulty attracting immigrants.

ALCOHOLISM
Since the fall of the USSR, alcoholism has increased. It killed 98,000 Russians in 2011 alone.

HIV/AIDS
Uncommon in the USSR, HIV boomed after its fall and continues to spread. The number of Russians living with HIV doubled from 2006 to 2011.

BRAIN DRAIN
Due to a lack of employment, many educated Russians leave the country. The vast majority who do are under 35 years old.

FEWER BIRTHS
A low birthrate of 1.61 births per woman and a high infant mortality rate of 7.2 deaths per 1,000 live births contribute to Russia's shrinking natural increase.

Tim E White/Photolibrary/Getty Images

R Reading Skills

Reading Graphs As a class, discuss each label to ensure that students know how to read the graph and understand what it is describing. Review as needed the meaning of the numbers on the X-axis and Y-axis. *(X-axis: the rising numbers measure the growth of population, the declining numbers measure the decrease of population: Y-axis shows how the population has changed over time from 1971 to 1991 to 2011)* **How might you evaluate the efforts made by the government in 2006?** *(The graph shows a slight increase in the population increase and a slight decrease in the population decrease, particularly since 2011, so the government efforts seem to be having a small but positive effect on halting the problem of a shrinking population in Russia.)* **AL Visual/Spatial, Logical/Mathematical**

W Writing Skills

Informative/Explanatory Have students write a short essay summarizing the causes of the declining Russian population and what the government is doing to solve the crisis. The essays should focus on which cause or causes students consider most important. Encourage students to share their essays with another student to compare their evaluations of the situation. **Verbal/Linguistic**

CLOSE & REFLECT

Reaching Conclusions Review how the Russian government is attempting to solve the shrinking population problem. Invite students to evaluate the seriousness of the problem and explain to a partner whether they think the government's reaction has been strong enough or whether the government should be doing more to fix the situation.

DIGITAL WORKSHEET

Assessing Background Knowledge

Activating Prior Knowledge Use this digital worksheet to assess students' prior knowledge about the Russian Core. This worksheet includes activities that will introduce the chapter content to the students and gets them thinking about the concept and topics. Distribute the worksheet to the students and have them complete the worksheets individually. After students have had time to complete the worksheet, lead a class discussion about each of the questions. Invite student volunteers to provide answers for questions before sharing them with the class. **Verbal/Linguistic, Logical/Mathematical**

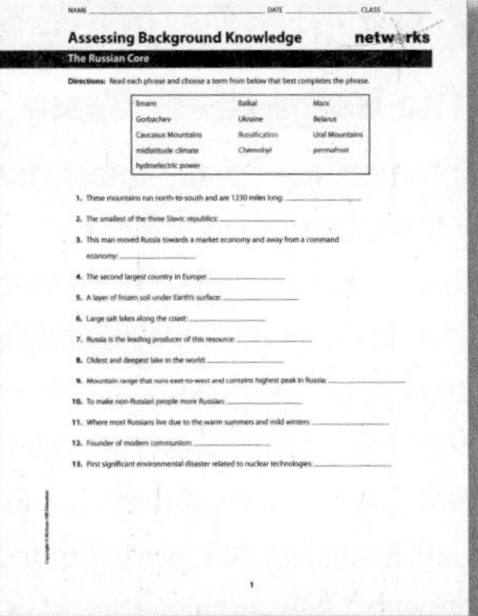
Assessing Background Knowledge
The Russian Core

ENGAGE

C1 Critical Thinking Skills

Considering Advantages and Disadvantages Display a physical map of the Russian Core found in the online Teacher Lesson Center and challenge students to identify features such as major waterways, mountain ranges, and other landforms. Have students note the overall size of the Russian Core. Lead a discussion on the advantages and disadvantages of living in such a large area when trade and travel to other areas may be involved.

TEACH & ASSESS

C2 Critical Thinking Skills

Comparing and Contrasting Have students list the similarities and differences of the Ural Mountains and the Caucasus Mountains. Suggest that they design a graphic organizer to arrange the information. **Ask:** What is one similarity between these two mountain ranges? *(Possible answer: Both form a natural barrier.)* How do these mountain ranges differ? *(Possible answers: The Ural Mountains run north to south and separate European Russia from Siberian Russia, while the Caucasus Mountains run east to west and separate Russia from the countries to the south such as Georgia, Azerbaijan, and Armenia; the Ural Mountains help the economy by being rich in natural resources such as iron ore and mineral fuels, while the Caucasus Mountains help the economy through tourism.)*
BL Verbal/Linguistic

networks

There's More Online!

- **IMAGE** Russia's Shipping Industry
- **IMAGE** The Ural Mountains
- **INFOGRAPHIC** The Volga River Basin—Heart of Russia
- **INTERACTIVE SELF-CHECK QUIZ**
- **VIDEO** Physical Geography of the Russian Core

RUSSIA
MOSCOW
KAZAN
VOLGOGRAD
SAMARA

LESSON 1
Physical Geography of the Russian Core

Reading **HELP**DESK

Academic Vocabulary (Tier Two Words)
- **corresponding**
- **challenge**

Content Vocabulary (Tier Three Words)
- **chernozem**
- **permafrost**
- **continentality**

TAKING NOTES: ***Key Ideas and Details***

PARAPHRASING Use a chart like the one below to take notes about the landforms, waterways, climates, biomes, and resources of the Russian Core.

Physical Geography of the Russian Core		
Landforms	Water Systems	Climate, Biomes, and Resources

ESSENTIAL QUESTION • *How do physical systems and human systems shape a place?*

IT MATTERS BECAUSE

C1 *The lowlands, plains, and plateaus of the Russian Core—Russia, Ukraine, and Belarus—helped shape human activity for centuries. In some cases, the harsh climate of the subregion made it a forbidding environment for people to settle and live in. Some were drawn to the few mountainous areas found in this region for their beauty and abundant natural resources despite difficult winters. Certainly the diverse topography of the Russian Core makes for some of the most beautiful geography in the world.*

Landforms

GUIDING QUESTION *How do interconnected mountain ranges and plains shape human activities in the Russian Core?*

C2 Russia has two notable mountain ranges, the Ural Mountains and the Caucasus Mountains. The other distinct landforms that dominate Russia are plains, hills, and plateaus. The Ural Mountains form a natural barrier between European Russia and Siberian Russia. Rich in iron ore and mineral fuels, they run in a north-to-south direction and span 1,230 miles (2,000 km) from the Arctic Ocean almost to the Caspian Sea. The Caucasus Mountains run east to west along the southwestern portion of the country, forming a natural barrier between Russia and countries to the south. The highest peak of the Caucasus Mountains is Mount Elbrus, which soars to 18,510 feet (5,642 m). It is the highest mountain in Russia and Europe. Mount Elbrus is also a popular tourist destination for skiing and mountain climbing.

To the west of the Ural Mountains is the Northern European Plain. The southern part of the plain has navigable waterways and rich, black soil called **chernozem** that supports agriculture. As a result, the majority of Russia's population lives here. This vast plain is an extension of the plain that begins in France and stretches across Northwestern Europe. This eastern part of the plain is sometimes called the Russian Plain

ANSWERS, p. 336

TAKING NOTES: Landforms—Ural Mountains, Caucasus Mountains, Northern European Plain, West Siberian Plain, other vast plains, hills, and plateaus, Isthmus of Perekop, swamps, and wetlands; **Water Systems**—major rivers include the Volga River, Dnieper River, Southern Bug River, Dniester River; there are freshwater lakes, saltwater lakes, and limans; Lake Baikal in Siberia is the oldest lake in the world; **Climate, Biomes, and Resources**—high latitudinal location yields cold, snowy winters for most of the region; the tundra has weeks of continuous darkness and of continuous light, and only small plants can grow; subarctic climate has only four months of temperatures over 50°F (10°C), but boreal forests thrive; midlatitude climates have milder winters and summers and deciduous forests; steppe climate produces open grasslands; southern Ukraine has a humid subtropical climate; Belarus has a cool continental climate.

networks *Online Teaching Options*

INTERACTIVE BELLRINGER

The Volga River Basin

Interpreting Use the introductory text and the infographic to identify the importance of the Volga River to the economic and social development of Russia. Have students form small groups and discuss their prior knowledge of Russia's economic and social development. Then have them discuss each question. Ask each group to write agreed-upon answers to the questions. Then in a class discussion, have each group share its answers. AL Interpersonal, Verbal/Linguistic

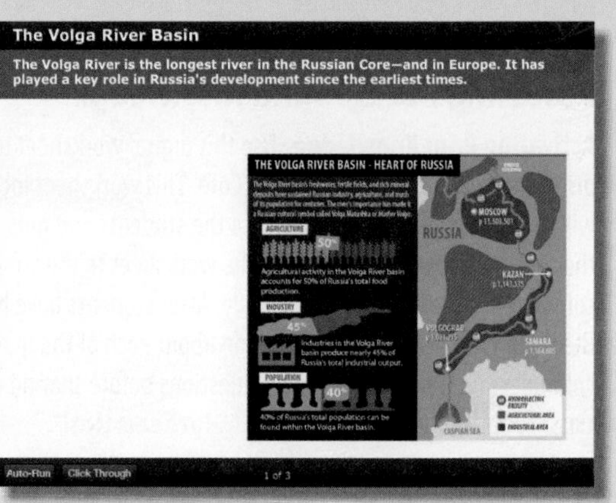
The Volga River Basin
The Volga River is the longest river in the Russian Core—and in Europe. It has played a key role in Russia's development since the earliest times.
THE VOLGA RIVER BASIN · HEART OF RUSSIA
RUSSIA
MOSCOW
KAZAN
SAMARA
Auto-Run
Click Through
1 of 3

because as it reaches the Russian Core it broadens and becomes very expansive.

East of the Ural Mountains and extending to the Pacific Ocean are the vast stretches of plains and plateaus that make up much of Siberia. The West Siberian Plain covers about one-third of Siberia and is one of the largest low-lying flatlands in the world. It is known for its harsh continental climate and some of the world's largest swamps and wetlands.

Ukraine is the second-largest country in Europe, occupying the southwest portion of the Russian Plain. Its two main landforms are vast plains and plateaus, with mountains found only in small areas in the west and south, accounting for less than five percent of the country's landmass. In the south, the Isthmus of Perekop connects the Crimean Peninsula to the mainland.

Belarus is the smallest of the three Slavic republics that were once part of the Soviet Union. Belarus is a landlocked country and lies entirely on the Northern European Plain. Glacier scarring accounts for the flat terrain and some 11,000 lakes found in Belarus. There are also numerous swamps and rivers.

The Ural Mountains extend for well over a thousand miles, cutting through many varied landscapes.

Evgeny Prokofyev/Alamy

▲ **CRITICAL THINKING**

1. ***Classifying*** Why are the Ural Mountains considered a natural boundary?
2. ***Speculating*** How might the Ural Mountains have influenced settlement patterns in the areas they span?

V

✓ **READING PROGRESS CHECK**

Naming Which mountains form a natural boundary between European Russia and Siberian Russia?

Water Systems

GUIDING QUESTION *What role do rivers of the Russian Core play in the economic activities of the region?*

The combined waterways of the Russian Core have played important roles in its social and economic development from early times. The rivers and lakes of Russia, Ukraine, and Belarus are key to the subregion's growth, expansion, and success. Included in the water system is the Volga River, one of the world's greatest rivers.

The Volga River and its many tributaries make up the Volga River system. Draining most of western Russia, the Volga travels 2,293 miles (3,690 km), making it the longest river in Europe. It starts in the Valdai Hills west of Moscow and travels across much of southern Russia before emptying into the Caspian Sea. The Volga River system is an important commercial, transportation, and hydroelectric resource for millions of Russians.

In Ukraine, the Dnieper River is the longest in the country, stretching 609 miles (908 km) beginning in the northwestern plains and traversing southeast to drain into the Black Sea. Other major waterways in Ukraine include the Southern Bug, Dniester, and even a small portion of the Danube River. Like the Volga in Russia, the Dnieper provides hydroelectric power and transportation as well as enabling commerce. But the most important function of these rivers collectively is to supply water to Ukrainians. This is done through an intricately constructed series of canals.

W

chernozem rich, black topsoil found in the Northern European Plain, especially in Russia and Ukraine

GAME

Physical Geography of the Russian Core

Monitoring Organize the class into pairs and have the students play this True/False Game to review the physical geography of the Russian Core. After they have completed the game, ask students to rewrite all false statements to make them true statements. Then have students share their statements with their partner to check for accuracy. **ELL** **Verbal/Linguistic**

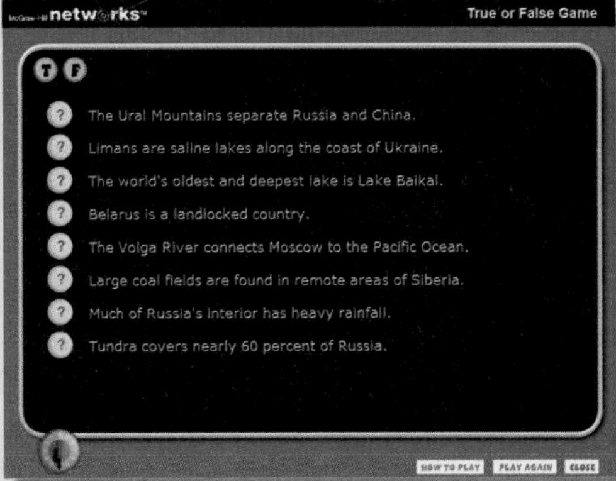

networks
True or False Game
The Ural Mountains separate Russia and China.
Limans are saline lakes along the coast of Ukraine.
The world's oldest and deepest lake is Lake Baikal.
Belarus is a landlocked country.
The Volga River connects Moscow to the Pacific Ocean.
Large coal fields are found in remote areas of Siberia.
Much of Russia's interior has heavy rainfall.
Tundra covers nearly 60 percent of Russia.
HOW TO PLAY
PLAY AGAIN
CLOSE

Physical Geography of the Russian Core

V Visual Skills

Locating Display a physical map that shows the geography of the Russian Core. Have students identify and observe the expanse of the Ural Mountains compared to the Caucasus Mountains. **Ask:** **Which mountain range is longer?** *(Ural Mountains)* Have students note the location of each mountain range in relation to Russia, Ukraine, and Belarus. **Ask:** **In which countries are the Caucasus Mountains located?** *(Russia, Georgia, Azerbaijan, and Armenia)* **AL** **Visual/Spatial**

Making Connections

Both the Russian Core and the United States contain large plains. The Great Plains of North America covers an area of about 1,125,000 square miles (2,914,000 square kilometers). As part of the Northern European Plain, the Russian Plain covers about 1,500,000 square miles (3,885,000 square kilometers) and runs from eastern Poland to the Ural Mountains. The Great Plains touch parts of ten states and three Canadian Provinces, and the Russian Plain covers Finland, Russia, Belarus, Ukraine, Latvia, Lithuania, and Estonia. While the land on the Russian Plain rests below 1,500 feet (457 meters) in elevation, the altitude of the Great Plains ranges from 5,000 to 6,000 feet (1,524–1829 meters) at the base of the Rocky Mountains to only a bit above sea level near the Arctic Ocean in the north. Both the Russian Plain and the Great Plains have a continental climate with more rain during the warmer times of the year, which is conducive for agriculture, although growing crops becomes more difficult at the eastern end of the Russian Plain.

W Writing Skills

Narrative Have students imagine that they are traveling along one of the major waterways in Russia, Ukraine, or Belarus. Students should use information from the book or online and print resources to write a journal of their journey along the river or lake. Students should include information about the path that their travels take, using descriptive words and phrases that tell about the sights they see. Encourage students to include drawings or printed images in their narratives. **ELL** **Verbal/Linguistic**

ANSWERS, p. 337

✓ **READING PROGRESS CHECK** The Ural Mountains

CRITICAL THINKING

1. They form a long range that is difficult to traverse. They run north to south from the Arctic Ocean almost to the Caspian Sea, separating European Russia from Siberian Russia.
2. Possible answer: Being difficult to cross, they limited migration.

V Visual Skills

Analyzing Visuals Have students study the visual and consider its parts and the information it is conveying. **Ask:**

- **What do the green and brown icons on the left tell you?** *(They visually represent the percentage of each economic activity and the total population accounted for within the Volga River Basin.)*
- **What generalization can these icons help you make?** *(The Volga River Basin is vital to life in Russia because it supports about half the agricultural activity, industry, and population of the whole country.)*
- **What information does the map on the right display?** *(It shows the location of hydroelectric facilities along the Volga River and the areas of land that are used for agriculture or industrial activities.)*
- **What information do the map labels provide about each city?** *(the name, location, and population of each city)*
- **What does the map help you better understand about the location of economic activities?** *(Possible answer: The hydroelectric facilities are located along the river because they rely on running water to generate power. The industrial areas are located along the river as well, while the areas of agriculture stretch farther out into the country.)* BL **Visual/Spatial**

R1 Reading Skills

Inferring Have students consider the associations that go along with the term *mother* and think of other symbols that use *mother* in their name, such as *Mother Earth or Mother Nature.* **Ask:** **Why might Russians call the Volga River *Mother Volga?*** *(Like a mother who provides life and food to her children, the Volga River supplies Russians with the resources they need to live and to make a living.)* **Verbal/Linguistic, Logical/Mathematical**

R2 Reading Skills

Understanding Relationships Have students work with a partner to review the information about how the waterways of Siberia change form over the course of a year. Then have partners write a series of brief statements explaining the cause-and-effect relationships that power this seasonal cycle. ELL **Interpersonal**

ANSWERS, p. 338

CRITICAL THINKING

1. Seven hydroelectric power facilities located along the Volga River harness its energy and make vital contributions to Russia's power supply.
2. Half of Russia's food supply and nearly half of its industrial output is produced in the river's basin. A large percentage of the population lives in the basin. The river connects Moscow to the Caspian Sea.

V

THE VOLGA RIVER BASIN—Heart of Russia
The Volga River basin's freshwater, fertile fields, and rich mineral deposits have sustained Russian industry, agriculture, and much of its population for centuries. The river's importance has made it a Russian cultural symbol called Volga Matushka or Mother Volga.
AGRICULTURE
50%
Agricultural activity in the Volga River basin accounts for 50% of Russia's total food production.
INDUSTRY
45%
Industries in the Volga River basin produce nearly 45% of Russia's total industrial output.
POPULATION
40%
40% of Russia's total population can be found within the Volga River basin.
RYBINSK RESERVOIR
MOSCOW
p 11,503,501
RUSSIA
KAZAN
p 1,143,535
VOLGOGRAD
p 1,021,215
SAMARA
p 1,164,685
CASPIAN SEA
HYDROELECTRIC FACILITY
AGRICULTURAL AREA
INDUSTRIAL AREA

R1 Western Russia's Volga River connects Moscow to the Caspian Sea. Called *Matushka Volga*, or "Mother Volga," the river is vital to Russia.

▲ **CRITICAL THINKING**

1. ***Assessing*** Based on the infographic, describe the importance of the Volga River to Russia in regard to hydropower generation.
2. ***Identifying Central Issues*** Why is the Volga River called *Mother Volga?* Provide at least two reasons.

There are few freshwater lakes across Ukraine. Small saltwater lakes can be found in the Black Sea Lowland and Crimea, while *limans*, or large saline lakes, are found along the coast. In recent years Ukraine has created some artificial lakes and reservoirs.

Belarus was once an important passage route for inland navigation between the Baltic Sea and the Black Sea. Each with its own tributaries, the largest rivers in the country include the Dnieper River, Berezina River, Pripyat' River, Neman River, Bug River, and Western Dvina. Narach is the country's largest lake, measuring 31 square miles (79.6 sq. km).

R2 Waterways are also a prominent feature of Siberia. Rivers such as the Ob', Irtysh, Yenisey, and Lena begin in the south of Siberia and flow northward,

networks Online Teaching Options

GRAPH

Russia's Oil Reserves: A World Comparison

Examining Information After students have had the opportunity to study "The Volga River Basin" infographic in the text, display this interactive graph to further discuss Russia's natural resources. Explain that Russia's oil reserves play a role in the country's economy, just as agriculture, mineral deposits, and industry influence the economy. Ask students to calculate what percentage of the global oil supply comes from Russia. Based on this, ask students whether Russia has a lot of political influence, some influence, or little influence over oil prices. Have students examine Russia's world economic standing and whether Russia's oil reserves affects its world standing. Lead a class discussion on this topic. BL **Logical/Mathematical**

PROVED OIL RESERVES BY COUNTRY 2010*

Country	Billions of barrels
Saudi Arabia	264.6
Canada	175.2
Iran	137.6
Iraq	115.0
Kuwait	104.0
U.A.E.	97.8
Venezuela	97.7
Russia	74.2
Libya	47.0
Nigeria	37.5
China	20.3
U.S.	19.1

0 20 40 60 80 100 120 140
BILLIONS OF BARRELS

*Proved reserves are estimated with reasonable certainty to be recoverable with present technology and prices.

Source: CIA *The World Factbook*

emptying into the Arctic Ocean. Ice in the Arctic Ocean blocks the rivers from reaching the ocean for much of the year. This is problematic in the springtime when the ice blockage prevents the surging rivers from reaching the ocean. Instead, the water floods out across the low-lying plains, causing extensive areas of swamps and floodlands.

One of the most renowned Siberian lakes is Lake Baikal. Located in southeast Russia, Lake Baikal is the oldest lake in the world (25 million years). It is also the deepest at 5,715 feet (1,742 m). It holds one-fifth of all unfrozen freshwater found on the planet. Known as the "Galapagos of Russia" because of its age and isolation, Lake Baikal has many unusual freshwater marine species, which are of exceptional value to scientists who study how species evolve.

☑ READING PROGRESS CHECK

Identifying Which river provides western Russia with hydroelectric power?

Climate, Biomes, and Resources

GUIDING QUESTION *What are the general climate conditions in much of the Russian Core?*

Russia's vast expanse of land extends from east to west, and all of the country lies in the same high latitude range. The result is that the dominant characteristic of the subregion is cold, snowy winters. There is, however, variation in how cold and how long the winters last, and the warmth and length of the summers. These variations in climate have shaped settlement patterns from the earliest times.

Climate Regions and Biomes

The tundra occupies the parts of the subregion that are farthest north and covers about 10 percent of Russia. Here, the sky stays dark for many weeks before and after the winter solstice that occurs around December 22 each year. Then, for several weeks during the summer, there is continuous sunlight. Its short growing season and thin, acidic soil lying just above the **permafrost** limit the kinds of plants that can grow there. Only mosses, lichens, algae, and dwarf shrubs thrive in the tundra. R

permafrost a permanently frozen layer of soil beneath the surface of the ground

South of the tundra lies the subarctic climate zone. While not as severe as the tundra climate, this zone only has four months of the year when the temperature rises above 50°F (10°C). The rest of the year is cold. The biome here is boreal forest, or taiga, which consists of broad expanses of coniferous evergreen trees.

Russia's midlatitude climates, found in the western region, are not as severe and have milder winters and warmer summers. Although still relatively cold, these climates are where most Russians live and where much of Russia's agricultural production takes place. The natural biome here is deciduous forest, although much of it has been cleared for agriculture and construction. T

An area between the Black and Caspian Seas north of the Caucasus Mountains and along Russia's border with Kazakhstan make up Russia's steppe climate region. The steppe is a broad, open grassland in which seas of grass stretch to the horizon in every direction. The region's chernozem soil supports the production of wheat, barley, rye, oats, and other crops. Sunflowers, mint, and beans also flourish here.

The southern part of Ukraine lies in a humid continental climate zone where warmer, humid air from the Atlantic Ocean makes the climate milder than farther north. The greatest amount of precipitation falls in the warmer summer season, with the maximum precipitation occurring in late June and July.

Belarus has a humid continental climate moderated by maritime influences from the Atlantic Ocean. Average January temperatures range from the mid-20°sF (about −4°C) in the southwest to about 17°–19° F (about −8°C) in the

VIDEO

Lake Baikal

Explanatory/Informative Use this video about Lake Baikal in southeastern Russia to discuss the importance of protecting ecosystems and freshwater supplies. Encourage students to consider what they know and have learned about freshwater shortages. Tell them that Lake Baikal is the world's oldest and deepest lake, and it contains one-fifth of Earth's unfrozen freshwater, making it a valuable resource for Russia and the world. Then have students write a brief essay explaining the importance of protecting Lake Baikal from environmental disaster. BL **Naturalist, Verbal/Linguistic**

Content Background Knowledge

Lake Baikal Similar to the way the Galápagos Islands isolated species, Lake Baikal in southeastern Siberia has protected its own unique flora and fauna from undue outside influence. The old age of Lake Baikal and the way its surface water regularly cycles through all of the levels of the lake has created an environment where many species that are found only there were able to develop. A rare freshwater seal called a nerpa and a fish that gives birth to live young are two of the more famous life forms that make their home in Lake Baikal. Because the shores of the lake support industries such as mining and paper mills, the Russian government and public are working to set controls that will keep this special area from becoming polluted.

R Reading Skills

Using Word Parts Have students examine the word *permafrost*. **Ask:** **What does the word *permanent* mean?** *("unchanging, without end")* **What root word can you identify in *permafrost*?** *(frost)* **What does the addition of the prefix *perma-* to the word *frost* tell you about the meaning of *permafrost*?** *(that the layer being described as permafrost will always be frozen)* ELL **Verbal/Linguistic**

T Technology Skills

Depicting Have students work in small groups to create a map that depicts the climate regions of the Russian Core. Have groups use information from the text and from online and print resources to compile their maps. Encourage students to use different colors and images to represent higher and lower temperatures, levels of precipitation, and the kinds of vegetation, soil, and landforms in each biome. Invite groups to present their finished maps to the class. **Visual/Spatial**

ANSWERS, p. 339

☑ READING PROGRESS CHECK the Volga River

CHAPTER 14, Lesson 1

Physical Geography of the Russian Core

R Reading Skills

Summarizing Have students review the information found in the section *Natural Resources*. **Ask: Why is Russia's physical geography both a blessing and a curse?** *(Blessing because the land is filled with many natural resources but a curse because these natural resources are often in remote, difficult to access, climatically unfavorable areas.)* AL **Verbal/Linguistic**

T Technology Skills

Comparing and Contrasting Organize students into three groups, assigning each Russia, Ukraine, or Belarus. Have groups conduct online research about the natural resources and their location. Groups should create a thematic map that includes a key or legend to present to the class. Use the maps to hold a class discussion comparing and contrasting the natural resources in each part of the Russian Core. BL **Visual/Spatial**

CLOSE & REFLECT

Assessing Review with students how geography has affected where people live and earn a living in the Russian Core. Discuss the relationship between a country's natural resources and the way people live.

ANSWERS, p. 340

READING PROGRESS CHECK As a result of being located in the high latitudes, cold, snowy winters are the region's dominant characteristic.

CRITICAL THINKING

1. The biggest coal fields are located in remote areas of eastern Siberia
2. Russia leads the world in nickel production and ranks among the top three producers of aluminum and platinum-group metals.

Russia's shipping industry includes both river- and sea-going vessels.

▲ CRITICAL THINKING

1. ***Speculating*** Why is Russia's coal, although abundant, difficult to produce?
2. ***Describing*** Where does Russia rank in the production of nickel, aluminum, and platinum-group metals?

northeast, but thaw days are frequent. **Corresponding** to these temperature differences, the frost-free period decreases from more than 170 days in the southwest to 130 days in the northeast. Maximum temperatures in July are generally in the mid-60°sF (about 18°C). Rainfall is moderate, although higher than over most of the vast Russian Plain.

Warmer air from the Atlantic Ocean moderates temperatures in western Russia. Most of Russia, however, lies well within the Eurasian landmass, far away from any moderating ocean influences. As a result, much of the country's interior has more extreme variations in temperature and little precipitation. This climatic effect within the interior areas of a landmass is called **continentality**.

corresponding showing a direct connection between two things

continentality effect of extreme variation in temperature and very little precipitation within the interior portions of a landmass

challenge to arouse or stimulate especially by presenting with difficulties

Natural Resources

R Russia's physical geography benefits but also **challenges** its people. The country has an abundance of natural resources, including one-fifth of the world's forests. Much of this wealth, however, lies in remote and climatically unfavorable areas and is difficult to tap or utilize. For example, Russia holds large petroleum deposits and 16 percent of the world's coal reserves; however, the country's biggest coalfields lie in remote areas of eastern Siberia. Russia is also a leading producer of natural gas, but much of it is located in northern Siberia. It also leads the world in nickel production and ranks among the top three producers of aluminum, gemstones, and platinum-group metals. Russia's rivers make it a leading producer of hydroelectric power.

T There are considerable resources of iron and other ores in parts of Ukraine. Other resources such as mountain wax, granite, and graphite are among the country's most abundant. Ukraine also produces various salts and has a rich base for metallurgical, porcelain, and chemical industries.

Natural resources in Belarus include fuel sources such as peat, oil, and natural gas deposits. The country also contains small quantities of a variety of rocks and minerals, such as chalk, sand, clay, gravel, granite, and limestone.

READING PROGRESS CHECK

Classifying How does Russia's location in the high latitudes affect its climate?

LESSON 1 REVIEW (CCSS)

Reviewing Vocabulary (Tier Three Words)

1. ***Explaining*** Explain the significance of permafrost and continentality. RH.9–10.4

Using Your Notes

2. ***Listing*** Use your chart to list and describe the locations of the major landforms of the Russian Core.

Answering the Guiding Questions

3. ***Identifying*** How do interconnected mountain ranges and plains shape human activities in the Russian Core?
4. ***Describing*** What role do rivers of the Russian Core play in the economic activities of the region?
5. ***Explaining*** What are the general climate conditions in much of the Russian Core?

Writing Activity

6. ***Informative/Explanatory*** Think about the locations of Russia's seas. Write a paragraph describing how the locations of these seas affect Russia's economy. WHST.9–10.2

340

LESSON 1 REVIEW ANSWERS

Reviewing Vocabulary

1. Both represent climactic effects on an environment. Permafrost is a permanently frozen layer of underground soil. In the tundra, it is a contributing factor in limiting the vegetation that can grow there. Continentality is the climactic effect of being located in the interior of a large landmass, far from moderating factors such as ocean winds. The location leads to extreme variations in temperature and little precipitation.

Using Your Notes

2. Major landforms include the Ural Mountains, the Caucasus Mountains, the Northern European Plain, and the West Siberian Plain.

Answering the Guiding Questions

3. Possible answer: The diverse topography creates a beautiful landscape, which gives rise to income through tourism. Mountains inspire recreational activities such as skiing and mountain climbing. Because the Northern European Plain has many rivers and extremely fertile soil, the majority of Russians live there today.
4. They are important commercial, transportation, and hydroelectric resources.
5. The region is characterized by cold, snowy winters. High and low temperatures vary significantly throughout the region, as does the length of summers and winters.

Writing Activity

6. Paragraphs will vary, but should be logical and strongly supported by lesson content. Paragraphs should include at least two seas and their effect on Russia's economy. The Caspian Sea, reachable via the Volga River, is used for trade. The Black Sea, reachable via the Dnieper River, is also used for trade.

networks
There's More Online!

- **GRAPHS** Ethnic Composition of the Russian Core
- **GRAPH** GDP Per Capita in the Russian Core
- **TIME LINE** Soviet Era of the Russian Core
- **INTERACTIVE SELF-CHECK QUIZ**
- **VIDEO** Human Geography of the Russian Core

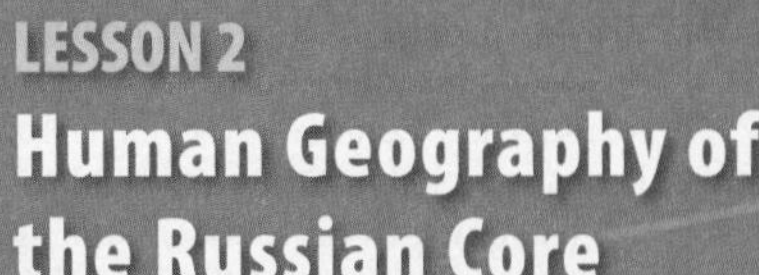

LESSON 2
Human Geography of the Russian Core

ESSENTIAL QUESTION • *How do physical systems and human systems shape a place?* R1

Reading **HELP**DESK

Academic Vocabulary (Tier Two Words)
- **acquire**
- **trigger**
- **decline**

Content Vocabulary (Tier Three Words)
- **czar**
- **Russification**
- **satellite**
- **perestroika**
- **glasnost**
- **black market**
- **privatization**

TAKING NOTES: ***Key Ideas and Details***

IDENTIFYING Use a graphic organizer like the one below to take notes on society and culture today in the Russian Core.

Human Geography of the Russian Core: Society and Culture Today
- Lasting effects of Soviet government policies →
- Family and Status of Women →
- The Arts →

It Matters Because

The Russian Revolution, the Soviet era, and the collapse of the Soviet Union have had profound effects on the Russian Core's economies, politics, and people. This subregion's countries have been forced to redefine who they are and to restructure their economies based on new ideas about political and economic systems.

History and Government

GUIDING QUESTION *How have the Russian Core's historical roots and modern ideas influenced the history and government of the region?*

For most of the last century, Russia was part of the Soviet Union. Ruled by a Communist government, it challenged the United States and other democracies for global influence. Then the Soviet Union collapsed, and Russia, Belarus, and Ukraine emerged as independent countries.

Early History

Russia's historical roots go back to the A.D. 600s when Slav farmers, hunters, and fishers settled near the waterways of the Northern European Plain. The Slav communities were once organized into a loose union of city-states known as Kievan Rus. Ruled by princes, the leading city-state, Kiev, controlled a prosperous trading route, using Russia's western rivers to link seaports and trade centers on the Baltic and Black Seas.

In the early 1200s, Mongols from Central Asia invaded Kiev and many of the Slav territories. Although the Mongols allowed the Slavs self-rule, they continued to control the area militarily for more than 200 years. T

In the late 1600s, **Czar** Peter I—known as Peter the Great—came to power, determined to modernize Russia. Under his rule, Russia enlarged its territory, built a strong military, and developed trade with Western Europe. To **acquire** seaports, Russia gained land along the Baltic Sea from Sweden. St. Petersburg became the new capital and a major port city. It was carved out of the wilderness along the Gulf of Finland, providing access to the Baltic Sea and giving Russia "a window on the West." R2

ENGAGE

R1 Reading Skills

Previewing Have students read the Guiding Question and quickly flip through the lesson to preview the visuals and headings. Then have students write three predictions about how the history of Russia and the Soviet Union has affected the human and physical geography of the Russian Core.

TEACH & ASSESS

T Technology Skills

Sequencing Have students work in pairs to create time lines to sequence the most important events in Russia's history. Have students record similar types of information for each event, such as who was ruling the territory at the time and why each event is important. Students should augment their time lines by searching the Internet or library resources to add additional facts about each period on their time lines. Invite volunteers to share their time lines with the class. **Interpersonal, Visual/Spatial**

R2 Reading Skills

Interpreting Review that metaphors such as "a window on the West" are not to be understood literally. **Ask: Why might this phrase be used to explain St. Petersburg?** *(Possible answers: By establishing this port city and a strong sea trade, Peter opened his country up to Western ideas and goods. The port let Western ideas enter Russia the way a window lets light illuminate a room.)* **Why did Peter I work so hard to establish this port city?** *(He wanted to maintain communication avenues and strong trade relationships with European countries. The location of St. Petersburg made doing both easier.)* **ELL Verbal/Linguistic**

networks ***Online Teaching Options***

INTERACTIVE BELLRINGER

GDP Per Capita in the Russian Core

Analyzing Graphs This interactive bellringer includes a graph that will allow students to identify how the economy of the Russian Core has changed since 1991. Have students work with a partner to analyze the data in the graph. Have pairs note the similarities and differences of the economies of Belarus, Russia, and Ukraine. Then tell each pair of students to discuss and answer the questions. After pairs have had time to complete the activity, display the answers and then as a class discuss any concerns. **AL Interpersonal, Visual/Spatial**

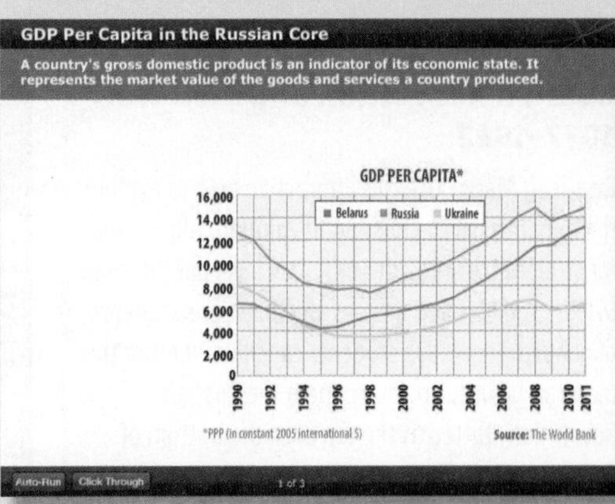

ANSWERS, p. 341

TAKING NOTES: Lasting Effects of Soviet Government policies—The Soviet government discouraged religion, and Russians have only been openly returning to their faiths since the 1980s; some of Russia's ethnic minority groups still seek to become independent countries, but Russia continues to prevent this; Russia is still struggling to establish its role in the global market after so many years of practicing communism; **Family and Status of Women**—Families live in small apartments in large apartment blocks as a result of a housing shortage, but options are improving; the status of women today is similar to during Soviet law, under which women were to be treated equally but in reality received lower pay, fewer career advancements, and decreased political representation; **Art**—Russian visual art, literature, ballet, and theater have an international reputation.

Human Geography of the Russian Core

G1 Critical Thinking Skills

Understanding Relationships Among Events Review with students the information about how and why Russian rulers expanded their territories. **Ask: What great accomplishment did Empress Catherine the Great achieve?** *(a warm-water port on the Black Sea)* **What did Russia accomplish under Czar Alexander III?** *(the construction of the Trans-Siberian Railroad, which made it easier to travel and settle Russian lands to the east and provided access to the eastern port of Vladivostok)*
AL **Logical/Mathematical**

G2 Critical Thinking Skills

Considering Perspectives Have students review the information about the social and economic problems facing the people of Russia before the Russian Revolution. **Ask: How effective were the reforms of Czar Alexander II?** *(Possible answer: The reforms caused many serfs to move to cities, which caused problems because there the serfs were not paid well and their quality of life suffered.)* **How did the principles championed by Karl Marx differ from the way regular people lived in Russia before the Revolution of 1917?** *(Possible answer: Marx wrote that all the people in a society should own the land of a country together and that everyone should share wealth equally. Before the Revolution, Russia was ruled by a royal family who controlled much of the land and wealth.)* Have students discuss the ethics of the Revolution of 1917 and ask them to draw their own conclusions about its methods and results.
BL **Verbal/Linguistic**

V Visual Skills

Analyzing Visuals Review the time line with students. Then have student pairs discuss the information it provides about the history and development of the Russian Core during the Soviet era. Have pairs finish by writing summaries that describe in their own words what the time line is explaining about this period. **Visual/Spatial, Interpersonal**

ANSWERS, p. 342

CRITICAL THINKING

1. It gave the Soviet Union control of Estonia, Latvia, Lithuania, and eastern Poland. Additionally, Germany and the Soviet Union promised not to attack each other.
2. Postwar agreements gave the USSR influence over Eastern and Southeastern Europe.

---

czar ruler of Russia until the 1917 revolution; originally from Latin word *Caesar,* title of Roman emperors

acquire to gain possession

Russification in nineteenth and twentieth century Russia and the Soviet Union, a government program that required everyone in the empire to speak Russian and to become a Christian; assignment of some Russian-speaking people to non-Russian ethnic regions

trigger to set off

satellite a country controlled by another country, notably Eastern European countries controlled by the Soviet Union by the end of World War II

During the late 1700s, Empress Catherine the Great continued to expand Russia's empire and gained a long-desired warm-water port on the Black Sea. A later royal family of Russia, the Romanovs, continued expansion, resulting in acquisitions in both Eastern and Central Europe. These new territories and their people brought many non-Russians under Russian rule. A program known as **Russification** was begun to make those peoples more "Russian."

G1 Czar Alexander II's limited reforms caused many former serfs to move to cities. There they faced the poor conditions and low wages of factory work. Non-Russian peoples from newly colonized regions of the Russian Empire faced prejudice. The government also insisted colonized people become like Russians. Russification became government policy, and people were required to speak Russian and follow Eastern Orthodox Christianity to receive jobs and benefits.

Beginning in 1891, under Czar Alexander III, Russia expanded into Siberia with the construction of the Trans-Siberian Railroad. Nearly 6,000 miles (9,700 km) long, it connected Moscow to Vladivostok. Once completed in 1916, the railroad opened Russia's Asian eastern region to settlement.

Revolution and Change

G2 One of the biggest proponents for greater economic equality was the German philosopher Karl Marx, the founder of modern communism. He advocated two principles: the public ownership of all land and means of production, and a classless society with an equal sharing of wealth. During World War I, which began in 1914, numerous strikes and demonstrations were organized by Russian workers who suffered hardships because of the war. They protested, demanding "bread and freedom." This unrest **triggered,** or set off, the Russian Revolution of 1917. Czar Nicholas and his family were murdered, signaling the demise of Europe's last absolute monarchy. What emerged was the Communist-controlled Union of Soviet Socialist Republics (USSR), or the Soviet Union.

The Soviet Union played a pivotal role in the Allied victory over Germany during World War II. Following the war, the Soviet Union occupied much of Eastern Europe. Several countries in the region were controlled as **satellites** under Communist rule. Following World War II, the Communist Soviet Union was engaged in a political and ideological war with the West, particularly the United

TIME LINE

V SOVIET ERA of the Russian Core

Discontent with inequality in Russian society led to revolution and freedom from generations of czarist rule in the early 1900s. This was followed by new ideas about political and economic systems that led to changes in Russia in the 1990s.

1910

1917 Revolution forces Czar Nicholas II to abdicate the throne. Vladimir Lenin becomes leader of Russia.

1922 The Union of Soviet Socialist Republics (USSR) is established.

1924 Lenin dies. Joseph Stalin emerges as new leader.

German-Soviet Nonaggression Pact gives Soviet Union a sphere of influence in Estonia, Latvia, Lithuania, and eastern Poland.

1939 Germany invades western Poland, starting World War II. The Soviets occupy eastern Poland.

▶ CRITICAL THINKING

1. ***Explaining*** What did the Soviet Union gain from the Nazi-Soviet Nonaggression Pact?
2. ***Describing*** How did post-World War II agreements change Russia's influence in Europe?

networks Online Teaching Options

INTERACTIVE MAP

Russian Revolution and Civil War, 1917–1922

Reading Maps Use this interactive map to explore the dynamics of the Russian Revolution. Allow time for students to study the different layers of this map. Discuss the text and answer any questions students may have. Then have students consider whether this map can be used to determine if the Russian Revolution started at the top or at the bottom of Russian society. If so, how? Have students discuss this question in small groups. Ask them to share within the group any evidence they can find in the map.
ELL **Visual/Spatial, Interpersonal**

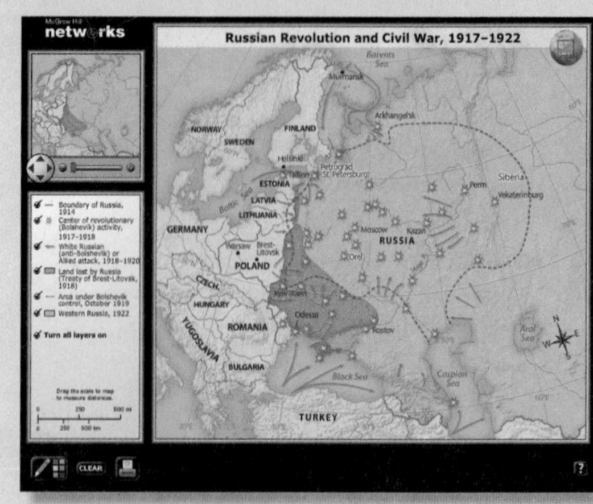

States, in the Cold War. Tensions during this time brought the world to the brink of nuclear war and shaped modern economic and political policies.

The enormous costs of the Soviet Union's military and inefficient economic policies weakened its role in the world. In 1985 Mikhail Gorbachev, a reform-minded official, became the leader of the Soviet Union. He instituted a policy of economic restructuring called **perestroika** (PEHR•uh•STROY•kuh) and a policy of greater political openness called **glasnost** (GLAZ•nohst). Political reform was set in motion. Satellites controlled by the Soviet Union began to replace their Communist governments in 1989. In 1991 a failed coup led to the collapse of the Soviet government and regions of the country began declaring their independence. Today there are 15 independent countries, including Russia, Ukraine, and Belarus. **T**

perestroika in Russian, "restructuring"; part of Gorbachev's plan for reforming the Soviet economy and government

glasnost Russian term for new openness in areas of politics, social issues, and media; part of Gorbachev's reform plans

The newly independent countries emerged from a long period of both imperial Russian and Soviet domination. Belarus is a good example. Although Belarusians share an ethnic identity and language, they had never enjoyed unity and political sovereignty, except during a brief period in 1918. Belarusian history is a study of regional conflicts and territorial claims by neighbors to the east and west. **R**

Since the beginning of Russian occupation, Chechnya has unsuccessfully sought independence. Several oil and gas pipelines vital to the Russian economy run through Chechen territory. In May 2000, Russian president Vladimir Putin established direct rule of Chechnya to try to stop the rebels. In 2003 a new constitution was passed that gave Chechnya a significant amount of autonomy. The new Chechen government is now struggling to recover from the violence waged by the Chechen rebels and to bring stability and peace to Chechnya.

☑ READING PROGRESS CHECK

Explaining How was St. Petersburg important to the expansion of the Russian Empire?

Population Patterns

GUIDING QUESTION *What factors have shaped population patterns in the Russian Core?*

About 80 percent of all Russians live west of the Ural Mountains. This is due in part to the rich soils, waterways, and a milder climate than that of eastern Russia, also known as Siberia. Densely settled western Russia includes the country's

1940

1941 Germany attacks the Soviet Union, drawing it into World War II.

1943 Germany fails to take Stalingrad. Soviet troops launch a counter-offensive. Berlin is eventually captured.

1945 Germany is defeated in World War II. USSR gains influence over Eastern Europe.

1953 Joseph Stalin dies. Nikita Khrushchev becomes Communist party leader.

1962 Cuban missile crisis erupts over presence of Soviet missiles in Cuba.

1985 Mikhail Gorbachev comes to power and proposes perestroika.

1990

1991 The USSR is dissolved.

T Technology Skills

Acquiring Information Have small groups of students research the policy of perestroika instituted by Mikhail Gorbachev. Assign each group a different aspect to research, such as the history of how the term *perestroika* was used before Gorbachev, the reasons why Gorbachev enacted this policy of restructuring, specific reforms he made to the Soviet economic system, or the short- and long-term effects of the policy. Once groups have completed their research, have them create and deliver a multimedia presentation that includes illustrations, video clips, and charts or graphs organizing their information. Finish with a class discussion about the value and effects of perestroika. **BL Verbal/Linguistic, Visual/Spatial**

R Reading Skills

Inferring Have students reread the information about Chechnya's attempts to gain independence. **Ask: Why was Russia unwilling to let Chechnya become an independent nation?** *(Oil and gas pipelines vital to the Russian economy run through Chechen lands. If Russia does not control Chechnya, it will lose control of those pipelines and the natural resources of oil and gas.)* **Logical/Mathematical**

Making Connections

Because they followed different systems of government and championed different lifestyle beliefs, the United States and the Soviet Union were locked in a nonmilitary conflict for several decades until the USSR broke apart in 1991. Caught up in an arms race with each other, each country focused on showing that it possessed superior weapons so as to dissuade the other country from trying to start a major conflict. However, preventing direct fighting was in the interests of both countries because the potential use of nuclear weapons may have escalated and set off global destruction.

INTERACTIVE MAP

Breakup of the Soviet Union, 1991

Interpreting Maps Use this interactive map on the Soviet Union breakup in 1991 to examine a claim. Tell the students to examine this statement: "Belarusian history is a study of regional conflicts and territorial claims by neighbors to the east and west." Have students write a paragraph, using the map to answer the following questions about the statement:

- **How does the map reinforce this statement?**
- **Who are the "neighbors" the statement refers to?**

AL Verbal/Linguistic

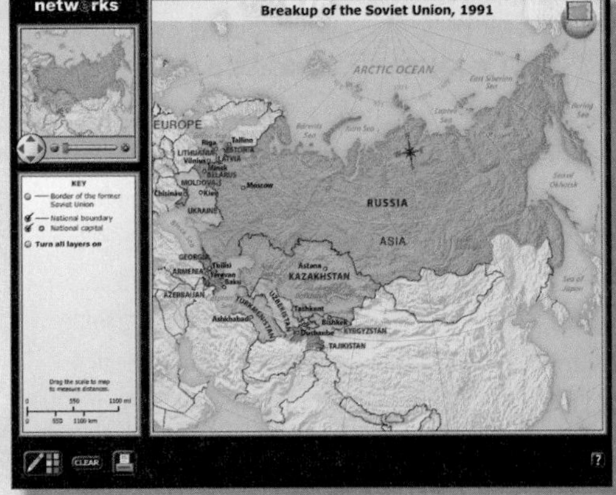

ANSWERS, p. 343

☑ **READING PROGRESS CHECK** As a major port city on the Baltic Sea, St. Petersburg allowed Russia to advance, but perhaps of greater importance was its ability to serve as a point from which Russia could observe the West.

V Visual Skills

Interpreting Visuals Have students examine the graphs. **Ask:** **What do these graphs represent about the formation of the countries of Belarus, Russia, and Ukraine?** *(The pie charts illustrate just how dominant each ethnic group—Belarusian, Russian, or Ukrainian—is in each individual country.)* **What generalization can you draw from looking at all three pie charts about the Russian ethnic group?** *(It is the largest group in the Russian Core, and it makes up the largest ethnic percentage after the main ethnic group in both the Belarus and Ukraine charts.)* AL **Visual/Spatial**

C1 Critical Thinking Skills

Speculating Have students think about what they have read so far about the history of the Russian Core and the different ethnic groups that have lived within it. **Ask: Why might different ethnic groups be demanding self-rule or independence now?** *(Possible answer: Especially if they are greatly outnumbered by much larger and dominant ethnic groups such as Russians, these smaller ethnic groups may now want to contribute to decision making regarding their own culture. Because Russia has a history of mandating that settlers from outside become more "Russian," these small ethnic groups may still feel oppressed.)* BL **Logical/Mathematical**

C2 Critical Thinking Skills

Synthesizing Have students examine the information about the society under the heading *Society and Culture Today*. Then have students evaluate the way issues such as religious practices have changed under the new government in the Russian Core. *(Possible answer: Under the Soviet Union, people's religious and cultural beliefs were strongly limited. For example, the government discouraged religious practices and promoted atheism.)* **Logical/Mathematical**

ANSWERS, p. 344

READING PROGRESS CHECK Rich soil, many waterways, and a mild climate are all incentives to live west of the Ural Mountains.

CRITICAL THINKING

1. Russian and Ukrainian
2. Russia has the highest percentage of "Other" ethnic groups. This is likely because many of the ethnic groups that lived in areas acquired by the expanding Russian empire still live in the region today.

GRAPH SKILLS Ethnic Composition of the Russian Core

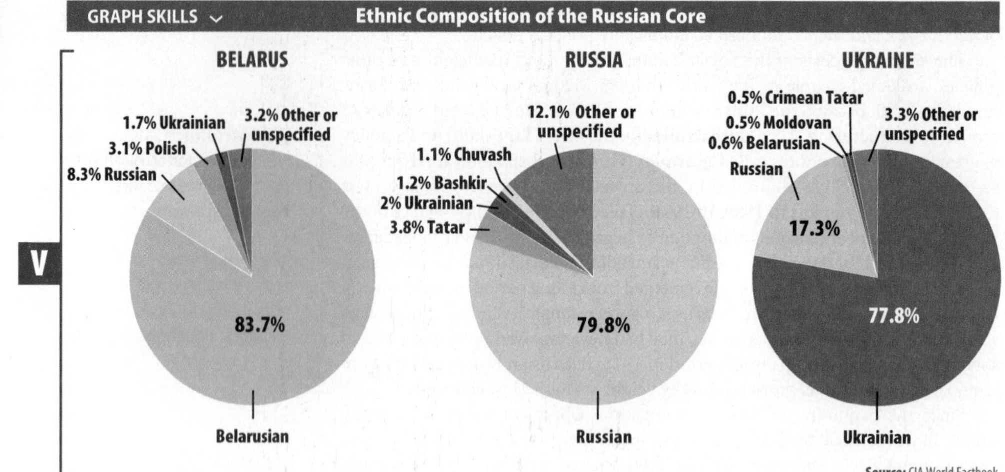

Source: CIA World Factbook

C1 The diversity of people in Russia has led to many ethnic groups demanding greater self-rule or independence. In some places, like Chechnya, some groups have resorted to violent methods, such as terrorism.

▲ **CRITICAL THINKING**

1. ***Analyzing*** Which groups make up over 10 % of the Ukrainian population?
2. ***Categorizing*** Which country shown has the largest population of "Other" ethnic groups? What factors may account for the higher percentage?

industrialized cities. The major industrial city is Moscow, Russia's capital. Following the reestablishment of Russia as a country in 1991, the controls over where people could live were removed. People migrated where there were jobs and other opportunities. As a result, Russian cities experienced increases in population. By 2000 the population of ethnic Russians began to **decline** due to a greatly reduced birthrate. The decline has continued into the twenty-first century.

decline to become less in amount or number

A shrinking population is a major problem for Russia. To offset falling birthrates, there are government programs that pay monthly allowances to parents with babies and children. The birthrate of 1.4 babies per woman in 2010 is far below the 2.1 needed to naturally maintain the population. Reducing mortality rates is also necessary. Death rates, particularly among males between the ages of 25 and 45, have increased to levels that outpace new births. As a result of having fewer younger people, Russia's overall population has been simultaneously decreasing and growing older.

READING PROGRESS CHECK

Making Connections Why do most Russians live west of the Ural Mountains?

Society and Culture Today

GUIDING QUESTION *How have past policies affected the Russian Core today?*

C2 The policies of the past have had lasting effects on Russia's culture. The Soviet government severely discouraged religious practices and discriminated against different ethnic groups. It actively promoted atheism, or the belief that God or another supreme being does not exist. In the late 1980s, however, the government relaxed its restrictions on religion. Since then, millions of Russians are rediscovering their religious faiths and traditions. Similarly, more than 100 languages are spoken in the country today, but Russian is the official language.

344

networks Online Teaching Options

INTERACTIVE GRAPHS

Ethnic Composition of the Russian Core

Considering Advantages and Disadvantages Use these graphs to discuss the diversity of people in Russia with students. Call on volunteers to suggest the advantages of diversity. Write out the suggested advantages. Then have several students suggest some of the disadvantages of diversity and write these in a separate list. Have students form small groups to debate whether the advantages of diversity outweigh the disadvantages. Invite groups to share the results of their debates. BL **Interpersonal, Logical/Mathematical**

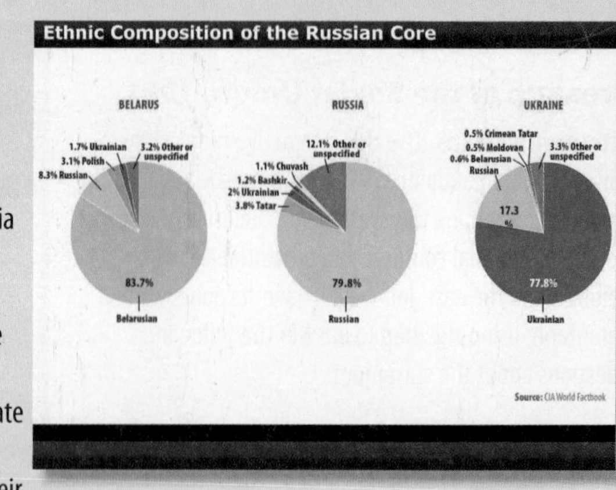

During the Soviet era, education was free and mandatory. The emphasis was on math, science, and engineering rather than on language, history, and literature. The curriculum changed dramatically after Russian independence. Schools began to emphasize a more balanced approach to learning, including language, history, and literature. Today, students have a choice of different types of schools, but the country's economy has limited funding for schools.

Family and Status of Women

Living conditions in Russia affect family life. Due to a housing shortage, most people live in large apartment blocks. While space in the traditional apartments is tight, new housing developments since 1991 offer space and living conditions similar to those in Western Europe and the United States.

R The status of women in Russian society is a combination of the past and the present. Women have always had a very important role working in industry. During World War II, women not only fought in every branch of the Soviet military but also took jobs in the wartime industrial workforce. That trend continued into the 1970s. In the 1990s, there were increasing financial pressures and shrinking government programs in Russia. This meant more women entered the workforce out of necessity. Full-time employment of women contributed to Russia's declining birthrate. Higher education, better-paying jobs, and feminist groups and social organizations have resulted in greater rights for women. As a consequence, many women marry later in life, many have careers, and they expect to be treated as equals in a society that has traditionally been dominated by men.

The Arts

T Russian arts are characterized by a list of well-known artists. Painters such as Viktor Vasnetsov and composers such as Pyotr (Peter) Tchaikovsky contributed to the richness of Russian culture. The works of poets Aleksandr Pushkin, Boris Pasternak, and Anna Akhmatova and novelists Lev (Leo) Tolstoy and Fyodor Dostoyevsky have made Russian literature famous. Russian ballet and theater also have an international reputation.

The period of communism limited individual artistic expression and directed artists to glorify the government's achievements in their works, an approach known as socialist realism. Artists who did not follow these guidelines were punished. Accounts of imprisonment and punishment among artists during the period are shown in works such as Aleksandr Solzhenitsyn's *The Gulag Archipelago.*

Beginning in the mid-1980s, activity in the arts renewed as loosening government controls allowed the printing of previously unpublished works and new materials. During the height of Communist repression, books were smuggled from Russia and printed in other languages, becoming best sellers in other countries. Many were not available to Russian readers until after 1991.

✓ READING PROGRESS CHECK

Analyzing What contributed to a resurgence of the arts in the 1980s?

Economic Activities

GUIDING QUESTION *How has the economy of the Russian Core changed since 1991?*

Under Communist leaders, the Soviet Union operated as a command economy in which the government made key economic decisions. The government owned banks, factories, farms, mines, and transportation systems. The government decided what and how much to produce, where and how to produce it, and who would benefit from the profits. It also controlled the pricing of most goods and decided where they would be sold.

Analyzing PRIMARY SOURCES CCSS

Poetry in Contemporary Russia

"Since the collapse of the Soviet empire in 1991, Russian poetry has begun to resemble American poetry in ways that are both fascinating and sad. What's fascinating is how talented, and how different from one another, Russia's young poets are. What's sad is how little they are read, and how little they matter. Whatever reach contemporary poetry had in Russian society has vanished like wood smoke."

—Dwight Garner, "When Poets Rocked Russia's Stadiums," *New York Times*, June 3, 2010

DBQ ***SPECULATING*** Why do you think poetry has lost its importance in Russian society today? RH.9–10.1

SLIDE SHOW

St. Basil's, the Kremlin, and Red Square

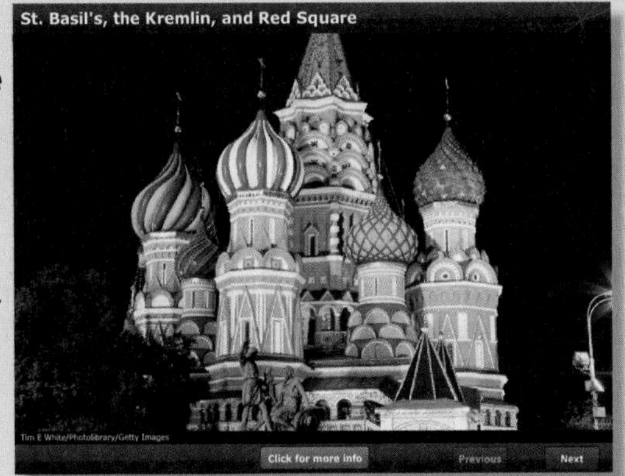

Making Generalizations This slide show can be used to introduce students to the changes in the Russian arts before and after 1991. Have students study the image of the Kremlin and then ask them to make generalizations about the image, including what this building symbolizes. Guide a class discussion about the limitation placed on artists before 1991. Explain that under the Communist regime, the arts were very limited and that the government controlled what was written, painted, and depicted artistically in Russia. Many writers and artists smuggled their works into other countries to be published or viewed. After 1991, many works that had been previously published in other countries were finally available to Russians. Have students write a paragraph about how artistic limitations affects education. BL **Visual/Spatial, Logical/Mathematical**

R Reading Skills

Explaining Have students review the information about the status of women in Russian society. **Ask: How might women's status be explained as a combination of the past and the present?** *(Possible answer: In both the past and the present, women have made important contributions to the workforce and been involved in industries. More recently, women gained greater rights, leading to better-paying jobs and improved education.)* AL **Verbal/Linguistic**

Content Background Knowledge

The Gulag Archipelago Written in three volumes published between 1973 and 1975, Aleksandr Solzhenitsyn's *The Gulag Archipelago* describes in great detail what it was like to live in a Soviet labor camp. Exposing the brutality of Stalinist policies, Solzhenitsyn, who lived in such prison camps himself for eight years, used his writing to bring the attention of the world outside the USSR to how the Soviet government was trying to control its people by imprisoning them and silencing their voices. The work takes its title from the image of a system of camps spread across the vast Russian lands like the islands of an archipelago.

T Technology Skills

Identifying Perspectives Have students explore the rich tradition of Russian arts in greater depth. Allow each student to choose a Russian artist, painter, composer, novelist, poet, or dancer. Have students conduct online research to gather information about the artist and the art's perspective on Russian life. Then in a multimedia presentation, students will present their research along with illustrations, video, or audio clips of the art and explain how the artist expressed his or her perspectives in their work. Have students make formal presentations to the class. BL **Visual/Spatial, Auditory/Musical**

ANSWERS, p. 345

✓ READING PROGRESS CHECK In the mid-1980s, the government began loosening control over what could be published. This allowed the printing of previously unpublished works and of new works.

DBQ Possible answer: People are so worried about meeting basic needs that they have little time or energy to enjoy poetry.

C Critical Thinking Skills

Comparing and Contrasting Have students work in pairs to make a graphic organizer that compares and contrasts information about the state of the Soviet economy under Communist leaders, under Mikhail Gorbachev and Boris Yeltsin, and today. Students should record information about the beliefs that underpinned each system of organization and how the economy fared in each case. Invite pairs to share their completed graphic organizers with the class and hold a discussion during which students explain how the economy changed and developed over the last few decades. **Visual/Spatial, Interpersonal**

W Writing Skills

Argument Once students have thoroughly examined the changes that the economy of the Russian Core has undergone over the last few decades, have them decide which changes in policies were most helpful and which were most harmful. Then have students write essays explaining their viewpoints, using facts and details to support their opinion.
BL Intrapersonal, Verbal/Linguistic

R Reading Skills

Reading Graphs Provide time for students to analyze and interpret the line graph. Remind students that GDP stands for Gross Domestic Product, or the value of all of the goods and services produced in a country at a given time. **Ask: How would you describe the growth of the country's economy after 1990?** *(The economies of all three countries declined.)* **When did the economy begin to turn around?** *(The economies of all three countries started to improve around 1998)* **How does this line graph represent the relationship between the economies of the three countries?** *(Possible answer: Because the lines generally move in the same direction, the economies seem to be linked. However, slight variations exist between countries, such as Russia and Ukraine experienced a dip in 2008, and Belarus experienced a plateau.)* **AL Visual/Spatial**

ANSWERS, p. 346

CRITICAL THINKING

1. Russia
2. 1994

black market illegal trade of scarce or illegal goods, usually sold at high prices

Unemployment was nearly nonexistent, but wages were low. Some people could not afford consumer goods, or goods needed for everyday life. Even when people had enough money, such goods were hard to find. Scarce products could be bought on the **black market**, illegal trade in which scarce or illegal goods are sold at high prices. Most workers, however, could not afford such high prices.

When Mikhail Gorbachev came to power in 1985, the Soviet command economy was under strain. He began to move the country toward a market economy, in which businesses became owned by private individuals and companies. Gorbachev reduced government controls, allowed people to start small businesses, and encouraged foreign investment. Boris Yeltsin, Gorbachev's successor, expanded this process.

privatization a change to private ownership of state-owned companies and industries

C Russia's economy continued to change after 1991. Yeltsin removed governmental price controls and encouraged **privatization**—a shift to private ownership—of state-owned companies. This favored wealthy people or businesses with money to purchase large companies. Those who made money sometimes invested their profits outside the country in Europe and the United States. Most Russians were not able to benefit from this new wealth at the time.

The Russian economy experienced many successes throughout the 1990s. More consumer goods were available to meet pent-up demands. Greater demands resulted in prices that soared, and many people could not afford to buy the goods. Between 1990 and 1995, Russia experienced an economic depression as its GDP fell by 50 percent. Following a 1998 financial crisis, the ruble—Russia's currency—lost 71 percent of its value. The international community issued loans and credit to help the country.

W Russia has experienced steady economic growth since 1998, due in part to increases in productivity, wages, consumption, and a growing middle class. The anchor in the economic success has been its vast supplies of natural resources that are marketed to industrialized countries.

Resources, Power, and Industry

The fertile triangle is the most productive agricultural area of western Russia, extending into Ukraine. With its tip at St. Petersburg and its base stretching from Novosibirsk to Odessa, the triangle has rich soils and a favorable climate. Ukraine's crop production is highly developed. It is referred to as a breadbasket because of the grain crops it grows. Yields of grain and potatoes are among the highest in Europe.

The Russian manufacturing and service sectors are expanding, while the oil and gas sector has grown rapidly. Russia's most important industry is petroleum extraction and processing, and the country is one of the world's largest producers of crude oil. While energy resources dominate Russian exports, minerals also provide important export income. Russian forests produce one-fifth of the world's softwood, and Russian supertrawlers, or fish-factory ships, process catches from the Atlantic and Pacific Oceans for sale on the global market.

Belarus is the one country that has remained closely aligned with Russia since 1991. The two countries remain industrially integrated as a carryover from the past. After 1991 Belarus experienced less privatization of industry and land. Instead, Belarus looked to Russia to be a strong trading partner in exchanging its agricultural products for oil and natural gas.

The gross domestic products (GDPs) of the Russian Core countries have fluctuated since the breakup of the Soviet Union.

▼ CRITICAL THINKING

1. ***Analyzing Visuals*** Which Russian Core country has consistently had the highest GDP since 1990?
2. ***Assessing*** In approximately what year did the GDP of Belarus surpass the GDP of the Ukraine?

R

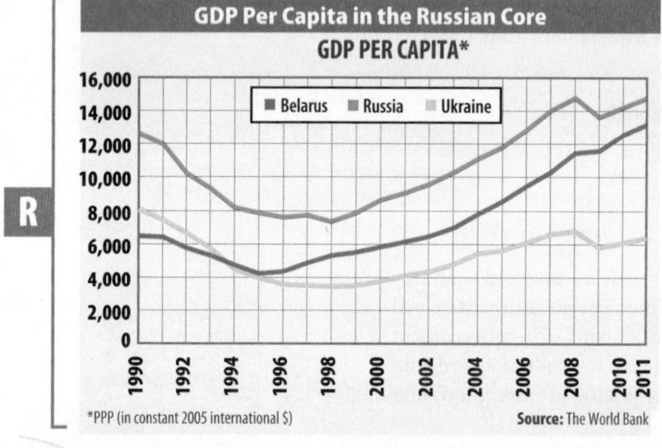

networks Online Teaching Options

VIDEO

The Beginning of Communist Russia

Monitoring Use this video on the rise and fall of Communist Russia to monitor students' understanding about the Soviet political and economic era. In a class discussion, ask students to use information from the video and what they already know to provide information about the fall of the Soviet Union. Discuss what happened when the Soviet Union fell and how it changed the lives of people around the world. Reinforce that this region continues to experience a volatile economy and a decrease in population. **Verbal/Linguistic**

Trade and Interdependence

Russia has focused on becoming a full partner in the global community by expanding trade and building international relationships. The country is a major source of oil and natural gas. These resources account for more than 50 percent of Russia's exports.

R Relationships with neighboring countries are important to Russia. Ukraine imports petroleum, petroleum products, and natural gas, as well as many other products. Ukraine has the major seaport on the Black Sea and exports grain, sugar, iron ore, coal, and manganese. In the twenty-first century, Russia and Ukraine remain dependent upon one another for trade. However, Ukraine is wary of past Russian dominance of the Ukrainian people. Therefore, Ukraine's government has discussed making application to join the European Union (EU), which would switch its closest relationships from Russia to Europe. However, acceptance to the EU is dependent on economic, political, and social criteria on which Ukraine must make progress. In the meantime, Ukraine is developing its economy and its national identity within the region.

W A major highway system links Moscow with other major cities in Russia, but winters are severe on roadways and repairs are both necessary and expensive. Because of its size and climate extremes, Russia depends on railroads and waterways for much of its transportation needs. Major cities are found where the Trans-Siberian Railroad and other railroads cross large rivers. Millions of tons of goods travel along thousands of miles of navigable inland waterways, which include seaports and inland cities. Pipelines are effective in transporting petroleum products, although constructing and maintaining them is challenging in large regions, such as Siberia, with a harsh climate.

Russia, Ukraine, and Belarus experience the effects of pressure for rapid modernization of their economies. Some of the world's best software companies are operated by people in Ukraine. Belarus is a crossroads for trade from Western Europe to Moscow and the rest of Russia. It has had to improve highways, communications, and repair services for long-haul trucks and railroads that transport goods both to and from Russia. All three countries are in the process of identifying their future roles in Europe and the world. All have traditions and cultures going back for centuries. However, they are each new countries, having become independent after 1991, and face political, economic, and social changes.

✓ READING PROGRESS CHECK

Identifying What economic transition has Russia been making since the mid-1980s?

Connecting Geography to **ECONOMICS**

Privatization

After 1991, private ownership of companies in Russia was allowed. The government established a stock exchange and gave vouchers to citizens enabling them to purchase shares in private companies, but these were often sold for cash instead. In 2001 the sale of land was legalized. These changes were a challenge for Russians who were accustomed to government control of nearly every aspect of their lives. It was complicated by a poor economy, inflation, and a drop in personal income. Corruption and organized crime have become issues in Russia, and they hinder investment by international businesses.

SPECULATING Why has the transition from a command to a market economy after 1991 affected Russia in both positive and negative ways?

LESSON 2 REVIEW 

Reviewing Vocabulary (Tier Three Words)

1. ***Explaining*** Explain the significance of black market and privatization. RH.9–10.4

Using Your Notes

2. ***Describing*** Use your graphic organizer to describe how the policies of the Soviet era affect society and culture in the Russian Core today.

Answering the Guiding Questions

3. ***Identifying Cause and Effect*** How have the Russian Core's historical roots and modern ideas influenced the history and government of the region?
4. ***Identifying*** What factors have shaped population patterns in the Russian Core?
5. ***Describing*** How have past policies affected the Russian Core today?
6. ***Explaining*** How has the economy of the Russian Core changed since 1991?

Writing Activity

7. ***Informative/Explanatory*** Write a paragraph describing the conditions in Russian society that led to the Revolution of 1917. Be sure to include the influence of German philosopher Karl Marx in your answer. WHST.9–10.2

Human Geography of the Russian Core

R Reading Skills

Understanding Relationships Review with students the interdependent relationship between Russia and Ukraine. **Ask:** What does Ukraine provide to Russia? *(It provides access to a major seaport on the Black Sea.)* Why might Ukraine want to break away from Russia economically? *(In the past, Russia has dominated other ethnic groups, and Ukraine may worry that Russia will again use its greater strength of numbers to dominate.)* How might Ukraine break free from dependence on Russia? *(by gaining admission to the EU)* **AL** **Logical/Mathematical**

W Writing Skills

Informative/Explanatory Have students write a paragraph describing the importance of transportation to life and the economy in the Russian Core and the problems people face maintaining a good system of transportation. **Verbal/Linguistic**

CLOSE & REFLECT

Transferring Tell students to review the predictions they wrote earlier. Then write a brief essay explaining whether their predictions were accurate, including new information they learned about the Russian Core.

ANSWERS, p. 347

✓ READING PROGRESS CHECK Russia is transitioning from a command economy to a market economy.

Connecting Geography Possible answer: Russians were used to the government controlling most aspects of their lives, but privatization allowed citizens to purchase shares in stock and land. Corruption and organized crime have hindered investment by international businesses.

LESSON 2 REVIEW ANSWERS

Reviewing Vocabulary

1. The black market is a system of illegal trade in which scarce or illegal goods can be bought at high prices. It became common in Russia as a result of the government's price and product controls. Privatization makes companies private and passes the control from the government to the company, which is able to reduce the need for a black market.

Using Your Notes

2. Soviet policies repressed religious and ethnic groups, so citizens have recently been returning to their faiths and traditions. The arts have been rebounding since the end of communist limitations on individual expression. Russia is still struggling to establish its role in the global market after so many years of practicing communism.

Answering the Guiding Questions

3. Under czarist rule, Russification was enforced to strengthen the nation, but it oppressed people of various ethnicities, pushing them to fight for autonomy. Inequality culminated in revolution inspired by the communist ideas of Marx. The Communist Soviet Union emerged and fought to defend its ideologies. Unable to sustain itself, it eventually split into 15 independent countries.
4. Rich soils and mild climate mean that the majority of the population lives west of the Ural Mountains.
5. Religious and ethnic discrimination is no longer prevalent. Many are reestablishing their traditions and languages other than Russian are thriving. Education once repressed language, history, and literature, but are valued today. The arts are thriving since the government has stopped regulating them.
6. Privatization was encouraged. Few Russians benefited because wealthy company owners often invested profits in other countries. After an economic depression and a financial crisis, the international community helped Russia achieve stability and its economy has been steadily growing.

Writing Activity

7. Paragraphs should include principles of Karl Marx and conditions such as low worker wages, poor working conditions, repression and prejudice by the government, and overall economic inequality.

ENGAGE

C Critical Thinking Skills

Predicting Have students recall what they previously learned about Arctic drilling, how it would benefit Russia, and why some groups are opposed to it. Remind them that vast deposits of minerals, oil, and gas are located under the Arctic Ocean. Then have students work with a partner to make a prediction about what might happen when several nations all want to take advantage of the natural resources located in the Arctic Ocean. Have students check how accurate their predictions are as they read this feature.

TEACH & ASSESS

R Reading Skills

Analyzing Text Structure Read aloud the last sentence, stressing the words in the question *worth the risk*. **Ask:** **How is the phrase *worth the risk* being used here?** *(Possible answer: It is a question that is being used to emphasize the point that the loss of the Amazon rain forest may not be worth the rewards of the oil extraction.)* **ELL Verbal/Linguistic**

V Visual Skills

Analyzing Visuals Have students study the map key and map labels and interpret the meaning of this map in a class discussion. **Ask:** **What do the dotted lines and colors on the map indicate?** *(The red dotted lines indicate international waters, and the blue dotted lines indicate agreed boundaries or the parts of the Arctic Ocean that each country claims.)* **What do the triangles indicate?** *(the locations where countries or companies plan to drill for oil and gas in the future)* **How does the map make it easier to understand the importance of settling the question of who will be allowed to drill for natural resources in the Arctic Ocean?** *(The map shows which countries are closest to this area and which are already claiming rights to its natural resources. The map helps illustrate the size of each country's claim compared to the claims of other countries and shows just what is at stake.)* **AL Visual/Spatial**

T Technology Skills

Acquiring Information Have small groups conduct online research to collect more information about new extraction techniques for collecting minerals, oil, and gas from beneath the Arctic Ocean. Remind groups to research the obstacles facing drilling operations in this area, how technology can overcome these obstacles, and which method various countries are using. Once groups have completed their research, have them create multimedia presentations using maps, illustrations, charts, or graphs to organize their information. Have each group present its findings to the class in a short verbal report.
BL Verbal/Linguistic, Visual/Spatial

Global Connections: **Europe**

C Arctic Oil Frontiers

R *Some of Earth's largest oil and natural gas fields lie under the icy waters of the Arctic Ocean. As extraction technology has improved and as demand for these resources has increased, states that border the Arctic Ocean have staked their claims and energy companies have begun to plan for drilling operations. But are energy companies prepared for the hazards involved in Arctic drilling? Are the rewards worth the risk?*

V
Int'l Waters | Agreed Borders
Danish Claim | Russian Claim
Canadian Claim | US Claim
Future Oil Field | Future Gas Field

GREENLAND
NORWAY

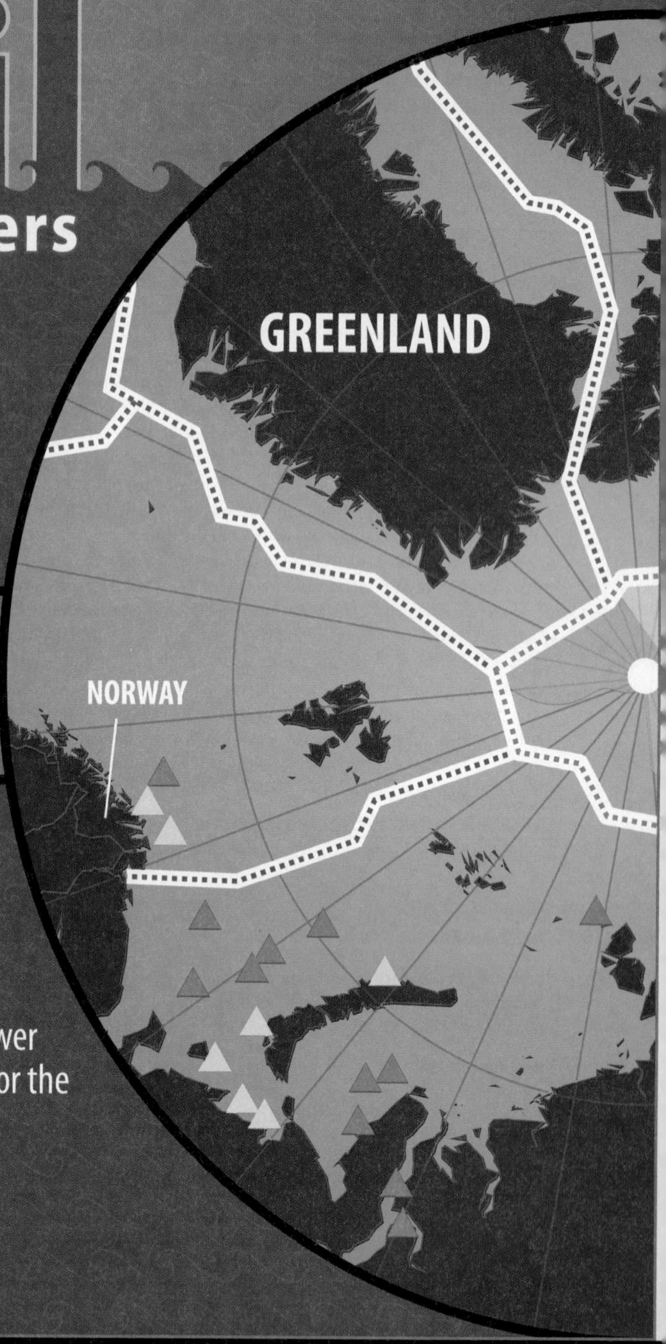

T HOW MUCH OIL IS THERE?

160 BILLION BARRELS

It could power the world for the next **5 years.**

348

networks ***Online Teaching Options***

INTERACTIVE SLIDE SHOW

How to Analyze Visuals

Analyzing Visuals Organize the class into small groups, and have each group review the materials about analyzing visuals. Tell them to follow the steps in the slide show to analyze the visual in the feature. Have them answer these questions: **What is the subject of the visual?** *(Oil in the Arctic Ocean)* **What are the four main parts of the visual?** *(Who claims waters in the Arctic Ocean? How much oil is there? How do the Arctic oil reserves compare to oil reserves in other places? Is the oil in the Arctic Ocean safe to extract?)* **What general statement can you make about oil in the Arctic Ocean based on information in this visual?** Allow the groups to share their analyses with the class. **Visual/Spatial, Logical/Mathematical**

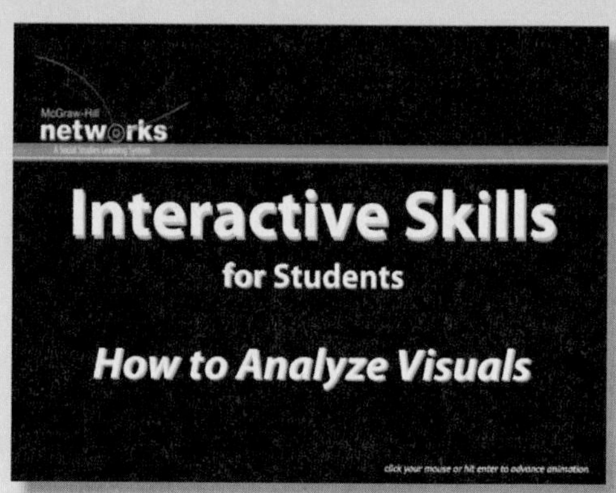

CANADA

UNITED STATES

ARCTIC OCEAN

RUSSIA

HOW DOES IT COMPARE?

256 BILLION BARRELS — SAUDI ARABIA

160 BILLION BARRELS — ARCTIC OIL

60 BILLION BARRELS — RUSSIA

20 BILLION BARRELS — UNITED STATES

IS IT SAFE TO EXTRACT? C

Extensive construction could alter the ecologically pristine environment.

Sound vibrations could disturb marine habitats. W

Oil spills could harm marine and coastal wildlife.

Narwhal

Making Connections

1. ***Speculating*** Besides harm to the environment, what other risks with Arctic drilling can you foresee?
2. ***Human Systems*** What patterns do you notice about the claims made on the Arctic Ocean by bordering states? Explain why you think these claims are fair or unfair.
3. ***Considering Advantages and Disadvantages*** Using what you know about the risks and rewards of Arctic drilling, write a one-page summary statement explaining why you think plans for drilling in the Arctic Ocean are positive or negative.

*Interact with **Global Connections** Online*

C Critical Thinking Skills

Analyzing Cause and Effect Have students review the information about the potential hazards of extracting oil. **Ask:** **What danger is described in the first case and what would cause it?** *(To drill for oil, people must construct huge oil rigs, which could cause land and water to become polluted.)* **What danger is described in the second case and what would cause it?** *(Noise from the working oil equipment will cause vibrations in the air and water, which could disturb local habitats.)* **What danger is being described in the third case and what would cause it?** *(Oil spilled from the rigs could spread and pollute the ocean and coasts.)* AL **Logical/Mathematical**

W Writing Skills

Argument Have students write a short essay arguing their opinion about which possible dangers posed by oil drilling in the Arctic Ocean are more likely to pose a true problem and explaining how people might decrease the chance that these scenarios might occur or cause harm. BL **Verbal/Linguistic**

CLOSE & REFLECT

Assessing Tell students to review the predictions they made before reading this section and check whether their predictions were correct. Then have students consider what they have learned about the main issues surrounding the Arctic oil frontiers and use specific information from this spread to summarize what is happening because of the interest that nations and companies are taking in the natural resources located in this area.

MAP

Regional Atlas: Europe

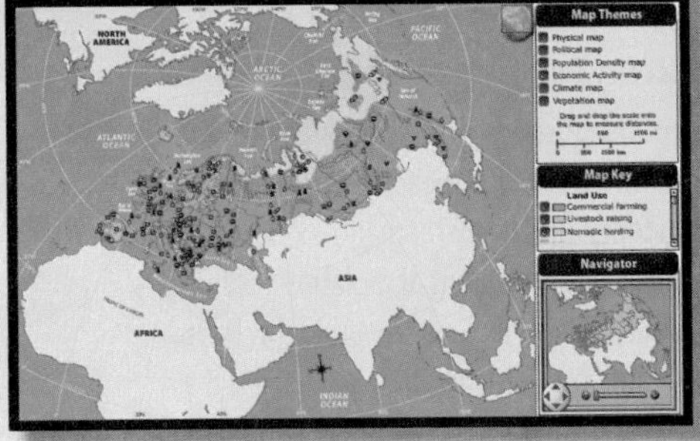

Drawing Conclusions Display the Unit 4 map of Europe showing the resources of the region and have students note the locations of the region's existing oil and natural gas resources. Have students study the Land Use key and to find the European areas on the map that meet ocean waters. **Ask: What are the primary kinds of land use for most of these areas?** *(forests and nomadic herding)* Discuss as a class the relationship of this land use and the concerns about the safety of extracting oil and natural gas from the Arctic Ocean, including how extracting activities might change the environments of these areas. Talk about how these environmental changes might affect the land and people of the region. AL BL **Visual/Spatial, Naturalist**

ANSWERS, p. 349

Making Connections

1. Possible answers: risks associated with the climate of the Arctic Ocean, the remote location, and the ocean environment.
2. Students should note that states have claimed those parts of the Arctic Ocean nearest to their coastlines. Students may consider this arrangement to be fair, as those states are nearest to those sections of the ocean. Students may consider this arrangement unfair as these areas are uninhabitable and far from the coast.
3. Student answers should include clearly thought-out arguments that take both the advantages and disadvantages of Arctic drilling into account. Students may include increased access to natural resources, increase in jobs, and economic development as advantages to Arctic drilling. Students may include increased environmental risks and dangerous working conditions as disadvantages to Arctic drilling.

ENGAGE

R1 Reading Skills

Activating Prior Knowledge Have small groups discuss what they already know about the harmful effects that industrialization and the invention of new ways to harvest and use Earth's resources can have on the environment of a country. Then have groups discuss solutions that individuals, governments, and organizations may have proposed for repairing past damages and for avoiding future harm. Invite students to share their knowledge with the class.

TEACH & ASSESS

C Critical Thinking Skills

Identifying Perspectives Have students think about the reasons why Arctic drilling would benefit Russia and the reasons why other groups would oppose Russia's accessing minerals, oil, and gas from beneath the Arctic Ocean. Ask students to summarize the main points in this conflict of interests and identify the perspective from which each side views the issue. **AL Logical/Mathematical**

R2 Reading Skills

Defining Ask students what the word *reverse* means *("able to be changed, to go backwards, or to be turned back the way it was to begin with")*. Ask students what the suffix *-able* means *("has the capacity to")*. Explain that the prefix *ir-* means "not." Then point out the word *irreversible* in the text. **Ask:** **How might you use these word parts to define *irreversible*?** *(Possible answer: "not able to be changed back to its original state")* **Why would environmentalists fear irreversible damage?** *(This kind of damage could never be fixed, and the environment would be permanently damaged.)* **ELL Verbal/Linguistic**

ANSWERS, p. 350

TAKING NOTES: Industrialization—Petroleum industry has required Arctic drilling and pipeline building, both of which threaten surrounding environments; other industries also release pollutants into the air; **Nuclear Wastes**—Many storage facilities were inadequate and leaked radioactive material; other industries dumped it directly into waterways; 1986 fire in a nuclear reactor released tons of radioactive particles into the environment; **Forest Destruction**—Forests are shrinking due to logging and wildfires; **Global Warming**—causing thawing of the world's largest peat bog, which will cause release of billions of metric tons of methane into the atmosphere

networks

There's More Online!

- **IMAGE** Grassroots Efforts
- **MAP** Environmental Issues in the Russian Core
- **MAP** Extent/Reach of Chernobyl Disaster
- **INTERACTIVE SELF-CHECK QUIZ**
- **VIDEO** People and Their Environment: The Russian Core

LESSON 3
People and Their Environment: The Russian Core

Reading HELPDESK 

Academic Vocabulary (Tier Two Words)
- radical
- stable

Content Vocabulary (Tier Three Words)
- nuclear wastes
- radioactive material
- pesticide

TAKING NOTES: ***Key Ideas and Details***

SUMMARIZING Use a chart like the one below to take notes about the human impact on the environment in the Russian Core.

The Human Impact on the Environment: The Russian Core	
Industrialization	Nuclear Wastes
Forest Destruction	Global Warming

ESSENTIAL QUESTION • *How do physical systems and human systems shape a place?*

IT MATTERS BECAUSE

R1 *Industrialization and economic progress in the Russian Core have had both positive and negative impacts on the subregion. Russia has to deal with considerable past damage to the environment. At the same time, it is working to manage natural resources and encourage economic growth while minimizing further harm.*

Managing Resources

GUIDING QUESTION *How do economic development and environmental protection cause conflict in the Russian Core?*

In general, Russia's economy is expanding, with robust growth in the areas of manufacturing and services and rapid growth in the oil and gas sector. Over time, this expansion has led to conflicts with organizations seeking to protect the environment and human populations from the negative aspects of industrialization and economic development.

C Russia's most important industry—petroleum extraction and processing—has made the country one of the world's largest producers of crude oil. It is no secret that Russia, by Arctic drilling, is trying to access the vast minerals, oil, and gas that lie beneath the Arctic Ocean. The area north of the Arctic Circle contains more than 90 billion barrels of oil and more than 1.5 trillion cubic feet of gas. There is much resistance, however, as environmentalist groups such as Greenpeace are protesting the drilling. Additionally, pipelines built to transport oil and gas pass through wilderness areas and threaten the surrounding environment. In 2006 Russia began constructing a highly controversial pipeline to carry oil from eastern Siberia to the Pacific Ocean. It will bring Russia billions of dollars from countries in the Asia-Pacific region. The pipeline will pass through a protected wilderness area near Lake Baikal (by•KAWL). R2 President Vladimir Putin ordered that the proposed route be diverted farther away from the lake, but environmentalists still fear the irreversible damage that could be caused by an oil spill.

350

(tl)Andrey Rudakov/Bloomberg/Getty Images, (tr)Heinrich Hoffmann/Hulton Archive/Getty Images

networks *Online Teaching Options*

 **INTERACTIVE BELLRINGER**

Extent of Chernobyl Disaster

Exploring Issues Have students view this the map to discuss the impact of nuclear reactor accidents on the environment. Explain that this map shows the extent of radiation resulting from the Chernobyl nuclear accident. Have students consider how they would feel if a nuclear reactor in a neighboring country accidentally released tons of radioactive particles into the environment. Then have students work with a partner to complete the activity by answering the questions. **Verbal/Linguistic, Visual/Spatial**

Extent of Chernobyl Disaster

The Chernobyl nuclear accident of 1986 released more than 400 times the radiation than was released by the nuclear bomb dropped on Hiroshima, Japan, in 1945.

Auto-Run Click Through 1 of 3

Another source of conflict is the subregion's fishing industry. Fish are a crucial component to the Russian diet and economy. Salmon from the Pacific Ocean and herring, cod, and halibut from the Arctic Ocean support a flourishing fishing industry. Russia's ocean fishing fleet contains what are known as supertrawlers that tow huge trawl nets—large enough to scoop up a whale. The ships can catch and process more than 40 tons (36 t) of fish a day. Because supertrawlers want only certain kinds of fish, everything else hauled up in the nets gets discarded. Millions of fish and other marine animals die unnecessarily every year as a result of supertrawling, and there are organizations working actively to stop this practice.

Another fish product from the region is the world-famous Russian caviar that comes from the eggs of sturgeon fish that inhabit freshwater rivers and lakes. The sturgeon population has declined, however. It is in danger because of dams built on the Volga River, which have interrupted the migration and disturbed the habitat of these fish.

✓ READING PROGRESS CHECK

Assessing Why is a new pipeline linking eastern Siberia to the Asia-Pacific region controversial?

Human Impact

GUIDING QUESTION *What impact did Soviet-era ideas and actions have on the environment of the Russian Core?*

The environmental damage caused by Soviet-era industrialization, including the region's affiliation with nuclear technologies, continues to pose risks to natural resources and human health. The Soviets' disregard for the environmental effects of industrialization has damaged Russia's water, air, soil, and forests. **V**

GEOGRAPHY CONNECTION

The Russian Core countries have many environmental issues including nuclear contamination, pollution, and deforestation.

1. ***THE WORLD IN SPATIAL TERMS*** Which part of Russia is most affected by industrial pollution?
2. ***PLACES AND REGIONS*** How does Belarus compare to Ukraine in regards to environmental issues? Use specific examples from the map to support your answer.

C

People and Their Environment: The Russian Core

Content Background Knowledge

Russian Caviar After the Soviet Union collapsed in 1991, poachers, unrestricted by the government, began to overfish the population of sturgeon in the Caspian and Azov Seas. Sellers could make huge profits by selling black caviar made from the sturgeon eggs. To try to save the fish, Russia passed increasingly stricter bans in 2001 and 2002 that forbade people from exporting caviar to Europe or commercially fishing for sturgeon. The government also started farms where the fish could be artificially cultivated. These strategies were so successful that Russia lifted the ban on exports of black caviar, at least from fish farms, in 2011.

V Visual Skills

Identifying Cause and Effect Have students create a graphic organizer that will help them record information about the many cause-and-effect relationships in this lesson that explain how Russia's water, air, soil, and forests have become damaged. Students should continue to add more information to their charts as they read the lesson. **AL** **Visual/Spatial**

C Critical Thinking Skills

Analyzing Visuals Have students study the map and interpret it in a class discussion. **Ask:** **Where is most industrial pollution found and why?** *(Most industrial pollution is found in the western area of the country because that is where the greatest population and industrial centers are located.)* **Which part of the country is least at risk for environmental issues and why?** *(The northeast section is the least at risk because it is sparsely populated and not very industrialized.)* **AL** **Visual/Spatial, Logical/Mathematical**

INTERACTIVE MAP

Environmental Issues in the Russian Core

Interpreting Issues Have students view the map to introduce the effects of human impact to the environment during the Soviet-era industrialization. As a class activity, ask volunteers to read the text as each interactive layer on the map is revealed. Then have students interpret the map by writing a statement that summarizes the amount of environmental damage caused by nuclear contamination, industrial pollution, water pollution, and extensive deforestation. Invite students to share their statements with the class. **Verbal/Linguistic, Visual/Spatial**

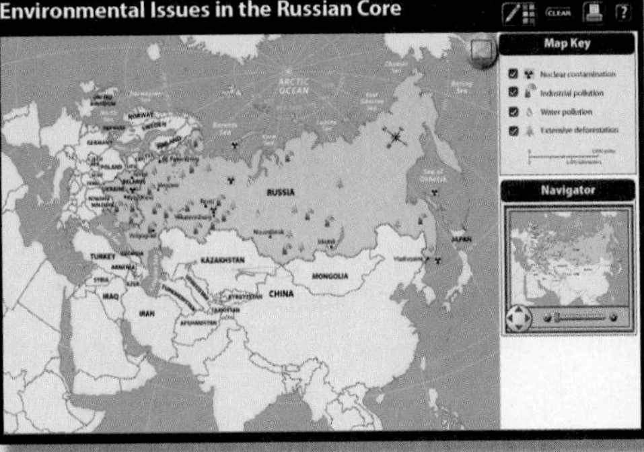

ANSWERS, p. 351

✓ **READING PROGRESS CHECK** It will allow Russia to transport oil and gas to Asia-Pacific countries, bringing in billions of dollars. However, it will pass through a protected wilderness area near Lake Baikal, where a spill would be environmentally disastrous.

GEOGRAPHY CONNECTION

1. Western Russia is most affected by industrial pollution.
2. Belarus has less environmental issues than Ukraine. The map indicates that Ukraine has water, industrial pollution, and nuclear contamination while Belarus suffers from nuclear contamination.

V Visual Skills

Analyzing Visuals Have students study the map key, labels, scale, and other parts of this map. **Ask:** What do the colors in this map indicate? *(how much radiation each area was exposed to)* Which countries were most affected? *(Russia, Belarus, Ukraine, Finland, Sweden, Norway, and Austria)* Why were countries located directly next to Chernobyl not affected? *(The winds transported radiation farther away.)* Have students use the map to continue discussing the widespread effects of Chernobyl on Europe and Asia. BL Visual/Spatial

Making Connections

Like the Soviet Union, the United States has also experienced nuclear power plant accidents. The Three Mile Island accident in Pennsylvania in 1979 was the worst nuclear accident to affect the United States. Where the Chernobyl incident was caused by a faulty reactor design, the Three Mile Island accident was caused by equipment failure. In Chernobyl, about 5 percent of the radioactive reactor core was released into the atmosphere. At Three Mile Island, very little radioactive gas was released, and the dose was not high enough to raise the normal atmospheric levels. Chernobyl caused the immediate deaths of 32 people and the subsequent deaths of thousands through radiation sickness. The Three Mile Island accident did not cause any deaths, but it did raise concerns about the safety of nuclear power.

W Writing Skills

Informative/Explanatory Have students review what they have read about Soviet generation and use of nuclear power and weapons. Then have them research and write an informative essay describing the benefits and risks of relying on nuclear technology. AL Verbal/Linguistic

ANSWERS, p. 352

GEOGRAPHY CONNECTION

1. Norway, Sweden, Finland, Austria, and Romania
2. Students may answer that the prevailing winds carried the fallout east, but they may also note that the extent was far-reaching to the north and west as well.

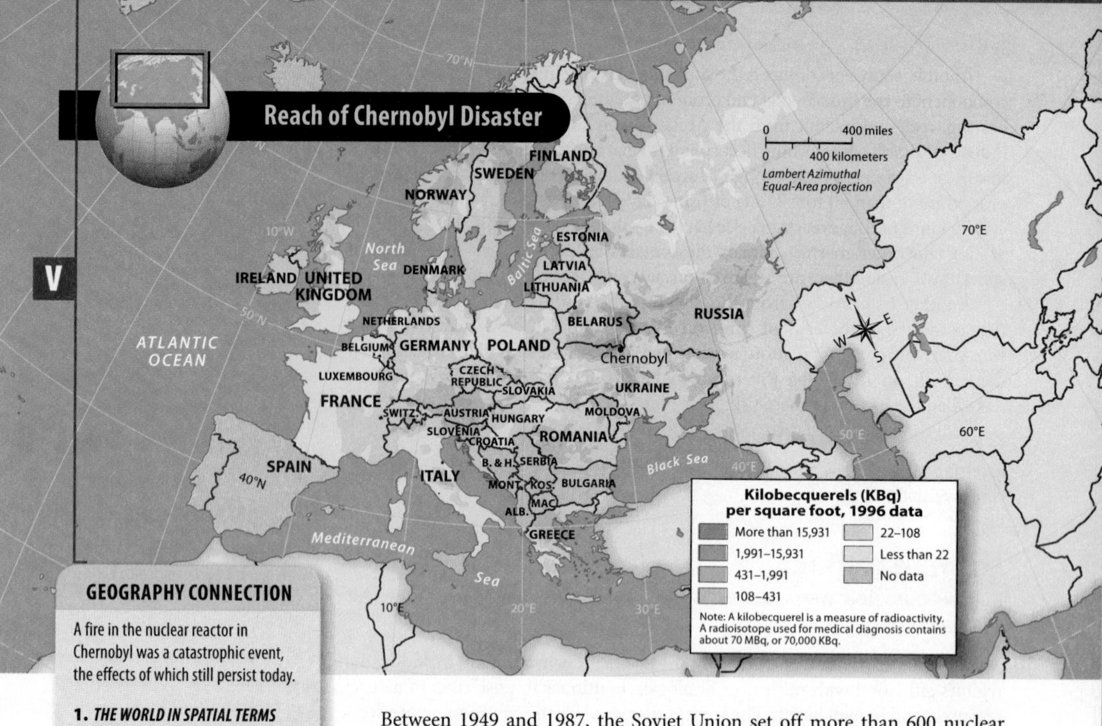

GEOGRAPHY CONNECTION

A fire in the nuclear reactor in Chernobyl was a catastrophic event, the effects of which still persist today.

1. ***THE WORLD IN SPATIAL TERMS*** Which countries outside the Russian Core had Kbq levels of 431–1,991 or greater?
2. ***PHYSICAL SYSTEMS*** Based on the data shown, which way were the winds blowing that carried the nuclear fallout?

nuclear wastes by-products of producing nuclear power and weapons

radioactive material material contaminated by residue from the generation of nuclear energy and weapons

radical fundamental or extreme; drastic

Between 1949 and 1987, the Soviet Union set off more than 600 nuclear explosions to test and improve its nuclear technologies and weapons. Soviets developed and then stockpiled nuclear weapons throughout the Cold War. Today, the condition and fate of those weapons concern Russia and the rest of the world. **Nuclear wastes** are the by-products of producing nuclear power and weapons. Some nuclear wastes can remain radioactive for thousands of years, posing danger to people and the environment. The Soviets placed most nuclear wastes in storage facilities, but some **radioactive materials**—materials contaminated by residue from the generation of nuclear energy and weapons—were dumped directly into the Barents, Baltic, and Bering Seas. **Radical** changes in these practices have been slow in coming.

The first significant environmental disaster in the Soviet Union related to nuclear technologies occurred in 1986. A fire in a nuclear reactor in the town of Chernobyl (chuhr•NOH•buhl), 60 miles (97 km) north of Kiev, Ukraine, released tons of radioactive particles into the local environment. The amount of radioactivity released was 400 times more than what was released when the nuclear bomb was dropped on Hiroshima, Japan, in 1945. Radiation covered tens of thousands of square miles of farmland and forests in the Soviet republics of Belarus, Ukraine, and Russia. Because of prevailing winds, other countries suffered as well. Millions of people were exposed to deadly levels of radiation because Soviet officials were slow to alert the public to the crisis and did not evacuate people soon enough. Thousands of people died as a direct result of radiation poisoning. Tens of thousands more continue to suffer from cancer, stomach diseases, cataracts, and immune system disorders. Approximately 350,000 people were displaced from their homes. Today, there is a tightly controlled exclusion zone surrounding the Chernobyl Nuclear Power Plant.

After the accident, international pressure prompted Soviet leaders to improve nuclear safety standards and to shut down dangerous plants. Despite

networks Online Teaching Options

GRAPH

The Nuclear Arms Race

Examining Ethical Issues Have students examine this graph to begin a discussion about the nuclear arms race and the dynamics and ethics of the Cold War. Then have students analyze the graph to identify which peaks first. Have students form small groups to discuss the following questions:

- Does it appear that the Soviet accumulation of nuclear arms was a response to the U.S. accumulation?
- What responsibility does the United States bear for current problems with Soviet waste disposal?

Ask groups to write agreed-upon responses to these questions. BL Interpersonal

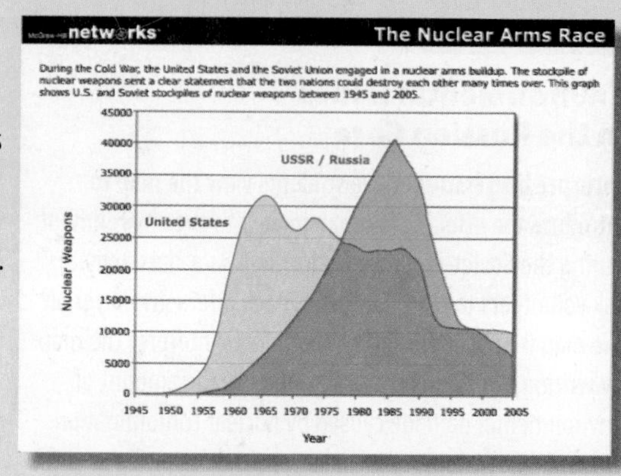

concerns, 29 nuclear reactors continue to provide some of the country's electricity. Experts think that many remaining Soviet-era reactors are poorly designed and unsafe. Russia plans to expand its nuclear power industry by building more reactors and new power plants. In 2009 over 10 percent of Russia's total electricity output was generated through radioactive decay of nuclear fuel, and Ukraine ranked third in the world with over 25 percent of its electricity produced by nuclear fuels.

In addition to the impact of nuclear technologies on the Russian Core, the region's industrialization—which began during the Soviet era and continues today—has polluted much of Russia's lakes, rivers, and soils. Fertilizer runoff, sewage, and radioactive material all contribute to poor water quality. The waters of the Moskva and Volga Rivers pose health risks, and dams along the Volga River trap contaminated water. Pollution also threatens the Caspian Sea.

Lake Baikal, the world's deepest and oldest lake, called the Pearl of Siberia, is considered a natural wonder with more than 1,500 different native species of aquatic plants and animals. In 1957 the Soviet Union announced a plan to build a paper-pulp factory along Lake Baikal's shores. Although this plan was opposed by people in the area, their protests were ignored and the factory was built. This factory and others that followed dumped industrial waste into the lake.

For decades, toxic waste dumps and airborne pollution have also posed problems for Russia's soil. In the rush to industrialize, little effort had been made to store toxic wastes properly. Thus, aging storage containers cracked and toxic wastes leaked into the soil. Petroleum pipelines often broke, allowing petroleum to ruin the land. In addition, overuse of fertilizers and **pesticides**—chemicals used to kill crop-damaging insects, rodents, and other pests—pollute farmland and water.

Russia's forests are also at risk from harmful practices. About one-fifth of the world's forest lands lie in Russia—75 percent of them in Siberia. Second only to the Amazon rain forest in the amount of oxygen returned to the atmosphere, the Russian boreal, or northern, forest also supplies much of the world's timber. The boreal is the southern part of the taiga biome. As a result of commercial logging, illegal poaching of trees, and wildfires, however, Russian forests shrink by almost 40 million acres (16 million ha) each year—a rate of loss higher than that of the Amazon Basin.

R

PRIMARY SOURCE

"If the tropical forests, which contain half the planet's woodlands, are one lung of the Earth, then the boreal forest is the other. Both play a vital role in regulating climate as they—along with the ocean, Earth's largest carbon repository—filter out billions of tons of carbon dioxide and other greenhouse gases during photosynthesis, storing the carbon in trees, roots, and soils."

—Fen Montaigne, "The Great Northern Forest," *National Geographic*, June 2002

The widespread effects of global warming are becoming visible in western Siberia because climate change more readily affects temperatures at higher northern latitudes. The warming is likely to produce an unprecedented thawing of the world's largest peat bog that would release into the atmosphere billions of metric tons of methane, a powerful greenhouse gas. Where permafrost once covered the subarctic regions of western Siberia, shallow lakes are now more prevalent. In addition, air pollution has contributed to increased temperatures in both the subregion and around the world. The human population is also affected in several ways. Increased health risks due to heat waves and changes in infectious diseases are present. In addition, activities such as hunting and travel over snow and ice are affected.

W

✓ READING PROGRESS CHECK

Evaluating What factors contribute to poor air quality in Russia?

Analyzing PRIMARY SOURCES (CCSS)

The Long Shadow of Chernobyl

"Early estimates that tens or hundreds of thousands of people would die from Chernobyl have been discredited. But genetic damage done 20 years ago is slowly taking a toll. No one can be sure of the ultimate impact, but an authoritative report estimated last year that the cancer fuse lit by Chernobyl will claim 4,000 lives. Alexei Okeanov of the International Sakharov Environmental University in Minsk, Belarus, who studies the health effects of the accident, calls it 'a fire that can't be put out in our lifetimes.'"

—Richard Stone, "The Long Shadow of Chernobyl," *National Geographic*, April 2006

T

DBQ ***INTERPRETING*** How does the description of the Chernobyl disaster as a lit fuse and a "fire that can't be put out" help you understand the problem? RH.9–10.1

pesticide chemicals used to kill crop-damaging insects, rodents, and other pests

VIDEO

Russian Forest Under Threat

Finding the Main Idea Use this video about the boreal forest to discuss environmental issues in Russia. As students view the video, have them write down the important concepts. Have students work with a partner to share their written concepts and identify details that support a larger idea or issue. Partners should then assess which concepts are the most important and write the main idea of the video and complete the accompanying video worksheet. **AL Interpersonal, Verbal/Linguistic**

People and Their Environment: The Russian Core

R Reading Skills

Using Context Clues Remind students to use context clues to define terms. **Ask: What context clue helps you understand the meaning of *boreal*? *(northern)* What other word or term can help you remember this meaning?** *(Aurora borealis, or the northen lights)* Have students reread the quote by Fen Montaigne. Guide a class discussion on the analogy between tropical forests, the boreal forest, and the lungs of Earth. **ELL Verbal/Linguistic**

W Writing Skills

Informative/Explanatory Have students do additional research to learn more about the damage that has been caused to Russia's air, water, soil, and forests. Then ask students to pick one of these endangered resources and write an essay using facts and details to describe the environmental situation. Tell them to propose concrete solutions that might fix the damage and address the underlying problem so no further harm is caused. Invite students to share their essays with the class and then lead a discussion about the value of each proposed solution. **BL Intrapersonal, Verbal/Linguistic**

T Technology Skills

Acquiring Information Have student pairs use online resources to gather in-depth information about the new business prospects raised by the melting of Arctic ice and the potential pollution threats that could be caused by these businesses. Have partners research a different business possibility such as extracting natural gas or oil, mining for minerals, fishing, traveling sea trade routes, or setting up tourist opportunities. Students should use photographs, illustrations, text, sound, and video clips to create a multimedia presentation about the pros and cons of the business venture. Have students share their presentations with the class. Then hold a class discussion about the dangers posed to the Arctic wilderness and whether the benefits of the business opportunities outweigh these dangers. **BL Auditory/Musical, Visual/Spatial**

ANSWERS, p. 353

✓ READING PROGRESS CHECK Radioactive particles have been released due to improper management of nuclear reactors. Also, industries emit pollutants into the air. Predictions are that in the future, global warming will cause the thawing of the world's largest peat bog, resulting in the release of billions of metric tons of methane into the atmosphere.

DBQ It emphasizes the silent, irreversible effects of contact with radiation.

People and Their Environment: The Russian Core

W Writing Skills

Argument Have students choose an environmental issue in the Russian Core to write a few paragraphs describing what has been done or needs to be done and then argue why this is the best solution. Students may need to do additional research to support their opinion. BL **Verbal/Linguistic**

R Reading Skills

Inferring Review with students the proposed mining operation in Kamchatka. **Ask: Why would the fishing industry be against the proposed mine?** *(If the spawning grounds are affected, not enough new fish will hatch and pollution from the mine may also cause extensive damage to the habitat.)* **Why are people tempted to open mines even when environmental groups are against them?** *(Mines can bring great profits making environmental concerns seem trivial.)* **Logical/Mathematical**

CLOSE & REFLECT

Recognizing Relationships Have students write three statements describing how the problems facing the Russian Core today are largely effects of past decisions.

ANSWERS, p. 354

READING PROGRESS CHECK Russia is trying to balance its natural resources with environmental protection through management techniques such as monitoring pollution levels, conservation, and international regulation.

CRITICAL THINKING

1. It reduces carbon emissions that contribute to global warming. Global warming is causing peat bogs to thaw.
2. Governments could give rebates and incentives to the manufacturers and to people who purchase these vehicles.

Driving vehicles fueled by electricity and natural gas provides a way for Russian citizens to help in reducing carbon emissions.

Andrey Rudakov/Bloomberg/Getty Images

▲ CRITICAL THINKING

1. ***Identifying Cause and Effect*** How does driving an electric or natural gas-fueled vehicle help protect the peat bogs in western Siberia?
2. ***Assessing*** In what ways can governments help to increase the use of electric and natural gas-fueled vehicles?

Addressing the Issues

GUIDING QUESTION *How are people and the governments in the Russian Core working to change ideas about the environment?*

W The balance between using natural resources and preserving the environment can be viewed from several different perspectives. Solutions that are available are environmental protection and wise management through monitoring pollution levels, conservation, and international regulation. For example, people have come together to oppose a mining operation in remote Kamchatka in eastern Russia. R Environmental groups have demanded that the mining company meet strict environmental standards. The possible threat to the area's salmon spawning grounds prompted the local fishing industry to support the effort. The mine also caused concern among local residents because it was close to a protected wildlife area. Even with growing environmental awareness, economic pressure continues to open other sensitive regions to development.

In September 2012, a British parliamentary committee called for a halt to drilling in the Arctic Ocean until necessary steps are taken to protect the region from the potentially catastrophic consequences of an oil spill. Another successful outside effort was Greenpeace's organization of an independent forum on the protection of sites in the Russian Core. Other outside groups are working to protect wildlife and the region's ecosystems.

In the case of Lake Baikal, all was not lost. Efforts from concerned citizens and environmental organizations have met with moderate success. In response to ongoing protests, the most serious polluters have been closed, and others are working to reduce pollution. Pollution levels in the lake are now relatively low compared with many lakes in Europe.

Additionally, the World Bank's Sustainable Forestry Pilot project is helping Russia manage its forests. Using land more wisely, protecting forests, planting new trees, and increasing private investment all help Russia's environment and economy. Increased employment opportunities in the forest industry and more **stable** economies will be possible only if steps are taken to conserve the forests.

stable not changing or fluctuating

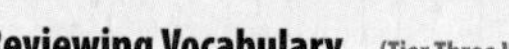

READING PROGRESS CHECK

Analyzing How is Russia trying to reverse past damage to its natural resources as well as manage them responsibly today?

LESSON 3 REVIEW (CCSS)

Reviewing Vocabulary (Tier Three Words)

1. ***Explaining*** Explain the difference between nuclear waste and radioactive material. RH.9–10.4

Using Your Notes

2. ***Describing*** Use your chart to describe the major threats to the forests of the Russian Core.

Answering the Guiding Questions

3. ***Explaining*** How do economic development and environmental protection cause conflict in the Russian Core?
4. ***Discussing*** What impact did Soviet-era ideas and actions have on the environment of the Russian Core?
5. ***Explaining*** How are people and governments in the Russian Core working to change ideas about the environment?

Writing Activity

6. ***Informative/Explanatory*** Think about the challenges Russia faces concerning water quality. Write a paragraph explaining why Russians do not use more water from Lake Baikal to supply their freshwater needs. WHST.9–10.2

354

LESSON 3 REVIEW ANSWERS

Reviewing Vocabulary

1. Nuclear waste is a by-product of producing nuclear power and weapons, and radioactive material is any material that becomes contaminated after contact with nuclear waste or residue.

Using Your Notes

2. As a result of commercial logging and wildfires, Russian forests shrink by almost 40 million acres each year, a rate of loss higher than that of the Amazon Basin.

Answering the Guiding Questions

3. Economic development can result in tapping into natural resources in ways that can damage the environment. For example, a new pipeline linking eastern Siberia to the Asia-Pacific region is controversial because although it will bring Russia billions of dollars, it will pose a great threat to the protected wilderness area near Lake Baikal.
4. The Soviets' embracing of industrialization and nuclear technologies with no regard to environmental effects poisoned the population with radiation and polluted the water, air, soil, and forests with industrial toxins.
5. People are joining together for action and seeing results. One group formed to demand that a mining company meet strict environmental standards. Protests by citizens led to the closing of the main polluters of Lake Baikal. Britain stepped in to postpone Arctic drilling until proper spill prevention measures were in place. The World Bank's Sustainable Forestry Pilot project is helping Russia manage its forests.

Writing Activity

6. Paragraphs will vary but should be logical and supported by information in the lesson. Explanations should include the lake's status as a natural wonder.

CHAPTER 14 Assessment 

Directions: On a separate sheet of paper, answer the questions below. Make sure you read carefully and answer all parts of the questions.

Lesson Review

Lesson 1

1. ***Describing*** Describe Russia's midlatitude climate regions. Why do such climate regions support most of the country's agricultural production?
2. ***Explaining*** How do Russia's climates and short growing season affect food production?
3. ***Assessing*** Discuss the importance of rivers in the Russian Core.

Lesson 2

4. ***Evaluating*** What area of Russia has the greatest population density? Why is the population concentrated there?
5. ***Drawing Inferences*** Why were satellite states eager to declare their independence from the Soviet Union in 1991? Provide an example.
6. ***Summarizing*** How did the fall of the Soviet Union affect religion in Russia?

Lesson 3

7. ***Discussing*** How are Russia's fishing practices affecting the fish populations in the oceans and rivers of the Russian Core? Provide specific examples.
8. ***Exploring the Issues*** Describe the Chernobyl disaster and how it affected the people of the region. WHST.9–10.2
9. ***Explaining*** How has industrialization of the Russian Core damaged the environment? What steps have local and international governments taken to combat the problem?

Critical Thinking

10. ***Identifying Central Issues*** What actions has Russia taken to become part of the global economy?
11. ***Identifying Cause and Effect*** How did the transition from a command economy to a market economy affect the Russian people?
12. ***Explaining*** How did the migration of the Slavs and their interactions with other peoples influence the history of Russia?
13. ***Exploring the Issues*** Discuss one way in which Russia is working with international agencies to manage its forests.

Research and Presentation

14. ***Research Skills*** Use the Internet and other resources to investigate Russian and American cooperative involvement with the International Space Station. What have both countries contributed to this project? Who are some of the key individuals? WHST.9–10.6, WHST.9–10.7

21st Century Skills

Telephone Use in Russia (2011)

	Main Lines	Mobile Cellular
Number of Telephones	44.181 million	256.117 million
World Ranking	5	4

Source: CIA World Factbook

Use the chart to answer the following questions.

15. ***Assessing*** How does the number of main lines compare to the number of cellular users in Russia?
16. ***Speculating*** How might the disparity in cell phone usage compared to main line usage be a reflection of the population structure of Russia today?

Need Extra Help?

If You've Missed Question	1	2	3	4	5	6	7	8	9	10	11	12	13	14	15	16
Go to page	339	338	337	334	343	344	351	352	353	347	346	341	354	343	355	355

CHAPTER 14 Assessment Answers

Lesson Review

Lesson 1

1. Midlatitude climates are characterized by milder winters and warmer summers. They also support deciduous forests. The mild climate is the most beneficial to agriculture.
2. Food production occurs mainly in the western region since the rest of Russia has harsher climates. Even in the west, it is limited by short growing seasons.
3. Russia's waterways have played important roles in its social and economic development. The Volga River and the Dnieper River are commercial, transportation, and hydroelectric power resources, and they also supply the people with water.

Lesson 2

4. The greatest population density is west of the Ural Mountains because this is the area with the richest soils, most waterways, and mildest climate.
5. The satellite states were not faring well under the communist policies of the Soviet Union. Belarus, for example, wanted political sovereignty so its people would be able to preserve their shared ethnic identity and language.
6. People began reclaiming their faiths and openly practicing their religions since it was no longer against government policy to do so.

Lesson 3

7. Supertrawlers use huge nets that haul in tons of fish, both wanted and unwanted, and many unwanted species are discarded and die unnecessarily. Dam building has contributed to the endangerment of the sturgeon population.
8. A fire in a nuclear reactor sent tons of radioactive particles into the environment of Chernobyl, covering thousands of square miles of farms and forests and exposing millions of people to deadly levels of radiation. Thousands died and tens of thousands still suffer health conditions caused by the radiation.
9. Industries release pollutants into the air. The petroleum industry threatens the environment with oil spills. The fishing industry threatens fish populations. The logging industry is shrinking the region's forests. Governments have been managing resources more closely by monitoring pollution levels, attempting conservation, and establishing regulations for industries.

Critical Thinking

10. Russia has transitioned to a market economy, expanded trade, and worked on building international relationships.
11. The wealthy profited from private ownership of companies. More consumer goods were available, but demand kept rising, which made prices increase too. Eventually Russians experienced an economic depression and financial crisis.
12. Slavs settled near waterways and established prosperous trading routes using Russia's rivers, which are still used in much the same way today.
13. Russia is part of the World Bank's Sustainable Forestry project, which is aimed at helping Russia manage its forests wisely and plant new trees.

Research and Presentation

14. Paragraphs will vary but should include an overview of Russia's and America's roles in the International Space Station and each country's significant contributions. Names of key individuals should also be included.

21st Century Skills

15. There are more than five times more cellular lines than main lines.
16. One phone line would not serve the needs of many people living in the same apartment or house.

Assessment Answers

DBQ Analyzing Primary Sources

17 The main threat is poaching, but habitat reduction caused by fires and logging is also part of the problem.

18 It helps the team reduce slaughter by allowing them to monitor the tigers in a timely manner.

Exploring the Essential Question

19 Paragraphs will vary but may include characteristics of the Ural and Caucasus Mountains, the Northern European and the Siberian Plains, swamps, and wetlands, and how these have shaped Russia.

Applying Map Skills

20 Northern Dvina, Ob'R, Irtysh, Yenisey, Kolyma, and Lena

21 coal, natural gas, and petroleum

22 Maps should show the basic political boundaries of Russia, the tundra climate region with a label, and major lines of latitude with labels.

College and Career Readiness

23 Paragraphs will vary but should include basic characteristics of education during the Soviet era, such as a focus on math, science, and engineering. These should be contrasted with characteristics of Russian education today, such as more balanced instruction that includes language, history, and literature.

24 Reports will vary but should be logical and supported by information from the chapter. They should include specific causes, the likelihood of reversibility, and current solutions being employed.

Writing About Geography

25 Essays will vary but should be logical and supported by information from the chapter. Physical features and their influence on culture may include such features as mountains as barriers, water systems as unifiers, or plains as agricultural centers.

CHAPTER 14 Assessment 

Directions: On a separate sheet of paper, answer the questions below. Make sure you read carefully and answer all parts of the questions.

DBQ Analyzing Primary Sources

Use the document to answer the following questions.

PRIMARY SOURCE

"As director of the Phoenix Fund, a small, environmental NGO that he has headed for 12 years, [Sergei] Bereznuk and his team of six people are carrying out an impressive range of activities to preserve the Amur [Siberian] tiger over a territory of 166,000 km^2. These include support of anti-poaching units, awareness-raising among local people, reversing habitat reduction due to fires and logging and resolution of human-animal conflicts, along with providing compensation for damage and monitoring invasive industrial projects in the region.

'Poaching remains the principal threat to the tigers' survival,' Rolex adds. The animals are killed in retaliation, mainly for loss of cattle and wild prey and as hunting trophies. There is also demand for their skin, bones and body parts, used primarily in Chinese traditional medicine. Despite international laws banning the sale of tiger parts there is a lucrative market that fuels poaching. In their campaign to reduce the slaughter, Bereznuk and the Vladivostok-based Phoenix Fund provide anti-poaching teams with software—the Management Information System (MIST)—developed specifically for this purpose by the Wildlife Conservation Society. Up-to-date, relevant and timely information is an integral part of effective protected area management."

—David Brau, *National Geographic Daily News*, November 25, 2012

17 ***Exploring the Issues*** What are the major threats to the Siberian tiger?

18 ***Interpreting*** In what ways does technology assist the protection efforts of the Phoenix Fund? WHST.9–10.2

Exploring the Essential Question

19 ***Making Connections*** Write a paragraph describing how the landforms of the Russian Core have helped shape it as a place.

Applying Map Skills

Use the Unit 4 Atlas to answer the following questions.

20 ***Human Systems*** What rivers serve as links to the Arctic Ocean in the Russian Core?

21 ***Environment and Society*** What natural resources are most abundant in the Russian Core?

22 ***Physical Systems*** Sketch your mental map of Russia. Then label the tundra climate region and label the major lines of latitude.

College and Career Readiness

23 ***Examining Information*** Use the Internet and other resources to research education in Russia today and how it compares with education during the Soviet era. Write a few paragraphs comparing and contrasting education during the two time periods. WHST.9–10.7

24 ***Change and Continuity of Groups*** As a social scientist conducting research in the Russian Core, you have been asked to write a brief report on the causes of demographic decline. Can this decline be reversed? What is being done to solve this critical problem? WHST.9–10.7

Writing About Geography

25 ***Informative/Explanatory*** Use standard grammar, spelling, sentence structure, and punctuation to write a one-page essay considering how physical geography has influenced culture in Russia. WHST.9–10.4

David Brau/National Geographic Stock

Need Extra Help?

If You've Missed Question	17	18	19	20	21	22	23	24	25
Go to page	356	356	336	242	245	244	345	344	341

356

networks Online Teaching Options

WORKSHEET

Chapter Test and Lesson Quizzes

Assessing Have students complete the Chapter Test and Lesson Quizzes to assess student understanding throughout the chapter. These assessment tools offer chapter and lesson evaluation through a variety of question formats, including document-based questions.

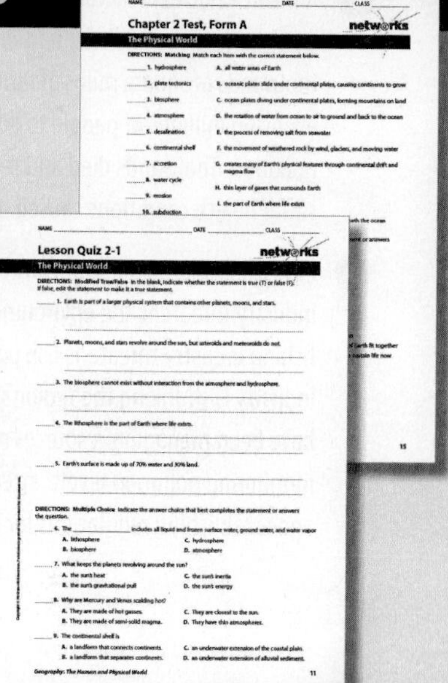

UNIT **5**

NORTH AFRICA, SOUTHWEST ASIA, AND CENTRAL ASIA Planner

UNDERSTANDING BY DESIGN®

Enduring Understandings

- *The physical environment affects people and their activities.*
- *The characteristics and distribution of cultures influence human systems.*
- *Culture influences people's perceptions of places and regions.*
- *Cooperation and conflict among people influences the division and control of Earth's surface.*
- *Places reflect the relationship between humans and the physical environment.*

Essential Question

- *How do physical systems and human systems shape a place?*

Students will know:

- *the landforms, water systems, climate regions, biomes, and natural resources in this region.*
- *how the history of North Africa, Southwest Asia, and Central Asia was shaped by migrations, religion, trade, and invasions.*
- *how physical geography and human activities contribute to water scarcity issues in the region.*
- *how religion and ethnic diversity conflicts have influenced population patterns.*
- *ways in which people and governments are addressing environmental issues in the region.*
- *the causes and effects of the uneven development of economies, including the influence of oil and petroleum income and water resources.*

Students will be able to:

- ***analyze*** *the influence of religion and ethnic diversity on North Africa's, Southwest Asia's, and Central Asia's population patterns and history.*
- ***explain*** *how conflicts that have led to political unrest and negative perceptions.*
- ***identify*** *factors that affect landforms, water systems, climate, and natural resources.*
- ***describe*** *causes of environmental issues and how they are being addressed.*
- ***analyze*** *how geography and human activities contribute to water scarcity issues.*

Predictable Misunderstandings

- *The desert forms the majority of the landscapes in North Africa.*
- *The physical geography of Southwest Asia is the same as in Central Asia.*
- *Southwest Asia has just one major world religion.*
- *Oil is found only in the Arabian Peninsula.*
- *Countries in the Arabian Peninsula have one culture.*
- *Conflict in this region is mostly due to government and economic issues.*
- *Water scarcity issues are the same in all areas within the region.*
- *Countries rich in oil resources are economically wealthy, and few people living there struggle with poverty.*

Assessment Evidence

Performance Tasks:

- *Environmental Case Study*
- *GeoLab Activity*
- *GIS Simulation*
- *Hands-On Chapter Projects*

Other Evidence:

- *Location Activity*
- *Self-Check Quizzes*
- *Lesson Quizzes*
- *Participation in Interactive Whiteboard Activities*
- *Contribution to small-group activities*
- *Interpretation of slide show images*
- *Participation in class discussions about North Africa, Southwest Asia, and Central Asia*
- *Analysis of graphic organizers, graphs, and charts*
- *Lesson Reviews*
- *Chapter Assessments*

Key for Using the Teacher Edition

SKILL-BASED ACTIVITIES

Types of skill activities found in the Teacher Edition.

* **V Visual Skills** require students to analyze maps, graphs, charts, and photos.

R Reading Skills help students practice reading skills and master vocabulary.

C Critical Thinking Skills help students apply and extend what they have learned.

W Writing Skills provide writing opportunities to help students comprehend the text.

T Technology Skills require students to use digital tools effectively.

*Letters are followed by a number when there is more than one of the same type of skill on the page.

DIFFERENTIATED INSTRUCTION

All activities are written for the on-level student unless otherwise marked with the leveled labels below.

BL Beyond Level
AL Approaching Level
ELL English Language Learners

All students benefit from activities that utilize different learning styles. Many activities are marked as below when a particular learning style is highlighted.

Intrapersonal	**Naturalist**
Logical/Mathematical	**Kinesthetic**
Visual/Spatial	**Auditory/Musical**
Verbal/Linguistic	**Interpersonal**

SUGGESTED PACING GUIDE

Introducing the Unit	1 Day
Chapter 15: North Africa	4 Days
Global Connections: The Arab Spring	1 Day
Chapter 16: The Eastern Mediterranean	4 Days
Chapter 17: The Northeast	4 Days
Case Study: How Have Sunni and Shia Beliefs Led to Conflict?	1 Day
Chapter 18: The Arabian Peninsula	5 Days
Chapter 19: Central Asia	4 Days
TOTAL TIME	**24 Days**

PLANNER

☑ Print Teaching Options

V Visual Skills

- ☐ **p. 357** Students analyze an image to discuss the landscape of the region. **Naturalist, Visual/Spatial**
- ☐ **p. 360** Students create a chart that shows the extreme geography in the region. **BL Logical/Mathematical**
- ☐ **p. 363** Students create a graph that displays the land use by country based on information on an economic map. **Logical/Mathematical**

R Reading Skills

- ☐ **p. 358** Students express themselves through songs or raps about the region's religious influences. **Verbal/Linguistic, Auditory/Musical**
- ☐ **p. 360** Students explain the effects that low and high elevations have on temperature. **ELL Verbal/Linguistic**
- ☐ **p. 363** Students make inferences about the manufacturing locations based on information on a map. **Visual/Spatial**

C Critical Thinking Skills

- ☐ **p. 358** Students formulate and answer questions about the region and then use them to play a review game. **AL Verbal/Linguistic**
- ☐ **p. 361** Students classify countries in the Transition Zone by subregion. **ELL Visual/Spatial**
- ☐ **p. 362** Students create an analysis of the vegetation within a specific climate zone. **AL Visual/Spatial, Naturalist**

W Writing Skills

- ☐ **p. 359** Students write to the economic leaders of the region about the current economic practices of reliance on oil. **AL Verbal/Linguistic**
- ☐ **p. 361** Students write an informative essay about a boundary dispute in the region. **AL Verbal/Linguistic, Logical/Mathematical**

T Technology Skills

- ☐ **p. 359** Students conduct research to compare and contrast three ancient kingdoms that thrived in the region. **BL Verbal/Linguistic**
- ☐ **p. 362** Students research and write a blog about the climate and vegetation in the region. **BL Logical/Mathematical, Musical/Auditory**
- ☐ **p. 364** Students create a multimedia presentation about an assigned metropolitan city to plan housing, infrastructure, and other building projects. **BL Logical/Mathematical**

☑ Online Teaching Options

V Visual Skills

- **INTERACTIVE MAP** **Economic Activity Map: North Africa, Southwest Asia, and Central Asia**—Students consider which natural resources are the most valuable to each area or subregion. **BL Verbal/Linguistic, Visual/Spatial**

R Reading Skills

- **INTERACTIVE FEATURE** **Explore the Region: North Africa, Southwest Asia, and Central Asia**—Students discuss the culture, history, and landscapes of the region. **AL Naturalist, Verbal/Linguistic**
- **GEO @ WORK** **Thinking Like a Geographer**—Students explore specific examples of geography principles and skills. **Visual/Spatial, Logical/Mathematical**
- **INTERACTIVE MAP** **Climate and Vegetation Maps: North Africa, Southwest Asia, and Central Asia**—Students discuss the climate and vegetation information on a map. **ELL Visual/Spatial**

C Critical Thinking Skills

- **INTERACTIVE MAP** **Physical Map: North Africa, Southwest Asia, and Central Asia**—Students calculate low and high elevations and then write questions for each other based on elevation. **AL Visual/Spatial, Logical/Mathematical**

W Writing Skills

- **INTERACTIVE MAP** **Political Map: North Africa, Southwest Asia, and Central Asia**—Students write about the official and claimed boundary lines in the Transition Zone. **AL Visual/Spatial**
- **INTERACTIVE MAP** **Population Density Map: North Africa, Southwest Asia, and Central Asia**—Students write about why some areas are sparsely populated. **AL Verbal/Linguistic**

☑ Printable Digital Worksheets

V Visual Skills

- **WORKSHEET** **Location Activity**—Students locate countries, water systems, and physical features of North Africa, Southwest Asia, and Central Asia.

C Critical Thinking Skills

- **WORKSHEET** **Environmental Case Study**—Students complete a study about invasive marine species and investigate whether the United States government should join other nations in ratifying the 2004 Ballast Water Management Convention guidelines.
- **WORKSHEET** **GeoLab Activity**—Students explore how a disease discovered in Tunisia is inherited.
- **WORKSHEET** **GIS Simulation**—Students play the part of disaster-risk-management decision makers and use GIS to evaluate the potential for different areas in the Eastern Mediterranean region to experience natural disasters.

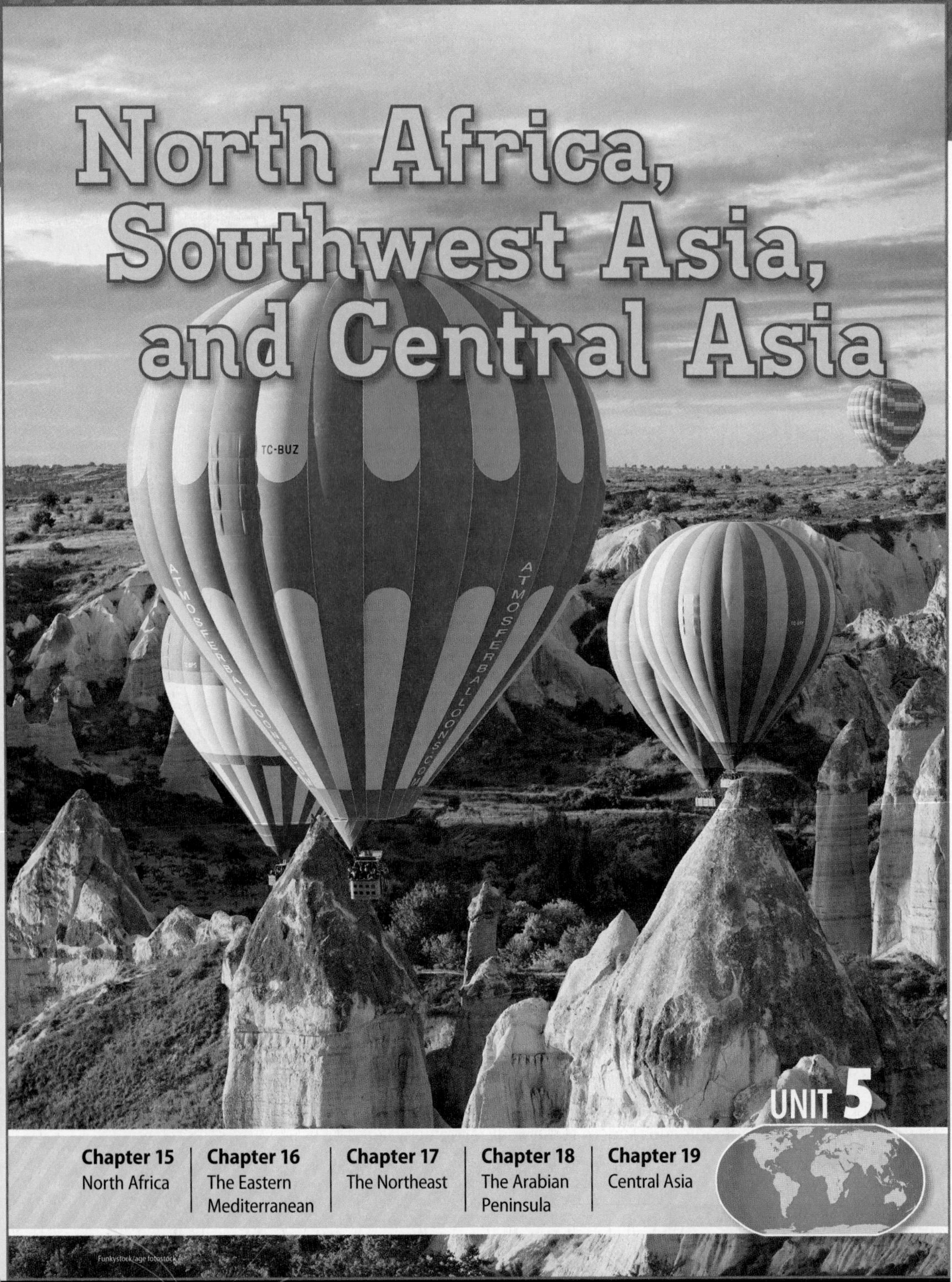

North Africa, Southwest Asia, and Central Asia

UNIT 5

Chapter 15	Chapter 16	Chapter 17	Chapter 18	Chapter 19
North Africa	The Eastern Mediterranean	The Northeast	The Arabian Peninsula	Central Asia

Funkystock/age fotostock

networks Online Teaching Options

GEO @ WORK

Thinking Like a Geographer

Problem Solving Explore specific examples of the principles and skills of geography applied to real-world challenges that impact people's lives. From agriculture to urban planning, to wiping out disease and managing changes in society—geography plays a key role in understanding relationships and generating solutions that make sense. **Visual/Spatial, Logical/Mathematical**

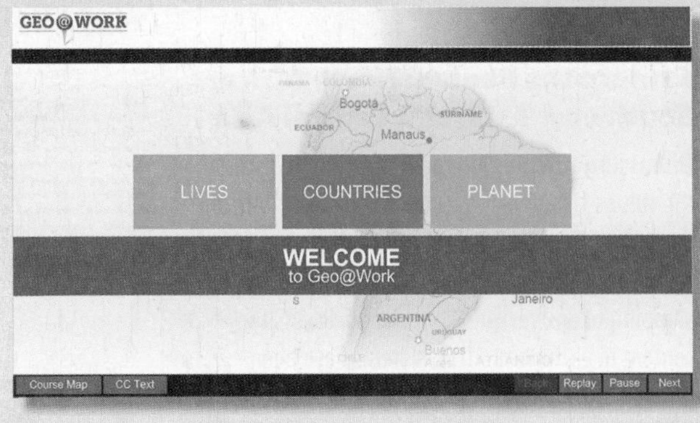

UNIT 5

North Africa, Southwest Asia, and Central Asia

ENGAGE

Activating Background Knowledge Invite volunteers to share what they already know about the physical, political, and cultural features that make North Africa, Southwest Asia, and Central Asia unique from other regions of the world. Have students sketch a map of the region based on what they think it comprises. As students look through the maps in the unit, have them check their sketches for accuracy and add physical features and political boundaries to it.

TEACH & ASSESS

Making Connections

Explain to students how the land and climate of the region of North Africa, Southwest Asia, and Central Asia is diverse and spans parts of two continents. Make a list of the land and climate features on the board. Then ask students to make connections between the land and climate where they live or other areas of the United States with those of North Africa, Southwest Asia, or Central Asia.

Analyzing Images Ask students to examine the unit opener image. Discuss the unique landscape, which serves as a backdrop for the balloons. **Ask:** **Where do you think this image was taken—in North Africa, Southwest Asia, or Central Asia, and why?** *(Possible answer: Central Asia; because of the rocky terrain)* **Why do you think people are viewing the land and rocks from balloons?** *(Possible answer: because the terrain is not good for road transportation)* **Do the rocks look like they were once part of something else? How do you know?** *(Possible answer: Yes, some of the rocks look like they were once towers or part of a larger structure such as a palace or temple.)* Invite students to describe other details in the image that might help to identify this place. **Naturalist, Visual/Spatial**

CLOSE & REFLECT

Listing Have students make a list of the unique physical, political, and cultural characteristics of the region. Tell students they will be learning more about North Africa, Southwest Asia, and Central Asia in this unit.

ENGAGE

R Reading Skills

Expressing Explain to students that the region's culture is diverse and made up of many countries and ethnic and religious groups. Have students read the callout and predict where in the region these men are playing music and singing. *(North Africa)* **Ask:** **Why do you think Islam is the dominant religion in this region?** *(Possible answer: because Islam began in Southwest Asia and was spread by people, especially traders, throughout the region)* Have students work with a partner to write a song or rap that describes how being the birthplace of the three major world religions has affected the entire region's cultural development. **Verbal/Linguistic, Auditory/Musical**

TEACH & ASSESS

V Visual Skills

Visualizing Have students visualize the region based on the phrases that are used to describe it. Ask them to draw a sketch or diagram that includes all of these details—area of contrasts, plentiful oil, scarce water, bustling cities, large expanses of uninhabited land, soaring mountains, flat plains, ancient landmarks, modern technology, extreme wealth and struggling poverty. Point out that students may use the map they sketched in the activity on the previous page.
ELL **Visual/Spatial**

C Critical Thinking Skills

Formulating Questions Discuss with students how the natural resources, religious history, and physical features of the region have made it unique but also a region of conflict. Ask students to write five questions they have about this region that they would like to have answered as they read through the unit. Tell students their questions should be varied and touch on different aspects of life in the region, such as physical, political, cultural, economic, and social. Have students place their questions in a chart so as they read through the chapters they can write answers directly in the chart. When students reach the end of the unit, use all of their questions in a unit review game of Jeopardy. AL **Verbal/Linguistic**

R

1 Culture Southwest Asia is the birthplace of three major world religions—Christianity, Islam, and Judaism. Islam is the dominant religion in the region, as Muslims form the majority in most countries.

EXPLORE the REGION

Stretching from the Atlantic Ocean in the west to the borders of China in the east, **NORTH AFRICA, SOUTHWEST ASIA,** and **CENTRAL ASIA** are three distinct but similar subregions. This is a vast area of contrasts, with plentiful oil and scarce water, bustling cities and large expanses of uninhabited land, soaring mountains and flat plains, ancient landmarks and modern technology, extreme wealth and struggling poverty.

C V

THERE'S MORE ONLINE

358

Frans Lemmens/Alamy

networks Online Teaching Options

INTERACTIVE FEATURE

Explore the Region: North Africa, Southwest Asia, and Central Asia

Discussing Use this interactive feature to discuss the culture, history, and landscapes of North Africa, Southwest Asia, and Central Asia with students. As a class, click through each of the interactive features, stopping to answer questions and to discuss the content in each item. After all items have been discussed, ask students to discuss what surprised them or interested them the most about this region.
AL **Naturalist, Verbal/Linguistic**

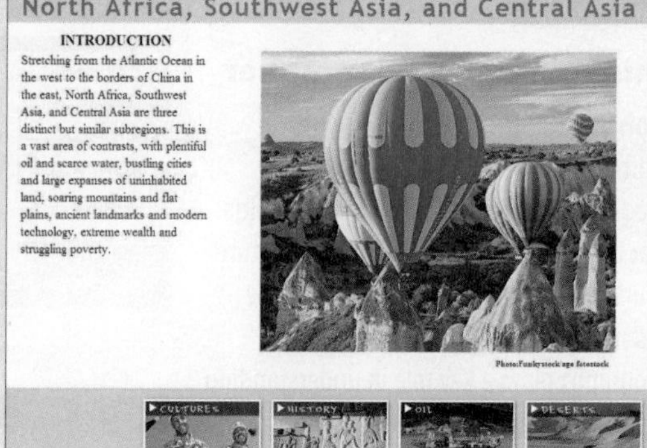

3 Deserts The Rub' al-Khali covers more than 250,000 square miles (650,000 sq. km) and is one of the major deserts found in the region.

4 History Home to ancient kingdoms and empires that rose and fell thousands of years ago, the region has left a lasting mark on history as the source of such common practices as farming wheat and writing with an alphabet.

2 Oil Much of the energy used around the world comes from this region, which includes six of the top ten countries with the most oil reserves and five of the top ten oil producers.

(t)Mustafa Ozer/AFP/Getty Images, (tc)Bemo Büchel/age fotostock, (b)Tim Barker/Lonely Planet Images/Getty Images

W Writing Skills

Argument Point out the oil derrick to students. Ask a volunteer to explain the advantages and disadvantages of the extraction and economic development of oil. Discuss with students how critical oil is to the economies of the region and how other countries around the world depend on this oil. **Ask:** What risks does the region take with its reliance on oil as a resource? *(Possible answer: Oil will run out one day because it is a nonrenewable resource.)* What might happen to the region's economies if oil is no longer an available resource? *(Possible answer: Their economies might decline rapidly.)* Have students write to the economic leaders of the region about their current economic practices of reliance on oil with one or two recommendations for changes to prevent economic collapse when the oil runs out.
AL Verbal/Linguistic

V Visual Skills

Locating Discuss with students the characteristics of a desert, as well as its effects on population distribution and economic development. Ask students to look at a map of the region and locate the Rub' al-Khali desert (southern Arabian Peninsula). Tell students that the largest oil field in the world was discovered here in 1948. Ask students to search online to find out more about the desert and if oil is still a major commodity that is developed in the area. Visual/Spatial

T Technology Skills

Researching Ask students to use online and library resources to research three major ancient kingdoms that thrived in this region. Have them compare and contrast the kingdoms, including their location, history, leaders, and significance. Ask students to trace the legacies of these kingdoms to the region today. Invite students to share their findings with the class.
BL Verbal/Linguistic

CLOSE & REFLECT

Summarizing Discuss with students the main physical, political, and cultural features of the region. Ask them to write a summary of these aspects. Have students exchange their summaries with a partner.

DIGITAL WORKSHEETS

North Africa, Southwest Asia, Central Asia

Demonstrating Use these online digital unit worksheets to have students demonstrate their depth of knowledge and comprehension and to provide them with extended unit content through project-based activities.

- **Environmental Case Study**
- **GIS Simulation**
- **Location Activity**
- **GeoLab Activity**

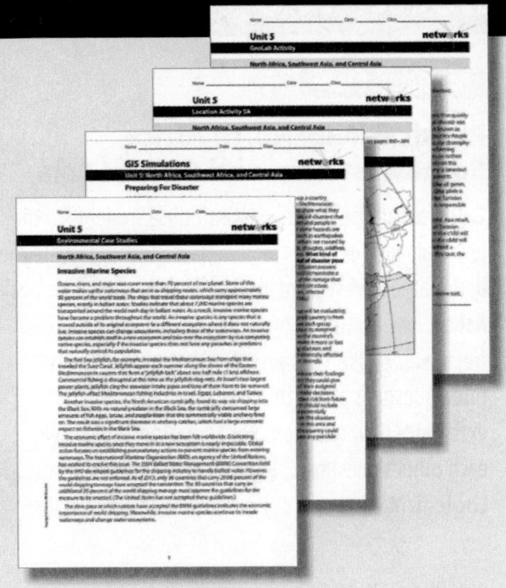

ENGAGE

C Critical Thinking Skills

Making Generalizations Point out to students that this region includes parts of two different continents. Have students study the map, examining the subregions carefully. Ask them to identify physical features that are similar or different among the subregions. Based on what students identified, have them make generalizations about the physical features of each subregion as well as the region as a whole. Explain to students that they will be learning more about how the physical features of each subregion affect the way people live.

TEACH & ASSESS

R Reading Skills

Reading Maps Ask students to study the map key, noting the different elevations. **Ask:** **Which areas have the highest elevation?** *(Tian Shan, Pamirs, Hindu Kush)* **Which physical feature has the highest elevation?** *(mountains)* **Which areas have the lowest elevation?** *(Possible answer: They are largely in northwestern Africa, northeastern Africa, and northern Southwest Asia.)* Have students write a paragraph to explain what effects low elevation and high elevation have on the temperature of a place. Then ask them to read their paragraphs to a partner and discuss the effects that they both chose. ELL Verbal/Linguistic

V Visual Skills

Creating Charts Discuss with students how this region of the world is one of extremes, related to its physical geography, political geography, cultural geography, and economic geography. Point out the inset map, and ask students what the map illustrates. Ask them to identify a physical feature that could be characterized as an extreme of the region (example: Dead Sea is 1,312 feet below sea level). Then have students work in pairs to create a chart that shows the extremes of the region. Students may use the map as a reference for the Physical column but should also conduct additional research using print and electronic resources. Point out that students should include columns for Political, Economic, and Cultural, and add to their charts as they study the other unit maps. BL Logical/Mathematical

North Africa, Southwest Asia, and Central Asia

Physical

0 — 1,000 miles
0 — 1,000 kilometers
Lambert Azimuthal Equal-Area projection

The red dashed line represents the northern boundary of a region known as the Transition Zone, an area of increasing Islamic influence.

Elevations

10,000 ft. (3,000 m)
5,000 ft. (1,500 m)
2,000 ft. (600 m)
1,000 ft. (300 m)
0 ft. (0 m)
Below sea level

National boundary
Mountain peak
Lowest point
Mountain pass

360

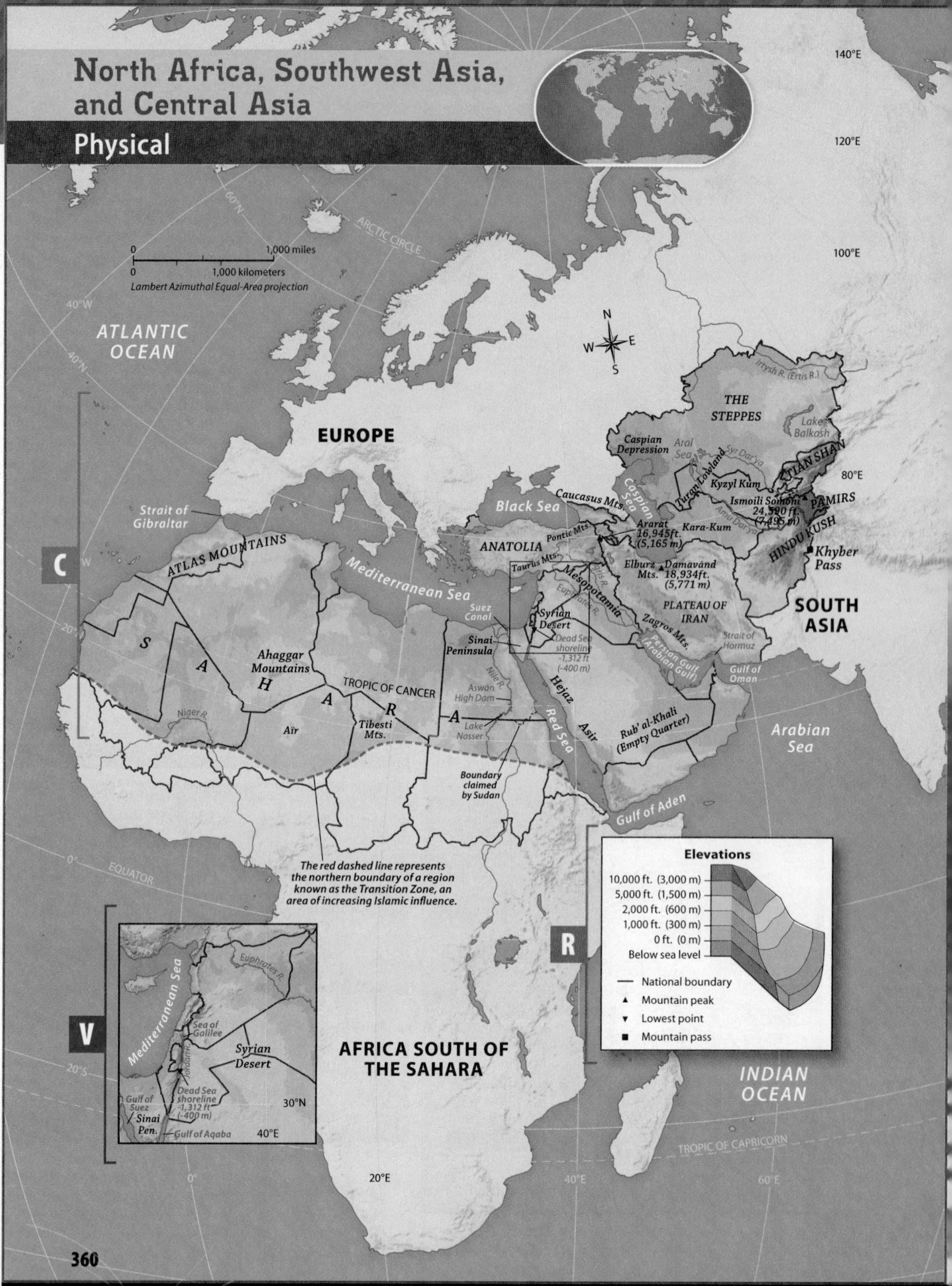

networks Online Teaching Options

INTERACTIVE MAP

Physical Map: North Africa, Southwest Asia, and Central Asia

Calculating Use this map to introduce students to the physical features in this region. Have students locate the designated lowest point and the highest mountain peak. **Ask:** **What is the difference in feet and meters between these two points?** Have students write three questions about this map. Then have them exchanges their questions with a partner and answer each other's questions. AL Visual/Spatial, Logical/Mathematical

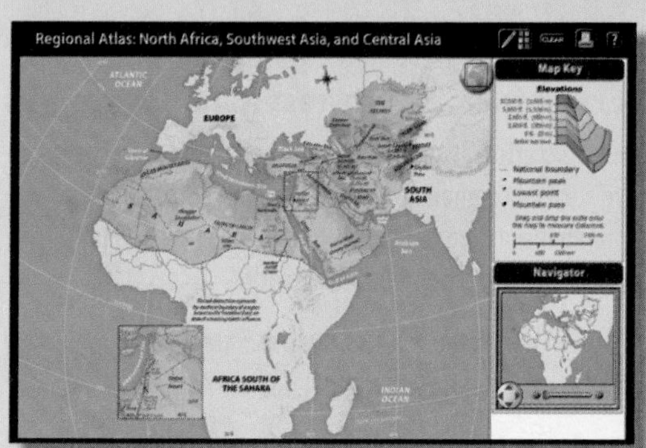

North Africa, Southwest Asia, and Central Asia

Political

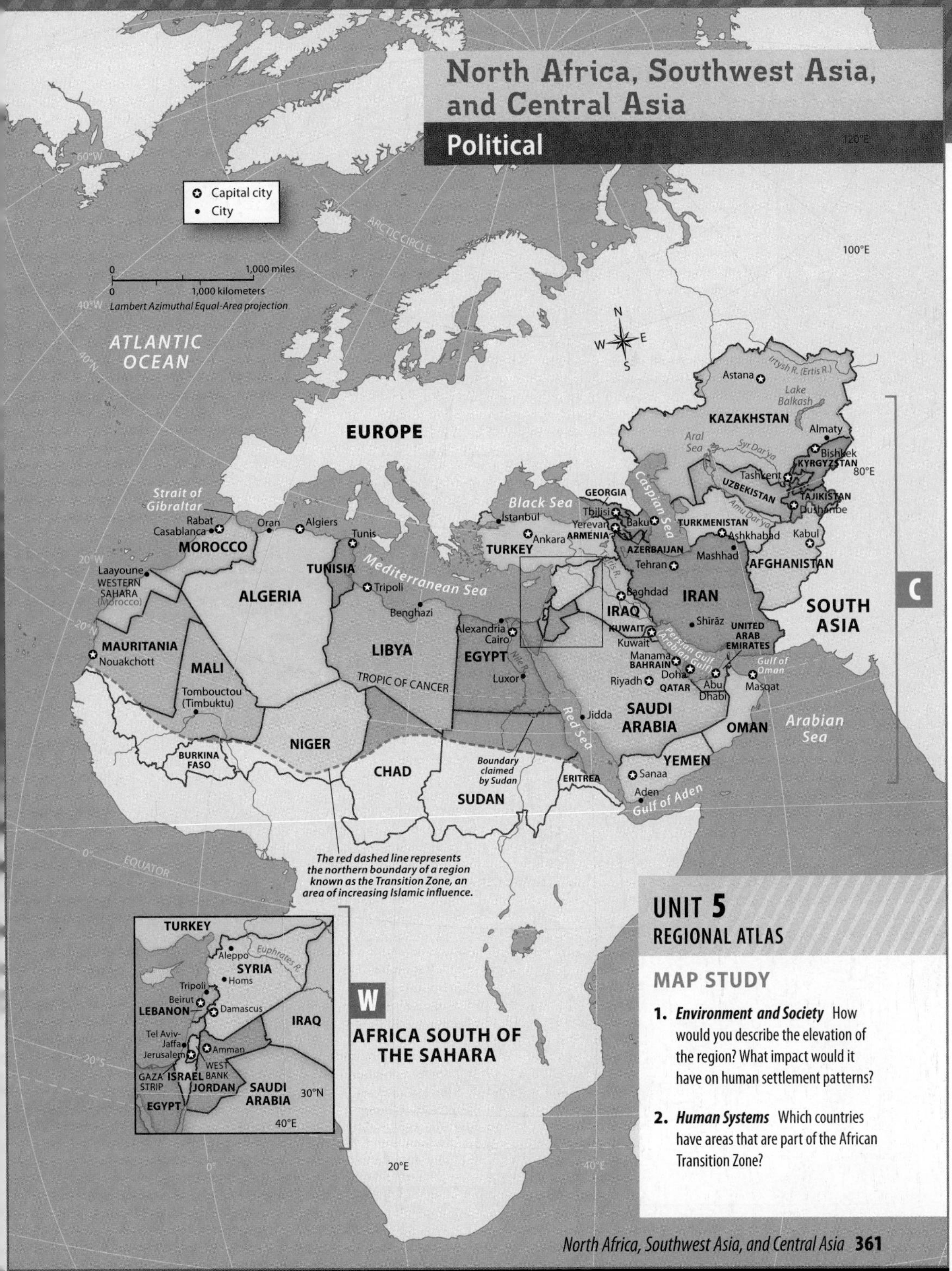

Capital city
City

Lambert Azimuthal Equal-Area projection

The red dashed line represents the northern boundary of a region known as the Transition Zone, an area of increasing Islamic influence.

UNIT 5
REGIONAL ATLAS

MAP STUDY

1. ***Environment and Society*** How would you describe the elevation of the region? What impact would it have on human settlement patterns?
2. ***Human Systems*** Which countries have areas that are part of the African Transition Zone?

UNIT 5

North Africa, Southwest Asia, and Central Asia

C Critical Thinking Skills

Classifying Discuss with students how many different subregions are shown on the map. Invite a volunteer to point out the difference between a country border and a cultural border such as the red dashed line marking the location of the Transition Zone. **Ask:** **Why are only parts of several countries in North Africa separated by the Transition Zone?** *(Possible answer: Islamic influence has not expanded into the entire country for these countries.)* **Do you think the line that marks the Transition Zone will move? Why or why not?** *(Possible answer: Yes, it may move as Islam continues to have a growing influence in North Africa.)* Have students work with a partner to classify the countries shown on the map by subregion. **ELL Visual/Spatial**

Content Background Knowledge

The area near and including the area inside the inset map is the birthplace of three monotheistic religions—Judaism, Christianity, and Islam. In 1000 B.C. King David made Jerusalem the holy city of Judaism and this city continues to be the holiest of cities for Jews. Just north of Jerusalem is Nazareth, where Christians believe Jesus grew to manhood. The Islamic faith began in the 600s in Mecca, several hundred miles southeast of Jerusalem and Nazareth. This city is where Muslims believe Muhammad received his first revelation from Allah (God).

W Writing Skills

Informative/Explanatory Explain to students that political maps often include information about disputed boundaries. Ask students to identify a disputed boundary on the map (Sudan). Have students research what the boundary dispute is, which countries are involved, and outlooks on how the dispute might be resolved. Then ask students to write an informative piece on their findings and to include inferences about when the dispute might be resolved. **AL Verbal/Linguistic, Logical/Mathematical**

INTERACTIVE MAP

Political Map: North Africa, Southwest Asia, and Central Asia

Inferring Use the political map of North Africa, Southwest Asia, and Central Asia to introduce the students to political boundaries in this region. Direct students' attention to the red dotted line denoting the northern boundary of the Transition Zone. Then point out the much smaller black dotted line showing the boundary claimed by the Sudan. Ask students to write an inference about how having one official boundary line and another claimed boundary line could affect relations among groups of people in the area. Write a paragraph explaining their inference.
AL Visual/Spatial

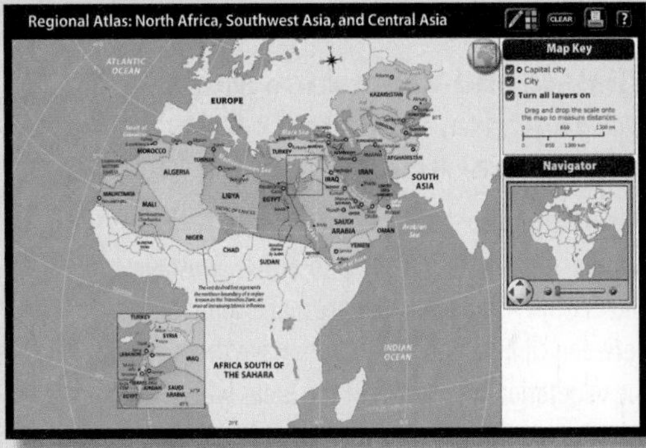

ANSWERS, p. 361

MAP STUDY

1. High mountains in the northeast region have impacted settlements by isolating communities.
2. Eritrea, Sudan, Chad, Niger, Mali, Mauritania, and Burkina Faso.

C Critical Thinking Skills

Analyzing Have students review the climate zones of the region and then make comparisons between this region and those of other regions they have studied. **Ask:** What factors affect climate zones? *(Possible answers: elevation, wind patterns, latitude, physical features, climate change)* Ask them to make inferences about how these factors affect the vegetation that is characteristic of a climate zone. Then have students select a climate zone and make an analysis of what vegetation is common in that area. Ask them to provide details that support their analyses. Invite students to share their analyses with the class. **AL Visual/Spatial, Naturalist**

Content Background Knowledge

Red Sea Situated between two lands that are primarily desert, the Red Sea not only has hot water but salty water. Coral reefs thrive here. In fact, the Red Sea has the second largest coral environment in the world. The vegetation of the Red Sea area includes mangrove swamps, salt marshes, and coastal desert plains and mountains.

T Technology Skills

Considering Advantages and Disadvantages Ask students what data on the map would be most relevant to:

- a traveler
- a manager of a company that wants to build an oil pipeline
- a city planner
- a food engineer

Then have students choose one of the people listed above and write a blog entry from their perspective. Ask students to create a digital presentation using images and audio to express their point of view regarding their concerns and interests in the region based on the climate and vegetation. Provide an opportunity for students to show their presentations to the class. **BL Logical/Mathematical, Musical/Auditory**

W Writing Skills

Narrative Have students suppose they have traveled to two distinct and different climate zones in the region. Then instruct them to write a narrative to describe how the climate affected their visit, including travel, clothing, food, and activities. Remind students to present their ideas in an engaging narrative that uses sensory language and dialogue. **AL Naturalist, Verbal/Linguistic**

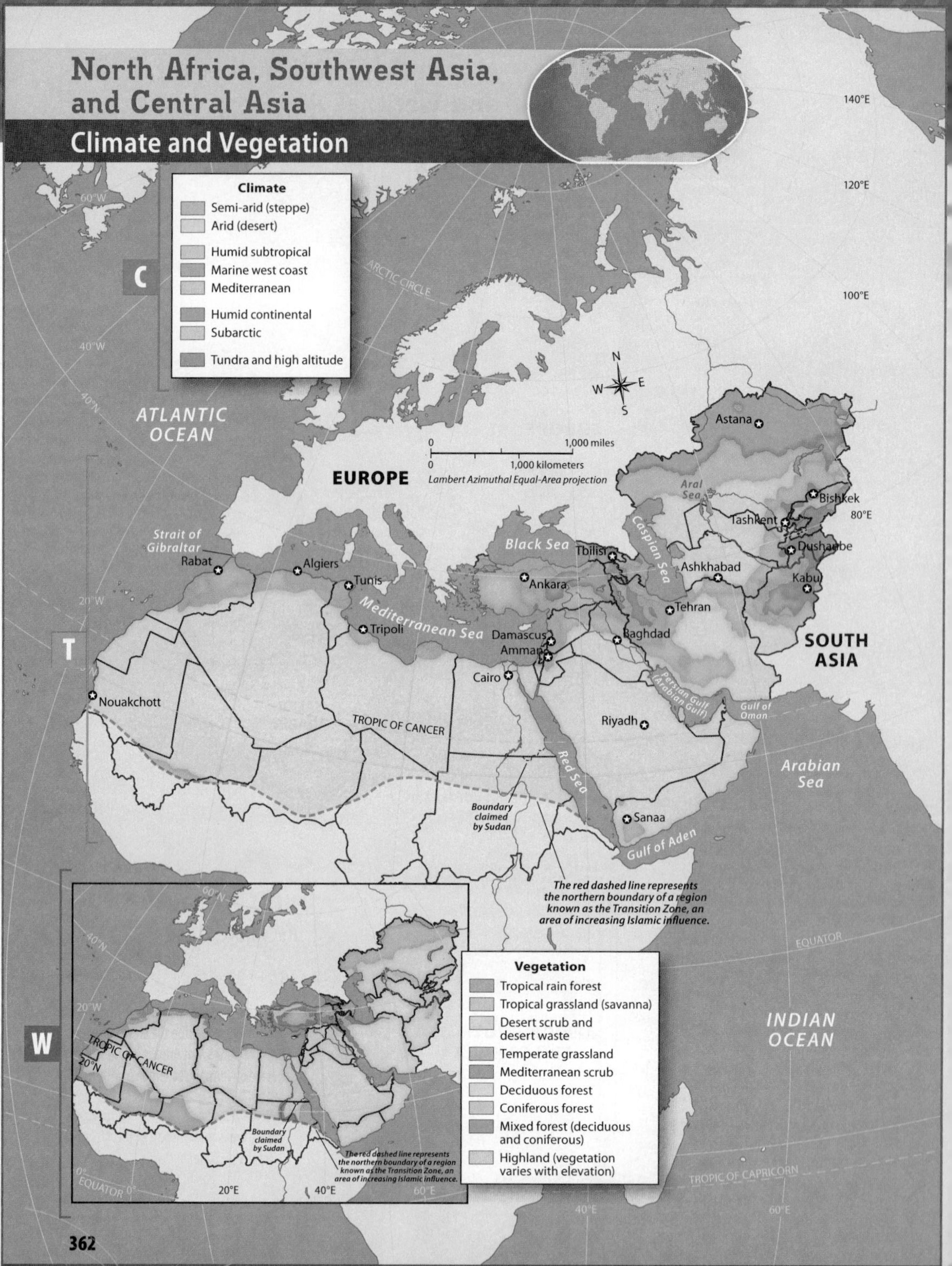

North Africa, Southwest Asia, and Central Asia
Climate and Vegetation

Climate
- Semi-arid (steppe)
- Arid (desert)
- Humid subtropical
- Marine west coast
- Mediterranean
- Humid continental
- Subarctic
- Tundra and high altitude

ATLANTIC OCEAN
EUROPE
0 — 1,000 miles
0 — 1,000 kilometers
Lambert Azimuthal Equal-Area projection
Strait of Gibraltar
Rabat
Algiers
Tunis
Tripoli
Mediterranean Sea
Black Sea
Tbilisi
Ankara
Caspian Sea
Aral Sea
Astana
Bishkek
Tashkent
Dushanbe
Ashkhabad
Kabul
Tehran
Baghdad
Damascus
Amman
Cairo
Riyadh
Persian Gulf
Arabian Gulf
Gulf of Oman
SOUTH ASIA
Nouakchott
TROPIC OF CANCER
Red Sea
Boundary claimed by Sudan
Sanaa
Gulf of Aden
Arabian Sea
INDIAN OCEAN
EQUATOR
TROPIC OF CAPRICORN

The red dashed line represents the northern boundary of a region known as the Transition Zone, an area of increasing Islamic influence.

Vegetation
- Tropical rain forest
- Tropical grassland (savanna)
- Desert scrub and desert waste
- Temperate grassland
- Mediterranean scrub
- Deciduous forest
- Coniferous forest
- Mixed forest (deciduous and coniferous)
- Highland (vegetation varies with elevation)

362

networks Online Teaching Options

INTERACTIVE MAP

Climate and Vegetation Maps: North Africa, Southwest Asia, and Central Asia

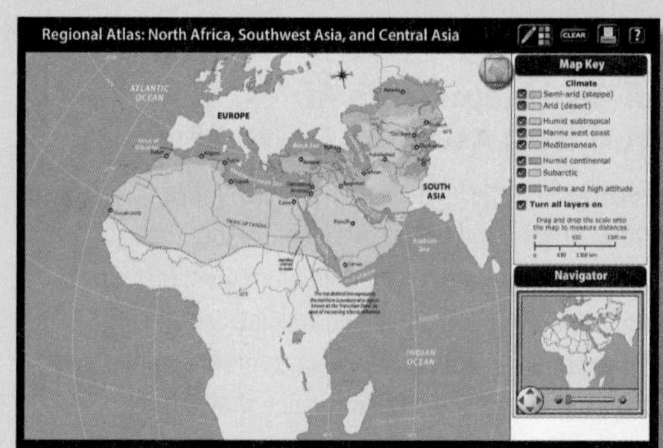

Observing Display the interactive map to discuss the climate and vegetation of North Africa, Southwest Asia, and Central Asia. Help students make connections between climate and vegetation. Have them analyze the vegetation map and find the areas where a mixed forest exists. Then look at the climate map and determine what climate conditions are present in those areas. Have students share their observations with a partner. **ELL Visual/Spatial**

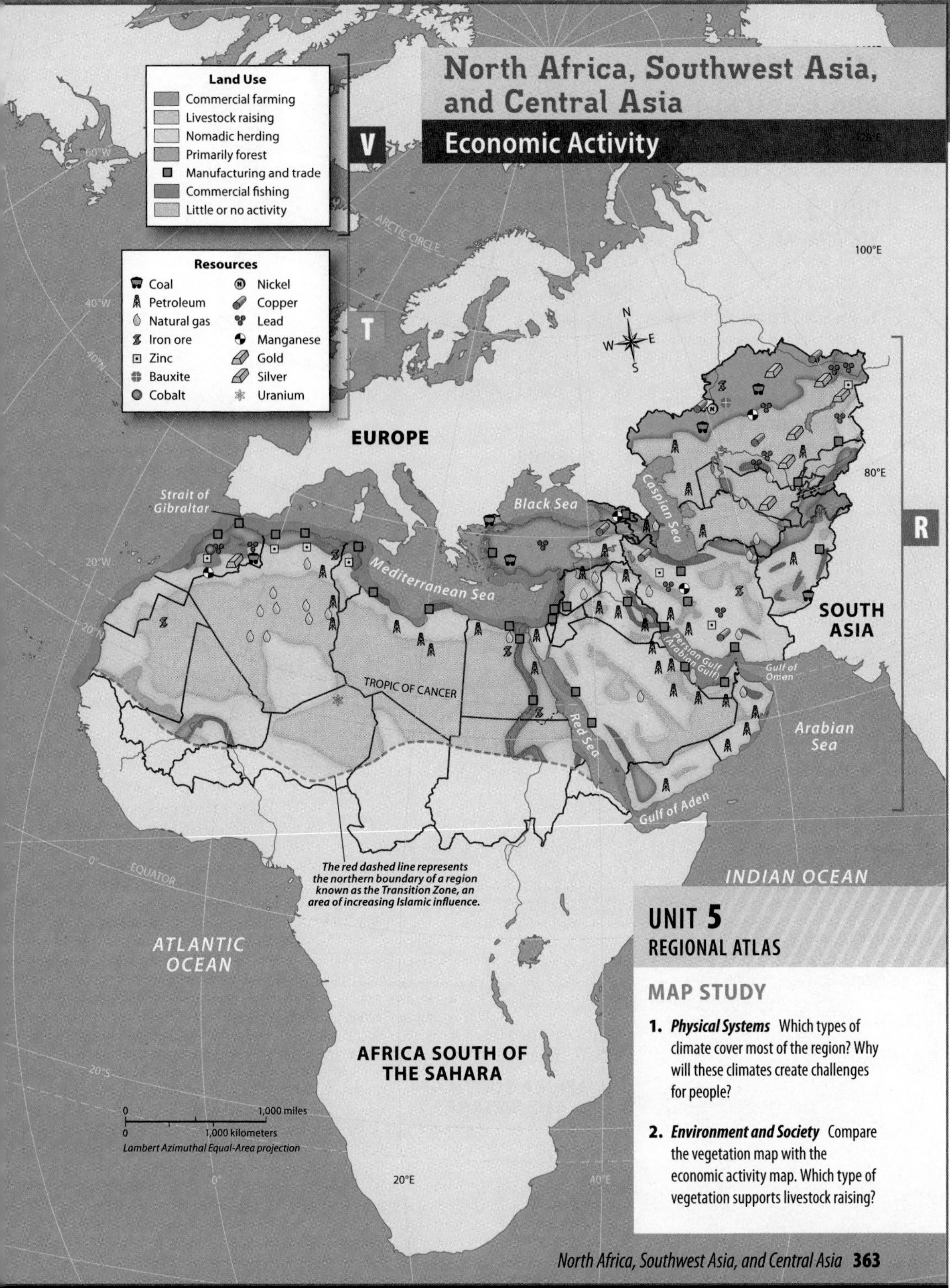

North Africa, Southwest Asia, and Central Asia

Economic Activity

V

Land Use
- Commercial farming
- Livestock raising
- Nomadic herding
- Primarily forest
- Manufacturing and trade
- Commercial fishing
- Little or no activity

Resources
- Coal
- Petroleum
- Natural gas
- Iron ore
- Zinc
- Bauxite
- Cobalt
- Nickel
- Copper
- Lead
- Manganese
- Gold
- Silver
- Uranium

T

R

EUROPE

Strait of Gibraltar

Black Sea

Caspian Sea

Mediterranean Sea

Persian Gulf (Arabian Gulf)

Gulf of Oman

SOUTH ASIA

Arabian Sea

TROPIC OF CANCER

Red Sea

Gulf of Aden

ARCTIC CIRCLE

EQUATOR

INDIAN OCEAN

ATLANTIC OCEAN

AFRICA SOUTH OF THE SAHARA

The red dashed line represents the northern boundary of a region known as the Transition Zone, an area of increasing Islamic influence.

0 — 1,000 miles
0 — 1,000 kilometers
Lambert Azimuthal Equal-Area projection

60°W 40°W 20°W 0° 20°E 40°E 80°E 100°E 120°E 40°N 20°N 0° 20°S

UNIT 5
REGIONAL ATLAS

MAP STUDY

1. ***Physical Systems*** Which types of climate cover most of the region? Why will these climates create challenges for people?
2. ***Environment and Society*** Compare the vegetation map with the economic activity map. Which type of vegetation supports livestock raising?

INTERACTIVE MAP

Economic Activity Map: North Africa, Southwest Asia, and Central Asia

Determining Importance Display the interactive map to discuss the economic activities including land use and the available natural resources of North Africa, Southwest Asia, and Central Asia. Working in groups, ask students to consider which natural resources they feel are the most valuable. Then tell groups to focus on the areas where petroleum is a natural resource, and discuss with students why these areas are important not only to the region, but to many other parts of the world. Have groups share their answers with the class.
BL **Verbal/Linguistic, Visual/Spatial**

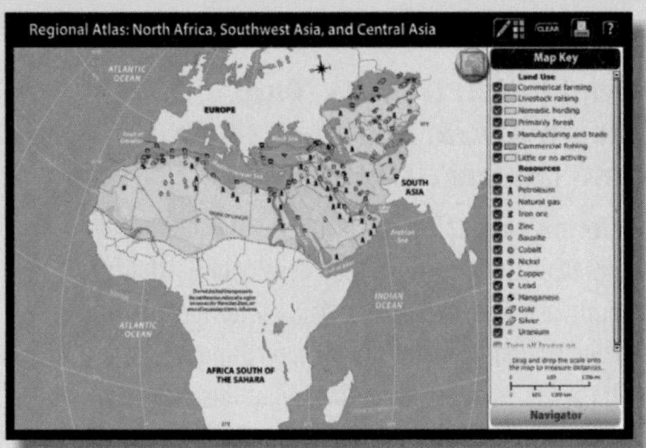

V Visual Skills

Creating Graphs Have students create a graph after studying the map key of land use. Ask students to work with a partner to estimate the percentage of land used in the region for each category shown in the key. Discuss with them ways in which they can calculate the percentages, such as determining the percentage of land use by country and then finding an average for the region. After they create their graphs, ask each student to write two to three paragraphs explaining what factors affect land use, such as climate, elevation, water resources, and so forth. **Logical/Mathematical**

T Technology Skills

Researching Point students to the map key on resources and ask them to cover the map. **Ask:** **Based on what you have already learned about the climate and land use of the region and prior knowledge, where do you think petroleum is prominent?** *(Southwest Asia)* **Gold, copper, and silver?** *(Central Asia)* **What resources do you think are found in North Africa?** *(Possible answer: petroleum, natural gas)* Working with a partner, have students choose one of the resources in the key to research. Ask them to find out how important that resource is to the economies of the region. Explain to students that they should gather economic data for the resource over the last 5–10 years and any data on projections. Then instruct students to write a report based on their findings. Challenge pairs to make recommendations in their reports on economic diversification or alternative methods of extracting the resources based on environmental concerns. **Interpersonal, Verbal/Linguistic**

R Reading Skills

Inferring Ask students to study the map, paying particular attention to the symbols that stand for manufacturing and trade. **Ask:** **Where are most manufacturing and trade centers located?** *(along the coast or near waterways)* **Why do you think that many of these centers are located here?** *(Possible answer: because they are near transportation resources for exports and a water source for power)* **Visual/Spatial**

ANSWERS, p. 363

MAP STUDY

1. Arid; the region is dry and lacks freshwater for people and agriculture.
2. Temperate grassland supports livestock raising in the region.

T Technology Skills

Presenting Explain to students that metropolitan areas are cities and the surrounding area. Invite students to name metropolitan areas that are familiar to them in the state and country. Explain to students that Istanbul, for example, has a population of about 5 million, but with its metropolitan area it has nearly double that number. Then divide the class into small groups and assign each group a city on the map. Have them research statistics for the city as well as the metropolitan area of that city, such as the differences in population and population density, demographics, and resources. Encourage students to create a multimedia presentation with their findings, using video, still images, audio, and graphics. Point out to students that in their presentation they should address how city developers might use this information when planning housing, infrastructure, and other building projects.
BL Logical/Mathematical

W Writing Skills

Argument Point out to students that there are advantages and disadvantages to living in urban areas versus rural areas. Have students support either living in urban or rural areas based on the data shown on the map. Ask them to use details to support their perspective. Guide students to additional resources to help them gather facts and data for their argument. Instruct students to write an essay to present and support their argument, as well as address any counterarguments. Invite students to share their argumentative papers with the class. **AL Intrapersonal**

CLOSE & REFLECT

Categorizing Ask students to work with a partner to review the unit maps and categorize important information from each map in a chart. Allow students to choose their own headings but explain to students that all of the topics that are covered in this section should be included in the chart. Then ask students to exchange their charts with another pair to evaluate them.

ANSWERS, p. 364

MAP STUDY

1. Turkey, Jordan, Iran, Iraq, and Israel are the most densely populated areas.
2. along the Atlantic and Mediterranean coasts

North Africa, Southwest Asia, and Central Asia
Population Density

UNIT 5
REGIONAL ATLAS

MAP STUDY

1. ***Places and Regions*** Which countries in the region are the most densely populated?
2. ***The World in Spatial Terms*** What are North Africa's largest cities? Where are they located?

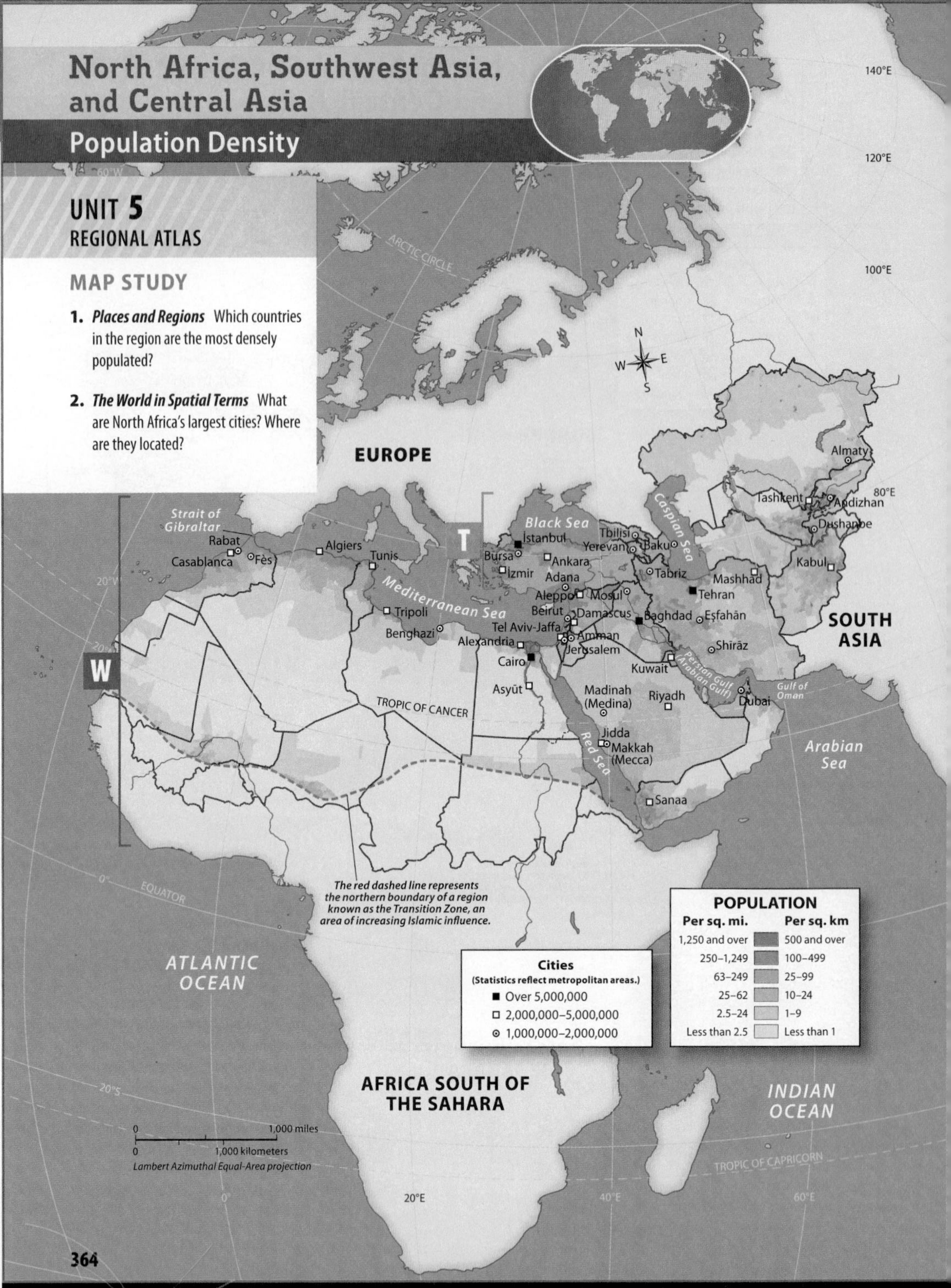

The red dashed line represents the northern boundary of a region known as the Transition Zone, an area of increasing Islamic influence.

Cities
(Statistics reflect metropolitan areas.)
- ■ Over 5,000,000
- □ 2,000,000–5,000,000
- ⊙ 1,000,000–2,000,000

POPULATION Per sq. mi.	Per sq. km
1,250 and over	500 and over
250–1,249	100–499
63–249	25–99
25–62	10–24
2.5–24	1–9
Less than 2.5	Less than 1

0 — 1,000 miles
0 — 1,000 kilometers
Lambert Azimuthal Equal-Area projection

364

networks Online Teaching Options

INTERACTIVE MAP

Population Density Map: North Africa, Southwest Asia, and Central Asia

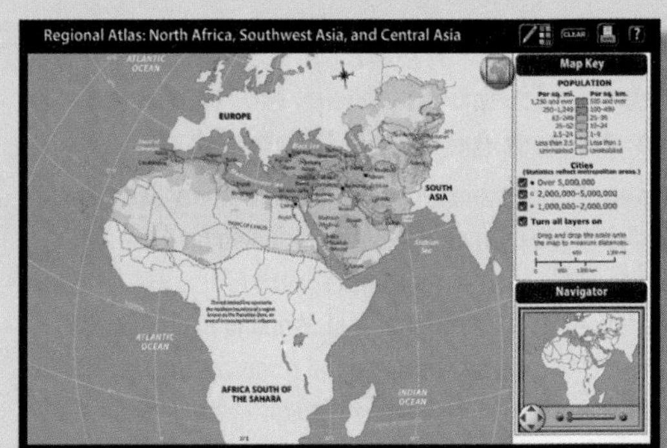

Informative/Explanatory Display the interactive map to discuss the population density of North Africa, Southwest Asia, and Central Asia. Have students analyze population density map, focusing on North Africa. Ask students to consider what they have learned so far about that part of the continent. Then have them consider why so much of that area is so sparsely populated. Have students write a paragraph explaining their thoughts. **AL Verbal/Linguistic**

CHAPTER **15**

North Africa Planner

UNDERSTANDING BY DESIGN®

Enduring Understandings

- *The physical environment affects people and their activities.*

Essential Question

- *How do physical systems and human systems shape a place?*

Predictable Misunderstandings

Students may think:

- *Countries in North Africa are very poor and mostly rural. While many people live in rural areas, there are many large cities with thriving economies.*
- *North Africa is populated by ethnic African groups. Explain that the percentage of the population that belongs to traditional ethnic groups is quite small. The vast majority of the population are Islam-practicing Arabs.*

Assessment Evidence

Performance Tasks:

- *Hands-On Chapter Project*

Other Evidence:

- *Guided Reading Activities*
- *Vocabulary Activities*
- *Lesson Quizzes*
- *Chapter Tests, Forms A and B*

SUGGESTED PACING GUIDE

Introducing the Chapter	½ Day	Global Connections	1 Day
Lesson 1	1 Day	Lesson 3	1 Day
Lesson 2	1 Day	Chapter Wrap-Up and Assessment	½ Day

TOTAL TIME 5 Days

Key for Using the Teacher Edition

SKILL-BASED ACTIVITIES

Types of skill activities found in the Teacher Edition.

* **V** **Visual Skills** require students to analyze maps, graphs, charts, and photos.

R **Reading Skills** help students practice reading skills and master vocabulary.

C **Critical Thinking Skills** help students apply and extend what they have learned.

W **Writing Skills** provide writing opportunities to help students comprehend the text.

T **Technology Skills** require students to use digital tools effectively.

*Letters are followed by a number when there is more than one of the same type of skill on the page.

DIFFERENTIATED INSTRUCTION

All activities are written for the on-level student unless otherwise marked with the leveled labels below.

BL **Beyond Level**
AL **Approaching Level**
ELL **English Language Learners**

All students benefit from activities that utilize different learning styles. Many activities are marked as below when a particular learning style is highlighted.

Intrapersonal	**Naturalist**
Logical/Mathematical	**Kinesthetic**
Visual/Spatial	**Auditory/Musical**
Verbal/Linguistic	**Interpersonal**

National Geography Standards covered in "North Africa"

The student knows and understands:

(3) How to analyze the spatial organizations of people, places, and environments on Earth's surface

3.1 The meaning and use of complex spatial concepts, such as connectivity, networks, hierarchies, to analyze and explain the spatial organizations of human and physical phenomena

(4) The physical and human characteristics of places

(8) The characteristics and spatial distribution of ecosystems and biomes on Earth's surface

8.3 The distribution and characteristics of biomes change over time

(9) The characteristics, distribution, and migration of human populations on Earth's surface

9.2 Population distribution and density are a function of historical, environmental, economic, political, and technological factors

9.3 Migration is one of the driving forces for shaping and reshaping the cultural and physical landscape of places and regions

(11) The patterns and networks of economic interdependence on Earth's surface

11.3 Economic systems are dynamic organizations of interdependent economic activities for production, exchange, distribution, and consumption of goods and services

(14) How human actions modify the physical environment

(15) How physical systems affect human systems

15.1 Depending on the choice of human activities, the characteristics of the physical environment can be viewed as both opportunities and constraints

(16) The changes that occur in the meaning, use, distribution, and importance of resources

16.3 Policies and programs that promote the sustainable use and management of resources impact people and the environment

(17) How to apply geography to interpret the past

17.1 Geographic contexts (the human and physical characteristics of places and environments) can explain the connections between sequences of historical events

(18) How to apply geography to interpret the present and plan for the future

18.1 Geographic contexts (the human and physical characteristics of places and environments) provide the bases for analyzing current events and making predictions about future issues

CHAPTER OPENER PLANNER

Students will know:

- *how the landscape was formed and the importance of the Nile River.*
- *how physical geography, migrations, and religion have influenced the history, population patterns, society, and cultures of North Africa.*
- *the characteristics of the modern economies of North Africa.*
- *how physical geography and human activities contribute to water scarcity issues and how these issues are being addressed.*
- *why Egypt built the Aswān High Dam and the resulting environmental effects.*
- *how oil production and distribution impact the environment.*

Students will be able to:

- ***describe** North Africa's landscape, how it was formed, and its importance to physical and human systems.*
- ***identify** factors that have influenced the history, population patterns, society, and cultures of North Africa.*
- ***identify** the characteristics of North Africa's modern economies.*
- ***analyze** water scarcity issues and how they are being addressed.*
- ***analyze** the purpose and results of the Aswān High Dam.*
- ***discuss** the environmental impacts of oil production and distribution.*

UNDERSTANDING BY DESIGN®

Print Teaching Options

V Visual Skills

- [ ] **p. 365** Students consider how physical and human systems have shaped different areas in North Africa.

R Reading Skills

- [ ] **p. 367** Students write statements that paraphrase the importance of the Suez Canal. **Verbal/Linguistic**

C Critical Thinking Skills

- [ ] **p. 366** Students record potential advantages and disadvantages of the Suez Canal. **AL Logical/Mathematical**

W Writing Skills

- [ ] **p. 366** Students write an essay explaining what might happen if the Suez Canal were blocked. **Verbal/Linguistic**

T Technology Skills

- [ ] **p. 366** Students research how water transportation is integral to trade in North Africa and report on their findings. **BL Visual/Spatial**

Online Teaching Options

C Critical Thinking Skills

- **INTERACTIVE MAP** **Sea Routes Before and After the Suez Canal**—Student discuss sea routes near North Africa before and after the Suez Canal, research the lengths of these routes, and calculate the miles that are saved when ships use the canal. **BL Logical/Mathematical**
- **MAP** **Interactive Regional Atlas**—Students use the interactive regional atlas to understand the physical and human geography of North Africa.

Printable Digital Worksheets

- **WORKSHEET** **Assessing Background Knowledge**—Determine the level of prior knowledge students have about North Africa.
- **WORKSHEET** **Chapter Summaries**—Students review the main idea of each lesson of the chapter content.
- **WORKSHEET** **Reteaching Activity**—These worksheets provide students with an opportunity for remedial practice and review of vital chapter content.

Project-Based Learning 

Hands-On

Current Affairs: North African Newspaper

Working in groups, students will write a local, regional, or national newspaper about the current events in one of the North African countries. Groups will conduct research and then decide what content their newspapers will contain. Each student will be responsible for one aspect of the newspaper and then the group will combine their articles, ads, political cartoons, and visuals into a newspaper format.

Digital Hands-On

Create Online Projects

Find an additional activity online that incorporates technology for this project. Visit the EdTech Teacher Web sites for more links, tutorials, and other resources.

Print Resources

ANCILLARY RESOURCES

This ancillary is available for every chapter and lesson.

- **Chapter Tests and Lesson Quizzes**

PRINTABLE DIGITAL WORKSHEETS

These printable digital worksheets are available for every chapter and lesson.

- **Assessing Background Knowledge**
- **Chapter Summaries**
- **Guided Reading Activities**
- **Hands-On Chapter Projects**
- **Quizzes and Tests**
- **Reading Essentials and Study Guide** **AL**
- **Reteaching Activities**
- **Video Activities**
- **Vocabulary Activities**

More Media Resources

SUGGESTED VIDEOS MOVIES

- **Global Treasures Marrakesh Morocco** (11 min.)
- **The World Atlas North Africa** (51 min.)
- **Mystery of the Nile** (48 min.)

SUGGESTED READING 

- ***Lifting the Veil: Two Centuries of Travelers, Traders and Tourists in Egypt,*** by Anthony Sattin
- ***Libya: From Colony to Revolution,*** by Ronald Bruce St. John
- ***Parting the Desert: The Creation of the Suez Canal,*** by Zachary Karabell

LESSON 1 PLANNER

PHYSICAL GEOGRAPHY OF NORTH AFRICA

Students will know:

- *that North Africa's landscape is the result of its location where four tectonic plates meet.*
- *the importance of the Nile River to North Africa's physical and human systems.*
- *how aridity affects the climates and biomes of North Africa.*

Students will be able to:

- ***explain*** *how tectonic plates affect landscape.*
- ***describe*** *why the Nile River is important to North Africa.*
- ***describe*** *the effects of aridity on climates and biomes.*

UNDERSTANDING BY DESIGN®

☑ *Print Teaching Options*

V Visual Skills

- ☐ **p. 368** Students write sentences that relate what images reveal about North Africa's physical geography.
- ☐ **p. 369** Students create a Venn diagram to visualize positive and negative impacts of damming the Nile River. AL Visual/Spatial
- ☐ **p. 370** Students label key climate zones in North Africa on an outline map. ELL Visual/Spatial, Interpersonal
- ☐ **p. 371** Students discuss how variations in climate affect human activity. AL Visual/Spatial

R Reading Skills

- ☐ **p. 368** Students create a chart to organize information about landforms and waterways. ELL Visual/Spatial
- ☐ **p. 369** Students write sentences using the term "gave birth to" literally and figuratively. ELL Verbal/Linguistic

C Critical Thinking Skills

- ☐ **p. 368** Students identify different landforms and what formed them. AL Verbal/Linguistic
- ☐ **p. 370** Students discuss the ways that water scarcity affects climate variations. AL Visual/Spatial

W Writing Skills

- ☐ **p. 370** Students write a travel blog imagining they are on a trip to the Sahel. Verbal/Linguistic

T Technology Skills

- ☐ **p. 371** Students create a multimedia presentation about the advantages and disadvantages of petroleum exports. BL Interpersonal

☑ *Online Teaching Options*

V Visual Skills

- VIDEO **Nile–Gift of the Nile**—Students watch the video, create a map of the Nile, and add a flowchart to show how weather patterns in Ethiopia affect life downstream in Egypt. Naturalist, Visual/Spatial
- INTERACTIVE IMAGE **Mediterranean Climate**—Students discuss climate and agriculture and infer and create charts that describe the types of climate in each region. Visual/Spatial, Naturalist

C Critical Thinking Skills

- INTERACTIVE BELLRINGER **Production of Phosphate Rock**—Students discuss the importance and distribution of phosphate rock in North Africa. ELL AL Interpersonal, Visual/Spatial
- INTERACTIVE WHITEBOARD ACTIVITY **The Great Nile and Sahara**—Students identify features or effects of the Nile River and the Sahara and move them to an appropriate column in the chart.

☑ *Printable Digital Worksheets*

R Reading Skills

- WORKSHEET **Guided Reading Activity**—Students use the Guided Reading Activity worksheets to review their comprehension of the content.

C Critical Thinking Skills

- WORKSHEET **Video Activity**—Students answer questions related to a topic in the chapter content after they have viewed a lesson video.

LESSON 2 PLANNER

HUMAN GEOGRAPHY OF NORTH AFRICA

Students will know:
- *how physical geography has influenced the history and population patterns of North Africa.*
- *the ways in which migrations and religion have shaped the population patterns, society, and cultures of North Africa.*
- *the characteristics of the modern economies of North Africa.*

Students will be able to:
- ***analyze** the impact of geography on history and population patterns.*
- ***analyze** the impact of migrations and religion on population patterns, society, and cultures in the region.*
- ***identify** characteristics of modern economies in North Africa.*

UNDERSTANDING BY DESIGN®

☑ Print Teaching Options

V Visual Skills

☐ **p. 373** Students compare the impact of the boundaries created by colonial powers to the physical boundaries that are often used to designate borders. ELL Visual/Spatial

☐ **p. 374** Students create a diagram to show how one event led to another in the Arab Spring. Visual/Spatial, Interpersonal

☐ **p. 375** Students discuss the importance of seacoasts and rivers to the development of cities. AL Visual/Spatial

R Reading Skills

☐ **p. 372** Students search for and jot down time, order, and sequence words as they read. ELL Verbal/Linguistic

☐ **p. 376** Students consider how religion has shaped population patterns, society, and cultures of North Africa. AL Verbal/Linguistic

C Critical Thinking Skills

☐ **p. 373** Students discuss how invasions and migrations impacted the history of North Africa. AL

☐ **p. 375** Students discuss how migrations have influenced population patterns in North Africa. Logical/Mathematical

☐ **p. 377** Students discuss the factors that have contributed to economic development in North Africa. Interpersonal

W Writing Skills

☐ **p. 373** Students write an argumentative essay either in favor of ethnic groups or in favor of colonial empires controlling a country. BL Verbal/Linguistic

☐ **p. 376** Students write a journal entry from the point of view of a person living in North Africa. Verbal/Linguistic

T Technology Skills

☐ **p. 374** Students choose an event from the time line to research and create a multimedia presentation about. BL Interpersonal, Visual/Spatial

☐ **p. 376** Students conduct research for a presentation about an assigned topic as it relates to the arts of different North African countries. BL Auditory/Musical, Kinesthetic

☐ **p. 377** Students research a specific topic on a North African country and present their findings to the class. BL Logical/Mathematical

☑ Online Teaching Options

V Visual Skills

VIDEO **Egypt Revolution**—Students watch a video about Egypt's Revolution in 2011 and discuss how Wael Ghonim's use of social media was able to bring about political change. AL Verbal/Linguistic

R Reading Skills

GAME **Human Geography of North Africa**—Students play a game to jump-start a discussion about the relationship between North Africa's location and its history. BL Interpersonal, Logical/Mathematical

C Critical Thinking Skills

INTERACTIVE BELLRINGER **The Status of Women in North Africa**—Students discuss what life might be like for women in North Africa. Intrapersonal, Verbal/Linguistic

INTERACTIVE MAP **Population of Egypt**—Students study the population map and discuss concerns large cities face because of rapid growth. AL Logical/Mathematical

W Writing Skills

INTERACTIVE WHITEBOARD ACTIVITY **North Africa's Modern Economy**—Students discuss North Africa's resources and economy and then write a summarizing paragraph.

☑ Printable Digital Worksheets

R Reading Skills

WORKSHEET **Guided Reading Activity**—Students use Guided Reading Activity worksheets to review their comprehension of the content.

WORKSHEET **Reading Essentials and Study Guide**—Students complete the study guide and answer Reading Progress Check and vocabulary questions. AL

C Critical Thinking Skills

WORKSHEET **Video Activity**—Students answer questions related to a topic in the chapter content after they have viewed a lesson video.

LESSON 3 PLANNER

PEOPLE AND THEIR ENVIRONMENT: NORTH AFRICA

Students will know:

- *how physical geography and human activities contribute to water scarcity issues in North Africa.*
- *the ways in which water scarcity issues are being addressed.*
- *why Egypt built the Aswān High Dam and the resulting environmental effects.*
- *how oil production and distribution impact the environment.*

Students will be able to:

- ***analyze** water scarcity issues in North Africa.*
- ***explain** how water scarcity issues are being addressed.*
- ***discuss** the environmental effects of the Aswān High Dam.*
- ***analyze** the environmental effects of oil production in the region.*

UNDERSTANDING BY DESIGN®

☑ Print Teaching Options

V Visual Skills

- ☐ **p. 382** Students create a visual report that shows the impact of oil production, fishing, and mass tourism on regions in North Africa. BL Visual/Spatial, Interpersonal
- ☐ **p. 383** Students create a web diagram to show concerns about the human impact on North Africa's environment.

R Reading Skills

- ☐ **p. 380** Students create outlines to show the impact of water scarcity in certain regions. AL Visual/Spatial
- ☐ **p. 383** Students discuss threats posed to the environment and write a paragraph predicting how pollutants could adversely affect ecosystems. AL Verbal/Linguistic

C Critical Thinking Skills

- ☐ **p. 381** Students conduct a mock debate in which they defend or refute providing water for Libya's population using water extraction. BL Logical/Mathematical, Interpersonal
- ☐ **p. 382** Students analyze the benefits and drawbacks shown in the diagram of Egypt's Aswān High Dam. Visual/Spatial, Logical/Mathematical
- ☐ **p. 383** Students discuss the advantages and disadvantages of Egypt's Aswān High Dam. Logical/Mathematical
- ☐ **p. 384** Students discuss how political unrest and foreign relations can play a part in the development and distribution of natural resources. Logical/Mathematical

W Writing Skills

- ☐ **p. 384** Students research the various efforts made by the World Bank as it relates to irrigation, water supplies, and agriculture and write an essay based on their findings. BL Verbal/Linguistic

T Technology Skills

- ☐ **p. 381** Students discuss desalination and other ways in which water scarcity issues are being addressed. BL Interpersonal
- ☐ **p. 382** Students conduct research on an oil spill and create a slide show to show its impacts on the surrounding environment. BL Visual/Spatial, Verbal/Linguistic

☑ Online Teaching Options

V Visual Skills

- ☐ INTERACTIVE CHART **Population: North Africa**—Students analyze the chart and relate the data to the importance of managing resources, especially water, and brainstorm ideas about providing water for the current population and conserving for future generations. BL Logical/Mathematical
- ☐ VIDEO **Libyan Oil Profits**—Students list the advantages and disadvantages that oil production brings to the economy and environment of a country and write either a positive or negative summarizing statement about the human impact of oil extraction. BL Logical/Mathematical, Verbal/Linguistic

C Critical Thinking Skills

- ☐ INTERACTIVE BELLRINGER **Egypt's Aswān High Dam**—Students discuss why Egypt built the dam and the resulting environment and social effects. Interpersonal, Verbal/Linguistic
- ☐ INTERACTIVE WHITEBOARD ACTIVITY **The Impact of the Aswān High Dam**—Students assess statements about the impact of the dam and then discuss the environmental impact of human modification to nature. Logical/Mathematical, Verbal/Linguistic

☑ Printable Digital Worksheets

R Reading Skills

- ☐ WORKSHEET **Guided Reading Activity**—Students use Guided Reading Activity worksheets to review their comprehension of the content.
- ☐ WORKSHEET **Reading Essentials and Study Guide**—Students complete the study guide and answer Reading Progress Check and vocabulary questions. AL
- ☐ WORKSHEET **Vocabulary Activity**—Students review the chapter content and academic vocabulary words.
- ☐ WORKSHEET **Chapter Summary**—Students review the main ideas of the chapter content.

C Critical Thinking Skills

- ☐ WORKSHEET **Video Activity**—Students answer questions based on a lesson video.
- ☐ WORKSHEET **Reteaching Activity**—Students use this activity worksheet to review and reteach chapter content and vocabulary. This worksheet can be used with struggling students who need additional help with difficult content concepts.

Intervention and Remediation Strategies

LESSON 1 Physical Geography of North Africa

Reading and Comprehension

To help students organize and comprehend the concepts discussed in this lesson, have them work in pairs to create a pictorial outline using the lesson's main headings and subheadings. As partners gather information, have them note key ideas and details under each heading, as well as content vocabulary terms. Encourage students to illustrate their outlines to develop a coherent understanding of each concept. For example, students may draw a picture of a streambed to represent the term *wadi.* Or they may wish to use a graphic organizer like the one on the Lesson Opener to organize their ideas about North Africa's water systems. Ask volunteers to present their outlines to the class.

Text Evidence

Organize students into small groups. Have each group identify evidence from the lesson that supports the following statement from the It Matters Because paragraph: *The physical geography of a region directly determines what natural resources are available to the people who live there.* Tell groups to work together to create a cause-and-effect chart that illustrates the evidence they identified in the text to support the statement. Students may wish to conduct additional research for their charts if desired. Have groups share their charts with the class.

LESSON 2 Human Geography of North Africa

Reading and Comprehension

Have students work in pairs to look up the definition of each of the content vocabulary terms in a print or online dictionary. For the two-word term *geometric boundary,* have students look up each individual word and use context clues in the text to determine the term's meaning. Have students write sentences using each content vocabulary term, showing a clear understanding of each word's meaning as it is used in the lesson. Encourage students to use the Academic Vocabulary words in their sentences.

Text Evidence

To ensure that students have a firm grasp of lesson content, have them write a summary of a topic or issue discussed in the lesson. You may wish to assign topics to students to avoid duplication. For example, students might describe various aspects of Egyptian culture or the development of an urban middle class in North Africa. Remind students to support claims in their summaries with evidence from the text. Encourage students to use content vocabulary words in their summaries.

LESSON 3 People and Their Environment: North Africa

Reading and Comprehension

Have student pairs identify cause-and-effect relationships as they read about the tenuous balance between North Africa's economic development and the need for water throughout the region. Tell partners to read through the lesson to locate the answer to this Guiding Question: *Why are water resources in such demand in North Africa?* Have student pairs collaborate to write a one-sentence summary explaining which places in North Africa are the most dependent on water sources. Remind students that identifying signal words such as *however, as a result,* and *consequences* can help them find the effects of an issue or event. Have pairs share their statements with the class.

Text Evidence

Assign student groups one of the challenges discussed in this lesson such as dependency on outside food sources, environmental challenges involving Libya's Great Man-Made River, the impact of economic activities such as oil extraction and fishing, and the impact of Egypt's Aswān High Dam. Have students in each group work together to summarize the problems related to their topic and how or if the problems are being addressed or solved. Students may wish to conduct online research to provide sufficient evidence in support of claims made in their summaries. Encourage students to use content vocabulary terms in their summaries.

Online Resources

Leveled Reader

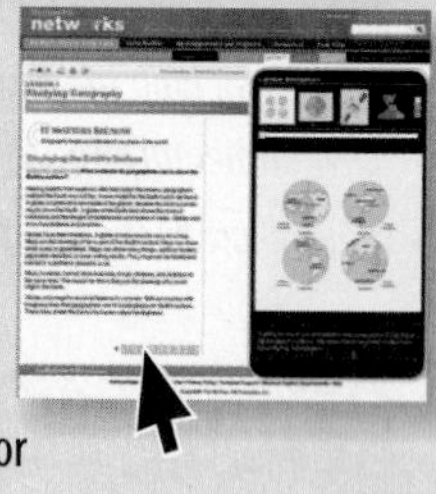

Use this online approaching-level text that corresponds directly to the text in the Student Edition. It also includes additional reading and comprehension support for English Language Learners.

Guided Reading Activities

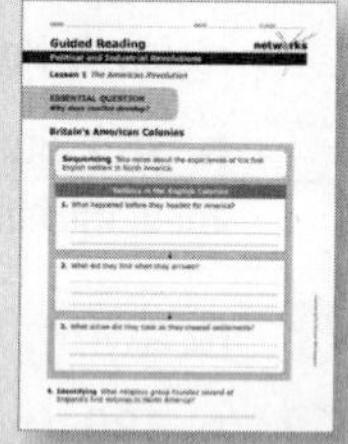

This resource uses guiding questions to help students with comprehension.

Reteaching Activities

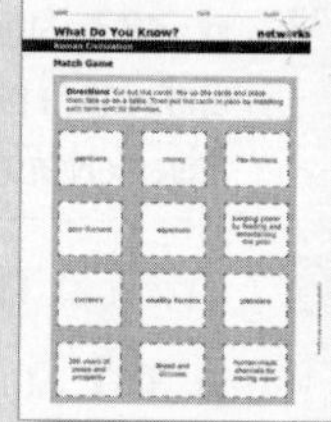

These worksheets provide students with an opportunity for remedial practice and review of vital chapter content.

Reading Essentials and Study Guide

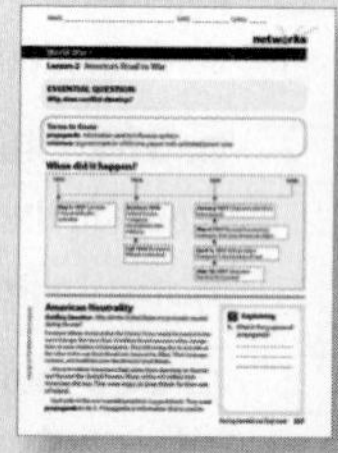

This resource offers writing and reading activities for the approaching-level student.

Self-Check Quizzes

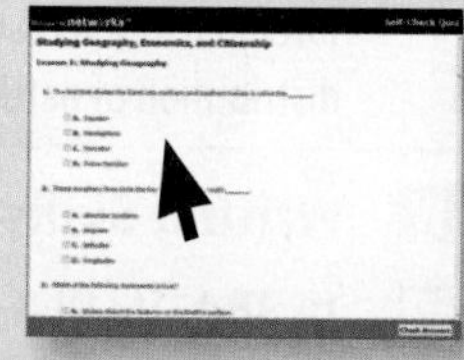

This online assessment tool provides instant feedback for students to check their progress.

Chapter Summaries

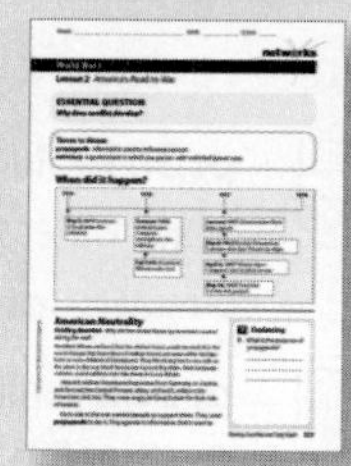

Summaries are provided for each chapter that thoroughly condense core content into manageable chunks.

North Africa

ESSENTIAL QUESTION • *How do physical systems and human systems shape a place?*

networks
There's More Online about North Africa.

CHAPTER 15

Why Geography Matters
Choke Point: Suez Canal

Lesson 1
Physical Geography of North Africa

Lesson 2
Human Geography of North Africa

Lesson 3
People and Their Environment: North Africa

Geography Matters...

North Africa is home to the Sahara, the world's largest hot desert, and the Nile Delta, the outflow of the world's longest river. North Africa also has access to thousands of miles of coastline and many favorable trade routes. There is a long history of trade across the subregion, with various ethnic groups moving in and out of North Africa. Today the culture of North Africa has developed as an eclectic mix of the indigenous Berbers and those of their trading partners throughout Europe and Asia.

◀ This young man is a Berber, one of the oldest ethnic groups in the region. Many Berbers live in the Atlas Mountains and in the Sahara.

Kimberley Coole/Lonely Planet Images/Getty Images

365

ENGAGE

Drawing Inferences Provide students with a recent news story involving North Africa's political or economic status. For example, you may want to share an article about the road to independence or the economic impact of the Arab Spring. Ask students to write a short paragraph inferring how the events of the news story might impact the country in which it occurred.

TEACH & ASSESS

Analyzing Visuals Display the unit physical map of North Africa. Invite volunteers to point out key geographic features such as the Nile River and the Sahara. Have students consider how physical and human systems have shaped different areas in North Africa. Ask students to explain possible challenges and benefits to living in this region. *(Possible answer: Regions near the Sahara may be challenging to live in because of their hot and dry climate. It would be a benefit to live near the Nile River, which is an important waterway for agriculture and transportation and provides freshwater.)* BL **Logical/Mathematical**

Making Connections

Use the photograph of the young Berber man as a launch point for a discussion about ethnic groups and cultural traditions and events. Explain that Berbers were the indigenous people of North Africa before Arab invasions and that most Berbers live in agrarian communities and speak their own language. Some Berbers continue to be pastoral nomads.

CLOSE & REFLECT

Questioning Have students prepare a list of questions they want to have answered as they study the chapter. Have them keep these questions in mind as they read, using outside resources to find answers to any unanswered questions.

Letter from the Author

Dear Geography Teacher,

The Great Man-Made River offers your class the chance to engage in an intriguing "environment and society" debate. Divide the class into two groups; one group becomes advocates (pros) for the "River" and the other detractors (cons). Students should examine: How did Libya get its water before the Man-Made River? How much did it cost? How might climate change affect this "River"? Also, your class might wish to consider whether or not this project impacts surrounding countries. Water rights are often at the forefront of political confrontations between countries in Southwest Asia: an example is the issue of water as a critical resource involving Turkey, Iraq, and Syria.

Richard G. Boehm

ePals GlobalCommunity
Where learners connect™

Extend the project-based learning experience globally through our partnership with ePals. EPals allows you to connect with classrooms around the world in a safe online environment for real-life lessons and projects in virtual study groups.

ENGAGE

C Critical Thinking Skills

Drawing Conclusions Note that transportation is a key ingredient of successful trade. Have students consider how the need to facilitate transportation in different parts of the world can have benefits as well as disadvantages by creating a two-column chart to record potential advantages and drawbacks of the Suez Canal, its control, and its use by different countries. **Ask:** **What could be a downside to having one country control a key trade route used by many different countries?** *(Possible answers: If one country controls an important trade route, then other countries that use that route might have problems accessing it. Conflict can result if the controlling country is geographically or politically unsafe.)* AL **Logical/Mathematical**

TEACH & ASSESS

T Technology Skills

Researching Draw students' attention to the introductory text, noting that shorter trade routes are a key factor in facilitating trade. Have students work in teams to conduct online research about how water transportation has been integral to trade in North Africa throughout history. Have teams choose from topics such as construction of the Suez Canal, trade on the Nile River, trade in the Mediterranean, or the Barbary Pirates and trade limitations. Students should create reports for the class, using presentation software. BL **Visual/Spatial**

W Writing Skills

Narrative Display the physical map of North Africa found in the online Teacher Resource Center that shows the Suez Canal linking the Mediterranean with the Red Sea. Briefly discuss as a class the significance of the Suez Canal to its surrounding regions. Then have students review the last sentence of the introductory paragraph. Tell students to write a short narrative essay that describes what might happen if the Suez Canal were blocked. **Verbal/Linguistic**

Why Geography Matters: **North Africa**

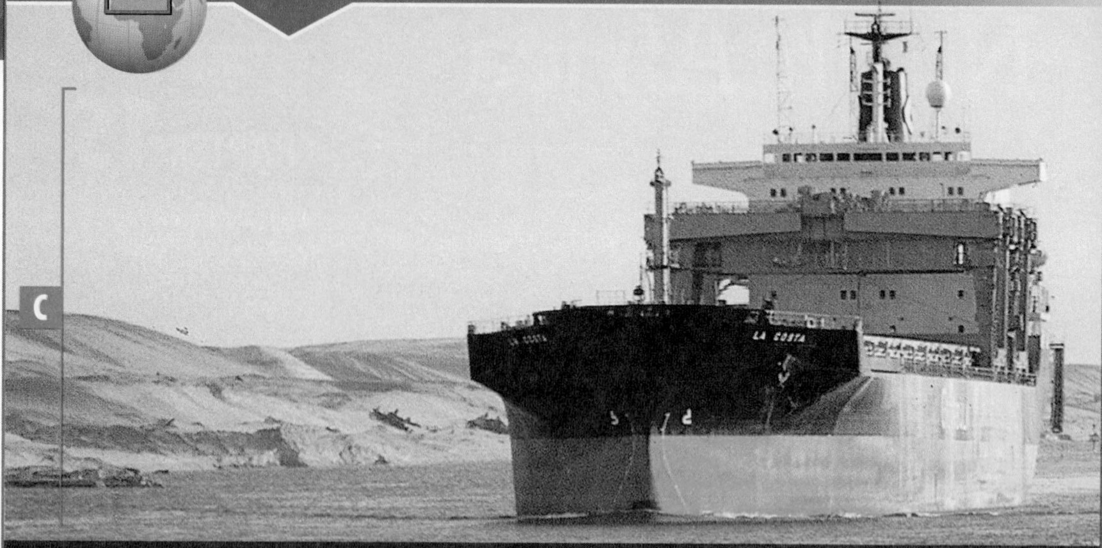

choke point: Suez Canal

For thousands of years, countries have sought shorter trade routes to boost imports and exports. Seafaring traders for all countries have looked for shortcuts called choke points. The ***Suez Canal,*** *linking the Mediterranean with the Red Sea, is a good example. If the Suez Canal were blocked, economies worldwide would be affected.*

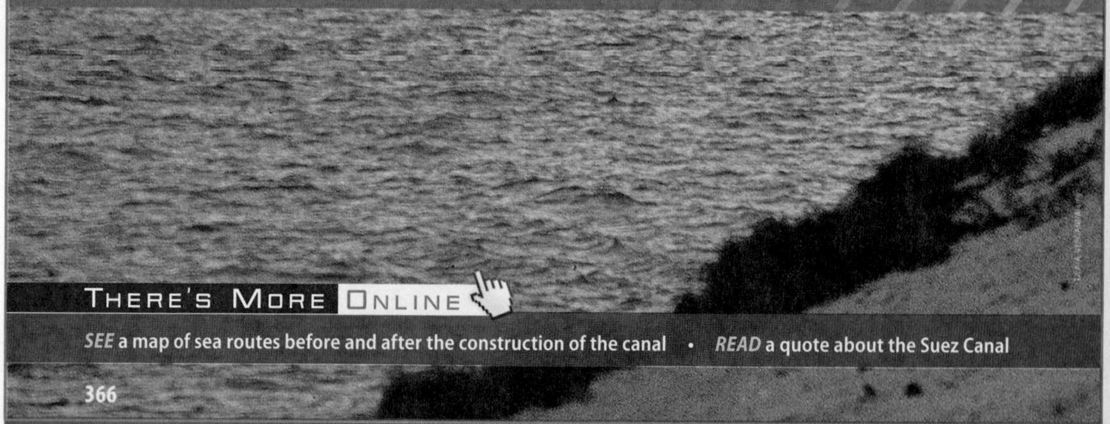

THERE'S MORE ONLINE

SEE a map of sea routes before and after the construction of the canal • *READ* a quote about the Suez Canal

366

Project-Based Learning

Hands-On

Current Events Newspaper

Student groups will write a newspaper article about the current events in one of the countries in North Africa. They will research and gather materials to decide what content and visuals their newspapers will contain. Each group member will be responsible for an element within the newspaper. Once the elements are written and visuals are selected, the group will decide how to lay out and organize their newspaper.

Digital Hands-On

Create Online Projects

Find an additional activity online that incorporates technology for this project. Visit the EdTech Teacher Web sites for more links, tutorials, and other resources.

What is a choke point?

A choke point is a narrow channel or canal that connects two larger bodies of water. Choke points are valuable trading routes that save vessels from traveling thousands of miles to reach a destination. Historically, countries have used choke points to create a trade monopoly by restricting trade through the narrow passage.

Today, choke points are a part of major trade networks for oil and petroleum products. In an energy-dependent world, these integral passageways power our daily lives. Roughly half of the world's oil production is shipped and moved through a choke point. Any disruption in shipment would add thousands of miles to shipping distance, raise energy prices worldwide, and possibly increase political tensions.

1. Environment and Society How have choke points influenced modern maritime trade routes?

Where is the Suez Canal?

The Suez Canal is in northern Egypt and connects the Red Sea to the Mediterranean Sea. The canal is 101 miles (163 km) long but is only 179 feet (55 m) wide at its narrowest point. Its depth has been increased over time to accommodate larger vessels. Before the completion of the canal in 1869, maritime traders were forced to sail around the tip of Africa, known as the Cape of Good Hope, which added some 4,000 miles (6,437 km) to their journey.

The canal was constructed as a shorter route between Europe and Asia. Today the Suez Canal's importance has increased due to the rise of the oil trade in the region. It now serves as a major passage for ships carrying oil and petroleum products from North Africa and Southwest Asia to Europe, North America, and the rest of the world. The canal is also a major source of revenue for Egypt. Ships pay a toll for passing through the strategic waterway. Each year the Suez Canal generates about $5 billion in foreign currency for Egypt.

2. Human Systems How has the purpose of the Suez Canal changed since its construction?

Why is the Suez Canal important?

The Suez Canal is one of the world's most important passageways for oil and petroleum products. Northbound transit through the canal supplies part of Europe's and North America's energy needs. In recent years, southbound transit has delivered more of the energy resources needed by Asia's growing economies.

Egypt controls the Suez Canal. Thus, the internal political stability of Egypt affects the world's energy security. Conflict in Egypt could jeopardize the security of the canal or shippers' confidence in the canal's safety. This could force vessels to use alternate routes to ensure that cargo reaches intended locations. Increased shipping times and costs would have a direct impact on oil and petroleum prices worldwide.

3. The World in Spatial Terms How could conflict in one country affect an uninvolved country far away?

Why Geography Matters

V Visual Skills

Analyzing Visuals Before students read the text, have them analyze the photographs and attempt to answer the questions beneath each image based solely on the photographs. Then discuss how the Suez Canal impacts human activity. Encourage students to revise their answers after they read this feature. **AL** **Visual/Spatial**

C Critical Thinking Skills

Identifying Cause and Effect Guide a class discussion about the importance of the Suez Canal to the economies of North African countries. Have students create a cause-and-effect chart that shows the economic impact a disruption in shipping would have on the region. **Ask:** **Why would a disruption in shipping have an impact on the economies of North African countries?** *(Possible answer: These countries are dependent on energy, so they rely on oil production. Shipping disruption could have a dramatic impact on the region because energy prices would go up.)* **BL** **Logical/Mathematical**

R Reading Skills

Paraphrasing Have students write three or four statements that paraphrase the importance of the Suez Canal and how the internal political stability of Egypt impacts the larger global community. **Verbal/Linguistic**

CLOSE & REFLECT

Global Analysis Review the significance of the Suez Canal. Have students consider the potential impact on global economies if the canal were blocked or compromised in some way. Guide students to brainstorm possible solutions to preventing the canal's security from being jeopardized.

INTERACTIVE MAP

Sea Routes Before and After the Suez Canal

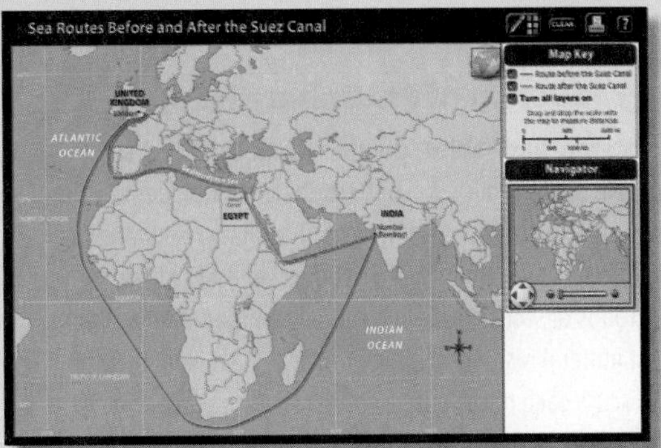

Calculating This map can be used to discuss popular sea routes near North Africa before and after the construction of the Suez Canal. Explain that these routes were and are used by countries all over the world. Allow students to work with a partner to conduct online research to find the length of the sea routes before and after the Suez Canal. Have pairs calculate the distance in miles that is saved when ships use the canal. Guide a class discussion on the economic importance of the Suez Canal to trade ships. **BL** **Logical/Mathematical**

ANSWERS, p. 367

Why Geography Matters

1. Countries that control choke points have historically created trade monopolies by restricting travel through these channels and canals. Today, about half of the world's oil production is moved through choke points. Without this access, shipping distances would increase causing rising energy prices and increased political tensions.
2. Originally constructed as a shorter route between Asia and Europe, the Suez Canal is now the major passageway for ships carrying petroleum from North Africa and Southwest Asia to Europe, North America, and the rest of the world. It is a major revenue source for Egypt.
3. Conflict in one country can cause disruptions in trade,shipping times, and raise costs of goods for other countries. This is particularly true for petroleum and oil being shipped worldwide.

ENGAGE

V Visual Skills

Analyzing Visuals Before beginning the lesson, have students study the images at the top of the page. Have them write two or three sentences that relate what these images reveal about North Africa's physical geography.

TEACH & ASSESS

R Reading Skills

Organizing After students read the paragraph, have them create a chart to organize the information in this lesson about North Africa's landforms and waterways. Suggest that students create a three-column chart labeled *Landforms, Waterways*, and *Impact*. Then have students complete their charts as they read. Encourage students to save their charts to use as a study tool when reviewing the lesson. **ELL Visual/Spatial**

C Critical Thinking Skills

Identifying Cause and Effect Guide students to understand the physical process that has shaped North Africa's landscape. Have them identify different landforms and what formed them. Remind students to look for cause-and-effect signal words and phrases such as *cause* and *as a result*. **Ask: What caused the formation of landforms in Northern Africa?** *(the action of four tectonic plates: the African, Arabian, Anatolian, and Eurasian plates)* **What happened when the African and Eurasian plates interacted?** *(The Atlas Mountains were formed.)* **How does rainfall affect the Atlas Mountains?** *(Both sections of the Atlas Mountains have deep gorges that cut through the sediment as a result of runoff from annual rainfall.)* **AL Verbal/Linguistic**

ANSWERS, p. 368

TAKING NOTES: The Nile River begins in the highlands of Ethiopia and Uganda and flows north through the desert. It is the world's longest river. The Aswān High Dam and other dams were built in the 1950s to control the flow of the Nile and reduce flooding.

networks
There's More Online! V

- IMAGE Nile River Valley
- MAP Tectonic Plates
- INTERACTIVE SELF-CHECK QUIZ
- VIDEO Physical Geography of North Africa

LESSON 1
Physical Geography of North Africa

ESSENTIAL QUESTION • *How do physical systems and human systems shape a place?*

Reading HELPDESK CCSS

Academic Vocabulary (Tier Two Words)
- **derive**
- **pose**

Content Vocabulary (Tier Three Words)
- **alluvial soil**
- **wadi**
- **phosphate**

TAKING NOTES: ***Key Ideas and Details***

ORGANIZING Use a graphic organizer like the one below to take notes on the water systems of North Africa.

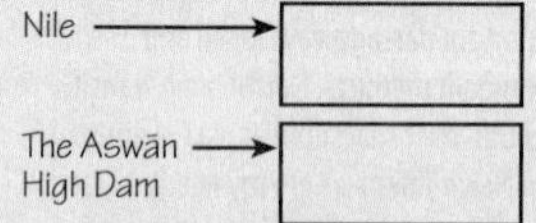

IT MATTERS BECAUSE

R *The physical geography of an area directly determines what natural resources are available to the people who live there. Physical features such as mountain ranges act as natural barriers to the rainfall and water that support human settlement. Rivers and oases provide water for irrigation and farming. Variations in climate influence local living conditions, which can affect the rate of economic and population change.*

Landforms

GUIDING QUESTION *What physical process is responsible for shaping the landscape in North Africa?*

C The landscapes of North Africa have been shaped by the action of four tectonic plates: the African, Arabian, Anatolian, and Eurasian plates. The movements and interactions among these plates build mountains, shift landmasses, and cause earthquakes. Africa's longest mountain range, the Atlas Mountains, was the result of the interaction of the African and Eurasian plates. The Atlas Mountains extend from southwest Morocco to northeast Tunisia in a region known as the Maghreb. The range consists of a northern section, the Tell Atlas, and a southern section, the Saharan Atlas. Both sections of the Atlas Mountains have deep gorges that cut through the sediment as a result of runoff **derived** from annual rainfall.

Western Sahara and Mauritania occupy a large region in northwest Africa on the edge of the Sahara. The picturesque, sandy, dune-covered areas in the desert are called *ergs*. However, the majority of the desert is not covered by sand. Two desert features are *regs*—stony plains covered with rocky gravel also known as "desert pavement"—and *hamadas*—flat, sandstone plateaus.

The Ahaggar is a large, mountainous plateau region in the north-central Sahara. The highest mountain in the Ahaggar is Mount Tahat at 9,573 feet (2,918 m) in southeastern Algeria. Parts of the plateau also extend into Niger in the south and Libya in the northeast. Black volcanic

networks Online Teaching Options

INTERACTIVE BELLRINGER

Production of Phosphate Rock

Interpreting Tables Use the introductory text and table of the production of phosphate rock to identify the importance and distribution of phosphate rock in North Africa as determined by its production. Have small groups of students discuss the information in the table of mineral resources in North Africa. Then have them discuss each question. Ask each group to write agreed-upon answers to the questions. Then in a class discussion, have each group share its answers. **ELL**
AL Interpersonal, Visual/Spatial

Production of Phosphate Rock

One of North Africa's most significant natural resources is phosphate, which is mined as a phosphate rock ore.

	2007	2008	2009	2010	2011
Algeria	1,800,025	1,805,000	1,017,000	1,525, 234	1,281,100
Egypt	2,290,295	2,356,523	6,227,424	3,021,335	1,392,990
Morocco	27,834,000	24,861,000	18,307,000	26,603,000	28,052,000
Tunisia	8,002,000	7,691,700	7,409,000	8,148,500	2,479,400
World Total	159,000,000	165,000,000	162,000,000	182,000,000	203,000,000

Auto-Run Click Through 1 of 3

landforms and a pink granite massif are found in the rocky desert of the Ahaggar plateau. Volcanic necks formed as magma cooled when the volcanoes were active, creating impressive landforms in the Ahaggar.

The Tibesti Mountains in northeastern Niger and southern Libya rise steeply above the surrounding plains. The mountain range is about 300 miles (480 km) long and about 175 miles (280 km) at its widest point. The Tibesti Mountains are the location of the highest point in the Sahara—the volcanic summit of Emi Koussi in northern Chad. It has an elevation of 11,204 feet (3,415 m).

derive to receive or obtain from a specified source

✓ READING PROGRESS CHECK

Identifying What major landform has been created by the interaction of the Eurasian and African plates?

Water Systems

GUIDING QUESTION *How has the Nile River been the lifeblood of North Africa?*

Rivers are the lifeblood of North Africa. They support the growth of plant and animal life. Rivers also promote human settlement and development. At 4,160 miles (6,693 km) in length, the Nile River is the world's longest river. It originates in the highlands of Ethiopia and Uganda and flows north through the desert. **R1**

The fertile land along the river's banks and the Nile Delta gave birth to some of the world's earliest civilizations. Today more than 90 percent of Egypt's people live in the Nile Delta or along the course of the river even though the area covers only 3 percent of Egypt's land. **R2**

Before the 1950s, the people in Egypt anticipated and depended on the annual flooding of the Nile River. The floodwaters carried sediments that were deposited along the river banks and formed rich **alluvial soil** that made for productive agricultural lands.

Beginning in the 1950s, the Aswān High Dam and other dams were built farther upstream along the Nile River. The dams were built to control the river's flow and reduce flooding. Dams were also built to provide year-round irrigation and hydroelectric power in Egypt. However, without the annual deposition of new alluvial material, soil fertility diminishes and requires the use of fertilizers. Away from the Nile, in deserts, infrequent but intense rainstorms can create **wadis** (WAH•dees), or streambeds that remain dry until a heavy rain. The rainstorms often produce flash flooding. During a flash flood, wadis fill with so much sediment that they can rapidly become mudflows, or moving masses of wet soil. The mudflows **pose** a danger to humans and animals. **V**

Bodies of water also help define boundaries in the subregion. For example, edging the coast of North Africa, the Mediterranean Sea separates Africa and Europe. To the region's east, Egypt's Sinai Peninsula, the Red Sea, and the Gulf of Aden separate North Africa from the Arabian Peninsula.

alluvial soil rich soil made up of sand and mud deposited by running water

wadi in the desert, a streambed that is dry except during a heavy rain

pose to present

✓ READING PROGRESS CHECK

Naming Which river in North Africa is the world's longest river?

The meeting of four tectonic plates shapes the landscape of North Africa.

▼ CRITICAL THINKING

1. ***Identifying Cause and Effect*** What landforms were created as a result of tectonic activity in North Africa?
2. ***Explaining*** Why does North Africa experience such a significant amount of tectonic activity?

R1 Reading Skills

Using Context Clues Read aloud the Guiding Question and ask students whether they know what the term *lifeblood* means. *("vital component, important factor")* Then have students read the first paragraph under the heading *Water Systems.* **Ask:** **What context clues help you understand the meaning of the word *lifeblood*?** *("support the growth of plant and animal life," "promote human settlement and development")* Then have students look up the word in a dictionary to verify its meaning. **ELL Verbal/Linguistic**

R2 Reading Skills

Using Correct Terminology and Grammar Ask students to reread the paragraph. Point out the phrase *gave birth to* and ask a volunteer to explain its meaning in the sentence. *("ushered in, allowed for")* Explain that the term is being used in a figurative manner and not a literal one. Have student write two sentences, one using the term figuratively and one using the term's literal meaning. **Ask:** **Why do you think the Nile Delta was so important to early civilizations?** *(With fertile land and a water source, early civilizations had land for growing crops.)* **ELL Verbal/Linguistic**

V Visual Skills

Diagramming Have students consider how the Nile River changed after dams were constructed. To help them understand how construction of dams on the river had both a positive and negative impact, have students complete a Venn diagram to visualize the information. Have students label one oval *Positive Impact* and one oval *Negative Impact.* **Ask:** **How did the Nile River change after the 1950s?** *(Dams constructed on the Nile caused streambeds to remain dry until rainstorms occurred, wadis filled with sediment, and flash flooding created dangerous mudflows.)* **AL Visual/Spatial**

VIDEO

Nile—Gift of the Nile

Creating Visuals Use this video on the Nile River to introduce water systems and to discuss the importance of climate biomes in North Africa. Have students work with a partner to create a map of the Nile flowing from Ethiopia to Egypt. Next, have them add a flowchart to their maps illustrating how the weather patterns in Ethiopia eventually affect life downstream in Egypt. Students' visuals should show the climate biome of the two seasons, wet and dry, found along this branch of the Nile. Have pairs present their visuals and explain where and why people settled along the Nile and how people adapt to varying climates. **Naturalist, Visual/Spatial**

ANSWERS, p. 369

✓ **READING PROGRESS CHECK** The Atlas Mountains are the result of collisions between the Eurasian and African plates.

✓ **READING PROGRESS CHECK** The Nile River is the world's longest river.

CRITICAL THINKING

1. The Atlas Mountains, the Tibesti Mountains, and the Ahaggar were all formed by tectonic activity.
2. North Africa experiences tectonic activity due to the movements of the African, Anatolian, Arabian, and Eurasian plates.

C Critical Thinking Skills

Explaining Continuity and Change Direct a class discussion about the ways that water scarcity affects the region's climate variations. **Ask:** **What did the ancient cave paintings reveal about the African continent?** *(The images revealed that the region was once wet and green.)* **How does this compare with the way North Africa's landscape appears today?** *(It conflicts with today's landscape, which consists of vast stretches of sand with only an occasional watering hole.)* **AL** **Visual/Spatial**

Making Connections

As students discuss the climate regions and biomes of North Africa, have them explain which parts of the United States might compare to these regions. For example, students might compare desert regions of Nevada, Arizona, or other parts of the southwestern United States to North African deserts.

V Visual Skills

Labeling Display a physical map of North Africa and provide student pairs with an outline map of Africa, which is available online at the Teacher Resource Center. Have partners use information in the text to label and name the key climate zones in North Africa. Then discuss how the arid conditions impact North Africa's climates and biomes. **Ask:** **How does the dry, harsh climate of North Africa's desert regions impact plant life?** *(Vegetation growth is sparse and freshwater is scarce.)* **ELL** **Visual/Spatial, Interpersonal**

W Writing Skills

Narrative After discussing the Sahel, ask students to imagine that they are travel writers taking an imaginary trip to the Sahel region in North Africa. Tell students to describe the flora, fauna, and other features that they pass and to add illustrations to their travel blogs. Encourage students to conduct additional research in books or online. **Verbal/Linguistic**

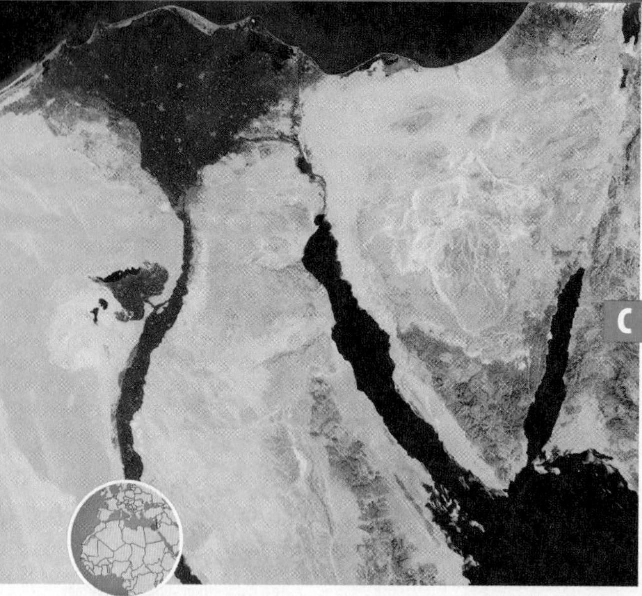

This true-color image shows the Nile River valley, the Nile Delta, and the strategic location of the Suez Canal.

NASA/Alamy

CRITICAL THINKING ▲

1. ***Identifying Cause and Effect*** What factors influence the green vegetation in the region shown in the image?
2. ***Categorizing*** Describe the landscapes that appear as tan and brown areas in the image.

phosphate a natural mineral containing chemical compounds often used in fertilizers

Climate, Biomes, and Resources

GUIDING QUESTION *How does water scarcity define the climate of North Africa?*

C North Africa has a varied climate because it is the meeting place of humid and cold air masses that come from the north and hot, tropical air masses that come from the south. Despite the region's ample amount of rainfall in some parts during the rainy season, desert is the dominant feature of the North African environment.

Climate Regions and Biomes

Water scarcity defines the subregion's variations in climate. Today's North African landscape is most commonly associated with vast stretches of sand and the occasional watering hole. Meanwhile, ancient cave paintings show that this part of the African continent was once wet and green. These opposing views of the landscape indicate changing climates over time because of physical processes. Moreover, changes in climates across the region have affected natural vegetation and human activities in the past and continue to influence the region.

The entire area covered by the Sahara is classified as desert because its annual precipitation averages 10 inches (25 cm) or less. The Sahara, the largest hot desert in the world, is about 3.5 million square miles (9.1 million sq. km) and covers almost 75 percent of North Africa. In recent decades, droughts have expanded the extent of the Sahara.

V The desert regions of North Africa experience extreme changes in climate. The Sahara mostly consists of two types of climates: an arid (desert) and a semi-arid (steppe) climate. Northern parts of the Sahara have winters with freezing temperatures, while the southern Sahara is characterized by milder, dry winters and summer rains. The harsh desert climate makes vegetation growth sparse.

Despite their arid conditions, the North African deserts can support some vegetation, such as cacti and drought-resistant shrubs. Small-scale farming is possible in oases, places in the desert where underground water surfaces. Oases are very fertile due to the ready availability of water. Because they are a source of water and can support the growth of trees— such as olive trees and date palms— many oases in the Sahara are also the sites of villages, towns, and cities.

W The Sahel is a flat plain that stretches about 3,300 miles (5,400 km) across the subregion from Senegal to Sudan south of the Sahara. The narrow band of semi-arid land forms a transition zone between the Sahara and the savannas to the south. The most common animal in the Sahel is the Senegal gerbil. Baobab and acacia trees are also found in the transition zone. Cattle feed on the Sahel's prickly cram-cram grass.

A long belt of grassland that spans nearly 5,000 miles (8,046 km) runs east to west, south of the Sahara and the Sahel. Precipitation in this semi-arid climate region usually averages less than 14 inches (36 cm) annually. This amount of rain is enough to support the growth of shrubs and some trees, as well as short grasses that feed sheep, goats, and camels.

370

networks Online Teaching Options

INTERACTIVE IMAGE

Mediterranean Climate

Integrating Visual Information Display the interactive image showing the Mediterranean landscape to discuss the climate and agriculture. Have students compare this image to the photo of the Nile River Valley in their textbooks on page 370. Divide the class into pairs. Have each pair identify the various kinds of landforms and biomes found in both images. Then ask pairs to use visual clues to infer and create charts that describe the types of climate in each region. **Visual/Spatial, Naturalist**

Kay Maeritz/LOOK/Getty Images

ANSWERS, p. 370

CRITICAL THINKING

1. The Mediterranean climate areas in the north as well as the Nile River and the Nile Delta areas have the most vegetation, as there are adequate water supplies.
2. The Sahel is a plain of semi- arid land that is between the Sahara and the savannas to the south. The Sahel has shrubs and cram-cram grass. The Sahara is part desert, or arid, and part semi-arid, or steppe. Vegetation is very sparse in the Sahara. The savannas to the south have short grasses, shrubs and some trees.

Some parts of North Africa enjoy the benefits of a mild Mediterranean climate. Occurring in parts of Morocco, Tunisia, and Libya, this climate consists of cool, rainy winters and hot, dry summers. Countries with Mediterranean climates boost their economies by exporting citrus fruits, olives, and grapes. They are mostly exported to Europe and North America. Some of these countries also benefit from tourism. People from colder climates seek the sunshine and warmth of the North African Mediterranean climate. **V**

Coastal and highland areas near mountain ranges usually receive the most rainfall. Warm, moist air driven off the sea by prevailing winds condenses as it rises over the mountains and returns to Earth as rainfall. The North African coast near the Atlas Mountains, for example, averages more than 30 inches (76 cm) of rain each year. The rainfall is enough to support agriculture and forests. **T**

In areas where more than 14 inches (36 cm) of rain falls yearly, farmers can raise food grains such as barley, oats, and wheat. These crops can be grown without irrigation. Areas with this much rainfall have an abundance of trees. Unfortunately, deforestation for agriculture has reduced tree cover in the Atlas ranges. The reduced tree cover has had negative effects on animal life.

Natural Resources

North Africa boasts an abundance of natural resources. The region's most significant resources are **phosphates**, natural gas, and petroleum. Morocco is one of the leading exporters of phosphates. Algeria has the tenth-largest natural gas reserves in the world. Additionally, it ranks sixteenth in oil reserves and sixth among the world's gas exporters.

Petroleum exports have enriched some of the countries of North Africa, particularly Algeria and Libya. Heavy reliance on petroleum exports can be risky, however. When oil prices go up and down on world markets, as they did in the late 1990s and after the Arab Spring in 2011, the region's economies suffer.

Some countries in North Africa are trying to make their economies more diverse as a way to decrease their reliance on oil and mineral exports. Algeria has tried to attract increased investment in business and industry. Libya is investing in infrastructure, agriculture, and fisheries.

Minerals also provide revenue for North African countries. Deposits of chromium, gold, lead, manganese, and zinc are sprinkled across the region. Discoveries of iron ore and copper deposits indicate that the region may contain up to 10 percent of the world's iron ore reserves.

✓ READING PROGRESS CHECK

Specifying What natural resources are most prevalent in North Africa?

Analyzing PRIMARY SOURCES (CCSS)

Saving Mediterranean Habitats Worldwide

"Mediterranean climate regions cover only 2.2 percent of Earth's land surface, yet they account for 20 percent of all known plant species. Only the tropical rainforests of the western hemisphere and southeast Asia have a greater density of plant species. Mediterranean climates are found in only five places on Earth: California and northern Baja California, the basin of the Mediterranean Sea, southwestern Australia, the western cape of South Africa and the central coast of Chile.

They all share similar landscapes. Mediterranean climates are characterized by hot, dry summers and mild, wet winters. . . ."

—Rebecca Shaw, Nature Conservancy, *Saving Mediterranean Habitats Worldwide*, February 25, 2011

DBQ ***IDENTIFYING CENTRAL ISSUES*** Why is it important to protect Mediterranean biomes? RH.9–10.1

LESSON 1 REVIEW

Reviewing Vocabulary (Tier Three Words)

1. ***Interpreting*** What physical forces cause the creation of wadis? RH.9–10.4

Using Your Notes

2. ***Describing*** Use your graphic organizer to describe the Nile Delta.

Answering the Guiding Questions

3. ***Summarizing*** What physical process is responsible for shaping the landscape in North Africa?
4. ***Evaluating*** How has the Nile River been the lifeblood of North Africa?
5. ***Paraphrasing*** How does water scarcity define the climate of North Africa?

Writing Activity

6. ***Informative/Explanatory*** Identify a climate in the North African subregion that has supported agricultural production and human growth. Identify another climate in this subregion that has restricted the establishment of settlement or agriculture. What physical features and specific natural resources differentiate these two types of climates? WHST.9–10.2

V Visual Skills

Transferring Information Discuss with students how variations in climate affect human activity in North Africa. Then have students transfer this information into a visual such as a word web or flowchart. Assess their comprehension of the benefits of a Mediterranean climate. **Ask:** **How does a Mediterranean climate help the economies of some North African countries?** *(Possible answers: The climate allows the growth of citrus fruits, olives, and grapes, which are exported by countries such as Morocco, Tunisia, and Libya. The warm climate benefits tourism in some North African countries.)*

AL Visual/Spatial

T Technology Skills

Presenting Have students work in small groups to gather additional facts about the advantages and disadvantages of petroleum exports. Have group members collaborate to create a multimedia presentation showing the results of their research. Presentations should include visuals, such as a graph or chart showing the economic impact of petroleum exports on North African countries. Groups should consider the impact of the "Arab Spring" on oil prices. Remind students to use reliable online sources when conducting their research.

BL Interpersonal

CLOSE & REFLECT

Theorizing Have students formulate a theory about how the landforms, water systems, climates, biomes, and natural resources of North Africa impact the way of life there. For example, students may theorize about how the long belt of grassland in the Sahel region and the animals and vegetation found there affect the local population.

LESSON 1 REVIEW ANSWERS

Reviewing Vocabulary

1. Intense rainstorms in the desert create wadis, or streambeds that are dry except during a heavy rain.

Using Your Notes

2. The fertile land along the banks of the Nile River and in the Nile Delta is where more than 90 percent of Egypt's population lives. The land in the Nile Delta is good for agriculture.

Answering the Guiding Questions

3. Tectonic activity between the African, Anatolian, Arabian, and Eurasian plates builds mountains, causes earthquakes, and shifts landmasses.
4. The Nile River supports plant and animal life and has promoted human settlement and development. Some of the world's earliest civilizations were built along the Nile.
5. The Sahara receives less than 10 inches of rain per year, classifying it as a desert climate. The Sahara dominates the subregion as it covers almost 75 percent of North Africa.

Writing Activity

6. Possible answers: The Mediterranean climate produces fruits, olives and grapes; the North African coast near the Atlas Mountains receives enough rain for growing barley, wheat, and oats; and the Nile Delta supports agricultural production. The desert/arid climate of the Sahara or Sahel produces little agriculture. Water supply/precipitation, temperature, and location of fertile soil differentiate the climates.

ANSWERS, p. 371

✓ READING PROGRESS CHECK Phosphates, natural gas, and petroleum are the most significant resources in North Africa.

DBQ It is important to protect Mediterranean biomes because they are found in only five places on Earth yet they contain 20 percent of all known plant species.

ENGAGE

V Visual Skills

Analyzing Visuals Direct students' attention to the images at the top of the page. Have students analyze each image and turn to a partner to share how they think each image relates to the *Essential Question*. Tell students to keep this question in mind as they work through the lesson.

TEACH & ASSESS

R Reading Skills

Sequencing Information Encourage students to look for time, order, and sequence words as they read about important historical events that occurred in North Africa. Have students jot down words and phrases that indicate when something happened. *(about 10,000 years ago, during dry seasons, each year)* **Ask:** **How were Egyptians in the Nile River valley able to grow crops during the dry seasons?** *(They developed sophisticated irrigation systems.)* **How did early Egyptians communicate?** *(They used a form of writing called hieroglyphics.)* **How do you think farming developments impacted the population in the Nile River valley?** *(Possible answer: Growing more crops allowed early Egyptians to feed more people and may have caused an increase in the population.)* **AL Verbal/Linguistic**

ANSWERS, p. 372

TAKING NOTES: Early Peoples and Civilizations—Hunters and gathers settled here about 10,000 years ago. The Berbers, historically pastoral nomads, are the indigenous people of North Africa. Egyptian civilization developed in the Nile River valley about 6,000 years ago; Arab armies invaded around A.D. 600, spreading Islam and the Arabic language; some were nomadic bedouins. Muslims and Jews fled into Morocco to escape the Spanish Inquisition. The Ottoman Empire invaded and took control in the 1500s; **Invasions and Independence**—After the invasions, European countries established colonies. By the 1800s, nationalism began. Egypt gained independence from Britain in 1922, Algeria from France in 1962, and Libya from Italy in 1951, and Morocco won independence from France in 1956. Egypt, Libya, and Tunisia recently experienced protests leading to new government elections.

networks

There's More Online!

- ☑ **IMAGE** Traditional Crafts of North Africa
- ☑ **MAP** North Africa: Invasions and Migrations
- ☑ **TIME LINE** North Africa: Path to Independence
- ☑ **INTERACTIVE SELF-CHECK QUIZ**
- ☑ **VIDEO** Human Geography of North Africa

V

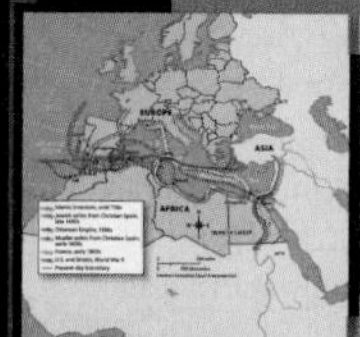

(t)Transcendental Graphics/Hulton Archive/Getty Images, (tcl)Keystone-France/Gamma-Keystone/Getty Images, (tcr)STR/AFP/Getty Images, (tr)Stefan Kiefer/Alamy

LESSON 2
Human Geography of North Africa

ESSENTIAL QUESTION • *How do physical systems and human systems shape a place?*

Reading HELPDESK CCSS

Academic Vocabulary (Tier Two Words)
- **principal**
- **partner**

Content Vocabulary (Tier Three Words)
- **domesticate**
- **hieroglyphics**
- **geometric boundary**
- **nationalism**
- **nomad**
- **bedouin**

TAKING NOTES: ***Key Ideas and Details***

IDENTIFYING Use a graphic organizer like the one below to take notes on the indigenous peoples and independence movements of North African countries.

Human Geography of North Africa

Early Peoples and Civilizations	Invasions and Independence

IT MATTERS BECAUSE

For centuries, North Africa has been the birthplace and meeting place of cultures, from the Maghreb area in the west to the Nile Valley in the east. Today the subregion exhibits a cultural vibrancy that rests on this deep historical foundation. Ethnic groups, religious changes, and political movements such as the Arab Spring make this a dynamic and important part of the world.

History and Government

GUIDING QUESTION *How have the Sahara, the Nile River valley, and multiple invasions influenced the history and government of North Africa?*

North Africa has a long history. Some of the oldest human civilizations began in the fertile Nile River valley. People from nearby places, including Greece, Rome, Arabia, and Europe, have all influenced North Africa.

Early Peoples and Civilizations

R

Hunters and gatherers settled throughout North Africa about 10,000 years ago. The subregion's farmers were among the first to **domesticate** plants and animals. Under this process, plants and animals once wild became raised by people for food, clothing, and transportation.

The Egyptian civilization developed in the fertile Nile River valley about 6,000 years ago. Annual floods from the Nile deposited rich soil on the floodplain. During dry seasons, Egyptians used sophisticated irrigation systems to water crops. This enabled farmers to grow two crops each year. The Egyptians also developed a calendar with a 365-day year and a system of writing known as **hieroglyphics** (HY•ruh•GLIH•fihks). The large pyramids the Egyptians built were used as tombs for their rulers and demonstrate their abilities in mathematics and engineering.

In the A.D. 600s, invasions of Arab armies moved westward from the Arabian Peninsula. These invasions heavily influenced the cultures of North Africa. As Arab rule spread across North Africa, so did the Muslim religion. Muslim and Jewish exiles fleeing persecution by the Spanish Inquisition

372

networks ***Online Teaching Options***

 **INTERACTIVE BELLRINGER**

Status of Women in North Africa

Exploring Issues This interactive bellringer can be used to introduce and identify the status of women in North African society. Ask students to consider what they think life might be like for women in North Africa and how the women's lives may be similar to or different from the lives of women in the United States. Have students form small groups and discuss their prior knowledge of the status of women in North Africa. Then have groups discuss each question. Ask each group to write agreed-upon answers to the questions. Then in a class discussion, have each group share its answers. **Intrapersonal, Verbal/Linguistic**

Status of Women in North Africa
Women's issues have been a low priority in most North African countries, and women seldom experience the same rights as men.
The countries of North Africa continue to be marked by social practices that not only discriminate against women and are inconsistent with international treaties but also contravene their own national laws. For example, Egypt's constitution grants equality to all citizens, but Egypt's family law contradicts that equality by placing women under the guardianship, or legal control, of their fathers, husbands or other men in their families.

infused Morocco with Spanish culture in the 1400s. The Arabs retained control over much of North Africa until the early 1500s, when the Ottoman Empire began expanding westward from what is now Turkey. The Ottomans were Muslims, or followers of the Islamic faith. With time, the Ottomans were expelled from North Africa as ethnic groups took up military efforts to end their rule. Resistance to Ottoman rule was finally ended with World War I in 1918.

V Location enabled other cultural influences on the subregion. Europe was geographically nearby and established colonial control as the Ottomans left. Algeria was invaded by the French in the mid-1800s. French influence was imprinted on the country, but unrest simmered beneath the colonial surface. Italy colonized Libya, and France occupied additional territory south of the Atlas Mountains. There were disagreements over who would rule North Africa. As a result, the European colonial powers drew **geometric boundaries** that followed straight lines and did not account for natural and cultural features. The boundaries often created conflict between groups of people. Tensions occurred because the local methods of governance were not the same as European methods of governance.

domesticate to adapt plants and animals from the wild for human use

hieroglyphics an ancient writing system used in Egypt in which pictures and symbols represent words or sounds

geometric boundary a fixed limit or extent that typically follows straight lines

nationalism a belief in the right of a nation to be an independent state

Independence and Power Struggles

W In the 1800s, an educated, urban middle class developed in North Africa. This new middle class came in contact with worldwide anticolonial thought and adopted European ideas of **nationalism**. This development stirred demands for self-rule that provided the basis for the modern countries that emerged.

Egypt gained independence from the United Kingdom in 1922. Algeria won independence from the France in 1962 when a nationalist movement led a violent revolt. Since independence, Algeria has developed its resources and raised its living standards. Libya won independence from Italy in 1951 and was then ruled by a Western-friendly monarchy until 1969 when a coup led by Colonel Muammar

W GEOGRAPHY CONNECTION

North Africa's location near Europe and Southwest Asia has made it vulnerable to numerous migrations and invasions over the centuries.

1. ***PLACES AND REGIONS*** Which cities were affected by Islamic invasions until the 750s?
2. ***HUMAN SYSTEMS*** Which later migration route is similar to that of Islamic invasions?

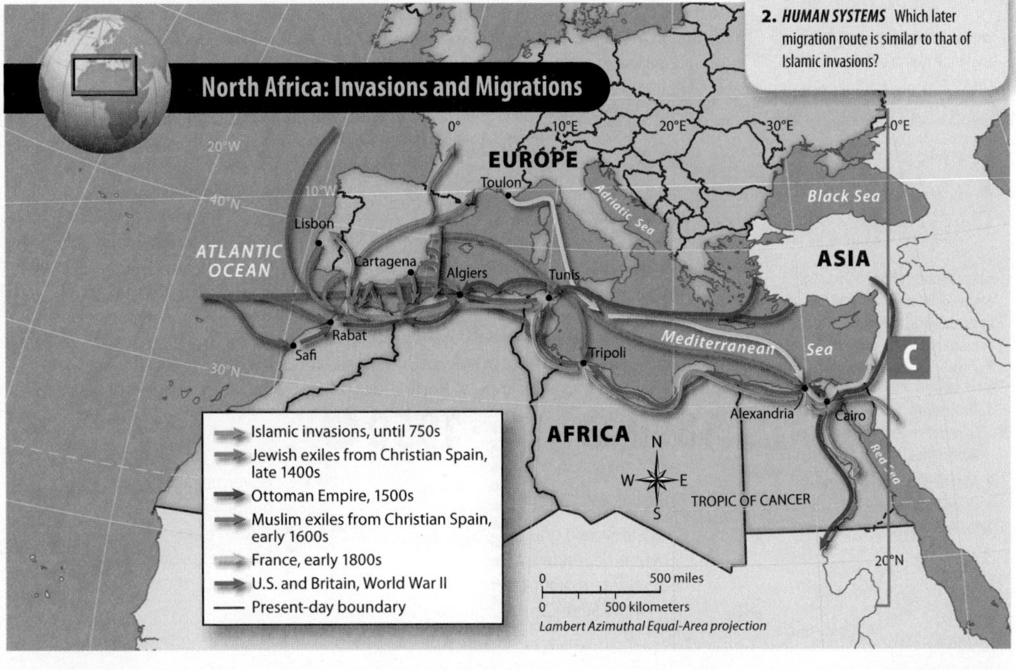

C

GAME

Human Geography of North Africa

Understanding Relationships Among Events Divide the class into pairs to play this Tic-Tac-Toe Game on the human geography of North Africa. After all of the students have finished the game, lead a class discussion about how North Africa's location made it vulnerable to invasions and migrations from Europe and Southwest Asia. Ask students to write three summarizing statements explaining the relationship between North Africa's location and events that have led to historical invasions and migrations. BL Interpersonal, Logical/Mathematical

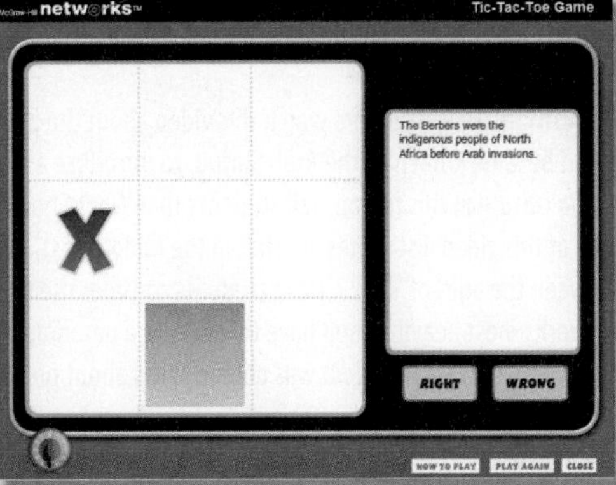

V Visual Skills

Interpreting Lead a class discussion on the impact of the geometric boundaries designated by colonial powers compared to physical boundaries that are often used to designate borders. Direct students to look at the map below and compare the boundaries of the countries in Europe to the southern boundaries of the countries in North Africa. **Ask:** Which continent utilizes physical boundaries? *(Europe)* On which continent are there more geometric boundaries? *(Africa)* ELL Visual/Spatial

W Writing Skills

Argument Discuss how the development of anticolonial thought led to the idea of nationalism. Have students write a short argumentative essay that is in favor of ethnic groups ruling their own country or in favor of colonial empires controlling a country while providing financial support for infrastructure and jobs. Students may find facts to support their opinions in online or library resources. Invite students to read their arguments to the class. BL Verbal/Linguistic

C Critical Thinking Skills

Changing Continuity of Groups Have students study the map of invasions and migrations of North Africa and lead a class discussion on how these actions have impacted the history of the region. Guide students to understand the cause-and-effect relationships involved with the changes that occurred during the nineteenth century. **Ask:** What is an example of how North Africa's location affected its people after Ottoman rule ended? *(Possible answer: Once the Ottoman rule decreased after WWI, location enabled other nearby countries in Europe to establish colonies. Then after WWII, the U.S. and Britain continued to invade and migrate farther into the region.)* How did physical and human systems play a role in the North African population that was ruled by European colonial powers? *(When European colonial powers drew geometric boundaries, they did not account for natural and cultural features, so the boundaries often created conflict for different groups of people.)* AL Logical/Mathematical

ANSWERS, p. 373

GEOGRAPHY CONNECTION

1. The cities of Cairo, Alexandria, Tripoli, Tunis, Rabat, Lisbon, and Cartagena were impacted by the Islamic invasions until the 750s.
2. The route of the U.S. and Britain during World War II is most similar to that of the Islamic invasion.

V Visual Skills

Creating Diagrams Have students read the paragraph and plan how to depict the information visually. Tell students to create a diagram to show how one event led to another in the development of the Arab Spring. Students should write a statement that summarizes the events on their diagrams. Ask volunteers to present their diagrams and statements to the class and use students' presentations as a springboard to discussion. **Ask: What event started the movement that became known as the Arab Spring?** *(A protest by a Tunisian citizen that resulted in his death in 2010 led to riots.)* **What happened as a result of this event?** *(People heard about the event, which led to revolts against oppressive government rule.)* **Visual/Spatial, Interpersonal**

R Reading Skills

Using Correct Terminology and Grammar Have students locate the word *principal* in the text and identify its meaning. **Ask: What is a synonym for the word *principal*?** *(main, primary)* Clarify for students that the word *principal* is a homonym, as it sounds the same as the word *principle* but has a different meaning. Have English language learners work with a partner who is a proficient English speaker to use both forms of the word in sentences, looking up their definitions in the dictionary if needed. Then have partners brainstorm a list of other homonyms. *(examples: affect, effect; ate, eight; allowed, aloud)* **ELL Verbal/Linguistic**

T Technology Skills

Presenting Have students review events and dates on the time line as they consider how migrations have shaped North Africa's population patterns. Have them work in small groups to choose an event from the time line to research and gather additional facts for a multimedia presentation. Presentations should include visuals, such as a graph or chart showing the impact of the event on population patterns, society, and cultures of North African countries. Remind students to use reliable online sources when conducting their research. Ask groups to present their findings to the class. **BL Interpersonal, Visual/Spatial**

ANSWERS, p. 374

READING PROGRESS CHECK Nationalism, the belief in the right for a nation to be independent, led the demand for self-rule in North African countries.

CRITICAL THINKING

1. Student answers may vary but should be supported by information from the lesson. Answers could include the war for independence in Algeria and the military leadership in Egypt and Libya.
2. Tunisia, Libya, and Egypt changed governments as a result of the Arab Spring.

al-Qaddafi overthrew the monarchy. Tunisia, one of the major fronts during World War II, separated from France in 1956. Its history is similar to Libya, with autocratic regimes ruling until 2011. Morocco also won independence from France in 1956. Today Morocco is a constitutional monarchy. Though most countries adopted constitutions, their elected presidents often ruled as dictators once they were in office. Their rule often stifled human rights and free speech.

V Political and ethnic tensions have risen often in North Africa. A protest by a Tunisian citizen that resulted in his death in 2010 led to riots. The act was to protest the lack of economic opportunities. News of the event resulted in revolts against oppressive, nondemocratic governments in Egypt, Libya, and Tunisia. The movement became known as the Arab Spring. Citizen protests in Morocco did not overthrow the government, but the king was forced to concede political and social reform. Beginning in 2011, new governments were elected in Egypt, Libya, and Tunisia.

READING PROGRESS CHECK

Examining What movement led the demand for self-rule in North African countries?

Population Patterns

GUIDING QUESTION *How have indigenous ethnic groups, migrations, and climate shaped population patterns in North Africa?*

nomad a member of a wandering pastoral people

principal most important, consequential, or influential

While European connections continue in the coastal regions of North Africa, a widespread influence throughout the subregion is a mix of indigenous and Arab cultures. The Berbers were the indigenous people of North Africa before the Arab invasions. They maintain their traditional non-Arabic language. Most of the 15 million Berbers live today as farmers. They had previously been pastoral **nomads**, groups of people who move from place to place with herds of animals depending on the season and the availability of grass for grazing and water. The other **principal** ethnic group in North Africa is the Arab people. United by language, Arabs first migrated from the Arabian Peninsula to North Africa in the

TIME LINE

NORTH AFRICA Path to Independence

The countries of North Africa share a common history of colonialism, independence, and journeys toward democracy.

CRITICAL THINKING

1. ***Describing*** Discuss the effects of colonization on the recent history of North Africa.
2. ***Identifying*** Which countries changed governments as a result of the Arab Spring?

1800

1800s France and Great Britain take control over areas of North Africa.

1922 Great Britain grants Egypt independence, but maintains control of the Suez Canal.

1950

1952 Military coup topples government of Egypt; military leader Gamal Abdel Nasser later becomes president of Egypt.

1954 Algerian nationalist group, the National Liberation Front, launches guerrilla war against France.

Transcendental Graphics/Hulton Archive/Getty Images

374

networks Online Teaching Options

VIDEO

Egypt Revolution

Explaining Have students watch this video about the Egyptian Revolution in 2011, which became known as the Arab Spring, to introduce a changing population and social media culture in this region. Tell students that Wael Ghonim was just 29 years old at the time of this video. Estimates are that in the Middle East, roughly 100 million people are between the ages of 15–29. Have students consider the age group that uses social networks most heavily. Then have them write a paragraph explaining why they think Ghonim's use of social media was able to bring about political change. **AL Verbal/Linguistic**

A.D. 600s. Some of the Arabic-speaking peoples are nomadic **bedouins** (BEH•duh•wuhns) who migrated to North Africa from deserts in Southwest Asia.

bedouin member of the nomadic desert peoples of North Africa and Southwest Asia

Geographic factors, especially the availability of water, have influenced settlement in the subregion. Because water is scarce, people have for centuries settled along seacoasts and rivers. The Mediterranean and Atlantic coasts and the Nile River valley hold most of the subregion's people. The Nile River valley is one of the world's most densely populated areas. Other population centers in North Africa include Casablanca, Tunis, Tripoli, and Cairo. Egypt's most populous city and its capital, Cairo, dominates the country's social and cultural life. Cities have grown rapidly as people migrate from rural areas in search of a better life. Cities face problems providing services because growth has occurred quickly.

Emigration to regions outside North Africa is high due to higher availability of employment opportunities in other regions. The region's close proximity and historical ties to European countries such as Spain and France pull migrants from Morocco, Algeria, and Tunisia. Migrants from Egypt, an ex-British colony, migrate to the United Kingdom and other English-speaking countries such as the United States, Canada, and Australia.

✓ READING PROGRESS CHECK

Naming Who are the people indigenous to North Africa?

Society and Culture Today

GUIDING QUESTION *How have Islam and the Arabic language helped define much of the culture and society of North Africa?*

When the Arabs invaded North Africa, they brought Islam. Calls to worship occur five times each day in countries with Muslim populations. A muezzin, or crier, delivers the call to prayer for each local mosque. Following the movements of the imam, or prayer leader, individuals bow and kneel, touching their foreheads to the ground in the direction of the holy city of Makkah (Mecca) in Saudi Arabia.

1956 March—France recognizes independence of Morocco and Tunisia.

1956 July—President Nasser of Egypt nationalizes Suez Canal, leading to Suez Crisis.

1962 Brutal Algerian war of independence with France ends; Algeria becomes an independent country.

1969 Libyan army overthrows king. Muammar al-Qaddafi becomes head of state.

2010 Young Tunisians launch protests that ultimately forces president to flee.

2010 ➔

2011 Arab Spring leads to regime change in Tunisia, Libya, and Egypt.

INTERACTIVE MAP

Egypt: Population Density

Identifying Trends Display this population map of Egypt. Ask students to identify the regions and cities on the map that are most densely populated. Have students write a brief statement identifying the trends that influence settlement in regions and subregions around the world. *(geographical factors, availability of water, temperate climates for growing seasons)* Then guide a class discussion about the concerns that large cities such as Cairo often face because of rapid growth, drawing from students' prior knowledge of rapid growth trends.
AL **Logical/Mathematical**

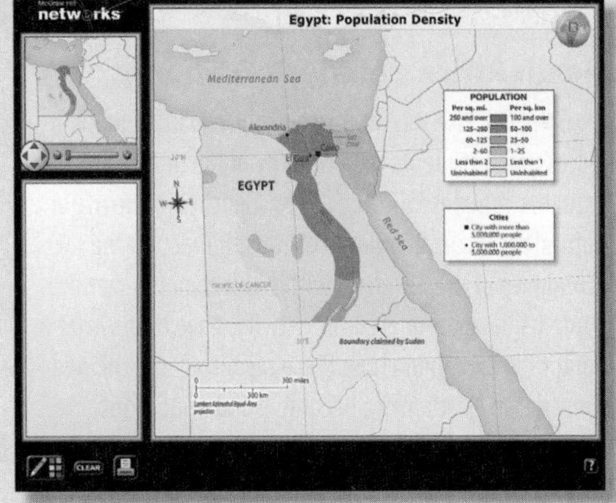

V Visual Skills

Using Graphs Have students refer to a physical map of North Africa. **Ask: What geographic factors impacted settlement in North Africa?** *(Proximity to bodies of water such as the Mediterranean Sea to the north and the Red Sea to the east influenced settlement.)* Guide a class discussion about the importance of seacoasts and rivers to the development of cities. **Ask: What are some examples of cities in the United States that benefit from their location close to bodies of water?** *(Student answers may vary, but might include New York, Boston, Los Angeles, Miami, and Chicago.)* AL **Visual/Spatial**

Content Background Knowledge

The Suez Canal The Suez Canal, which joins the Red Sea to the east of Egypt with the Mediterranean Sea to the north, was completed in 1869 and took more than 11 years to build. The canal allowed for a substantially shorter sailing route between Europe and Asia, Australia, and the eastern coast of Africa. At a length of more than 100 miles (161 kilometers), the canal is one of the busiest seaways in the world and a key route for shipping and trade.

C Critical Thinking Skills

Interpreting Significance Remind students that people who immigrate go into another country, while those who emigrate leave or exit their home country. Guide students to understand the ways in which migrations have influenced population patterns in North Africa and the surrounding regions. **Ask: How have changes in North Africa's population impacted its workforce?** *(People who seek jobs outside of North Africa have emigrated to other regions, which has caused a shift in the number of skilled workers available in North Africa.)* **What has been the result of opportunities within North African countries?** *(A growing middle class has emerged.)* **Logical/Mathematical**

ANSWERS, p. 375

✓ READING PROGRESS CHECK The Berbers are the indigenous people of North Africa.

R Reading Skills

Understanding Relationships Among Events After students read the paragraph, have them consider the ways in which religion has shaped population patterns, society, and the cultures of North Africa. Lead a discussion about the spread of Islam across North Africa and its impact on the people and culture. AL **Verbal/Linguistic**

W Writing Skills

Narrative Have students use the information in the text to write a journal entry from the point of view of a person living in North Africa. Tell students their journal entries should reveal the approximate age of the person, the region in which he or she lives, and the person's level of education. Allow time for students to conduct additional research to glean information for their journal entries. **Verbal/Linguistic**

T Technology Skills

Presenting Perspectives Organize students into pairs assigning them one of the following topics: music/dance, poetry/literature, art/crafts, and architecture. Have student pairs conduct research for a presentation about their assigned topic as it relates to the arts of different North African countries. Encourage partners to create a visual display in which students demonstrate art forms such as reading poetic lyrics or playing popular forms of music. Have pairs present their findings, encouraging them to create costumes and play music.
BL **Auditory/Musical, Kinesthetic**

Islamic patterns are found in weaving and embroidery throughout the subregion.

▲ **CRITICAL THINKING**

1. ***Analyzing Visuals*** Describe the designs shown in the picture above.
2. ***Making Connections*** Why are there no animals or people in the designs of traditional art in North Africa?

Stefan Kiefer/Alamy

R As Islam spread, so did the Arabic language. Non-Arab Muslims learned Arabic in order to read the Quran, Islam's holy book. Moroccans speak an Arabic dialect that is a result of Berber influence. Egyptians speak Arabic with a different accent than do Moroccans, Tunisians, and Algerians. People in Algeria and Morocco also speak French as a result of colonization and influence on education.

Family and Status of Women

W Since achieving independence in the 1950s and 1960s, North African countries have been redefining their political, social, and cultural systems. Class status influences family size. Upper-class families have fewer children than lower-class families. Historically, extended family members have lived nearby, so children usually grow up with many cousins, aunts, and uncles. Today, families are living more spread out and do not necessarily live close to one another.

Decades of urbanization have led nomadic peoples to settle in villages and cities. Very few groups still roam the desert as they did centuries ago. They have access to schools, transportation, and health care near where they live. Families have plans that educated children will earn enough money to support the older members of the family.

Although women participated in winning independence, women's issues were not priorities in the years immediately following independence. Government rule often stifled human rights. This affected women's issues as well, and many women are not permitted to accept jobs even when they have an education level higher than men.

The Arts

T From the earliest times, the peoples of North Africa have expressed themselves through the arts. The ancient Egyptians built huge pyramids that still stand as marvels of construction. One of Algeria's most popular forms of music, *raï*, involves various instruments and poetic lyrics. Contemporary Egyptian music blends traditional Arabic and Western styles. Egypt has experienced a revival of folkloric dance and traditional crafts. The arts of weaving, embroidery, and metalworking are heavily influenced by Islamic patterns found in local architecture. Elaborate geometric designs are featured in these works because of the traditional Islamic prohibition against the representation of living beings.

☑ **READING PROGRESS CHECK**

Assessing What has been the primary influence of language in North Africa?

Economic Activities

GUIDING QUESTION *What factors have helped many countries in North Africa become rising middle-income countries?*

North Africa, unlike other regions of the continent, has historically engaged in a range of manufacturing processes. By the end of the 1800s, much of the region, however, was regarded by European countries as a source of raw materials. Although manufacturing increased during World War II, output accelerated quickly only after the decline of European control. Despite expansion since the 1950s, manufacturing output among the countries varies greatly.

Only a small part of the subregion's land is arable, or suitable for farming. Agriculture plays a smaller role in countries with desert climates. It is also less important in countries with economies based on oil, such as Libya and Algeria.

376

networks Online Teaching Options

INTERACTIVE WHITEBOARD ACTIVITY

North Africa's Modern Economy

Explaining Use this interactive whiteboard activity to discuss with students the economy in North Africa. Have students complete the activity by identifying the major natural resources that have the most impact on the economies of the countries within this region. After the students have completed the activity, have them write a paragraph explaining how these resources have helped countries in North Africa become rising middle-income countries. Encourage several students to share their writing with the class. **Verbal/Linguistic**

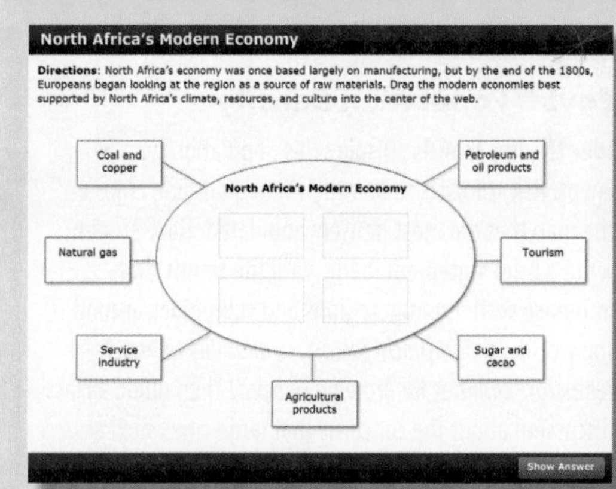

North Africa's Modern Economy
Directions: North Africa's economy was once based largely on manufacturing, but by the end of the 1800s, Europeans began looking at the region as a source of raw materials. Drag the modern economies best supported by North Africa's climate, resources, and culture into the center of the web.
Coal and copper
Petroleum and oil products
North Africa's Modern Economy
Natural gas
Tourism
Service industry
Sugar and cacao
Agricultural products
Show Answer

ANSWERS, p. 376

☑ **READING PROGRESS CHECK** The proliferation of Islam caused Arabic to spread throughout North Africa.

CRITICAL THINKING

1. The designs shown are traditional Islamic patterns, which are brightly colored and geometric.
2. Traditional Islamic beliefs prohibit any representation of living beings from being produced.

Areas of North Africa that have a Mediterranean climate are best suited for growing a variety of crops. Barley, wheat, citrus fruits, grapes, vegetables, olives, figs, dates, and almonds are grown. When rainfall is below normal, however, harvests of major crops such as wheat and barley seldom meet local needs, which increases dependence on imported food. Seafood is an important food source, and fishing vessels catch sardines and mackerel from the Atlantic Ocean.

Wealth from oil, natural gas, and mining has helped develop economies in the subregion. Petroleum and oil products are North Africa's main export commodities, or economic goods. Natural gas is also a major export. Coal and copper mining and cement production are important as well.

Tourism plays a significant role in the subregion's economies. Certain areas serve as popular travel destinations because of their historical importance, blend of religious history, or pleasant climates. The Valley of the Kings and the pyramids draw tourists to Egypt. Port el-Kantaoui near Sousse, Tunisia, is a vacation beach destination. Carthage, an ancient city, is rich in historical artifacts.

Advancements in transportation and communications have brought improvements to the subregion. However, the physical environment and government control have limited some development here. Water transportation is very important to North Africa. Ships load and unload cargo and passengers at ports on the Mediterranean Sea, Red Sea, and Atlantic Ocean, including oil, natural gas, minerals, and tourists. Because of its accessibility to Europe and low-cost labor, Morocco has become an appealing trading **partner**—especially for Spain, France, and Italy. Other North African countries also have significant trade relations with countries outside the region.

partner one associated with another, especially in an action

Despite economic progress within North Africa, its countries suffer from high rates of unemployment, poverty, wealth disparity, and political upheaval. Key economic challenges include reducing socioeconomic disparities in government spending, increasing available jobs for the young, and establishing more diverse industries. The Arab Spring has resulted in a number of stressful aftereffects in North Africa as well. These include high food and fuel prices that have strained many of the resources and budgets of the subregion's governments. Political instability, public unrest regarding dishonest elections, and the protection of human rights are concerns expressed in the new Arab Spring democracies.

☑ READING PROGRESS CHECK

Explaining How have North Africa's natural resources influenced economic growth?

LESSON 2 REVIEW 

Reviewing Vocabulary (Tier Three Words)

1. ***Locating*** Where did the bedouin people originate? RH.9–10.4
2. ***Defining*** What political concept introduced by North Africa's middle class is a response to the region's history of colonialism? RH.9–10.4

Using Your Notes

3. ***Summarizing*** Use your graphic organizer to describe the early peoples of North Africa.

Answering the Guiding Questions

4. ***Gathering Information*** How have the Sahara, the Nile River valley, and multiple invasions influenced the history and government of North Africa?
5. ***Explaining*** How have indigenous ethnic groups, migrations, and climate shaped population patterns in North Africa?
6. ***Summarizing*** How have Islam and the Arabic language helped define much of the culture and society of North Africa?
7. ***Describing*** What factors have helped many countries in North Africa become rising middle-income countries?

Writing Activity

8. ***Informative/Explanatory*** Identify two natural resources in North Africa crucial to economic activity and trade. In a paragraph, provide specific examples of how these resources increased trade and interdependence between North Africa and the world. WHST.9–10.2

C Critical Thinking Skills

Evaluating Lead a class discussion about the factors that have contributed to economic development in North Africa. Have students identify natural resources. *(oil, natural gas, coal, and copper mining)* **Ask: What other factors are important to the modern economies of North Africa?** *(Tourism is also a major factor in the development of economies.)* **Interpersonal**

T Technology Skills

Changing Continuity in Economics Organize the class into small groups and have them choose a North African country to research on one of the following topics: transportation, communication, physical environment, or government control. Remind students to use reliable online sources to research their assigned topic as it relates to trade relations in their chosen country. Have students present their findings to the class. **BL Logical/Mathematical**

CLOSE & REFLECT

Outlining Have students identify key factors that have led to the settlement and economic development of countries in North Africa. Suggest to students that they organize their notes into an outline and then use their outlines as a study tool to review the chapter.

ANSWERS, p. 377

☑ **READING PROGRESS CHECK** Natural gas and petroleum have helped develop the economies of the subregion.

LESSON 2 REVIEW ANSWERS

Reviewing Vocabulary

1. Bedouin people came from Southwest Asian deserts.
2. The belief in a nation's right to independence, called nationalism, was introduced by the middle class in response to colonialism.

Using Your Notes

3. Hunters and gatherers settled in North Africa about 10,000 years ago and domesticated plants and animals. The Berbers, the indigenous people of North Africa, were pastoral nomads. Egyptian civilization developed in the Nile River valley about 6,000 years ago. The Egyptians developed a 365-day calendar and writing systems. Arab armies invaded North Africa around A.D. 600, spreading Islam and the Arabic language. Some Arabic-speaking peoples were nomadic bedouins.

Answering the Guiding Questions

4. Student answers may vary, but could include settlements around the Nile River valley for access to water, lack of settlement in the desert, invasions brought Islam and Arabic across the subregion, colonialism, and independence.
5. Student answers may vary, but could include the Berbers, now living as farmers; Nile River valley settlements for water access; coastal development for trade access; rural-to-urban migration in search of better jobs and living conditions; and migration to other countries in search of better jobs.
6. Islam helps structure society and culture as it has five calls to worship each day. Islam spread Arabic across the subregion, which was needed to read the Quran, the holy book of Islam. Traditional art is influenced by Islam in that it cannot depict living beings.
7. Wealth from oil, natural gas, and mining have helped develop the economies of North African countries.

Writing Activity

8. Paragraphs may vary, but resources include: oil, natural gas, coal, and copper; North Africa is a major exporter of these resources, and many countries are increasingly dependent upon the subregion; examples may include Morocco, Mediterranean and Red Seas and Atlantic Ocean for shipping around the world.

ENGAGE

G1 Critical Thinking Skills

Activating Prior Knowledge Explain to students that they will be reading about how the events of the Arab Spring impacted various countries in North Africa and Southwest Asia. Have groups discuss what they already know from news media or other sources about these uprisings, where they took place, what happened, and why it happened. *(Student answers may vary but could include mention of large protests, the deposition of Arab leaders, or the holding of new elections.)* Have groups share their previous knowledge with the class.

TEACH & ASSESS

C2 Critical Thinking Skills

Understanding Relationships Among Events Have students scan the information boxes to find how one event influenced another. **Ask:** **What are two ways that the events in different countries were related?** *(The protests and change in government that took place in Tunisia and Egypt inspired the people of Yemen to protest their own leader; Both Syria and Bahrain organized a "Day of Rage.")* Continue the discussion, leading students to recognize other ways these events are linked. AL **Logical/Mathematical**

R Reading Skills

Making Inferences Explain that past uprisings such as the Prague Spring of 1968 and the French "springtime of the people" (a phrase used to describe the European 1848 revolutions) used the word *spring* in their labels. **Ask:** **What are characteristics of spring when compared to winter?** *(In spring, things that were cold and frozen bloom back to life. Spring is a time of new hope and life.)* **Why might people use *spring* to describe events such as those that took place during the Arab Spring?** *(Spring is a time of new beginnings, and these revolutionary events opened the possibility of new freedoms and a new kind of life in these places.)* ELL **Verbal/Linguistic**

V Visual Skills

Analyzing Visuals Have students study the symbols on the map key. **Ask:** **Why might each symbol have been chosen?** *(Possible answers: Fist for Major Protests: hand gesture often made by protesters that symbolizes resistance. Sign for Minor Protests: the signs peaceful protestors often carry. Riot gear helmet for Protests Suppressed: the way governments may violently suppress protests. Arrows for Change in Government: indicate movement. Crosshairs for Leader Killed: like the sight from a gun. Explosion for Civil War: largest and most violent internal conflict.)* Point out places where the events occurred. Talk about why the mapmaker chose these particular aspects of the Arab Spring to label the most prominently. BL **Visual/Spatial**

G1 The Arab Spring

C2 R *The Arab Spring was a series of protests and revolutions that began to spread across the Arab world in late 2010. All protesters shared the same general goals: less corruption in their country's leadership and more openly democratic forms of government. The outcomes of the Arab Spring have differed between countries. In some places, like Egypt, the protests have resulted in major changes in government. In others, like Syria, protests and government repression have broken down into full-scale civil wars. The lasting outcomes of the Arab Spring, positive or negative, are yet to be fully realized. Here we look at the beginnings of the Arab Spring.*

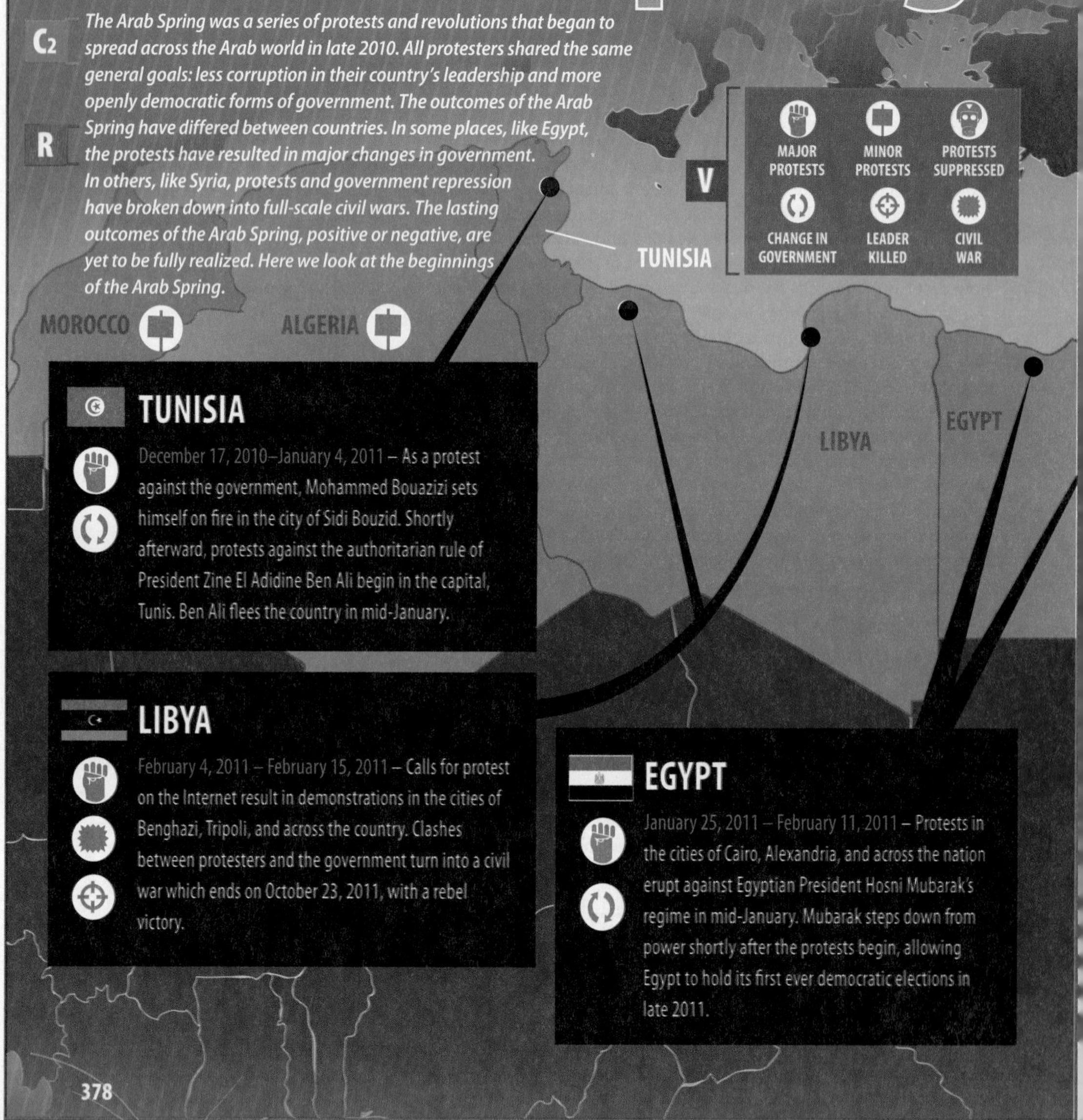

V
MAJOR PROTESTS
MINOR PROTESTS
PROTESTS SUPPRESSED
CHANGE IN GOVERNMENT
LEADER KILLED
CIVIL WAR

MOROCCO
ALGERIA
TUNISIA
LIBYA
EGYPT

TUNISIA

December 17, 2010–January 4, 2011 – As a protest against the government, Mohammed Bouazizi sets himself on fire in the city of Sidi Bouzid. Shortly afterward, protests against the authoritarian rule of President Zine El Adidine Ben Ali begin in the capital, Tunis. Ben Ali flees the country in mid-January.

LIBYA

February 4, 2011 – February 15, 2011 – Calls for protest on the Internet result in demonstrations in the cities of Benghazi, Tripoli, and across the country. Clashes between protesters and the government turn into a civil war which ends on October 23, 2011, with a rebel victory.

EGYPT

January 25, 2011 – February 11, 2011 – Protests in the cities of Cairo, Alexandria, and across the nation erupt against Egyptian President Hosni Mubarak's regime in mid-January. Mubarak steps down from power shortly after the protests begin, allowing Egypt to hold its first ever democratic elections in late 2011.

378

networks Online Teaching Options

VIDEO

Egypt Internet Freedom

Understanding Relationships Among Events Before students view this video about the role of social media in recent civilian uprisings in Egypt, ask students to write a statement about how they think the Internet affects current issues in North Africa. Have students view the video and then write a paragraph to summarize what they learned about the Internet and its effect on social unrest. Does their summary information support their statements about the Internet and current issues in North Africa that they made prior to viewing the video? If not, would students change their original statements and how? **Intrapersonal, Verbal/Linguistic**

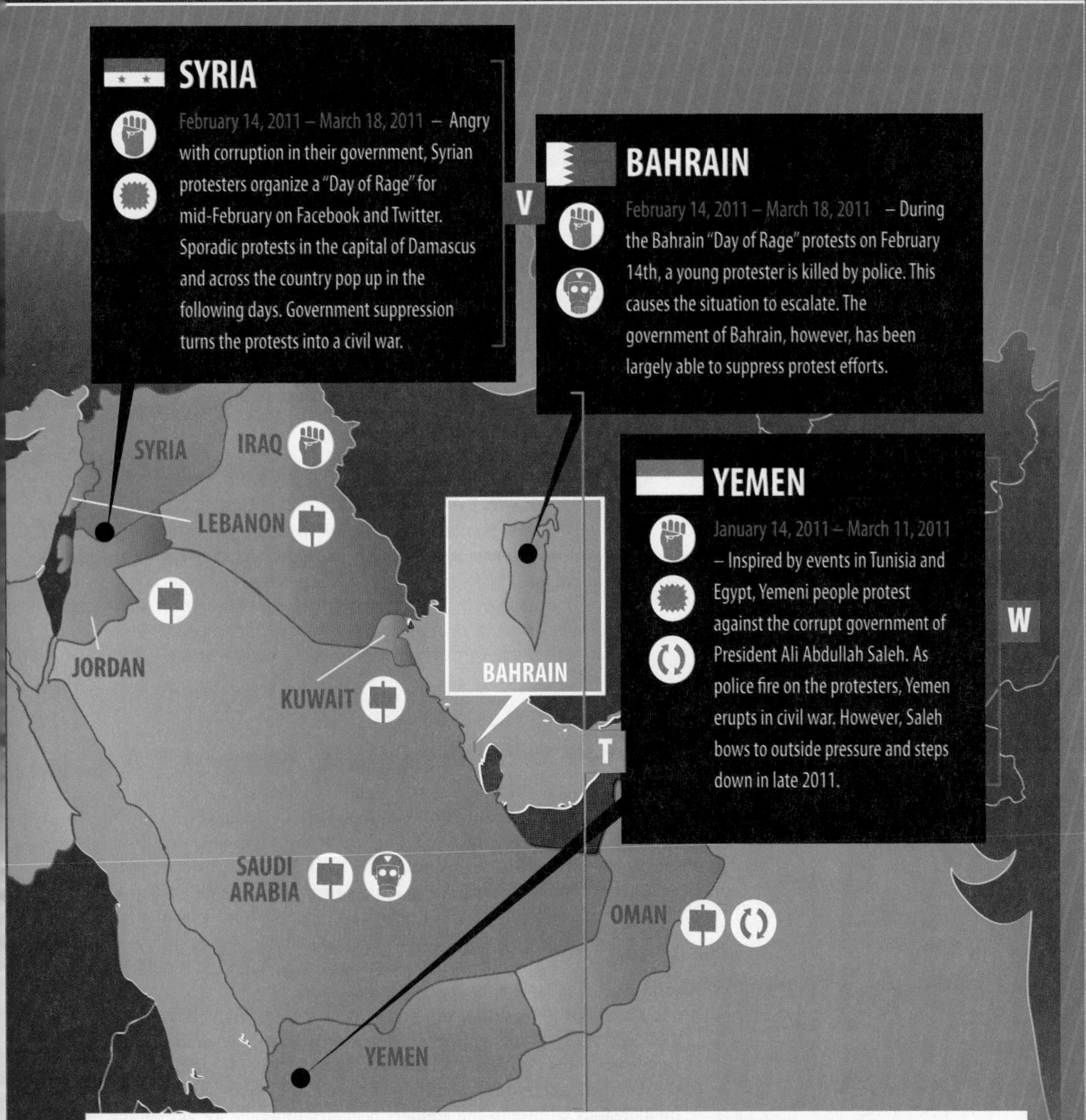

SYRIA

February 14, 2011 – March 18, 2011 – Angry with corruption in their government, Syrian protesters organize a "Day of Rage" for mid-February on Facebook and Twitter. Sporadic protests in the capital of Damascus and across the country pop up in the following days. Government suppression turns the protests into a civil war.

V

BAHRAIN

February 14, 2011 – March 18, 2011 – During the Bahrain "Day of Rage" protests on February 14th, a young protester is killed by police. This causes the situation to escalate. The government of Bahrain, however, has been largely able to suppress protest efforts.

YEMEN

January 14, 2011 – March 11, 2011 – Inspired by events in Tunisia and Egypt, Yemeni people protest against the corrupt government of President Ali Abdullah Saleh. As police fire on the protesters, Yemen erupts in civil war. However, Saleh bows to outside pressure and steps down in late 2011.

W

T

SYRIA
IRAQ
LEBANON
JORDAN
KUWAIT
BAHRAIN
SAUDI ARABIA
OMAN
YEMEN

Making Connections

1. ***Places and Regions*** What were the two most common outcomes of states experiencing major protests?
2. ***Human Systems*** Many protest groups used public sites like Facebook and Twitter to organize and communicate. How might this practice have inspired and encouraged protests elsewhere?
3. ***The Uses of Geography*** Create a time line of events for one of the states above, detailing some of the protests, changes in government, or conflicts. Then, write a short summary explaining the overall positive or negative effects of the movement on that state.

*Interact with **Global Connections** Online*

INTERACTIVE IMAGE

"Arab Spring"

Exploring Issues Display the interactive image of the Arab Spring protests. Discuss with students the role of technology in the protests. Ask students whether they think governments should be able to control technology information to prevent protests such as the Arab Spring. Then based on students' responses, organize the class into two groups—those that agree and those that disagree with government control. Have group members meet to organize information to support their opinion, researching online as necessary. Then hold a class debate about the topic. After the debate, survey the class to see whether any students have change their opinion.

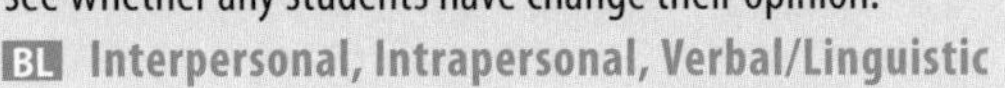
BL Interpersonal, Intrapersonal, Verbal/Linguistic

"Arab Spring"

V Visual Skills

Organizing Have students create a time line that shows when the Arab Spring uprisings took place in each country. The time line should mark off the often overlapping spans of time and note any linked events, such as the "Day of Rage" demonstrations planned for both Syria and Bahrain. Invite students to present their completed time lines to the class. **AL Logical/Mathematical, Visual/Spatial**

W Writing Skills

Informative/Explanatory Have students review the information about the uprisings in various countries. Ask them to write an informative paragraph describing the role of the Internet and social media in the events of the Arab Spring. **BL Verbal/Linguistic**

T Technology Skills

Acquiring Information Have small groups find online information about Arab Spring events in the countries on this map. Assign each group a country and remind them to gather information relating to the issues featured in the map key. Suggest they research details such as what role social media played in the events and caused the events in the first place. Have groups present their findings in a multimedia presentation and use the information to compare and contrast as a class the experiences of each country. **BL Interpersonal**

CLOSE & REFLECT

Making Generalizations Have students review the information about uprisings in each country and make a generalization about the effects of the Arab Spring. Invite volunteers to share their generalizations with the class.

ANSWERS, p. 379

Making Connections

1. States seeing major protests either saw a change in government or experienced a civil war.
2. Outsiders monitoring protest groups on Internet sites could see and hear about their experiences in the protesters' own words. Seeing these experiences firsthand could encourage others to form protest groups in their own countries or encourage them to organize and communicate via social media as well.
3. Student time lines should include minor and major protests, changes in government, and conflicts such as governmental crackdowns or civil wars. Summaries should support with evidence their assertion that the overall effect of the movement was positive or negative.

ENGAGE

V Visual Skills

Organizing Tell students to create a graphic organizer, such as a two-column chart, to organize information about the relationship between human activity and the environment in North Africa. Suggest that students label their chart *Effects of Advancements in Energy/Power Production* with the subheadings *Positive* and *Negative*.

TEACH & ASSESS

R Reading Skills

Understanding Relationships Have students consider the impact a high demand for freshwater has on human populations and how their own lives would change if they had little or no access to freshwater. Then have students create flowcharts or outlines showing the impact of water scarcity in certain regions. AL Visual/Spatial

Making Connections

As you discuss food production in North Africa, have students recall information about North Africa's vegetation. Review with students that some vegetation can grow in desert regions. Ask students what agricultural products from North Africa they enjoy. *(Students may say they enjoy olives, grapes, and citrus fruits.)* Remind students that olive trees and date palms can grow in deserts where there are oases.

ANSWERS, p. 380

TAKING NOTES: Desalination plants—turn salt water to freshwater; **Libya's Great Man-Made River**—a series of pumps and pipelines to access underground aquifers; the Aswān High Dam and the creation of Lake Nasser are ways North Africa is trying to manage water resources for irrigation and consumption.

networks

There's More Online!

- **IMAGE** Managing the Great Man-Made River project
- **IMAGE** Oasis in Tinghir, Morocco
- **INFOGRAPHIC** Aswān High Dam
- **INTERACTIVE SELF-CHECK QUIZ**
- **VIDEO** People and Their Environment: North Africa

LESSON 3
People and Their Environment: North Africa

ESSENTIAL QUESTION • *How do physical systems and human systems shape a place?*

Reading HELPDESK (CCSS)

Academic Vocabulary (Tier Two Words)
- subsequent
- relevant

Content Vocabulary (Tier Three Words)
- aquifer

TAKING NOTES: *Key Ideas and Details*

Summarizing Use a graphic organizer like the one below to summarize ways that North Africa is managing its resources.

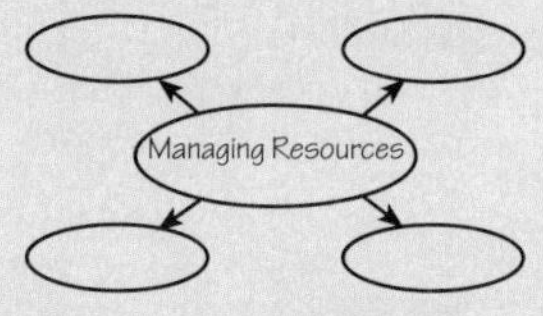

IT MATTERS BECAUSE

V *The relationship of humans with their environment is constantly changing. While humans have achieved impressive advancements in energy and power production, such innovation comes at a cost. For example, the need for freshwater and the process of oil extraction have often negatively affected the North African environment. The subregion's water scarcity and oil wealth make trade an essential activity for many North African countries.*

Managing Resources

GUIDING QUESTION *Why are water resources in such demand in North Africa?*

R As populations and economies grow, so does demand for water resources. Clean drinking water ensures the continued livelihood and development of human populations. Much water in North Africa is used for irrigation, which allows for continued food production. Places with fewer water resources, such as Western Sahara and Libya, are more dependent on trade to import food. This not only leaves populations dependent on outside food sources, but also creates a vulnerability to changes in market prices for food. Agricultural land loss due to urbanization and windblown sands is also an issue affecting food production.

Much of the freshwater in North Africa comes from rivers, oases, and **aquifers**, or underground sources of water. Aquifers can be problematic for countries with coastal access. As water is removed from the coastal aquifers, it is replaced by salty seawater. Water contaminated by increased salinity in the aquifers becomes unusable for agriculture. The contaminated water is also unfit to drink.

The source of water for consumption and agriculture in North Africa varies by country. Egypt, for example, gathers surface water from large rivers, particularly the Nile. Other countries, such as Algeria and Libya, have more limited water resources. As another form of water extraction, these countries use a process called desalination. Desalination is a

networks *Online Teaching Options*

INTERACTIVE BELLRINGER

Egypt's Aswān High Dam

Identifying Cause and Effect Use this bellringer activity to help students identify some causes and effects of the Aswān High Dam. Have students form small groups to discuss why Egypt built the dam and the dam's resulting environment and social effects since the dam was built. Then have groups discuss and answer the bellringer questions. Ask groups to share their answers in a class discussion. Interpersonal, Verbal/Linguistic

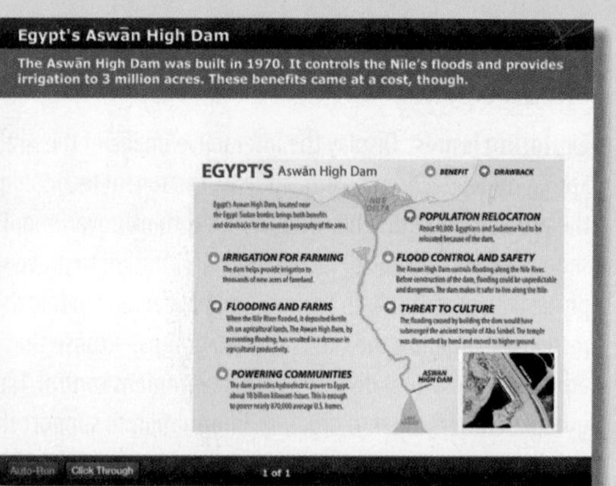

process in which the salt is removed from salt water. Building and maintaining desalination plants, however, can be expensive for most countries.

Libya's Great Man-Made River is an ambitious effort to supply freshwater to this country that consists of 95 percent desert and relies on food imports to feed its population. Nearly 40,000 years ago, when North Africa had a more temperate climate, rainwater collected in underground reservoirs beneath Libya. It was not until the mid-1950s that oil exploration in the southern Libyan Desert exposed these vast quantities of fresh, clean groundwater. The Great Man-Made River is a pumping and pipeline system that attempts to utilize this extensive source of groundwater.

The Great Man-Made River provides 70 percent of the Libyan population with water for drinking and irrigation. It was funded by profits from Libya's nationalized oil sector. The project uses two pipelines to pump water from large aquifers beneath the Sahara to farms along Libya's coastal region. The first two phases of the project were completed in 1993 and 1996. The third phase of the project, completed in 2009, links the pipelines of the first two phases. Two **subsequent** phases will extend the distribution network to the northeast coast and unite the two transporting systems into a single network.

However, environmental challenges exist for Libya's Great Man-Made River. Scientists fear that the pipelines could drain aquifers in Libya and neighboring countries. They also fear that pumping aquifers near the Mediterranean could draw in salt water from the sea. In most areas, the rate of water extraction far exceeds the rate at which water is replaced. Such rates of extraction cannot be sustained in the coming decades. Although providing water for the current population is important, an equally **relevant** concern is having water for future generations.

☑ READING PROGRESS CHECK

Specifying What is a project that has provided water to the region's inhabitants?

T

aquifer underground water-bearing layers of porous rock, sand, or gravel

R

subsequent later; following after another event

relevant having to do with the matter at hand

C

This dense palm oasis in Tinghir, Morocco, is irrigated by a network of pipes and irrigation canals.

CRITICAL THINKING ▼

1. ***Analyzing Visuals*** What environmental challenges does irrigation pose in North Africa?
2. ***Hypothesizing*** What type of water source is likely to be used to irrigate the oasis shown?

CHAPTER 15, Lesson 3

People and Their Environment: North Africa

T Technology Skills

Examining Information Guide a brief discussion about how desalination provides water for North African countries with limited freshwater resources. Organize students into small groups and assign each group one of the countries in North Africa. Have groups conduct research about ways in which water scarcity issues are being addressed in their assigned country. Tell students to present their findings in a report that includes visuals explaining the desalination process as well as other methods of water extraction or preservation used in their assigned country. **BL Interpersonal**

R Reading Skills

Defining Students who are mastering English may have trouble with some of the concepts and terms discussed in this paragraph. Have English language learners work with partners who are native English speakers to read through the paragraph and clarify any terms or phrases that might be confusing, such as *nationalized oil sector* and *distribution network*. To facilitate understanding, guide students to identify Spanish cognates, such as national *(nacional)* and distribution *(distribuci)*. **Ask: How does the Great Man-Made River provide water to the Libyan population?** *(It uses a series of pipelines to pump water from large aquifers beneath the Sahara.)* **ELL Verbal/Linguistic**

C Critical Thinking Skills

Creating and Analyzing Arguments Tell students to consider the pros and cons of Libya's Great Man-Made River. Have students work in groups to conduct a mock debate in which they defend or refute the following statement: It is important to provide water for Libya's current population using water extraction. Assign roles to students, such as scientists, farmers, engineers, environmental activists, and so on. Moderate the debate by having groups state their side of the issue, allowing each side to rebut the other's positions. After each group has presented its side of the issue, ask students which argument they found the most convincing and why. **BL Logical/Mathematical, Interpersonal**

ANSWERS, p. 381

☑ **READING PROGRESS CHECK** Libya's Great Man-Made River provides 70 percent of the Libyan population with water. It is a pumping and pipeline system that accesses the water in underground reservoirs for consumption and use in irrigation.

CRITICAL THINKING

1. North Africa is pumping groundwater for irrigation at rates faster than it can be replaced, leaving future water supplies in serious danger. Pumping near the Mediterranean could bring in salt water that could contaminate the freshwater supply.
2. Groundwater from aquifers is the likely source of water used for irrigation of the oasis in the picture.

CHART

Population: North Africa

Explaining This chart shows the population information for countries in North Africa. Have students analyze the chart and relate the data to the importance of managing resources, especially water in these countries. Lead a class discussion about the region's environmental challenges. Have students brainstorm ideas about providing water for the current population, as well as conserving water for future generations. Ask students to explain how the climate, biomes, and natural resources in this region will continue to cause environmental challenges. **BL Logical/Mathematical**

Population: North Africa

This chart contains population information for countries in North Africa.

	Population (in millions)	Population (world rank)	Population Growth Rate (in percent)	Population Growth Rate (world rank)
Algeria	37.4	34th	1.9	62nd
Egypt	83.7	15th	1.9	61st
Libya	5.6	109th	2.1	53rd
Morocco	32.3	38th	1.1	110th
Tunisia	10.7	79th	1.0	118th

V Visual Skills

Global Analysis Have students work in small groups to create a visual report that shows the impact of oil production, fishing, and mass tourism on regions in North Africa. Tell students to include the advantages and disadvantages of these activities in their reports, conducting additional research as needed. In their research, have students identify other parts of the world facing similar issues and what is being done there to remedy the issues. Guide students to understand how oil production and distribution impact the environment in North Africa as well as other parts of the world. BL **Visual/Spatial, Interpersonal**

T Technology Skills

Exploring Issues Discuss the impact that oil spills can have on the environment. Then have students conduct online research about one of the following topics: the current status of regions impacted by the *Kharg V* oil spill in 1990, such as the Canary Islands and Morocco's coastline, or an oil spill that has occurred in another part of the world. The impact on the surrounding environment and subsequent cleanup efforts should be included as students use presentation software to create slide shows. Tell students to relate both the economic and environmental impact of the oil spills in their reports. Have students present their slide shows to the class. BL **Visual/Spatial, Verbal/Linguistic**

C Critical Thinking Skills

Considering Advantages and Disadvantages Have students analyze the benefits and drawbacks shown in the diagram of Egypt's Aswān High Dam. **Ask: How would the dam pose a threat to the culture of the region, and what was done to prevent potential damage?** *(The flooding caused by building the dam could potentially harm the ancient temple of Abu Simbel. As a precaution, the temple was dismantled by hand and moved to higher ground.)* **Visual/Spatial, Logical/Mathematical**

ANSWERS, p. 382

CRITICAL THINKING

1. The Aswān High Dam benefits the people of North Africa by controlling flooding of the Nile, providing irrigation for farming, and supplying hydroelectric power.
2. Possible answers include questions regarding soil fertility/loss of agricultural productivity and changes to plants and animals of the ecosystem.

Human Impact

GUIDING QUESTION *How have modern economic activities impacted North Africa's environment?*

V North Africa faces many challenges related to economic activity and its effects on the environment. Oil and fishing are two very profitable economic sectors for the subregion. High-volume production for these economic sectors, however, can alter the physical environment. The plants and animals in the area also suffer when habitats are lost or damaged.

Mass tourism is another main cause behind ecological loss in the subregion. Areas along the coast that receive the most visits from tourists have suffered the greatest losses. Some locations that were once pristine are now severely damaged beyond repair. Increased use of water in hotels, swimming pools, and golf courses—especially during the summer—is also a concern since the subregion suffers from water shortages.

T North Africa's location puts it at risk for oil spills since tankers pass the subregion's coasts. Oil spills can occur on land or on the seas. Following an oil spill at sea, winds can sweep the oil slicks toward coastlines, affecting the ecosystems of the land as well as the marine environments. Past oil spills have

C

EGYPT'S Aswān High Dam

BENEFIT / DRAWBACK

NILE DELTA

Egypt's Aswān High Dam, located near the Egypt-Sudan border, brings both benefits and drawbacks for the human geography of the area.

POPULATION RELOCATION (drawback)
About 90,000 Egyptians and Sudanese had to be relocated because of the dam.

IRRIGATION FOR FARMING (benefit)
The dam helps provide irrigation to thousands of new acres of farmland.

FLOOD CONTROL AND SAFETY (benefit)
The Aswān High Dam controls flooding along the Nile River. Before construction of the dam, flooding could be unpredictable and dangerous. The dam makes it safer to live along the Nile.

FLOODING AND FARMS (drawback)
When the Nile River flooded, it deposited fertile silt on agricultural lands. The Aswān High Dam, by preventing flooding, has resulted in a decrease in agricultural productivity.

THREAT TO CULTURE (drawback)
The flooding caused by building the dam would have submerged the ancient temple of Abu Simbel. The temple was dismantled by hand and moved to higher ground.

POWERING COMMUNITIES (benefit)
The dam provides hydroelectric power to Egypt, about 10 billion kilowatt-hours. This is enough to power nearly 870,000 average U.S. homes.

ASWĀN HIGH DAM

LAKE NASSER

The Aswān High Dam and other modern dams constructed farther up the Nile control the river's flow, resulting in both positive and negative effects for the people of the subregion.

▲ **CRITICAL THINKING**

1. ***Assessing*** How does the Aswān High Dam benefit the people of North Africa?
2. ***Posing Questions*** What questions would you ask the government agency in charge of the dam about its effects on the environment of North Africa?

networks Online Teaching Options

VIDEO

Libyan Oil Profits

Considering Advantages and Disadvantages As students watch the video, ask them to note the various environmental scenes. Explain that Libya's oil industry has had both economic and environmental impacts on the region. After the video, ask small groups of students to discuss the environmental impacts they noticed. Have each group list the advantages and disadvantages that oil production brings to the economy and environment of a country. Then have groups write either a positive or negative summarizing statement about the human impact of oil extraction. Encourage groups to share their lists and statements with the class. BL **Logical/Mathematical, Verbal/Linguistic**

exposed the lack of safety precautions related to oil extraction and the necessity of establishing a faster response to oil spills. The need for greater cooperation between countries to prevent future spills is crucial to limit the disastrous effects of oil spills.

The combination of oil by-products, sewage, and industrial waste threatens the North African coast. Marine biodiversity is threatened by the pollutants. In Libya and Algeria, waste from petroleum refineries and raw sewage seeps into the rivers and coastal waters, damaging ecosystems. R

The European Union's 2010 bilateral trade agreement with Morocco allows for greater freedom in trade with Europe. The drawback of increased trade is that fish populations and other marine life may be endangered. Many fish populations have been in rapid decline in the Mediterranean during the past decade. For example, bluefin tuna have been overfished for decades and are at serious risk of extinction if overfishing and unsustainable fishing practices in the region are not stopped. Marine turtles have also been negatively affected by the destruction and disturbance of nesting sites.

The Great Man-Made River project uses pipelines to pump water from large aquifers beneath the Sahara to farms along Libya's coastal region.

▲ **CRITICAL THINKING**

1. ***Assessing*** How was the Great Man-Made project funded?
2. ***Evaluating*** What is the risk caused by pumping water from the underground aquifers?

In 1970 Egypt completed the Aswān High Dam, located about 600 miles (966 km) south of Cairo, Egypt. The dam controls the Nile's floods. It also created Lake Nasser and provides irrigation for about 3 million acres (1.2 million ha) of land while also increasing the Egyptian fishing industry. Electricity for Egypt is generated by the dam. The completion of the dam marked the first time in history that the Nile's annual flood could be controlled by humans.

Despite the economic boosts of the Aswān High Dam and Lake Nasser, these construction projects have had negative consequences. These negative impacts affect the health and livelihood of Egypt's people and their livestock. For instance, when the dam was built, it changed the ecosystem. Some plants and animals could adapt, but others could not. Ultimately, the new ecosystem provided the perfect environment for an increase in waterborne diseases such as malaria and dysentery. In addition, fertile silt has accumulated behind the dam, soil that formerly went downstream and revitalized farmland. C

There are three basic concerns in much of North Africa that relate to human impact on the environment: population growth, agricultural performance, and environmental degradation. Population growth—coupled with longer life spans and the ability to feed the population—is increasingly a challenge to the subregion. Making the matter worse is the low agricultural productivity faced by many farmers in North Africa.

Land degradation from desertification is an environmental issue in all of the North African countries and is human induced. Soil erosion as a result of farming, overgrazing, and destruction of vegetation contributes to desertification. Increasingly, evidence shows that land degradation is a driver of climate change. The other causes of land degradation include drought, population pressure, and local agricultural and land use policies. V

☑ **READING PROGRESS CHECK**

Identifying Cause and Effect How has tourism in North Africa negatively affected the environment?

ZUMA Press/Alamy

People and Their Environment: North Africa

R Reading Skills

Predicting Discuss the threats posed to the environment and ecosystems of the North African coast. Guide students to understand the potential impacts to different countries in North Africa. Then have students write a short paragraph predicting how pollutants could adversely impact ecosystems in different regions of North Africa. **AL** **Verbal/Linguistic**

C Critical Thinking Skills

Considering Advantages and Disadvantages Discuss the advantages and disadvantages of Egypt's Aswān High Dam. **Ask:** **How did the dam's construction impact the ecosystem?** *(The ecosystem was changed, and some plants and animals could not adapt to the changes.)* **What happened as a result?** *(A new ecosystem was created.)* **How did this have an impact on human systems?** *(The new ecosystem provided an ideal environment for an increase in waterborne diseases such as malaria and dysentery.)* **Logical/Mathematical**

V Visual Skills

Creating Diagrams Have students organize the information in the text by creating a web diagram that shows the three main concerns about the human impact on North Africa's environment. Ask volunteers to share their diagrams with the class, leading into a discussion about the impact of population growth and environmental degradation. **ELL** **Visual/Spatial**

INTERACTIVE WHITEBOARD ACTIVITY

The Impact of the Aswān High Dam

Assessing This interactive whiteboard activity can be used to discuss the environmental impact of the Aswān High Dam with students. Students will be asked to assess statements pertaining to the building of the dam and decide if these impact statements reflect positive or negative effects. Then guide a class discussion on how human modifications of the physical environment can have significant local and global impacts. **BL** **Logical/Mathematical, Verbal/Linguistic**

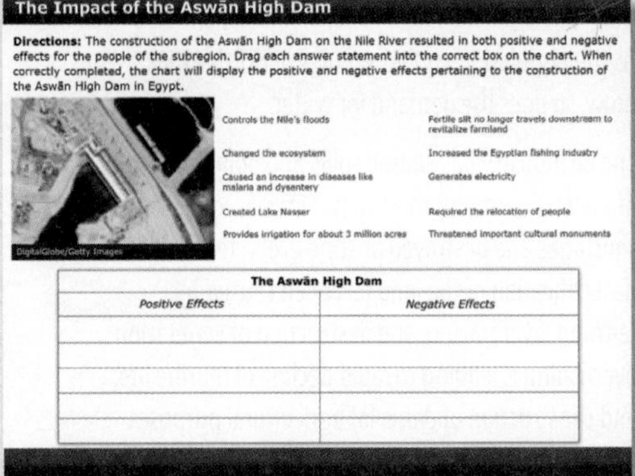

ANSWERS, p. 383

☑ **READING PROGRESS CHECK** Tourism is a main cause of ecological damage and loss. Some coastal areas are damaged beyond repair. The increasing use of water by hotels and golf courses to support tourism is contributing to water shortages.

CRITICAL THINKING

1. It was funded with profits from Libya's nationalized oil industries.
2. Water from underground aquifers is being pumped out at rates faster than it can be replaced, leaving future water supplies in serious danger. Pumping near the Mediterranean could bring in salt water, contaminating the water supply.

People and Their Environment: North Africa

C Critical Thinking Skills

Understanding Relationships Among Events Have students read the *Geopolitics* feature. Discuss how political unrest and foreign relations can play a part in the development and distribution of natural resources. **Ask: How did regional cooperation and international aid play a role in water scarcities during the Libyan conflict of 2011?** *(United Nations agencies and other international groups and countries such as Greece and Malta delivered millions of liters of water to Tripoli.)* **Logical/Mathematical**

W Writing Skills

Informative/Explanatory Organize students into groups, assigning each group a country in North Africa. Have them research the various efforts made by the World Bank in their assigned country as it relates to irrigation, water supplies, and agriculture. Groups will write an informative essay based on their findings and present it to the class. **BL Verbal/Linguistic**

CLOSE & REFLECT

Summarizing Assign each student a section of the lesson to write a one- or two-sentence summary. Then call on students in order of each section to read their summary to the class.

ANSWERS, p. 384

READING PROGRESS CHECK Student answers may vary but could include oil, fishing, and agriculture.

Connecting Geography When fuel and energy supplies are disrupted due to conflict and political unrest, countries are unable to supply power to pump underground water or operate desalination plants, leaving water supplies short or non-existent.

Connecting Geography to GOVERNMENT

Geopolitics

C Regional cooperation and international aid is important during times of regional unrest and government changes. Fuel scarcities due to the Libyan conflict in 2011 affected the amount of energy supplied to the Great Man-Made River and desalination plants. During the conflict, water shortages in Tripoli resulted from power outages, attacks on the staff managing the water network, and a reservoir held hostage by pro-al-Qaddafi fighters. United Nations agencies, the International Committee of the Red Cross, and neighboring countries such as Greece and Malta delivered millions of liters of water to Tripoli. Government resistance to change and the dependence of large populations on projects such as the Great Man-Made River exemplify how vulnerable Libya and other North African countries are to political and environmental crises.

EXPLAINING How can water supplies be vulnerable during times of political unrest and conflict?

Addressing the Issues

GUIDING QUESTION *How are environmental issues in North Africa being addressed?*

In North Africa, the environmental impacts of economic activities and growing populations is of increasing concern. Natural resources are important to economic activity, but resource extraction and harvesting are also major contributors to pollution and degradation in the region. The Middle East and North African countries (MENA) hold approximately 61 percent of the world's oil reserves. About 45 percent of the world's natural gas reserves are also located in these countries. Because the world relies on access to oil, global markets are affected by changes in the government policies of these countries. Therefore, cooperation among MENA countries can settle issues of fluctuating oil supplies to better meet the demand. Cooperation among countries can also help establish preventative measures related to oil spills and cleanup. The Partnership for African Fisheries (PAF) is working to strengthen the fishing industry. One goal of the partnership is to enforce stricter regulations to prevent overharvesting of certain species.

Determining water rights between countries is also a concern in North Africa. For example, Libya's Great Man-Made River receives water supplies from the Nubian Sandstone Aquifer System and other aquifers in the region. The aquifers are located beneath multiple political borders in the region. As a result, a joint authority for the management of the aquifer system was established in 1992. The joint authority encourages cooperation between Egypt and Libya in managing the Nubian Sandstone Aquifer System.

W At the international level, the World Bank is developing plans with several countries to invest in modern irrigation practices to address the needs of agriculture. The plans call for increasing water supply sources in North Africa. The World Bank is also working to develop water policies and institutions that will improve water quality in the region. Groundwater management and wastewater collection and treatment are central to these plans. Projects in Egypt and Morocco hope to increase irrigation efficiency and implement the reuse of treated wastewater. Improving the way farmers' associations are managed is another goal of projects in North Africa. In Algeria, the World Bank is promoting the creation of independent public companies that offer water supply delivery service to small cities and towns. The World Bank also supports organizations such as the Arab Water Council as a means to gather and share information related to water supply issues.

READING PROGRESS CHECK

Classifying Name two industries in North Africa that have required stricter regulation and enforcement to preserve natural resources.

LESSON 3 REVIEW 

Reviewing Vocabulary (Tier Three Words)

1. ***Defining*** What is an aquifer, and why is it important to the region? RH.9–10.4

Using Your Notes

2. ***Summarizing*** Use your graphic organizer to describe two human-made structures built to manage North Africa's resources.

Answering the Guiding Questions

3. ***Evaluating*** Why are water resources in such demand in North Africa?
4. ***Identifying Cause and Effect*** How have modern economic activities impacted North Africa's environment?
5. ***Synthesizing*** How are environmental issues in North Africa being addressed?

Writing Activity

6. ***Argument*** Using examples of economic activities or human-made projects, identify three ways in which natural resources in North Africa have been managed to profit and sustain the subregion's economies. WHST.9–10.1

LESSON 3 REVIEW ANSWERS

Reviewing Vocabulary

1. An aquifer is an underground layer of rock, sand, or gravel that holds water. Aquifers supply vital water to the region.

Using Your Notes

2. Student answers will vary, but could include desalination plants—removes salt from sea water; Libya's Great Man-Made River—series of pumps and pipelines that remove water from aquifers; Aswān High Dam and the creation of Lake Nasser—control flooding of the Nile.

Answering the Guiding Questions

3. As the population and economies of North Africa grow, so does the demand for water.
4. The oil industry has caused spills and pollution of the environment; tourism has increased water shortages and destroyed pristine ecosystems; desertification of the land has been caused by farming, overgrazing, and destruction of vegetation; overfishing is leading to rapid decline of marine life; and construction of dams for agricultural purposes has destroyed ecosystems.
5. Environmental issues are being addressed by a number of groups including: the Partnership for African Fisheries (PAF) is working on sustainable fishing practices; the World Bank is developing programs to improve and manage water resources; the Middle East and North African countries (MENA) is working to establish preventative measures to reduce oil spills.

Writing Activity

6. Student answers will vary but should be supported with information from the lesson. Possible examples include oil industry—developing economies; Aswān High Dam—increased fishing industry/agriculture; and the Great Man-Made River project—increased agriculture.

CHAPTER 15 Assessment 

Directions: On a separate sheet of paper, answer the questions below. Make sure that you read carefully and answer all parts of the questions.

Lesson Review

Lesson 1

1. ***Identifying Cause and Effect*** Briefly explain how tectonic activity has shaped the North African landscape. Provide an example of a land formation that illustrates its effects.
2. ***Explaining*** Why does such a great percentage of Egypt's population make a home on such a small percentage of the country's land? In your response, identify the area where this large population concentration lives.
3. ***Analyzing*** Explain whether this statement is accurate: "Sand covers most of the Sahara, and the Sahara and other deserts in North Africa are unable to support any substantial vegetation."

Lesson 2

4. ***Exploring Issues*** Provide a summary of why it has been difficult to maintain peace in North Africa.
5. ***Making Connections*** Discuss influences that have led to a change in lifestyle for nomadic peoples in North Africa.
6. ***Identifying Cause and Effect*** Identify at least three types of crops grown in North Africa, and name the type of climate that provides desirable conditions for crop growth. Explain why harvests of major crops sometimes fail to meet people's needs.

Lesson 3

7. ***Explaining*** Discuss how the location of North Africa makes the countries vulnerable to oil spills and what steps can be taken to prepare for such events.
8. ***Considering Advantages and Disadvantages*** Explain why petroleum refining and the Aswān High Dam can both be assessed as providing benefits and detriments.
9. ***Diagramming*** Create a graphic organizer to compare and contrast these organizations: Middle Eastern and North African countries (MENA) and Partnership for African Fisheries (PAF). Include the reasons for the formation of each organization as well as each organization's actions.

21st Century Skills

Use the graph to answer the questions that follow.

EGYPT: NATIONAL GAS PRODUCTION, CONSUMPTION AND EXPORTS FROM 2002–2010

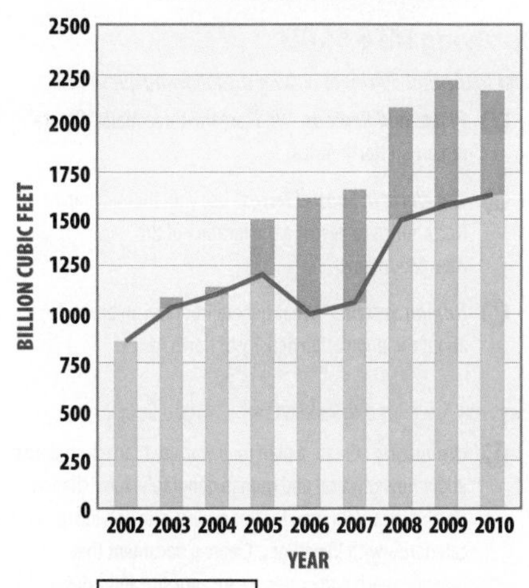

Source: US Energy Information Administration, *International Energy Statistics*

10. ***Creating and Using Graphs, Charts, Diagrams, and Tables*** Explain the relationship between Egypt's natural gas production and consumption during 2002.
11. ***Compare and Contrast*** Explain Egypt's natural gas consumption between 2002 and 2010.
12. ***Identifying and Explaining Continuity and Change*** Did Egypt's natural gas consumption rise, fall, or remain the same from 2009 to 2010? What impact, if any, did this have on exports of natural gas? What is a logical reason for this impact?

Need Extra Help?

If You've Missed Question	1	2	3	4	5	6	7	8	9	10	11	12
Go to page	368	369	370	372	374	377	382	382	384	385	385	385

CHAPTER 15 Assessment Answers

Lesson Review

Lesson 1

1. North Africa experiences tectonic activity such as earthquakes that build mountains and shift landmasses. This is due to the movements of the African, Anatolian, Arabian, and Eurasian plates. Possible examples of land formations include the Atlas Mountains, the Tibesti Mountains, and the Ahaggar.
2. The fertile land around the Nile River and the water it provides has attracted a large percentage of the population to the area.
3. The statement is not accurate. The desert does support some vegetation, including cacti and drought-resistant shrubs. Small-scale farming is possible around oases.

Lesson 2

4. Geometric boundaries were drawn by European colonial powers who failed to take into account the natural and cultural features of the subregion. As a result, conflicts between groups of people often arise.
5. The availability of water and grazing lands as well as the opportunities in urban areas and other countries have led to changes in lifestyle for nomadic peoples.
6. Possible answers: Barley, wheat, grapes, citrus fruits, vegetables, figs, almonds, and dates are grown in the Mediterranean climate. When rainfall is below normal amounts, crops fail to meet the needs of the people.

Lesson 3

7. North Africa is vulnerable to oil spills because oil tankers must pass along the subregion's coasts. Greater cooperation between countries in establishing safety precautions is needed to prevent future spills.
8. Petroleum refining provides needed jobs and money to the economy. The Aswān High Dam provides hydroelectric power, controls flooding, provides irrigation for agriculture, and increased the fishing industry. Petroleum refining pollutes the environment and creates the possibility of oil spills that harm marine life and ecosystems. The Aswān High Dam eliminated some forms of plants and wildlife, increased waterborne diseases, and prevents fertile deposits from being added to land downstream.
9. Graphic organizers will vary but should contain this information: Middle Eastern and North African countries (MENA)—involves multiple countries, established to ensure cooperation between countries; settles issues of fluctuating oil prices, supply and demand; establishes preventative measures for oil spills; and regulates cleanups. Partnership for African Fisheries (PAF)—involves multiple countries; established to ensure cooperation between countries, enforces regulations to prevent overfishing of certain species

21st Century Skills

10. Roughly the same amount of natural gas was produced as was consumed in 2002.
11. Consumption of natural gas increased from 2002 to 2010 except for 2006 and 2007 when less was used.
12. Natural gas consumption increased from 2009 to 2010. This increase caused the amount exported in 2010 to decrease because Egypt retained more to meet the increased demand within its own country.

Assessment Answers

Critical Thinking

13 Not all the food needed is able to be grown due to the limited groundwater supply in many countries. These countries rely on trade to import food. This reliance on imported food leaves the population and economy vulnerable based on the variable price of importing food.

Applying Map Skills

14 Arid, semi-arid, and Mediterranean are the three major climate regions.

15 The Atlas Mountains run through the middle of Morocco and the northern part of Algeria.

16 Populations densities are the highest along coastal areas and by water sources such as the Nile. The population densities are very low in interior areas that are primarily desert.

Exploring the Essential Question

17 Plans may vary but should be supported with information from the chapter. Each page must contain three links and must include items from the each of the following: Landforms—Atlas Mountains, Ahaggar, Tibesti Mountains; Water systems—Nile River, Mediterranean Sea, Red Sea, Gulf of Aden; Climates/Biomes—Mediterranean climate, desert -arid/semi-arid, savanna; History and Government—Egyptians, Arab invasions, the Berbers, bedouins, colonization (France, United Kingdom, Italy), independence; Language and Religion—Islam and spread of Arabic, French spoken due to colonization; Economic Activities and Trade—oil and natural gas, tourism; Environmental Issues—water scarcity, desertification, oil spills/pollution, overfishing.

College and Career Readiness

18 Student answers will vary but should be strongly supported from the chapter. The report must include a company overview explaining desalination and why it is important and contain a pro/con chart. Possible answers include a description of removing salt from seawater and explains that the process provides water for consumption and irrigation but is very expensive. Based on the overview, student should complete an opinion paragraph on why it is/is not a good idea for Libya and Algeria.

DBQ Analyzing Primary Sources

19 Student answers may vary but should indicate this would have been an accurate statement in earlier periods of history as well. Possible explanations could be early Egyptian civilization, British control, and oil supplies and production.

20 The events surrounding the Arab Spring would have prompted attention from then Secretary of State Clinton.

Research and Presentation

21 Presentations will vary but must include: charts, maps, diagrams, and pictures, a description of how and why the Great Man-Made River began, the accomplishments of the first three phases, the accomplishments of phases completed or in progress after the first three phases, suggestions that could effectively be incorporated into a current or future phase, and an analysis of the effectiveness of the Great Man-Made River.

Writing About Geography

22 Paragraphs will vary but could include that the dependence of the Algerian economy upon exporting oil could be problematic if prices go down or supplies become limited.

CHAPTER 15 Assessment 

Directions: On a separate sheet of paper, answer the questions below. Make sure that you read carefully and answer all parts of the questions.

Critical Thinking

13 ***Interpreting Significance*** Discuss the impact of groundwater availability on exports and the economy in general in North Africa.

Applying Map Skills

Refer to the Unit 5 Atlas to answer the following questions.

14 ***Places and Regions*** What are the three major climate regions in North Africa?

15 ***The World in Spatial Terms*** Use your mental map of North Africa to describe the location of the Atlas Mountains.

16 ***Human Systems*** What generalizations can be made about the population density of North Africa?

Exploring the Essential Question

17 ***Organizing*** Create a plan for a website to teach students about how physical and human geography have shaped North Africa. Your goal for this project is to provide general categories with hyperlinks. Create a document that describes each page category for your site and a design for the home page. Include at least three links for each page of the website. Include the following aspects of North Africa: landforms, water systems, climates, biomes, history and government, language and religion, economic activities and trade, and environmental issues.

College and Career Readiness

18 ***Reaching Conclusions*** Imagine you are an intern working for a company that is developing a report to analyze the pros and cons of desalination in Algeria and Libya. Write an overview for the company, briefly explaining the process of desalination and why it is important in Algeria and Libya. Your overview should include a chart listing the pros and cons of the process for these countries. Based on the overview, write a paragraph explaining whether you think desalination should be pursued in Algeria and Libya.

DBQ Analyzing Primary Sources

Use the quote to answer the following questions.

PRIMARY SOURCE

"Egypt is a large, complex, very important country . . . "

—Hillary Rodham Clinton, U.S. Secretary of State, CNN News interview, January 30, 2011

19 ***Evaluating*** Secretary of State Hillary Rodham Clinton made this statement in 2011. Explain whether this statement would have been equally accurate during earlier periods of history. RH.9–10.1

20 ***Identifying Central Issues*** What events in Egypt in 2011 would have given rise to the focus of Secretary of State Clinton and the world? RH.9–10.1

Research and Presentation

21 ***Problem Solving*** Utilize Internet and library sources to research information regarding the Great Man-Made River and create a multimedia presentation. Your presentation should explain the following: how and why the Great Man-Made River began, the accomplishments of the first three phases, the accomplishments of phases completed or in progress after the first three phases, and suggestions that could effectively be incorporated into a current or future phase. Within your presentation, provide an analysis as to whether the Great Man-Made River has provided effective solutions for the people of Libya. Include maps and images of places, as well as charts, diagrams, or graphs in your presentation. WHST.9–10.6; WHST.9–10.7

Writing About Geography

22 ***Argument*** Use standard grammar, spelling, sentence structure, and punctuation to write a paragraph explaining why Algeria should diversify its sources of revenue. WHST.9–10.1

Need Extra Help?

If You've Missed Question	13	14	15	16	17	18	19	20	21	22
Go to page	380	362	360	364	365	380	372	374	381	371

CHAPTER 16

The Eastern Mediterranean Planner

UNDERSTANDING BY DESIGN®

Enduring Understandings

- *The characteristics and distribution of cultures influence human systems.*

Essential Question

- *How do physical systems and human systems shape a place?*

Predictable Misunderstandings

Students may think:

- *The countries in the Eastern Mediterranean are very old. Explain that many of the cultural and historical landmarks in the Eastern Mediterranean have existed for hundreds and hundreds of years, but the modern countries of the region are relatively young, only having formed in the last century.*
- *The Eastern Mediterranean has experienced conflict in the past but is in a state of peace currently. Explain that the relationship between Palestine and Israel has always been and continues to be tense. Although many world leaders have attempted to work out peace agreements, none have been truly successful and the region is still prone to conflict.*

Assessment Evidence

Performance Tasks:

- *Hands-On Chapter Project*

Other Evidence:

- *Guided Reading Activities*
- *Vocabulary Activities*
- *Lesson Quizzes*
- *Chapter Tests, Forms A and B*

SUGGESTED PACING GUIDE

Introducing the Chapter	½ Day
Lesson 1	1 Day
Lesson 2	1 Day
Lesson 3	1 Day
Chapter Wrap-Up and Assessment	½ Day
TOTAL TIME	**4 Days**

Key for Using the Teacher Edition

SKILL-BASED ACTIVITIES

Types of skill activities found in the Teacher Edition.

* **V Visual Skills** require students to analyze maps, graphs, charts, and photos.

R Reading Skills help students practice reading skills and master vocabulary.

C Critical Thinking Skills help students apply and extend what they have learned.

W Writing Skills provide writing opportunities to help students comprehend the text.

T Technology Skills require students to use digital tools effectively.

*Letters are followed by a number when there is more than one of the same type of skill on the page.

DIFFERENTIATED INSTRUCTION

All activities are written for the on-level student unless otherwise marked with the leveled labels below.

BL Beyond Level

AL Approaching Level

ELL English Language Learners

All students benefit from activities that utilize different learning styles. Many activities are marked as below when a particular learning style is highlighted.

Intrapersonal	**Naturalist**
Logical/Mathematical	**Kinesthetic**
Visual/Spatial	**Auditory/Musical**
Verbal/Linguistic	**Interpersonal**

National Geography Standards covered in "The Eastern Mediterranean"

The student knows and understands:

(3) How to analyze the spatial organizations of people, places, and environments on Earth's surface

3.1 The meaning and use of complex spatial concepts, such as connectivity, networks, hierarchies, to analyze and explain the spatial organizations of human and physical phenomena

(4) The physical and human characteristics of places

(8) The characteristics and spatial distribution of ecosystems and biomes on Earth's surface

8.1 Ecosystems are dynamic and respond to changes in environmental conditions

(9) The characteristics, distribution, and migration of human populations on Earth's surface

(10) The characteristics, distribution, and complexity of Earth's cultural mosaics

10.3 Cultures changes through convergence and/or divergence

(11) The patterns and networks of economic interdependence on Earth's surface

11.3 Economic systems are dynamic organizations of interdependent economic activities for production, exchange, distribution, and consumption of goods and services

(14) How human actions modify the physical environment

14.1 Human modifications of the physical environment can have significant global impacts

(15) How physical systems affect human systems

15.1 Depending on the choice of human activities, the characteristics of the physical environment can be viewed as both opportunities and constraints

(16) The changes that occur in the meaning, use, distribution, and importance of resources

16.3 Policies and programs that promote the sustainable use and management of resources impact people and the environment

(17) How to apply geography to interpret the past

17.1 Geographic contexts (the human and physical characteristics of places and environments) can explain the connections between sequences of historical events

(18) How to apply geography to interpret the present and plan for the future

18.1 Geographic contexts (the human and physical characteristics of places and environments) provide the bases for analyzing current events and making predictions about future issues

CHAPTER OPENER PLANNER

Students will know:

- *the ways in which physical geography has affected human settlement and economic activities in the Eastern Mediterranean.*
- *the general characteristics of the climates and biomes.*
- *the role of religion in the history, politics, and culture.*
- *the causes and effects of the uneven development of economies.*
- *the factors threatening resources in the Eastern Mediterranean today.*
- *the ways in which people and governments are addressing environmental issues in the Eastern Mediterranean.*

Students will be able to:

- ***analyze** the effects of mountains and water systems on human and economic activities.*
- ***describe** the climates and biomes of the Eastern Mediterranean.*
- ***analyze** the influence of religion in the Eastern Mediterranean.*
- ***analyze** causes and effects of uneven development of economies in the region.*
- ***identify** how resources in the Eastern Mediterranean are threatened.*
- ***describe** how environmental issues in the region are being addressed.*

UNDERSTANDING BY DESIGN®

☑ Print Teaching Options

V Visual Skills

☐ **p. 388** Students write captions for photographs and discuss what they know about conflict.

R Reading Skills

☐ **p. 388** Students identify and sequence events in the conflict that has erupted in the Eastern Mediterranean.

C Critical Thinking Skills

☐ **p. 387** Students list factors that influence where people settle. **AL** **Logical/Mathematical**

W Writing Skills

☐ **p. 389** Students write an argument that the Oslo Agreement was either a poor or good solution to the Israeli-Palestinian conflict and hold a debate.

T Technology Skills

☐ **p. 389** Students research current events in the Gaza Strip and prepare a brief report from the perspective of a field reporter. **BL** **Verbal/Linguistic, Auditory/Musical**

☑ Online Teaching Options

C Critical Thinking Skills

☐ **INTERACTIVE IMAGE** **Rabin, Arafat, and Clinton**—Students research and discuss the Oslo Accord and other attempts at peace between Israel and Palestine. **BL** **Visual/Spatial, Logical/Mathematical**

☐ **MAP** **Interactive Regional Atlas**—Students use the interactive regional atlas to understand the physical and human geography of the Eastern Mediterranean.

☑ Printable Digital Worksheets

☐ **WORKSHEET** **Assessing Background Knowledge**—Determine the level of prior knowledge students have about the Eastern Mediterranean.

☐ **WORKSHEET** **Chapter Summaries**—Students review the main idea of each lesson of the chapter content.

☐ **WORKSHEET** **Vocabulary Activity**—Students apply their knowledge of content and academic vocabulary words.

Project-Based Learning

Hands-On

Time Line of the Eastern Mediterranean

Assign groups of students one of the Eastern Mediterranean countries to research. Groups will identify entries for a time line they will create. The time lines will include 20 events, which will each have a brief written summary and a visual. The visual can be a photo, diagram, portrait, graph, or drawing. Groups will give short oral presentations about their time lines.

Digital Hands-On

Create Online Projects

Find an additional activity online that incorporates technology for this project. Visit the EdTech Teacher Web sites for more links, tutorials, and other resources.

edtechteacher 21st Century Learning

Print Resources

ANCILLARY RESOURCES

This ancillary is available for every chapter and lesson.

- **Chapter Tests and Lesson Quizzes**

PRINTABLE DIGITAL WORKSHEETS

These printable digital worksheets are available for every chapter and lesson.

- **Assessing Background Knowledge**
- **Chapter Summaries**
- **Guided Reading Activities**
- **Hands-On Chapter Projects**
- **Quizzes and Tests**
- **Reading Essentials and Study Guide** **AL**
- **Reteaching Activities**
- **Video Activities**
- **Vocabulary**

More Media Resources

SUGGESTED VIDEOS MOVIES

- **Middle East: Trauma and Hopes of the Young** (65 min.)
- **Frontline: Syria Behind the Lines** (60 min.)
- **Jordan** (30 min.)

SUGGESTED READING

- ***Hidden Histories: Palestine And The Eastern Mediterranean,*** by Basem L. Ra'ad
- ***A New Euro-Mediterranean Energy Roadmap: Towards a sustainable energy transition in the Southern and Eastern Mediterranean region,*** by Manfred Hafner, Simone Tagliapietra, and El Habib El Andaloussi
- ***Israel,*** by Justin Dodge

LESSON 1 PLANNER

PHYSICAL GEOGRAPHY OF THE EASTERN MEDITERRANEAN

Students will know:

- *the ways in which mountains and water systems have affected human settlement and economic activities in the Eastern Mediterranean.*
- *the general characteristics of the climates and biomes of the Eastern Mediterranean.*

Students will be able to:

- ***analyze** the effects of mountains on human and economic activities.*
- ***identify** the influences of water systems on human settlement and economic activities.*
- ***describe** the climates and biomes of the Eastern Mediterranean.*

UNDERSTANDING BY DESIGN®

☑ Print Teaching Options

V Visual Skills

- ☐ **p. 391** Students research five major cities in an assigned country and organize statistics about the cities into a chart or table. AL Visual/Spatial
- ☐ **p. 392** Students discuss whether they believe the use of rivers has changed or remained the same over time. AL Visual/Spatial, Logical/Mathematical

R Reading Skills

- ☐ **p. 390** Students explain different meanings of the prefix *anti-*. ELL Verbal/Linguistic
- ☐ **p. 391** Students discuss the meaning of the term *rift valley*. ELL Verbal/Linguistic
- ☐ **p. 393** Students identify context clues to understand the meaning of *transform*. ELL Verbal/Linguistic

C Critical Thinking Skills

- ☐ **p. 390** Students discuss factors that pose challenges to the Eastern Mediterranean.
- ☐ **p. 392** Students work in groups to study an assigned body of water and give a short oral presentation about it. ELL Verbal/Linguistic
- ☐ **p. 393** Students categorize facts and details about climates, biomes, and natural resources by creating a table. AL Visual/Spatial, Naturalist
- ☐ **p. 393** Students write three questions about how rainfall affects agriculture based on a precipitation map. BL Visual/Spatial, Logical/Mathematical

W Writing Skills

- ☐ **p. 390** Students research and write an article about how skiing has impacted the tourism industry in Israel. Verbal/Linguistic
- ☐ **p. 394** Students choose a position about the development of oil and gas in the region and write an argumentative essay supporting their position. Naturalist, Intrapersonal

T Technology Skills

- ☐ **p. 394** Students research the significance of the cedar tree in the region and prepare a slide show to share their findings. BL Verbal/Linguistic, Naturalist

☑ Online Teaching Options

V Visual Skills

- ☐ VIDEO **Dead Sea Disappearing**—Students watch a video about the Dead Sea and learn about water systems and the physical geography of the region, then discuss ways that changes to water systems are influencing the economies of nearby countries. BL Logical/Mathematical, Verbal/Linguistic

C Critical Thinking Skills

- ☐ INTERACTIVE BELLRINGER **Eastern Mediterranean Precipitation**—Students discuss and answer questions about climate and biomes of this subregion. Visual/Spatial
- ☐ INTERACTIVE IMAGE **Tel Aviv Beach**—Students react to the image and discuss the availability of water in this subregion. AL Verbal/Linguistic, Visual/Spatial

W Writing Skills

- ☐ INTERACTIVE IMAGE **The Dying Dead Sea**—Students discuss the changes in the Dead Sea and then write predictions for the future. Visual/Spatial, Logical/Mathematical
- ☐ INTERACTIVE WHITEBOARD ACTIVITY **Waterways of the Eastern Mediterranean**—Students match the name of a major waterway in the Eastern Mediterranean to its description.

☑ Printable Digital Worksheets

R Reading Skills

- ☐ WORKSHEET **Guided Reading Activity**—Students use the Guided Reading Activity worksheets to review their comprehension of the content.

C Critical Thinking Skills

- ☐ WORKSHEET **Video Activity**—Students answer questions related to a topic in the chapter content after they have viewed a lesson video.

HUMAN GEOGRAPHY OF THE EASTERN MEDITERRANEAN

Students will know:

- *the role of religion in the history, politics, and culture of the Eastern Mediterranean.*
- *the factors affecting the population patterns.*
- *the causes and effects of the uneven development of economies.*

Students will be able to:

- ***analyze** the influence of religion in the Eastern Mediterranean.*
- ***identify** factors that affect the population of the region.*
- ***analyze** causes and effects of uneven development of economies in the region.*

UNDERSTANDING BY DESIGN®

☑ Print Teaching Options

V Visual Skills

- ☐ **p. 395** Students discuss how the subregion is a bridge between continents and why three major religions were founded in the subregion. AL Logical/Mathematical
- ☐ **p. 397** Students research and present a visual with information about Syria, Jordan, Lebanon, or Gaza Strip/West Bank/Golan Heights. ELL Visual/Spatial, Interpersonal
- ☐ **p. 398** Students discuss how climate and physical geography influence settlement patterns and then create a population density chart for a country. Visual/Spatial

R Reading Skills

- ☐ **p. 395** Students write three sentences to predict what they will learn in the lesson.
- ☐ **p. 396** Students discuss the changes in political borders and control after World War II. Verbal/Linguistic, Interpersonal
- ☐ **p. 400** Students create a three-column chart to list rights and regulations that women in the region have faced. ELL Visual/Spatial
- ☐ **p. 401** Students discuss the GDPs of countries in the region using a bar graph. AL Logical/Mathematical

C Critical Thinking Skills

- ☐ **p. 395** Students discuss the rise of Christianity.
- ☐ **p. 396** Students discuss how Islam was founded and its main beliefs and characteristics. AL Logical/Mathematical
- ☐ **p. 399** Students compare and contrast samples of Hebrew and Arabic with English. Auditory/Musical

W Writing Skills

- ☐ **p. 396** Students write a journal entry from the perspective of a young Palestinian or Jew living in Israel after World War II. Verbal/Linguistic, Intrapersonal
- ☐ **p. 400** Students write an article on common themes in the arts of the Eastern Mediterranean.

T Technology Skills

- ☐ **p. 397** Students research one of the military conflicts Israel was involved in and identify central issues of the conflict.
- ☐ **p. 398** Students discuss the Arab Spring and locate primary and secondary sources about it. Verbal/Linguistic
- ☐ **p. 401** Students research a tourist attraction in the region and create a tourism infomercial. Visual/Spatial

☑ Online Teaching Options

V Visual Skills

- VIDEO **Beginning of Islam**—Students watch the video and evaluate the different perspectives on the deep religious beliefs and ethnic attachments centered in the city of Jerusalem. ELL Visual/Spatial
- INTERACTIVE WHITEBOARD ACTIVITY **Ethnic Groups in Eastern Mediterranean**—Students analyze charts and answer questions about ethnicity. ELL Visual/Spatial
- GRAPHIC ORGANIZER **Human Geography of Eastern Mediterranean**—Students discuss the various reasons countries have struggled since gaining their independence as they complete the organizer. ELL Verbal/Linguistic, Visual/Spatial

R Reading Skills

- GAME **Human Geography of Eastern Mediterranean**—Students discuss the importance of family life in this subregion. Visual/Spatial, Verbal/Linguistic

C Critical Thinking Skills

- INTERACTIVE BELLRINGER **Israeli-Palestinian Conflict**—Students analyze a time line to answer questions about the conflict. ELL Visual/Spatial
- INTERACTIVE TIME LINE **Arab-Israeli Relations, 1948–1994**—Students learn about events on the time line and then choose one to research further and create a more detailed time line around the same time as the event. AL Visual/Spatial, Verbal/Linguistic

☑ Printable Digital Worksheets

R Reading Skills

- WORKSHEET **Guided Reading Activity**—Students use Guided Reading Activity worksheets to review their comprehension of the content.
- WORKSHEET **Reading Essentials and Study Guide**—Students complete the study guide and answer Reading Progress Check and vocabulary questions. AL

C Critical Thinking Skills

- WORKSHEET **Video Activity**—Students answer questions related to a topic in the chapter content after they have viewed a lesson video.

PEOPLE AND THEIR ENVIRONMENT: THE EASTERN MEDITERRANEAN

Students will know:

- *the factors threatening resources in the Eastern Mediterranean today.*
- *the causes and effects of the human impact on the environment in the Eastern Mediterranean.*
- *the ways in which people and governments are addressing environmental issues in the Eastern Mediterranean.*

Students will be able to:

- ***identify** how resources in the Eastern Mediterranean are threatened.*
- ***analyze** human impact on the environment in the region.*
- ***describe** how environmental issues in the region are being addressed.*

UNDERSTANDING BY DESIGN®

☑ Print Teaching Options

V Visual Skills

- ☐ **p. 403** Students discuss the infographic about how Israel manages its water resources. **AL** **Visual/Spatial, Logical/Mathematical**
- ☐ **p. 405** Students discuss an image of a landfill, how they work, and why they are used. **ELL** **Visual/Spatial, Naturalist**

R Reading Skills

- ☐ **p. 402** Students speculate about possible environmental effects of human activities.
- ☐ **p. 404** Students define *deforestation, desertification,* and *overgrazing.* **AL** **Verbal/Linguistic**
- ☐ **p. 406** Students discuss the importance and the impact of collaborative efforts to address environmental issues in the region. **AL** **Logical/Mathematical**

C Critical Thinking Skills

- ☐ **p. 402** Students compile a list of questions that need to be asked in order to examine the issues of overfishing and water pollution in the Mediterranean Sea and identify possible solutions. **AL** **Visual/Spatial, Logical/Mathematical**
- ☐ **p. 403** Students discuss air pollution. **BL** **Logical/Mathematical**
- ☐ **p. 404** Students discuss how the geography of the Eastern Mediterranean lends itself to deforestation and overgrazing. **AL** **Naturalist, Interpersonal**
- ☐ **p. 405** Students discuss how countries are working or not working together to address environmental issues. **AL** **Verbal/Linguistic**

W Writing Skills

- ☐ **p. 403** Students research and write an editorial about the importance of desalinating water. **Verbal/Linguistic**
- ☐ **p. 406** Students write an essay on energy-efficient transportation systems, sustainable fishing methods, or controlling and restricting agricultural runoff. **BL** **Verbal/Linguistic, Visual/Spatial**

T Technology Skills

- ☐ **p. 402** Students research tectonic plates that meet in the region and create and annotate diagrams to show the movement and how it affects landforms. **BL** **Naturalist**

☑ Online Teaching Options

V Visual Skills

- **VIDEO** **Israel-Palestine Water**—Students watch a video about freshwater usage and control and discuss how water scarcity concerns could lead to conflict or help to restore peace. **Verbal/Linguistic**
- **SLIDE SHOW** **Oasis**—Students write paragraphs explaining how human activities have affected an oasis in this subregion. **AL** **Verbal/Linguistic**
- **INTERACTIVE WHITEBOARD ACTIVITY** **Managing Israel's Water Resources**—Students reference a graph to answer statements that pertain to Israel's water resources. **Verbal/Linguistic**

C Critical Thinking Skills

- **INTERACTIVE BELLRINGER** **Desertification in Syria**—Students use text to answer and understand the causes and effects of the human impact on the environment in the subregion of Syria in the Eastern Mediterranean. **Interpersonal, Verbal/Linguistic**

☑ Printable Digital Worksheets

R Reading Skills

- **WORKSHEET** **Guided Reading Activity**—Students use Guided Reading Activity worksheets to review their comprehension of the content.
- **WORKSHEET** **Reading Essentials and Study Guide**—Students complete the study guide and answer Reading Progress Check and vocabulary questions. **AL**
- **WORKSHEET** **Vocabulary Activity**—Students review the chapter content and academic vocabulary words.

C Critical Thinking Skills

- **WORKSHEET** **Video Activity**—Students answer questions based on a lesson video.
- **WORKSHEET** **Reteaching Activity**—Students use this activity worksheet to review and reteach chapter content and vocabulary. This worksheet can be used with struggling students who need additional help with difficult content concepts.

INTERVENTION AND REMEDIATION STRATEGIES

LESSON 1 Physical Geography of the Eastern Mediterranean

Reading and Comprehension

To ensure comprehension of the concepts in this lesson, have students act as "virtual tour guides" for a region discussed in this lesson. Tell students they will write a short script for a tour through that region, noting unique landforms, waterways, and biomes. Students may write about a specific landform or waterway in the Eastern Mediterranean region, or they may wish to write about the various physical features of a specific subregion or country in the Eastern Mediterranean region. Have students share their scripts, acting as if their classmates are on a tour of the region. Encourage students to use visuals to accompany their scripts.

Text Evidence

Have students work in four groups to research an aspect of the Eastern Mediterranean's physical geography as it relates to one of the following topics discussed in the lesson: landforms, water systems, climate regions and biomes, and natural resources. Tell students to present an analysis of their findings, comparing information in the text with information found in their research. For example, students might research the significance of the Jordan River as it relates to irrigation and agriculture. Tell students to write an objective summary of their findings.

LESSON 2 Human Geography of the Eastern Mediterranean

Reading and Comprehension

Organize students into six groups. Assign a different content vocabulary word and Academic Vocabulary term to each group. Have students in each group work together to write a paragraph about a concept in the lesson, using their assigned term. For example, students may use the term *monotheism* in a paragraph about religion in the region and the influences from various cultural groups throughout history. After students have completed their paragraphs, ask a volunteer from each group to read the paragraph.

Text Evidence

Have students review the time line in this lesson, "Israeli-Palestinian Conflict: An Elusive Peace Process." Organize students into five groups and assign each group one of the following time periods: 1980-1989, 1990–1999, 2000–2005, 2006–2008, and 2009–present. Have students in each group work together to create a time line depicting key events in their assigned time period related to the Israeli-Palestinian conflict. Then have students in each group collaborate to write a summary of events that occurred during their assigned time period. Tell students to use textual evidence and online research to support ideas presented in their summaries.

LESSON 3 People and Their Environment: the Eastern Mediterranean

Reading and Comprehension

Have students work in pairs to compare and contrast two of the lesson's content vocabulary terms. Have partners write a compare-contrast paragraph in which they use each term and explain how the terms are similar to or different from each other. For example, students might compare the terms *fertilizer* and *pesticide* and discuss how each is used for agriculture. Or they may compare *desertification* and *overgrazing* and conduct additional research to determine their impact on specific regions in the Eastern Mediterranean.

Text Evidence

Have students work in small groups to create a visual diagram about an environmental issue facing the Eastern Mediterranean. You may wish to assign students topics to avoid duplication, such as commercial deep-sea fishing, water or air pollution, threats to wetlands, and so on. Have students collaborate to use evidence from the text on which to base their visual diagrams and present them to the class. Tell students their diagrams should address the following Guiding Question: *What human activities have affected the physical environment of the Eastern Mediterranean?* After students have presented their visuals, guide a discussion about how environmental issues are being addressed in the Eastern Mediterranean.

Online Resources

Leveled Reader

Use this online approaching-level text that corresponds directly to the text in the Student Edition. It also includes additional reading and comprehension support for English Language Learners.

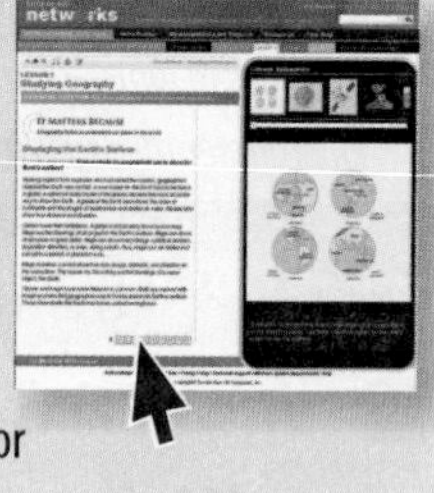

Guided Reading Activities

This resource uses guiding questions to help students with comprehension.

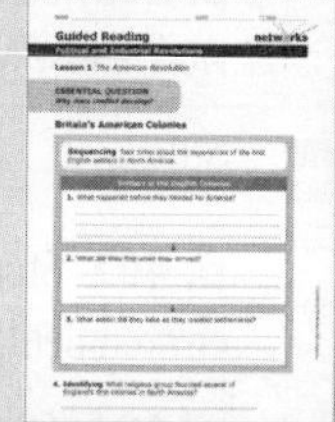

Reteaching Activities

These worksheets provide students with an opportunity for remedial practice and review of vital chapter content.

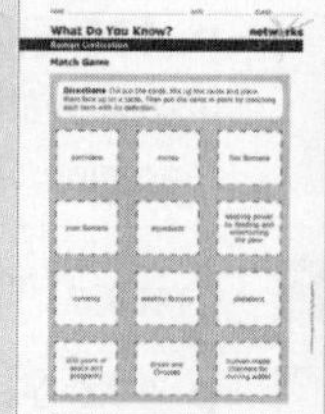

Reading Essentials and Study Guide

This resource offers writing and reading activities for the approaching-level student.

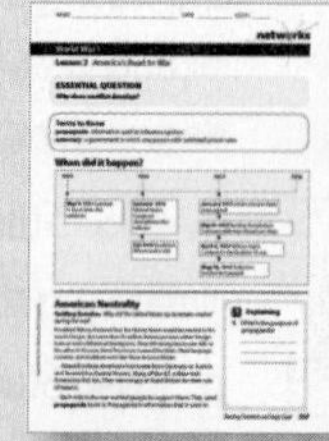

Self-Check Quizzes

This online assessment tool provides instant feedback for students to check their progress.

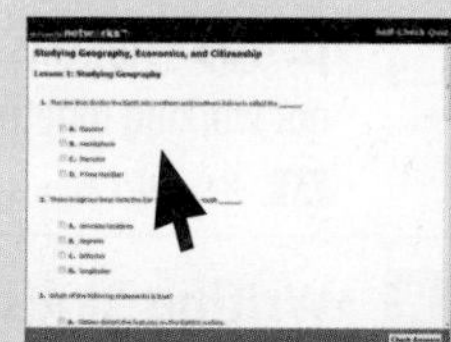

Chapter Summaries

Summaries are provided for each chapter that thoroughly condense core content into manageable chunks.

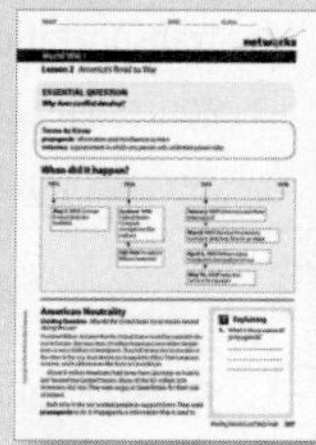

The Eastern Mediterranean

ESSENTIAL QUESTION • *How do physical systems and human systems shape a place?*

networks

There's More Online about the Eastern Mediterranean.

CHAPTER 16

Geography Matters...

Because its fertile land supported the development of agriculture, the Eastern Mediterranean became one of the birthplaces of civilization. Many of its cities have been continuously inhabited for thousands of years, and several of the world's most widespread religions have roots here. This subregion is marked by a deep, complex history of political and religious conflict. Modern tensions have developed many distinct ideologies that reside in close proximity.

◀ The Eastern Mediterranean is home to many ethnicities and religions.

387

Letter from the Author

Dear Geography Teacher,

Modern U.S. students take information technology (IT) for granted. They text, talk, tweet, and play music with their smartphones. They engage in social media and connect with the world daily. A recent researcher observed that teenagers often link themselves to places more remote than places that are closer to them, all because of the power of IT. If this is true, then is IT the secret to opening up dialogue in areas like the Eastern Mediterranean where religion, language, history, and culture seem to be loaded with social barriers that often lead to suspicion, misunderstanding, and sometimes war? Does IT offer the chance for sharing, understanding, and learning?

Richard G. Boehm

ENGAGE

Analyzing Visuals Have students closely examine the image of the woman. Guide a discussion about the human geography of the Eastern Mediterranean based on clues from the photograph. Ask students to explain what clues this photograph reveals about the culture and people of the Eastern Mediterranean. Discuss other ways that people might have adopted Western influences but still hold true to their traditions.

TEACH & ASSESS

Analyzing Cause and Effect Before beginning the chapter, have students list common factors that influence where people settle. *(Student answers may vary but might suggest that people tend to settle in areas that have a moderate climate, are near water, and have land for farming or development.)* **Ask:** **What reasons listed in the text may have contributed to the Eastern Mediterranean being an area of complexity and conflict?** *(Possible answers: variety of religious beliefs; political differences)* **AL** **Logical/Mathematical**

Content Background Knowledge

Jerusalem This ancient city in Israel is a sacred place to adherents of Judaism, Christianity, and Islam. For Jews, the city is considered holy because, among other reasons, King Solomon declared that Jerusalem should be the capital city of Judaism and he ordered the building of the first temple there in the tenth century B.C. For Christians, Jerusalem is considered holy because they believe it was where Jesus Christ preached and spoke to his followers, and where they believe he died and rose from the dead. Muslims believe the Dome of the Rock in Jerusalem is the first place where Muhammad ascended.

CLOSE & REFLECT

Problem Solving Tell students to review the reasons why the Eastern Mediterranean area is prone to religious and political conflict. Ask volunteers to suggest ways that countries in other regions can work with the people of the Eastern Mediterranean to help them resolve these conflicts.

Extend the project-based learning experience globally through our partnership with ePals. EPals allows you to connect with classrooms around the world in a safe online environment for real-life lessons and projects in virtual study groups.

ENGAGE

V Visual Skills

Analyzing Visuals Before they read the text, have students study the images and write a caption for each based on what they see. Ask students to share their captions. Then have them discuss what they know about conflict.

TEACH & ASSESS

R Reading Skills

Sequencing Information Have students explain the sequence of events leading to the conflicts in the Eastern Mediterranean. **Ask: What original group of people began immigrating back to Palestine?** *(European Jews)* **What event heightened conflict in the subregion?** *(the withdrawal of the British and the U.N-sponsored partitioning plan of Palestine, which led to the establishment of Israel)* **What occurred next?** *(Palestinians and nearby Arab states did not accept the plan; a series of wars occurred over Israel's right to exist and to ownership of areas such as the West Bank.)* **How has this long-term conflict affected relations among countries?** *(Relations have been tense between Arab states and Israel and between Israelis and Palestinians, resulting in continued political and military conflict.)* **ELL Verbal/Linguistic**

C Critical Thinking Skills

Identifying Perspectives Have students discuss the different perspectives of Israelis and Palestinians. **Ask: What point do both perspectives make that is a source of conflict?** *(Both Israelis and Palestinians want their own country for their people in the same location because they both claim that the area is holy to their religion and people.)* **Logical/Mathematical**

ANSWERS, p. 388

Why Geography Matters

1. The Zionist movement wanted to return Jews to their understood homeland in Palestine. Zionism increased Jewish immigration to Palestine and slowly introduced a large Jewish population to the region, leading to the Jewish state, Israel.
2. Israel, though not a state for thousands of years, has deep cultural ties to the region. Many Jews never left the region. Palestinians have also called the area home. Jerusalem as home to holy sites of both Judaism and Islam adds an additional layer of complexity.
3. Territory has changed hands between Israel and neighboring Arab states as a result of the wars they have fought. In addition, changes in land ownership associated with attempts to create a two-state solution have resulted in shifting areas of Palestinian and Israeli control and settlement.

Why Geography Matters: **The Eastern Mediterranean**

Israeli-Palestinian conflict

Conflict between Israelis and Palestinians has not evolved from one single factor such as a dispute over religion or land. Rather, the conflict has resulted from years of differences over cultural, religious, economic, and geographic issues. At the heart of the conflict lie the West Bank, the Gaza Strip, and East Jerusalem.

(l)Nir Kafri/AFP/Getty Images, (c)Uriel Sinai/Getty Images News/Getty Images, (r)Abbas Momani/AFP/Getty Images

What is the conflict?

In the 1880s and through the 1940s many European Jews immigrated to Palestine. This immigration took place in the context of the Zionist movement, which aimed to return Jews to what they saw as their homeland. Prior to World War I the Ottoman Empire controlled Palestine, and the British controlled it after. In 1948 the British withdrew and the State of Israel was established. Israel was then attacked by Arab states in the first of several wars. In 1967 Israel captured the West Bank, Gaza, and East Jerusalem, and these areas have become the focus of demands for the creation of a Palestinian state. Agreements like the Oslo Accords of the mid-1990s have attempted to resolve the conflict.

1. **Human Systems** How could the Zionist movement have led to the creation of the State of Israel?

What is the Israeli perspective?

Palestine, more properly "The Land of Israel," is the historic home of the Jewish people, from which they were expelled by force. Even after that expulsion, some Jews continued to live there, and the yearning for return was never abandoned. After centuries of persecution culminating in the Holocaust, this hope was finally realized. The Jews accepted a 1947 U.N.-sponsored plan to partition Palestine into two states; the Arabs did not accept this and instead attacked Israel. The conquests of 1967, which include East Jerusalem and other areas that are the heartland of historic Israel, resulted from an essentially defensive war. The fact that reasonable Israeli peace initiatives have been regularly rejected reinforces other evidence that many Palestinian leaders continue to strive not for peace but for the end of Israel as a Jewish state.

2. **Places and Regions** What issues make the conflict between the Israelis and the Palestinians so complex?

What is the Palestinian perspective?

Palestinian Arabs are the indigenous people of the area. Many were driven out during the war that followed the establishment of Israel, and those that remained are treated as second-class citizens and have been denied the right to self-determination. Israeli expansionism in the wake of the 1967 war has placed even larger sections of the Palestinian homeland under foreign rule. Settlement building in the occupied territories violates international law and makes it more and more difficult to bring about a two-state solution. This activity, along with Israel's insistence on retaining all of Jerusalem, demonstrates that Israel's assertions that it seeks peace and is willing to accept a Palestinian state are insincere.

3. **Human Systems** How has conflict resulted in changing borders and demographics?

388

Project-Based Learning

Hands-On

Create Time Line

Working in groups, students will compile a list of events and dates about their assigned country or territory in the Eastern Mediterranean. At least 20 major events, including visuals, should be gathered. Then have students work together within their groups to compile all of the events and visuals on a time line that they will present to the class.

Digital Hands-On

Create Online Projects

Find an additional activity online that incorporates technology for this project. Visit the EdTech Teacher Web sites for more links, tutorials, and other resources.

THERE'S MORE ONLINE

EXPLORE a map of Israel and the Palestinian territories • *VIEW* an image of the Oslo Accords

The Oslo Accords of 1993 and 1995 provided for different levels of authority in the Gaza Strip and the West Bank. Though the accords are still in effect they are unpopular with both the Palestinian and Israeli public.

W

GAZA STRIP

Double border fences and buffer zones

ISRAEL

T

WEST BANK

JERUSALEM

- Palestinian Civil and Security Control
- Palestinian Civil Control, Israeli Security Control
- Israeli Civil and Security Control
- Israeli Settlements
- Security Barrier
- Planned Security Barrier
- Border Crossing

JERUSALEM

WEST BANK

EAST JERUSALEM

WEST JERUSALEM

OLD CITY

ISRAEL

Why Geography Matters 389

W Writing Skills

Argument Organize students into two groups, assigning to each group one of the two perspectives—that the Oslo Agreement was either a poor or a good solution to the Israeli-Palestinian conflict. Have each group prepare an argument with supporting details that represents its assigned perspective. Before students begin writing, encourage them to discuss possible points to use in their argument, as well as counterclaims from the other perspective. After students write their argument, hold a debate in which the students use the details from their papers to support their perspective. **BL Verbal/Linguistic, Interpersonal**

T Technology Skills

Researching Have students conduct online research to identify current events in the Gaza Strip. Point out that the information they gather about an event should have occurred in the last ten years. Then ask students to prepare a brief report from the perspective of a field reporter. Provide an opportunity for them to present their reports to the class. Challenge students to use visual aids in their report. Then lead a class discussion in which students explain the event that has had the most impact on the Gaza Strip. **BL Verbal/Linguistic, Auditory/Musical**

CLOSE & REFLECT

Speculating Review with students the Israeli-Palestinian conflict in the West Bank and the Gaza Strip. Have students consider whether similar conflicts exist in other regions. Then discuss how the conflict in this area is unique and has a long history. Invite volunteers to suggest how decisions made in the past influenced conflict in the area and how different decisions could have alleviated conflict.

INTERACTIVE IMAGE

Rabin, Arafat, and Clinton

Researching Display the image of the three former leaders—Rabin, Arafat, and Clinton. Explain that in the mid-1990s, world leaders tried to bring about peace agreements between Israel and Palestine and that one such agreement was called the Oslo Accord. Have students work with a partner to research the Oslo Accord, as well as other attempts that have been made to resolve the conflict between these two countries. Ask each pair of students to summarize their findings in a class discussion. **BL Visual/Spatial, Logical/Mathematical**

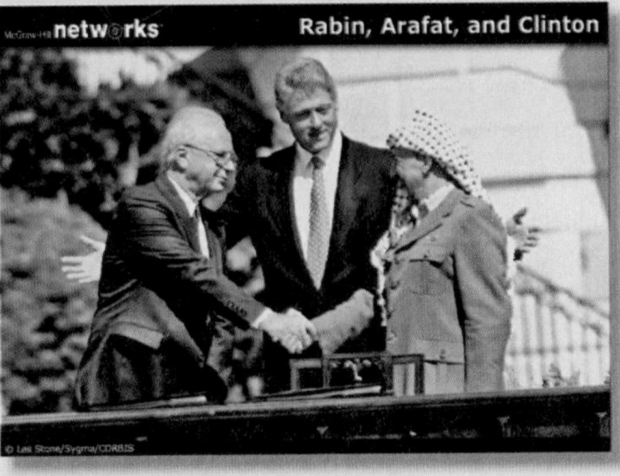

ENGAGE

C Critical Thinking Skills

Speculating Display the unit physical map of the Eastern Mediterranean and ask students to describe what they think the climate in this region is like, based on the landforms and its location. Discuss with students factors other than water shortages and increasing population that pose challenges to the subregion.

TEACH & ASSESS

R Reading Skills

Using Word Parts Ask students to explain different meanings of the prefix *anti-*. **Ask:** **Which meaning fits best with the term *Anti-Lebanon Mountains?* Explain.** *("opposite," because the Anti-Lebanon Mountains lie opposite of the Lebanon Mountains)* Have students write other words with the prefix *anti-* that could relate to the physical, human, and cultural geography of the Eastern Mediterranean. **ELL Verbal/Linguistic**

W Writing Skills

Informative/Explanatory Have students research the facts and details about Mount Hermon and how skiing has impacted the tourism industry in Israel. Then ask students to write an article to inform others about their findings. Consider having students create a website for the topic or post their articles on a class website. **Verbal/Linguistic**

ANSWERS, p. 390

TAKING NOTES: The Jordan River—flows through all of the countries in the Eastern Mediterranean and south into the Sea of Galilee; forms a border between the Israeli-occupied West Bank and Jordan before emptying into the Dead Sea; important for crop irrigation including bananas, beets, and other vegetables; **Sea of Galilee**—located in western Israel; relatively salty for freshwater; supported surrounding communities for centuries; **The Gulf of Aqaba**—located south of Israel and Jordan; connects Eastern Mediterranean countries with the Red Sea and the Indian Ocean

networks
There's More Online!
- **IMAGE** Fish Farm in Israel
- **IMAGE** Jordan River Valley
- **MAP** Eastern Mediterranean Precipitation
- **INTERACTIVE SELF-CHECK QUIZ**
- **VIDEO** Physical Geography of the Eastern Mediterranean

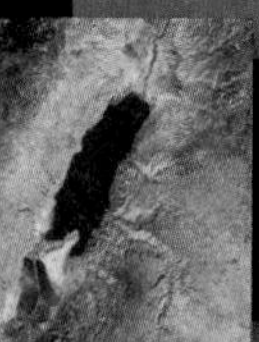

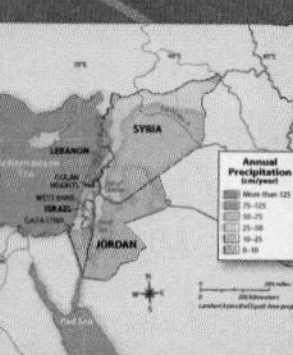

LESSON 1
Physical Geography of the Eastern Mediterranean

ESSENTIAL QUESTION • *How do physical systems and human systems shape a place?*

Reading HELPDESK (CCSS)

Academic Vocabulary (Tier Two Words)
- **range**
- **transform**

Content Vocabulary (Tier Three Words)
- **rift valley**
- **kibbutz**
- **moshav**

TAKING NOTES: ***Key Ideas and Details***

SUMMARIZING Use a graphic organizer like the one below to write about the water systems of the Eastern Mediterranean.

Water Systems of the Eastern Mediterranean		
The Jordan River	The Sea of Galilee	The Gulf of Aqaba

IT MATTERS BECAUSE

Landforms, waterways, and climate affect settlement and economic activities in any region. These factors interact in the Eastern Mediterranean, which has been home to people for centuries. It has a diverse and changing landscape. While the subregion is generally temperate, water scarcity greatly affects agricultural production and other aspects of life.

Landforms

GUIDING QUESTION *How have physical features affected the human geography of the Eastern Mediterranean?*

The Eastern Mediterranean subregion includes the countries of Syria, Jordan, Lebanon, and Israel and the Palestinian territories. This area is also known as the Levant, French for "rising," referring to the sun rising in the East. Some of the most prominent landforms in the area are the Anti-Lebanon Mountains, the Syrian Desert, the Jordan Rift Valley, and the Negev Desert.

Syria, the northernmost country in the Eastern Mediterranean, is bordered by Turkey on the north, Iraq on the east, Jordan on the south, and Lebanon and Israel on the southwest. To the southwest of Syria is a territory called the Golan Heights. This territory consists of a rocky plateau that is officially part of Syria, but most of it has been occupied by Israel since 1967.

The Anti-Lebanon mountain **range** runs along the border between Syria and Lebanon. The mountains have low population density since they have thin soil that is not useful for agriculture. They are frequented mainly by nomadic herders. The highest point in the Anti-Lebanon Mountains is Mount Hermon. At 9,232 feet (2,814 m), it is also the highest point on the land surrounding the Mediterranean Sea. The southern and western slopes of Mount Hermon, which are located in the Golan Heights, have been developed for tourist activities. A favorite tourist activity is skiing. The summit of the mountain is located in both Lebanon and Syria.

390

networks *Online Teaching Options*

INTERACTIVE BELLRINGER

Eastern Mediterranean Precipitation

Interpreting Maps Use the introductory text and map of the annual precipitation in the Eastern Mediterranean subregion. Have students form small groups and discuss their prior knowledge of the climate and biomes in the Eastern Mediterranean. Then have them discuss each question. Ask each group to write agreed-upon answers to the questions. Then in a class discussion, have each group share its answers. **Visual/Spatial**

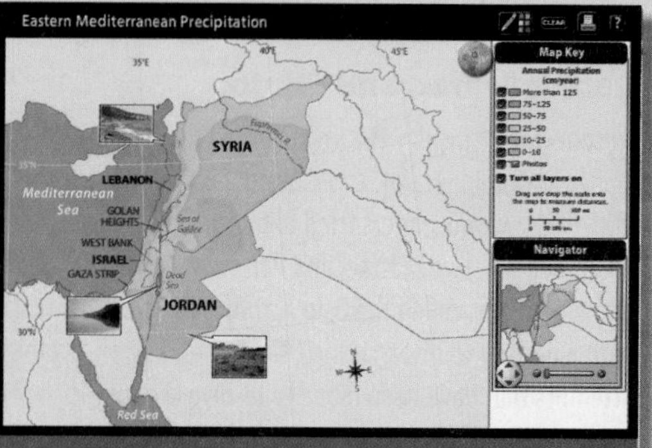

To the east of the Anti-Lebanon mountain range is the Syrian Desert. It covers parts of Saudi Arabia, Jordan, and Iraq. The desert is composed of gravel, not sand. Sparsely populated by nomadic tribes, the desert is used by the general public as a roadway. Southern Syria also includes high lava plains. Some of Syria's great cities, such as Aleppo, lie on the steppes, a semi-arid region east of the coastal country. Another feature is a narrow plain on the eastern edge of the Mediterranean Sea that stretches from the Turkish to the Lebanese borders.

V

range a series of things in a row; a series of mountains

The Syrian Desert takes up four-fifths of Jordan's total territory. The Jordan Rift Valley is located on the western border of the country. A **rift valley** is a valley formed by the separation of tectonic plates. The Jordan Rift Valley is deep, reaching 1,312 feet (400 m) below sea level on the coast of the Dead Sea. This is the lowest point on the Earth's land surface. Between the Syrian Desert and the Jordan Rift Valley is a large plateau where most cities in Jordan are located.

R

rift valley a valley formed by the separation of tectonic plates

Lebanon is mountainous. The Anti-Lebanon Mountains, which run from north to south, cover the eastern part of the country. The Lebanon Mountains lie in the western part of the country. They also run north to south and cover almost the entire length of the country. Both the Anti-Lebanon and Lebanon Mountains run parallel to the eastern coast of the Mediterranean Sea.

The northern and central parts of Israel, which border Lebanon, are hilly regions. The beaches of western Lebanon that border the eastern Mediterranean Sea continue south into Israel. The Galilee Mountains in the north of Israel are low in comparison with the Anti-Lebanon Mountains. The Galilee area consists of rocky terrain that is unsuitable for agriculture. The Negev Desert occupies most of southern Israel. The western side of the desert connects Israel with the Sinai Peninsula. The Negev Desert lies on top of fault lines and is geographically unique because of the erosion craters that dot the landscape.

Located in the Jordan River valley, the Dead Sea is fed by the Jordan River north of the sea as well as other smaller streams and springs.

▼ CRITICAL THINKING

1. ***Analyzing Visuals*** How can you tell that the Dead Sea is located in the Jordan Rift Valley?
2. ***Classifying*** What type of border does the Jordan River form between Jordan, Israel, and the West Bank?

Spacephotos/age fotostock

☑ READING PROGRESS CHECK

Identifying What factors have limited the settlement of the Anti-Lebanon Mountains?

Water Systems

GUIDING QUESTION *What role has water played in the human systems of the Eastern Mediterranean?*

There are several water bodies in the Eastern Mediterranean subregion. These include the Euphrates and Jordan Rivers, the Sea of Galilee, the Dead Sea, the Gulf of Aqaba, and the Mediterranean Sea itself. The Euphrates River, which originates in Turkey, is the most important river in Syria and provides the entire country with water. A complex irrigation network has watered the valley and supported farming there for some 7,000 years. The Euphrates helps irrigate Syria today. The river was dammed in the 1970s. Lake al-Assad was formed behind the dam. It was named after Syria's dictator.

T

The Jordan River, which has a tributary in Syria, flows through all of the countries in the Eastern Mediterranean. The river flows along

INTERACTIVE IMAGE

Tel Aviv Beach

Previewing Use this interactive image that shows a 360° view of the Tel Aviv Beach to introduce the water systems of the Eastern Mediterranean to students. After viewing the image, have students write down three points that interested or surprised them about the image. Then have students share their points. Lead a class discussion to explain that although this subregion consists of desert and some areas have very limited freshwater supplies, many of the beaches are quite beautiful and used for recreation and tourism. AL **Verbal/Linguistic, Visual/Spatial**

360° View: A Beach in Tel Aviv, Israel
Directions: Click on the image to see a 360° panorama view.

V Visual Skills

Creating Charts Assign students a country in the Eastern Mediterranean. Have them research five major cities in their assigned country, including the cities' location, population, and climate. Then have them include any unique or major landforms that are near the cities. Ask students to organize the statistics in a chart or table. Encourage students to present their charts to the class. AL **Visual/Spatial**

R Reading Skills

Defining Discuss the meaning of the term *rift valley.* Have students examine the picture of the Jordan Rift Valley. **Ask: Why is a valley, rather than a mountain, formed with the separation of tectonic plates?** *(A mountain would be formed by tectonic plates crashing together and raising the land. When the plates separate, the land moves downward and forms a valley.)* Have students consult a dictionary to explore the origin of the word *rift.* ELL **Verbal/Linguistic**

Content Background Knowledge

The Negev Desert The name of this desert comes from the Hebrew words meaning "to wipe dry." Records of the Negev Desert date back to the Old Testament of the Bible, and the desert has been a place where multiple civilizations and empires have expanded. Today, one of the largest Israeli cities, Beersheba, is considered the "capital of the Negev."

T Technology Skills

Gathering Information Discussion as a class that the Eastern Mediterranean has several bodies of water that are critical to supporting life in the region. Have students use online or library resources to create a time line that shows the development of civilizations in this area, dating back 7,000 years. Point out that students should include annotations in their time lines that explain the importance of water in these settlements, as well as list the civilizations and technology that people have developed over time to use and protect water resources. BL **Visual/Spatial, Logical/Mathematical**

ANSWERS, p. 391

☑ **READING PROGRESS CHECK** The soil in the Anti-Lebanon Mountains is thin and not good for agriculture, which has limited settlement.

CRITICAL THINKING

1. The Dead Sea is the lowest body of water on Earth. As shown in the picture, it appears to be at the bottom of a gorge within the Earth. This is the Jordan Rift Valley.
2. The Jordan River becomes a natural border between Jordan and the Israeli-occupied West Bank.

CHAPTER 16, Lesson 1
Physical Geography of the Eastern Mediterranean

V Visual Skills

Analyzing Visuals Have students study the image and consider whether they think the use of rivers has changed or remained the same over time. **Ask:** What is the most important role of rivers in the Eastern Mediterranean? *(irrigation)* What risks are involved in using large quantities of water for agriculture? *(Possible answers: The water supply will decrease and will not be able to support the population's drinking water needs. The rivers will become so low that they will no longer remain navigable.)* Have students work with their partner to discuss possible solutions to the water supply challenges that the Eastern Mediterranean faces. **AL Visual/Spatial, Logical/Mathematical**

C Critical Thinking Skills

Comparing and Contrasting Divide the class into three groups, assigning each group one of the following bodies of water: Sea of Galilee, Gulf of Aqaba, or Lake al-Assad. After groups read about their assigned body of water, encourage them to discuss what they read, and then have each group give a short oral presentation to the class. After all groups have presented, have students share an example of how the bodies of water are similar or different. Extend the discussion to include whether each of the bodies of water would be a good source for irrigation, transportation (goods or people), and recreation. **ELL Verbal/Linguistic**

ANSWERS, p. 392

READING PROGRESS CHECK The Gulf of Aqaba connects the Red Sea and the Indian Ocean.

CRITICAL THINKING

1. There appears to be oil drilling taking place in the picture.
2. The fish could be contaminated from oil spills or just the by-products from drilling so closely to the cages.

This fish farm in the Gulf of Aqaba in Israel once used cages to raise fish.

▲ CRITICAL THINKING

1. ***Analyzing Visuals*** What other activities can be seen in the photo?
2. ***Assessing*** How might the fish in the cages have been contaminated given their location?

Börje Olsson/Alamy

the Syrian-Lebanese border, through the Anti-Lebanon Mountains and near Mount Hermon. It then flows south into the Sea of Galilee. There the river becomes a natural border between the Israeli-occupied West Bank and Jordan before it empties into the Dead Sea. The river is important for irrigation and agriculture. Farmers grow oranges, bananas, beets, and other vegetables on the river's eastern banks.

Many of the streams in the desert regions of the Eastern Mediterranean subregion, mainly in inland areas, flow only intermittently, appearing suddenly and disappearing just as quickly. In the subregion's deserts, runoff from infrequent rainstorms creates wadis (WAH•dees), or streambeds that remain dry until a heavy rain. Irregular rainstorms often produce flash flooding. During a flash flood, wadis fill with so much sediment that they can rapidly become mudflows, or moving masses of wet soil. The mudflows pose dangers to humans and animals and can destroy agriculture.

The Sea of Galilee in western Israel supports some marine life, even though it is relatively salty for a freshwater body. The sea has supported communities of people for millennia due to its low elevation and moderate climate. The Dead Sea, which lies more than 1,300 feet (400 m) below sea level, is the lowest body of water on Earth. The salty waters make objects so buoyant that people can remain afloat in the sea without swimming.

The Gulf of Aqaba, located south of Israel and Jordan, connects the Eastern Mediterranean countries with the Red Sea and the Indian Ocean. The Mediterranean Sea allows people in the Eastern Mediterranean countries to navigate to Turkey and North Africa, as well as a number of countries in Western and Eastern Europe. Syria has a relatively short coastline that stretches between Turkey in the north and Lebanon in the south, while Lebanon and Israel have longer Mediterranean coastlines. The coastal areas are more densely populated than the interior areas of Syria and Lebanon.

Lake al-Assad is a large source of fish. It is also used for irrigation and agriculture in the surrounding lands and provides drinking water for the city of Aleppo. The southern part of the lake is home to trees such as the Aleppo pine. The lake is also a resting point for migrating birds.

READING PROGRESS CHECK

Identifying What bodies of water does the Gulf of Aqaba connect?

Climate, Biomes, and Resources

GUIDING QUESTION *What defines the climate of the Eastern Mediterranean?*

Rainfall is limited throughout the Eastern Mediterranean subregion. Much of the area contains semi-arid (steppe) and arid (desert) climates. Areas with slightly greater moisture include the Mediterranean, highland, and humid subtropical climates.

392

networks Online Teaching Options

VIDEO

Dead Sea Disappearing

Identifying Central Issues Use this video about the Dead Sea to introduce students to the water systems and the physical geography of the Eastern Mediterranean. Have students take notes on the information presented in this video. In a class discussion, ask students to identify ways that changes to the water systems in this region are affecting the physical geography and how these changes are influencing the economic activities in nearby countries. **BL Logical/Mathematical, Verbal/Linguistic**

Climate Regions and Biomes

The coastal regions of the Eastern Mediterranean have a Mediterranean climate with hot, dry summers and mild, rainy winters. Mediterranean climates support the growth of citrus fruits, olives, apples, apricots, and grapes. Natural vegetation is varied and includes oaks, evergreen conifers, and many types of wildflowers. Thickets of woody bushes and short trees known as Mediterranean shrub cover many parts of the region. Wildcats, wild boars, gazelles, hyenas, hares, badgers, and tiger weasels are found in the Eastern Mediterranean. The coastal areas are also important stopping places for more than 400 species of migratory birds. **G1**

Interior areas of the subregion have much less rainfall. As one moves inland, the climate becomes humid subtropical and then **transforms**, or changes, into semi-arid steppe and arid desert. The semi-arid climate zones usually receive about 14 inches (36 cm) of rain each year. Areas with less than 10 inches (25 cm) of rain per year are classified as deserts. Animal life in the deserts of the subregion includes geckos, lizards, and vipers. Plants in the deserts have adapted to the dry conditions and include a few scattered tree species, scrubs, and herbs. Overall, the landscape in Israel and Lebanon is extremely varied and can change within short distances. Syria and Jordan are dominated by semi-arid and arid climates. **R**

Soils vary across the subregion just as climates do. Eastern Mediterranean coastal soils are alluvial, making them richer than the inland soils. East of the coastal mountain ranges, in the more arid inland parts of Syria and Jordan, topsoil is often lost to strong winds. These dry areas need to be irrigated in order to produce agricultural products because of the lack of precipitation. The Syrian Desert, for example, receives less than 5 inches (13 cm) of rainfall each year. Similarly, the coast of the Dead Sea is desert and cannot support many types of plant life aside from halophytes, or plants that can grow in salty soil.

transform to change in form or appearance

kibbutz a communal farm or settlement in Israel

moshav a cooperative settlement of small individual farms in Israel

GEOGRAPHY CONNECTION

Differences in annual precipitation across the Eastern Mediterranean have affected and continue to affect vegetation and human activities.

1. ***PLACES AND REGIONS*** How does the annual precipitation in Israel compare to that of Jordan?
2. ***THE WORLD IN SPATIAL TERMS*** Describe how the physical geography of Israel and Lebanon influence precipitation in the two countries.

C2

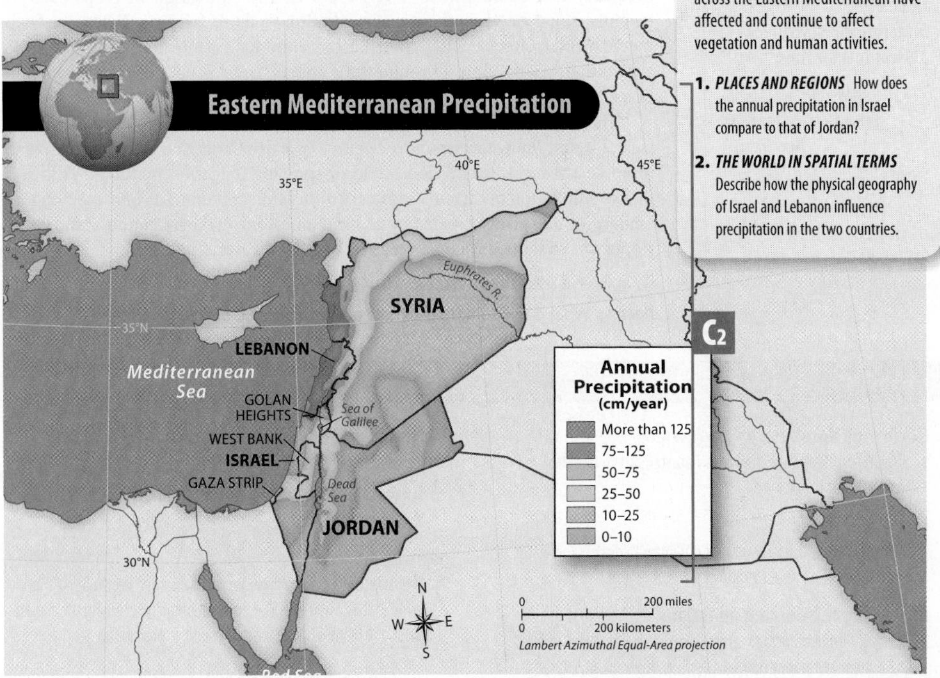

CHAPTER 16, Lesson 1

Physical Geography of the Eastern Mediterranean

G1 Critical Thinking Skills

Categorizing Have students categorize the facts and details about climates, biomes, and natural resources by creating a table. Suggest that students use the following headings: *Climate, Crops, Plants,* and *Animals.* Challenge students to compare these characteristics with those of another region that they have read about in the text. Discuss the factors that influence the vegetation and animals that inhabit both regions. **AL Visual/Spatial, Naturalist**

R Reading Skills

Using Context Clues Ask students to reread this section and to identify context clues that help to reveal the meaning of the word *transform.* **Ask:** **How does using the word *transforms* instead of *changes* help you to better understand the climate regions?** *(Possible answer: By using the word* transforms, *the explanation is more specific to climate. For example, the transformation in a climate region causes a physical change of appearance in the land and in the vegetation and animals that are supported by that climate region.)* **ELL Verbal/Linguistic**

C2 Critical Thinking Skills

Posing Questions Have students examine the map of precipitation in the Eastern Mediterranean. Based on the map, have them write three questions on how rainfall affects agriculture in this subregion. Suggest that students use some of the information in the text to help write their questions and answers. Then have students exchange their questions with a partner to answer each other's questions. Allow time for pairs to discuss the questions and answers. **BL Visual/Spatial, Logical/Mathematical**

INTERACTIVE IMAGE

The Dying Dead Sea

Predicting Have students view this image of the Dead Sea. As a class, discuss the changes that the sea has undergone in recent years and the causes for these extreme changes. Have students write a paragraph predicting what they think will happen to the region surrounding the Dead Sea over time. Remind them to consider the region's history of conflict as they write their predictions. Ask several volunteers to share their paragraphs. **Visual/Spatial, Logical/Mathematical**

ANSWERS, p. 393

GEOGRAPHY CONNECTION

1. Israel receives more precipitation at 25–50 cm per year while most of Jordan only receives 0–10 cm per year.
2. Lebanon is on the coast of the Mediterranean, which gives it a Mediterranean climate with rainy winters. Israel, with more inland semi-arid areas, receives less rain than Lebanon.

CHAPTER 16, Lesson 1
Physical Geography of the Eastern Mediterranean

T Technology Skills

Researching Have students research the significance of the cedar tree to each country in the Eastern Mediterranean. Challenge students to find current statistics on its production and how cedar trees are used in industry now and in the past. Have students prepare a slide show presentation to share their findings with the class. BL **Verbal/Linguistic, Naturalist**

W Writing Skills

Argument Have students choose a position about the development and production of oil and gas in the Eastern Mediterranean. Tell them to consider environmental, economic, and political factors and then write an argumentative essay supporting their position. Remind students to refute counter-argument points and statistics. **Naturalist, Intrapersonal**

CLOSE & REFLECT

Synthesizing To review this lesson, have students make a four-column chart with the heads: *Landforms, Water Systems, Climate Regions and Biomes, and Natural Resources.* Then guide a class discussion in which students add a fifth column with the head *Challenges* to their charts. Have them supply information for each column section.

ANSWERS, p. 394

✓ **READING PROGRESS CHECK** Arid and semi-arid climates dominate the Eastern Mediterranean.

DBQ The scrubby bushes and undergrowth in the forests were used in the past by villagers for cooking fuel. Electricity is now common, so undergrowth is no longer cleared, giving forest fires more fuel and adding to forest destruction.

Analyzing Primary Sources (CCSS)

Lebanon's Forests: Going up in Smoke

"In 2002 alone, there were over 15,000 fires that became out of control in this small country. The yearly fires are a huge threat to Lebanon's already vulnerable forests.

Most forest fires in Lebanon start when a fire set by a farmer to clear his orchards and fields of grasses and stubble gets out of control. The problem has become worse over the last decade because of changing land use.

In the past, villagers used scrubby bushes from the forests as fuel for cooking, which kept the dry undergrowth thin. Now there's electricity, so the undergrowth stays thick—perfect fuel for fires."

—World Wildlife Fund, "Lebanon's Forests: Facing New Threats"

DBQ ***ANALYZING PRIMARY SOURCES*** How has technological progress resulted in threats to the forests? RH.9–10.1

Natural Resources

T Many countries in the Eastern Mediterranean were once heavily wooded in the past, but have since cut down most of their trees. Cedar trees have been used by people in the region dating back to around 2500 B.C. The cedar trees are prized natural resources due to their fragrance and commercial value as a source of lumber. Most are found in the western part of the Anti-Lebanon Mountains. The cedar appears on the flag of Lebanon and is esteemed as a symbol of happiness and prosperity.

Minerals are also important to the economies of the Eastern Mediterranean subregion. Minerals—such as bromine and magnesium, gypsum from the Negev, and marble in the Galilee area—are produced. In addition, Syria produces chrome and manganese ores, asphalt, iron ore, and rock salt. Jordan has fewer mineral resources.

W Recently, large oil and natural gas reserves were discovered below the waters of the Mediterranean Sea in this region, including offshore parts of Israel. There have been other finds in the Palestinian territories. These finds are still being explored, and currently, production of oil and gas is of minor importance to these countries. While petroleum exports could enrich the region, they also would make the Eastern Mediterranean economies fluctuate, or rise and fall, in the global market. Some countries in the subregion seek to diversify their economies so that they are not reliant on single commodities. Many countries are also turning to tourism as a source of revenue.

All Eastern Mediterranean countries have relied on agriculture for centuries. However, the Israeli government has always made a specialized effort to create farming communities. They supply these communities with farming equipment and irrigation education. The two types of communities are the **kibbutz** and the **moshav**. The communities have supported the cultivation of crops such as peanuts, sugar beets, and cotton in addition to dairy farming. Extensive farm mechanization has recently contributed to the increase in the value of Israel's agricultural production. Through these efforts, Israel produces a major portion of its food supply and imports the remainder.

The biggest challenge for agriculture in the Eastern Mediterranean is the lack of water. Many farmers have begun to use drip irrigation as an alternative to more costly and wasteful flood-field or spraying irrigation methods. Thin soil makes cultivation of certain crops very difficult in certain parts of the subregion. Underground springs created by cracked limestone make irrigation of the lower slopes of Lebanon and Israel very successful, however.

✓ **READING PROGRESS CHECK**

Naming What is the dominant climate of the Eastern Mediterranean?

LESSON 1 REVIEW

Reviewing Vocabulary (Tier Three Words)

1. ***Specifying*** What geographical characteristics define the Negev Desert? RH.9–10.4

Using Your Notes

2. ***Summarizing*** Use your graphic organizer to discuss the water systems of the Eastern Mediterranean subregion.

Answering the Guiding Questions

3. ***Making Generalizations*** How have physical features affected the human geography of the Eastern Mediterranean?
4. ***Evaluating*** What role has water played in the human systems of the Eastern Mediterranean?
5. ***Synthesizing*** What defines the climate of the Eastern Mediterranean?

Writing Activity

6. ***Informative/Explanatory*** Write a paragraph describing plants found in the Eastern Mediterranean subregion, including the climate zones and biomes where they are found. WHST.9–10.2

394

LESSON 1 REVIEW ANSWERS

Reviewing Vocabulary

1. The Negev Desert is on top of fault lines in southern Israel. It has a unique landscape because of erosion craters that cover the area.

Using Your Notes

2. The Euphrates River helps irrigate Syria and was dammed to form Lake al-Assad, a large source of fish and irrigation for the area. The Jordan River flows through all of the countries of the Eastern Mediterranean and provides important irrigation for crops. The Sea of Galilee in western Israel supports the surrounding community. The Gulf of Aqaba connects Eastern Mediterranean countries with the Red Sea and the Indian Ocean.

Answering the Guiding Questions

3. Mountains and desert impact areas of settlement in the Eastern Mediterranean. The poor soil in the Anti-Lebanon Mountains and the rocky terrain in the Galilee area are unsuitable for agriculture and have low population densities.
4. Irrigation systems built in the Eastern Mediterranean have provided the water needed for agriculture for 7,000 years.
5. Semi-arid (steppe) and arid (desert) defines the climate of the Eastern Mediterranean.

Writing Activity

6. Paragraphs may vary but should include Mediterranean climate has hot, dry summers and mild, rainy winters; plants and trees include oak, evergreens, wildflowers, Mediterranean shrub, and cultivation of olives and fruits. Semi-arid and arid desert climates are very dry; plants include scrub bushes, few trees, and herbs. The coast of the Dead Sea is a desert where only halophytes grow in the salty soil.

netw@rks

There's More Online!

- **IMAGE** Family and Religion in the Eastern Mediterranean
- **GRAPHS** Ethnic Groups of the Eastern Mediterranean
- **GRAPH** GDP per Capita
- **INTERACTIVE SELF-CHECK QUIZ**
- **TIME LINE** Israeli-Palestinian Conflict: An Elusive Peace Process
- **VIDEO** Human Geography of the Eastern Mediterranean

LESSON 2

Human Geography of the Eastern Mediterranean

ESSENTIAL QUESTION • *How do physical systems and human systems shape a place?*

Reading HELPDESK (CCSS)

Academic Vocabulary
(Tier Two Words)

- **rely**
- **output**

Content Vocabulary
(Tier Three Words)

- **monotheism**
- **prophet**
- **mosque**
- **stateless nation**

TAKING NOTES: ***Key Ideas and Details***

SUMMARIZNG Use a graphic organizer like the one below to record details about how the settlement of Israel affected population patterns in the Eastern Mediterranean.

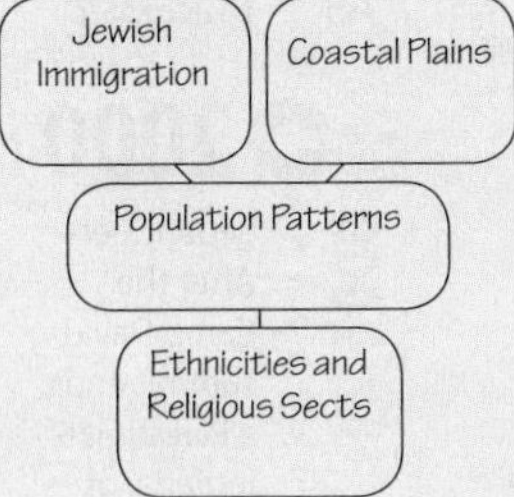

IT MATTERS BECAUSE

The Eastern Mediterranean is the birthplace of Judaism, Christianity, and Islam. Throughout history, including more recent times, the subregion has been characterized by political instability and conflict based on a combination of ethnic, religious, cultural, economic, and political factors. **R**

History and Government

GUIDING QUESTION *How have Judaism, Christianity, and Islam shaped the politics and culture of the Eastern Mediterranean?*

As a bridge between Europe, Africa, and Asia, the Eastern Mediterranean has been influenced by cultural groups from each of these continents throughout history. The rise of influential religions has profoundly affected its history, geography, and culture. **V**

Civilizations and Religion

The subregion has been under the control of powerful cultures and empires over the centuries. The capital city of Syria, Damascus, is one of the oldest continuously settled urban centers in the world. Judaism, Christianity, and Islam share the same territory, and they also share many beliefs, especially **monotheism**, or belief that there is only one God.

Judaism is the oldest of these monotheistic religions. Jews trace their origin to the ancient Israelites who created the kingdom of Israel along the Eastern Mediterranean coast. The kingdom, which included what is now Israel and the West Bank, had Jerusalem as its capital and religious center. Judaism teaches obedience to God's laws as the means for obtaining God's favor. These laws are described in the Hebrew Bible, which contains the Torah, the books of the prophets, and the sacred writings. **C**

A Jewish teacher named Jesus began preaching throughout Israel. His central teachings emphasized faith in God's grace as the means for obtaining God's favor and entry into heaven after death. After Jesus' death, his teachings became the basis of a new religion—Christianity.

ENGAGE

R1 Reading Skills

Predicting Have students page through the lesson, previewing the headings and the photographs. Then ask students to write three sentences predicting what they will learn in this lesson.

TEACH & ASSESS

V Visual Skills

Analyzing Visuals Display a physical map of the Eastern Mediterranean found in the online Teacher Resource Center. **Ask:** **How is the subregion a "bridge" between the continents?** *(It is situated between Europe, Asia, and Africa.)* **Why do you think three major religions were founded in this subregion?** *(Possible answer: Christianity was born from within the Jewish religion, and Islam developed from both the teachings of both Judaism and Christianity.)* **AL** **Logical/Mathematical**

C Critical Thinking Skills

Comparing and Contrasting Discuss the rise of Christianity with students. **Ask:** **What similarities do Judaism and Christianity share?** *(They are both monotheistic and were founded in the same geographic area. They also share some religious writings and teachings.)* **How are the two religions different?** *(Christians follow the teachings of Jesus, which focus on faith in God's grace in obtaining God's favor, while Jews believe in obedience to God's laws in obtaining God's favor.)* Invite students to share other details of what they know about both religions. **Verbal/Linguistic**

netw@rks *Online Teaching Options*

INTERACTIVE BELLRINGER

Israeli-Palestinian Conflict

Understanding Relationships Among Events Use the introductory text and time line showing events related to the Israeli-Palestinian conflict and peace process to help students understand the relationship between the events. Have them form small groups and then analyze each entry and event on the time line about the Israeli-Palestinian conflict and peace process. Ask each group to write an agreed-upon answer to the question. Then in a class discussion, have the groups share their answers. **ELL** **Visual/Spatial**

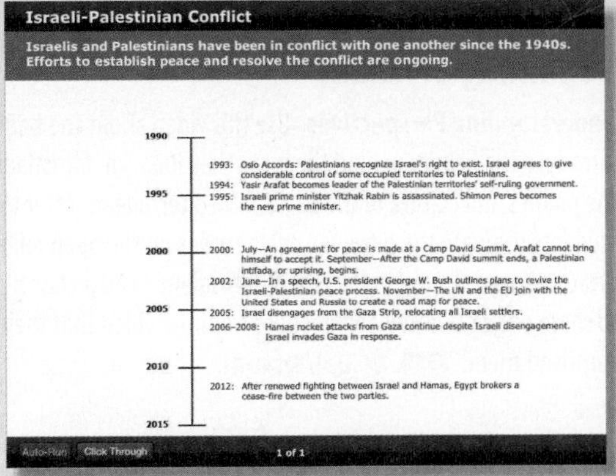

ANSWERS, p. 395

TAKING NOTES: Israel was created after World War II as a homeland for Jews. Palestine was populated by Arabs. The intent was to make a Jewish state of Israel and an Arab state for Palestinians. The Arab Palestinians rejected this, leading to many conflicts over the territory. These conflicts forced the Arabs living in Palestine to become refugees. The Palestinian people want an independent country of their own but are now a stateless nation. Palestinians are religously diverse, but most are Muslim with a number of Christians living near Jerusalem. Israel is largely populated by Jews with some Muslims and Christians.

C Critical Thinking Skills

Theorizing Review with students how Islam was founded and its main beliefs and characteristics. **Ask: Why did Islam spread throughout the subregion and into Europe and Africa by the A.D. 700s?** *(Possible response: Its spread to these areas was facilitated through conquest.)* **Did Christianity and Judaism spread in the same way during this time? Explain.** *(Possible response: No, Christianity spread through Jesus' followers, and Judaism did not spread outside of the subregion, although when Christians and Jews migrated to different regions and subregions, they brought their culture and religion with them).* **AL Logical/Mathematical**

R Reading Skills

Predicting If possible, show students maps of the Eastern Mediterranean subregion before and after World War II. Discuss the changes in political borders and control that resulted. **Ask: Why did Palestine continue to be a disputed territory unlike Jordan, Lebanon, and Syria?** *(Possible answer: Due to cultural and historic ties, Jews migrated to Palestine rather than Jordan, Lebanon, or Syria, resulting in disputed claims.)* Have students work in small groups to discuss what role the international community would take in helping to determine the fate of Palestine. **Verbal/Linguistic, Interpersonal**

W Writing Skills

Narrative Have students write a journal entry from the perspective of a young Palestinian or Jew living in Israel after World War II. Point out that students should include historical references but also the sentiments that a young person might be experiencing during this difficult time in the subregion. Remind students to use sensory details and vivid verbs in their narratives. Invite volunteers to share their journal entries with the class. **Verbal/Linguistic, Intrapersonal**

monotheism belief in one God

prophet person believed to be a messenger from God

mosque in Islam, a house of worship

The Christian Scriptures included the Old Testament, or Hebrew Bible, and the New Testament, a collection of works about the life of Jesus and the earliest Christian communities.

C Islamic tradition holds that in A.D. 610 revelations from God were received by Muhammad. He was a merchant in the city of Makkah (Mecca) in the Arabian Peninsula. Muhammad began preaching that people should turn away from sin and worship the one true God. His followers claimed that he was the last in a line of **prophets**, or messengers, that included Abraham and Jesus. Muslim beliefs were recorded in the Quran, the sacred text of Islam. By the A.D. 700s, Islam had spread through the subregion and into Europe and the eastern horn of Africa. Islam had profound influences in these areas. One of the new features in the land use of cities and villages was the **mosque**, or place of worship.

Independence and Conflict

R Over the centuries, Islamic empires in the Eastern Mediterranean rose and fell. Some were highly advanced civilizations that had great achievements in science, literature, and art. By the late 1800s, Western European powers conquered large areas of the subregion. These colonies generally provided few resources for the European powers until oil was discovered.

Following the defeat of the Ottomans in World War I, occupation of the Eastern Mediterranean was divided between Britain and France for protection from invasion, as well as for economic development, health and education. Lebanon and Syria gained independence from France in 1943 and 1946, respectively. Jordan gained independence from the British in 1946. The remaining disputed territory was Palestine.

W Soon after World War II, armed conflicts broke out among Jewish and Arab ethnic groups in Palestine. The Jews wanted an internationally recognized homeland in a part of Palestine. The Palestinians wanted all of Palestine. The Jews accepted a 1947 United Nations (UN) plan to divide Palestine into a Jewish

TIME LINE

ISRAELI-PALESTINIAN CONFLICT
An Elusive Peace Process

For decades, Israelis and Palestinians have been in conflict with one another.

1990

1993 Oslo Accords: Palestinians recognize Israel's right to exist. Israel agrees to give considerable control of some occupied territories to Palestinians.

1994 Yasir Arafat becomes leader of the Palestinian territories' self-ruling government.

1995 Israeli prime minister Yitzhak Rabin is assassinated. Shimon Peres becomes the new prime minister.

2000 July—An agreement for peace is made at a Camp David summit. Arafat cannot bring himself to accept it.

2000 September—After the Camp David summit ends, a Palestinian intifada, or uprising, begins.

2000

▶ CRITICAL THINKING

1. ***Analyzing*** What are the key issues that have created conflict between Israelis and Palestinians?
2. ***Explaining*** How have other world organizations tried to support the peace process?

396

networks Online Teaching Options

VIDEO

Beginning of Islam

Understanding Perspectives Use this video about the beginning of Islam to introduce the history behind the ways that Judaism, Christianity, and Islam have shaped the politics and culture of the Eastern Mediterranean. After they watch the video, have students evaluate the different perspectives on the deep religious beliefs and ethnic attachments centered in the city of Jerusalem. Lead a class discussion inviting students to share one or two key perspectives from the video that they found interesting or that surprised them. **ELL Visual/Spatial**

ANSWERS, p. 396

CRITICAL THINKING

1. Both groups feel they have a historic right to the land held by Israel. Both groups have a religious and ethnic attachment to the land. Conflicts led to Israel acquiring and settling more land, which continues to cause issues between Israelis and Palestinians.
2. Other world organizations have tried to broker peace agreements between Israel and the Palestinian territories. In 2002, the EU and UN joined with Russia and the United States to create a peace plan. In 2008, Egypt brokered a cease-fire.

state and an Arab state. The Arabs rejected it, thus setting up a struggle for control of the land. Both groups had a deep religious and ethnic attachment to the land. The British withdrew from the disputed Palestinian territory, and the Jews proclaimed the independent state of Israel in May 1948.

Between 1948 and 2013, tensions over Arab opposition to Israel and Israel's concern for its security led to seven military conflicts. They involved Israel in conflict with Egypt, Jordan, Syria, Lebanon, and Hezbollah, a paramilitary group dedicated to destroying Israel. In the 1967 Israeli-Palestinian conflict, Israel gained control of the West Bank, Gaza Strip, and Golan Heights.

The wars following the birth of Israel forced many Arabs living in Palestine and Jews living in various Southwest Asian and North African countries to become refugees. The status of Arab refugees is an ongoing issue in the Israeli-Palestinian dispute. In addition, the Palestinians want an independent country of their own in the West Bank. The Palestinian people have become a **stateless nation**, an ethnic group without a formal country. Although Palestinians are religiously diverse, today most are Muslim with a significant number of Christians living near Jerusalem.

stateless nation an ethnic group without a formal country

In 2006 Hamas, an Islamic political party, won elections in the West Bank and Gaza Strip. Hamas supported terrorist attacks on Israel. In 2012, in response to rocket attacks from Hamas-governed Gaza, the Israeli military launched air strikes followed by ground forces. Many targeted areas suffered extensive damage.

Independence in the 1940s was not smooth for Lebanon, Syria, or Jordan. By 1970 Lebanon had descended into a civil war based on religious politics between Christians and Muslims. Following the 1983 Israeli invasion, a group of Lebanese Shia clerics formed Hezbollah. Their goal was to drive Israel from Lebanon. The Syrian government intervened in the conflict, although Lebanese of all religions were opposed to Syrian interference. The civil war ended in 1989 with a new government that divided all administrative positions based on equal ratios of Christians and Muslims.

Ahmad Gharabli/AFP/Getty Images

2002 June— In a speech, U.S. president George W. Bush outlines plans to revive the Israeli-Palestinian peace process.

2002 November—The UN and the EU join with the United States and Russia to create a road map for peace.

2005 Israel disengages from the Gaza Strip, relocating all Israeli settlers.

2006–2008 Hamas rocket attacks from Gaza continue despite Israeli disengagement. Israel invades Gaza in response.

2012 After renewed fighting between Israel and Hamas, Egypt brokers a cease-fire between the two parties.

2002 ➔ 2008

CHAPTER 16, Lesson 2
Human Geography of the Eastern Mediterranean

T Technology Skills

Identifying Central Issues Divide the class up into seven groups. Assign each group one of the seven military conflicts that Israel was involved in over their concern for security. Allow time for students to conduct Internet research about the conflicts. Then have representatives from each group identify the central issues of each conflict in a class discussion.
BL Verbal/Linguistic, Logical/Mathematical

V Visual Skills

Time, Chronology, and Sequencing After students have read the brief history about the independence of Lebanon, Syria, and Jordan and the events following the creation of the state of Israel, organize students into four small groups and assign each group one of the following topics to research: Syria, Jordan, Lebanon, Gaza Strip/West Bank/Golan Heights. Ask students to use the Internet and library reference materials to locate additional information and events about their topic. Each group should create a visual, such as a time line or a slide show, to show important events from the 1940s to 1990. Have groups pull together photographs from primary and secondary sources for their presentations. Provide an opportunity for groups to share their chronologies using presentation software.
ELL Visual/Spatial, Interpersonal

Content Background Knowledge

Palestine Liberation Organization In 1964, Palestinians formed an umbrella group called the Palestine Liberation Organization (PLO). As a centralized group, the PLO used guerrilla tactics to wage war against Israel. In 1987, Palestinians launched a mass uprising called the First Intifada against Israel to control the Gaza Strip and the West Bank. Fighting continued until leaders from Israel, Arab countries, and Palestinians agreed to engage in peace talks in the 1990s. Another uprising called the Second Intifada began in 2000 and ended in 2005.

INTERACTIVE TIME LINE

Arab-Israeli Relations, 1948–1994

Spatial Understanding Display the time line to provide students with further information about the ongoing Arab and Israeli conflicts. Have student volunteers read each event as it is revealed and discuss it as a class. Ask students to choose one of the events and research it using the Internet. Then have students create a more detailed time line that includes events that occurred around the same time as the event that they chose. **AL**
Visual/Spatial, Verbal/Linguistic

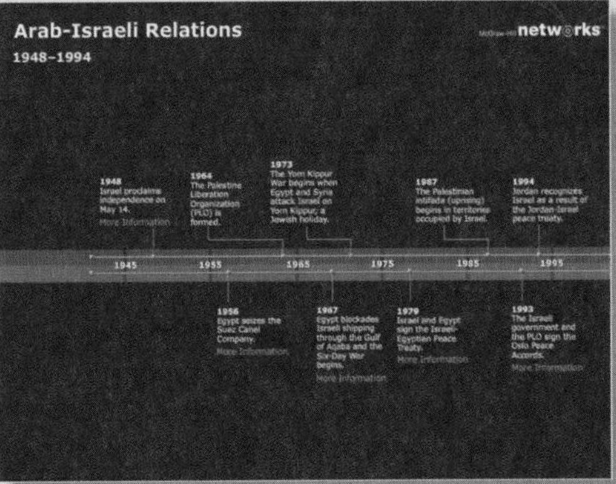

Human Geography of the Eastern Mediterranean

C Critical Thinking Skills

Drawing Conclusions Discuss with students possible reasons that Lebanon and Syria have a higher population of Armenians than does Israel or Jordan. **Ask: How do demographics in the subregion affect political stability?** *(Possible answer: Larger percentages of a certain religious or ethnic group may lead to more political stability, but if two main groups comprise the population, more political instability may result.)* Point out that demographics is an important factor that can contribute to political or religious conflict. **Logical/Mathematical, Interpersonal**

T Technology Skills

Changing Continuity in Politics Ask students what they already know about the Arab Spring. **Ask: Why did Jordan and Lebanon not experience an "Arab Spring"?** *(Student answers will vary but should provide logical reasoning, such as more political stability or moderate leadership in both countries.)* Consider having students locate some primary or secondary sources about the Arab Spring and why it did not occur in Lebanon and Jordan. Have students share their source finding in a class discussion. Ask students to explain any differences in the presentation of facts, perspectives, and ideas between the primary and secondary sources. **Verbal/Linguistic**

V Visual Skills

Creating Charts Review the unit population density map of the Eastern Mediterranean and discuss how climate and physical features can influence where people choose to live. Then have students work in pairs to create a population density chart that shows persons per square mile (coastal, inland, and desert) within one of the countries in this subregion. Remind students to label the *y*-axis and the *x*-axis appropriately and suggest that they represent in a map key or legend the following percentages: less than 25 percent, 25 percent, 50 percent, 75 percent, and 100 percent. ELL **Naturalist, Visual/Spatial**

ANSWERS, p. 398

READING PROGRESS CHECK The three monotheistic faiths of the Eastern Mediterranean are Judaism, Christianity, and Islam.

CRITICAL THINKING

1. Israel is mostly Jewish with official languages of Hebrew and Arabic. Most other Eastern Mediterranean countries are largely Arab populations that speak Arabic.
2. They share similar customs and speak Arabic.

GRAPH SKILLS Ethnic Groups in the Eastern Mediterranean

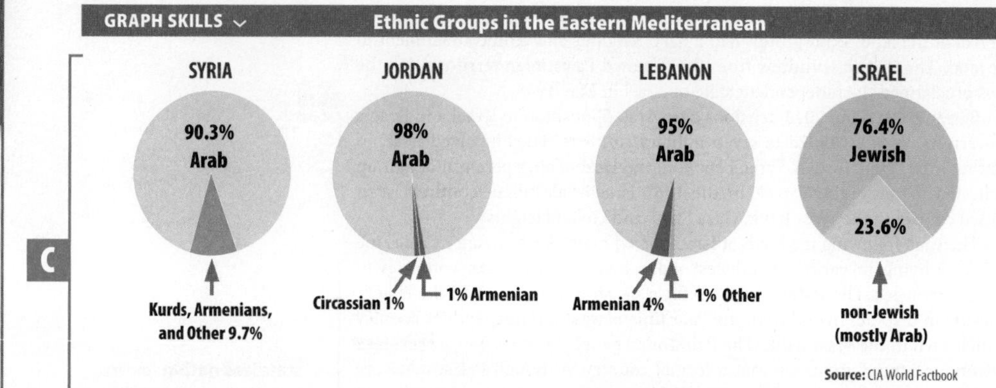

Source: CIA World Factbook

The Eastern Mediterranean is inhabited by millions of Arab and Jewish people. Arabs share similar customs and speak Arabic. Most Jewish people in the region live in Israel, where the official language is Hebrew.

▲ CRITICAL THINKING

1. ***Contrasting*** How is Israel's ethnic and religious composition different from that of other countries in the Eastern Mediterranean?
2. ***Comparing*** Other than large Arab populations, what do Syria, Lebanon, and Jordan have in common in terms of ethnic makeup?

While Syria was technically declared an independent country in 1946, it required a cultural convergence of ethnic groups. Territories with different religions and ethnicities that had been ruled separately by the French were joined under one government. Mergers of territory were disputed, and opposition to national independence persisted. Syria went through a series of military coups influenced by Egyptian and Iraqi politics. In 1971 Hafez al-Assad was elected president and remained in this position until 2000. His son, Bashar al-Assad, succeeded him.

In 2011, following a series of uprisings against dictators, prodemocracy Syrians rebelled against Bashar al-Assad's rule. This revolt grew out of the larger Arab Spring movement, but al-Assad's regime used lethal force against protesters and did not quickly collapse. In 2013 al-Assad's government was still resisting the revolutionary fighters.

Jordan is a constitutional monarchy. In 2012 people protested for lower food and gas prices and were successful. Jordan did not experience an "Arab Spring."

READING PROGRESS CHECK

Listing What are the three monotheistic faiths rooted in the Eastern Mediterranean?

Population Patterns

GUIDING QUESTION *How have migrations, claims to ancestral homes, and boundary disputes affected population patterns in the Eastern Mediterranean?*

The dry, desert climate causes the majority of people in the Eastern Mediterranean to live along coastal plains. For example, over 2 million of Lebanon's 4 million inhabitants live in its capital city, Beirut, on the Mediterranean coast. The two smallest countries in the subregion, Lebanon and Israel, are more densely populated. While Syria and Jordan have lower population densities, the majority of people live in the western parts of those countries. Few people live in the deserts of the east.

networks Online Teaching Options

INTERACTIVE WHITEBOARD ACTIVITY

Ethnic Groups in Eastern Mediterranean

Continuity of Groups This interactive whiteboard activity has students identify and answer questions about the various ethnic groups in the Eastern Mediterranean. Students will analyze graphs, then identify the country, using the information in the graph. Have students answer each question individually, first. Then have students work with a partner to check their answers. Guide a class discussion on whether ethnic groups in this subregion have changed, become diverse, or remained the same over the past fifty years.

ELL **Visual/Spatial**

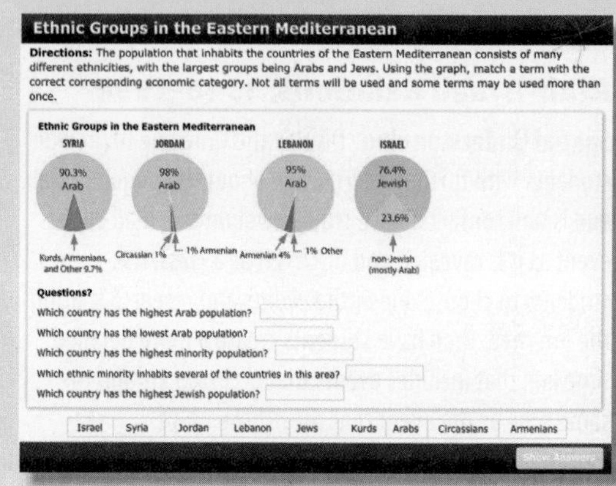

The population of the subregion includes many different ethnicities and religious sects. In Lebanon, Christians of various sects make up about 40 percent of the total population. Christians make up smaller percentages in Jordan and Syria. There is also a population of Kurds in Syria. A minority of Christians live among the Muslim majority in Gaza and the West Bank. Among the major Muslim groups, the largest number adhere to the Sunni branch of the religion. In Syria and Lebanon, there are Muslims who adhere to the teachings of the Shia branch.

The demographics of the Eastern Mediterranean have changed drastically in the past century. After 1990 nearly 900,000 immigrants moved to Israel from Russia. It was the largest immigration to Israel since independence in 1948. Today over 67 percent of Israel's Jews are native born. Due to military conflicts and resettlement programs, many Palestinians were displaced beginning with the war following Israel's declaration of independence. They relocated to refugee settlements in neighboring Arab countries. In 2012 the UN reported that there were 4,797,723 registered Palestinian refugees living in 58 camps in Syria, Lebanon, and Jordan. These include several generations of descendants of the original refugees. This has been a serious humanitarian issue that hampers peace talks between Israel and the Palestinians. G1

✓ READING PROGRESS CHECK

Discussing How have demographics in the Eastern Mediterranean changed?

Society and Culture Today

GUIDING QUESTION *How has history influenced the society and culture of the Eastern Mediterranean today?*

Hebrew and Arabic are both official languages in Israel. The primary language in all other areas of the subregion is Arabic. English is also spoken in some areas.

Public schools in the subregion are generally free. Private schools, which often offer a better standard of education, require fees. Education is mandatory, but the quality differs from country to country. Literacy rates vary from 80 percent in Syria to 97 percent in Israel. Most countries require schooling until the age of 15. G2

Family life in the Eastern Mediterranean often includes the extended family.

▼ CRITICAL THINKING

1. ***Classifying*** Would you characterize the family shown as a nuclear family or as an extended family?
2. ***Making Connections*** In what ways is the family in the picture similar to yours?

V

CHAPTER 16, Lesson 2
Human Geography of the Eastern Mediterranean

G1 Critical Thinking Skills

Differentiating Review the differences between refugees and immigrants by inviting volunteers to provide definitions for *refugee* and *immigrant*. **Ask:** **What key event caused so many people to immigrate to Israel from Russia after 1990?** *(the breakup of the Soviet Union)* Have students think about possible solutions to the refugee problem in the Eastern Mediterranean. Provide an opportunity for students to share their ideas and reasoning in small groups. **AL** **Logical/Mathematical, Verbal/Linguistic**

G2 Critical Thinking Skills

Critical Listening Ask volunteers to share any knowledge they may have of the Hebrew or Arabic languages. Provide an opportunity for students to listen to samples of spoken Hebrew and Arabic. Ask them to compare and contrast the languages with each other and then with English. Lead a class discussion on the importance of language to cultural identity and how language affects unity among common speakers in the subregion. **Auditory/Musical**

V Visual Skills

Analyzing Have students study the image of the family. **Ask:** **What does this image reveal about the culture of many families in the Eastern Mediterranean?** *(Possible answers: Many families include extended families in which grandparents and other family members may live with them; they live simply with limited furnishings.)* **What does this image reveal about the culture of these people?** *(Some people have adopted Western styles, as shown in the clothing the children wear. The man is wearing both traditional and Western styles, but the woman continues to wear traditional clothing.)* **ELL** **Visual/Spatial**

GRAPHIC ORGANIZER

Human Geography of the Eastern Mediterranean

Organizing Have students work with a partner to fill in this graphic organizer with content they have learned in this lesson. Students should consider how migrations, claims to ancestral homes, and boundary disputes have influenced population patterns in the Eastern Mediterranean. **ELL** **Verbal/Linguistic, Visual/Spatial**

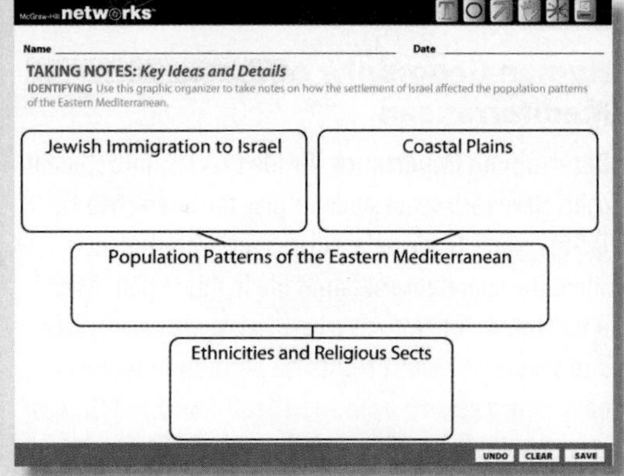

ANSWERS, p. 399

✓ READING PROGRESS CHECK After a large influx of Russian Jews in the 1990s, more than 67 percent of Israel's Jews are native born. Conflicts in the region and resettlement programs caused over four million Palestinians to settle in refugee camps in Syria, Lebanon, and Jordan.

CRITICAL THINKING

1. It appears to be an extended family.
2. Student answers will vary based on the family makeup of the student.

R Reading Skills

Organizing As students read the information in *Family and Status of Women,* have them complete a three-column chart with the headings *Political, Economic,* and *Social.* Have them list under each heading the important rights and regulations that women have faced in the subregion. Have students initiate small group discussions using their individual charts as guides. **ELL Visual/Spatial**

W1 Writing Skills

Informative/Explanatory Have students read the section *The Arts* and then write a one-page informative article on common themes in the arts of the Eastern Mediterranean. Provide this prompt to students: **How is art influenced by the subregion's history and ethnic and religious conflicts?** Point out that students should include information about historical and modern-day influences. Suggest that students search online or in library resources for specific examples of art, literature, poetry, or music to cite in their papers. **AL Verbal/Linguistic, Auditory/Musical**

W2 Writing Skills

Informative/Explanatory Have students read about the important resources and economic activities for each country in the subregion and study the unit economic activity map. Ask students to provide a brief summary about why certain economic activities are more prominent in some countries and to note which countries in the subregion have the most diversified economies. **BL Naturalist, Verbal/Linguistic**

Making Connections

Point out to students that in the last decade or more, high-tech industries have grown in the Eastern Mediterranean and in many other regions and subregions around the world. Invite volunteers to share specific examples of products or services supplied by high-tech industries. Have students determine whether their community and state have a large high-tech sector. Ask them to make a list of the major products and services that come from that sector.

ANSWERS, p. 400

READING PROGRESS CHECK Political themes are now the focus of painters in Jordan and Syria, literature is centered on social realism of the present, and Israeli art shows the insecurity and tensions the small country is experiencing.

Connecting Geography Internet-based information allowed people to be instantly informed of developments in Egypt, Libya, and Syria.

Connecting Geography to **ECONOMICS**

Development

Development projects sponsored by non-governmental organizations (NGOs) and private donors are introducing changes to the region. Two-thirds of Syrian homes have a satellite dish providing access to foreign television broadcasts. The role of the Internet and cellular phones in mobilizing people during the Arab Spring emphasized the importance of technology. The bloggers and social media users were informed instantly of developments in the revolts in Egypt, Libya, and later Syria. The Internet also improves the quality of life for individuals. Cell phones give access to information about health care, local food markets, and transportation. Investments in the communications infrastructures contribute to a more informed, connected society.

EXPLAINING How did access to Internet-based information affect the protest movements of the Arab Spring?

Affordable health care is something each country strives to achieve. Hospitals are often government-owned. However, such hospitals are crowded. As a result, Lebanon, Jordan, and Syria have private hospitals that provide equal or better health care at a higher cost. Both public and private health care facilities are generally located in urban areas. Rural dispensaries are available to treat minor health issues. In Israel medical insurance is mandatory for all citizens, partially subsidized by the government, and of high quality.

Family and Status of Women

R

Family life usually includes the extended family and often involves religious worship. Marriage, property, and in some cases divorce are a combination of civil and religious law. Religious laws differ among ethnic groups and guide arranged marriages and the division of property upon divorce.

In Israel, women generally enjoy equal rights. Women's rights in the Arab world have been changing drastically in the past few decades. In some countries women drive cars, own property, obtain advanced education, and pursue high-level jobs in government and industry. In other places, girls and women have few opportunities outside the home. They have restricted social interactions and attend schools set aside for girls. While government regulations provide legal rights for girls and women, the exercise of those rights may vary greatly from place to place. The greatest changes have been made in urban places where opportunities are more numerous. Women participated in large numbers in the Arab Spring in 2011. This participation was a clear indication of their increased influence on political and social issues.

The Arts

W1

For thousands of years, the peoples of the Eastern Mediterranean have expressed themselves through the arts and architecture. Artists and writers have also found inspiration in religion. Muslim scholars wrote about Islamic achievements and translated Greek writings into Arabic. These works later added to European knowledge about the ancient world. Syrian, Jordanian, and Lebanese poetry, which addressed themes such as female beauty, spirituality, and love, rivaled those of the Europeans. The poetry of the early people of the subregion also influenced Roman culture and thought. Arabs have been forging new methods for creativity and expression for centuries.

Paintings by Jordanian and Syrian artists have come to center on political themes. New expressions of romantic literature have removed the past and focused on the social realism of the present. Palestinian refugees have contributed to Syrian, Jordanian, and Lebanese social realism. The art forms of Israel reflect the insecurity and tensions of a country that occupies a relatively small area.

READING PROGRESS CHECK

Describing In what ways has art changed in Eastern Mediterranean countries?

W2 Economic Activities

GUIDING QUESTION *What has spurred economic growth in the Eastern Mediterranean?*

Large percentages of the world's known oil and natural gas reserves lie in North Africa, Central Asia, and Southwest Asia. However, oil resources are not distributed evenly. The Eastern Mediterranean is not well endowed with oil. Economic growth has been dependent upon agriculture, relatively small deposits of minerals, and manufacturing.

rely to be dependent

output something produced; a mineral, agricultural, or industrial production

400

networks ***Online Teaching Options***

GAME

Human Geography of the Eastern Mediterranean

Determining Importance Divide the class into student pairs. Have each set of students play the interactive Tic-Tac-Toe game. Guide a class discussion with students about the importance of family life in this region. **Ask: What importance does worship play in family life and tradition? What rights do women in Israel have compared to women in Arab families?** *(Student answers will vary, but should be supported by information supported in the text.)* **Visual/Spatial, Verbal/Linguistic**

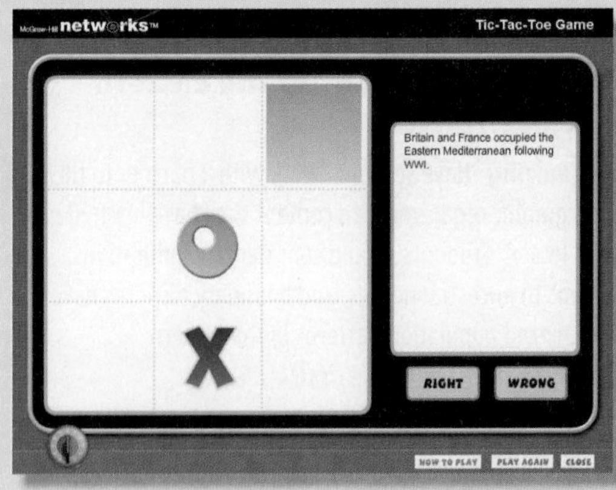

Resources, Power, and Industry

In recent years Israel has been exploring deposits of natural gas offshore in the Eastern Mediterranean. In addition to its investments in natural gas, Israel maintains a diversified economy with support from the international market. Lebanon and Jordan do not have significant natural resources to export. As a result, their economies **rely** on other exports, largely agricultural products, with the help of foreign investments.

Service industries play significant roles in the subregion's economies. For example, Israel's growing high-tech sector accounts for the largest share of the country's overall manufacturing **output**. Tourism is typically another profitable industry. Ancient monuments, sacred religious sites, sunny Mediterranean beaches, and archaeological sites attract visitors. However, conflicts and instability in Syria, Israel, the Palestinian territories, and Lebanon have negatively affected tourism.

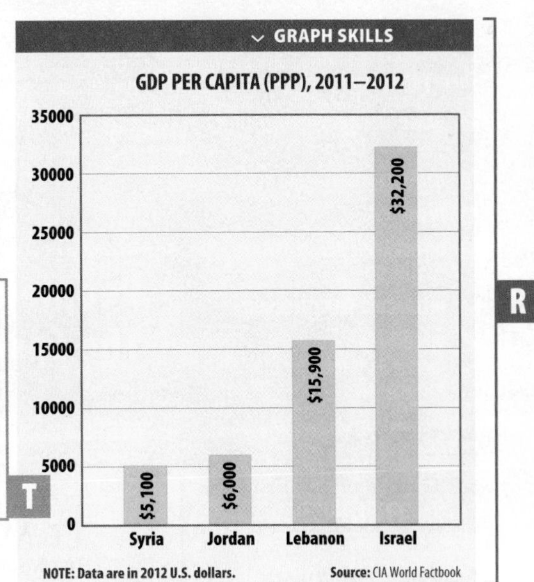

The economies of the Eastern Mediterranean countries are based on the resources available in each country.

▲ CRITICAL THINKING

1. ***Contrasting*** How does Israel's GDP compare to that of the other Eastern Mediterranean countries?
2. ***Assessing*** How can countries that lack natural resources maintain a high GDP?

Trade and Transport

Road systems are unevenly distributed across the subregion. In some countries, mountains and deserts make road building difficult and costly. In recent years, however, economic development and the growing number of vehicles have resulted in the construction of more roads. Since World War II, the growth of the air travel industry has benefited the Eastern Mediterranean. All major cities are transportation centers for goods and people.

Water transportation is vital to the subregion. Ships load and unload cargo at ports along the Mediterranean Sea. The Strait of Tirān—which links the Gulf of Aqaba and the Red Sea—is of strategic and economic importance. It is the gateway to Jordan's only port city, Aqaba. A pipeline transports oil from Iraq to Aqaba. Canned and processed fruits and fish products are exported to many places.

✓ READING PROGRESS CHECK

Describing How have Eastern Mediterranean countries diversified their economies?

LESSON 2 REVIEW (CCSS)

Reviewing Vocabulary (Tier Three Words)

1. ***Labeling*** Define the following terms and use each one appropriately in a sentence: monotheism, prophet, and mosque. RH.9–10.4

Using Your Notes

2. ***Summarizing*** Use your graphic organizer to describe how the settlement of Israel has affected the population patterns of the Eastern Mediterranean.

Answering the Guiding Questions

3. ***Stating*** How have Judaism, Christianity, and Islam shaped the politics and culture of the Eastern Mediterranean?
4. ***Classifying*** How have migrations, claims to ancestral homes, and boundary disputes affected population patterns in the Eastern Mediterranean?
5. ***Making Connections*** How has history influenced the society and culture of the Eastern Mediterranean today?
6. ***Synthesizing*** What has spurred economic growth in the Eastern Mediterranean?

Writing Activity

7. ***Informative/Explanatory*** Choose one Eastern Mediterranean country. Research to write a paragraph describing how the country's political history is linked to its economic activities today. WHST.9–10.2

T Technology Skills

Presenting Have small groups find out more about Eastern Mediterranean tourist attractions. Have them create a tourism infomercial for one of the attractions, using video clips, photographs, and audio. Have groups share their infomercials with the class. **Visual/Spatial, Verbal/Linguistic**

R Reading Skills

Reading Graphs Review that GDP measures all the goods and services produced in a country. **Ask:** **Why is Israel's GDP higher than that of Syria, Jordan, and Lebanon?** *(Israel has more resources available to develop into products and services.)* **What might happen to Israel's GDP if its natural gas deposits run out?** *(Israel may have to diversify its economy or its GDP may decrease.)* AL **Logical/Mathematical**

CLOSE & REFLECT

Summarizing Review how political instability and conflict have shaped the region's development. Have students summarize the subregion's primary economic activities and the affects of these activities to cultural traditions.

ANSWERS, p. 401

✓ READING PROGRESS CHECK Eastern Mediterranean countries have relied on the international market, natural gas and oil deposits, and exports to diversify their economies.

CRITICAL THINKING

1. Israel has a much higher GDP than other Eastern Mediterranean countries.
2. They must rely on other exports and foreign investments to increase their GDP.

LESSON 2 REVIEW ANSWERS

Reviewing Vocabulary

1. Sentence examples will vary but should fit the definitions of: **monotheism**—"the belief in one God"; **prophet**—"person believed to be a messenger from God"; **mosque**—"a house of worship for those who practice Islam"

Using Your Notes

2. Israel was created after World War II as a homeland for Jews. This resulted in a large influx of Jews from other places in the world and a displacement of Arab Palestinians to other countries in the Eastern Mediterranean.

Answering the Guiding Questions

3. Religion has often been the source of conflict both within and between countries. The religion of the ruling parties has influenced the daily lives of the people of the Eastern Mediterranean.
4. Claims to ancestral homes brought large numbers of Jews to Israel; this movement and boundary disputes led to the displacement of over four million Palestinians to Syria, Lebanon, and Jordan.
5. History has helped define the religions and languages of Eastern Mediterranean countries. Religious practices are often the center of family life, and religious laws often dictate what opportunities are available for women.
6. Economic growth has been dependent on agriculture, small mineral deposits, and manufacturing.

Writing Activity

7. Paragraphs will vary based on country chosen, but should describe political changes such as war or changes in government in connection to current economic activities.

ENGAGE

R Reading Skills

Speculating After students read *It Matters Because,* have them speculate about some of the possible effects of human activities on the environment in the Eastern Mediterranean. Ask them to make connections to their own region's environmental issues.

TEACH & ASSESS

C Critical Thinking Skills

Posing Questions Have students work with a partner to compile a list of questions that should be asked in order to examine the issues of overfishing and water pollution in the Mediterranean Sea. Ask pairs to share their questions with the class to create a two-column chart, listing the questions in the left column. As students work through the lesson, have them revisit the chart and identify possible solutions that can be added to the right column. AL **Visual/Spatial, Logical/Mathematical**

T Technology Skills

Creating Diagrams Have students work in small groups to research the tectonic plates that meet in the Eastern Mediterranean subregion. They should then create a diagram that shows the movement of the plates and how this movement affects the landforms in the subregion. Encourage students to use animation and computer presentation software. Explain that their diagrams should be annotated to explain how the process occurs and how it affects the subregion. Provide an opportunity for students to share their presentations with the class. BL **Naturalist**

networks *There's More Online!*

- **IMAGE** High-Tech Greenhouse in Israel
- **IMAGE** Landfill in Lebanon
- **IMAGE** Oases
- **INFOGRAPHIC** Managing Israel's Water Resources
- **INTERACTIVE SELF-CHECK QUIZ**
- **VIDEO** People and Their Environment: The Eastern Mediterranean

CONSERVATION

RAINFALL is scarce, leaving little fresh drinkable water.

DRIP IRRIGATION helps conserve water and is used in more than 90% of Israel's agriculture.

LESSON 3
People and Their Environment: The Eastern Mediterranean

ESSENTIAL QUESTION • *How do physical systems and human systems shape a place?*

Reading HELPDESK CCSS

Academic Vocabulary (Tier Two Words)

- **preliminary**
- **adequate**

Content Vocabulary (Tier Three Words)

- **fertilizer**
- **pesticide**
- **desertification**
- **overgrazing**

TAKING NOTES: ***Key Ideas and Details***

SUMMARIZING Use a graphic organizer like the one below to take notes on the ways agricultural pollutants affect the Eastern Mediterranean.

Eastern Mediterranean: People and Their Environment	
Agricultural Pollutants	Process of Desertification

It Matters Because

R *The Eastern Mediterranean subregion has a long and important history of human habitation and human impact on the environment. That impact has become an increasingly serious problem that some people and governments are currently addressing.*

Managing Resources

GUIDING QUESTION *What resources are at risk in the Eastern Mediterranean?*

C The Mediterranean Sea is at risk for a number of reasons. Overfishing, contamination, a rise in sea surface temperatures due to climate change, and the introduction of invasive species have all caused environmental damage. The Suez Canal connects the Red Sea to the Mediterranean Sea, allowing invasive species to enter. Invasive fish from the Red Sea have left Eastern Mediterranean reefs almost bare of native species and have greatly changed the ecology of the region. Also, the waters of the Eastern Mediterranean have been nearly depleted of fish due to overfishing. Another problem caused by human activity is water pollution. Sewage, oil spills, and chemical **fertilizers** and **pesticides** used for agriculture contaminate the Mediterranean Sea and have limited its use as a water source. The pollutants have also contributed to the vast depletion of marine life. Water pollution affects the limited number of freshwater supplies in the area and adds to the region's problem of water scarcity.

T Several tectonic plates meet in the Eastern Mediterranean Sea. This contact zone is an interesting deep-sea terrain with unique landforms and aquatic life. Scientists have only recently begun to study the ecosystems of these deep waters. They still have much to learn. However, because the fish resources of the continental shelf (the areas between the shoreline and the deeper waters) are seriously depleted, Mediterranean commercial fishers are turning to these deep-sea habitats as a new source of fish. This is putting additional strain on the natural resources of the Eastern Mediterranean subregion.

(tl)Paul Gapper/Alamy, (tc)©Tomasz Grzyb/Demotix/Corbis, (tr)©Pallava Bagla/Corbis

402

networks *Online Teaching Options*

INTERACTIVE BELLRINGER

Desertification in Syria

Analyzing Cause and Effect Use the introductory text to identify the causes and effects of the human impact on the environment in the Eastern Mediterranean. Have students form small groups and discuss their prior knowledge of overcropping and overgrazing in both the United States and other countries. Then have them discuss each question. Ask each group to write agreed-upon answers to the questions. Then in a class discussion, have each group share its answers. **Interpersonal, Verbal/Linguistic**

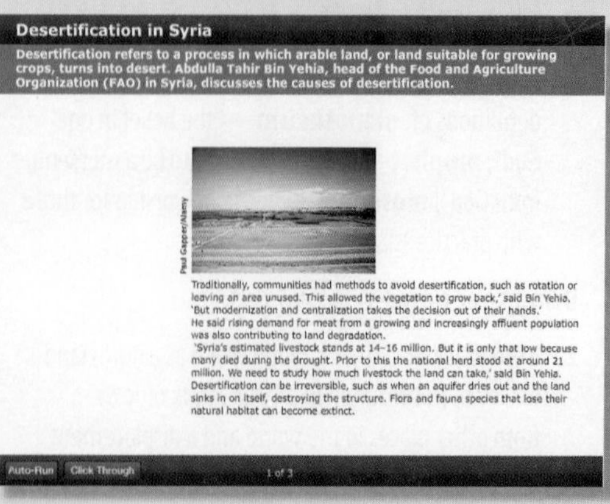

ANSWERS, p. 402

TAKING NOTES: Agricultural Pollutants—Fertilizers and pesticides used on crops run off into the water systems of the Eastern Mediterranean. This depletes marine life and pollutes the waters. **Process of Desertification**—process in which arable land is turned into desert by overgrazing and deforestation. Lebanon was once almost completely covered by forest. Today, only 5 percent remains forested.

Air pollution is also a serious problem in the Eastern Mediterranean. High levels of urbanization and immigration to the area in the past few decades have increased air pollution. Unplanned urbanization not only strains city services but also amplifies the air pollution problem produced largely by using old buses and taxis for transportation in densely populated urban communities. The unregulated burning of fossil fuels and wood for heating also contributes to air pollution. Air pollution problems have been difficult to address, mainly due to long-term unrest in the subregion and a resulting lack of environmental policies and services.

Heat waves in the subregion compound the problems of air pollution in these cities. Air pollutants have also been linked to health hazards. In the past few years, an increasing number of patients have been admitted to hospitals for respiratory diseases. Many cases of respiratory diseases are a result of poor air quality. **C**

The wetlands of the Eastern Mediterranean are another resource at risk. They serve as an important stopping place for over 250 species of migratory birds. In Lebanon, the Aammiq Wetland is the most significant remaining freshwater wetland in the country. The area covered by the Aammiq today is only a remnant of the marshes and lakes that once existed. Bird populations in the region also face serious threat from hunters. The government of Lebanon banned hunting in 1994, but environmental groups report that the hunting laws are ignored. Soaring aquatic birds and raptors are most at risk. This is a worldwide issue since these birds migrate to and from breeding grounds outside the subregion.

☑ READING PROGRESS CHECK

Identifying What risks to human health are posed by pollution in the Eastern Mediterranean?

fertilizer a chemical or natural substance added to soil or land to increase its fertility

pesticide a chemical used to kill insects, rodents, and other pests

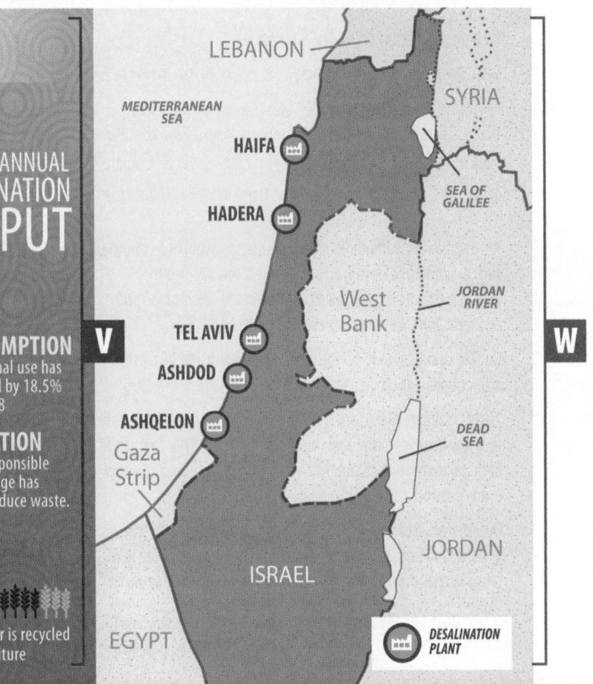

V **W**

Although desalination is expensive, more countries are using it as alternative water sources become scarce.

▼ CRITICAL THINKING

1. ***Assessing*** What is Israel's annual desalination output? How much of the country's drinking water is obtained from desalination?
2. ***Evaluating*** Describe the progress Israel has made in regard to water conservation.

CHAPTER 16, Lesson 3
People and Their Environment: The Eastern Mediterranean

C Critical Thinking Skills

Recognizing Counter Arguments Point out that air pollution is caused by different factors, including human actions and climate change. **Ask:** **What are some examples of human actions that cause air pollution?** *(urbanization, transportation, burning of fossil fuels)* **What are some examples of the climate causing air pollution?** *(heat waves)* Explain that environmentalists argue that human actions affect air pollution and climate change through global warming. **Ask:** **What counter argument could you make to refute this claim?** *(Possible answer: Some climate change is the result of natural causes.)* Challenge students to think of other causes of climate change that are not related to the burning of fossil fuels. **BL** **Logical/Mathematical**

V Visual Skills

Interpreting Visuals Direct students to the infographic about how Israel manages its water resources. **Ask:** **Why do you think Israel is the world leader in water recycling?** *(Possible answer: Israel's leaders realize the importance of reusing and conserving water.)* **What is a logical reason for Israel taking this initiative?** *(Possible answer: Water is scarce in the subregion and yet vital to the country's agriculture. Due to the political instability of this subregion, Israel must be self-reliant.)* **AL** **Visual/Spatial, Logical/Mathematical**

W Writing Skills

Argument Have students research how desalination is being used in the subregion. Ask them to write an editorial about the importance of desalinating water, using specific examples from this subregion as supporting points. Remind students to address counterarguments with rebuttals and to clearly state their thesis. **Verbal/Linguistic**

INTERACTIVE WHITEBOARD ACTIVITY

Managing Israel's Water Resources

Analyzing Visuals This interactive whiteboard activity has students reference an infographic to answer statements that pertain to Israel's water resources. Explain to students that as alternative water sources become scarce, more countries are using desalination to increase water supply. Have students work in small groups to research one of the conservation measures listed in the infographic. Then ask groups to share their findings with the class. **Verbal/Linguistic**

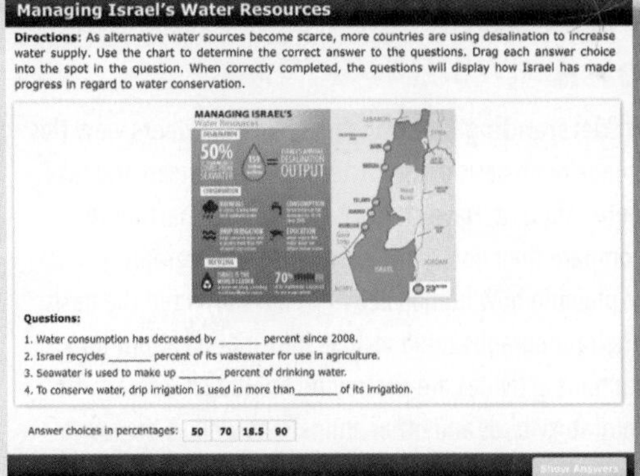

ANSWERS, p. 403

☑ READING PROGRESS CHECK Air pollution is causing an increasing number of respiratory illnesses and diseases.

CRITICAL THINKING

1. Israel produces 159 billion gallons of water through desalination each year. Fifty percent of the country's drinking water is obtained through desalination.
2. Israel is the world leader in water recycling, using 70 percent of its wastewater in agriculture. Israel also conserves water by practicing drip irrigation for crops. Education programs have led to an 18.5 percent decrease in water consumption since 2008.

CHAPTER 16, Lesson 3

People and Their Environment: The Eastern Mediterranean

R Reading Skills

Specifying As a class, discuss and define *deforestation, desertification,* and *overgrazing.* **Ask:** Based on what you have read about deforestation, desertification, and overgrazing in the subregion, which one is the effect of the other two? *(Desertification is caused by overgrazing and deforestation.)* If overgrazing and deforestation are controlled, how will the physical environment be impacted? *(Possible answer: Desertification will decrease, and more land will be available for agriculture as long as a source for irrigation is available.)* Ask students to work with a partner to write an action plan for the people of the Eastern Mediterranean to help control overgrazing and deforestation. AL Verbal/Linguistic

C Critical Thinking Skills

Understanding Relationships Among Events Discuss with students how the geography of the Eastern Mediterranean lends itself to deforestation and overgrazing. **Ask:** In what geographical area are trees and vegetation a limited resource? *(near the coast and in the desert)* Discuss how a lack of vegetation and a semi-arid climate can contribute to desertification and how the need for resources that are competitive in the global market affects human activities. Have students form small groups to discuss how replanting cedars and conservation efforts could impact the subregion. AL Naturalist, Interpersonal

Content Background Knowledge

Early Deforestation of Lebanon's Cedar The destruction of Lebanon's cedar trees was described by the Greek poet Homer, the Greek philosopher Plato, the Roman writer Pliny, and the writers of the Old Testament of the Bible. They described a vast sea of cedar trees in this area. Rulers ordered that they be cut down in order to use the wood to build temples and monuments. King Solomon built the first temple in Jerusalem with cedars from Lebanon. After the trees were chopped down, workers transported them by raft on the sea to Israel. Cedar trees continue to be an important resource in this region.

ANSWERS, p. 404

DBQ Document-Based Questions

1. Crop rotation or leaving land unused allowed for natural vegetation to grow back, which prevented desertification.
2. Desertification can be irreversible when an aquifer dries out and the land collapses in on itself.

Human Impact

GUIDING QUESTION *What human activities have affected the physical environment of the Eastern Mediterranean?*

desertification process in which arable land becomes desert

overgrazing grazing so heavily that the vegetation is damaged and the ground erodes

R Long-term deforestation and desertification are other problems in the Eastern Mediterranean. **Desertification** refers to a process in which arable land, or land that is suitable for growing crops, turns into desert. Desertification is caused by a number of factors, such as **overgrazing** and deforestation. Overgrazing in certain areas of Syria and Jordan has led to the desertification of grasslands and deforestation of the mountain ranges. This change has contributed to climate change in the subregion. Overgrazing is also a significant cause of soil erosion.

C Lebanon's legendary forests have a long history of exploitation. During the Middle Ages the forests were cleared for farmland, and trees were used for fuel and construction. In the early 1900s, the Ottomans controlled much of the Eastern Mediterranean. They pursued a policy of very aggressive deforestation in order to fuel their railways and keep up with industrialized Europe. The forests continue to face threats from overgrazing, unregulated tourism, and a high occurrence of forest fires. Lebanon had once been almost completely covered in forests, but by 2012 just 5 percent of the land was covered with forest. The Lebanese cedar—long a prized symbol of the country—survives today only in a small number of patches, although there have been efforts to conserve

ANALYZING PRIMARY SOURCES CCSS

Desertification in Syria

The UN has stated that 80 percent of Syria's land is at risk for desertification. The causes include both human-made and natural factors. Abdulla Tahir Bin Yehia, head of the Food and Agriculture Organization (FAO) in Syria, discusses the causes of desertification.

"'Traditionally, communities had methods to avoid desertification, such as rotation or leaving an area unused. This allowed the vegetation to grow back,' said Bin Yehia. 'But modernization and centralization takes the decision out of their hands.'

He said rising demand for meat from a growing and increasingly affluent population was also contributing to land degradation.

'Syria's estimated livestock stands at 14–16 million. But it is only that low because many died during the drought. Prior to this the national herd stood at around 21 million. We need to study how much livestock the land can take,' said Bin Yehia.

Desertification can be irreversible, such as when an aquifer dries out and the land sinks in on itself, destroying the structure. Flora and fauna species that lose their natural habitat can become extinct."

—United Nations, "Syria: Act Now to Stop Desertification, Says FAO," *Humanitarian News and Analysis*, June 15, 2010

Modern farming practices in Syria do not allow fields to lie fallow. This puts them at risk for desertification when droughts occur.

Paul Gapper/Alamy

DBQ ▲ CRITICAL THINKING

1. ***Assessing*** How did traditional methods protect the land from desertification? RH.9–10.1
2. ***Describing*** How can desertification become irreversible? RH.9–10.1

404

networks Online Teaching Options

SLIDE SHOW

Oasis

Understanding Relationships Have students view this image of an oasis in the Eastern Mediterranean and take notes about it. Have students work with a partner to compare their notes, and then write a paragraph explaining how human activities have affected the oasis. Their paragraphs could include information about how humans activities are destroying habitats necessary for migratory birds and other animals, as well as the loss of flora and fauna species. Invite pairs to share their paragraphs in a class discussion. AL Verbal/Linguistic

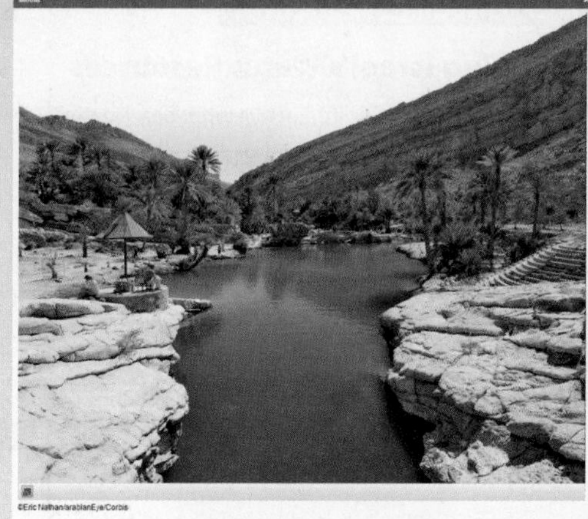

©Eric Nathan/arabianEye/Corbis

and protect these trees. This deforestation destroys animal habitats. As a result, large mammals such as wolves and wild boars—as well as migratory birds that stop in the forests on their way from Europe to Africa—are endangered.

Agriculture is one of Israel's most highly developed economic activities. It remains successful despite the lack of freshwater resources in the country. Israeli lands are not naturally suited to large-scale agricultural production. Only about 15 percent of Israel's land is arable. One major source of water for irrigation is from Lake Tiberias (the Sea of Galilee). It is an important freshwater source for the subregion. In Israel, water is carried through canals in the National Water Carrier project built in the 1960s. Desalination plants and water recycling programs also provide water for agricultural irrigation. Israel will need to find new sources of freshwater as its agricultural sector grows. New agricultural methods to increase crop yields will also become important as land is exhausted.

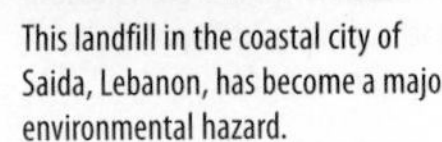

This landfill in the coastal city of Saida, Lebanon, has become a major environmental hazard.

▲ CRITICAL THINKING

1. ***Hypothesizing*** Why might a city locate a landfill along the coast?
2. ***Sequencing*** How do landfills cause the pollution of waterways?

V

✓ READING PROGRESS CHECK

Explaining Why has Lebanon experienced so much deforestation?

Addressing the Issues

GUIDING QUESTION *How are environmental issues being addressed in the Eastern Mediterranean?*

In recent years, Eastern Mediterranean governments have made real attempts to address serious environmental issues. In 2011 the Israeli Clean Air Law came into effect. This legislation provides a framework for reducing air pollution by imposing responsibilities on national and local government authorities and the country's industrial plants. The law aims to improve air quality and protect biodiversity. Also in 2011, the Ministry of the Environment in Lebanon, working with the United Nations Environmental Program, launched a project whose goal is sustainable management of marine and coastal biodiversity.

C

The Jordanian government has instituted an environmental education program in schools to address that country's severe water shortage. The importance of maintaining biodiversity in the country is also taught as part of the program. The Royal Society for the Conservation of Nature (RSCN) is an organization in Jordan with broad authority to manage the natural resources of the country. It has outlawed semiautomatic hunting weapons in Jordan. The government has determined how many and what types of animals can be hunted in any given season. The RSCN has also addressed biodiversity by planning a system of wildlife reserves. One success story is that of the Arabian oryx, a type of antelope with large horns. The Arabian oryx was extinct in the

©Tomasz Gzyb/Demotix/Corbis

VIDEO

Israel-Palestine Water

Identifying Bias Use this video about freshwater usage and control to discuss the water crisis issue between Israel and the Palestinian territories. As they view the video, ask students to list varying points of view or what may be considered bias views about water rations and the environmental effects of the Sea of Galilee. Have them write a sentence or two summarizing each bias and identify whether it is an Israeli or Palestinian point of view. Then discuss how water scarcity concerns in this region could lead to conflict or help to restore peace. **Verbal/Linguistic**

V Visual Skills

Problem Solving Discuss the image with students, explaining how landfills work and why they are used. If possible, show a diagram or a cross-section of a closed landfill. **Ask: Why do you think people in this area resorted to dumping trash along the coastline as shown in this image?** *(Possible answer: Landfills are full, and there is nowhere else to put the trash. Programs are not in place to recycle plastic, paper, and metals.)* **Ask: What risks do illegal landfills pose?** *(Possible answers: contamination of groundwater, land degradation, water pollution)* As a class, brainstorm possible solutions to the problem of illegal landfills. **ELL Visual/Spatial, Naturalist**

Content Background Knowledge

Cloud Seeding Israel has implemented cloud seeding to produce rain. To perform cloud seeding, a plane sprays silver iodide crystals into clouds in winter. These crystals help to form water droplets, which produce precipitation. Israel has had much success with cloud seeding. Scientists have been able to increase rainfall by about 15 percent in the area around Galilee. Cloud seeding has its opponents, however, and many scientists believe that weather patterns, not cloud seeding, bring larger amounts of precipitation.

C Critical Thinking Skills

Evaluating Invite a volunteer to read the section *Addressing the Issues.* **Ask: Which countries in the subregion are taking action to protect the environment, as described in the text?** *(Israel, Lebanon, Jordan)* Discuss with students what efforts have been made. **Ask: Do you think there have been enough collaborative efforts, in the subregion, region, and globally? Explain.** *(Possible answer: Yes, there has been some subregional and global collaboration, but more action is needed. Many countries in the region face similar environmental problems and may benefit from working together.)* **What factors might influence collaboration?** *(Possible answers: political, ethnic, and religious conflict)* Have students select one issue mentioned in the text and write a paragraph persuading the leaders of the countries in this subregion to work together to resolve the issue. **AL Verbal/Linguistic**

ANSWERS, p. 405

✓ **READING PROGRESS CHECK** The forests have been cleared throughout history for farmland, fuel, and construction, particularly during the reign of the Ottomans, who used timber to fuel railways. Deforestation continued with overgrazing, unregulated tourism, and forest fires.

CRITICAL THINKING

1. A landfill might be located along the coast because it is outside the city away from the majority of the population.
2. Landfills located too close to waterways can cause trash and other pollutants to enter into the water system.

R Reading Skills

Interpreting Continue the dialogue with students about the importance and the impact of collaborative efforts to address environmental issues in the subregion. **Ask:** What does the presence of so many international organizations in the Eastern Mediterranean indicate? *(that the international community is concerned and is committed to helping the subregion address these issues)* Why do you think the initial step in addressing these issues has focused on legislation? *(Possible answer: Once laws are in place, governments can take action if they are broken.)* Why have governments been reluctant to push ahead with environmental projects? *(lack of funding, other issues to deal with such as political, ethnic, and religious conflicts)* AL Logical/Mathematical

W Writing Skills

Informative/Explanatory Discuss with students that a lot of work is still ahead, despite some action by governments to protect the environment. Provide one of the following topics for students to write an essay: energy-efficient transportation systems, sustainable fishing methods, or controlling and restricting agricultural runoff. Ask students to research any legislation, action plans, and initiatives that countries in the subregion have taken in the past five years or plan to take in the next five years. Challenge students to include charts, graphs, or other visuals to illustrate data. BL Verbal/Linguistic, Visual/Spatial

CLOSE & REFLECT

Outlining To close the lesson, have students look back through the headings and subheadings in each section and use them to outline the main ideas and details of the lesson. Remind students to include only the main or central ideas and important supporting details. Have them compare their outlines with those of a partner for accuracy.

New agricultural methods, such as those in this high-tech greenhouse in Israel, are being developed to increase crop yields.

▲CRITICAL THINKING

1. ***Assessing*** Why is it important for governments to collaborate with international organizations in developing new agricultural methods?
2. ***Speculating*** How could research help increase agricultural yields?

preliminary something done in preparation for something more important

adequate satisfactory or acceptable

wild but was reintroduced to the wild in the Azraq wetlands in the deserts of eastern Jordan in 1978. The populations have since thrived under legal protection from hunters and habitat loss.

R A number of international organizations have offices throughout the Eastern Mediterranean. These include the United Nations Development Program (UNDP), the World Wildlife Fund (WWF), and the International Union for the Conservation of Nature (IUCN). Their urgent projects address desertification, unsustainable water extraction and use, biodiversity and habitat loss, and threats to sensitive marine ecosystems. The **preliminary** plan for most of these organizations is to address environmental issues by introducing legislation. They have been unsuccessful in getting most governments to take environmental projects seriously because most projects that are put on legislative agendas are severely underfunded. Local nongovernmental organizations, such as the Society for the Protection of Nature in Lebanon, also address environmental issues. However, these organizations are generally smaller and less effective than international environmental organizations.

In 2003 the WWF began a campaign to protect the cedar trees of Lebanon from fires and destruction caused by overgrazing. Fires threaten about 28 percent of Lebanon's forests. The project, which has met with some success, utilizes information and communication technologies (ICTs) to achieve its goal of protecting the endangered forests.

W All governments in the subregion could more **adequately** address air and water pollution. Investing in energy-efficient public transportation systems would help alleviate the air pollution caused by urbanization. Furthermore, marine life could gradually increase in the Mediterranean Sea if countries would employ sustainable fishing methods and legislate to protect the sea from agricultural runoff and other pollution.

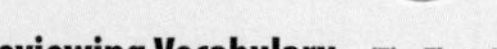

✓ **READING PROGRESS CHECK**

Describing How has the Jordanian government addressed the issue of water scarcity in the country?

LESSON 3 REVIEW CCSS

Reviewing Vocabulary (Tier Three Words)

1. ***Naming*** Define overgrazing and desertification and write two sentences describing the connection between them. RH.9–10.4

Using Your Notes

2. ***Explaining*** Use your notes from your graphic organizer to describe the impact of agricultural pollutants in the Eastern Mediterranean.

Answering the Guiding Questions

3. ***Stating*** What resources are at risk in the Eastern Mediterranean?
4. ***Categorizing*** What human activities have affected the physical environment of the Eastern Mediterranean?
5. ***Differentiating*** How are environmental issues being addressed in the Eastern Mediterranean?

Writing Activity

6. ***Informative/Explanatory*** Pick one of the international organizations discussed in the lesson. Using the Internet to search its website, pick one of its Eastern Mediterranean projects. Write a paragraph identifying the main issue that the project seeks to address, why the issue is important, and what the organization plans to do about the issue. WHST.9–10.2

406

ANSWERS, p. 406

✓ **READING PROGRESS CHECK** The government created an educational program in schools to address the water shortages facing the country.

CRITICAL THINKING

1. Collaboration with international organizations is useful to find ways to increase crop yields that also protect the environment and make the best use of natural resources.
2. Student answers may vary but could include finding new crops that thrive with little water and discovering ways to make crops drought, disease, and pest resistant.

LESSON 3 REVIEW ANSWERS

Reviewing Vocabulary

1. **overgrazing**—grazing by livestock to such an extent that the vegetation is destroyed and the ground erodes; **desertification**—process in which arable land becomes desert

Using Your Notes

2. Fertilizers and pesticides used on crops run off into the waters of the Eastern Mediterranean. This depletes marine life and pollutes the water systems.

Answering the Guiding Questions

3. Fish, coral reefs, forests, wetlands, and water supplies are all at risk in the Eastern Mediterranean.
4. Unregulated tourism, overfishing, deforestation for farmland and fuel, and desertification from overgrazing and poor agricultural methods are ways human activities have impacted the environment.
5. Jordan created educational programs to address water shortages and the RSCN manages its natural resources. The Israeli Clean Air Law (2011) reduces air pollution and protects biodiversity. The UNDP, the WWF, and the IUCN are working to introduce legislation to protect the environment. In Lebanon, the WWF is working to protect cedar trees and the Society for the Protection of Nature to protect the environment.

Writing Activity

6. Paragraphs will vary, but must describe an organization and project that involve an Eastern Mediterranean country.

CHAPTER 16 Assessment 

Directions: On a separate sheet of paper, answer the questions below. Make sure you read carefully and answer all parts of the questions.

Lesson Review

Lesson 1

1. ***Making Generalizations*** How do water systems and water scarcity affect economic activities in the Eastern Mediterranean?

2. ***Describing*** How does the climate change as one travels inland, away from coastal regions, in the Eastern Mediterranean?

3. ***Explaining*** Why do some economies in the Eastern Mediterranean subregion often fluctuate, or rise and fall, in the global market?

Lesson 2

4. ***Exploring Issues*** How have political activities affected settlement and population patterns in the Eastern Mediterranean?

5. ***Analyzing*** What activities have encouraged economic growth in the economies of the Eastern Mediterranean?

6. ***Making Connections*** Why is the Eastern Mediterranean an important connection between Judaism, Christianity, and Islam?

Lesson 3

7. ***Finding the Main Idea*** How have human activities affected the Eastern Mediterranean environment?

8. ***Making Connections*** What efforts have been made to preserve natural resources in the Eastern Mediterranean?

9. ***Evaluating*** How successful have international organizations been at addressing environmental issues in the Eastern Mediterranean?

21st Century Skills

Use the graph to answer the following questions.

ETHNIC GROUPS IN ISRAEL

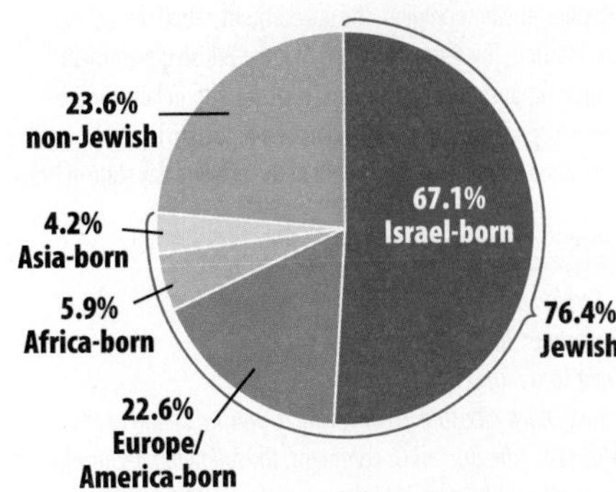

Source: CIA World Factbook

10. ***Creating and Using Graphs, Charts, Diagrams, and Tables*** From what part of the world have most non-native Israeli Jews emigrated?

11. ***Time, Chronology, and Sequencing*** What factors might be responsible for attracting non-native Jews to Israel?

Exploring the Essential Question

12. ***Drawing Conclusions*** Using a map of the Eastern Mediterranean, describe the locations of the physical features that exist in those countries—such as lakes, mountains, and rivers—and the major capital cities. Based on this information, write a paragraph describing how geographic features and urbanization in those countries are related. WHST.9–10.2

College and Career Readiness

13. ***Problem Solving*** Think about the issue of water scarcity in the Eastern Mediterranean. As an environmental geographer, where would you recommend desalination plants be built? Consider population centers, energy needs, and water sources. Explain your reasoning.

Need Extra Help?

If You've Missed Question	1	2	3	4	5	6	7	8	9	10	11	12	13
Go to page	391	393	394	398	400	395	402	405	406	407	407	390	391

CHAPTER 16 Assessment Answers

Lesson Review

Lesson 1

1. The Jordan River and Euphrates River are used to irrigate crops. The Mediterranean Sea, Sea of Galilee, Gulf of Aqaba, and Lake al-Assad help support the fishing industry. Desalination is needed to supply enough water for consumption and irrigation.

2. The coast has a Mediterranean climate with hot, dry summers and mild, rainy winters. Moving inland, the climate changes to humid subtropical and then to semi-arid steppe and arid desert with little to no rainfall.

3. Economies that rely on a single product fluctuate as the prices for that product rise and fall.

Lesson 2

4. Political activities brought large numbers of immigrants to Israel and displaced Palestinians to Syria, Lebanon, and Jordan.

5. Deposits of natural gas, exports, foreign investments, and service industries are encouraging economic growth in the economies of the Eastern Mediterranean.

6. All three religions share the same Eastern Mediterranean territory and many of the same beliefs.

Lesson 3

7. Unregulated tourism, overfishing, deforestation for farmland and fuel, and desertification from overgrazing and poor agricultural methods are some of the ways human activities have impacted the environment in the Eastern Mediterranean.

8. Jordan has created educational programs to address water shortages and the Royal Society for the Conservation of Nature (RSCN) to manage its natural resources. The Israeli Clean Air Law went into effect in 2011 to reduce air pollution and protect biodiversity. The United Nations Development Program (UNDP), the World Wildlife Fund (WWF), and the International Union for the Conservation of Nature (IUCN) are working throughout the Eastern Mediterranean to introduce legislation to protect the environment. The WWF is also working in Lebanon to protect cedar trees from fires and overgrazing. The Society for the Protection of Nature in Lebanon is also working to protect the environment.

9. International organizations have not been very successful because most projects are seriously underfunded.

21st Century Skills

10. Most non-native Israeli Jews have emigrated from Europe and America.

11. World War II, persecution in other parts of the world, and the emotional and historic ties to Israel have historically attracted non-native Jews to Israel.

Exploring the Essential Question

12. Paragraphs may vary but should be based on the information in the chapter and a map of the Eastern Mediterranean, should indicate that cities and capitals are located along the coast and by sources of water and not in desert or mountainous areas.

College and Career Readiness

13. Student answers may vary but should be supported from the chapter and indicate areas that are near water sources and close to cities for energy needs, and that have shorter distances to serve the population.

Assessment Answers

DBQ Analyzing Primary Sources

14 It promised that the British government would support the Zionist effort in securing a homeland for the Jewish people.

15 The British indicated that nothing should be done that would harm the civil and religious rights of the existing non-Jewish communities.

Critical Thinking

16 Displacement of Palestinians following the creation of Israel, ongoing military conflicts, and resettlement programs have all caused a need for Palestinian refugee camps in the subregion.

17 More people of Jewish descent are living in Israel. Other countries in the Eastern Mediterranean have experienced an influx of Palestinian refugees. After 1990, almost 900,000 immigrants arrived in Israel from Russia. The UN reported in 2012 that 4,797,723 Palestinians were living in refugee camps in Syria, Lebanon, and Jordan.

18 Israel could run out of water as its agricultural sector expands. It also has little arable land and must find ways to increase crop yields without harming the environment.

Applying Map Skills

19 Beirut, Damascus, Jerusalem, and Amman

20 The Anti-Lebanon Mountains, the Lebanon Mountains, and the Galilee Mountains are mountain ranges in the Eastern Mediterranean.

21 Areas in Israel along the coast of the Mediterranean and along the Jordan River have the most conflict.

Research and Presentation

22 Presentations will vary but should include: information on the civil war, the current political system (republic with a parliamentary system), economy, environmental issues including deforestation, the diverse culture and ethnicities, facts, figures, and images.

Writing About Geography

23 Essays will vary but should be supported with information from the chapter, and should indicate that international organizations could be effective in brokering a peaceful resolution to the conflict.

CHAPTER 16 Assessment 

Directions: On a separate sheet of paper, answer the questions below. Make sure you read carefully and answer all parts of the questions.

DBQ Analyzing Primary Sources

Use the document to answer the following questions.

In 1917, when Great Britain ruled parts of the Eastern Mediterranean subregion, the government issued the Balfour Declaration. This letter promised that the British government would support the Zionist effort to secure a homeland for the Jewish people. In time, the Declaration helped to lay the foundation for the establishment of the present-day state of Israel.

PRIMARY SOURCE

"Foreign Office
November 2nd, 1917
Dear Lord Rothschild,

I have much pleasure in conveying to you, on behalf of His Majesty's [the British] Government, the following declaration of sympathy with Jewish Zionist aspirations which has been submitted to, and approved by, the Cabinet:

'His Majesty's Government view with favour the establishment in Palestine of a national home for the Jewish people, and will use their best endeavours to facilitate the achievement of this object, it being clearly understood that nothing shall be done which may prejudice the civil and religious rights of existing non-Jewish communities in Palestine, or the rights and political status enjoyed by Jews in any other country.'

I should be grateful if you would bring this declaration to the knowledge of the Zionist Federation.

Yours sincerely
Arthur James Balfour"

—The Balfour Declaration, November 2, 1917

14 ***Evaluating*** How did the Balfour Declaration contribute to the formation of a Jewish state? RH.9–10.3

15 ***Identifying Central Issues*** What did the British say about the rights of the people who already lived in this area? RH.9–10.1

Critical Thinking

16 ***Identifying Cause and Effect*** What factors have created the need for Palestinian refugee camps in the subregion?

17 ***Evaluating*** How have demographics in the subregion changed since 1947? Be sure to use examples from the chapter.

18 ***Drawing Inferences*** What might result if the Israeli agriculture industry does not focus on immediate environmental issues?

Applying Map Skills

Refer to the Unit 5 Atlas to answer the following questions.

19 ***Human Systems*** Which capital cities of the Eastern Mediterranean are located near major waterways?

20 ***Physical Systems*** Name the major mountain ranges in the Eastern Mediterranean.

21 ***Environment and Society*** Think about your mental map of Israel. Using this mental map, describe the location of major areas of conflict.

Research and Presentation

22 ***Evaluating*** Use Internet and library resources to gather information about the factors that have shaped Lebanon's current political system. Create a multimedia presentation outlining the country's current political structure, its interaction with the global economy, and the most pressing environmental issues the country is facing. The presentation should include facts, figures, and images regarding ethnic and religious diversity in the country. WHST.9–10.7

Writing About Geography

23 ***Informative/Explanatory*** Use standard grammar, spelling, sentence structure, and punctuation to write a one-page essay describing the origins of the Israeli-Palestinian conflict. What role might international organizations play in resolving this conflict? WHST.9–10.2

Need Extra Help?

If You've Missed Question	14	15	16	17	18	19	20	21	22	23
Go to page	408	408	399	399	405	361	360	361	397	396

408

networks Online Teaching Options

WORKSHEET

Chapter Test and Lesson Quizzes

Assessing Have students complete the Chapter Test and Lesson Quizzes to assess student understanding throughout the chapter. These assessment tools offer chapter and lesson evaluation through a variety of question formats including document-based questions.

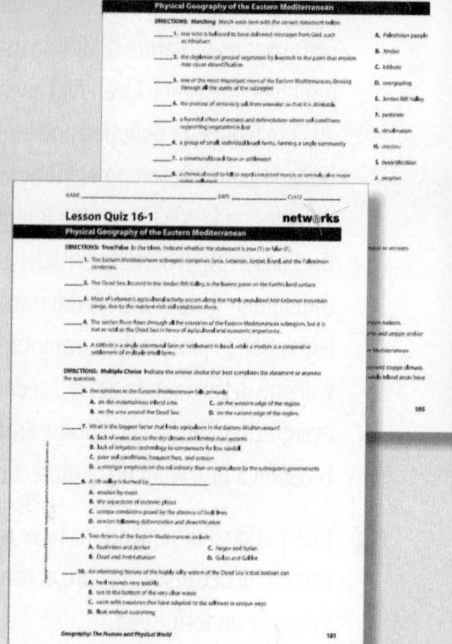

CHAPTER 17

The Northeast Planner

UNDERSTANDING BY DESIGN®

Enduring Understandings

- *Culture influences people's perceptions of places and regions.*

Essential Question

- *How do physical systems and human systems shape a place?*

Predictable Misunderstandings

Students may think:

- *Countries in the Northeast are populated with people from the same ethnic groups. Explain that there are several different ethnic groups living in Iran, Iraq, and Turkey. The majority in Turkey consists of Turks, the majority in Iraq consists of Iraqi Arabs, and the majority in Iran consists of Persians.*
- *Governments in the Northeast have been stable since the Iraq War. Explain that there continues to be conflict in the region that is heightened by the differences in ethnic groups and religions.*

Assessment Evidence

Performance Tasks:

- *Hands-On Chapter Project*

Other Evidence:

- *Guided Reading Activities*
- *Vocabulary Activities*
- *Lesson Quizzes*
- *Chapter Tests, Forms A and B*

SUGGESTED PACING GUIDE

Introducing the Chapter	½ Day	Case Study	1 Day
Lesson 1	1 Day	Lesson 3	1 Day
Lesson 2	1 Day	Chapter Wrap-Up and Assessment	½ Day

TOTAL TIME 5 Days

Key for Using the Teacher Edition

SKILL-BASED ACTIVITIES

Types of skill activities found in the Teacher Edition.

* **V Visual Skills** require students to analyze maps, graphs, charts, and photos.

R Reading Skills help students practice reading skills and master vocabulary.

C Critical Thinking Skills help students apply and extend what they have learned.

W Writing Skills provide writing opportunities to help students comprehend the text.

T Technology Skills require students to use digital tools effectively.

*Letters are followed by a number when there is more than one of the same type of skill on the page.

DIFFERENTIATED INSTRUCTION

All activities are written for the on-level student unless otherwise marked with the leveled labels below.

BL Beyond Level
AL Approaching Level
ELL English Language Learners

All students benefit from activities that utilize different learning styles. Many activities are marked as below when a particular learning style is highlighted.

Intrapersonal	**Naturalist**
Logical/Mathematical	**Kinesthetic**
Visual/Spatial	**Auditory/Musical**
Verbal/Linguistic	**Interpersonal**

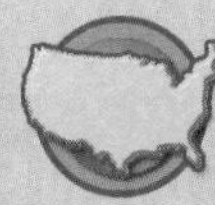

National Geography Standards covered in "The Northeast"

The student knows and understands:

(3) How to analyze the spatial organizations of people, places, and environments on Earth's surface

(4) The physical and human characteristics of places

(7) The physical processes that shape the patterns of Earth's surface

7.3 Physical processes interact over time to shape particular places on Earth's surface

(8) The characteristics and spatial distribution of ecosystems and biomes on Earth's surface

8.1 Ecosystems are dynamic and respond to changes in environmental conditions

8.3 The distribution and characteristics of biomes change over time

(9) The characteristics, distribution, and migration of human populations on Earth's surface

9.2 Population distribution and density are a function of historical, environmental, economic, political, and technological factors

(10) The characteristics, distribution, and complexity of Earth's cultural mosaics

(11) The patterns and networks of economic interdependence on Earth's surface

11.3 Economic systems are dynamic organizations of interdependent economic activities for production, exchange, distribution, and consumption of goods and services

(14) How human actions modify the physical environment

14.1 Human modifications of the physical environment can have significant global impacts

(15) How physical systems affect human systems

(16) The changes that occur in the meaning, use, distribution, and importance of resources

16.3 Policies and programs that promote the sustainable use and management of resources impact people and the environment

(17) How to apply geography to interpret the past

17.1 Geographic contexts (the human and physical characteristics of places and environments) can explain the connections between sequences of historical events

(18) How to apply geography to interpret the present and plan for the future

18.1 Geographic contexts (the human and physical characteristics of places and environments) provide the bases for analyzing current events and making predictions about future issues

CHAPTER OPENER PLANNER

Students will know:

- *what landforms and waterways form the physical geography.*
- *the factors that influence climate, history, and government.*
- *the ways that religion and ethnic diversity have shaped population patterns in the Northeast.*
- *that oil income and water resources have shaped the economies.*
- *the environmental issues that threaten the Northeast.*
- *the actions taken by people and governments to address environmental issues.*

Students will be able to:

- ***analyze** the importance of the physical geography of the Northeast.*
- ***identify** factors that affect climate, history, and government in the Northeast.*
- ***analyze** how religion and ethnic diversity have influenced population patterns.*
- ***analyze** how the economies of the Northeast are shaped by oil income and water resources.*
- ***identify** reasons why the environment is at risk in the region.*
- ***discuss** how governments and people are addressing threats to the environment.*

UNDERSTANDING BY DESIGN®

☑ Print Teaching Options

V Visual Skills

- ☐ **p. 410** Students record potential advantages and disadvantages of being a "stateless nation." ELL

R Reading Skills

- ☐ **p. 410** Students write a prediction about the Kurdish people.

C Critical Thinking Skills

- ☐ **p. 409** Students review the difference between human and physical systems. BL Logical/Mathematical
- ☐ **p. 410** Students formulate questions about the Kurdish people and answer each other's questions. BL Interpersonal

W Writing Skills

- ☐ **p. 411** Students write and perform a report for a newscast based on one or more events. AL Kinesthetic

T Technology Skills

- ☐ **p. 411** Students research the current status of Kurds within Iraq. BL Visual/Spatial, Verbal/Linguistic

☑ Online Teaching Options

C Critical Thinking Skills

- INTERACTIVE IMAGE **The Kurds**—Students discuss how cultures are tied to religion and list all of the information that they have learned about the Kurds, then write possible solutions to the Kurds' goal toward achieving an autonomous nation-state. BL Visual/Spatial
- MAP **Interactive Regional Atlas**—Students use the interactive regional atlas to understand the physical and human geography of the Northeast.

☑ Printable Digital Worksheets

- WORKSHEET **Assessing Background Knowledge**—Determine the level of prior knowledge students have about the Northeast.
- WORKSHEET **Chapter Summaries**—Students review the main idea of each lesson of the chapter content.
- WORKSHEET **Reteaching Activity**—These worksheets provide students with an opportunity for remedial practice and review of vital chapter content.

Project-Based Learning 

Hands-On

Disaster Preparedness Plans

Working in groups, students will create plans to reduce physical damage and loss of life related to natural disasters. Each group will identify and study tectonic activity in a particular part of the Northeast. They will use their research to develop disaster preparedness plans for their area. Their compiled plans will be placed into a portfolio with a title page and table of contents.

Digital Hands-On

Create Online Projects

Find an additional activity online that incorporates technology for this project. Visit the EdTech Teacher Web sites for more links, tutorials, and other resources.

ePals GlobalCommunity Where learners connect™ 

Print Resources

ANCILLARY RESOURCES

This ancillary is available for every chapter and lesson.

- **Chapter Tests and Lesson Quizzes**

PRINTABLE DIGITAL WORKSHEETS

These printable digital worksheets are available for every chapter and lesson.

- **Assessing Background Knowledge**
- **Chapter Summaries**
- **Guided Reading Activities**
- **Hands-On Chapter Projects**
- **Quizzes and Tests**
- **Reading Essentials and Study Guide** AL
- **Reteaching Activities**
- **Video Activities**
- **Vocabulary Activities**

More Media Resources

SUGGESTED VIDEOS MOVIES

- **Turkey** *New Dimension Media* (25 min.)
- **Iran Then and Now** (1 h. 24 min.)
- **Iraq and Beyond** *Dan Hare, David S. Dawson* (49 min.)

SUGGESTED READING 

- ***Understanding Iran: Everything You Need to Know, from Persia to the Islamic Republic, from Cyrus to Ahmadinejad,*** by William R. Polk
- ***A Brief History of Iraq,*** by Eric Gustafson
- ***The New Cultural Climate in Turkey,*** by Nurdan Gurbilek

LESSON 1 PLANNER

PHYSICAL GEOGRAPHY OF THE NORTHEAST

Students will know:

- *why the landscape of the Northeast is dominated by mountains.*
- *the importance of water to the human systems of the Northeast.*
- *the factors affecting climate in the Northeast.*

Students will be able to:

- ***analyze** why mountains are numerous in the Northeast.*
- ***explain** why water is important to human systems in the region.*
- ***identify** factors that affect climate in the Northeast.*

UNDERSTANDING BY DESIGN®

☑ Print Teaching Options

V Visual Skills

- ☐ **p. 412** Students identify key landforms and bodies of water on a map and describe how they might shape the region's human systems.
- ☐ **p. 412** Students create a three-column chart to organize key information about Iran, Iraq, and Turkey. AL Visual/Spatial
- ☐ **p. 415** Students create a flowchart for each country in the Northeast and complete it with information about climates, biomes, and resources. Visual/Spatial

R Reading Skills

- ☐ **p. 414** Students discuss the significance of the Tigris and Euphrates Rivers. ELL Visual/Spatial, Interpersonal

C Critical Thinking Skills

- ☐ **p. 412** Students identify how landforms were created and the ongoing impact of tectonic plate activity.
- ☐ **p. 413** Students discuss the impact of the mountainous landscape of the Northeast. AL Logical/Mathematical

W Writing Skills

- ☐ **p. 413** Students write an informative essay about Iraq's alluvial plain. BL Verbal/Linguistic
- ☐ **p. 414** Students write an article for a travel magazine about a trip along the coastal plains of Turkey. BL Verbal/Linguistic

T Technology Skills

- ☐ **p. 415** Students prepare a report about Iraq's energy resources and evaluate a statement by the International Energy Agency's chief economist in their reports. BL Logical/Mathematical, Interpersonal

☑ Online Teaching Options

V Visual Skills

SLIDE SHOW **The Northeast's Physical Geography**—Students learn about the physical geography of the Northeast and how volcanic activity contributed to the mountainous terrain. AL Verbal/Linguistic, Visual/Spatial

VIDEO **Iraq Geography**—Students learn about the geography of Iraq, identify physical distinct regions, and discuss the importance of the Tigris-Euphrates river system. ELL Visual/Spatial, Verbal/Linguistic

C Critical Thinking Skills

INTERACTIVE BELLRINGER **Water Systems of the Northeast**—Students discuss how control of the waterways in this region may have affected the rise and decline of past civilizations as well as how they give countries military and commercial benefits today. ELL Interpersonal, Visual/Spatial

INTERACTIVE WHITEBOARD ACTIVITY **Landforms of the Northeast**—Students locate and name various landforms of the Northeast on a map, and then identify the landforms' characteristics in a chart.

☑ Printable Digital Worksheets

R Reading Skills

WORKSHEET **Guided Reading Activity**—Students use the Guided Reading Activity worksheets to review their comprehension of the content.

C Critical Thinking Skills

WORKSHEET **Video Activity**—Students answer questions related to a topic in the chapter content after they have viewed a lesson video.

LESSON 2 PLANNER

HUMAN GEOGRAPHY OF THE NORTHEAST

Students will know:

- *the factors that have influenced history and government in the Northeast.*
- *the ways that religion has shaped population patterns.*
- *how ethnic diversity affects population patterns.*
- *that oil income and water resources have shaped the economies.*

Students will be able to:

- ***identify*** *factors that have affected history and government of the Northeast.*
- ***analyze*** *how religion and ethnic diversity have influenced population patterns.*
- ***analyze*** *how the economies of the Northeast are shaped by oil income and water resources.*

UNDERSTANDING BY DESIGN®

☑ Print Teaching Options

V Visual Skills

☐ **p. 418** Students create graphs to depict ethnic diversity in the Northeast. BL Visual/Spatial, Logical/Mathematical

☐ **p. 420** Students discuss the reasons for varying household sizes and create a graph to show household size data for various countries. ELL Logical/Mathematical

R Reading Skills

☐ **p. 419** Student groups are assigned a country and formulate questions about their country after analyzing events on the time line. Interpersonal

☐ **p. 421** Student discuss the term *interdependence.* AL Interpersonal

C Critical Thinking Skills

☐ **p. 416** Students discuss how the discovery of oil might impact a region. BL Logical/Mathematical

☐ **p. 416** Students create a flowchart or diagram to depict the series of events that led to the emergence of civilization. Visual/Spatial

☐ **p. 417** Students discuss the formation of an Islamic Republic in Iran and why modern-day Iran may have strained relations with other countries. AL Logical/Mathematical

☐ **p. 421** Students discuss the impact of OPEC on the global economy.

W Writing Skills

☐ **p. 417** Students review the vocabulary terms and write one or two paragraphs to demonstrate their understanding. ELL Verbal/Linguistic

☐ **p. 420** Students write a short argumentative essay on whether or not they agree with government policies that regulate family size. BL Verbal/Linguistic

T Technology Skills

☐ **p. 419** Students research recent population patterns of an assigned city, the reasons for the population changes, and the social and cultural impacts of those changes and present their findings. BL Logical/Mathematical, Verbal/Linguistic

☐ **p. 420** Students research arches and domes in Sumerian architecture and write an essay to compare and contrast this architecture with those of other civilizations. Visual/Spatial

☑ Online Teaching Options

V Visual Skills

☐ SLIDE SHOW **The Kurds**—Students use the time line and slide show to outline reasons for the Kurdistan Workers' Party's revolt against Turkey. AL Visual/Spatial, Verbal/Linguistic

R Reading Skills

☐ INTERACTIVE BELLRINGER **Ethnic Groups of the Northeast**—Students use the graphs to identify how ethnic diversity affects population patterns in the Northeast. Verbal/Linguistic, Visual/Spatial

☐ INTERACTIVE WHITEBOARD ACTIVITY **From Mesopotamia to Modern Day**—Students examine how civilizations and empires of the past developed and led to development of the Northeast countries today. BL Logical/Mathematical, Visual/Spatial

C Critical Thinking Skills

☐ INTERACTIVE MAP **Civilizations and Empires of the Northeast**—Students discuss the chronology of different civilizations and empires in the Northeast and their influence on modern culture. ELL Verbal/Linguistic

☐ VIDEO **The Challenge of the Past Ottoman Empire**—Students discuss Turkey's history, what it means for many in Turkey today to practice their Muslim beliefs, and whether it is possible for the region to have a balance between religion and politics in the modern era. BL Verbal/Linguistic

☑ Printable Digital Worksheets

R Reading Skills

☐ WORKSHEET **Guided Reading Activity**—Students use Guided Reading Activity worksheets to review their comprehension of the content.

☐ WORKSHEET **Reading Essentials and Study Guide**—Students complete the study guide and answer Reading Progress Check and vocabulary questions. AL

C Critical Thinking Skills

☐ WORKSHEET **Video Activity**—Students answer questions related to a topic in the chapter content after they have viewed a lesson video.

LESSON 3 PLANNER

PEOPLE AND THEIR ENVIRONMENT: THE NORTHEAST

Students will know:
- *that water resources in the Northeast are at risk for several reasons.*
- *the causes and effects of soil degradation and erosion.*
- *the causes and effects of air pollution.*
- *the actions taken by people and governments to address environmental issues.*

Students will be able to:
- ***identify** reasons why water resources are at risk.*
- ***analyze** causes of soil degradation, erosion, and air pollution.*
- ***identify** effects of soil degradation, erosion, and air pollution.*
- ***discuss** how governments and people are addressing threats to the environment.*

UNDERSTANDING BY DESIGN®

☑ Print Teaching Options

V Visual Skills

- ☐ **p. 425** Students create cause-and-effect diagrams showing the cause and effect of the drainage of marshlands on the Marsh Arabs and their culture. **Visual/Spatial**
- ☐ **p. 426** Students create a visual report that shows the impact of oil and gas production on the Caspian Sea. **BL Visual/Spatial, Interpersonal**
- ☐ **p. 427** Students create a display that shows the impact of soil erosion in Iraq. **Visual/Spatial, Interpersonal**

R Reading Skills

- ☐ **p. 424** Students jot down questions about the material as they skim through the lesson.

C Critical Thinking Skills

- ☐ **p. 424** Students consider the impact of the development of hydroelectric power. **Logical/Mathematical**
- ☐ **p. 426** Students discuss the war-related causes of pollution in the Persian Gulf. **Logical/Mathematical**
- ☐ **p. 427** Students discuss the various threats to the environment of the Caspian Sea. **AL Logical/Mathematical**

W Writing Skills

- ☐ **p. 428** Students write an informative essay about environmental damage in Turkey and efforts to improve things that explains the short-term and long-term costs of some of these efforts. **BL Verbal/Linguistic**

T Technology Skills

- ☐ **p. 425** Students research an assigned topic related to drought or irrigation in the region and present a slide show about their topic. **BL Interpersonal, Naturalist**

☑ Online Teaching Options

V Visual Skills

- ☐ **INFOGRAPHIC** **Caspian Energy**—Students create a chart to compare and contrast the positive and negative impacts of drilling in the Caspian Sea. **AL Visual/Spatial**

R Reading Skills

- ☐ **INTERACTIVE BELLRINGER** **Caspian Energy**—Students learn about water pollution in the Caspian Sea. **Verbal/Linguistic**

C Critical Thinking Skills

- ☐ **VIDEO** **Marsh Arabs**—Students consider the various environmental, migration, and population impacts of the Marsh Arabs in Iraq and discuss how water-controlled sanctions and genocide issues related to the former Iraqi government impacted the environment. **ELL Visual/Spatial**
- ☐ **INTERACTIVE WHITEBOARD ACTIVITY** **Human Impact on the Environment**—Students compare human factors and physical factors using a graphic organizer. **AL Kinesthetic, Visual/Spatial**

☑ Printable Digital Worksheets

R Reading Skills

- ☐ **WORKSHEET** **Guided Reading Activity**—Students use Guided Reading Activity worksheets to review their comprehension of the content.
- ☐ **WORKSHEET** **Reading Essentials and Study Guide**—Students complete the study guide and answer Reading Progress Check and vocabulary questions. **AL**
- ☐ **WORKSHEET** **Vocabulary Activity**—Students review the chapter content and academic vocabulary words.

C Critical Thinking Skills

- ☐ **WORKSHEET** **Video Activity**—Students answer questions based on a lesson video.
- ☐ **WORKSHEET** **Reteaching Activity**—Students use this activity worksheet to review and reteach chapter content and vocabulary. This worksheet can be used with struggling students who need additional help with difficult content concepts.

INTERVENTION AND REMEDIATION STRATEGIES

LESSON 1 Physical Geography of the Northeast

Reading and Comprehension

Display a physical map of countries in the Northeast for students to see. Organize students into five groups and assign each team one of the following topics: *Landforms, Water Systems, Climate Regions, Biomes,* and *Natural Resources.* Have teams collaborate to develop three quiz questions based on the text for their assigned topic. After students have had time to develop and write down their quiz questions (and answers on a separate sheet of paper), have teams exchange papers. Allow time for each team to answer the quiz questions.

Text Evidence

Have students review the text to identify examples of how and why mountains dominate the Northeast and have shaped its history. Tell students to write at least one example of how the physical geography of the Northeast has changed, using evidence from the lesson. For example, students might discuss the formation of the Zagros Mountains. Encourage students to conduct an online search to identify the appearance of regions in the Northeast thousands of years ago to compare it to a current physical map of the region today. Ask volunteers to share their examples with the class.

LESSON 2 Human Geography of the Northeast

Reading and Comprehension

Have students work with a partner to scan the lesson and create flashcards for each content vocabulary term. Have partners take turns quizzing each other, repeating those that may cause confusion. Challenge students to write sentences using each vocabulary term to demonstrate their understanding of each word's meaning. Then have students look up the definition of each Academic Vocabulary term and use each in a sentence. Challenge students to explain how the word *assume* can have more than one meaning, depending on its context.

Text Evidence

Organize students into pairs or small groups and assign them one of the following headings from the lesson: *Civilizations and Empires; Oil and the Modern Era; Population Patterns; Family and Status of Women; The Arts; Resources, Power, and Industry;* and *Trade and Interdependence.* Have groups write a summary about their topic, using information from the lesson. Encourage students to conduct additional research if desired to identify supporting evidence of information presented in the text. Have students present their findings to the class.

LESSON 3 People and Their Environment: the Northeast

Reading and Comprehension

Have students work in pairs to identify an environmental danger or potential threat facing the region, such as the impact of hydroelectric stations planned along the Tigris and Euphrates Rivers. Have partners create a graphic organizer or flowchart that illustrates the cause-and-effect relationship of their chosen issue and its impact on surrounding regions. Have student pairs share their diagrams or charts with the class.

Text Evidence

Have student groups choose an issue or problem discussed in the lesson. Tell students to design a website that addresses their chosen issue by providing information and links to groups that are working to improve or remedy the problem. For example, students might choose to design a website addressing the loss of wetlands in Iraq and provide links to organizations such as Wetlands International and the International Wetlands Conference. Tell students to present their website design, acting as if their classmates are potential sponsors. Encourage students in the "audience" to ask pertinent question of presenters that relate to the group's selected issue, its mission, and the purpose and content of the website.

Online Resources

Leveled Reader

Use this online approaching-level text that corresponds directly to the text in the Student Edition. It also includes additional reading and comprehension support for English Language Learners.

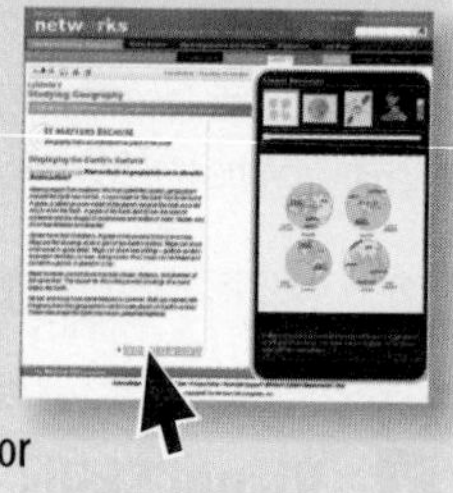

Guided Reading Activities

This resource uses guiding questions to help students with comprehension.

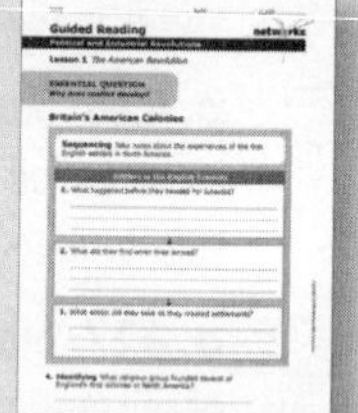

Reteaching Activities

These worksheets provide students with an opportunity for remedial practice and review of vital chapter content.

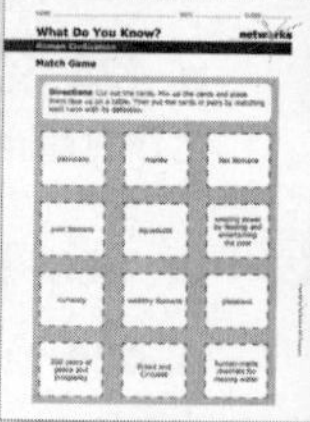

Reading Essentials and Study Guide

This resource offers writing and reading activities for the approaching-level student.

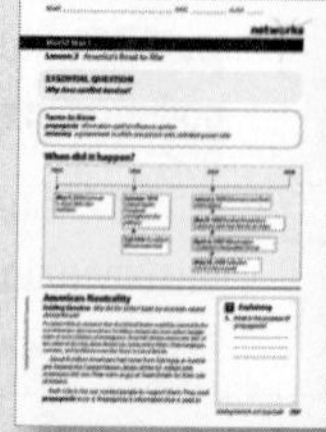

Self-Check Quizzes

This online assessment tool provides instant feedback for students to check their progress.

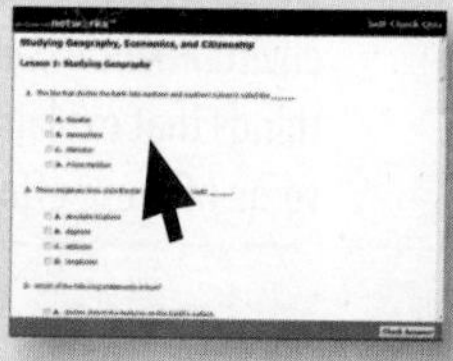

Chapter Summaries

Summaries are provided for each chapter that thoroughly condense core content into manageable chunks.

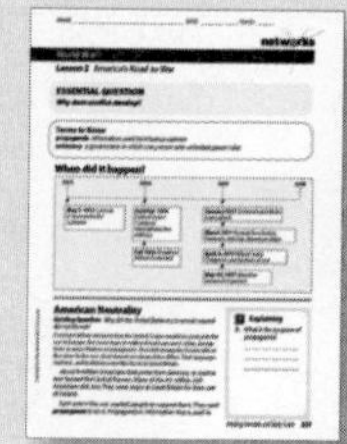

The Northeast

networks

There's More Online about the Northeast.

CHAPTER 17

ESSENTIAL QUESTION • *How do physical systems and human systems shape a place?*

Geography Matters...

In the Northeast, cultures are fundamentally tied to religion. Islam is the most widely practiced of them all. For hundreds of years, it has defined people's lives in the subregion. The Northeast is not homogenous, however. Many different ethnic groups live in the Northeast, including Arabs, Persians (Iranians), Turks, and Kurds.

◀ Turkish youth in an outdoor market in İstanbul, Turkey

Rebecca Erol/Alamy

409

Letter from the Author

Dear Geography Teacher,

The Turkish Straits— the Dardanelles, the Sea of Marmara, and the Bosporus— connect the Black Sea with the Mediterranean and create one of the most critical "choke points" in the world. A "choke point" is a narrow stretch of water or land that could easily be blocked or cut off entirely, thereby disrupting important international trade and everyday commerce. The Turkish Straits are actually three or more "choke points," depending on where the impediments are placed. Have your students develop scenarios of where these "choke points" might be located and how they might affect countries such as Turkey, Russia, Ukraine, and others surrounding the Mediterranean Sea.

Richard G. Boehm

ENGAGE

Drawing Inferences Provide students with a recent news article about an event involving one or more of the countries in the Northeast. The article may relate to the country's political situation or to issues involving its society, education, natural resources, or economic problems such as unemployment, debt, or poverty. Challenge students to infer how the issue discussed in the article relates to the geography of the Northeast.

TEACH & ASSESS

Hypothesizing Review the difference between physical and human systems and invite volunteers to give examples of each. **Ask: Based on the location of countries in the Northeast, how do you think this region has been impacted by both physical and human systems?** *(Possible answer: The region may have been impacted by seismic activity due to its mountainous location. It may also be affected by natural resources in the region, such as oil. The resources in turn can lead to human systems developing these resources.)* BL **Logical/Mathematical**

Making Connections

Have students locate the word *homogenous* in the *Geography Matters...* text. Ask a volunteer to offer a definition. *("having similar traits, uniform")* Then ask students whether they have heard the expression "melting pot" used to describe the population of the United States. Have them offer a definition of the term. *("a group of people with different cultures, backgrounds, and beliefs")* Ask students to consider if this term could also apply to the population of the Northeast.

CLOSE & REFLECT

Questioning Have students think about aspects of a region's human population, such as how and where people live, their cultures, belief systems, and socioeconomic status. Have students write one or two sentences about how one or more of these factors might lead to conflict.

ePals GlobalCommunity
Where learners connect™

Extend the project-based learning experience globally through our partnership with ePals. EPals allows you to connect with classrooms around the world in a safe online environment for real-life lessons and projects in virtual study groups.

ENGAGE

R Reading Skills

Predicting Have students read the introductory paragraph about the Kurdish people and their distribution. Tell students to write a prediction about the Kurdish people. Explain that they may study the map to formulate their predictions if needed. After reading the rest of this feature, have students return to their predictions to see if they are correct.

TEACH & ASSESS

C Critical Thinking Skills

Formulating Questions Have students discuss the information in the left box on the far left of the map. Have students work with a partner to formulate questions about the Kurdish people, their history, and their distribution. Then in a class discussion, ask each pair to share one of their questions with the class; allow time for other students to try to answer the question. If the question cannot be answered, assign the pair that asked the question to research the answer and then report their findings back to the class. BL Interpersonal, Logical/Mathematical

V Visual Skills

Analyzing Visuals Review the definitions of a nation and a country. **Ask:** What is the difference between a country and a nation? *(Student answers may vary, but should reflect that a country is a political unit and that a nation is a group of people with similar characteristics but who are not necessarily living within the same country.)* Explain that the Kurds are considered a "stateless nation." Have students analyze the map with a partner and then create a two-column chart to record potential advantages and disadvantages of being a "stateless nation." Have student pairs share their responses in a class discussion. Encourage students to add or revise information in their charts after they read this feature. ELL Visual/Spatial

Why Geography Matters: **The Northeast**

a stateless nation: *the* Kurds

R *A nations is a group of people who share a common language, religion, culture, and common institutions. When a national group has a state or country of its own, it is called a nation-state. Albania, Iceland, and Japan are examples of nation-states. Other nations, such as the Kurds of the Northeast, do not have their own country. They are considered "stateless nations."*

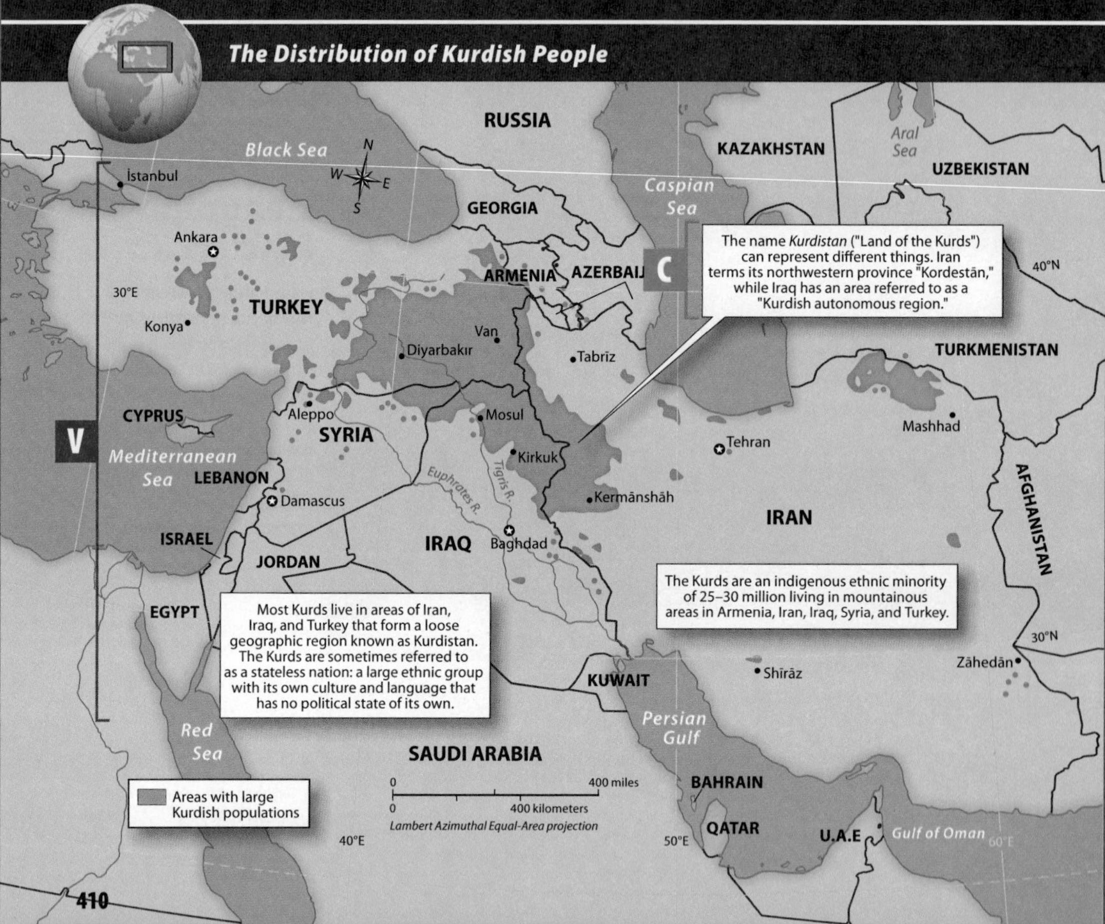
The Distribution of Kurdish People
RUSSIA
KAZAKHSTAN
Aral Sea
UZBEKISTAN
Black Sea
Istanbul
Caspian Sea
GEORGIA
Ankara
ARMENIA
AZERBAIJ
TURKEY
Konya
Van
Diyarbakır
Tabrīz
TURKMENISTAN
CYPRUS
Aleppo
SYRIA
Mosul
Kirkuk
Mashhad
Tehran
Mediterranean Sea
LEBANON
Damascus
Kermānshāh
IRAN
ISRAEL
JORDAN
IRAQ
Baghdad
AFGHANISTAN
EGYPT
KUWAIT
Shīrāz
Zāhedān
Persian Gulf
Red Sea
SAUDI ARABIA
BAHRAIN
QATAR
U.A.E.
Gulf of Oman
The name *Kurdistan* ("Land of the Kurds") can represent different things. Iran terms its northwestern province "Kordestān," while Iraq has an area referred to as a "Kurdish autonomous region."
The Kurds are an indigenous ethnic minority of 25–30 million living in mountainous areas in Armenia, Iran, Iraq, Syria, and Turkey.
Most Kurds live in areas of Iran, Iraq, and Turkey that form a loose geographic region known as Kurdistan. The Kurds are sometimes referred to as a stateless nation: a large ethnic group with its own culture and language that has no political state of its own.
Areas with large Kurdish populations
400 miles
400 kilometers
Lambert Azimuthal Equal-Area projection
30°E
40°E
50°E
60°E
40°N
30°N
410

Project-Based Learning

Hands-On

Disaster Preparedness Plans

Working in groups, students will research tectonic activity in an assigned area of the Northeast. Groups will compile their research to develop a disaster preparedness plan for their area that includes proposed evacuation routes, a diagram of items needed in an emergency kit, a list of recommendations for safer structures, and an illustrated brochure providing school safety tips.

ePals GlobalCommunity Where learners connect™

Digital Hands-On

Create Online Projects

Find an additional activity online that incorporates technology for this project. Visit the EdTech Teacher Web sites for more links, tutorials, and other resources.

edtechteacher
21st Century Learning

Why Geography Matters

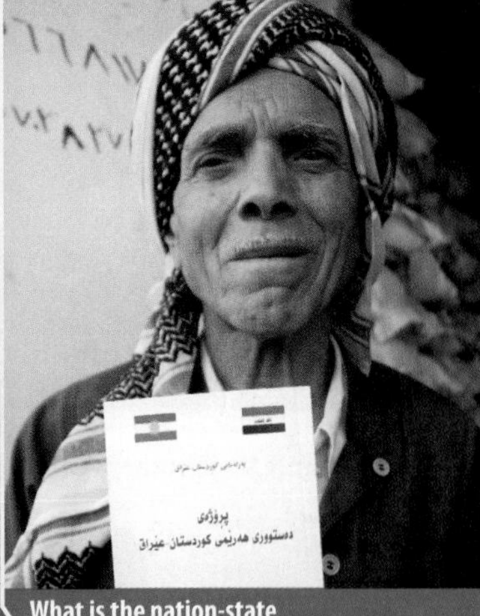

(l)Ahmad Al-Rubaye/AFP/Getty Images, (c)©Peter Turnley/Corbis, (r)Safin Hamed/AFP/Getty Images

What is a stateless nation?

The term *stateless nation* refers to a group that identifies itself as a nation based on common ethnic, linguistic, and religious identity, but that lacks majority status in any nation-state. Some stateless nations are native minority populations within a larger state. Examples of such minority populations include the Uyghur people in China and the Catalan people in Spain. Others are dispersed across several countries in numbers insufficient to form a majority in any one state. The Yoruba people of Nigeria, Benin, and Togo are an example of this latter category. Another such group is the Kurdish people. The Kurds are an Islamic pastoral people who have lived in parts of the Northeast for at least three thousand years, but have never achieved the status of a nation-state. Today they constitute a stateless nation of an estimated 25 to 30 million people. The Kurds are the largest ethnic group in the world that does not have its own country.

1. **Human Systems** Why are the Kurds considered a stateless nation?

Who are the Kurds?

The Kurds are the fourth-largest ethnic group in the Northeast, after Arabs, Persians, and Turks. The majority are Sunni Muslims, although some are Shia Muslims, Christians, or followers of other faiths. Kurds speak dialects of the Indo-European language family that are related to Persian. They live in an area that straddles mountain and plateau regions of eastern Turkey, northeastern Iran, northern Iraq, northwestern Syria, southern Armenia, and eastern Azerbaijan. There are also Kurdish communities in Georgia, Kazakhstan, Lebanon, and parts of Europe. For centuries, their lands were part of the vast multiethnic Ottoman and Persian Empires. After World War I, an independent Kurdish state was proposed, but that plan was abandoned. The Kurds found their lands divided among several new nation-states. Since then, Kurdish nationalist movements have led to conflicts with those countries. During the Iran-Iraq War (1980–1988), the Iraqi regime of Saddam Hussein embarked on a campaign to crush Kurdish resistance. This included the use of chemical weapons against Iraqi Kurdish civilians. Land mines planted during the war continue to take the lives of Kurds who live along the Iran-Iraq border. **T**

2. **Places and Regions** Why do the Kurds want their own state?

What is the nation-state of Kurdistan?

Kurdistan literally means "Land of the Kurds." Calls for an independent Kurdish state date back to at least the 1800s. In 1880 a Kurdish sheikh in Turkey wrote to an American missionary, explaining the need for an independent Kurdish state: "We are . . . a nation apart. We want our affairs to be in our own hands." In the twenty-first century, however, there is still no Kurdish nation-state. Some Kurds (particularly educated urban residents) have formed a nationalist movement aimed at gaining autonomous (self-governing) rule. After years of brutal suppression and the fall of the regime of Saddam Hussein, Iraqi Kurds were able to gain autonomous civil authority over a section of northern Iraq, and in 2005 a Kurdish parliament was formed. Kurdish populations in Syria, Turkey, and Iran—encouraged by the success of the Iraqi Kurds—continue to push for more political autonomy. **W**

3. **Human Systems** What progress have Kurds made toward achieving the goal of an autonomous nation-state?

THERE'S MORE ONLINE

READ a primary source quote about Kurds in Iraq • *VIEW* an image of the Kurdish people

T Technology Skills

Researching Have students conduct online research to identify the current status of Kurds within Iraq. Challenge students to investigate how past conflicts have impacted the economy of Iraq and the health and education of the Kurds and other Iraqi people. Provide an opportunity for students to present their findings to the class, inviting them to enhance their presentations with visual displays. BL
Visual/Spatial, Verbal/Linguistic

W Writing Skills

Informative/Explanatory Organize students into small groups and have them write and perform a "live" report for a mock television newscast based on one or more events described in the text. Tell students the focus of their reports should relate to the idea of the nation-state of Kurdistan. Encourage students to assign roles to each member of their group, including reporters, people interviewed (a Kurdish sheikh, an "educated urbanite," a member of the Kurdish parliament, an Iraqi Kurd, etc.), and anchors on the "news desk." Allow time for students to prepare interview questions and to rehearse their newscasts before presenting them to the class.
AL **Kinesthetic, Interpersonal**

CLOSE & REFLECT

Understanding Relationships Review with students the meaning and significance of the term *stateless nation*. Have students consider the disadvantages for native minority populations. Discuss why the Kurdish people continue to strive for political autonomy.

INTERACTIVE IMAGE

The Kurds

Determining Importance Use this interactive image to help students understand the importance of relationships in the Northeast region. After students have viewed the image, remind them that the cultures in this region are fundamentally tied to religion; however, they are not homogenous. Have students form small groups to discuss and list all the information that they have learned about the Kurds. Then have each group write a possible solution to the Kurds' goal toward achieving an autonomous nation-state. Allow students time to research ideas or concepts, if needed. Then have each group present its solutions to the class.
BL **Visual/Spatial**

The Kurds

Bulent Kilic/AFP/Getty Images

ANSWERS, p. 411

Why Geography Matters

1. The Kurds share an ethnic, religious, and linguistic identity and have an estimated population of 25 to 30 million, but they do not have their own country.
2. The Kurds have historically occupied lands that are now divided among many countries. This situation has caused conflicts for Kurds within those countries, and they want a state where they can be in control of their own affairs.
3. The Kurds have been able to gain autonomous civil authority over a portion of northern Iraq, and in 2005 a Kurdish parliament was formed. This success is encouraging Kurds in other countries to push for autonomy.

ENGAGE

V1 Visual Skills

Analyzing Visuals Have students look at the images at the top of the page and write one or two sentences that explain what these images reveal about the physical geography of the Northeast. Then display a physical map of the region. Ask volunteers to identify key landforms and bodies of water shown on the map. Have students describe how these landforms and waterways might shape the region's human systems.

TEACH & ASSESS

V2 Visual Skills

Creating Charts Ask a volunteer to read the *It Matters Because* paragraph. Elicit from students what they know about the Northeast based on information they have read or seen in the news. Suggest that students create a three-column chart labeled *Iran, Iraq,* and *Turkey*. As students work through the lesson, have them fill in their charts with key information about each country. Suggest that students use their charts as a study guide when reviewing the lesson. AL Visual/Spatial

C Critical Thinking Skills

Identifying Cause and Effect Have students read the paragraph to identify how landforms were created and what the ongoing impact is of tectonic plate activity in the region. **Ask:** What region in the United States compares to the North Anatolian Fault? *(the San Andreas Fault of California)* What sort of activity has been caused by the North Anatolian Fault? *(It has been very active and has led to nearly a dozen high-magnitude earthquakes.)* How has the East Anatolian Fault impacted Turkey in recent years? *(It has caused several large earthquakes in eastern Turkey.)*

ANSWERS, p. 412

TAKING NOTES: Landforms of the Northeast: Turkey—Pontic Mountains (highest peak at 12,900 ft) and Taurus Mountains (many peaks exceed 10,000 ft), North Anatolian Fault, Anatolian Plateau; Iran—Elburz (highest peak is Mount Damavand at 18,934 ft) and Zagros (highest peak is Zard Kūh at 14,921 ft) mountain ranges; Iraq—central and southern third covered by an alluvial plain, Zagros Mountains extend from Iran

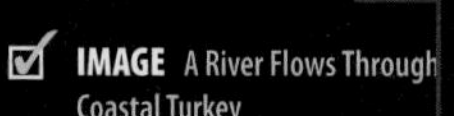

There's More Online! V1

- IMAGE A River Flows Through Coastal Turkey
- MAP Physical Map: Turkey, Iran, and Iraq
- INTERACTIVE SELF-CHECK QUIZ
- VIDEO Physical Geography of the Northeast

Reading HELPDESK 

Academic Vocabulary (Tier Two Words)
- exceed
- sustain

Content Vocabulary (Tier Three Words)
- pastoralism

TAKING NOTES: *Key Ideas and Details*

IDENTIFYING As you read about the physical geography of the Northeast, use a graphic organizer like the one below to record the major features of the subregion.

Landforms of the Northeast

LESSON 1

Physical Geography of the Northeast

ESSENTIAL QUESTION • *How do physical systems and human systems shape a place?*

IT MATTERS BECAUSE

V2 *The mountains that dominate the Northeast have shaped and continue to shape human history. Some of the earliest civilizations sprang from this ancient land. Today, the Northeast subregion is home to the countries of Iran, Iraq, and Turkey.*

Landforms

GUIDING QUESTION *What features dominate the physical geography of the Northeast?*

The Northeast is a largely mountainous area, but it also features a range of other significant landforms and environments, particularly the broad plain of the Tigris and Euphrates Rivers in Iraq. The subregion occupies a part of the Earth where several tectonic plates converge. The movement of these plates has produced the many mountain ranges that dominate the Northeast. Movement along the fault lines produces earthquakes.

C The North Anatolian Fault extends much of the distance across Turkey. At about 750 miles (1,200 km) long, it rivals the San Andreas Fault of California in length. As the plates slide past each other in an east-west direction, they can rupture and cause destructive earthquakes. Over the last seven decades, the North Anatolian Fault has been among the most active faults in the world, with nearly a dozen quakes **exceeding** 6.7 on the Richter scale of earthquake magnitude. Recently, the East Anatolian Fault in eastern Turkey has also become more active, causing several large quakes in the twenty-first century. Earthquakes are also frequent in Iran. In recent years, several devastating quakes have taken tens of thousands of lives.

Ancient volcanic activity also contributed to the mountainous terrain of the Northeast. Even today, a number of volcanoes dot the region. Turkey alone has over a dozen volcanoes within its borders.

The Pontic Mountains and the Taurus Mountains rise from the Turkish landscape. The highest peak in the Pontic range rises to 12,900 feet (3,932 m). The Taurus Mountains have many peaks which

networks Online Teaching Options

 INTERACTIVE BELLRINGER

Water Systems of the Northeast

Interpreting a Map Use the introductory text and map of the waterways of the Northeast to identify the importance of water to the human systems of the Northeast. Have students form small groups to discuss how control of the waterways in this region may have affected the rise and decline of past civilizations and how they provide countries with military and commercial benefits today. Have groups discuss and answer each question. Then review the answers in a class discussion. ELL Interpersonal, Visual/Spatial

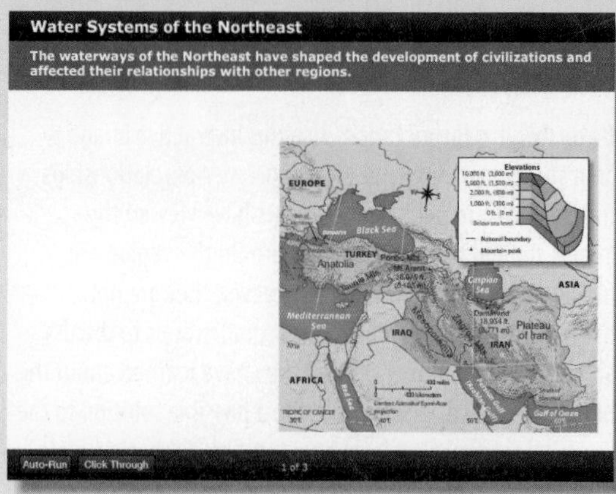

exceed 10,000 feet (3,048 m). Between these ranges lies the Anatolian Plateau, or central massif. It stands 2,000 to 5,000 feet (610 to 1,524 m) above sea level. The plateau also has extensive sections of relatively flat terrain. East of the Pontic range, camel-backed Mount Ararat—at a height of 16,945 feet (5,165 m)—overlooks the Turkish-Iranian border.

exceed to be greater than

To the east of Turkey, in Iran, lie the mountains of the Elburz and Zagros ranges. The Elburz Mountains cover the northern portion of Iran with a series of peaks that often exceed 9,000 feet (2,743 m). The tallest of these mountains is Iran's highest peak—the volcanic Mount Damāvand, which rises to 18,934 feet (5,771 m). The Zagros Mountains were formed by the collision of the Eurasian and Arabian plates. This mountain system stretches for 932 miles (1,500 km) from southwestern Iran and extending into Iraq at its northwestern end. The tallest peak in this range, Zard Kūh in Iran, is 14,921 feet (4,548 m) high. **C**

In the western part of the subregion lies the Anatolian Peninsula, the location where the continents of Europe and Asia meet. This great peninsula is surrounded to the north by the Black Sea, to the east and south by the eastern Taurus Mountains and the Mediterranean Sea, and to the west by the Aegean Sea. It was historically referred to as Asia Minor. Today, it constitutes the Asian part of Turkey.

sustain to give support to

Over thousands of years, rivers created an alluvial plain that covers the central and southern third of Iraq. This alluvial plain is a low-lying area that is frequently marshy and covered with lakes and swamps. It is this land that produced and **sustained** the earliest civilizations in human history. **W**

✓ READING PROGRESS CHECK

Describing How has tectonic activity shaped the Northeast?

GEOGRAPHY CONNECTION

The Northeast is a largely mountainous area that includes some of the most important waterways in the world.

1. ***PHYSICAL SYSTEMS*** Name the two major mountain ranges in Turkey and describe their locations.
2. ***ENVIRONMENT AND SOCIETY*** On the map, find the Dardanelles, Sea of Marmara, and Bosporus. How are these features important to trade?

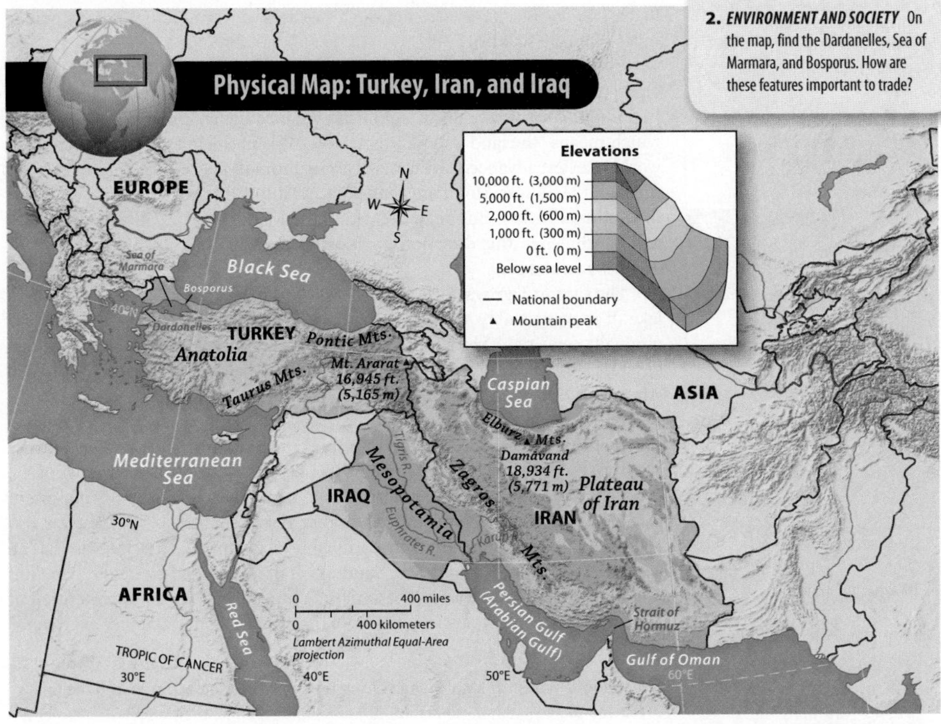

Content Background Knowledge

The Moment Magnitude and the Richter Magnitude Scales The Richter scale, invented by Charles Richter, was first used in 1935 to study earthquakes in California. It is based on a scale of 10 to measure an earthquake's magnitude. The moment magnitude is based on a scale of 30 or more to measure the energy released by an earthquake. It was developed in 1979 to measure larger intensity earthquakes in Southern California. The Richter scale is best used when measuring smaller earthquakes because it records responses of seismographs and the distance from the epicenter. The moment magnitude scale accurately records the energy of an earthquake when it occurs more than 370 miles (600 km) from the epicenter.

C Critical Thinking Skills

Differentiating Guide a discussion on the impact of the Northeast's mountainous landscape. **Ask:** What region do the Elburz Mountains cover? *(northern portion of Iran)* How were the Zagros Mountains formed? *(by the collision of the Eurasian and Arabian plates)* What might be an advantage and a disadvantage of the region's physical geography with regard to transportation? *(Possible answers: advantage—waterways provide transportation for shipping goods; Disadvantage—mountains can make road transportation difficult)* AL Logical/Mathematical

W Writing Skills

Informative/Explanatory Have students write an essay about changes in Iraq's Alluvial Plain over many years. Tell them to describe the land as it existed thousands of years ago and to chronicle the changes in the region up to present day. Students should use online or library resources to gather information about the alluvial plain in central and southern Iraq, its history, and physical changes. Encourage students to illustrate their essays and present them to the class. BL Verbal/Linguistic

SLIDE SHOW

The Northeast's Physical Geography

Stating Use the interactive slide show to introduce students to the varied physical geography of the Northeast. Explain that ancient volcanic activity contributed to the mountainous terrain found in this region. After viewing the slide show, have students write three statements they learned that surprised or interested them. Invite students to share their statements and then answer any questions students may have about the information in the slides. AL Verbal/Linguistic, Visual/Spatial

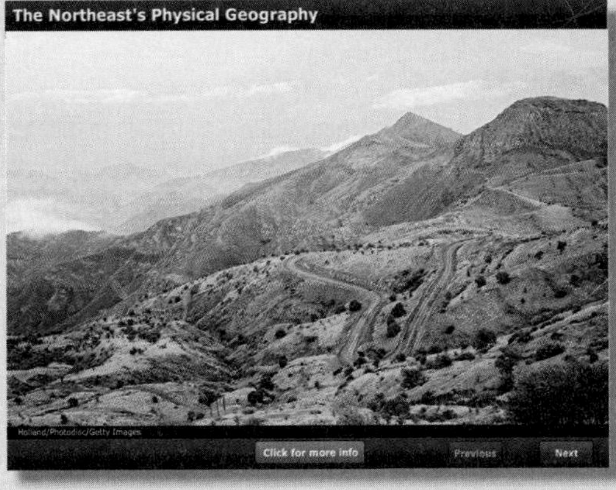

ANSWERS, p. 413

✓ READING PROGRESS CHECK Several tectonic plates converge in the area causing earthquakes and volcanic activity that created the mountainous terrain. The Zagros Mountains were formed by the Eurasian and Arabian plates colliding.

GEOGRAPHY CONNECTION

1. Pontic Mountains are in northern Turkey along the Black Sea. The Taurus Mountains are in southern Turkey along the Mediterranean coast.
2. The Dardanelles provide access from the Sea of Marmara to the Mediterranean for trade. The Bosporus provides access from the Sea of Marmara to the Black Sea for trade.

W Writing Skills

Narrative Draw students' attention to the image of the river on this page. Tell students that they have been hired by a travel magazine to document a trip along the coastal plains of Turkey for a special issue about the Northeast. Tell students to use the photograph as a launching point for their articles, as well as using information from the text and conducting additional research. In their articles, students should describe the landscape, waterways, flora, fauna, and other natural features they pass on their trip. Encourage students to use their imaginations to provide travel tips to potential tourists, such as what essential items to pack based on the physical geography and climate of the region. BL Verbal/Linguistic

R Reading Skills

Describing Have students read the paragraph to learn about the characteristics of the Tigris and Euphrates Rivers. Then discuss the significance of the two rivers. **Ask:** What was the region called in ancient times? *(Mesopotamia)* What did this name mean? *("land between the rivers")* Across what regions does the Euphrates River flow? *(through the Taurus Mountains, southwest toward the Mediterranean coast in southern Turkey, across Syria and Iraq where it converges with the Tigris River)* Why do you think some of the world's earliest advanced civilizations arose near these rivers? *(Possible answer: Human civilizations need access to freshwater to thrive, to cultivate farmland for agriculture, and to raise livestock.)* ELL Visual/Spatial, Interpersonal

ANSWERS, p. 414

READING PROGRESS CHECK The Dardanelles and the Bosporus provide access from the Sea of Marmara to the Mediterranean and the Black Sea, which has been historically important for trade and military advantages.

CRITICAL THINKING

1. Student answers may vary but could include for agricultural/irrigation purposes and for transportation of goods and people.
2. It can be used to transport trade goods to ports along the Mediterranean coast.

W

A river flows through the Turkish plains near the Mediterranean coast.

▲ CRITICAL THINKING

1. ***Analyzing Visuals*** Based on the photo, what human purposes might this river serve?
2. ***Interpreting Significance*** What is the significance of this river's close proximity to the sea?

Water Systems

GUIDING QUESTION *How is the Tigris-Euphrates river system important to the human geography of the Northeast?*

The waterways of the Northeast have supported the birth of great civilizations and played vital roles in the fates of nations and empires. Linking the Aegean Sea and the Black Sea is a key waterway known as the Turkish Straits. It marks the border between Asia and Europe and consists of three smaller waterways called, from west to east, the Dardanelles, the Sea of Marmara, and the Bosporus. Through history, control of this waterway has produced military and commercial advantages for those who possessed it. The ability to stop or profit from traffic between the Mediterranean Sea and the Black Sea has been fought over repeatedly.

The Dardanelles is a narrow strait. At one point, it is only three-fourths of a mile (1 km) in width and at no point along its 38 miles (61 km) is it greater than 4 miles (6 km) wide. It opens on its eastern end to the small but deep Sea of Marmara. To the east of that point begins the Bosporus, which is another long, narrow strait. The Bosporus runs for 19 miles (31 km) before emptying into the Black Sea. The Black Sea encompasses a vast area, covering about 180,000 square miles (466,200 sq. km).

R

In the mountains of far eastern Turkey, within 50 miles (80.5 km) of each other, two great rivers begin their descent to the sea. These are the Tigris and the Euphrates. The rivers bound a region known since ancient times as Mesopotamia, which means "the land between the rivers." It is in this region that some of the world's earliest advanced civilizations arose. From its source, the Euphrates flows through the Taurus Mountains and southwest toward the Mediterranean coast in southern Turkey. But before reaching the Mediterranean, it turns southeast and continues in this direction for most of its 2,235-mile (3,596 km) journey across Syria and Iraq.

The shorter Tigris, at 1,180 miles (1,900 km) in length, flows from a mountain lake. It moves steadily southeast into Iraq. There, the Tigris and the Euphrates gradually converge. They almost touch near the Iraqi capital, Baghdad. They then separate and converge again. The two rivers eventually meet to form the Shatt al Arab. This river then flows the final 120 miles (193 km) to the Persian Gulf.

The dominant water feature in northern Iran is the Caspian Sea, which is slowly shrinking because of evaporation and a reduction of water flowing into the sea from the Volga River. This great inland sea forms the northern border of the country, where its waters are salty. The Caspian Sea serves as an important transportation link between Iran and other Asian countries. The Caspian also yields a number of valuable resources, notably oil and natural gas. Iran also has an active fishery in the Caspian Sea. Southern Iran is bounded by the Persian Gulf (or Arabian Gulf) and the Gulf of Oman. Between these lies the narrow Strait of Hormuz, a vital and strategic outlet from the Persian Gulf to the Indian Ocean.

READING PROGRESS CHECK

Explaining What is the significance of the Dardanelles, the Bosporus, and the Sea of Marmara?

networks Online Teaching Options

VIDEO

Iraq Geography

Identifying Before watching the video, explain that Iraq's geography is very diverse and that the Tigris-Euphrates river system flows through the country. As they watch the video, have students identify the physical regions *(alluvial plains, upland, deserts, highlands)* and the importance of the river system to Iraq. After viewing the video, have students share their information with a partner. Then as a class, have students discuss what they know or have learned about Iraq and its relationship within the region.
ELL Visual/Spatial, Verbal/Linguistic

Climate, Biomes, and Resources

GUIDING QUESTION *How do mountains influence climate in Turkey and Iran?*

The climate of the Northeast is heavily influenced by two major factors: mountain ranges and proximity to major bodies of water. Coastal and highland areas near mountain ranges usually receive the most rainfall. This is because moist, warm air is driven off the sea by the prevailing winds.

Climate Regions and Biomes

In Turkey, the areas along the coast enjoy a Mediterranean climate. Temperatures are subtropical, and typical Mediterranean scrub plants are native to the subregion. The summers are warm and dry, and the winters are mild and rainy. A similar climate prevails in the northern part of Iran along the Caspian Sea. The most valuable soils in Turkey are the alluvial soils found in the valleys, deltas, and basins of the lowland areas.

V

The interior of Turkey features a semi-arid steppe climate, which means it is generally dry with mild temperatures. Grasslands are the dominant vegetation type in the interior areas. This climate supports **pastoralism**—the raising of livestock—which is widely practiced in these areas. Western Iran also has an area of semi-arid steppe, although the temperatures are generally higher than in Turkey.

The high mountains of the subregion form barriers that block moisture from the major bodies of water from penetrating far inland. Thus, apart from the coasts, much of the Northeast experiences arid or semi-arid climates. Deserts cover western and southern Iraq and eastern and southern Iran.

Natural Resources

The most significant resources of the Northeast today are fossil fuels and the vital waterways that transport them. Iraq and Iran are among the world's leading producers of petroleum and natural gas. Iraq has many untapped mineral resources. Known reserves include sulfur and phosphates. Iran's major natural resources include chromium, copper, iron ore, lead, manganese, zinc, and sulfur. In addition to hydroelectric power, Turkey's natural resources include coal, iron ore, copper, mercury, and gold.

Turkey's geographic location is also an asset. In 2006 a pipeline that carries oil from an oil field in the Caspian Sea to the Mediterranean opened. Turkey benefits substantially from the transit fees. Other pipeline projects are planned to transport oil to Europe through Turkey from other countries.

✓ **READING PROGRESS CHECK**

Identifying What are the key natural resources of the Northeast subregion?

Iraq's Energy Resources

"Among all oil exporters, Iraq in 20 years' time will vault past Russia from third to second place, behind only Saudi Arabia, says IEA. The agency expects Iraq single-handedly to provide 45 percent of global production growth between now and 2035.
Iraq is 'very, very rich' in energy assets, said Fatih Birol, IEA chief economist and the report's main author. Iraq benefits from having some of the lowest production costs in the world and 'easy geography,' he said."

—Thomas K. Grose, "Iraq Poised to Lead World Oil Supply Growth, but Obstacles Loom," *National Geographic Daily News*, October 9, 2012

T

DBQ ***DRAWING CONCLUSIONS*** Why would the IEA chief economist say that Iraq has "easy geography"? RH.9–10.2, RH.9–10.4

pastoralism the raising of animals for food and other products

LESSON 1 REVIEW (CCSS)

Reviewing Vocabulary (Tier Three Words)

1. ***Identifying*** Write a sentence or two explaining pastoralism and how the geography of Turkey supports it. RH.9–10.4

Using Your Notes

2. ***Listing*** Use your graphic organizer to describe the significance of the North Anatolian Fault.

Answering the Guiding Questions

3. ***Describing*** What features dominate the physical geography of the Northeast?
4. ***Evaluating*** How is the Tigris-Euphrates river system important to the human geography of the Northeast?
5. ***Making Connections*** How do mountains influence climate in Turkey and Iran?

Writing Activity

6. ***Informative/Explanatory*** Write a paragraph explaining why the alluvial soils of the Northeast have been so central to the development of the human geography of the subregion. WHST.9–10.2

V Visual Skills

Transferring Information Ask a volunteer to read aloud the Guiding Question. Tell students to create a concept web for each country in the Northeast region labeled *Climate, Biomes,* and *Resources* with arrows between each heading. After students have had time to complete their webs, discuss their responses. **Ask: How does physical geography influence the climate of the Northeast?** *(The mountain ranges and proximity to bodies of water have a major impact on the region. Areas near mountains receive more rainfall than other areas because prevailing winds bring moist, warm air to the region.)* **How do waterways play a role in the region's natural resources?** *(Waterways provide a means of transportation of fossil fuels.)* **Visual/Spatial**

T Technology Skills

Evaluating Primary Sources After students read the *Analyzing Primary Sources* feature, have them work in groups to prepare a report about Iraq's energy resources. Tell students to evaluate the statement by the International Energy Agency's (IEA) chief economist in their reports. Have group members collaborate to find facts that support the title of the article, "Iraq Poised to Lead World Oil Supply Growth, but Obstacles Loom." Students should identify information that supports both the first and the second part of the title. **BL Logical/Mathematical, Interpersonal**

CLOSE & REFLECT

Speculating In a class discussion, have students speculate about how one or more aspects of the Northeast's physical geography might play a role in impacting relations between countries in the region. Then have students make speculations about potential environmental issues the physical geography might present.

LESSON 1 REVIEW ANSWERS

Reviewing Vocabulary

1. Sentences will vary but should include that pastoralism is the raising of livestock and it is supported in Turkey by the mild temperatures and abundant grasslands of the interior.

Using Your Notes

2. The North Anatolian Fault is one of the most active faults in the world, causing many devastating earthquakes in the last seven decades.

Answering the Guiding Questions

3. The Anatolian Plateau and mountain ranges, such as the Taurus and Pontic in Turkey, the Elburz in Iran, and Zagros in Iran and Iraq, dominate the landscape in the Northeast.
4. The Tigris-Euphrates river system created an area where the world's earliest civilizations could rise and flourish.
5. The high mountains block moisture from penetrating inland areas. This causes the interior areas of Turkey and western Iran to have a semi-arid climate. Southern Iran is covered by desert.

Writing Activity

6. Paragraphs will vary but should be strongly supported with information from the lesson, including that the alluvial plain covers the central and southern third of Iraq and sustained some of the earliest civilizations in history.

ANSWERS, p. 415

✓ **READING PROGRESS CHECK** The key natural resources include fossil fuels and waterways to transport resources.

DBQ Iraq has relatively easy access geographically to its oil.

ENGAGE

V Visual Skills

Interpreting Visuals Direct students' attention to the images at the top of the page. Have partners create a list of topics and issues about the human geography of the Northeast that they think relate to the photos. Tell students to skim through the lesson to check whether their lists are correct.

TEACH & ASSESS

C1 Critical Thinking Skills

Drawing Inferences Ask a volunteer to read aloud the Guiding Question. **Ask:** **What are some ways that the discovery of oil might impact a region?** *(Possible answer: The discovery can ultimately lead to great wealth, but it can also cause conflict. For example, conflicts might arise over who will control the resource and profit from revenue generated by the sale of the oil. The development of oil resources could also have a negative impact on the environment.)* **BL** **Logical/Mathematical**

C2 Critical Thinking Skills

Identifying Continuity and Change Have students review the text and depict the information in a flowchart or diagram. Students should indicate the series of events that led to the emergence of civilization. Explain that before early humans settled in permanent communities, they were primarily nomadic hunters and gatherers. **Ask:** **What led to the development of permanent villages in the Northeast?** *(The rich soil of Mesopotamia supported agriculture, which allowed early humans to grow a surplus of food. This in turn allowed the support of growing populations, and larger, settled communities formed. With this food surplus, early humans could focus on activities other than farming, such as developing tools and organizing communities.)* **Visual/Spatial**

ANSWERS, p. 416

TAKING NOTES: Sumerian civilization—developed in Mesopotamia around 5,000 years ago; grew crops year-round and used irrigation systems, developed an early writing system based on cuneiform; created a system of mathematics and a code of law; **Persian Empire**—arose east of Mesopotamia across the Zagros Mountains in what is now Iran; by 500 B.C. Persians had captured the territory that is modern-day Iraq and Turkey; built qanats (underground canals); **Ottoman Empire**—began on the Anatolian Plateau; empire extended into North Africa, western Asia, and southeastern Europe at its peak; defeat of the Ottomans and Germans in WW I ended some 600 years of rule

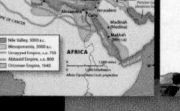

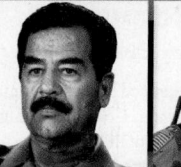

networks
There's More Online! **V**

- **IMAGE** Women Wearing Burkas
- **MAP** Civilizations and Empires of the Northeast
- **TIME LINE** Independence and Turmoil
- **INTERACTIVE SELF-CHECK QUIZ**
- **VIDEO** Human Geography of the Northeast

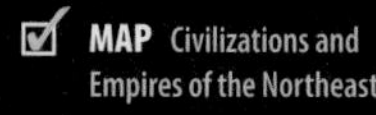

(tl)Thomas Hartwell/TIME & LIFE Images/Getty Images, (tc)Tom Stoddart Archive/Hulton Archive/Getty Images, (tc)Janet Wishnetsky/Alamy, (tr)Ali Al-Saadi/AFP/Getty Images

LESSON 2
Human Geography of the Northeast

ESSENTIAL QUESTION • *How do physical systems and human systems shape a place?*

Reading HELPDESK (CCSS)

Academic Vocabulary (Tier Two Words)
- **assume**
- **participate**

Content Vocabulary (Tier Three Words)
- **natural boundary**
- **culture hearth**
- **cuneiform**
- ***qanat***
- **ziggurat**
- **embargo**

TAKING NOTES: ***Key Ideas and Details***

IDENTIFYING As you read about the human geography of the Northeast, use a graphic organizer like the one below to list the subregion's historical civilizations and empires and record their characteristics.

The Northeast

Ancient Civilizations	Characteristics

IT MATTERS BECAUSE

In the Northeast, cultures are fundamentally tied to religion. Islam is the most widely practiced religion in the subregion. For hundreds of years, it has defined people's lives. Today, Islam is the fastest-growing religion in the world.

History and Government

C1 **GUIDING QUESTION** *How have ancient civilizations and the discovery of oil impacted the Northeast?*

The Northeast saw the rise of several great civilizations. The earliest was Sumer, followed by the Babylonian, Persian, and Ottoman civilizations. More recently, the subregion's rich oil resources have helped make it the focus of the international quest to obtain and control energy supplies.

Civilizations and Empires

The Tigris and Euphrates Rivers formed a **natural boundary** around a historical region known as Mesopotamia. Mesopotamia was one of the world's first **culture hearths**. A culture hearth is a center from which cultures develop and then spread to other places.

C2 The rich alluvial soils of Mesopotamia supported the development of agriculture. As humans learned to raise their own food, they were able to settle in permanent villages. Farmers could produce a surplus, which supported growing populations. In larger, settled communities, people now had time to develop new tools and organize and govern communities. In this way, civilizations emerged.

Mesopotamia was home to the Sumerian civilization that developed some 5,000 years ago. The Sumerians grew crops year-round and used canals to irrigate their fields. To keep records, they developed an early system of writing based on **cuneiform** which consists of wedge-shaped symbols pressed into clay tablets. In time the Sumerians created a system of mathematics and a code of law. About 1900 B.C., the Babylonian civilization emerged and dominated Mesopotamia.

416

networks Online Teaching Options

INTERACTIVE BELLRINGER

Ethnic Groups of the Northeast

Reading Graphs and Inferring These graphs can be used to help students identify how ethnic diversity affects population patterns in the Northeast. Have students work with a partner to answer the questions. Ask each pair to record their answers. Compile a list of all responses, and then have the class discuss the answers. **Verbal/Linguistic, Visual/Spatial**

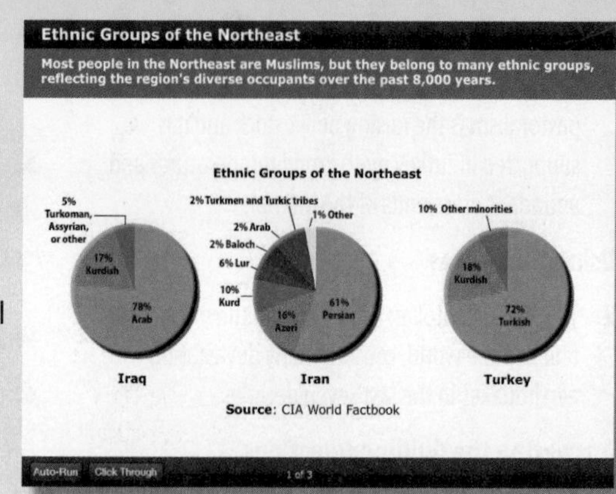

The Persian Empire arose to the east of Mesopotamia, in what is now Iran. By 500 B.C. the Persians had conquered nearly all of the present-day territory of Iraq, Jordan, Israel, and Turkey. One of their great engineering achievements was the building of **qanats**, or underground canals. *Qanats* reduced the evaporation of water as it flowed from the mountains to farmlands. **W**

The Ottoman Empire has its roots on the Anatolian Plateau. At its peak, the empire extended into North Africa, western Asia, and southeastern Europe. The defeat of the Ottomans and Germans in World War I ended some 600 years of rule.

Oil and the Modern Era

From the remnants of the Ottoman Empire, the modern country of Turkey was established. Turkey is aligned militarily with Western Europe as a member of the North Atlantic Treaty Organization (NATO). It has applied for EU membership.

Once part of the Ottoman Empire, Iraq became an independent state in 1932. It has experienced considerable turmoil since. This includes a war with Iran (1980–1988) and two wars against the United States and coalition forces. The most recent occurred between 2003 and 2011. It resulted in the arrest, conviction, and execution of dictator Saddam Hussein and the establishment of a parliamentary democracy.

The last Persian Empire lost most of its territory to the Ottoman Empire, but the core of Persia—modern-day Iran—remained an independent country. In 1979 a revolution overthrew the secular government headed by the shah, and an Islamic Republic was formed. Islamic scholars, known as mullahs, came to power. They continue to dominate Iranian politics. Recently, international tensions have risen as Iran is suspected of developing nuclear weapons. **C**

Fossil fuels are a major natural resource in the subregion. Oil was discovered near the Persian Gulf in 1908. By 1911 the first commercial oil well was operating in Iran. Over time, the wells produced large quantities of oil and came under the control of countries and national oil companies, benefiting their economies.

natural boundary a boundary created by a physical feature, such as a mountain, river, or strait

culture hearth a center in which cultures develop and from which they are spread

cuneiform a system of writing using wedge-shaped symbols that were pressed into clay tablets

qanat an underground canal first built by the ancient Persians

GEOGRAPHY CONNECTION

The Northeast produced several great civilizations and empires.

1. ***PLACES AND REGIONS*** Which present-day country in the Northeast was not part of the Ottoman Empire?
2. ***PHYSICAL SYSTEMS*** Which area benefited from its physical geography, which included the Tigris and Euphrates Rivers?

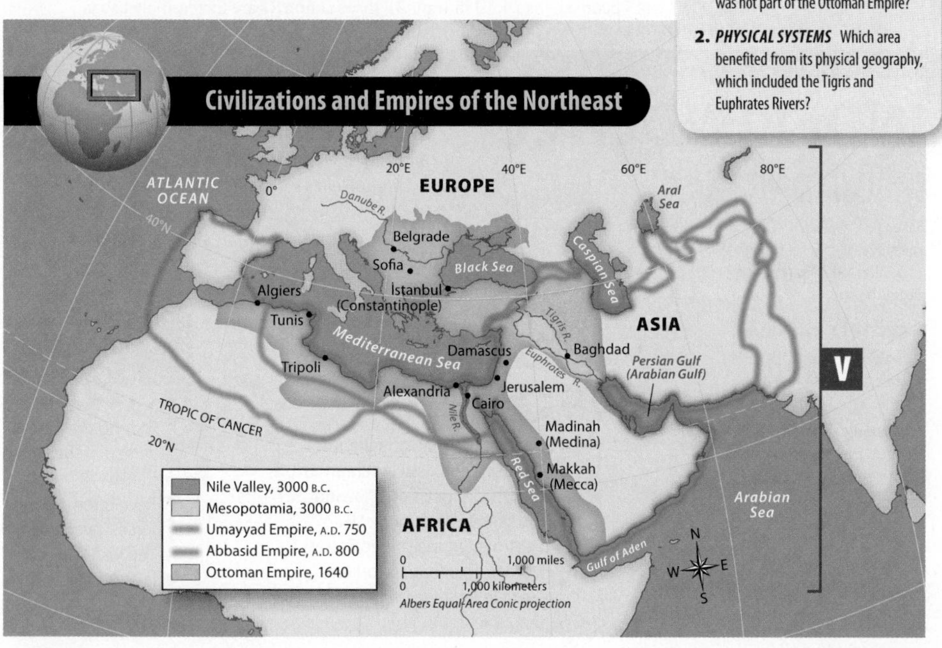

V

INTERACTIVE MAP

Civilizations and Empires of the Northeast

Sequencing Information Point out the key presented on the Civilizations and Empires of the Northeast interactive map. Review with students the significance of the abbreviations "B.C." and "A.D." Ask students to determine whether the civilizations and empires in the key are listed in chronological order. Once students have determined the chronology, ask them to discuss which of the civilizations/empires may have had the most impact on present-day conditions in the Northeast, and to explain why they chose their answer.

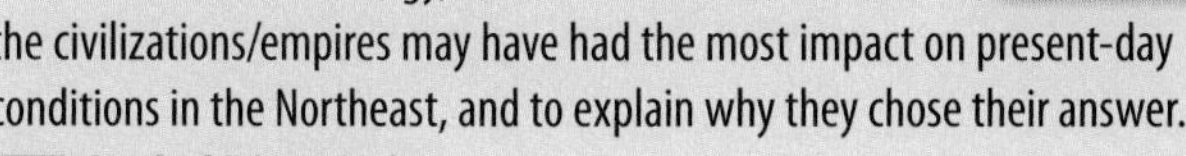

ELL Verbal/Linguistic

W Writing Skills

Informative/Explanatory Have students review each of the sections' four vocabulary terms and their meanings. Challenge students to write one or two paragraphs to use and show their understanding of the terms. Ask volunteers to read their paragraphs to the class. **Ask:** **How did cuneiform and *qanats* contribute to the development of societies in the Northeast?** *(Cuneiform gave the Sumerians a system of writing that allowed them to keep records and communicate. By building qanats, Persians developed an underground water-supply system that lasted longer than aboveground canals would have.)*
ELL Verbal/Linguistic

C Critical Thinking Skills

Identifying Central Issues Have students read the paragraph, noting the various issues in Iran's past and present. **Ask:** **What led to the formation of an Islamic Republic in Iran?** *(The Shah of Iran was overthrown in a revolution.)* **Why might modern-day Iran have strained relations with other countries?** *(Possible answer: Other countries may be suspicious of Iran's suspected development of nuclear weapons.)*
AL Logical/Mathematical

V Visual Skills

Global Analysis Have students work in pairs to analyze the map, noting the different regions where civilizations and empires developed. Then have partners identify the modern-day countries that exist in these regions today. Have students sketch a similar map showing where today's countries are located. You may wish to provide each pair with an outline map of the region, which can be found in the online Teacher Resource Center. Have students present their maps to the class along with a summarizing statement about the modern-day countries located in the Northeast. **Visual/Spatial**

ANSWERS, p. 417

GEOGRAPHY CONNECTION

1. Iran was not part of the Ottoman Empire.
2. Mesopotamia benefited from its location between the Tigris and Euphrates Rivers.

V Visual Skills

Creating Graphs After students have read the Guiding Question and the paragraphs about population patterns, have them work in small groups to create a graph that shows the ethnic diversity using current population percentages. Suggest that students conduct online research to identify ethnic populations in the Northeast. After students have had time to gather the information and create their graphs, tell them to write a statement that summarizes the information in their charts. Have groups present their graphs to the class, and then use students' presentations as a springboard to discussion. **Ask: Why does the Northeast have a diverse population even though the majority of its people are Muslims?** *(Over the past 8,000 years, many people have occupied the subregion from different ethnic groups including Turks, Iranians, Arabs, and Kurds.)* **What might be the effect of this diversity on the culture of the Northeast?** *(Many different languages are spoken and different customs practiced among the ethnic groups.)* **BL Visual/Spatial, Logical/Mathematical**

Making Connections

As you review the time line with students, have them recall previous chapters they have studied in which independence is linked to conflict and turmoil. Then have them recall what they know about the history of the United States and its road to independence. Discuss some of the reasons that countries seek independence and how the quest for independence often results in struggles and conflict.

ANSWERS, p. 418

READING PROGRESS CHECK Sumerians grew crops year-round and developed an early system of writing based on cuneiform in order to keep records.

CRITICAL THINKING

1. Iraq feared the spread of the Iranian Revolution and invaded Iran. The Iraq-Iran War lasted eight years.
2. The U.S. led airstrikes against Iraq in 1991 that began the Persian Gulf War, which ended six weeks later with the defeat of Iraq. The U.S. invaded Iraq in 2003, which led to the overthrow of Saddam Hussein and the installation of an interim government. U.S. troops were not withdrawn from Iraq until 2011.

In 1960 Iran and Iraq joined with several oil-producing neighbors to form the Organization of Petroleum Exporting Countries (OPEC). This group agreed to regulate oil production to keep oil prices high. As the global demand for oil grew, OPEC **assumed**, or gained, more power over global oil prices.

assume to gain or acquire

READING PROGRESS CHECK

Explaining How did agriculture contribute to the formation of the Sumerian civilization?

Population Patterns

GUIDING QUESTION *How have ethnic diversity and Islam shaped the population patterns of the Northeast?*

The majority of people in the Northeast are Muslims. Their religion, Islam, has a significant role in their cultures. While Islam is the primary religion, the population is ethnically diverse. Major ethnic groups include Turks, Iranians, Arabs, and Kurds.

V This ethnic diversity persists because over the past 8,000 years many peoples have occupied the subregion. Each group added its own customs and beliefs to the local culture. Turkic peoples migrated to the western Anatolian Plateau from Central Asia in the A.D. 1000s. The name *Iran* means "land of the Aryans" (AR•ee•uhnz), from the ancient Indo-European people who settled in Iran.

Today the majority of people living in Iraq are Arabs, with ethnic ties to the Arabian Peninsula. The Kurds are an ethnic group that has lived for thousands of years in the mountainous border areas of Turkey, Iraq, and Iran. Kurds have no country of their own, though they call the land they live in Kurdistan. Some Kurds **participate** in efforts to achieve independence and have their own country.

participate to take part in

Turkey and Iran each have populations of about 80 million people, while about 31 million people live in Iraq. Population density ranges from about 246 people per square mile (95 people per sq. km) in Turkey to about 117 people per square mile (45 people per sq. km) in Iran. All three countries are increasingly urban.

TIME LINE

INDEPENDENCE and Turmoil

Turkey, Iran, and Iraq have experienced decades of struggles for political and military power in the Northeast.

CRITICAL THINKING

1. ***Analyzing*** How did the Iranian Revolution affect Iran and its neighbors?
2. ***Describing*** What role has the United States played in events in this region?

1979

1979 January—Shah of Iran forced to flee due to Iranian Revolution. Ayatollah Ruhollah Khomeini takes over as Iran's supreme leader.

1979 July—Saddam Hussein becomes president of Iraq and begins work to secure his power as a dictator.

1979 November—Iranian militants seize U.S. embassy in Tehran to protest U.S. decision allowing the shah to seek medical treatment in the United States. Dozens of embassy workers are held hostage for more than a year.

1980 Fearing the spread of the Iranian Revolution, Iraqi forces invade Iran. The Iraq-Iran War lasts eight years.

networks Online Teaching Options

VIDEO

The Challenge of the Past Ottoman Empire

Summarizing Use this video about the Ottoman Empire to discuss Turkey's history. Have students summarize the role religion has played in the history and politics of Turkey. Review that Muslims are followers of Islam. Lead a class discussion on what it means for many in Turkey today to practice their Muslim beliefs. Ask students if they believe it is possible for this region to have a balance between religion and politics in the modern era. **BL Verbal/Linguistic**

The cities of Istanbul, Turkey; Tehran, Iran; and Baghdad, Iraq, dominate social and cultural life in their respective countries. These cities have become overcrowded due to the rapid influx of villagers seeking opportunities available in the urban centers. Iran has tried to address this problem by moving some of its government offices to towns away from the capital, Tehran. T

READING PROGRESS CHECK

Identifying What are the major ethnic groups in the Northeast?

Society and Culture Today

GUIDING QUESTION *How do religion and language influence life in the Northeast today?*

The legacies of the ancient civilizations of the Northeast can be seen today. Languages and customs differ depending on ancestral homes. Arabic is the most commonly spoken language in Iraq. Most Iraqi Arabs are Shia Muslims, but about 35 percent are Sunni Muslims. A small percentage is Christian or another faith. Iranians speak Farsi, also called Persian, and the majority are Shia. Turks speak Turkish, and most practice Islam. Modern Turkish culture blends Turkish, Islamic, and Western elements. Most Kurds are Sunni Muslims and speak Kurdish, a language distinct from, but related to, Farsi.

Turkey, Iraq, and Iran all support systems of free public education. The amount of education a child receives in a lifetime is 13 years in Iran, 12 years in Turkey, and 10 years in Iraq. Iran has made great strides in educating its population since the Islamic Revolution. Before the revolution, its literacy rate was under 50 percent. Today, the literacy rate is 77 percent in Iran, more than 78 percent in Iraq, and over 87 percent in Turkey.

Health care varies in the subregion. Iraq is still struggling to rebuild hospitals after years of war. In other countries, hospitals are government-owned and may suffer from doctor shortages, especially in rural areas. In recent years, private

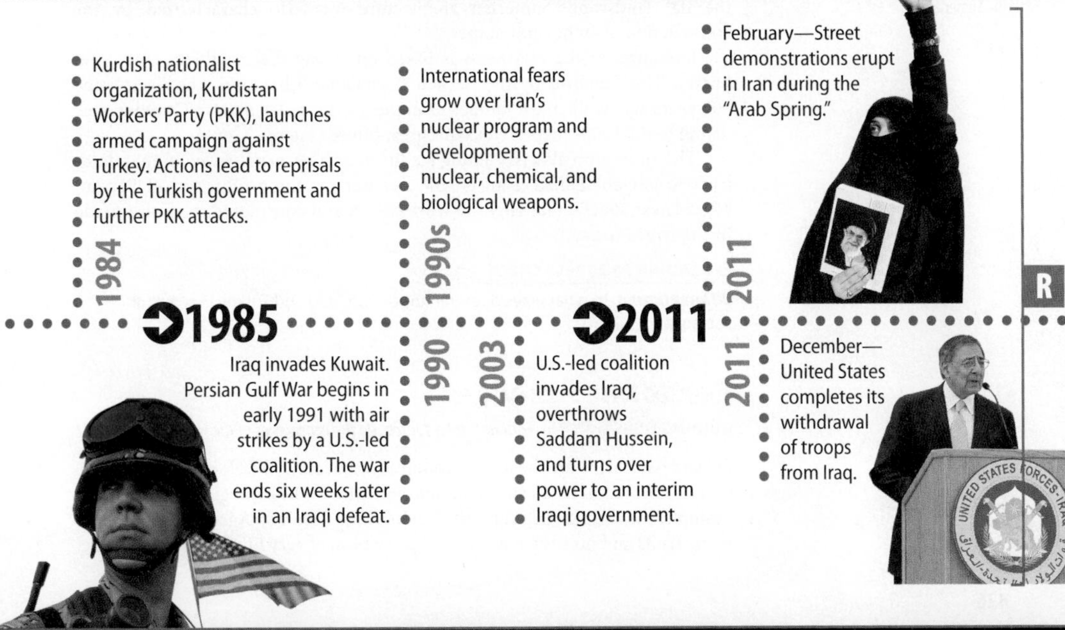

1984
Kurdish nationalist organization, Kurdistan Workers' Party (PKK), launches armed campaign against Turkey. Actions lead to reprisals by the Turkish government and further PKK attacks.
1985
1990
Iraq invades Kuwait. Persian Gulf War begins in early 1991 with air strikes by a U.S.-led coalition. The war ends six weeks later in an Iraqi defeat.
1990s
International fears grow over Iran's nuclear program and development of nuclear, chemical, and biological weapons.
2003
U.S.-led coalition invades Iraq, overthrows Saddam Hussein, and turns over power to an interim Iraqi government.
2011
2011
February—Street demonstrations erupt in Iran during the "Arab Spring."
2011
December—United States completes its withdrawal of troops from Iraq.
R

SLIDE SHOW

The Kurds

Outlining After reviewing the slide show, direct students' attention to the time line. Note the 1984 entry relating the Kurds' campaign against Turkey. Have students use the information from the slide show and the time line to outline the reasons why the Kurdistan Workers' Party decided to revolt against Turkey. Then challenge students to write a thesis statement for their outlines. AL **Visual/Spatial, Verbal/Linguistic**

T Technology Skills

Changing Continuity of Groups Have students read the information about major cities in countries of the Northeast. Guide students to understand how population patterns can shift according to migrations of different groups of people. Organize students into small groups and have each group choose a major city in the subregion to research. Students may choose one of the cities discussed in the text or another major city in the region. Have groups conduct online research to identify recent population patterns of their city, the reasons for the population changes, and the social and cultural impacts of those changes. Have students present their findings to the class in a report that includes visuals to support the information. BL **Logical/Mathematical, Verbal/Linguistic**

R Reading Skills

Questioning Organize students into three groups, assigning each group to Turkey, Iran, or Iraq. After they analyze the events on the time line, have students in each group collaborate to formulate questions about their assigned country. Questions may be about a fact on the time line that students want to learn more about, or students may address an issue that is confusing or requires clarification. Once students have compiled a list of questions, have them reread information in the text to answer their questions. Then have students conduct online research to address any unanswered questions. After groups have answered each question on their lists, call on groups to discuss one of their questions and its answer, describing what information they found most interesting or surprising. **Interpersonal**

ANSWERS, p. 419

READING PROGRESS CHECK Turks, Iranians, Arabs, and Kurds are the major ethnic groups of the Northeast.

V Visual Skills

Creating Charts After students read the paragraph, have them consider the reasons for the different average household sizes and how the various sizes might impact society and the economies of the Northeast. Lead a discussion about the reasons for varying household sizes in Turkey, Iran, and Iraq. To reinforce students' understanding, have them create a bar graph to show the number of people in the average household for each country. **ELL Visual/Spatial, Logical/Mathematical**

W Writing Skills

Argument Have students review the information in the text about family life and the status of women in the Northeast. Have students conduct research about the impact that government-supported family planning programs have had on population patterns in countries in the Northeast. Then have students write a short argumentative essay based on whether or not they agree with government policies that regulate family size. Allow time for students to conduct additional research to locate supporting evidence for their argument. Ask volunteers to present their essays to the class, which can lead into a class discussion about the issue of women's rights with regard to family size. **BL Verbal/Linguistic**

T Technology Skills

Researching Have students conduct research to identify the use and significance of arches and domes in Sumerian architecture. Tell students to draw parallels to the use of arches and domes in other civilizations, such as ancient Greece and Rome. Have students use information from their research to prepare a compare-and-contrast essay in which they describe the similarities and differences of Sumerian architecture with that of other civilizations. Have students include visual samples of the arches and domes in their essays. **Visual/Spatial**

ANSWERS, p. 420

READING PROGRESS CHECK Iran is an Islamic republic, which means it adheres strictly to Islamic laws. Women have fewer rights than in Turkey and Iraq and must dress and act according to Islamic law.

CRITICAL THINKING

1. The chador limits women's interactions in public as it makes them indistinguishable from one another and inhibits any kind of contact.
2. The chador reveals that even in countries that claim there is equality for women, religious law still hinders women's rights.

Some Muslim women wear a chador—a long, loose garment that covers the body—in public.

▲ CRITICAL THINKING

1. ***Analyzing Visuals*** How would wearing the chador affect women's interactions in public?
2. ***Inferring*** What does the chador reveal about the status of women?

Janet Wishnetsky/Alamy

hospitals in Turkey have begun competing with state hospitals. The competition has led to improvements in state-owned hospitals.

Family and Status of Women

V Family life usually includes the extended family. In Turkey, the average household consists of a nuclear family with 3.8 persons, but the extended family remains important. The average household size in Iran is similar, with 3.6 persons per household. In recent years, family size in Iran has decreased due to a government-supported family planning program and the economic effects of embargoes intended to stop Iran's nuclear program. The average household in Iraq is much larger than in Turkey and Iran, with an average of 6.7 persons.

W The conservative Islamic culture of the Northeast defines the roles and opportunities available to women. Government policies in some countries have improved the status of women. In Turkey, a 2002 law gave women equal rights with men for marriage, divorce, and property. In Iran, however, women's rights were curtailed after the establishment of the Islamic Republic in 1979. Many public places were segregated by sex, and female government workers were required to observe an Islamic dress code. In the more secular state of Iraq, women and men have equal rights under the law. However, lack of women's rights and gender equity are issues that hinder development in much of the Northeast.

The Arts

T The early civilizations of the Northeast created sculptures, fine metalwork, and large buildings. In Mesopotamia the Sumerians built large, mud-brick temples called **ziggurats**. These temples were shaped like pyramids and rose high above the flat landscape. Sumerian architecture was also characterized by the construction of arches and domes.

ziggurat a large temple built by the Sumerians

Literature in the Northeast is based on strong oral tradition, epics, and poetry. The *Rubáiyát* by the Persian poet Omar Khayyám, who lived some 900 years ago, is the most famous example. *Osman's Dream* is an Ottoman epic dating to the 1200s that foretells of a great future empire.

The subregion also has a long tradition of fine carpet weaving that dates back to ancient Persia. Iran is still a center for the production of Persian rugs. These spectacular rugs are works of art and considered the finest made in the world today.

READING PROGRESS CHECK

Differentiating In what ways does Iran differ from Iraq and Turkey in terms of society and culture?

Economic Activities

GUIDING QUESTION *On what natural resources do the economies of the Northeast depend?*

Oil and natural gas are the major economic resources in the Northeast. There are other valuable resources and economic activities in the subregion, however. For example, the Caspian Sea supports Iran's fishing industry. Agriculture produces many fruits and nuts, such as figs and pistachios, of very high quality and value.

420

networks Online Teaching Options

INTERACTIVE WHITEBOARD ACTIVITY

From Mesopotamia to Modern Day

Identifying Continuity and Change Use this interactive whiteboard activity to have students examine how civilizations and empires of the past developed and led to development of the Northeast countries today. Students will identify historical events of past empires and civilizations and then relate these present events to the countries in the Northeast today. After the activity, ask students to make observations about trends or connections between the past and today. **BL Logical/Mathematical, Visual/Spatial**

From Mesopotamia to Modern Day

Directions: Three empires once occupied the Northeast subregion that is modern-day Turkey, Iraq, and Iran. Drag the events or characteristics into the empire column to which each belongs. Each description will be used only once. Not all columns will be filled.

Sumerian Empire	Persian Empire	Ottoman Empire

Built mud-brick temples called ziggurats
Lost all territory except the land that makes up Iran today
Began in the region known as the Anatolian Plateau
Part of one of the world's first culture hearths
Built underground canals called qanats
Extended into North Africa, western Asia, and southeastern Europe
Developed communities that farmed year-round
Arose originally in the area that is present-day Iran
Designed a system of writing based on cuneiform
By 500 B.C., conquered much of present-day Turkey and Iraq
Ruled for 600 years until defeat by the Germans
Built canals to irrigate their farmland
Gave rise to modern-day Turkey and Iraq

Show Answers

Resources, Power, and Industry

Both Iran and Iraq produce far more oil than they need for domestic consumption, and so are leading exporters of oil. Revenues from oil exports are enormously important to their economies. As members of OPEC, Iran and Iraq have considerable influence in global affairs. For example, OPEC raised oil prices during the 1970s and placed an **embargo** on oil shipments to the United States and other industrialized countries. OPEC actions can also have positive effects. OPEC restored stability to the oil market and supported economic recovery during the global recession in 2009. Events unrelated to OPEC also show the influence that Iraq and Iran can have in global affairs. For example, in 2006 and 2008, oil prices rose sharply due to the ongoing conflict in Iraq and tensions over Iran's nuclear ambitions. C

embargo a ban on trade

Turkey does not have the oil or natural gas resources that its regional neighbors do, but it does produce hydroelectric power. Other key industries in Turkey include textiles, food processing, and manufacturing autos and electronics. Turkey's service sector also forms a significant part of the economy.

Trade and Interdependence

The countries of the Northeast and the rest of the world depend on one another. Industrialized countries need oil from the region; the region needs industrial products for its markets. Iran operates oil-refining facilities, although Iraq's oil-refining facilities were closed or greatly restricted during the 2003–2011 U.S.-led war. Natural gas and oil pipelines are examples of the advanced transportation systems that crisscross this subregion. Much of this network is designed to move oil and gas from the fields to various ports. Since Turkey has access to the Mediterranean and the rest of Europe, many pipelines from oil fields end in Turkish ports. Other lines deliver oil to ports on the Persian Gulf and the Gulf of Oman. Much of the oil shipped from the Persian Gulf must pass through the Strait of Hormuz. The narrow strait is a choke point for shipping. Military action, a shipping accident, or political decisions could possibly close the strait. During most years, there are about 17 supertankers passing through the strait each day. R

Television and radio broadcasting is expanding in the subregion, though government control of the media in many places limits programming. Advances in satellite technology are improving communication services. Wireless service and solar-powered radiophones are bringing telephone service to more people. Cell phones are now common, and many people have computer and Internet access.

☑ READING PROGRESS CHECK

Identifying What is the most significant natural resource in the Northeast?

LESSON 2 REVIEW

Reviewing Vocabulary (Tier Three Words)

1. ***Applying*** Write a paragraph about the history of the Northeast that includes the words *culture hearth, cuneiform,* qanat, *natural boundary, embargo,* and *ziggurat.* RH.9–10.4

Using Your Notes

2. ***Summarizing*** Use your notes from the graphic organizer to write two paragraphs summarizing the history of the Northeast.

Answering the Guiding Questions

3. ***Explaining*** How have ancient civilizations and the discovery of oil impacted the Northeast?
4. ***Describing*** How have ethnic diversity and Islam shaped the population patterns of the Northeast?
5. ***Making Connections*** How do religion and language influence life in the Northeast today?
6. ***Identifying*** On what natural resources do the economies of the Northeast depend?

Writing Activity

7. ***Informative/Explanatory*** Write a paragraph comparing and contrasting modern Turkey, Iran, and Iraq. Include aspects of their economies, cultures and population patterns. WHST.9–10.2

C Critical Thinking Skills

Evaluating Discuss with the class the impact of OPEC on the global economy. **Ask: How has OPEC influenced the global economy in past years?** *(The members of OPEC raised oil prices and placed a ban on oil shipments to the United States and other countries in the 1970s.)* **What have been some positive effects of OPEC's actions?** *(The organization has worked to restore stability to the oil market and has supported economic recovery and stabilization during the global recession in 2009.)*

R Reading Skills

Identifying Trends Discuss the term *interdependence* with students. Ask students to volunteer a scenario in their own lives that could be described as interdependent. Have students work in pairs to read the information in the paragraph to be sure they understand the concepts being discussed. **Ask: Why do many pipelines and oil fields end in Turkish ports?** *(Turkey has access to the Mediterranean Sea and the rest of Europe.)* AL **Interpersonal**

CLOSE & REFLECT

Summarizing Have students review the lesson. Tell them to write a summarizing paragraph about the impact that the discovery of oil has had on the societies, cultures, and economies of the countries in the Northeast region.

ANSWERS, p. 421

☑ **READING PROGRESS CHECK** Oil is the most significant resource for Iran and Iraq in the Northeast. Turkey has hydroelectric power.

LESSON 2 REVIEW ANSWERS

Reviewing Vocabulary

1. Student answers may vary but should include the words *culture hearth, cuneiform, qanat, natural boundary, embargo,* and *ziggurat.*

Using Your Notes

2. Student answers may vary but should include information on the Sumerian civilization and the Persian and Ottoman Empires.

Answering the Guiding Questions

3. Ancient civilizations helped form and determine the settlement of the modern countries of Iran, Iraq, and Turkey. The discovery of oil has changed the economies, making them dependent on exports. Many international efforts have been made to control the vast energy supplies available in Iran and Iraq.
4. Most people are Muslim, yet they are ethnically diverse. Turkish people migrated to the Anatolian Plateau. Indo-Europeans settled Iran. The majority of Iraqis are Arabs with ties to the Arabian Peninsula. The Kurds have lived for thousands of years in the mountainous border areas of Turkey, Iraq, and Iran, and call the region Kurdistan.
5. Language and religion vary; most Iraqi Arabs are Shia Muslim but 35 percent are Sunni Muslim, Iranians are mostly Shia Muslim but speak Farsi, Turks speak Turkish and practice Islam, Kurds are Sunni Muslim and speak Kurdish.
6. Northeast economies depend upon oil and natural gas, especially in Iran and Iraq. Iran also depends on its fishing industry. Agriculture such as figs and pistachios are important in the region as well.

Writing Activity

7. Student answers may vary, but should include: **economies**—world trade is important; oil exports for Iran and Iraq, service sector for Turkey; **cultures**—Arabic is the most common language; religions include Shia Muslims, Sunni Muslims, small percentage of Christians and other faiths; greater women's rights in Iraq and Turkey than Iran; average household size of 3.8 in Turkey, 3.6 for Iran, and 6.7 for Iraq; **population patterns**—major ethnic groups: Turks, Iranian, Arabs, and Kurds; all three countries are increasingly urban; Turkey and Iran have populations of about 80 million, Iraq has about 31 million people

ENGAGE

V Visual Skills

Analyzing Visuals Before students read this Case Study, direct their attention to the title of this feature and the photographs on each page. **Ask:** **What do you think the people in the photographs are protesting?** *(Student answers may vary, but based on the feature's title and images, they should infer that the people in the photographs are probably speaking out for their religious rights or against oppression or discrimination.)* As students read about the different beliefs of the Sunni and Shia in this Case Study, have them consider how deep religious faith as well as struggles for political power can lead to conflict.

TEACH & ASSESS

C Critical Thinking Skills

Understanding Historical Interpretation After students have read the first paragraph, discuss the deep-seated division between the Sunni and Shia. **Ask:** **What is the primary difference between the two branches within Islam?** *(The Shia originally believed that a descendant of Muhammad should be the Muslim leader, but the Sunni believed that the leader should be chosen by the Islamic community based on personal qualities and abilities.)* **How do these factors play a role in modern-day conflicts between the two branches?** *(Possible answer: These two factors likely played a larger role in the early years of the religion but may now have more to do with political power or overall religious freedom.)* **Logical/Mathematical**

Making Connections

To help students make connections to the theme of religious discrimination and persecution discussed in this Case Study, remind them that early European settlers escaped to this country seeking religious freedom. Explain that religious differences have been the cause of persecution in other parts of the world for centuries.

Case Study: **Culture** 

HOW HAVE SUNNI AND SHIA BELIEFS LED TO CONFLICT?

C Within Islam, there are two main branches—Sunni and Shia. The divisions between these groups go back to the early years of the religion. The death of Muhammad in A.D. 632 led to a dispute over the succession of leadership in Islam. What we today call the Shia insisted that the Muslim leader, or caliph, be a descendant of Ali, the son-in-law and cousin of Muhammad, and his wife Fatima, Muhammad's daughter. Conversely, the Sunni believed that the leader should be selected by the Islamic community on the basis of personal qualities and abilities.

The split between the two groups has persisted over the centuries. Today Sunnis are the majority of Muslims. It is estimated that between 85 and 90 percent of all Muslims worldwide are Sunni. Only in Iran, Iraq, Bahrain, and Azerbaijan do Shias make up the majority of Muslims.

Iran is a country dominated by Shia Muslims. With this dominance has come some conflict—and not all of it having to do purely with matters of deeply held religious faith. In many places, Sunnis and Shias have vied for political power and sought to advance their people's interests at the expense of others.

After the Iranian Revolution, Islamic law was reintroduced. Although the new government was a republic with elements of a parliamentary democracy, it was also a theocracy. Shia clerics have final approval of legislation, with the intention of ensuring compliance with Islamic law. Iran does permit and have religious minorities. These include a small but significant Sunni Muslim population (many of whom are Kurds), Zoroastrians, Christians, and Baha'is. However, relations between the government and its Sunni minority have been complicated, and members of religious minorities are treated as second-class citizens.

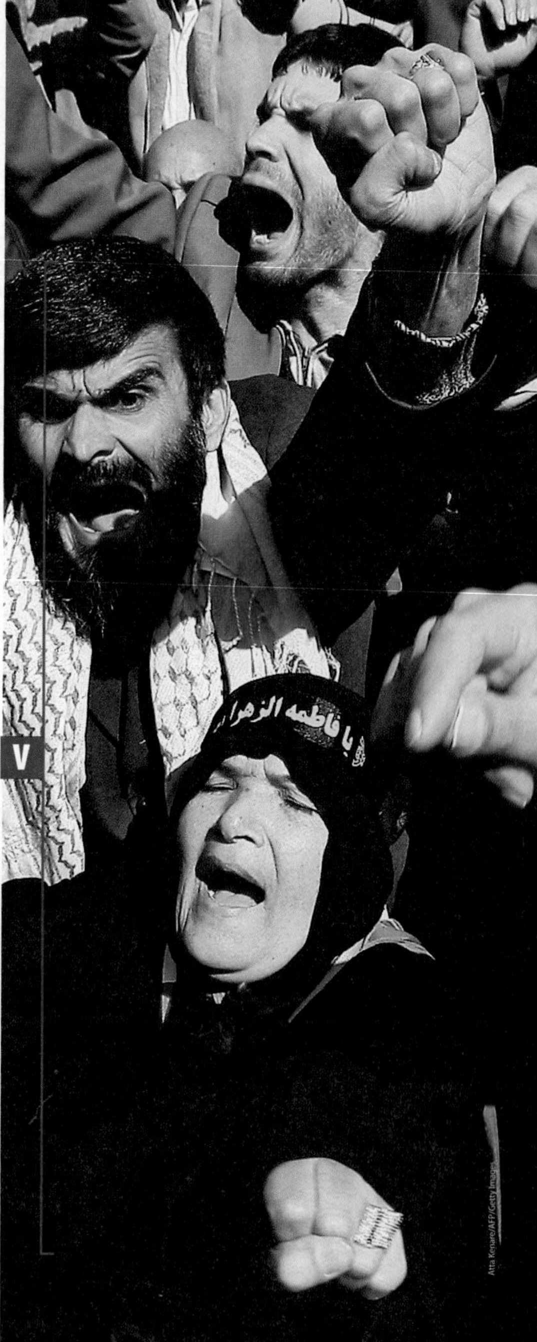

V

Atta Kenare/AFP/Getty Images

422

networks Online Teaching Options

INTERACTIVE MAP

Islamic Expansion

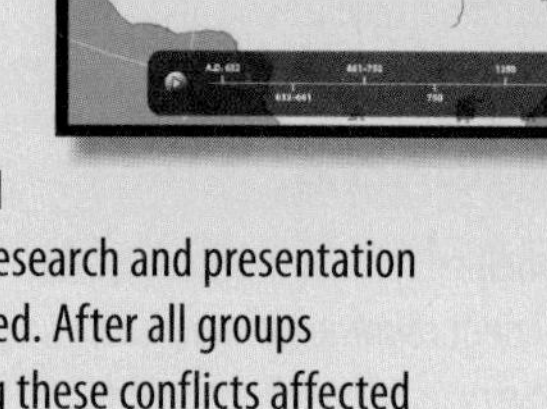

Explaining Continuity and Change Display the interactive map and its time line. Have volunteers click on each date on the time line and read aloud the pop-up text to show the spread of Islam from Arabia to other parts of the world. Then click on the various buttons in the map key to summarize the spread of Islam. Have small groups of students choose one of the conflicts from the time line and research online for additional information to prepare a visual presentation about the conflict. Tell students to focus their research and presentation on how the conflicts affected the rights of the groups involved. After all groups complete their presentations, discuss whether actions during these conflicts affected what is happening in Iraq today. **AL** **Visual/Spatial, Verbal/Linguistic**

Case Study

Charges of Sunni Mistreatment in Iran

PRIMARY SOURCE

"Iran's Sunni Muslims . . . face widespread discrimination by Iranian authorities. The United States Commission on International Religious Freedom 2012 Report states that 'Sunni leaders have reported . . . abuses and restrictions on their religious practice, including detentions and abuse of Sunni clerics . . . and bans on Sunni teachings in public schools and Sunni religious literature, even in predominantly Sunni areas'. Sunnis are not allowed to build mosques in large cities and have been banned from conducting separate Eid prayers. **W**

Attacks in Sunni-populated areas are not unusual. In May, one person was killed and two injured after police forces opened fire on protestors in Sistan-Baluchistan province. They were protesting against the recent arrest of local Sunni clerics. Last year, at least 12 people believed to be Sunni protestors were killed in Ahwaz, a southwestern city in the Khuzestan province, in clashes with security forces. Several Sunni mosques have been destroyed—the Abu Hanifa Mosque in Sistan-Baluchistan was bulldozed in 2008—or converted into parks."

—Mona Moussavi, *ISS Voices*, October 10, 2012

Charges of Sunni Terrorism in Iran **T**

PRIMARY SOURCE

"Jundallah [a pro-Sunni group] was designated as a Foreign Terrorist Organization on November 4, 2010. Since its inception in 2003, Jundallah, a violent extremist organization that operates primarily in the province of Sistan va Balochistan of Iran, has engaged in numerous attacks resulting in the death and maiming of scores of Iranian civilians and government officials. Jundallah's stated goals are to secure recognition of Balochi cultural, economic, and political rights from the government of Iran and to spread awareness of the plight of the Balochi situation through violent and nonviolent means. In October 2007, Amnesty International reported that Jundallah has by its own admission, carried out gross abuses such as hostage-taking, the killing of hostages, and attacks against non-military targets." **R**

—The United States Institute of Peace, *U.S. Terrorism Report: MEK and Jundallah*, August 23, 2011

What do you think? DBQ

1. ***Drawing Conclusions*** How might religious differences affect how countries interact? RH.9–10.1
2. ***Identifying Cause and Effect*** How might the actions of a group like Jundallah promote the denial of rights to Sunni groups in Iran? RH.9–10.2
3. ***Identifying Cause and Effect*** How might the actions of the Iranian government promote the activities of groups like Jundallah? RH.9–10.2

W Writing Skills

Informative/Explanatory Pair English language learners with native speakers to read the paragraph together, rereading if necessary to clarify the meaning of terms such as *discrimination, restrictions, detentions,* and *predominantly.* Have partners write a two- or three-sentence summary of the paragraph. Ask volunteers to read their summaries. Provide corrective guidance if needed or clarify any misconceptions. **ELL Interpersonal, Verbal/Linguistic**

T Technology Skills

Making Presentations Organize the class into groups and have each group research one of the religious groups discussed. Tell students to use reliable online sources to identify facts that either defend or refute one of the quotes. Have students present their findings to the class. Guide a discussion about the impact of the ongoing conflict over religious differences has on people living in the subregion. **AL Interpersonal**

R Reading Skills

Examining Primary Resources Ask: **Based on Moussavi's article, how have Iran's Sunni Muslims been treated?** *(According to the article, Iran's Sunni Muslims have been discriminated against and have experienced "abuses and restrictions" on their religious beliefs.)* **How does the excerpt from the *U.S. Terrorism Report* compare to Moussavi's article?** *(Student answers may vary but should note that Moussavi's article claims widespread abuse of Sunnis, while the U.S. Terrorism Report describes "attacks" by a pro-Sunni group.)* **BL Logical/Mathematical**

CLOSE & REFLECT

Summarizing Have students write a summarizing paragraph describing the issue discussed in this Case Study and how it presents a challenge to politics and leadership in Iran.

ANSWERS, p. 423

DBQ What do you think?

1. Countries may not be able to communicate effectively because of a failure to understand and respect each other's religious differences, which can lead to conflict.
2. It is a pro-Sunni organization that admits to carrying out attacks against non-military targets and the taking and killing of hostages. Because of these actions, the Iranian government might further deny rights to Sunni groups.
3. The Iranian government restricts the religious practices of Sunni Muslims, detains clerics, bans literature and teaching of religion in schools, bans the building of Sunni mosques, and promotes attacks on Sunni areas, all of which lead to Sunni Muslims forming an organization to combat these practices by the government.

GRAPHIC NOVEL

The Five Pillars

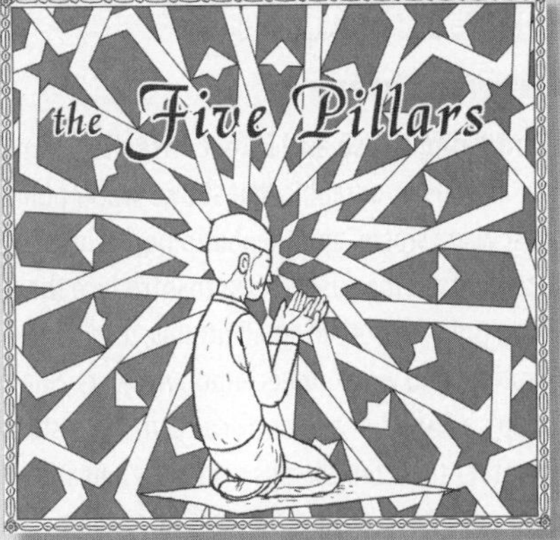

Comparing and Contrasting Students can read this graphic novel to gain knowledge about the Five Pillars of Islam, which are the most important traditions of the religion. After students have read the novel, have student pairs prepare a two-column chart. Tell them to label the left column *Islam* and then to choose another religion and label the right column with that name. Next, have students list the five pillars of Islam in the left column of the chart. In the right column, have them list similar traditions for the religion they chose. After all students have completed their charts, discuss the traditions that are common to all or most religions and those that are unique to Islam. **BL Interpersonal**

ENGAGE

R Reading Skills

Questioning Have students skim through the lesson and look at the visuals. Tell them to jot down any questions they have about the material and to note any unfamiliar terms. Tell students to keep these questions in mind as they read. Suggest that students return to their questions after working through the lesson to write the answers.

TEACH & ASSESS

Making Connections

Read aloud the Guiding Question and lead students to recall places they have learned about in other chapters that have had water-management issues. For example, students may recall the human impact of Egypt's Aswān High Dam on the surrounding environment, population, and culture. Have students consider how the management of water resources plays a role in the economy and environment of a region.

C Critical Thinking Skills

Analyzing Cause and Effect Have students read the information and then consider the impact of the development of hydroelectric power. **Ask:** **How can the development of hydroelectric power have both positive and negative effects on a region? Provide examples from the text to support your answer.** *(It can have a positive effect by bringing much-needed power to a region. In the case of GAP, it can also boost the region's economic development and benefit poor regions of Turkey. Developing hydroelectric power can also have a negative impact by threatening water systems. For example, the construction of dams can alter the course and ecology of rivers, forever changing their habitats.)* **Logical/Mathematical**

ANSWERS, p. 424

TAKING NOTES: Air Pollution—Urban areas are heavily polluted from cars; heavy pollution from oil industry; Iraq's dust storms spread air contaminated with lead from untreated gasoline; **Land Pollution**—Iraq has issues with overgrazing and deforestation has caused soils to erode; heavy irrigation has caused high salinity of the soil, making it unsuitable for agriculture; Iran and Turkey have issues with deforestation, causing soil to erode; **Water Pollution**—Caspian Sea is polluted with untreated waste from the Volga River, chemicals from industries along its shores, pesticides and fertilizers used in agriculture, garbage dumped by Iran, hydrocarbons and heavy metals from oil and gas operations; Black Sea is polluted by oil spills, agricultural runoff, and industrial waste; Tigris and Euphrates Rivers are polluted from agricultural runoff and industrial waste.

networks

There's More Online!

- **IMAGE** Drained Marshland
- **INFOGRAPHIC** Water Pollution in the Northeast
- **MAP** Tigris-Euphrates River Basin
- **INTERACTIVE SELF-CHECK QUIZ**
- **VIDEO** People and Their Environment: The Northeast

LESSON 3
People and Their Environment: The Northeast

ESSENTIAL QUESTION • *How do physical systems and human systems shape a place?*

Reading **HELP**DESK

Academic Vocabulary (Tier Two Words)
- **link**
- **monitor**

Content Vocabulary (Tier Three Words)
- **feeder stream**
- **marsh**

TAKING NOTES: ***Key Ideas and Details***

IDENTIFYING As you read about people and their environment in the Northeast, use a graphic organizer like the one below to record the environmental dangers facing the subregion.

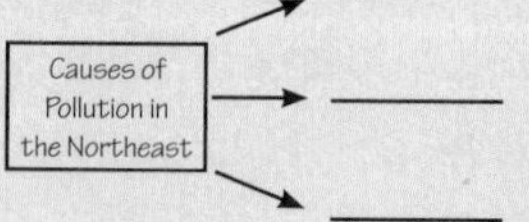

It Matters Because

The Northeast contains valuable natural resources. Human utilization of those resources, however, can sometimes place other aspects of the environment at risk. Countries in the subregion attain variable levels of success in maximizing the benefits from their resources while minimizing the costs associated with obtaining them.

Managing Resources

GUIDING QUESTION *How and why are water resources at risk in the Northeast?*

Turkey has long utilized its many rivers for hydroelectric power and other purposes. In recent years, Turkey has been engaged in a regional development project called the Southeast Anatolia Project. The project is known as GAP in Turkey. GAP involves the construction of nearly two dozen dams along the Tigris and Euphrates Rivers and a number of their **feeder streams**, or tributaries. The plan also calls for a large number of hydroelectric stations capable of generating huge amounts of energy. The project will divert water to irrigate about 4.2 million acres (1.7 million ha) of land. Finally, GAP is also an economic development program that provides a number of benefits to a poor region of Turkey.

Such massive projects threaten existing water systems in a number of ways. The dams change the course and ecology of rivers. They also inundate lands that were once dry and divert water that would otherwise flow downstream. The effect on water quality and quantity is significant. Many ecosystems and habitats are disturbed or even destroyed.

Southern Iraq is characterized by **marshes**. The lower portions of the Tigris and Euphrates feature the Mesopotamian Marsh, which covers 15,000 square miles (38,850 sq. km). It is the largest wetlands area in the Northeast. In recent decades the Iraqi government has undertaken the draining of many of these marshlands. Marsh drainage was used to create farmland and divert water for agricultural purposes.

networks *Online Teaching Options*

INTERACTIVE BELLRINGER

Caspian Energy

Identifying Cause and Effect Use the introductory text and the infographic that shows water pollution from oil, sewage waste, and the dumping of chemicals and detergents in the Caspian Sea to introduce the lesson. Have students work in small groups, discuss each question, and write agreed-upon answers. Share each group's answers in a class discussion. Ask a student volunteer to record the answers and then add any additional items during the class discussion. **Verbal/Linguistic**

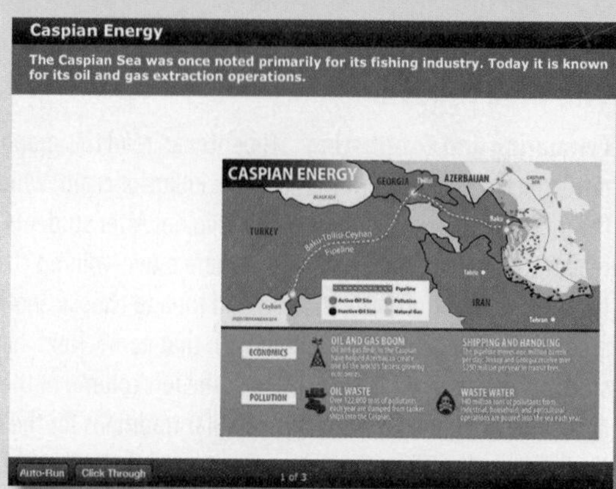

Some marshlands were also drained for political reasons. The people who historically lived on these lands—the Marsh Arabs—had developed a culture and economy based upon the marsh. The Marsh Arabs became involved in uprisings against the regime of Saddam Hussein in the early 1990s. During the uprisings they took refuge in the tall reeds. The Iraqi government retaliated and drained large portions of the marshlands. The Marsh Arabs, whose cultural **link** to the land went back thousands of years, were forced to relocate.

V

More recently, another threat to the marshes has become a concern: drought. The problem is made worse by the heavy diversion of water for irrigation projects for agriculture in places like Turkey. These factors have lowered water levels in many wetlands areas to dangerous levels. Drought has also led to wetlands destruction in Iran.

T

feeder stream a tributary that feeds a larger river

marsh a wetland typically covered with grasses

link a connecting structure

✓ READING PROGRESS CHECK

Explaining How did politics play a part in the destruction of the Mesopotamian Marsh in the 1990s?

Human Impact

GUIDING QUESTION *What human activities result in air, land, and water pollution in the Northeast?*

Human activity impacts the environment in many ways. A major threat is the pollution of air, land, and water. Human activity can also lead to the loss or degradation of natural resources, such as soils and forests. War has also had

GEOGRAPHY CONNECTION

The Tigris and Euphrates Rivers define the boundaries of the historical region known as Mesopotamia.

1. ***PLACES AND REGIONS*** In what country is the Southeast Anatolia Project located?
2. ***THE WORLD IN SPATIAL TERMS*** What region of the Tigris-Euphrates Basin has the most irrigated land?

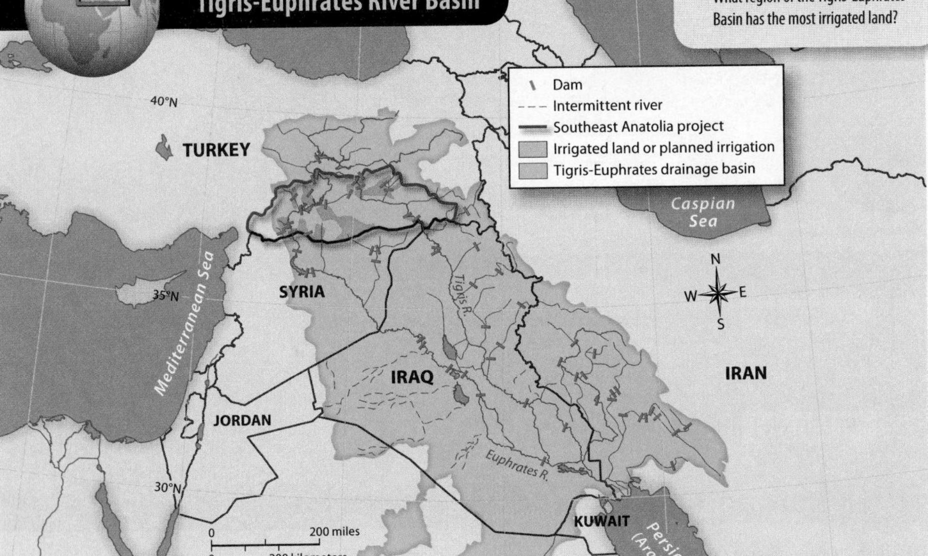

VIDEO

Marsh Arabs

Analyzing Visuals As students watch this video about the Marsh Arabs in Iraq, have them consider the various environmental, migration, and population impacts. Ask students to write down facts or information from the video that they found interesting or that surprised them. Have students share this information with the class. Then guide a class discussion that analyzes how the former Iraqi government water-controlled sanctions and genocide issues have environmentally impacted this region and the rest of the world. **ELL** **Visual/Spatial**

V Visual Skills

Creating Diagrams Have students work with a partner to read the information about the history of the Marsh Arabs. Students should then conduct additional research to find more information about the Marsh Arabs, their culture, and the impact that Saddam Hussein's regime had on them in the early 1990s. To reinforce students' understanding, have them create cause-and-effect diagrams showing the effect of the drainage of marshlands on the Marsh Arabs and their culture. Ask volunteers to share their diagrams with the class, leading into a class discussion about how political and geographic issues are often intertwined. **Visual/Spatial**

T Technology Skills

Exploring Issues Have students read the information about the impact of drought on wetlands in regions in the Northeast. Then organize students into six groups and assign each group one of the following topics: impact of drought in Iran, Turkey, or Iraq or impact of irrigation projects in Iran, Turkey, or Iraq. Have groups conduct online research about their assigned topic for a slide show presentation. Presentations should identify the impact of drought or irrigation projects on the surrounding environment and on the region's economy and culture. Have students use presentation software to create their slide shows, assigning members different tasks such as researching, fact-checking, writing, creating slides, and presenting. In relating both the economic and environmental impact of drought and irrigation projects, encourage students to incorporate visuals such as graphs and diagrams into their reports. Have groups present their slide shows to the class. Guide a class discussion about the factors that have had a detrimental impact on wetlands in the Northeast. **BL** **Interpersonal, Naturalist**

ANSWERS, p. 425

✓ **READING PROGRESS CHECK** Saddam Hussein drained large portions of the marsh in retaliation when the Marsh Arabs took refuge there during a political uprising against the government.

GEOGRAPHY CONNECTION

1. The Southeast Anatolia project is located in Turkey.
2. The northern region has the most irrigated land.

C Critical Thinking Skills

Interpreting Significance Lead students in a class discussion about the war-related causes of pollution in the Persian Gulf. **Ask:** **What has been the environmental impact of these actions?** *(Setting fire to the oil wells caused huge black clouds of smoke to pollute the air and threatened millions of birds. Dumping oil into the Persian Gulf killed thousands of fish and other marine life.)* **How might such disasters be prevented in the future?** *(Student answers may vary but might include suggestions such as making international agreements on pollution and monitoring, and establishing resources to quickly deal with accidental or intentional environmental problems.)* **Logical/Mathematical**

V Visual Skills

Spatial Analysis Have students work in pairs or small groups to create a visual report that shows the impact of oil and gas production on the Caspian Sea. Tell students to use the map in the text as the basis for their reports. Reports should indicate the threat to environmental habitats and activities such as fishing and tourism in the Caspian region.

Allow students to complete their reports as a homework assignment. Reports should answer the following questions:

- **What impact has the development, production, and distribution of oil and gas had on the Caspian Sea's marine habitat?**
- **Have these activities had an impact on tourism in the region? If so, explain why.**
- **How have these activities impacted the population and economy of the region?**

Have students present their findings to the class, allowing for a question-and-answer session following each presentation. Guide students to understand how oil and gas development, production, and distribution impact the environment in the Caspian Sea and other regions of the Northeast. BL **Visual/Spatial, Interpersonal**

ANSWERS, p. 426

CRITICAL THINKING

1. Student answers may vary but could include details on how pollution limits the amount of uncontaminated water that can be used for consumption and in agriculture, and how it causes areas to be unsuitable for marine life, tourism, the fishing industry, and recreational activities.
2. Student answers may vary but should include regulating the oil and gas industry, restricting the use of pesticides and fertilizers in agriculture, and stopping the dumping of household and industrial waste into waterways.

C negative effects on the environment. During the Persian Gulf War in 1991, Iraqi troops retreating from Kuwait set fire to more than 700 oil wells. Huge black clouds of smoke polluted the area. Iraqi troops also dumped about 250 million gallons (946 million l) of oil into the Persian Gulf. Thousands of fish and other marine life died when the oil spill spread along the coastal areas of the Persian Gulf. Smoke from the oil well fires threatened millions of birds. Oil pollution from routine shipping also adversely affects the environment of the Persian Gulf.

Water pollution in the Caspian Sea is an issue. The Caspian Sea is the world's largest inland body of water, measuring 750 miles (1,200 km) from north to south with an average width of 200 miles (320 km). It has historically served as a key fishery, notable for its sturgeon and the valuable caviar. Today, however, pollution threatens these fish populations.

There are several sources of biological and chemical pollutants in the Caspian Sea. Untreated waste from the Volga River flows into the sea. The river also receives chemicals that run off from industries located along its shores, which then flow into the Caspian. In Iran it has been common practice to dump garbage from seaside cities and towns directly into the Caspian Sea. Runoff from farms—carrying pesticides, fertilizers, and detergents—also flows into the sea, adding to what is a major environmental problem.

V

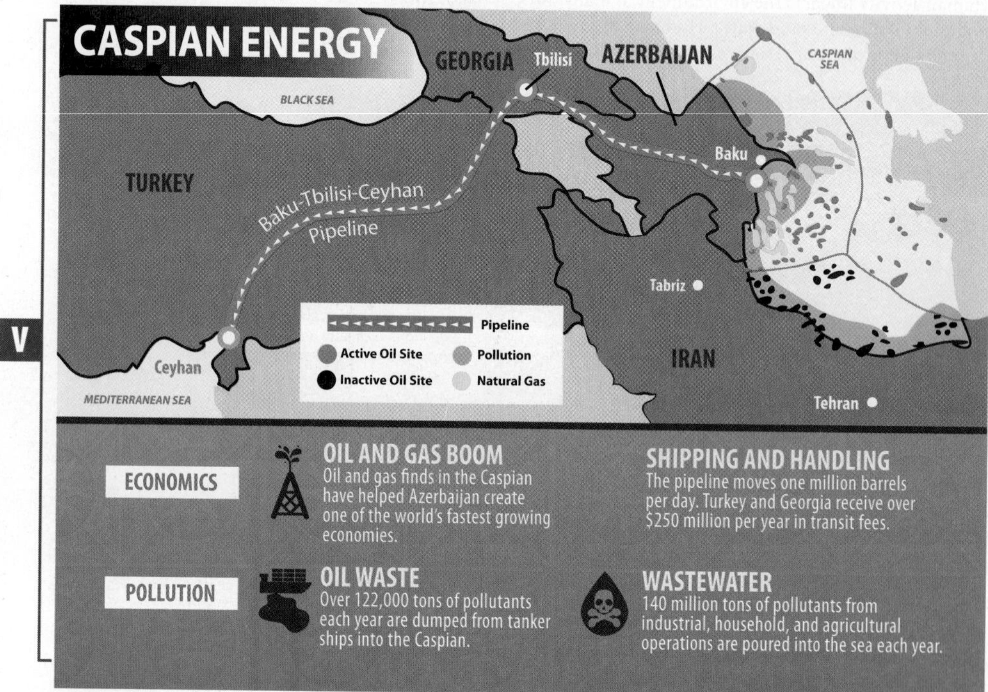

The Caspian Sea has experienced a boom in oil and natural gas finds in recent decades. The processes used to extract these resources, however, have contributed to the increasing levels of pollution in the Caspian Sea.

▲ **CRITICAL THINKING**

1. ***Evaluating*** How might the pollution of water sources limit their value to people?
2. ***Problem Solving*** What steps could governments or individuals take to reduce water pollution in the Northeast?

426

networks Online Teaching Options

INTERACTIVE INFOGRAPHIC

Baku-Tblisi-Ceyhan Pipeline

Creating Charts With students, note that the infographic presents both visual information (a map with corresponding key) and text. The text breaks down the economic and environmental impacts of oil drilling in the Caspian Sea. Have students determine which impacts are beneficial and which are detrimental. Ask them to create a chart that shows the positive impacts of the drilling and what entities benefit from it, as well as the negative impacts of the drilling and what entities are affected by it. AL **Visual/Spatial**

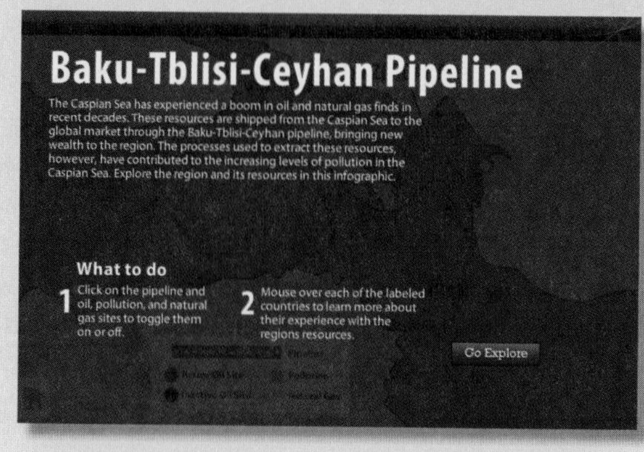

Perhaps the biggest threat to the Caspian's waters comes from the large oil-extraction operations that take place throughout the sea. Much of this work is carried on by countries other than Iran that rim the Caspian. The effects of pollution from oil and gas operations have been devastating. Each year, thousands upon thousands of tons of hydrocarbons and heavy metals are spilled into the Caspian. This pollution is likely to get worse as Iran and other countries increase their exploitation of the large reserves of oil and gas beneath the Caspian Sea.

The Black Sea, which forms Turkey's northern border, is also plagued by severe pollution. The contributors are agricultural runoff and industrial pollution related to the shipping of oil. Much of this pollution comes from countries other than Turkey. Of particular concern to Turkey is the danger of an oil spill in the Bosporus. This major shipping channel sees a great deal of traffic by oil tankers. With a population of more than 10 million, Turkey's largest city—İstanbul—straddles the Bosporus. Thus, the potential for environmental disaster is high. In addition, Turkey's ability to regulate traffic in the strait is limited by international agreements designed to ensure the free flow of shipping.

In Iraq, the Tigris and the Euphrates have also suffered a serious decline in water quality. Some of this comes from agricultural runoff, as water used for irrigation flows back into the rivers. Pollution from industrial sources and sewage also threatens the rivers.

Air pollution is a problem in all of the countries of the Northeast, especially in urban areas. The population of these areas has been growing. With that increase have come concerns about air quality. Streets and roadways are frequently clogged with cars, many of which are older or poorly maintained models that produce heavy exhaust. Iran's capital, Tehran, has especially suffered from severe air pollution. In recent years there have been many instances of school and public office closures due to high air pollution levels. The Iranian government has blamed air pollution for thousands of deaths in the city.

In Iraq problems with air pollution raised the concern of U.S. military officials, who worried about the effects on American soldiers stationed there. Iraq's frequent dust storms produce large amounts of airborne particulates, many contaminated with substances such as lead, a toxin still used in Iraqi gasoline. Iraq has traditionally done little to ensure good air quality.

The health of forests and soils is threatened in several parts of the Northeast. In Iraq, for example, soils in many areas have become increasingly saline—salty—to the point that many areas have been abandoned for agricultural use. High salinity results from heavy irrigation in a place where evaporation happens quickly. Iraq has also had major problems with overgrazing and deforestation, which have left the soil exposed to seasonal rains. Many tons of soil have been carried down the Tigris and the Euphrates and been deposited in the Persian Gulf.

Iran has sizable forests in the northern part of the country. These, however, have been heavily exploited, especially in recent decades. Loss of forest resources is a major concern in the country. In 1963 Iran nationalized its forests, but that failed to stop deforestation.

Turkey also has seen many of its historical forest resources destroyed. Areas once covered with forests are now open plains. The loss of forests has brought a loss of soil. Erosion in hillier areas is a serious problem for a country that depends heavily on agriculture.

✓ READING PROGRESS CHECK

Describing In what ways does oil extraction pose an environmental threat to the Northeast?

Connecting Geography to **SCIENCE**

Soil Erosion in Iraq

Iraq is an ancient land that has supported agriculture and pastoralism longer perhaps than any other land on Earth. The removal of trees and the cultivation of soil began thousands of years ago. This has exposed soils in the mountain and foothill regions of northern Iraq to erosion. Massive amounts of soil have flowed down these mountains and hills over the centuries. These soils have been deposited at the mouth of the Shatt al Arab, the river formed where the Tigris and Euphrates meet and an area long contested by Iraq and Iran. Over the years, the river's delta has extended many miles into the Persian Gulf. The Iranian city of Ābādān, for example, was located on the Persian Gulf 1,000 years ago. Today it is some 30 miles (50 km) inland, situated on an island in the Shatt al Arab.

IDENTIFYING CAUSE AND EFFECT What led to the extension of the alluvial deposits at the mouth of the Shatt al Arab?

People and Their Environment: The Northeast

C Critical Thinking Skills

Analyzing Cause and Effect Continue to guide students in a discussion about the various threats to the environment of the Caspian Sea. Have students use information in the text to create a flowchart showing the causes and effects of threats posed to the Caspian Sea and its surrounding ecosystems. **Ask: What is the primary threat to the Caspian Sea and its environment?** *(The Caspian Sea has experienced devastating pollution caused by oil and gas operations.)* **What are the effects of large-scale oil extraction in the Caspian Sea?** *(A huge amount of hydrocarbons and heavy metals have been spilled into the Caspian Sea.)* **What is the long-term outlook of this activity?** *(The problem is likely to get worse as Iran and other countries continue to exploit and develop large reserves of oil and gas beneath the Caspian Sea.)* **AL Logical/Mathematical**

V Visual Skills

Spatial Understanding Have students work in pairs or small groups to create a display that shows the impact of soil erosion in Iraq. Tell students to use the information in the text and from online research for their displays. In their research, students should locate images that show how the Tigris and Euphrates Rivers and their feeder rivers have eroded soil along their paths and carried it to the delta of the Shatt al Arab River. Encourage students to find "before" and "after" images that show how the delta has changed. Students' displays should show how cities such as Ābādān in Iraq have changed and how those changes have impacted the people who live there. Allow time for students to present their visual displays to the class. Culminate the presentations in a discussion about soil erosion in other parts of the world and what can be done to remedy these situations. **Visual/Spatial, Interpersonal**

INTERACTIVE WHITEBOARD ACTIVITY

Human Impact on the Environment

Identifying Cause and Effect Using the graphic organizer provided, have students drag items categorized as human factors and physical factors into the appropriate spots. Once the graphic organizer is completed, have students identify each cause and its corresponding effect. Then lead a class discussion on how human activities are affecting the environment in the Northeast. **AL Kinesthetic, Visual/Spatial**

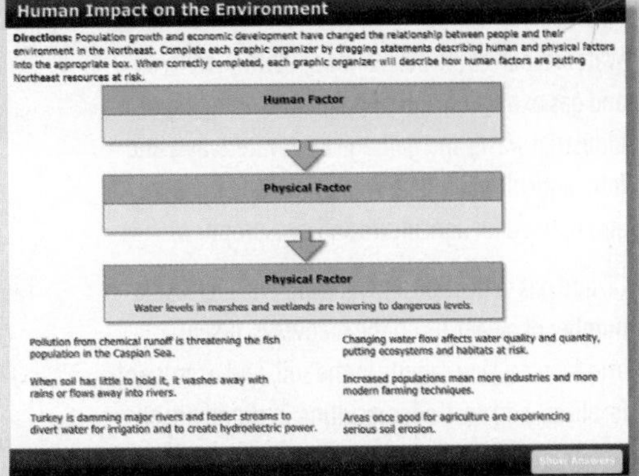

ANSWERS, p. 427

✓ READING PROGRESS CHECK Oil extraction causes hydrocarbons, heavy metals, and oil spills during shipping to pollute the waterways of the Northeast.

Connecting Geography The removal of trees and cultivation of the land has caused erosion in the mountains and foothills of the region. This erosion caused large amounts of soil to wash down the mountains where it has been deposited at the mouth of the Shatt al Arab. Over centuries, it has extended the land many miles into the Persian Gulf.

People and Their Environment: The Northeast

W Writing Skills

Informative/Explanatory Have students research the damage that has affected Turkey's air, water, and soil and what strategies are in place to improve the environment. Tell students to write an informative essay that explains the short- and long-term costs of some of these efforts. Tell them to to address the underlying problems that threaten Turkey's environment and to offer possible solutions to prevent further damage. Invite students to share their essays with the class. Then **ask**: **How can the desire to enter the European Union potentially benefit Turkey's environment?** *(Turkey has stepped up its environmental laws to meet EU standards.)* BL **Verbal/ Linguistic**

CLOSE & REFLECT

Understanding Relationships Have small groups reflect on the use and misuse of natural resources and the resulting impact on the Northeast's environment. Ask them to examine a source of environmental problems and then present a proposal to reduce its negative environmental impact while maintaining its benefit to the Northeast's people and economy. Have the class discuss, revise, and prioritize the proposals.

ANSWERS, p. 428

☑ **READING PROGRESS CHECK** Turkey must balance the need for cleaner power generated by hydropower and the economic benefits for some regions with the destruction of archaeological treasures and the opposition of those who question the benefits GAP is supposed to supply.

CRITICAL THINKING

1. The land is now dry, rocky, and lacking any vegetation.
2. The Marsh Arabs have lost income, food sources, and their traditional way of life due to the loss of the marshland.

Iraqi Marsh Arabs examine their canoes in what had once been marshland.

Essam Al-Sudani/AFP/Getty Images

▲ **CRITICAL THINKING**

1. ***Analyzing Visuals*** How would you describe the land shown in the photo that was once covered with marshes?
2. ***Making Connections*** How might the changed landscape affect the lives and livelihoods of the Marsh Arabs?

monitor to watch closely, evaluate

Addressing the Issues

GUIDING QUESTION *How are environmental issues being addressed in the Northeast?*

In Turkey there are many active groups working to address environmental issues. Opposition to GAP has been strong. In Turkish universities, scientists have questioned some of the claimed benefits of the project. Activists have also sought to prevent the destruction of archaeological treasures that would occur if land is flooded for GAP. Supporters of GAP point out that hydropower is a relatively clean way to address rising energy needs. Environmentalists have placed a heavy emphasis on reducing Turkey's historical dependence on coal, which is highly polluting. There is lively debate in Turkey about the best ways to balance competing interests.

W Political forces from outside Turkey are also having an impact. Turkey continues to make its case for entry into the European Union (EU). In an effort to attain this goal, it has strengthened certain environmental laws to meet EU standards.

The loss of wetlands in Iraq has prompted action from Iraqis as well as from people around the world. Organizations such as Wetlands International and the International Wetlands Conference are working on solutions to the threats. Iran has also been acting to protect its many valuable wetlands. In 1971 Iran hosted the Ramsar Convention. This meeting produced an international treaty, the Ramsar Convention on Wetlands, to **monitor**—or closely watch—and preserve wetlands resources around the world. Today, this convention brings together governments and nongovernmental organizations (NGOs) from around the world to protect wetlands of all types.

The Iranian government has also been vocal in raising concerns about pollution in the Caspian Sea. Many of these complaints, however, have been aimed at other nations who contribute to the problem. In 2013, for example, Iran threatened to sue the government of Azerbaijan over pollution coming from its oil platforms in the Caspian.

☑ **READING PROGRESS CHECK**

Evaluating What factors must Turkey balance when evaluating the benefits of its GAP project?

LESSON 3 REVIEW 

Reviewing Vocabulary (Tier Three Words)

1. ***Applying*** Using the words *feeder stream* and *marsh*, explain the environmental challenges facing the Northeast. RH.9–10.4

Using Your Notes

2. ***Describing*** Use your graphic organizer to write a paragraph describing the major causes of pollution in the Northeast.

Answering the Guiding Questions

3. ***Analyzing*** How and why are water resources at risk in the Northeast?
4. ***Describing*** What human activities result in air, land, and water pollution in the Northeast?
5. ***Problem Solving*** How are environmental issues being addressed in the Northeast?

Writing Activity

6. ***Argument*** Write an argument either for or against the development of the Southeast Anatolia Project, or GAP, in Turkey. WHST.9–10.1

428

LESSON 3 REVIEW ANSWERS

Reviewing Vocabulary

1. Student answers may vary but must include the terms *feeder stream* and *marsh*. Possible response could include that the diversion of water for irrigation decreases the amount in feeder streams and marshes.

Using Your Notes

2. Student answers may vary but should be strongly supported with information from the chapter. Answers could include information on oil and gas extraction, agricultural runoff, dumping of waste, urbanization, and car traffic.

Answering the Guiding Questions

3. Water resources are at risk from pollution from oil and gas extraction and shipping, the dumping of industrial waste and garbage into waterways, and from agricultural runoff. Waterways and marshes are also drained for agriculture and consumption.
4. Oil and gas extraction and refining, the increasing number of older cars on the roadways, heavy irrigation causing salinity in the soil, and overuse of fertilizers and pesticides resulting in runoff are all causing pollution in the Northeast.
5. Turkey is working to provide hydropower to reduce pollution from coal; Iraq is working with Wetlands International to protect wetlands; and Iran hosted the Ramsar Convention on Wetlands to help preserve wetlands and is actively trying to combat pollution in the Caspian Sea from other countries.

Writing Activity

6. Student answers may vary but should be strongly supported with information from the lesson. Answers could include the issues with damming the rivers and the associated flooding, the possible economic benefits, the benefit of hydropower versus coal, possible damage to archaeological finds, and opposition groups.

CHAPTER 17 Assessment 

Directions: On a separate sheet of paper, answer the questions below. Make sure that you read carefully and answer all parts of the questions.

Lesson Review

Lesson 1

1. ***Analyzing*** What is the meaning of the word *Mesopotamia*? Based on the location of Mesopotamia, explain whether this name is logical for the region.
2. ***Interpreting Significance*** Identify the dominant water feature in northern Iran. Explain its significance to the area.
3. ***Making Decisions*** Imagine you are considering the possibility of pursuing agricultural interests in the Northeast subregion. Would you select the steep slopes or the river basin? Explain.

Lesson 2

4. ***Identifying Cause and Effect*** In Mesopotamia, humans learned to raise their own food. How and why did this change population and settlement patterns?
5. ***Describing*** When did Turkic peoples migrate to the Anatolian Peninsula? Provide an overview of the cultural blend that constitutes modern Turkish culture and identify the language spoken and religion practiced by most Turks.
6. ***Identifying Perspectives*** Explain why other countries in the Northeast could benefit by following Turkey's example of an alternative energy source. Within your response, identify the specific alternative energy source used in Turkey and explain at least one likely reason that Turkey developed it.

Lesson 3

7. ***Identifying Central Issues*** Discuss one human factor and one factor of the physical environment that has posed threats to marshlands in Iraq.
8. ***Summarizing*** Summarize the threats to the Caspian Sea, explaining which is likely the greatest threat and why.
9. ***Making Connections*** Identify the causes and consequences of soil erosion in the Northeast.

21st Century Skills

Use the graph below to answer the following questions.

CRUDE OIL PRODUCTION AND CONSUMPTION PER DAY, 2010

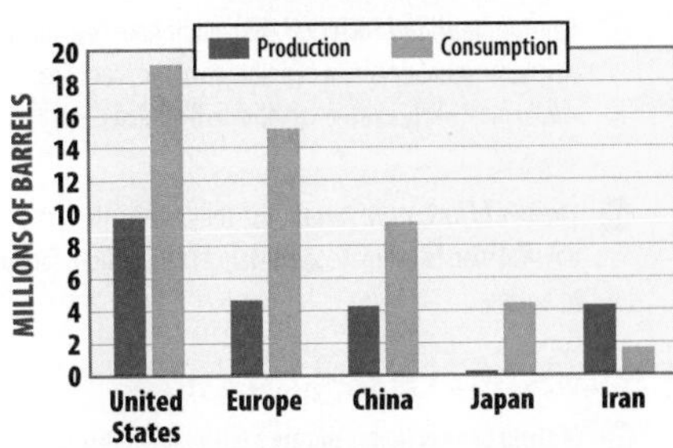

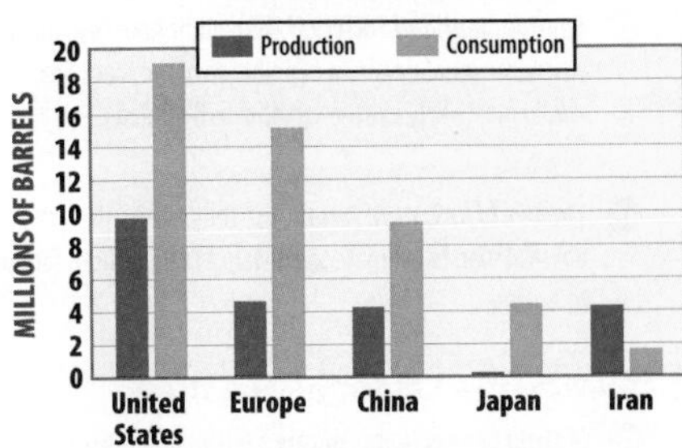

Source: U.S. Department of Commerce Economics & Statistics Administration, http://www.esa.doc.gov/Blog/2012/02/22/crude-oil-and-gasoline-prices-2012

10. ***Using Graphs, Charts, Diagrams, and Tables*** Which country shown on the graph produced the most barrels of crude oil per day in 2010? How did this relate to its consumption?
11. ***Compare & Contrast*** Other than Japan and China, which country produced the fewest barrels of crude oil per day in 2010? How did this relate to its consumption? Discuss the relationships among production, consumption, and likelihood of exports. Then tie this to the likely imports of the country that produced the most barrels of crude oil per day.

Critical Thinking

12. ***Exploring Issues*** Write a one-page essay explaining this statement: "The modern-day Northeast is a product of early historical events in the region, though more recent events threaten the human and physical geography of the area."

Need Extra Help?

If You've Missed Question	1	2	3	4	5	6	7	8	9	10	11	12
Go to page	414	414	415	416	419	421	424	426	427	429	429	419

CHAPTER 17 Assessment Answers

Lesson Review

Lesson 1

1. *Mesopotamia* means "the land between the rivers." This name is logical because Mesopotamia is bounded by the Euphrates and Tigris Rivers.
2. The Caspian Sea is the dominant water feature of northern Iran. It is an important transportation route between Iran and other Asian countries and a source of resources such as oil, natural gas, and fish.
3. The river basin would be best for agriculture as it has deposits of alluvial soils and a water source.

Lesson 2

4. Raising food allowed people to live in permanent villages and grow a surplus of food that supported a growing population. As everyone wasn't needed to grow food, people could spend time pursuing other activities, such as organizing and governing, which caused civilizations to emerge and spread.
5. Turkic people first migrated to the Anatolian Peninsula from Central Asia in the A.D. 1000s. Turks speak Turkish and practice Islam. Modern Turkish culture blends Turkish, Islamic, and Western elements. The Kurds, who are mostly Sunni Muslims, also occupy parts of Turkey.
6. Responses will vary but should explain that Turkey makes use of hydroelectric power because it has access to rivers and fewer oil and natural gas resources than Iran and Iraq. Responses should also include the benefits of hydroelectric power, such as being less harmful to the environment than the extraction and refining of oil and natural gas.

Lesson 3

7. Answers may include the human factors of draining swamps for farmland, irrigation, development, and political reasons such as retaliation against the Marsh Arabs. Droughts are the major threat to marshlands from the physical environment.
8. The Caspian Sea is polluted with untreated waste from the Volga River, chemicals from industries along its shores, pesticides and fertilizers used in agriculture, and garbage dumped by Iran. The biggest threat is from oil extraction that spills thousands of tons of hydrocarbons and heavy metals into the Caspian Sea.
9. Heavy irrigation has caused high salinity of the soil, making it unsuitable for agriculture or natural vegetation. Overgrazing and deforestation have also left the soil exposed to heavy rains and wind that cause erosion. This impacts the ability to grow crops in these areas.

21st Century Skills

10. The United States produced the most barrels of crude oil per day in 2010. However, the United States consumed about twice the amount it produced.
11. Iran produced the fewest barrels of oil besides Japan and China. However, Iran still produced more than twice what it consumed. The United States produces the most barrels of oil per day, but it consumes double that amount. Therefore, the United States must import oil to meet its consumption rate.

Critical Thinking

12. Essays will vary but should be strongly supported with information from the chapter. Essays should explain how the modern-day language, culture, and religion are products of historical events. Answers could include: Even though Islam is the dominant religion of the region, there are a variety of ethnic groups—Turks, Iranians, Arabs, and Kurds; Iraqi Arabs speak Arabic and are largely Shia Muslims; Iranians speak Farsi but are also mostly Shia; Turks speak Turkish and practice Islam; Kurds speak Kurdish, which is related to Farsi, have inhabited mountainous border of Turkey, Iraq, and Iran for thousands of years, are largely Sunni Muslims; Iran adheres to Islamic law in government, which restricts the rights of women in society

CHAPTER 17
Assessment Answers

CHAPTER 17 Assessment 

Directions: On a separate sheet of paper, answer the questions below. Make sure that you read carefully and answer all parts of the questions.

Applying Map Skills

Refer to the Unit 5 Atlas to answer the following questions.

13. ***The World in Spatial Terms*** Use your mental map of Turkey and Iraq to describe the course of the Euphrates River.

14. ***Environment and Society*** Use the Unit Atlas to explain where the greatest threat of pollution of the Black Sea would most likely exist—İstanbul or Baghdad—and why.

15. ***The World in Spatial Terms*** Use the scale on the physical map to estimate the distance in miles from Tehran to Ankara.

Exploring the Essential Question

16. ***Making Connections*** You are a television broadcast journalist who has been assigned a broadcast segment focusing on the following statement: "The ongoing conflicts between Shia Muslims and Sunni Muslims can be viewed through the perspectives of the physical and human geography of the region." Your broadcast report must open with a broad overview of the interaction between physical and human systems of the subregion. Write your report, and deliver it orally to the class. Include visuals, such as maps and photos. WHST.9–10.4, WHST.9–10.7

College and Career Readiness

17. ***Examining Information*** You are working for a firm that has interests in Turkey. Your boss is concerned about the possibility of oil spills in the Bosporus Strait, and you have been asked to write a memo to summarize the following: the likelihood of oil spills in the Bosporus; the reasons for this likelihood; issues with cleaning up after an oil spill in the Bosporus. Within your memo, you have been asked to reference at least two other oil spills that have occurred in the world—with an explanation as to the causes and the mitigation after the spills. Prepare the memo for your boss, clearly and logically supporting your statements. WHST.9–10.4, WHST.9–10.7

DBQ Analyzing Primary Sources

Use the excerpt to answer the following questions.

PRIMARY SOURCE

"Iraq's energy sector holds the key to the country's future prosperity and can make a major contribution to the stability and security of global energy markets. Iraq is already the world's third-largest oil exporter and has the resources and plans to increase rapidly its oil and natural gas production as it recovers from three decades punctuated by conflict and instability. Success in developing Iraq's hydrocarbon potential and effective management of the resulting revenues can fuel Iraq's social and economic development. Failure will hinder Iraq's recovery and put global energy markets on course for troubled waters."

—International Energy Agency, "Executive Summary," *Iraq Energy Outlook*, 2012

18. ***Interpreting Significance*** Reread the following statement from the quote: "Failure will hinder Iraq's recovery and put global energy markets on course for troubled waters." What did the writer most likely mean by this statement? RH.9–10.1

19. ***Drawing Conclusions*** Why would oil exports alone fail to hold the key to Iraq's future prosperity? RH.9–10.2

Research and Presentation

20. ***Gathering Information*** Use Internet and library sources to research the Southeast Anatolia Project, known as GAP, in Turkey. Identify the purpose of GAP and note the reasons for opposition to GAP within Turkey. WHST.9–10.7; WHST.9–10.8

Writing About Geography

21. ***Narrative*** Use standard grammar, spelling, sentence structure, and punctuation to write a paragraph that describes what you might see around you if you were to fly in an airplane from Ankara to an area near the summit of Mount Ararat. WHST.9–10.2

Need Extra Help?

If You've Missed Question	13	14	15	16	17	18	19	20	21
Go to page	360	360	360	409	427	430	430	424	413

430

Applying Map Skills

13. The Euphrates River flows through the Taurus Mountains in Turkey through Syria and Iraq.

14. The greatest threat of pollution would come from İstanbul as it is located on the Black Sea, while Baghdad is not located nearby.

15. Tehran is between 1,000–1,500 miles from Ankara.

Exploring the Essential Question

16. Reports will differ but should be strongly based on information from the chapter. Reports may include information about the Kurds (majority Sunni Muslim), who live in the mountains and plateau regions of eastern Turkey, northeastern Iran, and northern Iraq, and their desire for an independent state, or the Iraqi and Iranian majority population of Shia Muslims and the conflicts because of this distribution. Reports should include maps and photos to support the content.

College and Career Readiness

17. Memos will differ but must include the likelihood and reasons for oil spills in the Bosporus, what issues there might be in cleaning up after an oil spill, and references to at least two other oil spills with an explanation as to the causes and the mitigation after the spills. Memos could include the high traffic of oil ships in the Bosporus that Turkey is unable to regulate due to international agreements, the narrow aspect of the strait, and the location of İstanbul that makes spills potentially disastrous and cleanup difficult. Oil spill references could include the 2010 BP spill that impacted the coasts of Alabama, Mississippi, and Louisiana; the 1989 *Exxon Valdez* spill in Alaska; and the 2009 West Atlas spill off the northwest Australian coast.

DBQ Analyzing Primary Sources

18. The writer most likely means that if Iraq fails in developing its hydrocarbon potential or in managing the resulting revenues, it will become unstable. Instability in Iraq that results in the interruption of the supply of oil to world markets could result in price increases or shortages that would have serious impacts on nations around the world.

19. Iraq must also manage the revenues it receives from exporting oil effectively in order to grow the economy and solve social issues within the country.

Research and Presentation

20. Answers will differ but should identify that GAP is a project that involves the construction of almost two dozen dams along the Tigris and Euphrates Rivers and their tributaries. This construction is being done to generate hydroelectric power and to divert water for irrigation. While the project is also designed to increase economic development, concerns exist about damage to the environment and archaeological sites.

Writing About Geography

21. Paragraphs will differ but should include information from the chapter such as flying over the Taurus Mountains, Anatolian Plateau (relatively flat), and Pontic Mountains before seeing the camel-backed Mount Ararat.

CHAPTER 18

The Arabian Peninsula Planner

UNDERSTANDING BY DESIGN®

Enduring Understandings

- *Cooperation and conflict among people influence the division and control of Earth's surface.*

Essential Question

- *How do physical systems and human systems shape a place?*

Predictable Misunderstandings

Students may think:

- *Arabia is a single country. Explain that the Arabian Peninsula, which is also known as Arabia, is a region, not a country, and includes the countries of Saudi Arabia, Yemen, Oman, the United Arab Emirates, Kuwait, Qatar, and Bahrain.*
- *The Arabian Peninsula is completely covered by desert. Explain that while a large portion of the peninsula is desert and receives very little rainfall, there are mountain ranges with cooler, wetter climates, and the coastal plains along the coastlines are fertile and can sustain agriculture.*

Assessment Evidence

Performance Tasks:

- *Hands-On Chapter Project*

Other Evidence:

- *Guided Reading Activities*
- *Vocabulary Activities*
- *Lesson Quizzes*
- *Chapter Tests, Forms A and B*

SUGGESTED PACING GUIDE

Introducing the Chapter	½ Day
Lesson 1	1 Day
Lesson 2	2 Days
Lesson 3	1 Day
Chapter Wrap-Up and Assessment	½ Day
TOTAL TIME	**5 Days**

Key for Using the Teacher Edition

SKILL-BASED ACTIVITIES

Types of skill activities found in the Teacher Edition.

*V **Visual Skills** require students to analyze maps, graphs, charts, and photos.

R **Reading Skills** help students practice reading skills and master vocabulary.

C **Critical Thinking Skills** help students apply and extend what they have learned.

W **Writing Skills** provide writing opportunities to help students comprehend the text.

T **Technology Skills** require students to use digital tools effectively.

*Letters are followed by a number when there is more than one of the same type of skill on the page.

DIFFERENTIATED INSTRUCTION

All activities are written for the on-level student unless otherwise marked with the leveled labels below.

BL **Beyond Level**
AL **Approaching Level**
ELL **English Language Learners**

All students benefit from activities that utilize different learning styles. Many activities are marked as below when a particular learning style is highlighted.

Intrapersonal **Logical/Mathematical** **Visual/Spatial** **Verbal/Linguistic** **Naturalist** **Kinesthetic** **Auditory/Musical** **Interpersonal**

National Geography Standards covered in "The Arabian Peninsula"

The student knows and understands:

(7) The physical processes that shape the patterns of Earth's surface

7.1 The interaction of Earth's physical systems (the atmosphere, biosphere, hydrosphere, and lithosphere) vary across space and time

7.2 Earth-Sun relationships are variable over time resulting in changes in physical processes and patterns on Earth

7.3 Physical processes interact over time to shape particular places on Earth's surface

(9) The characteristics, distribution, and migration of human populations on Earth's surface

9.2 Population distribution and density are a function of historical, environmental, economic, political, and technological factors

9.3 Migration is one of the driving forces for shaping and reshaping the cultural and physical landscape of places and regions

(11) The patterns and networks of economic interdependence on Earth's surface

11.3 Economic systems are dynamic organizations of interdependent economic activities for production, exchange, distribution, and consumption of goods and services

11.4 Improvements in transportation and communication networks reduce the effects of distance and time on the movements of people, products, and ideas

(14) How human actions modify the physical environment

14.1 Human modifications of the physical environment can have significant global impacts

14.2 The use of technology can have both intended and unintended impacts on the physical environment which may be positive or negative

14.3 People can either mitigate and/or adapt to the consequences of human modifications of the physical environment

(15) How physical systems affect human systems

15.3 Societies use a variety of strategies to adapt to changes in the physical environment

(16) The changes that occur in the meaning, use, distribution, and importance of resources

16.3 Policies and programs that promote the sustainable use and management of resources impact people and the environment

CHAPTER OPENER PLANNER

Students will know:

- *the landforms of and the role of climate on the Arabian Peninsula.*
- *how bodies of water both isolate and connect the peninsula to other regions.*
- *how the Arabian Peninsula developed politically.*
- *the factors that affect population distribution and life.*
- *how the petroleum industry has affected the environment.*
- *how population growth is creating a water crisis in the region and how it is being addressed.*

Students will be able to:

- ***identify** landforms of the Arabian Peninsula and their locations and describe climate.*
- ***analyze** how the locations of bodies of water affect the connection of the peninsula to other regions.*
- ***explain** the political development of the Arabian Peninsula.*
- ***identify** factors that affect population distribution and life in the region.*
- ***discuss** the effects of the petroleum industry in the Arabian Peninsula.*
- ***analyze** how population growth is leading to a water crisis and what is being done about it.*

UNDERSTANDING BY DESIGN®

☑ *Print Teaching Options*

V Visual Skills

☐ **p. 432** Students describe the image of migrant workers and hypothesize where it is and what is happening. **Visual/Spatial**

R Reading Skills

☐ **p. 433** Students list the push factors that make migrant workers leave their home countries. **AL Verbal/Linguistic**

C Critical Thinking Skills

☐ **p. 431** Students describe how the Arabian Peninsula has changed in recent times. **AL Verbal/Linguistic**

W Writing Skills

☐ **p. 433** Students write a letter from the perspective of a female migrant worker who lives in Saudi Arabia.

T Technology Skills

☐ **p. 433** Students prepare arguments explaining why basic human rights should be extended to all workers. **BL Logical/Mathematical, Verbal/Linguistic**

☑ *Online Teaching Options*

C Critical Thinking Skills

☐ **SLIDE SHOW** **Wanted: Migrant Workers**—Students list the advantages and disadvantages of being a migrant worker, as well as being a country that employees large numbers of migrant workers. **AL Verbal Linguistic**

☐ **MAP** **Interactive Regional Atlas**—Students use the interactive regional atlas to understand the physical and human geography of the Arabian Peninsula.

☑ *Printable Digital Worksheets*

☐ **WORKSHEET** **Assessing Background Knowledge**—Determine the level of prior knowledge students have about the Arabian Peninsula.

☐ **WORKSHEET** **Chapter Summaries**—Students review the main idea of each lesson of the chapter content.

☐ **WORKSHEET** **Vocabulary Activity**—Students apply their knowledge of content and academic vocabulary words.

Project-Based Learning 

Hands-On

Arabian Tour Books

Students will create tour books that describe the climate, physical features, cultural features, and events and current issues that affect the Arabian Peninsula. Groups will conduct research to compile and organize their reports into a cohesive tour book. Then groups will present brief oral summaries about their countries, using information from their tour books.

Digital Hands-On

Create Online Projects

Find an additional activity online that incorporates technology for this project. Visit the EdTech Teacher Web sites for more links, tutorials, and other resources.

Print Resources

ANCILLARY RESOURCES

This ancillary is available for every chapter and lesson.

- **Chapter Tests and Lesson Quizzes**

PRINTABLE DIGITAL WORKSHEETS

These printable digital worksheets are available for every chapter and lesson.

- **Assessing Background Knowledge**
- **Chapter Summaries**
- **Guided Reading Activities**
- **Hands-On Chapter Projects**
- **Quizzes and Tests**
- **Reading Essentials and Study Guide** AL
- **Reteaching Activities**
- **Video Activities**
- **Vocabulary Activities**

More Media Resources

SUGGESTED VIDEOS 

- **Global Treasures Nizwa Oman** (11 min.)
- **The Hanging Gardens of Arabia** (52 min.)
- **Women of the Holy Kingdom** (50 min.)

SUGGESTED READING 

- ***Water and Food Security in the Arabian Gulf,*** The Emirates Center for Strategic Studies and Research
- ***A History of Saudi Arabia,*** by Madawi Al-Rasheed
- ***Coral Reefs of the Gulf: Adaptation to Climatic Extremes,*** by Bernhard Riegl, Sam J. Purkis

LESSON 1 PLANNER

PHYSICAL GEOGRAPHY OF THE ARABIAN PENINSULA

Students will know:

- *the location of and landforms of the Arabian Peninsula.*
- *how bodies of water both isolate and connect the peninsula to other regions.*
- *the role of climate on the landscape of the peninsula.*

Students will be able to:

- ***identify** landforms of the Arabian Peninsula and their locations.*
- ***analyze** how the locations of bodies of water affect the connection of the peninsula to other regions.*
- ***analyze** how climate affects the landscape of the peninsula.*

UNDERSTANDING BY DESIGN®

☑ Print Teaching Options

V Visual Skills

☐ **p. 434** Students use maps to discuss the impact of tectonic plate movement in the region. AL Visual/Spatial

R Reading Skills

☐ **p. 434** Students write three or four sentences predicting what they will learn about the physical geography of the Arabian Peninsula.

☐ **p. 434** Students use maps to explain how wind currents, distance from the shore, latitude, and landforms may affect climates on the Arabian Peninsula. BL Verbal/Linguistic

☐ **p. 435** Students pronounce the names of the two great deserts of the Arabian Peninsula and create a pronunciation dictionary. ELL Verbal/Linguistic

C Critical Thinking Skills

☐ **p. 435** Students discuss the advantages of being located on a coast. AL Logical/Mathematical

☐ **p. 437** Students debate the issue of whether oil or freshwater is a more important resource to modern life. BL Verbal/Linguistic

W Writing Skills

☐ **p. 436** Students imagine they are hotel owners in an Arabian city and write a promotional piece to attract tourists to their hotel, touting its amenities. ELL Interpersonal, Verbal/Linguistic

T Technology Skills

☐ **p. 436** Students research information about the location of the oases of the Arabian Peninsula. BL Verbal/Linguistic

☐ **p. 437** Students research the coral reefs of the Red Sea and make a presentation describing an imaginary diving adventure in the region. BL Kinesthetic, Auditory/Musical

☑ Online Teaching Options

V Visual Skills

☐ INTERACTIVE MAP **Physical Geography: The Arabian Peninsula**—Students study the formation of the Arabian Peninsula through tectonic plate movement and draw a map of what the area may have looked like beforehand. BL Verbal/Linguistic, Visual/Spatial

C Critical Thinking Skills

☐ INTERACTIVE BELLRINGER **Physical Geography: The Arabian Peninsula**—Students analyze how bodies of water that surround the Arabian Peninsula both isolate it from and connect it to the African continent and the rest of the Asian continent. AL Interpersonal, Visual/Spatial

☐ INTERACTIVE WHITEBOARD ACTIVITY **Landforms and Water Systems of the Arabian Peninsula**—Students make vocabulary words with features on a map of the Arabian Peninsula. ELL AL Visual/Spatial, Naturalist

☑ Printable Digital Worksheets

R Reading Skills

☐ WORKSHEET **Guided Reading Activity**—Students use the Guided Reading Activity worksheets to review their comprehension of the content.

C Critical Thinking Skills

☐ WORKSHEET **Video Activity**—Students answer questions related to a topic in the chapter content after they have viewed a lesson video.

HUMAN GEOGRAPHY OF THE ARABIAN PENINSULA

Students will know:
- *how the Arabian Peninsula developed politically.*
- *the factors that affect population distribution.*
- *the ways in which Islam affects life on the Arabian Peninsula.*
- *how oil influences the human geography of the Arabian Peninsula.*

Students will be able to:
- ***explain** the political development of the Arabian Peninsula.*
- ***identify** factors that affect population distribution in the region.*
- ***analyze** the effect of Islam on life of the people of the Arabian Peninsula.*
- ***analyze** the influence of oil on human geography of the region.*

UNDERSTANDING BY DESIGN™

Print Teaching Options

V Visual Skills

- **p. 443** Students compare maps of the Arabian Peninsula and make correlations between landforms, climate, population distribution, industry, and agriculture. Verbal/Linguistic

R Reading Skills

- **p. 438** Students identify questions about the history and government of the Arabian Peninsula that they hope to answer as they read this lesson.
- **p. 439** Students explain how the chart of country statistics can be used to indicate the economy of a country and discuss why the median age of a country is important to an economist. BL Verbal/Linguistic
- **p. 440** Students discuss how and why the discovery of oil changed population patterns and brainstorm why large regions of the peninsula remain sparsely populated. AL Verbal/Linguistic

C Critical Thinking Skills

- **p. 438** Students list key facts about the history, culture, and government of the bedouins and other groups.
- **p. 441** Students discuss how medical practices vary between Arabian countries. Logical/Mathematical
- **p. 442** Students present sides in a debate about whether women should be granted more rights and why. Interpersonal, Logical/Mathematical
- **p. 443** Students imagine they are on the economic development commission of a city in Kuwait or Yemen and debate whether money should be spent on a major project. Verbal/Linguistic, Interpersonal

W Writing Skills

- **p. 439** Students summarize how population patterns in the Arabian Peninsula have changed over time. AL

T Technology Skills

- **p. 441** Students research the religious pilgrimage taken by Muslims to Makkah and present their findings to the class. BL Interpersonal, Verbal/Linguistic
- **p. 442** Students research and create a multimedia presentation about an art form of the Arabian Peninsula. BL Auditory/Musical, Visual/Spatial

Online Teaching Options

V Visual Skills

GRAPHIC ORGANIZER **Human Geography of the Arabian Peninsula**—Students use a graphic organizer to classify the many different ethnic groups living in the Arabian Peninsula. ELL AL Verbal/Linguistic

R Reading Skills

INTERACTIVE WHITEBOARD ACTIVITY **Impact of Islam on the Arabian Peninsula**—Students determine which statements about the effect of Islam on the Arabian Peninsula are true and which are inaccurate. AL Verbal/Linguistic

VIDEO **Saudi Women: Jobs**—Students summarize the changing roles of Saudi women and discuss how this has affected the country. AL Verbal/Linguistic

C Critical Thinking Skills

INTERACTIVE BELLRINGER **Arabian Peninsula Country Statistics**—Students use the table to interpret the significance of the population distribution of ethnic groups in countries of the Arabian Peninsula and make calculations to find the country with the highest per capita income. BL Logical/Mathematical

W Writing Skills

INTERACTIVE IMAGE **Foods of Ramadan**—Students describe the religious significance of Ramadan and write a paragraph about what they have learned. Verbal/Linguistic, Visual/Spatial

Printable Digital Worksheets

R Reading Skills

WORKSHEET **Guided Reading Activity**—Students use Guided Reading Activity worksheets to review their comprehension of the content.

WORKSHEET **Reading Essentials and Study Guide**—Students complete the study guide and answer Reading Progress Check and vocabulary questions. AL

C Critical Thinking Skills

WORKSHEET **Video Activity**—Students answer questions related to a topic in the chapter content after they have viewed a lesson video.

LESSON **3 PLANNER**

PEOPLE AND THEIR ENVIRONMENT: THE ARABIAN PENINSULA

Students will know:

- *how the petroleum industry has affected the environment of and around the Arabian Peninsula.*
- *how population growth is creating a water crisis in the region.*
- *what steps people and governments of the Arabian Peninsula are taking to address their environmental concerns.*

Students will be able to:

- ***discuss*** *the effects of the petroleum industry in the Arabian Peninsula.*
- ***analyze*** *how population growth is leading to a water crisis.*
- ***identify*** *ways in which people and governments are working to improve the environment.*

UNDERSTANDING BY DESIGN®

☑ *Print Teaching Options*

V Visual Skills

- ☐ **p. 445** Students discuss a photograph showing air pollution in a city. AL Visual/Spatial
- ☐ **p. 446** Students create a line graph showing how the populations of the countries of the Arabian Peninsula are expected to increase over time and predict how this will affect the countries economically. BL Visual/Spatial

R Reading Skills

- ☐ **p. 444** Students name some environmental issues facing the United States today.
- ☐ **p. 445** Students discuss what is meant by the statement "oil extraction comes with a price" and explain where the United States has experienced oil spill disasters and the costs of those disasters. ELL Verbal/Linguistic

C Critical Thinking Skills

- ☐ **p. 445** Students list the changes that have occurred in the different countries on the Arabian Peninsula and identify their effects. AL Logical/Mathematical
- ☐ **p. 446** Students compare a rainfall map to an economic activities map and predict where water shortages may happen. BL Logical/Mathematical
- ☐ **p. 447** Students discuss short- and long-term measures to deal with Saudi Arabia's growing water problems. AL Verbal/Linguistic
- ☐ **p. 448** Students hold a debate about who should be responsible for managing a community's water resources. Interpersonal, Logical/Mathematical

W Writing Skills

- ☐ **p. 444** Students write two or three paragraphs summarizing why oil is a crucial commodity in the world economy. AL Verbal/Linguistic
- ☐ **p. 448** Students write a report evaluating how a country is dealing with the problem of overconsumption.

T Technology Skills

- ☐ **p. 444** Students conduct further research beyond what they know about the Arab Spring and the 1991 Persian Gulf War, construct a time line of events, and predict future developments. BL Interpersonal, Logical/Mathematical

☑ *Online Teaching Options*

V Visual Skills

- ☐ INTERACTIVE GRAPHIC ORGANIZER **People and Their Environment: The Arabian Peninsula**—Students use a graphic organizer to summarize the lesson. ELL AL Visual/Spatial, Verbal/Linguistic

C Critical Thinking Skills

- ☐ INTERACTIVE BELLRINGER **Smoke Plumes Over Kuwait, 1991**—Students draw inferences about the effect of the oil fires on the environment and human activities based on the image and imagine what it might be like to have similar plumes of smoke over their city or community for an extended period of time. Intrapersonal, Visual/Spatial
- ☐ INTERACTIVE IMAGE **Polluting the Air**—Students brainstorm causes of air pollution in Dubai and write a proposal on how to reduce emissions. BL Visual/Spatial, Logical/Mathematical
- ☐ INTERACTIVE WHITEBOARD ACTIVITY **Impact of the Petroleum Industry on the Environment**—Students match a list of causes and effects of the petroleum industry on the Arabian Peninsula.

W Writing Skills

- ☐ VIDEO **Why Much of the World's Oil Supply Is in Southwest Asia**—Students write an essay describing the positive and negative effects of the prevalence of oil in Southwest Asia. Verbal/Linguistic

☑ *Printable Digital Worksheets*

R Reading Skills

- ☐ WORKSHEET **Guided Reading Activity**—Students use Guided Reading Activity worksheets to review their comprehension of the content.
- ☐ WORKSHEET **Reading Essentials and Study Guide**—Students complete the study guide and answer Reading Progress Check and vocabulary questions. AL
- ☐ WORKSHEET **Vocabulary Activity**—Students review the chapter content and academic vocabulary words.

C Critical Thinking Skills

- ☐ WORKSHEET **Video Activity**—Students answer questions based on a lesson video.
- ☐ WORKSHEET **Reteaching Activity**—Students use this activity worksheet to review and reteach chapter content and vocabulary. This worksheet can be used with struggling students who need additional help with difficult content concepts.

INTERVENTION AND REMEDIATION STRATEGIES

LESSON 1 Physical Geography of the Arabian Peninsula

Reading and Comprehension

Have students work in pairs to create an illustrated outline using the lesson's headings and subheadings. As partners gather information from each section, have them note key ideas and details under each heading. Encourage students to illustrate their outlines to show their understanding of lesson concepts and content vocabulary terms. For example, students may wish to draw a picture of a peninsula under their outline subheading *Landforms.* Or they may choose to use a graphic organizer like the one on the Lesson Opener to organize information about the climates and biomes of the Arabian Peninsula. Ask volunteers to present their outlines to the class.

Text Evidence

Assign student groups a region or country located on the Arabian Peninsula. Tell groups they will create a travel brochure about their region that answers one of the Guiding Questions in the lesson. For example, students may include information about interesting landforms such as the Arabian Shield in a brochure that answers the first Guiding Question: *What are the major physical characteristics of the Arabian Peninsula?* Students should use simple sketches and phrases to describe the region's physical features and a list of reasons tourists might want to visit. Students may wish to conduct additional research about their region to enhance their brochures. Have groups present their brochures to the class.

LESSON 2 Human Geography of the Arabian Peninsula

Reading and Comprehension

To help students comprehend the population and ethnic makeup of countries on the Arabian Peninsula, assign student pairs or small groups one of the countries shown on the chart in this lesson that outlines statistics in the region. Have partners work together to add a column to the chart that includes key facts about their assigned region's history and government. Students may conduct research using print or online sources to verify or add to information gleaned from the lesson. Tell students to write a short summary of the information and present it to the class.

Text Evidence

To ensure that students have a firm grasp of lesson content, have them create a "living" time line of the lesson. Have students review the time line in this lesson depicting events related to Islam and Saudi Arabia. Tell students to choose an event from the time line (or assign students specific events to avoid duplication) and have them conduct research about it. As students research their event, tell them to take notes and write a summarizing sentence that explains its significance. After students have had time to prepare their sentences, organize students in sequential order and have them recite their sentences.

LESSON 3 People and Their Environment: the Arabian Peninsula

Reading and Comprehension

Assign student groups one of the challenges discussed in this lesson such as management of petroleum reserves, oil extraction, climate change, the impact of population on resources such as water, and so on. Have students in each group work together to summarize the problems related to their topic and how or if the problems are being addressed or solved. Tell students their summaries should answer the Guiding Question: *How have people and governments on the Arabian Peninsula addressed the environmental challenges they face?* Have students share their summaries with the class, guiding a discussion about the significance of oil and water management in the region.

Text Evidence

Have students work in pairs or small groups to identify evidence from the lesson that supports one of the following statements: 1. *Physical, human, and economic geography can influence government policy.* 2. *Yemen shows that an increasing population and the effects of climate change can contribute to political instability.* 3. *By far the greatest overconsumption in the region has been in the practice of agriculture.* Ask students to share their evidence with the class and guide a class discussion about the topics to reinforce students' understanding. Discuss the fragile balance between managing development and resources and preserving the natural environment of the Arabian Peninsula's land and water.

Online Resources

Leveled Reader

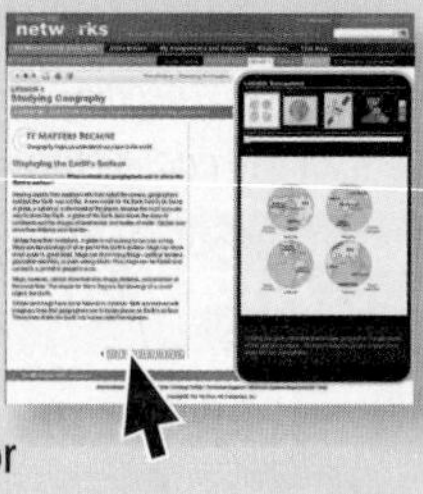

Use this online approaching-level text that corresponds directly to the text in the Student Edition. It also includes additional reading and comprehension support for English Language Learners.

Guided Reading Activities

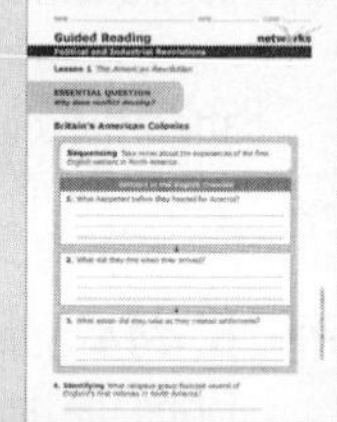

This resource uses guiding questions to help students with comprehension.

Reteaching Activities

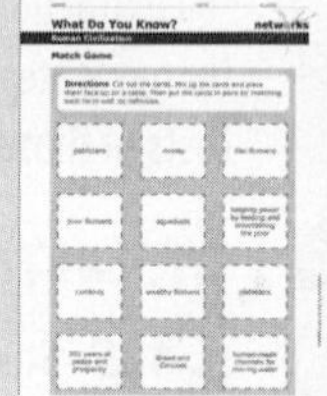

These worksheets provide students with an opportunity for remedial practice and review of vital chapter content.

Reading Essentials and Study Guide

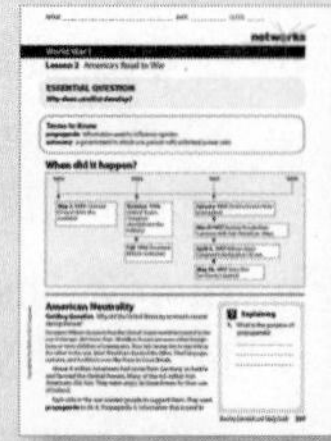

This resource offers writing and reading activities for the approaching-level student.

Self-Check Quizzes

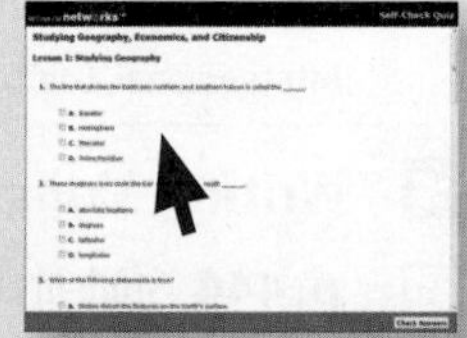

This online assessment tool provides instant feedback for students to check their progress.

Chapter Summaries

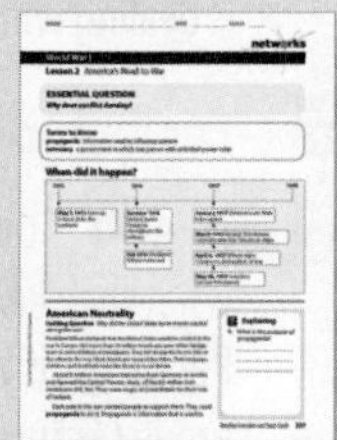

Summaries are provided for each chapter that thoroughly condense core content into manageable chunks.

The Arabian Peninsula

ESSENTIAL QUESTION • *How do physical systems and human systems shape a place?*

networks

There's More Online about the Arabian Peninsula's geography.

CHAPTER 18

Geography Matters...

Once a land of nomadic herders, the Arabian Peninsula entered the modern world during the twentieth century with a sudden burst of wealth and power created by the vast deposits of oil beneath its land. It is a region of contrasts. Its teeming cities perch on the edge of the sea or on inland oases, surrounded by seemingly endless deserts. The oil beneath those deserts has created almost boundless wealth. However, it is not the most precious resource on the peninsula. The most sought-after resource of all is water.

◀ Herding sheep and goats is an ancient tradition on the Arabian Peninsula.

Morales/age fotostock

431

Letter from the Author

Dear Geography Teacher,

The two holiest cities in Saudi Arabia are Makkah (Mecca) and Madinah (Medina). The story of these two cities is intertwined with the life and teachings of the prophet Muhammad. Have students research to learn about the role Makkah and Madinah played in the origins of Islam. Also have students explore the role these two cities played in the early struggles that Muhammad endured to get people to listen to his messages based on the words and guidance of Allah.

Richard G. Boehm

ENGAGE

Defining Write these questions on the board: **Who are the Arabs? Where do Arabs live? Why are they called Arabs? What language do Arabs speak? What is the Arabian Peninsula? Which term was used first, Arab or Arabia?** Encourage students to be on the lookout for answers to these questions as they study the chapter.

TEACH & ASSESS

Interpreting Call students' attention to the photograph of a girl holding a goat and have them describe in detail what they see. *(Possible answer: a young girl, probably an Arab; wearing short-sleeved dress and gold jewelry; holding a goat)* **Ask: Based on this photograph, what assumptions can you make about the girl? The Arabian Peninsula?** *(Possible answer: The girl lives on a farm; goats are raised on the farm; goats are important to the Arabian people; climate is warm or warm part of the year.)* **AL Visual/Spatial**

Explaining Have students read the paragraph under the "Geography Matters" heading and explain how the Arabian Peninsula has changed in recent times. **Ask: What caused these abrupt changes?** *(discovery of vast deposits of oil)* **Why would the discovery of oil change the life of nomads?** *(Student answers may vary, but students might note that new opportunities would arise.)* **Why do geographers say that water is more precious than oil on the Arabian Peninsula?** *(Student answers may vary, but students should understand that people cannot live without water and that water is necessary for raising crops and livestock.)* **AL Verbal/Linguistic**

CLOSE & REFLECT

Synthesizing Have students list terms that characterize the Arabian Peninsula. **Ask: What words come to mind when you think of the Arabian Peninsula?** *(Possible answers: dry, hot, oil, Arabs, Islam, wealth, power, nomads)* Have students use these words to review the lesson.

ePals **GlobalCommunity**
Where learners connect™

Extend the project-based learning experience globally through our partnership with ePals. EPals allows you to connect with classrooms around the world in a safe online environment for real-life lessons and projects in virtual study groups.

ENGAGE

C Critical Thinking Skills

Drawing Conclusions Have students read the text under the title "Migrant Workers in the Arabian Peninsula." Then ask a volunteer to locate the Arabian Peninsula on a globe or large world map. Have another volunteer locate Indonesia and the Philippines on the map and trace the path a migrant from the South Pacific would follow to reach a city in the Arabian Peninsula. Have students estimate the distance. Discuss the difficulties a poor migrant would have in traveling so far from home to seek a job.

TEACH & ASSESS

V Visual Skills

Interpreting Visuals Call students' attention to the photograph on page 432. Have students describe the photograph and hypothesize where the scene takes place and what is going on. *(Student answers may vary, but students might guess that these are migrant workers who have come to the Arabian Peninsula to get a job.)* **Ask:** Who is the woman and why is she dressed as she is? *(Possible answers: She is a clerk who is processing paperwork. She is a Muslim and is wearing traditional garb.)* What clues does the photograph give you about old and new ways in the Arabian Peninsula? *(old: woman wearing traditional garb; new: using a computer)* Visual/Spatial

Content Background Knowledge

The Promise of Work

- The influx of foreign workers in the Arabian Peninsula started soon after oil was discovered there in the late 1930s.
- The first workers to arrive were Arab and Western technical, professional, and administrative personnel.
- Today workers from these areas generally hold the highest positions not held by the Arabs themselves. For professionals, working in an Arab country can be lucrative and pleasant.
- Most guest workers from poor countries get low-paying jobs in the agriculture, cleaning, and domestic service industries.

Why Geography Matters: **The Arabian Peninsula**

migrant workers *in the* Arabian Peninsula

C *The Arabian Peninsula is flanked by the Red Sea and the Persian Gulf, far from the island countries of Indonesia and the Philippines. Yet this peninsula has drawn thousands of migrants from these and other countries who migrate here in search of work. This "guest" population, however, faces several other difficulties in addition to living thousands of miles from their homes and families.*

V

Karim Sahib/AFP/Getty Images

432

Project-Based Learning

Hands-On

Arabian Tour Books

Working in groups, students will create tour books that describe the climate, physical and cultural features, events, and current issues that affect the Arabian Peninsula. Each group will research and write a tour book about an assigned country. Tour books will include a title page, table of contents, written reports about tour topics, and visuals. Groups will present their tour books to the class by reading selected excerpts from their written reports.

ePals GlobalCommunity
Where learners connect™

Digital Hands-On

Create Online Projects

Find an additional activity online that incorporates technology for this project. Visit the EdTech Teacher Web sites for more links, tutorials, and other resources.

Why Geography Matters

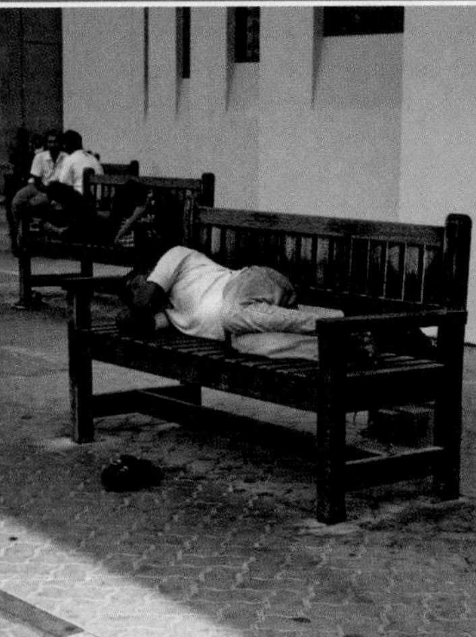

Why are migrant workers coming to the Arabian Peninsula?

Migrant workers are pushed out of their homelands because of increasing poverty and unemployment. This was especially true after the global financial crisis that broke out in 2007–2008. Many migrant workers flock to the Arabian Peninsula because of the promise of wages that are much higher than they could ever earn in their native countries. Even Yemen, which has high levels of poverty, sends many workers to Saudi Arabia.

In 2010 Saudi Arabia was the world's second-largest source of jobs for migrant workers, followed by the United States. Another reason Muslim migrants in particular are attracted to the Arabian Peninsula is that they will be able to fulfill one of the pillars of Islam—the pilgrimage to Makkah (Mecca).

1. **Human Systems** What are the push and pull factors influencing migration to the Arabian Peninsula? How do similar religious beliefs affect the cultural geography of the subregion?

Who makes up the majority of migrant workers, and what challenges do they face?

In Indonesia, about 90 percent of the total population is Muslim, and nearly half of all migrant workers in Saudi Arabia are from Indonesia. The millions of migrant workers include women who travel each year in search of domestic work. They come from such Asian countries as the Philippines, Sri Lanka, and Indonesia, and from some African countries including Ethiopia, Egypt, and Madagascar.

R

Many are products of the *kafala* system, in which an employer sponsors a migrant worker by paying travel expenses and providing room and board. In some cases, however, the system is abused, and the sponsor exercises tight control over the migrant worker. Sometimes sponsors confiscate, or take control of, workers' passports. Some of the challenges migrant workers face include unsanitary living conditions, hunger, low wages, a lack of health care, and discrimination. All too often, they become the victims of human rights violations. Some critics say the system closely resembles slavery; female migrant workers, especially, are treated like property.

2. **Human Systems** What challenges do female migrant workers face, and what influence does the *kafala* system have on their rights?

What actions can be taken to help migrant workers?

W

Migrant workers have few rights and are not protected under most labor laws. Many work nearly 100 hours per week with little or no compensation for overtime work; few are given leisure time. Under the *kafala* system, they are indebted to their sponsors, who prevent them from leaving to visit family in their home countries. The workers are also prevented from seeking other employment.

International groups such as Amnesty International and other organizations are pressuring governments and organizations in the region to take action to crack down on human rights abuses. The United Nations is also investigating court rulings that have favored and empowered employers in labor disputes that involve migrant workers.

T

3. **Human Systems** Write a paragraph explaining how government and community action could improve the lives of female migrant workers in the Arabian Peninsula.

THERE'S MORE ONLINE

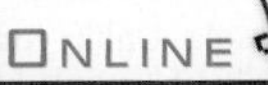

VIEW a map of migrant worker home countries • *READ* about issues of migrant workers' rights in Saudi Arabia

R Reading Skills

Listing Have students list two reasons why migrants are pushed from their home countries *(increasing poverty; unemployment)* and two reasons why they are drawn to the Arabian Peninsula *(promise of higher wages; chance to make the pilgrimage to Mecca)*. Discuss which factor is probably the strongest motivation and why. AL **Verbal/Linguistic**

W Writing Skills

Narrative Have students imagine the life of a female migrant worker who is the product of the *kafala* system in Saudi Arabia. Have students write a letter back home describing how life differs from what the migrant worker expected and/or was promised. ELL **Interpersonal, Verbal/Linguistic**

T Technology Skills

Constructing Arguments Have students imagine they are a representative of a human rights organization. After researching online or in library resources, have students prepare arguments explaining why basic human rights should be extended to all workers in the Arabian Peninsula. BL **Logical/Mathematical, Verbal/Linguistic**

CLOSE & REFLECT

Finding the Main Idea Have students list important points presented in this feature and then use their lists to write brief statements that express the main idea.

SLIDE SHOW

Wanted: Migrant Workers

Comparing and Contrasting After students view this slide show about migrant workers in the Arabian Peninsula, discuss how migrant workers contribute to the economic growth of this area. Then ask students why people become migrant workers. Have students list the advantages and disadvantages of being a migrant worker. Then have them list the advantages and disadvantages for a country that employs a large number of migrant workers. AL **Verbal/Linguistic**

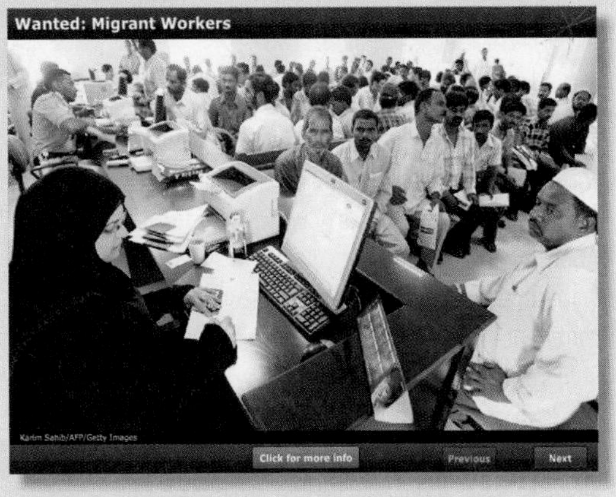

ANSWERS, p. 433

Why Geography Matters

1. Push factors: high unemployment and increasing poverty in home countries of migrant workers; Pull factors: jobs, higher wages, and the ability to make the pilgrimage to Makkah (Mecca). Muslim migrants come in high numbers to share common beliefs and to complete a pillar of Islam.
2. Female migrant workers face low wages, lack of health care and freedom, unsanitary living conditions, possible confiscation of their passport, discrimination, and human rights violations. The *kafala* system can result in women being treated as property as the employer pays their travel expenses.
3. Paragraphs may vary but could include that governments and communities should protect migrant workers under labor laws, reduce work hours, mandate fair wages, and take action against human rights abuses.

ENGAGE

R Reading Skills

Predicting After reading *It Matters Because*, have students page through the lesson, looking at the headings and photos. Have students write three or four sentences predicting what they will learn about the physical geography of the Arabian Peninsula.

TEACH & ASSESS

V Visual Skills

Analyzing Visuals Provide students with a map showing tectonic plate movement in the Middle East. Have students compare a physical map with the tectonic plate map to imagine how the Arabian Peninsula had once been more firmly connected to Africa. Lead a discussion about the impact of plate movement, which causes earthquakes, rifts, and mountains to form. AL Visual/Spatial

ANSWERS, p. 434

TAKING NOTES: The Arabian Shield—runs north to south along the coast of the Red Sea; forms a tall mountain range; western side contains a steep escarpment that runs along the Red Sea; extinct volcanoes cover its surface; lava beds from ancient volcanoes created wide black bands on the landscape; **The Najd**—central plateau of the Arabian Peninsula; lies east of the Arabian Shield; gently slopes from west to east, ending on the coast of the Persian Gulf; **An Nafūd**—northern desert of the Arabian Peninsula; covered in reddish sand and crescent-shaped dunes; stretches 25,000 square miles; **Rub' al-Khali**—known as "the Empty Quarter"; south of the An Nafūd; ten times larger than An Nafūd; is the world's largest uninterrupted area of sand

networks *There's More Online!*

- IMAGE Red Sea Coral Reef
- MAP Physical Geography: The Arabian Peninsula
- INTERACTIVE SELF-CHECK QUIZ
- VIDEO Physical Geography of the Arabian Peninsula

Reading **HELP**DESK CCSS

Academic Vocabulary (Tier Two Words)
- **nonetheless**
- **estimate**

Content Vocabulary (Tier Three Words)
- **peninsula**
- **arid**
- **dune**
- **monsoon**
- **simooms**
- ***shamal***

TAKING NOTES: ***Key Ideas and Details***

IDENTIFYING As you read about the landforms of the Arabian Peninsula, use a graphic organizer like the one below to identify the characteristics of each major area.

Arabian Peninsula

Area	Characteristics

LESSON 1
Physical Geography of the Arabian Peninsula

ESSENTIAL QUESTION • *How do physical systems and human systems shape a place?*

IT MATTERS BECAUSE

R *The physical systems of the Arabian Peninsula affect the distribution of its two greatest resources, oil and water. The location and types of landforms contribute to extremes of climate. Human activities shape the peninsula through the movement of people, the creation of settlements, and the use of natural resources.*

Landforms

GUIDING QUESTION *What are the major physical characteristics of the Arabian Peninsula?*

V About 20 to 30 million years ago, Africa and Arabia formed a single tectonic plate. Over the millennia, tectonic forces created a rift valley which separated the plate into two landmasses. The valley filled with water, becoming the Red Sea. Positioned almost equally north and south of the Tropic of Cancer, this area east of the Red Sea is now the Arabian Peninsula.

The Red Sea became the western and southwestern boundaries of the newly formed **peninsula**. A peninsula is an area of land almost entirely surrounded by water. The waters of the Gulf of Aden, the Arabian Sea, the Gulf of Oman, and the Persian Gulf form natural boundaries on the southern and eastern parts of the peninsula. The southern borders of Israel, Jordan, and Iraq make up its northern boundary.

On the west, the Arabian Shield runs from north to south along the Red Sea coast. A shield is a landform composed of hard, ancient rocks. Here the Shield forms a tall mountain range. Along the western side of the Shield there is a steep escarpment, or cliff, that looms above the narrow strip of coastal plain that runs the length of the Red Sea. Extinct volcanoes cover the surface of the Shield. The lava beds produced by once-active volcanoes create the wide black bands typical of the western Arabian landscape.

To the east of the peaks of the Arabian Shield lies the Najd, the central plateau of the Arabian Peninsula. Unlike most plateaus, it does not end abruptly with a steep cliff. Instead, it slopes gently from west to east and ends at sea level on the Persian Gulf coast.

networks *Online Teaching Options*

INTERACTIVE BELLRINGER

Physical Geography: The Arabian Peninsula

Interpreting Maps Use the introductory text and map to identify the bodies of water that surround the Arabian Peninsula and to explain how these bodies of water both isolate it from and connect it to the African continent and the rest of the Asian continent. Have students form small groups and view the bellringer. Ask each group to answer the questions, form a consensus on the answers, and then record their answers. Review the questions as a class.
AL Interpersonal, Visual/Spatial

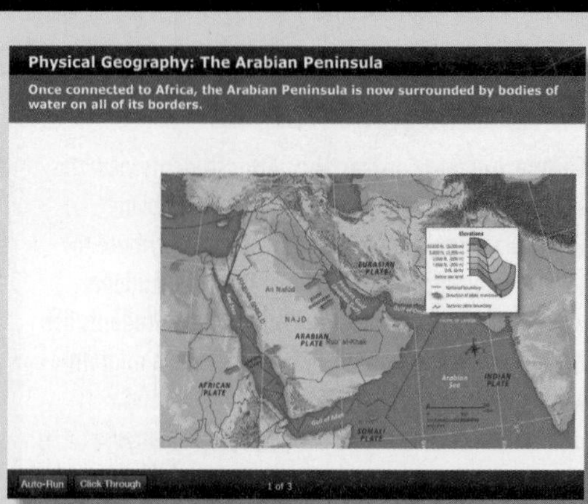

The Arabian Peninsula is a region dominated by the **arid**, or very dry, land of its interior. The 1.2 million square miles (3 million sq. km) of the peninsula are mostly unsuitable for human settlement. In much of the peninsula, silt and dust left by winds and sediment deposited by ancient seas have created soil suitable for agriculture. **Nonetheless**, a lack of water has meant that less than two percent of the peninsula is used for agriculture.

R The Arabian desert has two areas with distinct characteristics. The northern desert, An Nafūd, consists of reddish, crescent-shaped **dunes**—ridges of sand formed by wind. This desert stretches across an area of 25,000 square miles (65,000 sq. km). Far to the south of An Nafūd is the Rub' al-Khali. Known as "the Empty Quarter," the Rub' al-Khali has ten times the area of the northern desert. It is the world's largest uninterrupted area of sand. It is also one of the driest regions on Earth. These four areas—the central plateau, the northern desert, the Rub' al-Khali, and the Arabian Shield—make up most of the Arabian Peninsula.

peninsula a portion of land nearly surrounded by water

arid excessively dry

nonetheless in spite of; nevertheless

dune a mound or ridge of sand formed by the wind

READING PROGRESS CHECK

Describing How did tectonic activity form the Red Sea?

Water Systems

GUIDING QUESTION *How do the waters surrounding the Arabian Peninsula affect life there?*

Thousands of miles of mostly tropical seas surround three sides of the Arabian Peninsula. The Red Sea runs south along the western edge of the Arabian Shield and then to the southeast, where it meets the waters of the Gulf of Aden. The Arabian Sea lies to the southeast of the peninsula. On the northeast lie the Gulf of Oman and the Persian Gulf. These bodies of water isolate the peninsula from

GEOGRAPHY CONNECTION

The Arabian Plate broke free of Africa millions of years ago. It is still moving northeast at a rate of approximately .039 inches (4 mm) per year.

1. ***PHYSICAL SYSTEMS*** What physical characteristics might the Arabian Peninsula share with the African continent?
2. ***PHYSICAL SYSTEMS*** What will eventually happen to the Persian Gulf as the Arabian Plate moves northeast over time?

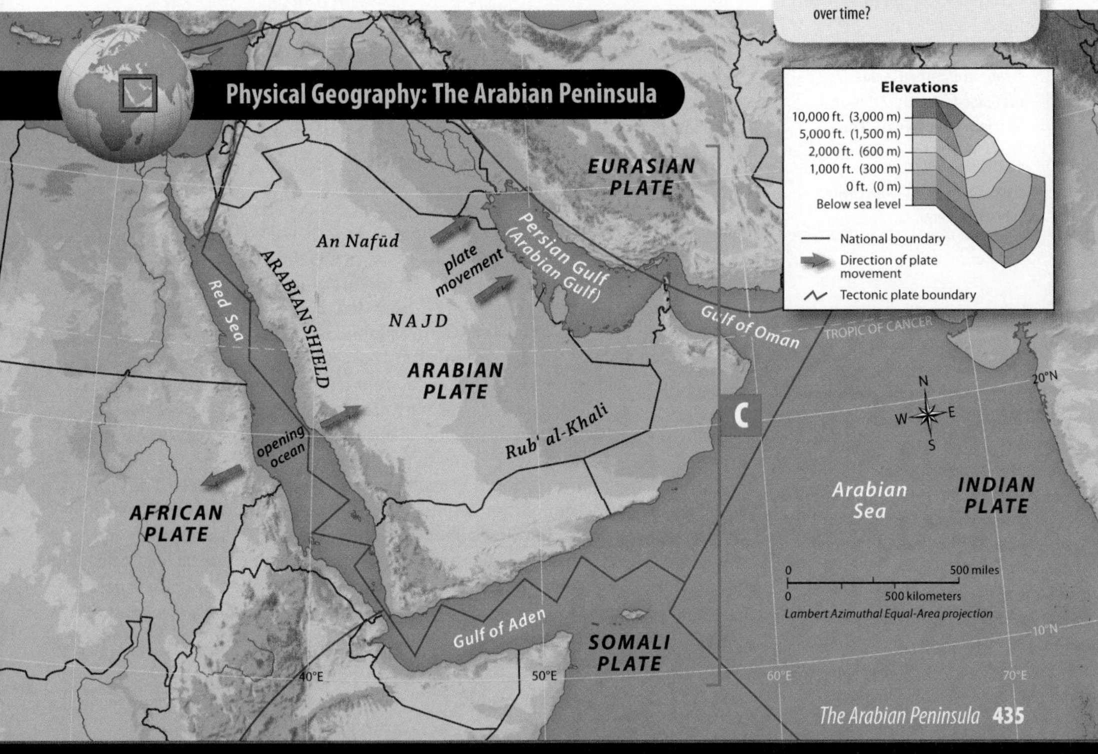

C

INTERACTIVE MAP

Physical Geography: The Arabian Peninsula

Speculating With students, explore this interactive map highlighting the current physical landscape of the Arabian Peninsula and how this peninsula was formed long ago. Pay special attention to the arrows depicting tectonic plate movement and to the waterways surrounding the peninsula. Have students draw a map showing what the area probably looked like before movement of the tectonic plates, and then have them write a paragraph describing how the area's economics would be different today if the plate movement had not occurred and the peninsula did not exist. BL **Verbal/Linguistic, Visual/Spatial**

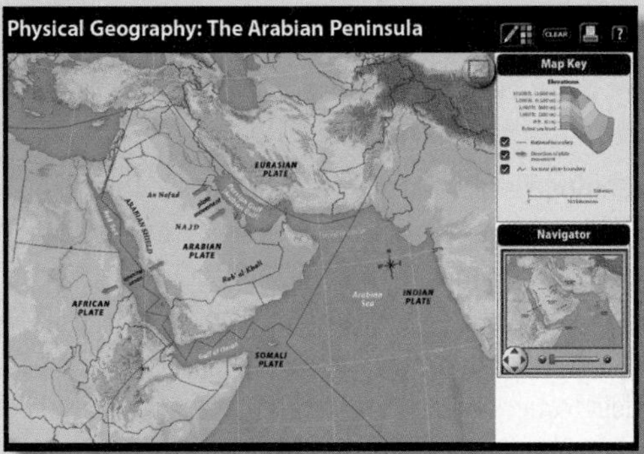

CHAPTER 18, Lesson 1

Physical Geography of the Arabian Peninsula

R Reading Skills

Naming Challenge students to pronounce the names of the two great deserts of the Arabian Peninsula—Al-Nafud *(na·fūd; rhymes with food)"* and Rub' al-Khali *(rŭb-al-`kä-lē; "Rub" rhymes with tube; "Khali" with holly)."* Suggest that students create a pronunciation dictionary of Arabic names and places to keep close at hand as they study this chapter. ELL **Verbal/Linguistic**

C Critical Thinking Skills

Analyzing Visuals Draw students' attention to the map. Have students note the relationship of the Arabian Plate to the surrounding water systems. Discuss the advantages of an area being located on a coast. *(Student answers will vary but may include transportation and source of water.)* Point out that these bodies of water are occasionally scenes of global conflict. **Ask: How might the narrow openings to the Red Sea and Persian Gulf be important in times of conflict?** *(Student answers will vary but may relate to the narrow openings being easy to block or defend.)* AL **Logical/Mathematical**

Making Connections

Encourage students to locate and name the deserts of North America on a map. Have students describe how the North American deserts are similar to and different from the deserts of the Arabian Peninsula. Encourage students who have visited one of these deserts to describe their experiences.

ANSWERS, p. 435

READING PROGRESS CHECK Tectonic activity formed the Red Sea by creating a rift valley that separated into the African and Arabian plates and then filled with water.

GEOGRAPHY CONNECTION

1. The Arabian Peninsula and the African continent might share physical characteristics such as mountains, plateaus, and coastal lowlands.
2. As the Arabian Plate moves northeast, the Persian Gulf will get smaller and eventually disappear.

CHAPTER 18, Lesson 1
Physical Geography of the Arabian Peninsula

T Technology Skills

Researching Organize students into pairs or small groups. Have groups research online and elsewhere to learn about the oases of the Arabian Peninsula. Have student consider the following questions: Where are they? What do they look like? How are they used? Are towns built around them? Are other sources of freshwater available in oases? Have students report their findings to the class. Encourage students to include visuals such as maps, photos, and diagrams to develop a multimedia presentation. BL **Verbal/Linguistic**

W Writing Skills

Informative/Explanatory Have students imagine they are hotel owners in an Arabian city. To attract visitors to their hotel, have them write a promotional piece touting the many amenities the hotel offers, particularly its new air-conditioning system. Then have them explain how tourists will benefit from this amenity. ELL **Interpersonal, Verbal/Linguistic**

ANSWERS, p. 436

READING PROGRESS CHECK The Red Sea, Persian Gulf, Gulf of Aden, Arabian Sea, and Gulf of Oman all border the Arabian Peninsula.

Connecting Geography Air-conditioning increases productivity in hot weather by allowing people to work comfortably.

Connecting Geography to SCIENCE

Air-Conditioning

W In 1902 an American named Willis Carrier invented air-conditioning. At first it was used commercially in the United States in public buildings like movie theaters and hotels. It was a boon to productivity in the summertime. Air-conditioning allowed cities in the southern United States to attract industries from other parts of the country. On the Arabian Peninsula, air-conditioning made it possible for people from temperate climates to work during the summers in the hot, steamy coastal cities or on the oil pipelines that cross the deserts. In recent years, the demand for air-conditioning on the Arabian Peninsula has increased as industries and tourism have expanded.

ANALYZING How does air-conditioning affect productivity in hot weather?

its neighbors to the east and west. However, they are vital to the life of the peninsula. The Red Sea and the Persian Gulf, in particular, are necessary to the economies of the region.

The Red Sea, on the western side of the Arabian Peninsula, is the northernmost tropical sea in the world. It is also an important shipping route. Ships entering from the Suez Canal in the north carry goods through the Red Sea to the Gulf of Aden. Most of the products transported between Europe and Asia pass through the long and narrow Red Sea.

On the east, the Persian Gulf serves the international shipping needs of all the oil-producing countries of the peninsula. The warm waters of the Persian Gulf are crowded with traffic. Huge tankers bring oil from Saudi Arabia, Kuwait, Qatar, Bahrain, and the United Arab Emirates to the rest of the world.

T Although oil is plentiful on the Arabian Peninsula, freshwater is scarce. The subregion receives little rainfall. Rapidly growing populations are quickly using up groundwater, the water in the earth that supplies wells and springs. Dotted across the Arabian landscape are small oases, which are gradually going dry as groundwater is depleted. Small, temporary rivers form in wadis when there is rain. Wadis are streambeds that remain dry when no rain falls. They are not reliable sources of water because rainfall is unpredictable.

READING PROGRESS CHECK

Locating Where are the principal bodies of water that border the Arabian Peninsula?

Climate, Biomes, and Resources

GUIDING QUESTION *How does the climate of the Arabian Peninsula affect its biomes?*

For the most part, the Arabian Peninsula is a desert with an extremely dry climate. In much of the peninsula, the average rainfall is less than 4 inches (10 cm) per year. The temperature in some places has been recorded as high as 129°F (54°C). The noontime sun is directly overhead at least once a year for land on or south of the Tropic of Cancer. The heat of the sun combined with the lack of moisture for cloud cover makes the peninsula one of the hottest places on Earth.

Climate Regions and Biomes

A hot and dry desert biome like the Rub' al-Khali has little rainfall. There is no surface water. The little rain that falls often evaporates before it reaches the ground. The Rub' al-Khali has few forms of animal or plant life. Some of the desert areas in the northern part of the peninsula have a greater abundance of plants and animals. These areas are similar to the Mojave and Sonoran Deserts in the United States.

The dry heat of the desert areas in summer contrasts with the extreme humidity of some coastal areas, which are affected by their closeness to water. Dew and fog add to the humidity. Seasonal **monsoon** winds bring heavy rains in the summer.

Wind is a significant factor in the climate of the Arabian Peninsula. The heat of the deserts in the summer sometimes generates hot, suffocating winds called **simooms**. The simooms last only about 20 minutes, but they destroy plant and animal life. These winds are so dangerous, in fact, that the word *simoom* actually means "poison" in Arabic. In areas near the Persian Gulf, sand- and dust-laden winds called ***shamals*** occur in midwinter and early summer. The word *shamal* means "north," and the winds blow from the north or northwest. These winds carry millions of tons of sand and silt into the Rub' al-Khali.

monsoon a seasonal wind that brings warm, moist air from the oceans in summer and cooler, dry air from inland in winter

simoom a hot, dry, suffocating wind that blows from time to time in the Arabian Peninsula

shamal a northwesterly wind in the Persian Gulf area

436

networks Online Teaching Options

INTERACTIVE WHITEBOARD ACTIVITY

Landforms and Water Systems of the Arabian Peninsula

Analyzing Visuals This interactive whiteboard activity will help students review terms associated with the physical geography of the Arabian Peninsula within a visual context. Students will be presented with a map of the Arabian Peninsula, along with a set of labels for the various features on the map. Have students drag the names of landforms and water systems to the map. Then ask students to locate some of the features in the Key Words list by clicking on the correct areas of the map. ELL AL **Visual/Spatial, Naturalist**

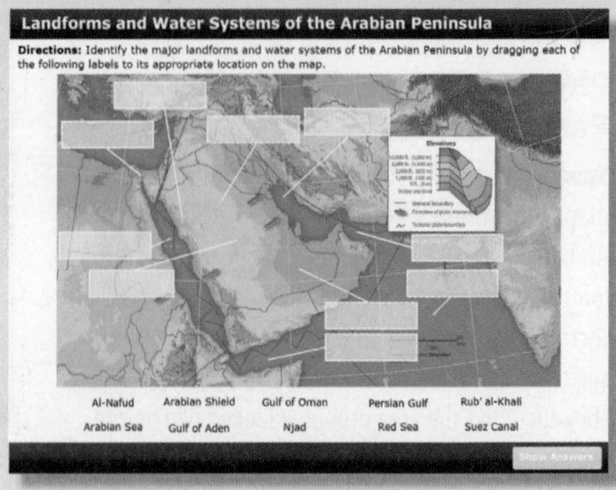

The Red Sea is an aquatic biome. The coral reefs shelter about 1,200 different species of fish and many species of plants. About 10 percent of the species found in the Red Sea are not found in any other marine environment. This aquatic biome is unique because its corals can endure extreme heat and salinity. The salinity is high because of high rates of evaporation and a lack of rain over the area. Violent, dust-laden winds churn the waters in ways that would prove fatal to other reefs. In spite of their hardiness, the reefs are subject to the same threats as other aquatic biomes: heavy pollution and overuse. **T**

Natural Resources

At one time, the Earth was a huge aquatic biome. Animal and plant life teemed in ancient seas. Over time, the remains of these organisms were buried under the sedimentary rock. Millions of years of intense heat and pressure eventually transformed the remains of these organisms into crude oil. This fossil fuel is one of the world's most sought-after resources.

The Arabian deserts lie over a vast deposit of crude oil. This deposit is **estimated** to be at least 25 percent of the world's proven reserves, and oil is the region's principal export. Discovered in Saudi Arabia in 1938, rapid expansion of the oil industry did not occur until after World War II. Of the seven countries of the Arabian Peninsula, only Bahrain does not have significant petroleum reserves.

The Arabian Peninsula has few other significant resources. Some of these resources include fish, pearls, and salt and gypsum produced from saline flats. Mineral resources include iron ore, gold, copper, limestone, and some marble.

The resource that is most crucial to the peninsula, however, is freshwater. Drinkable water is rapidly being depleted because the population has grown dramatically. Aquifers beneath the desert sands cannot be replenished at the rate they are being used. The countries of the area are looking for ways to increase their supplies of this critical resource. **C**

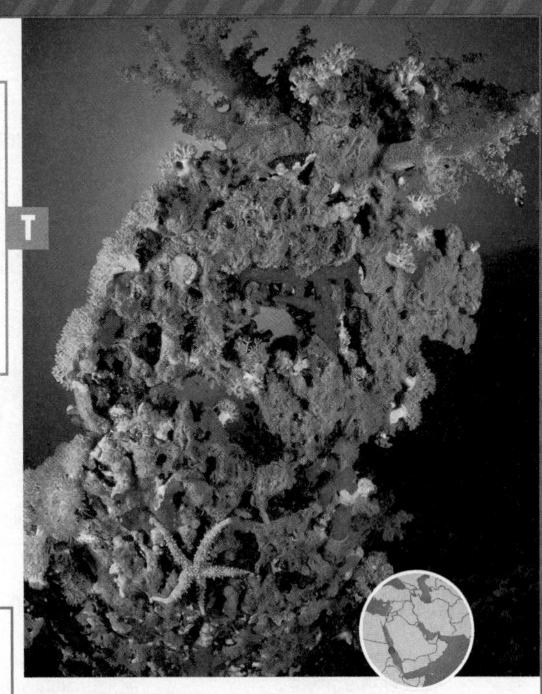

The Red Sea is known for its extensive coral reefs.

▲ **CRITICAL THINKING**

1. ***Hypothesizing*** Why would it be important to protect the Red Sea reefs?
2. ***Describing*** What resources does the Red Sea provide?

estimate to judge approximately; to determine roughly

☑ **READING PROGRESS CHECK**

Classifying What characteristics of the Rub' al-Khali make it a desert biome?

LESSON 1 REVIEW 

Reviewing Vocabulary (Tier Three Words)

1. ***Comparing*** What do *shamals* and simooms have in common? RH.9–10.4
2. ***Contrasting*** How do monsoons differ from *shamals* and simooms? RH.9–10.4

Using Your Notes

3. ***Analyzing*** Use your graphic organizer on the Arabian Peninsula's landforms to write a paragraph analyzing the characteristics that make some areas of the peninsula more suitable for some activities than others.

Answering the Guiding Questions

4. ***Differentiating*** What are the major physical characteristics of the Arabian Peninsula?
5. ***Evaluating*** How do the waters surrounding the Arabian Peninsula affect life there?
6. ***Making Connections*** How does the climate of the Arabian Peninsula affect its biomes?

Writing Activity

7. ***Explanatory*** In a paragraph, discuss why the Red Sea and the Persian Gulf are vital to the economy of the Arabian Peninsula. WHST.9–10.4, WHST.9–10.9

Franco Banfi/WaterFrame/Getty Images

T Technology Skills

Presenting Have students research the coral reefs of the Red Sea. Suggest that students imagine they have gone on a Red Sea dive. Have students make a presentation to the class describing their imaginary adventure. They should include coral species and other species living in the water and any threats to the aquatic ecosystem. Encourage students to use photographs, drawings, maps, and music in their presentations. **BL** **Kinesthetic, Auditory/Musical**

Content Background Knowledge

Oil and Natural Gas Formation

- When they lived, plants absorbed energy from the sun and stored it in molecules made of carbon, the main element in oil. Their plant remains were buried under rock.
- The amount of pressure, the degree of heat, and the type of biomass determined which material became oil and which became natural gas.
- After oil and natural gas were formed, some escaped upward through pores in the rock.
- Other deposits were caught under impermeable layers of rock or clay and form the deposits we find today.

C Critical Thinking Skills

Constructing Arguments Organize the class into two groups to debate this issue: **Which resource is more important to modern life: oil or freshwater?** Encourage students to make clear in their arguments how each resource is used and how the absence or scarcity of one or the other would affect people's lives. **BL** **Verbal/Linguistic**

CLOSE & REFLECT

Summarizing Ask students to identify one or two places on the Arabian Peninsula that they would most like to visit. Have them describe the geography of the region. Ask students to exchange the information with classmates as they review the lesson.

LESSON 1 REVIEW ANSWERS

Reviewing Vocabulary

1. *Shamals* and simooms are both seasonal winds that cause damage.
2. Monsoons bring heavy rain, while *shamals* and simooms are dry winds that carry sand and silt.

Using Your Notes

3. Most of the interior is uninhabitable due to lack of water; less than 2 percent of the peninsula is suitable for agriculture; oases and groundwater provide freshwater; the Red Sea and Persian Gulf are important shipping routes; and under the deserts lie vast deposits of crude oil.

Answering the Guiding Questions

4. The major physical characteristics of the Arabian Peninsula are the vast arid deserts, the central plateau, and the Arabian Shield with its steep escarpments and extinct volcanoes.
5. The waters surrounding the Arabian Peninsula isolate it from other countries to the east and west but are essential to the economies of the peninsula.
6. The dry climate of the Arabian Peninsula causes its biomes to have little water and vegetation and also creates winds that are very destructive to life.

Writing Activity

7. The Red Sea is an important shipping route for goods between the peninsula and Europe and Asia; the Persian Gulf serves as the point where oil from the region is shipped to the rest of the world.

ANSWERS, p. 437

☑ **READING PROGRESS CHECK** The Rub' al-Khali has few forms of plants or animal life, little rainfall, and no surface water, making it a desert biome.

CRITICAL THINKING

1. The Red Sea reefs provide a home for 1,200 species of fish and many types of plants, some of which are not found in any other marine environment. Without protection, these species would become extinct.
2. The Red Sea provides many species of fish and contains oil deposits.

ENGAGE

R Reading Skills

Previewing Ask students to flip through the pages of the lesson, noting titles, subtitles, vocabulary words, and visuals. Have students identify questions about the history and government of the Arabian Peninsula that they hope to answer as they read this lesson. After they complete the lesson, have them review their questions and answer as many as possible.

TEACH & ASSESS

C Critical Thinking Skills

Drawing Inferences Ask students to read the paragraphs relating to the history of tribal and family groups of the Arabian Peninsula. Have students list key facts about the history, culture, and government of the bedouins and other groups. **Ask: How did the lack of a formal, centralized government impact the peoples of the Arabian Peninsula?** (*Student answers may vary but should include details such as: no fixed borders, shared culture but no common rules or laws, tribal leader had absolute control of his group, no collaborative defense against invaders)* **Logical/Mathematical**

ANSWERS, p. 438

TAKING NOTES: Tribes, or social groups based on family relationships, became the first organized groups on the peninsula. Individual tribes, or sheikdoms, controlled specific parts of the region, bedouin nomads of Saudi Arabia followed a tribal structure but were nomadic; different nomadic tribes became powerful at times, dominating the area; no formal government as tribal leaders had absolute power; powerful families controlled areas along the coast; the Ottoman Empire was a strong presence on the peninsula for several hundred years until the Saud family drove them out in the early twentieth century. Most governments on the peninsula are monarchies today; Saudi Arabia, Oman, and Qatar are absolute monarchies; Kuwait and Bahrain are constitutional monarchies; the United Arab Emirates is a federation ruled by emirs (Arab rulers); North Yemen and South Yemen, united in 1990 to form a republic, continue to cause conflict that has destabilized the government.

networks

There's More Online!

- **TIME LINE** Islam and Saudi Arabia
- **CHART** Arabian Peninsula Country Statistics
- **IMAGE** Sanaa, Yemen
- **INTERACTIVE SELF-CHECK QUIZ**
- **VIDEO** Human Geography of the Arabian Peninsula

LESSON 2

Human Geography of the Arabian Peninsula

Reading HELPDESK CCSS

Academic Vocabulary (Tier Two Words)
- **document**
- **strategy**

Content Vocabulary (Tier Three Words)
- **sheikdoms**
- **laws of migration**
- **Sunni**
- **Shia**
- **Ibadhism**
- **shari'ah**
- **hajj**
- **choke point**

TAKING NOTES: ***Key Ideas and Details***

ORGANIZING As you read the lesson, take notes on how the people of the Arabian Peninsula have been governed in the past and how they are governed today.

Arabian Peninsula: Government

Past	Today

ESSENTIAL QUESTION • *How do physical systems and human systems shape a place?*

IT MATTERS BECAUSE

R *History and physical geography have had profound effects on the Arabian Peninsula. A similar history, religion, and culture have shaped the lives of its people. The discovery of vast oil and natural gas resources in the twentieth century produced widespread changes and major challenges to the human population, as well as effects on the physical environment.*

History and Government

GUIDING QUESTION *How did history, culture, and geography help influence the types of governments on the Arabian Peninsula?*

The people of the Arabian Peninsula are overwhelmingly ethnic Arabs and religious Muslims. Religion, ethnicity, and a shared culture unite and define the subregion. From the earliest times, the people of the peninsula lived in tribes—social groups based on family relationships. Individual tribes controlled specific areas of the region, called **sheikdoms**. Some tribes were sedentary, and others were nomadic.

C The bedouin nomads of Saudi Arabia had a tribal structure but were not confined to a single place. Bedouins occupied most of the Arabian Peninsula. Primarily herders of camels, goats, and sheep, the bedouin tribes moved throughout the Arabian Peninsula and beyond. Different tribes of nomads became powerful from time to time and dominated much of the area. Nevertheless, there was no formal government. Each tribal leader had absolute power, and there was no authority above him.

Similarly, powerful families controlled the settled areas along the eastern and southern coasts. These lands were more vulnerable to foreign control than the vast area of the interior. Throughout history, foreigners invaded these areas. The ancient Greeks established a trade center in the Persian Gulf near what is now Kuwait. The Ottoman Empire was a strong presence on the Arabian Peninsula for several hundred years until the

networks ***Online Teaching Options***

INTERACTIVE BELLRINGER

Arabian Peninsula Country Statistics

Calculating This introductory text and table showing population, ethnic groups, and GDP statistics for countries in the Arabian Peninsula can be used to help students interpret the significance of the population distribution of ethnic groups in the countries of the Arabian Peninsula. Students will make calculations to identify the country with the highest per capita income. Tell students to use calculators for part of this activity. Have students pairs discuss each question. Ask student pairs to calculate and record their answers. Then in a class discussion, have volunteers read aloud each question and ask other students to show how they determined the answer for the question about per capita income. Guide the discussion, assisting students as necessary. BL **Logical/Mathematical**

Arabian Peninsula Country Statistics

Arabs once made up the majority population of the Arabian Peninsula. Today, many immigrants move to the Arabian Peninsula for job opportunities.

Arabian Peninsula Country Statistics

Country	Population	Median Age	Principle Ethnic Groups	GDP Billions
Bahrain	1,248,349	30	Bahrainis, Asians	$31.5
Kuwait	2,646,314	28	Kuwaiti, other Arabs, South Asians, Iranians	155.5
Oman	3,090,150	25	Arabs, Baluchis, South Asians, Africans	82.8
Qatar	1,951,591	32	Arabs, South Asians, Iranians	184.3
Saudi Arabia	26,534,504	26	Arabs, Asians, Africans	691.5
United Arab Emirates	5,314,317	30	South Asians, other Arabs and Iranians, Emiratis	262.1
Yemen	24,771,809	17	predominantly Arabs	58.7

Source: World Almanac and Book of Facts 2013

Auto-Run Click Through 1 of 3

Saud family finally drove them from the northern part of the peninsula in the early twentieth century. Despite the interference of foreigners, however, the power of the families remained.

Today, the majority of governments in the Arabian Peninsula are monarchies. Saudi Arabia, Oman, and Qatar are absolute monarchies. Kuwait and Bahrain are constitutional monarchies. The United Arab Emirates is a federation of emirates, formed from seven smaller states that were headed by emirs, or Arab rulers. In 1990 North Yemen and South Yemen were united to form a republic. However, southern secessionists and northern insurgents have continued to oppose the union. By 2012, civil unrest and violence had destabilized the government. The activities of al-Qaeda militants increased in number in recent years, and ocean piracy along the coasts remains a problem.

sheikdom territory ruled by an Arab tribal leader

✓ **READING PROGRESS CHECK**

Drawing Conclusions How has the role of nomadic tribes affected the way that most people are governed in the Arabian Peninsula?

Population Patterns

GUIDING QUESTION *How have climate and history helped determine the population patterns of the Arabian Peninsula?*

The harsh climate of the Arabian Peninsula has had a strong influence on human settlement. Most of the subregion's population lives along the coasts of the Persian Gulf and the Red Sea. Bedouin herders once moved from oasis to oasis in the arid interior of the peninsula. Today, most bedouins have settled in towns and cities.

The population of the Arabian Peninsula was once almost exclusively Arab. The makeup of the population began to change with the development of the petroleum industry. The oil fields and construction jobs attracted guest workers from South Asia, mainly from India and Bangladesh. Poverty and unemployment in South Asia pushed these workers toward the oil-wealthy Arab countries. The prospect of high wages continues to pull guest workers to the subregion despite **laws of migration** that allow long work hours and crowded housing conditions.

laws of migration rules governing the employment of foreign workers within different countries

Arabian Peninsula Country Statistics

Country	Population	Median Age	Principal Ethnic Groups	GDP Billions $
Bahrain	1,248,349	30	Bahrainis, Asians	31.5
Kuwait	2,646,314	28	Kuwaiti, other Arabs, South Asians, Iranians	155.5
Oman	3,090,150	25	Arabs, Baluchis, South Asians, Africans	82.8
Qatar	1,951,591	32	Arabs, South Asians, Iranians	184.3
Saudi Arabia	26,534,504	26	Arabs, Asians, Africans	691.5
United Arab Emirates	5,314,317	30	South Asians, other Arabs and Iranians, Emiratis	262.1
Yemen	24,771,809	17	predominantly Arabs	58.7

Source: World Almanac and Book of Facts 2013

CHART SKILLS

This chart shows some population statistics for countries of the Arabian Peninsula. It also gives each country's GDP, or gross domestic product. GDP is a measure of a country's wealth.

CRITICAL THINKING

1. ***Differentiating*** In what ways does Yemen's population differ from that of other Arabian Peninsula countries?
2. ***Hypothesizing*** Why might few immigrants be attracted to Yemen?

Human Geography of the Arabian Peninsula

W Writing Skills

Informational/Explanatory Have students write a paragraph summarizing how population patterns in the Arabian Peninsula have changed over time. Then lead a class discussion about why the population patterns have shifted. Have students add a summarizing statement to their paragraph that explains why the population patterns in the Arabian Peninsula have changed. **AL** **Verbal/Linguistic**

R Reading Skills

Reading Charts Have students explain how the chart on page 439 can be used to indicate the economy of a country. Discuss why the median age of a country is important to an economist. Explain that GDP is one way of figuring the wealth of a country but that GDP per capita is also an important indicator. Have students use the information on the chart to figure the GDP per capita for each country. **Ask: Which country has the highest GDP per capita? The lowest?** *(Saudi Arabia's GDP per capita (691.5 billion ÷ 26,534,504 people = $26,060) is about 10 times greater than the per capita GDP of Yemen (58.7 billion ÷ 24,771,809 people = $2,440).)* **BL** **Verbal/Linguistic**

GRAPHIC ORGANIZER

Human Geography of the Arabian Peninsula

Organizing Students can use the interactive graphic organizer to organize information about how people of the Arabian Peninsula have been governed in the past and how they are governed today. Students should try to identify specific examples of governance from the past and the present. **ELL** **AL** **Verbal/Linguistic, Visual/Spatial**

networks

Name ______ Date ______

KEY IDEAS AND DETAILS

ORGANIZING As you read the lesson, take notes on how the people of the Arabian Peninsula have been governed in the past and how they are governed today.

Arabian Peninsula Government

Past	Today

UNDO CLEAR SAVE

ANSWERS, p. 439

✓ **READING PROGRESS CHECK** Most countries of the Arabian Peninsula are monarchies with some being absolute monarchies. This type of government is similar to that of the nomadic tribes that had a single leader with absolute power.

CRITICAL THINKING

1. Yemen has the second largest population of these countries, and its population is largely homogeneous; the other countries contain multiple ethnic groups.
2. Yemen has a high population that is largely homogeneous and has a very low median age. This might indicate to immigrants that they would have a hard time assimilating into a homogeneous culture where they would stand out. Also, Yemen has the second lowest GDP despite its large number of people, indicating it does not have a good economy and much of the population must live in poverty. This would not be attractive to immigrants who are looking for work.

R Reading Skills

Reading Maps Have students read the first three paragraphs on the page. Supply students with a population density map of the Arabian Peninsula. Discuss how and why the discovery of oil changed population patterns in the region and led to the growth of cities. Have students locate the major cities and the areas of dense population. Ask students to brainstorm why large regions of the peninsula remain sparsely populated. *(Possible answers: unfavorable climate, lack of vegetation and water, no industry)* Encourage volunteers to find a population density map of the Arabian Peninsula that was published before the discovery of oil. How do the population patterns compare? **AL Verbal/Linguistic**

Content Background Knowledge

Population of Capital Cities of the Arabian Peninsula

Bahrain: Al-Manámah, 527,000 (metro area), 149,900 (city proper)

Kuwait: Kuwait City, 1,709,800 (metro area), 32,600 (city proper)

Oman: Muscat, 797,000 (metro area), 54,800 (city proper)

Qatar: Doha, 550,700 (metro area), 318,500 (city proper)

Saudi Arabia: Riyadh, 3,724,100

United Arab Emirates: Abu Dhabi, 539,800

Yemen: Sanaa, 1,778,900

W Writing Skills

Informative/Explanatory Ask students to study the time line at the bottom of the page. Have students use the time line to write a paragraph about the history of Islam in Saudi Arabia from A.D. 570 to the present. Students may include additional information from the text if they wish. **AL Verbal/Linguistic**

ANSWERS, p. 440

READING PROGRESS CHECK The coast is heavily populated because it is the location of most cities in the region. Cities are important centers for their countries' oil industries, which provide jobs for both people from the region and immigrant workers.

CRITICAL THINKING

1. Islam divided into Sunni and Shia Muslims groups when a disagreement occurred about who should take over after Muhammad's death.
2. Millions of Muslims make the pilgrimage to the holiest city of Islam, Makkah (Mecca), in Saudi Arabia each year. They also come to visit the city of Madinah, where the tomb of the prophet Muhammad is located.

R

Before the discovery of oil in 1932, the cities of the Arabian Peninsula were already important economic centers. Their populations were small, however, compared to the numbers of people living in rural areas and in desert towns and villages. In addition, there were smaller clans of nomads grazing sheep, camels, and goats where there was vegetation for the animals.

Today about 80 percent of the population in the Arabian Peninsula lives in cities. Most of these cities, like Jidda (Saudi Arabia), Kuwait (Kuwait), and Doha (Qatar), are located on either the Red Sea or the Persian Gulf. They thrive because they are important centers of their countries' oil industries.

One major city is located in the interior, away from the coast. Riyadh, a center of oil refining, is also the capital of Saudi Arabia and home to the royal palace of the king. Other important cities are near the coast. Makkah (Mecca) is the holiest city of Islam. Millions of religious pilgrims visit the city every year. Lying 50 miles (80 km) from the Red Sea, it houses the Grand Mosque. Madinah (Medina), which is farther inland, is several hundred miles north of Makkah. The tomb of Muhammad is in Madinah. The city is considered a holy city second in importance only to Makkah.

READING PROGRESS CHECK

Drawing Conclusions Why does most of the population live along the coast?

Society and Culture Today

GUIDING QUESTION *How does Islam affect life on the Arabian Peninsula?*

Arabic is the language common to all Arab people of the Arabian Peninsula. Many people also speak a second language, often English. Immigration to the peninsula has added to the number of languages spoken, but most immigrants learn the Arabic necessary to function in their jobs and everyday life.

Hassan Ammar/AFP/Getty Images

TIME LINE

ISLAM and Saudi Arabia

In the seventh century, Islam originated in Makkah, a city on the Arabian Peninsula. Islam had a profound influence over the culture and governance of the peoples of the Arabian Peninsula.

CRITICAL THINKING

1. ***Describing*** Why did Islam split into two branches?
2. ***Analyzing*** Why do millions of Muslims travel to Saudi Arabia each year?

W

500

570 Muhammad is born in the city of Makkah.

610 According to Islamic teachings, an angel tells Muhammad that he is chosen to be Allah's prophet.

622 To escape persecution, Muhammad and his followers leave Makkah and travel to Madinah.

630 Muhammad leads his followers from Madinah to Makkah. Muslims dedicate the Kaaba to worship of Allah.

632 Muhammad dies. Much of the Arabian Peninsula is united under Islam.

networks Online Teaching Options

INTERACTIVE WHITEBOARD ACTIVITY

Impact of Islam on the Arabian Peninsula

Listing Have students complete this interactive whiteboard activity to further their knowledge of Islam. Students are presented with a list of statements describing the effects of Islam on the Arabian Peninsula. Students will choose the accurate statements to place in their new list while disregarding the inaccurate statements. At the end of the activity lead a class discussion about how the impacts of Islam will continue to be felt on the Arabian Peninsula in the future. **AL Verbal/Linguistic**

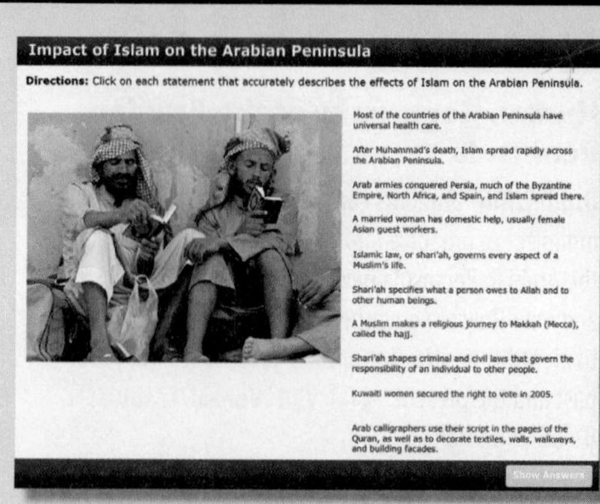

The majority of immigrants are Muslims. When Muhammad founded Islam, the new religion spread rapidly across the peninsula. Arab armies conquered Persia, much of the Byzantine Empire, North Africa, and Spain. Their military successes eventually ended, but Islam continued to diffuse across Asia and Africa.

The unifying fervor of the early years of Islam was broken by a growing conflict within the religion. After Muhammad's death, arguments arose over who would succeed him. As a result, Islam broke into two branches, the **Sunni** and the **Shia**. The conservative sect of **Ibadhism** broke off from the main branches of Islam in A.D. 657. Ibadhites became the major religious group in Oman.

Islamic law, or **shari'ah**, governs every aspect of a Muslim's life. Shari'ah specifies what a person owes to Allah, or God, and what he or she owes to other human beings. A Muslim's duty to Allah is satisfied by observing such practices as making a religious journey to Makkah, called the **hajj**, at least once in one's lifetime. Shari'ah also shapes criminal and civil laws that govern the responsibility of an individual to other people.

With the exception of Yemen, the countries of the Arabian Peninsula have universal health care. However, medical practice varies greatly. Qatar spends large amounts on health care, and its citizens are the most satisfied with their health care system. People in Yemen, which does not offer universal health care, receive little or no preventive care. Overall, in Yemen it is estimated that 48 percent of women and 37 percent of men have the necessary access to health care.

Education for males is compulsory in all of the countries of the subregion. Boys and girls attend separate schools, and higher education is not as available to women as it is to men. For example, in Saudi Arabia there were no schools for girls until the 1960s, a situation that changed by the twenty-first century.

Saudis must attend school from the ages of six to eleven. Saudi Arabia has a literacy rate of 86.6 percent. Qatar, with a literacy rate of 96 percent, requires children to attend school until they are seventeen. In Yemen, a much poorer

Sunni a branch of Islam that regards the first four successors of Muhammad as his rightful successors

Shia a branch of Islam that regards Muhammad's son-in-law Ali and the imams as his rightful successors

Ibadhism a conservative form of Islam distinct from Sunni and Shia sects

shari'ah Islamic law derived from the Quran and the teachings of Muhammad

hajj in Islam, the yearly pilgrimage to Makkah that Muslims must make at least once in a lifetime

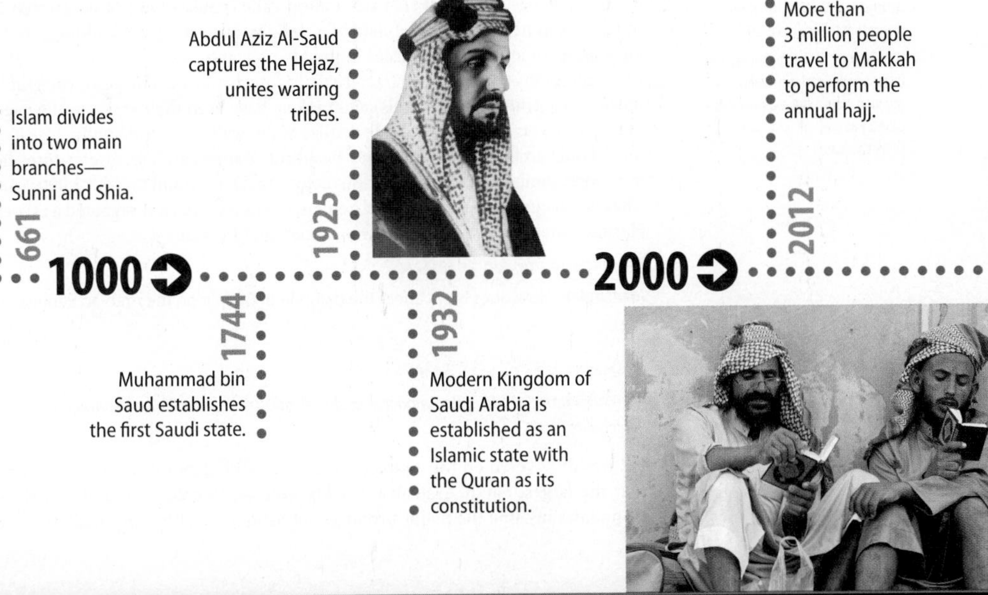

661
Islam divides into two main branches—Sunni and Shia.
1000
1744
Muhammad bin Saud establishes the first Saudi state.
1925
Abdul Aziz Al-Saud captures the Hejaz, unites warring tribes.
1932
Modern Kingdom of Saudi Arabia is established as an Islamic state with the Quran as its constitution.
2000
2012
More than 3 million people travel to Makkah to perform the annual hajj.

T Technology Skills

Presenting Organize students into small groups to research the religious pilgrimage taken by Muslims to Makkah (Mecca). Have groups make a visual presentation to the class describing the event. Some students might present as if they were observers of the hajj. Others might present as if they themselves had taken part in it. Encourage students to use photographs, maps, and music in their presentation. Students might choose to read a passage from the Quran relating to the experience.
BL Interpersonal, Verbal/Linguistic

Making Connections

Review with students the role religion plays in the Arab world. Have students imagine how a government-enforced religion in this country might impact people's lives.

C Critical Thinking Skills

Exploring Issues Discuss how medical practices vary from one Arabian country to another. Have students explore the question of whether health care is a basic right and who should pay for it. Encourage students to consider the different views Americans have on this issue. **Logical/Mathematical**

INTERACTIVE IMAGE

Foods of Ramadan

Questioning Have students view this interactive image of the traditional foods of Ramadan. Ask a student volunteer to explain the religious significance of Ramadan. Then have students write a paragraph describing what they found interesting or learned from viewing and discussing the image. Have students share their paragraphs with a partner.
Verbal/Linguistic, Visual/Spatial

C Critical Thinking Skills

Constructing Arguments Organize students into teams, one side representing Arab Muslims with traditionalist views about the status of women and the other side with more progressive views. Have students debate whether women should be granted more rights and why. Each side should support its position with solid reasons. **Interpersonal, Logical/Mathematical**

Making Connections

Have students consider how the controversy over women's rights on the Arabian Peninsula compares to the battle over women's suffrage in the United States in the 1920s. What were the arguments for and against suffrage then? How has life changed for American women since that time? Are other issues still facing women in the United States? Students may conduct research to learn more about these issues.

T Technology Skills

Presenting Organize students into small groups to research the arts of the Arabian Peninsula. Each group might select a different country or a different art form—poetry, folk art, religious art, architecture, calligraphy, and the like. Have students make multimedia presentations to the class using photographs and other visuals and music. **BL Auditory/Musical, Visual/Spatial**

country without oil resources, students are supposed to stay in school until they are age fourteen. Only about 64 percent of Yemen's population is literate.

Family and the Status of Women

Most marriages in the subregion are arranged between families. Although not required, the arranged marriages of cousins have been a tradition. Once they are married, most women are expected to stay at home to take care of the children and provide a comfortable home for their husbands. In most countries, a married woman has domestic help, usually female Asian guest workers. The male head of household is the ultimate authority in the home.

Throughout the peninsula, men and women socialize separately. They are also segregated in public, particularly in Saudi Arabia. Usually women wear an *abaya*, a long black robe, over their clothing. In most of the countries, women cover their hair but are permitted to show their faces. In most of Saudi Arabia, however, women are considered immodest if their faces are not covered by a veil.

There has been political progress for women in several countries in the subregion. Most countries guarantee women equal rights, although equality is not enforced. Women in Saudi Arabia are denied voting rights, but King Abdullah recently granted women the right to vote in municipal elections. Kuwaiti women secured the right to vote in 2005. Elsewhere in the region, women's suffrage is permitted, but women have little political power.

Sanaa, Yemen, is a UNESCO World Heritage City and famous for its ancient architecture.

▲ **CRITICAL THINKING**

1. ***Analyzing Visuals*** What clues reveal that this is an old city?
2. ***Analyzing*** Sanaa's population has increased dramatically and is growing almost twice as fast as the country as a whole. Why do you think this is so?

The Arts

The Arabian Peninsula has produced many art forms. There is a strong oral tradition, and the culture is rich in poetry and folk art. The founding of Islam was accompanied by the flowering of religious art. In order to glorify the words of Allah, artists produced rich decoration called arabesques, often created in intricate geometric designs. Inlaid tile designs were used on buildings as far away as Spain and in other places in the Mediterranean.

Calligraphy is another characteristic Islamic art form. The word *calligraphy* means "beautiful writing." Arab calligraphers have used their script in the pages of the Quran, as well as to decorate textiles, walls, walkways, and building facades.

Islamic architecture is uniquely beautiful. Yemen's architecture features tall buildings, sometimes tinted in various colors, that have stood for over 2,000 years. The capital city, Sanaa, and several Yemeni towns have been designated as World Heritage sites because of their extraordinary architecture.

☑ **READING PROGRESS CHECK**

Identifying How does Islam affect the daily life of people on the Arabian Peninsula?

Economic Activities

GUIDING QUESTION *What impact does the oil industry have on life on the Arabian Peninsula?*

Oil was discovered on the Arabian Peninsula in 1932, but it was not until 1938 that the largest Saudi Arabian oil fields were discovered. U.S. and British oil companies became the major producers of Saudi oil. With time, Saudi Arabian

networks Online Teaching Options

VIDEO

Saudi Women—Jobs

Summarizing Students can gain a better understanding of the role of Saudi Arabian women by viewing this video, which explores traditional customs and cultural reform in this country. Have students summarize how the roles of women in Saudi Arabia have changed over the years. Guide a class discussion with students asking them to consider how these changing roles have affected the country. **AL Verbal/Linguistic**

ANSWERS, p. 442

☑ **READING PROGRESS CHECK** Shari'ah, or Islamic law, governs every part of a Muslim's life, including personal actions and criminal and civil laws.

CRITICAL THINKING

1. The design of the structures and building materials used reveal this city to be old.
2. Sanaa could have some type of economic development creating jobs or could be capitalizing on its status as a World Heritage City to attract tourism, which would attract people to the city and boost its economy. Rural people could also be coming to the city in search of work or better living conditions.

engineers were trained, often in the United States and the United Kingdom, so they could fill management positions in the oil fields. By the end of the twentieth century, the Saudi Arabian government was in control of the production and export of its oil. In 1960 Saudi Arabia joined with Kuwait and other oil-producing countries to form the Organization of the Petroleum Exporting Countries (OPEC). Later Qatar and the United Arab Emirates and other countries outside the peninsula joined OPEC. The members of OPEC meet regularly to set production quotas. Every five years, OPEC **documents** its **strategy** for dealing with the long-term demands for oil.

The Arabian Peninsula is one of the most strategically important regions in the world for oil. Maintaining good relations with its neighbors is important. This is because two strategic waterways, the Strait of Hormuz on the Persian Gulf and the Bab el Mandeb, a strait on the Red Sea, are two of the world's leading oil-shipping **choke points**. Choke points are strategically located narrow passages between two bodies of water. Blocking either of these straits would prevent the export by shipping of the crude oil and petroleum products from the Arabian Peninsula.

document to put in writing in order to have as a record

strategy a plan or method

choke point a strategic, narrow waterway between two larger bodies of water

Oil has produced great wealth for some countries on the peninsula. Some countries have used this wealth wisely. Saudi Arabia, with its enormous oil income, has made large investments in infrastructure and education. Bahrain, with relatively small reserves of oil, has successfully diversified its economy into banking and finance. Oman and the United Arab Emirates have invested their oil revenue. The investments help to soften the effects of fluctuations in oil prices in the international markets. Despite its oil wealth, Kuwait has not invested in its infrastructure. Yemen's oil production is small compared to other countries in the subregion. It has an unstable government and poorly developed economy. It has also been affected by internal division and conflict between Sunni and Shia groups, each wanting to control the country.

V

Although petroleum is the major product of the peninsula, there are other important industries. Cement manufacturing is a leading industry, as is ship repair. Bahrain and Oman have fishing industries, and commercial aquaculture is being developed. Tourism is important to both Bahrain and the United Arab Emirates. The Red Sea coastline of Saudi Arabia is a growing magnet for tourists because of its white sand beaches and its magnificent coral reefs. Yemen has a small textile industry.

Although arable land is scarce and precipitation is limited, a variety of fruits, vegetables, and some grains are grown. Agriculture consumes most of the water in the subregion. Food crop production is being developed that uses less water and has a high yield. Water is the subregion's most important natural resource issue.

✓ READING PROGRESS CHECK

Explaining How has Saudi Arabia used its oil wealth to improve life in the country?

LESSON 2 REVIEW (CCSS)

Reviewing Vocabulary (Tier Three Words)

1. ***Determining Importance*** What is the significance of shari'ah? RH.9–10.4

Using Your Notes

2. ***Explaining*** Use your graphic organizer on the governments of the Arabian Peninsula to explain how the governments of the subregion have or have not changed throughout history.

Answering the Guiding Questions

3. ***Inferring*** How did history, culture, and geography help influence the types of governments on the Arabian Peninsula?
4. ***Evaluating*** How have climate and history helped determine the population patterns of the Arabian Peninsula?
5. ***Explaining*** How does Islam affect life on the Arabian Peninsula?
6. ***Drawing Conclusions*** What impact does the oil industry have on life on the Arabian Peninsula?

Writing Activity

7. ***Argument*** In a paragraph, discuss the advantages and disadvantages of monarchy as a form of government for a country in the Arabian Peninsula. Conclude with your opinion supported by reasons. WHST.9–10.4, WHST.9–10.9

C Critical Thinking Skills

Constructing Arguments Have students read the paragraph about how different countries have used their oil wealth. Have students imagine that they serve on the economic development commission of a city in Kuwait or Yemen. A business group is proposing that money be spent for a major project, perhaps a new highway, hospital, university, or port. Organize students into two teams and have the teams debate whether this investment wold be good for the city, with each team taking an opposing side of the issue. **Verbal/Linguistic, Interpersonal**

V Visual Skills

Spatial Analysis After they have read the last three paragraphs of the lesson, have students compare agricultural, resources, climate, and population maps of the Arabian Peninsula. Have students make correlations between landforms, climate, and the distribution of people, industry, and agriculture in the Arabian Peninsula. **Ask: What might help make more of the land area of the Arabian Peninsula usable?** *(Student answers may vary but might include finding new sources of water, desalination, irrigation, and infrastructure development.)* **Verbal/Linguistic**

CLOSE & REFLECT

Listing Ask students to look back over the lesson and list the major changes that the Arabian Peninsula has experienced since oil was discovered there in the 1930s. Have students use their list to review the lesson.

ANSWERS, p. 443

✓ **READING PROGRESS CHECK** Saudi Arabia has used its wealth to invest in its infrastructure and education.

LESSON 2 REVIEW ANSWERS

Reviewing Vocabulary

1. Shari'ah, or Islamic law, governs every part of Muslim life and also shapes criminal and civil laws.

Using Your Notes

2. Historically, tribal structures with individual tribes called sheikdoms were the predominant governments of nomadic peoples, while powerful families controlled coastal regions. The control of areas by individuals led to the rise of monarchies, both constitutional and absolute, that are found in the region today.

Answering the Guiding Questions

3. Being surrounded on three sides by water and having vast interior deserts, the region was isolated in its early history. This isolation gave rise to tribal structures with single leaders of interior regions and control by powerful families in the coastal areas. This type of rule and the largely homogenous culture driven by Islam led to the monarchies, both constitutional and absolute, that control the countries of the peninsula today.
4. The very dry climate of the Arabian Peninsula helped establish the early nomadic lifestyles of the people as they moved to find water and food for themselves and their herds. Populations settled along coasts as they were historic centers for trade and have more rainfall than the vast interior deserts. The discovery of oil and oil refining has attracted populations to areas where these activities occur.
5. Shari'ah, or Islamic law, governs every part of Muslim life and not only directs individual actions such as hajj and acceptable dress for women but also shapes criminal and civil laws.
6. The oil industry provides jobs for people within the region, produces great wealth for oil-producing countries, and attracts guest workers and immigrants from other areas of the world to the peninsula.

Writing Activity

7. Paragraphs may vary but should include that monarchy promotes a strong ethnic identity and that many of the countries are a constitutional monarchy, with elected officials as opposed to the absolute monarchies of Saudi Arabia, Oman, and Qatar that rule with absolute power. Opinions presented by students must be supported by reasons.

ENGAGE

R Reading Skills

Activating Prior Knowledge Have students name some environmental issues facing the United States today. Direct students to list the sources and effects of these problems. Tell students that the countries of the Arabian Peninsula are dealing with many of the environmental problems our country faced in the past or is dealing with now. Have students look for comparisons as they study the lesson.

TEACH & ASSESS

W Writing Skills

Informative/Explanatory Have students note the multiple ways oil is used by people and industry and its importance to the Arabian Peninsula and the world at large. Have students use their notes to write two or three paragraphs summarizing why oil is a crucial commodity in the world economy. AL **Verbal/Linguistic**

T Technology Skills

Chronological Reasoning Review with students what they know about the Arab Spring and the 1991 Persian Gulf War and, if necessary, have them research to gather additional information. Students may seek to answer various questions: **Which countries were involved in the Persian Gulf War? What countries of the Arabian Peninsula have experienced an Arab Spring? How were the United States and other countries involved, if at all?** Have students create a time line of these events. Ask them to predict future developments in the region and discuss how these developments may impact the United States. BL **Interpersonal, Logical/Mathematical**

ANSWERS, p. 444

TAKING NOTES: Oil extraction, processing, and spills release pollutants into the air where rain carries them to the ground contaminating groundwater and soil; Processing and extraction of oil as well as carbon emissions from use of fossil fuels for desalination, air conditioning has also led to climate changes including increases in temperature, higher winds, reduced rainfall, rising sea levels, and rising sea temperatures; Increasing populations are using more water which is in limited supply in aquifers and when water is removed it is often replaced by seawater; Increasing population, reduced rainfall, mismanagement of the land by overuse, and increased temperatures reducing the fertility of the land are all leading to desertification.

networks *There's More Online!*

- IMAGE Dubai's Air Pollution
- IMAGE Golf Course in the Desert
- IMAGE Drilling Equipment
- INTERACTIVE SELF-CHECK QUIZ
- VIDEO People and Their Environment: The Arabian Peninsula

LESSON 3

People and Their Environment: The Arabian Peninsula

Reading **HELP**DESK

Academic Vocabulary (Tier Two Words)
- **furthermore**
- **coincide**

Content Vocabulary (Tier Three Words)
- **geopolitics**
- **desalination**

TAKING NOTES: ***Key Ideas and Details***

IDENTIFYING As you read about environmental concerns of the Arabian Peninsula, use a graphic organizer like the one below to identify the causes and effects of the environmental problems.

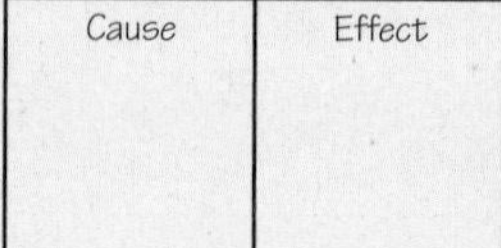
Environmental Concerns
Cause
Effect

ESSENTIAL QUESTION • *How do physical systems and human systems shape a place?*

IT MATTERS BECAUSE

R *The petroleum industry has had an enormous impact on the environment of the Arabian Peninsula. The growth of the population, due partly to the arrival of millions of foreign workers, is putting a serious strain on the subregion's water supplies. In addition to the scarcity of water, environmental concerns such as pollution and climate change are an ongoing challenge to the people and governments of the peninsula.*

Managing Resources

GUIDING QUESTION *How has the extraction of petroleum resources impacted the environment of the Arabian Peninsula?*

W Oil is the most widely used energy source in the modern world. For industrialized nations, oil is one of the most sought-after natural resources. Petroleum products are used for the generation of power and the operation of vehicles. Oil is a fossil fuel, created over millions of years, and thus is a nonrenewable resource. The relative scarcity of this resource makes it an important factor in the economies of the Arabian Peninsula. The peninsula's vast petroleum reserves also make it a focus of international interest.

Events in the oil-producing countries generate concern throughout the world. Unrest, such as that generated by the series of uprisings known as the Arab Spring, is magnified in importance by the effect it might have on oil production or transportation.

T Physical, human, and economic geography can influence government policy. Such **geopolitics** determines how world powers respond to shifts in power on the peninsula. The 1991 Persian Gulf War is an example of such a response. In late 1990, Iraq invaded Kuwait, a neighbor of Saudi Arabia. The presence of Iraqi forces in Kuwait was not only a violation of international law, but it was also a threat to oil-rich Saudi Arabia. The United States, heading a large multinational force, pushed Iraq's forces back and restored the control of Kuwait to the Kuwaitis.

(tl)Sorge/Alamy, (tc)Barry Iverson/arabianEye/Getty Images, (tr)©Bryan Denton/Corbis

networks ***Online Teaching Options***

INTERACTIVE BELLRINGER

Smoke Plumes over Kuwait, 1991

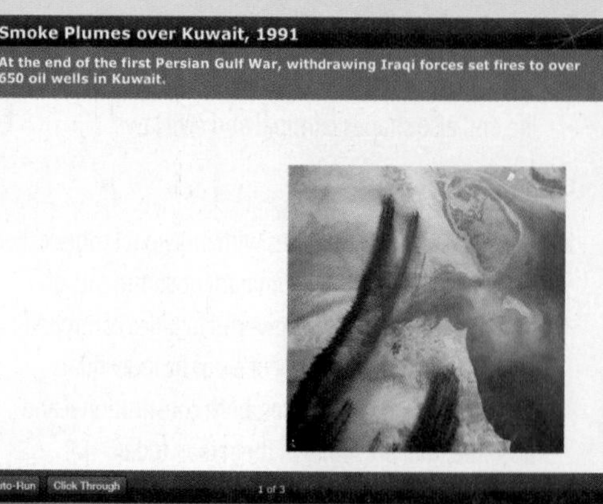
Smoke Plumes over Kuwait, 1991
At the end of the first Persian Gulf War, withdrawing Iraqi forces set fires to over 650 oil wells in Kuwait.
Auto-Run
Click Through
1 of 3

Drawing Inferences This image of the smoke plumes over Kuwait in 1991 can be used to help students draw inferences about the effect of oil fires on the environment and human activities. Ask students to study the image and imagine what it might be like to have similar plumes of smoke over their city or community for an extended period. Have small groups discuss the bellringer questions. Ask groups to generate as many details as possible for each question. Note that it is likely that students will come up with more details than shown as answers. After they have answered the questions, invite groups to share their answers. Ask a student volunteer to list the responses so that they may be used to further a class discussion about this topic. **Intrapersonal, Visual/Spatial**

Oil extraction comes with a price. Oil pollution, whether from extraction, processing, or spills, releases hundreds of chemical gases into the air. These pollutants linger in the air until rain carries them to the ground, where they contaminate the groundwater and the soil.

R

One of the most dramatic examples of oil pollution occurred during the Persian Gulf War. In a successful attempt to sabotage Kuwait's oil industry, Iraqi forces set fire to oil wells and released 250 million gallons of oil into the Persian Gulf. Hundreds of miles of coastline were soaked with oil. The fishing industry, a vital part of the Persian Gulf economy, was dealt a serious blow.

The extraction and processing of petroleum has other consequences. Climate studies show that the average temperature of the peninsula has increased over the past three decades. All of the countries of the subregion have been affected by climate change.

Rainfall has decreased over much of Saudi Arabia. Persian Gulf countries like Oman are experiencing flash floods that erode the topsoil. Drought has affected the fertility of the soil and altered times for planting crops. Farmers report that increased temperatures have led to an increase of insect pests and plant diseases. Higher temperatures also increase the evaporation of water used for irrigation.

C

Kuwait has experienced both a sharp drop in rainfall and a dramatic rise in average temperature. The country has experienced tornado winds and an increase in sandstorms and flooding. Offshore, seawater temperatures have risen at three times the global rate.

Climate change is also causing a rise in sea level. The archipelago country of Bahrain is particularly vulnerable to rising sea levels. A significant rise would be a disaster for the small country, whose population lives mainly on the coasts, as well as for its marine ecology.

Most scientists think that these changes can be attributed, at least in part, to human activities. The burning of fossil fuels releases carbon dioxide into the air. These carbon emissions are called greenhouse gases because they contribute to

geopolitics government policy as it is influenced by physical, human, and economic geography

Air pollution creates a dense blanket over Dubai, United Arab Emirates.

▼ CRITICAL THINKING

1. ***Drawing Inferences*** How does air pollution affect the lives of people?
2. ***Explaining*** Why is air pollution such a problem on the Arabian Peninsula?

V

CHAPTER 18, Lesson 3
People and Their Environment: the Arabian Peninsula

R Reading Skills

Discussing Have students read the first two paragraphs. Discuss what is meant by the statement "Oil extraction comes with a price." Have students note some "prices" paid by the countries of the Arabian Peninsula. Ask students where the United States has experienced oil spill disasters like those that occurred in the Persian Gulf and what the costs of those disasters were. *(Student answers may vary but might include the 2010 oil rig disaster in the Gulf of Mexico, the 1989 tanker* Exxon Valdez *collision off the Alaska coast, and the 2013 pipeline rupture in Arkansas, etc.)* ELL **Verbal/Linguistic**

C Critical Thinking Skills

Analyzing Cause and Effect Have students list the changes that have occurred in the different countries on the Arabian Peninsula and identify their effects. For instance, decreased rainfall leads to drought, loss of soil fertility, and altered planting times. Discuss the human activities that have caused many of these changes. AL **Logical/Mathematical**

V Visual Skills

Analyzing Visuals Have students study the photograph at the bottom of page 445. **Ask:** What do you notice about the city and its skyline? *(Possible answers: covered by haze; low visibility; can hardly see the buildings in the distance)* Imagine you are a traveler flying into this city. What do you see and feel as you leave the plane? *(Student answers will vary but may include that air pollution may burn eyes and affect breathing.)* AL **Visual/Spatial**

INTERACTIVE IMAGE

Polluting the Air

Problem Solving Display the image of air pollution over Dubai and allow time for students to analyze the content. Organize students into small groups, and have them use information provided in the text to brainstorm specific causes of air pollution and ways to alleviate toxic emissions. Ask each group to write a fictional proposal to the leaders in Dubai. This proposal should contain a list of several possible actions that the people of Dubai could take to reduce the amount of pollution in the air over their city. Have groups share their proposals with the class. BL **Visual/Spatial, Logical/Mathematical**

ANSWERS, p. 445

CRITICAL THINKING

1. Air pollution contributes to climate changes, including decreased rainfall and increased temperatures. This climate change has caused the people of the peninsula to struggle with drought, decreased soil fertility, increased insects, and diseased plants, impacting crop yields. The increased temperatures in countries such as Kuwait are causing higher winds and more sandstorms. The increased sea temperatures and rising levels are impacting marine life. Bahrain, with a large coastal population, is in danger from flooding and land loss due to rising sea levels.
2. The high amounts of oil extraction and processing and the burning of fossil fuels by the oil industry and for air conditioning, desalination, transportation, and shipping cause the Arabian Peninsula to have a large air-pollution problem.

People and Their Environment: the Arabian Peninsula

V Visual Skills

Creating Graphs Have students create a line graph showing how the populations of the countries of the Arabian Peninsula are expected to increase over time. Tell students to imagine they are population forecasters. Have them use their graphs to predict which nations are likely to experience the gravest economic hardships in the future and why. BL Visual/Spatial

Content Background Knowledge

Population Projections by Country: Arabian Peninsula

The following are population projections made by the World Bank:

Country	2010	2025	2050
Bahrain	1,262,000	1,609,000	1,811,000
Kuwait	2,736,000	3,720,000	4,989,000
Oman	2,783,000	3,540,000	4,016,000
Qatar	1,759,000	2,424,000	2,861,000
Saudi Arabia	27,448,000	35,495,000	43,160,000
UAE	7,512,000	9,954,000	13,308,000
Yemen	24,053,000	36,631,000	61,196,000

C Critical Thinking Skills

Acquiring Information Have students compare a rainfall map and an economic activities map of the Arabian Peninsula. Ask them which regional areas are likely to have devastating drought and/or water shortages in the future and to give reasons for their predictions. BL Logical/Mathematical

ANSWERS, p. 446

READING PROGRESS CHECK The large oil deposits in the area have created a pollution problem. Pollutants released during extraction and refining contaminate groundwater and soil. Oil processing and extraction and carbon emissions from use of fossil fuels have led to climate changes. The Red Sea and Persian Gulf are becoming increasingly polluted by spills and by oil transport.

DBQ The speaker means that pollution has caused the Gulf to be in danger of being unable to support life.

CRITICAL THINKING

1. Maintaining a golf course in the middle of a desert is not a good use of water because the limited water supply could be better used to support crops or for consumption.
2. The golf course is not suited for its environment because it is in the middle of dry, barren landscape with no visible water sources.

Threats to the Gulf

"You have thousands of tankers entering the Gulf and washing their tanks illegally. Between the tankers, pollution from urban centres and the brine disposed of from desalination plants, the Gulf is almost dead."

—Dr. Shawki Barghouti, director-general of the International Centre for Biosaline Agriculture, from "Desalination Threat to the Growing Gulf," *The National,* August 31, 2009

DBQ ***ANALYZING*** What does the speaker mean by "the Gulf is almost dead"? RH.9–10.4

the warming climate. Heavy use of fossil fuels for desalination, air-conditioning, and oil processing add greenhouse gases to the atmosphere. Carbon emissions were the topic of a special meeting of a United Nations convention on climate change in December 2012. The meeting was held in Qatar, which has the highest rate of carbon dioxide emissions per capita of any country in the world.

READING PROGRESS CHECK

Identifying How have the advantages of the Arabian Peninsula's resources created a problem for its environment?

Human Impact

GUIDING QUESTION *How has a growing population created a set of related environmental challenges in the subregion?*

V In 2012 the Arabian Peninsula was home to approximately 68 million people, and the population is expected to reach 120 million by 2050. Saudi Arabia's population alone is projected to grow by 333 percent over the next 34 years. The population of Kuwait is increasing at an annual rate of 1.88 percent, and Oman's is increasing at a rate of 4.93 percent. Yemen's population is growing by about 700,000 people each year. As the number of people increases, so does the human impact on the environment.

C The need for water is critical. Surface water created by rainfall exists in only a few places, and the evaporation rate is high because of the hot, arid climate. **Furthermore**, climate change is reducing the amount of rainfall in some areas, while increasing it in others. As weather patterns change, severe flooding can occur. These increases in rainfall overwhelm the existing drainage system, eroding the soil and endangering the human population.

furthermore besides; in addition

Every country in the peninsula extracts increasingly higher annual percentages of water from its aquifers every year. This increase is not sustainable. The aquifers contain fossil water—water trapped in the underground rocks millions of years ago. Only minute amounts of surface water reach these depths

A golf course has been carved out of the barren desert of the Arabian Peninsula.

▶ CRITICAL THINKING

1. ***Assessing*** Is maintaining a golf course in the middle of a desert a good use of water? Why or why not?
2. ***Analyzing Visuals*** How can you tell that this golf course is not suited to the environment?

Barry Iverson/arabianEye/Getty Images

446

networks Online Teaching Options

VIDEO

Why Much of the World's Oil Supply Is in Southwest Asia

Identifying Cause and Effect Have students view this video to provide them with an overview of why there is a prevalence of oil in Southwest Asia. As they view the video, have students consider how this abundance of oil affects the region. After viewing the video, ask students to write an essay describing the positive and negative effects that the oil supply has on the countries of Southwest Asia. Verbal/Linguistic

over time. Not only is the water virtually a nonrenewable resource, removing it from the aquifers draws in seawater. The seawater contaminates the aquifer and makes it unfit for drinking. The impact of the rising population on water resources has reached a crisis stage in many countries. For example, Sanaa, the capital city of Yemen, is estimated to have only a three-year supply of water left.

Yemen shows that an increasing population and the effects of climate change can contribute to political instability. Warring factions, coupled with widespread corruption and a weak government, prevent Yemen from enacting solutions to its problems. A 40 percent unemployment rate and widespread poverty are made worse by decreased rainfall and a resulting water crisis. Without governmental leadership, individuals and groups are extracting water as quickly as they can in order to make easy short-term profits. Meanwhile, the large rural population, which depends on agriculture, is starved for water. Yemen is at the point of collapse.

The Arabian Peninsula is facing growing desertification. There are many factors that **coincide** to turn arable land into desert. Reduced rainfall can gradually extend a desert into a once fertile area. Mismanagement of the land is another factor. As the population of farmers has increased, so have the herds of sheep and goats. Domestic animals take a heavy toll on vegetation that anchors topsoil. Increasing temperatures reduce the fertility of the soil, and unusually violent rainstorms wash it away. All the countries of the peninsula are affected to some degree by these conditions, but the four Persian Gulf States—Bahrain, Kuwait, Qatar, and the United Arab Emirates—are the most desertified countries on the Arabian Peninsula. **G1**

Drilling equipment sits at a farm in Yemen. Yemen faces a water crisis due to overconsumption and mismanagement. Illegal drilling in aquifers is rampant.

▲ **CRITICAL THINKING**

1. ***Analyzing*** What factors have led to Yemen's water shortage?
2. ***Making Predictions*** What are some ways Yemen might address water shortages?

coincide to happen in the same place and at the same time

✓ **READING PROGRESS CHECK**

Identifying Which challenges to the environment are related to population?

Addressing the Issues

GUIDING QUESTION *How have people and governments on the Arabian Peninsula addressed the environmental challenges they face?*

Water use in most countries of the Arabian Peninsula is similar to that of more developed countries with far greater supplies of freshwater. Saudi Arabia uses the same amount of water per capita as other more developed countries. Qatar uses almost twice that amount.

One response to the need for water has been to build **desalination** plants. Desalination removes salt from seawater, as well as minerals from undrinkable groundwater. Current methods of desalination require enormous amounts of energy. For example, desalination accounts for 25 to 30 percent of the energy used in Saudi Arabia. **G2**

As groundwater has been depleted, the countries of the subregion have greatly increased their dependence on desalination. Qatar is an extreme example of this dependence. It relies on desalination for 99 percent of its water needs. Yemen, on the other hand, has just recently begun to use desalination.

desalination the removal of salt from seawater or from brackish groundwater to make it usable for drinking and irrigation

People and Their Environment: the Arabian Peninsula

G1 Critical Thinking Skills

Identifying Cause and Effect Have students explain the sequence of events that can lead to desertification. Students might create diagrams to illustrate these sequences. Discuss what people in the United States learned about poor agricultural practices during the Dust Bowl years. Have students brainstorm three factors necessary for good agriculture. *(sufficient water, fertile soil, favorable growing season)* Suggest that students research to find out how much water precipitation is needed to raise different crops and then make a visual representation of the information. **AL** **Verbal/Linguistic, Visual/Spatial**

Making Connections

Have students imagine that hydrologists estimate that their community has only a three-year supply of water left. How should individuals and the community respond and why?

G2 Critical Thinking Skills

Evaluating Have students suppose that they are members of an environmental protection agency of Saudi Arabia. What short- and long-term measures would they put in place to deal with the nation's growing water problems? Have students read the section "Addressing the Issues." Discuss whether building desalination plants is the only or best solution. **AL** **Verbal/Linguistic**

INTERACTIVE GRAPHIC ORGANIZER

People and Their Environment: The Arabian Peninsula

Summarizing This interactive graphic organizer can be used to help students summarize all of the information contained in this lesson. Have students review the lesson, and as they do so, complete the graphic organizer with the appropriate facts and details requested. When the graphic organizer is completed, ask individual students to verbally summarize the material presented in this lesson. **ELL** **AL** **Visual/Spatial, Verbal/Linguistic**

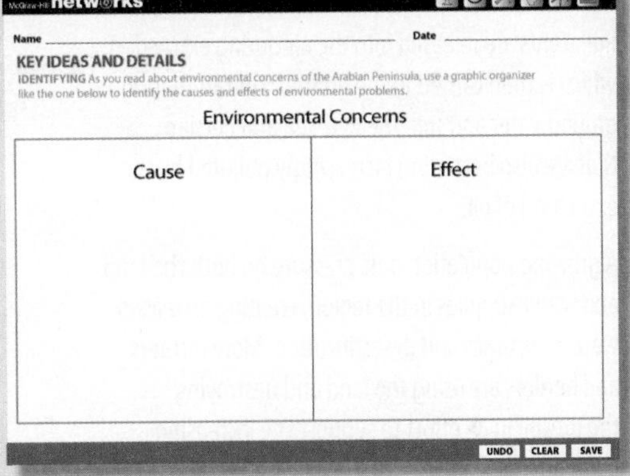
networks
Name
Date
KEY IDEAS AND DETAILS
IDENTIFYING As you read about environmental concerns of the Arabian Peninsula, use a graphic organizer like the one below to identify the causes and effects of environmental problems.
Environmental Concerns
Cause
Effect
UNDO
CLEAR
SAVE

ANSWERS, p. 447

✓ **READING PROGRESS CHECK** Water supply and desertification are challenges to the environment related to population.

CRITICAL THINKING

1. A rapidly increasing population, climate change, corruption, and conflict are factors in Yemen's water shortage.
2. Yemen should stop people from extracting water for short-term profits. They also should eliminate the corruption and conflict within the country so they can devote time and resources to conserving what water they have and devise new strategies for increasing the water supply.

People and Their Environment: the Arabian Peninsula

C Critical Thinking Skills

Constructing Arguments Have students read the sidebar titled "Water Management." Have students hold a debate about who should be responsible for managing a community's water resources—government, businesses, or individuals. **Interpersonal, Logical/Mathematical**

W Writing Skills

Explanatory/Informative Have students imagine they are journalists reporting on the problem of overconsumption of water in a country of the Arabian Peninsula. Have them write a report evaluating how the country is dealing with the issue. Students might research news stories online for ideas. **Logical/Mathematical, Verbal/Linguistic**

CLOSE & REFLECT

Summarizing To close the lesson, have students list the many environmental problems facing the countries of the Arabian Peninsula. Have students share their lists as they review the lesson.

ANSWERS, p. 448

Connecting Geography A national government should work to educate its citizens about conservation of natural resources. Regulations established by the government are also important to ensure the wise use and protection of natural resources.

☑ **READING PROGRESS CHECK** Desalination can turn undrinkable water into drinkable. However, the process requires large amounts of energy and has environmental costs associated with disposal of the brine (leftover water) that include contamination and ecological imbalance.

Connecting Geography to GOVERNMENT

Water Management

Yemen, like the other countries of the Arabian Peninsula, has a limited water supply. Farmers use 90 percent of that water every year, irrigating their crops as they have done for centuries. Plentiful groundwater supplies exist in eastern Yemen, but the cost of transporting it to other parts of the country is too high.

C Yemen's water problems stem in part from the lack of a stable government. In other parts of the peninsula, governments reach out to farmers, teaching them how to use water effectively. Yemen does not have an agricultural service, nor does the government have the ability to regulate consumption of water. Without a stable government, there can be no countrywide solutions to the water problem.

ASSESSING What should be government's role in managing a country's resources?

Desalination is not a perfect solution. Desalinated water must be blended with water from aquifers to make it drinkable. Even then, many people prefer the taste of imported bottled water to that of their local tap water.

Perhaps more important, desalination has environmental costs. Disposal of the brine that results from the desalination process presents problems. If it is collected in pools, it can seep into the groundwater and contaminate the aquifer. If it is piped into the sea, it increases the salinity of the water, interfering with the ecology of the coastal waters.

Historically, all of the governments of the Arabian Peninsula have subsidized the cost of water, and cheap water has led to overconsumption. To cater to wealthy citizens and attract tourists, the Persian Gulf countries have built resorts and spas that feature swimming pools and waterfalls, among other water-intensive attractions. Even the less wealthy are accustomed to using water freely to wash their cars and water their gardens.

W By far the greatest overconsumption, however, has been in the practice of agriculture. During the 1970s, the demand for meat and dairy products increased as the urban population grew richer. An effort was made to supply meat from local ranches, but within 10 years most meat was imported. Many governments became alarmed by increasing prices on the world market and concerned about their countries' dependence on foreign food. In response, the governments of Kuwait, Bahrain, the United Arab Emirates, and Saudi Arabia joined in an effort to encourage agriculture. However, about 85 percent of the region's annual water supply is used for agriculture, and much of it is wasted due to inefficient irrigation. Yemen provides another example of impractical water use. Much of its groundwater goes toward khat cultivation, the leaves of which are chewed as a mild stimulant.

Today, many countries on the Arabian Peninsula, particularly Saudi Arabia, are promoting a variety of changes in how agriculture is practiced. Greenhouse agriculture, which uses much less water than other methods of growing food, is being encouraged. Scientists are developing salt-tolerant plants that can make use of water that is too salty for drinking. Several countries are also looking abroad to find new solutions to their food problems. They are investing in land overseas. They plan to use the natural resources and labor of the host countries to produce food for import to the peninsula. Qatar, for example, is purchasing farmland in such distant places as Sudan, Australia, Kenya, Brazil, Argentina, Turkey, and Ukraine.

☑ **READING PROGRESS CHECK**

Explaining What are the advantages and disadvantages of desalination as a solution for water scarcity issues in the subregion?

LESSON 3 REVIEW

Reviewing Vocabulary (Tier Three Words)

1. ***Explaining*** Write a paragraph explaining how geopolitics can create conflict between countries. RH.9–10.4

Using Your Notes

2. ***Summarizing*** Use your graphic organizer on the environmental concerns in the Arabian Peninsula to write a paragraph summarizing the environmental situation in the subregion.

Answering the Guiding Questions

3. ***Evaluating*** How has the extraction of petroleum resources impacted the environment of the Arabian Peninsula?
4. ***Making Connections*** How has a growing population created a set of related environmental challenges in the subregion?
5. ***Explaining*** How have people and governments on the Arabian Peninsula addressed the environmental challenges they face?

Writing Activity

6. ***Argument*** In a paragraph, take the position of a water resource manager of a city in the subregion, and explain to citizens why it is necessary to conserve water. WHST.9–10.1a, WHST.9–10.4, WHST.9–10.9

LESSON 3 REVIEW ANSWERS

Reviewing Vocabulary

1. Students' paragraphs should show an understanding of the economic and political issues that can arise between countries over resources.

Using Your Notes

2. Paragraphs may vary but should include lack of water; the encroachment of seawater as freshwater is removed from aquifers; the heavy pollution of air and water by oil extraction and refining; the high levels of carbon emissions from desalination plants, air conditioning, and vehicles; climate change with increasing temperatures, winds, sea levels, and sea water temperatures.

Answering the Guiding Questions

3. Pollutants are released into the air during extraction, which is then carried to the ground, contaminating groundwater and soil. The Red Sea and Persian Gulf are also becoming increasingly polluted by the extraction of oil.
4. A growing population puts pressure on both the land and water supplies in the region, creating increased water shortages and desertification. More farmers and herders are using the land and destroying the topsoil in an effort to support the increasing population, which leads to desertification.
5. Many countries are changing agricultural practices to use less water and investing in land in other countries for growing crops. Desalination is used in Saudi Arabia and Qatar to create usable water. In December 2012, a meeting on climate change was held in Qatar.

Writing Activity

6. Paragraphs may vary based on the city chosen but should include lack of available water, encroaching seawater as freshwater is removed from aquifers, monetary and environmental costs of desalination, and reduced rainfall in the region further straining water supplies.

CHAPTER 18 Assessment 

Directions: On a separate sheet of paper, answer the questions below. Make sure you read carefully and answer all parts of the questions.

Lesson Review

Lesson 1

1. ***Describing*** Describe how the Red Sea interacted with a single tectonic plate to create the Arabian Peninsula.
2. ***Explaining*** Why is wind such a significant factor in the climate of the Arabian Peninsula? How do simooms and *shamals* affect plant and animal life there?
3. ***Contrasting*** The two greatest resources in the Arabian Peninsula are oil and water. Why is freshwater even more crucial than oil to countries in the subregion?

Lesson 2

4. ***Identifying Cause and Effect*** How did the development of the petroleum industry affect the makeup of the population on the Arabian Peninsula?
5. ***Evaluating*** Why is the Arabian Peninsula considered one of the most strategically important regions in the world?
6. ***Identifying*** What countries in the Arabian Peninsula belong to OPEC? What is the role of that organization?

Lesson 3

7. ***Making Connections*** How does the extraction of oil cause damage to air, land, and water throughout the Arabian Peninsula?
8. ***Summarizing*** What are some of the drawbacks associated with current methods of desalination?
9. ***Explaining*** Why is the 1991 Persian Gulf War an example of the importance of oil production to geopolitics?

Critical Thinking

10. ***Hypothesizing*** Oil is a nonrenewable resource. How might the economies of the Arabian Peninsula be different if oil were renewable?
11. ***Drawing Conclusions*** Why do you think millions of immigrants have been drawn to the Arabian Peninsula even though their employers may treat them unfairly?

21st Century Skills

Use the graph to answer the following questions.

HUMAN EFFECTS ON OIL SUPPLY

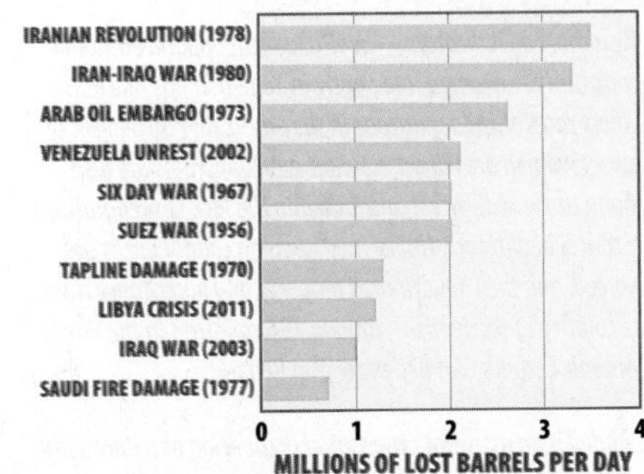

Sources: Energy Information Administration (EIA), Bank of America Merrill Lynch Global Commodities Research, Money Morning staff research

12. ***Understanding Relationships Among Events*** According to the graph, how do war, revolution, and social unrest affect global oil production?
13. ***Drawing Conclusions*** What other factors may also have affected daily oil production during these events?

College and Career Readiness

14. ***Multicultural Societies*** Tourism has become an important way to diversify the economy in Bahrain and the United Arab Emirates. Choose one of these countries. Imagine that you have been hired by a travel agency to design a three-day tour of that country. Research the major tourist destinations, cultural highlights, and other activities. Write a travel itinerary for each day of the trip.

WHST.9.10.4, WHST.9.10.5, WHST.9.10.6

Need Extra Help?

If You've Missed Question	1	2	3	4	5	6	7	8	9	10	11	12	13	14
Go to page	434	436	437	439	443	443	445	447	444	444	439	449	444	443

CHAPTER 18 Assessment Answers

Lesson Review

Lesson 1

1. The single plate of Arabia and Africa was split into two by tectonic forces, forming a rift that filled with water to become the Red Sea. The Red Sea created the western and southwestern boundaries of the Arabian Peninsula.
2. Winds are such a significant factor of the climate in the Arabian Peninsula because of the damage they cause. The simooms blow hot, dry air with such force that they destroy plants and animals, and *shamals* create dust and sand storms that carry millions of tons of sand and silt into the Rub' al-Khali desert.
3. Freshwater is more crucial than oil because such a limited supply is available, the population is growing creating more need for water, and existing aquifers cannot be replenished at the rate they are currently being used.

Lesson 2

4. The petroleum industry created jobs that attracted guest workers from South Asian countries, diversifying the homogeneous population of the peninsula.
5. The Arabian Peninsula is strategically important because the vast amounts of oil it transports to other countries must go through either the Strait of Hormuz on the Persian Gulf or the Bab el Mandeb on the Red Sea. Maintaining good relations with its neighbors is important for the Arab Peninsula to prevent blocking of these passages.
6. Saudi Arabia, Kuwait, Qatar, and the United Arab Emirates belong to OPEC. The role of OPEC is to set oil production quotas and develop strategies for dealing with the long-term demand for oil.

Lesson 3

7. Oil extraction releases gases into the air that are eventually brought to the ground by rain, polluting the groundwater and the soil. Oil extraction also causes spills and other by-products to be released into the waters surrounding the peninsula, destroying marine life.
8. Desalination is expensive, requires large amounts of energy, still requires the use of some freshwater to make drinkable water, and creates brine that must be disposed of without contaminating aquifers or raising the salinity of coastal waters.
9. The Persian Gulf War illustrates how world powers will respond when oil production is threatened by conflict.

Critical Thinking

10. Student answers may vary but could include that the price of oil would be lower if it were a renewable resource, which would result in less money in the economies of the Arabian Peninsula and more diversification of the economies of these countries if they were not as focused on oil production.
11. Immigrants have been drawn to the Arabian Peninsula for jobs and the promise of high wages as their own countries are experiencing high unemployment rates.

21st Century Skills

12. War, revolution, and social unrest cause the number of available barrels of oil on the market to decrease.
13. The Iranian Revolution in 1978 resulted in the greatest loss of oil production. About 3 and a half million barrels per day were taken off the market.

College and Career Readiness

14. Travel itineraries will vary based on the country chosen but could include major cities, beaches, museums, and archaeological sites.

DBQ Analyzing Primary Sources

15 Marriage typically means women are expected to stay home and care for children and the home. This isolates women and makes them financially dependent on their husbands. Divorce is uncommon because of these issues and because it is not easily permitted by the government in Yemen, leaving women with little to no opportunities.

16 Better access to education could lead to improved economic conditions for women, increased awareness of issues, and the ability to change laws that limit property and inheritance rights.

17 Student answers may vary but could include dreams of better education, health care, economic opportunities, and equality for women.

Applying Map Skills

18 The Red Sea is on the west side of the Arabian Peninsula, the Persian Gulf borders the east side of the peninsula, and the Arabian Sea is off the tip of the peninsula to the south.

19 The overall population density of the Arabian Peninsula is low, with the greatest area having between 2.5–24 people per square mile. The cities in coastal areas have the highest population densities.

20 The Bab el Mandeb on the Red Sea and the Strait of Hormuz on the Persian Gulf are both narrow straits that are strategic for shipping oil and petroleum from the Arabian Peninsula to other parts of the world.

Exploring the Essential Question

21 Diagrams will vary, but students should label the human and physical systems of the region interacting in relation to oil deposits. Diagrams could include: population patterns/population density information—about 80 percent of the population resides in cities along the Persian Gulf and Red Sea and in the refining city of Riyadh; guest workers; and use of the Strait of Hormuz and Bab el Mandeb for shipping oil worldwide.

Research and Presentation

22 Multimedia presentations will vary, but students could include that bedouin tribes traveled from place to place; were primarily herders of camels, goats, and sheep; had tribal leaders that held absolute power; and that bedouins mostly live in cities today.

Writing About Geography

23 Essays will vary but should be strongly supported with information from the chapter, including that relying heavily on oil could be dangerous if the prices or demand drop, shipping channels are unavailable, or conflict within the region causes production to be shut down. Examples of countries that have diversified their economies include Bahrain using the finance and banking industries, Bahrain, Saudi Arabia, and the United Arab Emirates using tourism, Bahrain and Oman using the fishing industry, the small textile industry in Yemen, and many countries having ship repair and cement manufacturing industries.

CHAPTER 18 Assessment

Directions: On a separate sheet of paper, answer the questions below. Make sure you read carefully and answer all parts of the questions.

DBQ Analyzing Primary Sources

Use the document to answer the following questions.

Strict interpretations of Islamic law and tradition on the Arabian Peninsula have created many restrictions for women. This is particularly the case in Yemen, the country with the least developed infrastructure.

PRIMARY SOURCE

"By almost all indicators—health, education, and economic opportunity—women fare poorly in Yemen. It has one of the highest rates of child marriage in the world, and 60 percent of Yemeni women are illiterate. Infant mortality rates are also among the world's worst, attributed to the lack of prenatal and postnatal health care. Unlike men, women cannot easily get divorced, and they have limited property and inheritance rights. The country ranks dead last among 135 countries in the World Economic Forum's Global Gender Gap Report.

Al Abdeli is an assistant professor of accounting at a university in Taizz, and she enjoys more freedoms than most of her peers. She credits this to growing up in Taizz and having an open-minded father who 'did not go to university but is knowledgeable about the world.' She is also a poet who for years openly expressed her loathing for Ali Abdullah Saleh's regime. 'I put some of my dreams in my poetry and implanted them in the minds of my students,' she said."

—Joshua Hammer, "Days of Reckoning," *National Geographic*, September 2012

15 ***Analyzing*** How do traditions of marriage and divorce contribute to the difficulties women face in Yemen? RH.9–10.1

16 ***Problem Solving*** How might greater access to education improve the condition of women in Yemen? RH.9–10.1

17 ***Interpreting*** What dreams do you think Al Abdeli implanted in the minds of her students? RH.9–10.1

Applying Map Skills

Use the Unit 5 Atlas to answer the following questions:

18 ***Physical Systems*** Use your mental map of the Arabian Peninsula to describe the location of the Red Sea, the Arabian Sea, and the Persian Gulf.

19 ***Places and Regions*** Describe the overall population density pattern of the Arabian Peninsula.

20 ***Environment and Society*** What physical and human features help explain why the Bab el Mandeb and the Strait of Hormuz are called choke points?

Exploring the Essential Question

21 ***Diagramming*** Design two diagrams showing how vast deposits of crude oil under the sands of the Arabian deserts have affected the human and physical systems of the Arabian Peninsula. In each diagram, label the factors involved, and explain how the human and physical systems interact. WHST.9–10.2

Research and Presentation

22 ***Research Skills*** Using the Internet and other resources, research the history and culture of nomadic bedouin tribes in the Arabian Peninsula. Describe how bedouin culture evolved to meet the demands of life in the enormous central deserts of the interior. How do bedouins live today? Create a multimedia presentation to share your findings. WHST.9–10.2, WHST.9–10.6

Writing About Geography

23 ***Argument*** Use standard grammar, spelling, sentence structure, and punctuation to write an essay arguing the benefits of a diverse economy for countries in the Arabian Peninsula. Give examples of how countries in the subregion have successfully diversified their economies, and discuss the potential consequences of relying too heavily on oil. WHST.9–10.1

Need Extra Help?

If You've Missed Question	15	16	17	18	19	20	21	22	23
Go to page	442	441	442	360	364	360	439	438	443

450

CHAPTER **19**

Central Asia Planner

UNDERSTANDING BY DESIGN®

Enduring Understandings

- *Places reflect the relationship between humans and the physical environment.*

Essential Question

- *How do physical systems and human systems shape a place?*

Predictable Misunderstandings

Students may think:

- *Central Asia is made up of Russian states. Explain that many countries in Central Asia were part of the Soviet Union at one time, but when the Soviet Union dissolved in 1991, they became separate, independent states.*
- *People that live in Central Asia come from the same ethnic background. Explain that there are many different ethnic groups in Central Asia and that this is one of the main reasons for conflict in the area – tension between ethnic groups.*

Assessment Evidence

Performance Tasks:

- *Hands-On Chapter Project*

Other Evidence:

- *Guided Reading Activities*
- *Vocabulary Activities*
- *Lesson Quizzes*
- *Chapter Tests, Forms A and B*

SUGGESTED PACING GUIDE

Introducing the Chapter	½ Day
Lesson 1	1 Day
Lesson 2	1 Day
Lesson 3	1 Day
Chapter Wrap-Up and Assessment	½ Day
TOTAL TIME	**4 Days**

National Geography Standards covered in "Central Asia"

The student knows and understands:

5.1 Regions are defined by different sets of criteria and places can be included in multiple regions of different types

(7) The physical processes that shape the patterns of Earth's surface

7.1 The interaction of Earth's physical systems (the atmosphere, biosphere, hydrosphere, and lithosphere) vary across space and time

7.3 Physical processes interact over time to shape particular places on Earth's surface

(9) The characteristics, distribution, and migration of human populations on Earth's surface

9.1 Culture, economics, and politics influence the changing demographic structure of different populations

9.2 Population distribution and density are a function of historical, environmental, economic, political, and technological factors

(14) How human actions modify the physical environment

14.1 Human modifications of the physical environment can have significant global impacts

14.3 People can either mitigate and/or adapt to the consequences of human modifications of the physical environment

(15) How physical systems affect human systems

15.1 Depending on the choice of human activities, the characteristics of the physical environment can be viewed as both opportunities and constraints

15.2 Human perceive and react to environmental hazards in different ways

15.3 Societies use a variety of strategies to adapt to changes in the physical environment

Key for Using the Teacher Edition

SKILL-BASED ACTIVITIES

Types of skill activities found in the Teacher Edition.

* **V Visual Skills** require students to analyze maps, graphs, charts, and photos.

R Reading Skills help students practice reading skills and master vocabulary.

C Critical Thinking Skills help students apply and extend what they have learned.

W Writing Skills provide writing opportunities to help students comprehend the text.

T Technology Skills require students to use digital tools effectively.

*Letters are followed by a number when there is more than one of the same type of skill on the page.

DIFFERENTIATED INSTRUCTION

All activities are written for the on-level student unless otherwise marked with the leveled labels below.

BL Beyond Level
AL Approaching Level
ELL English Language Learners

All students benefit from activities that utilize different learning styles. Many activities are marked as below when a particular learning style is highlighted.

Intrapersonal	**Naturalist**
Logical/Mathematical	**Kinesthetic**
Visual/Spatial	**Auditory/Musical**
Verbal/Linguistic	**Interpersonal**

CHAPTER OPENER PLANNER

Students will know:
- *the physical geography of Central Asia.*
- *how water systems, climate, and natural resources are important.*
- *how Central Asia has been claimed by many peoples and how ethnic groups are distributed.*
- *the ways of life of the peoples of Central Asia.*
- *how the people manage natural resources to create economies.*
- *the environmental challenges of the region and how they are being addressed.*

Students will be able to:
- ***describe** the physical geography of Central Asia.*
- ***analyze** how water systems, climate, and natural resources affect human activity in the region.*
- ***identify** peoples who have claimed Central Asia and describe population distribution.*
- ***describe** how peoples of Central Asia live.*
- ***analyze** how Central Asian economies are created from natural resources.*
- ***describe** environmental challenges and possible solutions in Central Asia.*

UNDERSTANDING BY DESIGN®

☑ Print Teaching Options

V Visual Skills
- ☐ **p. 452** Students write paragraphs that explain why Afghanistan has had a troubled history.

R Reading Skills
- ☐ **p. 453** Students consider how a diverse population can have both positive and negative impacts. **Verbal/Linguistic**

C Critical Thinking Skills
- ☐ **p. 452** Students record internal and external forces and consider how they contribute to instability in Afghanistan.

W Writing Skills
- ☐ **p. 452** Students write a journal entry describing a day on a trade mission in Central Asia.

T Technology Skills
- ☐ **p. 453** Students research specific examples of government corruption in Afghanistan and what is being done to remedy the situation.

☑ Online Teaching Options

R Reading Skills
- **IMAGE** **Soviet Invasion of Afghanistan**—Students take notes on the information presented in the image and organize it into an outline with the heads "External Forces" and "Internal Forces." **ELL** **Verbal/Linguistic**
- **MAP** **Interactive Regional Atlas**—Students use the interactive regional atlas to understand the physical and human geography of Central Asia.

☑ Printable Digital Worksheets

- **WORKSHEET** **Assessing Background Knowledge**—Determine the level of prior knowledge students have about Central Asia.
- **WORKSHEET** **Chapter Summaries**—Students review the main idea of each lesson of the chapter content.

Project-Based Learning 

Hands-On

Mural of Events

Students will create a mural that highlights important events of Central Asia. Pairs will be responsible for researching and illustrating an event, which they will add to a class time line. Pairs will also present a brief summary explaining how their event relates to the physical and human geography of Central Asia.

Digital Hands-On

Create Online Projects

Find an additional activity online that incorporates technology for this project. Visit the EdTech Teacher Web sites for more links, tutorials, and other resources.

Print Resources

ANCILLARY RESOURCES

This ancillary is available for every chapter and lesson.
- **Chapter Tests and Lesson Quizzes**

PRINTABLE DIGITAL WORKSHEETS

These printable digital worksheets are available for every chapter and lesson.
- **Assessing Background Knowledge**
- **Chapter Summaries**
- **Guided Reading Activities**
- **Hands-On Chapter Projects**
- **Quizzes and Tests**
- **Reading Essentials and Study Guide** **AL**
- **Reteaching Activities**
- **Video Activities**
- **Vocabulary Activities**

More Media Resources

SUGGESTED VIDEOS MOVIES
- **Silk Road Journey From China Through Central Asia** (48 min.)
- **Central Asia: Markets at the Crossroads** (20 min.)
- **Through the Desert Goes Our Journey** (57 min.)

SUGGESTED READING 
- ***Inside Central Asia: A Political and Cultural History of Uzbekistan, Turkmenistan, Kazakhstan, Kyrgyzstan, Tajikistan, Turkey, and Iran,*** Dilip Hiro
- ***Central Asia: In Search of a New Identity,*** by Igor P. Lipovsky
- ***Palgrave Concise Historical Atlas of Central Asia,*** by Rafis Abazov

LESSON 1 PLANNER

PHYSICAL GEOGRAPHY OF CENTRAL ASIA

Students will know:
- *the location of and landforms of Central Asia.*
- *what water systems are important to the people of Central Asia.*
- *how climate and natural resources affect human activity in Central Asia.*

Students will be able to:
- ***identify** landforms of Central Asia and their locations.*
- ***identify** important water systems in the region.*
- ***analyze** how climate and natural resources affect human activity in the region.*

UNDERSTANDING BY DESIGN®

☑ Print Teaching Options

V Visual Skills

- ☐ **p. 454** Students create a diagram labeled *Eastern* and *Western* and complete it with information from the text. AL Visual/Spatial
- ☐ **p. 457** Students create a diagram or annotated map to show how the climate of the region impacts human activity. ELL Visual/Spatial, Interpersonal

R Reading Skills

- ☐ **p. 455** Students create a picture of the region Strabo describes in *Geography.* Verbal/Linguistic

C Critical Thinking Skills

- ☐ **p. 454** Students consider how different landforms and waterways might affect where people settle and how they make a living. Visual/Spatial
- ☐ **p. 454** Students discuss what countries in Central Asia have in common.
- ☐ **p. 457** Students consider the similarities and differences of the human activity shown in the images of agriculture. Visual/Spatial
- ☐ **p. 458** Students develop charts or visuals depicting the resources and other benefits available in each country in Central Asia for a group of investors looking to invest in the area. BL Verbal/Linguistic

W Writing Skills

- ☐ **p. 456** Students write a paragraph in which they describe the differences between the Aral Sea and the Caspian Sea. AL Verbal/Linguistic

T Technology Skills

- ☐ **p. 456** Students research the advantages and disadvantages of the location of an assigned country that borders the Caspian Sea and create a visual that maps out the resources of their assigned country. Visual/spatial

☑ Online Teaching Options

V Visual Skills

- ☐ INTERACTIVE GRAPHIC ORGANIZER **Physical Geography of Central Asia**—Students use this interactive graphic organizer to help them classify the many landforms and waterways that make up Central Asia. ELL AL Verbal/Linguistic, Visual/Spatial
- ☐ VIDEO **Aral Sea is Slowly Drying Out**—Students view the video about water policies and their effect on the Aral Sea and think of a way that a water policy could be revised or replaced to the benefit of the Aral Sea. AL BL Verbal/Linguistic, Visual/Spatial
- ☐ SLIDE SHOW **Herding in Central Asia**—Students view a slide show about herding in Central Asia and describe herding as a livelihood in Central Asia. AL Verbal/Linguistic

R Reading Skills

- ☐ INTERACTIVE BELLRINGER **Central Asia's Water Tower**—Students discuss how climate affects the water supply, which affects human activity in Central Asia. BL Interpersonal, Visual/Spatial
- ☐ INTERACTIVE WHITEBOARD ACTIVITY **Central Asia Water Systems**—Students locate and attach labels to name waterways on the map.

☑ Printable Digital Worksheets

R Reading Skills

- ☐ WORKSHEET **Guided Reading Activity**—Students use the Guided Reading Activity worksheets to review their comprehension of the content.

C Critical Thinking Skills

- ☐ WORKSHEET **Video Activity**—Students answer questions related to a topic in the chapter content after they have viewed a lesson video.

LESSON 2 PLANNER

HUMAN GEOGRAPHY OF CENTRAL ASIA

Students will know:

- *how Central Asia has been claimed by many peoples.*
- *how ethnic groups are distributed in Central Asia.*
- *the ways of life of the peoples of Central Asia.*
- *how people in Central Asia use the region's natural resources.*

Students will be able to:

- ***identify** peoples who have claimed Central Asia.*
- ***describe** the population patterns of ethnic groups in the region.*
- ***describe** how peoples of Central Asia live.*
- ***analyze** the use of natural resources in Central Asia.*

UNDERSTANDING BY DESIGN®

Print Teaching Options

V Visual Skills

- **p. 459** Students create a web diagram with the name of each country in Central Asia and use it to record key facts. ELL Visual/Spatial
- **p. 462** Students create a graph that shows the population of Central Asia's major cities. AL Logical/Mathematical

R Reading Skills

- **p. 461** Students discuss the definitions of the words *mujahideen, Taliban,* and *al-Qaeda.* ELL Verbal/Linguistic

C Critical Thinking Skills

- **p. 461** Students formulate questions based on the dates and events of the second half of the time line. AL Visual/Spatial, Interpersonal
- **p. 462** Students discuss the reasons that the concentration and distribution of different ethnic groups across Central Asia has led to conflict. BL Logical/Mathematical
- **p. 463** Students discuss how conflicts can impact people in different regions of Central Asia. AL Logical/Mathematical
- **p. 465** Students explore the relationship between a country's reliance on its natural resources and its economic productivity. AL Logical/Mathematical

W Writing Skills

- **p. 465** Students write a short summary on the economy and natural resources of a country in Central Asia. Verbal/Linguistic

T Technology Skills

- **p. 461** Students research how a country in Central Asia was impacted by invasions, becoming part of the Soviet Union, and the collapse of the Soviet Union. BL Verbal/Linguistic
- **p. 463** Students listen to a sample of Russian, and then do research to locate audio excerpts of other languages spoken in Central Asia. BL Auditory/Musical
- **p. 464** Students research, prepare, and present a "Central Asian Art and Culture Exhibit." BL Visual/Spatial, Auditory/Musical

Online Teaching Options

C Critical Thinking Skills

- INTERACTIVE BELLRINGER **Economic Productivity in Central Asia**—Students learn about productivity in the region and discuss what life might be like for people living in countries in which the average income is just a few thousand dollars a year. AL Logical/Mathematical, Verbal/Linguistic
- VIDEO **Trading Domes of Bukhara, Uzbekistan**—Students watch a video about trade in Central Asia and make a simple chart identifying the similarities and differences between Central Asian trade years ago and today. AL Verbal/Linguistic
- INTERACTIVE WHITEBOARD ACTIVITY **Historical Events That Shaped Central Asia**—Students drag letters into the correct sequence on a time line. ELL AL Verbal/Linguistic, Visual/Spatial
- INTERACTIVE MAP **Ethnic Groups in Central Asia**—Students consider how much of the land in Central Asia either has very few residents or is completely uninhabited based on the map. AL Verbal/Linguistic, Visual/Spatial
- INTERACTIVE IMAGE **Women Who Weave**—Students gather information from the image of a woman weaving and predict what she may be producing. ELL Visual/Spatial
- GAME **Human Geography of Central Asia**—Students play the fill-in-the blank game and write a paragraph explaining how human systems shape Central Asia. AL Verbal/Linguistic

Printable Digital Worksheets

R Reading Skills

- WORKSHEET **Guided Reading Activity**—Students use Guided Reading Activity worksheets to review their comprehension of the content.
- WORKSHEET **Reading Essentials and Study Guide**—Students complete the study guide and answer Reading Progress Check and vocabulary questions. AL

C Critical Thinking Skills

- WORKSHEET **Video Activity**—Students answer questions related to a topic in the chapter content after they have viewed a lesson video.

PEOPLE AND THEIR ENVIRONMENT: CENTRAL ASIA

Students will know:

- *that the people of Central Asia manage natural resources to create economies.*
- *what environmental challenges the people of Central Asia face.*
- *how governments and international groups are addressing environmental challenges.*

Students will be able to:

- ***analyze*** *how Central Asian economies are created from natural resources.*
- ***describe*** *environmental challenges in the region.*
- ***identify*** *ways in which people and governments are working to improve the environment.*

UNDERSTANDING BY DESIGN®

☑ Print Teaching Options

V Visual Skills

- ☐ **p. 466** Students create a visual display that shows how countries in Central Asia manage their natural resources. AL Visual/Spatial, Interpersonal
- ☐ **p. 468** Students analyze a visual about the Aral Sea. AL Logical/Mathematical
- ☐ **p. 469** Students create a diagram or flowchart that depicts the various causes of damage to the Caspian and Aral Seas. AL Visual/Spatial, Interpersonal

R Reading Skills

- ☐ **p. 466** Students predict the types of errors in resource management countries may make.

C Critical Thinking Skills

- ☐ **p. 467** Students consider the advantages and disadvantages of different uses of natural resources in Central Asia and work in groups to conduct mock debates on the use of a particular resource. BL Verbal/Linguistic, Interpersonal
- ☐ **p. 468** Students consider how the Aral Sea has changed and calculate its lost area and volume. AL Logical/Mathematical

W Writing Skills

- ☐ **p. 469** Students work in small groups to conceptualize, write, and rehearse a skit that portrays a family living in one of the regions impacted by environmental problems. Kinesthetic, Interpersonal

T Technology Skills

- ☐ **p. 467** Students research how water scarcity issues are being addressed in a country in the region. Logical/Mathematical, Interpersonal
- ☐ **p. 470** Students should research what their assigned country is doing to manage its water resources, the impact of the problem on the surrounding environment and on the region's economy, and present a slide show with their findings. BL Interpersonal

☑ Online Teaching Options

V Visual Skills

- ☐ VIDEO **In the Wake of the USSR**—Students view the video about environmental damage caused by the Soviet Union's invasion of Afghanistan in 1979 and the challenges that still exist today. Verbal/Linguistic, Logical/Mathematical

R Reading Skills

- ☐ INTERACTIVE BELLRINGER **Aral: A Sea Sacrificed**—Students learn about environmental challenges in Central Asia and consider how their lives might be affected if they lived in the Midwest and suddenly the Great Lakes lost a significant volume of water. Visual/Spatial, Verbal/Linguistic
- ☐ GRAPHIC ORGANIZER **People and Their Environment**—Students learn how people in Central Asia manage natural resources and thereby impact their environment and use the graphic organizer as a note-taking tool. AL BL Verbal/Linguistic, Interpersonal
- ☐ SLIDE SHOW **The Effects of Economic Development**—Students view the slide show, take notes on the positive and negative effects of economic development on the countries featured, and create a concept web showing how these effects may impact other countries in the region. AL Verbal/Linguistic, Visual/Spatial
- ☐ INTERACTIVE WHITEBOARD ACTIVITY **Addressing Environmental Issues in Central Asia**—Students complete sentences about environmental challenges that Central Asia faces.

☑ Printable Digital Worksheets

R Reading Skills

- ☐ WORKSHEET **Guided Reading Activity**—Students use Guided Reading Activity worksheets to review their comprehension of the content.
- ☐ WORKSHEET **Reading Essentials and Study Guide**—Students complete the study guide and answer Reading Progress Check and vocabulary questions. AL
- ☐ WORKSHEET **Vocabulary Activity**—Students review the chapter content and academic vocabulary words.

C Critical Thinking Skills

- ☐ WORKSHEET **Video Activity**—Students answer questions based on a lesson video.
- ☐ WORKSHEET **Reteaching Activity**—Students use this activity worksheet to review and reteach chapter content and vocabulary. This worksheet can be used with struggling students who need additional help with difficult content concepts.

INTERVENTION AND REMEDIATION STRATEGIES

LESSON 1 Physical Geography of Central Asia

Reading and Comprehension

Copy on the board the graphic organizer labeled Physical Geography from the first page of this lesson. Organize students into four groups and assign them one of the four topics in each oval. Have groups add labeled ovals to their part of the web diagram with related topics. For example, students assigned to the Landforms oval might add two additional bubbles labeled Western Section and Eastern Section. Have students in each group work together to complete their portion of the graphic organizer. Then have groups take turns drawing their portion of the graphic organizer on the board. Invite volunteers to add more ovals with details about each topic.

Text Evidence

Have student pairs choose a region of Central Asia and create a visitor's guide to the region based on information from the lesson. Tell students their guides should inform visitors to the region about its climate zones, biomes, waterways, vegetation, wildlife, and natural resources. Students may wish to conduct online research to enhance their guides. Invite groups to present their finished guides to the class, encouraging them to include visuals such as maps and illustrations. Have students list positive and negative aspects of living in the region, defending each side with evidence from the text.

LESSON 2 Human Geography of Central Asia

Reading and Comprehension

Have students work in pairs to create time lines or other graphic organizers to help them sequence and organize information about the different groups of people who formed kingdoms or empires in regions of Central Asia. Have students record information such as the dates when each group first conquered or settled the land, where the settlements were mainly located, and the impact this group had on the other groups. In addition to using information from the time line in this lesson, invite students to enhance their organizers with more facts about each cultural group using online or library resources. Ask volunteers to share their completed graphic organizers with the class.

Text Evidence

Have student groups review the chart in this lesson outlining statistics about economic productivity in Central Asia as compared to the United States. Have students collaborate to write a paragraph that summarizes the economic activities in Central Asian countries, assigning each group a country from the region. Remind students to use information from the lesson to support statements in their paragraphs. Then guide students in a discussion to answer the Guiding Question: *How do the people of Central Asia use resources to create economies?*

LESSON 3 People and Their Environment: Central Asia

Reading and Comprehension

Have students review information in the lesson about the management of oil, water and other resources in Central Asia and the environmental issues resulting from economic activities in the region. Have students work with a partner to develop a problem-solution chart, listing an environmental issue facing the region in the left column and how it is being addressed in the right column. Ask partners to share their charts with the class to compile a class chart on the board. As students work through the lesson, tell them to revisit the class chart and identify possible solutions that can be added to the right column.

Text Evidence

Have students work in pairs to identify evidence from the lesson that supports one of the following statements: 1. *Because of the generally dry climate of Central Asia, water and other resources have to be managed carefully.* 2. *Mistakes in the past have posed several challenges to some aspects of the environment.* 3. *Since some resources are shared by several countries, they need to work together to solve these problems and manage their resources.* Students may conduct online research to identify facts to support their chosen statement. Invite pairs to share their statements with the class.

Online Resources

Leveled Reader

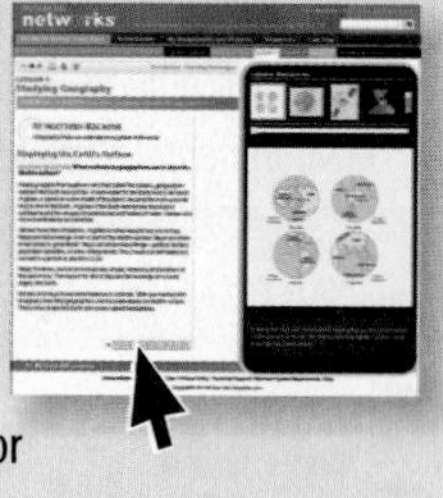

Use this online approaching-level text that corresponds directly to the text in the Student Edition. It also includes additional reading and comprehension support for English Language Learners.

Guided Reading Activities

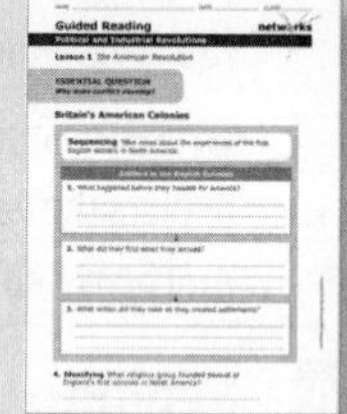

This resource uses guiding questions to help students with comprehension.

Reteaching Activities

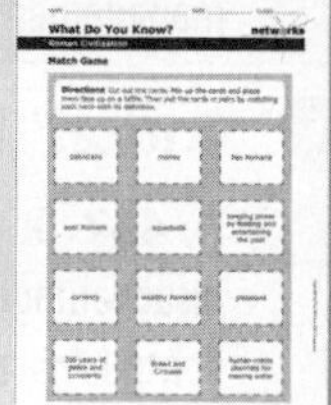

These worksheets provide students with an opportunity for remedial practice and review of vital chapter content.

Reading Essentials and Study Guide

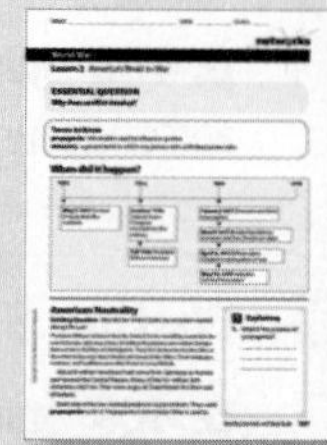

This resource offers writing and reading activities for the approaching-level student.

Self-Check Quizzes

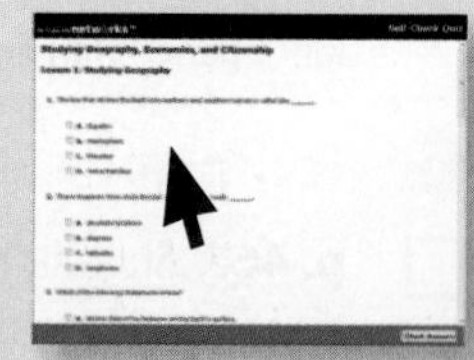

This online assessment tool provides instant feedback for students to check their progress.

Chapter Summaries

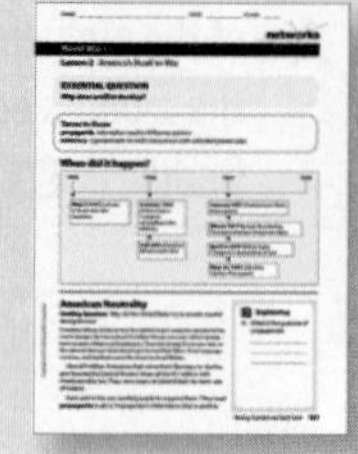

Summaries are provided for each chapter that thoroughly condense core content into manageable chunks.

Central Asia

networks

There's More Online about Central Asia's geography.

CHAPTER 19

ESSENTIAL QUESTION • *How do physical systems and human systems shape a place?*

Geography Matters...

Central Asia can be a challenging area in which to live. Much of it is arid. Farmers rely on snowmelt from the mountains to provide water to farm land in the valleys. Rocky highlands prevent farming in many areas but provide pasture for sheep. Forbidding deserts stretch over large expanses.

However, much of Central Asia is quite beautiful. Snow-covered mountains tower over deserts of stark beauty. Dazzling tiles adorn buildings. In some cities, centuries-old mosques stand alongside gleaming glass skyscrapers.

◀ This man in Kabul, Afghanistan, faces traditional and modern ways.

ENGAGE

Activating Prior Knowledge Tell students that this subregion includes Georgia, Armenia, Azerbaijan, and the six *stans*—an ancient Persian word that means "land of." Explain that different ethnic groups inhabit many of the countries in the region. For example, Kazakhstan is the "land of Kazakhs." Have small groups discuss any stories in the news they may have heard or seen involving countries in Central Asia, such as news about ongoing conflicts that have plagued Afghanistan. Tell students to think about the connection between the region's physical location and the challenges faced by the people who live in Central Asian countries.

TEACH & ASSESS

Drawing Inferences Have students read the text and consider the physical limitations of the region. **Ask:** **What challenges do you think people in Central Asia face?** *(Possible answer: Living in an arid or semi-arid region can present challenges to farmers who need water for irrigating their crops and for raising livestock. Mountainous areas also limit the amount of arable land in the region.)* **How might the beauty of Central Asia help its economy?** *(Possible answer: The physical beauty of the region could benefit the economy by increasing tourism.)* **AL** **Verbal/Linguistic Logical/Mathematical**

Content Background Knowledge

Kazakhstan The largest country in Central Asia by area is Kazakhstan, measuring more than 1,800 miles (almost 3,000 kilometers) east to west, and about 960 miles (1,545 kilometers) north to south. In comparison, if a map of the country were placed over a map of the United States, Kazakhstan would extend east to west from Ohio to Nevada, and north to south from North Dakota to Texas. By population, Kazakhstan is the third largest in the region.

Letter from the Author

Dear Geography Teacher,

The United States has withdrawn most of its military forces from Afghanistan, and procedures are in place to turn over Afghan security to local military and police forces. Have students map U.S. military infrastructure that will remain in Central Asia. Also consider the Russians during their 10 year war in Afghanistan. What were they after? How do you think they feel about current U.S. air bases and missiles in Central Asia? Are the Russians likely to start something, now that the Americans are gone? These are huge geopolitical questions, and the U.S. State Department, and the Pentagon, who have a geographical perspective, will be called upon to answer them.

Richard G. Boehm

CLOSE & REFLECT

Posing Questions Have students think about aspects of Central Asia's human population or physical geography that they would like to know more about. Tell students to write two or three questions and refer back to them, filling in answers as they work through the chapter.

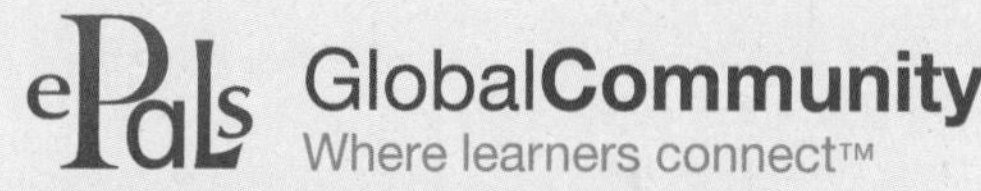

Extend the project-based learning experience globally through our partnership with ePals. EPals allows you to connect with classrooms around the world in a safe online environment for real-life lessons and projects in virtual study groups.

ENGAGE

C Critical Thinking Skills

Diagramming Have students read the paragraph and draw their attention to the phrases *external forces* and *internal forces*. Have students consider how each of these forces contributes to the instability of Afghanistan. Tell students to create a two-column chart labeled *External Forces* and *Internal Forces* and to record examples of these forces in their chart as they examine the map. Have students share their responses. Encourage students to add or revise information in their charts after they read this feature. **Logical/Mathematical**

TEACH & ASSESS

W Writing Skills

Narrative Have students imagine they are embarking on a trade mission in Central Asia. Using the map as a guide, have students write a journal entry describing a day or two along their journey. Students should write about their method of transportation and what they encounter along the way. Tell students to use adjectives to describe the terrain and the people of the regions through which they travel. Encourage students to share their journal entries with the class.
AL Verbal/Linguistic, Intrapersonal

V Visual Skills

Analyzing Visuals Have students work with a partner to read the map's title and callouts, and to examine the regions outlined on the map. Have partners collaborate to write a summary paragraph that explains why Afghanistan has had a troubled history. Challenge students to address the positive and negative impact of being at "the crossroads of Central Asia" for thousands of years. **BL Interpersonal, Verbal/Linguistic**

Afghanistan's troubled history

C

Located on trade routes that link areas from East Asia, South Asia, Southwest Asia, and Europe, Afghanistan has been "the crossroads of Central Asia" for thousands of years. Becoming an independent country in 1747, Afghanistan has had a troubled history. In recent decades, Afghanistan has faced the external forces of invasion, as well as the internal forces of ethnic and tribal diversity. Both threaten the country's stability.

W *Ethnic Groups of Afghanistan*

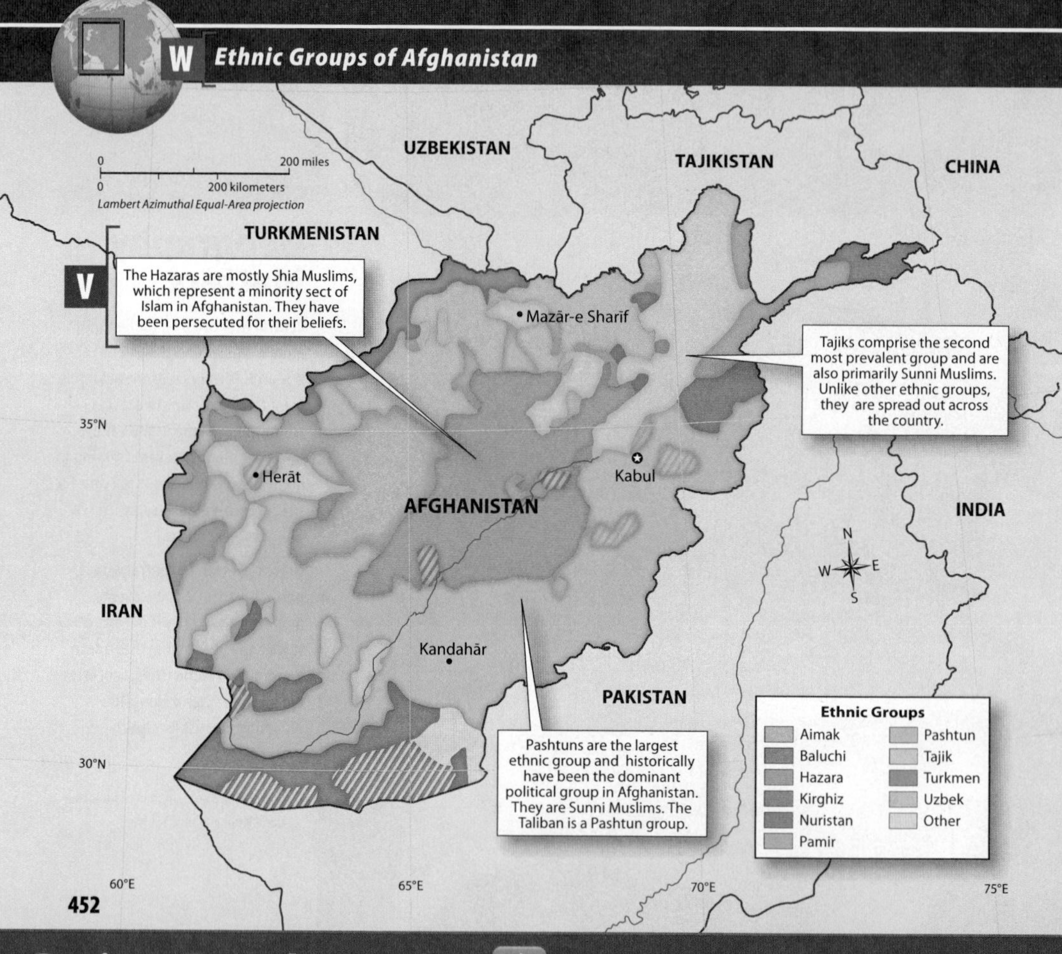
UZBEKISTAN
TAJIKISTAN
CHINA
0 200 miles
0 200 kilometers
Lambert Azimuthal Equal-Area projection
TURKMENISTAN
V
The Hazaras are mostly Shia Muslims, which represent a minority sect of Islam in Afghanistan. They have been persecuted for their beliefs.
Mazār-e Sharif
Tajiks comprise the second most prevalent group and are also primarily Sunni Muslims. Unlike other ethnic groups, they are spread out across the country.
35°N
Herāt
Kabul
AFGHANISTAN
INDIA
N
W
E
S
IRAN
Kandahār
PAKISTAN
Ethnic Groups
Aimak
Baluchi
Hazara
Kirghiz
Nuristan
Pamir
Pashtun
Tajik
Turkmen
Uzbek
Other
Pashtuns are the largest ethnic group and historically have been the dominant political group in Afghanistan. They are Sunni Muslims. The Taliban is a Pashtun group.
30°N
60°E
65°E
70°E
75°E

Project-Based Learning

Hands-On

Mural of Events

Working in pairs, students will create a mural that highlights important events of Central Asia. Each student pair will be assigned to research one of the important events. Pairs will sketch an illustration of their assigned event on a large classroom mural. Students will also present to the class a brief summary explaining how their event relates to the physical and human geography of Central Asia.

ePals GlobalCommunity
Where learners connect™

Digital Hands-On

Create Online Projects

Find an additional activity online that incorporates technology for this project. Visit the EdTech Teacher Web sites for more links, tutorials, and other resources.

edtechteacher
21st Century Learning

Who are the people of Afghanistan?

Afghanistan has a complex human geography. The country is home to dozens of different ethnic groups and subgroups. The map shows only the largest. While Pashtuns form the largest group, even they do not make up a majority of the country's people. Afghanistan's people speak about 50 languages. The two most widely spoken are Pashto and Dari. Pashto is the language of the Pashtun. Dari is a Farsi, or Persian, dialect. Dari often serves as a lingua franca (common language) in Afghanistan.

Ethnic differences are not necessarily strong divisions. People from different ethnic groups marry one another and live in the same areas. Perhaps the strongest tie Afghanistan's people feel is to their local tribes. For many people, their bond to the tribe is stronger than their feeling of national identity, which has made it difficult to organize them into a single modern country. **R**

1. **Human Systems** How might tribal loyalties affect a leader's ability to govern Afghanistan?

Who has invaded and tried to rule Afghanistan?

For thousands of years, Afghanistan has been the target of foreign invaders. Persians ruled the area until Alexander the Great conquered it around 330 B.C. Alexander was followed by the Scythians, then the Huns, and then the Turks. Later, Arabs conquered the area. Persians ruled again, followed by the Turks once more. Then two different Mongol conquerors invaded Afghanistan.

The Soviet Union invaded Afghanistan in 1979. However, the Soviets withdrew after ten years of costly fighting. In the 1990s, a fundamentalist Islamic group took control of Afghanistan. They began to shelter Islamic terrorists. The terrorists established training camps for their fighters, some of whom attacked the United States on September 11, 2001. When the government refused to close the terrorist camps and even refused to hand over the terrorist leader, the United States and other countries sent troops to fight them. The government was quickly defeated and an elected government eventually took office. However, rebels have continued to fight against the new regime.

2. **Places and Regions** Why do you think Afghanistan has been invaded by outside forces so frequently?

Why does Afghanistan continue to suffer?

Afghanistan is among the poorest countries in the world. More than three-fourths of its workforce makes its living by farming using traditional methods. As a result, incomes are low. For example, more than a third of the people live in poverty. Just over a third of the workforce is unemployed.

Afghanistan's economy has begun to recover since the fundamentalists were ousted, and the economy has the potential for development. The country has reserves of natural gas and petroleum, precious metals such as gold and silver, and gems. However, conflict has hampered efforts to develop the country's natural resources. For example, continuing conflict has interfered with infrastructure development. Government corruption has also been a significant problem in trying to develop the economy and a stable society. As a result, Afghanistan still depends heavily on aid from the international community. **T**

3. **Environment and Society** What opportunities and what challenges does Afghanistan face today?

THERE'S MORE ONLINE 

READ about Afghanistan's place in the world • *VIEW* an image of the Soviet invasion of Afghanistan

R Reading Skills

Determining Importance Have students read the paragraph and consider the "ethnic differences" of people in Afghanistan. Tell students to consider how a diverse population can have both positive and negative impacts on the region. **Ask:** **Why is it difficult for Afghanistan to maintain a national identity?** *(The country is made up of many local tribes, to which many people identify more closely than to their national identity.)* **Verbal/Linguistic**

T Technology Skills

Researching Have students research to identify specific examples of government corruption in Afghanistan and what, if anything, is being done to remedy the situation. Challenge students to investigate the international efforts to provide aid to the region and what the success rate has been. Tell students to identify reasons that certain relief efforts have had more success than others. Provide an opportunity for students to present their findings to the class, inviting them to enhance their presentations with visual displays. **BL** **Interpersonal, Logical/Mathematical**

CLOSE & REFLECT

Understanding Relationships Have students review the text in each column. Have students write a paragraph that correlates the events in the United States on September 11, 2001, with the ongoing conflicts in Afghanistan today.

IMAGE

Soviet Invasion of Afghanistan

Outlining Use this interactive image of the Soviet invasion of Afghanistan to introduce students to the struggles the people of Afghanistan face to follow their traditional beliefs. Explain to students that Afghanistan has long been viewed as the "crossroads of Central Asia"; however, government stability has been faced with many challenges. As they view the interactive image, have students take notes on the information that is presented. Afterward, have them organize their notes into an outline, using two main section heads—*External forces* and *Internal forces*. Tell students to leave room to add details to their outlines as they continue to gather more information about Afghanistan in this chapter. **ELL** **Verbal/Linguistic**

ANSWERS, p. 453

Why Geography Matters

1. Many people identify more strongly with their tribal identity than with a national identity, making it difficult for a leader to unify people to work towards common goals.
2. Afghanistan has been invaded so frequently because it is located on trade routes that link East Asia, South Asia, Southwest Asia, and Europe. Other countries want access to these routes.
3. Afghanistan has opportunities for economic development given its reserves of oil, natural gas, gold, silver, and gems. However, it faces challenges due to continuing conflict hampering efforts to extract resources and develop infrastructure.

ENGAGE

C1 Critical Thinking Skills

Considering Advantages and Disadvantages Before students begin the lesson, have them consider how different landforms and waterways might affect where people settle and how they make a living. Display a map of Central Asia and challenge students to identify features such as major waterways, mountain ranges, and other landforms. Guide a discussion about the advantages and disadvantages of living in this region. **Visual/Spatial**

TEACH & ASSESS

C2 Critical Thinking Skills

Comparing Have students read about the formation of Central Asia's cultures. **Ask: What do the countries in Central Asia have in common?** *(Geographically, all the countries in the subregion, except Georgia, are landlocked. Historically, every country in the region, except for Afghanistan, was once a part of the Soviet Union and gained their independence in the 1990s.)*

V Visual Skills

Creating Diagrams Display a world map that includes the physical geography of Central Asia. To help students visualize the two sections of the region, have them create a diagram or chart labeled *Eastern* and *Western.* Have students use the information in the text to complete their diagrams. **Ask: Which countries make up Central Asia's eastern section?** *(Georgia, Armenia, and Azerbaijan)* As you discuss countries that comprise the western section, clarify pronunciation of the country names. Encourage students to continue filling in their diagrams with details about each country as they work through this lesson. **AL Visual/Spatial**

ANSWERS, p. 454

TAKING NOTES: Landforms—Caucasus Mountains composed of two ranges, the Greater and Lesser Caucasus; Tian Shan mountain range; Altay Shan mountain range; Pamirs; Hindu Kush; Fergana Valley basin; Kara-Kum and Kyzyl Kum; **Water Systems**—Caspian Sea; Lake Balkhash; Aral Sea; Amu Dar'ya and Syr Dar'ya Rivers; **Climate**—mainly dry, Caucasus area wetter; Kara-Kum and Kyzyl Kum deserts have sparse vegetation; Steppes border desert areas across Kazakhstan; areas along southern Caspian Sea have Mediterranean climate; Caucasus region to the north has semi-arid climate; Caucasus region to the south has humid subtropical climate; higher latitude areas of Caucasus Mountains and eastern portion of subregion have highland climate that is wetter and colder; **Resources**—oil and natural gas; Kazakhstan: uranium, copper, zinc, and iron ore; Uzbekistan: gold; Kyrgyzstan: gold; Tajikistan: gold, silver, tungsten, and uranium; Georgia: manganese, copper, gold, agricultural products, and hydroelectricity

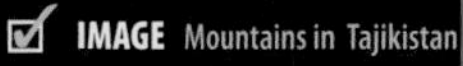

networks
There's More Online!

- **IMAGE** Mountains in Tajikistan
- **IMAGE** Resort on Caspian Sea
- **IMAGE** Herding in Armenia
- **IMAGE** Farming in Afghanistan
- **INTERACTIVE SELF-CHECK QUIZ**
- **VIDEO** Physical Geography of Central Asia

C1

LESSON 1
Physical Geography of Central Asia

ESSENTIAL QUESTION • *How do physical systems and human systems shape a place?*

Reading **HELP**DESK

Academic Vocabulary (Tier Two Words)
- **unique**
- **reverse**

Content Vocabulary (Tier Three Words)
- **steppe**
- **cereal**

TAKING NOTES: ***Key Ideas and Details***

IDENTIFYING As you read about the physical geography of Central Asia, use a graphic organizer like the one below to identify major features of the subregion.

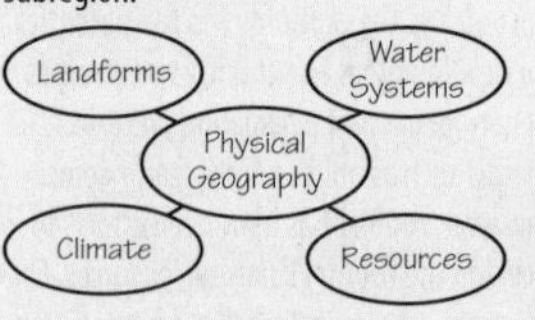

IT MATTERS BECAUSE

Central Asia has long been home to varied peoples. It has also served as the location of trade routes connecting Asia and Europe. For thousands of years, the people of this subregion have carved a life from a rugged land of mountains, deserts, and grasslands.

Landforms

GUIDING QUESTION *What are the major landforms of Central Asia?*

C2 Central Asia stretches from the Black Sea to China. It is bounded on the north by Russia, on the east by China and Pakistan, and on the south by Iran and Turkey. It is a distinct subregion defined by its physical and human geography. The land is challenging, marked mainly by highlands, a dry climate, and vast expanses of desert. All the countries of the subregion, except Georgia, are landlocked, meaning they have no access to the sea. The many cultures of the subregion share some **unique**, or distinctive, characteristics. They have been formed by the ethnic traditions and ways of life of the people and largely by Islam. All the countries in Central Asia, except Afghanistan, have something of a common history as well. They were part of the Soviet Union, gaining their independence in the 1990s.

V Central Asia can be divided into two sections. The western section, sometimes called the Caucasus, lies between the Black Sea and the Caspian Sea. It consists of the three small countries of Georgia, Armenia, and Azerbaijan. The eastern section, reaching from the eastern shores of the Caspian Sea to China and Pakistan, includes the six "stans": Kazakhstan, Uzbekistan, Turkmenistan, Kyrgyzstan, Tajikistan, and Afghanistan. The suffix *-stan* is an ancient Persian word that means "land of" or "place of." In most of these countries, the first part of the name identifies the major ethnic group living there.

The western section gets its name from the Caucasus Mountains, which straddle the area between the Black Sea and Caspian Sea. The mountains actually consist of two ranges. The higher peaks, called the

networks *Online Teaching Options*

INTERACTIVE BELLRINGER

Central Asia's Water Tower

Analyzing Visuals This image of the Tian Shan will help students become familiar with the landform of Central Asia and to identify the region's climates. Students will answer questions about how climate affects the water supply, which affects human activity in Central Asia. Have students form small groups. Ask them to discuss each question and agree on the answer to each question. Then ask groups to share their answers in a class discussion.

BL Interpersonal, Visual/Spatial

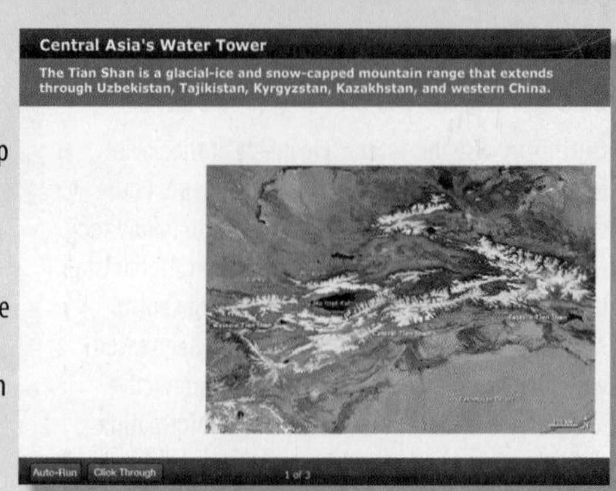

Central Asia's Water Tower
The Tian Shan is a glacial-ice and snow-capped mountain range that extends through Uzbekistan, Tajikistan, Kyrgyzstan, Kazakhstan, and western China.
Auto-Run
Click Through
1 of 3

Greater Caucasus, are to the north. They include Mount Shkhara, in Georgia. At 17,063 feet (5,201 m), it is the third-highest peak in the Caucasus. The lower mountain range, the Lesser Caucasus, is to the south.

The Central Asian countries have several high mountain ranges. Like the Caucasus, they were formed and continue to rise because of the collision of tectonic plates. The eastern ranges include the high Tian Shan of Kazakhstan and Kyrgyzstan; the Altay Shan, which run through those countries and Tajikistan; the Pamirs of Tajikistan; and the Hindu Kush of Afghanistan. Some of the peaks in these chains, like Nowshak in the Hindu Kush, soar over 24,000 feet (7,315 m) above sea level. These mountains dominate the eastern part of the subregion. They are separated by high plateaus and basins. Some of these basins, like the Fergana Valley of eastern Uzbekistan, have water and fertile soil. The Fergana, which covers an area about the size of Massachusetts, is thickly settled and marked by farms. Other basins are vast, dune-covered *kums* (KOOMZ), or deserts.

While the eastern part of the subregion has mountains that soar miles high, the western part slopes downward. The Turan Plain, around the Aral Sea, is only 200 to 300 feet (61 to 91 m) above sea level. The Caspian Depression, on the north shore of the Caspian Sea in southwestern Kazakhstan, is below sea level.

The Kara-Kum, or black-sand desert, covers most of Turkmenistan. The Kyzyl Kum, or red-sand desert, blankets the western half of Uzbekistan. These deserts are each about the size of Arizona. The deserts are sparsely settled. Afghanistan has a fertile plateau to the north of the Hindu Kush and a dry plateau to the south.

The Caucasus section is dominated by the Caucasus Mountains. Small patches of lowland plains lie along the shores of the Black and Caspian Seas. The mountains are flanked north and south by foothills and divided by valleys.

Tectonic activity built the mountains of this subregion. As is typical along plate boundaries, earthquakes frequently strike here. Afghanistan, surrounded by active plate boundaries, has an estimated 500 significant earthquakes a year. Tajikistan averages a major destructive quake every 10 or 15 years. A 1948 earthquake in Turkmenistan destroyed the capital city of Ashkhabad and killed about 176,000 people. Forty years later, a quake shook Armenia and caused such damage that its manufacturing capacity fell by 25 percent. T

READING PROGRESS CHECK

Explaining How do the landforms of Central Asia affect where people live?

Analyzing PRIMARY SOURCES (CCSS)

Ancient Geography Text

"In proceeding from the [Caspian] Sea towards the east, on the right hand are the mountains . . . extending as far as India. They . . . stretch to this part from the west in a continuous line, bearing different names in different places." R

—Strabo from *Geography,* Book XI, Chapter 8, C.A.D. 21

DBQ ***MAKING CONNECTIONS*** Through what present-day countries would you pass if following the route through Central Asia as described by this ancient geographer?
CCSS.RS.9–10.1

unique distinctive

Fertile areas of Central Asia are dwarfed by the arid deserts and high, rocky mountains.

◀ CRITICAL THINKING

1. ***Analyzing Visuals*** Do you think this is the Kara-Kum or the Kyzyl Kum? Why do you think so?
2. ***Hypothesizing*** What challenges might this landscape pose to the people of the subregion?

CHAPTER 19, Lesson 1

Physical Geography of Central Asia

R Reading Skills

Examining Primary Sources Have students work with a partner to review the *Ancient Geography Text,* an excerpt from Strabo's *Geography.* Ask partners to collaborate to create a picture of the region Strabo describes. Then relate to students the information in the *Content Background Knowledge* below. **Ask:** **How might a physical geographer's writings differ from those of a historian?** *(Possible answer: A physical geographer would likely pay more attention to accurate distances on maps, climate zones, and so on, whereas a historian would be more interested in describing a region's culture and history.)* **Verbal/Linguistic**

Content Background Knowledge

Strabo Greek historian Strabo was born about 64 B.C. and died after A.D. 21. In *Geography,* Strabo relates the history and geography of the Greeks and Romans during the reign of the Roman emperor Augustus. His first major work, *Historical Sketches,* provides a history of the world from 145 B.C. During the last years of his life, Strabo began writing *Geographical Sketches,* which historians believe he wrote after a visit to Egypt. Strabo stated that his writings were meant to provide information about the natural resources and customs of various countries, not to serve as scientific or mathematic descriptions.

T Technology Skills

Researching Have students read the paragraph on tectonic activity in the Central Asian region. Then have students work in pairs to use the Internet to research earthquakes in this area. Student pairs should develop detailed time lines that show major earthquakes and their impact. Students should then write a letter from the perspective of a resident of the region describing what is being done or what needs to be done to decrease the damage and loss of life from future earthquakes.
BL **Logical/Mathematical, Verbal/Linguistic**

INTERACTIVE GRAPHIC ORGANIZER

Physical Geography of Central Asia

Classifying Students can use this interactive graphic organizer to help them classify the many landforms and waterways that make up Central Asia. Ask students to provide the names of mountains, valleys, seas, and deserts as they read. Once the graphic organizers are completed, have students share their graphic organizers in small groups to ensure that each student has correctly classified the various parts of Central Asia.
ELL **AL** **Verbal/Linguistic, Visual/Spatial**

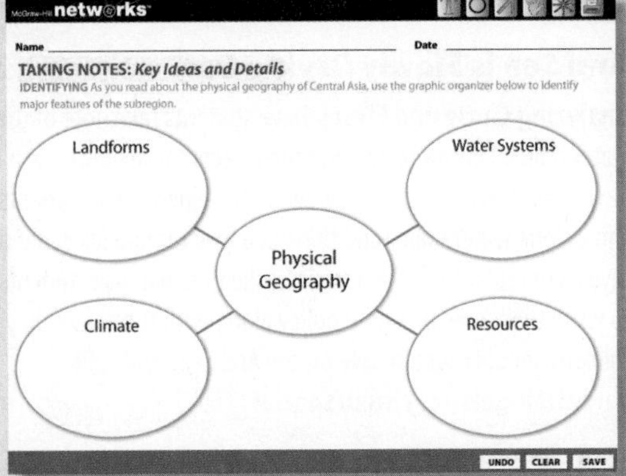

ANSWERS, p. 455

READING PROGRESS CHECK People live where there is fertile soil and water, such as in the Fergana Valley. The deserts of Kara-Kum and Kyzyl Kum are sparsely populated.

DBQ Turkmenistan, Afghanistan, Pakistan, and India

CRITICAL THINKING

1. This is the Kyzyl Kum because of the mountains and lack of black sand.
2. Student answers may vary but should include a lack of water for drinking and agriculture as well as sparse vegetation for livestock.

T Technology Skills

Considering Advantages and Disadvantages Have students read the first paragraph and then look at the image at the top of the page. Display a map of the region that includes the Caspian Sea. **Ask:** **What countries border the Caspian Sea and where are they in relationship to the sea?** *(Kazakhstan to the northeast, Turkmenistan to the southeast, Iran to the south, Azerbaijan to the southwest, and Russia to the northwest)* Organize students into three groups and assign each group one of the three countries in Central Asia that borders the Caspian Sea. Have groups use information from the text and from Internet or library resources to research the advantages and disadvantages of their assigned country's location. Have students consider the natural resources in the region and the issues related to the development and transportation of those resources. Have students create a map, using colors and symbols to show the location of the resources in their assigned country. Have groups present their maps to the class. Use the presentations to guide a class discussion about the advantages and disadvantages for these Central Asian countries. **Visual/Spatial**

W Writing Skills

Informative/Explanatory After students read the paragraph, discuss the Aral Sea with students and how it contrasts with the Caspian Sea. Tell students to write a paragraph in which they describe the differences between the two bodies of water. Students may wish to conduct additional research to support their essays. Call on volunteers to read their paragraphs to the class. Discuss how water supply issues present a problem for people who live in regions that border the Aral Sea. **I**
AL **Verbal/Linguistic**

Resorts, such as this one in Baku, Azerbaijan, dot some parts of the coast of the Caspian Sea, where people go to vacation.

▲ CRITICAL THINKING

1. ***Identifying*** Which countries in the subregion border on the Caspian Sea?
2. ***Summarizing*** What economic benefits does the Caspian Sea provide?

reverse the opposite

Water Systems

GUIDING QUESTION *What water features are important to the people of Central Asia?*

Central Asia is home to a large inland sea, the Caspian Sea, and a large lake, Lake Balkhash. The Caspian is the world's largest inland sea. Thousands of years ago it was connected to the Black Sea and, through it, to the Mediterranean. When the climate is warmer and precipitation is low, the Caspian Sea loses more water from evaporation than it gains from rivers emptying into it. In cooler, rainier times, the **reverse**, or opposite, is true.

T Three countries from the subregion, plus Russia and Iran, border the Caspian Sea. Sturgeon fishing has long been an important industry. The sturgeon's eggs are eaten as caviar, an expensive delicacy. In recent years, oil and natural gas found under the Caspian Sea have become very important. Along some coastal areas of the sea are beaches and resort hotels.

W East of the Caspian Sea is the Aral Sea. Until the 1960s, it was one of the world's largest inland seas. Today the sea is several small, shallow, disconnected bodies of water separated by dry land. This drying of the Aral Sea began in the 1960s when water from the main tributary was diverted to irrigate fields. This diminished the water supply to the Aral Sea. Also, the sea sits in a hot, dry region where high temperatures evaporate the water faster than rainfall replaces it.

Similar problems have hurt Lake Balkhash, in eastern Kazakhstan. The Ile River provided most of the lake's water. When the river was dammed, the lake's water level began to drop. The water also grew more saline, or salty.

The subregion's main rivers are the Amu Dar'ya and Syr Dar'ya. Both form in the subregion's center, fed by mountain rivers. Both rivers flow into the Aral Sea. Turkmenistan's Karakum Canal connects the Amu Dar'ya to the Caspian Sea.

☑ READING PROGRESS CHECK

Identifying Cause and Effect How have humans affected the water systems of Central Asia?

networks Online Teaching Options

VIDEO

Aral Sea Is Slowly Drying Out

Analyzing Cause and Effect Have students take note of the water policies in this region and the effects these policies are having on the Aral Sea. After viewing the video, have students choose one water policy and think of a way that policy could be revised or replaced to the benefit of the Aral Sea. Ask students to write their new or revised policy along with the effect they think their policy would have on the Aral Sea. **AL** **BL**
Verbal/Linguistic, Visual/Spatial

ANSWERS, p. 456

☑ READING PROGRESS CHECK Humans have used the water systems for irrigation of crops, causing the water levels to drop, become more saline, and dry up in places.

CRITICAL THINKING

1. Kazakhstan, Turkmenistan, and Azerbaijan border the Caspian Sea.
2. Tourism, the sturgeon fishing industry including caviar, and oil and natural gas extraction all boost the economies of countries around the Caspian Sea.

Climate, Biomes, and Resources

V

GUIDING QUESTION *How does the climate affect human activity in Central Asia?*

Central Asia sits in the midst of continental Asia. It is far from any major oceans. As a result, the subregion has mainly dry climates, although the Caucasus area is generally wetter. The subregion's sparse scrub vegetation reflects this dryness.

While vegetation in the Kara-Kum and Kyzyl Kum deserts is sparse, these deserts are not completely desolate. Scrub grasses can grow in some areas. For centuries, the people of the region have lived there by practicing pastoralism, or the raising of livestock. The people drive herds of sheep, horses, camels, and cattle to graze on brush. Karakul sheep provide milk, meat, wool, and pelts. The wool of the Karakul sheep is used to weave carpets common to the region. The pelts of newborn sheep, often referred to as Persian lamb, are used for clothing.

Some farming is carried out on oases. Oases are areas where underground water naturally comes to the surface. Farming also takes place where irrigation has supplied water to the area, expanding the amount of arable land.

Steppes border desert regions across eastern Kazakhstan. **Steppes** form the wide, grassy plains of Central Asia. Precipitation in this semi-arid climate region usually averages from 8 to 12 inches (20 to 30 cm) annually. This amount is enough to support shrubs and short grasses, providing pasturage for sheep, horses, goats, and camels. Forests are rare in Central Asia. For example, only 3 percent of Kazakhstan's land is wooded. Small forests dot the islands of the Amu Dar'ya and on some of the foothills of the region's mountains. Temperatures are warm in summer and cold in winter. Temperatures are even hotter in Uzbekistan.

Because the soil is fertile, some parts of the steppe have been turned over to growing crops. Much of this farmed area is watered by irrigation. The major crops are **cereals**—grains like barley, oats, or wheat grown for food. Inhabitants also grow a great deal of cotton on the irrigated land of the steppes. Nomads use the steppes to graze their herds. In spring and summer, nomads lead their sheep and goats up into the mountains, where grasses grow in that season and where temperatures are cooler than in the lowlands.

Central Asia also has other climate zones. Areas on the shores of the southern part of the Caspian Sea have a Mediterranean climate. The Caucasus region has a semi-arid climate to the north of the mountains and a humid subtropical climate to the south. Although it is a small area, the Caucasus has great variation in climate. Western Georgia, on the shores of the Black Sea, receives from 40 to

steppe wide, grassy plains of Eurasia; also, similar semi-arid grassy areas elsewhere

cereal any grain like barley, oats, or wheat that is grown for food

People in Central Asia have adapted their agricultural practices to the climate and biomes where they live.

▼ CRITICAL THINKING

1. ***Explaining*** What seasonal pattern of movement do the subregion's pastoral nomads follow?
2. ***Hypothesizing*** Why can farmers of the Caucasus grow fruits and vegetables more easily than people in the rest of Central Asia?

C

(l)Kim Karpeles/Alamy; (c)Mark/National Geographic Society/Corbis; (r)Andrew Peacock/Lonely Planet Images/Getty Images

CHAPTER 19, Lesson 1
Physical Geography of Central Asia

V Visual Skills

Transferring Information Ask a volunteer to read aloud the Guiding Question. Tell students they will work in small groups to use the information from this section about Central Asia's climates, biomes, and resources to create a diagram or annotated map that shows how the climate impacts human activity. After groups have completed their visual displays, ask volunteers to present their displays to the class. Discuss the unique challenges of living in certain regions of Central Asia. **Ask: How is land farmed in desert regions of Central Asia?** *(Some farming is done in oases where underground water comes to the surface. Other desert regions are bordered by steppes, which receive enough rainfall to support grazing grass for sheep, horses, goats, and camels; or some parts of steppes are adequate for growing crops.)* **ELL Visual/Spatial, Interpersonal**

C Critical Thinking Skills

Analyzing Visuals Have students analyze the photographs on this page and consider the similarities and differences of the human activity shown in the images. **Ask: How does the land shown in the image on the far left differ from the land shown in the middle photograph?** *(Possible answers: The land shown on the far left is not as lush or green as the land shown in the middle image, which appears to be rich farmland.)* **What can you infer about the climate based on these images?** *(Possible answers: The climate of the grazing land on the left is likely semi-arid, which receives enough rainfall to support shrubs and short grasses that are adequate for grazing sheep. The climate of the image in the middle appears to have higher rainfall so that land can be irrigated.)* **What do the women in the image on the far right appear to be doing?** *(They are weaving carpets or tapestry out of sheep's wool.)* **Visual/Spatial**

SLIDE SHOW

Herding in Central Asia

Describing This slide show highlights the role of the physical landscape of Central Asia in the practice of herding in the region. Review with students what types of areas are necessary to practice herding. Have students note the reasons why herding is vital to the economy of Central Asia. Ask them to consider the non-monetary benefits of herding to the herders and their families. After viewing the slide show, lead a class discussion describing the livelihood of herding in Central Asia.
AL Verbal/Linguistic

ANSWERS, p. 457

CRITICAL THINKING

1. Nomads lead their livestock into the mountains during the spring and summer because it is cooler and more grasses grow there during these seasons.
2. Parts of the Caucasus have more rainfall and milder weather than the rest of Central Asia, making it possible to grow fruits and vegetables.

Physical Geography of Central Asia

C Critical Thinking Skills

Comparing and Contrasting Tell students to suppose that they have been hired by a group of investors who are looking for a good place to invest in new manufacturing companies. Using the information in this section, students should work in small groups to develop charts or visuals depicting the resources and other benefits available in each country. The visuals will support their recommendation as to which country the investors should consider. Students may wish to do additional research on existing manufacturing and trade in the region. Ask volunteers to present their proposals to the class. Have students in the audience act as members of the investment firm by asking questions of each presenter. BL **Verbal/Linguistic**

CLOSE & REFLECT

Assessing Tell students to review what they have learned about the landforms, water systems, climates, biomes, and resources of countries in Central Asia. Have students evaluate how one or more of these aspects of Central Asia's physical geography has both helped and presented challenges to the people who live in the subregion. Guide a discussion about the relationship between Central Asia's natural resources and the way people live there.

ANSWERS, p. 458

READING PROGRESS CHECK The main resource of Central Asia is oil.

100 inches of rain (102 to 254 cm) a year. Winds over the Black Sea provide much of this moisture. Eastern Georgia, on the other hand, receives only 16 to 28 inches (41 to 71 cm) of rain on average. Winters in the mountain foothills are mild. This climate allows the people of the Caucasus to grow different crops than people can on the steppes of the region. Many farmers here raise fruits and vegetables. Tea and citrus fruits are commercially important crops. The greater rainfall and milder weather in Georgia also supports forests of deciduous trees such as oak and beech on the mountainsides.

Higher areas, like the Caucasus Mountains and the mountains of the eastern subregion, have highland climates. It is generally wetter and colder than in other parts of the subregion. The highland climate varies, however, with elevation and exposure to wind and sun.

C

The major resources in the subregion are oil and natural gas. The largest deposits are found under the Caspian Sea, benefiting Kazakhstan, Turkmenistan, and Azerbaijan. Pipelines carry the oil to other parts of the world, allowing these landlocked nations to export these valuable resources.

Kazakhstan has the most abundant resources of the Central Asian countries. In addition to oil and gas, it has uranium, copper, zinc, iron ore, and other metals. Oil and oil products generate three-fifths of Kazakhstan's export earnings. Metals account for nearly another fifth. According to one estimate, Turkmenistan has the fourth-largest natural gas reserves in the world. While all those reserves have not yet been tapped, natural gas is a major export. In addition, Uzbekistan has the world's fourth-largest gold reserves; gold and natural gas are major exports.

Kyrgyzstan also has large supplies of gold, its number one export. Tajikistan also has gold as well as silver, tungsten, and uranium. These resources are not fully developed, however. None of them figures as a major export of Tajikistan. Afghanistan possesses natural resources, but few have been developed.

Among the Caucasus countries, Azerbaijan has the largest oil and gas resources. Its economy relies heavily on oil and oil products, which form 90 percent of its exports.

Georgia has no oil, but is taking advantage of its location. It has benefited by allowing pipelines to be built through it so that Caspian Sea oil can be transported to Europe. Georgia relies on hydroelectric power for electricity. The Georgians mine the metals manganese, copper, and gold. With its favorable climate, Georgia also grows fruits, vegetables, and other agricultural products. Tiny Armenia has few natural resources.

READING PROGRESS CHECK

Synthesizing What is the main natural resource of Central Asia?

LESSON 1 REVIEW

Reviewing Vocabulary (Tier Three Words)

1. ***Explaining*** Write a paragraph explaining the connection between the steppes and cereals in Central Asia. RI.9–10.1

Using Your Notes

2. ***Summarizing*** Use your graphic organizer on the physical systems of Central Asia to write a paragraph explaining how landforms and climates in the subregion are related.

Answering the Guiding Questions

3. ***Identifying*** What are the major landforms of Central Asia?
4. ***Identifying*** What water features are important to the people of Central Asia?
5. ***Describing*** How does the climate affect human activity in Central Asia?

Writing Activity

6. ***Informative/Explanatory*** In a paragraph, discuss how the landforms and climates of Central Asia shape people's lives in the subregion. RH.9–10.2

LESSON 1 REVIEW ANSWERS

Reviewing Vocabulary

1. Paragraphs should describe how the steppes have fertile soil that with the help of irrigation is used to grow barley, oats, and wheat, which are collectively referred to as cereals.

Using Your Notes

2. Students' paragraphs should describe how areas around the Caspian Sea have a Mediterranean climate, the area north of the Caucasus has a semi-arid climate, and areas south of the Caucasus have a humid subtropical climate, higher latitudes in the Caucasus and mountains in the east have a highland climate that is wetter and colder than the rest of the subregion.

Answering the Guiding Questions

3. The major landforms of Central Asia are the mountains including the Caucasus, deserts such as the Kara-Kum and Kyzyl Kum, and basins such as the Fergana Valley.
4. The Caspian Sea, Lake Balkhash, the Aral Sea, and the rivers of Amu Dar'ya and Syr Dar'ya are important to the people of Central Asia for irrigation, economic activities, and consumption.
5. The subregion has mainly dry climates. While few people live in the deserts, sparse vegetation grows there, which allows for some raising of livestock largely by pastoral nomads who must travel with the seasons to find food and water for livestock. Agriculture is supported only in oases or in places with irrigation except for areas with a Mediterranean climate along the Caspian Sea or in the Caucasus region.

Writing Activity

6. Paragraphs will vary but should be strongly supported with information from the lesson. Paragraphs should explain how mountains, deserts, water resources, and fertile soil help determine where people will live and how they make a living. Students could also include details on the seasonal migration of nomads in their paragraphs.

networks

There's More Online!

- **IMAGE** Rug Weaving
- **MAP** Ethnic Groups in Central Asia
- **IMAGE** Potato Farming
- **IMAGE** Oil in Azerbaijan
- **TIME LINE** A Significant Crossroads
- **INTERACTIVE SELF-CHECK QUIZ**
- **VIDEO** Human Geography of Central Asia

R

LESSON 2
Human Geography of Central Asia

ESSENTIAL QUESTION • *How do physical systems and human systems shape a place?*

Reading **HELP**DESK 

Academic Vocabulary (Tier Two Words)
- **restrain**
- **virtually**

Content Vocabulary (Tier Three Words)
- **mujahideen**
- **Taliban**
- **exclave**
- **enclave**

TAKING NOTES: ***Key Ideas and Details***

ORGANIZING As you read about the human geography of Central Asia, use a graphic organizer like the one below to identify examples of the influence of native and foreign cultures on the subregion.

	Influences
History	
People/Culture	
Economy	

It Matters Because

Over the centuries Central Asia has been a crossroads of cultures and empires, as well as a home for people seeking independence. While other countries have ruled the subregion, the diverse peoples of Central Asia have created their own distinct cultures. C

History and Government

GUIDING QUESTION *How have the countries of Central Asia been governed over the centuries?*

The peoples of Central Asia have a long and very old history. Some established their own countries in ancient times. Other peoples were herders and moved often in search of pasture. The subregion has been conquered many times by various empires. With some countries recently independent, the countries of Central Asia are working to find economic and political stability.

Kingdoms and Conquests

Both Georgia and Armenia formed kingdoms more than 2,000 years ago. Both places were Christianized under the Roman Empire in the A.D. fourth century. They were the first countries in the world to declare Christianity as the national religion. The Armenian and Georgian churches remain important today. V

The peoples in the eastern part of the subregion lived largely as nomads in ancient times. Beginning about 100 B.C., the Silk Road was established for trade between Europe and China. The Silk Road crossed Central Asia. Locations along the road, such as Samarqand in present-day Uzbekistan, became rich trading centers.

The Silk Road made Central Asia a crossroads, and because Central Asia is surrounded by powerful neighbors, it has come under the control of various empires. In the seventh through the ninth centuries, Arabs conquered such areas as Azerbaijan, Turkmenistan, Uzbekistan, and Tajikistan. They brought Islam to the region. That religion later spread to other parts of the subregion. Armenia and Georgia remained Christian in a vast area dominated by Islam.

ENGAGE

R Reading Skills

Previewing Have students skim through the lesson to preview the images and headings. Tell students to consider what they already know about the history and government of countries in Central Asia and how this history has affected the human geography of the subregion. Then have students write three questions they have about the region's history and its people. As students work through the lesson, have them return to their questions to see if they can answer them.

TEACH & ASSESS

C Critical Thinking Skills

Making Predictions Have student partners use clues from the text to brainstorm and write a list of predictions about the human geography of Central Asia. For example, students might infer from the phrase *seeking independence* that some countries in the region have struggled to gain their independence. Guide them to consider how culture plays a part in the region's history. Encourage students to return to their predictions to check for accuracy after they read this lesson. AL **Visual/Spatial**

V Visual Skills

Creating Diagrams Have students read about the development of kingdoms and trade in Central Asia. Have student pairs create a web diagram with the name of each country in a circle. Tell them to add key facts that led to each country's formation in surrounding circles. ELL **Visual/Spatial**

INTERACTIVE BELLRINGER

Economic Productivity in Central Asia

Drawing Conclusions and Making Generalizations Use the introductory text and table to introduce students to the economic productivity in Central Asia countries. Ask students to discuss what life might be like for people living in countries in which the average income is just a few thousand dollars a year. Have students work in pairs to answer the questions on the bellringer activity. Then have a class discussion in which students share their answers. Compile a list of responses to discuss. AL **Logical/Mathematical, Verbal/Linguistic**

Economic Productivity in Central Asia

The countries of Central Asia have little industrialization, relying primarily on natural resources and agriculture for exports despite the lack of arable land.

Productivity in Central Asia

Country	Per Capita GDP	Percentage of Population Below Poverty Line	Percentage of Workforce in Agriculture
United States	$48,300	15.1%	1.2%
Kazakhstan	$13,000	8.2%	25.9%
Azerbaijan	$10,200	11.0%	38.3%
Turkmenistan	$7,800	30.0%	48.2%
Georgia	$5,500	9.7%	55.6%
Armenia	$5,400	35.8%	44.2%
Uzbekistan	$3,300	26.0%	44.0%
Kyrgyzstan	$2,400	33.7%	48.0%
Tajikistan	$2,100	46.7%	49.8%
Afghanistan	$1,000	36.0%	78.6%

Source: CIA World Factbook

Auto-Run Click Through 1 of 3

ANSWERS, p. 459

TAKING NOTES: History—Georgia and Armenia formed Christian kingdoms 2,000 years ago. The eastern portions were largely nomadic until the Silk Road; Arabs conquered areas bringing Islam; Genghis Khan conquered region in 1200s; Russian Empire took control in 1800s except for Afghanistan, which was held by British; **People/Culture**—people were traditionally farmers, herders, and nomadic; Urbanization is slow; Islam is major religion, except in Armenia and Georgia where Christianity is major religion; Most people speak a Turkic language, but Russian is official language in Kazakhstan and Kyrgyzstan. **Economy**—Countries are less developed, rely on agriculture and natural resources for exports. Uzbekistan produces silk, as a result of Silk Road. Kazakhstan has increased oil exports; Uzbekistan and Turkmenistan produce and export natural gas; Georgia has pipelines that export oil and gas; Countries that were part of Soviet Union have command economies and have not moved to market economy.

W Writing Skills

Narrative Have students write a journal entry from the perspective of a Mongol invader or someone living in one of the countries in the subregion around A.D. 1200. Encourage students to consider the Mongols' motivations for conquests and the perceptions a person might have about the conquests. Remind students to use descriptive details to convey former life in Mongolia or along the Silk Road. Invite volunteers to share their journal entries with the class. AL **Verbal/Linguistic, Intrapersonal**

R Reading Skills

Identifying Cause and Effect Have students read the paragraph and ask them to consider the Guiding Question: *How have the countries of Central Asia been governed over the centuries?* **Ask:** **What was the effect of expansion by the Russian Empire into Central Asia?** *(The Russian Empire first invaded Georgia and part of Azerbaijan and then conquered all other countries in the subregion except Afghanistan.)* **How did British forces impact conquests by the Russian Empire?** *(The British prevented Russia from seizing Afghanistan and advancing into South Asia.)* **What was the effect of the Communist revolution?** *(All of Central Asia, except Afghanistan, became republics within the Soviet Union.)* AL **Verbal/Linguistics**

C Critical Thinking Skills

Formulating Questions Have students work with a partner to formulate questions based on the dates and events on the time line. Tell students to take turns quizzing each other about Central Asia's history of different rulers. Students may wish to investigations further one or more of the conquerors. **Ask:** **Why have different rulers tried to control Central Asia throughout the region's history?** *(Central Asia's location is an important crossroads between the eastern and western regions.)* **Interpersonal**

ANSWERS, p. 460

CRITICAL THINKING

1. The Silk Road was a trade route between Europe and China.
2. The location of Central Asia has made it important to other regions as a trade route from east to west and has also made it an area of great conflict as many other countries have conquered and controlled areas for centuries.

W In the A.D. 1200s, Genghis Khan led Mongol forces—members of nomadic tribes that previously lived north of China—to conquer Central Asia. While tens of thousands of people died, the Mongols eventually established control over the region. The Mongol period revived trade and brought prosperity. Parts of the region benefited greatly from renewed Silk Road trade. Later, Mongol control weakened and ethnic groups in the region came to power. Georgia emerged as a new kingdom and gained power in the eleventh and twelfth centuries.

R Later, the Russian Empire expanded into Central Asia. It invaded Georgia and part of Azerbaijan in the early 1800s. Then it conquered all the countries in the eastern subregion except Afghanistan. The British, who held India and what is now Pakistan, prevented Russia from seizing Afghanistan and advancing into South Asia. After the Communist revolution in Russia in 1917, all of Central Asia, except Afghanistan, became Soviet Socialist Republics (SSRs) within the Soviet Union.

restrain to hold down or back; to limit

For several decades, Central Asia was under strict Soviet control. The Soviets tried to **restrain**, or hold down, the subregion's native cultures. At the same time, they improved literacy and standards of living. Georgia prospered. Kazakhstan saw both its industry and agriculture grow rapidly because of Soviet policies.

Independence and Conflict

virtually almost; nearly

The eight Soviet republics in the subregion gained independence at **virtually**, or almost, the same time the Soviet Union dissolved in 1991. While leaders in most of these countries said they would adopt democracy, they have not fully delivered on this promise. The leaders have generally ruled harshly, ignored human rights, and suppressed dissent. Elections are held, but the process of voting is questioned. Georgia has been hurt by the attempts of separatist groups to secede and form new countries. Tajikistan also has been troubled by ethnic conflict.

Starting in 2011, Armenia's government took steps to become more democratic. Kyrgyzstan, in 2011, held largely fair elections that produced the first democratic transfer of power in any of these countries. Still, dictatorial rule has maintained strong influences across the subregion.

TIME LINE

A Significant CROSSROADS

Over its long history, many rulers have tried to control Central Asia because its location made it an important crossroads between east and west.

C ▶ CRITICAL THINKING

1. ***Describing*** What was the Silk Road?
2. ***Analyzing*** How has the location of Central Asia affected its relationship with other regions?

300s B.C.

300s B.C. Alexander the Great conquers Central Asia.

1st Century B.C. Central Asia becomes a major crossroads due to the Silk Road.

A.D. 600s Arabs conquer Central Asia and convert its inhabitants to Islam.

1200s Genghis Khan conquers Central Asia, which becomes part of the Mongol Empire.

World History Archive/Alamy

networks Online Teaching Options

VIDEO

Trading Domes of Bukhara, Uzbekistan

Identifying Continuity and Change Use this video to further students' knowledge of trade, both past and present, in Central Asia. As they view Trading Domes of Bukhara, Uzbekistan, have students note how much the barter system has changed or stayed the same over the years in this region. When the video ends, ask students to make a simple chart identifying the similarities and differences between Central Asian trade hundreds of years ago and today. AL **Verbal/Linguistic**

In 1979 the Soviet Union invaded Afghanistan. That prompted Afghan freedom fighters known as the **mujahideen** to fight the Soviets. More than a million Afghans died before the Soviets left in 1989. Then the Islamic fundamentalist **Taliban** gained control of most of the country. The Taliban imposed an extremely strict interpretation of Islam on the people of Afghanistan.

That government also sheltered al-Qaeda, a terrorist group, and its leader, Osama bin Laden. Al-Qaeda claimed responsibility for the September 11, 2001, terrorist attacks on the United States. The United States demanded that the Taliban turn over bin Laden. When they refused, American and coalition forces entered Afghanistan and overthrew the Taliban-led government. A new Afghan government was formed after elections were held in 2009. Afghanistan still faces many challenges in ruling its territory and providing basic services for its people.

R

mujahideen Islamic guerrilla fighters

Taliban from Arabic for "seeker" or "student"; name of a fundamentalist Sunni Muslim group, active in Afghanistan, which controlled the Afghan government from 1996 to 2001

✓ READING PROGRESS CHECK

Explaining Why has Central Asia been conquered so often?

Population Patterns

GUIDING QUESTION *How have population patterns changed over time in Central Asia?*

The population of Central Asia is diverse and complex. Settlement patterns are strongly affected by the landforms and climates of the region. Many different ethnic groups live in the subregion. Though several countries are named for one particular group, most have a very complex mix of ethnic groups.

The countries of Central Asia have very different total populations. Afghanistan has the largest population, with more than 33 million people. Uzbekistan has under 30 million and Kazakhstan is under 17 million. The other five countries of the subregion all have fewer than 10 million. Due to low birthrates, the populations of Armenia and Georgia are shrinking and are expected to have smaller populations by 2025. In contrast, Afghanistan's population may more than double by 2050.

T

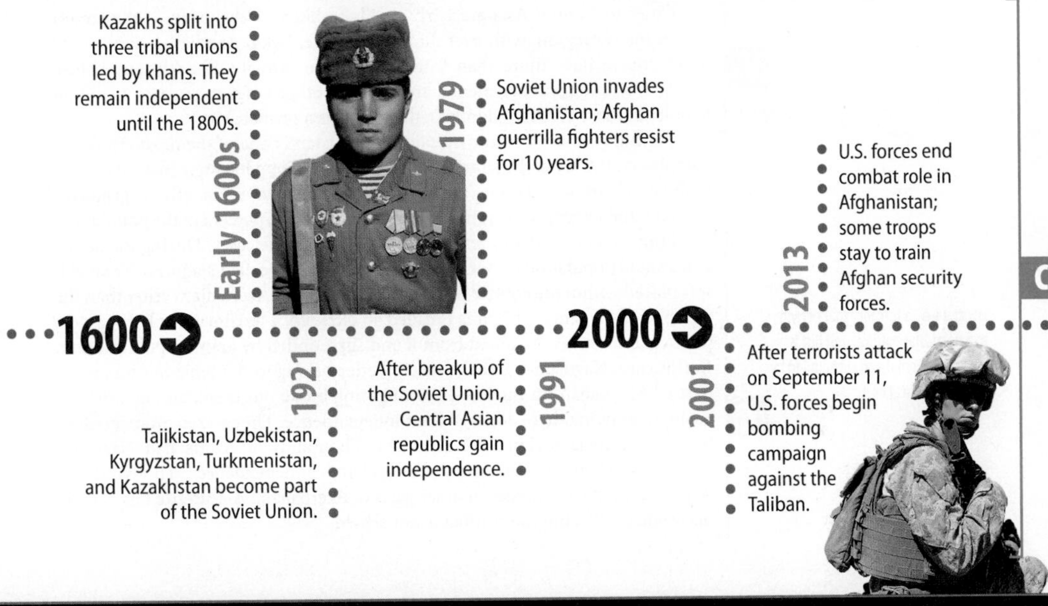

Early 1600s
Kazakhs split into three tribal unions led by khans. They remain independent until the 1800s.
1979
Soviet Union invades Afghanistan; Afghan guerrilla fighters resist for 10 years.
2013
U.S. forces end combat role in Afghanistan; some troops stay to train Afghan security forces.
1600
2000
1921
Tajikistan, Uzbekistan, Kyrgyzstan, Turkmenistan, and Kazakhstan become part of the Soviet Union.
1991
After breakup of the Soviet Union, Central Asian republics gain independence.
2001
After terrorists attack on September 11, U.S. forces begin bombing campaign against the Taliban.

C

CHAPTER 19, Lesson 2
Human Geography of Central Asia

R Reading Skills

Defining Have students note the definitions of the words *mujahideen, Taliban,* and *al-Qaeda.* Guide a discussion to help students understand the meaning of each word. **Ask:** **How did the 1979 Soviet invasion impact Afghanistan?** *(More than a million Afghans died over the course of the next ten years as a result of the Soviet invasion.)* **What is the difference between al-Qaeda and the Taliban?** *(al-Qaeda is a terrorist group once led by Osama bin Laden; the Taliban is a fundamentalist Sunni Muslim group that once controlled the Afghan government)* **ELL** **Verbal/Linguistic**

T Technology Skills

Changing Continuity of Groups Assign student groups a country in Central Asia. Have groups read the paragraph on populations and the time line below. Then students should research how the countries were impacted by invasions, by becoming part of the Soviet Union, and by the collapse of the Soviet Union in 1991. Students should conduct research to identify how the transition to independence impacted the countries' borders. Have students present their findings to the class. Discuss how invasions and quests for independence affected the region. **BL** **Verbal/Linguistic**

C Critical Thinking Skills

Time, Chronology, and Sequencing Have students work with the same partner with whom they performed the time line activity on the previous page to formulate questions based on the dates and events on the second half of the time line. Tell students to take turns quizzing each other on facts related to Central Asia's history between 1600 and 2013. **Ask:** **What caused U.S. forces to begin a bombing campaign against the Taliban in 2001?** *(Terrorists attacked the United States on September 11, 2001.)* **AL** **Visual/Spatial, Interpersonal**

INTERACTIVE WHITEBOARD ACTIVITY

Historical Events that Shaped Central Asia

Sequencing Information Students will create their own time line in this Interactive White Board Activity. Students will be presented with letters representing historical events that occurred in Central Asia. Have students drag the letters into the correct sequence on the time line. The completed time line will display significant Central Asian events over time. When the time line is finished, ask students to briefly state each historical event shown. **ELL** **AL** **Verbal/Linguistic, Visual/Spatial**

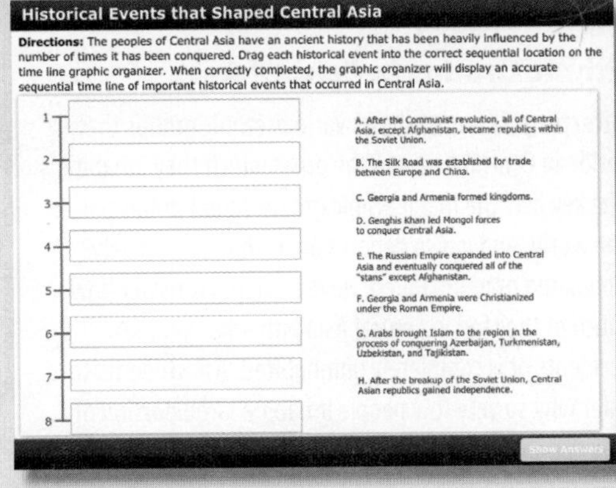

ANSWERS, p. 461

✓ READING PROGRESS CHECK Central Asia is surrounded by powerful neighbors who wanted access to the area because it is an important crossroad or trade route between east and west.

V1 Visual Skills

Analyzing Visuals Have students study the map with a partner. Reinforce students' knowledge by having pairs take turns asking questions based on the distribution of ethnic groups in the region shown. Suggest that students ask "more or less" or "higher or lower" questions to compare the ethnic groups. Also invite students to describe regions where ethnic groups are concentrated using cardinal directions. **Ask: Why might ethnic groups tend to cluster in Central Asia's northwestern and southeastern countries and only inhabit certain areas of more central countries? Explain.** *(Student answers should include responses about climate and physical features such as river valleys or mountains that encourage or deter settlements.)* **AL Visual/Spatial**

V2 Visual Skills

Creating Graphs Have students work with a partner to create a bar graph that shows the population of Central Asia's major cities. Have students conduct online research to include other cities in their graphs. Recommend that students visit specific websites, such as the CIA World Factbook, which lists ethnic groups and population figures for each country in the region. You may wish to provide students with examples of bar graphs. Tell students to include a summarizing statement about Central Asian cities and have pairs present their graphs to the class. **AL Visual/Spatial, Logical/Mathematical**

C Critical Thinking Skills

Drawing Inferences Discuss with students the reasons that the concentration and distribution of different ethnic groups across Central Asia has led to conflict. **Ask: How might an exclave be vulnerable to conflict?** *(Possible answer: Being surrounded by but separate from another political unit would make an exclave vulnerable because there could be issues with borders and territorial claims.)* **BL Logical/Mathematical**

ANSWERS, p. 462

GEOGRAPHY CONNECTION

1. Answers will vary but could include Kyrgyzstan exporting gold, Uzbekistan exporting uranium and gold, or Azerbaijan and Kazakhstan exporting natural gas and oil.
2. There is a significant Russian population due to the shared border with Russia in Kazakhstan and because of the control of the subregion, with the exception of Afghanistan, by the Russian Empire and the Soviet Union.

V1

GEOGRAPHY CONNECTION

The distribution of ethnic groups in Central Asia reflects its complex history.

1. ***PLACES AND REGIONS*** How does the ethnic diversity in the three Caucasus countries compare to that of the six countries in the east?
2. ***HUMAN SYSTEMS*** Why is there a significant Russian population in many countries of Central Asia?

Overall population density is generally low. However, population density per acre of arable land is high. Population density is strongly influenced by the land and climate of the subregion. Mountainous and desert areas are sparsely settled. River valleys are much more densely populated. That is especially true of the lower reaches of the Amu Dar'ya in Uzbekistan.

As the people of Central Asia traditionally lived by farming and herding, it is not a highly urbanized region. Armenia has the highest level of urbanization at about 64 percent. Azerbaijan, Georgia, Kazakhstan, and Uzbekistan are the only other countries in which more than half of the people live in urban areas. Afghanistan's rate of urbanization is the lowest. Fewer than 25 percent of Afghans live in cities.

V2 Cities in Central Asia are fairly small. Tashkent, Uzbekistan, is the largest city in the subregion, with over 2 million people. Baku, Azerbaijan, is the only other city to have more than 2 million people. Almaty, Kazakhstan; Tbilisi, Georgia; and Yerevan, Armenia, are the only other cities to surpass 1 million people. In most of these countries, the capital is a primate city.

Central Asia is an ethnic mosaic. Afghanistan is one of the most ethnically complex countries in the subregion, with no one group having a majority of the population. In Kazakhstan and Kyrgyzstan the two main ethnic groups—Kazakhs and Kyrgyz (or Kirghiz)—include less than 66 percent of the population.

exclave a territory that belongs to a particular political unit but is separated from it and surrounded by another political unit

C Ethnic complexity has resulted in conflict in some cases. During the Soviet era, a small population of Armenians living in an area called Nagorno-Karabakh was placed within the control of the Soviet republic of Azerbaijan rather than the republic of Armenia. This area is called an **exclave**, a territory that belongs to a political unit but is separated from it and surrounded by another political unit. In this case, Nagorno-Karabakh might better belong to Armenia but was made part of Azerbaijan. In the late 1980s, fighting broke out there, and in 1991 the Armenians living there declared their independence. They seized more territory to connect their region with Armenia. Thousands of Azeris fled Nagorno-Karabakh when Armenians there declared independence. Thousands of Armenians left their homes in other parts of Azerbaijan. A ceasefire has been in place since 1994, but the conflict is not settled.

462

networks Online Teaching Options

INTERACTIVE MAP

Ethnic Groups in Central Asia

Inferring This map shows various ethnic groups that reside in Central Asia and the areas which they inhabit. The key lists the major ethnic groups found in this part of the world, and it also denotes areas that are sparsely populated or uninhabited. Have students consider how much of the land in Central Asia either has very few residents or is completely uninhabited. Ask students to infer why so very few people inhabit a large portion of this region. **AL Verbal/Linguistic, Visual/Spatial**

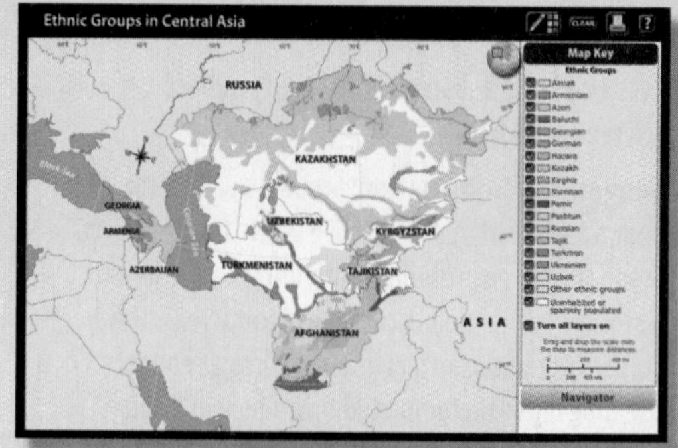

The Fergana Valley is one of Central Asia's most ethnically diverse areas. A patchwork of poorly defined and disputed borders, it includes several enclaves. An **enclave** is a territory surrounded by another political unit that it does not belong to. For example, the enclave of Sokh is controlled by Uzbekistan, entirely surrounded by Kyrgyzstan, and populated mostly by Tajiks, who are minorities in both Uzbekistan and Kyrgyzstan. These differences have led to several border clashes.

C

The conflicts in Nagorno-Karabakh and Sokh are not the only ones in the subregion that have resulted in thousands of displaced persons. These are people uprooted from their homes by conflict or fear and forced to live elsewhere. Two decades of fighting in Afghanistan have left more than 250,000 people displaced as refugees. Many rely on the help of the United Nations and other organizations to survive. Ethnic fighting in the south of Kyrgyzstan in 2010 forced some 300,000 people from their homes. Only about half have returned.

☑ READING PROGRESS CHECK

Drawing Conclusions How has ethnic conflict in Azerbaijan changed population patterns there?

Rug weaving is a traditional craft still practiced in Central Asia.

▲ CRITICAL THINKING

1. ***Speculating*** Do you think rug weaving is more likely to be done in rural or urban areas? Why?
2. ***Making Connections*** Which group of people in the subregion is most likely to weave, farmers or nomadic pastoralists? Why?

enclave a distinct territorial or cultural area that is within a foreign territory

Society and Culture Today

GUIDING QUESTION *What are some aspects of the cultures of the people of Central Asia?*

T

Most people in Central Asia speak one of the Turkic languages. Russian remains an official language in Kazakhstan and Kyrgyzstan and is still widely spoken in other countries. Georgia has a unique language and alphabet. Islam is the predominant religion throughout Central Asia, although Christianity is the majority religion in Armenia and Georgia. The Russian Orthodox faith is present mostly in Kazakhstan.

Education is universal across Central Asia, and in most countries students have 11 years of school. Literacy is at 98 percent or more except in Afghanistan, where it is less than 30 percent. The average schooling there is 9 years, and much less for females. Except for Georgia, health care spending is generally low. The rate of infant mortality—or death before a child's first birthday—is high in Afghanistan, and life expectancy is lower than elsewhere in the subregion.

Family and the Status of Women

Life in Central Asia today is characterized by a mix of traditional and modern features. People who live in rural areas tend to follow centuries-old ways of life. For instance, the Aimak people of Afghanistan live in yurts, a traditional form of housing made of fabric and skins stretched over wooden poles. Those living in cities are more likely to use cell phones and connect to the Internet. The Internet is available in many places, but use is highest in the more urban countries and those with more prosperous economies, such as Georgia and Kazakhstan.

Women's rights are a significant issue in some countries of the subregion. In Soviet times, the government mandated equality for women in education and opened career opportunities for them. After the republics gained independence, however, the shift to traditional Islamic practices resulted in women losing rights and opportunities in some of these countries. Women's situations in Afghanistan under the Taliban were worse. Women were prevented from getting an education and from working outside the home. The government that formed after the fall of the Taliban has reversed these policies, but traditions change slowly.

C Critical Thinking Skills

Theorizing Review with students how conflicts can impact people in different regions of Central Asia. **Ask:** **Why did the conflict in Nagorno-Karabakh and other places lead to the displacement of thousands of people?** *(Possible answer: During times of conflict and violence, people feared for their lives so they fled the region, hoping to keep their families safe.)* **Do you think the people who have fled their homes in Afghanistan or Kyrgyzstan are likely to return? Why or why not?** *(Possible answers: Yes, people want to return to their homeland, but probably not until they know it is safe. No, people will not return because their homes have likely been destroyed and they have nothing to go back to).* AL **Logical/Mathematical**

T Technology Skills

Critical Listening Ask student volunteers to share any knowledge they may have of the Russian language and have students listen to samples of spoken Russian. Then have students conduct research to locate audio excerpts of other languages spoken in different regions of Central Asia. Ask students to compare and contrast the languages with each other, Russian, and English. Discuss how language is important to cultural identity. Consider local examples of diverse ethnic groups as an example of how a language can create unity among people who speak it. BL **Auditory/Musical**

Making Connections

After students have read the paragraph on education and health care in Central Asia, ask them to think about how life is different than in the United States. Ask students to use the Internet to look up statistics about literacy, health care coverage, and infant mortality in the United States, Afghanistan, Georgia, and Kazakhstan. Have students compare these statistics for these four countries. Discuss how health and education may impact the lives of school-aged children in these countries.

INTERACTIVE IMAGE

Women Who Weave

Making Predictions Display the image of the woman weaving. Tell students that the apparatus she is using is called a loom. Ask students to note details about the photograph, such as the construction of the loom, how it is being operated by the woman, and the material that she is using to weave. Based on the information they have gathered from the photo, have students make predictions about what the woman may be producing (a rug, a piece of clothing, etc.). ELL **Visual/Spatial**

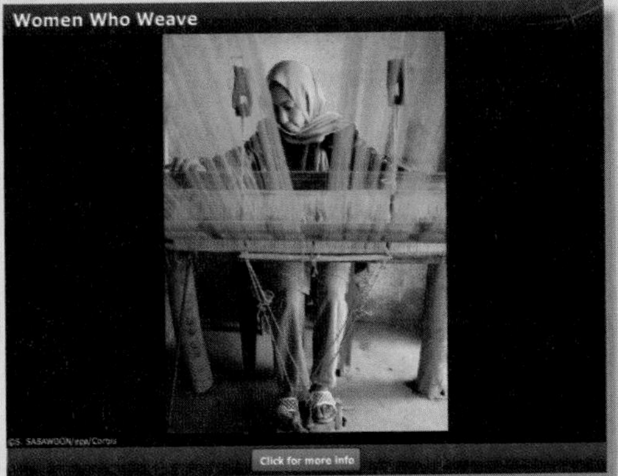

ANSWERS, p. 463

☑ **READING PROGRESS CHECK** The conflict between Armenians and Azeris caused Azeris to flee Nagorno-Karabakh and Armenians to leave their homes in other parts of Azerbaijan.

CRITICAL THINKING

1. Rug weaving is more likely to be done in rural areas where traditional ways of life are more common.
2. Pastoralists are more likely to weave as they have access to the livestock needed to provide the wool for such projects.

T Technology Skills

Explaining Continuity and Change After students have read the information about the arts in Central Asia, tell them they will research, prepare, and present a "Central Asian Art and Culture Exhibit." Organize students into groups, assigning each group a country in Central Asia. Have groups conduct additional research to identify the artwork and cultural aspects that are representative of each region. Tell students to trace the origins of art and architecture in their assigned country and its influence on later cultures. Students may wish to focus on one element of art, such as architecture, literature, dance, or the visual arts. Have students prepare a presentation in which they display reproductions of an original work from their assigned region. Students may also wish to present their information in a slide show using presentation software. Encourage artistically inclined students to perform a poetry reading, play a musical piece, create a drawing, and so on. **BL Visual/Spatial, Auditory/Musical**

C Critical Thinking Skills

Evaluating Have students read the text and then discuss the challenges and benefits of farming in the region. **Ask: What region is suitable for farming in Central Asia?** *(The steppes provide fertile soil for growing crops and supporting the grasslands that nomadic herders use for their livestock.)* **What products help the economy in Uzbekistan?** *(cotton and silk)* **What farm product helps the economy in Kazakhstan?** *(wheat)* **Why does Tajikistan have to import much of its food?** *(The region is mountainous and not ideal for farming, as it has limited land that can be used for agriculture.)* **ELL Logical/Mathematical**

ANSWERS, p. 464

READING PROGRESS CHECK The people in rural areas follow centuries-old ways of life. The people in urban areas follow more modern ways of life, including using the Internet and cell phones.

CRITICAL THINKING

1. Kazakhstan and Azerbaijan have the highest per capita output in Central Asia.
2. Kazakhstan and Azerbaijan have the lowest percentage of the workforce involved in agriculture of the countries in Central Asia.

The Arts

T Georgia and Armenia have literary histories that reach back more than two thousand years, and classic works from then and later are still treasured in both countries. The building styles of both these ancient kingdoms influenced the architecture of the Byzantine Empire. The six countries in the eastern subregion have a rich oral literature centered on epic poems that relate the adventures of cultural heroes. Like several countries in Southwest Asia, they also have a tradition of weaving brilliantly colored and intricately designed rugs. Bukhara and Samarqand in Uzbekistan have some magnificent mosques and tombs that are many centuries old.

READING PROGRESS CHECK

Identifying Cause and Effect How are society and culture in Central Asia today different in urban and rural areas?

Economic Activities

GUIDING QUESTION *How do the people of Central Asia use resources to create economies?*

The countries of Central Asia are less developed. Most are not very industrialized and rely instead on agriculture and natural resources exports. Monetary output for these countries is a fraction of that of the United States, a more developed country.

Much of the land in this subregion has limited uses for agriculture. Yet for most of these countries, nearly half the workforce lives by farming. The high percentage of agricultural workers, the lack of good land, and the reliance on traditional farming methods help explain the countries' low economic output.

C While many areas are not well suited for farming, the steppes of Central Asia do provide fertile soil for growing crops and supporting the grasslands that nomadic herders use in colder months for grazing their livestock. Uzbekistan is one of the world's largest cotton producers and one of the top exporters of cotton. Uzbekistanis also produce fine clothing from silk, a skill they learned as a result of their location along the Silk Road. Turkmenistan is another major cotton producer and is also a wheat producer. Uzbekistan and Turkmenistan rely on irrigation to grow crops in dry regions. Kazakhstan is among the world's top ten wheat producers. Its nomadic herders and farmers also produce dairy products, meat, and wool. Kyrgyzstan produces grains, wool, meat, and two export crops—cotton and tobacco. Tajikistan is mountainous and must import more than half of its food. Georgia's humid subtropical climate is good for growing citrus fruits, grapes, and hazelnuts. Farmers in Azerbaijan grow wheat, cotton, rice, fruits and

Economic Productivity in Central Asia

Country	Per Capita GDP	Percentage of Population Below Poverty Line	Percentage of Workforce in Agriculture
United States	$48,300	15.1%	1.2%
Kazakhstan	$13,000	8.2%	25.9%
Azerbaijan	$10,200	11.0%	38.3%
Turkmenistan	$7,800	30.0%	48.2%
Georgia	$5,500	9.7%	55.6%
Armenia	$5,400	35.8%	44.2%
Uzbekistan	$3,300	26.0%	44.0%
Kyrgyzstan	$2,400	33.7%	48.0%
Tajikistan	$2,100	46.7%	49.8%
Afghanistan	$1,000	36.0%	78.6%

A traditional potato farmer in Afghanistan cultivates his field by hand.

CRITICAL THINKING

1. ***Identifying*** Which countries in Central Asia have the highest per capita economic output?
2. ***Comparing and Contrasting*** How does the workforce of these countries compare to that of other countries in the subregion?

networks Online Teaching Options

GAME

Human Geography of Central Asia

Monitoring Have students play this Fill in the Blank Game with a partner until all questions are correctly answered. Then have each set of students join another pair to form groups of four. Have each group write a paragraph explaining how human systems shape Central Asia. Invite groups to share their paragraphs with the class. **AL Verbal/Linguistic**

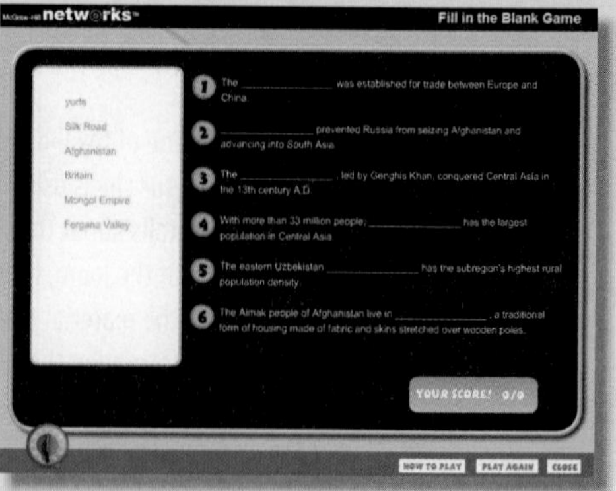

vegetables, and tea, with cotton as a major export. Armenians grow fruits and vegetables and raise livestock.

Energy resources fuel Kazakhstan's economy. Oil accounts for some three-fourths of its export earnings. Oil and gas sales helped the country rebound from the worldwide economic crisis of 2008. Kazakhstan aims to substantially increase production.

Uzbekistan and Turkmenistan produce and export natural gas. Uzbekistan also exports gold and uranium. Kyrgyzstan is a major gold exporter. Azerbaijan, an important oil producer, is improving its exports of natural gas. Pipelines and train lines built through Georgia have helped Azerbaijan export its oil and gas to European markets. The lines have also benefited Georgia. Georgia has developed hydroelectric power and exports some of the electricity. **C**

Manufacturing has a small role in Central Asia. Uzbekistan's factories make automobiles, most of which are exported to Russia. Kazakhstan produces tractors and agricultural equipment. Tajikistan produces aluminum and cement. Armenia's economy was geared more toward manufacturing when it was part of the Soviet Union. Much of that activity ended after independence. Armenia still has economic ties to Russia and depends on that country for natural gas. In addition, some businesses in Armenia are Russian owned. Tajikistan relies on Russia as a source of employment income, with nearly a million Tajikistani guest workers sending their earnings back home.

When the countries of Central Asia were part of the Soviet Union, they were also part of its command economy. Some of the countries in the subregion have not yet moved to a market economy. In Turkmenistan, for instance, the government owns the land, which it leases to farmers while also telling them what crops to grow. Along with government control of the economy, Turkmenistan is plagued by government corruption. These same problems have hurt Azerbaijan's economy, as has too much reliance on oil and gas revenues. **W**

Uzbekistan has made more of a shift to a market economy. Still, the largest firms are government owned. Kazakhstan and Kyrgyzstan have moved more fully to market economies. Kyrgyzstan and Georgia have adopted reforms aimed at fixing government corruption, which has helped their economies develop.

Central Asia is not as rich in energy resources as nearby Southwest Asia, although some countries such as Azerbaijan have sizable reserves of oil and natural gas.

▲ CRITICAL THINKING

1. ***Hypothesizing*** In which country of Central Asia do you think this photograph was taken? Why?
2. ***Analyzing*** Why have the energy-producing countries in the subregion focused on building pipelines in recent years?

Michael Runkel/Alamy

 READING PROGRESS CHECK

Describing Explain how one country in Central Asia has used its resources to build its economy.

LESSON 2 REVIEW (CCSS)

Reviewing Vocabulary (Tier Three Words)

1. ***Explaining*** Write a paragraph explaining the difference between an enclave and an exclave. RI.9–10.1

Using Your Notes

2. ***Summarizing*** Use your graphic organizer on Central Asia's human geography to write a paragraph summarizing the influence of Soviet rule on the subregion's history, people, and economies.

Answering the Guiding Questions

3. ***Summarizing*** How have the countries of Central Asia been governed over the centuries?
4. ***Explaining*** How have population patterns changed over time in Central Asia?
5. ***Describing*** What are some aspects of the cultures of the people of Central Asia?
6. ***Explaining*** How do the people of Central Asia use resources to create economies?

Writing Activity

7. ***Persuasive*** In a paragraph, discuss whether you think traditional culture, Islam, or Soviet rule had the strongest influence on the subregion. WHST.9–10.1

C Critical Thinking Skills

Comparing and Contrasting Guide students to understand the relationship between a country's reliance on its natural resources and its economic productivity. **Ask: How is Kazakhstan's economy different from other regions in Central Asia?** *(Its energy resources fuel its economy; it benefits from oil and gas exports and leads the region in per capita GDP.)* **What natural resource similarities do Uzbekistan and Turkmenistan share?** *(Both produce and export natural gas.)* **What do Georgia and Azerbaijan have in common?** *(Both benefit from pipelines and train lines that transport oil and natural gas.)* **AL** **Logical/Mathematical**

W Writing Skills

Informative/Explanatory Have students write a short summary on the economy and natural resources of one of the countries in Central Asia. Then discuss the economic challenges that currently face Central Asian countries. **Verbal/Linguistic**

CLOSE & REFLECT

Summarizing Ask students to explain how conquests have influenced Central Asia's development. Then have students summarize aspects of the region's society, culture, and current economic activities.

ANSWERS, p. 465

READING PROGRESS CHECK Possible answers: Kyrgyzstan exporting gold; Uzbekistan exporting uranium and gold; Azerbaijan and Kazakhstan exporting natural gas and oil.

CRITICAL THINKING

1. Kazakhstan may want to become one of the top-ten oil producers as oil accounts for three-fourths of its exports.
2. Pipelines will help these countries export oil and gas, which will grow their economies.

LESSON 2 REVIEW ANSWERS

Reviewing Vocabulary

1. Student answers must explain that an exclave is a territory belonging to one political unit but surrounded by a different political unit. An enclave is a distinct territory or cultural area surrounded by a foreign territory.

Using Your Notes

2. Student answers may vary but may include: the ongoing influence of a command economy that the Soviets implemented in these countries except Afghanistan; continued ownership of land by the Turkmenistan government and leasing land to farmers and dictating what crops to grow; the largest firms in Uzbekistan are government owned; Russian is the official language in Kyrgyzstan and Kazakhstan and is spoken throughout the subregion.

Answering the Guiding Questions

3. Numerous empires and countries have ruled the countries of Central Asia over the centuries, including the Arabs, the Mongols, and the Russian Empires. The British ruled Afghanistan for a period. The countries have become independent, but dictatorial rule has maintained a strong influence in many countries.
4. Traditionally, most people in Central Asia lived in rural areas as herders and farmers. It is slowly becoming more urban. Afghanistan's rate of urbanization is lowest with less than 25 percent living in cities. Overall, the population density of Central Asia is low, but the population density per acre of arable land is high.
5. Islam is the predominant religion in the subregion except in Armenia and Georgia where Christianity is practiced. Russian is widely spoken throughout the region and is the official language in Kyrgyzstan and Kazakhstan. Traditional and modern ways of life are mixed throughout Central Asia.
6. The people of Central Asia export resources to create economies.

Writing Activity

7. Student answers may vary depending on the influence chosen but could include the long period of Soviet rule and ongoing impact of the command economy in the subregion, the influence of Islam on all the countries except Armenia and Georgia, or the traditional ways of life still practiced in rural areas.

ENGAGE

R Reading Skills

Predicting Have students read the *It Matters Because* text and look at the images at the top of the page. Have students predict the types of "mistakes" they will read about in this lesson, and whether and how countries have worked together to solve problems regarding resource management. Tell students to return to their predictions after they read through this lesson to see if they were correct.

TEACH & ASSESS

V Visual Skills

Global Analysis Remind students that the physical geography of Central Asia is dominated by mountainous terrain, such as the Caucasus mountain range. After students read the information on this page, have them work in pairs to create a visual display that shows how countries in Central Asia manage their natural resources. Invite students to conduct additional research to describe the benefits and challenges of harnessing and managing the region's resources. **Ask:** **How do Georgia and Kyrgyzstan benefit from their physical geography?** *(Mountainous terrain provide swiftly flowing rivers that can be tapped for hydroelectric power.)* **How does Tajikistan hope to improve its energy issues?** *(Tajikistan hopes to expand its hydroelectric power by building a dam on a tributary of the Amu Dar'ya, but the project has created conflict.)* AL **Visual/Spatial, Interpersonal**

networks

There's More Online!

- **IMAGE** Central Asian Steppe
- **INFOGRAPHIC** Aral: A Sea Sacrificed
- **IMAGE** Kazakh Factory
- **INTERACTIVE SELF-CHECK QUIZ**
- **VIDEO** People and Their Environment: Central Asia

LESSON 3
People and Their Environment: Central Asia

Reading **HELP**DESK

Academic Vocabulary (Tier Two Words)
- concentrated
- expose

Content Vocabulary (Tier Three Words)
- radioactive material

TAKING NOTES: ***Key Ideas and Details***

EXPLORING ISSUES As you read about the environment of Central Asia, use a graphic organizer like the one below to identify environmental issues and steps being taken to address them.

Issue	Steps

ESSENTIAL QUESTION • *How do physical systems and human systems shape a place?*

It Matters Because

R *Because of the generally dry climate of Central Asia, water and other resources have to be managed carefully. Mistakes in the past have posed several challenges to some aspects of the environment. Since some resources are shared by several countries, they need to work together to solve these problems and manage their resources.*

V Managing Resources

GUIDING QUESTION *How do the people and governments manage the natural resources of Central Asia?*

Several countries in Central Asia are well supplied with natural resources, including fossil fuels and minerals. Others have few of these resources, and must try to find alternative sources to meet their energy and other needs. The strong role of agriculture in all the economies places demands on soil and water, while the fairly dry climate of the eastern subregion puts limits on the growth of agricultural output.

Kazakhstan, Azerbaijan, Turkmenistan, and Uzbekistan all have substantial oil or natural gas reserves, or both. Though these countries are landlocked, pipelines connect them to other parts of the world. One carries oil from Azerbaijan to the Black Sea coast of Georgia. Turkmenistan recently opened a pipeline to transport its natural gas to China, an important market because of its growing economy and increasing demand for energy.

The mountainous terrain of Georgia and Kyrgyzstan gives them swiftly flowing rivers that can be tapped for hydroelectric power. With very little of their own oil and gas, these countries rely on hydroelectric power. In fact, they generate enough electricity to not only meet their own needs, but to export power to neighboring countries as well.

Tajikistan often faces energy shortages, leaving many of its people without electricity for long periods of time. The country hopes to expand its hydroelectric power by building a dam on a tributary of the Amu Dar'ya, but this project has created conflict. Uzbekistan fears that the

466

networks Online Teaching Options

INTERACTIVE BELLRINGER

Aral: A Sea Sacrificed

Analyzing Cause and Effect This introductory text and infographic of the Aral Sea can be used to help students understand the environmental challenges that the people of Central Asia face. Have students form small groups and ask them to consider how their lives might be affected if they lived in the Midwest and suddenly the Great Lakes lost a significant volume of water. Prompt them, if necessary, to consider the effects on the transportation of goods and the economic activity of the United States as a whole. Then have groups discuss each question. Ask each group to write all possible answers to the questions. Then in a class discussion, have groups share their answers. **Visual/Spatial, Verbal/Linguistic**

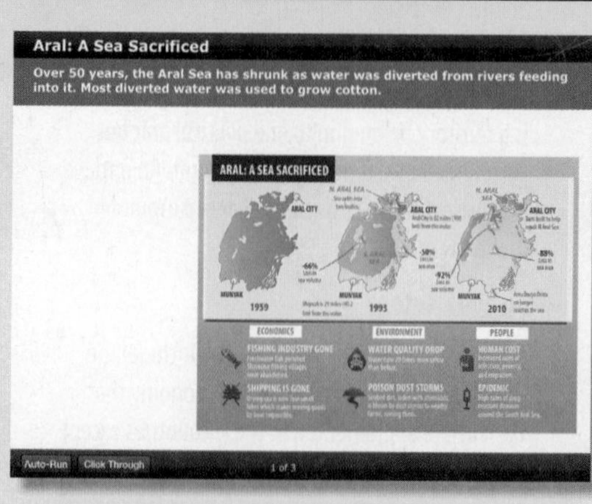

ANSWERS, p. 466

TAKING NOTES: Issues—agriculture, livestock, and humans use increasing amounts of water; deforestation and desertification in Afghanistan; cutting trees for fuel; livestock overgraze land; pollution and overfishing threaten Caspian Sea; air, water, and soil pollution from oil and gas industry, pesticides, and fertilizers have made Apsheron Peninsula of Azerbaijan the most environmentally damaged place on Earth; **Steps**—USAID works with countries to protect the Syr Dar'ya river basin; governments and European universities work to manage water resources; In 2006, the Convention for the Protection of the Marine Environment of the Caspian Sea was signed to reduce pollution and conserve marine life. Afghanistan works with several NGOs to safely locate and dispose of landmines; governments are working to find efficient ways to irrigate.

dam would limit its own ability to use the river's water to irrigate its profitable cotton fields. In response, Uzbekistan cut off sale of natural gas to Tajikistan. Tajikistan's government complained that Uzbekistan also shut down rail service carrying needed food imports. Another concern is the impact of reduced water flow on the quality of the river's water. The World Bank has urged Tajikistan to halt construction until further study of the dam's environmental impact is completed.

Despite small amounts of arable land, farming remains an important economic activity in all countries of the subregion. Herding can take place in hilly areas that are not suitable for farming, but some livestock herds graze on flatter grasslands. Given the low levels of rainfall in much of the area, carefully managing water resources for farming, grazing, and other uses is vitally important. Underscoring this need is the estimate by World Bank experts that more than three-fourths of the water used for irrigation in the subregion is lost. Inefficient practices will have to change if governments in the subregion want to farm more productively and save water. **T**

Deforestation and desertification are problems in Afghanistan. People needing fuel sources have been cutting down trees to burn the wood. The loss of trees along with overgrazing by livestock are contributing to desertification. **C**

Heavy reliance on exporting just one or two resources—however vital they may be—can be risky for an economy. For example, because of their dependence on oil exports, both Azerbaijan and Kazakhstan suffered in recent years when oil prices fell. Aware of this problem, Azerbaijan has taken steps to develop a more varied economy. It has increased investment in tourism as well as information and communications industries to develop new sources of jobs and revenue.

Of course, the reverse is also true: lack of resources poses problems for other countries. Armenia depends on natural gas from Russia. When the price goes up or supply falters, its economy suffers. Armenia could try to buy natural gas from neighboring Azerbaijan, but relations between those two countries are poor because of the dispute over Nagorno-Karabakh. Armenia recently opened a new pipeline that allows it to import natural gas from Iran. However, overreliance on Iran could become a problem in the future.

✓ READING PROGRESS CHECK

Identifying What is one example of how countries in the subregion are taking steps to properly manage their resources?

Irrigation is essential to supplying the cotton fields growing on the Central Asian steppe in Uzbekistan.

◀ CRITICAL THINKING

1. ***Explaining*** Why is it necessary to irrigate these fields?
2. ***Identifying*** Where does the water come from?

T Technology Skills

Problem Solving Guide a brief discussion about the need for Central Asian countries to carefully manage limited water resources. **Ask: Why is water management a key factor in farming and grazing in regions across Central Asia?** *(Much of the region receives little rainfall, so water management is vitally important in providing irrigation for crops and grassland for grazing.)* Organize students into small groups and assign each group one country in Central Asia. Have groups research how water scarcity issues are being addressed in their assigned country. Tell students to identify problems created by inefficient practices and then brainstorm solutions to these problems and present their findings in a report. Tell students to include visuals showing how the problems are created and how they could be reduced or solved. Have groups present their reports to the class. **Logical/Mathematical, Interpersonal**

C Critical Thinking Skills

Creating and Analyzing Arguments Tell students to consider the advantages and disadvantages of different uses of natural resources in Central Asia. Have students work in groups to conduct mock debates on the use of a particular resource. Students could focus on whether the Amu Dar'ya should be used for irrigation or be dammed for hydroelectric power. Alternately, students could focus on whether forests in Afghanistan should be preserved or cut for fuel and grazing land. Assign roles to students, such as scientists, farmers, Uzbekistan rail operators, spokesperson from the World Bank, environmentalists, and so on. Moderate the debate by having groups state their side of the issue, allowing each side to rebut the other positions. Remind students to use information from the text and additional research to support their arguments. After each group has presented its side of its issue, ask students which argument they found the most convincing and why.
BL Verbal/Linguistic, Interpersonal

GRAPHIC ORGANIZER

People and Their Environment: Central Asia

Defending Use this graphic organizer to show students how people in Central Asia manage natural resources and thereby impact their environment. Have students work in small groups to use the graphic organizer as a note-taking tool as they read. When the graphic organizers are complete, have groups write what they think are the most significant impacts that Central Asian people have made in their region, using evidence from the slide show and the text. Then ask groups to share their ideas with the rest of the class and defend their reasoning with the evidence they found.
AL BL Verbal/Linguistic, Interpersonal

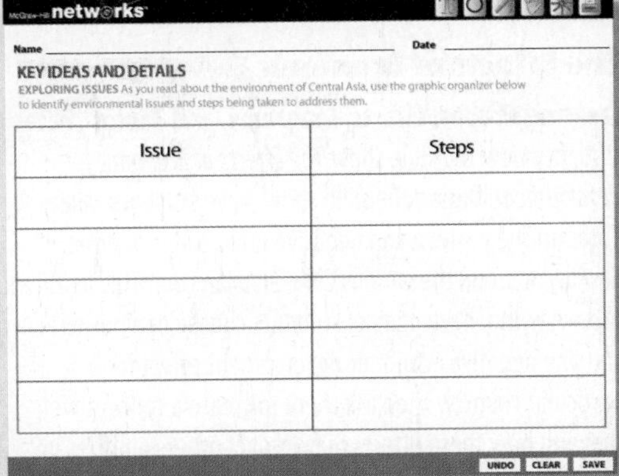

ANSWERS, p. 467

✓ READING PROGRESS CHECK Student answers will vary but could include Georgia and Kyrgyzstan using rivers to generate hydroelectric power not only to meet their energy needs but for export to other countries as well; Azerbaijan is taking steps to diversify its economy so it is less dependent upon oil; the use of pipelines by Kazakhstan, Azerbaijan, Turkmenistan, and Uzbekistan to transport oil and natural gas to other countries.

CRITICAL THINKING

1. The steppe areas of Central Asia have a generally dry climate, which makes the cotton fields pictured require irrigation to be productive.
2. The water most likely comes from the Amu Dar'ya or one of its tributaries.

People and Their Environment: Central Asia

Making Connections

As you discuss the impact of the Soviet era, help students make the connection between environmental issues and economic policies. Have students recall information they learned about the Caspian Sea from Lesson 1. Review with students that during the warmer months the Caspian Sea loses more water from evaporation than it gains from rivers emptying into it. Remind students of the significance of sturgeon fishing in the Caspian as well as oil and natural gas found beneath the sea. Using the Caspian and Aral Seas as examples, guide students to understand the balance between preserving an ecosystem's environment and harvesting that ecosystem's resources for economic gain.

C Critical Thinking Skills

Identifying Cause and Effect Have students read the information about water supply to the Aral Sea. **Ask: How has the size of the Aral Sea changed over the years?** *(It is now a fraction of its former size.)* **What caused this change?** *(During the Soviet era, the Soviets took water from the Syr Dar'ya and Amu Dar'ya to irrigate fields in order to boost cotton production in the area. The size was also reduced because of evaporation during hot summers.)* **What was the effect of this change to the Aral Sea's size?** *(It dramatically reduced water supply to the Aral Sea.)* **AL Logical/Mathematical**

V Visual Skills

Calculating Have students analyze the visual about the Aral Sea at the bottom of the page. Discuss the economic, environmental, and human impact caused by the damage to the Aral Sea. Have students work with a partner to calculate the Aral Sea's loss in area and volume in approximate fractions. Ask students to complete the following sentence as an example: **In 1993, the Aral Sea lost approximately __ of its volume.** *(2/3 or 66 percent)* **ELL Logical/Mathematical, Interpersonal**

ANSWERS, p. 468

CRITICAL THINKING

1. The southern Aral Sea is currently the most damaged or depleted.
2. The generally dry climate in areas surrounding the Aral Sea caused people to divert water for irrigation purposes. This water came from rivers that feed the sea. This diversion, combined with evaporation due to the dry climate, caused the sea to largely disappear.

Human Impact

GUIDING QUESTION *How have modern economic activities impacted Central Asia?*

The Soviet era left a legacy of environmental issues resulting from Soviet economic policies. The subregion's major bodies of water face severe environmental challenges. Pollution in the Caspian Sea is severe. Pollution and overfishing threaten fish, like sturgeon, which provide important exports as well as serve important roles in maintaining the ecology of the sea. Scientists from the area say that the Apsheron Peninsula of Azerbaijan is the most environmentally damaged place on Earth. The damage is the result of air, water, and soil pollution from the oil and gas industries and from the overuse of pesticides and other harmful chemicals for agriculture.

Perhaps nowhere has the environmental damage of the Soviet era been more profound than in the area around the Aral Sea. This body of water, once the fourth-largest inland sea in the world, is now a fraction of its former size—in fact, it is no longer one sea but several very small bodies of water. The Soviets took water from the Syr Dar'ya and Amu Dar'ya—the two rivers that feed the Aral Sea—to irrigate fields in their push to boost cotton production. The result was a sharp reduction in the supply of water reaching the sea. Evaporation during the hot summers increased the loss of water from the sea. Over decades, the sea's levels

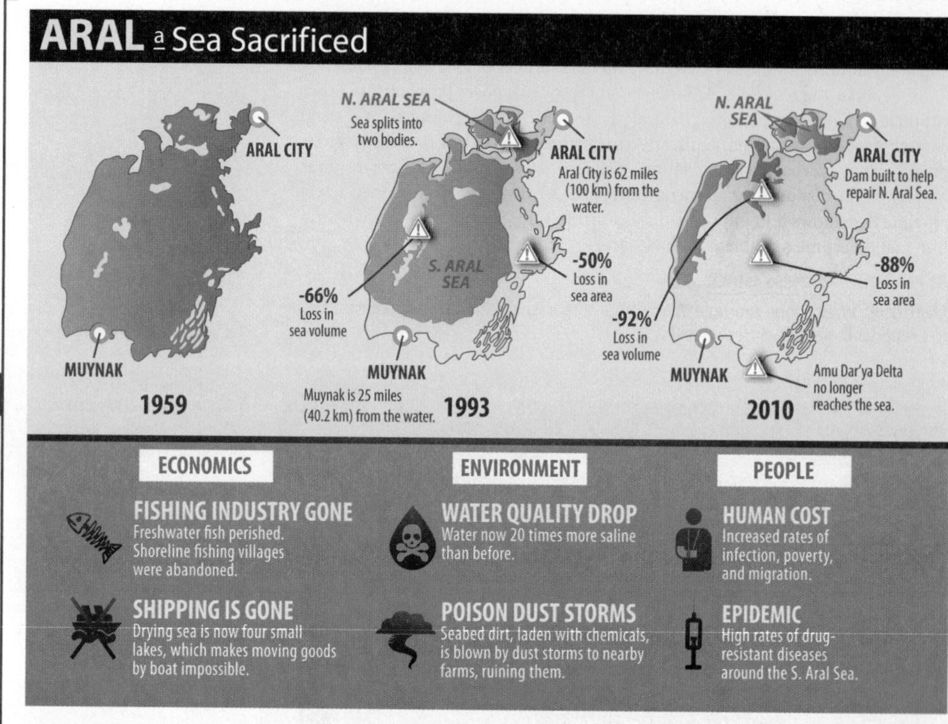

The Aral Sea is in peril because too much water has been diverted from the rivers that feed into the sea. Most of the diverted water has been used to grow cotton.

▲ CRITICAL THINKING

1. ***Analyzing Visuals*** Which part of the sea is now in the most danger?
2. ***Making Connections*** How did the climate of the area around the Aral Sea contribute to the environmental problem there?

networks Online Teaching Options

SLIDE SHOW

The Effects of Economic Development

Creating Graphs, Charts, Diagrams, and Tables Have students view the slide show *The Effects of Economic Development.* During the slide show, have students take notes on the positive and negative effects of economic development on the various Central Asian countries featured. After viewing, have pairs of students choose one positive and one negative economic development effect for a particular country. Then ask them to create a concept web showing how these effects may impact other countries in the region. **AL Verbal/Linguistic, Visual/Spatial**

decreased dramatically, and water quality also fell as levels of salt and of harmful chemicals in the water became more **concentrated**, or stronger.

While those problems were bad enough, worse occurred. Winds blew salt and harmful chemicals from the dry seabed to nearby areas. These substances damaged the soil where they landed, ruining farmland. The salt and chemicals in the air also caused cancer and respiratory diseases in people.

V

Problems with the Caspian and Aral Seas are not the only environmental issues in Central Asia. Kazakhstan was home to nuclear bases during the Soviet era. During the Cold War, the Soviet government tested nuclear, chemical, and biological weapons there. As a result, northeastern Kazakhstan remains severely affected by radiation given off by the **radioactive material** after the Soviets tested nearly 500 nuclear weapons. In many instances, local populations were not warned or evacuated before the testing took place. In 1989 it was discovered that this weapons testing had caused radiation leaks. Scientists think many years will pass before all the resulting contamination disappears.

W

Soviet planners also chose Kazakhstan as a site for heavy industry, which polluted the air with toxic chemicals. Scientists have linked increased infant mortality in Kazakhstan directly to industrial pollution. The people of Kyrgyzstan, another site of heavy Soviet industry, have suffered similar effects. Soviet-era agriculture also caused serious environmental damage from heavy use of pesticides all across the region.

Armenia has been strongly criticized by environmental activists for continuing to run a nuclear power plant in an area prone to earthquakes. Activists worry that a quake could lead to a serious nuclear accident. The country, however, relies on that plant to generate 40 percent of its electricity, and the government has chosen to build a new plant rather than to abandon nuclear power completely. Armenia has also been criticized for deforestation of the Teghut Forest in northern Armenia as a result of mining activity there.

Land mines put into the ground during periods of war are a serious problem in Afghanistan. In 2001 and 2002, an average of 176 people were killed or injured as a result of the inadvertent explosion of land mines or other ammunition each month. More than three-fourths of those victims were children. While these rates of death and injury dropped dramatically in the following ten years, the problem remains and tragedies continue to take place.

Land mines and unexploded ammunition do not just **expose** humans to major life and health threats. They also hamper economic activity. They prevent farmers from working fields because of the fear of mines. They also interfere with the delivery of goods and services when explosive devices on roadways explode.

While Central Asia is not highly industrialized, factories like these in Kazakhstan have created a serious pollution problem.

▲ **CRITICAL THINKING**

1. ***Making Connections*** Is this kind of pollution more likely to affect urban or rural areas? Why?
2. ***Hypothesizing*** Based on the information in this lesson, how concerned do you think Soviet leaders were about environmental issues? Explain your response.

concentrated less dilute, stronger

radioactive material material contaminated by residue from the generation of nuclear energy or the testing of nuclear weapons

expose to make vulnerable

Lynn Johnson/National Geographic/Getty Images

✓ **READING PROGRESS CHECK**

Identifying Cause and Effect What were the causes and effects of one of the environmental challenges facing the subregion?

VIDEO

In the Wake of the USSR

Posing Questions This video depicts the environmental damage caused by the Soviet Union's invasion of Afghanistan in 1979 and the challenges that still exist today, long after the collapse of the Soviet Union. As students view the video, have them write questions they may have regarding any historical issues that are unclear to them or about why challenges still exist so long after the initial invasion, especially in light of the fact that the invading country no longer exists as a whole. Guide students to find answers to their questions using the Internet or print resources.
AL BL **Verbal/Linguistic, Logical/Mathematical**

V Visual Skills

Creating Diagrams Have students review the information in the text about the damage that has been caused to the Caspian and Aral Seas over the years. Tell students to work with a partner to create a diagram or flowchart that depicts the various causes of the damage and its effects. Have student pairs share their diagrams with the class, challenging them to incorporate illustrations to convey the information.
AL **Visual/Spatial, Interpersonal**

W Writing Skills

Narrative Have students read the information in the text and then imagine what it might be like to live in a region where pollution from heavy industry has caused environmental damage. Organize students into small groups and assign the following activity: conceptualize, write, and rehearse a skit that portrays a family living in one of the regions impacted by environmental problems. Tell students to relate how the problems have impacted each family member. Students' skits may take place as "a day in the life" of a family or may show a progression over months or years. Tell students to keep their skits approximately 10 to 15 minutes long.

Remind students to consider how the heads of the household earn a living. For example, the father or mother might work in a factory that results in industrial pollution. Encourage students to create costumes and props for their skits and to make the dialogue realistic, using the text for clues as to what life might be like in that region. Have groups perform their skits for the class. **Kinesthetic, Interpersonal**

ANSWERS, p. 469

✓ **READING PROGRESS CHECK** Kazakhstan is polluted with radioactive material from nuclear testing, which has harmed the air, soil, water, and health of residents; rivers that feed the Aral Sea for irrigation of farmland have caused the sea to become isolated bodies of water; pollution and overfishing of the Caspian Sea have caused many species of fish to become depleted or extinct; air, water, and soil pollution from the oil and natural gas industries, pesticides, and fertilizers have made the Apsheron Peninsula the most environmentally damaged area on Earth.

CRITICAL THINKING

1. Rural areas are more likely to be affected as the pollutants become trapped in the soil and water.
2. At the time, the Soviets were more concerned about the Cold War than they were about possible environmental damage from nuclear testing and heavy industry in the area.

People and Their Environment: Central Asia

T Technology Skills

Exploring Issues Have students read about the need for international cooperation with regard to environmental issues in Central Asia. **Ask:** **How might mismanagement of water resources in Central Asia create conflict with other nations?** *(Possible answer: Other nations would likely resent having to spend resources to help fix a problem they did not cause.)* Organize students into five groups and assign each group one of the five northern "stans." Then have groups conduct online research about the assigned country for a slide show using presentation software. Students' presentations should identify what each country is doing to manage its water resources, and the impact of the problem on the surrounding environment and on the region's economy. Have groups present their slide shows to the class. BL **Interpersonal**

CLOSE & REFLECT

Outlining Have students review the headings and subheadings in each section of the text and use them to create a lesson outline. Tell students to include an example to support the main ideas. Suggest that students save their outlines to use as a study tool when reviewing the chapter.

ANSWERS, p. 470

✓ **READING PROGRESS CHECK** Countries within the subregion must work together as they often do not have the resources to develop and implement solutions on their own. Some issues, such as water supply and pollution, also affect multiple countries.

Connecting Geography Student answers could include that the water supplied to and kept in the northern portion of the Aral Sea would not have been enough to help the severely damaged southern portion or that Uzbekistan must make an effort to solve the problem in the southern portion of the sea.

Connecting Geography to GOVERNMENT

Saving the Aral Sea

Efforts to save the Aral Sea began in the 1990s when the mayor of a town on the northern shore had a dam built. The dam prevented the loss of water from the northern part of the sea by blocking it from flowing into the more seriously damaged southern part. Later, the government of Kazakhstan built a higher, sturdier dam. The World Bank has helped Kazakhstan with this program. Since then, sea levels in the north have risen, salt levels have declined, and fish have returned to the Northern Aral Sea from the Syr Dar'ya. The southern portion of the sea is still in serious danger, however, in part because Uzbekistan has not acted to solve the problem.

DEFENDING Do you think Kazakhstan was selfish in saving the northern part of the Aral Sea and doing nothing for the southern part? Why or why not?

Addressing the Issues

GUIDING QUESTION *How are environmental issues in Central Asia being addressed?*

The environmental problems of Central Asia must be addressed for the health and economic future of the countries in the subregion. Governments in the subregion, which often do not have enough resources, have sought outside help in developing and implementing solutions. As the dispute between Tajikistan and Uzbekistan over water resources highlights, some of the problems cross borders, which means regional governments must cooperate.

The governments of the United States and other countries and also nongovernmental organizations (NGOs) have taken part in efforts to solve environmental problems in Central Asia. For example, the United States Agency for International Development (USAID) has joined with the affected countries to work to protect the river basin of the Syr Dar'ya. A group formed by several universities in Europe and most of the governments of the eastern subregion is dedicated to managing water resources. One of the early steps in this program has been to found water-management centers in each of the countries involved. The program's goal is to train local people in water-management techniques. The group also hopes to build cooperation among the countries involved.

In 2006 the countries around the Caspian Sea agreed to the legally binding Convention for the Protection of the Marine Environment of the Caspian Sea. The agreement commits them to reducing agricultural and industrial pollution into that troubled sea. It also commits the countries to conserve fish and other marine life. In addition, another international agreement called the Convention on International Trade in Endangered Species has placed all sturgeon species from the Caspian Sea on its list of threatened animals. Strict quotas have been set for sturgeon fishing. Sturgeon eggs, or caviar, are very profitable, however, which has led to poaching. Poaching is the illegal harvesting of wild animals.

Afghanistan has joined with other countries and NGOs to try to solve the landmine problem. Many of the NGOs use an approach called "community-based demining." Experienced workers recruit and train local people in the skills needed to identify and to disable mines so they cannot explode. The NGOs work closely with local communities to find people to do this dangerous work and to support their activities. One possible future benefit of this approach is that trained Afghanis will be available to help other countries with the same problem.

✓ **READING PROGRESS CHECK**

Evaluating Why do the countries of the subregion need to cooperate with each other and with other countries to address their environmental issues?

LESSON 3 REVIEW (CCSS)

Reviewing Vocabulary (Tier Three Words)

1. ***Explaining*** Write a paragraph explaining why radioactive materials are so dangerous. RI.9–10.1

Using Your Notes

2. ***Explaining*** Use your graphic organizer on Central Asia's environmental issues to write a paragraph explaining how each solution chosen aims to solve the targeted environmental challenge.

Answering the Guiding Questions

3. ***Explaining*** How do the people and governments manage the natural resources of Central Asia?
4. ***Summarizing*** How have modern economic activities impacted Central Asia?
5. ***Explaining*** How are environmental issues in Central Asia being addressed?

Writing Activity

6. ***Argument*** In a paragraph, discuss which environmental problem in the subregion you think is the worst, and defend your reasoning. WHST.9–10.1

LESSON 3 REVIEW ANSWERS

Reviewing Vocabulary

1. Student answers may vary but could include information on diseases caused by radiation exposure, soil contamination by radiation making it unfit to grow food, and radioactive material remaining in the water supply, making it unsafe for use.

Using Your Notes

2. Student answers may vary but should be supported with information from the lesson. Possible responses include: USAID is working with affected countries to protect the Syr Dar'ya river basin. Governments and several European universities are working on training people in water-management techniques. In 2006, the countries around the Caspian Sea signed the Convention for the Protection of the Marine Environment of the Caspian Sea that commits them to reducing pollution and conservation of fish and marine life. The Convention on Trade in Endangered Species has placed all sturgeon on its list of threatened animals and limits the amount that may be fished. Afghanistan is working with other countries and several NGOs on training local communities to safely locate and dispose of landmines. Governments are working to find more efficient ways to irrigate, as almost three-fourths of the water used for irrigation is lost.

Answering the Guiding Questions

3. Oil and natural gas are extracted and transported through pipelines for export, Georgia and Kyrgyzstan use rivers for hydroelectric power, and water resources are used for irrigation of crops.
4. Modern economic activities such as oil and gas extraction have polluted the air and water, exports of sturgeon and caviar have led to overfishing, and irrigation for crops threatens the water supplies.
5. Governments of the subregion are working with other countries and NGOs to protect the Caspian Sea, improve water management, and clear landmines.

Writing Activity

6. Student answers may vary based on environmental problem chosen but should be supported with information from the lesson. Possible environmental issues could be the shrinking of the Aral Sea, pollution and overfishing of the Caspian Sea, radioactive and industrial waste in Kazakhstan, landmines in Afghanistan, and pollution of the Apsheron Peninsula.

CHAPTER 19 Assessment CCSS

Directions: On a separate sheet of paper, answer the questions below. Make sure that you read carefully and answer all parts of the questions.

Lesson Review

Lesson 1

1. ***Identifying Cause and Effect*** Explain how and why the Aral Sea has changed since the 1960s.
2. ***Describing*** What makes up the western section and the eastern section of Central Asia?
3. ***Examining*** Despite a lack of oil resources, Georgia has profited from oil, and it has managed to create power to generate its electricity. How has it been successful in these endeavors?

Lesson 2

4. ***Considering Advantages and Disadvantages*** Why is it accurate to describe Central Asia as an ethnic mosaic? Explain why this "ethnic mosaic" is both a benefit and a detriment.
5. ***Making Connections*** Why was Afghanistan never a Soviet republic?
6. ***Analyzing*** Explain whether this statement is accurate: "The percentage of the workforce in Central Asia earning its living by farming is disproportionate to the amount of fertile farmland in the region."

Lesson 3

7. ***Identifying Cause and Effect*** What was the impact on Azerbaijan and Kazakhstan when oil prices recently fell dramatically? What has Azerbaijan done since then to prevent a similar outcome should oil prices drop again?
8. ***Summarizing*** Summarize the nuclear and chemical pollution in Kazakhstan. Explain the origins of this pollution.
9. ***Evaluating*** What are the impacts of land mines and unexploded ammunition in Afghanistan?

21st Century Skills

Use the cartoon below to answer the questions that follow.

"Wow! The Ukraine, Moldavia, Uzbekistan, Kazakhstan, Byelorussia, Tadzhikistan, Kirgizia, Turkmenistan . . ."

10. ***Using Primary Sources*** The teacher in the cartoon has just discussed information about these countries and the Soviet Union. What do all of these countries have in common, as related to the Soviet Union, that would likely have given rise to the comment in the caption?
11. ***Identifying Perspectives*** Create a new editorial cartoon to illustrate another point about one or all of the countries mentioned in the caption above. The cartoon should clearly depict a point about one or all of these countries. Write a short paragraph to explain your cartoon.

Joseph Farris/The New Yorker Collection/www.cartoonbank.com

Need Extra Help?

If You've Missed Question	1	2	3	4	5	6	7	8	9	10	11
Go to page	456	454	458	462	460	464	467	469	469	454	454

CHAPTER 19 Assessment Answers

Lesson Review

Lesson 1

1. Until the 1960s, the Aral Sea was one of the world's largest inland seas. However, the main rivers that feed the sea were diverted in order to provide water for irrigation. The diversion of water coupled with evaporation due to the climate in the area has caused the sea to now be several small bodies of water separated by dry land.
2. The western section or Caucasus area of Central Asia consists of Georgia, Armenia, and Azerbaijan. The eastern section consists of Kazakhstan, Uzbekistan, Turkmenistan, Kyrgyzstan, Tajikistan, and Afghanistan.
3. Georgia has taken advantage of its location and allowed profitable pipelines to be built to transport oil from the Caspian Sea to Europe. Georgia uses hydroelectric power to generate electricity.

Lesson 2

4. It is accurate to describe Central Asia as an "ethnic mosaic" because many different ethnic groups live in the subregion. This causes conflict in some cases but also results in diverse contributions to art and society.
5. The British prevented Russia from seizing Afghanistan.
6. The statement is accurate because while the subregion has little arable land, nearly half of the workforce lives by farming.

Lesson 3

7. The economies of Azerbaijan and Kazakhstan suffered when oil prices fell. Azerbaijan is trying to diversify the economy by investing in the tourism, information, and communications industries.
8. The Soviet government tested nuclear, chemical, and biological weapons in Kazakhstan. They also made Kazakhstan a site for heavy industry. The testing of weapons has left the area with radioactive material that is still giving off radiation. There were also leaks of radiation into the environment. Heavy industry polluted the air with toxic chemicals, which has been linked to infant mortality in the area.
9. Land mines and unexploded ammunition are a serious threat to human life and health as well as to the economy. Farmers are unable to work fields for fear of land mines and transport of goods is often disrupted due to explosions on the roadways.

21st Century Skills

10. All of the countries mentioned were part of the Soviet Union until they gained their independence in the 1990s.
11. Cartoons and paragraphs will differ but should be strongly supported with information from the chapter regarding at least one country mentioned in the original cartoon.

CHAPTER 19
Assessment Answers

CHAPTER 19 Assessment 

Directions: On a separate sheet of paper, answer the questions below. Make sure that you read carefully and answer all parts of the questions.

Critical Thinking

12 ***Exploring Issues*** Write a one-page essay to explain this statement: "Early historical and geographical events in Central Asia are clearly evident in the region today, though events in recent history have given rise to perils to the human and physical geography, perils that would not have been foreseen during the early history of the region."

Applying Map Skills

Refer to the Unit 5 Atlas to answer the following questions.

13 ***The World in Spatial Terms*** Use your mental map of Central Asia to generally describe the subregion's two sections and their relationship to the Black Sea, Caspian Sea, China, Pakistan, and the Caucasus Mountains.

14 ***Human Systems*** Which subregion of North Africa, Southwest Asia, and Central Asia is the most densely populated?

15 ***The World in Spatial Terms*** Identify the sea that is located partially in Kazakhstan and partially in Uzbekistan.

Exploring the Essential Question

16 ***Making Connections*** Summarize the conflicts over resources between Tajikistan and Uzbekistan. Explain how this conflict is emblematic of the types of conflicts faced in the subregion. Your summary should reference the ways physical and human systems interact to shape a place.

College and Career Readiness

17 ***Change and Continuity in Economics*** You have been hired to conduct research for a company that provides data about the world's oil producers. Use your research to develop a memo and a graph to explain Kazakhstan's current level of oil production in relation to the world's top ten oil producers. Explain where Kazakhstan's oil production falls within the graph and whether it is likely to change during the next five years compared to other countries included in the graph.

DBQ Analyzing Primary Sources

Read the excerpt and use it to answer the following questions.

PRIMARY SOURCE

Despite Government efforts, deficiencies in the administration of justice continue to pose a major impediment to the attainment of justice . . . Trials monitored by OHCHR staff in Kyrgyzstan—from city courts to the Supreme Court—continue to reveal concerns about due process, the independence of the judiciary, security for defendants, their lawyers and court officials . . . Reports of continuing discriminatory practices towards . . . national and ethnic minorities are deeply troublesome.

—Rupert Colville, UN Office of the High Commissioner for Human Rights (OHCHR), June 10, 2011, UN News Centre

18 ***Interpreting Significance*** What do Colville's comments indicate about the pursuit of justice in Kyrgyzstan? RH.9–10.2

19 ***Drawing Conclusions*** Why would the UN and news agencies be interested in comments from Rupert Colville regarding 2010 events in Kyrgyzstan? RH.9–10.1, RH.9–10.2

Research and Presentation

20 ***Gathering Information*** Research the work of the various organizations to protect the Syr Dar'ya river basin. With a partner, create a multimedia presentation to explain the problems affecting the river basin, current efforts to solve the problems, and additional solutions you would propose. Include map and images and charts, diagrams, or graphs in your presentation. WHST.9–10.7; WHST.9–10.8, WHST.9–10.1; WHST.9–10.6; WHST.9–10.7

Writing About Geography

21 ***Argument*** Use standard grammar, spelling, sentence structure, and punctuation to write an editorial explaining why nuclear power plants in Armenia should be shut down. Be certain to anticipate and rebut the opposing viewpoint. WHST.9–10.1

Need Extra Help?

If You've Missed Question	12	13	14	15	16	17	18	19	20	21
Go to page	454	360	360	360	466	465	472	463	470	469

472

Critical Thinking

12 Essays will vary but should be strongly supported with information from the chapter, including the historic significance of ethnic traditions and ways of life of the people, influences of Islam, physical geography of landforms and water systems, and perils of recent history including conflicts, oil and gas extraction causing environmental damage, damage from nuclear testing, and depletion of the Aral Sea through use of water sources.

Applying Map Skills

13 Descriptions will vary but must include some reference to: the western section is known as the Caucasus because of the Caucasus Mountains that lie between the Black Sea and the Caspian Sea; the eastern section of the subregion is located on the eastern shore of the Caspian Sea and reaches to China and Pakistan.

14 the Northeast (Turkey, Iran, and Iraq)

15 The Aral Sea is located partially in Kazakhstan and partially in Uzbekistan.

Exploring the Essential Question

16 Summaries will vary but should include information on the conflict between Tajikistan and Uzbekistan over the damming of a tributary of the Amu Dar'ya and the way in which this human system impacts the physical systems of the subregion. Summary should also include how this conflict is emblematic of those within the subregion. Tajikistan wishes to build the dam to make use of hydroelectricity to address its energy needs. Uzbekistan is concerned the dam will limit the water available to irrigate its cotton fields. As a result of this dispulte, Uzbekistan cut off the sale of natural gas to Tajikistan and shut down rail service that imported food to the country. There are also concerns that the dam could harm the water quality of the river. This conflict is emblematic of many within the region as it is over the control and supply of natural resources.

College and Career Readiness

17 Memo and graphs may vary but should show that the oil production in Kazakhstan is likely to increase in the next five years as the country is trying to become one of the top ten oil producers in the world.

DBQ Analyzing Primary Sources

18 Colville's comments indicate that the justice system in Kyrgyzstan discriminates against national and ethnic minorities, making justice impossible to attain for minority groups.

19 In 2010, ethnic fighting forced some 300,000 people from their homes in Kyrgyzstan and only half have returned. The UN and news agencies are interested in finding out why this fighting occurred and why people feel they can't return to their homes.

Research and Presentation

20 Presentations will vary but should include maps, images, charts, graphs, and/or diagrams to show what problems are affecting the Syr Dar'ya river basin and how the organizations chosen are protecting it. The presentation should also supply additional solutions to the problems affecting the river basin.

Writing About Geography

21 Paragraphs will vary but should be strongly supported with information from the chapter, including that Armenia runs a nuclear power plant in an earthquake-prone area and that an earthquake could cause a serious nuclear accident. The government has also chosen to build another nuclear plant rather than find another energy source. Opposing viewpoints could include that the country relies on nuclear power for 40 percent of its electricity, which makes it difficult to abandon this power source.

UNIT 6

AFRICA SOUTH OF THE SAHARA Planner

UNDERSTANDING BY DESIGN®

Enduring Understandings

- *Places reflect the relationship between humans and the physical environment.*
- *The characteristics and distribution of human populations affect physical and human systems.*
- *The physical environment affects people and their activities.*

Essential Question

- *How do physical systems and human systems shape a place?*

Students will know:

- *that Africa south of the Sahara has a diverse landscape that includes shoreline, low plains, highlands, major rivers, and tropical rain forest.*
- *that a wide variety of climates supports various biomes in the region.*
- *how cultures and conflict coexist in the region today.*
- *how economic activities and conflict in the region intersect.*
- *how government, politics, resource management, and democracy influence the region.*
- *how geography helps shape settlement patterns in the region.*
- *how a growing population presents challenges.*
- *the serious environmental issues that affect life in the region, including water scarcity and desertification.*

Students will be able to:

- ***analyze** how the influence of democracy affects the economy, resource management, and conflict.*
- ***identify** factors that affect climate, vegetation, and population patterns.*
- ***describe** the influence of water systems on population density and settlement.*
- ***explain** how economic activities, changes in government, and cultural differences cause conflict.*
- ***describe** the ways that ancient and modern life coexist.*
- ***analyze** the severe environmental issues in this region and how they are being addressed.*

Predictable Misunderstandings

- *The dominant climate in Africa is hot and dry.*
- *People in Equatorial Africa live in villages in the rain forest and have little contact with the outside world.*
- *Africa south of the Sahara has a similar geography to North Africa.*
- *Southern Africa and South Africa are the same place.*
- *The Transition Zone has little impact on the global economy.*
- *The ethnic groups of Africa south of the Sahara are largely insulated in their own villages.*
- *People in Africa have little need for cell phones or technology.*

Assessment Evidence

Performance Tasks:

- *Environmental Case Study*
- *GeoLab Activity*
- *GIS Simulation*
- *Hands-On Chapter Projects*

Other Evidence:

- *Location Activity*
- *Self-Check Quizzes*
- *Lesson Quizzes*
- *Participation in Interactive Whiteboard Activities*
- *Contribution to small-group activities*
- *Interpretation of slide show images*
- *Participation in class discussions about Africa south of the Sahara*
- *Analysis of graphic organizers, graphs, and charts*
- *Lesson Reviews*
- *Chapter Assessments*

Key for Using the Teacher Edition

SKILL-BASED ACTIVITIES

Types of skill activities found in the Teacher Edition.

* **V Visual Skills** require students to analyze maps, graphs, charts, and photos.

R Reading Skills help students practice reading skills and master vocabulary.

C Critical Thinking Skills help students apply and extend what they have learned.

W Writing Skills provide writing opportunities to help students comprehend the text.

T Technology Skills require students to use digital tools effectively.

*Letters are followed by a number when there is more than one of the same type of skill on the page.

DIFFERENTIATED INSTRUCTION

All activities are written for the on-level student unless otherwise marked with the leveled labels below.

BL Beyond Level
AL Approaching Level
ELL English Language Learners

All students benefit from activities that utilize different learning styles. Many activities are marked as below when a particular learning style is highlighted.

Intrapersonal	**Naturalist**
Logical/Mathematical	**Kinesthetic**
Visual/Spatial	**Auditory/Musical**
Verbal/Linguistic	**Interpersonal**

SUGGESTED PACING GUIDE

Introducing the Unit	1 Day
Chapter 20: The Transition Zone	4 Days
Chapter 21: East Africa	4 Days
Case Study: Should the Blue Nile Dam Be Built?	1 Day
Chapter 22: West Africa	4 Days
Global Connections: Conflict Diamonds	1 Day
Chapter 23: Equatorial Africa	4 Days
Chapter 24: Southern Africa	4 Days
TOTAL TIME	**23 Days**

PLANNER

☑ Print Teaching Options

V Visual Skills

- ☐ **p. 474** Students draw a sketch of the region based on a passage description. ELL Visual/Spatial
- ☐ **p. 479** Students analyze an economic map to answer questions about population growth and settlement. AL Logical/Mathematical, Visual/Spatial

R Reading Skills

- ☐ **p. 474** Students preview the unit by studying an image and answering questions about it.
- ☐ **p. 475** Students discuss colonial legacy in Africa and weigh the consequences of European influences. Interpersonal, Verbal/Linguistic
- ☐ **p. 477** Students identify political units on a map and create a mnemonic device to remember them. ELL Verbal/Linguistic, Auditory/Musical

C Critical Thinking Skills

- ☐ **p. 479** Students make generalizations about climate and land use in the region. AL Logical/Mathematical, Visual/Spatial
- ☐ **p. 480** Students explore the social, economic, and cultural issues that cities in the region face. Logical/Mathematical, Visual/Spatial

W Writing Skills

- ☐ **p. 475** Students compare and contrast two images and write about their similarities and differences. AL Visual/Spatial, Verbal/Linguistic
- ☐ **p. 477** Students write a narrative to explain their experiences as a student ambassador in a country in the region. BL Verbal/Linguistic, Intrapersonal
- ☐ **p. 478** Students write a report about the vegetation found in climate zones. AL Naturalist, Verbal/Linguistic
- ☐ **p. 479** Students assume the role of a co-owner of a mineral extraction company and write argumentative reports about areas in the region where it would be advantageous to start a branch of the company. BL Intrapersonal

T Technology Skills

- ☐ **p. 475** Students gather information to write a formal essay about ecotourism and environmental preservation in the region. BL Verbal/Linguistic
- ☐ **p. 478** Students research how vegetation affects land use in Africa south of the Sahara and then present their findings in graphs or charts. BL Visual/Spatial

☑ Online Teaching Options

V Visual Skills

- INTERACTIVE FEATURE **Explore the Region: Africa South of the Sahara**—Students compare and contrast the physical and human geography where they live with this region. Verbal/Linguistic
- INTERACTIVE MAP **Political Map: Africa South of the Sahara**—Students discuss the political boundaries of countries in a current map and then compare them to a map of the region from fifty years ago. Visual/Spatial
- INTERACTIVE MAP **Physical Map: Africa South of the Sahara**—Students identify the river systems in the region and then predict how water systems impact population density. AL Visual/Spatial, Logical/Mathematical

R Reading Skills

- INTERACTIVE MAP **Population Density Map: Africa South of the Sahara**—Students study the unit maps to draw conclusions about population growth. BL Interpersonal
- INTERACTIVE MAP **Economic Activity Map: Africa South of the Sahara**—Students rank the resources located on the map that provide the most economic value for a country. BL Verbal/Linguistic, Logical/Mathematical

C Critical Thinking Skills

- GEO @ WORK **Thinking Like a Geographer**—Students explore principles and skills of geography to see the importance of geography in understanding relationships and generating solutions.

W Writing Skills

- INTERACTIVE MAP **Climate and Vegetation Maps: Africa South of the Sahara**—Students choose a city in the region and write an article about it, focusing on the climate, from the perspective of a travel magazine reporter. BL Verbal/Linguistic

☑ Printable Digital Worksheets

V Visual Skills

- WORKSHEET **Location Activity**—Students locate countries, water systems, and physical features of Africa south of the Sahara.
- WORKSHEET **GeoLab Activity**—Students explore how to construct a model showing how the atoms in a diamond are arranged to give it its properties.

C Critical Thinking Skills

- WORKSHEET **Environmental Case Study**—Students complete a study about whether they think agricultural biotechnology in Africa south of the Sahara should be used.

T Technology Skills

- WORKSHEET **GIS Simulation**—Students use the techniques of GIS to understand the changes in physical, political, and cultural factors in the African region south of the Sahara from the pre-colonial period to the present.

Africa South of the Sahara

UNIT 6

Chapter 20	Chapter 21	Chapter 22	Chapter 23	Chapter 24
The Transition Zone	East Africa	West Africa	Equatorial Africa	Southern Africa

GEO @ WORK

Thinking Like a Geographer

Problem Solving Explore specific examples of the principles and skills of geography applied to real-world challenges that impact people's lives. From agriculture to urban planning, to wiping out disease and managing changes in society—geography plays a key role in understanding relationships and generating solutions that make sense.

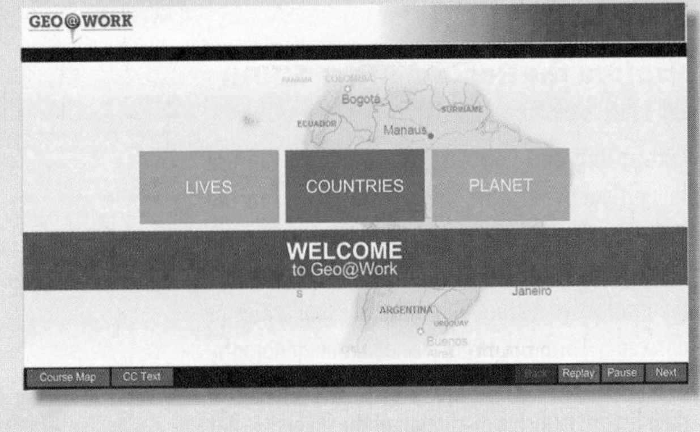

ENGAGE

Creating Charts Have students locate the Sahara on a map of Africa. Then ask them to think about why geographers have divided Africa by this physical feature, considering physical, political, cultural, and economic factors. Have students make a chart with these terms as headings and make inferences to fill in each column. As students read through the unit, have them go back to their charts to add information.

TEACH & ASSESS

Making Connections

Explain to students how the physical and human geography of Africa south of the Sahara is quite distinct from North Africa. Have students think about the physical and human geography of North America. Ask if there are any comparable physical features that divide our continent as the Sahara separates Africa. Then ask them to compare and contrast those features with the Sahara.

Drawing Inferences Ask students to examine the unit opener image. Discuss the landforms, flora, and fauna. **Ask:** **In which subregion of Africa south of the Sahara do you think this image was taken?** *(Possible answer: East Africa).* **How do you know?** *(Possible answer: Giraffes live in East Africa, and the mountains and land are similar to those that are found in that subregion.)* **What inferences can you make about the climate?** *(Possible answer: It is mostly warm and dry on the flatland but cooler and wetter in the mountains.)* **Visual/Spatial, Naturalist**

CLOSE & REFLECT

Identifying Have students identify on a map of Africa the different subregions that comprise this region. Invite them to identify characteristics of the region that make it distinctive from North Africa. Ask students to keep a record of these characteristics and features and add to it as they learn more about the region. Have students discuss which characteristics and features are most conducive to supporting population growth and the economy.

ENGAGE

R Reading Skills

Previewing Point out the image of the Masai women and the callout labeled number 1 on the map. **Ask:** **How does previewing the image of the Masai women and seeing where the Masai people live on the map help you to better understand aspects about the Masai culture?** *(Possible answer: I see that the Masai live in East Africa and that red is an important color to their culture. I can also see that beaded jewelry is important to their culture and is possibly a tradition or shows status.)* **Why do you think that the women sing to visitors?** *(Possible answer: It is their custom to welcome visitors in this way and is a part of their culture.)* Have students work with a partner to research the location and history of Maasai Mara National Reserve.

TEACH & ASSESS

V Visual Skills

Spatial Analysis Have a student volunteer read aloud the section "Explore the Region." As the student is reading, ask students to listen closely and draw a sketch of the region based on what they hear. Ask students to include an outline map, physical features, and subregions. Have students locate areas that are hot and wet and make educated guesses about the location of the densest population centers in the region.
ELL Visual/Spatial

C Critical Thinking Skills

Speculating After students have read the last sentence, **ask:** **Why do you think each subregion has a blend of traditional cultures?** *(Possible answer: The European powers ignored tribal areas and lands and therefore combined diverse tribes into one country. After the countries gained independence, these tribes were forced to live together but have still tried to maintain their traditional cultures.)* Have students write a short poem that describes the diversity of physical, human, and cultural geography of Africa south of the Sahara. Invite several volunteers to recite their poems to the class.
BL Auditory/Musical, Verbal/Linguistic

R ① Culture Women of the Masai ethnic group sing to welcome tourists to their village in Kenya's Maasai Mara National Reserve.

EXPLORE the REGION

AFRICA SOUTH OF THE SAHARA includes some of the driest and wettest spots on Earth. A region of physical and human diversity, Africa south of the Sahara includes the Transition Zone, with its mix of Islamic and African influences; the ethnic complexity of West Africa; the savannas and mountains of East Africa; the dense, lush rain forests of Equatorial Africa; and mineral-rich Southern Africa. Each subregion has a mix of large and small countries and a blend of traditional cultures deeply marked by a colonial past.

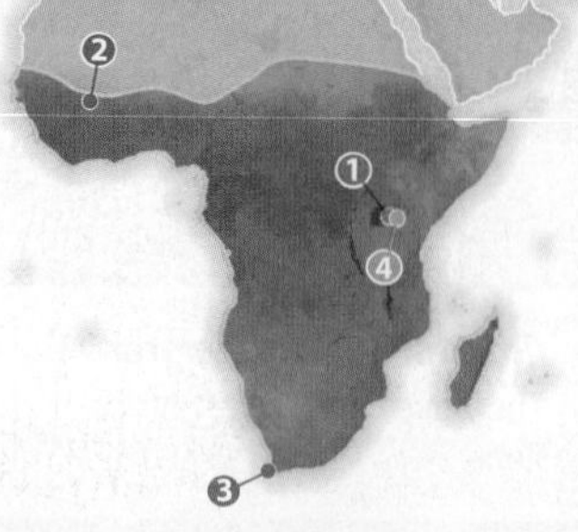

THERE'S MORE ONLINE 

474

networks Online Teaching Options

INTERACTIVE FEATURE

Explore the Region: Africa South of the Sahara

Comparing and Contrasting Students can use this interactive feature as an introduction to the culture, colonial legacy, people, and resources of Africa south of the Sahara. Have student pairs view the interactive feature and note any similarities or differences with the physical and human geography of the area in which they live. Have students share their lists to launch a discussion of the diversity that exists in this region. **Verbal/Linguistic**

Africa South of the Sahara

INTRODUCTION

Africa south of the Sahara includes some of the driest and wettest spots on Earth. A region of physical and human diversity, Africa south of the Sahara includes the Transition Zone, with its mix of Islamic and African influences; the ethnic complexity of West Africa; the savannas and mountains of East Africa; the dense, lush rain forests of Equatorial Africa; and mineral-rich Southern Africa. Each subregion has a mix of large and small countries and a blend of traditional cultures deeply marked by a colonial past.

2 **The People** Africa south of the Sahara has hundreds of ethnic groups, each with rich cultural and artistic traditions and distinct ways of life.

3 **Colonial Legacy** Beginning in the late 1800s, European powers took possession of most of Africa. The lasting impact of European colonization is still evident today in language, culture, politics, and economic and social issues.

4 **The Resources** Africa south of the Sahara is famous for its captivating wildlife, for being rich in mineral resources, and for its lush rain forests. Countries in the region work to balance the use of these resources, seeking to spur economic development while still preserving the environment.

UNIT 6

Africa South of the Sahara

W Writing Skills

Informative/Explanatory Have students contrast this image of women with the image on page 474. **Ask:** **How and why are these women dressed differently?** *(Possible answer: The women in image #2 are wearing wrappings on their head and their clothing is a different color. The two groups of women are from different ethnic groups, so they have their own styles and traditions of dress.)* **Do you think that differences among ethnic groups bring conflict or cooperation in this region? Explain.** *(Possible answer: It most likely has brought conflict because some ethnic groups may not be able to embrace different traditions or may want to have power and influence over other ethnic groups.)* Have students write about which group of women they would like to meet and explain their reasoning. **AL Visual/Spatial, Verbal/Linguistic**

R Reading Skills

Observing Discuss with students how this image reveals a colonial legacy in Africa. Divide the class into small groups, instructing students to discuss how European colonialism was beneficial to the infrastructure of Africa, such as buildings and roads, using this image as an example. Then have students weigh the consequences of the European colonial legacy on Africa. **Interpersonal, Verbal/Linguistic**

T Technology Skills

Researching Ask students to research ecotourism and environmental preservation in Africa south of the Sahara. As students do Internet searches, have them answer these three questions to guide their research:

- Where is ecotourism and environmental preservation prevalent in the region?
- Are they beneficial to the economy? How?
- What challenges do they pose?

Have students compile their data to write a formal essay using software technology. Remind them to include a thesis statement and to support their main points with facts and details. **BL Verbal/Linguistic**

CLOSE & REFLECT

Posing Questions Ask students to write down the main physical and cultural characteristics of Africa south of the Sahara. Have them write three or four questions they would like to investigate about this region. Then have students find the answers to the questions as they read through the unit.

DIGITAL WORKSHEETS

Africa South of the Sahara

Demonstrating Use these online digital unit worksheets to have students demonstrate their depth of knowledge and comprehension and to provide them with extended unit content through project-based activities.

- **Environmental Case Study**
- **GeoLab Activity**
- **GIS Simulations**
- **Location Activity**

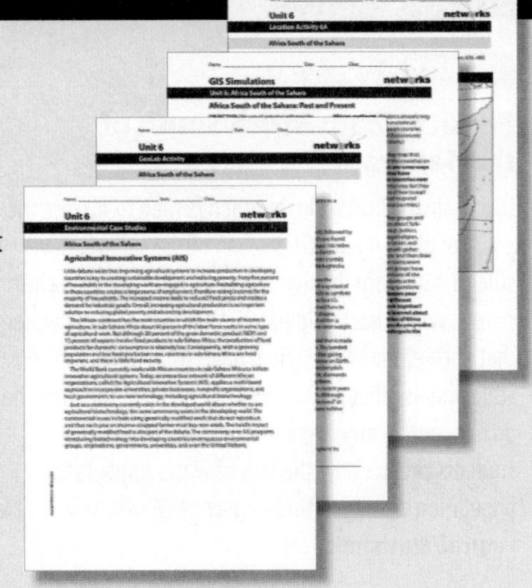

ENGAGE

C Critical Thinking Skills

Transferring Information Have students examine the physical map of Africa South of the Sahara in groups, discussing different physical features and comparing and contrasting them to those of North Africa. Challenge students to be creative in creating a game in which they have to identify physical features of the region. Point out that students may need to conduct some research to gain enough information for the game.

TEACH & ASSESS

V Visual Skills

Using Diagrams Point to the map key and ask students to study it. Review with students how to read latitude and longitude lines on the map. Provide an example such as the location of Mount Kenya being about 15°S, 37°E. **Ask:**

- **What is the approximate location of the lowest point on the map and the name of the geographic feature?** *(11°N, 42°E 500 feet below sea level, Lake Assal)*
- **What is the region's highest mountain?** *(Kilimanjaro)*
- **Which area has a higher elevation, Lake Chad or Lake Victoria?** *(Lake Victoria)*
- **How does the map key help you to better understand where the countries of the region are located?** *(The key includes a symbol for national boundaries, and those boundaries are included on the map for each country of the region.)*
- **What other symbol might you add to the map key to illustrate information and data about the physical features of the region?** *(Possible answer: a symbol for bodies of water that are freshwater or salt water)*

ELL Visual/Spatial

R Reading Skills

Reading Maps Draw students' attention to the dotted red lines on the map. **Ask:** **Why do you think these lines are dotted and not solid?** *(The dotted red lines represent a transitional area.)* **Do any physical features align with these boundaries? Explain.** *(Possible answer: No, not really, because this area is not based on physical features but more on cultural divisions.)* AL Visual/Spatial, Logical/Mathematical

C Africa South of the Sahara
Physical

Elevations
10,000 ft. (3,000 m)
5,000 ft. (1,500 m)
2,000 ft. (600 m)
1,000 ft. (300 m)
0 ft. (0 m)
Below sea level

— National boundary
▲ Mountain peak
▼ Lowest point

EUROPE
CENTRAL ASIA
Mediterranean Sea
NORTH AFRICA
SOUTHWEST ASIA
Boundary represents January 1, 1956, alignment; final alignment pending negotiations.
SAHARA
SAHEL
Cape Verde Islands
Lake Chad
Darfur
Red Sea
Gulf of Aden
Lake Assal -500 ft. (-152 m)
ETHIOPIAN HIGHLANDS
Boundary in dispute
Gulf of Guinea
Bioko
Principe
São Tomé
Pagalu
The red dashed lines represent the northern and southern boundaries of a region known as the Transition Zone, an area of increasing Islamic influence.
CONGO BASIN
Great Rift Valley
Mt. Kenya 17,058 ft. (5,199 m)
Serengeti Plain
Kilimanjaro 19,341 ft. (5,895 m)
Lake Victoria
Lake Tanganyika
Pemba I.
Zanzibar I.
Seychelles
Amirante Is.
BIÉ PLATEAU
Katanga Plateau
Comoro Is.
Farquhar Is.
ATLANTIC OCEAN
INDIAN OCEAN
Lake Malawi
Lake Kariba
Mozambique Channel
Madagascar
Mauritius
Réunion
Victoria Falls
Okavango Delta
Namib Desert
Kalahari Desert
Drakensberg
Cape of Good Hope
Cape Agulhas
TROPIC OF CANCER
EQUATOR
TROPIC OF CAPRICORN
0 — 1,000 miles
0 — 1,000 kilometers
Lambert Azimuthal Equal-Area Conic projection

476

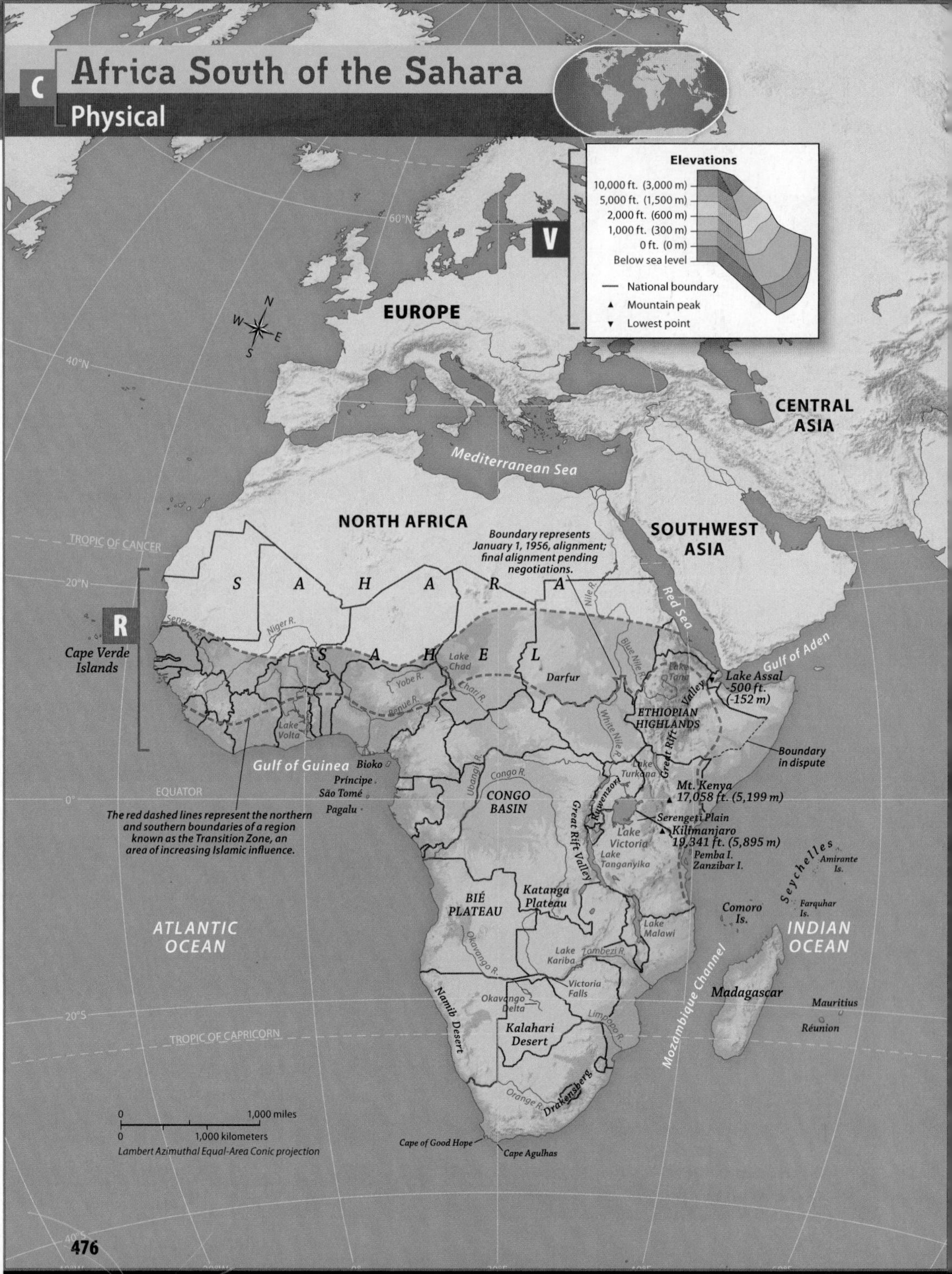

networks Online Teaching Options

INTERACTIVE MAP

Physical Map: Africa South of the Sahara

Discussing Display the interactive map to discuss the physical diversity of Africa south of the Sahara. Have students identify the rivers that flow throughout the region, where each originates, and the bodies of water that each empties into. Then have students note the scale and ask them to identify the areas of the map that do not contain any rivers or water systems. Have students predict how the lack of water impacts the population density in these areas. AL Visual/Spatial, Logical/Mathematical

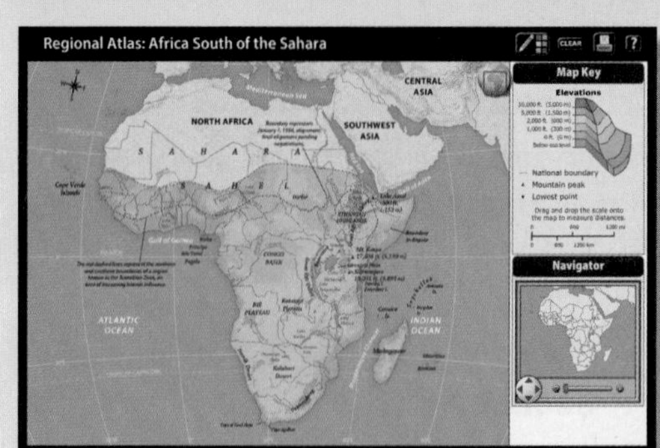

Africa South of the Sahara

Political

UNIT 6
REGIONAL ATLAS

MAP STUDY

1. ***Physical Systems*** Where is the Great Rift Valley located? Which lakes are part of the Great Rift Valley?
2. ***Human Systems*** Which of the region's countries are landlocked? How might this characteristic affect their economies?

- ○ National capital
- • Major city

R

EUROPE

NORTH AFRICA

SOUTHWEST ASIA

The red dashed lines represent the northern and southern boundaries of a region known as the Transition Zone, an area of increasing Islamic influence.

Boundary represents January 1, 1956, alignment; final alignment pending negotiations.

Boundary in dispute

CAPE VERDE, MAURITANIA, MALI, NIGER, CHAD, SUDAN, ERITREA, DJIBOUTI, SENEGAL, GAMBIA, GUINEA-BISSAU, GUINEA, SIERRA LEONE, LIBERIA, CÔTE D'IVOIRE, BURKINA FASO, GHANA, TOGO, BENIN, NIGERIA, CAMEROON, CENTRAL AFRICAN REPUBLIC, SOUTH SUDAN, ETHIOPIA, SOMALIA, EQUATORIAL GUINEA, SÃO TOMÉ & PRÍNCIPE, GABON, CONGO, DEMOCRATIC REPUBLIC OF THE CONGO, UGANDA, KENYA, RWANDA, BURUNDI, TANZANIA, CABINDA (Angola), ANGOLA, ZAMBIA, MALAWI, MOZAMBIQUE, ZIMBABWE, NAMIBIA, BOTSWANA, SOUTH AFRICA, SWAZILAND, LESOTHO, MADAGASCAR, COMOROS, SEYCHELLES, MAURITIUS, Mayotte (France), Réunion (France), Ascension (U.K.), St. Helena (U.K.)

ATLANTIC OCEAN · INDIAN OCEAN · Mediterranean Sea · Red Sea · Gulf of Aden · Gulf of Guinea · Mozambique Channel

0 — 1,000 miles
0 — 1,000 kilometers
Lambert Azimuthal Equal-Area Conic projection

W T

INTERACTIVE MAP

Political Map: Africa South of the Sahara

Visualizing Display this interactive political map of the region to discuss with students the changes in map boundaries. Explain the Making Connections section on this page to students. Provide a political map of the region from fifty years ago and make numerous copies to distribute to students. Have students visually compare the map from fifty years ago to this current political map, and then list as many visual differences as possible. Ask several students to share their lists with the class. **Visual/Spatial**

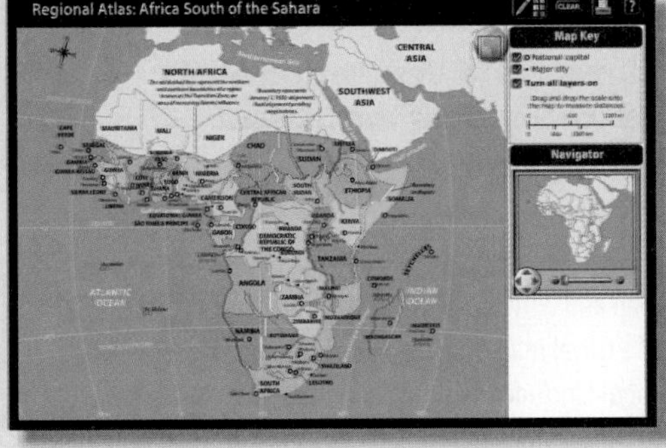

UNIT 6

Africa South of the Sahara

R Reading Skills

Listing Explain to students that political maps show boundaries and borders. They can also be useful in locating capital cities and other political units. Have students make a list of each country and capital city in the region. Then have students work in small groups to create a jingle as a mnemonic device to remember the capitals of each country. When students have practiced their jingle, invite them to share it as a group with the class. **ELL Verbal/Linguistic, Auditory/Musical**

Making Connections

Explain to students that the political map of this region has changed significantly as a result of European colonization—borders, boundaries, and national capitals included. Names have changed, and different ethnic groups were forced to live within certain boundaries that European countries drew randomly or to meet their own needs.

W Writing Skills

Narrative Explain to students that they will be serving as a student ambassador to one of the countries in the region. Ask them to write a narrative about their experience. Guide students to resources that will provide information about what ambassadors do and specific details about the work of ambassadors in countries in the region. Invite students to share their narratives with the class. **BL Verbal/Linguistic, Intrapersonal**

T Technology Skills

Researching Remind students that the colonial legacy left a mixture of small and large countries in this region. Assign students a country in the region. Have them find out when the country was colonized, by which country, and when the African country gained its independence. If their assigned country was never colonized, ask students to find out what factors led to this situation. Have students create a fact file about their country based on their findings and record the information digitally on a class website or blog posting. **Verbal/Linguistic**

ANSWERS, p. 477

MAP STUDY

1. eastern Africa; Lakes Turkana, Victoria, Tanganyika, and Malawi are part of the Great Rift Valley.
2. Mali, Burkina Faso, Niger, Chad, South Sudan, Central African Republic, Ethiopia, Uganda, Rwanda, Democratic Republic of the Congo, Malawi, Zambia, Zimbabwe, Botswana, Swaziland, Lesotho; could limit trade because of lack of access to the sea

R Reading Skills

Observing Explain to students that the Sahel is a semi-arid grassland that separates the Sahara in the north from the tropical grasslands in the south. Have students use the climate map key to describe the climates of this region (arid and semi-arid to tropical wet/dry). Ask students to work in pairs to use the map and key to make other observations of a drastic change from one climate area or zone to another. ELL **Verbal/Linguistic, Visual/Spatial**

T Technology Skills

Presenting Point out the vegetation map key at the bottom left of the main map, as well as the inset map. Assign pairs of students different countries or subregions of Africa south of the Sahara to determine how vegetation affects land use. Guide students to online resources that will provide the most current data on land use and economic activities for their assigned country or region. Challenge students to find or create charts and graphs to illustrate the data they find. Then provide an opportunity for students to deliver their presentations to the class. Ask students who are in the audience to take notes for use in a class discussion about the effects of vegetation and land use on the respective economies. BL **Visual/Spatial**

W Writing Skills

Informative/Explanatory Have students compare the climate map to the vegetation map of Africa South of the Sahara. Ask them to write a short informative report that describes the vegetation that is dominant within each climate zone. Instruct students to draw conclusions in their writing about the effects of climate on the types of vegetation that thrive in an area. Challenge them to make comparisons to other world regions that have similar vegetation and climate zones. AL **Naturalist, Verbal/Linguistic**

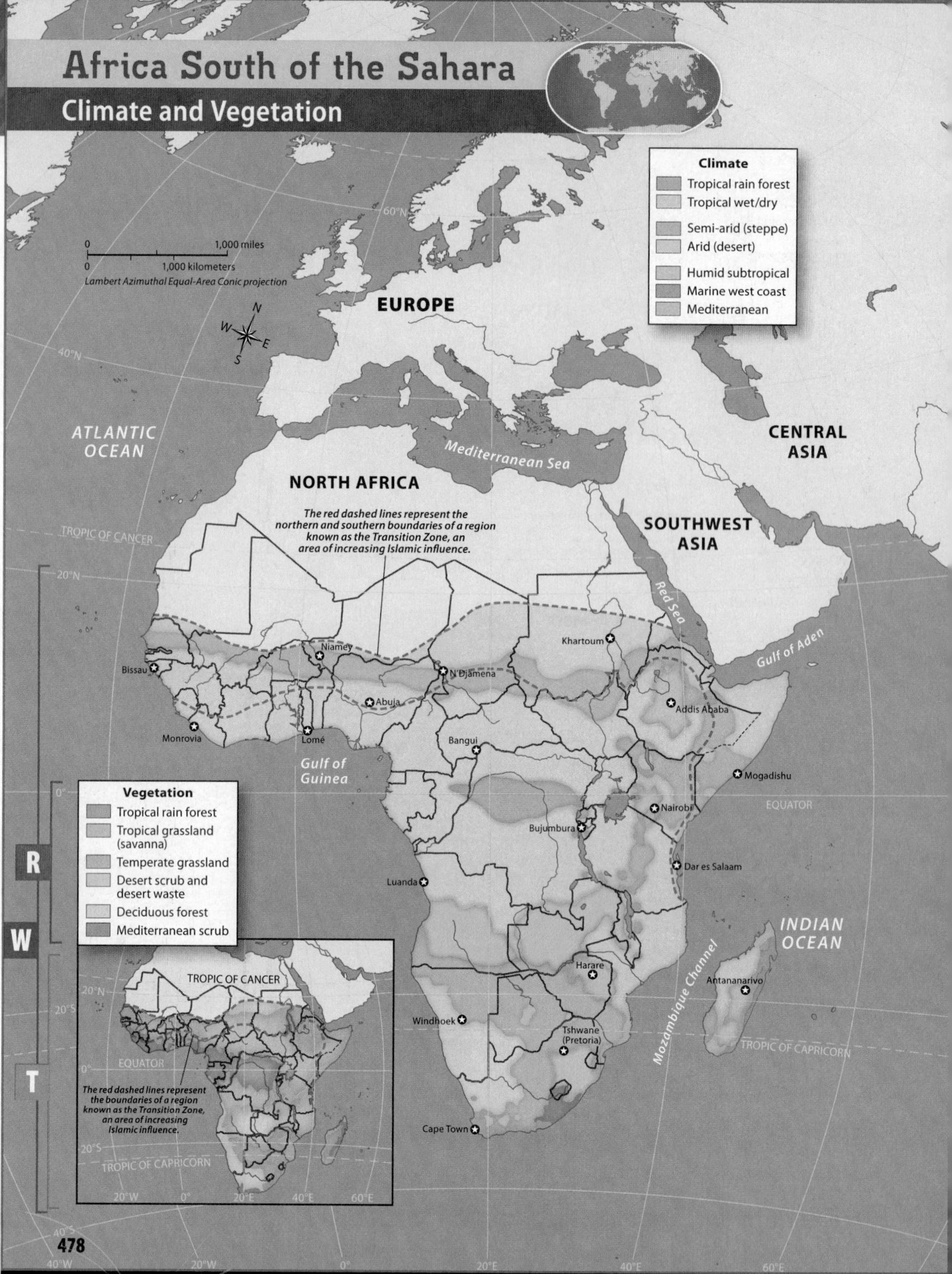

Africa South of the Sahara

Climate and Vegetation

Climate
- Tropical rain forest
- Tropical wet/dry
- Semi-arid (steppe)
- Arid (desert)
- Humid subtropical
- Marine west coast
- Mediterranean

0 — 1,000 miles
0 — 1,000 kilometers
Lambert Azimuthal Equal-Area Conic projection

EUROPE
ATLANTIC OCEAN
Mediterranean Sea
NORTH AFRICA
CENTRAL ASIA
SOUTHWEST ASIA
TROPIC OF CANCER
Red Sea
Gulf of Aden

The red dashed lines represent the northern and southern boundaries of a region known as the Transition Zone, an area of increasing Islamic influence.

Khartoum, Niamey, Bissau, N'Djamena, Abuja, Addis Ababa, Monrovia, Lomé, Bangui, Mogadishu, Gulf of Guinea, Nairobi, EQUATOR, Bujumbura, Dar es Salaam, Luanda, INDIAN OCEAN, Mozambique Channel, Harare, Antananarivo, Windhoek, Tshwane (Pretoria), TROPIC OF CAPRICORN, Cape Town

Vegetation
- Tropical rain forest
- Tropical grassland (savanna)
- Temperate grassland
- Desert scrub and desert waste
- Deciduous forest
- Mediterranean scrub

TROPIC OF CANCER
EQUATOR
The red dashed lines represent the boundaries of a region known as the Transition Zone, an area of increasing Islamic influence.
TROPIC OF CAPRICORN

478

networks Online Teaching Options

INTERACTIVE MAP

Climate and Vegetation Maps: Africa South of the Sahara

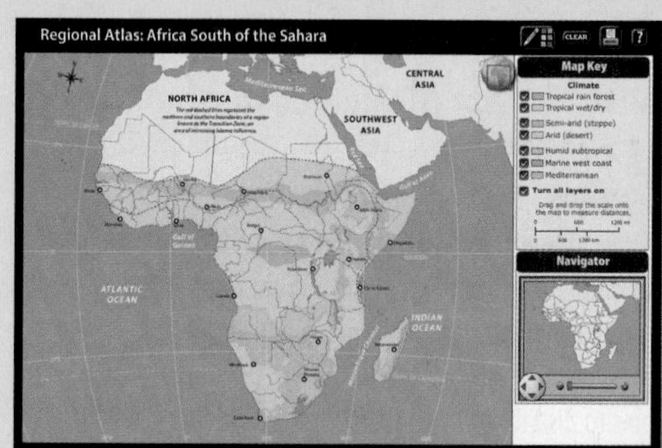

Narrative Use these maps to discuss with students the variations in climate and vegetation within the region. Have students choose one of the cities on the map and write a story about it from the perspective of a travel magazine reporter. Students' travel articles should include the sights and sounds of the city, as well as the weather and climate information. Their narratives should also recommend what travelers should wear and bring along with them. Allow students to conduct research to complete their magazine articles and encourage them to include one visual of their chosen city. BL **Verbal/Linguistic**

Africa South of the Sahara

Economic Activity

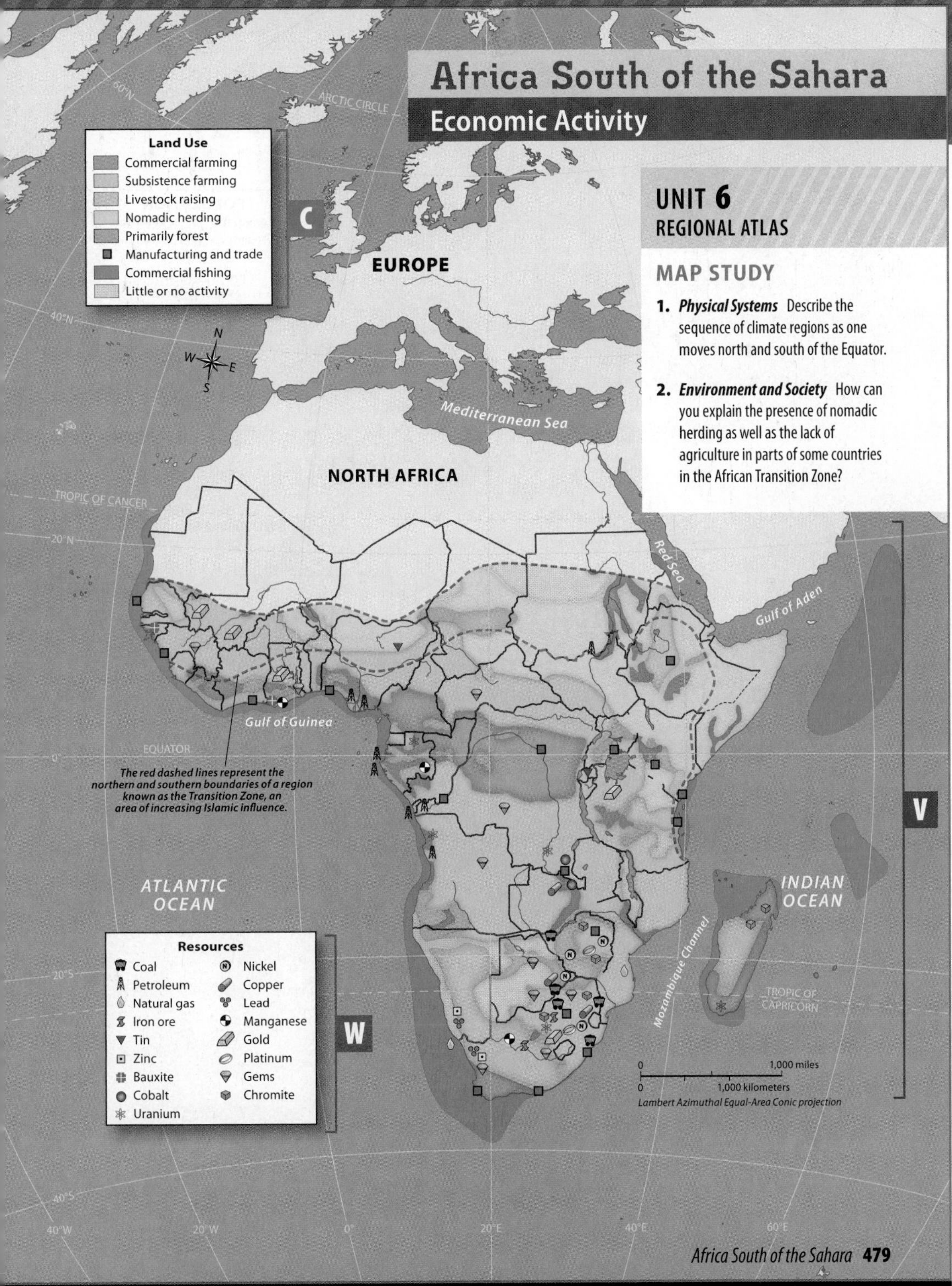

Land Use
- Commercial farming
- Subsistence farming
- Livestock raising
- Nomadic herding
- Primarily forest
- Manufacturing and trade
- Commercial fishing
- Little or no activity

UNIT **6**
REGIONAL ATLAS

MAP STUDY

1. ***Physical Systems*** Describe the sequence of climate regions as one moves north and south of the Equator.
2. ***Environment and Society*** How can you explain the presence of nomadic herding as well as the lack of agriculture in parts of some countries in the African Transition Zone?

EUROPE

NORTH AFRICA

Mediterranean Sea

Red Sea

Gulf of Aden

Gulf of Guinea

ATLANTIC OCEAN

INDIAN OCEAN

Mozambique Channel

ARCTIC CIRCLE

TROPIC OF CANCER

EQUATOR

TROPIC OF CAPRICORN

The red dashed lines represent the northern and southern boundaries of a region known as the Transition Zone, an area of increasing Islamic influence.

Resources
- Coal
- Petroleum
- Natural gas
- Iron ore
- Tin
- Zinc
- Bauxite
- Cobalt
- Uranium
- Nickel
- Copper
- Lead
- Manganese
- Gold
- Platinum
- Gems
- Chromite

0 — 1,000 miles
0 — 1,000 kilometers
Lambert Azimuthal Equal-Area Conic projection

Africa South of the Sahara **479**

INTERACTIVE MAP

Economic Activity Map: Africa South of the Sahara

Classifying Use this interactive map to discuss resources and land uses within the region. Review with students the harsh desert climate and limited water sources found in some of the subregions. Then ask several volunteers to identify some of the predominant resources and land uses in Africa. Have the class rank which resources are the most plentiful and which resources are noticeably lacking. Have students consider what they have learned about resources and their connection to a country's economy. Ask them to discuss which resources might have the most impact on a country's economy. BL **Verbal/Linguistic, Logical/Mathematical**

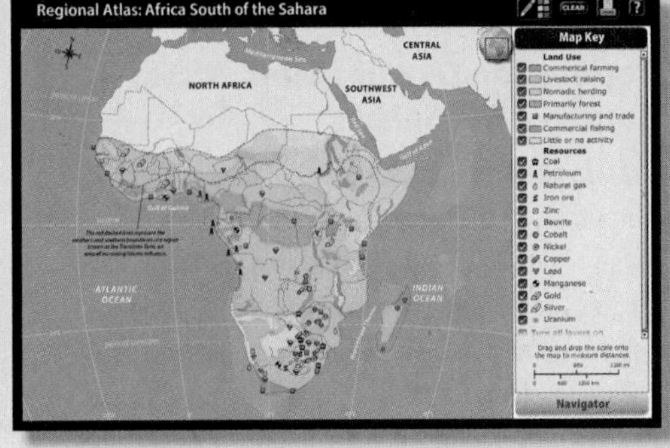

UNIT 6

Africa South of the Sahara

C Critical Thinking Skills

Making Generalizations Have students compare the land use data with that of the climate data on the map on the previous page. **Ask:** **What generalizations can you make about climate and land use from looking at the maps?** *(Possible answer: Tropical rain forest and tropical wet/dry is used for commercial and subsistence farming and forestry; arid is used for nomadic herding.)* **What one land use activity is used throughout the region regardless of climate?** *(commercial fishing)* **How can you explain the areas where there is little to no land use or economic activity?** *(Possible answer: The population is too low or the climate is too challenging in these areas to support economic activity.)* Ask students to write a paragraph to make generalizations about the dominant land use activities in the region, noting climatic conditions when applicable. AL **Logical/Mathematical, Visual/Spatial**

V Visual Skills

Analyzing Visuals Divide the class into small groups. Ask students to identify areas that are rich in resources and to name those resources. Then instruct them to study the areas of the map where the dotted red lines fall. Have students use the following guiding questions for their group discussions: **Do you think that other factors, besides Islamic influence, have affected population growth and settlement here? Do you think that the lack of resources has had any effect on the area's cultural development?** As students discuss these questions, have someone record their responses. Ask each group to form a consensus and then report its point of view to the class. AL **Logical/Mathematical, Visual/Spatial**

W Writing Skills

Argument Ask students to take the role of a co-owner of a foreign mineral extraction company. Have students identify areas of the region where it may be advantageous to start a branch of the company, considering mineral resources, climate, and accessibility. Ask students to make their case for a certain location by writing an argumentative report to the other co-owner of the company. Remind students that both owners must agree on a location, so their argument must be clear, supported, and convincing. BL **Intrapersonal**

ANSWERS, p. 479

MAP STUDY

1. Equator north: tropical rain forest, tropical wet/dry, semi-arid (steppe); arid (desert); Equator south: tropical rain forest, tropical wet/dry, humid subtropical, semi-arid (steppe), arid (desert)
2. These are areas of semi-arid or arid climate and do not support agriculture.

C Critical Thinking Skills

Exploring Issues Ask students to study the map and determine the most densely populated versus the lowest populated areas. Have students make a list of social, economic, and cultural issues that both areas face. **Ask:** **What do you think is the greatest issue that areas with high population density are trying to solve?** *(Possible answers: overcrowding, overpopulation, not enough social services, unsanitary conditions)* **What do you think is the greatest issue that areas with low population density face?** *(Possible answer: lack of resources for economic development)* Have students identify cities that are located in densely populated and not as densely populated areas and then explore whether these cities face the issues that were suggested. Have students take turns presenting their findings to the class. **Logical/Mathematical, Visual/Spatial**

R Reading Skills

Locating Have students locate those cities with a population under 2 million. **Ask:** **Where are most of these smaller cities located?** *(in western Africa and central Africa)* **What factors influence where people settle?** *(Possible answer: resources, job opportunities, family, climate)* **Do you think that these cities will eventually grow larger and become metropolitan areas of 5 million or more? Explain.** *(Possible answer: Yes, they most likely will grow and expand, as more and more people move from rural areas to urban areas to seek opportunities.)* Have students consider what they know about the land, climate, and resources of the region and identify other locations where cities might expand. **Interpersonal, Visual/Spatial, Logical/Mathematical**

CLOSE & REFLECT

Diagramming Have students work with a partner to review the content that the unit maps show and to create a diagram that illustrates the most relevant information for someone who wants a snapshot of Africa south of the Sahara. Show some examples of infographics to students to get them thinking about how to visually show the information. Remind students to cover physical features, political borders, population density, vegetation, land use, climate, and resources. Suggest that students share their diagrams with the class and select the most comprehensive one to use as a study aid for the unit.

ANSWERS, p. 480

MAP STUDY

1. West Africa
2. southwestern portion of continent; the Namib and Kalahari deserts

Africa South of the Sahara
Population Density

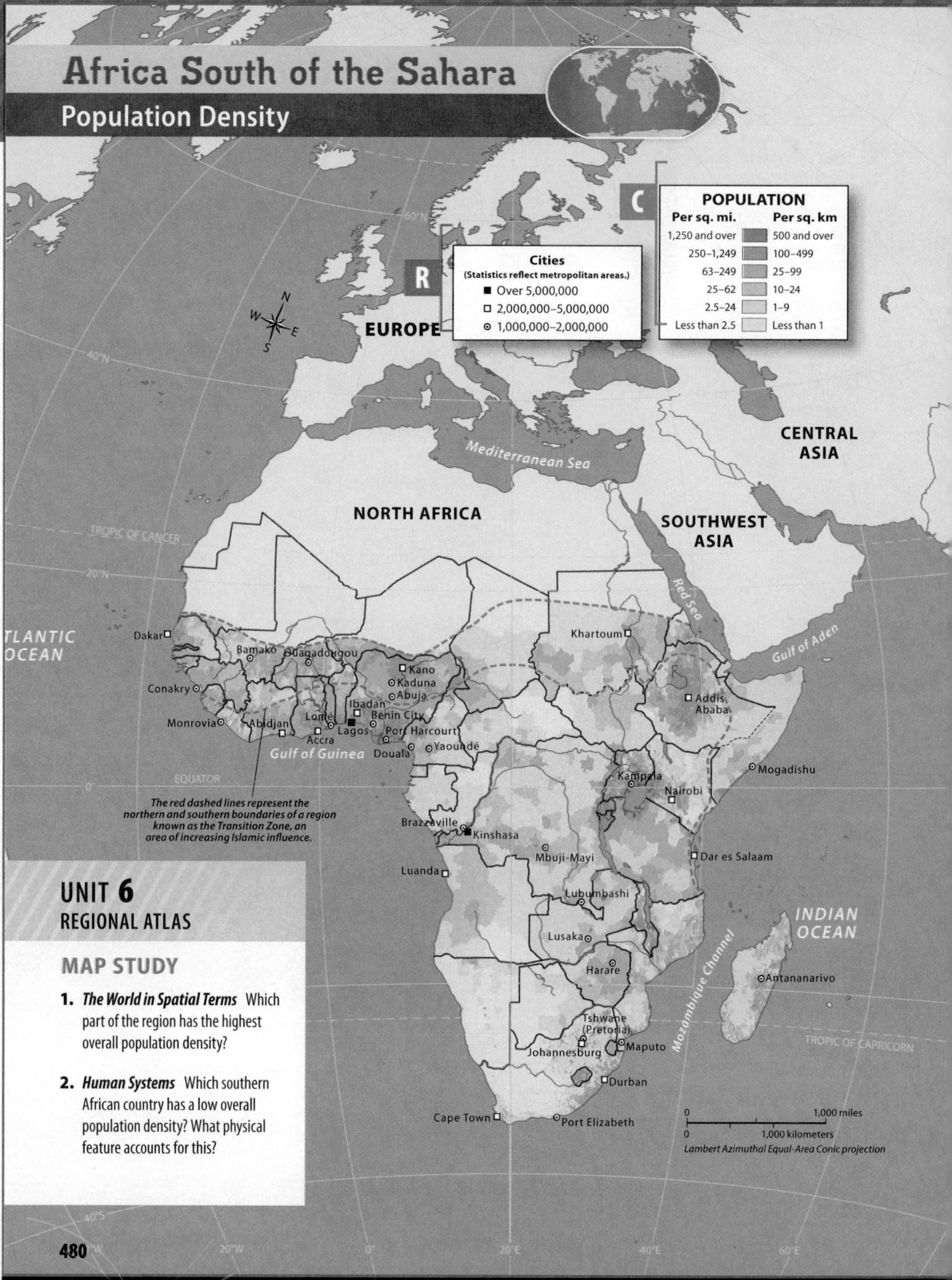

POPULATION

Per sq. mi.	Per sq. km
1,250 and over	500 and over
250–1,249	100–499
63–249	25–99
25–62	10–24
2.5–24	1–9
Less than 2.5	Less than 1

Cities
(Statistics reflect metropolitan areas.)
- ■ Over 5,000,000
- □ 2,000,000–5,000,000
- ⊙ 1,000,000–2,000,000

EUROPE
CENTRAL ASIA
NORTH AFRICA
SOUTHWEST ASIA
Mediterranean Sea
ATLANTIC OCEAN
INDIAN OCEAN
Gulf of Guinea
Gulf of Aden
Red Sea
Mozambique Channel
Dakar, Bamako, Ouagadougou, Conakry, Monrovia, Abidjan, Accra, Lomé, Ibadan, Lagos, Benin City, Port Harcourt, Kano, Kaduna, Abuja, Douala, Yaoundé, Khartoum, Addis Ababa, Mogadishu, Kampala, Nairobi, Dar es Salaam, Brazzaville, Kinshasa, Mbuji-Mayi, Luanda, Lubumbashi, Lusaka, Harare, Antananarivo, Tshwane (Pretoria), Johannesburg, Maputo, Durban, Cape Town, Port Elizabeth

The red dashed lines represent the northern and southern boundaries of a region known as the Transition Zone, an area of increasing Islamic influence.

0 — 1,000 miles
0 — 1,000 kilometers
Lambert Azimuthal Equal-Area Conic projection

UNIT 6
REGIONAL ATLAS

MAP STUDY

1. ***The World in Spatial Terms*** Which part of the region has the highest overall population density?
2. ***Human Systems*** Which southern African country has a low overall population density? What physical feature accounts for this?

480

networks Online Teaching Options

INTERACTIVE MAP

Population Density Map: Africa South of the Sahara

Drawing Conclusions Display this interactive map of Africa south of the Sahara to discuss population density in this region with students. Working in groups, have students analyze population issues in parts of Africa. Ask groups to identify the city that contains over five million residents. Then have groups use the previous four maps to gather information to determine factors that may have contributed to this city's growth. Ask them to consider how this growth may or may not have an effect on the surrounding cities and towns. Groups should work together to write a statement summarizing their conclusions. **BL Interpersonal**

CHAPTER 20

The Transition Zone Planner

UNDERSTANDING BY DESIGN®

Enduring Understandings

- *Geographers organize Earth into regions that share common characteristics.*

Essential Question

- *How do physical systems and human systems shape a place?*

Predictable Misunderstandings

Students may think:

- *The Transition Zone of Africa is entirely rural with people living mostly in small villages. Explain that there are relatively few cities in the Transition Zone, but there are several important ones such as Niamey, Khartoum, and Port Sudan.*
- *Transition refers only to the climate of the area. Explain that this area is not just a transition zone from desert to tropical climate, but also a transition zone from Muslim to animist and Christian and other non-Muslim groups, so it is also a cultural/religious transition zone.*

Assessment Evidence

Performance Tasks:

- *Hands-On Chapter Project*

Other Evidence:

- *Guided Reading Activities*
- *Vocabulary Activities*
- *Lesson Quizzes*
- *Chapter Tests, Forms A and B*

SUGGESTED PACING GUIDE

Introducing the Chapter...............½ Day
Lesson 1............................ 1 Day
Lesson 2............................ 1 Day
Lesson 3............................ 1 Day
Chapter Wrap-Up and Assessment......½ Day

TOTAL TIME 4 Days

Key for Using the Teacher Edition

SKILL-BASED ACTIVITIES

Types of skill activities found in the Teacher Edition.

* **V Visual Skills** require students to analyze maps, graphs, charts, and photos.

R Reading Skills help students practice reading skills and master vocabulary.

C Critical Thinking Skills help students apply and extend what they have learned.

W Writing Skills provide writing opportunities to help students comprehend the text.

T Technology Skills require students to use digital tools effectively.

*Letters are followed by a number when there is more than one of the same type of skill on the page.

DIFFERENTIATED INSTRUCTION

All activities are written for the on-level student unless otherwise marked with the leveled labels below.

BL Beyond Level
AL Approaching Level
ELL English Language Learners

All students benefit from activities that utilize different learning styles. Many activities are marked as below when a particular learning style is highlighted.

Intrapersonal
Logical/Mathematical
Visual/Spatial
Verbal/Linguistic
Naturalist
Kinesthetic
Auditory/Musical
Interpersonal

National Geography Standards covered in "The Transition Zone"

The student knows and understands:

(4) The physical and human characteristics of places

4.2 The interaction of physical and human systems result in the creation of and changes to places

(7) The physical processes that shape the patterns of Earth's surface

7.3 Physical processes interact over time to shape particular places on Earth's surface

(8) The characteristics and spatial distribution of ecosystems and biomes on Earth's surface

8.2 The characteristics and geographic distribution of ecosystems

(9) The characteristics, distribution, and migration of human populations on Earth's surface

9.1 Culture, economics, and politics influence the changing demographic structure of different populations

9.2 Population distribution and density are a function of historical, environmental, economic, political, and technological factors

(10) The characteristics, distribution, and complexity of Earth's cultural mosaics

10.2 Cultural landscapes exist at multiple scales

10.3 Cultures changes through convergence and/or divergence

(11) The patterns and networks of economic interdependence on Earth's surface

11.2 Patterns exist in the spatial organization of economic activities

11.3 Economic systems are dynamic organizations of interdependent economic activities for production, exchange, distribution, and consumption of goods and services

(12) The process, patterns, and functions of human settlement

(13) How the forces of cooperation and conflict among people influence the division and control of Earth's surface

(14) How human actions modify the physical environment

14.1 Human modifications of the physical environment can have significant global impacts

14.2 The use of technology can have both intended and unintended impacts on the physical environment which may be positive or negative

14.3 People can either mitigate and/or adapt to the consequences of human modifications of the physical environment

CHAPTER OPENER PLANNER

Students will know:
- *the physical features that are included in the Transition Zone.*
- *how the climate affects the biomes and human activities.*
- *the Transition Zone has been home to many peoples, empires, and kingdoms for centuries.*
- *how differing cultures have come into conflict in the Transition Zone.*
- *how subsistence farming and nomadic herding have been practiced for centuries.*
- *the causes and effects of desertification and how it is addressed.*

Students will be able to:
- ***identify*** *landforms and physical features that are important to the Transition Zone.*
- ***describe*** *the effects of climate on biomes and human activities in the Transition Zone.*
- ***describe*** *the peoples, empires, and kingdoms that have populated the Transition Zone.*
- ***explain*** *conflicts between differing cultures in the region.*
- ***describe*** *livelihoods such as subsistence farming and nomadic herding.*
- ***explain*** *desertification, the threats it poses, and how it is being addressed.*

UNDERSTANDING BY DESIGN®

☑ Print Teaching Options

V Visual Skills

☐ **p. 483** Students locate the countries that make up the Transition Zone on a map. AL Visual/Spatial

R Reading Skills

☐ **p. 483** Students classify characteristics that are found south of the Sahara and those found north of the Sahara.

C Critical Thinking Skills

☐ **p. 481** Students contrast the Sahara with the Tropics.

☐ **p. 482** Students raise questions about why having different religions in a region could create problems.

☐ **p. 482** Students make inferences about life in the Transition Zone. AL Interpersonal

T Technology Skills

☐ **p. 483** Students research an area of the Transition Zone that has experienced conflict and create a multimedia presentation to explain the reasons and any resolutions. Verbal/Linguistic

☑ Online Teaching Options

C Critical Thinking Skills

INTERACTIVE MAP **Animist, Muslim, and Christian Believers in the Transition Zone**—Students use the map to learn about the politically and religiously drawn borders in the Transition Zone and then make predictions about what they expect to learn in the chapter. Logical/Mathematical

MAP **Interactive Regional Atlas**—Students use the interactive regional atlas to understand the physical and human geography of the Transition Zone.

☑ Printable Digital Worksheets

WORKSHEET **Assessing Background Knowledge**—Determine the level of prior knowledge students have about the Transition Zone.

WORKSHEET **Chapter Summaries**—Students review the main idea of each lesson of the chapter content.

WORKSHEET **Reteaching Activity**—These worksheets provide students with an opportunity for remedial practice and review of vital chapter content.

Project-Based Learning 

Hands-On

Documentary

Students will create a documentary about the causes and effects of desertification. Have students research about the environmental issues in the Transition Zone and then as a group, they will compile their information to create a 10-minute documentary about desertification, its causes, and effects.

Digital Hands-On

Create Online Projects

Find an additional activity online that incorporates technology for this project. Visit the EdTech Teacher Web sites for more links, tutorials, and other resources.

Print Resources

ANCILLARY RESOURCES

This ancillary is available for every chapter and lesson.

- **Chapter Tests and Lesson Quizzes**

PRINTABLE DIGITAL WORKSHEETS

These printable digital worksheets are available for every chapter and lesson.

- **Assessing Background Knowledge**
- **Chapter Summaries**
- **Guided Reading Activities**
- **Hands-On Chapter Projects**
- **Quizzes and Tests**
- **Reading Essentials and Study Guide** AL
- **Reteaching Activities**
- **Video Activities**
- **Vocabulary Activities**

More Media Resources

SUGGESTED VIDEOS MOVIES

- **Sahel A West African Journey** (1 h. 17 min.)
- **Nature Parks: Keoladeo Ghana Rajasthan** (46 min.)
- **Baka: People of the Forest** (45 min.)

SUGGESTED READING 

- ***African Landscapes: Interdisciplinary Approaches,*** by Michael Bollig and Olaf Bubenzer
- ***Women Writing Africa: West Africa and the Sahel,*** by Esi Sutherland-Addy and Aminata Diaw
- ***Living on the Edge: Wetlands and Birds in a Changing Sahel,*** by Leo Zwarts, Rob Blijlsma, Jan Van der Kamp, and Eddy Wymenga

LESSON 1 PLANNER

PHYSICAL GEOGRAPHY OF THE TRANSITION ZONE

Students will know:
- *the physical features that are included in the Transition Zone.*
- *what water features are important to the people of the Transition Zone.*
- *how the climate affects the biomes and human activities of the Transition Zone.*

Students will be able to:
- ***identify** landforms and physical features in the Transition Zone.*
- ***analyze** the importance of water features in the region.*
- ***describe** the effects of climate on biomes and human activities in the Transition Zone.*

UNDERSTANDING BY DESIGN®

☑ Print Teaching Options

V Visual Skills

☐ **p. 484** Students create a 3-D map of the Sahel in the classroom to demonstrate its size. AL Kinesthetic/Naturalist

☐ **p. 486** Students locate Lake Volta and the Volta River system on a detailed map. AL Verbal/Linguistic, Interpersonal

☐ **p. 488** Students find data on annual precipitation in the Transition Zone in the past decade and use it to create a graph. ELL Logical/Mathematical, Visual/Spatial

R Reading Skills

☐ **p. 484** Students discuss what they know about the physical geography of the African Transition Zone.

C Critical Thinking Skills

☐ **p. 484** Students discuss how culture changes over time as new cultures are added to an area. AL Logical/Mathematical

☐ **p. 485** Students discuss how a drought can cause a famine. Interpersonal

☐ **p. 486** Students construct a thesis that explains why standing water instead of running water and annual floods would lead to an increase in disease. BL Naturalist, Logical/Mathematical

☐ **p. 487** Students compare and contrast the effects of damming the Volta River with the effects of damming the Senegal River. Logical/Mathematical, Naturalist

W Writing Skills

☐ **p. 486** Students research and write a one-page summary on desertification in this region. Verbal/Linguistic, Naturalist

☐ **p. 488** Students construct a narrative based on the diverse population of animals found in the African Transition Zone. AL Verbal/Linguistic

T Technology Skills

☐ **p. 485** Students research overgrazing and present a step-by-step description of how land turns from grassland to barren steppe or desert. AL Visual/Spatial, Auditory/Musical

☐ **p. 487** Students research hydroelectric production at four dams and evaluate how each has affected or will affect the region. AL Logical/Mathematical

☑ Online Teaching Options

V Visual Skills

INTERACTIVE IMAGE **Lake Chad**—Students use the image of a shrinking Lake Chad to discuss how the loss of a large lake threatens the diversity of animal, plant, and even human life in this region. BL Visual/Spatial

INTERACTIVE WHITEBOARD ACTIVITY **The African Transition Zone**—Students will complete a chart about the physical features that are included in the Transition Zone.

C Critical Thinking Skills

INTERACTIVE BELLRINGER **Average Rainfall in Transition Zone Cities**—Students use a table of annual rainfall in certain African cities to identify how rainfall affects the biomes and human activities of the Transition Zone. AL Interpersonal, Visual/Spatial

SLIDE SHOW **The Shrinking Lake Chad**—Students view this slide show to gain a better understanding of how Lake Chad drying out is affecting the surrounding areas and consider what life was like for people before it began drying out and what life may be like when the lake is gone. Visual/Spatial, Naturalist

W Writing Skills

VIDEO **Storm Sahel**—Students watch a video about the harsh climate of the Sahel and write about how the climate would affect their lives, what they would do differently than they do now, and what the positive and negative effects of living in this region might be. AL Intrapersonal, Verbal/Linguistic

☑ Printable Digital Worksheets

R Reading Skills

WORKSHEET **Guided Reading Activity**—Students use the Guided Reading Activity worksheets to review their comprehension of the content.

C Critical Thinking Skills

WORKSHEET **Video Activity**—Students answer questions related to a topic in the chapter content after they have viewed a lesson video.

LESSON 2 PLANNER
HUMAN GEOGRAPHY OF THE TRANSITION ZONE

Students will know:
- *the Transition Zone has been home to many peoples, empires, and kingdoms for centuries.*
- *there are both nomadic peoples and large cities in the region.*
- *how differing cultures have come into conflict in the Transition Zone.*
- *how subsistence farming and nomadic herding have been practiced for centuries in the Transition Zone.*

Students will be able to:
- ***describe** the peoples, empires, and kingdoms that have populated the Transition Zone.*
- ***describe** life for nomadic peoples and life in large cities.*
- ***explain** conflicts between differing cultures in the region.*
- ***describe** livelihoods such as subsistence farming and nomadic herding.*

UNDERSTANDING BY DESIGN®

☑ Print Teaching Options

V Visual Skills
- ☐ **p. 490** Students discuss the map of kingdoms and empires of the Transition Zone. AL Visual/Spatial
- ☐ **p. 492** Students explore population density by using a map of their community. Visual/Spatial
- ☐ **p. 492** Students discuss events on the time line. ELL

R Reading Skills
- ☐ **p. 489** Students discuss reasons for Egypt's power weakening and a civilization's desire to expand. AL Verbal/Linguistic
- ☐ **p. 492** Students simulate what it would be like for the population of the African Transition Zone to double in thirty years. AL Kinesthetic

C Critical Thinking Skills
- ☐ **p. 489** Students discuss the domestication of animals. ELL Verbal/Linguistic
- ☐ **p. 491** Students discuss what it would be like to live in a region that has been summarily divided up by another country or countries. AL Verbal/Linguistic, Intrapersonal
- ☐ **p. 491** Students discuss the ethical issues involved in African colonization. Verbal/Linguistic, Interpersonal
- ☐ **p. 495** Students discuss the central issues related to subsistence farming. Naturalist, Logical/Mathematical

W Writing Skills
- ☐ **p. 490** Students research and write an informative paper about Makkah. AL Verbal/Linguistic
- ☐ **p. 493** Students write a persuasive letter in favor of investment in infrastructure, particularly sanitation. ELL Interpersonal, Verbal/Linguistic

T Technology Skills
- ☐ **p. 491** Students create a time line of conflict in Sudan using presentation software. AL Visual/Spatial
- ☐ **p. 494** Students research to find audio samples of oral tradition in the cultures of the Transition Zone and summarize a story and retell it to a classmate. Auditory/Musical, Intrapersonal

☑ Online Teaching Options

V Visual Skills
- ☐ INTERACTIVE MAP **Kingdoms and Empires of the Transition Zone**—Students locate and name the various kingdoms and empires denoted on the map. AL Visual/Spatial, Logical/Mathematical
- ☐ GRAPHIC ORGANIZER **Human Geography of the Transition Zone**—Students use the graphic organizer to list the main idea and important details about the human geography of the African Transition Zone. ELL Visual/Spatial
- ☐ INTERACTIVE WHITEBOARD ACTIVITY **Empires of the Transition Zone**—Students drag place names to the correct locations on a map and drag facts about the Mali and Songhai empires to a chart. ELL Visual/Spatial, Kinesthetic

C Critical Thinking Skills
- ☐ INTERACTIVE BELLRINGER **Kingdoms and Empires of the Transition Zone**—Students draw conclusions about the empires and kingdoms of the Transition Zone and their trade practices. BL Verbal/Linguistic
- ☐ INTERACTIVE ART **Refugees of Sudan**—Students discuss the religious and economic concerns facing refugees of Sudan and the lasting impact that violence and forced relocation can have on the culture of a civilization. Intrapersonal, Visual/Spatial

W Writing Skills
- ☐ INTERACTIVE IMAGE **The Golden Ground Under the Transition Zone**—Students examine the image and discuss how the gold that is being mined would impact the excavators' lives, then write a narrative about the image. BL Verbal/Linguistic

☑ Printable Digital Worksheets

R Reading Skills
- ☐ WORKSHEET **Guided Reading Activity**—Students use Guided Reading Activity worksheets to review their comprehension of the content.
- ☐ WORKSHEET **Reading Essentials and Study Guide**—Students complete the study guide and answer Reading Progress Check and vocabulary questions. AL

C Critical Thinking Skills
- ☐ WORKSHEET **Video Activity**—Students answer questions related to a topic in the chapter content after they have viewed a lesson video.

LESSON 3 PLANNER

PEOPLE AND THEIR ENVIRONMENT: THE TRANSITION ZONE

Students will know:
- *what desertification is and what causes it.*
- *how desertification threatens ways of life in the Transition Zone.*
- *what steps are being taken to combat desertification.*

Students will be able to:
- ***explain** desertification and how it happens.*
- ***describe** the threats posed by desertification.*
- ***identify** how desertification is being addressed.*

UNDERSTANDING BY DESIGN®

☑ Print Teaching Options

V Visual Skills

- ☐ **p. 497** Students use a map to discuss the rainy season's effect on the Sahel. AL Visual/Spatial

R Reading Skills

- ☐ **p. 496** Students discuss the word parts of the word *desertification.* ELL Verbal/Linguistic
- ☐ **p. 498** Students paraphrase a paragraph about human activity exacerbating desertification. ELL Verbal/Linguistic

C Critical Thinking Skills

- ☐ **p. 496** Students list what they think people do to solve problems of poverty and hunger.
- ☐ **p. 496** Students predict the conditions of the Sahel 50 and 100 years from now. AL Verbal/Linguistic
- ☐ **p. 499** Students discuss the infographic of the Great Green Wall. AL Visual/Spatial
- ☐ **p. 500** Students research and discuss the concept of adding bacteria to sand dunes to calcify the sand and reduce desertification. BL Logical/Mathematical

W Writing Skills

- ☐ **p. 499** Students research how traditional planting pits can help reclaim severely dry land and write about the process. AL Interpersonal, Verbal/Linguistic

T Technology Skills

- ☐ **p. 497** Students research images that show the various stages of desertification and create a display with captions. Naturalist
- ☐ **p. 498** Students brainstorm ideas about how to battle desertification. BL Interpersonal
- ☐ **p. 499** Students research more information about an organization that is combating desertification and create a presentation of their information. Visual/Spatial, Verbal/Linguistic

☑ Online Teaching Options

V Visual Skills

- INTERACTIVE MAP **Desertification of the Sahel**—Students use the supporting text in the infographic and information in the map to create illustrations showing what a part of the Sahel may look like now and 50 years from now. ELL AL Visual/Spatial

C Critical Thinking Skills

- INTERACTIVE BELLRINGER **Great Green Wall of Africa**—Students study the infographic to analyze the causes and effects of desertification and how they are being addressed. ELL Interpersonal, Visual/Spatial, Verbal/Linguistic
- INTERACTIVE WHITEBOARD ACTIVITY **Environmental Challenges of the Transition Zone**—Students decide whether statements concerning particular environmental challenges in the Transition Zone are a cause, a problem, an impact, or a solution. AL Kinesthetic, Logical/Mathematical

W Writing Skills

- INTERACTIVE MAP **The Sahel's Vulnerable Zone**—Students write a short list of factors that make the Vulnerable Zone of the Sahel vulnerable. AL Visual/Spatial, Verbal/Linguistic

☑ Printable Digital Worksheets

R Reading Skills

- WORKSHEET **Guided Reading Activity**—Students use Guided Reading Activity worksheets to review their comprehension of the content.
- WORKSHEET **Reading Essentials and Study Guide**—Students complete the study guide and answer Reading Progress Check and vocabulary questions. AL
- WORKSHEET **Vocabulary Activity**—Students review the chapter content and academic vocabulary words.

C Critical Thinking Skills

- WORKSHEET **Video Activity**—Students answer questions based on a lesson video.
- WORKSHEET **Reteaching Activity**—Students use this activity worksheet to review and reteach chapter content and vocabulary. This worksheet can be used with struggling students who need additional help with difficult content concepts.

INTERVENTION AND REMEDIATION STRATEGIES

LESSON 1 Physical Geography of the Transition Zone

Reading and Comprehension

To ensure students understand the concept of a transition zone, discuss the meaning of the word *transition,* asking volunteers to offer synonyms of the word. Have students work with a partner to take turns explaining how Africa not only transitions from north to south in its physical geography, but culturally as well. Then have partners choose a key concept, place, or vocabulary term from the lesson to explain to the rest of the class. Have students make a brief presentation to "teach" the topic or term, using visuals if desired. Tell students they may use the board to draw diagrams or charts to better explain their assigned concept.

Text Evidence

Have students review the lesson and write five paragraphs, each one summarizing the information under the five headings in the text. Tell students their paragraphs should include a topic sentence, a main idea, and key details. Students should use textual evidence to support ideas presented in their paragraphs, using the lesson narrative and graphics for ideas. Ask volunteers to read their paragraphs to the class. Then have students quiz a partner, using terms and concepts described in their paragraphs.

LESSON 2 Human Geography of the Transition Zone

Reading and Comprehension

Have students work with a partner to create a time line based on one of the subheadings in the lesson, conducting additional research if needed. For example, students may wish to create a time line showing the evolution of kingdoms in the region, the ongoing conflict in Sudan, or the development of trade in the region. Instruct students to use visuals to accompany their time lines and present them to the class. Guide a class discussion about the natural resources in the Transition Zone and how they impact the region's economy.

Text Evidence

Have student groups review the lesson to choose a topic for a skit depicting a historical or cultural aspect of a region in the Transition Zone. Tell students in each group to collaborate on a script for their skit, which should depict a scene in the country today or in the past. Encourage students to write a realistic scene that depicts a family living in their chosen region. Tell students to conduct additional research to identify additional information about their region to make their skits more realistic. Allow time for groups to rehearse their skits before performing them for the class.

LESSON 3 People and Their Environment: The Transition Zone

Reading and Comprehension

Have students work with a partner to create a graphic organizer like the one shown in the lesson opener to outline key facts about problems facing regions in the Transition Zone and possible solutions. Tell students they may wish to conduct additional research about a topic discussed in the text to identify the status of that issue today. For example, students might find information about the Great Green Wall and its impact on desertification. After partners have shared their graphic organizers with the class, allow time for a question-and-answer session in which students from each pair answer questions about their topic.

Text Evidence

Have students call out different issues or problems discussed in the lesson as you write them on the board. Tell students to form groups that will pretend to be a delegation for the United Nations stationed in the Transition Zone. Have students work in their groups to brainstorm solutions to an issue they feel needs the most attention and write a summary listing textual evidence to support their proposed solution. Call on groups to explain their solution to the rest of the class. Have the class vote on each group's proposal and decide which "delegation" should be approved to move forward with its solution.

Online Resources

Leveled Reader

Use this online approaching-level text that corresponds directly to the text in the Student Edition. It also includes additional reading and comprehension support for English Language Learners.

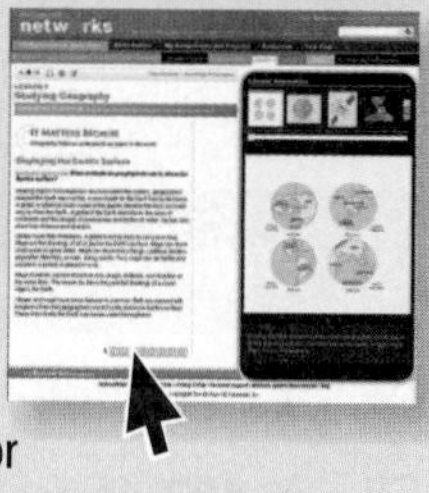

Guided Reading Activities

This resource uses guiding questions to help students with comprehension.

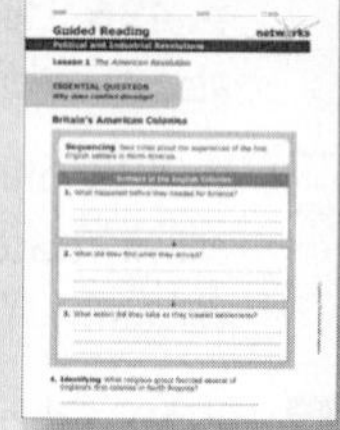

Reteaching Activities

These worksheets provide students with an opportunity for remedial practice and review of vital chapter content.

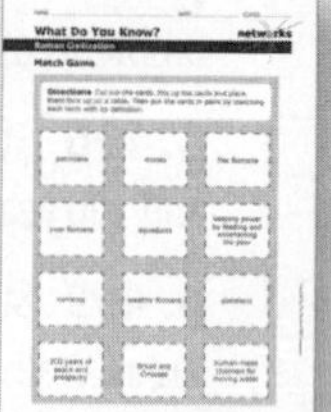

Reading Essentials and Study Guide

This resource offers writing and reading activities for the approaching-level student.

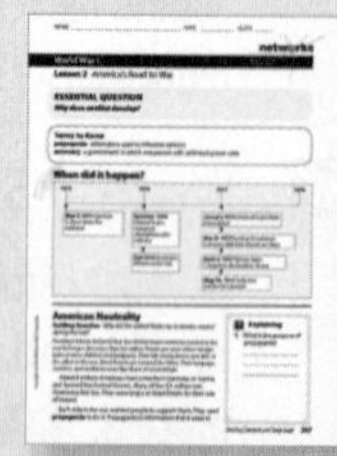

Self-Check Quizzes

This online assessment tool provides instant feedback for students to check their progress.

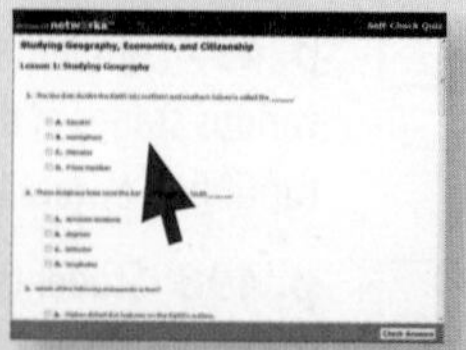

Chapter Summaries

Summaries are provided for each chapter that thoroughly condense core content into manageable chunks.

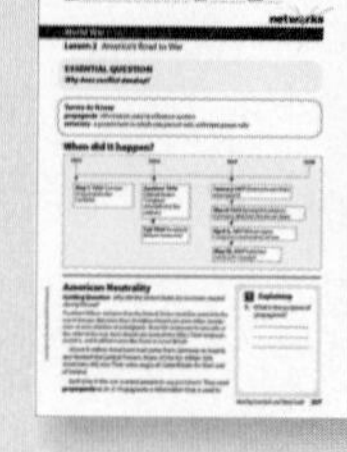

The Transition Zone

ESSENTIAL QUESTION • *How do physical systems and human systems shape a place?*

networks

There's More Online about the Transition Zone.

CHAPTER 20

Geography Matters...

The Transition Zone is a challenging land because of transitions in both the human and physical geography. It is a mix of Muslim, Christian, and animist cultures. It is also a transition from the Sahara to the Tropics. Climate and geography, as well as the legacy of colonialism, have led to turmoil in the subregion.

In recent decades, the Transition Zone has experienced extended periods of drought. Overpopulation has contributed to the problem. People are trying to find new ways to cope with or to reverse the damage to the land and face the environmental challenge.

◄ A Muslim woman in Lomé, Togo

Godong/age fotostock

481

Letter from the Author

Dear Geography Teacher,

For Westerners, particularly those of us from the United States, Timbuktu has had a magical ring to it. At one time, it was one of the most prominent cities in the world. Its geographical location helped to create the importance of a place that today we would say was off the beaten path. When camel caravans were the only means of crossing the Sahara, Timbuktu held sway, and maintained that position for centuries. Your students will benefit by researching and then creating a time line for Timbuktu. Have students compile information on this geographical location, that even today brings images of Arabs, the desert, camels, salt flats, and probably some nostalgia for past times.

Richard G. Boehm

ENGAGE

Making Predictions Invite students to share what they know about the Transition Zone of Africa. Then have them scan the photographs and maps throughout the lesson. Ask students which photographs and maps caught their attention and why. Have them make a list of predictions about what they will study in this chapter.

TEACH & ASSESS

Making Connections

Students may be surprised to find that a number of Africans are Muslim. According to oral tradition, Muslim refugees fleeing persecution in the Arabian Peninsula brought Islam to the continent. Discuss with students the similarity between this and how many of the first settlers of the United States were also fleeing religious persecution.

Contrasting Have students contrast the Sahara with the Tropics. **Ask:** **How are the climates of the two areas different?** *(The desert is very dry with extreme temperatures, and the Tropics are temperate and humid.)* **Ask:** **How does the vegetation differ?** *(The desert has very little vegetation, while the Tropics have lush, green vegetation.)* Point out that the Transition Zone between the Sahara and the Tropics is relatively small compared to the other two zones. **Ask:** **What kind of climate and vegetation would you expect to see in the Transition Zone?** *(Possible answer: The climate is likely more temperate than the desert and not as humid as the Tropics. The Transition Zone likely has more vegetation than the desert but not as much as the Tropics.)* **BL** **Naturalist**

CLOSE & REFLECT

Discussing Explain that desertification is the major challenge facing the Transition Zone. Have students share what they have learned previously about desertification. Write *desertification* in the middle of a concept map and add students' ideas about its causes and effects.

ePals GlobalCommunity
Where learners connect™

Extend the project-based learning experience globally through our partnership with ePals. EPals allows you to connect with classrooms around the world in a safe online environment for real-life lessons and projects in virtual study groups.

ENGAGE

C1 Critical Thinking Skills

Formulating Questions After students have read the introduction, have them raise questions about why having different religions in a region could create problems. Have them share their questions and write several of them on the board. As students work through the chapter, revisit their list of questions to see which ones can be answered from information in the chapter. Verbal/Linguistic

TEACH & ASSESS

V Visual Skills

Identifying Perspectives **Ask:** Which person in the photograph might you identify as being Muslim? Explain. *(the woman because she is wearing the required dress)* Explain that the woman is wearing a hijab. This is the name of the traditional covering for the hair and neck of Muslim women. There are many different varieties of hijab. Some are more traditional, while others are more modern. ELL Visual/Spatial

C2 Critical Thinking Skills

Drawing Inferences Have students use both the text and the photograph to draw inferences about life in the Transition Zone. **Ask:** What challenges exist when a society has different religions? *(Possible answers: Sometimes, some groups can have little religious tolerance for other groups, which can create conflict.)* How is African society similar to American society with regard to religion? *(Possible answers: People practice different religions in Africa just as they do in the United States. In the United States, freedom of religion is a guaranteed right. That is not necessarily the case in other countries around the world.)* AL Interpersonal

Why Geography Matters: **The Transition Zone**

diffusion: Muslim and non-Muslim cultures

C1 *Africa is a continent with great diversity in its physical, cultural, and economic geography. The Transition Zone is a region that lies south of the Sahara and has been increasingly influenced by Islam. At the same time, Christian and traditional religions are also practiced. Some countries in this zone are predominantly Muslim, while others are more religiously mixed.*

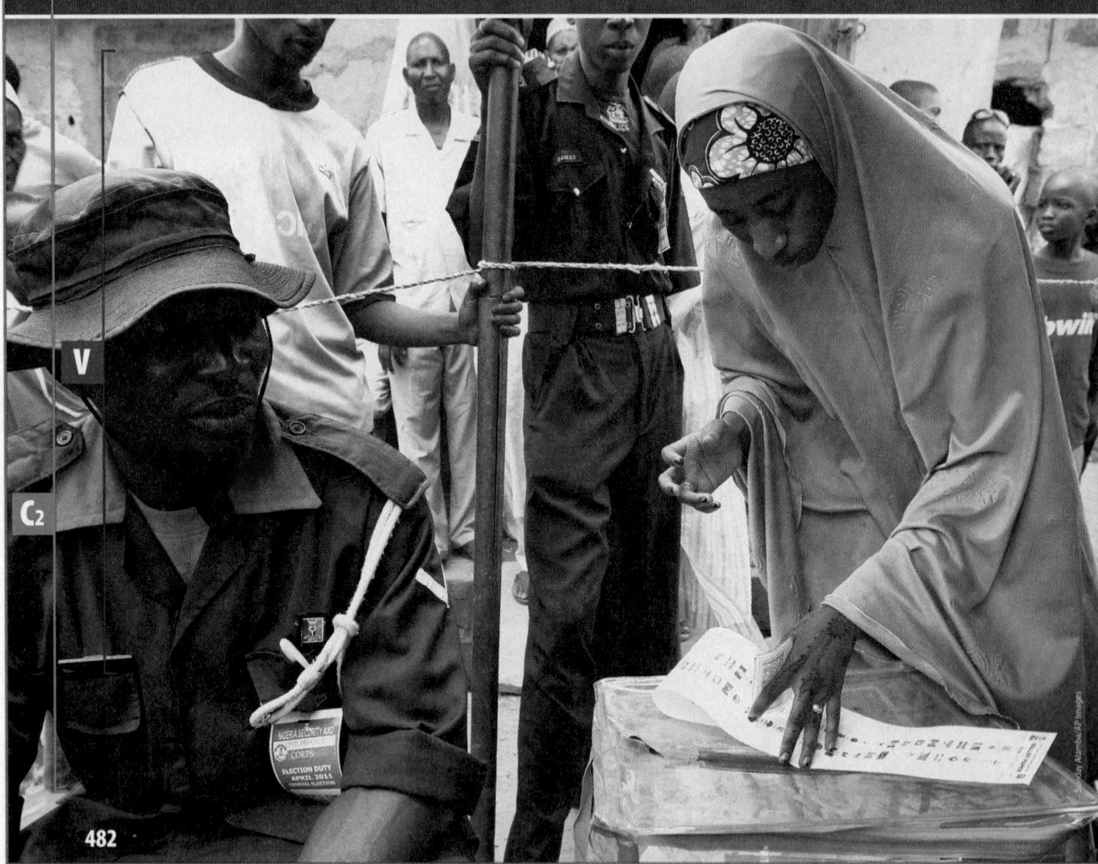

V

C2

482

Project-Based Learning

Hands-On

Documentary

Working in small groups, students will research environmental issues in the Transition Zone. Based on their research, students will use technology to create a short documentary—about 10 minutes in length—that includes narration and visuals about desertification in the Transition Zone. The documentary should also include the causes and effects of desertification.

ePals GlobalCommunity
Where learners connect™

Digital Hands-On

Create Online Projects

Find an additional activity online that incorporates technology for this project. Visit the EdTech Teacher Web sites for more links, tutorials, and other resources.

Why Geography Matters

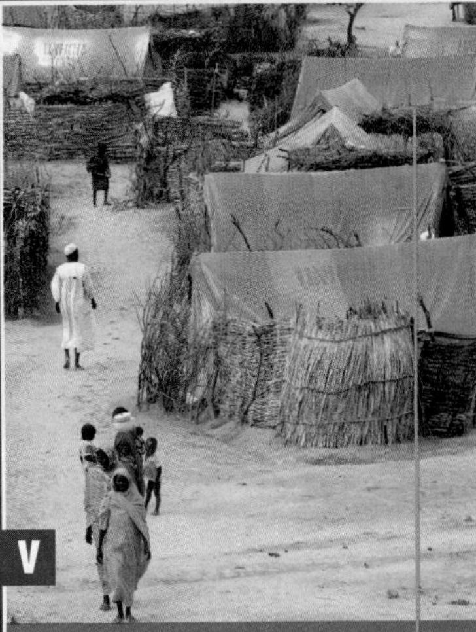

Why do Muslim and non-Muslim cultures exist in Africa?

The Sahel, which means "shore" in Arabic, serves as a cultural and ecological gateway. To the north are primarily Muslim countries and more arid land. To the south are mostly non-Muslim countries with less arid to tropical environments. This cultural gateway exists because of the continent's long history of interaction with other cultures.

When trade flourished in the West African kingdoms and East African kingdoms between 800 and the 1500s, the region encountered new cultures. Arab and Berber traders exchanged trade goods with the people of these kingdoms. They also shared ideas, including their Islamic faith. Christianity also spread in different parts of the region through trade with merchants from the Mediterranean. In Axum (Ethiopia), an East African trading state, Christianity became the official religion in the fourth century.

1. **The World in Spatial Terms** How did the location of Africa's kingdoms and trading states influence its cultural and religious diversity?

What happens when these distinct cultures encounter each other?

The slave trade, European colonialism, and independence also contributed to cultural diffusion in Africa. All of the following countries make up the Transition Zone: Somalia, Djibouti, Guinea, Guinea-Bissau, Gambia, and Senegal, as well as parts of Eritrea, Ethiopia, Sudan, Chad, Cameroon, Niger, Nigeria, Benin, Togo, Ghana, Burkina Faso, Côte d'Ivoire, Liberia, Sierra Leone, Mali, and Mauritania. Ethnic conflicts occurred in post-colonial Africa because Europeans drew these political borders with **R** no regard for ethnic borders.

As a result, the Transition Zone has seen cultural and ethnic conflicts in many countries. In Nigeria, a civil war rooted in ethnic tensions erupted not long after independence. The "Biafran War" resulted in the deaths of about a million Ibo people, mainly from starvation. In Senegal, a rebellion spurred by religious and cultural differences began in 1984. The area's residents were mainly Christian or followers of traditional religions—unlike the majority of Senegalese, who were Muslim. The conflict ended in 1998.

2. **Human Systems** Has cultural diffusion in Africa through interaction with other cultures been positive or negative for the Transition Zone? Explain.

V

How are distinct cultures encountering one another today?

The Transition Zone is still a hotbed for conflict. Sudan, for example, has experienced ongoing conflicts since its independence in 1956. The government has oppressed its Christian population, which mainly lives in the south. Even though South Sudan became independent from Sudan in 2011, conflict continues. **T**

In the Darfur region of Sudan, fighting broke out in 2003 between Muslim villagers, who identified themselves as African, and government-backed militias. The militias were made up of Muslim nomads who identified themselves as Arab. Since then, nearly 3 million people have been displaced and hundreds of thousands killed. Many of the Darfur refugees have fled to the neighboring country of Chad, but refugee camps there have swelled beyond capacity. Peace deals have been signed and a peacekeeping force tries to maintain peace. Critics predict, however, that change will be slow.

3. **Environment and Society** Write a paragraph explaining how the environment of Darfur might be contributing to this conflict.

(l)Lissa Harrison, (c)MC-PHOTO/age fotostock, (r)Scott Nelson/Getty Images News/Getty Images

THERE'S MORE ONLINE

VIEW an interactive image of Lake Chad • *EXPLORE* a map of religions in the Transition Zone

INTERACTIVE MAP

Animist, Muslim, and Christian Believers in the Transition Zone

Making Predictions Display this interactive map of the Transition Zone to introduce the politically and religiously drawn borders. Explain that Europeans decided to draw these political borders for the African countries without taking any ethnic borders into consideration; therefore, religious and ethnic conflicts occur in many countries within the Transition Zone. Have students write three predictions about what they expect to learn in this chapter. Ask students to keep these predictions in a notebook and to refer to them at the end of the chapter. **Logical/Mathematical**

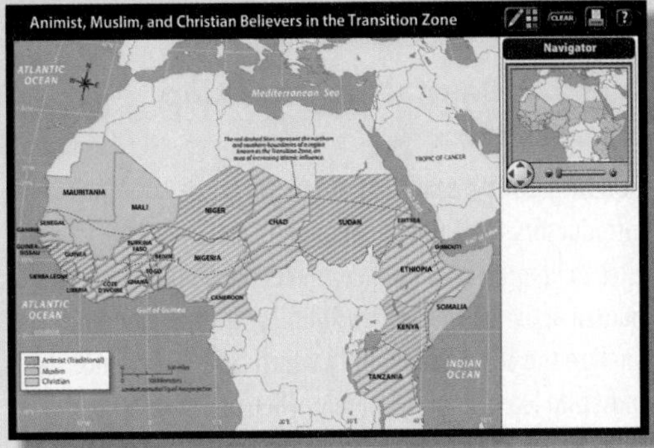

R Reading Skills

Classifying Have students divide a piece of paper in half by drawing a horizontal line across the middle. Ask them to classify each of the characteristics that are primarily found south of the Sahara and those found north of the Sahara. The top half of the sheet of paper should be north and the bottom half should be south. **AL** **Kinesthetic, Logical/Mathematical**

V Visual Skills

Reading Maps Display a political map of Africa and have students locate the countries that make up the Transition Zone. **Ask:** **What is the smallest country found entirely in the Transition Zone?** *(Gambia)* **How does Somalia differ geographically from other countries in the Transition Zone?** *(It is farther south.)* **AL** **Visual/Spatial**

T Technology Skills

Presenting Have students choose an area of the Transition Zone that has experienced conflict. Ask them to research a specific conflict. Then create a multimedia presentation that includes information about the reason(s) and any resolutions for the conflict. Have students present their findings to the class. **Verbal/Linguistic**

CLOSE & REFLECT

Speculating Have students speculate about what they will learn in this chapter, based on the introduction to Muslim and non-Muslim cultures, differences in culture, and conflicts. Have them make notes about their speculations and refer back as they study the chapter. Tell them to make adjustments as necessary based on what they learn.

ANSWERS, p. 483

Why Geography Matters

1. The location of African kingdoms and trading states influenced their ideas and religious faiths. Arab and Berber traders spread Islam. Traders from the Mediterranean spread Christianity. Areas such as Axum (Ethiopia) adopted Christianity as the official religion in the fourth century.
2. The cultural diffusion in Africa has been negative for the Transition Zone. While the slave trade, European colonialism, and independence resulted in cultural diffusion, the political boundaries Europeans made in the area had no regard for ethnic or religious borders. This has resulted in ongoing conflicts between people of different religions and cultures.
3. The standard the government sets in oppressing people of different faiths sets a precedent to militias that identify as Arab to have ongoing conflicts with villagers that identify as African.

ENGAGE

R Reading Skills

Activating Prior Knowledge Before students read, have them discuss what they know about the physical geography of the African Transition Zone. Discuss the different wildlife found in this area and speculate on what climates in the area would support this wildlife.

TEACH & ASSESS

C Critical Thinking Skills

Hypothesizing Discuss how culture changes over time as new cultures are added to an area. **Ask:** How do you think European cultures affected religion in Africa? *(Possible answer: Europeans were Christians, so it is likely they introduced Christianity to Africa.)* From which cultures did the animist views most likely come—African, Islamic, or Christian? *(African)* Do you think these cultures mixed easily together or were there difficulties? Why? *(Possible answer: There were likely difficulties because some of the cultures were very different from each other.)* **AL Logical/Mathematical**

V Visual Skills

Spatial Understanding Have students use the description of the elevation range in the Sahel, and its length and width, to create a 3-D map in the classroom to demonstrate its size. Tell students to use the length of the classroom as the length from the northern border of Africa to its southern tip and then map out the Sahel relative to this. To show elevation, students should mark the floor as 650 feet (200 m) above sea level. They can use the same scale as for the length and width to calculate how high above the floor 1300 feet (400 m) is.
AL Kinesthetic, Naturalist

ANSWERS, p. 484

TAKING NOTES: Land—Part of the Transition Zone is called the Sahel; vegetation makes a coastline along the sands of Sahara; mainly flat with a series of plateaus; **Water**—Lake Chad was largest wetland in Africa but has been shrinking since 1970s drought; Lake Volta was made by damming Volta River and is used for hydroelectric power, fishing, and irrigation; Niger River extends from Guinea for about 2,600 miles (4,183 km) and is important for transportation and agriculture; Niger River makes several deltas along its course that create wetlands; Senegal River forms border between Senegal and Mauritania and has dams to generate hydroelectric power and for irrigation; Blue Nile and White Nile feed the Nile River but supply power and water to the region before reaching Egypt; **Climate**—humid, subtropical; rainy season is from May to August; harmattan is a hot, dry wind that carries dust and sand from the Sahara; the Sahel grows grasslands, baobab tree, and the jujube

networks
There's More Online!

- **IMAGE** Lake Chad in 1973
- **IMAGE** Lake Chad in 2001
- **MAP** The African Transition Zone
- **INTERACTIVE SELF-CHECK QUIZ**
- **VIDEO** Physical Geography of the Transition Zone

LESSON 1
Physical Geography of the Transition Zone

ESSENTIAL QUESTION • *How do physical systems and human systems shape a place?*

Reading HELPDESK (CCSS)

Academic Vocabulary (Tier Two Words)
- area
- benefit

Content Vocabulary (Tier Three Words)
- **transition zone**
- **Sahel**
- **delta**
- **harmattan**

TAKING NOTES: ***Key Ideas and Details***

IDENTIFYING As you read about the geography of the African Transition Zone, use a graphic organizer like the one below to note the characteristics of the land, water, and climate of the area.

The African Transition Zone		
Land	Water	Climate

It Matters Because

R *The African Transition Zone lies south of the Sahara, almost entirely within tropical latitudes, and marks the shift from desert to tropical forests, as well as from Muslim to Christian and animist cultures. The subregion is known for its remarkable wildlife and extraordinary physical geography. It also has the world's fastest-growing population and hundreds of ethnic groups.*

Landforms

GUIDING QUESTION *What is the Transition Zone?*

Africa immediately south of the Sahara is an **area** of land that transitions between the desert climate of North Africa and the tropical savanna of Equatorial Africa. This subregion, with a total area of 1,178,800 square miles (3,053,200 sq. km), in the widest part of Africa is known as the African Transition Zone. A **transition zone** is a physical area in which the land undergoes a radical change such as from arid to tropical.

C The African Transition Zone also represents a transition between the Islamic cultures of North Africa and the Christian and animist cultures to its south. Extending east to west from Senegal to Somalia, this region is home to a very diverse population. Hundreds of ethnic groups coexist in an area influenced by the African cultures that originated in the region and by the Arab and European cultures that came later.

V Part of the Transition Zone is a geographical area called the **Sahel**, which means "shore" or "coast" in Arabic. The word describes the appearance of vegetation in the Sahel as a "coastline" marking the border of the sands of the Sahara. The topography is mainly flat with a series of plateaus that range in elevation from about 650 feet (200 m) to about 1,300 feet (400 m). This steppe region runs in a band across Africa from the Atlantic Ocean in the west to the Red Sea in the east. It spans more than 3,000 miles (4,800 km) and ranges in width from about 125 miles (200 km) to 250 miles (400 km). East of the Sahel is a region known as the Horn of Africa for its shape.

networks ***Online Teaching Options***

INTERACTIVE BELLRINGER

Average Rainfall in Transition Zone Cities

Reading Charts and Drawing Inferences Use the introductory table of annual rainfall in certain African cites to identify how rainfall affects the biomes and human activities of the Transition Zone. Have students analyze the chart and identify which cities experience the most and least amounts of rain. Then ask them to consider what living in an environment where it seldom rained would be like. Have students form small groups and discuss each bellringer question.
AL Interpersonal, Visual/Spatial

Average Rainfall in Transition Zone Cities (in inches)

The climate of the Transition Zone is dry, with average rainfall of 4 to 8 inches a year.

City	Jan–Mar	Apr–Jun	Jul–Sept	Oct–Dec
Bamako, Mali	0.1	8.3	28.9	5.6
Khartoum, Sudan	0	0.4	7.3	0.2
N'Djamena, Chad	0.0	3.9	18	0.9
Niamey-Aero, Niger	0.1	4.5	16.6	0.6
Suakin, Sudan	0.7	0.1	0.5	4.8

Auto-Run Click Through 1 of 3

The Sahel receives little rainfall. On average, 4 to 8 inches (10 to 20 cm) of rain falls annually, mostly in June, July, and August when the sun is high in the sky and the temperatues are hot. The rest of the year is a little cooler but very dry, so only low-growing grasses, shrubs, and acacia trees can grow there. Most people in the Transition Zone have traditionally herded livestock. The short grasses of the Sahel provide one of the largest pastoral and herding zones in the world. Overgrazing, however, has stripped the land bare in some places.

READING PROGRESS CHECK

Identifying Describe the human and geographic features that characterize the African Transition Zone.

area a geographical region; the amount of space that the surface of a place covers

transition zone an area in which the properties of the land undergo a radical change

Sahel steppe region extending from Senegal to Somalia that receives little rainfall

Water Systems

GUIDING QUESTION *What rivers flow through the Transition Zone?*

The African Transition Zone experiences dryness, infrequent rainfall, and often drought. A drought in the 1970s caused a famine that killed thousands of people. Over the past century, annual precipitation has decreased. This, in turn, is shrinking some of the subregion's natural lakes. However, the Sahel still has a number of lakes, rivers, and wetlands. These water resources, in addition to rain, are important to the livelihood of many people.

At the southern edge of the Sahara, Lake Chad is bordered by Nigeria, Niger, Chad, and Cameroon. It was once the second-largest wetland in Africa and supported a rich diversity of animal and plant life. It has been important to

GEOGRAPHY CONNECTION

The African Transition Zone is both a physical transition between desert and savanna and a cultural transition from Muslim cultures to Christian and animist cultures in the south.

1. ***THE WORLD IN SPATIAL TERMS*** What three bodies of water does the Transition Zone meet in the east?
2. ***HUMAN SYSTEMS*** What countries in the Transition Zone may be more influenced by Muslim culture than by Christian culture? Explain.

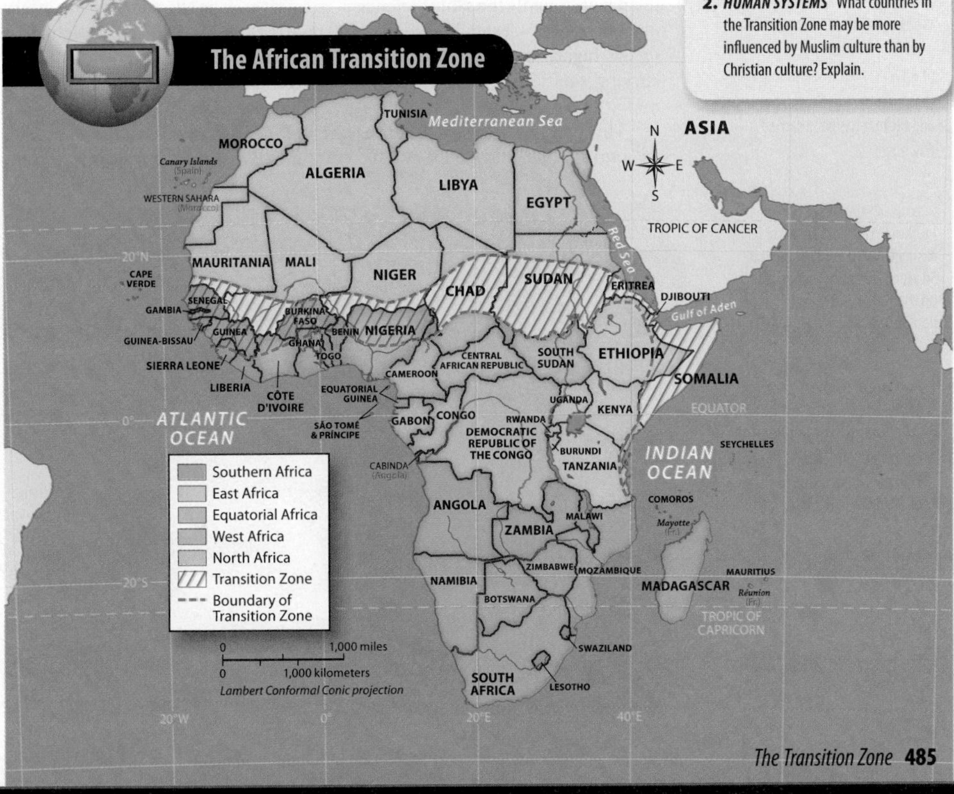

Physical Geography of the Transition Zone

T Technology Skills

Presenting Have students research overgrazing and present a step-by-step description of how land turns from grassland to barren steppe or desert. Encourage students to include animation and sound in their presentations to fully demonstrate the process. **AL Visual/Spatial, Auditory/Musical**

C Critical Thinking Skills

Identifying Cause and Effect Discuss with students how a drought can cause a famine. **Ask:** **How was the famine in the late 1970s caused by drought?** *(Possible answer: A drought is a lack of rain. Without rain, crops won't grow. Without crops, people will starve.)* **How did countries in the Transition Zone most likely recover from famine and drought?** *(Possible answer: They likely had international aid. Eventually, the drought ended, and they were able to produce food again.)* **Interpersonal**

Content Background Knowledge

Sahelian Drought The drought that occurred in this area in the 1970s actually lasted from 1972 to 1984. It is one of the worst droughts on record for the Sahel. More than 100,000 people died during this period due to the drought. Over 750,000 people in the countries of Mali, Niger, and Mauritania were completely dependent on food aid sent from other countries. In addition, power shortages existed due to the lack of water to power hydroelectric plants.

VIDEO

Storm Sahel

Making Connections Have students view this video about the Sahel to help them understand the harsh climate found in this region of Africa. Ask students to imagine living in the Sahel, a part of the Transition Zone, as they write a brief essay about how the climate would affect their lives, what they would do differently than they do now, and what the positive and negative effects of living in this region might be. **AL Intrapersonal, Verbal/Linguistic**

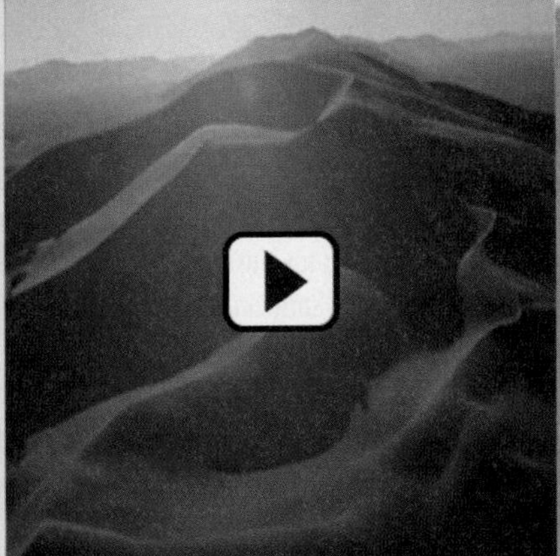

ANSWERS, p. 485

READING PROGRESS CHECK The African Transition Zone is a mainly flat area with plateaus. It is fairly dry for most of the year, but grasses and shrubs can grow, which allows people to raise livestock. It is one of the largest pastoral and herding zones in the world. It also represents a transition between the Islamic cultures of North Africa and the Christian and animist cultures to the south, as well as a transition from a desert or arid climate to a tropical climate.

GEOGRAPHY CONNECTION

1. The Red Sea, the Gulf of Aden, and the Indian Ocean meet the Transition Zone in the east.
2. The countries that share a border with North African countries that are predominantly Muslim are more likely to be influenced by this culture. These countries in the Transition Zone could include Chad, Sudan, and Nigeria.

Physical Geography of the Transition Zone

W Writing Skills

Informative/Explanatory Have students research and write a one-page summary on desertification in this region, such as at Lake Chad. They should include causes and effects of desertification and the steps that are being taken to prevent desertification. **Verbal/Linguistic, Naturalist**

V Visual Skills

Locating On a detailed map of the Transition Zone, have students locate Lake Volta in Ghana. Ask them to identify the six countries that share the Volta River system—Benin, Burkina Faso, Côte d'Ivoire, Ghana, Mali, and Togo. Then have them locate the approximate place where the river was dammed south of Ajena in Ghana. **Ask:** **Where do you think more than 70,000 people moved when they were displaced by the flooding?** *(Possible answer: They likely moved to just outside of the flooded area.)* **What do you think it would be like to be forced to leave your home and, in some cases, your livelihood?** *(Possible answer: It would be very difficult to move all of my possessions and start over again.)* AL **Verbal/Linguistic, Interpersonal**

C Critical Thinking Skills

Constructing a Thesis Review with students the aspects of a thesis. Ask them to consider the increase in disease due to the damming of the Volta River. Have them construct a thesis that explains why standing water instead of running water and annual floods would lead to an increase in disease. Have them conduct research to see if the thinking they used in their theses is correct. BL **Naturalist, Logical/Mathematical**

ANSWERS, p. 486

CRITICAL THINKING

1. The surface of Lake Chad has shrunk about 90 percent.
2. The desert area has increased, and the amount of vegetation has decreased.

the livelihoods of more than 20 million people but is threatened with extinction. Although fed by three rivers—the Chari, the Logone, and the Yobe—the lake is shrinking. The drought of the 1970s completely dried up the northern portion of the lake. Even during years of normal rainfall, the water level remains low. Because of the dry climate, much of the lake's water evaporates or becomes increasingly saline. The land is left dry and unable to support life. As Lake Chad shrinks, the desert expands.

Lake Volta in Ghana is one of the largest human-made lakes in the world. It is about 250 miles (400 km) long and covers 3,275 square miles (8,482 sq. km). The lake itself lies entirely in Ghana. However, six countries—Benin, Burkina Faso, Côte d'Ivoire, Ghana, Mali, and Togo—share the Volta River system. Lake Volta was created in the 1960s by damming the Volta River south of Ajena in Ghana. The new lake flooded more than 700 villages, forcing more than 70,000 people to find new homes. It was originally created as a reservoir to store water for generating hydroelectric power. People **benefit** from the lake because it supplies irrigation for farming and has several fisheries. It also serves as a transportation route linking different parts of the country. The hydroelectric plant also generates electricity used throughout Ghana.

benefit to gain

Unfortunately, there are negative consequences of this reservoir. These include reduced agricultural productivity because annual floods no longer occur and bring new silt, and because the land higher up on the current lake shore is not as fertile as the land now on the lake bottom. Also, the ecology of the river is completely different because running water and annual floods were replaced by standing water. This has resulted in an increase in disease.

The Niger (NY•juhr) River is known by many names along its course. All of them have roughly the same meaning—"great river." The Niger is the main artery in western Africa, extending about 2,600 miles (4,183 km) in length. Originating in the highlands of Guinea, the river forms an arc flowing northeast, then curving southeast to its mouth on the Nigerian coast. In addition to being important to agriculture, the Niger River is a major means of transportation.

delta an often triangular-shaped section of land formed as the waters of a river slow down and split into many channels as they deposit sand and silt that has been carried downriver

This great river does not flow as one well-defined stream all the way along its course to the Atlantic Ocean. In central Mali, the river spreads out across a

Once nearly the size of Lake Erie, the surface area of Lake Chad has declined dramatically in the last 50 years. The photo on the left was taken in 1973 and the one on the right in 2001.

▶ **CRITICAL THINKING**

1. ***Assessing*** By about what percentage does the surface area of Lake Chad appear to have shrunk?
2. ***Making Connections*** How do you suppose the lake's shrinkage has affected the surrounding land?

486

networks ***Online Teaching Options***

INTERACTIVE IMAGE

Lake Chad

Analyzing Visuals This interactive image showing the dramatic decline of the surface area of Lake Chad can be used to have students consider the effects of the dry climate. Have them study the image and jot down notes about why the lake is shrinking. *(infrequent rainfall, drought conditions, water evaporation rate)* Then have students form small groups to discuss how the loss of a large lake, such as Lake Chad, threatens the diversity of animal, plant, and even human life in this region. Ask each group to write a statement about what, if anything, can be done to slow Lake Chad from shrinking. BL **Visual/Spatial**

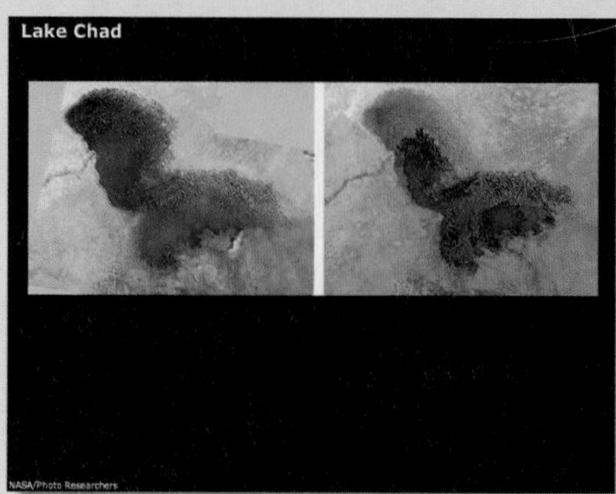

broad plateau and inland **delta**, an area where a river slows down and spreads out into many smaller channels. These small river channels create a large wetland that supports wildlife. This inland delta also provides local farmers with water. Further downstream, at Aboh in southern Nigeria, the Niger splits into a delta that stretches 150 miles (241 km) north to south and extends to a width of about 200 miles (322 km) where the river empties into the Gulf of Guinea.

The Senegal River is 1,015 miles (1,633 km) long in West Africa and forms the border between Senegal and Mauritania. The sources of the river are in Guinea and the wetter, southwestern part of Mali. Its drainage basin encompasses some 174,000 square miles (450,000 sq. km). Roughly 3.5 million people live near the river. In 1972 Mali, Mauritania, and Senegal founded an organization to manage the river basin. Guinea joined in 2005. Two dams have helped the inhabitants of the area make better use of the river. The Manantali Dam, built in 1986, helps prevent flooding during the rainy season and provides freshwater during the dry season. In 2002 the dam began generating hydroelectric power. The Diama Dam was built near the mouth of the river in 1988. It helps prevent the intrusion of salt water during the dry season. The dam also creates reserves for irrigation. C

Two major tributaries of the Nile River pass through the Transition Zone. These are the Blue Nile and the White Nile. The Blue Nile, the main source of the fertile soil along the banks of the Nile River, stretches 850 miles (1,368 km) and originates in the mountains of Ethiopia. In 2012 Ethiopia began construction of a 6000-megawatt hydroelectric dam on the river. Expected to be completed in 2015, the Grand Millennium Dam will be the largest hydroelectric power plant in Africa. It will also create Ethiopia's largest artificial lake. T

The White Nile River, which is longer than the Blue Nile River, originates in the mountains to the west of Lake Victoria in Burundi. The Blue Nile and the White Nile meet at the city of Khartoum in Sudan. From there, the famous Nile River flows northward into Egypt on a winding course across the desert to the Mediterranean Sea.

READING PROGRESS CHECK

Summarizing How is Lake Volta used by the residents of the region?

Connecting Geography to MATH

Geometry

The Sahel is a deceptively huge area—1,178,800 square miles (3,053,200 sq. km). Consider the area of Texas, Tennessee, and the contiguous United States in relation to the area of the Transition Zone.

Texas:
268,800 square miles (696,200 sq. km)

Tennessee:
42,180 square miles (109,200 sq. km)

United States:
3,718,710 square miles (9,631,420 sq. km)

Compare Tennessee and Texas. How many times larger is Texas than Tennessee? Now answer the questions below.

ANALYZING How many times larger is the Sahel than Texas? How many times smaller is the Sahel than the United States?

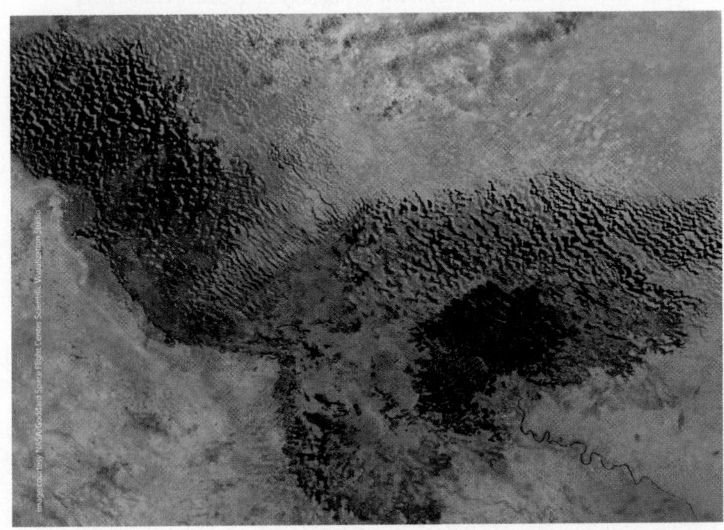

SLIDE SHOW

The Shrinking Lake Chad

Explaining Have students view this slide show to gain a better understanding of how Lake Chad drying out is affecting the surrounding areas. As the slide show is playing, have students consider what life was like for residents of the areas near Lake Chad before it began drying out. Also have them consider what life is like for the residents of those same areas today, now that Lake Chad is a fraction of the size it once was. When the slide show is completed, ask students to predict what life will be like for residents in surrounding areas when the lake ceases to exist. **Visual/Spatial, Naturalist**

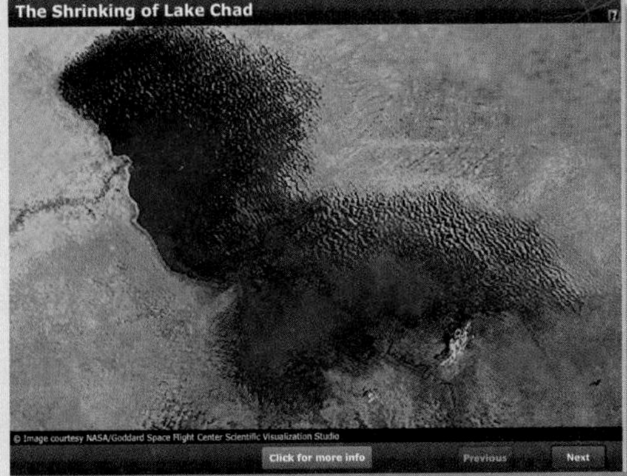

Physical Geography of the Transition Zone

C Critical Thinking Skills

Comparing and Contrasting Have students compare and contrast the effects of damming the Volta River with the effects of damming the Senegal River. **Ask:** What is similar about the effects of the dams? *(They provide hydroelectric power and water for irrigation.)* What effects have been different? *(Possible answer: It seems that the damming of the Volta River has had more negative effects such as changing the ecology of the river and reducing agricultural productivity. Only positive effects are described for the Senegal River dams, such as making better use of the river and preventing floods and the intrusion of salt water.)* **Logical/Mathematical, Naturalist**

T Technology Skills

Researching Organize students into small groups and have them research hydroelectric production at the Grand Millennium Dam, the Manantali Dam, the Diama Dam, and the Volta River Dam. They should first look specifically at how the energy of moving water is converted into electricity. Then have them evaluate how each dam has affected or will affect the region. Have them use presentation software to create a brief presentation for the class. **AL** **Logical/Mathematical**

Content Background Knowledge

Ethiopia and Hydroelectric Power Ethiopia is in a unique position to harness hydroelectric power and sell it to its neighbors. The Ethiopian highlands are at a higher elevation and receive large amounts of rainfall. This difference in elevation and precipitation creates a large potential for hydropower. Ethiopia currently has more than 20 dams either operating or under construction—more than any other African country. The building of dams is filled with controversy, especially the environmental concerns and human costs of building the Grand Millennium Dam. Historically, Ethiopia's track record in dam building is tarnished. The government has pushed tribal people from their ancestral lands so dams can be built, leaving them with no place to live and often no source of livelihood, which has led to an increase in armed conflicts in the region.

ANSWERS, p. 487

READING PROGRESS CHECK Lake Volta is used as a transportation route for the residents and also generates hydroelectric power, supplies water for irrigation, and has several fisheries.

Connecting Geography The Sahel is over four times larger than Texas but three times smaller than the entire area of the United States.

Physical Geography of the Transition Zone

V Visual Skills

Creating Graphs Have students use the Internet to find data on annual precipitation in areas of the Transition Zone in the past decade. Have them use the data to create a graph that clearly shows decreasing annual precipitation. Ask them to write two critical thinking questions that can be answered using data on their graphs. **ELL Logical/Mathematical, Visual/Spatial**

W Writing Skills

Narrative Have students construct a narrative, either fiction or nonfiction, based on the diverse population of animals found in the African Transition Zone. They may choose to write about one animal or include many, such as a narrative that revolves around a watering hole. Encourage students to be creative and to research additional information about the animals. **AL Verbal/Linguistic**

CLOSE & REFLECT

Summarizing Review with students the importance of water to the economies of the Transition Zone and the difficulties encountered when the region is affected by drought. Encourage students to complete a cause-and-effect graphic organizer to tie together how water and rain affects climates, biomes, and economies in the Transition Zone.

ANSWERS, p. 488

✓ **READING PROGRESS CHECK** The Transition Zone has few resources, and those such as water must be managed carefully as droughts and famines can occur. Recently discovered mineral, oil, and gas deposits could help the region develop their economies, but extraction and processing must be done carefully so as not to damage the already fragile environment.

Climates, Biomes, and Resources

GUIDING QUESTION *How does the climate affect life and resources in the Transition Zone?*

There are two hot seasons in the African Transition Zone. One occurs between February and April and the other between September and October. The rainy season occurs between May and August, with most of the rain falling in the southern part of the subregion. Some years, this results in a fair amount of rain. However, the rain may be isolated to one area or be so intense that it damages crops. Most of the rain occurs during the summer months. During December and January, a hot, dry wind known as the **harmattan** blows from the north. It often carries dust and sand from the Sahara. In western Africa, the harmattan is sometimes referred to as "the doctor" because its dryness—in contrast to the typical humid air of the subregion—is considered invigorating.

harmattan a hot, dry wind that blows from the northeast or east in the western Sahara

In most countries of the Transition Zone, water is such a precious resource that rain and life are one and the same. Rain helps determine climate, and in turn vegetation, in most parts of the subregion. In many areas, rainfall is the only water source. Over the past century, annual precipitation has decreased. For example, parts of interior Eritrea get almost no rainfall. Sadly, a vicious cycle of soil erosion, insufficient water, deforestation, and drought has plagued the area for decades. Long periods of drought and overuse of the land destroyed vegetation, making the land unusable. Droughts have caused crops to fail, killed livestock, and led to famines.

This vast biome is also an important home to a diverse population of flora and fauna. For much of the year, the African Transition Zone is a vast expanse of dry soil. During the rainy season, however, the Sahel comes alive with plant life. In addition to grasslands, the Sahel is home to the baobab tree and the jujube, whose fruit is used to feed herds. Although the summer months provide abundant food for animal life, at other times of the year wildlife must remain constantly on the move, foraging for water and vegetation. The diverse population of animals includes migratory birds, which use the wetlands as a rest and feeding area. Wild dogs, cheetahs, lions, elephants, giraffes, warthogs, and gerbils are some of the many different animals that roam the African Transition Zone.

Farming and nomadic herding remain the important traditional economies of the subregion. Unfortunately, deforestation and drought are making these lifestyles more difficult. However, new discoveries and better use of oil, natural gas, and coal, as well as the mining of uranium, gold, and iron deposits may help the people of the Transition Zone develop new economies.

✓ **READING PROGRESS CHECK**

Determining Importance Why is it important that the people of the Transition Zone manage their resources in the most efficient way?

LESSON 1 REVIEW

Reviewing Vocabulary (Tier Three Words)

1. ***Making Connections*** Why is the Sahel called a transition zone? RH.9–10.4

Using Your Notes

2. ***Summarizing*** Use your graphic organizer on the geography of the African Transition Zone to write a paragraph summarizing how the land supports the people, flora, and fauna of the subregion.

Answering the Guiding Questions

3. ***Finding the Main Idea*** What is the Transition Zone?
4. ***Classifying*** What rivers flow through the Transition Zone?
5. ***Identifying Central Issues*** How does the climate affect life and resources in the Transition Zone?

Writing Activity

6. ***Informative/Explanatory*** In a paragraph, discuss how the climate affects the people and the flora and fauna of the Transition Zone. WHST.9–10.2

LESSON 1 REVIEW ANSWERS

Reviewing Vocabulary

1. The Sahel is called a transition zone because this is where the land changes from arid to tropical. It also represents a transition between the Islamic cultures of North Africa and the Christian and animist cultures to the south.

Using Your Notes

2. Paragraphs will vary but should be strongly supported with information from the lesson. Possible answers could include: grasslands support herding livestock; the rainy season replenishes water sources and supports growth of plants; wetlands support all animals, particularly migratory birds; water resources have been dammed to generate power, provide water for irrigation, and support fisheries.

Answering the Guiding Questions

3. The Transition Zone is the physical area in which the land undergoes a radical change. It is also the area that represents a transition from Islamic culture to Christian and animist cultures.
4. The Niger, the Senegal, White Nile, and Blue Nile Rivers flow through the Transition Zone. The Chari, the Logone, and the Yobe feed Lake Chad and are important to that area of the Transition Zone.
5. For much of the year, the Transition Zone is dry. However, during the rainy season, plants, animal, and people thrive. Water is the most valuable resource as lands must be irrigated to grow crops to feed the population. Nomadic peoples use the changes of seasons from dry to wet in this climate zone to travel to areas in order to find grazing lands for their livestock.

Writing Activity

6. Paragraphs will vary but should be strongly supported with information from the lesson. Possible answers could include: the rainy season replenishes water sources and supports growth of plants; wetlands support all types of plants and animals; and nomadic herding is common as grasslands are supported in the rainy season, but travel is necessary to find grazing land in the dry season.

networks

There's More Online!

- **IMAGE** Dogon Mask
- **IMAGE** Mine Workers
- **MAP** Kingdoms and Empires of the Transition Zone
- **INTERACTIVE MAP** Crisis in Darfur
- **TIME LINE** Droughts and Hunger
- **INTERACTIVE SELF-CHECK QUIZ**
- **VIDEO** Human Geography of the Transition Zone

LESSON 2

Human Geography of the Transition Zone

ESSENTIAL QUESTION • *How do physical systems and human systems shape a place?*

Reading **HELP**DESK 

Academic Vocabulary (Tier Two Words)
- **enhance**
- **potential**

Content Vocabulary (Tier Three Words)
- **domesticate**
- **animist**
- **sanitation**
- **patriarchal**
- **clan**
- **nuclear family**
- **oral tradition**
- **subsistence farming**

TAKING NOTES: ***Key Ideas and Details***

IDENTIFYING As you read about the human geography of the African Transition Zone, use a graphic organizer like the one below to identify examples of how history, culture, and economics have worked together to create the Transition Zone of today.

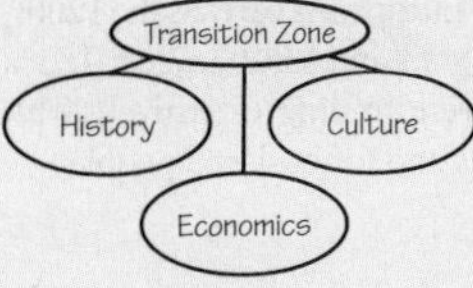

(tl)Stapleton Collection/Corbis, (tcl)Alain Nogues/Sygma/Corbis, (tc)Daphne Ouwersloot/Alamy, (tcr)Ton Koene/Alamy, (tr)Eric Feferberg/AFP/Getty Images

It Matters Because

The Transition Zone has been home to many peoples, empires, and kingdoms for millennia. European colonization in the late 1800s and early 1900s had lasting effects on the subregion. The peoples of the Sahel maintain their distinct cultures and traditions but face many similar challenges. R1

History and Government

GUIDING QUESTION *What factors influenced the formation of the countries of the Transition Zone?*

Between about 9000 B.C. and 4000 B.C., the northern half of Africa received greater amounts of rain than today. At that time, what is now the Sahara was a savanna of extensive grasslands, lakes, and rivers. Nomadic people who once hunted for food settled in places, adopted agriculture, and **domesticated**, or tamed, animals. Around 4000 B.C., however, a climate shift began to occur. It became hotter and drier. Some scientists think that this shift happened quite abruptly, perhaps in as few as 400 years beginning in about 2000 B.C. As a result of the changes, the people in the farming communities migrated south. C

Although much of the area became desert, the Nile Valley remained well watered, giving rise to Egypt and its civilization. Between about 2000 B.C. and 1000 B.C., the Egyptians pushed south, bringing various peoples along the Nile under their control. When Egypt's authority weakened, these peoples rose to power. R2

One of the civilizations Egyptians encountered as they pushed south was Kush. Around 2000 B.C., the Kush river civilization became a powerful kingdom in what is now Sudan. From about 2000 B.C. to about 1500 B.C., the Kushites controlled the Egyptian territory to the north. After retreating from Egypt, the Kushites pushed south and built a civilization around a new capital, Meroë. Kush flourished until about A.D. 300, when Meroë was attacked by Axum, a trading empire in Ethiopia. Axum was a great trading power from about A.D. 100 to A.D. 700.

ENGAGE

R1 Reading Skills

Determining Importance Have students read the *It Matters Because* section. Then have them think about how colonization affects cultures. Discuss the difficulties that go along with maintaining distinct cultures and traditions in modern times when the global world is more connected.

TEACH & ASSESS

C Critical Thinking Skills

Assessing Discuss with students the domestication of animals. **Ask:** **What kinds of animals do you think nomads most likely domesticated?** *(Possible answer: They likely domesticated animals that are similar to the ones that are domesticated today, such as goats, chickens, horses, and cattle.)* **What benefits do you think domesticating animals provided?** *(These animals could either help people work or could provide food, such as milk or eggs.)* ELL **Verbal/Linguistic**

R2 Reading Skills

Inferring Point out that as Egyptian authority weakened, the peoples they had brought under their control began to rise to power again. **Ask:** **What are some possible reasons for Egypt's power weakening?** *(Possible answer: Controlling large numbers of people is more difficult than controlling smaller numbers of people. The more people they brought under their control, the more difficult maintaining that control became.)* **Throughout history, in general, how has a civilization's desire to expand and conquer ultimately turned out in the end? Why?** *(Possible answer: That civilization eventually loses power because they are unable to control such a large number of people in a vast area or because specific groups consistently strive for independence.)* AL **Verbal/Linguistic**

ANSWERS, p. 489

TAKING NOTES: History—Kush was a powerful kingdom in what is now Sudan; Axum, a powerful trading empire in Ethiopia, attacked the Kush kingdom; Mali Empire became legendary for its wealth and conquering of surrounding territories; Songhai Empire capitalized on the salt trade and took over Mali; by 1200s, Timbuktu was an important trade center between Africa and Europe; **Culture**—all the Sahel was under European control by 1914; Europeans created boundaries with no regard for ethnic or religious groups; animist cultures and Islam were predominant religions; the introduction of Christianity increased tensions; conflicts are common between religious and ethnic groups; **Economics**—salt and gold were traditional ways kingdoms and empires built their economies; today, oil, natural gas, gold, coal, and other minerals are found in the region; most live in traditional economies of seminomadic herding and subsistence farming.

networks *Online Teaching Options*

 INTERACTIVE BELLRINGER

Kingdoms and Empires of the Transition Zone

Drawing Conclusions Use the introductory text and map of the empires and kingdoms of the Transition Zone to draw conclusions about the empires and kingdoms of the Transition Zone and their trade practices. Have students form small groups and discuss each question. Ask group to come to a consensus on the answers and write agreed-upon explanations to the questions. Then in a class discussion, have groups share their answers. BL **Verbal/Linguistic**

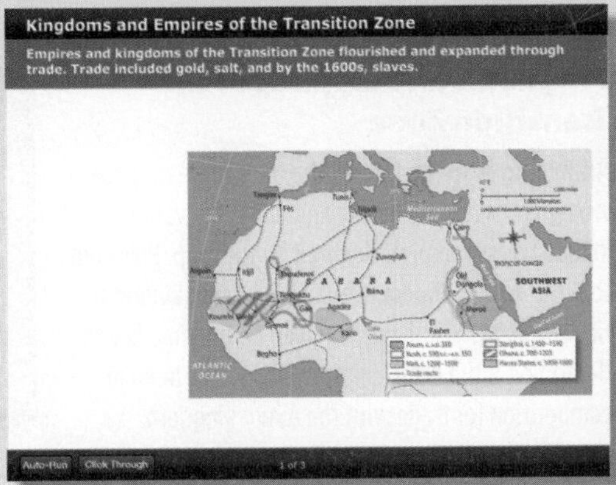

Kingdoms and Empires of the Transition Zone
Empires and kingdoms of the Transition Zone flourished and expanded through trade. Trade included gold, salt, and by the 1600s, slaves.
SAHARA
SOUTHWEST ASIA
ATLANTIC OCEAN
Auto-Run
Click Through
1 of 3

Human Geography of the Transition Zone

V Visual Skills

Examining Have students study the map. **Ask:** **What is common to every kingdom or empire in reference to trade routes?** *(Possible answer: Each kingdom or empire contains at least one city that is along a trade route.)* **Why did the Kush and Axum empires develop earlier than empires on the western side of Africa?** *(Possible answer: They were physically closer to Egypt and the Nile River valley.)* **According to the dates shown on the map, which empire existed for the longest period?** *(the Hausa states)*
AL **Visual/Spatial, Logical/Mathematical**

W Writing Skills

Informative/Explanatory Have students research and write an informative paper about Makkah. Ask them to explore its history, particularly its role in Islam at the time of Mansa Musa. Have them explain why a pilgrimage to Makkah is important and how Musa's pilgrimage helped Mali to become legendary in the Islamic world. **AL** **Verbal/Linguistic**

C Critical Thinking Skills

Identifying Perspectives Discuss early European contact with Africa. **Ask:** **How would you describe the initial relationship between Africa and Europe?** *(Possible answer: It was likely beneficial to both sides. They traded with each other.)* **How did European countries quickly begin to view Africa?** *(as a source of raw materials and a market for finished products)* **Which word best describes Europe's interest in Africa—*economic, political,* or *cultural*? Explain.** *(Europe's interest in Africa was economic. Europe wanted to get raw materials from the region and then turn around and make money selling finished products back to them.)* **Logical/Mathematical**

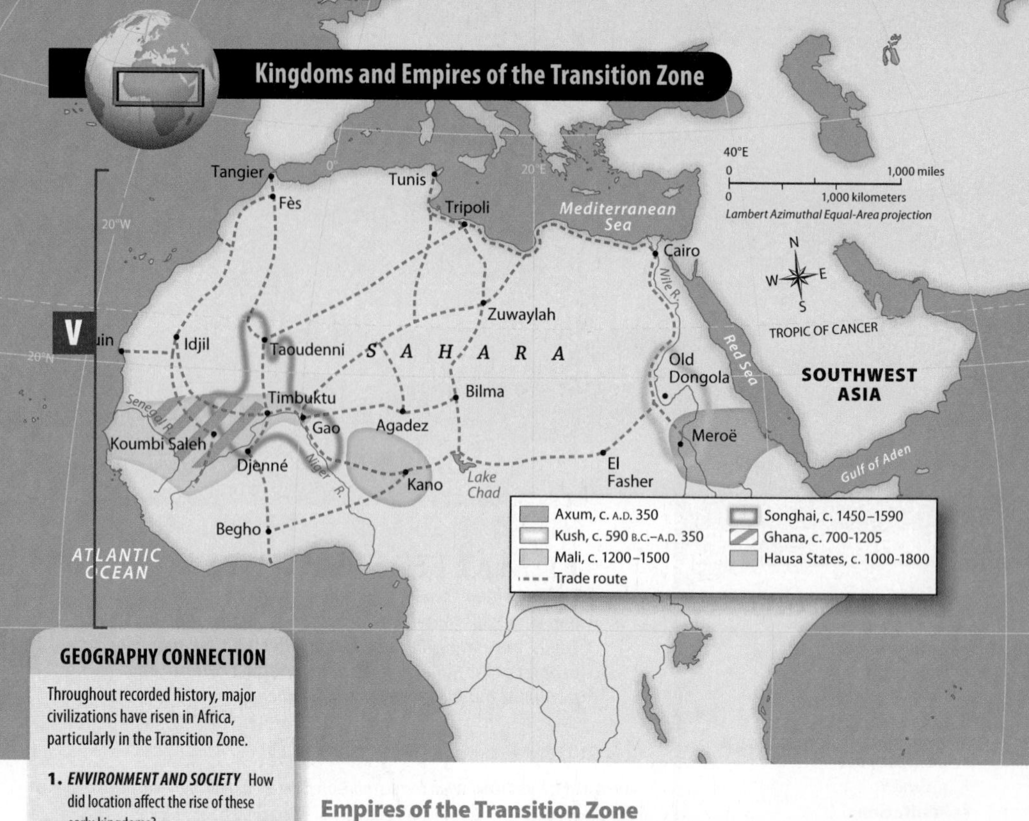

GEOGRAPHY CONNECTION

Throughout recorded history, major civilizations have risen in Africa, particularly in the Transition Zone.

1. ***ENVIRONMENT AND SOCIETY*** How did location affect the rise of these early kingdoms?
2. ***HUMAN SYSTEMS*** Which kingdom overtook the Kushites?

domesticate to adapt plants and animals from the wild for human use

enhance to improve or increase

Empires of the Transition Zone

In addition to the kingdoms of Kush and Axum in the eastern part of the Transition Zone, new trading empires gained strength in the western part. The present-day country of Mali is named after one of them, the Mali Empire. One of Mali's early kings, Sundiata Keita, helped Mali flourish by expanding trade routes for gold and salt. He also conquered many of the surrounding territories. The most famous ruler of the Mali Empire was Mansa Musa. A Muslim, Musa **enhanced** the prestige and power of Mali through a famous pilgrimage to Makkah (Mecca). Accompanied by a huge entourage, Musa apparently dispensed so much gold on his journey to Makkah that the price of gold fell drastically in places he visited.

The Mali Empire became legendary in the Islamic world and Europe, and helped Islam spread. Mali, which extended west to the Atlantic, had as its center the wealthy city of Timbuktu. Another empire, Songhai (SAWNG•hy), grew rich from the gold-for-salt trade started in the western empire of Ghana. Songhai eventually took over Mali and expanded east. It prospered until about A.D. 1600, when the Moroccans overran it.

Word of the wealth of Africa's kingdoms reached Europe. As early as the 1200s, Timbuktu became an important center of trade in gold and salt between Africa and Europe. By the 1600s and 1700s, Europeans were trading extensively with Africa. They traded for African gold and other goods and for enslaved people.

Colonization and Independence

In the 1800s, European powers regarded the region as a source of raw materials and as a **potential** market for finished goods. European countries also laid claim

networks Online Teaching Options

INTERACTIVE MAP

Kingdoms and Empires of the Transition Zone

Analyzing Visuals Display the interactive map for students. Have them locate and name the various kingdoms and empires denoted on the map. Point out that the Kush kingdom overlaps the Axum kingdom. Have students use the dates given on the map key to determine if the Kush kingdom could have been in competition for trade with the Axum kingdom.
AL **Visual/Spatial, Logical/Mathematical**

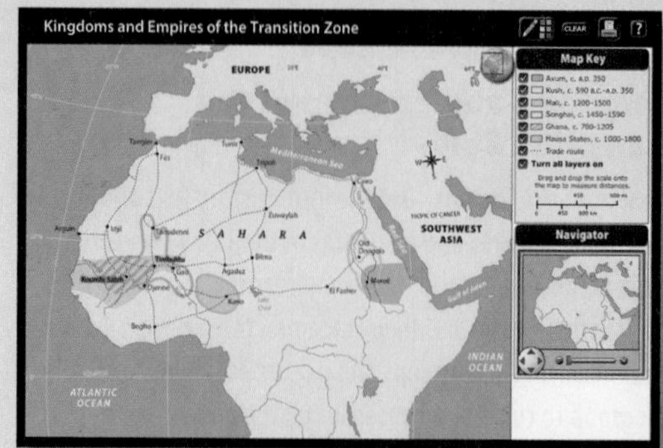

ANSWERS, p. 490

GEOGRAPHY CONNECTION

1. Early kingdoms rose along trade routes.
2. The Axum kingdom of Ethiopia overtook the Kushites.

to African territory. A conference, known as the Berlin Conference, was held between 1884 and 1885 to regulate European colonization. All of the Sahel was under European control by 1914.

G1 European rulers knew little about Africa's political and social systems, and no Africans participated at the Berlin Conference. As a result, Europeans created colonial boundaries that often cut across cultural, religious, or traditional boundaries, merging **animist** cultures with Muslim societies. Animist cultures believe all elements of nature, such as animals and mountains, have spirits. The introduction of Christianity added to the tension. Religious friction set African peoples against one another and strengthened European rule.

C2 In the mid-1900s, Africans began to demand a share in government. Educated Africans launched independence movements. In the second half of the century, the colonies became independent of European rule.

These new countries faced difficult challenges, often the result of their colonial legacy. European powers, for example, set up colonial economies that met European, rather than African, needs. In addition, colonial governments did not involve Africans much in government, nor did they give Africans models for democracy. At independence, many of the new countries kept the political boundaries set by the colonial powers. Within the new countries, rival ethnic groups struggled for power. Civil wars erupted.

Conflicts also arose between countries in the Sahel. Border disputes have lasted for years between Somalia and Ethiopia. The collapse of governments as a result of warring factions, drought, and famine further weakened the newly independent countries. While some countries in the African Transition Zone continue to struggle, new opportunities from the discoveries of oil, gas, and uranium deposits may help to bring stability if governments can manage these resources properly.

Conflict in Sudan

T The countries in the Transition Zone are teeming with cultural differences. At times, these differences have led to conflicts such as between Sudan's north and south. Arabic-speaking Muslims live mostly in the northern cities and favor Islamic-oriented governments. People in the south live mostly in rural areas, are focused on a subsistence economy, and prefer a secular government. These differences led to a conflict in which nearly 300,000 people died and an estimated 2.7 million people were displaced between 1983 and 2005.

A peace agreement was finally signed in 2005, which provided considerable independence for Sudan's southern provinces. Although the agreement ended the conflict between the north and the south, it did not address the conflict in the western Darfur region of the country. The civil war in Darfur occurred because non-Arab Sudanese accused the government of favoring Sudanese Arabs. Finally, in 2011, the southern provinces of Sudan held a referendum and voted for independence. South Sudan is now an independent country, with Juba as its capital.

More recently, in January 2011, South Sudan shut down all of its oil fields after a disagreement about the fees Sudan demanded to transport the oil. In May 2011, Sudan seized control of Abyei, a disputed oil-rich border region, after three days of clashes with South Sudanese forces. On September 27, 2011, the presidents of Sudan and South Sudan signed agreements of cooperation. The status of Abyei, however, was not addressed. The future of the region is still uncertain.

✓ READING PROGRESS CHECK

Identifying Cause and Effect In what ways has colonialism affected the countries of the Transition Zone?

Analyzing PRIMARY SOURCES (CCSS)

The Conflict in Sudan

"We left because of war. For the last one and a half years we have been bombed by planes every day. We lived in the forest; there was no chance for school for the children, no healthcare or medicine. We got food from the ground, but not corn. We would collect water in the early mornings. This has happened all seasons."

—a 36-year-old mother of nine at the Jamam refugee camp in South Sudan, from Médecins Sans Frontières, January 18, 2013

DBQ ***IDENTIFYING CAUSE AND EFFECT*** In what ways did the people of Sudan suffer from the conflict between the north and the south? RH.9–10.2

animist pertaining to traditional religious beliefs in which nature and objects, such as animals and mountains, are thought to have spirits

G1 Critical Thinking Skills

Making Predictions Emphasize to students that no Africans participated at the Berlin Conference. Discuss with students what it would be like to live in a region that is summarily divided up by another country or countries. Explore predictions of what may have happened had Africans been represented at the Berlin Conference. **Ask:** Do you think Europeans would have listened to Africans while determining how to colonize the continent? Why or why not? *(Possible answer: No, they would not have listened to Africans. They saw the economic opportunities in Africa, so they might not have listened to African opinions if they opposed the Europeans' plans.)* AL **Verbal/Linguistic, Intrapersonal**

C2 Critical Thinking Skills

Analyzing Ethical Issues Discuss with students the ethical issues involved in African colonization. **Ask:** What were some of the ethical issues involved in the beginning of colonization? *(Possible answer: The European countries made decisions on how to divide Africa without regard for physical or cultural and ethnic boundaries.)* What are some of the ethical issues regarding making people live under colonial rule? *(Possible answers: People do not have any say in their own government. Decisions are made for them that may not be in their best interests.)* What ultimately led to independence for African countries? *(Possible answers: Educated Africans began speaking out and demanding independence.)* **Verbal/Linguistic, Interpersonal**

T Technology Skills

Sequencing Have students create a time line of conflict in Sudan using presentation software. Have them locate online photos and videos to add to their time lines. Encourage them to research further to add details more specific than those mentioned in the text. AL **Visual/Spatial**

INTERACTIVE ART

Refugees of Sudan

Analyzing Visuals Have students analyze and discuss the religious and economic concerns that refugees of Sudan are faced with. Remind students that Sudan has been involved in civil war for many years as they review the art. Discuss with student the genocide and forced relocation in South Sudan. Have students share their thoughts and feelings with a partner. Be sure to discuss with students the lasting impact that violence and forced relocation can have on the culture of a civilization. **Intrapersonal, Visual/Spatial**

Refugees of the Sudan

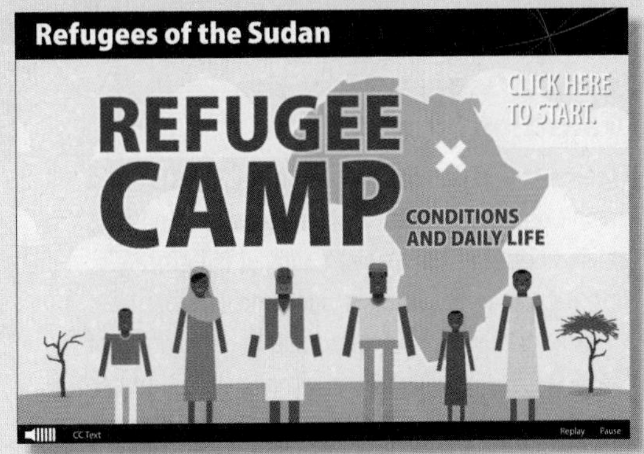

ANSWERS, p. 491

✓ READING PROGRESS CHECK Europeans set up boundaries that cut across cultural, religious, and traditional boundaries. The boundaries stayed in place even after these areas became independent. This has created ongoing conflict throughout the region. The introduction of Christianity during the colonial period added to the tensions within the region. Colonial governments set up economies that met only the needs of Europeans, did not involve the Africans in government, and failed to set up democratic models in the countries of the Transition Zone.

DBQ People in Sudan were displaced from their homes, had little food, and had no access to health care or education.

V1 Visual Skills

Spatial Analysis To help students relate to a population density of 58 people per square mile, have them draw a square mile on a map of their community or neighborhood. Then ask them to describe what having 58 people in that area would be like. **Ask:** **Would it be crowded in this area?** *(Possible answer: No, there is lots of room for people. They would not be right next to each other.)* **Visual/Spatial**

R Reading Skills

Simulating Have students simulate what it would be like for the population of the African Transition Zone to double in thirty years. The classroom space can represent the Transition Zone. Encourage students to use a certain number of seconds to represent a year and have them work together to simulate this growth in population. AL **Kinesthetic**

V2 Visual Skills

Using Charts Refer students to the time line. **Ask:** **When did the first recognized problem related to drought occur?** *(1640)* **Why would a large migration of people disrupt trade?** *(Possible answer: Shopkeepers are no longer around to tend stores, and herders have to move to other pastures.)* ELL **Verbal/Linguistic**

ANSWERS, p. 492

READING PROGRESS CHECK Islam, Christianity, and traditional animist religions are found in the Transition Zone.

CRITICAL THINKING

1. Droughts have brought famine and the fall of empires in the Sahel. They have caused the deterioration or elimination of wetlands and have substantially reduced the size of Lake Chad.
2. Various organizations are working to determine how human activities may contribute to drought, implement water management techniques, and provide food to relieve famines caused by drought.

Population Patterns

GUIDING QUESTION *What are the population patterns of the Transition Zone?*

The African Transition Zone is more than just a geographical transition—it is also a cultural transition between Muslim North Africa and the animist and Christian south. Many different cultural groups inhabit the changing environment of the Transition Zone.

V1 There are not only differences in religious beliefs, but also differences in ways of life. Herders, farmers, nomads, and city dwellers make up the people of the Transition Zone. Despite rapid population growth, population density currently remains low. The average population density of the subregion is about 58 people per square mile (23 people per sq. km). Only a small portion of the total land area, however, is suitable for agriculture. Thus, population throughout the subregion is not evenly distributed.

R According to some studies, the population of the countries in the Transition Zone will reach 100 million by 2020 and 200 million by 2050. More than half of these people are expected to live in Burkina Faso, Mali, and Niger. It is difficult to imagine how the environment can support such a large population.

While there are relatively few cities, there are several important ones. The ancient city of Timbuktu, now known as Tombouctou, is still standing. Nouakchott, the capital of Mauritania, has a population of about 710,000 people. Sudan has two important cities as well. Khartoum, its capital, has a population of over 5 million. The second, Port Sudan, handles the bulk of Sudan's external trade.

Cities in the Sahel will continue to grow in the years to come. Increasing drought and environmental damage have spurred people who once lived in rural areas to migrate to cities such as Niamey in Niger and Bamako in Mali.

READING PROGRESS CHECK

Gathering Information Which religions can be found in the Transition Zone?

TIME LINE

DROUGHTS and HUNGER

For centuries, the peoples of the Sahel have experienced famine brought about by droughts. As the droughts have become more severe in recent years, climate scientists have collected evidence to determine if they are, in part, caused or intensified by human activities.

CRITICAL THINKING

1. ***Identifying Cause and Effect*** What have been some of the effects of the droughts in the Sahel?
2. ***Analyzing*** What efforts have been made to deal with the effects of drought?

V2

1600

1640 European travelers observe a major drought in the Sahel and create the first modern record.

1740s–1750s The Great Famine in northern Nigeria, Niger, and Mali leads to massive migration and disruption of trade.

1800

1820s–1830s Major droughts lead to famine from Senegal to Chad and contribute to decline of Bornu Empire

networks Online Teaching Options

GRAPHIC ORGANIZER

Human Geography of the Transition Zone

Finding the Main Idea Have students use this graphic organizer to list the main idea and important details about the human geography of the African Transition Zone. Encourage students to consider structuring their main ideas around the main ideas of the lesson, *History*, *Culture*, and *Economics*. Tell students that these organizers may serve as a study tool for the chapter assessment. ELL **Visual/Spatial**

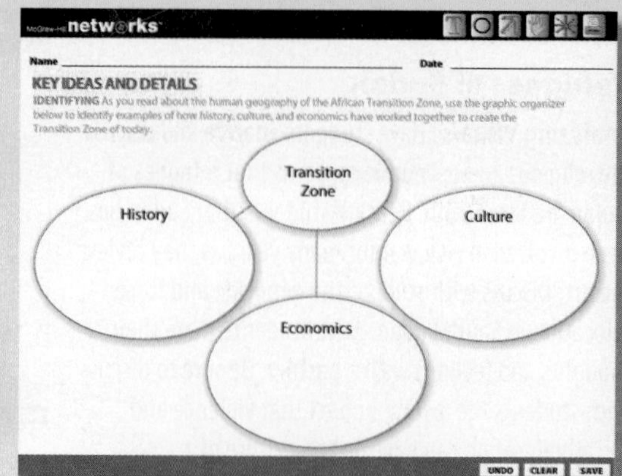

Society and Culture Today

GUIDING QUESTION *What cultural conflicts affect life in the Transition Zone?*

As you have seen, the Transition Zone includes more than 20 countries. There are more than 200 distinct ethnic groups in Chad alone. These groups coexist in an area influenced by Arab, European, and indigenous African cultures. Some of the major ethnic groups include the Mandé peoples of Senegal and Mali, the Wolof of Senegal, and the Hausa of Niger. The Fulani and the Berber peoples both live throughout the Sahel. The many ethnic groups of the Transition Zone speak languages from several African language groups: Afro-Asiatic, Nilo-Saharan, and Congo-Kordofanian. Because of European colonial rule, French is also widely spoken throughout the subregion. C1

The dominant religion among the peoples of the Transition Zone is Islam. Christianity, however, is also practiced in varying degrees in Chad, Sudan, Niger, and Senegal. Additionally, many ethnic groups in the region have maintained many of their indigenous religious practices. These usually involve belief in the existence of a supreme being and a hierarchy of lesser beings. C2

Many issues essential for development and for meeting basic needs revolve around education, health, and urbanization. Rural-to-urban migration has increased in the Transition Zone as drought and overworked land force farmers to look for work in cities. Sometimes men leave their families behind. Money sent home by these migrant workers is often the most important source of income in rural households. But many families choose to move to the cities as well.

Poverty is a key factor in access to health care in the Transition Zone. Some of the major health concerns are high mortality rates and infectious diseases. Lack of adequate health care during pregnancy and childbirth also results in high female and infant mortality rates. Only a small number of rural Africans have access to clean water, and only one-fourth live where there is adequate **sanitation**, or disposal of waste products. 

sanitation the disposal of waste products

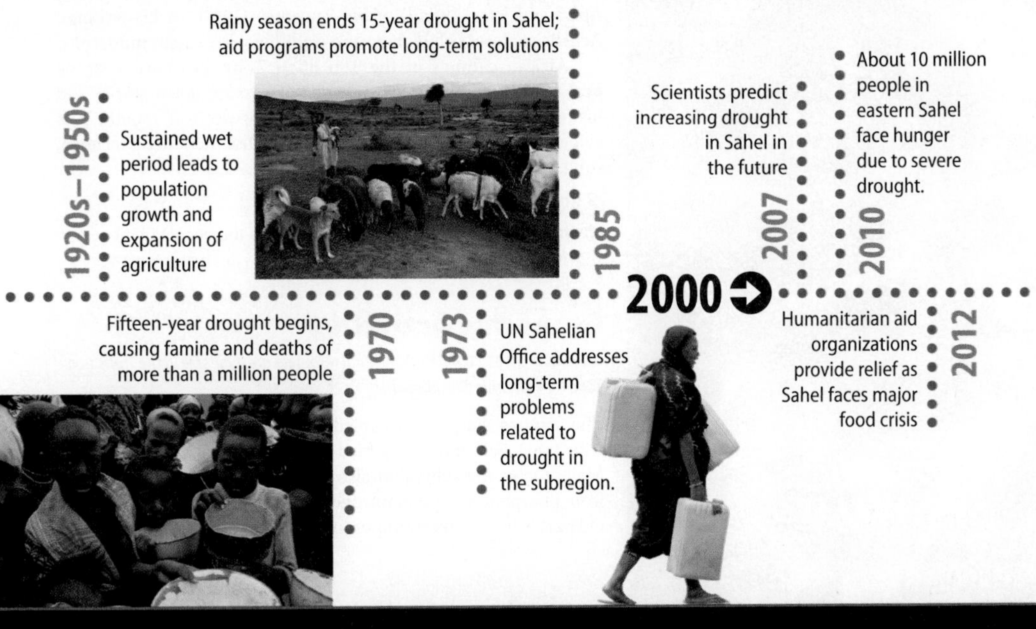

1920s–1950s
Sustained wet period leads to population growth and expansion of agriculture
1970
Fifteen-year drought begins, causing famine and deaths of more than a million people
1973
UN Sahelian Office addresses long-term problems related to drought in the subregion.
1985
Rainy season ends 15-year drought in Sahel; aid programs promote long-term solutions
2000
2007
Scientists predict increasing drought in Sahel in the future
2010
About 10 million people in eastern Sahel face hunger due to severe drought.
2012
Humanitarian aid organizations provide relief as Sahel faces major food crisis

C1 Critical Thinking Skills

Evaluating Discuss with students what it would be like to live in an area like the Transition Zone where many different cultures and languages exist. Have students relate this situation to situations in their own lives when they encounter other languages. **Ask:** **Do you speak a language other than English?** *(Student answers will vary.)* **What are your thoughts when you hear two people speaking a language with which you are not familiar?** *(Student answers may vary but should explain their feelings about not being able to understand what others are saying.)* **Is learning foreign languages important for Americans? Why or why not?** *(Possible answer: Yes, it is important for cultural understanding.)* **AL Intrapersonal**

C2 Critical Thinking Skills

Comparing and Contrasting Have students use a Venn diagram to compare and contrast Islam and Christianity. Tell them to use reference materials and the Internet to find basic characteristics of each religion and use them to complete the Venn diagram. **AL Visual/Spatial**

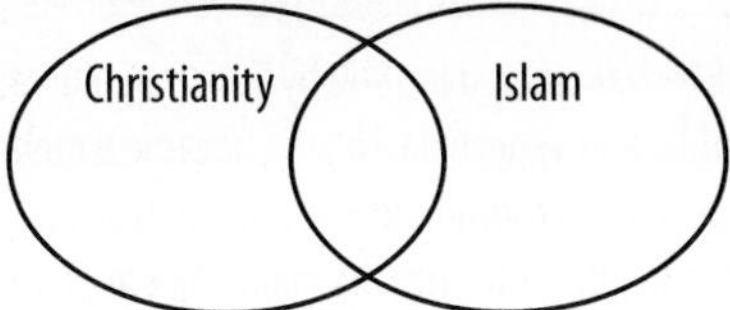

W Writing Skills

Argument Have students construct a persuasive letter to the government of a country in the Transition Zone. They should argue in favor of investment in infrastructure, sanitation in particular. Encourage them to research specific information about the sanitation in their chosen country and to find data and statistics to back up their claims. They should attempt to provide specific ideas for how to solve sanitation problems in the region. **ELL Interpersonal, Verbal/Linguistic**

INTERACTIVE WHITEBOARD ACTIVITY

Empires of the Transition Zone

Locating and Categorizing Students can use this whiteboard activity as a review to broaden their understanding of the Mali and Songhai empires. Have students drag place names to the correct locations on the map. Also have them drag facts about the Mali and Songhai empires to the chart provided. When the activity is completed, have pairs of students read one location and one fact about either empire, until all locations have been identified and all facts have been read. **ELL Visual/Spatial, Kinesthetic**

Empires of the Transition Zone

Directions: New trading empires gained strength in the western part of the African Transition Zone. First label the Mali and Songhai Empires on the map by dragging the words from the text box to the correct locations on the map. Then drag pertinent facts about each empire underneath the appropriate empire. When correctly completed, the Mali and Songhai Empires will be correctly labeled on the map and the chart will display facts about each empire.

- Mali Empire
- Eventually took over a rival empire and expanded east
- Mansa Musa enhanced the empire's power and prestige through a famous pilgrimage to Mecca
- Sundiata Keita helped the empire flourish by expanding trade routes for gold and salt and conquering many surrounding territories
- Grew rich from the gold-for-salt trade started in Ghana
- Songhai Empire
- Became legendary in both the Islamic world and Europe, and helped Islam to proliferate
- Prospered until Moroccans overran it in A.D. 1600

Mali Empire

Songhai Empire

CHAPTER 20, Lesson 2
Human Geography of the Transition Zone

R Reading Skills

Defining Discuss the definition of *nuclear family* with students. **Ask:** How does the text describe a nuclear family? *(a husband, a wife, and children)* In what other ways have you heard the term *nuclear* used? *(Possible answer: in nuclear energy and as in the nucleus of an atom or the nucleus of a cell)* How could you define *nuclear* based on the nucleus of a cell? *(Possible answers: in the center, the control center)* Emphasize to students the relationship between the term *nuclear* and the term *nuclear family.* ELL Verbal/Linguistic

T Technology Skills

Critical Listening Have students conduct online research to find audio samples of oral tradition in the cultures of the Transition Zone. Have students listen to a sample only one time. Then ask them to summarize the story and retell it to a classmate after the one hearing. Point out that stories told by oral tradition are told over and over. Auditory/Musical, Intrapersonal

Content Background Knowledge

OPEC OPEC was created in 1960 by Iran, Iraq, Kuwait, Saudi Arabia, and Venezuela. Nigeria became a member in 1971. OPEC aims to coordinate and unify petroleum policies among its member countries. Its main objectives are to secure fair and stable prices for producers of petroleum and a regular supply of petroleum to countries that consume it.

patriarchal a family that is headed by a male family member

clan a large group of people descended from the same ancestor

nuclear family a family unit made up of a husband, wife, and children

oral tradition the practice of passing down stories from generation to generation by word of mouth

Dogon masks represent certain animals that symbolize their ancestors' spirits. This Dogon mask is worn at a rite that celebrates the passage of the dead into the spirit world.

▼ CRITICAL THINKING

1. ***Analyzing Visuals*** Describe the dominant features of the Dogon mask.
2. ***Making Connections*** How does this mask compare with modern abstract artistic representations of humans and animals?

School enrollment and literacy rates in the Transition Zone are generally low. In countries such as Niger and Mali, only a small percentage of children go to school. When children do go to school, they still face unemployment upon graduation. The education system has not yet adapted to the economic conditions and development that lead to jobs. However, governments are working to increase school enrollment.

Family and the Status of Women

No matter how different their ways of life, most Africans in the Transition Zone value strong family ties. Most people still live in extended families in rural areas. Women are very involved in supporting the family, often doing much of the farmwork. However, most families are **patriarchal**, or headed by a male family member, and descent is traced through the male line. Families are organized into **clans**, large groups of people descended from an early common ancestor. R People often marry only within their clan. In the cities, however, extended families are more difficult to maintain. As a result, the **nuclear family**—made up of husband, wife, and children—is rapidly replacing the extended family.

The Arts

African art comes in many forms, from ritual masks to rhythmic drum music to folktales. These various art forms often express traditional religious beliefs. Visual arts include the ceremonial masks and wooden figures of the Dogon people of Mali. Music is also an important part of Dogon culture. Traditionally, the Dogon use music at ceremonies honoring their loved ones who have died. Rich musical T traditions of the region include percussion and the five-string guitar. The talking drum is also popular, so called because it can reproduce the tone changes that are part of the Dogon language. By combining different tones and rhythms, the drumming creates messages that can be understood like the language.

Literature has also become an important art in the Transition Zone. Notable writers include Nafissatou Niang Diallo, whose 1975 autobiography was one of the first literary works to be published by a Senegalese woman. Chinua Achebe, from Nigeria, was a celebrated novelist and poet. He is most well known for his 1958 novel *Things Fall Apart* and later *Anthills of the Savannah* (1987). In his writings, Achebe explores colonialism and traditional life versus modernity.

African cultures of the Transition Zone also have a strong **oral tradition**. This is the practice of passing down stories and history from generation to generation by word of mouth. It is evident in folktales, myths, and proverbs. Oral literature is chanted, sung, or recited.

☑ READING PROGRESS CHECK

Identifying Central Issues What challenges do the people of the Transition Zone face today?

Economic Activities

GUIDING QUESTION *What natural resources are available in the Transition Zone for economic development?*

The empires that once occupied this region built their kingdoms with trade. Salt and gold added to the wealth of empires such as Mali. Today, the subregion also has rich deposits of oil and gas, iron, phosphates, copper, tin, and uranium to explore and develop. Oil has been particularly important in attracting outside investment.

Daphne Ouwersloot/Alamy

494

networks Online Teaching Options

INTERACTIVE IMAGE

The Golden Ground Under the Transition Zone

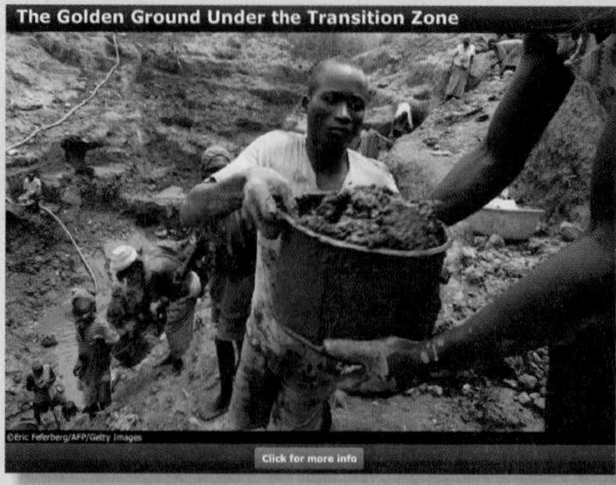

Narrative Display the interactive image of The Golden Ground Under the Transition Zone. Students may be surprised to learn that what they are viewing is a gold mine. Have students examine the photograph and think about whether or not the gold that is being mined would impact the excavators' lives. Ask students to use details from the photograph and from the text to write a narrative about one of the persons shown working in the gold mine. Have them write a journal entry describing his work in the mine and what it means to him.

BL Verbal/Linguistic

ANSWERS, p. 494

☑ READING PROGRESS CHECK The people of the African Transition Zone face challenges of urbanization and providing the basic needs of health care and education. Drought is an ongoing issue that creates challenges in supplying food for the population and also increases rural-to-urban migration.

CRITICAL THINKING

1. An elongated face with prominent teeth, white eyebrows and beard, and a yellow and red mane/hair are the dominant features of the Dogon mask.
2. Answers may vary but could indicate a combining of features such as hair and teeth or the use of color.

Eric Feferberg/AFP/Getty Images

Workers form a human chain to pass buckets of mud and stones in a gold mine.

◀ CRITICAL THINKING

1. *Analyzing Visuals* How would you characterize the level of technology in this gold mine?

2. *Making Connections* What can you infer about the mine, given the level of technology used?

Immense oil reserves make Nigeria the region's only member of the Organization of Petroleum Exporting Countries (OPEC). In 2003 Chad became one of the subregion's oil-producing countries. Another country in the Sahel that has attracted investors is Niger. It has some of the world's largest deposits of uranium. Niger also has oil, gold, coal, and other mineral deposits, while Eritrea has gold and copper. In Senegal, the mineral industry—primarily petroleum products and phosphates—makes up about 20 percent of the country's exports.

Nonetheless, most people make their living in the traditional economies of the Transition Zone, primarily seminomadic herding and **subsistence farming**. In subsistence farming, the farmer and his or her family consume most of what is produced, leaving little to sell at market. Usually, subsistence farms are small and farming technology is labor-intensive. Typically, yields are low. Subsistence farmers decide what to plant based on what the family will need rather than on market prices. Much of what is grown in the Transition Zone is millet and sorghum. However, for countries such as Eritrea, subsistence farming often does not yield enough food even for their own populations.

subsistence farming farming that provides the basic needs of a family with little surplus

C

 READING PROGRESS CHECK

Categorizing What economic activities can be found in the Transition Zone?

LESSON 2 REVIEW (CCSS)

Reviewing Vocabulary (Tier Three Words)

1. *Making Connections* Write a paragraph using the terms *patriarchal, clan,* and *nuclear family* to describe families in the Transition Zone. RH.9–10.4

Using Your Notes

2. *Describing* Use your graphic organizer about the human geography of the Transition Zone to write a paragraph about the complexity of the subregion and the difficulties it faces.

Answering the Guiding Questions

3. *Drawing Conclusions* What factors influenced the formation of the countries of the Transition Zone?

4. *Classifying* What are the population patterns of the Transition Zone?

5. *Exploring Issues* What cultural conflicts affect life in the Transition Zone?

6. *Evaluating* What natural resources are available in the Transition Zone for economic development?

Writing Activity

7. *Informative/Explanatory* In a paragraph, discuss how the people of the Transition Zone, both past and present, have shaped the subregion. WHST.9–10.2

C Critical Thinking Skills

Identifying Central Issues Discuss the central issues related to subsistence farming. **Ask:** **How vulnerable are subsistence farmers? To what are they most vulnerable?** *(Possible answer: They are very vulnerable to the weather. If the weather is poor, they may lose their crops and not have enough to eat.)* **Is subsistence farming the best use of land in the Transition Zone? Explain.** *(Possible answer: No, small pieces of land are used to feed small numbers of people. If the land was used more efficiently to grow crops, it could supply food for larger numbers of people.)* **Naturalist, Logical/Mathematical**

CLOSE & REFLECT

Summarizing Review with students the history and governments of the Transition Zone including the various empires and kingdoms. Have students complete a cause-and-effect chart to organize information surrounding conflicts in the region, beginning with colonization. Discuss other challenges faced by the region.

ANSWERS, p. 495

READING PROGRESS CHECK Most people in the Transition Zone make their living from seminomadic herding and subsistence farming. However, Nigeria, Chad, Niger, and Senegal also have economic activities surrounding oil, natural gas, and mineral extraction.

CRITICAL THINKING

1. The level of technology is low. It does not have any machinery to aid the miners.
2. The mine is probably unsafe to work in.

LESSON 2 REVIEW ANSWERS

Reviewing Vocabulary

1. Paragraphs will vary but must include the terms *patriarchal, clan,* and *nuclear family* in a description of families of the Transition Zone. Possible answers could state that families are mostly patriarchal, or led by male family members, and are sometimes organized into clans, or larger groups descended from a common ancestor; nuclear families, or husband, wife, and children, are more common in urban settings.

Using Your Notes

2. Paragraphs will vary but should be strongly supported with information from the lesson. Possible answers could include: the large numbers of countries in the subregion, the mix of Islam, Christianity, and animist religions, ongoing conflicts based on these differences, high likelihood of droughts and famine, the need of the subregion to develop its natural resources such as oil and natural gas, and the improvements needed in supplying basic needs such as health care and education.

Answering the Guiding Questions

3. The early kingdoms and empires of the region established some areas as trading centers and drew the attention of Europe. European colonialism and the boundaries drawn by Europeans influenced the formation of countries of the Transition Zone.

4. The population is not evenly distributed in the Transition Zone because most of the land is not suitable for agriculture. The highest numbers of people are expected to live in Burkina Faso, Mali, and Niger in the future.

5. Cultural conflicts between ethnic and religious groups affect life in the Transition Zone.

6. The Transition Zone has gold, oil, natural gas, phosphates, copper, tin and uranium deposits that could be used for economic development.

Writing Activity

7. Paragraphs will vary but should be strongly supported with information from the lesson. Possible answers could include: the Axum, Kush, Mali, and Songhai people and the empires and trading centers they established; colonialism; and the creation of boundaries that did not take into account the ethnic, religious, and cultural traditions of the people that has created ongoing conflicts for the subregion.

ENGAGE

G1 Critical Thinking Skills

Making Generalizations Have students list what they think people do to solve problems of poverty and hunger. Discuss how poverty leads to hunger, hunger leads to conflict, and conflict leads to war. Have students generalize about the causes of war based on this information. *(Possible answer: War happens when basic needs of a population are not being met.)*

TEACH & ASSESS

G2 Critical Thinking Skills

Making Predictions Have students predict the conditions of the Sahel 50 and 100 years from now if the annual amount of precipitation continues to drop and the population continues to increase. *(People will have to deal with the same issues of less rainfall, fewer crops, and an increasing population to feed.)* **If this trend continues, what do you predict will happen to the population of the Sahel? What will be the cause?** *(Possible answer: Eventually, the population will decline; many people will be lost to the devastation of famine.)* AL Verbal/Linguistic

R Reading Skills

Using Word Parts Write *desertification* on the board and break it into *desert/ifi/cation*. Have students define *desert*. *(a dry area)* **Ask:** **What does the suffix *–ify* do to a noun? Think about the words *classify* and *modify*.** *(It changes a noun into a verb.)* **How does adding *–ify* change *desert*?** *(It changes from a noun into a verb, meaning "to make into desert.")* **How does the suffix *–cation* change a word?** *(It changes a verb into a noun.)* Explain that *desert* is changed into a verb by adding *–ify*, and back into a noun by adding *–cation*. ELL Verbal/Linguistic

ANSWERS, p. 496

TAKING NOTES: Problems: desertification caused by water shortages, overgrazing, poor agricultural practices, increasing population, and inefficient water management. **Solutions:** the International Atomic Energy Association is working with countries to better manage the freshwater aquifers in the Sahel; the United Nations Convention to Combat Desertification is working to reduce effects of drought and desertification and restore land productivity; the Permanent Interstate Committee for Drought Control in the Sahel improves food security, living conditions, water, land, and natural resource management; the Great Green Wall project involves many countries of the Sahel creating a wall of trees to stop the spread of the Sahara.

✓ **READING PROGRESS CHECK** Chaotic shifts in rainfall make the dry soil unable to absorb heavy rainfall fast enough. As a result, water collects in fields, which then causes crops to rot.

networks *There's More Online!*

- ✓ **IMAGE** A Town in Darfur
- ✓ **IMAGE** Combating Desertification
- ✓ **INFOGRAPHIC** Great Green Wall
- ✓ **MAP** The Sahel's Vulnerable Zone
- ✓ **INTERACTIVE SELF-CHECK QUIZ**
- ✓ **VIDEO** People and Their Environment: The Transition Zone

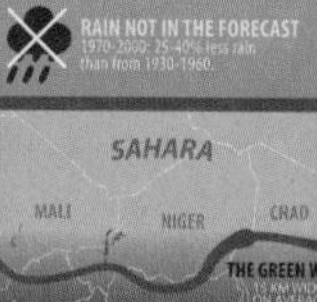

LESSON 3
People and Their Environment: The Transition Zone

ESSENTIAL QUESTION • *How do physical systems and human systems shape a place?*

Reading HELPDESK 

Academic Vocabulary (Tier Two Words)
- **circumstance**
- **stress**

Content Vocabulary (Tier Three Words)
- **desertification**

TAKING NOTES: ***Key Ideas and Details***

IDENTIFYING As you read about people and their environment in the Transition Zone, use a graphic organizer like the one below to identify environmental problems faced by the people of the subregion and different ways in which people are trying to address these problems.

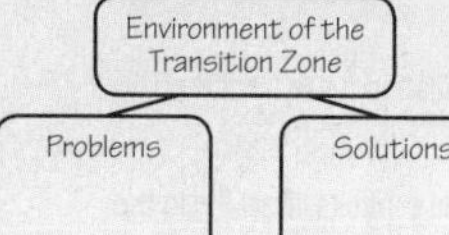

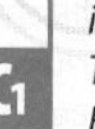

It Matters Because

The Transition Zone is faced with multiple challenges. These include drought, overpopulation, and the loss of arable land. These conditions can lead to poverty, hunger, conflict, and war. Finding solutions to these problems may help to reverse the loss of land and end both health and political crises that afflict the countries of the Transition Zone.

Managing Resources

GUIDING QUESTION *What water challenges do people of the Sahel face?*

Recall that the most vital resources of the Transition Zone, water and arable land, are at risk. While precipitation has decreased and become erratic, the number of people depending on it has increased. In the last several decades, the Sahel has experienced a rapid growth in population. Increasing at about 3 percent a year, the population will double about every 20 years. This rapid population growth makes the problem of inadequate rainfall that much worse.

One problem with chaotic shifts in rainfall is that extremely dry ground cannot absorb a heavy rain fast enough. Water that is not absorbed and does not drain pools up on the surface, causing crops to rot at the stem. By far the biggest problem, however, is a water shortage, which leads to **desertification**. Desertification is the destruction of land in arid and semi-arid areas, often caused by variations in climate. Human activity adds to the destruction. Desertification often causes poverty, food insecurity, and further water shortages. In these **circumstances**, the best hope for the subregion is to adopt new ways to manage existing water supplies. Furthermore, the adoption of agricultural methods that put less **stress** on the land could produce positive results.

✓ **READING PROGRESS CHECK**

Understanding Relationships What are the effects of the chaotic shifts in rainfall?

496

networks ***Online Teaching Options***

INTERACTIVE BELLRINGER

Great Green Wall of Africa

Analyzing Cause and Effect Before showing students this bellringer, ask them to discuss what the title might mean. Then have pairs of students study the infographic of the Great Green Wall of Africa to analyze the causes and effects of desertification and how people in the Transition Zone are hoping to stem the damages caused by it. Ask pairs to discuss and answer each question. Then, in a class discussion, have students share their answers. ELL Interpersonal, Visual/Spatial, Verbal/Linguistic

Human Impact

GUIDING QUESTION *What causes desertification and water shortages?*

Desertification puts pressure on the people that live in the Transition Zone. Agriculture and livestock suffer, as does the natural biodiversity of the area. In addition to infrequent rainfall, various human activities also cause desertification. One example of harmful human management is overgrazing.

T

Overgrazing is caused by an excessive number of livestock feeding too long in one area. Overgrazing kills plant roots. Too many animals in one area also compact the soil, thus reducing its capacity to hold water. Other detrimental human activities include poor agricultural practices and deforestation, which include the stripping of trees for firewood and clearing of land for farming. The main trigger of these harmful human activities is overpopulation. When more people live on the land, more livestock and crops are needed for food and more trees are needed for use as fuel. Just as drought and poor land use practices led to the Dust Bowl in the Great Plains of the United States, these factors have hastened desertification in the Sahel. A growing population dependent on the land in an already arid region puts further stress on that land. This stress triggers even more harm to the environment, in turn leading to more desertification.

Human activity in the Transition Zone has exacerbated desertification and created water management problems. For example, the availability of water in the Lake Chad Basin has decreased not only because of climate change but also because of over-demand. Planners have recognized that because of very high evaporation rates, it will not be enough to efficiently manage the water supply. The quality of the water that remains is also a concern. Commercial cotton and rice farmers are using agricultural chemicals that are polluting the water in Lake Chad. In other areas, poorly planned irrigation projects have pumped out too much groundwater, which causes wells to go dry. After the drought of the late

desertification the destruction of land in arid and semi-arid climates

circumstance an event or fact that accompanies or determines another

stress pressure or strain

GEOGRAPHY CONNECTION

The risk for desertification in the Sahel varies but overall is increasing.

1. ***THE WORLD IN SPATIAL TERMS*** Which biomes border the fragile zone?
2. ***ENVIRONMENT AND SOCIETY*** Why would it be important for people and governments to know which areas were in the high risk fragile zone?

The Sahel's Vulnerable Zone

20°W 0° 20°E 20°N

0 500 miles
0 500 kilometers
Lambert Conformal Conic projection

WESTERN SAHARA (Morocco), ALGERIA, TROPIC OF CANCER, LIBYA, MAURITANIA, MALI, NIGER, CHAD, SUDAN, Nouakchott, Dakar, Banjul, SENEGAL, GAMBIA, Bissau, GUINEA-BISSAU, GUINEA, Bamako, Niamey, Ouagadougou, BURKINA FASO, BENIN, NIGERIA, TOGO, GHANA, CÔTE D'IVOIRE, SIERRA LEONE, LIBERIA, Lake Chad, N'Djamena, ATLANTIC OCEAN, 50 days, 110 days

50 days Length of rainy season
Limit of the fragile zone
Desert region (nomadic herding)
High risk fragile zone
Average risk fragile zone
Capital city

V

T Technology Skills

Examining Information Have students look online for images of land at various stages of desertification. Challenge them to find images of the same place several years apart so they can assess the changes evident due to desertification. Have them put together their images for display. For each image, students should write a caption describing the changes they see due to desertification. **Naturalist**

V Visual Skills

Interpreting Direct students to the map showing the Sahel's vulnerable zone. **Ask: Is the majority of the land between the length of rainy season lines at higher or lower risk of desertification?** *(higher risk)* **How does the length of the rainy season affect the fragility of the land?** *(the longer the rainy season, the less fragile the land)* **AL Visual/Spatial**

Content Background Knowledge

Desertification Estimates are that dry lands cover more than 40 percent of Earth's surface. Nearly one-third of the world's population—nearly two billion people—live on these dry lands. In African countries south of the Sahara, the farm economy makes up 25 to 50 percent of gross domestic product, making maintaining soil fertility an even more pressing issue.

INTERACTIVE MAP

The Sahel's Vulnerable Zone

Examining Display the interactive map of The Sahel's Vulnerable Zone. As students examine the map and the corresponding key, review with them that the terms *vulnerable* and *fragile* are synonyms meaning "weak." Have students use the supporting text to determine why these terms accurately describe the area in question. Ask students to write a short list of factors that make this portion of the Sahel vulnerable. **AL Visual/Spatial, Verbal/Linguistic**

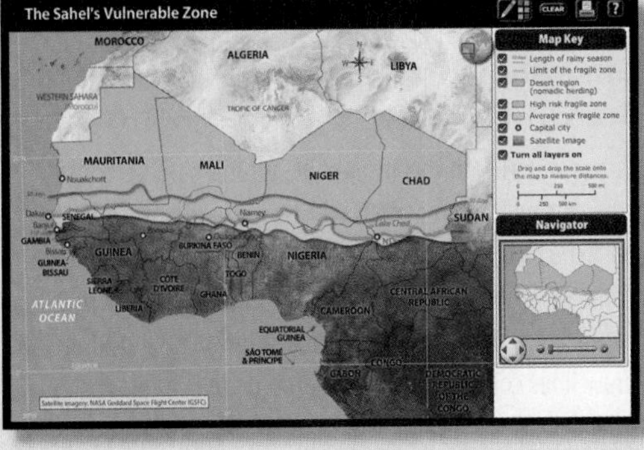

ANSWERS, p. 497

GEOGRAPHY CONNECTION

1. The desert borders the fragile zone.
2. It is important to know which areas are in the high risk fragile zone as people and governments could extend the greatest efforts in those areas since they are most at risk from desertification.

R Reading Skills

Paraphrasing Have students read the paragraph about human activity exacerbating desertification and creating water management problems. Then students them paraphrase the information to a partner. Remind them that paraphrasing is the rewording of a text, but summarizing condenses the information in the text into a concise form. Paraphrasing the text will help them to better summarize the text to answer the Reading Progress Check question. **ELL Verbal/Linguistic**

T Technology Skills

Problem Solving Have students work in small groups to brainstorm ideas about how to battle desertification. Tell them to think small-scale, i.e., what changes can a small farming village in Africa in the average-risk fragile zone make to fight desertification. Have each group choose one of their ideas to research further. Ask them to present their findings to the class. **BL Interpersonal**

Content Background Knowledge

Urbanization and Water Management Cities in Africa are growing at 3.9 percent each year. This growth rate is the highest in the world. About 320 million Africans live in cities. By 2030, it is expected that the African urban population will be 654 million. As a result, demand for water will almost quadruple. Innovative ideas will be a major part of solutions to Africa's water management problems. These ideas include harvesting rainwater and recycling grey water (wastewater generated from laundry and washing dishes).

ANSWERS, p. 498

READING PROGRESS CHECK Human activities such as overgrazing livestock, deforestation, and poor agricultural practices lead to desertification and water management problems. Irrigation systems that were built could not withstand droughts, attracted disease-carrying insects, and interrupted the natural water flow. Wells and boreholes dug in areas that were not well suited for agriculture and livestock led to overcrowding of areas, resulting in more overgrazing and desertification.

CRITICAL THINKING

1. The landscape is dry and devoid of vegetation.
2. Reversing desertification is necessary if the countries in the Transition Zone want to improve food security and living conditions.

R 1960s—which lasted until the 1980s—humanitarian aid poured into the region in an effort to create water resources for the people. Though well-intentioned, the results were not beneficial. The irrigation systems that were built attracted disease-carrying insects and could not withstand the frequent droughts. The systems also interrupted the natural flow patterns of water. Boreholes and wells that were dug also added to the problem. Many boreholes and wells were dug in areas unsuitable for livestock and agriculture. This led to larger herds occupying smaller areas and resulted in further overgrazing and desertification.

READING PROGRESS CHECK

Summarizing How has human activity affected the Transition Zone?

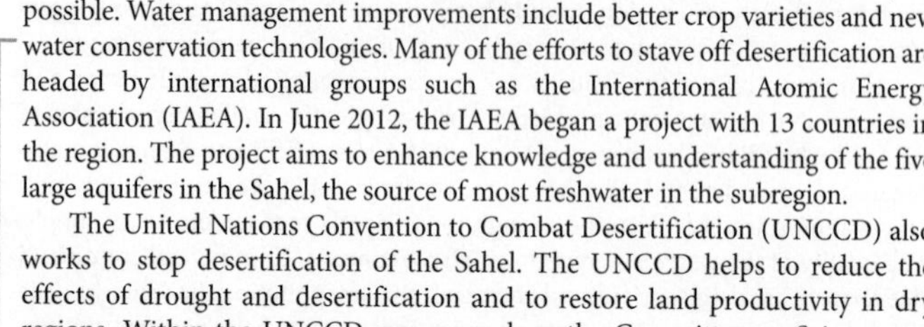

Addressing the Issues

GUIDING QUESTION *How are environmental problems in the Sahel being addressed?*

Once an ecosystem is damaged, it is difficult to reverse the effects. However, by improving water management and land use practices, some remediation may be possible. Water management improvements include better crop varieties and new water conservation technologies. Many of the efforts to stave off desertification are headed by international groups such as the International Atomic Energy Association (IAEA). In June 2012, the IAEA began a project with 13 countries in the region. The project aims to enhance knowledge and understanding of the five large aquifers in the Sahel, the source of most freshwater in the subregion.

T The United Nations Convention to Combat Desertification (UNCCD) also works to stop desertification of the Sahel. The UNCCD helps to reduce the effects of drought and desertification and to restore land productivity in dry regions. Within the UNCCD, groups such as the Committee on Science and Technology and a Roster of Experts create action plans or programs to combat specific aspects of desertification.

This aerial view of a town in the Darfur region of Sudan shows the barren landscape produced by desertification.

▼ CRITICAL THINKING

1. ***Analyzing Visuals*** As shown in this photograph, describe the landscape of areas affected by desertification.
2. ***Drawing Conclusions*** Why is it important to reverse desertification in the Transition Zone?

©Richard Baker/In Pictures/Corbis

networks Online Teaching Options

INTERACTIVE WHITEBOARD ACTIVITY

Environmental Challenges of the Transition Zone

Categorizing In this interactive whiteboard activity, students will be presented with statements concerning particular environmental challenges in the Transition Zone. Have them determine whether each statement is a cause, a problem, an impact, or a solution. Ask students to draw lines connecting the statements to the categories provided. When finished, ask students to consider whether more problems or solutions exist for individual challenges. **AL Kinesthetic, Logical/Mathematical**

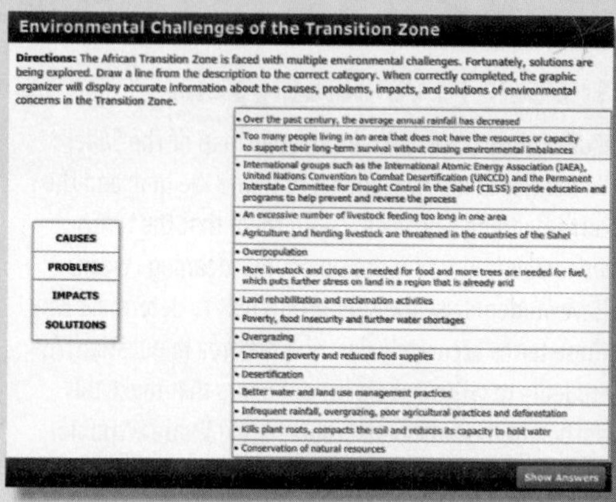

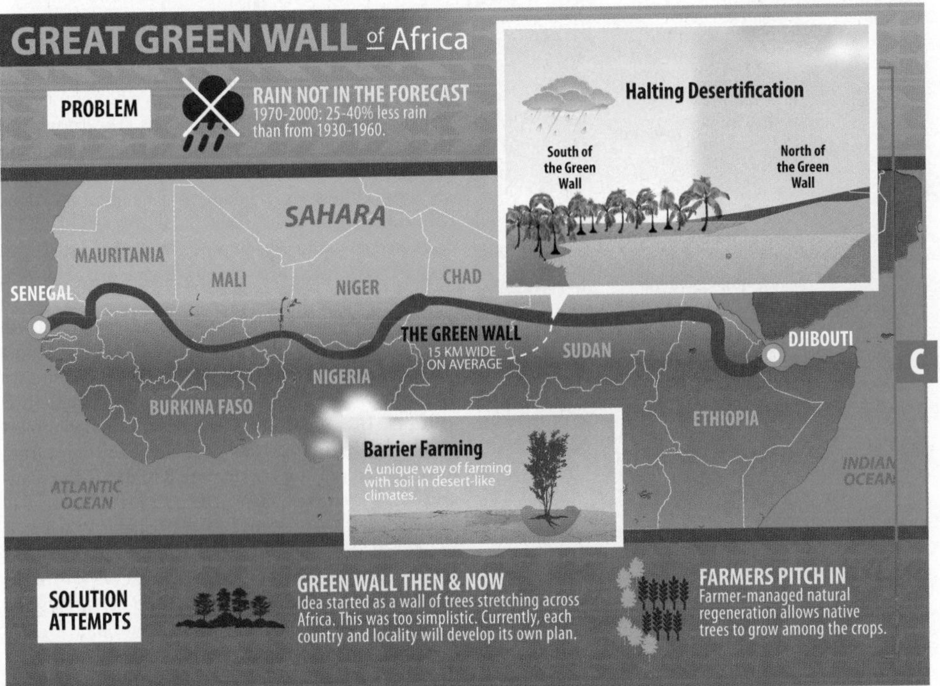
GREAT GREEN WALL of Africa
PROBLEM
RAIN NOT IN THE FORECAST
1970-2000: 25-40% less rain than from 1930-1960.
Halting Desertification
South of the Green Wall
North of the Green Wall
SAHARA
MAURITANIA
MALI
NIGER
CHAD
SENEGAL
THE GREEN WALL
15 KM WIDE ON AVERAGE
SUDAN
DJIBOUTI
NIGERIA
BURKINA FASO
ETHIOPIA
Barrier Farming
A unique way of farming with soil in desert-like climates.
ATLANTIC OCEAN
INDIAN OCEAN
SOLUTION ATTEMPTS
GREEN WALL THEN & NOW
Idea started as a wall of trees stretching across Africa. This was too simplistic. Currently, each country and locality will develop its own plan.
FARMERS PITCH IN
Farmer-managed natural regeneration allows native trees to grow among the crops.

The Great Green Wall is an ambitious project on the part of 11 countries to combat desertification. It will stretch across the continent. Expectations are high. One way the wall is expected to help is by blocking desert winds, which dry the soil.

▲ CRITICAL THINKING

1. ***Analyzing Visuals*** How will the Great Green Wall combat desertification?
2. ***Drawing Conclusions*** Why is it important for farmers to support the project?

Another group is the Permanent Interstate Committee for Drought Control in the Sahel (CILSS). The CILSS was established in 1973 following the severe drought that struck the region. Current member states include Gambia, Guinea-Bissau, Mauritania, Senegal, Burkina Faso, Mali, Niger, Chad, and Cape Verde. The CILSS works to improve food security and living conditions, water and land management, and natural resources management in the Sahel.

Small-scale efforts that local farmers can employ have been the most successful changes to date. Exchange of information on best farming and water management practices can be particularly helpful. Simple water-saving irrigation techniques, such as drip irrigation, have also proved useful. However, the challenge to adapt new technologies to local circumstances remains.

On a small scale, local people are also discovering ways to improve their land. After the drought in the 1980s, farmers in Burkina Faso started to experiment with traditional planting pits to reclaim severely dry land. These farmers increased the depth and width of the pits and began adding manure at the bottom before planting. These changes improved soil fertility and production. The techniques allowed farmers to increase their yield, prevent further soil erosion, and improve the soil quality. This technique has spread throughout the surrounding countries and has helped to rehabilitate between 500,000 and 750,000 acres (200,000 and 300,000 ha).

C Critical Thinking Skills

Analyzing Have students study the infographic. **Ask: Why do you think the original idea of a green wall was too simplistic? What were some of its likely drawbacks?** *(Possible answers: The Sahel is very wide, stretching all across Africa. To simply plant a line of trees doesn't take into account the different factors in different areas. Planting a line of trees may be a good solution for some areas but not necessarily for all areas.)* **What is the advantage of having each country and locality make its own plan?** *(Possible answer: Countries and localities can better address the specific issues in their area.)* **Why is it important that farmers participate in conservation efforts?** *(Possible answer: Farmers are the people who are most directly connected to the land. Their livelihoods depend on the land so they need to be a part of its management.)*
AL Visual/Spatial

T Technology Skills

Presenting Have students work in small groups and choose one of the organizations that is combating desertification. Have them research more information on their selected group and the group's efforts in the Sahel. Ask groups to create a presentation to introduce the class to the organization and its work. **Visual/Spatial, Verbal/Linguistic**

W Writing Skills

Informative/Explanatory Have students research how traditional planting pits can help reclaim severely dry land. Then have students write two or three paragraphs explaining the process and why they think it is important for small farmers to come up with plans for their own land as opposed to having a large international group tell them what to do.
AL Interpersonal, Verbal/Linguistic

INTERACTIVE MAP

Desertification of the Sahel

Making Predictions Display this interactive map of the Desertification of the Sahel and compare it to the ambitious project known as the Great Green Wall of Africa. Point out the "Problem" and "Solution Attempts" sections of the infographic. Ask students to imagine that the Great Green Wall is successful in its attempts to halt desertification. Have students use the supporting text in the infographic and information in the map to create illustrations showing what a particular area in the Sahel may look like now and 50 years from now. Students may label their pictures "Before" and "After". **ELL AL Visual/Spatial**

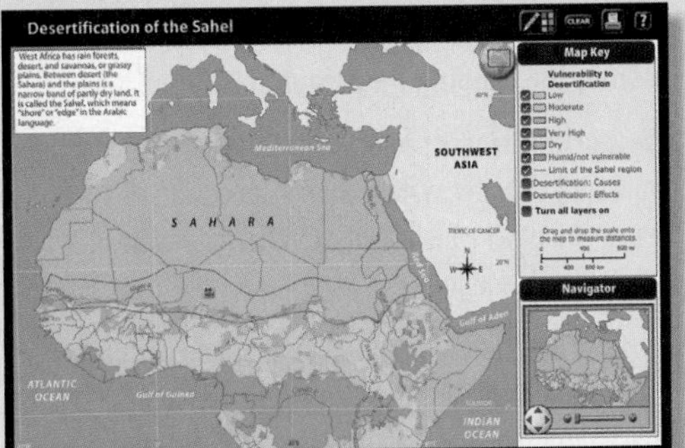
Desertification of the Sahel
Map Key
Navigator
SAHARA
SOUTHWEST ASIA
ATLANTIC OCEAN
INDIAN OCEAN

ANSWERS, p. 499

CRITICAL THINKING

1. The Great Green Wall will combat desertification by blocking desert winds from the Sahara, help hold moisture in the soil, and help reduce soil erosion.
2. Farmers will manage the natural regeneration, which allows native trees to grow among the crops. This along with other plantings will help prevent soil erosion, increase moisture levels in the soil, and possibly increase rainfall, all helping crop production and decreasing desertification.

People and Their Environment: The Transition Zone

C Critical Thinking Skills

Drawing Conclusions Have students conduct online research to explore the concept of adding bacteria to sand dunes to calcify the sand. Then hold a class discussion about whether this process is a viable practice for reducing desertification. Have students provide their researched solutions.
BL **Logical/Mathematical**

V Visual Skills

Observing Direct students to the photograph. **Ask:** How are the plants planted? *(They are in pits.)* How are the pits similar to pots and containers? *(They keep the soil and plant together.)* How does this method prevent water loss? *(Water does not run off the soil because the sides keep it in.)*
AL **Visual/Spatial**

CLOSE & REFLECT

Explaining Continuity and Change Review that many of the reasons for African desertification have been going on for hundreds of years. Then discuss that most people have lived as herders, nomads, and farmers and the changes needed to preserve this way of life.

ANSWERS, p. 500

READING PROGRESS CHECK The Permanent Interstate Committee for Drought Control in the Sahel was established in 1973 to improve food security, living conditions, water, land, and natural resource management.

CRITICAL THINKING

1. The trenches could serve to hold in water and help prevent drying of the soil by winds.
2. The environment pictured appears to be dry and barren, except in irrigated areas where crops are being grown.

Various projects are underway to combat desertification. This man in Tombouctou, Mali, is irrigating a field.

▲ CRITICAL THINKING

1. ***Analyzing Visuals*** What purpose do you suppose the shallow trenches serve?
2. ***Classifying*** How would you describe the environment shown in the photograph?

There are differing techniques and views on how to combat desertification, and the problem is not confined to the Sahel. In some areas, such as Australia, scientists are monitoring when and where desertification occurs to better understand why it happens. They hope this information will aid in finding an appropriate solution that can be applied no matter where desertification is a problem. Others are thinking about radical solutions such as adding bacteria to sand dunes that would calcify, or harden, the sand. The hope is that the hardened sand would create a wall between the deserts and semi-arid land on the other side.

Others think that applying better water and land use management can reverse the problem. This has led to a unique initiative by many of the African countries within the Sahel to stop the spread of the Sahara. It is called the Great Green Wall, and it is a $2 billion project backed by the United Nations. The name comes from the plan that calls for a wall of trees to divide the semi-arid Sahel from the Sahara. The goal is for the trees to stop the southward spread of the Sahara. When it is completed, the Great Green Wall will stretch 4,970 miles (8,000 km) from Senegal to Djibouti in a band roughly 9 miles (15 km) wide. Planners expect that the barrier will be wide enough to block desert winds and will help hold moisture in the soil and also help to reduce soil erosion.

Senegal was one of the first countries to support the Great Green Wall project, and it has already benefited from the initiative. Senegal hopes that the project will help increase food security and prevent poverty. The planners hope to support local community efforts to sustainably manage the trees that are planted. To help build local support, seven varieties of acacia tree—including one that produces a fruit that can be used as animal food—were planted. People in local communities have harvested vegetables from gardens planted near the trees and fenced to keep out livestock. People have improved their nutrition, and they been able to sustain themselves throughout the year without having to leave for work in towns.

READING PROGRESS CHECK

Making Connections How is the Permanent Interstate Committee for Drought Control in the Sahel working to combat desertification in the Transition Zone?

LESSON 3 REVIEW

Reviewing Vocabulary (Tier Three Words)

1. ***Determining Importance*** Write a paragraph discussing some of the causes of desertification. RH 9–10.4

Using Your Notes

2. ***Applying*** Use your graphic organizer on the environment in the Transition Zone to write a paragraph evaluating the problems and some possible solutions.

Answering the Guiding Questions

3. ***Identifying Central Issues*** What water challenges do people of the Sahel face?
4. ***Identifying Cause and Effect*** What causes desertification and water shortages?
5. ***Finding the Main Idea*** How are environmental problems in the Sahel being addressed?

Writing Activity

6. ***Argument*** In a paragraph, explain what may happen if the environmental problems of the Transition Zone are not resolved. WHST. 9–10.1

500

LESSON 3 REVIEW ANSWERS

Reviewing Vocabulary

1. Paragraphs will vary but should be supported with information from the lesson. They should include causes such as overgrazing, deforestation, poor agricultural practices, increasing population, growth of the Sahara, drought, and inefficient water management.

Using Your Notes

2. Paragraphs will vary but should be supported with information from the lesson. They should include problems such as desertification, food security, health, education, and water management. Solutions could include: Permanent Interstate Committee for Drought Control, International Atomic Energy Association, United Nations Convention to Combat Desertification, and governments of multiple countries working together on projects such as the Great Green Wall.

Answering the Guiding Questions

3. The water challenges people of the Sahel face include availability of water, water pollution, poor water management with inefficient or outdated irrigation systems, and drought.
4. Causes of desertification and water shortages include overgrazing, increasing population, deforestation, poor agricultural practices, growth of the Sahara, drought, and inefficient water management.
5. Environmental problems are being addressed by: International Atomic Energy Association (to increase understanding and better management of freshwater aquifers in the Sahel); United Nations Convention to Combat Desertification (to reduce effects of drought and desertification and restore land productivity); Permanent Interstate Committee for Drought Control in the Sahel (to improve food security, living conditions, water, land, and natural resource management); Great Green Wall project (to stop the spread of the Sahara); efforts by farmers to manage water more effectively; and a return to planting pits to prevent erosion and improve soil fertility.

Writing Activity

6. Paragraphs will vary but should be strongly supported with information from the lesson including increasing desertification, increasing droughts, more famine, and a continual decline in the health and living conditions in the Transition Zone.

CHAPTER 20 Assessment

Directions: On a separate sheet of paper, answer the questions below. Make sure you read carefully and answer all parts of the questions.

Lesson Review

Lesson 1

1. ***Defining*** Why is the region immediately south of the Sahara called the Transition Zone?
2. ***Identifying Cause and Effect*** How has the climate of the Sahel affected Lake Chad?
3. ***Problem Solving*** What are some ways that countries in the Transition Zone manage water resources?

Lesson 2

4. ***Describing*** Describe how culture changes as one moves from north to south in the Transition Zone.
5. ***Making Predictions*** Why are urban populations in the Sahel likely to grow in the years to come?
6. ***Identifying Cause and Effect*** What are some ways that poverty affects people in the Transition Zone?

Lesson 3

7. ***Explaining*** How has human activity in the Transition Zone contributed to desertification?
8. ***Evaluating*** After the drought that lasted from the late 1960s to the 1980s, irrigation systems were built to create water resources for people. Why were these systems ineffective?
9. ***Analyzing*** What steps have international organizations taken to reduce desertification in the Sahel?

Critical Thinking

10. ***Explaining*** In the mid-1900s, colonies in the Sahel gained independence from European powers. How did the legacy of colonialism create problems for the new countries?
11. ***Comparing and Contrasting*** Compare the Great Green Wall project to the proposal to create a wall of hardened sand. Which project do you think is more likely to stop the Sahara from moving south?

21st Century Skills

Use the chart to answer the questions that follow.

Country	Imports	Exports
Burkina Faso	Capital goods, foodstuffs, petroleum	Gold, cotton, livestock
Chad	Machinery & transport equipment, industrial goods, foodstuffs, textiles	Oil, cattle, cotton
Senegal	Food & beverages, capital goods, fuels	Fish, groundnuts, petroleum products, phosphates, cotton
Sudan	Foodstuffs, manufactured goods, refinery & transport equipment, medicines & chemicals, textiles, wheat	Gold, oil & petroleum products, cotton, sesame, livestock, groundnuts, sugar

Source: CIA World Factbook

12. ***Economics*** What general statement can you make about the types of commodities these four countries export?
13. ***Compare and Contrast*** How do Chad's imports differ from Senegal's imports? How are Senegal's imports similar to those of Burkina Faso?

Need Extra Help?

If You've Missed Question	1	2	3	4	5	6	7	8	9	10	11	12	13
Go to page	484	486	486	491	492	493	497	498	498	491	500	501	501

CHAPTER 20 Assessment Answers

Lesson Review

Lesson 1

1. The region south of the Sahara is called the Transition Zone because it is where the land changes dramatically from arid to tropical. It is also the area that transitions from the Islamic cultures of North Africa and the Christian and animist cultures of the south.
2. The dry climate of the Sahel causes the water in Lake Chad to evaporate or to become increasingly saline. This has caused Lake Chad to continue to shrink.
3. Rivers in the Transition Zone are dammed for a variety of uses. For example, the Volta River was dammed in the 1960s to create Lake Volta, a reservoir for hydroelectricity, irrigation, and fishing.

Lesson 2

4. The culture changes from the Islamic cultures in North Africa to the Christian and animist cultures in the south.
5. Droughts and environmental damage are likely to make traditional ways of life more difficult in rural areas, causing people to move to urban areas.
6. Poverty causes there to be little access to health care in the Transition Zone. This leads to high infant and female mortality rates and high numbers of infectious diseases. There is also limited access to clean water and sanitation.

Lesson 3

7. Human activities such as overgrazing, poor agricultural management, deforestation, and overpopulation contribute to desertification.
8. These systems were ineffective because they were not built to endure the frequent droughts, interrupted the natural flow of patterns of water, and attracted disease-carrying insects.
9. International organizations have taken steps to improve water management and create better land use practices by introducing different crops and new ways to conserve water, all of which will reduce desertification.

Critical Thinking

10. During colonialism, European governments set up economies that only met European needs, failed to involve Africans in the government, did not provide a democratic model for African countries, and set political boundaries that did not take into account the cultural or religious differences of the population, which created problems for the new countries.
11. Answers will vary but should be strongly supported with information from the chapter. Possible answers could include that the 9-mile-wide, 4,970-mile-long band of trees of the Great Green Wall project is more likely to block winds, hold moisture in the soil, and prevent soil erosion than a wall of hardened sand, which is made by adding chemicals to sand dunes that could be harmful to the environment.

21st Century Skills

12. All four countries export cotton and either gold or petroleum products.
13. Chad imports machinery and transport equipment, industrial goods, and textiles while Senegal imports capital goods and fuel. Both countries import foodstuffs. Senegal's imports are similar to Burkina Faso in that they also import capital goods, food, and petroleum or fuel.

CHAPTER 20
Assessment Answers

College and Career Readiness

14 Reports will vary but should include information on digging and expansion of traditional planting pits, the addition of manure to the pits, the increasing amount of cereal crops, the prevention of soil erosion, and the increase in trees due to the use of these pits to rehabilitate dry land.

DBQ Analyzing Primary Sources

15 The author states that "food is power" in Somalia because food is a valuable commodity and those in power will seize the food supply either directly from fields or from ships that are sending food aid.

16 Somalia is largely a desert region, making the cultivation of food difficult. While its long coastline could provide opportunities for imports of food, pirates have seized these shipments. Since it shares relatively few borders with other countries, land trade is not as easy as in other countries.

17 Food aid is not an effective way to address hunger. The problem of hunger is caused in part by the militia and pirates seizing food supplies. Until these issues are addressed and stability is restored to the region, food aid will continue to be ineffective.

Applying Map Skills

18 Answers could include: the Senegal River which connects Mali, Mauritania, Senegal, and Guinea; the Niger River which begins in Guinea and flows through Mali and Nigeria; the Blue Nile which begins in Ethiopia and flows through Sudan; the White Nile which starts in Burundi and flows through Sudan.

19 The regions directly south of the Sahara are most likely to be affected by drought.

20 Population density is much higher near bodies of water.

Exploring the Essential Question

21 Posters will vary but must include drought, human activity, and desertification as part of a cycle. They should indicate how both drought and human activities such as overgrazing, deforestation, population growth, poor agricultural practices, and poor water management lead to desertification.

CHAPTER 20 Assessment 

Directions: On a separate sheet of paper, answer the questions below. Make sure you read carefully and answer all parts of the questions.

College and Career Readiness

14 ***Problem Solving*** As a researcher for the United Nations Convention to Combat Desertification, you have been asked to report on how farmers in Burkina Faso used traditional planting pits to reclaim severely dry land. Write a two-page report describing their techniques. Do you recommend that these techniques be used more widely? Why or why not? WHST.9–10.4

DBQ Analyzing Primary Sources

Use the document to answer the following questions.

Long regarded as a failed state, Somalia has had persistent problems dealing with hunger.

PRIMARY SOURCE

"Food is power in Somalia. Militia groups have routinely descended on the arable lands of central Somalia during harvest and claimed the crops for themselves. Pirates on the Indian Ocean have waylaid dozens of foreign vessels bearing food aid. Food prices were high here even before last year's worldwide spike, thanks to drought, militia roadblocks, and a devalued currency. The result is that millions now depend on food aid. The fresh fighting is pushing the country toward an unprecedented humanitarian crisis."

—Robert Draper, "Shattered Somalia," *National Geographic Magazine*, September 2009

15 ***Interpreting*** Why does the author say that in Somalia "food is power"?

16 ***Speculating*** How might geography have affected the availability of food in Somalia? RH.9–10.1

17 ***Evaluating*** Is food aid an effective way to address the problem of hunger? Why or why not? RH.9–10.5

Applying Map Skills

Use the Unit 6 Atlas to answer the following questions.

18 ***Physical Systems*** Use your mental map of Africa to describe the location of two or more major rivers in the Transition Zone. What countries do they connect?

19 ***Environment and Society*** What regions in the Transition Zone are most likely to be affected by desertification in the coming years?

20 ***Human Systems*** How do bodies of water affect population density in the Transition Zone?

Exploring the Essential Question

21 ***Making Connections*** Recall what you have learned about the problem of water shortage in the Transition Zone. Create a poster showing how drought, human activity, and desertification interact as part of a cycle.

Research and Presentation

22 ***Research Skills*** Use Internet and other resources to gather information and write a report about recent developments in the conflict in Sudan. What has happened since the presidents of Sudan and South Sudan signed agreements of cooperation? Has the conflict in Darfur been resolved? WHST.9–10.7

Writing About Geography

23 ***Informative/Explanatory*** Use standard grammar, spelling, sentence structure, and punctuation to write an essay describing how drought has affected population patterns in the Transition Zone. How do these patterns reflect changes in traditional rural life and in the extended family? WHST.9–10.2

Need Extra Help?

If You've Missed Question	14	15	16	17	18	19	20	21	22	23
Go to page	499	502	502	502	476	476	480	497	491	492

502

Research and Presentation

22 Reports will vary but should include that while the peace agreement provided more independence for the southern provinces and ended the conflict between north and south, ultimately resulting in South Sudan becoming an independent country, it did not address the conflict in Darfur. The civil war in Darfur is ongoing. Sudan has also seized regions of South Sudan and signed a new agreement of cooperation since the initial peace agreement.

Writing About Geography

23 Essays will vary but should be strongly supported with information from the chapter, including rural-to-urban migrations due to lack of arable land for farming, the transition to a nuclear family in urban settings rather than the clan and extended families of rural settings, and men often leaving families behind when leaving rural settings to find work in urban areas.

CHAPTER **21**

East Africa Planner

UNDERSTANDING BY DESIGN®

Enduring Understandings

- *Places reflect the relationship between humans and the physical environment.*

Essential Question

- *How do physical systems and human systems shape a place?*

Predictable Misunderstandings

Students may think:

- *The dominant climate in East Africa is hot and dry. Explain that East Africa covers a great range in latitude and therefore has many different climates and biomes including desert, steppe, highland, and tropical wet/dry. In addition, many inland lakes are found in and near the Great Rift Valley.*
- *The ethnic groups of East Africa are largely insulated in their own villages. Explain that the population of East Africa is actually genetically diverse with Arabs having colonized the coast in the 700s and the region engaging in trade with Arabs, Chinese, and Indians.*

Assessment Evidence

Performance Tasks:

- *Hands-On Chapter Project*

Other Evidence:

- *Guided Reading Activities*
- *Vocabulary Activities*
- *Lesson Quizzes*
- *Chapter Tests, Forms A and B*

SUGGESTED PACING GUIDE

Introducing the Chapter	½ Day	Case Study	1 Day
Lesson 1	1 Day	Lesson 3	1 Day
Lesson 2	1 Day	Chapter Wrap-Up and Assessment	½ Day

TOTAL TIME 5 Days

Key for Using the Teacher Edition

SKILL-BASED ACTIVITIES

Types of skill activities found in the Teacher Edition.

* **V Visual Skills** require students to analyze maps, graphs, charts, and photos.

R Reading Skills help students practice reading skills and master vocabulary.

C Critical Thinking Skills help students apply and extend what they have learned.

W Writing Skills provide writing opportunities to help students comprehend the text.

T Technology Skills require students to use digital tools effectively.

*Letters are followed by a number when there is more than one of the same type of skill on the page.

DIFFERENTIATED INSTRUCTION

All activities are written for the on-level student unless otherwise marked with the leveled labels below.

BL Beyond Level

AL Approaching Level

ELL English Language Learners

All students benefit from activities that utilize different learning styles. Many activities are marked as below when a particular learning style is highlighted.

Intrapersonal	Naturalist
Logical/Mathematical	Kinesthetic
Visual/Spatial	Auditory/Musical
Verbal/Linguistic	Interpersonal

National Geography Standards covered in "East Africa"

The student knows and understands:

(4) The physical and human characteristics of places

4.2 The interaction of physical and human systems result in the creation of and changes to places

(8) The characteristics and spatial distribution of ecosystems and biomes on Earth's surface

8.2 The characteristics and geographic distribution of ecosystems

8.3 The distribution and characteristics of biomes change over time

(9) The characteristics, distribution, and migration of human populations on Earth's surface

9.1 Culture, economics, and politics influence the changing demographic structure of different populations

9.2 Population distribution and density are a function of historical, environmental, economic, political, and technological factors

(10) The characteristics, distribution, and complexity of Earth's cultural mosaics

10.2 Cultural landscapes exist at multiple scales

10.3 Cultures changes through convergence and/or divergence

(11) The patterns and networks of economic interdependence on Earth's surface

11.2 Patterns exist in the spatial organization of economic activities

11.3 Economic systems are dynamic organizations of interdependent economic activities for production, exchange, distribution, and consumption of goods and services

(12) The process, patterns, and functions of human settlement

12.1 The numbers, types, and range of the functions of settlement change

12.2 Settlements can grow and/or decline over time

(13) How the forces of cooperation and conflict among people influence the division and control of Earth's surface

(14) How human actions modify the physical environment

14.2 The use of technology can have both intended and unintended impacts on the physical environment which may be positive or negative

14.3 People can either mitigate and/or adapt to the consequences of human modifications of the physical environment

CHAPTER OPENER PLANNER

Students will know:

- *that East Africa is a collection of diverse landscapes and waterways.*
- *that a wide variety of climates support various biomes in the region.*
- *why many different ethnic groups live in East Africa and how the population is distributed.*
- *what life is like for the people of East Africa.*
- *how the economy of the region is changing.*
- *environmental threats the region faces and how they are addressed.*

Students will be able to:

- ***identify*** *the landscapes of East Africa.*
- ***analyze*** *how climates support biomes in East Africa.*
- ***explain*** *why East Africa is composed of many different ethnic groups.*
- ***describe*** *how the economy is changing.*
- ***explain*** *why East Africa has had difficulties managing natural resources.*
- ***describe*** *environmental threats to the region and how they are being addressed.*

UNDERSTANDING BY DESIGN®

☑ *Print Teaching Options*

V Visual Skills

☐ **p. 504** Students research crops that people in East Africa grow for food and make a chart to list the most prevalent foods.

R Reading Skills

☐ **p. 504** Students describe what the photograph of the woman outside her home shows about life in East Africa.

C Critical Thinking Skills

☐ **p. 505** Students discuss how a country's reliance on a single export crop is risky. AL **Verbal/Linguistic**

W Writing Skills

☐ **p. 505** Students write a letter arguing in favor of the farmers that use modern farm technologies.

T Technology Skills

☐ **p. 505** Students research one of the international organizations that addresses the problem of subsistence farmers and present their results. BL **Verbal/Linguistic, Logical/Mathematical**

☑ *Online Teaching Options*

R Reading Skills

☐ INTERACTIVE MAP **Resources in East Africa**—Students locate the resources in each area on the map and write down how these resources may or may not benefit the residents of the specific area or areas in which the resources are found. AL **Interpersonal, Visual/Spatial**

V Visual Skills

☐ MAP **Interactive Regional Atlas**—Students use the interactive regional atlas to understand the physical and human geography of East Africa.

☑ *Printable Digital Worksheets*

☐ WORKSHEET **Assessing Background Knowledge**—Determine the level of prior knowledge students have about East Africa.

☐ WORKSHEET **Chapter Summaries**—Students review the main idea of each lesson of the chapter content.

☐ WORKSHEET **Vocabulary Activity**—Students apply their knowledge of content and academic vocabulary words.

Project-Based Learning 

Hands-On

Educational Brochures

Students create brochures that highlight important issues in the subregion. Students research and gather information about issues facing girls and women in East Africa. Groups then compile their information to create educational brochures that aim to resolve the problem of girls in East Africa not continuing their education beyond primary school.

Digital Hands-On

Create Online Projects

Find an additional activity online that incorporates technology for this project. Visit the EdTech Teacher Web sites for more links, tutorials, and other resources.

Print Resources

ANCILLARY RESOURCES

This ancillary is available for every chapter and lesson.

- **Chapter Tests and Lesson Quizzes**

PRINTABLE DIGITAL WORKSHEETS

These printable digital worksheets are available for every chapter and lesson.

- **Assessing Background Knowledge**
- **Chapter Summaries**
- **Guided Reading Activities**
- **Hands-On Chapter Projects**
- **Quizzes and Tests**
- **Reading Essentials and Study Guide** AL
- **Reteaching Activities**
- **Video Activities**
- **Vocabulary Activities**

More Media Resources

SUGGESTED VIDEOS MOVIES

- **Wildlife of East Africa** (36 min.)
- **The Great Rift: Africa's Greatest Story** (150 min.)
- **Discoveries…Africa, Tanzania: Arusha and Lake Manyara** (51 min.)

SUGGESTED READING 

- ***East Africa: An Introductory History,*** by Robert M. Maxon
- ***Serengeti Spy: Views from a Hidden Camera on the Plains of East Africa,*** by Anup Shah
- ***The Great Rift Valley,*** by National Geographic

LESSON 1 PLANNER

PHYSICAL GEOGRAPHY OF EAST AFRICA

Students will know:
- *that East Africa is a collection of diverse landscapes.*
- *how the Indian Ocean and lakes help shape life in the region.*
- *that a wide variety of climates support various biomes in the region.*

Students will be able to:
- ***identify** the landscapes of East Africa.*
- ***explain** how the Indian Ocean affects the region.*
- ***analyze** how climates support biomes in East Africa.*

UNDERSTANDING BY DESIGN®

☑ Print Teaching Options

V Visual Skills

- ☐ **p. 507** Students identify countries in the Great Rift Valley on a map. AL Visual/Spatial

R Reading Skills

- ☐ **p. 506** Students identify geographical features on a map and in the lesson.
- ☐ **p. 507** Students define the word *escarpment.* ELL Verbal/Linguistic
- ☐ **p. 508** Students discuss lakes and rivers. ELL Visual/Spatial
- ☐ **p. 509** Students read the definition of the word *survive.* ELL Verbal/Linguistic

C Critical Thinking Skills

- ☐ **p. 506** Students discuss a political map of East Africa. AL Verbal/Linguistic
- ☐ **p. 509** Students review the physical map of East Africa. AL Visual/Spatial

W Writing Skills

- ☐ **p. 508** Students write an essay explaining how two of the water systems in the Great Rift Valley influence the economy in East African countries. AL Verbal/Linguistic
- ☐ **p. 510** Students write a one-page essay discussing how the diverse landforms and climates of East African countries make for a variety of resources in each country. BL Verbal/Linguistic

T Technology Skills

- ☐ **p. 507** Students research the Afar Depression and create a multimedia presentation about it. BL Verbal/Linguistic, Logical/Mathematical
- ☐ **p. 508** Students conduct Internet research to design a chart comparing and contrasting the positive and negative effects bordering the Indian Ocean has had on the development of Tanzania or Kenya. BL Verbal/Linguistic, Logical/Mathematical
- ☐ **p. 510** Students research the current status of the Serengeti Plain and create a multimedia presentation. Verbal/Linguistic, Interpersonal

☑ Online Teaching Options

V Visual Skills

- INTERACTIVE BELLRINGER **The Great Rift Valley**—Students use the introductory text and the infographic to visualize the diverse landscapes of East Africa and identify how physical processes shape patterns in the physical environment. ELL Visual/Spatial, Interpersonal
- VIDEO **Wild Wonders of Africa**—Students watch a video about Mount Kenya and discuss its climate and habitat. ELL Intrapersonal, Visual/Spatial
- SLIDE SHOW **East Africa Climate Zones**—Students discuss the climate zones and create a chart to organize information about the climate zones. Visual/Spatial, Naturalist

R Reading Skills

- INTERACTIVE WHITEBOARD ACTIVITY **Physical Geography of East Africa**—Students define and identify terms pertaining to the physical geography of East Africa.

☑ Printable Digital Worksheets

R Reading Skills

- WORKSHEET **Guided Reading Activity**—Students use the Guided Reading Activity worksheets to review their comprehension of the content.

C Critical Thinking Skills

- WORKSHEET **Video Activity**—Students answer questions related to a topic in the chapter content after they have viewed a lesson video.

LESSON **2 PLANNER**

HUMAN GEOGRAPHY OF EAST AFRICA

Students will know:

- *why so many different ethnic groups live in East Africa.*
- *how the population of the region is distributed.*
- *what life is like for the people of East Africa.*
- *how the economy of the region is changing.*

Students will be able to:

- ***explain** why East Africa is composed of many different ethnic groups.*
- ***analyze** the population distribution of East Africa.*
- ***describe** how the economy is changing.*

UNDERSTANDING BY DESIGN®

☑ *Print Teaching Options*

V Visual Skills

- ☐ **p. 512** Students research the foreign cultures that have influenced an assigned country and create a chart that includes dates, types of governments, boundary changes, and other significant historical events for the country.
- ☐ **p. 515** Students research the literacy rates in East African countries in the past ten years and make a bar or line graph to show the data. **Logical/Mathematical**
- ☐ **p. 516** Students gather images that contrast urban and rural life in a country they select. **ELL** **Visual/Spatial**

R Reading Skills

- ☐ **p. 514** Students learn the definition of *lingua franca* and write a short essay explaining what colonialism had to do with the lingua franca of East Africa. **AL** **Verbal/Linguistic**
- ☐ **p. 517** Students discuss overfarming and exports in reference to food supply issues. **ELL** **Verbal/Linguistic**

C Critical Thinking Skills

- ☐ **p. 513** Students discuss issues surrounding colonization and independence. **Verbal/Linguistic**

W Writing Skills

- ☐ **p. 512** Students choose a time period in which they would have liked to live in East Africa and write an essay about why. **AL** **Verbal/Linguistic**
- ☐ **p. 513** Students write an essay about how they think the events on the time line affected the population of East Africa. **BL** **Logical/Mathematical**
- ☐ **p. 515** Students decide what they would recommend about the UNICEF study and write an essay expressing their recommendation to the government. **BL** **Intrapersonal**

T Technology Skills

- ☐ **p. 511** Students research the archaeological discoveries of the Awash River Valley. **BL** **Verbal/Linguistic**
- ☐ **p. 514** Students create a slide show that provides a chart or diagram indicating where each tribe or ethnic culture is concentrated in an assigned country, as well as a graph that shows the percentage of people speaking the languages spoken. **BL** **Visual/Spatial, Auditory/Musical**
- ☐ **p. 516** Students research the origins of Taarab music and its status in the world today. **Auditory/Musical**

☑ *Online Teaching Options*

V Visual Skills

- ☐ **GRAPHIC ORGANIZER** **Human Geography of East Africa**—Students complete the graphic organizer and write a short paragraph differentiating two of the groups in the organizer. **Visual/Spatial, Verbal/Linguistic**

C Critical Thinking Skills

- ☐ **INTERACTIVE BELLRINGER** **East Africa: European Colonization**—Students use the introductory text and a table of East African countries to discuss the influence of European colonialism on the people of East Africa today. **ELL** **Visual/Spatial, Interpersonal**
- ☐ **VIDEO** **Ancient Lives–Masai**—Students note differences between the Masai culture and their own culture. **BL** **Verbal/Linguistic**
- ☐ **TIME LINE** **A Cultural Crossroads**—Students review the time line and list possible reasons why the time line does not continue after 1840. **AL** **Verbal/Linguistic**

W Writing Skills

- ☐ **INTERACTIVE WHITEBOARD ACTIVITY** **Key Events in the History of East Africa**—Students identify events and dates on a time line and and write a brief summary of the milestones in East Africa. **ELL** **Logical/Mathematical**
- ☐ **INTERACTIVE IMAGE** **The Stonebreakers**—Students analyze the photograph and determine what they may find unusual about it. Ask them to think about the elements they find unusual and write down what they can infer about why those elements may be considered typical in East Africa. **Verbal/Linguistic**

☑ *Printable Digital Worksheets*

R Reading Skills

- ☐ **WORKSHEET** **Guided Reading Activity**—Students use Guided Reading Activity worksheets to review their comprehension of the content.
- ☐ **WORKSHEET** **Reading Essentials and Study Guide**—Students complete the study guide and answer Reading Progress Check and vocabulary questions. **AL**

C Critical Thinking Skills

- ☐ **WORKSHEET** **Video Activity**—Students answer questions related to a topic in the chapter content after they have viewed a lesson video.

LESSON 3 PLANNER

PEOPLE AND THEIR ENVIRONMENT: EAST AFRICA

UNDERSTANDING BY DESIGN®

Students will know:

- *why proper management of resources has proved a challenge in East Africa.*
- *the variety of environmental threats the region faces.*
- *that national and international groups are working to combat these threats.*

Students will be able to:

- ***explain** why East Africa has had difficulties managing natural resources.*
- ***describe** environmental threats to the region.*
- ***identify** how environmental threats are being addressed.*

☑ Print Teaching Options

V Visual Skills

- ☐ **p. 521** Students list three things a photo of refugees shows about the people and their circumstances. AL **Verbal/Linguistic, Intrapersonal**

R Reading Skills

- ☐ **p. 520** Students skim through the lesson content to provide a list of challenges people in East Africa face.
- ☐ **p. 521** Students define the term *intervene.* ELL **Verbal/Linguistic**
- ☐ **p. 522** Students discuss the term *carrying capacity.* AL **Verbal/Linguistic, Logical/Mathematical**

C Critical Thinking Skills

- ☐ **p. 520** Students make a chart showing the cause and effect of one of the problems the Human Development Index identifies for a country in the region. **Verbal/Linguistic, Logical/Mathematical**
- ☐ **p. 522** Students discuss the problem of deforestation in East Africa. **Verbal/Linguistic, Intrapersonal**
- ☐ **p. 523** Students research sustainable farming in East Africa. BL **Verbal/Linguistic, Visual/Spatial**
- ☐ **p. 524** Students identify the problems countries in East Africa are trying to resolve. **Verbal/Linguistic**

W Writing Skills

- ☐ **p. 522** Students write an essay describing how the interaction of environmental factors and human factors is causing desertification in areas of East Africa. BL **Verbal/Linguistic, Interpersonal**

T Technology Skills

- ☐ **p. 521** Students research a recent or continual strife in an assigned country and create a multimedia report that includes both perspectives on the strife. BL **Verbal/Linguistic, Visual/Spatial, Interpersonal**
- ☐ **p. 523** Students identify one action that is being taken to stem the pollution of shoreways and waterways and write a few paragraphs describing whether it is successful. AL **Verbal/Linguistic**

☑ Online Teaching Options

V Visual Skills

- VIDEO **Postcards from Kenya: Tourism**—Students watch the video and identify one or two ways in which the lives of Africans are depicted somewhat differently in the video than in the text. AL BL **Intrapersonal**
- GRAPHIC ORGANIZER **People and Their Environment: East Africa**—Students use this graphic organizer to help them better understand how the actions of people in the past and in the present have shaped the environment of East Africa. AL **Verbal/Linguistic, Visual/Spatial**

C Critical Thinking Skills

- INTERACTIVE BELLRINGER **Africa's Shrinking Elephant Population**—Students analyze text and a map of the range and populations of elephants in Africa between 1979 and 2007 to discuss their opinions about hunting for sport and trade. **Verbal/Linguistic, Visual/Spatial**
- SLIDE SHOW **Animals in East Africa**—Students watch the slide show and write any questions they may have about the different animals that live in East Africa, and factors that may or may not threaten their survival. AL **Verbal/Linguistic, Naturalist, Interpersonal**
- INTERACTIVE WHITEBOARD ACTIVITY **Human Impact of Environmental Challenges in East Africa**—Students complete a chart to create accurate statements about the human impact/cause and environmental outcome/effects of environmental challenges in East Africa.

☑ Printable Digital Worksheets

R Reading Skills

- WORKSHEET **Guided Reading Activity**—Students use Guided Reading Activity worksheets to review their comprehension of the content.
- WORKSHEET **Reading Essentials and Study Guide**—Students complete the study guide and answer Reading Progress Check and vocabulary questions. AL
- WORKSHEET **Vocabulary Activity**—Students review the chapter content and academic vocabulary words.
- WORKSHEET **Chapter Summary**—Students review the main ideas of the chapter content.

C Critical Thinking Skills

- WORKSHEET **Video Activity**—Students answer questions based on a lesson video.
- WORKSHEET **Reteaching Activity**—Students use this activity worksheet to review and reteach chapter content and vocabulary. This worksheet can be used with struggling students who need additional help with difficult content concepts.

Intervention and Remediation Strategies

LESSON 1 Physical Geography of East Africa

Reading and Comprehension

Assign each of six student groups one of the following topics: unique features of plateaus in East Africa, the Great Rift Valley, Lake Turkana, Lake Victoria, Lake Tanganyika, and East Africa's wettest areas. Tell groups to review the lesson to identify key facts about their topic for an outline. Encourage students to define content vocabulary terms in their outlines if pertinent to their topic. Tell students to leave a space under their main headings. After students have completed their outlines, have groups exchange papers and quiz each other on facts about their topics. Discuss how landforms, water systems, and climate impact life in the region.

Text Evidence

Have students work in the same groups, using their outlines as a "roadmap" to explore the region in more depth. Tell students to conduct online research to identify important information that supports key ideas and concepts noted in their outlines. Have students develop a rating system for the facts gleaned from their research on a scale of one to five, from the most to least important supporting evidence of the main headings. Tell students to add the information to their outlines. Ask volunteers to share one or two pieces of information identified in their research, how they rated its importance, and reasons for their ratings.

LESSON 2 Human Geography of East Africa

Reading and Comprehension

Have students review the lesson to identify a topic about which they will write a journal entry from the point of view of someone living in the past or present-day East Africa. Encourage students to use their imaginations to envision what it might have been like to live in the region long ago or what it is like there today. In their journal entries, students should refer to key events that occurred during their chosen time period. Invite students to use sensory adjectives to convey a picture of what life in East Africa was like during that time period. Ask volunteers to share their journal entries with the class.

Text Evidence

Have students work in small groups and tell them they will act as archaeologists surveying a region in East Africa to identify clues about its history, government, culture, or economy. Using the text as a guide, students should imagine what types of artifacts they might find if they were to conduct an archaeological dig. After reviewing the lesson, have students collaborate to select a "found object" and explain its significance to the class. Encourage students to identify evidence from the text to support the significance of their artifact, fossil, or found object, explaining how it provides clues about the region.

LESSON 3 People and Their Environment: East Africa

Reading and Comprehension

Ensure students' understanding of the factors that contribute to the challenging way of life for so many East Africans. Have student groups create a diagram or flowchart that demonstrates how poverty, hunger, drought, corruption, and conflict are inextricably linked in exacerbating the region's problems. Students should work together to create and complete their diagrams and present them to the class, using content vocabulary words where possible.

Text Evidence

Organize students into groups of four or five students. Tell groups they will create and perform a television talk show titled "East Africa Today," featuring key figures who will discuss an issue from the lesson. Assign each group one of the following Guiding Questions to discuss: *What makes effective resource management in East Africa especially challenging? What environmental challenges does East Africa face today? What steps are being taken to combat these environmental challenges?* Encourage students to have a range of opinions represented by "guests" on their talk shows, such as a government official, a person living in a refugee camp, a pastoralist, a hunter, an ecotourism guide, and so on. Allow time for students to prepare their talk shows before presenting them for their classmates, who will act as the "studio audience."

Online Resources

Leveled Reader

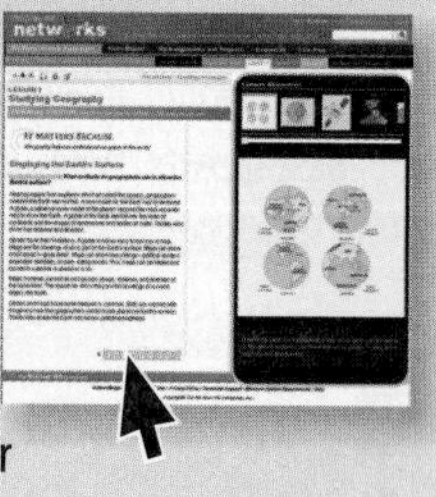

Use this online approaching-level text that corresponds directly to the text in the Student Edition. It also includes additional reading and comprehension support for English Language Learners.

Guided Reading Activities

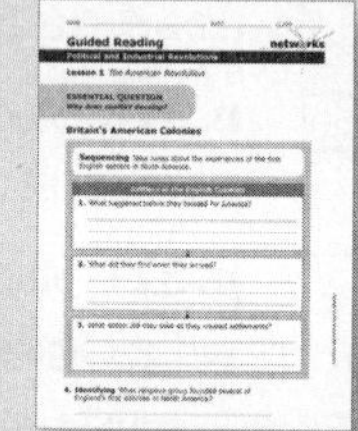

This resource uses guiding questions to help students with comprehension.

Reteaching Activities

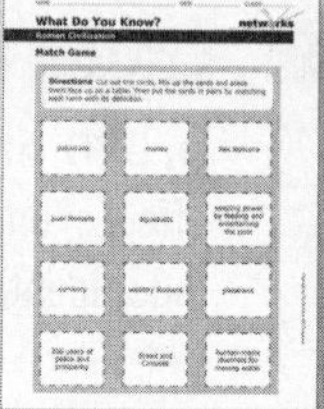

These worksheets provide students with an opportunity for remedial practice and review of vital chapter content.

Reading Essentials and Study Guide

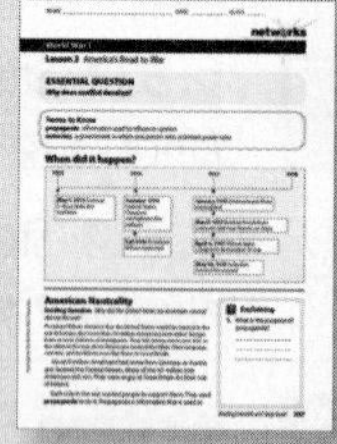

This resource offers writing and reading activities for the approaching-level student.

Self-Check Quizzes

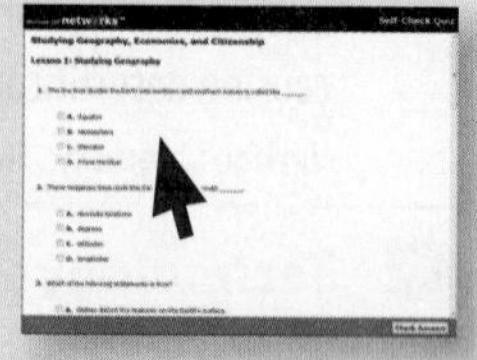

This online assessment tool provides instant feedback for students to check their progress.

Chapter Summaries

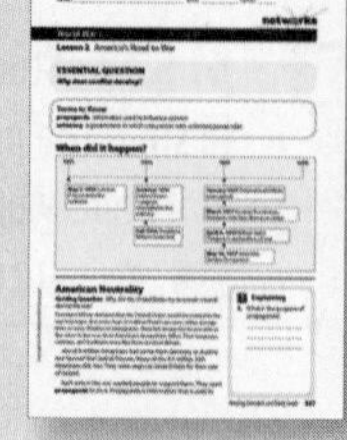

Summaries are provided for each chapter that thoroughly condense core content into manageable chunks.

East Africa

networks

There's More Online about East Africa's geography.

CHAPTER 21

ESSENTIAL QUESTION • *How do physical systems and human systems shape a place?*

Geography Matters...

East Africa is a land of magnificent landscapes, from the volcanic peak of Kilimanjaro to the lakes of the Great Rift Valley. It is also, however, a land of desert and drought.

East Africa has attracted many countries over the centuries. Its prime location on the Red Sea and Indian Ocean drew the interest of people looking for trade outposts and entrances into the continent. Outsiders colonized almost all the land. Today, East Africa is working toward improving its economies, environments, and standards of living in the face of challenges such as population growth, corruption, and environmental degradation.

◀ Many young East Africans enjoy both tradition and modern ways of life.

Roy Toft/National Geographic Stock

503

Letter from the Author

Dear Geography Teacher,

The Blue Nile Dam seems to be exactly what Ethiopia needs for water development and hydroelectric generation. But the Blue Nile is a main branch of the much larger Nile River, which passes through many different countries in this dry region. What are the national interests in the dam? What can be done? Is Ethiopia interested in cooperating with its neighbors? Who has the water rights? What do upstream partners owe downstream countries? This is a big problem if several countries are involved and this situation is a metaphor for many of the river systems of the world.

Richard G. Boehm

ENGAGE

Activating Prior Knowledge Have student pairs brainstorm what they know about East Africa, whether it be the physical or human geography of the area or the history of the area. Then have pairs look at the photographs and headings in the chapter to add items to their lists.

TEACH & ASSESS

Making Connections

The East African coast has a long history of being a vital trading area in the world. The earliest written accounts of the East African coast, the *Periplus,* was written by a Greek merchant living in Egypt in the first century A.D. The *Periplus* describes in some detail the shore of what was to become northern Somalia. Ships sailed from there to western India to bring back cotton cloth, grain, oil, and sugar. Other ships moved down the Red Sea coast bringing cloaks, tunics, copper, and tin. Tortoiseshell, ivory, and enslaved persons were traded in return. A consequence of this international trade was that markets became focused on urban centers along the coast with concentrations of wealth and power. The colonization of the area by outsiders led to the merging of African, Arab, and Indian peoples from southern Somalia to northern Mozambique and produced a unique language, Swahili, or Kiswahili, and culture which still exist today.

Hypothesizing Emphasize to students that physical systems such as the Red Sea and the Indian Ocean have historically influenced trade and cultural development in East Africa. **Ask:** **What is a positive result of this interaction and what is a negative result?** *(Possible answers: Positive: the sharing of cultural and technological achievements; Negative: the colonization of the area and a loss of original cultures)*

CLOSE & REFLECT

Summarizing Have students summarize what they know of the history of East Africa and the challenges the area faces in the twenty-first century. Have a student volunteer write the key concepts on the board as the discussion evolves.

ePals GlobalCommunity
Where learners connect™

Extend the project-based learning experience globally through our partnership with ePals. EPals allows you to connect with classrooms around the world in a safe online environment for real-life lessons and projects in virtual study groups.

ENGAGE

R1 Reading Skills

Listing Have students consider the title and the photograph showing an East African woman outside her home. Have student pairs write a short list describing what the photograph shows about life in East Africa. Have pairs share their lists in a class discussion.

TEACH & ASSESS

V Visual Skills

Creating Charts Have small groups of students research online or in the library about the crops that people grow in East Africa for their food supply. Have them create a chart that lists and describes the most prevalent foods in the East African diet. Have groups share their charts with the class.
BL Visual/Spatial

R2 Reading Skills

Defining Write the term *subsistence farming* on the board. **Ask:** What does the phrase *subsistence farming* mean? *(It is a form of farming in which nearly all the crops or livestock raised are used to maintain the farmer and his family, leaving little surplus for sale or trade.)* What happens to the crops of subsistence farmers when there is a drought? *(Crops fail and there is a shortage of food.)* ELL Verbal/Linguistic

Content Background Knowledge

Drought in East Africa Poor rains during the 2011 and 2012 rainy seasons led to severe drought in Kenya, Ethiopia, Somalia, and Uganda. The drought left over 13 million people in need of humanitarian assistance. As the crisis peaked in mid 2011, families saw their crops fail and their livestock die from lack of pasture to graze. And while 2012 brought some rains, they were not sufficient to enable people to recover. The severe drought and escalating food prices led to a declaration of famine in Somalia in 2011. The situation in Somalia remains volatile; more than 320,000 children remain malnourished and in need of urgent assistance.

Why Geography Matters: **East Africa**

V export crops and East Africa

R2 *About 80 percent of East Africa's population relies on subsistence farming. However, the subregion's per capita agricultural income and production is one of the lowest in the world. Still, agriculture is of vital importance and makes up about 40 percent of the subregion's gross domestic product (GDP). Even when local farmers try to produce agricultural commodities, the global market is highly competitive, which makes it difficult for them to access.*

R1

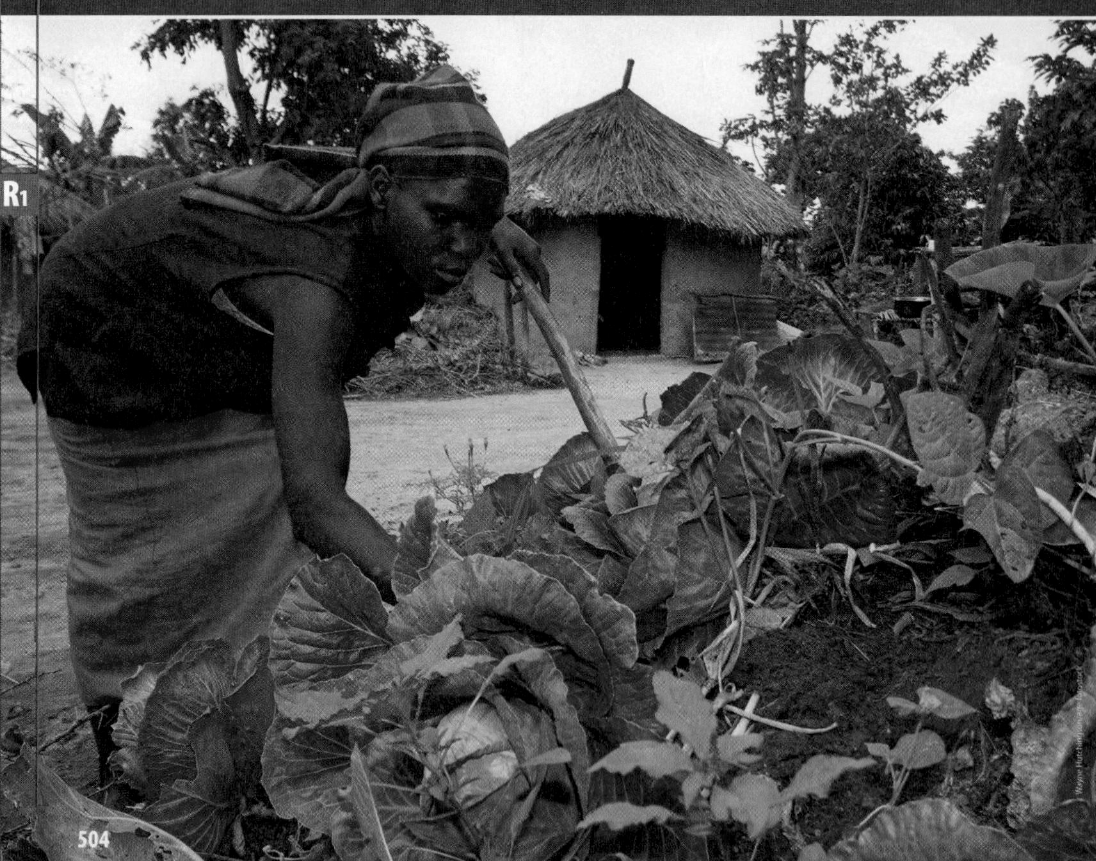

504

Project-Based Learning

Hands-On

Educational Brochures
Working in small groups, students will create educational brochures that aim to resolve the problem of girls in East Africa not continuing their education beyond primary school. Each group will focus on proposing solutions to one obstacle that prevents girls from continuing their education. Groups will be responsible for researching and illustrating their proposals and presenting them in the form of a brochure.

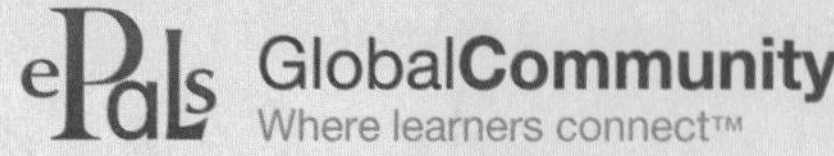

Digital Hands-On

Create Online Projects
Find an additional activity online that incorporates technology for this project. Visit the EdTech Teacher Web sites for more links, tutorials, and other resources.

Why do farmers in East Africa grow certain crops?

Many of the crops that are grown in East Africa are the legacy of colonialism. Colonial powers made the economic decisions about what crops would be grown for consumption and for export. They based these decisions on profit for themselves, not for the benefit of the African people. Many colonial governments set up plantations that each produced a single crop for export because export crops brought in the most income for the colonial government.

In East Africa, export crops included tea, coffee, tobacco, cotton, cashews, copra, and sisal. After decolonization, it was difficult or even impossible for the newly independent governments to modify this system. The result is the current situation, in which these countries are dependent on agricultural exports and there is little support for small-scale subsistence farmers.

1. **Human Systems** How has East Africa's colonial legacy influenced what crops are produced?

How has growing single crops for export affected the people in East Africa?

Reliance on the success of a single export crop can be risky. For example, if climate conditions are extreme—too hot or cold, or too dry or wet—a crop might be wiped out or limited for a season. Sometimes the single crop grown for export requires more labor or resources such as water and fertilizer to cultivate and harvest. Essentially, the crop requires a large investment in terms of human and capital resources. These factors can affect the return on investment.

Another factor is the fluctuation in market demand and price. If demand for a product is low, then the price at which a farmer can sell will be low as well. The decision to produce one single crop over another may result in the loss of resources that could have been used elsewhere. If the government decides that the best land should be devoted to growing one export crop, that land might be unavailable for growing food. Because many farmers in East Africa rely on subsistence farming for their livelihood, they are most affected by agricultural decisions.

2. **The World in Spatial Terms** How have agricultural decisions about export crops affected subsistence farmers in East Africa?

What steps have been taken to help farmers?

To achieve better crop yields in East Africa, some organizations are working on solutions. For example, the goal of the Smallholder Cash and Export Crops Development Project is to help small growers of coffee in Rwanda by setting up cooperatives. The hope is that by working together, they can produce high-quality coffee that will fetch a high price. In another project, public land is being made available to small growers of tea.

Also, East African governments have encouraged the use of modern farm technology, such as genetically engineered seeds, soil conservation, and fertilizers. However, these actions have created new marketing problems. Some countries in Europe have boycotted certain crops from East Africa to protest the use of some of these techniques.

3. **Environment and Society** Write a paragraph evaluating the actions taken to improve crop yields in East Africa. Propose an idea that governments or other organizations can initiate to help farmers in the subregion.

READ about cash crops in East Africa • *EXPLORE* a map of East African natural resources

C Critical Thinking Skills

Analyzing Have students read column two and discuss how a country's reliance on a single export crop is risky and even affects subsistence farmers. **Ask:** **What are two risks of relying on a single export crop?** *(If the market for that crop fluctuates or if there are extreme weather conditions that damage the crop, farmers have nothing to fall back on.)* **How are subsistence farmers affected in countries that rely on a single export crop?** *(The government can allocate the best farmland to growing the single export crop, thereby making less land available for subsistence farmers.)* **AL Verbal/Linguistic**

T Technology Skills

Researching Have students go online to research one of the international organizations that address the problems of subsistence farmers. Students should present the results of their research, focusing on assistance provided in the last five years. **BL Verbal/Linguistic, Logical/Mathematical**

W Writing Skills

Argument Have students research one of the modern farm technologies being used in East Africa. Then have students write a letter to the head of a European country that has been boycotting these products, arguing in favor of the farmers. **AL Verbal/Linguistic**

CLOSE & REFLECT

Summarizing Review how colonialism affected countries in East Africa and the problems countries faced when they gained independence. Have students write a paragraph summarizing these problems.

INTERACTIVE MAP

Resources in East Africa

Locating Have students use this map for a visual representation of where particular natural resources are located throughout East Africa. Working with a partner, have students locate the resources in each area. Ask pairs to write down how these resources may or may not benefit the residents of the specific area or areas in which the resources are found. **AL Interpersonal, Visual/Spatial**

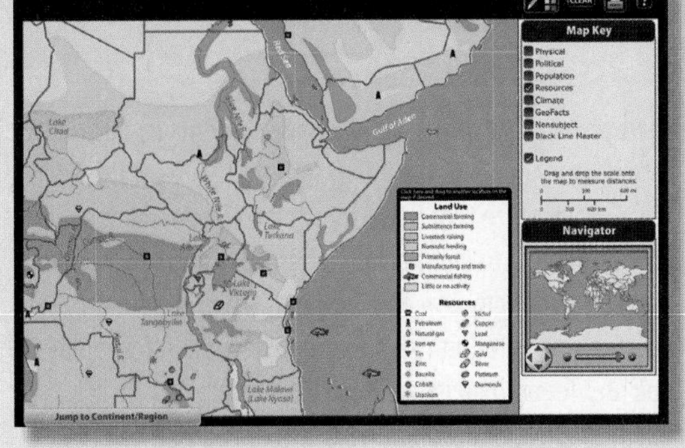

ANSWERS, p. 505

Why Geography Matters

1. Colonial powers made decisions about what crops to grow; since export crops made the most profits, plantations were often set up to grow a single export crop while ignoring traditional crops used as food sources.
2. Export crops are grown on lands that could be used for subsistence farming. Export crops are also labor and resource intensive, leaving fewer people and resources for subsistence farming.
3. Paragraphs will differ but should include an idea that can be implemented to help farmers in the region and an evaluation of cooperatives and public land use for small growers of crops, as well as the use of genetically engineered seeds, soil conservation, and fertilizers.

ENGAGE

R Reading Skills

Activating Prior Knowledge Display a physical map of East Africa. Have students identify geographical features that they are familiar with, such as the Red Sea and the Indian Ocean. Then have students browse the lesson to identify different geographical features of East Africa.

TEACH & ASSESS

C Critical Thinking Skills

Inferring Display on the board a political map of East Africa. **Ask:** What countries in East Africa are located along the coast? *(Eritrea and a tip of Djibouti border the Red Sea; Kenya and Tanzania border the Indian Ocean.)* What countries are landlocked? *(Ethiopia, Uganda, Rwanda, and Burundi are landlocked.)* What can you infer about the role that oceans and seas played in the development of those countries? *(The Red Sea and Indian Ocean played a significant role in the economic and cultural development of those countries.)* AL Verbal/Linguistic

Content Background Knowledge

Rift Valleys on Earth When plates below Earth's crust move apart, the Earth's crust separates, or rifts. Rift valleys can lead to the creation of entirely new continents or deepen valleys in existing ones. Many rift valleys have been found underwater along the large ridges that run throughout the oceans. This occurs along the northern crest of the Mid-Atlantic Ridge, where the North American plate and the Eurasian plate are splitting apart. In the Pacific Ocean, the East Pacific Rise has created rift valleys where the Pacific plate is separating from the North American plate. There are only two rift valleys on Earth within the continental crust, the Baikal Rift Valley in Russia and the Great Rift Valley. Tectonic activity splits continental crust much in the same way it does along mid-ocean ridges.

ANSWERS, p. 506

TAKING NOTES: Landforms: the Great Rift Valley has two branches: the Western Rift Valley and the Eastern Rift Valley; two major volcanic mountains, Kilimanjaro and Mount Kenya; long coastlines along the Red Sea and Indian Ocean; plateaus; and grassy plains such as the Serengeti; **Water Systems:** the Indian Ocean, Lake Victoria, Lake Tanganyika, Lake Turkana, and Lake Baringo; **Climates, Biomes, and Resources:** East Africa has a wide range of latitudes and elevations creating diverse climates and biomes such as desert, semi-arid steppe (which contains low grasses, shrubs, and acacia trees), tropical grassland, or savanna, and highlands climate; East Africa has many resources, including gold, natural gas, copper, soda ash, diamonds, and tanzanite.

networks

There's More Online!

- **INFOGRAPHIC** The Great Rift Valley
- **IMAGE** Lake Turkana
- **IMAGE** Subtropical Climate
- **IMAGE** Arid Climate
- **INTERACTIVE SELF-CHECK QUIZ**
- **VIDEO** Physical Geography of East Africa

LESSON 1
Physical Geography of East Africa

ESSENTIAL QUESTION • *How do physical systems and human systems shape a place?*

Reading **HELP**DESK 

Academic Vocabulary (Tier Two Words)
- **constitute**
- **survive**

Content Vocabulary (Tier Three Words)
- **rift valley**
- **fault**
- **escarpment**
- **cataract**

TAKING NOTES: ***Key Ideas and Details***

IDENTIFYING As you read about the physical geography of East Africa, use a graphic organizer like the one below to identify examples of its key physical features.

East Africa's Physical Systems		
Landforms	Water Systems	Climates, Biomes, and Resources

IT MATTERS BECAUSE

With a variety of landscapes stretching from the Red Sea to south of the Equator and from the heart of the African continent to the Indian Ocean, East Africa can claim many natural wonders. These natural features range from mountains to deep rift valleys and from deserts to great lakes. It is an area of rich resources and, at the same time, a land of dusty, barren desert.

Landforms

GUIDING QUESTION *What physical features are part of the diverse landscape of East Africa?*

East Africa has a considerable range of landforms that include plains of differing types, volcanic mountains, and plateaus cut by a tremendous valley, marked by rivers and lakes. The subregion is home to the Serengeti Plain, as well as Kilimanjaro, Mount Kenya, and the Great Rift Valley. This subregion, which includes Burundi, Ethiopia, Kenya, Rwanda, Tanzania, and Uganda, has a strikingly diverse landscape.

A significant part of the landscape of East Africa is the Great Rift Valley. This long geologic feature begins well north of the subregion in Syria in Southwest Asia, and it extends south of the subregion to Mozambique (moh•zahm•BEEK) in the southeastern part of Africa. This natural wonder cuts through much of East Africa and is a defining feature of the landscape. A **rift valley** is a crack in Earth's surface formed by shifting and separating tectonic plates. The formation of the Great Rift Valley began millions of years ago when **faults**, or breaks in Earth's crust, were formed by the movement of plates below Earth's surface.

In East Africa, the Great Rift Valley is made up of two branches, each of which lies within a set of fault lines. The Western Rift Valley cuts through Tanzania, Burundi, Rwanda, and Uganda. Running the length of the rift, through the center of the Western Rift Valley, is Lake Tanganyika, one of the deepest and longest freshwater lakes in the world. The Eastern Rift Valley cuts through Tanzania and Kenya and north into Ethiopia. It is flanked in the east by two major volcanic mountains, Kilimanjaro and Mount Kenya.

506

networks ***Online Teaching Options***

INTERACTIVE BELLRINGER

The Great Rift Valley

Interpreting an Infographic Have students use the introductory text and the infographic of the Great Rift Valley to visualize that East Africa is a collection of diverse landscapes and to identify how physical processes shape patterns in the physical environment. Have students meet in small groups. Ask them to review the infographic and answer each question. Have each group record all answers to each question. Then, in a class discussion, share answers. ELL Visual/Spatial, Interpersonal

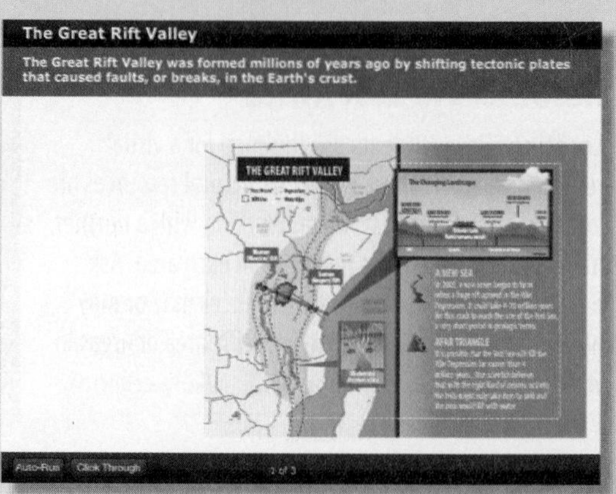

The Great Rift Valley
The Great Rift Valley was formed millions of years ago by shifting tectonic plates that caused faults, or breaks, in the Earth's crust.
THE GREAT RIFT VALLEY
A NEW SEA
AFAR TRIANGLE

East Africa has long coastlines along both the Red Sea and Indian Ocean. This coastal access has been of great economic importance. For example, Kenya and Tanzania have major ports on the Indian Ocean. The major rivers of Kenya and Tanzania drain into the Indian Ocean, linking the interior with the coast.

East Africa is made up of plateaus and cliffs. Plateaus, ranging in elevation from 500 feet (152 m) in the west to 8,000 feet (2,438 m) or more in the east, **constitute** much of the landscape. They are edged in **escarpments**, or steep cliffs. Rivers crossing the plateaus plunge down the escarpments in **cataracts**, or large waterfalls. The Ethiopian Plateau includes gorges, river channels, and *ambas,* or steep-sided, flat-topped land. East Africa also contains many grassy plains. Most notable is the Serengeti Plain, much of which is now a nature preserve in Tanzania and Kenya. R

A mountainous region of East Africa is known as the Eastern Highlands. These highland areas include the Ethiopian Highlands, as well as the volcanic Kilimanjaro and Mount Kenya. These volcanoes are no longer active. East Africa is also home to the Ruwenzori Mountains, which divide Uganda and the Democratic Republic of the Congo. Covered with snow and cloaked in clouds, they are also known as the "Mountains of the Moon."

rift valley a crack in Earth's surface created by the shifting of tectonic plates

fault a crack or break in Earth's crust

constitute to compose or form

escarpment a steep cliff or slope between a higher and lower land surface

cataract a large waterfall

READING PROGRESS CHECK

Identifying What are some unique features of the plateaus in East Africa?

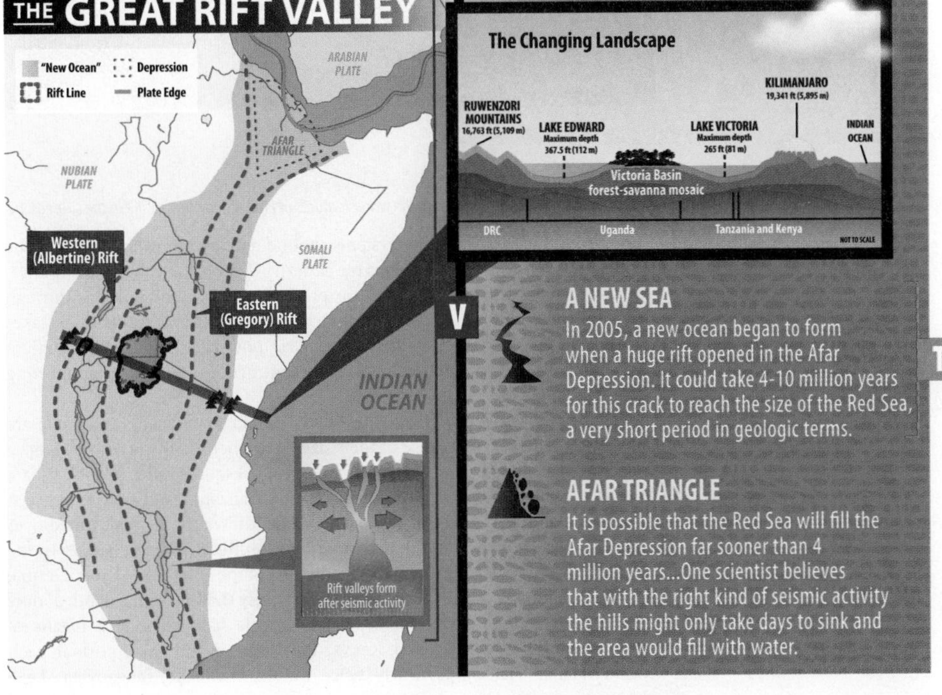

The Great Rift Valley formed millions of years ago and is a defining feature of the East African landscape.

▲ **CRITICAL THINKING**

1. ***Analyzing Visuals*** What happened beneath Earth's surface during the formation of the Great Rift Valley?
2. ***Identifying Cause and Effect*** How did the formation of the Great Rift Valley change the face of East Africa?

R Reading Skills

Defining Write the word *escarpment* on the board. Have students define and discuss the term in their own words. Have them use the word in a paragraph that describes how *escarpments* are one part of the diverse geography of East Africa. ELL **Verbal/Linguistic**

V Visual Skills

Analyzing Visuals Draw students' attention to the political map of East Africa posted on the board. Then have students look at the map of the Great Rift Valley in East Africa. **Ask:** **What country has both the eastern and western branch of the Great Rift Valley running through it?** *(Tanzania)* **In what country does the Great Rift Valley enter a major waterway?** *(Eritrea)* AL **Visual/Spatial**

T Technology Skills

Researching Have small groups of students research the Afar Depression. Have each group create a multimedia presentation for the class. Group presentations should include visuals. After the student presentations, discuss the theories about the Afar Depression and the significance and effects the depression has on everyday life in East Africa. BL **Verbal/Linguistic, Logical/Mathematical**

VIDEO

Wild Wonders of Africa

Identifying Have students view this video about Mount Kenya. Have students take notes about the various physical features that are highlighted in the video. After viewing, lead a class discussion in which students discuss the climate and habitat of Mount Kenya, as well as why the makers of the video consider these features "wonders." Ask students to identify the elements of Mount Kenya that they believe are "wonders." ELL **Intrapersonal, Visual/Spatial**

ANSWERS, p. 507

READING PROGRESS CHECK Plateaus in East Africa are edged in steep cliffs called escarpments with rivers that run over them in cataracts, or large waterfalls. They also contain gorges, river channels and *ambas,* or flat-topped land with steep sides.

CRITICAL THINKING

1. Tectonic plates beneath the Earth's surface began forming faults, or breaks in the Earth's crust making a crack in the surface.
2. The formation of the Great Rift Valley changed the face of East Africa by creating valleys where lakes lie and mountains such as the Ruwenzori Mountains and the volcanic Kilimanjaro and Mount Kenya.

W Writing Skills

Informative/Explanatory Display the physical map of East Africa. Emphasize to students that the Great Rift Valley has created a variety of inland water systems in East Africa. Have students write an essay explaining how two of these water systems influence the economy in East African countries.
AL **Verbal/Linguistic**

T Technology Skills

Comparing and Contrasting Have students discuss the information about the Indian Ocean in this section with a partner. Then assign student pairs either Tanzania or Kenya. Have each pair conduct Internet research to design a chart comparing and contrasting the positive and negative effects that bordering the Indian Ocean has had on the economic and cultural development of their assigned country. Have pairs present their charts in a class presentation. BL **Verbal/Linguistic, Logical/Mathematical**

R Reading Skills

Understanding Relationships Have a student volunteer read the last paragraph. **Ask:** **What is the relationship between Lake Victoria and the White Nile River?** *(Lake Victoria is the source of the White Nile River.)* **What lake lies between the Democratic Republic of the Congo and Tanzania?** *(Lake Tanganyika)* **Why do you think Lake Victoria and Lake Tanganyika are the most heavily populated areas in Africa?** *(Both lakes provide a source for food; people can either grow food in the rich soil around the lakes or catch fish in the lakes.)* In a class discussion have students link the Great Rift Valley and the various internal water systems of East Africa.
ELL **Visual/Spatial**

ANSWERS, p. 508

CRITICAL THINKING

1. Lake Turkana has no outlet for drainage, making it a good site for hydroelectric power.
2. Lake Turkana separated from Lake Baringo because of the dry conditions in the area, which caused the lakes to shrink and become two distinct bodies of water.

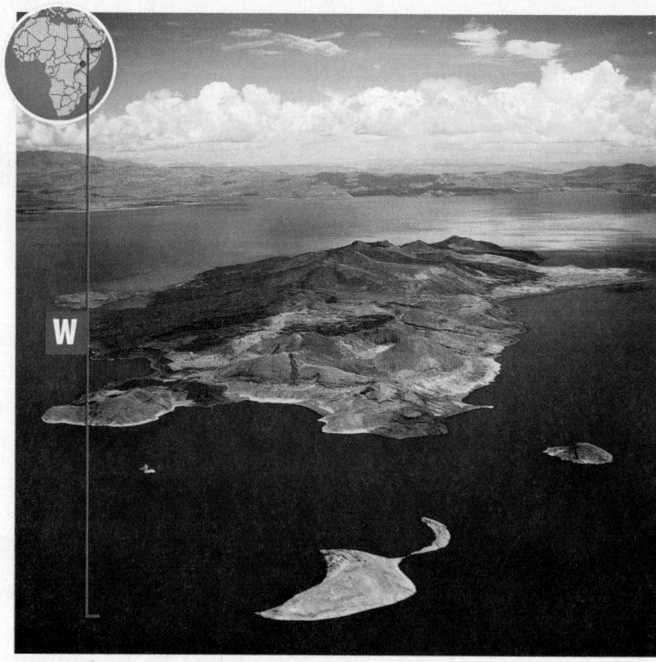

South Island in Lake Turkana is the largest island in the lake. Located at the southern and deepest part of the lake, it is part of a ridge of extinct volcanoes and hills poking above the surface.

▶ CRITICAL THINKING

1. ***Making Inferences*** How might the geography around Lake Turkana make it a good site for generating hydroelectric power?
2. ***Identifying Cause and Effect*** What caused Lake Turkana to separate from Lake Baringo?

Nigel Pavitt/AWL Images/Getty Images

Water Systems

GUIDING QUESTION *How have the water features of East Africa affected life in the subregion?*

Throughout East Africa, water systems abound and are important to life in the subregion. The Indian Ocean forms the eastern border of Tanzania and of Kenya. The ocean provides an entry point for products, people, and cultures through these countries and into the subregion. East Africa is known for its many lakes and rivers, which are used for hydroelectric power, fishing, transportation, supporting agriculture, and even as tourist attractions, as well as supporting natural ecosystems.

The two arms of the Great Rift Valley contain many lakes, and some are considered great lakes because of their size. Lake Victoria is the second-largest freshwater lake in the world, with an area of 26,828 square miles (69,485 square km). It is located along the borders of Uganda, Tanzania, and Kenya, between the eastern and western branches of the Great Rift Valley. It was formed over 100,000 years ago when the flow of water was shifted through changes in the western rift. Lake Victoria lies at the headwaters of the White Nile River. Despite its large surface area, Lake Victoria is comparatively shallow with a depth of only 270 feet (82 m). Since the 1900s, Lake Victoria has provided a means of transportation between Uganda, Kenya, and Tanzania with ferry ports in each country. Lake Victoria is nearly twice the size of Lake Tanganyika. Lake Tanganyika, in the Western Rift Valley, is one of the deepest freshwater lakes in the world. It is located between Tanzania and the Democratic Republic of the Congo and is within the drainage basin of the Congo River. The rich soil around Lake Victoria and the abundant fishing on Lake Tanganyika make the land around these lakes among the most heavily populated areas in Africa.

508

networks Online Teaching Options

INTERACTIVE WHITEBOARD ACTIVITY

Physical Geography of East Africa

Defining Students will increase their vocabulary and be better able to visualize the physical geography of East Africa through the completion of this interactive whiteboard activity. Display the activity and ask students to match the terms to the definitions provided. Once they have completed the activity, have students pair up. One student can turn away from the display, and the other student can read a definition from the whiteboard. The first student will then provide the correct term.
ELL **Verbal/Linguistic**

Physical Geography of East Africa

Directions: East Africa has a diverse physical geography that includes a considerable range of landforms. Drag terms to the appropriate definition. When correctly completed, a list of terms pertaining to the physical geography of East Africa and their definitions will be displayed.

	A crack in Earth's surface formed by shifting tectonic plates
	Breaks in Earth's crust that was formed by the movement of plates below Earth's surface
	Runs the length of the rift, through the center of the Western Rift Valley
	Cuts through Tanzania and Kenya and north into Ethiopia
	Large waterfalls
	Comprised of Burundi, Eritrea, Ethiopia, Kenya, Rwanda, Tanzania, and Uganda
	Volcanic mountains that flank the Eastern Rift Valley on the east
	Cuts through Tanzania, Burundi, Rwanda, and Uganda
	Steep cliffs
	Comprised of two branches, each of which lies within a set of fault lines, this long geologic feature begins well north of the subregion in Syria and extends south of the subregion to Mozambique

Cataracts	Eastern Rift Valley	Fault	Kilimanjaro and Mount Kenya	Rift Valley
East African Subregion	Escarpments	Great Rift Valley	Lake Tanganyika	Western Rift Valley

Show Answers

Lake Turkana, in Kenya, with its northern border in Ethiopia, is a source of growing wind-power and hydroelectric industries in Kenya. Lake Turkana has rocky shores in the east and south due to volcanic outcrops. It lies in a part of the Eastern Rift Valley that gets so little rain it is a hot desert. The lake had once been a part of a larger lake, along with Lake Baringo, but dry conditions caused the lakes to shrink and become two distinct bodies. In the west and north, it is marked by sand dunes, sandpits, and mudflats and has no outlet for drainage.

✓ READING PROGRESS CHECK

Determining Importance Describe key features of Lake Victoria and Lake Tanganyika.

Climates, Biomes, and Resources

GUIDING QUESTION *How does the climate affect life in East Africa?*

East Africa covers a wide range of latitudes and elevations, resulting in a diverse set of climates and biomes. Tropical heat characterizes much of the subregion, with savanna vegetation predominant. North of the savanna is the semi-arid steppe. North of the semi-arid steppe is the arid desert. Finally, the high mountains of the subregion have warm, humid subtropical climates.

Hot, dry weather prevails in the desert areas of East Africa. The northeastern area of the subregion, known as the Horn of Africa, is largely desert. Located in the Horn of Africa are parts of Eritrea, Ethiopia, Djibouti, Somalia, Kenya, and Uganda. Some areas receive only limited summer rain. Parts of Kenya may receive almost no rain. Thus the vegetation and wildlife must be able to **survive** on limited water.

Separating the deserts from the tropical savanna is a semi-arid, steppe transition zone. The northern steppe is called the Sahel—which means "shore" or "edge" in Arabic. The Sahel has pastures of low-growing grasses, shrubs, and acacia trees.

survive to manage to stay alive

These images demonstrate different climate zones in East Africa. East Africa's climate is as diverse as its landscape.

▼ CRITICAL THINKING

1. ***Exploring Issues*** How does climate impact life in East Africa?
2. ***Contrasting*** How are these climate zones different?

East Africa 509

SLIDE SHOW

East Africa Climate Zones

Creating Charts and Tables As students view the slide show, have them take notes on the many and varied climate zones of East Africa. After viewing, lead a class discussion about the different zones. Then ask students to create a chart of the climate zones featured in the slide show, using their notes and points brought up in the discussion. This chart will help them clarify and organize all of the information presented in the slide show and lesson content. **Visual/Spatial, Naturalist**

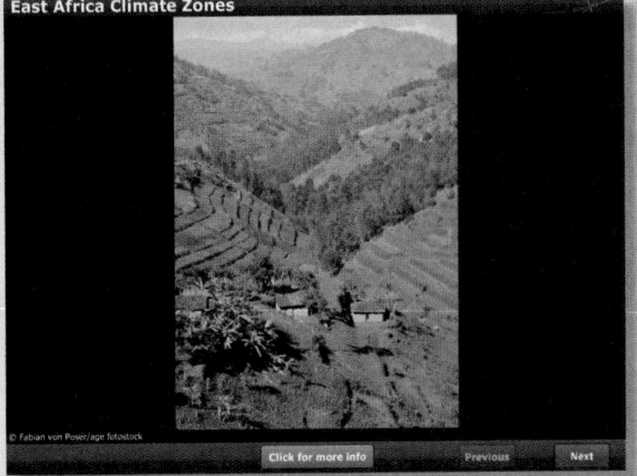

C Critical Thinking Skills

Analyzing Before students read this section, have them review the physical map of East Africa that includes latitude lines. **Ask:** **Given the latitudes in which East Africa is located, what can you conclude about the climate? Give specific reasons for your answer.** *(East African countries are located on or near the Equator, which means that most of the climate is tropical wet/dry, semi-arid, or arid, and humid subtropical in the highlands.)* **What are some of the geographic elements affecting the climate in East Africa?** *(the elevation varies in East Africa due to the Great Rift Valley; high mountains have warm, humid subtropic climates and desert flatlands have hot, dry weather)* Then have students read about the climates and biomes of East Africa and discuss the information with a partner. AL **Visual/Spatial**

Making Connections

The Horn of Africa is a peninsula and the easternmost projection of the African continent. The peninsula juts into the Gulf of Aden in the north and into the Indian Ocean in the southeast. It is named the Horn of Africa because it resembles a rhinoceros horn. The countries of Somalia, Djibouti, and parts of Eritrea, Ethiopia, and Kenya are located on the peninsula.

R Reading Skills

Defining Have students read the definition of the word *survive*. **Ask:** **What has vegetation and wildlife done in order to *survive* in many areas of East Africa?** *(They have adjusted to living on limited water.)* Have students write a short paragraph describing a living organism they are familiar with that is able to adjust in order to survive. Encourage students to share their paragraphs. ELL **Verbal/Linguistic**

ANSWERS, p. 509

✓ READING PROGRESS CHECK Lake Victoria is the second-largest freshwater lake in the world and is surrounded by fertile soil. It is about twice the size of Lake Tanganyika, which is much deeper, being one of the deepest and longest freshwater lakes in the world. Lake Tanganyika supports a large fishing industry.

CRITICAL THINKING

1. Climate impacts where people live, what kind of and how much food they can grow, and availability of water for both people and animals.
2. The midlatitudes look almost lush and green. They are good places for farming as they have sufficient rainfall and moderate temperatures. The savanna is mainly grassland and some trees. While there is rainfall here for part of the year, the rest of the year is dry.

T Technology Skills

Exploring Issues Have student pairs research the current status of the Serengeti Plain. Using primary sources, have students create a multimedia presentation. Tell pairs to include at least one positive element about the Serengeti Plain and one of the challenges it faces today. Have pairs display their presentation to the class. **Verbal/Linguistic, Interpersonal**

W Writing Skills

Informative/Explanatory Have students write a one-page essay discussing how the diverse landforms and climates of East African countries make for a variety of resources in each country in the subregion. Have students share their essays in class discussion. BL **Verbal/Linguistic**

CLOSE & REFLECT

Creating Charts Have students summarize the physical diversity of East Africa by making a chart that identifies East Africa's diverse biomes and geographic features according to the countries discussed in the lesson.

Connecting Geography to HISTORY

Naming Places

What is in a name? Names of places have meaning. Sometimes places are named for famous people. Sometimes names describe something about a place or its location. In 1858 Lake Victoria was named for Britain's Queen Victoria by British explorer John Speke. Lake Turkana used to be known as Lake Rudolf. This European name came from an Austrian explorer who named it for an Austrian prince. After Kenya gained independence, it changed the name to Lake Turkana, after the people who lived there. The lake has also been known as the Jade Sea, due to its color, and Basso Narok, which means "black lake." Anam Ka'alakol, meaning "sea of many fish," was the name given to the lake by the Turkana people.

SUMMARIZING Why has Lake Turkana had so many names?

On average, 4 to 8 inches (10 to 20 cm) of rain falls annually, mostly in June, July, and August. The rest of the year is very dry. This band of dry land extends across the whole continent, from Senegal to Sudan, and into Eritrea and Ethiopia. The Sahel has been plagued with soil erosion, deforestation, desertification, and drought. Overpopulation of the area has made these problems worse.

Savanna, or tropical grassland with scattered trees, lies south of the steppe and extends east to west across the subregion. Rainfall is seasonal in this tropical climate zone, with alternating wet and dry seasons. The wettest areas are closest to the Equator. There, six months of almost daily rain is followed by a six-month dry season. Average annual rainfall is about 35 to 45 inches (90 to 115 cm). These tropical areas include Kenya, Uganda, Tanzania, Rwanda, and Burundi.

T Vegetation varies in the savanna depending on the amount of rainfall and the length of the dry season. Trees are the main feature of the landscape in parts of the savanna with greater rain and a mild dry season, while tall grasses cover areas that are drier. In general, the soils are not very fertile. On the Serengeti Plain, one of the world's largest savanna plains, there are three types of grasses: short, medium, and tall. These grasslands make this area a suitable home for millions of animals such as zebras, gazelles, hyenas, lions, giraffes, and cheetahs.

Although less extensive than the tropical and dry climate regions, midlatitude climates are also found in East Africa. The midlatitude climate zone is found in the highlands of Ethiopia and western Tanzania. The highland areas enjoy a moderate climate with comfortable temperatures and adequate rainfall for farming. Temperatures are somewhat lower, snow is not uncommon at high elevations, and there is plenty of vegetation. The highland areas, with green farmlands and protected forests, can seem almost lush.

W The diversity of landforms and climates of East Africa contributes to its diversity of resources. Tanzania contains significant deposits of gold and natural gas. Diamonds and tanzanite, used as a gemstone, are found in Tanzania. Ethiopia and Burundi have stores of gold. Copper is found in Uganda. Kenya is also rich in minerals, such as soda ash, which is used in glassmaking. The biggest agricultural exports of the subregion are coffee and cotton. In Kenya, agriculture is a major part of the economy due to the fertile soil in locations like the Lake Victoria basin. Burundi has rich pastureland as well as farmland, and is well-known for its coffee. Rwanda's major resources are agricultural, but natural gas has also been discovered there.

✓ **READING PROGRESS CHECK**

Summarizing Where are the wettest areas of East Africa?

LESSON 1 REVIEW 

Reviewing Vocabulary (Tier Three Words)

1. ***Explaining*** Write a paragraph explaining how faults are connected to the formation of a rift valley. WHST.9–10.9

Using Your Notes

2. ***Describing*** Use your graphic organizer on East Africa's physical systems to write a paragraph identifying the major aspects of the subregion's physical geography.

Answering the Guiding Questions

3. ***Classifying*** What physical features are part of the diverse landscape of East Africa?
4. ***Identifying Cause and Effect*** How have the water features of East Africa affected life in the subregion?
5. ***Differentiating*** How does the climate affect life in East Africa?

Writing Activity

6. ***Informative/Explanatory*** In a paragraph, discuss the impact of the Great Rift Valley and its features on life in East Africa. WHST.9–10.1

LESSON 1 REVIEW ANSWERS

Reviewing Vocabulary

1. Paragraphs will differ but should include how faults in Earth's crust were formed when tectonic plates beneath the surface began to move, then became a rift valley as cracks began to form in the surface.

Using Your Notes

2. Paragraphs will differ but should include plains such as the Serengeti; plateaus like the Ethiopian Plateau with gorges; the Ruwenzori Mountains and the volcanic Kilimanjaro and Mount Kenya; the Great Rift Valley; Lake Victoria, Lake Tanganyika, and Lake Turkana.

Answering the Guiding Questions

3. Mountains, plateaus, plains, escarpments, *ambas*, gorges, coastlines, rivers, and lakes.
4. The water features in East Africa help determine where people will live because they support farming and fishing, provide power and transportation, and water for humans and animals.
5. The climate and how much rainfall an area receives determines where people will live, what crops can be grown, and the economic activities in the area.

Writing Activity

6. Paragraphs will differ but should include the creation of valleys where lakes lie, such as Lake Victoria and Lake Tanganyika, and mountains such as the Ruwenzori Mountains and the volcanic Kilimanjaro and Mount Kenya.

ANSWERS, p. 510

✓ **READING PROGRESS CHECK** The wettest areas are close to the Equator in the savanna, or tropical grasslands area, and in the midlatitude areas of the highlands.

Connecting Geography Lake Turkana has had many names that reflect the different peoples that have occupied the area from European colonialism to independence, including a variety of names given to it by local peoples.

networks
There's More Online!

- ☑ **TIME LINE** A Cultural Crossroads
- ☑ **IMAGE** Traditional Villagers
- ☑ **IMAGE** Colorful City Bus
- ☑ **IMAGE** Mining
- ☑ **INTERACTIVE SELF-CHECK QUIZ**
- ☑ **VIDEO** Human Geography of East Africa

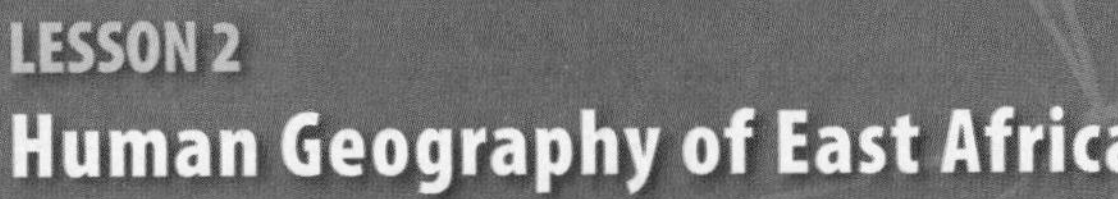

LESSON 2
Human Geography of East Africa

ESSENTIAL QUESTION • *How do physical systems and human systems shape a place?*

Reading **HELP**DESK 

Academic Vocabulary (Tier Two Words)
- **approximately**
- **incorporate**
- **export**

Content Vocabulary (Tier Three Words)
- **indigenous**
- **lingua franca**
- **overfarming**

TAKING NOTES: ***Key Ideas and Details***

SUMMARIZING As you read about the human geography of East Africa, use a graphic organizer like the one below to identify key events in the history of the subregion.

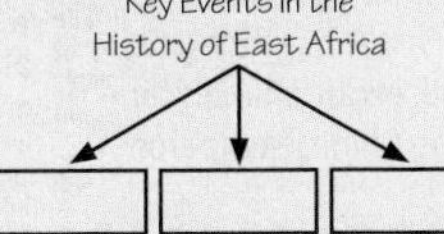

It Matters Because

The population of East Africa dates far back in the archaeological record to the first humans. Much later, traders introduced cultures from other parts of the world, and eventually Europeans colonized the subregion. The current countries of East Africa gained independence beginning in 1962. 

History and Government

GUIDING QUESTION *What cultures have influenced life in East Africa?*

East Africa contains fossils of prehumans that date back millions of years. Archaeologists have uncovered such fossils that are more than 3.2 million years old in the Awash River Valley in Ethiopia. In Kenya, in the area of Lake Turkana, they have found prehuman fossils that are 2.6 million years old. Other groundbreaking discoveries have been made in East Africa, including footprints of prehumans who walked the land approximately 1.5 million years ago. **T**

In more recent times, East Africa's location, with borders on the Red Sea and the Indian Ocean, has made trade important. Living along the Red Sea coast near the Arabian Peninsula, its peoples have long had trade relationships with Arabian, Asian, and Mediterranean peoples. This contact resulted in a culturally and genetically diverse population. People from southern Arabian kingdoms invaded and absorbed Eritrea in 1000 B.C., establishing the Kingdom of Axum. This kingdom stretched west into the Ethiopian Highlands. By A.D. 600 the power center shifted to Ethiopia, which then controlled much of the Red Sea coast, linking Axum to Mediterranean cultures.

Traders from the Arabian Peninsula established colonies along the coast of East Africa in the A.D. 700s, bringing with them the Arabic language and the Islamic religion. They also established the slave trade. Persians, too, began settling along coastal areas from about the A.D. 700s. Even Chinese explorers made contact with East Africa in the early 1400s. Then, in the late 1400s, the Portuguese claimed control of the area.

ENGAGE

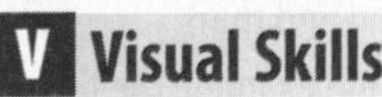

V Visual Skills

Sequencing Information Have students create a flowchart that displays how East Africa's long history of interacting with both the Western and Eastern worlds affects the life of the people of East Africa. Tell students that they will add more elements to these charts as they read this lesson.

TEACH & ASSESS

T Technology Skills

Acquiring Information Have student conduct research about the archaeological discoveries in the Awash River Valley. Their research should specifically identify the most recent archaeological discoveries and explain how that discovery fits into the history of human origins. **BL** **Verbal/Linguistic**

Content Background Knowledge

Kingdom of Axum Axum was a civilization in Africa south of the Sahara that flourished toward the end of the period of the great Mediterranean empires. It had its own writing systems and coinage and had an international reputation. It was as advanced as the Western European societies of the time. During the 1st millennium B.C. the indigenous people of northern Ethiopia developed close ties with their neighbors across the Red Sea, absorbing elements of Arabian culture into their local traditions. By A.D. 100 Arabs had exploited this ideal trading location, between the Red Sea and the Indian Ocean, to found Axum. At the height of its power, from the A.D. 3rd to the 6th centuries, Axum was the dominant trading power in eastern Africa. Its Red Sea port, Adulis, received a continuous stream of merchants from Egypt, Greece, Rome, and Arabia.

networks Online Teaching Options

 **INTERACTIVE BELLRINGER**

East Africa: European Colonization

Interpreting a Table Working with a partner, have students use the introductory text and the table of East African countries to discuss the influence of European colonialism on the people of East Africa today. Ask pairs to discuss and answer each question. Then, review each question in a class discussion. **ELL** **Visual/Spatial, Interpersonal**

East Africa: European Colonization

Beginning in the 1880s, European powers divided Africa into colonies. Countries later gained their independence, but colonial influences remain.

Country	Independence	From	Official Language(s)	Other Language(s)
Burundi	1962	Belgian administered UN trusteeship	Kirundi, French, Swahili	
Eritrea	1993	UN-established autonomous region within Ethiopia	Tigrinya, Arabic, English	Tigre, Kunama, Afar, other Cushitic languages
Ethiopia	NA	only colonial rule was Italian occupation, 1936-1941	Amarigna, English, Arabic	Oromigna, Somaligna, Tigrigna, others
Kenya	1963	UK	English, Swahili	Numerous indigenous languages
Rwanda	1962	Belgian administered UN trusteeship	Kinyarwanda, French, English	Swahili
Tanzania*	1960s	UK, and UK-administered UN trusteeship	Swahili, English	Arabic, local languages
Uganda	1962	Great Britain	English	Niger-Congo languages, Nilo-Saharan languages, Swahili, Arabic

* Tanzania formed from merger of Tanganyika and Zanzibar, 1964

Auto-Play | Click Through | 1 of 3

ANSWERS, p. 511

TAKING NOTES: East Africa has prehuman fossils that date back millions of years; East Africa has had long trade relationships with Arabian, Asian, and Mediterranean peoples; People from Arabian kingdoms established the Kingdom of Axum in 1000 B.C. and by A.D. 600 controlled much of the Red Sea coast, linking Axum and Mediterranean cultures; Traders from the Arabian Peninsula established colonies in East Africa in the A.D. 700s, bringing Arabic and Islam as well as establishing the slave trade; Chinese explorers came in the early 1400s; The Portuguese claimed control of the area in the late 1400s, leading to the decline of Arab influence and bringing Roman Catholicism to Ethiopia; Britain, France, Portugal, and Germany settled in the area in the 1800s; Eritrea came under control of Italy, the British took control of Kenya and Uganda, Germany took over Tanzania, Rwanda, and Burundi; In the 1960s, most countries won independence.

East Africa

W Writing Skills

Narrative Have students read the second and third paragraphs about European colonialism and examine the time line at the bottom of the page. Tell them to think about what age in East Africa they would have liked to live in—ancient times, when the Greeks established trade networks, later when the Arabs and Iranians developed trading stations, or in the 1400s when the Europeans arrived in East Africa. Have them write an essay discussing why they chose this time period. Encourage students to include drawings with their essays.
AL Verbal/Linguistic

V Visual Skills

Creating a Chart Divide the class into small groups of students. Assign each group one of the countries of East Africa. Using the library or online sources, have students research what foreign cultures have heavily influenced their countries and how these countries were colonized. Charts should include dates, types of governments, boundary changes, and other significant historical events. Have each group present their charts in a class discussion. BL Visual/Spatial, Logical/Mathematical

R Reading Skills

Reading Time Lines Direct students' attention to the time line. **Ask:** What does the title of the time line, *A Cultural Crossroads,* tell you about East Africa? *(The region was an area where traders from many different parts of the world came to trade.)* What three cultures traded with East Africa before A.D. 1000? *(the Greeks, Arabs, and Persians)*
ELL Visual/Spatial, Verbal/Linguistic

ANSWERS, p. 512

CRITICAL THINKING

1. Merchants came from East Asia, Southwest Asia, and Europe to trade in East Africa.
2. East Africa's long coastlines along the Red Sea and Indian Ocean helped it become a center of trade and cultural exchange.

European Colonization

W

Vasco da Gama's voyage around the Cape of Good Hope in the late 1400s began the Portuguese exploration of the East African coast. The Portuguese established control over the Indian Ocean and brought Roman Catholicism to Ethiopia. Portuguese dominance led to the decline of Arab influence there, as well as to hostility toward foreign Christians and Europeans that lasted into the 1900s.

Others also made their way to East Africa. Railroads were built inland from the coast of the Indian Ocean. New medicines were discovered to treat tropical diseases and reduce health risks. Interior Africa gradually opened to immigrants from Europe and Asia who settled the region in the 1800s. A famous European explorer to the subregion was a British doctor and missionary David Livingstone. One of his goals was to end the slave trade, but he also called for Europeans to spread commerce, Christianity, and their civilization throughout Africa.

V

European powers—mainly Britain, France, Portugal, and Germany—took advantage of new opportunities. They competed fiercely to expand their empires and to protect their trade routes. In less than 40 years following 1880, Africa was divided into more than 40 colonial divisions with borders that ignored traditional tribal territories. In East Africa, present-day Eritrea came under Italy's control. With the opening of the Suez Canal, Eritrea's Red Sea location made it a valuable prize. Italy tried to establish itself in Ethiopia but was never fully successful. The British took control of Kenya and Uganda, while the Germans took control of Tanzania, Rwanda, and Burundi. Europeans also disrupted African village life by replacing traditional farming with plantation agriculture. New colonial economies focused on cash crops, such as coffee and tea, for export to world markets and ignored the crops relied upon by the people.

Colonialism created enormous problems for Africa's peoples. Some Africans attempted to resist colonial rule. Most, however, failed. Independence movements began to change the geopolitics of Africa in the 1950s. The colonies began winning self-government. Under increasing pressure, European powers granted

TIME LINE

A Cultural CROSSROADS

For centuries, traders came to East Africa from Europe, East Asia, and Southwest Asia. This trade resulted in significant cultural exchanges, as traders from these far-flung places worked with African traders.

R

▶ CRITICAL THINKING

1. ***Describing*** From which parts of the world did merchants come to trade in East Africa?
2. ***Analyzing*** How did the location of East Africa lead to it becoming a center of trade and cultural exchange?

1 A.D.

1–100 Greeks have an established trade network along the East African coast.

600s Arabs develop trading stations along the coast of East Africa and begin spreading Islam.

late 900s Settlers from Arabia and Persia found the trading city of Kilwa on an island off the coast of Tanzania.

c. 1420s Zheng He travels to East Africa, bringing back exotic animals for the Chinese emperor.

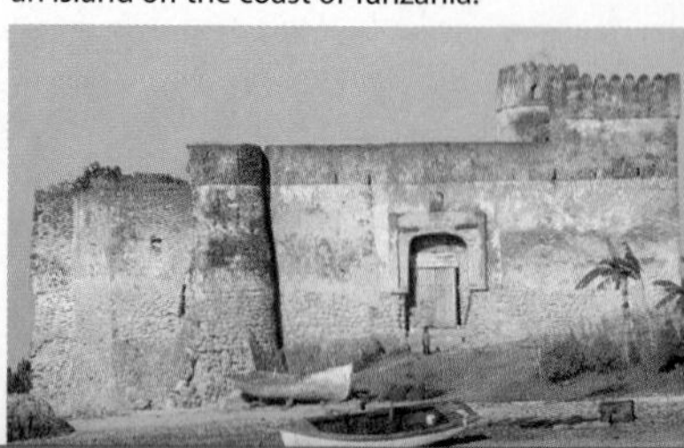

Paul Joynson Hicks/age fotostock

networks Online Teaching Options

INTERACTIVE WHITEBOARD ACTIVITY

Key Events in the History of East Africa

Summarize To reinforce information from the time line and the text, have students complete this interactive whiteboard activity. Display the graphic organizer. Have students drag each event presented to the correct location. When the time line is completed, ask students to write a brief summary of the milestones in East Africa from 2.6 million years ago through the late 1400s.
ELL Logical/Mathematical

Key Events in the History of East Africa

Directions: The population of East Africa dates back to the first humans. Later, traders introduced cultures from other parts of the world before European colonization. Drag answer choices to the appropriate box on the graphic organizer. When correctly completed, an accurate chronology of key events in the history of East Africa will be displayed.

3.2 million years old	
2.6 million years old	
1.5 million years ago	
1000 B.C.	
A.D. 600	
A.D. 700	
Early 1400s	
Late 1400s	

- Archaeologists have uncovered fossils in Ethiopia's Awash River Valley.
- Chinese explorers made contact.
- Footprints have been found of people who walked the land in East Africa.
- People from southern Arabian kingdoms invaded and absorbed Eritrea, establishing the kingdom of Aksum.
- Portuguese claimed control.
- Power center shifted to Ethiopia.
- Near Lake Turkana in Kenya, scientists have found fossils.
- Traders from the Arabian Peninsula established colonies along the coast of East Africa and began the slave trade; Persians also settled in the area.

Show Answers

a large number of colonies their independence in the 1960s. Independence, however, was not a simple cure for long-standing issues. These newly independent countries often faced internal strife and leadership issues. In Uganda, a dictator ruled for eight years in the 1970s, causing social disintegration, human rights violations, and economic decline. **C**

Conflict between **indigenous** peoples resulted in extraordinary dislocations. In Rwanda and Burundi, the colonial powers had favored the Tutsi people and had given them positions of power over the majority Hutu. In 1959, the resentment among the Hutus sparked a violent rebellion. Conflict between the two peoples continued for decades. The country erupted in violence over the discrimination against Hutus in 1994. In this violent outbreak, called the Rwanda genocide, the Hutus killed hundreds of thousands of Tutsi people. **R**

indigenous native to a place

Conflict also arose between several African countries. Major issues include the location of national borders and control of natural resources. Governments collapsed and periods of military rule followed. Famine and drought further weakened some of the newly independent countries. However, people continued to work toward nation building and improving the quality of life for citizens.

READING PROGRESS CHECK

Describing Describe some effects of European colonization on East Africa.

Population Patterns

GUIDING QUESTION *How is the population of the subregion distributed?*

With many different indigenous peoples and so many peoples coming to East Africa over the centuries, the population of the subregion is as diverse as the terrain. East Africa's population today reflects the many languages, belief systems, and ways of life that originated here and that have been introduced into this subregion. For example, European and Arab influences are everywhere. **W**

1450
1498
Portuguese explorer Vasco da Gama reaches Tanzania.
1506
The Portuguese control most of the East African coast.
1527
Portuguese cartographer Diego Ribero is the first to depict the Comoros Islands on a map.
1699
The Portuguese are driven out of Zanzibar by Omani Arabs.
1800
1840s
Muslim traders from the Indian Ocean coast exchange weapons, cloth, and beads for ivory and slaves in Uganda.

C Critical Thinking Skills

Examining Information Remind students that the colonization of East Africa created enormous problems for Africans, especially when the colonies gained their independence. **Ask: What were two issues among newly independent African nations that stemmed from colonial rule?** *(The newly independent countries of Africa fought over their national borders and the control of valuable natural resources, two issues that had previously been decided by colonial powers.)* **Ask: What can you conclude about colonial rule in East Africa? Give reasons for your answer.** *(The colonial powers made mistakes in governing. They created borders without considering traditional tribal territories, causing violent conflict after independence, such as in Rwanda and Burundi. They decided on cash crops for exports, rather than on providing farming practices necessary to sustain the needs of the people, causing economic ruin and widespread famine.)* In a class discussion, have students consider if there were any positive aspects of the colonization of East Africa for the Africans. **Verbal/Linguistic**

R Reading Skills

Defining Write the word *indigenous* on the board. Invite a student volunteer to read and define the term in his or her own words. Have students write a paragraph using the term to explain how independence affected some *indigenous* people in East Africa. Encourage students to share their paragraphs. **ELL Verbal/Linguistic**

W Writing Skills

Informative/Explanatory Have students read the paragraph under *Population Patterns* and look at the time line. Discuss with the class the various events marked on the time line. Have students write an essay discussing how they think the events shown affected the population of East Africa. **BL Logical/Mathematical**

TIME LINE

A Cultural Crossroads

Speculating As students review the time line, point out the last entry, which describes events that occurred in the 1840s. Ask students to speculate why the time line ends here and does not continue to the present day. Have pairs of students compose a short list of possible reasons, and then have them share their lists with the whole class. **AL Verbal/Linguistic**

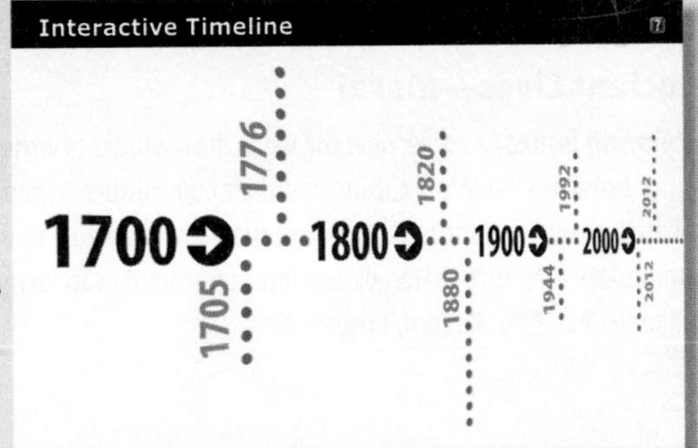

ANSWERS, p. 513

READING PROGRESS CHECK Possible answers: the creation of colonial divisions that ignored traditional tribal borders resulting in conflict; the disruption of African village life by replacing locally centered agriculture with cash crops for export that ignored crops relied on by Africans; the introduction of Christianity and conflicts it created; and the creation of national borders and control of natural resources resulting in conflict between countries.

T Technology Skills

Changing Continuity of Groups Divide the class into enough groups for each to select one of the East African countries. Explain that there are various tribes or ethnic groups that are distinct to each country. Also emphasize to students that the language traditions of East Africa are diverse and each tribe or ethnic culture often has its own language or dialect. Each group member should be assigned a specific role in this assignment, such as presenter, researcher, visual compiler, or writer. Have students conduct online research to create a slide show that provides a chart or diagram indicating where each tribe or ethnic culture is concentrated in the country, as well as a graph that shows the percentage of people speaking the languages spoken within their assigned country in the twenty-first century. Encourage students to include music or audio with their slide shows. Have groups present their multimedia slide shows to the class. **BL Visual/Spatial, Auditory/Musical**

R Reading Skills

Defining Have a student read the definition for *lingua franca* in the margin of the text. **Ask: What languages are the lingua francas of East Africa?** *(English and French)* Have students write a short essay explaining what colonialism had to do with determining the lingua franca of East Africa. In a class discussion, encourage students to share their essays. **AL Verbal/Linguistic**

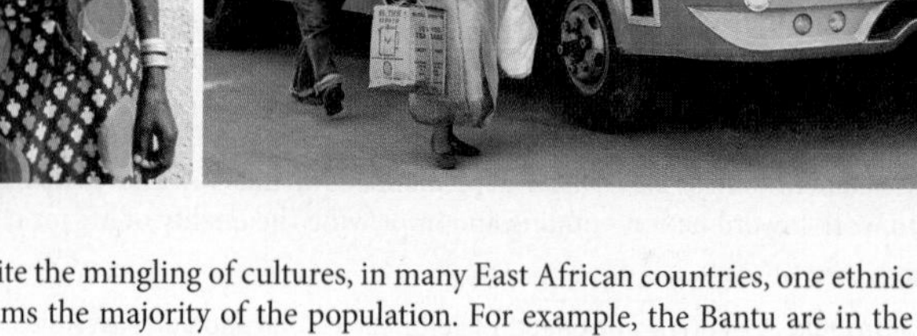

East Africa's population can be found in the cities as well as in the countryside.

▲ CRITICAL THINKING

1. ***Contrasting*** What are some differences between the nomad and the city dweller?
2. ***Drawing Conclusions*** Why do you think that most people of European descent in East Africa live in the cities?

approximately about or nearly

Despite the mingling of cultures, in many East African countries, one ethnic group forms the majority of the population. For example, the Bantu are in the majority in Uganda and Tanzania. In Rwanda and Burundi, the Hutu are the majority. In contrast, Ethiopia has more than ten distinct ethnic groups.

T East Africa is home to city dwellers, nomads, and farmers. Geography has played an important role in population distribution. Due to widely diverse land and climate characteristics, settlement is varied. Most urban centers lie along the ocean coasts or along major rivers. However, some inland cities—such as Nairobi in Kenya and Addis Ababa in Ethiopia—have developed along trade routes. Urbanization is low in East Africa, varying from **approximately** 26 percent of the population in Tanzania to 11 percent in Burundi. Fresh water is the magnet for people in East Africa. Population densities are high on the fertile lands near water since crop irrigation increases yields.

☑ READING PROGRESS CHECK

Understanding Relationships What are some ethnic groups who still influence the subregion today?

Society and Culture Today

GUIDING QUESTION *What is life like for the people of East Africa?*

With the movement of many ethnic groups through East Africa over the centuries, languages, religions, and ways of life are a mosaic of influences. However, many indigenous traditions and languages, differing religious practices, and vibrant forms of art remain in the culture of today.

lingua franca a common language used among people with different native languages

incorporate to blend or thoroughly combine

R There are hundreds of indigenous languages spoken in East Africa. Because of European colonization, however, English and French often serve as a **lingua franca**, or common language. They are spoken throughout the subregion. In addition to their religion, Islam, Arab settlers brought their language, Arabic, to East Africa, and it is a secondary language in the region. Some indigenous languages have **incorporated** European, Arabic, and other elements and are widely spoken. An example is Swahili in Kenya and Tanzania. Swahili combines elements from local Bantu languages, Arabic, Persian, Portuguese, Hindi, and English. It has tens of millions of speakers in East Africa and other areas as well.

Because of the Arab and European influences of the past, most people in the subregion are either Muslim or Christian. But traditional animist religions are

514

networks Online Teaching Options

VIDEO

Ancient Lives—Masai

Exploring Issues As they view the video, have students write down differences they notice between the Masai culture and their own culture. When the video is completed, ask them to choose one issue that they would like to know more about. Guide them to appropriate reference materials and Internet resources to further their understanding of the issues. **BL Verbal/Linguistic**

ANSWERS, p. 514

☑ READING PROGRESS CHECK The Bantu in Uganda and Tanzania and the Hutu in Rwanda and Burundi still influence the subregion today.

CRITICAL THINKING

1. The nomad lives a more traditional lifestyle, travels seasonally, and wears more traditional clothing while a city dweller uses modern technology and transportation, lives mostly in one place, and dresses in a more modern/Western fashion.
2. Most cities are along the coast, rivers, and trade routes. These are places where Europeans first settled, making them more densely populated with the descendants of those settlers. Additionally, people of European descent do not follow the traditional lifestyles found in rural areas.

also practiced. Christian beliefs spread across East Africa during the colonial period, especially along the coast where Africans had more contact with foreigners. In contrast, the Ethiopian Orthodox Church predates European contact. It is one of the world's oldest Christian churches. It began in the fourth century, when two brothers from Tyre, Lebanon, brought Christianity to the area and were allowed to evangelize by King Ezana, a powerful king in northern Ethiopia. It was the official religion until the fall of the Ethiopian monarchy in 1974. Today, more than 40 percent of the Ethiopian population belongs to the Ethiopian Orthodox Church, while about 30 percent is Muslim. Christianity remains a dominant religion in the rest of East Africa, though shifts are taking place. For example, since the end of European colonialism, Tanzania's population is fairly evenly divided among Islam, Christianity, and animist beliefs.

Levels of education vary throughout East Africa. Literacy rates are higher in urban areas, but literacy rates among rural Africans have steadily increased since independence. Literacy ranges from approximately 43 percent in Ethiopia to 87 percent in Kenya, with literacy among men consistently higher than among women. In East African countries, most children complete elementary school. However, fewer than 40 percent of students enroll in secondary school. After elementary school, students begin working to contribute to the family's income.

ANALYZING PRIMARY SOURCES

Secondary Education for Girls

Officials in East Africa are concerned about the large number of students, particularly girls, who fail to make the transition from primary to secondary school.

"Kenya's Assistant Minister of Education Honorable Beth Mugo attributes the poor transition rates to poverty, poor funding to schools, not enough secondary school teachers, inadequate classroom facilities, underemployment of school leavers, and HIV/AIDS. For girls, puberty, and early marriage are major barriers, with only one in five girls enrolling in secondary school. Any approaches to improve post primary education need to address these barriers but should equally focus specifically on girls....

'Girls who have a secondary education tend to have fewer and healthier children,' said Aster Haregot, UNICEF's Focal Point on the UN Girls Education Initiative for Eastern and Southern Africa. 'Studies ... have also shown that girls who received primary and some secondary education had lower HIV infection rates than those who did not attend school. Secondary education for girls therefore is an effective barrier against HIV.'

There are encouraging signs that countries are beginning to act. Last week, Uganda became the first country in sub-Saharan Africa to provide free secondary education to a potential target of 250,000 students. Others may soon follow suit."

—"Concerted efforts needed to improve Post-Primary Education in Eastern and Southern Africa," United Nations Girls' Education Initiative, February 27, 2007

W

Ton Koene/age fotostock

In East Africa, it is mainly women who work in the fields raising crops. This makes it more difficult for older girls to attend high school.

DBQ ▲ CRITICAL THINKING

1. ***Explaining*** How does poverty contribute to low rates of transition to secondary school among students? RH.9–10.1
2. ***Drawing Conclusions*** Why do you think girls who make the transition to secondary school have fewer and healthier children? RH.9–10.1

GRAPHIC ORGANIZER

Human Geography of East Africa

Differentiating Have students complete the graphic organizer. When it is completed, ask students to choose two of the groups of people mentioned in their notes in the graphic organizer. Ask them to write a short paragraph differentiating the two groups. Then ask them to consider the many groups of people who live in East Africa and think about how all of these varying groups coexist in the region. **Visual/Spatial, Verbal/Linguistic**

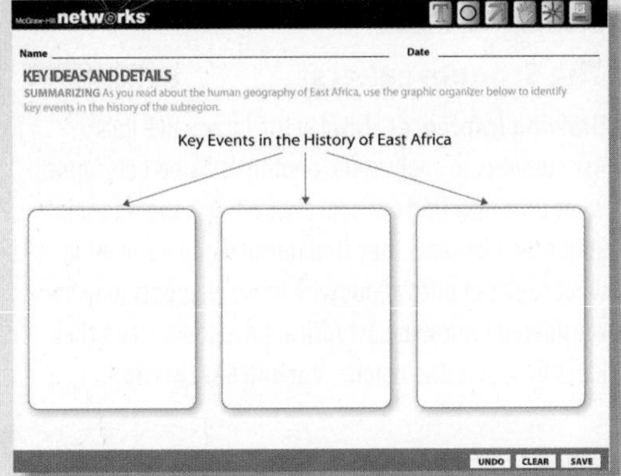

V Visual Skills

Creating Graphs Have student pairs research the literacy rates in East African countries over the past ten years. Have partners make a bar or line graph to show the statistics they find. Then in a class discussion, **ask**: **Do the countries that have more urban areas show a higher literacy rate?** *(Student answers may vary, but should name specific countries in their answers.)* **Logical/Mathematical, Visual/Spatial**

Making Connections

In approximately the A.D. 700s, it is thought that Islam had first taken hold in the East African coast, though it is not known exactly how Islam came to the region. One tradition states that the first Muslims came from Shiraz in Persia; however, most believe that Islam came from the Arabian Peninsula. This belief is widely held because the Horn of Africa is less than fifty miles away and Muslim traders often made this sea journey. These Muslim traders started settling in the area, but were not intentionally spreading their Islamic beliefs. However, they intermarried and soon the Swahili, with their unique style of dress, music, and architecture, formed a new coastal society.

W Writing Skills

Argument Tell students to imagine they are Education Commissioners in an East African government and have read the results of the UNICEF study. Some of the leading politicians do not accept the UNICEF study and there is a government debate. Students, as Education Commissioners, have to make a recommendation to the government about the study. Have students decide what they would recommend and write an essay expressing their recommendation and the reasons for their argument. BL **Intrapersonal, Logical/Mathematical**

ANSWERS, p. 515

DBQ Document-Based Questions

1. In poor families, children begin working after elementary school in order to help support the family, making attending secondary school an impossibility.
2. Girls who make the transition to secondary school marry later and become more educated, resulting in better opportunities and fewer and healthier children.

W Writing Skills

Informative/Explanatory Emphasize to students that East African people have persistent population, nutrition, and economic issues to cope with. Write an essay that identifies one of the problems East African people cope with and suggest a realistic solution that could be enacted through the United Nations or another international agency or institution. **Verbal/Linguistic, Intrapersonal**

V Visual Skills

Contrasting Visuals Tell students that they will select one country in East Africa and research images of everyday life in urban and rural areas. Have students gather a variety of images that contrast urban and rural life in the country they select. Have students present their images to the class. **ELL Visual/Spatial**

T Technology Skills

Interpreting Significance Invite a small group of student volunteers to research the origins of Taarab music and its status in the world today. Have students share their findings, as well as audio recordings of the music with the class. Then in a class discussion compare and contrast Taarab pop music to popular music in the United States. **Auditory/Musical**

ANSWERS, p. 516

CRITICAL THINKING

1. To support economic growth, East Africans use the mining of gold, copper, and other minerals; the lakes of the Great Rift Valley to support the fishing industry; wind power as an energy source for businesses; and Kilimanjaro and the Serengeti National Park to support ecotourism.
2. Some mining that takes place in East Africa is still labor intensive with people doing most of the work, using techniques and tools that have not changed over time. Hydroelectric power uses modern technologies, computers, and construction techniques to harness and control the power of a river in order to generate power.

Women in Uganda break rock to be used in construction materials.

▲ **CRITICAL THINKING**

1. ***Making Generalizations*** How are East Africans using their natural resources to support economic growth?
2. ***Contrasting*** In what way are the technologies for mining and hydroelectric power different?

Poor nutrition, famine, overpopulation, and the inability to treat common diseases are persistent issues for people in East Africa. AIDS (acquired immunodeficiency syndrome), a disease caused by the HIV (human immunodeficiency virus) has reached epidemic proportions. In Kenya, Tanzania, and Uganda, more than 5 percent of adults, the majority of them women, are infected with HIV. This disease has drastically cut average life expectancy throughout East Africa. However, new medications as well as government policies and funding have begun to change the outlook for infected people. Rwanda has been particularly successful. Most HIV-infected Rwandans are receiving treatment. In contrast, fewer than one-third of Burundi's people with HIV infection receive treatment. Access to health care, inadequate medical facilities, and a shortage of medical personnel and supplies in many East African countries remain a persistent challenge.

Family and the Status of Women

Housing varies greatly between urban and rural areas. In urban areas, most people live in high-rise apartment buildings with modern conveniences. In rural areas, many people live in thatched-roof dwellings with few, if any, conveniences.

Ways of life in East Africa are as varied as the ethnic groups who live there. In Kenya, urbanization has resulted in a more cosmopolitan population. In the capital city of Nairobi, nightclubs, movie theaters, and water parks are the norm. A very different lifestyle is found in rural communities, where 77 percent of Kenyans live. The Masai of Kenya and Tanzania are pastoralists and tend herds of cattle. They live in hierarchically organized settlements where elders make the important decisions. The growth of tourism around the national parks and game reserves, however, has brought the rural population greater access to modern conveniences, such as shopping centers and clean water supplies.

In rural farming communities, women do most of the farmwork but rarely own land. Women engage in commercial activities too, selling goods in local markets, aided by cell phones. Women's roles have remained traditional, with often-limited access to education. However, many groups are trying to change this situation. Tanzania Women's Bank, for example, was established to offer small loans and start-up capital to women. While change takes time, East Africa is seeing an increasing number of women in positions of power in business, government, and the arts.

The Arts

The visual arts of masks and textiles and music, dance, theater, and oral traditions are all expressions of East African cultures. Crafts such as basketry, ceramics, and ironwork are still important to East African tradition. African music is known around the world for its strong rhythms and unique instruments. Taarab is one type of music unique to East African. Tanzania is the home of Taarab,

networks Online Teaching Options

INTERACTIVE IMAGE

The Stonebreakers

Drawing Inferences Display the interactive image. Ask students to analyze the photograph and determine what they may find unusual about it. Ask them to think about the elements they find unusual and write down what they can infer about why those elements may be considered typical in East Africa. Have them share their ideas in a class discussion. **Verbal/Linguistic**

which blends African, Arab, and Indian musical elements played on instruments from each of these cultures. Taarab is a well-known form of pop music today in Africa and around the world.

✓ READING PROGRESS CHECK

Inferring What is the significance of the literacy rates in East Africa?

Economic Activities

GUIDING QUESTION *How is the economy of East Africa changing?*

Despite development, the majority of jobs in East Africa are in agriculture. In Rwanda and Burundi, agriculture makes up as much as 90 percent of total employment. Much of the farming in East Africa is done for **export**. Cash crops—particularly coffee, tea, spices, and cashews—are sold to other countries. In addition to **overfarming**, the emphasis on growing cash crops has created food-supply issues in East Africa. Drought and rapid population growth have made this problem more urgent. Even in countries practicing subsistence farming, food is often in short supply. R1

export a commodity produced and sent from one country to another for purposes of trade

overfarming situation in which land is repeatedly farmed so that the soil nutrients are depleted

The lakes in the Great Rift Valley support an important fishing industry. Lake Turkana is rich with a variety of fish, including tilapia, Nile perch, tigerfish, and bichir. Mining for gold, copper, and minerals is also a lucrative activity in some East African countries, such as Tanzania. The development of hydroelectric power, as well as wind power, is an increasingly important source of energy to power new businesses. R2

Tourism in East Africa is an important part of the economy, particularly ecotourism, or tourism based on concern for the environment. Kenya's ecotourism revolves around its many game reserves. In countries like Tanzania, where Kilimanjaro is located, as well as in reserves like the Serengeti National Park and other conservation areas, ecotourism is growing.

Trade between China and East Africa is centuries old. In recent years, foreign direct investment by China in East Africa's infrastructure has skyrocketed. Between 2001 and 2006, trade between Africa and China increased from about $10 billion to about $55 billion. In 2011, China accounted for 18 percent of Africa's trade, up from 10 percent in 2008.

✓ READING PROGRESS CHECK

Sequencing Information How is the economy of East Africa changing?

LESSON 2 REVIEW

Reviewing Vocabulary (Tier Three Words)

1. ***Identifying Trends*** Write a paragraph explaining how the lingua franca in East Africa is connected to the movement of peoples into the subregion. WHST.9–10.2

Using Your Notes

2. ***Summarizing*** Use your graphic organizer of key events in the history of East Africa to write a paragraph explaining the long-term effects that immigrants have had on the subregion.

Answering the Guiding Questions

3. ***Understanding Historical Interpretation*** What cultures have influenced life in East Africa?
4. ***Analyzing*** How is the population of the subregion distributed?
5. ***Identifying Perspectives*** What is life like for the people of East Africa?
6. ***Drawing Conclusions*** How is the economy of East Africa changing?

Writing Activity

7. ***Informative/Explanatory*** In a paragraph, discuss how either religion, education, or health care has impacted life in East Africa. WHST.9–10.2

R1 Reading Skills

Describing Emphasize to students that agriculture is a major industry in East African countries, yet there are food supply issues in East Africa. **Ask:** What does the word *export* have to do with food supply issues in East Africa? *(An export is a commodity traded from one country to another and East African countries export much of the food they grow.)* What does the word *overfarming* have to do with food supply issues in East Africa? *(Overfarming is when the land is repeatedly farmed so it depletes the nutrients in the soil; these crops get less nutrients from the soil, resulting in lower yields which cause food supply issues.)* ELL Verbal/Linguistic

R2 Reading Skills

Identifying As students identify the industries of East Africa, write them on the board, such as agriculture, fishing, mining, and tourism. AL Verbal/Linguistic

CLOSE & REFLECT

Sequencing Information Have students complete the flow chart they started at the beginning of the lesson. Tell students that their charts should include the history of East Africa, as well as the prominent characteristics of its people, languages, and culture.

ANSWERS, p. 517

✓ READING PROGRESS CHECK Literacy rates vary throughout East Africa but have increased steadily since independence. However, it is significant that men have a much higher literacy rate than women as a result of different standards of education.

✓ READING PROGRESS CHECK Ecotourism, the development of hydroelectric and wind power sources, and increased trade with China have changed the economy of East Africa.

LESSON 2 REVIEW ANSWERS

Reviewing Vocabulary

1. Paragraphs will differ but should include that English and French often serve as the lingua franca of the subregion, which is a direct result of European colonization.

Using Your Notes

2. Paragraphs will differ but should include that Arabia established the Kingdom of Axum and by A.D. 600 controlled the Red Sea coast, linking Axum and Mediterranean cultures; Traders from the Arabian Peninsula established colonies in A.D. 700s, bringing Arabic and Islam and establishing slave trade; Chinese explorers came in the 1400s; the Portuguese claimed control in the late 1400s bringing Catholicism to Ethiopia; Britain, France, Portugal, and Germany settled in 1800s; Italy controlled Eritrea, the British controlled Kenya and Uganda, and Germany took over Tanzania, Rwanda, and Burundi.

Answering the Guiding Questions

3. East Africa has been influenced by Arab, Asian, and a variety of European cultures including Portuguese, English, French, and German.
4. Settlement is varied, most urban centers lie along the coasts, rivers, and trade routes, but the availability of freshwater has the greatest effect on settlement.
5. Poor nutrition, famine, overpopulation, and lack of health care are common. Literacy rates vary greatly with Kenya having the highest and men overall having a much higher rate of literacy than women. Rural people are farmers and pastoralists who live in organized settlements where elders make decisions and women hold traditional roles. In urban areas there is a more modern lifestyle with opportunities in business and government for women.
6. Ecotourism, the development of hydroelectric and wind power sources, and increased trade with China have changed the economy of East Africa.

Writing Activity

7. Paragraphs will differ based on topic but could include the impacts of Christianity, Islam, and animist religions and conflict between them; lack of education especially for girls and effect on literacy and number of children; and lack of health care especially for HIV/AIDS and impact on life expectancy.

ENGAGE

V Visual Skills

Analyzing Visuals Before students read this feature, have them look at the image and, without reading any of the text, write a brief paragraph explaining what they see and how this image makes them feel. Ask several volunteers to share their paragraphs. Then tell students that sometimes first impressions can be deceiving, as they will learn in this feature.

TEACH & ASSESS

T Technology Skills

Identifying Central Issues Have students work in small groups to conduct online research to find additional background information on the Blue Nile's Millennium Dam. Remind students to use reliable sources, encouraging them to glean information from different news organizations' Web sites. Have groups take notes on the issues they identify and ask volunteers to present their findings to the class. Then have students keep their research in mind as they read this Case Study to better understand the central issues involving the Blue Nile Dam's construction.

Making Connections

To help students relate to the size of the Blue Nile Dam, ask them to think of dams near your region or dams in the United States that they have heard of such as the Hoover Dam. Then share the following information about dams to help students draw comparisons with the Blue Nile Dam.

- The 730-foot-(223-meter-) high Hoover Dam, which was constructed in 1936 on the Colorado River in Nevada, is the largest human-made reservoir in the United States.
- Egypt's Aswān Dam, which took 10 years to build and cost more than $1 billion, has a hydroelectric power plant that supplies Egypt with half its electricity.
- Completed in 2012, China's Three Gorges Dam houses the world's largest hydropower station; however, the dam has caused an increase in the risk of landslides.
- The Itaipu Dam, built between 1975 and 1982 at the Brazil-Paraguay border, is 643 feet (196 meters) high and crosses almost 5 miles (8 kilometers) over the Alto Paraná River.

C Critical Thinking Skills

Identifying Perspectives and Different Interpretations Discuss the pros and cons of the Millennium Dam. **Ask: Why do some people oppose the dam's construction?** *(They fear that the dam will reduce water available to countries downstream, such as Sudan and Egypt. Others have criticized the dam's cost and its potential negative impact on Ethiopians due to land used for agriculture.)* **Verbal/Linguistic**

SHOULD THE BLUE NILE DAM BE BUILT?

The Blue Nile River is nearly 907 miles (1460 km) long. It begins in northwestern Ethiopia and is one of the sources of the Nile River. In fact, the Blue Nile supplies two-thirds of the Nile's water. However, before it reaches the Nile, it flows over a series of rapids, making it ideal for producing hydroelectric power. In 2011 Ethiopia started construction of the Millennium Dam on the Blue Nile. When complete, this dam will be one of the largest in the world, and the water flowing through it will generate nearly 6,000 megawatts of hydroelectric power. Some of this electricity will be used in Ethiopia; some of it will be sold to nearby countries. The dam will also form one of the world's largest human-made reservoirs. When full, the reservoir will be almost twice the size of the largest lake in Ethiopia. The dam is part of a plan to reduce poverty and to secure a better economic future for Ethiopia. The government thinks that in addition to providing electricity, building the dam will create jobs.

Although support for the dam is strong in Ethiopia, there is opposition. Some critics include International Rivers, an organization that works to protect the world's rivers. This group and other critics argue that the amount of water available to countries downstream, such as Sudan and Egypt, will be greatly reduced. They are concerned that, along with a trend of decreased rainfall in the region, the dam will make water even scarcer. In addition, some fear that the more than $4 billion cost will make the project too expensive for Ethiopia. Still others believe that the dam will be harmful to Ethiopians. They predict that more and more people will be displaced as the dam is built, and that surrounding land will be used for agriculture. In spite of its many critics, building on the dam continues.

networks Online Teaching Options

MAP

Physical Map: Africa South of the Sahara

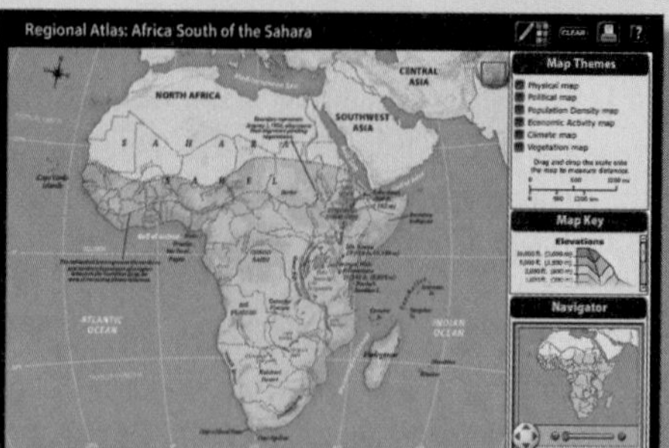

Drawing Conclusions Before students read the feature, display the physical map of the region, and have volunteers point out the Nile, Blue Nile, and White Nile Rivers. Ask students what the relationship is among these three rivers. *(The Blue Nile and White Nile feed the Nile River.)* **What is the source of the Blue Nile?** *(Lake Tana)* Discuss how the people of the countries through which these rivers flow depend on the rivers. Talk about what might happen to the land the people if one or more of the rivers changed so that less water flowed.

AL **Visual/Spatial, Verbal/Linguistic, Logical/Mathematical**

Transform Ethiopia

PRIMARY SOURCE

"When the Millennium Dam becomes operational, communities all along the riverbanks and surrounding areas, particularly in Sudan, will be permanently relieved from centuries of flooding. These countries will have the opportunity to obtain increased power supplies at competitive prices. The Millennium Dam will increase the amount of water resources available, reducing the wastage from evaporation, which has been a serious problem in these countries. It will in fact ensure a steady year-round flow of the Nile. This, in turn, should have the potential to amicably resolve the differences, which currently exist among riparian (countries near the Nile River) states over the issue of equitable utilization of the resource of the Nile water.

In other words, the Millennium Dam will not only provide benefits to Ethiopia. It will also offer mutually beneficial opportunities to Sudan and to Egypt."

—Meles Zenawi, the former Prime Minister of Ethiopia, at the official commencement of the Millennium Dam, 2011

Protect World Rivers

PRIMARY SOURCE

"While there are no known studies about the dam's impacts on the river's flow, filling such a huge reservoir (it will hold up to 67 billion cubic meters of water, and likely take up to seven years to reach capacity) will certainly impact Egypt, which relies almost totally on the Nile for its water supply. *Development Today* magazine reports that the Nile flow into Egypt could be cut by 25% during the filling period. Many fear the project could set off a water war in the region. Climate change could increase the project's many risks. **R**

The potential for conflict is probably the main reason international funders have shown no interest in supporting the project. The government says it will fund the dam itself: it has devised a scheme to sell bonds for the project, is raising taxes, and is encouraging Ethiopians to support the dam with their paychecks." **W**

—"Grand Ethiopian Renaissance Dam," International Rivers (organization whose aim is to protect rivers)

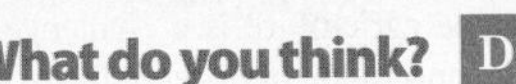

1. ***Drawing Conclusions*** Why might there be so little opposition in Ethiopia to building the dam? RH.9–10.1
2. ***Identifying Central Issues*** According to critics, what are some potential drawbacks of building the dam? RH.9–10.5
3. ***Hypothesizing*** Why do you think International Rivers warns that building the dam could result in water wars? RH.9–10.6

Case Study **519**

R Reading Skills

Using Case Studies Have students read the paragraph and list reasons in opposition to the dam's construction. **Ask:** **What evidence does International Rivers cite in support of its position?** *(A report from* Development Today *magazine states that the Nile flow "could be cut by 25% during the filling period.")* **What statement in this paragraph weakens its position?** *("...there are no known studies about the dam's impacts on the river's flow.")* **Verbal/Linguistic**

W Writing Skills

Argument Have students write an argument defending one of the primary sources in this Case Study. Students' arguments should clearly state why they think the Millennium Dam will either transform Ethiopia in a positive way or have a detrimental impact on surrounding rivers and communities. Students may wish to conduct additional research to provide supporting evidence for their arguments, but they should use only reliable online sources. Invite students to share their arguments with the class. **Verbal/Linguistic**

CLOSE & REFLECT

Summarizing Have students write a summarizing paragraph about one of the primary sources in this Case Study. Remind students to include only the main points with strong supporting evidence. Then guide a class discussion about the balance between providing power and jobs to a community and protecting and preserving its water sources.

ANIMATION

Hydroelectric, Wind, and Geothermal Power

Evaluating Use this animation to explain how renewable resources can be used to generate electricity. After students view the animation, ask which of the three types of electricity generation they think is most easily available in Ethiopia and why. If necessary, have them review the physical geography of Ethiopia before they answer the question. Discuss how generating electrical power from the water of the Blue Nile could help improve the economy and the lives of the people of Ethiopia. **Visual/Spatial, Interpersonal**

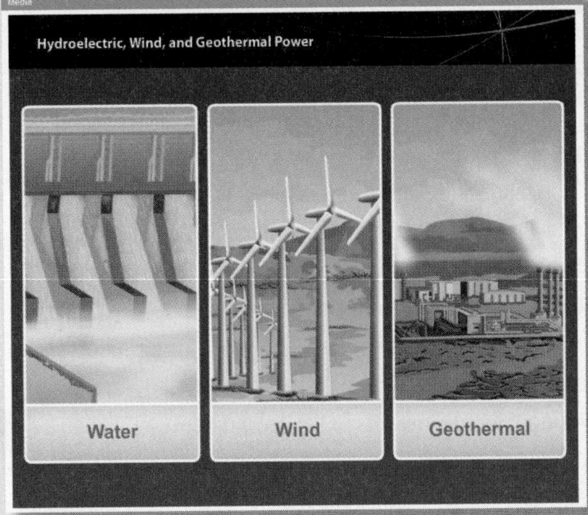

ANSWERS, p. 519

DBQ What do you think?

1. There might be little opposition to the dam in Ethiopia because it will generate huge amounts of hydroelectric power, create jobs that reduce poverty, and create a reservoir that is twice the size of Ethiopia's largest lake.
2. Some potential drawbacks to the dam are reduction of water to countries downstream such as Sudan and Egypt, displacement of people, and the cost to Ethiopia.
3. The dam and the filling of the reservoir could cause countries like Sudan and Egypt to lose a substantial amount of water that they rely on, causing conflict between the countries. Climate change that results in less rainfall would increase the risk of water shortages for these countries.

ENGAGE

R Reading Skills

Skimming Before students arrive, write **Challenges facing the people of East Africa** on the board. Have students skim through the lesson content to provide a list of these challenges. Then have students share their lists in a class discussion.

TEACH & ASSESS

Content Background Knowledge

Review HDI The *Human Development Report* is an independent publication commissioned by the United Nations Development Program (UNDP). Launched in 1990, its single goal is putting people back at the center of the development process in terms of economic debate, policy, and advocacy. It emphasizes that the goals of development are choices and freedoms. The report addresses the question of how economic growth translates, or fails to translate, into human development. The focus is on people and on how development enlarges their choices. It summarizes the record of human development over the past decades, analyzing the experience of 187 countries in managing economic growth in the interest of the broadest possible number of people.

C Critical Thinking Skills

Identifying Cause and Effect Divide the class into pairs. Assign each set of students to look up the Human Development Index report of one the countries in East Africa. Have partners make a chart showing the cause and effect of one of the problems the Human Development Index identifies for the country. In a class discussion, have each pair present its chart. **Verbal/Linguistic, Logical/Mathematical**

ANSWERS, p. 520

TAKING NOTES: War is a major cause of hunger and malnutrition as it halts economic development and causes large refugee populations which strain food supplies; Government corruption keeps aid from reaching those in need; About half of the tropical forests have been destroyed for export or fuel, destroying habitats; Savannas have been plowed for farmland to support the population, destroying wildlife areas; Hunting and poaching have also decimated the animal population; Poor farming practices, overgrazing, and deforestation have led to desertification and a reduction in the carrying capacity of the land; Rapid population growth continues to strain resources and put pressure on the land; Pollution from industrialization, urbanization, agricultural runoff, and shipping is destroying coastal and freshwater sources.

networks

There's More Online!

- ☑ **IMAGE** Refugees in Rwanda
- ☑ **IMAGE** Mountain Gorilla
- ☑ **IMAGE** White Rhinoceros
- ☑ **IMAGE** Grevy's Zebra
- ☑ **IMAGE** African Elephant
- ☑ **INTERACTIVE SELF-CHECK QUIZ**
- ☑ **VIDEO** People and Their Environment: East Africa

LESSON 3

People and Their Environment: East Africa

ESSENTIAL QUESTION • *How do physical systems and human systems shape a place?*

Reading HELPDESK

Academic Vocabulary (Tier Two Words)

- **intervene**
- **prohibit**

Content Vocabulary (Tier Three Words)

- **habitat**
- **carrying capacity**
- **poaching**

TAKING NOTES: *Integration of Knowledge and Ideas*

SUMMARIZING As you read about the people of East Africa and their environment, use a graphic organizer like the one below to summarize what you learn about how humans have affected and changed this subregion.

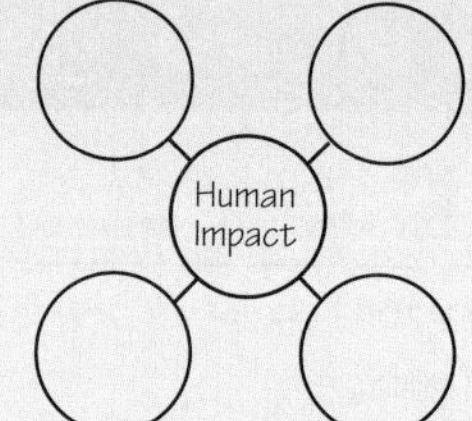

IT MATTERS BECAUSE

R *Overcoming adversity in East Africa continues to remain a significant challenge for its people. Factors such as conflict, corruption, and mismanagement compound the issues of illiteracy, health crises, and climatic problems. The will of the people to overcome adversity remains a powerful tool in meeting these challenges.*

Managing Resources

GUIDING QUESTION *What makes effective resource management in East Africa especially challenging?*

Poverty, hunger, drought, corruption, and strife all create a precarious outlook for the people of East Africa. Rising above such challenges has tested the will of these countries for decades. Survival tends to take precedence over environmental concerns. However, the failure to deal with environmental issues contributes to poverty and hunger. The Human Development Index (HDI) is a measure created by the United Nations that ranks countries based on their health, education, and living standards. East African countries rate among the lowest on this scale. Of 187 countries measured, Burundi ranked 185, while Kenya ranked the highest in the subregion at only 143. This means life expectancy, literacy, and standard of living in East Africa are among the lowest in the world.

C Developing sustainable agriculture is a challenge in this subregion. Poor cultivation practices and frequent drought have only exacerbated the problem. With the exception of Ethiopia, all East African countries were at one time European colonies. The end of the colonial period had an impact on the economy and environment in East Africa. In Tanzania, for example, under German control, farming coffee, rubber, and cotton for export flourished. After World War I and a British blockade of this German colony, the economy was left in shambles. When the Germans withdrew from their colony, the people returned to subsistence farming, rather than farming for export, and that is not sufficient to maintain a national economy.

520

networks ***Online Teaching Options***

INTERACTIVE BELLRINGER

Africa's Shrinking Elephant Population

Exploring Issues Use the introductory text and the map of the range and populations of elephants in Africa between 1979 and 2007 to understand an environmental issue facing East Africa, and to examine it from a global perspective. Have students form small groups. Ask them to briefly discuss their opinions about hunting wildlife for sport and trade. Then have them discuss both questions, writing down all answers to the second question. Have each group share its answers in a class discussion. Record responses to the second question on a flipchart or board. **Verbal/Linguistic, Visual/Spatial**

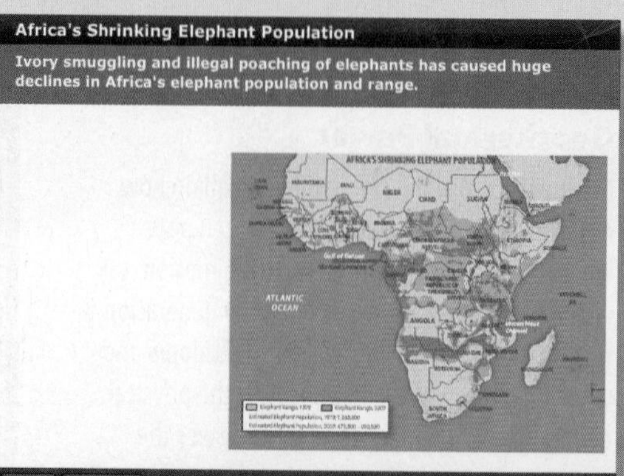

Africa's Shrinking Elephant Population
Ivory smuggling and illegal poaching of elephants has caused huge declines in Africa's elephant population and range.
ATLANTIC OCEAN
ANGOLA
Auto-Run
Click Through
1 of 2

After Eritrea gained its independence from Ethiopia in 1993, farmers in both countries worked to improve the land. In the Ethiopian province of Tigray, farmers terraced more than 250,000 acres (101,172 ha) of land. Then they planted 42 million young trees to hold the soil in place. They also built earthen dams to store precious rainwater. Grain crops thrived in their fields. In Eritrea, crops were so abundant that the government was able to reduce its request for relief from other countries by 50 percent. This all changed when Ethiopia and Eritrea went to war over their shared border. At the end of that war, Eritrea faced many challenges. The government controlled the economy, and the military was slow in allowing agriculturalists to help get farming back on track. In addition to a devastating drought, subsistence farmers were not able to produce enough food to feed themselves. The country is still working to undo this damage. T

War continues to be a major cause of hunger and malnutrition in East Africa. Since 1990, conflicts in countries such as Rwanda have halted economic development, caused widespread starvation, and cost the lives of countless Africans. Huge refugee populations fleeing war-torn areas and crossing borders into neighboring countries strain already limited food resources. The civil war in Rwanda in the 1990s between the Hutu and Tutsi resulted in the genocide of over 800,000 people, most of whom were Tutsi. Over 2 million people became refugees. Since then, Rwanda has **intervened** in neighboring countries to limit the ethnic extremism that led to genocide within its borders. This involvement, however, has taken a toll on the country by preventing attention from being devoted to managing resources and getting its economy moving. While Rwanda is a heavily agricultural society, its exports focus on coffee and tea, which are processed there. R

intervene to take action to change what is happening

East Africa has also seen government corruption. In Burundi, government corruption has kept much-needed aid from flowing into the cash-strapped country. Even in Kenya, the regional trade and finance center for East Africa, corruption has been rampant. The International Monetary Fund (IMF) stopped lending money to Kenya because it failed to put anticorruption measures in place. There was a change in government in 2002. Just when it looked as if the corruption tide was turning, Kenya went through another major corruption scandal. Despite the government's failure to prevent corruption in its ranks, lending has resumed, and the economy is slowly recovering.

☑ READING PROGRESS CHECK

Making Connections How has conflict impacted farming in East Africa?

V

The war in Rwanda, as with many conflicts in the subregion, created a refugee crisis.

◀ CRITICAL THINKING

1. ***Analyzing*** What has been the human and economic impact of war in East Africa?
2. ***Drawing Conclusions*** How do refugees destabilize surrounding countries?

R Reading Skills

Defining Write on the board the word *intervene*. Ask student volunteers to define the term and use it in a sentence. **Ask:** Can you think of a world event in the past year that caused a country or organization to intervene to change that event? *(Student answers may vary, but the event should be within the past year.)* ELL **Verbal/Linguistic**

T Technology Skills

Identifying Perspectives and Differing Interpretations Divide the class into small groups. Assign each group an East African country and have them conduct research about a recent or continual strife that has plagued their assigned country. Then divide each group into two smaller groups. Have one of the smaller groups represent the perspective of the people affected by the strife and the other group represent the people or government on the opposite side of the issue. Each smaller group should provide graphics such as photos and maps to help explain their side of the issue. Then groups should combine their work to create a multimedia report on the strife in their assigned country, identifying both perspectives to the class. Be sure groups include efforts to resolve the strife. BL **Verbal/Linguistic, Visual/Spatial, Interpersonal**

V Visual Skills

Analyzing Visuals Direct students' attention to the image of the refugees. Have students list three things the photo shows about the people and the circumstances they face. Ask students to consider what they might need to do if faced with these circumstances. Have students write a paragraph describing what they think they would do. AL **Verbal/Linguistic, Intrapersonal**

GRAPHIC ORGANIZER

People and Their Environment: East Africa

Making Predictions Students can use this graphic organizer to help them better understand how the actions of people in the past and in the present have shaped the environment of East Africa. They can also predict how people's actions may shape the environment in the future. Have students complete the graphic organizer as they read, using different colored highlighters to differentiate between past and present events. After it is complete, ask students to look at events that are currently taking place in East Africa and write a prediction about how those events will impact the subregion's future.

AL BL **Verbal/Linguistic, Visual/Spatial**

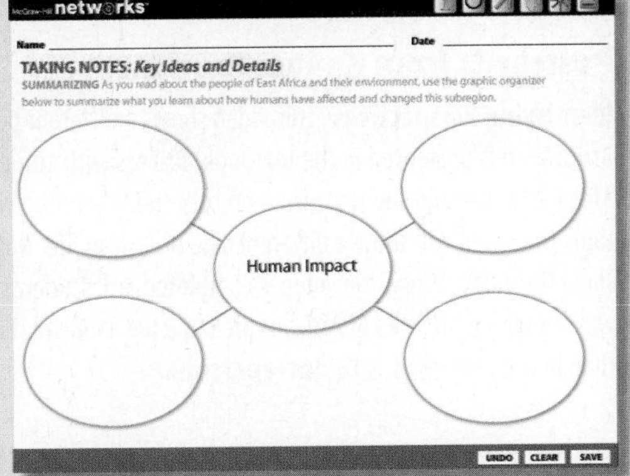

ANSWERS, p. 521

☑ **READING PROGRESS CHECK** The war between Eritrea and Ethiopia stopped the efforts of farmers to improve the land and government control after the war resulted in a slow return to farming. In Rwanda, war halted development and caused large numbers of people to flee leading to the inability to feed populations.

CRITICAL THINKING

1. War causes hunger, malnutrition, large numbers of refugees, genocide, prevents management of resources, and halts economic development.
2. Refugees strain the already limited food supply, cost the economy, and slow development in surrounding countries.

C Critical Thinking Skills

Drawing Conclusions Have students read the first paragraph on the page about tropical rain forests and deforestation. Discuss with the class the problem of deforestation in East Africa. **Ask:** **What are two causes of deforestation in East Africa?** *(The logging industry cuts valuable timber for export and because of a lack of electricity, many rural areas use wood and charcoal for heating, cooking, and light.)* **What do you think needs to be done to stem deforestation in East Africa?** *(The logging industry needs to be regulated and electricity has to be provided to rural areas.)* Based on what students have learned so far about East Africa, have them provide several reasons why they are optimistic or pessimistic that these efforts will have an impact. **Verbal/Linguistic, Intrapersonal**

R Reading Skills

Defining Discuss the definition of the term *carrying capacity* with students. Emphasize that the issue of carrying capacity is faced by every nation in the world. Have students write a brief essay in which they consider how population growth affects the carrying capacity of a land area. **AL Verbal/Linguistic, Logical/Mathematical**

W Writing Skills

Informative/Explanatory Have students write an essay describing how the interaction of environmental factors and human factors is causing desertification in areas of East Africa. Encourage students to do additional research as necessary. Then guide a class discussion in which students brainstorm possible solutions to this problem. **BL Verbal/Linguistic, Interpersonal**

ANSWERS, p. 522

CRITICAL THINKING

1. Hunting animals for sport, profit, and food along with deforestation which has destroyed animal habitats is causing many species to be in danger of extinction.
2. Students' answers will vary but they may include organized conservation efforts and increased educational programs.

Human Impact

GUIDING QUESTION *What environmental challenges does East Africa face today?*

C In 1990, tropical forests covered almost 1.5 billion acres (608 million ha) in the region. By 2000, 126 million acres (51 million ha) had disappeared, mostly due to loggers and farmers clearing the land. On the continent as a whole, about half the original tropical forests are gone. The most valuable woods have been logged for export. Also, the lack of infrastructure in many countries has resulted in the need for wood to make charcoal for cooking and heating. Lack of electricity in villages in Tanzania, for example, means people have to depend on wood for light and heat. One goal of the effort to expand access to electricity in the country is to cut back on deforestation. Various countries have also created forest reserves to protect tropical forests. Logging companies are also becoming involved, using scientific tree farming and replanting projects to protect and renew forests.

Another consequence of deforestation is the destruction of animal **habitats**, or living areas, causing many species to be in danger of extinction, or disappearance from Earth. As the subregion's population grows, farmers have moved into and cleared some forested areas. Some savannas—home to huge herds of animals, such as elephants, giraffes, antelopes, and lions—are also being plowed for farming. Hunting also threatens wildlife. During the colonial period, European hunters reduced animal populations significantly. In recent years, hunters have continued to pursue African game for sport, profit, and food.

R A combination of environmental factors and human factors, such as severe drought and poor farming practices, has been a major cause of desertification in areas of East Africa. Outdated agricultural techniques have stripped the soil of nutrients, while destruction of forests and wetlands has caused erosion. Rapid population growth has made these problems worse. As a result, in this subregion **carrying capacity**—the number of people an area of land can support on a sustained basis—has already been greatly exceeded. Despite this fact, the population growth rate remains high, further straining resources. Kenya was the first country in the subregion to recognize the problem and to put a population policy in place. Family size has been somewhat reduced since, but is still larger than in the West.

habitat area with conditions suitable for certain plants or animals to live

carrying capacity the population that an area will support without undergoing deterioration

Wildlife like the mountain gorilla, the white rhinoceros, Grevy's zebra, and the African elephant face loss of habitat and possible extinction as a result of human activities like hunting and poaching.

▼ **CRITICAL THINKING**

1. ***Drawing Conclusions*** How has the face of East African wildlife changed due to the impact of humans?
2. ***Hypothesizing*** How can human beings change the fate of these species?

W

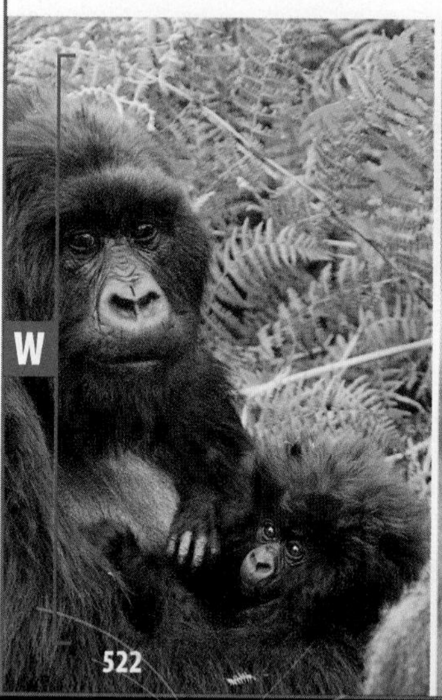

(l)Giles Breton/Flickr/Getty Images, (r)Radius Images/Getty Images

522

networks ***Online Teaching Options***

VIDEO

Postcards from Kenya: Tourism

Identifying Perspectives This video shows a different perspective of life in Africa than is presented in the textbook. Discuss with students their impression of Africa after reading the text. Then present the title of the video. Ask them if they think the video will show a different side of African life. Note their answers and show the video. When the video is completed, ask students to identify one or two ways in which the lives of Africans are depicted somewhat differently in the video than in the text. **AL BL Intrapersonal**

Because traditional pastoralists have been pushed out of the area, the soil that their animals used to fertilize while grazing has become nutrient-deprived. The lack of sustainable pasture management plans has led to the overgrazing of livestock, which has taken a toll on soil quality and prevented vegetation growth. The semi-arid areas of East Africa are most at risk for desertification.

In the early 1970s, 2 million elephants roamed the subregion. Today fewer than 600,000 remain, largely because of **poaching**, or illegal hunting. Despite being **prohibited**, the poaching of elephants for their ivory tusks causes as many as 80,000 elephants to be killed each year. Such drastic reduction in numbers put the African elephant on the endangered species list starting in 1989. Other animals at risk include the mountain zebra, the mountain gorilla, and the rhinoceros. Rhinoceroses face extinction because of the demand for their horns, which are used in traditional Asian medicine. The price of rhinoceros horn far exceeds the price of gold, which makes them a prime target for poaching.

Pollution of East Africa's shorelines and waterways is creating new challenges for the subregion. The East African coast is well traveled by oil tankers, and this is causing pollution in the reef-fishing zone. Without adequate environmental safeguards in place, increasing urbanization and industrialization are also causing damage to East Africa's waterways. Sewage treatment is inadequate. Agricultural chemicals such as fertilizers and pesticides pollute runoff water, which flows unchecked into waterways.

As the population increases in the fertile areas around East Africa's lakes, so does pollution. Lake Victoria, which provides fishing and freshwater for Uganda, Tanzania, and Kenya, has become polluted. Uganda's supply of drinking water has been extremely threatened by this pollution. Authorities have warned that part of the lake suffers from severe pollution, which will be difficult to combat. "As more algal blooms, phosphates, nitrates, heavy metals, and fecal matter all pile into the lake, it's going to be harder and harder to clean the water," warned Gerald Sawula, deputy executive director of Uganda's state-run National Environmental Management Authority (NEMA).

✓ READING PROGRESS CHECK

Understanding Relationships Describe one way in which humans have affected the environment in East Africa.

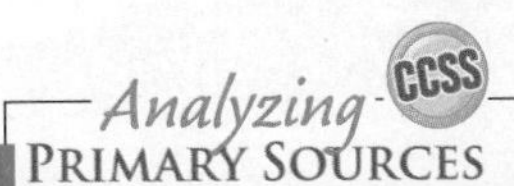

Analyzing CCSS PRIMARY SOURCES

Contrasting Views of Tanzania's Landscape

"We walked for miles over burnt out country. . . . Then I saw the green trees of the river, walked two miles more and found myself in paradise."

—Stewart Edward White, American hunter describing the Serengeti in Tanzania, 1913

"Since it takes wood to produce charcoal, Tanzania suffers an annual loss of 400,000 hectares of forests with the main culprit behind this depletion of its major natural resources being the domestic fuel demand."

—IPP Media, describing Tanzania, September 28, 2012

DBQ ***CONTRASTING*** How has deforestation changed Tanzania over time? RH.9–10.1

C Critical Thinking Skills

Evaluating Have students work with a partner to research sustainable farming in East Africa. Pairs should identify at least one problem regarding sustainable farming, describe it, and prepare an oral report on current actions being taken to resolve the problem. Pairs should include whether those actions are currently successful. Encourage pairs to include images, charts, or graphs with their oral reports. BL **Verbal/Linguistic, Visual/Spatial**

T Technology Skills

Researching Emphasize to students that as East Africa's population and industries grow, pollution of its shorelines and waterways grows as well. Have students identify one action that is currently being taken to stem the pollution of East Africa's shorelines and waterways. Have them write a few paragraphs describing that action and whether it is successful. AL **Verbal/Linguistic**

Content Background Knowledge

Initiative Global Partnership The motto for TerraAfrica is "Our Land—Our Wealth, Our Future, in Our Hands" This global partnership is spread over 23 countries south of the Sahara in Africa, located in West Africa and the Sahel, that depend on soil and water to promote their economies. However, due to large populations and poor resource management in these countries, many rivers and lakes are drying up, soil is eroding, and overused land is producing less vegetation. TerraAfrica's program goal is to integrate natural resource management in order to expand sustainable land and water management (SLWM). Its efforts are leading to economic growth and more food production.

SLIDE SHOW

Animals in East Africa

Formulating Questions This slide show highlights various animals that are indigenous to East Africa and which may be threatened by the actions of humans. As they view the slide show, instruct students to write any questions they may have regarding the different species of animals that live in East Africa, and factors which may or may not threaten their survival. When the slide show is completed, have students form small groups and share the questions they have formulated. AL **Verbal/ Linguistic, Naturalist, Interpersonal**

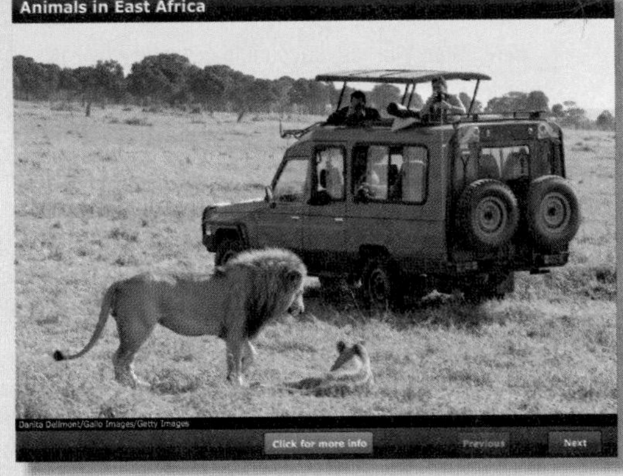

ANSWERS, p. 523

✓ **READING PROGRESS CHECK** Possible answers: hunting and poaching; deforestation for fuel and farmland; desertification by deforestation, poor agricultural practices, overgrazing; and waterway pollution by shipping, agricultural runoff, industry, and inadequate sewage treatment.

DBQ Deforestation has changed Tanzania from a paradise filled with green trees to an area that loses 400,000 hectares of forest a year, leaving the landscape dry and barren.

C Critical Thinking Skills

Identifying Continuity and Change In a class discussion have students identify the problems countries in East Africa are trying to resolve. **Ask:** **What has been a result of East Africa's preserving wildlife areas?** *(The number of tourists traveling to the area has increased.)* **What effect does the ecotourism business have on the people of East Africa?** *(The industry creates jobs.)* **Do you think ecotourism helps the protection of wildlife?** *(Student answers may vary, but should provide specific reasons to support their answers.)* **Verbal/Linguistic**

Making Connections

The African Conservation Foundation is working towards the protection and conservation of endangered wildlife and their habitats. Their mission is to change the approach of the management and utilization of natural resources through training, support, and technical assistance for conservation, nongovernment, and grassroots organizations. It also supports sustainable community projects linked with conservation and ground conservation projects.

CLOSE & REFLECT

Summarizing Review with students the challenges and issues facing the countries of East Africa. Ask students to identify two interrelated issues and describe solutions that would help resolve those issues.

Ecotourism is a growing industry in East African countries.

▲ **CRITICAL THINKING**

1. ***Drawing Inferences*** What draws people to ecotourism in East Africa?
2. ***Identifying Central Issues*** How do the profits from ecotourism help to drive conservation?

poaching illegal hunting

prohibit to forbid from doing through a law or rule

Addressing the Issues

GUIDING QUESTION *What steps are being taken to combat these environmental challenges?*

East African countries are taking major steps to preserve the environment. For example, the protection of tropical forests has become a priority. In 1999, leaders from six central African countries signed an agreement to preserve the forests. Rwanda has put effort into reforestation, planting fast-growing eucalyptus trees in previously deforested areas to help combat erosion.

Much of the land in Uganda once devastated by deforestation has been turned into national parks. One of the ten national parks there is the Bwindi Impenetrable Forest, which is home to about half the world's population of endangered mountain gorillas. This park, along with others in Uganda, was designated a UNESCO world heritage site in 1994. This designation has been applied in other areas of East Africa, bringing more attention to the subregion.

Wildlife reserves—which include Tanzania's Serengeti National Park and Kenya's Maasai Mara—have helped some animals make a comeback. Rhinoceroses and elephants stand a chance at survival because wildlife reserves are providing protection. The battle against poaching, however, will continue as long as the demand for tusks and horns exists.

The parks also attract millions of tourists each year. Ecotourism has become a big business in parts of the subregion, bringing millions of dollars into regional economies. The benefits of income and job opportunities provided by the parks are strong motivations for the local people to continue measures aimed at protecting wildlife. Ecotourism also raises international interest in the ecological concerns of the region and brings international aid and support for conservation.

✓ **READING PROGRESS CHECK**

Identifying How are people working to solve environmental issues in East Africa?

LESSON 3 REVIEW (CCSS)

Reviewing Vocabulary (Tier Three Words)

1. ***Summarizing*** Write a paragraph describing why East Africa is exceeding its carrying capacity. WHST.9–10.2

Using Your Notes

2. ***Summarizing*** Use your graphic organizer on human impact in East Africa to write a paragraph summarizing the effects people have had on the environment of the subregion over the years.

Answering the Guiding Questions

3. ***Interpreting*** What makes effective resource management in East Africa especially challenging?
4. ***Identifying Central Issues*** What environmental challenges does East Africa face today?
5. ***Drawing Conclusions*** What steps are being taken to combat these environmental challenges?

Writing Activity

6. ***Argument*** In a paragraph, explain how human interaction with the environment has exacerbated East Africa's environmental problems. WHST.9–10.1

LESSON 3 REVIEW ANSWERS

Reviewing Vocabulary

1. Paragraphs will vary but should describe why East Africa is exceeding its carrying capacity.

Using Your Notes

2. Paragraphs will vary but should describe the effects of people on the environment, including the loss of wildlife by hunting and poaching; deforestation; desertification; and waterway pollution.

Answering the Guiding Questions

3. War, corruption, and effects from colonization make resource management in East Africa challenging.
4. East Africa faces challenges with deforestation, desertification, pollution of freshwater and coastal waters, and loss of wildlife.
5. Six central African countries signed agreements to preserve tropical rain forests. Rwanda is making efforts at reforestation. Uganda has turned large amounts of land into national parks including one for mountain gorillas. Wildlife reserves along with ecotourism are helping endangered animals.

Writing Activity

6. Paragraphs will vary but should include how poor farming and grazing practices have led to desertification; how deforestation for fuel, farmland, and export destroys forests and animal habitats, and leads to desertification; how ineffective sewage treatment, agricultural runoff, shipping, and industry pollute the waterways; and how hunting and poaching has destroyed wildlife populations.

ANSWERS, p. 524

✓ **READING PROGRESS CHECK** Six central African countries signed an agreement to preserve the tropical rain forests. Wildlife reserves along with ecotourism are helping animals make a comeback.

CRITICAL THINKING

1. The opportunity to see animals that are unique to East Africa in their natural habitat draws large numbers of people to the subregion.
2. Ecotourism supports the local economy and supplies jobs to people in the area, making local populations more interested in conservation. It also draws international attention, interest, aid, and support for conservation efforts.

CHAPTER 21 Assessment 

Directions: On a separate sheet of paper, answer the questions below. Make sure that you read carefully and answer all parts of the questions.

Lesson Review

Lesson 1

1. ***Discussing*** Discuss the relationship between escarpments and cataracts.
2. ***Comparing and Contrasting*** Create a Venn diagram to compare and contrast Lake Victoria and Lake Tanganyika.
3. ***Describing*** Describe the proximity of the wettest areas of the savanna in East Africa to the Equator. Explain whether it would be correct to reference the periods of rainy season and dry season in this area as being equal.

Lesson 2

4. ***Organizing*** Create a time line that depicts invaders and power centers in East Africa from 1000 B.C. into the 1400s.
5. ***Summarizing*** Summarize the conflict between the Tutsi and the Hutu, and explain the significance of the conflict to the history of East Africa.
6. ***Summarizing*** Explain whether it would be accurate to state that literacy rates are similar across East Africa.

Lesson 3

7. ***Making Connections*** What is the Human Development Index (HDI)? Where does it rank the countries of East Africa?
8. ***Describing*** Describe the impact of deforestation on the tropical forests in East Africa.
9. ***Evaluating*** Why does poaching still exist even though wildlife preserves are working to halt this practice?

Critical Thinking

10. ***Exploring Issues*** Write a one-page essay to explain how the current-day issues in East Africa are tied to East Africa's physical geography and early history.

21st Century Skills

Use the diagrams below to answer the questions that follow.

The Great Rift Valley—A

The Great Rift Valley—B

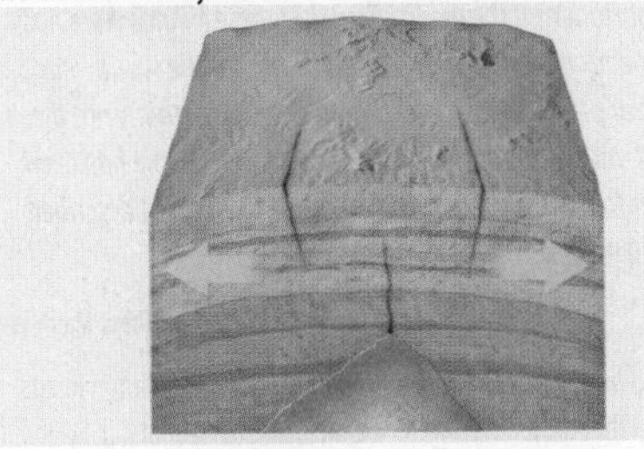

11. ***Using Primary Sources*** Describe the tectonic action depicted in these images. Explain which of the images depicts events that occurred earlier—Image A or Image B—and how you are able to tell.
12. ***Geography Skills*** Does Image A depict the Western Rift Valley or the Eastern Rift Valley? How is it possible to make this determination based on the information in the image?

Need Extra Help?

If You've Missed Question	1	2	3	4	5	6	7	8	9	10	11	12
Go to page	507	508	510	511	512	515	520	522	523	506	506	506

CHAPTER 21 Assessment Answers

Lesson Review

Lesson 1

1. Cataracts are large waterfalls formed by rivers flowing over escarpments, or steep cliffs, in East Africa.
2. Lake Victoria, as the world's second largest freshwater lake, is almost twice the size of Lake Tanganyika. Lake Victoria is shallow while Lake Tanganyika is one of the deepest lakes in the world. Both lakes are surrounded by densely populated areas, Lake Victoria for the rich soils and Lake Tanganyika for the abundant fish.
3. The wettest areas of East Africa are those closest to the Equator. It would be correct to reference the rainy and dry seasons as being equal as there are six months of rain followed by a six-month dry season.

Lesson 2

4. Time lines will vary but should include: people from Arabian kingdoms established the Kingdom of Axum in 1000 B.C. and by A.D. 600 controlled much of the Red Sea coast, linking Axum and Mediterranean cultures; Traders from the Arabian Peninsula established colonies in East Africa in the A.D. 700s, bringing Arabic and Islam as well as establishing the slave trade; Chinese explorers came in the early 1400s; The Portuguese claimed control of the area in the late 1400s, leading to the decline of Arab influence and bringing Roman Catholicism to Ethiopia.
5. Summaries will vary but should include that the colonial powers of Rwanda and Burundi favored the Tutsi people and put them in positions of power over the Hutu even though the Hutu were the majority. Once independence was gained, conflict broke out between the two groups that continued for decades. In one episode known as the Rwanda genocide, Hutus killed hundreds of thousands of Tutsi people. The conflict between these two groups has caused the dislocation of great numbers of people, strained resources and food supplies, and stalled economic growth.
6. It would not be accurate to state that literacy rates are similar across East Africa as they vary widely across the subregion with Kenya having an 87 percent literacy rate and Ethiopia having 43 percent literacy.

Lesson 3

7. The Human Development Index (HDI) was created by the United Nations as a ranking system of countries based on health, education, and living standards. East African countries rank the lowest on the scale, making the life expectancy, literacy, and standard of living in East Africa the lowest in the world.
8. About half of the forests on the continent have been destroyed for fuel and export, causing destruction of habitats and have led to animals being endangered as well as desertification and a reduction in the carrying capacity of the land.
9. Poaching still exists because of the high prices being paid for items such as rhinoceros horn, which is used in Asian medicine. Sometimes the price for horns and tusks exceed the price of gold.

Critical Thinking

10. Essays will vary but should be strongly supported with information from the chapter. Essays could include colonization based on resources, which also led to borders being set that had no regard for traditional and ethnic boundaries, resulting in conflicts that are ongoing today. War causes hunger, malnutrition, large numbers of refugees, genocide, prevents management of resources, and halts economic development on the subregion. Essays should also include the impact of colonial rule on agriculture, including the growing of cash crops while ignoring traditional food crops grown by East Africans, which still impacts agriculture and economies today.

21st Century Skills

11. Both images show the process of spreading. Image B depicts events that occurred eariler. It shows the beginnings of the tectonic plates moving away from each other.
12. Image A depicts the western branch because Lake Tanganyika is located here.

Assessment Answers

Analyzing Primary Sources

13 The killings were not the result of ancient tribal struggles as the Tutsi and Hutu had lived together for centuries before the killings took place.

14 The comparison suggests that the Rwandan genocide happened faster and was more violent.

Applying Map Skills

15 Descriptions may vary but must include the following: the Western Rift Valley cuts through Tanzania, Burundi, Rwanda, and Uganda and contains Lake Tanganyika; the Eastern Rift Valley cuts through Tanzania and Kenya and is flanked by Mount Kenya and Kilimanjaro.

16 Kilimanjaro is the highest mountain in East Africa.

17 It is approximately 800 miles across the widest part of Tanzania.

College and Career Readiness

18 Memos will differ but could include locations such as Serengeti National Park in Tanzania and Maasai Mara in Kenya to see animals of the savanna, Bwindi Impenetrable Forest to see mountain gorillas or one of the 9 other national parks in Uganda. Trips could be worthwhile because they bring attention and funds to the area, improving the economy and helping to preserve the animals. The travel to these places could leave a large carbon footprint leading to further damage, however.

Research and Presentation

19 Multimedia presentations will vary but should include maps, photos, audio, and video. It must identify Idi Amin as the dictator, explain how and why he came to power, how his reign came to an end, a summary of the impacts of the economic decline and black market on the country after his rule ended, and if a dictator with similar goals could come to power today.

Writing About Geography

20 Paragraphs will vary but should include that the mountains divide Uganda and the Democratic Republic of Congo, and that the peaks are covered in snow and shrouded by clouds, leading to them being called the "Mountains of the Moon" as they seem to touch the sky.

CHAPTER 21 Assessment

Directions: On a separate sheet of paper, answer the questions below. Make sure that you read carefully and answer all parts of the questions.

DBQ Analyzing Primary Sources

In 1998 President Clinton arrived in Kigali, Rwanda, and spoke to survivors of the Rwandan genocide.

PRIMARY SOURCE

"The government-led effort to exterminate Rwanda's Tutsi and moderate Hutus, as you know better than me, took at least a million lives. Scholars of these sorts of events say that the killers, armed mostly with machetes and clubs, nonetheless did their work five times as fast as the mechanized gas chambers used by the Nazis.

It is important that the world know that these killings were not spontaneous or accidental. It is important that the world hear what your president just said; they were most certainly not the result of ancient tribal struggles. Indeed, these people had lived together for centuries before the events the president described began to unfold."

—President Bill Clinton, Associated Press, March 1998

13 ***Interpreting*** Why do you think President Clinton insists that the killings "were not the result of ancient tribal struggles"?

14 ***Comparing*** What does the comparison President Clinton makes to the Nazis suggest about the Rwandan genocide?

Applying Map Skills

Refer to the Unit 6 Atlas to answer the following questions.

15 ***The World in Spatial Terms*** Use your mental map of East Africa to describe the locations of the two branches of the Great Rift Valley. Include the following in your description: Tanzania, Burundi, Rwanda, Uganda, Lake Tanganyika, Kenya, Ethiopia, Kilimanjaro, and Mount Kenya.

16 ***Places and Regions*** What is the highest mountain in East Africa? RI.9–10.1

17 ***The World in Spatial Terms*** Estimate the distance in miles across the widest part of Tanzania. RI.9–10.5

College and Career Readiness

18 ***Decision Making*** You've been hired by an ecotourism company. Your boss explains that she wants to develop trips to East Africa. She believes that ecotourism to this location would be worthwhile, from both an economic perspective and an environmental perspective, and she has asked you to research the potential destinations. You have been asked to develop a memo identifying at least five potential stops and the activities ecotourists would engage in at each one. The memo should also include your opinion on whether these trips would be worthwhile based on economic and environmental considerations. Prepare the memo for your boss. RHI.9–10.1

Research and Presentation

19 ***Gathering Information*** Read this statement from the chapter: "In Uganda, a dictator ruled for eight years in the 1970s, causing social disintegration, human rights violations, and economic decline." Conduct research to identify this dictator and explain how and why he came to power; a summary of the action this dictator took while in office; events that led to the end of the dictatorship; a summary of the impact of the dictator's rule; and an explanation as to whether a dictator with similar goals and objectives is likely to come to rule Uganda in the near future. With a partner, create a multimedia presentation to explain all the points above. The presentation should include maps and photos, as well as video and/or audio. WHST.9–10.1; WHST.9–10.6; WHST.9–10.7, WHST.9–10.8

Writing About Geography

20 ***Narrative*** Use standard grammar, spelling, sentence structure, and punctuation to write a narrative paragraph that describes the area around you as you travel to the top of the Ruwenzori Mountains. Describe the border created by these mountains, and explain why you think they are referred to as the "Mountains of the Moon." WHST.9–10.3

Need Extra Help?

If You've Missed Question	13	14	15	16	17	18	19	20
Go to page	513	513	476	476	476	524	526	507

526

networks Online Teaching Options

WORKSHEET

Chapter Test and Lesson Quizzes

Assessing Have students complete the Chapter Test and Lesson Quizzes to assess student understanding throughout the chapter. These assessment tools offer chapter and lesson evaluation through a variety of question formats including document-based questions.

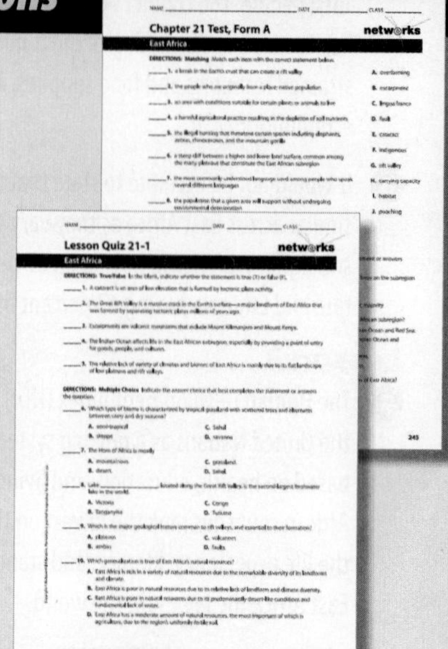

CHAPTER 22

West Africa Planner

UNDERSTANDING BY DESIGN®

Enduring Understandings

- *The characteristics and distribution of human populations affect physical and human systems.*
- *Natural resources enable the economies of West Africa to be more independent. Explain that many areas in Africa are rich in natural resources, but corruption has led to only a very small number of people benefitting from these resources.*

Essential Question

- *How do physical systems and human systems shape a place?*

Predictable Misunderstandings

Students may think:

- *The ocean is not an integral part of life in West Africa. Explain that the Atlantic Ocean provides fish, which provides food for the people of the region and is also a key source of revenue. In addition, lagoons and mangrove swamps along the coast are also an important source of crabs, clams, oysters, and fish.*

Assessment Evidence

Performance Tasks:

- *Hands-On Chapter Project*

Other Evidence:

- *Guided Reading Activities*
- *Vocabulary Activities*
- *Lesson Quizzes*
- *Chapter Tests, Forms A and B*

SUGGESTED PACING GUIDE

Introducing the Chapter	½ Day	Global Connections	1 Day
Lesson 1	1 Day	Lesson 3	1 Day
Lesson 2	1 Day	Chapter Wrap-Up and Assessment	½ Day

TOTAL TIME 5 Days

Key for Using the Teacher Edition

SKILL-BASED ACTIVITIES

Types of skill activities found in the Teacher Edition.

* **V Visual Skills** require students to analyze maps, graphs, charts, and photos.

R Reading Skills help students practice reading skills and master vocabulary.

C Critical Thinking Skills help students apply and extend what they have learned.

W Writing Skills provide writing opportunities to help students comprehend the text.

T Technology Skills require students to use digital tools effectively.

*Letters are followed by a number when there is more than one of the same type of skill on the page.

DIFFERENTIATED INSTRUCTION

All activities are written for the on-level student unless otherwise marked with the leveled labels below.

BL Beyond Level
AL Approaching Level
ELL English Language Learners

All students benefit from activities that utilize different learning styles. Many activities are marked as below when a particular learning style is highlighted.

Intrapersonal	**Naturalist**
Logical/Mathematical	**Kinesthetic**
Visual/Spatial	**Auditory/Musical**
Verbal/Linguistic	**Interpersonal**

National Geography Standards covered in "West Africa"

The student knows and understands:

(9) The characteristics, distribution, and migration of human populations on Earth's surface

9.1 Culture, economics, and politics influence the changing demographic structure of different populations

9.2 Population distribution and density are a function of historical, environmental, economic, political, and technological factors

(10) The characteristics, distribution, and complexity of Earth's cultural mosaics

10.2 Cultural landscapes exist at multiple scales

10.3 Cultures changes through convergence and/or divergence

(11) The patterns and networks of economic interdependence on Earth's surface

11.2 Patterns exist in the spatial organization of economic activities

11.3 Economic systems are dynamic organizations of interdependent economic activities for production, exchange, distribution, and consumption of goods and services

11.4 Improvements in transportation and communication networks reduce the effects of distance and time on the movements of people, products, and ideas

(12) The process, patterns, and functions of human settlement

12.1 The numbers, types, and range of the functions of settlement change

12.2 Settlements can grow and/or decline over time

(13) How the forces of cooperation and conflict among people influence the division and control of Earth's surface

13.3 Changes within, between and among countries regarding division and control of Earth's surface may result in conflict

(14) How human actions modify the physical environment

14.1 Human modifications of the physical environment can have significant global impacts

14.2 The use of technology can have both intended and unintended impacts on the physical environment which may be positive or negative

14.3 People can either mitigate and/or adapt to the consequences of human modifications of the physical environment

CHAPTER OPENER PLANNER

Students will know:

- *that West Africa has a diverse landscape and is largely a tropical region.*
- *that both salt- and freshwater features are important to the people.*
- *how a colonial history has affected governments in West Africa.*
- *how a growing population presents challenges.*
- *how economic and political factors have led to mismanagement of resources in the region.*
- *the several serious environmental issues West Africa faces and how they are being addressed.*

Students will be able to:

- ***identify** the landscapes of West Africa and its major climate.*
- ***analyze** how water sources are important to the region.*
- ***describe** colonial influence on West African governments.*
- ***analyze** challenges posed by increasing populations.*
- ***analyze** the effects of economic and political factors on mismanagement of resources.*
- ***identify** serious environmental threats to West Africa and how they are being addressed.*

UNDERSTANDING BY DESIGN®

☑ Print Teaching Options

V Visual Skills

☐ **p. 529** Students list reasons why women in many West African communities tolerate discrimination and violence.

R Reading Skills

☐ **p. 528** Students consider what gender equality may mean for women in West Africa. ELL Verbal/Linguistic

C Critical Thinking Skills

☐ **p. 528** Students discuss the meaning of *empower*.

W Writing Skills

☐ **p. 529** Students brainstorm how being in a polygamous marriage may create inequality. Verbal/Linguistic

T Technology Skills

☐ **p. 529** Students research an organization addressing gender inequality issues in a West African country. BL

☑ Online Teaching Options

C Critical Thinking Skills

INTERACTIVE MAP **Literacy Rates Among Young African Women**—Students explore the map showing literacy rates and write three statements explaining how this map relates to some of the economic challenges facing many West African countries. BL Visual/Spatial, Logical/Mathematical

MAP **Interactive Regional Atlas**—Students use the interactive regional atlas to understand the physical and human geography of West Africa.

☑ Printable Digital Worksheets

WORKSHEET **Assessing Background Knowledge**—Determine the level of prior knowledge students have about West Africa.

WORKSHEET **Chapter Summary**—Students review the main idea of each lesson of the chapter content.

WORKSHEET **Reteaching Activity**—These worksheets provide students with an opportunity for remedial practice and review of vital chapter content.

Project-Based Learning 

Hands-On

Artistic Presentation

Students will create multimedia presentations that examine the connection between place and people as seen in West African art, music, and literature. As they research, groups should gather facts and appropriate visual, auditory, and interactive content, and ideas for their presentations based on important issues in the subregion. Groups will present their projects to the class.

Digital Hands-On

Create Online Projects

Find an additional activity online that incorporates technology for this project. Visit the EdTech Teacher Web sites for more links, tutorials, and other resources.

ePals GlobalCommunity Where learners connect™

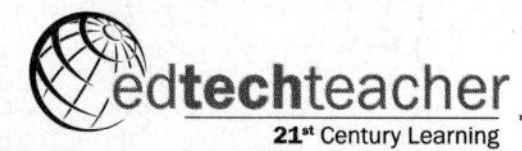

Print Resources

ANCILLARY RESOURCES

This ancillary is available for every chapter and lesson.

- **Chapter Tests and Lesson Quizzes**

PRINTABLE DIGITAL WORKSHEETS

These printable digital worksheets are available for every chapter and lesson.

- **Assessing Background Knowledge**
- **Chapter Summaries**
- **Guided Reading Activities**
- **Hands-On Chapter Projects**
- **Quizzes and Tests**
- **Reading Essentials and Study Guide** AL
- **Reteaching Activities**
- **Video Activities**
- **Vocabulary Activities**

More Media Resources

SUGGESTED VIDEOS 

- **West Africa (Worlds Together)** (25 min.)
- **Tubabs in Africa** (58 min.)
- **The Majesty of West African History** (90 min.)

SUGGESTED READING 

- ***The Portuguese in West Africa, 1415–1670: A Documentary History,*** by Malyn Newitt
- ***Onions Are My Husband: Survival and Accumulation by West African Market Women,*** by Gracia Clark
- ***West African Agriculture and Climate Change,*** edited by Robert Zougmoré, Harold Roy-Macauley, Timothy S. Thomas, Gerald C. Nelson, and Abdulai Jalloh

PHYSICAL GEOGRAPHY OF WEST AFRICA

Students will know:

- *that West Africa has a diverse landscape that includes shoreline, low plains, and highlands.*
- *that both salt- and freshwater features are important to the people of the region.*
- *that West Africa is largely a tropical region.*

Students will be able to:

- ***identify*** *the landscapes of West Africa.*
- ***analyze*** *how water sources are important to the region.*
- ***identify*** *the major climate of West Africa.*

☑ Print Teaching Options

V Visual Skills

- ☐ **p. 530** Students organize information about the major landforms found in West Africa. ELL Visual/Spatial
- ☐ **p. 531** Students create a physical map of the region, labeling major landforms. Visual/Spatial
- ☐ **p. 533** Students create maps of one of the river systems of West Africa. AL Visual/Spatial

R Reading Skills

- ☐ **p. 530** Students name and locate on a map the countries of West Africa.
- ☐ **p. 532** Students organize information about the salt water and freshwater resources of West Africa, either in note or chart form. ELL Verbal/Linguistic

C Critical Thinking Skills

- ☐ **p. 533** Students explain how an inland delta differs from a delta that empties into the sea. BL Verbal/Linguistic, Logical/Mathematical
- ☐ **p. 533** Students discuss how the discovery of oil has impacted the Niger Delta region. Logical/Mathematical
- ☐ **p. 534** Students imagine they are members of an NGO and hold a community meeting to persuade the executives of a diamond company to stop dealing in conflict diamonds.

W Writing Skills

- ☐ **p. 531** Students study the elevation profile and diagram and write a paragraph explaining the information. AL ELL Verbal/Linguistic
- ☐ **p. 532** Students write a travel brochure touting Lake Volta as a tourist destination. BL Verbal/Linguistic, Naturalist
- ☐ **p. 534** Students imagine that they are taking a trip from north to south across West Africa and create a journal describing the landscape and what they encounter. AL Verbal/Linguistic

T Technology Skills

- ☐ **p. 531** Students research the location of major lagoons and create a multimedia presentation. BL Naturalist
- ☐ **p. 532** Students research and create a multimedia presentation about how large reservoirs like Lake Volta are created. Visual/Spatial

☑ Online Teaching Options

R Reading Skills

- ☐ INTERACTIVE WHITEBOARD ACTIVITY **Water Systems of West Africa**—Students identify the location and characteristics of major waterways in West Africa.

C Critical Thinking Skills

- ☐ INTERACTIVE BELLRINGER **West African Coastlines**—Students compare the lengths of the coastlines of West African countries and explain the advantages and disadvantages of living near a water system. ELL Interpersonal, Verbal/Linguistic
- ☐ INTERACTIVE IMAGE **Lake Volta**—Students determine whether the benefits reaped from the Akosombo Dam and Lake Volta outweigh the damage caused during their creation. Verbal/Linguistic, Interpersonal

W Writing Skills

- ☐ VIDEO **Desert Camels**—Students watch a video about desert camels in the Sahara to discuss the harsh climate and landscape, and then write a brief essay about what it might be like to live in this area. AL Intrapersonal, Verbal/Linguistic
- ☐ SLIDE SHOW **West Africa's Variety of Land**—Students learn about the diverse landscape features and write a paragraph about the landform they find most interesting. AL Verbal/Linguistic

☑ Printable Digital Worksheets

R Reading Skills

- ☐ WORKSHEET **Guided Reading Activity**—Students use the Guided Reading Activity worksheets to review their comprehension of the content.
- ☐ WORKSHEET **Chapter Summary**—Students review the main ideas of the chapter content.

C Critical Thinking Skills

- ☐ WORKSHEET **Video Activity**—Students answer questions related to a topic in the chapter content after they have viewed a lesson video.

LESSON 2 PLANNER

HUMAN GEOGRAPHY OF WEST AFRICA

Students will know:

- *how a colonial history has affected governments in West Africa.*
- *how a growing population presents challenges.*
- *how ancient and modern life ways coexist in West Africa.*
- *how economic activities and conflict in the region intersect.*

Students will be able to:

- ***describe*** *colonial influence on West African governments.*
- ***analyze*** *challenges posed by increasing populations.*
- ***explain*** *how ancient and modern ways of life coexist.*
- ***analyze*** *the ways in which economics and conflict intersect.*

UNDERSTANDING BY DESIGN®

☑ Print Teaching Options

V Visual Skills

- ☐ **p. 535** Students sketch a time line of the precolonial history of West Africa. **AL** **Visual/Spatial**
- ☐ **p. 539** Students imagine they are walking along a crowded street in Lagos, Nigeria, and describe what they see. **Intrapersonal, Visual/Spatial**
- ☐ **p. 541** Students create a chart or graph that explains the differences between the three types of farming practiced in West Africa. **ELL** **Visual/Spatial**

R Reading Skills

- ☐ **p. 535** Students read and explain excerpts from Ibn Battuta's writing. **BL** **Verbal/Linguistic**
- ☐ **p. 536** Students make a list showing which West African countries were colonized, the colonizing countries, and the dates the West African countries gained independence. **AL** **Verbal/Linguistic**
- ☐ **p. 536** Students discuss events on the time line of West Africa's history. **ELL** **Verbal/Linguistic**

C Critical Thinking Skills

- ☐ **p. 536** Students discuss the ways Europeans drew colonial boundaries. **BL** **Logical/Mathematical**
- ☐ **p. 537** Students analyze Liberia's independence. **AL** **Logical/Mathematical**
- ☐ **p. 540** Students identify conditions that influence population movement. **AL** **Logical/Mathematical**

W Writing Skills

- ☐ **p. 538** Students use the information "Today's Nigerian Family" to write a population profile of Nigeria.

T Technology Skills

- ☐ **p. 537** Students find recent online news stories about West Africans dealing with tensions between ethnic groups.
- ☐ **p. 539** Students research one of the major ethnic groups of West Africa and create a multimedia presentation about the group. **Auditory/Musical, Visual/Spatial**
- ☐ **p. 540** Students gather information about the traditional arts and crafts of West Africa and create a multimedia presentation. **BL** **Auditory/Musical, Visual/Spatial**

☑ Online Teaching Options

V Visual Skills

- **GRAPHIC ORGANIZER** **Influences on African Religions**—Students discuss the major religions of West Africa, and what factors may or may not have influenced and continue to influence those religions. **Visual/Spatial**

R Reading Skills

- **INTERACTIVE MAP** **Independent Africa**—Students learn which colonies existed in Africa in 1914 and note how long it took for each country to become independent. **AL** **Kinesthetic, Visual/Spatial**
- **INFOGRAPHIC** **Today's Nigerian Family**—Students use the infographic to explore life expectancy and list possible reasons for the relatively short life span of people born in Nigeria. **AL** **Visual/Spatial, Logical/Mathematical**
- **GAME** **Human Geography of West Africa**—Students match place names or terms with their correct descriptions. **ELL** **AL** **Verbal/Linguistic**
- **INTERACTIVE WHITEBOARD ACTIVITY** **Internal Strife: Liberia**—Students match events with dates on a time line about the struggle for power in Liberia.

C Critical Thinking Skills

- **INTERACTIVE BELLRINGER** **Today's Nigerian Family**—Students use Nigerian population statistics to make inferences about the cultural values that influence the population boom and the challenges Nigeria faces as a result of it. **BL** **Interpersonal**

W Writing Skills

- **CHART** **Ethnic Groups in West Africa**—Students learn about ethnic groups, choose one group, and write a narrative describing what they think a day in the life of a member of that group might be like. **BL** **Verbal/Linguistic**

☑ Printable Digital Worksheets

R Reading Skills

- **WORKSHEET** **Guided Reading Activity**—Students use Guided Reading Activity worksheets to review their comprehension of the content.
- **WORKSHEET** **Reading Essentials and Study Guide**—Students complete the study guide and answer Reading Progress Check and vocabulary questions **AL**

C Critical Thinking Skills

- **WORKSHEET** **Video Activity**—Students answer questions related to a topic in the chapter content after they have viewed a lesson video.

People and Their Environment: West Africa

Students will know:
- *how economic and political factors have led to mismanagement of resources in the region.*
- *the several serious environmental issues West Africa faces.*
- *the ways in which national and international groups are working to resolve these issues.*

Students will be able to:
- ***analyze** the effects of economic and political factors on mismanagement of resources.*
- ***identify** serious environmental threats to West Africa.*
- ***identify** how environmental threats are being addressed by national and international groups.*

UNDERSTANDING BY DESIGN®

☑ Print Teaching Options

V Visual Skills
- ☐ **p. 547** Students explain how they might use an image of poor sanitation to argue for changes in sanitation practices.

R Reading Skills
- ☐ **p. 545** Students write a paragraph summarizing the corruption problem in West Africa. Verbal/Linguistic
- ☐ **p. 546** Students note the main causes of deforestation and how it impacts biodiversity. AL Verbal/Linguistic
- ☐ **p. 548** Students discuss how sanitation and clean water projects in the region are likely to improve the economic and social welfare of the people. AL Verbal/Linguistic

C Critical Thinking Skills
- ☐ **p. 544** Students explain the characteristics of poor sanitation and its impact. AL Logical/Mathematical
- ☐ **p. 545** Students discuss how colonialism is partly responsible for the mismanagement of natural resources.
- ☐ **p. 546** Students compare and contrast traditional systems of agriculture with large-scale commercialized farming systems. BL Logical/Mathematical
- ☐ **p. 547** Students choose a natural resource for which there is competition and brainstorm groups that are vying for it and why. BL Logical/Mathematical

W Writing Skills
- ☐ **p. 545** Students write a paragraph describing the story behind an image of women carrying firewood. AL
- ☐ **p. 547** Students research modern agricultural practices that farmers are using to improve food production.
- ☐ **p. 548** Students imagine they are living in an area of West Africa without a source of clean water and write a letter to an official explaining the effects of water scarcity and asking for help in resolving the situation.

T Technology Skills
- ☐ **p. 544** Students research a disease associated with poor sanitation. BL Verbal/Linguistic
- ☐ **p. 548** Students research water treatment processes.

☑ Online Teaching Options

V Visual Skills
- INTERACTIVE BELLRINGER **West African Street Scene**—Students discuss what environmental concerns they see in an image of sanitation issues in a West African city. ELL Visual/Spatial, Interpersonal

R Reading Skills
- INTERACTIVE WHITEBOARD ACTIVITY **Challenges of West Africa**—Students identify impact statements to match challenges depicted in photographs. Visual/Spatial, Logical/Mathematical
- INTERACTIVE IMAGE **Sanitation Problems**—Students consider the causes of poor sanitation. BL Visual/Spatial, Logical/Mathematical

C Critical Thinking Skills
- INTERACTIVE IMAGE **Deforestation in Ghana: The Next Frontier**—Students view the image and compose *Who, What, Where, Why,* and *How* questions about deforestation in Ghana. ELL AL Visual/Spatial, Verbal/Linguistic

☑ Printable Digital Worksheets

R Reading Skills
- WORKSHEET **Guided Reading Activity**—Students use Guided Reading Activity worksheets to review their comprehension of the content.
- WORKSHEET **Reading Essentials and Study Guide**—Students complete the study guide and answer Reading Progress Check and vocabulary questions. AL
- WORKSHEET **Vocabulary Activity**—Students review the chapter content and academic vocabulary words.
- WORKSHEET **Chapter Summary**—Students review the main ideas of the chapter content.

C Critical Thinking Skills
- WORKSHEET **Video Activity**—Students answer questions based on a lesson video.
- WORKSHEET **Reteaching Activity**—Students use this activity worksheet to review and reteach chapter content and vocabulary. This worksheet can be used with struggling students who need additional help with difficult content concepts.

INTERVENTION AND REMEDIATION STRATEGIES

LESSON 1 Physical Geography of West Africa

Reading and Comprehension

Assign one of the academic and content vocabulary terms to each of five groups. Have students collaborate to create a visual that relates to the meaning of their assigned term. Encourage students to get creative in their efforts to convey the term's meaning. In their visuals, students should include a sentence that demonstrates an understanding of the word and whether it has more than one meaning. Challenge students to include an example of the term and how the term relates to the lesson content.

Text Evidence

Assign student pairs one of the 12 West African countries discussed in the lesson. Tell partners to review the text to identify examples of landforms, water systems, climates, biomes, and resources in their assigned country. Tell students to present their findings in a graphic organizer, providing specific examples from the text. Ask partners to share their charts and examples with the class. Guide a discussion that allows students to compare and contrast the physical geography of different West African countries.

LESSON 2 Human Geography of West Africa

Reading and Comprehension

Have student pairs choose either the topic of colonization or decolonization and scan the text for information about their topic. Tell students to identify how their chosen topic has had an impact on the countries of West Africa. Then have students write a list of quiz questions about their topic with the answers on a separate sheet of paper. After students have had time to write their questions and answers, have them switch papers with a partner to answer each other's questions.

Text Evidence

Organize students into five groups and assign each group one of the following five ethnic groups: Yoruba, Hausa, Fulani, Ibo, and Akan. Tell students to conduct research about their assigned group to answer the following questions for a short report: In what regions does this group predominantly reside? What language or languages does the group speak? What are some of its cultural and religious beliefs? Tell students to include a visual display with their reports and present their findings to the class. Then discuss the following Guiding Question as a class: *How is life in West Africa a mix of the ancient and the modern?*

LESSON 3 People and Their Environment: West Africa

Reading and Comprehension

Have students work in pairs to use the lesson content to complete a diagram with the following headings: Health and Wellness and Environmental Issues. Tell partners to show the cause-and-effect relationship of West Africa's poor health and wellness conditions and issues involving the environment in their diagrams. Challenge students to consider poverty, polluted water, and health care costs when completing their diagrams. Invite partners to share their diagrams with the class.

Text Evidence

To help students understand the complexities of West Africa's environmental challenges, have small groups choose one of the following topics from the lesson to describe and summarize in a paragraph: drought, increasing population, deforestation, and degradation of water resources. Tell groups to explain how these factors contribute to poverty, hunger, conflict, and war in the region. Instruct students to identify evidence from the text to support their statements. Challenge students to offer one or more solutions to one of the problems outlined in their paragraphs.

Online Resources

Leveled Reader

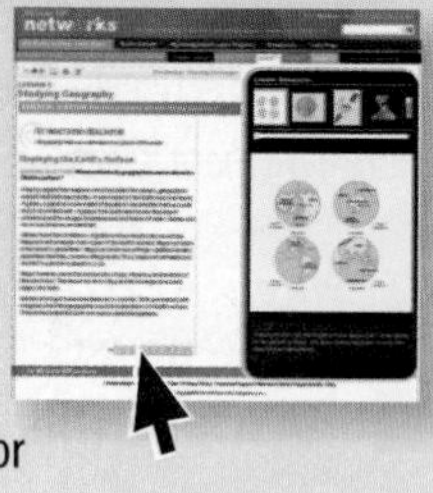

Use this online approaching-level text that corresponds directly to the text in the Student Edition. It also includes additional reading and comprehension support for English Language Learners.

Guided Reading Activities

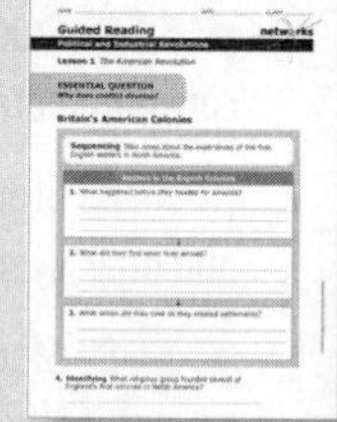

This resource uses guiding questions to help students with comprehension.

Reteaching Activities

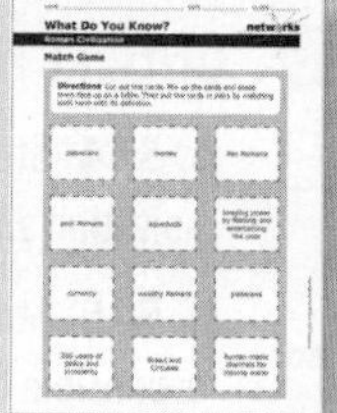

These worksheets provide students with an opportunity for remedial practice and review of vital chapter content.

Reading Essentials and Study Guide

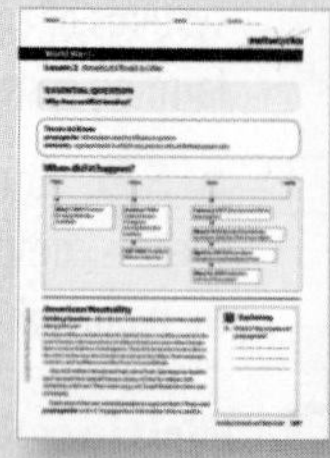

This resource offers writing and reading activities for the approaching-level student.

Self-Check Quizzes

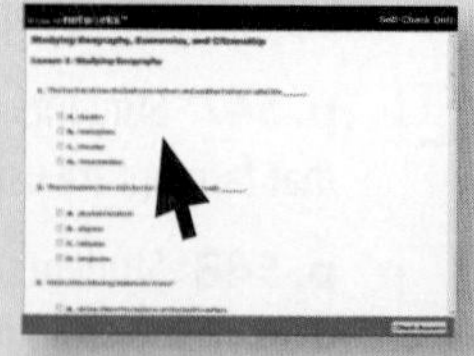

This online assessment tool provides instant feedback for students to check their progress.

Chapter Summaries

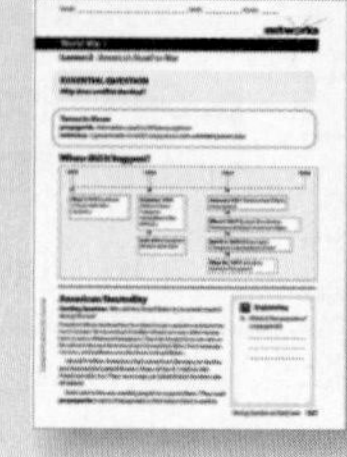

Summaries are provided for each chapter that thoroughly condense core content into manageable chunks.

West Africa

networks

There's More Online about West Africa's geography.

CHAPTER 22

ESSENTIAL QUESTION • *How do physical systems and human systems shape a place?*

Geography Matters...

West Africa is a rich land with many natural resources and a diverse cultural heritage. Thousands of years of history have influenced the many cultures throughout the subregion and continue to do so today.

West Africa, however, faces many challenges. Increasing populations, drought, deforestation, reduction in the quality of farmland, and diminishing water resources place burdens on the land and the people.

West African countries have made strides in addressing these issues, but problems persist. With the help of individuals and national and international organizations, progress is being made.

◀ A Nigerian woman in Lagos dances in an annual festival held the day after Easter.

527

ENGAGE

Drawing Inferences Display recent news stories relating to some of West Africa's pressing regional issues, such as economic growth, foreign aid, agricultural production, food or water crises, human rights violations, population growth, environmental concerns, and civil war. Challenge students to explain what clues these stories provide about the geography of West Africa.

TEACH & ASSESS

Interpreting Call students' attention to the photograph. Have students write a paragraph describing in detail what they see. Ask several students to share their written descriptions with the class. Then ask students to brainstorm what the photograph suggests about life in West Africa. **Visual/Spatial**

Hypothesizing Invite a student volunteer to read aloud the *Geography Matters* section. Lead a class discussion in which students hypothesize in what ways West Africa is both rich and poor. **Ask:** **Based on the challenges that West Africa faces, in what ways is this region rich?** *(Possible answers: It is rich in natural resources and cultural heritage)* **In what ways is this region poor?** *(Possible answers: It faces many challenges, including population pressures, drought, deforestation, loss of productive farmland, and diminishing water resources. All these challenges create economic hardship.)* **Logical/Mathematical**

CLOSE & REFLECT

Questioning Have students skim through the chapter and write four questions about West Africa that they would like answered. They should refer to the questions after studying the chapter to make sure they were answered. If not, have students do independent research to answer their questions. Use these questions to review the lesson.

Letter from the Author

Dear Geography Teacher,

Many Americans have volunteered and have helped to bring about modernization in rural areas of West Africa through participation in the Peace Corps. One of the first countries to receive Peace Corps Volunteers was Sierra Leone. You may want to use Sierra Leone as a case study to help answer the questions: Where are volunteers located? What do they do? What changes have these Americans helped to bring about in this small African country? The Peace Corps website is a good place to begin your search.

Richard G. Boehm

ePals GlobalCommunity Where learners connect™

Extend the project-based learning experience globally through our partnership with ePals. EPals allows you to connect with classrooms around the world in a safe online environment for real-life lessons and projects in virtual study groups.

ENGAGE

C Critical Thinking Skills

Analyzing Cause and Effect Discuss the meaning of the word *empower.* **Ask: What would give disadvantaged women more economic, political, and social power?** *(Possible answers: power to vote, make and control their own money, receive equal pay and job opportunities, own property, get an education, run for public office)* Then direct students' attention to the photograph. In a class discussion, **ask: Does this photograph reflect positively or negatively on life for women in West Africa?** *(Possible answer: Most would consider this a positive achievement about life in West Africa since it shows girls attending school.)*

TEACH & ASSESS

R Reading Skills

Defining Ask a student to define *gender inequality.* Then ask several students to provide examples they may have seen or experienced of the term. Broaden the discussion to what gender inequality may mean for the women in West Africa, including women who are considered economically, politically, and socially disadvantaged. **ELL Verbal/Linguistic**

Content Background Knowledge

Global Gender Gap Index The World Economic Forum's Global Gender Gap Index measures gender equality by these criteria: income, economic participation and opportunity, educational attainment, health and survival, and political empowerment. The top-ranked countries in 2012 were: Iceland, Finland, Norway, Sweden, and Ireland; the United States ranked 22. The only West African country to rank in the top 50 percent was Cape Verde at 35. All other West African countries ranked in the bottom 50 percent, with Mali and Côte d'Ivoire near the very bottom of the list.

Why Geography Matters: **West Africa**

C empowering women in West Africa

R *According to the United States Agency for Gender Development, many West African countries rank high in measures of gender inequality. Other international agencies have reported lower statistics, but the fact remains that many women in this subregion are economically, politically, and socially disadvantaged. At the same time, some West African countries and organizations are working to provide a more positive environment for women. The goal of these efforts is to empower women to boost economic development in West Africa.*

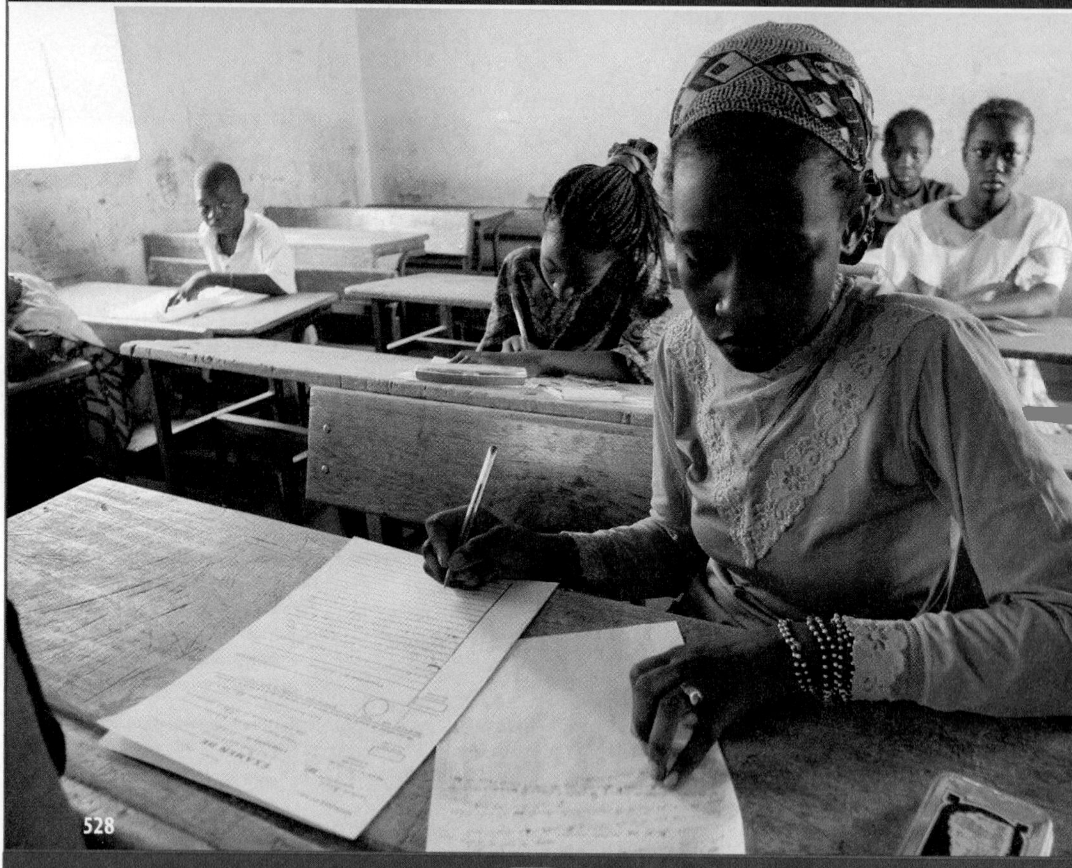

528

Project-Based Learning

Hands-On

Artistic Presentation

Working in small groups, students will create presentations that examine the connection between place and people as seen in West African art, music, and literature. Each group will focus on either art, music, or literature and will trace its origins and influences to its present form. Each group will be responsible for researching and sharing their findings with the class in a multimedia presentation.

ePals GlobalCommunity Where learners connect™

Digital Hands-On

Create Online Projects

Find an additional activity online that incorporates technology for this project. Visit the EdTech Teacher Web sites for more links, tutorials, and other resources.

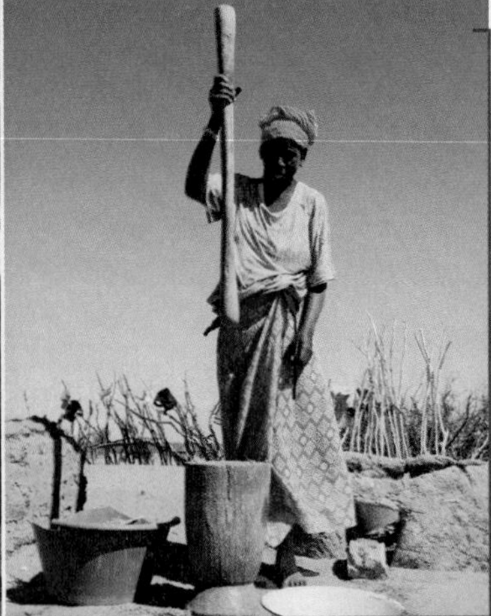

(l)Kimberley Coole/Lonely Planet Images/Getty Images, (c)Christian Aslund/Lonely Planet Images/Getty Images, (r)©Godong/Robert Harding World Imagery/Corbis

What challenges do women in West Africa face?

Women in West Africa are equal to men under the law. In reality, however, they face many hardships. Many are forced into marrying much older men at a young age. When women marry early, they have few opportunities for education. Some of these women are in polygamous marriages. Polygamy is the practice of having more than one spouse at a time. While illegal in some parts of the world, polygamy is a cultural and religious tradition in many others. It is legal in parts of West Africa. Polygamy is particularly common in agricultural societies where women do most of the farmwork. Multiple wives and their children provide the labor necessary for a man to expand his agricultural holdings. Polygamous marriages offer little financial security to women. **W**

Studies show that when women are able to earn income or receive benefit payments, they spend more money on education and health care for their children. This promotes economic growth and development.

1. **Human Systems** How does tradition in West Africa affect women's rights?

Why do these conditions exist?

Despite efforts to improve the status of women, discrimination and other challenges persist. Many gender inequalities are deeply rooted in cultural and religious beliefs and practices across West Africa. These traditions support limiting opportunities for women and girls in education, the economy, and political life. Rural areas of West Africa are more likely to hold onto traditional ways of life. Additionally, it is more difficult to monitor and enforce laws in rural areas. Fewer opportunities for education and health care are available in the countryside, and transportation to cities is often difficult and expensive. Isolated, the women of rural West Africa have few options.

These deeply held traditions and beliefs have prevented some countries from signing the Maputo Protocol (also known as the Protocol to the African Charter on Human and Peoples' Rights on the Rights of Women in Africa), which took effect in 2005. The goal of the protocol is to end discrimination and violence against women while also promoting women's rights in Africa. However, some countries have refused to sign or ratify the protocol, citing issues with its stances on polygamy, contraception, and abortion.

2. **Human Systems** Why have some West Africans been resistant to supporting the equality of women?

What steps have been taken to address these issues?

Organizations such as the Office of the United Nations High Commissioner for Refugees are working to change the nationality laws for states that do not provide equal rights to women. Gender inequality in nationality laws can prevent women from passing on their citizenship to their children. Children without citizenship face many problems, including little or no access to education and health care. Sierra Leone is one West African country that has made partial reform in this area.

V In 2012 the New Partnership for Africa's Development (NEPAD) and the Economic Community for West African States (ECOWAS) signed an agreement for the empowerment of West African women who live in rural areas. This grant of one million euros will offer funding for an organization that supports African female entrepreneurs in agriculture and related endeavors. **T**

3. **Places and Regions** How have other regions around the world worked to promote change and boost economic development for West African women?

THERE'S MORE ONLINE 

VIEW a West African gender population map • *READ* about the changing lives of West African women

Why Geography Matters **529**

W Writing Skills

Argument Challenge students to explain how women in West Africa could be equal to men under the law, yet in reality not equal at all. Have students brainstorm how being in a polygamous marriage creates inequality. Then have students write two or three paragraphs describing the reasons for polygamous practices in West Africa. **Verbal/Linguistic**

V Visual Skills

Analyzing Visuals Working with a partner, have students use the information in the text and gleaned from the image to make a list of reasons why women in many West African communities tolerate discrimination and violence. **Ask:** **Why would living in rural areas make it more difficult for women to gain equality?** *(rooted to old ways, difficult to monitor and enforce laws, isolation, etc.)* **AL** **Interpersonal, Logical/Mathematical**

T Technology Skills

Identifying Perspectives Divide the class into small groups. Assign each group a country and one of the organizations mentioned in the text. Have groups conduct research to learn how these organizations are addressing the issues facing gender inequality in their assigned country. Then have groups present a report on their country and organization to the class. **BL** **Verbal/Linguistic**

CLOSE & REFLECT

Summarizing Have students write a paragraph summarizing the status of women in West Africa and the measures being taken to address gender inequality.

INTERACTIVE MAP

Literacy Rates Among Young West African Women

Understanding Relationships Display this interactive map showing the literacy rates of women in West African countries. Click on each interactive element, discussing each section. Have students work with a partner to write three statements explaining how this map relates to some of the economic challenges facing many West African countries. Have pairs share their statements in a class discussion. Then challenge students to explain how empowering women could boost development in West Africa. **BL** **Visual/Spatial, Logical/Mathematical**

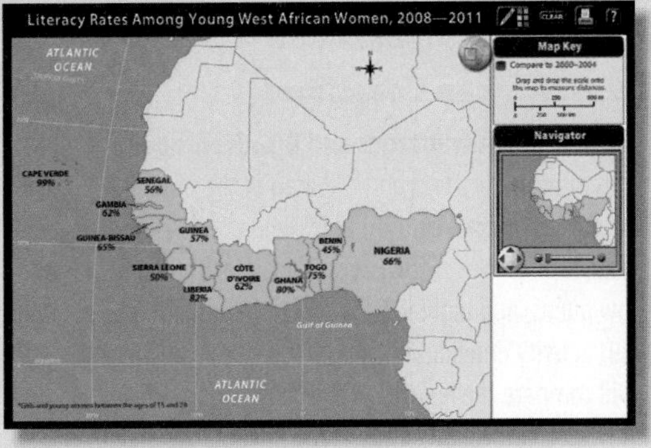

ANSWERS, p. 529

Why Geography Matters

1. Forced marriages between young women and much older men, as well as polygamous marriages, are common in West Africa. These practices keep women from being educated and having financial security.
2. Some West Africans have been resistant to supporting equality due to traditions and religious beliefs. Some of these beliefs are against contraception and abortion, which many women's rights groups support. Others are resistant because these groups support an end to polygamy.
3. Organizations like the United Nations High Commissioner for Refugees are working to change nationality laws to allow women to pass their citizenship to their children, improving the children's opportunities for education and health care. Other groups are providing funding to support female entrepreneurs in agriculture and other businesses.

ENGAGE

R Reading Skills

Naming Before students open their texts, write the first letter or letters of the countries of West Africa (B_, C_V_, C_d'_, Ga_, Gh_, Gu_, G_-B_, L_, S_, S_L_, T_). Challenge students to name the countries. Display a map of the region and ask students to locate the countries of West Africa. Point out that West Africa takes up the southern half of what is called Africa's "bulge."

TEACH & ACCESS

V Visual Skills

Organizing Have students create a chart to organize information about the major landforms found in West Africa. Students should identify the landform and its location, and describe the major characteristics of each landform. As they read the chapter, encourage students to add information to their charts. ELL Visual/Spatial

Landform	Location	Description/Characteristics
Coastal region	Atlantic Coast	sandy beaches, mangrove swamps, lagoons, coastal plains

ANSWERS, p. 530

TAKING NOTES: Land—desert, shoreline, low plains, highlands, grasslands, and rain forests; long coastlines have mangrove swamps, lagoons, and coastal plains; **Water Systems**—the Atlantic Ocean, the Gulf of Guinea, Lake Chad, Lake Volta, the Volga River, the Senegal River, the Niger River, lagoons, and mangrove swamps; **Biomes**—environments change from north to south: beginning in the north with desert which changes to semi-arid steppe, savanna grassland, and finally tropical forest

networks
There's More Online!

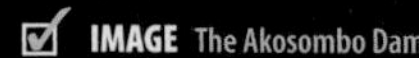

- IMAGE The Akosombo Dam
- IMAGE The Senegal River
- IMAGE Oases
- INFOGRAPHIC Elevation Profile of West Africa
- INTERACTIVE SELF-CHECK QUIZ
- VIDEO Physical Geography of West Africa

LESSON 1
Physical Geography of West Africa

ESSENTIAL QUESTION • *How do physical systems and human systems shape a place?*

Reading HELPDESK

Academic Vocabulary (Tier Two Words)
- parallel
- environment

Content Vocabulary (Tier Three Words)
- reservoir
- river plain
- conflict diamonds

TAKING NOTES: *Key Ideas and Details*

IDENTIFYING As you read about the physical geography of West Africa, use a graphic organizer like the one below to note the characteristics of the land, water, and biomes of the subregion.

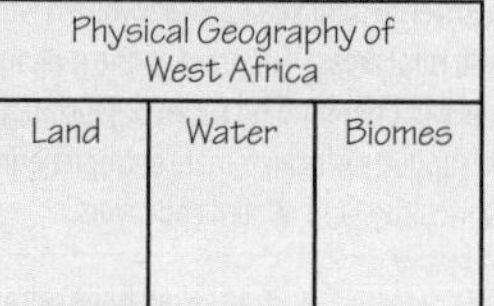

IT MATTERS BECAUSE

West Africa has a rich and diverse landscape, which includes shoreline, lakes, rivers, low plains, and highlands. These landscapes and the subregion's resources are important to the people for many reasons. West Africa is rich in resources and minerals such as oil, natural gas, uranium, gold, and diamonds.

Landforms

GUIDING QUESTION *What landforms dominate the West African landscape?*

R West Africa includes the southern half of the bulge of the African continent that extends west into the Atlantic Ocean. West African countries include Benin, Cape Verde, Côte d'Ivoire, Gambia, Ghana, Guinea, Guinea-Bissau, Liberia, Nigeria, Senegal, Sierra Leone, and Togo. The African Transition Zone cuts through the northern part of this subregion. The land in the African Transition Zone changes from deserts to a tropical savanna. All of the countries of West Africa, except Cape Verde, have part of their territory in the Transition Zone. The northern border of West Africa is the Sahara.

West Africa is a large area. Its size contributes to its considerable diversity, as does its location in the Transition Zone. West Africa is largely a tropical region with a landscape that includes desert, shoreline, low plains, highlands, and rain forests.

V West Africa has a long coastline. The coastal region is made up of sandy beaches, thick mangrove swamps, lagoons, and broad coastal plains. Lagoons are shallow bodies of water that are separated from the ocean by islands, which lie **parallel** to the shoreline. The Ebrié Lagoon is the largest lagoon in West Africa with a surface area of 218 square miles (566 sq. km). Rain forests once covered much of the West African coast. However, rain forests have been drastically reduced as land was cleared for agriculture and logging of prized hardwood trees such as African mahogany and iroko, also known as African teak.

networks Online Teaching Options

INTERACTIVE BELLRINGER

West African Coastlines

Considering Advantages and Disadvantages
This introductory text and the map of the coastline of West Africa can be used to explain the diverse landscape of West Africa, which includes shorelines, low plains, and highlands. Have students complete this activity individually or with a partner. Students will compare the lengths of the coastlines of West African countries and explain the advantages and disadvantages of living near a water system. Review each question in a class discussion.
ELL Interpersonal, Verbal/Linguistic

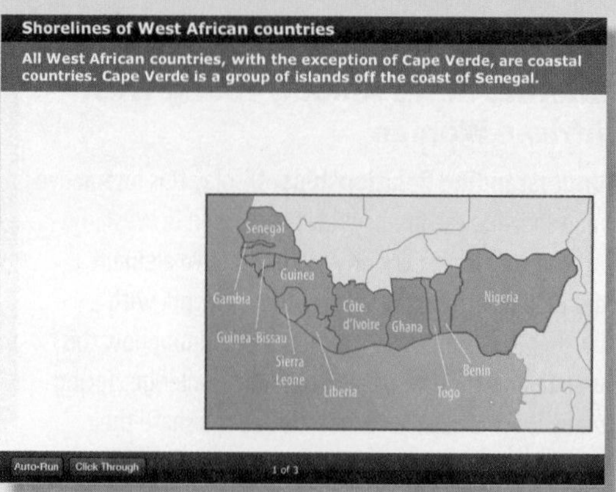

Mountains rise up behind the broad coastal plains of the subregion. In the south-central part of West Africa are the Guinea Highlands. This mountainous plateau rises several thousand feet above the coastal plains in southeastern Guinea, northern Sierra Leone, Liberia, and northwestern Côte d'Ivoire. The plateau contains the Nimba Range, the Loma Mountains, and the Tingi Mountains. These highlands are covered with savanna and rain forest.

In the southeast are the Cameroon Highlands, which lie between Nigeria and Cameroon. Forest and grasslands with a rich biodiversity cover these highlands. They form part of a chain of former volcanoes that stretch inland from the sea. The largest and only active one of these volcanoes is Mount Cameroon, which rises to a height of 13,353 feet (4,070 m).

Low plains, sandy soil, and grasslands cover much of inland West Africa. The Sahara, the largest desert in Africa, is in the north. It is a vast and nearly uninhabited region. The landforms here are shaped mostly by winds and infrequent rainstorms. They include sand dunes, salt flats, gravel plains, stone plateaus, and dry valleys.

V

parallel lying in the same direction with an equal distance between

✓ READING PROGRESS CHECK

Identifying What types of landscapes are found in coastal regions?

Water Systems

GUIDING QUESTION *How are saltwater and freshwater resources important to the people of West Africa?*

The water systems of West Africa are not only important to wildlife but to people as well. The lagoons and mangrove swamps are important parts of the coastal ecosystem of the subregion. They provide food and shelter for fish, shellfish, mollusks, wildfowl, and marine mammals. Flounder and bluefish use the

Elevation Profile: West Africa ⌄ DIAGRAM SKILLS

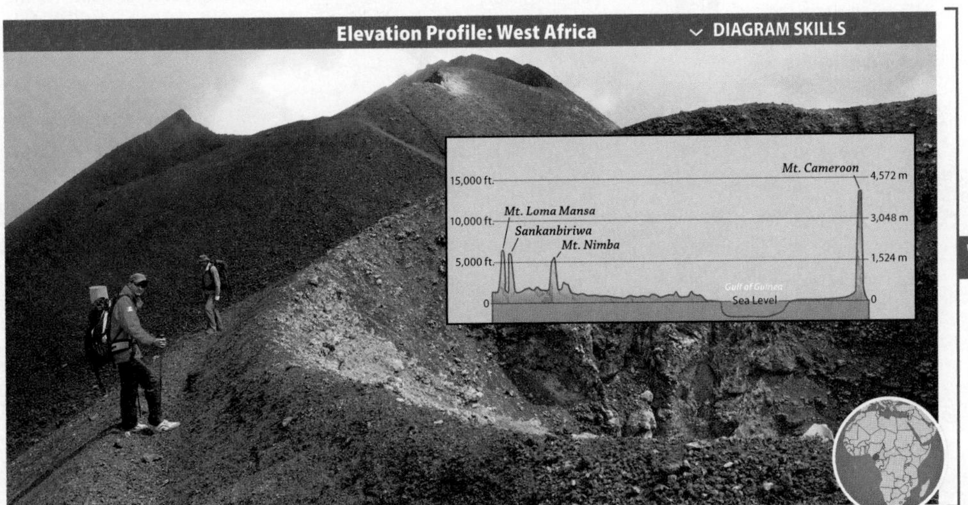

W

Mount Cameroon is the highest point in West Africa and an active volcano. It is much higher than the peaks in the Guinea Highlands.

▲ CRITICAL THINKING

1. ***Classifying*** What is the second-highest peak shown in the diagram?
2. ***Analyzing Visuals*** What appears to coat the surface of the mountain on which the hikers are standing?

V Visual Skills

Creating Maps Provide student pairs with outline maps of West Africa available in the Resource Library of the Teacher Lesson Center. Have each set of students use these maps to create a physical map of the region, indicating the location of major landforms such as any desert or coastal regions, low plains, highlands, and rain forests. Have students create a key for their maps and label major mountains and other significant landform features. **Visual/Spatial**

T Technology Skills

Researching Have students research online the location of West Africa's major lagoons and their importance to West Africa's coastal ecosystem and create a multimedia presentation. Encourage students to include images, maps, and diagrams to illustrate their reports. Have students present their reports to the class, and then use their presentations to discuss the human activities that threaten these delicate ecosystems. **BL Verbal/Linguistic, Naturalist**

Content Background Knowledge

West African Lagoons

- A lagoon is a shallow body of water protected from a larger body of water (usually an ocean) by sandbars, barrier islands, or coral reefs.
- There are no generally accepted criteria that distinguish a lagoon from a bay, estuary, or sound.
- Lagoons are highly productive ecosystems.
- Lagoons contain mostly brackish water, a mix of salt water from an ocean and freshwater from a river. Those with significant protection from the open ocean have a more freshwater habitat.

W Writing Skills

Informative/Explanatory Have students study the elevation profile and diagram at the bottom of the page. Have students write a paragraph explaining the information depicted on these visuals. **AL ELL Verbal/Linguistic**

VIDEO

Desert Camels

Making Connections Have students view this video about the desert camels found in the Sahara to introduce them to the harsh climate and landscape found in sections of West Africa. Ask students to imagine living in this region, as they write a brief essay about how the climate would affect their lives, what they would do differently than they do now, and what the positive and negative impacts of living in this region might be. **AL Intrapersonal, Verbal/Linguistic**

ANSWERS, p. 531

✓ READING PROGRESS CHECK Mangrove swamps, lagoons, coastal plains, and sandy beaches are found in coastal regions.

CRITICAL THINKING

1. Mt. Loma Mansa is the second-highest peak shown in the diagram.
2. Ash or soot appears to coat the surface of the mountain.

R Reading Skills

Taking Notes Have students organize information about the salt water and freshwater resources of West Africa, either in note or chart form. Their notes should include details about lagoons, mangrove swamps, the Atlantic Ocean, Lake Chad, and Lake Volta. Students should list the importance of each water resource to the wildlife and people of West Africa. ELL Verbal/Linguistic

T Technology Skills

Presenting Divide students into pairs or small groups. Have students research how large reservoirs like Lake Volta are created. Have groups create multimedia presentations for the class showing their online research. Presentations might include visuals showing the various phases of the construction process, from clearing the basin and relocating the residents to building a dam and releasing the water to fill the basin. **Visual/Spatial**

Making Connections

Nearly every region in the United States has water reservoirs, some on a relatively small scale and some quite large, like Lake Mead in Nevada and Arizona, which was created by damming the Colorado River (Hoover Dam). Encourage students to relate what they know about the creation and purpose of reservoirs in their region, such as flood control, hydroelectric generation, water storage, or recreation.

W Writing Skills

Informative/Explanatory Have students imagine they work for the tourist bureau of Ghana. Working in pairs, have them gather additional information about Lake Volta and then write a travel brochure touting it as a tourist destination. BL **Verbal/Linguistic, Naturalist**

ANSWERS, p. 532

CRITICAL THINKING

1. Student answers may vary, but should include that the area behind the dam would have been covered in water instead of trees and dry land, and that the area that is now lake was once covered in trees.
2. Hydroelectricity is an important resource as it is a cleaner source of energy than fossil fuels and it allows Ghana to have a more consistent power supply.

marshes as nurseries and winter habitats. Ducks, geese, and other wild birds stop over during migration. Unfortunately, due to environmental disasters such as oil spills, global warming, and clearing of the mangrove for the farming of shrimp, these swamps are slowly disappearing.

The mangrove swamps are also very important to coastal people. They provide a source of food such as crabs, clams, oysters, and fish. Even the mangrove fruits themselves can be eaten. The mangrove trees are also useful. They are often collected for firewood and can be used for construction.

The Atlantic Ocean provides an important resource for the people of West Africa—fish. Fishing not only provides food for the people of the subregion, but is also a key source of revenue. Commercial fishing is particularly important in the Gulf of Guinea, which is part of the eastern tropical Atlantic Ocean system off the coast of western Africa. In 2006 a fishery committee was established to manage fishing among the countries of Liberia, Côte d'Ivoire, Ghana, Togo, Benin, and Nigeria. All these countries share fish stocks in the Gulf of Guinea.

reservoir a natural or artificial lake used as a source of water

R Lake Chad, in west-central Africa, is bordered by Nigeria, Niger, Chad, and Cameroon. Lake Chad was once the second-largest wetland in Africa, supporting a great diversity of animal and plant life. Although Lake Chad has since shrunk by about 90 percent, it is still vital to the region for irrigation of farmland and fishing.

T Lake Volta is a human-made lake and is the fourth-largest **reservoir** in the world. A reservoir is an artificial or natural lake where water is stored and used to supply farms, homes, and businesses in the area with freshwater. The lake was made by damming the Volta River, and its creation flooded more than 700 villages, forcing over 70,000 people to find new homes. The trade-off is that W it has provided a consistent source of freshwater and electricity. Recently a project has begun to try to harvest the trees that were submerged when the lake was created. This project will provide additional revenue and work for the people of the region. Another new industry in the region is tourism. The town of Akosombo, which grew around the dam, is the starting point for many fishing excursions and for water sports. Fishing for Volta perch, African tiger fish, Nile tilapia, and several varieties of catfish is a favorite of charter expeditions.

Lake Volta, an artificial lake, was formed by the Akosombo Dam. Today the dam provides electricity for most of Ghana's needs.

▼ CRITICAL THINKING

1. ***Analyzing Visuals*** How do you suppose the landscape shown in the photo contrasts with its appearance before the construction of the Akosombo Dam?
2. ***Explaining*** Why is hydroelectricity an important resource in Ghana?

532

networks Online Teaching Options

SLIDE SHOW

West Africa's Variety of Land

Describing Have students view the slide show of West Africa's landforms. Ask students to jot down notes about the diverse landscape, which includes shoreline, lakes, rivers, low plains, and highlands. Then have students use their notes to write a paragraph describing one of the landform features that they found most interesting. Invite student volunteers to share their descriptions with the class. AL **Verbal/Linguistic**

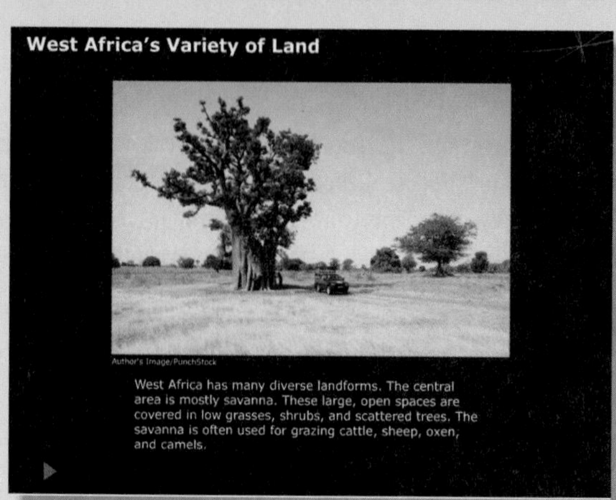

West Africa's Variety of Land
West Africa has many diverse landforms. The central area is mostly savanna. These large, open spaces are covered in low grasses, shrubs, and scattered trees. The savanna is often used for grazing cattle, sheep, oxen, and camels.

The number of fish in the Senegal River has increased since the Senegal River Basin Multi-Purpose Water Resources Development project began managing irrigation and water resources in the area.

◀ CRITICAL THINKING

1. ***Analyzing*** How can the health of waterways affect surrounding communities?
2. ***Making Inferences*** In what other ways can water resource management benefit surrounding communities?

While the Atlantic Ocean, Lake Chad, and Lake Volta are important to the economy and people of West Africa, the subregion also has a number of significant rivers. The Volta River, the main river system in Ghana, runs 1,000 miles (1,600 km) long. The northern four-fifths of the Volta River valley are now covered by Lake Volta, which was formed by the Akosombo Dam. The Volta River Basin covers an estimated area of 154,440 square miles (400,000 sq. km).

The Senegal River flows north from the Guinea Highlands through four countries: Guinea, Mali, Mauritania, and Senegal. The best agricultural land along the river is the **river plain** between the towns of Bakel and Dagana in Senegal. A river plain, also known as an alluvial plain, is a plain formed by the deposit of sediment over a long period of time by one or more rivers. After the yearly floods have retreated, crops such as millet, rice, and vegetables are sown. While agriculture is the largest economic activity along the river, fishing is the second largest. Additionally, two dams along the river, the Manantali and the Diama, provide electricity to the subregion.

river plain a plain formed by the deposit of sediment over a long period of time by one or more rivers

The Niger (NY•juhr) River, which runs about 2,600 miles (4,183 km), is the third-longest river in Africa. The Niger is the main river of western Africa. Commercial shipping takes place on about 80 percent of the river. Fishing is also an important industry to the people who live along the Niger. The Benue River, the longest tributary of the Niger River, is about 673 miles (1,083 km) long. A considerable amount of trade moves along the Benue River, including petroleum, cotton, and peanuts.

The Niger River has two deltas, a vast inland delta and a delta where the river empties into the Atlantic Ocean. The inland delta is in Mali, where the river spreads out across the plains, creating a large wetland and agricultural area. The delta at the river's mouth is in Nigeria. At one time, fishing and the production of palm oil were strong industries in the region. However, the discovery of oil in the 1950s in the Niger Delta region has changed that. Oil production and spills have polluted the land and water. This pollution has destroyed the livelihoods of farmers and fishers of the Niger Delta.

☑ READING PROGRESS CHECK

Understanding Relationships How do the water systems of West Africa benefit the people of the subregion?

Physical Geography of West Africa

V Visual Skills

Creating Maps Have students work in pairs or small groups to create maps of one of the river systems of West Africa. Have students present their maps to the class, explaining the intricate nature of the system and how it drains the basin it traverses.
AL Visual/Spatial

C1 Critical Thinking Skills

Comparing and Contrasting Lead a class discussion in which students explain how an inland delta differs from a delta that empties water and sediment into a sea, which is more common. Invite a small group of students to research how the Niger River deltas compare to other famous deltas, such as the Nile or Mississippi River Deltas, or the Volga Delta (the largest inland delta in Europe), and then present their findings to the class.
BL Verbal/Linguistic, Logical/Mathematical

C2 Critical Thinking Skills

Analyzing Cause and Effect Discuss how the discovery of oil has impacted the Niger Delta region. **Ask:** **How has oil production in the Niger Delta affected the region?** *(Numerous oil spills have damaged and polluted the land and the water.)* **How do you suppose oil production in the United States compares to that of the Niger Delta region?** *(Student answers may vary, but they should understand that despite recent oil disasters in the United States, it has stricter environmental laws governing oil production than are in place in West Africa.)* Have students brainstorm steps Nigerians might take to address the environmental problems caused by oil production. **Interpersonal, Logical/Mathematical**

INTERACTIVE IMAGE

Lake Volta

Constructing Arguments Display the image of Lake Volta for students. Reiterate that this is a human-made lake created by the construction of the Akosombo Dam. Using the text as support, have students determine whether the benefits reaped from the dam and the lake outweigh the damage caused during their creation. Ask students to work in small groups to write arguments defending or criticizing the construction of the Akosombo Dam. Students may present their arguments for the entire class. **Verbal/Linguistic, Interpersonal**

ANSWERS, p. 533

☑ **READING PROGRESS CHECK** The water systems of West Africa supply water for irrigation and consumption, are a means for transportation of goods and people, and support the fishing and tourism industries.

CRITICAL THINKING

1. A healthy water system supplies more food and income from the fishing industry.
2. Better water resource management can help to improve the quality and amount of water available for irrigation and consumption.

W Writing Skills

Narrative Have students imagine that they are taking a trip from north to south across West Africa. Have them create a journal describing the landscape and what they encounter during their trip. Encourage artistic students to include maps showing the route they follow on their trip. AL Verbal/Linguistic

C Critical Thinking Skills

Constructing Arguments Ask students to imagine that they are members of a nongovernmental organization, or NGO, trying to stop the trafficking of conflict diamonds in West Africa. Have students hold a community meeting in which they try to persuade the executives of a diamond company to stop dealing in conflict diamonds. BL Logical/Mathematical

CLOSE & REFLECT

Identifying Have students identify important facts about the physical geography of West Africa, including specific details about its landforms, water systems, climates, biomes, and resources.

ANSWERS, p. 534

✓ READING PROGRESS CHECK Oil, natural gas, gold, coal, uranium, and diamonds are some of the natural resources in West Africa.

Climates, Biomes, and Resources

GUIDING QUESTION *How do the tropical climates of West Africa support different biomes?*

environment natural surroundings

The **environment** of West Africa changes dramatically along a north-to-south latitudinal climate pattern. In the north it begins with the desert, which transitions into the semi-arid steppe, savanna grassland, and finally tropical forest. These environments have different climates, biomes, and resources.

W

In the north, where some countries of West Africa border the Sahara, the climate is hot and dry with very little rainfall. Parts of the African Transition Zone are steppe, with low-growing grasses, shrubs, and acacia trees. This area receives about 4 to 8 inches (10 to 20 cm) of rainfall a year.

As one moves farther south in West Africa, the land slowly becomes savanna. During the rainy season, the average rainfall here is about 15 to 25 inches (38 cm to 64 cm) a month. The rainy season begins in May and ends in November as warm, moist air is drawn from the Gulf of Guinea. At other times of the year, when the wind reverses and blows from the Sahara, rainfall averages about 4 inches (10 cm) a month. The land is covered with grasses and trees, such as the acacia and baobab. Many types of mammals and birds—such as giraffe, gerbils, foxes, elephants, and pygmy hippos—live in the savanna.

Still farther south, West Africa has tropical forests. Its tropical wet and dry forests, also known as tropical seasonal forests, receive rainfall during the rainy season followed by the dry and hot months. These tropical dry forests have less densely growing trees than the tropical wet forests farther south. The tropical wet forests receive plentiful rain and are abundant with semideciduous trees, evergreens, or semievergreens. They are also rich in spices, nuts, and legumes. These forests are at risk for deforestation as the human population increases.

conflict diamonds diamonds that are mined in war-torn areas and are used to finance wars

C

Oil, natural gas, coal, gold, and uranium deposits are just some of the natural resources found in West Africa. Another major resource is diamonds. In recent years, diamonds from Africa have been referred to as **conflict diamonds**, or blood diamonds. Conflict diamonds are diamonds that are mined in a war zone. Often the money from the sale of diamonds in these areas is used to finance war. For example, during the conflict in Sierra Leone in the 1990s, rebels used forced labor to mine diamonds. These diamonds were then sold in neighboring countries and then in European markets. The money earned from these sales was used to finance the civil war in Sierra Leone. As people around the world became aware of conflict diamonds, efforts were made to prevent their purchase.

✓ READING PROGRESS CHECK

Summarizing What are some of the natural resources in West Africa?

LESSON 1 REVIEW CCSS

Reviewing Vocabulary (Tier Three Words)

1. ***Describing*** Write a paragraph describing how reservoirs are used in West Africa. RH.9–10.4

Using Your Notes

2. ***Summarizing*** Use your graphic organizer on the physical geography of West Africa to write a paragraph summarizing the characteristics of the land, water, and biomes of the subregion.

Answering the Guiding Questions

3. ***Categorizing*** What landforms dominate the West African landscape?
4. ***Identifying Central Issues*** How are saltwater and freshwater resources important to the people of West Africa?
5. ***Analyzing*** How do the tropical climates of West Africa support different biomes?

Writing Activity

6. ***Informative/Explanatory*** In a paragraph, discuss how the land of West Africa affects life in the subregion. WHST.9–10.2

534

LESSON 1 REVIEW ANSWERS

Reviewing Vocabulary

1. Paragraphs will differ but could include the use of reservoirs to supply homes, farms, and businesses with freshwater, as well as being sources of hydroelectric power and supporting industries such as tourism and fishing.

Using Your Notes

2. Paragraphs will differ but should include characteristics of: desert, low plains, coastal areas with mangrove swamps and lagoons, highlands/mountains, and rain forests; water systems such as Lake Chad, Lake Volta, Atlantic Ocean, the Volta, Niger, and Senegal Rivers, and Niger River Delta; dramatic climate changes from north to south beginning with desert, moving to semi-arid steppe, savanna grassland, and tropical wet/dry forest.

Answering the Guiding Questions

3. Coastal regions are dominated by lagoons, beaches, low plains, mangrove swamps, and the remaining rain forests. The area behind coastal plains is dominated by mountainous highlands, and inland areas are mostly covered in low sandy plains and grasslands.
4. Saltwater and freshwater resources are important sources of food and income for the fishing industry and tourism. Freshwater provides drinking water, irrigation of crops, and transportation.
5. The climates support different biomes depending on the amount of rain they receive. The steppe has little rainfall, which can support low-growing grasses, shrubs, and the acacia tree; the savanna has 15 to 25 inches of rainfall and can support trees, grasses, and many mammals and birds; tropical dry areas have a rainy season followed by hot, dry months but is able to support a thick forest; tropical wet areas receive the most rainfall, have a much denser forest than tropical dry areas and are rich in spices, nuts and legumes.

Writing Activity

6. Paragraphs will differ but include how life clusters around sources of water that supply food, income, and transportation; the use of fertile soil in the river plain along the Senegal River for crops; and how pollution of the Niger Delta has impacted the livelihoods of fishers and farmers.

netw@rks
There's More Online!

- **IMAGE** Lagos, Nigeria
- **INFOGRAPHIC** Today's Nigerian Family
- **TIME LINE** Struggle for Power
- **INTERACTIVE SELF-CHECK QUIZ**
- **VIDEO** Human Geography of West Africa

LESSON 2
Human Geography of West Africa

ESSENTIAL QUESTION • *How do physical systems and human systems shape a place?*

Reading **HELP**DESK 

Academic Vocabulary (Tier Two Words)
- **convert**
- **scope**

Content Vocabulary (Tier Three Words)
- **infrastructure**
- **griot**
- **e-commerce**

TAKING NOTES: ***Key Ideas and Details***

IDENTIFYING As you read about the human geography of West Africa, use a graphic organizer like the one below to identify examples of how history, a growing population, and economic activities affect life today.

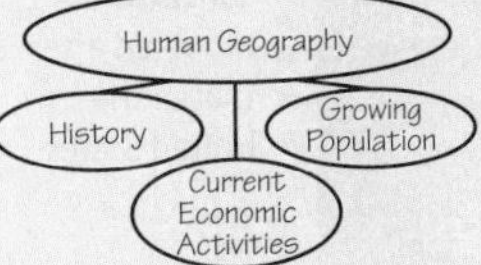

It Matters Because

West Africa has seen many peoples, empires, and kingdoms flourish. The peoples of West Africa are incredibly diverse. Colonial rule brought changes and challenges to West Africa, and the cultures of the subregion modified. Some aspects of traditional cultures were destroyed, while others remained intact, often incorporating elements of European culture, such as a language. **C**

History and Government

GUIDING QUESTION *How does the legacy of colonialism affect governments in West Africa today?*

Thousands of years ago, the Sahara was a much wetter area that supported considerable plant and animal life and, in turn, human populations. As the climate of the Sahara changed, however, people adapted by moving south to greener and more habitable regions. These seminomadic peoples herded animals and developed a system of agriculture. As populations grew, settlements grew into cities and empires.

Empires of West Africa **V**

The first empire to emerge in West Africa was the Ghana Empire. It became one of the richest trading civilizations of West Africa. Ghana profited from its location midway between the salt mines in the Sahara and the gold mines farther south. Archaeologists believe the empire began around A.D. 300. It lasted until about the thirteenth century. During its time as a trading empire, the kingdom prospered by imposing taxes on trade goods. Muslim traders from North Africa sent caravans of goods and salt across the Sahara to Ghana. Gold from Ghana was traded for salt. Muslim traders also brought Islamic beliefs and customs to the kingdom. Eventually, many Ghanaians **converted** to Islam.

The Mali Empire developed after the small state of Kangaba broke away from Ghana. Sundiata Keita, one of Mali's early kings, helped Mali flourish. He took over Timbuktu and made it an important center of trade and scholarship. By the fourteenth century, the power of the Mali Empire began to wane and another empire, Songhai (SAWNG•hy), arose. **R**

ENGAGE

C Critical Thinking Skills

Speculating Review that West Africa is a region of incredible diversity. Challenge students to estimate how many ethnic groups are indigenous to West Africa *(hundreds; 200 in Nigeria alone)* and how many languages are spoken there *(over 700; more than 500 in Nigeria alone).* Ask students to speculate why they think so many languages are indigenous to West Africa. **Logical/Mathematical**

TEACH & ASSESS

V Visual Skills

Time, Chronology, and Sequencing Have students sketch a time line of the precolonial history of West Africa, beginning with the emergence of the Ghana Empire in A.D. 300. Have students add to the time line as they read about the rise of other empires. Encourage interested students to go online to provide additional information to their time lines. **AL Visual/Spatial**

R Reading Skills

Examining Primary Sources Explain that Ibn Battuta was an Arab traveler and scholar who visited West Africa during the fourteenth century. Provide students with several selections of Battuta's writing. Divide students into small groups and assign each group a selection of his writings to examine. Have students read and explain excerpts from their selection to the class. Explore how Battuta's writings help add knowledge about West Africa's precolonial history. **BL Verbal/Linguistic**

netw@rks ***Online Teaching Options***

 **INTERACTIVE BELLRINGER**

Today's Nigerian Family

Inferring This infographic shows current statistics of Nigeria's population. Have students make inferences about the cultural values that influence the population boom and the challenges Nigeria faces as a result of it. Then have students form small groups to analyze the infographic and to discuss each question. Have students record all group members' answers to each question. Then, have groups share their responses in a class discussion. **BL Interpersonal**

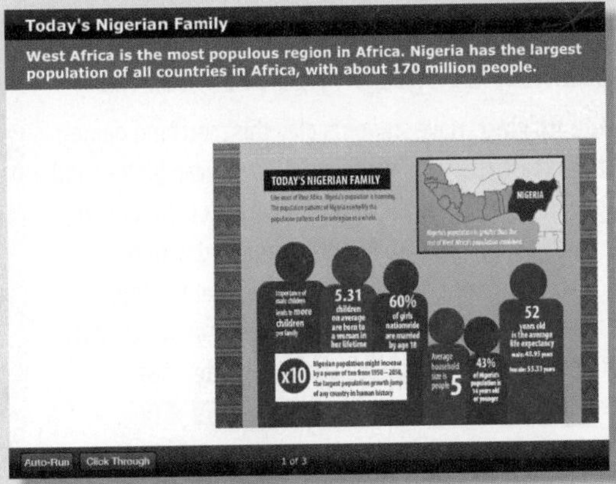

ANSWERS, p. 535

TAKING NOTES: History—Early empires traded with Muslim traders, who brought Islam; Europeans colonized the region for its resources, bringing Christianity and resulting in drawn boundaries that have no regard for traditional ethnic or religious borders, causing conflicts even today; **Growing Population**—West Africa has one of the world's fastest rates of urbanization, straining the infrastructure of cities, which limits economic development, education, health care, and availability of services; increasing populations put demands on an already limited food supply; **Economic Activities**—Internet allows small businesses to sell merchandise around the world; subsistence farmers are not involved in a wage-earning economy; commercial farmers employ a small portion of the growing cash crops; mining is dangerous but an important economic activity; oil has been discovered in the region; Nigeria is the only member of OPEC due to its large reserves; diamonds are an important resource, but conflict diamonds have also financed wars.

Content Background Knowledge

Timbuktu Timbuktu is an ancient city in Mali established by the nomadic Tuareg perhaps in the tenth century. Its geographical setting made it a natural meeting point for West Africans and traders from the north and beyond. Its long history as a faraway trading outpost gave it a fabled status and inspired the phrase "from here to Timbuktu," a metaphor for remote and distant lands.

R1 Reading Skills

Listing Explain that Britain, France, Spain, Belgium, and Germany established colonies in West Africa. Have students make a list showing which West African countries were colonized, the colonizing countries, and the dates the West African countries gained independence. Discuss why each European country wanted to establish colonies in West Africa. AL Verbal/Linguistic

C Critical Thinking Skills

Analyzing Ethical Issues Many historians criticize the Europeans for drawing the boundaries of Africa without regard for ethnic boundaries. **Ask:** Why do you suppose the Europeans were not more respectful of ethnic differences? *(Possible answers: more interested in the resources to be exploited; were not planning to create stable, integrated societies or relationships)* Was the way the boundaries were drawn ethical? Why or why not? *(Student answers may vary, but they might bring out that a disregard for the rights and needs of others is never ethical.)* What long-term effect have Europeans caused to this region? *(Student answers may vary, but they should understand that West Africa has experienced one kind of upheaval after another, beginning with outside conquerors and continuing with colonial neglect.)* BL Logical/Mathematical

R2 Reading Skills

Determining Importance Have students study the time line. **Ask:** What does this time line show? *(events in Liberia's history)* What important facts about Liberia's relations with the United States are reflected on this time line? *(Many enslaved Africans came from Liberia to the Americas; its constitution is patterned after the U.S. Constitution; Americans helped establish it.)* Continue to discuss and ask students questions about the events in the time line. ELL Verbal/Linguistic

ANSWERS, p. 536

CRITICAL THINKING

1. Liberia was established on land purchased by the American Colonization Society for freed slaves to return to Africa. The first constitution of Liberia is modeled after that of the United States.
2. The political situation since 1980 has been volatile with the government being overthrown twice and civil war erupting.

convert to change from one system, use, or method to another that is quite different

Songhai broke from Mali after the death of Mali's most well-known king, Mansa Musa. Sunni Ali Ber conquered the cities of Timbuktu and Djenné, expanding his empire to include most of the West African savanna. The empire prospered until about A.D. 1600, when it fell to the Moroccans.

The Hausa city-states were located between the Niger River in what is now northern Nigeria and ended at Lake Chad in the east. These independent states, the first of which emerged around A.D. 1000, formed loose alliances. The Hausa city-states remained independent for the most part, until they were conquered in the early 1800s by the Fulani. Each of the states served a different role within the alliance. Some provided goods, others soldiers or access to trade. As a result, the states became important to international trade.

The kingdom of Benin, which occupied the area of present-day Nigeria, developed into an important power from the thirteenth to the nineteenth century. Benin became an extremely organized state by the late 1400s. Between the fifteenth and eighteenth centuries, the kingdom grew in wealth and power through trade with the Portuguese and Dutch. By the nineteenth century, however, infighting weakened the kingdom. At the same time, suppression of the slave trade, from which Benin had greatly profited, led to the kingdom's decline.

The Colonization of Africa

R1 As contact with Europe increased, word of the riches to be found in Africa spread. Europeans soon began to view Africa as a source of resources and opportunities. As European countries laid claim to territories in Africa, disputes over territory arose. At the Berlin Conference between 1884 and 1885, 14 European countries met in an effort to sort out how territory would be divided.

C With no African input at the Berlin Conference, colonial boundaries were drawn with little regard for African ethnic boundaries. One example of this is in Nigeria, where boundaries were drawn that merged Muslim societies with animist cultures. As Christianity was introduced, additional tensions emerged. These and other issues set African peoples against one another and strengthened European rule.

TIME LINE

Struggle for POWER

The oldest republic in Africa, Liberia has experienced a lengthy period of warfare as warlords vie for power.

▶ CRITICAL THINKING

1. ***Explaining*** How was Liberia influenced by the United States?
2. ***Analyzing*** How would you characterize the political situation in Liberia since 1980?

R2

1400 — 1900

1461 Portuguese traders first arrive in Liberia

1500s Portuguese and British traders transport Africans to the Americas as part of the transatlantic slave trade.

1816 American Colonization Society (ACS) is formed in the United States to send free blacks to Africa.

1847 Liberia becomes independent with a constitution modeled after that of the United States.

networks *Online Teaching Options*

GAME

Human Geography of West Africa

Identifying Have students play this matching game to increase their knowledge of West African history and geography. Display the game and instruct students to match each place name or term provided with the correct description. When the game is completed, students receive instant feedback. Encourage students to correct any errors they may have made, thus reinforcing the concepts presented. ELL AL Verbal/Linguistic

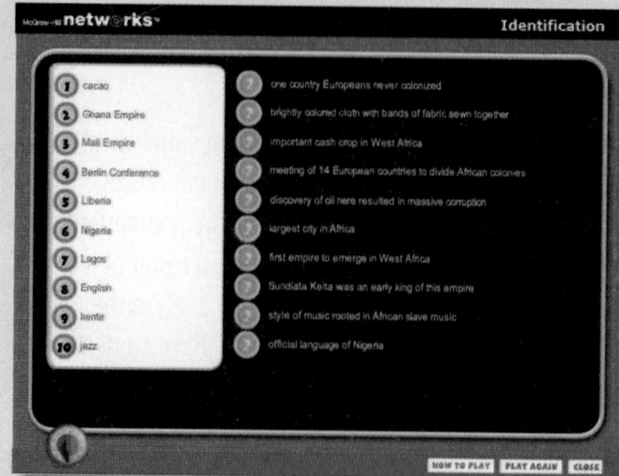

The one country Europeans never colonized is Liberia. African Americans freed from slavery established it on land purchased for them by the American Colonization Society. The African Americans who relocated to Liberia had a different culture from the indigenous people who already lived in the area. Over time, the differences widened, causing conflicts between the people of Liberia. In 1847 Liberia declared independence. Soon after, a constitution was written. **C**

Decolonization and Difficulties

Europeans maintained their colonies in West Africa until the mid-1900s. But even after attaining independence, these new countries faced daunting challenges. Years of strife afflicted many of the countries. In Nigeria, for example, the ill-conceived boundaries drawn by the colonial powers led to increasing tensions between Muslims and Christians. In 2009 the Nigerian government began fighting against a militant Islamist group that sought to establish an Islamist state in Nigeria. **T**

Another problem is corruption. In Nigeria, for example, the discovery of oil and gas made the country particularly vulnerable. Nigerian leaders used their offices to steal billions of dollars paid by foreign companies for oil extraction rights. To give an idea of the **scope**, or extent, of the problem, some estimate that close to $400 billion was stashed in foreign bank accounts between 1960 and 1999. In the early 2000s, Nigerians and new leaders waged a war against corruption.

scope the extent of an activity or influence

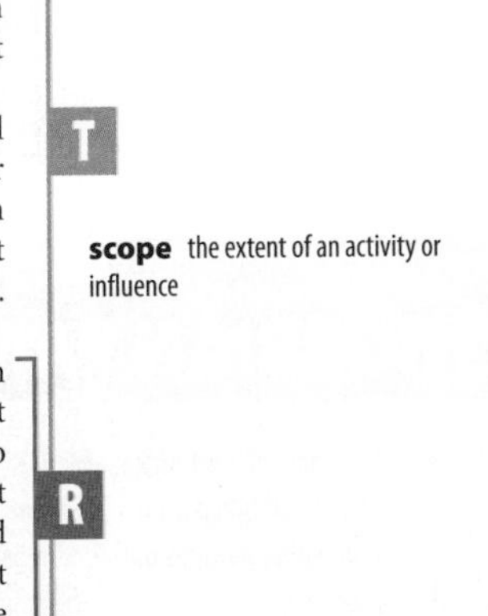

Changes in infrastructure and culture produced by European colonization persisted even after independence. The countries' economies were still dependent on providing raw materials to European countries. They were largely unable to revive their traditional cultural knowledge and practices that had been lost during colonization. As a result, they had to adopt the market economy and consumer culture of the European powers. These lasting changes made it impossible for the new countries to chart an independent course that would be more beneficial to their own interests. **R**

✓ **READING PROGRESS CHECK**

Evaluating In what ways has colonialism affected the countries of West Africa?

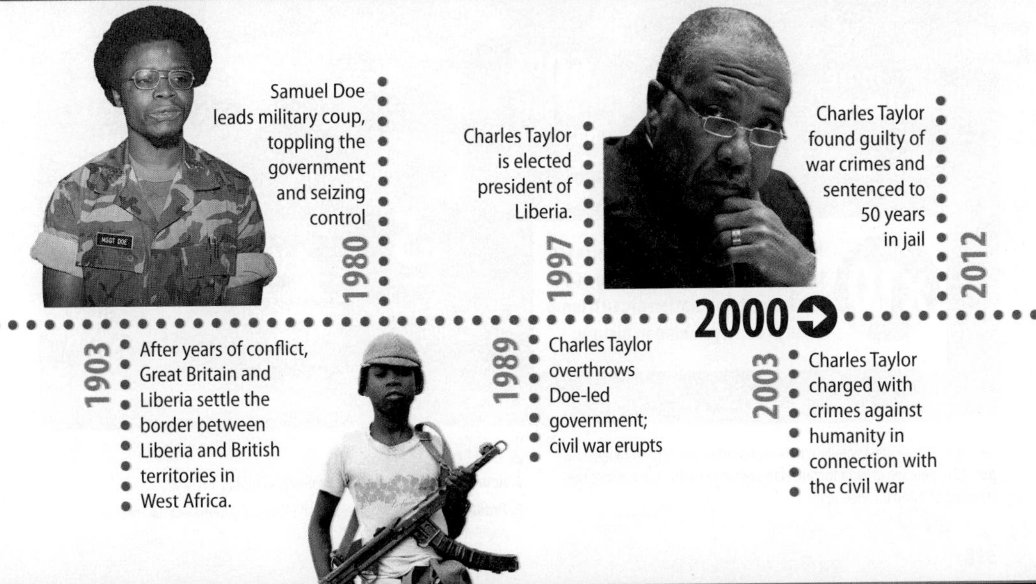

1903
After years of conflict, Great Britain and Liberia settle the border between Liberia and British territories in West Africa.
1980
Samuel Doe leads military coup, toppling the government and seizing control
1989
Charles Taylor overthrows Doe-led government; civil war erupts
1997
Charles Taylor is elected president of Liberia.
2000
2003
Charles Taylor charged with crimes against humanity in connection with the civil war
2012
Charles Taylor found guilty of war crimes and sentenced to 50 years in jail

C Critical Thinking Skills

Comparing and Contrasting Have students analyze Liberia's independence. **Ask:** **How was the country of Liberia founded?** *(the land purchased by the American Colonization Society and settled by freed African Americans)* **How was the founding of Liberia different from the founding of the other nations of West Africa?** *(It was never colonized by the Europeans or under the jurisdiction of another country.)* **Why do you suppose this situation led to conflicts with the indigenous people of the area?** *(Student answers may vary, but they should understand that the freed African Americans had a very different culture from the indigenous people.)* **AL** **Logical/Mathematical**

R Reading Skills

Explaining Have a student read the third paragraph under "Decolonization and Difficulties" aloud. Have students form small groups to discuss the negative effects European colonization had on the new countries' ability to chart a viable course for themselves. Then have groups brainstorm how and why many countries lost traditional cultural knowledge and practices during the colonial period, listing several ideas to share in a class discussion. **Verbal/Linguistic, Interpersonal**

T Technology Skills

Explaining Continuity and Change Display the political map of West Africa for students. Have students note where political boundaries cut across ethnic enclaves that they have read about in this chapter. Have students find recent online news stories from countries of West Africa dealing with tensions between ethnic groups. Remind students a *country* is a political unit and a *nation* is a group of people with similar characteristics, but not necessarily living within the same country. Then use the students' news stories to guide a class discussion about how these divisions might have led to tensions between countries and between nations. **BL** **Verbal/Linguistic**

INTERACTIVE MAP

Independent Africa

Classifying Display the interactive map for students. First, have students click on the colored boxes to highlight the colonies that existed in Africa in 1914. Then, have them click on the country names on the map to see when each country gained its independence. Ask students to note how long it took for each country to become independent, as well as which countries, if any, were never colonized. **AL** **Kinesthetic, Visual/Spatial**

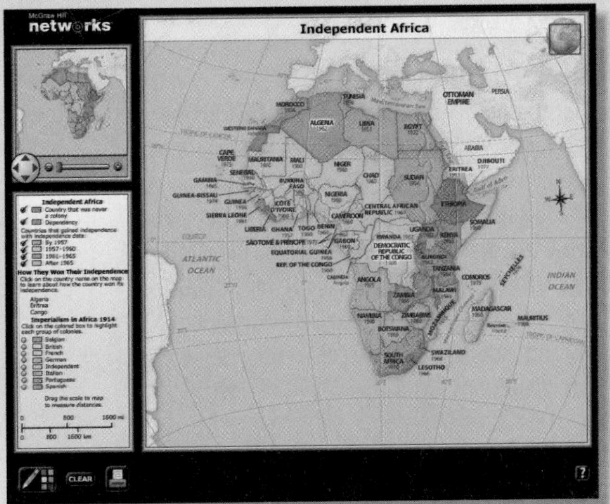

ANSWERS, p. 537

✓ **READING PROGRESS CHECK** Colonialism introduced Christianity to West Africa and created boundaries that had no regard for African ethnic boundaries. This created tensions and conflicts. European changes to culture and infrastructure resulted in a loss of traditional cultural knowledge and practices, making the independent countries of today have little choice but to adopt the market economy and consumer culture of European powers as they are dependent on trade with Europe.

C Critical Thinking Skills

Explaining Have students identify conditions that influence population movement. Have them consider what they have learned about the reasons people move to urban areas.
Ask: **Why do you think West Africa is one of the most populous regions in Africa?** *(Possible answers: many people live along the coast and river plains in West Africa because other areas of Africa are less hospitable; there are limited birth control efforts; cultural or society traditions of large families; children are needed to help with agricultural activities)* **What conditions in rural areas cause people to leave their homes?** *(Possible answers: deforestation, decreasing food supplies, poverty)* **Why do many West Africans living in rural areas move to the cities?** *(Possible answer: West Africans move to the city with the hope that they will find a better life, better jobs, educational opportunities, better health care and public services; however, many are disappointed. Life in the cities of West Africa can be harsh. Many people live in abject poverty.)* Encourage interested students to research what life is like in a West African city today. Have students report their findings to the class. AL
Verbal, Linguistic, Logistic/Mathematical

W Writing Skills

Informational/Explanatory Have students study the infographic "Today's Nigerian Family." Working with a partner, have students use the information to write a population profile of Nigeria. Pairs should include a paragraph that theorizes about what life might be like in the future should the population increase tenfold by 2050 in Nigeria, as projected.
BL **Verbal/Linguistic**

Population Patterns

GUIDING QUESTION *How is a booming population affecting life in West Africa?*

C Africa's population is increasing rapidly. Most people in West Africa live along the coast and river plains. About half of the people in West Africa live in crowded urban locations. West Africa is one of the most populous regions of Africa, and the country of Nigeria has the largest population of any country in Africa. Lagos, the commercial center of Nigeria, is Africa's largest city with an estimated population of more than 20 million. In 2012, about 170 million people lived in Nigeria. By 2025, the country's population is projected to exceed 190 million.

Demands created by climate change, deforestation, increasing population, and decreasing food supplies have prompted many Nigerians to move to urban areas. This pattern is also occurring in other parts of West Africa. People are moving to urban areas in hopes of finding better job opportunities, health care, public services, and education.

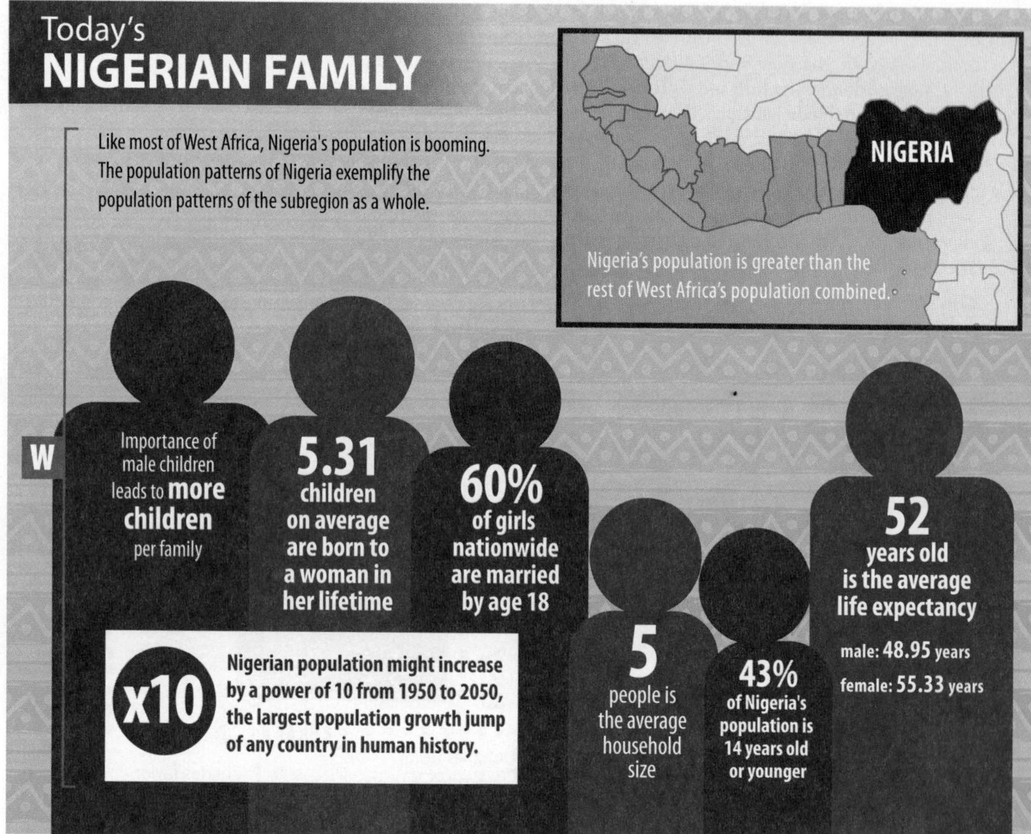

Today's
NIGERIAN FAMILY
Like most of West Africa, Nigeria's population is booming. The population patterns of Nigeria exemplify the population patterns of the subregion as a whole.
NIGERIA
Nigeria's population is greater than the rest of West Africa's population combined.
W
Importance of male children leads to more children per family
5.31 children on average are born to a woman in her lifetime
60% of girls nationwide are married by age 18
52 years old is the average life expectancy
male: 48.95 years
female: 55.33 years
x10
Nigerian population might increase by a power of 10 from 1950 to 2050, the largest population growth jump of any country in human history.
5 people is the average household size
43% of Nigeria's population is 14 years old or younger

Nigeria is Africa's most populous nation and continues to grow rapidly. The pace of population growth threatens to undermine efforts to improve the standard of living for Nigerians.

▲ **CRITICAL THINKING**

1. ***Analyzing*** What are the consequences of having a very young population?
2. ***Problem Solving*** What steps could Nigeria's government take to slow population growth?

538

networks Online Teaching Options

INFOGRAPHIC

Modern Nigerian Families

Speculating Have students study and discuss the infographic *Modern Nigerian Families* with a partner. Direct their attention to the average life expectancy for a Nigerian. Have partners list reasons why they believe the average life span of a person born in Nigeria is relatively short compared with persons born in other industrialized nations in the world. Students may use the text as support, if necessary.
AL **Visual/Spatial, Logical/Mathematical**

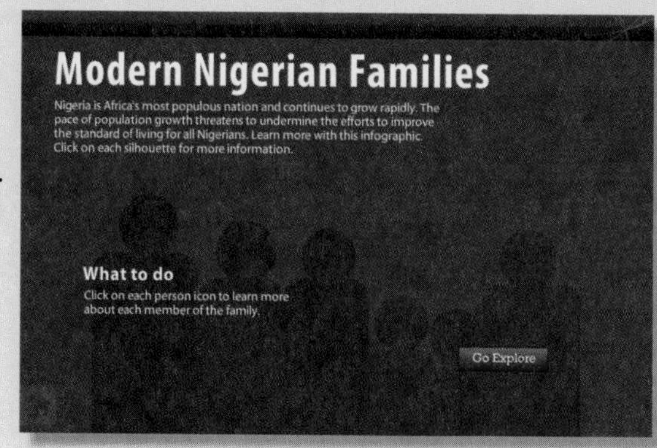

Modern Nigerian Families
What to do
Click on each person icon to learn more about each member of the family.
Go Explore

ANSWERS, p. 538

CRITICAL THINKING

1. Having many young people in a population puts a strain on the country's infrastructure such as health care and education. This segment of the population does not contribute to the economy, therefore, the infrastructure is unable to support the population as there are fewer wage earners than people that require services.
2. Access to and creation of education and health care programs that promote family planning, a later marrying age, and a change in the attitudes toward the importance of having male children could help slow population growth.

Human Geography of West Africa

The Nigerian city of Lagos is the most populous city in Africa and one of the fastest growing.

CRITICAL THINKING

1. ***Analyzing Visuals*** How does the photograph illustrate the effects of rapid urbanization?
2. ***Drawing Inferences*** How does rapid urbanization affect the daily lives of a city's residents?

V1

West Africa's rate of urbanization, or movement of people from rural areas to cities, is among the world's fastest. New population growth has caused cities to spread out into the countryside. This expansion of population in urban areas in West African countries has placed a strain on existing **infrastructure**—which includes electricity, water, roads, and information and communications technology. Limitations on infrastructure reduce productivity and limit economic development. However, with the help of international investors, West African countries are attempting to improve infrastructure to meet the demands of their ever-increasing populations.

R

infrastructure the set of systems that affect how well a place or organization operates, such as telephone or transportation systems, within a country

READING PROGRESS CHECK

Evaluating How has West Africa been affected by population growth?

Society and Culture Today

GUIDING QUESTION *How is life in West Africa a mix of the ancient and the modern?*

West Africa is home to a very large number of ethnic groups—about 500 in Nigeria alone. This immense diversity includes peoples that have lived in West Africa for centuries. It also includes groups that have settled there more recently. Some ethnic groups that live in West Africa have been divided into different countries by political boundaries originally established by European colonial powers.

Of the ethnic groups in West Africa, the five largest are the Yoruba, Hausa, Fulani, Ibo, and Akan. Estimated at more than 30 million, the Yoruba live in areas of Nigeria, Benin, Togo, and Ghana. Some 30 million Hausa live in the West African countries of Nigeria, Ghana, and Côte d'Ivoire as well as in Chad, Niger, and Cameroon.

T

Hundreds of languages are spoken in West Africa. Arabic is common in the northern areas of the subregion. Yoruba and its many dialects, which are part of the Congo-Kordofanian language group, are widely spoken. In the southern region of West Africa, Yoruba is taught in primary and secondary schools, at universities, and in television and radio broadcasting schools. It is also commonly used in printed materials such as books, newspapers, and pamphlets. Part of the legacy of colonial rule was the introduction of European languages. Thus, English and French are widely spoken. In Nigeria, English is the official language. Using English facilitates communication in a country where more than 500 languages are spoken.

V2

V1 Visual Skills

Analyzing Visuals Direct students' attention to the photograph of Lagos, Nigeria. Ask students to imagine that they are walking along this crowded street. Invite several volunteers to describe what they see and what it might be like to visit or live in Africa's largest city. **Intrapersonal, Visual/Spatial**

R Reading Skills

Sequencing Information Have students use the information in the paragraph to make a flowchart describing the domino effects caused by rapid urbanization. **Ask:** **What are some ways countries can improve the negative effects of rapid urbanization?** *(Possible answer: anticipate infrastructure needs)* **How would improving infrastructure help?** *(Possible answer: with a better infrastructure, cities would be able to accommodate more people)* AL **Verbal/Linguistic**

T Technology Skills

Presentation Working in small groups, have students research one of the major ethnic groups of West Africa. They should gather data about population, location, and famous people of each ethnicity to create multimedia presentations that include images, diagrams, and music or other auditory enhancements. **Auditory/Musical, Visual/Spatial**

V2 Visual Skills

Creating Visuals Point out that with the arrival of new people to West Africa came new languages. **Ask:** **With all these languages, how are people able to communicate?** *(Possible answers: Many people speak multiple languages or dialects; As a result of colonial rule, many West Africans speak French or English)* Have students work with a partner to research and then create a map or chart showing the official languages spoken in each West African country. **Verbal/Linguistic**

CHART

Ethnic Groups in West Africa

Narrative Have students study and discuss this chart on the ethnic groups within West Africa. Point out that this chart lists the five largest ethnic groups that currently reside in West Africa. Have students read each "Did You Know?" fact about the five groups. Ask them to choose one group and write a narrative describing what they think a day in the life of a member of that group might be like, using the information provided in the chart and in the text. BL **Verbal/Linguistic**

Ethnic Groups in West Africa

Group	Location	Did you know?
Ibo	Nigeria	The Ibo have no single ruler or king. Almost everyone in an Ibo village takes part in making important decisions.
Fulani	Throughout West Africa	The Fulani are the largest nomadic group in the world. They established many of the trade routes in West Africa.
Wolof	Senegal	Hospitality is important to the Wolof. They share lodgings and meals with visitors and ask nothing in return.
Senufo	Mali, northern Cote d'Ivoire	The Senufo follow a caste system. They place farmers at the highest level of their caste system.
Yoruba	Southwest Nigeria, Benin	The Yoruba worship hundreds of gods. Some are worshiped by all. Others are worshiped by certain families or towns.

ANSWERS, p. 539

READING PROGRESS CHECK West Africa has one of the world's fastest rates of urbanization resulting from rapid population growth. The urban infrastructure has become overwhelmed, limiting the productivity and economic development. The growing population also increases the risk of food insecurity within the subregion.

CRITICAL THINKING

1. The traffic jam and people crowding the street illustrate how rapid urbanization causes the infrastructure of roadways and people to be overwhelmed.
2. Rapid urbanization causes the city's residents to be less productive. They are unable to get from place to place efficiently, lack basic access to services, and must deal with increasing amounts of waste and pollution.

C Critical Thinking Skills

Analyzing Have students consider why literacy rates and infant mortality rates are indicators of a region's welfare. **Ask:** **Why are literacy rates low in many West African nations?** *(lack of education)* **Why are infant mortality rates high?** *(poverty; lack of health care)* **Which parts of West Africa's population are most likely to have a low standard of living and poor health care?** *(people in rural areas and in urban slums)* AL **Logical/Mathematical**

R Reading Skills

Applying Have students read the section titled "Family and the Status of Women." Ask students to explain the difference between a nuclear family and an extended family and the role of women in each. Brainstorm reasons why the nuclear family household is likely to prevail in cities. **Ask:** **How will the lives of women change as they enter into professions and establish small businesses?** *(Student answers may vary, but should include that women will gain economic independence and the ability to participate in politics and assume leadership roles.)* **Verbal/Linguistic**

T Technology Skills

Presenting Have students gather information about the traditional arts and crafts of West Africa. Students may wish to concentrate on one of the arts such as music, weaving, or mask creation. Or students may choose a specific ethnic group or tribe and research art or music that the group produces. Have students create a multimedia presentation showing their research that include visuals and/or music, depending upon the chosen art form. BL **Auditory/Musical, Visual/Spatial**

Connecting Geography to SOCIOLOGY

Social Norms

Sociology is the study of the development, structure, and function of humans in society. As more West Africans move from rural to urban areas in search of better health care, sanitation, and work, social norms are changing. West Africans have had to adapt to new ways of life in an urban setting. One example of this is the shift from living with extended families to living in nuclear families. This often leads to cultural changes and lost traditions.

ANALYZING What examples of change in social norms do you see in your own society?

Regardless of ethnic group or language, the diverse people of West Africa value religion and strong family ties. The dominant religions practiced in the subregion are Islam, Christianity, and the traditional animist religions of Africa. Although followers of different religions often coexist peacefully, conflict sometimes occurs.

C Education in West Africa is inconsistent. Literacy rates in West Africa are one of the lowest in the world. As of 2010, for example, the literacy rate in Sierra Leone was only 42 percent. In Ghana, however, education has been a priority, and government spending on education has steadily increased since the 1960s. As of 2010, the literacy rate in Ghana was 67 percent, the highest in the subregion.

Poverty is a key factor in determining access to health care in West Africa. Health care is uneven and limited. As a result, infant mortality rates are high throughout the subregion. In Sierra Leone, for example, 185 children out of every 1,000 die before they reach the age of five. High death rates are caused by poor sanitation, health conditions, and inadequate nutrition.

Family and the Status of Women

R Many people in West Africa still live in extended families made up of parents, children, grandparents, and sometimes aunts, uncles, and cousins. Generally in these traditional societies, men and women have different roles. Traditionally, women look after children and the home while men earn a living to support the family. In the cities, however, the nuclear family—made up of husband, wife, and children—is rapidly replacing the extended family. The role of women is also beginning to change.

Women in West Africa play a vital role in the family. In recent years, men have begun to move away from home to find jobs, leaving women and children behind. Yet, in traditional societies, there are few jobs available for women that would provide income to care for a family. Things are beginning to change, however. Women are beginning to enter into professions and establish small businesses like selling vegetables in local markets or opening a local beauty salon. These small businesses give women control over their own lives and pave the way for participation in other aspects of their society such as politics. For example, the Women Peace Security Network Africa (WIPSEN-Africa) was established in 2006 in Ghana to promote women's strategic participation and leadership in peace and security governance in Africa.

The Arts

T Much of the art in West African culture expresses religious beliefs. Music and dance are a part of everyday life, and entire communities participate. Dancers wear masks honoring specific deities, the spirits of their ancestors, or to honor special occasions, such as a birth. West African music has become popular around the world and has influenced contemporary Western music. Kanye West and Sting are only two of the popular Western musicians who have borrowed from African music. In fact, the entire blues and jazz tradition of the United States has its roots in the music enslaved Africans brought with them. **Griots** are an ancient tradition and an important part of the history of art in West Africa. They are oral historians, storytellers, singers, and musicians. Their songs, music, and stories help the people remember their cultural heritage.

griots traditional oral historians, storytellers, singers, and musicians of West Africa

Another art form is weaving. The Ashanti of Ghana are expert weavers, known for kente cloth. Kente is a brightly colored cloth consisting of bands of fabric sewn together. The Ashanti king and royal family have worn this cloth for centuries. Today people around the world also wear kente. Kente has become a symbol of Africa for many African Americans.

☑ **READING PROGRESS CHECK**

Evaluating What ancient tradition can be found in West Africa today?

networks Online Teaching Options

GRAPHIC ORGANIZER

Influences on African Religions

Identifying Continuity and Change Display the graphic organizer. Discuss with students the major religions of West Africa, and what factors may or may not have influenced and continue to influence those religions. Then have small groups of students discuss which of those factors have remained in place over the years and which have changed. After discussion, students may complete the graphic organizer. **Visual/Spatial**

networks **Influences on African Religions**

	Influence of Islam on African Religions	Influence of Christianity on African Religions
How It Spread in Africa	• Muslim traders from nearby Arabia brought Islam to Africa. • Islam was spread by Muslim conquerors and missionaries.	• Missionaries spread Christianity in Africa. • Christianity was the official religion of the Roman Empire, which included parts of northern Africa. • Axum embraced Christianity as early as the fourth century.
How It Was Received in Africa	• Many African rulers allowed their people to convert to Islam. • Islam did not demand conversion and was very tolerant of existing and different religions.	• Missionaries converted kings, who then converted their people. • Christianity spread into less populated areas of the country, often because of trade.
Examples of Syncretism (blending of religions)	• Tradition of spirit worship maintained from African religions • Belief in a single creator god in Islam and many African religions • Traditional roles of men and women maintained	• Syncretism was less common between Christianity and African religions because Christianity was not tolerant of blending ideas. • Africans used their own cultural practices as a means for interpreting Christianity. • Belief in a single creator god

ANSWERS, p. 540

☑ **READING PROGRESS CHECK** The ancient tradition of griots, or oral historians, storytellers, singers, and musicians that help people remember their cultural heritage can be found in West Africa.

Connecting Geography Students' examples will vary but they should describe, in detail, the change in social norms they observe in their local communities.

Economic Activities

GUIDING QUESTION *What natural resources are available in West Africa for economic development?*

People in West Africa earn their living in many different ways. Some West Africans run small businesses selling locally made products such as baskets, art, and jewelry. Using **e-commerce**, or buying and selling on the Internet, people sell their products to customers around the world. The Internet broadens the market for locally made products. Agriculture, however, is the main economic activity of more than half of the people in West Africa.

e-commerce buying and selling on the Internet

Many of the people in West Africa live by subsistence farming in which people focus on growing food to feed themselves and their families. These people are largely self-sufficient, growing their own food and building their own houses. They are generally not involved in a wage-earning economy.

A small percentage of the population works at commercial farming. Commercial farmers produce crops on a large scale. These cash crops are grown and sold for profit. One important cash crop in West Africa is cacao, which is used to make cocoa powder and chocolate. Côte d'Ivoire is the world's largest exporter of cacao, as well as a major exporter of palm oil and coffee beans. Cacao trees are native to Central and South America, and the crop was introduced to West Africa during the colonial period. Small family-run farms have the greatest success in growing cacao. A very small percentage of people along the coast also work in commercial fishing.

Although difficult and risky, mining is also an important economic activity in the region. Coal, gold, uranium, and natural gas are some of the natural resources found in West Africa. Oil has also been discovered in some countries. Immense oil reserves make Nigeria the region's only member of the Organization of Petroleum Exporting Countries (OPEC). Nigeria's economy has been heavily dependent on this single resource, but Nigerian leaders have tried to diversify the economy in recent years. Diamonds, another important resource for West Africa, have a sordid history. Conflict diamonds have financed wars in Sierra Leone, Liberia, and Côte D'Ivoire.

Trade groups have helped increase trade within the region. Various countries have formed regional trade associations, such as the Economic Community of West African States (ECOWAS). This group of 15 countries was founded in 1975 to promote economic integration across the region. ECOWAS is expanding trade within the region and outside of Africa. In 2012 ECOWAS signed an agreement with China for cooperation in infrastructure development, trade, and investment.

READING PROGRESS CHECK

Evaluating What economic activities can be found in West Africa?

LESSON 2 REVIEW (CCSS)

Reviewing Vocabulary (Tier Three Words)

1. ***Describing*** Write a paragraph describing how griots contribute to the culture of West Africa. RH.9–10.4

Using Your Notes

2. ***Analyzing*** Use your graphic organizer about the human geography of West Africa to write a paragraph about the complexity and difficulties the subregion faces.

Answering the Guiding Questions

3. ***Drawing Conclusions*** How does the legacy of colonialism affect governments in West Africa today?
4. ***Evaluating*** How is a booming population affecting life in West Africa?
5. ***Making Connections*** How is life in West Africa a mix of the ancient and the modern?
6. ***Listing*** What natural resources are available in West Africa for economic development?

Writing Activity

7. ***Informative/Explanatory*** In a paragraph, discuss how the people of West Africa, both past and present, have shaped the subregion. WHST.9–10.2

V Visual Skills

Comparing and Contrasting Have students create a chart or graph that explains the differences between the three types of farming practiced in West Africa: subsistence, commercial, and small family. Encourage students to consult an agricultural map to determine what crops are grown in each ecological zone and incorporate this information into their charts.
ELL Visual/Spatial

R Reading Skills

Explaining Have students reread the section and then review the unit economic activity map showing where important deposits of mineral and energy resources are found in West Africa. Then have students write a brief statement explaining the importance of each resource and if they feel the resource helps or hinders the economy of the region.
Logical/Mathematical/Visual/Spatial

CLOSE & REFLECT

Taking Notes Have students look back over the lesson and note important historical, political, cultural, and economic information they have gained about West Africa. Then tell students to write brief summaries of the human geography of West Africa to review the chapter.

ANSWERS, p. 541

READING PROGRESS CHECK Economic activities such as small businesses selling locally made products, subsistence farming, small amounts of commercial farming, and mining can all be found in West Africa.

LESSON 2 REVIEW ANSWERS

Reviewing Vocabulary

1. Paragraphs will vary but should include that griots are traditional oral historians, storytellers, singers, and musicians that help the people of West Africa remember their cultural heritage.

Using Your Notes

2. Paragraphs will vary but should include the large ethnic diversity with hundreds of spoken languages, the legacy of colonialism, problems of population growth, and the impact of rapid urbanization on infrastructure.

Answering the Guiding Questions

3. The boundaries created by Europeans during colonialism results in many conflicts. Economic dependence on trade with European countries and loss of traditional knowledge and practices have made governments adopt practices that are not beneficial to economies and often leads to corruption.
4. A growing population is resulting in rapid urbanization as people leave rural areas to find jobs, health care, and education, resulting in a strain on the existing infrastructure in urban areas. It is also increasing food insecurity, leading to deforestation, desertification, and drought.
5. Traditional extended families are common throughout the region, but women are taking on more modern roles in starting businesses and entering professions. Traditional arts are being sold via the Internet. While over 500 languages are spoken, English and French as a result of colonization are also widely spoken.
6. Oil, natural gas, coal, gold, and uranium are available for economic development in West Africa.

Writing Activity

7. Paragraphs will vary but could include the early empires that initiated trade that brought Islam to the region; European colonization that established boundaries that did not take into account the traditional ethnic borders of the subregion resulting in conflict; how colonization changed culture and infrastructure, and influenced the economies of today; the ethnic diversity in the subregion; the influence of family and expanding roles of women; and how population growth influences rapid urbanization.

ENGAGE

G1 Critical Thinking Skills

Previewing Have students quickly preview the visuals and headings of this diagram as they consider what they already know about the diamond business and issues surrounding how diamonds are mined and sold to the public. Then have students write a prediction for what they will learn about from examining this diagram more closely.

TEACH & ASSESS

R Reading Skills

Using Context Clues Have students read the introductory text. **Ask:** **What context clues help you understand the meaning of "conflict diamonds"?** *(The text explains that these diamonds were also once known as "blood diamonds" and notes that miners and people near the mines were often subject to violence.)* **Why do you think these diamonds are called "conflict diamonds"?** *(Possible answer: They are mined in places full of violent conflict and often become a part of the conflict as people fight to control them or use them to fund future conflicts.)* ELL Verbal/Linguistic

V Visual Skills

Analyzing Visuals Have students study the colors and symbols used in this diagram and use them to interpret the meaning of the diagram in a class discussion. **Ask:** **What is the topic of this diagram?** *(how and why conflict diamonds move around the world)* **What do the colors and symbols indicate?** *(They show the reasons why diamonds move from place to place. For example, the diamond symbol paired with the blue line shows how some diamonds are prepared and sold to consumers in the United States.)* **How does the diagram make understanding conflict diamonds easier?** *(The diagram shows how widely spread the industry is and how even people in Europe and the United States have ties to the situation in Africa.)* AL Visual/Spatial

G2 Critical Thinking Skills

Identifying Cause and Effect As students read the first step of this diagram, have them identify the cause-and-effect relationships that fuel this situation. **Ask:** **Why do rebel groups steal uncut diamonds or take over diamond mines?** *(Possible answer: They need or want money to buy weapons and to fund their civil wars and attempts to take over the governments of various countries, so they steal and sell the diamonds.)* Have students continue to note cause-and-effect relationships in other steps. AL Logical/Mathematical

Global Connections: **Africa South of the Sahara**

Conflict DIAMONDS

Diamonds are one of Africa's most important natural resources. Today, about $8.5 billion annually worth of rough diamonds are from Africa. Groups have found ways to exploit this natural resource for their own gain. Conflict diamonds, also known as blood diamonds, are ones that are mined in rebel-controlled areas. The miners, and those who lived near the mines, have often been threatened, harmed, or even killed.

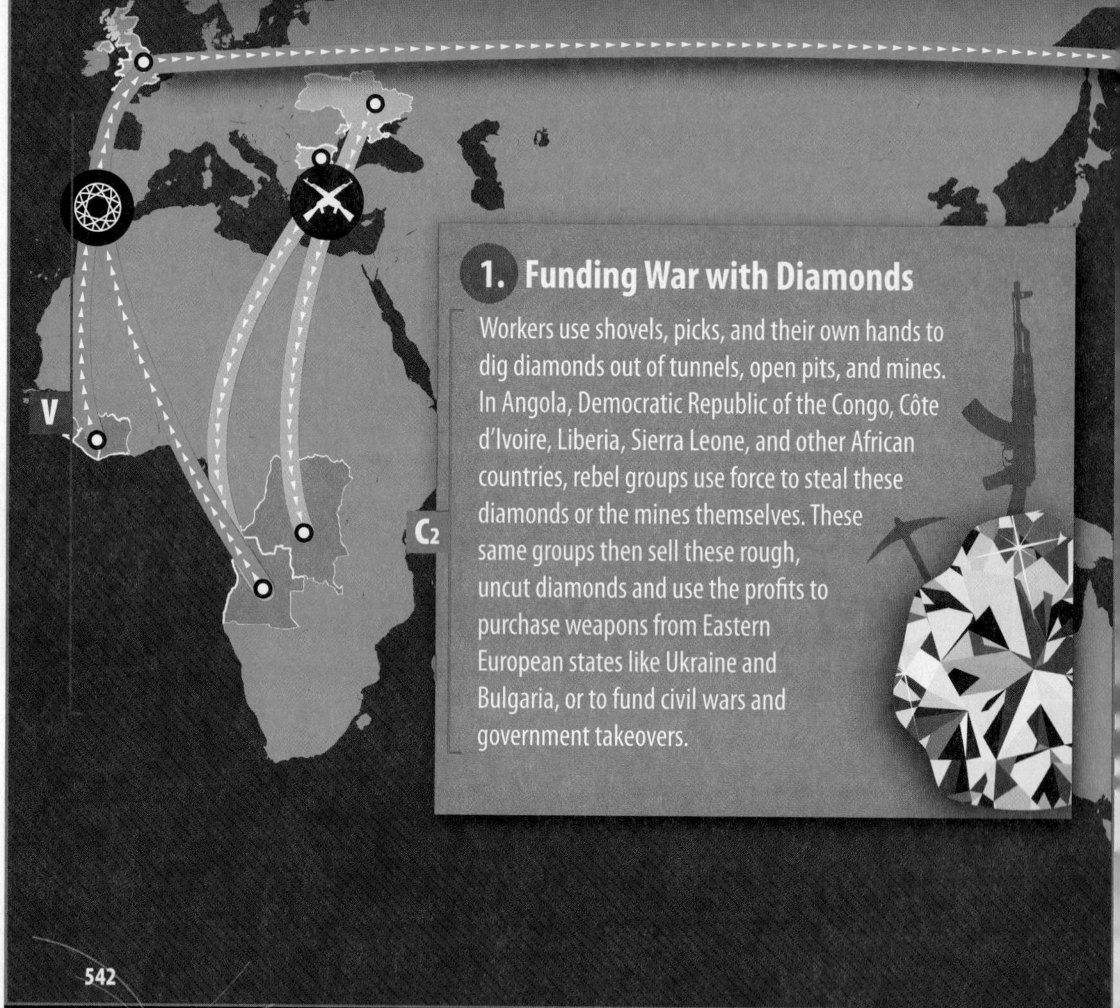

1. Funding War with Diamonds

Workers use shovels, picks, and their own hands to dig diamonds out of tunnels, open pits, and mines. In Angola, Democratic Republic of the Congo, Côte d'Ivoire, Liberia, Sierra Leone, and other African countries, rebel groups use force to steal these diamonds or the mines themselves. These same groups then sell these rough, uncut diamonds and use the profits to purchase weapons from Eastern European states like Ukraine and Bulgaria, or to fund civil wars and government takeovers.

542

networks Online Teaching Options

INTERACTIVE SLIDE SHOW

Diamonds

Applying Have students view the first slide as you read aloud the caption. Ask students how the diamond in the photo differs from the diamonds they are familiar with. Next, display the second slide and read aloud the text. Discuss with students what they know about the process that is used to turn the rough diamond shown on the previous slide into the brilliant stone in this ring. Display the third slide and read aloud the caption. Emphasize that diamonds are important for many important uses other than jewelry. Discuss how these other uses might create a large demand for diamonds in fields such as manufacturing and technology. Verbal/Linguistic

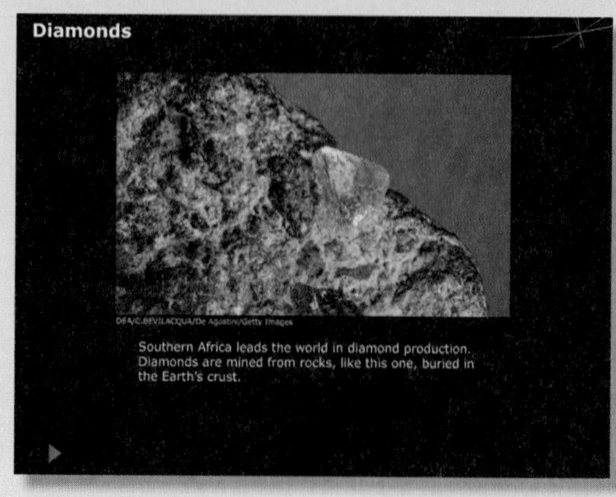

Diamonds
Southern Africa leads the world in diamond production. Diamonds are mined from rocks, like this one, buried in the Earth's crust.

2. Selling Conflict Diamonds

Some conflict diamonds are smuggled into neighboring African countries. These diamonds are then mixed with diamonds hat have been mined legally, making the illegal gems undetectable. Buyers in London and other large diamond markets then purchase the diamonds unaware of their source.

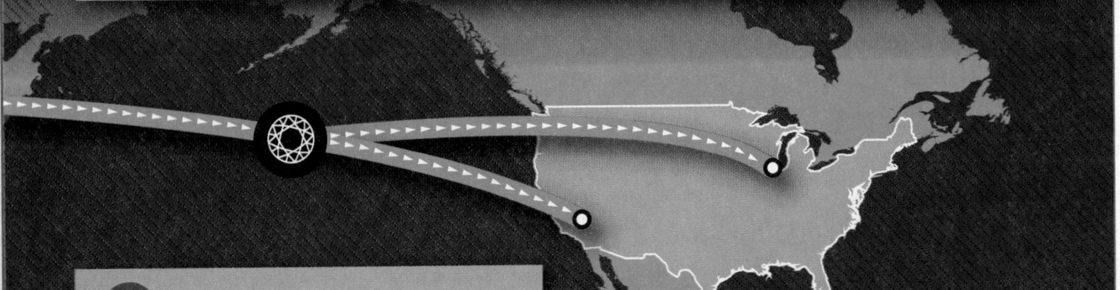

3. Cutting Diamonds

Diamonds are then cut and polished and sold to consumers throughout the world. Some of these diamonds are used in jewelry while others are used for industrial purposes.

Establishing the Kimberley Process

W

The United Nations established the Kimberley Process to reduce the amount of conflict diamonds. In this process a diamond must be certified that it is "conflict-free" before it can be sold.

T

Making Connections

1. ***Places and Regions*** How does the demand for diamonds in other parts of the world fuel civil war and conflict in Africa?
2. ***Human Systems*** Why has it been difficult to stop the flow of conflict diamonds?
3. ***The Uses of Geography*** Using what you know about the trade in conflict diamonds, write a one-page letter to the United Nations suggesting additional steps that could be taken to address the issue of conflict diamonds.

*Interact with **Global Connections** Online*

INTERACTIVE SLIDE SHOW

How to Write a Letter

Gathering Information Before students write their letter to complete the Making Connections question 3, have them view this interactive slide show to review the parts of a letter. Then have students write a draft of their letter and trade it with a partner. Have partners review each other's letters and make suggestions for improvement. Have students review their partner's suggestions and revise their letters before submitting them. **Verbal/Linguistic, Interpersonal, Intrapersonal**

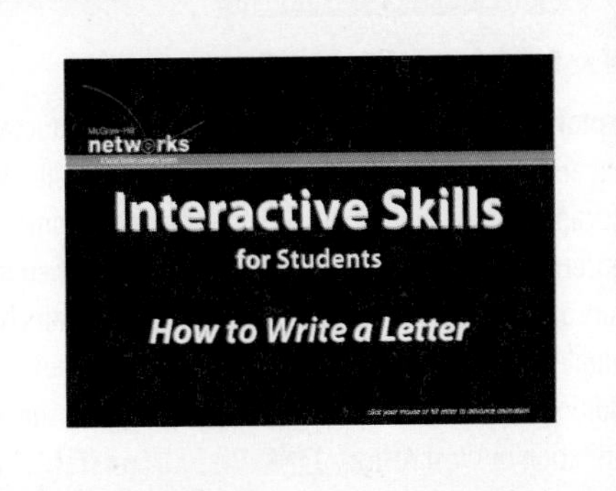

W Writing Skills

Problem Solving Have students discuss the issues surrounding the potential sale of conflict diamonds. **Ask: What is the problem with conflict diamonds?** *(Profits go to fund violent activity. Sometimes they are smuggled out of the country and mixed with legal diamonds, which makes it harder for buyers to know what they are purchasing.)* **What is one solution people have devised for this problem?** *(The UN has set up a process that makes it necessary to certify that a diamond is conflict-free before it is sold.)* Ask students to write essays to describe the problem of conflict diamonds and propose concrete solutions that might address the underlying problems and fix the situation. BL **Logical/Mathematical**

T Technology Skills

Exploring Issues Explain that although the Kimberley Process was set up to ensure that diamonds sold are conflict-free, some people question how well the system actually works in certifying only conflict-free diamonds. Organize the class into small groups. Have groups conduct online research to learn more about different viewpoints on the Kimberley Process. Tell groups to decide for themselves how good a job the Kimberley Process is doing at ensuring that people know where the diamonds for sale are coming from and whether they are conflict diamonds. Have each group present their findings to the class. **Interpersonal, Verbal/Linguistic**

CLOSE & REFLECT

Recognizing Relationships Have students review the information about conflict diamonds and then write three sentences describing ways the actions of people in one place affect the actions of people elsewhere in this situation. Then have students summarize what might need to change to reduce or eliminate the issue of conflict diamonds.

ANSWERS, p. 543

Making Connections

1. Diamonds are in demand around the world for their value as jewelry and their use in industry. Money spent on diamonds is often used by competing interests in Africa to purchase weapons, ammunition, or other supplies.
2. Many groups obtaining African diamonds through force are groups outside the control of any government. Many African countries have difficulty containing or subduing them, and many of these groups pose very real threats to current governments. Any outside country attempting to solve the problem without the cooperation of local authorities runs the risk of starting a larger war. The overall value of diamonds, the willingness of some to purchase conflict diamonds, and the lack of knowledge regarding conflict diamonds mean that demand — and the money to be made — remains very high.
3. Student letters should include ideas and plans for realistic potential solutions to the problem of conflict diamonds.

ENGAGE

R Reading Skills

Previewing Share a news story or headline relating one of West Africa's environmental challenges with the class. Encourage students to explain what these stories indicate about life in West Africa today. Tell students to consider this information as they read the lesson.

TEACH & ASSESS

C Critical Thinking Skills

Analyzing Cause and Effect Have students explain the characteristics of poor sanitation and its impact on people's health. **Ask:** What are some of the illnesses related to poor sanitation? *(infant diarrhea, cholera, malaria, respiratory infections)* How do you suppose poor sanitation contributes to these illnesses? *(polluted water and polluted surfaces carry bacteria)* AL **Logical/Mathematical**

T Technology Skills

Researching Divide students into pairs to research a disease associated with poor sanitation, such as infant diarrhea, cholera, malaria, or respiratory infections. Have students describe the symptoms of the diseases, how they are transmitted, what countries they are prevalent in, and what segments of the population are most likely affected by them. Have students share their research with the class. BL **Verbal/Linguistic**

ANSWERS, p. 544

TAKING NOTES: Problems—Sanitation issues result in illness, premature death, and loss of productivity; corruption leads to conflicts and wars (financed by exploiting natural resources) and stops economic development; failure to manage natural resources leads to food insecurity; high population growth leads to depletion of resources; overgrazed and overworked fields cause soil erosion and desertification; pollution and dynamite practices destroy water systems and depletes fish supplies; **Solutions**—Farmers and organizations such as Oxfam International are reviving traditional land management practices to reclaim land, reduce erosion and desertification, and increase soil fertility; Nigeria is working to reduce water shortages; the Global Water Initiative is working to improve access to clean water and sanitation; the United Nations is working with the Integrated Water Resources Management to increase availability of water for health and sanitation issues; efforts are being made to encourage governments to reduce corruption to bring stability and end conflicts.

networks

There's More Online!

- **IMAGE** Deforestation in Ghana
- **IMAGE** Sanitation Problems
- **INTERACTIVE SELF-CHECK QUIZ**
- **VIDEO** People and Their Environment: West Africa

Reading **HELPDESK** 

Academic Vocabulary (Tier Two Words)
- **goal**
- **demonstrate**

Content Vocabulary (Tier Three Words)
- **carrying capacity**
- **erosion**
- **fishery**

TAKING NOTES: *Key Ideas and Details*

IDENTIFYING As you read about the people and their environment in West Africa, use a graphic organizer like the one below to identify problems and the different ways in which groups are trying to address these problems.

People and Their Environment: West Africa
Problems | Solutions

LESSON 3
People and Their Environment: West Africa

ESSENTIAL QUESTION • *How do physical systems and human systems shape a place?*

IT MATTERS BECAUSE

R *West Africa is faced with multiple challenges. These include drought, increasing population, deforestation, and the degradation of water resources. These challenges have contributed to poverty, hunger, conflict, and war. Finding solutions to these problems may help to reverse the losses and end the crises that afflict the countries of West Africa.*

Managing Resources

GUIDING QUESTION *What challenges resource management in West Africa?*

The poor health and wellness conditions of many West Africans makes survival a chief **goal**, or aim—well ahead of environmental concerns. And yet, many of the environmental issues contribute to poor health and wellness. The ongoing water and sanitation crisis kills large numbers of people and limits economic development. The poor, especially women and children in rural areas, are most at risk. Water and sanitation problems also threaten the growing informal settlements near cities where the poor have migrated seeking work. C

Sanitation problems include the lack of toilets and polluted water supplies. These problems result in illness, premature death, and loss of productivity while people are sick or looking for health care. Some of the illnesses that result from poor sanitation are infant diarrhea, cholera, malaria, and respiratory infections. Poor sanitation also costs countries money through such things as health care and lost hours of work. T For example, poor sanitation costs Benin $104 million per year. Ghana loses $209 million per year, and the cost to Nigeria is $3 billion per year. Tackling these problems by providing better health care, education, and sanitation would help improve the quality of life for everyone in the subregion.

One obstacle to change and economic efficiency in some countries of West Africa is corruption. Corruption has a negative impact on social and economic development as well as on the environment and resource

(t)Max Milligan/AWL Images/Getty Images, (tcl)Jean-Marc Giboux/Getty Images News/Getty Images, (tcr)Kimberley Coole/Lonely Planet Images/Getty Images, (tr)©Godong/Robert Harding World Imagery/Corbis

544

networks *Online Teaching Options*

INTERACTIVE BELLRINGER

West African Street Scene

Exploring Issues Have students read the introductory text and examine the image of sanitation issues in a West African city. Ask students to discuss what environmental concerns they see in the image with a partner. Then have pairs discuss and answer each question. When pairs have completed the activity, invite students to contribute additional comments about the image and the issue of sanitation in West Africa.  **Visual/Spatial, Interpersonal**

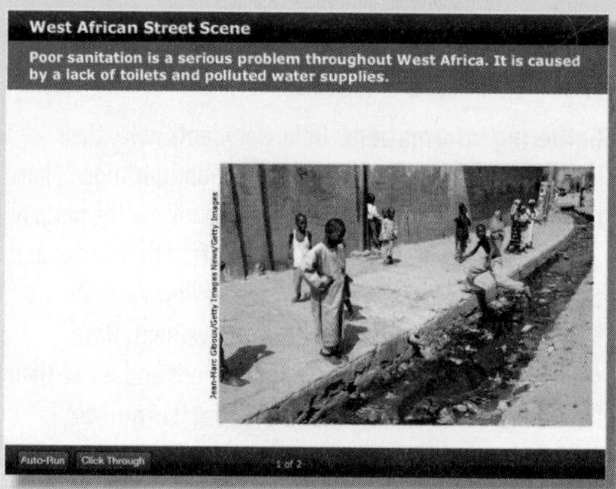

management. Corruption in West African countries has often led to violent political conflict. These conflicts are financed by the unlawful sale of weapons or the illegal extraction and sale of natural resources such as diamonds, gold, and timber. The use of money and natural resources to fund these conflicts hinders economic development. Fortunately, national and international groups are making efforts in West African countries to address corruption, health, sanitation, and access to education and health care. R

goal the aim of an activity

These are not the only problems West Africans face, however. Difficulty in meeting the needs of the people also leads to the mismanagement of natural resources. Such mismanagement is part of a legacy of colonialism, during which massive numbers of people were forced to migrate from mainly rural areas to other rural areas or even urban areas. This resulted in the abandonment of long-held practices learned over generations that were no longer relevant in the new areas and which ultimately caused environmental harm in some places. G1

Many of the countries in West Africa depend on natural resources for economic development. However, the failure to properly manage soils, forests, lakes, rivers, and wildlife will only lead to further problems. There is great concern that the mismanagement of resources will lead to food insecurity for large numbers of West Africans.

READING PROGRESS CHECK

Explaining How does poor sanitation affect the people and countries of West Africa?

Human Impact

GUIDING QUESTION *What environmental challenges does West Africa face today?*

The population of countries south of the Sahara is increasing at a rate of 3.2 percent a year. While that may not sound high, it means—if the rate stays the same—that the population will double in about 22 years. This rate of population C2

Ghana has the highest rate of deforestation in Africa.

▼ CRITICAL THINKING

1. ***Analyzing*** Why is it important to stop deforestation?
2. ***Identifying Cause and Effect*** How has the issue of management of resources affected deforestation?

W

R Reading Skills

Summarizing Ask students to read about corruption in West Africa. Then have students write a paragraph summarizing the corruption problem and its negative impact on social and economic development in West Africa. **Verbal/Linguistic**

G1 Critical Thinking Skills

Analyzing Cause and Effect Have students read the paragraph about the mismanagement of natural resources in West Africa. Lead a class discussion about how colonialism is partly responsible for this mismanagement. **Ask: Why were the pressures on the environment greater during the colonial period than in the precolonial period?** *(Student answers may vary, but they should understand that in precolonial times people practiced sustainable agriculture and did not engage in large-scale extraction of natural resources.)* BL **Logical/Mathematical**

G2 Critical Thinking Skills

Hypothesizing Have students think about what it means for a population to double in 22 years. Have students imagine what effect a population boom of this magnitude would have on the environment, on natural resources, and on communities and their ability to deliver services. Have students give evidence to support their hypotheses. **Logical/Mathematical**

W Writing Skills

Informative/Explanatory Have students study the photograph of women carrying firewood and then write a paragraph describing the story behind the image. Ask students to consider what might be going on here and why, as well as what the result would be. AL **Visual/Spatial**

INTERACTIVE IMAGE

Deforestation in Ghana: The Next Frontier

Formulating Questions Have students view the image and compose *Who, What, Where, Why,* and *How* questions about deforestation in Ghana. Ask students which of those questions can be answered simply by looking at the image and which cannot. Suggest that students conduct further research to answer all the questions, including any others they may have concerning the actions depicted in the photograph. ELL AL **Visual/Spatial, Verbal/Linguistic**

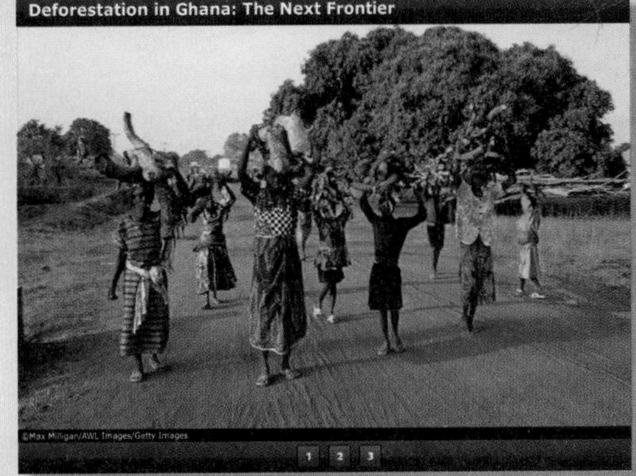

ANSWERS, p. 545

READING PROGRESS CHECK Poor sanitation results in illness, premature death, and loss of productivity of people while they are ill or looking for health care. This loss of productivity and health care expenses cost countries millions to billions of dollars a year across the subregion.

CRITICAL THINKING

1. Deforestation leads to soil erosion and desertification, which causes livestock and agriculture to suffer. This impacts the ecosystem as well as food production of the subregion, making it impossible to produce enough food to feed the population.
2. Since there is little management of resources deforestation continues as land is cleared for housing, farmland, and mining. Timber also provides funds for conflicts. This mismanagement of resources is likely to lead to food insecurity for large numbers of people.

People and Their Environment: West Africa

G1 Critical Thinking Skills

Comparing and Contrasting Have students compare and contrast traditional systems of agriculture with large-scale commercialized farming systems. Discuss which farming practices are more likely to result in deforestation and desertification. **Ask:** **What are the long-term effects on food production when poor farming practices are employed?** *(decreased food production)* **Are there modern farming techniques that do not harm the environment and destroy farmland? Explain.** *(Student answers may vary, but should explain that some modern farming practices are sustainable, especially those that rely on diversification.)* BL **Logical/Mathematical**

R Reading Skills

Identifying Trends Ask students to read the paragraph about deforestation and to note its main causes. Lead a class discussion about how deforestation impacts biodiversity and why this is a problem. AL **Verbal/Linguistic**

T Technology Skills

Presenting Have students research the fishing industry in West Africa. Students might focus on the fishing industry of a single nation or of a particular ecosystem—ocean, lagoon, river, or lake. Challenge students to find out how these industries are dealing with competition, overfishing, and other problems. Suggest that students add photographs, charts, and graphs to illustrate their reports. Have students present their findings to the class. **Verbal/Linguistic**

G2 Critical Thinking Skills

Constructing Arguments Have students imagine that they represent different interest committees in the Lake Chad controversy, such as farming, fishing, tourism, or environmental protection members. Have students conduct a debate on what should be done to save Lake Chad as a committee member. Provide students with time to research their interest in order to present an adequate argument in the debate. BL **Interpersonal, Logical/Mathematical**

ANSWERS, p. 546

READING PROGRESS CHECK Population growth leads to unsustainable practices such as overgrazing, deforestation, poor agricultural practices, overfishing, and pollution, which reduces the already overburdened carrying capacity of the land. This leads to food insecurity and loss of natural resources.

DBQ Drought and desertification have caused the waters available to fish to shrink and fish numbers to dwindle. Fishers are forced to move to other waters to find fish, which results in conflicts over territory and their equipment sometimes being seized.

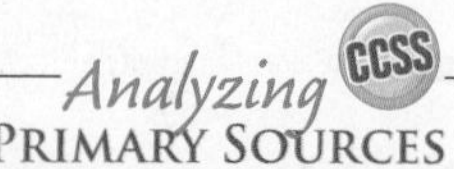

Analyzing Primary Sources

Local Fishermen Near Lake Chad

"There are constant arguments over territory between fishermen. . . . It's difficult to determine boundaries on water, yet the gendarmes [police from Cameroon and Chad] always come after us and seize our fishing nets and traps and we have to pay heavily to get them back."

—Muhammad Sanusi, a fisher in Dogon Fili, "Lake Chad fishermen pack up their nets," BBC News, January 15, 2007

DBQ ***IDENTIFYING CAUSE AND EFFECT*** How has drought and desertification affected fishers in some areas?
RH. 9–10.1

carrying capacity the maximum population of any given species that an environment can sustain

erosion the wearing away of soil

fishery a place for catching fish; the fishing industry

increase is one of the highest in the world. Such rapid growth has placed tremendous pressure on the **carrying capacity** of the land. Carrying capacity is the maximum population of a species the environment can sustain without depleting or degrading the resources available. The growth in population has already led to an environmental crisis in many parts of Africa. One hopeful idea is that humans can increase the carrying capacity of the land by employing more sustainable technologies. Examples include solar cooking technology that reduces the need to burn wood and small-scale irrigation pumps that work like bicycle pedals and allow subsistence farmers to irrigate their fields.

In addition to the heavy load on the environment caused by the increase in population, the breakdown of traditional systems of agriculture is also causing environmental deterioration on a massive scale. This deterioration, in turn, contributes to widespread poverty, malnutrition, and famine. In some countries, the breakdown in farming is contributing to political instability and civil war.

G1 Overgrazed and overworked soils make farming difficult and can damage the long-term health of the soil. The use of heavy farm machinery, frequent tilling, and the clearing of forests have caused **erosion** and desertification. Together with the mismanagement of the land, drought and infrequent rainfall in West Africa also cause desertification. Once desertification begins, it puts pressure on the people that live in the area. Agriculture and livestock suffer, as well as the area's natural biodiversity. All these problems result in food production that has fallen short of the needs of the West African population.

R Another problem facing West Africa is deforestation. Logging creates serious consequences, but the lumber industry maintains a relatively small output. Coastal countries with rain forests, such as Ghana and Côte d'Ivoire, export significant amounts of valuable hardwoods, such as teak, ebony, African walnut, and rosewood. Forests are also cut down to make room for farming, mining, and settlement. Unfortunately, most of this logging is not done sustainably, which threatens the natural biodiversity of the area and also contributes to desertification and erosion.

T Fishing is an important industry in West Africa. **Fisheries** in the West African Marine Ecoregion (WAMER) generate about $400 million a year, making them a key source of revenue. In Senegal alone, over 600,000 people depend directly on fishing and related industries. Here, individual fishers catch over 80 percent of the fish while industrial fishing fleets catch about 20 percent. However, in Senegal and other West African countries, unsustainable fishing practices are leading to dwindling stocks in the ocean fisheries. More and more boats are searching for fewer fish. The competition is leading to even more destructive methods of fishing. These methods include the use of chemicals, dynamite, and bottom trawling. Pollution has also negatively affected fishing in countries such as Nigeria. Oil spills in the Niger Delta, where the local people are fishers and farmers, has led to dwindling fish stocks and reduced soil quality.

G2 Lake Chad is another resource that has been affected by human activity. Drought, desertification, and climate change have caused Lake Chad to shrink. But there are other causes for the changes to the size of the lake as well. The need for water to irrigate farmland as well as for consumption has led to the damming of the rivers that supply Lake Chad. This has also contributed to the reduction in the size of the lake. The shrinking lake has led to smaller fish stocks and, in turn, to arguments over territory between fishers. Conflicts also arise between farmers and fishers over the use of the water from Lake Chad for irrigation. At times, these arguments have led to violence.

READING PROGRESS CHECK

Summarizing How does human activity impact the carrying capacity of the land?

546

networks Online Teaching Options

INTERACTIVE WHITEBOARD ACTIVITY

Challenges of West Africa

Interpreting In this activity, students will use their critical thinking skills to interpret the challenge depicted in each of a series of photographs. Have students carefully view each photograph. Then ask them to read the list of statements that accompanies each image. Ask them to consider the impact on West Africa society the image depicts. When they believe they have correctly identified the correct impact statement, they may click on it. If students have chosen an incorrect statement, have them choose a different statement, until they have correctly identified the challenge represented in the photograph. **Visual/Spatial, Logical/Mathematical**

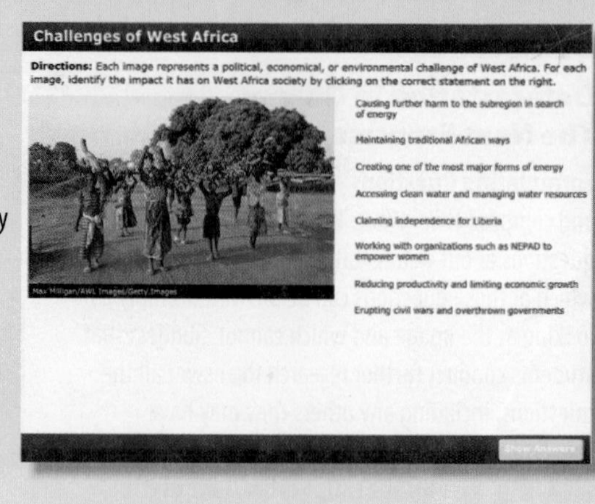

Lack of sanitation and access to clean water are major problems for some areas in West Africa.

▲ CRITICAL THINKING

1. ***Analyzing*** How can poor sanitation affect a community?
2. ***Making Connections*** How would people benefit from better management of water resources?

Addressing the Issues

GUIDING QUESTION *What steps are being taken to combat these environmental challenges?*

West African countries face many environmental problems. These include the degradation of land, desertification, drought, pollution, and the reduction of fish stocks and water resources that reduce the availability of food for both humans and animals. These problems increase the likelihood for conflicts to arise over competition for natural resources. Many individuals, cities, countries, and national and international organizations are working to combat the problems the subregion is facing. Some farmers, for example, have started to practice conservation farming, a land-management technique that helps protect farmland. By planting different crops where they will grow best, farmers protect farmland. Better fertilizers, seeds, and irrigation practices have increased crop yields and production.

Some farmers have begun to revive traditional land-management practices to reverse desertification and have **demonstrated** that these practices can be effective. Such practices include using planting pits to reclaim severely dry land. Additionally, help has come from Oxfam International, a nongovernmental organization (NGO). Oxfam International is a confederation of 17 organizations working together in more than 90 countries around the world to end poverty. Together with Oxfam, farmers in the Yatenga Province of Burkina Faso are building stone contour bunds, or embankments, to control rainwater runoff. This technique has rehabilitated about 740,000 acres (300,000 ha) of land. The additional food produced on the land helps feed about 500,000 people. Other farmers in the region have started to plant native plants in and around crop fields. These food-producing, drought-resistant trees and shrubs help improve soil fertility, retain moisture, and reduce erosion.

demonstrate to clearly show

INTERACTIVE IMAGE

Sanitation Problems

Analyzing Visuals As students view this image, ask them to consider the causes of the poor sanitation seen therein. Ask, also, if they believe this poor sanitation is part of the day-to-day life of the children captured in the photograph, or if the children are being exposed to these conditions for the first time. Have students provide plausible justifications with their responses.
BL Visual/Spatial, Logical/Mathematical

People and Their Environment: West Africa

V Visual Skills

Analyzing Visuals Tell students to imagine that they are NGOs working to improve sanitation in West Africa. Ask students to explain how they might use the photograph at the top of page to make their argument for changes in sanitation practices.
AL Visual/Spatial

C Critical Thinking Skills

Identifying Perspectives Have students choose a West African resource over which there might be competition—perhaps water, farmland, a fishery, or a forest. Have students brainstorm what groups might be vying for control over the resource and why. Then ask students to work with a partner to list ways such conflicts might be resolved. **BL Logical/Mathematical**

W Writing Skills

Informative/Explanatory Have students select one of the practices farmers are starting to use to improve food production and research that practice using the Internet or other library resources. Have students write a short essay explaining in detail how the practice will affect land management and food production. **Verbal/Linguistic**

Content Background Knowledge

Oxfam International Millions of people across West Africa struggle with poverty and are facing serious food shortages. Oxfam is one of many NGOs working in West Africa to end hunger and poverty. At times of acute crisis, Oxfam distributes emergency food to people facing starvation. Among its ongoing programs, Oxfam supports small-scale farmers so they can produce more food, supports the incomes of the poorest people through cash-for-work programs, and builds systems of food reserves. It also works to increase access to safe water and sanitation and promotes good hygiene. In all Oxfam's actions, its ultimate goal is to enable people to exercise their rights and manage their own lives. Oxfam works to influence the powerful to ensure that these goals are realized.

ANSWERS, p. 547

CRITICAL THINKING

1. Communities with poor sanitation have high rates of illness, premature death, and loss of productivity.
2. Better water management would lead to economic and social development of the subregion.

People and Their Environment: West Africa

T Technology Skills

Researching Ask students to research water treatment processes. Encourage them to create diagrams showing the steps to convert dirty water into clean water and what is accomplished by each step. Then have students share their reports with the class. BL Visual/Spatial

R Reading Skills

Explaining Have students read about the large-scale sanitation and clean water projects under way in West Africa. Have students note the purpose, location, and scale of each project. Discuss how the projects are likely to improve the economic and social welfare of the people of the region. AL Verbal/Linguistic

W Writing Skills

Argument Have students imagine they are living in an area of West Africa without a source of clean water. Have students write a letter to an official explaining how water scarcity affects the people of the community and asking for help in resolving the situation. ELL Verbal/Linguistic, Interpersonal

CLOSE & REFLECT

Listing To close the lesson, have students list key ideas from each section of the lesson: "Managing Resources," "Human Impact," and "Addressing the Issues." Have students share their lists as they review the lesson.

ANSWERS, p. 548

✓ READING PROGRESS CHECK Farmers have started to practice conservation farming by reviving traditional land management practices, including the planting of native trees around crops and use of embankments to reclaim land, reduce erosion and desertification, and increase soil fertility.

T

In Nigeria, President Goodluck Jonathan is attempting to address water shortages in the state of Benue through the Greater Makurdi Water Works project. The water treatment plant is designed to bring clean water daily to the people of Benue. However, corruption is hampering this and other projects within the region. For example, in the case of the Makurdi Water Works project, the government council agreed to a water treatment plant with a capacity of 26 million gallons (98 million l). However, the governor of Benue state signed a contract for a treatment plant of half the capacity at the same price of full capacity, raising questions about corruption. Additionally, the plant and the state of Benue do not have the pipe structure necessary to supply the water. The people of Benue will continue to suffer with insufficient clean drinking water until more contracts are signed and the government spends additional money.

R

On a larger scale, the Global Water Initiative (GWI) works in various regions around the world to improve access to clean water and sanitation. In West Africa, GWI works with Burkina Faso, Ghana, and Senegal as well as Mali and Niger. One of the main objectives of the GWI in West Africa is to improve access to clean water and sanitation for vulnerable populations in the region. The group has six projects in West Africa that focus on these objectives in the countries surrounding the Gambia, Volta, and Niger River basins. In villages in Ghana where the GWI initiated projects, the rate of access to safe water has increased by an estimated 50–80 percent.

The United Nations (UN) is working on the use and availability of water in the subregion through the Integrated Water Resources Management (IWRM) project. The IWRM recognizes that water is key to economic and social development in West Africa and elsewhere. The project promotes the coordinated development and management of water, land, and related resources in order to maximize the economic and social welfare of people in the region without harming the environment.

W

Other projects around the region are working to improve access to clean water, thereby improving health and sanitation. Efforts by farmers and larger organizations to improve soil quality will help increase crops, thus reducing hunger. These improvements will encourage governments to make greater efforts to reduce corruption and to increase access to health care and education. These changes and others will help bring stability and security to the people of the region and reduce the incidences of conflict.

✓ READING PROGRESS CHECK

Evaluating In what ways are West Africans trying to combat their environmental problems?

LESSON 3 REVIEW

Reviewing Vocabulary (Tier Three Words)

1. ***Describing*** In what ways has the human population put pressure on the land? RH.9–10.4

Using Your Notes

2. ***Summarizing*** Use your graphic organizer on the people and their environment in West Africa to write a summary of the problems the subregion faces and to propose possible solutions.

Answering the Guiding Questions

3. ***Synthesizing*** What challenges resource management in West Africa?
4. ***Evaluating*** What environmental challenges does West Africa face today?
5. ***Classifying*** What steps are being taken to combat these environmental challenges?

Writing Activity

6. ***Informative/Explanatory*** In a paragraph, write about the cause-and-effect relationship between people and the environment in West Africa. WHST.9–10.2

548

LESSON 3 REVIEW ANSWERS

Reviewing Vocabulary

1. The human population of West Africa puts pressure on the land by growing at a rapid rate, which has led to overgrazing, using unsustainable agricultural and fishing practices, and deforesting areas for housing, timber, farmland and mining.

Using Your Notes

2. Summaries will vary, but could include: **Problems**—population growth, poor sanitation, corruption, conflict, deforestation, soil erosion, desertification, unsustainable agricultural and fishing practices, drought, food insecurity, poverty, and malnutrition; **Solutions**—conservation farming or return to traditional agricultural practices, better water management including irrigation practices, improvements to infrastructure to provide better sanitation, more regulation on the fishing industry, and efforts to reduce corruption and conflict.

Answering the Guiding Questions

3. Corruption and population growth challenge resource management.
4. West Africa faces environmental challenges of deforestation, soil erosion, desertification, unsustainable agricultural and fishing practices, drought, and climate change.
5. Farmers and organizations such as Oxfam International have started to revive traditional land management practices to reclaim land, reduce erosion and desertification, and increase soil fertility. Nigeria is working to reduce water shortages with the Makurdi Water Works project and the United Nations is working through the Integrated Water Resources Management to manage use and increase availability of water throughout the subregion.

Writing Activity

6. Paragraphs will differ but should be strongly supported with information from the lesson illustrating the cause-and-effect relationship between people and the environment. Possible answers could include: the growing population requires more food and housing which causes unsustainable agricultural practices, overfishing, and deforestation; conflicts and corruption leads to depletion of natural resources to finance activities.

CHAPTER 22 Assessment (CCSS)

Directions: On a separate sheet of paper, answer the questions below. Make sure you read carefully and answer all parts of the questions.

Lesson Review

Lesson 1

1. ***Explaining*** Why are mangrove swamps an important part of the ecosystem of West Africa?
2. ***Evaluating*** How successful was the damming of the Volta River at providing benefits for people in the area?
3. ***Comparing and Contrasting*** Describe how biomes and climates change as one moves from north to south in West Africa.

Lesson 2

4. ***Identifying Cause and Effect*** How did the colonial boundaries drawn by European countries at the Berlin Conference affect people in the region?
5. ***Assessing*** Why has the discovery of oil and gas reserves in Nigeria made the country more vulnerable?
6. ***Summarizing*** West Africa has one of the fastest rates of urbanization in the world. What are some of the reasons for this population trend?

Lesson 3

7. ***Describing*** Describe how the ongoing sanitation and water crisis affects the economy and health of people in the subregion.
8. ***Making Connections*** How does the clearing of forests contribute to desertification in West Africa? What are some of the economic and social consequences of this process?
9. ***Problem Solving*** What steps are some West African farmers taking to manage resources more effectively?

Critical Thinking

10. ***Hypothesizing*** How might diamonds purchased in Europe fuel political and social instability in West Africa?
11. ***Drawing Conclusions*** Why do you think e-commerce has become a popular way for West Africans to market locally produced goods?

21st Century Skills

Use the chart to answer the questions that follow.

People Vulnerable to Food Insecurity, March 2012

Country	Number of People Food Insecure
Burkina Faso	2,852,280 food insecure
Chad	3,622,200 food insecure, of which 1,180,300 severe
Gambia	713,433 in areas at risk
Mauritania	700,000 food insecure, of which 290,000 severe
Niger	6,112,089 food insecure, of which 1,916,855 severe
Senegal	850,000 food insecure

Source: www.oxfam.org

12. ***Geography Skills*** Which country in West Africa has the highest number of people vulnerable to severe food insecurity? What is the number?
13. ***Creating and Using Graphs, Charts, Diagrams, and Tables*** How does food insecurity in Senegal compare to Burkina Faso? Why does the table describe Gambia as at risk?

College and Career Readiness

14. ***Problem Solving*** Imagine that you have been hired by Oxfam to help identify potential food shortages in West Africa. Choose a country from the region. Use the Internet to research food production and population growth in that country. How fast is the population growing? Does the production of food meet the needs of the growing population? Write a brief response assessing whether or not the country faces a food shortage. WHST.9–10.2; WHST.9–10.7

Need Extra Help?

If You've Missed Question	1	2	3	4	5	6	7	8	9	10	11	12	13	14
Go to page	532	532	534	536	537	538	544	546	547	534	541	549	549	547

CHAPTER 22 Assessment Answers

Lesson Review

Lesson 1

1. Mangrove swamps provide food and shelter for fish, mollusks, waterfowl, and marine mammals. They are also an important stop for migratory birds.
2. Damming the Volta River has been very successful at providing hydroelectric power and water for drinking and irrigation, and supporting the fishing and tourism industries of the area.
3. From the north to south the land changes from dry desert with little vegetation to steppe, which has very little rainfall and can only support low-growing grasses, shrubs, and the acacia tree. It then changes to savanna, which receives 15 to 25 inches of rainfall and can support trees, grasses, and many mammals and birds. It then changes to tropical dry, which has a rainy season followed by hot, dry months but is able to support a thick forest. It finally changes to tropical wet, which receives the most rainfall and has a much denser forest than tropical dry areas. Tropical wet areas are rich in spices, nuts, and legumes.

Lesson 2

4. The 14 European countries at the Berlin Conference determined boundaries with no regard for African ethnic boundaries, resulting in conflicts and wars.
5. The discovery of oil and gas reserves allowed corrupt government officials to steal billions of dollars paid by foreign companies for oil extraction rights. This not only cost the country revenue but contributed to environmental damage and caused conflicts and wars.
6. Climate change, deforestation, increasing population, and decreasing food supplies have prompted many people to migrate to urban areas seeking jobs, health care, public services, and education. This has caused West Africa to have a rapid rate of urbanization.

Lesson 3

7. The sanitation and water crisis contributes to illness, premature death rates, and a loss of productivity while people are ill or seeking medical attention. It also costs the governments millions to billions of dollars in health care and lost productivity.
8. The clearing of forests exposes the land to erosion as there are no trees or vegetation to hold the soil in place and retain moisture. This leads to desertification. Desertification makes lands unusable for crops or grazing, meaning less food can be grown or supported. This leads to food insecurity, famine, poverty, high prices for existing food, and drought, and slows or stops economic development.
9. Farmers have revived traditional land management practices, including the planting of native trees around crops and use of embankments to reclaim land, reduce erosion and desertification, and increase soil fertility.

Critical Thinking

10. When diamonds from conflict areas are sold in Europe, the proceeds are used to finance the wars in West Africa, continuing the political and social instability in the subregion.
11. E-commerce allows West Africans to offer their products to customer around the world, increasing their market area and revenues.

21st Century Skills

12. Chad has the highest percentage of people vulnerable to severe food insecurity at 32.6 percent.
13. There are a higher number of people that are food insecure in Burkina Faso than in Senegal. Gambia is described as at risk because conditions exist in some areas that could make people vulnerable to food insecurity.

College and Career Readiness

14. Student answers may vary depending on the country chosen, but should include the rate at which the population is growing in the country, if food production within the country supports the population, and if the country is facing a food shortage.

Assessment Answers

DBQ Analyzing Primary Sources

15 The author's observation of what climate change "costs" women farmers in lack of medical care, resulting in possible loss of limbs and the inability to feed their families, helps make the title *"Sahel Food Crisis: the Cost of Climate Change"* understandable.

16 Climate change results in limited or lost crops, which causes food shortages. With no food to eat or sell, there are no funds to pay for medical treatment. There are also no funds to purchase food. A lack of food and no way to obtain medical care result in a loss of productivity as people are unable to work or supply goods and money to the economy.

17 Student answers may vary, but could include that the author begins her description this way because the inability to treat injuries to the hands and feet are the example she uses to illustrate the cost of climate change to individuals in Senegal.

Applying Map Skills

18 The Niger is the main river in West Africa and is 2,600 miles long. It begins in Guinea and flows through Mali, Niger, and Nigeria before emptying into the Atlantic Ocean. The Niger has two deltas, one inland in Mali and one where it empties into the Atlantic Ocean

19 The infrastructures of cities are unable to support the growing population, so they are expanding outward into what was a once untouched land. Examples could include Lagos, Kano, and Ibadan in Nigeria, Accra in Ghana, and Abidjan in Côte d'Ivoire.

20 Lake Chad, Lake Volta, the Volta River, the Senegal River, and the Niger River are important freshwater resources in West Africa. They support the fishing industry, supply water for irrigation of crops, support the tourism industry (Lake Volta), provide transportation for goods and people, and are a source of hydroelectricity, providing power to homes and businesses.

Exploring the Essential Question

21 Time lines will vary based on the country chosen by the student, but should include time line entries for who colonized the country and when, what ethnic boundary lines were crossed, and events since the country gained independence.

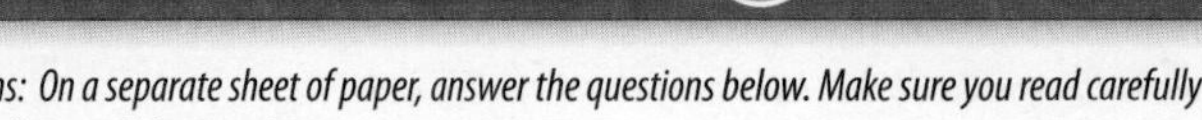

Directions: On a separate sheet of paper, answer the questions below. Make sure you read carefully and answer all parts of the questions.

DBQ Analyzing Primary Sources

Use the document to answer the following questions.

The ongoing food crisis in West Africa has many causes and consequences. Below are the observations of a journalist who has written about Oxfam's work in West Africa.

PRIMARY SOURCE

"Some of my most vivid images of the Sahel food crisis are of hands and feet.

When I traveled to Senegal recently to document Oxfam's work on the crisis, I met with women farmers who lost their last harvest to erratic rains. Several times I noticed an injury to a woman's foot or finger—usually something simple that without medical care had become so serious that it was disabling or worse: from the look of it, some would require amputation. But none of the women had any food stocks left and, with prices on the rise, none could afford to purchase enough for her family to eat, so a visit to the doctor was out of the question."

—Elizabeth Stevens, "Sahel Food Crisis: The Cost of Climate Change," October 2012

15 ***Interpreting*** How does the author's observation of women farmers in Senegal help you understand the title of the article? RH.9–10.6

16 ***Making Connections*** Describe how climate change, inadequate medical care, and food shortages combine to create problems in productivity. RH.9–10.1

17 ***Analyzing Primary Sources*** Why do you think the author begins her description of the food crisis with the image of hands and feet? RH.9–10.4

Applying Map Skills

Use the Unit 6 Atlas to answer the following questions.

18 ***Places and Regions*** Use your mental map of West Africa to describe the length and location of the Niger River and the Niger Delta.

19 ***Human Systems*** How has rapid population growth caused cities to spread out into the countryside in West Africa? Give examples.

20 ***Environment and Society*** What are some of the freshwater resources in West Africa? How important are they to the economies of the subregion?

Exploring the Essential Question

21 ***Analyzing*** Use the Internet and library resources to research the colonial history of a country in West Africa. Who colonized the region? Did colonial boundaries cut across ethnic lines? What happened when colonial rule ended? Create a time line showing how colonial rule affected people in the country you chose. WHST.9–10.2; WHST.9–10.7

Research and Presentation

22 ***Research Skills*** The Niger Delta is one of the world's most important ecosystems. However, the discovery of oil in the 1950s has created problems. Use the Internet to research the environmental and social impact oil has had on the Niger Delta. How severe is the problem of pollution? How have oil companies and the Nigerian government responded? Write your conclusions in paragraph form and share them with the class. WHST.9–10.1; WHST.9–10.7

Writing About Geography

23 ***Informative/Explanatory*** Use the Internet to research challenges facing a city in West Africa. Using standard grammar, spelling, sentence structure, and punctuation, write a two-page essay describing the ways rapid urbanization creates pressure on infrastructure. WHST.9–10.2; WHST.9–10.7

Need Extra Help?

If You've Missed Question	15	16	17	18	19	20	21	22	23
Go to page	550	550	550	476	476	476	537	533	538

550

Research and Presentation

22 Paragraphs will vary but should include that the pollution of the land and water is very severe and has destroyed the livelihood of farmers and fishers in the area. Oil companies have largely blamed sabotage, theft, and illegal refining for the spills. Efforts are ongoing to partner government and oil companies in attempts to clean up the spills.

Writing About Geography

23 Essays will vary depending on the country the student chooses. Essays could include issues cities have in providing sanitation services, clean and adequate water supplies, electricity, health care, education, transportation, and food supplies.

CHAPTER **23**

Equatorial Africa Planner

UNDERSTANDING BY DESIGN®

Enduring Understandings

- *The physical environment affects people and their activities.*

Essential Question

- *How do physical systems and human systems shape a place?*

Predictable Misunderstandings

Students may think:

- *People in Equatorial Africa live in villages in the rain forest and have little contact with the outside world. Explain that remote villages are becoming less so with technology such as cell phones.*
- *Poaching is well-controlled and animals are no longer in danger of becoming extinct. Explain that the demand for products from species like the African elephant continues to fuel the poaching of elephants, even in protected areas, and it continues to be difficult to police despite a worldwide ban on the trade of ivory.*

Assessment Evidence

Performance Tasks:

- *Hands-On Chapter Project*

Other Evidence:

- *Guided Reading Activities*
- *Vocabulary Activities*
- *Lesson Quizzes*
- *Chapter Tests, Forms A and B*

SUGGESTED PACING GUIDE

Introducing the Chapter	½ Day	Lesson 3	1 Day
Lesson 1	1 Day	Chapter Wrap-Up and Assessment	½ Day
Lesson 2	1 Day		

TOTAL TIME 4 Days

Key for Using the Teacher Edition

SKILL-BASED ACTIVITIES

Types of skill activities found in the Teacher Edition.

* **V Visual Skills** require students to analyze maps, graphs, charts, and photos.

R Reading Skills help students practice reading skills and master vocabulary.

C Critical Thinking Skills help students apply and extend what they have learned.

W Writing Skills provide writing opportunities to help students comprehend the text.

T Technology Skills require students to use digital tools effectively.

*Letters are followed by a number when there is more than one of the same type of skill on the page.

DIFFERENTIATED INSTRUCTION

All activities are written for the on-level student unless otherwise marked with the leveled labels below.

BL Beyond Level

AL Approaching Level

ELL English Language Learners

All students benefit from activities that utilize different learning styles. Many activities are marked as below when a particular learning style is highlighted.

Intrapersonal
Logical/Mathematical
Visual/Spatial
Verbal/Linguistic
Naturalist
Kinesthetic
Auditory/Musical
Interpersonal

National Geography Standards covered in "Equatorial Africa"

The student knows and understands:

(5) That people create regions to interpret Earth's complexity

5.1 Regions are defined by different sets of criteria and places can be included in multiple regions of different types

(7) The physical processes that shape the patterns of Earth's surface

7.1 The interaction of Earth's physical systems (the atmosphere, biosphere, hydrosphere, and lithosphere) vary across space and time

7.3 Physical processes interact over time to shape particular places on Earth's surface

(9) The characteristics, distribution, and migration of human populations on Earth's surface

9.1 Culture, economics, and politics influence the changing demographic structure of different populations

9.2 Population distribution and density are a function of historical, environmental, economic, political, and technological factors

(10) The characteristics, distribution, and complexity of Earth's cultural mosaics

10.2 Cultural landscapes exist at multiple scales

(11) The patterns and networks of economic interdependence on Earth's surface

11.4 Improvements in transportation and communication networks reduce the effects of distance and time on the movements of people, products, and ideas

(12) The process, patterns, and functions of human settlement

12.1 The numbers, types, and range of the functions of settlement change

12.2 Settlements can grow and/or decline over time

(13) How the forces of cooperation and conflict among people influence the division and control of Earth's surface

13.3 Changes within, between and among countries regarding division and control of Earth's surface may result in conflict

(14) How human actions modify the physical environment

14.1 Human modifications of the physical environment can have significant global impacts

14.2 The use of technology can have both intended and unintended impacts on the physical environment which may be positive or negative

14.3 People can either mitigate and/or adapt to the consequences of human modifications of the physical environment

CHAPTER OPENER PLANNER

Students will know:
- *that the Congo Basin and Congo River shape life in Central Africa.*
- *how the many life forms of the tropical rain forest form a system.*
- *challenges to democratic governments in the region.*
- *how cultures and conflict coexist in the region today.*
- *how economic and political factors have led to mismanagement of resources in the region.*
- *the several serious environmental issues Equatorial Africa faces and how they are being addressed.*

Students will be able to:
- ***analyze*** *the effect the Congo River and Congo Basin have on life in the region.*
- ***analyze*** *the life forms of the tropical rain forest and how they are connected.*
- ***identify*** *challenges faced by democratic governments.*
- ***analyze*** *how cultures and conflict exist together.*
- ***identify*** *factors that contribute to the mismanagement of resources.*
- ***identify*** *serious environmental threats to Equatorial Africa and how they are being addressed.*

UNDERSTANDING BY DESIGN®

☑ Print Teaching Options

V Visual Skills
- ☐ **p. 552** Students discuss the conflict over oil fields in Sudan and South Sudan using a map. AL Visual/Spatial

R Reading Skills
- ☐ **p. 553** Students create a time line of events in the text.

C Critical Thinking Skills
- ☐ **p. 551** Students consider factors that influence where people settle and compare the Congo and Nile Rivers.
- ☐ **p. 552** Students consider what they know about other countries that have split and the sources of conflict these countries have experienced.
- ☐ **p. 552** Students draw inferences about the nature of conflicts in Equatorial Africa. AL Interpersonal
- ☐ **p. 553** Students classify each of the ethnic, religious, and political characteristics of Sudan and South Sudan.

T Technology Skills
- ☐ **p. 553** Students research challenges the people of Sudan and South Sudan face and potential resolutions.

☑ Online Teaching Options

C Critical Thinking Skills
- GAME **Refugees in Sudan**—Students play a game to further understand the challenges facing Sudan. ELL Interpersonal
- MAP **Interactive Regional Atlas**— Students use the interactive regional atlas to understand the physical and human geography of Equatorial Africa.

☑ Printable Digital Worksheets
- WORKSHEET **Assessing Background Knowledge**—Determine the level of prior knowledge students have about Equatorial Africa.
- WORKSHEET **Chapter Summary**—Students review the main idea of each lesson of the chapter content.
- WORKSHEET **Vocabulary Activity**—Students apply their knowledge of content and academic vocabulary words.

Project-Based Learning 

Hands-On

Nongovernmental Organization
Students research and decide on an issue. They then work together to create a plan to solve it by developing a fictional nongovernmental organization.

Digital Hands-On

Create Online Projects
Find an additional activity online that incorporates technology for this project. Visit the EdTech Teacher Web sites for more links, tutorials, and other resources.

Print Resources

ANCILLARY RESOURCES
This ancillary is available for every chapter and lesson.
- **Chapter Tests and Lesson Quizzes**

PRINTABLE DIGITAL WORKSHEETS
These printable digital worksheets are available for every chapter and lesson.
- **Assessing Background Knowledge**
- **Chapter Summaries**
- **Guided Reading Activities**
- **Hands-On Chapter Projects**
- **Quizzes and Tests**
- **Reading Essentials and Study Guide** AL
- **Reteaching Activities**
- **Video Activities**
- **Vocabulary**

More Media Resources

SUGGESTED VIDEOS 

- **The World Atlas: Equatorial Africa** *Createspace* (45 min.)
- **60 Minutes: The Orphanage** (12 min.)
- **The Mists of Mwanenguba** (62 min.)

SUGGESTED READING 
- ***Foreign Intervention in Africa: From the Cold War to the War on Terror,*** by Elizabeth Schmidt
- ***Forests of Belonging: Identities, Ethnicities, and Stereotypes in the Congo River Basin,*** by Stephanie Rupp
- ***Elephant Hunting in East Equatorial Africa,*** by Arthur H. Neumann

LESSON 1 PLANNER
PHYSICAL GEOGRAPHY OF EQUATORIAL AFRICA

Students will know:
- *that the Congo Basin is the dominant landform of Equatorial Africa.*
- *how the Congo River system shapes life in the subregion.*
- *how the many life forms of the tropical rain forest form a system.*

Students will be able to:
- ***identify** the dominant landform of Equatorial Africa.*
- ***analyze** the effect the Congo River has on life in the region.*
- ***analyze** the life forms of the tropical rain forest and how they are connected.*

UNDERSTANDING BY DESIGN®

☑ Print Teaching Options

V Visual Skills
- ☐ **p. 554** Students create a mental map of Equatorial Africa and label physical features. AL **Visual/Spatial**
- ☐ **p. 555** Students create a map to show areas of high and low population density and compare settlement in Equatorial Africa to another region in Africa. BL **Visual/Spatial**
- ☐ **p. 556** Students discuss the role of rapids and falls in the region. **Visual/Spatial, Naturalist**
- ☐ **p. 557** Students discuss the different layers and the role of each layer in the rain forest. ELL **Visual/Spatial**

R Reading Skills
- ☐ **p. 555** Students discuss the meaning of the term *highlands.* ELL **Verbal/Linguistic**
- ☐ **p. 556** Students select a river from the chart in the text and determine if it is navigable. ELL **Logical/Mathematical**

C Critical Thinking Skills
- ☐ **p. 554** Students describe the geography and climate of Equatorial Africa and how it affects how people live.
- ☐ **p. 557** Students create a chart that compares and contrasts a tropical rain forest climate, a tropical wet/dry climate, and a montane climate. AL **Visual/Spatial, Naturalist**

W Writing Skills
- ☐ **p. 555** Students write an article about Mount Stanley. AL **Logical/Mathematical**
- ☐ **p. 558** Students write a proposal that argues for the development of a particular alternative energy source as if they are working with an organization to develop these sources. BL **Intrapersonal**

T Technology Skills
- ☐ **p. 556** Students research four rivers and bodies of water, record their statistics in a chart or diagram, and use them to summarize the economic importance of each to particular countries. BL **Visual/Spatial, Verbal/Linguistic**
- ☐ **p. 558** Students research a species that is endangered or threatened in the rain forest of the Congo Basin and create a report using presentation software. BL **Visual/Spatial, Naturalist**

☑ Online Teaching Options

V Visual Skills
- INTERACTIVE IMAGE **The Congo River**—Students use the image to learn about the importance of the Congo River to Equatorial Africa. AL **Verbal/Linguistic, Visual/Spatial**

R Reading Skills
- INTERACTIVE WHITEBOARD ACTIVITY **Landforms of Equatorial Africa**—Students drag terms to appropriate locations on a map. AL **Visual/Spatial**

C Critical Thinking Skills
- INTERACTIVE BELLRINGER **Anatomy of the Rain Forest**—Students analyze the infographic to understand how the layers and life forms of the tropical rain forest form a system. ELL **Interpersonal, Visual/Spatial**

W Writing Skills
- INFOGRAPHIC **Anatomy of the Rain Forest**—Students choose an animal in the infographic and imagine that they are that animal living in the rain forest, and write a narrative describing the rain forest from the animal's point of view. **Verbal/Linguistic, Interpersonal**

☑ Printable Digital Worksheets

R Reading Skills
- WORKSHEET **Guided Reading Activity**—Students use the Guided Reading Activity worksheets to review their comprehension of the content.

C Critical Thinking Skills
- WORKSHEET **Video Activity**—Students answer questions related to a topic in the chapter content after they have viewed a lesson video.

HUMAN GEOGRAPHY OF EQUATORIAL AFRICA

Students will know:
- *challenges to democratic governments in the region.*
- *how geography helps shape settlement patterns in Equatorial Africa.*
- *how cultures and conflict coexist in the region today.*
- *how diverse resources lead to a variety of economic activities in Equatorial Africa.*

Students will be able to:
- ***identify** challenges faced by democratic governments.*
- ***analyze** how geography influences settlement patterns.*
- ***analyze** how cultures and conflict exist together.*
- ***identify** the different economic activities and the resources that support them.*

UNDERSTANDING BY DESIGN®

☑ Print Teaching Options

V Visual Skills

- ☐ **p. 560** Students discuss a slave trade map. AL Visual/Spatial, Logical/Mathematical
- ☐ **p. 562** Students research where different ethnic groups live and create maps to show their locations. Visual/Spatial
- ☐ **p. 564** Students research the GDP of an assigned country and create a circle graph to show the data. AL Visual/Spatial, Logical/Mathematical
- ☐ **p. 565** Students review the importance of the development of hydroelectricity in the region. BL Visual/Spatial

R Reading Skills

- ☐ **p. 559** Students discuss the transatlantic slave trade in Africa. ELL Interpersonal, Naturalist

C Critical Thinking Skills

- ☐ **p. 561** Students discuss the treatment of Africans by European colonists. AL Logical/Mathematical
- ☐ **p. 562** Students research the various ethnic groups of São Tomé and Príncipe and how some are unique. AL Logical/Mathematical
- ☐ **p. 563** Students discuss crime and homelessness in the Democratic Republic of the Congo. ELL Auditory/Musical
- ☐ **p. 564** Students consider how foreign-owned plantations are similar to and different from colonial plantations.

W Writing Skills

- ☐ **p. 560** Students write a journal entry from the perspective of a person living in Equatorial Africa during the time of the transatlantic slave trade.
- ☐ **p. 563** Students write an informative paper on how governments and other groups in the region are working to improve health care. BL Verbal/Linguistic

T Technology Skills

- ☐ **p. 559** Students research the Mbuti and create a multimedia presentation about them. BL Interpersonal
- ☐ **p. 561** Students discuss political instability after independence and find primary sources about human rights violations in Equatorial Africa. BL Verbal/Linguistic, Logical/Mathematical

☑ Online Teaching Options

V Visual Skills

- INTERACTIVE BELLRINGER **The Atlantic Slave Trade**—Students review a map of trade routes and discuss challenges posed to democratic governments by the slave trade. Visual/Spatial, Verbal/Linguistic
- TIME LINE **Conflict in the Congo**—Students discuss the events surrounding the name change of the Republic of Congo. Interpersonal, Visual/Spatial
- GRAPHIC ORGANIZER **Human Geography of Equatorial Africa**—Students learn about ethnic groups, choose one group, and write a narrative describing what they think a day in the life of a member of that group might be like. AL Verbal/Linguistic

R Reading Skills

- GAME **Human Geography of Equatorial Africa**—Students play a game in which they decide if statements about the human geography of the region are right or wrong. AL Kinesthetic, Verbal/Linguistic
- VIDEO **Rwanda Macy**—Students watch a video to learn the reasons why so many Rwandan women are widowed, why they have forged a bond with each other, how their woven goods came to be sold at Macy's, and how these sales contribute to the economic well-being of Equatorial Africa. AL Logical/Mathematical, Verbal/Linguistic
- INTERACTIVE WHITEBOARD ACTIVITY **Slavery and European Colonization in Equatorial Africa**—Students identify the location of some of the political challenges to democratic governments in the region.

C Critical Thinking Skills

- INTERACTIVE MAP **The Atlantic Slave Trade**—Students study the slave trade map and consider why routes for sugar, tobacco, and manufactured goods are included on the map. AL Verbal/Linguistic

☑ Printable Digital Worksheets

R Reading Skills

- WORKSHEET **Guided Reading Activity**—Students use Guided Reading Activity worksheets to review their comprehension of the content.
- WORKSHEET **Reading Essentials and Study Guide**—Students complete the study guide and answer Reading Progress Check and vocabulary questions. AL

C Critical Thinking Skills

- WORKSHEET **Video Activity**—Students answer questions related to a topic in the chapter content after they have viewed a lesson video.

People and Their Environment: Equatorial Africa

Students will know:

- *how economic and political factors have led to mismanagement of resources in the region.*
- *the several serious environmental issues Equatorial Africa faces.*
- *the ways in which national and international groups and social entrepreneurs are working to resolve these issues.*

Students will be able to:

- ***identify** factors that contribute to the mismanagement of resources.*
- ***identify** serious environmental threats to Equatorial Africa.*
- ***identify** how environmental threats are being addressed by different groups.*

UNDERSTANDING BY DESIGN®

Print Teaching Options

V Visual Skills

- **p. 566** Students research the production of copper, cobalt, and diamonds in Equatorial Africa over the past decade and create a graph to illustrate their findings. BL **Logical/Mathematical**
- **p. 569** Students discuss how events or actions can have multiple causes and effects and create a cause-and-effect diagram. **Interpersonal, Visual/Spatial**

R Reading Skills

- **p. 566** Students identify examples of natural resources in Equatorial Africa.
- **p. 568** Students discuss and define *deforestation*, *desertification*, and *pollution*. AL **Verbal/Linguistic**

C Critical Thinking Skills

- **p. 566** Students create a list of issues and challenges most people in the region face in their daily lives. AL **Verbal/Linguistic**
- **p. 569** Students discuss the effect poverty has had on hunting in Equatorial Africa. ELL **Verbal/Linguistic**
- **p. 570** Students discuss the causes and effects of human actions on the environment and steps being taken to reduce the problems. **Logical/Mathematical**

W Writing Skills

- **p. 567** Students write an editorial about the importance of sustainable practices to prevent soil erosion. **Verbal/Linguistic**
- **p. 570** Students write a report on the struggle that one NGO faces to eradicate poaching in the wake of rising poverty levels. BL **Verbal/Linguistic**

T Technology Skills

- **p. 567** Students track the GDP and the level of poverty of one of the Equatorial African countries over the last several years and discuss the data. AL **Visual/Spatial, Logical/Mathematical**
- **p. 568** Students look online for images of tropical rain forests in the region at various stages of logging and use them to create a slide show. ELL **Visual/Spatial**

Online Teaching Options

V Visual Skills

GRAPH **Elephant Poaching in 2011**—Students use the graph to consider reasons why elephant poaching is so prevalent in many parts of Africa. BL **Logical/Mathematical, Verbal/Linguistic**

R Reading Skills

INTERACTIVE WHITEBOARD ACTIVITY **Environmental Threats in Equatorial Africa**—Students draw lines to match the correct relationships between some of the natural features of Equatorial Africa and the threats these features face. **Kinesthetic, Naturalist**

GAME **People and the Environment: Equatorial Africa**—Students determine whether statements concerning the people and environment of Equatorial Africa are true or false. AL **Verbal/Linguistic**

C Critical Thinking Skills

INTERACTIVE BELLRINGER **Refugees and Internally Displaced Persons in the CAR**—Students explore economic and political factors that have led to the mismanagement of resources in the Central African Republic. BL **Logical/Mathematical, Verbal/Linguistic**

Printable Digital Worksheets

R Reading Skills

WORKSHEET **Guided Reading Activity**—Students use Guided Reading Activity worksheets to review their comprehension of the content.

WORKSHEET **Reading Essentials and Study Guide**—Students complete the study guide and answer Reading Progress Check and vocabulary questions. AL

WORKSHEET **Vocabulary Activity**—Students review the chapter content and academic vocabulary words.

WORKSHEET **Chapter Summary**—Students review the main ideas of the chapter content.

C Critical Thinking Skills

WORKSHEET **Video Activity**—Students answer questions based on a lesson video.

WORKSHEET **Reteaching Activity**—Students use this activity worksheet to review and reteach chapter content and vocabulary. This worksheet can be used with struggling students who need additional help with difficult content concepts.

INTERVENTION AND REMEDIATION STRATEGIES

LESSON 1 Physical Geography of Equatorial Africa

Reading and Comprehension

Assign student pairs one of Equatorial Africa's subregions discussed in the text. Have partners use the map of the Congo Basin in the lesson to identify key physical features of their assigned region. Using information from the text, have partners develop a descriptive summary of their region. Students may wish to include visuals to accompany their summaries. Encourage students to use one or more content vocabulary terms in their summaries.

Text Evidence

Have students review the It Matters Because paragraph at the beginning of the lesson. Tell students to choose one of the statements and use it as a topic for an outline, chart, or map. Students should identify evidence from the text to support their chosen statement. For example, if students choose the first statement in the paragraph, they might create a map that shows the vast area encompassed by Equatorial Africa and include a description from the text of a "stunning landscape." Then have students share their outlines, charts, and maps with the class.

LESSON 2 Human Geography of Equatorial Africa

Reading and Comprehension

To ensure that students fully comprehend the varied economies of Equatorial Africa, have them review the information under the heading Economic Activities in the lesson. Have student pairs choose one of the economic activities listed in the text and summarize its importance to the region. Challenge students to draw inferences about the economic benefits or the environmental consequences of their chosen activity in their summaries.

Text Evidence

Organize students into small groups to create a pictorial time line based on information in the lesson about Equatorial Africa's history, government, culture, and economy. Students may choose either a concept or region on which to focus their time lines, but remind students that they should use textual evidence to support the events listed on their time lines. After each group has gathered facts for its time line, have groups present their time lines to the class. Discuss as a class how conflict has shaped life in Equatorial Africa.

LESSON 3 People and Their Environment: Equatorial Africa

Reading and Comprehension

Assign student pairs one of the subregions of Equatorial Africa. Have partners identify cause-and-effect relationships as they read about the human impact on the environment of their subregion. Remind students to look for signal words and phrases such as *cause, effect, as a result,* and *consequently.* Tell partners to create a diagram or flowchart that illustrates the cause-and-effect relationship in their assigned subregion. Have student pairs share their diagrams or charts with the class.

Text Evidence

Have students review the lesson to write a journal entry from the point of view of a teenager living in Equatorial Africa. Tell students their journal entries should reveal where the teenager lives and should refer to the positive and negative aspects of living in that region. Encourage students to incorporate facts about the region and daily life there, based on evidence from the lesson. Students may wish to conduct research to find additional information about their region to enhance their writing. Invite students to read their journal entries to the class.

Online Resources

Leveled Reader

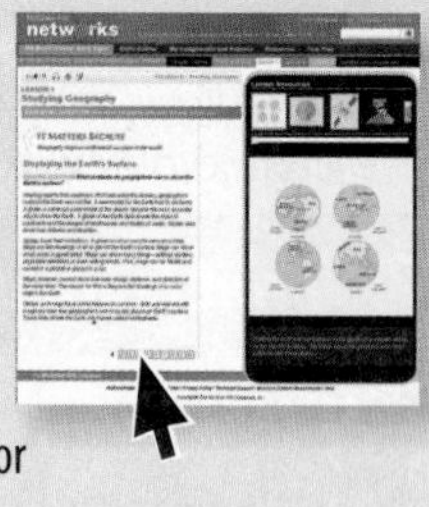

Use this online approaching-level text that corresponds directly to the text in the Student Edition. It also includes additional reading and comprehension support for English Language Learners.

Guided Reading Activities

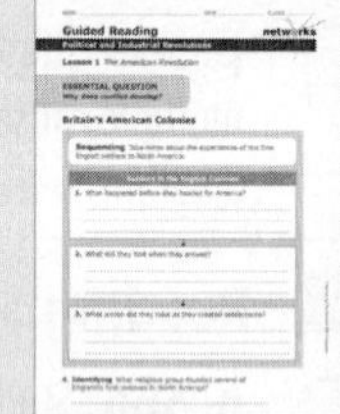

This resource uses guiding questions to help students with comprehension.

Reteaching Activities

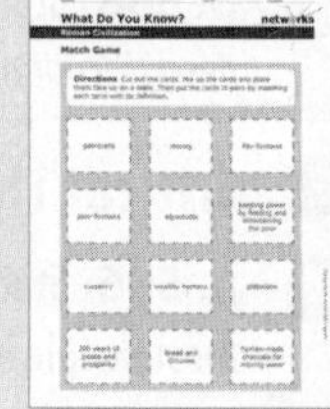

These worksheets provide students with an opportunity for remedial practice and review of vital chapter content.

Reading Essentials and Study Guide

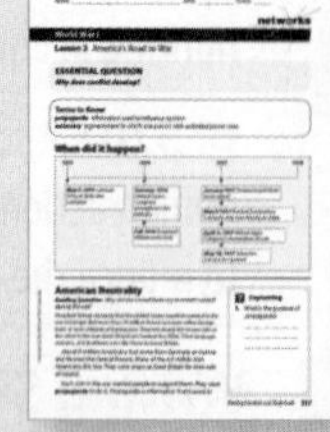

This resource offers writing and reading activities for the approaching-level student.

Self-Check Quizzes

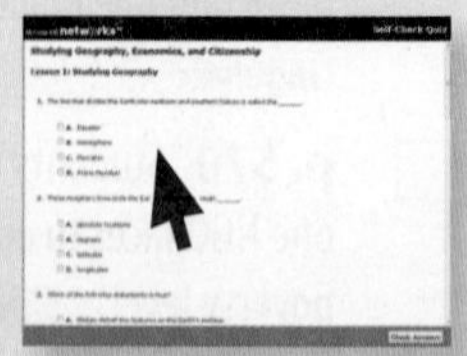

This online assessment tool provides instant feedback for students to check their progress.

Chapter Summaries

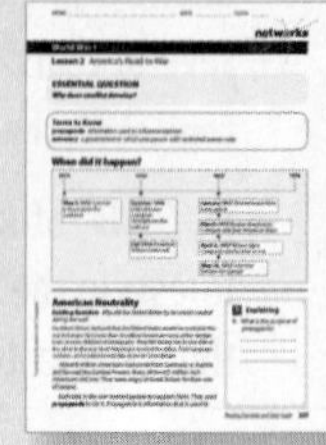

Summaries are provided for each chapter that thoroughly condense core content into manageable chunks.

Equatorial Africa

ESSENTIAL QUESTION • *How do physical systems and human systems shape a place?*

networks

There's More Online about Equatorial Africa's geography.

CHAPTER 23

Geography Matters...

Equatorial Africa lies in the heart of Africa. Great expanses of rain forest teem with wildlife. Through the forest flows the mighty Congo River—one of the longest in the world—and its many tributaries. These waterways form a vast transportation network that the people of Equatorial Africa have used for centuries.

Along these streams are many villages. Most of the people of these villages make their living as farmers. Others work in the region's many mines, extracting gold, diamonds, and other minerals. Still others live and work in huge port cities, where the rivers of the heart of Africa flow into the Atlantic Ocean.

◀ A chief from Ndian and Koupe-Manengouba in Cameroon

551

Letter from the Author

Dear Geography Teacher,

The elephant issue in Equatorial Africa is a bit more complicated than most people think. Poaching is bad, it is illegal, and it is what we hear about in the media. But there is another side to the issue. Elephants are protected and breeding quite well in some game preserves. But a herd of elephants can destroy plants and trees in a tropical rain forest, upsetting the ecological balance. Game wardens "thin the herd," by killing elephants to protect the overall physical environment. In fact, game wardens sometimes kill whole herds so as to not destroy the social relationships within the herd.

Richard G. Boehm

ENGAGE

Drawing Conclusions Have students think about the area of Africa that comprises the Equatorial subregion. Then invite a volunteer to explain how a location's climate is affected by being situated near the Equator. Ask students to write a paragraph that draws conclusions about how the climate of Equatorial Africa affects how the people live as compared to climates in other subregions of Africa.

TEACH & ASSESS

Making Predictions Have students consider what factors influence where people settle. **Ask:** **Do you think the climate, land, resources, and availability of water affected where people have settled in Equatorial Africa?** *(Student answers may vary, but might suggest that more people usually settle in areas that have a moderate climate, are near water, have resources to develop, and have available land to farm.)* **Which of the factors that you predicted affected settlement in this subregion? Which did not?** *(Congo River and resources such as gold, diamonds, and other minerals would attract settlers; rain forests rather than open land to farm would discourage settlement)*

Comparing and Contrasting Have students compare the Congo River with the Nile River. **Ask:** **How are the Congo and Nile Rivers similar?** *(They are both located in Africa and are both among the longest in the world. Both are used for transportation.)* Discuss with students the flow and course of the Congo River. Explain that it flows generally to the northwest, west, and southwest. **Ask:** **How are the rivers different or unique?** *(The Nile River flows northward and empties into the Mediterranean Sea, while the Congo River generally flows westward and empties into the Atlantic Ocean.)* **BL** **Naturalist**

CLOSE & REFLECT

Problem Solving Explain that natural resources are a major point of contention and have caused civil war in Equatorial Africa. Ask students if the subregion's natural resources can be divided fairly. Then have them make a list of possible solutions to this challenge.

ePals GlobalCommunity Where learners connect™

Extend the project-based learning experience globally through our partnership with ePals. EPals allows you to connect with classrooms around the world in a safe online environment for real-life lessons and projects in virtual study groups.

ENGAGE

C1 Critical Thinking Skills

Predicting Before students open their texts, read the title aloud to students. Ask them to consider what they know about other countries that have split and the sources of conflict these countries have experienced. Tell students to write three predictions on what this feature will be about based on this title. Have several volunteers share their answers with the class.

TEACH & ASSESS

V Visual Skills

Identifying Invite a volunteer to read the callouts. **Ask:** **Where are the oil-producing areas located?** *(They are in disputed or border areas between Sudan and South Sudan in two places.)* **What solution could you suggest to the governments of Sudan and South Sudan regarding the conflict over oil fields and the building of a pipeline?** *(Possible answer: The government of South Sudan could try to work out an agreement with the neighboring countries such as Kenya to build a pipeline to the Indian Ocean.)* **How would your solution solve the conflict?** *(Possible answer: By building the pipeline in a neighboring country and one which is bordered by a different body of water, it might help to ease tensions.)* Invite students to share their solutions.

AL Visual/Spatial, Logical/Mathematical

C2 Critical Thinking Skills

Drawing Inferences Have students use both the callouts and map to draw inferences about the nature of conflicts in Equatorial Africa. **Ask:** **Do you think similar conflicts over resources exist in the subregion or just in the Sudan and South Sudan?** *(Possible answers: There are probably other disputes that are similar and related to resources.)* **Why is the conflict over oil and pipelines in the Sudan and the South Sudan so heated?** *(Possible answers: because South Sudan created an independent nation from the Sudan, which probably caused conflict to begin with)* **AL Interpersonal**

Why Geography Matters: **Equatorial Africa**

South Sudan: independence and conflict

South Sudan declared its independence from Sudan in 2011, after centuries of ethnic and religious conflict. The celebration of newly won freedom did not last long, however. This break only fueled tensions, as both countries continue to dispute borders, which affects in part the economic survival of South Sudan.

Sudan and South Sudan Conflicts

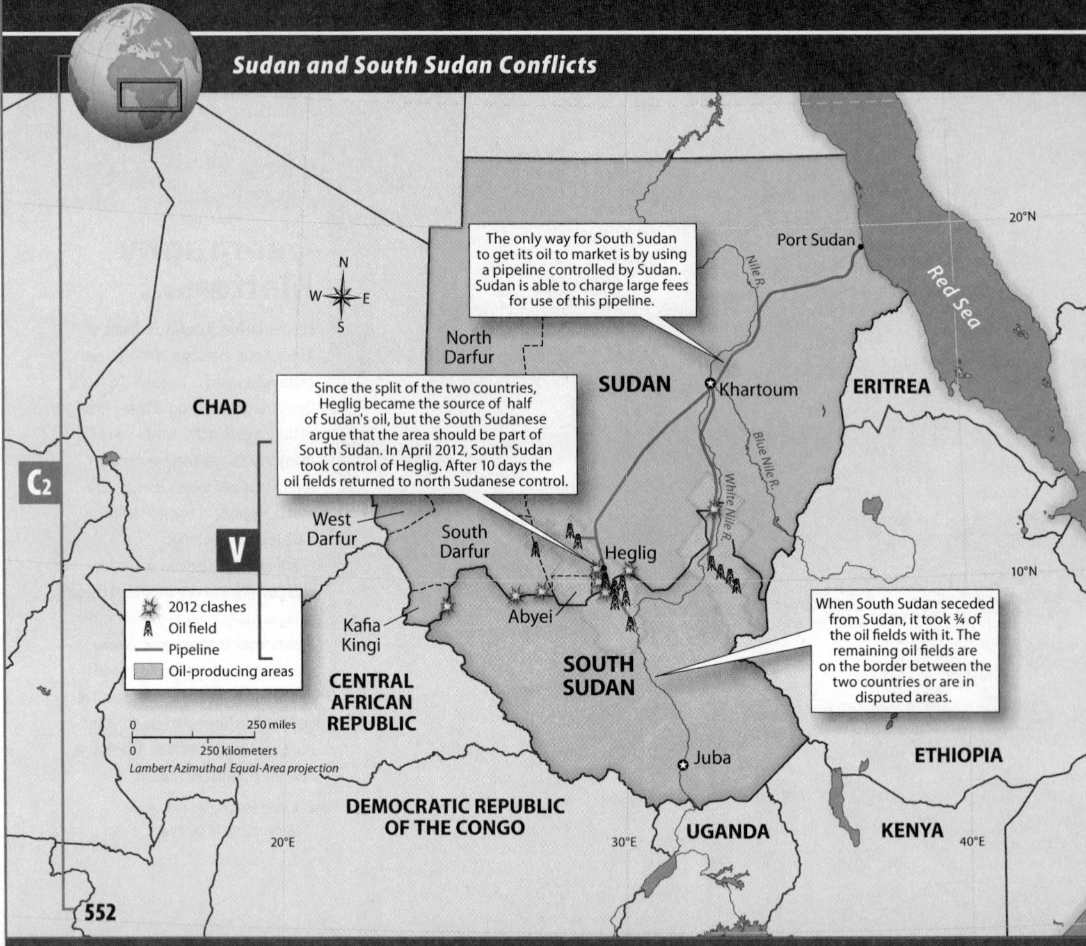
The only way for South Sudan to get its oil to market is by using a pipeline controlled by Sudan. Sudan is able to charge large fees for use of this pipeline.
Since the split of the two countries, Heglig became the source of half of Sudan's oil, but the South Sudanese argue that the area should be part of South Sudan. In April 2012, South Sudan took control of Heglig. After 10 days the oil fields returned to north Sudanese control.
When South Sudan seceded from Sudan, it took ¾ of the oil fields with it. The remaining oil fields are on the border between the two countries or are in disputed areas.
2012 clashes
Oil field
Pipeline
Oil-producing areas
0 250 miles
0 250 kilometers
Lambert Azimuthal Equal-Area projection
N
S
W
E
Port Sudan
Red Sea
Nile R.
Blue Nile R.
White Nile R.
North Darfur
West Darfur
South Darfur
SUDAN
Khartoum
ERITREA
CHAD
Heglig
Abyei
Kafia Kingi
CENTRAL AFRICAN REPUBLIC
SOUTH SUDAN
Juba
ETHIOPIA
DEMOCRATIC REPUBLIC OF THE CONGO
UGANDA
KENYA
20°N
10°N
20°E
30°E
40°E
552

Project-Based Learning

Hands-On

Nongovernmental Organization

Working in small groups, students will research, decide on an issue, and create a plan to solve it. Each group will develop a fictional nongovernmental organization created to combat environmental issues while addressing the needs of the people. The plan should state the issue and describe the geographical features, resources, and historical events that contribute to the issue, and propose a plan of action to address the issue.

ePals GlobalCommunity
Where learners connect™

Digital Hands-On

Create Online Projects

Find an additional activity online that incorporates technology for this project. Visit the EdTech Teacher Web sites for more links, tutorials, and other resources.

edtechteacher
21st Century Learning

What is the history of Sudan?

The modern country of Sudan emerged from a history that dates back thousands of years to the Kush civilization in the fourth century B.C. The kingdoms of Kush, Nubia, Axum, and Egypt vied for power in the region until the A.D. 600s, when the Arab Muslim conquest of Egypt and what is now northern Sudan began. By the mid-1300s, Arab Muslims had dethroned the last Christian king of Nubia, replacing him with a Muslim ruler. The last Christian kingdom in Sudan fell in the early 1500s.

In the 1800s Egyptian forces—and later, British and Egyptian forces—conquered Sudan. In 1899 the two countries consolidated their rule of Sudan. In 1916 they annexed Darfur to Sudan. Even though Britain and Egypt shared control of Sudan, the British sought to limit Egyptian power. Sudan was essentially a British colony. After decades of protests and uprisings, Britain recognized Sudan as an independent, sovereign country in 1956.

1. **Human Systems** How did other civilizations and countries influence Sudan's history?

What conditions led to the country splitting in two?

Civil war broke out in 1983 when the Sudanese government tried to enforce Islamic law throughout the country. The seeds of this conflict were planted centuries ago. The northern part of the country was dominated by Arabic-speaking Muslims. In the southern part of Sudan, however, the majority of the people were Christians or animists and spoke a variety of African languages. Differences had long brewed between the northern and southern regions of Sudan. Under British colonial rule, this tension increased. Sudanese Arabs in the north racially **R** discriminated against the black Sudanese farmers in the south. In response to the attempt to impose Islamic law on non-Islamic southern Sudan, leaders in the south organized the Sudan People's Liberation Movement. Civil war and strife continued for decades until a peace agreement was signed in 2005.

Finally, after nearly 4 million people had been displaced and nearly half that number had died, the vast majority of registered voters in southern Sudan voted for secession from Sudan in January 2011. The Republic of South Sudan was born, but independence did not solve all the region's problems.

2. **Places and Regions** In what ways did northern Sudan differ from southern Sudan?

What challenges does the new country of South Sudan face?

Refugees who fled Sudan during the civil war have returned to their homeland, but the country faces many challenges. One hurdle is the country's devastated economy, which is linked to its landlocked status. After South Sudan seceded, economic and political conflict erupted over rights to its oil fields, because the pipeline to export oil runs through Sudan. South Sudan struggled to pay the fees to use the pipeline. In 2012 leaders from both countries met to sign a series of agreements. One part of the agreement would enable South Sudan to export oil through the pipeline in Sudan. **T**

C Other challenges have slowed efforts to rebuild. Armed rebels and militias and warring ethnic groups continue to challenge efforts to promote economic and political stability. Poverty is widespread but could be reduced or controlled if both countries cooperate and make economic decisions that will benefit the region.

3. **Places and Regions** How can Sudan and South Sudan work together to achieve economic growth and strength for the region?

(l)Comstock Images/Getty Images, (c)Roberto Schmidt/AFP/Getty Images, (r)Karel Prinsloo/AP Images

THERE'S MORE ONLINE 

CONNECT with the lives of refugees in Sudan • *EXAMINE* a map of the Darfur crisis

Why Geography Matters

R Reading Skills

Sequencing Information After students have read the text, **ask:** **What time period is discussed in the paragraph?** *(fourth century B.C. to 1956)* In pairs, have students create a time line of the events. **Ask: How did the people of Sudan respond to British control?** *(They protested British control.)* **How did Darfur become part of Sudan?** *(In 1916 Britain annexed Darfur to Sudan.)* **Why did Britain limit Egypt's control of the Sudan?** *(Britain and Egyptian forces both ruled Sudan, but Sudan was a British colony, so Britain wanted full control.)* Explain that Sudan struggled for many decades before it achieved independence. **AL** **Visual/Spatial**

C Critical Thinking Skills

Classifying Have students divide a piece of paper into two columns by folding and creasing it in the middle. Ask students to classify each of the ethnic, religious, and political characteristics of Sudan and South Sudan. If there are any characteristics that are prominent in both countries, they should list them on both halves. **ELL** **Logical/Mathematical**

T Technology Skills

Gathering Information Ask students to select one of the challenges the people of Sudan and South Sudan face and then research about this challenge. Have students write an essay about their research and any potential resolutions. Have students present their information to the class. **Verbal/Linguistic**

CLOSE & REFLECT

Identifying Trends Based on what students have learned about Sudan and South Sudan, ask them to predict whether similar conflicts could be trends in the entire subregion.

GAME

Refugees of Sudan

Transferring Information This game about the refugees of Sudan can be used to provide further understanding about the challenges facing the country. Divide students into pairs or groups of four to play the game as teams of two. Allow time for students to play the game, and then ask them to discuss information in the game within their groups. After their discussion, have students individually write out the information that they learned about the refugees of Sudan while playing the game and discussing this issue. **ELL** **Interpersonal**

ANSWERS, p. 553

Why Geography Matters

1. Many kingdoms vied for power in the region and eventually Arab Muslims took over the Christian kingdoms. Britain and Egypt combined forces to conquer Sudan, eventually annexing Darfur as well in 1916. The British limited Egypt's power making Sudan essentially a British colony until their independence in 1956.
2. Northern Sudan was largely Arabic-speaking Muslims while the south followed Christian or animist religions and spoke a variety of African languages.
3. The countries could work together to make agreements for the export of oil from South Sudan through Sudan that is profitable for both countries as well as reducing ethnic conflict, which is making the region unstable.

ENGAGE

C Critical Thinking Skills

Analyzing Display a physical and climate map of Equatorial Africa for students and ask them to describe the geography and climate. Invite a volunteer to read *It Matters Because.* Discuss the contrasts in climate between the tropical wet and tropical dry climates. Ask students how the climate and land affect how people live and use the resources of the region.

TEACH & ASSESS

V Visual Skills

Creating Visuals Have students create a mental map of Equatorial Africa, keeping in mind that it is about the size of Australia. Have them label any physical features that they may know. **Ask:** **What do the names of the countries in this subregion reveal about its physical features?** *(Equatorial Guinea includes the name of the subregion and relates to its proximity to the Equator. Two countries include the word* Congo, *relating to Congo River. Central African Republic reveals its central location.)* **Why are physical features often found in the names of places?** *(They define a location and reveal descriptive information about a place.)* AL Visual/Spatial

Content Background Knowledge

Congo Basin Rain Forest The Congo Basin is located on the Equator, bounded by high elevations. The center of the basin is called the *cuvette,* which means "saucer" or "shallow bowl" in French. A rain forest sits within the basin. The second largest in the world, the rain forest is surrounded by stretches of savanna; 10,000 tropical plants thrive here, about 30 percent are indigenous to the subregion.

ANSWERS, p. 554

TAKING NOTES: Landforms—The Atlantic coastal region of the Republic of the Congo and Gabon is a low plain; the coast of Cameroon is mountainous; the islands of São Tomé and Príncipe are extinct volcanoes; the Congo Basin is a rain forest; to the south is Katanga Plateau; to the southwest are the highlands of Gabon and the Republic of Congo, containing the Chaillu Mountain ranges; the Ruwenzori Mountains separate the Congo Basin from the Nile River; to the northwest lie the Grotel Mountains with an active volcano, Mount Cameroon. **Water Systems**—The Gulf of Guinea borders Equatorial Africa and contains the islands of São Tomé and Príncipe; five countries have coastlines on the gulf; the Congo River is part of the border between the Republic of Congo and the Democratic Republic of Congo and drains to the Atlantic Ocean, navigable by oceangoing ships; the Congo River, its tributaries, and Lake Tanganyika serve as sources of transportation.

networks *There's More Online!*

- IMAGE Fishing at Boyoma Falls
- INFOGRAPHIC Anatomy of the Rain Forest
- MAP Physical Geography: The Congo Basin
- INTERACTIVE SELF-CHECK QUIZ
- VIDEO Physical Geography of Equatorial Africa

LESSON 1

Physical Geography of Equatorial Africa

ESSENTIAL QUESTION • *How do physical systems and human systems shape a place?*

Reading HELPDESK CCSS

Academic Vocabulary (Tier Two Words)
- **navigable**
- **abundant**

Content Vocabulary (Tier Three Words)
- **basin**
- **montane**
- **canopy**
- **understory**

TAKING NOTES: ***Key Ideas and Details***

IDENTIFYING Use a graphic organizer like the one below to take notes about landforms and water systems in Equatorial Africa.

Landforms	Water Systems

C

IT MATTERS BECAUSE

Equatorial Africa is a huge area that displays some of the most stunning landscapes on the planet. One of the world's great rivers courses through the heart of this region of plains, hills, mountains, and dense rain forests. It is a land of abundant natural resources and exotic wildlife. Everything from active volcanoes to lagoons can be found in this hot and humid tropical subregion.

Landforms

GUIDING QUESTION *What huge landform covers most of Equatorial Africa?*

Equatorial Africa is another of the five subregions that make up the larger region of Africa south of the Sahara. It is located on and near the Equator in central Africa. This tropical subregion is also called Central Africa or the Heart of Africa. Much of the land is covered by thick rain forest and is home to some of Africa's most famous and colorful wildlife.

V

The subregion covers a huge area. It stretches from about ten degrees north to ten degrees south of the Equator and covers about 2.6 million square miles (6.7 million sq. km)—nearly the size of Australia. It includes the countries of the Democratic Republic of the Congo, Cameroon, Central African Republic, Gabon, Equatorial Guinea, Republic of the Congo (or Congo), South Sudan, and the southern part of Chad. The island country of São Tomé and Príncipe, located in the Gulf of Guinea, is also part of the subregion. The Democratic Republic of the Congo, at about 1.5 million square miles (3.9 million sq. km), is by far the largest country in Equatorial Africa.

This large subregion also has a diverse landscape. The Atlantic coastal region of the Republic of the Congo and Gabon is mostly a low plain with lagoons and beaches, while the coast of Cameroon is mountainous. The two islands that comprise São Tomé and Príncipe are both extinct volcanoes. Each island is steep in the west and gradually slopes to the northeast.

Equatorial Africa is dominated by the Congo Basin. A **basin** is an area of land that is drained by a river and its tributaries. Water from rainfall in the Congo Basin flows downhill and collects into streams.

networks ***Online Teaching Options***

INTERACTIVE BELLRINGER

Anatomy of the Rain Forest

Acquiring Information Have students analyze this infographic showing the layers of the rain forest to understand how the many life forms of the tropical rain forest form an ecosystem. Have students discuss and examine the infographic with a partner. Then, have pairs discuss each question. Ask each set of students to agree on the answer to the question and to record their answers. Then in a class discussion have partners share and explain their answers. ELL Interpersonal, Visual/Spatial

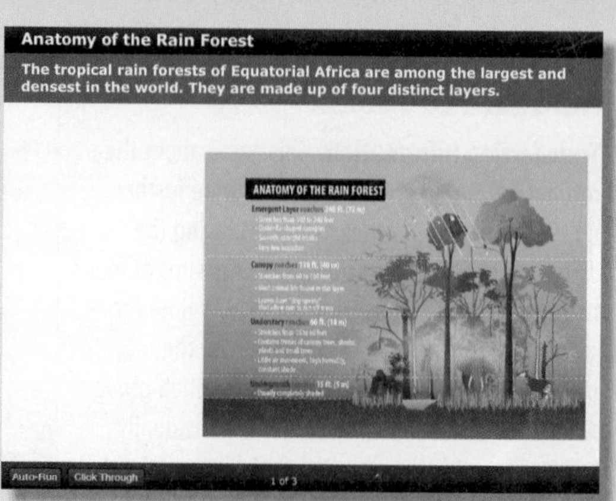

These streams meet with larger streams, which flow into rivers that empty into the Congo River. The Congo Basin is the second-largest river basin on Earth. Most of the basin is flatland covered by rain forest.

The Congo Basin is surrounded by higher country. To the southeast lie the Congo highlands. These highlands include plateaus and mountains. South of the Congo Basin is a high, flat area called the Katanga Plateau. Southwest of the Congo Basin lie the highlands of Gabon and the Republic of the Congo. This is a region of low hills, plateaus, and mountain ranges, including the Chaillu Mountains.

North of the Congo Basin lies another plateau. It makes up most of the Central African Republic. This plateau has an average elevation of about 2,000 feet (600 m). To its east, on the northeast side of the Congo Basin, highlands separate the Congo Basin from a plain of another drainage basin, that of the Nile River. The Ruwenzori Mountain range is found here. Covered with snow and cloaked in clouds, they are also called the "Mountains of the Moon." Moist air from the Indian Ocean creates the clouds that wrap around the Ruwenzori Mountains. The highest mountain in the region is Mount Stanley, named after the famous British explorer, Sir Henry Morton Stanley. The top of Mount Stanley, Margherita Peak, soars 16,763 feet (5,109 m) into the sky.

To the northwest of the Congo Basin lie the Gotel Mountains of western Cameroon. At the southern end of this range, Mount Cameroon, at 13,353 feet (4,070 m), is Cameroon's highest point. Mount Cameroon is an active volcano that lies just a few miles inland from the Atlantic coast.

✓ READING PROGRESS CHECK

Describing What is the Congo Basin?

basin an area drained by a river and its tributaries

R

W

GEOGRAPHY CONNECTION

The Congo Basin is covered by lush tropical rain forests, swamps, and plains.

1. ***PLACES AND REGIONS*** What are the major tributaries of the Congo River?
2. ***HUMAN SYSTEMS*** What might encourage human settlement in the Congo Basin? What might discourage it?

Physical Geography: The Congo Basin

V

R Reading Skills

Defining Discuss the meaning of the term *highlands* and reinforce that highlands include both plateaus and mountains. Direct students' attention to the map on the page. **Ask: Which areas mark plateaus in Equatorial Africa?** *(The yellow and orange areas on the map.)* Then ask students to define what a *plateau* is and also explain where on the map plateaus lie within the subregion. Have students write a brief encyclopedic entry for *highlands* and *plateau,* including elevation ranges. Guide students to additional resources to help them with their entries. **ELL Verbal/Linguistic**

W Writing Skills

Informative/Explanatory Discuss with students how Mount Stanley is the third tallest mountain in Africa. Explain how it attracts climbers from around the world. Have students research facts and details about climbing Mount Stanley, including the gear needed, transportation (distance to the closest city), and other relevant information that a climber preparing to scale the mountain might want to know. Then ask students to write an article about their findings and post it on a blog. **AL Logical/Mathematical**

V Visual Skills

Transferring Information Have students study the map and map key. Ask them to think about how physical geography influences climate and how both of those factors affect human settlement. Have students use this knowledge and information from the map to create a sketch of the subregion that includes areas of high and low population density. After students finish their maps, have them use the maps as a reference in a class discussion. Challenge students to compare settlement in Equatorial Africa to settlement in another subregion of Africa. Ask them to explain specifics about the climate and other factors such as physical features that affect settlement in that subregion. **BL Visual/Spatial**

INTERACTIVE WHITEBOARD ACTIVITY

Landforms of Equatorial Africa

Labeling Students complete this interactive whiteboard activity to give them a better sense of the various landforms that make up Equatorial Africa. Display the activity. Have students drag bolded text terms to the appropriate locations on the map. When the map is complete, ask students to look at the key and determine the elevations of the various landforms. **AL Visual/Spatial**

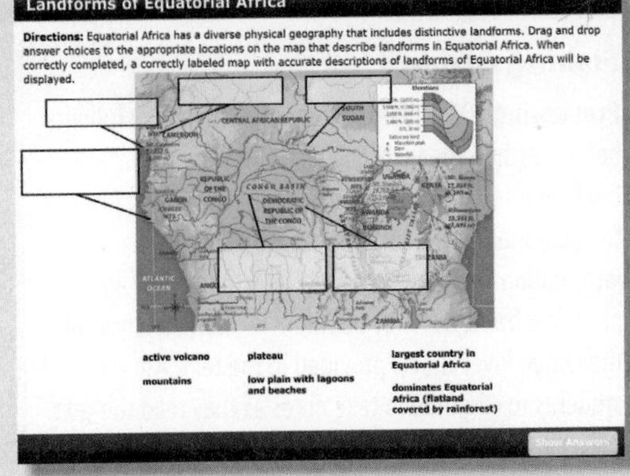
Landforms of Equatorial Africa
Directions: Equatorial Africa has a diverse physical geography that includes distinctive landforms. Drag and drop answer choices to the appropriate locations on the map that describe landforms in Equatorial Africa. When correctly completed, a correctly labeled map with accurate descriptions of landforms of Equatorial Africa will be displayed.
active volcano
plateau
largest country in Equatorial Africa
mountains
low plain with lagoons and beaches
dominates Equatorial Africa (flatland covered by rainforest)

ANSWERS, p. 555

✓ **READING PROGRESS CHECK** The Congo Basin is the second largest river basin in the world and is flatland covered by rain forest. This large area collects water that then flows downhill through the basin to the Congo River.

GEOGRAPHY CONNECTION

1. The Ubangi River, Aruwimi River, Kasai River, Lomami River, and Lulonga River are major tributaries of the Congo River.
2. The access to water for consumption, crops, and transportation of goods and people might encourage settlement of the Congo Basin. The dense rain forest might discourage settlement.

V Visual Skills

Analyzing Perspectives Have students study the image and work with a partner to discuss the role of rapids and falls, such as the one pictured here. **Ask:** Why is fishing an important economic activity? *(Possible answer: Fishermen need to feed their families or sell the fish.)* Discuss with students the challenges fishermen face, such as overfishing, and how these issues might affect the subregion's economy. **Visual/Spatial, Naturalist**

T Technology Skills

Acquiring Information Have students work with a partner to research four rivers and bodies of water in the subregion, including their location, size or length, and economic uses. Point out additional online and print resources that students may use to acquire the information. Have them record their statistics in a chart or diagram. Then have each set of students take turns summarizing the economic importance of each to particular countries in the subregion and the subregion itself in a class discussion. BL **Visual/Spatial, Verbal/Linguistic**

R Reading Skills

Inferring Explain to students that the Congo River is navigable. Have students select one of the rivers from the chart, other than the Congo River, and determine if it is a navigable river. Ask them to identify what obstacles prevent a river from being navigable. **Ask:** What effect does a river not being navigable have on the people and economy? *(Possible answer: A navigable river can provide people with transportation and opportunities to trade. Without a navigable river, an area might have a weaker or smaller economy as a result.)* ELL **Logical/Mathematical**

ANSWERS, p. 556

READING PROGRESS CHECK The Congo River and its many tributaries provide transportation for goods and people throughout the Congo Basin. While some portions are not navigable, it does provide an estuary to the Atlantic Ocean that oceangoing boats can navigate.

CRITICAL THINKING

1. The fast-moving waters of Boyoma Falls require large and sturdy nets to catch fish that are being pushed downstream.
2. Student answers may vary, but could include that since all the people fishing are men that this is traditionally a male-dominated occupation/activity.

Local people have been trapping fish at Boyoma Falls on the Lualaba River for centuries.

▲ CRITICAL THINKING

1. ***Analyzing*** Why are the fish traps so large?
2. ***Inferring*** What can you infer by the gender of the people fishing?

T Water Systems

GUIDING QUESTION *How is the Congo River central to life in Equatorial Africa?*

The part of the Atlantic Ocean that borders Equatorial Africa is called the Gulf of Guinea. It is the part of the ocean south of where Africa bulges to the west. A gulf is a part of the ocean that is partially enclosed by land. The island country of São Tomé and Príncipe lies in the heart of the gulf. European colonizers once used the islands to prevent the Africans they enslaved from escaping. Today, many people on the islands work on fishing boats.

On the mainland, five countries of Equatorial Africa have coastlines on the Gulf of Guinea. Fishing is important in all of them. Major ports include Libreville in Gabon and Pointe-Noire in the Republic of the Congo. At the southern edge of Equatorial Africa's coast, where the Democratic Republic of the Congo borders Angola, the freshwater of the world's mightiest river, the Congo, flows into the salt water of the Atlantic Ocean.

The Congo River serves as much of the border between the Republic of the Congo and the Democratic Republic of the Congo as it journeys to its outlet in the Atlantic Ocean. The Congo reaches the Atlantic through an estuary (EHS•chuh•WEHR•ee), or passage where freshwater meets seawater. The Congo's estuary is 7 miles (11 km) wide, and oceangoing ships can navigate its deep waters. The Congo River is nearly 3,000 miles (4,800 km) long, which makes it the second-longest river in Africa and the fifth-longest river in the world. More water flows in the Congo than any other river except for the vast Amazon River in South America.

The Congo River begins where the Lualaba and the Luvua Rivers meet. Downstream, the water flows through Boyoma Falls, near Kisangani. Boyoma Falls is a series of seven cataracts that stretch for 60 miles (97 km) down the river. For generations, local people have used the falls to catch fish in giant triangular traps.

Downstream from Kisangani, the Congo River flows in a great arc. Near Kinshasa, the Congo widens, creating a lake called Stanley Pool. Like Mount Stanley, the pool is named for the British explorer, Sir Henry Morton Stanley, who traveled the length of the Congo River in 1877.

navigable able to be traveled by boat

R The Congo River and its many tributaries form a large network of "natural highways" that are **navigable** by smaller boats. Some parts, however, have rapids and waterfalls that present serious obstacles to boat traffic and have limited the flow of goods and people along the full length of the river. The river plunges almost 900 feet (274 m) in numerous cataracts not far from where it meets the Atlantic Ocean.

The eastern border of Equatorial Africa is marked, in part, by the second-largest and second-deepest lake in the world. Lake Tanganyika is 420 miles (680 km) long and is nearly a mile deep in some places. Fish from the lake serve as a major source of food. Like the Congo, the huge Lake Tanganyika also serves as a means of transportation, as ferry boats cross its blue waters.

READING PROGRESS CHECK

Explaining How is the Congo River an important transportation system?

SuperStock

networks Online Teaching Options

INTERACTIVE IMAGE

Fishing Around

Previewing Display the interactive image for students before reading the textbook page. The labels contain brief summaries of the importance of the Congo River to Equatorial Africa. Ask students to read the information and take notes as a way to preview and provide a framework for the more in-depth analysis of the Congo River that is provided in the text. Ask students to continue to take notes as they read the text. AL **Verbal/Linguistic, Visual/Spatial**

Fishing Around
There are three hotspots on this image. Click to find them all.
Label

Climates, Biomes, and Resources

GUIDING QUESTION *How is the rain forest structured and how does this affect plant and animal life?*

Equatorial Africa is called "equatorial" because it is located on and near the Equator. It is a region of high temperatures and tropical climates. Most of the subregion has a tropical rain forest climate. There is a smaller area that has a tropical wet/dry (savanna) climate. The highland areas that surround most of the Congo Basin experience highland or **montane** climates. The word *montane* comes from the Latin word for "mountain," and it simply means "of mountainous country."

montane referring to a mountainous area

Warm temperatures prevail in the tropical wet climate zone of Equatorial Africa. More than 60 inches (150 cm) of rainfall per year soak the land. Rainfall varies seasonally, but there is not a truly dry season. Daily, rain falls on an amazing number and variety of life-forms. The tropical rain forests of Equatorial Africa are among the biggest—covering about half of the subregion—and densest in the world.

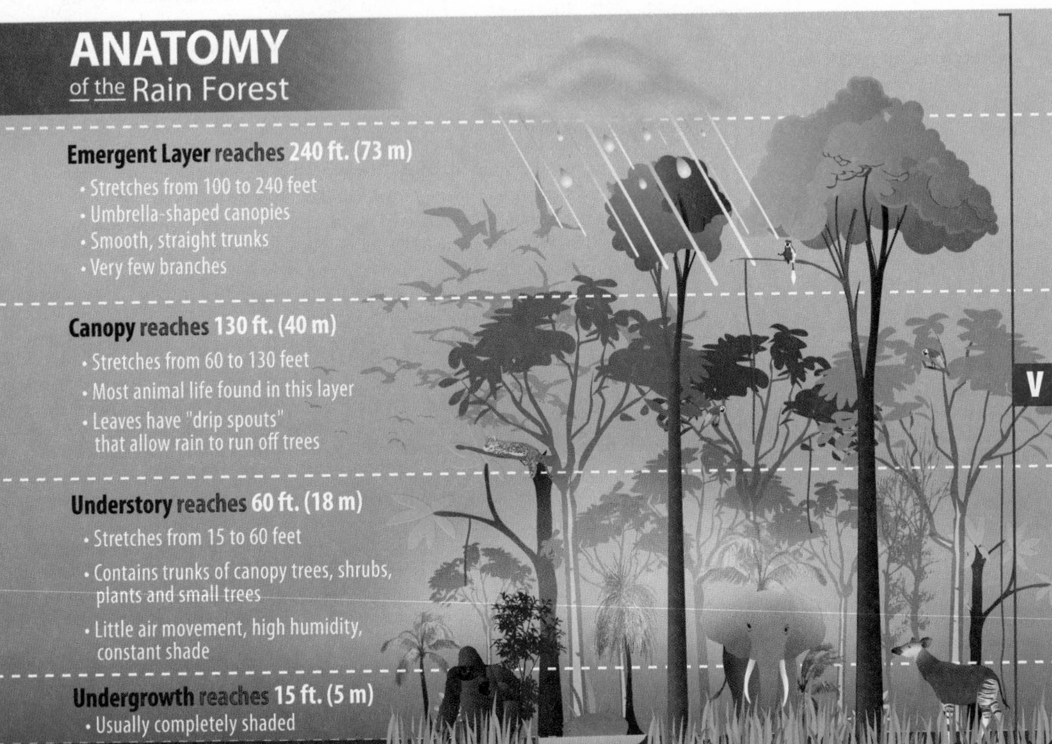

ANATOMY
of the Rain Forest
Emergent Layer reaches 240 ft. (73 m)
• Stretches from 100 to 240 feet
• Umbrella-shaped canopies
• Smooth, straight trunks
• Very few branches
Canopy reaches 130 ft. (40 m)
• Stretches from 60 to 130 feet
• Most animal life found in this layer
• Leaves have "drip spouts" that allow rain to run off trees
Understory reaches 60 ft. (18 m)
• Stretches from 15 to 60 feet
• Contains trunks of canopy trees, shrubs, plants and small trees
• Little air movement, high humidity, constant shade
Undergrowth reaches 15 ft. (5 m)
• Usually completely shaded
V

The rain forest is not a simple forest, but a complex web of life. Distinct forms of vegetation grow at different layers.

▲ CRITICAL THINKING

1. ***Hypothesizing*** Why might there be little growth on the rain forest floor?
2. ***Differentiating*** What is the difference between the understory and the canopy?

INFOGRAPHIC

Anatomy of the Rain Forest

Narrative Have students study the characteristics of the four layers of the rain forest provided on this infographic. Guide a class discussion, asking students to note the different animals that appear in the illustration. Then, have students choose one animal and imagine that they were that animal living in the rain forest. Have them write a narrative describing the rain forest from that animal's point of view, making sure to use factual evidence from the infographic in their stories. **Verbal/Linguistic, Interpersonal**

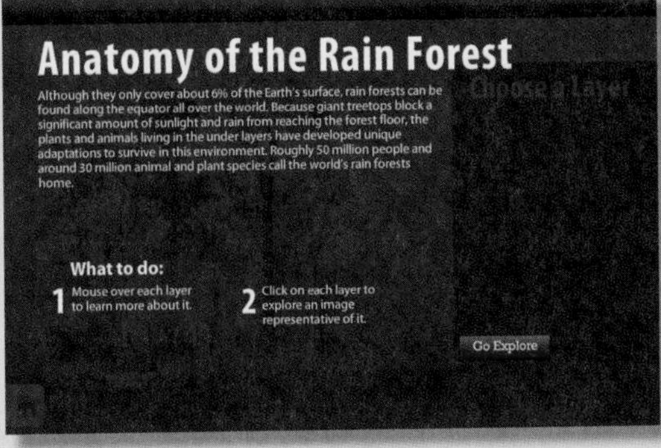

Anatomy of the Rain Forest
Although they only cover about 6% of the Earth's surface, rain forests can be found along the equator all over the world. Because giant treetops block a significant amount of sunlight and rain from reaching the forest floor, the plants and animals living in the under layers have developed unique adaptations to survive in this environment. Roughly 50 million people and around 30 million animal and plant species call the world's rain forests home.
What to do:
1 Mouse over each layer to learn more about it.
2 Click on each layer to explore an image representative of it.
Go Explore

C Critical Thinking Skills

Comparing and Contrasting Once students have read the page, have them create a chart that compares and contrasts the characteristics of a tropical wet climate, a tropical dry savanna climate, and a montane climate. **Ask: Which climate region would be ideal for agriculture? Explain.** *(Possible answer: None of the areas are ideal for agriculture because they are too wet or too dry, but irrigation could be used in the tropical dry climate to make agriculture more successful.)* **AL** **Visual/Spatial, Naturalist**

Content Background Knowledge

Animals of the Congo Basin Rain Forest The Congo Basin comprises an area about the size of the state of Alaska. Although the basin is filled with animals such as monkeys, elephants, and gorillas, many animal species are endangered. These include chimpanzees, forest elephants, mountain gorillas, and bonobos. In addition, the rain forest is home to about 1,000 different species of birds and hundreds of species of fish. The extraction of minerals and construction of roads and buildings threatens the environment.

V Visual Skills

Interpreting Have students study the infographic. Discuss the different layers and role of each rain forest layer. Explain how the rain forest recycles carbon dioxide into oxygen. **Ask: Why is preserving the rain forest and its environment so important?** *(Possible answer: If people do not preserve and protect the rain forest, it can no longer "clean" the air that people, animals, and plants need to live.)* Explain to students that because the rain forest of the Congo Basin is such an important recycler of carbon dioxide into oxygen, people and groups are working to maintain it. **Ask: What happens to the rain forest environment when loggers cut down trees for construction?** *(Possible answer: Animals and plants lose their habitats.)* **ELL** **Visual/Spatial**

ANSWERS, p. 557

CRITICAL THINKING

1. The rain forest floor is normally completely shaded, limiting the amount of growth that can occur here.
2. The canopy contains most of the animal life in the rain forest and has space for air movement and for rain to run off of the leaves. The understory has little air movement and constant shade.

CHAPTER 23, Lesson 1

Physical Geography of Equatorial Africa

T Technology Skills

Researching Have students work with a partner to research a species—either endangered or threatened—in the rain forest of the Congo Basin. Ask them to find out what actions are being taken to help that species. Then have students create a report using presentation software to provide information, images, and even audio of sounds the species makes, as well as a persuasive argument to prompt others to take action. **BL Visual/Spatial, Naturalist**

W Writing Skills

Argument Ask students to discuss how nonrenewable resources in Equatorial Africa will one day run out. Then have students imagine they are working with an organization in the subregion to help to develop alternative energy sources. Based on the climate and the resources that are available, ask students to write a proposal that argues for the development of a particular alternative energy source. Point out that students may need to do additional research before they begin planning their argument. Remind students to address counterarguments and to use specific details, facts, and examples to support their thesis. **BL Intrapersonal**

CLOSE & REFLECT

Summarizing Review with students the landforms, water systems, climates and biomes, and resources of Equatorial Africa. Discuss the importance of the rain forest and the subregion's resources to the area's economy. Encourage students to write a summary explaining how the water resources of Equatorial Africa are unique on the continent as water is in abundance in this subregion and scarce in many other subregions.

ANSWERS, p. 558

READING PROGRESS CHECK The tropical rain forest climate areas have no dry season and receive daily rain. Tropical wet/dry areas have seasonal rainfall with alternating wet and dry seasons such as near the Equator where there is six months of rain followed by a dry season of six months.

Rain forests are complex biomes. They are home to a wide variety of animal life, including birds, bats, rodents, monkeys, baboons, chimpanzees, elephants, wild boar, and okapi. A huge number and variety of insects also live there. Some of these, such as the tsetse fly and mosquito, carry diseases.

canopy top layer of a rain forest, where the tops of tall trees form a continuous layer of leaves

understory a lower layer of the rain forest

T

Rain forests have four basic layers. The topmost layer of the rain forest is the emergent layer, where trees stick out of, or emerge from, the canopy—the next highest layer. The **canopy** is a layer of trees and leaves with a maximum height of 130 feet (39.6 m). Orchids, ferns, and mosses grow among the branches of the canopy, which provide most of the plant food for rain forest animals. Below the canopy is the layer called the **understory**. Shrubs, ferns, and mosses grow together at this level of the rain forest, which rises 15 to 60 feet (4.6 to 18 m). The lowest layer is the undergrowth, where little sunlight penetrates and consequently few shrubs and herbs can grow. The soils in the tropical rain forest biome are typically not very fertile because the heavy rains leach, or dissolve and carry away, nutrients from the soil. Here animals feed mostly on insects.

Tropical grassland with scattered trees—known as savanna—covers much of southern Equatorial Africa. Rainfall is seasonal in this climate zone, with alternating wet and dry seasons. In the wettest areas, which are closest to the Equator, six months of almost daily rain is followed by a six-month dry season. Average annual rainfall is about 35 to 45 inches (90 to 115 cm).

abundant present in large amounts; plentiful

W

Mineral resources are **abundant** through much of Equatorial Africa. In the Democratic Republic of the Congo alone, the following are mined: cadmium, cobalt, copper, gold, manganese, petroleum, silver, tin, and zinc. The value of these mineral resources is estimated to be about $25 trillion. The Congo Basin also holds major diamond deposits. Gabon, the Republic of the Congo, Cameroon, and Equatorial Guinea have oil and natural gas reserves.

Water is a major natural resource in the subregion. Equatorial Africa receives abundant rainfall. Yet controlling water for practical uses, such as irrigation and hydroelectric power, is difficult because the amounts of rainfall are irregular and unpredictable. These challenges, combined with a lack of financial support, result in untapped hydroelectric power potential in parts of the subregion.

Solar power is another renewable energy source that has been harnessed in Equatorial Africa. Rural electrification programs involve installing small-scale solar power systems. These continue to expand in some parts of the subregion.

The rain and the sun together give rise to the massive tropical rain forests, which may be Equatorial Africa's most important natural resource. Tropical rain forests are a rich source of food, medicine, fibers, oils, rubber, and, wood. Deforestation, however, is threatening many of the forests in the subregion.

READING PROGRESS CHECK

Differentiating What is the difference between the tropical rain forest and tropical wet/dry areas of Equatorial Africa?

LESSON 1 REVIEW

Reviewing Vocabulary (Tier Three Words)

1. ***Describing*** Describe the layers of a rain forest using the words *canopy* and *understory.* RH.9–10.4

Using Your Notes

2. ***Identifying*** Use your graphic organizer to write a paragraph describing the major land and water features of Equatorial Africa.

Answering the Guiding Questions

3. ***Identifying*** What huge landform covers most of Equatorial Africa?

4. ***Describing*** How is the Congo River central to life in Equatorial Africa?

5. ***Explaining*** How is the rain forest structured and how does this affect plant and animal life?

Writing Activity

6. ***Informative/Explanatory*** Think about the physical features of Equatorial Africa. Write a paragraph describing how specific landforms affect the course of the subregion's rivers. WHST.9–10.2

558

LESSON 1 REVIEW ANSWERS

Reviewing Vocabulary

1. Student answers will vary, but should include a description of the canopy as the top layer containing the food for animals and the understory as the layer below the canopy where shrubs and mosses grow.

Using Your Notes

2. Paragraphs will vary, but could include the Congo, Basin; the Katanga Plateau; the Chaillu Mountains; the Ruwenzori Mountains; the Grotel Mountains; Mount Stanley; Mount Cameroon; the extinct volcanoes forming the islands of São Tomé and Príncipe; the Congo River, Atlantic Ocean, Gulf of Guinea; Lake Tanganyika; Boyoma Falls; and Stanley Pool.

Answering the Guiding Questions

3. The Congo Basin covers most of Equatorial Africa.

4. The Congo River and its tributaries provide transportation for goods and people and an estuary to the Atlantic Ocean that ships can navigate.

5. The rain forest is structured into four layers: the emergent or uppermost layer; the canopy; the understory; and the undergrowth.

Writing Activity

6. Paragraphs will vary but should include how the Congo Basin collects water that drains to form the Congo River, the drop of almost 900 feet of the Congo River that forms numerous cataracts, and the creation of Stanley Pool where the Congo flows in a large arc.

networks
There's More Online!

- ☑ **GRAPH** Democratic Republic of the Congo 2008 GDP
- ☑ **IMAGE** Cell Phone Use
- ☑ **IMAGE** Harvest in Central Africa
- ☑ **MAP** The Atlantic Slave Trade
- ☑ **MAP** Independent Africa
- ☑ **TIME LINE** Conflict in the Congo
- ☑ **INTERACTIVE SELF-CHECK QUIZ**
- ☑ **VIDEO** Human Geography of Equatorial Africa

LESSON 2

Human Geography of Equatorial Africa

ESSENTIAL QUESTION • *How do physical systems and human systems shape a place?*

Reading **HELP**DESK 

Academic Vocabulary (Tier Two Words)
- **intermittent**
- **hub**

Content Vocabulary (Tier Three Words)
- **cash crop**
- **plantation**

TAKING NOTES: ***Key Ideas and Details***

IDENTIFYING Use a graphic organizer like the one below to take notes about the human geography of Equatorial Africa.

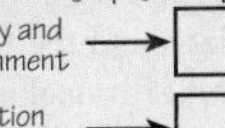

(bl)Jacques Pavlovsky/Sygma/Corbis, (tcl)Brennan Linsley/AP Images, (tc)Themba Hadebe/AP Images, (tcr)Giovanni Mereghetti/age fotostock, (tr)Lionel Healing/AFP/Getty Images

It Matters Because

Equatorial Africa reflects a wide variety of cultures. The arrival of Europeans fundamentally affected life for the Africans and led to a long struggle for freedom. The legacy of European colonization is still felt in the subregion. Today, Equatorial Africa is a rich mix of African and European influences, ancient and modern lifestyles, and challenges and hope. R1

History and Government

GUIDING QUESTION *What challenges does democracy face in Equatorial Africa?*

Thousands of years ago, people lived nomadic lifestyles across Africa. They eventually settled to grow food and livestock. By the time Europeans began to arrive in the 1400s, peoples of the region had established enduring cultures.

The first inhabitants of the Congo Basin are thought to be the Mbuti, once known as Pygmies, whose descendants still live in the region today. They were already living there when the great migration of Bantu-speaking peoples arrived in the region. The Bantu-speaking peoples, who were farmers and herders, had established settlements by A.D. 800. Although the origins of the Bantu and their migration routes are debated, historians believe that they spread across one-third of the continent. The Bantu founded the kingdoms of Kongo (Congo), Luba, and Lunda. 

Slavery and European Colonization

When European explorers landed along Equatorial Africa's coasts in the late 1400s, they were interested in trade. They sought gold, ivory, textiles, and enslaved Africans. European ships carried away enslaved people from areas that are now the Republic of the Congo, Gabon, and Cameroon. Gabon later became a center of the slave trade.

Millions of people from the African interior were sold into slavery. Nzinga Mbemba, the king of Kongo, deplored the actions of some African rulers. He also complained to the king of Portugal about Portuguese slave merchants: R2

ENGAGE

R1 Reading Skills

Determining Importance Have students consider how colonization affects cultures. Discuss the difficulties that go along with maintaining distinct cultures and traditions. Ask students how modern living and technology affect cultures and what challenges they pose to preserving cultural identity.

TEACH & ASSESS

T Technology Skills

Presenting Ask students to find out more about the Mbuti. Have them research statistics on their population today and during colonial times, language spoken, and traditions. Have students create a multimedia presentation based on their research and present it to the class. **BL Interpersonal**

R2 Reading Skills

Activating Prior Knowledge Before reading this section, ask students to share what they know about the transatlantic slave trade in Africa. **Ask:** **How did the physical geography of Equatorial Africa make it vulnerable to the transatlantic slave trade?** *(It borders the coast, providing easy access.)* **Why did many of the enslaved people come from the interior?** *(African rulers on the coast made money by selling people of the interior to slave traders.)* Have students work in small groups to discuss how the interior would have been a good hiding place for people trying to avoid capture. Provide a map of the subregion and ask students to indicate where they would have hidden and what challenges slave traders would have had trying to locate them. **ELL Interpersonal, Naturalist**

networks Online Teaching Options

 **INTERACTIVE BELLRINGER**

The Atlantic Slave Trade

Interpreting a Map Have students review the map of trade routes for the slave trade. Have students identify some of the possible challenges that the slave trade brought to the democratic governments in Equatorial Africa. Continue the class discussion by asking students to explain what they know about the slave trade from Africa to the Americas. Have them form small groups and discuss this issue. Then have groups answer the bellringer questions. Have students agree on the answer to each question and write it down. Then, review the answers in a class discussion. **Visual/Spatial, Verbal/Linguistic**

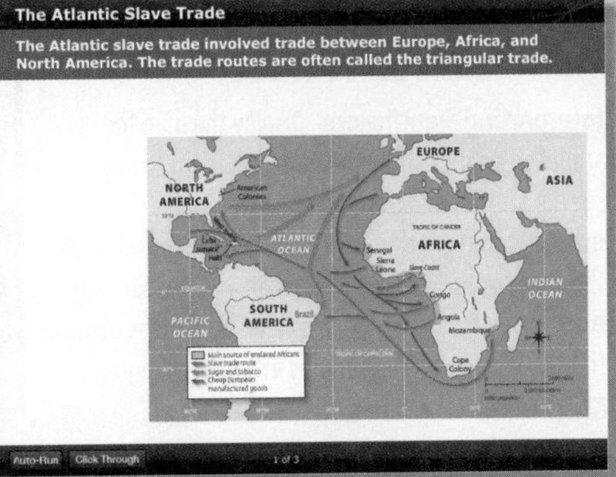

ANSWERS, p. 559

TAKING NOTES: History and Government—first inhabitants thought to be the Mbuti; the Bantu founded Kongo (Congo), Luba, and Lunda; Europeans brought slavery and conflict, weakened culture, traditions, and independence; **Population Patterns**—largely rural with the lowest population density on the continent; influenced by tropical forest; mostly rural except in Gabon; capital cities are more heavily populated; **Society Today**—hundreds of ethnic groups; over 200 in Democratic Republic of Congo; Bantu, the largest, speaks hundreds of languages; the Mbuti live in the rain forest, remain untouched, and diverse; Islam, Christianity, and traditional animist religions are practiced; family and religion are interwoven; health care and safe drinking water are primary concerns.

V Visual Skills

Examining Have students study the map. **Ask:** **What is common among the trade routes?** *(Possible answer: They form a triangular pattern, with slaves leaving Africa and being taken to the Americas; then cash crops and raw materials are sent to America with cheap manufactured goods from Europe going back to Africa and the Americas.)* **Ask:** **Why do you think certain areas of the African coast along the Atlantic were not significant sources of enslaved Africans? Explain.** *(Possible answer: There may have been resistance or too small a population of Africans living there. For example, the physical geography and climate of northwestern Africa is hot and dry and would not support as large a population as Equatorial Africa.)* AL **Visual/Spatial, Logical/Mathematical**

C Critical Thinking Skills

Analyzing Primary Sources Ask students what context clues they could use to determine the meaning of unfamiliar words such as *licentiousness*. **Ask:** **Why did the Portuguese think it was morally justified to sell and trade human beings from Africa?** *(Possible answer: The Portuguese were probably driven by profit and gain and disregarded moral restraints.)* Have students work in small groups to discuss what role other European countries could have taken at this time to stop or limit the slave trade. Have them discuss the specific words that King Nzinga Mbemba uses to describe the actions and effect of the slave trade on the Kongo. ELL **Verbal/Linguistic, Interpersonal**

W Writing Skills

Narrative Have students write a journal entry from the perspective of a person living in Equatorial Africa during the time of the transatlantic slave trade. They can write the narrative from the perspective of an observer, a slave trader, or a person trying to escape capture. Remind them to use sensory details and vivid verbs in their narratives. Invite volunteers to share their completed narratives with the class. **Verbal/Linguistic, Intrapersonal**

ANSWERS, p. 560

GEOGRAPHY CONNECTION

1. South America, Central America, and the American Colonies in North America were major destination points for enslaved people.
2. Historians can use maps to see how landforms, climate, natural resources, and locations impact historical events.

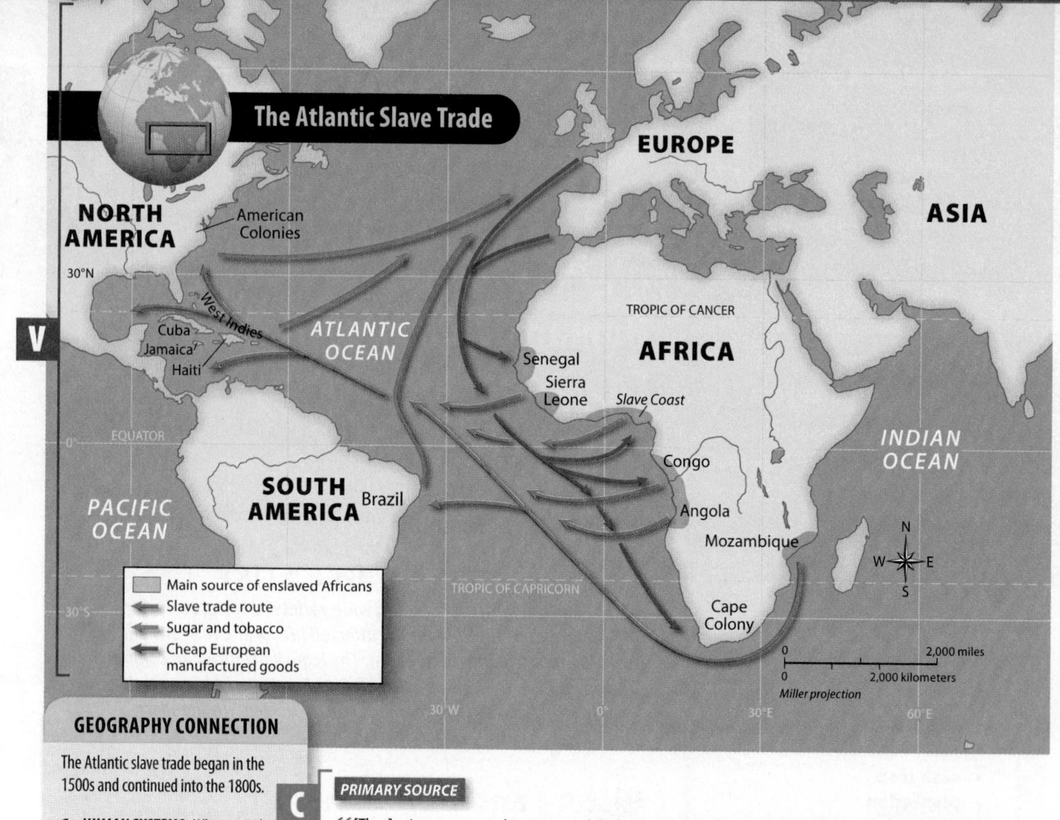

GEOGRAPHY CONNECTION

The Atlantic slave trade began in the 1500s and continued into the 1800s.

1. ***HUMAN SYSTEMS*** What were the major destination points for enslaved people leaving Africa?
2. ***THE USES OF GEOGRAPHY*** How can maps help historians understand the past?

PRIMARY SOURCE

"[They] seize upon our subjects, sons of the land and sons of the noblemen, and cause them to be sold; and so great, Sir, is their corruption and licentiousness that our country is being utterly depopulated."

—Nzinga Mbemba, the king of Kongo, quoted in *East Along the Equator*, 1987

Once captured and sold, enslaved Africans faced a terrible trip across the Atlantic Ocean as human cargo in a ship's hold. The passage from Africa claimed millions of lives. The loss of so many young people to the slave trade did great harm to the societies they left behind.

Large areas of Equatorial Africa were not colonized until the 1800s. Various obstacles had previously prevented colonization, including malaria and the Congo River cataracts. By the 1900s, however, European powers held colonies throughout the subregion. Colonizers were Spain, Germany, France, Belgium, Britain, and Portugal.

France gained control of what is now the Republic of the Congo in the late 1800s by engineering treaties with local rulers who wanted protection against Belgium, France's main rival in the region. The French changed the local economy into one based on income from resource extraction and growing **cash crops** for export. In 1878 King Leopold II of Belgium began establishing trade posts along the Congo River. He soon convinced other European powers to grant him control of what was then termed the Congo Free State and what is today called the Democratic Republic of the Congo. This territory and its people were considered the king's personal property. He treated the people terribly.

cash crop a farm crop grown to be sold or traded rather than used by the farm family

European rulers, traders, and missionaries promoted European culture, weakened traditional African cultures, and often treated Africans harshly. African village life was also disrupted by the replacing of locally centered

560

networks Online Teaching Options

INTERACTIVE MAP

The Atlantic Slave Trade

Interpreting Significance Display the map for students. As they study the map, ask them to pay special attention to the sugar, tobacco, and manufactured goods routes. Ask them to consider why these routes have been included on a map depicting the slave trade. Have students write their ideas about the significance of these routes in a brief paragraph. AL **Verbal/Linguistic, Visual/Spatial**

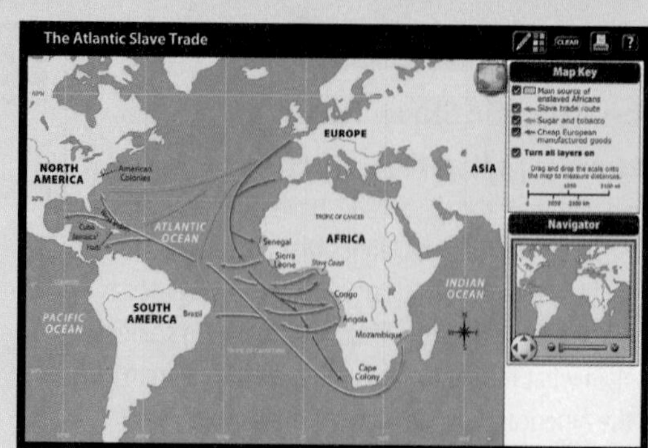

agriculture with large commercial farms, called **plantations,** that grew cash crops. This harsh treatment of native peoples by European colonists led to the many struggles for independence across Africa during the twentieth century.

C

T

Independence

Resistance to colonial rule in Africa was growing by the mid-1900s. In one year alone, 1960, all of the countries of Equatorial Africa achieved independence. Thus, 1960 is remembered as "the year of independence."

People in most of the new countries experienced periods of ethnic strife, harsh rule, and human rights abuses after independence. In the Democratic Republic of the Congo, serious instability led to the reign of the dictator Mobutu Sese Seko from the late 1960s until the 1990s. Although the countries of the subregion were technically democracies, this period saw human rights abuses, one-party rule, and **intermittent** civil war.

Today the governments of Equatorial Africa have varying degrees of stability. Gabon is a stable republic. It has been developing its economy through the creation of a national park system (to promote ecotourism), developing industry, and educating its residents to work in financial services, education, and health care. In contrast, the Central African Republic has experienced military coups and periods of instability. Although today it is nominally a democracy, rebel groups, not the government, control land and people in the countryside. Abundant natural resources in the subregion have helped some countries achieve relative stability, but problems persist. Oil revenues helped Equatorial Guinea achieve greater stability, but most residents have a low standard of living, and the government has a history of human rights abuses.

✓ READING PROGRESS CHECK

Theorizing Why might the countries of Equatorial Africa have suffered harsh rule after independence?

Population Patterns

GUIDING QUESTION *How does geography influence where the people of Equatorial Africa live?*

Life for people in Equatorial Africa is influenced by the subregion's tropical climates, thick tropical forests, and tropical grasslands. Equatorial Africa is mostly rural, despite having prominent urban centers. The dense growth of natural vegetation in this equatorial region makes large-scale intensive plantation agriculture difficult. Most people exist by subsistence agriculture or raising cattle. In some places, coffee, rubber, and cacao are grown for export.

As a whole, Equatorial Africa is one of the least densely populated regions on the continent. The northern part of the Democratic Republic of the Congo, for example, is tropical forest. Large tracts of government forest reserves discourage cities, although there are scattered villages along the Congo and its tributaries. The southern part of the country, however, has millions of people. Kinshasa, the capital city, is the political, cultural, and economic **hub** of the region. It is home to some 8 million people. Just across the Congo River is Brazzaville, the capital of the Republic of the Congo, which is home to 1.2 million. In contrast, the largest city in São Tomé and Príncipe is the capital, São Tomé, with only 60,000 residents. Overall, Gabon is the most urbanized country in Equatorial Africa, with 86 percent of its population living in urban areas. At the other extreme is the newly independent South Sudan, where only 22 percent of the population lives in urban areas.

✓ READING PROGRESS CHECK

Explaining Why is much of Equatorial Africa thinly populated?

Connecting Geography to HISTORY

Slave Forts

European colonizers built a series of forts along coastal Africa. These were fortified trading posts from which they conducted their trade in gold and enslaved Africans. Built by the Portuguese in 1482, Elmina Castle was the first such fort in Africa south of the Sahara. Africans captured in the interior of the continent were held in the fortress until ships arrived to transport them across the Atlantic in chains. This trip, known as the "Middle Passage," could last from three to six weeks. Located in present-day Ghana, Elmina Castle is a national museum and has been declared a World Heritage Monument. Over 100,000 tourists visit the site annually.

UNDERSTANDING HISTORICAL INTERPRETATION How would touring Elmina Castle help a visitor understand the history of Equatorial Africa?

plantation a large commercial farm growing crops for export

intermittent occurring at irregular intervals; occasional

hub the center of an activity or region

GAME

Human Geography of Equatorial Africa

Evaluating Pairs of students can test their knowledge with this geography-based game. Have students take turns choosing a symbol and then a square. After each square is chosen, a statement regarding some aspect of the human geography of Equatorial Africa will appear. Direct students to use what they have learned to decide if the statement is right or wrong, and then click on the corresponding label. Have students play two games in a row to give each partner an equal chance at success.
AL **Kinesthetic, Verbal/Linguistic**

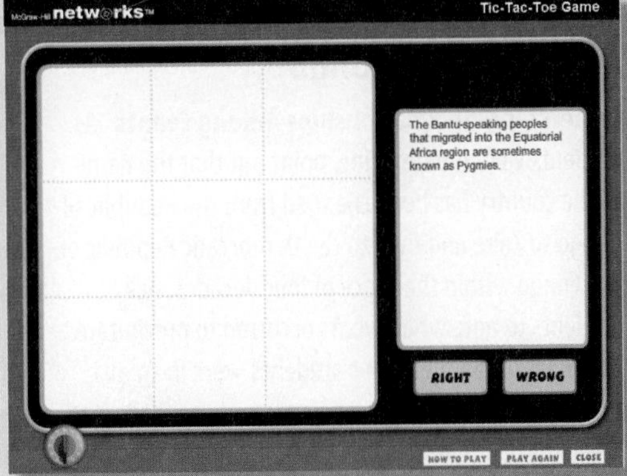
networks
Tic-Tac-Toe Game
The Bantu-speaking peoples that migrated into the Equatorial Africa region are sometimes known as Pygmies.
RIGHT
WRONG
HOW TO PLAY
PLAY AGAIN
CLOSE

Human Geography of Equatorial Africa

C Critical Thinking Skills

Analyzing Cause and Effect Discuss with students the treatment of Africans by European colonists. **Ask:** **Why do you think European colonies thought they had a right to colonize and exploit Africa?** *(Possible answer: They thought only about economic gain and not about the impact of their actions on the people of Africa.)* **Besides exploiting Africa's resources, how did colonization affect the livelihood of Africans?** *(Possible answer: For many, it forced them to give up their ways of life to work on plantations for European owners.)*
AL **Logical/Mathematical**

T Technology Skills

Speculating Discuss with students what global events may have contributed to the countries of Equatorial Africa gaining independence by 1960. Then ask them to speculate why the people of the subregion continued to experience political instability and strife after independence. **Ask:** **Were the European colonial powers to blame for this political instability? If so, why?** (*Possible answer: The European colonial powers did nothing to prepare the people of each country for independence and self-governance.)* Ask students to work with a partner to find primary sources about human rights violations in Equatorial Africa using electronic resources. **BL**
Verbal/Linguistic, Logical/Mathematical

Content Background Knowledge

Diversifying to Maintain Stability Unlike many other countries of Equatorial Africa, Gabon has enjoyed more political stability since its independence in 1960. This country is diverse, with dozens of different ethnic groups. Its secret to success is its economy, which is fueled in part by its oil industry. However, decreasing supplies of oil have prompted the government to diversify the economy by focusing on ecotourism. Rain forest comprises about ten percent of the land area. Gabon is sparsely populated, which provides an opportunity for growth and development. In 2002, thirteen national parks were created, but efforts to develop ecotourism were slowed by the country's inexperience in international tourism.

ANSWERS, p. 561

✓ READING PROGRESS CHECK The countries of Equatorial Africa may have suffered harsh rule because the unstable economies and ethnic conflicts after independence left them vulnerable to one-party or dictatorial rule.

✓ READING PROGRESS CHECK The dense tropical forests and government forest reserves keep Equatorial Africa less densely populated than other areas of the continent.

Connecting Geography Touring Elmina Castle would help visitors understand the history and impact of the slave trade on Equatorial Africa.

Content Background Knowledge

Swahili The descendants of the Bantu make up hundreds of different ethnic groups and speak about 400 different languages. Swahili is one of the most well-known Bantu languages that survived over time. For those who speak Swahili, it could be their first or second language. Historically, Swahili was used by Arab traders in Africa; therefore, many dialects developed that were influenced by Arabic. As Arab traders traveled farther into the interior, they brought Swahili to the people of Equatorial Africa.

V Visual Skills

Creating Maps To help students understand the ethnic distribution of Equatorial Africa, ask them to work in pairs researching where different groups such as the Mbuti, Fang, Bantu, and other ethnic groups live. Have them list the top ten ethnic groups in the subregion and create maps showing where those groups predominantly live. Point out that students may create their maps digitally using computer software or may use paper. **Ask:** **What conclusions can you draw about the major ethnic groups and where they have chosen to settle?** *(Possible answer: The Bantu are scattered throughout the subregion and large numbers live along the coast.)*
Visual/Spatial

C Critical Thinking Skills

Changing Continuity of Groups Direct students to research the various ethnic groups of São Tomé and Príncipe and how some are unique. **Ask:** **Who are the *forros* and why are they considered the country's elite? Is physical geography a factor? Explain.** *(Possible answer: Forros are Portuguese Africans or descendants of Portuguese settlers and freed enslaved Africans. They have brought together the two dominant cultures of the islands and are isolated from the mainland, therefore not as influenced by other groups in Equatorial Africa.)*
AL Logical/Mathematical

Society and Culture Today

GUIDING QUESTION *How does conflict shape life in Equatorial Africa?*

V Equatorial Africa contains hundreds of ethnic groups. The Democratic Republic of the Congo alone has more than 200 groups. The largest ethnic groups in that country are Bantu, peoples who speak one of the hundreds of Bantu languages. One indigenous group, the Mbuti, lives in the rain forest of eastern Democratic Republic of the Congo and is relatively unchanged by outside influences. In the northwestern part of the country, Fang and Bantu ethnic groups are the dominant ethnic groups.

C The approximately 200,000 people of the islands of São Tomé and Príncipe are from many different ethnic groups. Many of the people are descendants of Portuguese settlers and people freed from slavery in Africa. These Portuguese Africans are known as *forros* and compose the country's elite. Much of the population is descended from groups that migrated to the islands in the late 1400s.

Along with hundreds of ethnic groups come hundreds of languages. About 700 local languages are spoken in the Democratic Republic of the Congo alone. French is widely spoken throughout most of Equatorial Africa, reflecting its colonial heritage. It is the official language of the Democratic Republic of the Congo and the Republic of the Congo. People from different sublanguage groups often communicate in pidgin, a simplified speech used among people who speak different languages.

Christianity, Islam, and indigenous religions are practiced in Equatorial Africa. Traditional indigenous religions are numerous and diverse, but they have many common elements. For example, most traditional religions profess a belief in the existence of a supreme being and a ranked order of deities. Animism, or the belief that natural or inanimate objects possess spirits, is also widespread.

European colonialism greatly influenced Equatorial Africa's religious practices. In many areas today, a majority of people observe different forms of Christianity. Roman Catholicism, brought by Belgian and French colonists and

TIME LINE

Conflict in the CONGO

Since independence, the history of the Democratic Republic of the Congo has been one of corruption and civil war.

CRITICAL THINKING

1. ***Describing*** How would you describe the political climate of the Democratic Republic of the Congo from 1960 to 2006?
2. ***Analyzing*** How has the history of the Democratic Republic of the Congo been affected by nearby countries?

1960 — 1990

1960 Republic of the Congo becomes an independent country.

1965 In a military coup, Mobutu Sese Seko overthrows the government and renames the country Zaire.

1996 Mobutu leaves the country for medical treatment; Tutsi rebels capture eastern Zaire.

1997 Tutsi rebels oust Mobutu; Zaire becomes Democratic Republic of Congo, and Laurent Kabila becomes president.

networks Online Teaching Options

TIME LINE

Conflict in the Congo

Understanding Relationships Among Events As students view the time line, point out that the name of the country has been changed from the Republic of Congo to Zaire and then to the Democratic Republic of the Congo within the space of four decades. Ask students to note what events occurred to precipitate these name changes. Have students work in small groups to discuss the reason or reasons the leaders of the country at one particular time made the decision to change the name of the country. Students may then share their ideas with the rest of the class.
AL Interpersonal, Visual/Spatial

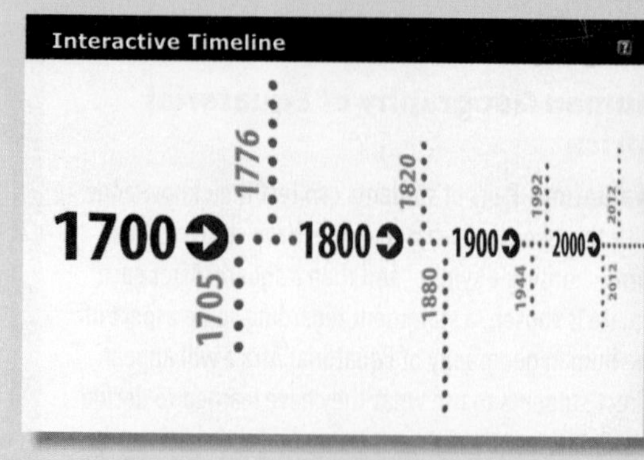

ANSWERS, p. 562

CRITICAL THINKING

1. The political climate was unstable with military coups, rebel fighting, and presidential assassination until free elections were held in 2006.
2. Nearby countries have helped finance rebellions against the government, creating conflicts and influencing who holds the power in the Democratic Republic of the Congo.

missionaries, is common. About half of the population of the Democratic Republic of the Congo is Roman Catholic. The subregion is home to an increasing number of Muslims, as well.

Religion and family life are interwoven in Equatorial Africa. Some ethnic groups in the Democratic Republic of the Congo, for example, live according to a mix of indigenous and Christian beliefs. Many observe strict divisions of labor between men and women, depending on whether they farm or raise livestock. Several generations—and even people from different families—might share the same dwelling.

During the colonial era, religion dominated education systems in the subregion. After countries gained their independence, efforts were made to modernize education, but many rural areas still lacked sufficient support. Today, literacy ranges from about 56 percent in the Central African Republic to about 94 percent in Equatorial Guinea. Literacy among women is commonly lower than that of men.

W Under Spanish rule, Equatorial Guinea achieved a high literacy rate as well as a decent health-care system. In general, however, Equatorial Africa's countries lack the resources to halt preventable diseases that Western countries have been able to stop. The lack of safe drinking water, the shortage of vaccines for curable diseases, and the rising rate of HIV infection and number of AIDS victims remain primary health concerns.

Ethnic conflicts continue to plague parts of Equatorial Africa. In the Democratic Republic of the Congo (once known as Zaire) the long dictatorship of Mobutu Sese Seko was followed by ethnic strife and one of the bloodiest conflicts since World War II. Ethnic conflict spiked after 1994, when the country received a heavy influx of refugees who were fleeing the fighting in the neighboring countries of Rwanda and Burundi.

✓ READING PROGRESS CHECK

Hypothesizing How might Equatorial Africa's ethnic and linguistic diversity be an obstacle to political stability?

Analyzing Primary Sources

Crime in Kinshasa

C "Most reported criminal incidents in Kinshasa involve crimes of opportunity, which include pick-pocketing and petty theft. The majority of the crimes are committed by 'sheggehs,' who are generally homeless street children. Travel in certain areas of Kinshasa, Kisangani, Lubumbashi and most other major cities is generally safe during daylight hours, but travelers are urged to be vigilant against criminal activity that targets non-Congolese."

—U.S. Department of State, International Travel for U.S. Citizens

DBQ ***ANALYZING PRIMARY SOURCES*** Who are "sheggehs"? RH.9–10.4

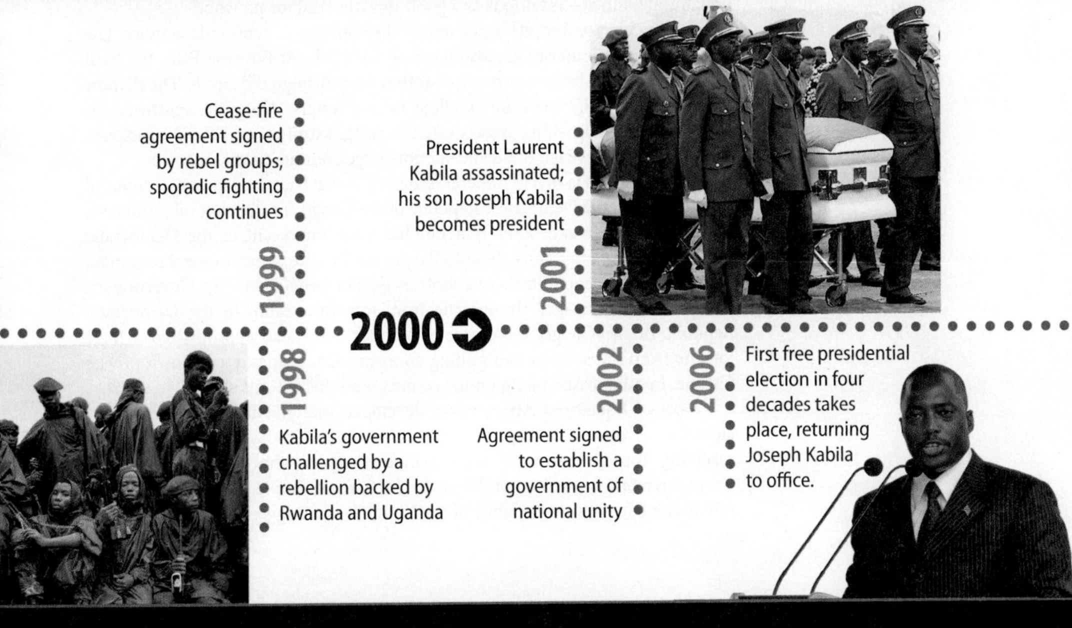

1998
Kabila's government challenged by a rebellion backed by Rwanda and Uganda
1999
Cease-fire agreement signed by rebel groups; sporadic fighting continues
2000
2001
President Laurent Kabila assassinated; his son Joseph Kabila becomes president
2002
Agreement signed to establish a government of national unity
2006
First free presidential election in four decades takes place, returning Joseph Kabila to office.

GRAPHIC ORGANIZER

Human Geography of Equatorial Africa

Taking Notes Have students complete this interactive graphic organizer to gain a clearer picture of the diverse groups of people who live in Equatorial Africa. As students work, ask them to take notes on some of the groups featured in this activity. When the graphic organizer is complete, have students use it, their notes, and their texts to write a brief informative paragraph about one or more of the groups of people who call this region their home. AL **Verbal/Linguistic**

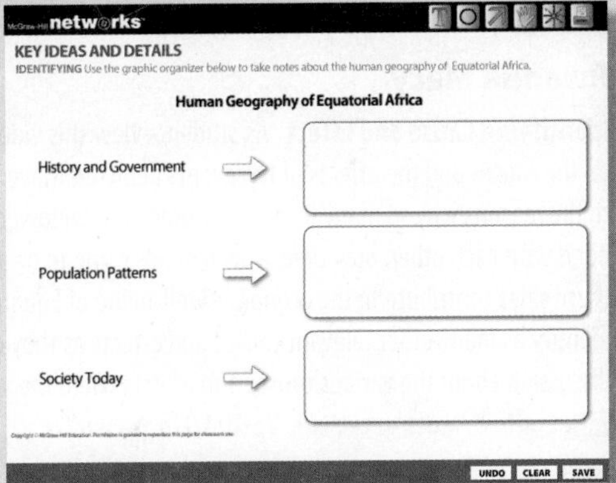

networks
KEY IDEAS AND DETAILS
IDENTIFYING Use the graphic organizer below to take notes about the human geography of Equatorial Africa.
Human Geography of Equatorial Africa
History and Government
Population Patterns
Society Today
UNDO
CLEAR
SAVE

W Writing Skills

Informative/Explanatory Discuss with students how colonization and post-colonization have affected the subregion's education and health care. Then ask students to do some additional research on how the governments of Equatorial Africa and international groups are working to improve educational opportunities, literacy, and health care. Instruct them to write a multi-paragraph informative paper on their findings. Remind students to use current facts and data whenever possible as supporting details. Point out that they should state their thesis clearly in the introduction and restate it in the conclusion. BL **Verbal/Linguistic**

C Critical Thinking Skills

Analyzing Primary Sources Ask a volunteer to read the primary source excerpt on crime in Kinshasa. Then have students review the events in the time line. Explain that Kinshasa is the capital of the Democratic Republic of the Congo. **Ask: Based on what you have learned about the social, economic, and political conditions in the DRC, are you surprised by the fact that crime is high in this country? Why do you think there are so many homeless children?** *(Possible answer: No. There are probably a lot of homeless children because fighting in the country has killed many people, including parents of some of these children.)* Have students work with a partner to write a song that expresses the plight of the *sheggehs,* including what factors led to them becoming homeless and what their hopes are for the future. ELL **Auditory/Musical**

ANSWERS, p. 563

✓ **READING PROGRESS CHECK** Equatorial Africa's ethnic and linguistic diversity are obstacles to political stability because this keeps groups from establishing a national identity, complicates communication between groups, and is a source of conflict between groups.

DBQ Sheggehs are homeless street children.

V Visual Skills

Creating Graphs Discuss the graph with students. Divide the class into small groups, assigning each to research the GDP of a different country in Equatorial Africa. Students should create a circle graph similar to the graph on the page. Ask students to compare the data in each graph, and then write a summary based on the comparison. Then have students share the information about their country's GDP. Have students make a chart of all of the countries' GDPs in the subregion, and then hold a discussion about the factors that influence a country's GDP. **AL Visual/Spatial, Logical/Mathematical**

C Critical Thinking Skills

Analyzing Ethical Issues After students read about agriculture in Equatorial Africa, ask them to consider these questions in a debate: **Are foreign-owned plantations similar to or different from the colonial plantations of the past? Do you think foreign-owned companies are following ethical practices by growing cash crops on plantations, or is it an exploitation of the subregion's resources?** Divide the class into two groups, with one group supporting the foreign-owned plantations and the other representing local farmers. Provide an opportunity for students to gather information for the debate. Remind them to be prepared for counterarguments and to gather evidence to support their point of view. Hold the debate, giving each group an opportunity to present and give a rebuttal. **BL Interpersonal, Logical/Mathematical**

Making Connections

Point out to students that artisanal, or small-scale, mining of gold and diamonds in Equatorial Africa has become prominent and difficult to regulate. The tools that artisanal miners use are basic and often not mechanized. Invite volunteers to explain what impact artisanal mining has on the economy and the environment. Ask them to explain why artisanal mining continues and what solutions they can recommend to reduce or limit it.

ANSWERS, p. 564

CRITICAL THINKING

1. The country's smallest economic sector is Government Services, Defense, and Social Security.
2. Agriculture, hunting, forestry, and fishing make up the largest economic sector, which shows the colonial legacy of growing cash crops for export.

GRAPH SKILLS

DEMOCRATIC REPUBLIC OF THE CONGO 2008 GDP

Government services, Defense and social security 2%
Agriculture, hunting, forestry and fishing 38%
Market services 6%
Transport, storage and communications 6%
Electricity, water and gas 1%
Wholesale and retail trade 22%
Mining and quarrying 14%
Construction 7%
Manufacturing 4%

Source: http://focusafrica.gov.in/Sector_Profile_DRC.html

Agriculture is the most important economic activity in the Democratic Republic of the Congo, accounting for more than one-third of the country's GDP.

▲ CRITICAL THINKING

1. ***Analyzing Visuals*** What is the country's smallest economic sector?
2. ***Drawing Conclusions*** How does the economy of the Democratic Republic of the Congo exemplify Equatorial Africa's colonial legacy?

Economic Activities

GUIDING QUESTION *Why is the economic activity of Equatorial Africa so varied?*

The lives of people throughout Equatorial Africa are changing. The region is becoming more closely tied to the global economy. Like the countries in which they live, individuals face challenges, yet changing economic activities also offer new opportunities.

Farming is the main economic activity in Equatorial Africa. Some countries still depend on single-crop economies; others produce a variety of agricultural goods. Most farmers are subsistence farmers, providing primarily for the needs of their family or village. After they meet their own needs, farmers often sell or trade any extra harvest or livestock at a local market. Common crops are bananas, cacao, cassava (a root), corn, sweet potatoes, and yams.

A smaller percentage of the population works in commercial farming, in which farms produce crops on a large scale. These cash crops are grown and exported to global markets. Most commercial farms are large, foreign-owned plantations. They produce palm oil, peanuts, cacao, and sisal (a vegetable fiber used in rope, drywall and car interiors).

The colonial economic systems played an important role in the growth of commercial crops in Equatorial Africa. Today these same crops are the subregion's main agricultural exports. Most cash crops leave Africa to be processed elsewhere, just as during the colonial period. In the Democratic Republic of the Congo, crops and other goods are exported from Matadi, a port on the Congo River.

Logging has serious consequences, but the lumber industry maintains a relatively small output. Coastal countries with rain forests, such as Gabon, export significant amounts of ebony, mahogany, and natural rubber. Wood from the Okoume tree—found mainly in Gabon, the Republic of the Congo, and Equatorial Guinea—is famous as a good raw material for plywood.

Fishing also represents a portion of the subregion's economic activity. The Congo and its tributaries are also teeming with fish. At Boyoma Falls, the local fishers use conical baskets to trap fish as they pass through the rapids. The shallow ocean area near the coast are excellent fishing waters. Along the southwestern coast, commercial fishing vessels catch herring, sardines, and tuna for export. Few countries, however, build and support large commercial fishing fleets.

The subregion is rich in mineral resources. Equatorial Guinea, the Republic of the Congo, and the Democratic Republic of the Congo are all major oil producers. Mining of copper and other minerals has been important in the Democratic Republic of the Congo since the colonial period. In spite of rich mineral resources, however, many people in these countries do not benefit directly. Governments have often mismanaged the income from mineral wealth. In the Democratic Republic of the Congo, for example, Mobutu Sese Seko appropriated a huge fortune from the state-owned mining company, Gécamines, for his own private fortune. In other cases, foreign mine owners send their profits abroad.

Most of Equatorial Africa never developed manufacturing industries and lacks the infrastructure to process natural resources. Today many countries are receiving foreign loans to industrialize. Progress, however, is slow and unemployment is a major problem. In 2010, for example, the unemployment rate in the Democratic Republic of the Congo was a staggering 61 percent.

networks Online Teaching Options

VIDEO

Rwanda Macy

Identifying Cause and Effect As students view this video, ask them to take notes on the causes and the effects of the events depicted. Have them pay special attention to the reasons why so many Rwandan women are widowed, why they have forged a bond with each other, how their woven goods came to be sold at Macy's, and how these sales contribute to the economic well-being of Equatorial Africa. Ask them to identify as many other relevant causes and effects as they can, as well. Lead a group discussion about the various causes and effects when the video is completed.

AL Logical/Mathematical, Verbal/Linguistic

Demand for manufactured goods has increased, and locally produced goods have replaced some imported items. Today the subregion's industrial workers process food or produce textiles, paper goods, leather products, and cement. Some assemble electric motors, tractors, electronics, and automobiles.

Equatorial Africa faces many obstacles to industrialization. Educational systems are still developing, and more people must gain new skills. Hydroelectric resources are plentiful but untapped, and electrical outages occur. Political conflicts interrupt economic planning and divert resources from development projects. **V**

The use of cell phones and smart phones has grown dramatically in Equatorial Africa.

▲ **CRITICAL THINKING**

1. ***Considering Advantages and Disadvantages*** What advantages do you think cell phones offer over land lines in this region? Might there be any disadvantages to their use?
2. ***Making Predictions*** Would you expect smart phone use to increase or decrease in the future? Why?

Well-developed transportation and communications systems are essential to industry and trade. However, creating and maintaining such systems is difficult. Roads and railways must cross vast distances and varied terrain in the region. Many countries lack modern roads and transport systems except in urban areas.

Some Africans run small businesses selling local products such as baskets, art, and jewelry. Using e-commerce, or selling and buying on the Internet, people sell their products. Thus, the Internet broadens the market for local products.

The subregion has long relied on radio, with state-run stations providing broadcast programming. Television reaches fewer people because the land-relay systems for transmitting TV signals are costly and less available outside urban areas. Satellite technology is helping to expand the reach of television.

Land-line telephone service is also limited, especially in rural areas. However, cell phone usage is increasing. According to a United Nations report, Africa has the highest growth rate of cell phone subscriptions. Satellite and wireless technology have broadened access to phone service and the Internet. Today, more than half of the people in large cities in the region have access to the Internet. Because it is less expensive to set up cell phone towers than to connect telephone wire over vast distances, some areas now have cell phone service where they never before had access to a telephone. Increasingly, these cell phones are smart phones with Internet access which opens new opportunities. **T**

Giovanni Mereghetti/age fotostock

☑ **READING PROGRESS CHECK**

Identifying Cause and Effect Why has it been difficult to develop transportation and communications networks in Equatorial Africa?

LESSON 2 REVIEW (CCSS)

Reviewing Vocabulary (Tier Three Words)

1. ***Explaining*** What effect did the introduction of colonial cash crops have in Equatorial Africa? RH.9–10.4

Using Your Notes

2. ***Summarizing*** For each section of the graphic organizer, write one sentence that summarizes your notes.

Answering the Guiding Questions

3. ***Expressing*** What challenges does democracy face in Equatorial Africa?
4. ***Identifying Cause and Effect*** How does geography influence where the people of Equatorial Africa live?
5. ***Identifying Central Issues*** How does conflict shape life in Equatorial Africa?
6. ***Assessing*** Why is the economic activity of Equatorial Africa so varied?

Writing Activity

7. ***Informative/Explanatory*** Write a paragraph describing how technology is changing how people in Equatorial Africa communicate. WHST.9–10.2

V Visual Skills

Spatial Analysis Review the importance of the development of hydroelectricity in Equatorial Africa. **Ask:** **Why do you think hydroelectric resources have not been developed?** *(Many countries do not have the technology, funds, and other resources needed.)* Tell students to propose a plan for building a dam and hydroelectric plant in Equatorial Africa. They should consider population density, water resources, and potential obstacles when choosing their locations. BL **Visual/Spatial**

T Technology Skills

Explaining Continuity and Change Point out the image of the young woman using a cell phone. **Ask:** **What effect will advancements in technology have as people gain Internet access and acquire cell phones?** *(Communication and information sharing will improve, which may help the economy to foster foreign investment and other aid.)* **Visual/Spatial**

CLOSE & REFLECT

Summarizing Review how the history and people of Equatorial Africa have influenced the economy, politics and government, and culture. Have them summarize their influence on its primary economic activities today.

ANSWERS, p. 565

☑ **READING PROGRESS CHECK** Constructing and maintaining transportation and communication networks is difficult given the large areas and different terrains.

CRITICAL THINKING

1. Advantages: cell phone towers are constructed easier than land lines and provide service in rural areas. Disadvantages: impact to culture by providing smart phone service and access to the Internet .
2. Smart phone use will increase as more towers are constructed and access to technology becomes available.

LESSON 2 REVIEW ANSWERS

Reviewing Vocabulary

1. The cash crops grown for export today are the same as the crops put into place during the colonial period and are still grown on large foreign-owned plantations.

Using Your Notes

2. Summary sentences could include: **History**—history of Bantu and Mbuti; colonization; slavery; weakening of culture and traditions; independence and conflicts; **Population Patterns**—influenced by geography with tropical forest/reserves being sparsely populated; a mostly rural population except in Gabon; capital cities are more heavily populated; **Society and Culture**—extremely diverse with more than 700 languages spoken and more than 200 ethnic groups; Islam, Christianity, and traditional animist religions are practiced; family and religion are interwoven; literacy rates vary; health care and safe drinking water are primary concerns.

Answering the Guiding Questions

3. Democracy faces challenges due to the instability in many countries caused by ethnic conflicts, lack of education and health care, and poverty.
4. The dense tropical forests and forest reserves make these areas sparsely populated with villages clustered along the Congo River and its tributaries.
5. Conflicts cause countries to be unstable and slow economic growth and development. Many countries also see large numbers of refugees due to conflict, such as those entering the Democratic Republic of the Congo from Rwanda and Burundi. An influx of refugees can introduce strife between ethnic groups.
6. The economic activity varies based on the geography and development of the countries of Equatorial Africa. For example, countries with coastal forests export lumber, the countries along the southwest coast have commercial fishing industries, and those countries along the Congo River fish to support the local economy.

Writing Activity

7. Students' paragraphs will vary but should clearly explain how technology is changing how people in the subregion communicate.

ENGAGE

R Reading Skills

Identifying After reading *It Matters Because,* have students identify examples of natural resources in Equatorial Africa. Ask them to make connections to their own region's natural resources. Then discuss different approaches that can be used to manage natural resources effectively.

TEACH & ASSESS

C Critical Thinking Skills

Identifying Central Issues Have students create a list of issues and challenges most people in Equatorial Africa face in their daily lives. Have students jot down possible actions or strategies that can be taken to resolve these issues. Then have students use their lists in small groups to conduct a round-table discussion. After five minutes, ask each group to report on the most viable solutions to these issues. **AL Verbal/Linguistic**

V Visual Skills

Creating Graphs Working with a partner, have students research the production (in terms of exports and quantities) of copper, cobalt, and diamonds in countries in Equatorial Africa over the past decade. Ask them to find data projections for the production of these minerals. Have students create a graph to illustrate their findings. Display the graphs for the class to analyze. **Ask: Which mineral is probably worth investing in the most, and why?** *(Students answers may vary depending on the results of their research, but should be supported with data.)* **BL Logical/Mathematical**

ANSWERS, p. 566

TAKING NOTES: Natural Feature: management of resources; water; land; air; animals **Threat:** poverty, hunger, conflict, corruption; dumping of sewage; deforestation, soil erosion, climate change; burning of biofuels for cooking, vehicle emissions; poaching and hunting for sport; loss of biodiversity.

networks
There's More Online!
- **IMAGE** Cooking With Biofuels
- **IMAGE** Refugee Camp
- **INFOGRAPHIC** Poaching of the African Elephant
- **INTERACTIVE SELF-CHECK QUIZ**
- **VIDEO** People and Their Environment: Equatorial Africa

LESSON 3
People and Their Environment: Equatorial Africa

ESSENTIAL QUESTION • *How do physical systems and human systems shape a place?*

Reading HELPDESK CCSS

Academic Vocabulary (Tier Two Words)
- **priority**
- **hamper**

Content Vocabulary (Tier Three Words)
- **internally displaced person**
- **biofuel**

TAKING NOTES: ***Key Ideas and Details***

IDENTIFYING Use a graphic organizer like the one below to take notes about threats to natural resources in Equatorial Africa.

Equatorial Africa: Managing Resources and Human Impact	
Natural Feature	Threat

IT MATTERS BECAUSE

R *The dense rain forest of Equatorial Africa is an area of abundant resources. Banana, orange, and mango trees grow wild. The rain forest is alive with the sounds of wildlife, and a vast treasure in mineral wealth lies beneath the ground. Such resources can provide a bright future to this often-troubled region, but managing them in a sustainable way poses challenges.*

Managing Resources

GUIDING QUESTION *What makes managing resources in Equatorial Africa especially challenging?*

C The people of Equatorial Africa face tremendous difficulties in achieving a better life. Many environmental challenges threaten the subregion's supply of food, the health of its people, and its plant and animal life. Yet its people, like their neighbors around the globe, look to the future with hope.

Today many of the people in Equatorial Africa must focus on survival. While there is wealth in the subregion, it tends to be concentrated in the hands of the few. Poverty and hunger are bitter enemies for most of the population. When the focus is on survival, management of natural resources can be less of a **priority**.

V And yet, Equatorial Africa has a great number of natural resources. The Democratic Republic of the Congo, for example, has tremendous amounts of fertile land. Rapidly moving streams are resources that could be harnessed to generate electricity. The country also has many mineral resources, including large reserves of copper, cobalt, and industrial diamonds. Although mining is extensive, the full economic benefits that could be gained from mining have not been realized.

Extensive conflict in the subregion is a major cause of misery. Fighting and looting severely **hamper** food distribution and normal economic activity. In the Democratic Republic of the Congo, rival

networks ***Online Teaching Options***

INTERACTIVE BELLRINGER

Refugees and Internally Displaced Persons in the CAR

Hypothesizing Use this chart showing internally displaced persons and the Central African Republic refugees in other countries to help students understand how economic and political factors have led to the mismanagement of resources in the region. Then explain to students that this bellringer activity includes two questions that require them to hypothesize reasons without having detailed background information. Thus, there are no right or wrong answers for the questions, but the answers should be reasonable and based on available facts. Discuss the questions as a class. **BL Logical/Mathematical, Verbal/Linguistic**

Refugees and Internally Displaced Persons in the CAR

From December 2012 to March 2013, thousands of people fled their homes in the Central African Republic to escape violence from rebel forces.

	Before Dec 2012	From Dec 2012 - March 2013
Internally Displaced Persons	51,679	173,274
Refugees in Other Countries:		
Cameroon	87,092	2,000
Chad	70,664	5,000
Democratic Republic of the Congo	29,000	25,400
South Sudan	1,143	--
Total Refugees	187,899	32,400

Auto-Run Click Through 1 of 3

factions fight for control of regions and wealth. In South Sudan, ethnic groups bent on eliminating other groups terrorize the countryside. In the Central African Republic, pockets of the countryside are lawless.

The Office of the United Nations High Commissioner for Refugees estimates the "population of concern" in Equatorial Africa is about four million people. These are refugees and **internally displaced persons**, individuals who have been forced from their homes but remain in their own country. Humanitarian organizations such as Doctors Without Borders (Médecins Sans Frontières) and the International Red Cross have helped by sending medical teams and relief workers, but the persistence of the conflicts limits their effectiveness. **C**

Along with conflict, poverty takes an enormous toll on the people of the subregion. Africa south of the Sahara is the poorest region in the world, and some of the countries in Equatorial Africa are the poorest of the poor. With a per capita gross domestic product (GDP) of $300, the Democratic Republic of the Congo is arguably the poorest country in the world. For comparison, the United States has a per capita GDP of about $48,000. The reality of the region's deep and widespread poverty demands that attention be focused on meeting immediate human needs rather than on managing natural resources. **T**

A further challenge to the management of natural resources is widespread corruption in the governments of the region. Government officials who might work to manage natural resources are subject to bribery by businesses who want to maximize profits. Enforcement of environmental regulations is also hampered by corruption.

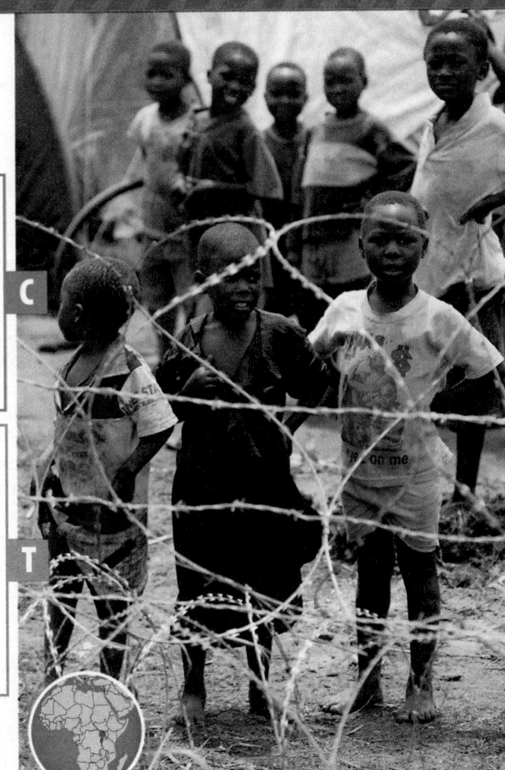

These children live in a refugee camp in the Democratic Republic of the Congo. The country has endured decades of civil war and ethnic strife.

▲ **CRITICAL THINKING**

1. ***Analyzing Visuals*** Based on the photograph, what hardships are experienced by refugees from ethnic conflicts? What other basic needs might these children lack?
2. ***Making Connections*** How does ethnic strife contribute to the region's poverty?

Jack Guez/AFP/Getty Images

✓ **READING PROGRESS CHECK**

Identifying Cause and Effect Why has effective resource management been given a low priority in Equatorial Africa?

Human Impact

GUIDING QUESTION *How have human activities impacted the environment in Equatorial Africa?*

Equatorial Africa is a beautiful region of forests, rivers, mountains, plains, and wildlife. The natural resources of this land are vast. Unfortunately, human activities have placed much of this land in jeopardy. Water pollution, for example, is a major issue in much of the region. This is partly due to the dumping of raw sewage. In the Central African Republic, Equatorial Guinea, and the Republic of the Congo, tap water is not potable, or suitable for drinking.

Soil erosion has become a major ecological problem in Equatorial Africa. In the Democratic Republic of the Congo, for example, soil erosion affects agricultural productivity and thus causes food shortages. Soil erosion also leads to landslides and mud flows. These can have devastating consequences when they happen near rapidly growing cities, such as Bamenda City in Cameroon. Mudslides can destroy buildings that were hastily and poorly constructed. **W**

priority something given or meriting attention before competing alternatives

hamper to make difficult; to impede

internally displaced person a refugee within his or her own country

CHAPTER 23, Lesson 3
People and Their Environment: Equatorial Africa

C Critical Thinking Skills

Differentiating Invite a volunteer to provide definitions and descriptions for *refugee* and *internally displaced persons.* Discuss the differences between them. **Ask:** **Are internally displaced persons unique to this subregion where internal strife is rampant? Explain.** *(Possible answer: No, the term is not unique to the subregion, but there are many internally displaced people in Equatorial Africa where there is political instability.)* Ask students to think of possible solutions to the problem of a growing number of refugees and internally displaced people in Equatorial Africa. Discuss with them if immigration to other subregions or regions is a possibility, and what effect such immigration would have on not only the individuals who immigrate but also the places that receive them. **BL** **Logical/Mathematical, Verbal/Linguistic**

T Technology Skills

Changing Continuity in Economics Have students work independently or in pairs to track the GDP and the level of poverty of one of the countries in Equatorial Africa over the last several years. Discuss the data and make connections between some of the factors that are considered in calculating a country's GDP: consumption, investment/incomes, government spending, exports, and imports. **Ask:** **How can the countries of Equatorial Africa break this continuum of having a low GDP and high poverty?** *(Possible answer: They need more investment in helping people to have their basic needs met.)* **AL** **Visual/Spatial, Logical/Mathematical**

W Writing Skills

Argument Have students research information about how soil erosion is being managed to reduce its effects on poor agricultural output. Tell them to write an editorial about the importance of sustainable practices to prevent soil erosion, citing specific examples from the subregion as supporting points. Remind them to address counterarguments with rebuttals and to clearly state their thesis. **Verbal/Linguistic**

INTERACTIVE WHITEBOARD ACTIVITY

Environmental Threats in Equatorial Africa

Understanding Relationships This interactive helps students to understand the relationships between some of the natural features of Equatorial Africa and the threats these features faces. As students are presented with descriptions of the features and the threats, ask them to draw lines matching the correct relationships. If necessary, students may use their text for support. When they have completed the activity, have them click the button to show the correct answers. Encourage students to compare any incorrect guesses they may have made with the correct answers displayed. **Kinesthetic, Naturalist**

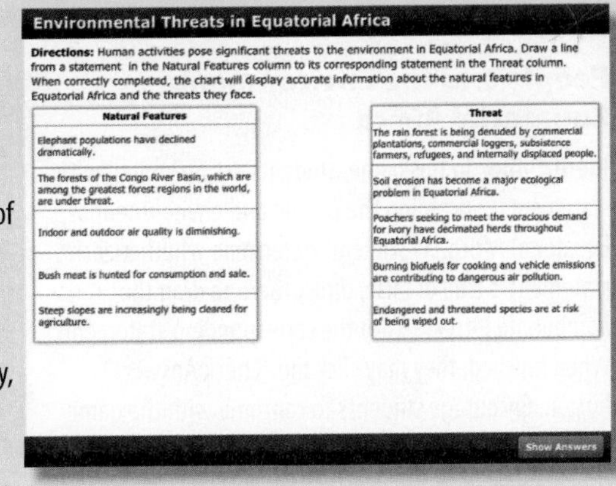

Environmental Threats in Equatorial Africa
Directions: Human activities pose significant threats to the environment in Equatorial Africa. Draw a line from a statement in the Natural Features column to its corresponding statement in the Threat column. When correctly completed, the chart will display accurate information about the natural features in Equatorial Africa and the threats they face.
Natural Features
Elephant populations have declined dramatically.
The forests of the Congo River Basin, which are among the greatest forest regions in the world, are under threat.
Indoor and outdoor air quality is diminishing.
Bush meat is hunted for consumption and sale.
Steep slopes are increasingly being cleared for agriculture.
Threat
The rain forest is being denuded by commercial plantations, commercial loggers, subsistence farmers, refugees, and internally displaced people.
Soil erosion has become a major ecological problem in Equatorial Africa.
Poachers seeking to meet the voracious demand for ivory have decimated herds throughout Equatorial Africa.
Burning biofuels for cooking and vehicle emissions are contributing to dangerous air pollution.
Endangered and threatened species are at risk of being wiped out.
Show Answers

ANSWERS, p. 567

✓ **READING PROGRESS CHECK** The focus has been on survival as issues of poverty and hunger are a higher priority for countries of Equatorial Africa than resource management.

CRITICAL THINKING

1. Student answers may vary, but could include hardships such as living in tents, confinement, lack of shoes and clothing. Other basic needs that are lacking could include food, education, and health care.
2. Ethnic conflict displaces people, hampers food distribution, and interferes with normal economic activity, all of which contributes to the region's poverty.

People and Their Environment: Equatorial Africa

T Technology Skills

Examining Information Have students look online for images of tropical rain forests in Equatorial Africa at various stages of logging. Challenge them to find images where logging has been carried out at the same place several years apart so they can assess the loss of the rain forest habitat. Have them put together their images in a slide show. For each image, they should write a brief description of the environmental changes resulting from logging and the lumber industry. **ELL Visual/Spatial**

R Reading Skills

Specifying As a class, discuss and define *deforestation, desertification,* and *pollution.* **Ask:** **Based on what you have read about these terms, are any of them causing the other? If so, which ones?** *(Desertification is partly caused by deforestation, but is also a result of climate change and other human activities such as irrigation methods.)* **If deforestation is controlled, how will the physical environment be impacted?** *(Possible answer: Desertification may decrease, but other factors may also need to be controlled or slowed; some of the effects of deforestation have already caused factors of climate change, so even a slow down or stop to deforestation is not enough, since it may be impossible to change or decrease the average world temperature or to refreeze the glaciers.)* Ask students to work with a partner to write an action plan for the governments of Equatorial Africa to help control deforestation. **AL Verbal/Linguistic**

Making Connections

Many countries in Equatorial Africa are taking the initiative to invest in and produce biofuels. These alternative fuels are made from agricultural products such as jatropha or palm oil. Jatropha is a common plant in Cameroon, where it is used as food. People eat the seeds and leaves of the plant after it has been cooked. They also use the plant in traditional medicine. The government is studying which biofuel—palm oil or jatropha—is a better environmental choice and which one is the most cost effective to produce. Ask a small group of volunteers to research businesses or government agencies in the United States that have invested or are interested in producing biofuels. Then have the students report their findings to the class.

ANSWERS, p. 568

CRITICAL THINKING

1. There does not appear to be any way to vent the pollution caused by burning biofuels for cooking, which would cause respiratory problems for the inhabitants of the dwelling in the image as well as the danger of fire or injury from the open flame.
2. Possible answers: solar cooking technologies, increasing electricity throughout the region by use of hydroelectric power, and improved construction and filtering technologies to filter and vent pollutants.

T The Congo Basin is one of the great forest regions of the world. Forests cover close to half of the basin's 2 million square miles (5.2 million sq. km). These forests, however, are under threat. Bananas, pineapples, cocoa, tea, coffee, and cotton are grown as cash crops on large commercial plantations. As farmers clear more land to grow these crops, the rain forest is seriously denuded, or stripped of trees. Commercial loggers also diminish the rain forest, as do local people who clear the land for small farming plots. Millions of refugees and internally displaced persons are forced to live off the land. They take wood for heating and cooking fires. About 3,500 square miles (9,100 sq. km) of the forest are lost each year.

Deforestation does not mean simply the loss of trees. It means less wood for the lumber industry, a loss of biodiversity, and accelerating climate change. It also leads to desertification, which in this case refers not to the advancing of a desert, but to the degradation of a formerly forested area. Many areas of Equatorial Africa that used to be forestland are now considered part of the savanna. Deforestation also contributes to soil erosion.

R Air pollution, both inside and outdoors, is also a growing issue. In many parts of Equatorial Africa, household cooking is still done by burning **biofuels**—fuels such as charcoal or wood that are made from living matter. These pose a health threat as the smoke they produce pollutes household air. Household air pollution is much higher in countries that burn biofuels than in industrialized countries. Women, because they do most of the cooking, are especially at risk for the respiratory illnesses that pollution from burning biofuels can cause. Outdoor air pollution is also a problem. Vehicle emissions in growing, crowded cities, such as Kinshasa, pose a health threat to residents.

biofuel fuel created from living matter, such as trees

The Ivory Trade

African elephants once roamed in great numbers across the continent. Biologists estimate that in 1930, Africa was home to between 5 and 10 million elephants. During the last century, however, elephants were slaughtered by the tens of thousands for meat, for sport, and especially for their ivory tusks. Both male and female African elephants grow tusks—the world's main source of ivory. Ivory is a form of dentin that is excellent for carving and valued for its beauty. The trade in ivory dates back thousands of years. In the 1800s and 1900s, however, the demand for ivory from India, Europe, and the United States grew dramatically. By the mid-1900s, elephant populations had declined sharply. When the price of ivory soared in the 1970s, elephant tusks increased in value. Poachers began illegally killing elephants for their tusks. As many as 80,000 elephants a year were shot.

The ivory trade has had devastating consequences for the African elephant. During the 1980s, approximately half of Africa's elephant population was wiped out by poachers and only about 600,000 elephants remained. In 1989 African elephants were placed on the endangered species list by the

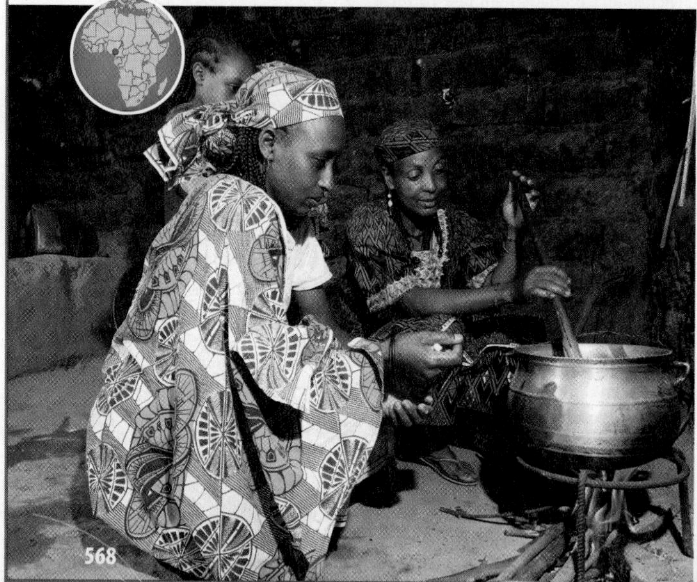

Millions of people in Equatorial Africa, such as these Mbororo women in Cameroon, rely on wood to make fires for cooking and heating. This accelerates deforestation and causes indoor air pollution.

Heiner Heine/age fotostock

▼ CRITICAL THINKING

1. ***Analyzing Visuals*** Based on the photo, what dangers are posed by indoor cooking with biofuels?
2. ***Problem Solving*** What technologies might be used to combat this problem?

568

networks Online Teaching Options

GAME

People and the Environment: Equatorial Africa

Identifying In this game, students are presented with statements concerning the people and environment of Equatorial Africa. As students determine whether each statement is true or false, direct them to drag the appropriate letter next to the corresponding statement. When finished, they may click the "Check Answers" button. Encourage students to continue with the game until they have correctly identified each statement as true or false. **AL Verbal/Linguistic**

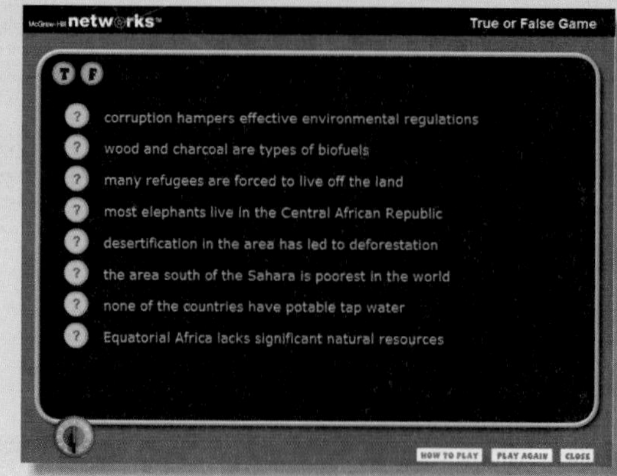

Convention on International Trade in Endangered Species (CITES). Trade in ivory was banned worldwide. Organizations were established to coordinate the ban on the ivory trade and help African countries stop the poaching of elephants. The ban has only been partly successful, however. In recent years, the demand for ivory has surged. This is due in part to the huge demand for ivory ornaments in China.

Most elephants in Equatorial Africa are found in Cameroon. Armed poachers travel to Cameroon on horseback from Sudan and Chad across the Central African Republic, where almost all the elephants have already been wiped out. Even in protected areas, such as Cameroon's Bouba N'Djida National Park, more than half of the park's 400 elephants have been killed by poachers.

Hunting

In Equatorial Africa, local people do not hunt wild animals for sport as much as they hunt them for food. Warfare in the subregion has led to a widespread availability of firearms. It has also displaced millions of people who are extremely poor. This has proved a deadly combination for the subregion's wildlife. People hunt to feed themselves, and a growing number of people hunt to sell the meat to others.

The term *bushmeat* refers to the meat of animals hunted in "the bush," or forest. Among these animals are endangered or threatened species. Hunted animals include monkeys, antelopes, gorillas, and bonobos. In the Democratic Republic of the Congo, it is estimated that more than one million pounds of bushmeat are consumed each year.

C

V

READING PROGRESS CHECK

Identifying Cause and Effect How has conflict in Equatorial Africa put pressure on the subregion's resources?

Marcel Pepeira/age fotostock

An area's elephant population will decline if more than 50 percent of the deaths are due to poaching. In 2011 all subregions in Africa south of the Sahara exceeded 50 percent. Some experts believe this rise in poaching could lead to the extinction of elephants by 2025. The loss of elephants could lead to ecosystem collapse in some areas.

▲ CRITICAL THINKING

1. ***Exploring Issues*** Do you think that the poachers or the people who buy ivory from poachers should be targeted by officials trying to stop the ivory trade? Explain.
2. ***Hypothesizing*** In what region are the most elephants killed by poachers? Why do you suppose more elephants are killed there than in other parts of Africa?

Equatorial Africa **569**

Content Background Knowledge

Poaching: Here and There Poaching of elephants is a problem that is not unique to Africa. However, the African elephant is unique to the continent. In India, the Indian elephant is also killed for its ivory. Asian elephants are smaller than African elephants. In about 1900, there were approximately 100,000 Asian elephants in the world. Today, that number is less than half. Unlike African elephants, Asian elephants are important in the Hindu worship of deities.

C Critical Thinking Skills

Analyzing Cause and Effect Invite a volunteer to read about hunting in Equatorial Africa. **Ask:** **What effect has poverty had on hunting?** *(Hunting has increased because people do not have enough food. People hunt to feed themselves and their families or to sell the meat to others. People also hunt elephants for their valuable ivory tusks.)* Explain to students that *bushmeat* is a term that is unique to Africa and Asia. The consumption of bushmeat can cause diseases, such as Ebola and foot-and-mouth disease.

ELL Verbal/Linguistic

V Visual Skills

Analyzing Cause and Effect Discuss with students how events or actions can have multiple causes and effects. Have students complete a cause-and-effect diagram on their own. Then have them exchange their diagrams with a partner. **Ask:** **Should the governments of Equatorial Africa outlaw or regulate hunting? Explain. What long-term effects will nonregulated hunting have on the population?** *(Possible answers: More people will contract diseases and perish. More species will become endangered or extinct.)* Then have students work with a partner to create a cost-benefit analysis of hunting in Equatorial Africa based on their diagrams and the class discussion. **Interpersonal, Visual/Spatial**

GRAPH

Elephant Poaching in 2011

Comparing and Contrasting Have students look carefully at the graph and consider the reasons why elephant poaching is so prevalent in many regions of Africa. Have them consider, also, the measures taken to prevent this poaching and how effective or not these measures have been. Then ask students to imagine that these elephants lived in a more economically developed and politically stable area elsewhere in the world. Do they think the poaching would be so rampant? If so, what measures would be taken, and would those measures be effective? Have students discuss their ideas in small groups.

BL Logical/Mathematical, Verbal/Linguistic

Elephant Poaching in 2011

ELEPHANT POACHING IN 2011
PERCENTAGE OF DEATHS DUE TO POACHING
100
90
80
70
60
50
40
30
20
10
0
Central Africa
Eastern Africa
Southern Africa
Western Africa
NOTE: Central Africa is sometimes referred to as Equatorial Africa.
Sources: http://www.cntraveler.com/2010; http://ngm.nationalgeographic.com/2012

ANSWERS, p. 569

READING PROGRESS CHECK Conflicts in Equatorial Africa have led to there being large numbers of firearms available, which contributes to the destruction of wildlife as people displaced by conflicts and those in poverty also hunt the wildlife for food.

CRITICAL THINKING

1. Student answers will vary, but could include targeting the people who buy from poachers because if there are no buyers, there would be no purpose in poaching; or targeting poachers to make the penalty so high that poaching decreases.
2. Central Africa has the most elephants killed by poachers. Answers may vary, but reasons for this could include the increased value of ivory combined with the high poverty in the region as well as elephants have already been greatly reduced in other areas by poaching.

C Critical Thinking Skills

Considering Advantages and Disadvantages Lead a class discussion about the causes and effects of human actions on the environment and what people of Equatorial Africa, Western governments, and nongovernmental organizations (NGOs) are doing to reduce the problems. Discuss the importance of collaborative efforts. **Ask: Why is it important to the global community that the rain forests are protected?** *(They help clean the air and produce oxygen.)* **Logical/Mathematical**

W Writing Skills

Informative/Explanatory Discuss efforts that the subregion has taken to combat poachers. Ask students to use information from the text and additional resources to write a report on the struggle that one NGO wrestles with to eradicate poaching in the wake of rising poverty levels. Students should include primary source excerpts and data. BL **Verbal/Linguistic**

CLOSE & REFLECT

Outlining Have students look back through the headings and subheadings used in each section and use them to outline the main ideas and details of the lesson. Remind them to include only the main or central ideas and important supporting details.

ANSWERS, p. 570

READING PROGRESS CHECK Many countries have created forest reserves to protect tropical forests, logging companies are using tree farming technologies and replanting trees, and the Central Africa Forest Commission is working on conservation and sustainable management of the forests with countries in the region.

Addressing the Issues

GUIDING QUESTION *What steps are being taken to combat these environmental challenges?*

C Increasingly, the protection of tropical rain forests is a priority in the subregion. Various countries have created forest reserves to protect tropical forests. Logging companies are also getting involved, using scientific tree farming and replanting projects to protect and renew forests. In one program, more than 10 million trees were planted on a tree plantation outside Virunga National Park in the Democratic Republic of the Congo. The Central African Forest Commission (COMIFAC) is an international organization coordinating the conservation and sustainable management of the forest ecosystem in the region. COMIFAC works in conjunction with a network of member countries, international institutions, and nongovernmental organizations (NGOs).

Some NGOs and other charitable organizations, along with Western governments and entrepreneurs, are working with local African communities to solve the indoor air pollution problem. New technologies may offer a solution to this serious health issue. Some organizations are inventing ways to make biofuel cookstoves cleaner and more efficient. Others have developed solar-powered cookstoves. Some are developing clean technologies to provide lighting. One of the most recent innovations is the development of gravity-powered lighting. This type of light uses gravity to power a small light for a short period of time. It has the potential to offer cheap lighting that is safe for both people and the environment.

W To counter the ivory trade, governments in Equatorial Africa have deployed troops and special police forces to combat poachers. Unfortunately, they are often too few in number and poorly trained. Private groups like the World Wildlife Fund support local people's efforts to oppose poachers and pressure governments in the region to devote resources to antipoaching efforts. Nongovernmental organizations and conservationists have, however, come under criticism for allegedly disregarding the poverty and human suffering that exist in the region. The widespread economic hardship in Equatorial Africa creates a situation in which poaching is a tempting way of making a living. This makes the antipoaching campaign even more of a challenge.

Similarly, decreasing the trade in bushmeat is a difficult task given the ongoing political and economic struggles in the region. Humanitarian and development efforts aim to increase people's standard of living in hopes that this will in turn decrease the demand for hunted wildlife.

READING PROGRESS CHECK

Identifying What actions are being taken to protect Africa's tropical forests?

LESSON 3 REVIEW

Reviewing Vocabulary (Tier Three Words)

1. ***Expressing*** What problem does the use of biofuels create? RH.9–10.4

Using Your Notes

2. ***Expressing*** Use the notes in your graphic organizer to write a paragraph about environmental issues in Equatorial Africa.

Answering the Guiding Questions

3. ***Identifying Central Issues*** What makes managing resources in Equatorial Africa especially challenging?
4. ***Identifying Cause and Effect*** How have human activities impacted the environment in Equatorial Africa?
5. ***Listing*** What steps are being taken to combat these environmental challenges?

Writing Activity

6. ***Argument*** Write an e-mail to a United Nations official arguing for or against the creation of more protected wildlife areas in Equatorial Africa. WHST.9–10.1

570

LESSON 3 REVIEW ANSWERS

Reviewing Vocabulary

1. The use of biofuels contributes to both indoor and outdoor air pollution, which leads to respiratory illnesses.

Using Your Notes

2. Paragraphs will vary, but should be strongly supported with information from the lesson including poaching, water pollution, hunting, air pollution, deforestation, and soil erosion that leads to landslides and mud flows.

Answering the Guiding Questions

3. Managing resources is especially challenging in Equatorial Africa because of conflict, corruption, and the focus on survival because there are high rates of hunger and poverty.
4. The dumping of raw sewage has caused water pollution making much of the water unsuitable for drinking, burning of biofuels for cooking and vehicle emissions are leading to indoor and outdoor air pollution, poaching and hunting is endangering many species, and deforestation for logging and farming not only destroys the forests but contributes to soil erosion. Soil erosion in turn leads to food shortages, mud flows, and landslides.
5. Some NGOs are working to find ways to reduce the use of biofuels and make cooking cleaner and safer, governments have sent troops and special forces to combat poachers, humanitarian groups are working to increase the standard of living to eliminate the need to hunt bushmeat for food, many countries have created forest reserves to protect tropical forests, logging companies are using scientific tree farming technologies and replanting trees to renew forests, and the Central Africa Forest Commission is working on conservation and sustainable management of the forests with a number of countries in the region.

Writing Activity

6. E-mails will vary, but should include the protection of endangered animals and risk of extinction of species in those arguing for protected wildlife areas or the poverty and need for income from these areas for those against more wildlife reserves.

Directions: *On a separate sheet of paper, answer the questions below. Make sure you read carefully and answer all parts of the questions.*

Lesson Review

Lesson 1

1. ***Explaining*** What physical feature dominates Equatorial Africa? What functions does it serve?
2. ***Making Connections*** What is the economic value of the subregion's rain forests?
3. ***Identifying Cause and Effect*** Why do Equatorial Africa's water resources remain underdeveloped, despite abundant rainfall?

Lesson 2

4. ***Sequencing*** Create a graphic organizer showing the rise and fall of colonial powers in what is now the Republic of the Congo.
5. ***Explaining*** What role did colonialism play in the development of commercial agriculture?
6. ***Identifying Central Issues*** Describe the quantity of mineral resources in Equatorial Africa. Explain why the people of the area see few benefits from these resources.

Lesson 3

7. ***Summarizing*** Why is Africa south of the Sahara the poorest region in the world, despite its many resources?
8. ***Identifying Cause and Effect*** Develop a diagram with labels to show the causes and effects of soil erosion in Equatorial Africa. Write a paragraph to explain the information in your diagram.
9. ***Making Connections*** Discuss the connection between deforestation and desertification in Equatorial Africa.

Critical Thinking

10. ***Organizing*** After studying Equatorial Africa, you have decided you would like to write a book about the people, land, and climate of this subregion. Write a one-page outline for your book to show the major topics you will include. WHST.9–10.4

21st Century Skills

Use the cartoon below to answer the questions that follow.

"'Born in conservation,' if you don't mind. 'Captivity' has negative connotations."

11. ***Evaluating Primary Sources*** Explain why you think elephants were chosen as the topic of this cartoon. What conservation efforts are taking place in Equatorial Africa?
12. ***Understanding Relationships Among Events*** What relationship does poverty have to conservation in Equatorial Africa?

Applying Map Skills

Use the Unit 6 Atlas to answer the following questions.

13. ***The World in Spatial Terms*** Use your mental map of Equatorial Africa to describe the spatial relationship among the Congo Basin, the Katanga Plateau, and the Republic of the Congo.
14. ***Places and Regions*** What is the largest country in Equatorial Africa? Provide the approximate size of this country in square miles.
15. ***Environment and Society*** Discuss the connections between the population of Kinshasa, Democratic Republic of the Congo, and the pollution levels from vehicle emissions.

Need Extra Help?

If You've Missed Question	1	2	3	4	5	6	7	8	9	10	11	12	13	14	15
Go to page	554	558	558	560	564	564	567	567	568	551	571	571	476	476	476

CHAPTER 23 Assessment Answers

Lesson Review

Lesson 1

1. The Congo Basin dominates Equatorial Africa and serves to collect rainfall that drains through various tributaries to form the Congo River.
2. The minerals mined out of the forests of the Democratic Republic of the Congo are estimated to be worth about $25 trillion.
3. Equatorial Africa's water resources are underdeveloped because of a lack of financial resources and due to the irregular and unpredictable amounts of rainfall.

Lesson 2

4. Graphic organizer should show that in 1878, the king of Belgium had trading posts set up along the Congo River by explorer Henry M. Stanley. He convinced other European powers to grant him control of what was called the Congo Free State and treated the people who lived there horribly. France gained control of the Republic of the Congo in the late 1800s through negotiations with local rulers who were concerned about threats from Belgium.
5. Colonialism established the cash crops that are the main exports of Equatorial Africa today and also created the large foreign-owned plantations that operate commercial farms.
6. The subregion is very rich in minerals, but the people see very few benefits as the income generated is mismanaged by the government or lost to corruption. Many countries also lack the infrastructure and funds to develop these resources.

Lesson 3

7. Conflict and corruption hamper economic development and management of resources, which keep the region from effectively using its resources to decrease poverty.
8. Diagrams and paragraphs will vary, but should be strongly supported with information from the chapter, including how deforestation leads to erosion and how soil erosion causes a loss in agricultural productivity, food shortages, landslides, and mud flows.
9. Desertification occurs when forested land changes to savanna because trees have been removed. This deforestation changes the climate, which also adds to desertification.

Critical Thinking

10. Outlines will vary, but should be supported with information from the chapter which could include: the Congo Basin; mountains and plateaus; volcanoes both active and inactive; Congo River; rain forests; savanna; hundreds of ethnic groups such as the Fang, Bantu, and Mbuti; hundreds of languages spoken; Christianity, Islam, and traditional animist religions; colonization; and conflicts.

21st Century Skills

11. Explanations will vary but should include that elephants are endangered due to poachers who sell the tusks as a source of ivory. Conservation efforts include worldwide bans on the selling of ivory, creating protected areas for elephants, and governments sending troops and special police to combat poaching.
12. Conservation efforts are difficult due to the extreme poverty in Equatorial Africa, ivory is worth a lot of money so it attracts the threat of poachers, and the need to hunt for food endangers other animals, thus hampering conservation efforts.

Applying Map Skills

13. The Congo Basin is surrounded by highlands that include the Katanga Plateau to the south and the Republic of the Congo to the southwest.
14. The Democratic Republic of the Congo is the largest country in Equatorial Africa at approximately 1.5 million square miles.
15. The northern portion of the Democratic Republic of the Congo is sparsely populated due to tropical forests. However, the southern portion is heavily populated, including the capital city of Kinshasa, which has a population of around 8 million. Kinshasa serves as the cultural, political, and economic hub of the region, making it have high pollution levels from vehicle emissions.

Assessment Answers

DBQ Analyzing Primary Sources

16 Conflict is causing food prices to rise, interrupting trade and deliveries of food, and keeping farmers from working in fields due to insecurity.

17 Rebels have taken control over areas of land and disrupted trade for food supplies and created feelings of insecurity among the farmers. The government has increased the price of food by 40 percent in areas they control, which causes people to be unable to afford food.

Exploring the Essential Question

18 Brochures will differ but should be strongly supported with information from the chapter, including the following headings: History, Politics, Population, Society and Culture, and Economics.

College and Career Readiness

19 Essays will vary, but should be strongly supported with information from the chapter on problems facing refugees, including that there is estimated to be four million refugees and internally displaced people in the region, there is widespread poverty and hunger, ongoing ethnic conflicts cause the issue and also keep it from being resolved, corruption also hampers relief efforts, and the necessity of efforts to bring badly needed health care to the region by groups like Doctors Without Borders and the International Red Cross.

Research and Presentation

20 Multimedia presentations will vary, but should include audio/video/printed excerpts from news reports, maps, and diagrams to define conflict diamonds, explain why they are called conflict diamonds, identify issues related to conflict diamonds, and explain how the issues are being addressed.

Writing About Geography

21 Paragraphs will vary, but should include descriptions of how elements of the rain forest look, sound, taste, smell, and feel to the student. They could include descriptions of the emergent layer, canopy, understory, and undergrowth or floor of the rain forest; wildlife including birds, bats, monkeys, and elephants; the daily rain and humidity; and differing amounts of light on each level of the forest.

CHAPTER 23 Assessment 

Directions: On a separate sheet of paper, answer the questions below. Make sure you read carefully and answer all parts of the questions.

DBQ Analyzing Primary Sources

Conflict is a major contributor to poverty in Equatorial Africa. Read the news report below to see how conflict in the Central African Republic affects access to and production of food.

PRIMARY SOURCE

"The U.N. World Food Program [WFP] expressed concern about a potential food crisis in CAR [the Central African Republic]. It said conflict that erupted during a rebellion . . . had sparked the situation.

The WFP said trade has been interrupted in parts of the country controlled by the rebel group. Basic food prices for areas under government control, meanwhile, have increased 40 percent since December.

WFP called on the rebel group to let humanitarian workers into its parts of CAR. An estimated 800,000 people live in areas under rebel control.

'We are very concerned about prospect for the 2013 growing season, which is due to start in just a few weeks,' Rockaya Fall, the Food and Agriculture Organization's country representative, said in a statement. 'Land preparation, which should have begun, is behind schedule in many places, due to insecurity.'"

—"Food Crisis Plagues War-Torn CAR," United Press International, February 18, 2013

16 ***Identifying Cause and Effect*** In what ways is conflict contributing to a food crisis in the Central African Republic? RH.9–10.1

17 ***Differentiating*** Distinguish between the roles played by the rebels and the government in the food crisis. RH.9–10.2

Exploring the Essential Question

18 ***Synthesizing*** Create a short guide in the form of a brochure to provide an overview of the ways physical systems and human systems shape Equatorial Africa. Within your brochure, include the following headings: *History, Politics, Population, Society, Culture,* and *Economics.* WHST.9–10.4

College and Career Readiness

19 ***Clear Communication*** Imagine that you are applying for a position as an intern with the Office of the United Nations High Commissioner for Refugees (UNHCR). The focus of this internship is on helping refugees and internally displaced persons in Equatorial Africa. Write a one-page essay to explain why you should be chosen to serve in this position. Within your essay, provide the following: your knowledge of the relevant problems in the subregion, including the conditions that have led to the problems and the relevance of the work of Doctors Without Borders (Médicins Sans Frontières) and the International Red Cross in the subregion. WHST.9–10.4

Research and Presentation

20 ***Gathering Information*** With a partner, conduct research to learn more about conflict diamonds, also known as blood diamonds, mined from Africa. Develop a multimedia presentation to answer the following questions: What are conflict diamonds? Why are they known as conflict diamonds? What are some issues related to conflict diamonds? What steps are being taken to address these issues? Include the following in your multimedia presentation: audio and video of relevant news reports, maps, diagrams, and excerpts from printed news reports. WHST.9–10.1; WHST.9–10.6; WHST.9–10.7; WHST.9–10.8

Writing About Geography

21 ***Narrative*** Use standard grammar, spelling, sentence structure, and punctuation to write a paragraph that describes a visit to the equatorial rain forest. In your paragraph, include details that relate to all five senses and to the wildlife, plant life, and resources of the rain forest. WHST.9–10.2

Need Extra Help?

If You've Missed Question	16	17	18	19	20	21
Go to page	572	572	551	567	566	558

572

networks Online Teaching Options

ASSESSMENT

Chapter Test and Lesson Quizzes

Assessing Have students complete the Chapter Test and Lesson Quizzes to assess their understanding throughout the chapter. These assessment tools offer chapter and lesson evaluation through a variety of question formats including document-based questions.

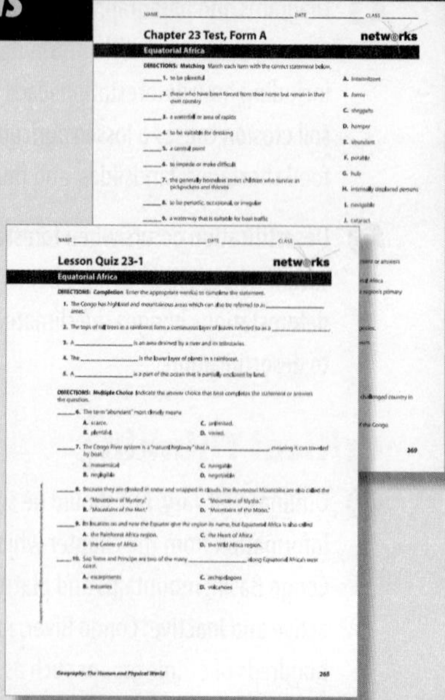

CHAPTER 24

Southern Africa Planner

UNDERSTANDING BY DESIGN®

Enduring Understandings

- *The characteristics and distribution of human populations affect physical and human systems.*

Essential Question

- *How do physical systems and human systems shape a place?*

Predictable Misunderstandings

Students may think:

- *Southern Africa and South Africa are the same place. Explain that South Africa is a country in Southern Africa at the very southern tip of Africa. Other countries in the region of Southern Africa include Zambia, Zimbabwe, Malawi, Mozambique, Swaziland, Namibia, Lesotho, Madagascar, Angola, Comoros, Botswana, and Mauritius.*
- *Most laborers in Southern Africa work in diamond and gold mining. Explain that although mining is an important economic activity, most people in Southern Africa are farmers. Most of the farms are used for subsistence farming, but commercial farming is also important.*

Assessment Evidence

Performance Tasks:

- *Hands-On Chapter Project*

Other Evidence:

- *Guided Reading Activities*
- *Vocabulary Activities*
- *Lesson Quizzes*
- *Chapter Tests, Forms A and B*

SUGGESTED PACING GUIDE

Introducing the Chapter .... ½ Day
Lesson 1 .... 1 Day
Lesson 2 .... 1 Day
Lesson 3 .... 1 Day
Chapter Wrap-Up and Assessment ...... ½ Day

TOTAL TIME 4 Days

Key for Using the Teacher Edition

SKILL-BASED ACTIVITIES

Types of skill activities found in the Teacher Edition.

* **V Visual Skills** require students to analyze maps, graphs, charts, and photos.

R Reading Skills help students practice reading skills and master vocabulary.

C Critical Thinking Skills help students apply and extend what they have learned.

W Writing Skills provide writing opportunities to help students comprehend the text.

T Technology Skills require students to use digital tools effectively.

*Letters are followed by a number when there is more than one of the same type of skill on the page.

DIFFERENTIATED INSTRUCTION

All activities are written for the on-level student unless otherwise marked with the leveled labels below.

BL Beyond Level
AL Approaching Level
ELL English Language Learners

All students benefit from activities that utilize different learning styles. Many activities are marked as below when a particular learning style is highlighted.

Intrapersonal	Naturalist
Logical/Mathematical	Kinesthetic
Visual/Spatial	Auditory/Musical
Verbal/Linguistic	Interpersonal

National Geography Standards covered in "Southern Africa"

The student knows and understands:

(5) That people create regions to interpret Earth's complexity

5.1 Regions are defined by different sets of criteria and places can be included in multiple regions of different types

(7) The physical processes that shape the patterns of Earth's surface

7.3 Physical processes interact over time to shape particular places on Earth's surface

(9) The characteristics, distribution, and migration of human populations on Earth's surface

9.1 Culture, economics, and politics influence the changing demographic structure of different populations

(10) The characteristics, distribution, and complexity of Earth's cultural mosaics

10.2 Cultural landscapes exist at multiple scales

(11) The patterns and networks of economic interdependence on Earth's surface

11.2 Patterns exist in the spatial organization of economic activities

11.3 Economic systems are dynamic organizations of interdependent economic activities for production, exchange, distribution, and consumption of goods and services

11.4 Improvements in transportation and communication networks reduce the effects of distance and time on the movements of people, products, and ideas

(12) The process, patterns, and functions of human settlement

12.1 The numbers, types, and range of the functions of settlement change

12.2 Settlements can grow and/or decline over time

(13) How the forces of cooperation and conflict among people influence the division and control of Earth's surface

13.3 Changes within, between and among countries regarding division and control of Earth's surface may result in conflict

(14) How human actions modify the physical environment

14.1 Human modifications of the physical environment can have significant global impacts

14.2 The use of technology can have both intended and unintended impacts on the physical environment which may be positive or negative

14.3 People can either mitigate and/or adapt to the consequences of human modifications of the physical environment

CHAPTER OPENER PLANNER

Students will know:

- *the region's dramatic landforms and non-navigable but valuable rivers.*
- *how the climates affect the biomes of Southern Africa.*
- *that Southern Africa has been affected by many different cultures in which family is important.*
- *that mining is a major economic activity of the region and the difficulties of resource management.*
- *how environmental issues affect life and how they are being addressed.*

Students will be able to:

- ***describe** the physical geography of Southern Africa and the value of its rivers.*
- ***describe** how the biomes are affected by the climates in Southern Africa.*
- ***analyze** the effects of different cultures on Southern Africa and the importance of family.*
- ***identify** mining as a major economic activity in the region and analyze why it is difficult to manage resources.*
- ***describe** the impact of environmental issues on life in Southern Africa and how the issues are being addressed.*

UNDERSTANDING BY DESIGN®

☑ Print Teaching Options

V Visual Skills

- ☐ **p. 574** Students discuss and answer questions about HIV/AIDS map. AL Visual/Spatial

R Reading Skills

- ☐ **p. 575** Students consider what they have learned about how HIV/AIDS spreads. AL Verbal/Linguistic

C Critical Thinking Skills

- ☐ **p. 574** Students analyze what it means to a country to face an epidemic and identify the more serious aspects of the HIV/AIDS epidemic facing Southern Africa.
- ☐ **p. 575** Students make a cause-effect graphic organizer to record the different reasons why HIV/AIDS is being transmitted at a high rate. BL Logical/Mathematical

W Writing Skills

- ☐ **p. 575** Students write an essay summarizing what is being done to combat HIV/AIDS in Southern Africa.

T Technology Skills

- ☐ **p. 574** Students research factors that affect the rate of HIV infection. BL Verbal/Linguistic, Visual/Spatial

☑ Online Teaching Options

C Critical Thinking Skills

- INTERACTIVE MAP **World Distribution of HIV, 2010**—Students hypothesize about whether the HIV epidemic has increased or decreased in Southern Africa. AL Logical/Mathematical, Visual/Spatial
- MAP **Interactive Regional Atlas**—Students use the interactive regional atlas to understand the physical and human geography of Southern Africa.

☑ Printable Digital Worksheets

- WORKSHEET **Assessing Background Knowledge**—Determine the level of prior knowledge students have about Southern Africa.
- WORKSHEET **Chapter Summary**—Students review the main idea of each lesson of the chapter content.
- WORKSHEET **Reteaching Activity**—These worksheets provide students with an opportunity for remedial practice and review of vital chapter content.

Project-Based Learning 

Hands-On

Educational Materials

Students create environmental educational materials related to a specific environmental issue for students and teachers in Southern African countries.

Digital Hands-On

Create Online Projects

Find an additional activity online that incorporates technology for this project. Visit the EdTech Teacher Web sites for more links, tutorials, and other resources.

Print Resources

ANCILLARY RESOURCES

This ancillary is available for every chapter and lesson.

- **Chapter Tests and Lesson Quizzes**

PRINTABLE DIGITAL WORKSHEETS

These printable digital worksheets are available for every chapter and lesson.

- **Assessing Background Knowledge**
- **Chapter Summaries**
- **Guided Reading Activities**
- **Hands-On Chapter Projects**
- **Quizzes and Tests**
- **Reading Essentials and Study Guide** AL
- **Reteaching Activities**
- **Video Activities**
- **Vocabulary**

More Media Resources

SUGGESTED VIDEOS MOVIES

- **Exploring the Wildlife of Southern Africa** *National Geographic* (44 min.)
- **Today the Hawk Takes One Chick** Jane Gillooly (72 min.)
- **War Elephants** (45 min.)

SUGGESTED READING 

- ***Transforming the Frontier: Peace Parks and the Politics of Neoliberal Conservation in Southern Africa,*** by Bram Büscher
- ***Southern Africa: Living Landscapes,*** by David Rogers
- ***South Africa: The Rise and Fall of Apartheid,*** by Nancy L. Clark and William H. Worger

LESSON 1 PLANNER

PHYSICAL GEOGRAPHY OF SOUTHERN AFRICA

Students will know:
- *that Southern Africa is a large area of high land and dramatic landforms.*
- *that the region's major rivers are non-navigable but still valuable resources.*
- *how the climates affect the biomes of Southern Africa.*

Students will be able to:
- ***describe*** *the physical geography of Southern Africa.*
- ***analyze*** *the value of Southern Africa's rivers.*
- ***describe*** *how the biomes are affected by the climates in Southern Africa.*

UNDERSTANDING BY DESIGN®

☑ *Print Teaching Options*

V Visual Skills

- ☐ **p. 576** Students name and locate each country on a political map. ELL Visual/Spatial
- ☐ **p. 577** Students design a chart or graphic organizer to compare and contrast the landforms in each country in the region. Verbal/Linguistic, Visual/Spatial
- ☐ **p. 579** Students create a visual guide to the biomes of the countries of Southern Africa. BL Visual/Spatial

R Reading Skills

- ☐ **p. 576** Students list and describe any landforms, waterways, climates, and biomes they already know can be found in Southern Africa.
- ☐ **p. 577** Students read about the terrain in Madagascar. ELL Verbal/Linguistic
- ☐ **p. 577** Students write a description of what happens at the end of the Okavango River. AL Verbal/Linguistic, Visual/Spatial
- ☐ **p. 578** Students define the word *navigable.* ELL Verbal/Linguistic

C Critical Thinking Skills

- ☐ **p. 578** Students review the information about how people in Southern Africa use rivers differently. AL Logical/Mathematical
- ☐ **p. 579** Students discuss rain shadows. AL Verbal/Linguistic
- ☐ **p. 580** Students discuss the ways foreign companies run their businesses of extracting minerals and gemstones from Southern Africa compared to how multinational companies do business. AL Logical/Mathematical

W Writing Skills

- ☐ **p. 578** Students write a narrative to describe animals they see as if they are visiting an area in Southern Africa to protect the native wildlife. BL Verbal/Linguistic

T Technology Skills

- ☐ **p. 580** Students research the importance of the baobab tree to people in Southern Africa and present their findings in a multimedia display. Interpersonal, Naturalist

☑ *Online Teaching Options*

V Visual Skills

- ☐ VIDEO **Around the World—Botswana**—Students watch this video about Botswana and then summarize what they have learned. AL Interpersonal, Verbal/Linguistic

R Reading Skills

- ☐ INTERACTIVE BELLRINGER **Topography of Southern Africa**—Students answer questions about the topography of the region. AL Visual/Spatial, Interpersonal
- ☐ INTERACTIVE IMAGE **Reserving Game**—Students create a list of ideas about how to preserve wildlife and natural reserve game farms in this region. Verbal/Linguistic, Interpersonal
- ☐ INTERACTIVE WHITEBOARD ACTIVITY **Southern Africa Landforms**—Students complete a chart and sentences about the landforms of Southern Africa. ELL AL Verbal/Linguistic

☑ *Printable Digital Worksheets*

R Reading Skills

- ☐ WORKSHEET **Guided Reading Activity**—Students use the Guided Reading Activity worksheets to review their comprehension of the content.

C Critical Thinking Skills

- ☐ WORKSHEET **Video Activity**—Students answer questions related to a topic in the chapter content after they have viewed a lesson video.

HUMAN GEOGRAPHY OF SOUTHERN AFRICA

Students will know:
- *that Southern Africa has been affected by many different cultures.*
- *the factors that have influenced settlement patterns.*
- *the ways in which family is crucial to the cultures of Southern Africa.*
- *that mining is a major economic activity of the region.*

Students will be able to:
- ***analyze*** *the effects of different cultures on Southern Africa.*
- ***identify*** *factors that influence settlement patterns.*
- ***describe*** *the role of the family in Southern Africa cultures.*
- ***identify*** *mining as a major economic activity in the region.*

UNDERSTANDING BY DESIGN®

☑ Print Teaching Options

V Visual Skills

- ☐ **p. 582** Students interpret the map of European colonization in Africa. BL Visual/Spatial
- ☐ **p. 587** Students analyze and interpret a bar graph about gold production. AL Visual/Spatial

R Reading Skills

- ☐ **p. 583** Students consider pidgin languages and the development of Afrikaans. ELL Verbal/Linguistic
- ☐ **p. 585** Students review the ways physical geography influences where people settle. AL Logical/Mathematical
- ☐ **p. 586** Students discuss efforts by organizations to improve the financial status of women. AL Verbal/Linguistic

C Critical Thinking Skills

- ☐ **p. 582** Students discuss the influence of the Portuguese on life in Southern Africa. AL Verbal/Linguistic
- ☐ **p. 583** Students review why slavery was practiced in Southern Africa in the past. BL Interpersonal
- ☐ **p. 584** Students review the events of the time line and write summaries that explain the effect of apartheid on people living in Southern Africa. AL Visual/Spatial

W Writing Skills

- ☐ **p. 583** Students write an essay summarizing the information about Shaka's life and discussing how his past might have affected his style of leadership. Verbal/Linguistic
- ☐ **p. 587** Students write essays to explain why the land reform program in Zimbabwe was enforced and what happened to damage Zimbabwe's agriculture sector. BL Verbal/Linguistic

T Technology Skills

- ☐ **p. 581** Students create time lines to sequence the different groups of people who originated in, migrated to, or colonized the lands of Southern Africa. AL Visual/Spatial
- ☐ **p. 584** Students research the road to independence for Southern African countries and present a multimedia display on the history of an assigned country. BL
- ☐ **p. 585** Students research the end of apartheid and subsequent efforts to investigate abuses under the system and stage a debate about the success of post-apartheid efforts. BL Interpersonal, Kinesthetic

☑ Online Teaching Options

C Critical Thinking Skills

- INTERACTIVE BELLRINGER **Gold Production**—Students study a graph about gold production and use it to answer calculation questions. Interpersonal, Logical/Mathematical
- INTERACTIVE WHITEBOARD ACTIVITY **European Colonization of Southern Africa**—Students locate and identify map locations related to European colonization in the region. ELL Visual/Spatial, Verbal/Linguistic, Kinesthetic
- INTERACTIVE IMAGE **Shaka**—Students study an image of the statue of Shaka and then research what an artist's intention was when carving the statue. BL Visual/Spatial, Verbal/Linguistic
- VIDEO **Apartheid**—Students view and discuss this emotional video on the apartheid in Southern Africa. AL Visual/Spatial, Interpersonal
- TIME LINE **Apartheid and Its Legacy**—Students use the time line to discuss actions taken by people to show their opposition to apartheid. BL Verbal/Linguistic
- GAME **Identification**—Students play this game to assess their knowledge of the group and place names presented in the lesson. ELL AL Kinesthetic, Verbal/Linguistic

☑ Printable Digital Worksheets

R Reading Skills

- WORKSHEET **Guided Reading Activity**—Students use Guided Reading Activity worksheets to review their comprehension of the content.
- WORKSHEET **Reading Essentials and Study Guide**—Students complete the study guide and answer Reading Progress Check and vocabulary questions. AL

C Critical Thinking Skills

- WORKSHEET **Video Activity**—Students answer questions related to a topic in the chapter content after they have viewed a lesson video.

LESSON 3 PLANNER

People and Their Environment: Southern Africa

Students will know:

- *the difficulties of resource management in Southern Africa.*
- *how environmental issues affect life in the region.*
- *steps regional organizations are taking to address environmental issues.*

Students will be able to:

- ***analyze** why it is difficult to manage resources in Southern Africa.*
- ***describe** the impact of environmental issues on life in Southern Africa.*
- ***identify** ways in which organizations are addressing environmental issues.*

UNDERSTANDING BY DESIGN®

☑ Print Teaching Options

V Visual Skills

☐ **p. 592** Students design graphic organizers to compare and contrast NGOs. AL Visual/Spatial

R Reading Skills

☐ **p. 588** Students discuss the reasons why people think it is important to focus on conservation and preserve the environment.

☐ **p. 588** Students discuss the causes of deforestation in Africa. BL Logical/Mathematical

C Critical Thinking Skills

☐ **p. 588** Students review information about habitat destruction. AL Verbal/Linguistic

☐ **p. 589** Students discuss the problems of poaching. ELL Logical/Mathematical

☐ **p. 590** Students discuss the reasons why it is difficult to find a clear solution to the problem of how to conserve and share the natural resources of the region. AL Logical/Mathematical

☐ **p. 590** Students review the details about global climate change and groundwater. Logical/Mathematical

☐ **p. 591** Students review the measures Zimbabwe and Angola have taken to help their environments and save their resources. AL Intrapersonal

W Writing Skills

☐ **p. 591** Students write essays explaining their viewpoint on whether it is a good idea to have environmental rights built into a country's constitution. BL Verbal/Linguistic

☐ **p. 592** Students write essays to describe how corruption can inhibit the attempts of NGOs to help people and propose solutions to this problem. BL Verbal/Linguistic

T Technology Skills

☐ **p. 589** Students research additional information about the potential for conflict over water and other natural resources. BL Kinesthetic, Logical/Mathematical

☑ Online Teaching Options

V Visual Skills

INTERACTIVE BELLRINGER **Loss or Gain of Natural Forests**—Students study a graph and answer questions about environmental issues in Southern African countries. AL Visual/Spatial

INTERACTIVE IMAGE **Dumping Grounds**—Students study an image to discuss and decide whether the title reflects the image and then they create their own titles for the image. BL Visual/Spatial, Interpersonal

GRAPHIC ORGANIZER **People and Their Environment: Southern Africa**—Students complete a graphic organizer about the human impact on the environment of Southern Africa. BL Logical/Mathematical, Verbal/Linguistic

R Reading Skills

GAME **True or False**—Students play this game to review lesson content. AL Verbal/Linguistic

INTERACTIVE WHITEBOARD ACTIVITY **Environment of Southern Africa**—Students complete a chart about the natural features, damage, and factors that contribute to damage of the environment of Southern Africa.

☑ Printable Digital Worksheets

R Reading Skills

WORKSHEET **Guided Reading Activity**—Students use Guided Reading Activity worksheets to review their comprehension of the content.

WORKSHEET **Reading Essentials and Study Guide**—Students complete the study guide and answer Reading Progress Check and vocabulary questions. AL

WORKSHEET **Vocabulary Activity**—Students review the chapter content and academic vocabulary words.

WORKSHEET **Chapter Summary**—Students review the main ideas of the chapter content.

C Critical Thinking Skills

WORKSHEET **Video Activity**—Students answer questions based on a lesson video.

WORKSHEET **Reteaching Activity**—Students use this activity worksheet to review and reteach chapter content and vocabulary. This worksheet can be used with struggling students who need additional help with difficult content concepts.

INTERVENTION AND REMEDIATION STRATEGIES

LESSON 1 Physical Geography of Southern Africa

Reading and Comprehension

Have students choose one of the three biomes in Southern Africa: tropical, desert, and temperate regions. Tell students to work with a partner to identify information in the text about their chosen biome for writing a descriptive paragraph about the biome. Encourage students to incorporate academic and content vocabulary in their paragraphs. When students have completed their paragraphs, have students present them to the class by having one partner slowly read each sentence of the paragraph, while the other partner draws a visual of the description on the board.

Text Evidence

Organize students into small groups and have students in each group work to complete a graphic organizer like the one shown at the beginning of this lesson. Tell students they may wish to conduct additional research to learn more about an aspect of Southern Africa's physical geography to extend the graphic organizer. Challenge students to include headings for wildlife and natural resources in their diagrams. Have groups present a summary of their findings, comparing information in the text with information found in their research.

LESSON 2 Human Geography of Southern Africa

Reading and Comprehension

To help students understand the interrelationship between Southern Africa's colonization and its diverse population and cultural makeup, have students review the section under the heading *History and Government* in this lesson. Then have students work with a partner to study the map in this lesson showing the colonization of Africa. Have partners collaborate to write a response to this Guiding Question: *What cultures have influenced life in Southern Africa?* Ask volunteers to share their responses and discuss the varied colonial control throughout the history of Southern Africa.

Text Evidence

Have students choose a key figure or group discussed in the lesson, such as Shaka, Cecil Rhodes, Robert Mugabe, Nelson Mandela, or a member of a group such as the Shona peoples. Tell students not to reveal who they have chosen to their classmates. Have students use information in the text and additional research to create a "living museum." Tell students they will use facts gleaned from the text and their research to write a short speech by their chosen person or group. Tell students to use textual evidence to support ideas presented in their speeches. After students have written their speeches, allow time for them to present their speeches, challenging classmates to guess the figure or group.

LESSON 3 People and Their Environment: Southern Africa

Reading and Comprehension

To ensure comprehension of the concepts in this lesson, have students work in small groups to write a summarizing paragraph for each of the three sections in the text: managing resources, human impact, and addressing the issues. Tell students their paragraphs should mention one or more issues facing Southern Africa and should identify what is being done to solve the problem. Have students share their paragraphs with the class and discuss the impact of shortages and mismanagement of Southern Africa's many resources.

Text Evidence

Have students work in small groups to create a skit that conveys how environmental degradation has impacted life in Southern Africa. Have students assign roles to each group member and have them create a script for their skit. Tell students to use clues from the text to enhance their scenes and use their imaginations to convey how they envision daily life in the region. After students have had time to write their scripts and rehearse their scenes, have groups present their skits to the class. Guide a discussion about what is being done to improve the environment in the region.

Online Resources

Leveled Reader

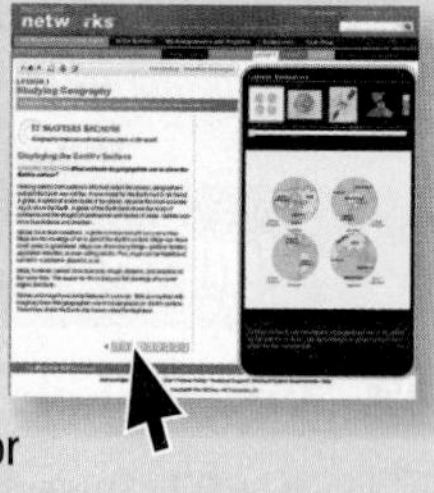

Use this online approaching-level text that corresponds directly to the text in the Student Edition. It also includes additional reading and comprehension support for English Language Learners.

Guided Reading Activities

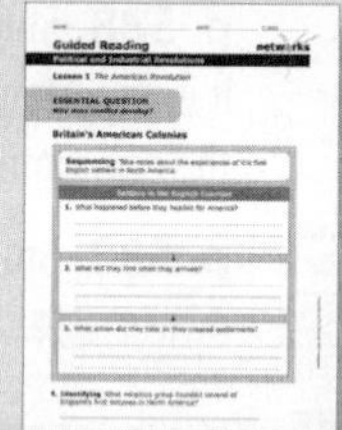

This resource uses guiding questions to help students with comprehension.

Reteaching Activities

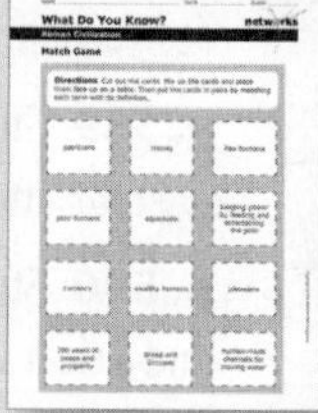

These worksheets provide students with an opportunity for remedial practice and review of vital chapter content.

Reading Essentials and Study Guide

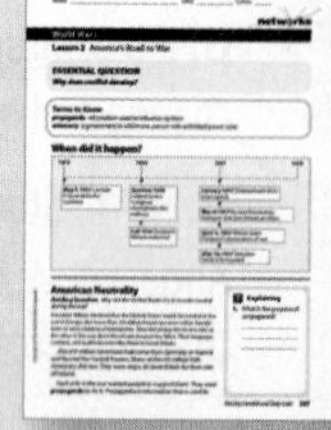

This resource offers writing and reading activities for the approaching-level student.

Self-Check Quizzes

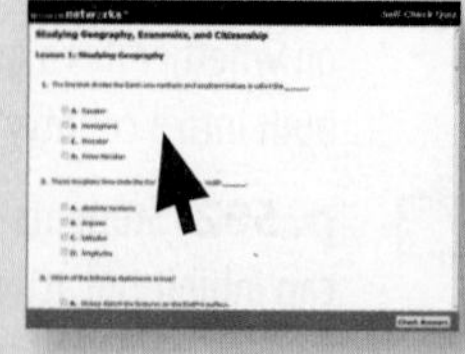

This online assessment tool provides instant feedback for students to check their progress.

Chapter Summaries

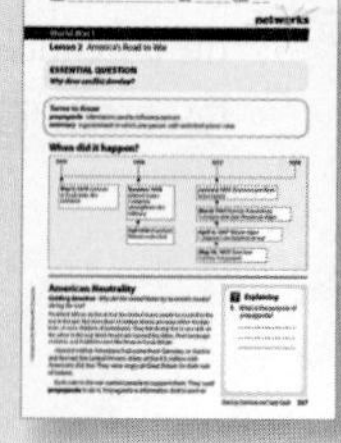

Summaries are provided for each chapter that thoroughly condense core content into manageable chunks.

Southern Africa

networks

There's More Online about Southern Africa's geography.

CHAPTER 24

ESSENTIAL QUESTION • *How do physical systems and human systems shape a place?*

Geography Matters...

Southern Africa is a difficult land to categorize. Most of it is located on a continent, but it also consists of a large island and several small islands. The continental part is surrounded on three sides by ocean, but most of its landforms are plateaus and highlands.

The people of Southern Africa have a history that goes back tens of thousands of years. Yet their culture has been heavily influenced by Europeans who arrived just a few centuries ago. Some people in Southern Africa live in densely packed cities. Others live in the desert much the same way as their ancestors did. Christianity is widespread, but many traditional religions are still practiced as well.

◀ Jeffreys Bay in South Africa is one of the world's top destinations for surfers.

573

ENGAGE

Activating Prior Knowledge Tell students they will read about how the unique geography and mixture of cultures in Southern Africa have influenced human life in this area. Have pairs discuss what they already know about Southern Africa and the problems people there face.

TEACH & ASSESS

Geography Matters Have students read the text. **Ask:** **Why is the land of Southern Africa difficult to categorize?** *(Possible answer: It has a continental part, a large island, and several small islands, all of which contain unique indigenous groups and varied landforms.)* **How might the physical geography of this area have affected settlements?** *(Possible answer: The ocean probably made it easier for people from other places, such as Europe, to travel to Southern Africa to colonize and settle there.)*

Making Connections

Explain to students that Europeans coming to Southern Africa clashed with and displaced indigenous groups such as the San just as European colonists conflicted with Native Americans. The San were hunter-gatherers who had migrated around Southern Africa for over 20,000 years. European settlers restricted San migration and raised cattle that consumed the San's food resources. As did Native Americans, the San proved susceptible to smallpox and other unfamiliar European diseases and many died. Today, the few remaining San are making decisions about how to preserve what is left of their unique culture and heritage.

CLOSE & REFLECT

Questioning Have students consider the contrasts of religions, cultures, and types of settlements found in Southern Africa. Then have them list specific questions about problems different cultures might have faced as they interacted in Southern Africa. Students should keep these questions in mind as they read the chapter.

Letter from the Author

Dear Geography Teacher,

For a great map related to a special report on "Emerging Africa," look to the March 2, 2013, issue of the *The Economist*. Writers and cartographers have cooperated to display graphically that much of Africa is experiencing strong, positive economic development. Too often, our perception is of ethnic and religious conflict, political corruption, refugees, poverty, the ravages of HIV/AIDS infections, and the continuing problems associated with throwing off the colonial past. While many countries across Africa continue to experience these problems, there is much good to report in many areas of Africa, as well.

Richard G. Boehm

ePals GlobalCommunity
Where learners connect™

Extend the project-based learning experience globally through our partnership with ePals. EPals allows you to connect with classrooms around the world in a safe online environment for real-life lessons and projects in virtual study groups.

ENGAGE

C Critical Thinking Skills

Evaluating Have students work with a partner to consider what it means to a country to face an epidemic. Have partners review the information in the introductory text and identify the more serious aspects of the HIV/AIDS epidemic facing Southern Africa and any facts that offer hope for the future.

TEACH & ASSESS

V Visual Skills

Analyzing Maps Have students examine the map key. **Ask:** According to the map, what color indicates areas with the highest percentage of adult population infected with HIV? *(dark purple)* Smallest percentage? *(yellow)* How does the map help you understand the effect that HIV has had on Southern Africa? *(The tip of Africa is dark purple and the areas above it are red. No other areas in the world are these colors, showing how hard hit by HIV infection this area has been.)* Aside from Southern Africa, what other areas of the world are the most affected by HIV infection? *(Russia and the United States are also tinted colors that indicate a high rate of HIV infection.)* AL **Visual/Spatial**

T Technology Skills

Researching Have students review the information in this caption to identify factors that affect the spread of HIV in parts of Southern Africa such as Botswana, Lesotho, and Swaziland. Then assign small groups each a country from the map to research, such as the United States, Russia, Australia, or Canada. Pick a mix of countries with high and low rates of infection. Then have groups research what effect the factors listed in the map caption have on the rate of infection in their assigned countries. Tell them to identify other factors that make HIV spread at a lower or higher rate in their countries. Finally, have groups design and make a chart that compares and contrasts the spread of HIV in their countries with that in parts of Southern Africa. BL **Verbal/Linguistic, Visual/Spatial**

Southern Africa and HIV/AIDS

In Africa, HIV/AIDS has reached epidemic proportions. Southern Africa has the highest number of people infected with HIV/AIDS on the continent. Nearly one in five people in the region is suffering from the disease. New incidences of HIV infections have declined somewhat, but the disease is still devastating the economic and social health of Southern Africa.

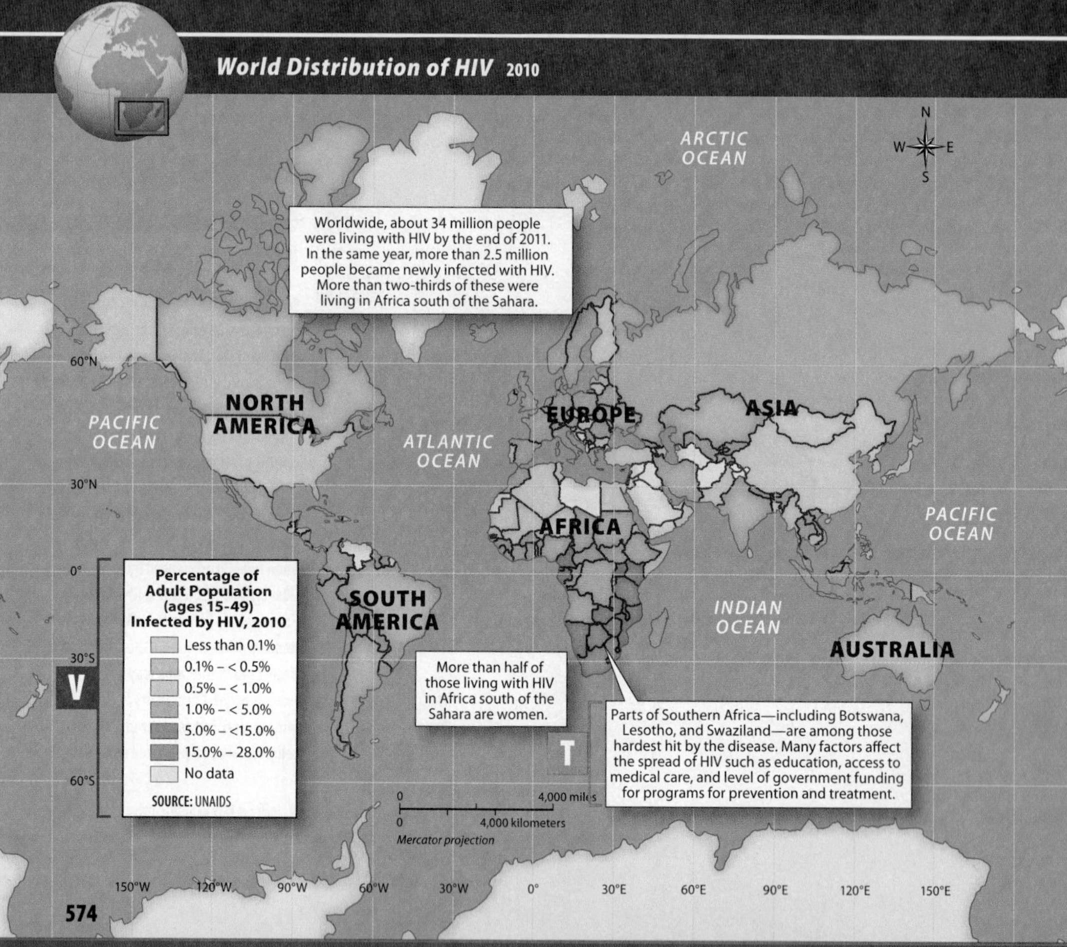
World Distribution of HIV 2010
ARCTIC OCEAN
N
W
E
S
Worldwide, about 34 million people were living with HIV by the end of 2011. In the same year, more than 2.5 million people became newly infected with HIV. More than two-thirds of these were living in Africa south of the Sahara.
60°N
NORTH AMERICA
PACIFIC OCEAN
ATLANTIC OCEAN
EUROPE
ASIA
30°N
AFRICA
PACIFIC OCEAN
0°
Percentage of Adult Population (ages 15-49) Infected by HIV, 2010
Less than 0.1%
0.1% – < 0.5%
0.5% – < 1.0%
1.0% – < 5.0%
5.0% – <15.0%
15.0% – 28.0%
No data
SOURCE: UNAIDS
SOUTH AMERICA
INDIAN OCEAN
AUSTRALIA
30°S
More than half of those living with HIV in Africa south of the Sahara are women.
Parts of Southern Africa—including Botswana, Lesotho, and Swaziland—are among those hardest hit by the disease. Many factors affect the spread of HIV such as education, access to medical care, and level of government funding for programs for prevention and treatment.
60°S
0
4,000 miles
0
4,000 kilometers
Mercator projection
150°W
120°W
90°W
60°W
30°W
0°
30°E
60°E
90°E
120°E
150°E

574

Project-Based Learning

Hands-On

Educational Materials

Working in groups, students will create environmental education materials related to a specific environmental issue for hypothetical students and teachers in Southern African countries. Possible materials include posters, fact sheets, quizzes with answers, or booklets that describe environmental issues and possible solutions.

ePals GlobalCommunity
Where learners connect™

Digital Hands-On

Create Online Projects

Find an additional activity online that incorporates technology for this project. Visit the EdTech Teacher Web sites for more links, tutorials, and other resources.

edtechteacher
21st Century Learning

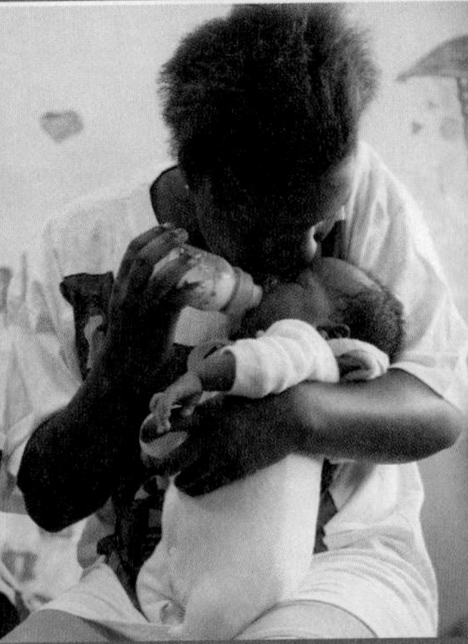

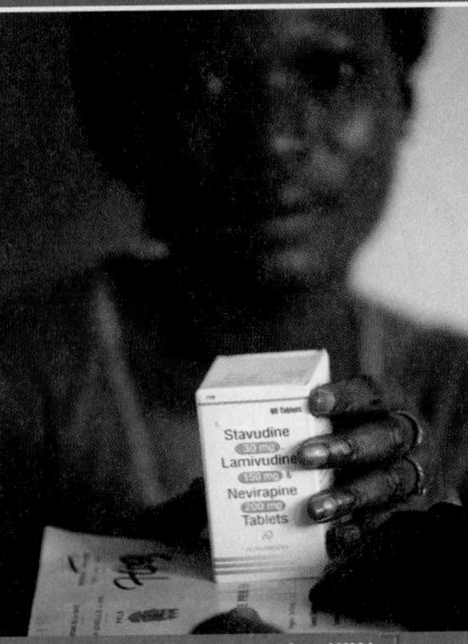

What are HIV and AIDS?

HIV (human immunodeficiency virus) is an infection that can be spread from one person to another. Over time, the disease attacks a person's immune system and can advance to AIDS (acquired immunodeficiency syndrome). The disease can be spread through blood or other bodily fluids, as well as from a pregnant mother to her unborn child. In a few instances, the disease has spread through organ transplants. Symptoms of HIV/AIDS range from flulike symptoms to none at all. In some cases, people who are infected with HIV show no symptoms for years, so without annual medical exams it can be difficult to diagnose in its early stages. **R**

Southern African countries have the highest number of people living with HIV/AIDS on the continent. It is believed to have emerged in the Democratic Republic of the Congo in the 1970s. However, the disease did not become an epidemic in Africa until the following decade. It first spread east and then south within the continent. By the late 1980s, the virus had become a regional epidemic.

1. Human Systems Why is HIV/AIDS so dangerous to humankind?

Why have the people of Southern Africa been so badly affected by HIV/AIDS?

Much of the population of Southern Africa lives in poverty. Literacy is low. Medical care is limited or too expensive for the majority of the population. These factors weigh heavily into the high rates of HIV/AIDS in the subregion. In some countries of Southern Africa, about 40 percent of the adult population is living with HIV/AIDS. Percentages are over 40 percent in some urban areas. More than a million Southern Africans die each year because of HIV/AIDS, resulting in lower life expectancy and a rise in the number of orphans. Some scientists believe that differences between HIV subtypes have an effect on transmission rates. There is also some evidence that genetic factors and parasitic worm infections, which are common in Africa south of the Sahara, may contribute to the epidemic in the region.

There are other factors that may contribute to the high rate of HIV/AIDS cases in Southern Africa. These include social instability, rapid urbanization, labor migration, gender inequality, and sexual violence. Additionally, ineffective political leadership failed to address the crisis in the 1990s when the disease became an epidemic in the region. **C**

2. Human Systems Why are the people of Southern Africa so vulnerable to HIV/AIDS?

What is being done to combat HIV/AIDS in Southern Africa?

Some governments in Southern Africa, as well as organizations such as the World Health Organization (WHO), have been working to educate people on how the disease is contracted and passed to others. This includes counseling programs, controlling incidences of other sexually transmitted diseases, which can cause the spread of HIV, and caring for people living with HIV/AIDS. Efforts have also been made to improve the safety of blood supplies. **W**

Early testing for HIV has helped identify cases that can then be treated with antiretroviral drugs (ARVs). These drugs delay the progression of HIV to AIDS. WHO began a program in 2003 to treat 5 million people in the region with ARVs. Even though WHO failed to reach its goal, it set a precedent for countries in Southern Africa such as Botswana, Namibia, and South Africa to make ARVs accessible to those living with HIV.

3. Human Systems How are people working to combat HIV/AIDS, and how successful are their efforts?

THERE'S MORE ONLINE

SEE a map of HIV infection rates in Africa • *READ* a quote about efforts to fight HIV/AIDS in Southern Africa

INTERACTIVE MAP

World Distribution of HIV, 2010

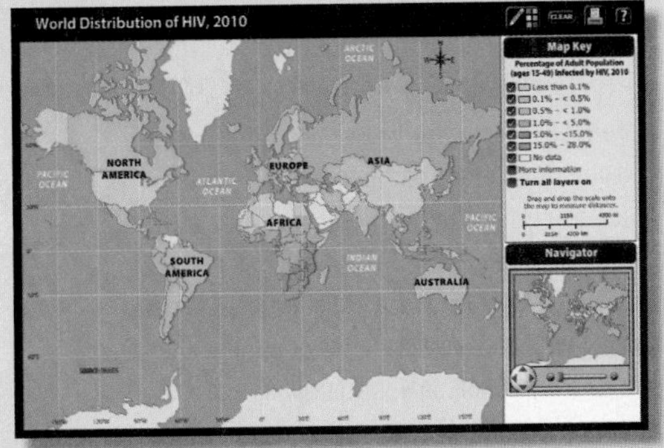

Hypothesizing This interactive map delineates for students the reasons why HIV is more prevalent in Southern Africa than in the rest of the world. Have students study the key and the map. Ask them to read each label carefully. Point out that the map reflects conditions in 2010. Ask students to hypothesize whether the HIV epidemic has lessened in Southern Africa at the present time. Have them provide evidence from the text with their hypotheses. **AL** **Logical/Mathematical, Visual/Spatial**

Why Geography Matters

R Reading Skills

Inferring Have students consider what they have learned about how HIV/AIDS spreads. **Ask:** **What inference can you make about what might be happening when people who are infected with HIV show no symptoms for years?** *(Possible answer: Because the people do not show symptoms, they do not know they are infected and could unknowingly spread the disease to other people.)* **AL** **Verbal/Linguistic**

C Critical Thinking Skills

Identifying Cause and Effect Have students review the information about why the people of Southern Africa have been so badly affected by HIV/AIDS. Have pairs make a cause-effect graphic organizer to record the reasons why HIV/AIDS is being transmitted at such a high rate. Then have each pair pick one reason, research it in more detail, and share their findings with the class. **BL** **Logical/Mathematical**

W Writing Skills

Argument Have students write a short essay summarizing what is being done to combat HIV/AIDS in Southern Africa, explaining briefly why each approach might help and identifying the solution they think is likely to be most effective. Encourage students to share their essays with another student to compare their evaluations of the approaches being used. **AL** **Interpersonal, Verbal/Linguistic**

CLOSE & REFLECT

Reaching Conclusions Tell students to review what they have read about the spread of HIV/AIDS in Southern Africa and consider how governments and organizations are attempting to solve this problem. Invite student pairs to discuss whether they think enough is being done to help the people of Southern Africa deal with this epidemic and whether other things could be done.

ANSWERS, p. 575

Why Geography Matters

1. HIV/AIDS has become a deadly epidemic as it may show no symptoms for years, preventing diagnosis and treatment.
2. The people of Southern Africa are so vulnerable to HIV/AIDS because of the high rate of poverty, low literacy rates, and limited and expensive medical care.
3. Governments and organizations such as the World Health Organization are working to educate people on the disease, controlling the spread, implementing early testing, and improving blood supplies. Efforts are helping, and the antiretroviral drugs which delay the progression from HIV to AIDS are now much more accessible.

ENGAGE

R Reading Skills

Activating Prior Knowledge Before students begin the lesson, have pairs work together to list and describe what they know about the landforms, waterways, climates, and biomes of Southern Africa *(such as plateaus, the Zambezi River, tropical rain forest, highland, savannas, and desert)* and any well-known places *(such as the Cape of Good Hope or Victoria Falls).*

TEACH & ASSESS

V Visual Skills

Locating Display a political map of Southern Africa. Have students name and locate each country. **Ask:** **Which three countries are not part of the mainland?** *(Comoros, Madagascar, and Mauritius)* **How is Comoros different from Madagascar and Mauritius?** *(Comoros is a series of islands and reefs, the other two countries are single islands.)* **How is Lesotho different from the other countries?** *(Its boundaries place it entirely inside another country.)* **ELL Visual/Spatial**

Content Background Knowledge

The Great Escarpment An escarpment is any place where two sections of land at different elevations meet. It forms either through faulting or by erosion. The Great Escarpment was formed over millions of years by the movement of rivers flowing over the land. This erosion continues today. Across the Great Karoo, in a large basin south of the Great Escarpment, European colonists once kept large numbers of sheep and cattle. The widespread grazing by these animals removed much of the vegetation necessary to prevent erosion. Though now fewer animals are on the land, it continues to erode, especially during heavy rains.

ANSWERS, p. 576

TAKING NOTES: Landforms—Coastal plains run along Angola, Namibia, and South Africa; the Great Escarpment forms an almost unbroken U-shape behind the coastal plains; the Highveld is a plateau over a mile high; the Drakensberg Range is part of the Great Escarpment; Madagascar is a plateau surrounded by an escarpment and scattered with volcanoes; **Rivers**—Okavango River runs from central Angola to northern Botswana; Orange River flows from Lesotho, through South Africa and Namibia into the Atlantic; the Zambezi River begins in eastern Angola, forming a border with Namibia, Botswana, and Zimbabwe; Zambezi drops sharply, forming Victoria Falls, and empties in the Indian Ocean; Limpopo River begins in northern South Africa and forms border of Botswana and Zimbabwe.

networks

There's More Online!

- **CHART** Wildlife Reserves in Southern Africa
- **IMAGE** Baobab Tree
- **IMAGE** The Long Wall of Namib
- **IMAGE** Moremi Game Reserve
- **INTERACTIVE SELF-CHECK QUIZ**
- **VIDEO** Physical Geography of Southern Africa

LESSON 1
Physical Geography of Southern Africa

ESSENTIAL QUESTION • *How do physical systems and human systems shape a place?*

Reading HELPDESK CCSS

Academic Vocabulary (Tier Two Words)
- **altitude**
- **source**

Content Vocabulary (Tier Three Words)
- **escarpment**
- **delta**
- **Mediterranean climate**
- **rain shadow**

TAKING NOTES: ***Key Ideas and Details***

IDENTIFYING As you read about the physical geography of Southern Africa, use a graphic organizer like the one below to keep track of its physical features.

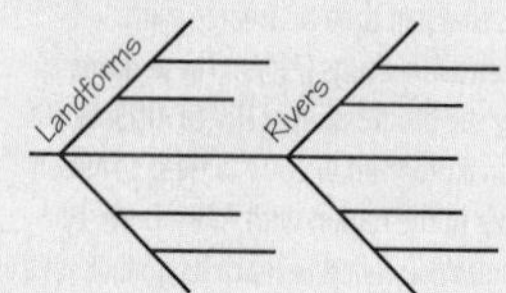

IT MATTERS BECAUSE

R *The terrain of Southern Africa produces a wide variety of biomes—tropical, desert, and temperate regions. Life and culture are very different in each of these areas. In addition, Southern Africa's rivers are essential for both the natural environment and human activity in the subregion.*

Landforms

GUIDING QUESTION *What is the most dominant physical feature of Southern Africa?*

Southern Africa consists of 14 countries, 10 of which are on the mainland. The other four are island countries. Imagine a line drawn roughly along the northern borders of Angola, Zambia, Malawi, and Mozambique. Everything south of that line is part of Southern Africa. Extend the line out into the Indian Ocean, and it runs just above Comoros and Madagascar. Mauritius is east of Madagascar, while Seychelles is northeast of Madagascar.

V If Angola, Zambia, Malawi, and Mozambique form the "top row" of Southern Africa, then Namibia, Botswana, Zimbabwe, and the southern half of Mozambique form the "second row." At the southern tip of the continent is South Africa. The country of Lesotho (luh•SOO•too) lies entirely within South Africa. Swaziland is on the South Africa-Mozambique border.

The mainland of Southern Africa is surrounded on three sides by ocean. Most of the land sits at a high **altitude**, or height above sea level, of over 2,000 feet (610 m). Along the coasts of Angola, Namibia, and South Africa lies the coastal plain, a narrow strip of land that varies from a few miles wide to a few dozen miles wide. Looming up behind this coastal plain are high steep cliffs known as the Great **Escarpment**. These cliffs form an almost unbroken U-shape. They run from the west coast south to the Cape of Good Hope and then curve northeast to the South Africa-Mozambique border. The Drakensberg Range is part of the Great

576

networks Online Teaching Options

INTERACTIVE BELLRINGER

Topography of Southern Africa

Acquiring Information Use the introductory text and the photographic image of the topography of Southern Africa to learn about the landforms of this region. Working with a partner, have students and discuss each question. Ask each pairs to write out answers to the questions. Then in a class discussion, share the answers and list responses on a flipchart or on the board.
AL Visual/Spatial, Interpersonal

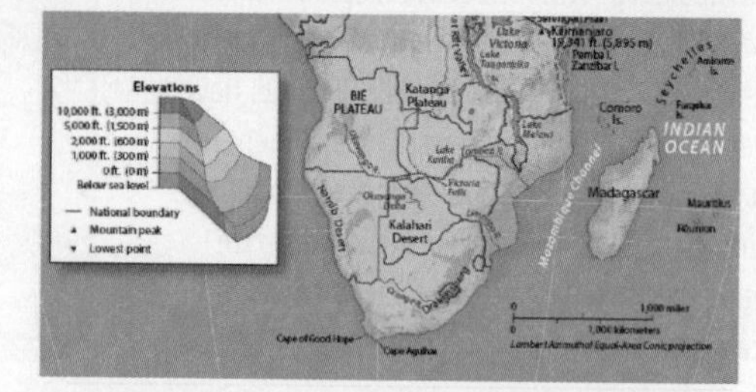

Topography of Southern Africa
The topography of eastern South Africa includes the Great Escarpment, which are high, steep cliffs that include hills, mountain ranges, and plateaus.
Auto-Run
Click Through
1 of 3

Escarpment. The range rises to more than 11,000 feet (3,353 m) and runs along the southern edge of South Africa. As the escarpment reaches Mozambique, it turns north to follow along Mozambique's western border and on through Malawi. Because most of Mozambique lies outside of the Great Escarpment, its landscape is mainly made up of soft, rolling hills. Only in the northwestern interior of the country does the land rise above 600 feet (183 m).

The land inside the Great Escarpment is mostly hills and plateaus. A plateau, or "tableland," is a stretch of flat land that is higher than its surroundings. The most striking part of the Southern African landscape is a plateau that is over a mile high. The Highveld, as it is called, sits more than 50 miles (80 km) from the coast. However, given its 6,000 foot (1,829 m) altitude, it is visible from a long distance.

V

The highest parts of Namibia and Angola are near the coast, along the Great Escarpment. Zimbabwe's highest terrain is in the center of the country. Zambia's high points are in the northeast, where they merge with Mozambique's highlands along the Great Escarpment. In contrast, most of Botswana sits in a great basin. While still much higher than the coastal lands, it is lower than the surrounding landforms.

The landforms surrounding Botswana on the west into Namibia or northwest into Angola are once again hills and plateaus. This undulating terrain continues westward until it rises up over the Great Escarpment. It then drops down onto the narrow Atlantic coastal plain.

R1

In a sense, the terrain of Madagascar is a smaller version of that on the mainland. The middle of the island, like the mainland, is a series of plateaus surrounded by an escarpment. Unlike the mainland, groups and masses of volcanoes are strewn among the Madagascar plateaus. Tsiafajavona, one of these volcanic peaks, is 8,671 feet (2,643 m) high.

In the north, the plateaus give way to volcanoes that slope down to the sea. The southern edges of the plateaus tower above the Indian Ocean. To the east and west are escarpments. The escarpments, some of which are impassable, separate the highlands from the lower areas on either side. The eastern part of the island is a narrow coastal strip, rather like the Atlantic coast of Southern Africa. The western side is more varied, with low plateaus and rolling hills.

✓ **READING PROGRESS CHECK**

Describing Where is the highest terrain in Southern Africa found?

Water Systems

GUIDING QUESTION *How do people harness the power of the subregion's rivers?*

R2

The Okavango River runs southeast from central Angola to northern Botswana. It starts on a plateau, and for a while it flows along the border between Angola and Namibia. Then it turns south and heads into Botswana. Most rivers empty into a lake or ocean, but the Okavango ends inland. The river just spreads wider and wider until it forms an inland **delta** and swamps.

The Orange River flows nearly from one side of Southern Africa to the other. It starts in Lesotho, on the Highveld, just over 100 miles (161 km) from the coast. It flows west across South Africa, then forms part of the border between South Africa and Namibia before it empties into the Atlantic Ocean.

altitude height above sea level

escarpment a long cliff that separates lands at two different altitudes

delta an often triangular-shaped section of land formed as the waters of a river slow down and split into many channels as they deposit silt and sediment

The Long Wall of Namib is a section of the Namib Desert that runs along the coast of southern Namibia.

▼ **CRITICAL THINKING**

1. ***Making Connections*** Less than 100 miles (161 km) inland from this spot is fertile land. Why does that fertile land not extend to the ocean?
2. ***Analyzing Visuals*** Why is the water in this picture not being used to irrigate the arid land?

Juan Carlos Muñoz/age fotostock

V Visual Skills

Comparing and Contrasting Have students examine the similarities and differences between the landforms in each country in Southern Africa. Have students design a chart or graphic organizer to arrange the information. Then have them use the charts to make comparisons and contrasts. **Ask:** **How is Mozambique similar to Botswana?** *(Possible answer: Both countries contain hills.)* **How is Zambia like Mozambique?** *(Possible answer: They both have high parts that border the Great Escarpment.)* **How is Botswana different from Mozambique and Zambia?** *(Most of Botswana sits in a basin, whereas the other two countries have highlands.)* **Verbal/Linguistic, Visual/Spatial**

R1 Reading Skills

Explaining Have students read about the terrain in Madagascar. **Ask:** **What does it mean to say that the terrain of Madagascar is like a smaller version of that on the mainland?** *(The middle of the mainland and the middle of Madagascar both are covered with plateaus surrounded by an escarpment.)* **How is Madagascar different from the mainland?** *(The middle of Madagascar does not have just plains. It also has volcanoes.)* **ELL** **Verbal/Linguistic**

R2 Reading Skills

Understanding Relationships Have students review the information about what a delta is and how the Okavango River differs from many other rivers. Then have student pairs write a description in their own words of what happens at the end of the Okavango River. Allow students to research the subject further if they need more information. Suggest that artistically inclined students draw a diagram of the river's end. **AL** **Verbal/Linguistic, Visual/Spatial**

INTERACTIVE WHITEBOARD ACTIVITY

Physical Geography of Southern Africa

Using Correct Terminology and Grammar This interactive whiteboard activity utilizes sentence-completion skills to reinforce students' comprehension of the various landforms of Southern Africa. Students will be presented with the beginnings of sentences. Direct students to complete the sentences by dragging and dropping the correct ending into the appropriate box. When completed, have students read each sentence aloud to ensure that each sentence is grammatically correct. If the sentence is not grammatically correct, suggest that students choose a different answer that is. **ELL** **AL** **Verbal/Linguistic**

Physical Geography of Southern Africa

Directions: Southern Africa is a distinctive area comprised of high land and dramatic landforms. Drag and drop answer choices to the appropriate boxes on the table to display sentences pertaining to the physical geography of Southern Africa along with their definitions. When correctly completed, accurate sentences pertaining to the physical geography of Southern Africa will be displayed.

Southern Africa consists of a total of	
Southern Africa has 10	
The four island countries of Southern Africa are	
The top row of countries in Southern Africa are	
The second row of countries in Southern Africa are	
The southernmost country in Southern Africa is	
Lesotho is located	
Swaziland is located on the	

South Africa.
Namibia, Botswana, Zimbabwe, and the southern half of Mozambique.
Comoros, Madagascar, Seychelles, and Mauritius.
South Africa-Mozambique border.
Angola, Zambia, Malawi, and Mozambique.
Mainland countries.
entirely within South Africa.
14 countries.

ANSWERS, p. 577

✓ **READING PROGRESS CHECK** The highest terrain in Southern Africa is the Highveld, which is a plateau that is 6,000 feet high.

CRITICAL THINKING

1. The fertile land does not extend to the ocean because of the Great Escarpment.
2. The water in the image is the Atlantic Ocean, which could not be used for irrigation unless it was desalinated.

Physical Geography of Southern Africa

R Reading Skills

Defining Ask students what the word *navigate* means. *(to travel on a course)* Ask students what the suffix *-able* means. *(capable of)* Then point out the word *navigable* in the text. **Ask:** **How might you use these word parts to define *navigable*?** *(Possible answer: able to be traveled upon)* **Why would it matter whether a river was navigable or not?** *(If a river is not navigable, it cannot be used for transportation of people or goods.)* ELL Verbal/Linguistic

C Critical Thinking Skills

Assessing Have students review the information about how people in Southern Africa use their different rivers. **Ask:** **Why do the features of the African rivers described in the text make them unsuitable for transportation?** *(Conditions such as rapids and waterfalls would break apart boats or make them fall and crash. These conditions make the rivers unsafe for travel.)* **How have people adapted to make the rivers useful?** *(The rivers are a good source of hydroelectric power.)* AL Logical/Mathematical

W Writing Skills

Narrative Have students imagine that they are visiting an area in Southern Africa to protect the native wildlife, such as the Moremi Game Reserve or the Great Limpopo Transfrontier Park. Encourage them to use the information in the text and from additional research to describe the animals they see there. Students should include descriptive words and phrases about what they might see and why the sanctuaries exist. They could also include drawings or photographs to illustrate their narratives. BL Verbal/Linguistic

ANSWERS, p. 578

READING PROGRESS CHECK Rivers that run along steep terrain and have rapids and waterfalls are suitable for generating electricity.

CRITICAL THINKING

1. The area can be arid and hot but fed by a river that relies on water sources outside the desert biome.
2. Most rivers empty into a lake or ocean as an outlet, but the Okavango River ends inland forming an inland delta.

Wildlife abounds in the Moremi Game Reserve in Botswana.

▲ **CRITICAL THINKING**

1. ***Constructing a Thesis*** How can an area that is as wet as a swamp be part of a desert?
2. ***Identifying Cause and Effect*** Why do the waters of the Okavango River collect in northern Botswana and not flow into some other area?

The Zambezi River comes into contact with several countries along its course to the sea. Starting in eastern Angola, it flows south through western Zambia. It forms the border between Zambia and the countries of Namibia, Botswana, and Zimbabwe. Along the southern stretch of the border with Zimbabwe, the river suddenly drops straight down, forming Victoria Falls. Once it has cleared the northern tip of Zimbabwe, the Zambezi heads east through Mozambique, where it flows near the southern tip of Malawi before emptying into the Indian Ocean.

The Limpopo River begins in northern South Africa and flows north for a distance before it turns eastward and forms the border between South Africa and Botswana and the border between South Africa and Zimbabwe. Then it flows across Mozambique to the ocean.

R C None of these rivers are navigable, except for short stretches across the coastal plain. They originate in highlands and as they flow through the steep, terrain, rapids and waterfalls mark their courses. These conditions are not suitable for transportation, but they are useful for generating electricity. Two of the largest hydroelectric dams in Africa—the Kariba Dam and the Cahora Bassa Dam—are located on the Zambezi River.

W Aquatic wildlife such as hippopotamuses and crocodiles thrive in and along these rivers. The northeastern part of the Okavango Delta is set aside as the Moremi Game Reserve. Hundreds of species including lions, cheetahs, hippopotamuses, buffalo, wild dogs, and many types of birds and fish live there. Two wildlife areas on either side of the Limpopo, in South Africa and in Mozambique, recently joined with each other and with several sanctuaries in Zimbabwe to form the Great Limpopo Transfrontier Park. This extended preserve provides a safe haven for lions, leopards, hippopotamuses, elephants, giraffes, and many other species.

READING PROGRESS CHECK

Explaining What makes a river suitable for generating electricity?

Climates, Biomes, and Resources

GUIDING QUESTION *How do the climates of Southern Africa affect its biomes?*

Southern Africa is large with many different landforms. The result is a great variety of climates. These different climates and landforms create a number of different biomes with distinct characteristics.

networks ***Online Teaching Options***

INTERACTIVE IMAGE

Reserving Game

Transferring Have students view the image. Using information they have learned about other areas of Africa and details from the photograph, have students think about why game reserves may be necessary in Southern Africa. Ask pairs of students to work together to write a list of ideas. Then have students share their ideas with the whole class. Verbal/Linguistic, Interpersonal

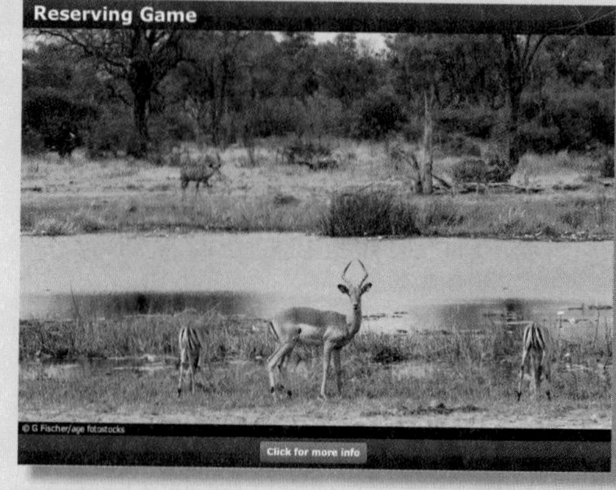

Climate Regions and Biomes

The coastal areas of Southern Africa have marine climates, which means they are greatly affected by weather conditions and systems that blow in from the open ocean. The Cape of Good Hope and the area to its immediate northeast have a **Mediterranean climate** similar to that of Greece and Italy. It is not typical of Southern Africa, however. Moving up the eastern coast to Mozambique, the climate becomes tropical wet/dry. The winters are warm and the summer rainy season stretches from November through March. The western coast up through Namibia and Angola has an arid, or desert, climate.

The interior of the subregion is generally hot, although temperatures can dip below freezing in the higher elevations. The eastern areas experience a fair amount of precipitation, but toward the west the rainfall drops off. The deserts of Botswana and Namibia receive very little rain.

C The climate of Madagascar is determined by its central plateau and the warm, wet winds off the open ocean. The eastern coast of the island has a tropical wet climate, while the interior plateau has a highland climate. The western side is in a **rain shadow**, and much of it is desert.

V Given the number of different climates in the subregion, Southern Africa has many different biomes. Much of the coastal plain along the Atlantic coast is a desert biome. On the Indian Ocean side, grassland biomes give way to forest as one moves north. In the interior of the continent, on the highlands inside the Great Escarpment, the vast majority of the land falls into one of two types, savanna or desert.

The north and the east are covered with savanna—vast grasslands dotted with small stands of trees. Many of the most recognized African mammals, such as giraffes, zebra, and jackals, live on the savanna. This biome is also home to animals known as the Big Five: lions, leopards, elephants, Cape buffalo, and rhinoceroses. These animals became known as the Big Five because they were so dangerous and difficult to hunt. However, they are now the five species most tourists want to see while on safari.

The south and the west of the inland area are mostly desert biome. The Kalahari Desert occupies much of the Botswana basin. It stretches southwest to where Botswana meets Namibia and South Africa. Here, it blends into the Namib Desert. The Namib continues down to the coast, then runs north between the ocean and the Great Escarpment through all of Namibia and into southern Angola.

Most of the Namib Desert is quite arid. The southern parts are covered with seemingly endless sand dunes—brick red inland and yellow along the coast—some of which can be 800 feet (244 m) tall and 20 miles (32 km) long. Inland, bushes and tall grasses have adapted to grow in the sand dunes. Antelope and ostriches live here as well. Farther north in the interior desert, rivers can be found, and with them elephants, rhinoceroses, hyenas, and more.

The arm of the Namib Desert that runs along the coast is quite different. It is almost completely arid, with little or no plant life. Some reptiles and insects have adapted to this biome, but no larger animals live here. As in the interior portion, though, the most northern reaches have more water. Succulents grow here, and it is home to various marine birds, such as pelicans, flamingos, and even penguins.

In the southern part of the Kalahari, rain is scarce. Drought-tolerant grasses and scrub are all that can take root. Herds of antelope such as wildebeest and springbok roam the area. The central part of the Kalahari gets some rain, and shrubs can grow there. Acacia trees provide homes for birds, rodents, and insects. The northern Kalahari is hardly desertlike at all because of the rivers that flow through it. Many smaller animals, such as wild dogs, foxes, anteaters, and porcupines, live here. Plants such as pond lilies and reeds thrive here as well.

Connecting Geography to MATH

Output of the Kariba Hydroelectric Dam

The Kariba Dam, located on the Zambezi River between the countries of Zambia and Zimbabwe, produces 6.7×10^8 kilowatt-hours (kWh) of electricity per year. Some of that electricity goes to Zambia and some to Zimbabwe. Average per capita electricity use in Zimbabwe is approximately 850 kWh.

APPLYING If half the output of Kariba Dam were sent to Zimbabwe, how many people's electricity needs could be met? Round your answer to the nearest thousand.

Mediterranean climate a climate marked by warm, dry summers and cool, rainy winters

rain shadow a condition created when winds blow in primarily one direction over mountains or other elevated terrain: the altitude change causes clouds to drop their precipitation on the near side of the mountain, leaving the land on the far side, where winds descend, with little rain or snow

VIDEO

Around the World—Botswana

Paraphrasing Have students view the video about Botswana in Southern Africa. Ask them to pay careful attention to the narration and to take notes on what they hear. After the video ends, ask students to write a summary of what they learned, using their notes to paraphrase the information presented. Have them share their summaries with a partner. Ask students to add any details that they may have left out. AL **Interpersonal, Verbal/Linguistic**

C Critical Thinking Skills

Analyzing Cause and Effect Have students read the definition and review the information about rain shadows. **Ask:** **What happens when winds blow mostly in one direction over high ground?** *(Because the altitude is changing, the winds are pushed upward and the rising air cools, releasing moisture or precipitation on the windward side of the mountain.)* **What happens when precipitation drops on one side of a mountain?** *(The winds become warmer and drier on the leeward side, producing little precipitation and making the climate on the other side dry and sometimes deserts.)* AL **Verbal/Linguistic**

V Visual Skills

Depicting Have students work in small groups to create a visual guide to the biomes of the countries of Southern Africa. Have groups use information from the text and information gathered from Internet and print resources. Encourage students to use colors to indicate the kinds of landforms and symbols to indicate the different kinds of plants and animals in each place. Invite groups to present their finished guides to the class. BL **Visual/Spatial**

Making Connections

Although dams help countries by generating inexpensive hydroelectric power, the process of constructing a dam has an impact on the environment and wildlife in the area. For example, when the United States diverted the flow of the Colorado River to build the Hoover Dam, the plant and animal habitats that ran alongside the river were destroyed or flooded when Lake Mead was created. Reptiles and amphibians had to find new places to lay their eggs, and the composition of the fish population in the water changed. The construction of the Kariba Dam also affected life in that area of Southern Africa. Although planners evacuated people from the villages that would be inundated, the local animals were not considered. As the dam filled to make Lake Kariba, the waters rose higher and higher and thousands of animals were stranded on newly created islands. Many of the animals were in danger of drowning, so operation Project Noah was launched to rescue over 7,000 animals and relocate them to Matusadona National Park.

ANSWERS, p. 579

Connecting Geography Approximately 353,000 people's electricity needs could be met if half of the output of Kariba Dam were sent to Zimbabwe.

CHAPTER 24, Lesson 1
Physical Geography of Southern Africa

T Technology Skills

Researching Organize students into groups to conduct online research about the importance of the baobab tree to people in Southern Africa, the many ways people use it, and the cultural myths associated with it. Have groups present their findings to the class in a multimedia display. **Interpersonal, Naturalist**

C Critical Thinking Skills

Identifying Perspectives Have students consider ways that foreign companies extract minerals and gemstones from Southern Africa and how this method of doing business compares to the way De Beers runs its business. Discuss how each method affects the economies of countries in Southern Africa and why each company most likely does business the way it does. **AL Logical/Mathematical**

CLOSE & REFLECT

Summarizing Have students review what they have learned about the physical environments of Southern Africa. Ask individuals to pick one area of the subregion and use information from this lesson to describe the life, landforms, waterways, and plant and animals in that area.

ANSWERS, p. 580

READING PROGRESS CHECK Desert, savanna, and tropical forest are biomes found in Southern Africa.

CRITICAL THINKING

1. The baobab tree might be used as a symbol for the entire continent because of its striking appearance and longevity.
2. The bark can be used to make rope, fabric, strings for instruments, trunk hollowed out for shelter or to collect rainwater; the fruit of the tree can be eaten or used to make drinks; the leaves can be eaten or used to make medicine.

The fruit of the baobab tree is eaten or used to make a soft drink. The bark is used to make rope, fabric, and strings for instruments. The leaves are eaten or used to make medicines.

▲ **CRITICAL THINKING**

1. ***Constructing a Thesis*** Why might Africans like to use the baobab tree as a symbol for the entire continent?
2. ***Drawing Conclusions*** Why might someone living in or near the desert like to have a baobab tree growing nearby?

source a point of origin

T

The most striking tree found in the northern Kalahari is the baobab. The baobab tree is often used as a symbol for all of Africa. Its thick trunk stretches high before splitting into a tangle of skinny branches, making the tree look as if it is upside-down with its roots in the air. Baobabs can live for hundreds of years and reach a diameter of 30 feet (9 m). The trunks can be hollowed out and used to collect rainwater or even as a shelter.

Natural Resources

C

Southern Africa's most important resource is its vast mineral wealth. Gold and copper are mined today, just as they were by ancient peoples. Coal, nickel, iron, cobalt, manganese, and uranium are found in abundance. Deposits of gemstones, especially diamonds, have drawn miners for several centuries. Additionally, Southern Africa's mineral wealth made it attractive to countries for colonization.

Unfortunately, Southern Africa's valuable resources are a **source** of controversy. In most cases, foreign companies own the mines that extract minerals and gemstones. They hire local workers and pay them very little money to work in dangerous conditions. The profits the foreign companies make are taken out of Southern Africa and do little to benefit the subregion.

One major exception is found in Botswana. In 1978 the government formed a partnership with a multinational company called De Beers. The partnership, known as Debswana, mines and sells Botswana's diamonds. The profits are split between the country and the company. This has given Botswana one of the healthiest, fastest-growing economies in all of Southern Africa.

The history of diamond mining can be seen in Kimberley, South Africa, at a site called the Big Hole. It was a hill until diamonds were discovered. From 1871 to 1914, 22.5 million tons (20.4 million t) of dirt and rock were removed, with picks and shovels. Today, the 700-foot- (213-m-) deep hole is a tourist destination.

READING PROGRESS CHECK

Evaluating What types of biomes are found in Southern Africa?

LESSON 1 REVIEW (CCSS)

Reviewing Vocabulary (Tier Three Words)

1. ***Applying*** Write a paragraph describing the altitudes of the various areas in Southern Africa. Be sure to mention the Great Escarpment. RH.9–10.4

Using Your Notes

2. ***Synthesizing*** Use your graphic organizer on the features of Southern Africa's physical geography to write a paragraph describing the four major rivers of the subregion and their courses.

Answering the Guiding Questions

3. ***Identifying*** What is the most dominant physical feature of Southern Africa?
4. ***Explaining*** How do people harness the power of the subregion's rivers?
5. ***Applying*** How do the climates of Southern Africa affect its biomes?

Writing Activity

6. ***Informative/Explanatory*** In a paragraph, describe the major biomes of Southern Africa. WHST.9–10.2

LESSON 1 REVIEW ANSWERS

Review Vocabulary

1. Paragraphs will vary but should be strongly supported with information from the lesson, including the Great Escarpment, which forms an almost unbroken U-shape behind the coastal plains and includes the Drakensberg Range that rises to more than 11,000 feet. The Highveld is a plateau that sits more than 50 miles high inside the Great Escarpment. The highest parts of Namibia and Angola are along the coast, while Zimbabwe's highest terrain is in the center of the country. Zambia has higher land in the northeast where it meets with Mozambique's highlands along the Great Escarpment.

Using Your Notes

2. Paragraphs will vary but could include identifying the Okavango, Orange, Zambezi, and Limpopo Rivers. Answers could include that the Okavango River runs from central Angola to northern Botswana, ending inland in a delta and swamps. The Orange River flows from Lesotho, through South Africa and Namibia before emptying into the Atlantic Ocean. The Zambezi River begins in eastern Angola and then flows through Zambia, forming its border with Namibia, Botswana, and Zimbabwe. In Zimbabwe, the Zambezi drops sharply, forming Victoria Falls, before running through Mozambique near the southern tip of Malawi and emptying into the Indian Ocean. The Limpopo River begins in northern South Africa and forms the border with Botswana and Zimbabwe.

Answering the Guiding Questions

3. The Highveld is the most dominant feature of Southern Africa.
4. The people use the rivers to generate hydroelectric power.
5. The different climates provide different types of biomes, including savanna and desert, with a wide variety of plant and animal life.

Writing Activity

6. Paragraphs will vary but should include information from the lesson on the desert and savanna biomes in Southern Africa.

networks

There's More Online!

- **GRAPH** Gold Production
- **IMAGE** Cecil Rhodes
- **IMAGE** Johannesburg
- **IMAGE** Shaka Zulu
- **MAP** European Colonization of Africa
- **TIME LINE** Apartheid and Its Legacy
- **INTERACTIVE SELF-CHECK QUIZ**
- **VIDEO** Human Geography of Southern Africa

LESSON 2

Human Geography of Southern Africa

ESSENTIAL QUESTION • *How do physical systems and human systems shape a place?*

Reading **HELP**DESK

Academic Vocabulary (Tier Two Words)

- **policy**
- **prohibit**

Content Vocabulary (Tier Three Words)

- **urbanization**
- **sanitation**
- **subsistence farming**
- **commercial farming**

TAKING NOTES: ***Integration of Knowledge and Ideas***

IDENTIFYING As you read about the human geography of Southern Africa, use a graphic organizer like the one below to identify examples of how history, population, culture, and economics have worked together to create the subregion as it is today.

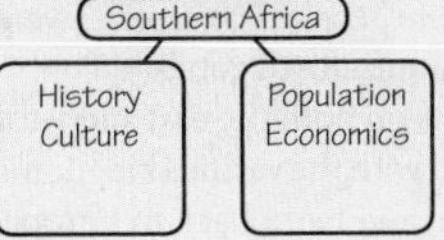

It Matters Because

Southern Africa's human geography blends components from the very earliest humans, traditional African cultures, and European influences. Southern Africa today is full of contrasts—white and black, traditional and modern, wealth and poverty, urban and rural. **R**

History and Government

GUIDING QUESTION *What cultures have influenced life in Southern Africa?*

Fossils that predate those of modern humans can be found in Southern Africa. Fossils of the first true humans are found north of the subregion in the valleys of Tanzania and Kenya. The first people to live in Southern Africa were the San, who arrived more than 20,000 years ago. Today, their descendants live in Botswana, Namibia, and Angola.

The Bantu peoples originated in central Africa, but began spreading across the continent some 3,500 years ago. The term *Bantu* refers to a group of about 500 related languages and to the various peoples who speak them. By about A.D. 300, Bantu peoples had migrated to Southern Africa.

One of the Bantu peoples, the Shona, established a city called Great Zimbabwe. By A.D. 1000, Great Zimbabwe had a population of between 12,000 and 20,000 people. The inhabitants farmed, raised cattle, and mined and traded gold. For 400 years, Great Zimbabwe was the center of a huge trading empire. Sometime in the 1400s, however, the city was abandoned. No one knows why. All that remains are ruins in southeastern Zimbabwe.

Madagascar's population is also the result of migration. Around A.D. 800, a small group of people sailed in outrigger canoes from islands in Southeast Asia to Madagascar. These people were the Malagasy, and their descendants populated the entire island, later mixing with migrants from the African continent. DNA tests confirm the ancestry of Madagascar is evenly split between Indonesia and East Africa. Despite sharing ancestry, as well as the many political and economic ties to Africa, many Malagasy do not consider themselves to be African.

ENGAGE

R Reading Skills

Previewing Have students quickly skim the lesson to preview the visuals and headings as they consider what they already know about the different cultural groups that settled Southern Africa over time. Ask students to speculate on the social and economic issues that may result from the mixing of this diverse group of people. Then have students write three predictions for what they will read and learn about in this lesson.

TEACH & ASSESS

T Technology Skills

Sequencing Have students work in pairs to create time lines that will help them sequence the many different groups of people who originated in or migrated to colonize the lands of Southern Africa. Have students record information such as the dates when each group first settled the land, where their settlements were mainly located, or any effect groups had on the other groups. Suggest that students use Internet or library resources to add additional facts about each cultural group. Invite volunteers to share their completed time lines. AL **Visual/Spatial**

Content Background Knowledge

Great Zimbabwe Although no one knows the actual answer, scientists have a few theories about why Great Zimbabwe was deserted. Some think that so many people were living in the area that the natural resources became depleted. Some feel the enormous number of grazing cattle exhausted the nutrients in the soil, leading to famine. Another explanation is that the most popular routes for trade shifted away from Great Zimbabwe, so the people moved to other areas where they could make a better living.

ANSWERS, p. 581

TAKING NOTES: History/Culture—Bantu migrated around A.D. 300; the Shona, one of the Bantu peoples, established Great Zimbabwe, thriving by A.D. 1000; Madagascar populated by the Malagasy around A.D. 800, though many do not consider themselves African; Portuguese established slave and trading posts on the coasts by the 1500s; in the 1700s, Dutch and British expanded settlement aided by the spread of European diseases; British took over Cape Colony in the 1800s, outlawed the slave trade, but did not free those enslaved; Germany lost its colonies after WWI; Independence for countries came in different ways, problems from colonization persisted after independence; hundreds of local languages are spoken and French, English, and German are common. Christianity is the most common religion, but traditional religions are practiced. **Population/Economics**—Generally, population increases from the Atlantic to the Indian Ocean. Much of the western areas are desert. Location of natural resources, such as gold, also influenced settlement. Most people are farmers but some areas support mining operations. Manufacturing is small, but is growing economically.

networks *Online Teaching Options*

INTERACTIVE BELLRINGER

Gold Production

Interpreting Significance Use the introductory text and the graph of gold production to understand that mining is a major economic activity in South Africa. Inform students they will need to use calculators for this activity. Have students form small groups. Ask them to discuss where they think most of the world's gold comes from. Then, have them answer each question and write agreed-upon answers for each one. Review the answers in a whole-class discussion. **Interpersonal, Logical/Mathematical**

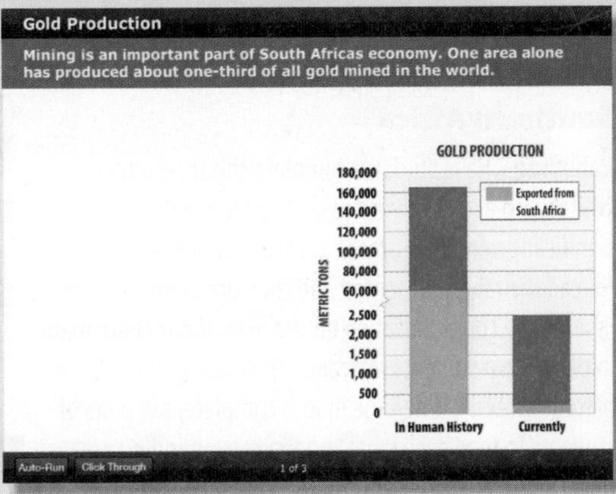

V Visual Skills

Analyzing Visuals Have students study the map key, labels, scale, and inset map and interpret them in a class discussion. **Ask:** What do the colors on the main map indicate? *(foreign countries that controlled the various parts of Africa as their colonies in 1913)* What do the numbers on the inset map tell you? *(in which year each African country became independent)* What does the larger map help you understand about foreign countries' influence on Southern Africa? *(It makes it easy to see at a glance which countries established colonies in this area.)* BL Visual/Spatial

C Critical Thinking Skills

Understanding Relationships Among Events Discuss with students the information about the Portuguese influence on life in Southern Africa. **Ask:** What were the first European settlers in Southern Africa like? *(They were Portuguese explorers, priests, and traders who established peaceful relations with the people native to the Kingdom of Kongo.)* How did the relationship change by the mid-1550s? *(A slave trade was set up where kings who lived on the coasts would capture and enslave people who lived farther inland and then trade these enslaved people to the Portuguese.)* How did this relationship further develop by the 1600s? *(The trading relationship of Portuguese goods for native resources such as enslaved people, gold, silver, and ivory was so well established that the Portuguese built slave and trading posts on both the east and the west coasts.)* AL Verbal/Linguistic

Making Connections

The Dutch East India Company wanted to find easier ways to travel to and from East Asia. After failing to find a good northeast sailing route, English sailor Henry Hudson searched for a northwest route, a journey that led him to find and explore what is now New York in North America. Dutch settlers, sent by a newly chartered West India Company, followed Hudson and established New Netherland, a series of trading posts and towns that became parts of New York. The Dutch East India Company established a settlement on the Cape of Good Hope to provide their trading ships a place to refuel on the long journey around the southern tip of Africa to India.

ANSWERS, p. 582

GEOGRAPHY CONNECTION

1. The Dutch initially governed Cape Colony until the British took it over in 1806.
2. The British controlled much of inland Southern Africa.

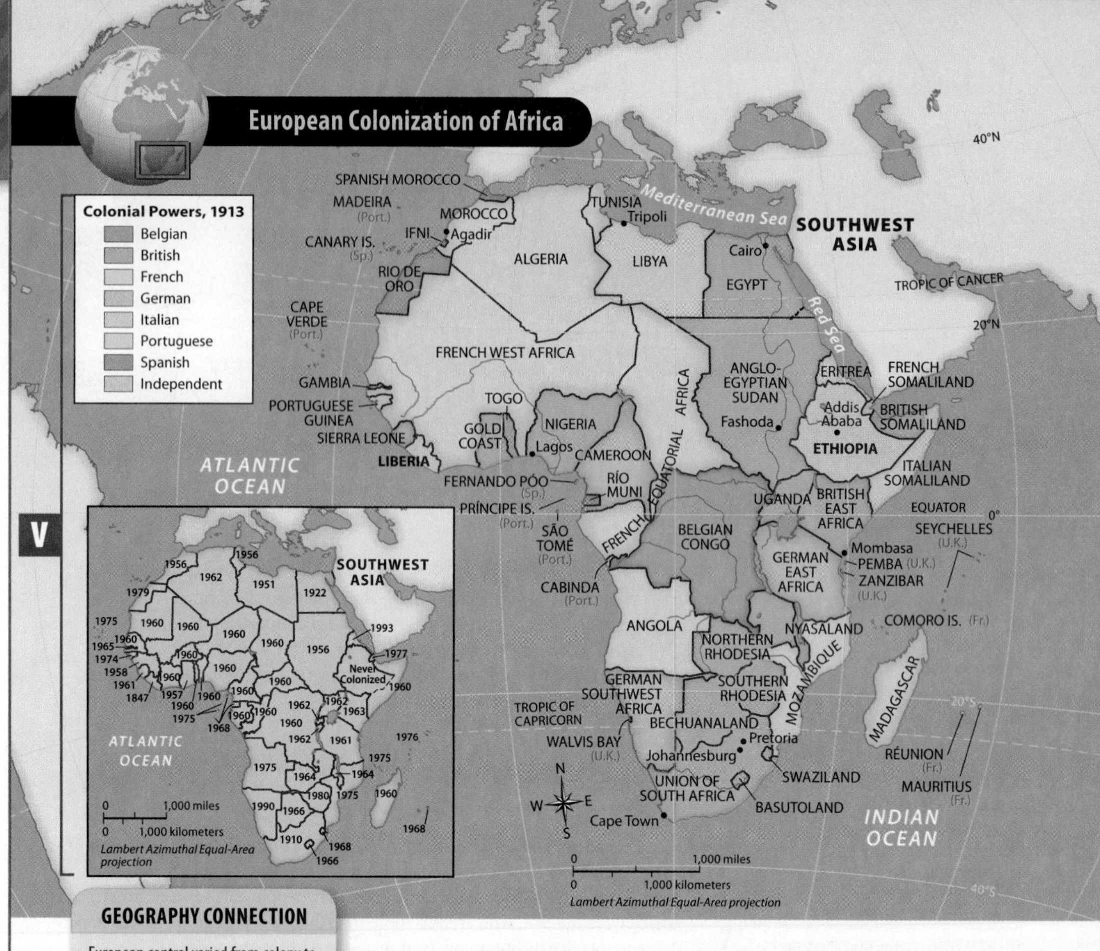

GEOGRAPHY CONNECTION

European control varied from colony to colony. For example, Cape Colony (South Africa) had a strong central government. In Angola, however, the Portuguese had little control over the people who lived in the inland areas.

1. ***HUMAN SYSTEMS*** Which European country governed Cape Colony?
2. ***HUMAN SYSTEMS*** Which European country controlled most of inland Southern Africa?

European Influences

Great Zimbabwe had faded away by the time the first Europeans arrived in Southern Africa. In the 1480s, Portuguese explorers, priests, and traders sailed into the Kingdom of Kongo in what is now the northern tip of Angola. At first, relations between the Portuguese and Kongo were peaceful, but it did not last.

By the mid-1500s, an active slave trade was running throughout Southern Africa. Coastal African kings sent raiding parties inland to capture people. The captives were then traded to the Portuguese for firearms and other manufactured goods.

The Portuguese established slave and trading posts on both the east and west coasts of Southern Africa. They either traded or warred with the various kingdoms they encountered, and they shipped much gold, silver, and ivory back to Europe. In the 1600s, other European powers expanded into Africa, causing Portuguese power to wane. By the mid-1700s, Dutch, British, and local African forces had confined the Portuguese to Angola and Mozambique. Only small settlements near the coast remained subject to Portuguese control.

In 1652 the Dutch East India Company established a settlement on the Cape of Good Hope. Dutch settlers took more and more land from the local African inhabitants, expanding well beyond the influence of the Dutch East India Company.

networks Online Teaching Options

INTERACTIVE WHITEBOARD ACTIVITY

European Colonization of Southern Africa

Labelling Have students complete this interactive whiteboard activity to increase their knowledge of significant colonial events in Southern Africa. Ask students to read the labels presented and then drag and drop each label to the correct location on the map. If errors are made initially, have students rearrange their labels until all are placed correctly. When the map is complete, ask pairs of students to read each label and the corresponding area name aloud to each other. ELL Visual/Spatial, Verbal/Linguistic, Kinesthetic

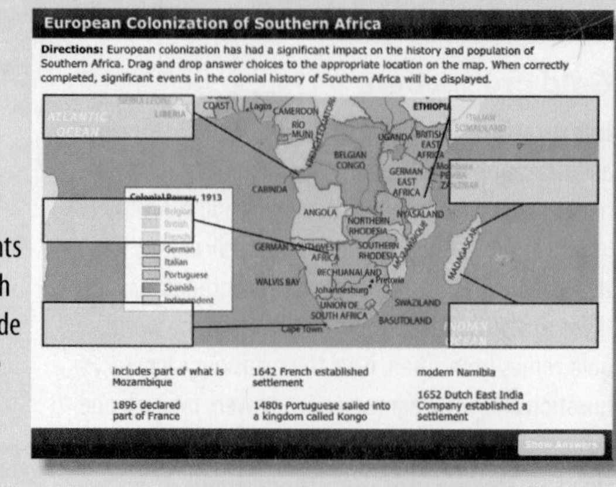

The Dutch were aided in their expansion by disease. As in the Americas, the local population had no immunity to European diseases and many died. After a few generations, the Dutch settlers referred to themselves as Afrikaners, which means "Africans." They were also called Boers, the Dutch word for "farmers."

Most of the Boers used slave labor on their farms. At first, enslaved people were brought in from areas farther north, but later the Boers enslaved local people as well. In order to communicate, the Afrikaners and the Africans developed a pidgin dialect that eventually evolved into Afrikaans, a new language.

At the start of the 1800s, Cape Colony was home to 22,000 whites, 25,000 enslaved blacks, and tens of thousands of free blacks. In 1806 Great Britain seized control of Cape Colony. A year later, Britain outlawed the slave trade in all its colonies. This had a positive effect in that the British and Afrikaners were now prohibited from capturing and enslaving Africans. It did not benefit people already enslaved, who were not freed by the ending of the trade.

C

European contact with Madagascar was sporadic and varied. The Portuguese, British, and French tried to gain influence on the island. The French established a settlement in 1642, but it did not last. Trade continued, and both the French and the British allied themselves with various local groups and leaders. In 1896 Madagascar became a French colony.

In 1884 Germany's new colonial goals led to the establishment of two colonies on the mainland of Africa. One, German East Africa, was farther north on the continent but did include some of what is today Mozambique. The other, German Southwest Africa, later became the country of Namibia. After losing World War I, Germany was stripped of all its African colonies. German East Africa was divided between Great Britain and Belgium. German Southwest Africa was renamed Southwest Africa, and it was placed under the control of South Africa.

Shaka

One of the most important Africans in the history of Southern Africa was Shaka. He was the son of a Zulu chief and a Langeni princess. Shaka was raised by his mother among the Langeni and the Mthethwa. Both Shaka and his mother were treated cruelly and resented by both groups.

Shaka's father died in 1816, when Shaka was about 30 years old. He took over the Zulu clan his father had led. He reorganized, rearmed, and retrained the Zulu army. He also instituted a draft system.

The new weapons and tactics were devastatingly effective against the other clans. Shaka's army killed hundreds of thousands of other African people. Refugees fled inland and those who remained were incorporated into the Zulu empire.

W

After his assassination in 1828, the Zulu empire lived on, ruled by various relatives of Shaka. Over time, the Boers and the British began encroaching on Zulu territory. The Boers captured much of southern Zululand, but were forced to give it back. Then, in 1879, the British declared war. The Zulu army of 50,000 soldiers won the first battle in an enormous victory, but it prompted the British to send even more soldiers and supplies. The war ended with the division of the Zulu empire into 13 smaller territories. Even so, Zulu resistance to British rule continued until the first decade of the 1900s.

Cecil Rhodes

One of the most important Europeans in the history of Southern Africa was Cecil Rhodes. He moved from England to Cape Colony (South Africa) in 1870, at the age of 17. He bought up gold and diamond mines throughout the area. By 1891, the company he started, De Beers, produced 90 percent of the world's diamonds.

Shaka created a modern African empire and built an army that fought colonial powers for more than 50 years.

▼ CRITICAL THINKING

1. ***Identifying Perspectives*** What do you think Shaka thought of the Europeans in Africa?
2. ***Assessing*** Was Shaka a successful leader? Why or why not?

Tim Gainey/Alamy

R Reading Skills

Defining Explain that a pidgin language is a simple language that groups who do not have a common language create to try to communicate with one another. Pidgin might use gestures, simplified grammar structures, and simplified versions of words from the languages spoken by the people trying to communicate. **Ask:** **Who were the two groups who created Afrikaans?** *(the Boers and the enslaved Southern African people)* **How might the development of Afrikaans have affected life in Southern Africa?** *(Establishing a common pidgin language drew the two cultures of Africans and Boers closer together.)* ELL **Verbal/Linguistic**

C Critical Thinking Skills

Exploring Issues Have students review the information about why slavery was practiced in Southern Africa in the past. Then **ask:** **How were people enslaved in the first place?** *(Possible answer: Some people were captured and enslaved by other people native to Africa, while others were captured and enslaved by Afrikaners.)* **How did the situation change when the British took control of the Cape?** *(Possible answer: The slave trade in the colonies stopped, which meant that no more people could become enslaved. However, people who were already enslaved were not freed.)* Have students discuss the British decision to end the slave trade in the colonies.
BL **Interpersonal, Verbal/Linguistic**

W Writing Skills

Informative/Explanatory Have students think about the relationship between Shaka's childhood experiences and the actions he took as the leader of the Zulu clan. Have students write a short essay summarizing the information about Shaka's life and discussing how his past might have shaped and affected his style of leadership. Allow students to use print or online resources to do additional research. **Verbal/Linguistic**

INTERACTIVE IMAGE

Shaka

Describing Have students view the interactive image of Shaka. Ask students to list adjectives that they think describe Shaka based on the photograph of his statue. Ask students to consider the artist's intention when carving the statue, and how that intention may relate to the students' descriptions. Ask a small group of volunteers to research information about Shaka and report their findings to the class. BL **Visual/Spatial, Verbal/Linguistic**

ANSWERS, p. 583

CRITICAL THINKING

1. Student answers may vary but could include that he did not like Europeans because they encroached on his territory and he fought against them.
2. Student answers may vary but should be supported by information in the section and could include that he was successful because he organized, armed, and trained his people to build an empire. Others might indicate that he killed hundreds of thousands of Africans while building the Zulu empire.

T Technology Skills

Acquiring Information Have small groups of students use online resources to collect more in-depth information about the road to independence in the countries that make up Southern Africa. Assign each group a specific country's history to research. Remind them to include facts such as which European country or countries had colonized it and what different systems of government it might have experienced along the road to freedom. Once groups complete their research, have them create multimedia presentations using maps, illustrations, charts, or graphs to organize their information. Invite groups to present their findings to the class. Finish with a class discussion in which students compare and contrast the different paths to independence that these countries took. **BL**
Verbal/Linguistic, Visual/Spatial

C Critical Thinking Skills

Chronological Reasoning Review the events of the time line with students. Then have pairs work together to read each entry and consider what type of information it provides about the history and legacy of apartheid. Have pairs finish by writing summaries that explain in their own words what the time line is explaining about the effect apartheid had on people living in South Africa. *(Possible answer: The events on the time line show how injustice permeated life in this area from the very beginning when native people were imported from West Africa and other places. It provides information about the history of protests, the ensuing violence, and the effectiveness of an economic boycott, as well as how South Africa moved past apartheid. Looking at the flow of events as a whole helps the viewer understand how many years it took to overturn apartheid and begin to heal the society.)*
AL **Verbal/Linguistic, Visual/Spatial**

In his will, Cecil Rhodes used most of his fortune to establish a scholarship program that would bring students, regardless of race, to Oxford University.

▲ CRITICAL THINKING T
1. ***Identifying Perspectives*** Why would Cecil Rhodes want to send students to Oxford rather than to local universities?
2. ***Hypothesizing*** Why do you think Rhodes specified that scholarships would not be restricted by race?

Rhodes was elected to the parliament of Cape Colony in 1881 and remained in government the rest of his life. He served as prime minister of the colony from 1890 to 1896. A committed imperialist, he used his wealth and power to further his dream of expanding British control to all of Africa.

Rhodes tried to reconcile the Dutch Boers and the British, but under British rule. He expanded British influence north into what is today Botswana, Zambia, and Zimbabwe. The latter two were once combined as the colony of Rhodesia, which was named after Rhodes.

Rhodes's life can be seen as a metaphor for European involvement in Africa. To him, Africa was a resource to be exploited and brought under "civilized" control. Local populations were dealt with ruthlessly—although, in Rhodes's case, generally without violence—and then ignored. The land and riches Africans once controlled were taken over by Europeans.

Independence

After World War I, unrest against colonial rule began to grow across Africa. In 1910 the Union of South Africa was created from four British colonies. Most other countries in Southern Africa were freed from European control in the 1960s and 1970s. Namibia became independent from South Africa in 1990.

Each country had a different road to independence. In Botswana, for example, independence was quick and peaceful. In Angola, however, guerrilla forces fought the Portuguese army for 14 years. Mozambique gained independence in 1976, but fought a civil war until 1992.

In some countries, problems continued after independence. Rhodesia divided into two parts. The northern part became Zambia in 1964 with a black African majority government. In Southern Rhodesia whites took control and declared an independent country in 1965. Black Africans living there did not win the right to vote or run for office until 1978. It came only after a long period of civil war. Once black majority rule was established, the country was renamed Zimbabwe. Robert Mugabe became its first prime minister in 1980. His rule has become more brutal and repressive as political opposition to him has increased.

TIME LINE

APARTHEID and Its Legacy

South Africa's long history of racial discrimination, enshrined in law during the era of apartheid, left deep, long-lasting scars on its people.

CRITICAL THINKING ▶
1. ***Describing*** How did white settlers secure their power in South Africa?
2. ***Analyzing*** How has South Africa tried to heal the wounds caused by apartheid?

C

1750

1756 Afrikaners begin to import slaves from West Africa, Malaysia, and India.

1948 The National Party comes to power and continues a policy of racial segregation they call apartheid.

1960 Police open fire on protest in Sharpeville; 69 black demonstrators killed

1962 African National Congress (ANC) leader Nelson Mandela is arrested, sentenced to life imprisonment two years later

584

networks Online Teaching Options

VIDEO

Apartheid

Applying Ethical Issues Explain to students that apartheid is an emotional topic in South Africa. Show them the video. Lead a class discussion regarding the ethics of separating and treating people differently based upon skin color. Play the video again, and this time ask students to focus on the attitudes of the woman leading the tour of the Apartheid Museum and the man—himself a former prisoner—who provided the tour of the political prison. Ask students if they believe these attitudes have been helpful or harmful in resolving the wounds caused by apartheid.
AL **Visual/Spatial, Interpersonal**

ANSWERS, p. 584

CRITICAL THINKING
Cecil Rhodes
1. Rhodes felt that Africans were uncivilized, thus making education in Britain better than anything offered at a local level.
2. Student answers may vary but could include that he was interested in expanding European influence and "civilizing" Africans, and education would be one way to do this.

CRITICAL THINKING
Apartheid and Its Legacy
1. They established slavery and then put in place laws that controlled and discriminated against the local peoples.
2. It has set up commissions to have public hearings on crimes committed during apartheid and make restitutions.

In South Africa, society had been segregated into blacks, whites, and South African coloured (mixed race) since colonial days. In 1948 the government established a **policy** called apartheid, an Afrikaans word meaning "separateness." Under apartheid, blacks and coloureds were required to live in specific places. They were allowed certain jobs, needed permits to leave their neighborhoods, and were **prohibited** from having social contact with whites. Civil protests and international boycotts during the 1970s and 1980s ended the policy of white minority rule and apartheid. In 1994 South Africa's first black president, Nelson Mandela, was elected. In 1995 he established a Truth and Reconciliation Commission to reveal the abuses that occurred under apartheid and provide restitution to its victims. South Africa had its first black majority government in modern times. T

policy an overall plan that establishes goals and determines procedures, decisions, and actions

prohibit to prevent or forbid by authority

✓ READING PROGRESS CHECK

Listing How many different European powers established colonies in Southern Africa?

Population Patterns

GUIDING QUESTION *How have natural resources helped to determine the location of many settlements in Southern Africa?*

Parts of the Southern Africa subregion are heavily populated while others are practically uninhabited. In general, the population increases as one moves from west to east, from the Atlantic to the Indian Ocean. Madagascar follows the same pattern of a west-to-east increase. The explanation for most of the sparsely populated western areas is physical geography. Much of Botswana and Namibia is desert that can support few people.

Throughout history, major cities have often grown up along trade routes. Until the mid-1800s, trade routes mostly involved waterways. Since Southern Africa has almost no navigable rivers, the first trade centers were located along the coast. R

A second factor that affected population distribution was natural resources. In 1886 the discovery of gold in the interior of Cape Colony led to a gold rush. One town that was established near the mines, Johannesburg, is now the largest and most important city in South Africa. Many settlements in the subregion

1980s
International campaign to boycott South Africa in protest of apartheid cripples its economy
1990
Nelson Mandela released after 27 years in prison
1994
First free elections held in post-apartheid South Africa; Mandela elected president as the ANC candidate
2012
Capital city of Tshwane (Pretoria) renames streets after leaders of anti-apartheid movement
STEVE BIKO ST
JOHANNES RAMOKHOASE ST
1990
2000
1976
More than 600 people killed in clashes between black protesters and government forces during Soweto uprising
1996
Truth and Reconciliation Commission begins public hearings on crimes committed during apartheid era

(l)Per-Anders Pettersson/Getty Images News/Getty Images, (r)Alexander Joe/AFP/Getty Images, (b)Africa Media Online/The Image Works

CHAPTER 24, Lesson 2
Human Geography of Southern Africa

T Technology Skills

Constructing Arguments Have students review what they already know and what they have read about apartheid. **Ask: What were some effects of apartheid?** *(Whites and nonwhites were kept separate. Nonwhites could not live in most parts of the country, hold certain jobs, or mingle socially with whites.)* **How was apartheid finally repealed?** *(Internal and external pressure on the government, including an economic boycott, convinced the government to get rid of apartheid.)* Have small groups of students use the Internet to research the end of apartheid and the subsequent efforts to investigate the abuses that happened under the system. Direct student groups to structure a debate, each with a differing viewpoint about the success of post-apartheid efforts to make amends and restitution to the victims. Have students consider current events in South Africa. **Ask: Does the end of apartheid mean the end of discrimination? How do you think the death of Nelson Mandela in December 2013 might affect future race relations in South Africa?** *(Student answers will vary, but should be supported with logical reasoning.)* Allow class time for groups to construct their arguments. Then have the students present their views in classroom debates. Use the debate presentations to further discuss apartheid and its long-term effects. BL **Interpersonal, Kinesthetic**

R Reading Skills

Understanding Relationships Have students work in pairs to review the ways physical geography influences where people settle. **Ask: What characterized most trade routes until the mid-1800s?** *(Most trade routes were located along waterways.)* **What are most rivers in Southern Africa like?** *(They are full of rapids, waterfalls, and other elements that make them difficult to travel on safely.)* **Why did many people settle on the coast of Southern Africa?** *(Because the rivers were not navigable, people who wanted to participate in trade had to settle near the ocean.)* AL **Logical/Mathematical**

TIME LINE

Apartheid and Its Legacy

Determining Importance Explain to students that apartheid in South Africa began to meet its end in the 1970s and 1980s. Have students read the entries related to those decades. Using the information from the entries and from the text, ask students to identify the types of actions taken by people to show their opposition to apartheid. After careful consideration of the entire time line, ask them which action they believe was more effective and why. BL **Verbal/Linguistic**

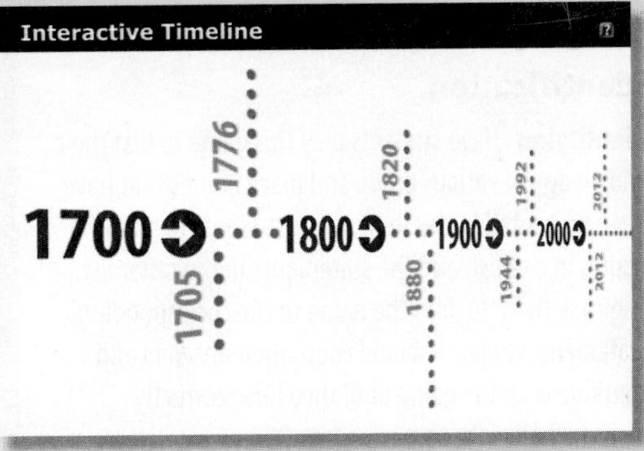
Interactive Timeline
1700
1776
1705
1800
1820
1880
1900
1944
1992
2000
2012

ANSWERS, p. 585

✓ **READING PROGRESS CHECK** The Dutch, French, British, Portuguese, and Germans all established colonies in Southern Africa.

C Critical Thinking Skills

Drawing Inferences Have students read the quote about poverty tourism and consider the reasons for and effects of this industry. **Ask:** What does it mean to say that these township tours sprang up more by accident, arising from demand? *(Possible answer: These tours were not planned at first. Because tour buses traveling to other attractions were passing through these areas out of curiosity, the locals took the opportunity to make some money by scheduling actual "safe" tours.)* What might happen as more tourists take these tours and see the townships? *(Possible answer: Witnessing the conditions that people living in poverty actually experience might help others who are better off gain an understanding for how poor people live and might drive new attempts to improve these conditions and reduce poverty.)* **Logical/Mathematical**

R Reading Skills

Explaining Have students recall what they have read about the status of women in other African countries. **Ask:** Why might local and foreign organizations have to take special steps to improve the financial status of women in Southern Africa? *(Possible answer: Despite the fact that many Southern African countries have laws that state that men and women should be treated equally, many places revert to following traditional laws that do not allow women to inherit or own property.)* In addition to loaning the women money to start small businesses, what can or should be done to help the women? *(Possible answer: Local governments should enforce laws. International businesses should establish trade relationships with women-owned businesses. Women should protest inequalities.)* AL **Verbal/Linguistic**

ANSWERS, p. 586

☑ **READING PROGRESS CHECK** Johannesburg developed and grew when gold was discovered and mining industries were established.

DBQ The areas without water and electricity are referred to as townships.

Analyzing PRIMARY SOURCES

Touring South Africa's Townships

"The township tours around Soweto, for example, seemed to spring up more by accident, arising from demand. Bus loads of tourists bound for other tourist attractions drove through the townships to stop and take a look from the safety of their buses. A few locals decided to offer tours around the townships so they could make some money out of the passing trade. With security tightened for visitors, they can see the huts where people live without water or electricity, and understand what tiny and cramped conditions the people live in."

—Amanda Kendle, "Poverty Tourism: Exploring the Slums of India, Brazil and South Africa," www.vagabondish.com

DBQ ***DRAWING INFERENCES*** What name is applied to the urban slums in South Africa? RH.9–10.4

urbanization the migration of people from rural areas to urban areas

sanitation the disposal of trash and human waste

were established due to the discovery of gold. Pretoria (Tshwane), the administrative capital of South Africa, was first settled by Boers who were attracted not to mineral wealth but to the fertile farmland in the valley and the favorable climate.

Like many other places, Southern Africa has been affected by **urbanization**. People hoping to better their lives migrate to cities in search of jobs. The most populated urban areas are Cape Town, Port Elizabeth, Durban, and Johannesburg in South Africa and Maputo in Mozambique. Some neighborhoods in these cities are wealthy and modern, with expensive homes and fashionable shopping areas. Others are very poor, and many people live without electricity or **sanitation**.

☑ **READING PROGRESS CHECK**

Explaining Why did Johannesburg develop and grow at its location?

Society and Culture Today

GUIDING QUESTION *How do traditions play a role in the lives of the peoples of the subregion?*

The effects of centuries of European influence are still felt in Southern Africa. Colonizing powers divided the continent among themselves with no regard for the traditional territories occupied by the local people. As a result, most of the major ethnic groups—Shona, San, Ambo, Makua, and Ndebele—are distributed in different countries with no defined national territories.

Hundreds of local languages are spoken. However, many countries use the European language of their colonizers to facilitate communication. As a result, French, German, and English are spoken in many places. In South Africa, white Afrikaners form an ethnic group. Their language, Afrikaans, is one of the country's 11 official languages, along with English and 9 local languages such as Zulu.

Christian missionaries worked throughout Africa during colonial times. As a result, Christianity is the most common religion in Southern Africa. Many people still practice traditional religions, however, which involve nature spirits, animal sacrifice and worship, and worshiping the spirits of one's ancestors.

In urban areas, people attend movies, shop in malls, watch television, surf the Internet, and listen to music by African artists. Those living in poverty, both in urban and rural areas, do not have these opportunities. Their leisure activities center on the family and traditional activities such as games, singing, and dancing.

Poverty is an issue throughout the subregion. In Mozambique in 2008, protests against the high prices of necessities such as fuel led to deadly riots. The pattern repeated itself in 2010. When the price of bread rose by 30 percent, there was rioting, Thirteen people were killed and more than 400 were arrested.

Poverty also affects life expectancy, which has been decreasing for decades because of the HIV/AIDS epidemic that was severe in Africa. The situation is improving, however. In 2012, researchers announced that life expectancy in South Africa had increased by five years since 2005. The increase is due to the world's largest drug treatment effort for people with HIV/AIDS.

Education also varies with income. Large cities have colleges and universities, and the children of wealthy families generally get a good education. However, the children of poor families attend school for only a few years, if at all, and often leave school early. Girls, in particular, usually get much less schooling than boys do.

The status of girls and women is an issue in many parts of Southern Africa. In rural areas, women generally do not have the same rights as men. For example, traditional laws often prohibit women from inheriting or even owning property. Most Southern African countries have laws that require gender equality, but traditional laws are often observed instead. To help women, local and international organizations have been working to improve the financial status of African women.

networks Online Teaching Options

GAME

Identification

Identifying Have students play this game to test their knowledge of various group and place names that have been presented in this lesson. Ask students to read the names in one list, and the statements in the other list. Then ask them to drag the name to the corresponding statement. Students should check their answers and continue with the game until they have correctly identified all eight names. ELL AL **Kinesthetic, Verbal/Linguistic**

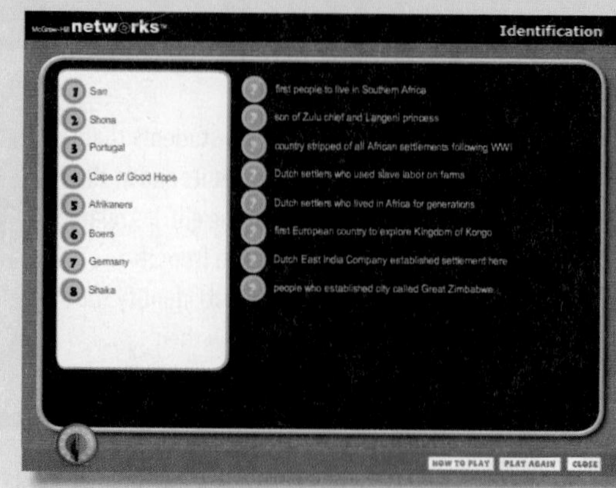

The organizations make small loans to help women set up small businesses, such as growing vegetables or making clothes. These loans are mostly made to women in rural areas, and often lead to women becoming the business leaders in a village or community.

☑ READING PROGRESS CHECK

Describing How does tradition affect women in Southern Africa?

Economic Activities

GUIDING QUESTION *What role does mining play in the economy of Southern Africa?*

Most people in Southern Africa are farmers. Over 80 percent of the residents of Angola and Mozambique are agricultural workers. Most of the farms are used for **subsistence farming**. With increased global markets, **commercial farming** has gained in importance. For example, sugar plantations dot the coasts of Angola, South Africa, and Mozambique, while oil palm, cacao, and peanuts are grown in South Africa and Zimbabwe. Fresh flowers and vegetables are grown on commercial farms and exported to European cities.

Control of farmland is a big issue in much of Africa. European colonists claimed much of the best land. A land reform program in Zimbabwe gave land owned by white farmers back to Africans. The result was chaos, violence, and corruption. The land reform led to the failure of Zimbabwe's economy. Zimbabwe's agricultural workforce includes about 50 percent of the country's people.

Mining has always been important to the economy of Southern Africa. One section of the Highveld in South Africa, the Witwatersrand, has been mined since the 1880s. This area has produced about one-third of the gold ever mined in the world. Gold is also found in other parts of South Africa and in Zimbabwe. Most of the world's diamonds come from mines near the Witwatersrand, Botswana, and along the coast near the Namibia-South Africa border. Copper and cobalt are mined in Zimbabwe, Namibia, and Zambia.

Since the 1960s, many countries in Southern Africa have been trying to encourage and support manufacturing. Foreign loans have financed the development of manufacturing. Today, factories produce materials such as paper goods, cement, electric motors, and tractors. Compared to other developing regions, Southern Africa's manufacturing sector is still small, but it is growing.

☑ READING PROGRESS CHECK

Explaining From what one area does much of the world's gold come?

GRAPH SKILLS

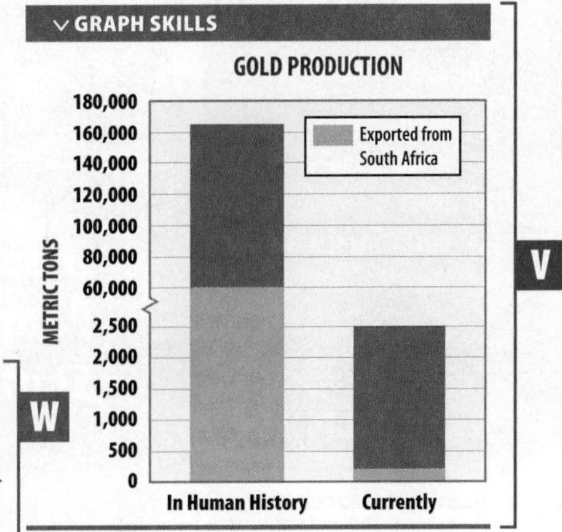

Gold mining has long been a central part of South Africa's economy.

▲ CRITICAL THINKING

1. ***Using Graphs*** About what percentage of the world's gold exports currently come from South Africa?
2. ***Making Connections*** How has gold influenced South Africa's history?

subsistence farming small-scale agriculture that provides for the needs of a family or village, but little more

commercial farming growing large quantities of crops or livestock in order to sell them for a profit

LESSON 2 REVIEW (CCSS)

Reviewing Vocabulary (Tier Three Words)

1. ***Applying*** Write a paragraph describing the difference between subsistence farming and commercial farming. RH.9–10.4

Using Your Notes

2. ***Summarizing*** Use your graphic organizer on Southern Africa's human geography to write a paragraph summarizing how the history of the subregion affected the people and their culture.

Answering the Guiding Questions

3. ***Identifying*** What cultures have influenced life in Southern Africa?
4. ***Making Connections*** How have natural resources helped to determine the location of many settlements in Southern Africa?
5. ***Drawing Inferences*** How do traditions play a role in the lives of the peoples of the subregion?
6. ***Evaluating*** What role does mining play in the economy of Southern Africa?

Writing Activity

7. ***Informative/Explanatory*** In two or three paragraphs, describe how European control in Southern Africa began and ended. WHST.9–10.2

V Visual Skills

Using Graphs Provide time for students to analyze and interpret the bar graph. **Ask:** What is being measured on the vertical axis? *(metric tons of gold)* Horizontal axis? *(different periods)* What do the colors tell you? *(how much gold is being exported at different times)* About how much gold exported over the course of human history came from South Africa? *(about half, or 60,000 metric tons)* AL Visual/Spatial

W Writing Skills

Informative/Explanatory Have students research the forced land reform program in Zimbabwe to write an essay explaining why the program was enforced and what happened to damage Zimbabwe's agriculture sector. Then have students propose solutions that might improve the situation and make the agricultural industry run in ways that build up, rather than destroy, the lives of the labor force. BL Verbal/Linguistic

CLOSE & REFLECT

Summarizing Have students write a few paragraphs summarizing the development of the different industries, both good and bad, and how these industries have been affected by issues such as European colonization and apartheid.

ANSWERS, p. 587

☑ READING PROGRESS CHECK Traditional laws often keep women from owning or inheriting property; poor women are given less education and are held to traditional roles.

☑ READING PROGRESS CHECK The Witwatersrand has produced about one-third of the gold mined in the world.

CRITICAL THINKING

1. About 200 metric tons of the world's gold exports currently come from South Africa, accounting for about 8 percent.
2. Gold has influenced settlements and colonization.

LESSON 2 REVIEW ANSWERS

Review Vocabulary

1. Paragraphs will vary but should include that subsistence farming is to feed a family while commercial farming is for profit.

Using Your Notes

2. Paragraphs should be supported with information from the lesson including: Bantu migrated to Southern Africa around A.D. 300; Shona established Great Zimbabwe that was thriving by A.D. 1000; Madagascar was populated by the Malagasy around A.D. 800; many Malagasy do not consider themselves African; Portuguese established slave and trading posts on coasts by the 1500s; by the 1700s, Dutch and British expanded settlement aided by the spread of European diseases; British took over Cape Colony in the 1800s, outlawed slave trade, but did not free those already enslaved; Germany lost its colonies after WWI; Independence for Southern African countries came in different ways; problems from colonization persisted after independence; hundreds of local languages are spoken; French, English, and German are common languages in many places; Christianity is the most common religion, but traditional religions are also practiced.

Answering the Guiding Questions

3. French, German, and British cultures and traditional cultures of the people influence life in Southern Africa.
4. Settlements were often founded when natural resources such as gold were found in the area.
5. Traditions show in the variety of local languages, practice of traditional religions, lack of education, and restriction of women owning and inheriting property.
6. Mining has always been important to Southern Africa as the Witwatersrand has produced about one-third of the gold ever mined in the world and diamonds and copper are also found throughout the subregion.

Writing Activity

7. Paragraphs should include information from the lesson including that the Portuguese began with slave and trading posts and then colonized areas before being pushed out and limited to small areas by the Dutch and British. Germans also established colonies that they held until the end of WWI. Independence came in various ways; in Botswana it was peaceful, but Angola fought the Portuguese for 14 years.

ENGAGE

R1 Reading Skills

Discussing Discuss with students the reasons why people think it is important to focus on conservation and preservation of the environment. Have them identify negative outcomes that can occur when people do not take care of the land and its natural resources.

TEACH & ASSESS

C Critical Thinking Skills

Explaining Have students review the information about habitat destruction. **Ask: What is a possible explanation of the conflict between people's needs and the necessity of protecting the environment?** *(Possible answer: On the one hand, it is important not to cut too many trees down because deforestation will lead to soil erosion, which will hurt the land. On the other hand, many people do not have gas or electricity so they have to burn wood to cook their food.)* AL **Verbal/Linguistic**

R2 Reading Skills

Problem Solving Have students discuss deforestation in Africa. **Ask: What are the causes of deforestation in Southern Africa?** *(Possible answers: The regulations that might control the logging industry and keep it from cutting down too many trees have not been updated in 40 years; businesses ignore the regulations; even when they are punished for breaking the law, they do not pay large fines.)* Have students work with a partner to come up with a solution that might slow or stop the rate of deforestation. BL **Logical/Mathematical**

networks

There's More Online!

- **IMAGE** LifeStraws
- **IMAGE** Poor Urban Sanitation
- **IMAGE** Well in Mozambique
- **INTERACTIVE SELF-CHECK QUIZ**
- **VIDEO** People and Their Environment: Southern Africa

Reading **HELP**DESK

Academic Vocabulary (Tier Two Words)

- **cite**
- **administer**

Content Vocabulary (Tier Three Words)

- **shifting cultivation**
- **groundwater**

TAKING NOTES: ***Key Ideas and Details***

IDENTIFYING As you read about the environment of Southern Africa, use a graphic organizer like the one below to identify features that are being damaged.

Southern Africa	
Feature	Damage

588

LESSON 3

People and Their Environment: Southern Africa

ESSENTIAL QUESTION • *How do physical systems and human systems shape a place?*

IT MATTERS BECAUSE

R1 *Southern Africa is a land of mineral wealth, great natural beauty, and many of the most awe-inspiring animal species on the planet. But if that is to be true a hundred years from now, the governments and people of Southern Africa must increase their focus on conservation and preservation of the environment.*

Managing Resources

GUIDING QUESTION *Why are many resources in Southern Africa not managed closely?*

C In Southern Africa, as in other parts of the world, poverty is the underlying reason behind much of the failure to manage resources. Most of the people living in Southern Africa are subsistence farmers. In general, these people have little income, poor health care, and little education. The main concern for the people in this region is their families' welfare, not conservation.

Habitat destruction occurs when people collect firewood. While collecting firewood contributes to deforestation, the people have no other choice. Outside of urban areas, people do not have gas or electric stoves, so they use wood for cooking. As the population increases, more pressure is put on forest resources.

R2 Development is not necessarily the major cause of environmental degradation, however. Commercial logging is responsible for most of the deforestation in Southern Africa. The regulations that affect the logging industry have not been changed in 40 years. Furthermore, these regulations are usually ignored. When logging companies are **cited**, or summoned to appear in court, the fines they pay are tiny by today's standards.

Poaching, or illegal hunting, threatens some of Southern Africa's most notable species. Elephant tusks are made of ivory, which is a precious commodity around the world. Many countries have outlawed the importation or sale of ivory, but an illegal market still exists.

networks *Online Teaching Options*

INTERACTIVE BELLRINGER

Loss or Gain of Natural Forests in Southern African Countries

Reading Graphs Use the introductory text and the graph showing loss and gain of natural forest land in Southern African countries to understand an environmental issue facing the region. Have students meet in small groups. Have them discuss and answer each question. Have each group record its answers. Then, discuss the answers as a class. AL **Visual/Spatial**

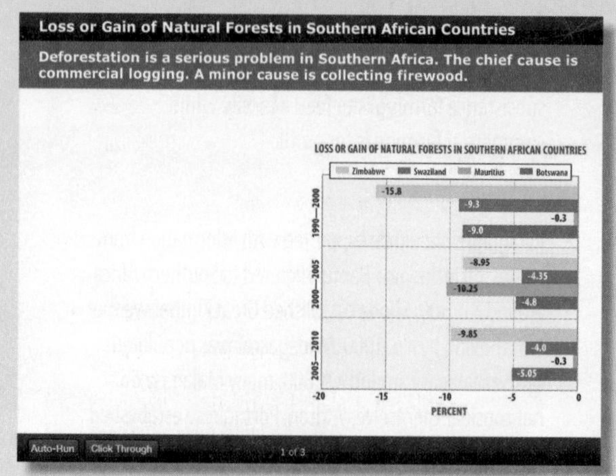

ANSWERS, p. 588

TAKING NOTES: Deforestation by logging companies and by people collecting wood for heat and cooking is destroying habitats. Poaching has driven elephants and rhinos to near extinction. Soils are being depleted of their nutrients by subsistence farming methods. Food and clean water shortages put pressure on communities and lead to conflicts.

Rhinoceroses are another species that may soon be hunted to extinction. Many Asians believe that the horn of the rhinoceros has powerful medicinal properties, even though there is no scientific proof of this claim. In much of Southern Africa, hunting endangered animals, including elephants and rhinoceroses, is illegal. However, because economic conditions are difficult and because it is so profitable, poaching continues to threaten these species.

C

Access to clean water is another serious issue. In both rural and urban areas, many residents do not have running water in their homes. They either dig their own wells or walk—sometimes for many miles—to collect water from a river or stream. These water sources can be and often are contaminated. During the rainy season, water abounds. However, even unclean water can be difficult to find during winter or in times of drought. Lack of access to clean water has serious health consequences. Many diseases are spread by contaminated water.

These women in Mozambique are drawing water from a well.

▲ **CRITICAL THINKING**

1. ***Analyzing Visuals*** How might relying on well water affect daily life?
2. ***Assessing*** What health risks might relying on well water pose?

In most developed countries, farmers attempt to prevent soil erosion and replenish the nutrients in their soil. Subsistence farmers in less developed countries often cannot and usually do not do this. The result is farmland that becomes unusable for growing crops after just a few years. For example, farmers on the volcanic islands of Comoros face loss of soil fertility and erosion where terraced farming is not practiced.

Shortages of food and water put pressure on communities.What is more likely, though, is that pressure from shortages pushes groups that are already at odds into conflict. For example, both Mozambique and Angola suffered through decades of civil war. The fighting may be over, but shortages of food, water, or other resources could easily drive them back into war.

cite to summon to appear in a court of law

T

Resources are not confined by political boundaries. In fact, many of the borders in Southern Africa are defined by rivers—important resources themselves. What starts as a conflict over resources can lead to larger wars between groups, resulting in many casualties and destabilizing the societies and economies of countries where they occur. Resource shortages can thus have effects that extend far beyond the borders of the regions where they occur.

☑ **READING PROGRESS CHECK**

Explaining Why are rhinoceroses endangered?

Human Impact

GUIDING QUESTION *How has environmental degradation affected life in the subregion?*

Human activity is affecting Southern Africa's environment in large and small ways. For example, many subsistence farmers engage in **shifting cultivation**. In this system, farmers cut and then burn brush and trees. After the land is cleared they plant crops in the ash-enriched soil. Once the soil is no longer productive, farmers clear a new plot. They return to the original plot once the fertility is restored. This method of agriculture works if the population is

shifting cultivation a system in which farmers plant a field for several years until its resources are depleted, then abandon it and clear a new field

People and Their Environment: Southern Africa

C Critical Thinking Skills

Interpreting Discussion the problems of poaching. **Ask:** **Why is poaching such a large problem in Southern Africa?** *(Possible answer: People can make money selling bushmeat and parts of the animals such as elephant tusks.)* **Ask:** **What can countries do to stop poachers?** *(Possible answer: provide other jobs, provide protected areas for the animals, impose heavy fines or jail for poachers)* **ELL** **Logical/Mathematical**

Making Connections

Southern Africans rely on groundwater to provide a high percentage of their water needs. In the Southern African Development Community (a group of 15 Southern African countries), at least 70 percent of about 250 million people rely on groundwater. Therefore, it is a grave problem if the groundwater becomes contaminated with sewage or other pollutants. In the United States, many people also rely on groundwater to meet their needs. Of all the community water systems across the U.S., 77 percent use groundwater as their primary source to supply 90 million citizens with drinking water. Additionally, about 15 million U.S. citizens get their water from private wells. The U.S. Environmental Protection Agency regulates the amount of pollutants allowed in community water systems. Private wells are not subject to these same regulations, so homeowners must check the safety and cleanliness of their water themselves.

T Technology Skills

Constructing Arguments Have students review the information about whether people will likely develop conflicts over limited natural resources. **Ask:** **Why might some people in Southern Africa fight over natural resources?** *(Possible answers: Some groups are already at odds with one another, and a clash over a resource might motivate them to fight.)* Have students work in small groups research online additional information about the potential for conflict over water and other natural resources in Southern Africa. Direct groups to structure a debate, each with a differing viewpoint, about whether it is likely that groups and/or countries will end up going to war over resources. Have students present their views in classroom debates. **BL** **Kinesthetic, Logical/Mathematical**

GRAPHIC ORGANIZER

People and Their Environment: Southern Africa

Identifying Cause and Effect Students will gain an overview of environmental issues in Southern Africa by completing this graphic organizer. As students work, have them consider the causes of damage to the natural environment. They should identify examples of specific physical features that have been affected and the damage to that feature. When their graphic organizers are complete, ask students to write a paragraph highlighting how the damage to one physical feature has impacted the lives of people in Southern Africa. **BL** **Logical/Mathematical, Verbal/Linguistic**

networks

KEY IDEAS AND DETAILS

IDENTIFYING As you read about the environment of Southern Africa, use the graphic organizer below to identify features that are being damaged.

Southern Africa	
Feature	Damage

UNDO CLEAR SAVE

ANSWERS, p. 589

☑ **READING PROGRESS CHECK** Rhinoceroses are endangered because they are being hunted for their horns, which are bought for large sums of money for use in traditional Asian medicines.

CRITICAL THINKING

1. Water would have to be drawn from the well and carried back to where it is needed, taking considerable time and effort.
2. Wells could be contaminated and spread diseases to anyone who uses the water.

G1 Critical Thinking Skills

Identifying Perspectives Have students discuss why it is difficult to find a clear-cut solution to the problem of how to conserve and share the natural resources of Southern Africa. **Ask:** **What conflict of interests exists when it comes to conserving the forests of Zimbabwe?** *(Possible answer: On the one hand, preserving the forests will stop deforestation and save the land from soil erosion. On the other hand, individuals have to use wood for heating and cooking, and businesses use wood for curing tobacco since wood is cheaper than coal.)* **What conflict exists when it comes to sharing the waters of the Zambezi, Orange, and Okavango Rivers?** *(Possible answer: Many towns and villages must figure out how to share these waters for irrigation and other uses because if one town diverts the water, other people downstream will have less to use. Unfortunately, people with wealth and power often dictate the water usage, leaving poor people with no say in the matter.)* **AL Logical/Mathematical**

G2 Critical Thinking Skills

Drawing Inferences Have students review the details about global climate change and groundwater. **Ask:** **Why would a change in the global climate affect the amount of groundwater?** *(Possible answer: If the climate changes so that temperatures get hotter, more water might evaporate into the atmosphere, leaving less groundwater available on Earth.)* **Logical/Mathematical**

Content Background Knowledge

LifeStraw Along with an individual portable water filter product, LifeStraw also offers a family water filter that can be installed and used in a home. Its various products are designed to protect people from otherwise preventable diseases such as cholera, dysentery, typhoid, and gastroenteritis.

ANSWERS, p. 590

☑ READING PROGRESS CHECK Farmers clear new areas of land when the old one is no longer productive, leaving it to return to a fertile state. However, population growth is causing more land to be used and not allowing enough time for land to recover, which is stressing the land further and causing erosion.

CRITICAL THINKING

1. Student answers may vary but could include: the company should give LifeStraws away for free as it would save many thousands of lives; the company should charge for the LifeStraws given that they have production and development costs.
2. The LifeStraws do not eliminate everything that is potentially harmful in contaminated water.

---

small enough to allow the land time to recover. However, rapid population growth is stressing the land because the land is not allowed enough time to rest. This method leaves depleted soil and empty fields in its wake, which can lead to soil erosion.

Deforestation causes habitat destruction on a large scale. Agricultural companies clearing fields and lumber companies collecting timber are cutting down the tropical forests. Madagascar, for example, has only 10 percent of its forests left. Zimbabwe is also hard hit, but for a different reason. Between 1990 and 2005, 21 percent of Zimbabwe's forests were cut down. Since then, the rate has increased. Almost all of the cut trees are being used for firewood, both by individuals and by the country's tobacco industry. Tobacco is cured over fire, and in Zimbabwe, firewood is cheaper than coal.

G1 The Zambezi, Orange, and Okavango Rivers all flow through different regions and even different countries. When one town or village diverts some of the water, such as to irrigate its fields, all of the people downstream have less water to use. In Southern Africa, richer, more powerful groups often hoard natural resources such as water, leaving even less available to the poor and disenfranchised. On some occasions, arguments about access to water have led to violent conflict.

groundwater water that lies underground and feeds wells and springs

Most people in the countryside in Southern Africa do not live near a major river. They rely on wells to get the water they need. Since there is no management system in place, people simply tap into the **groundwater** wherever they can. Groundwater is water that lies underground and feeds wells and springs. G2 The increasing use of groundwater in rural areas is reducing the amount of water available in the region. Furthermore, as the global climate changes and temperatures increase, groundwater may become even more limited.

In the past several decades, one of the major changes Southern Africa has experienced is urbanization. Many different factors have contributed to this trend. People in rural areas often perceive cities as having better housing conditions and better job opportunities. Climate change, exhausted farmland, or several consecutive years of bad crops may convince people to give up farming and to move to cities.

Sometimes the people's need to leave rural areas is more pressing. During the late twentieth century in Angola and Mozambique, armed rebels involved in civil war took control of large sections of the countryside. Millions of people fled to the relative safety of urban areas.

Several recent inventions have been developed to allow people to purify contaminated water. LifeStraw, shown here, was one of the first. It removes 99.9 percent of the sediment, bacteria, and viruses in the water that passes through it.

▼ CRITICAL THINKING

1. ***Analyzing Ethical Issues*** Should the company that makes LifeStraws give them away for free? Why or why not?
2. ***Evaluating*** What are the limits on the usefulness of this product?

Courtesy of Vestergaard Frandsen/Newscom

Most of the cities in Southern Africa have not been able to keep up with this rapid population growth. The natural resources in these areas are nearly gone. Urban areas are increasingly polluted and sanitation is often nonexistent, leading to widespread disease. Clean water and even trash removal are simply not available in many areas.

☑ READING PROGRESS CHECK

Explaining What do farmers do when their farmland is depleted?

590

networks Online Teaching Options

GAME

True or False

Skimming Have students play this true/false game to reinforce the topics presented in this lesson. Encourage them to use the text as they play. Have pairs of students work together to skim the lesson before they determine whether a statement is true or false. Remind them to check their answers and to rewrite all false statements to make them correct. **AL Verbal/Linguistic**

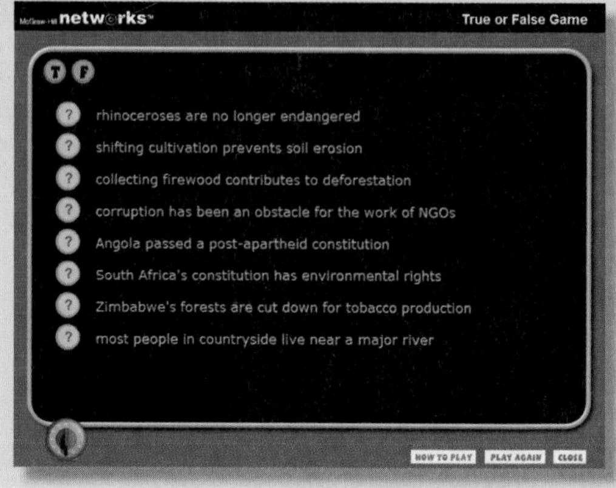

networks
True or False Game
rhinoceroses are no longer endangered
shifting cultivation prevents soil erosion
collecting firewood contributes to deforestation
corruption has been an obstacle for the work of NGOs
Angola passed a post-apartheid constitution
South Africa's constitution has environmental rights
Zimbabwe's forests are cut down for tobacco production
most people in countryside live near a major river
HOW TO PLAY
PLAY AGAIN
CLOSE

Despite the end of apartheid, many black South Africans still live in crowded, impoverished townships with poor sanitation.

▲ **CRITICAL THINKING**

1. ***Analyzing Visuals*** What environmental problems can you see in this photo?
2. ***Identifying Central Issues*** What do you think could be done to help solve those problems?

Addressing the Issues

GUIDING QUESTION *What steps are being taken to combat these environmental challenges?*

Many people realize that the environmental problems in Southern Africa must be addressed. Many countries are working to combat the problems the region is facing. International organizations, such as nongovernmental organizations (NGOs), are also tackling these issues.

South Africa is one of only a handful of countries in the world that have environmental rights built into their constitutions. Section 24 of the country's post-apartheid constitution says that "everyone has the right—(a) to an environment that is not harmful to their health or well-being; and (b) to have the environment protected, for the benefit of present and future generations, through reasonable legislative and other measures." **W**

South Africa recently adopted the National Strategy for Sustainable Development and Action Plan (NSSD1). The action plan describes more than 100 steps the government and private organizations can take to sustain the country's resources and ecosystems, develop a green economy, build sustainable communities, and respond to climate change. The NSSD1 and its action plan are guidelines and suggestions, not laws. They do, however, show that the government recognizes that action is required.

In the 1970s and 1980s, Zimbabwe adopted a number of laws designed to reduce air and water pollution, protect wildlife and other natural resources, regulate hazardous materials, and promote land management. Some of these laws have had positive results. Others, such as the Forest Act, which was designed to prevent deforestation, are largely ignored. **C**

In 2011 Angola's president, José Eduardo dos Santos, signed two presidential decrees. One decree is on water quality, and the other requires any person or company that damages the environment to pay for repairing the damage. It remains to be seen how effective these decrees will be in reducing damage to the natural environment.

INTERACTIVE IMAGE

Dumping Grounds

Analyzing Visuals Display the image for students. Tell them that the title of the photograph is Dumping Grounds. Ask them why the authors of the text may have chosen that title. Have students form small groups and challenge them to think of another title for the image. They should be able to provide one or more sound reasons for their choice of a new title. Have students share their titles and reasons behind the titles with the rest of the class. **BL** **Visual/Spatial, Interpersonal**

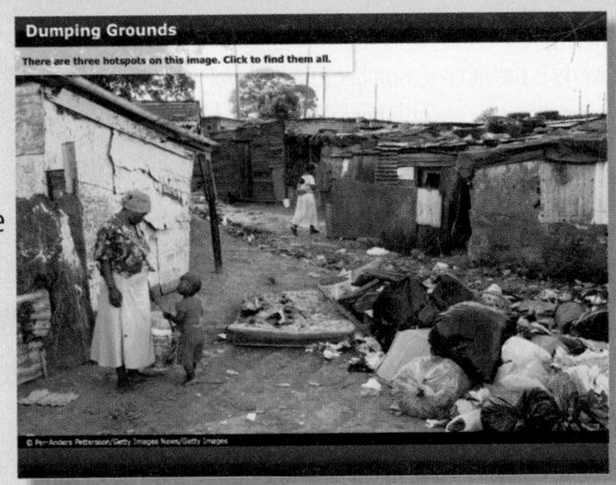

Dumping Grounds
There are three hotspots on this image. Click to find them all.
© Per-Anders Pettersson/Getty Images News/Getty Images

W Writing Skills

Argument Have students reread the information about how South Africa is one of only a handful of countries in the world to have environmental rights built into its constitution. Have small groups discuss whether this is a good idea and whether it should be necessary or desired for other countries to follow suit. Then have students write essays explaining their viewpoints, using facts and details to support their opinions. Allow students to use Internet and print resources to do further research if they wish. **BL** **Verbal/Linguistic**

C Critical Thinking Skills

Analyzing Have students review the measures Zimbabwe and Angola have taken to help their environments and save their resources. **Ask:** **In your opinion, how seriously is the Zimbabwe government treating the issue?** *(Possible answer: They are taking it seriously insofar as they are trying to protect their air and water. However, to truly secure their future, they must do better at enforcing laws against deforestation.)* Then **ask:** **In your opinion, how seriously is the Angolan government treating the issue?** *(Possible answer: It sounds like they are treating it seriously by passing laws to ensure water quality and to punish people and companies that break the law. However, the proof will be in how well they enforce these laws and whether they actually fine and punish lawbreakers.)* **AL** **Intrapersonal**

ANSWERS, p. 591

CRITICAL THINKING

1. No trash and waste removal seems to be practiced in the photo, which results in pollution and the spread of disease.
2. Possible answers: better infrastructure to set up services such as proper waste disposal and running water; education programs to help the people understand better methods of disposal

People and Their Environment: Southern Africa

V Visual Skills

Creating Diagrams To help students compare and contrast the NGOs, have students design and fill in a graphic organizer to record information about each organization, such as the Musokotwane Environment Resource Centre for South Africa, the Southern African Development Community, and the Nature Conservancy. Then have them point out similarities and differences between the aims of the organizations and the actual work and programs they support. AL **Visual/Spatial**

W Writing Skills

Informative/Explanatory Reread the description of how corruption in national and local governments can inhibit the attempts of NGOs to help people. Then have students write essays to describe the situation and propose solutions that help NGOs prevent corruption and provide people with the equipment, services, and resources they need. Invite students to share their essays with the class and discuss the value of each proposed solution. BL **Verbal/Linguistic**

CLOSE & REFLECT

Recognizing Relationships Discuss the environmental challenges facing Southern Africa. Have students write three statements describing conflicts between the different groups and then a paragraph explaining what needs to be done to help resolve the conflicts in order to guide Southern Africa to a brighter future.

ANSWERS, p. 592

☑ **READING PROGRESS CHECK** Musokotwane Environment Resource Centre for Southern Africa, the African Adaption Knowledge Network, the Nature Conservancy, and World Wildlife Fund are all NGOs working in Southern Africa.

Southern Africa has many NGOs that work on environmental issues in the region as a whole. One such group is the Musokotwane Environment Resource Centre for Southern Africa, which is based in Zimbabwe. Its aim is to "inform, motivate, and empower" decision-makers to take positive action on issues such as water resource management, sanitation, and climate change. In 2012 the United Nations Environment Program created the Africa Adaptation Knowledge Network to collect and distribute data for research, information, and strategies for adapting to climate change.

administer to manage; to supervise

V The South Africa–based Southern African Development Community **administers** many programs, such as the Regional Environmental Education Programme (SADC REEP), which develops environmental education materials for students and teachers from grade school to the college level. These materials are used in schools in Mauritius, South Africa, Botswana, Lesotho, Swaziland, and Zambia.

The Nature Conservancy, an international organization, has partnered in Southern Africa with a number of local and international organizations. For example, it has teamed with the Zambia Wildlife Authority to reverse the decline in wildlife populations in that country. It is also working with the World Wildlife Fund to protect coral reef ecosystems off Mozambique from climate change. The Conservancy has also partnered with Save the Rhino Trust Namibia to help save the black rhinoceros from extinction. These organizations and many more are working hard to protect Southern Africa's resources and improve the lives of the people who live there. They face two major obstacles.

As discussed above, one of these obstacles is the region's poverty; the other is corruption. In many Southern African countries, national and local governments are corrupt. Officials are more concerned with staying in power and enriching themselves and their friends than with improving conditions for their citizens and their country. Often, this means that help does not reach the people who need it.

W As an example, suppose an NGO donates 10,000 propane cookstoves and propane bottles so that people in a rural area can stop cutting firewood. Now imagine that various government officials refuse to distribute the stoves unless they get payoffs from the NGO. Then suppose that 8,000 of the stoves disappear from the warehouse and are sold by friends of a local official. The NGO has spent far more money than it planned, and only 2,000 families got stoves.

Increasingly, NGOs are trying to work directly with the people they want to help, bypassing corrupt officials whenever possible. In addition, new methods and equipment are being developed that will be within the capabilities of even the poorest of people.

☑ **READING PROGRESS CHECK**

Listing What NGOs are working to protect the environment of Southern Africa?

LESSON 3 REVIEW 

Reviewing Vocabulary (Tier Three Words)

1. ***Identifying*** Write a paragraph explaining the effects of shifting cultivation. RH.9–10.4

Using Your Notes

2. ***Summarizing*** Use your graphic organizer on managing Southern Africa's resources to write a paragraph summarizing the habitat destruction that has been taking place.

Answering the Guiding Questions

3. ***Summarizing*** Why are many resources in Southern Africa not managed closely?
4. ***Explaining*** How has environmental degradation affected life in the subregion?
5. ***Identifying*** What steps are being taken to combat the environmental challenges?

Writing Activity

6. ***Argument*** In a paragraph, discuss what you think needs to be done to preserve Southern Africa's resources. WHST.9–10.1

592

LESSON 3 REVIEW ANSWERS

Review Vocabulary

1. Paragraphs should be supported with information from the lesson including that shifting cultivation involves clearing land by cutting and burning of trees, which initially enriches the soil with ash. Once the land is no longer productive, it is left to regain its fertility, and new land is cleared. This results in deforestation. The growing population accelerates this process, which results in further soil erosion.

Using Your Notes

2. Paragraphs should be supported with information from the lesson including: deforestation; poaching due to high prices paid for ivory and tusks for Asian medicines: farming techniques that use land without replenishing the soil.

Answering the Guiding Questions

3. Poverty is the main reason because survival takes precedence over environmental concerns.
4. Deforestation and shifting cultivation are causing erosion and habitat destruction; water is contaminated and becoming limited by climate change; conflicts in the subregion are leading to high rates of urbanization, which overwhelms infrastructure and causes extreme pollution and widespread disease.
5. Many countries and organizations are working on programs to address water, sanitation, and climate change issues; NGOs are working with locals to preserve and reverse the decline of wildlife and marine life; South Africa's National Strategy for Sustainable Development and Action Plan aims to sustain resources and ecosystems, develop a green economy, build communities, and address climate change; Angola has made decrees on water quality and imposes fines for damage to the environment; Zimbabwe has laws that regulate hazardous materials and promote land management and some have had positive results but others are largely ignored.

Writing Activity

6. Paragraphs should include ending government corruption that stops aid and programs from being implemented; creation and enforcement of laws protecting habitats and wildlife; creation of reserves for wildlife and marine life, conservation for local people; better infrastructure to deal with waste and water issues.

CHAPTER 24 Assessment (CCSS)

Directions: On a separate sheet of paper, answer the questions below. Make sure you read carefully and answer all parts of the questions.

Lesson Review

Lesson 1

1. ***Describing*** Describe the location and physical features of the Great Escarpment in Southern Africa.
2. ***Hypothesizing*** Why do you think many of the most recognizable African mammals live on the savanna? Give examples of the mammals that live there.
3. ***Explaining*** Southern Africa has vast resources of mineral wealth. Why are these resources often a source of controversy?

Lesson 2

4. ***Making Connections*** How do Southern Africa's rivers help explain why the first sizable communities developed along the coast?
5. ***Hypothesizing*** Why do you think many Southern African countries experienced conflict after gaining independence from colonial rule?
6. ***Analyzing*** Why do people in many countries in Southern Africa continue to use the language of their colonizers?

Lesson 3

7. ***Discussing*** Discuss how global demand for animal products threatens some of Southern Africa's most notable species.
8. ***Identifying Cause and Effect*** How might the use of a scarce resource such as river water by one village affect other communities downstream?
9. ***Summarizing*** What are some factors that have fueled urbanization in Southern Africa?

Critical Thinking

10. ***Explaining*** Why does subsistence farming in Southern Africa contribute to the mismanagement of resources? Give examples.
11. ***Interpreting*** Discuss how the life of Cecil Rhodes provides a metaphor for European involvement in Africa.

21st Century Skills

Use the document to answer the following questions.

"Look, I'd rather be free, too, but at least we're not in a zoo anymore."

12. ***Identifying Central Issues*** What problem does the cartoon address? How do you know? RH.9–10.2
13. ***Hypothesizing*** Why do you think the gorillas are in an urban wildlife conservation park rather than their native habitat? RH.9–10.2
14. ***Interpreting*** What does the cartoon suggest about efforts to protect African animals? RH.9–10.2

Need Extra Help?

If You've Missed Question	1	2	3	4	5	6	7	8	9	10	11	12	13	14
Go to page	576	579	580	585	584	586	588	590	590	588	584	593	593	593

CHAPTER 24 Assessment Answers

Lesson Review

Lesson 1

1. The Great Escarpment forms a nearly unbroken U-shape of high steep cliffs behind the coastal plains from the west coast south to the Cape of Good Hope and northeast to the South Africa-Mozambique border. The Drakensberg Range is also part of the Great Escarpment.
2. The savanna has grasslands and small stands of trees and receives enough rainfall to support the life there, making it a good home for many mammals including lions, leopards, elephants, rhinoceroses, Cape buffalo, giraffes, zebra, and jackals.
3. Minerals are often a source of controversy because they are mined by foreign-owned companies that employ local workers at a very low wage to do the dangerous work. Most of the profits are then taken out of the countries they are mined in with no benefit to the local economies.

Lesson 2

4. Southern Africa has no navigable rivers, resulting in trade centers and communities developing along the coast.
5. Many Southern African countries experienced conflict after independence because white Europeans that had settled in these countries still held the power and government offices. They were able to make laws that continued to discriminate and suppress the black Africans, which resulted in many conflicts.
6. Many countries still use the language of their colonizers to easily communicate between multiple groups of people because hundreds of local languages are spoken.

Lesson 3

7. The poaching of elephants and rhinoceroses to sell their tusks and horns for ivory and use in Asian medicines threatens their existence.
8. When one community diverts water for irrigation and consumption, villages downstream receive less water. This results in increased poverty and sometimes violent conflict between peoples.
9. Urbanization has been fueled by rural people going to cities to find better jobs, opportunities, and housing because farming is no longer a viable option in some places due to climate change and exhausted farmland. Conflicts also cause people to leave the countryside for the relative safety of urban areas.

Critical Thinking

10. Subsistence farmers are poor with little education or access to health care, which makes them more concerned with survival than management of resources. Examples include poaching to increase income, which endangers wildlife, deforestation for firewood and farmland, shifting cultivation, which causes soil erosion and loss of habitats, and accessing groundwater with wells that contaminate groundwater.
11. Like the involvement of the Europeans in Africa, Rhodes felt that Africa should be used for its resources and that its people needed to become "civilized" and brought under control.

21st Century Skills

12. The problem being addressed is how to conserve wildlife in a manner that is effective with development expanding and encroaching in wildlife areas. You know this because of the backdrop of a city in the cartoon and the caption of gorillas speaking of preferring to be free.
13. Student answers may vary, but could include protection from poachers and hunters and increasing development and destruction of their native habitat.
14. The cartoon suggests that habitats are not being protected, but that animals are instead being removed and placed in parks.

College and Career Readiness

15 Reports will vary, but should include ways to address some of the following: slash-and-burn agriculture, soil erosion, and soil degradation.

DBQ Analyzing Primary Sources

16 Mandela insists that poverty is man-made as it can be overcome and eliminated by the actions of people.

17 Mandela uses the metaphor of prison to describe the effects of poverty because he wants to illustrate that people are trapped and unable to escape poverty by themselves.

18 Mandela makes the distinction because charity is something that is given while justice is a right that is deserved by all people.

Applying Map Skills

19 Angola, Zambia, Malawi, and Mozambique are the northernmost countries of the subregion.

20 Rural areas with no river access such as the south and west of the inland areas of Southern Africa would rely on wells. These areas might have increased health problems because well water can easily be contaminated, spreading disease.

21 The location of mineral resources has prompted settlements and cities to arise around their locations as the resources create jobs. Examples include: Johannesburg, Cape Town, Lusaka, Durban, Port Elizabeth, and Gaborone.

Exploring the Essential Question

22 Posters will vary based on the Southern African country chosen by the student. Posters should illustrate the history, politics, art, and economics of the country and can include photos, graphs, charts, and maps.

Research and Presentation

23 Summaries will vary, but must include the factors that led to the land reform program, the effectiveness of the program, and what challenges the country faces today. Possible answers can include this is a forced redistribution of farmland from white landowners to native peoples in an effort to reverse inequalities that began in colonial times. There have been great losses in agricultural production to the extent that Zimbabwe no longer exports food and must now import and rely on aid to meet food demands.

CHAPTER 24 Assessment

Directions: On a separate sheet of paper, answer the questions below. Make sure you read carefully and answer all parts of the questions.

College and Career Readiness

15 ***Problem Solving*** You are an environmentalist working for the Nature Conservancy in Madagascar. Use the Internet to research the causes and consequences of severe deforestation. Write a brief report exploring ways to address the problem. WHST.9–10.2; WHST. 9–10. 7

DBQ Analyzing Primary Sources

Use the document to answer the following questions.

Before becoming South Africa's first black president, Nelson Mandela struggled for decades to end apartheid in his country. In 2005 he delivered a speech in London comparing apartheid to poverty today.

PRIMARY SOURCE

"But in this new century, millions of people in the world's poorest countries remain imprisoned, enslaved, and in chains.

They are trapped in the prison of poverty. It is time to set them free.

Like Slavery and Apartheid, poverty is not natural. It is man-made and it can be overcome and eradicated by the actions of human beings.

And overcoming poverty is not a task of charity, it is an act of justice. It is the protection of a fundamental human right, the right to dignity and a decent life."

—Nelson Mandela, February 3, 2005

16 ***Identifying Perspectives*** Why does Mandela insist that poverty is man-made rather than natural? RH.9–10.6

17 ***Analyzing Arguments*** What metaphor does Mandela use to describe the effects of poverty on people? Why does he use this metaphor? RH.9–10.4

18 ***Identifying Perspectives*** Why do you think Mandela makes a distinction between charity and justice? RH.9–10.6

Applying Map Skills

Use the Unit 6 Atlas to answer the following questions.

19 ***Places and Regions*** Use your mental map of Southern Africa to name the northernmost countries in the subregion.

20 ***Environment and Society*** Identify areas in Southern Africa where people are most likely to rely on wells to access groundwater. Why might people in these areas have health problems?

21 ***Human Systems*** Describe how the location of mineral resources has affected the development of cities in Southern Africa. Give examples.

Exploring the Essential Question

22 ***Making Connections*** Choose one of the countries in Southern Africa. Use what you have learned about its history, politics, art, and economics to create a poster illustrating how human systems have shaped it as a place. Posters should be visual and can include photos, graphs, charts, and maps. WHST.9–10.7

Research and Presentation

23 ***Research Skills*** Research the legacy of colonial rule in Zimbabwe. What factors led President Robert Mugabe to institute a forced land reform program? How effective was the program? What challenges does the country face today? Write a multi-paragraph summary of your findings and present it to the class. WHST.9–10.7

Writing About Geography

24 ***Argument*** Using Botswana as an example, write an essay suggesting steps other African countries can take to create a healthy economy. What measures have the people of Botswana taken to strengthen the country's economy? How might other countries benefit from this example? Remember to use standard grammar, spelling, sentence structure, and punctuation in your response. WHST.9–10.1

Need Extra Help?

If You've Missed Question	15	16	17	18	19	20	21	22	23	24
Go to page	590	594	594	594	476	476	476	576	584	580

594

Writing About Geography

24 Essays will vary, but should be strongly supported with information from the chapter, including that Botswana formed a partnership with the diamond company DeBeers so that the country would benefit from the mining of diamonds. This has created one of the best and fastest-growing economies in Southern Africa. Other countries would benefit by using this example to allow only foreign companies that they are partnered with to extract minerals.

UNIT 7

SOUTH ASIA Planner

UNDERSTANDING BY DESIGN®

Enduring Understandings

- *The characteristics and distribution of human populations affect physical and human systems.*
- *Certain patterns, processes, and functions help determine where people settle.*
- *Places reflect the relationship between humans and the physical environment.*

Essential Question

- *How do physical systems and human systems shape a place?*

Students will know:

- *what landforms and water systems help shape life and support human activities in South Asia.*
- *how South Asia's modern economies and modern governments were formed.*
- *how monsoon winds affect the weather in different seasons in India.*
- *how topography affects settlement patterns and climate in Nepal and Bhutan.*
- *how a high population density affects life in India, Pakistan, and Bangladesh.*
- *that agriculture, farming, and fishing are key economic activities in many countries in the region.*
- *what efforts national governments of countries and regional organizations have taken to address environmental issues.*

Students will be able to:

- ***analyze** how landforms and waterways help shape and support life.*
- ***describe** how modern economies and governments were formed.*
- ***identify** factors that affect climate, economic, and population patterns.*
- ***explain** why high population density is affecting the environment.*
- ***identify** why agriculture and fishing are vital economic and natural resources.*

Predictable Misunderstandings

- *The physical geography of South Asia is consistent throughout the region.*
- *All of South Asia has the same warm climate.*
- *Maldives and Sri Lanka are isolated and do not have any environmental concerns.*
- *People in India are all Hindu.*
- *Sri Lanka is a territory of India.*
- *India only experiences pollution concerns in its large cities.*
- *Few crops are grown in this region because it lacks fertile soil.*
- *There are no resources in this region.*

Assessment Evidence

Performance Tasks:

- *Environmental Case Study*
- *GeoLab Activity*
- *GIS Simulation*
- *Hands-On Chapter Projects*

Other Evidence:

- *Location Activity*
- *Self-Check Quizzes*
- *Lesson Quizzes*
- *Participation in Interactive Whiteboard Activities*
- *Contribution to small-group activities*
- *Interpretation of slide show images*
- *Participation in class discussions about South Asia*
- *Analysis of graphic organizers, graphs, and charts*
- *Lesson Reviews*
- *Chapter Assessments*

Key for Using the Teacher Edition

SKILL-BASED ACTIVITIES

Types of skill activities found in the Teacher Edition.

* **V Visual Skills** require students to analyze maps, graphs, charts, and photos.

R Reading Skills help students practice reading skills and master vocabulary.

C Critical Thinking Skills help students apply and extend what they have learned.

W Writing Skills provide writing opportunities to help students comprehend the text.

T Technology Skills require students to use digital tools effectively.

*Letters are followed by a number when there is more than one of the same type of skill on the page.

DIFFERENTIATED INSTRUCTION

All activities are written for the on-level student unless otherwise marked with the leveled labels below.

BL Beyond Level
AL Approaching Level
ELL English Language Learners

All students benefit from activities that utilize different learning styles. Many activities are marked as below when a particular learning style is highlighted.

Intrapersonal	**Naturalist**
Logical/Mathematical	**Kinesthetic**
Visual/Spatial	**Auditory/Musical**
Verbal/Linguistic	**Interpersonal**

SUGGESTED PACING GUIDE

Introducing the Unit	1 Day
Chapter 25: India	4 Days
Case Study: What is the Future of Kashmir?	1 Day
Chapter 26: Pakistan and Bangladesh	4 Days
Global Connections: South Asia on the Brink	1 Day
Chapter 27: Bhutan, Maldives, Nepal, and Sri Lanka	4 Days
TOTAL TIME	**15 Days**

PLANNER

☑ Print Teaching Options

V Visual Skills

- ☐ **p. 596** Students analyze an image and then find out more about festivals in South Asia.
- ☐ **p. 598** Students calculate distances and determine elevations on a map. **Logical/Mathematical, Visual/Spatial, Interpersonal**
- ☐ **p. 602** Students identify similar cities in the region based on population density. **ELL Visual/Spatial**

R Reading Skills

- ☐ **p. 596** Students discuss the advantages and disadvantages of mountains to the region's development. **AL Verbal/Linguistic**
- ☐ **p. 597** Students discuss the relationship between weather patterns and agriculture. **AL Verbal/Linguistic**
- ☐ **p. 599** Students read a map to explain political map features and to compare locations. **ELL Visual/Spatial**

C Critical Thinking Skills

- ☐ **p. 597** Students sketch a regional map and discuss various spatial aspects. **Visual/Spatial, Logical/Mathematical**
- ☐ **p. 598** Students consider how the region's history, dominant religions, and cultures contribute to boundary lines disputes. **BL Verbal/Linguistic, Visual/Spatial**
- ☐ **p. 600** Students examine and answer questions about climate zones. **ELL Kinesthetic, Visual/Spatial**
- ☐ **p. 601** Students reason about which resources contribute the most to the economy of the region. **Logical/Mathematical, Verbal/Linguistic**

W Writing Skills

- ☐ **p. 597** Students write a narrative as if they are climbing Mount Everest. **BL Verbal/Linguistic**
- ☐ **p. 599** Students write about the government and political tensions of a country. **BL Verbal/Linguistic**
- ☐ **p. 601** Students write about whether the region should promote subsistence over commercial farming. **BL Intrapersonal**

T Technology Skills

- ☐ **p. 596** Students create a time line showing the development of Hinduism, Buddhism, and Islam in the region. **BL Logical/Mathematical**
- ☐ **p. 601** Students create a presentation on resources and land use in South Asia. **Logical/Mathematical, Visual/Spatial**
- ☐ **p. 602** Student make predictions about population projections of major cities in the next 25 and 50 years. **Interpersonal, Visual/Spatial**

☑ Online Teaching Options

V Visual Skills

- INTERACTIVE MAP **Population Density Map: South Asia**—Students develop a cause-and-effect chart about population patterns. **Verbal/Linguistic, Logical/Mathematical**

R Reading Skills

- GEO @ WORK **Thinking Like a Geographer**—Students explore principles and skills of geography applied to real-world challenges.
- INTERACTIVE MAP **Political Map: South Asia**—Students identify factors that might have led to the location of major cities. **Visual/Spatial, Verbal/Linguistic**

C Critical Thinking Skills

- INTERACTIVE MAP **Climate and Vegetation Maps: South Asia**—Students use a climate map to speculate about human activities. **Interpersonal, Visual/Spatial**
- INTERACTIVE FEATURE **Explore the Region: South Asia**—Students compare the physical and human geography aspects of South Asia. **AL Verbal/Linguistic**

T Technology Skills

- INTERACTIVE MAP **Physical Map: South Asia**—Students research a mountain and report their findings to the class. **BL Visual/Spatial, Logical/Mathematical**
- INTERACTIVE MAP **Economic Activity Map: South Asia**—Students research and write a report about the financial status of various locations within the region. **BL Visual/Spatial, Verbal/Linguistic**

☑ Printable Digital Worksheets

V Visual Skills

- WORKSHEET **Location Activity**—Students locate countries, water systems, and physical features of South Asia.
- WORKSHEET **GeoLab Activity**—Students use a model to understand what happens when a nuclear reaction takes place.

C Critical Thinking Skills

- WORKSHEET **Environmental Case Study**—Students complete a study about India's Ganges River and its pollution concerns, and then debate whether they are for or against building dams on the Ganges River.

T Technology Skills

- WORKSHEET **GIS Simulation**—Students use GIS to identify and evaluate the severity of certain health risks present in various areas of India.

South Asia

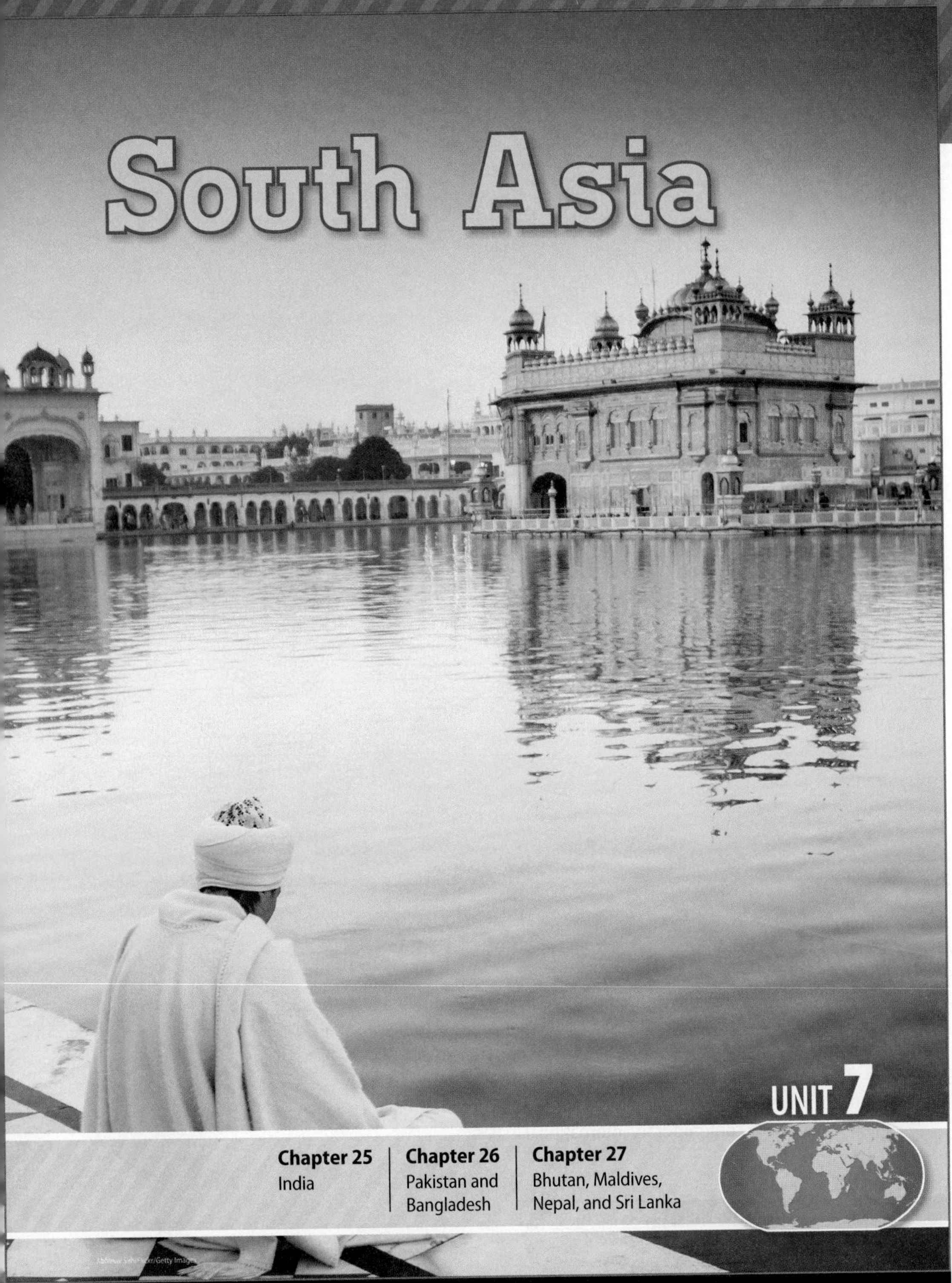

UNIT 7

Chapter 25	Chapter 26	Chapter 27
India	Pakistan and Bangladesh	Bhutan, Maldives, Nepal, and Sri Lanka

GEO @ WORK

Thinking Like a Geographer

Problem Solving Explore specific examples of the principles and skills of geography applied to real-world challenges that impact people's lives. From agriculture to urban planning, to wiping out disease and managing changes in society—geography plays a key role in understanding relationships and generating solutions that make sense.

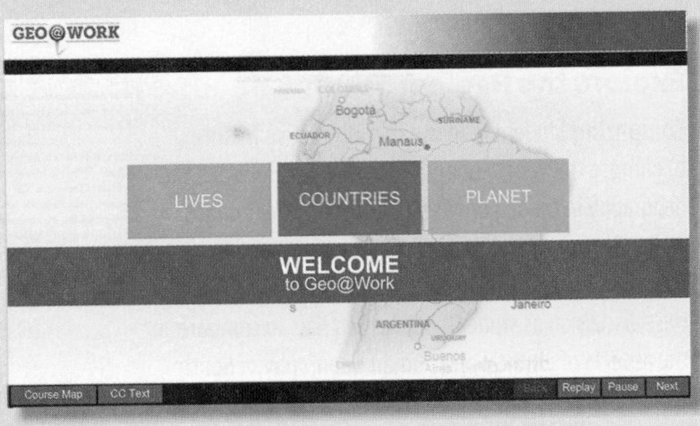

ENGAGE

Assessing Before calling students' attention to the list of chapter titles at the bottom of the page, challenge students to name the countries of South Asia—India, Pakistan, Bangladesh, Bhutan, Maldives, Nepal, and Sri Lanka. Invite a student volunteer to locate each country on a globe or map and share one fact about its physical or human geography. Assess students' knowledge about South Asia by asking them to list facts and details about each country, including its history. Ask students to share what they know about British and European colonialism in this region and its effect on the social, cultural, and economic development of the individual countries.

TEACH & ASSESS

Expressing Have students study the photograph and determine whether the image expresses the cultural heritage of the region. Ask students to look at the architecture and clothing style. **Ask:** **Do the details in the photograph express European or South Asian influence? Explain.** *(Possible answer: The architecture of the buildings appears to be a blend of European and South Asian influence. The man is wearing traditional clothing of the region. The clothing may be connected to his religious beliefs. The bridge appears to have a European style.)* **Where do you think this image was taken, India or Bhutan? Why?** *(India; India was colonized by Britain, but Britain never colonized Bhutan.)* Tell students that this image shows a man praying at the Harmandir Sahib Temple in Amritsar, India. It is the holiest of temples in Sikhism. Ask them to find out more about Sikhism and its history in the region. BL **Visual/Spatial**

Content Background Knowledge

The Former Golden Temple of Amritsar

- Once known as the Golden Temple, Harmandir Sahib is located in Amritsar, Punjab. It was given its new name in 2005. It was built in the late 1500s.
- Sikhs from around the globe make pilgrimages to the temple.
- About 220 pounds (100 kg) of gold was added to the dome in the early 1800s.

CLOSE & REFLECT

Summarizing Have students write a summary that includes what they already know about South Asia's geography, culture, and history. Have them revisit their summaries at the end of the unit to revise them based on what they learned in the unit.

ENGAGE

V Visual Skills

Analyzing Visuals Invite students to guess what festival the children shown in this image are celebrating. Explain to students that the children are celebrating Holi, which takes place in March on the full moon day. One custom during this festival is that children spray colors on each other to celebrate. **Ask: What do you think Holi festival celebrates?** *(the arrival of spring)* **Why do you think bright colors are connected to the celebration?** *(Possible answers: because spring is a time of flowers in bloom)* **What does this image reveal about the Hindu culture of India?** *(Possible answers: They celebrate the natural world and change of seasons.)*

Ask students to work with a partner to find out more about Holi festival or about a similar festival that is celebrated by another cultural group within or outside South Asia.

TEACH & ASSESS

T Technology Skills

Presenting Discuss with students why they think Islam is a predominant religion in the region even though it did not begin here. Have students work in small groups to create a time line of Hinduism, Buddhism, and Islam in this region. Point out to students that they can create a digital chart to show the sequence of when each religion started in the region or when it spread to South Asia. Challenge students to incorporate maps in their presentations to show the inception and spread of each religion. Invite students to present their completed work to the class. **BL Logical/Mathematical**

R Reading Skills

Visualizing Have a student volunteer read the section called *Explore the Region.* **Ask: What mountains separate South Asia from other regions of Asia?** *(Himalaya, Hindu Kush, and Sulaiman Range)* Have students visualize these mountain chains and how they isolated South Asia from other civilizations in ancient times. **Ask: How do you think South Asia's culture would have developed without these mountain chains? Would its development have been different? Explain.** *(Possible answer: Yes, South Asia may have been more prone to invasions and may be more culturally and religiously diverse than it is today without these mountains.)* Instruct students to write a one-page extended response to the above question, stating whether they think the mountains were more advantageous or disadvantageous to the region's development.
AL Verbal/Linguistic

V

T

① **Religion** These children have been painted as part of a religious festival. Hinduism and Buddhism began in the region, which also has three of the four most populous Muslim countries in the world.

EXPLORE the REGION

R

Though seemingly isolated from the rest of Asia by mountains, **SOUTH ASIA** has long-practiced religious and cultural traditions that have influenced—and been shaped by—other parts of Asia. With roots in ancient civilizations, the region today is home to vibrant software and film industries, rising economic powers, and countries that play an important role in contemporary international issues.

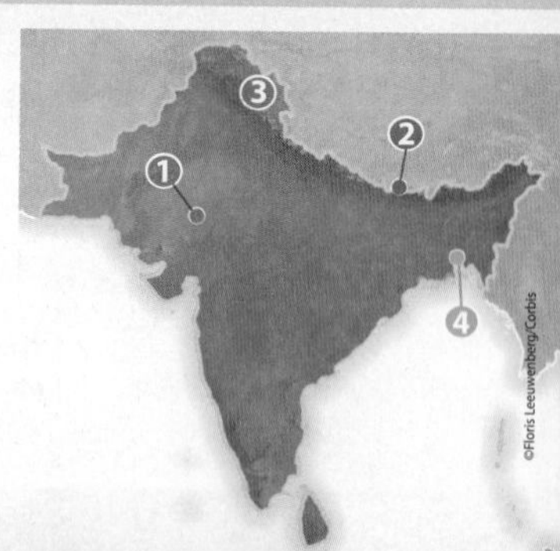

THERE'S MORE ONLINE

596

networks Online Teaching Options

INTERACTIVE FEATURE

Explore the Region: South Asia

Comparing Students can use this interactive feature to glimpse the variety of human and physical geography in the region. As students view the images and text, have them note any characteristics of the region that they can infer from them. Then guide a class discussion as students share their lists to compare the aspects of physical and human geography of South Asia. **AL Verbal/Linguistic**

South Asia

INTRODUCTION

Though seemingly isolated from the rest of Asia by mountains, South Asia has long-practiced religious and cultural traditions that have influenced—and been shaped by—other parts of Asia. With roots in ancient civilizations, the region today is home to vibrant software and film industries, rising economic powers, and countries that play an important role in contemporary international issues.

RELIGION MOUNTAINS RIVERS CLIMATE

3 Rivers Major rivers that drain the region—such as the Indus, Ganges, and Brahmaputra—flow from their source high in the Himalaya in the north to the floodplains in the south, carrying fertile soil used to grow food for the region's large population.

2 Mountains As the Indian subcontinent moves slowly and steadily into Asia, it pushes up the highest mountains in the world, the 1,500-mile- (2,414-km-) long Himalaya, which have individual peaks that reach more than 5 miles (8 km) high.

4 Climate Strong winds traveling across warm seas bring the wet season to South Asia, providing rain vitally needed by the region's farms but also causing flooding in low-lying areas.

(t)SDBWP Sundeep Bhardwaj World Photography 50+ Countries/Flickr/Getty Images, (bl)Pal Teravagimov Photography/Flickr/Getty Images, (br)Munir Uz Zaman/AFP/Getty Images

UNIT 7

South Asia

W Writing Skills

Narrative Explain to students that the highest peak in the world is Mount Everest in the Himalaya. Have students find firsthand accounts from people who have climbed Mount Everest to learn about their experiences. Then ask students to write a narrative about climbing Mount Everest, including the challenges, climate, natural beauty, and culture of the area. Have students describe the view from the top, the experience of traveling with Sherpas, and the risks taken on the ascent and descent. BL **Verbal/Linguistic**

C Critical Thinking Skills

Spatial Analysis Have students work with a partner to locate and sketch the three major rivers of the region—the Indus, Ganges, and Brahmaputra. Ask them to add the Himalaya to their sketches. Then discuss with students how these physical features combine to provide the region with the water it needs to support agriculture. Instruct partners to mark areas on their map that would be ideal for agriculture and settlement. Then have them compare their sketches to the unit maps that show land use and population density to check for accuracy. **Visual/Spatial, Logical/Mathematical**

R Reading Skills

Understanding Relationships After students have read the text about South Asia's climate, **ask:** **What is the relationship between the wet season in South Asia that brings strong winds and heavy rain and agriculture?** *(Possible answer: These rains can be detrimental to farm fields, but they also provide much needed water for crops. Without the crops, the people of South Asia would not be able to feed its population. But with the excess water, farmers risk losing their crops.)* AL **Verbal/Linguistic**

CLOSE & REFLECT

Reaching Conclusions Review the various factors that have influenced South Asian physical, human, and cultural geography. Ask students to consider all of these factors and write a concluding statement about how each factor contributed to the region's development.

DIGITAL WORKSHEETS

South Asia

Demonstrating Use these online digital unit worksheets to have students demonstrate their depth of knowledge and comprehension and to provide them with extended unit content through project-based activities.

- **Environmental Case Study**
- **GIS Simulation**
- **Location Activity**
- **GeoLab Activity**

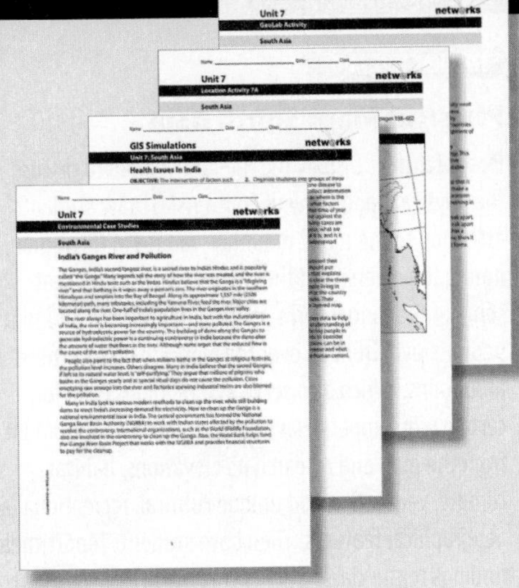

ENGAGE

R Reading Skills

Examining Ask students to describe South Asia's location and to identify the region's features and characteristics, such as its shape, bodies of water, and landforms. Ask students to describe what a subcontinent is and why it is unique to South Asia. Tell students that they will be learning more about South Asia's unique geography as they study the maps in this unit.

TEACH & ASSESS

V Visual Skills

Calculating Review the map key with students, including the elevation data and symbols. **Ask:** **In what subregion of South Asia does the elevation change dramatically?** *(northeast)* **By how much?** *(0–1,000 feet to 10,000 feet)* **What is a pass?** *(a low area in a mountain range)* **What is the elevation of Khyber Pass?** *(2,000–5,000 feet range)* **How do you think the location of the Khyber Pass affected the region's development?** *(It probably served as a gateway between South Asia and Southwest Asia and was an avenue for cultural interaction and trade.)* Have students work with a partner to ask each other questions about calculating distance and determining differences in elevation. **Logical/Mathematical, Visual/Spatial, Interpersonal**

C Critical Thinking Skills

Hypothesizing Have students study the disputed boundaries on the map. Ask students to consider how the region's history, religions, and cultures may have contributed to the existence of these boundaries. Make a list on the board of students' suggestions. Then have them think about how these boundary disputes might be resolved, such as through international intervention, regional cooperation, war, or other possibilities. Organize the class into small groups and have them investigate the historical background and prospects for these boundary disputes. Then ask groups to write an essay that outlines their findings and offers possible solutions. BL **Verbal/Linguistic, Visual/Spatial**

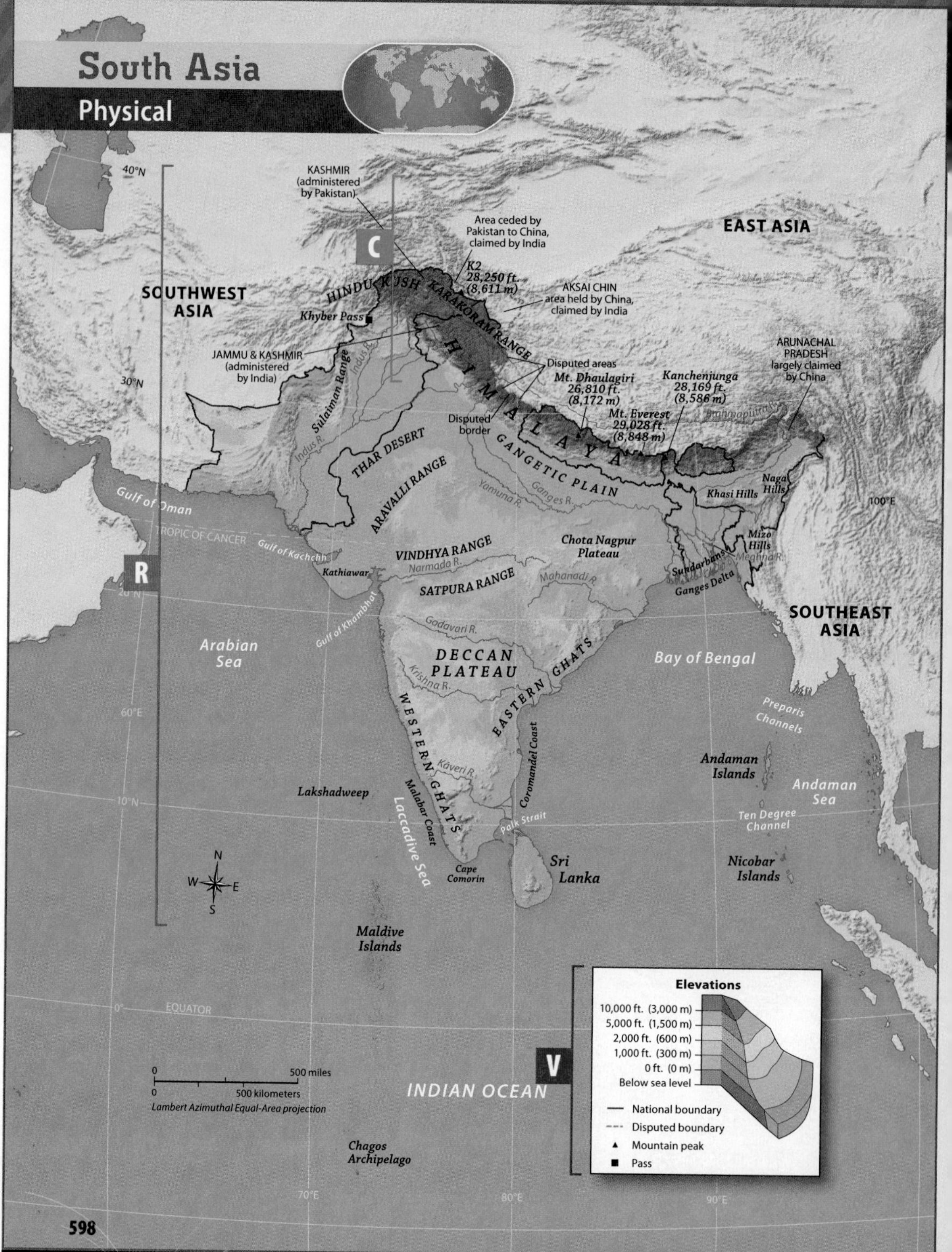

South Asia
Physical

KASHMIR (administered by Pakistan)
Area ceded by Pakistan to China, claimed by India
EAST ASIA
K2 28,250 ft. (8,611 m)
AKSAI CHIN area held by China, claimed by India
SOUTHWEST ASIA
HINDU KUSH
KARAKORAM RANGE
Khyber Pass
JAMMU & KASHMIR (administered by India)
HIMALAYA
Disputed areas
Mt. Dhaulagiri 26,810 ft. (8,172 m)
Kanchenjunga 28,169 ft. (8,586 m)
ARUNACHAL PRADESH largely claimed by China
Mt. Everest 29,028 ft. (8,848 m)
Sulaiman Range
Indus R.
Disputed border
THAR DESERT
ARAVALLI RANGE
GANGETIC PLAIN
Yamuna R.
Ganges R.
Brahmaputra R.
Khasi Hills
Naga Hills
Gulf of Oman
TROPIC OF CANCER
Gulf of Kachchh
Kathiawar
VINDHYA RANGE
Narmada R.
Chota Nagpur Plateau
Mizo Hills
Meghna R.
SATPURA RANGE
Mahanadi R.
Sundarbans
Ganges Delta
Gulf of Khambhat
Arabian Sea
Godavari R.
SOUTHEAST ASIA
DECCAN PLATEAU
Krishna R.
EASTERN GHATS
Bay of Bengal
WESTERN GHATS
Coromandel Coast
Preparis Channels
Kaveri R.
Andaman Islands
Andaman Sea
Lakshadweep
Malabar Coast
Laccadive Sea
Palk Strait
Ten Degree Channel
Cape Comorin
Sri Lanka
Nicobar Islands
Maldive Islands
EQUATOR
INDIAN OCEAN
Chagos Archipelago
40°N
30°N
20°N
10°N
0°
60°E
70°E
80°E
90°E
100°E

0 — 500 miles
0 — 500 kilometers
Lambert Azimuthal Equal-Area projection

Elevations
10,000 ft. (3,000 m)
5,000 ft. (1,500 m)
2,000 ft. (600 m)
1,000 ft. (300 m)
0 ft. (0 m)
Below sea level

National boundary
Disputed boundary
▲ Mountain peak
■ Pass

598

networks Online Teaching Options

INTERACTIVE MAP

Physical Map: South Asia

Researching Display the interactive map to discuss the physical geography of South Asia. Draw students' attention to the many mountain ranges in the region, noting the diversity of their significance. Note that some of the ranges form political boundaries and that people travel from all over the world to hike in these mountains, which also serve as a religious exile for certain worshippers. Have students select a mountain from the map and research its elevations, habitat, climate, vegetation and unique cultural, recreational and geographical features. Then have students report their findings to the class. BL **Visual/Spatial, Logical/Mathematical**

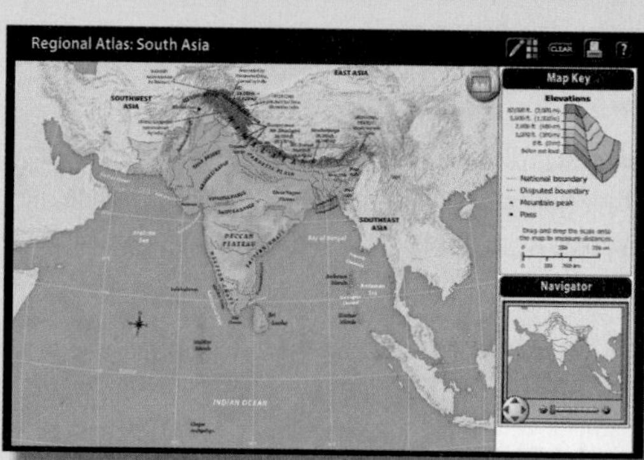

South Asia
Political

R

KASHMIR (administered by Pakistan)
Area ceded by Pakistan to China, claimed by India
AKSAI CHIN area held by China, claimed by India
JAMMU & KASHMIR (administered by India)
Disputed areas
ARUNACHAL PRADESH largely claimed by China
SOUTHWEST ASIA
EAST ASIA
SOUTHEAST ASIA
PAKISTAN
INDIA
NEPAL
BHUTAN
BANGLADESH
SRI LANKA
MALDIVES
Islamabad
Rawalpindi
Lahore
Karachi
Delhi
New Delhi
Jaipur
Kanpur
Lucknow
Kathmandu
Thimphu
Dhaka
Chittagong
Kolkata (Calcutta)
Ahmadabad
Mumbai (Bombay)
Pune
Hyderabad
Bengaluru (Bangalore)
Chennai (Madras)
Colombo
Male
Indus R.
Brahmaputra R.
Ganges R.
Yamuna R.
Meghna R.
Narmada R.
Mahanadi R.
Godavari R.
Krishna R.
Kaveri R.
Gulf of Oman
Gulf of Kachchh
Gulf of Khambhat
TROPIC OF CANCER
Arabian Sea
Bay of Bengal
Andaman Sea
Laccadive Sea
Palk Strait
Ten Degree Channel
Lakshadweep (India)
Andaman Islands (India)
Nicobar Islands (India)
INDIAN OCEAN
British Indian Ocean Territory (U.K.)
EQUATOR
40°N
30°N
20°N
10°N
0°
70°E
80°E
100°E

National capital
Major city
Disputed boundary

0 500 miles
0 500 kilometers
Lambert Azimuthal Equal-Area projection

W

C

UNIT 7
REGIONAL ATLAS

MAP STUDY

1. ***Physical Systems*** What physical features would isolate South Asia from other parts of Asia? What features would allow contact between this and other regions?
2. ***Human Systems*** Which South Asian countries are involved in disputes over borders in the region?

R Reading Skills

Reading Maps Have students explain the purpose of a political map to a partner using the key to help them. **Ask:**

- What is the capital of India? *(New Delhi)*
- Which city in Pakistan lies nearest to the Arabian Sea? *(Karachi)*
- Which two countries in the region have disputed boundaries? *(Pakistan and India)*
- Which countries in the region are landlocked? *(Nepal and Bhutan)*
- Which countries have capitals that are centrally located? *(Bangladesh and Nepal)*

Challenge students to make comparisons about the countries using the features of the political map. **ELL** Visual/Spatial

W Writing Skills

Informative/Explanatory Assign students a South Asian country to explore. Ask students to find out what type of government the country has and any recent online news articles about political tensions. Have students write about their findings in an informative paper and then present what they learned about their country to the class. Make a chart on the board that categorizes the information. Use the chart for a class discussion on the political systems and tensions in the region. **BL** Verbal/Linguistic

C Critical Thinking Skills

Comparing and Contrasting Ask students to use the map scale to compare and contrast geographic information on the map. **Ask:** About how many miles apart are Kathmandu and Islamabad? *(about 900 miles)* Which capital city is the closest to New Delhi, and about how far away is it? *(Islamabad; about 400 miles)* Are Colombo and Male closer together than the next closest capital is to New Delhi? How far apart are they? *(Male and Colombo are about the same distance from each other as New Delhi and Islamabad are; they are about 400 miles apart.)* Have students choose one city from each country in the region to find out what its population is. Then ask them to make a chart or graph to illustrate the data. **AL** Logical/Mathematical, Visual/Spatial

INTERACTIVE MAP

Political Map: South Asia

Summarizing Display this political map and have students locate and identify the capital cities of countries in South Asia, especially New Delhi, Kathmandu, and Dhaka. Organize students into small groups and assign each group a different capital city. Have groups identify factors that might have contributed to the location of their capital city, using online resources if needed. Have students report their findings to the class, and then lead a discussion that summarizes the effects of various factors on the establishment of cities and capitals. Visual/Spatial, Verbal/Linguistic

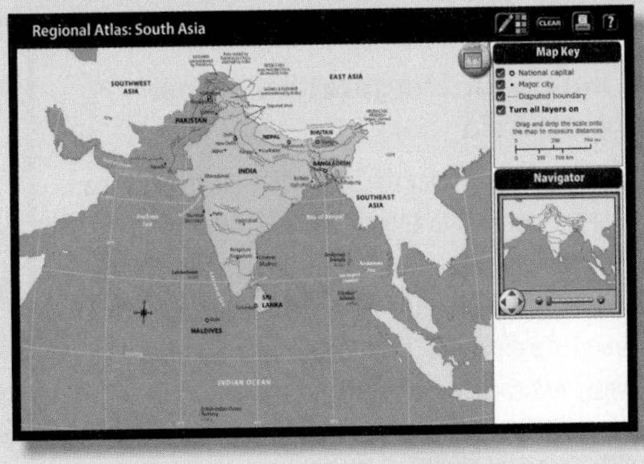

ANSWERS, p. 599

MAP STUDY

1. Mountains (the Himalaya) would isolate South Asia; water (oceans and rivers) would allow contact with other regions
2. India and Pakistan

C Critical Thinking Skills

Interpreting Have students examine the map key and use it to identify the major climate zones of South Asia. Assign different students specific climate regions. Then, call out names of cities and if that city lies within a particular climate zone, students should stand up if it is their assigned climate and identify the climate zone. Provide an opportunity to students to answer several questions to become familiar with what lies within their assigned climate region and the location of major cities on the map. **Ask:**

- **What is the climate zone of Kolkata?** *(tropical wet/dry)*
- **What is the climate zone of Ahmadabad?** *(semi-arid)*
- **Which city has a cooler climate zone, Islamabad or Dhaka?** *(Islamabad)*
- **What city lies in an arid climate zone?** *(Karachi)*
- **Which capital cities lie near the tundra zone?** *(Kathmandu and Thimphu)*

ELL Kinesthetic, Visual/Spatial

W Writing Skills

Narrative Have students describe the major vegetation zones in South Asia by writing a narrative in which they are traveling by train around the region. Explain to them that they should note the cities where the train stops and the vegetation that they see. Challenge students to include creative dialogue and detailed descriptions that will help them write an engaging story. Point out that they may use additional resources to gather information on the vegetation of the region. Invite students to share their narratives in small groups. **Naturalist, Verbal/Linguistic**

Content Background Knowledge

Cyclones Abound

Cyclones are the name that hurricanes have been given in the Southwest Indian Ocean. They have caused much destruction and damage to South Asia since the late twentieth century.

- In 1970, more than 1 million people lost their lives in East Pakistan when a cyclone hit. Ten thousand were killed the following year in Orissa, India.
- In 1977, 10,000 people died after a cyclone hit Andhra and Orissa, India, and West Bengal.
- In 1991, a cyclone hit Bangladesh, killing about 100,000 people.
- In May 2013, a cyclone hit Bangladesh and forced the evacuation of 1 million people.

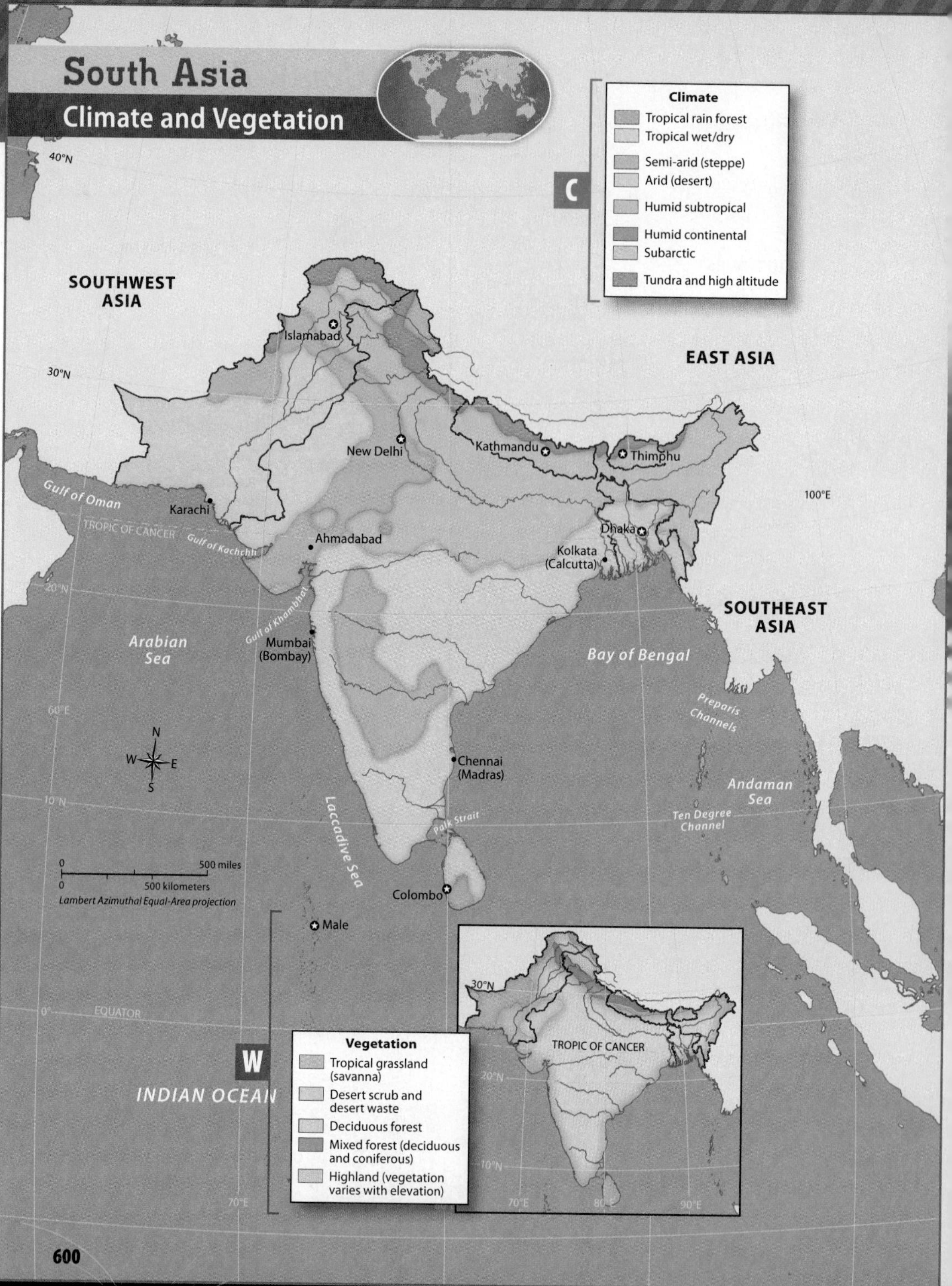

South Asia
Climate and Vegetation
Climate
Tropical rain forest
Tropical wet/dry
Semi-arid (steppe)
Arid (desert)
Humid subtropical
Humid continental
Subarctic
Tundra and high altitude
C
SOUTHWEST ASIA
EAST ASIA
SOUTHEAST ASIA
Islamabad
New Delhi
Kathmandu
Thimphu
Karachi
Ahmadabad
Dhaka
Kolkata (Calcutta)
Mumbai (Bombay)
Chennai (Madras)
Colombo
Male
Gulf of Oman
Gulf of Kachchh
Gulf of Khambhat
TROPIC OF CANCER
Arabian Sea
Bay of Bengal
Preparis Channels
Andaman Sea
Ten Degree Channel
Palk Strait
Laccadive Sea
INDIAN OCEAN
EQUATOR
40°N
30°N
20°N
10°N
0°
60°E
70°E
100°E
0 500 miles
0 500 kilometers
Lambert Azimuthal Equal-Area projection
W
Vegetation
Tropical grassland (savanna)
Desert scrub and desert waste
Deciduous forest
Mixed forest (deciduous and coniferous)
Highland (vegetation varies with elevation)
30°N
TROPIC OF CANCER
20°N
10°N
70°E
80°E
90°E
600

networks Online Teaching Options

INTERACTIVE MAP

Climate and Vegetation Maps: South Asia

Regional Atlas: South Asia
Map Key
Navigator

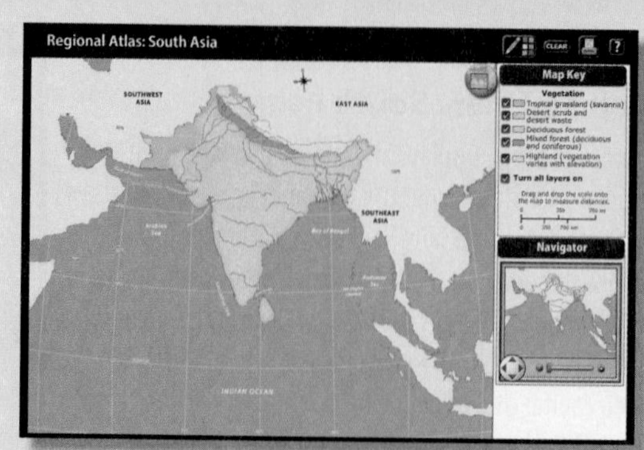

Speculating Display the interactive maps, allowing time for students to analyze and discuss the climate patterns and vegetation in the various regions. Organize students into four groups, assigning each group to a division of the region (north, south, east, west). Ask each group to use the map to speculate on the weather conditions, food, and outdoor activities of the people who live in each of the four divisions. Invite a volunteer from each group to share the group's ideas with the class. **Interpersonal, Visual/Spatial**

South Asia
Economic Activity

Resources
- Coal
- Petroleum
- Natural gas
- Iron ore
- Zinc
- Bauxite
- Uranium
- Copper
- Lead
- Manganese

0 — 500 miles
0 — 500 kilometers
Lambert Azimuthal Equal-Area projection

SOUTHWEST ASIA
EAST ASIA
SOUTHEAST ASIA
Gulf of Oman
TROPIC OF CANCER
Gulf of Kachchh
Gulf of Khambhat
Arabian Sea
Bay of Bengal
Andaman Sea
Ten Degree Channel
Palk Strait
Laccadive Sea
INDIAN OCEAN

Land Use
- Commercial farming
- Subsistence farming
- Nomadic herding
- Primarily forest
- Manufacturing and trade
- Commercial fishing
- Little or no activity

UNIT 7 REGIONAL ATLAS

MAP STUDY

1. ***Places and Regions*** What generalization can you make to describe the climate of this region?
2. ***Environment and Society*** How do the climate and vegetation maps help explain the presence of nomadic herding in the northwestern part of the region?

INTERACTIVE MAP

Economic Activity: South Asia

Informative Have students use this map to discuss the land use and resources of various areas within South Asia. After students review the map, guide a class discussion about how a country's land uses and resources affect its economy. Then assign each student to a country or location. Have students research its financial status to write a brief report about their findings. Invite several volunteers to share their reports with the class. **BL Visual/Spatial, Verbal/Linguistic**

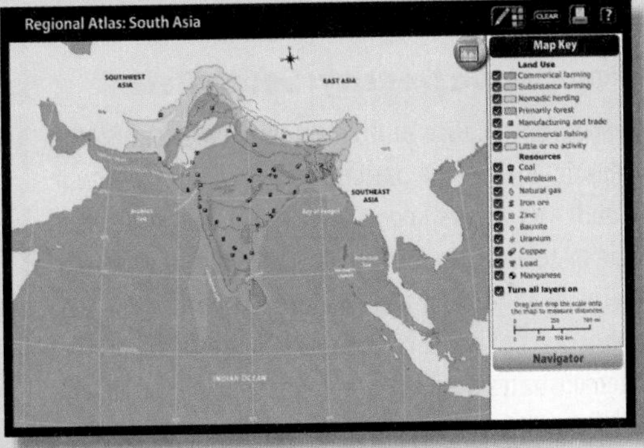

C Critical Thinking Skills

Evaluating Challenge students to identify uses of each resource. **Ask: Which resources are the most widely distributed?** *(iron ore, manganese, and bauxite)* **Which resources are *not* abundant with regard to distribution?** *(uranium, coal, and zinc)* Then lead a class discussion, asking students to explain which resources they think contribute the most to the economy of the region. Have them explain their reasoning using examples and supporting details. **Logical/Mathematical, Verbal/Linguistic**

T Technology Skills

Transferring Information Review with students the difference between subsistence and commercial farming, as well as nomadic herding. Challenge students to make connections between land use and climate. **Ask: How is most of the land used in the northeast?** *(subsistence farming)* **Where are manufacturing and trade primary activities?** *(throughout the region, primarily along or near rivers or the coast and near major cities and capitals)* **Why do you think commercial fishing is more substantial in some areas of the region versus others?** *(Possible answer: because there are more fish or better access to fish in these areas)* Have students work in pairs or small groups and use data from this map to create a digital presentation on the relationship between resources and land use in South Asia.
Logical/Mathematical, Visual/Spatial

W Writing Skills

Argument Have students take a stand on whether the region should promote more subsistence farming over commercial farming. Ask students to research the topic and find facts, details, and examples to support their point of view. Remind them that in writing their argumentative papers they should address counterarguments and clearly state their supporting reasons. Divide the class into two groups based on the viewpoints expressed in the papers. Provide an opportunity for students to hold a class debate. **BL Intrapersonal**

ANSWERS, p. 601

MAP STUDY

1. It has a varied climate, although most parts of the region are generally warm.
2. The northwest is arid grassland that can support nomadic herding but not long-term, fixed agriculture.

V Visual Skills

Naming Have students study the key that shows population density data. Then have them name two cities on the map with the same population density for as many population density ranges as possible. Challenge students to name more than two per range and to tell if the city's population is more than 5 million, between 2 million and 5 million, or between 1 million and 2 million. ELL **Visual/Spatial**

T Technology Skills

Making Predictions Discuss with students how South Asia has a very high population growth compared to other regions of the world. Have students work with a partner to create a graph that shows the population of the ten largest cities in South Asia, using this map as a reference. Ask students to predict which of these ten cities is projected to have the greatest growth in the next 25 years and 50 years. Then ask them to research population projections for these cities. Have them plot the data they compile on a graph, and then invite them to share their graphs with the class. **Interpersonal, Visual/Spatial**

Content Background Knowledge

Population Growth and Megacities Population growth in South Asia, notably India, is the highest in the world. About one-third of India's population lives in urban areas, but more people are migrating to cities because of economic opportunities. The average urban population around the globe is about 50 percent. Megacities, or cities with a population over 10 million, are expanding in this region. In 2010, there were 58 in the region. Projections for 2020 show that the number of South Asian megacities will climb to 73.

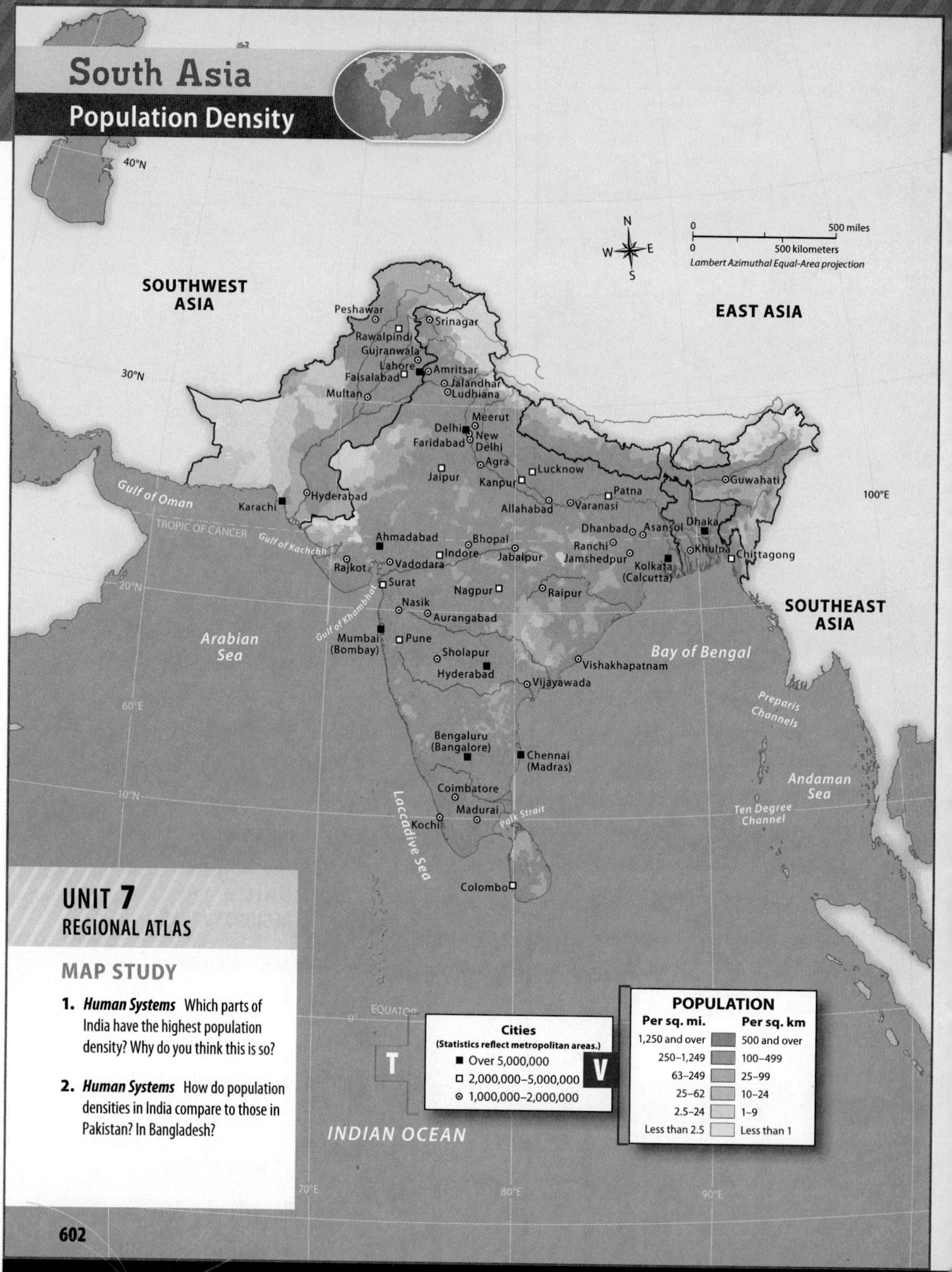

CLOSE & REFLECT

Listing Have students make a list of the topics and information covered in each of the maps. Ask them to choose three topics from the list and then write one question about each topic that they would like answered as they read the unit.

ANSWERS, p. 602

MAP STUDY

1. the northeast because of the Ganges River
2. Overall, India is more densely populated than Pakistan. And Bangladesh is more densely populated than India.

South Asia
Population Density

SOUTHWEST ASIA
EAST ASIA
SOUTHEAST ASIA
Arabian Sea
Bay of Bengal
INDIAN OCEAN
Gulf of Oman
Gulf of Kachchh
Gulf of Khambhat
Laccadive Sea
Palk Strait
Andaman Sea
Preparis Channels
Ten Degree Channel
TROPIC OF CANCER
EQUATOR
40°N
30°N
20°N
10°N
0°
60°E
70°E
80°E
90°E
100°E
0 500 miles
0 500 kilometers
Lambert Azimuthal Equal-Area projection

Peshawar, Srinagar, Rawalpindi, Gujranwala, Lahore, Amritsar, Faisalabad, Jalandhar, Multan, Ludhiana, Meerut, Delhi, New Delhi, Faridabad, Agra, Jaipur, Lucknow, Kanpur, Patna, Guwahati, Karachi, Hyderabad, Allahabad, Varanasi, Dhaka, Ahmadabad, Bhopal, Dhanbad, Asansol, Indore, Ranchi, Khulna, Chittagong, Rajkot, Vadodara, Jabalpur, Jamshedpur, Kolkata (Calcutta), Surat, Nagpur, Raipur, Nasik, Aurangabad, Mumbai (Bombay), Pune, Sholapur, Hyderabad, Vishakhapatnam, Vijayawada, Bengaluru (Bangalore), Chennai (Madras), Coimbatore, Madurai, Kochi, Colombo

Cities
(Statistics reflect metropolitan areas.)
■ Over 5,000,000
□ 2,000,000–5,000,000
⊙ 1,000,000–2,000,000

POPULATION	
Per sq. mi.	Per sq. km
1,250 and over	500 and over
250–1,249	100–499
63–249	25–99
25–62	10–24
2.5–24	1–9
Less than 2.5	Less than 1

UNIT 7
REGIONAL ATLAS

MAP STUDY

1. ***Human Systems*** Which parts of India have the highest population density? Why do you think this is so?
2. ***Human Systems*** How do population densities in India compare to those in Pakistan? In Bangladesh?

602

networks Online Teaching Options

INTERACTIVE MAP

Population Density: South Asia

Identifying Cause and Effect Students can use this map to analyze the patterns of population density in South Asia. Have students view the interactive layers of the map, and then work in pairs to discuss density patterns in South Asia and possible reasons for the patterns. Ask pairs to develop a cause-and-effect chart that demonstrates the influences for population settlement. **Verbal/Linguistic, Logical/Mathematical**

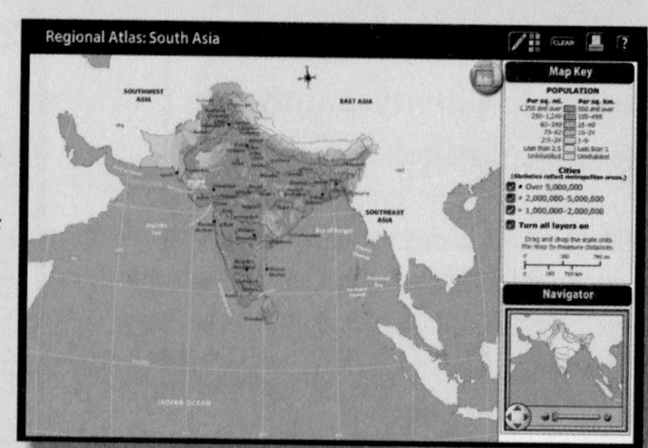

CHAPTER 25

India Planner

UNDERSTANDING BY DESIGN®

Enduring Understandings

- *The characteristics and distribution of human populations affect physical systems and human systems.*

Essential Question

- *How do physical systems and human systems shape a place?*

Predictable Misunderstandings

Students may think:

- *India's large size can accommodate its large population. Explain that even though most of India's population lives in rural areas with lower population density, the population is so large that there are over 50 cities with populations of 1 million or more, leading to many issues related to population.*
- *Indians are all part of the same ethnic group. Explain that India is ethnically diverse with over 1,000 languages being spoken in the country.*

Assessment Evidence

Performance Tasks:

- *Hands-On Chapter Project*

Other Evidence:

- *Guided Reading Activities*
- *Vocabulary Activities*
- *Lesson Quizzes*
- *Chapter Tests, Forms A and B*

SUGGESTED PACING GUIDE

Introducing the Chapter	½ Day	Case Study	1 Day
Lesson 1	1 Day	Lesson 3	1 Day
Lesson 2	1 Day	Chapter Wrap-Up and Assessment	½ Day

TOTAL TIME 5 Days

Key for Using the Teacher Edition

SKILL-BASED ACTIVITIES

Types of skill activities found in the Teacher Edition.

* **V Visual Skills** require students to analyze maps, graphs, charts, and photos.

R Reading Skills help students practice reading skills and master vocabulary.

C Critical Thinking Skills help students apply and extend what they have learned.

W Writing Skills provide writing opportunities to help students comprehend the text.

T Technology Skills require students to use digital tools effectively.

*Letters are followed by a number when there is more than one of the same type of skill on the page.

DIFFERENTIATED INSTRUCTION

All activities are written for the on-level student unless otherwise marked with the leveled labels below.

BL Beyond Level
AL Approaching Level
ELL English Language Learners

All students benefit from activities that utilize different learning styles. Many activities are marked as below when a particular learning style is highlighted.

Intrapersonal	Naturalist
Logical/Mathematical	Kinesthetic
Visual/Spatial	Auditory/Musical
Verbal/Linguistic	Interpersonal

National Geography Standards covered in "India"

The student knows and understands:

(5) That people create regions to interpret Earth's complexity

5.1 Regions are defined by different sets of criteria and places can be included in multiple regions of different types

(7) The physical processes that shape the patterns of Earth's surface

7.3 Physical processes interact over time to shape particular places on Earth's surface

(9) The characteristics, distribution, and migration of human populations on Earth's surface

9.1 Culture, economics, and politics influence the changing demographic structure of different populations

9.2 Population distribution and density are a function of historical, environmental, economic, political, and technological factors

(10) The characteristics, distribution, and complexity of Earth's cultural mosaics

10.3 Cultures changes through convergence and/or divergence

(11) The patterns and networks of economic interdependence on Earth's surface

11.2 Patterns exist in the spatial organization of economic activities

11.3 Economic systems are dynamic organizations of interdependent economic activities for production, exchange, distribution, and consumption of goods and services

11.4 Improvements in transportation and communication networks reduce the effects of distance and time on the movements of people, products, and ideas

(12) The process, patterns, and functions of human settlement

12.2 Settlements can grow and/or decline over time

(13) How the forces of cooperation and conflict among people influence the division and control of Earth's surface

13.3 Changes within, between and among countries regarding division and control of Earth's surface may result in conflict

(14) How human actions modify the physical environment

14.1 Human modifications of the physical environment can have significant global impacts

14.2 The use of technology can have both intended and unintended impacts on the physical environment which may be positive or negative

CHAPTER OPENER PLANNER

Students will know:
- *that an alluvial plain and the sea are vital to the people of India.*
- *how monsoon winds affect the weather in different seasons.*
- *how India gained its independence from British rule.*
- *how population pressures affect all aspects of life in India.*
- *how vital Indian agriculture is to the country and the world.*
- *what issues make resource management difficult and how environmental issues are being addressed.*

Students will be able to:
- ***examine** how people in India use the alluvial plain and the sea.*
- ***explain** how monsoon winds affect the weather.*
- ***describe** how India gained its independence.*
- ***analyze** how population pressures affect life in India.*
- ***describe** the importance of Indian agriculture.*
- ***analyze** the effects of environmental and resource management issues in India.*

UNDERSTANDING BY DESIGN®

☑ Print Teaching Options

V Visual Skills
- ☐ **p. 605** Students discuss age structure in India.

R Reading Skills
- ☐ **p. 604** Students explain the rate of growth in India's population and display the population data in a visual. ELL

C Critical Thinking Skills
- ☐ **p. 603** Students consider what factors have helped India's economy expand and how that growth has affected its culture.
- ☐ **p. 604** Students list challenges posed by India's population and how the government and people are addressing them.

W Writing Skills
- ☐ **p. 604** Students write about whether the government should do more about the population problem in India. AL

T Technology Skills
- ☐ **p. 605** Students research the labor forces of India and China and create graphs to display their findings. BL Visual/Spatial

☑ Online Teaching Options

C Critical Thinking Skills
- ☐ SLIDE SHOW **India's Growing Population**—Students write three predictions about what they will learn about India's growing population as they watch the slide show. AL Visual/Spatial, Verbal/Linguistic
- ☐ MAP **Interactive Regional Atlas**—Students use the interactive regional atlas to understand the physical and human geography of India.

☑ Printable Digital Worksheets

- ☐ WORKSHEET **Assessing Background Knowledge**—Determine the level of prior knowledge students have about India.
- ☐ WORKSHEET **Chapter Summary**—Students review the main idea of each lesson of the chapter content.
- ☐ WORKSHEET **Vocabulary Activity**—Students apply their knowledge of content and academic vocabulary words.

Project-Based Learning 

Hands-On

Writing a Graphic Novel
Students explore India's experiences with colonialism and its quest for independence. Then as a group, they create a graphic novel to bring together information about India's physical and human geography.

Digital Hands-On

Create Online Projects
Find an additional activity online that incorporates technology for this project. Visit the EdTech Teacher Web sites for more links, tutorials, and other resources.

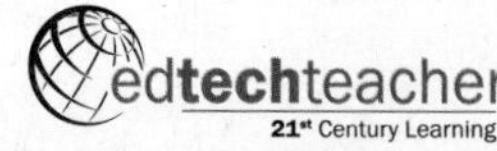

Print Resources

ANCILLARY RESOURCES
This ancillary is available for every chapter and lesson.
- **Chapter Tests and Lesson Quizzes**

PRINTABLE DIGITAL WORKSHEETS
These printable digital worksheets are available for every chapter and lesson.
- **Assessing Background Knowledge**
- **Chapter Summaries**
- **Guided Reading Activities**
- **Hands-On Chapter Projects**
- **Quizzes and Tests**
- **Reading Essentials and Study Guide** AL
- **Reteaching Activities**
- **Video Activities**
- **Vocabulary**

More Media Resources

SUGGESTED VIDEOS MOVIES
- **The Story of India** *PBS* (360 min.)
- **Mystic India: A Child's Incredible Journey of Inspiration** (45 min.)
- **Just the Facts: World History: India** (30 min.)

SUGGESTED READING 
- ***India: A Sacred Geography,*** by Diana L. Eck
- ***India Becoming: A Portrait of Life in Modern India,*** by Akash Kapur
- ***History of India: From Ancient Times to the 20th Century*** by William W. Hunter

LESSON 1 PLANNER

PHYSICAL GEOGRAPHY OF INDIA

Students will know:

- *that an alluvial plain is vital to the people of India.*
- *that the sea has important effects on life in this peninsular country.*
- *how monsoon winds affect the weather in different seasons.*

Students will be able to:

- ***examine** how people in India use the alluvial plain.*
- ***analyze** the effects of the sea on life in India.*
- ***explain** the effects monsoon winds have on the seasonal weather.*

UNDERSTANDING BY DESIGN®

☑ Print Teaching Options

V Visual Skills

- ☐ **p. 606** Students explain the difference between a continent and a subcontinent. ELL Kinesthetic, Visual/Spatial
- ☐ **p. 608** Students discuss the role of monsoons on India's climate. BL Logical/Mathematical, Visual/Spatial

R Reading Skills

- ☐ **p. 606** Students brainstorm what they already know about India's physical geography, its shape and location.
- ☐ **p. 607** Students sketch the water flowing from the sources of three major river systems and delivering fertile soil to the floodplains. ELL Visual/Spatial
- ☐ **p. 608** Students create a sequence of the monsoon seasons and outline when and how they affect the Indian subcontinent. ELL Kinesthetic, Musical/Auditory
- ☐ **p. 609** Students discuss cyclones, hurricanes, and tsunamis and identify which natural hazard each of a series of images shows. ELL Logical/Mathematical, Visual/Spatial

C Critical Thinking Skills

- ☐ **p. 606** Students discuss the differences between a plateau and a plain. BL Logical/Mathematical, Naturalist
- ☐ **p. 609** Students categorize the location, climate, and vegetation of different parts of India in a chart. AL Naturalist, Visual/Spatial

W Writing Skills

- ☐ **p. 609** Students write a personal narrative from the perspective of a farmer whose lands are dry and who is awaiting summer monsoon rains. BL Intrapersonal, Verbal/Linguistic
- ☐ **p. 610** Students write an essay on an animal common to India. AL Naturalist, Verbal/Linguistic

T Technology Skills

- ☐ **p. 607** Students research a river or body of water and its importance to India's economics and culture. AL Verbal/Linguistic, Visual/Spatial
- ☐ **p. 610** Students research which mineral resource and crop are the most valuable in terms of exports in India and respond to whether India should continue to invest in these resources. BL Verbal/Linguistic

☑ Online Teaching Options

V Visual Skills

- VIDEO **India Collides with Asia**—Students watch a video about the Himalaya and take notes on the theory of how the featured area of the mountain range has formed. AL Visual/Spatial, Verbal/Linguistic
- INTERACTIVE GRAPHIC ORGANIZER **Physical Geography of India**—Students complete the graphic organizer about how physical geography affects the daily lives of people in India. AL Visual/Spatial, Verbal/Linguistic, Interpersonal

R Reading Skills

- INTERACTIVE BELLRINGER **Brahmaputra River Valley, India**—Students use the text and photograph to understand that water has important effects on life in India. ELL AL Visual/Spatial, Verbal/Linguistic, Interpersonal
- INTERACTIVE WHITEBOARD ACTIVITY **Climates of India**—Students determine whether each climate activity is affected by summer or winter monsoons or mountain ranges. AL Verbal/Linguistic, Kinesthetic

☑ Printable Digital Worksheets

R Reading Skills

- WORKSHEET **Guided Reading Activity**—Students use the Guided Reading Activity worksheets to review their comprehension of the content.

C Critical Thinking Skills

- WORKSHEET **Video Activity**—Students answer questions related to a topic in the chapter content after they have viewed a lesson video.

LESSON 2 PLANNER

HUMAN GEOGRAPHY OF INDIA

Students will know:
- *how India gained its independence from British rule.*
- *how population pressures affect all aspects of life in India.*
- *what village life is like for hundreds of millions of Indian villagers.*
- *how vital Indian agriculture is to the country and the world.*

Students will be able to:
- ***describe** how India gained its independence.*
- ***identify** the effects of pollution in India.*
- ***describe** village life in India.*
- ***analyze** the importance of Indian agriculture to India and the world.*

UNDERSTANDING BY DESIGN®

☑ Print Teaching Options

V Visual Skills

- ☐ **p. 611** Students discuss how the Aryans invaded and culturally influenced India. AL Visual/Spatial
- ☐ **p. 613** Students describe how an image of an overloaded train expresses the population issues of India.

R Reading Skills

- ☐ **p. 612** Students discuss a primary source about Gandhi's salt march. AL Interpersonal, Verbal/Linguistic
- ☐ **p. 614** Students break the word *reincarnation* into parts and define each part. ELL Verbal/Linguistic
- ☐ **p. 617** Students review the three basic economic questions that countries ask and discuss how they pertain to India. AL Logical/Mathematical

C Critical Thinking Skills

- ☐ **p. 611** Students compare the example of Britain in India with that of another European country at this time that adopted an imperialist policy. BL Verbal/Linguistic
- ☐ **p. 614** Students compare and contrast life in rural versus urban areas in India. BL Logical/Mathematical
- ☐ **p. 616** Students create a chart with the headings *Economic Activity, Government Actions,* and *Challenges.* ELL

W Writing Skills

- ☐ **p. 612** Students write a newspaper article about Gandhi's actions, the momentum he gained for Indian independence, and biographical information. Verbal/Linguistic
- ☐ **p. 613** Students consider what it would be like to live in one of India's cities and write a narrative about daily life.
- ☐ **p. 615** Students discuss the roles of women over time and write an essay that states a position on the role and status of women in India. BL Verbal/Linguistic

T Technology Skills

- ☐ **p. 612** Students find primary sources that discuss the foreign relations between Indian leaders and the Soviet Union and the United States. BL Verbal/Linguistic
- ☐ **p. 614** Students research a minority religious group's issues and numbers in India over time and present their findings in a presentation or report. Interpersonal, Visual/Spatial

☑ Online Teaching Options

R Reading Skills

- INTERACTIVE BELLRINGER **Population Growth in India**—Students identify population growth and patterns in India between 1992 and 2003. ELL AL Verbal/Linguistic, Visual/Spatial, Interpersonal
- GAME **Human Geography of India**—Students play a game to better understand various groups of people who live in India. ELL Kinesthetic, Visual/Spatial
- INTERACTIVE WHITEBOARD ACTIVITY **Village and City Life**—Students will enhance the information they already have about the similarities and differences of village and city lives in India. ELL AL Visual/Spatial

C Critical Thinking Skills

- VIDEO **Visions of India—Days of Raj**—Students watch a video about the Days of Raj, think about the positive and negative influences the British had on India, and discuss the British raj and its lasting effects. BL Verbal/Linguistic
- TIME LINE **Women's Rights in India**—Students consider how four entries on the time line are related to each other. BL Verbal/Linguistic
- INFOGRAPHIC **All Aboard in India**—Students look at the amount of time it takes to move from one city to another by train and infer the physical size of the subcontinent based on this information. ELL Visual/Spatial, Logical/Mathematical

☑ Printable Digital Worksheets

R Reading Skills

- WORKSHEET **Guided Reading Activity**—Students use Guided Reading Activity worksheets to review their comprehension of the content.
- WORKSHEET **Reading Essentials and Study Guide**—Students complete the study guide and answer Reading Progress Check and vocabulary questions. AL

C Critical Thinking Skills

- WORKSHEET **Video Activity**—Students answer questions related to a topic in the chapter content after they have viewed a lesson video.

LESSON 3 PLANNER

PEOPLE AND THEIR ENVIRONMENT: INDIA

Students will know:
- *what difficulties are involved in the management of resources in India.*
- *the ways in which environmental issues affect life in the region.*
- *the steps that regional organizations are taking to address environmental issues.*

Students will be able to:
- ***identify** challenges in managing resources in India.*
- ***analyze** the effects of environmental issues in India.*
- ***identify** how environmental threats are being addressed by different groups.*

UNDERSTANDING BY DESIGN®

☑ Print Teaching Options

V Visual Skills

- ☐ **p. 621** Students use a graph to explain the difference between water and sanitation and then explore another way to show the data visually. ELL Visual/Spatial, Logical/Mathematical

R Reading Skills

- ☐ **p. 620** Students predict the impacts of India's population on the environment.
- ☐ **p. 622** Students discuss soil productivity. ELL Verbal/Linguistic
- ☐ **p. 624** Students read about the significance of the Forest Rights Act and stage a debate between the mining and timber companies and the people of the forests. BL Verbal/Linguistic

C Critical Thinking Skills

- ☐ **p. 622** Students discuss an image of a polluted river and what it indicates about the poverty level. Visual/Spatial
- ☐ **p. 623** Students discuss what the Indian government is doing to protect the environment. AL Verbal/Linguistic

W Writing Skills

- ☐ **p. 620** Students write an essay that addresses the advantages and disadvantages that colonialism brought to India's economy. Verbal/Linguistic
- ☐ **p. 621** Students research how states or areas in India are tackling the need for clean water and write a position paper that argues how one of the areas in India should be used as a model in the country's attempts to clean up the water supply. BL Verbal/Linguistic
- ☐ **p. 623** Students write an essay that explains the Bhopal environmental disaster. BL Verbal/Linguistic

T Technology Skills

- ☐ **p. 620** Students research progress made under the previous and current Five-Year Plan in India and produce a presentation to show the information. BL Visual/Spatial
- ☐ **p. 624** Students research the differences among national parks, wildlife sanctuaries, conservation reserves, and community reserves and find statistics on the change in populations of protected animals. AL Naturalist

☑ Online Teaching Options

V Visual Skills

- INTERACTIVE IMAGE **Pollution and Recycling**—Students find items in the photo they think are recyclable and write a story describing recyclable items the man in the photo has found and how he will use them for himself and his family. AL Verbal/Linguistic

R Reading Skills

- INTERACTIVE BELLRINGER **Water and Sanitation in India**—Students use the text and bar graphs showing sanitation statistics to identify ways in which environmental issues affect the population. BL Verbal/Linguistic, Logical/Mathematical, Interpersonal
- INTERACTIVE WHITEBOARD ACTIVITY **Pressures of Population Growth**—Students read human impact statements and choose the environmental effect that results from each impact. Kinesthetic, Logical/Mathematical
- GAME **People and Their Environment: India**—Students complete a crossword puzzle and consider how each term relates to the people and environment of India. ELL AL Verbal/Linguistic

☑ Printable Digital Worksheets

R Reading Skills

- WORKSHEET **Guided Reading Activity**—Students use Guided Reading Activity worksheets to review their comprehension of the content.
- WORKSHEET **Reading Essentials and Study Guide**—Students complete the study guide and answer Reading Progress Check and vocabulary questions. AL
- WORKSHEET **Vocabulary Activity**—Students review the chapter content and academic vocabulary words.
- WORKSHEET **Chapter Summary**—Students review the main ideas of the chapter content.

C Critical Thinking Skills

- WORKSHEET **Video Activity**—Students answer questions based on a lesson video.
- WORKSHEET **Reteaching Activity**—Students use this activity worksheet to review and reteach chapter content and vocabulary. This worksheet can be used with struggling students who need additional help with difficult content concepts.

INTERVENTION AND REMEDIATION STRATEGIES

LESSON 1 Physical Geography of India

Reading and Comprehension

Have students work with a partner to create an outline of the lesson that highlights key facts related to India's landforms, water systems, climate, biomes, and resources. To ensure comprehension of the topics, have partners create a slide show, using presentation software, that explains a topic or process. For example, students might explain the formation and significance of the Gangetic Plain. Students may wish to conduct additional research to enhance their presentations. After each group presents its slide show to the class, allow time for groups to conduct a question-and-answer session in which students from each group answer questions about their topic.

Text Evidence

Organize students into five groups and assign each group one of the lesson's content vocabulary terms. Have students in each group work together to create statements for a Jeopardy-style game show that relate to their assigned term. After students have had time to compile a list of statements, moderate a class game show by organizing groups into categories based on lesson headings. Then have students select a representative from their group to compete against other group members, using the group's statements as clues. Remind "contestants" to answer in the form of a question.

LESSON 2 Human Geography of India

Reading and Comprehension

Have students choose one of the lesson's content vocabulary words to describe silently to a partner using pantomime or by drawing on the board. Then have pairs play a guessing game in which one partner conveys clues to describe the chosen term for the other partner to guess. After students have guessed each other's terms, have them each write a sentence using both words correctly. Tell students their sentences should relate to India's history, government, culture, or economy.

Text Evidence

Have students review the graphic in the lesson that depicts India's railroad system. Tell students to imagine they are taking a tour of India and to map out their trip, including each of the destinations shown on the map. Have students describe their journey using information from the lesson to enhance their descriptions. For example, in writing about various segments of their trip, students should incorporate descriptions of village and city life they see along the way. Encourage students to use both textual and visual evidence from the lesson to support their descriptions.

LESSON 3 People and Their Environment: India

Reading and Comprehension

Have students work with a partner to take turns paraphrasing segments of the text. As students come across a confusing term or phrase, tell one partner to write it down and brainstorm its meaning based on context clues. Have the other partner look up the term in an online or print dictionary. For example, students may be confused by terms such as *sustainability, facilitated,* or *degradation.* After students have clarified the terms, have them go back and paraphrase the segment of the text.

Text Evidence

Tell students to create and complete a flowchart or diagram that conveys how India's population impacts its environment. In addition to identifying evidence from the text, students may conduct online research to find information that supports facts listed in their visuals. Have students take turns presenting their diagrams to the class, allowing students to brainstorm possible solutions as a class. Then guide a discussion about the viability and cost of students' proposed solutions.

Online Resources

Leveled Reader

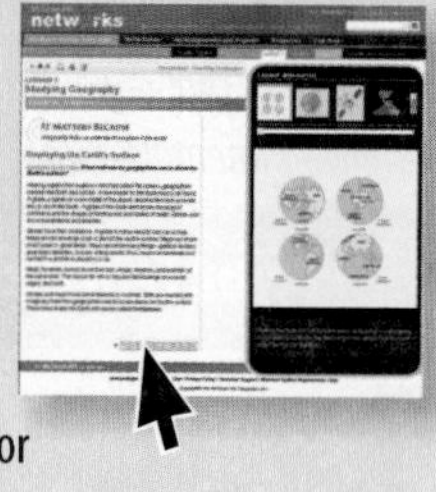

Use this online approaching-level text that corresponds directly to the text in the Student Edition. It also includes additional reading and comprehension support for English Language Learners.

Guided Reading Activities

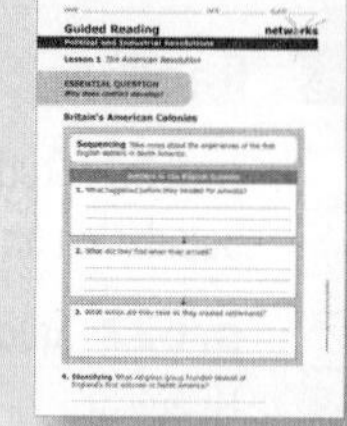

This resource uses guiding questions to help students with comprehension.

Reteaching Activities

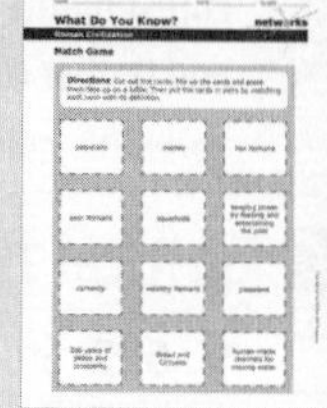

These worksheets provide students with an opportunity for remedial practice and review of vital chapter content.

Reading Essentials and Study Guide

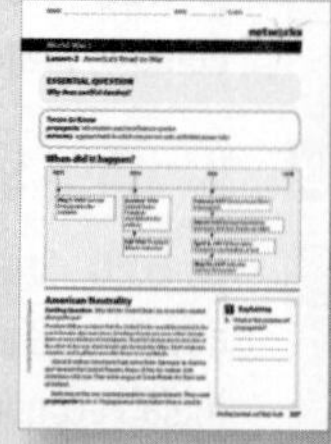

This resource offers writing and reading activities for the approaching-level student.

Self-Check Quizzes

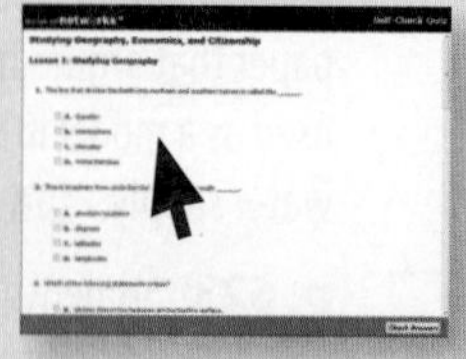

This online assessment tool provides instant feedback for students to check their progress.

Chapter Summaries

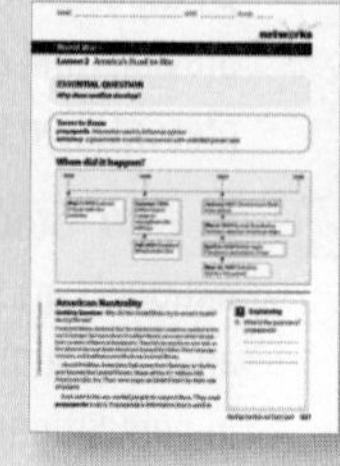

Summaries are provided for each chapter that thoroughly condense core content into manageable chunks.

India

ESSENTIAL QUESTION • *How do physical systems and human systems shape a place?*

networks

There's More Online about India's geography.

CHAPTER 25

Geography Matters...

India is an ethnically diverse country whose population practices a wide range of religions and speaks more than a dozen major languages. Laws have helped to lessen the injustice formerly faced by members of "untouchable" castes, ethnic minorities, and women. But many problems and tensions remain. Despite the challenges of great economic inequality, India's economic power is growing. It has one of the world's largest pools of trained scientists and engineers. India's films, literature, and music have attracted a global following. While some 70 percent of its people live in rural villages, India has three of the world's largest cities.

◀ This woman in Pushkar, India, is wearing traditional dress and jewelry.

603

Letter from the Author

Dear Geography Teacher,

The United States has a growing relationship with India. As a result, parts of American culture have spread to India, and characteristics of Indian culture are woven into American culture. To help students understand India's influence in American culture today, ask students to interview two adults for homework. Have them identify and record examples of evidence of Indian culture in the United States. Then have students list each example on a sticky note and attach it to a map of South Asia. The number of notes on the map will reveal the importance of India in students' lives today.

Richard G. Boehm

ENGAGE

Analyzing Visuals Guide a discussion about the human geography of India based on details from the image. **Ask:** **What details might imply that it is a woman from India?** *(Possible answers: her clothing and jewelry)* **Do you see any Western influences in this image or influences from any other region? Explain.** *(No, the woman appears to be dressed in traditional clothing.)* Discuss with students how rural versus urban life might affect traditions and customs.

TEACH & ASSESS

Analyzing Cause and Effect Have students consider what factors have helped India's economy expand and how that growth has affected its culture. **Ask:** **Why do you think India has the three largest cities in the world?** *(Many people have been moving to the cities from rural areas for jobs and education.)* **Why is India's population still concentrated largely in rural areas? Is it possible that the population distribution will change in the next decade or more?** *(Possible answer: India's population is mostly rural, but the population distribution is shifting because of the country's economy and job growth.)* BL **Logical/Mathematical**

Content Background Knowledge

Untouchables The unofficial fifth caste that was established in India centuries ago is no longer called the *Untouchables*. The caste still exists, but today in India, people refer to the group as *Dalit*. The word means "broken people" and constitutes about one-sixth of India's population. Even though the Indian Constitution outlaws social injustice and inequality, it is enforced only some of the time. Many *Dalits* are discriminated against and continue to perform menial and even degrading tasks.

CLOSE & REFLECT

Speculating Have students speculate about ways that India's diversity contributes to its economic strength. Discuss how India's physical and human geography might be impacted by the country's growing economy.

Extend the project-based learning experience globally through our partnership with ePals. EPals allows you to connect with classrooms around the world in a safe online environment for real-life lessons and projects in virtual study groups.

ENGAGE

C Critical Thinking Skills

Problem Solving Ask students to read the title of this feature and examine each photograph. Have them make a list of the challenges posed by India's population. Then discuss how the government and people of India are addressing the challenges. Have students identify what they think is the best possible solution to India's overpopulation issue and invite them to share the reasons for their choice.

TEACH & ASSESS

R Reading Skills

Explaining Have students read the information in the text about India's population growth rate. Ask volunteers to explain the rate of growth, including the age groups that have swelled the most. Encourage students to display the population data in a visual format. **Ask:** **What age groups have increased greatly?** *(the two youngest age groups)* **How does India's growth rate compare to that of the rest of the world?** *(It is higher than the global growth rate.)* **What has been the trend of India's population growth rate in the last decade, and how does that trend compare to the global trend?** *(It has decreased in India, but it is still higher than the world's average growth rate.)* **ELL Logical/Mathematical**

W Writing Skills

Argument Have students examine the image and read the text about how India is responding to its population problem. Have students consider whether India's government is doing enough to curtail the growth rate. Students should write two or three paragraphs stating whether they think the government should do more. If they think the government should do more, they should state what. Likewise, if they think the government need do nothing more, students should state their reasonings. **AL Interpersonal, Verbal/Linguistic**

ANSWERS, p. 604

Why Geography Matters

1. The high population growth rate makes India have a large young population.
2. The young, growing population could increase India's economy.
3. Various state governments in India are trying to control population growth by distributing birth control, providing information about birth control methods, offering payments to people who wait to have children, and barring people that have too many children from running for public office.

Why Geography Matters: **India**

India's population structure

In the third decade of this millennium, India may become the world's most populous country. China is in the lead, but its policies to limit population growth are rigorous, and the population growth rate has declined. India's population growth rate also has fallen. But the population is still large and, unlike China, young. Together, these two countries contain nearly 40 percent of the world's population.

What are the main characteristics of India's population?

India's population growth rate is higher than the world average. In 2012 the number of male children age 4 or under was about 64 million. This age group alone grew by about 8 percent between 1992 and 2012. India's two youngest age groups dominate. Males and females ages 10–24 make up as much as one-third of the country's population.

Over the past decade, India's growth rate has declined. But in 2012 the growth rate was 1.5 percent, which leads to population increase. This rate still exceeds the world's average annual growth rate of 1.2 percent in 2011. Fertility rates also have dropped. Still, the U.S. Census Bureau predicts that by 2025 India will outrank China as the world's most populous country.

1. **Human Systems** Why does India have such a large young population?

What are the consequences of this population structure?

The structure and size of India's population produces multiple effects. The population will continue to grow as the large number of young people start families of their own. Additionally, a large population in a poor country leads to poverty. About one-third of the total population lives in poverty. Social services, health care, and education are difficult to provide to a population of this size. With such a young population, India's workforce has expanded, but so too has its need to provide jobs.

At the same time, India faces what some experts think may be a positive effect of its large and growing population. They think a young and growing workforce could fuel India's economy. Much of the young population yearns for educational opportunities and training. However, the country faces a monumental task in providing education and social services as an investment for the future.

2. **Places and Regions** How might its young, growing population benefit India's future?

How is India responding to its population situation?

To reduce population growth, India's national government has launched an initiative to distribute contraceptives. India's National Family Planning Program has trained service providers to introduce other birth control methods. However, action at the national level may not be enough.

Some Indian states are responding to India's population challenges. They have issued incentives to control the birthrate and offered payments for people who delay having children. In some states, people who have many children are barred from running for political office. However, not all states are implementing programs to slow population growth. This uneven response could thwart efforts to achieve national goals.

3. **Human Systems** How are governments in India important in controlling population growth?

Project-Based Learning

Hands-On

Writing a Graphic Novel

Students will explore India's experiences with colonialism and its quest for independence. Working with a group, they will create a graphic novel that will bring together information from all lessons about physical and human geography in India. Groups will use the chapter lessons along with library or online research to gather information for their graphic novels.

Digital Hands-On

Create Online Projects

Find an additional activity online that incorporates technology for this project. Visit the EdTech Teacher Web site for more links, tutorials, and other resources.

THERE'S MORE ONLINE

EXPLORE a graph of population structure in India's largest cities • *COMPARE* India and U.S. population structure

1 person is born per second (approx.)

Average household size is 5 PEOPLE

Age Structure

MALE FEMALE

Median Age: 26.5 years

0-14 years: 28.9%
15-24 years: 18.2%
25-54 years: 40.4%
55-64 years: 6.9%
65 years and over: 5.7%

V

India total population: 1,220,800,359

Second Highest Population In The World (China Is Higher, U.S. Is Third)

Population Growth 1.3%
89TH IN THE WORLD

Urban Population 30%

Largest Cities
Delhi 20.4 Million
Mumbai 20.5 Million
Chennai 5 Million

Labor Force 498.4 million

53% agriculture
28% services
19% industry
2nd largest in the world

T

Unemployment Rate 9.90%

Population below the poverty line 29.8%

CHAPTER 25

Why Geography Matters

V Visual Skills

Creating Graphs Have students locate the data on age structure in the infographic. **Ask: At a glance, what generalizations can you make about the age structure of India's population?** *(The bulk of the population is 25–54 years of age, but a substantial part is in the 0–14-year range. The median age is young.)* Have students create a circle graph that illustrates this information. Point out that students may draw a graph on paper or use software to create it digitally.
AL Visual/Spatial

T Technology Skills

Gathering Information Review with students the part of the infographic on the labor force of India. **Ask: What inference can you make about which country has the largest labor force in the world?** *(China most likely has the largest labor force because it has the largest population in the world.)* **How is a country's population and the size of its labor force related?** *(The countries with the highest population generally have large labor forces.)* Have students research online or in other library resources the number of people in India and in China employed in agriculture, services, and industry. Have them create a set of graphs showing each country's labor force as well as a comparison chart or graph. **BL Visual/Spatial Interpersonal**

CLOSE & REFLECT

Researching Review with students how the local and national governments of India are working to resolve challenges posed by its growing population. Ask students to work in groups to research one area of India that has successfully lowered its population growth rate. Invite them to share the solution with the class and discuss whether this solution could work in other areas of India.

SLIDE SHOW

India's Growing Population

Predicting Have students view the slide show. As they watch, have students write three predictions about what they will learn in this chapter regarding India's increasing population. When the slide show is finished, have students share their predictions with a partner. At the end of the chapter, ask students to revisit their predictions to see how close their predictions matched the material presented.
AL Visual/Spatial, Verbal/Linguistic

Physical Geography of India

ENGAGE

R Reading Skills

Activating Prior Knowledge Have students brainstorm what they already know about India's physical geography, its shape, and its location. Show students the unit physical map of the region and invite volunteers to describe different landforms and bodies of water.

TEACH & ASSESS

V Visual Skills

Demonstrating After students have read about the formation of the Indian subcontinent, invite a volunteer to explain the difference between a continent and subcontinent. **Ask: Do you think the hypothesis that geologists made about how the Indian subcontinent formed is feasible? Why?** *(Possible answer: Yes, it seems feasible because it looks as if the subcontinent could have broken off from Africa and collided into Asia.)* Organize the class into small groups and ask them to model how geologists think the subcontinent and the Himalaya formed. Challenge students to be creative. Point out that they may use available resources to demonstrate the process, including digital resources. Provide an opportunity for students to show the class their demonstrations. **ELL Kinesthetic, Visual/Spatial**

C Critical Thinking Skills

Considering Advantages and Disadvantages After students read the last two paragraphs, discuss the differences between a plateau and a plain. **Ask: What are the advantages of living on a plain versus a plateau?** *(A plain is flatter and probably more fertile versus a plateau, which rises from a flat surface.)* **Which area in India do you think poses more of a challenge to live in, the Gangetic Plain or the Deccan Plateau? Why?** *(Possible answer: The Gangetic Plain has rich soil from floodwaters, but it would be challenging to deal with floods. The plateau has rich soil as well, so it may be easier to live there.)* **BL Logical/Mathematical, Naturalist**

ANSWERS, p. 606

TAKING NOTES: Factor: Shape; proximity to Equator; Indian Ocean **Influence on Climate:** Landforms affect amount of rainfall monsoon winds bring to different areas; mostly tropical climates; differences in air temperature over the Indian Ocean and the Asian landmass creates monsoon winds

networks

There's More Online!

- **IMAGE** Forest in Goa
- **IMAGE** Pilgrims at the Ganges
- **MAP** South Asia: Monsoons
- **INTERACTIVE SELF-CHECK QUIZ**
- **VIDEO** Physical Geography of India

LESSON 1
Physical Geography of India

ESSENTIAL QUESTION • *How do physical systems and human systems shape a place?*

Reading HELPDESK 

Academic Vocabulary (Tier Two Words)
- **fluctuate**
- **annual**

Content Vocabulary (Tier Three Words)
- **subcontinent**
- **alluvial plain**
- **monsoon**
- **cyclone**
- **tsunami**

TAKING NOTES: ***Key Ideas and Details***

LISTING As you read about the physical geography of India, use a graphic organizer like the one below to list factors that influence the climate of India.

Factors	Influence on Climate

IT MATTERS BECAUSE

Rugged mountains have isolated parts of India, while its rivers and monsoon winds have brought both benefits and catastrophic floods. Its huge population depends on the land, water, and other resources of India to meet its growing needs.

Landforms

GUIDING QUESTION *Why is the Gangetic Plain important?*

India's shape and position is the result of the movement of the Earth's tectonic plates. About 160 million years ago, geologists think that a large piece of land broke away from the landmass that is now Africa. This landmass collided with the southern edge of Asia about 50 million years ago. Over time, the force of this collision thrust up the world's highest mountains, the Himalaya. This mountain range stretches about 1,500 miles (2,414 km) from west to east and includes Mount Everest, Kanchenjunga, and over 100 other peaks that are more than 24,000 feet (7,300 m) above sea level. The Himalaya meet the Karakoram Range in northwestern South Asia, which in turn connects to the Hindu Kush farther west. These mountains separate South Asia from the rest of Asia, forming a **subcontinent**. India occupies most of the subcontinent.

At the foot of the Himalaya lies the Gangetic Plain. This plain is the world's longest **alluvial plain**, an area of fertile soil deposited by river floodwaters. It is also India's most densely populated area. West of the alluvial plain is the Thar Desert, bordered by the mineral-rich Aravalli Range. In eastern India, the Chota Nagpur Plateau is another mineral-rich region.

The Vindhya and Satpura Ranges divide India into northern and southern regions. To the south lies the Deccan Plateau, which has a relatively flat surface but rises to hundreds of feet high. It is covered with rich, black soil. Bordering the Deccan Plateau on the east are the Eastern Ghats, a low mountain range. Another range of low mountains, the Western Ghats, borders the western edge of the Deccan Plateau. The Nilgiri Hills, a fertile region for growing tea and coffee, are part of the Western Ghats.

606

networks *Online Teaching Options*

 **INTERACTIVE BELLRINGER**

Brahmaputra River Valley, India

Analyzing Visuals Use the introductory text and the photograph of the Brahmaputra River Valley to understand that water has important effects on life in India. Have students form small groups. Ask them to study the photograph and locate as many rivers as possible. Then, have them discuss both questions. Have each group write agreed-upon answers to the questions. Review answers as a class. **ELL AL Visual/Spatial, Verbal/Linguistic, Interpersonal**

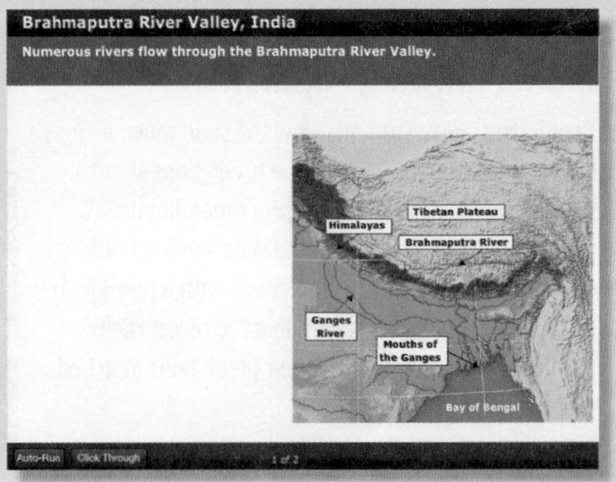

India's long coastline includes the Malabar Coast on the west and the Ganges Delta and Coromandel Coast in the east. India also includes Lakshadweep, a group of about three dozen islands in the Arabian Sea, as well as the Andaman and Nicobar Islands at the southeastern edge of the Bay of Bengal. The southernmost tip of the subcontinent, Cape Comorin, marks the division between the Arabian Sea and the Bay of Bengal.

☑ READING PROGRESS CHECK

Explaining Why is South Asia called a subcontinent?

Water Systems

GUIDING QUESTION *How does water affect life in India?*

R From sources high in the Himalaya, three major river systems—the Ganges, the Brahmaputra, and the Indus—fan out over the northern part of the subcontinent. These rivers carry fertile soil from the mountain slopes of the Himalaya and Karakoram onto the floodplains as the rivers swell with seasonal rains.

The Ganges River draws waters from a basin covering about 400,000 square miles (about 1 million sq. km). The Ganges flows throughout the year, even during the dry season from December to June. During the summer **monsoon**, heavy rains can cause devastating floods along the Ganges. Named for the Hindu deity Ganga, the Ganges is sacred to Hindus. A number of major cities, including Kanpur, Varanasi, and Kolkata (Calcutta), are located on its shores. The Brahmaputra River forms a broad delta as it joins the Ganges in Bangladesh and empties into the Bay of Bengal. The Indus flows mainly through Pakistan and empties into the Arabian Sea. The Indus is an important source of irrigation and a major transportation route.

Many other rivers begin in the Western Ghats. These rivers' many rapids and gorges make navigation impossible but make them suitable for hydropower. Many of India's major cities, such as Mumbai (Bombay) on the Arabian Sea and Chennai (Madras) on the Bay of Bengal, are port cities. People fish all along India's coastline and on nearly all of its rivers. However, it is getting harder for small fishing families to compete with larger commercial enterprises. Aquaculture, of both fish and shrimp, is increasing.

☑ READING PROGRESS CHECK

Identifying Which rivers come together to form a delta before emptying into the Bay of Bengal?

Analyzing PRIMARY SOURCES (CCSS)

Hindu Pilgrims

"Lines of Indian pilgrims walk barefoot through the alleys, drawn by occasional glimpses of the holy river. At last, the alleys fall away, and the sluggish green river appears, smooth as a sheet of glass. From here the view extends to the distant eastern bank, hazed with brown dust. This year, the monsoon rains have been below average, and the Ganges lies low and tame between the banks.

Tens of narrow steps shine wetly. The pilgrims sigh, picking their way down the steps to the water's edge. It's sunrise, the most fortunate hour, and they're here to take a dip in the Ganges."

—Anika Gupta, "The Holy City of Varanasi," *Smithsonian.com* August 20, 2009

DBQ ***IDENTIFYING CENTRAL ISSUES*** Why do the pilgrims sigh as they walk to the river's edge? RH.9–10.2

subcontinent a large landmass that is part of a continent but still distinct from it

alluvial plain a floodplain on which flooding rivers have deposited silt

T Pilgrims gather at the Ganges.

◀ CRITICAL THINKING

1. ***Interpreting*** What draws pilgrims to the Ganges River?
2. ***Identifying*** The Ganges is sacred to people of which religion?

Physical Geography of India

R Reading Skills

Visualizing Have students visualize what is being described about water flowing from the sources of three major river systems and then delivering fertile soil from the mountains to the floodplains. Have students sketch what they visualize and include labels for each geographic feature. Have students exchange their sketches with a partner to check for accuracy. **Ask: Based on the description, what can you infer about the main economic activities on the floodplains?** *(Agriculture is an important activity.)* Discuss with students the location of India and how its physical geography might put the country at risk for severe flooding. Remind students to use their sketches as a resource in the discussion. **ELL Visual/Spatial**

Content Background Knowledge

Life with Monsoons The Indian subcontinent experiences two monsoon seasons, a wet one in summer and a dry one in winter. Monsoons are seasonal winds, not rain, that bring vast amounts of precipitation that drench the land. Some areas receive more than 300 inches (about 8 meters) of rainfall, while others receive about one-third that amount. The people of India rely on the rainfall brought by the monsoons to irrigate their fields. When the monsoons bring too much rain, crops are lost, homes and businesses are flooded, and people can lose their lives. In winter, monsoon winds blow opposite the direction they do in summer. They are called "dry monsoons," yet they still produce rainfall.

T Technology Skills

Transferring Information Discuss how rivers provide more than irrigation and drinking water. Assign partners a river or body of water of India and have them research its importance to the country's economics and culture. Ask students to provide visuals of and data on the water system to illustrate its importance. Have students present their findings to the class. **AL Verbal/Linguistic, Visual/Spatial**

INTERACTIVE GRAPHIC ORGANIZER

Physical Geography of India

Explaining Students can use this graphic organizer to help them understand the physical geographic factors that influence climate in India. Have students complete the graphic organizer. As they work, ask them to think about how the different climates might affect life in India. When the organizer is complete, have students discuss their thoughts in small groups. **AL Visual/ Spatial, Verbal/Linguistic, Interpersonal**

networks

Name ______ Date ______

KEY IDEAS AND DETAILS

LISTING As you read about the physical geography of India, use the graphic organizer below to list factors that influence the climate of India.

Factors	Influence on Climate

UNDO CLEAR SAVE

ANSWERS, p. 607

☑ **READING PROGRESS CHECK** South Asia is separated from the rest of Asia by the Himalaya, the Karakoram Range, and the Hindu Kush, forming a subcontinent.

☑ **READING PROGRESS CHECK** The Brahmaputra and Ganges form a delta in Bangladesh.

DBQ The pilgrims sigh because they are completing their journey to what they consider to be a holy river at the most fortunate hour of the day.

CRITICAL THINKING

1. Hindu pilgrims come to bathe in the Ganges as part of their religious practices.
2. The Ganges is sacred to Hindus.

Physical Geography of India

V Visual Skills

Creating Charts Have students work with a partner to discuss the role of monsoons on India's climate, using the map as a reference. Ask them to create a chart or similar visual that illustrates which cities on the map would be most affected by the summer and winter monsoons. Point out that students should use what they already know and have learned about how landforms and other physical features affect the climate. **Ask: Which of these cities probably receives the most rainfall during the monsoon seasons? Why?** *(Student answers may vary but should be supported by the content in the visuals.)* Have students check their charts and their response to the question by conducting research. Ask them to report back to the class and use their findings in a class discussion. BL **Logical/Mathematical, Visual/Spatial**

R Reading Skills

Sequencing Information Have students read about the monsoon seasons and then work with a partner to create a sequence, showing each month of the year and when the monsoon seasons affect the Indian subcontinent. Then ask students to show the sequence they have created by presenting it to the class in a unique way. Challenge students to be creative, such as performing a skit, singing a song or rap, or reciting a poem. Provide an opportunity for students to deliver their presentations to the class. Ask students in the audience to evaluate each sequence for content, presentation, and originality. ELL **Kinesthetic, Musical/Auditory**

Content Background Knowledge

Gangetic Plain Rice and wheat are two important crops that farmers cultivate on the Gangetic Plain. Because of its landforms and climate, notably the monsoon season, the western part of the plain often produces high crop yields, while the eastern part does not. The east has a much higher chance of flooding. However, climate change and human factors such as population growth are affecting the productivity of the western part of the plain.

ANSWERS, p. 608

GEOGRAPHY CONNECTION

1. Rainfalls and temperatures fluctuate, causing South Asia to have wet and dry climates.
2. Summer monsoon winds bring wet weather because hot air rises over the land, which brings moist ocean air from the south and southwest. The winter monsoons bring drier weather because they blow from the Asian interior in the north across India to the ocean.

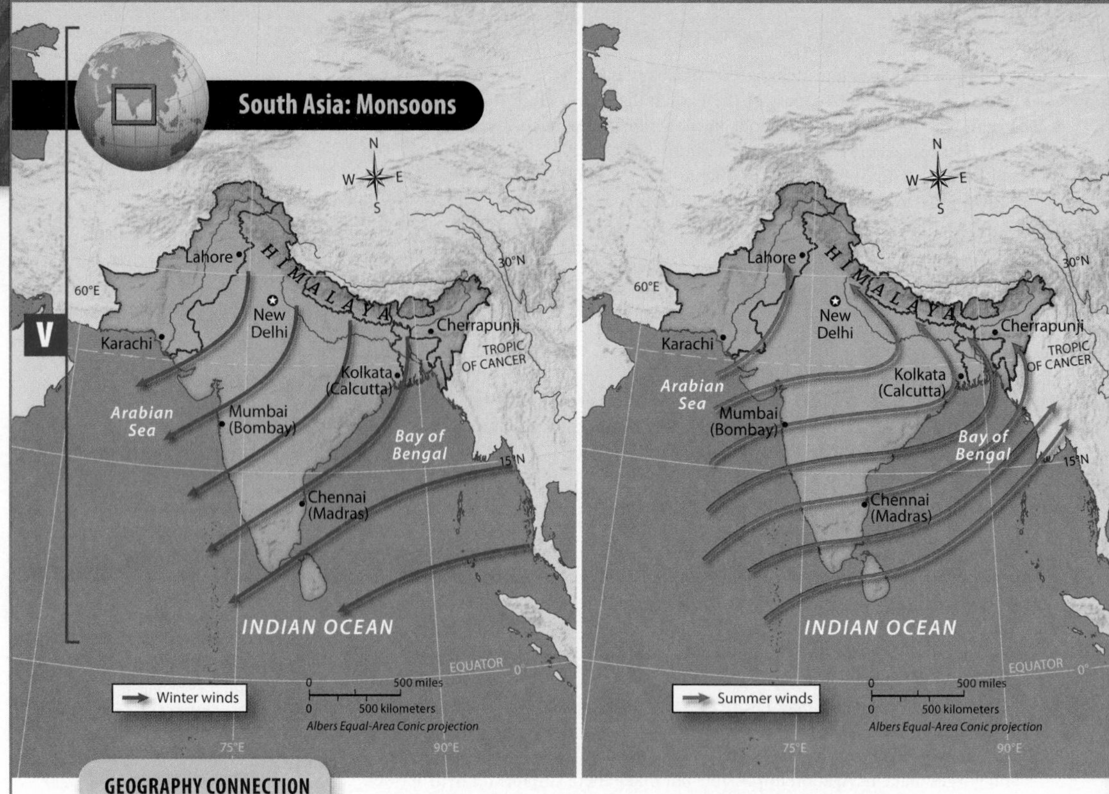

GEOGRAPHY CONNECTION

Seasonal wind patterns called monsoons influence the subregion's climate.

1. ***PHYSICAL SYSTEMS*** What generalization can you make to describe the climate of South Asia?
2. ***PHYSICAL SYSTEMS*** Which monsoon winds are likely to bring wet weather? Which monsoons bring drier weather? Why?

monsoon in Asia, a seasonal wind that brings warm, moist air from the oceans in summer and reverses direction in the winter, bringing cold, dry air from Asia's interior

fluctuate to ebb and flow in waves

Climates, Biomes, and Resources

GUIDING QUESTION *How do monsoons affect India's weather and climate?*

India's climate is influenced by the shape of the subcontinent, its proximity to the Equator, and the Indian Ocean. The difference in temperatures of the air over the ocean and the air over the landmass creates the monsoon winds. These winds cause rainfall and temperature to **fluctuate**, creating wet and dry seasons.

From about mid-June to the end of September, the winds bring hot, wet weather. This occurs during the summer period because heated air rises over the land, which pulls in the moist ocean air from the south and southwest. The monsoon winds cause heavy rains and flooding across the subcontinent during these months. Then, from early October to February, the winds change direction. In these winter months, air from the Asian interior in the north is drawn across the subcontinent toward the ocean. The air is dry and cool compared to the wet season. The weather turns hot and humid with little rainfall from March to mid-June and the winds turn calm. The weather becomes hot with little rainfall but high humidity in the south and dry conditions in the north.

Landforms and location affect the amount of rain that monsoon winds bring to different areas. Different amounts of rain create different biomes. When rain sweeps over the Ganges-Brahmaputra Delta, the Himalaya block rain clouds from moving north. Instead, the rain moves west to the Gangetic Plain. Farmers in this densely populated plain depend on these rains.

When summer monsoons rise over the Western Ghats, the air cools and releases heavy rains that create rain forests in this part of the country. As the

608

networks Online Teaching Options

INTERACTIVE WHITEBOARD ACTIVITY

Climates of India

Understanding Relationships This activity will help students make connections among the landforms of India and the country's climate and seasonal monsoon winds. Display the chart with climate descriptions. Ask students to determine whether each climate activity is affected by summer or winter monsoon winds or mountain ranges. Students should place a check mark in the corresponding column and check their answers when the chart is complete. AL BL **Verbal/Linguistic, Kinesthetic**

Climates of India

Directions: India's climate and biomes are affected by its landforms and seasonal monsoon winds. For each characteristic of India's climate described in the chart, use the writing tool to draw a check mark beside the primary cause at the right: Summer Monsoons, Winter Monsoons, or Mountain Ranges.

Climate Description	Summer Monsoons	Winter Monsoons	Mountain Ranges
Climate becomes hotter from mid-June to September.			
Winds from the Asian interior blow cool air across the subcontinent.			
Rain shadow creates a drier area of deciduous forests.			
The Ganges River experiences heavy flooding.			
Dry steppe region supports thorny scrub, acacia, and palm trees.			
The subcontinent's climate becomes drier from October to February.			
The Eastern and Western Ghats support a semiarid steppe region.			
Heavy rains soak the farms on the Gangetic Plain and feed rain forests.			
Heavy rains over the Ganges-Brahmaputra are blocked from reaching the drier north.			
Farmlands receive the heat and rain needed for			
Flooding in low-lying lands kills people and livestock and ruins crops.			

Show Answers

winds go over the mountains, they lose most of their moisture. This rain shadow makes a dry area of scrub and deciduous forests. The center of the Deccan Plateau, between the Eastern and Western Ghats, is semi-arid steppe. The driest area of India is the Thar Desert, east of the Indus River. The vegetation here is desert scrub of low, thorny trees, and grasses. The rest of the area around the Thar Desert is semi-arid grassland. Few trees grow in this steppe. The northeastern coast of India is quite different, however. It receives considerable rainfall and has a forested biome, including the world's largest protected mangrove forest. **C**

Natural Disasters

Temperature and rainfall affect agriculture in the subregion. High temperatures and ample water allow farmers to produce plentiful crops, especially on the alluvial plains. These crops include the rice that many people in India depend on year-round. The extreme heat, however, can dry the fields, and without rainfall there is drought.

The summer monsoons bring problems as well as benefits. Rainfall waters crops, but areas outside the path of the monsoon may suffer from drought. Large amounts of rain from the monsoons cause flooding in low-lying land. The floods deposit rich silt on the floodplains which renews soil fertility. But the floods can also kill people and livestock, ruin crops, and leave thousands homeless. **W**

Cyclones are a natural hazard in South Asia. They begin in the Bay of Bengal or the Arabian Sea. Much like hurricanes that originate in the Atlantic Ocean, they can be dangerous and destructive. Tropical cyclones bring torrential rains and winds that can reach speeds of more than 100 miles (161 km) per hour. Cyclones often cause storm tides, or surges of high water along the coasts.

Coastal regions also face the threat of **tsunamis**. Tsunamis are triggered by underwater earthquakes. The huge waves of the 2004 Indian Ocean tsunami destroyed entire villages and killed hundreds of thousands of people. **R**

cyclone a storm with heavy rains and high winds that blow in a circular pattern around an area of low atmospheric pressure

tsunami originally a Japanese term, is a huge sea wave caused by an undersea earthquake

Alan Lagadu/E+/Getty Images

This forest is located in the Indian state of Goa.

▼ CRITICAL THINKING

1. ***Analyzing Visuals*** What is the dominant type of tree that grows in this forest? What does that tell you about its climate?
2. ***Making Connections*** Why is it difficult for India to protect its forests?

VIDEO

India Collides with Asia

Taking Notes Students will gain a unique perspective on the Himalaya by viewing this video. As the video is playing, have students take notes on the theory of how the featured area of the mountain range has formed. Ask higher-level students to work with lower-level and ELL students to improve their note-taking skills. When the video is completed, ask students how the title of the video relates to its subject matter.
AL **Visual/Spatial, Verbal/Linguistic**

Physical Geography of India

C Critical Thinking Skills

Categorizing Have students read about the vegetation of the Eastern and Western Ghats, Deccan Plateau, and Thar Desert. Then ask them to categorize the location, climate, and vegetation of each area, using a chart like the one shown. Discuss with students the factors that influence the vegetation of a place or region. **AL** **Naturalist, Visual/Spatial**

	Location	Climate	Vegetation
Eastern Ghats			
Western Ghats			
Deccan Plateau			
Thar Desert			

W Writing Skills

Narrative Instruct students to write a personal narrative from the perspective of a farmer whose lands are dry and who is awaiting the summer monsoon rains. Explain to students that their narratives should evoke emotions such as impatience, frustration, or hope as the farmer waits for the rainfall to arrive. Invite students to share their personal narratives on a blog. **BL** **Intrapersonal, Verbal/Linguistic**

R Reading Skills

Identifying Ask students to share experiences about cyclones, hurricanes, or tsunamis, either a personal experience or a current event. Then invite a volunteer to explain the similarities and differences between a cyclone, hurricane, and a tsunami, and why the Indian subcontinent is at risk of being hit by them. Show students several images from print or electronic resources, and ask them to write which natural hazard each image shows. Then **ask: How can the people of India prepare for these natural disasters?** *(Possible answer: They can alert people to stay in a safe place and take cover. They can build stronger buildings that can withstand the high winds and tidal surges of these storms.)* Have students work together to devise an emergency plan that will help people to recover and rebuild in the event that one of these three disasters hits India. **ELL** **Logical/Mathematical, Visual/Spatial**

ANSWERS, p. 609

CRITICAL THINKING

1. Palm trees dominate this forest, which indicates that it has a tropical climate with plenty of rainfall.
2. It is difficult for India to protect its forests because timber is illegally cut and used for fuel and trees are cleared to make farmland.

Physical Geography of India

W Writing Skills

Informative/Explanatory Ask students to select and research an animal common to India that may or may not be mentioned in the text. Challenge them to choose an animal that is unique to India or endangered. Then have them write an essay on the animal, including its habitat, population, status, and importance to the subregion. **AL** **Naturalist, Verbal/Linguistic**

T Technology Skills

Researching Have students research which mineral resource is the most valuable in terms of exports in India. Then ask students to find the most important crop export in terms of value. Challenge students to find the most current statistics on both, as well as whether the mineral resource and crop have maintained that top position for some time or whether they have more recently increased their position. **Ask: What factors affect how valuable an export is to a country's economy?** *(Possible answer: price, production, competition)* Based on what students learned from their research, ask them to take the role of an economic adviser to the government of India. Have them respond to the prompt: **Would you recommend that the country continue to invest in developing these two resources?** Remind students that they need to support their responses with specific data and facts. Suggest that they conduct additional research to aid in their responses. Invite students to share their responses with the class and use them to further discuss the topic. **BL** **Verbal/Linguistic**

CLOSE & REFLECT

Comparing and Contrasting Have students make a T-chart comparing the wet and dry monsoon seasons that affect India, including how landforms and other physical features affect and are influenced by them. Their charts should include details about when monsoon seasons occur, where monsoon winds blow, rainfall produced, areas affected, and crops that benefit from them.

ANSWERS, p. 610

READING PROGRESS CHECK Hot, wet weather would be found in the Gangetic Plain in July.

Climates and Biomes

annual occurring once a year

The climates of different areas of India make diverse biomes of vegetation and animal life. About one-fourth of India's land is forest, but the types of trees and plants vary with rainfall. The heartland of northern India is a humid subtropical zone. Areas that receive more than 80 inches (203 cm) of rainfall on an **annual** basis have generally tropical evergreen and mixed evergreen-deciduous forests. Areas with 60 to 80 inches (152 to 203 cm) of annual rainfall have mostly tropical deciduous trees, while areas that receive less than 60 inches (152 cm) are dry deciduous forests. Tropical palms and bamboo are found throughout the country. Much of the land along the coast is tidal marsh or wetland, with mangrove forests in some areas. Wetlands are used for growing rice and are important wildlife habitats.

Northwestern India receives less than 20 inches (51 cm) of rain in some desert areas. Regions in the northwest and the central southern subcontinent that receive 20 to 40 inches (51 to 102 cm) of rain are steppe, covered largely with thorny scrub, acacia, and palm trees.

W

India has a wide diversity of animals. Among the large mammals are the Indian elephant, the Indian rhinoceros, and several species of tiger. The numbers of some of these mammals have decreased to such low levels that the animals are in danger of extinction. There are many species of monkeys and other primates. India is home to more than 1,200 species of birds, including cranes, herons, flamingos, and peacocks, the national bird. Many species of lizards and snakes—especially cobras—are widespread. Crocodiles and turtles are found in the country's rivers, swamps, and coastal regions.

Natural Resources

T

India's mineral resources are numerous and widespread. Iron ore is abundant. Other important mineral resources include copper, bauxite (used to make aluminum), zinc, lead, gold, and silver. Petroleum is one of India's most valuable resources. Oil reserves are located along India's northeast coast, near the Ganges Delta, and in the Arabian Sea. India produces a slight surplus of coal from about 500 mines in many different areas of the country. India also produces a small amount of uranium.

The country has large areas of rich soil that support agriculture and timber. Timber resources include India's sandalwood, sal, and teak woods. Nearly any type of wood is used for fuel, often illegally. More than half of India's total land area is used for growing crops. Given the population of India, however, the country does not have a large amount of high-quality cropland.

READING PROGRESS CHECK

Applying What kind of weather would you expect to find in the Gangetic Plain in July?

LESSON 1 REVIEW

Reviewing Vocabulary (Tier Three Words)

1. ***Summarizing*** Write a paragraph summarizing weather patterns created by monsoon winds. RH.9–10.4

Using Your Notes

2. ***Listing*** Use your graphic organizer on India's climate to write a paragraph about the factors that influence rainfall in India.

Answering the Guiding Questions

3. ***Drawing Conclusions*** Why is the Gangetic Plain important?
4. ***Speculating*** How does water affect life in India?
5. ***Finding the Main Idea*** How do monsoons affect India's weather and climate?

Writing Activity

6. ***Informative/Explanatory*** In a paragraph, explain how the Himalaya affect the climate of India. WHST.9–10.2

610

LESSON 1 REVIEW ANSWERS

Reviewing Vocabulary

1. Paragraphs should include: heated air rises over land, which pulls moist ocean air from the south and southwest, creating summer monsoons with heavy rain and flooding; air from the Asian interior in the north is pulled across India to the ocean, creating winter monsoons that are cool and dry; winds are calm from March to mid-June, leaving the area dry and humid in the south and dry in the north.

Using Your Notes

2. Paragraphs should include: difference in temperature of air over land; ocean creates winds that bring wet and dry seasons; mountains (Himalaya) and the Eastern and Western Ghats create rain shadow effects by blocking rain from reaching some areas.

Answering the Guiding Questions

3. The Gangetic Plain is the world's longest alluvial plain and the most densely populated area in India. It has fertile soil for growing crops.
4. Rivers provide transportation, irrigation, hydroelectric power, fish for food and the economy, and deposit fertile soil in the plains during seasonal flooding.
5. They cause rainfall and temperature to fluctuate and cause wet and dry climate areas.

Writing Activity

6. The Himalaya affect the amount of rain monsoon winds bring to areas; block rain from moving north, causing rainfall and wet climates in Gangetic Plain and drier climates in north.

Human Geography of India

There's More Online!

- **CHART** India's Political Parties
- **IMAGE** Passenger Train in Lucknow
- **INFOGRAPHIC** All Aboard in India
- **MAP** Partition of India
- **TIME LINE** Women's Rights in India
- **INTERACTIVE SELF-CHECK QUIZ**
- **VIDEO** Human Geography of India

LESSON 2

Human Geography of India

ESSENTIAL QUESTION • *How do physical systems and human systems shape a place?*

Reading HELPDESK

Academic Vocabulary (Tier Two Words)
- **dominate**
- **neutral**

Content Vocabulary (Tier Two Words)
- ***jati***
- **mercantilism**
- **imperialism**
- **reincarnation**
- **karma**
- ***panchayat***
- **green revolution**
- **cottage industry**

TAKING NOTES: ***Key Ideas and Details***

ORGANIZING As you read about the human geography of India, use a graphic organizer like the one below to organize information about India's culture and economy.

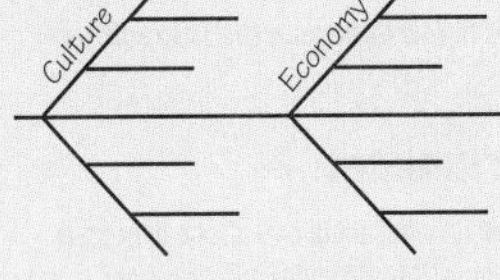

(tl)Dinodia Photos/Alamy, (tcl)©Pawan Kumar/Reuters/Corbis, (tc)Hulton Archive/Archive Photos/Getty Images, (tcr)akg-images/British Library/Newscom, (tr)©Jens Kalaene/dpa/Corbis

IT MATTERS BECAUSE

As the world's most populous democracy, India is rich in human resources and has large amounts of natural resources. Meeting the basic needs of many of its people is a challenge even though it is one of the largest economies in the world. **R**

History and Government

GUIDING QUESTION *How did modern India gain its independence?*

India's history dates back more than 4,500 years to the Indus Valley civilization, located in what is now modern-day Pakistan. Later the Aryans, a group of hunters and herders from the northwest, settled in India in the 2000s B.C. The Aryans created a rigid social structure based on castes. A caste, or ***jati***, is the social position into which a person is born. The Aryans' sacred writings, the Vedas, outline Aryan ideas about social structure. These writings also form a basis of the Hindu religion. **V** India's religions are key to understanding its history and culture.

Around A.D. 320, the Gupta Empire united much of India and built one of the world's most advanced civilizations. In the 700s Muslim invaders began arriving. A Muslim dynasty of mixed Mongol and Turkish heritage, the Moguls, ruled most of India from 1526 to the 1800s. During this period of Muslim rule, many Indians converted to Islam.

The final group of invaders were Europeans. Beginning in the 1490s, Europeans came to trade. Eventually, the British East India Company tightened control over India. They employed a policy of **mercantilism**. Under this economic system, colonies supplied raw materials to the colonizing country, which then sold finished goods back to to the colony. The **imperialist** policy of the British government led it to take direct control of India. The British called their Indian empire the British raj, the Hindi word for "empire." The British **dominated** India. They introduced the English language, restructured the educational system, built railroads, and developed a civil service and judiciary. Indians, however, were not treated as equal citizens and were forced to pay the costs of British domination. **C**

ENGAGE

R Reading Skills

Activating Prior Knowledge Have students brainstorm what they already know about India's history, culture, society, population, and economy. Discuss how India's history included interactions with other groups that influenced its people, society, and culture. Ask students if they can identify any of these interactions and describe how they affected India's society and culture, making it the diverse country it is today.

TEACH & ASSESS

V Visual Skills

Spatial Understanding Discuss with students how the Aryans invaded India and their cultural influence in India. Invite a volunteer to show on a map where the Aryans came from and entered the area. **Ask: What landforms did the Aryans have to cross to reach India?** *(Indus River and Thar Desert)* **If the Aryans had lived to the northeast of India, do you think they would have tried to invade or have been successful in invading India? Explain.** *(Possible answer: They may have tried, but they would have had to face more daunting physical challenges, such as the Himalaya.)* Have students write two or three paragraphs describing how Indian culture and society might have been different had the Aryans not invaded. **AL Logical/Mathematical, Visual/Spatial**

C Critical Thinking Skills

Identifying Cause and Effect Point out the relevance of mercantilism and imperialism in India's history. **Ask: How did mercantilism drive imperialism?** *(In order to carry out a policy of mercantilism, Britain had to find new places to colonize. To colonize, Britain adopted a policy of imperialism.)* Ask students to compare the example of Britain in India with that of another European country at this time that adopted an imperialist policy and exploited raw materials in its colonies for its own economic expansion and strength. **BL Verbal/Linguistic**

networks Online Teaching Options

INTERACTIVE BELLRINGER

Population Growth in India

Analyzing Visuals Use the introductory text and the composite satellite image of city lights in India to identify population growth and patterns in India between 1992 and 2003. Inform students to use the map on page 608 in their textbooks to answer one of the questions. Have students form small groups and discuss each question. Tell each group to write agreed-upon answers to the questions. Then have each group share its answers in a class discussion. **ELL AL Verbal/Linguistic, Visual/Spatial, Interpersonal**

Population Growth in India
In this composite of satellite images, the white area shows city lights visible before 1992. Colored areas show lights that later became visible.

ANSWERS, p. 611

TAKING NOTES: Culture—speak more than 1,000 languages, Hindi and English most widely used; many religions including Hinduism, Islam, Buddhism, Sikhism, Jainism, Christianity; majority are Hindus who identify by *jati;* has small, rural villages and large, densely populated cities; artistic expression reflects religious beliefs, includes "Bollywood"; family life of extended families; arranged and "love" marriages; male heads of household; **Economy**—half of people work in agriculture; green revolution attempts to increase crops to reduced hunger, also introduced environmental hazards; high-technology services and software workers important to economy; cottage industries, manufacturing, and mining jobs.

W Writing Skills

Informative/Explanatory Tell students to take the role of a newspaper reporter at the time that Mohandas Gandhi was leading Indians in a nonviolent protest against Britain. Ask students to gather more facts and details about Gandhi's actions, the momentum that he gained for Indian independence, and other interesting biographical information. Have them publish their newspaper articles on a class blog or website. **Verbal/Linguistic**

T Technology Skills

Examining Information Instruct students to read the text on India after independence. Then ask students to locate primary sources that discuss the foreign relations between Indian leaders Jawaharlal Nehru or Indira Gandhi and the Soviet Union and the United States. **Ask: Do you think that India under Nehru and Gandhi did a good job of balancing its relations with both countries, or did they lean toward one side?** *(Student answers may vary, but their answers should be supported by the primary source selected.)* **What factors do you think influenced India's government to maintain friendly relations with both countries?** *(Possible answer: India's colonial past with Britain could have been a factor, as well as wanting to maintain peace during a volatile time.)* Have students trade primary sources with a classmate and analyze any differing viewpoints. **BL Verbal/Linguistic**

R Reading Skills

Examining Primary Sources Ask students to read the primary source excerpt from *Time* magazine. **Ask: Which policy, mercantilism or imperialism, is described in the excerpt? Support your answer with specific facts and details.** *(Possible answer: mercantilism—"a regime of monopolies over commodities like tea, textiles, and even salt"; "Indians were forbidden to extract and sell their own salt.")* Have students work in small groups to discuss the response of Indians such as Mohandas Gandhi to British rule. **AL Interpersonal, Verbal/Linguistic**

ANSWERS, p. 612

✓ READING PROGRESS CHECK Jawaharlal Nehru and Indira Gandhi wanted to have friendly relations with the United States.

DBQ Document-Based Questions

1. Gandhi and his followers marched from Ahmedabad to Dandi. They choose the march because it attracted attention, culminating with the symbolic act of removing salt from the sea as the British did not permit them to extract, process, and use their own salt.
2. The British had monopolies on most of the commodities including tea, textiles, and salt, which forced Indians to pay high prices for the goods imported from the UK even though they were made using materials and raw goods from India. Money and power motivated the British policy.

jati in India, a group that defines one's occupation and social position

mercantilism the theory or practice of merchant or trading pursuits

imperialism the actions by which one country is able to extend power to control another country

dominate to have a commanding position

neutral not favoring either side in a quarrel, contest, or war

W By the late nineteenth century, the Indian National Congress was calling for independence. After British troops fired on unarmed protesters at Amritsar in 1919, Mohandas K. Gandhi led Indians to seek freedom using nonviolent methods of civil disobedience. India won its independence in 1947. Britain divided the region into Hindu India and Muslim Pakistan. Conflicts between Pakistan and India over the territorial division of the state of Kashmir continue today.

T Following independence, India launched a series of five-year plans to guide economic development under its first prime minister, Jawaharlal Nehru. Throughout the Cold War era, Nehru tried to keep India nonaligned, or **neutral**. He wanted to maintain friendly relations with both the United States and the Soviet Union. Two years after Nehru's death in 1964, his daughter, Indira Gandhi, became prime minister and continued this policy. She held office for a total of 15 years until her assassination in 1984. Her son Rajiv then became prime minister. He pursued a closer relationship with the United States until his assassination in 1991.

Today India is the world's most populous democracy. Ruled by a coalition, the government has been trying to improve life for farmers and rural Indians. The government approved the country's twelfth Five-Year Plan in October 2012.

✓ READING PROGRESS CHECK

Interpreting What was the attitude of Jawaharlal Nehru and Indira Gandhi toward the United States?

ANALYZING PRIMARY SOURCES (CCSS)

The Last Straw: Salt Satyagraha, 1930

Mohandas Gandhi's Salt March is considered one of the most influential protests in history. Gandhi demonstrated how civil disobedience could be used to fight social and political injustices. His peaceful methods were a strong influence on American civil rights leader Martin Luther King, Jr.

R "Britain's centuries-long rule over India was, in many ways, first and foremost a regime of monopolies over commodities like tea, textiles and even salt. Under colonial law, Indians were forbidden to extract and sell their own salt and instead were forced to pay the far higher price of salt processed in and imported from the U.K. In March 1930, Mohandas Gandhi, the charismatic and enigmatic independence leader, embarked on a 24-day march from the city of Ahmedabad to the small seaside town of Dandi, attracting followers along the way. The assembled throngs watched as he and dozens of others dipped into the sea to obtain salt. That act—for which more than 80,000 Indians would be arrested in the coming months—sparked years of mass civil disobedience that came to define both the Indian independence struggle and Gandhi himself. Known as the salt *satyagraha* —a Sanskrit term loosely meaning 'truth-force'—it carried the emotional and moral weight to break an empire."

—Ishaan Tharoor, "Top 10 Most Influential Protests," *Time*, June 28, 2011

Mohandas Gandhi (center) leads fellow Indians in the 1930 Salt Satyagraha.

DBQ ▲ CRITICAL THINKING

1. ***Identifying Central Issues*** In what act of civil disobedience did Gandhi and his followers engage? Why do you think they chose this action? RH.9–10.1; RH.9–10.2
2. ***Identifying Cause and Effect*** What actions by the British government led to the protests? What do you think motivated British policy? RH.9–10.1; RH.9–10.2

networks Online Teaching Options

VIDEO

Visions of India—Days of Raj

Exploring Issues As students view this video about a pivotal part of India's history, have them think about the influences, both positive and negative, that the British had on the country of India and how the division of India affects its relations with Pakistan to this day. When the video is completed, lead the class in a discussion about the British raj and its lasting effects on India. Students should cite information from the textbook as well as the video in their discussions. **AL BL Verbal/Linguistic**

Population Patterns

GUIDING QUESTION *Why are population patterns so important in India?*

One of the most significant characteristics of India's population is its size. With over 1.2 billion people, it is second only to China in population. It is estimated that India will surpass China to become the world's most populous country in the next 20 years.

Most Indians belong to one of two ethnic groups. About 22 percent are descended from the Dravidians, who have lived in the south of India for 8,000 years. About 75 percent are Indo-Aryan, descended from the Aryans, who migrated from Central Asia some 4,000 years ago. Most Indo-Aryans live in the north. Indians traditionally identify themselves by their religion as Hindus, Muslims, Buddhists, Sikhs, Jains, or Christians.

India has a relatively high average population density of about 1,050 people per square mile (325 per sq. km), but it is much higher in some places. The distribution of population varies from place to place due to factors such as climate, vegetation, and physical features that affect the number of people the land can support. The population density on the Gangetic Plain can be more than 2,000 people per square mile (800 people per sq. km). On the other hand, the Thar Desert and some mountain regions are very sparsely populated.

India's cities are among the world's largest and most densely populated. More than 50 urban areas in India have populations of more than a million. There are several megalopolises—super-sized cities that may include a chain of closely linked metropolitan areas—that are far larger. India's largest megalopolises are Delhi (DEH•lee), Mumbai, and Kolkata, each with populations of between 15 and 22 million people.

Although the cities are large, most of India's population is rural—about 70 percent of the people live in villages. They farm and work to grow enough food for their families. Part of their crops often goes to the owners of the fields they farm. In recent years, growing numbers of Indians have been migrating to urban areas, drawn by the hope of better jobs and higher wages. As urban populations grow, they strain public resources and facilities.

READING PROGRESS CHECK

Identifying Central Issues How can India's cities be so large when most people live in rural areas?

Passengers travel on an overcrowded train in the Indian city of Lucknow on the occasion of World Population Day, an annual event designed to draw attention to global population issues.

▲ CRITICAL THINKING

1. ***Considering Advantages and Disadvantages*** As people move from villages to large cities, what are some advantages and disadvantages for them?
2. ***Making Predictions*** How will India's population growth affect transportation systems?

Society and Culture Today

GUIDING QUESTION *What is life in Indian villages like?*

The people of India speak more than 1,000 languages. There are 22 official languages, with Hindi being the most widely spoken. English, the common language for national, political, and business communication, is also widely spoken in India.

Human Geography of India

Content Background Knowledge

Population Projections Scientists that study population are called demographers. They project that, even though the birthrate in India has declined, India will still take over the top position from China in the next 20 years. How are population projections determined? Demographers consider three factors when making projections: mortality, fertility, and migration. National governments usually make their own projections, but outside organizations such as the United Nations (UN) and the World Bank do too. Accuracy rates are not formally tracked, but the UN has correctly projected the world population a dozen times since 1950.

V Visual Skills

Expressing Prompt students to study the image and read the caption. Then read the first three paragraphs of text that describes the population patterns and distribution in India. **Ask:** **How does this image express the population issues that India faces?** *(Possible answer: The image shows an overfilled train with people hanging off the side and top.)* **How is the image symbolic of India's population challenge?** *(Possible response: India is running out of space for its large and growing population.)* **Does the image express anything about ethnicity and diversity in India? Explain.** *(Possible answer: No, the people in the image look similar or united, even though they are different and may come from different ethnic groups.)* **ELL Visual/Spatial**

W Writing Skills

Narrative Ask students to consider what it would be like to live in one of India's most densely populated cities. Discuss how this might affect daily life, such as going to school, participating in activities, working, and using transportation. Have students write a narrative about daily life in one of the megalopolises of India. Point out that they should describe the setting and include dialogue to make their narratives more interesting and engaging for the reader. Allow students to do additional research as needed. **Intrapersonal**

GAME

Human Geography of India

Classifying Students can get a better idea of the various groups of people who live in India by playing this game. Encourage students to use the information in their textbooks to complete the activity. When the game is completed, students should check their answers and correct any errors that may have been made.

ELL Kinesthetic, Visual/Spatial

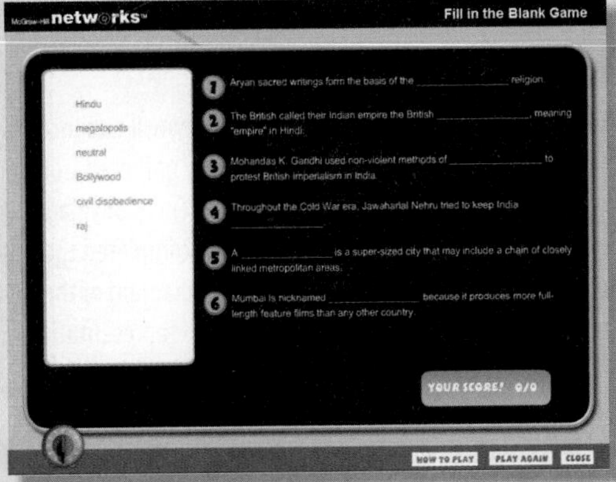

ANSWERS, p. 613

READING PROGRESS CHECK Even though about 70 percent of the population live in rural areas, the total population that lives in India is so large that the 30 percent that live in cities is a big enough number to create megalopolises.

CRITICAL THINKING

1. Advantages for some people moving to cities could be finding jobs with higher pay and more opportunities such as education. Disadvantages could be homelessness or living in slums as housing is expensive and the growing urban population has strained resources and the infrastructure.
2. India's population growth will overload the already strained public transportation system.

Human Geography of India

R Reading Skills

Using Word Parts Have students break the word *reincarnation* into parts—a prefix, base word, and suffix. Ask them to define each part. **Ask:** **Which definition of the base word *incarnate* best relates to the concept of reincarnation?** *(Possible answer:* Incarnate *means "invested with bodily form," which relates to the concept of rebirth in a new body or form of life.)* Ask students to brainstorm other forms of the word *reincarnation* (reincarnate, reincarnating). **ELL** **Verbal/Linguistic**

T Technology Skills

Changing Continuity of Groups Divide students into small groups and assign each group one of the minority religious groups in India (Christian, Sikh, and Buddhist). Instruct students to use online resources to track the group's issues and numbers in India over time and to present their findings in a digital presentation or research report. Suggest that students find out what factors led to their migration or existence in India and their current status. Challenge students to create charts and graphs to illustrate data and use audio and video clips to make their presentations more engaging. **Interpersonal, Visual/Spatial**

C Critical Thinking Skills

Diagramming Ask students to create a Venn diagram to compare and contrast life in rural versus urban areas in India. **Ask:** **Do you think it is difficult for people in India who live in rural areas to move to cities and adjust to urban life? Explain.** *(Possible answer: Yes, it would probably be quite an adjustment for them because they would not have access to open spaces like they do in rural areas. Also, they may need to adjust to the crowded communities and to the possibility of having electricity and running water.)* Have students form small groups to describe how the government in India could help people from rural areas better assimilate into urban areas, not only culturally but also economically and socially. Ask each group to come up with a list of possible solutions that they can share with the class. **BL** **Logical/Mathematical**

ANSWERS, p. 614

CRITICAL THINKING

1. An increase in the literacy rate for women improves their chances of getting a job and allows them to be more informed about rights and health care, all of which improve their quality of life.
2. Women may have equal status under the law, but they are expected to follow traditional ways in daily life, including obeying their husbands and participating in arranged marriages.

---

reincarnation rebirth in new bodies or forms of life

karma in Hindu belief, the sum of good and bad actions in one's present and past lives

panchayat village council

R Indians identify with a variety of religions. Some 80 percent of people in India are Hindus, and many Hindus also identify themselves by a *jati,* a group that defines one's occupation and social position by birth. The highest *jati* is the Brahmans; the lowest is the Shudras. Hindus believe that after death people undergo **reincarnation**, or rebirth. By moving through multiple reincarnations, Hindus strive to overcome personal weaknesses. The law of **karma** states that good deeds—actions in accord with dharma, or rules of conduct—lead one to break the cycle of birth and death and attain salvation.

T A little over 13 percent of Indians practice Islam, and much smaller numbers are Christian or Sikh. Only about 1 percent of Indians are Buddhist, even though Buddhism began in India. Most Sikhs live in northwestern India; many want an independent Sikh state there.

Village Life and City Life

In rural India, Hindus of the higher *jatis* live in the core or center of the village, while Muslims and those of lower *jatis* generally live in areas that surround the core. Village streets are narrow and twisting, but people gather in open spaces next to temples or mosques, at a water well, or in front of the home of a wealthy or powerful villager. These open spaces could be public areas such as the ***panchayat*** (village council) hall, shops, a tea stall, a public radio hooked up to a loudspeaker, or a post office. The village school is usually on the edge of the village so that children have room to play outside the school building.

C Most village houses are small with just one or two rooms. People and animals live in the same shelter, and few people have electricity or running water. The design of roofs and the materials used for building vary depending on an area's rainfall. Houses in rainy areas have sloped roofs and are likely to be made of bamboo and covered with metal or plastic; they may be built on stilts to protect from flooding. In drier regions, homes may be made of mud and have flat roofs. Brahmans and wealthier people also tend to live in the core areas of cities. As in villages, streets are narrow and winding, with gathering places near businesses

TIME LINE

WOMEN'S RIGHTS in India

Despite considerable progress in recent generations, women in India continue to struggle for equality in society.

CRITICAL THINKING

1. ***Analyzing*** How can the increase in the literacy rate for women affect their quality of life in India?
2. ***Hypothesizing*** What might explain the difference between the legal status of women and the reality of their daily lives?

500s *Sati,* the practice of widows killing themselves by fire, begins in parts of India.

1829 East India Company prohibits *sati* in British-ruled India, but enforcement proves difficult.

1917 First women's delegation meets with India's secretary of state to demand women's political rights.

1929 Child Marriage Restraint Act prohibits the marriage of girls younger than 12.

networks Online Teaching Options

INTERACTIVE WHITEBOARD ACTIVITY

Village and City Life

Comparing and Contrasting This activity will enhance the information that students have already gathered from their texts about the similarities and differences of village and city lives in India. After students have completed the activity, ask them to create a simple Venn diagram of their own so that they can have a personal visual representation of some of the features of Indian village life and city life. Students can include details such as class, housing, markets, and artistic expression in their Venn diagrams. **ELL** **AL** **Visual/Spatial**

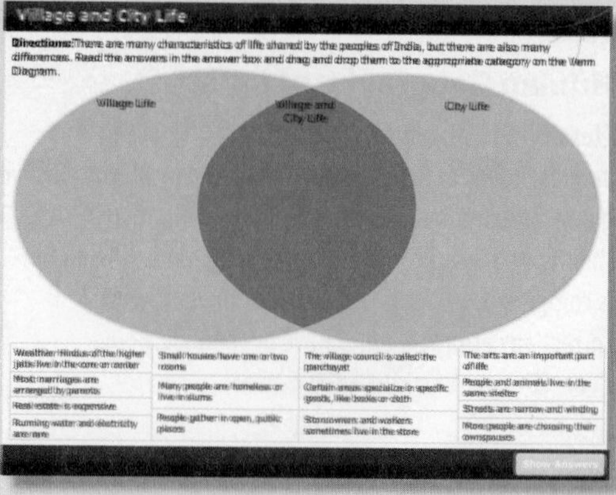

and public buildings. Markets in the city specialize in certain goods. For example, one street may include stores that sell books and stationery, while another market may sell cloth. Store owners and their employees may live in the store building.

Housing is a problem in India's largest cities. Real estate in Delhi, Kolkata, and Mumbai is very expensive. Many people are homeless and others live in slums. According to a 2011 report by the government of India, more than 7.6 million children under the age of 6, or more than 13 percent of the urban population for this age group, live in slums. **V**

Artistic expression is important to Indians whether they live in cities or villages. The arts are as much a part of Indian life as religious practice. Two great epic poems—the *Mahābhārata* (muh•hah•BAH•ruh•tuh) and the *Rāmāyana* (rah•MAH•yah•nuh)—combine Hindu social and religious beliefs. India has numerous classical dance styles, most of which are based on themes from Hindu mythology. India's film industry is the world's largest, producing more full-length feature films each year than any other country. It is centered in Mumbai and is nicknamed "Bollywood," a combination of Bombay (Mumbai) and Hollywood.

Family Life

The family unit is very important to Indians of all religions. Many people live in extended families in which people of several generations make up a household. The oldest man in the household—whether father, grandfather, or uncle—is usually the head of the family, and his wife assigns tasks to the women of the household. Nearly all Indians marry and have children. Women are still expected to obey their husbands in all things. Divorce is rare. Parents or older relatives arrange most marriages, but more people in cities are choosing their own spouses in "love marriages." Hindus who belong to the same *jati* treat one another as relatives, even when there is no kinship connection. People are also expected to marry within their *jati*. **W**

✔ READING PROGRESS CHECK

Comparing How are India's villages and cities similar?

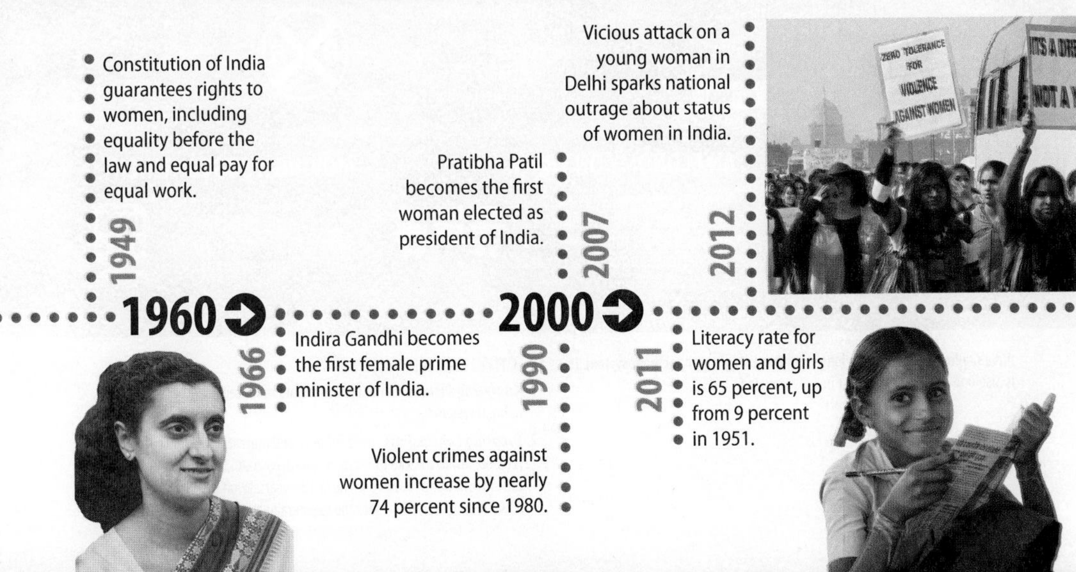

1949
Constitution of India guarantees rights to women, including equality before the law and equal pay for work.
1960
1966
Indira Gandhi becomes the first female prime minister of India.
1990
Violent crimes against women increase by nearly 74 percent since 1980.
2000
2007
Pratibha Patil becomes the first woman elected as president of India.
2011
Literacy rate for women and girls is 65 percent, up from 9 percent in 1951.
2012
Vicious attack on a young woman in Delhi sparks national outrage about status of women in India.
ZERO TOLERANCE FOR VIOLENCE AGAINST WOMEN

TIME LINE

Women's Rights in India

Understanding Relationsohips Among Events As students view the time line, point out the 1917, 1949, 1966, and 2007 entries. Have students consider how the four entries are related to each other. Lead a class discussion focusing on how each entry builds on the other, although each event is decades apart from its predecessor. **BL** **Verbal/Linguistic**

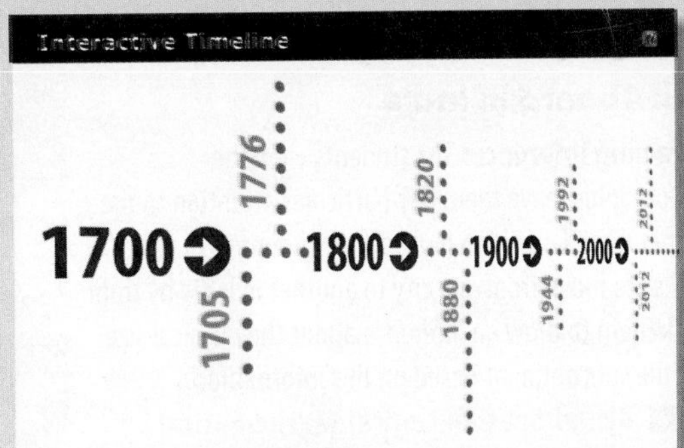

V Visual Skills

Displaying Discuss with students how many people who live in Indian cities are forced to live in slums because of the cost of real estate. Have students work in pairs to search for the median price range of a home in their community and the home's specs (square footage, number of bedrooms, number of bathrooms, location). Remind students that they learned earlier in the chapter that the average size of a family in India is five persons. Then have students research the cost and specs of a comparable house (in terms of size and price) in Delhi, Kolkata, or Mumbai. **Ask:** **Was it difficult to find a comparable house? How did the houses compare?** *(Student answers may vary but houses should be comparable in size depending on the primary source selected; however, the prices might vary greatly.)* Ask students what factors they need to consider if there are large differences in price. *(income, cost of living)* Have students display their findings in the form of a real estate brochure or advertisement and include a visual for each home.
AL **Visual/Spatial**

W Writing Skills

Argument Discuss with students how the roles of women in India have evolved but that there are still many limitations, especially in rural areas. Tell students to read the events and study the content in the time line. Then have students write an essay that states a position on the role and status of women in India. Have them think about the effects that educating women and granting them more political opportunities will have on the population growth of India. At the same time, ask students to weigh the cultural practices that have been upheld for centuries in India and how recognizing rights for women might affect Indian society. **BL** **Verbal/Linguistic**

ANSWER, p. 615

✔ **READING PROGRESS CHECK** India's cities and villages both have narrow, winding streets with people of higher *jatis* living in the central areas and those of lower *jatis* living in the surrounding areas.

C Critical Thinking Skills

Organizing As students read the information in "Economic Activities," have them complete a three-column chart with the headings *Economic Activity*, *Government Actions*, and *Challenges*. Have them list information from the text under these three headings. **Ask: What factors would benefit agricultural growth, and what factors currently limit it?** *(Possible answer: New technology would benefit the agriculture sector because much of the equipment and methods used are outdated and limit the output. Environmental factors such as flooding also help and hinder agriculture practices.)* Then ask students to brainstorm solutions to the challenges that India faces with regard to its main economic activity. Ask them to consider how foreign investment and deregulation benefited India's economy. **ELL Visual/Spatial**

Making Connections

Point out to students that through foreign investment, India's agricultural output has grown at an average annual rate of 3.6 percent. Explain that foreign investment in agriculture is not unique to India and that about 2 percent of U.S. farmland is foreign-owned. Have students find out how much foreign investment has gone into agriculture in other countries in different regions of the world.

V Visual Skills

Calculating Distribute blank outline maps of India to students. Then have them label the cities that are shown on the map in the infographic (New Delhi, Kolkata, Mumbai, Bangalore, and Chennai). Ask them to use the map legend to estimate the distances between each city. Then have them add the total distances between the five cities and subtract that number from 71,000, which is the total number of miles of railroad track in India. Ask students to find the percentage that this number represents of India's total miles of railroad track. **AL Logical/Mathematical, Visual/Spatial**

ANSWERS, p. 616

CRITICAL THINKING

1. Factors that might influence passenger miles on a railroad system are ticket costs, amount of time it takes to get from place to place, and the other modes of transportation that are available.
2. The adding of such quantities of track indicates that the government feels that the number of people and the amount of goods transported by the railroad system is going to continue to increase.

Economic Activities

GUIDING QUESTION *What role does agriculture play in the Indian economy?*

C The Indian government opened its economy to direct foreign investment in the 1990s. It also deregulated many industries and turned over government-run companies to private owners. These changes sparked economic growth that helped expand the middle class. However, these changes also contributed to a growing economic inequality.

About half of India's people work in agriculture. Many farmers rely on labor-intensive methods. They use digging sticks or hand plows to break up the soil. Many fields have irrigation, but in some fields, farmers must hand-carry water from a river or well. Most farmers use oxen and water buffalo to pull plows and carts with heavy loads and turn waterwheels for irrigation. Motorbikes and small tractors are increasingly used by rural people for transportation and farming.

V

ALL ABOARD in India
NEW DELHI
KOLKATA
MUMBAI
CHENNAI
BANGALORE
TIMETABLES *
New Delhi to Mumbai: 16 hours, 45 minutes
Kolkata to Chennai: 11 hours, 45 minutes
Bangalore to New Delhi: 33 hours, 30 minutes
Mumbai to Kolkata: 26 hours, 20 minutes
*Travel times will vary. Listed times represent fastest travel times on a given day.
LINKING INDIA TOGETHER
With over 71,000 miles of track, nearly 10,000 locomotives, and 7,500 stations, India has one of the world's largest railway networks.
R R
AN ECONOMY ON TRACK
70% of India's railways are used to ship nearly half the country's freight. Freight profits are used to make passenger fares cheaper.
MOVING A SUBCONTINENT
India's passenger rail system moves nearly 25 million people daily and almost 9 billion people annually.

India's railroad system is the longest under a single management system. It is also one of the world's most heavily traveled.

▲ **CRITICAL THINKING**

1. ***Analyzing Visuals*** What factors might influence passenger miles on a railroad system?
2. ***Drawing Conclusions*** India plans to add more than 15,000 miles (24,000 km) of track to its railroad system by 2020. This is more than twice the amount of track added in the last 50 years. What does this tell you about how India's government sees the role of railroads in the country's future?

616

networks Online Teaching Options

INFOGRAPHIC

All Aboard in India

Drawing Inferences As students view the infographic, have them pay particular attention to the timetable. Have them look at the amount of time it takes to move from one city to another in India by train. Ask them to draw an inference about the physical size of the subcontinent based on this information. **ELL Visual/Spatial, Logical/Mathematical**

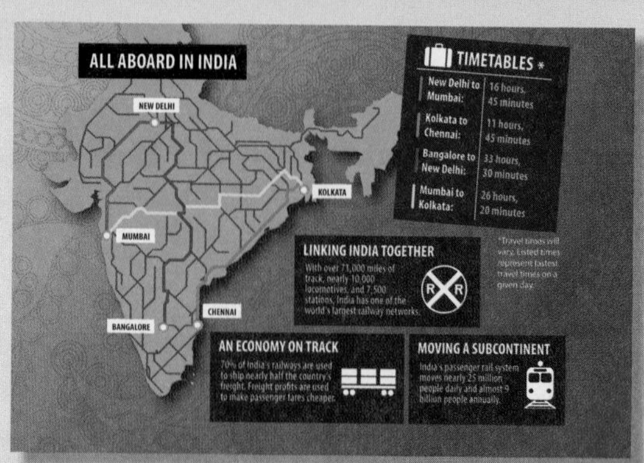
ALL ABOARD IN INDIA
TIMETABLES *
LINKING INDIA TOGETHER
AN ECONOMY ON TRACK
MOVING A SUBCONTINENT

The most important crops on India's farms are rice, wheat, and other grains. Pulses, which include legumes such as chickpeas and lentils, are grown. Large plantations grow commercial agricultural products such as bananas, coffee, tea, and cotton.

Since the 1960s, an effort known as the **green revolution** has sought to increase crop yields in India with high-yielding varieties of crops. These varieties require carefully managed irrigation, fertilizers, and pesticides. The green revolution has stirred controversy, however. Supporters point out that it has increased food production and alleviated hunger in a country that once suffered devastating famines. Opponents argue that excessive use of chemicals pollutes waters, poses health hazards, and leads to pest resistance, requiring farmers to use more and more chemicals to grow crops.

Despite problems of poverty in the country as a whole, India has millions of well-educated, English-speaking people who work in the growing high-technology industry. India is one of the world's largest exporters of high-technology services and software workers. Increasing numbers of schools offer training in technology and engineering. Indian computer professionals are in high demand around the world.

Although India has large oil reserves, it uses more and more energy every year. As more Indians buy cars and trucks, and as electricity serves more homes and businesses, energy consumption increases. According to the U.S. Energy Information Administration, India's oil production held fairly steady at 950,000 barrels of oil per day between 2000 and 2010. However, consumption of oil rose from a little over 2 million barrels a day in 2000 to over 3 million barrels a day in 2010. India must buy the energy from other countries that it does not produce itself.

Many people in India work in **cottage industries**, businesses that employ workers in their homes. These workers work on a variety of tasks. They weave textiles and make shoes, jewelry, woodcarvings, furniture, and bowls. The biggest number of manufacturing jobs comes from India's textile industries, which employ people in turning cotton, jute, wool, silk, and synthetic fibers into fabrics. Nearly every large Indian city has at least one cotton mill.

Heavy industry provides jobs as well. India manufactures iron, steel, cement, and heavy machinery. The Gangetic Plain and parts of eastern India have rich deposits of iron ore, low-grade coal, bauxite, and copper. Many Indians are employed in mining these resources, while others work in India's fishing industry.

READING PROGRESS CHECK

Making Connections Why is farming the occupation of so many of India's people?

Connecting Geography to MATH

India's GDP

In 2011 India's gross domestic product (GDP), or the value of the goods and services produced by its people in a year, was $4.421 trillion. India's GDP was the world's fifth highest after the European Union, the United States, China, and Japan.

Divide India's GDP by its population of 1.2 billion to figure out the per capita GDP, or the value of goods and services produced per person in a year.

R ***EVALUATING*** Based on the per capita GDP, do you think the average Indian is wealthy? Explain your answer.

green revolution a program begun in the 1960s to produce higher-yielding, more productive strains of wheat, rice, and other food crops

cottage industry a business that employs workers in their homes

LESSON 2 REVIEW

Reviewing Vocabulary (Tier Three Words)

1. ***Drawing Inferences*** Write a paragraph discussing how the green revolution has affected India. RH.9–10.4

Using Your Notes

2. ***Summarizing*** Use your graphic organizer on India's economy to write a paragraph summarizing the types of work available to most Indians.

Answering the Guiding Questions

3. ***Summarizing*** How did modern India gain its independence?
4. ***Evaluating*** Why are population patterns so important in India?
5. ***Understanding Perspectives*** What is life in Indian villages like?
6. ***Assessing*** What role does agriculture play in the Indian economy?

Writing Activity

7. ***Informative/Explanatory*** Write a paragraph describing the features of a typical Indian village. WHST.9–10.2

R Reading Skills

Questioning Review with students the three basic economic questions that countries ask: ***What should be produced? How and for whom should the goods be produced?*** Then **ask:** **How is India both a leader in the tech industry but also maintains a workforce in cottage industries?** *(Possible answer: India is very diverse with a large population still living in rural areas where cottage industries most likely are common and megalopolises where manufacturing centers and industries thrive.)* **What additional economic questions might India need to consider as it continues to expand its economy and resolve the overpopulation issues in urban areas?** *(Possible answers: Should cottage industries be replaced with factories? Should manufacturing centers be located in rural areas?)* **AL Logical/Mathematical**

CLOSE & REFLECT

Summarizing Review with students how Indian society and culture were influenced by other groups and civilizations during its history. Discuss how these cultural influences continue to influence Indian culture but also cause conflict. Ask students to write a few sentences that summarize the subregion's society and culture today, as well as its economic activities.

ANSWERS, p. 617

READING PROGRESS CHECK Farming is the occupation of so many of India's people because of the food needs of a large population and the lack of development, which not only would modernize farming methods so they require less labor but would also supply jobs elsewhere for the large numbers of farmers.

Connecting Geography No, the average GDP per capita is $3,684, which means most Indians live in poverty.

LESSON 2 REVIEW ANSWERS

Reviewing Vocabulary

1. Paragraphs may vary but should include that the green revolution is an attempt to produce more food by increasing crop yields through irrigation, fertilizers, and pesticides. This movement has helped reduce hunger but has also introduced new environmental hazards.

Using Your Notes

2. Paragraphs may vary but should include that about half of India's people work in agriculture; many people work in cottage industries, which includes textiles, shoes, jewelry, furniture, and wood carvings; and the well-educated, English-speaking people work in the high technology industry, including software and technology services.

Answering the Guiding Questions

3. Gandhi led people to seek freedom using methods of nonviolent civil disobedience, which eventually led to independence in 1947 with the creation of Hindu India and Muslim Pakistan.
4. The population is still growing and it is important to know when more people are living in an area than the land can support.
5. People in villages live in small houses that they share with animals and that rarely have running water or electricity. People of higher *jatis* live near the center of the village, and those of lower *jatis* live in the surrounding areas. The streets are narrow and twisting, and people gather in open spaces. The school is on the edge of town so children have room to play.
6. Almost half of the workforce is involved in agriculture, making it important to the economy. Plantations grow commercial crops such as bananas, coffee, tea, and cotton.

Writing Activity

7. Paragraphs may vary but should include that the features of a typical Indian village are small houses with one or two rooms that are shared with animals; houses may be on stilts and have sloped roofs in flood-prone areas or be made of mud and have flat roofs in drier areas; the streets are very narrow and winding; and the schoolhouse generally sits on the edge of town.

ENGAGE

V Visual Skills

Identifying Perspectives Have students read the title and first sentence of the Case Study. To help students organize information as they read, have them create a web diagram with the center oval labeled *Perspectives* and three surrounding ovals labeled *Pakistanis, Indians,* and *Kashmiris.* As students read about the differing perspectives about the future of Kashmir and who should govern it, have them write notes about each perspective in the appropriate oval.

TEACH & ASSESS

R Reading Skills

Sequencing Information Ask volunteers to take turns reading aloud each sentence, beginning with "The dispute began. . . ." **Ask:** **What words or phrases indicate a time order or sequence?** *("in 1947 when India and Pakistan became independent," "when Britain withdrew from the region," "until a cease-fire agreement went into effect on January 1, 1949")* **What words or phrases indicate a cause-and-effect relationship?** *(as a result, in response, in return)* Have students work in pairs to create a time line that shows the sequence of events discussed in the text. **Ask:** **What caused Pakistanis to invade Kashmir?** *(The invasion resulted from an ideological conflict between the maharaja of Kashmir, who wanted Kashmir to be an independent country, and many Pakistanis, who believed that Kashmir should become part of Pakistan because it included many Muslims.)* As students read further, encourage them to add events to their time lines.
AL Verbal/Linguistic, Interpersonal

T Technology Skills

Changing Continuity of Groups Organize the class into small groups. Have each group research one of the positions outlined in the text about who should govern Kashmir. Tell students to use reliable online sources to identify the current status of the conflict in the region. Students should note what their chosen group is doing to make its opinion about Kashmir known. Have students present their findings to the class. Guide a discussion about the impact of the ongoing conflict on people in the region. **Interpersonal**

Case Study: **Geopolitics** 

WHAT IS THE FUTURE OF KASHMIR?

V Pakistanis, Indians, and Kashmiris today all have widely different views about who should govern Kashmir, a region in northern India. R The dispute began in 1947 when India and Pakistan became independent from Britain. When Britain withdrew from the region, the Princely states ruled by maharajas were given the choice of joining either India or Pakistan. Hari Singh, the maharaja of Kashmir, wanted Kashmir to be an independent country. Many Pakistanis, however, believed that Kashmir should become part of Pakistan because it included many Muslims. As a result, Pakistanis invaded Kashmir on October 22, 1947. In response, the maharaja signed an agreement to make Kashmir part of India. In return, India agreed to provide military help to force out the Pakistanis. However, India and Kashmir were not successful. Conflict continued until a cease-fire agreement went into effect on January 1, 1949. The United Nations urged Pakistani forces to withdraw until a plebiscite, or vote, could be held to allow Kashmiris to choose between India and Pakistan. However, the Pakistanis did not withdraw and a plebiscite was not held. On July 27, 1949, Pakistan and India signed the Karachi Agreement, which established a line of control (LOC) that divided the territory. Neither Pakistan nor India, however, recognizes the LOC as an international border. Fighting between the two countries intensified when China took parts of northern Kashmir in the 1960s. In 1965 protests in Kashmir against the Indian government stirred unrest in Pakistani cities. Pakistan launched a covert operation, which quickly failed, against Indian forces in Kashmir. The United Nations Security Council became involved and India and Kashmir signed a cease-fire agreement on January 10, 1966. Today, tensions near the LOC continue as both Pakistan and India maintain a large military presence there.

T Not only are Pakistan and India divided on who should govern Kashmir, but so are many Kashmiris. Some want to stay part of India. Others are tired of the conflicts and military presence in the area and want to form their own country as the maharaja wanted. Still others support the Pakistani position.

618

networks Online Teaching Options

IMAGE

An Emerald Set in Pearls

Analyzing Visuals Project the image and ask the following questions to encourage students to improve visual analysis.

- **What do you see? What action is taking place?**
- **What choices has the photographer made in taking the picture—such as the scene or camera placement—that convey a point of view?**
- **What is the subject's point of view? Does she know that she is being photographed?**
- **Why is the title of this image *An Emerald Set in Pearls?***

(Students should be able to identify significant details of the image and properly understand a possible goal of the photographer and the title.) **Visual/Spatial**

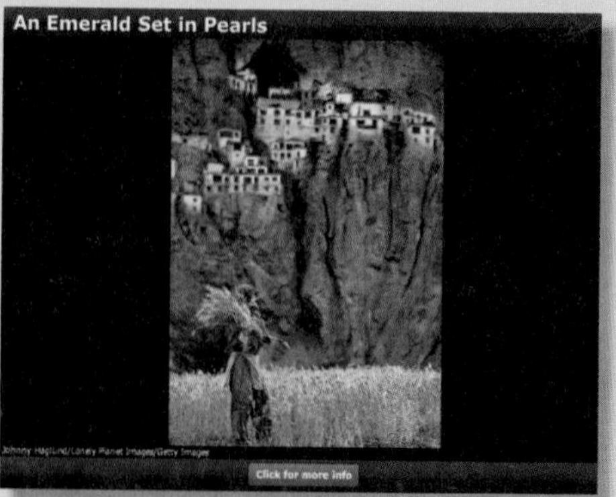

Johnny Haglund/Lonely Planet Images/Getty Images

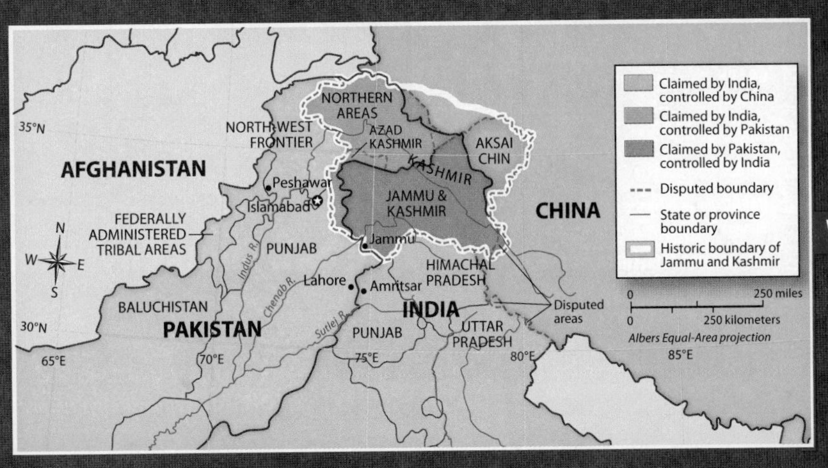

A New Government is Needed

PRIMARY SOURCE

"We know that there is armed struggle going on in Kashmir since 1988, and we Kashmiris can sit down to analyse what progress we have made. India and Pakistan had armed conflicts over Kashmir, they were not only indecisive but they created more problems to all the parties to the dispute. In other words by use of force alone we cannot be successful in finding lasting solution. We need to sit down with open mind and see how we can bring peace, stability and prosperity to the region. Peace and stability can only return to Indian Sub-Continent if Kashmir dispute is resolved according to the wishes of the Kashmiri people."

—Shabir Choudhry, Director of the Institute of Kashmir Affairs

Support for the Indian Government

PRIMARY SOURCE

"Government of India has expressed its willingness to accommodate the legitimate political demands of the people of the state of J&K [Jammu and Kashmir]. However, Pakistan sponsored terrorists have terrorised the population and hindered political dialogue by intimidating or silencing voices of moderation that wish to engage in dialogue. The human rights of the people of J&K have been systematically violated by such terror tactics and the kidnappings and killings of innocent people by terrorists.

Jammu & Kashmir is an integral part of India. There can be no compromise on India's unity and integrity." C

—Ministry of External Affairs, India

What do you think? DBQ

1. ***Drawing Conclusions*** Why might Kashmiris want both Pakistan and India out of Kashmir? RH.9–10.2
2. ***Identifying Central Issues*** On what basis does India defend its claims to Kashmir? RH.9–10.2
3. ***Hypothesizing*** Why might it be dangerous for Kashmir to become an independent country? RH.9–10.1

Case Study **619**

Content Background Knowledge

Ongoing Conflict Border disputes in the Kashmir region erupted in violence over the conflict about who should govern the region. In January 2013, Indian troops killed three Pakistani soldiers and two Indian soldiers. The next month, they killed another Pakistani soldier. Despite curfews imposed by Indian officials, the deaths ignited protests in Kashmir's Indian-controlled areas and subsequent arrests.

V Visual Skills

Spatial Understanding Have student partners analyze the map, noting which region is controlled by which group. Tell pairs to identify the geographic size of the disputed areas. Have then draw comparisons between the regions shown on the map and geographic locations with which they are familiar. Ask them to present their comparisons to the class. **Visual/ Spatial, Interpersonal**

C Critical Thinking Skills

Evaluating Primary Sources Review how the differences in opinion regarding Kashmir have led to conflict over the years. **Ask: What does Choudhry believe will help resolve the conflict?** *(He believes that the use of force will not solve the conflict and that the Kashmiri people need to have a voice for the conflict to be resolved.)* **Who do supporters of the Indian government fault for preventing a "compromise on India's unity and integrity"?** *(Pakistan sponsored terrorists)*

CLOSE & REFLECT

Argument Instruct students to write an argument defending one of the primary sources in this Case Study. Have students conduct additional research to provide supporting evidence for their arguments. Invite students to share their arguments with the class.

PRIMARY SOURCES

A New Government is Needed/ Support for the Indian Government

Exploring Issues Project the primary sources and discuss the main issues within each source. **Ask: Why is a new government needed? Why is the Indian government supported?** *(Students' answers may vary, but they should be able to identify significant details from the sources and properly understand the goal of each source.)* Then have students write a paragraph explaining which source they tend to agree with and why. Organize student into groups based on their agreement with a source. Lead a class debate in which each group represents one side of the issue as portrayed in the sources. Tell students to use the information in the Case Study to support their views. **BL Logical/ Mathematical, Verbal/Linguistic**

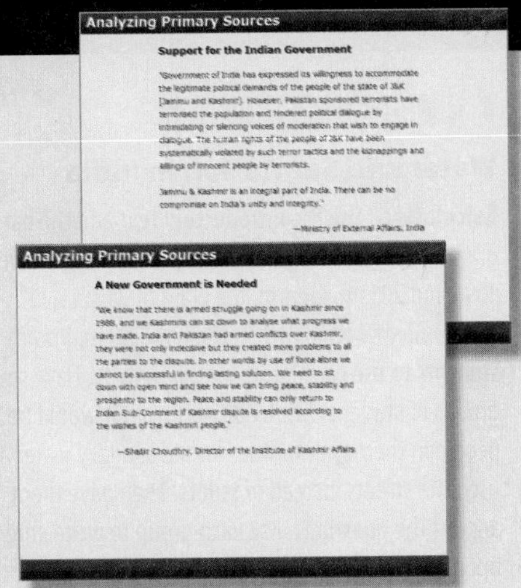

ANSWERS, p. 619

DBQ What do you think?

1. Both India and Pakistan have caused many conflicts within Kashmir and maintain a strong military presence there, which might cause the people of Kashmir to want to be an independent country.
2. India feels that Kashmir is an integral part of their country as the maharaja signed an agreement in 1949 to be part of India.
3. It could be dangerous for Kashmir to be an independent country as China, Pakistan, and India could cause conflict in the country or with each other, which could make the country strategically important to each of them.

ENGAGE

R Reading Skills

Predicting Have students predict the effects of India's population on the environment after reading *It Matters Because.* Ask them to consider the impact of population on physical features, resources, animals, and plants.

TEACH & ASSESS

T Technology Skills

Researching Explain to students that India's government has followed a Five-Year Plan since 1951. **Ask: Why do you think India's government chooses to implement an economic plan that is five years long?** *(Possible answer: India's government wants to plan ahead but not too far into the future. Long-term planning is more effective than short-range planning.)* Have students work in small groups to research progress made under the previous and current Five-Year Plan. Ask them to gather facts and data to produce a presentation that shows this information using visuals such as infographics, graphs, or charts. Instruct them to include information about poverty, economic development, and resource management.
BL **Visual/Spatial**

W Writing Skills

Considering Advantages and Disadvantages After students read about how human activities have negatively affected the environment in India, have students weigh the advantages and disadvantages that colonialism brought to India's economy. Ask them to write an essay that addresses both, using specific examples. Invite students to share their ideas with the class and use them as a discussion starter. **Verbal/Linguistic**

ANSWERS, p. 620

TAKING NOTES: Managing Resources—Deforestation: damaged an estimated 40 percent of forests, increases erosion and flooding. Farmland overuse: removes soil nutrients. Groundwater pollution: increasing. Industrial and human waste: pollute water supply. Overcrowding and lack of sanitation: lead to air pollution and disease. **Human Impact**—Illegal cutting of trees for firewood: leads to soil erosion, flooding, temperature increase, loss of habitats. Rapid growth of cities: straining resources. Overuse, plowing, and improper irrigation: causing farmland depletion. The 1984 Bhopal chemical leak: still affects people's health. **Addressing the Issues**—India's government involved in environmental protection, constitutional amendments, court rulings, and laws of protection and prohibition. Endangered species protected by law. India's Five-Year Plan: improving standard of living and environmental protection.

networks
There's More Online!

- ☑ **GRAPH** Water and Sanitation in India
- ☑ **IMAGE** Bengal Tiger
- ☑ **IMAGE** Busy Street in Kolkata
- ☑ **IMAGE** Pollution in the Yamuna River
- ☑ **INTERACTIVE SELF-CHECK QUIZ**
- ☑ **VIDEO** People and Their Environment: India

LESSON 3
People and Their Environment: India

ESSENTIAL QUESTION • *How do physical systems and human systems shape a place?*

Reading HELPDESK (CCSS)

Academic Vocabulary (Tier Two Words)
- **environment**
- **prohibit**

Content Vocabulary (Tier Three Words)
- **pesticide**
- **ecotourism**

TAKING NOTES: ***Key Ideas and Details***

FORMULATING QUESTIONS As you read about India's people and environment, use a graphic organizer like the one below to list details about India's environment. Then formulate a question about each section.

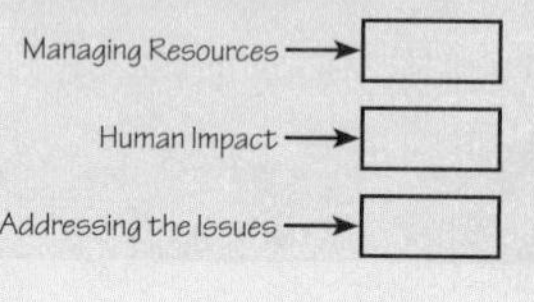

IT MATTERS BECAUSE

R *India is among the most biologically diverse countries in the world. Although it has less than 2.5 percent of the Earth's land area, it has nearly 17 percent of its human population. It also has the world's largest population of wild tigers and a number of other rare and endangered species. India's ability to manage its resources while raising the standard of living for its entire population will affect hundreds of millions of people, as well as many species of animals and plants.*

Managing Resources

GUIDING QUESTION *Why are many resources in India not managed closely?*

T In recent years, India's economy has grown rapidly, and the country has made significant advances in reducing poverty and improving the education and health of its citizens. Despite these advances, India's people still face high levels of poverty and inequality. The government's latest Five-Year Plan (2012–2017) calls for sustainable growth. In the past, India has often favored economic development over resource management and sustainability.

W Development policies have put many of India's resources at risk. Forests provide a good example. India's forests are an important natural resource, providing a livelihood for some 250 million people. It is estimated, however, that 40 percent of India's forests are degraded. Deforestation began in the colonial era. The construction of the country's railways, which facilitated moving crops to market, encouraged the development of cash crop agriculture and the clearing of land.

Removal of forests also affects farmland by increasing erosion and flooding. Erosion degrades farmland by washing away the nutrients that make farmland productive. This in turn leads to further degradation because farmers overuse the soil in an effort to increase their harvests. Overuse further depletes nutrients. Erosion caused by wind is also a problem in drier areas of India.

620

networks ***Online Teaching Options***

INTERACTIVE BELLRINGER

Water and Sanitation in India

Calculating Use the introductory text and the bar graphs showing sanitation statistics for India between 1990 and 2011 to identify the ways in which environmental issues affect the population. Inform students to use calculators for this activity. Have small groups of students briefly discuss what it would be like if people in their communities lacked sanitary water and used the streets instead of toilets. Then have them answer the questions. Ask each group to write agreed-upon answers to the questions. Review the answers as a class, asking students to share how they calculated the answers. BL **Verbal/Linguistic, Logical/Mathematical, Interpersonal**

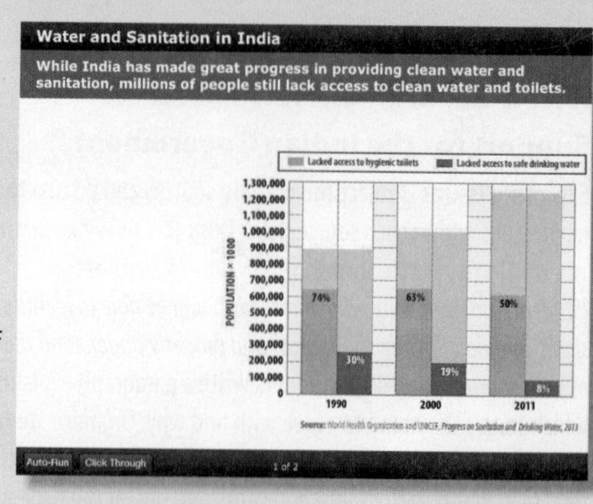

No resources are more basic to human life than air and water. Yet these important resources are also threatened in India. Pollution of groundwater is a growing health threat. Much of India's water has high levels of chemicals that make it unsafe to drink because as water supplies are depleted, people draw water from deeper and deeper in the ground, where it is polluted by arsenic, fluoride, and heavy metals. Excessive fertilizer runoff and pollution from human and industrial wastes also contaminate water supplies. **W**

Air pollution is another serious problem. A number of India's cities, including its capital, New Delhi, are among the world's most polluted. Overcrowding in urban areas leads to air pollution as a result of increased use of fossil fuels for transportation and industry.

✔ **READING PROGRESS CHECK**

Summarizing What resources in India are threatened?

Human Impact

GUIDING QUESTION *How has pollution affected the quality of life in India?*

The size and density of India's population creates a significant human impact on the **environment**. Ten percent of the world's population (about half of India's population) lives in the Ganges River valley. Although the Indian economy is growing rapidly, the country also holds a large concentration of people living in poverty, especially in the states of Chhattisgarh, Jharkhand, and Maniput. Large numbers of people cut down trees illegally because they need fuel for cooking. Removal of forests creates many other problems. In addition to soil erosion and flooding, loss of trees can cause temperatures to rise. Loss of forests destroys habitats for wildlife, including birds and other creatures that eat insects, snakes, and rodents.

environment the complex of physical, chemical, and biotic factors (as climate, soil, and living things) that act upon an organism or an ecological community and ultimately determine its survival

India's already large cities continue to grow rapidly. Their growing populations have water and energy needs. To supply the residents of northern India with water and power, the Tehri Dam was built in the Himalaya. Located

GRAPH SKILLS

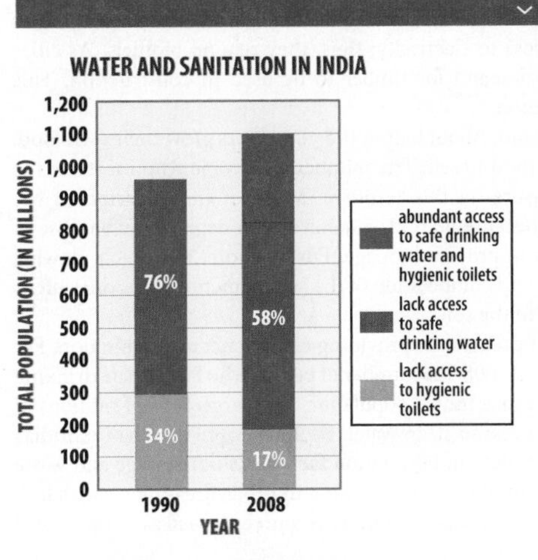

Source: *New York Times*, March 21, 2012 "Liter by liter, Indians get cleaner water," Amy Yee

India provided more of its people with clean water and better hygiene between 1990 and 2008.

CRITICAL THINKING

1. ***Analyzing Visuals*** Which improvement—access to safe drinking water or access to hygienic toilets—affected the greatest number of people?
2. ***Synthesizing*** Why is access to clean water still a problem even though over 80 percent of Indians have it?

V

W Writing Skills

Argument Have students research additional information about the chemical pollution of India's water resources and its effect on safe water supplies that are needed for drinking, cooking, and other needs. Ask them to find out how one state or area within India is trying to tackle the problem. Then have students write a position paper that argues how that state or area should be used as a model in the country's attempts to clean up the water supply. BL Verbal/Linguistic

Content Background Knowledge

Air Moves and Pollutes Even though efforts have been made in New Delhi to combat air pollution, the situation has worsened. Population growth has fueled transportation pollution. Thousands of automobiles and buses crowd city streets each day, resulting in more air pollution. Tests have indicated that fine-particle pollution has increased nearly 50 percent and nitrogen dioxide even more. Another problem is the nearby areas that have more lenient controls on air emissions. Air moves from one area to the next. The government of New Delhi realizes that limiting air pollution is going to take a united approach, rather than a single city trying to implement changes.

V Visual Skills

Applying Direct students to the graph about water and sanitation in India. Invite a volunteer to explain the difference between water and sanitation. **Ask:** **What conclusion can you draw from the data in this chart?** *(Possible answer: India is making strides in improving water and sanitation needs.)* **How do you think this chart might look twenty years from now?** *(Possible answer: The percentage of abundant access to safe drinking water and hygienic toilets will increase but perhaps not as significantly as it has in the past eighteen years.)* Ask students to work with a partner to figure out another way to display this data. ELL Visual/Spatial, Logical/Mathematical

INTERACTIVE WHITEBOARD ACTIVITY

Pressures of Population Growth

Analyzing Cause and Effect This activity will highlight for students how a growing population can affect a country's resources. Display the activity for students. Have them read each human impact statement carefully, and then choose the environmental effect that results from the impact. Remind students to check their answers when they are finished, and to correct any errors that they may have made in order to get a complete and accurate picture of the causes and effects of a growing population on the environment. Kinesthetic, Logical/Mathematical

Pressures of Population Growth

Directions: Though India is rich in natural resources, the needs of its growing population are exceeding what the land can support. Match the impact of the growing population with the environmental effect it creates by using the writing tool to draw a checkmark in the appropriate column. Some descriptions may match more than one column.

Impact of Growing Population	Deforestation	Water Pollution	Air Pollution	Depleted Farmland
Farmers over-irrigate without proper drainage.	☐	☐	☐	☐
More people without electricity cut down trees for biofuel.	☐	☐	☐	☐
Growing cities lack proper sewage and waste disposal.	☐	☐	☐	☐
Farmers over-plow, changing structure and composition of soil.	☐	☐	☐	☐
Growing cities need more timber.	☐	☐	☐	☐
Growing number of cars produce more dangerous emissions.	☐	☐	☐	☐
Greater use of fertilizers produces more runoff.	☐	☐	☐	☐
The need for cash crops requires clearing more land.	☐	☐	☐	☐
Clearing forests causes soil erosion, which washes away nutrients.	☐	☐	☐	☐

Show Answers

ANSWERS, p. 621

✔ **READING PROGRESS CHECK** The forests, soil, air, and water are resources that are threatened in India.

CRITICAL THINKING

1. Access to clean drinking water has affected the greatest number of people.
2. India's population is so large that even though more than 80 percent have access to clean water, tens of millions of people are still without clean water.

C Critical Thinking Skills

Analyzing Visuals As a class, discuss the image and how the Yamuna River flows though Delhi, one of the most polluted and populous cities in India. **Ask:** **What does this image indicate about the poverty level in India?** *(Possible answer: It is high and people are willing to risk their health by entering polluted waters to find valuable items that have been discarded.)* **Take a close look at the kinds of wastes that have been dumped in the river. Why have people thrown these items in the river versus disposing of them properly?** *(Possible answer: There is probably limited garbage collection because it is an overwhelming job, and the city does not have the resources to provide such services.)* Lead a class discussion asking students to think of solutions to help clean up the Yamuna River. **Visual/Spatial**

Make Connections

Explain to students that the government recently ruled that the Yamuna River was no longer a river but rather a drain because of its high pollution levels. Discuss with students how dumping pollution affects the flow of waterways and the organisms that rely on it. Ask students to make connections to a waterway or body of water in their area that is or was threatened because of pollution. Have them figure out what actions were (or are) being taken and then discuss whether those actions could be used and successful for the Yamuna River.

R Reading Skills

Defining As a class, discuss soil productivity. If possible, show students examples of productive and nonproductive soil. **Ask:** **How is soil productivity important in agriculture?** *Productive soil is healthy and strong so that it can support crops.)* **What does the term *composition* mean?** *(Composition refers to the parts that make up a whole.)* **How does this definition relate to productivity?** *(The soil's composition helps to determine whether it will be productive.)* ELL **Verbal/Linguistic**

ANSWERS, p. 622

CRITICAL THINKING

1. The photograph indicates that the sanitation systems in major cities are overwhelmed and unable to support the amount of waste created by a growing urban population.
2. The growing population: deforests land for fuel, construction, and farmland; mismanages soil resources by overworking land and by excessive irrigation; pollutes the air with auto emissions, construction dust, fires for heating and cooking, and industry; pollutes water with raw sewage, agricultural runoff, and industrial waste.

C

A man looks for recyclable items in the polluted waters of the Yamuna River in New Delhi.

Andrew Caballero-Reynolds/AFP/Getty Images

▲ **CRITICAL THINKING**

1. ***Analyzing Visuals*** What does this photograph indicate about sanitation systems in India's major cities?
2. ***Identifying Cause and Effect*** How does India's growing population affect its environment?

on the Bhagirathi River, the Tehri Dam is India's highest dam. The dam was designed to increase the flow of water during the dry season. The poor in India's cities often also lack access to electricity; thus, they rely on biofuels. As cities grow, they increase the demand for timber to be used in construction. This further adds to deforestation.

R India is rich in farmland. About half of India's farmers grow their own food, and the other half grow food to sell. The numbers of people who must use the farmland put great pressure on this resource. Much of India's farmland has become less productive because its nutrients have been depleted or because of excessive irrigation with improper drainage. Furthermore, too much plowing can change the structure and composition of the soil. Sometimes it is difficult or impossible to grow food in the soil.

India has made great progress in providing clean water and sanitation. For example, between 1990 and 2008, the number of people who lacked safe drinking water fell by half. But because India's population is so large, tens of millions of people still do not have access to clean water. By 2008, more than half of India's people still did not have toilets and sanitation facilities. Poor sewage and waste disposal threatens water supplies. Overcrowding in urban areas along with lack of sanitation leads to pollution of air and water resources as well as to the spread of disease.

The large population contributes to air pollution as well. Fires used for cooking and heating create smoke. In densely populated cities, construction dust and auto

networks Online Teaching Options

INTERACTIVE IMAGE

Pollution and Recycling

Narrative As students view the photo, ask them to find items that they think are recyclable. Have them write a story describing one or two recyclable items that the man in the photo has found and how he will use these items for himself and his family. When students have completed their narratives, they may share them with the class. AL **Verbal/Linguistic**

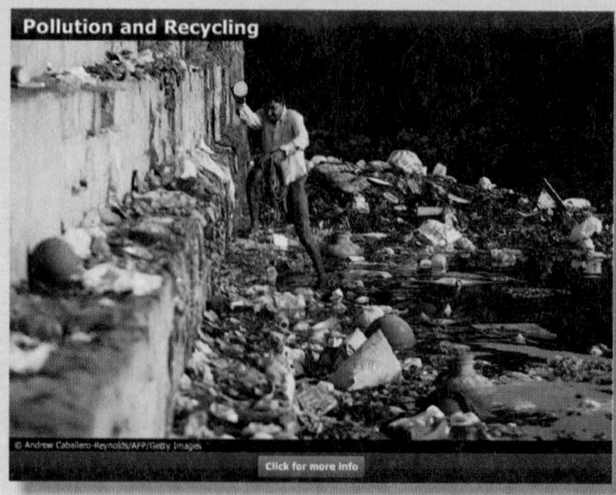

emissions create smog that can cause respiratory and heart problems, especially in children and older people. New Delhi has more than 7 million registered vehicles. Each day, another 1,400 cars and trucks get on the city's roads.

One of the worst environmental disasters in history occurred in December 1984 in Bhopal, a city in central India. A dangerous chemical leaked from a factory that made insecticides. It drifted over densely populated areas around the plant and killed between 15,000 and 20,000 people. Hundreds of thousands of others were blinded or suffered respiratory problems or other injuries. By the early twenty-first century, testing found that the soil and water around the factory site was still contaminated. This soil pollution has been blamed for high rates of birth defects and chronic health problems among people living near the factory. **W**

prohibit to prevent from doing something

pesticide a chemical used to kill insects, rodents, and other pests

✓ READING PROGRESS CHECK

Making Generalizations How did the 1984 Bhopal accident continue to affect people near the site in the early 2000s?

Addressing the Issues

GUIDING QUESTION *What steps has the Indian national government taken to combat pollution?*

Although India's environmental problems are severe, the national government has been involved in environmental protection. In 1976 India's constitution was amended to require the government to protect the environment. India's Supreme Court has made many decisions designed to protect India's air, water, ecosystems, and wildlife. It has considered a proposal to charge an extra tax on diesel cars because of the pollution they cause. In 2011 the Indian Supreme Court **prohibited** the production, distribution, and use of a **pesticide** called endosulfan because of its toxicity and its persistence in the environment. **C**

Almost 5 percent of India's land area falls within protected areas to ensure that the habitat of Bengal tigers is preserved.

▼ CRITICAL THINKING

1. ***Speculating*** How has the growth of India's human population caused the Bengal tiger to become an endangered species?
2. ***Defending*** Do you think it is important for India's government to protect tigers, elephants, and snow leopards? Defend your position.

Mike Ledwith/Flickr/Getty Images

GAME

People and Their Environment: India

Defining Students can strengthen their vocabulary skills by completing this crossword puzzle. As students play the game, have them consider how each term relates to the people and the environment of India. Have students check their answers at the end of the activity, and correct any errors, if necessary. ELL AL Verbal/Linguistic

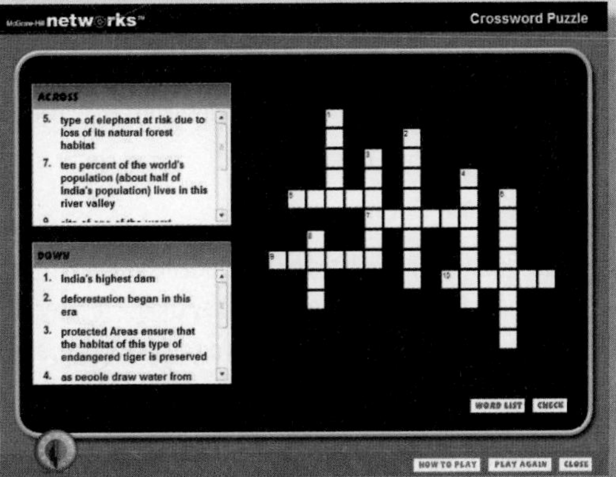

W Writing Skills

Informative/Explanatory Discuss the Bhopal environmental disaster with students. Then have them write an essay that explains more about the incident, such as how it happened, how people responded, and what measures were put in place after the incident to prevent it from reoccurring in Bhopal or elsewhere. Suggest to students that they take a particular angle in their papers such as political, economic, or social. Remind students to use reliable sources when using the Internet to gather information. BL Verbal/Linguistic

Content Background Knowledge

Diesel With gasoline prices on the rise, many people have chosen diesel cars as an alternative. Gas mileage is much better in diesel cars, and the price of diesel is often lower or very competitive with other fuels. The downside is the air pollution that diesel cars cause. India's government is considering placing an extra tax on diesel cars and possibly even on SUVs. However, if diesel cars are more fuel-efficient, they are likely to burn less fuel than nondiesel cars.

C Critical Thinking Skills

Evaluating Invite a volunteer to read the paragraphs under "Addressing the Issues." **Ask:** **What is the Indian government doing to protect the environment?** *(It has prohibited the production, distribution, and use of a pesticide.)* Discuss with students what additional actions have been proposed. **Do you think adding a tax on diesel cars can be enforced? Explain.** *(Possible answer: It will be difficult for India to enforce this tax. It may not make much of a difference in emissions of diesel cars.)* **Which action do you think better protects the environment, limiting the use of a dangerous pesticides or placing a tax on diesel cars? Why?** *(Possible answer: Limiting the use of the pesticide will be easier to enforce and will decrease pollution of the environment, including water resources).* AL Verbal/Linguistic

ANSWERS, p. 623

✓ READING PROGRESS CHECK In the early 2000s, the soil and water were still contaminated, leading to high rates of birth defects and chronic health problems among people living around the site.

CRITICAL THINKING

1. The growing population has increased development, causing a loss of habitat for the Bengal tiger.
2. Answers will differ based on the position students choose on preservation but should be supported with information from the lesson, including that India has unique and diverse animals that are at great risk from loss of habitat and poaching.

T Technology Skills

Gathering Information After students read about India's efforts to protect plants and animals, have them use additional resources to find out the differences among national parks, wildlife sanctuaries, conservation reserves, and community reserves. **Ask: Are all of the animals mentioned in the text protected in one of these four protected areas?** *(Student answers may vary based on their findings but should include that the animals are protected in these areas.)* Suggest that students work with a partner. Provide them with links to websites and other electronic resources that will provide statistics on the change in populations of protected animals over the past several decades. **Ask: Has placing these animals in the protected areas made a difference? Include statistics to support your answer.** *(Student answers may vary, but their data should support their response based on the most recent data they are able to locate.)* **AL Naturalist**

R Reading Skills

Determining Importance Have students read about the significance of the Forest Rights Act. **Ask: Why do you think the act was such landmark legislation?** *(Possible answer: because it had its roots in the women's movement, and it gave people living in the forest the right to stand up to protect their resources against companies that wanted to exploit them)* Provide an opportunity for students to stage a debate between the mining and timber company management and the people of the forests in India. After each group has presented an argument and rebuttal, ask them if they have changed their point of view. **BL Verbal/Linguistic**

CLOSE & REFLECT

Summarizing To close the lesson, have students write a summary for each section or feature in the lesson. Ask them to include the most important ideas that were covered, as well as what they learned.

ANSWERS, p. 624

READING PROGRESS CHECK India's twelfth Five-Year Plan wants economic growth that occurs more quickly than in the past and is more environmentally sustainable.

T

In 1972 the government of India passed a law to protect wildlife from poaching and smuggling. In 2003 this law was amended to increase punishment and penalties. The law was also expanded to protect plants and ecosystems as well as endangered animals. India has the world's largest population of wild tigers and many other endangered species such as the Asian elephant, the one-horned rhinoceros, and snow leopards. While the African elephant is endangered primarily as a result of poaching of the animals for their ivory tusks, the Asian elephant is at risk due to loss of its natural forest habitat. The clearing of forests for timber and agricultural purposes continues to threaten the viability of this species. To protect its unique biological heritage, India has created a network of 668 protected areas. These include national parks, wildlife sanctuaries, conservation reserves, and community reserves.

ecotourism the practice and business of recreational travel based on a concern for the environment

In 2012 the court restricted **ecotourism** in India's tiger reserves. Although ecotourism is designed to protect wildlife and ecosystems by increasing appreciation, environmentalists argued that tourists were threatening tiger habitat. After a temporary ban on any tourism, the court allowed tourism in the reserves but with far more restrictions.

In 2006 India's government passed the Forest Rights Act. This law gives authority to people living in the forest areas to prohibit forest clearance by large timber and mining companies. This law can trace its origins to a movement in the 1970s among Himalayan women. In what is considered one of India's first environmental movements, the women protected trees that were marked for logging. The women were determined to protect the trees that provided them with firewood and prevented soil erosion.

India continues its efforts to improve the quality of life for its people. The government, however, recognizes that sustainable development and economic growth are related. These principles guided India's Planning Commission as it prepared the near final draft of its twelfth Five-Year Plan. This latest plan states that India must improve living standards "through a growth process which is faster than in the past, more inclusive, and also more environmentally sustainable." The draft went on to say that India cannot "neglect the environmental consequences of economic activity, or allow unsustainable depletion and deterioration of natural resources."

READING PROGRESS CHECK

Analyzing What perspective does India's twelfth Five-Year Plan take toward economic growth?

LESSON 3 REVIEW (CCSS)

Reviewing Vocabulary (Tier Three Words)

1. ***Hypothesizing*** Write a paragraph to form a hypothesis about why India's Supreme Court put a temporary ban on the pesticide endosulfan. RH.9–10.4

Using Your Notes

2. ***Formulating Questions*** Choose one of the questions you formulated as you completed your graphic organizer. List three additional questions you might ask to begin researching the answer to the first one.

Answering the Guiding Questions

3. ***Identifying Cause and Effect*** Why are many resources in India not managed closely?
4. ***Finding the Main Idea*** How has pollution affected the quality of life in India?
5. ***Classifying*** What steps has the Indian national government taken to combat pollution?

Writing Activity

6. ***Informative/Explanatory*** Based on the information covered in this lesson, what environmental challenges are posed by India's rapid population growth? WHST.9–10.2

LESSON 3 REVIEW ANSWERS

Reviewing Vocabulary

1. Paragraphs may vary but should include the toxicity and the length of time that endosulfan can remain in the environment.

Using Your Notes

2. Questions formulated by the students will vary based on the initial question they choose to research, but could include information on deforestation, air pollution, water pollution, and soil erosion.

Answering the Guiding Questions

3. India has put more emphasis on economic development than resource management due to its large and growing population.
4. A lack of clean drinking water and increased illness and disease from poor sanitation and air pollution are lowering the quality of life in India.
5. The national government has amended the constitution to require the government to protect the environment and the Supreme Court has made many decisions to protect the air, water, and ecosystems of India.

Writing Activity

6. India's rapid population growth: puts a strain on the infrastructure, leading to water and air pollution; leads to deforestation for fuel, construction, and farmland; leads to soil erosion and degradation due to overworking the soil, excessive irrigation, and excessive chemical use; and leads to destruction of habitats for many unique plants and animals.

CHAPTER 25 Assessment 

Directions: On a separate sheet of paper, answer the questions below. Make sure that you read carefully and answer all parts of the questions.

Lesson Review

Lesson 1

1. ***Diagramming*** Create a diagram to show the following movements that affected India's shape and position: a major tectonic event about 160 million years ago, a major tectonic event about 50 million years ago, and the thrusting up of the Himalaya.
2. ***Assessing*** What is a monsoon? Discuss the positive and negative effects of monsoons in India.
3. ***Identifying Cause and Effect*** Identify three types of timber resources in India. Explain the conditions that affect the supply of these resources in India.

Lesson 2

4. ***Analyzing Cause and Effect*** Discuss the effects of British imperialist policy in India. Explain how the eventual push by Indians for self-rule was in response to this policy.
5. ***Summarizing*** Provide an overview of the concept of *jati*.
6. ***Identifying Central Issues*** What is the green revolution? Why has it given rise to controversy?

Lesson 3

7. ***Identifying Cause and Effect*** What is the approximate percentage of farmers in India that grow their own food or grow food to sell? Create a graphic organizer to show the cause and effect of this pressure on India's farmland.
8. ***Summarizing*** Summarize efforts taken by the Indian government to address environmental protection since 1976. Explain why these efforts have not achieved all of the desired results.
9. ***Evaluating*** How did an act passed by India's government in 2006 connect to action among Himalayan women during the 1970s? What does this tell you about the determination of these Himalayan women? Within your response, include the name of the referenced act.

21st Century Skills

Use the document to answer the following questions.

INDIA: OIL PRODUCTION AND CONSUMPTION

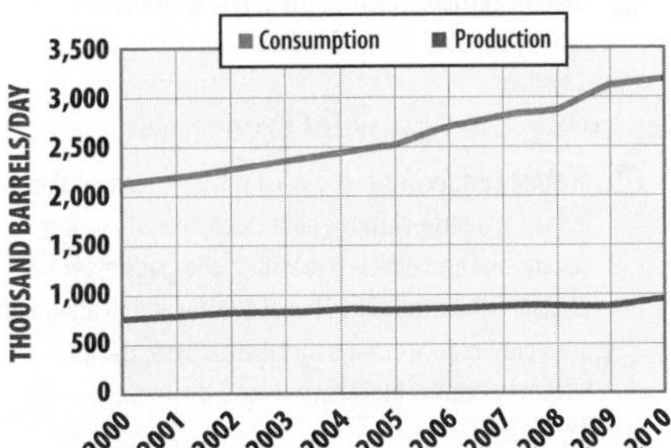

Source: U.S. Energy Information Administration

10. ***Compare & Contrast*** Compare and contrast India's oil production and consumption in 2000 and in 2010.
11. ***Using Graphs*** Explain whether it would be logical to conclude, based on the data in the graph, that India was reliant on oil imports from 2000 to 2010.

Critical Thinking

12. ***Exploring Issues*** Suppose you are a geologist who is writing a full-page blog to identify and describe the three major river systems in India and their importance to life in India. Within your blog, include an explanation of at least four types of pollution that could threaten these river systems—and action that might be taken to address the threats.

Need Extra Help?

If You've Missed Question	1	2	3	4	5	6	7	8	9	10	11	12
Go to page	606	608	610	611	611	617	622	623	624	625	625	607

CHAPTER 25 Assessment Answers

Lesson Review

Lesson 1

1. Diagrams should show a large landmass breaking away from Africa 160 million years ago, landmass colliding with the southern edge of Asia 50 million years ago, and the Himalaya being thrust up between the two landmasses.
2. It is a seasonal wind that brings wet ocean air in summer and reverses direction to bring cool, dry air in winter. Positive effects include bringing rain for crops and creating rain forests and causing cooler, drier winter weather. Negative effects include heavy rains causing floods.
3. Timber resources in India include sandalwood, sal, and teak. The supply of these types of wood is affected by people illegally cutting them for fuel and clearing the land of timber to create farmland.

Lesson 2

4. The British imperialist policy led them to take control of India. Under this policy they employed mercantilism where they took raw goods from India and then forced India to buy back the finished products made with these goods. This led to Indians pushing for self-rule as they were not permitted to have control or use of the raw goods of their country under this system.
5. A *jati* is a caste or social position into which a person is born. It determines where a person can live, what kind of job and education her or she may receive, and who he or she is able to marry.
6. The green revolution is a program to produce higher-yielding crops. It is controversial because some people believe that the fertilizers and pesticides used to produce higher-yielding crops are harming the environment.

Lesson 3

7. About half of all farmers grow their own food; the other half grow food to sell. Graphic organizers should be supported with information from the chapter, including that farmland has become less productive due to overuse and excessive irrigation. This causes the soil to lack the nutrients and structure to grow food.
8. The Indian government amended the constitution in 1976 to require government environmental protection. Since then, the Supreme Court has made many decisions to protect the air, water, ecosystems, and wildlife, including a ban on the pesticide endosulfan and laws against wildlife poaching and smuggling. In 2006, the government passed the Forest Rights Act, which allows people living in forested areas to prohibit forest clearance. These efforts have not had total success because the needs of the large and growing population have come before environmental needs.
9. The Forest Rights Act passed in 2006 gave people living in forested areas the right to prohibit others from removing trees. This is similar to the actions of Himalayan women in the 1970s when they protected trees that were marked by logging. This indicates that the Himalayan women were very determined and outspoken, and garnered great deal of attention for their cause.

21st Century Skills

10. In 2000, India consumed more than twice the amount of oil it produced. In 2010, it consumed more than three times what it produced. Oil production has remained relatively the same while consumption has increased.
11. As India is consuming more oil than it is producing, it is logical to conclude that it is reliant upon oil imports.

Critical Thinking

12. Blog entries will vary but should: identify the Ganges, Brahmaputra, and Indus Rivers; describe the rivers' importance in irrigation, transportation, hydroelectric power, drinking water, and fishing; and identify at least four types of pollution that threaten the rivers (industrial waste, agricultural runoff, raw sewage, soil and silt washed from the mountains due to deforestation).

Assessment Answers

Applying Map Skills

13 The Vindhya and Satpura Ranges divide India into northern and southern regions with the Deccan Plateau to the south. The Eastern Ghats lie on the east of the Deccan Plateau while the Western Ghats lie on the western side of the plateau.

14 The highest elevations in India are in the Himalaya.

15 The Gangetic Plain is the most densely populated area of India.

Exploring the Essential Question

16 Essays will vary but should be strongly supported with information from the chapter, including that the large and densely populated cities and lack of regulation led to hundreds of thousands of people being killed and injured, with problems ranging from birth defects to chronic health problems still affecting the people living near the site. This is representative of how the large population and lack of enforcement of laws and regulations continues to affect the country today.

College and Career Readiness

17 Memos will vary based on the grassroots efforts that the student chooses but could include: protection of forests and wildlife, including the creation of national parks, sanctuaries, and reserves; protection of trees and forested areas by the Forest Rights Act; and restrictions on ecotourism.

Writing About Geography

18 Articles will vary but should include that the Gupta Empire united most of India and was one of the most advanced civilizations of its time, contributing mathematics, astronomy, and metallurgy, and great art and poetry to the culture.

Analyzing Primary Sources

19 The author criticizes the new constitution for keeping the fundamental liberties under control of the government and for reforms that are to be financed by taxes, which will place an even greater burden on the poor.

20 The views of the author seem to align with those of Gandhi, who felt that the people should be in control of the resources of the country and that the government should not have absolute power.

CHAPTER 25 Assessment

Directions: On a separate sheet of paper, answer the questions below. Make sure that you read carefully and answer all parts of the questions.

Applying Map Skills

Use the Unit 7 Atlas to answer the following questions.

13 ***The World in Spatial Terms*** Use your mental map of India to describe the spatial relationship among the following: Deccan Plateau, Eastern Ghats, Western Ghats, and the Vindhya and Satpura Ranges.

14 ***Places and Regions*** Name the location of highest elevation in India.

15 ***Human Systems*** Identify the plain that is the most densely populated area of India.

Exploring the Essential Question

16 ***Making Connections*** Use what you have learned about human systems—history, politics, population, society, culture, and economics—to write a one-page essay explaining how the 1984 Bhopal disaster and its aftermath are representative of ways the physical systems and human systems of India have shaped the country. WHST.9–10.2

College and Career Readiness

17 ***Reaching Conclusions*** Imagine that you work for an organization that is interested in advancing environmental protection efforts in India. Your boss has asked you to research recent legislation and grassroots efforts related to environmental concerns in India. Provide a one-page memo to identify and explain the focus of the legislation and grassroots local efforts that you find the most effective. Your memo should explain why you find these to be the most effective. WHST.9–10.2; WHST.9–10.4

Writing About Geography

18 ***Informative/Explanatory*** Do research and then use standard grammar, spelling, sentence structure, and punctuation to write an article explaining why the Gupta Empire was one of the world's most advanced civilizations of its time—and why it ceased to exist. WHST.9–10.2

DBQ Analyzing Primary Sources

Use the document to answer the following questions.

PRIMARY SOURCE

"The new constitution gives no scope for retrenchment and therefore no scope for measures of social reform except by fresh taxation, the heavy burden of which on the poor will outweigh all the advantages of any reforms.

The reformed constitution keeps all the fundamental liberties of person, property, press, and association completely under bureaucratic control. All those laws which give to the irresponsible officers of the Executive Government of India absolute powers to override the popular will, are still unrepealed."

—C. Rajagopalachar, Introduction to *Freedom's Battle: Being a Comprehensive Collection of Writings and Speeches on the Present Situation,* 1922

19 ***Understanding Historical Interpretation*** What criticisms does the author make of the new constitution? RH.9–10.1

20 ***Interpreting Significance*** Explain whether the author's views align with Gandhi's general political and social views regarding the people of India. RH.9–10.1

Research and Presentation

21 ***Gathering Information*** With a partner, conduct research to learn more about the slum problem in India. Create a multimedia presentation to explain why and how these slums developed, the living conditions within the slums, and the complex problems that have resulted in them. Propose at least two actions that might ultimately lead to the decline of slums and a better quality of life for those who currently live in slums. Within your presentation, include video and audio clips, maps, photographs, and diagrams or graphs. WHST.9–10.1; WHST.9–10.6; WHST.9–10.7; WHST.9–10.8

Need Extra Help?

If You've Missed Question	13	14	15	16	17	18	19	20	21
Go to page	598	598	598	623	624	611	626	626	615

626

Research and Presentation

21 Multimedia presentations will vary but should be supported with information from the chapter as well as video and audio clips, maps, photographs, and diagrams or graphs that help illustrate the slum problem in India and must include information on how and why the slums developed, describe the living conditions and what problems led to these conditions, and propose at least two actions that would lead to the decline of the slums. Answers could include the high cost of living; increasing population and migration to cities; lack of jobs, infrastructure, and education; no electricity, running water, or sanitation services; solutions include education of people on proper waste disposal, building appropriate housing, improving infrastructure, and building a better economy.

CHAPTER 26

Pakistan and Bangladesh Planner

UNDERSTANDING BY DESIGN®

Enduring Understandings

- *Certain patterns, processes, and functions help determine where people settle.*

Essential Question

- *How do physical systems and human systems shape a place?*

Predictable Misunderstandings

Students may think:

- *Bangladesh and Pakistan gained their independence from Britain at the same time as India. Explain that in 1947, Pakistan was granted independence from Britain at the same time as India, but Pakistan was divided into East and West. In 1971, East Pakistan became independent from West Pakistan and became Bangladesh.*
- *All Pakistanis belong to the same ethnic group, and all Bengali belong to the same ethnic group. Explain that this is largely true of Bangladesh, but Pakistan has five main ethnic groups and that nearly 100 languages are spoken in the country.*

Assessment Evidence

Performance Tasks:

- *Hands-On Chapter Project*

Other Evidence:

- *Guided Reading Activities*
- *Vocabulary Activities*
- *Lesson Quizzes*
- *Chapter Tests, Forms A and B*

SUGGESTED PACING GUIDE

Introducing the Chapter	½ Day	Global Connections	1 Day
Lesson 1	1 Day	Lesson 3	1 Day
Lesson 2	1 Day	Chapter Wrap-Up and Assessment	½ Day

TOTAL TIME 5 Days

Key for Using the Teacher Edition

SKILL-BASED ACTIVITIES

Types of skill activities found in the Teacher Edition.

* **V Visual Skills** require students to analyze maps, graphs, charts, and photos.

R Reading Skills help students practice reading skills and master vocabulary.

C Critical Thinking Skills help students apply and extend what they have learned.

W Writing Skills provide writing opportunities to help students comprehend the text.

T Technology Skills require students to use digital tools effectively.

*Letters are followed by a number when there is more than one of the same type of skill on the page.

DIFFERENTIATED INSTRUCTION

All activities are written for the on-level student unless otherwise marked with the leveled labels below.

BL Beyond Level
AL Approaching Level
ELL English Language Learners

All students benefit from activities that utilize different learning styles. Many activities are marked as below when a particular learning style is highlighted.

Intrapersonal	**Naturalist**
Logical/Mathematical	**Kinesthetic**
Visual/Spatial	**Auditory/Musical**
Verbal/Linguistic	**Interpersonal**

National Geography Standards covered in "Pakistan and Bangladesh"

The student knows and understands:

(5) That people create regions to interpret Earth's complexity

5.1 Regions are defined by different sets of criteria and places can be included in multiple regions of different types

(7) The physical processes that shape the patterns of Earth's surface

7.3 Physical processes interact over time to shape particular places on Earth's surface

(9) The characteristics, distribution, and migration of human populations on Earth's surface

9.2 Population distribution and density are a function of historical, environmental, economic, political, and technological factors

(10) The characteristics, distribution, and complexity of Earth's cultural mosaics

10.2 Cultural landscapes exist at multiple scales

10.3 Cultures changes through convergence and/or divergence

(11) The patterns and networks of economic interdependence on Earth's surface

11.2 Patterns exist in the spatial organization of economic activities

11.3 Economic systems are dynamic organizations of interdependent economic activities for production, exchange, distribution, and consumption of goods and services

11.4 Improvements in transportation and communication networks reduce the effects of distance and time on the movements of people, products, and ideas

(12) The process, patterns, and functions of human settlement

12.1 The numbers, types, and range of the functions of settlement change

12.2 Settlements can grow and/or decline over time

(13) How the forces of cooperation and conflict among people influence the division and control of Earth's surface

13.3 Changes within, between and among countries regarding division and control of Earth's surface may result in conflict

(14) How human actions modify the physical environment

14.1 Human modifications of the physical environment can have significant global impacts

14.3 People can either mitigate and/or adapt to the consequences of human modifications of the physical environment

CHAPTER OPENER PLANNER

Students will know:

- *what landforms and rivers are important to Pakistan and Bangladesh.*
- *how modern Pakistan and Bangladesh formed.*
- *how a high population density affects life in each country.*
- *the major industries that contribute to the economies of Pakistan and Bangladesh.*
- *why sustainable development and a shortage of potable water are challenges.*
- *what efforts the national governments of the two countries have taken to improve the environment.*

Students will be able to:

- ***identify** the landforms and rivers that are important to the region.*
- ***explain** how Pakistan and Bangladesh were formed.*
- ***identify** the effects of a high population density.*
- ***identify** the major industries in the two countries.*
- ***identify** challenges to sustainable development and sufficient potable water.*
- ***identify** how governments are working to improve the environment.*

UNDERSTANDING BY DESIGN®

☑ Print Teaching Options

V Visual Skills

- ☐ **p. 628** Students gather data online to create a chart about floods in their assigned country. **Logical/Mathematical**

R Reading Skills

- ☐ **p. 628** Students think and write about how a large flood affects economic progress in developing countries.

C Critical Thinking Skills

- ☐ **p. 627** Students compare Pakistan and Bangladesh.
- ☐ **p. 629** Students discuss how floods affect the lives of people and whether the governments are prepared to help people affected by floods. **AL** **Verbal/Linguistic**

W Writing Skills

- ☐ **p. 628** Students write an essay suggesting solutions to prevent massive flooding in the region. **BL** **Verbal/Linguistic**

T Technology Skills

- ☐ **p. 629** Students research an assigned river and create a multimedia report about it. **BL** **Visual/Spatial**

☑ Online Teaching Options

C Critical Thinking Skills

- ☐ **CHART** **Effects of Floods, 2001–2012**—Students review a table showing the number of people affected by floods in the region and work in groups to discuss and list the short-term effects of repeated flooding, or the long-term effects of the repeated devastation. **AL** **Visual/Spatial, Verbal/Linguistic**
- ☐ **MAP** **Interactive Regional Atlas**—Students use the interactive regional atlas to understand the physical and human geography of Pakistan and Bangladesh.

☑ Printable Digital Worksheets

- ☐ **WORKSHEET** **Assessing Background Knowledge**—Determine the level of prior knowledge students have about Pakistan and Bangladesh.
- ☐ **WORKSHEET** **Chapter Summary**—Students review the main idea of each lesson of the chapter content.

Project-Based Learning 

Hands-On

Create a Website

Working in groups, students create a website that includes visuals and text about four different political, social, economic, and environmental issues facing Pakistan and/or Bangladesh.

Digital Hands-On

Create Online Projects

Find an additional activity online that incorporates technology for this project. Visit the EdTech Teacher websites for more links, tutorials, and other resources.

Print Resources

ANCILLARY RESOURCES

This ancillary is available for every chapter and lesson.

- **Chapter Tests and Lesson Quizzes**

PRINTABLE DIGITAL WORKSHEETS

These printable digital worksheets are available for every chapter and lesson.

- **Assessing Background Knowledge**
- **Chapter Summaries**
- **Guided Reading Activities**
- **Hands-On Chapter Projects**
- **Quizzes and Tests**
- **Reading Essentials and Study Guide** **AL**
- **Reteaching Activities**
- **Video Activities**
- **Vocabulary Activities**

More Media Resources

SUGGESTED VIDEOS MOVIES

- **Between the Tides** (51 min.)
- **60 Minutes: The Shipbreakers** (14 min.)
- **The Killing of Kashmir** (50 min.)

SUGGESTED READING 

- ***Pakistan: A Hard Country,*** by Anatol Lieven
- ***Shooting for a Century: The India-Pakistan Conundrum,*** by Stephen P. Cohen
- ***Bangladesh: Politics, Economy, and Civil Society,*** by David Lewis

PHYSICAL GEOGRAPHY OF PAKISTAN AND BANGLADESH

Students will know:
- *what landforms dominate the landscape of Pakistan and Bangladesh.*
- *that rivers are vital to life in Pakistan and Bangladesh.*
- *that Pakistan and Bangladesh each rely on one major natural resource.*

Students will be able to:
- ***identify** the landforms that dominate Pakistan and Bangladesh.*
- ***analyze** how rivers are important to the two countries.*
- ***identify** the major natural resources that Bangladesh and Pakistan rely on.*

UNDERSTANDING BY DESIGN®

☑ Print Teaching Options

V Visual Skills

☐ **p. 630** Students identify and list prominent geographical features of each country from a physical map.

☐ **p. 632** Students draw or digitally create their own maps that show the point(s) of origin of the Padma and Jamuna Rivers and how they join and flow into the Bay of Bengal, creating a delta. Naturalist, Visual/Spatial

☐ **p. 633** Students create a chart for Bangladesh and one for Pakistan to show the months of the three distinct seasons, the role of the winds, and whether each season is wet or dry. ELL Logical/Mathematical, Visual/Spatial

R Reading Skills

☐ **p. 631** Students write a list of countries in the world they have studied that are subject to earthquakes and compare lists. ELL Verbal/Linguistic

C Critical Thinking Skills

☐ **p. 631** Students discuss the map of Pakistan and how it relates to Pakistan's development. Visual/Spatial

☐ **p. 632** Students discuss major rivers in Pakistan and Bangladesh. Logical/Mathematical, Verbal/Linguistic

W Writing Skills

☐ **p. 630** Students write an essay discussing the relationship between continental drift and the geography of Pakistan and its borders. AL Verbal/Linguistic

T Technology Skills

☐ **p. 630** Students research who controlled the Khyber Pass during their assigned historical period and evaluate how important it was during this time, and then create a multimedia presentation. BL Verbal/Linguistic, Visual/Spatial

☐ **p. 632** Students research an important river and create a multimedia presentation about it. AL Verbal/Linguistic, Visual/Spatial

☑ Online Teaching Options

V Visual Skills

INTERACTIVE BELLRINGER **Landforms of Pakistan**—Students use a map showing the mountain ranges and passes of Pakistan to understand and identify some of the landforms of Pakistan. AL Interpersonal, Visual/Spatial, Verbal/Linguistic

VIDEO **Saira Khan's Pakistan Adventure: Kara Koram Highway**—Students watch a video tour of Pakistan's landscape and complete a graphic organizer to understand how the physical geography of Pakistan affects the daily lives of the people who live there. AL Visual/Spatial

INTERACTIVE MAP **Monsoons in India**—Students make connections between the waterways of India and the waterways in Pakistan and Bangladesh, as well as compare each country's climate and seasonal monsoon winds. BL Naturalist, Verbal/Linguistic

INTERACTIVE WHITEBOARD ACTIVITY **Landforms of Pakistan and Bangladesh**—Students identify characteristics of landforms that dominate the landscape of Pakistan and Bangladesh and then label the landforms on a map.

☑ Printable Digital Worksheets

R Reading Skills

WORKSHEET **Guided Reading Activity**—Students use the Guided Reading Activity worksheets to review their comprehension of the content.

C Critical Thinking Skills

WORKSHEET **Video Activity**—Students answer questions related to a topic in the chapter content after they have viewed a lesson video.

HUMAN GEOGRAPHY OF PAKISTAN AND BANGLADESH

Students will know:
- *how modern Pakistan and Bangladesh formed.*
- *how a high population density affects life in each country.*
- *how life in Pakistan is similar to and different from life in Bangladesh.*
- *the major industries that contribute to the economies of Pakistan and Bangladesh.*

Students will be able to:
- ***explain** how Pakistan and Bangladesh were formed.*
- ***identify** the effects of a high population density.*
- ***compare and contrast** life in Pakistan and Bangladesh.*
- ***identify** the major industries in the two countries.*

UNDERSTANDING BY DESIGN®

Print Teaching Options

V Visual Skills
- [ ] **p. 635** Students make charts comparing and contrasting the people of East Pakistan with the people of West Pakistan. BL Logical/Mathematical, Visual/Spatial
- [ ] **p. 639** Students research the economic activities and industries of one of the countries and create a graph to show the data. BL Visual/Spatial

R Reading Skills
- [ ] **p. 635** Students sequence the events from Pakistan gaining its independence to today. ELL Verbal/Linguistic
- [ ] **p. 636** Students discuss what it might be like to live in one of the most populous countries of the world. AL Verbal/Linguistic
- [ ] **p. 637** Students compare the two countries in ethnic background, language, and religion. ELL Verbal/Linguistic

C Critical Thinking Skills
- [ ] **p. 636** Students discuss events on the time line.

W Writing Skills
- [ ] **p. 635** Students write a narration of what it may have been like to be in East Pakistan in 1970 when a severe cyclone hit. AL Intrapersonal
- [ ] **p. 636** Students write a short essay explaining what Bangladesh is doing to curtail its growing population. Verbal/Linguistic
- [ ] **p. 637** Students write a one-page narrative about what they think they would have done if they lived in Pakistan or Bangladesh at a date on the time line of their choice. Intrapersonal, Verbal/Linguistic

T Technology Skills
- [ ] **p. 634** Students research the archaeological discoveries of the ancient city of Mohenjo Daro and create a multimedia presentation about it. BL Verbal/Linguistic
- [ ] **p. 637** Students research a problem facing Pakistan or Bangladesh, find solutions that have been enacted to solve it, and then create a presentation. BL Visual/Spatial
- [ ] **p. 638** Students research and prepare a presentation about a salvage industry in the region. AL Visual/Spatial

Online Teaching Options

V Visual Skills
- VIDEO **Saira Khan's Pakistan Adventure, Islamabad**—Students view a video about the changing political process in Pakistan, listen to the interviews, and take notes about the views of the demonstrators and leaders. AL Visual/Spatial
- INTERACTIVE IMAGE **Risky Work**—Students view an image of a dangerous work environment and discuss how culture, politics, and economic conditions contribute to the work environment in an area. BL Verbal/Linguistic, Visual/Spatial
- INTERACTIVE WHITEBOARD ACTIVITY **Comparing and Contrasting Pakistan and Bangladesh**—Students complete a Venn diagram comparing and contrasting modern-day Pakistan and Bangladesh.

C Critical Thinking Skills
- INTERACTIVE BELLRINGER **Bangladesh: The Road to Independence**—Students use the introductory text and the time line showing dates and events leading up to the independence of Bangladesh to understand how Pakistan and Bangladesh formed. BL Interpersonal, Visual/Spatial
- MAP **Partition of India, 1947**—Students discuss the shifting populations of Hindus and Muslims during the partition and hypothesize about what life might have been like for families at this time by listing three hypotheses about the effects relocation would have on a family. ELL Verbal/Linguistic

W Writing Skills
- TIME LINE **Unity and Division**—Students study the time line, research what makes Kashmir so valuable, and write a brief summary of their findings. Visual/Spatial

Printable Digital Worksheets

R Reading Skills
- WORKSHEET **Guided Reading Activity**—Students use Guided Reading Activity worksheets to review their comprehension of the content.
- WORKSHEET **Reading Essentials and Study Guide**—Students complete the study guide and answer Reading Progress Check and vocabulary questions. AL

C Critical Thinking Skills
- WORKSHEET **Video Activity**—Students answer questions related to a topic in the chapter content after they have viewed a lesson video.

LESSON 3 PLANNER

PEOPLE AND THEIR ENVIRONMENT: PAKISTAN AND BANGLADESH

Students will know:
- *why sustainable development has not taken hold in Pakistan and Bangladesh.*
- *why a shortage of potable water afflicts the two countries.*
- *what efforts the national governments of the two countries have taken to improve the environment.*

Students will be able to:
- ***identify** challenges to sustainable development in the region.*
- ***explain** why there is a water shortage in Pakistan and Bangladesh.*
- ***identify** how governments are working to improve the environment.*

UNDERSTANDING BY DESIGN®

Print Teaching Options

V Visual Skills

- [ ] **p. 644** Students design a chart or diagram using presentation software to show the cycle of water in the two countries that leads to water pollution. AL Logical/Mathematical, Visual/Spatial
- [ ] **p. 646** Students research data and design graphs showing the total number of CNG vehicles in the United States, Italy, and Pakistan. Visual/Spatial

R Reading Skills

- [ ] **p. 642** Students discuss the environmental challenges due to the high population rate in the region.
- [ ] **p. 643** Students identify the problems the two countries face in succeeding in sustainable development. Logical/Mathematical
- [ ] **p. 645** Students discuss the bar graph showing the world's worst cities for air pollution. ELL Logical/Mathematical, Visual/Spatial

C Critical Thinking Skills

- [ ] **p. 642** Students discuss whether the economies of Pakistan and Bangladesh could be called *fragile.* AL Verbal/Linguistic
- [ ] **p. 644** Students discuss and design a solution or solutions to the problem of water pollution and its ramifications. Interpersonal, Logical/Mathematical
- [ ] **p. 646** Students discuss climate change. Verbal/Linguistic

W Writing Skills

- [ ] **p. 642** Students select one of the principles of sustainable development and write a narrative of a hypothetical program that is working in the region. Verbal/Linguistic
- [ ] **p. 644** Students write an essay describing how soil erosion interconnects with economic problems in either Pakistan or Bangladesh. BL Verbal/Linguistic

T Technology Skills

- [ ] **p. 643** Students research and create a photo library of the Sundarbans and the threats to them. BL Visual/Spatial
- [ ] **p. 645** Students research one project the World Bank has funded in the region and create a presentation about it. BL Verbal/Linguistic, Visual/Spatial

Online Teaching Options

V Visual Skills

- [ ] VIDEO **Bangladesh River Erosion**—Students watch the video to learn about the effects of environmental change on people's lives and list the causes and impact of the erosion of the land in Bangladesh. AL Visual/Spatial
- [ ] INTERACTIVE IMAGE **Water Pollution in Bangladesh**—Students use the image to discuss the impact of polluted water on daily life for the boy in the picture. BL Visual/Spatial, Logical/Mathematical
- [ ] INTERACTIVE WHITEBOARD ACTIVITY **Environment Dangers**—Students complete graphic organizers with efforts the national governments of the two countries have taken to improve the environment.
- [ ] INTERACTIVE BELLRINGER **World's Worst Cities for Air Pollution**—Students study the graph of the world's worst cities for air pollution and discuss their experiences with air pollution to describe a time when they were adversely affected by poor air quality. BL Interpersonal, Visual/Spatial, Verbal/Linguistic

R Reading Skills

- [ ] GAME **People and Their Environment: Pakistan and Bangladesh**—Students play an identification game to strengthen their knowledge of the environment in Pakistan and Bangladesh. AL ELL Verbal/Linguistic

Printable Digital Worksheets

R Reading Skills

- [ ] WORKSHEET **Guided Reading Activity**—Students use Guided Reading Activity worksheets to review their comprehension of the content.
- [ ] WORKSHEET **Reading Essentials and Study Guide**—Students complete the study guide and answer Reading Progress Check and vocabulary questions. AL
- [ ] WORKSHEET **Vocabulary Activity**—Students review the chapter content and academic vocabulary words.
- [ ] WORKSHEET **Chapter Summary**—Students review the main ideas of the chapter content.

C Critical Thinking Skills

- [ ] WORKSHEET **Video Activity**—Students answer questions based on a lesson video.
- [ ] WORKSHEET **Reteaching Activity**—Students use this activity worksheet to review and reteach chapter content and vocabulary. This worksheet can be used with struggling students who need additional help with difficult content concepts.

INTERVENTION AND REMEDIATION STRATEGIES

LESSON 1 Physical Geography of Pakistan and Bangladesh

Reading and Comprehension

To help students organize and comprehend the concepts discussed in this lesson, have them work in pairs to create an outline using the lesson's main headings. As partners gather information, encourage students to note cause-and-effect relationships in their outlines. Have students note key ideas and details under each heading as well as content vocabulary terms. Encourage students to illustrate their outlines to develop a coherent understanding of each concept. For example, students may wish to use a graphic organizer like the one on the Lesson Opener to organize their notes about cause-and-effect relationships. Ask volunteers to present their outlines to the class.

Text Evidence

Have students choose one of the following statements from the It Matters Because text: *Pakistan and Bangladesh are two of the ten most populous countries in the world. The landforms and climates of this subregion pose major challenges to the people living there.* Tell students to create a web diagram that provides textual evidence from the lesson to support their chosen statement. For example, if students choose the second statement, their diagrams should cite the high, rugged mountains in Pakistan. After students complete their diagrams, guide a discussion about what makes the physical geography of the region unique.

LESSON 2 Human Geography of Pakistan and Bangladesh

Reading and Comprehension

To help students comprehend the lesson content, assign students pairs a different segment of the text in this lesson. Tell students to work as a team to paraphrase their assigned portion, looking up confusing or unknown words in a dictionary or defining terms using context clues. Remind students that paraphrases should be in their own words. After students have had time to write their paraphrases, organize pairs in order of the text segments as they appear in the lesson. Tell students to read their paraphrases one after the other, interjecting to provide corrective guidance if needed.

Text Evidence

Organize students into small groups and tell each group to write a compare-contrast paragraph that describes the quest for independence by Pakistan and Bangladesh. Tell students their paragraphs should include information about the struggles endured by both countries since independence. Remind students to support claims in their summaries with evidence from the text. Encourage students to provide a visual to accompany their paragraphs, such as the Venn diagram at the beginning of the lesson.

LESSON 3 People and Their Environment: Pakistan and Bangladesh

Reading and Comprehension

Have students read the definition in the text of the term *sustainable development.* Ask a volunteer to paraphrase the definition in his or her own words. Have student pairs create a problem-solution graphic organizer with the heading "Sustainable Development." Tell students to fill in the chart as they read about issues facing Pakistan and Bangladesh. Ask volunteers to present their charts to the class. Guide a discussion about the fragile balance between economic growth and the ability of impoverished societies to meet their own needs.

Text Evidence

Tell student groups they will act as members of a committee being sent to Pakistan or Bangladesh to determine where to provide economic and environmental relief. Have students review the text to identify challenges faced by the region, and which they believe are the most pressing. Tell students to prepare a brief report that explains which issue requires the most attention, using evidence from the text to support their statements. Students may wish to conduct online research to provide sufficient evidence in support of claims made in their reports. Ask groups to present their reports, allowing for discussion following each one that allows for constructive criticism.

Online Resources

Leveled Reader

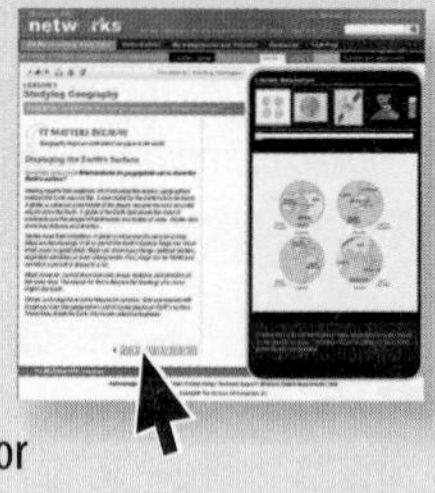

Use this online approaching-level text that corresponds directly to the text in the Student Edition. It also includes additional reading and comprehension support for English Language Learners.

Guided Reading Activities

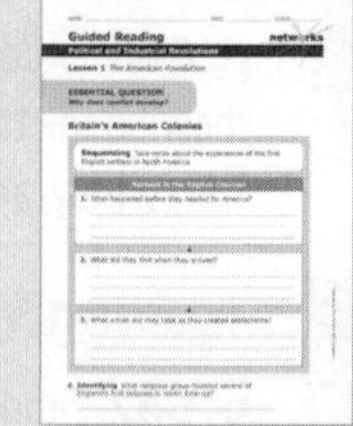

This resource uses guiding questions to help students with comprehension.

Reteaching Activities

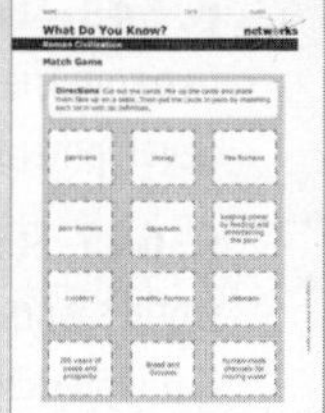

These worksheets provide students with an opportunity for remedial practice and review of vital chapter content.

Reading Essentials and Study Guide

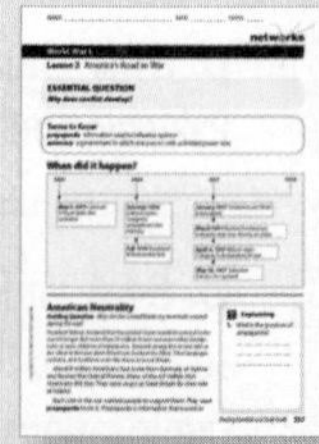

This resource offers writing and reading activities for the approaching-level student.

Self-Check Quizzes

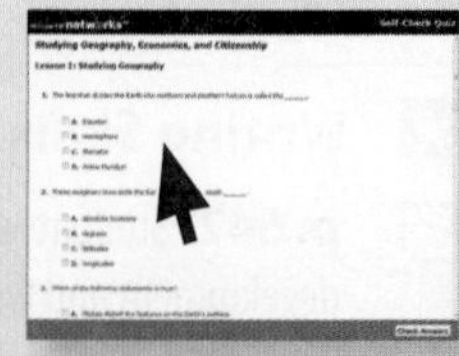

This online assessment tool provides instant feedback for students to check their progress.

Chapter Summaries

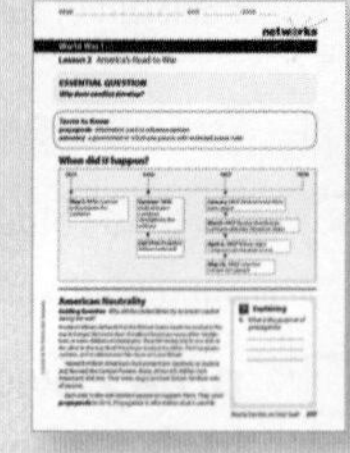

Summaries are provided for each chapter that thoroughly condense core content into manageable chunks.

Pakistan and Bangladesh

ESSENTIAL QUESTION • *How do physical systems and human systems shape a place?*

networks

There's More Online about Pakistan's and Bangladesh's geography.

CHAPTER 26

Geography Matters...

Pakistan and Bangladesh are lands of contrast. Northern Pakistan is home to K2, the world's second-tallest mountain, which is nearly 5.4 miles (8.7 km) high. Coastal Bangladesh is at sea level. Bangladesh has enough water to grow rice. In Pakistan, farmers must use dry-farming methods to grow crops.

Culturally, Pakistan and Bangladesh have similarities. They are both highly populous countries with strong Muslim cultures. Both share some of their history with neighboring India. Both countries are also struggling to develop their economies to overcome extreme poverty.

◀ Boy in Cox's Bazar, Bangladesh

627

Letter from the Author

Dear Geography Teacher,

It seems like a necessary exercise for this chapter would be to have your students, using the text first and Internet later, do a comparative analysis of West and East Pakistan (later to become Bangladesh). Go back to 1947 and the partitioning of the subcontinent by the British. Why was Pakistan created in two disparate areas over 1,000 miles apart? What problems did that decision create? How are the two countries alike? How are they different? How do they operate politically with their neighbors? What environmental problems do they face?

Richard G. Boehm

ENGAGE

Activating Prior Knowledge Display a map showing of South Asia. Direct students' attention to Pakistan and Bangladesh. Then have students brainstorm a list of what they know about Pakistan and Bangladesh. Review their lists in class.

TEACH & ASSESS

Content Background Knowledge

History Tell students that Pakistan and Bangladesh have had a long and varied history as you read the following:

- Both Pakistan and Bangladesh are countries that were established after World War II. Both countries were controlled by the Moguls, a Muslim dynasty that originated in Turkestan. The dynasty ruled South Asia from the early 1500s to the early 1800s. By 1835, the British had defeated the Mogul Empire.
- Pakistan was established in 1947 when it was partitioned from British India. The partition established West Pakistan, which was west of India between India and Afghanistan, and East Pakistan, which was east of India between India and Myanmar (Burma). In 1971 a war between India and Pakistan established the new country of Bangladesh from what had been East Pakistan.

Hypothesizing Emphasize to students that Pakistan and Bangladesh share similarities and differences. **Ask:** **Do you think there are more similarities or differences that exist between the two countries? Explain.** *(Possible answers: Similarities—both are Muslim countries, both have large populations, both suffer from extreme poverty. Differences—Pakistan has a more diverse geography with mountains, rivers, and plains. Bangladesh is mostly flat plains with many rivers and wetlands, which are good for growing rice.)*

CLOSE & REFLECT

Summarizing In a class discussion, have students briefly summarize the history of Pakistan and Bangladesh and the challenges both countries face in the twenty-first century.

Extend the project-based learning experience globally through our partnership with ePals. EPals allows you to connect with classrooms around the world in a safe online environment for real-life lessons and projects in virtual study groups.

ENGAGE

R Reading Skills

Interpreting Have students examine the image of the flood scene. Tell students to think about how a flood of such magnitude affects economic progress in developing countries like Pakistan and Bangladesh. Have them write one or two paragraphs describing those effects. In a class discussion, have students share their paragraphs.

TEACH & ASSESS

V Visual Skills

Creating a Chart Assign small groups of students either Pakistan or Bangladesh and have them research online or in the library what recent floods have hit their assigned country. Then, have them create a chart about floods in their assigned country that shows the river or rivers that flooded, the date and length of time of the flood, and the number of people it affected. Have groups share their charts with the class. **Logical/Mathematical**

W Writing Skills

Informative/Explanatory Have students write a brief essay suggesting possible solutions to prevent massive flooding in Pakistan and Bangladesh. Encourage students to share their essays. **BL** **Verbal/Linguistic**

Content Background Knowledge

The UN South Asia Water Initiative

- The overall objectives of the UN South Asia Water Initiative (SAWI) are to reduce poverty, stimulate economic growth, and help countries adapt to climate change.
- The main goal is to greatly improve water security in the region, and to do that, SAWI addresses some of the long-term challenging problems of the region.
- SAWI works at all three levels—international, regional, and national—in nine countries in South Asia, including Pakistan and Bangladesh.

R

V flood-prone Pakistan and Bangladesh

W *Floods are a common and major natural disaster in these two countries. In 2010 more than 18 million Pakistanis experienced terrible floods. In 1984 about 30 million Bangladeshis suffered through floods. Other major floods hit in 1992, 1993, 1995, 1998, 2004, 2005, 2007, and 2012. Why are floods so terrible here? What can Pakistan and Bangladesh do to mitigate them?*

THERE'S MORE ONLINE

VIEW a chart about flooding in Pakistan and Bangladesh • *EXPLORE* a map of flood zones in Bangladesh

Project-Based Learning

Hands-On

Create a Website

Working in groups, students will create a website that includes visuals and text about four different political, social, economic, and environmental issues facing Pakistan and/or Bangladesh. Students will investigate the issues facing modern Pakistan and Bangladesh, and then groups will create a website that will bring together this information.

ePals GlobalCommunity
Where learners connect™

Digital Hands-On

Create Online Projects

Find an additional activity online that incorporates technology for this project. Visit the EdTech Teacher websites for more links, tutorials, and other resources.

Why Geography Matters

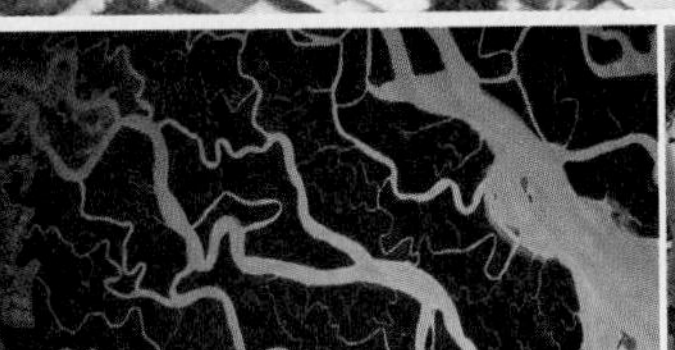

Why do floods threaten Pakistan and Bangladesh?

Pakistan and Bangladesh experience at least two floods a year, many of which are devastating. In Pakistan, heavy rains cause the Indus River to overflow its banks. Poor water management adds to the problem. Since population density is high along the river, these floods affect millions of people.

Many factors combine to cause floods in Bangladesh. The country has a very low elevation. Four major rivers—the Ganges, the Brahmaputra, the Jamuna, and the Meghna—flow through Bangladesh's plains, raising the probability of flooding. These floods strike when snow in the Himalaya melts, filling the rivers. The problem is made worse during the wet monsoon season or when cyclones hit.

1. **Physical Systems** In which country do you think flooding occurs more often? Why?

How has flooding harmed these two countries?

Flooding causes a host of problems in Pakistan and Bangladesh. Hundreds of people can die in a flood. In 1988 floods in Bangladesh resulted in the deaths of more than 2,000 people. In 2010 record flooding in Pakistan killed some 1,700 people and destroyed almost 2,000 homes. The economic cost can rise to billions and billions of dollars.

T The danger comes from more than the flood waters alone. The water washes away crops, reducing harvests, and stored food becomes wet and spoils more quickly. With reduced food supplies, people suffer from hunger. Ironically, too much water means too little drinkable water. River water is muddy and contaminated by chemicals washed off farmland and by the decomposition of the bodies of dead animals and other waste. This kind of contamination also raises the likelihood of deadly diseases.

2. **Environment and Society** How are these problems affected by high population density in these countries?

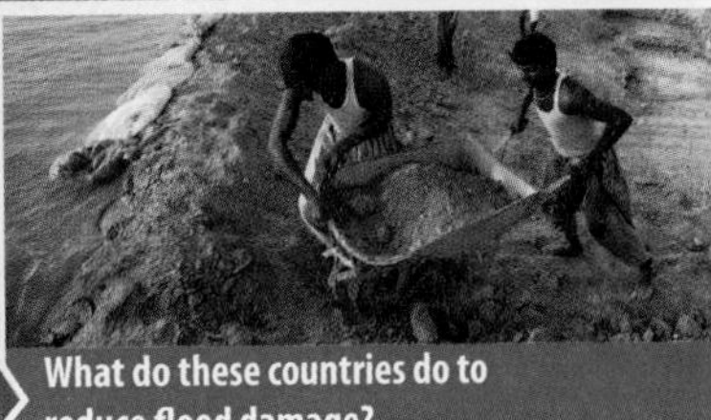

What do these countries do to reduce flood damage?

Other countries faced with frequent flooding have taken steps to prevent it. They have built dikes and levees to hold water back, and put limits on building on floodplains or other flood-prone areas. They also have evacuation plans.

C In 2005 world leaders met to discuss ways to prevent and recover from disasters like the floods in Pakistan and Bangladesh. They adopted a set of recommendations called the Hyogo Framework for Action. Both Pakistan and Bangladesh have tried to implement some of the recommendations. However, their efforts are hampered by the lack of funding.

3. **Human Systems** What conditions prevent Pakistan and Bangladesh from taking more steps to address flooding?

(l)NASA/JSC, (c)Rizwan Tabassum/AFP/Getty Images, (r)©Gideon Mendel For Action Aid/In Pictures/Corbis

Why Geography Matters **629**

T Technology Skills

Researching Assign each of the student groups a river in Bangladesh. Have student groups research on the Internet their assigned river and, using maps and charts, create a multimedia report. The reports should include each river's origin, where the river flows, and where it ends. In addition, encourage students to identify and show photos of cities along each river. **BL Visual/Spatial**

C Critical Thinking Skills

Analyzing Encourage students whose family or friends may have experienced a flood to share their experiences. **Ask:** **How do floods affect the daily life of people in Pakistan or Bangladesh?** *(Possible answers: Floods affect every aspect of life including the houses where people live; there would be a lack of food and drinkable water; there would be a lack of medical care; schools and business would be adversely affected; all the daily routines would be affected.)* **Do you think that the Pakistan and Bangladesh governments are well prepared to help people affected by the floods? Explain.** *(Student answers may vary, but could point out that both Pakistan and Bangladesh are developing nations with politically unstable governments, large populations, and widespread poverty, so the governments may not necessarily be well prepared.)* **AL Verbal/Linguistic**

CLOSE & REFLECT

Summarizing Direct students to consider the reasons why Pakistan and Bangladesh are unable to enact a proactive program to prevent floods. Have students write an essay summarizing those problems and share their essays in a class discussion.

CHART

Effects of Floods, 2001–2012

Activating Prior Knowledge Have students view the table listing the major floods in Pakistan and Bangladesh between 2001 and 2012. As students review the number of people affected by the floods, divide the class into two groups. Ask one group to discuss and list the short-term effects of repeated flooding, while the other lists and considers the long-term effects of the repeated devastation. Remind them to call upon their knowledge from earlier lessons about the effects of water on landforms, soil and the environment. Once the group discussions are complete, ask each group to share its list with the class. **AL Visual/Spatial, Verbal/ Linguistic**

Effects of Floods, 2001-2012

Effects of Floods, 2001–2012

Year	Place	Number of Deaths	Number of People Affected
2001	Pakistan	210	400,000
2003	Pakistan	162	1,300,000
2004	Bangladesh	700+	30,000,000
2005	Pakistan	520	7,000,000
2007	Pakistan Bangladesh	330 500+	2,500,000 10,000,000
2008	Pakistan	55	2,100,000
2010	Pakistan	2,000	20,000,000
2011	Pakistan	520	5,400,000
2012	Pakistan Bangladesh	400 140	4,800,000 5,000,000

ANSWERS, p. 629

Why Geography Matters

1. Bangladesh might experience more flooding as the major rivers flow through its plains, whereas Pakistan experiences flooding primarily from the Indus River.
2. The high population density causes more people to die in floods, as well as to be affected by unsafe drinking water, hunger caused by loss of crops and food supplies, and disease from contamination.
3. Pakistan and Bangladesh lack the money needed to implement any of the needed steps to prevent flooding.

ENGAGE

V Visual Skills

Interpreting Display a physical map of Pakistan and Bangladesh for students. Ask them to work with a partner to identify and list the prominent geographical features of each country. Then have students share their lists in a class discussion.

TEACH & ASSESS

W Writing Skills

Informative/Explanatory Ask: **What landforms dominate Pakistan?** *(high mountains, rivers, plains)* Tell students to consider ways that continental drift affects the geography of Pakistan. Have students write an essay discussing the relationship between continental drift and the geography of Pakistan and its borders. Students may want to do additional research. **AL Verbal/Linguistic**

T Technology Skills

Evaluating Emphasize to students that the Khyber Pass has influenced events in Pakistan for thousands of years. Divide the class into groups and assign each a period in history: Persian Empire, Greek Empire, Mughal (or Mogul) Empire, and the British Empire. Have each group research who controlled the Khyber Pass and evaluate how important it was during their assigned historical period. Be sure groups identify the dates of their historical period. Have student groups create a multimedia presentation to present to the class, which includes a summary of their time period. **BL Verbal/Linguistic, Visual/Spatial**

ANSWERS, p. 630

TAKING NOTES: The high mountains in Pakistan are generally impassable, but the Khyber Pass in northwest Pakistan has allowed armies to enter South Asia. The mountainous northern and western regions of Pakistan are prone to earthquakes, which cause destruction and loss of lives. Bangladesh is very low and flat with wetlands and many rivers. The lowlands have depressions that fill with water that can be used for irrigation during dry seasons. However, the many rivers cause destructive floods. The low landscape also keeps rivers from being used for hydroelectric power. Both Pakistan and Bangladesh have coastal areas that are prone to floods. Bangladesh suffers from cyclones and tsunamis, which may cause damage and loss of life.

networks

There's More Online!

- **IMAGE** Flood Damage in Bangladesh
- **MAP** Mountain Passes of Pakistan
- **INTERACTIVE SELF-CHECK QUIZ**
- **VIDEO** Physical Geography of Pakistan and Bangladesh

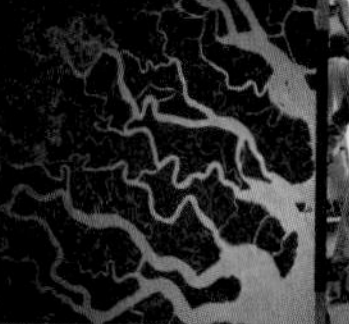

LESSON 1
Physical Geography of Pakistan and Bangladesh

ESSENTIAL QUESTION • *How do physical systems and human systems shape a place?*

Reading HELPDESK 

Academic Vocabulary (Tier Two Words)
- **generate**
- **maintain**

Content Vocabulary (Tier Three Words)
- **delta**
- **floodplain**

TAKING NOTES: ***Key Ideas and Details***

IDENTIFYING CAUSE AND EFFECT
As you read about the physical geography of Pakistan and Bangladesh, use a graphic organizer like the one below to identify examples of how physical systems shape human systems.

Cause	Effect

IT MATTERS BECAUSE

V *Pakistan and Bangladesh are two of the ten most populous countries in the world. The landforms and climates of this subregion pose major challenges to the people living there.*

Landforms

GUIDING QUESTION *How do landforms in Pakistan and Bangladesh affect human activities?*

Pakistan lies toward the northwestern edge of the Indian subcontinent, and Bangladesh lies toward the northeastern edge. Pakistan borders Afghanistan in Central Asia to the west and China to the north. Bangladesh is almost surrounded by India, but also shares a small border with Myanmar (Burma).

Physically, the two countries have few similarities and many differences. Bangladesh is almost entirely low and flat. Pakistan has large areas of low, flat plains as well as high mountains.

W According to the theory of continental drift, the Indian subcontinent is slowly and steadily pushing into the southern edge of Asia. This collision thrust up the Himalaya mountain ranges. The Himalaya cover part of northern Pakistan, as do, farther north, the Karakoram Mountains. Farther west, the Hindu Kush range frames the northwest edge of Pakistan. In Pakistan, these mountain systems range from about 13,000 feet (3,962 m) to more than 19,500 feet (5,944 m) high. A few peaks soar more than 25,000 feet (7,620 m). One peak in the Karakoram, named K2, towers 28,250 feet (8,611 m). It is the second-highest mountain in the world.

T These mountains are generally impassable, but the Hindu Kush have several wide, very high passes. The most important is the Khyber Pass in northwest Pakistan along the Afghanistan border. This pass has allowed armies to enter the Indian subcontinent. A highway through the Khunjerab Pass in the Karakoram is being modernized by China as a link to Pakistan.

Three lower mountain ranges run in a north-to-south direction from the western half of Pakistan and toward the Arabian Sea. These are, from north to south, the Salt Range, the Sulaiman Range, and the Kirthar Range.

networks *Online Teaching Options*

 **INTERACTIVE BELLRINGER**

Landforms of Pakistan

Interpreting a Map Use the introductory text and the map showing the mountain ranges and mountain passes of Pakistan to understand and identify some of the landforms of Pakistan. Have students pair with a partner and answer each question. Have students write agreed-upon answers to the questions. Then, review the answers with the class as a whole. **AL Interpersonal, Visual/Spatial, Verbal/Linguistic**

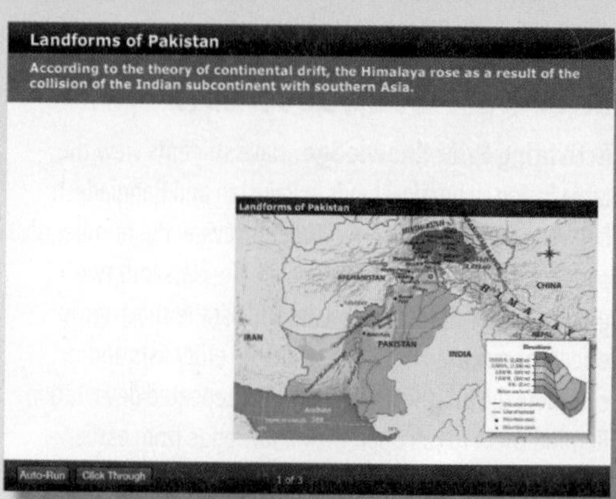

West of the Kirthar Range is a highland region, the Baluchistan Plateau. The mountainous northern and western regions of Pakistan are prone to earthquakes. A major earthquake in northwestern Pakistan in 2005 killed more than 80,000 people.

To the east is the Indus River valley, which has rich alluvial soil. The Indus and its tributaries form two alluvial plains, the Punjab in the north and the Sind in the south. The Sind includes part of the sandy Thar Desert.

R

Bangladesh is very flat and low, reaching only about 30 feet (9 m) above sea level. The land is cut deeply by the Ganges and the Brahmaputra. In Bangladesh, these rivers are called the Padma and Jamuna, respectively. After joining, the rivers flow through central Bangladesh to empty into the Bay of Bengal in a **delta** system that is the largest in the world. Islands are scattered along the Bay of Bengal. The land is low, so the rivers often change course, altering the landscape.

delta an alluvial deposit at a river's mouth that is shaped roughly like the Greek letter *delta* (Δ)

Bangladesh has few hilly areas. The Chittagong Hills are the largest and the highest. Mount Keokradong, the highest point in the country, is located here, rising about 4,035 feet (1,230 m) high. Bangladesh also has lowland depressions. The Haor Basin, which covers 9,459 square miles (24,500 sq. km), has hundreds of depressions that form wetlands in the rainy months.

Along the southwest coast of Bangladesh is a massive wetland called the Sundarbans. This region is crossed by many waterways that are part of the Ganges Delta. It is thick with mangrove trees that live in the mixture of salt water and freshwater found in this coastal marshland.

✓ **READING PROGRESS CHECK**

Comparing How are the landforms of Pakistan and Bangladesh similar?

GEOGRAPHY CONNECTION

Pakistan has some of the highest and most rugged mountains in the world.

1. ***PLACES AND REGIONS*** Which pass allows travel into Pakistan through the Karakoram Range?
2. ***ENVIRONMENT AND SOCIETY*** Which pass was most likely used by armies invading South Asia from Central Asia?

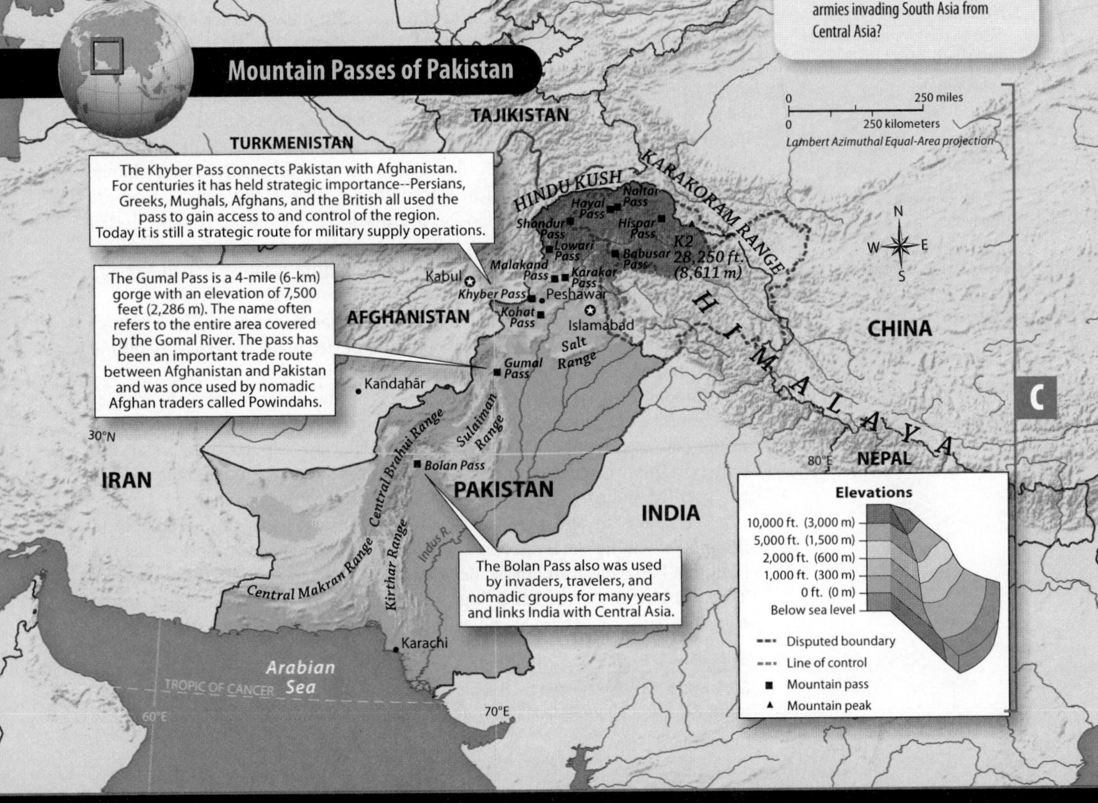

Mountain Passes of Pakistan
TAJIKISTAN
TURKMENISTAN
The Khyber Pass connects Pakistan with Afghanistan. For centuries it has held strategic importance--Persians, Greeks, Mughals, Afghans, and the British all used the pass to gain access to and control of the region. Today it is still a strategic route for military supply operations.
The Gumal Pass is a 4-mile (6-km) gorge with an elevation of 7,500 feet (2,286 m). The name often refers to the entire area covered by the Gomal River. The pass has been an important trade route between Afghanistan and Pakistan and was once used by nomadic Afghan traders called Powindahs.
HINDU KUSH
KARAKORAM RANGE
Naltar Pass
Hayal Pass
Shandur Pass
Hispar Pass
Lowari Pass
Babusar Pass
K2 28,250 ft. (8,611 m)
Malakand Pass
Karakar Pass
Kabul
Khyber Pass
Peshawar
Kohat Pass
Islamabad
Salt Range
AFGHANISTAN
CHINA
HIMALAYA
Gumal Pass
Kandahār
Sulaiman Range
Central Brahui Range
Bolan Pass
30°N
IRAN
PAKISTAN
INDIA
NEPAL
80°E
Central Makran Range
Kirthar Range
Indus R.
Karachi
Arabian Sea
TROPIC OF CANCER
60°E
70°E
The Bolan Pass also was used by invaders, travelers, and nomadic groups for many years and links India with Central Asia.
0 250 miles
0 250 kilometers
Lambert Azimuthal Equal-Area projection
N
S
E
W
Elevations
10,000 ft. (3,000 m)
5,000 ft. (1,500 m)
2,000 ft. (600 m)
1,000 ft. (300 m)
0 ft. (0 m)
Below sea level
Disputed boundary
Line of control
Mountain pass
Mountain peak

C

VIDEO

Saira Khan's Pakistan Adventure: Kara Koram Highway

Identifying Details Show students this video tour of Pakistan's dramatic landscape. When it is finished have students identify the details in a graphic organizer to help them understand how the physical geography of India affects the daily lives of the people who live there. Have students complete the graphic organizer. As they work, ask them to think about how the landforms and water systems might affect an individual's or a family's day-to-day activities. When the organizer is complete, have students discuss the landform details in small groups. **AL Visual/Spatial**

Physical Geography of Pakistan and Bangladesh

R Reading Skills

Explaining Have students read the first few lines on the page. **Ask: Why do you think some mountainous regions in Pakistan are prone to earthquakes?** *(There are earthquakes in Pakistan because of the movement of the tectonic plates.)* **According to continental drift, what created the Himalaya and increases the number of earthquakes in this area?** *(The Indian subcontinent is pushing into the southern edge of Asia.)* Have students work with a partner to write a list of countries in the world they have studied that are subject to earthquakes. Then have each pair share their lists with another pair. **ELL Verbal/Linguistic**

C Critical Thinking Skills

Analyzing Visuals Draw students' attention to the map of Pakistan on the page. **Ask: What countries have a major influence on Pakistan's development?** *(Afghanistan and India)* **Do you think the land along the Indus River is arable and why?** *(The map shows the land along the Indus River has a low elevation and is a plain, thus is arable.)* **What might this mean in regards to the distribution of the population in modern Pakistan?** *(Most of the population lives near the Indus River.)* **Visual/Spatial**

Content Background Knowledge

The Sundarbans in Bangladesh

- The Sundarbans, West, East, and South, make up three wildlife sanctuaries that were first listed on the UNESCO World Heritage List in 1997.
- The UNESCO Committee identified the Sundarbans as a wetland that nurtures the largest ecosystem of mangrove in the world. The forest ranges over 345,947 acres (140,000 ha) and provides a habitat for a number of marine and freshwater species. In addition, it is a habitat for the Bengal tiger, which currently is an endangered species.
- The wetland is located just west of where the Ganges, Brahmaputra, and Meghna Rivers flow into the Bay of Bengal.

ANSWERS, p. 631

✓ **READING PROGRESS CHECK** Bangladesh and Pakistan both have low, flat plains.

GEOGRAPHY CONNECTION

1. The Hispar Pass allows travel through the Karakoram Range.
2. The Bolan Pass was likely used by armies invading South Asia.

T Technology Skills

Researching Assign student pairs one of the three important rivers mentioned in the text: the Indus, the Ganges, and the Brahmaputra. Have partners conduct online or library research to find images or photos of cities, towns, and populations along their assigned river. Have them organize their findings into a class presentation using presentation software.
AL **Verbal/Linguistic, Visual/Spatial**

C Critical Thinking Skills

Analyzing Invite a student to read aloud the second paragraph under Water Systems. **Ask:** **What is the source of the Indus River?** *(the Himalaya)* **What is the relationship of the Indus to the Jhelum, Chenab, Ravi, and Sutlej rivers?** *(These four rivers feed the Indus River in its upper regions and together the five rivers are called the Punjab.)* **What is the importance of the Punjab?** *(It is an agricultural area.)* **Logical/Mathematical, Verbal/Linguistic**

V Visual Skills

Interpreting Maps From the Teacher Lesson Center, make copies of the outline map of South Asia showing national boundaries. Make sure each set of students has a copy. Have student pairs conduct library or Internet research about the Bay of Bengal delta system in Bangladesh. Then have pairs draw or digitally create their own maps that show the point(s) of origin of the Padma and Jamuna Rivers and how they join and flow into the Bay of Bengal, creating a delta. Encourage students to include a map key and to use color variations. **Naturalist, Visual/Spatial**

ANSWERS, p. 632

READING PROGRESS CHECK The Ganges and the Brahmaputra flow through the lowlands of Bangladesh, which does not provide high enough terrain to generate electricity, whereas the Indus flows out of the Himalaya, creating steep drops that are good for creating power.

CRITICAL THINKING

1. Cyclones are more of a problem in Bangladesh as its location on the Bay of Bengal makes it prone to an average 16 cyclones every 10 years.
2. Flooding is beneficial as it provides fertile soil for agriculture, but it is also destructive as it damages homes and other properties.

Powerful cyclones can deliver driving rains to the region and contribute to the causes of flooding. This house in Bangladesh collapsed when the Padma River flooded.

Shawkat Khan/AFP/Getty Images

▲ **CRITICAL THINKING**

1. ***Comparing and Contrasting*** Do you think cyclones are more of a problem in Pakistan or Bangladesh? Why?
2. ***Explaining*** How is flooding in this region both beneficial and destructive?

floodplain the low-lying land along a river, formed mainly by sediment that has been deposited by floodwaters

generate to produce

maintain to support

Water Systems

GUIDING QUESTION *How are rivers important to the peoples of Pakistan and Bangladesh?*

From their sources high in the Himalaya, three major river systems—the Indus, the Ganges, and the Brahmaputra—supply Pakistan and Bangladesh with water. These three rivers swell with seasonal snowmelt and rains, overflowing their banks and depositing fertile soil on their **floodplains**. People rely on these rivers for farming, transportation, and power. However, the floods can be destructive.

The Indus flows south from the Himalaya through Pakistan, watering wheat and rice crops before emptying into the Arabian Sea. In its upper reaches, the Indus is fed by four tributaries—the Jhelum, Chenab, Ravi, and Sutlej. Together these five rivers give the region its name, Punjab, from a Persian word for "five waters." To the north, the Mangla Dam on the Jhelum and the Tarbela Dam on the Indus are used to **generate** electricity.

The Ganges and Brahmaputra Rivers both retain a flow of water throughout the year. The Ganges is the most important river in South Asia, drawing waters from a basin covering about 400,000 square miles (1 million sq. km). The Brahmaputra is a major waterway for the subregion. Boats can navigate the river inland from the Bay of Bengal some 800 miles (1,290 km). In Bangladesh, these rivers move through lowlands and thus cannot be used for hydroelectric power. Some electricity is generated from rivers that flow through the Chittagong Hills, however.

Depressions in Bangladesh form freshwater wetlands that range from small lakes to marshes. *Haors,* the largest of these features, are bowl-like basins that flood during the wet monsoon. *Beels* are more like saucers that fill with water and then support plant growth. *Baors* are lakes that form after rivers change course. Many *baors* are found in the southwest. In the dry season, they are tapped for irrigation. All these bodies **maintain** fish life that adds to the diet of the people of Bangladesh. They offer potential for developing commercial fisheries, too. Recently, however, commercial shrimp farming has threatened wild fish populations.

Pakistan's lakes are threatened by environmental degradation. The country's largest freshwater lake, Lake Manchar, once supported many fishers. Agricultural runoff in the lake, however, has caused a decline in fish populations.

Karachi, Pakistan's largest city, is located on the Arabian Sea and serves as the country's most important port. Rail lines and highways connect it to the rest of the country, making it possible to move Pakistani exports overseas and to transport imports received at the port around the country. Karachi is also home to a shellfish industry that provides another export for Pakistan.

Both Pakistan and Bangladesh have coastal areas that are vulnerable to flooding when the wet monsoons are strong. Cyclones are a very serious natural hazard in Bangladesh and India. Bangladesh averages 16 cyclones every 10 years. These powerful storms bring high winds and heavy rains. Another coastal danger is tsunamis. These are huge waves caused by underwater earthquakes.

READING PROGRESS CHECK

Explaining Why is Pakistan more able to generate hydroelectric power from the Indus River than Bangladesh can from the Ganges and the Brahmaputra?

networks Online Teaching Options

INTERACTIVE MAP

Monsoons in India

Understanding Relationships This activity will help students make connections between the waterways of India and the waterways in Pakistan and Bangladesh, as well as compare the countries' climate and seasonal monsoon winds. Display the map showing the monsoons. Explain that the Ganges, Brahmaputra, and Indus Rivers carry fertile soil from the mountains to the floodplains of the rivers, which swell during seasonal rains. Have students write a paragraph explaining how the monsoon winds are important to this process in each country. **BL** **Naturalist, Verbal/Linguistic**

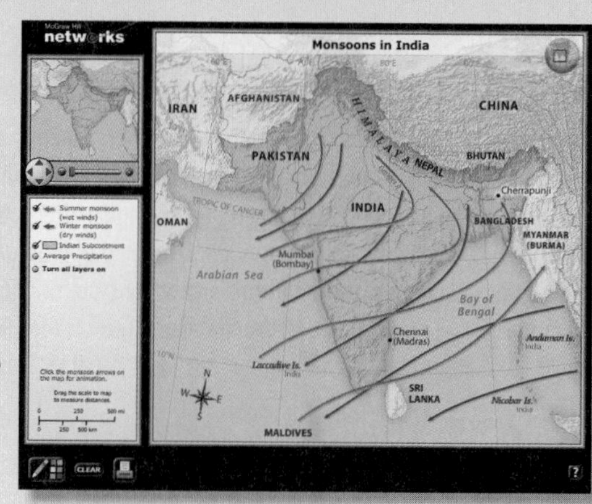

Climates, Biomes, and Resources

GUIDING QUESTION *What are the most important natural resources in Pakistan and Bangladesh?*

Pakistan and Bangladesh are subject to seasonal monsoons. These winds create three distinct seasons: hot (from late February to June), hot and wet (from June or July until September), and cool (from October to late February). In the hot and wet season, moist monsoon winds from the ocean bring rain. During the cool season, dry, cool monsoon winds from the Asian interior blow across the subcontinent toward the ocean.

Southeastern Bangladesh has a tropical wet climate. Most of Bangladesh receives as much as 60 inches (152 cm) of rain a year. In the wet monsoon months, rain forests absorb great amounts of moisture. In the hot, damp Sundarbans, tropical mangrove forests thrive. The Himalaya block the cold winds blowing from Central Asia. As a result, a band of humid subtropical climate extends across northern Bangladesh. The Hakaluki Hoar wetland in the east is home to rare and endangered fish, bird, and plant species.

Monsoon rains are not nearly as heavy in Pakistan as in Bangladesh. The wettest part of Pakistan, in the northeast, receives about half the rain of Bangladesh. Much of Pakistan only gets a fraction of that. Most rain falls in the hot months and evaporates quickly. Along the lower Indus in southern Pakistan, a desert climate keeps the land arid and windswept. East of the Indus in the Thar Desert, the vegetation is desert scrub. Though irrigation makes it possible to grow wheat in some parts, much of this area remains sandy with little vegetation.

South Asian rivers are important for basic needs, as well as for economic needs. They provide drinking water, alluvial soil, transportation, and hydroelectric power. They also provide fish for local use and export.

Pakistan and Bangladesh have few mineral resources. Of these, Pakistan has large amounts of limestone. It has oil in the north and natural gas in the south. Pakistan has very small amounts of iron ore, copper, coal, and other minerals.

The most abundant resource in Bangladesh, besides water, is natural gas. Most of that is burned by people for heat or used to make fertilizer, rather than exported. Bangladesh has small amounts of oil and coal. Some of these resources are inaccessible because they are buried too deep. Bangladesh does have valuable plant resources in the bamboo that grows in the Chittagong Hills and the high-quality mangrove wood of the Sundarbans.

✓ READING PROGRESS CHECK

Explaining In which country would it be easier to irrigate fields? Why?

Analyzing PRIMARY SOURCES

Flooding in Bangladesh

"That is how I felt in Sukkur 10 days ago. Overwhelmed.

People were flowing into the city at a ferocious pace, a ragged river of humanity, with shocked faces and frightened eyes.

They were fleeing on trucks, donkey carts, bicycles and on foot, clutching whatever was precious—electric fans, bedding, pots and pans, chickens and goats. Behind them, a great sinister mass of floodwater was pouring in."

—Jill McGivering, "'Elation' and 'Unease' at Helping Pakistan Flood Child," *BBC News*, September 4, 2010

DBQ ***MAKING PREDICTIONS*** What kind of help will these fleeing people need both immediately and in the future? RH.9–10.2

LESSON 1 REVIEW (CCSS)

Reviewing Vocabulary (Tier Three Words)

1. ***Identifying*** Write a paragraph explaining how the people of Pakistan and Bangladesh benefit from the floodplain. RH.9–10.4

Using Your Notes

2. ***Describing*** Use your graphic organizer on the physical systems of Pakistan and Bangladesh to write a paragraph describing one example of how landforms or waterways shape life in these countries.

Answering the Guiding Questions

3. ***Drawing Conclusions*** How do landforms in Pakistan and Bangladesh affect human activities?
4. ***Explaining*** How are rivers important to the peoples of Pakistan and Bangladesh?
5. ***Analyzing*** What are the most important natural resources in Pakistan and Bangladesh?

Writing Activity

6. ***Informative/Explanatory*** In a paragraph, discuss how the rivers of Pakistan and Bangladesh are both an advantage and a disadvantage. WHST.9–10.2

V Visual Skills

Creating Charts Have students identify the three seasons created by the monsoons. Then have students create a chart for Pakistan and a chart for Bangladesh showing three things about the climates of each country: the months of the three distinct seasons, the role of the winds, and whether each season is wet or dry. Students can use draw, sketch, or create their charts on the computer. Have students share their charts with the class.

 **Logical/Mathematical, Visual/Spatial**

Content Background Knowledge

Hydroelectricity in Pakistan and Bangladesh In Pakistan the main source of hydroelectricity is the Tarbela Dam, built on the Indus River and located west of the capital city of Islamabad. The dam was built from 1968 to 1976 and is the largest rock-filled dam in the world. It is 469 feet (143 m) high and at its crest is 8,997 feet (2,743 m) wide. Besides providing hydroelectricity, it controls the seasonal high and low flows of the Indus River. In Bangladesh, one dam generates hydroelectricity. The Kaptai Dam was built on the Karnaphuli River and is located approximately 40 miles (65 km) upstream of Chittagong, which is on the Bay of Bengal. It was built from 1957 to 1962 and is an earth-filled dam. It is 149 feet high (45.7 m) and 149 feet wide (45.7 m) at its foundation. In addition to producing hydroelectricity, it stores water in the reservoir, controlling 50 percent of the downstream flow in peak flood periods of the Karnaphuli River.

CLOSE & REFLECT

Summarizing To summarize the lesson, have students create a graphic organizer that compares and contrasts land forms and natural resources of Pakistan and those of Bangladesh. Students should share their lists as the class discusses the lesson in review.

LESSON 1 REVIEW ANSWERS

Reviewing Vocabulary

1. Paragraphs will vary, but should include that the fertile soil on the floodplain is good for growing crops.

Using Your Notes

2. Paragraphs will vary based on the example chosen by the student but could include the generally impassable mountains of Pakistan or the flooding of low-lying Bangladesh.

Answering the Guiding Questions

3. Mountains affect how people can travel and transport goods through Pakistan; the western and northern mountainous regions of Pakistan have earthquakes; the low plains in both countries have fertile soil which affects where people live and grow crops.
4. Rivers are important for drinking water, transportation, hydroelectric power, and for the flooding that deposits fertile soil on the plains.
5. The most important natural resources in Pakistan include limestone, oil, and natural gas. Bangladesh has important natural resources in its rivers, natural gas, and bamboo.

Writing Activity

6. Paragraphs will vary, but should include rivers being used for transportation, irrigation, fishing, and a source of power (largely Pakistan). Rivers are also the source of destructive floods during seasonal snowmelt and rains.

ANSWERS, p. 633

✓ **READING PROGRESS CHECK** Bangladesh would be easier to irrigate because it has more rain, is much less arid, has more rivers, and has lowlands covered with depressions. These depressions also fill with water for irrigation use during dry seasons.

DBQ Immediate needs could include food, shelter, and medical care. Future needs could include education and employment.

ENGAGE

C Critical Thinking Skills

Exploring Issues Have student pairs browse the lesson and read the headings on each page. Ask them to make a list of the topics they will be learning about in the lesson. Have pairs compare and discuss their lists with other pairs.

TEACH & ASSESS

T Technology Skills

Researching Divide the class into small groups and have them conduct Internet research about the archaeological discoveries of the ancient city of Mohenjo Daro. Their research should cover the history of discovering the city, the history of the Indus River valley, and should include that Mohenjo Daro is a designated UNESCO World Heritage site. Then have groups create a multimedia presentation. **BL Verbal/Linguistic**

Content Background Knowledge

Sikhism Founded in the 1400s by Guru Nanak, the religion is based on the Hindu devotion to Vishnu and the Muslim Sufis, or mystics. Sikhs believe there is one God who created the world. In order to perceive God, believers follow a discipline of meditation. Nanak believed in reincarnation. He taught that the soul is born many times until it is freed, and reaches unity with God. There are approximately 27 million Sikhs today. About 83 percent live in the Punjab in India.

W Writing Skills

Information/Explanatory Have students select one of the countries and write a short essay about the religious preference of that area during a specific time period. Allow students to do additional research as needed. **Verbal/Linguistic**

ANSWERS, p. 634

TAKING NOTES: Pakistan has been home to civilizations since about 2500 B.C. in the Indus River valley, where the culture developed a writing system, a central government, and overseas trade. A Buddhist kingdom ruled Bangladesh in the A.D. 600s. Hinduism was also practiced. Many traveled and settled in what became Pakistan and Bangladesh. Muslim invaders brought Islam to Pakistan in the A.D. 700s. Muslim traders brought Islam to Bangladesh in the A.D. 800s. Both areas are now predominantly Muslim. Both Pakistan and Bangladesh were part of the Mogul Empire and British colonization from 1500s to 1800s. The British introduced English, restructured the education system, built railroads, and developed civil service. Pakistan has conflicts between Hindus and Muslims since independence and disputes with India over control of Kashmir. Both are parliamentary republics. Bangladesh's people are ethnically Bengali and speak Bangla, which led to its independence.

networks *There's More Online!*

- **IMAGE** Microloans in Bangladesh
- **IMAGE** Ship-Breaking in Bangladesh
- **MAP** Partition of India, 1947
- **TIME LINE** Unity and Division
- **INTERACTIVE SELF-CHECK QUIZ**
- **VIDEO** Human Geography of Pakistan and Bangladesh

LESSON 2
Human Geography of Pakistan and Bangladesh

ESSENTIAL QUESTION • *How do physical systems and human systems shape a place?*

Reading HELPDESK (CCSS)

Academic Vocabulary (Tier Two Words)
- **infrastructure**
- **available**

Content Vocabulary (Tier Three Words)
- **total fertility rate**
- **jute**

TAKING NOTES: ***Key Ideas and Details***

COMPARING AND CONTRASTING As you read about the human geography of Pakistan and Bangladesh, use a graphic organizer like the one below to identify similarities and differences in the countries' histories.

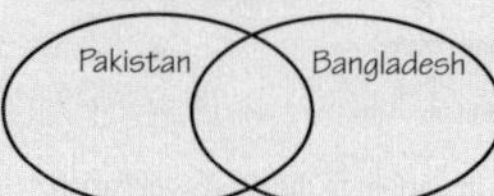

IT MATTERS BECAUSE

C *Pakistan and Bangladesh share a similar history of Muslim influence, British colonialism, and the pursuit of independence. Both have struggled since independence to build stable governments and overcome poverty.*

History and Government

GUIDING QUESTION *How did contemporary Pakistan and Bangladesh form?*

T The area we know today as Pakistan has been home to civilizations for thousands of years. One of the earliest settlements here was at Mehrgarh, near the Bolan Pass. Evidence dating back to 7000 B.C. shows that agriculture was being practiced. Around 2500 B.C. a great civilization arose in the Indus River valley. This culture developed a writing system, a strong central government, and a thriving overseas trade. Ruins of the walled city of Mohenjo Daro include evidence of plumbing and other advanced technology.

Beginning in the A.D. 600s, a Buddhist kingdom ruled over what is today Pakistan and Bangladesh for several centuries. Hinduism from India was also practiced. However, the diversity of the two countries suggests that both were crossroads for other groups seeking trade and territorial control. Over the centuries, many peoples crossed or settled in the regions that later became Pakistan and Bangladesh.

W Coming of Islam

Muslim invaders and traders brought Islam to southeast Pakistan in the A.D. 700s. About a century later, Muslim traders brought Islam to Bangladesh. Over time, Islam became the majority religion in both areas.

From the 1500s to the 1800s, Pakistan and Bangladesh were part of the Mogul Empire that also ruled much of India. Early in this period, Sikhism, which blends elements of Hinduism and Islam, arose in the Punjab in northwestern India. In the early 1800s, a Sikh named Ranjit Singh established a kingdom in northern Pakistan, but it fell apart after his death.

networks Online Teaching Options

INTERACTIVE BELLRINGER

Bangladesh: The Road to Independence

Interpreting a Time Line Use the introductory text and the time line showing dates and events leading up to the independence of Bangladesh to understand how Pakistan and Bangladesh formed. Have students form small groups and discuss each question. Ask each group to list all possible answers for questions 2 and 3. Then, as a class, review the answer to the first question and have each group shares its answers to the other two questions. **BL Interpersonal, Visual/Spatial**

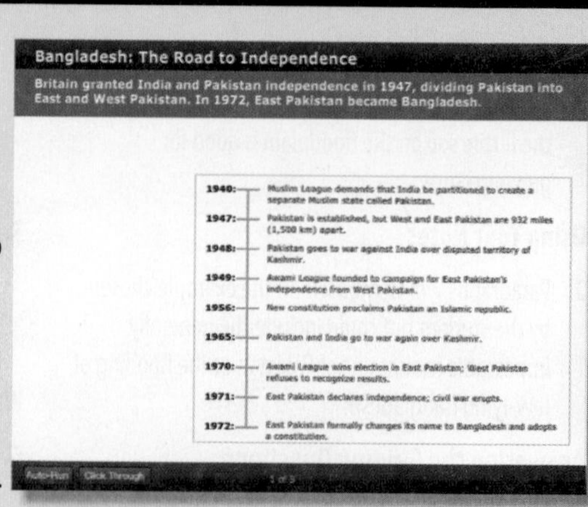

Bangladesh: The Road to Independence
Britain granted India and Pakistan independence in 1947, dividing Pakistan into East and West Pakistan. In 1972, East Pakistan became Bangladesh.
1940: Muslim League demands that India be partitioned to create a separate Muslim state called Pakistan.
1947: Pakistan is established, but West and East Pakistan are 932 miles (1,500 km) apart.
1948: Pakistan goes to war against India over disputed territory of Kashmir.
1949: Awami League founded to campaign for East Pakistan's independence from West Pakistan.
1956: New constitution proclaims Pakistan an Islamic republic.
1965: Pakistan and India go to war again over Kashmir.
1970: Awami League wins election in East Pakistan; West Pakistan refuses to recognize results.
1971: East Pakistan declares independence; civil war erupts.
1972: East Pakistan formally changes its name to Bangladesh and adopts a constitution.
Auto-Run
Click Through

In the middle 1800s, the British included both Pakistan and Bangladesh within their colony of India. Together they formed a single colonial administrative unit called India. The British introduced English, restructured the educational system, built railroads, and developed a civil service. During their rule, tension between Muslims and Hindus in South Asia grew. While Hindus formed a group to campaign for independence, Muslims, who feared domination by the majority Hindus, created a similar organization of their own.

Pakistan Since Independence

By the 1930s, the idea of a Muslim state separate from India had taken hold among South Asia's Muslims. When Hindu and Muslim leaders could not agree on a constitution for a single state, in 1947 the British granted independence to two states based upon the dominant religion. India was formed as a predominantly Hindu state and Pakistan as a predominantly Muslim state. The latter consisted of two sections, known at the time as East Pakistan and West Pakistan. They were separated by about 1,000 miles (1,609 km) of Indian territory.

Independence from Britain was marked by a massive movement of Hindus and Muslims between India and Pakistan. During this time, there were outbreaks of violence between followers of the two religions. Adding to the tension, both countries claimed the area of Kashmir. It was part of India by tradition, but had a majority Muslim population. The two countries fought wars for control of Kashmir in 1948, 1965, and 1999. Tensions over Kashmir and other issues became more worrisome in the 1990s after India and Pakistan both developed nuclear weapons. Relations between the two countries have improved in recent years, but the situation remains uneasy.

Pakistan is a parliamentary republic, but instability and military rule have prevailed since 1971. In the early 2000s, General Pervez Musharraf allied Pakistan with the United States in its war on terror. His rule became increasingly unpopular, however, and he was forced to step down in 2008. Asif Ali Zardari, the widower of former prime minister Benazir Bhutto, was elected president in 2008. He introduced reforms to try to establish civilian government, but poverty and rebel activity in the west plague the country. In 2013 Nawaz Sharif took office as Pakistan's prime minister after a sweeping victory of his Pakistan Muslim League party.

R

Bangladesh: Independence and After

The people of East Pakistan were culturally different from the people in West Pakistan long before independence from the British. In Bangladesh they are ethnic Bengali and speak Bangla. After independence, West Pakistan wanted to impose a national language, Urdu, on all of Pakistan. Bengali leaders believed that their ethnic majority was treated unfairly by the government, which was dominated by leaders from West Pakistan. They formed a protest movement.

V

After wins in the 1970–1971 elections, Bengali nationalists pushed for self-rule. Pakistan sent its army to suppress the nationalists, which prompted them to declare independence for Bangladesh—which means "Bengal country." India entered the war on behalf of independent Bangladesh, and Pakistan surrendered.

Bangladesh is also a parliamentary republic. Political and ethnic rivalries have made stable rule difficult. Discontent has continued in recent years.

READING PROGRESS CHECK

Making Connections How was the movement that led to the independence of Bangladesh similar to the movement that led to the formation of Pakistan?

Connecting Geography to HISTORY

Natural Disaster

When does a storm create a political movement? Since Pakistan's independence in 1947, many people in East Pakistan were unhappy with domination by those in West Pakistan. In the 1960s, some groups began calling for an independent state. Then a devastating cyclone smashed into East Pakistan in 1970, flooding large areas and killing as many as 500,000 people. The West Pakistan-dominated government was slow to provide desperately needed relief to the suffering Bengalis. The smoldering anger over this slow response contributed to the Bengali declaration of independence the following year and the establishment of Bangladesh.

W

EVALUATING What effect did the 1970 cyclone have on the history of Bangladesh?

VIDEO

Saira Khan's Pakistan Adventure, Islamabad

Taking Notes As students view this video about the changing political process in Pakistan, have them listen to the interviews, taking notes about the views of the demonstrators and leaders. When the video is completed, lead the class in a discussion about Pakistan's current political climate and hopes for the future. Students should cite information from the textbook as well as the video in their discussions.
AL Visual/Spatial

Human Geography of Pakistan and Bangladesh

R Reading Skills

Sequencing Information Have students read the paragraphs under *Pakistan Since Independence*. Emphasize to students the number of events occurring in Pakistan from its independence to current day. Using the text as well as additional resources, have students list the sequence of events from Pakistan gaining its independence to today. Have students share their lists with another student to check for accuracy. **ELL Verbal/Linguistic**

V Visual Skills

Creating a Chart Tell students to consider the similarities and differences people of West Pakistan and East Pakistan had. Using computers, have pairs make charts comparing and contrasting the people of East Pakistan with the people of West Pakistan. Charts should include dates as well as facts. Have each set of students present its chart in a class discussion. Then lead the class to conclude whether the people of West and East Pakistan had more differences than similarities. **BL Logical/Mathematical, Visual/Spatial**

W Writing Skills

Narrative Direct students' attention to how a natural event can influence history. Tell students to imagine they were in East Pakistan in 1970 when a severe cyclone hit. Have them write a narration of what it was like and to describe how they felt when the West Pakistan government was slow to send relief. Have students read their narratives to the class. **AL Intrapersonal**

ANSWERS, p. 635

READING PROGRESS CHECK The ethnic cohesiveness of the Bengali of East Pakistan led them to declare independence from the predominantly Muslim West Pakistan, which is similar to the British creating the division so that India would be a Hindu state and Pakistan a Muslim state.

Connecting Geography The slow response of the West Pakistan-dominated government to the cyclone contributed to East Pakistan declaring independence and the establishment of Bangladesh.

R Reading Skills

Examining Information Lead a class discussion about what it might be like to live in one of the most populous countries in the world. **Ask:** What are two characteristics of the population in Pakistan? *(One-third of the people in Pakistan are under 15 years of age and most of the population lives in the Indus River valley.)* What population changes are occurring in Pakistan? *(Many people are migrating to cities.)* Why is this shift causing problems? *(The cities do not have the infrastructure to support a growing population.)* AL Verbal/Linguistic

W Writing Skills

Informative/Explanatory Emphasize that Bangladesh is the most densely populated country in South Asia. Have students write a short essay explaining what Bangladesh is doing to curtail its growing population. Encourage students to use the information in the text as well as Internet resources to learn if there have been any additional programs that may affect the fertility rate. Verbal/Linguistic

C Critical Thinking Skills

Interpreting Visuals Direct students' attention to the time line. **Ask:** What does the title of the time line, *Unity and Division,* suggest about the history of Pakistan and Bangladesh? *(Possible answer: It suggests that the countries' history was once unified and then turned divisive.)* Why do you think creating a West and East Pakistan was a solution that would not last? *(Student answers may vary, but should include that since West and East Pakistan were separated by such a great distance and since the populations were different culturally, it was unlikely the solution would work.)* Logical/Mathematical, Visual/Spatial

Population Patterns

GUIDING QUESTION *How does high population density affect life in Pakistan and Bangladesh?*

Pakistan, with its population numbering 180 million, is the sixth most populous country in the world. Bangladesh, with a population of 153 million, ranks eighth. In Pakistan, more than one-third of the people are under the age of 15. In Bangladesh, just under one-third are under age 15.

R Physical geography shapes settlement in Pakistan, where most of the population lives in the Indus River valley. Although Pakistan is one of South Asia's most urbanized countries, only about 35 percent of the population lives in urban areas. Many people are migrating to cities, however, including Islamabad, Lahore, and Karachi. This growing urban population is straining resources. Migrants to the cities are forced to live in makeshift structures pulled together from scrap material. The **infrastructure** that makes urban life more livable, such as public water and sewage removal, is undeveloped in these poor areas.

infrastructure system of public services such as power, water and sewage, transportation and communication networks, and schools and health care facilities

total fertility rate the average number of children a woman has in her lifetime

W In Pakistan the **total fertility rate**, or the average number of children a woman has in her lifetime, is 3.6. This is 50 percent higher than the world average. As a result, its population is growing rapidly, at 2 percent a year.

Bangladesh is the most densely populated country in South Asia, with 3,256 people per square mile (1,257 people per sq. km). The highest population densities occur in cities, such as Dhaka. However, density is generally high throughout the country. Only the Sundarbans in the southwest and the Chittagong Hills in the southeast have lower population densities.

To encourage Bengali women to have fewer children, private and government programs give women small loans to start their own businesses. The programs have achieved some success. While the total fertility rate was 4.4 in 1991, by 2011 it had declined to 2.2, just below the world average. Fertility rates have decreased as women become more educated and have more economic opportunities.

READING PROGRESS CHECK

Explaining How did the government of Bangladesh address its high fertility rate?

TIME LINE

UNITY and Division

The state of Pakistan was born out of a desire of Muslims in India for national unity, but geographic and demographic challenges caused further disunity, leading to the creation of Bangladesh.

C **CRITICAL THINKING**

1. ***Explaining*** Why did the Muslim League call for a separate state to be created for Muslims?
2. ***Comparing*** In what ways are the histories of Pakistan and Bangladesh similar?

1900

1906 Muslim League is founded to protect Muslim rights in India under British rule

1940 Muslim League demands that India be partitioned to create a separate Muslim state called Pakistan

1947 Pakistan is established, but West and East Pakistan are about a thousand miles apart. First governor-general is Mohammed Ali Jinnah.

1948 Pakistan goes to war against India over disputed territory of Kashmir

Bert Brandt/AFP/Getty Images

636

networks Online Teaching Options

INTERACTIVE MAP

Partition of India, 1947

Hypothesizing Display the map while discussing the shifting populations of Hindus and Muslims during the Partition. Have students hypothesize about what life might have been like for families as the countries were divided and people relocated to new areas by listing three hypotheses about the effects relocation would have on a family. Then ask students to share their lists in a class discussion. ELL Verbal/Linguistic

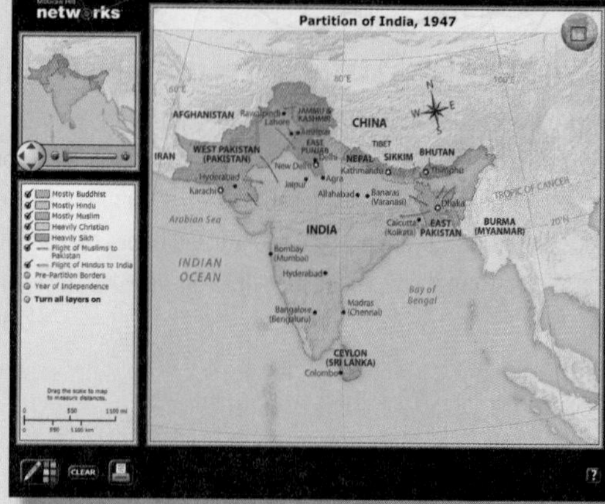

ANSWERS, p. 636

READING PROGRESS CHECK The government addressed the high fertility rated by providing more education and economic opportunities to women.

CRITICAL THINKING

1. The Muslim League called for a separate state for Muslims to ensure that Muslim rights were protected and because they also had a strong desire for national unity.
2. Bangladesh was created as the Bengalis wanted a country where their ethnic majority dominated just as the Muslim majority of Pakistan wanted separation from the Hindus of India.

Society and Culture Today

GUIDING QUESTION *How is life in Pakistan similar to and different from life in Bangladesh?*

Pakistan and Bangladesh became separate countries because of their diverse ethnic heritages. Pakistan is diverse in large part because it experienced invasions and migrations over many centuries. Pakistan has six main ethnic groups: Punjabis, Pashtuns, Sindhis, Sariakis, Muhajirs, and Balochis. Punjabis make up about 45 percent of the country's people. No other group has more than 16 percent. Urdu is the official language of Pakistan, but only 8 percent of the population speaks it. More Pakistanis speak Punjabi than any other language. English, also an official language, is typically spoken by members of the elite, including government officials. **R**

In Bangladesh the majority of the people are Bengali, a term describing both an ethnic and a language group. It is something they share with some of their Hindu neighbors in the Indian state of Bengal. Non-Bengalis, mostly smaller indigenous groups, make up only a small percentage of Bangladesh's population.

Islam is the main religion in both countries. The two countries also have some Hindus and small Christian populations. Most Muslims are Sunnis, but about one-fifth of Pakistan's Muslims are Shias.

Literacy rates in Pakistan and Bangladesh are very low, at less than 60 percent. In Bangladesh, the literacy rate for men is about 10 percentage points higher than for women. In Pakistan, the gap between male and female literacy is much greater. Schooling in Bangladesh is free and required for all children to age ten, but only about half of children actually attend. School is not required in Pakistan, where the educational system is a mix of government-run, Islamic, and private schools. **T**

Lack of health care is a major problem in both countries, mainly because of their large populations and high poverty rates. Spending on health care ranks toward the bottom of priorities, and there are relatively fewer doctors or hospital beds than are needed. Several diseases, including tuberculosis and malaria, have long been problems in both countries. Bangladesh has succeeded in reducing malaria but still faces many public health issues.

- **1949** Awami League is founded to campaign for East Pakistan's independence from West Pakistan
- **1950**
- **1956** New constitution proclaims Pakistan an Islamic republic
- **1965** Pakistan and India go to war again over Kashmir.
- **1970** Awami League wins election in East Pakistan; West Pakistan refuses to recognize results.
- **1971** East Pakistan declares independence; civil war erupts.
- **1972** East Pakistan formally changes its name to Bangladesh and adopts a constitution.
- **1975**

W

R Reading Skills

Listing Have students use the text and make a T-chart with one column entitled Pakistan and the other Bangladesh. Have students list the differences and similarities of the two countries in ethnic background, language, and religion. Have students compare their T-charts in pairs. **ELL Verbal/Linguistic, Visual/Spatial**

T Technology Skills

Researching Emphasize to students that Pakistan and Bangladesh have similar challenges in the twenty-first century. Divide the class into small groups and assign each group a country and have them identify one problem the country faces. The problems could be literacy, water (flooding and potable water), health care, or economic, including the problems of building a sustainable economy. Have students research in the library or on the Internet what solutions have been enacted to resolve that problem. Solutions could include UN programs such as literacy programs and the UN South Asia Water Initiative, World Bank financial investment programs, or work done by private nonprofit organizations such as Doctors Without Borders. Have each group make a presentation showing the problem and attempted solutions. **BL Visual/Spatial**

W Writing Skills

Narrative Tell students to select one date on the time line and write a one-page narrative about what they think they would have done if they had lived in East or West Pakistan during that time. Tell them to consider, for example, that if they lived in East Pakistan whether they would have joined the Awami League to campaign for East Pakistan's independence or whether they would have supported the East Pakistanian civil war. Have students share their narratives. Encourage students to include drawings with their essays. **Intrapersonal, Verbal/Linguistic**

TIME LINE

Unity and Division

Understanding Conflict This time line graphic notes the key events on the path toward the independence of Pakistan and Bangladesh, including two wars between India and Pakistan over the disputed territory of Kashmir. Mention to students that fighting still goes on about this disputed territory and ask them to use the Internet to research what makes Kashmir such a valuable territory for both Indians and Pakistanis. Have students write a brief summary of their findings. **Visual/Spatial**

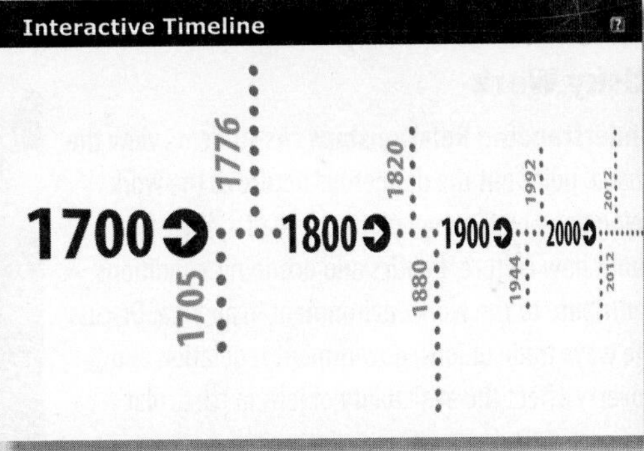

W Writing Skills

Argument Emphasize that Pakistan and Bangladesh have employment, literacy, and health care issues. Tell students that they are to think like an executive director of an international nonprofit organization charged with helping one of these countries. In small groups, ask students to decide whether to design a program to reduce literacy, improve health care, or create jobs in either Pakistan or Bangladesh. Have groups select one area and write a persuasive argument about why this is the nonprofit direction. Have groups with opposing viewpoints argue their points in a class debate. **BL Verbal/Linguistic**

T Technology Skills

Exploring Issues Direct students' attention to the photo of the ship-breaking industry. Have student pairs research other salvage industries in Bangladesh or Pakistan. They should create a presentation using illustrations and graphs of the industry or of projects that indicate the amount of work done, number of workers, and so forth. **AL Visual/Spatial**

Content Background Knowledge

Pakistan–Bangladesh: Prime Ministers

- Both Benazir Bhutto, former Pakistan Prime Minister, and Sheikh Hasina, the Prime Minister of Bangladesh, came from prominent political families. Both of their fathers held the office of prime minister either of Pakistan or Bangladesh.
- Benazir Bhutto was the first woman to serve as prime minister of an Islamic country. Her tenure as prime minister was marred by strong opposition from the Islamic fundamentalist movement in Pakistan. In 2008, she was killed in Pakistan.
- Sheikh Hasina has served two terms as prime minister of Bangladesh. She was elected to her first term in 1996. While serving as prime minister she has worked to alleviate the poverty of Bangladesh. Also during her tenure, Bangladesh signed a peace treaty with India.

ANSWERS, p. 638

READING PROGRESS CHECK The people of Pakistan are comprised of six main ethnic groups speaking multiple languages. The people of Bangladesh are all Bengali and speak Bangla.

CRITICAL THINKING

1. People take such dangerous jobs because they have no choice as poverty is widespread and jobs outside of agriculture are limited.
2. Bangladesh does not have the kind of heavy industry, manufacturing, or resources needed to be part of the ship building industry whereas ship-breaking mostly requires labor.

Family and the Status of Women

Family is the social basis in both countries. Extended families live close, often in the same home. Many marriages are arranged, though increasing numbers of educated people choose their own partners. After marriage, the wife typically lives with the husband's family.

In traditional families in Pakistan, women stay in separate parts of the house when nonfamily males visit. This is more common among urban and middle-class Pakistanis than rural or poor people, where women must work to help the family survive. Some Muslim women also wear the burka, a loose garment that covers the face and body, when they are in public.

Both Pakistan and Bangladesh have had women leaders. Benazir Bhutto was twice prime minister of Pakistan. Sheikh Hasina served as prime minister of Bangladesh from 1996 to 2001 and took that office again in 2009.

The Arts

Literature and dance are very important in Bangladesh. In 1913 Bengali Rabindranath Tagore became the first non-European writer to win the Nobel Prize in Literature. The poetry and plays of Kazi Nazrul Islam, "the voice of Bengali nationalism," have inspired poor farmers with themes about the oppression of Muslims. Bangladesh also has developed original and creative traditional dances in classical as well as folk styles.

Music and literature are the richest of all Pakistani art forms. *Qawwali,* a form of devotional singing, is popular. People recite poetry at public *musha'irahs* that are organized like music concerts. The classical music tradition can be traced to the thirteenth-century poet and musician Amir Khosrow, who composed the traditional rhythmic form known as the raga.

READING PROGRESS CHECK

Contrasting How are the people of Pakistan more diverse than those of Bangladesh?

These men at a shipyard in Bangladesh, on the Bay of Bengal, work in the ship-breaking industry. They face dangerous conditions, including accidents and exposure to toxic materials.

CRITICAL THINKING

1. ***Drawing Conclusions*** Why do people take such dangerous jobs?
2. ***Making Inferences*** Why do you think Bangladesh has a ship-breaking industry, but not a ship-building industry?

networks Online Teaching Options

INTERACTIVE IMAGE

Risky Work

Understanding Relationships As students view the image, point out the dangerous nature of the work being done by the men pictured. Lead a discussion about how culture, politics and economic conditions contribute to the work environment in an area. Discuss the ways trade unions, government regulation and poverty affect the availability of jobs in particular regions. **BL Verbal/Linguistic, Visual/Spatial**

Economic Activities

GUIDING QUESTION *What are the dominant economic activities in Pakistan and Bangladesh?*

Pakistan and Bangladesh have traditionally relied on agriculture. Industrial activity is increasing in the twenty-first century. Poverty is widespread. The economic situation has worsened in recent years due mainly to inflation.

About one-fifth of Pakistan's gross domestic product (GDP) comes from agriculture, and about two-fifths of the workforce is in agriculture. Cash crops, including rice, cotton, and sugarcane, bring much-needed income. Pakistan also has a fishing industry, exporting shrimp, lobster, and fish. Despite reforms in the last 50 years, land distribution remains highly unequal. Most farmers continue to use draft animals on small farms. Since the 1980s, service industries have grown. Today, more than half the country's GDP is from the service sector. **V**

Industry constitutes about one-fourth of Pakistan's GDP. The most important are cotton textiles and clothing for export. Other exports include rice, leather, sporting goods, chemicals, and carpets. Most exports are shipped out of the Port of Karachi. Pakistan has become a major trading partner of the United States. Small-scale production, or cottage industries, has played an important role in Pakistan's industrialization. They employ many craftspeople and provide at-home employment for women.

As in India, railways are the principal mode of transportation. The state-owned Pakistan Railways moves both people and cargo throughout Pakistan. Highways are increasing in importance. The Makran Coastal Highway runs along the Arabian Sea and integrates economic activities in the area.

Rural areas in both countries often lack electricity and other modern services. The spread of cell phones has made communications more widely **available** even in rural areas. That is more the case in Pakistan than Bangladesh, however.

available able to be obtained

In Bangladesh most people are sharecroppers. Rice is the major crop. In some areas, farmers can grow three crops a year, alternating rice, wheat, and other crops. **Jute**, a fiber used to make string, rope, and cloth, is also a major cash crop.

jute a fiber used to make string, rope, and cloth

The garment industry has expanded and clothing is now Bangladesh's top export. As in Pakistan, much of Bangladesh's textile manufacturing relies on cottage industries. Dhaka is a center for weaving muslin, a lightweight cotton cloth. Nearly 2 million women work in Bangladesh's garment industry. Other craft goods include jute products, such as upholstery, and leather goods. **W**

Bangladesh is one of the world's largest aquaculture-producing countries. It has many inland fisheries that cultivate fish and shrimp. These proteins are part of a staple diet that also relies heavily on rice and lentils.

☑ **READING PROGRESS CHECK**

Explaining How are cottage industries important in Pakistan and Bangladesh?

LESSON 2 REVIEW

Reviewing Vocabulary (Tier Three Words)

1. ***Identifying*** Write a paragraph explaining what jute is and why it could be called the "golden crop" of Bangladesh. RH.9–10.4

Using Your Notes

2. ***Comparing and Contrasting*** Use your graphic organizer on the human geography of Pakistan and Bangladesh to write a paragraph explaining how their histories are similar and different.

Answering the Guiding Questions

3. ***Explaining*** How did contemporary Pakistan and Bangladesh form?
4. ***Assessing*** How does high population density affect life in Pakistan and Bangladesh?
5. ***Comparing and Contrasting*** How is life in Pakistan similar to and different from life in Bangladesh?
6. ***Identifying*** What are the dominant economic activities in Pakistan and Bangladesh?

Writing Activity

7. ***Argument*** In a few paragraphs, discuss challenges Pakistan and Bangladesh face and how they might be tackled. WHST.9–10be.1

LESSON 2 REVIEW ANSWERS

Reviewing Vocabulary

1. Paragraphs should explain that jute is a major cash crop used to make rope, cloth, and string.

Using Your Notes

2. Paragraphs will differ but could include Muslim invaders brought Islam to Pakistan while Muslim traders brought Islam to Bangladesh. Both Pakistan and Bangladesh were part of the Mogul Empire and British colonization of India.

Answering the Guiding Questions

3. Contemporary Pakistan and Bangladesh formed from West and East Pakistan when the Bengali of East Pakistan wanted fair treatment and their own state.
4. High population density puts a strain on the infrastructure particularly in cities where housing and sanitation are issues.
5. In both countries the major religion is Islam, there is a lack of health care, and widespread poverty. The people of Pakistan are ethnically diverse and several languages are spoken. Bangladesh is ethnically homogeneous.
6. The dominant economic activities are agriculture followed by textile manufacturing.

Writing Activity

7. Paragraphs will vary, but could include the challenges of poverty, lack of health care, low literacy rates, and high populations along with solutions of education, economic growth, and development.

V Visual Skills

Creating Graphs In pairs, have students research the economic activities and industries of Pakistan or Bangladesh. They should list each activity's percentage of the total economy in a graph showing the data they gathered. Remind pairs to use credible websites. BL **Visual/Spatial**

Content Background Knowledge

Nobel Peace Prize Muhammad Yunus is a Bangladeshi economist who started a new type of banking known as micro-credit. This type of banking gives small loans to poor people who are unable to get conventional bank loans. This program has helped millions of people in Bangladesh, mostly women, to buy things they need, such as cell phones to run their own businesses. He started Grameen Bank in 1976 when he lent $27 (in U.S. dollars) from his own money to a group of 42 women in a Bangladesh village who made bamboo furniture. The loan gave the women the boost they needed to succeed in establishing their business. In 2006 Muhammad Yunus won the Nobel Peace Prize.

W Writing Skills

Argument Tell students to assume they work for the World Bank and have been assigned to design a program that would promote one aspect of economic growth in Pakistan or Bangladesh. What solution would they recommend? Why? Have students write an essay describing their solution, including reasons why their solution will work. Have students present their solutions. Then have the class debate whether the solutions will work. BL **Intrapersonal**

CLOSE & REFLECT

Outlining Have students create an outline with two main sections: Pakistan and Bangladesh. Tell students to include items in the outline about the history, population, economy, and the culture and arts for each country. Have student pairs exchange outlines and review the lesson together.

ANSWERS, p. 639

☑ **READING PROGRESS CHECK** Cottage industries have played an important role in industrialization by employing craftspeople and providing at-home employment for women.

ENGAGE

Formulating Questions Have students identify the countries shown on the map. Ask a volunteer to identify and explain the symbols and what each means. Then have students work with a partner to brainstorm and list questions they have about nuclear weapons. *(Sample questions: Why do some countries have nuclear weapons programs? What are the dangers of these types of weapons to humans? To the environment?)* Have students save their questions and write in answers after reading this Global Connections feature.

TEACH & ASSESS

R Reading Skills

Discussing Point to the phrase *on the brink* in the title of this feature and guide students to understand its meaning. Offer an example of the phrase in a different context, such as: "I was on the brink of giving up on the math homework, when my classmate called me to explain the assignment." **Ask: How can understanding the phrase *on the brink* help you understand this feature?** *(Possible answer: The phrase is helpful to understand because it conveys how disputes between countries such as India and Pakistan can escalate into war.)* **Verbal/Linguistic**

Content Background Knowledge

Tense Relations In 1998, Pakistan reacted to India's nuclear weapons testing by conducting its own tests. Relations between the two countries have been tense ever since terrorist attacks in Mumbai, India, killed at least 100 people in 2008. In June 2013, five soldiers were killed and seven others were wounded when an army convoy was attacked in Kashmir, which is controlled by India.

V Visual Skills

Calculating Direct students' attention to the visual on this page titled "Regional Nuclear Arsenals." Have students work in pairs to calculate the percentage of nuclear arsenals in China compared to those in Pakistan and India. Guide a discussion about the size of each country as it relates to its nuclear arsenals. **Logical/Mathematical**

Global Connections: **South Asia**

South ASIA on the BRINK

R

The nuclear weapons programs of India and Pakistan began in the late 1960s and early 1970s and produced nuclear weapons for both countries. India and Pakistan have over 100 missiles between them. India's Agni-V missile is capable of striking a target more than 3,100 miles (4,989 km) away. Although the two countries' nuclear arsenals are small relative to those of the United States and Russia, they nonetheless pose a threat to the rest of the world.

PAKISTAN

INDIA

1,550 mi (2,500 km)

REGIONAL NUCLEAR STOCKPILES

V

CHINA 200

PAKISTAN 60

INDIA 50

640

networks Online Teaching Options

INTERACTIVE MAP

Kashmir

Creating Time Lines Use this map of the Kashmir region to illustrate and introduce students to this location of much of the turmoil. Have students identify possible reasons why this location is vital to both India and Pakistan. Invite a small group of volunteers to research more information about the northern Kashmir border dispute, and then report their findings to the class. Based on the gathered data, create a time line as a class that reviews the history of the dispute. Ask several students to write statements and to draw or collect illustrations to enhance the class time line. **Interpersonal, Visual/Spatial**

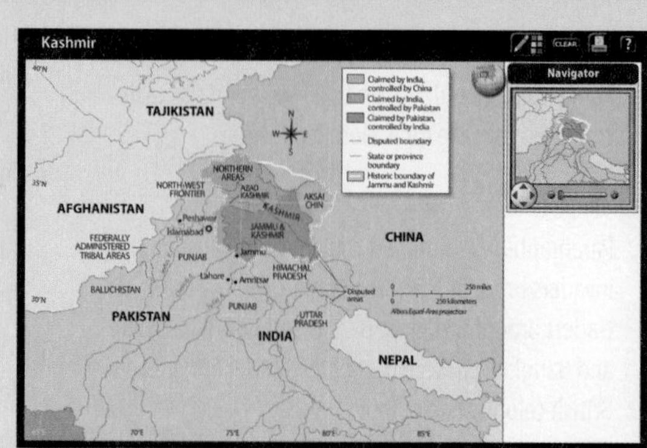

THREATS

KASHMIR DISPUTE

India and Pakistan have both claimed ownership of the northern Kashmir border region. War has erupted over the area twice in the past, and there are worries that if there was ever a third it would go nuclear.

CHINA

CHINA DISPUTE

China and India too have border disputes. Both countries having nuclear arms raises fears of nuclear war.

TERRORISM

Pakistan's political instability causes some concern. Should its government fall, nuclear materials could fall into the hands of terrorist cells in neighboring countries and within Pakistan itself.

— PAKISTANI MAXIMUM RANGE
— INDIAN MAXIMUM RANGE

3,107 mi (5,000 km)

NUCLEAR WINTER

Should both India and Pakistan detonate their arsenals, it could result in a 20% depletion of global ozone levels. The resulting increase in UV radiation could seriously impact human health across the globe.

Making Connections

1. ***Places and Regions*** What ongoing regional conflicts increase the risk of nuclear war?
2. ***The World in Spatial Terms*** According to the map, about how many countries are in range of Pakistan's nuclear weapons?
3. ***Environment and Society*** What effects could a nuclear conflict have on the environment and the people of the region?

*Interact with **Global Connections** Online*

INTERACTIVE SLIDE SHOW

How to Analyze the News

Analyzing Have small groups of students view the slide show lesson about analyzing the news. Then have each group prepare a checklist for analyzing the news, based on the information in the slide show lesson. Have each group compare its checklist with that of another group and revise the lists as needed. Then tell groups to search the Internet or other media for current news reports about the nuclear weapons programs in South Asia. Tell groups to choose one report and to use their checklist to analyze it. Have each group share its news report and checklist with the class and tell what they learned from the news report. **Verbal/Linguistic, Logical/Mathematical**

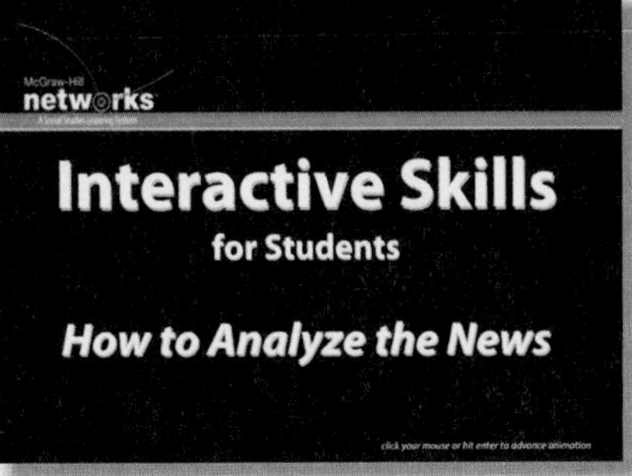

T Technology Skills

Changing Continuity of Groups Help students visualize the size of the countries by offering examples in comparison, such as Pakistan is almost twice the size of California. Then have students research the types of weapons programs and the military capabilities in one of the countries shown on the map. Have students present their findings in a short report using presentation software. Encourage students to include a time line. BL **Visual/Spatial, Interpersonal**

C Critical Thinking Skills

Interpreting Significance Have students read the information about Pakistan's political instability. **Ask: How do you think Pakistan's tenuous political situation could impact its relations with neighboring countries?** *(Student answers should demonstrate an understanding of the cause-and-effect relationship between a country's nuclear capabilities and a deteriorating government.)* **Verbal/Linguistic**

W Writing Skills

Narrative Ask a volunteer to read aloud the text under the *Nuclear Winter* heading. **Ask: What do you think is the likelihood that India or Pakistan will detonate its nuclear arsenals?** *(Possible answer: The chances are slim because the impact would be so devastating.)* Have students write a narrative that conveys how the physical and human systems in surrounding regions would be impacted by a detonation. BL **Verbal/Linguistic**

CLOSE & REFLECT

Constructing Arguments Have students review this feature and formulate an opinion as to the value of nuclear arsenals. Then guide a discussion about possible solutions to remedy the fears of nuclear deployment discussed in this feature.

ANSWERS, p. 641

Making Connections

1. Ongoing tension between Pakistan and India is seen as the greatest risk of nuclear war. In addition to this, the conflict in Pakistan and neighboring Afghanistan involving the United States has increased the risk of nuclear arms falling into the hands of terrorist groups. Finally, conflicting land claims between India and China are also seen as a nuclear risk.
2. Roughly 16 countries. These include: India, Bangladesh, Sri Lanka, Maldives, China, Mongolia, Myanmar, Bhutan, Nepal, Afghanistan, Iran, Turkestan, Uzbekistan, Kazakhstan, Kyrgyzstan, and Tajikistan.
3. A nuclear conflict would have an immediate impact on the environment of the region and the health of its people through deaths in attacks and then through the effects of radiation.

ENGAGE

R Reading Skills

Listing When students enter the class, have the following question written on the board: **How does the high population rate of Pakistan and Bangladesh create environmental challenges for the two governments?** Have student pairs browse through the lesson to list the environmental challenges discussed.

TEACH & ASSESS

C Critical Thinking Skills

Drawing Conclusions Discuss with students whether the economies of Pakistan and Bangladesh could be called *fragile.* **Ask: What are the difficulties of relying heavily on one aspect of an economy, such as agriculture?** *(Student answers may vary, but should point out that if the growing season is challenged, that greatly affects the success of the economy.)* **What do you conclude would be a key to a healthy economy for Pakistan and Bangladesh?** *(A healthy economy for Pakistan and Bangladesh would include greater diversification in goods and services for internal use and to export to the world market.)* **AL Verbal/Linguistic**

W Writing Skills

Narrative Have students select one of the principles of sustainable development and write a narrative of a hypothetical sustainable development program that is working in Pakistan or Bangladesh. For example, they might think of a program that would protect the environment in the Bay of Bengal. Or they might think of a program that would create a cottage industry in which women in Pakistan could work. Emphasize to students that their hypothetical example has to have adequate funding from an international or national organization. Use student narratives to continue a class discussion on sustainable development programs in developing countries. **Verbal/Linguistic**

ANSWERS, p. 642

TAKING NOTES: The Sundarbans is a wetland area in southwestern Bangladesh and northeastern India with the world's largest mangrove forest; it is threatened by rising sea levels and saltwater flooding from the Bay of Bengal and deforestation from the Himalaya which allows more soil and silt to wash into the area, restricting water flow to the trees. Deforestation of the mangrove forest itself for fuel or land use is also an issue. Both lack clean drinking water due to raw sewage and agricultural runoff and soil erosion due to deforestation. Pakistan is working to protect the soil, make irrigation efficient, and improve forest management but political turmoil has interrupted. Bangladesh has adopted a climate change policy, is composting for fertilizer and using the by-product of methane gas.

networks

There's More Online!

- **GRAPH** World's Worst Cities for Air Pollution
- **IMAGE** Compressed Natural Gas Vehicle
- **IMAGE** The Sundarbans
- **IMAGE** Water Pollution in Bangladesh
- **INTERACTIVE SELF-CHECK QUIZ**
- **VIDEO** People and Their Environment: Pakistan and Bangladesh

LESSON 3
People and Their Environment: Pakistan and Bangladesh

ESSENTIAL QUESTION • *How do physical systems and human systems shape a place?*

Reading HELPDESK (CCSS)

Academic Vocabulary (Tier Two Words)
- **principle**
- **accumulate**

Content Vocabulary (Tier Three Words)
- **sustainable development**
- **hydroelectric power**

TAKING NOTES: ***Key Ideas and Details***

IDENTIFYING As you read about the environments of Pakistan and Bangladesh, use a graphic organizer like the one below to identify threats to the environment and responses to those threats.

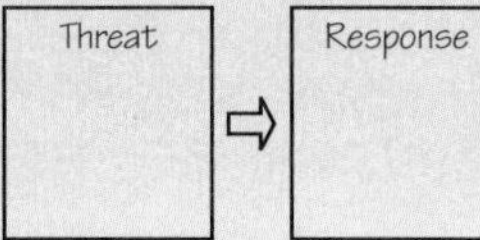

IT MATTERS BECAUSE

Pakistan and Bangladesh are two of the most populous countries in the world. They are also among the world's poorest countries. Their governments need to find solutions to environmental problems to provide their people with health and opportunity. Finding the resources for these solutions is difficult, however.

Managing Resources

GUIDING QUESTION *Why has sustainable development been given a low priority in Pakistan and Bangladesh?*

The economies of Pakistan and Bangladesh are heavily agricultural. The water from their mighty rivers and their fertile soils are very important resources. Agriculture does not generate a great deal of wealth, however. As a result, these countries have huge numbers of people living in poverty and little national income to use to build stronger economies.

In the 1970s and 1980s, people around the world began to notice the environmental damage caused by modern economic activities. Factory smokestacks and vehicle exhaust fouled the air. Chemical and industrial waste poisoned the water. Pumping oil from the ground and mining coal and other resources scarred the landscape. In response, economists and environmentalists began to advocate, or promote, the idea of sustainable development.

When first introduced, **sustainable development** was defined as economic growth that meets the needs of present populations without hampering the ability of people in the future to meet their own needs. Over time, a third goal was added. This was to promote progress in less developed countries and to reduce the gap between those who are wealthy and those who are poor. Sustainable development, then, rests on these **principles**:

- promoting economic development
- protecting the environment
- promoting social fairness

642

networks ***Online Teaching Options***

INTERACTIVE BELLRINGER

World's Worst Cities for Air Pollution

Analyzing Visuals Use the introductory text and the graph of the world's worst cities for air pollution to understand the impact of human activities on the environment in Pakistan. Have students form small groups. Ask them to discuss their experiences with air pollution and to describe a time when they were adversely affected by poor air quality. Then, have students discuss the questions. Have each group record its answers to each question. Then, in a class discussion, have each group share its answers. List responses for questions 2 and 3 on a flipchart or board.

BL Interpersonal, Visual/Spatial, Verbal/Linguistic

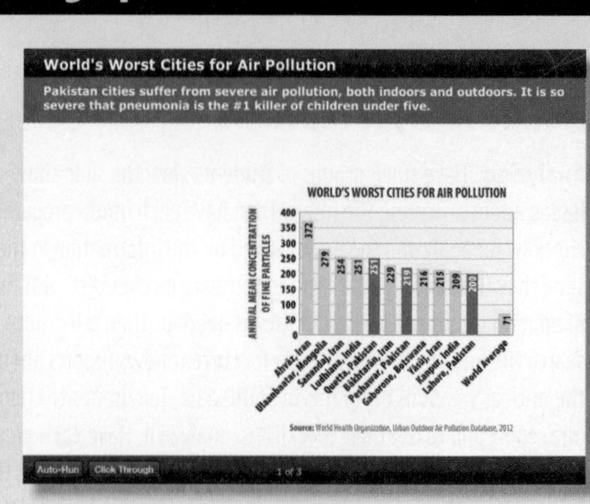

World's Worst Cities for Air Pollution
Pakistan cities suffer from severe air pollution, both indoors and outdoors. It is so severe that pneumonia is the #1 killer of children under five.
WORLD'S WORST CITIES FOR AIR POLLUTION
Auto-Run
Click Through
1 of 3

While many people agree on the goals of sustainable development, achieving them is not an easy task. Poorer countries—which need economic development to give their people a better standard of living—have few financial resources to invest in building a more modern economy. For instance, such countries lack the technology or the knowledge needed to create and use more efficient or cleaner production methods.

Less developed countries face another obstacle in achieving sustainable development. For survival, people living in these low-income countries often make short-term choices that can have long-term negative consequences. For example, to gain money by selling valuable wood, they may cut down trees too rapidly to replace them. To expand agricultural output, they may use fertilizers and pesticides that, over time, hurt the soil or leach into the water, damaging drinking supplies.

Both Pakistan and Bangladesh need to develop their economies. One-fourth of Pakistan's people and one-third of Bangladesh's population live in poverty. The rankings of these countries in education and health statistics also reflect their low standards of living. At the same time, both countries suffer from obstacles to development. These include an overreliance on agriculture, a lack of capital to invest, corruption, and the unwise use of resources.

Perhaps the most threatened environmental region in these two countries is the Sundarbans. This wetland area in southwestern Bangladesh and the northeastern coast of India has the world's largest mangrove forest. This forest is threatened due to rising sea levels and the constant floods of salt water from the Bay of Bengal. Mangroves can grow in somewhat salty water, but if the concentration of salt increases too much, they will not thrive. The forest is threatened by action upriver as well. Because of deforestation in the Himalaya, the rivers that flow into Bangladesh now carry more silt and soil than before. Some of this soil reaches the Sundarbans, where it is building up and reducing the easy flow of water on which the trees depend.

sustainable development economic growth that meets the needs of present populations without hampering the ability of people in the future to meet their own needs and that benefits people and societies

principle a fundamental characteristic

The most threatened area in Bangladesh—the Sundarbans— is also the site of the largest mangrove forest in the world. These boats are hauling harvested mangrove for export.

▼ CRITICAL THINKING

1. ***Making Connections*** What problems threaten this vast forest?
2. ***Identifying Cause and Effect*** What might be some effects of the death of the mangrove forest?

Tim Laman/National Geographic/Getty Images

VIDEO

Bangladesh River Erosion

Identifying Cause and Effect This dramatic video highlights the efforts of people in Bangladesh to save their homes and livelihoods. Use the video to demonstrate the effects of environmental change on people's lives. Ask students to list the causes and impact of the erosion of the land in Bangladesh, pointing out that if the people pictured are displaced, they will have to find new homes. AL Visual/Spatial

People and Their Environment: Pakistan and Bangladesh

R Reading Skills

Explaining Have students identify the problems the two countries face in succeeding in sustainable development. **Ask:** **What do poor countries need to have to reach the goal of sustainable development?** *(Possible answer: They need adequate financial resources to build a modern economy.)* **How does the human factor impact sustainable development?** *(People living in poor countries often make short-term choices to solve a problem that have long-term negative effects.)* After identifying these problems, have students debate which problem is important to solve. **Logical/Mathematical**

T Technology Skills

Researching Have student groups research the Sundarbans and the threats to this area. Each group should determine the current threats to the wetlands, as well as the current attempts made to alleviate environmental degradation. Encourage students to create a photo library of before and after pictures of the Sundarbans. Students should also include a summary paragraph describing the most recent problems and efforts to solve them. BL **Visual/Spatial**

V Visual Skills

Analyzing Visuals Direct students' attention to the photo on the page. Have students list three things the photo shows about the people and what they are doing. After students have made their list, **Ask:** **Are any of the things you listed problems that prevent sustainable development?** *(Student answers may vary but should include one problem, such as harvesting large quantities of wood from the mangrove forest and causing deforestation.)* ELL **Visual/Spatial, Verbal/Linguistic**

Content Background Knowledge

Forests in Pakistan While Bangladesh has the largest mangrove forest in the world, Pakistan has the world's second largest juniper forest. The forests in Pakistan are mostly concentrated in the Himalaya, Hindu Kush and Karakoram mountain regions, areas which contain 60 percent of Pakistan's forests. Juniper trees are one of the oldest species of trees found on Earth and a juniper forest can exist for some three thousand years.

ANSWERS, p. 643

CRITICAL THINKING

1. This area is threatened by rising sea levels and saltwater flooding from the Bay of Bengal as well as deforestation in the Himalaya which allows more soil and silt to wash into the area, restricting water flow to the trees. Deforestation of the mangrove forest itself for fuel or land use is an issue.
2. Mangrove forests can grow in salty water and therefore provide a barrier that does not allow the salt water to move upriver.

V Visual Skills

Creating Charts Have student pairs design a chart or diagram using presentation software to show the cycle of water in the two countries that leads to water pollution. Have pairs present their charts to the class. AL **Logical/Mathematical, Visual/Spatial**

W Writing Skills

Informative/Explanatory Have students read the last paragraph on the page about soil erosion. Have students write an essay describing how soil erosion interconnects with economic problems in either Pakistan or Bangladesh. BL **Verbal/Linguistic**

C Critical Thinking Skills

Drawing Conclusions Point out to students that the cycle of water pollution leads to other problems for people of Bangladesh. Direct students' attention to the photo on the page, and then pose this series of questions for students to consider; **ask: Do the fish the boy is holding look healthy? What do you think he will do with the fish? What can you conclude will possibly happen to the boy when he eats the fish? Since the boy lives in Bangladesh, do you think he will receive adequate medical attention if he gets sick?** Divide the class into small groups. Have groups discuss and design a solution(s) to the problem of water pollution and its ramifications. Tell groups to include reasons why their solution would help resolve the problem of water pollution. Encourage groups to use graphics and photos to explain their solutions. **Interpersonal, Logical/Mathematical**

Local deforestation is a problem for the mangrove forest as well. About half the trees have been cut down over the years as people seek wood for fuel or clear the land for other uses. The forest faces yet another threat. Wastewater from shrimp farms located just north of the forest is raising concerns about damage it might do to the water quality of the Sundarbans.

Another resource at risk in Pakistan and Bangladesh is water. Most of the population of Pakistan does not have regular access to potable, or drinkable, water. A lack of clean water leads to a host of health problems.

Bangladesh could benefit more than it does from its abundant supply of natural gas by exporting it. Most of it, however, is used locally. Bangladeshis burn natural gas as a fuel, and much of the rest is used in fertilizer factories.

Hydroelectric power, an important source of energy in Pakistan, is also at risk. Pakistan's two hydroelectric power dams in the north are affected by physical geography. The Indus River carries a heavy load of soil as it flows south. While this fertile soil benefits farmers, it **accumulates**, or builds up, behind the dam. This clogs the Tarbela Dam, making it unable to generate power.

hydroelectric power electrical energy generated by falling water

accumulate to build up

✓ READING PROGRESS CHECK

Explaining What are the three principles on which sustainable development rests?

Human Impact

GUIDING QUESTION *What kinds of human activity have affected the environment in Pakistan and Bangladesh?*

The threatened Sundarbans is just one example of the way the people of Pakistan and Bangladesh affect the physical environment of these countries. The struggle to survive has created several environmental issues. For example, Pakistan suffers from severe water pollution, which has several different causes. Sewage treatment facilities are scarce, and raw sewage enters the country's rivers and water supply. Industrial pollution is another contributor, as is agricultural runoff of pesticides and fertilizers from farmland. Water pollution is a problem that plagues Bangladesh as well.

With its fairly dry climate, Pakistan has to manage its water. Farmers use irrigation to bring water to areas that receive little rainfall but have fertile soil. However, because of the relatively high temperatures during Pakistan's growing season, some of this water evaporates, leaving minerals and salt in the soil, which makes the land less fertile.

Along with salinity, or saltiness, of the soil, these countries also have problems with soil erosion. This is particularly a problem in Pakistan, where erosion occurs in highlands that are losing their tree cover.

Agricultural runoff and industrial pollutants in both countries lead to water pollution. People, like this boy in Dhaka, Bangladesh, still rely on fish from the dying rivers for food.

▼ CRITICAL THINKING

1. ***Explaining*** What are other causes of water pollution in these countries?
2. ***Identifying Cause and Effect*** How do you think this kind of pollution affects humans?

©mhasan/Demotix/Corbis

644

networks Online Teaching Options

INTERACTIVE IMAGE

Water Pollution in Bangladesh

Creating Charts After viewing the image, have students discuss the impact of polluted water on daily life for the boy in the picture. Then ask students to research the sources of clean water in their region, the key uses for those water sources, and have them develop a risk assessment chart, outlining the key risks for contamination and the negative effects of polluted water to daily life. Be sure to discuss industrial and agricultural wastes, as well as other environmental hazards to help them understand the relationships between food, jobs, waste, and more.

BL **Visual/Spatial, Logical/Mathematical**

ANSWERS, p. 644

✓ READING PROGRESS CHECK Sustainable development rests on the principles of promoting economic development, promoting social fairness, and protecting the environment.

CRITICAL THINKING

1. Raw sewage from inadequate sewage treatment facilities also pollutes the water.
2. Water pollution leaves humans with no safe drinking water, limits the food supply by destroying fish, and spreads disease.

The crowded cities of Pakistan have serious air pollution problems. Car ownership has increased at a rapid rate in the past few decades. Many vehicles burn diesel fuel or leaded gas, which are heavy pollutants.

Pakistan's people cannot escape this problem by staying indoors. Air within homes is polluted, too, because people burn wood and animal dung for fuel. Both of these release smoke and dust that harm the respiratory system. A World Health Organization (WHO) report relates heavy indoor air pollution to the high rates of death and pneumonia that afflict many of Pakistan's children.

Deforestation is not only a problem in Bangladesh's Sundarbans, but also in Pakistan. Several decades of tree cutting in the north has left mountain slopes bare. In one area, about 15 percent of the forest was lost in just 10 years. This deforestation has had an impact on Pakistan's people. The loss of trees means that heavy rains are more likely to cause devastating floods.

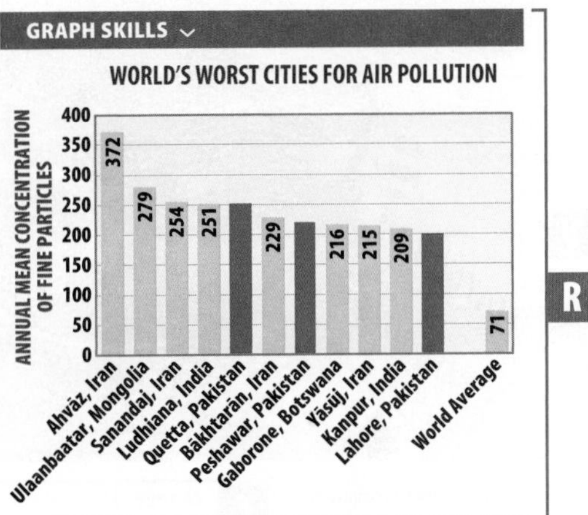

Air pollution is high in some of Pakistan's cities.

▲ CRITICAL THINKING

1. ***Analyzing Visuals*** Which cities in Pakistan rank among the world's worst cities for particulate air pollution?
2. ***Explaining*** Why is this air pollution a problem for Pakistan's people?

 READING PROGRESS CHECK

Evaluating What human actions have hurt the environments of these countries?

Addressing the Issues

GUIDING QUESTION *What steps have the governments of Pakistan and Bangladesh taken to improve the environment?*

Pakistan and Bangladesh have not been able to promote major efforts of sustainable development. They have not completely ignored environmental issues, however. Both countries have taken several steps to address their environmental issues, but the efforts have been inconsistent and the success marginal.

Pakistan began making efforts to improve the environment in the 1990s, when it issued the National Conservation Strategy Report. This report set goals that included protecting the soil, increasing the efficiency of irrigation to prevent water loss, improving forest management, and a host of other steps. The country also issued an action plan in 2001 and a new environmental policy in 2005. However, ongoing political turmoil in Pakistan and the continuing emphasis on economic growth have not allowed these ambitious plans to be fully implemented.

Pakistan's government, using funds from the World Bank, tried to solve the problem of soil salinity in the Indus River valley by digging a long channel parallel to the river. The goal was to carry salt-heavy water away from fields to empty into the Arabian Sea. Unfortunately, the engineering at the outlet was poorly executed. Instead of carrying salty water away, even more saline seawater was allowed to enter the channel. So much water came in that crops and fisheries in the southeastern corner of Pakistan were destroyed. The people of the region asked the government to shut down the channel. As late as 2012, the polluted water still threatened southern areas.

To combat air pollution, Pakistan has promoted the use of compressed natural gas (CNG) vehicles, which pollute less than other vehicles. The country is among the world's leaders in CNG vehicles. However, it lacks enough fueling stations to encourage consumers to buy more of these vehicles.

Many scientists have argued that the world's climate is undergoing significant change. This change, they say, may result in warmer overall temperatures, changes in patterns of rainfall, as well as more frequent and more powerful storms.

R Reading Skills

Reading Graphs Direct students' attention to the bar graph showing the world's worst cities for air pollution. **Ask:** **What does the graph express about Pakistan's air pollution problems?** *(Pakistan has a severe air pollution problem, as three cities in Pakistan are included in the world's worst cities for air pollution.)* **How could you describe the pollution rate of Pakistani cities in relation to the world average shown on the graph?** *(The pollution rate is high above the world average. Two of Pakistan's cities have triple the world average of air pollution and one, Lahore, has double the world average.)* Have students locate the cities on a map of Pakistan. **ELL** **Logical/Mathematical, Visual/Spatial**

T Technology Skills

Researching Assign student pairs to research in the library or on the Internet one project the World Bank has funded in the last five years in either Pakistan or Bangladesh. The project should be one that is designed to help that country promote sustainable development. Examples for Pakistan include the extension of a hydropower project and an irrigation improvement system for the Punjab. Examples for Bangladesh include the extension of electricity in rural areas, including the development of solar home systems. Have pairs create a presentation with photos, if possible, of their project funded by the World Bank. Have pairs present to the class their multimedia report. **BL** **Verbal/Linguistic, Visual/Spatial**

Content Background Knowledge

Compressed Natural Gas This energy source is widely used throughout the world. Compressed Natural Gas (CNG) is used in more and more vehicles rather than gasoline or diesel. CNG is clean burning, and CNG automobiles and trucks generate little exhaust or greenhouse emissions. CNG is made up of methane and in CNG vehicles is stored in high-pressure fuel cylinders. There are approximately 10 million CNG vehicles in the world.

GAME

People and Their Environment: Pakistan and Bangladesh

Summarizing Students can strengthen their knowledge of the environment in Pakistan and Bangladesh by playing this Identification game. As students play the game, pair higher-level students with lower-level and ELL students to ensure optimal comprehension and success. Have students report their at the end of the activity, and review any information that seemed problematic, if necessary. Ask students to write sentences to summarize any difficult information. **AL** **ELL** **Verbal/Linguistic**

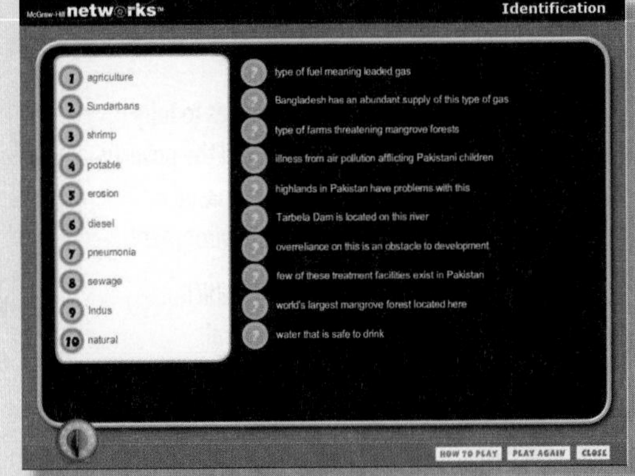

ANSWERS, p. 645

READING PROGRESS CHECK Human actions have led to water pollution from raw sewage, industry, and agricultural runoff; air pollution from vehicles and burning of wood; overirrigation in Pakistan leading to high soil salinity; and soil erosion and flooding from deforestation.

CRITICAL THINKING

1. The cities of Quetta, Peshawar, and Lahore in Pakistan rank among the world's worst cities for air pollution.
2. The air pollution is a problem for the people of Pakistan because it causes damage to respiratory systems and is linked to high death rates and pneumonia in many Pakistani children.

People and Their Environment: Pakistan and Bangladesh

V Visual Skills

Creating Graphs Have students research the number of CNG vehicles in Pakistan, Italy, and the United States. Have them design graphs showing the total number of CNG vehicles in the United States, Italy, and Pakistan. **Visual/Spatial**

C Critical Thinking Skills

Identifying Central Issues Discuss climate change. **Ask: Why did Sheikh Hasina encourage other countries to be more proactive in reducing greenhouse gases?** *(Bangladesh produces low amounts of greenhouse gases, but may experience extreme damage.)* **Verbal/Linguistic**

W Writing Skills

Argument Have students write a blog arguing whether developing nations like Bangladesh should work to reduce their emissions of greenhouse gases. Then have them debate the various points they argue in their blogs. **BL Intrapersonal**

CLOSE & REFLECT

Summarizing Review current issues that Pakistan and Bangladesh face. Ask students to write a brief summary about two interrelated issues in either Pakistan or Bangladesh and describe solutions that might help to resolve these issues.

ANSWERS, p. 646

☑ READING PROGRESS CHECK Political turmoil, a lack of funds, and widespread poverty have resulted in governments being unable to fully implement their plans.

CRITICAL THINKING

1. The benefit of CNG vehicles is the low amount of pollutants.
2. Lack of funds and infrastructure to build CNG filling stations.

V

Pakistan is a leading country in the use of CNG vehicles. However, more filling stations are needed to encourage people to buy more of the vehicles.

▲ **CRITICAL THINKING**

1. ***Identifying*** What are the benefits of CNG vehicles?
2. ***Drawing Conclusions*** Why do you think that Pakistan has not yet installed enough filling stations for CNG vehicles?

While all scientists do not agree on these conclusions, climate change could be a problem for Bangladesh. The low-lying country could experience worse damage and a higher loss of life if floods increase or cyclones grow stronger. Rising sea levels caused by climate change could also be catastrophic.

Bangladesh moved to adopt an environmental policy in the 1990s and adopted a climate-change strategy and plan in 2009. Bangladesh's prime minister, Sheikh Hasina, has urged countries around the world to take more active steps to fight climate change. Her government points out that Bangladesh produces relatively low amounts of the greenhouses gases said to cause this climate change. C

Bangladesh has also taken steps at home. Rather than allowing animal waste to release climate-changing methane gas into the atmosphere, the people of Bangladesh are composting the waste to make organic fertilizer. A by-product of that process is a gas, which is used for cooking, that pollutes less when burned. The country has also made progress in reducing other gases that damage the air and water. The growing ship-breaking industry, however, is a major source of air pollution. Bangladesh recently issued regulations to try to reduce that effect, but they have not yet been enforced. W

Bangladesh has also moved to protect the Sundarbans. The government has set aside several areas of the vast forest as reserves. These are aimed, not only at protecting the trees of the Sundarbans, but also the remaining population of Bengal tigers that live and hunt there. Bangladesh has targeted 5 percent of its land and sea area to be set aside as nature reserves. However, by 2011 it had only managed to preserve about 2 percent. This gap is attributed to a lack of resources to attain the goal.

☑ READING PROGRESS CHECK

Explaining Why have these governments not acted to implement all their plans to improve the environment?

LESSON 3 REVIEW 

Reviewing Vocabulary (Tier Three Words)

1. ***Identifying*** Write a paragraph explaining what sustainable development is and why it is especially challenging to countries with limited resources. RH.9–10.4

Using Your Notes

2. ***Summarizing*** Use your graphic organizer on the environment of Pakistan and Bangladesh to write a paragraph describing one effective response and one ineffective response to an environmental threat one of them faces.

Answering the Guiding Questions

3. ***Identifying*** Why has sustainable development been given a low priority in Pakistan and Bangladesh?
4. ***Summarizing*** What kinds of human activity have affected the environment in Pakistan and Bangladesh?
5. ***Evaluating*** What steps have the governments of Pakistan and Bangladesh taken to improve the environment?

Writing Activity

6. ***Informative/Explanatory*** Write a letter to the prime minister of either Pakistan or Bangladesh, suggesting what can be done to address environmental issues even when their resources are limited. WHST.9–10.2

646

LESSON 3 REVIEW ANSWERS

Reviewing Vocabulary

1. Paragraphs will vary, but should include a description of sustainable development as economic growth that promotes both development and social fairness while protecting the environment, and the challenges of implementation including lack of funds, political turmoil, and widespread poverty dictating choices for survival rather than the good of the environment.

Using Your Notes

2. Paragraphs will differ based on country and environmental threat chosen by the student but should include environmental threats such as deforestation; destruction of the Sundarbans; water pollution from agriculture, industry, and sewage; air pollution from vehicles and burning of firewood; soil erosion; or soil salinity.

Answering the Guiding Questions

3. Bangladesh and Pakistan lack the resources to fully implement sustainable development, and the poverty of their people cause choices to be made based on survival rather than the welfare of the environment.
4. Human activities such as deforestation, vehicle emissions, burning of firewood, agricultural mismanagement, industry, and inadequate sewage treatment have affected the environment in Pakistan and Bangladesh.
5. Pakistan is working to protect the soil, make irrigation more efficient, and improve forest management but political turmoil has caused concerns. Pakistan is also promoting the use of vehicles using compressed natural gas. Bangladesh has adopted a climate change policy and is composting animal waste for fertilizer, then using the by-product of methane gas as a cooking fuel. It is trying to reduce air pollution caused by the ship-breaking industry, and has set aside reserves to protect the Sundarbans and the Bengal tiger.

Writing Activity

6. Letters will vary, but should include environmental issues from the lesson such as water pollution, air pollution, deforestation, destruction of the Sundarbans, soil erosion, and soil salinity and provide ways to address the issues regardless of resources.

CHAPTER 26 Assessment CCSS

Directions: On a separate sheet of paper, answer the questions below. Make sure you read carefully and answer all parts of the questions.

Lesson Review

Lesson 1

1. ***Explaining*** How does the theory of continental drift explain the formation of the Himalaya mountain ranges?
2. ***Identifying Cause and Effect*** Where do the three major river systems in Pakistan and Bangladesh originate? What causes them to flood seasonally?
3. ***Summarizing*** What are some ways that South Asian rivers help people meet their basic and economic needs?

Lesson 2

4. ***Explaining*** Why did Bengali nationalists push for independence from Pakistan?
5. ***Comparing and Contrasting*** How are population patterns in Pakistan similar to and different from those in Bangladesh?
6. ***Hypothesizing*** Why do you think health care in Bangladesh and Pakistan is a major problem?

Lesson 3

7. ***Defining*** What are the characteristics and goals of sustainable development?
8. ***Identifying Cause and Effect*** How does deforestation in the Himalaya affect the mangrove forest of the Sundarbans?
9. ***Evaluating*** What are some steps Pakistan has taken to improve the environment? How effective have they been?

Critical Thinking

10. ***Analyzing*** Why is poverty a major obstacle to sustainable development in Pakistan and Bangladesh?
11. ***Assessing*** Which one of the environmental challenges facing Pakistan is most urgent? Explain your answer.

21st Century Skills

Review the graph and answer the questions that follow.

MOST DENSE WORLD URBAN AREAS OVER 2.5 MILLION POPULATION: 2012

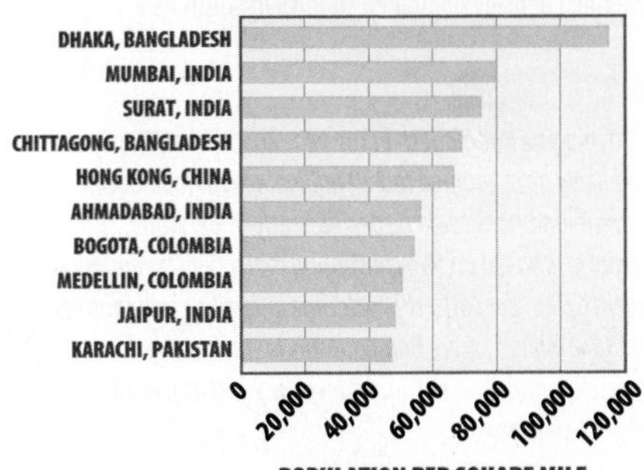

Source: http://www.newgeography.com/files/cox-worldurban-2.png

12. ***Compare and Contrast*** How does population density in Dhaka compare to that of Karachi? About how many people live per square mile in each city? RH.9–10.1
13. ***Create and Analyze Arguments and Draw Conclusions*** What does the bar graph suggest about overall population patterns in Bangladesh? RH.9–10.7
14. ***Creating and Using Graphs, Charts, Diagrams, and Tables*** Why do you think the bar graph focuses on cities with populations of more than 2.5 million? RH.9–10.7

College and Career Readiness

15. ***Change and Continuity in Economics*** As an economist for the United Nations, you have been asked to report on the role of cottage industries in Pakistan. What benefits do cottage industries provide to local populations? How do they affect the environment and economy? Use the Internet to conduct research, and write a two-page report describing your findings. WHST.9–10.2; WHST.9–10.7

Need Extra Help?

If You've Missed Question	1	2	3	4	5	6	7	8	9	10	11	12	13	14	15
Go to page	630	632	633	635	636	637	642	643	645	643	644	636	636	636	639

CHAPTER 26 Assessment Answers

Lesson Review

Lesson 1

1. The theory of continental drift explains that the Indian subcontinent is pushing against the southern edge of Asia and the collision between the two caused the Himalaya to rise.
2. The three major river systems originate in the Himalaya. The floods are caused by seasonal snowmelts and rains.
3. Rivers provide transportation, drinking water and hydroelectric power, and deposit alluvial soil in the flood plains which supports agriculture.

Lesson 2

4. Bengali leaders pushed for independence because they felt their ethnic group, which held the majority in East Pakistan, was being ruled and treated unfairly by the government dominated by West Pakistan.
5. In Pakistan, more than one-third of the population is under 13, the population is more rural than urban, and the fertility rate is 3.6, well above the world average. Bangladesh also has a higher fertility rate than the world average, but has managed to lower it to 2.2 percent. Just one-third of the population is under 13 and the population density is highest in cities.
6. Health care is a major problem because of the large population and high poverty rates in both countries.

Lesson 3

7. Characteristics and goals of sustainable development are promoting social fairness and economic development while protecting the environment in order to ensure the ability of people in the future to meet their own needs.
8. Deforestation in the Himalaya causes more silt and soil to be washed into the forests, which blocks the flow of water to the mangrove trees.
9. Pakistan is working to protect the soil, make irrigation more efficient, and improve forest management, but political turmoil has kept some plans from being implemented. Pakistan is also promoting the use of vehicles that use compressed natural gas which cause less air pollution, but it lacks sufficient fueling stations.

Critical Thinking

10. Poverty causes people to make choices based on survival that are not consistent with sustainable development.
11. Answers will vary based on the environmental challenge chosen by the student, but should be strongly supported with information from the chapter. Possible challenges could include water pollution, air pollution, deforestation, erosion, and soil salinity.

21st Century Skills

12. The population density in Bangladesh is more than twice that of Karachi. About 118,000 people per square mile live in Bangladesh, compared to about 50,000 people per square mile in Karachi.
13. The graph suggests that Bangladesh has a very high population density with concentrations in urban areas.
14. The graph focuses on cities with more than 2.5 million people, as these cities are more likely to have high population densities.

College and Career Readiness

15. Reports will differ but should be strongly supported with information from the chapter. Answers should describe the benefit to the local population and the impact to the environment and economy of cottage industries. Possible answers could include the benefits of employment of both craftspeople and women who must work from home, the influx of money to the economy, and the support of industrialization cottage industries provide.

Assessment Answers

Analyzing Primary Sources

16 The rising sea levels are going to cause people in the coastal areas to migrate inland creating higher population densities in other areas.

17 He means that the infrastructure and government services will not be able to support the influx of people that will migrate due to rising sea levels, particularly given the already growing population numbers.

18 Student answers may vary, but could include food and housing shortages, overwhelmed services such as water and sewage, and an inability to provide education and health care to the number of people migrating.

Applying Map Skills

19 Bangladesh is largely low and flat with many rivers. This makes the entire country heavily populated as there are abundant sources of water and farmland. The city of Dhaka is heavily populated since it lies near several rivers.

20 The Karakorum are the mountains farthest north in Pakistan, not as far north are the Himalaya, and the Hindu Kush are along the northwest area of Pakistan.

21 Pakistan has less agriculture than Bangladesh due to the mountains and arid regions. Bangladesh relies more heavily on agriculture due to its flat landscape and abundant water.

Exploring the Essential Question

22 Posters will differ but should be strongly supported with information from the chapter on obstacles to sustainable development and contain visual elements such as photos, charts, graphs, and maps. Challenges could include lack of funds and widespread poverty, causing choices to be made for survival rather than long-term environmental goals.

Research and Presentation

23 Reports will differ but should be strongly supported with information from the chapter, including the factors that led to Bengali nationalists declaring independence, the role of India, and the current state of relations between Bangladesh and Pakistan. Answers should include that while both countries are predominantly Muslim, the Bengalis are a cohesive ethnic group that speak Bangla and felt they were being mistreated and imposed upon by the government, which was dominated by West Pakistan. India supported independence for Bangladesh, which contributed to the surrender of Pakistan.

CHAPTER 26 Assessment 

Directions: On a separate sheet of paper, answer the questions below. Make sure you read carefully and answer all parts of the questions.

DBQ Analyzing Primary Sources

Use the document to answer the following questions.

Population density is already a major concern in Bangladesh, the most densely populated country in South Asia.

PRIMARY SOURCE

"So imagine Bangladesh in the year 2050, when its population will likely have zoomed to 220 million, and a good chunk of its current landmass could be permanently underwater. That scenario is based on two converging projections: population growth that, despite a sharp decline in fertility, will continue to produce millions more Bangladeshis in the coming decades, and a possible multifoot rise in sea level by 2100 as a result of climate change.

'Globally, we're talking about the largest mass migration in human history,' says Maj. Gen. Muniruzzaman. . . . 'By 2050 millions of displaced people will overwhelm not just our limited land and resources but our government, our institutions, and our borders.'"

—Don Belt, "The Coming Storm," *National Geographic*, May 2011

16 ***Making Connections*** Based on the article, how is climate change likely to affect population density in Bangladesh in the coming decades? RH.9–10.1

17 ***Interpreting*** What does Maj. Gen. Muniruzzaman mean when he says that Bangladesh will be overwhelmed by "the largest mass migration in human history"? RH.9–10.4

18 ***Making Predictions*** How might the mass migration of Bangladeshis affect the resources and infrastructure of neighboring countries? RH.9–10.2

Applying Map Skills

Use the Unit 7 Atlas to answer the following questions.

19 ***Environment and Society*** Describe how the physical geography of Bangladesh affects population density. Give examples.

20 ***Places and Regions*** Use your mental map of South Asia to describe the location of the major mountain ranges in Pakistan: the Himalaya, the Hindu Kush, and the Karakoram.

21 ***Environment and Society*** How does agriculture in Pakistan compare with that in Bangladesh? Which country relies more heavily on agriculture?

Exploring the Essential Question

22 ***Exploring Issues*** Pakistan and Bangladesh face many obstacles to sustainable development. Use what you have learned about the human and physical systems in these countries to create a poster showing the challenges they face. Posters should be visual and can include photos, graphs, charts, and maps. WHST.9–10.4

Research and Presentation

23 ***Research Skills*** Use the Internet to research relations between Bangladesh and Pakistan. What ethnic, linguistic, and political factors led Bengali nationalists to declare independence? What was the role of India? What are relations between Pakistan and Bangladesh like today? Explain your findings in a short research report. WHST.9–10.7; WHST.9–10.8

Writing About Geography

24 ***Informative/Explanatory*** Use standard grammar, spelling, sentence structure, and punctuation to write a multi-paragraph essay describing the problem of water pollution in Pakistan. What factors contribute to the problem? How does water pollution affect people? How does it affect the environment and economy? What steps has the government taken to solve the problem? How effective have they been? WHST.9–10.2; WHST.9–10.7

Need Extra Help?

If You've Missed Question	16	17	18	19	20	21	22	23	24
Go to page	636	636	636	598	598	598	643	635	644

648

Writing About Geography

24 Paragraphs will differ, but should be strongly supported with information from the chapter. Paragraphs should describe the factors that contribute to water pollution in Pakistan; how the pollution affects people, the environment, and the economy; and what steps have been taken by the government and how effective those steps have been. Factors could include agricultural runoff, raw sewage, and industrial waste. Impacts could include lack of clean water for drinking, spread of disease, loss of fish for food and export, and destruction of wildlife habitats. Steps taken by the government include issuing the National Conservation Strategy Report. Efforts have not been very effective due to political turmoil.

CHAPTER **27**

Bhutan, Maldives, Nepal, and Sri Lanka Planner

UNDERSTANDING BY DESIGN®

Enduring Understandings

- *Places reflect the relationship between humans and the physical environment.*

Essential Question

- *How do physical systems and human systems shape a place?*

Predictable Misunderstandings

Students may think:

- *Nepal and Bhutan are near the Indian Ocean and have tropical climates. Explain that Nepal and Bhutan are actually north of India and Bangladesh and are very mountainous, landlocked countries. Because of their location and the mountainous terrain, they have a variety of climates.*
- *That Maldives is part of Sri Lanka, not a separate country. Explain that both countries were at one time under British rule, but gained independence as two separate countries, although the Sinhalese from Sri Lanka most likely settled in the Maldive Islands many years ago.*

Assessment Evidence

Performance Tasks:

- *Hands-On Chapter Project*

Other Evidence:

- *Guided Reading Activities*
- *Vocabulary Activities*
- *Lesson Quizzes*
- *Chapter Tests, Forms A and B*

SUGGESTED PACING GUIDE

Introducing the Chapter...............½ Day
Lesson 1............................ 1 Day
Lesson 2............................ 1 Day
Lesson 3............................ 1 Day
Chapter Wrap-Up and Assessment......½ Day

TOTAL TIME 4 Days

Key for Using the Teacher Edition

SKILL-BASED ACTIVITIES

Types of skill activities found in the Teacher Edition.

* **V Visual Skills** require students to analyze maps, graphs, charts, and photos.

R Reading Skills help students practice reading skills and master vocabulary.

C Critical Thinking Skills help students apply and extend what they have learned.

W Writing Skills provide writing opportunities to help students comprehend the text.

T Technology Skills require students to use digital tools effectively.

*Letters are followed by a number when there is more than one of the same type of skill on the page.

DIFFERENTIATED INSTRUCTION

All activities are written for the on-level student unless otherwise marked with the leveled labels below.

BL Beyond Level
AL Approaching Level
ELL English Language Learners

All students benefit from activities that utilize different learning styles. Many activities are marked as below when a particular learning style is highlighted.

Intrapersonal	**Naturalist**
Logical/Mathematical	**Kinesthetic**
Visual/Spatial	**Auditory/Musical**
Verbal/Linguistic	**Interpersonal**

National Geography Standards covered in "Bhutan, Maldives, Nepal, and Sri Lanka"

The student knows and understands:

(5) That people create regions to interpret Earth's complexity

5.1 Regions are defined by different sets of criteria and places can be included in multiple regions of different types

(7) The physical processes that shape the patterns of Earth's surface

7.3 Physical processes interact over time to shape particular places on Earth's surface

(9) The characteristics, distribution, and migration of human populations on Earth's surface

9.1 Culture, economics, and politics influence the changing demographic structure of different populations

9.2 Population distribution and density are a function of historical, environmental, economic, political, and technological factors

(10) The characteristics, distribution, and complexity of Earth's cultural mosaics

10.2 Cultural landscapes exist at multiple scales

10.3 Cultures changes through convergence and/or divergence

(11) The patterns and networks of economic interdependence on Earth's surface

11.2 Patterns exist in the spatial organization of economic activities

11.3 Economic systems are dynamic organizations of interdependent economic activities for production, exchange, distribution, and consumption of goods and services

11.4 Improvements in transportation and communication networks reduce the effects of distance and time on the movements of people, products, and ideas

(12) The process, patterns, and functions of human settlement

12.1 The numbers, types, and range of the functions of settlement change

12.2 Settlements can grow and/or decline over time

(13) How the forces of cooperation and conflict among people influence the division and control of Earth's surface

13.3 Changes within, between and among countries regarding division and control of Earth's surface may result in conflict

(14) How human actions modify the physical environment

14.2 The use of technology can have both intended and unintended impacts on the physical environment which may be positive or negative

Chapter Opener Planner

Students will know:
- *what landforms, rivers, and oceans help shape life in the region.*
- *how topography affects the climate and settlement patterns in Nepal and Bhutan.*
- *how modern Nepal, Bhutan, Sri Lanka, and Maldives were formed.*
- *that farming and fishing are key economic activities in the region.*
- *how decentralization challenges resource management in Nepal and Bhutan.*
- *that the four countries face similar environmental challenges and the steps taken to address them.*

Students will be able to:
- ***identify** landforms, rivers, and oceans and how they affect life in the region.*
- ***explain** how topography, climate, and settlement are connected.*
- ***explain** how modern countries in the region were formed.*
- ***identify** key economic activities in the region.*
- ***analyze** decentralization and its effect on resource management in Nepal and Bhutan.*
- ***identify** the environmental challenges in the region and efforts to address them.*

UNDERSTANDING BY DESIGN®

☑ Print Teaching Options

V Visual Skills
- ☐ **p. 651** Students speculate why a photo of the Dalai Lama was included in the text. AL Visual/Spatial

R Reading Skills
- ☐ **p. 650** Students discuss the meaning of the term *buffer*, and predict how Nepal's location could be a political advantage or disadvantage. ELL Verbal/Linguistic

C Critical Thinking Skills
- ☐ **p. 651** Students consider the impact of the McMahon Line and summarize the importance of the border disputes involving Tibet, China, and India. Verbal/Linguistic

W Writing Skills
- ☐ **p. 650** Students explain how Nepal might be "caught in the middle" between China and India. Verbal/Linguistic

T Technology Skills
- ☐ **p. 651** Students research other examples of Nepal's dependence on India for trade and explore its role as a buffer state in border disputes. BL Verbal/Linguistic, Visual/Spatial

☑ Online Teaching Options

C Critical Thinking Skills
- SLIDE SHOW **Nepal: A Buffer State**—Students choose one of the images from the slide show to write a descriptive paragraph explaining cultural diversity. BL Verbal/Linguistic
- MAP **Interactive Regional Atlas**—Students use the interactive regional atlas to understand the physical and human geography of Bhutan, Maldives, Nepal, and Sri Lanka.

☑ Printable Digital Worksheets

- WORKSHEET **Assessing Background Knowledge**—Determine the level of prior knowledge students have about Bhutan, Maldives, Nepal, and Sri Lanka.
- WORKSHEET **Chapter Summary**—Students review the main idea of each lesson of the chapter content.
- WORKSHEET **Reteaching Activity**—These worksheets provide students with an opportunity for remedial practice and review of vital chapter content.

Project-Based Learning 

Hands-On

Journal

Students will write a fictional journal as if they were members of a family in Nepal or Maldives dealing with environmental issues.

Digital Hands-On

Create Online Projects

Find an additional activity online that incorporates technology for this project. Visit the EdTech Teacher Web sites for more links, tutorials, and other resources.

Print Resources

ANCILLARY RESOURCES

This ancillary is available for every chapter and lesson.
- **Chapter Tests and Lesson Quizzes**

PRINTABLE DIGITAL WORKSHEETS

These printable digital worksheets are available for every chapter and lesson.
- **Assessing Background Knowledge**
- **Chapter Summaries**
- **Guided Reading Activities**
- **Hands-On Chapter Projects**
- **Quizzes and Tests**
- **Reading Essentials and Study Guide** AL
- **Reteaching Activities**
- **Video Activities**
- **Vocabulary Activities**

More Media Resources

SUGGESTED VIDEOS MOVIES
- **When the Mountain Calls—Nepal, Tibet, Bhutan** (57 min.)
- **Discover the World Sri Lanka** (30 min.)
- **Maldives 2013** (20 min.)

SUGGESTED READING 
- ***Bhutan: The Land of Serenity,*** by Matthieu Ricard
- ***Nepal—A Brief History,*** by James Grissom
- ***Katie Goes to the Maldives: A View of Paradise Beyond the Glossy Image,*** by Catherine Black
- ***The Sri Lanka Reader: History, Culture, Politics*** by John Clifford Holt

Physical Geography of Bhutan, Maldives, Nepal, and Sri Lanka

Students will know:

- *what landforms help shape life in Nepal, Bhutan, Sri Lanka, and Maldives.*
- *how rivers and the ocean support human activities in these countries.*
- *how topography affects the climate in Nepal and Bhutan.*

Students will be able to:

- ***identify** landforms and how they affect life in the region.*
- ***describe** dependence on rivers and oceans.*
- ***explain** how topography and climate are connected.*

UNDERSTANDING BY DESIGN®

☑ Print Teaching Options

V Visual Skills

- ☐ **p. 652** Students work with a partner to read and transfer information in the text into a map. **AL** **Visual/Spatial**
- ☐ **p. 653** Students create a four-column chart with information about Nepal's four geographic zones. **ELL** **Visual/Spatial**
- ☐ **p. 653** Students create a four-column chart with information about Bhutan's geographic zones. **AL** **Visual/Spatial**

R Reading Skills

- ☐ **p. 655** Students read information in a graphic about ecotourism, and then create a time line that sequences information from the graphic. **ELL** **Verbal/Linguistic, Visual/Spatial**

C Critical Thinking Skills

- ☐ **p. 653** Students compare and contrast Sri Lanka's two regions. **AL** **Logical/Mathematical**
- ☐ **p. 654** Students visualize five square miles, offering examples from their community. **AL** **Visual/Spatial**
- ☐ **p. 655** Students consider the impact that topography has on the region's climate. **AL** **Logical/Mathematical**
- ☐ **p. 655** Students debate whether climbing tourism is vital to Nepal's economy. **BL** **Interpersonal, Verbal/Linguistic**

W Writing Skills

- ☐ **p. 654** Students write a journal entry describing a day on the final leg of the route up to the summit of Mount Everest. **Intrapersonal, Verbal/Linguistic**
- ☐ **p. 656** Students research a hydroelectric project that exists in the region, identify any issues related to the project or other resources that could be developed to benefit the region's economy, then report the information to the class. **BL** **Verbal/Linguistic**

T Technology Skills

- ☐ **p. 654** Students research a river discussed in the text and present their findings in a visual display. **BL** **Interpersonal**

☑ Online Teaching Options

V Visual Skills

- ☐ **INTERACTIVE WHITEBOARD ACTIVITY** **Landforms of Bhutan, Maldives, Nepal, and Sri Lanka**—Students complete a chart about how landforms shape life in Bhutan, Maldives, Nepal, and Sri Lanka.
- ☐ **INTERACTIVE BELLRINGER** **Highest Mountain Peaks of Five Continents**—Students study a diagram of the highest mountain peaks of five continents to help them understand what landforms impact humans in Nepal. **Interpersonal, Visual/Spatial**
- ☐ **INTERACTIVE IMAGE** **Mount Everest**—Students create a Venn diagram comparing and contrasting Mount Everest with the rest of the Himalaya. **ELL** **Visual/Spatial**

C Critical Thinking Skills

- ☐ **INTERACTIVE MAP** **China, India, Nepal: Boundary Disputes**—Students make speculations about how boundary disputes may affect tourism in Nepal. **BL** **Logical/Mathematical**

W Writing Skills

- ☐ **VIDEO** **Natural World–Himalaya**—Students write a fictional journal entry as if they are climber on a Himalaya mountain peak. **Verbal/Linguistic, Visual/Spatial**

☑ Printable Digital Worksheets

R Reading Skills

- ☐ **WORKSHEET** **Guided Reading Activity**—Students use the Guided Reading Activity worksheets to review their comprehension of the content.

C Critical Thinking Skills

- ☐ **WORKSHEET** **Video Activity**—Students answer questions related to a topic in the chapter content after they have viewed a lesson video.

HUMAN GEOGRAPHY OF BHUTAN, MALDIVES, NEPAL, AND SRI LANKA

Students will know:

- *how modern Nepal, Bhutan, Maldives, and Sri Lanka were formed.*
- *how settlement patterns follow topography in Nepal and Bhutan.*
- *how cultures coexist and clash in Nepal, Bhutan, and Sri Lanka.*
- *that farming and fishing are key economic activities in all four countries.*

Students will be able to:

- ***explain** how modern countries in the region were formed.*
- ***describe** how topography affects settlement patterns in the region.*
- ***analyze** the coexistence and conflicts between cultures in the region.*
- ***identify** key economic activities in the region.*

UNDERSTANDING BY DESIGN®

☑ Print Teaching Options

V Visual Skills

- ☐ **p. 657** Students create a flowchart with key information about the development of Nepal and Bhutan. AL Visual/Spatial
- ☐ **p. 660** Students create a two-column chart that shows different aspects of Sri Lanka's two main ethnic groups, the Sinhalese and the Tamils. Visual/Spatial

R Reading Skills

- ☐ **p. 660** Students write a short summary about the importance of religion in the region. ELL Verbal/Linguistic
- ☐ **p. 661** Students write down what they think the meaning of the word *invocation* is. ELL Verbal/Linguistic

C Critical Thinking Skills

- ☐ **p. 658** Students consider the factors that influenced the present-day governments of the countries in the region. AL Logical/Mathematical
- ☐ **p. 659** Students write down facts about ethnic strife that occurred in a time period they are assigned and then create a "living" time line with the class. ELL Kinesthetic, Logical/Mathematical
- ☐ **p. 662** Students discuss the challenges and benefits of having few natural resources.

W Writing Skills

- ☐ **p. 661** Students write an argumentative essay about women's role in one of the four countries. BL Intrapersonal, Verbal/Linguistic
- ☐ **p. 661** Students write an informative paragraph about the relationship between art and religion in a specific culture of the region. AL Verbal/Linguistic

T Technology Skills

- ☐ **p. 659** Students research population density to create a multimedia presentation of their findings. Verbal/Linguistic
- ☐ **p. 662** Students research the impact of the 2004 tsunami, specifically on an assigned economic activity, and present their findings in a slide show. BL Visual/Spatial

☑ Online Teaching Options

V Visual Skills

- ☐ **INTERACTIVE WHITEBOARD ACTIVITY** **Patterns of the Populace**—Students match and identify the modern countries of Bhutan, Maldives, Nepal, and Sri Lanka with their populations.
- ☐ **INTERACTIVE BELLRINGER** **Percentage of Seats Held by Women in National Parliaments**—Students interpret a table about national parliaments in this region and then answer questions about it. AL Interpersonal, Logical/Mathematical, Verbal/Linguistic
- ☐ **GRAPHIC ORAGANIZER** **Human Geography of Bhutan, Maldives, Nepal, and Sri Lanka**—Students complete a graphic organizer about the human geography of this region. AL Visual/Spatial, Verbal/Linguistic

R Reading Skills

- ☐ **GAME** **Fill in the Blank**—Students play this interactive game by completing sentences about the lesson content. AL ELL Verbal/Linguistic, Interpersonal
- ☐ **TIME LINE** **Ethnic Strife**—Students discuss the time line and then write a summarizing paragraph about the relationship between the Sinhalese and Tamils. AL Verbal/Linguistic

T Technology Skills

- ☐ **INTERACTIVE IMAGE** **Prayer Flags**—Students discuss the image and then research the origin and significance of prayer flags in Bhutan. AL Verbal/Linguistic

☑ Printable Digital Worksheets

R Reading Skills

- ☐ **WORKSHEET** **Guided Reading Activity**—Students use Guided Reading Activity worksheets to review their comprehension of the content.
- ☐ **WORKSHEET** **Reading Essentials and Study Guide**—Students complete the study guide and answer Reading Progress Check and vocabulary questions. AL

C Critical Thinking Skills

- ☐ **WORKSHEET** **Video Activity**—Students answer questions related to a topic in the chapter content after they have viewed a lesson video.

LESSON 3 PLANNER

PEOPLE AND THEIR ENVIRONMENT: BHUTAN, MALDIVES, NEPAL, AND SRI LANKA

Students will know:

- *how decentralization challenges resource management in Nepal and Bhutan.*
- *that Nepal, Bhutan, Maldives, and Sri Lanka face similar environmental challenges.*
- *what efforts the national governments of the four countries have taken to address environmental issues.*

Students will be able to:

- ***analyze** decentralization and its effect on resource management in Nepal and Bhutan.*
- ***identify** the environmental challenges in the region.*
- ***describe** ways in which governments are addressing environmental issues.*

UNDERSTANDING BY DESIGN®

☑ *Print Teaching Options*

V Visual Skills

- ☐ **p. 663** Students create a web diagram that shows the reasons that the subregion struggles to implement sustainable development. **Visual/Spatial**

R Reading Skills

- ☐ **p. 663** Students look up word definitions to clarify the meaning of confusing words and then paraphrase the paragraph. **ELL** **Verbal/Linguistic**

C Critical Thinking Skills

- ☐ **p. 663** Students create a two-column chart to list the advantages and disadvantages of development.
- ☐ **p. 664** Students identify causes and effects of deforestation in the subregion. **BL** **Logical/Mathematical**

W Writing Skills

- ☐ **p. 665** Students write an informative essay about coral bleaching in Maldives. **AL** **Verbal/Linguistic, Visual/Spatial**
- ☐ **p. 666** Students write an argumentative essay in which they defend or refute whether Nepal's government has taken adequate steps to protect the country's environment. **BL** **Verbal/Linguistic**

T Technology Skills

- ☐ **p. 664** Students research the phrase *Gross National Happiness* as it applies to Bhutan and present their findings. **Interpersonal, Verbal/Linguistic**
- ☐ **p. 666** Students research what their assigned country is doing to address climate change and present visuals showing how their country's response to climate change compares with that of other countries. **BL** **Verbal/Linguistic, Interpersonal**

☑ *Online Teaching Options*

V Visual Skills

- INTERACTIVE BELLRINGER **Two Atolls in Maldives**—Students identify and answer questions about environmental issues in Maldives. **Interpersonal, Verbal/Linguistic**
- SLIDE SHOW **Paradise Lost**—Students discuss the effectiveness of the Maldives government to influence conservation efforts in the area. **BL** **Naturalist, Verbal/Linguistic**

R Reading Skills

- GAME **True or False**—Students identify the accuracy of statements regarding the subregion's natural resources. **ELL** **AL** **Verbal/Linguistic, Naturalist**
- INTERACTIVE WHITEBOARD ACTIVITY **Endangered Environment**—Students match the countries with the environmental issues that are threatening them.

☑ *Printable Digital Worksheets*

R Reading Skills

- WORKSHEET **Guided Reading Activity**—Students use Guided Reading Activity worksheets to review their comprehension of the content.
- WORKSHEET **Reading Essentials and Study Guide**—Students complete the study guide and answer Reading Progress Check and vocabulary questions. **AL**
- WORKSHEET **Vocabulary Activity**—Students review the chapter content and academic vocabulary words.
- WORKSHEET **Chapter Summary**—Students review the main ideas of the chapter content.

C Critical Thinking Skills

- WORKSHEET **Video Activity**—Students answer questions based on a lesson video.
- WORKSHEET **Reteaching Activity**—Students use this activity worksheet to review and reteach chapter content and vocabulary. This worksheet can be used with struggling students who need additional help with difficult content concepts.

CHAPTER 27 Bhutan, Maldives, Nepal, and Sri Lanka

INTERVENTION AND REMEDIATION STRATEGIES

LESSON 1 Physical Geography of Bhutan, Maldives, Nepal, and Sri Lanka

Reading and Comprehension

Organize students into four groups, assigning one of the countries in the region to each group. Have students in each group work together to complete a graphic organizer like the chart shown at the beginning of this lesson. After groups have completed their charts, allow groups to compare their charts, noting similarities and differences among the countries. Guide a class discussion about the various challenges and benefits of each country's physical geography.

Text Evidence

Have students remain in the same four groups but this time, assign a different country to each group. Tell students to research an aspect of their country's physical geography as it relates to one of the following topics discussed in the lesson: landforms, water systems, climate regions and biomes, and natural resources. Tell students to prepare an analysis of their findings, comparing information in the text with information found in their research. For example, students assigned to Nepal might research the significance of ecotourism and its impact on the country's economy. Ask each group to present its findings to the class.

LESSON 2 Human Geography of Bhutan, Maldives, Nepal, and Sri Lanka

Reading and Comprehension

Have students write sentences using the lesson's content vocabulary. Tell students that their sentences should show an understanding of the meaning of each word and how it applies to the lesson content. Encourage students to look up unknown or confusing words in the text associated with the vocabulary terms. For example, students might need to clarify the meaning of the word *shrines* when defining stupas or the meaning of the word *fortified* when writing a sentence about dzongs. Have students work in pairs to conduct a peer review by sharing their sentences to check each word's meaning.

Text Evidence

Have students review the time line *Ethnic Strife* in this lesson. Organize students into four groups and assign each group a country in the region. Have students in each group work together to create an illustrated time line depicting key events to enhance the time line shown in the text. Then have students in each group collaborate to write a summary about the events shown on their time line. Encourage students to explain the significance of one or more events related to the history of their country, such as its conflicts regarding independence and hostilities that still exist between countries.

LESSON 3 People and Their Environment: Bhutan, Maldives, Nepal, and Sri Lanka

Reading and Comprehension

To ensure comprehension of the concepts in this lesson, have students write a summarizing sentence for each of the three sections in the text: managing resources, human impact, and addressing the issues. Tell students that their sentences should touch on one or more issues facing each of the four countries in the region and should identify what is being done to solve the problem. Have students share their sentences with the class, leading into a discussion about the challenges that face regions with few resources.

Text Evidence

Have students work in small groups to create a television commercial or public service announcement for one of the countries in the region. Suggest topics students may wish to focus on, such as tourism, the environment and ecosystems of the region, or the impact of human activity. For example, students might write a public service announcement by Bhutan's government touting the benefits of organic farming or a message from Sri Lanka's government promoting sustainable development. Allow time for students to prepare and rehearse their commercials before presenting them to the class. Tell students in the audience to rate the effectiveness of their peers' commercials based on adequate supporting evidence.

Online Resources

Leveled Reader

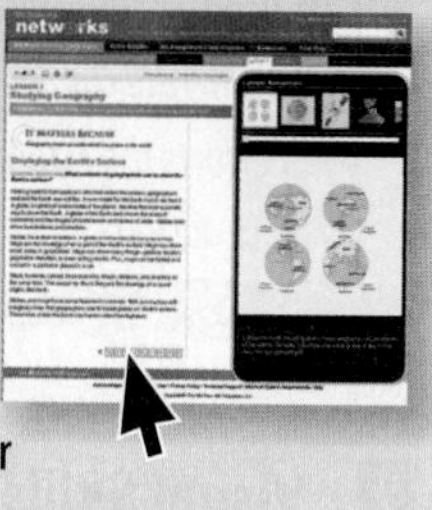

Use this online approaching-level text that corresponds directly to the text in the Student Edition. It also includes additional reading and comprehension support for English Language Learners.

Guided Reading Activities

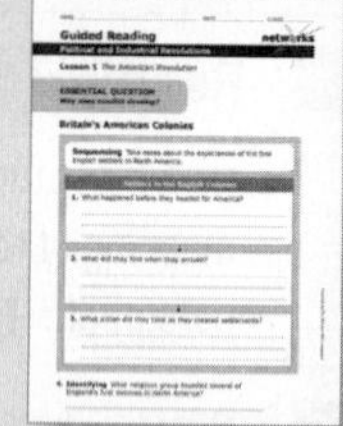

This resource uses guiding questions to help students with comprehension.

Reteaching Activities

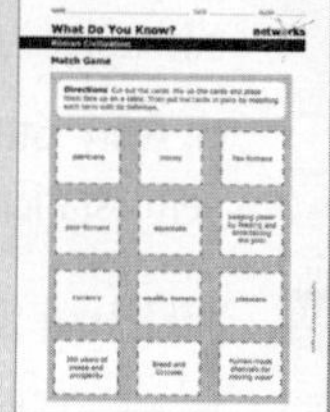

These worksheets provide students with an opportunity for remedial practice and review of vital chapter content.

Reading Essentials and Study Guide

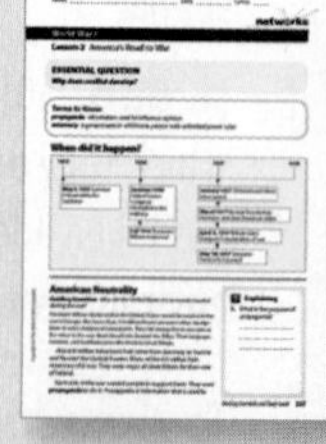

This resource offers writing and reading activities for the approaching-level student.

Self-Check Quizzes

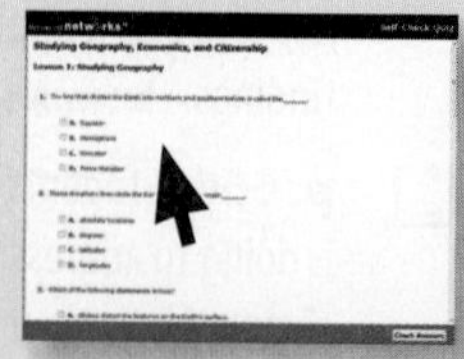

This online assessment tool provides instant feedback for students to check their progress.

Chapter Summaries

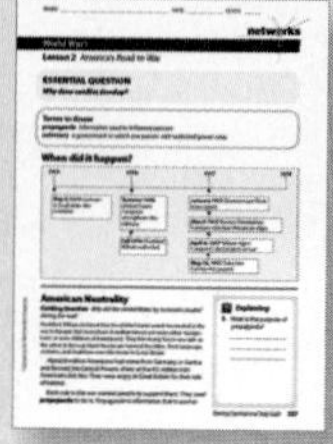

Summaries are provided for each chapter that thoroughly condense core content into manageable chunks.

Bhutan, Maldives, Nepal & Sri Lanka

ESSENTIAL QUESTION • *How do physical systems and human systems shape a place?*

networks

There's More Online about the geography of Bhutan, Maldives, Nepal, and Sri Lanka.

CHAPTER 27

Geography Matters...

The four countries of South Asia profiled in this chapter offer a great variety of natural beauty and human culture and more. They include the world's highest mountain, tropical forests, and beautiful coral reefs. Mountainous Nepal and Bhutan and tropical Sri Lanka and Maldives possess cultures that are centuries old as well as natural wonders that have existed for millions of years.

◀ This Hindu holy man in Nepal wears traditional facial painting.

ENGAGE

Drawing Inferences Have students look at a physical map of the region. Ask volunteers to offer information they know about the physical geography of the countries discussed in this chapter. For example, students might mention Mount Everest as a popular mountain climbing destination. Tell students to infer how the region's physical geography might have both a positive and negative impact.

TEACH & ASSESS

Geography Matters Have students read the text and consider the physical geography of the region. **Ask:** **What "natural wonders" do you think exist in the region?** *(Possible answers: the towering Himalaya, waterfalls created by rivers that flow from high elevations)* **How might the region's location impact its people?** *(Possible answer: The physical beauty of the region could benefit the economy by increasing tourism, but a country like Nepal might struggle politically being in between the two large countries of India and China.)* **Verbal/Linguistic**

Content Background Knowledge

Mount Everest Nepal's Mount Everest is the world's highest mountain and is therefore a destination for ardent mountain climbers. The mountain presents often insurmountable challenges, especially its frigid climate. In the summer months, the average temperature on Mount Everest is only about –2° F (–60° C). In the winter, temperatures can drop to –76° F (–76° C) and winds can blow more than 100 miles per hour.

CLOSE & REFLECT

Posing Questions Have students write three questions about aspects of Bhutan, Maldives, Nepal, and Sri Lanka that they would like to know more about. Tell students to refer back to their questions, filling in answers as they read the chapter.

ePals GlobalCommunity Where learners connect™

Extend the project-based learning experience globally through our partnership with ePals. EPals allows you to connect with classrooms around the world in a safe online environment for real-life lessons and projects in virtual study groups.

Letter from the Author

Dear Geography Teacher,

When I was last in Kathmandu, I became interested in the city's urban infrastructure and the environmental consciousness of its citizens. Cattle roamed the streets, small businesses operated openly on sidewalks and the side of the road. Butcher shops were scattered throughout the city, and food was prepared in a primitive manner. The Bagmati valley was a mass of trash, garbage, animal and human waste, all contributing to a stench that could be smelled a half mile away. For an alternative view, have students research the Chhuk ha Hydel project in Bhutan. Here the river has been tamed and a hydroelectric complex supplies much of the country's power.

Richard G. Boehm

ENGAGE

R Reading Skills

Predicting Draw students' attention to the term *buffer*. **Ask:** **What does this term mean?** If students have trouble coming up with a logical response based on the context, allow them to use a dictionary. **How does the term relate to the geography of a place?** *(something that acts as a protective barrier)* Have students write a short paragraph predicting how Nepal's location could be a political advantage or disadvantage. Ask volunteers to share their paragraphs with the class. Tell students to review their paragraphs after they have read this feature, checking to see if their predictions were accurate. **ELL Verbal/Linguistic**

TEACH & ASSESS

V Visual Skills

Spatial Analysis Have students work with a partner to analyze the disputed boundaries shown on the map. Have students conduct online research to identify how long these disputed boundaries have been in place and how these boundaries have impacted relations among countries in the region. Challenge students to identify how the border disputes in South Asia have impacted the people who live there. **BL Interpersonal, Visual/Spatial**

W Writing Skills

Informative/Explanatory Have students read the callouts. Then have them respond in an explanatory paragraph to the following prompt: Explain how Nepal might be "caught in the middle" between China and India. Students should use the border dispute involving Tibet to explain their response. Invite students to revise their paragraphs after reading the entire *Why Geography Matters* feature. **Verbal/Linguistic**

Why Geography Matters: **Bhutan, Maldives, Nepal & Sri Lanka**

Nepal's role as a buffer state

Nepal is located high in the rugged Himalaya. Nepal's geographic isolation makes trade and travel difficult. In order to survive, Nepal has forged important political and economic alliances with its neighbors. At times, maintaining friendly relationships with surrounding countries has proved challenging.

Buffer States and Border Disputes in South Asia

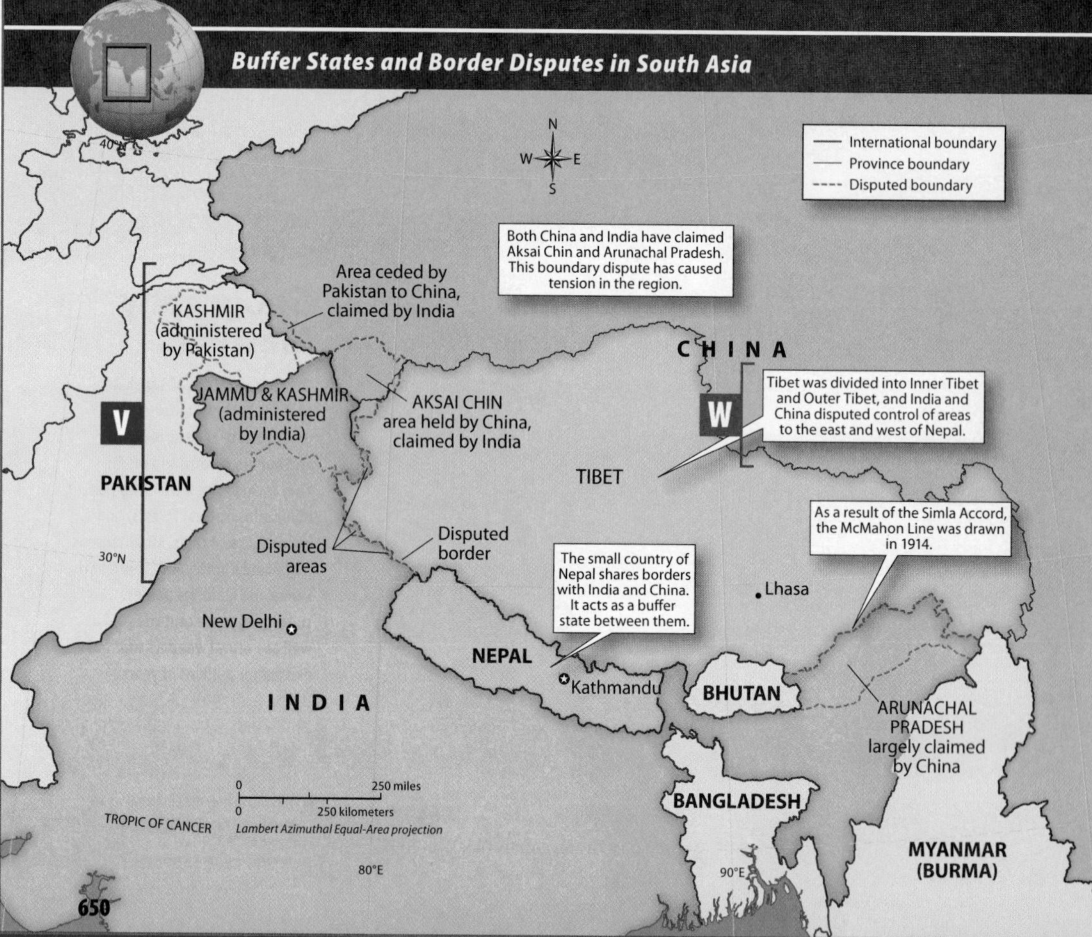

650

Project-Based Learning

Hands-On

Journal

Students will work individually to write a fictional journal about a Sherpa's family in Nepal or a family that depends on fishing for a living in Maldives. Students will research the economic-related issues that affect the highlands and lowlands of Bhutan, Maldives, Nepal and Sri Lanka. The journal should touch upon environmental issues as well as relate to the fictional journal writer.

ePals GlobalCommunity
Where learners connect™

Digital Hands-On

Create Online Projects

Find an additional activity online that incorporates technology for this project. Visit the EdTech Teacher Web sites for more links, tutorials, and other resources.

Why Geography Matters

(l)Bartosz Hadyniak/E+/Getty Images, (c)Ilya S. Savenok/FilmMagic/Getty Images, (r)China Photos/Getty Images News/Getty Images

What is a buffer state?

A *buffer* is something that acts as a protective barrier. A *buffer state* is a smaller, independent country sandwiched between larger, more powerful rivals. In the 1800s, Thailand—then called Siam—was a buffer between the British empire in India and the French empire in Southeast Asia. A buffer state serves to prevent conflict between its neighbors. To function as a buffer state, a country must remain neutral and resist pressure from neighboring powers. A buffer state gains trading partners and other advantages from its alliances. It also literally keeps the peace in a region.

A buffer state is vulnerable to instability. It can be caught in the middle if a simmering conflict between its neighbors heats up. Being heavily dependent on other countries, a buffer state also loses the freedom to act as it chooses. A buffer state that is more influenced by one country can lose its independence and become a satellite state.

1. **The World in Spatial Terms** How does the location of a country make it a buffer state, and what purpose does a buffer state serve?

Why is Nepal considered a buffer state?

Small, landlocked Nepal stands between two much larger countries, China and India. In 1775 a Nepalese king described his country's location as "a yam between two boulders." Nepal is considered a buffer state because these two "boulders"—which combined have more than one-third of the world's population—are rivals.

Their hostility largely began with the 1959 Tibetan uprising against China, when the Dalai Lama and other Tibetans took refuge in India. In 1914 British colonial officials had drawn the McMahon Line, which divided Tibet and gave more territory to British-ruled India. India accepted the boundary as legal, but China did not. Since then, the two countries have disagreed about control of areas to the east and west of Nepal and have had an unclear border. In October 1962, Chinese soldiers launched a surprise invasion, crossing the Himalaya and seizing India's territory. Although this Sino-Indian War ended quickly, these quarreling countries have maintained an uneasy peace ever since, putting Nepal's interests at risk.

2. **Places and Regions** What physical and political characteristics of a buffer state does Nepal exhibit?

What does Nepal's status as a buffer state mean for its future?

For years, Nepal benefited from close relations with both China and India. With each country, Nepal shares historical, economic, cultural, and religious bonds. Yet being in the middle means that Nepal must constantly perform a delicate balancing act. Political and economic changes in China and India affect Nepal and its future. Although trading partners, China and India still view one another with suspicion. India's awareness that China is capable of launching a surprise attack led to militarization of the region. Having Nepal as a buffer reduces tensions.

After years of depending heavily on India for trade, Nepal is strengthening its economic ties with China. In 2007, for example, China began constructing a railway extension to link Tibet and Nepal and improve trade. As China and India themselves develop stronger economic ties, there is hope that one day Nepal will become a bridge between them.

3. **Environment and Society** In what way does being a buffer state affect Nepal's future?

THERE'S MORE ONLINE

READ a time line of Nepal's history • *SEE* a map of disputed territory claimed by China, India, and Nepal

SLIDE SHOW

Nepal: A Buffer State

Analyzing Visuals This slide show presents information about the cultural and political role of Nepal in the subregion. As a class, have students view and read the information in the slide show. After the presentation, ask students to choose one of the images that interested them to write a descriptive paragraph that explains the cultural diversity of Nepal. Encourage volunteers to share their paragraphs with the class. BL Verbal/Linguistic

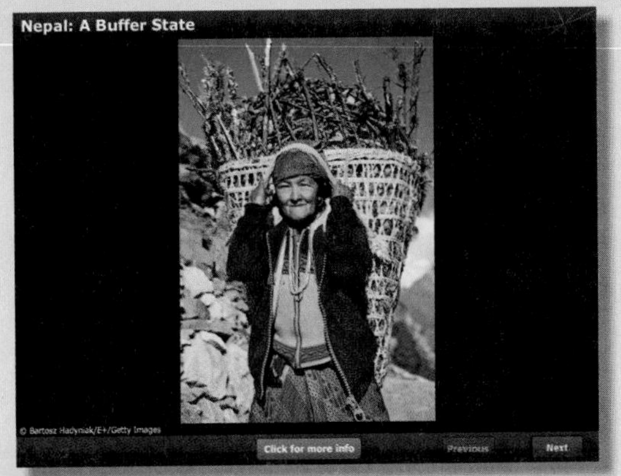

V Visual Skills

Speculating Have students speculate why a photo of the Dalai Lama was included here. **Ask:** **What is the Dalai Lama doing in this photo?** *(He appears to be praying.)* **After looking at the map on the previous page and reading this column, why do you think the Dalai Lama and other Tibetans left Tibet?** *(Possible answer: They were probably fearful for their lives after the uprising against China.)* **How would this uprising and the fleeing of Tibetans to India impact Nepal?** *(Possible answer: Nepal is physically inbetween two countries where people are not agreeing, which could put Nepal and its citizens at risk.)* AL **Logical/Mathematical, Visual/Spatial**

C Critical Thinking Skills

Determining Importance Have students consider the impact of the British-drawn McMahon Line. Have students collaborate with a partner to summarize the importance of the border disputes involving Tibet, China, and India. After students share their summaries with the class, **ask:** **Why was the McMahon Line originally drawn?** *(British colonial officials set the border in 1914, dividing Tibet and giving more territory to India, which was controlled by Britain.)* **What happened in 1962?** *(Chinese soldiers crossed the Himalaya in a surprise attack and seized India's territory.)* **Verbal/Linguistic**

T Technology Skills

Researching Have students conduct online research to identify other examples of Nepal's dependence on India for trade. Tell students to pose and answer questions in their research about Nepal as a buffer state and the ongoing border disputes that impact the region. Provide an opportunity for students to present their findings in a report to the class and ask them to enhance their presentations with visual displays. BL **Verbal/Linguistic, Visual/Spatial**

CLOSE & REFLECT

Evaluating Have students review the text in each column and write a summarizing paragraph that relates the challenges that Nepal continues to face because of its geographic location.

ANSWERS, p. 651

Why Geography Matters

1. The location of a country between two larger and more powerful rival countries make it a buffer state. A buffer state serves as a barrier to conflict between rival countries.
2. Nepal physically is a buffer state because of its location between China and India.
3. The political and economic changes in China and India, as well as their relations with each other, have an effect on the future of Nepal.

Physical Geography of Bhutan, Maldives, Nepal & Sri Lanka

ENGAGE

C Critical Thinking Skills

Comparing and Contrasting Show students a physical map of South Asia that includes Bhutan, Maldives, Nepal, and Sri Lanka. Challenge students to identify features such as major waterways, mountain ranges, and other landforms. Have students create a two-column chart that compares and contrasts the highest and lowest countries in the region. **Ask: How do you think life for people who live in Maldives differs from those who live near the Himalaya?** *(Student answers may vary, but should infer that the climate on the islands is less harsh than the Himalaya, and that living on low islands would be different than living in a landlocked country.)*

TEACH & ASSESS

V Visual Skills

Transferring Information Have students work with a partner to read and transfer information in the text into a map. Tell students to create a key that indicates approximate distances. **Ask: Where is the island country of Maldives located?** *(to the southwest of India in the Indian Ocean)* Then have students compare their drawings to a physical map of the region. Encourage students to continue adding information to their maps as they work through this lesson. AL **Visual/Spatial**

T Technology Skills

Researching Have students work with a partner to research facts about the Greater Himalaya mountain range and present their findings in a visual report to the class. Students should show the varying sizes of the range's tallest mountains in feet and meters, comparing them to a U.S. mountain such as Alaska's Mount McKinley. **Logical/Mathematical, Visual/Spatial**

ANSWERS, p. 652

TAKING NOTES: Nepal – mountains and valleys—high mountains limit settlement while valleys are locations of cities; rivers—rivers attract tourists for rafting **Bhutan** – valleys—population concentrated in valleys; rivers—rivers used for hydroelectric power **Maldives** – islands—low islands don't support agriculture or large populations, most people work in fishing industry; location in Indian Ocean—location is popular with tourists but threatened by cyclones and tsunamis **Sri Lanka** – highlands—tea is grown in highlands; tropical climate—tropical climate supports rice and rubber crops; rivers—rivers are used for irrigation; location in Indian Ocean—location is popular with tourists but threatened by cyclones and tsunamis

networks *There's More Online!*

- **IMAGE** Kathmandu, Nepal
- **IMAGE** Mount Everest
- **INFOGRAPHIC** Ecotourism
- **INTERACTIVE SELF-CHECK QUIZ**
- **VIDEO** Physical Geography of Bhutan, Maldives, Nepal & Sri Lanka

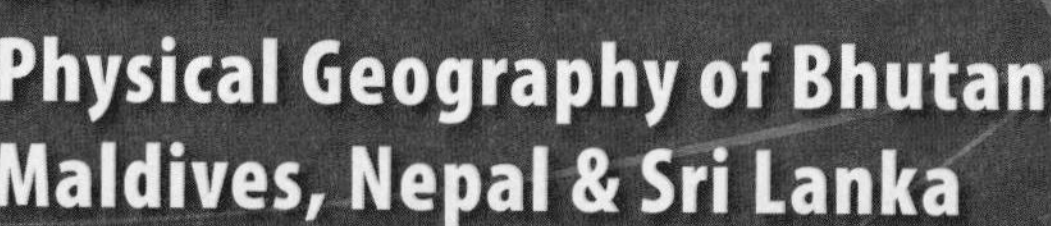

Reading **HELP**DESK CCSS

Academic Vocabulary

- **potential**
- **exploit**

Content Vocabulary

- **aquifer**
- **cowrie shell**

TAKING NOTES: ***Key Ideas and Details***

IDENTIFYING As you read about the physical geography of Bhutan, Maldives, Nepal, and Sri Lanka, use a graphic organizer like the one below to give examples of how a landform, water system, or resource affects life in each country.

How Physical Geography Affects Life

Country	Physical Characteristics	Impact on Life

LESSON 1
Physical Geography of Bhutan, Maldives, Nepal & Sri Lanka

ESSENTIAL QUESTION • *How do physical systems and human systems shape a place?*

IT MATTERS BECAUSE

C *The northern and southern fringes of South Asia are among the highest and lowest countries in the world. Mountainous Nepal and Bhutan contain the sources of some of South Asia's mighty rivers. Sri Lanka is an island country. Maldives, a collection of low islands, faces the danger of rising sea levels.*

Landforms

GUIDING QUESTION *What landforms help shape life in Bhutan, Maldives, Nepal, and Sri Lanka?*

V While these four countries are unique, their locations on the fringe of South Asia have meant that their physical and human geographies have been influenced by the South Asian core. Nepal and Bhutan sit on the northern fringe of South Asia, amid the lofty Himalaya. They are bordered by India to the south and China to the north. Far to the south, in the Indian Ocean, sit the island countries of Maldives and Sri Lanka. Sri Lanka is off the southeastern coast of India. Maldives is a collection of islands southwest of India. Its islands stretch over 500 miles (805 km) from north to south and 80 miles (129 km) from east to west. The country's nearly 1,200 islands have a total area of about 115 square miles (298 sq. km).

The Indian subcontinent is a large landmass that is slowly and steadily colliding with the southern edge of Asia. This collision thrust up several mountain ranges, including the Himalaya, which dominate much of Nepal and Bhutan. These ranges spread about 1,500 miles (2,414 km) across the northern edge of South Asia and are hundreds of miles from T north to south. The Himalaya are divided into three ranges: the Greater Himalaya to the north, the Lesser Himalaya in the center, and the Outer Himalaya to the south. The Greater Himalaya soar the highest, averaging over 20,000 feet (6,096 m) in elevation. In Nepal, the Greater Himalaya range has eight of the highest mountains in the world. Among them is Mount Everest, the world's highest mountain, which rises to 29,028 feet (8,848 m) above sea level along the border between Nepal and China.

networks ***Online Teaching Options***

INTERACTIVE BELLRINGER

Highest Mountain Peaks of Five Continents

Interpreting a Diagram Use the introductory text and the diagram of the highest mountain peaks of five continents to understand what landforms help shape life in Nepal. Have students work in pairs. Ask each pair to answer the questions and record their answers. Then, review the answers with the class as a whole. **Interpersonal, Visual/Spatial**

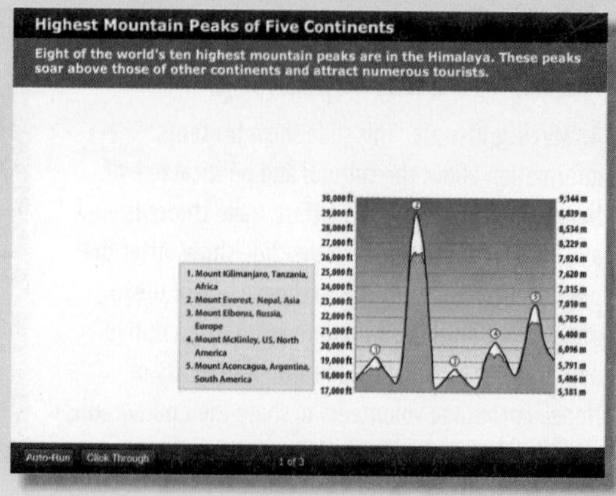

Nepal has four geographic zones: the Tarai Plain on its southern border, the Churia and Mahabharat Ranges north of it, the Lesser Himalaya north of them, and the Greater Himalaya on its northern rim. The Tarai was originally forested marshland, but much of the plain has been drained for farming. The low Churia Range includes flat valleys that have been cleared of trees for farming. Between the Mahabharat Range and the Lesser Himalaya are more valleys where cities such as Kathmandu are located. Few people live in the Greater Himalaya. **V1**

Bhutan has four geographic zones. A narrow lowland called the Duars Plain sits on the southern edge of the country. This area receives heavy rainfall and is thick with vegetation and wild animals. On its northern edge are several passes into the mountains called *dwars,* meaning "doors," which gave their name to the plain. The southern part of the Duars Plain is flat land used for growing rice. A dramatic change in altitude occurs as the Lesser Himalaya and then the Greater Himalaya rise steeply above the plain. Many of Bhutan's people live in the several wide, level valleys that cut through the Lesser Himalaya. The valleys of the Greater Himalaya, found from 12,000 to 18,000 feet (3,658 to 5,486 m) above sea level, are sparsely populated. The Black Mountain range runs north and south from the Greater to the Lesser Himalaya in west-central Bhutan. Few people live in these rugged mountains. **V2**

Sri Lanka has two regions. The first is a triangle-shaped mountain range in the south-central part of the island called the Central Highlands. The second is a plain that covers most of the island. The Central Highlands has a few peaks that reach about 7,000 feet (2,134 m), including the island's highest point, Mount Pidurutalagala, with an elevation of 8,281 feet (2,524 m). The plain ranges from sea level at the coast to about 1,000 feet (305 m) high. Many inlets called lagoons lie along the coast, as well as Mannar Island. To the north of the Central Highlands, low ridges cross the plain. To the west, there are higher ridges and deeper valleys. Highland areas are used for growing tea, and the wetter southwest is home to plantations growing rubber plants. Rice is grown in the wet southwest, but irrigation projects have increased rice cultivation in other areas. **C**

Maldives is a scattered collection of about 1,200 islands grouped into 13 atolls with barrier reefs. These atolls are coral reefs formed at the edge of volcanoes that have since sunk beneath the ocean. Colonies of tiny polyps secrete calcium carbonate to form the coral that builds the reefs. Over time, rubble from the reefs and sediment build up low islands. These islands have a very low elevation, mainly reaching no more than 6 feet (1.8 m) above the surrounding water.

Kathmandu, Nepal's capital and most populous city, sits in a valley more than 4,300 feet (1,311 m) above sea level.

◀ CRITICAL THINKING

1. ***Identifying Cause and Effect*** How do the mountains of Nepal and Bhutan influence where people in those countries live?
2. ***Hypothesizing*** Do you think these two countries have much farmland? Why or why not?

VIDEO

Natural World–Himalaya

Narrative Have students watch this video to learn more about the physical processes that continue to shape the Himalaya. After viewing the video, ask students to imagine that they are mountain climbers about to leave on an expedition to a Himalayan peak. Tell them to write journal entries as if it is the first night after they have started the ascent. Their entries should include a description of the scenery as well as descriptions of the variation in climate and elevation. Invite several volunteers to share their narratives.
Verbal/Linguistic, Visual/Spatial

V1 Visual Skills

Creating Charts Have students work with a partner to create a four-column chart with information about Nepal's four geographic zones. After students have completed their charts, have pairs exchange their charts with other pairs, checking for accuracy and revising as needed. **Ask: How has the Tarai Plain changed over time?** *(The Tarai Plain is on the southern border of Nepal and was originally marshland, but much of the land has been drained for farming.)* **Where is Kathmandu located?** *(between the Mahabharat range and the Lesser Himalaya)* ELL **Visual/Spatial**

V2 Visual Skills

Creating Charts Have students work in the same pairs as they did for the above activity, creating a similar four-column chart, but completing it with information about Bhutan's geographic zones. **Ask: What is the climate of the Duars Plain?** *(The Duars Plain has a humid subtropical climate which receives heavy rainfall, so the region is thick with vegetation and wild animals.)* **What part of the Himalaya is inhabited by people?** *(the valleys that cut through the Lesser Himalaya)*
AL **Visual/Spatial**

C Critical Thinking Skills

Comparing and Contrasting Have students read the text and compare and contrast Sri Lanka's two regions. **Ask: What is a distinguishing feature of the Central Highlands?** *(a triangle-shaped mountain range in the south-central part of the island)* **What is the island's highest peak?** *(Mount Pidurutalagala)* **What crops are grown on the island?** *(tea in the highland areas, rubber plants and rice in the wetter southwest)* AL **Logical/Mathematical**

ANSWERS, p. 653

CRITICAL THINKING

1. The mountains of these countries are sparsely populated while the valleys contain much larger populations.
2. Farmland is a low proportion of total land of these countries because of their very mountainous and rough terrain.

C Critical Thinking Skills

Drawing Inferences Have students read the text and ask them to visualize five square miles, offering examples from your community. **Ask:** What do you think living on an island of this size must be like? *(Student answers may vary, but students might mention that life on islands of this size would lack a number of activities that people enjoy in major cities, such as sporting events, theater, and so on.)* What are the drawbacks? Benefits? *(A drawback is that resources are limited, as fishing is the primary activity. A benefit is that the islands are in a warm climate and have sandy beaches.)* AL Visual/Spatial

T Technology Skills

Critical Listening Have small groups conduct online research about a river in one of the regions discussed in the text. Have groups use information in the text, as well as online or library resources, to research how the river contributes to life in the region. Tell students to present their findings in a visual display. Have groups present their visuals to the class, allowing time for a question-answer session after each presentation. Remind students to listen carefully to their classmates' responses. BL Interpersonal

W Writing Skills

Narrative After students read Norgay's quote, discuss the challenges and logistics involved with climbing Mount Everest. Have students write a journal entry describing a day on the final leg of the route up to the summit. Tell students to describe the scenery as well as the physical and emotional toll the journey might have on climbers, guides, and animals. Call on volunteers to read their journal entries to the class. Intrapersonal, Verbal/Linguistic

ANSWERS, p. 654

READING PROGRESS CHECK Bhutan, Sri Lanka, and Nepal all have mountains, and while Maldives has a very low elevation, its islands were formed from volcanoes that sank beneath the ocean.

READING PROGRESS CHECK Maldives has no rivers and depends upon the aquifers for freshwater.

DBQ The snow had created such deep drifts that the Sherpas were afraid the yaks would not survive. The yaks were worth more to the Sherpas than any amount of money.

Climbing Mount Everest

W "From Dingboche, Ed Viesturs, Jangbu, and I went ahead of the team to check on the condition of the trail [up Mount Everest]. Reports had reached us that fresh snow had fallen between the settlement of Lobuche and Base Camp, making the final leg of the route impossible for yaks. The yak drivers were refusing to lead their animals through the deep drifts. Hazard pay can tempt the Sherpas [people of Nepal who assist mountain climbers], but they won't risk their yaks for any price. We had nearly one hundred of the animals, but the loads would have to be carried by porters."

—Jamling Tenzing Norgay, *Touching My Father's Soul*, 2002

DBQ ***DRAWING INFERENCES*** Why were the Sherpas unwilling to use their yaks? RH.9–10.1

potential having a capacity that could be developed

aquifer an underground water-bearing layer of porous rock, sand, or gravel

C The highest point on the islands is less than 8 feet (2.4 m) above sea level. Barrier reefs off many of these islands protect the sandy beaches from high seas. Many of the atolls are tiny; no island is larger than 5 square miles (13 sq. km). Only about 200 atolls are inhabited; most have fewer than 1,000 people. With little land for growing crops, fishing is a major activity.

READING PROGRESS CHECK

Comparing How are the landforms of Bhutan, Maldives, Nepal, and Sri Lanka similar?

Water Systems

GUIDING QUESTION *How are rivers and the sea vital to human life in Bhutan, Maldives, Nepal, and Sri Lanka?*

Three major river systems—the Ganges, the Brahmaputra, and the Indus—fan out across the northern part of the Indian subcontinent. These rivers begin high in the Himalaya and carry fertile soil from mountain slopes onto their floodplains as the rivers swell with seasonal rains. The rivers of Nepal and Bhutan help feed the Ganges and the Brahmaputra.

T Several rivers cut through the mountains of Nepal and Bhutan, generally flowing from the north to the south. The chief rivers in Nepal are the Baghmati, the Kosi, the Gandak, and the Karnali. These rivers eventually feed into the Ganges. Some of Nepal's rivers cut deep gorges running north and south through the mountains. Many rivers have fast-flowing streams through rocky channels that make them ideal for white-water rafting. This activity attracts many tourists who are eager for adventure. Nepal's fast rivers have great **potential** for hydroelectric power, but that resource has not been fully developed. The main rivers of Bhutan are the Torsa, the Raidak, the Sankosh, and the Manas. All join the Brahmaputra.

Sri Lanka has a dozen major rivers, most of which flow from the Central Highlands directly to the sea. The exception is the longest river, the Mahaweli, which begins flowing west of the Central Highlands but then follows a northward and eastward path to empty on the northeast coast. The Mahaweli, which swells in the rainy season, is tapped for water to irrigate fields. Rivers that drop from high elevations in the Central Highlands to lower-lying areas give Sri Lanka many spectacular waterfalls. Nearly 20 of them fall more than 348 feet (100 m).

Tiny Maldives has no rivers, but it does have underground aquifers that provide it with freshwater. **Aquifers** are underground water-bearing layers of porous rock, sand, or gravel.

The Indian Ocean surrounds both Maldives and Sri Lanka. The ocean provides rich resources to the people of these islands and affects the climate of all four countries, even far-off Nepal and Bhutan. Ocean waters also represent a threat to low-lying areas of Sri Lanka and to all of Maldives. Powerful cyclones—storms like hurricanes—can bring not only heavy rains but also high seas that can flood Sri Lanka's coastal lowlands and Maldives' low-lying islands.

Another danger comes from earthquakes that occur on the floor of the Indian Ocean. These events can unleash towering waves called tsunamis that can travel and flood far inland. A 2004 tsunami killed more than 31,000 people in Sri Lanka.

The ocean may cause problems for these countries in the future as well. Some climate scientists are forecasting that sea levels may rise as much as several feet during this century. If that does happen, the people of Maldives face a grim future, as the waters could submerge these low islands.

READING PROGRESS CHECK

Drawing Inferences Why are aquifers important in Maldives?

networks Online Teaching Options

INTERACTIVE IMAGE

Mount Everest

Comparing and Contrasting Allow students ample time to analyze this interactive image of Mount Everest. Then ask students to form small groups of three or four to create a Venn diagram that compares and contrasts Mount Everest with the rest of the Himalaya. Students should use information from the lesson, as well as other resources as needed. Have groups share the information in their diagrams in a class discussion. ELL Visual/Spatial

Harry Kikstra/Flickr/Getty Images

Climates, Biomes, and Resources

GUIDING QUESTION *How does topography affect the climate in Nepal and Bhutan?*

As with the rest of South Asia, the monsoons strongly affect the climate of these four countries. However, the locations and landforms of these countries give them different climate zones. Elevation is also an important factor in climate.

Nepal and Bhutan have four climate zones. The Tarai in Nepal and lowlands in Bhutan have a humid subtropical climate. The lower hills and mountains have a warm temperate climate with summer rain and dry winters. The higher mountains have a highland climate with cool temperatures. Areas above 16,000 feet (4,877 m) have an arctic climate with year-round ice. Winters in the Himalaya are long and harsh. Bhutan is directly in the path of wet monsoon winds.

Vegetation varies by elevation and is related to the climate zones. Tropical forests cover the lowlands. Deciduous trees are found at the next elevation level, and conifers appear higher up. Grasses cover the next level, up to about 15,000 feet (4,572 m). Above that is the snow line, where nothing grows. Elephants, rhinoceroses, deer, and tigers roam the lowland areas.

ECOTOURISM IN NEPAL

LOW IMPACT
Ecotourism is responsible travel to areas of natural significance that attempts to conserve the environment and improve the well-being of local people.

INTERNATIONAL
Ecotourism is a growing industry, increasing by 5% each year. It represents 6% of the world's gross domestic product and 11.4% of all consumer spending worldwide.

PRE-TOURIST
Prior to the 1920s, the area was inhabited by the Sherpa people and largely undisturbed by Westerners. Climbing began in the 1920s, and the first successful attempt was in 1953.

TOURIST
Since 1990, climbing has become a popular tourist activity. Unfortunately, these tourists have made a habit of littering the mountain with gear and equipment after use.

ECOTOURIST
Today climbers are encouraged to be more responsible with their waste and unused gear. Since 2008, yearly "eco-climbs" occur to remove trash and raise awareness.

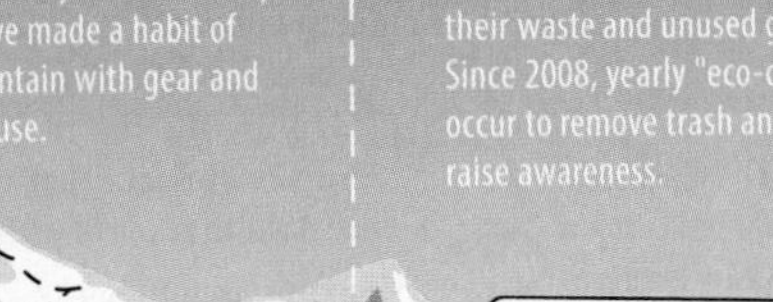

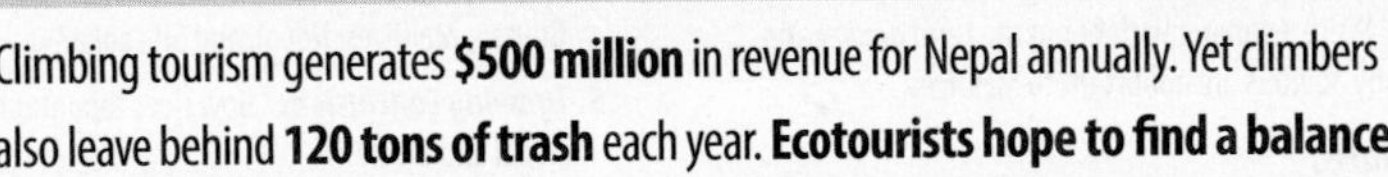

Climbing tourism generates **$500 million** in revenue for Nepal annually. Yet climbers also leave behind **120 tons of trash** each year. **Ecotourists hope to find a balance.**

Ecotourism based on the climate and natural beauty of the Himalaya is a growing industry. Mount Everest, the tallest mountain in the world, is an especially popular destination.

▲ CRITICAL THINKING

1. ***Considering Advantages and Disadvantages*** How does Nepal benefit from tourism? What are the negative effects of tourism?
2. ***Hypothesizing*** Why might someone decide to take part in an "eco-climb"?

G1 Critical Thinking Skills

Analyzing Cause and Effect Have students read the information and consider the impact that topography has on the region's climate. **Ask: How do monsoons impact the climate of Bhutan?** *(The wet monsoon winds impact Bhutan, which is directly in their path.)* **Why is elevation a key factor in the region's climate?** *(The climate varies according to the elevation of a particular region. For example, the Tarai in Nepal and lowlands in Bhutan have a humid subtropical climate, whereas the higher mountains have a highland climate with cooler temperatures.)* **How is vegetation impacted by elevation?** *(Vegetation in the climate zones varies by elevation. Tropical forests cover lowlands, the next level has deciduous trees, conifers are located at higher elevations, and nothing grows above the snow line.)* **AL Logical/Mathematical**

R Reading Skills

Sequencing Information Have students work with a partner to read the facts presented in the infographic. Ask students to point out words and phrases that signal sequential time order *(prior to, in the 1920s, in 1953, since 1990, today, since 2008)*. Have students collaborate to create a time line that sequences relevant information about Nepal's ecotourism based on the infographic. **ELL Verbal/Linguistic, Visual/Spatial**

C2 Critical Thinking Skills

Considering Advantages and Disadvantages Have students read the information about climbing tourism. Then moderate a class debate in which students defend or refute the following statement: *Climbing tourism is vital to Nepal's economy.* Remind students to use information from the text to support their arguments. **BL Interpersonal, Verbal/Linguistic**

INTERACTIVE MAP

China, India, Nepal: Boundary Disputes

Speculating Use this interactive map to discuss both the political boundaries and natural boundaries of China, India, and Nepal. Working with a partner, have students speculate about how boundary disputes may affect tourism in Nepal. Have each set of students write out a statement speculating the effect, then ask them to share their statements with another pair. Have students discuss their speculation, and then encourage a small group of volunteers to research whether the boundary disputes cause tourism concerns. **BL Logical/Mathematical**

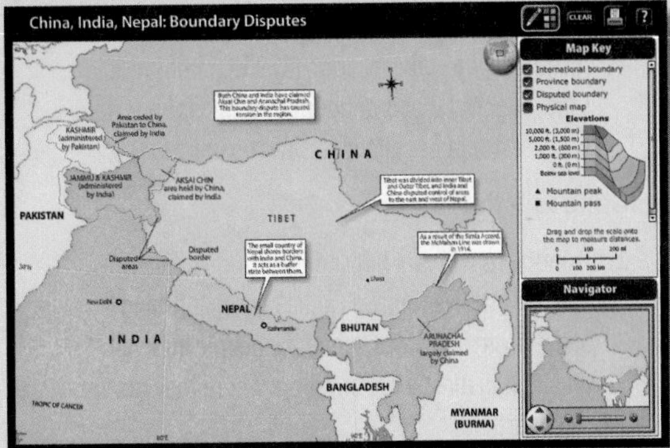

ANSWERS, p. 655

CRITICAL THINKING

1. Tourism brings money to Nepal's economy but litters the mountains with gear, equipment, and trash.
2. Someone might choose to take an eco-climb to be able to travel responsibly in a way that conserves the environment and improves life for local people by adding money to the economy.

Physical Geography of Bhutan, Maldives, Nepal & Sri Lanka

W Writing Skills

Informative/Explanatory Tell students to act as reporters covering a story about the region's natural resources and hydroelectric power. Students may choose a particular country or region to research. Then have students conduct online research to identify a hydroelectric project that exists in their chosen region. Students should also identify any issues or problems related to the project, as well as other resources that could be developed to benefit the region's economy. Have students gather the information for a report to the class. Encourage students to provide visuals, such as a map or diagram, to accompany their articles. BL **Verbal/Linguistic**

Content Background Knowledge

Stilt Fishing Along Sri Lanka's southern coast, fishermen sit perched on tall wooden poles to catch fish. The fishermen wade into the water to reach their stilts, which are wooden poles that have been lodged in the ocean floor. They then climb up the pole, sit on a small bamboo board, and use a rod to catch the fish from above the water's surface. The fish are placed in a small bag or basket, which can be hung from the stilts.

CLOSE & REFLECT

Evaluating Tell students to review what they have learned about the landforms, water systems, climates, biomes, and resources of Bhutan, Maldives, Nepal, and Sri Lanka. Have students evaluate how the region's physical geography has both helped and presented challenges to the people who live in the subregion.

Maldives has a humid tropical climate with a hot monsoon season and a warm dry season. Coconut palms and breadfruit trees grow on the islands. Tropical fish dart among the coral reefs, and tuna and sea turtles swim in the deeper waters.

Sri Lanka has a similar climate in lowland areas. Temperatures are warm or hot throughout the year. The Central Highlands are much cooler. The country has a tropical wet climate in the west which supports rain forests, but becomes tropical dry in the east with evergreen and deciduous forests and upland grasslands. Drier areas have low bushes and scrub plants. Sri Lanka's forests are teeming with wildlife, including elephants, sloth bears, buffalo, and a variety of birds.

Nepal's rivers have great potential for hydroelectric power, but only a tiny fraction of the country's energy is provided in this way. It does have some power-generating dams, and plans for more are underway. If the country can develop this resource, it could export surplus electricity to India. Mineral resources include deposits of coal, iron ore, copper, and limestone. Nepal's forests contain a variety of trees, but overcutting has resulted in massive soil erosion, prompting the government to implement conservation and reforestation projects.

exploit to make use of a resource

W Bhutan has been much more successful in **exploiting** its hydroelectric potential. Electricity is its most valuable export. The Chhukha hydroelectric project began operating in the 1980s. Proceeds from selling power to India paid for the project. Another project completed in 2007 has also been successful, and the country has signed agreements with India to build four more dams. Bhutan has mineral resources, but transportation difficulties have limited its ability to use them.

Bhutan has worked to preserve its forests and has been more successful than Nepal in protecting this resource. While logging is important, it has not resulted in deforestation. Bhutan has taken cautious steps toward promoting tourism. While the government has encouraged tourists, it has also limited their number. The government fears damage to the land or to its culture if too many tourists visit.

Sri Lanka is a major producer of graphite, the material used for the "lead" in pencils. Other mineral resources include precious and semiprecious stones, which are important exports. Among Sri Lanka's most valuable resources, though, are its climate and rich variety of plant and animal life. These resources can attract tourists. Much of the forests have been cut down for farming or for timber, however.

Most of Maldives's resources derive from its ocean location. Tourism and fishing are the top two economic activities. For many centuries, the people of Maldives took another resource from the sea: **cowrie shells**. These shells were once sold to traders who used them for money in India, China, and Africa.

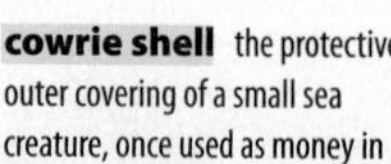

cowrie shell the protective outer covering of a small sea creature, once used as money in Asia and Africa

☑ READING PROGRESS CHECK

Explaining How are the climate zones of Nepal and Bhutan related to their landforms?

LESSON 1 REVIEW

Reviewing Vocabulary

1. ***Identifying*** Write a paragraph defining the term *aquifer* and explaining why aquifers are important to Maldives.

Using Your Notes

2. ***Summarizing*** Use your graphic organizer on these countries' physical systems to write a paragraph explaining how life in Nepal and Bhutan differs from that in Sri Lanka and Maldives.

Answering the Guiding Questions

3. ***Drawing Conclusions*** What landforms help shape life in Bhutan, Maldives, Nepal, and Sri Lanka?
4. ***Identifying*** How are rivers and the sea vital to human life in Bhutan, Maldives, Nepal, and Sri Lanka?
5. ***Drawing Conclusions*** How does topography affect the climate in Nepal and Bhutan?

Writing Activity

6. ***Informative/Explanatory*** In a paragraph, explain how the mountains of Nepal or Bhutan or the oceans surrounding Sri Lanka or Maldives both benefit and cause problems for people of those countries.

656

LESSON 1 REVIEW ANSWERS

Reviewing Vocabulary

1. An aquifer is a water-bearing layer of porous rock, sand, or gravel that is underground, and is important because it supplies all the freshwater in Maldives.

Using Your Notes

2. Paragraphs will vary but should include differences such as: Maldives and Sri Lanka have rich fishing and tourism industries, while the people in Nepal and Bhutan mostly live in valleys where they can cultivate land.

Answering the Guiding Questions

3. Nepal and Bhutan's mountains, Sri Lanka's highlands, and the reefs of Maldives determine where people live and the economic opportunities available.
4. The rivers provide drinking water, irrigation, hydroelectric power potential, and tourism opportunities, while the ocean supports the fishing and tourism industries of Sri Lanka and Maldives.
5. The topography causes the climates to get progressively cooler as the elevation rises, until becoming an arctic climate above 16,000 feet.

Writing Activity

6. Paragraphs will vary, but could include that the mountains in Nepal and Bhutan limit settlement and farming, but provide tourism income and headwaters for rivers that are capable of producing hydroelectric power. The ocean provides a rich fishing and tourism industry for Sri Lanka and Maldives, but causes significant hazards with cyclones and tsunamis.

ANSWERS, p. 656

☑ READING PROGRESS CHECK The mountains and lowlands dictate the climate zones with the Tarai in Nepal and lowlands of Bhutan having a humid subtropical climate, the low mountains and hills having a warm temperate climate, higher mountains having a highland climate with cool temperatures, and mountain areas above 16,000 feet having an arctic climate.

networks

There's More Online!

- **IMAGE** Prayer Flags
- **CHART** South Asian Human Development Index
- **TIME LINE** Ethnic Strife
- **INTERACTIVE SELF-CHECK QUIZ**
- **VIDEO** Human Geography of Bhutan, Maldives, Nepal & Sri Lanka

Reading **HELP**DESK

Academic Vocabulary (Tier Two Words)

- **portion**
- **recover**

Content Vocabulary (Tier Three Words)

- **lama**
- **mantra**
- **stupa**
- ***dzong***

TAKING NOTES: *Key Ideas and Details*

IDENTIFYING CENTRAL ISSUES As you read about the human geography of the subregion, use a graphic organizer like the one below to identify the main points about the history, government, people, and economy of one country.

I. Bhutan
  A.
  B.
  C.
II. Nepal
  A.
  B.
  C.
  D.
III. Maldives
  A.
  B.
  C.
  D.
IV. Sri Lanka
  A.
  B.
  C.
  D.

(tl)Keystone-France/Gamma-Keystone/Getty Images, (tcl)©Roger Hutchings/In Pictures/Corbis, (tcr)STR/AFP/Getty Images, (tr)David Min/Flickr/Getty Images

LESSON 2
Human Geography of Bhutan, Maldives, Nepal & Sri Lanka

R

ESSENTIAL QUESTION • *How do physical systems and human systems shape a place?*

IT MATTERS BECAUSE

The cultural geography of Bhutan, Maldives, Nepal, and Sri Lanka is widely varied. Each country's unique history and geographic location have determined the current political situation and religious practices.

History and Government

GUIDING QUESTION *What factors influenced the present-day governments of Bhutan, Maldives, Nepal, and Sri Lanka?*

There is little recorded Bhutan history before the introduction of Buddhism by monks fleeing Tibet in the A.D. 800s. These Tibetan monks gained control over the region. In the 1600s, a Tibetan high-level monk, or **lama**, named Ngawang Lopsang Gyatso merged religious and political power and created a system of law. After his death, however, chaos enveloped the country until 1885, when Ugyen Wangchuck began to establish order and unify the country. In 1907 he was proclaimed king. He adopted ideas from Britain regarding foreign affairs. Bhutan remained isolated. After Indian independence in 1947, India gained influence over Bhutan. V

Bhutan began to emerge from its isolation in the 1950s. In 1972 Jigme Singye Wangchuck, great-grandson of the first king, took the throne and began to modernize the country. However, his policies favoring Buddhist culture angered thousands of Nepalese Hindus. There were violent protests in the 1990s; some Hindus fled to Nepal. The king instituted more democratic reforms and abdicated the throne in 2006. His son Jigme Khesar Namgyal Wangchuck became king with less power. In 2008 Bhutan became a constitutional monarchy and held its first general elections.

For thousands of years, small and medium kingdoms have existed in Nepal. Modern Nepal was founded in 1769, when Prithvi Narayan Shah conquered rival lands and declared a dynasty. While his heirs continued to rule as kings, the family isolated the country from the world. Nepal's skilled, disciplined soldiers, called Gurkhas, were recruited to serve in the British and Indian armies.

ENGAGE

R Reading Skills

Predicting Have students skim through the lesson to preview the images and headings. Ask students to consider what they might learn about Bhutan, Maldives, Nepal, and Sri Lanka. Then have students write two predictions about what they will learn about the region as it relates to the history and culture of the people who live there. As students work through the lesson, have them return to their predictions to see if they were accurate. **Verbal/Linguistic**

TEACH & ASSESS

V Visual Skills

Time, Chronology, and Sequencing To help students visualize the development of Nepal and Bhutan, have students work with a partner to create a flowchart with key information separated by arrows indicating the sequence of events. **Ask: Why do you think there is little recorded Bhutan history before the A.D. 800s?** *(Possible answer: Bhutan's mountainous terrain likely made it impervious to the outside world. It was not until the A.D. 800s that Tibetan Buddhist monks recorded Bhutan's history.)* **AL Visual/Spatial**

Making Connections

Bhutan's History Very little is known about Bhutan's history before the A.D. 800s. Historians have pieced together information about the development of the region based on archaeological artifacts such as tools, weapons, and the remains of stone structures. Based on these findings, historians believe that a tribal group known as the Monpa lived in the region as far back as 2000 B.C.

ANSWERS, p. 657

TAKING NOTES: Bhutan—became isolated in the 1900s after Wangchuck was elected king; became a constitutional monarchy in 2008; about 700,000 people live in Bhutan; the Nepalese practice Hinduism and the Bhote practice Tibetan Buddhism; **Nepal**—founded in 1769 by Prithvi Narayan Shah; his heirs ruled until the 1950s; in 1996, a new constitution was approved; people live in Tarai Plain or in the hills and valleys, two main ethnic groups are the Indo-Nepalese and the Tibeto-Nepalese; **Maldives**—Settled by Buddhists from South Asia; became controlled by the Portuguese, Dutch, and British; in 1965, they became a republic; in 2008, they became a democracy; many islands are uninhabited and a third of the population lives in Male; **Sri Lanka**—Sinhalese people from India arrived during the 400s B.C., but the British had control of the island by 1815; Sri Lanka became independent in 1948 but had a civil war until 2009; Sri Lanka has a population of about 21.2 million people: The Sinhalese are the majority and live in the southwest, while the Tamils live mostly in the north.

INTERACTIVE BELLRINGER

Women in National Parliaments

Interpreting a Table and Identifying Trends

Use the introductory text and the table showing the percentages of women participating in national parliaments in Bhutan, Maldives, Nepal, and Sri Lanka to identify how cultures coexist and clash in these countries. Have students form small groups and discuss each question. Ask each group to come to a consensus on the answer to each question and record the answer. Then, review the answers with the class as a whole. **AL Interpersonal, Logical/Mathematical, Verbal/Linguistic**

Women in National Parliaments

Traditionally, women in Nepal, Sri Lanka, Bhutan, and Maldives often had a second-class status. This is reflected in their participation in government.

Percentage of Seats Held by Women in National Parliaments

	1990	2000	2010
Bhutan	2	9	9
Maldives	6	6	7
Nepal	6	6	33
Sri Lanka	5	5	5

Auto-Run Click Through 1 of 3

C Critical Thinking Skills

Identifying Cause and Effect Have students read the paragraph and tell them to consider the Guiding Question as they read: *What factors influenced the present-day governments of Nepal, Bhutan, Maldives, and Sri Lanka?* **Ask:** What was the effect of Nepal's king overthrowing the Ranas? *(The king began to rule the country directly, but Nepal's government fluctuated between a representative government and direct rule by the king; as a result, democratic protests ensued.)* What was the impact of the king allowing the election of parliament in 1990? *(It was largely unsuccessful because party rivalries prevented any government from gaining stability.)* What was the effect of the Communist revolt in 1996? *(The conflict lasted more than ten years and left thousands dead. Eventually the king and parliament approved a new constitution and the conflict ended.)* AL Logical/Mathematical

W Writing Skills

Narrative Have students write a journal entry from the perspective of a European leader, a Portuguese merchant, a Dutch trader, a British soldier, or someone living in Sri Lanka during the time period discussed in the text, such as a member of the Sinhalese or Tamil people. Using information in the text as clues, have students write about what life must have been like in Sri Lanka during this time. Encourage students to consider the Europeans' motivations for control of the region, as well as the perceptions that a member of the Sinhalese or Tamil people might have about the conflicts. Remind students to use descriptive details to convey life in the region, what items might have been traded, and so on. Invite volunteers to share their journal entries with the class. Intrapersonal, Verbal/Linguistic

ANSWERS, p. 658

READING PROGRESS CHECK The conflicts and one-party or one-person rule has made it difficult for these countries to form democracies.

CRITICAL THINKING

1. The relationship between the Sinhalese and the Tamils has been full of tension and conflict.
2. The Sinhalese majority held most of the power in the postcolonial government, causing increased tension and protests from the Tamils that eventually led to a long civil war.

lama Buddhist monk

C In the 1950s, the Narayan descendants were overthrown. The king then ruled directly. For the next 40 years, Nepal's government wavered between representative government and direct rule, which provoked democratic protests. In 1990 the king yielded and allowed election of a parliament, but party rivalries prevented stability. This gave Communist Mao rebels the chance to increase their activities. In 1996 a conflict between Maoist rebels and government troops lasting more than a decade left thousands dead. In 2008 Nepal abolished the monarchy, but political parties have been unable to agree on a new constitution.

Buddhists from South Asia first settled the Maldive Islands, followed by Muslims in the twelfth century. The islands came under the control of the Portuguese in the late 1500s and later the Dutch. In 1887 the islands became a British protectorate. After gaining independence in 1965, Maldives became a republic, but had the same person and political party in power for four decades. In 2008 the country adopted a democratic government, but rival groups struggle for power.

The Sinhalese probably arrived in Sri Lanka from India during the 400s B.C. Subsequently, the Tamil people settled in Sri Lanka from southern India. For nearly a thousand years, these two groups have been rivals for control of the island.

W From the 1500s, European powers fought for control of Sri Lanka and its strategic location along trade routes. Portuguese merchants were followed by Dutch traders. The British had control of the entire island by 1815. They developed an economy based on growing coffee, tea, rubber, and coconuts. They brought in more Tamils to work on plantations. In 1948 Britain gave independence to Sri Lanka, at that time called Ceylon. The country adopted a parliamentary form of government. In 1972 it changed its name to the traditional form of Sri Lanka.

Sri Lanka was torn for decades by a civil war. The Tamil minority demanded a separate Tamil state, and many died in the fighting. The government declared an end to hostilities in 2009. Since then, Sri Lanka has had peace, but the underlying issues are unresolved and tension remains.

READING PROGRESS CHECK

Analyzing Why have these countries had difficulties forming democratic governments?

TIME LINE

ETHNIC Strife

Historically, the Sinhalese and the Tamils competed for power and influence in Sri Lanka, but after independence, their relationship grew increasingly hostile.

CRITICAL THINKING

1. ***Evaluating*** What has been the relationship between the Sinhalese and the Tamils in Sri Lanka?
2. ***Explaining*** How did the end of the colonial era change the relationship between the Sinhalese and the Tamils?

400s B.C.

400s B.C. Buddhist Sinhalese begin migrating to Sri Lanka from India, forming majority in Sri Lanka

200s B.C. Hindu Tamils begin to migrate to Sri Lanka from India, forming a minority in Sri Lanka

1505 Colonial period begins when the Portuguese arrive in Sri Lanka; Britain controls all of Sri Lanka by 1815.

1948 Sri Lanka gains independence; cooperation between Sinhalese and Tamils breaks down.

networks Online Teaching Options

GRAPHIC ORGANIZER

Human Geography of Bhutan, Maldives, Nepal, and Sri Lanka

Taking Notes Have students use this graphic organizer to improve their note-taking skills. As they read through the text, have them place the name of the country being discussed in the middle of the web, and then list details about the history, government, people, and economy of that country. Have them repeat this exercise for each of the four countries featured. AL Visual/Spatial, Verbal/Linguistic

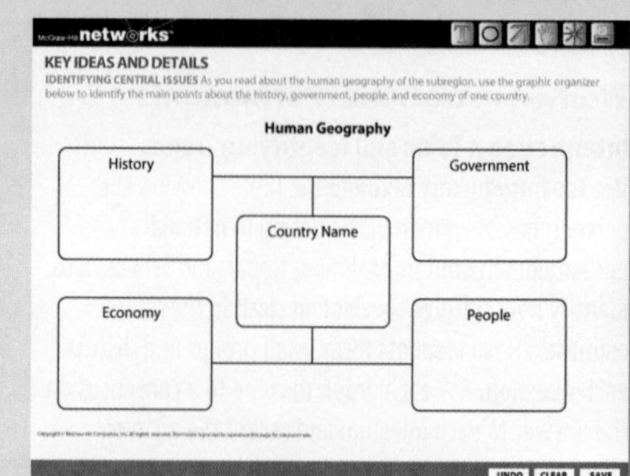

Population Patterns

GUIDING QUESTION *How do population density maps of Nepal and Bhutan reflect the rugged landscape of the two countries?*

Of the four countries in the subregion, Nepal is the most populous country with 30.9 million people. As population density maps of the country show, the population distribution reflects Nepal's physical geography. Nearly half of all Nepalese live in the Tarai Plain in the southeast, and just over 40 percent live in the midlevel elevation hills and valleys, such as the valley of Kathmandu.

Bhutan, with about 700,000 people, has a rugged terrain with people living in isolated pockets. Some parts of the Duars Plain are less populated even though they are in lowlands because they are swampy and harbor malaria-carrying mosquitoes. About 35 percent of Bhutan's people are of Nepalese ancestry. They live mainly in the south of the country, speak Nepali, and practice Hinduism. In 1988 Bhutan's government declared that many of these people were living in Bhutan illegally. Protests and demands for equal rights arose, and thousands of people fled. Today about 85,000 of these former residents of Bhutan live in Nepal in refugee camps. T

Sri Lanka has a population of 21.2 million people. Its highest population density is along the southwest coast near the capital, Colombo. Other areas of high density are around the Central Highlands city of Kandy, an important religious and commercial center, and on the northern part of the island. A chain of smaller cities runs along the west coast from Negombo to the north. Another cluster of cities is in the southeast from Batticoloa to Akkaraipattu.

About 200 of the islands in Maldives are inhabited. Another 100 islands have been reserved as tourist resorts. The most populous settlement is Male, the capital, with more than a third of the country's population. Maldives has 300,000 people, with another 100,000 living and working in foreign countries.

✓ READING PROGRESS CHECK

Identifying Cause and Effect What is the connection between the landforms and population density patterns in Nepal and Bhutan?

1950

1956 Prime Minister Solomon Bandaranaike declares Sinhalese the official language. Tamils rise in violent protest.

1965 Tamil-dominated United National Party wins election.

1970 Sirimavo Bandaranaike, widow of Solomon, comes to power and reinstates pro-Sinhalese policies.

1983 Thirteen Sinhalese soldiers killed in ambush by Tamil Tigers; civil war erupts

2000

2002 Cease-fire agreement signed. Ban against Tamil Tigers ends; Tamils drop demand for a separate state.

2006 New clashes erupt between government forces and Tamil Tigers.

C

TIME LINE

Ethnic Strife

Summarizing Have students read through the entire time line. Discuss with the class each event that is presented and how they relate to each other. Then, have students write a paragraph summarizing the relationship between the Sinhalese and Tamils from ancient times, when both groups migrated to Sri Lanka from India, until the present. AL **Verbal/Linguistic**

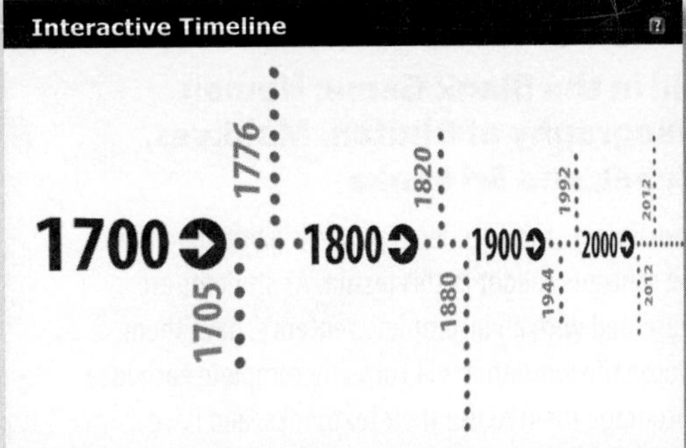

T Technology Skills

Changing Continuity of Groups Discuss with students the information about the population patterns in Nepal, Bhutan, Sri Lanka, and Maldives. Organize students into four groups and assign each group one of the four countries. Have each group research population density in their assigned country. Students should consult population density maps to identify the correlation between the region's physical geography and its impact on settlement patterns and population. Groups should present their findings in a multimedia presentation to the class. **Verbal/Linguistic**

C Critical Thinking Skills

Understanding Relationships Among Events Organize students into six groups and give each group a folded-up piece of paper with a year from the time line on it (either 1956, 1965, 1970, 1983, 2002, or 2006). Have students write down facts about ethnic strife that occurred during their assigned year based on the dates and events shown on the time line. Students may wish to conduct additional research to identify other key events that occurred in the region during that year. After students have had time to write down the information, collect the pieces of paper. Reinforce students' understanding of hostility between ethnic groups in Sri Lanka by having them recite their key facts in a "living" time line. Tell students in each group to arrange themselves in correct sequential order without referring to the time line in the text. Provide corrective guidance as needed. ELL **Kinesthetic, Logical/Mathematical**

ANSWERS, p. 659

✓ READING PROGRESS CHECK Few people live in the mountains and rugged terrain of Nepal and Bhutan or in the swampy areas of the Duars Plain in Bhutan. Most people in Nepal live in the Tarai Plain and midlevel elevation hills and valleys.

R Reading Skills

Determining Importance Have students write a short summary about the importance of religion in the region. Assess students' knowledge by having them use one or more content vocabulary terms in their responses. **Ask:** **What is an example of how Nepal has a blended culture?** *(Buddhism and Hinduism are blended since some Hindus and Buddhists both recite mantras.)* **How has the importance of Buddhism left its mark on Bhutan?** *(Bhutan is home to thousands of lamas and stupas, or Buddhist shrines, as well as fortified monasteries called dzongs that dot the countryside.)* ELL **Verbal/Linguistic**

V Visual Skills

Creating Charts Have students create a two-column chart that shows different aspects of Sri Lanka's two main ethnic groups, the Sinhalese and the Tamils. After students complete their charts, discuss the differences between Sri Lanka's ethnic groups. **Ask:** **What is the official language of Sri Lanka?** *(Sinhalese)* **What religion or philosophy do the Sinhalese practice?** *(Buddhism)* **What religion do the Tamils practice, and what language do they speak?** *(Tamils are Hindu and they speak Tamil, which has its origins in southern India.)* **What has caused these ethnic groups to clash over the years?** *(In addition to their different beliefs and languages, some members of the Tamils have sought an independent Tamil state, which has likely caused conflict in the region.)* **Visual/Spatial**

ANSWERS, p. 660

Connecting Geography Student answers will vary, but could include records and databases of births and deaths, travel and migration documents, and comparing art and literature of different cultures.

Connecting Geography to SCIENCE

Genetics

Social scientists research where the people living in a place come from—and how peoples from different areas mix. Now biochemists have a new tool to help them: detailed comparison of the genetic makeup of different peoples. Previous studies of the Nepalese showed that they have genetic connections to ancient populations from both South Asia and East Asia. Still unknown was whether the East Asian peoples came directly or went to India first, with their descendants moving into Nepal. In a study published in 2012, a team of scientists concluded, based on genetic similarities between Nepalese and Tibetans, that the migrants came directly from Tibet.

SPECULATING What other tools can geographers use to study the connections between peoples?

Society and Culture Today

GUIDING QUESTION *How do different cultures and religions coexist in Bhutan, Maldives, Nepal, and Sri Lanka?*

The populations of these four countries reveal ethnic and religious diversity as the result of centuries of population movement and cultural influence from surrounding regions. Ethnic diversity has sometimes led to clashes between peoples. It has also contributed to unique and fascinating cultures.

R The two main ethnic groups in Nepal are the Indo-Nepalese, whose ancestors migrated from India, and the Tibeto-Nepalese, whose ancestors came from Tibet. Sherpa are a Tibeto-Nepalese people known for their mountaineering skills. About half the people speak Nepali, but other languages are also spoken. Most of Nepal's people are Hindu. About 10 percent are Buddhists. Some aspects of Nepal's culture blend both Buddhism and Hinduism. Some Hindus and Buddhists recite **mantras**, sacred words or phrases that are repeated in prayers or chants. About four out of every five people live and work in rural areas, where they farm crops they sell in villages, herd animals, or produce traditional handicrafts.

The Bhote, who are also called Bhutia and Ngalops, make up about half the population of Bhutan and are descendants of Tibetan peoples. They practice Tibetan Buddhism, as do the Sharchops of eastern Bhutan. The official language of Bhutan, called Dzongka, is of Tibetan origin. Most people, however, speak other languages. Buddhism has left a strong mark on the country, which is home to about 4,500 monks, and thousands of **stupas**, or Buddhist shrines. In addition, the countryside is dotted by ***dzongs***, fortified monasteries that once served as administrative and commercial centers. A little over one-third of Bhutan's people live in cities, the largest of which is the capital of Thimphu, with only about 40,000 people. Rural people farm and raise livestock. Illiteracy has long been a problem in Bhutan. The government has recently devoted a major **portion**, or share, of its national budget to education. As a result, school enrollment and literacy rates are on the increase.

V Sri Lanka's two main ethnic groups are deeply divided along religious as well as ethnic lines. The Sinhalese majority, found mainly in the southwest, are Buddhist and speak Sinhalese, the official language of Sri Lanka. The Tamils live chiefly in the northern region of the island. They are Hindu and speak Tamil, which is related to the Dravidian languages of southern India. The move for an independent Tamil state arose among members of this group. Most of Tamils are descended from Indians brought to the island in the 1800s to work on plantations.

The earliest-known settlers in the Maldive Islands were probably from southern India, followed by the Sinhalese from Sri Lanka. Later, people from East Africa and Arab traders settled in the Maldives. Today people of Maldives speak the official language of Dhivehi, which is based on Sinhalese, as well as English.

Family and the Status of Women

The chiefly rural populations of these countries followed traditional lifestyles and family patterns for many centuries. In Sri Lanka, parents typically arranged marriages and brides were generally quite young. Married children lived in the same household as their parents, although the wives in the household tended to cook separately for their own smaller family unit. These patterns have changed in recent decades. About 1.6 million Sri Lankans live and work in other countries, and about 100,000 leave their homes to work in plantations on the island. About half the overseas workers are women. Sri Lanka's government is concerned that these women have few protections in the countries where they work and can be exploited and harassed. The number of migrant workers combined with other economic changes has altered family patterns in Sri Lanka. People tend to marry

mantra sacred words or phrases that are repeated in prayers or chants

stupa a dome-shaped structure that serves as a Buddhist shrine

dzong a fortified monastery that also served as an administrative and commercial center

portion a share of a whole

660

networks Online Teaching Options

GAME

Fill in the Blank Game: Human Geography of Bhutan, Maldives, Nepal, and Sri Lanka

Specifying Have students play this game to reinforce the concepts taught in this lesson. As students are presented with an incomplete sentence, have them choose the word that will correctly complete each idea. Encourage them to use their textbooks, and have higher-level students work with lower-level students to ensure success for all. When the game is completed, students can check their answers and make corrections as necessary. ELL AL BL **Verbal/Linguistic, Interpersonal**

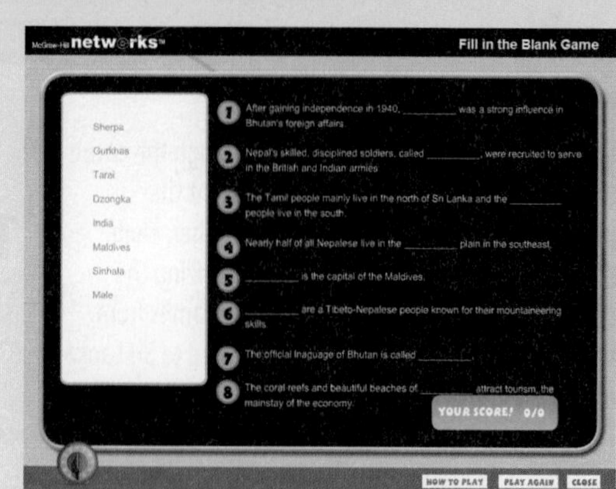

later than in the past, have fewer children, and live in nuclear families rather than extended families. People are living longer than in the past as well, which creates the need for support from family members and for government pensions and health care.

In traditional cultures, women often are second-class in status. Society in Nepal has long had a caste system similar to that of India, in which social status is set at birth. Males belonging to the highest caste—a tiny minority of the country's people—dominated society. Women, members of the lower castes, Muslims, and others had few rights. The country has tried to change this by making women's equality before the law a fundamental part of the constitution. Women have yet to make much progress. Women are pushing for laws that would give them the rights to own and inherit property.

In Bhutan, women traditionally enjoyed more rights. In fact, women in the family inherited property to ensure their economic security and make sure that they could care for both children and elderly family members. Women were as likely as men to be the head of the household and their work was valued equally with that of men. However, Bhutanese women play a very small role in government and politics—only one-fourth of the seats in the national legislature are held by women, compared to one-third of those in Nepal. In both Sri Lanka and Maldives, less than 10 percent of lawmakers are women. W1

Women's rights activists say the situation for women is worsening in Maldives. The rise of religious fundamentalism there threatens women's rights. Violence against women is a major problem, and the government is slow to enact a law against it.

The Arts

The artistic spirit is part of daily life in each of these countries. The Buddhist stupas of Nepal and Sri Lanka and the dzongs of Bhutan are works of art and architecture. They also reveal the importance of religion to these cultures. Dance is a popular cultural expression in Bhutan and Nepal and often tells religious or mythical stories. The Newar people of Nepal have a rich architectural and artistic tradition and built many religious shrines. In literature, Michael Ondaatje, who was born in Sri Lanka, won England's prestigious Booker Prize for his novel *The English Patient.* W2

✓ **READING PROGRESS CHECK**

Making Connections Why is it thought that the Tamils of Sri Lanka originated in southern India?

In Bhutan and Nepal, people fly colorful prayer flags, and prayer wheels twirl on many corners, sending out invocations. Monks chant mantras, or repetitive prayers. R

◄ **CRITICAL THINKING**

1. ***Drawing Conclusions*** Why is religion a strong force in these people's lives? Explain your answer.
2. ***Comparing*** What do other religions use that is similar to prayer flags? Why do you think Buddhists use prayer flags?

INTERACTIVE IMAGE

Prayer Flags

Researching Display the image. Ask students if they are familiar with prayer flags. Discuss the purpose of these flags as a class, using information from the text. Then have students research the origin, significance, and use of prayer flags in Bhutan and Nepal. When their research is complete, have students present their findings to the rest of the class. **AL Verbal/Linguistic**

Human Geography of Bhutan, Maldives, Nepal & Sri Lanka

W1 Writing Skills

Argument Have students choose one of the four countries in the subregion and write an argumentative essay about women's role in that country. Tell students to think about women's rights and equality in that society. Students should use information in the text to support their arguments but may also conduct online research if desired to identify specific examples of how that society treats women. Encourage students to form their own opinions about the issues facing women in their chosen country, but to base their opinions on facts gleaned from their research. Tell students to write a concluding statement that supports the argument presented in their essays. **BL Intrapersonal, Verbal/Linguistic**

W2 Writing Skills

Informative/Explanatory Have students write an informative paragraph about the relationship between art and religion in a specific culture in the region. For example, students might write about the Buddhist stupas of Bhutan or the significance of dance as a way to convey religious stories in Bhutan or Nepal. Suggest that students conduct research using online or library sources for examples of art, literature, architecture, dance, or music to cite in their paragraphs. **AL Verbal/Linguistic**

R Reading Skills

Defining Have students write down what they think is the meaning of the term *invocation.* Then have students look up the definition in an online or print dictionary. *(requesting help or support through prayer)* **ELL Verbal/Linguistic**

ANSWERS, p. 661

✓ **READING PROGRESS CHECK** The Tamils speak a language that is related to the Dravidian languages of southern India, and many people from southern India were brought to Sri Lanka to work on the plantations in the 1800s.

CRITICAL THINKING

1. Bhutan was controlled by Tibetan monks who introduced Buddhism early in its history; the country is still home to about 4,500 monks and numerous monasteries.
2. Other religions may use candles or rosaries to represent prayers or good wishes.

Human Geography of Bhutan, Maldives, Nepal & Sri Lanka

C Critical Thinking Skills

Evaluating Have students discuss the challenges and benefits of having few natural resources in the region. **Ask:** **How do these four countries of South Asia make up for having few resources?** *(The countries benefit economically from the tourism industry. Some export goods or services, and they all receive aid from wealthier countries.)*

T Technology Skills

Acquiring Information Have small groups of students conduct online resources to research the impact of the 2004 tsunami on the region. Assign each group an economic activity to research, such as farming or fishing, and have them collect information about the tsunami's impact on specific products, such as rice, shellfish, or tuna. Tell students to assign specific roles to each member of the group, and then present their findings in a slide show using presentation software. Culminate the activity with a class discussion that compares the tsunami to a natural disaster in the United States, such as Hurricane Katrina's impact on the Gulf Coast shrimp industry in 2005.
BL **Visual/Spatial**

CLOSE & REFLECT

Summarizing Ask students to describe the different aspects of the various cultures in the countries of the subregion and the influence of the subregion's history on that diversity. Have them summarize society and culture today and primary economic activities in the region.

ANSWERS, p. 662

✓ READING PROGRESS CHECK Agriculture and fishing provide not only food but make up a good portion of the exports of these countries. The tourism industry is also important in all these countries but particularly Maldives, which has few other options for economic development.

CRITICAL THINKING

1. The four countries of this subregion are not well developed economically, leading to low levels of education and health care and a low standard of living.
2. Factors such as environmental measurements, which include air and water pollution levels, or access to Internet, radio, and television.

South Asian Human Development Report

Country	Rank
United States (comparison)	3
Sri Lanka	92
Maldives	104
India	136
Bhutan	140
Pakistan	146
Bangladesh	146
Nepal	157

Source: United Nations Development Programme, 2013

The Human Development Index is based on three dimensions: health (life expectancy at birth); education (mean years of schooling and expected years of schooling); and standard of living (gross national income per capita).

▲ CRITICAL THINKING

1. ***Comparing and Contrasting*** Why do you think the four countries of this subregion rank where they do?
2. ***Analyzing*** Are there any other factors that you think should be included in a measure of a country's development? Why or why not?

recover to return to a previous level of performance after a decline

Economic Activities

GUIDING QUESTION *How important are farming and fishing to the people of Bhutan, Maldives, Nepal, and Sri Lanka?*

C The countries of South Asia have relatively few resources and are somewhat remote. As a result, they are not very economically well developed. Nevertheless, all these countries are connected to the world economy as tourist destinations. Some also export goods or services, and all receive development aid from more developed countries. All joined with Bangladesh, India, and Pakistan in 1985 to form the South Asian Association for Regional Cooperation (SAARC).

In the highlands of Nepal, farmers practice terracing, making use of arable land on the steep slopes. They also cultivate the highland valleys and the low-lying Tarai Plain. Almost three-fourths of the workforce is engaged in agriculture and herding. Chief crops are rice, wheat, and corn. Bhutan, like Nepal, also practices terracing to increase its arable area. Farmers in Bhutan also grow wheat and rice, as well as barley, vegetables, and fruit.

T Sri Lanka exports tea, rubber, and coconuts, as well as shrimp, lobsters, and fish. Rice is grown for domestic consumption. In 2004 a tsunami in the Indian Ocean caused widespread destruction in Sri Lanka and Maldives, including the devastation of the fishing industry. Fish catches of tuna and bonitos have declined because large-scale fishing operations from other countries are taking more fish and depleting the supply. The people of Maldives export fruits, vegetables, and coconut for food and oil.

Few major industries exist in these countries due to their lack of technical development. Sri Lanka mines and exports graphite. Precious and semiprecious stones are also mined. Food, tea, and rubber processing plants sell products globally. Bhutan has developed hydroelectric projects and sells electricity to India.

Hiking and white-water rafting are popular activities for tourists in Nepal, which also attracts visitors to its religious sites. Bhutan has moved in recent years to expand tourism. To protect the environment and its traditional culture, however, Bhutan restricts the number of tourists who may visit. In Sri Lanka, the tourism industry has **recovered** since relative peace has been restored. Tourism is a mainstay of the economy of Maldives, which attracts visitors with beautiful beaches and colorful coral reefs. The tourism industry was set back by the 2004 tsunami, which damaged some resorts, but it has since rebounded.

✓ READING PROGRESS CHECK

Summarizing How important is agriculture, fishing, and industry to the people of these countries?

LESSON 2 REVIEW

Reviewing Vocabulary (Tier Three Words)

1. ***Identifying*** Write a paragraph explaining how *dzongs*, lamas, mantras, and stupas are related to one another. RH.9–10.4

Using Your Notes

2. ***Considering Advantages and Disadvantages*** Use your graphic organizer on one of these countries to write a paragraph explaining the country's greatest advantages and its biggest challenges.

Answering the Guiding Questions

3. ***Explaining*** What factors influenced the present-day governments of Bhutan, Maldives, Nepal, and Sri Lanka?
4. ***Comparing and Contrasting*** How do population density maps of Nepal and Bhutan reflect the rugged landscape of the two countries?
5. ***Explaining*** How do different cultures and religions coexist in Bhutan, Maldives, Nepal, and Sri Lanka?
6. ***Comparing and Contrasting*** How important are farming and fishing to the people of Bhutan, Maldives, Nepal, and Sri Lanka?

Writing Activity

7. ***Argument*** In a paragraph, explain what you think can be done to settle conflicts between groups in Sri Lanka or Bhutan and why you think it would work. WHST.9–10.1

662

LESSON 2 REVIEW ANSWERS

Reviewing Vocabulary

1. Paragraphs will vary, but must include that lamas are Buddhist monks, *dzongs* are Buddhist monasteries that were historically administrative and commercial centers in Bhutan, mantras are sacred words or phrases that are repeated in prayers or chants by Buddhists, and stupas are Buddhist shrines.

Using Your Notes

2. Paragraphs will vary based on country, but challenges for all could include lack of health care and education, low standards of living, and lack of economic development. Advantages for all can be tourism, such as mountain climbing and rafting in Nepal and Bhutan or the beaches and scuba diving in Maldives and Sri Lanka.

Answering the Guiding Questions

3. Historic rule by kings and colonization influenced the modern-day governments of these countries.
4. Population density maps would show that Nepal and Bhutan are sparsely populated.
5. They often live in separate areas, as these differences have been a source of conflict.
6. Farming and fishing are very important as they provide food and exports for these countries.

Writing Activity

7. Paragraphs will vary depending on the country chosen, but could include increasing education, literacy, and understanding between peoples, and ensuring equal representation in government.

There's More Online!

- GRAPH Deforestation
- IMAGE Deforestation in Sri Lanka
- IMAGE Underwater Cabinet Meeting
- INTERACTIVE SELF-CHECK QUIZ
- VIDEO People and Their Environment: Bhutan, Maldives, Nepal & Sri Lanka

LESSON 3

People and Their Environment: Bhutan, Maldives, Nepal & Sri Lanka

Reading **HELP**DESK 

Academic Vocabulary

- extract
- generate

Content Vocabulary

- clear-cutting
- organic farming

TAKING NOTES: *Key Ideas and Details*

EVALUATING As you read about environmental issues in Bhutan, Maldives, Nepal, and Sri Lanka, use a graphic organizer like the one below to list key environmental issues facing each country.

Key Environmental Issues

Country	Issues
Bhutan	
Maldives	
Nepal	
Sri Lanka	

ESSENTIAL QUESTION • *How do physical systems and human systems shape a place?*

It Matters Because

As countries with developing economies, Bhutan, Maldives, Nepal, and Sri Lanka want to promote economic development so their people have better lives. At the same time, they have unique and fragile natural environments. They work to balance economic development and preservation of those environments. C

Managing Resources

GUIDING QUESTION *Why has sustainable development been given a low priority in the subregion?*

The countries of Bhutan, Maldives, Nepal, and Sri Lanka have few resources and are not well developed economically. With limited resources, there are few opportunities to pursue traditional methods of economic development such as industrialization. However, these countries do have the ability to protect their existing natural resources by managing them wisely.

In recent years, environmentalists and some economists have pushed the idea of sustainable development. This concept emphasizes seeking economic development in concert with other goals. These other goals include a more equal distribution of the benefits of economic development and reduced damage to the environment. R

There are obstacles to implementing sustainable development in the subregion. Countries are generally poor and lack advanced technology. They do not have the capital to invest in new technologies, and the population lacks the education needed to make use of the technology. People in the subregion live in scattered communities with strong local traditions that are sometimes at odds with the goals of sustainable development. Their isolation also makes communication difficult. In some places, government turmoil and conflicts have delayed development. These factors make it difficult to unite people in common approaches to the goals of sustainable development. V

ENGAGE

C Critical Thinking Skills

Considering Advantages and Disadvantages Have students read the paragraph. Tell students to create a two-column chart in which they list the advantages of development in one column and the disadvantages in the other. **Ask: Why do you think economic development might pose a threat to the region's natural environments?** *(Possible answer: Industrialization may help develop the region's economy, but it can harm the natural environment.)*

TEACH & ASSESS

R Reading Skills

Paraphrasing Have students work in pairs to read the paragraph, jotting down unknown or confusing words and phrases. Have students look up the definitions of the words and then use the words in sentences to clarify their meaning. Then have partners reread the paragraph and take turns paraphrasing it in their own words. **Ask: Why do you think "sustainable development" is not a top priority for governments in the subregion?** *(Student answers may vary, but might include that the economic benefits outweigh the costs of preserving natural environments.)* **ELL** **Verbal/Linguistic**

V Visual Skills

Expressing To reinforce students' understanding, have them create a web diagram that shows the reasons that the subregion struggles to implement sustainable development. **Ask: How does a region's geographic location impact its ability to grow its economy?** *(Possible answer: If a community is in a remote location, communication and transportation challenges add to its isolation, prohibiting it from becoming economically independent.)* **Visual/Spatial**

INTERACTIVE BELLRINGER

Two Atolls in Maldives

Interpreting Significance Use the introductory text and the image of two atolls in Maldives to identify the environmental challenges that Maldives faces due to its low-lying elevation and understand the efforts the national government of Maldives has taken to address environmental issues. Have students form small groups. Then have them discuss each question. Ask each group to record all possible answers to each question, but to come to a consensus on the best answer for each question. Have each group share its answers in a class discussion. **Interpersonal, Verbal/Linguistic**

Two Atolls in Maldives

Maldives is a chain of 1,192 small coral islands. It is the world's lowest-lying country, with an average elevation of 6 feet above sea level.

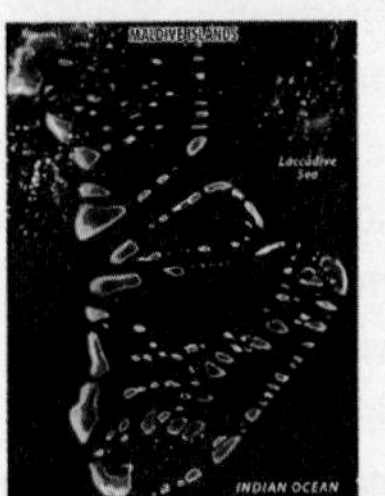

Auto-Run Click Through 1 of 3

ANSWERS, p. 663

TAKING NOTES: Bhutan—Deforestation, soil erosion, water pollution, and poaching; **Maldives**—Extraction of coral for building and jewelry making, climate change raises sea levels, which threaten all the low-lying islands as well as the reefs, coral reefs and other sea animals that feed in the reef are also lost when sea temperatures rise, increased demand for water straining the existing supplies in aquifers; **Nepal**—Deforestation by clear-cutting used by lumber companies as well as by people for fuel and farmland, soil erosion from deforestation, loss of food and habitat for animals, indoor air pollution from burning wood, poaching further threatens animals, water pollution threatens water supplies; **Sri Lanka**—Deforestation, including mangrove and tropical forests, leading to soil erosion and severe flooding, loss of habitat and food for animals, water pollution.

T Technology Skills

Acquiring Information Organize the class into small groups. Point out the term "Gross National Happiness" (GNH) to students. **Ask:** **What phrase does this term refer to as a play on words?** *(gross national product; gross national income)* Have students search the term "Gross National Happiness" online to acquire more in-depth information about the phrase as it applies to the country of Bhutan. They should identify specific information about the GNH Index, what it reveals about the people and government of Bhutan, and if the GNH Index could be applied to other countries in the subregion. Tell students to gather research to answer the following questions: What is the current status of Bhutan's GNH? Would King Jigme Singye Wangchuck be pleased with this status? Why, or why not? Invite groups to present their findings to the class in a summary paragraph. They should include their opinion as to whether or not the GNH is an effective tool for implementing sustainable development. **Interpersonal, Verbal/Linguistic**

C Critical Thinking Skills

Analyzing Cause and Effect Have students identify some of the causes and effects of deforestation in the subregion. **Ask:** **What human activities have caused deforestation to accelerate in recent years?** *(Commercial timber companies have used clear-cutting to harvest logs, and areas of forest have been cleared to make room for expanding settlements, agriculture, and to provide fuel for woodstoves.)* **What are the effects of these activities?** *(Burning wood indoors can lead to indoor air pollution and respiratory problems. Deforestation can cause temperatures to rise, exacerbating climate change.)*
BL Logical/Mathematical

ANSWERS, p. 664

READING PROGRESS CHECK The countries in the subregion lack the technology and the money to invest in new technologies for sustainable development. The people are generally poor with little education, which makes implementing new technology difficult. The relative isolation of communities also makes communication of new ideas and education difficult.

Nevertheless, these countries also have some advantages. The Buddhist and other traditions place value on all forms of life and teach respect for nature—ideas that are consistent with protecting the environment. The relative lack of modern technology means that they are not tied to more developed countries' production methods—methods that have often led to heavy pollution.

T The idea of sustainable development has taken hold in Bhutan. In 1972 King Jigme Singye Wangchuck coined the phrase "Gross National Happiness." This phrase describes his vision for Bhutan's future, a future that focuses not only on economic growth but also on broader social, cultural, and environmental concerns. Although King Jigme Singye Wangchuck stepped down from the throne in 2006, the country continues to focus on these concerns.

Although the countries of this subregion do not have abundant resources, they do have some. Forests cover much of Bhutan, and about one-third of both Nepal and Sri Lanka's land is forested. Bhutan has been more successful in protecting its forests than Nepal and Sri Lanka, where deforestation is a major problem. Both Nepal and Sri Lanka have tried to step up their efforts to protect the environment in recent years after years of political conflict absorbed government attention. Their efforts are still too recent to yield strong results, however. Maldives has moved to ban mining of coral and dredging of sand. In 2012 it announced an ambitious plan to turn the entire country into a biological reserve that would allow only sustainable fishing and other resource use. The government hopes to achieve this goal in just a few years. All of the countries have areas of natural beauty that attract visitors. Because it is an island, Sri Lanka is home to many unique plant and animal species that face extinction unless protected. These assets will only attract tourists if their natural beauty is protected and maintained.

READING PROGRESS CHECK

Summarizing What are the obstacles to sustainable development in this subregion?

Human Impact

GUIDING QUESTION *What environmental threats do these countries face?*

Human activity has had a devastating impact on the fragile environments of the countries in this subregion. Major environmental problems include deforestation and soil and water issues. Beaches and marine life have also been damaged.

clear-cutting the removal of all trees in a stand of timber

Centuries ago, much of South Asia was covered with forests. Today the region is in an environmental crisis, as deforestation has accelerated in recent years. According to some estimates, Sri Lanka lost as much as 20 percent of its forest cover between 1990 and 2010. Damage in Nepal was even worse—a decline of 25 percent over the same period. Commercial timber companies have used **clear-cutting**, or the removal of all trees in a stand of timber, to harvest logs. Areas of forest are also cleared to make way for agriculture and expanding settlements, as well as to provide fuel for woodstoves. Burning wood indoors for cooking and heating leads to indoor air pollution and respiratory problems. C

Whatever the reasons behind deforestation, the results are devastating. Environmentalists believe the destruction of mangrove forests in Sri Lanka made the coast more vulnerable to the devastation caused by the December 2004 tsunami. Losing tropical rain forests, as in Sri Lanka, has many damaging effects. Rain forests usually grow in poor soil where the complex root systems of trees efficiently absorb water and hold the topsoil in place. Additionally, as rainfall slowly filters through layers of leafy branches, the surrounding air is cooled. When rain forests disappear, soil erodes, rains produce floods, and temperatures rise.

664

networks Online Teaching Options

SLIDE SHOW

Paradise Lost

Interpreting Significance Play the slide show for students. Ask them if they find anything unique or surprising about the content. Have them discuss the significance of government members holding an underwater conference for an island nation dealing with environmental threats. Ask them if they believe this was an effective method to influence cabinet members to increase conservation efforts in the area.
BL Naturalist, Verbal/Linguistic

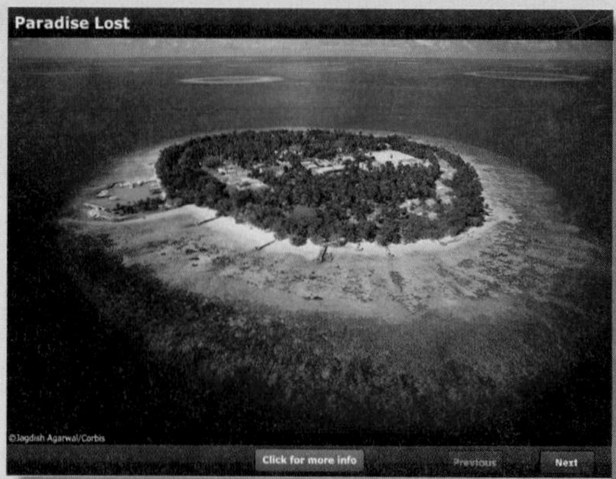

Soil erosion is also a problem when trees are cut in mountainous Nepal and Bhutan, where tree roots are also needed to hold soil in place to sustain agriculture.

Deforestation also affects South Asia's wildlife, which depend on the forests and other ecosystems for food and habitat. The region is home to an astonishing variety of wildlife. Elephants, water buffalo, and monkeys flourish in the rain forests of Sri Lanka. The Himalaya are home to the endangered snow leopard, musk deer, Himalayan black bear, red panda (firefox), and others. Bhutan's national animal, the takin, which is most closely related to the musk ox, is threatened by overhunting and habitat loss. All these animals are threatened by the spread of settlement that further reduces and fragments their habitat. Poaching, or illegal hunting, is also a threat.

Bhutan, Nepal, and Sri Lanka suffer from soil erosion, which means lost farmland, the possibility of mudslides, and the pollution of freshwater supplies. Industrial waste, agricultural runoff, and untreated human and animal waste threaten water supplies in Nepal and Sri Lanka. Groundwater in Nepal's Kathmandu and Pokhara valleys is so polluted that it is unhealthy to drink. The growing demand for water threatens the supply of freshwater in Maldives's aquifers.

Maldives is also seriously threatened by other problems. Coral is being **extracted**, or removed, from the coral reefs just offshore in order to make jewelry and to use as a building material. By depleting the coral reef, however, people have made the low-lying islands more vulnerable to high seas when major storms hit.

The government of Maldives has also grown increasingly concerned about the possibility of climate change. The rising sea levels would be a serious threat to a country that is generally only about 6 feet (1.8 m) above sea level. Warming also threatens the coral that protect Maldives. When ocean waters become too warm, the coral organisms that make up the reefs expel the algae that live inside them. The loss of algae causes the coral to lose its color, a process known as coral bleaching. Coral feed off the nutrients that the algae produce, and their loss often leads to death because of the reduced food supply. Since the coral is the foundation of the reef, other plants and animals are also threatened. A temperature spike in 1998 wiped out almost all the coral around Maldives. While the reefs recovered over time, high temperatures in 2010 caused another loss. **W**

Deforestation is a major environmental problem in Sri Lanka where timber companies have used clear-cutting.

▲ **CRITICAL THINKING**

1. ***Analyzing Visuals*** How does deforestation change habitats?
2. ***Making Connections*** What other problems does deforestation cause?

extract to withdraw or remove

☑ **READING PROGRESS CHECK**

Analyzing What are the most pressing environmental issues? Why?

Addressing the Issues

GUIDING QUESTION *What steps have the governments of Bhutan, Maldives, Nepal and Sri Lanka taken to improve the environment?*

The countries of this subregion have taken some steps to address environmental problems. Bhutan and Maldives have also become leading voices urging action toward sustainable development.

Bhutan's constitution requires that the country keep a minimum of 60 percent of its land forested. The government has stated its goals of relying on organic farming and having no emissions of carbon dioxide. **Organic farming** is the use

organic farming the use of natural substances rather than chemical fertilizers and pesticides to enrich the soil and grow crops

Eco Images/Universal Images Group/Getty Images

People and Their Environment: Bhutan, Maldives, Nepal & Sri Lanka

Making Connections

Guide students to understand that deforestation not only has a negative impact on humans but on wildlife as well. Have students read the information in the text about the impact of deforestation on South Asia's wildlife. Have students think about the wildlife of the region where they live. Have them identify ways that human activity can have a negative impact on the food and ecosystems of this wildlife. Then have students identify the similarities and differences between the impact in South Asia's wildlife and on their own home wildlife and ecosystems. If students are unable to identify wildlife in the region where they live, have them consider wildlife in other parts of the country where the detrimental human impact is evident. Have students discuss the comparisons as a class.

W Writing Skills

Informative/Explanatory Point out the term *coral bleaching*. Have students conduct online research about coral bleaching in Maldives. Tell students to gather facts and figures that convey the cause-and-effect relationship between climate change and coral ecosystems in Maldives. Instruct students to present their findings in an informative essay that includes online images, photos, or other visuals to support their findings. Encourage students to present their information to the class.
AL **Verbal/Linguistic, Visual/Spatial**

GAME

True or False Game: People and Their Environment: Bhutan, Maldives, Nepal, and Sri Lanka

Synthesizing Have students play this game to help them synthesize the information they have been presented with in this lesson. Have them read the statements regarding natural resources in Bhutan, Maldives, Nepal, and Sri Lanka, and decide whether the statements are accurate or not. After they have correctly identified each item, have them list at least one positive measure that each country has taken to protect its environment. **ELL** **AL** **Verbal/Linguistic, Naturalist**

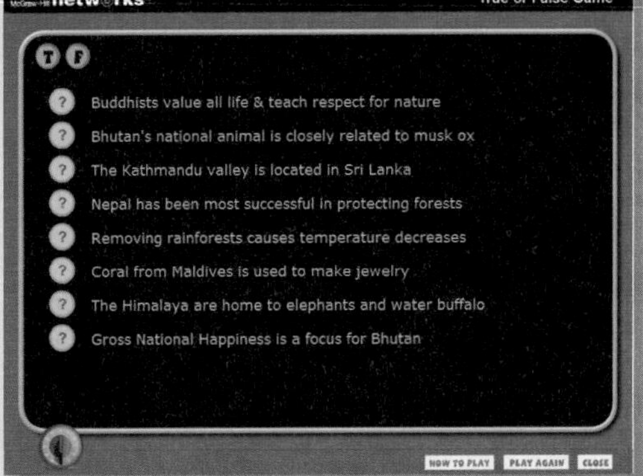
networks
True or False Game
Buddhists value all life & teach respect for nature
Bhutan's national animal is closely related to musk ox
The Kathmandu valley is located in Sri Lanka
Nepal has been most successful in protecting forests
Removing rainforests causes temperature decreases
Coral from Maldives is used to make jewelry
The Himalaya are home to elephants and water buffalo
Gross National Happiness is a focus for Bhutan
HOW TO PLAY
PLAY AGAIN
CLOSE

ANSWERS, p. 665

☑ **READING PROGRESS CHECK** Pressing environmental issues include deforestation, pollution of freshwater supplies, climate change, and destruction of the coral reefs in Maldives. Deforestation leads to soil erosion, loss of habitat, destructive mudslides, loss of farmland, and water pollution. Water pollution from erosion, industry, and waste threatens the limited supplies in Maldives aquifers and pollutes the many sources in other countries. The destruction of the coral reefs by people and warming sea temperatures threaten many other forms of sea life that depend on the reef for survival. Climate change could also cause sea levels to rise to the point that people could no longer live in Maldives.

CRITICAL THINKING

1. Deforestation removes the shelter and food sources for animals, which leads to animals becoming endangered.
2. Deforestation leads to soil erosion, which causes loss of farmland, increases mudslides, and pollutes water supplies.

W Writing Skills

Argument Have students consider if Nepal's government has done enough to implement plans for protecting the environment and preserving the nation's resources. Have students write an argumentative essay in which they defend or refute the following statement: Nepal's government has taken adequate steps in protecting the country's environment. Encourage students to conduct online research to identify specific facts to support their arguments. Have students present their essays to the class, using them to launch a discussion about government's dual role in economic development and preservation of resources. BL Verbal/Linguistic

T Technology Skills

Identifying Perspectives Guide students to understand the relationship between a country's economic status and its ability to reduce or limit threats due to climate change. Organize the class into four groups, assigning each group one of the countries in the subregion. Using reliable online sources, have groups identify what their assigned country's government is doing to address climate change. In gathering information, students should also identify how countries outside of the subregion are responding to the issue of reducing carbon emissions. Tell students to present a comparison using visuals, such as charts or graphs, to show how their assigned country's response to climate change compares with that of other countries. Students should also address how or if their assigned country has contributed to the Climate Change Trust Fund. Invite groups to present their findings to the class. I BL Verbal/Linguistic, Interpersonal

CLOSE & REFLECT

Problem Solving Have students review the various environmental issues discussed in this lesson. Tell students to choose one issue and brainstorm a possible solution with a partner. Have students share their solutions with the class.

ANSWERS, p. 666

READING PROGRESS CHECK Student answers may vary, but could include Maldives for taking a lead in addressing climate change and reducing carbon emissions; Sri Lanka for generating more than half of its electricity using hydroelectricity and other renewable sources; and Bhutan for its goal of keeping 60 percent of its land forested, commitment to organic farming, and emphasis on social and environmental issues rather than economic growth.

CRITICAL THINKING

1. Maldives is only a few feet above sea level, so rising sea levels pose a serious threat to the existence of the islands.
2. It draws attention to the issue of climate change and the very serious problems it can create, not just for Maldives, but for coastal communities around the world, motivating other governments to reduce their carbon emissions.

In 2009, to emphasize the threat posed by rising seas that might result from climate change, the government of Maldives held an underwater cabinet meeting.

▲ CRITICAL THINKING

1. ***Explaining*** Why would climate change be a particular threat to Maldives?
2. ***Analyzing*** What impact do you think an action like this will have on other governments? Why?

of natural substances rather than chemical fertilizers and pesticides to enrich the soil and grow crops. Carbon dioxide emissions are thought to add to climate change. The government has also urged other countries to move away from an emphasis on economic growth while ignoring its social and environmental costs. In 2012 Bhutan led a conference promoting these ideas. Bhutan has also worked with donor countries and outside experts, including the European Union, to promote its environmental policies.

W Nepal's government has also put in place policies aimed at protecting the environment and preserving resources. Critics say it has not gone far enough in actually implementing these plans. According to a recent report, the government has not followed through on its commitments. Nepal relies on foreign aid to fund more than half of its development efforts. Many of these donors have pushed for environmentally-friendly projects to bolster Nepal's efforts in this area.

Sri Lanka began to take steps to care for its environment in 1981, when it created the Central Environmental Authority. Twenty years later, it formed the Ministry of Environment and Natural Resources, raising environmental action to the cabinet level of government. Along with protecting some areas, the government has launched efforts to reduce household and plastic waste and promote environmental education among students. Recently the government began an initiative aimed at promoting sustainable development in ten areas. It points to some progress, including the fact that renewable resources **generate** more than half of its electricity, primarily hydroelectricity. It has also increased efforts to fight river water pollution.

T Maldives, worried that climate change threatens its very existence, has launched programs to try to limit the use of fossil fuels. Like Bhutan, its goal is to have no carbon dioxide emissions by 2020. To achieve that goal, it is pushing for increased use of solar energy, and it is importing more electric cars. Other countries are helping by contributing to a Climate Change Trust Fund set up by the World Bank. In addition, the leaders of Maldives are very active in all international discussions of the climate change issue, urging other countries—especially developed countries—to take steps to reduce their own carbon emissions.

READING PROGRESS CHECK

Analyzing Which country do you think has made the most progress in addressing environmental issues? Why?

generate to bring into existence

(t)Jagdish Agarwal/Corbis, (b)HO/Reuters/Corbis

LESSON 3 REVIEW 

Reviewing Vocabulary

1. ***Identifying*** Write a paragraph explaining why organic farming is thought to help the environment.

Using Your Notes

2. ***Comparing and Contrasting*** Use your graphic organizer on the key environmental issues of these countries to explain which country you think faces the most serious environmental issues.

Answering the Guiding Questions

3. ***Summarizing*** Why has sustainable development been given a low priority in the subregion?
4. ***Explaining*** What environmental threats do these countries face?
5. ***Summarizing*** What steps have the governments of Bhutan, Maldives, Nepal, and Sri Lanka taken to improve the environment?

Writing Activity

6. ***Argument*** Write a speech that the leader of Bhutan or Maldives might give urging developed countries to take steps to adopt sustainable development or to address climate change.

666

LESSON 3 REVIEW ANSWERS

Reviewing Vocabulary

1. Paragraphs will vary, but should include that organic farming uses natural substances instead of chemical fertilizers and pesticides that can run off into the water supply or build up in the soil.

Using Your Notes

2. Student answers may vary, but could describe the destruction of coral reefs in Maldives or deforestation in Nepal, Bhutan, and Sri Lanka.

Answering the Guiding Questions

3. Sustainable development has been given a low priority in the subregion due to lack of funds.
4. These countries face climate change, deforestation, soil erosion, poaching, and water pollution.
5. Bhutan requires 60 percent of its land to be forested, relies more on organic farming, and strives to have no carbon emissions. Nepal's government has put environmental policies in place. Sri Lanka created the Central Environmental Authority and formed the Ministry of Environment and Natural Resources. It is also generating more than half of the country's electric needs using hydroelectric power or renewable sources. Maldives is increasing solar energy use and importing electric cars, and has a goal of zero carbon emissions.

Writing Activity

6. Speeches will vary, but should address rising sea levels and temperatures in Maldives or loss of habitats for endangered animals in Bhutan.

CHAPTER 27 Assessment CCSS

Directions: On a separate sheet of paper, answer the questions below. Make sure that you read carefully and answer all parts of the questions.

Lesson Review

Lesson 1

1. ***Explaining*** Explain whether people living in Maldives are more likely to make a living through farming or fishing.
2. ***Assessing*** How have Nepal's rivers with fast-flowing streams been effectively used as a resource? What potential resource of fast rivers has not been fully developed?
3. ***Drawing Conclusions*** Is Bhutan's attitude toward tourism contradictory? Why or why not?

Lesson 2

4. ***Identifying Cause and Effect*** What was the main cause of European powers fighting for control of Sri Lanka?
5. ***Making Connections*** Identify three of the principal crops in Nepal. Explain whether it would be correct to state that the percentage of the Nepalese workforce engaging in agricultural work is not proportionate to the amount of farmland in Nepal.
6. ***Explaining*** Explain why industry is limited in Bhutan, Maldives, Nepal, and Sri Lanka.

Lesson 3

7. ***Describing*** What are the causes of the deforestation in Sri Lanka?
8. ***Identifying*** What are two major reasons the government of Maldives is extremely concerned about the possibility of climate change?
9. ***Summarizing*** Summarize Sri Lanka's environmental efforts from 1981 to the present day.

21st Century Skills

Use the image below to answer the questions that follow.

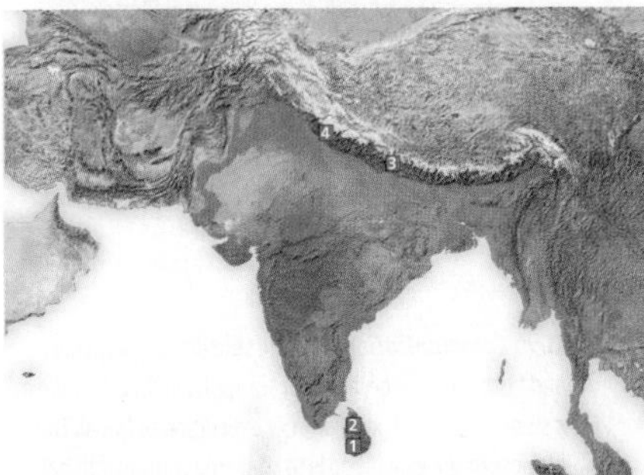

10. ***Geography Skills*** Identify the mountain range indicated by the number 3.
11. ***Creating Diagrams*** Explain the tectonic activity that resulted in this mountain range and create a diagram to show this tectonic activity.

Critical Thinking

12. ***Exploring Issues*** Explain how rising sea levels threaten Maldives. Discuss ways in which countries can cooperate to address this issue.

Applying Map Skills

Use the Unit 7 Atlas to answer the following questions.

13. ***Human Systems*** Of Bhutan, Maldives, Nepal, and Sri Lanka, identify the country with the greatest population density.
14. ***The World in Spatial Terms*** Use your mental map of South Asia to describe the following: the spatial relationship between the Himalaya and South Asia; the spatial relationship among the three major ranges of the Himalaya.
15. ***Places and Regions*** Identify the longest river in Sri Lanka.

Need Extra Help?

If You've Missed Question	1	2	3	4	5	6	7	8	9	10	11	12	13	14	15
Go to page	653	654	656	658	662	662	664	665	666	667	667	665	598	598	598

CHAPTER 27 Assessment Answers

Lesson Review

Lesson 1

1. The people of Maldives are more likely to make a living through fishing because they are surrounded by the Indian Ocean. Also, the islands have little land for growing crops.
2. Nepal has used its fast-flowing rivers to attract tourists interested in white-water rafting, but has yet to fully develop their potential for supplying hydroelectric power.
3. Bhutan's attitude is more cautious than contradictory toward tourism, as it desires the boost to the economy tourism can provide but does not want to damage the land or the culture of its people.

Lesson 2

4. European powers wanted control of Sri Lanka because of its location along important trade routes.
5. The three principal crops of Nepal are wheat, rice, and corn. It would be correct to state that the number of people working in agriculture is not proportionate to the amount of farmland, as most people work in farming but only a small amount of land is actually able to be farmed.
6. Industry is limited in these countries because they lack technical development.

Lesson 3

7. Deforestation is caused by timber companies who export wood and by people clearing land for farmland, development, and firewood.
8. The possibility of rising sea levels and increasing temperatures of seawater associated with climate change are concerns of the government.
9. Sri Lanka created the Central Environmental Authority more than 20 years ago and has since formed the Ministry of Environment and Natural Resources to help protect the environment and initiate programs to reduce household and plastic waste and to promote environmental education. It is also meeting more than half of the country's electric needs using hydroelectric power or renewable sources.

21st Century Skills

10. The Himalaya mountain range runs across the northern edge of South Asia.
11. The Himalaya range was formed by tectonic activity causing the Indian subcontinent to collide with the southern edge of Asia. Diagrams should show the collision between the two and the Himalaya being thrust up at the southern edge of Asia.

Critical Thinking

12. Maldives is generally only about six feet above sea level, which puts the islands at great risk from rising sea levels. Countries can cooperate to reduce carbon emissions, which are thought to contribute to climate change.

Applying Map Skills

13. Sri Lanka has the greatest population density.
14. The Himalaya mountain range runs across the northern edge of South Asia. The Greater Himalaya is the farthest north, the Lesser Himalaya is in the center, and the Outer Himalaya is to the south.
15. The Mahaweli is the longest river in Sri Lanka.

Assessment Answers

Exploring the Essential Question

16 Posters will vary, but must include a map of each country with the capital, major waterways and mountains, and locations of natural resources labeled, as well as a statement on a major challenge for each country. **Bhutan**—capital is Thimpu, Lesser and Greater Himalaya and Black Mountains, Torsa, Raidak, Sankosh, and Manas Rivers; **Maldives**—capital is Male, Indian Ocean, no rivers or mountains; **Nepal**—capital is Kathmandu, Churia, Mahabharat Ranges, Lesser and Greater Himalaya, Baghmati, Kosi, Gandak, and Karnali Rivers; **Sri Lanka**—capital is Colombo, Mount Pidurutalagala, Mahaweli River and Indian Ocean.

College and Career Readiness

17 Essays will vary, but should provide current environmental challenges and the culture of Nepal, including the two main ethnic groups: Indo-Nepalese from India and Tibeto-Nepalese from Tibet; about half of the people speak Nepali and most of the population is Hindu but about 10 percent are Buddhist; some parts of the culture are a result of the blending of Hinduism and Buddhism; four out of five people live and work in rural areas; Sherpa are a Tibeto-Nepalese people known for their mountain-climbing abilities; environmental challenges include deforestation, water pollution, and soil erosion.

Research and Presentation

18 Multimedia presentations will vary, but should explain the formation, initial work, current activities, and future plans of SAARC. Presentation should include maps, photographs, diagrams or graphs.

DBQ Analyzing Primary Sources

19 The quote helps to understand the excitement and desire to push the physical limits of the body to reach the top of Mount Everest.

20 Whittaker made repeated efforts to climb Mount Everest, just as the people of Nepal must keep trying to overcome the obstacles they face.

Writing About Geography

21 Editorials will vary, but should include arguments for and against increased tourism, which could include boosting the economy, harming the environment, and changing the culture of the people of Bhutan.

CHAPTER 27 Assessment 

Directions: On a separate sheet of paper, answer the questions below. Make sure you read carefully and answer all parts of the questions.

Exploring the Essential Question

16 ***Identifying Central Issues*** Create a poster divided into four sections, one for each of the following: Bhutan, Maldives, Nepal, and Sri Lanka. For each country, sketch a map and include labels to identify major features such as the capital, waterways, mountains, and locations of natural resources. Provide a brief statement for each country about a major challenge faced today.

College and Career Readiness

17 ***Clear Communication*** You are studying anthropology and history in college, and you are applying for a position as a student assistant on a summer expedition to Nepal. The purpose of the expedition is to study the culture of Nepal and report on the current interaction between the Nepalese and their physical environment. Write a one-page application essay to your professor to explain why you should be selected for the expedition. In your essay, detail your knowledge of the culture of Nepal and current environmental benefits and challenges in the country, explaining how you will be respectful of the culture as you conduct observation and research.

Research and Presentation

18 ***Gathering Information*** With a partner, conduct research to learn about the roots, development, and current activity of the South Asian Association for Regional Cooperation (SAARC). Provide a multimedia presentation to explain the following: when and why the organization was formed, initial work of the organization, growth of the organization, members of the organization, current activity, and planned future activity. Within your presentation, include maps, photographs, and diagrams or graphs.

DBQ Analyzing Primary Sources

Use the document to answer the following questions.

Mount Everest has attracted climbers who hope to scale its famously steep summit for decades. It is a difficult mountain to get to, and it is even more difficult to climb. However, despite the danger, many continue to attempt to ascend Mount Everest.

PRIMARY SOURCE

"Off in the distance, Everest's three-thousand-foot summit pyramid looms, nearly invisible in the night but unmistakably there. Its steep ribs of stone and ice gullies are not so much seen as conjured up in a brain starved for oxygen weary from driving a dying body up into the upper reaches of the ionosphere. Every time I see this peak—or even get close to it—the reaction never varies: excitement, intimidation, dread."

—Tom Whittaker, *Higher Purpose: The Heroic Story of the First Disabled Man to Conquer Everest*, 2001

19 ***Synthesizing*** How does the quote help you understand why so many people travel to Nepal to try to climb Mount Everest?

20 ***Analyzing*** How is Whittaker's effort to climb Mount Everest symbolic of the struggle of the people in Nepal to try to overcome obstacles?

Writing About Geography

21 ***Argument*** Use standard grammar, spelling, sentence structure, and punctuation to write an editorial of five to seven paragraphs about whether or not to support increased tourism in Bhutan. Be sure to address opposing arguments in your editorial.

Need Extra Help?

If You've Missed Question	16	17	18	19	20	21
Go to page	649	660	662	668	668	656

networks Online Teaching Options

WORKSHEET

Chapter Test and Lesson Quizzes

Assessing Have students complete the Chapter Test and Lesson Quizzes to assess student understanding throughout the chapter. These assessment tools offer chapter and lesson evaluation through a variety of question formats including document-based questions.

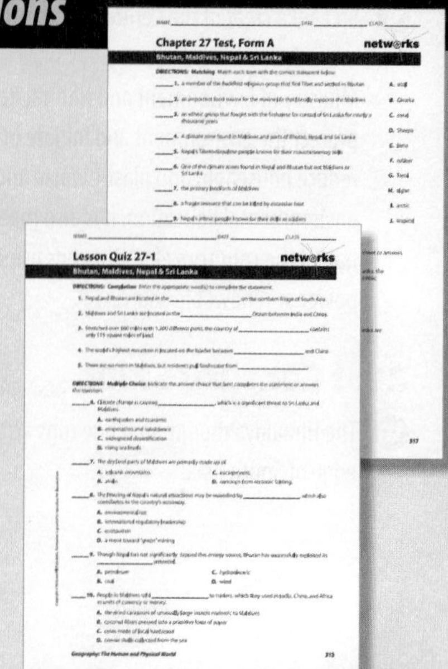

UNIT 8

EAST ASIA Planner

UNDERSTANDING BY DESIGN®

Enduring Understandings

- *The characteristics and distribution of human populations affect physical and human systems.*
- *Culture influences people's perceptions of places and regions.*
- *Cooperation and conflict among people influence the division and control of Earth's surface.*

Essential Question

- *How do physical systems and human systems shape a place?*

Students will know:

- *how physical geography varies from North Korea to South Korea and how this impacts human geography.*
- *how tectonic activity formed and affects life on the islands of Japan.*
- *the characteristics of culture and conflict and how they influence population patterns.*
- *the major influences to culture and art in this region.*
- *the types of minerals and resources important to each country's economy in East Asia.*
- *the economic activities and trade relations between the countries of East Asia and other countries.*
- *the effects of rapid industrialization on the environment in China and other East Asian countries.*

Students will be able to:

- ***analyze** the influence of ancient beliefs, cultures, and traditions on East Asia's history.*
- ***identify** factors that affect climate, vegetation, and population patterns.*
- ***explain** how industrialization and technology impact humans and the environment.*
- ***describe** environmental issues and how they are being addressed.*
- ***analyze** the trade relationships between countries inside and outside of East Asia.*

Predictable Misunderstandings

- *The countries of North Korea and South Korea are very similar.*
- *Ancient beliefs and religions have slowed industrialization and technology in this region.*
- *Most Asians share the same culture.*
- *China is densely populated.*
- *Japan is located on one island.*
- *Most Asian countries still have communist governments.*
- *Taiwan and Hong Kong are part of China. Tell students that while Hong Kong was returned to China by Britain in 1997, Taiwan's political status is less clearcut: most countries have accepted China's claim that Taiwan is one of its 23 provinces, but the United States maintains that Taiwan has been an independent republic since the Nationalists fled there in 1949.*

Assessment Evidence

Performance Tasks:

- *Environmental Case Study*
- *GeoLab Activity*
- *GIS Simulation*
- *Hands-On Chapter Projects*

Other Evidence:

- *Location Activity*
- *Self-Check Quizzes*
- *Lesson Quizzes*
- *Participation in Interactive Whiteboard Activities*
- *Contribution to small-group activities*
- *Interpretation of slide show images*
- *Participation in class discussions about East Asia*
- *Analysis of graphic organizers, graphs, and charts*
- *Lesson Reviews*
- *Chapter Assessments*

Key for Using the Teacher Edition

SKILL-BASED ACTIVITIES

Types of skill activities found in the Teacher Edition.

*V **Visual Skills** require students to analyze maps, graphs, charts, and photos.

R **Reading Skills** help students practice reading skills and master vocabulary.

C **Critical Thinking Skills** help students apply and extend what they have learned.

W **Writing Skills** provide writing opportunities to help students comprehend the text.

T **Technology Skills** require students to use digital tools effectively.

*Letters are followed by a number when there is more than one of the same type of skill on the page.

DIFFERENTIATED INSTRUCTION

All activities are written for the on-level student unless otherwise marked with the leveled labels below.

BL Beyond Level
AL Approaching Level
ELL English Language Learners

All students benefit from activities that utilize different learning styles. Many activities are marked as below when a particular learning style is highlighted.

Intrapersonal	**Naturalist**
Logical/Mathematical	**Kinesthetic**
Visual/Spatial	**Auditory/Musical**
Verbal/Linguistic	**Interpersonal**

SUGGESTED PACING GUIDE

Introducing the Unit	1 Day
Chapter 28: China	5 Days
Case Study: Are Limits on Growth Best for China?	1 Day
Chapter 29: Japan	5 Days
Global Connections: The Tohoku Earthquake and Tsunami	1 Day
Chapter 30: North Korea and South Korea	5 Days
TOTAL TIME	**18 Days**

PLANNER

Print Teaching Options

V Visual Skills

- ☐ **p. 671** Students analyze an image and discuss the importance of rivers. **ELL** Visual/Spatial
- ☐ **p. 672** Students study a map to answer questions about elevations. **AL** Visual/Spatial, Logical/Mathematical
- ☐ **p. 676** Students create graphs about the population density in East Asia. **BL** Visual/Spatial

R Reading Skills

- ☐ **p. 671** Students identify objects in the classroom that are manufactured in East Asia. **AL** Kinesthetic
- ☐ **p. 674** Students make inferences about human activity based on a map showing climate and vegetation. **AL** Visual/Spatial, Logical/Mathematical

C Critical Thinking Skills

- ☐ **p. 672** Students study a map to answer a question about agriculture and elevation. **AL** Logical/Mathematical, Visual/Spatial
- ☐ **p. 673** Students use a map scale to compare geographical information. Logical/Mathematical, Visual/Spatial
- ☐ **p. 675** Students study a map to make generalizations relating climate and land use. Logical/Mathematical, Visual/Spatial

W Writing Skills

- ☐ **p. 671** Students write an essay about ways in which one culture can influence other cultures. Verbal/Linguistic
- ☐ **p. 673** Students write a journal entry as if they were a teenager living in a city in East Asia. Verbal/Linguistic
- ☐ **p. 675** Students write a television or radio commercial to advertise a manufactured product from one of the countries in this region. **AL** Interpersonal, Verbal/Linguistic

T Technology Skills

- ☐ **p. 670** Students research a major city in East Asia and draw comparisons to a major city in the United States. Interpersonal
- ☐ **p. 674** Students research how vegetation affects land use in East Asia and then present their findings to the class. **BL** Visual/Spatial, Interpersonal
- ☐ **p. 675** Students research to present class reports on the economic benefits of resources in an area of East Asia. **BL** Visual/Spatial

Online Teaching Options

V Visual Skills

INTERACTIVE FEATURE **Explore the Region: East Asia**—Students write a statement about each of the images presented in the feature. Visual/Spatial, Verbal/Linguistic

INTERACTIVE MAP **Population Density Map: East Asia**—Students make a cause-and-effect graphic organizer highlighting the population issues in many East Asian countries. **BL** Logical/Mathematical, Visual/Spatial

INTERACTIVE MAP **Political Map: East Asia**—Students create a chart about the current political systems of East Asia's countries. **ELL** Visual/Spatial, Verbal/Linguistic

C Critical Thinking Skills

GEO @ WORK **Thinking Like a Geographer**—Students explore principles and skills of geography applied to real-world challenges. Visual/Spatial, Logical/Mathematical

INTERACTIVE MAP **Economic Activity Map: East Asia**—Students compare the nomadic herding activity in East Asia to another region in the world. Visual/Spatial, Logical/Mathematical, Verbal/Linguistic

W Writing Skills

INTERACTIVE MAP **Physical Map: East Asia**—Students write an informative essay about a Mt. Everest climbing expedition. **BL** Visual/Spatial, Verbal/Linguistic, Naturalist

INTERACTIVE MAP **Climate and Vegetation Maps: East Asia**—Students write a travel article about the climate and vegetation found in one of the cities in this region. Intrapersonal, Verbal/Linguistic

Printable Digital Worksheets

V Visual Skills

WORKSHEET **Location Activity**—Students locate countries, water systems, and physical features of East Asia.

WORKSHEET **GeoLab Activity**—Students explore how to use a model to understand how a tsunami forms and what affects the speed at which the tsunami waves travel.

C Critical Thinking Skills

WORKSHEET **Environmental Case Study**—Students complete a study about whether they think nuclear power is safe and should be used to generate electricity.

T Technology Skills

WORKSHEET **GIS Simulation**—Students utilize the techniques of GIS to research and prepare reports evaluating the effect that geography has on the transportation networks of China and Japan.

East Asia

Chapter 28
China

Chapter 29
Japan

Chapter 30
North Korea and South Korea

UNIT 8

WanRu Chen/Flickr/Getty Images

GEO @ WORK

Thinking Like a Geographer

Problem Solving Explore specific examples of the principles and skills of geography applied to real-world challenges that impact people's lives. From agriculture to urban planning, to wiping out disease and managing changes in society—geography plays a key role in understanding relationships and generating solutions that make sense. **Visual/Spatial, Logical/Mathematical**

ENGAGE

Creating Charts Have students read the list of chapter titles at the bottom of the page. Ask students to share what they know about one or more of the countries. Then have students create a four-column chart with the country's names as column headings. Tell students to label the rows with one or two topics that they would like to know more about. As students read through the unit, have them go back to their charts to add information.

TEACH & ASSESS

Inferring Direct students' attention to the photograph and have them analyze its details. **Ask:** **What can you infer about the people of East Asia based on this photograph?** *(Possible answer: The photograph of a pagoda in a natural setting indicates that people of East Asia value nature as well as ornamental architecture.)* **For what purpose do you think the building is used?** *(Possible answer: The building may be used for religious or spiritual purposes, or possibly as a museum.)* **Visual/Spatial**

Content Background Knowledge

Pagodas

- Pagodas are a common type of structure in Japan, China, and Korea.
- The structures, often associated with Buddhist temples, were first used in ancient India to symbolize mountains that were considered sacred.
- The domed shape of a Buddhist stupa was later used in China, where it evolved into an underground structure called a "dragon palace."
- In Japan, the pagoda style is represented by towering structures that are associated with the most popular form of pagodas.

CLOSE & REFLECT

Predicting Have students predict what they expect to learn about the physical geography, culture, and history of East Asia. Have students write their predictions to review after studying the unit.

ENGAGE

C Critical Thinking Skills

Comparing and Contrasting Call students' attention to the photograph and encourage them to analyze it by asking the following questions. **Ask:** **How does the image of this city compare to those you have seen of cities in the United States? Describe the similarities.** *(Possible answer: It is similar to pictures of cities in the United States. The city shown here has tall, modern skyscrapers that are similar to those in U.S. cities such as New York, San Francisco, and Chicago.)* **What does the appearance of this city tell you about the people who work in cities of East Asia?** *(Possible answer: People who work in East Asian cities are technologically advanced and value industry and business.)* **How does this city differ from how you picture rural life in East Asia?** *(Possible answer: Life in this city is much more hectic and fast-paced than life in rural regions of East Asia.)* **What employment opportunities might exist in a city like this as opposed to jobs found in the countryside of subregions in East Asia?** *(Possible answer: There are more job opportunities and a better selection of jobs, as there appears to be industry, technology, services, businesses, and infrastructure in the city shown. Rural areas have limited employment opportunities, as they may lack transportation or modern conveniences.)*

TEACH & ASSESS

T Technology Skills

Presenting Discuss with students how life in East Asian cities might be similar to or different from city life in the United States. Have students work in small groups to research a major city in East Asia for a short report (or assign groups specific cities to avoid redundant presentations). Encourage students to draw comparisons between their assigned city and a U.S. city with which their classmates may be familiar. Invite students to present their visual reports to the class. **Interpersonal**

1 Cities East Asia has several cities with many millions of people, where traditional culture is combined with modern skyscrapers and technology.

EXPLORE the REGION

A dynamic region of booming economies and bustling cities, **EAST ASIA** is also home to one of the world's oldest civilizations and to centuries-old traditions. Several countries in the region are major trading partners with the United States, and by virtue of their size and economic output, some countries in East Asia are among the most powerful and influential in the world.

Bob Charlton/Lonely Planet Images/Getty Images

THERE'S MORE ONLINE 

670

networks Online Teaching Options

INTERACTIVE FEATURE

Explore the Region: East Asia

Expressing Students can use this interactive feature as an introduction to the culture, cities and economies of East Asia. Have student pairs view the interactive feature and write a statement about each of the images presented in the feature. Have students share their statements to launch a discussion on the diversity found in this region. **Visual/Spatial, Verbal/Linguistic**

East Asia

INTRODUCTION

A dynamic region of booming economies and bustling cities, East Asia is also home to one of the world's oldest civilizations and to centuries-old traditions. Several countries in the region are major trading partners with the United States, and by virtue of their size and economic output, some countries in East Asia are among the most powerful and influential in the world.

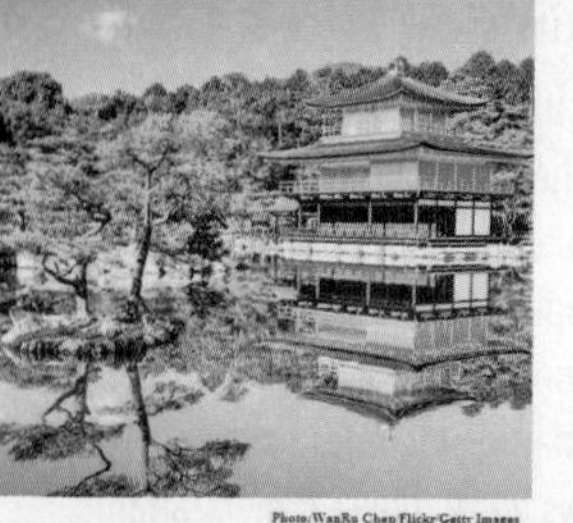

3 Economy Manufacturing and trade are major economic activities in East Asia, a region that includes four of the most productive economies in the world.

2 Farming The people of East Asia have relied on its rivers for thousands of years to bring water and fertile soil to their fields. Rice, long cultivated here, is a major staple of the diet, but China is also a major producer of wheat.

4 Culture China's culture, thousands of years old, has influenced other countries in the region. But those countries have also maintained their own traditions, like this Korean dance.

UNIT 8

East Asia

V Visual Skills

Explaining Point out to students that the photograph shows people in rice fields in East Asia. **Ask:** **Based on the photograph, why do you think rivers are so important to rice farmers in East Asia?** *(Possible answer: Judging from the photograph, rice needs a watery environment in which to grow, so rivers are important to producing a healthy rice crop.)* **ELL** **Visual/Spatial**

R Reading Skills

Identifying Trends Have a student volunteer read the text next to "Economy" on this page. Then ask students to stand next to or hold an object in the classroom or at their desks that may have been manufactured in an East Asian country. Ask one or two volunteers to see whether they can identify one that was produced in an East Asian country, reading a label if possible. Explain that while China is one of the world's most productive economies, it is also one of the largest export markets for products made in and shipped from the United States. **AL** **Kinesthetic**

W Writing Skills

Explanatory/Informative Have students read the information about culture and examine the photograph. Tell students to work with a partner to brainstorm examples of cultural influences in major U.S. cities. Explain that students may cite Chinatown in New York or San Francisco. Have students write a short essay about ways in which one culture can influence other cultures. **Verbal/Linguistic**

CLOSE & REFLECT

Formulating Questions Ask students to write two or three questions they would like to have answered in this unit. Then have students find the answers to the questions as they read through the unit.

DIGITAL WORKSHEETS

East Asia

Demonstrating Use these online digital unit worksheets to have students demonstrate their depth of knowledge and comprehension and to provide them with extended unit content through project-based activities.

- **Environmental Case Study**
- **GIS Simulation**
- **Location Activity**
- **GeoLab Activity**

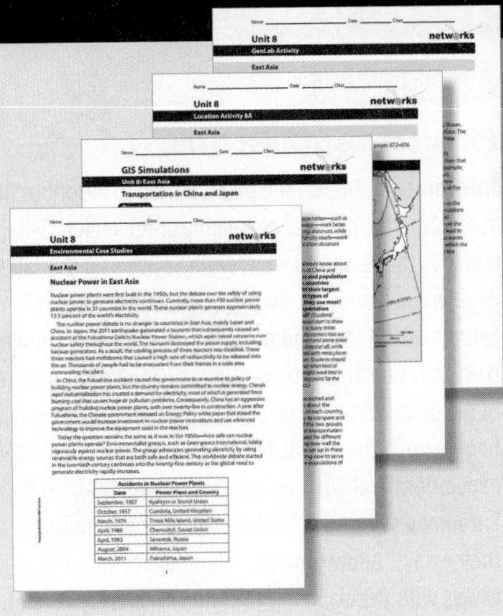

ENGAGE

R Reading Skills

Activating Prior Knowledge Have students examine the map and look for places they may have heard of, such as the Himalaya, Mt. Everest, or the Gobi. Ask volunteers to share information they may know about each place, such as the country in which it is located or a story about it from a book or in the news. Tell students that they will be learning more about these and other geographical features of East Asia as they study the maps in this unit.

TEACH & ASSESS

V Visual Skills

Reading Maps Have students work with a partner to locate each mountain in the Plateau of Tibet region. **Ask:** **What is the highest mountain peak in the region?** *(Mt. Everest)* **What do you think the climate is like in the region where these mountains are located?** *(Possible answer: The climate is probably colder at higher elevations with snow and ice covering the mountains.)* **What is the lowest point shown on the map?** *(the Turpan Depression)* **AL Visual/Spatial, Logical/Mathematical**

C Critical Thinking Skills

Evaluating Remind students to note the information in the map key. **Ask:** **How do you think daily life and agriculture differ in regions where elevations are 5,000 to 10,000 feet from those that are 1,000 to 5,000 feet?** *(Possible answer: Daily life for people who live in higher elevations is probably more challenging, since farming, a main occupation in rural areas, would be difficult in a mountainous terrain.)* **AL Logical/Mathematical, Visual/Spatial**

ANSWERS, p. 672

MAP STUDY

1. the Gobi
2. Chongqing, Wuhan, Nanjing, Shanghai

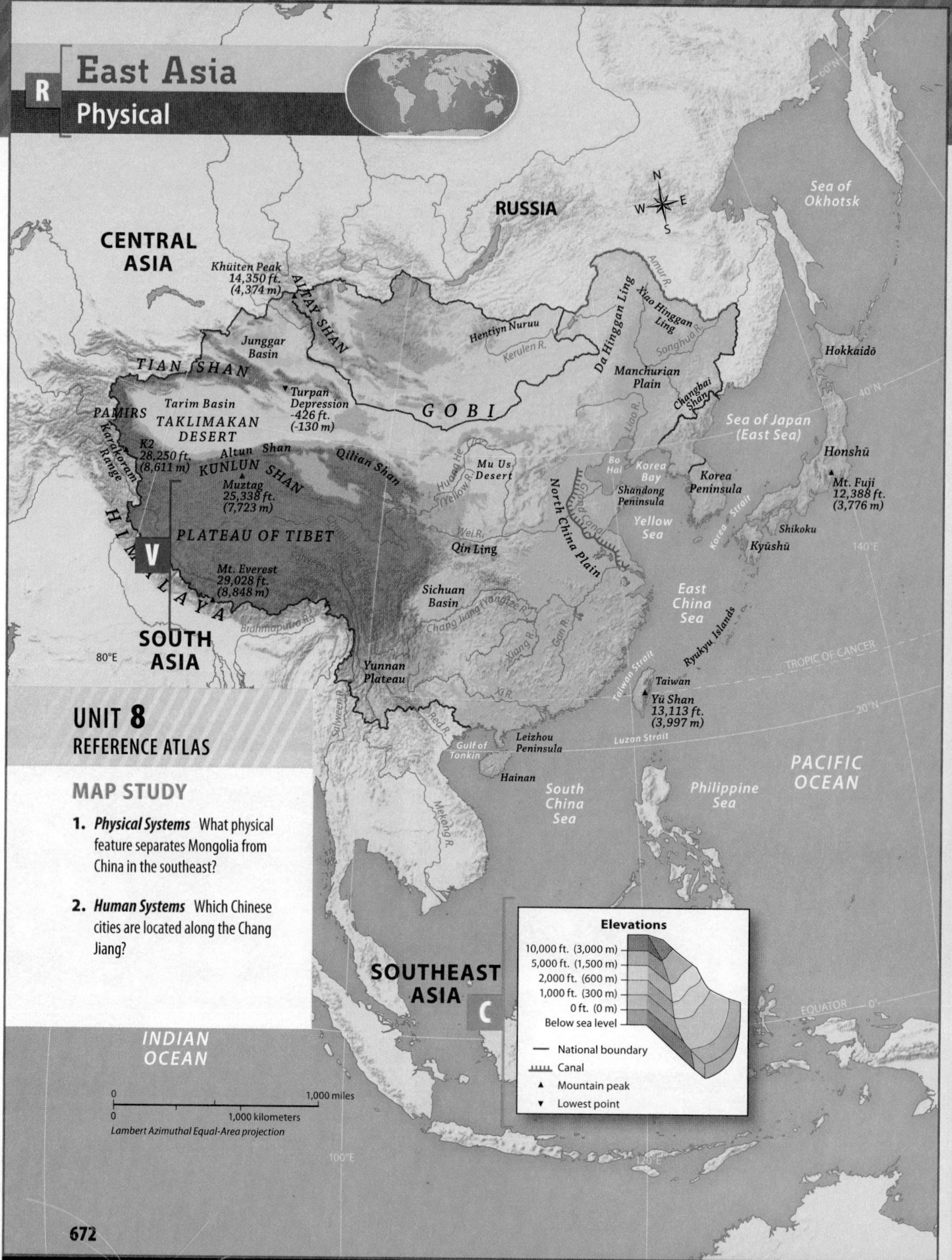

R
East Asia
Physical
RUSSIA
CENTRAL ASIA
Khüiten Peak 14,350 ft. (4,374 m)
ALTAY SHAN
Junggar Basin
TIAN SHAN
Tarim Basin
Turpan Depression -426 ft. (-130 m)
PAMIRS
TAKLIMAKAN DESERT
Karakoram Range
K2 28,250 ft. (8,611 m)
Altun Shan
KUNLUN SHAN
Muztag 25,338 ft. (7,723 m)
Qilian Shan
PLATEAU OF TIBET
HIMALAYA
V
Mt. Everest 29,028 ft. (8,848 m)
SOUTH ASIA
80°E
Hentiyn Nuruu
Kerulen R.
GOBI
Da Hinggan Ling
Xiao Hinggan Ling
Amur R.
Songhua R.
Manchurian Plain
Changbai Shan
Sea of Okhotsk
Hokkaidō
Sea of Japan (East Sea)
Honshū
Mt. Fuji 12,388 ft. (3,776 m)
Mu Us Desert
Huang He (Yellow R.)
Bo Hai
Korea Bay
Korea Peninsula
Shandong Peninsula
North China Plain
Grand Canal
Yellow Sea
Korea Strait
Shikoku
Kyūshū
Wei R.
Qin Ling
Sichuan Basin
Chang Jiang (Yangtze R.)
East China Sea
Ryukyu Islands
Brahmaputra R.
Yunnan Plateau
Taiwan Strait
Taiwan
Yü Shan 13,113 ft. (3,997 m)
TROPIC OF CANCER
Salween R.
Red R.
Xi R.
Gulf of Tonkin
Leizhou Peninsula
Luzon Strait
Hainan
South China Sea
Philippine Sea
PACIFIC OCEAN
Mekong R.
SOUTHEAST ASIA
C
INDIAN OCEAN
EQUATOR
Elevations
10,000 ft. (3,000 m)
5,000 ft. (1,500 m)
2,000 ft. (600 m)
1,000 ft. (300 m)
0 ft. (0 m)
Below sea level
National boundary
Canal
Mountain peak
Lowest point
0 1,000 miles
0 1,000 kilometers
Lambert Azimuthal Equal-Area projection
100°E
120°E
140°E
40°N
20°N
60°N

UNIT 8
REFERENCE ATLAS

MAP STUDY

1. ***Physical Systems*** What physical feature separates Mongolia from China in the southeast?
2. ***Human Systems*** Which Chinese cities are located along the Chang Jiang?

672

networks Online Teaching Options

INTERACTIVE MAP

Physical Map: East Asia

Regional Atlas: East Asia
Map Key
Elevations
Navigator
CENTRAL ASIA
RUSSIA
GOBI
SOUTH ASIA
SOUTHEAST ASIA
PACIFIC OCEAN

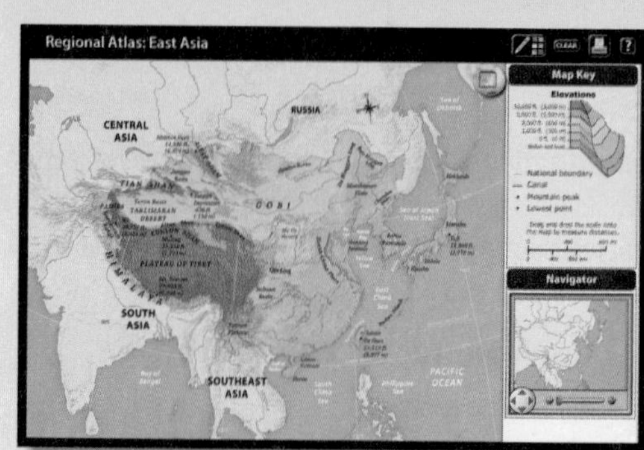

Informative Display the physical map to introduce the students to the physical geography of the region. Tell students that East Asia shares wih South Asia the tallest peak in the world, Mt. Everest. Have them locate Mt. Everest on the map and note its elevation. Ask student pairs to research the many famous expeditions or ascent of the mountain that have taken place over the years, beginning in the 1800s. Tell them to choose one of these expeditions and write an informative essay about it. Encourage students to include maps or other visuals with their essays. Allow time for volunteers to share their essays with the class. **BL Visual/Spatial, Verbal/Linguistic, Naturalist**

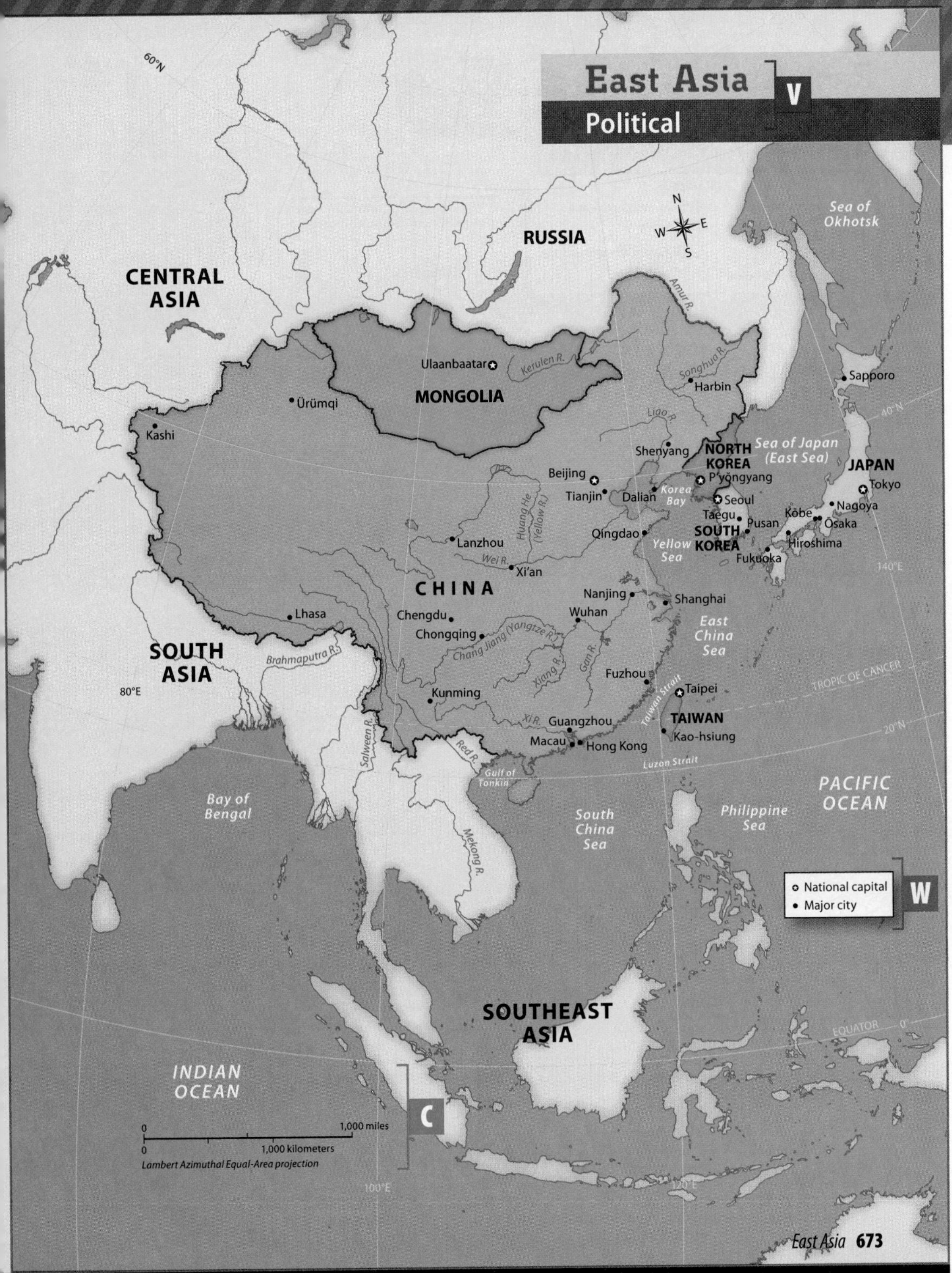

East Asia
Political

RUSSIA
CENTRAL ASIA
MONGOLIA
CHINA
NORTH KOREA
SOUTH KOREA
JAPAN
TAIWAN
SOUTH ASIA
SOUTHEAST ASIA
Ulaanbaatar
Ürümqi
Kashi
Harbin
Shenyang
Beijing
Tianjin
Dalian
P'yŏngyang
Seoul
Taegu
Pusan
Sapporo
Tokyo
Nagoya
Kobe
Osaka
Hiroshima
Fukuoka
Qingdao
Lanzhou
Xi'an
Nanjing
Shanghai
Wuhan
Chengdu
Chongqing
Lhasa
Kunming
Fuzhou
Taipei
Kao-hsiung
Guangzhou
Macau
Hong Kong
Sea of Okhotsk
Sea of Japan (East Sea)
Korea Bay
Yellow Sea
East China Sea
South China Sea
Philippine Sea
PACIFIC OCEAN
INDIAN OCEAN
Bay of Bengal
Gulf of Tonkin
Luzon Strait
Taiwan Strait
Amur R.
Songhua R.
Kerulen R.
Liao R.
Huang He (Yellow R.)
Wei R.
Chang Jiang (Yangtze R.)
Gan R.
Xiang R.
Xi R.
Red R.
Mekong R.
Salween R.
Brahmaputra R.
TROPIC OF CANCER
EQUATOR
60°N
40°N
20°N
0°
80°E
100°E
140°E

○ National capital
• Major city

0 — 1,000 miles
0 — 1,000 kilometers
Lambert Azimuthal Equal-Area projection

East Asia 673

V Visual Skills

Creating Charts Discuss the location of different cities shown on the map. **Ask:** **What can you infer about the countries of China and Mongolia based on the number of major cities?** *(Possible answer: China is a larger country so it has many more major cities than Mongolia, but Mongolia has only one major city, its capital.)* Have students choose one city from each country in the region to identify its population. Have students create a chart or graph to organize the data. Then have students add to their charts information such as which country is biggest, smallest, coastal, landlocked, and other facts. **AL Visual/Spatial**

W Writing Skills

Narrative Ask students to choose a city on the map and conduct research about its geographic size, population, industries, educational opportunities, and other facts. Then have students write a journal entry describing a day in the life of a teenager living in that city, using information from their research to enhance their stories. **Verbal/Linguistic**

C Critical Thinking Skills

Comparing Ask students to use the map scale to compare geographic information on the map. **Ask:** **About how many miles is Beijing from Hong Kong?** *(just over 1,200 miles, or 1,931 kilometers)* **What geographic advantages does Hong Kong have compared to Beijing?** *(Student answers may vary, but should include that Hong Kong is a port city, which benefits shipping and trade, whereas Beijing is inland.)* **Compare the geographic locations of Taipei and Tokyo.** *(Possible answer: Both are capital cities located on islands in the Pacific Ocean.)* **Logical/Mathematical, Visual/Spatial**

INTERACTIVE MAP

Political Map: East Asia

Creating Charts Display the political map to discuss the countries of East Asia with students. Have students work with a partner to research the current political system in place for each country. Tell them to create a chart listing the country name, its political system, and the dates showing how long that system has been in place for the country. Have partners share their charts with another set of students to compare their findings. Then guide a class discussion asking students to explain which country appears to have the most stable government based on the length of time it has been in place. **ELL Visual/Spatial, Verbal/Linguistic**

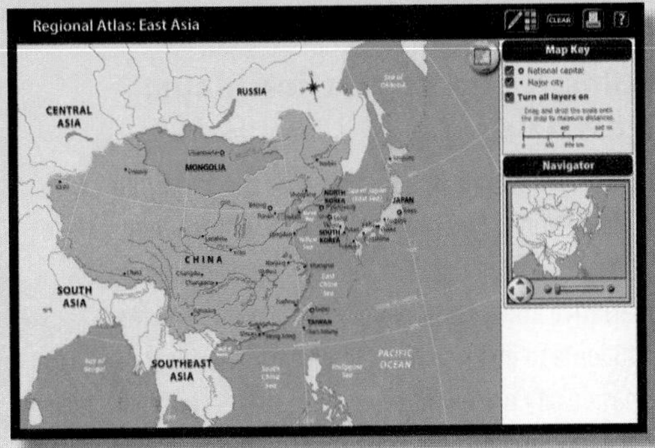

C Critical Thinking Skills

Drawing Conclusions Have students use the map key to identify the major climate zones in East Asia. **Ask:** **Why do you think there are so few cities located in the yellow regions shown on the map?** *(These areas have arid climates with vegetation made up of desert scrub and desert waste, so it would be difficult for cities to develop in those regions.)* **AL Visual/Spatial, Logical/Mathematical**

T Technology Skills

Presenting Point out the inset map at the bottom left of the larger map. Assign student pairs different countries or subregions of East Asia to determine how vegetation affects land use. Invite students to research data on land use and economic activities for their assigned country or region, recommending specific websites if needed. Have partners present their findings to the class in a short report, including visuals. Then have students revisit their inferences made in the activity above to see whether they were correct. **BL Visual/Spatial, Interpersonal**

R Reading Skills

Inferring Have students review the Vegetation map key and identify the different regions shown on the map. **Ask:** **How do you think vegetation impacts human activity in the different regions shown on the map? Provide at least one example.** *(Possible answer: Vegetation, or a lack of it, can impact human activity in a variety of ways. For example, regions with desert scrub are likely to have less human activity because the land is not adequate for farming. Regions with grasslands and forests will likely have more human activity because they are more suitable for raising stock and crops.)* **AL Visual/Spatial, Logical/Mathematical**

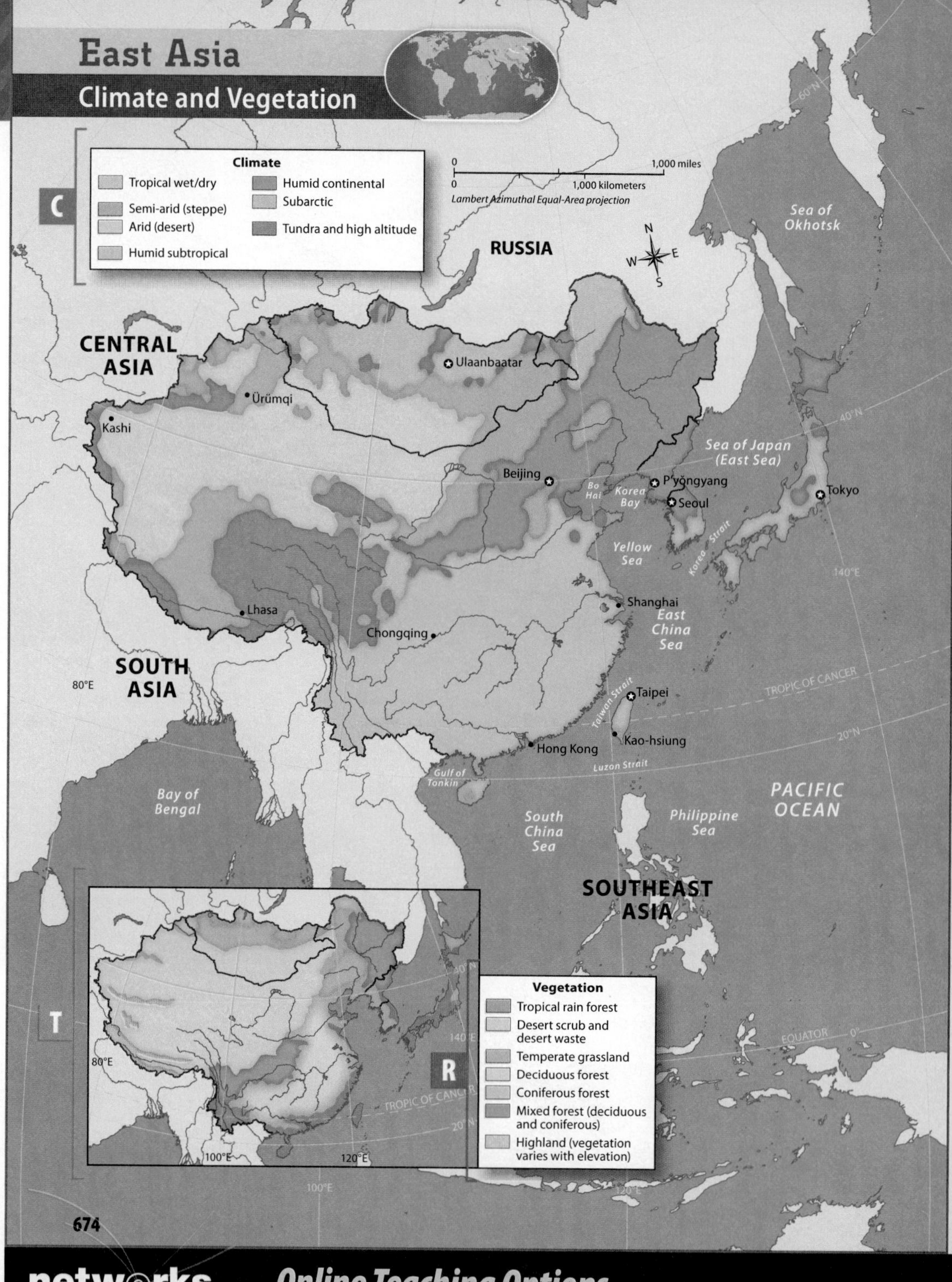

networks Online Teaching Options

INTERACTIVE MAP

Climate and Vegetation Maps: East Asia

Narrative Use this map to discuss the variations in climate and vegetation of East Asia with students. Have them choose one of the cities on the map and write a narrative about the city for a travel magazine. Ask students to imagine what it might be like to travel to a seaside city or one that is located in a desert scrub area. Their narratives should describe the sights, sounds, smells, and textures of the city, as well as climate information. Have students share their narrative with a small group of classmates. Have each group decide, based on the narratives, which city they would like to visit. **Intrapersonal, Verbal/Linguistic**

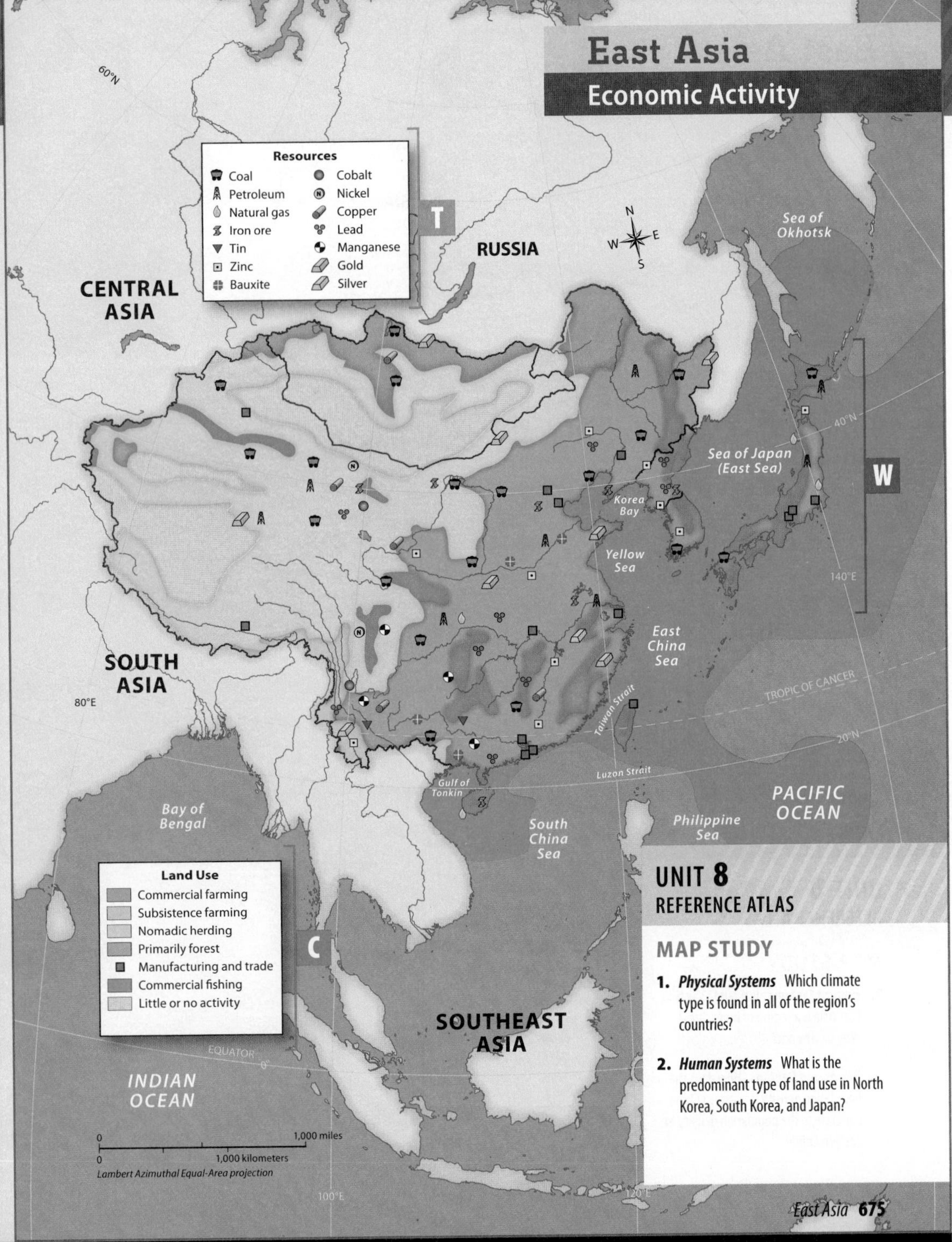

East Asia
Economic Activity

Resources
- Coal
- Petroleum
- Natural gas
- Iron ore
- Tin
- Zinc
- Bauxite
- Cobalt
- Nickel
- Copper
- Lead
- Manganese
- Gold
- Silver

Land Use
- Commercial farming
- Subsistence farming
- Nomadic herding
- Primarily forest
- Manufacturing and trade
- Commercial fishing
- Little or no activity

CENTRAL ASIA
RUSSIA
SOUTH ASIA
SOUTHEAST ASIA
Sea of Okhotsk
Sea of Japan (East Sea)
Korea Bay
Yellow Sea
East China Sea
Taiwan Strait
Luzon Strait
Gulf of Tonkin
South China Sea
Philippine Sea
PACIFIC OCEAN
Bay of Bengal
INDIAN OCEAN
TROPIC OF CANCER
EQUATOR
60°N 40°N 20°N 0° 80°E 100°E 120°E 140°E

0 — 1,000 miles
0 — 1,000 kilometers
Lambert Azimuthal Equal-Area projection

UNIT 8
REFERENCE ATLAS

MAP STUDY

1. ***Physical Systems*** Which climate type is found in all of the region's countries?
2. ***Human Systems*** What is the predominant type of land use in North Korea, South Korea, and Japan?

East Asia 675

T Technology Skills

Changing Continuity in Economics Assign students (or pairs) one of the 14 resources listed in the resources map key. Have students conduct online research to identify products that are made or manufactured from their assigned resource and how the resource or products benefit the region's economy. Have students present the information in a report that incorporates graphs and charts to show the economic benefits of their resource. Tell students to note in their reports whether availability of certain resources has played a role in the region's economy. **BL Visual/Spatial**

W Writing Skills

Narrative As a class, discuss how climate, vegetation, and the presence of natural resources can impact a region's economy. Point to Japan as an example, discussing its various resources. Then organize students into groups and assign each group a subregion of East Asia. Tell students to use their imaginations to write a television or radio commercial advertising one of the products manufactured in their assigned subregion. Have groups present their commercials to the class.
AL Interpersonal, Verbal/Linguistic

C Critical Thinking Skills

Making Generalizations Have students compare the land-use data with that of the climate data on the map on the previous page. **Ask: What generalizations can you make about East Asia's climate and land use from looking at the two maps?** *(Possible answer: Humid subtropical and humid continental climates are suitable for commercial farming and forestry, while arid regions are used for nomadic herding.)* **Why do you think land along coastal regions is used for manufacturing and trade more than inland areas?** *(Possible answer: Coastal regions are closer to ports where shipping is key to transporting manufactured goods.)* **Logical/Mathematical, Visual/Spatial**

INTERACTIVE MAP

Economic Activity Map: East Asia

Comparing and Contrasting Display this map to introduce the economic activities of East Asia to students. Ask students to study the map and the land use key. Point out that nomadic herding is an important economic activity in East Asia. Tell students to look back at the climate and vegetation map to find the climate types associated with the regions in which nomadic herding is popular. Then ask them to find another part of the world in which nomadic herding is an essential economic activity today. Have students write two paragraphs comparing and contrasting those two areas. **Visual/Spatial, Logical/Mathematical, Verbal/Linguistic**

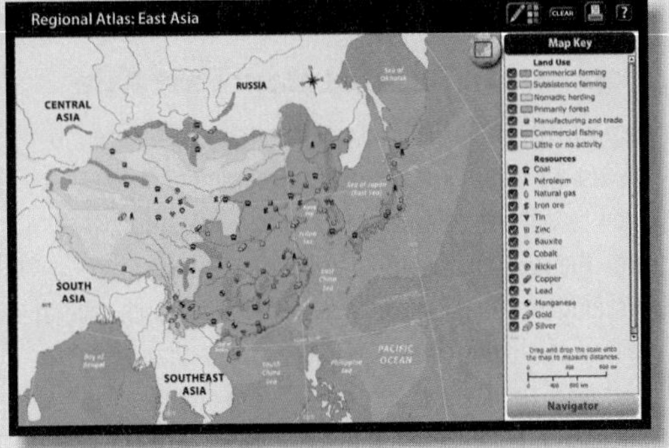

ANSWERS, p. 675

MAP STUDY

1. humid continental
2. commercial farming (could also be commercial fishing)

V Visual Skills

Creating Graphs Discuss with students how subregions in East Asia have varied populations, depending on a number of factors. Have students work in pairs to create a graph that shows the population density of a region in East Asia and how it relates to that region's topography, climate, and natural resources. Encourage students to use the other maps in this unit as a reference for their information. Invite partners to present their graphs to the class. **BL Visual/Spatial**

C Critical Thinking Skills

Comparing and Contrasting Have students locate the largest cities in East Asia shown on the map. **Ask:** **How do you think life in Japanese cities differs from life in Ürümqi, based on the region's cities and populations?** *(Possible answer: Japan has many more populated cities, so they are probably more crowded, whereas life in Ürümqi is less crowded because it is in a region with 63–249 people per square mile.)* **Visual/Spatial, Logical/Mathematical**

Making Connections

To help students understand the relative populations of East Asian cities, provide them with comparisons to the five most populous U.S. cities:

- New York, New York: 8,269,639
- Los Angeles, California: 3,823,316
- Chicago, Illinois: 2,705,248
- Houston, Texas: 2,126,196
- Philadelphia, Pennsylvania: 1,538,567

*2011 estimates

CLOSE & REFLECT

Summarizing Organize students into five groups, assigning each group one of the unit maps. Have groups collaborate to write a paragraph summarizing of their assigned map as it relates to East Asia, and then share it with the class.

ANSWERS, p. 676

MAP STUDY

1. Yes, the region has 11 cities over 5,000,000.
2. Western China is less densely populated.

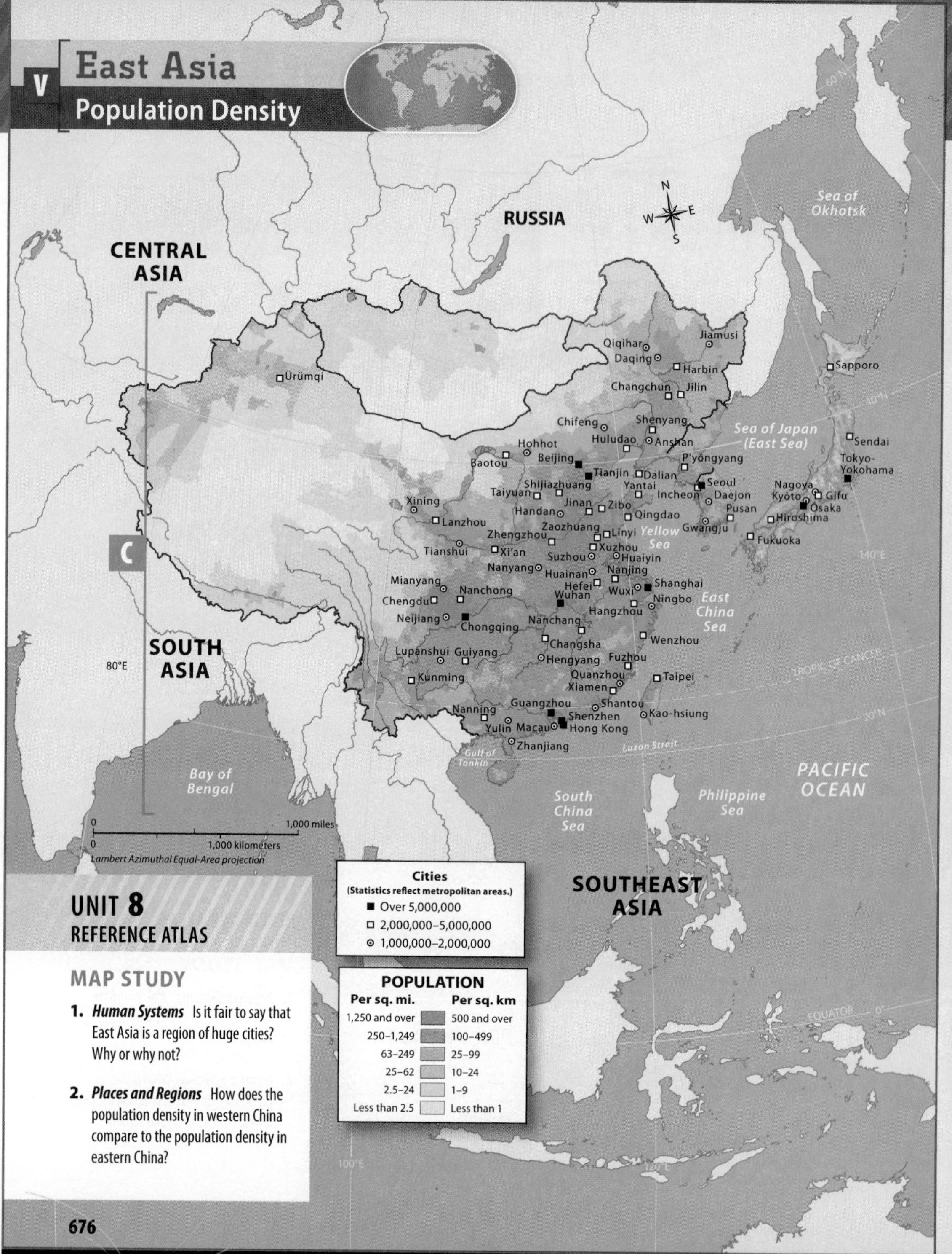

UNIT 8
REFERENCE ATLAS

MAP STUDY

1. ***Human Systems*** Is it fair to say that East Asia is a region of huge cities? Why or why not?
2. ***Places and Regions*** How does the population density in western China compare to the population density in eastern China?

networks Online Teaching Options

INTERACTIVE MAP

Population Density Map: East Asia

Exploring Issues This interactive map can be used to discuss with students the issue of rapid population growth in many countries of East Asia. Ask students to note the most densely populated areas on the map. Working in small groups, have students research several effects of rapid growth, specifically those that apply to East Asia. Then as a group, tell them to organize the information they gather into a cause-and-effect graphic organizer. Ask groups to choose the two effects that they think are most important for the region to address. Have groups share their choices and reasoning with the class. **BL Logical/Mathematical, Visual/Spatial**

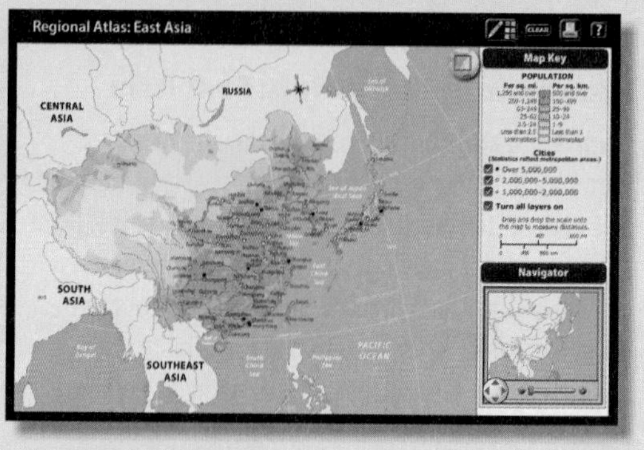

CHAPTER 28

China and Mongolia Planner

UNDERSTANDING BY DESIGN®

Enduring Understandings

- *The characteristics and distribution of human populations affect physical and human systems.*

Essential Question

- *How do physical systems and human systems shape a place?*

Predictable Misunderstandings

Students may think:

- *China and Mongolia are communist countries. Explain that Mongolia adopted a democratic constitution when Soviet communism collapsed in the 1990s and that China has been pursuing modernization and limited capitalism since the 1970s.*
- *Chinese people speak Chinese. Explain that a majority of Chinese people are of Han ethnicity and speak Mandarin, as there is no official language known as "Chinese." Mandarin is the language taught in schools. In addition, there are many ethnic minorities, each with their own language.*

Assessment Evidence

Performance Tasks:

- *Hands-On Chapter Project*

Other Evidence:

- *Guided Reading Activities*
- *Vocabulary Activities*
- *Lesson Quizzes*

SUGGESTED PACING GUIDE

Introducing the Chapter	½ Day	Case Study	1 Day
Lesson 1	1 Day	Lesson 3	1 Day
Lesson 2	2 Days	Chapter Wrap-Up and Assessment	½ Day

TOTAL TIME 6 Days

National Geography Standards covered in "China and Mongolia"

The student knows and understands:

(4) The physical and human characteristics of places

4.1 The effects of place-based identities on personal, community, national, and world events

4.2 The interaction of physical and human systems result in the creation of and changes to places

(7) The physical processes that shape the patterns of Earth's surface

7.3 Physical processes interact over time to shape particular places on Earth's surface

(9) The characteristics, distribution, and migration of human populations on Earth's surface

9.2 Population distribution and density are a function of historical, environmental, economic, political, and technological factors

(11) The patterns and networks of economic interdependence on Earth's surface

11.4 Improvements in transportation and communication networks reduce the effects of distance and time on the movements of people, products, and ideas

(12) The process, patterns, and functions of human settlement

12.2 Settlements can grow and/or decline over time

(13) How the forces of cooperation and conflict among people influence the division and control of Earth's surface

13.3 Changes within, between and among countries regarding division and control of Earth's surface may result in conflict

(14) How human actions modify the physical environment

14.1 Human modifications of the physical environment can have significant global impacts

14.3 People can either mitigate and/or adapt to the consequences of human modifications of the physical environment

(16) The changes that occur in the meaning, use, distribution, and importance of resources

16.2 The spatial distribution of resources affects patterns of human settlement and trade

(17) How to apply geography and interpret the past

17.1 Geographic contexts (the human and physical characteristics of places and environments) can explain the connections between sequences of historical events

17.2 The causes and processes of change in the geographic characteristics and spatial organizations of places, regions, and environments in the past

Key for Using the Teacher Edition

SKILL-BASED ACTIVITIES

Types of skill activities found in the Teacher Edition.

* **V Visual Skills** require students to analyze maps, graphs, charts, and photos.

R Reading Skills help students practice reading skills and master vocabulary.

C Critical Thinking Skills help students apply and extend what they have learned.

W Writing Skills provide writing opportunities to help students comprehend the text.

T Technology Skills require students to use digital tools effectively.

*Letters are followed by a number when there is more than one of the same type of skill on the page.

DIFFERENTIATED INSTRUCTION

All activities are written for the on-level student unless otherwise marked with the leveled labels below.

BL Beyond Level
AL Approaching Level
ELL English Language Learners

All students benefit from activities that utilize different learning styles. Many activities are marked as below when a particular learning style is highlighted.

Intrapersonal	Naturalist
Logical/Mathematical	Kinesthetic
Visual/Spatial	Auditory/Musical
Verbal/Linguistic	Interpersonal

CHAPTER OPENER PLANNER

Students will know:

- *the location of landforms and rivers in China and Mongolia and how they affect life.*
- *the types of minerals and resources that are important to the economies.*
- *the factors affecting climate and vegetation in China and Mongolia.*
- *rural and urban population patterns and major ethnic groups.*
- *China's economic activities and trade relations with other countries.*
- *the effects of rapid industrialization on the environment and how environmental threats are being addressed in the region.*

Students will be able to:

- ***identify*** *the landforms and major rivers in China and Mongolia and how they influence life.*
- ***identify*** *minerals and resources that are important to the region.*
- ***identify*** *factors that influence climate and vegetation in the region.*
- ***describe*** *urban and rural population patterns and ethnic groups.*
- ***analyze*** *China's economic activity in relation to other countries.*
- ***explain*** *how rapid industrialization affects the environment and how issues are being addressed in the region.*

UNDERSTANDING BY DESIGN®

☑ Print Teaching Options

V Visual Skills

- ☐ **p. 679** Students discuss China's plans for meeting its energy needs in the future based on an infographic. ELL

R Reading Skills

- ☐ **p. 678** Students consider how energy needs differ between agricultural- and industrial-based economies.

C Critical Thinking Skills

- ☐ **p. 677** Students discuss causes and effects of environmental problems that result from a country's rapid growth.
- ☐ **p. 678** Students discuss the steps China is taking to meet its growing demand for energy.

W Writing Skills

- ☐ **p. 679** Students write an article describing positive and negative effects of using their selected energy resource. AL **Verbal/Linguistic**

T Technology Skills

- ☐ **p. 679** Students create a chart to compare energy use in the region. **Verbal/Linguistic**

☑ Online Teaching Options

C Critical Thinking Skills

- ☐ GRAPH **Energy Use in China Per Capita**—Students use a graph to examine how China's per capita energy use has increased between 1995 and 2009. AL **Visual/Spatial**
- ☐ MAP **Interactive Regional Atlas**—Students use the interactive regional atlas to understand the physical and human geography of China and Mongolia.

☑ Printable Digital Worksheets

- ☐ WORKSHEET **Assessing Background Knowledge**—Determine the level of prior knowledge students have about China and Mongolia.
- ☐ WORKSHEET **Chapter Summary**—Students review the main idea of each lesson of the chapter content.
- ☐ WORKSHEET **Vocabulary Activity**—Students apply their knowledge of content and academic vocabulary words.

Project-Based Learning 

Hands-On

Create Ideogram Report

Students create ideogram reports that bring together information about the physical and human geography of China and the interactions between people and the environment.

Digital Hands-On

Create Online Projects

Find an additional activity online that incorporates technology for this project. Visit the EdTech Teacher Web sites for more links, tutorials, and other resources.

Print Resources

ANCILLARY RESOURCES

This ancillary is available for every chapter and lesson.

- **Chapter Tests and Lesson Quizzes**

PRINTABLE DIGITAL WORKSHEETS

These printable digital worksheets are available for every chapter and lesson.

- **Assessing Background Knowledge**
- **Chapter Summaries**
- **Guided Reading Activities**
- **Hands-On Chapter Projects**
- **Quizzes and Tests**
- **Reading Essentials and Study Guide** AL
- **Reteaching Activities**
- **Video Activities**
- **Vocabulary Activities**

More Media Resources

SUGGESTED VIDEOS MOVIES

- **China's Century of Humiliation** (1 h. 17 min.)
- **China from the Inside** (240 min.)
- **China: The Rebirth of an Empire** (86 min.)

SUGGESTED READING 

- ***China Goes Global: The Partial Power,*** by David Shambaugh
- ***China: A History,*** by John Keay
- ***China: Portrait of a People,*** by Tom Carter

Physical Geography of China and Mongolia

Students will know:
- *the location and characteristics of China's and Mongolia's landforms.*
- *the location and influence of China's major rivers on how people live.*
- *the types of minerals and resources that are important to China's and Mongolia's economies.*
- *factors affecting climate and vegetation in China and Mongolia.*

Students will be able to:
- ***identify** the landforms in China and Mongolia.*
- ***analyze** how major rivers influence how people live.*
- ***identify** minerals and resources that are important in China's and Mongolia's economies.*
- ***identify** factors that influence climate and vegetation in the region.*

UNDERSTANDING BY DESIGN®

☑ Print Teaching Options

V Visual Skills

- ☐ **p. 682** Students create a chart to compare the major climate regions and biomes of China. AL Visual/Spatial
- ☐ **p. 683** Students analyze a map to help them explain monsoon activity in China. Verbal/Linguistic
- ☐ **p. 684** Students describe an image showing terraced farmland in China. AL Visual/Spatial

R Reading Skills

- ☐ **p. 682** Students create a written flowchart explaining the sequence involved in transforming rock into fertile soil. ELL Visual/Spatial
- ☐ **p. 684** Students make a list of China's natural resources and how they are used. Verbal/Linguistic

C Critical Thinking Skills

- ☐ **p. 681** Students discuss important river systems in China. ELL Verbal/Linguistic
- ☐ **p. 683** Students describe the rain shadow phenomenon in their own words. BL Logical/Mathematical
- ☐ **p. 684** Students gather news stories about recent typhoons in East Asia or hurricanes in the Western Hemisphere in order to compare and contrast the storms and the damage done by them. BL Logical/Mathematical

W Writing Skills

- ☐ **p. 681** Students write about a water system in the region. Verbal/Linguistic

T Technology Skills

- ☐ **p. 680** Students research a physical feature and how it affects China and then use presentation software to share pictures of the feature. BL Verbal/Linguistic, Visual/Spatial
- ☐ **p. 682** Students research the importance of bamboo or the mulberry tree to the Chinese people and their economy. BL Naturalist

☑ Online Teaching Options

V Visual Skills

- ☐ INTERACTIVE BELLRINGER **East Asian Monsoons**—Students use the text and map showing the direction of seasonal winds to identify the factors affecting climate in China and Mongolia. Interpersonal, Visual/Spatial, Verbal/Linguistic
- ☐ INTERACTIVE WHITEBOARD ACTIVITY **Mountains, Rivers, and Plains**—Students identify the names of China's major landforms in a chart, match the characteristic given, and slide the characteristics of three rivers into the correct columns. AL Visual/Spatial

R Reading Skills

- ☐ INTERACTIVE MAP **Physical Geography of China and Mongolia**—Students analyze the map to understand how China and Mongolia have a variety of landforms and discuss their prior knowledge of these landforms. AL Visual/Spatial
- ☐ GAME **Physical Geography of China and Mongolia**—Students complete a crossword puzzle about human or physical geography in China and Mongolia. AL Verbal/Linguistic

☑ Printable Digital Worksheets

R Reading Skills

- ☐ WORKSHEET **Guided Reading Activity**—Students use the Guided Reading Activity worksheets to review their comprehension of the content.

C Critical Thinking Skills

- ☐ WORKSHEET **Video Activity**—Students answer questions related to a topic in the chapter content after they have viewed a lesson video.

LESSON 2 PLANNER

HUMAN GEOGRAPHY OF CHINA AND MONGOLIA

Students will know:

- *rural and urban population patterns in China and Mongolia.*
- *major ethnic groups and where most people live.*
- *government and beliefs in ancient times.*
- *how modern times have brought changes in government and the economy.*
- *China's economic activities and trade relations with other countries.*

Students will be able to:

- ***describe** urban and rural population patterns.*
- ***identify** major ethnic groups in China and Mongolia.*
- ***describe** the government structures.*
- ***analyze** modern changes to government and the economy.*
- ***analyze** China's economic activity in relation to other countries.*

UNDERSTANDING BY DESIGN®

☑ Print Teaching Options

V Visual Skills

- ☐ **p. 691** Students analyze graphs to compare U.S. exports to China with U.S. imports from China. Verbal/Linguistic

R Reading Skills

- ☐ **p. 688** Students locate areas of dense and sparse populations on physical and population density maps of China. Verbal/Linguistic
- ☐ **p. 690** Students list the ways communism and a changing economy have impacted families and women in China. AL Verbal/Linguistic

C Critical Thinking Skills

- ☐ **p. 685** Students make comparisons between the Shang and the Zhou dynasties. ELL Logical/Mathematical
- ☐ **p. 685** Students brainstorm what they know about Confucianism. AL Verbal/Linguistic
- ☐ **p. 688** Students discuss China's ethnic makeup. ELL Logical/Mathematical
- ☐ **p. 689** Students discuss the positive and negative aspects of living under a communist regime. BL Logical/Mathematical
- ☐ **p. 690** Students describe the changes China's agricultural sector has experienced since 1949. BL Verbal/Linguistic

W Writing Skills

- ☐ **p. 686** Students use the time line to write a brief paragraph about the history of China from 1940 to the present. ELL Verbal/Linguistic
- ☐ **p. 688** Students imagine they are citizens of China and write a letter to a government official explaining why they believe that all children should go to school. ELL Intrapersonal, Verbal/Linguistic

T Technology Skills

- ☐ **p. 686** Students create a time line to show the rise and fall of Chinese dynasties over time. ELL Verbal/Linguistic
- ☐ **p. 689** Students research an art form of China, such as poetry, opera, or pottery, and make a multimedia presentation to show the art form. Auditory/Musical, Visual/Spatial

☑ Online Teaching Options

V Visual Skills

- ☐ VIDEO **Around the World–Shanghai**—Students watch a video to learn more about rapid development in modern Chinese cities such as Shanghai and complete a worksheet about the video. AL Visual/Spatial
- ☐ INTERACTIVE TIME LINE **Modern China**—Students examine events on the time line that show how China transformed from an impoverished agrarian society to the economic powerhouse of Asia. AL Visual/Spatial

R Reading Skills

- ☐ PRIMARY SOURCE **The Spread of Rap and Hip-Hop in China**—Students read the primary source to better understand the popularity of hip-hop and rap music in China. AL Visual/Spatial

C Critical Thinking Skills

- ☐ INTERACTIVE BELLRINGER **U.S. and China Trade**—Students discuss whether China is becoming a superpower based on its economic activities and trade relations with the United States. AL Interpersonal, Logical/Mathematical, Verbal/Linguistic
- ☐ CHART **Grain Production in China, 1950–1970**—Students study a chart about grain production and analyze how the Great Leap Forward affected the production or rice, wheat, and soybeans. AL Visual/Spatial
- ☐ INTERACTIVE WHITEBOARD ACTIVITY **Changes in the Farm Economy**—Students identify how modern times have brought changes to China's farming economy and affected population patterns.

☑ Printable Digital Worksheets

R Reading Skills

- ☐ WORKSHEET **Guided Reading Activity**—Students use Guided Reading Activity worksheets to review their comprehension of the content.
- ☐ WORKSHEET **Reading Essentials and Study Guide**—Students complete the study guide and answer Reading Progress Check and vocabulary questions. AL

C Critical Thinking Skills

- ☐ WORKSHEET **Video Activity**—Students answer questions related to a topic in the chapter content after they have viewed a lesson video.

LESSON 3 PLANNER

People and Their Environment: China and Mongolia

UNDERSTANDING BY DESIGN®

Students will know:
- *the effects of rapid industrialization on the environment in China and Mongolia.*
- *how the governments and the people are addressing environmental issues.*

Students will be able to:
- ***explain** how rapid industrialization affects the environment in China and Mongolia.*
- ***identify** how the governments and the people are addressing environmental issues.*

☑ *Print Teaching Options*

V Visual Skills

- [ ] **p. 696** Students explain how the infographic adds to information about Three Gorges Dam in the text. AL Visual/Spatial
- [ ] **p. 697** Students discuss the impact of China's economic boom on its environment. AL Verbal/Linguistic

R Reading Skills

- [ ] **p. 695** Students summarize a paragraph about how China's future is threatened by its physical geography. AL Verbal/Linguistic

C Critical Thinking Skills

- [ ] **p. 694** Students discuss the consequences of China's growing demand for electric power. AL Logical/Mathematical
- [ ] **p. 694** Students consider the advantages and disadvantages of nuclear power. BL Logical/Mathematical
- [ ] **p. 697** Students discuss how China is dealing with its environmental problems. BL Logical/Mathematical
- [ ] **p. 698** Students discuss China's growing demand for products derived from rare or exotic animals. Logical/Mathematical

W Writing Skills

- [ ] **p. 695** Students write an entry in their journal explaining what their day at a factory is like from the perspective of a woman working in the factory. ELL Intrapersonal, Verbal/Linguistic
- [ ] **p. 697** Students write a paragraph about China's forest industry and the problems associated with its need for lumber. Verbal/Linguistic

T Technology Skills

- [ ] **p. 696** Students research what effect the Three Gorges Dam will have on people and the environment and hold a debate about the issue. BL Logical/Mathematical
- [ ] **p. 698** Students research the animals impacted by China's trade in rare or exotic animals and the steps taken in China and elsewhere to protect these animals from extinction. BL Naturalist, Verbal/Linguistic

☑ *Online Teaching Options*

V Visual Skills

- [ ] VIDEO **Pollution in China**—Students watch a video to see one of the consequences of pollution in Shanghai, China. AL Visual/Spatial
- [ ] IMAGE **Flooding in China**—Students view an image that shows the effects of a flood in Guangdong Province in 2007. AL Visual/Spatial

R Reading Skills

- [ ] INTERACTIVE BELLRINGER **Three Gorges Dam: Harnessing the Yangtze**—Students explore the infographic of the Three Gorges Dam and discuss how they would feel if their family were forced to relocate so a dam could be built. AL Interpersonal, Intrapersonal, Visual/Spatial, Verbal/Linguistic
- [ ] INTERACTIVE WHITEBOARD ACTIVITY **Economic Growth and the Environment**—Students drag a human or a physical factor into a cause-and-effect graphic organizer to show how industrialization and economic growth are impacting the environment and health in China.

☑ *Printable Digital Worksheets*

R Reading Skills

- [ ] WORKSHEET **Guided Reading Activity**—Students use Guided Reading Activity worksheets to review their comprehension of the content.
- [ ] WORKSHEET **Reading Essentials and Study Guide**—Students complete the study guide and answer Reading Progress Check and vocabulary questions. AL
- [ ] WORKSHEET **Vocabulary Activity**—Students review the chapter content and academic vocabulary words.
- [ ] WORKSHEET **Chapter Summary**—Students review the main ideas of the chapter content.

C Critical Thinking Skills

- [ ] WORKSHEET **Video Activity**—Students answer questions based on a lesson video.
- [ ] WORKSHEET **Reteaching Activity**—Students use this activity worksheet to review and reteach chapter content and vocabulary. This worksheet can be used with struggling students who need additional help with difficult content concepts.

INTERVENTION AND REMEDIATION STRATEGIES

LESSON 1 Physical Geography of China and Mongolia

Reading and Comprehension

Have students work in four groups to write an informational paragraph about one of the four content vocabulary terms from the lesson to demonstrate their understanding of the word's meaning. Instruct students to leave out the term in their paragraph, inserting a blank space. Have groups switch papers to see if students can determine the correct content vocabulary term based on context clues in the paragraph. After groups have determined the correct word for each passage, discuss how physical features and climate impact life in China and Mongolia.

Text Evidence

Have students review the text to identify examples of how and why China's major rivers influence human systems. Tell students to work with a partner to analyze the map in this lesson, *Physical Geography of China and Mongolia*. Encourage students to conduct an online search to identify additional information about how the rivers impact the region. Challenge students to analyze Mongolia's rivers and take notes on their impact as well. Then have students write a paragraph that summarizes their findings. Ask volunteers to share their notes with the class, instructing them to include supporting evidence from the text or their research.

LESSON 2 Human Geography of China and Mongolia

Reading and Comprehension

Organize students into six pairs or groups and assign each team two of the twelve academic and content vocabulary terms listed on the first page of the lesson. Have teams collaborate to develop three quiz questions based on the text for their assigned terms. After students have had time to develop and write down their quiz questions, have teams exchange papers. Allow time for each team to answer the quiz questions. Challenge teams to write a sentence for each of their assigned terms.

Text Evidence

To help students comprehend the impact of various dynasties discussed in the lesson, have students team up to create a web diagram with the center oval titled "China's Dynasties." Tell students to complete their diagrams based on information in the text. As students fill in each oval, have them write a summarizing statement that relates the impact of each dynasty. Challenge students to accompany their web diagrams with a time line that shows the time period during which each dynasty ruled. Tell students that their visuals should answer the question: How was the country of Mongolia created? *(After China's Qing dynasty was overthrown in 1911, Mongolia was created. Mongolians refused to be part of the new China and adopted a democratic constitution when Soviet communism collapsed.)*

LESSON 3 People and Their Environment: China and Mongolia

Reading and Comprehension

Have students work in pairs to identify cause-and-effect relationships between human activity and managing resources as they read this lesson. Have partners choose a concept from the text to illustrate, such as China's economic growth and its impact on the need for electric power. Have pairs create a diagram or flowchart that illustrates the cause-and-effect relationship of their chosen concept. Have student pairs share their diagrams or charts with the class.

Text Evidence

Organize students into six groups and assign each group one of the following topics as it relates to China's environmental issues: Land, Present; Land, Future; Water, Present; Water, Future; Air, Present; Air, Future. Draw the chart shown on the first page of this lesson on the board. Have groups collaborate to research their topic and complete their portion of the chart. After students complete the chart, ask volunteers to make predictions about the long-term impacts of environmental issues discussed in the lesson.

Online Resources

Leveled Reader

Use this online approaching-level text that corresponds directly to the text in the Student Edition. It also includes additional reading and comprehension support for English Language Learners.

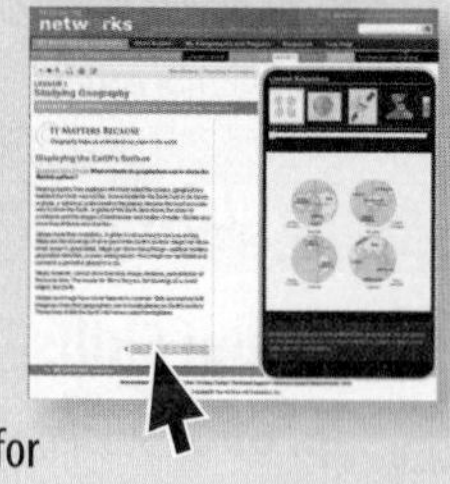

Guided Reading Activities

This resource uses guiding questions to help students with comprehension.

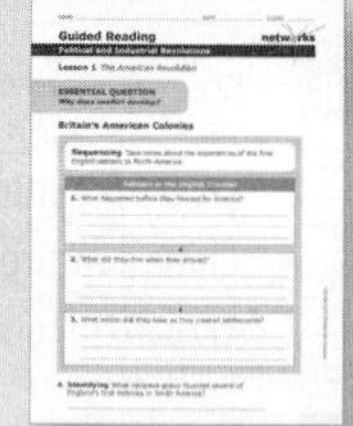

Reteaching Activities

These worksheets provide students with an opportunity for remedial practice and review of vital chapter content.

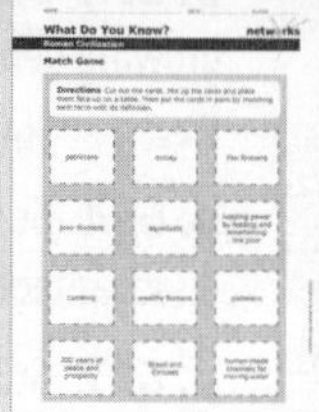

Reading Essentials and Study Guide

This resource offers writing and reading activities for the approaching-level student.

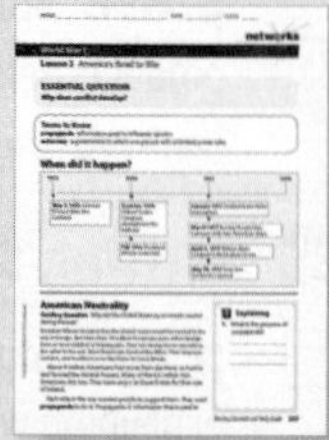

Self-Check Quizzes

This online assessment tool provides instant feedback for students to check their progress.

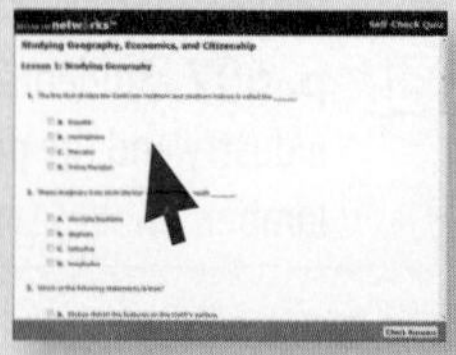

Chapter Summaries

Summaries are provided for each chapter that thoroughly condense core content into manageable chunks.

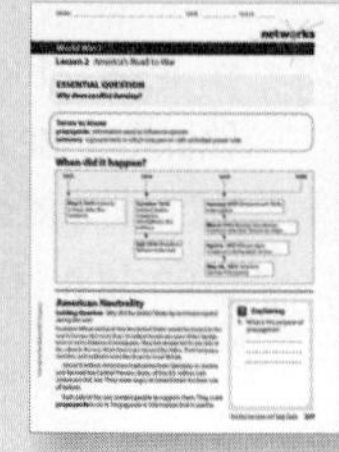

China and Mongolia

ESSENTIAL QUESTION • *How do physical systems and human systems shape a place?*

networks

There's More Online about the geography of China and Mongolia.

CHAPTER 28

Geography Matters...

China is one of the largest and most influential countries in the world. With a civilization thousands of years old, this country of geographical contrasts has more than a billion people.

China's mammoth economy exports goods globally. However, environmental problems resulting from the country's rapid growth have given rise to domestic and international challenges.

The center of a vast empire, Mongolia was later ruled by China. A land of windswept plains and mountains, today independent Mongolia faces challenges of urbanization and development.

◀ This woman stands in the Forbidden City located in the center of Beijing, China.

Letter from the Author

Dear Geography Teacher,

China and Taiwan are economic dynamos with growing stature in the world. China has expanded military strength and has entered the world of advanced technology. These actions have caused the United States to turn its international policy emphasis from Europe to the Western Pacific Basin. For a creative way to help students learn about East Asia beyond this chapter, visit the Grosvenor Center for Geographic Education series "Geography: Teaching with the Stars" at www.geoteach.org. Access the unit on *Globalization* for lessons on globalization that focus on East Asia.

Richard G. Boehm

ENGAGE

Previewing After students have read the opening paragraphs about China, have them consider that:

- China is the world's fourth-largest country in terms of land area.
- It is the world's most populous country.
- It is the world's largest exporter and has the second-largest economy.

Challenge students to add other superlatives to this list as they study the chapter.

TEACH & ASSESS

Identifying Cause and Effect Have students read the *Geography Matters* text. **Ask: What are some of the environmental problems that often result from a country's rapid growth?** *(air and water pollution, overcrowding, loss of open space and wildlife habitat, loss or deterioration of farmland, deforestation)* **What ramifications might these problems have?** *(Students should note that all these situations negatively affect people's lives and livelihoods.)* **What are some benefits that rapid growth might bring?** *(Benefits depend on the type of growth. A burgeoning population coupled with increased industrialization would have a much different effect than a rapidly growing population dependent on a farming economy.)* **BL** **Logical/Mathematical**

Making Connections

Have students make a list of superlatives that apply to the United States. Then have them compare and contrast their list to a list for China. Have students consider what could change in those superlatives for both countries in the future.

CLOSE & REFLECT

Taking Notes Ask students to keep a notebook while studying the chapter for recording important facts about China's physical geography, human geography, and environment. Students can use these notebooks as a review at the end of the chapter.

Extend the project-based learning experience globally through our partnership with ePals. EPals allows you to connect with classrooms around the world in a safe online environment for real-life lessons and projects in virtual study groups.

ENGAGE

R1 Reading Skills

Identifying Have students consider how energy needs differ between an agricultural-based economy and an industrial-based economy. **Ask:** **Which kind of economy would have the greatest energy needs and why?** *(Student answers may vary, but they should understand that powering factories and running cities takes a tremendous amount of energy.)*

TEACH & ASSESS

R2 Reading Skills

Understanding Relationships Have students consider what it means to have the world's second-largest economy. **Ask:** **How is the size of an economy measured?** *(Possible answers: measuring gross domestic product, estimating purchasing power parity)* **What is the relationship between a burgeoning economy and energy use?** *(Generally, a growing economy has a high demand for energy.)* ELL Verbal/Linguistic

C Critical Thinking Skills

Comparing and Contrasting Discuss the steps China is taking to meet its growing demand for energy. **Ask:** **Why does China need to rely on outside energy sources to meet its energy demands?** *(It does not have enough resources so it must supplement its own reserves.)* **What is China doing to lessen its need for outside energy sources?** *(It is developing new products and technologies, such as solar and wind power, that use and create energy more efficiently.)* Have students write a paragraph describing China as the largest consumer of coal in the world and the second-largest consumer of oil and compare and contrast those statistics with what is needed to lessen its energy consumption. AL Logical/Mathematical

ANSWERS, p. 678

Why Geography Matters

1. The increasing large population and industrialization has caused increased energy consumption in China.
2. China must supply enough affordable energy to its people and industries to ensure continued economic growth.
3. Developing new energy sources can help China meet its energy demands by reducing its dependence on coal.

China's growing energy demands

R1 *Since 1978 China has been shifting from an agriculture-based economy to an industrial economy. Today, Chinese workers manufacture clothes, shoes, cars, bicycles, ships, planes, washing machines, televisions, computers, cement, steel, iron, toys, and many other products for export. China's surging industrial growth has resulted in an increasing demand for energy, which is needed to power thriving cities and bustling factories from Guangzhou to Shenyang.*

Why is China consuming more energy resources?

Since the 1970s, China's consumption of oil, natural gas, coal, and other sources of energy has climbed steadily. One reason for this increase in demand is China's population. With more than 1.3 billion people, China has the largest population in the world. An even more important factor is that China has developed its economy through industrialization, which causes energy demand to increase. Following this path of development, China will continue to require more energy to generate electricity for homes, schools, and businesses and to fuel cars, trucks, and buses. R2 As of 2013, China had the second-largest economy in the world, behind the United States.

1. **Human Systems** What has caused increased consumption of energy in China?

How can China meet the growing demand for energy?

Currently, China uses more of the world's energy than any other country. In 2011, for example, China was the largest consumer of coal and the second-largest consumer of oil in the world. To meet its demand for energy that will keep its economy growing, China must supply enough affordable oil, coal, and other types of energy to its people and industries. C To supplement its own reserves of oil, coal, and natural gas, China must also import these fuels. In addition, the Chinese are investing in products and technologies—such as solar power, LED lighting, fuel-efficient cars, and advanced coal technology—that either use or provide energy more efficiently. By improving energy efficiency, China can shrink its energy consumption and make sure it has adequate supplies of energy for the future.

2. **Places and Regions** How can China ensure continued economic growth?

What challenges does China face in supplying its future energy needs?

China uses coal to generate nearly 80 percent of its electricity. In 2010 its demand for coal caused a 75-mile traffic jam involving 10,000 trucks carrying coal from Inner Mongolia. The government's twelfth Five-Year Plan lays out guidelines for reducing consumption, increasing efficiency, and developing alternative sources such as solar, nuclear, water, and wind. China—one of the world's largest producers of electricity from wind power—can harness the wind energy created by its long coastline and large landmass. With many rivers and mountains, China has become the world's leading producer of hydroelectric power, or energy from flowing water.

3. **Environment and Society** How could developing new energy sources help China meet its energy demands?

Project-Based Learning

Hands-On

Create Ideogram Report

Students will create in a group setting ideograms to write a report that brings together information from all lessons about the physical geography and human geography of China and the interactions between people and the environment.

Digital Hands-On

Create Online Projects

Find an additional activity online that incorporates technology for this this project. Visit the EdTech Teacher Web sites for more links, tutorials, and other resources.

THERE'S MORE ONLINE

WATCH a video on health effects of factory emissions in China • *SEE* how Shanghai looks under heavy smog

YESTERDAY ca. 1980s

As China industrialized, it relied heavily on fossil fuels and non-renewable resources such as oil, natural gas, and coal. Emissions from vehicles remained low, as many relied on animal transportation in rural areas or bicycles in urban areas.

* 85% 14% 1%

- COAL
- OIL
- HYDROELECTRIC

TODAY

While China is making strides in the implementation of green technology, it continues to have issues with pollution due to a heavy reliance on fossil fuels. Greater access to cars and trucks has also increased emissions.

70% 19% 6% 4% 1%

- COAL
- OIL
- HYDROELECTRIC
- NATURAL GAS
- NUCLEAR

TOMORROW

In the future, China has planned to increase its usage of solar, nuclear, and wind energy sources. However, as its population continues to grow, China's ability to reduce overall emissions remains in question.

* 65% 22% 8% 3% 2%

- COAL
- OIL
- HYDROELECTRIC
- NUCLEAR
- RENEWABLES

*Data for Yesterday and Tomorrow are approximations.

GRAPH

Energy Use in China Per Capita

Reading Graphs Have students use the graph to examine how China's per capita energy use increased between the years 1995 and 2009. Ask students to identify the year when energy use dramatically increased.
AL Visual/Spatial

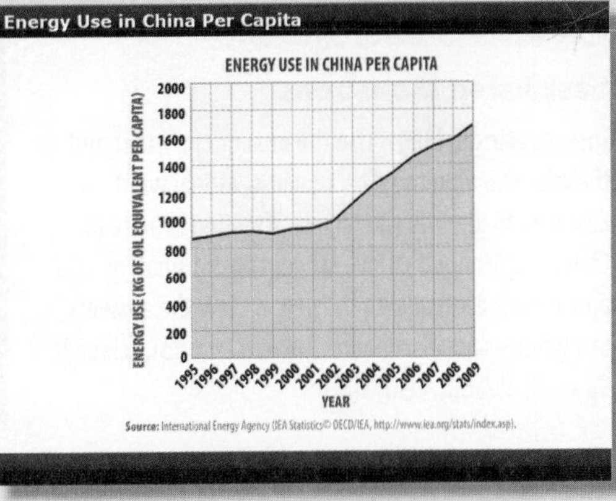

Source: International Energy Agency (IEA Statistics© OECD/IEA, http://www.iea.org/stats/index.asp).

CHAPTER 28

Why Geography Matters

T Technology Skills

Gathering Information To facilitate making comparisons, ask students to create a chart like the one below. Have students use the information from the first panel titled "YESTERDAY ca. 1980s" to complete the first column of the chart. Have students add to the chart as they read the other panels. Permit students to do additional research online to determine what specific renewable energy sources China is using. Verbal/Linguistic

	Percentage of Total Energy Use		
Resource	**1980s**	**Today**	**Tomorrow**
Coal	85%		
Oil	14%		
Hydroelectricity	1%		
Nuclear	-		
Renewables	-		

W Writing Skills

Narrative Tell students to imagine they are international reporters visiting China to investigate how China's use of fossil fuels is affecting climate change. Have students select one of the energy resources from the panel to research its environmental effects. Students should then write an article describing the negative and positive effects of using that energy source. AL Verbal/Linguistic

V Visual Skills

Analyzing Visuals Direct students attention to the panel titled "TOMORROW." Ask: **According to the caption, how has China planned to meet its energy needs in the future?** *(increase usage of solar, nuclear, and wind energy sources)* **How is this reflected in the graphic?** *(It shows more wind energy, more nuclear power plants, more solar energy, greater pollution, and more buildings and homes than the graphic depicting "TODAY.")* ELL Visual/Spatial

CLOSE & REFLECT

Finding the Main Idea Have students list important points presented in this feature. Have students use their lists to write a brief statement that expresses the main idea.

ENGAGE

R Reading Skills

Previewing Collect several brochures about traveling to China. Invite student pairs to peruse the brochures and scan the lesson to make observations about China's geography. Have partners search for facts about China that interest or surprise them. Have pairs share their thoughts with the class.

TEACH & ASSESS

V Visual Skills

Analyzing Visuals Have students locate China on a globe or world map. Have volunteers name the countries and bodies of water that border China on the west *(Afghanistan, Kazakhstan, Kyrgyzstan, Tajikistan, Pakistan, India)*; east *(Russia, North Korea, Sea of Japan, Yellow Sea, Taiwan, East China Sea)*; north *(Russia, Mongolia)*; and south *(Nepal, Bhutan, India, Myanmar, Laos, Vietnam, South China Sea)*. **Ask:** **What landforms does China share with other countries?** *(Possible answer: The Himalaya are shared with India, Nepal, Bhutan, and Bangladesh.)* **Why might these landforms be politically and culturally important?** *(Possible answer: The Himalaya separate China's borders, acting as political protection and a barrier to preserve cultural traditions.)* **AL** **Visual/Spatial**

T Technology Skills

Gathering Information Organize the class into nine groups and assign each group one physical feature mentioned in paragraphs two and three. Have students research their assigned feature to learn how it affects China as a source of natural resources, as a barrier, and so forth. Direct students to use presentation software to share pictures of their assigned feature and additional information. **BL** **Verbal/Linguistic, Visual/Spatial**

ANSWERS, p. 680

Landforms: mountains and plateaus in the west and plains and hills in the east; Kunlun Shan and Tian Shan connected to Pamirs in western China; Tarim Basin between the Kunlun Shan and Tian Shan and covered by Taklimakan desert; Gobi stretches across north-central China and southern Mongolia; Altay Shan on border of China and Mongolia; China separated from South Asia by Himalaya. **Water Systems:** China's major rivers begin on Plateau of Tibet; Huang He is major river in northern China; Chang Jiang (Yangtze River) is longest river in China; Xi River is largest in southern China; Orhon River is longest in Mongolia. **Climate Regions:** China's climate ranges from tropical in the south to subarctic in the north; Plateau of Tibet has a very high elevation and cool temperatures; Mongolia has continental climate with long, cold winters and short, cool-to-hot summers.

networks

There's More Online!

- **IMAGE** Giant Panda Eating Bamboo
- **IMAGE** Terraced Rice Fields
- **MAP** China's River: Huang He
- **MAP** East Asian Monsoons
- **MAP** Physical Geography of China and Mongolia
- **INTERACTIVE SELF-CHECK QUIZ**
- **VIDEO** Physical Geography of China and Mongolia

LESSON 1
Physical Geography of China and Mongolia

ESSENTIAL QUESTION • *How do physical systems and human systems shape a place?*

Reading **HELP**DESK CCSS

Academic Vocabulary (Tier Two Words)
- **symbol**

Content Vocabulary (Tier Three Words)
- **range**
- **loess**
- **monsoon**
- **typhoon**

TAKING NOTES: ***Key Ideas and Details***

IDENTIFYING China's landforms and bodies of water are regularly affected by weather systems. As you read, use a graphic organizer like the one below to note the main landforms, water systems, and climate regions.

China's Physical Geography		
Landforms	Water Systems	Climate Regions

It Matters Because

China is a large land of many contrasts: high mountains, grassy steppes, broad plains, tropical rain forests, and cold, dry deserts. Great rivers nourish the soil to support agriculture that feeds millions, but monsoons can cause dangerous floods. Mongolia has large areas of upland plateau that are deserts, as well as mountainous regions and basins. Most of its land consists of extensive grasslands used for livestock herding.

Landforms

GUIDING QUESTION *What physical features dominate China and Mongolia, and how have they affected human geography?*

East Asia spans the snowy peaks of the Himalaya in the west all the way to the Japanese islands in the east. China makes up the majority of the landmass in this subregion. Rivers, hills, and plains occupy the east. The southwest contains high plateaus, and the northwest stretches wide into dry deserts. Mongolia is mostly an upland plateau with mountains in the north and south interrupted by basins.

The landforms of China can be divided into two parts: the mountains and plateaus of the west and the plains and hills of the east. In far western China, a mountain **range** called the Pamirs forms a node from which several other ranges radiate. This remote interior region includes the Kunlun Shan and Tian Shan ranges. Between them stretches the Tarim Basin, characterized by deserts and salt marshes. A desert, the Taklimakan, covers most of the Tarim Basin. Another massive desert, the Gobi, is found in north-central China and southern Mongolia. It is the source of frequent dust storms that plague these areas. Rain seldom falls in the Gobi—less than 3 inches (7.5 cm) a year.

The Altay Shan range, farther north, lies along part of the border between China and Mongolia. China is separated from South Asia by the Himalaya, the world's highest mountains and the location of the world's tallest peak, Mount Everest, at 29,028 feet (8,848 m) on the border of China and Nepal. The country's lowest point, the Turpan Depression, is found in western China near Mongolia and lies 426 feet (130 m) below sea level.

680

networks ***Online Teaching Options***

INTERACTIVE BELLRINGER

East Asian Monsoons

Interpreting a Map Use the introductory text and the map showing the direction of seasonal winds in East Asia to identify the factors affecting climate in China and Mongolia. Have students form small groups and answer each question. Then, review the answers in a whole-class discussion. **Interpersonal, Visual/Spatial, Verbal/Linguistic**

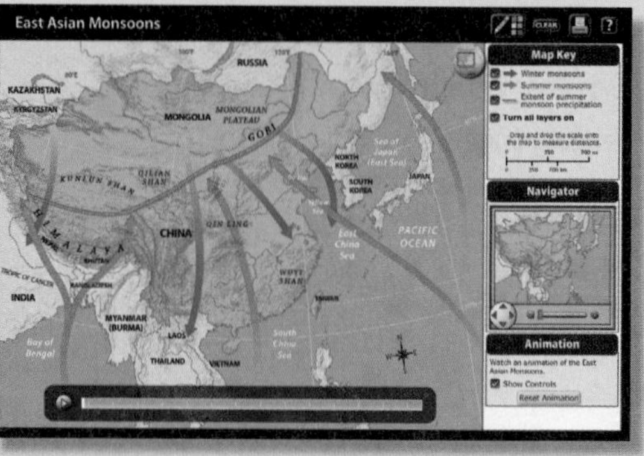

The highest plateau in East Asia is the Plateau of Tibet (or the Plateau of Xizang), which forms a large part of China's southwest. It has an average elevation of 16,000 feet (4,875 m). North and east of the Plateau of Tibet lie other rugged highlands, although with lower elevations.The mountains, plateaus, and great deserts in China's west and south have formed natural barriers that helped protect its inhabitants from land invasion for thousands of years, but also isolated China from peaceful contact with foreigners. For centuries China's isolation served to protect the country, allowing it to develop its unique culture.

range a group of mountains

V

The eastern part of China is characterized by vast lowland plains and some hills. It contains most of China's population because the land is conducive to farming and settlement. The Manchurian Plain (or Northeast Plain) and the North China Plain are two of the most important of the numerous plains areas.

In addition to the southern upland plateau and deserts, Mongolia has areas of mountains in the north and the south with basins in between. Some contain remnants of extinct volcanoes, also found on the far eastern plateau.

✓ **READING PROGRESS CHECK**

Identifying Which mountain ranges originate in the Pamirs?

Water Systems **W**

GUIDING QUESTION *How do China's major rivers influence human systems?*

China's major rivers originate on the Plateau of Tibet and flow eastward, down from the plateau and across the lowland plains to the Pacific Ocean. In northern

GEOGRAPHY CONNECTION

China's immense size covers many types of landforms and physical features.

1. ***THE WORLD IN SPATIAL TERMS*** Approximately how wide is the Plateau of Tibet?
2. ***PLACES AND REGIONS*** Which desert spans both Mongolia and China? What is the elevation of this desert?

Physical Geography of China and Mongolia

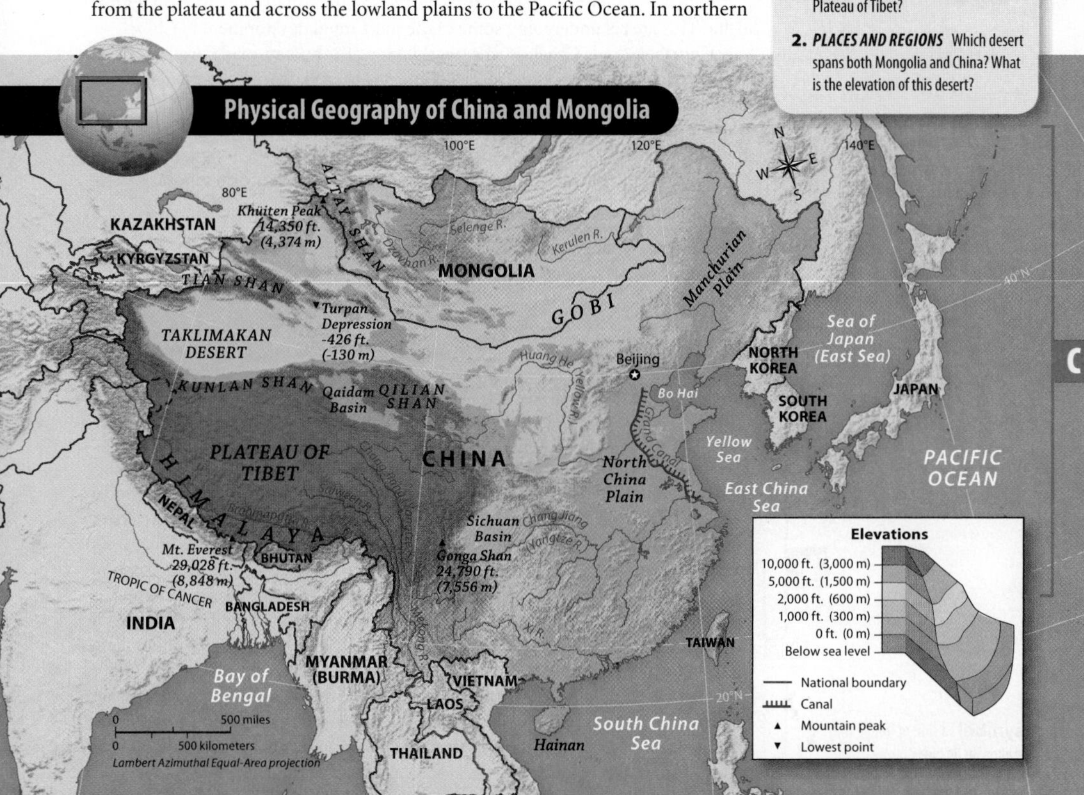

INTERACTIVE MAP

Physical Geography of China and Mongolia

Interpreting a Map Use this interactive map to introduce the physical geography of China and Mongolia. Have students analyze the map to understand how China and Mongolia have a variety of landforms. Have students form small groups and discuss their prior knowledge of these landforms, such as deserts, plateaus, rivers, and mountains. **AL Visual/Spatial**

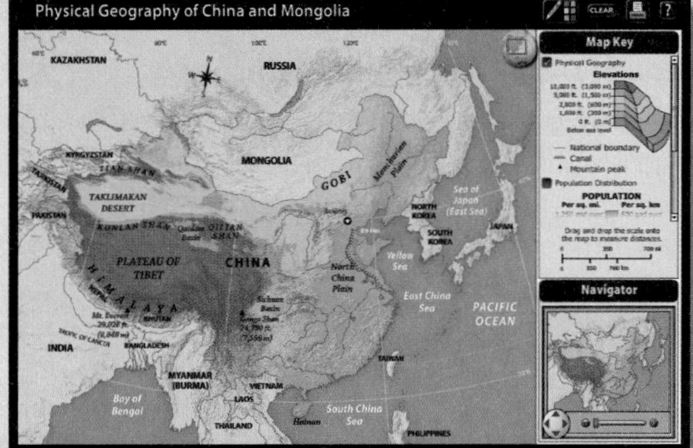

CHAPTER 28, Lesson 1
Physical Geography of China and Mongolia

V Visual Skills

Observing Have students imagine they are taking an trip across China, either from west to east, south to north, or from one major city to another. Using the map on this page as a reference, have students verbally describe to another student the landforms and other features they would see along the way. Encourage students to use the scale bar to calculate distances between landforms and cities. Then have students switch roles, ensuring that each student has a chance to describe an imaginary trip. **AL Visual/Spatial**

Content Background Knowledge

North China Plain The North China Plain is a large alluvial plain located in the river basins and highlands of eastern China. The plain was built up by deposits of the Huang He and other rivers. Most of the plain is less than 160 feet (50 m) above sea level. It is one of the world's most densely populated regions and one of its most fertile and productive farming regions. Beijing and Tianjin, an important industrial city and port, are located in this region.

W Writing Skills

Informative/Explanatory Organize students into small groups. Have each group choose a different water system to describe, noting the route the river follows from its source to its mouth and the landforms it cuts through on the way. Tell students that they may consult more detailed maps if they choose. **Verbal/Linguistic**

C Critical Thinking Skills

Questioning Ask: What important river systems, if any, does China share with other countries? *(Student answers will vary, but should note that several rivers originate on the Plateau of Tibet and flow into Southeast Asia, including the Mekong.)* **Why might this be important?** *(It is important to transportation, communication, and trade between countries.)* Divide students into pairs. Ask students to read and answer the *Geography Connection* questions. Then have pairs write their own questions about China's physical geography or waterways that can be answered by studying the map. Have students answer each other's questions. **ELL Verbal/Linguistic**

ANSWERS, p. 681

✓ **READING PROGRESS CHECK** Kunlun Shan and Tian Shan begin in the Pamirs

GEOGRAPHY CONNECTION

1. approximately 1,500 miles wide
2. The Gobi, which is about 2,000 feet in elevation, lies in north-central China and southern Mongolia.

Physical Geography of China and Mongolia

R Reading Skills

Sequencing Have students create a written flowchart explaining the sequence involved in transforming rock into fertile soil. Then guide a class discussion by asking several students to explain why this phenomenon is critical to the people of China. **ELL Verbal/Spatial**

V Visual Skills

Creating Charts Have students use their text to create a chart like the one below to compare the major climate regions and biomes of China. Encourage volunteers to gather additional details from a world atlas or other library resources to use on their charts. **AL Visual/Spatial**

Climate Zone	Description	Vegetation	Locations
Humid, subtropical	Hot summers and heavy rains	Deciduous trees and evergreens with broad leaves; bamboo; mulberry	Mid-latitudes

T Technology Skills

Researching Divide students into small groups. Have groups research the importance of bamboo or the mulberry tree to the Chinese people and their economy. Encourage students to report where and how these plants are grown, how they are harvested, their various uses, and the industries that have built up around them. The students researching bamboo will want to include the importance of bamboo to the giant and red panda. Have students report their findings to the class.
BL Naturalist

ANSWERS, p. 682

✓ READING PROGRESS CHECK The flooding of the Huang He, which carries nutrient-rich loess onto the North China Plain, makes it so fertile.

CRITICAL THINKING

1. Bamboo is important because it is used for food, medicine, and building as well as being the sole source of food for the giant panda and red panda.
2. Bamboo can grow as much as a foot per day, making it a quickly replenishing resource as well as being a hardy building material.

Bamboo is an important plant to people and animals.

▲ CRITICAL THINKING

1. ***Identifying Central Issues*** Why is bamboo so important to China?
2. ***Analyzing*** What characteristics of bamboo make it so useful?

loess fine, yellowish-brown topsoil made up of particles of silt and clay, carried by the wind

symbol a sign or image that stands for an idea

R China, the major river system is the Huang He, or Yellow River. The river gets its name from the sediment load of yellowish-brown topsoil it carries. This fine topsoil is called **loess**, and it covers large areas in northern China. The loess was created by wind erosion that deposited the fine soil at the end of the last ice age. When the soil is eroded by the Huang He, the yellow loess is carried into the water. The combination of nutrient-rich loess and water flowing into the North China Plain makes this area ideal for farming wheat and soybeans. Over the years, though, flooding of the Huang He has killed hundreds of thousands of people, earning it the nickname "China's sorrow."

The longest of central China's rivers is the Chang Jiang, or Yangtze River, which flows for 3,434 miles (5,525 km) through dramatic gorges as it comes off the Plateau of Tibet and then across the wide plains of eastern China. It empties into the ocean near Shanghai. More than half of China's rice and other grains are watered by the Chang Jiang, which is also a major transportation route. The recent construction of the Three Gorges Dam helps control flooding along the lower portions of the river and provides water for irrigation and hydroelectric power.

The Xi River and its tributaries form the largest major river system in southern China. This river system is also known as the Pearl River. The ports of Guangzhou, Hong Kong, and Macau benefit from fertile soil deposited there to form a great delta. This area is undergoing some of the most rapid development in China.

China's Grand Canal is the world's longest human-made waterway. Its construction was begun in the 400s B.C. and has been expanded and rebuilt. Today it carries goods and people from Beijing to Hangzhou, some 1,000 miles (1,609 km).

Most of Mongolia's rivers are located in the north and are difficult to harness for transportation or hydroelectric power. The Orhon is the longest, at almost 700 miles (1,130 km). Lakes in Mongolia are often saltwater or temporary.

✓ READING PROGRESS CHECK

Summarizing What process makes the North China Plain so fertile?

Climates, Biomes, and Resources

GUIDING QUESTION *What defines the climates, natural resources, and biomes of China?*

China's climates are extremely diverse, ranging from tropical in the south to subarctic in the north. Climates are shaped by the interaction of latitude and physical features such as mountains, highlands, and coastal regions. Each type of climate supports different vegetation. Temperate, humid forests dominate the south and east, while the north and west are characterized by dry highlands and grasslands.

A humid subtropical climate, with hot summers and heavy rains, characterizes the midlatitudes of much of eastern China and the island of Taiwan. Deciduous trees **V** and evergreens with broad leaves both flourish here. The tree-like grass bamboo grows in many warmer areas. This fast-growing plant—some species can grow as much as one foot per day—is also hardy and versatile. It is used for everything from **T** medicine, food, and decoration to building material. It also provides the only source of food for two rare mammals: the giant panda and the smaller red panda. Other native plants with important economic value are the mulberry tree, whose leaves are food for silkworms, and the tea bush. Tea, silk, and bamboo have long been important in China and have come to stand as **symbols** of Chinese culture, as has the panda.

networks Online Teaching Options

INTERACTIVE WHITEBOARD ACTIVITY

Mountains, Rivers, and Plains

Categorizing Have students drag the names of China's major landforms into a chart to match the characteristic given, and then slide the characteristics of three rivers into the correct river columns. **AL Visual/Spatial**

Mountains, Rivers, and Plains

Directions: China's landforms can be divided into two parts: the western mountains and plateaus and the eastern plains and hills. Match each term with its corresponding definition or description by dragging the term into the appropriate category on the chart.

Description/Definition	Term
a mountain range in China from which other ranges branch out	
deserts and salt marshes located between the Kunlun Shan and Tian Shan ranges	
part of the border between China and Mongolia	
a desert that covers most of the Tarim Basin	
separates China from South Asia and includes Mount Everest	
a massive desert in north-central China that causes frequent dust storms	
forms the lowest point in China at 426 feet (130 m) below sea level	
forms a large part of China's southwest at an elevation of 16,000 feet (4875 m)	
lands that host the largest population and are conducive to farming	

Altay Shan | Pamirs | Taklimakan
Gobi | Plateau of Tibet | Tarim Basin
Himalaya | Northeast Plain and North China Plain | Turpan Depression

Show Answers

Deserts have formed in China's north and west where surrounding mountains create a rain shadow, blocking the moist coastal winds. These deserts stretch across Mongolia into inland northern China. Deserts—such as the Gobi and the Taklimakan—and the steppe lands experience temperature extremes. Daytime temperatures can fall as much as 55°F (30.5°C) overnight. Temperatures in the Gobi range from 100°F to –30°F (38°C to –34°C), although they average 73°F (23°C) in summer and 0°F (–18°C) in winter. The large steppe climate regions east of the Gobi display a natural vegetation of grasses, with few trees.

The climate in mountainous areas changes according to elevation. In most cases, the higher the elevation, the cooler the temperature is. For example, the average annual high temperature on the Plateau of Tibet is a cool 58°F (14°C), because the elevation is very high—averaging about 16,000 feet (4,875 m). Lower mountain slopes bloom with meadows, grass, flowers, and trees. No trees grow above the timberline; only mosses and colorful lichens survive here.

C

monsoon in Asia, a seasonal wind that brings warm, moist air from the oceans in summer and cold, dry air from land in winter

Lush rain forest covers much of Hainan, an island off China's southern coast. This tropical wet climate has high temperatures year-round. In summer, the rainy **monsoons**, or seasonal winds, blow in. Palms and tropical hardwoods grow alongside tropical fruit trees and broad-leaved evergreens.

Seasonal weather patterns in China are created by the interactions that occur between the air mass above the continent and the air mass above the Pacific Ocean. The meeting of these air masses results in monsoons that blow in the same direction for about half the year before switching directions. Heat and humidity from the Pacific Ocean arrive in China during the summer monsoon, which blows from southeast to northwest. As a result, more than 80 percent of the subregion's

GEOGRAPHY CONNECTION

In China, monsoons blowing westward bring warm, moist air in the summer. Monsoons blowing eastward bring cold, dry air in the winter.

1. ***PHYSICAL SYSTEMS*** Winds originating on the Plateau of Tibet have what characteristics?
2. ***ENVIRONMENT AND SOCIETY*** How do summer monsoon rains affect farms near the coast?

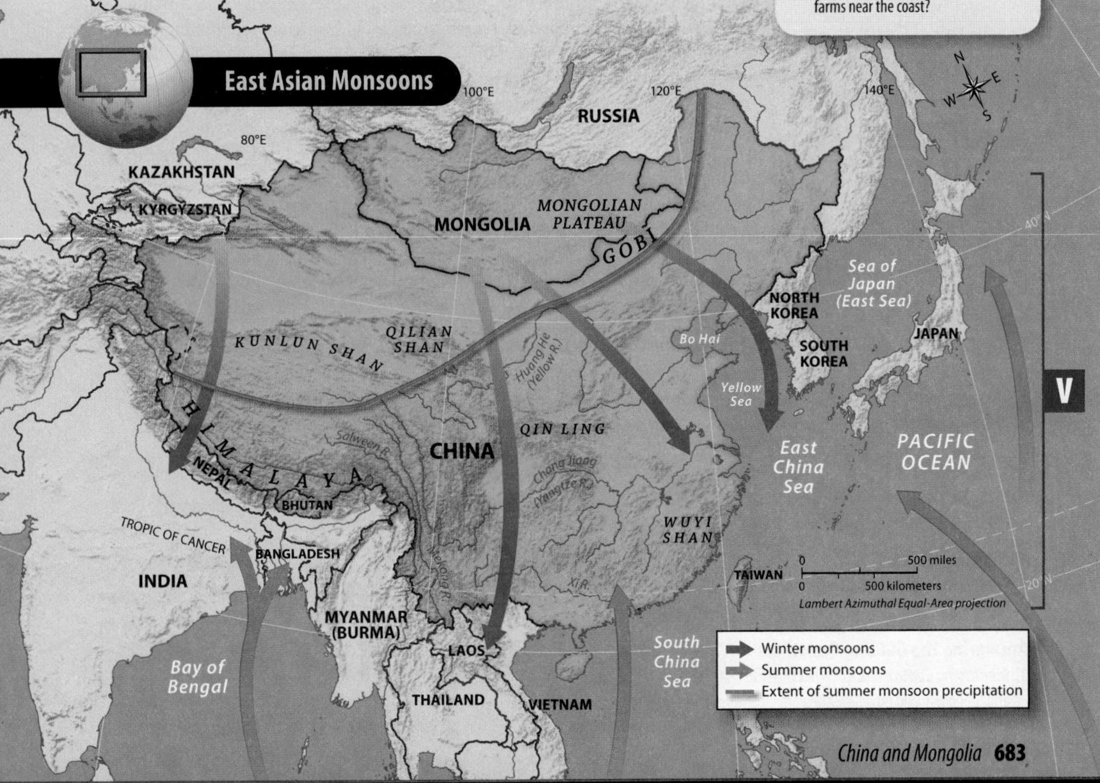

CHAPTER 28, Lesson 1
Physical Geography of China and Mongolia

C Critical Thinking Skills

Identifying Cause and Effect Review the rain shadow effect with students. Have them describe the rain shadow phenomenon in their own words and the role it plays in creating deserts. Ask students to create a diagram to illustrate the phenomenon. **BL Logical/Mathematical**

Making Connections

Have students think about places in the United States where mountains create a rain shadow that keeps moist coastal winds from reaching inland areas. Have students describe what they know about these areas. *(Most deserts in the United States are the result of a rain shadow effect, including the Mojave Desert and the Great Basin. Dry areas of eastern Washington State were also created by a rain shadow effect as are the leeward sides of volcanoes in the Hawaiian Islands.)*

V Visual Skills

Reading Maps Have students reread this paragraph, paying particular attention to the term *monsoon*. Then ask students to read and analyze the map to help them explain monsoon activity in China. **Ask:** Which ways do winds blow in summer? *(from southeast to northwest)* How does this affect weather? Why? *(The wind blows over water and brings rain, heat, and humidity inland.)* Is this a beneficial or destructive occurrence? *(Both: the monsoons bring rain for crops but that rain sometimes causes flooding.)* How does the wind pattern change in winter? *(The cold, arctic winds blow across the continent from north to south.)* What effect do winter monsoons have on weather? *(They bring cold, usually dry winds.)* **Verbal/Linguistic**

GAME

Physical Geography of China and Mongolia

Assessing Divide the class into student pairs. Have each set of students fill in this crossword puzzle about human or physical geography in China and Mongolia. Once students have completed this crossword puzzle, have students write a sentence using each term. **AL Verbal/Linguistic**

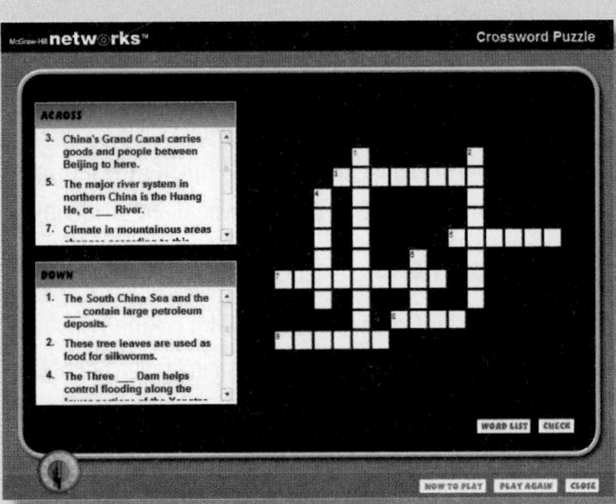

ANSWERS, p. 683

GEOGRAPHY CONNECTION

1. They are cold and dry.
2. They bring rain that is necessary to grow crops near the coast. However, too much or too little rain can cause crops to fail.

Physical Geography of China and Mongolia

V Visual Skills

Analyzing Visuals Direct students' attention to the photograph at the top of page 684. Ask students to describe the scene. **Ask:** **Why is so much of China's farmland terraced?** *(Possible answers: There is a great need for farmland; much of China is hilly and mountainous.)* **AL** **Visual/Spatial**

C Critical Thinking Skills

Comparing and Contrasting Have students describe what they know about hurricanes and typhoons. **Ask:** **What is the difference between a monsoon and a typhoon?** *(monsoon: seasonal winds that blow in the same direction; typhoon: a violent storm with strong winds and rain)* **Are there positive effects from these weather events?** *(Possible answers: Yes, summer monsoons bring much-needed rain; typhoons, however, like hurricanes, are mainly destructive.)* Students should gather news stories about any recent typhoons in East Asia or hurricanes in the Western Hemisphere in order to compare and contrast the storms and the damage done by them. **BL** **Logical/Mathematical**

R Reading Skills

Listing Have students make a list of China's major resources. Divide students into small groups to brainstorm how each resource is used and how it is important to the Chinese economy. **Verbal/Linguistic**

CLOSE & REFLECT

Planning Ask students to review the landforms in China and identify one or two places they would most like to visit. Have students jot down a few words that describe the place. Ask students to exchange the information with classmates as they review the lesson.

ANSWERS, p. 684

✓ READING PROGRESS CHECK Summer monsoons that are late or bring less rain cause crops to fail.

CRITICAL THINKING

1. Terracing allows more crops to be grown as it utilizes land more efficiently and enables land on slopes and mountainsides to be farmed.
2. China's fertile river plains, monsoon rains, and the climate in the south that allows two harvests of rice per year make China a successful crop producer.

There are many areas of rich farmland in China. In the photo, rice fields have been planted on terraced slopes in Guangxi.

▲ CRITICAL THINKING

1. ***Analyzing*** What is the benefit of terracing?
2. ***Synthesizing*** What geographic conditions make China such a successful crop producer?

typhoon a violent tropical storm that forms in the western Pacific Ocean, usually in late summer

annual rainfall occurs in heavy downpours from April through October. Farmers depend on these summer monsoons to water their crops. If monsoons come late or bring less rainfall, crops fail. When too much rain comes, flooding can result. From November to March, the winter monsoon brings cold, dry arctic air across China as it blows from the land onto the ocean.

Large, violent storms with high winds, known as **typhoons**, result when warm, humid air over the Pacific Ocean moves onto land. Typhoons are also called tropical cyclones and are similar to hurricanes. These intense spiral storms with their storm surges can raise coastal waters up to 20 feet (6 m) above normal, creating serious flooding along the coasts. As with hurricanes in the Atlantic and Caribbean, typhoon season peaks between late August and October.

Far from the ocean, Mongolia has a continental climate with long, cold winters and short, cool-to-hot summers. Mostly arid to semi-arid, annual rainfall in desert areas is less than 4 inches (10 cm), with 14 inches (35 cm) in the northern forested mountains.

China has a wealth of mineral resources, including iron ore, tin, tungsten, and gold. The South China Sea and the Taklimakan contain large petroleum deposits. Northeastern China has abundant coal deposits. Other natural resources include natural gas, mercury, aluminum, lead, zinc, and uranium. Mongolia has a number of minerals, including coal, gold, and copper, as well as oil and uranium deposits.

China is the world's leading producer of rice. The "rice bowl" in southern China yields two harvests of rice per year. Agricultural income as a percentage of gross domestic product (GDP) equaled 10 percent in 2011. In fact, China is the world leader in the gross value of its farm output for rice, wheat, potatoes, corn, peanuts, tea, millet, barley, apples, cotton, oilseed, pork, and fish. East Asia, including China, boasts the world's biggest deep-sea fishing industries.

✓ READING PROGRESS CHECK

Making Connections How can monsoons affect China's agricultural output?

LESSON 1 REVIEW

Reviewing Vocabulary (Tier Three Words)

1. ***Using Context Clues*** Write a sentence explaining how loess affects agriculture in China. RH.9–10.4

Using Your Notes

2. ***Comparing and Contrasting*** How do the water systems in China affect its climates compared to the effects of weather systems?

Answering the Guiding Questions

3. ***Identifying Central Issues*** What physical features dominate China and Mongolia, and how have they affected human geography?
4. ***Analyzing*** How do China's major rivers influence human systems?
5. ***Synthesizing*** What defines the climates, natural resources, and biomes of China?

Writing Activity

6. ***Informative/Explanatory*** In a paragraph, explain the possible effects of typhoons and monsoons on the Chinese people and their economy. WHST.9–10.2

684

Rodrigo A. Torres/Glowimages

LESSON 1 REVIEW ANSWERS

Reviewing Vocabulary

1. Sentences should include that loess is a nutrient-rich topsoil that is eroded by the Huang He and carried to the North China Plain where it enriches the farmland, producing abundant crops of wheat and soybeans.

Using Your Notes

2. The Pacific Ocean is responsible for creating the summer monsoons which result in 80 percent of the region's annual rainfall, creating a greater effect than weather systems alone on China.

Answering the Guiding Questions

3. Mongolia is an upland plateau with mountains in the north and south separated by basins. China has mountains and plateaus in the west and plains and hills in the east. These features have isolated as well as protected China and have been factors in settlement, farming, and economic development.
4. China's rivers provide water for drinking, irrigation of farmland, hydroelectric power, deposit fertile soil, and provide transportation for goods and people.
5. Climates, biomes, and resources are defined by the interaction of latitude and physical features.

Writing Activity

6. Paragraphs should be supported with information from the lesson: summer monsoons bring 80% of annual rainfall, a light or late monsoon season can cause crop failure; typhoons can cause damage and coastal flooding, resulting in loss of life and property.

networks
There's More Online!

- **GRAPHS** Grain Production in China, 1950–1970
- **GRAPHS** U.S. Exports to China and Imports from China
- **IMAGE** Chinese Schoolgirl
- **IMAGE** Mongolian Flag
- **TIME LINE** Modern China
- **INTERACTIVE SELF-CHECK QUIZ**
- **VIDEO** Human Geography of China and Mongolia

LESSON 2

Human Geography of China and Mongolia

ESSENTIAL QUESTION • *How do physical systems and human systems shape a place?*

Reading **HELP**DESK (CCSS)

Academic Vocabulary
(Tier Two Words)

- **impact**
- **institute**
- **dominate**

Content Vocabulary
(Tier Three Words)

- **dynasty**
- **aborigine**
- **ideogram**
- **atheist**
- **commune**
- **merchant marine**
- **dissident**
- **economic sanctions**
- **Special Economic Zone (SEZ)**

TAKING NOTES: ***Key Ideas and Details***

DESCRIBING As you read about the human geography of China, use a graphic organizer like the one below to identify how history, population, culture, and economics have created the China of today.

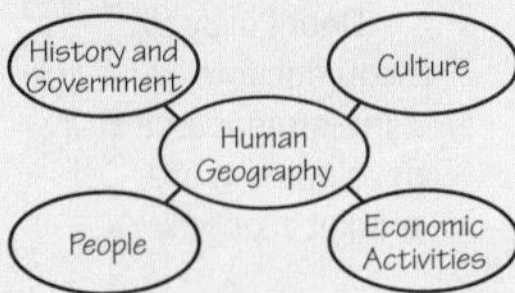

It Matters Because

China's long history and geography have shaped its culture. The ideas on which its government is based have had long-lasting effects. The country's economic life reveals how it fulfills the daily needs of its citizens and interacts with the larger world. Mongolia, once the world's largest land empire, today faces modern challenges. R

History and Government

GUIDING QUESTION *What influence did ancient Chinese history have on government, culture, and daily life in modern times?*

Many powerful transformations have occurred during China's history. Under leaders ranging from nomadic warriors to long-ruling **dynasties**, the country has endured profound political and cultural changes.

China's culture spans more than 5,000 years. Archaeological evidence indicates it began in the Wei River valley. Historical records were begun when invaders established a dynasty, or ruling family, around 1766 B.C. This Shang dynasty arose on the North China Plain. They faced attacks by nomads from Central Asia, rebellions by local nobles, and natural disasters. In China, dynasties were believed to rule under the "mandate of heaven," or the approval of the gods and goddesses. When the people suffered, it was assumed that the dynasty had lost its mandate. The Shang dynasty ruled for over 700 years, coming to an end in 1046 B.C. G1

The Zhou (JOH) dynasty then took control of the region, and continued for the next 800 years. Under its rule, trade grew, Chinese culture spread, and the making of iron tools began. Crossbows, ox-drawn plows, and horseback riding were introduced, as were widespread irrigation and other efforts to control water. This helped to increase crop yields.

China's most famous teacher and philosopher, Confucius (or Kongfuzi), lived during the Zhou dynasty. He founded a system of thought called Confucianism. It is based on discipline and proper moral conduct, and continues to have an **impact** in China and other Asian civilizations to the present day. C2

ENGAGE

R Reading Skills

Activating Prior Knowledge Write out this list of names and ask students to identify each: Confucius, Laozi, Zheng He, Sun Yat-sen, Chiang Kai-shek, Mao Zedong, Deng Xiaoping. Have students brainstorm what they know about each of these people. Explain that students will learn about the role each person played in China's history in this lesson.

TEACH & ASSESS

G1 Critical Thinking Skills

Comparing and Contrasting Ask students to read the paragraphs relating to the rise and fall of the Shang and Zhou dynasties. Have students make comparisons between the two dynasties. **Ask:** **Which lasted longer?** *(Zhou)* **Which was the most tumultuous and why?** *(Shang; They faced many attacks, rebellions, and natural disasters.)* **Which did the most to improve life in China? Explain.** *(Student answers may vary, but should note that under the Zhou dynasty, trade grew, Chinese culture spread, crop yields increased, and many new technologies were developed.)* **ELL** **Logical/Mathematical**

C2 Critical Thinking Skills

Differentiating Have students brainstorm what they know about the philosophy of Confucianism. **Ask:** **What is unique about Confucianism?** *(It is based on discipline and a code of moral conduct.)* **How did Confucianism begin?** *(It was based on the teachings and philosophy of Confucius, who lived during the Zhou dynasty.)* **AL** **Verbal/Linguistic**

ANSWERS, p. 685

HISTORY AND GOVERNMENT: Shang was first dynasty; Confucius lived during Zhou dynasty; Laozi founded Daoism; first emperor of Qin dynasty built walls to defend China; in 1911 a revolution ended dynasties and civil war began; Communists took power in 1949; The People's Republic of China was founded; Mongolia was created by fall of Qing dynasty; Mongolia adopted democratic constitution in 1990s.
People: Han Chinese are 92% of population; China took over Tibet in 1959; most people in Taiwan emigrated from China; most people in Mongolia are ethnic Mongolians; most people in China live along major rivers; rural-to-urban migration has caused overcrowding in the cities.
Culture: Literacy is increasing; most people in China speak Mandarin; written Chinese uses pictures; health care is paid for by the government; there are atheists, Buddhists, and Daoists; government maintains power over religion; the bond with the state is considered most important; women traditionally did not hold positions of power; boys are preferred, so there are more men than women.
Economic Activities: 1 in 3 Chinese people work in agriculture; in 2010 China became world's largest exporter; China's waterways are important for movement of goods; China and the U.S. want to increase trade; dissidents in China are fighting for human rights; economic sanctions against China to encourage improvement in human rights; Hong Kong has strong economy because it is close to the Special Economic Zone; Mongolia's grasslands are used to graze livestock; mining has become a major economic activity in Mongolia.

networks ***Online Teaching Options***

INTERACTIVE BELLRINGER

U.S. and China Trade Activities

Reading Graphs Use the introductory text and graphs showing trade between the United States and China to identify China's economic activities and trade relations with the United States. Have students form small groups. Ask students to discuss this question: Is China becoming a superpower? Then, have them answer each question to identify China's growing economic power as demonstrated by its exports to the United States. Have each group write its agreed-upon answers to the questions. Review the answers as a class.

AL **Interpersonal, Logical/Mathematical, Verbal/Linguistic**

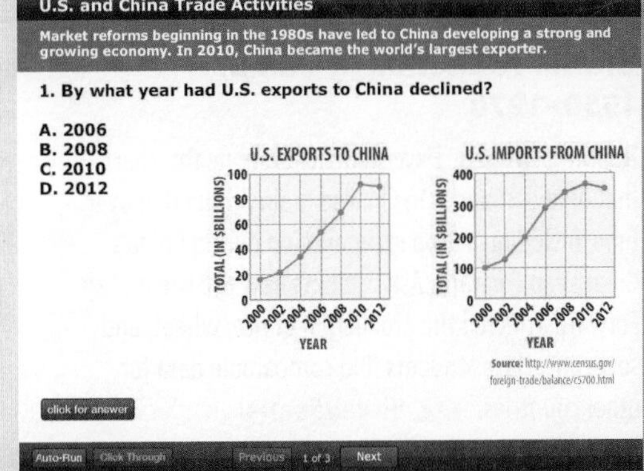

T Technology Skills

Sequencing Have students create a time line to show the rise and fall of Chinese dynasties over time. Direct students to conduct further online research about the accomplishments of each dynasty to evaluate how each impacted China's history. Use the time lines as a basis for a class discussion on the dynasties of China. **ELL** **Verbal/Linguistic**

C Critical Thinking Skills

Identifying Cause and Effect Once students have read the text under *China Today,* have them describe the events leading up to the Communist revolution inspired and led by Mao Zedong. **Ask:** **What events in China led to Mao's rise to power?** *(Student answers will vary, but they should understand that a period of tumult followed the collapse of the last Chinese dynasty in 1911. Mao was able to defeat Chiang Kai-shek by winning support of China's farmers.)* **What was Mao's appeal?** *(He had a vision of industrializing China and promised a better life for China's farmers and workers. He talked of creating a classless society and promised to root out capitalism.)* **Logical/Mathematical**

W Writing Skills

Informative/Explanatory Ask students to study the time line at the bottom of pages 686–687. Have students use the time line to write a brief paragraph about the history of China from 1940 to the present. Students may include additional information from the text or from additional research if they wish. **ELL** **Verbal/Linguistic**

ANSWERS, p. 686

CRITICAL THINKING

1. The government launched the Great Leap Forward in a massive effort to industrialize China.
2. China has faced problems with lower crop production and starvation during the establishment of communes, growing population numbers until the one-child policy was enacted, human rights protests, and pollution.

dynasty a ruling house or continuing family of rulers

impact an effect on something

Around the same time, a thinker named Laozi (or Lao-Tzu) helped found another major Chinese philosophy called Daoism. This philosophy emphasizes harmony with nature and simple living. Daoism is still followed in modern China.

T Qin Shihuangdi, the first emperor of the Qin dynasty (221–206 B.C.), was the first to unify the country. To ward off attacks from peoples from Central Asia, he joined together and added sections to existing defensive walls, thus establishing the Great Wall of China. Traders and missionaries under the Han (206 B.C.–A.D. 220) and Tang (A.D. 618–907) dynasties spread Chinese culture throughout East Asia. The explorer Zheng He (JUHNG HUH) sailed as far as the coast of East Africa under the Ming dynasty in the early 1400s. From the mid-1600s to the early 1900s, the Qing dynasty ruled China.

By the 1600s, Europeans had set up trade routes to China and other parts of East Asia to gain access to the region's silk and tea trade. China rejected these efforts. In the 1800s, frustration prompted some European countries to force China to open more ports. Later, European governments and Japan divided large areas of China into spheres of influences, or areas over which they had exclusive trading rights.

China Today

C The Chinese dynasties ended in 1911 after a revolution led by Sun Yat-sen. A tumultuous period followed in which warlords competed for control. When Sun died in 1925, Chiang Kai-shek came to power and formed the Nationalist government of the Republic of China. Chiang's rival, however, a Communist named Mao Zedong, won the support of China's farmers. Civil war erupted, and the Communists eventually took power in 1949. They set up the People's Republic of China on the mainland. The Republic of China was on Taiwan, where Nationalists had fled after the war.

institute to organize and establish

In the 1950s, the Communist government **instituted** the "Great Leap Forward." Small-scale farms were replaced by large government farms as part of economic and social change. However, the economy faltered and the new farms failed to produce enough food, causing millions to die of starvation.

Despite these failures, Mao still dreamed of a classless society. He believed that only an atmosphere of constant revolutionary fervor could enable the Chinese to

TIME LINE

Modern CHINA

Since the mid-twentieth century, China has been transformed from an impoverished agrarian society to the economic powerhouse of Asia. However, these profound changes have come at a great cost.

CRITICAL THINKING

1. ***Describing*** How did China try to speed up its change from an agrarian society to an industrial society?
2. ***Analyzing*** What challenges has China faced during its transformation?

W **1940**

1949 Mao Zedong proclaims the establishment of the People's Republic of China.

1958 Great Leap Forward begins a massive government effort to industrialize China.

1966 Cultural Revolution begins with the aim of strengthening communism in China by rooting out capitalist and traditionalist elements.

1986 China issues Open Door Policy to encourage foreign investment and development of a market economy.

©Hulton-Deutsch Collection/Corbis

networks Online Teaching Options

GRAPH

Grain Production in China, 1950–1970

Reading Graphs Have students examine this chart that details changes in Chinese grain production over time, including a drop in production during China's Great Leap Forward. Ask students how the Great Leap Forward affected the production of rice, wheat, and soybeans. Have students find comparable data for other countries. **AL** **Visual/Spatial**

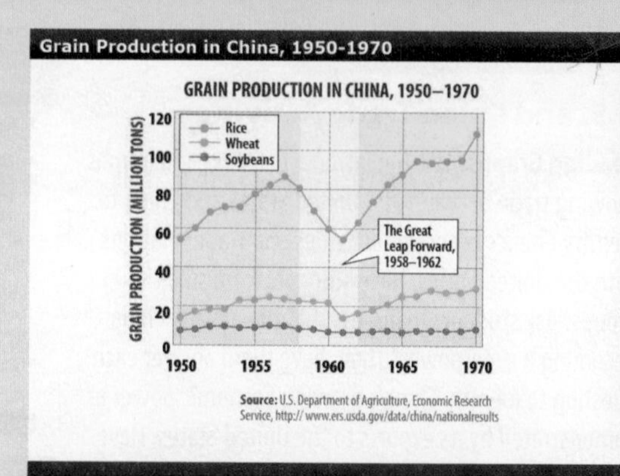

achieve the final stage of communism. In 1966 Mao launched the Great Proletarian Cultural Revolution in which urban and educated Chinese were sent to work on rural farms. The goal was to cleanse Chinese society of elements thought to be guilty of embracing capitalist ideas.

In the late 1970s, Deng Xiaoping, with other new government leaders, encouraged modernization and limited capitalism. They made some businesses and farms available for private ownership. Officials also began to allow foreign businesses and technology into the country. Free-market influences and the modernization they represented have gradually opened China's economy and society further.

G1

Mongolia became an independent country in 1921. The current flag was adopted in 1992, when Mongolia became a democracy.

▲ **CRITICAL THINKING**

1. ***Drawing Conclusions*** Why do you think Mongolians did not want to be part of the People's Republic of China?
2. ***Making Inferences*** Why might the Soviet Union have wanted Mongolia to be a Communist state?

Taiwan and Mongolia

Tensions have remained high between the Republic of China on Taiwan and the People's Republic of China on the mainland. Both have desired to reunite since the 1950s, but they cannot agree on how this might occur. Taiwan has embraced democracy and industry, but China has not reached the same levels of change. In recent years, Taiwan has invested billions of dollars in factories located on the mainland. China receives key computer and electronics parts from Taiwan. Such business interests have created an intermingling of the Chinese and Taiwanese economies.

G2

Early inhabitants of Mongolia were the Xiongnu, a contemporary rival empire of the Qin and Han dynasties in China. Later, under Genghis Khan, the Mongol Empire with its capital in Karakorum took over much of China, Russia, and Central Asia. After the empire fell, the Qing claimed it as the Chinese province of Outer Mongolia. When China's Qing dynasty was overthrown in 1911, the modern country of Mongolia was created. The Mongolians had been loyal to the Qing dynasty, but they refused to be part of the new China. From 1924 to 1991, the Soviet Union pressured Mongolia to become and remain a Communist state. When Soviet communism collapsed in the 1990s, however, Mongolia adopted a democratic constitution.

✓ **READING PROGRESS CHECK**

Describing How did the Great Leap Forward affect China?

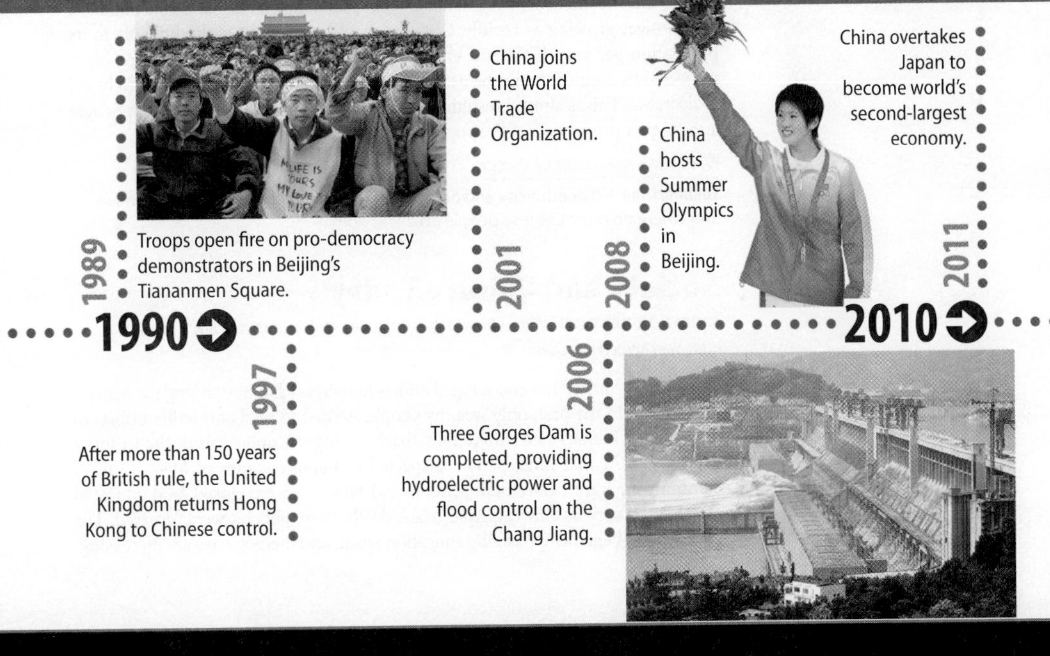

1989 Troops open fire on pro-democracy demonstrators in Beijing's Tiananmen Square.
2001 China joins the World Trade Organization.
2008 China hosts Summer Olympics in Beijing.
2011 China overtakes Japan to become world's second-largest economy.
1990
2010
1997 After more than 150 years of British rule, the United Kingdom returns Hong Kong to Chinese control.
2006 Three Gorges Dam is completed, providing hydroelectric power and flood control on the Chang Jiang.

CHAPTER 28, Lesson 2

Human Geography of China and Mongolia

G1 Critical Thinking Skills

Constructing Arguments Have students read the information about Mao Zedong. **Ask: Was Mao a failure or a visionary?** *(Student answers may vary, but they should understand that while Mao dreamed of a classless society, he was a dictator who brutally imposed his will on the Chinese people. However, Mao unified China after the revolution (except for Taiwan), and raised the status of peasants and industrial workers, but many of his agricultural policies failed.)* **Did Deng Xiaoping put China on a better path? Explain.** *(Student answers may vary, but they should understand that while Deng embraced modernization, the free market, private ownership, and an improved economy, human rights violations remained a problem in China.)* BL **Logical/Mathematical**

G2 Critical Thinking Skills

Comparing and Contrasting Have students compare and contrast the histories of Taiwan and Mongolia, noting their relations with the People's Republic of China. **Ask: Why do tensions remain between China and Taiwan?** *(Possible answers: China is a communist regime; Taiwan is a democracy. China does not recognize Taiwan's independence.)* **Why did Outer Mongolia refuse to become part of the new China after 1911?** *(The Mongolians had been loyal to the Qing dynasty.)* AL **Verbal/Linguistic**

Content Background Knowledge

Mongolia and Inner Mongolia Mongolia, sometimes called Outer Mongolia, is an independent nation. It is populated mainly by ethnic Mongolians. Inner Mongolia is an autonomous region in northern China. It has a small population of ethnic Mongolians, many of whom hold on to traditional ways. From time to time, mainly because of human rights disputes, tensions break out between the People's Republic of China and Inner Mongolia. Some citizens have pushed for independence from China.

INTERACTIVE TIME LINE

Modern China

Sequencing Have students examine the time line that displays events in China, showing its transformation from an impoverished agrarian society to the economic powerhouse of Asia. AL **Visual/Spatial**

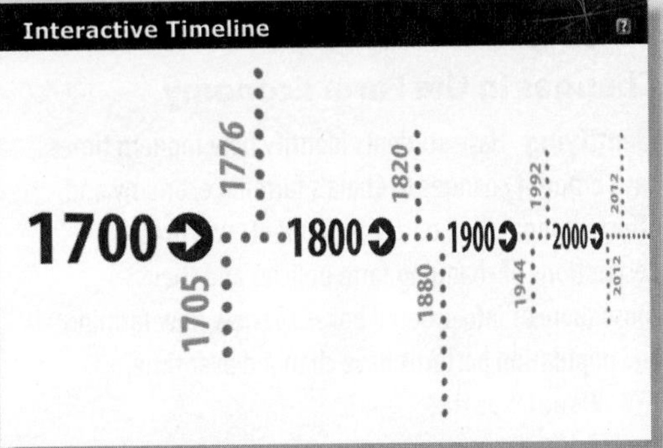

ANSWERS, p. 687

✓ **READING PROGRESS CHECK** The Great Leap Forward caused the economy to fail and lowered food production, causing widespread starvation.

CRITICAL THINKING

1. Answers may include loyalty to the Qing dynasty and being ethnically and culturally different from the Chinese.
2. Answers may include that the Soviets wanted it to be a communist state, given its location between the Soviet Union and China, because having a democracy in the region could create tensions.

C1 Critical Thinking Skills

Synthesizing Have students read the information about China's ethnic makeup. **Ask:** **What is unique about China's ethnic makeup?** *(It is composed mainly of one ethnic group, Han Chinese; only 8% of China's population is composed of other ethnic groups.)* **ELL** **Logical/Mathematical**

R Reading Skills

Reading Maps Supply students with a physical map and a population density map of China. Have students locate the areas of dense and sparse populations. **Ask:** **Why do large regions of China remain sparsely populated?** *(Possible answer: unfavorable climate and terrain)* **Why are many rural people moving to the cities?** *(Possible answers: hope for a better life, scarcity of land, and lack of services in the countryside)* **Verbal/Linguistic**

C2 Critical Thinking Skills

Constructing Arguments Divide students into teams, one side representing people who support China's one-child policy and the other side representing people who oppose it. Have students debate the issue. Each side should give reasons for their positions. **Ask:** **What would have happened to China's population if the one-child policy had not been put into effect?** *(Possible answer: the population might have increased beyond China's capacity to sustain it.)* **AL** **Interpersonal, Logical/Mathematical**

W Writing Skills

Argument Ask students to imagine that they are citizens of China. Have them write a letter to a government official explaining why they believe that all children should go to school and be taught to read and write. **ELL** **Intrapersonal, Verbal/Linguistic**

Population Patterns

GUIDING QUESTION *How has the migration of rural dwellers to urban areas affected China's population?*

C1 The Han dynasty gave its name to what is today the largest ethnic group in China. Ethnic Han Chinese comprise approximately 92 percent of China's more than 1.3 billion people. About 55 ethnic groups make up the remaining 8 percent.

Non-Chinese ethnic groups governed by China have their own distinct cultures and histories. Tibet, once a Buddhist kingdom, was taken over by China in 1959. Tensions between the Chinese and the Tibetans continue to simmer.

Taiwan and China share a long history. Chinese people who immigrated to Taiwan hundreds of years ago make up the majority of the inhabitants there. Only about 2 percent of Taiwan's people are **aborigines**, or original inhabitants.

aborigine an area's original inhabitant

R Like China, Mongolia has a largely homogeneous population. Most inhabitants of Mongolia are ethnic Mongolians. About 80 percent are Khalka Mongols who speak Mongolian. Other Mongolians belong to different linguistic groups.

Although China covers a large territory, 90 percent of the people live on just one-sixth of the land. Much of this is in the fertile valleys and plains of the Huang He, Chang Jiang, and Xi, China's three great rivers. River valleys and coastal plains are the location of many large urban centers, such as Shanghai, Beijing, Tianjin, and Guangzhou. In contrast, Mongolia claims a population density of only 5 people per square mile (2 people per sq. km) over its vast steppe regions. Most of Mongolia's 2.7 million people live in the north-central part of the country.

C2 While many Chinese still live and work on farms, the migration of millions of people to quickly growing urban areas continues to increase. This urbanization has resulted in overcrowding in cities. Because so many people have left the countryside to live in cities, farms are experiencing labor shortages. To remedy this, China has built dozens of new agricultural towns in remote areas. Such towns provide more social services to attract rural people, with a higher quality of life.

The Chinese government has reduced population growth. A policy of one child per married couple was begun in 1979. This policy has reduced the number of people born since then. While the current population of China is 1.36 billion, it is no longer growing as rapidly. China now adds about 5.3 million people to its population per year. If the one-child policy is maintained, population growth is projected to decline within the next 10 years, and the population is likely to begin to decrease. This is already resulting in an aging population in which older people are a higher proportion of the population.

✓ **READING PROGRESS CHECK**

Summarizing What ethnicity and occupation does a typical Chinese person have, and where do most Chinese people live?

Society and Culture Today

GUIDING QUESTION *What cultural beliefs, practices, and distinctive achievements and attitudes characterize China?*

W China's government has encouraged efforts to increase literacy among the general population. In the past, only wealthy people learned to read and write. Efforts to improve the literacy rate suffered a setback during the upheavals of the Cultural Revolution. At that time, people suspected of being enemies of Mao's form of communism were persecuted. Schools and factories were closed, and educated people were seen as a threat. After Mao's death, these policies were reversed. The government began emphasizing education again, and literacy rates are increasing.

688

networks Online Teaching Options

INTERACTIVE WHITEBOARD ACTIVITY

Changes in the Farm Economy

Identifying Have students identify how modern times have brought changes to China's farming economy and affected population patterns. Students will drag descriptions of changing farm policies and their consequences into ordered boxes to show how farming and population patterns have changed over time. **AL** **Visual/Spatial**

Changes in the Farm Economy

Directions: Agriculture is the largest segment of China's economy, employing one-third of the workforce, but has undergone many changes with shifting government policies. Place in order the ways in which farming as well as population patterns have changed over time by dragging the descriptions into the ordered boxes at the right.

Descriptions	Correctly Ordered Descriptions
China builds agricultural towns to draw city dwellers back to rural life as farms face labor shortages.	1.
Growing urban populations create a greater demand for food.	2.
A surplus of farmers from government communes move to cities for work.	3.
Crop production plunges and many people starve.	4.
Farmers meet growing urban demand by selling locally, increasing their profits.	5.
Great Leap Forward organizes farmers into government-owned communes where work and profit is shared.	6.
Government encourages small family farms over communes, allowing farmers to keep extra crops for their own profit.	7.

ANSWERS, p. 688

✓ **READING PROGRESS CHECK** Most people are Han Chinese, work in agriculture, and live in the fertile valleys of the Huang He, Chang Jiang, and Xi River with urban centers also in coastal plains.

Mandarin, a dialect of Han Chinese, **dominates** spoken language in China. Written Chinese uses **ideograms**, symbolic pictures that stand for ideas, unlike Western languages, which use letters to represent sounds. Compared to letters, ideograms have both an advantage and a disadvantage. The advantage is that people who do not speak the same dialect can still communicate through writing. The disadvantage is that Chinese writing is difficult to learn, since there are thousands of ideograms. However, the written language has been a major factor in China's cultural unity.

dominate to exert influence over

ideogram a pictorial character or symbol that represents a specific meaning or idea

Life expectancy has risen to over 70 years due to better health care. As a general rule, Communist governments pay for medical treatment for their people. Economic reforms, however, have resulted in the Chinese government covering fewer services than before.

Some Chinese are identified as **atheists**, or those who do not believe in a deity, but others practice Buddhism, Daoism, and Islam. The government controls religious freedom. Since 1962, ruling Chinese officials have restricted the practice of Buddhism in Tibet. In 2012 the government began stationing officials in Tibetan monasteries to oversee what is taught there. Mongolia's people are largely Tibetan Buddhist (Lamaist), but some are Muslim or atheist or shamanist. **C**

atheist a person who believes there is no god

The Arts

China has a rich history of artistic and literary accomplishments. These include ancient poetry, which describes nature's beauty, and traditional opera, which features costumes and martial arts. Under the Tang dynasty, potters created fine porcelain, known as "china" in the West. During the Cultural Revolution, the government nearly destroyed traditional arts, but it did not crush all artistic endeavors. China is now enjoying a resurgence in the arts. **T**

ANALYZING PRIMARY SOURCES 

The Spread of Rap and Hip-Hop in China

Chinese youth interpret rap music in their own way by changing its language and instrumentation. They have made it unique to their culture.

"... Chinese students admitted to not fully understanding the lyrics of the American songs they loved. But the love for hip-hop was not solely for the lyrics. It was the music, the emotions conveyed in the lyrics, that made hip-hop such a unifying force that overcame any barrier—linguistic or geographic.

Still, the music did not come so easily. 'You can't rap in Chinese, it's a tonal language.' 'You can't rap in China, they'll censor you.' ... all sentiments that kept Chinese hip-hop from taking off with a running start. But hip-hop could not be stopped. ...

To this day, hip-hop still comes head-to-head with censorship and doubts on the ability to rap in Chinese dialects and creativity. Yet, these obstacles provide listeners with the best form of hip-hop music Chinese youth can offer."

—Carla Amurao, "From West to Far East: Rappin' and Rockin' the House," *Tavis Smiley: China Week, PBS California*, July 2011

Hip-hop dancing started in the early 1970s in the United States in the Bronx in New York City. It has become increasingly popular among youth in China's major cities, as the country has opened its borders to other cultural influences.

DBQ ▲ CRITICAL THINKING

1. ***Identifying Central Issues*** Describe the difficulties that people may face creating rap music in China. RH.9–10.2
2. ***Speculating*** How do you think the Internet and social media have influenced the growth of hip-hop in China? RH.9–10.2

C Critical Thinking Skills

Comparing and Contrasting Remind students that health care and freedom of religion are quality-of-life issues. Have students discuss the positive and negative aspects of living under a communist regime like China's that provides health care to its citizens but limits their right to practice their own religion. Have students speculate why Chinese officials restrict the practice of Buddhism in Tibet. **Ask:** **What might it be about Buddhism that many officials fear?** *(Student answers may vary, but they should understand that religious leaders often are supporters of human rights. Buddhist monks have been deeply involved in Tibet's push for autonomy and human rights.)* **BL** **Logical/Mathematical**

Content Background Knowledge

Demographic Data: China

Urban population: 47% (2010)
Infant mortality: 15.2 deaths per 1,000 live births; 116th in the world
Life expectancy: 74.99; 100th in the world
Health expenditures: 5.1% of GDP (2010); 138th in the world
Literacy: 92.2%; male, 96%; female, 88.5% (2007)
GDP per capita: $9,100 (2012 est.); 122nd in the world
Population below the poverty line: 13.4%

T Technology Skills

Presenting Divide students into small groups to research the literary and artistic accomplishments of China. Each group might select a different art form to research—poetry, opera, pottery, and the like. Have students make multimedia presentations to the class that include photographs, other visuals, and music. **Auditory/Musical, Visual/Spatial**

PRIMARY SOURCE

The Spread of Rap and Hip-Hop in China

Analyzing Primary Sources Chinese youth interpret rap music in their own way by changing its language and instrumentation. They have made it unique to their culture. Have students read the primary source to better understand the popularity of hip-hop and rap music in China. **AL** **Visual/Spatial**

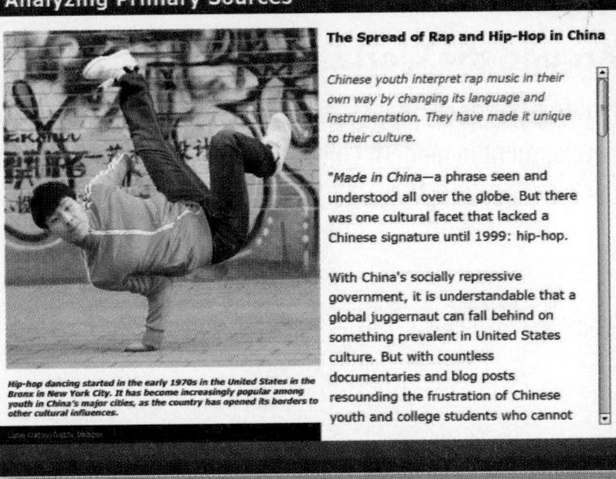

ANSWERS, p. 689

DBQ Document-Based Questions

1. Difficulties include creating rap in a tonal language with multiple dialects and government censorship.
2. Answers may differ but could include that the Internet and social media have increased the visibility and availability of hip-hop and allowed it to be more easily listened to and accessed in China.

CHAPTER 28, Lesson 2
Human Geography of China and Mongolia

T Technology Skills

Implementing After students have read the caption under the photo, have pairs work together to research how well females are doing in the areas of education and the workforce in China. Students should do additional research to learn if the advances in education are limited to urban areas or if rural schools are permitting female students as well. Have student pairs write a brief proposal for improved educational quality for girls in China. Proposals should lead to a class discussion about the rights of women in China. **Visual/Spatial**

R Reading Skills

Listing Have students list the ways communism and a changing economy have impacted families and women in China. **Ask:** **Why is the reliance on extended families decreasing while nuclear families are increasing?** *(Possible answers: More families are moving to cities; nuclear families are more adaptable to urban living.)* **AL Verbal/Linguistic**

C Critical Thinking Skills

Analyzing Cause and Effect Have students describe the changes China's agricultural sector has experienced since 1949. **Ask:** **Why did the Great Leap Forward initiative fail?** *(Possible answers: Farmers did not like working in communes; they did not benefit from their toils; bureaucrats, not farmers, were setting policies.)* **What happened after the new policies restored small family farms and why?** *(Possible answers: production increased; farmers profited from their own labor and were able to make their own decisions based on individual circumstances.)* **BL Verbal/Linguistic**

Today in China, females are receiving more education and gaining places in the workforce.

▲ CRITICAL THINKING

1. ***Analyzing*** How has the position of women and girls improved in China?
2. ***Drawing Conclusions*** What long-term effects might the one-child policy have on China's families?

Family and the Status of Women

The most important social unit in China's history has been the family. It monitors the behavior of its members and their welfare and provides work. Communism changed family bonds, weakening them in favor of loyalty to the state. The government provided jobs. Husbands and wives were sometimes separated in different regions to work. Family size was generally limited to one child.

Economic growth has brought changes to Chinese families. While most rural families remain traditional, families in urban areas are changing. Extended families are decreasing, while nuclear families are increasing. People are marrying and having their only child later in life. Divorce rates are climbing.

Traditionally, Chinese women have had a low position in society. Men have had all the power in the family, society, and government. Modern governments have worked to improve women's status, with some success. Women participate in the Chinese workforce at a relatively high level. However, few have achieved powerful positions in business or government.

The traditional preference for boys, combined with the one-child policy, has resulted in the death of many female infants through purposeful neglect. Girls are put up for adoption at high rates. Population figures from 2012 show that there are 93 women for every 100 men in China. In contrast, there are 102 women for every 100 men in the United States.

✓ READING PROGRESS CHECK

Making Connections What features of the Chinese written language have helped unify the culture?

Economic Activities

GUIDING QUESTION *How do domestic activities, government policy, trade, and international relations interact to form modern China's economy?*

commune a collective farming community

merchant marine a country's shipping fleet that engages in trade

dissident a citizen who speaks out against government policies

A little more than one-third of China's workforce is involved in agriculture, making it the largest segment of the economy. No country produces more rice, wheat, and tea than China. China's farmers also produce soybeans, cotton, and silk.

Since 1949, the agricultural sector has seen many changes enforced by the government. The Great Leap Forward organized farmers into **communes**, or large farming communities. The government decided what and how much to grow, and commune members shared work and products. The results were disastrous. Crop production plunged, and starvation resulted during this time.

Chinese leaders instituted new policies in the 1980s. Such policies encouraged the development of small family farms. Farmers could sell and keep the profits when they produced extra crops or livestock.

At the beginning of the twenty-first century, Chinese farms began operating under different conditions. China's growing urban population now consumes crops through markets supplied by the country's farms as well as imports. Farmers' earnings have improved substantially as a result. These reforms, however, created a surplus of farmworkers who had previously been employed by larger collective farms. Many of these workers have moved to cities.

Market reforms have increased the growth of China's economy at a strong rate. In 2010 China became the world's largest exporter. However, challenges exist. Areas on the coast are wealthier than the interior agricultural regions. This economic gap brings new migrants from the countryside to the cities.

networks Online Teaching Options

VIDEO

Around the World–Shanghai

Making Connections Have students watch this video to learn more about rapid development in modern Chinese cities such as Shanghai. Then have them complete the corresponding Video Activity worksheet. **AL Visual/Spatial**

ANSWERS, p. 690

✓ READING PROGRESS CHECK The Chinese written language uses ideograms, or pictures, allowing people who do not speak the same dialect to still communicate, unifying the culture.

CRITICAL THINKING

1. The government has worked to improve the status of women and many are now in the workforce at relatively high levels.
2. There are fewer extended families; people are waiting longer to have their one child, resulting in an aging population; and there are fewer women than men, which will also result in a decline in population.

China's waterways provide important routes for the transportation of goods to seaports like Shanghai near the outlet of the Chang Jiang. Large, oceangoing ships can navigate to the port of Wuhan in central China. The **merchant marine** fleet is used for commercial transport. Major ports are Hong Kong, Tianjin, and Guangzhou.

Both China and the United States seek increased trade, but obstacles exist. The United States wants increased trade to take advantage of China's growing economy. China's undervalued currency, established to keep export prices down, has resulted in a flood of inexpensive Chinese goods to other countries.

Although China's economy is strong and its global trade aspirations ambitious, positive political reforms have lagged. Human rights issues are of particular concern. **Dissidents**, or citizens who speak out against government policies, are harshly treated. In 1989, when Chinese students held a protest for democratic reforms in Beijing's Tiananmen Square, government troops responded brutally. China's major trade partners—the United States, Japan, and the European Union—have encouraged China to respect human rights. They imposed **economic sanctions**, or trade restrictions, on China in response to the events at Tiananmen Square. When China released several imprisoned dissidents, the United States relented on some sanctions.

The United States hopes that trade may stimulate democratic reforms in China. The U.S. Congress granted full trading privileges to China in 2000. The next year, China became a member of the World Trade Organization (WTO), an international body overseeing trade agreements and disputes.

Hong Kong's robust economy is due in large part to its proximity to Shenzhen, a **Special Economic Zone (SEZ)** that welcomes foreign investment. Such areas experience only minimal interference by the government. China has established SEZs, and uses the income to expand manufacturing. Taiwan has one of the strongest export-based economies in the world. Textiles, plastics, and electronic goods are specialties. Taiwan's depends heavily on exports. When demand decreased in 2009, it weakened the economy, which began to improve in 2010.

Mongolia's extensive grasslands are used for grazing huge numbers of livestock—sheep, goats, cattle, camels, and horses. Only 1 percent of its land can be farmed. Land is often government-owned, although efforts to privatize it have boosted economic growth. In the last few decades mining has become a major activity, with coal, copper, and fluorite as exports. Some textile and food production takes place, and tourism is on the rise. In addition, foreign investors have shown interest in the country's mineral deposits, which include gold, copper, and oil found in the Gobi.

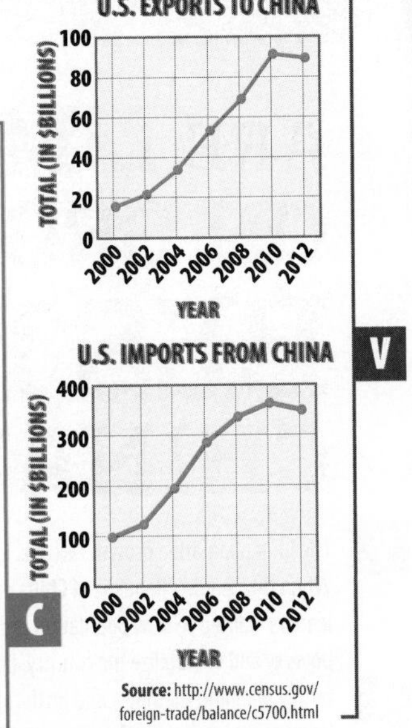

Source: http://www.census.gov/foreign-trade/balance/c5700.html

China is one of the United States's leading trading partners.

▲ **CRITICAL THINKING**

1. ***Drawing Inferences*** Describe the U.S.-China trade relationship.
2. ***Predicting*** How will these graphs look in 10 years? Explain.

economic sanctions trade restrictions

Special Economic Zone (SEZ) a relatively small district in China that is fully open to global commerce

✓ **READING PROGRESS CHECK**

Inferring How has life changed for Chinese farmers since the 1980s?

LESSON 2 REVIEW 

Reviewing Vocabulary (Tier Three Words)

1. ***Identifying*** What is an ideogram and how is it used? RH.9–10.4
2. ***Summarizing*** Who are dissidents? What role did they play in the Tiananmen protests of 1989? RH.9–10.4

Using Your Notes

3. ***Interpreting*** Use your graphic organizer to write a paragraph about how China's culture has affected the way it carries out economic activities.

Answering the Guiding Questions

4. ***Drawing Conclusions*** What influence did ancient Chinese history have on government, culture, and daily life in modern times?
5. ***Evaluating*** How has the migration of rural dwellers to urban areas affected China's population?
6. ***Identifying Perspectives*** What cultural beliefs, practices, and distinctive achievements and attitudes characterize China?
7. ***Assessing*** How do domestic activities, government policy, trade, and international relations interact to form modern China's economy?

Writing Activity

8. ***Argument*** In a paragraph, take the Chinese government's position and defend their policies, economic reforms, and attitude toward human rights. WHST.9–10.1

V Visual Skills

Analyzing Graphs Direct students to analyze the two graphs. Note that the vertical axis figures differ on each graph. **Ask:** How much did the United States export to China in 2000? *(nearly $20 billion)* How much did it import from China? *($100 billion)* Was this a favorable trade balance? Explain. *(No; The U.S. imported 5 times more than it exported.)* Did the situation improve or worsen in 2012? Explain. *(It improved slightly for the U.S.; it worsened slightly for China, but the balance of trade was still in China's favor.)* **Verbal/Linguistic**

C Critical Thinking Skills

Analyzing Ethical Issues Ask: How is China's undervalued currency an obstacle to trade with the United States? *(China is able to flood the market with cheap goods.)* Why are human rights issues an obstacle to trade? *(The United States sometimes restricts trade in response to egregious human rights violations.)* Why do China's trading partners care about its human rights policies and should they? *(Student answers may vary, but they should understand that as a democracy, the United States champions democratic institutions and human rights around the world. It hopes to pressure China into reforming its policies.)*
BL Verbal/Linguistic

CLOSE & REFLECT

Listing Ask students to look back over the lesson and list the major changes that China experienced between 1949 and the late 1970s and between the 1970s and the present. Have students use their lists to review the lesson.

LESSON 2 REVIEW ANSWERS

Reviewing Vocabulary

1. An ideogram is a picture that represents an idea that is used in the written Chinese language. Ideograms allow people who do not speak the same language but know the written language to communicate.
2. Dissidents are people who speak out against the government or its policies. Dissidents gathered in Tiananmen Square to protest for democratic reforms.

Using Your Notes

3. Paragraphs may include: historic isolationism, treatment of dissidents, exports, and importance of agriculture.

Answering the Guiding Questions

4. Confucius and Laozi founded the philosophies of Confucianism and Daoism, which still influence China today. Historic dynasties set the stage for one-party and communist rule of modern times.
5. Cities are becoming overcrowded and farms are experiencing labor shortages.
6. Some Chinese are atheists, but others practice Buddhism, Daoism or Islam; traditional opera and making of porcelain "china"; a traditional preference for boys; loyalty to the state; increasing education; and a common written language using ideograms.
7. Agriculture employs one-third of the workforce. Market reforms and ambitions of global trade aspirations have increased economic growth.

Writing Activity

8. Paragraphs should include a discussion of economic sanctions and the Chinese government's response.

ANSWERS, p. 691

✓ **READING PROGRESS CHECK** Farmers are now earning more money from their crops, but the need for many farmworkers was eliminated as larger collective farms ceased to exist, causing an influx of these workers to cities.

CRITICAL THINKING

1. The U.S. imports more than it exports to China.
2. These graphs will likely show increased trade because the U.S. and China are working toward this goal.

ENGAGE

V Visual Skills

Identifying Perspectives Have students read the title and first sentence of this Case Study. To help students organize information as they read, have them create a visual time line that includes key dates and events discussed in this feature. Students may wish to conduct additional research to identify when certain events occurred that were integral to China's efforts to slow population growth.

TEACH & ASSESS

R Reading Skills

Using Case Studies Ask volunteers to take turns reading aloud each sentence, beginning with "When the People's Republic of China came to power. . . ." **Ask:** **What were the reasons the Chinese government wanted to slow population growth?** *(to reduce poverty and to stabilize the country)* **Were the government's initial tactics effective?** *(No; the government had to impose a one-child policy after the population neared 1 billion people.)* AL **Verbal/Linguistic, Interpersonal**

T Technology Skills

Analyzing Ethical Issues Organize the class into small groups. Have each group conduct research to learn more about China's one-child policy, assigning one of the following groups discussed in the text to each group of students: minority groups, people whose first child has disabilities, people in rural areas, or people who pay a fine for each additional child. Have groups identify facts and figures that show the percentage of people who make up their assigned group. Then have students in each group compile their findings in a summary and present their findings to the class. Guide a discussion about the ethical issues involved in China's one-child policy. BL **Logical/Mathematical, Interpersonal**

Content Background Knowledge

Population Limitations The country of India has a planning commission that has set forth guidelines to limit population growth. However, reasons for India's restrictions on its population relate to reducing the spread of disease and lowering the infant mortality rate. For example, the Health, Nutrition and Family Welfare division of the commission has outlined specific reasons for limiting population growth. These include the ability to provide clean drinking water, reduce malnutrition among children, and reduce anemia among women and girls by 50 percent.

Case Study: **Culture** CCSS

ARE LIMITS ON GROWTH BEST FOR CHINA?

V The high population growth rate has long been a concern in China. When the People's Republic of China came to power in 1949, its leaders wanted to slow population growth in order to reduce poverty and to stabilize the country. R People were exposed to new family planning methods, and birth control was encouraged. However, once the population neared 1 billion in the 1970s, leaders wanted people to have no more than two children. By 1980, a one-child policy was put in place and continues today.

T Most people must follow the one-child policy and are often rewarded for doing so. However, there are exceptions. Some minority groups, people whose first child has disabilities, and people in rural areas may have more than one child. Also, people may pay a fine for each additional child. However, those who knowingly go against the policy are required to pay large fines. Some have reported that if the fine is not paid, families can lose their homes or jobs.

Demographers and others think that China should end the one-child policy. These critics warn that if it continues, China will have a shortage of workers and fewer people available to take care of an aging population.

China's National Population and Family Planning Commission manages the one-child policy. Their goal is to make sure that the country can sustain development. To meet this goal, they monitor the effects of population changes on the economy, society, natural resources, and the environment. The Family Planning Commission is currently reexamining the one-child policy. They will only make changes if the revisions benefit the continued growth of the country.

networks Online Teaching Options

INTERACTIVE IMAGE

Nanjing Road

Using Case Studies Use this interactive image to introduce students to the Case Study topic of population growth rate. Before viewing the image, ask students to share what they have read or heard about the limits of growth in China. List the statements that they discuss. Then click through the interactive components of the image to discuss the content. Have students write a paragraph about one aspect of the image that was interesting or surprising to them. Ask several volunteers to share their paragraphs with the class.
AL **Visual/Spatial, Verbal/Linguistic**

Benefits of Population Limits

PRIMARY SOURCE

"Henan has much to teach the world in family planning, but it is a hard lesson to learn. Officials from Africa and India come to study what we are doing in China, but I'm not sure that they can apply it the same way. That's because they don't have a Communist party so it is difficult for them to take such strong steps."

—Liu Shaojie, Vice Director of the Population Commission in Henan province, China, quoted in *The Guardian,* October 25, 2011

End Population Limits

PRIMARY SOURCE

"Everyone has blindly accepted the fact that population control has helped China's economy, but it has never been proven. . . . In fact, by 2030, no matter what policy China adopts the population will start to shrink. And I have never seen a country with a shrinking population and sound economic development. Western countries may have shrinking populations, but they have immigrants to make up their labour force. China does not have large immigration, so aiming for a zero or negative birth rate is very risky."

—Liang Zhongtang, a former committee member of the National Family Planning Commission, quoted in *The Telegraph,* September 25, 2010

"We have been discussing the one-child policy since 2000. . . . It is just a matter of finding the right solution. Making the jump to two children is only a matter of time now. . . . If China sticks to the one-child policy, we are looking at a situation as bad as the one in southern Europe. Old people will make up a third of the population by 2050."

—Li Jiamin, a specialist in population studies at Nankai University, quoted in *The Telegraph,* October 31, 2012

What do you think? DBQ

1. ***Drawing Conclusions*** Why might Chinese people hesitate to speak out against China's one-child policy? RH.9–10.2
2. ***Identifying Central Issues*** According to critics of the one-child policy, what are the risks of keeping the policy as it is? RH.9–10.2; RH.9–10.6
3. ***Hypothesizing*** Why might Chinese people in urban areas and Chinese people in rural areas have different opinions on the one-child policy? RH.9–10.2

Case Study 693

W Writing Skills

Informative Have students research about China's one-child policy, its impact on girls and women, and the cost of fines for violating the policy. In addition to reliable, unbiased reports, have students identify an opinion piece about the policy from a respected news organization such as *The New York Times.* Have students present their findings in an informational essay. Ask volunteers to present their essays to the class, voicing their own opinions about the policy if desired. **Visual/Spatial, Interpersonal**

C Critical Thinking Skills

Evaluating Primary Sources Have students reread each quote, taking notes about the differences in opinion regarding China's one-child policy. Ask students to share their notes with the class, allowing them to voice their opinions as to whether they agree with each quote. **Ask: Why does Li Jiamin believe that China should not stick to its one-child policy?** *(Li Jiamin believes that if China continues to enforce its one-child policy, it will end up with a population like that of southern Europe in which a third of the population is made up of "old people.")* **Verbal/Linguistic**

CLOSE & REFLECT

Argument Instruct students to write an argument defending one of the primary sources in this Case Study. Have students conduct additional research to provide supporting evidence for their arguments. Invite students to share their arguments with the class. Guide a class discussion about China's one-child policy and its ethical implications.

INTERACTIVE IMAGE

Busy Street in Calcutta, India

Comparing Have students view this interactive image of a busy street in India and compare it to the image of the busy street of China in their texts. Organize students into small groups and then read aloud the Content Background Knowledge section of the Teacher Edition that explains India's population limits. Ask groups to use this information, the information in the Case Study, and the images to compare the population issues in China and India. Then guide a class discussion in which groups share their comparisons. **Logical/Mathematical, Interpersonal**

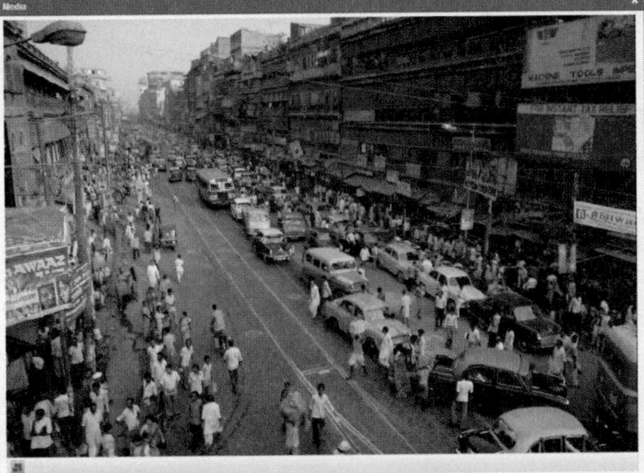

ANSWERS, p. 693

DBQ What do you think?

1. There are risks to speaking out against government policies, and communism has long functioned by creating loyalty between the people and the state.
2. The risks of keeping the one-child policy include a shrinking and aging population, an insufficient number of workers, and a lack of economic development.
3. Some people in rural areas are allowed to have more than one child, making them less likely to have a poor opinion of the policy.

ENGAGE

R Reading Skills

Identifying Have students list ways people in the United States and other developed countries have been impacted by industrialization and economic development. Then have students brainstorm ideas about how rapid industrialization and economic development might be affecting the people of China.

TEACH & ASSESS

C1 Critical Thinking Skills

Analyzing Cause and Effect Have students read about the consequences of China's growing demand for electric power. **Ask:** How and why has economic prosperity increased demand for electric power in China? *(As industry and populations grow and standards of living increase, more electricity is needed.)* What are China's two main sources of electrical power today? *(hydroelectricity and coal-burning power plants)* How does building hydroelectric plants affect the environment? *(Changing the natural flow of rivers has led to endangerment and extinction of plants and animals.)* Is power produced in a coal-burning plant less or more harmful to the environment than other energy sources? *(Student answers may vary, but should include that burning coal produces a host of environmental problems including acid rain, air pollution, and climate change.)* AL Logical/Mathematical

C2 Critical Thinking Skills

Hypothesizing Have students consider the advantages and disadvantages of nuclear power. **Ask:** Why is China planning to build many more nuclear power plants in the future? *(because of the growing need for electricity; hydroelectric and coal-burning power plants have many negative environmental effects)* What is one of the advantages of nuclear power plants? *(little air pollution)* Are there any negative effects? *(nuclear waste disposal problems; the possibility of meltdowns and malfunctions)* BL Logical/Mathematical

ANSWERS, p. 694

READING PROGRESS CHECK The large local supplies, low cost, and lack of other power sources make China dependent on coal.

TAKING NOTES: Present: Land – desertification from overgrazing and soil erosion, erosion and flooding from desertification; Water – pollution of lakes and rivers; access to clean water because of problems with waste disposal; Air – air pollution and acid rain due to old technology and use of coal; **Future:** Land – barren and dry, loss of agriculture, loss of biodiversity; Water – loss of aquatic life, illness; Air – illness, continued climate change, damage to buildings

networks *There's More Online!*

- **GRAPH** Daily Oil Production and Consumption in China
- **IMAGE** Chinese Timber Plant
- **IMAGE** Smog and Traffic in Beijing
- **IMAGE** Electronics Factory
- **INFOGRAPHIC** Three Gorges Dam: Harnessing the Yangtze
- **INTERACTIVE SELF-CHECK QUIZ**
- **VIDEO** People and Their Environment: China and Mongolia

1.21
Gwtz
Powers 200
Homes

LESSON 3
People and Their Environment: China and Mongolia

ESSENTIAL QUESTION • *How do physical systems and human systems shape a place?*

Reading HELPDESK 

Academic Vocabulary (Tier Two Words)
- **utilize**
- **consequence**

Content Vocabulary (Tier Three Words)
- **nuclear**

TAKING NOTES: ***Integration of Knowledge and Ideas***

MAKING PREDICTIONS
As you read about the people and environment of China, use a graphic organizer like the one below to record the country's current environmental issues and predict what might happen if steps are not taken to address them.

China's Environmental Issues	Present	Future
Land		
Water		
Air		

It Matters Because

R *China's economic success has generated many critical issues that must be addressed so that people can live healthy and safe lives. Environmental issues in both China and Mongolia affect not only people, but also animals and the natural environment.*

Managing Resources

GUIDING QUESTION *How do China and Mongolia use fossil fuels as energy sources?*

China's growing economic prosperity has fueled a demand for more electric power. The country is now the number one consumer of electricity worldwide. Increasing living standards mean that more people can afford appliances and electronic devices. Meeting this increasing demand has become an issue for both the government and the public. A massive dam project known as the Three Gorges Dam was built on the Chang Jiang, or Yangtze River, to supply hydroelectric power to China's interior with its expanding population.

C1 While hydroelectric plants provide some power to China, the country's main source of power comes from burning fossil fuels. China and Mongolia both **utilize** large local reserves of coal. Rising oil prices make it difficult to end this dependency on cheaper coal. However, burning coal has serious **consequences** for the environment, including acid rain, air pollution, and climate change.

Power from **nuclear** plants is an option for many countries, but China has been slow to embrace it. Nuclear power provides only 1 percent of China's electricity. Future plans, however, involve the construction of at least 100 more nuclear power plants.

C2 Mongolia's valuable mineral deposits are putting its environment at risk. Mining often has long-term detrimental effects such as water sources contaminated with toxins and dead zones around open-pit mines. Yet economic development is sorely needed in the country to benefit its people.

READING PROGRESS CHECK

Summarizing Why is China so dependent on coal?

694

networks Online Teaching Options

INTERACTIVE BELLRINGER

Three Gorges Dam: Harnessing the Yangtze

Analyzing Visuals Use the introductory text and the infographic of the Three Gorges Dam to identify how the people and the government of China are addressing environmental issues. Have students form small groups. Ask them to discuss this question: How would you feel if everyone in your town or city—and the surrounding towns—was forced to relocate so a dam could be built that would provide more energy than that produced by most electric companies today? Then have students discuss each question. Ask each group to record all answers to each question. Then, in a class discussion, have each group share its answers. Compile a list of the answers on a flipchart or board.

AL Interpersonal, Intrapersonal, Visual/Spatial, Verbal/Linguistic

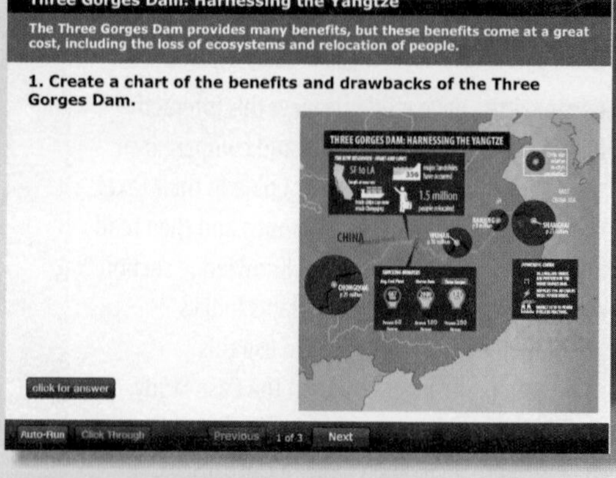
Three Gorges Dam: Harnessing the Yangtze
The Three Gorges Dam provides many benefits, but these benefits come at a great cost, including the loss of ecosystems and relocation of people.
1. Create a chart of the benefits and drawbacks of the Three Gorges Dam.
THREE GORGES DAM: HARNESSING THE YANGTZE
SF to LA
1.5 million
CHINA
click for answer
Auto-Run
Click Through
Previous
1 of 3
Next

Human Impact

GUIDING QUESTION *What special challenges come with globalization, and how will they affect China's future?*

In a world increasingly connected by the Internet and business and cultural exchanges, globalization exerts a stronger influence on Chinese life than ever before. In most periods of change in Chinese history, the country has tended to look within rather than seek out the cultures and trends of the outside world. This attitude was largely due to strong national pride, suspicion of outsiders, and more recently, rigid Communist rule.

When the Communists triumphed in 1949, the only area of the country able to maintain international connections was Hong Kong, ruled by the British. During the 1970s and early 1980s, Communist rulers instituted new policies, making an effort to open their economy to foreigners. Foreign influence began to be felt first on the coasts. Nightclubs, karaoke bars, fast-food restaurants, and theme parks began to appear. The Internet also began to have an impact on Chinese society.

The loosening of government control has resulted in the rise of regional identities, which had been suppressed before the late 1970s. This is especially apparent in southeastern China, where most people do not speak the dominant Mandarin language, making their culture distinctive. The Guangdong region of China, including Hong Kong—which was turned over to China by the British in 1997—is the main gateway for the entrance of foreign influences into the country.

Since the end of the Cold War, the balance of power in East Asia has shifted, with China rising to the top. It has the largest army in the world, a nuclear arsenal, and complex missile technology. All of this has combined to worry China's neighbors.

China's physical geography could potentially cause major problems in the future. Two of China's great rivers, the Huang He and Chang Jiang, have often produced disastrous floods. Flood control of the rivers has been attempted by constructing drainage channels and irrigation canals to carry away or redirect the water. Levees, dikes, and dams have also been built. Still, terrible flooding

Analyzing CCSS PRIMARY SOURCES

Speaking Manchu

"For decades, China's authoritarian policies kept a lid on ethnic expression. Now, as the party loosens control over society, individuals are defining themselves by their culture —embracing who they are, what language they speak and what their ancestors accomplished. 'This is not a hobby or an interest,' says Hukshen, a 22-year-old Manchu language student."

—Ian Johnson, "In China, the Forgotten Manchu Seek to Rekindle Their Glory," *The Wall Street Journal*, October 3, 2009

DBQ ***Identifying Cause and Effect*** Why was Manchu suppressed and why are some people working to preserve it?

RH.9–10.2

utilize to make use of

consequence the result of an action

nuclear of, relating to, or using the atomic nucleus, atomic energy, the atomic bomb, or atomic power

STR/AFP/Getty Images

The increasing demand for technology has offered new challenges and benefits to China and its people.

◀ **CRITICAL THINKING**

1. ***Identifying Perspectives*** How has the world's demand for technology affected China's citizens?
2. ***Synthesizing*** How do you think the Internet might contribute to changes in Chinese society?

VIDEO

Pollution in China

Analyzing Have students watch this video to see one of the consequences of pollution in Shanghai, China. **AL** **Visual/Spatial**

C Critical Thinking Skills

Analyzing Cause and Effect Review with students the history of China's relationships with the outside world. **Ask:** **Why was China reluctant to engage with the outside world for most of its history?** *(national pride, suspicion of outsiders, rigid Communist rule beginning under Mao)* **Why did Communist rulers after Mao do more to open China's economy to foreigners?** *(They hoped to improve China's economy. They needed trading partners.)* **How has this more open policy changed China?** *(It affected its society and culture: introduction of nightclubs, karaoke bars, fast-food restaurants, theme parks, Internet; rise of regional identities.)* **What might Mao have said about these changes?** *(Student answers will vary, but students should understand that Mao wanted to root out capitalist elements and ideas.)* **Logical/Mathematical**

R Reading Skills

Summarizing Have students read and summarize the paragraph about how China's future is threatened by its physical geography. **Ask:** **In what way is China's physical geography a threat to its future?** *(Possible answers: It is periodically subject to disastrous floods, which lead to loss of life and property. There is destruction of farmland and infrastructure, and it costs a lot of money to recover.)* **What flood control measures has China taken to mitigate the problem?** *(It has built drainage channels and irrigation canals to carry away or redirect water and levees, dikes, and dams to hold back water.)* **Are these efforts working?** *(Possible answer: These measures have probably helped the situation but not solved it. Many of the infrastructures are outdated and need maintenance.)*
AL **Verbal/Linguistic**

W Writing Skills

Narrative Have students imagine they are one of the women working in this factory. Have them write an entry in their journal explaining what their day at the factory is like, how they feel about working in the factory, and what hopes they have for the future. **ELL** **Intrapersonal, Verbal/Linguistic**

ANSWERS, p. 695

DBQ The authoritarian government policies forbade ethnic expression and culture such as language. People are now working to preserve Manchu because people use it to define themselves as individuals and members of a culture group.

CRITICAL THINKING

1. The world's demand for technology has increased job opportunities, created economic growth, and raised the standard of living.
2. Answers will vary, but could include that increased communication and information have resulted in society demanding more changes and becoming more open.

T Technology Skills

Constructing Arguments Have students read the information about the Three Gorges Dam project and its positive and negative effects. Divide students into teams to research more information about the effect it will have on people and the environment. Have students hold a debate in which one side supports the project and the other opposes it.
BL Logical/Mathematical

Content Background Knowledge

Hydroelectric Power in China Despite the adverse effects on Chinese society and the environment caused by the Three Gorges Dam project, China's leaders are planning to build more hydroelectric power plants in the years to come. By 2015 the government expects hydroelectric power capacity to reach 290 gigawatts (GW). In 2013 China's environment ministry authorized the construction of what will be the country's tallest hydroelectric dam. The dam, will be 1,030 feet (314 m) tall and will be built on the Dadu River in southwestern Sichuan Province. The ministry acknowledges that the dam will have negative environmental effects, but says that developers have promised to take steps to mitigate the adverse effects.

V Visual Skills

Analyzing Visuals Direct students' attention to the visual *Three Gorges Dam: Harnessing the Yangtze*. Have students explain how the graphic augments the information in the text. Have students describe what additional data it gives about the dam that does not appear in the text. **AL Visual/Spatial**

continues to occur. Thousands of dams built rapidly during the 1950s and 1960s are now damaged and at risk of failure.

T To deal with these problems, China has invested more in flood-control projects. The Three Gorges Dam created a huge reservoir almost 400 miles (644 km) long. The project has been controversial due to the relocation of over a million people. Countless farms, villages, and historic temples were submerged. Natural ecosystems have been damaged with some animal and plant species now endangered or extinct. Changing the flow of the river may interfere with migratory paths of fish species. Pollutants in the soil and chemicals in abandoned factories may leach into the soil as the water rises in the reservoir. Supporters of the project point to the energy created by the dam and its commercial benefits. The dam will help to ease China's future power shortages that could potentially be crippling. The reservoir behind the dam holds an enormous amount of water for farming.

✓ **READING PROGRESS CHECK**

Understanding Relationships How does China's physical geography influence flooding?

V

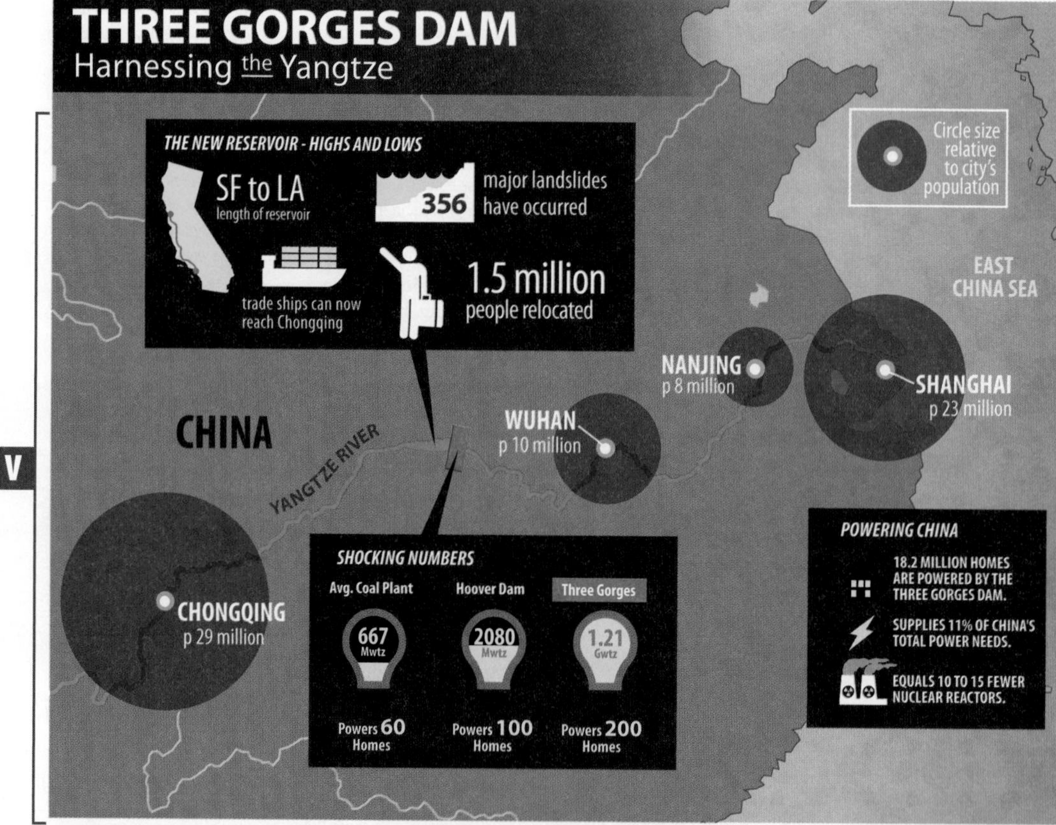

The Three Gorges Dam was a major engineering project. The dam was designed to serve several purposes: to prevent flooding along the Yangtze; to generate electricity; to increase the water supply for agriculture, industry, and homes; and to improve navigation along the river.

▲ **CRITICAL THINKING**

1. ***Analyzing*** What are the benefits of the Three Gorges Dam for China?
2. ***Formulating Questions*** Write three questions that you would ask the engineers of the Three Gorges Dam.

696

networks Online Teaching Options

IMAGE

Flooding in China

Analyzing-Visuals China has experienced devastating floods in recent years that have destroyed homes, and farmland, and taken many lives. This image shows the effects of a flood in Guangdong Province in 2007. Students will view an image to support understanding of natural disasters in China.
AL Visual/Spatial

ANSWERS, p. 696

✓ **READING PROGRESS CHECK** The Huang He and Chang Jiang are not easily controlled and cause disastrous floods.

CRITICAL THINKING

1. The Three Gorges Dam powers 18.2 million homes, supplying 11 percent of China's electrical needs, increases the water supply, helps reduce flooding, and allows trade ships to reach additional ports.
2. Questions will vary but could include questions on how the flow of the river was changed, how to increase its energy output, why the construction has caused mudslides, and what can be done about chemicals leaching into the water supply.

Addressing the Issues

GUIDING QUESTION *How are the Chinese people and government addressing the effects of industrial and economic growth on the environment?*

Industrial and economic growth has created very real benefits for the Chinese people. This growth has also created a host of environmental problems. The impact of China's economic boom on the environment and human health has been enormous. Urban areas are plagued by serious air pollution created by old technology in transportation and industry. One major reason for such severe pollution is China's heavy use of the country's coal supply. In addition to its abundance, coal is relatively cheap, making it attractive. But coal produces high amounts of several types of pollution. Blowing coal dust in the northern industrial areas worsens air pollution and causes many people to suffer from lung diseases. These same problems affect the inhabitants of Mongolia's few cities, where coal is burned for heating and cooking in homes and by factories.

Burning coal creates not only air pollution, but also acid rain. It has become a major problem in China and has also affected other areas of Asia. Mercury from the burning of coal has been found in the Pacific Ocean and as far away as the western United States. Ashes that remain in the coal furnaces after burning occurs, called bottom ash, must be removed and stored in large ponds that can leak or spill.

Like other rapidly urbanizing countries, China has trouble disposing of wastes. About one-third of China's population lacks access to clean water. Many tons of sewage are discharged annually into the Chang Jiang—30 billion tons in 2006. Seventy percent of the country's lakes and rivers are polluted. Two-thirds of China's cities lack clean water, forcing millions of people to boil their drinking water to make it safe to consume.

Pollution has made cancer the leading cause of death in China. Industrial waste is mostly to blame. One metal company in Shenyang spewed clouds of sulfur dioxide and other hazardous chemicals into the atmosphere for many years. City residents affected by health problems from the plant's toxic emissions prompted the government, for the first time, to shut down a state-run factory. In early 2013, a state of emergency was declared in Beijing due to terrible air quality. Mongolia's capital, Ulaanbaatar, is also among cities with the worst air pollution in the world.

Efforts to regulate polluters have been slow for many reasons. In China, one reason is the industries' reluctance to support stricter laws. More importantly, the overwhelming focus on economic growth encourages governments at both the national and local levels to ignore pollution regulations. Record-high pollution levels in Beijing in 2012 caused temporary emergency measures. The Beijing government shut down 103 factories and took 30 percent of government vehicles off the road. Despite such measures, air quality remains extremely hazardous. **C**

China's large population and thriving industry depend on huge quantities of lumber. Each year China cuts down thousands of acres of forests, but also plants many trees to replace this resource. However, the replacement forests **W**

Increasingly, air pollution is a major health concern in today's large Chinese cities. **V**

▲ **CRITICAL THINKING**

1. ***Identifying Cause and Effect*** Why is coal creating a health problem in China?
2. ***Analyzing*** How effectively has China dealt with air pollution?

narvikk/E+/Getty Images

CHAPTER 28, Lesson 3

People and Their Environment: China and Mongolia

V Visual Skills

Interpreting Have students read the first paragraph and then discuss the impact of China's economic boom on its environment. **Ask:** **How has China's economic boom impacted its environment?** *(It has created air pollution, acid rain, mercury pollution, and water pollution.)* **What is the main cause of China's air pollution problems?** *(the use of coal and old technologies; factories spewing industrial waste into the air)* **How has air pollution affected human health?** *(There are significant incidences of lung diseases and cancer.)* **AL** **Verbal/Linguistic**

C Critical Thinking Skills

Evaluating Discuss how China is dealing with its environmental problems. **Ask:** **What are some measures China could take to correct its environmental problems?** *(Possible answers: pass tough air, water, and waste pollution laws; outlaw or reduce the use of coal; employ new technologies that are less polluting)* **Why has China not done more to regulate polluters?** *(Chinese industries are reluctant to support stricter environmental laws. Governments, too, fear regulations will inhibit economic growth.)* **BL** **Logical/Mathematical**

W Writing Skills

Informative/Explanatory Have students write a paragraph about China's forest industry and the problems associated with its growing need for lumber. Allow students to do additional research if they desire on China's use of its own lumber and how much it purchases from the United States and Canada. **Verbal/Linguistic**

INTERACTIVE WHITEBOARD ACTIVITY

Economic Growth and the Environment

Synthesizing Have students complete this interactive whiteboard activity. Students will drag a human factor or a physical factor into a cause-and-effect graphic organizer to show how industrialization and economic growth are impacting the environment and health in China.

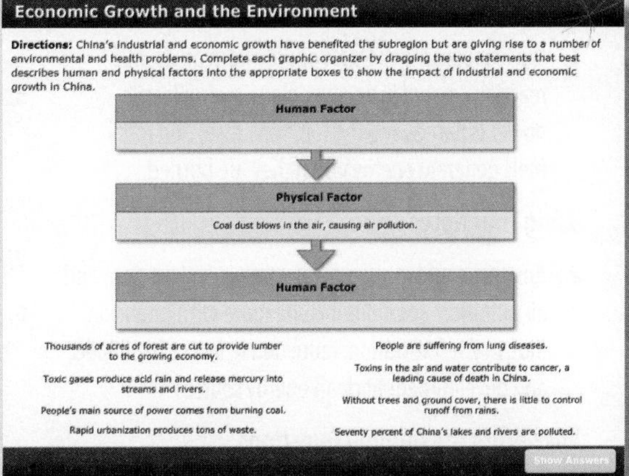

Economic Growth and the Environment
Directions: China's industrial and economic growth have benefited the subregion but are giving rise to a number of environmental and health problems. Complete each graphic organizer by dragging the two statements that best describes human and physical factors into the appropriate boxes to show the impact of industrial and economic growth in China.
Human Factor
Physical Factor
Coal dust blows in the air, causing air pollution.
Human Factor
Thousands of acres of forest are cut to provide lumber to the growing economy.
Toxic gases produce acid rain and release mercury into streams and rivers.
People's main source of power comes from burning coal.
Rapid urbanization produces tons of waste.
People are suffering from lung diseases.
Toxins in the air and water contribute to cancer, a leading cause of death in China.
Without trees and ground cover, there is little to control runoff from rains.
Seventy percent of China's lakes and rivers are polluted.
Show Answers

ANSWERS, p. 697

CRITICAL THINKING

1. The burning of coal releases pollutants into the air, causing an increase in lung diseases, and ash that remains from burning coals must be stored in ponds that could leak or spill into water supplies.
2. China has not been very effective in dealing with air pollution because the focus is on economic growth, not the environment. Industry as well as government officials ignore regulations and refuse to pass stricter rules.

C Critical Thinking Skills

Exploring Issues Have students read the information about China's growing demand for products derived from rare or exotic animals. **Ask: Why are these animal products in demand and why is the demand growing?** *(They are used in traditional Chinese medicines; people have more money to purchase these medicines.)* **What are the environmental effects of China's demand for these products?** *(It is decimating its own wildlife population.)* **What is the international impact?** *(China is importing these products from other countries, thus affecting wildlife populations worldwide.)* **What are some steps China is taking to protect wildlife?** *(It is establishing wildlife preserves in some areas.)* **Are there other measures it could take?** *(Possible answers: write stronger laws to protect wildlife and enforce them; work with international organizations to end illegal poaching and trade; institute educational campaigns; promote alternative medicines)* **Logical/Mathematical**

T Technology Skills

Presenting Divide students into small groups. Have groups research the animals impacted by China's trade in rare or exotic animals and the steps taken in China and elsewhere to protect these animals from extinction. Have students present their findings to the class using photographs, maps, and other visuals. Students might divide up the pieces of the project between researchers, writers, presenters, visual producers, and so forth. **BL Naturalist, Verbal/Linguistic**

CLOSE & REFLECT

Listing To close the lesson, have students list the many environmental problems facing China. Have students note how China is dealing with the problems and share their notes as they review the lesson.

Each year, China meets its demand for lumber by cutting down thousands of acres of forest.

▲ **CRITICAL THINKING**

1. ***Identifying Cause and Effect*** What are the effects of the huge demand for lumber in China?
2. ***Exploring Issues*** Why does reforestation not completely solve the problems of deforestation?

are much less diverse than the original forests. In addition, reforestation efforts have not kept up with demand for timber. China has become a major importer of lumber, pulp, and paper. Clear-cutting timber has led to soil erosion, which in turn, leads to deforestation. Trees and other types of living ground cover help to slow runoff from rain. When they are destroyed, large-scale soil erosion and flooding occur.

A succession of unusually heavy rains in the late 1990s caused flooding of the Chang Jiang and the Huang He. The consequences of such flooding included the deaths of thousands, widespread destruction of property, and damage to the landscape.

Disasters such as these prompted China to plant trees on millions of acres of deforested riverbanks. A major dam was constructed along the Huang He to control flooding. Nature and wetland reserves and wildlife protection zones have also been created.

Western China is experiencing desertification. Much of the vegetation has been depleted by overgrazing and soil erosion, leaving the land bare and dry. Desertification has worsened sandstorms and dust storms that travel from the Gobi through southern Mongolia, northern and western China, and to the Pacific Ocean.

C Traditional Chinese medicines often utilize products derived from rare or exotic animals. Deer antlers, rhinoceros horns, and bear gallbladders contain desirable substances that are often worth incredible sums of money. As wealth grows in the country, the demand for these products has increased. Because China has little wildlife remaining, many animal products are imported. The consequences of this increased demand have affected exotic and endangered animal populations worldwide.

T Some areas in China are protected, however. These include forests at high altitudes and bamboo groves in the western Sichuan province, where pandas need the bamboo to survive. A surviving population of Siberian tigers was found in the far northeast in 1997. Wildlands there and in northwestern Yunnan have been protected as well.

☑ **READING PROGRESS CHECK**

Identifying How has industrialization affected the health of Chinese and Mongolian people living in cities?

LESSON 3 REVIEW (CCSS)

Reviewing Vocabulary (Tier Three Words)

1. ***Analyzing Text Structure*** How does nuclear power differ from hydroelectric or fossil fuel power sources? RH.9–10.4

Using Your Notes

2. ***Organizing*** Using your graphic organizer, list three environmental issues in China and efforts to address them.

Answering the Guiding Questions

3. ***Analyzing*** How do China and Mongolia use fossil fuels as energy sources?
4. ***Hypothesizing*** What special challenges come with globalization, and how will they affect China's future?
5. ***Exploring Issues*** How are the Chinese people and government addressing the effects of industrial and economic growth on the environment?

Writing Activity

6. ***Narrative*** In two or three paragraphs, discuss the possible effects of environmental problems on a fictional Chinese person. Be sure to include relevant details from the lesson. WHST.9–10.2

698

ANSWERS, p. 698

☑ **READING PROGRESS CHECK** Industrialization caused serious air pollution, resulting in many people suffering from lung diseases.

CRITICAL THINKING

1. Demand for lumber has led to deforestation, which causes soil erosion and increased flooding.
2. Replacement forests are less diverse than the original forests, and not enough trees are able to be planted to replace the ones that have been cut.

LESSON 3 REVIEW ANSWERS

Reviewing Vocabulary

1. Nuclear power generates energy from an atomic reaction created in a power plant, hydroelectric power is harnessing the force of a river, and fossil fuels generate energy when they are burned.

Using Your Notes

2. Answers could include deforestation, soil erosion, and air pollution; solutions include more regulations on industry, reforestation, reduction in use of fossil fuels, and development of clean energy sources

Answering the Guiding Questions

3. They burn fossil fuels, particularly coal, for energy.
4. Challenges with globalization include influences on China's society and culture that are leading to a rise in cultural identities and a continuing rise in industry, resulting in a need for more energy sources.
5. They are protecting some forests and wildlands, creating nature and wetland preserves, undertaking reforestation projects including those on riverbanks, and closing a heavily polluting state-run factory.

Writing Activity

6. Paragraphs will differ but must be strongly supported with information from the lesson on the effects of environmental problems on an individual. Possible problems include: lung diseases from air pollution; lost homes and crops because of flooding due to deforestation; and issues with water pollution due to inadequate sanitation in crowded cities, industry, and agriculture.

CHAPTER 28 Assessment

Directions: On a separate sheet of paper, answer the questions below. Make sure you read carefully and answer all parts of the questions.

Lesson Review

Lesson 1

1. ***Describing*** What are some ways in which the Chang Jiang influences human systems in China?
2. ***Explaining*** Why do monsoons form in China? How do they change during the summer and winter months?
3. ***Evaluating*** China has a wealth of natural resources. How important is the production of rice to the Chinese economy?

Lesson 2

4. ***Summarizing*** Describe some of the challenges facing farms and cities in China as a result of urbanization.
5. ***Considering Advantages and Disadvantages*** What are some of the advantages and disadvantages of using ideograms for written language?
6. ***Hypothesizing*** Why do you think the creation of farming communes during the Great Leap Forward led to starvation?

Lesson 3

7. ***Making Connections*** Why has China's growing economic prosperity created more demand for electric power?
8. ***Making Generalizations*** How has the balance of power in East Asia shifted since the end of the Cold War?
9. ***Explaining*** How has burning coal affected the health of urban populations in China and Mongolia? Give examples.

Critical Thinking

10. ***Analyzing*** Why has globalization led to the rise of regional identities in China?
11. ***Hypothesizing*** China currently has a population with more boys than girls. What problems might this imbalance cause in coming years?

21st Century Skills

Use the cartoon below to answer the following questions.

PRIMARY SOURCE

Michael Shaw/The New Yorker Collection/www.cartoonbank.com

12. ***Identifying Perspectives*** What do you think the "Made in China" sign means to the cartoonist?
13. ***Explaining Continuity and Change*** What does the cartoon suggest about how China's booming economy will affect its tradition of isolation?

College and Career Readiness

14. ***Decision Making*** Imagine that you have been asked to advise the Chinese government on the construction of a new dam. Research the controversy surrounding the Three Gorges Dam. Write a two-page report summarizing the controversy and offering your recommendations. Should China go forward with the new dam project? Explain. WHST.9–10.2; WHST.9–10.7

Need Extra Help?

If You've Missed Question	1	2	3	4	5	6	7	8	9	10	11	12	13	14
Go to page	682	683	684	688	689	690	694	695	697	695	690	690	695	696

CHAPTER 28 Assessment Answers

Lesson Review

Lesson 1

1. The Chang Jiang provides water for more than half of China's rice and other grains as well as providing hydroelectric power.
2. Monsoons form in China due to the mixing of the air masses above the Pacific Ocean. Summer monsoons bring rain while winter monsoons bring dry, cool air.
3. China leads the world in rice production, producing two harvests a year in the southern areas of the country.

Lesson 2

4. Farms are facing a shortage of labor due to urbanization, while cities are experiencing overcrowding.
5. The disadvantage of ideograms includes how difficult it is to learn, while advantages include that people who do not speak the same dialect are still able to communicate through writing which also contributes to cultural unity.
6. Student answers may vary, but should include that farming communes were run by the government, which determined what and how much to grow, resulting in poorly planned crops and yields.

Lesson 3

7. The number of people that have electronic appliances and devices has increased with greater prosperity, causing the demand for energy to soar.
8. China has become the most powerful country in East Asia since the end of the Cold War with the largest army in the world and a nuclear arsenal.
9. The burning of coal creates air pollution and blowing coal dust, which cause people to suffer from lung diseases.

Critical Thinking

10. Globalization has led to the loosening of government control, which has included less suppression of regional identities.
11. Student answers may vary, but should be strongly supported with information from the chapter, including that the disproportionate amount of women coupled with the one-child policy could result in a population decline in coming years as well as a decrease in the labor force and an aging population.

21st Century Skills

12. Student answers may vary, but could include that with China having become the world's largest exporter that everything, including the Great Wall, has a "Made in China" label.
13. The cartoon suggests that the booming economy will make it impossible to be isolated as globalization is already exerting a strong influence on life in China.

College and Career Readiness

14. Reports will vary, but should be strongly supported with information from the chapter regarding the problems of the dam, including relocation of over a million people; damage to ecosystems; some plants and animals becoming endangered or extinct; changing the course of the river interferes with the path of migratory birds and fish; and pollutants from factories leaching into the reservoir. Student should also supply a supported opinion on whether or not China should proceed with a new dam project.

Assessment Answers

Analyzing Primary Sources

15 The author states the greening of China is a "dark picture" because the actions they are taking are not enough to prevent the dramatic warming that scientists predict will have drastic consequences.

16 Seligsohn thinks the U.S. should take actions to drastically reduce carbon emissions, which would spur China to do the same.

17 The description helps show how rapidly China's economy is growing and that the "green" actions they are taking amount to little more than sparks in comparison.

Applying Map Skills

18 The Mongolian mountains to the north and south, along with the Gobi in the south, cause limited settlement in these areas.

19 Possible answers include Chongqing, Nanchong, Neijiang, Chengdu, and Mianyang as cities receiving immigrants due to the construction of the Three Gorges Dam.

20 The Gobi is in the north-central part of China and the southern portion of Mongolia. The Taklimakan is between the Kunlun Shan and Tian Shan mountain ranges in western China.

Exploring the Essential Question

21 Paragraphs will vary but could include that 90 percent of the population lives in the fertile river valleys of the Huang He, Chang Jiang, and Xi; urban centers have risen from port cities on these rivers; the rivers provide transportation for goods and people, water for crops and consumption, and deposit fertile soil in the river plains.

Research and Presentation

22 Posters will differ but should include photos and quotes to illustrate human rights issues in China and if economic sanctions have been useful in encouraging political reforms. Examples could include Tiananmen Square and the corresponding sanctions, censorship of Internet and press, and limitations of religious freedom; sanctions could include the ban of some exports such as munitions and arms, the limits on U.S. assistance, and the restriction of Chinese government–affiliated businesses from operating inside the United States.

CHAPTER 28 Assessment CCSS

Directions: On a separate sheet of paper, answer the questions below. Make sure you read carefully and answer all parts of the questions.

DBQ Analyzing Primary Sources

Use the document to answer the following questions.

China has taken significant measures to deal with threats to its environment. But these measures haven't kept pace with the rapid growth of its economy.

PRIMARY SOURCE

"Given what scientists now predict about the timing of climate change, the greening of China will probably come too late to prevent more dramatic warming, and with it the melting of Himalayan glaciers, the rise of the seas, and the other horrors Chinese climatologists have long feared.

It's a dark picture. Altering it in any real way will require change beyond China—most important, some kind of international agreement that transforms the economics of carbon. At the moment China is taking green strides that make sense for its economy. 'Why would they want to waste energy?' Deborah Seligsohn of the World Resources Institute asked, adding that 'if the U.S. changed the game in a fundamental way—if it really committed to dramatic reductions—then China would look beyond its domestic interests and perhaps go much further.' Perhaps it would embrace more expensive and speedier change. In the meantime China's growth will blast onward, a roaring fire that throws off green sparks but burns with ominous heat."

—Bill McKibben, "Can China Go Green?" *National Geographic,* June 2011

15 ***Interpreting*** Why does the author say that the greening of China is a "dark picture"? RH.9–10.4

16 ***Problem Solving*** What does Deborah Seligsohn think the United States should do to help China go green? RH.9–10.6

17 ***Analyzing*** How does the description of China's economy as a "roaring fire that throws off green sparks" help you understand the problem? RH.9–10.4

Applying Map Skills

Use the Unit 8 Atlas to answer the following questions:

18 ***Environment and Society*** What features of Mongolia's geography help explain why some areas have lower density populations than others?

19 ***Human Systems*** Locate the area that was submerged by the construction of the Three Gorges Dam. To what neighboring towns and cities did people most likely relocate?

20 ***Physical Systems*** Use your mental map of China to describe the location of the Gobi and Taklimakan deserts.

Exploring the Essential Question

21 ***Making Connections*** Write a paragraph describing how China's three great rivers have shaped population patterns. How have rivers influenced the location of urban centers? WHST.9–10.2

Research and Presentation

22 ***Understanding Relationships*** Use the Internet and other resources to research the debate over human rights in China. What are the major issues? How effective have economic sanctions been at encouraging positive political reforms? Use your findings to create a poster that includes photos and quotes and present it to the class. WHST.9–10.7

Writing About Geography

23 ***Informative/Explanatory*** Use standard grammar, spelling, sentence structure, and punctuation to write three paragraphs describing the problems of erosion and deforestation in China. How has economic growth fueled these problems? WHST.9–10.2

Need Extra Help?

If You've Missed Question	15	16	17	18	19	20	21	22	23
Go to page	696	696	694	672	672	672	688	691	697

Writing About Geography

23 Paragraphs will vary, but could include that economic growth has spurred the demand for timber in construction and manufacturing, which has led to widespread deforestation; without trees to hold topsoil in place, it is eroded by wind and rain; eroded soil washes into rivers causing problems with dams and harming wildlife; dust storms are becoming more severe; erosion causes some land to become unable to grow crops; and erosion contributes to desertification of the land.

CHAPTER 29

Japan Planner

UNDERSTANDING BY DESIGN®

Enduring Understandings

- *Culture influences people's perceptions of places and regions.*

Essential Question

- *How do physical systems and human systems shape a place?*

Predictable Misunderstandings

Students may think:

- *Japan does not produce its own agricultural products. Explain that although the terrain is not ideal for agriculture, rice is a major crop, grown in flooded paddies on small farms along rivers. In addition, grains, vegetables, fruits, potatoes, and tea are grown in Japan.*
- *Japan is ruled by an emperor. Explain that while Japan does still have an emperor, this person is a ceremonial figurehead, or symbol of state, with very limited powers. Executive power is held by the prime minister.*

Assessment Evidence

Performance Tasks:

- *Hands-On Chapter Project*

Other Evidence:

- *Guided Reading Activities*
- *Vocabulary Activities*
- *Lesson Quizzes*
- *Chapter Tests, Forms A and B*

SUGGESTED PACING GUIDE

Introducing the Chapter .... ½ Day	Lesson 2 .... 2 Days
Lesson 1 .... 1 Day	Lesson 3 .... 1 Day
Global Connections .... 1 Day	Chapter Wrap-Up and Assessment ...... ½ Day

TOTAL TIME 6 Days

Key for Using the Teacher Edition

SKILL-BASED ACTIVITIES

Types of skill activities found in the Teacher Edition.

* **V Visual Skills** require students to analyze maps, graphs, charts, and photos.

R Reading Skills help students practice reading skills and master vocabulary.

C Critical Thinking Skills help students apply and extend what they have learned.

W Writing Skills provide writing opportunities to help students comprehend the text.

T Technology Skills require students to use digital tools effectively.

*Letters are followed by a number when there is more than one of the same type of skill on the page.

DIFFERENTIATED INSTRUCTION

All activities are written for the on-level student unless otherwise marked with the leveled labels below.

BL Beyond Level

AL Approaching Level

ELL English Language Learners

All students benefit from activities that utilize different learning styles. Many activities are marked as below when a particular learning style is highlighted.

Intrapersonal	**Naturalist**
Logical/Mathematical	**Kinesthetic**
Visual/Spatial	**Auditory/Musical**
Verbal/Linguistic	**Interpersonal**

National Geography Standards covered in "Japan"

The student knows and understands:

(3) How to analyze the spatial organizations of people, places, and environments on Earth's surface

3.2 Complex processes change over time and shape patterns in the distribution of human and physical phenomena

(8) The characteristics and spatial distribution of ecosystems and biomes on Earth's surface

8.1 Ecosystems are dynamic and respond to changes in environmental conditions

(9) The characteristics, distribution, and migration of human populations on Earth's surface

9.2 Population distribution and density are a function of historical, environmental, economic, political, and technological factors

(10) The characteristics, distribution, and complexity of Earth's cultural mosaics

10.3 Cultures changes through convergence and/or divergence

(11) The patterns and networks of economic interdependence on Earth's surface

11.2 Patterns exist in the spatial organization of economic activities

(12) The process, patterns, and functions of human settlement

12.2 Settlements can grow and/or decline over time

(14) How human actions modify the physical environment

14.1 Human modifications of the physical environment can have significant global impacts

(15) How physical systems affect human systems

15.2 Humans perceive and react to environmental hazards in different ways

(16) The changes that occur in the meaning, use, distribution, and importance of resources

16.3 Policies and programs that promote the sustainable use and management of resources impact people and the environment

(17) How to apply geography and interpret the past

17.2 The causes and processes of change in the geographic characteristics and spatial organizations of places, regions, and environments in the past

(18) How to apply geography to interpret the present and plan for the future

18.1 Geographic contexts (the human and physical characteristics of places and environments) provide the bases for analyzing current events and making predictions about future issues

CHAPTER OPENER PLANNER

Students will know:

- *how tectonic activity formed and affects life on the islands of Japan.*
- *the climate and biomes and how oceanic currents affect the weather.*
- *how Japan has experienced periods of being an open and a closed country.*
- *that both ancient and modern traditions and population density shape the culture and life in Japan.*
- *the ways in which industrialization has shaped the economy.*
- *the factors that are threatening resources and how they are addressed.*

Students will be able to:

- ***analyze** the effect of tectonic activity on life in Japan.*
- ***identify** the major climate regions and biomes and how oceanic winds affect weather.*
- ***explain** why Japan has been both an open and a closed country at different times.*
- ***describe** the impacts of ancient and modern traditions on culture and population density on life.*
- ***describe** how the economy of Japan has been shaped by industrialization.*
- ***identify** threats to Japan's environment and resources and how they are being addressed.*

UNDERSTANDING BY DESIGN®

Print Teaching Options

V Visual Skills

- ☐ **p. 703** Students discuss a population pyramid for Japan.

R Reading Skills

- ☐ **p. 702** Students contrast the life expectancy today with that in 1950. **AL Logical/Mathematical**

C Critical Thinking Skills

- ☐ **p. 701** Students discuss how an ethnically homogeneous population influences culture differently than a diverse ethnic population. **BL Logical/Mathematical**
- ☐ **p. 702** Students list comparisons between Japan's aging population and the United States's aging population.

W Writing Skills

- ☐ **p. 702** Students write about the advantages and disadvantages of spending two more years in the workforce. **BL Intrapersonal, Verbal/Linguistic**

T Technology Skills

- ☐ **p. 702** Students research the expected effects of a shrinking workforce in Japan. **Verbal/Linguistic**

Online Teaching Options

C Critical Thinking Skills

- **SLIDE SHOW** **Japanese Demographics**—Students learn about the demographics of Japan. **AL Visual/Spatial**
- **MAP** **Interactive Regional Atlas**—Students use the interactive regional atlas to understand the physical and human geography of Japan.

Printable Digital Worksheets

- **WORKSHEET** **Assessing Background Knowledge**—Determine the level of prior knowledge students have about Japan.
- **WORKSHEET** **Chapter Summary**—Students review the main idea of each lesson of the chapter content.
- **WORKSHEET** **Reteaching Activity**—These worksheets provide students with an opportunity for remedial practice and review of vital chapter content.

Project-Based Learning

Hands-On

Create News Interviews

Students create news interviews that bring together information about the physical and human geography of Japan.

Digital Hands-On

Create Online Projects

Find an additional activity online that incorporates technology for this project. Visit the EdTech Teacher Web sites for more links, tutorials, and other resources.

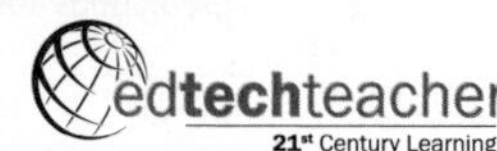

Print Resources

ANCILLARY RESOURCES

This ancillary is available for every chapter and lesson.

- **Chapter Tests and Lesson Quizzes**

PRINTABLE DIGITAL WORKSHEETS

These printable digital worksheets are available for every chapter and lesson.

- **Assessing Background Knowledge**
- **Chapter Summaries**
- **Guided Reading Activities**
- **Hands-On Chapter Projects**
- **Quizzes and Tests**
- **Reading Essentials and Study Guide** **AL**
- **Reteaching Activities**
- **Video Activities**
- **Vocabulary Activities**

More Media Resources

SUGGESTED VIDEOS MOVIES

- **Japan: Memoirs of a Secret Empire** (170 min.)
- **21 Up Japan** (1 h. 30 min.)
- **Living Treasures of Japan** (60 min.)

SUGGESTED READING 

- ***Japan,*** by Kim Sata
- ***Japan and the Culture of the Four Seasons: Nature, Literature, and the Arts,*** by Haruo Shirane
- ***2:46: Aftershocks: Stories from the Japan Earthquake,*** by The Quakebook Community and Our Man in Abiko

LESSON 1 PLANNER

PHYSICAL GEOGRAPHY OF JAPAN

Students will know:

- *how tectonic activity formed and affects life on the islands of Japan.*
- *the two major climate regions of the country.*
- *how oceanic currents affect seasonal weather patterns.*
- *the major biomes found in the country.*

Students will be able to:

- ***analyze*** *the effect of tectonic activity on life in Japan.*
- ***identify*** *the major climate regions of Japan.*
- ***explain*** *the effect of oceanic currents on seasonal weather patterns.*
- ***identify*** *major biomes in Japan.*

UNDERSTANDING BY DESIGN®

Print Teaching Options

V Visual Skills

- ☐ **p. 705** Students use a physical map to identify elevations, major cities, and areas prone to earthquakes. **Naturalist, Visual/Spatial**
- ☐ **p. 706** Students find two pieces of Japanese art that depict cherry blossoms and compare and contrast the perspectives and interpretations of the artists. **BL Naturalist**

R Reading Skills

- ☐ **p. 706** Students discuss the context clues that help them define *predominant*. **ELL Verbal/Linguistic**
- ☐ **p. 707** Students discuss how a traditional Japanese diet is different from a typical American diet. **ELL Interpersonal**

C Critical Thinking Skills

- ☐ **p. 704** Students discuss whether Japan should rebuild massive seawalls in coastal cities after the 2011 tsunami. **BL Verbal/Linguistic**
- ☐ **p. 705** Students discuss the challenges Japan faces in providing water for agriculture, industry, and drinking. **AL Logical/Mathematical**
- ☐ **p. 706** Students use a Venn diagram to contrast winter and summer monsoons and another Venn diagram to contrast the two climates in Japan. **AL Visual/Spatial, Logical/Mathematical**
- ☐ **p. 707** Students discuss the fact that copper and iron mines have virtually ceased production and that these minerals are imported today. **AL Logical/Mathematical**

W Writing Skills

- ☐ **p. 705** Students write an informative paragraph on one of Japan's famous waterfalls. **Verbal/Linguistic**

T Technology Skills

- ☐ **p. 704** Students research how the activity around the Ring of Fire affects Earth and people in the area as well as globally. **BL Naturalist, Visual/Spatial**
- ☐ **p. 707** Students research the main types of fish and seafood that are staples of the Japanese diet and present a multimedia presentation about three of them. **Verbal/Linguistic, Visual/Spatial**

Online Teaching Options

V Visual Skills

- **VIDEO** **Skyscraper Japan**—Students watch a video that explains how Japan prepares for earthquakes and designs buildings to withstand them. **AL Verbal/Linguistic**
- **INTERACTIVE BELLRINGER** **Physical Map of Japan**—Students use the text and map to learn how tectonic activity formed and affects life on the islands of Japan. **AL Visual/Spatial**
- **INTERACTIVE WHITEBOARD ACTIVITY** **Major Climates and Forest Biomes**—Students drag descriptions of climates and forest biomes to the appropriate locations on a map of Japan. **AL Visual/Spatial**

Printable Digital Worksheets

R Reading Skills

- **WORKSHEET** **Guided Reading Activity**—Students use the Guided Reading Activity worksheets to review their comprehension of the content.

C Critical Thinking Skills

- **WORKSHEET** **Video Activity**—Students answer questions related to a topic in the chapter content after they have viewed a lesson video.

LESSON 2 PLANNER

HUMAN GEOGRAPHY OF JAPAN

Students will know:

- *how Japan has experienced periods of being an open and a closed country.*
- *that both ancient and modern traditions shape the culture in Japan.*
- *how population density impacts life and technology in Japan.*
- *the ways in which industrialization has shaped the Japanese economy.*

Students will be able to:

- ***explain*** *why Japan has been both an open and a closed country at different times.*
- ***describe*** *the impacts of both ancient and modern traditions on culture in Japan.*
- ***analyze*** *the impact of population density on life and technology.*
- ***describe*** *how the economy of Japan has been shaped by industrialization.*

UNDERSTANDING BY DESIGN®

☑ *Print Teaching Options*

V Visual Skills

- ☐ **p. 714** Students create simple origami pieces. **Kinesthetic, Naturalist**
- ☐ **p. 715** Students discuss the double-line graph that displays the Japanese balance of trade with the United States. **Logical/Mathematical, Visual/Spatial**

R Reading Skills

- ☐ **p. 711** Students make a list of countries and lands that Japan conquered during the Meiji Restoration and into the World War II era. **Verbal/Linguistic**
- ☐ **p. 712** Students discuss what it would be like to live in the Tokaido corridor. **Interpersonal**
- ☐ **p. 713** Students define the word *polytheistic* using word parts. **ELL Verbal/Linguistic**
- ☐ **p. 714** Students discuss the changes happening in families in Japan and how they may conflict with the traditional values of revering ancestors. **ELL Interpersonal, Logical/Mathematical**

C Critical Thinking Skills

- ☐ **p. 711** Students brainstorm a list of questions about what is happening in the painting of Commodore Perry's arrival in Japan. **BL Visual/Spatial**
- ☐ **p. 712** Students simulate the population density of the Tokyo-Yokohama urban area. **BL Logical/Mathematical**
- ☐ **p. 716** Students discuss the decisions Japan has made to place tariffs on some imports and not others. **BL Logical/Mathematical**

W Writing Skills

- ☐ **p. 714** Students write a scene for a Kabuki play. **Auditory/Musical, Kinesthetic**

T Technology Skills

- ☐ **p. 710** Students research and create a presentation about a particular Japanese dynasty. **BL Verbal/Linguistic**
- ☐ **p. 713** Students explore how magnetic levitation trains work and research how other countries may also use this type of train. **BL Verbal/Linguistic**

☑ *Online Teaching Options*

V Visual Skills

- **VIDEO Japan Labor**—Students watch a video to learn more about the changing nature of work in Japan. **AL Verbal/Linguistic**
- **INTERACTIVE GRAPHIC ORGANIZER Human Geography of Japan**—Students complete the graphic organizer to identify major turning points in Japan's history. **AL Visual/Spatial**
- **INTERACTIVE WHITEBOARD ACTIVITY Modern Culture and Society**—Students identify how population density has impacted Japan's modern cities and the characteristics of Japan's modern culture. **AL Visual/Spatial**
- **INTERACTIVE TIME LINE Shifting Power**—Students examine the time line that shows how the real power in Japan has shifted from emperors to warlords to the people. **AL Verbal/Linguistic**

R Reading Skills

- **PRIMARY SOURCE The History of Origami**—Students read and answer the question about the history of origami. **AL Verbal/Linguistic**

C Critical Thinking Skills

- **INTERACTIVE BELLRINGER Japanese Balance of Trade with the United States**—Students use the graph of the Japanese balance of trade with the United States to understand the ways in which industrialization shaped the Japanese economy. **BL Interpersonal, Logical/Mathematical, Verbal/Linguistic**

☑ *Printable Digital Worksheets*

R Reading Skills

- **WORKSHEET Guided Reading Activity**—Students use Guided Reading Activity worksheets to review their comprehension of the content.
- **WORKSHEET Reading Essentials and Study Guide**—Students complete the study guide and answer Reading Progress Check and vocabulary questions. **AL**

C Critical Thinking Skills

- **WORKSHEET Video Activity**—Students answer questions related to a topic in the chapter content after they have viewed a lesson video.

LESSON 3 PLANNER

PEOPLE AND THEIR ENVIRONMENT: JAPAN

Students will know:
- *the factors that are threatening resources in Japan today.*
- *how humans impact the environment in Japan.*
- *how people and the government are addressing environmental issues.*

Students will be able to:
- ***identify** threats to Japan's resources.*
- ***analyze** human impact on the environment in Japan.*
- ***explain** actions being taken to address environmental issues.*

UNDERSTANDING BY DESIGN®

☑ Print Teaching Options

V Visual Skills
- ☐ **p. 718** Students discuss the location of nuclear power plants on a map. ELL Logical/Mathematical, Visual/Spatial

R Reading Skills
- ☐ **p. 718** Students discuss pollution from vehicle emissions in Japan. Logical/Mathematical

C Critical Thinking Skills
- ☐ **p. 717** Students categorize energy resources as renewable or nonrenewable. AL Naturalist, Verbal/Linguistic
- ☐ **p. 718** Students discuss the environmental issues related to Japan's rapid industrialization. AL Verbal/Linguistic
- ☐ **p. 719** Students discuss the issues surrounding overfishing. BL Verbal/Linguistic
- ☐ **p. 720** Students conduct additional research and give a speech on aquaculture. ELL Auditory/Musical

W Writing Skills
- ☐ **p. 719** Students research and write an essay about supertrawlers and their effects. AL Verbal/Linguistic
- ☐ **p. 720** Students write an argument directed at fishers in favor of adhering to fishing quotas. BL Logical/Mathematical

T Technology Skills
- ☐ **p. 717** Students research the Fukushima nuclear disaster and present their findings. Verbal/Linguistic

☑ Online Teaching Options

V Visual Skills
- VIDEO **Many in Japan Worried About Nuclear Meltdown**—Students watch a video about the fears of radioactive contamination in Japan after the 2011 earthquake. AL Verbal/Linguistic
- INTERACTIVE WHITEBOARD ACTIVITY **Resource Problems and Solutions**—Students identify the missing cause, effect, or potential solution to Japan's resource problems and drag it into the correct column of the chart. AL Verbal/Linguistic

C Critical Thinking Skills
- INTERACTIVE BELLRINGER **Japan's Nuclear Power Plants**—Students use the text and map of nuclear power plants to identify factors that are threatening resources in Japan today. AL Interpersonal, Intrapersonal, Visual/Spatial, Verbal/Linguistic

☑ Printable Digital Worksheets

R Reading Skills
- WORKSHEET **Guided Reading Activity**—Students use Guided Reading Activity worksheets to review their comprehension of the content.
- WORKSHEET **Reading Essentials and Study Guide**—Students complete the study guide and answer Reading Progress Check and vocabulary questions. AL
- WORKSHEET **Vocabulary Activity**—Students review the chapter content and academic vocabulary words.
- WORKSHEET **Chapter Summary**—Students review the main ideas of the chapter content.

C Critical Thinking Skills
- WORKSHEET **Video Activity**—Students answer questions based on a lesson video.
- WORKSHEET **Reteaching Activity**—Students use this activity worksheet to review and reteach chapter content and vocabulary. This worksheet can be used with struggling students who need additional help with difficult content concepts.

Intervention and Remediation Strategies

LESSON 1 Physical Geography of Japan

Reading and Comprehension

Have students work in pairs to create an outline using the lesson's headings and subheadings. As partners gather information from each section, have them note key ideas and details under each heading. Encourage students to illustrate their outlines to help explain each content vocabulary term. For example, students may wish to draw a picture of an archipelago or tsunami under their outline subheading *Landforms*. Encourage students to view the physical map of Japan in this lesson to understand the impact of tectonic plates. After volunteers present their outlines to the class, discuss how volcanic activity has impacted Japan's formation.

Text Evidence

Assign four student groups one of the four main islands of Japan discussed in this lesson. Tell groups that they will create a travel brochure about their island that answers one of the Guiding Questions in the lesson. For example, students may include information about the Ring of Fire and its impact on their island to answer the first Guiding Question: *How has volcanic activity changed the land?* Students should include simple sketches and phrases to describe the region's physical features and a list of reasons tourists might want to visit. Students may wish to conduct additional research about their island to give them ideas for their brochures. Have students present their brochures to the class.

LESSON 2 Human Geography of Japan

Reading and Comprehension

To help students comprehend the turning points in Japan's history and their impact, assign student pairs one of the dates shown in the graphic organizer at the beginning of this lesson. Have partners work together to identify the date's significance, the event or series of events that occurred during that time, and the impact on Japan's development. Then have students conduct research using print or online sources to find out more about their assigned time period. Tell students to write a short summary of the information and present it to the class.

Text Evidence

Have students write a paragraph that answers the Guiding Question: *How do ancient and modern traditions influence life in Japan?* After volunteers share their paragraphs, guide a class discussion to reinforce students' understanding. Then have students review the section from the lesson about Japan's society and culture today. Have students work with a partner to identify how ancient and modern traditions impact family life and art in Japan.

LESSON 3 People and Their Environment: Japan

Reading and Comprehension

Have student groups choose one of the challenges discussed in this lesson, such as management and safety of Japan's nuclear power plants, the impact of economic growth on the region, reliance on supertrawlers, or the impact of commercial whaling in the region. Have students in each group work together to summarize the problems related to their topic and how or whether the problems are being addressed or solved. Students may wish to conduct online research to provide sufficient evidence in support of claims made in their summaries. Encourage students to use content vocabulary terms in their summaries.

Text Evidence

Have students work in teams and tell them that they will prepare for a class debate. Tell students that their team should use supporting evidence from the text to defend or refute the following statement: *Nuclear power is a benefit to the islands of Japan.* Have teams choose whether they will refute or defend the statement and then take notes from the lesson to provide supporting evidence for their chosen claim. After students have had time to prepare their arguments, moderate a class debate. Encourage students to allow teams to state their case without interrupting.

Online Resources

Leveled Reader

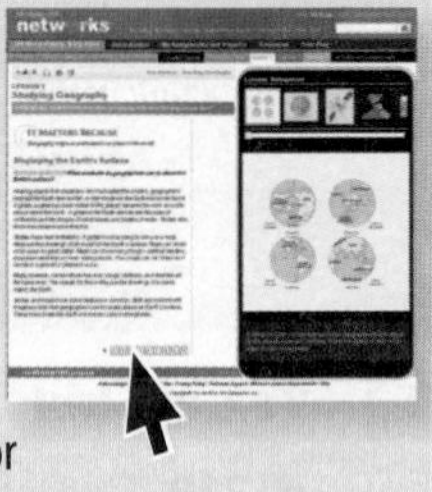

Use this online approaching-level text that corresponds directly to the text in the Student Edition. It also includes additional reading and comprehension support for English Language Learners.

Guided Reading Activities

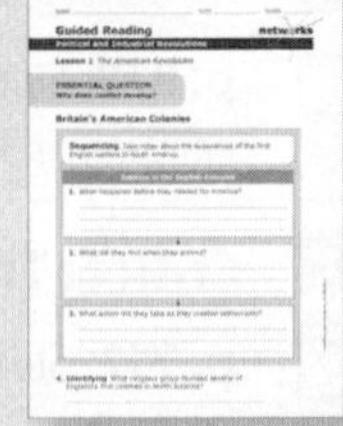

This resource uses guiding questions to help students with comprehension.

Reteaching Activities

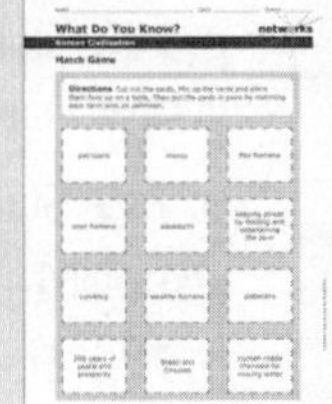

These worksheets provide students with an opportunity for remedial practice and review of vital chapter content.

Reading Essentials and Study Guide

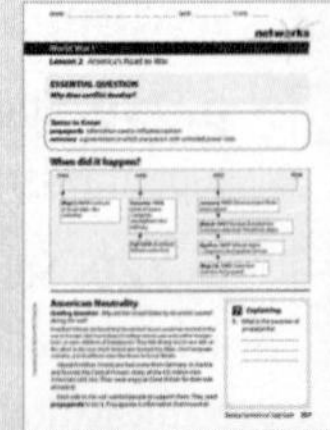

This resource offers writing and reading activities for the approaching-level student.

Self-Check Quizzes

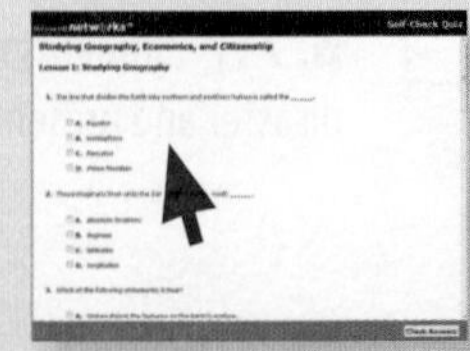

This online assessment tool provides instant feedback for students to check their progress.

Chapter Summaries

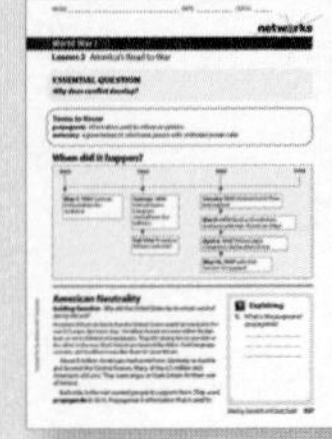

Summaries are provided for each chapter that thoroughly condense core content into manageable chunks.

Japan

ESSENTIAL QUESTION • *How do physical systems and human systems shape a place?*

networks

There's More Online about Japan's geography.

CHAPTER 29

Geography Matters...

The rugged island country of Japan, punctuated by volcanic mountains formed over millions of years, is home to a population that is ethnically homogenous compared to most industrialized countries. With its ancient culture and complex traditions, Japan also has a leading world economy that is highly advanced technologically. One of Asia's most successful democracies, Japan has become a strong ally of the United States and a force of stability in the region.

◀ Nobu Matsuhisa is the chef and owner of one of Tokyo's most famous restaurants.

Letter from the Author

Dear Geography Teacher,

A critical factor in geography is space, and nowhere is a country more conscious of the lack of space than in Japan. The physical geography is dominated by mountains and small, narrow coastal plains. Add millions of people concentrated in cities and villages, and soon there simply is not enough space. In rural areas, every square inch of land is cultivated. More creative yet are what urban planners are up to. Tokyo now has apartment complexes that extend down into the ground. Underground shopping is a way of life. Hotel rooms can be one half the size of a prison cell! Space has to be created.

Richard G. Boehm

ENGAGE

Activating Prior Knowledge Invite students to share what they know about Japan. Make a list of items students associate with Japan and discuss whether or not those associations are accurate. Help students recognize that many items that may be associated with Japan may have been developed elsewhere. Have students keep the list in mind and look for items that are authentic as they study the chapter.

TEACH & ASSESS

Making Connections There are many Japanese restaurants in the United States, some more authentic than others. In Japan, restaurants often specialize in one type of food, such as sushi, curry rice, or freshwater eel dishes. Most restaurants in Japan display models of their menu items. This "plastic food" looks exactly like the real thing and is very useful for foreigners who are unfamiliar with Japanese cuisine.

Inferring Point out that the population of Japan is ethnically homogenous. **Ask:** **How does the fact that Japan is an island nation likely contribute to the homogeneity of the population?** *(Possible answer: It is more difficult to travel to an island than it is to travel across land, so it is likely that fewer different peoples came to Japan.)* **Ask:** **How does an ethnically homogenous population influence culture differently than a diverse ethnic population?** *(Possible answer: It is likely that traditions will be carried on through the generations with less change than in cultures with many ethnic backgrounds.)* **BL** **Logical/Mathematical**

CLOSE & REFLECT

Predict Ask students to write three predictions—one about the physical geography of Japan, one about the human geography of Japan, and one about environmental issues that Japan is currently facing. Have them share their predictions and then refer back to them as they study the chapter.

ePals GlobalCommunity
Where learners connect™

Extend the project-based learning experience globally through our partnership with ePals. EPals allows you to connect with classrooms around the world in a safe online environment for real-life lessons and projects in virtual study groups.

ENGAGE

C Critical Thinking Skills

Comparing Have students read the title and introductory paragraph. Then ask them to work with a partner to list several comparisons between Japan's aging population and what they know about the United States's aging population. Then have each set of students join another set of students to discuss their lists.

TEACH & ASSESS

R Reading Skills

Contrasting Have students contrast the life expectancy today with that in 1950. **Ask:** **How much longer are women living now than they were in 1950?** *(23 years longer)* **How much longer are men living now than they were in 1950?** *(19 years)* AL **Logical/Mathematical**

T Technology Skills

Researching Have students conduct online research about the expected effects of a shrinking workforce in Japan. Ask them to find real predictions about just how much and how fast the workforce is expected to shrink and the ramifications for the economy. Then use the students' research as a basis for a class discussion on Japan's shrinking workforce. **Verbal/Linguistic**

W Writing Skills

Informative/Explanatory Ask students to think about how they would feel if the generation before them were allowed to retire at age 65, but they had to wait until they were 67 to retire. Have students write 2–3 paragraphs about the advantages and disadvantages of spending two more years in the workforce. Then ask volunteers to share their paragraphs with the class. BL **Intrapersonal, Verbal/Linguistic**

ANSWERS, p. 702

Why Geography Matters

1. The current fertility rate is causing Japan's population to decline and age.
2. Paragraphs may vary but should include that the increasing dependency ratio causes more people to draw from government services such as health care and pensions; there are fewer people working to fund government services; more people may be asked to work longer; there may be fewer services available to all people; and the economy may suffer.
3. Raising the retirement age is important in keeping government services like pensions and health care available for all people and to keeping people in the workforce to support the economy.

Why Geography Matters: **Japan**

Japan's aging population

After a post–World War II baby boom, Japan experienced declining birthrates and slower overall population growth. The current population is declining and aging. Aging populations mean that a smaller percentage is working to support those in retirement. This could pose a threat to Japan's economic future.

How is the population of Japan changing?

In Japan, the fertility rate is declining as women marry later, delay having children, or never marry at all. (Most Japanese babies are born to married women.) At the same time, life spans are lengthening. The Japanese have the longest life spans in the world. In 1950, on average, Japanese women lived to age 63 and Japanese men to 60. Today Japanese women are expected to live to age 86 and Japanese men to 79. In 2012 more than 50,000 Japanese were centenarians, or people who are more than 100 years old. That number is projected to be at least six times as great by 2030. The combination of lower fertility rates and lengthening life spans has caused the population of Japan to decline and age.

1. **Human Systems** What effect is Japan's current fertility rate having on its population?

What are the long-term effects of an aging population?

As Japan's population decreases and ages, the workforce shrinks. Statistics indicate that the number of Japanese workers peaked in 1999 and has shrunk 2.5 percent since then. Therefore, there is a possibility of a shortage of workers in the future, as well as an increase in the dependency ratio. The dependency ratio refers to the ratio of economically dependent persons to economically active persons. As the dependency ratio increases, more retired people are drawing on government services, such as pensions and health care, and fewer people are paying taxes to fund those services. Interestingly, the lengthening life span of the Japanese does not necessarily mean increased sickness and debility. Japan's men appear to be healthier longer than men in other countries, and its women are generally vigorous for much of old age.

2. **Human Systems** Write a paragraph describing how the increased dependency ratio may change the way the Japanese people live in the future.

How are people in Japan and across the world finding solutions?

Many Japanese men—almost one-third of the workforce—continue to work beyond the usual retirement age. If more Japanese women also worked longer, the dependency ratio and the burden on the younger workforce would be reduced. Internationally, some governments are taking steps to make it easier for people over 65 to continue working. Others are considering raising the retirement age from 65 to 67—or possibly higher—and even linking the retirement age to life expectancy. Other options include increasing taxes to pay for government pensions and social security systems or reducing payouts in these systems.

3. **Human Systems** Why is raising the retirement age in Japan and other countries an important response to aging populations?

Project-Based Learning

Hands-On

Create News Interviews

Have students create news interviews that bring together information from all lessons about the physical geography and human geography of Japan, including environment concerns.

Digital Hands-On

Create Online Projects

Find an additional activity online that incorporates technology for this project. Visit the EdTech Teacher Web sites for more links, tutorials, and other resources.

THERE'S MORE ONLINE

VIEW a chart of population distribution in Japan • *READ* a quote about Japan's aging population

Folding the traditional population pyramid in order to compare male and female populations more closely

FEMALE MALE RETIRED AGE WORKING AGE SCHOOL AGE

AGE

⊖ SINO-JAPANESE WAR
The beginning of the Sino-Japanese war in 1937 results in a declining birth rate.

⊖ END OF WWII
Birth rates, already low, tumble due to the hardships in Japan at the end of World War II.

⊕ FIRST BABY BOOM
Much like the rest of the world, Japan experienced a baby boom after World War II from 1947 to 1949.

⊖ YEAR OF HINOEUMA
Female babies born every sixtieth year in the Japanese lunar calendar are considered bad luck. This resulted in a 26% drop in the birth rate in 1966.

⊕ SECOND BABY BOOM
A large number of births from 1971 to 1974 results in a birth rate peak.

⊖ DEMOGRAPHIC CRISIS

A trend is developing where each year a smaller number of Japanese men and women are marrying and having children.

As more and more Japanese retire, the workforce will shrink.

Fewer people in the workforce will result in a smaller tax base for the support of social programs.

WWII WOMEN
Due to World War II casualties, there are significantly more women aged 75 and older than men.

RECORD LOW
Low annual birthrates are narrowing the base of Japan's population pyramid.

100 90 80 70 60 50 40 30 20 10 0

1200 1000 800 600 400 200 0

THOUSANDS OF PEOPLE

C

R

V

SLIDE SHOW

Japanese Demographics

Analyzing Visuals Have students examine the slide show to understand the demographics of Japan.
AL **Visual/Spatial**

CHAPTER 29

Why Geography Matters

V Visual Skills

Analyzing Visuals Direct students to the population pyramid age grid. **Ask:** **Are there more males or females under age 50 in Japan?** *(males)* Have a student read the trend "Year of Hinoeuma." **Ask:** **If tradition is followed, what is the next year in which you would expect a significant drop in the birth rate due to cultural beliefs?** *(2026)* **Verbal/Linguistic**

C Critical Thinking Skills

Speculating Have students draw conclusions about why the birthrate is declining and population growth rate is slow. **Ask:** **What are some reasons why the population would be aging?** *(Possible answers: Women are waiting longer to have children or not having children at all because they have careers. People are choosing to have smaller families due to economic pressures. Life expectancy has increased.)* **Verbal/Linguistic**

R Reading Skills

Summarizing Have a volunteer read the trends in the "Demographic Crisis" section. **Ask:** **What risk does Japan's changing population face?** *(It is possible that there will not be enough money in the economy to support all of the people who are leaving the workforce.)* **Verbal/Linguistic**

CLOSE & REFLECT

Formulating Questions Based on the introduction to the chapter, have students write three questions they have about what they might learn in this chapter. Have them share their questions with a partner and attempt to answer the questions as they study the chapter.

Physical Geography of Japan

ENGAGE

C1 Critical Thinking Skills

Speculating Have students locate the Ring of Fire on a world map. Ask them to describe what they know about the Ring of Fire and then to speculate on how living in close proximity to an area prone to earthquakes, volcanic eruptions, and tsunamis might affect life in Japan.

TEACH & ASSESS

T Technology Skills

Global Analysis Have students work in small groups to explore the Ring of Fire. Have them research how the activity around the Ring of Fire affects Earth and people in the area as well as how it affects the world globally. Ask them to focus on a particular effect and give a classroom presentation on that effect. BL Naturalist, Visual/Spatial

C2 Critical Thinking Skills

Defending Tell students that in Japan there are different opinions on how to rebuild the damaged coastal cities after the 2011 tsunami. Many places in Japan have large seawalls made of concrete to help protect them in the event of a tsunami. Tell students that some people wish to rebuild the seawalls, while others argue that building enormous seawalls damages and changes the natural environment beyond repair. Discuss with students the two sides to this issue. **Ask:** **Which do you believe should receive higher priority—possibly protecting cities from a tsunami by building large seawalls or preserving the environmental habitats and natural shoreline? Do you think there is a way to compromise? How?** *(Student answers may vary, but should support their thoughts and ideas such as there may be a way to build more natural seawalls that will both protect a city and do less harm to the natural environment.)* BL Verbal/Linguistic

networks

There's More Online!

- IMAGE Fuji Fishing Harbor
- IMAGE Japanese Macaques
- MAP Physical Map of Japan
- INTERACTIVE SELF-CHECK QUIZ
- VIDEO Physical Geography of Japan

LESSON 1

Physical Geography of Japan

ESSENTIAL QUESTION • *How do physical systems and human systems shape a place?*

Reading HELPDESK 

Academic Vocabulary (Tier Two Words)
- **consist**
- **affect**
- **predominant**

Content Vocabulary (Tier Three Words)
- **archipelago**
- **tsunami**

TAKING NOTES: ***Key Ideas and Details***

SUMMARIZING As you read about the physical geography of Japan, use a graphic organizer like the one below to take notes on the climate.

Climate of Japan

IT MATTERS BECAUSE

The islands of Japan form an arc of 1,500 miles (2,400 km) across the North Pacific Ocean, rocky evidence of the Ring of Fire and its powerful volcanic action. Japan's waterways have been essential to transportation and agriculture. Although much of Japan is mountainous, its people have benefited from proximity to the ocean as a rich natural resource.

Landforms

GUIDING QUESTION *How has volcanic activity changed the land?*

Although there are more than 6,800 islands in its **archipelago**, most of Japan's land area **consists** of four main islands: Hokkaidō, Honshū, Shikoku, and Kyūshū. The islands of Japan formed during the last 15 to 20 million years. They were thrust upward and layered by the force of volcanic action from the Pacific Ring of Fire, the volcanic zone that runs along the edges of the Pacific. The resulting landscape of mostly rugged mountains **affects** where people live. The majority of the population dwells in the Japanese coastal lowlands.

Japan's location in the Ring of Fire causes some 50 Japanese volcanoes to remain active and frequent earthquakes. Japan's tallest peak, Mount Fuji, is a volcano not currently active. In a typical year more than 1,000 small earthquakes occur, with major quakes occurring less frequently but with more destruction and often causing deaths. When a powerful undersea earthquake occurs nearby, a major **tsunami**, or huge wave, can form, bringing terrible consequences. Tsunamis can travel more than 250 miles per hour (400 km per hour) and be more than 30 feet (10 m) high. In 2011 an earthquake off the coast of Honshū rocked the island and launched a series of tsunamis that flooded the coastline in massive waves. More than 19,000 people died, property damage was enormous, and a serious accident occurred at a nuclear power station. The cleanup and reconstruction effort was predicted to take ten years and cost upwards of $150 billion.

READING PROGRESS CHECK

Summarizing How does the Ring of Fire affect Japan?

704

networks *Online Teaching Options*

INTERACTIVE BELLRINGER

Physical Map of Japan

Acquiring Information Use the introductory text and the physical map of Japan to know how tectonic activity formed and affects life on the islands of Japan. Have students work in pairs. Have each pair discuss each question. Ask pairs to write agreed-upon answers to the questions. Then, have each pair share its answers in a class discussion. AL Visual/Spatial

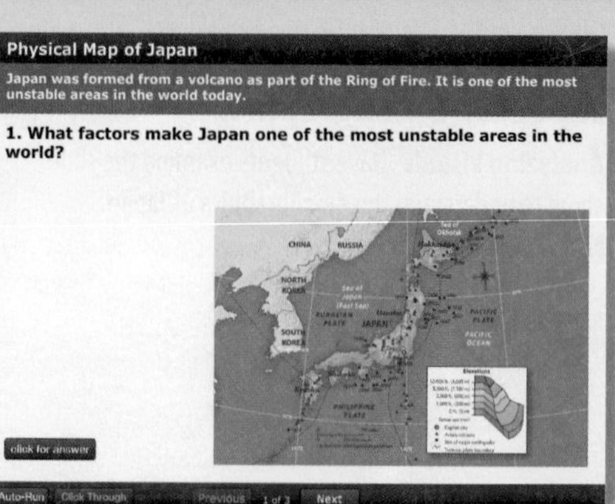
Physical Map of Japan
Japan was formed from a volcano as part of the Ring of Fire. It is one of the most unstable areas in the world today.
1. What factors make Japan one of the most unstable areas in the world?
click for answer
Auto-Run
Click Through
Previous
1 of 3
Next

ANSWERS, p. 704

READING PROGRESS CHECK The Ring of Fire is responsible for the volcanic action that formed Japan and created the mountainous landscape that affects where people are able to live.

TAKING NOTES: A mild climate and abundant rainfall prevail in Japan. Different latitudes have different climates and biomes. Northern Japan has a humid continental climate with cold, snowy winters and warm summers. Southern Japan has a humid subtropical climate with hot summers and heavy rain. Monsoon winds bring rain and dry conditions seasonally.

Waterways

GUIDING QUESTION *What makes the waterways in Japan unique?*

A distinctive feature of Japan is its short, swift rivers that flow from the mountains, often plunging over cliffs as stunning waterfalls. Typically, Japanese rivers rise in forested mountains, flow through steep valleys, and then cross alluvial plains to empty into the sea. The lower regions of these rivers are often used for farming rice. In the coastal lowlands, where rivers slow and pass through cities, some waterways are used for transportation, including carrying passenger water buses. These uses often involve damming the rivers or altering their original courses. Increasing demand for water—for agriculture, industry, and drinking—remains a challenge. The lack of natural or easily constructed reservoirs makes it difficult to contain rapid runoff from rainfall.

Japan's longest rivers, the Shinano and the Tone, flow from mountain heights on Honshū and can be very destructive when they flood. The Shinano is 225 miles (360 km) long. The Tone is 200 miles (322 km) long and supplies Tokyo with drinking water. On Hokkaidō, the Ishikari and the Teshio flow into the Sea of Japan (East Sea). The Yoshino River on Shikoku flows through a deep gorge and is known for its rapids.

Japan's largest lake, Lake Biwa, is in the central part of Honshū. It was created from a depression along a fault. Many of Japan's coastal lakes are simply drowned river valleys that reached the sea and were dammed over time by accumulating silt and sandbars.

✓ READING PROGRESS CHECK

Identifying Name three ways in which Japan's waterways have changed over time and identify whether the processes were natural or caused by humans.

archipelago a group or chain of islands

consist to be composed of

affect to have an effect on

tsunami a huge wave resulting from undersea earthquake or volcanic activity that gets higher and higher as it approaches the coast

GEOGRAPHY CONNECTION

More than four-fifths of Japan's surface area consists of mountains.

1. ***PHYSICAL SYSTEMS*** Why does Japan experience frequent earthquakes and occasional tsunamis?
2. ***PLACES AND REGIONS*** Name the four major bodies of water that border the islands of Japan.

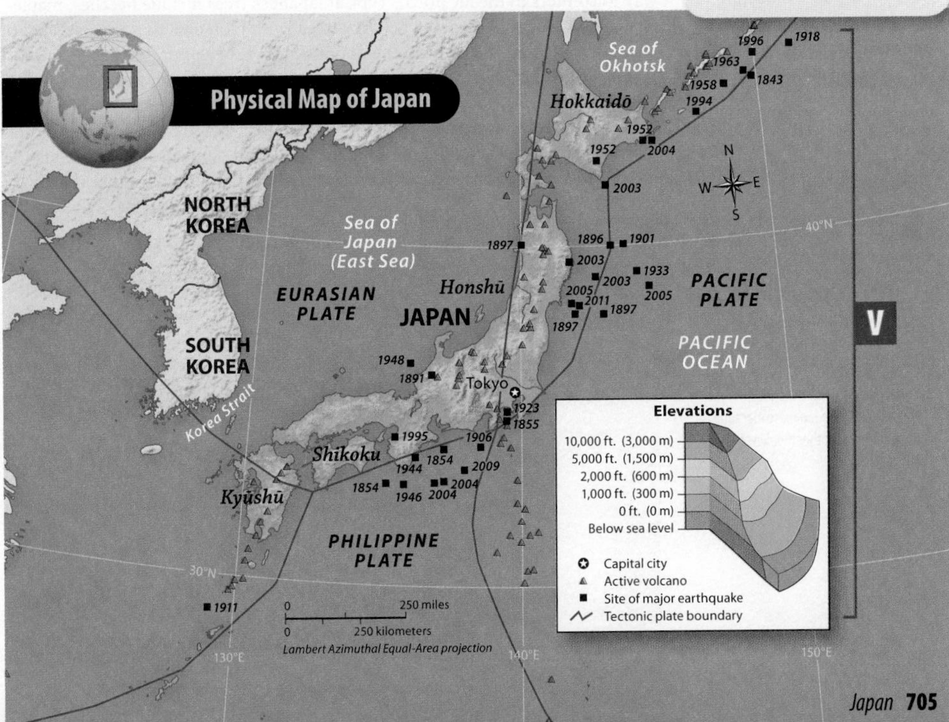

VIDEO

Skyscraper Japan

Examining Have students watch this video that explains how Japan prepares for earthquakes and designs buildings to withstand them. Then have them answer the corresponding questions on the Video Activity worksheet. **AL** **Verbal/Linguistic**

Physical Geography of Japan

W Writing Skills

Informative/Explanatory Explain that Japan's waterfalls draw many tourists. Ask students to research and write an informative paragraph on one of Japan's most famous waterfalls. Tell them to include interesting statistics and data about the waterfall, including information about its source. **Verbal/Linguistic**

Content Background Knowledge

Kegon Waterfall One of the most famous waterfalls in Japan is the Kegon Waterfall found in Nikko, which is just north of Tokyo. It is nearly 100 meters tall and can be seen from an observation platform, or one can take an elevator to the base of the falls. In the winter months, the waterfall freezes nearly solid.

C Critical Thinking Skills

Problem Solving Discuss the challenges Japan faces in providing water for agriculture, industry, and drinking. Have students brainstorm ideas of how to solve this problem. **Ask:** **What sources of water are available in Japan?** *(rivers, rainfall, ocean)* **What main challenges must be overcome to provide water?** *(Possible answer: It is difficult to capture freshwater from rain through reservoirs because of the terrain. There are fewer freshwater sources than in larger countries.)* **Is the ocean a viable source of water? Explain.** *(Possible answer: If desalinization becomes a simpler and less expensive process, it could become a viable option for Japan.)* **AL** **Logical/Mathematical**

V Visual Skills

Analyzing Visuals Direct students to the physical map of Japan. **Ask:** **Land is found at which two main elevations in Japan?** *(0 m and between 600 m and 1,500 m)* **Based on these elevations, where in Japan would you expect to find major cities?** *(Possible answer: Major cities are most likely found along the coastal lowlands.)* **Where in Japan might a person who wants to avoid earthquakes settle?** *(Possible answers: Kyūshū or western parts of Hokkaidō or Shikoku)* **Naturalist, Visual/Spatial**

ANSWERS, p. 705

✓ READING PROGRESS CHECK Rivers are dammed or have their courses changed by humans and are also dammed by nature through the accumulation of silt and sandbars, which creates coastal lakes.

GEOGRAPHY CONNECTION

1. because it is located along the Ring of Fire
2. The Pacific Ocean, the East China Sea, the Sea of Japan, and the Philippine Sea border the islands of Japan.

Physical Geography of Japan

R Reading Skills

Using Context Clues Discuss with students the context clues that help them determine the meaning of *predominant*. **How does the word *influences* and the listing of the four predominant influences help to determine the meaning of *predominant*?** *(Possible answer: Influences tells me that predominant is an adjective that describes the influences. The fact that there are four influences listed and it tells how they combine to make Japan monsoonal tells me that they are important or main influences.)* **ELL** **Verbal/Linguistic**

C Critical Thinking Skills

Contrasting As students study the two main climates found in Japan, have them construct a Venn diagram to contrast winter and summer monsoons, and another to contrast the two climates found in Japan. **Ask: Which part of Japan is most likely to experience cold, snowy winters?** *(northern Japan)* **How does the vegetation change as you move from southern Japan to northern Japan?** *(Possible answers: The semitropical rain forests have broad-leaved evergreen trees. As you move north, these mix with deciduous trees, and then further north conifers are found.)* **AL** **Visual/Spatial, Logical/Mathematical**

V Visual Skills

Differing Interpretations Explain to students that nature is a recurring theme in Japanese art. Have them find two pieces of Japanese art that depict cherry blossoms. Ask them to compare and contrast the two pieces and identify the possible perspectives and interpretations of each artist. Have them share the two pieces with the class and describe the artist's interpretations. **BL** **Naturalist**

ANSWERS, p. 706

Connecting Geography Answers may differ but could include that the celebrations act as a way to bring society together in celebration and appreciation of a symbol that also represents their national pride.

CRITICAL THINKING

1. The Japanese macaque appears to have a thick coat as an adaption to living farther north than any other primate.
2. The Japanese macaque differs from other monkeys in the color of its fur and face.

Climates, Biomes, and Resources

GUIDING QUESTION *How does the climate in Japan change from north to south?*

Japan generally has a mild climate and abundant rainfall. Nevertheless, there are startling contrasts in climate and biomes. The northern latitudes of Hokkaidō are much colder and experience deep winter snows and howling winds, while far to the south, Okinawa has a subtropical climate.

Climate Regions and Biomes

R The **predominant** influences on Japan's climate are latitude, the proximity of the great Asian landmass to the west, the mountainous terrain, and ocean currents. The combination of these factors makes Japan monsoonal, or C influenced by seasonal winds that bring either precipitation or dry air. The cold winter monsoon drops rain or snow on the western slopes of Japan's mountains, leaving the eastern region drier. The warmer summer monsoon reverses this action, bringing warm rains to the eastern slopes and dry air to the west. The warm waters of the Japan Current, which is similar to the flow of the Atlantic Gulf Stream, provide moisture for the summer monsoon. The cold Kuril Current is responsible for dense fogs off Hokkaidō. Tropical storms called typhoons, similar to hurricanes, generally occur in late summer, forming over warm tropical waters. They bring torrential rains, high winds, and frequently great destruction to Japanese islands.

Northern Japan has a humid continental climate with warm summers and cold, snowy winters. Southern Japan has a humid subtropical climate with hot summers and heavy rain. Most of Japan is forested, or was once. Semitropical rain forests in the south consist of broad-leaved evergreen trees. Transitioning north, broad-leaved evergreens mix with deciduous trees, which eventually give way to conifers in the far north. Typical Japanese trees include beeches, maples, V oaks, and spruces. A variety of cherry trees, with blossoms that are a symbol of Japan, are planted throughout the country. Much of the original vegetation of Japan is gone, however, supplanted by agriculture and foreign flora.

Despite great concentrations of people in Japan, large land mammals and birds still thrive in isolated mountain regions. Bears, wild boars, deer, and antelope are common in remote mountains. The Japanese macaque, a kind of wild monkey, also dwells as far north as Honshū. Ocean animals along the coasts

Connecting Geography to SOCIOLOGY

Hanami: Viewing of Flowers

The Japanese tradition of viewing cherry tree *(sakura)* blossoms in springtime dates back a thousand years. The beautiful tree and its flowers symbolize the natural cycle of human life and became revered as a symbol of good luck. Today cherry blossom festivals are held throughout Japan, timed to match the local blooms. People picnic under the blossoming trees and hold tea ceremonies, welcoming spring together with food, drink, and song.

SPECULATING What effect might *hanami* celebrations have on Japanese society as a whole?

predominant present as the strongest or main characteristic

The Japanese macaque lives farther north than any other wild primate.

▶ **CRITICAL THINKING**

1. ***Analyzing Visuals*** How is the Japanese macaque well adapted to its natural environment?
2. ***Contrasting*** How does the appearance of the Japanese macaque differ from most other monkeys?

networks Online Teaching Options

INTERACTIVE WHITEBOARD ACTIVITY

Major Climates and Forest Biomes

Classifying Have students drag descriptions of climates and forest biomes to the appropriate location on a map of Japan. **AL** **Visual/Spatial**

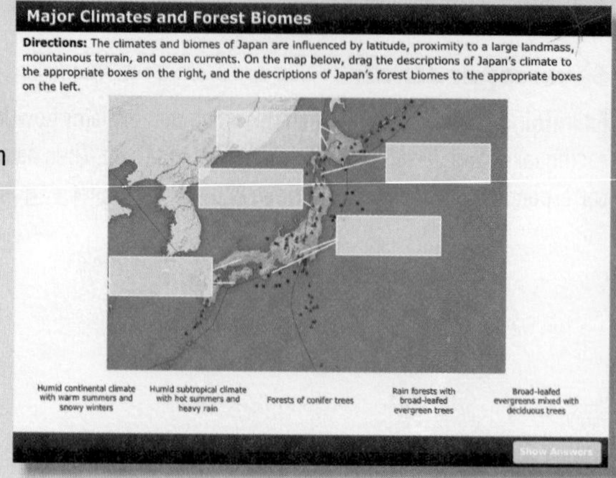

include sea turtles, sea snakes, abundant water birds, fish, whales, dolphins, and porpoises. The rich sea life is made possible, in part, by the meeting of the warm and cold currents.

Natural Resources

Despite extensive mountains and poor soil, Japanese agriculture makes the most of reliable rainfall and irrigation from rivers to grow most of the rice the country needs. The main crop is rice, cultivated in flooded paddies and principally on small farms. Other crops include a variety of grains, vegetables, fruits, potatoes, and tea. Dairy cattle are raised on Hokkaidō. Beef cattle are raised in feed lots, where they are carefully nurtured to provide high-fat meat. R

This busy fishing harbor lies at the base of Mount Fuji, Japan's highest mountain at 12,388 feet (3,776 m). There are about 200,000 vessels in Japan's entire fishing fleet.

▲ CRITICAL THINKING

1. ***Analyzing Visuals*** What details in the photo reflect how Japan's physical geography shapes its human geography?
2. ***Hypothesizing*** How may Japan's economy be affected if fisheries continue to decline?

Because Japan is an island country, the resources of the sea have always been an important source of food for the Japanese. Modern sources come from both deep sea fishing and human-made seafood farms. Japan is a world leader in harvesting and importing fish. The country consumes some 7.5 billion tons of fish annually, which amounts to nearly 15 percent of the world's catch, and reaps about $14 billion a year from the fishing industry. Ocean pollution and overfishing, however, have jeopardized the fisheries on which Japan depends. Such overfishing has seriously depleted marine life. 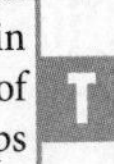

The mining industry is small and declining, with the exception of gold. Limestone is still widely quarried. Coal was historically the most important mineral mined in Japan. However, various factors—such as foreign competition, high production costs, and increasing reliance on oil—have lessened the importance of the industry. The last coal mine in Japan closed in 2002. Most of Japan's limited oil and natural gas resources come from Niigata Prefecture several hundred miles north of Tokyo. Since the beginning of this century, copper and iron mines have virtually ceased production, and these minerals are imported. C

READING PROGRESS CHECK

Determining Importance Which of Japan's natural resources are most closely related to Japan's being an island country? What is threatening these resources?

LESSON 1 REVIEW (CCSS)

Reviewing Vocabulary (Tier Three Words)

1. ***Making Connections*** How is a tsunami different from an ordinary ocean wave? RH.9–10.4

Using Your Notes

2. ***Listing*** Use your graphic organizer from this lesson to list the characteristics of Japan's climate.

Answering the Guiding Questions

3. ***Examining*** How has volcanic activity changed the land?
4. ***Describing*** What makes the waterways in Japan unique?
5. ***Summarizing*** How does the climate in Japan change from north to south?

Writing Activity

6. ***Informative/Explanatory*** Write a paragraph describing how latitude affects the climate and biomes of Japan. WHST.9–10.2

Physical Geography of Japan

R Reading Skills

Inferring Discuss how a traditional Japanese diet is different from a typical American diet. **What food is a staple in Japan and not in the United States?** *(rice)* Point out that rice is an integral part of Japanese culture—most meals include rice. **What can you infer about beef and dairy in Japan? Is it consumed at the same rate as in the United States? Explain.** *(Possible answer: The Japanese eat less beef and dairy than in the United States. They have much less land area on which to raise cattle. They refer to dairy cattle only being raised on Hokkaidō. With only a small number of dairy cows, it is not possible to supply enough dairy products to be considered an integral part of the Japanese diet.)* ELL **Interpersonal**

T Technology Skills

Researching Have students conduct online research about the main types of fish and seafood that are staples of the Japanese diet. Ask them to choose three of the fish or seafood types and write a paragraph giving information about each one. Students should provide visuals for each food item. Have them present their information to the class using multimedia presentation software. **Verbal/Linguistic, Visual/Spatial**

C Critical Thinking Skills

Hypothesizing Discuss with students the fact that copper and iron mines have virtually ceased production in Japan and that these minerals are imported. Have students brainstorm a list of ideas as to why this is the case and then write a hypothesis. Ask them to find evidence to support their hypotheses. AL **Logical/Mathematical**

CLOSE & REFLECT

Summarizing Review with students the climate, biomes, and geography of Japan. Discuss how geography influences where and how people live, what crops can be cultivated, and the economic resources of Japan.

LESSON 1 REVIEW ANSWERS

Reviewing Vocabulary

1. Tsunamis form due to the occurrence of an undersea earthquake which causes a wave that is higher than normal. Tsunamis may travel great distances, causing a massive wave to wash inland for miles.

Using Your Notes

2. Characteristics of Japan's climate include: cold, snowy winters; warm, wet summers; monsoons; and typhoons.

Answering the Guiding Questions

3. Volcanic activity formed the mountainous landscape.
4. Japan has short, fast rivers that flow from the mountain regions, often dropping off cliffs in stunning waterfalls.
5. The climate becomes warmer as one travels from the humid continental climate in northern areas to the subtropical climate of southern areas.

Writing Activity

6. Paragraphs will differ but should be strongly supported with information from the lesson including: northern latitudes have a humid continental climate while southern latitudes have a humid subtropical climate; semitropical forests grow in the south; broad-leaved evergreens and mixed deciduous trees grow in the midlatitudes; conifers grow in the far north; winter monsoons drop snow on western mountain slopes and bring drier air to the east; warm summer monsoons bring rains to the eastern slopes and dry air to the west.

ANSWERS, p. 707

READING PROGRESS CHECK Fish and other sea life are the natural resource most closely related to Japan being an island country. Pollution and overfishing are threatening these resources.

CRITICAL THINKING

1. The mountains in the background with only coastal development of houses, fishing, and shoreline industries shows how the rugged landscape shapes where people live and industry develops.
2. The decline of fisheries will negatively affect Japan's economy.

CHAPTER 29

Global Connections

ENGAGE

Analyzing Cause and Effect Have students work with a partner to create a cause-and-effect diagram or flowchart to organize information depicted in this feature. As students work through the feature, have them work with their partner to complete the chart. Then have students collaborate to write a summarizing paragraph that explains the causes and effects of the Tohuku earthquake and resulting tsunami.

TEACH & ASSESS

R Reading Skills

Discussing Point to the phrase *recorded earthquake* in the first sentence and read aloud the information in the Content Background Knowledge below. **Ask:** **How do you think the ability to measure and record earthquakes has helped scientists over the years?** *(Possible answer: Scientists can likely learn more about the cause and frequency of earthquakes by measuring them.)* **What do you think can be learned from the severity of the Tohoku earthquake?** *(Possible answer: If earthquakes are a common occurrence in a particular region, then additional safety precautions should be taken to protect people and the surrounding environment. For example, scientists and seismologists should advise companies and governments seeking to construct nuclear power plants in a highly seismic region.)* **Verbal/Linguistic**

Content Background Knowledge

First Recorded Earthquake According to the United States Geological Survey, the first reported earthquake in California was in 1769. The quake occurred approximately 30 miles (48 km) southeast of Los Angeles. To date, the USGS reports that the world's largest earthquake, which registered a 9.5 on the Richter scale, was in Chile on May 22, 1960. The largest recorded earthquake in the United States occurred in 1964 in Alaska, registering a magnitude 9.2.

V Visual Skills

Interpreting Direct students' attention to the diagram on this page showing the process of faulting. Ask a few student volunteers to describe the diagram in their own words. **Verbal/Linguistic**

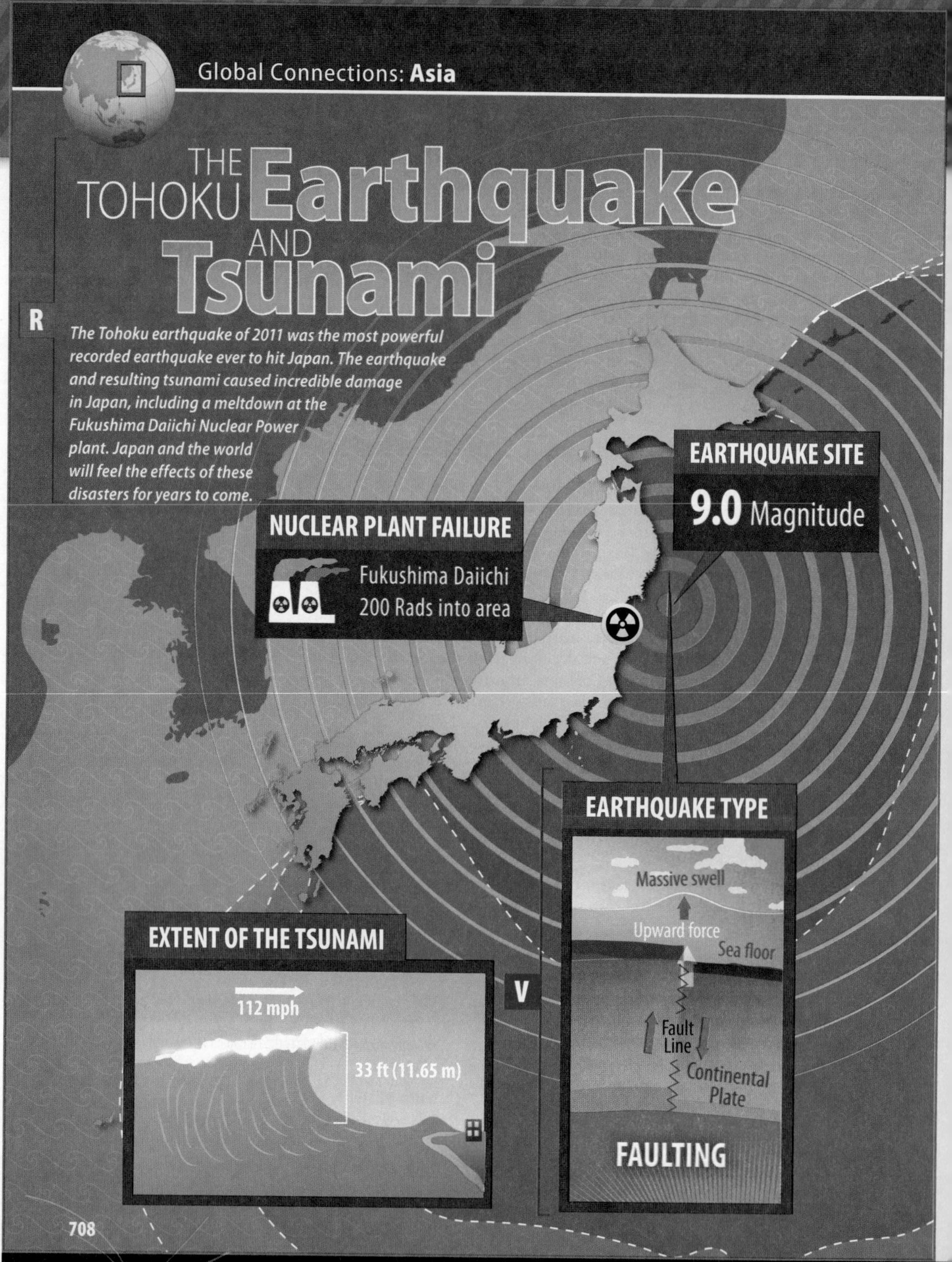

Global Connections: **Asia**

THE TOHOKU Earthquake AND Tsunami

R *The Tohoku earthquake of 2011 was the most powerful recorded earthquake ever to hit Japan. The earthquake and resulting tsunami caused incredible damage in Japan, including a meltdown at the Fukushima Daiichi Nuclear Power plant. Japan and the world will feel the effects of these disasters for years to come.*

EARTHQUAKE SITE
9.0 Magnitude

NUCLEAR PLANT FAILURE
Fukushima Daiichi
200 Rads into area

EARTHQUAKE TYPE
Massive swell
Upward force
Sea floor
Fault Line
Continental Plate
FAULTING

V **EXTENT OF THE TSUNAMI**
112 mph
33 ft (11.65 m)

708

networks Online Teaching Options

ANIMATION

How Tsunamis Form

Creating Charts Allow time for students to interact and analyze this interactive animation on how tsunamis form. Have students work with a partner to create a flowchart or graph that explains the process of tsunami formation. Students may want to conduct Internet research. Tell students that their charts should include visuals that are either hand drawn or computer generated. Invite students to display their charts in the classroom. **Visual/Spatial**

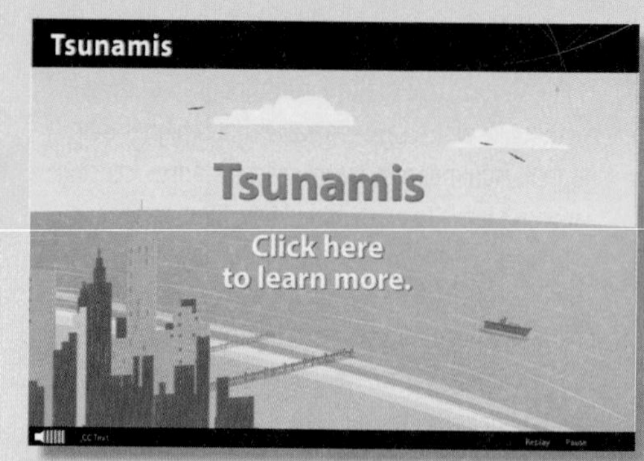

RELIEF EFFORTS

In total, 116 countries and 28 international organizations offered assistance to Japan after the earthquake and tsunami.

C

As of early 2012, over 5 billion dollars for relief and recovery had been donated from people in Japan and across the globe.

700 million

Private donations from the United States exceeded 700 million dollars, the third highest U.S. donations total for any overseas disaster.

W

WORLD IMPACT

4–10 inches off axis

At a magnitude of 9.0, the earthquake was so strong it shifted Earth on its axis by estimates of 4 to 10 inches (10–25 cm).

High tsunami waters from the Tohoku earthquake hit several other places, such as Hawaii, Peru, Chile, Oregon and California.

As of early 2013, twelve pieces of Japanese debris from the tsunami, including a 20-foot (6.1-m) boat, had washed onto U.S. and Canadian shores.

T

Making Connections

1. ***The World in Spatial Terms*** How did the location of the Tohoku earthquake contribute to the destructive power of the tsunami?
2. ***Physical Systems*** Outside of Japan, the tsunami impacted areas in the southern and eastern Pacific Ocean the most. Explain why areas in the western Pacific were largely spared.
3. ***Environment and Society*** Numerous images and video of the Tohoku earthquake and subsequent tsunami were posted on the Internet almost immediately following the disaster. How do you think these visuals contributed to international relief efforts?

*Interact with **Global Connections** Online*

INFOGRAPHIC

Tohoku Earthquake and Tsunami

Making Connections Display the infographic on the Tohoku earthquake and tsunami to explain the effects and devastation that these types of natural disasters can cause. Ask students to consider the types of natural disasters that have or could have occurred where they live, such as hurricanes, tornadoes, or floods. Guide a class discussion about these types of disasters. Then discuss community warning devices that alert people to severe weather or natural disasters. Have students provide any information they know about these systems and ask them to explain whether they think these devices are helping to save lives or whether more needs to be done within their communities. BL **Interpersonal**

The Tohoku Earthquake and Tsunami

The Tohoku Earthquake of 2011 was the most powerful recorded earthquake ever to hit Japan. The earthquake and resulting tsunami caused incredible damage in Japan, including a meltdown at the Fukushima Daiichi nuclear power plant. Japan and the world will feel the effects of these disasters for years to come.

What to do:

Click on the buttons along the bottom to learn more about this aspect of the disaster and its aftermath.

Go Explore

C Critical Thinking Skills

Interpreting Significance Ask a volunteer to read aloud the paragraph about the assistance to Japan from other countries. **Ask: How do you think the earthquake and tsunami impacted the economies of the countries that offered financial assistance to Japan?** *(Students' responses will vary but should infer that countries may have been negatively impacted economically.)* AL **Logical/Mathematical**

W Writing Skills

Informative Read aloud the text about U.S. donations to Japan. Have students conduct research to identify where some of the donations went and how they impacted Japanese students and their families who were affected by the earthquake and tsunami. Tell students to write an informative essay that details their findings and ask volunteers to share their essays with the class. BL **Verbal/Linguistic**

T Technology Skills

Analyzing Cause and Effect Read aloud the paragraph and organize students into six groups. Assign each group one of the following countries or states: Japan, Hawaii, Peru, Chile, Oregon, or California. Have each group research the tsunami's impact on their assigned region, noting the cost of damage and cleanup to that region, the impact on the environment, and the status of cleanup efforts in that region today. Have groups present their findings in a short report. Then discuss the impact of the Tohoku earthquake and resulting tsunami on the immediate and surrounding regions. BL **Visual/Spatial, Interpersonal**

CLOSE & REFLECT

Reaching Conclusions Guide a discussion about the status of the Fukushima Daiichi Nuclear Power plant and how Japan and other parts of the world will continue to feel the impact of the earthquake and tsunami for many years.

ANSWERS, p. 709

Making Connections

1. The earthquake was underwater and just offshore from Japan. As a result, the subsequent tsunami hit the shoreline at a high speed, broad width, and tall height. These combined elements caused the tsunami to be far more destructive than is typical.
2. The islands of Japan absorbed the impact of the tsunami's western flow, meaning many areas on the western Pacific shore were largely spared.
3. Visuals from the tsunami, posted so quickly, allowed the world to see the impact of the disaster. As a result, worldwide awareness was high and could have led individuals to respond far more rapidly than before.

ENGAGE

R Reading Skills

Transferring Ask students to think about the concept of traditional and modern existing comfortably together. Have students write a paragraph explaining the influences of both traditional and modern in their own community and how they mix. Then, **ask:** **What is the value or purpose in holding on to traditional society?** *(Possible answer: Traditions give people a sense of shared history and stability.)*

TEACH & ASSESS

T Technology Skills

Researching Have students research a particular Japanese dynasty. Ask them to collect information about how the dynasty came to power, how long it ruled, and what the transition from this dynasty was to the next form of government. Have students create a short presentation for the class about their chosen dynasty. **BL Verbal/Linguistic**

C Critical Thinking Skills

Identifying Perspectives and Differing Interpretations Discuss with students the shoguns' unwillingness to allow foreigners into Japan. **Ask:** **What was the perspective of the shoguns?** *(Possible answer: They were afraid of an attack from the outside.)* **How did they interpret the visits of Roman Catholic missionaries and European traders?** *(Possible answer: as a threat)* **What might your reaction be if unexpected strangers invaded your country?** *(Possible answer: It would be frightening because people would not know what the other country's motivations for coming were.)* **Interpersonal, Verbal/Linguistic**

networks

There's More Online!

- ☑ **GRAPH** Japanese Balance of Trade with the United States
- ☑ **IMAGE** Commodore Perry in Japan
- ☑ **IMAGE** Japan and the West
- ☑ **IMAGE** Port of Tokyo
- ☑ **TIME LINE** Shifting Power
- ☑ **INTERACTIVE SELF-CHECK QUIZ**
- ☑ **VIDEO** Human Geography of Japan

LESSON 2
Human Geography of Japan

ESSENTIAL QUESTION • *How do physical systems and human systems shape a place?*

Reading HELPDESK CCSS

Academic Vocabulary (Tier Two Words)
- **approximate**
- **generation**
- **unique**
- **overseas**

Content Vocabulary (Tier Three Words)
- **clan**
- **samurai**
- **acculturation**
- **trade surplus**

TAKING NOTES: Key Ideas and Details

IDENTIFYING As you read about the human geography of Japan, use a graphic organizer like the one below to identify major turning points in Japan's history.

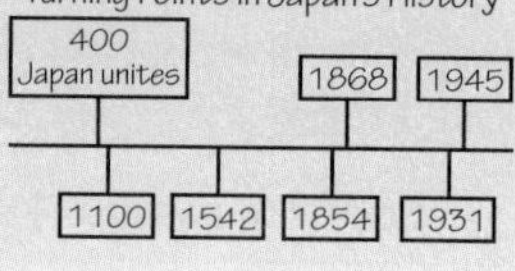

IT MATTERS BECAUSE

R *Japan's early human geography reflects influences from ancient China and Korea. The Japanese civilization that developed from these two countries then isolated itself well into the 1800s. Since then, the forces of modernization and globalization have influenced Japanese society. Yet the traditional and the modern exist comfortably together.*

History and Government

GUIDING QUESTION *How do ancient and modern traditions influence life in Japan?*

Japan's history combines tradition with transformation. Japan has maintained its cultural traditions while leaping toward modernization over the last century.

Japan Through the Ages

T Because they are so close, China and Korea had a significant impact on Japan. Once ruled by many **clans,** in the A.D. 400s Japan united under the Yamato dynasty. Yamato rulers adopted China's philosophy, writing system, art, sciences, and governmental structure. Korean scholars also influenced the Japanese.

Japan was ruled by dynasties for centuries. Japanese society evolved, developing a government and establishing an emperor as absolute monarch. In the 1100s, warring armies brought about the shogunate, a feudal society under the control of a shogun, or military ruler. Professional warriors known as **samurai** supported the shogun's rule, although the emperor was the official ruler of Japan.

C The first documented contact with the West occurred in 1542. A Portuguese ship sailing to China was blown off course and landed in Japan. Roman Catholic missionaries and European traders followed, raising concerns that military conquest might follow. To prevent this, shoguns restricted foreigners. They expelled all but a few European merchants who traded at Nagasaki.

During the 1800s, the United States worked to open Japan to trade. In 1854, following a show of strength, Commodore Matthew C. Perry of

710

networks ***Online Teaching Options***

INTERACTIVE BELLRINGER

Japanese Balance of Trade with the United States

Determining Importance Use the introductory text and the graph of the Japanese balance of trade with the United States to understand the ways in which industrialization shaped the Japanese economy. Have students form small groups and discuss each question. Have each group write agreed-upon answers to each question. Then, have each group share its answers in a class discussion. **BL Interpersonal, Logical/ Mathematical, Verbal/Linguistic**

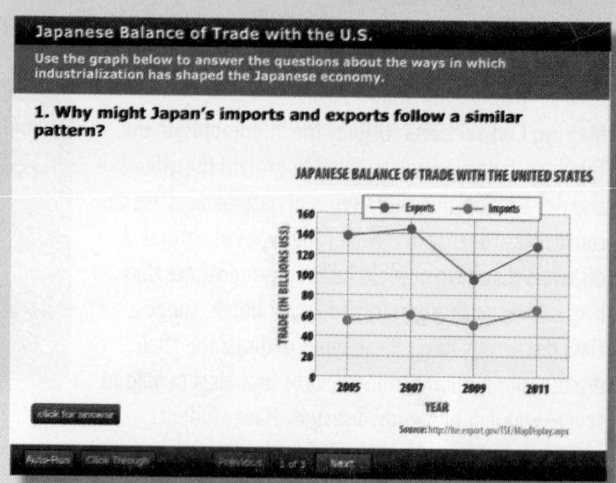

ANSWERS, p. 710

TAKING NOTES: Japan was ruled by many groups before being united under the Yamato dynasty in the A.D. 400s. In the 1100s, the shogunate was established by warring armies. A Portuguese ship blown off course in 1542 was Japan's first documented contact with the West. Commodore Perry of the U.S. Navy opened Japan to trade with the U.S. in 1854. Japan underwent a period of rapid modernization from 1868 to 1912. In 1910 Japan took control of Korea and became Asia's most powerful empire. In 1931 Japan invaded China. In WWII, Japan sided with the Axis Powers and surrendered when atomic bombs were dropped in 1945.

the U.S. Navy negotiated opening Japanese ports to U.S. ships. A trade agreement followed that benefited the United States. This action eventually sparked a samurai rebellion that returned full authority to the emperor.

clan a family group

samurai a professional warrior of preindustrial Japan

A Changing Government

R

The return of authority to the emperor was a turning point in Japanese history. Called the Meiji Restoration, this period—which lasted from 1868 to 1912—involved the rapid modernization of Japanese society, including its government, economy, military, education, and legal systems. Japan became a modern country set on building an empire. In a war with China, Japan conquered the island of Formosa (Taiwan). Japan also fought Russia for control of Korea and gained rights to Manchuria and the Russian island of Sakhalin. By the time Japan took control of Korea in 1910, it had become the most powerful empire in Asia.

During World War I, Japan sided with the Allies, profiting from exports to Allied countries and expanding its influence in Asia. Following the war, Japan continued to prosper and extend its reach. Though Japan steered toward a democracy, military leaders gained influence over the government. In 1931 they invaded northeast China; in 1937 they invaded northern China. By 1939, Japan had joined with Germany and Italy as the Axis Powers. Japan's 1941 attack on Pearl Harbor drew the United States into World War II, in which some 3 million Japanese lost their lives. The war ended when Japan surrendered after the United States dropped atomic bombs on Hiroshima and Nagasaki in 1945.

The American occupation of Japan that followed stripped the empire of its territories and military. It also set the country back on the road to democracy. Out of the ruins, a vibrant economy emerged. Several decades later, Japan

Commodore Perry's steamships, anchored in Edo Bay (now Tokyo Bay) and bristling with huge guns, convinced the Japanese government to sign a trade treaty with the United States and open two ports and a trade agreement.

▼ CRITICAL THINKING

1. ***Identifying Central Issues*** What caused the Japanese to end years of isolation abruptly?
2. ***Defending*** Provide a main reason to justify Commodore Perry's pressure on Japan to open trade with the United States. Then provide a main reason to justify Japanese resistance to opening their country to foreign influences.

C

R Reading Skills

Listing Have students make a list of countries and lands that Japan conquered during the Meiji Restoration and through the first half of the twentieth century and into the World War II era. **Ask:** **What was the main goal of the Japanese government in taking over nearby lands and countries?** *(Japan wanted to build an empire and obtain natural resources.)* **How was Japan's dominance brought to an end?** *(It ended after World War II when Japan surrendered to the United States.)* **Verbal/Linguistic**

C Critical Thinking Skills

Posing Questions Direct students to the painting of Commodore Matthew C. Perry's arrival in Japan. Brainstorm with students a list of questions they have about what is happening in the painting. Have them do further research to learn more about Perry's pressuring Japan to open the country for trade. Discuss the details of the painting that most effectively portray this relationship. BL **Visual/Spatial**

Content Background Knowledge

Japan's Response to Commodore Perry Although the Japanese did not want to open up their country for trade with the United States, they also had no navy with which to defend themselves. They realized that the U.S. ships were only the beginning, and soon Russia, Britain, and France would all use their navies to force Japan to sign trade treaties. The trade treaties signed between Japan and the United States were the beginning of the downfall of the shogunate. The influx of foreign currency disrupted the Japanese monetary system, which ultimately led to the samurai rebellion.

INTERACTIVE GRAPHIC ORGANIZER

Human Geography of Japan

Organizing Have students complete the graphic organizer to identify major turning points in Japan's history. AL **Visual/Spatial**

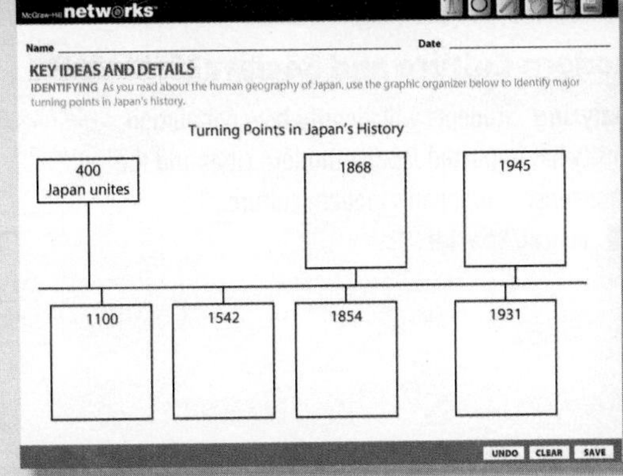

ANSWER, p. 711

CRITICAL THINKING

1. The United States made a show of force to compel them to open their ports to trade.
2. Reasons provided may differ but could include: trade was mutually beneficial for both countries, prevented conflict, and allowed Japan to grow its economy; resistance could be justified as a desire to keep their culture intact, did not wish to have foreign interference in governmental affairs, and a fear of conquest by those coming to trade.

Human Geography of Japan

T Technology Skills

Gathering Information Have students work with a partner to gather information about a constitutional monarchy. Ask them to find out what, if any, power the emperor has. Have them write a short explanation or design a one-page presentation about constitutional monarchies. Ask pairs to include a list of other countries that also have constitutional monarchies. **Verbal/Linguistic**

C Critical Thinking Skills

Simulating Have students simulate the population density of the Tokyo-Yokohama urban area. **Ask:** **What is the population density in this area?** *(11,300 people per square mile or 4,300 people per square kilometer)* **What are some ways to simulate this population density on a smaller scale, such as in the classroom?** *(Possible answers: calculate the number of people per square meter and map out a square meter in the classroom and place the number of people per square meter in that area; draw a scaled map of a square kilometer, and then draw dots to show the number of people.)* BL **Logical/Mathematical**

R Reading Skills

Examining Have students think about what it would be like to live in the Tokaido corridor. **Ask:** **What are some of the advantages of living in this huge urban environment?** *(Possible answers: easy access to work and shopping, not having to own a car, public transportation options, lots of cultural activities)* **What are some possible disadvantages to living in this type of urban environment?** *(Possible answers: small houses or apartments, need to always use public transportation, less privacy)* **Interpersonal**

ANSWERS, p. 712

READING PROGRESS CHECK The role of the Japanese emperor began as one of an absolute monarch, moved to a figurehead under the shogun, transitioned back to an absolute monarch after the U.S. opened its ports, and finally settled as a head of state as part of a constitutional monarchy.

CRITICAL THINKING

1. Either through hereditary rights or military power.
2. In the past, military power brought Japan under the control of a shogun, brought power to warlords, and helped lead to WWII.

T became a global economic power. Today, Japan has the third-largest economy in the world, surpassed only by China and the United States. As a constitutional monarchy, Japan has an emperor who is the head of state.

READING PROGRESS CHECK

Sequencing Information How has the role of the Japanese emperor changed over time?

Population Patterns

GUIDING QUESTION *How does population density influence life in parts of Japan?*

The majority of Japanese—99 percent—belong to the same ethnic group. They are descendants of migrating people from Asia who pushed out most of the indigenous people of Japan, the Ainu (EYE•noo). Some Ainu still live on Hokkaidō today.

C Since most of Japan is mountainous, there is limited land area suitable for habitation. Most people are concentrated in the lowlands along the seacoasts, or in valleys and plains. The urban concentrations are great, and Tokyo-Yokohama is one of the largest megacities in the world, with more than 37 million people. The population density in this urban area is 11,300 people per square mile (4,300 people per sq. km). The average population density in Japan is about 907 people per square mile (350 per sq. km). The lowest density is on Hokkaidō.

approximate close to, but not exact

R **Approximately** four-fifths of Japanese live in urban areas, and a majority of these people live near the Tokaido megalopolis. This corridor is a 750-mile-(1,200-km-) long urbanization zone and is concentrated along rail lines. Extreme urbanization affects many aspects of Japanese life. This includes not only the lifestyles of the Japanese, but architecture, transportation, housing, and daily activities. In Tokyo, crowded streets with immense skyscrapers and numerous commercial areas are located within easy walking distance of subway stations. Bicycles are widely used by Japanese of all ages to ride to

TIME LINE

Shifting POWER

Although Japan's monarchy has endured longer than that of any other country, the real power in Japan has shifted from emperors to shoguns to the people. The emperor plays an important symbolic role in Japan, but wields little power.

CRITICAL THINKING

1. ***Describing*** In Japan's history, how has power passed from one leader to another?
2. ***Analyzing*** What role has the military played in Japan's government in the past?

700

710 Japan's capital moves to Nara, the emperor emerges as leader, and Buddhism becomes the state religion.

794 Capital moves to Heian-kyo; powerful Fujiwara family dominates political and cultural life

1185 Minamoto Yoritomo becomes first shogun, or military leader, and establishes capital at Kamakura

1300

1392 During the Muromachi period, provincial warlords hold real power in Japan.

networks Online Teaching Options

INTERACTIVE WHITEBOARD ACTIVITY

Modern Culture and Society

Analyzing Students will identify how population density has impacted Japan's modern cities and the characteristics of Japan's modern culture. AL **Visual/Spatial**

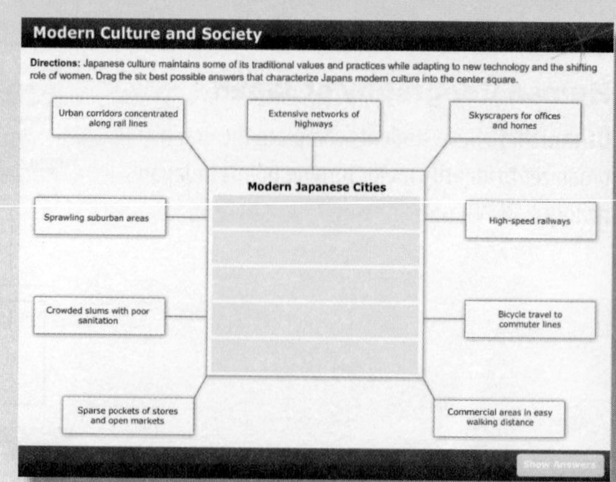

school or to commute to work or subway stations. These stations link to a system of railroads. This system includes a network of long-distance, high-speed electric bullet trains. In 2012 a Japanese railroad company unveiled plans for a magnetic levitation train. It would float above the tracks, levitated by the force of powerful magnets. This train is expected to travel at 311 miles per hour (500 km per hour). Due to its emphasis on convenient public transportation, Tokyo has developed very differently from cities that are heavily reliant on privately owned vehicles. It has no slums and is considered environmentally friendly. **T**

✓ **READING PROGRESS CHECK**

Summarizing What is the largest urban area in the world?

Society and Culture Today

GUIDING QUESTION *How do traditions influence family life and art?*

The written form of Japanese began around A.D. 400, when Chinese writing was first introduced and adapted to Japanese. The Japanese borrowed words from Chinese and have more recently borrowed thousands of English words for concepts that do not exist in Japanese.

Japan's indigenous religion, Shinto, is often practiced in a mix with Buddhism and even Christianity. Shinto emphasizes reverence for nature and is polytheistic. While it is unusual for Japanese children to receive formal religious instruction, many households have both a Buddhist altar and a Shinto alter. **R**

Modern Japanese society has a high regard for education. By law, children must attend school until age 15. Many begin at a very young age to focus on getting into the best schools and eventually the best universities. Adults often continue to seek instruction long after formal schooling is completed, studying **C**

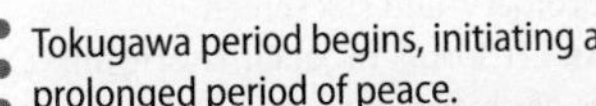

1600 Tokugawa period begins, initiating a prolonged period of peace.

1868 In response to pressure from Western nations, Japan begins rapidly modernizing during Meiji Restoration.

1900 ➔

1912 Yoshihito becomes emperor; Japan becomes more democratic as more men gain the vote.

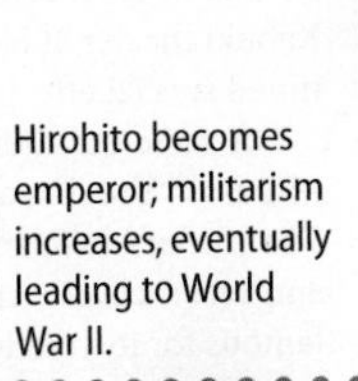

1926 Hirohito becomes emperor; militarism increases, eventually leading to World War II.

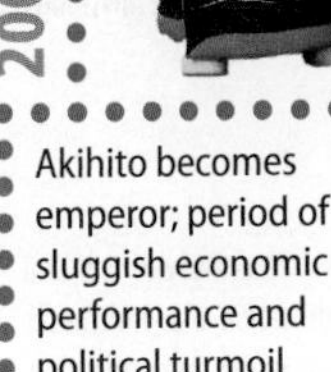

1989 Akihito becomes emperor; period of sluggish economic performance and political turmoil

2006 Prince Hisahito is born and becomes third in line for the Japanese throne.

INTERACTIVE TIME LINE

Shifting Power

Evaluating Information Have students examine the time line that displays how the real power in Japan has shifted from emperors to shoguns to the people.

AL Verbal/Linguistic

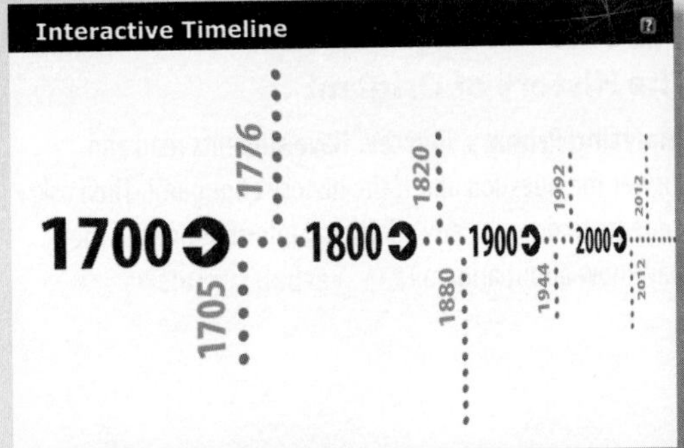

T Technology Skills

Researching Ask a small group of student volunteers to explore how a magnetic levitation train works and why they are being considered as the next step in modernizing trains. Ask them to describe the science behind magnetic levitation trains and why this is a viable option for Japan. Then have them research how other countries may also use this type of train and provide an estimate of when this type of train may be found in use throughout Japan and other countries.

BL Verbal/Linguistic

R Reading Skills

Using Word Parts Point out the word *polytheistic* to students. Explain that some words can be completely broken down into prefixes, suffixes, and root words that help to define the word itself. **Ask: What is the prefix and what does it mean?** *(poly-: many)* **What are the suffixes and what do they each mean?** *(-ist: a person or group who practices something or has certain principles; -ic: it forms an adjective of the word to which it is attached)* **What is the root word in *polytheistic* and what is its meaning?** *(the-: God or gods)* **What is the meaning of *polytheistic*?** *(a person or group that worships many gods)* **What word means worshipping one god?** *(monotheistic)* **What word means worshipping no gods?** *(atheistic)*

ELL Verbal/Linguistic

C Critical Thinking Skills

Comparing and Contrasting Discuss with students how education and the importance of education is similar and different between Japan and the United States. **Ask: Until what age must a child in our state attend school?** *(This varies by state. It is often sixteen or seventeen years old.)* **How does this compare to the age in Japan?** *(Possible answer: It is older in the United States.)* **How do you think society's view on education differs between Japan and the United States? Explain.** *(Possible answer: Education may be more highly regarded in Japan than it is in the United States. In the United States, school is important, but overall a smaller percentage of students are focused on getting into the best schools or universities.)* **Interpersonal, Verbal/Linguistic**

ANSWERS, p. 713

✓ **READING PROGRESS CHECK** Tokyo-Yokohama is one of the largest megacities in the world. The majority of people live near the Tokaido megalopolis.

Human Geography of Japan

V Visual Skills

Applying Have students work on simple origami pieces. There are many images and instructions available online. Have students all try the same piece. Then have them explore on their own to see what creations they can make. **Ask: Now that you have tried origami, why do you think it became popular in Japan?** *(Possible answer: It is fun and challenging to see what creations you can make simply from a piece of flat paper.)* **What types of objects were most likely made into origami in ancient Japan when it was used only for ceremonial purposes?** *(Possible answers: cranes, flowers, animals)* **Kinesthetic, Naturalist**

R Reading Skills

Examining Discuss the changes happening in families in Japan and how they may or may not conflict with the traditional values of being part of a group and the revering of ancestors. **Ask: Are modern views likely or unlikely to conflict with these traditional values? How?** *(Possible answer: They are likely to conflict with traditional values because they are very different. Technology has changed the way people interact, and they are more likely to regard being part of a group as less important. They are also less likely to revere their ancestors because of the technological divide between younger people and their older ancestors.)* ELL **Interpersonal, Logical/Mathematical**

W Writing Skills

Narrative Have students work in small groups to explore the characteristics of Kabuki theater. Then challenge them to write a scene for a Kabuki play, incorporating as many characteristics of Kabuki theater as possible. Emphasize that Kabuki incorporates singing, dancing, and elaborate costumes. Tell students to incorporate singing and dancing in their narratives by writing them in the form of a script. Motivated students may wish to put on a performance of their scene. **Auditory/Musical, Kinesthetic**

ANSWERS, p. 714

READING PROGRESS CHECK Answers may include: origami–paper folding; tea ceremony–ritual artistry combining literary and artistic expression into an elaborate tea service; Kabuki theater–music, dancing, elaborate costumes/makeup, and special effects; haiku–strictly formed descriptive poetry; silk screening–painting delicate scenes traditionally of rugged mountains on silk fabric.

DBQ Once paper became affordable and widely available due to mass production, origami was able to be practiced as an art.

The History of Origami

"Composed of the Japanese words *oru* (to fold) and *kami* (paper), origami has a rich and complex history that spans culture, class and geography.

Paper was first invented in China around 105 A.D., and was brought to Japan by monks in the sixth century. Handmade paper was a luxury item only available to a few, and paper folding in ancient Japan was strictly for ceremonial purposes, often religious in nature.

By the Edo period (1603–1868), paper folding came to be regarded as a new form of art that was enabled by the advent of paper both mass-produced and more affordable."

—"Between the Folds," *PBS Independent Lens*, November 30, 2009

DBQ ***ANALYZING PRIMARY SOURCES*** Why did the advent of mass-produced paper change origami from a ceremonial practice to a new form of art? **RH.9–10.1**

anything from foreign languages to technology. The Japanese are also avid travelers and tourists.

In addition to a high standard of living, the Japanese enjoy corresponding general good health and the longest life expectancy in the world. National health insurance covers all citizens. However, high life expectancy combined with a low birthrate means the Japanese population is aging disproportionately, which strains health and social services. A smaller workforce is a future issue for Japan.

Family and the Status of Women

Family in Japan remains a source of stability but is undergoing changes. Families are smaller than in the past. Many children are still taught the importance of being part of a group, as opposed to being an individual. They are also taught to revere their ancestors. But as new **generations** are more likely to be raised in urban settings, rather than in villages, they tend to have more modern views and changing values. In a technologically advanced and consumer-driven society, less social conformity and increasing individual choice is apparent in ordinary Japanese people. Young Japanese are among the world's major users of technology.

Some of the changes in Japanese families are due to the changing role of women in society. There is growing dissatisfaction with traditional roles in which women are expected to bear major responsibility for the household tasks. Women make up about two-fifths of Japanese workers. As they enter the workforce in larger numbers, they often delay marriage and childbearing. This has contributed to the trend of smaller families and Japan's declining population. Female role models, such as Japan's first female foreign minister, have helped to change perceptions. Many women work only part-time jobs, however, and those in careers often find it difficult to win promotion to high-level positions.

The Arts

The Japanese have developed their own art forms. Traditional Japanese art rejects what is showy and emphasizes delicacy, exquisite forms, and simplicity. Poets, writers, and artisans throughout the centuries have portrayed the beauty of the seasons, the changing environment, and the rugged mountains through poetry, theater, painting, pottery, embroidery, and silk screen.

Among the enduring and **unique** art forms of Japan is origami. Origami uses folded paper to depict the shapes of objects of nature, such as animals and birds. The Japanese tea ceremony is also a time-honored tradition. Still practiced as a hobby today, the tea ceremony combines literary and artistic traditions into a ritual of great artistry. Another tradition that remains popular is the classical Kabuki theater. It blends music, dancing, costumes, elaborate makeup, and well-timed special effects to bring characters to life.

A taste for literature among educated Japanese has a long history. Lady Murasaki Shikibu, a Japanese noblewoman, wrote one of the world's first novels, *The Tale of Genji*, around A.D. 1010. It tells the story of an imperial prince in the emperor's court. Another well-known form of Japanese poetry, the haiku, is famous for its concise and exact use of words and nature imagery that appeals to the senses.

Japan's rich artistic history does not hinder the Japanese from enjoying and excelling at art and cultural forms that developed in other places. Such **acculturation** is apparent in many ways. Western classical music is popular, and major Japanese cities may have more than one symphony orchestra. Western-style painting, sculpture, architecture, and cinema are also very popular.

READING PROGRESS CHECK

Identifying List five of Japan's unique art forms and describe two of them.

generation a group of individuals born and living at the same time

unique unlike anything else

acculturation cultural modification of an individual, group, or people by adapting to or borrowing traits from another culture

714

networks Online Teaching Options

PRIMARY SOURCE

The History of Origami

Analyzing Primary Sources Have students read and answer the question about the history of origami. Then ask students to describe any additional information that they may know about origami. AL **Verbal/Linguistic**

Analyzing Primary Sources

The History of Origami

"Composed of the Japanese words *oru* (to fold) and *kami* (paper), origami has a rich and complex history that spans culture, class and geography.

Paper was first invented in China around 105 a.d., and was brought to Japan by monks in the sixth century. Handmade paper was a luxury item only available to a few, and paper folding in ancient Japan was strictly for ceremonial purposes, often religious in nature.

By the Edo period (1603–1868), paper folding came to be regarded as a new form of art that was enabled by the advent of paper both mass-produced and more affordable."

—"Between the Folds," *Independent Lens*, November 30, 2009

Economic Activities

GUIDING QUESTION *How have industry and trade transformed the country?*

Japan's industrial economy is based on a mixed market system. Such a system emphasizes private ownership of the means of production and distribution. The government plays a key role, however. It carefully coordinates with industry and regulates all sectors of the economy, including imports.

Industry and Manufacturing

Japan has seen extraordinary economic growth since World War II. High demand for trade goods around the world has made it a global economic power since the 1980s. Lacking ample natural resources, such as fossil fuels and minerals, Japan has focused on trade to sustain its industries. It has highly skilled and educated workers and newly advanced technology. This has helped Japan to become a leading producer of consumer goods such as cars, electronic devices, and computers.

Telecommunications industries, particularly mobile communications leaders NTT and KDDI, rank among the largest Japanese corporations. Other huge conglomerates include Canon, which makes office and consumer products, and Honda, which builds automobiles and motorcycles. Nippon Steel is Japan's leading steel producer. Mitsubishi is a major multinational company with diverse business interests. These and many other important companies earn billions in annual profits.

Apart from their economic role, Japanese corporations play an important societal role. Although this practice is beginning to change, most employees expect to stay with their company until retirement. This culture of lifetime employment creates very strong bonds between company and workers. Politeness, sensitivity, and good manners are basic elements in the workplace. Executives and their families are ranked socially by the importance of the company for which they work.

R

Trade

To sustain its economy, Japan imports raw materials such as fossil fuels and minerals from other countries. Japanese industries turn these resources into finished products that they sell in huge quantities **overseas**. For example, China, the United States, South Korea, Taiwan, Singapore, Thailand, and Germany all buy Japanese cars and high-tech devices.

overseas relating to a foreign country, especially one across the ocean

Japanese Balance of Trade with the United States

Exports — Imports

TRADE (IN BILLIONS US$): 0, 20, 40, 60, 80, 100, 120, 140, 160

YEAR: 2005, 2007, 2009, 2011

Source: http://tse.export.gov/TSE/MapDisplay.aspx

V

GRAPH SKILLS

Japan relies heavily on exports to drive economic growth.

CRITICAL THINKING

1. ***Analyzing Visuals*** Describe the difference between Japan's exports to and imports from the United States.
2. ***Constructing a Thesis*** Give a logical reason for why Japan's imports and exports both dipped in 2009. Explain your reasoning.

R Reading Skills

Identifying Discuss with students the reasons why Japan became an industry and manufacturing leader. **Ask:** What role has Japan's geography played in its economy? *(Possible answer: Japan's rugged mountain landscape means it has fewer available natural resources. So it has focused on manufacturing and industry by using resources acquired through trade.)* What are some of Japan's leading products? *(Possible answers: automobiles, motorcycles, steel, electronic devices, computers, office products)* What practices are expected in the workplace in Japan? *(politeness, sensitivity, good manners)* What creates strong bonds between employers and employees? *(Most employees stay with their company until they retire.)* **AL Logical/Mathematical, Interpersonal**

V Visual Skills

Using Graphs Discuss with students the double-line graph that displays the Japanese balance of trade with the United States. Point out that when a country's exports exceed its imports, it is said to have a trade surplus. When its imports exceed its exports, it is said to have a trade deficit. **Ask:** Does Japan have a trade deficit or a trade surplus when trading with the United States? *(It has a trade surplus because its exports to the United States exceed its imports from the United States.)* In which year was Japan's trade surplus with the United States the lowest? *(in 2009)* Does the United States experience a trade deficit or a trade surplus when trading with Japan? *(a trade deficit because its imports exceed its exports)* **Logical/Mathematical, Visual/Spatial**

Content Background Knowledge

Japan's Trade Balance There are many factors that affect the trade balance of a country that are outside of the country's control. In the years since the 2011 tsunami, Japan ultimately shut down most of its nuclear reactors due either to damage done by the tsunami or to outdated designs. During this time, imports of fossil fuels rose dramatically to account for the loss of energy that was previously provided by nuclear reactors. This huge shift is one factor that led to an overall trade deficit for Japan in 2012 and 2013.

VIDEO

Japan Labor

Examining Have students watch this video to learn more about the changing nature of work in Japan. Then have them answer questions from the corresponding Video Activity worksheet. **AL Verbal/Linguistic**

ANSWERS, p. 715

CRITICAL THINKING

1. The number of exports is much higher than the number of imports but is balanced–as exports rise, so do imports.
2. Imports and exports dipped in 2009 due to the recession which decreased the demand for Japanese goods, resulting in fewer exports and less money to spend on imports.

Human Geography of Japan

V Visual Skills

Analyzing Visuals Discuss the photograph of the Port of Tokyo with students. **Ask:** **What can you infer about how exports and imports travel from and to Japan?** *(Possible answer: Many of the exports and imports are shipped by sea.)* **How does Japan's geography influence this?** *(Possible answer: Since it is an island nation, it is easily accessible to ships.)* **How do you think the 2011 tsunami affected exports from and imports to Japan? Why?** *(Possible answer: It likely disrupted them because the coastline and some ports were damaged by the tsunami.)* **Visual/Spatial**

C Critical Thinking Skills

Drawing Conclusions Discuss the decisions Japan has made to place tariffs on some imports and not others. **Ask:** **What imports have tariffs?** *(manufactured goods)* **What imports do not have tariffs?** *(raw materials)* **Why is there no tariff on raw materials but on manufactured goods?** *(Possible answer: Japan needs raw materials to produce manufactured goods. It needs to make it easy to get these raw materials from other countries, so there is no tariff. However, Japan wants to protect its companies from foreign competition, which it does by attaching a tariff to imported manufactured goods.)*
BL Logical/Mathematical

CLOSE & REFLECT

Reaching Conclusions Review with students the great influence the geography of Japan has on the inhabitants, where and how they live, and what they produce. Since many millions of people often live and work in a small area, they have developed cultural traditions and expectations as well as infrastructures that allow them to be successful.

ANSWERS, p. 716

READING PROGRESS CHECK Answers may vary but could include that tariffs protect jobs and corporations, keep Japan's economy growing, and lead to new technology as more resources can be devoted to development.

CRITICAL THINKING

1. Japan relies on trade to acquire fossil fuels and minerals as well as many raw materials required to produce goods sold for export.
2. Japan has highly skilled and educated workers who utilize new technology, making its consumer goods highly sought after around the world.

This freighter is docked at the Port of Tokyo. Japan's economy depends on imports of raw materials and exports of finished products.

▲ **CRITICAL THINKING**

1. ***Finding the Main Idea*** Why is Japan's economy so reliant on trade?
2. ***Evaluating*** Why are Japanese finished goods in high demand globally?

trade surplus earning more money from export sales than spending for imports

Although the global demand for Japanese goods is high, the Japanese government protects local industries from foreign competition. It places tariffs, or taxes, on the manufactured goods imported from foreign countries (but not on raw materials). This restricts foreign sales in Japan and helps tip the balance of trade in Japan's favor. Balance of trade is the difference between a country's imports and exports. Japan has a **trade surplus** in its balance of trade because the value of its exports is greater than the value of its imports. This makes Japan wealthy. However, it lowers profits for trading partners, such as the United States, which import from Japan more than they export. Efforts to persuade Japan to drop tariff protections on finished products have yet to be completely successful.

In the 1990s, an economic downturn occurred in Japan. This was brought about, in part, by poor banking practices. As banks failed, production slowed, exports dropped, and unemployment rose. The Japanese government took steps to reform unsafe economic practices. By 2003, the situation had stabilized and was improving. The recession that began in 2008, however, reduced global demand for Japanese goods and slowed the economy. Things began to improve again in 2013.

READING PROGRESS CHECK

Inferring What might a Japanese official say to defend the practice of placing tariffs on finished goods imported from overseas countries?

LESSON 2 REVIEW

Reviewing Vocabulary (Tier Three Words)

1. ***Identifying*** Write several sentences indicating the role of the clan and the samurai in Japan's early history. RH.9–10.4

Using Your Notes

2. ***Sequencing*** Use your graphic organizer to write a paragraph describing the major turning points in Japan's history.

Answering the Guiding Questions

3. ***Drawing Conclusions*** How do ancient and modern traditions influence life in Japan?
4. ***Evaluating*** How does population density influence life in parts of Japan?
5. ***Making Connections*** How do traditions influence family life and art?
6. ***Synthesizing*** How have industry and trade transformed the country?

Writing Activity

7. ***Informative/Explanatory*** In a paragraph, discuss the advantages and disadvantages of living in Tokyo-Yokohama, the largest urban area in the world. WHST.9–10.2

LESSON 2 REVIEW ANSWERS

Reviewing Vocabulary

1. Sentences will differ but should include that many clans once ruled Japan before being united under the Yamato dynasty. Dynasties ruled for centuries with emperors as absolute monarchs until warring armies brought the shogunate to power with the support of samurai, leaving the emperor as a figurehead.

Using Your Notes

2. Paragraphs will differ but should be strongly supported with information from the lesson.

Answering the Guiding Questions

3. The tradition of dynasties and emperors still influences government today as Japan has a constitutional monarchy with an emperor who is head of state.
4. High urban concentrations have led to megacities that have massive transportation systems and large commercial areas.
5. Respect for ancestors and the importance of being part of a group are still taught to children and traditional arts such as origami, tea ceremonies, and Kabuki theater are still practiced.
6. Industry and trade have combined to make Japan a global economic power with corporations also playing a strong societal role.

Writing Activity

7. Paragraphs will differ but should be strongly supported with information from the lesson.

networks
There's More Online!

- GRAPH Total Whale Catch
- IMAGE Aquaculture
- IMAGE Bluefin Tuna
- MAP Japan's Nuclear Power Plants
- INTERACTIVE SELF-CHECK QUIZ
- VIDEO People and Their Environment: Japan

LESSON 3
People and Their Environment: Japan

Reading **HELP**DESK 

Academic Vocabulary (Tier Two Words)
- **sustain**
- **widespread**
- **issue**
- **strategy**

Content Vocabulary (Tier Three Words)
- **aquaculture**
- **supertrawler**
- **chlorofluorocarbon (CFC)**

TAKING NOTES: ***Key Ideas and Details***

ORGANIZING Use a graphic organizer like the one below to take notes on Japan's environment as you read the lesson.

Japan: Managing Resources

Human Activity	Impact on Environment	Addressing the Issues
Build nuclear reactor		

ESSENTIAL QUESTION • *How do physical systems and human systems shape a place?*

IT MATTERS BECAUSE
Because of its economic strength, Japan has an impact on the world disproportionate to its size. The choices the Japanese make about energy, ocean harvesting, and consumption resonate far beyond their island home. G1

Managing Resources
GUIDING QUESTION *What resources are at risk in Japan?*

Because of its limited supply of fossil fuels, Japan has long depended on foreign oil imports. To reduce this dependence, the Japanese people turned to nuclear technology to provide electrical energy. Today Japan has more than 50 nuclear reactors with the capacity to supply the country with some 30 percent of its energy. A series of nuclear accidents at Japanese reactors, however, exposed people to radiation. The first accident occurred in 1978. A more recent one happened in 2011. T

Following the earthquake and resulting tsunami in 2011, a damaged nuclear reactor had a meltdown. The perils of operating nuclear reactors in a region prone to earthquakes and tsunamis were made clear. In response, Japan temporarily shut down most of its reactors. This prompted calls to reverse Japan's reactor-building program and focus instead on renewable energy sources. Japanese businesses and industries resisted such a change, however. They pointed out that rising fossil fuel prices could cripple the Japanese economy and add substantially to pollution. Japan continues searching for answers and alternatives that will allow it to **sustain** its energy needs safely. Investment in solar power, wind, biomass, and small hydroelectric and geothermal projects has expanded. Increasingly, Japanese companies are building wind turbines and developing solar cell technology. There is some discussion of building floating wind turbines to be anchored in the sea because Japan has limited land area for wind projects. G2

READING PROGRESS CHECK

Identifying What are the pros and cons of using nuclear power in Japan?

(tl)Sue Flood/The Image Bank/Getty Images, (tr)Gyro Photography/amanaimagesRF/Getty Images

ENGAGE

G1 Critical Thinking Skills

Interpreting Significance Discuss with students the global reaches of Japan's economy. **Ask:** **What items do you own that were made in Japan or by a Japanese company?** *(Possible answer: electronics and automobiles)* **How would a downturn in the world's second-largest economy affect the global economy?** *(Possible answer: It would have a negative effect on the global economy.)*

TEACH & ASSESS

T Technology Skills

Researching Have students work in small groups to research the Fukushima nuclear disaster. Ask them to gather information about what happened, why it happened, and how it unfolded. Have them examine the risks to the health of individuals living near the nuclear power plant. They should also explain what precautions are being taken to prevent such accidents from happening again. Ask them to present their findings to the class. **Verbal/Linguistic**

G2 Critical Thinking Skills

Categorizing As students discuss the different resources available for energy in Japan, have them categorize each as renewable or nonrenewable. Then have them rank the renewable resources in order from most environmentally friendly to least environmentally friendly. As students share their lists, ask them to justify why they ranked one resource ahead of or behind another. **AL** **Naturalist, Verbal/Linguistic**

networks ***Online Teaching Options***

INTERACTIVE BELLRINGER

Japan's Nuclear Power Plants

Analyzing Ethical Issues Use the introductory text and the map of nuclear plants in Japan to identify factors that are threatening resources in Japan today. Have students form small groups. Ask them if they are familiar with the earthquake and tsunami that hit Japan in 2011. If the majority of students have prior knowledge of this event, have them briefly discuss what they recall about it. Then, have each group answer the questions. Ask them to write an agreed-upon answer to question 1 and to list all answers to question 2. Then, in a class discussion, have each group share its answers. List the responses to the second question on a flipchart or board. **AL** **Interpersonal, Intrapersonal, Visual/Spatial, Verbal/Linguistic**

Japans Nuclear Power Plants

Nuclear reactors allow Japan to avoid dependence on foreign oil imports. They pose a risk, however, as Japan is prone to earthquakes and tsunamis.

1. If the winds blew northwest and east after the 2011 nuclear accident in Fukushima, Japan, what country would be most at risk of radioactive fallout?

ANSWERS, p. 717

READING PROGRESS CHECK Using nuclear power reduces Japan's dependence on imported fossil fuels and supplies the country with 30 percent of its energy, but nuclear accidents can be devastating, exposing people and the environment to harmful radiation.

TAKING NOTES: Human Activity: Build nuclear reactor; industrialization; commercial fishing/supertrawlers
Impact on Environment: Reactors built in earthquake- and tsunami-prone areas can result in meltdown; air and water pollution, loss of biodiversity; overfishing, ecosystem unbalanced
Addressing the Issues: Explore renewable energy resources, investment in solar power, wind, biomass, hydroelectricity, and geothermal projects; strict regulations, Kyoto Protocol; aquaculture, economic zones, international bans

V Visual Skills

Locating Direct students to the map of nuclear power plants. **Ask:** Which power plant is closest to Tokyo? *(Tokai Daini)* In general, where in Japan are nuclear power plants located? *(along the coasts)* Explain that nuclear power plants require tremendous amounts of water for cooling and this is why they are most often located near water sources.
ELL **Logical/Mathematical, Visual/Spatial**

C Critical Thinking Skills

Analyzing Ethical Issues Discuss with students the environmental issues brought about by Japan's rapid industrialization. **Ask:** In the 1960s, why did companies expand without regard to pollution? *(Possible answer: They likely did not understand the full environmental effects of what they were doing and because they were rapidly growing the economy.)* Is it ethical for factories and businesses to cause pollution? Explain. *(Possible answer: Businesses and factories must cause a certain amount of pollution to produce their products. It is most ethical for them to try to create as little pollution as they can.)* **AL** **Verbal/Linguistic**

R Reading Skills

Inferring Discuss pollution from vehicle emissions with students. **Ask:** What inferences can you make about the public transportation systems in Japan, based on the information in this paragraph? *(Possible answer: it could be inferred that a main reason for investing in and building efficient and accessible mass transportation systems is to reduce the number of vehicles on the road.)* Where in Japan would you expect pollution to be the least problematic? Why? *(Possible answer: in rural areas that have fewer vehicles)* **Logical/Mathematical**

ANSWERS, p. 718

GEOGRAPHY CONNECTION

1. Power plants are located along the coasts for access to water and because the mountainous terrain makes it difficult to build plants in the interior of Japan.
2. Major cities, including the capital of Japan, are located within a few hundred miles of the largest clusters of nuclear power plants.

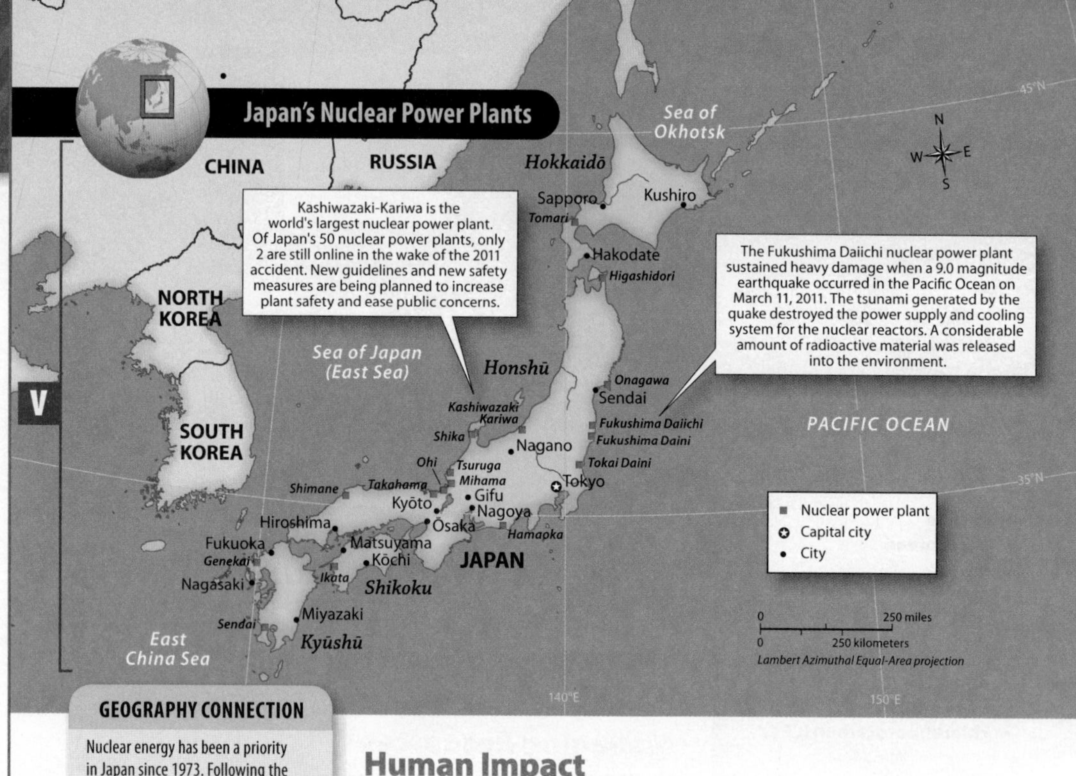
Japan's Nuclear Power Plants
CHINA
RUSSIA
NORTH KOREA
SOUTH KOREA
Sea of Okhotsk
Hokkaidō
Sapporo
Tomari
Kushiro
Hakodate
Higashidori
Kashiwazaki-Kariwa is the world's largest nuclear power plant. Of Japan's 50 nuclear power plants, only 2 are still online in the wake of the 2011 accident. New guidelines and new safety measures are being planned to increase plant safety and ease public concerns.
The Fukushima Daiichi nuclear power plant sustained heavy damage when a 9.0 magnitude earthquake occurred in the Pacific Ocean on March 11, 2011. The tsunami generated by the quake destroyed the power supply and cooling system for the nuclear reactors. A considerable amount of radioactive material was released into the environment.
Sea of Japan (East Sea)
Honshū
Onagawa
Sendai
Kashiwazaki Kariwa
Shika
Fukushima Daiichi
Fukushima Daini
Nagano
Tokai Daini
Ohi
Tsuruga
Mihama
Tokyo
Shimane
Takahama
Kyōto
Gifu
Nagoya
Hiroshima
Ōsaka
Hamaoka
Fukuoka
Genkai
Matsuyama
Kōchi
JAPAN
Ikata
Nagasaki
Shikoku
Sendai
Miyazaki
Kyūshū
East China Sea
PACIFIC OCEAN
Nuclear power plant
Capital city
City
0 250 miles
0 250 kilometers
Lambert Azimuthal Equal-Area projection
45°N
35°N
140°E
150°E

GEOGRAPHY CONNECTION

Nuclear energy has been a priority in Japan since 1973. Following the earthquake and tsunami that caused a nuclear accident in 2011, however, this policy came under review.

1. ***THE WORLD IN SPATIAL TERMS*** Why do you think Japan's nuclear power plants are located along the coasts?
2. ***ENVIRONMENT AND SOCIETY*** What are located within a few hundred miles of the largest clusters of nuclear power plants?

sustain to continue without interruption

widespread found over a large area

Human Impact

GUIDING QUESTION *What human activities have affected the physical environment of Japan?*

Japan's rapid industrialization brought with it severe and **widespread** environmental problems. Economic growth took priority over health and safety. The result was increasing air and water pollution and declining populations of aquatic animals.

Following World War II and into the 1960s, Japan's major industries—iron and steel, cement, paper and pulp—expanded without regard to pollution. Power plants vented noxious pollutants into the air. Industry and agriculture tainted rivers, lakes, and surrounding ocean with chemicals and raw sewage. Air and water quality suffered, creating health risks. In the 1970s, smog alerts were frequent. Acid rain became a serious problem. It damaged lakes, crops, and trees; threatened animal species; and corroded buildings and bridges. By the mid-1990s, Japan was the world's fourth-largest emitter of carbon dioxide.

Starting in the 1970s, Japan began adopting stricter rules to protect air and water quality. Today, it has some of the strictest regulations in the world. Yet despite improvements in the levels of soot and smoke emissions from factory smoke stacks, motor vehicle emissions remain a serious problem. Diesel engines, in particular, foul the air of Japan's major cities. Regulations to further tighten control of emissions from diesel engines and buses have been passed. Japanese industries have been at work on fuel-cell engines, which produce no dangerous emissions.

The problem of acid rain is particularly troubling. Even as Japan has tightened regulations on emissions, the acidity of the rain has remained largely unchanged. Researchers believe that massive sulfur dioxide emissions in China contribute to acid rain in Japan. China and Japan signed a preliminary treaty to address acid

networks ***Online Teaching Options***

VIDEO

Many in Japan Worried About Nuclear Meltdown

Making Connections Have students watch this video to learn more about the fears of radioactive contamination in Japan after the 2011 earthquake.
AL **Verbal/Linguistic**

rain in 1994. Evidence suggests, however, that acid rain that originates in China will reach disastrous levels in Japan by 2020.

For centuries, the Japanese have depended on the abundance of the sea for food. Fish are an integral part of the Japanese diet, and the Japanese consume large amounts of fish and other seafood. Japan's most internationally famous food specialty, sushi, usually includes thin slices of raw fish called sashimi. Overfishing—resulting from catching too many fish of particular species—has seriously depleted fish stocks around the Japanese islands and around the world. Water pollution has also contributed to declining fish stocks. **C**

Mature bluefin tuna reach 6.5 feet (2 m) and live up to 15 years in the wild. These endangered and valuable fish are prized for food in Japan even as their stocks have plummeted worldwide. A premium fish sold for $1.76 million in 2013.

Sue Flood/The Image Bank/Getty Images

▲ CRITICAL THINKING

1. ***Making Connections*** Why did fish become a staple in the Japanese diet?
2. ***Analyzing Ethical Issues*** Is it ethical to consume endangered species? Explain your answer.

Some 40,000 people use Japan's Inland Sea—a narrow body of salt water surrounded by Honshū, Shikoku, and Kyūshū—for fishing and **aquaculture**, which is the farming of seafood. Wild fish stocks such as red sea bream, anchovies, and mackerel have declined dramatically in this area in recent decades. The number of jellyfish—which negatively affect other species—is increasing in these waters because the plankton on which they feed thrive in polluted water.

Globally, the huge Japanese demand for seafood has contributed to declining fish stocks in fisheries in the Atlantic and the Pacific. Many countries, including Japan, rely on powerful deep-sea **supertrawlers**. These huge ships are equipped to serve as modern factories at sea, harvesting distant fisheries. Harvesting huge catches using supertrawlers leads to overfishing. It also causes the killing and waste of tons of unwanted sea life. To protect fisheries from foreign commercial fishing, many countries claim an economic zone extending to 200 nautical miles off their shores. Public opposition to supertrawlers is gaining strength globally, particularly as numerous fish stocks are rapidly declining. **W**

Despite a 1986 international ban on commercial whaling, Japan remains the largest consumer of whale meat in the world. Centuries of overhunting by many countries caused serious declines in whale populations globally, severely endangering many species. By the 1960s, only Japan, Russia, and a few other countries continued to hunt whales on a large scale. Following the 1986 ban, Japan, Iceland, and Norway used a loophole for scientific research to continue to capture whales. Hundreds are still killed and eaten each year. Japan and the other whale-hunting countries are widely criticized for their whaling practices.

aquaculture the cultivation of seafood

supertrawler an ocean-going factory ship with facilities for processing and freezing fish

☑ READING PROGRESS CHECK

Understanding Relationships Explain why fish stocks in Japan's Inland Sea have declined in recent years.

Total Whale Catch

Total | Japan | Iceland | Norway

NUMBER OF WHALES: 0; 5,000; 10,000; 15,000; 20,000; 25,000; 30,000; 35,000; 40,000

YEAR: 1946; 1956; 1966; 1976; 1986; 1996; 2009

Source: http://awionline.org/sites/default/files/uploads/flash/whaling_stats/main.swf.

GRAPH SKILLS

Whales have been hunted and eaten by the Japanese, Icelanders, and Norwegians for centuries.

◀ CRITICAL THINKING

1. ***Analyzing Visuals*** What was the largest total number of whales captured by Japan, Iceland, and Norway after 1946?
2. ***Constructing a Thesis*** Give a logical reason for why all three countries' whale hunting dipped sharply in 1986.

C Critical Thinking Skills

Identifying Perspectives Discuss the issues surrounding overfishing. **Ask:** What are the two perspectives involved in fishing? *(The perspective of the fisher who is trying to make a living and the perspective of the environmentalist who wants to see the levels of fish recover to healthy levels.)* What are some ideas on how to balance these two perspectives? *(Possible answer: Fishing, but not overfishing, should be allowed so that fishers may make a living, but not deplete the supply of fish.)* **BL** Verbal/Linguistic

W Writing Skills

Informative/Explanatory Discuss supertrawlers with students. Have students work with a partner to research the use of supertrawlers, the positive and negative reasons for using them, and the countries with fishing industries that use them the most. Direct students to write an essay describing their research. **AL** Verbal/Linguistic

Content Background Knowledge

Sushi Sushi has evolved and changed over many centuries. The sushi we think of today first came about in the early 1800s. A man named Hanaya Yohei added rice vinegar and salt to freshly cooked rice and then topped a small ball of rice with a thin slice of raw fish. The fish was so fresh that there was no need to ferment it. Prior to this time, making sushi was sometimes a months-long endeavor. When salted fish is placed in cooked rice, it ferments and is preserved. Thus, originally sushi was made as a way to preserve fish. Over time, new methods were developed to make the process much faster. In the 1970s, advances in refrigeration allowed fresh fish to be shipped over long distances, leading to a boom in the sushi business.

INTERACTIVE WHITEBOARD ACTIVITY

Resource Problems and Solutions

Problem Solving Have students use this interactive whiteboard activity to drag the missing cause, effect, or potential solution to Japan's resource problems into the correct column of the chart. **AL** Verbal/Linguistic

Resource Problems and Solutions

Directions: After a period rapid industrialization with an emphasis on economic growth, Japan adopted some of the strictest regulations in the world to reduce its water and air pollution and protect the environment. Drag the missing cause, effect, or potential solution to the correct column to complete the chart.

Cause	Effect	Potential Solution
	Depletion of the ozone	The Kyoto Protocol treaty to reduce greenhouse gases
Motor vehicle emissions		Development of fuel cell engines
Sulfur dioxide emissions blowing overseas	Acid rain	
Overfishing and water pollution	Depleted fish supplies	
	People exposed to dangerous radiation	Use of alternative forms of energy, such as solar and wind

Air pollution and acid rain

Chlorofluorocarbons (CFCs) used in liquid coolants

A treaty between Japan and China to address pollution

Nuclear reactor accidents and meltdowns

Increasing aquaculture practices

Show Answers

ANSWERS, p. 719

☑ READING PROGRESS CHECK Overfishing and pollution in the Inland Sea have led to declines in fish stocks, as has the rise in the number of jellyfish which feed on the plankton that thrive in polluted waters.

CRITICAL THINKING

1. Fish became a staple of the Japanese diet due to a lack of arable land and its island location.
2. Answers may vary, but should be strongly supported with information from the lesson which could include that consuming endangered species affects the economy, impacts availability for future generations, and disrupts the natural ecosystem.

CRITICAL THINKING

1. The largest total number of whales captured after 1946 is about 38,000.
2. Whale hunting dropped because it was banned in 1986 and is only continued today by Norway, Japan, and Iceland through a loophole for research.

C1 Critical Thinking Skills

Assessing Discuss with students the complete phaseout of CFCs that Japan is working toward. **Ask:** **Why is it not possible to eliminate CFCs immediately?** *(Possible answers: Industries must find environmentally sustainable substitutes for CFCs in their products. This takes research and money.)* **What would happen to many companies if a ban was instituted immediately on products containing CFCs? Why?** *(Possible answer: Many would go out of business because they do not have economical substitutes for CFCs.)* **BL** **Logical/Mathematical**

C2 Critical Thinking Skills

Communicating Have students do additional research and then give a brief speech on aquaculture. They should explain what aquaculture is and how it benefits Japan and the fishing industry. Ask them to include statistics specific to the industry in Japan. **ELL** **Auditory/Musical**

W Writing Skills

Argument Explain that a major reason quotas that limit fish harvests do not work is that fishing boats will not comply with the limits and they are difficult to enforce. Have students write an argument in favor of adhering to fishing quotas directed at fishers. Tell them to include information about how restoring fish stocks to sustainable levels is good for everyone in the long term, despite short-term losses. **BL** **Logical/Mathematical**

CLOSE & REFLECT

Identifying Central Issues Review with students the central environmental issues discussed in the lesson. Make a class list of these issues and then add ways in which Japan is working to improve these issues.

ANSWERS, p. 720

READING PROGRESS CHECK Answers may differ but could include that Japan has been a leader in addressing issues and supporting sustainable growth, but its carbon emissions are still increasing and whaling and fishing limits have not been effective. However, aquaculture is preventing some overfishing and the use of CFCs has been almost completely phased out.

CRITICAL THINKING

1. Fish farms are floated or anchored to the sea floor, making the relatively calm waters of a bay a good spot to set up a farm.
2. Fish farms are likely to increase in the future, given the declining natural fish stocks and the increasing demand for seafood.

This fish farm is located in Ago Bay, along the south coast of Honshū. Aquaculture provides the Japanese with about 22 percent of their seafood.

▲ **CRITICAL THINKING**

1. ***Assessing*** Why would it be advantageous to create a fish farm in a bay?
2. ***Making Predictions*** Do you think the number of fish farms will increase in the future? Why or why not?

issue a topic for debate and discussion

chlorofluorocarbon (CFC) a chemical substance, found mainly in liquid coolants, that damages the Earth's protective ozone layer

strategy a plan of action to achieve an aim

Addressing the Issues

GUIDING QUESTION *How are environmental issues being addressed in Japan?*

Japan ignored the environmental problems caused by rapid economic growth for many years. In the 1970s, however, the Japanese government began to encourage industries to address environmental **issues** more responsibly.

Today Japan is a leader in addressing environmental issues and supporting industries that profit from sustainable growth. For example, the Japanese have taken steps to reduce emissions of **chlorofluorocarbons (CFCs)**. CFCs were widely used in industry in the liquid coolants for refrigerators and air conditioners during the mid-1900s. Released into the atmosphere, they deplete Earth's stratospheric ozone layer that protects the planet from harmful ultraviolet solar radiation. Japan is working toward a complete phase-out of CFCs.

Japan is also working to mitigate climate change. In 1997 Japan hosted an international meeting under the United Nations Framework Convention on Climate Change. The treaty that resulted is known as the Kyoto Protocol. It defined ways to reduce the carbon emissions that contribute to global warming. It was ratified by 37 industrial countries, including Japan (but not the United States). The treaty set binding targets to reduce greenhouse gas emissions, including carbon dioxide. Nevertheless, by 2007 carbon dioxide emissions in Japan had increased by more than 10 percent from 1990 levels.

One **strategy** Japan has used to offset declining fish stocks and other sea products has been to increase aquaculture. Fish farmers raise fish by floating fish cages in the sea or anchoring them to the sea floor. Floats and ropes are used to cultivate shellfish such as oysters, scallops, pearl oysters, and abalone, as well as kelp. Although aquaculture production has declined somewhat since 1990, nearly 1.2 million tons of fish and seaweed were farmed in Japan in 2010.

Another strategy for maintaining fish populations has been to prevent overfishing by establishing quotas that limit fish harvests. Like the ban on whaling, however, quotas have limited effectiveness.

READING PROGRESS CHECK

Inferring Has Japan been generally successful in addressing environmental problems? Explain your answer.

LESSON 3 REVIEW

Reviewing Vocabulary (Tier Three Words)

1. ***Making Connections*** Write a paragraph describing the relationship of supertrawlers to Japanese aquaculture. RH.9–10.4

Using Your Notes

2. ***Transferring Information*** Use your graphic organizer to identify a human activity that has been destructive to Japan's environment and write a paragraph about ways in which the issue is being addressed.

Answering the Guiding Questions

3. ***Differentiating*** What resources are at risk in Japan?
4. ***Assessing*** What human activities have affected the physical environment of Japan?
5. ***Drawing Conclusions*** How are environmental issues being addressed in Japan?

Writing Activity

6. ***Argument*** Write an introductory paragraph for a personal essay that will argue whether you think Japan is doing enough to address environmental issues and why. WHST.9–10.1

720

LESSON 3 REVIEW ANSWERS

Reviewing Vocabulary

1. Paragraphs will differ but should be supported with information from the lesson including: supertrawlers are a major cause of overfishing and also kill many other types of sea life; and aquaculture has been developed to deal wth some of the shortages brought about by supertrawling.

Using Your Notes

2. Answers could include issues such as overfishing, whaling, carbon emissions from cars/ industry and the Kyoto Protocol, acid rain, and industrial pollution of waterways especially after WWII. Addressing the issues could include: fish and whaling limits, strict regulations, Kyoto Protocol, aquaculture, and elimination of CFCs.

Answering the Guiding Questions

3. Fish and other sea life, water, and air are all at risk in Japan.
4. Overfishing, whaling, industrial pollution of waterways and air after WWII, and carbon emissions from cars and industry.
5. Japan supports sustainable development and addresses environmental issues by setting fishing and whaling limits, reducing and phasing out CFCs, introducing the Kyoto Protocol to work on climate change, and increasing aquaculture.

Writing Activity

6. Paragraphs will differ but should be strongly supported with information from the lesson.

CHAPTER 29 Assessment

Directions: On a separate sheet of paper, answer the questions below. Make sure you read carefully and answer all parts of the questions.

Lesson Review

Lesson 1

1. ***Identifying Cause and Effect*** How does the Pacific Ring of Fire affect human settlement in Japan?
2. ***Explaining*** What combination of factors makes Japan monsoonal?
3. ***Assessing*** Generally, where does Japan rank in oil production and oil exporting in the world? Why?

Lesson 2

4. ***Describing*** How did the United States "open up" Japan in 1854?
5. ***Explaining*** Explain whether it would be accurate to state that the emperor is the government official in Japan who makes or approves the major governmental decisions for the country.
6. ***Identifying Central Issues*** Where does Japan rank in life expectancy among all countries of the world? Explain the reasons that have greatly contributed to this ranking and discuss problems that are arising in relation to it.

Lesson 3

7. ***Explaining*** What events in 2011 caused Japan to reconsider its reliance on nuclear energy? Why?
8. ***Interpreting Significance*** Explain the significance of economic zones to fisheries.
9. ***Evaluating*** Explain whether it would be accurate to state that the level of carbon dioxide emissions in Japan in 2007 poses an irony to its role relative to the Kyoto Protocol.

21st Century Skills

Use the cartoon below to answer the questions that follow.

PRIMARY SOURCE

"Before you do something you may regret, I think you should know that I contain six parts of mercury per million."

10. ***Using Primary Sources*** How does the cartoon provide a whimsical look at a serious issue plaguing Japan and other countries around the world? Why might this cartoon be more effective than long lists of statistics in attracting the attention of some readers?
11. ***Drawing Conclusions*** What effect do you think the artist hoped to gain through this cartoon? Explain whether you think this effect is evident in Japan.

Critical Thinking

12. ***Exploring Issues*** You are preparing a Web site about the current economy of Japan—and the connection of the current economy to the country's history, physical geography (including natural resources), human geography (including population patterns), and environmental concerns. Lay out the main page of the Web site, including at least 10 links to information for the content detailed above. For each link, provide a short paragraph to summarize the main content that will be accessed through the link.

Need Extra Help?

If You've Missed Question	1	2	3	4	5	6	7	8	9	10	11	12
Go to page	704	706	707	710	712	714	717	719	720	721	721	701

CHAPTER 29 Assessment Answers

Lesson Review

Lesson 1

1. The Pacific Ring of Fire created the mountainous terrain of Japan, causing most settlements to be in the coastal lowlands.
2. The ocean currents, mountainous landscape, location close to the Asian landmass, and its latitude combine to make Japan monsoonal.
3. Japan ranks at the bottom of oil production and exports because it has very few oil resources and must import most of its oil.

Lesson 2

4. The United States Navy made a show of strength in Japan's ports, convincing them to negotiate a trade agreement with the United States and thus "opening" Japan for trade.
5. It would not be accurate to state that the emperor makes or approves the major governmental decisions since Japan is a constitutional monarchy.
6. Japan has the longest life expectancy in the world. Reasons could include: the high standard of living, good health care, and active lifestyle. An aging population and smaller workforce are issues that are arising from the long life expectancy.

Lesson 3

7. The earthquake and resulting tsunami caused a meltdown of a nuclear reactor, prompting Japan to rethink its use of nuclear energy, given the risks of great damage and loss of life that could occur from having such power plants in an earthquake-prone zone.
8. Economic zones extend a country's claim on ocean waters 200 nautical miles from its shoreline, protecting its fisheries from foreign commercial fishing vessels that overfish the waters.
9. Japan's carbon dioxide emissions increased by 10 percent from 1990 to 2007, making it accurate to state that this poses an irony relative to the Kyoto Protocol, which called for a reduction in emissions.

21st Century Skills

10. The cartoon is whimsical because it has a fish explaining that it would not be a good thing to eat due to the high levels of mercury it contains. The cartoon might be more effective as it illustrates that not only do the mercury levels of fish affect humans, but the entire marine ecosystem as well.
11. Explanations may differ but could include that the artist is hoping to draw attention to the high levels of mercury and that these levels impact humans and the entire marine ecosystem. Evidence that Japan is aware of the issues could be assumed due to it being a leader in addressing environmental issues.

Critical Thinking

12. Website designs on the current economy of Japan and its connection to history, physical and human geography, and environmental concerns will differ. They should include at least 10 links with a short paragraph detailing the information found when the link is accessed. Possible information could include a lack of natural resources, mountainous terrain, technology, communications, highly urban population, aging workforce, and water and air pollution.

Assessment Answers

Analyzing Primary Sources

13 The quotes are in disagreement about whether the bombs should have been dropped on Japan. The first looks at the situation from a viewpoint of Japan surrendering regardless of the use of the bombs, and the second argues that Germany and Japan would have certainly used them given the same opportunity.

14 Opinions and explanations will differ but should be strongly supported as to why the student believes Churchill's statement that other countries would use these types of weapons if they had the same ability to do so.

Exploring the Essential Question

15 Time lines will differ but must include at least five entries explaining major milestones as being influenced or isolated from other countries. They could include dates such as: 1542 Japan's first documented contact with the West; 1854 Japan was opened to trade with the U.S.; 1910 Japan took control of Korea and became Asia's most powerful empire; 1931 Japan invaded China; 1945 Japan surrendered when atomic bombs were dropped.

Applying Map Skills

16 Ōsaka lies close to the Pacific Ocean.

17 Hokkaidō is the farthest north followed by Honshū with Kyūshū running from its tip to cover the most southern areas while Shikoku is nestled in between Honshū with Kyūshū.

18 Tokyo-Yokohama and Ōsaka are the most densely populated cities in Japan.

College and Career Readiness

19 Reports will vary but should include that the original trees in Washington, D.C., were a gift from Japan, the trees bloom from late March through mid-April, and activities could include picnics, kite flying, concerts, and sightseeing.

Research and Presentation

20 Multimedia presentations will differ but should contain audio, video, and maps to help detail the development of the bullet train and magnetic levitation train, including information such as: the magnetic levitation train is expected to travel at least 311 miles per hour and would float above the tracks; the bullet train has had no accidents and currently runs as fast as 170 miles per hour.

CHAPTER 29 Assessment 

Directions: On a separate sheet of paper, answer the questions below. Make sure you read carefully and answer all parts of the questions.

DBQ Analyzing Primary Sources

Use the excerpts to answer the questions that follow.

PRIMARY SOURCE

"Based on a detailed investigation of all the facts, and supported by the testimony of the surviving Japanese leaders involved, it is the Survey's opinion that certainly prior to 31 December 1945, and in all probability prior to 1 November 1945, Japan would have surrendered even if the atomic bombs had not been dropped, even if Russia had not entered the war, and even if no invasion had been planned or contemplated."

—United States Bombing Survey, July 1, 1946, President's Secretary's File, Truman Papers

"... There are voices which assert that the bomb should never have been used at all. I cannot associate myself with such ideas. Six years of total war have convinced most people that had the Germans or Japanese discovered this new weapon, they would have used it upon us to our complete destruction with the utmost alacrity.... Future generations will judge these dire decisions, and I believe that if they find themselves dwelling in a happier world from which war has been banished, and where freedom reigns, they will not condemn those who struggled for their benefit amid the horrors and miseries of this gruesome and ferocious epoch."

—Winston Churchill, "Why Should We Fear for Our Future?" House of Commons, August 16, 1945

13 ***Understanding Historical Interpretation*** Explain whether these quotes provide statements that are essentially in agreement with one another. RH.9–10.1

14 ***Interpreting Significance*** Explain whether you think Churchill's anticipation of potential future events related to weapons of mass destruction were valid. RHI.9–10.1

Exploring the Essential Question

15 ***Sequencing*** Conduct research on Japan's history and the periods in which the island country was influenced by or isolated from other countries. Use your research to create a time line of at least five entries explaining major milestones.

Applying Map Skills

Refer to the Unit 8 Atlas to answer the following questions.

16 ***Places and Regions*** Identify the major body of water nearest Ōsaka.

17 ***The World in Spatial Terms*** Use your mental map of Japan to describe the spatial relationship among the islands of Hokkaidō, Honshū, Kyūshū, and Shikoku.

18 ***Human Systems*** Which two cities in Japan are the most densely populated?

College and Career Readiness

19 ***Examining Information*** You are located in Washington, D.C., and wish to host a traditional Japanese cherry blossom festival. Conduct research to determine the connection between Japan and the cherry blossom trees in your location, as well as the optimal time of the year to have a festival. Write a report explaining why you have chosen this time of the year and the activities that will be included in the experience.

Research and Presentation

20 ***Gathering Information*** With a partner, conduct research to learn more about the Shinkansen and the development of the bullet train and the magnetic levitation train in Japan. Create a multimedia presentation to detail development of the bullet train and the magnetic levitation train—and the importance of rapid mass transit to Japan. Include audio, video, and maps in your presentation. WHST.9–10.1; WHST.9–10.6; WHST.9–10.7; WHST.9–10.8

Writing About Geography

21 ***Argument*** Use standard grammar, spelling, sentence structure, and punctuation to write an editorial to support the pro or con side of this statement: "Supertrawlers should be banned." Focus your argument on the effects of such a ban. Support your statements with information from the chapter and address opposing arguments in your editorial. WHST.9–10.1

Need Extra Help?

If You've Missed Question	13	14	15	16	17	18	19	20	21
Go to page	722	722	710	672	672	676	706	713	719

722

Writing About Geography

21 Arguments will vary based on whether the student chooses to support or argue against the banning of supertrawlers. Answers should be strongly supported with information from the chapter and could include that fishing is an important part of the economy, the people of Japan consume large amounts of fish and seafood, large amounts of other sea life are killed by supertrawlers, overfishing is causing fish stocks to drop, and negative effects on the environment and future generations by supertrawling.

CHAPTER **30**

North Korea and South Korea Planner

UNDERSTANDING BY DESIGN®

Enduring Understandings

- *Cooperation and conflict among people influence the division and control of Earth's surface.*

Essential Question

- *How do physical systems and human systems shape a place?*

Predictable Misunderstandings

Students may think:

- *North Korea and South Korea have similar climates, biomes, and physical geography. Explain that latitude plays a large role in the differences between the north and south, with the climate getting colder the further north one travels on the peninsula.*
- *North Koreans and South Koreans come from different ethnic backgrounds. Explain that North Korea and South Korea are split based on political differences, not ethnic differences. People in both countries come from the same ethnic background and they all speak Korean.*

Assessment Evidence

Performance Tasks:

- *Hands-On Chapter Project*

Other Evidence:

- *Guided Reading Activities*
- *Vocabulary Activities*
- *Lesson Quizzes*
- *Chapter Tests, Forms A and B*

SUGGESTED PACING GUIDE

Introducing the Chapter .... ½ Day
Lesson 1 .... 1 Day
Lesson 2 .... 2 Days
Lesson 3 .... 1 Day
Chapter Wrap-Up and Assessment ...... ½ Day

TOTAL TIME 5 Days

National Geography Standards covered in "North Korea and South Korea"

The student knows and understands:

(3) How to analyze the spatial organizations of people, places, and environments on Earth's surface

3.1 The meaning and use of complex spatial concepts, such as connectivity, networks, hierarchies, to analyze and explain the spatial organizations of human and physical phenomena

(6) How culture and experience influence people's perceptions of places and regions

6.2 Changing perceptions of places and regions have significant economic, political and cultural consequences in an increasingly globalized and complex world

(8) The characteristics and spatial distribution of ecosystems and biomes on Earth's surface

8.1 Ecosystems are dynamic and respond to changes in environmental conditions

(10) The characteristics, distribution, and complexity of Earth's cultural mosaics

10.3 Cultures changes through convergence and/or divergence

(11) The patterns and networks of economic interdependence on Earth's surface

11.1 The scale and organization of economic activities change over time

(13) How the forces of cooperation and conflict among people influence the division and control of Earth's surface

13.1 The function and consequences of territorial divisions

13.2 Cooperation between countries and organizations may have lasting influences on past, present, and future global issues

(15) How physical systems affect human systems

15.2 Humans perceive and react to environmental hazards in different ways

(16) The changes that occur in the meaning, use, distribution, and importance of resources

16.3 Policies and programs that promote the sustainable use and management of resources impact people and the environment

Key for Using the Teacher Edition

SKILL-BASED ACTIVITIES

Types of skill activities found in the Teacher Edition.

* **V Visual Skills** require students to analyze maps, graphs, charts, and photos.

R Reading Skills help students practice reading skills and master vocabulary.

C Critical Thinking Skills help students apply and extend what they have learned.

W Writing Skills provide writing opportunities to help students comprehend the text.

T Technology Skills require students to use digital tools effectively.

*Letters are followed by a number when there is more than one of the same type of skill on the page.

DIFFERENTIATED INSTRUCTION

All activities are written for the on-level student unless otherwise marked with the leveled labels below.

BL Beyond Level
AL Approaching Level
ELL English Language Learners

All students benefit from activities that utilize different learning styles. Many activities are marked as below when a particular learning style is highlighted.

Intrapersonal **Naturalist**
Logical/Mathematical **Kinesthetic**
Visual/Spatial **Auditory/Musical**
Verbal/Linguistic **Interpersonal**

CHAPTER OPENER PLANNER

Students will know:
- *how the land, climates, and biomes of the Korean Peninsula change from north to south.*
- *the natural resources that are shared and separate.*
- *the population patterns of North Korea and South Korea.*
- *the major influences on the culture and art in both countries.*
- *how the major industries have changed over time.*
- *what factors are threatening resources on the Korean Peninsula today and how they are being addressed.*

Students will be able to:
- ***describe** the physical geography, climates, and biomes of the Korean Peninsula.*
- ***identify** shared and separate natural resources.*
- ***describe** where people live on the Korean Peninsula.*
- ***identify** influences on art and culture in the region.*
- ***explain** how the major industries have changed.*
- ***identify** current threats to the Korean Peninsula and how they are being addressed.*

UNDERSTANDING BY DESIGN®

☑ Print Teaching Options

V Visual Skills
☐ **p. 724** Students use the image of a major city to discuss what life there might be like. **Interpersonal, Visual/Spatial**

R Reading Skills
☐ **p. 724** Students explore the term *complementarity.* **AL Verbal/Linguistic**

C Critical Thinking Skills
☐ **p. 725** Students make generalizations about the importance of resources and agriculture. **Logical/Mathematical**

W Writing Skills
☐ **p. 725** Students research the status of the Trans-Siberian Railway extension project. **AL Verbal/Linguistic**

T Technology Skills
☐ **p. 725** Students research specific ways that North Korea and South Korea have found "common ground." **BL Interpersonal, Visual/Spatial**

☑ Online Teaching Options

C Critical Thinking Skills
☐ **SLIDE SHOW** **Relations Between North Korea and South Korea**—Students use the slide show to learn more about the relationships between North Korea and South Korea. **AL Visual/Spatial**

☐ **MAP** **Interactive Regional Atlas**—Students use the interactive regional atlas to understand the physical and human geography of North Korea and South Korea.

☑ Printable Digital Worksheets
☐ **WORKSHEET** **Assessing Background Knowledge**—Determine the level of prior knowledge students have about North Korea and South Korea.

☐ **WORKSHEET** **Chapter Summary**—Students review the main idea of each lesson of the chapter content.

☐ **WORKSHEET** **Reteaching Activity**—These worksheets provide students with an opportunity for remedial practice and review of vital chapter content.

Project-Based Learning 

Hands-On
Create Posters

Students create posters that compare and contrast geographic systems in North Korea and South Korea.

Digital Hands-On
Create Online Projects

Find an additional activity online that incorporates technology for this project. Visit the EdTech Teacher Web sites for more links, tutorials, and other resources.

ePals GlobalCommunity Where learners connect™ 

Print Resources

ANCILLARY RESOURCES

This ancillary is available for every chapter and lesson.
- **Chapter Tests and Lesson Quizzes**

PRINTABLE DIGITAL WORKSHEETS

These printable digital worksheets are available for every chapter and lesson.
- **Assessing Background Knowledge**
- **Chapter Summaries**
- **Guided Reading Activities**
- **Hands-On Chapter Projects**
- **Quizzes and Tests**
- **Reading Essentials and Study Guide** AL
- **Reteaching Activities**
- **Video Activities**
- **Vocabulary Activities**

More Media Resources

SUGGESTED VIDEOS MOVIES
- **Inside North Korea** *National Geographic* (51 min.)
- **Discoveries...Asia Collection, Ep. 3 "Dicoveries: Asia Korea, Seoul, Gyeongju, Busan, and Jeju Island** (51 min.)
- **7 Days South Korea** (53 min.)

SUGGESTED READING 
- ***Korea: The Impossible Country,*** by Daniel Tudor
- ***Nothing to Envy: Ordinary Lives in North Korea,*** by Barbara Demick
- ***Brothers at War: The Unending Conflict in Korea,*** by Sheila Miyoshi Jager

LESSON 1 PLANNER

PHYSICAL GEOGRAPHY OF NORTH KOREA AND SOUTH KOREA

Students will know:

- *how the land of the Korean Peninsula changes from north to south and the impact on human geography.*
- *how the climate gets colder the farther north you travel.*
- *how the biomes differ in the north and the south.*
- *the natural resources that are shared and separate.*

Students will be able to:

- ***describe** the physical geography of the Korean Peninsula.*
- ***explain** the change in climate as one travels north.*
- ***describe** how the biomes are different in the north and the south.*
- ***identify** shared and separate natural resources.*

UNDERSTANDING BY DESIGN®

Print Teaching Options

V Visual Skills

- **p. 726** Students examine images and list some features of North Korea and South Korea, based on their observations. AL Visual/Spatial
- **p. 726** Students transfer the information in the text about landforms, waterways, and bordering countries onto an outline map of the Korean Peninsula. Visual/Spatial
- **p. 728** Students create diagrams or drawings that show how deforestation impacts animals mentioned in the text. ELL Visual/Spatial, Interpersonal

R Reading Skills

- **p. 726** Students use word parts to define *homogenous.* ELL Verbal/Linguistic

C Critical Thinking Skills

- **p. 727** Students discuss the impact of most of the peninsula's major rivers being in South Korea. AL Logical/Mathematical

W Writing Skills

- **p. 727** Students choose one of the physical features from the text and conduct additional research, writing a paragraph, poem, or song about the place. BL Auditory/Musical, Intrapersonal
- **p. 729** Students write an informative essay in which they identify positive and negative aspects of cooperatives, or communal farms. BL Verbal/Linguistic

T Technology Skills

- **p. 727** Students create a diagram that shows how North Korea's and South Korea's waterways are similar and different. AL Visual/Spatial
- **p. 728** Students research deforestation on the Korean Peninsula and why specific trees are developed and for what purposes, and create a chart or graph that depicts the total area of forestland that has been deforested. BL Logical/Mathematical, Visual/Spatial

Online Teaching Options

V Visual Skills

- VIDEO **Rituals of South Korea**—Students watch this video to learn more about a secretive South Korean group living high in the mountains that is trying to preserve traditional Korean values. ELL Verbal/Linguistic
- INTERACTIVE BELLRINGER **Waterways of the Korean Peninsula**—Students use the introductory text and the map of North Korea and South Korea to identify the major waterways of both countries. AL Interpersonal, Visual/Spatial
- INTERACTIVE WHITEBOARD ACTIVITY **Landforms, Biomes, and Resources**—Students identify which landforms, climates, biomes, and natural resources are shared by North Korea and South Korea and which are separate to each region. ELL Visual/Spatial

Printable Digital Worksheets

R Reading Skills

- WORKSHEET **Guided Reading Activity**—Students use the Guided Reading Activity worksheets to review their comprehension of the content.

C Critical Thinking Skills

- WORKSHEET **Video Activity**—Students answer questions related to a topic in the chapter content after they have viewed a lesson video.

HUMAN GEOGRAPHY OF NORTH KOREA AND SOUTH KOREA

Students will know:
- *how the countries with similar histories move in different directions today.*
- *the population patterns of North Korea and South Korea.*
- *what are the major influences on the culture and art in both countries.*
- *how the major industries have changed over time.*

Students will be able to:
- ***analyze** the different directions North and South Korea are taking.*
- ***describe** where people live on the Korean Peninsula.*
- ***identify** influences on art and culture in the region.*
- ***explain** how the major industries have changed.*

UNDERSTANDING BY DESIGN®

☑ Print Teaching Options

V Visual Skills
- ☐ **p. 730** Students create a flowchart or time line to show the series of events that led to the Korean War and the division of Korea into two states. AL Visual/Spatial
- ☐ **p. 736** Students create a chart to show the events that led to the economic transformation in South Korea. Visual/Spatial

R Reading Skills
- ☐ **p. 733** Students discuss the term *cultural divergence.* AL Verbal/Linguistic
- ☐ **p. 733** Students analyze the time line and summarize information about Korea's quest for independence. ELL Verbal/Linguistic, Visual/Spatial
- ☐ **p. 735** Students discuss how a command economy works. BL Logical/Mathematical

C Critical Thinking Skills
- ☐ **p. 730** Students infer what factors might lead up to the division of a country. BL Logical/Mathematical
- ☐ **p. 734** Students discuss the differences between health care systems in North Korea and South Korea. AL Verbal/Linguistic
- ☐ **p. 736** Students discuss the term *self-reliance* and how it relates to North Korea's economy. Verbal/Linguistic

W Writing Skills
- ☐ **p. 732** Students summarize the current relationship between North Korea and South Korea. BL Verbal/Linguistic
- ☐ **p. 734** Students write a scene about a day in the life of a family living in either country. BL Verbal/Linguistic

T Technology Skills
- ☐ **p. 733** Students research recent population patterns in a major city in the region and present their findings. BL Interpersonal, Logical/Mathematical
- ☐ **p. 734** Students identify the major influences on art in both North Korea and South Korea and present their findings in a multimedia presentation. Visual/Spatial
- ☐ **p. 735** Students identify specific examples of how mismanagement led to widespread starvation in North Korea and present their findings. BL Visual/Spatial

☑ Online Teaching Options

V Visual Skills
- ☐ INTERACTIVE IMAGE **North Korea's Nuclear Program**—Students examine an image of North Korean soldiers and explain the development of the country's nuclear program. BL Verbal/Linguistic
- ☐ VIDEO **South Korea as an Economic Power**—Students watch a video to learn how South Korea has become a modern, industrialized country in a short amount of time. Verbal/Linguistic

C Critical Thinking Skills
- ☐ INTERACTIVE BELLRINGER **Health Expenditures of Select Countries**—Students use the introductory text and the table showing the health expenditures of select countries to understand the major influences on the culture and art in both countries in terms of education. ELL Logical/Mathematical, Verbal/Linguistic
- ☐ INTERACTIVE WHITEBOARD ACTIVITY **Shared History, Divided Growth**—Students drag descriptions of historic events or cultural characteristics into a chart to show how both countries have changed. BL Verbal/Linguistic
- ☐ INTERACTIVE TIME LINE **Focus of Rival Interests**—Students examine the time line that displays how Korea maintained political and cultural independence for more than a thousand years. AL Visual/Spatial, Verbal/Linguistic
- ☐ INTERACTIVE IMAGE **Cultural Exchange**—Students examine the image of women performing the Fan Dance that explains the visit of the New York Philharmonic to North Korea in 2008. AL Verbal/Linguistic

☑ Printable Digital Worksheets

R Reading Skills
- ☐ WORKSHEET **Guided Reading Activity**—Students use Guided Reading Activity worksheets to review their comprehension of the content.
- ☐ WORKSHEET **Reading Essentials and Study Guide**—Students complete the study guide and answer Reading Progress Check and vocabulary questions. AL

C Critical Thinking Skills
- ☐ WORKSHEET **Video Activity**—Students answer questions related to a topic in the chapter content after they have viewed a lesson video.

LESSON 3 PLANNER

PEOPLE AND THEIR ENVIRONMENT: NORTH KOREA AND SOUTH KOREA

Students will know:

- *what factors are threatening resources on the Korean Peninsula today.*
- *what the human impact is on the environment in North Korea and South Korea.*
- *how people and both governments are addressing environmental issues.*

Students will be able to:

- ***identify** current threats to the Korean Peninsula.*
- ***describe** how people impact the environment in the region.*
- ***identify** ways in which governments and people are addressing environmental issues.*

UNDERSTANDING BY DESIGN®

☑ Print Teaching Options

V Visual Skills

- ☐ **p. 737** Students create a flowchart or illustration that shows how air pollution has an impact on different regions. AL Visual/Spatial

R Reading Skills

- ☐ **p. 737** Students create a K-W-L chart to complete about the people and environment of North Korea and South Korea. AL Visual/Spatial

C Critical Thinking Skills

- ☐ **p. 737** Students read about water and air pollution in North Korea and predict what will happen to the Taedong River over time. Naturalist
- ☐ **p. 738** Students create a two-column chart to record problems and solutions as they read the *Human Impact* section. AL Visual/Spatial
- ☐ **p. 739** Students discuss problems caused by North Korea's isolation and secrecy. AL Interpersonal, Naturalist

W Writing Skills

- ☐ **p. 740** Students write as scientists who are reviewing North Korea's environment to identify what their assigned country's scientists recommended at the P'yŏngyang conference. BL Verbal/Linguistic, Interpersonal

T Technology Skills

- ☐ **p. 738** Students research to prepare for a debate about by-catch methods and the use of FADs in the fishing industry. BL Intrapersonal, Verbal/Linguistic

☑ Online Teaching Options

V Visual Skills

- INTERACTIVE BELLRINGER **Fog and Aerosol Plume over the Yellow Sea**—Students use the introductory text and satellite image of fog and aerosol plume over the Yellow Sea to identify factors threatening resources on the Korean Peninsula today. ELL Interpersonal, Visual/Spatial
- INTERACTIVE WHITEBOARD ACTIVITY **Human Actions and the Environment**—Students identify and place descriptions of the human actions involved in deforestation, drift-net fishing, and urbanization and their environmental consequences in a chart. AL Verbal/Linguistic

C Critical Thinking Skills

- INTERACTIVE INFOGRAPHIC **Facing Empty Oceans**—Students explore the techniques commonly used by the South Korean fishing industry that threaten the sustainability of fish populations. BL Verbal/Linguistic

☑ Printable Digital Worksheets

R Reading Skills

- WORKSHEET **Guided Reading Activity**—Students use Guided Reading Activity worksheets to review their comprehension of the content.
- WORKSHEET **Reading Essentials and Study Guide**—Students complete the study guide and answer Reading Progress Check and vocabulary questions. AL
- WORKSHEET **Vocabulary Activity**—Students review the chapter content and academic vocabulary words.
- WORKSHEET **Chapter Summary**—Students review the main ideas of the chapter content.

C Critical Thinking Skills

- WORKSHEET **Video Activity**—Students answer questions based on a lesson video.
- WORKSHEET **Reteaching Activity**—Students use this activity worksheet to review and reteach chapter content and vocabulary. This worksheet can be used with struggling students who need additional help with difficult content concepts.

Intervention and Remediation Strategies

LESSON 1 Physical Geography of North Korea and South Korea

Reading and Comprehension

Have students work with a partner to analyze the map in this lesson and then create a graphic organizer to compare and contrast physical features or climates of the Korean Peninsula. For example, students might draw a Venn diagram that shows how North Korea's and South Korea's waterways are similar and different. After students have completed their diagrams, have pairs exchange their charts with other pairs, checking for accuracy and revising as needed.

Text Evidence

Have students work in four groups to research an aspect of the physical geography of North Korea and South Korea as it relates to one of the following topics discussed in the lesson: landforms, water systems, climate regions and biomes, and natural resources. For example, students might research the importance of fertilizer and irrigation to North Korea's agricultural production. Tell students to present an analysis of their findings, encouraging them to include visuals.

LESSON 2 Human Geography of North Korea and South Korea

Reading and Comprehension

Have students work in pairs to review the time line in this lesson. Discuss the meaning of the word *rival,* using the term *sibling rivalry* to explain the relationship between Korea and its larger neighbors, China and Japan. Tell students to conduct online research to identify important dates and events to add to the time line. Students may wish to research events that occurred during the time span shown on the time line or those after 1945. Have students present their additional dates and events to the class, encouraging them to include visuals in their presentations.

Text Evidence

Organize students into five groups and assign each group one of the following topics: education, the status of women, arts, religion, and family. Tell students in each group to collaborate on a script for a short skit about life in the country today or in the past, based on their topic. Encourage students to write a realistic scene that depicts a family living in their chosen country. Allow time for groups to rehearse their skits before performing them for the class. Guide students in a discussion to answer the Guiding Question: *What are the major influences on the culture and art in each country?*

LESSON 3 People and Their Environment: North Korea and South Korea

Reading and Comprehension

To ensure comprehension of the concepts in this lesson, have students write a summarizing sentence for each of the three sections in the text: *Managing Resources, Human Impact,* and *Addressing the Issues.* Tell students their sentences should touch on one or more issues facing North Korea or South Korea and should identify what is being done to solve the problem or problems. Have students share their sentences with the class, providing corrective guidance if needed.

Text Evidence

Tell student pairs to write a paragraph that identifies supporting evidence for one of the following statements from the *It Matters Because* text: 1. *The environments of North Korea and South Korea are affected by the air quality of other countries.* 2. *The actions of North Koreans and South Koreans, in turn, affect their own air and water, as well as the air and water of other countries.* In addition to identifying evidence from the text, students may conduct online research to provide facts to support their chosen statement. Encourage students to add visuals that enhance their paragraphs.

Online Resources

Leveled Reader

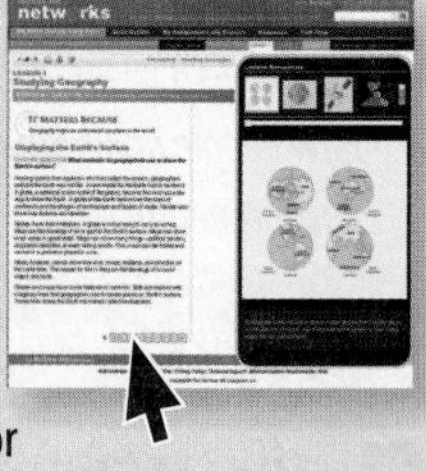

Use this online approaching-level text that corresponds directly to the text in the Student Edition. It also includes additional reading and comprehension support for English Language Learners.

Guided Reading Activities

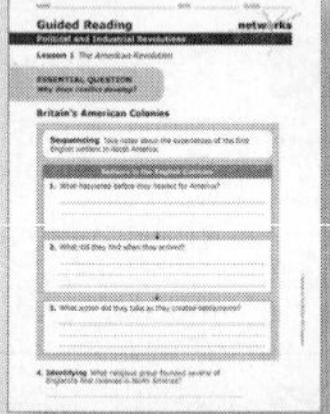

This resource uses guiding questions to help students with comprehension.

Reteaching Activities

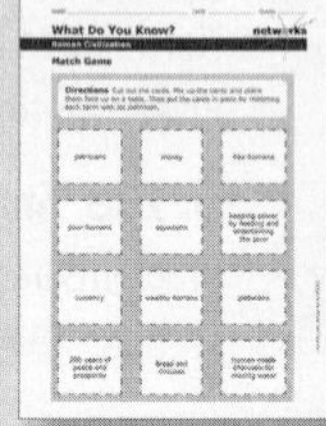

These worksheets provide students with an opportunity for remedial practice and review of vital chapter content.

Reading Essentials and Study Guide

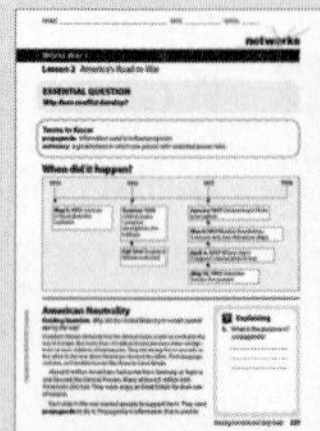

This resource offers writing and reading activities for the approaching-level student.

Self-Check Quizzes

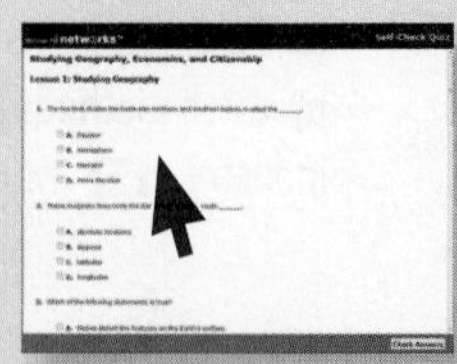

This online assessment tool provides instant feedback for students to check their progress.

Chapter Summaries

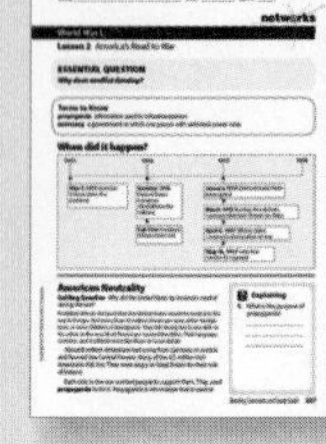

Summaries are provided for each chapter that thoroughly condense core content into manageable chunks.

North Korea and South Korea

ESSENTIAL QUESTION • *How do physical systems and human systems shape a place?*

networks

There's More Online about the geography of North Korea and South Korea.

CHAPTER 30

Geography Matters...

The Korean Peninsula is composed of North Korea and South Korea. The people of the peninsula share a language, a history, and a culture. War and politics, however, divided a single country into two. Political philosophies and decisions about resources have resulted in two very different economies and standards of living. Prosperity and scarcity threaten the environment in different ways. Urbanization, the increased use of technology and consumer goods, and the loss of rural culture threaten South Korea. Famine, erosion, and lack of freedom threaten North Korea.

◀ This young Korean woman wears traditional dress.

Letter from the Author

Dear Geography Teacher,

In 2013, the North Korean government began "rattling the saber" with a series of threats that included sending intercontinental ballistic missiles to targets in South Korea, Japan, and the United States. Whether these threats are attempts to gain economic concessions from other countries, or represent a flexing of North Korea's giant military muscle is unknown. One of the few remaining Communist countries, North Korea now must chart its own course without the assistance of the former Soviet Union and with the transformation of China's economy to a more Western-like appearance.

ENGAGE

Activating Prior Knowledge Explain to students that they will be reading about the physical and human systems of the Korean Peninsula and the vast differences between North Korea and South Korea. Have pairs discuss what they already know about the region's history and some of the problems and issues facing people there today.

TEACH & ASSESS

Geography Matters Explain that even though North Korea and South Korea share a peninsula, they have long been contentious enemies with different political and economic systems. **Ask: How do you think a "loss of rural culture" has impacted the people of South Korea?** *(Possible answer: Traditional ways of life in farming communities are likely threatened due to urbanization and modernization.)* **What might life be like for the people of North Korea with a "lack of freedom"?** *(Student answers may vary, but could include censorship or cultural and religious restrictions.)* **Verbal/Linguistic**

Making Connections

Help students make the connection between conflicts involving North Korea and South Korea to those between the North and the South in the U.S. Civil War. Explain that while the reasons behind the conflicts are quite different, a civil war can divide a country in dramatic ways. The U.S. Civil War resulted in four years of bloody battles, but the country eventually rebuilt. In the case of the Korean Peninsula, however, conflicts divided the region into two very different countries.

CLOSE & REFLECT

Predicting Have students write two or three predictions about aspects of North Korea and South Korea based on what they have learned about the region so far. Tell students to refer back to their predictions after completing the chapter to see if they were correct.

Extend the project-based learning experience globally through our partnership with ePals. EPals allows you to connect with classrooms around the world in a safe online environment for real-life lessons and projects in virtual study groups.

ENGAGE

R Reading Skills

Defining Have students read the title and opening paragraph, drawing their attention to the term *complementarity.* **Ask:** **What word or words might relate to the term?** *(complement, complementary)* **Based on your understanding of the word *complement,* what do you think the word *complementarity* means?** *(Possible answers: the balance or completion of something else; the state of being complementary or improved)* Have students look up the word in the dictionary to see if their definitions were correct. Then have students work with a partner to brainstorm sentences using the word *complementarity.* **Ask:** **Why do you think the Koreas are described as a complementarity?** *(Possible answer: They are each different, but could complement each other economically if they were not bitterly divided enemies.)*

AL Verbal/Linguistic

TEACH & ASSESS

V Visual Skills

Spatial Analysis Have students use the photograph to consider what life in a major city such as the one shown might be like. Discuss how a well-developed urban area such as the one pictured may contrast with a city in North Korea, which is not as well-developed industrially or economically. Have students work with a partner to complete a Venn diagram showing possible similarities and differences between the two countries. As each set of students completes its diagram, have pairs share their diagrams with another set of partners to discuss and compare. **Interpersonal, Visual/Spatial**

Why Geography Matters: **North Korea and South Korea**

complementarity: *two* Koreas

R

North Korea and South Korea share a peninsula, a history, and a culture, but they are enemies. The two countries are in a situation known as a complementarity in which two places are economically interdependent. North Korea has more natural resources and raw materials, while South Korea is more developed industrially and economically. Economic cooperation could occur if the countries were not bitterly divided.

V

724

Project-Based Learning

Hands-On

Create Posters

Have students create posters that bring together information from all lessons about the physical geography and human geography of North Korea and South Korea.

Digital Hands-On

Create Online Projects

Find an additional activity online that incorporates technology for this project. Visit the EdTech Teacher Web sites for more links, tutorials, and other resources.

How is life in both countries similar on the peninsula?

North Korea occupies the northern half of the Korean Peninsula and South Korea occupies the southern half. North Korea's rugged, mountainous terrain makes farming difficult, but yields coal and other valuable mineral resources such as gold, iron, copper, and zinc. Although North Korea has invested in mining, as well as other industries, it is one of the world's poorest countries. In contrast, South Korea's economy is one of the strongest in Asia. Like North Korea, South Korea is mountainous. However, fertile plains in the west and south are suitable for growing rice, barley, soybeans, corn, and other crops. Since the 1940s, South Korea's economy has been shifting from agricultural to industrial. Today, South Korea is the largest shipbuilder in the world. Its modern factories also manufacture cars, electronics, chemicals, and steel. **C**

1. **Places and Regions** How are North Korea and South Korea similar and different?

How has a shared history affected both countries?

North Korea and South Korea have common bonds and the ability to satisfy each other's economic needs. However, these two countries have political differences that make cooperation difficult. Communist North Korea is a dictatorship. It has ties to China and Russia. South Korea is a republic with ties to the United States, Western Europe, and Japan. Since the Korean War ended in 1953, relations between the two countries have remained tense. North Korea has threatened South Korea with military strikes and South Korea has vowed to strike back. In 2010 North Korea fired on South Korean forces stationed on Yeonpyeong Island. Despite hostile relations, the two countries have been able to find some common ground. **T** For instance, North Korea has been plagued by serious food shortages brought on by drought and flooding. To help solve this problem, North Korean leaders have accepted emergency food aid from South Korea. With few of its own resources, South Korea supports its growing industries by buying raw materials from North Korea.

2. **Human Systems** What prevents North Korea and South Korea from working together?

In a global economy, what do the two countries have in common?

To help one another, North Korea and South Korea can continue to work toward sharing resources. In the late 1990s, South Korea pursued the "Sunshine Policy" of economic cooperation, sharing aid and resources with North Korea. Later, the leaders of North Korea and South Korea attended inter-Korean summits to address political and economic issues. As a result, the two countries were able to launch a joint economic venture in 2006: the Kaesong Industrial Complex in North Korea. For this project, South Korea supplied money and technology. North Korea supplied land and labor. More than 100 South Korean-owned companies employ about 47,000 North Koreans. Other inter-Korean economic projects have been proposed, such as a natural gas pipeline from Russia to South Korea via North Korea. There is also a proposal to extend the Trans-Siberian Railway through North Korea to South Korea. **W**

3. **The World in Spatial Terms** What are the possible benefits of economic cooperation between North Korea and South Korea?

THERE'S MORE ONLINE

EXPLORE a map of the Korean War • *COMPARE* the populations of North Korea and South Korea

C Critical Thinking Skills

Making Generalizations After students read about the similarities and differences between North Korea and South Korea, have them collaborate with a partner to make a generalization about the importance of resources and agriculture to each region. Have students share their generalizations with the class. **Ask: How does the geography of North Korea and South Korea impact their respective economies?** *(North Korea is mountainous with very little farmland so it has food shortages, whereas South Korea has some fertile plains that are suitable for growing a variety of crops.)* **Logical/Mathematical**

T Technology Skills

Researching Have students conduct research to identify examples of specific ways that North Korea and South Korea have found "common ground." Allow time for students to present their findings in brief reports to the class, inviting them to enhance their presentations with visual displays. **BL Interpersonal, Visual/Spatial**

W Writing Skills

Informative/Explanatory Have students research the status of the Trans-Siberian Railway extension project or the natural gas pipeline project. Students should determine if negotiations between the two countries have resulted in approval for these projects and a start-up of construction. Have them respond in an explanatory essay, detailing the projected cost of the project and how long it will take to complete. Invite students to share their essays with the class. **AL Verbal/Linguistic**

SLIDE SHOW

Relations Between North Korea and South Korea

Analyzing Visuals Have students examine the slide show to see more about the relationships between North Korea and South Korea. **AL Visual/Spatial**

CLOSE & REFLECT

Problem Solving Guide a brainstorming session with students about some of the ways that North Korea and South Korea could collaborate to better meet each other's economic needs.

ANSWERS, p. 725

Why Geography Matters

1. North and South Korea are on the same peninsula and are both mountainous, but South Korea has fertile plains in the west and south. North Korea is one of the poorest countries in the world while South Korea has one of the strongest economies in Asia.
2. Political differences have kept the countries from working together. Communist North Korea is a dictatorship while South Korea is a republic, which has caused ongoing conflicts since the end of the Korean War.
3. Both countries could benefit by sharing aid and resources as North Korea could supply raw materials and labor while South Korea supplies funds and technology. A natural gas pipeline and an extension of the Trans-Siberian Railway to South Korea could help both countries economically.

ENGAGE

V1 Visual Skills

Observing Have students work with a partner to examine the images and list some features of North Korea and South Korea, based on their observations. Tell students to add to or revise their lists as they work through the lesson. **Ask: What are some characteristics of the region's physical geography?** *(Possible answer: The region has rolling green hills suitable for farmland and rugged, mountainous terrain.)* AL **Visual/Spatial**

TEACH & ASSESS

R Reading Skills

Using Word Parts Ask a volunteer to read aloud the paragraph. Direct students' attention to the word *homogenous*, noting that the word's meaning is difficult to determine based on context clues alone. Note that using word parts can provide clues to the word's meaning. **Ask: What word parts help you know the meaning of *homogenous*?** (Homo- *is a prefix that means "same."*) **What synonyms could replace the term in this sentence?** *(*similar, alike*)* ELL **Verbal/Linguistic**

V2 Visual Skills

Transferring Information Have students work with a partner to transfer the information in the text about landforms, waterways, and bordering countries onto an outline map of the Korean Peninsula. Tell students to gauge locations based on descriptions in the text. Then have students refer to a physical map of North Korea and South Korea to see whether the locations on their outline map are accurate. **Visual/Spatial**

ANSWERS, p. 726

TAKING NOTES: Landforms: T'aebaek Mountains begin in North Korea and follow the east coast into South Korea. Mount Paektu is on the border between North Korea and China. There are more than 3,000 islands off the coast of South Korea. Most of the rivers in the peninsula are in South Korea. South Korean rivers include the Han, the Kŭm, and the Naktong. **Climates:** continental climate with cold winters and warm or hot summers; the north has greater temperature variances and the southern part of the peninsula has a humid subtropical climate. Monsoon winds bring heavy rains to the whole peninsula during the summer. **Resources:** North Korea has most of the mineral resources on the peninsula: iron ore, coal, and magnesite. Hydroelectric power is the main source of electricity in North Korea. In South Korea, more than half of its power is generated by thermal electric plants, but nuclear power use is increasing. South Korea must import petroleum and most metals. Both countries lack large areas of farmland due to their mountainous terrain. South Korea has a large dairy industry. Both countries rely on fish and other seafood.

networks

There's More Online!

V1

- ☑ **CHART** Average Year-Round Temperatures in Select Korean Cities
- ☑ **IMAGE** Rural Town in South Korea
- ☑ **MAP** Waterways of the Korean Peninsula
- ☑ **INTERACTIVE SELF-CHECK QUIZ**
- ☑ **VIDEO** Physical Geography of North Korea and South Korea

LESSON 1

Physical Geography of North Korea and South Korea

ESSENTIAL QUESTION • *How do physical systems and human systems shape a place?*

Reading HELPDESK 

Academic Vocabulary (Tier Two Words)
- **vary**
- **cooperative**

Content Vocabulary (Tier Three Words)
- **islet**
- **aquaculture**

TAKING NOTES: ***Key Ideas and Details***

COMPARING As you read about the physical geography of the Korean Peninsula, use a graphic organizer like the one below to compare the landforms, climates, and natural resources of North Korea and South Korea.

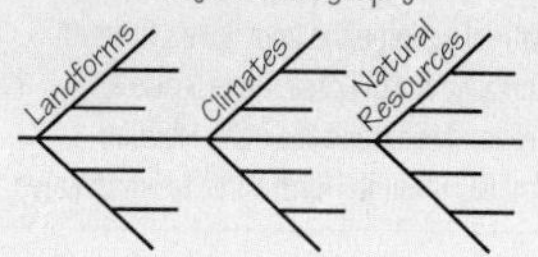

IT MATTERS BECAUSE

R *The Korean Peninsula lies between China and Japan, at the center of one of the world's most economically and strategically important regions—East Asia. The peninsula's rugged terrain was a barrier to invaders for many centuries, and the population of the peninsula is quite homogeneous. However, the peninsula's long coastline allowed contact with other civilizations. The two Koreas have great economic and geopolitical importance today.*

Landforms

GUIDING QUESTION *How does the land on the Korean Peninsula change from north to south?*

V2 The Korean Peninsula is about half the size of California. It is bordered by Russia and China to the north and surrounded by water on the other three sides. To the east is the Sea of Japan, which the Koreans call the East Sea. To the south, the Korea Strait lies between South Korea and Japan. To the southwest lies the East China Sea, which joins the Yellow Sea on the western coast. The Koreans call this the West Sea. After World War II, the peninsula was split into the Democratic People's Republic of Korea (North Korea) and the Republic of Korea (South Korea). The two countries have been divided by the Korean Demilitarized Zone (DMZ) since 1953. The DMZ is a strip of unoccupied land about 6 miles (9.7 km) wide.

The peninsula is very mountainous. The T'aebaek Mountains begin in North Korea and stretch along the Sea of Japan following the east coast into South Korea. Both North Korea and South Korea are mountainous, but North Korea is more mountainous with highlands and plateaus across its northern and eastern areas. North Korea has some of the highest peaks. Mount Paektu, the highest peak on the peninsula, is on the border between North Korea and China. Most of the rivers on the peninsula originate in the T'aebaek range and flow westward. This creates large river valleys on the western side of the peninsula. Most people live in these lowlands or along the coastline.

networks ***Online Teaching Options***

INTERACTIVE BELLRINGER

Waterways of the Korean Peninsula

Interpreting a Map Use the introductory text and the map of North Korea and South Korea to identify the major waterways of both countries. Have students work with a partner. Ask each pair to answer the questions and record their answers. Then lead a class discussion to review the answers.

AL **Interpersonal, Visual/Spatial**

Waterways of the Korean Peninsula

North Korea has the longest river on the peninsula, but rivers are more plentiful in South Korea.

1. Which river forms most of the border between North Korea and China?

A. Chaeryong
B. Taedong
C. Yesong
D. Yalu

click for answer

Auto-Run Click Through Previous 1 of 3 Next

The coastline has many small inlets and bays, especially in the south. There are more than 3,000 islands off the coast of South Korea. The two largest, Cheju and Ulleungdo, were formed by volcanic lava. Cheju, in the East China Sea south of the Korean Peninsula, is beloved by honeymooners, and is known as the "Hawaii of Korea." Ulleungdo, located to the north in the Sea of Japan, has fine fishing and forests. South Korea also claims a group of rocky **islets** that Koreans call the Tok Islands. Japan also claims them.

W

islet a very small island

✓ READING PROGRESS CHECK

Specifying Which country of the Korean Peninsula is more mountainous?

Waterways

GUIDING QUESTION *Which major waterways drain the land in the peninsula?*

Most of the peninsula's major rivers are in South Korea. The Han, the Kŭm, and the Naktong all begin in the T'aebaek Mountains. The northernmost of these rivers, the Han, flows through South Korea's capital, Seoul. Both the Han and the Kŭm flow west to reach the Yellow Sea. South Korea's longest river, the Naktong, flows south for 325 miles (523 km) to the Korea Strait.

North Korea's longest river is the Yalu, which forms most of the border between North Korea and China. The source of the Yalu is on the southern slope of Mount Paektu. The Yalu flows some 500 miles (800 km) to Korea Bay, an inlet of the Yellow Sea, on the western coast of North Korea. Several other rivers in North Korea—the Ch'ŏngch'ŏn, Taedong, Chaeryŏng, and Yesŏng—also drain into Korea Bay. These large river valleys are important farming areas in this mountainous land.

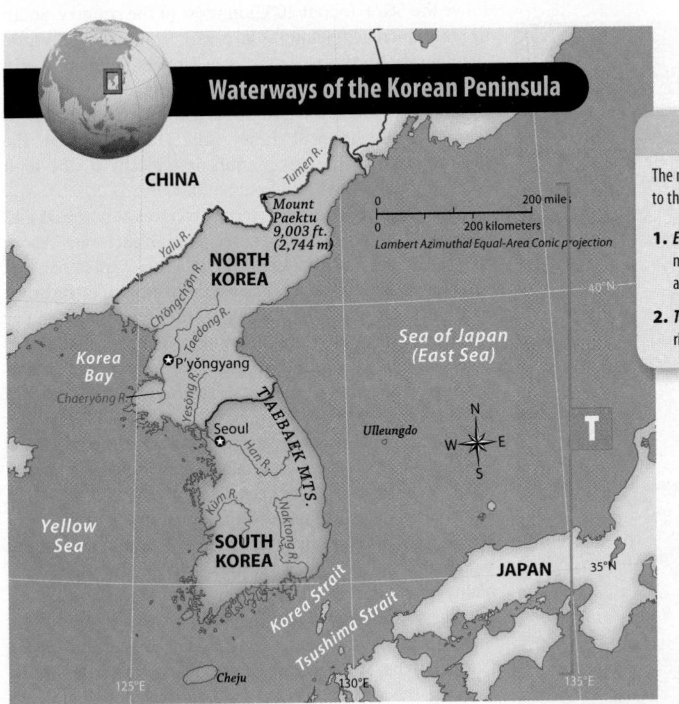

GEOGRAPHY CONNECTION

The major rivers of the Korean Peninsula flow to the west.

1. ***ENVIRONMENT AND SOCIETY*** Why are the major cities of the Korean Peninsula located along rivers?
2. ***THE WORLD IN SPATIAL TERMS*** On which river is P'yŏngyang located?

T

VIDEO

Rituals South Korea

Examining Have students watch this video to learn more about a secretive South Korean group living high in the mountains that is trying to preserve traditional Korean values. ELL **Verbal/Linguistic**

W Writing Skills

Narrative After students read the information about South Korea's coastline, ask them to choose one of the physical features discussed in the text. Have students conduct additional research about one of the places mentioned and then write a paragraph, poem, or song about the place. Tell students their writing should describe the place and its impact on human systems in the region. Call on volunteers to share their paragraphs, poems, or songs with the class. Encourage musically inclined students to enhance their songs and poems with a musical instrument. BL **Auditory/Musical, Intrapersonal**

C Critical Thinking Skills

Drawing Inferences Discuss with students the impact of most of the peninsula's major rivers being in South Korea. **Ask:** **How do you think North Korea has managed without the same amount of freshwater that South Korea has?** *(Possible answer: The lack of major rivers is another reason that North Korea does not do well in agriculture.)* **What can you infer about South Korea's use of its rivers?** *(Possible answer: South Korea has learned to use its rivers for irrigation and has been successful in providing food for its people.)* AL **Logical/Mathematical**

T Technology Skills

Diagramming Have students work with a partner to analyze the map and then create a diagram that shows how North Korea's and South Korea's waterways are similar and different. Students can create their diagram by using computer software. After students have completed their diagrams, ask them to exchange the diagrams with another student pair to check for accuracy. AL **Visual/Spatial**

ANSWERS, p. 727

✓ READING PROGRESS CHECK North Korea is the more mountainous country of the peninsula.

GEOGRAPHY CONNECTION

1. The major cities began as river ports as rivers were important trade and transportation routes.
2. P'yŏngyang is on the Taedong River.

T Technology Skills

Analyzing Cause and Effect After students read the text, discuss the significance of natural resources to both North Korea and South Korea. Have small groups conduct online research about why different regions on the Korean Peninsula have been deforested. Have groups use information in the text as well as online or in other library resources to research why specific trees are developed and for what purpose. Tell students to present their findings in a visual display. Tell students to create a chart or graph that depicts the total area of forestland in each country that has been lost due to deforestation. Have groups present their visuals to the class, explaining the significance of trees to the region's economy. **BL Logical/Mathematical, Visual/Spatial**

V Visual Skills

Depicting Have students create diagrams or drawings that show how deforestation impacts animals mentioned in the text. Students' diagrams should show the cause-and-effect relationship between various species of birds and animals on the peninsula and the impact of deforestation. Students may wish to conduct additional research to support their drawings. **ELL Visual/Spatial, Interpersonal**

ANSWERS, p. 728

READING PROGRESS CHECK North Korea has the longest river on the peninsula, the Yalu.

CRITICAL THINKING

1. Both countries rely on fish and seafood and rivers for hydroelectric power.
2. Terracing increases crop yields by creating more farmland by utilizing the mountainous terrain.

They have also been important to the settlement of the peninsula. Both South Korea's capital, Seoul, and P'yŏngyang, the capital of North Korea, began as river ports.

Rivers are no longer the main transportation routes in the two Koreas. However, they are still used for irrigation and for generating hydroelectricity. Water levels **vary** throughout the year. Rivers are shallow except during the summer rainy season. This means that the water supply and ability to generate power vary seasonally, as well.

vary to exhibit or undergo change

READING PROGRESS CHECK

Identifying Which country on the Korean Peninsula has the longest river?

Climates, Biomes, and Resources

GUIDING QUESTION *How does the climate change from north to south?*

The Korean Peninsula lies close to the landmass of Asia. Because of this, much of it has a continental climate of cold winters and warm or hot summers. The north is closer to the mainland, so it has the greater temperature extremes. The southern part of the peninsula has a humid subtropical climate, with temperatures moderated by the surrounding seas. Monsoon winds bring heavy rains to the entire peninsula in the summer.

This small rural town in South Korea is surrounded by fields that have been terraced for growing crops.

▼ CRITICAL THINKING

1. ***Comparing*** What resources do both countries have?
2. ***Drawing Conclusions*** How does terracing like this increase crop yields?

Topic Photo Agency/age fotostock

Climate Regions and Biomes

North Korea's winter lasts from December to March, and is generally cold and snowy. The average temperatures in January range from about −10°F (−23°C) in the northern interior to 20°F (−7°C) in the south. Mean July temperatures are above the 60s°F (about 20°C) in most of the country. South Korea's winter temperatures also vary from north to south. Seoul, in the northwest, has average January temperatures in the low 20s°F (−5°C), while in Pusan, in the southeast, winter temperatures are in the mid-30s°F (about 2°C). In summer, it is generally hot with heavy rain. During August, the warmest month, the temperature is typically in the high 70s°F (about 25°C) throughout South Korea.

T The Korean Peninsula typically receives between 35 and 60 inches (89 and 152 cm) of precipitation each year. About 60 percent falls as rain between June and September, the summer monsoon season. The northern plateau is the driest area, receiving about 24 inches (61 cm) of precipitation per year. Typhoons may bring heavy rains in the late summer, especially along the southern coast. The South Korean island of Cheju is the wettest area, receiving more than 70 inches (178 cm) per year.

There are many coniferous trees, such as the Siberian fir, spruce, and Korean pine, especially in the northern highlands. Much of the lowlands have been deforested in both countries, but small pine groves mixed with oaks, lindens, maples, and birches can be found in some areas. The humid subtropical regions of the south support over 4,500 known species of plants, including needle-leaved deciduous trees and broad-leaved evergreens, such as camellias and camphor trees.

V Due to deforestation, large predators such as tigers, leopards, lynx, and bears are nearly gone from the peninsula. Deer are the most common large mammals. The peninsula

networks Online Teaching Options

INTERACTIVE WHITEBOARD ACTIVITY

Landforms, Biomes, and Resources

Identifying Have students identify which landforms, climates, biomes, and natural resources are shared by North Korea and South Korea and which are separate to each region. **ELL Visual/Spatial**

Landforms, Biomes, and Resources

While North Korea and South Korea share many landforms, their climates and biomes differ due to their location. For each description below, click on North Korea, South Korea, or both to show the similarities and differences in landforms, climates, and biomes in the subregion.

Example	Element	
1. American Southwest	North Korea	South Korea
2. Cleveland is on Lake Erie	North Korea	South Korea
3. Climatology	North Korea	South Korea
4. Urban planning	North Korea	South Korea
5. Impact of hurricanes on humans	North Korea	South Korea
6. Movement of people and goods	North Korea	South Korea
7. Home to Siberian fir, spruce, and pine	North Korea	South Korea
8. Home to needle-leafed deciduous trees and broad-leafed evergreens	North Korea	South Korea

Show Answers

is home to many species of birds. These include wild pigeons, herons, and cranes. The Demilitarized Zone (DMZ) serves as an important nature preserve, where waterfowl, migratory birds, and mammals can flourish undisturbed by humans.

Natural Resources

Neither country on the peninsula has a great deal of farmland because of the mountainous landscape. North Korea has increased agricultural production through the use of fertilizers and irrigation. Since 1958, North Korea's farms have been administered as **cooperatives**, or communal farms. The country has more than 3,000 cooperatives. About 300 families work each farm on about 1,200 acres (500 ha) of land. These farms deliver produce to the government, which distributes food through state-owned stores. South Korea also has little arable land, but recent improvements in processes and commercialization of the farming industry have led to increased production. **W**

In both countries, rice is the most important crop. North Korea also grows corn, wheat, barley, potatoes, and fruit. The warmer climate areas, particularly in the southern regions of South Korea, are suitable for growing a variety of citrus fruits. These areas also produce vegetables, pears, and persimmons. Ginseng is an important export for South Korea. In North Korea, livestock is raised on land that cannot be used to grow crops. Livestock production, especially of poultry, has steadily increased over time. The raising of livestock is also important in South Korea. South Korea also has a large dairy industry. After rice, the top agricultural products of South Korea are pork, beef, and milk.

Both countries rely heavily on fish and seafood. In North Korea, deep-sea fishing supplies pollack, sardines, mackerel, and other fish. About one-fourth of the country's fish comes from **aquaculture**. South Korea is one of the world's major deep-sea fishing countries. Significant fish production there also comes from coastal fisheries and inland aquaculture.

Most of the peninsula's known mineral resources are in North Korea. Iron ore and coal are especially important. North Korea has the world's largest magnesite deposits, too. Magnesite is used to make many items, including fertilizers and rubber. The main source of electric power in North Korea is hydroelectric. While South Korea has one of the world's largest supplies of graphite and tungsten, it has very few other minerals. It must import all its petroleum and most metals. More than half of South Korea's electricity is generated through thermal electric plants. However, nuclear power generation is becoming more important in that country.

 READING PROGRESS CHECK

Identifying Which country on the Korean Peninsula has the warmest winters?

Connecting Geography to SCIENCE

The DMZ

The Demilitarized Zone, or DMZ, created as a buffer zone between warring North Korea and South Korea, has become an important nature preserve. Bordered by armies and landmines, the DMZ has been untouched by humans since 1953. Former farmland has been overgrown or slowly replaced by trees, wetlands, and estuaries. These habitats provide a home to rare species, including Asiatic black bears, Siberian musk deer, and the red-crowned crane, one of the rarest birds in the world. Naturalists are working on ways to protect the nature preserve if the two Koreas are ever reunited.

DRAWING CONCLUSIONS Why might reunification of Korea pose a threat to habitats and species in the DMZ?

cooperative an organization, often a farm, whose members work together and share expenses and profits

aquaculture the cultivation of seafood

LESSON 1 REVIEW (CCSS)

Reviewing Vocabulary (Tier Three Words)

1. ***Describing*** Write several sentences to describe how cooperative farming works in North Korea. WHST.9–10.4

Using Your Notes

2. ***Comparing and Contrasting*** Use your graphic organizer to write a paragraph comparing and contrasting the physical geography of North Korea and South Korea.

Answering the Guiding Questions

3. ***Drawing Conclusions*** How does the land on the Korean Peninsula change from north to south?
4. ***Identifying*** Which major waterways drain the land in the peninsula?
5. ***Analyzing*** How does the climate change from north to south?

Writing Activity

6. ***Argument*** In three paragraphs, formulate an argument about whether you think life would be easier in North Korea or South Korea, based only on physical geography and resources. WHST.9–10.1

W Writing Skills

Informative/Explanatory Tell students to use the information in the text as well as additional online research to learn more about cooperatives, or communal farms, in North Korea. Have students prepare an informative essay in which they identify positive and negative aspects of cooperatives. Students' reports should reveal any issues or problems related to working on cooperatives, as well as how cooperatives benefit the region's economy. BL **Verbal/Linguistic**

Making Connections

Direct students' attention to the last sentence on this page and then share the following information about nuclear power in South Korea.

Though nuclear power generation is becoming important in South Korea, it is not without problems. After a series of forced shutdowns in recent years, more problems surfaced in 2013 when South Korea's Nuclear Safety and Security Commission stopped the operations of two nuclear reactors. According to information provided by an anonymous tip to the government, components of reactors that had previously failed safety inspections were given false certificates of inspection.

CLOSE & REFLECT

Hypothesizing Tell students to review what they have learned about the landforms, waterways, climates, and resources of North Korea and South Korea. Have students describe what they think life is like in each country based on its physical geography.

LESSON 1 REVIEW ANSWERS

Reviewing Vocabulary

1. Sentences will vary but should include that cooperative farming in North Korea involves 3,000 farms with each having about 300 people working the land. The farms produce food that is delivered to the government, which then distributes it through state-owned stores.

Using Your Notes

2. Paragraphs will vary but should be strongly supported with information from the lesson. Answers could include that both countries are mountainous, surrounded by water, and have rivers. North Korea is the more mountainous with higher peaks while most of the major rivers are in South Korea.

Answering the Guiding Questions

3. The land becomes less mountainous with more major rivers as one moves south on the peninsula.
4. The Han, the Kŭm, and the Naktong in South Korea and the Yalu in North Korea drain the land in the peninsula.
5. The climate becomes warmer and wetter as one moves from north to south on the peninsula.

Writing Activity

6. Arguments will differ but should be strongly supported with information from the lesson. Answers could include the better climate and less mountainous terrain of South Korea and the greater number of mineral resources in North Korea.

ANSWERS, p. 729

READING PROGRESS CHECK South Korea has the warmest winters on the peninsula.

Connecting Geography The DMZ has been untouched since 1953, becoming a nature preserve for many rare species of animals and birds. This preserve could be destroyed by development should the countries be reunited.

ENGAGE

R Reading Skills

Previewing Have students jot down some facts they might know about the history, culture, politics, and people of North Korea and South Korea. Then have them skim through the lesson to preview the visuals and headings. Have students write two or three questions they have about the people and history of the region.

TEACH & ASSESS

C Critical Thinking Skills

Drawing Inferences Ask a volunteer to read aloud the Guiding Question. Before students read the information in the section about Korea's early history, guide them to infer what factors might lead up to the division of a country. **Ask: What do you think might have caused Korea to eventually become divided into two separate countries?** *(Possible answer: Political differences and influence from other countries could cause a rift and eventual division.)* Have students check to see if their inferences were correct after they read the section *Korea Divided.* **BL Logical/Mathematical**

V Visual Skills

Time, Chronology, and Sequencing To help students keep track of the series of events in Korea's early history, suggest that they depict the information visually in a flowchart or time line. Students should indicate the series of events that led to the Korean War and the division of Korea into two states.
AL Visual/Spatial

ANSWERS, p. 730

TAKING NOTES: History: China expanded into Korea in 108 B.C. Silla dynasty united Korea in A.D. 668. Became Japanese protectorate in 1905 and colony in 1910. Korea occupied by Soviet Union in the north and United States in the south after WWII. North Korea invaded South Korea, beginning the Korean War in 1950. Fighting ended in 1953 and DMZ separates the two countries. North Korea is communist and South Korea is democratic. **Population:** People trace heritage to China and Central Asia and share common Korean ethnicity. North Korea's population doubled between 1953 and 1993. Inland areas are sparsely populated. South Korea's population doubled during the last half of the 20th century, but birthrates have fallen in the 21st century. About 80 % of South Korea's population is urban. **Culture:** People of both countries speak Korean. Buddhism, Confucianism, shamanism, and Christianity are all practiced in South Korea. North Korea is atheist, religion is not permitted. Education is mandatory in both countries. **Economic Activities:** North Korea has a command economy, producing metal products, machinery, military equipment, and chemicals. Major trading partners are China, South Korea, Russia, Japan, and Thailand. South Korea is highly industrialized and produces machinery, electronics, textiles, and automobiles. Trade partners are the U.S., Japan, the EU, and countries of Southeast Asia.

networks
There's More Online!

- ☑ **CHART** North Korean Conflicts
- ☑ **IMAGE** North Korean Soldiers Celebrate
- ☑ **IMAGE** South Korean Aircraft Factory
- ☑ **IMAGE** Traditional Korean Fan Dance
- ☑ **TIME LINE** Focus of Rival Interests
- ☑ **INTERACTIVE SELF-CHECK QUIZ**
- ☑ **VIDEO** Human Geography of North Korea and South Korea

LESSON 2

Human Geography of North Korea and South Korea

ESSENTIAL QUESTION • *How do physical systems and human systems shape a place?*

Reading HELPDESK (CCSS)

Academic Vocabulary (Tier Two Words)
- principle
- isolation
- regime
- authority
- ethnicity

Content Vocabulary (Tier Three Words)
- coup
- cultural divergence

TAKING NOTES: *Key Ideas and Details*

LISTING As you read about the human geography of North Korea and South Korea, use a graphic organizer like the one below to list details about the history, population, culture, and economic activities of the two countries.

	North Korea	South Korea
History		
Population		
Culture		
Economic Activities		

IT MATTERS BECAUSE

R *Korea's ancient culture has influenced and been influenced by the cultures of China and Japan. The tense relationship between North Korea and South Korea and their different political systems have gained the two countries different major allies—China and the United States, respectively.*

History and Government

C **GUIDING QUESTION** *How has the decision to divide the Korean Peninsula into North Korea and South Korea affected the development of each country?*

V Before China expanded into Korea in 108 B.C. during the Han dynasty, the Korean people mostly belonged to village communities that were not united. Eventually three united kingdoms emerged that shared similar cultures, but were also rivals. These kingdoms traded with China and were greatly influenced by Chinese culture.

Buddhism was introduced to the peninsula from China in the fourth century A.D. It was widely adopted by ruling kingdoms. From Korea, Buddhism was introduced to Japan in the sixth century A.D. Confucianism came to the peninsula from China about a thousand years ago. At first, Korean rulers promoted Buddhism as the religion for personal enlightenment. Confucianism was adopted as a standard for political **principles**. Later, Buddhism was suppressed, and Confucianism provided the basis for a complex governmental bureaucracy.

The Silla dynasty drove out the Chinese and united Korea in A.D. 668. Other Korean dynasties came to power, which were largely supported by the Chinese and influenced by Chinese culture. The government of the Koryo dynasty, for example, used China's government as a model.

After resisting Mongol invaders, Korea became known as the Hermit Kingdom because of its **isolation**. In 1871 Korea declared an official policy of isolation, but Japanese warships arrived in 1876. This "gunboat diplomacy" by Japan forced Korea to open its ports for trade. After the Russo-Japanese War ended in 1905, Korea became a Japanese protectorate.

networks Online Teaching Options

INTERACTIVE BELLRINGER

Health Expenditures of Select Countries

Reading Charts Use the introductory text and the table showing the health expenditures of select countries to understand the major influences on the culture and art in both countries in terms of education. Have students form pairs. Ask pairs to answer each question and to record their answers. Then ask each set of students to join another set of students to review and check their answers for accuracy, before revealing the answers to the class.
ELL Logical/Mathematical, Verbal/Linguistic

Health Expenditures of Select Countries

Both North Korea and South Korea value healthcare, although they spend a vastly different percentage of their GDP on health expenditures.

1. What is the only country that spends less on health expenditures than North Korea?

A. Burma
B. Nepal
C. Qatar
D. South Korea

Ranking	Country	% of GDP
1	Marshall Islands	18.10
2	United States	17.90
35	Japan	9.50
83	Haiti	6.90
85	South Korea	6.90
86	Guatemala	6.90
89	Vietnam	6.80
122	Nepal	5.50
138	China	5.10
164	India	4.10
187	Congo, Republic of	2.50
188	Pakistan	2.20
189	North Korea	2.00
190	Burma	2.00
191	Qatar	1.80

click for answer

Auto-Run Click Through Previous 1 of 3 Next

Japan annexed Korea in 1910, making it a colony. Japanese occupation deprived the Korean people of many rights and freedoms. The Japanese attempted to assimilate Koreans into Japanese life and culture. They used Korea's resources to grow their own economy. Anti-Japanese feelings increased the desire to gain independence. G1

principle a rule or code of conduct

isolation state of being set or kept apart from others

Korea Divided

After Japan's defeat in World War II, the Korean Peninsula was jointly occupied by the Soviet Union and the United States. North of the 38th parallel, or line of latitude, the Soviets set up a Communist government. The new country that emerged was the Democratic People's Republic of Korea. The south was administered by the United States. The Republic of Korea was established there, with Seoul as its capital. G2

In June 1950, North Korean forces invaded South Korea. The conflict that followed became known as the Korean War. United Nations forces, mainly troops from the United States, came to the aid of the Republic of Korea (South Korea), while the Soviet Union and China supported the Democratic People's Republic of Korea (North Korea) with troops and equipment. Fighting concluded in 1953 with an armistice, or cease-fire, and the establishment of the Korean Demilitarized Zone (DMZ) separating the two countries.

United States military support of South Korea has continued since 1950. Soviet support for North Korea ceased with the fall of the Soviet Union and the end of the Cold War in 1991. Today, North Korea remains isolated from the global community. Its main supporter is China.

Kim Il Sung became the first premier under the North Korean Communist **regime** in 1948. His son succeeded him, and his grandson became premier in 2011. It is a family dynasty that rules the north. South Korea has become a democratic government. The first president of South Korea, Syngman Rhee, was elected in 1948. Strict governmental control, a military **coup**, and meeting economic over social needs continued until 1993, when civilian **authority** was restored. In 2012 South Korea elected a woman as its president for the first time.

regime a form of government

coup an overthrow of the government

authority the power to influence or command thought, opinion, or behavior

Korean Governments Today

The Korean Workers' Party controls North Korea's elections and provides lists of approved candidates—usually only one for each position. This legislative body meets for only one or two weeks a year. Most decisions are made by the 15-member Presidium of the Supreme People's Assembly (SPA). T

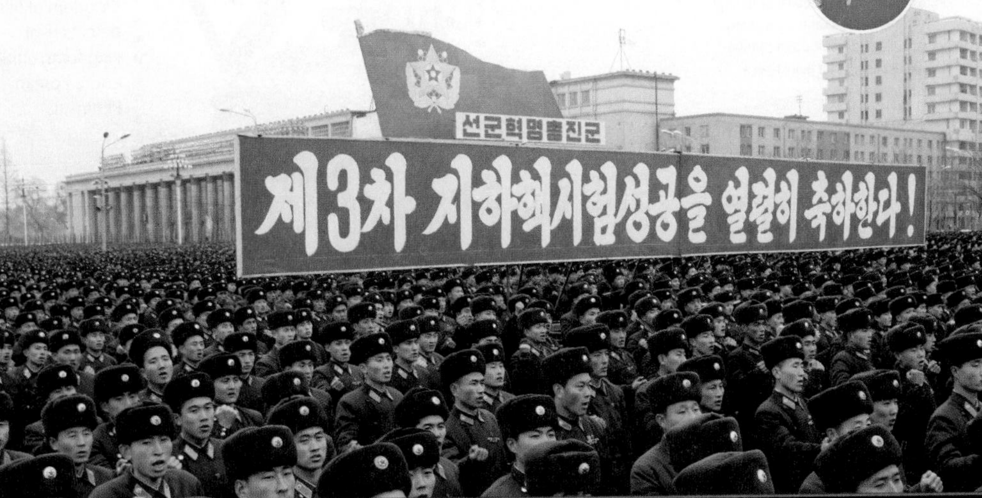

Jon Chol Jin/AP Images

North Korean soldiers celebrate their country's successful nuclear bomb test on February 13, 2013. Experts believe that North Korea's nuclear operations are being carefully planned to avoid detection.

▼ **CRITICAL THINKING**

1. ***Interpreting*** What may underground nuclear testing reveal about North Korea's intentions?
2. ***Making Inferences*** Why might North Korea want to hide its nuclear development?

G1 Critical Thinking Skills

Identifying Cause and Effect Have students note the role that geography has played in Korea's history. Display a political map of the region. **Ask:** How has Korea's geographic location affected its relations with other countries? *(Possible answer: Korea's close proximity to Japan led to its annexation by Japan and Japan's resulting influence over Korea. The neighboring countries of Russia and China also impacted Korea's history.)* AL **Logical/Mathematical, Visual/Spatial**

G2 Critical Thinking Skills

Understanding Relationships Among Events Have students read the information about Korea's separation. **Ask:** What event led to the division of Korea? *(The Communist Soviet Union set up a government in North Korea after World War II.)* What event led to the Korean War? *(North Korean forces invaded South Korea.)* What role did the United States play in the Korean War? *(U.S. and UN forces supported South Korea and continue to do so.)* Lead a discussion about the reasons that certain countries support or become allies with others. **Ask:** Why do you think the Soviet Union initially supported North Korea? *(Possible answer: The two countries were likely aligned politically.)* **Logical/Mathematical, Verbal/Linguistic**

T Technology Skills

Diagramming Have students work in pairs to learn more about the governments of North Korea and South Korea. After doing additional online research, have partners create a Venn diagram showing the similarities and differences of each country's government structure. Tell students to keep their diagrams in mind as they learn more about South Korea's relations with the global community and North Korea's isolation from it. AL **Visual/Spatial**

INTERACTIVE IMAGE

North Korea's Nuclear Program

Analyzing Visuals Have students examine the interactive image of North Korean soldiers gathered in P'yŏngyang that explains the development of the country's nuclear program. BL **Verbal/Linguistic**

ANSWERS, p. 731

CRITICAL THINKING

1. Nuclear testing may reveal that North Korea plans to violate international agreements and may be preparing to invade South Korea.
2. North Korea may want to hide that it has nuclear capabilities as this violates international agreements and may cause other countries to take military or economic action against it.

Human Geography of North Korea and South Korea

C Critical Thinking Skills

Evaluating Primary Sources Have students read the primary source about the Korean War. **Ask:** **Why do you think the Communist invasion of southern Korea was not a "surprise"?** *(Possible answer: Tensions between northern and southern Korea had been building for some time after the Soviet Union set up a government in northern Korea.)* **What can you infer about the role of the UN in the Korean War based on Jaisohn's letter and the war's outcome?** *(Answers may vary, but students should infer that the UN had limited control over the Communist forces, as the war's outcome resulted in Korea's formal division.)* BL **Logical/Mathematical**

W Writing Skills

Informative/Explanatory Discuss with students how the actions of one country can ultimately have a ripple effect and impact the actions of others. Have students write an informative essay that summarizes the current relationship between North Korea and South Korea, discussing the effects of specific events and conducting online research as needed. Challenge students to write a concluding statement in which they predict whether relations between the two countries will improve or deteriorate over the next few years. Remind students to provide supporting evidence to back up their claims. BL **Verbal/Linguistic**

Making Connections

After volunteers share their essays with the class, discuss the role that the global community has in enforcing international law and assisting other countries to preserve human rights or instill democracy. Use a current story in the news to launch a discussion, such as the UN's role in the fate of the nine North Korean defectors in 2013.

ANSWERS, p. 732

READING PROGRESS CHECK In 2010, North Korea used a submarine to sink a South Korean warship, killing 46 South Korean sailors.

DBQ The author hoped that the Communists would be driven out of Korean territory and that northern and southern Korea would be unified under one competent leader.

CRITICAL THINKING

1. The physical location of China to the north and Japan to the south made Korea a target for invasion by these countries.
2. Korea was annexed by Japan, becoming first a protectorate and later a colony.

Analyzing PRIMARY SOURCES (CCSS)

The Korean War

C "The invasion of Southern Korea by the Reds [Communists] was not altogether a surprise but it was shocking to us all just the same....I hope the UN forces will drive the Reds beyond the Korean territory and that they will unify the Korean Government under a competent person."

—Philip Jaisohn, letter dated September 14, 1950, to U.S. Lieutenant General John R. Hodge

DBQ ***IDENTIFYING CENTRAL ISSUES*** What did the author hope would be accomplished by the Korean War? RH.9–10.2

Since 1987, South Korea's government has had a structure like that of the United States. Power is balanced among legislative, executive, and judicial branches. South Korea has a multiparty system, although two parties usually dominate.

W In the early twenty-first century, relations between North Korea and South Korea seemed to improve. South Korean industrial firms opened plants in Kaesong, North Korea. The plants employed people from both countries. Leaders of both countries met in 2000 and in 2007. In 2010 hundreds of South Koreans crossed the border to meet North Korean relatives for the first time since the division.

There were also setbacks in relations, however. In December 2007 South Korea elected a conservative president. His policies offended North Korea, and North Korea closed the Kaesong facility in 2009 and 2013. In 2010 a North Korean submarine sank a South Korean warship, killing 46 sailors. In 2012 North Korea conducted two rocket-test fires in violation of international agreements. A successful underground nuclear test was carried out by North Korea in 2013. The United Nations and many countries around the world condemned the test. It also strained relations between North Korea and China, its closest ally.

READING PROGRESS CHECK

Explaining What 2010 incident increased distrust of North Korea by South Koreans?

Population Patterns

GUIDING QUESTION *How do settlement patterns and density differ in the two countries?*

Almost all of those who live on the Korean Peninsula can trace their heritage to China and Central Asia. The people all share a common Korean **ethnicity**. The peninsula is one of the most ethnically homogeneous regions in the world. The number of foreigners—mostly from Japan, the United States, and China—in South Korea is growing, especially in major urban areas.

TIME LINE

FOCUS of Rival Interests

Although often troubled by its larger neighbors China and Japan, Korea maintained political and cultural independence for more than a thousand years.

CRITICAL THINKING

1. ***Explaining*** How did geography play a role in the relationship between Korea, China, and Japan?
2. ***Analyzing*** How did Korea lose its independence in the early twentieth century?

300 B.C.

300 B.C. First Korean kingdom, Choson, emerges in northern Korean Peninsula

108 B.C. China conquers Choson and turns it into a Chinese colony.

668 Kingdom of Silla defeats rival kingdoms, uniting entire Korean Peninsula

935 Kingdom of Koryo overthrows Silla; takes control of Korean Peninsula

DEA Picture Library/age fotostock

networks Online Teaching Options

INTERACTIVE WHITEBOARD ACTIVITY

Shared History, Divided Growth

Analyzing Have students use this interactive whiteboard activity to drag descriptions of historic events or cultural characteristics into boxes labeled Early Korea, North Korea, and South Korea and to show how the countries have changed from their shared histories to new directions today. BL **Verbal/Linguistic**

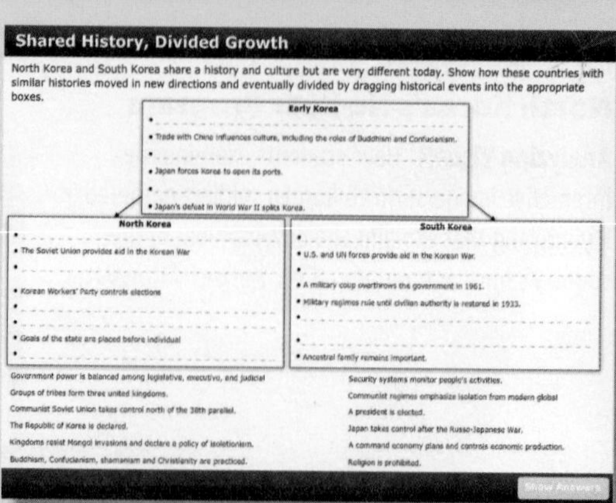

The countries' populations have had different growth rates. North Korea's population more than doubled between 1953 and 1993. The estimated 2011 population of North Korea was less than half that of South Korea's nearly 50 million. Food shortages, adequate health services, and living standards have been problems. Most of the rural population lives in the coastal lowlands and river valleys. Inland areas are very sparsely settled due to mountains and lack of arable land. Government expansion of industry has relocated people from rural to urban areas. P'yŏngyang is the largest city and capital of North Korea.

South Korea's population also doubled in the second half of the twentieth century. In the twenty-first century, although the birthrate has fallen, population density is high in urban areas. About 80 percent of South Korea's population is urban. Roughly half of that population lives in the country's seven largest cities. The capital city of Seoul is by far the largest city. Satellite cities encircle Seoul to form an extremely large urban region. These satellite cities include Anyang, Songnam, Suwŏn, Inch'ŏn, and Puch'on.

ethnicity relating to races or large groups of people classed according to common traits and customs

READING PROGRESS CHECK

Summarizing Describe the changes to South Korea's population since the 1950s.

Society and Culture Today

GUIDING QUESTION *What are the major influences on the culture and art in each country?*

People of both countries speak Korean. They use the alphabet known as hangul in South Korea and as *Choson muntcha* in North Korea. The heritage of Buddhism, Confucianism, shamanism, and Christianity are important in South Korea. North Korea is atheist, and religion is not permitted. Despite their shared ethnicity, the political divisions between the two countries have created **cultural divergence**, or contrasts in the development of culture.

cultural divergence a separation of people or societies, with regard to beliefs, values, and customs, due to a division under different political systems

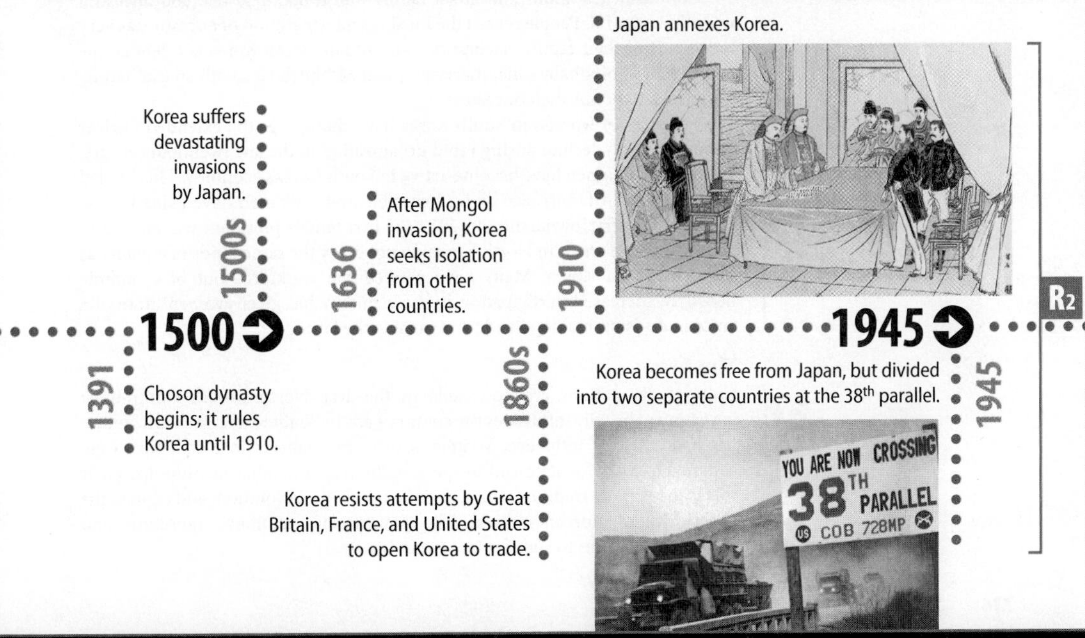

1391
Choson dynasty begins; it rules Korea until 1910.
1500s
Korea suffers devastating invasions by Japan.
1500
1636
After Mongol invasion, Korea seeks isolation from other countries.
1860s
Korea resists attempts by Great Britain, France, and United States to open Korea to trade.
1910
Japan annexes Korea.
1945
Korea becomes free from Japan, but divided into two separate countries at the 38th parallel.
1945
YOU ARE NOW CROSSING
38TH PARALLEL
COB 728MP

CHAPTER 30, Lesson 2
Human Geography of North Korea and South Korea

T Technology Skills

Changing Continuity of Groups Organize students into small groups and have each group choose a major city in either North Korea or South Korea. Students may choose one of the cities discussed in the text or another major city in the region or consider assigning a city to each group to avoid duplication. Then have groups conduct online research to identify recent population patterns in their city. Students should compile information that identifies the reasons for the population changes as well as the economic and social impacts of those changes. Have students present their findings to the class in a report that includes visuals to support the information. Challenge students to create charts or graphs comparing the shifts in population in their city over several years.

BL Interpersonal, Logical/Mathematical

R1 Reading Skills

Identifying Trends Discuss the term *cultural divergence* with students. Have students read the definition of the term in the side column of this page to be sure they understand the concept. Ask a volunteer to paraphrase the definition in his or her own words. **Ask: What cultural differences do you think have been caused by the cultural divergence between North Korea and South Korea?** *(Student answers may vary, but should include religious differences causing many of the cultural divergences.)* **AL Verbal/Linguistic**

R2 Reading Skills

Summarizing Have students analyze the time line and summarize the information about Korea's quest for independence. Guide students to understand the significance of trade as it relates to Korea's relations with other countries.

ELL Verbal/Linguistic, Visual/Spatial

INTERACTIVE TIME LINE

Focus of Rival Interests

Examining Have students examine the time line that displays how Korea maintained political and cultural independence for more than a thousand years.

AL Visual/Spatial, Verbal/Linguistic

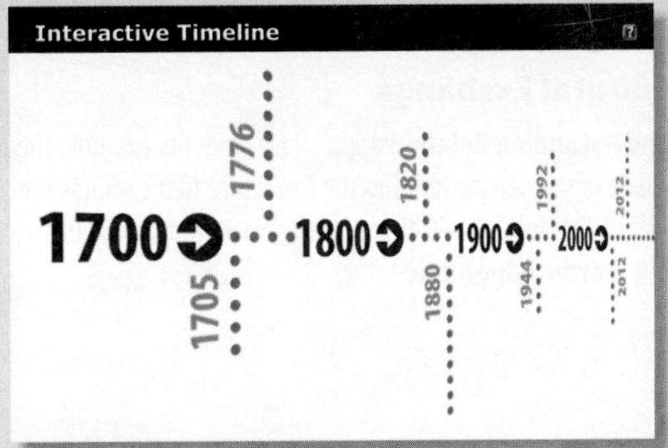

Interactive Timeline
1700
1705
1776
1800
1820
1880
1900
1944
1992
2000
2012

ANSWERS, p. 733

READING PROGRESS CHECK South Korea's population has more than doubled since the 1950s and the government has expanded industry by relocating rural populations to urban areas.

C Critical Thinking Skills

Defending Discuss the differences between North Korea's health care system and that of South Korea. **Ask: If you were a government official in North Korea, how would you defend the medical care for citizens?** *(Student answers may vary, but should include that the medical care is free and provided by the government with at least one clinic in every village.)* **If you were a North Korean citizen, what might you think about medical care?** *(Possible answer: The lack of quality medical care due to shortages of doctors and medical equipment would probably be felt, but not openly criticized.)* **AL Verbal/Linguistic**

W Writing Skills

Narrative Have students review the information in the text about family life and the status of women in South Korea and North Korea. Have students write a scene about a day in the life of a family living in either country. Tell students to use clues from the text to develop characters for their skits. Students may wish to conduct research from reliable sources to provide realistic situations for their characters. Allow time for students to write a script, rehearse, and perform their scenes for the class. Guide a class discussion about the similarities and differences in women's rights in North Korea versus South Korea. **BL Kinesthetic, Verbal/Linguistic**

T Technology Skills

Researching Have students conduct research to identify the major influences on art in both North Korea and South Korea. Tell students to present their findings to the class in a multimedia presentation that includes visuals to support the information. Encourage students to provide examples of artwork from each country. **Visual/Spatial**

C

While North Korea and South Korea share similar cultural traits, there are also major differences between them. Government-provided medical care is free in North Korea. There is at least one clinic in every village. However, there are shortages of physicians and equipment. Most people in South Korea have medical insurance. There, the basic health care needs of the citizens are generally met. The life expectancy at birth for North Korean males was 61.2 years in 2009; for females it was 66.5 years. In South Korea, life expectancy at birth for males in 2008 was 76.5 years; for females it was 83.3 years.

Both countries value education. In North Korea, students receive a free and compulsory education for 11 years, starting with a year of preschool. Some older students are required to work while they are in school. The emphasis of all education is on science and technology. Institutions of higher education offer an additional two to six years of education. The most important institution of higher education is Kim Il-Sung University in P'yŏngyang.

Nine years of primary and middle school are compulsory for South Koreans. Nearly all who graduate from middle school go to high school or technical school. About 80 percent of high school graduates continue their education at a college or university. High school students undergo strenuous preparation for the highly competitive entrance exams to top universities. Most of the prestigious universities are in Seoul. In the twenty-first century, more and more South Koreans have pursued higher education abroad, with many studying in the United States.

Family and the Status of Women

After World War II, the occupying Soviets destroyed the lineage records of North Koreans. Since awareness of ancestry is an important component of Confucian practice, the fabric of Korean tradition was destroyed in that country. People are encouraged to spend their leisure time in activities that support the communist state. An extensive internal security apparatus monitors people's activities. The Korean Central News Agency censors newspapers. Government controls radio and television broadcasts. Internet is restricted to a few people, although illegal cell phone and Internet connections are more common in recent years.

Confucian traditions still affect family life in South Korea, and ancestral worship is central. People regard the most recent generation of ancestors as very much part of their family celebrations and rituals. South Koreans celebrate the first 100 days of a baby's life, marriages, and 61st birthdays with special family gatherings to honor their ancestors.

W

The roles of women in South Korea have changed as the extended nuclear family began to decline during rapid urbanization in the late twentieth century. Increasingly, women have become active in South Korea's economy. This has led to a decrease in family size and a lower birthrate. Women have gained equal rights in property ownership. In 2012 the first female president was elected in South Korea. Women in North Korea do not enjoy the same kinds of equality as those in South Korea. Many have entered the workforce out of economic necessity. Increased participation in the economy has given women more of a voice in decision making inside and outside the family.

The Arts

Cultural distinctions are noticeable in the arts. North Korea's Communist government heavily influences the country's art. In South Korea, Western culture has had a strong influence. Writers, artists, and dancers in North Korea are assigned to work for state-run theaters, orchestras, and other institutions. Their role is to promote traditional arts, commemorate the revolution, and express the superiority of Korean culture. The government maintains museums and archaeological sites to support its communist goals.

734

networks Online Teaching Options

INTERACTIVE IMAGE

Cultural Exchange

Understanding Relationships Have students examine the image of women performing the Fan Dance that explains the visit of the New York Philharmonic to North Korea in 2008. **AL Verbal/Linguistic**

These North Korean women are performing a traditional fan dance.

◀ **CRITICAL THINKING**

1. ***Analyzing*** Why do you suppose the North Korean government supports traditional dance?
2. ***Comparing and Contrasting*** How are the goals of art similar and different in the two Koreas?

Mark Ralston/AFP/Getty Images

In South Korea, dancers, singers, and musicians preserve traditions. Dances with masked dancers and folk songs are still performed. Symphony orchestras, modern theater, rock concerts, and art galleries are also enjoyed by South Koreans. **W**

✓ **READING PROGRESS CHECK**

Evaluating What are advantages of North Korea's health care system?

Economic Activities

GUIDING QUESTION *What industries have grown in importance in North Korea and South Korea?*

North Korea has a command economy in which the state plans and controls all economic production. Today, the economy's main industries produce metal products, machinery, military equipment, and chemicals. In its initial years, the focus was on development of heavy industry. Later it worked to improve technology and infrastructure. It was not until the 1970s and 1980s that North Korea's government began to pay attention to the production of agricultural products and consumer goods. **R**

In the 1990s, a series of natural disasters occurred. These included floods and drought, which contributed to the problems of widespread starvation and malnutrition originally caused by government mismanagement. Subsequently, the North Korean government's highest priority has been to solve what it calls its "food problem." 

Since the 1960s, South Korea has transformed itself from one of the world's poorest states to a highly industrialized society. Government and business

Human Geography of North Korea and South Korea

W Writing Skills

Argument Have students write an argumentative paragraph defending or refuting the following statement: *It is important to a country's national heritage to preserve its art forms.* If students choose to refute the statement, have them provide reasons why they think preserving a country's art forms should not be a priority. Remind all students to support their claims with evidence. **Verbal/Linguistic**

R Reading Skills

Defining Have students read the Guiding Question. Then read aloud the first sentence under the head *Economic Activities.* Ask a volunteer to explain the way a command economy works, providing corrective guidance as needed. *(A command economy is an economic system that is controlled by a central authority or government.)* **Ask:** **Aside from North Korea, what is another example of a country that has a command economy?** *(Students' answers may vary, but they could cite Cuba, China, the former Soviet Union, or Iran.)* Discuss what these countries have in common with North Korea. **BL** **Logical/Mathematical**

T Technology Skills

Changing Continuity in Economics Have students read the information about North Korea's "food problem." Guide a discussion about what life must be like for the majority of citizens in North Korea. Have students conduct research to identify specific examples of how mismanagement by the North Korean government led to widespread starvation and malnutrition for many of North Korea's citizens. Have students present their findings to the class. **BL** **Visual/Spatial**

VIDEO

South Korea as an Economic Power

Making Connections Have students watch this video to learn how South Korea has become a modern, industrialized country in a short amount of time. **Verbal/Linguistic**

ANSWERS, p. 735

✓ **READING PROGRESS CHECK** The advantages of North Korean medical care is that it is provided for free from the government and there is at least one clinic in every village.

CRITICAL THINKING

1. The North Korean government promotes traditional dance as a way of expressing the superiority of Korean culture and to keep out Western influences in the arts.
2. Both North Korea and South Korea support the goal of preserving the traditional arts, but South Korea also enjoys and encourages art, music, and dance from other cultures.

CHAPTER 30, Lesson 2

Human Geography of North Korea and South Korea

V Visual Skills

Creating Charts Have students create a chart showing the events that led to the economic transformation in South Korea. Ask students to identify how South Korea's population has been impacted by the shift to an industrialized society. **Visual/Spatial**

C Critical Thinking Skills

Evaluating Ask a student what the term *self-reliance* means. *(to be independent and not have to rely on someone or something else)* Discuss the meaning of the term as it relates to North Korea's economy. **Ask: What are the advantages and disadvantages of a country striving to be economically self-reliant?** *(Advantage: not having to rely on another country; Disadvantage: if a country lacks resources, being self-reliant could present hardships, such as North Korea's "food problem")* **Verbal/Linguistic**

CLOSE & REFLECT

Summarizing Have students write a summarizing paragraph about the economic, cultural, and political differences between North Korea and South Korea.

ANSWERS, p. 736

READING PROGRESS CHECK Japan is a major trading partner with both North Korea and South Korea.

CRITICAL THINKING

1. Exports allow South Korea's economy to grow and expand as well as providing the needed funds to import the raw materials it requires to continue exporting high-value goods.
2. North Korea's goal of economic self-reliance failed due to natural disasters such as drought and floods as well as a failure to pay attention to agriculture and consumer goods.

These workers at a South Korean aircraft factory are building a helicopter. The same factory hopes to start constructing aircraft for the U.S. Air Force.

▲ **CRITICAL THINKING**

1. ***Making Connections*** Why are exports so important to South Korea's economy?
2. ***Drawing Conclusions*** Why did North Korea's goal of economic self-reliance fail?

leaders developed a strategy focused on exports. They targeted specific industries for development, beginning with textiles and light manufacturing, and then moving to heavy industries such as iron, steel, chemicals, ship building, and automobiles. Manufacturing occurs in the Seoul region. Heavy industry is located in the south with access to seaports. High-tech industries, such as aerospace, electronics, and information technology, have thrived. Industries with global consumers, including smart phones, computers, and tablets, are a specialty.

Since the 1950s, the government of North Korea has stressed self-reliance as a goal in its economic planning. Nonetheless, it had trade relations with the Soviet Union and its Eastern European satellites, as well as with China. The severe economic hardships of the 1990s forced North Korea to accept foreign aid, seek foreign investment, and expand its range of trade partners. Now North Korea exports live animals and agricultural products, textiles and apparel, machinery, and mineral fuels and lubricants. It imports beverages, food and other agricultural products, mineral fuels, machinery, and textiles. Its major trading partners include China, South Korea, Russia, Japan, and Thailand.

Exports have been important to South Korea's economic growth. Many industries produce goods such as machinery, electronics, textiles, automobiles, and footwear for export around the world. South Korea's trade partners include the United States, Japan, the European Union, and the countries of Southeast Asia. South Korea imports raw materials, such as textile fibers, metal ores, and mineral fuels. The raw materials are converted into high-value exports known for their high quality.

READING PROGRESS CHECK

Identifying Which country is a major trading partner with both countries?

LESSON 2 REVIEW

Reviewing Vocabulary (Tier Three Words)

1. ***Understanding Relationships*** Write a paragraph discussing the reasons for the cultural divergence of North Korea and South Korea. WHST.9–10.4

Using Your Notes

2. ***Listing*** Use your graphic organizer on the human geography of North Korea and South Korea to describe how physical and human systems have shaped these two countries.

Answering the Guiding Questions

3. ***Making Connections*** How has the decision to divide the Korean Peninsula into North Korea and South Korea affected the development of each country?
4. ***Contrasting*** How do settlement patterns and density differ in the two countries?
5. ***Comparing and Contrasting*** What are the major influences on the culture and art in each country?
6. ***Identifying*** What industries have grown in importance in North Korea and South Korea?

Writing Activity

7. ***Informative/Explanatory*** In a paragraph, explain how the Kaesong facility might have strengthened the relationship between the two Koreas had it continued to operate. WHST.9–10.2

736

SeongJoon Cho/Bloomberg/Getty Images

LESSON 2 REVIEW ANSWERS

Reviewing Vocabulary

1. Paragraphs will vary but should include factors of culture divergence such as: communist government of North Korea and the democratic government of South Korea; economic differences with a command economy in North Korea and a highly industrialized society in South Korea.

Using Your Notes

2. Descriptions will differ but should be strongly supported with information from the lesson, including how physical systems shape settlement with coastal regions and river valleys being the most densely populated areas of North Korea and South Korea's population being highly urban.

Answering the Guiding Questions

3. South Korea became a republic with many Western influences and support from the U.S., leading it to become highly industrialized with one of the best economies in Asia. North Korea has remained under communist control with a command economy where the government dictates what goods to produce, leading to many economic challenges.
4. Coastal regions and river valleys are the most densely populated areas of North Korea with the mountainous interior having low population density due to a lack of arable land. South Korea's population is 80 percent urban with over half of the population spread among the country's seven largest cities.
5. The Communist government of North Korea influences the art to be traditional and commemorate the revolution, whereas traditions as well as modern and Western influences are found in the art of South Korea.
6. High-tech industries have grown in importance in South Korea and the agriculture industry has become important to North Korea.

Writing Activity

7. Paragraphs will vary but should be strongly supported with information from the lesson. Answers could include improved communication, more funds and technology for North Korea, and more raw materials and workers for South Korea.

networks

There's More Online!

- **CHART** South Korean Exports
- **IMAGE** Drift-Net Fishing
- **INFOGRAPHIC** Facing Empty Oceans
- **INTERACTIVE SELF-CHECK QUIZ**
- **VIDEO** People and Their Environment: North Korea and South Korea

LESSON 3

People and Their Environment: North Korea and South Korea

ESSENTIAL QUESTION • *How do physical systems and human systems shape a place?*

Reading **HELPDESK** CCSS

Academic Vocabulary (Tier Two Words)
- **impact**
- **affect**

Content Vocabulary (Tier Three Words)
- **deforestation**
- **drift-net fishing**
- **fertilizer**

TAKING NOTES: ***Key Ideas and Details***

IDENTIFYING CAUSE AND EFFECT
As you read about the human geography of the Korean Peninsula, use a graphic organizer like the one below to identify causes of environmental problems.

Managing Resources	
Feature	Damage
Air	
Water	
Forests	
Fish	

It Matters Because

The environments of North Korea and South Korea are affected by the air quality of other countries. The actions of North Koreans and South Koreans, in turn, affect their own air and water, as well the air and water of other countries. **R**

Managing Resources

GUIDING QUESTION *What resources are at risk on the Korean Peninsula?*

Air pollution is a serious problem, especially in South Korea's cities. Because 80 percent of the population lives in cities, this problem has an **impact** on millions of people. Dust and pollutants that are carried by the winds from China and Mongolia are a big source of the problem. Pollutants from automobiles and industries also contribute to the poor air quality. A 2012 study found that South Korea had more pollutants in its air than either Japan or the United States. **V**

South Korea's large cities also have problems with sewage and sanitation. Sanitation systems built after the Korean War are failing because of the impact of the country's rapid urbanization. Sanitation companies are unable to keep up with and properly dispose of the increasing amount of waste materials. Instead, they pump untreated sewage directly into the Pacific Ocean. Sewer systems also overflow and pollute local rivers and streams. Pollution of the seas and other bodies of water has **affected** fish supplies.

Population density has also had a negative effect on garbage disposal and sanitation systems in Seoul and other South Korean cities. These cities have many rules for garbage disposal and recycling, but they are not enforced or followed. On some streets, uncollected garbage is left in stacks.

North Korea also continues to experience its own problems with water and air pollution. A 2004 report found that almost 30,000 cubic meters, or about 7,925 gallons, of industrial wastewater was being poured every day into the Taedong River. This river flows through the middle of **C**

ENGAGE

R Reading Skills

Setting a Purpose Tell students to create a K-W-L chart in which they list what they know about the people and environment of North Korea and South Korea in the first column and what they want to know in the middle column. After students work through the lesson, have them go back to their charts and fill in what they learned in the third column. **AL** **Visual/Spatial**

TEACH & ASSESS

V Visual Skills

Expressing To reinforce students' understanding of air pollution's widespread impact, have them create a flowchart or illustration that shows how air pollution has an impact on different regions. **Ask:** **What is the main source of air pollution in South Korea's cities?** *(dust and pollutants carried by winds from China and Mongolia)* **How do you think this impacts relations among countries in the region?** *(It likely has a negative impact and strains relations between countries that are affected by air pollution and those that are causing it.)* **AL** **Visual/Spatial**

C Critical Thinking Skills

Making Predictions Have students read the information about North Korea's water and air pollution problems. **Ask:** **What do you predict will happen to the Taedong River over time?** *(Student answers may vary, but should include that the river will become dangerously polluted over time, harming the river's ecosystems. People who live near the river could also be threatened if the industrial wastewater seeps into groundwater used for drinking.)* **Naturalist**

ANSWERS, p. 737

TAKING NOTES: Air: Pollutants and dust carried by winds from China and Mongolia are a large source of air pollution. Cars and industry contribute to the problem. North Korea uses coal for power and heat, which causes air pollution and acid rain. **Water:** Sanitation and sewage systems are failing in South Korea, causing raw sewage to be pumped directly into the ocean and also overflow into local rivers and streams. North Korea has about 7,925 gallons of industrial wastewater dumped daily into the Taedong River. **Forests:** Deforestation has destroyed almost all the forests on the Korean Peninsula. Trees are cut for fuel for heating and cooking, and land is cleared for farming and development. Deforestation has led to soil erosion, flooding, and loss of habitat for many animals. **Fish:** Drift-net fishing is used to catch fish and squid, but about 80 percent of what is caught is other sea life, causing a threat to the marine ecosystem by killing numerous dolphins, whales, turtles, and birds.

networks ***Online Teaching Options***

INTERACTIVE BELLRINGER

Fog and Aerosol Plume over the Yellow Sea

Analyzing Visuals Use the introductory text and the satellite image of fog and an aerosol plume over the Yellow Sea to identify factors threatening resources on the Korean Peninsula today. Have students form small groups to discuss each question. Ask each group to write agreed-upon answers to the questions. Then review the answers to the first two questions as a class. Ask each group to share their answers for the first two questions. Answer the third question in a class discussion. **ELL** **Interpersonal, Visual/Spatial**

Fog and Aerosol Plume over Yellow Sea

In March 2012, a satellite captured fog and an aerosol plume, most likely haze from industrial areas in China, over the Yellow Sea.

1. The fog and plume covered an area stretching from the Korea Bay to what city in China?

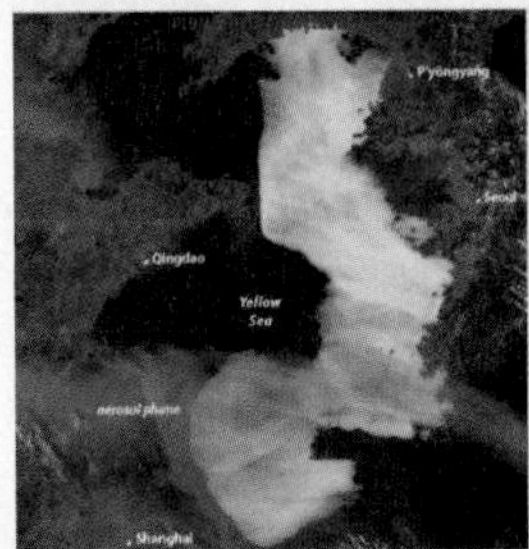

click for answer

Auto-Run Click Through Previous 1 of 3 Next

C Critical Thinking Skills

Problem Solving Have students create a two-column chart labeled *Problem* and *Solution.* Tell students that as they read the *Human Impact* section, to write each problem in the *Problem* column. Then have students use information in the text and additional online research to identify a possible solution to each problem and write it in the *Solution* column. Ask volunteers to present their problem-solution charts to the class, guiding a discussion about the viability of each solution. **Ask: What human activity has negatively impacted forests on the Korean Peninsula? Explain the effects.** *(Deforestation; nearly all forests are gone, habitats and animal species have vanished)* AL **Visual/Spatial**

T Technology Skills

Constructing Arguments After students examine the illustration, discuss South Korea's fishing industry. **Ask: Why is the topic of placing limits on overfishing so important to people in South Korea?** *(South Korea is the 12th largest fishery producer in the world. The industry would likely feel the economic impact of limits on overfishing.)* Tell students they will conduct research to prepare for a classroom debate. Organize students into small groups and have each group gather information and supporting evidence to defend or challenge by-catch methods and the use of FADs. In preparing their debates, students should consider the economic impact of placing limits on overfishing in South Korea. Students should also consider the perspective of people who rely on the fishing industry for their income. After students have prepared their arguments, moderate a classroom debate, reminding students to listen respectfully to each speaker. BL **Intrapersonal, Verbal/Linguistic**

impact a significant or major effect

affect to produce an effect upon

North Korea's most densely populated city and its capital, P'yŏngyang. In North Korea, too, coal is used to heat most homes and provides power for most industries. Coal burning is a major cause of air pollution and acid rain.

READING PROGRESS CHECK

Identifying What are two effects of pollution on natural resources in the Koreas?

Human Impact

GUIDING QUESTION *What human activities have affected the physical environment of North Korea and South Korea?*

deforestation the loss or destruction of forests, mainly from logging or farming

Deforestation has affected the entire Korean Peninsula. Forests once covered about two-thirds of South Korea and most of the western lowlands of North Korea. These forests are now nearly gone due to deforestation. Trees are cut for fuel for heating and cooking. Additionally, much land is also cleared

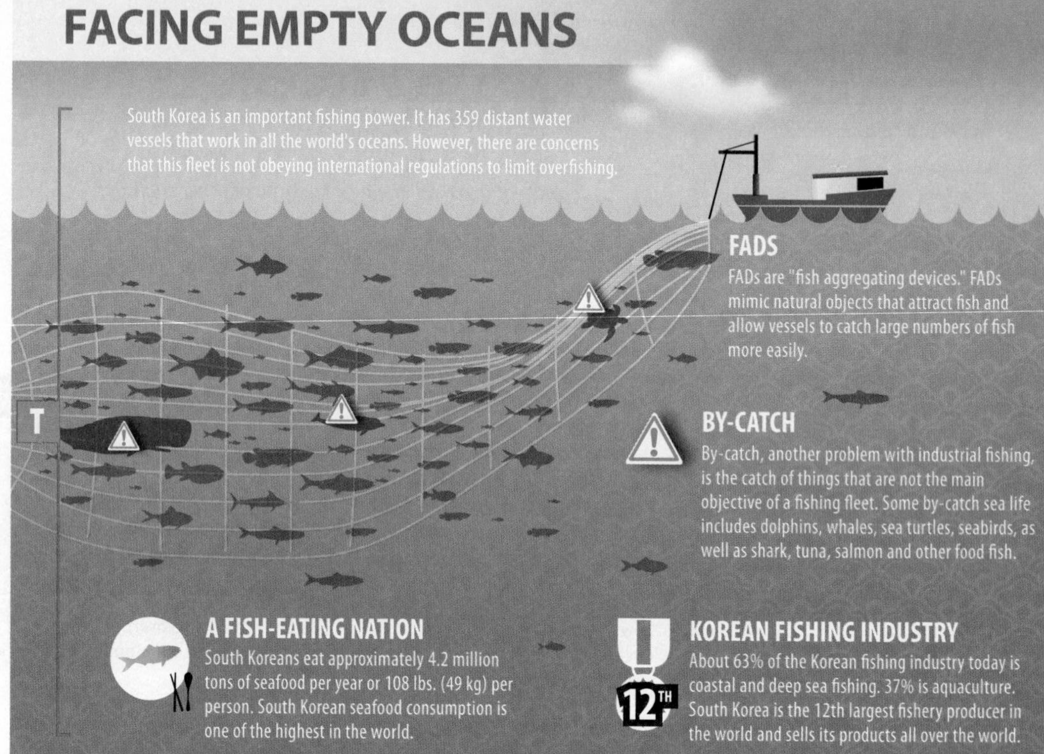

FACING EMPTY OCEANS
South Korea is an important fishing power. It has 359 distant water vessels that work in all the world's oceans. However, there are concerns that this fleet is not obeying international regulations to limit overfishing.
FADS
FADs are "fish aggregating devices." FADs mimic natural objects that attract fish and allow vessels to catch large numbers of fish more easily.
T
BY-CATCH
By-catch, another problem with industrial fishing, is the catch of things that are not the main objective of a fishing fleet. Some by-catch sea life includes dolphins, whales, sea turtles, seabirds, as well as shark, tuna, salmon and other food fish.
A FISH-EATING NATION
South Koreans eat approximately 4.2 million tons of seafood per year or 108 lbs. (49 kg) per person. South Korean seafood consumption is one of the highest in the world.
KOREAN FISHING INDUSTRY
About 63% of the Korean fishing industry today is coastal and deep sea fishing. 37% is aquaculture. South Korea is the 12th largest fishery producer in the world and sells its products all over the world.
12TH

Techniques commonly used by the South Korean fishing industry threaten the sustainability of fish populations in the region.

▲ **CRITICAL THINKING**

1. ***Making Predictions*** What could happen to South Korea's fishing industry if fishing practices are not changed?
2. ***Constructing a Thesis*** Do you think fish aggregating devices and drift-net fishing should be banned? Why or why not?

networks Online Teaching Options

INTERACTIVE INFOGRAPHIC

Facing Empty Oceans

Examining Have students examine this interactive infographic that explores the techniques commonly used by the South Korean fishing industry that threaten the sustainability of fish populations in the region. BL **Verbal/Linguistic**

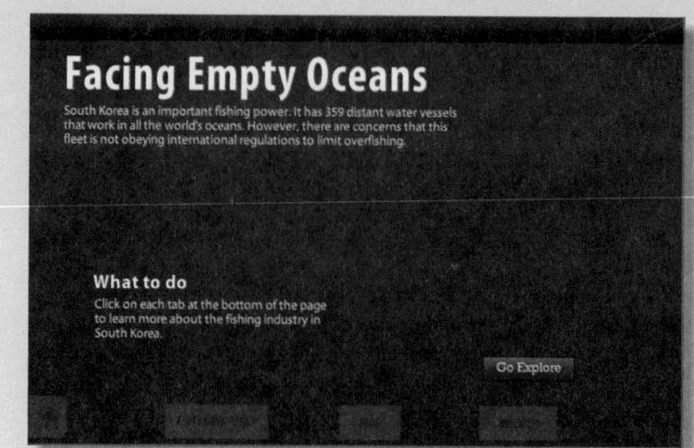

ANSWERS, p. 738

READING PROGRESS CHECK Answers could include: water pollution not only affects drinking water but kills fish and other marine life in the oceans and rivers; pollution from industry, cars, burning of coal, and other countries cause acid rain and other hazardous air pollution.

CRITICAL THINKING

1. If unsustainable fishing practices continue, the fishing industry will be diminished or destroyed.
2. Answers will vary but could include that aggregating devices and drift-net fishing enable the fishing industry to catch large numbers of fish. However, these practices also kill large amounts of other sea life. Additionally, the large numbers of fish being caught are not able to be replenished, resulting in overfishing of waters.

for cultivation and settlement as the population density increases in forested areas. The resulting loss of habitat has caused a decrease in the populations of many animals that once lived on the peninsula.

Deforestation has several terrible effects. For example, deforestation has led to soil erosion in North Korea. Trees and bushes hold soil in place during the heavy seasonal rains. Without them, soil washes down the steep hillsides of the mountainous terrain. This depletes nutrients that keep the soil healthy and make the land fertile for raising crops. Soil loss makes growing food more of a challenge for a country with ongoing food shortages.

Deforestation also leads to flooding. Aside from the direct loss of lives and property that floods can cause, flooding can also pollute drinking water. This occurs when a buildup of mud and debris is washed into the water supply. In 2012 severe floods polluted drinking water supplies in parts of North Korea. As a result, an estimated 50,000 families were left without potable, or drinkable, water.

C The isolation and secrecy of the North Korean government make it difficult to monitor the environmental problems facing the country. A 2004 report by the United Nations Environment Programme makes it clear that the country faces multiple environmental problems. Data from 2012 indicate that the average temperature in North Korea had increased by almost 2°C as a result of deforestation. During this period, the world average temperature increase was only about 0.7°C.

While Japan has the world's largest fleet of drift-net fishing vessels, South Korea and Taiwan also have sizable drift-net operations. Environmentalists, the United States Coast Guard, and the Canadian Department of Fisheries and Wildlife are concerned about **drift-net fishing**, or fishing with huge nets. Drift-net fishing is condemned by many countries because it is so destructive. Sometimes called "walls of death," the huge nets are suspended vertically in the ocean and allowed to drift with the currents. Some of these nets are as much as 37 miles (60 km) long.

They are intended to trap squid and fish. However, sea mammals, such as dolphins, porpoises and whales, also die in these nets. So do turtles and birds. Animals like these die in such numbers that the nets are considered a threat to the marine ecosystem. It is estimated that about 80 percent of the animals caught in the nets are not even their intended targets.

In 1992 the United Nations created a resolution to end drift-net fishing. At the same time, the Convention for the Conservation of Anadromous Stocks (fish that migrate from salt water to freshwater) in the North Pacific Ocean was formed. The governments of the United States, Canada, Russia, and Japan signed this convention. South Korea agreed to it in 2003. However, there are few resources to monitor compliance with this agreement, and it is not clear that such fishing has declined.

✓ READING PROGRESS CHECK

Hypothesizing What might be the long-term effect of drift-net fishing on the South Korean fishing industry if it is not controlled?

Although unintended, drift-net fishing kills sea life. Several countries continue to practice drift-net fishing even though it violates a United Nations resolution.

▲ CRITICAL THINKING

1. ***Drawing Conclusions*** Do you think South Korea will really stop drift-net fishing while other countries still practice it? Why or why not?
2. ***Identifying Cause and Effect*** Why is drift-net fishing so threatening to the marine ecosystem?

drift-net fishing the use of fishing nets of great length and depth

C Critical Thinking Skills

Identifying Perspectives and Differing Interpretations Launch a class discussion about problems caused by North Korea's isolation and secrecy. **Ask: How might North Korea's perspective about environmental problems differ from that of South Korea?** *(Student answers may vary, but could include that North Korea lacks a system of checks and balances so it may not enforce laws or restrictions pertaining to environmental issues. Due to its isolation and secrecy, North Korea can get away with ignoring policies meant to protect the environment. South Korea is more democratic minded, so it likely fosters a sense of responsibility when dealing with protecting the environment.)* **AL Interpersonal, Naturalist**

Making Connections

Tell students that in addition to South Korea's overfishing problems, Japan has also been criticized for overfishing and unethical fishing practices. The Japanese fishing industry was in the spotlight in 2009 with the release of "The Cove," an Academy Award–winning documentary film about a covert operation to expose questionable fishing practices in a remote cove in Japan. Led by known dolphin trainer Richard O'Barry, a team of activists used hidden cameras to reveal the capture and slaughter of dolphins, many sold for their meat. Critics of O'Barry's film say it unfairly editorializes about the use of dolphins, which are not an endangered species in Japan. However, dolphin meat, which is a delicacy in Japan, contains high levels of mercury.

INTERACTIVE WHITEBOARD ACTIVITY

Human Actions and the Environment

Identifying Have students complete this interactive whiteboard activity. Students drag descriptions of the human actions involved in deforestation, drift-net fishing, and urbanization and their environmental consequences into the appropriate columns of a chart. **AL Verbal/Linguistic**

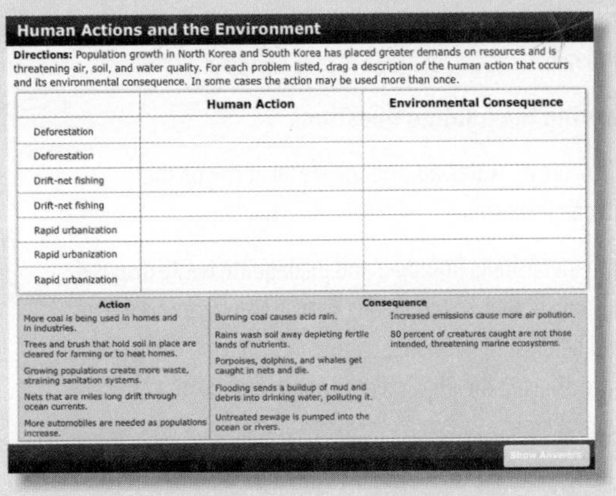

Human Actions and the Environment

Directions: Population growth in North Korea and South Korea has placed greater demands on resources and is threatening air, soil, and water quality. For each problem listed, drag a description of the human action that occurs and its environmental consequence. In some cases the action may be used more than once.

	Human Action	Environmental Consequence
Deforestation		
Deforestation		
Drift-net fishing		
Drift-net fishing		
Rapid urbanization		
Rapid urbanization		
Rapid urbanization		

Action

- More coal is being used in homes and in industries.
- Trees and brush that hold soil in place are cleared for farming or to heat homes.
- Growing populations create more waste, straining sanitation systems.
- Nets that are miles long drift through ocean currents.
- More automobiles are needed as populations increase.

Consequence

- Burning coal causes acid rain.
- Rains wash soil away depleting fertile lands of nutrients.
- Porpoises, dolphins, and whales get caught in nets and die.
- Flooding sends a buildup of mud and debris into drinking water, polluting it.
- Untreated sewage is pumped into the ocean or rivers.
- Increased emissions cause more air pollution.
- 80 percent of creatures caught are not those intended, threatening marine ecosystems.

ANSWERS, p. 739

✓ READING PROGRESS CHECK The South Korean fishing industry could be greatly diminished or destroyed if drift-net fishing isn't controlled as the number of fish could be seriously depleted.

CRITICAL THINKING

1. Answers will vary but could include that South Korea has a vested interest in stopping/not stopping drift-net fishing because of its high consumption of seafood and large fishing industry.
2. Drift-net fishing not only kills many other types of sea life but also catches such large quantities of fish that they are unable to be replenished, resulting in overfished waters.

CHAPTER 30, Lesson 3

People and Their Environment: North Korea and South Korea

W Writing Skills

Informative/Explanatory Organize students into eight small groups and assign each group one of the countries that attended the P'yŏngyang conference. Tell students they will act as scientists who are reviewing North Korea's environment. Using reliable online sources, have groups identify what their assigned country's scientists recommended at the P'yŏngyang conference. Tell students to collaborate to write an informative essay that outlines the suggested plans for restoring North Korea's environment and alleviating its food shortage. Groups may use visuals, such as charts or graphs, to show how their assigned country's response to environmental issues compares with that of other countries. Have groups present their essays to the class. BL **Verbal/Linguistic, Interpersonal**

CLOSE & REFLECT

Problem Solving Have students review the various environmental issues discussed in this lesson. Tell students to choose one issue and brainstorm a possible solution. Have students share their solutions with the class.

ANSWERS, p. 740

READING PROGRESS CHECK Life for North Koreans would improve with deforestation programs because there would be less flooding, soil erosion, and water pollution.

Addressing the Issues

GUIDING QUESTION *How are environmental issues being addressed in North Korea and South Korea?*

In 2012 North Korea invited scientists from eight countries to a conference in P'yŏngyang to review the condition of the country's environment. Scientists found barren landscapes on the brink of collapse, a result of decades of environmental degradation. They developed plans for restoring the environment and increasing food security in North Korea.

Deforestation has reached alarming levels in North Korea. According to one study, North Korea was the third most deforested country in the world, after Nigeria and Indonesia. However, North Korea has also started a series of reforestation programs. Such programs are planned for Kandong province, located outside P'yŏngyang. Other programs intend to reforest the western lower hillsides and eastern highlands.

South Korea, which has succeeded in restoring forests to nearly two-thirds of the country, is also attempting to promote reforestation in North Korea. South Korea's former president, Lee Myung-bak, pledged to send seedlings to North Korea. Many private South Korean citizens have donated trees to North Korea as well. Increasing forest coverage is a good step, but these young forests are very different from the old-growth forests that were cut down. They are much less diverse and offer minimal habitat for animals.

fertilizer a substance, such as manure or a chemical mixture, used to make soil more fertile

The North Korean government has also encouraged the use of **fertilizer** to restore soil nutrients to help the trees grow back healthy. The government has provided fertilizer to farmers. However, there is evidence that, rather than use the fertilizer, farmers are selling it to cover their costs.

South Korea is also working on increasing its energy efficiency. In the twenty-first century, the government announced a plan to change every lightbulb in every public building to energy-efficient LED lights.

An ambitious stimulus package launched in 2009 allocated money to research low-carbon technologies, build high-speed railways, and expand bus lanes. The effort also supports building one million "green" homes and improving the efficiency of one million existing homes. While South Korea has yet to solve all of its environmental problems, the country is making substantial progress.

READING PROGRESS CHECK

Predicting How might an effective reforestation program improve life for North Koreans?

LESSON 3 REVIEW

Reviewing Vocabulary (Tier Three Words)

1. ***Explaining*** Write a paragraph explaining the impact of deforestation on North Korea's agriculture. RH.9–10.4

Using Your Notes

2. ***Identifying Cause and Effect*** Use your graphic organizer on the effects of the Korean Peninsula's environmental problems to write a paragraph about the cause and effect of one type of pollution on the peninsula.

Answering the Guiding Questions

3. ***Evaluating*** What resources are at risk on the Korean Peninsula?
4. ***Analyzing*** What human activities have affected the physical environment of North Korea and South Korea?
5. ***Summarizing*** How are environmental issues being addressed in North Korea and South Korea?

Writing Activity

6. ***Informative/Explanatory*** Use reliable Internet sources to locate an article about environmental issues in North Korea or South Korea over the past year. Write a paragraph summarizing the main points of the article. WHST.9–10.2

740

LESSON 3 REVIEW ANSWERS

Reviewing Vocabulary

1. Paragraphs will differ but should be strongly supported with information from the lesson, including that deforestation causes soil erosion and flooding. As nutrients are removed or washed away from the soil, the land becomes unable to support as many crops. Flooding can also cause a total loss of crops and the soil can lose so many nutrients that it is unable to support any crops.

Using Your Notes

2. Paragraphs will differ but should be strongly supported with information from the lesson. Answers could include lack of or inadequate sewer and sanitation systems and industrial waste, leading to water pollution; deforestation leading to soil erosion and water pollution; industry pollutants, car emissions, burning of coal, and pollution from China and Mongolia, causing serious air pollution and acid rain.

Answering the Guiding Questions

3. Fish, forests, water, air, and soil are all at risk on the Korean Peninsula.
4. Drift-net fishing, improper and inadequate waste disposal, burning of coal, car emissions, industrial waste and smoke, and deforestation for fuel, farmland, and development have affected the physical environment of North Korea and South Korea.
5. South Korea has succeeded in restoring nearly two-thirds of its forests. It is also working on increasing its energy efficiency by changing all lightbulbs to LED lights, building green homes and light rail systems, increasing bus lanes, and improving the efficiency of one million existing homes. North Korea invited scientists from eight countries to a conference to review plans for restoring the environment and increasing food security. It is also encouraging the use of fertilizer to restore soil nutrients.

Writing Activity

6. Summaries will vary depending on the article chosen by the student, but should summarize the main points of an environmental issue in North Korea or South Korea.

CHAPTER 30 Assessment 

Directions: On a separate sheet of paper, answer the questions below. Make sure you read carefully and answer all parts of the questions.

Lesson Review

Lesson 1

1. ***Comparing*** Why do you think the capitals of North Korea and South Korea began as river ports?
2. ***Explaining*** How did the creation of the Demilitarized Zone affect wildlife in the area?
3. ***Drawing Conclusions*** Why does mountainous terrain make livestock production and fishing particularly important on the Korean Peninsula?

Lesson 2

4. ***Summarizing*** How has North Korea's population changed since the middle of the twentieth century?
5. ***Contrasting*** Describe how life expectancy in South Korea differs from life expectancy in North Korea.
6. ***Describing*** What are some methods the North Korean government uses to control free speech and limit individual freedoms?

Lesson 3

7. ***Explaining*** How does deforestation contribute to food shortages in North Korea?
8. ***Identifying Cause and Effect*** What are some problems caused by population density in South Korea's cities?
9. ***Analyzing*** Why do you think South Korea has taken steps to address the problem of deforestation in North Korea?

Critical Thinking

10. ***Making Predictions*** How might reunification on the Korean Peninsula affect the economy of South Korea?
11. ***Hypothesizing*** South Korea has taken steps to improve energy efficiency. How might these steps help improve air quality in urban areas?

21st Century Skills

Use the graph to answer the following questions.

NORTH KOREAN CHILDREN

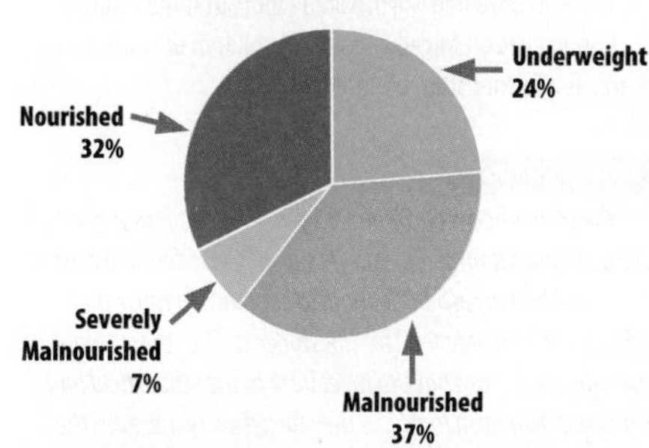

Source: http://han-schneider.org

12. ***Creating and Using Graphs, Charts, Diagrams, and Tables*** According to the circle graph, what percentage of children in North Korea faces problems with nourishment?
13. ***Creating and Using Graphs, Charts, Diagrams, and Tables*** Why do you think the graph includes the percentage of children who are underweight?
14. ***Identifying Perspectives and Differing Interpretations*** Based on the graph, how severe do you think the problem of malnutrition is among North Korean children?

College and Career Readiness

15. ***Problem Solving*** Imagine you have been hired by the United Nations World Food Program to find solutions to the problem of food shortages in North Korea. Use the Internet to research the causes and consequences of the problem. How have natural disasters affected the availability of food in that country? What role has the government played? Write a paragraph outlining steps the North Korean government can take to solve the problem. WHST.9–10.2; WHST.9–10.7

Need Extra Help?

If You've Missed Question	1	2	3	4	5	6	7	8	9	10	11	12	13	14	15
Go to page	728	729	729	733	734	734	739	737	740	735	740	734	734	734	734

CHAPTER 30 Assessment Answers

Lesson Review

Lesson 1

1. The capitals of North Korea and South Korea likely began as river ports because rivers were used to transport goods and people, making port cities areas of commerce and growth.
2. The creation of the DMZ in 1953 inadvertently made habitats for many rare species of animals and birds on the peninsula.
3. Livestock production can take place on land that is unable to be farmed because it is mountainous. Fishing also serves to supplement the food supply as there is little arable land.

Lesson 2

4. North Korea's population has more than doubled since the middle of the twentieth century.
5. Life expectancy in South Korea is much greater than North Korea, with men living on average 15 years longer and women on average living 16 years longer.
6. The government of North Korea controls the arts, including museums and archaeological sites, and only allows things that promote the traditional Korean arts, commemorate the revolution, or that show the superiority of the Korean culture. North Korea is an atheist country and does not permit religious practices.

Lesson 3

7. Deforestation leads to soil erosion as trees hold the soil in place during heavy rains. The loss of both soil and nutrients makes growing crops difficult or impossible in some areas, contributing to the food shortages.
8. The population density causes the sewage, garbage disposal, and sanitation systems to be overloaded, which leads to raw sewage and waste being dumped directly into the ocean and other waterways, causing pollution and declines in the fish supplies.
9. South Korea has taken steps to address deforestation in North Korea because it impacts the environmental health of the entire peninsula.

Critical Thinking

10. Reunification could help the South Korean economy as North Korea could provide raw materials and labor.
11. Improving energy efficiency would decrease air pollution by reducing the amount of energy that needs to be generated using methods that pollute the air, such as burning fossil fuels.

21st Century Skills

12. According to the graph, 44 percent (37 percent malnourished, 7 percent severely malnourished) face problems with nourishment.
13. Answers may differ but could include that underweight children are included in the graph as they are likely to become malnourished in the future or to illustrate the malnutrition problem may be related to food shortages.
14. Based on the graph, almost half of all children are malnourished, making this a very serious problem.

College and Career Readiness

15. Paragraphs will differ but must include the role of natural disasters and the government in the food shortage problems in North Korea and possible solutions the government could undertake. Natural disasters could include floods and droughts, leading to widespread famine and government control of farms. Solutions could include allowing family farms and more free enterprise, taking steps to address soil quality and deforestation issues, and accepting aid from other countries.

Assessment Answers

Analyzing Primary Sources

16 The use of children as labor implies that the economy is underdeveloped. For example, children are completing manual labor tasks that would otherwise be done with machines or be automated.

17 The requirement to bring your own tools further illustrates that the economy is underdeveloped because the government lacks the funds to provide even the basic tools needed for the task at hand.

18 The description that all the students are required to work on the farm but that it does not benefit their families would indicate it is a cooperative farm where the government takes the crops for distribution to state-run stores.

Applying Map Skills

19 South Korea is more urbanized.

20 South Korean rivers include the Han, the Kŭm, and the Naktong. North Korea has the Ch'ŏngch'ŏn, Taedong, Chaeryŏng, Yalu, and Yesŏng Rivers. The Yalu River forms the border between North Korea and China.

21 The mountainous terrain of the Korean Peninsula causes there to be little arable land. Terracing is used to increase the area that can be farmed.

Exploring the Essential Question

22 Paragraphs will differ but should be strongly supported with information from the chapter, including that South Korea became a highly industrialized society with most of the population living in urban areas. South Korea became a republic that encouraged a variety of religious and cultural influences as well as operating with a system of free enterprise. North Korea has maintained a Communist regime with a command economy, which has resulted in a less industrialized and more rural population. North Korea is an atheist country and does not allow religious or artistic freedoms.

Research and Presentation

23 Time lines will differ depending on events the student chooses but could include the beginning of the program with help from the Soviets in the 1950s; Yongbyon reactor going online in 1986; refusal to allow inspection of sites in 2002; the declaration in 2005 that they have nuclear weapons; testing conducted and UN sanctions imposed in 2006; more testing in 2009 that is condemned by various countries and coalitions; rockets launched in 2012 and new sanctions imposed; more tests in 2013 with China and other UN countries widely condemning the actions.

CHAPTER 30 Assessment 

Directions: On a separate sheet of paper, answer the questions below. Make sure you read carefully and answer all parts of the questions.

DBQ Analyzing Primary Sources

Use the document to answer the following questions.

People who have fled North Korea report that the country's economy relies on forced labor. Even children are forced to work, as a former student describes below.

PRIMARY SOURCE

"When I was between 11 and 15 years old I had to work on the government farm almost every day. . . . We finished class at 1 P.M. and had to rush back home to eat lunch because the school didn't provide food for the students. The school would announce that we'd have to meet back at the school field and bring our own farm tools. . . . They forced everyone, even the small children, to work. I felt bad because this didn't benefit our family and I had many responsibilities to do for my family but the government forced me to work for them. I was always very exhausted as a child."

—Human Rights Watch, "North Korea: Economic System Built on Forced Labor," June 13, 2012

16 ***Drawing Conclusions*** What does the use of children as forced labor imply about the North Korean economy? RH.9–10.1

17 ***Interpreting*** The students were told to bring their own tools from home. How does this detail help you understand the problem? RH.9–10.2

18 ***Analyzing*** What features of the farm in the description show that it is a cooperative? RH.9–10.4

Applying Map Skills

Use the Unit 8 Atlas to answer the following questions.

19 ***Human Systems*** Compare population density in North and South Korea. Which country is more urbanized?

20 ***Places and Regions*** Use your mental map of East Asia to identify the major rivers in North Korea and South Korea. Which river forms the border between North Korea and China?

21 ***Environment and Society*** How has the geography of the Korean Peninsula affected agricultural activity?

Exploring the Essential Question

22 ***Analyzing*** How has the division of Korea into two countries affected human systems on the Korean Peninsula? Write a paragraph describing the changes, including population density, use of resources, and culture. WHST.9–10.7

Research and Presentation

23 ***Research Skills*** Using the Internet, research the development of the North Korean nuclear program. How have other countries responded to these nuclear tests? Create a time line showing your findings and share it with the class. WHST.9–10.7

Writing About Geography

24 ***Narrative*** Use the Internet to research and write a two-page essay describing the Demilitarized Zone. How does the DMZ create a buffer between North and South Korea? What features of the DMZ make it an important nature preserve? WHST.9–10.2; WHST.9–10.7

Need Extra Help?

If You've Missed Question	16	17	18	19	20	21	22	23	24
Go to page	733	733	729	676	672	672	730	731	729

742

Writing About Geography

24 Essays will differ but must identify how the DMZ creates a buffer zone and why it is an important nature preserve. Answers can include that the 6-mile-wide DMZ is bordered by armies and landmines, creating a buffer between North Korea and South Korea but also keeping the land there untouched. With the extreme deforestation and other environmental issues on the peninsula, the DMZ has become one of the only sanctuaries for animals and birds.

UNIT 9

SOUTHEAST ASIA AND THE PACIFIC WORLD Planner

UNDERSTANDING BY DESIGN®

Enduring Understandings

- *The characteristics and distribution of cultures influence human systems.*
- *Certain patterns, processes, and functions help determine where people settle.*
- *Places reflect the relationship between humans and the physical environment.*

Essential Question

- *How do physical systems and human systems shape a place?*

Students will know:

- *how rivers, seas, and oceans support human and economic activities in the region.*
- *that Southeast Asia, Oceania, Australia, and New Zealand have both indigenous populations and immigrants from other countries, creating diverse cultures.*
- *how elevation and location influence climate.*
- *the changes brought by South Asians, East Asians, Europeans, and Americans.*
- *how tourism, industrialization, and trade have contributed to the destruction of the Great Barrier Reef.*
- *the steps being taken to address the issues of resource management and human impact on the environment in the region.*

Students will be able to:

- ***analyze** the influence of waterways on shaping and supporting life.*
- ***describe** how modern economies and governments were formed.*
- ***identify** factors that affect climate, economic, and population patterns.*
- ***explain** why some islands are culturally diverse, while others are virtually untouched.*
- ***analyze** the human and physical impacts on the environment and how these issues are being addressed.*

Predictable Misunderstandings

- *Life in Australia and New Zealand is basically the same.*
- *This entire region has a consistent geography and the same warm climate.*
- *China has had little effect on the isolated islands in Southeast Asia.*
- *The ecosystems on each island in the Pacific World are all the same.*
- *Oceania's geography is mostly ice.*
- *Other countries have very little interest in this region.*
- *There is little concern about environmental issues in this region.*

Assessment Evidence

Performance Tasks:

- *Environmental Case Study*
- *GeoLab Activity*
- *GIS Simulation*
- *Hands-On Chapter Projects*

Other Evidence:

- *Location Activity*
- *Self-Check Quizzes*
- *Lesson Quizzes*
- *Participation in Interactive Whiteboard Activities*
- *Contribution to small-group activities*
- *Interpretation of slide show images*
- *Participation in class discussions about Southeast Asia and the Pacific World*
- *Analysis of graphic organizers, graphs, and charts*
- *Lesson Reviews*
- *Chapter Assessments*

Key for Using the Teacher Edition

SKILL-BASED ACTIVITIES

Types of skill activities found in the Teacher Edition.

*V **Visual Skills** require students to analyze maps, graphs, charts, and photos.

R **Reading Skills** help students practice reading skills and master vocabulary.

C **Critical Thinking Skills** help students apply and extend what they have learned.

W **Writing Skills** provide writing opportunities to help students comprehend the text.

T **Technology Skills** require students to use digital tools effectively.

*Letters are followed by a number when there is more than one of the same type of skill on the page.

DIFFERENTIATED INSTRUCTION

All activities are written for the on-level student unless otherwise marked with the leveled labels below.

BL **Beyond Level**
AL **Approaching Level**
ELL **English Language Learners**

All students benefit from activities that utilize different learning styles. Many activities are marked as below when a particular learning style is highlighted.

Intrapersonal	**Naturalist**
Logical/Mathematical	**Kinesthetic**
Visual/Spatial	**Auditory/Musical**
Verbal/Linguistic	**Interpersonal**

SUGGESTED PACING GUIDE

Introducing the Unit	1 Day
Chapter 31: Southeast Asia	4 Days
Chapter 32: Australia and New Zealand	4 Days
Global Connections: Non-Native Species: Rabbits in Australia	1 Day
Chapter 33: Oceania	4 Days
Case Study: Who Owns the High Seas?	1 Day
TOTAL TIME	**15 Days**

PLANNER

Print Teaching Options

V Visual Skills

- ☐ **p. 747** Students use a political map to create a three-column chart that classifies the islands in the Pacific Ocean. ELL Verbal/Linguistic, Visual/Spatial

R Reading Skills

- ☐ **p. 744** Students discuss how various subregions might be influenced by other cultures in the region. AL ELL Visual/Spatial
- ☐ **p. 746** Students discuss inset maps and then relate them to Mercator projections. BL Logical/Mathematical

C Critical Thinking Skills

- ☐ **p. 745** Students formulate questions they would like to have answered about this region. AL Verbal/Linguistic
- ☐ **p. 748** Students identify the climate zones and then draw conclusions about human activities based on the climate and vegetation in each subregion. AL Visual/Spatial
- ☐ **p. 749** Students analyze an economic map and then consider how the region's economic activity could be negatively impacted by human activity. BL Logical/Mathematical, Visual/Spatial
- ☐ **p. 750** Students compare and contrast population density with island size. AL Logical/Mathematical, Visual/Spatial

W Writing Skills

- ☐ **p. 744** Students write a poem, song, or rap about cultural diversity. Verbal/Linguistic, Auditory/Musical
- ☐ **p. 747** Students research a subregion to write an essay about its government and political conflicts. BL Verbal/Linguistic
- ☐ **p. 749** Students write about how a resource affects the economy of a country, island, or subregion. Verbal/Linguistic, Logical/Mathematical

T Technology Skills

- ☐ **p. 745** Students research to create a graphic organizer about the environmental threats to countries in this region. AL Visual/Spatial
- ☐ **p. 748** Students study a climate map and then write a weather report about an island or subregion on the map. Verbal/Linguistic, Kinesthetic
- ☐ **p. 750** Students research a city in the region and then create a slide show about its climate, population, industry, and economy and whether they would like to live in that city. BL Intrapersonal

Online Teaching Options

V Visual Skills

- ☐ INTERACTIVE FEATURE **Explore the Region: Southeast Asia and the Pacific World**—Students create a Venn diagram that contrasts the landforms and diversity of two countries in the region. BL Visual/Spatial, Verbal/Linguistic
- ☐ INTERACTIVE MAP **Economic Activity Map: Southeast Asia and the Pacific World**—Students examine an economic map to determine the importance of raising livestock to the economies of various countries. AL Visual/Spatial, Logical/Mathematical
- ☐ INTERACTIVE MAP **Climate and Vegetation Maps: Southeast Asia and the Pacific World**—Students make predictions about Australia's population density based on information on a climate map. Interpersonal, Logical/Mathematical

R Reading Skills

- ☐ INTERACTIVE MAP **Population Density Map: Southeast Asia and the Pacific World**—Students study the population map and write down three questions that they would like answered about the region. Logical/Mathematical

C Critical Thinking Skills

- ☐ GEO @ WORK **Thinking Like a Geographer**—Students explore principles and skills of geography applied to real-world challenges. Visual/Spatial, Logical/Mathematical
- ☐ INTERACTIVE MAP **Physical Map: Southeast Asia and the Pacific World**—Students discuss landforms on a physical map and speculate about the ease of colonization of various areas in the region. Visual/Spatial, Logical/Mathematical

W Writing Skills

- ☐ INTERACTIVE MAP **Political Map: Southeast Asia and the Pacific World**—Students research a specific island or country to write an essay explaining when, how, and by whom it was colonized. BL Verbal/Linguistic

Printable Digital Worksheets

V Visual Skills

- ☐ WORKSHEET **Location Activity**—Students locate countries, water systems, and physical features of Southeast Asia and the Pacific World.

C Critical Thinking Skills

- ☐ WORKSHEET **GeoLab Activity**—Students explore what can happen when a non-native species is introduced into a geographic region.

T Technology Skills

- ☐ WORKSHEET **Environmental Case Study**—Students research the most recent negotiations the United States has had with PNA about tuna fishing in the Pacific Islands and then conclude whether these negotiations were beneficial or detrimental to U.S. fisheries.
- ☐ WORKSHEET **GIS Simulation**—Students research how Australia and New Zealand have developed different sectors of their economies, compare the countries' current economies, examine how the economies of the two countries are interlinked, and make suggestions for how the countries can further their economies in the future.

Southeast Asia and the Pacific World

UNIT 9

Chapter 31
Southeast Asia

Chapter 32
Australia and New Zealand

Chapter 33
Oceania

Alex Langham/Photolibrary/Getty Images

GEO @ WORK

Thinking Like a Geographer

Problem Solving Explore specific examples of the principles and skills of geography applied to real-world challenges that impact people's lives. From agriculture to urban planning, to wiping out disease and managing changes in society—geography plays a key role in understanding relationships and generating solutions that make sense.

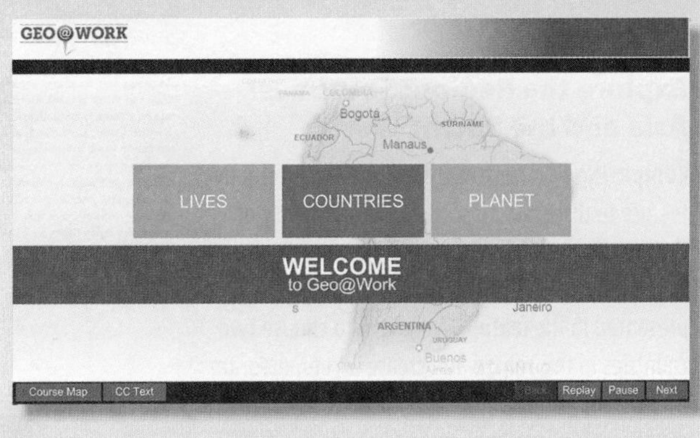

ENGAGE

Assessing Call students' attention to the list of chapter titles at the bottom of the page. Challenge students to see how many of the countries of Southeast Asia they can name. Assess students' knowledge about Southeast Asia and the Pacific World by asking a volunteer to locate each country on a globe or map and share a fact they may know about its physical or human geography.

TEACH & ASSESS

Analyzing Images Call students' attention to the photograph and have them analyze its details. **Ask:** **What clues from the photograph tell you about the past and present of this place?** *(Possible answer: The photograph depicts impressive architectural structures that appear to have been constructed many years ago. The telephone lines indicate that a modern society inhabits the place now.)* **What do the buildings tell you about the ancient civilization that once inhabited this place?** *(Possible answer: The people who lived during ancient times were knowledgeable about geometry and engineering based on the symmetric style of the architecture.)* **AL Visual/Spatial**

Making Connections

Have students consider what buildings or monuments they would choose to show a friend who had never visited the United States to give them an idea about the country's culture and people. Then have them consider what type of structure is shown in the photograph on this page. Explain that the buildings are representative of temples built in Southeast Asia in places that were once ancient cities or religious centers.

CLOSE & REFLECT

Organizing Have students create a two-column chart labeled *Human Geography* and *Physical Geography.* As they work through this unit, tell students to complete the chart, adding notes about characteristics of Southeast Asia and the Pacific World as they relate to each heading.

ENGAGE

V Visual Skills

Analyzing Visuals Ask students to study the photograph on this page. Guide them to analyze its details by asking the following series of questions. **Ask:** **What is happening in the photo?** *(Dancers are performing in some type of celebration that may be honoring their heritage.)* **What does this tell you about some of the cultures in Southeast Asia and the Pacific World?** *(Possible answer: People enjoy ceremonial celebrations to honor their ancestry, culture, or religious beliefs.)* **Can you find similarities between the people shown in the photograph and a cultural group in the United States? Explain.** *(Possible answer: The women wear headbands, feathers, and face paint similar to some Native American cultures in the United States.)*

TEACH & ASSESS

W Writing Skills

Informative/Explanatory Discuss with students the relevance of diversity in a region, explaining that Southeast Asia and the Pacific World is made up of people from different cultures and ethnic groups. Using the "melting pot" of the United States as an example, have students write a poem explaining how different cultures make up the United States. Students may also write a song or rap that describes a specific culture or ethnic group that they know about. Invite volunteers to share their poems and songs with the class, and discuss how different cultures influence a region. **Verbal/Linguistic, Auditory/Musical**

R Reading Skills

Reading Maps Ask students to examine the numbered inset map on this page. Have students work with a partner to discuss how each numbered location might influence, or be influenced by, another culture in the region. Then, **ask:** **How might geography impact one of the locations shown on this map?** *(Possible answer: The #4 location might be influenced by Chinese cultures as it is in close proximity to the country of China.)* **AL ELL Visual/Spatial**

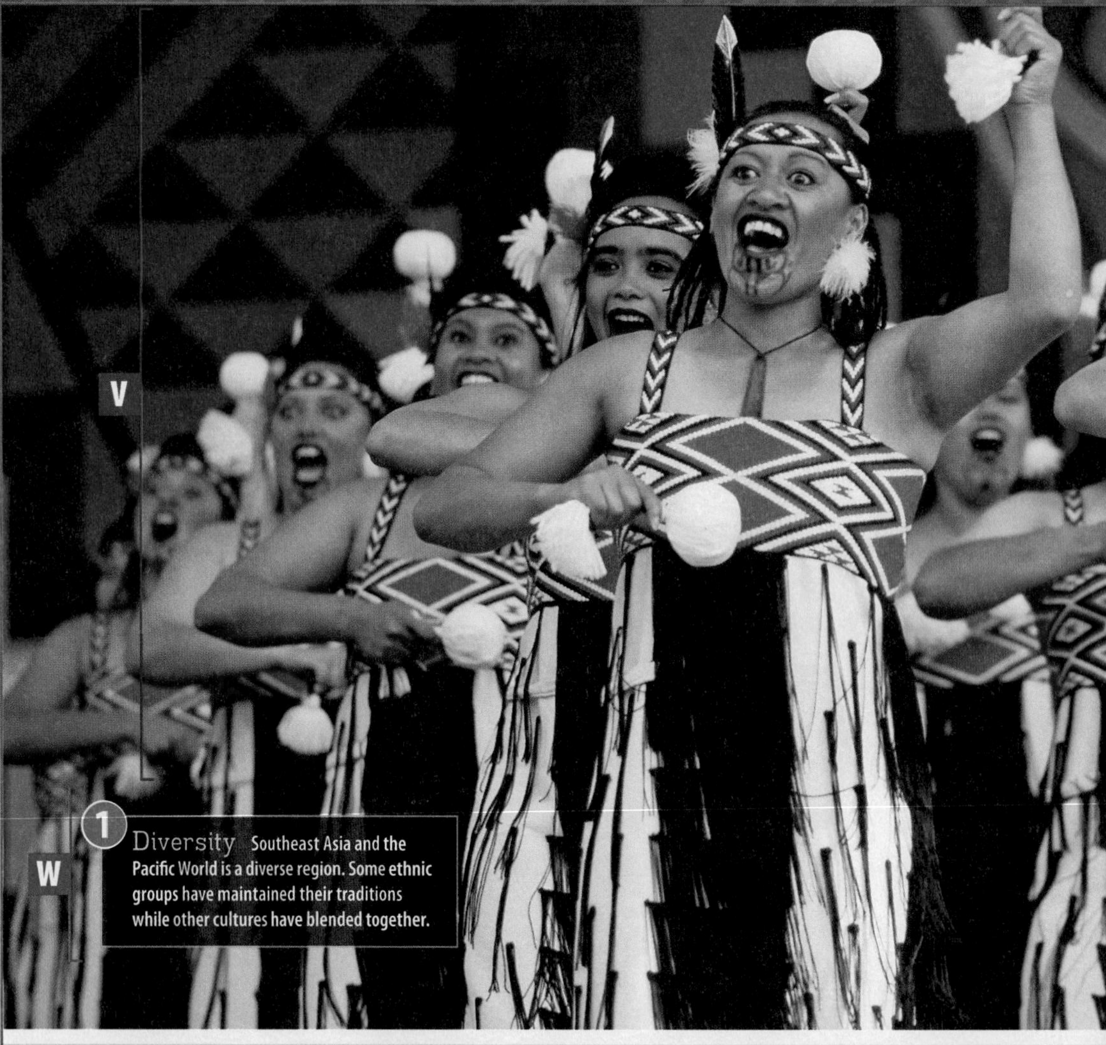

V

W

① Diversity Southeast Asia and the Pacific World is a diverse region. Some ethnic groups have maintained their traditions while other cultures have blended together.

EXPLORE the REGION

Stretching from the eastern border of India east nearly to South America, and from China in the north to the Southern Ocean, **SOUTHEAST ASIA** and the **PACIFIC WORLD** is a vast region dominated by the sea. With populous countries like Indonesia, countries with large land areas like Australia, and small island countries with few people, this region shows great variety of landforms, people, and cultures.

R

THERE'S MORE ONLINE

744

networks Online Teaching Options

INTERACTIVE FEATURE

Explore the Region: Southeast Asia and the Pacific World

Comparing and Contrasting Use this interactive feature to discuss with students the diversity of the landforms and environments in the region. Have students analyze the text and images presented in the feature. Ask them to choose two countries in this region and create a Venn diagram that contrasts the landforms and diversity of the countries. Students may need to conduct additional research to fill out their diagrams. **BL Visual/Spatial, Verbal/Linguistic**

Southeast Asia and the Pacific World

INTRODUCTION

Stretching from the eastern border of India east almost to South America, and from China in the north to the Southern Ocean, Southeast Asia and the Pacific World is a vast region dominated by the sea. With populous countries like Indonesia, countries with large land areas like Australia, and small island countries with few people, this region shows great variety of landforms, people, and cultures.

3 Environment The region has dense rain forests and unique plants and animals. Various countries are taking steps to protect these natural wonders from the threats they face.

4 Water Almost all of the countries in the region have coastlines, and some countries rely on rivers. Fishing and shipping are important activities in the region.

2 Landforms The region has many different landforms, from soaring, glacier-covered mountains to low islands that rise just a few feet above the sea.

(t)Purestock/PunchStock, (bl)Nora Carol Photography/Flickr/Getty Images, (br)Jonathan Saruk/Getty Images News/Getty Images

DIGITAL WORKSHEETS

Southeast Asia and the Pacific World

Demonstrating Use these online digital unit worksheets to have students demonstrate their depth of knowledge and comprehension and to provide them with extended unit content through project-based activities.

- **Environmental Case Study**
- **GeoLab Activity**
- **GIS Simulation**
- **Location Activity**

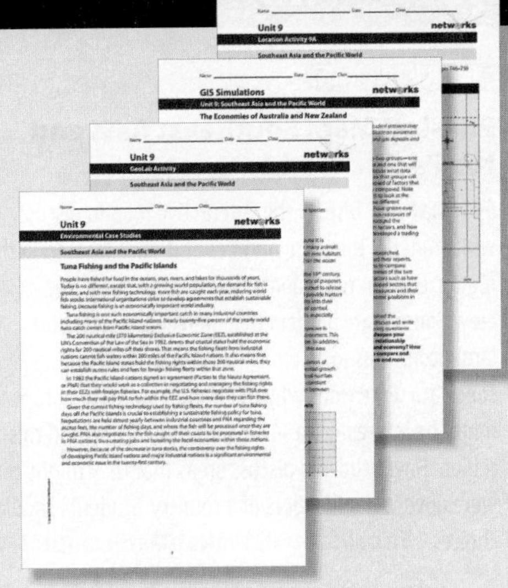

C Critical Thinking Skills

Formulating Questions Discuss with students how the physical features of a region can define a place and its way of life. Explain that much of Southeast Asia and the Pacific World is defined by its proximity to bodies of water. Ask students to write three to five questions about the region that they would like to have answered as they read through the unit, leaving room for an answer beneath each question. As students work through each chapter in this unit, have them periodically return to their questions to jot down the answers. Encourage students to save their list of questions and answers as a study guide for a unit review. **AL** **Verbal/Linguistic**

W Writing Skills

Informative/Explanatory Have students imagine that they are a travel writer for a newsmagazine visiting a region in Southeast Asia and the Pacific World and witness one of the scenes depicted in the images on this page. Tell students to write a short article telling about the scene, using descriptive words and sensory adjectives to describe what is happening in the picture. Invite students to share their articles with the class. **Naturalist, Verbal/Linguistic**

T Technology Skills

Researching Have students research some of the threats faced by countries in the region for a short report. Have students place their notes in a graphic organizer to add to as they work through each chapter of this unit. **AL** **Visual/Spatial**

CLOSE & REFLECT

Comparing and Contrasting Have students review the images shown in this Unit Opener, taking notes about each image. Have students write a short compare-contrast paragraph that describes the region's similarities to and differences from their own region based on the images.

ENGAGE

C Critical Thinking Skills

Making Generalizations Have students study the map, examining the proximity of the region to the Equator. Have students make generalizations about the physical features of each landmass and the region as a whole. Tell students to consider how the region's physical geography affects its climate, which in turn impacts human activity such as tourism and fishing, for example. Explain to students that they will be learning more about how the physical features of the region affect the way people live.

TEACH & ASSESS

R Reading Skills

Calculating Point out to students the inset at the bottom of the map, noting the scale. **Ask:** **Why do you think the mapmaker chose to include this portion of the map as an inset?** *(The region shown in the inset is too big to include in its true geographic location on the map.)* **How can you tell where the islands shown in the inset should appear on the map?** *(Student answers will vary but could include that the western islands shown on the inset—such as Fiji, Tonga, and the Gilbert Islands—also appear on the larger map, indicating the location of the region shown in the inset.)* Challenge interested students to research how a Mercator projection is calculated and to share their findings with the class, providing examples. **BL Logical/Mathematical**

ANSWERS, p. 746

MAP STUDY

1. Sumatra, Borneo, New Guinea, Java, Sulawesi
2. along the southeastern coast

Southeast Asia and the Pacific World
Physical

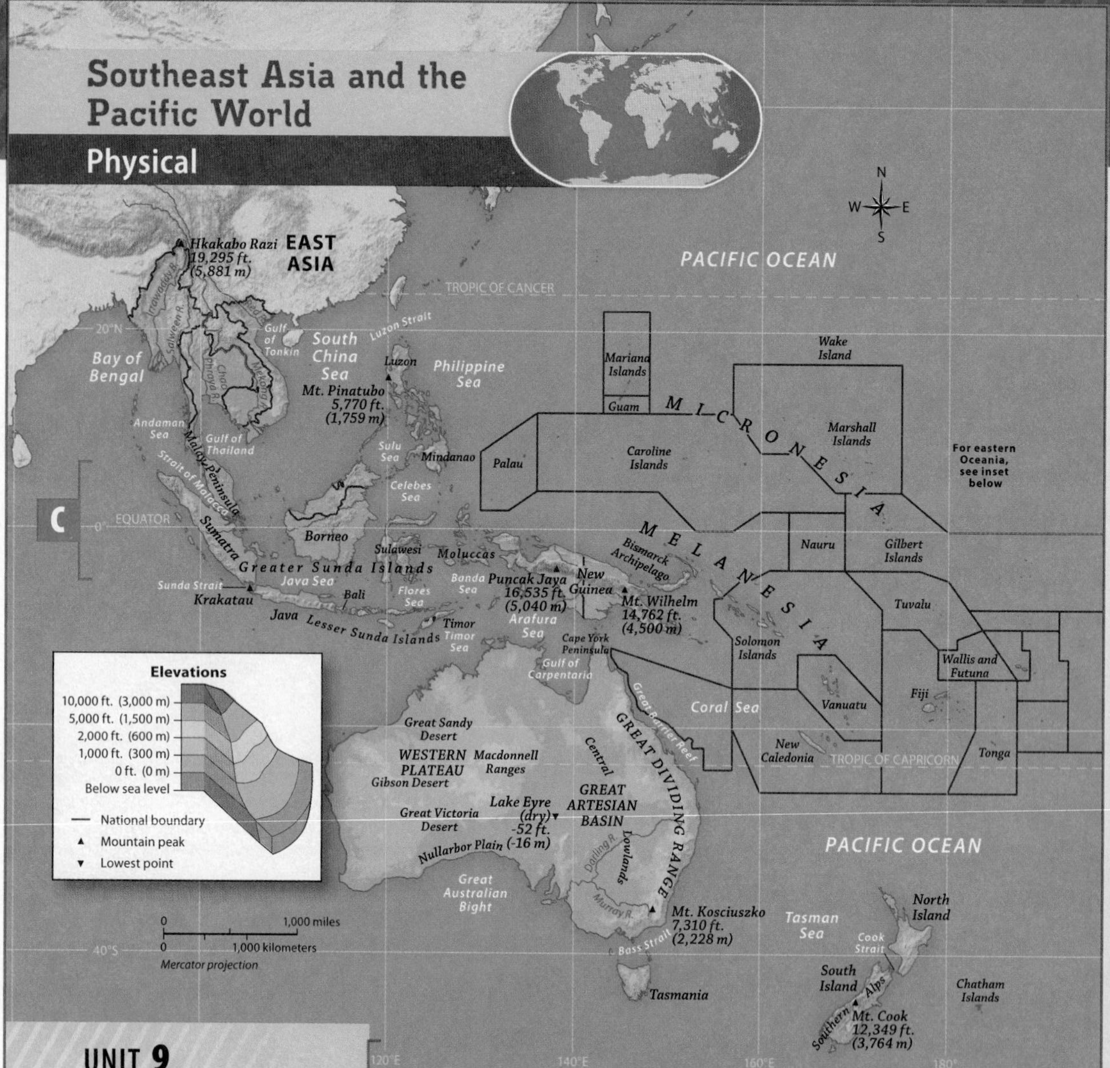

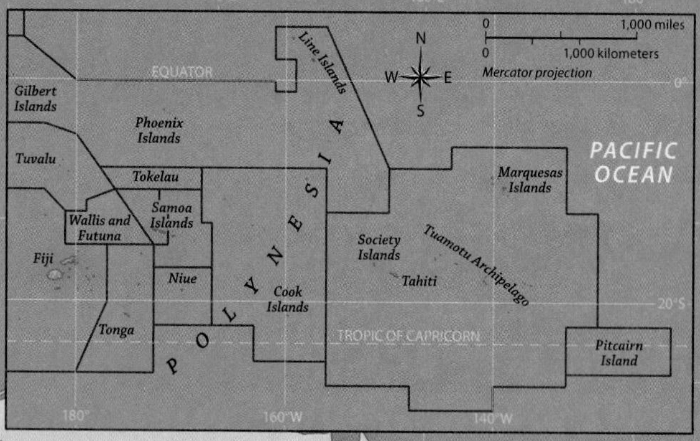

Elevations
10,000 ft. (3,000 m)
5,000 ft. (1,500 m)
2,000 ft. (600 m)
1,000 ft. (300 m)
0 ft. (0 m)
Below sea level
— National boundary
▲ Mountain peak
▼ Lowest point

Mercator projection

UNIT 9 REGIONAL ATLAS

MAP STUDY

1. ***Physical Systems*** What large islands make up the country of Indonesia?
2. ***Environment and Society*** Where are most major cities in Australia located? What about the physical geography of the country explains these settlement patterns?

746

networks Online Teaching Options

INTERACTIVE MAP

Physical Map: Southeast Asia and the Pacific World

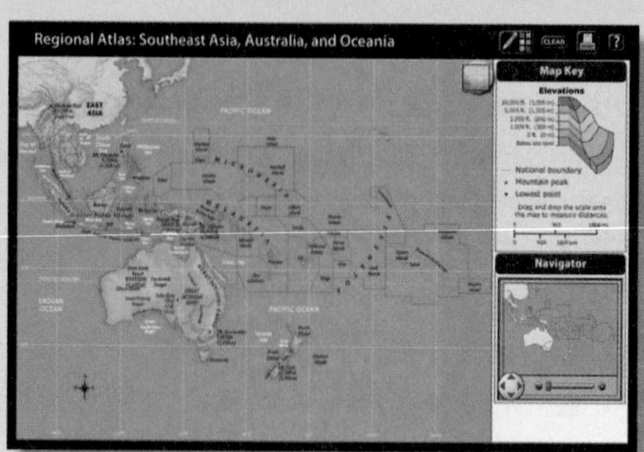

Speculating Display this interactive map to discuss with students the large number of islands located in this region. Explain to students that the relatively low elevations create borders that allow easy access for larger countries to colonization. Ask students to speculate on reasons why the United States or Europeans might be interested in setting up colonies within this region. Have students discuss areas that they might consider colonizing if they were government leaders of a country. Students should include reasons for their choices. **Visual/Spatial, Logical/Mathematical**

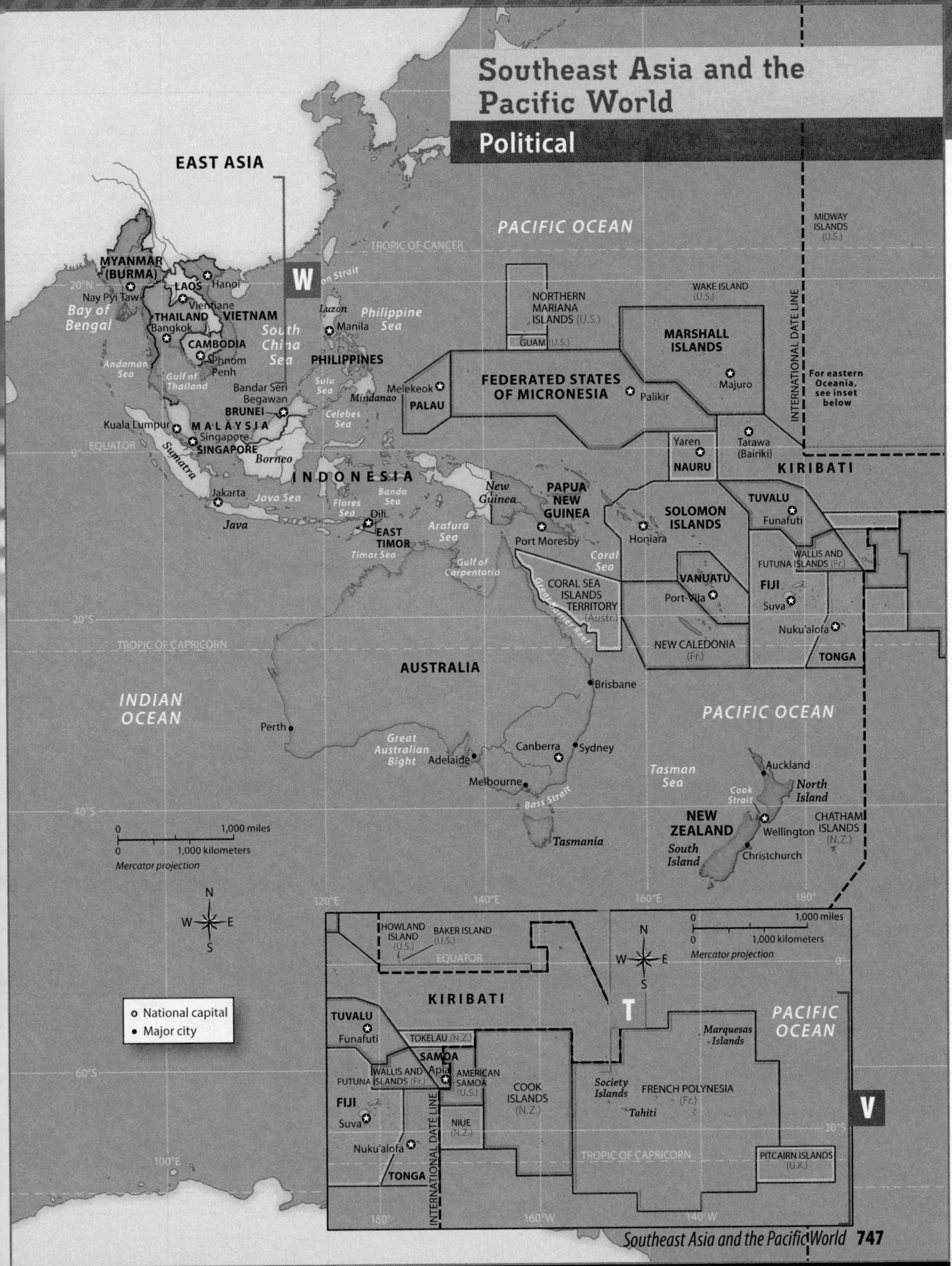

Southeast Asia and the Pacific World

Political

Southeast Asia and the Pacific World 747

Southeast Asia and the Pacific World

W Writing Skills

Informative/Explanatory Assign student pairs a subregion on the map to explore, such as the countries on the mainland in the west or the Marshall Islands to the east. Have students conduct online research to identify the type of government of a country or countries in the region, the political conflicts the region has endured, and how those conflicts have changed the region. Have students present their findings in a short essay that describes the causes and effects of political conflict in the subregion. **BL Verbal/Linguistic**

T Technology Skills

Identifying Continuity and Change Have students choose an island or country on the map, such as Kiribati, and consider how, or if, climate change is affecting the island. Tell students to conduct online research to locate news reports, scholarly articles, or government publications that outline the impact of climate change on the island or country's ecosystems and natural habitat. Invite students to present their findings to the class. **Naturalist, Verbal/Linguistic**

V Visual Skills

Creating Charts Point out the inset portion of the map to students, noting the islands that make up French Polynesia. Explain to students that the thousands of islands in the Pacific Ocean are divided into three broad regions: Micronesia, Polynesia, and Melanesia. Ask students to identify each word's meaning based on its word parts, looking up the words' etymologies in an online dictionary if needed. *(small islands, many islands, black islands)* Then ask them to create a three-column chart that lists the key islands shown on the map under the headings *Micronesia, Polynesia,* and *Melanesia.*
ELL Verbal/Linguistic, Visual/Spatial

INTERACTIVE MAP

Political Map: Southeast Asia and the Pacific World

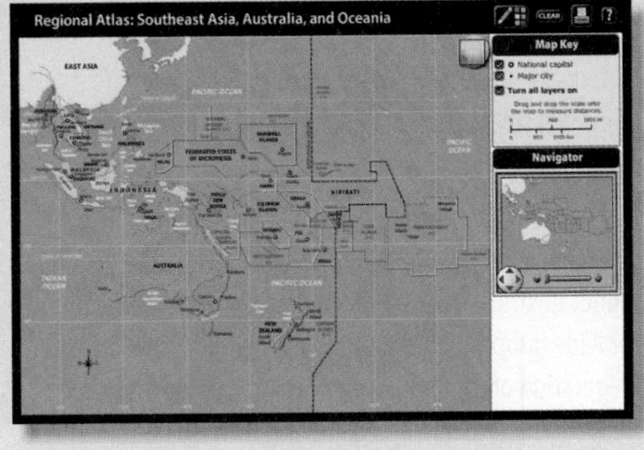

Informative/Explanatory Use this political map of Southeast Asia and the Pacific World to discuss territories and jurisdictions with students. Explain to them that several islands, or group of islands, in this part of the world are U.S. territories, while others are under the jurisdiction of France, Australia, New Zealand, and the United Kingdom. Have students choose one of the islands or group of islands and research its history to write an essay explaining how and when that area became the territory of a greater political power. Invite students to share their essays with the class. **BL Verbal/Linguistic**

T Technology Skills

Presenting Have students select an island or subregion shown on the map. Tell students they will act as meteorologists reporting on the week's weather in their chosen island or region. Have students use information from the map, as well as online research if desired, to write a weather report for a television news program. Invite students to perform their weather forecasts for the class, enhancing them with visuals. Challenge students to present their forecasts without revealing the region to see if their classmates can guess the region they are describing. **Verbal/Linguistic, Kinesthetic**

C Critical Thinking Skills

Drawing Conclusions Have students use the map key to identify the different climate zones shown on the map. **Ask:** **How might climate and vegetation impact population patterns and how people make a living in Australia compared to the islands to its north?** *(Possible answer: The dry areas in inland Australia are likely less populated than a thriving port city such as Singapore.)* **What conclusions can you draw about how vegetation affects human activities based on the map?** *(Student answers will vary but should include a connection between a region's vegetation, or lack of it, and its land use).* Invite students to brainstorm different human activities according to a region's climate. For example, fishing occurs in coastal communities, ranching occurs in favorable climates with adequate vegetation, and so on. Then have students refer to the economic activity map on the next page to see if their generalizations were accurate.
AL **Visual/Spatial**

ANSWERS, p. 748

MAP STUDY

1. Indonesia, parts of the Philippines, Papua New Guinea, Pacific island countries ; western and central Australia
2. They are located along the coasts.

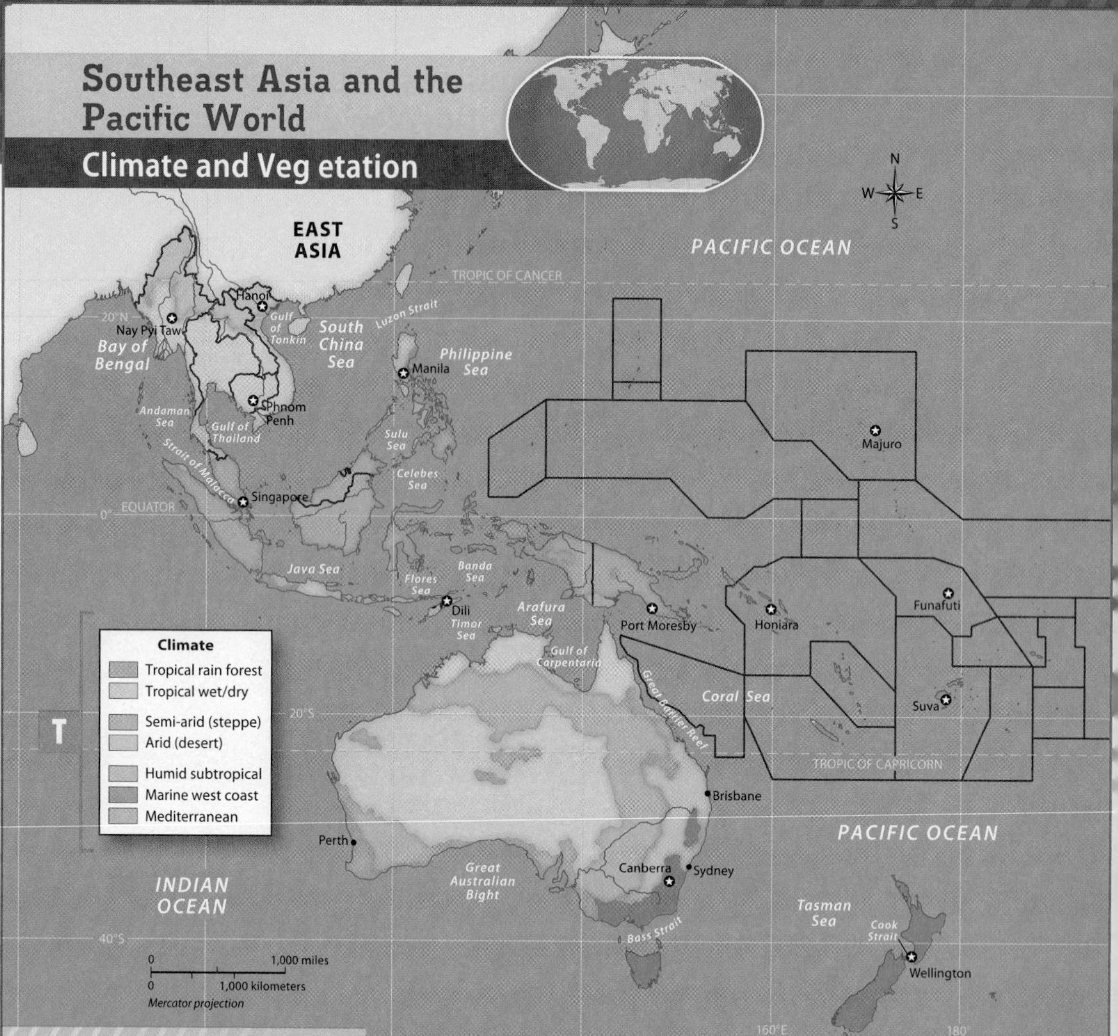

Southeast Asia and the Pacific World

Climate and Veg etation

Climate
- Tropical rain forest
- Tropical wet/dry
- Semi-arid (steppe)
- Arid (desert)
- Humid subtropical
- Marine west coast
- Mediterranean

0 — 1,000 miles
0 — 1,000 kilometers
Mercator projection

Vegetation
- Tropical rain forest
- Tropical grassland (savanna)
- Desert scrub and desert waste
- Temperate grassland
- Deciduous forest
- Mixed forest (deciduous and coniferous)

UNIT 9
REGIONAL ATLAS

MAP STUDY

1. ***Physical Systems*** Which parts of the region would you expect to have ample rainfall? Which would you expect to be dry?
2. ***The World in Spatial Terms*** What generalization can you make about the location of centers of manufacturing in the region?

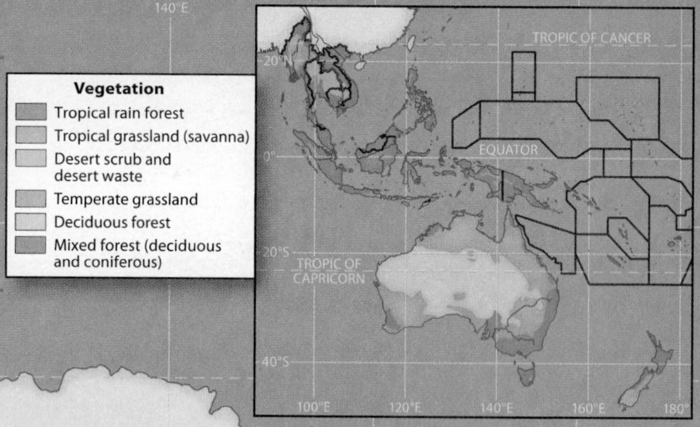

748

networks Online Teaching Options

INTERACTIVE MAP

Climate and Vegetation Maps: Southeast Asia and the Pacific World

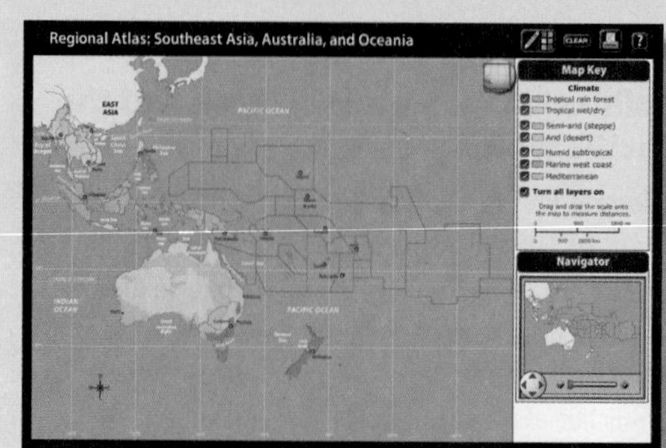

Predicting Display the climate and vegetation maps to introduce students to this diverse region. Direct students' attention to Australia. Lead a class discussion about Australia's varied climate zones. Have students provide information about the effects of landforms and vegetation on climate. Using this knowledge, ask several student volunteers to predict what the population density will be, based on the climate and vegetation of Australia. Turn to the population density map in the text to check students' predictions. **Interpersonal, Logical/Mathematical**

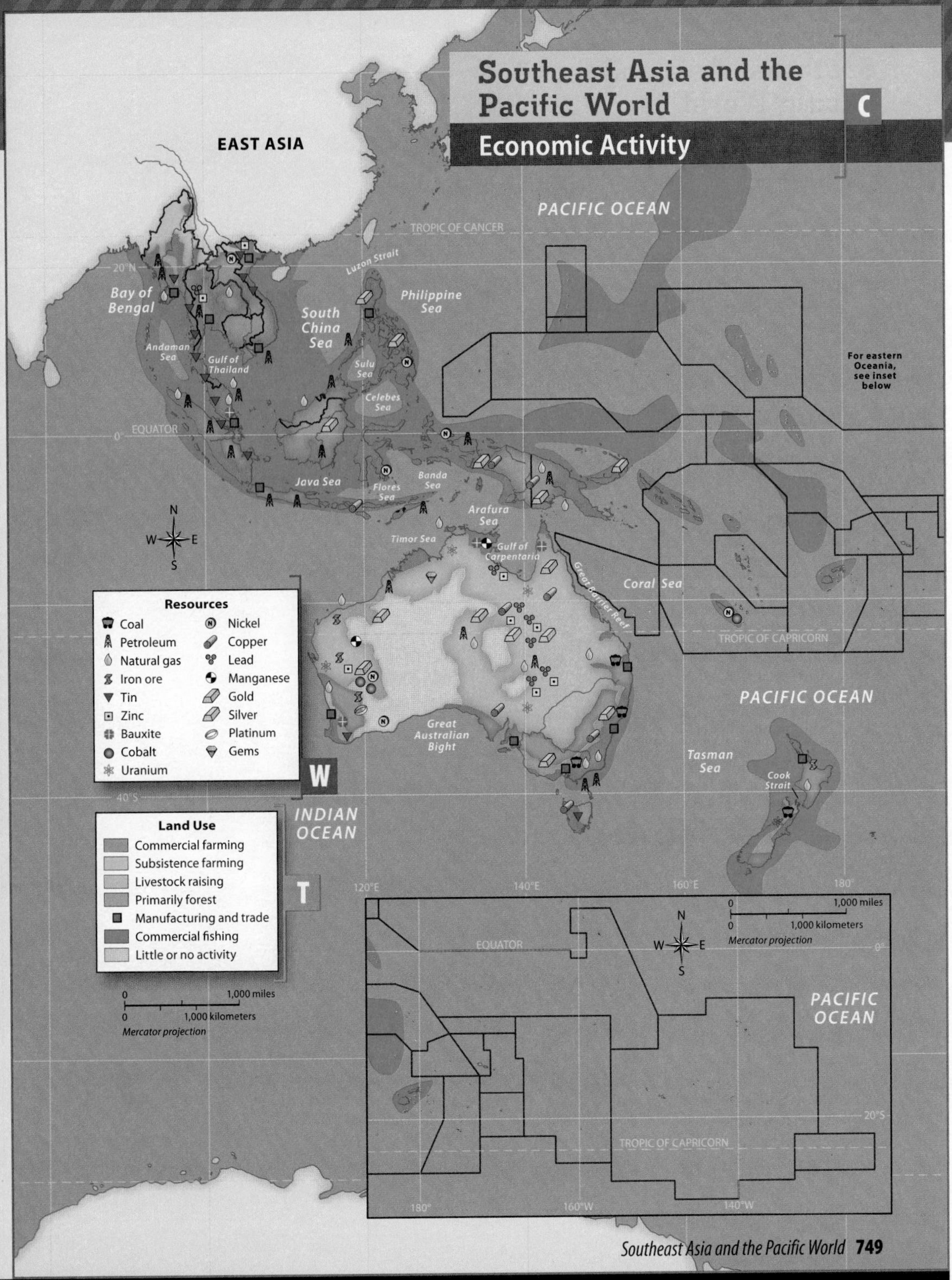

Southeast Asia and the Pacific World

Economic Activity

EAST ASIA

PACIFIC OCEAN

TROPIC OF CANCER

Luzon Strait

Bay of Bengal

Andaman Sea

South China Sea

Philippine Sea

Gulf of Thailand

Sulu Sea

Celebes Sea

EQUATOR

Java Sea

Flores Sea

Banda Sea

Arafura Sea

Timor Sea

Gulf of Carpentaria

Great Barrier Reef

Coral Sea

For eastern Oceania, see inset below

TROPIC OF CAPRICORN

PACIFIC OCEAN

Great Australian Bight

Tasman Sea

Cook Strait

INDIAN OCEAN

120°E 140°E 160°E 180°

Resources

- Coal
- Petroleum
- Natural gas
- Iron ore
- Tin
- Zinc
- Bauxite
- Cobalt
- Uranium
- Nickel
- Copper
- Lead
- Manganese
- Gold
- Silver
- Platinum
- Gems

Land Use

- Commercial farming
- Subsistence farming
- Livestock raising
- Primarily forest
- Manufacturing and trade
- Commercial fishing
- Little or no activity

0 1,000 miles
0 1,000 kilometers
Mercator projection

EQUATOR

PACIFIC OCEAN

TROPIC OF CAPRICORN

180° 160°W 140°W

UNIT 9

Southeast Asia and the Pacific World

C Critical Thinking Skills

Identifying Perspectives Have students analyze the map, considering how each region's economic activity could be negatively impacted by human activity. **Ask: How might the commercial fishing industry be adversely impacted by another industry in the same region?** *(Possible answer: Heavy industry and manufacturing could lead to water pollution that in turn could adversely impact the commercial fishing industry.)* Ask students to create a diagram that illustrates the positive and negative impacts of human activity on a specific region shown on the map. **BL Logical/Mathematical, Visual/Spatial**

W Writing Skills

Informative/Explanatory As a class, discuss how the presence of natural resources can benefit a country in terms of the exports it ships to other countries. Have students choose a resource listed in the Resources map key and write a paragraph explaining how that resource benefits the economy of a region shown on the map. Students may wish to conduct additional research about their region's economy by using credible online sources, such as the CIA World Factbook. **Verbal/Linguistic, Logical/Mathematical**

T Technology Skills

Understanding Relationships Among Events Divide the class into small groups, assigning each group to a subregion shown on the map. Explain to students they will produce a "nightly news" program about their subregion, using information from each of the maps in this unit. Instruct students to assign a segment of the program to each member of their group, for example: a "top story" involving a current event or political issue in the subregion, an economic report, a sports report, and a weather report. Students should conduct research about their subregion to enhance their news programs. Have groups present their newscasts to the class. **Verbal/Linguistic, Kinesthetic, Interpersonal**

INTERACTIVE MAP

Economic Activity Map: Southeast Asia and the Pacific World

Determining Importance Have students consider the economic activities of this region by examining the resources and land uses in this map. Working in groups, ask students to examine the economic importance of raising livestock in this region. **Ask: How important is raising livestock to the Australian economy? How important is it to the Tasmanian and New Zealand economies? To Southeast Asian countries? To other Pacific Islands?** Have groups discuss the answers to each question. Then in a class discussion, have groups share their answers. **AL Visual/Spatial, Logical/Mathematical**

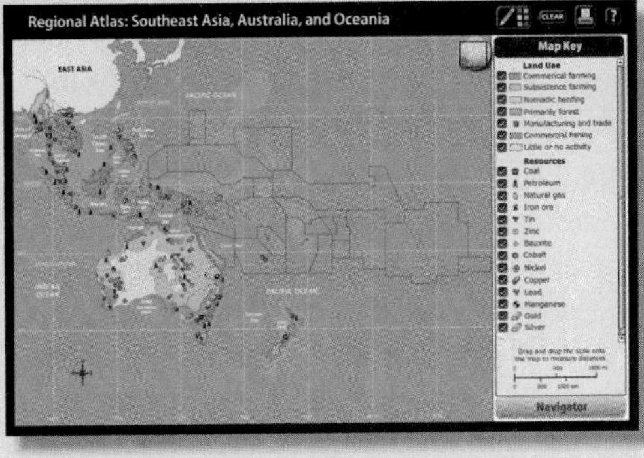

T Technology Skills

Presenting Have students choose a city on the map that they would like to research to find information about the city's way of life. Students should gather information that describes the city's population, climate, industry, and economy to compile into a slide show presentation. Have students present their slide show to the class, inviting them to include a summarizing paragraph about their selected city, explaining whether or not they would want to live there. Students should include illustrations in their slides and supporting evidence from reliable sources to back up their concluding statements.
BL **Intrapersonal**

C Critical Thinking Skills

Comparing and Contrasting Have students read the population map key and then analyze each subregion shown on the map. **Ask:** What is an example of a subregion with a large land area but a relatively small population? *(Possible answer: Australia has a large land area but a relatively small population.)* What is an example of a subregion with a small land area but a large population? *(Possible answer: Jakarta has a small land area but a large population.)*
AL **Logical/Mathematical, Visual/Spatial**

CLOSE & REFLECT

Categorizing Have students create a "Rate-a-Place" chart that lists advantages and disadvantages of a subregion, island, or city shown on one of the unit maps. Tell students to base their rating system on criteria such as climate and weather, economic activity, population density, and employment opportunity. Have students present their charts to the class, explaining their rating system.

ANSWERS, p. 750

MAP STUDY

1. Philippines, Thailand
2. The eastern coast has a more moderate climate.

Southeast Asia and the Pacific World
Population Density

Cities
(Statistics reflect metropolitan areas.)
■ Over 5,000,000
□ 2,000,000–5,000,000
⊙ 1,000,000–2,000,000

POPULATION	
Per sq. mi.	Per sq. km
1,250 and over	500 and over
250–1,249	100–499
63–249	25–99
25–62	10–24
2.5–24	1–9
Less than 2.5	Less than 1

EAST ASIA
PACIFIC OCEAN
INDIAN OCEAN
Mandalay, Hanoi, Haiphong, Yangon (Rangoon), Bay of Bengal, Bangkok, South China Sea, Philippine Sea, Manila, Luzon Strait, Andaman Sea, Gulf of Thailand, Phnom Penh, Ho Chi Minh City, Sulu Sea, Davao, Celebes Sea, Medan, Kuala Lumpur, Singapore, Palembang, Jakarta, Java Sea, Semarang, Surabaya, Bandung, Ujung Pandang, Banda Sea, Flores Sea, Timor Sea, Arafura Sea, Gulf of Carpentaria, Great Barrier Reef, Coral Sea, Brisbane, Perth, Great Australian Bight, Adelaide, Newcastle, Sydney, Melbourne, Bass Strait, Tasman Sea, Cook Strait, Auckland
TROPIC OF CANCER, EQUATOR, TROPIC OF CAPRICORN
For eastern Oceania, see inset below
0 — 1,000 miles
0 — 1,000 kilometers
Mercator projection

UNIT 9
REGIONAL ATLAS

MAP STUDY

1. ***Human Systems*** Which countries in Southeast Asia are the most densely populated?
2 ***Human Systems*** Why do you think the heaviest concentration of population in Australia is along the eastern coast?

750

networks Online Teaching Options

INTERACTIVE MAP

Population Density: Southeast Asia and the Pacific World

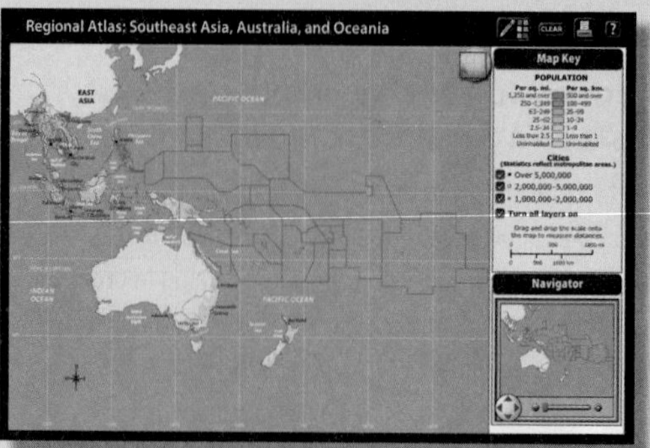

Predictions Display the population map of this region for students to analyze. Explain to them that just as there are a variety of cultures within this region, there are also great variances in populations. Have students consider what they would like to know about Southeast Asia and the Pacific Islands. Ask them to write out three predictions they have about environmental issues that an island, country, or subregion is facing in this unit. Tell students to keep these predictions in a notebook so that they can refer to them as they complete this unit. **Logical/Mathematical**

CHAPTER 31

Southeast Asia Planner

UNDERSTANDING BY DESIGN®

Enduring Understandings

- *The characteristics and distribution of cultures influence human systems.*

Essential Question

- *How do physical systems and human systems shape a place?*

Predictable Misunderstandings

Students may think:

- *Island countries in Southeast Asia are small and insignificant. Explain that Southeast Asia's island countries are quite large, their landmass being larger than that of the region's mainland countries. A few of the countries have emerging markets, while others have large economies with a lot of foreign investment.*
- *Few people live in Southeast Asia, particularly in the island countries. Explain that the mainland is the least densely populated and that millions of people live on the islands where there is rich volcanic soil. Java, an island in Indonesia, has a population of 150 million.*

Assessment Evidence

Performance Tasks:

- *Hands-On Chapter Project*

Other Evidence:

- *Guided Reading Activities*
- *Vocabulary Activities*
- *Lesson Quizzes*
- *Chapter Tests, Forms A and B*

SUGGESTED PACING GUIDE

Introducing the Chapter	½ Day
Lesson 1	1 Day
Lesson 2	1 Day
Lesson 3	1 Day
Chapter Wrap-Up and Assessment	½ Day
TOTAL TIME	**4 Days**

Key for Using the Teacher Edition

SKILL-BASED ACTIVITIES

Types of skill activities found in the Teacher Edition.

* **V Visual Skills** require students to analyze maps, graphs, charts, and photos.

R Reading Skills help students practice reading skills and master vocabulary.

C Critical Thinking Skills help students apply and extend what they have learned.

W Writing Skills provide writing opportunities to help students comprehend the text.

T Technology Skills require students to use digital tools effectively.

*Letters are followed by a number when there is more than one of the same type of skill on the page.

DIFFERENTIATED INSTRUCTION

All activities are written for the on-level student unless otherwise marked with the leveled labels below.

BL Beyond Level
AL Approaching Level
ELL English Language Learners

All students benefit from activities that utilize different learning styles. Many activities are marked as below when a particular learning style is highlighted.

Intrapersonal **Naturalist**
Logical/Mathematical **Kinesthetic**
Visual/Spatial **Auditory/Musical**
Verbal/Linguistic **Interpersonal**

National Geography Standards covered in "Southeast Asia"

The student knows and understands:

(3) How to analyze the spatial organization of people, places, and environments on Earth's surface

(4) The physical and human characteristics of places

4.2 The interaction of physical and human systems result in the creation of and changes to places

(7) The physical processes that shape the patterns of Earth's surface

7.3 Physical processes interact over time to shape particular places on Earth's surface

(8) The characteristics and spatial distribution of ecosystems and biomes on Earth's surface

8.3 The distribution and characteristics of biomes change over time

(9) The characteristics, distribution, and migration of human populations on Earth's surface

9.2 Population distribution and density are a function of historical, environmental, economic, political, and technological factors

(10) The characteristics, distribution, and complexity of Earth's cultural mosaics

10.3 Cultures changes through convergence and/or divergence

(11) The patterns and networks of economic interdependence on Earth's surface

11.3 Economic systems are dynamic organizations of interdependent economic activities for production, exchange, distribution, and consumption of goods and services

(14) How human actions modify the physical environment

14.1 Human modifications of the physical environment can have significant global impacts

(15) How physical systems affect human systems

15.3 Societies use a variety of strategies to adapt to changes in the physical environment

(17) How to apply geography to interpret the past

17.3 Historical events must be interpreted in the contexts of people's past perceptions of places, regions, and environments.

(18) How to apply geography to interpret the present and plan for the future

18.1 Geographic contexts (the human and physical characteristics of places and environments) provide the bases for analyzing current events and making predictions about future issues

CHAPTER OPENER PLANNER

Students will know:

- *the physical geography of Southeast Asia and how its location and elevation influence its climate.*
- *how water systems are important to economic development.*
- *that diverse ethnic groups, powerful neighbors such as China and Japan, and Europeans shaped the history, government, and culture.*
- *how population patterns in Southeast Asia have been affected by physical geography, migration, and urban growth.*
- *the modern economy is dominated by agriculture and natural resources, and mismanagement of resources leads to loss of biodiversity.*
- *the threats to the environment in the region and how they are being addressed.*

Students will be able to:

- ***describe*** *the physical geography of Southeast Asia and how its location affects its climate.*
- ***analyze*** *the importance of water systems to economic development in Southeast Asia.*
- ***identify*** *the different countries and groups that have influenced the history, government, and culture of Southeast Asia.*
- ***analyze*** *how physical geography, migration, and urban growth affect population patterns.*
- ***identify*** *industries that dominate Southeast Asia's economy and how mismanagement leads to loss of forests and biodiversity.*
- ***identify*** *threats to the environment in the region and how they are being addressed.*

UNDERSTANDING BY DESIGN®

☑ Print Teaching Options

V Visual Skills

- ☐ **p. 752** Students record details about the three causes that create an emerging market. AL Visual/Spatial

R Reading Skills

- ☐ **p. 752** Students describe what an emerging market is and why they develop. ELL Verbal/Linguistic
- ☐ **p. 752** Students discuss the "roaring tigers." ELL

C Critical Thinking Skills

- ☐ **p. 752** Students discuss a image of Kuala Lumpur. BL

W Writing Skills

- ☐ **p. 753** Students describe how fairly they think workers are treated in an emerging market. BL Verbal/Linguistic

T Technology Skills

- ☐ **p. 753** Students research the positive and negative effects of economic expansion and make a visual presentation. BL Logical/Mathematical, Visual/Spatial

☑ Online Teaching Options

C Critical Thinking Skills

- SLIDE SHOW **Development in Southeast Asia**—Students learn about economic developments in Southeast Asia. AL Visual/Spatial
- MAP **Interactive Regional Atlas**—Students use the interactive regional atlas to understand the physical and human geography of Southeast Asia.

☑ Printable Digital Worksheets

- WORKSHEET **Assessing Background Knowledge**—Determine the level of prior knowledge students have about Southeast Asia.
- WORKSHEET **Chapter Summary**—Students review the main idea of each lesson of the chapter content.
- WORKSHEET **Reteaching Activity**—These worksheets provide students with an opportunity for remedial practice and review of vital chapter content.

Project-Based Learning 

Hands-On

Create Conservation Plans

Students bring together information from all lessons about the physical geography and human geography of Southeast Asia to write a conservation plan for an endangered species.

Digital Hands-On

Create Online Projects

Find an additional activity online that incorporates technology for this project. Visit the EdTech Teacher Web sites for more links, tutorials, and other resources.

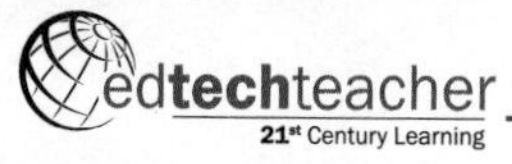

Print Resources

ANCILLARY RESOURCES

This ancillary is available for every chapter and lesson.

- **Chapter Tests and Lesson Quizzes**

PRINTABLE DIGITAL WORKSHEETS

These printable digital worksheets are available for every chapter and lesson.

- **Assessing Background Knowledge**
- **Chapter Summaries**
- **Guided Reading Activities**
- **Hands-On Chapter Projects**
- **Quizzes and Tests**
- **Reading Essentials and Study Guide** AL
- **Reteaching Activities**
- **Video Activities**
- **Vocabulary**

More Media Resources

SUGGESTED VIDEOS MOVIES

- **Rivers of Our Times Mekong River Thailand** (23 min.)
- **Terra Mystica Angkor** (27 min.)
- **Indochina: The Heart of Southeast Asia** (25 min.)

SUGGESTED READING 

- ***Southeast Asia in the New International Era,*** by Robert A. Dayley and Clark D. Neher
- ***Southeast Asia: Past and Present,*** by D.R. SarDesai
- ***Everyday Life in Southeast Asia,*** by Kathleen M. Adams and Kathleen A. Gillogly

LESSON 1 PLANNER

PHYSICAL GEOGRAPHY OF SOUTHEAST ASIA

Students will know:

- *how Southeast Asia's location on the Ring of Fire has impacted its physical geography.*
- *how Southeast Asia's water systems are important to economic development.*
- *how elevation and location influence Southeast Asia's climate.*

Students will be able to:

- ***describe** the physical geography of Southeast Asia and analyze the effects of the Ring of Fire.*
- ***analyze** the importance of water systems to economic development in Southeast Asia.*
- ***examine** how the climate of the region is influenced by elevation and location.*

UNDERSTANDING BY DESIGN®

☑ Print Teaching Options

V Visual Skills

- ☐ **p. 754** Students examine sizes of Southeast Asian countries and locate states or countries on a map. AL Visual/Spatial
- ☐ **p. 757** Students create a guide to the three types of tropical storms—cyclones, typhoons, and hurricanes. BL Visual/Spatial

R Reading Skills

- ☐ **p. 754** Students review the word *archipelago.* ELL Verbal/Linguistic
- ☐ **p. 755** Students discuss the relationship between volcanic eruptions and climate. ELL Logical/Mathematical, Verbal/Linguistic
- ☐ **p. 757** Students explain what a typhoon is. ELL Verbal/Linguistic

C Critical Thinking Skills

- ☐ **p. 754** Students consider effects the Ring of Fire might have on countries in Southeast Asia.
- ☐ **p. 755** Students discuss the map of volcanoes in Southeast Asia. AL Visual/Spatial
- ☐ **p. 756** Students review information about how life in Southeast Asia depends on water. BL Logical/Mathematical
- ☐ **p. 758** Students review information about plant growth in Southeast Asia. Logical/Mathematical

W Writing Skills

- ☐ **p. 757** Students imagine they are living in Southeast Asia for one year and describe the experience of living through the dry season and the rainy monsoon season. BL Verbal/Linguistic

T Technology Skills

- ☐ **p. 756** Students create an illustrated sequence of events that explains the process by which an undersea earthquake can cause a tsunami. AL Visual/Spatial
- ☐ **p. 758** Students research the natural resources in a country to create a visual that summarizes how people make a living and meet their needs. BL Visual/Spatial

☑ Online Teaching Options

V Visual Skills

- INTERACTIVE MAP **Volcanoes in Southeast Asia**—Students examine an interactive map of volcanoes in Southeast Asia. AL Visual/Spatial, Verbal/Linguistic
- VIDEO **Around the World–Borneo**—Students watch a video about the biodiversity of Borneo. AL Verbal/Linguistic

R Reading Skills

- INTERACTIVE WHITEBOARD ACTIVITY **Waterways and the Ring of Fire**—Students identify terms that best match the landforms and characteristics of Southeast Asia and list ways in which people use rivers. AL Visual/Spatial

C Critical Thinking Skills

- INTERACTIVE BELLRINGER **Eruption at Paluweh Volcano**—Students use the introductory text and the photography of an eruption at a volcano to know how Southeast Asia's location on the Ring of Fire impacts its physical geography. BL Interpersonal, Visual/Spatial, Verbal/Linguistic

☑ Printable Digital Worksheets

R Reading Skills

- WORKSHEET **Guided Reading Activity**—Students use the Guided Reading Activity worksheets to review their comprehension of the content.

C Critical Thinking Skills

- WORKSHEET **Video Activity**—Students answer questions related to a topic in the chapter content after they have viewed a lesson video.

LESSON 2 PLANNER

HUMAN GEOGRAPHY OF SOUTHEAST ASIA

Students will know:

- *that diverse Southeast Asian ethnic groups, powerful neighbors such as China and Japan, and Europeans shaped the history and government of Southeast Asia.*
- *how population patterns in Southeast Asia have been affected by physical geography, migration, and urban growth.*
- *the ways in which Southeast Asian ethnic groups, immigrants from South Asia and East Asia, and Europeans influenced the culture of Southeast Asia.*
- *that the modern economic geography of Southeast Asia is dominated by agriculture and natural resources.*

Students will be able to:

- ***identify** the different countries and groups that have influenced the history and government of Southeast Asia.*
- ***analyze** how physical geography, migration, and urban growth affect population patterns.*
- ***analyze** influences of different groups on the culture of Southeast Asia.*
- ***identify** industries that dominate Southeast Asia's economy.*

UNDERSTANDING BY DESIGN®

☑ Print Teaching Options

V Visual Skills

- ☐ **p. 759** Students create a map that shows European colonization of Southeast Asia and discuss how it changed boundaries. BL Visual/Spatial
- ☐ **p. 761** Students compare and contrast guerrilla independence movements in each country. AL Visual/Spatial

R Reading Skills

- ☐ **p. 763** Students discuss the various religions practiced in Southeast Asia. AL Logical/Mathematical
- ☐ **p. 765** Students restate the purpose of the Bangkok Declaration of the Association of Southeast Asian Nations in their own words. AL Verbal/Linguistic

C Critical Thinking Skills

- ☐ **p. 760** Students write summaries about how a time line explains the independence process. ELL Visual/Spatial
- ☐ **p. 763** Students discuss Southeast Asian women rising to positions of leadership. BL Logical/Mathematical
- ☐ **p. 764** Students explain what a free port is and how being one has changed Singapore. Interpersonal

W Writing Skills

- ☐ **p. 764** Students write an essay explaining the relationship between the geography of the countries in the region and meeting economic needs. AL Verbal/Linguistic
- ☐ **p. 765** Students evaluate groups that promote the economies of Southeast Asian countries. BL Verbal/Linguistic

T Technology Skills

- ☐ **p. 760** Students create a multimedia presentation with images and a time line about how countries gained their independence. BL Verbal/Linguistic, Visual/Spatial
- ☐ **p. 761** Students create a visual that classifies types of governments. BL Interpersonal
- ☐ **p. 763** Students research a specific kind of art in Southeast Asia and present a poster display. Visual/Spatial

☑ Online Teaching Options

V Visual Skills

- ☐ VIDEO **Thai Economy is Booming**—Students watch a video about Thailand's new manufacturing sector and its growing economy. AL Verbal/Linguistic
- ☐ TIME LINE **Colonization and Independence**—Students examine the events leading up to independence for many Southeast Asian countries. AL Visual/Spatial

R Reading Skills

- ☐ INTERACTIVE BELLRINGER **Contribution to GDP by Economic Sector**—Students use the introductory text and the graph to answer questions about how the modern economic geography of Southeast Asia is dominated by agriculture and natural resources. Interpersonal, Logical/Mathematical, Verbal/Linguistic
- ☐ INTERACTIVE WHITEBOARD ACTIVITY **Colonization and the Shatter Belt**—Students match European powers with the regions of Southeast Asia they colonized and descriptions of political unrest to countries. AL Kinesthetic, Visual/Spatial, Verbal/Linguistic

W Writing Skills

- ☐ VIDEO **World Treasures: Angkor Wat**—Students watch a video about the Khmer civilization and write a paragraph describing how the temple features of Angkor Wat relate to the Khmer people's way of life. BL Verbal/Linguistic

☑ Printable Digital Worksheets

R Reading Skills

- ☐ WORKSHEET **Guided Reading Activity**—Students use the Guided Reading Activity worksheets to review their comprehension of the content.
- ☐ WORKSHEET **Reading Essentials and Study Guide**—Students complete the study guide and answer Reading Progress Check and vocabulary questions. AL

C Critical Thinking Skills

- ☐ WORKSHEET **Video Activity**—Students answer questions related to a topic in the chapter content after they have viewed a lesson video.

LESSON 3 PLANNER

PEOPLE AND THEIR ENVIRONMENT: SOUTHEAST ASIA

Students will know:

- *how the mismanagement of forest resources results in the deterioration of biodiversity.*
- *the ways in which urban growth and industrialization impact the environment in Southeast Asia.*
- *examples of the efforts made to address environmental issues in Southeast Asia.*

Students will be able to:

- ***describe** how loss of forests leads to loss of biodiversity.*
- ***identify** impacts of urban growth and industrialization on the environment.*
- ***identify** ways in which environmental issues are being addressed.*

UNDERSTANDING BY DESIGN®

☑ *Print Teaching Options*

V Visual Skills

- ☐ **p. 766** Students create a graphic organizer to record cause-and-effect relationships in the lesson. AL Visual/Spatial, Logical/Mathematical
- ☐ **p. 767** Students study the visuals and read the captions of the diagram about palm oil cultivation. AL Visual/Spatial, Logical/Mathematical

R Reading Skills

- ☐ **p. 766** Students discuss possible side effects of industrialization and why it might be important for countries to manage their resources while industrializing.
- ☐ **p. 768** Students discuss the meaning of *siltation.* ELL Verbal/Linguistic

C Critical Thinking Skills

- ☐ **p. 766** Students consider the threats facing the forests of Sumatra and Borneo. AL Logical/Mathematical
- ☐ **p. 767** Students review the bulleted list of suggested solutions to problems with the cultivation of palm oil. AL Verbal/Linguistic
- ☐ **p. 768** Students review the information about the conflict between subsistence farmers and the need to combat deforestation. AL Logical/Mathematical
- ☐ **p. 769** Students discuss the reasons why it is difficult to balance the needs of different people that must share water resources. BL Logical, Mathematical
- ☐ **p. 769** Students discuss the threats to the mangrove trees of Thailand and the effects of the loss of the trees. AL Verbal/Linguistic

W Writing Skills

- ☐ **p. 768** Students write essays explaining how Thailand, Laos, and Cambodia are proposing to save the Mekong catfish and argue whether these solutions go far enough. BL Verbal/Linguistic

T Technology Skills

- ☐ **p. 770** Students evaluate Indonesia's response to pollution issues and create a presentation display. BL Verbal/Linguistic

☑ *Online Teaching Options*

V Visual Skills

- INFOGRAPHIC **An Oil That's Everywhere**—Students examine the infographic about the production of palm oil. BL Verbal/Linguistic

R Reading Skills

- INTERACTIVE BELLRINGER **Deforestation in Malaysian Borneo**—Students identify how the mismanagement of forest resources results in the deterioration of biodiversity and endangers the natural resources of the area. BL Interpersonal, Visual/Spatial, Verbal/Linguistic
- INTERACTIVE IMAGE **Vietnam's Polluted Rivers**—Students use the interactive image to discuss why water pollution has become a serious problem in parts of Southeast Asia. BL Visual/Spatial, Verbal/Linguistic
- INTERACTIVE WHITEBOARD ACTIVITY **Addressing Pollution and Deforestation**—Students complete sentences that explain how urban growth and industrialization are impacting the environment in Southeast Asia and the efforts being made to address the problems. BL Verbal/Linguistic

☑ *Printable Digital Worksheets*

R Reading Skills

- WORKSHEET **Guided Reading Activity**—Students use Guided Reading Activity worksheets to review their comprehension of the content.
- WORKSHEET **Reading Essentials and Study Guide**—Students complete the study guide and answer Reading Progress Check and vocabulary questions. AL
- WORKSHEET **Vocabulary Activity**—Students review the chapter content and academic vocabulary words.
- WORKSHEET **Chapter Summary**—Students review the main ideas of the chapter content.

C Critical Thinking Skills

- WORKSHEET **Video Activity**—Students answer questions based on a lesson video.
- WORKSHEET **Reteaching Activity**—Students use this activity worksheet to review and reteach chapter content and vocabulary. This worksheet can be used with struggling students who need additional help with difficult content concepts.

INTERVENTION AND REMEDIATION STRATEGIES

LESSON 1 Physical Geography of Southeast Asia

Reading and Comprehension

Have students work with a partner to analyze the map in this lesson, *Volcanoes in Southeast Asia.* Tell students to take turns making inferences about how the proximity of countries in Southeast Asia within the Ring of Fire impacts life in the region. Students may wish to conduct additional research to learn more about the impact of active volcanoes in the region. Have volunteers share their findings with the class, explaining whether they would want to live in the region, and why.

Text Evidence

Assign students, or student pairs, one of the countries of Southeast Asia. Have students use the text to compile a summary of the physical characteristics, climates, biomes, and resources of their country. Tell students to conduct additional research to learn more about an aspect of their assigned country's physical geography as it relates to the impact on human activities in Southeast Asia. Have students present their summaries. Guide students to compare and contrast physical aspects of countries in the region.

LESSON 2 Human Geography of Southeast Asia

Reading and Comprehension

Have students work in four groups, assigning each group one of the topics shown on the graphic organizer at the beginning of the lesson. Tell students in each group to work individually, scanning the text for information related to their assigned topic. Then have students compare their notes, agreeing on the most important information to include in the graphic organizer/chart. Have partners collaborate to write a summarizing paragraph about their assigned topic and present their summaries to the class.

Text Evidence

Organize students into small groups and assign each group one or two of the events shown on the time line in this lesson, *Colonization and Independence.* Have students in each group work together to determine the central idea in the text about their assigned event. Then have students in each group collaborate to write a response to one of the following questions: *How have conflicts between powerful neighbors affected the history of Southeast Asia? How did European colonialism affect the countries of Southeast Asia?* Remind students to support their answers with evidence from the text.

LESSON 3 People and Their Environment: Southeast Asia

Reading and Comprehension

To ensure comprehension of the concepts in this lesson, have student groups create a graphic organizer based on one of the sentences in the *It Matters Because* paragraph in this lesson. Suggest that students use the sentence or a key term or phrase from it as the heading or center of their organizers. For example, the term *biodiverse* could be the center oval of a web diagram. Tell students to complete their diagrams with key information about issues facing Southeast Asia. Have students share their visuals with the class.

Text Evidence

Have students work in pairs to write three cause-and-effect statements, one corresponding to each main heading in the lesson. Remind students to provide evidence from the text to support their statements. Tell students to provide a visual with their statements, such as the chart at the beginning of the lesson. As students read through each section, have them use evidence from the text on which to base their visual diagrams. After students have presented their statements and visuals, guide a discussion about the threats facing Southeast Asia's environment.

Online Resources

Leveled Reader

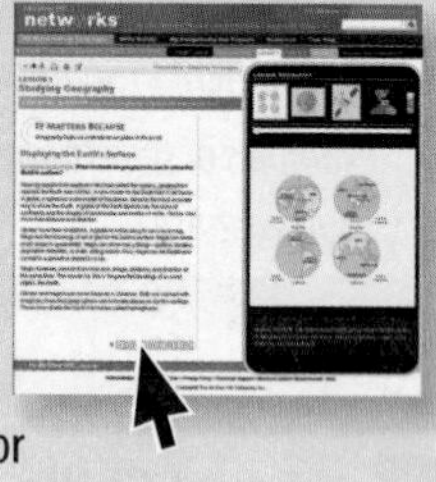

Use this online approaching-level text that corresponds directly to the text in the Student Edition. It also includes additional reading and comprehension support for English Language Learners.

Guided Reading Activities

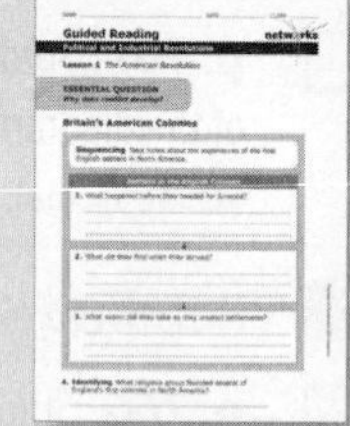

This resource uses guiding questions to help students with comprehension.

Reteaching Activities

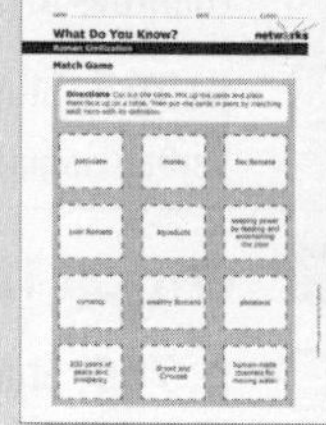

These worksheets provide students with an opportunity for remedial practice and review of vital chapter content.

Reading Essentials and Study Guide

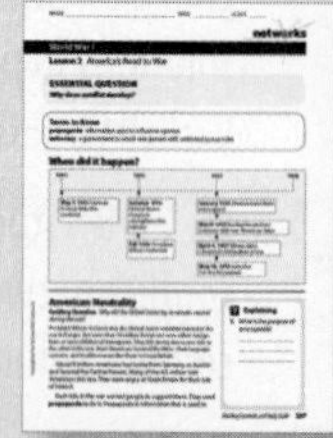

This resource offers writing and reading activities for the approaching-level student.

Self-Check Quizzes

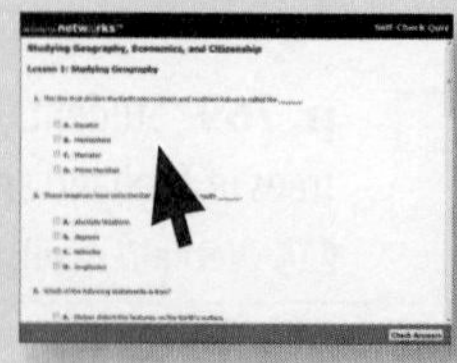

This online assessment tool provides instant feedback for students to check their progress.

Chapter Summaries

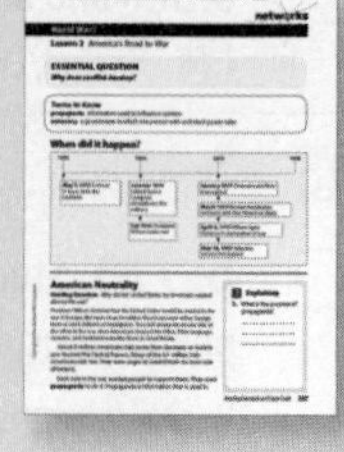

Summaries are provided for each chapter that thoroughly condense core content into manageable chunks.

Southeast Asia

ESSENTIAL QUESTION • *How do physical systems and human systems shape a place?*

networks

There's More Online about Southeast Asia's geography.

CHAPTER 31

Geography Matters...

Southeast Asia is one of the most diverse regions on Earth. All the world's religions, political systems, and economic systems can be found here—and so can hundreds of ethnic groups speaking hundreds of different languages. The physical geography is just as diverse, with towering volcanoes, broad river deltas, and a wide variety of tropical biomes and climates. The region includes a mainland area and two large island archipelagoes.

This young woman in Bali, Indonesia, wears an intricate gold headdress.

ENGAGE

Activating Prior Knowledge Explain to students that they will be reading about changing economies in three Southeast Asia countries—Indonesia, Malaysia, and Vietnam. Have pairs discuss what they already know about the economies of these countries, including what products are manufactured there and what each country imports and exports. Have pairs share their previous knowledge with the class.

TEACH & ASSESS

Making Generalizations Have students read the text. **Ask:** **What generalization can be made about Southeast Asia?** *(Possible answer: The diversity of this area of the world is reflected in its many religious systems, political systems, economic systems, ethnic groups, and physical geography.)* **Why might the religious, political, and economic systems be so diverse?** *(Possible answer: Because many ethnic groups live in this place, their different beliefs and cultures are expressed in different religions and ways of organizing governments.)*

CLOSE & REFLECT

Questioning Have students recall how Southeast Asia is made up of a diverse assembly of languages, religions, and cultures. Then have students identify specific questions they have about this diversity. For example, how might this diversity compare to the diversity found in a country formed by groups of immigrants, such as the United States? Are the different religious groups isolated by region or mixed together as part of one society? Have students record their questions and keep these questions in mind as they read the chapter, using outside resources to find answers to any questions that may remain unanswered.

Letter from the Author

Dear Geography Teacher,

Much of Southeast Asia is similar: rural, rainy, subject to seismic activity, a rich cultural history, and similar environmental problems. A few unique aspects to this intriguing region include the harsh military rule in Myanmar, the ravages of the Khmer Rouge in Cambodia, the establishment of a Communist government in Vietnam, and the rise of emerging markets in Malaysia, Indonesia, and Vietnam. Perhaps one of the most curious places in this region is the city-state of Singapore, one of the truly distinctive cities in the world.

Richard G. Boehm

ePals GlobalCommunity
Where learners connect™

Extend the project-based learning experience globally through our partnership with ePals. EPals allows you to connect with classrooms around the world in a safe online environment for real-life lessons and projects in virtual study groups.

ENGAGE

R1 Reading Skills

Defining Explain that when something emerges, it first comes to being or rises out of something. Have students describe in their own words what an emerging market is and why one might begin to develop in a country or area. ELL Verbal/Linguistic

TEACH & ASSESS

V Visual Skills

Creating Charts After students read the definition of *emerging market* and the three causes that create one—rapid industrialization, economic growth, and integration into the global economic system—have them organize the information visually by creating a three-column chart. Ask students to record important details about each of these causes in the three countries as they read the rest of this feature. AL Visual/Spatial

R2 Reading Skills

Examining Have students review the final part of the introductory text. **Ask:** What are "roaring 'tigers'"? *(They are three Southeast Asian countries whose economies are among the fastest-growing—Indonesia, Malaysia, and Vietnam.)* Why might these countries be referred to as "tigers"? *(Possible answers: Tigers are native to Southeast Asia. These animals are dominant predators, so they make a good symbol for a strong economy.)* ELL Verbal/Linguistic

C Critical Thinking Skills

Analyzing Visuals Have students examine the photograph of Kuala Lumpur. **Ask:** How does this photograph help you understand better about the effects of being an emerging market on life in a country? *(Student answers may vary, but should include aspects of the photo such as how well-developed this city is, with many tall modern buildings and a park area full of sophisticated landscaping, and how the city is clearly still booming with new construction.)* BL Visual/Spatial

Why Geography Matters: **Southeast Asia**

emerging markets *in* Southeast Asia

R1

V *A country that is moving toward a more complex economy as the result of rapid industrialization, economic growth, and integration into the global economic system is an emerging market. In **Southeast Asia**, emerging markets are booming.*
R2 *Indonesia, Malaysia, and Vietnam—three of Southeast Asia's roaring "tigers"—are among the fastest-growing economies in the region.*

C

752

Project-Based Learning

Hands-On

Create Conservation Plans
Have students create conservation plans that bring together information from all lessons about the physical geography and human geography in Southeast Asia.

Digital Hands-On

Create Online Projects
Find an additional activity online that incorporates technology for this project. Visit the EdTech Teacher Web sites for more links, tutorials, and other resources.

Why Geography Matters

Why are businesses investing in Indonesia, Malaysia, and Vietnam?

During the late twentieth century, Southeast Asia underwent an economic transformation. From the 1970s to the 1990s, traditionally agricultural countries began to industrialize. Today, Indonesia, Malaysia, and Vietnam manufacture shoes, clothing, electronics, and many other goods, most of which are exported around the world. Industrialization has led to economic growth in Southeast Asia. Between 1967 and 1997, Indonesia's gross domestic product (GDP) grew 6 percent per year. Since adopting a constitution in 1992 that encouraged the development of a market economy, Vietnam has experienced impressive economic growth. Vietnam's economy is growing about 7 percent each year. Both Vietnam and Malaysia have some of the lowest unemployment rates in the world. Thriving industries have boosted international trade and attracted European, Chinese, and American businesses to the region.

1. **Human Systems** What economic changes have taken place in these countries?

How did these three countries become classified as emerging markets?

Indonesia, Malaysia, and Vietnam share characteristics that helped them develop strong economies. First, each country has abundant natural resources. For example, Indonesia has oil, tin and other minerals, timber, coal, and natural gas. Second, these countries have plenty of highly skilled workers and low labor costs. Although several Southeast Asian countries raised the minimum wage in 2013, workers here still earn much less per hour compared to workers in Europe, North America, and many other parts of the world. Third, the location of these countries spurs trade. Southeast Asia is strategically located between the South China Sea and the Indian Ocean. The Strait of Malacca—a choke point that connects the two bodies of water—is one of the most important shipping routes in the world. Finally, the governments of Indonesia, Malaysia, and Vietnam adopted policies that foster trade and business. These policies include building new roads, airports, and ports; improving education; and streamlining processes to make it easier for people to start businesses.

2. **Places and Regions** What four factors led to Indonesia, Malaysia, and Vietnam becoming classified as emerging markets?

What are some risks of rapid economic growth?

Indonesia, Malaysia, and Vietnam have impressively expanded their economies, yet the widening gap between the rich and the poor in these countries often creates tensions. At times, economic inequality has led to labor unrest, corruption, violent clashes, and political and social instability. In 2011, for instance, copper miners at the Grasberg Mine in Indonesia went on strike for higher wages and large protests demanding political reforms erupted in Malaysia. Rapid growth can also involve uneven economic development. Indonesia, for example, has relied heavily on its oil and natural gas resources for economic growth, but its manufacturing sector has fallen behind. In addition, these emerging market countries have developed greater vulnerability to the ripple effects of the global recession. Even the most vibrant emerging markets can be negatively affected by a struggling worldwide economy.

3. **Human Systems** What are the economic challenges these countries face?

THERE'S MORE ONLINE

READ a chart of Southeast Asia's major exports • *VIEW* a graph showing GDP of Southeast Asian countries

W Writing Skills

Argument Have students write a paragraph expressing their opinion about how fairly they think workers in these emerging markets are being treated. Have students explain the situation in two or three paragraphs, detailing what workers contribute to the growing prosperity of these countries and how the workers are rewarded in return. They should then evaluate whether the current state of affairs is good for the futures of these countries or whether some aspects may need to change. Allow students to do additional research as needed. BL **Verbal/Linguistic**

T Technology Skills

Researching Assign small groups either Indonesia, Malaysia, or Vietnam to research more about these emerging markets and how their growth is affecting life in each country. Have groups work together to find out specific details about the positive and negative effects of economic expansion in each country. Encourage groups to research how the people in these countries feel about the new chances for prosperity and evaluate whether the more positive benefits are being experienced by everyone. Have groups finish by making and presenting a visual that weighs the positive and negative effects in their assigned country against one another. Hold a class discussion to talk about each group's findings and to compare and contrast the three emerging markets. BL **Logical/Mathematical, Visual/Spatial**

CLOSE & REFLECT

Reaching Conclusions Ask students to review the effects of emerging markets on their countries. Invite students to write a few sentences summarizing the overall current situation in one of these countries and evaluate whether this country has benefited from or been hurt more by becoming an emerging market.

SLIDE SHOW

Development in Southeast Asia

Analzying Visuals Ask students to examine the slide show about economic developments in Southeast Asia. AL **Visual/Spatial**

ANSWERS, p. 753

Why Geography Matters

1. Southeast Asia has become industrialized and has begun manufacturing many goods, including clothing and electronics, which has led to economic growth.
2. The four factors leading to these countries becoming emerging markets are plentiful natural resources, highly skilled workers and low labor costs, their locations which provide access to shipping routes, and government policies that promote trade and business.
3. Economic challenges in these countries include a large gap between the rich and poor, leading to corruption, violence, and instability; uneven development; and more vulnerability to changes in global economies.

ENGAGE

C Critical Thinking Skills

Interpreting Significance Before students begin the lesson, have pairs work together to recall what they have already learned about the Ring of Fire and how it has affected the geography and history of other places around the world. Have them consider what effects the Ring of Fire might have on countries in Southeast Asia, including the reasons why Southeast Asian countries might be mountainous, have volcanoes, and be prone to experiencing earthquakes.

TEACH & ASSESS

R Reading Skills

Explaining Have students read about how some countries in Southeast Asia can be classified as island archipelagoes. Review the term *archipelago.* **Ask:** **What is an archipelago?** *(It is a group of islands.)* **What kind of country would an island archipelago be?** *(a group of islands united under the same government)* **How are island archipelagoes different from the other type of countries found in Southeast Asia?** *(The other countries are found on the mainland and are each composed of one large area of land, rather than many islands scattered across the water.)* ELL Verbal/Linguistic

V Visual Skills

Locating Display a world map and provide students with their own copies. Have students review the information in the lesson about how the sizes of Southeast Asian countries compare to other areas of land in the world, such as U.S. states. Have them first examine the size of the Southeast Asian country and then locate the state or country to which it is being compared and check to see for themselves whether the text is making a fair comparison. Then have students find other countries or states that compare in size to various Southeast Asian countries. AL Visual/Spatial

ANSWERS, p. 754

TAKING NOTES: Mainland: Rivers such as the Mekong, the Red, the Irrawaddy, the Salween, and the Chao Phraya provide water for crops and transportation. **Islands and Archipelagoes:** The Pacific Ocean is important for transportation. **Mainland, Islands, and Archipelagoes:** With the exception of the island of Borneo, the countries of Southeast Asia experience volcanic eruptions, earthquakes, and tsunamis. This is especially true of the islands. All the countries are known for their mountains and hills. Monsoon winds create a dry season and a rainy season. Cyclones and typhoons occur during the rainy season. Average temperatures are around 80°F. Rain forests provide great biodiversity. Volcanic soil and the warm, wet climate are good for farming.

networks

There's More Online!

- **IMAGE** Mekong River Delta
- **IMAGE** Population Density in Southeast Asia
- **MAP** Volcanoes in Southeast Asia
- **INTERACTIVE SELF-CHECK QUIZ**
- **VIDEO** Physical Geography of Southeast Asia

LESSON 1
Physical Geography of Southeast Asia

ESSENTIAL QUESTION • *How do physical systems and human systems shape a place?*

Reading HELPDESK

Academic Vocabulary (Tier Two Words)
- **access**
- **differentiate**

Content Vocabulary (Tier Three Words)
- **tsunami**
- **cyclone**
- **typhoon**
- **biodiversity**

TAKING NOTES: ***Key Ideas and Details***

IDENTIFYING As you read about the physical geography of Southeast Asia, use a diagram like the one below to note similarities and differences between the features of the mainland and those of the islands and archipelagoes.

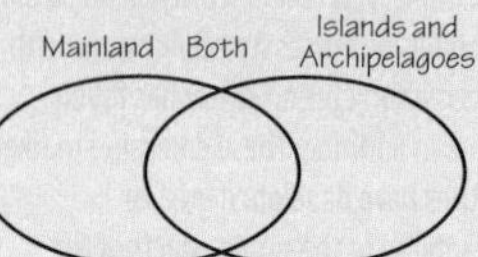

IT MATTERS BECAUSE

Few regions have such diverse physical features as Southeast Asia. The Pacific Ocean dominates this subregion where the combined landmass of island countries is greater than the combined landmass of countries on the mainland. Southeast Asia's physical geography also shows the effects of the Pacific Ring of Fire. Most Southeast Asian countries are mountainous, and many have volcanoes and are prone to earthquakes.

Landforms

GUIDING QUESTION *What are the major physical characteristics of Southeast Asia?*

The 11 countries of Southeast Asia can be divided into two areas: the countries of the mainland in the west, and island archipelagoes in the east. Cambodia, Vietnam, Thailand, Myanmar (Burma), Laos, and the city-state of Singapore make up most of the subregion's mainland. Malaysia is partly on the Malay Peninsula and partly on the island of Borneo. In the east, Indonesia, East Timor, Brunei, and the Philippines form island countries that stretch across the western half of the Pacific Ocean.

It is important to realize how large Southeast Asia's island countries are. Their landmass is actually larger than that of the subregion's mainland countries. Indonesia consists of more than 13,000 islands that span a distance of 1,000 miles (1,609 km) from north to south and 3,000 miles (4,828 km) from west to east—an area wider than the continental United States. The Philippines is a close second to Indonesia, with more than 7,000 islands and an area close in size to the state of Arizona. Countries on the mainland are also large. Myanmar is larger than the country of France, while Laos is almost as large as the entire United Kingdom.

Southeast Asia also includes some of the world's tiniest countries. On the Malay Peninsula, the tiny city-state of Singapore, at 433 square miles (697 sq. km), is approximately a third of the size of Rhode Island. Brunei, which borders Malaysia on the island of Borneo, is a little smaller than Delaware.

754

networks Online Teaching Options

INTERACTIVE BELLRINGER

Eruption at Paluweh Volcano

Analyzing Visuals Use the introductory text and the photograph of an eruption at a volcano on an Indonesian island to know how Southeast Asia's location on the Ring of Fire has impacted its physical geography. Have students form small groups. Ask them to discuss each question and record an agreed-upon answer to each one. Then, in a class discussion, have each group share its answers. BL Interpersonal, Visual/Spatial, Verbal/Linguistic

Eruption at Paluweh Volcano

Indonesia has the largest concentration of active volcanoes in the world. A volcano on the tiny island of Paluweh erupted in February 2013.

1. The path of the volcanos landslide runs from its summit to the ocean in what direction?

A. North
B. South
C. East
D. West

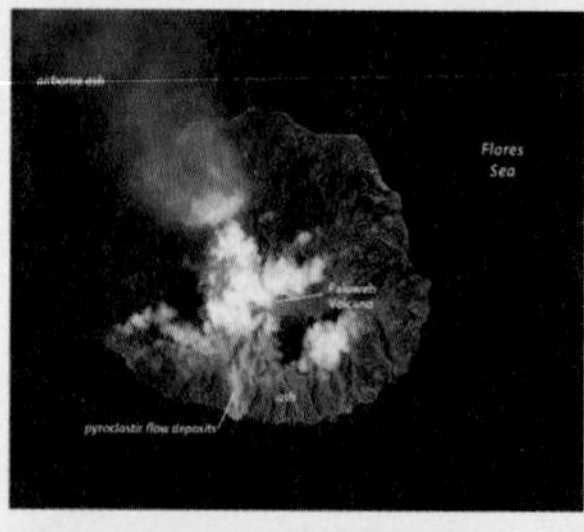

click for answer

Auto-Run Click Through Previous 1 of 3 Next

Southeast Asia's position along the Pacific Ocean places it within the Ring of Fire, a belt of volcanoes and tectonic plate boundaries that surrounds the Pacific. About 75 percent of the world's volcanoes are located along the Ring of Fire. Most of the world's strongest earthquakes also occur here because of the moving and colliding of Earth's tectonic plates. As tectonic plates move, they produce earthquakes and volcanoes. In much of Southeast Asia, earthquakes and volcanic eruptions are common. Volcanic eruptions are more typical in the subregion's island countries. One exception, however, is the large island of Borneo. Borneo is often called a mini-continent because it is so stable. This stability makes Borneo's physical geography an exception to the pattern of the rest of the subregion. Although it has mountains, Borneo has no volcanoes and rarely experiences earthquakes.

The rest of Indonesia, in contrast, has the largest concentration of active volcanoes in the world. In 2010 Mount Merapi erupted, sending hot gases high into the air and dropping hot ash and debris on nearby villages. As Merapi's explosions grew more violent, Indonesia's government evacuated nearby villages and cut off **access** to them. It was two weeks before villagers were able to return.

Eruptions in Indonesia have changed world history. In 1815 Mount Tambora sent so much ash into the sky that the year was dubbed "the year without a summer" because ash blocked so much solar energy. Crops failed and millions went hungry in places as far away as the United States, Europe, and northern Africa. In 1883 Krakatau exploded, killing some 36,000 people. Indonesia's most destructive volcanic eruption is thought to have occurred about 73,000 years ago, when Mount Toba exploded. That eruption changed weather patterns worldwide for the next 20 years.

Some of Southeast Asia's earthquakes occur under water. When this happens, they can produce **tsunamis**, dangerous huge waves that can flood inland areas with little warning. This is what happened in 2004, when an underwater

access a way to approach or enter a place

tsunami a dangerous large ocean wave caused by an underwater earthquake, a volcanic eruption, or a sudden displacement of the ocean floor

R

GEOGRAPHY CONNECTION

Southeast Asia is located along the Ring of Fire, an area of frequent volcanic eruptions and earthquakes.

1. ***THE WORLD IN SPATIAL TERMS*** What countries that are not part of Southeast Asia are also affected by the Ring of Fire around the Pacific Ocean?
2. ***ENVIRONMENT AND SOCIETY*** In what ways are people affected by volcanic eruptions?

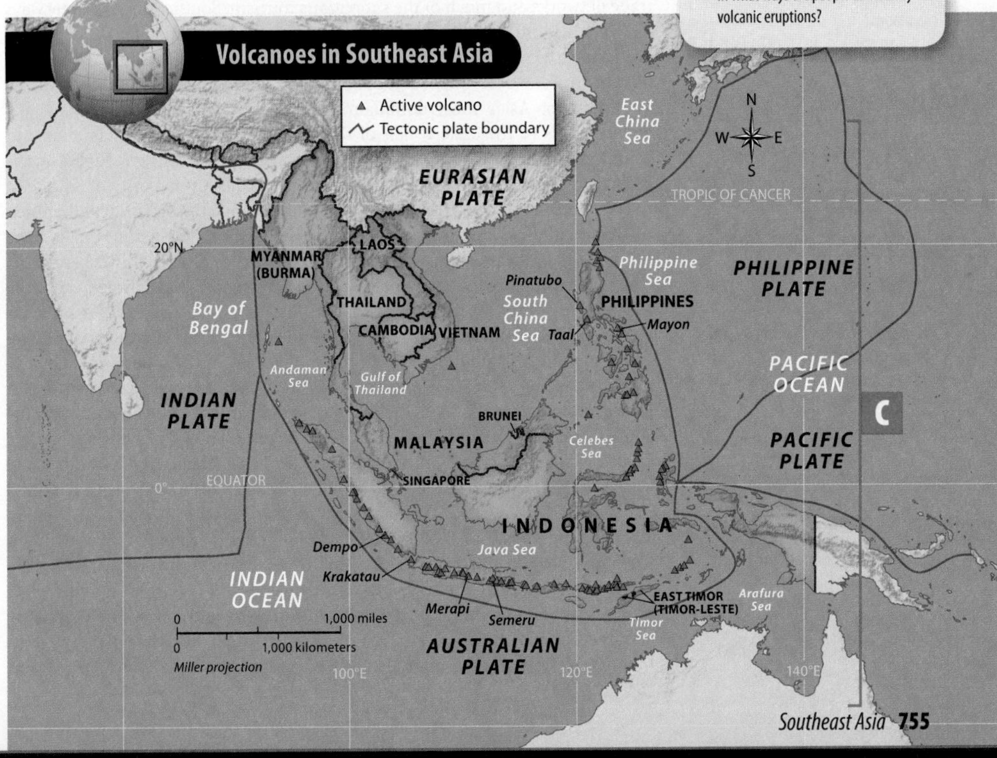

INTERACTIVE MAP

Volcanoes in Southeast Asia

Examining Have students examine the interactive map of volcanoes in Southeast Asia. Ask students to click on a volcano for more information. AL Visual/Spatial, Verbal/Linguistic

CHAPTER 31, Lesson 1
Physical Geography of Southeast Asia

R Reading Skills

Understanding Relationships Help students understand the relationship between volcanic eruptions and climate. **Ask:** What happens to ash when a volcano erupts? *(The ash is dispersed into the air.)* What happens to energy from the sun when it hits the ash in the atmosphere? *(The solar energy is blocked and cannot reach the surface of the Earth.)* What happens to the weather on the Earth when solar energy is blocked in this way? *(It becomes colder and cloudy.)* How can colder weather affect life on the Earth? *(The cold weather and lack of sun can make it harder to grow enough food.)* ELL Logical/Mathematical, Verbal/Linguistic

Making Connections

Even though Mount Tambora is located far away from the United States, people in the United States still felt effects from its eruption in 1815. It was the largest and most powerful eruption ever recorded by humans. During the "year without a summer," some places around the globe experienced temperatures as much as 5°F (3°C) colder than normal. People living in the northeastern United States at the time described the weather as "backward," because in May states ranging along the coast from the Northeast down to Virginia experienced frost. Virginia also experienced a June snowfall and a freezing spell that struck during July 4. Furthermore, some historians think that this eruption may be one reason that larger numbers of people from New England began leaving to settle the American Midwest. They speculate that the poor growing season caused by the bad weather convinced many farmers to emigrate west in search of a better climate for farming.

C Critical Thinking Skills

Analyzing Visuals Have students study the map and consider what information it is displaying. **Ask:** What do the purple lines indicate? *(the boundaries of each of the tectonic plates)* What do the triangles symbolize? *(the location of active volcanoes)* What is the relationship between the location of the active volcanoes and the boundaries of the tectonic plates? *(The majority of the volcanoes are clustered right next to the boundaries of tectonic plates.)* AL Visual/Spatial

ANSWERS, p. 755

GEOGRAPHY CONNECTION

1. Countries not in Southeast Asia that are also affected by the Ring of Fire include the west coast of the United States, Japan, Chile, New Zealand, and Mexico.
2. Volcanic eruptions can cause ash to block solar energy, causing crops to fail; destructive and unpredictable eruptions cause loss of property and life; and weather patterns can be disrupted for many years into the future.

Physical Geography of Southeast Asia

T Technology Skills

Sequencing Have students work in pairs to create an illustrated sequence of events that explains step by step the process by which an undersea earthquake can cause a tsunami. Students should use information in the text as well as information found online or in other library resources. Remind pairs to use features such as numbered pictures, labels, and captions to provide information about each step. Invite volunteers to share their completed visuals with the class. AL Visual/Spatial

Content Background Knowledge

Tsunami Preparedness By calculating how much stress has built up in different sections of underwater trenches, seismologists can try to predict how soon major earthquakes may strike in the future and cause tsunamis to batter the nearby coastlines. While scientists cannot calculate the exact time when an earthquake might happen, they can at least determine how likely it is that another earthquake will occur in the future. People who live in places prone to tsunamis can then take steps to prepare. One main strategy for preparing for a tsunami is to monitor conditions undersea and urge people to be responsible for evacuating themselves to higher ground as soon as experts sense that an undersea earthquake has hit.

C Critical Thinking Skills

Analyzing Cause and Effect Have students review the information in the text about how life in Southeast Asia depends on water. **Ask:** **How could you categorize the ways that everyday life in this subregion revolves around water?** *(People depend on the water for travel and trade, particularly in areas next to the Pacific Ocean that conduct international trade. People also depend on the rivers and oceans for tourism, fishing, and irrigation for crops.)* **How might life in Southeast Asia be different if the waterways were not as accessible?** *(Student answers may vary, but could include that the population would be distributed differently and that people would find other methods of traveling or make their living in other ways than by agriculture or fishing.)* BL Logical/Mathematical

ANSWERS, p. 756

READING PROGRESS CHECK The Ring of Fire is responsible for creating the mountains of the subregion.

Connecting Geography Earthquakes under the ocean displace water, which changes the waves at the surface, making them many feet taller by the time they reach a coast and thus producing a tsunami.

Connecting Geography to SCIENCE

Tsunamis

T Large earthquakes under the sea (those greater than 7.0 on the Richter Scale) may cause the ocean floor to move vertically, displacing water and changing the waves at the surface. At sea, waves may only be a few inches taller than usual. When these waves reach a coast, however, they may be many feet taller than usual, producing a tsunami. In 1883 earthquakes preceding Krakatau's eruption produced a 98-foot- (30-m-) high tsunami.

IDENTIFYING CAUSE AND EFFECT What is the connection between undersea earthquakes and tsunamis?

earthquake in Indonesia triggered a devastating tsunami in the Indian Ocean. The tsunami generated a series of waves, killing more than 300,000 people.

The same tectonic forces that produce volcanoes also produced the mountains for which this subregion is famous. Not all Southeast Asian countries are as vulnerable to volcanic eruptions as Indonesia. All, however, are known for their mountains and hills. These mountains have folded together into a fanlike shape as the Indian subcontinental plate has collided with the Eurasian plate over the past 50 million years. Mountain ranges on the mainland run from north to south and form a natural backbone for most mainland countries in this region. Mountains also form natural borders. For example, the border between Thailand and Myanmar is marked by a mountain range. So is Thailand's border with China. Another major mountain range divides Laos and Vietnam. The island archipelagoes and the Malay Peninsula are also mountainous. Many elevations in the region exceed 10,000 feet (3,000 m).

READING PROGRESS CHECK

Explaining How does the Ring of Fire affect the landforms of Southeast Asia?

Waterways

GUIDING QUESTION *What are the major waterways of Southeast Asia?*

C In much of Southeast Asia, everyday life revolves around water. Rivers provide water for crops and serve as navigable arteries for trade. Much of the subregion's population lives along the rivers. This is especially the case on the mainland, where the population has become concentrated in certain areas. The Pacific Ocean is also ideal for transportation, which has made it the basis of international trade networks and much of the subregion's tourism. Southeast Asia's waterways have made it one of the most accessible regions in the world. This accessibility has shaped the region's economy and its politics. Not surprisingly, waterways have historically been important to Southeast Asian cultures as well.

Southeast Asia's most dominant waterway, the Pacific Ocean, holds the archipelagoes of the eastern half of the region. But Southeast Asia's mainland countries also depend on the ocean for trade, fishing, and tourism. Rivers on the islands are mostly short, steep, and fast-flowing. The vast majority of Southeast Asia's population is concentrated on the islands of Indonesia and the Philippines.

The mainland has five major rivers: the Mekong (sometimes called the Danube of Southeast Asia), the Red River, the Irrawaddy, the Salween, and the Chao Phraya. Three of these rivers—the Irrawaddy, the Salween, and the Mekong—originate in the mountains of Tibet in China. Southeast Asia's river systems **differentiate** the farming economies of the lowland valley and delta areas from the hill and mountain communities that separate the river valleys.

differentiate to distinguish or recognize as different

The Mekong River is the longest river in Southeast Asia and the seventh longest in Asia. It flows south for some 2,600 miles (4,200 km) across the mainland to the South China Sea. As it progresses, the Mekong passes through or along the borders of five Southeast Asian countries: Myanmar, Laos, Thailand, Cambodia, and Vietnam. It forms Laos's border with Myanmar and part of its border with Thailand. Access to the Mekong and its tributaries is the basis of several international disputes. The countries most affected by the Mekong—Laos, Thailand, Cambodia, and Vietnam—have formed a committee to study water projects involving the river.

By contrast, the mainland's other four major rivers are shorter and each is mostly (though not entirely) contained within a single country. The Irrawaddy and the Salween form part of the drainage system for Myanmar's western mountains. The Chao Phraya is the shortest of the four rivers and drains

networks Online Teaching Options

IMAGE

Paddling the Mekong

Identifying Have students view the image of the woman paddling the small boat on the Mekong River. Ask them to list three ways in which people use rivers for economic development in Southeast Asia.

AL Visual/Spatial

Thailand's western mountains. Thailand's capital, Bangkok, is located on the Chao Phraya's delta. The Red River, though it has a smaller drainage area than the other rivers, provides Vietnam with a second river delta (in addition to that of the Mekong). Both of these deltas provide rich soil for farming.

READING PROGRESS CHECK

Explaining How do the major waterways of Southeast Asia affect population distribution?

Climates, Biomes, and Resources

GUIDING QUESTION *How does climate affect human activities in Southeast Asia?*

Southeast Asia's climate is tropical and subtropical. Its seasonal changes are based more on rainfall than on temperature. Most of Southeast Asia, like many tropical oceanic regions, divides the year into just two seasons: the dry season and the rainy monsoon season. These seasons are created by the changing wind patterns over the Indian and Pacific Oceans. For most of the mainland, the rainy season is from May to September when the monsoon winds blow from the Indian Ocean. Between November and March, the winds blow in a reverse direction and make the season drier. Some parts of Malaysia, Indonesia, and the Philippines have a rainy season that lasts all year, however. They are surrounded by the Pacific and Indian Oceans so that the winds bring rains no matter which way they are blowing. During the rainy season, rainfall is quite heavy. Most of Southeast Asia gets more than 60 inches (150 cm) of rain each year. Some areas get two or three times that amount. For example, Ranong, on the coast of Thailand, receives some 160 inches (400 cm) of rain each year.

During the rainy season, some weather systems become severe tropical storms. These storms are called **cyclones** in the Indian Ocean and **typhoons** in the western Pacific Ocean. They are the same kind of storm as Atlantic hurricanes. In late 2013, Typhoon Haiyan struck in what meteorologists refer to as the "typhoon belt" of the Philippines. Haiyan was among the strongest storms ever recorded. Besides devastating winds, it produced torrential rains that caused flash floods which destroyed villages. Thousands died and many more were left homeless.

Climate Regions and Biomes

Overall, the average annual temperature in most Southeast Asian countries is around 80°F (27°C). But temperatures in Southeast Asia, like temperatures around the world, tend to vary by elevation. Mountainous regions are differentiated from river lowland deltas not only by their different landforms, but also by their cooler temperatures. Air temperatures typically drop by about 0.9°F (0.5°C) for every 328 feet (100 m) climbed.

Some tourists to Southeast Asia head for the cooler highlands. Other tourists go to the coastal areas to experience the beaches and coral reefs. They find that the heat of these areas is somewhat mitigated by the sea breezes.

This satellite image helps show population density in Southeast Asia.

▲ CRITICAL THINKING

1. ***Comparing*** In what areas of Southeast Asia is the population most dense? What geographic features are common in areas of high population density?
2. ***Identifying*** Do you see a connection between Southeast Asia's waterways and the borders of countries? What countries seem to have been affected by the locations of rivers?

cyclone a spiral-shaped tropical storm with winds of at least 74 miles (119 km) per hour and with heavy rain; occurs in the western South Pacific or Indian Oceans

typhoon a cyclone that occurs in the western North Pacific Ocean (west of the International Date Line)

Physical Geography of Southeast Asia

W Writing Skills

Narrative Have students imagine that they are living in Southeast Asia over the course of one year. Have them describe the experience of living through this area's two seasons—the dry season and the rainy monsoon season. Encourage them to describe what they experience at different times of the year and to explain why these weather events happen. Students should include descriptive words and phrases about what they might see and encounter. They could also include drawings or photographs to illustrate their narratives. BL **Verbal/Linguistic**

V Visual Skills

Depicting Have students work in small groups to create a guide to the three types of tropical storms discussed in the text—cyclones, typhoons, and hurricanes. Have groups use information from the text and information gathered from the Internet and print resources. Make sure that students are clear in their guides that these are the same type of storm, just experienced in different parts of the world. Have students include references to historical events and scientific facts, as well as visuals such as maps, photographs, and satellite images to create their guides. Invite groups to present their finished guides to the class. BL **Visual/Spatial**

R Reading Skills

Defining Have students explain what a *typhoon* is. *(a spiral-shaped tropical storm located in the western Pacific Ocean)* Discuss other uses of "belt" in this lesson. *(The Ring of Fire is a "belt" of volcanoes and tectonic plate boundaries that surrounds the Pacific.)* **Ask:** What might a "typhoon belt" be? *(Possible answer: An imaginary line that surrounds an area like a belt to indicate where typhoons might be more likely to occur.)* ELL **Verbal/Linguistic**

VIDEO

Around the World - Borneo

Making Connections Have students watch this video to learn more about Borneo and its impressive biodiversity. AL **Verbal/Linguistic**

ANSWERS, p. 757

READING PROGRESS CHECK Most of the population, particularly on the mainland, live along the rivers as they provide irrigation for crops and transportation for goods.

CRITICAL THINKING

1. The population is concentrated on the islands of Indonesia and the Philippines. The population of Southeast Asia is most dense in coastal areas and along rivers.
2. Rivers often make up the borders between countries. Myanmar, Laos, Thailand, Cambodia, and Vietnam have been affected by the Mekong River.

C Critical Thinking Skills

Drawing Inferences Have students review the information about plant growth in Southeast Asia. **Ask: How do volcanoes affect the soil around them?** *(They enrich the soil with minerals.)* **Why would plants grow better in these places?** *(If a soil is rich with minerals, it is full of the nutrients that plants need to grow well.)* **Why don't more people farm near the volcanoes?** *(It is risky with the constant threat of volcanic eruptions and earthquakes.)* **Logical/Mathematical**

T Technology Skills

Comparing and Contrasting Divide students into several groups and assign each group one Southeast Asian country. Have each group use the Internet or library resources to research in more depth the natural resources found in their assigned country. Groups should create a visual that illustrates the different resources found in their country and summarizes how people make a living and meet their needs there. Have groups present their visuals to the class. Then use the presentations to hold a class discussion comparing and contrasting the resources of the different countries. BL **Visual/Spatial**

CLOSE & REFLECT

Summarizing Tell students to review what they have learned about how the physical environment of Southeast Asia has affected where people have established settlements and how they make a living. Have individual students pick one area of Southeast Asia and use specific information from this lesson to describe everyday life in this place and explain why people live there.

River deltas, such as the Mekong River Delta, are important to economies in Southeast Asia.

▲ **CRITICAL THINKING**
1. ***Analyzing Visuals*** What purposes do river deltas serve in Southeast Asia?
2. ***Explaining*** Describe the ways in which everyday life revolves around water in Southeast Asia.

biodiversity the diverse life forms in a habitat or ecosystem

Southeast Asia's warm, wet tropical climate is conducive to plant growth. Plants thrive even in areas where the soil is poor. Some soils are poor, but areas where volcanoes have enriched the soil with minerals have richer soils. In mainland areas that have a dry season, the vegetation is tropical-deciduous, or monsoon, forest. In areas that are wet and rainy all the time, the vegetation is tropical rain forest. In the monsoon forests, trees shed their leaves during the dry season and grow new ones during the rainy season.

Southeast Asia is one of the few regions in the world in which equatorial rain forests can still be found. These tropical rain forests get more than 70 to 100 inches (180 to 250 cm) of rainfall every year. Rain forests around the world are known for their exceptional **biodiversity**. Southeast Asia's rain forests are especially biodiverse. Scientists think that as much as 10 percent of Earth's plant and animal species can be found in Southeast Asia's rain forests, which are mainly found in Myanmar, Thailand, Malaysia, Indonesia's island of Sumatra, the Indonesian half of New Guinea, and the Philippines. The island of Borneo (which is part of Malaysia, Indonesia, and Brunei) is also covered with rain forest.

Natural Resources

Southeast Asia's river deltas, its areas of volcanic soil, and its warm, wet climate are good for farming. Agriculture is an important part of the economy for most countries in the subregion, although living near volcanoes also means living at risk of an eruption or an earthquake—and the risk of a tsunami if near the coast. Nevertheless, farming remains a critical part of Southeast Asia's economy.

Southeast Asia is also rich in minerals, including offshore oil. Indonesia, Malaysia, Brunei, and East Timor are some of the subregion's largest producers of oil and natural gas. Cambodia also has recently discovered offshore oil deposits, and Myanmar has a developing natural gas industry. Copper, gold, iron, and gems are also mined in various parts of Southeast Asia, particularly in Cambodia and Laos. In addition, Cambodia has deposits of bauxite, a mineral that is used in the manufacture of aluminum.

✓ **READING PROGRESS CHECK**

Evaluating How does Southeast Asia's elevation affect its climate?

LESSON 1 REVIEW

Reviewing Vocabulary (Tier Three Words)
1. ***Describing*** What is the difference between a cyclone and a typhoon? RH.9–10.4

Using Your Notes
2. ***Summarizing*** Use your graphic organizer on Southeast Asia's physical geography to write a paragraph summarizing the main physical differences between Southeast Asia's island archipelagoes and its mainland countries.

Answering the Guiding Questions
3. ***Identifying*** What are the major physical characteristics of Southeast Asia?
4. ***Identifying*** What are the major waterways of Southeast Asia?
5. ***Making Connections*** How does climate affect human activities in Southeast Asia?

Writing Activity
6. ***Informative/Explanatory*** In a paragraph, discuss how Southeast Asia's physical geography affects everyday life in the subregion. WHST.9–10.2

758

ANSWERS, p. 758

✓ **READING PROGRESS CHECK** The temperature drops as elevation increases by about .9° F for every 328 feet.

CRITICAL THINKING
1. They provide rich soils for farming.
2. Rivers provide water for crops and are arteries for trade. Much of Southeast Asia's population lives along rivers. Southeast Asia's location in the Pacific Ocean has made it the basis for international trade networks.

LESSON 1 REVIEW ANSWERS

Reviewing Vocabulary
1. Cyclones occur in the western South Pacific or Indian Oceans while typhoons occur in the western North Pacific Ocean.

Using Your Notes
2. Paragraphs will differ but should include that the island archipelagoes have short, fast rivers, and the island of Borneo has no active volcanoes.

Answering the Guiding Questions
3. The major physical characteristics are the mountains, volcanoes, rivers, and the Pacific Ocean.
4. The Pacific Ocean, Mekong River, Red River, Irrawaddy River, Salween River, and the Chao Phraya are the main waterways of Southeast Asia.
5. The monsoon winds bring the rainy season and storms such as cyclones and typhoons which cause great damage, the high temperatures often cause people to head to higher elevations where it is cooler or to the coast where there are breezes, and the warm, wet climate is good for farming.

Writing Activity
6. Paragraphs will differ but should be strongly supported with information from the lesson, including that people live along rivers and coastal regions for access to water for irrigation and transport of goods, the volcanic soil especially on the islands makes good farmland, and the mountains are not heavily populated.

networks
There's More Online!

- **IMAGE** Angkor Wat
- **IMAGE** Railroad Construction
- **IMAGE** Woman in Indonesian Market
- **TIME LINE** Colonization and Independence
- **TIME LINE** Movement Toward Democracy in Southeast Asia
- **INTERACTIVE SELF-CHECK QUIZ**
- **VIDEO** Human Geography of Southeast Asia

LESSON 2
Human Geography of Southeast Asia

ESSENTIAL QUESTION • *How do physical systems and human systems shape a place?*

Reading **HELP**DESK (CCSS)

Academic Vocabulary (Tier Two Words)
- dynamic
- interdependence

Content Vocabulary (Tier Three Words)
- shatter belt
- buffer zone
- emerging market
- free port

TAKING NOTES: ***Key Ideas and Details***

IDENTIFYING As you read about the human geography of Southeast Asia, use a graphic organizer like the one below to identify examples of how history, population, culture, and economics have worked together to create the Southeast Asia of today.

Southeast Asia			
History	Population	Culture	Economics

It Matters Because

Southeast Asia's waterways, a natural transportation network, have brought waves of immigrants. The subregion's dominant religions—Islam, Buddhism, and Christianity—were brought by immigrants from other parts of the world. Some of these waves of immigration are the result of Southeast Asia's position as a buffer zone between more powerful states. In addition, all of the countries of Southeast Asia, except Thailand, experienced European colonization. R1

History and Government

GUIDING QUESTION *How have conflicts between powerful neighbors affected the history of Southeast Asia?*

The mainland countries of Southeast Asia are positioned near two countries that have been historical centers of power: India and China. This position alone made the region a **shatter belt**, as larger and more powerful countries invaded. When Europe began to colonize the area, Southeast Asia was caught between powerful European powers as well. A shatter belt, though, can also serve as a **buffer zone**, a neutral area separating powerful nations from each other, and thereby reduce conflict. R2

Early Cultures and European Conquest

At the time of European contact in the 1500s, Southeast Asia was a patchwork of small kingdoms, principalities, and sultanates. The Dutch colonized Indonesia. Portugal colonized part of eastern Timor. The British, expanding from their empire in India, colonized Burma (now Myanmar), Malaysia, and several islands in the South China Sea. The French colonized what was once known as French Indochina and divided it into regions based on the boundaries of the cultural groups already living there. Today these regions are the countries of Vietnam, Cambodia, and Laos. Spain colonized the Philippines, which became a territory of the United States after the Spanish-American War in 1898. In some cases, European powers V

ENGAGE

R1 Reading Skills

Previewing Have students quickly flip through the lesson to preview the visuals and headings. Ask students to consider what they already know about the human geography and history of the countries of Southeast Asia. They should pay particular attention to how the United States has been involved with this subregion. Then have students write down three questions they would like to have answered in this lesson.

TEACH & ASSESS

R2 Reading Skills

Explaining Work with students to deepen their understanding of the term *shatter belt*. **Ask:** **What is the meaning of the word *shatter*?** *(to break violently into pieces)* **What is shattering or breaking apart in this case?** *(the alliances between different ethnic groups)* **How could you define *shatter belt* in your own words?** *(Possible answer: A* shatter belt *is a region that is populated by people who belong to different ethnic groups and finds itself becoming pulled in different directions and fragmented as the people try to group together or isolate themselves in different areas of land.)* **Verbal/Linguistic**

V Visual Skills

Depicting Have students work in small groups to draw and color a map that shows European colonization of Southeast Asia. Once the maps are done, use them as a starting point for a class discussion about how European colonization changed the boundaries of these countries. Have groups use their maps as visual aids during the discussion. **BL** **Visual/Spatial**

ANSWERS, p. 759

TAKING NOTES: History: India, China, and European powers invaded. The Dutch, French, British, and Spanish established colonies. Independence brought conflict. Today the region includes communist governments, military dictatorships, and emerging democracies. **Population:** Mainland is not densely populated. Islands and river plains are the most heavily populated. Indonesia is the 4th most populous country in the world. **Culture:** Hundreds of ethnic groups with most having their own language. Largest minority ethnic group is the Chinese. Religions reflect immigration patterns. Most common religion is Islam. It is dominant in Indonesia and Malaysia. Buddhism predominates in Myanmar, Thailand, and Cambodia. Philippines is largely Catholic. Vietnam has a mix of religions but more than 80% of the people claim no religion. **Economics:** Subregion has very wealthy areas such as Singapore and Brunei. Agriculture is leading economic activity but many countries are emerging markets. Southeast Asia has been important to ocean trade for centuries. Singapore is an important port and has attracted investors to build its economy. Asian Development Bank is helping poorer countries.

networks *Online Teaching Options*

INTERACTIVE BELLRINGER

Contribution to GDP by Economic Sector

Reading Graphs Use the introductory text and the graph showing the contribution to GDP by economic sector for ten countries in Southeast Asia to show that the modern economic geography of Southeast Asia is dominated by agriculture and natural resources. Have students work with a partner and answer each question. Have each pair write an agreed-upon answer to each question. Then, in a class discussion, review the answers **Interpersonal, Logical/Mathematical, Verbal/Linguistic**

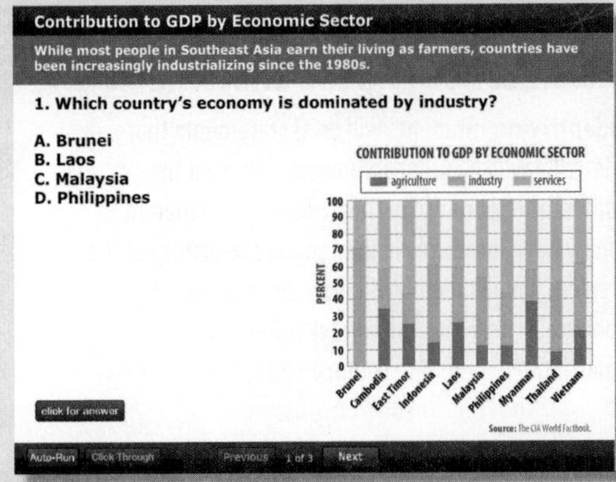

Content Background Knowledge

The United States and the Philippines One reason the United States annexed the Philippines was to protect U.S. trade interests in Southeast Asia. The United States wanted the Philippines to serve as a market for its manufactured goods. In return, the United States wanted to import raw materials such as sugar and coconut oil from the Philippines. Over the years, the United States has generally been the largest foreign investor in the Philippines. The largest categories of U.S. exports to the Philippines today include electrical machinery, regular machinery, wheat, dairy, and red meat. The largest categories of U.S. imports from the Philippines include electrical machinery, regular machinery, and knit and woven clothing items.

T Technology Skills

Acquiring Information Have small groups of students use online resources to collect more in-depth information about how the countries in Southeast Asia gained their independence. Assign each group a country mentioned in the text, such as Myanmar (Burma), Malaysia, Singapore, Indonesia, Cambodia, Laos, Vietnam, and the Philippines. Have groups examine issues such as how the country gained independence and how it is governed today. Once groups have completed their research, have them create multimedia presentations using photographs and a time line to organize their information. Have groups present their findings to the class. BL **Verbal/Linguistic, Visual/Spatial**

C Critical Thinking Skills

Analyzing Visuals Review the entries on the time line with students. As necessary, guide students to recognize how some entries discuss how an area was colonized in the first place, while others focus on how a country began to gain independence. Have students finish by writing summaries that explain in their own words what the time line is explaining about the sometimes turbulent process by which the countries won independence. ELL **Visual/Spatial**

ANSWERS, p. 760

CRITICAL THINKING

1. United States gained the Philippines as a territory after the Spanish-American War in 1898.
2. Laos and Vietnam were both colonized as part of Indochina by the French, who then divided Indochina into regions based on ethnicity. Both Laos and Vietnam had wars with their colonizers to establish independence and within their countries following independence.

shatter belt a region where political alliances are constantly splintering and fracturing based on ethnicity

buffer zone a neutral area serving to separate powerful countries or those that are hostile to each other

united hundreds of ethnic groups into one country. The British united Malaysia's nine sultanates with the indigenous groups of northern Borneo. The Dutch colonized indigenous people on hundreds of islands who spoke different languages. The colony became Indonesia. Thailand remained an independent country called Siam because it served as a buffer zone between the British and the French colonies.

Independence and Movements for Change

The era of European colonialism did not last. The first independence movement began in the Philippines. Following the Spanish-American War, the Filipino revolutionaries targeted the U.S. military. In World War II the Philippines were invaded by Japan. World War II ended in 1945, and the Philippines became independent in 1946. The last U.S. military base in the Philippines was closed in 1992 following the eruption of the Mount Pinatubo volcano.

T The end of World War II started the independence movement in Southeast Asia. Britain's colonies in the region gained independence: Myanmar in 1948; Malaysia and Singapore in the 1960s. Indonesia declared independence in 1946. French Indochina had a strong colonial administration that resisted independence movements. After 1946 the colonies of France became flash points for struggles between groups supporting either democratic or communist leaders.

Independence from colonial powers did not always lead to peace. Cambodia became independent in 1953. In the 1970s it fell to the Khmer Rouge, a brutal regime that murdered at least 1.5 million Cambodians. In Vietnam, France fought to keep control until it was finally defeated at Dien Bien Phu in 1954. Vietnam was divided between communist forces in the north and a U.S.-supported government in the south. U.S. support for the democratic Republic of Vietnam ended in 1975. In 1976 North and South Vietnam were unified under a communist government.

Cambodia and Vietnam were not the only countries in the region to have internal conflicts. Thailand had a military coup in 2006, followed by mass protests in the streets from 2008 to 2010. When Thailand held elections in 2011, the new government began reforming the Thai constitution to be more democratic.

AFP/Getty Images

TIME LINE

COLONIZATION and Independence

After decades or even centuries of colonization, Southeast Asian countries won their independence, but liberation brought problems of its own.

CRITICAL THINKING

C
1. ***Describing*** How did the United States gain territory in Southeast Asia?
2. ***Comparing*** How were the experiences of colonization and independence similar in Laos and Vietnam?

1521

1521 First Spaniards arrive in what they later name the Philippines in honor of the heir to the Spanish throne.

1602 Dutch colonists begin to settle Indonesia in order to control spice trade

1850s–1890s French colonial rule established in Indochina; United States wins Philippines from Spain

1930 Ho Chi Minh founds Indo-Chinese Communist Party in Vietnam.

760

networks Online Teaching Options

INTERACTIVE WHITEBOARD ACTIVITY

Colonization and the Shatter Belt

Identifying Students will drag statements that describe which European powers colonized the different regions of Southeast Asia onto a map to show how Europeans helped shape the history of the region. Then students will drag descriptions of political unrest into the correct column of a chart to match the appropriate country. AL **Kinesthetic, Visual/Spatial, Verbal/Linguistic**

Colonization and the Shatter Belt

Directions: The region of Southeast Asia became known as a shatter belt as larger powers colonized its principalities, small kingdoms, and sultanates. On the map, drag the European powers that colonized the different regions into the correct box to show the political effects of colonization. Drag the red star to countries that represent shatter belts. Drag the yellow star to countries that represent buffer zones. Click on the caption for more information.

• Dutch colonized Indonesia
• Portuguese colonized East Timor
• French colonized French Indochina (now Vietnam, Cambodia, and Laos)
• British colonized Burma (now Myanmar) and Malaysia
• Spain colonized the Philippines (later a U.S. territory)

Show Answers

The country also struggles with an armed separatist revolt in its southern provinces, where the population is ethnically Malay rather than Thai. In Burma, a military coup overthrew the government in 1988 and renamed the country Myanmar. A military junta has ruled ever since, although democratic elections were held in 1990. After the election, the junta put the leader of the winning opposition party, Aung San Suu Kyi, under house arrest. In 2007 the junta killed 13 people and arrested thousands more who participated in protests led by pro-democracy activists and Buddhist monks. Elections were held in 2010, and Myanmar is now slowly reforming its government. C

Several Southeast Asian countries such as Indonesia and the Philippines have guerrilla independence movements. The Philippines has struggled to achieve a peace accord with an ethnic group called the Moro in the south and is threatened by Maoist guerrillas throughout the entire country. Indonesia made peace with its separatists in 2005, though it still faces an independence movement in Papua. East Timor is an example of a local independence movement that succeeded. East Timor was invaded by Indonesia after declaring independence from Portugal in 1975. Over the next 24 years, hundreds of thousands of East Timorese died fighting for independence. In 1999 a majority of East Timorese voted for independence in an election supervised by the United Nations (UN). The Indonesian military violently retaliated, however. Later that year, Australian-led UN peacekeeping troops stopped the bloodshed. In 2002 East Timor became independent. East Timor continued to struggle with a rebel group for several more years, but most rebels surrendered in 2008 after unsuccessfully trying to attack East Timor's president and prime minister. V

Today, Southeast Asia's political map is diverse. The subregion includes communist governments, emerging democracies, and recent military dictatorships. There is also a sultanate (Brunei) and a city-state (Singapore). T

✓ READING PROGRESS CHECK

Explaining How did European colonialism affect the countries of Southeast Asia?

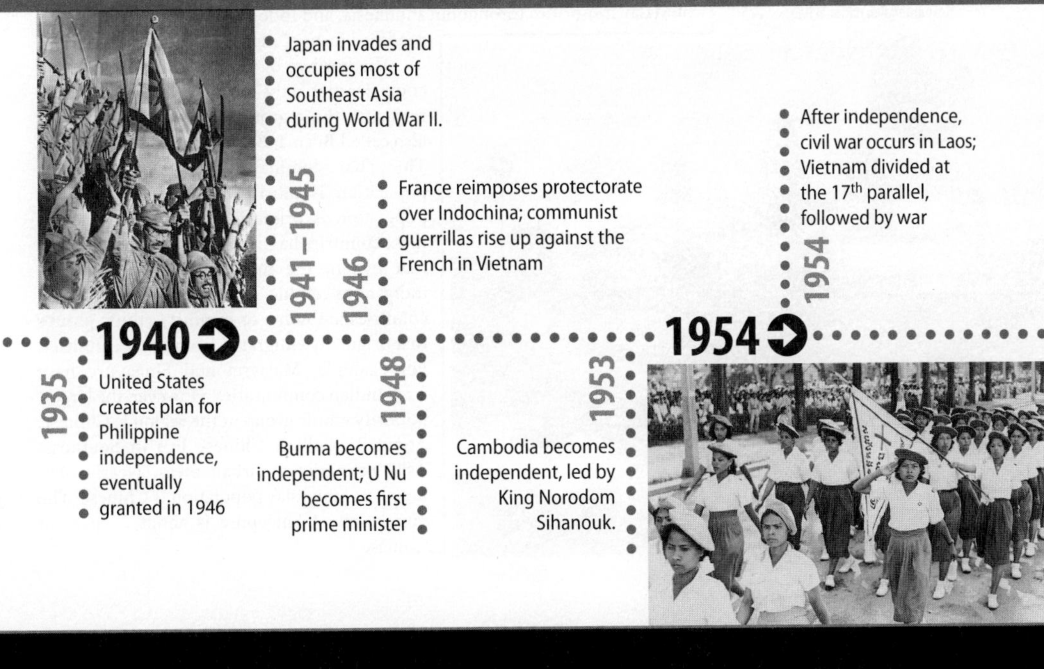

1935 United States creates plan for Philippine independence, eventually granted in 1946
1940
1941–1945 Japan invades and occupies most of Southeast Asia during World War II.
1946 France reimposes protectorate over Indochina; communist guerrillas rise up against the French in Vietnam
1948 Burma becomes independent; U Nu becomes first prime minister
1953 Cambodia becomes independent, led by King Norodom Sihanouk.
1954
1954 After independence, civil war occurs in Laos; Vietnam divided at the 17th parallel, followed by war

TIME LINE

Colonization and Independence

Evaluating Have students examine the time line that displays events leading up to independence for many Southeast Asia countries and problems associated with gaining that independence. AL Visual/Spatial

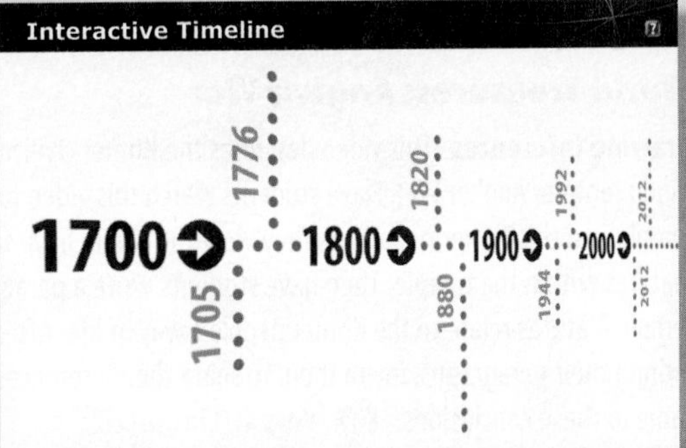

C Critical Thinking Skills

Exploring Issues Explain that a separatist movement is a group of people within a country that want to break away and form their own country or government within the country. **Ask:** **What kind of separatist movement is Thailand dealing with?** *(Possible answer: In the south, there are many citizens who are ethnically Malay, instead of Thai. Because they belong to a different ethnic group, some of these people want to break away.)* Have students discuss the ethics of a separatist movement and the pros and cons of organizing a country based on grouping people of the same ethnicity together. Have them draw their own conclusions about whether a separatist movement might be justified in agitating against a current system of government. BL **Verbal/Linguistic**

V Visual Skills

Comparing and Contrasting Review with students the Southeast Asian countries dealing with guerrilla independence movements. Have students create a chart that will help them compare and contrast what is happening in each country. Supply students with the following headings: *Country, Dissenting Group(s),* and *Outcome.* Once students have filled in the chart, work with them to compare and contrast the experiences of the countries. Invite students to do additional research to add more detailed information to their charts. AL **Logical/Mathematical, Visual/Spatial**

T Technology Skills

Classifying Divide students into pairs and, using the text as a starting point, have each pair identify the current system of government found in each Southeast Asian country. Partners can use the Internet or library resources to do additional research. Student pairs should create a visual that classifies the types of governments: emerging democracy, military dictatorship, sultanate, city-state, etc. Have groups present their visuals to the class. Use the presentations to further class discussion about systems of government in this area. BL **Interpersonal**

ANSWERS, p. 761

✓ READING PROGRESS CHECK Some countries were created based on ethnic groups, and others united hundreds of ethnic groups in one country during colonization. The countries were frequently caught between more powerful countries, creating a shatter belt.

R Reading Skills

Specifying Have students reread the first paragraph on the page. Review any of the vocabulary words or phrases that students may need help with, such as *alluvial soil. (rich soil made up of sand and mud deposited by running water)* **Ask: Why is the mainland sparsely populated?** *(The soil is not productive.)* **What factor contributes to the dense population on the island of Java?** *(Possible answer: Many of the people living on the island are farmers and the island has rich volcanic soil for agriculture.)* ELL **Verbal/Linguistic**

Content Background Knowledge

Angkor Wat The city of Angkor takes its name from the Sanskrit word *nagara,* which means "city" or "capital." It served as the capital of the Khmer Empire for about 600 years, from the ninth century to the fifteenth century. The world's largest religious building, Angkor Wat is actually only one of many monumental buildings that make up this huge city. Inside this temple, over a half mile of its walls are carved with scenes from the famous Indian epic poems *Mahabharata* and *Ramayana.*

C Critical Thinking Skills

Drawing Inferences Review the ethnic groups found in different areas of Southeast Asia. **Ask: Why might the greatest ethnic diversity be found in the island countries?** *(Possible answers: Because the islands have the highest population density. Because the islands are surrounded by water, making them geographically easier to invade, other ethnic groups could move in, adding to the diversity through invasion and intermarriage.)* **Ask: Why might mainland countries have smaller ethnic groups that live in the mountains?** *(Possible answer: Because the mountains were separated geographically, they isolated the people living there from the other parts of the countries. This separation would make it easier for unique cultures, populations, and ways of life to develop.)* **Ask: Why might there be such a large minority ethnic group of Chinese people in the region?** *(Possible answers: China is a huge country and a nearby neighbor, so more people probably immigrate to Southeast Asian countries from China than from other countries that are farther away; Since one-fourth of Malaysians are Chinese, it can be assumed that practicing Buddhist immigrants moved to the region.)* **Logical/Mathematical**

ANSWERS, p. 762

READING PROGRESS CHECK Islands and river plains have the highest population density.

CRITICAL THINKING

1. it is a distinctive and recognizable site that unifies Cambodians with a sense of pride and also is a tourist destination generating revenue for the area.
2. It is a recognizable symbol of the country and is a source of pride for Cambodians.

Population Patterns

GUIDING QUESTION *How has Southeast Asia's physical geography influenced its population patterns?*

R Southeast Asia's mainland countries are not densely populated. The soil on the volcanic islands tends to be more productive than soil in the region's mainland. River valleys and flood plains of major rivers, such as the Mekong, are the exception with rich alluvial soil. Islands and river plains are where the population density is greatest. Southeast Asia's largest population center is located on Java, an island in Indonesia. Almost 150 million people live on this one island in this country that is entirely made up of islands. More than half of all Indonesians live on Java, and more than half of the people on Java work as farmers.

Despite Indonesia's agrarian economy, it is the fourth most populous country in the world. After Indonesia, the next most populous country in Southeast Asia is the Philippines. Southeast Asia is becoming more urban as it industrializes. Each country has at least one large city: Kuala Lumpur in Malaysia; Bangkok in Thailand; Manila in the Philippines; Yangon(Rangoon) in Myanmar; Hanoi and Ho Chi Minh City in Vietnam; and the city-state of Singapore. All of these cities have become a thriving part of the global economy.

READING PROGRESS CHECK

Explaining What parts of Southeast Asia have the highest population density?

Angkor Wat is a Cambodian temple complex built in the twelfth century. It was built as a Hindu temple, but was later turned into a Buddhist temple.

CRITICAL THINKING

1. ***Drawing Conclusions*** Why do you think that the Angkor Wat temple continued to be important to Cambodians even after local religious traditions had changed?
2. ***Hypothesizing*** Why do you think an image of Angkor Wat appears on the Cambodian national flag?

Digital Vision/Punchstock

Society and Culture Today

GUIDING QUESTION *Why is Southeast Asia one of the world's most culturally diverse areas?*

C Southeast Asia encompasses hundreds of different ethnic groups. Most ethnic groups have their own language. The greatest ethnic diversity is found in the island countries. For example, Indonesia's ethnic groups include Javanese, Madurese, Sundanese, and Balinese. In addition, while Malays predominate in Malaysia, they have also emigrated to nearby areas. As a result, there are enclaves of Malay minorities throughout Indonesia, and Indonesia's official language is a modified form of Malay.

The borders of Southeast Asia's mainland countries match the locations of each country's majority ethnic group. In Myanmar, which is also called Burma, Burmans form the majority. The Thai dominate Thailand. Cambodia's population is mostly Khmer, and Vietnam's population is primarily Vietnamese. Each of these countries has other, smaller ethnic groups that live in the mountains. In addition to indigenous ethnic groups, Southeast Asian countries are home to minority ethnic groups that originally emigrated from other countries. For example, Malaysia and Singapore have large Indian communities. However, the largest minority ethnic group in the region is Chinese. About 32 million Chinese live in Southeast Asia, primarily in urban areas. Nearly one-fourth of Malaysia's population is Chinese. The population of Singapore is about 77 percent Chinese.

762

networks Online Teaching Options

VIDEO

World Treasures: Angkor Wat

Drawing Inferences This video describes the Khmer civilization and its landmark Hindu temple, Angkor Wat. Have students watch this video to learn more about the temple and the Khmer people. As they view the video, have students list the different features within the temple. Then have students write a paragraph relating how the temple features relate to the Khmer people's way of life. After students have finished writing their paragraphs, invite them to share their inferences and explain how they came to these conclusions. BL **Verbal/Linguistic**

Southeast Asia's religions reflect the waves of immigration that have reached this subregion. The most common religion in Southeast Asia is Islam. Muslim traders who traveled to the region in the twelfth and thirteenth centuries introduced the religion to Southeast Asia. Islam is the dominant religion in Southeast Asia's largest country, Indonesia. About 90 percent of Indonesian people are Muslim. So are most Malaysians. Malaysia's South Asian minority, though, tend to be Hindu, while Chinese Malaysians are mostly Buddhist. Buddhism predominates in the following mainland countries as well: Myanmar, Thailand, and Cambodia. Vietnam historically served as a religious crossroads for Buddhism, Catholicism, Daoism, Confucianism, and ancestor worship. In the last census, however, more than 80 percent of the people of Vietnam, a communist country, claimed no religion. In the Philippines, where Spanish missionaries accompanied colonists, most people are Catholic.

This woman is selling produce in a market in Bukittinggi on the Indonesian island of Sumatra. Originally the site of a Dutch fort and now an important commercial center, the town reflects a multiethnic heritage.

▲ **CRITICAL THINKING**

1. ***Drawing Conclusions*** How do you think that people of many different ethnic groups, speaking many different languages, are able to coexist peacefully and conduct transactions with each other in urban markets?
2. ***Considering Advantages and Disadvantages*** What are some of the advantages and disadvantages of Indonesia's ethnic diversity?

Tibor Bognár/age fotostock

Family and the Status of Women

Women in Southeast Asia have traditionally been responsible for raising families but are also a major part of the workforce. This produces a double burden for women who must both work outside the home and still keep up with the daily household responsibilities. In rural areas, women often work as farmers. In cities, women frequently work in factories, especially in industries such as textiles, food processing, and electronics.

Increasingly, Southeast Asian women are rising to positions of leadership as activists for change. In Myanmar, activist Aung San Suu Kyi leads a democratic opposition party that often wins national elections. But Aung San Suu Kyi has not become president of Myanmar. Instead, she has spent much of her life under house arrest because of her outspoken opposition to the military government. She was awarded the Nobel Peace Prize in 1991 for her work to bring democracy to Myanmar. After the government liberalized policies, she was elected to the lower house of the Myanmar parliament in 2012.

In 1991 a young Indonesian woman and law student, Dita Sari, began leading factory workers to strike for higher wages and better working conditions. She was jailed and beaten, but was later released as Indonesia became more democratic. Today Sari is still a union leader, but instead of leading strikes, she lobbies Indonesia's parliament for labor law reforms.

The Arts

The arts in Southeast Asia have been heavily influenced by religion, which can be seen through the architectural style of Buddhist and Hindu temples and monuments. Chinese and Indian styles are prevalent in Southeast Asian ceramics and bronze, as well as architecture. Elaborate Chinese-style pagodas and Indian-style *wats*, or temples, dot the landscape. Traditional crafts such as weaving and other textile techniques such as batik are still practiced.

☑ **READING PROGRESS CHECK**

Identifying What are the dominant religions of Southeast Asia?

WORKSHEET

Guided Reading Activity

Examining Have students complete this activity and discuss their answers in pairs. This worksheet uses guiding questions to help students with reading comprehension. **AL** **Verbal/Linguistic**

R Reading Skills

Understanding Relationships Have students review and discuss the information about the various religions practiced in Southeast Asia. **Ask:** **Why might more than 80 percent of the people in Vietnam now claim no religion?** *(Possible answer: Communist countries often suppress religion. Since Vietnam is now run by a communist regime, people may not practice any religion or may not admit to practicing a religion.)* **Why is Catholicism such a popular religion in the Philippines?** *(Catholicism was the religion brought to that area by the Spanish missionaries who settled there with the Spanish colonists.)* **AL** **Logical/Mathematical**

C Critical Thinking Skills

Exploring Issues Have students review the information about Southeast Asian women rising to positions of leadership. **Ask:** **What events happened in Aung San Suu Kyi's career?** *(She led a democratic opposition party that won elections, but she was not allowed to become the president of Myanmar. She was put under house arrest for opposing the military government.)* **What events happened in Dita Sari's career?** *(She led strikes to help factory workers win higher wages and better working conditions. She was jailed and beaten.)* **How are the pasts of these two women alike?** *(Possible answer: They both worked to win freedoms and were both jailed for their work.)* **How are these two women alike today?** *(Possible answer: The governments of their countries have undergone some changes, and now they are better able to work with the government. Aung San Suu Kyi has been elected to the lower house of the Myanmar parliament, and Dita Sari lobbies the parliament in Indonesia for labor law reforms.)* **BL** **Logical/Mathematical**

T Technology Skills

Acquiring Information Have groups of students research more about the arts in Southeast Asia. Assign each group a different kind of art, such as ceramics, metalwork, architecture, weaving, or batik. Students should present a poster displaying pictures of their assigned type of art. Students should also provide a summarizing paragraph describing their art form. **Visual/Spatial**

ANSWERS, p. 763

☑ **READING PROGRESS CHECK** Islam and Buddhism are the dominant religions of Southeast Asia.

CRITICAL THINKING

1. Answers may vary but could include that the people are able to effectively communicate based on sharing common needs and a mutual respect for each other.
2. Ethnic diversity brings cultural diversity in the form of languages, arts, religions, and ways of life. However, it can also bring conflict as different groups with different beliefs, traditions, and ways of life have to live in close proximity to one another.

W Writing Skills

Informative/Explanatory Have students review the information about how people in different regions of Southeast Asia make their living and the top exports from different countries. Then have students write a short essay explaining the relationship between the geography of the countries and how it helps people meet their economic needs. Allow students to use print or online resources to do additional research if necessary. **AL Verbal/Linguistic**

C1 Critical Thinking Skills

Analyzing Cause and Effect Discuss the information about mineral resources in Southeast Asia. **Ask: What did Indonesia do with its oil in the past?** *(It exported most of its oil.)* **What caused this state of affairs to change and why?** *(Now that the country is industrializing, it needs to keep more of its oil to power its new industries.)* **AL Logical/Mathematical**

C2 Critical Thinking Skills

Evaluating Have students examine the information explaining what a free port is and how being one has changed Singapore. **Ask: What are some benefits to doing business in a free port?** *(Because people can unload, store, and reload and reship merchandise without having to pay import duties, businesses can save money by preparing their goods to ship from here rather than other places.)* **What geographical features make Singapore a good choice to become a free port?** *(It is located at the crossing point of several large trade routes, and it has a large, deep natural harbor that can handle many ships.)* **How has Singapore benefited from being a free port?** *(It has attracted enough business to become the largest container port in the world.)* Have students finish by evaluating how Singapore's decision to become a free port has affected life there. **Interpersonal, Logical/Mathematical**

Workers are drilling in preparation for the construction of a railroad that will run from China into several Southeast Asian mainland countries.

▲ CRITICAL THINKING

1. ***Identifying Cause and Effect*** Why do you think Southeast Asian countries are cooperating with China to build a railroad? How do you think the new railroad will affect trade networks in the region?
2. ***Making Connections*** What characteristics of Southeast Asia's geography make the construction of railroads a challenge?

emerging market an economy that may not have been very strong in the recent past, but that is in transition to becoming a stronger market

free port a place where goods can be unloaded, stored, or reshipped free of import duties

Economic Activities

GUIDING QUESTION *How have Southeast Asia's location and natural resources contributed to its economic development?*

Southeast Asia is as diverse economically as it is politically. It holds one of the world's most prosperous cities, Singapore, and a wealthy sultanate, Brunei. The subregion also includes some countries that are among the world's poorest, such as Myanmar. During the 1980s, the industrializing countries of Southeast Asia enjoyed an economic boom. This boom was based on advantages of location, natural resources, inexpensive labor, and increased foreign investment. Some countries that did not have strong economies in the past—such as Indonesia, Malaysia, and Vietnam—are now considered to be **emerging markets**, ripe for foreign investment.

W Today agriculture remains Southeast Asia's leading economic activity. Most people in the subregion make their living as farmers. More than half of the subregion's arable land is used to grow rice. Thailand and Vietnam are among the world's top exporters of rice. Indonesia and Myanmar are also two of the region's major rice producers. Farmers in Southeast Asia also grow cassava, yams, corn, bananas, sugarcane, coffee, coconuts, and spices. Thailand, Indonesia, and Malaysia—the world's "rubber belt"—have many rubber plantations. Palm oil, a product of oil palm trees, is an important cash crop in Malaysia and Indonesia. Forestry and logging have also become important in Malaysia, the Philippines, Indonesia, and Thailand. Forests include teak and ebony trees, which are very valuable. The high value results in illegal logging and export to other countries. Along the coasts and rivers, many people make a living by fishing.

Resources, Power, and Industry

Southeast Asia is rich in mineral resources. Thailand, Malaysia, and Indonesia are three of the world's leading producers of tin. Iron ore is mined in Malaysia and the Philippines. Brunei, Malaysia, and Indonesia also produce oil. Indonesia once exported much of its oil. Now that it is industrializing, however, it has begun to import more oil than it exports. C1 Malaysia uses some of its resources for industries such as manufacturing electronics, cement, chemicals, and processed foods. Indonesia's industries focus on textile and garment manufacturing.

Economic Integration

Southeast Asia has long been the crossroads of major ocean trade routes. Today, most shipping between Europe and East Asia passes through the Strait of Malacca, near Singapore. The city-state of Singapore was originally founded as a British trading colony. Not only does Singapore have a strategic location at the crossing of trade routes, but it has a large, deep natural harbor. Historically, this harbor was used by British warships to displace the economic dominance of the Dutch in the region. Today, its location enables Singapore to prosper as a **free port**, C2 a place where goods can be unloaded, stored, and reshipped free of import duties. Its port is the largest container port in the world. These large metal containers may be stacked on ships for crossing oceans, and then carried by rail or truck after they reach ports. Singapore has also attracted foreign investors, especially in technology, consumer electronics, and pharmaceuticals. Singapore's efforts to build its economy have paid off. Its population has the highest standard of living in the subregion, and its per-capita income levels are comparable to those of the United States and Switzerland.

764

networks Online Teaching Options

VIDEO

Thai Economy is Booming

Analyzing Visuals Have students watch this video to learn more about Thailand's new manufacturing sector and its growing economy. **AL Verbal/Linguistic**

ANSWERS, p. 764

CRITICAL THINKING

1. Southeast Asian countries are cooperating with China to build a railroad because it will enable the countries to ship goods across the region and to ports where they can go all over the world. The new railroad will strengthen and increase trade networks in the region.
2. Rivers and mountains make the construction of railroads a challenge.

In contrast, the countries of Indonesia and the Philippines have much larger populations, but less than one-tenth of Singapore's per-capita income. Singapore is both a city and a country, which makes it a city-state. Of all the countries in the subregion, Singapore has the most **dynamic** economy. Because it is small, Singapore also tries to promote peaceful **interdependence** and international cooperation in the region. Other regional ports include Haiphong in Vietnam, Bangkok in Thailand, Jakarta in Indonesia, and Manila in the Philippines.

In 2010 several Southeast Asian countries signed a free trade agreement with China. They hope to cooperate to improve trade networks. Now work is underway to build railroads from the city of Kunming in China's Yunnan Province into Laos. From there, railroads will extend into Cambodia, Vietnam, Thailand, Malaysia, and Singapore. From Singapore goods can be shipped to world markets by sea.

W In recent decades, Southeast Asian countries have become more interdependent. Based in the Philippines, the Asian Development Bank (ADB) was founded in 1966 to promote regional economic development. The Association of Southeast Asian Nations (ASEAN) was formed in 1967 to promote regional stability.

The ADB provides international loans to aid the economies of Asian member countries. ADB's loans support agricultural, transportation, and industrial development projects. For example, in Indonesia, ADB funds are being used to improve infrastructure such as transportation networks. ADB is also currently working to develop financing and loans that are compliant with Islamic law. ADB is attempting to be more culturally sensitive to countries that have a high percentage of Muslims, such as Indonesia and Malaysia.

Indonesia, Malaysia, the Philippines, Singapore, and Thailand are ASEAN's founding members. ASEAN's mission is to promote regional economic growth. Brunei joined in 1984. In 1992 ASEAN's member nations agreed to form the ASEAN Free Trade Area (AFTA). This meant that ASEAN members agreed to cooperate economically by opening trade between member countries and by reducing tariffs on nonagricultural products. By the late 1990s, Vietnam, Cambodia, Laos, and Myanmar had all become members. Growth is increasing in these countries, but it is slowing in Indonesia because of political instability. In 2004 ASEAN's members signed a trade agreement with China. Now ASEAN's members hope to develop a regional trading market by 2015 that could operate as one interdependent unit, much like the European Union.

READING PROGRESS CHECK

Drawing Conclusions How has Southeast Asia's location along trade routes affected the histories and economies of countries in the subregion?

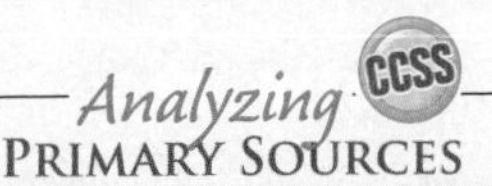

Analyzing PRIMARY SOURCES

Regional Cooperation

R "To collaborate more effectively for the greater utilization of their agriculture and industries, the expansion of their trade . . . the improvement of their transportation and communication facilities and the raising of the living standards of their peoples."

— Association of Southeast Asian Nations (ASEAN), Bangkok Declaration, 1967

DBQ ***MAKING CONNECTIONS*** Why are transportation and communication important areas in which to collaborate? How do you think the transportation and communication networks in one country might affect the people of another country? RH.9–10.2

dynamic energetic, characterized by constant change and progress

interdependence a condition in which people or groups rely on each other, rather than only relying on themselves

LESSON 2 REVIEW (CCSS)

Reviewing Vocabulary (Tier Three Words)

1. ***Identifying*** Write a paragraph explaining how Southeast Asia has historically functioned both as a shatter belt and a buffer zone. RH.9–10.4

Using Your Notes

2. ***Summarizing*** Use your graphic organizer on Southeast Asia's human geography to write a paragraph explaining why Southeast Asia is one of the world's most ethnically diverse regions.

Answering the Guiding Questions

3. ***Describing*** How have conflicts between powerful neighbors affected the history of Southeast Asia?

4. ***Identifying*** How has Southeast Asia's physical geography influenced its population patterns?

5. ***Summarizing*** Why is Southeast Asia one of the world's most culturally diverse areas?

6. ***Explaining*** How have Southeast Asia's location and natural resources contributed to its economic development?

Writing Activity

7. ***Informative/Explanatory*** In a paragraph, discuss how life in small towns might be affected if transportation and communication networks in Southeast Asia are expanded to reach more rural areas. WHST.9–10.2

R Reading Skills

Explaining Have students reread the quote and restate the purpose of the Bangkok Declaration of the Association of Southeast Asian Nations in their own words. *(Possible answer: The member countries are agreeing to work together to make sure they use their resources—like the things they are able to grow and the businesses they have developed—as wisely as possible. They also want to strengthen and expand their trade to do a better job of transporting people and goods, building and maintaining good communication, and improving the living conditions in all the countries.)* **AL** **Verbal/Linguistic**

W Writing Skills

Informative/Explanatory Have students do additional research to learn more about the groups that promote the economies of Southeast Asian countries, such as the Asian Development Bank and the Association of Southeast Asian Nations. Have students evaluate the methods by which these groups are trying to develop the economies of Southeast Asian countries. Invite students to share their essays with the class and lead discussions about how well the groups are doing at solving the problem of developing strong local economies. **BL** **Verbal/Linguistic**

CLOSE & REFLECT

Summarizing Review with students the different ways people in Southeast Asia have used human and physical resources to develop their economies. Have students write a few paragraphs summarizing the development of current economies in the subregion. Invite volunteers to share their paragraphs with the class.

LESSON 2 REVIEW ANSWERS

Reviewing Vocabulary

1. Paragraphs should include that Southeast Asia became a shatter belt as the Dutch, British, French, and Spanish invaded. It was a buffer zone between India and China.

Using Your Notes

2. Paragraphs should include the large diversity of islands, colonization, emigration between islands, and immigration including people from China and India.

Answering the Guiding Questions

3. Conflicts have caused the subregion to at times be a shatter belt and at others to be a buffer zone.

4. Islands with fertile volcanic soil and mainland alluvial river plains are densely populated since they are good for farming.

5. Great diversity is due to historical emigration between islands and from outside immigration. Mainland countries have populations of Chinese and Indians as well as single ethnicities that are largely contained within the borders of each country.

6. Agriculture is a leading economic activity because of the fertile volcanic soils, rain forests contribute lumber, the ocean and rivers support a fishing industry, and the access to rivers and the ocean for shipping goods enables economic development.

Writing Activity

7. Paragraphs will differ but could include that traditional farming lifestyles might change as well as greater influences from different cultures that occupy the subregion.

ANSWERS, p. 765

READING PROGRESS CHECK Singapore has used its historic importance being on trade routes and as an important port to its economic advantage, having the highest standard of living in the region while other countries are now considered to be emerging markets by being able to capitalize on their locations to transport goods.

DBQ Transportation and communication are important areas in which to collaborate because they are essential for economic growth. Answers may vary but could include that good transportation and communication in one country can improve the distribution of goods to people of another country, increasing their standard of living.

ENGAGE

R Reading Skills

Discussing Have students recall what they have read so far about the natural resources of Southeast Asia and how many of its countries are industrializing and developing their economies. Then have pairs discuss possible side effects of industrialization and identify reasons why it might be important for these countries to manage their resources to protect their environments while in the process of industrializing. Have pairs make a list of potential problems that can occur when people do not take the time to take care of their land and its natural resources.

TEACH & ASSESS

V Visual Skills

Identifying Cause and Effect Have students create a graphic organizer that will help them record information about the many cause-and-effect relationships described in this lesson. They should list the threats facing the environment of Southeast Asia, such as deforestation, water pollution, and air pollution. Have students record information about how these problems are caused and the negative effects they create. Point out that some issues may have many different relevant causes and effects to record. Students should continue to add more information to their charts as they read the lesson. AL **Visual/Spatial, Logical/Mathematical**

C Critical Thinking Skills

Drawing Inferences Have students consider the threats facing the forests of Sumatra and Borneo. **Ask:** **Why would only the forests bordering the national parks be in danger, not the forests in the national parks?** *(Possible answer: The national parks are most likely protected land, so the logging companies cannot cut down the trees located there.)* AL **Logical/Mathematical**

ANSWERS, p. 766

TAKING NOTES: Cause: commercial agriculture; mining; commercial fishing; urbanization, industrialization
Effect: deforestation, loss of biodiversity, soil erosion; water pollution; loss of biodiversity, destruction of coral reefs; strain on resources, sanitation systems, and infrastructure, air and water pollution

networks
There's More Online!

- ☑ **IMAGE** Air Pollution
- ☑ **IMAGE** Reforestation Efforts in Thailand
- ☑ **INFOGRAPHIC** An Oil That's Everywhere
- ☑ **INTERACTIVE SELF-CHECK QUIZ**
- ☑ **VIDEO** People and Their Environment: Southeast Asia

Reading **HELP**DESK

Academic Vocabulary (Tier Two Words)
- **generation**
- **intervene**

Content Vocabulary (Tier Three Words)
- **deforestation**
- **shifting cultivation**
- **sustainable development**
- **reforestation**

TAKING NOTES: ***Key Ideas and Details***

IDENTIFYING As you read about environmental issues in Southeast Asia, use a graphic organizer like the one below to identify examples of how economic development has contributed to environmental challenges.

Economic Development = Environmental Challenges	
Cause	Effect

LESSON 3
People and Their Environment: Southeast Asia

ESSENTIAL QUESTION • *How do physical systems and human systems shape a place?*

IT MATTERS BECAUSE

R *Southeast Asia contains some of the most biodiverse areas on Earth. The subregion's equatorial rain forests provide a habitat for hundreds of unique plant and animal species, some of which have never been documented or studied by scientists. Many of the rare plant and animal species of Southeast Asia's rain forests are now facing extinction. In addition, the people of Southeast Asia depend on their environment for clean air to breathe and clean water to drink.*

Managing Resources

GUIDING QUESTION *How has the management of natural resources impacted the environment in Southeast Asia?*

V Minerals, metals, and rain forest timber are among the natural resources most valued by the countries of Southeast Asia. They provide important sources of income. However, mining and harvesting these resources also involve shifting some parts of Southeast Asia from a rural economy to an urban one. These changes cause deforestation and pollution. This environmental damage threatens current and future **generations**. Southeast Asia still has some of the world's last remaining rain forests. However, large sections of the rain forests are being cut down. Countries such as Laos, Thailand, Malaysia, and Myanmar rely on teak and other timber as sources of income. Economies have benefited, but the widespread cutting of trees has diminished the region's forests. Scientists predict that many unique environments will be lost to **deforestation**, the cutting down or clearing of trees, within a few years. This threatens C plant and animal species that do not exist anywhere else on Earth. On the Indonesian islands of Sumatra and Borneo, logging has already destroyed much of the forests bordering national parks.

Agricultural activities pose another threat to Southeast Asia's forests. In some countries, forests are cleared to make room for rubber and palm tree plantations. Together, Malaysia and Indonesia produce 85 percent of

(tl)Suthep Kritsanavarin/AP Images, (tc)Terry Whittaker/FLPA/age fotostock, (tr)Eco Images/Universal Images Group/Getty Images

766

networks *Online Teaching Options*

INTERACTIVE BELLRINGER

Deforestation in Malaysian Borneo

Exploring Issues Use the introductory text and the image of forested land and cleared land in Malaysia to identify how the mismanagement of forest resources results in the deterioration of biodiversity and endangers the natural resources of the area. Have students form small groups and discuss each question. Ask each group to write down all reasonable answers to the questions. Then, in a class discussion, have each group share its answers. Compile a list of all possible answers to each question on a board or flipchart. BL **Interpersonal, Visual/Spatial, Verbal/Linguistic**

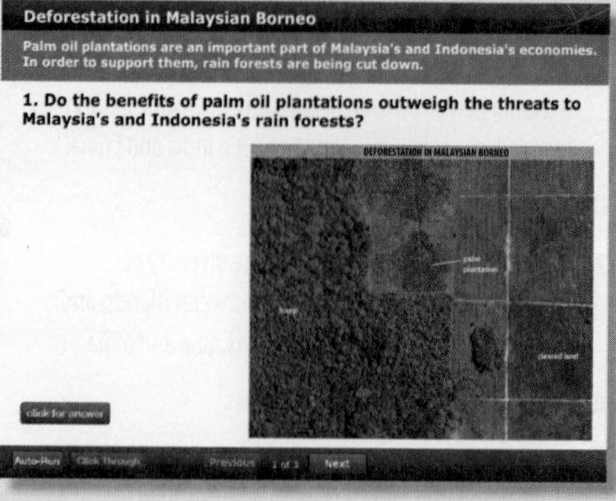
Deforestation in Malaysian Borneo
Palm oil plantations are an important part of Malaysia's and Indonesia's economies. In order to support them, rain forests are being cut down.
1. Do the benefits of palm oil plantations outweigh the threats to Malaysia's and Indonesia's rain forests?
DEFORESTATION IN MALAYSIAN BORNEO

the world's palm oil. Palm oil is a product that is used as a lubricant by industries. It is also an additive in more than half of foods sold in grocery stores. According to the United Nations, however, palm oil plantations now form the single largest threat to rain forests in these two countries. Southeast Asian palm oil plantations cover an area equivalent to the size of the country of Austria. Every day, about 30 square miles (48 sq. km) of rain forest are cleared from Indonesia's Sumatra, an island the size of Spain, and from Borneo, an island the size of Turkey that is shared by Malaysia, Indonesia, and Brunei.

The loss of forested lands is putting many unique plant and animal species in danger. Sumatra's rain forest is estimated to have 465 bird species, 194 mammal species, 217 reptile species, and 272 species of freshwater fish. It also is home to more than 10,000 plant species. Borneo is believed to have 420 bird species, 210 mammal species, 254 reptile species, and 368 freshwater fish species. Some 15,000 species of plants grow in Borneo's forests. Many unique animal species are in danger of becoming extinct. This may be avoided if governments **intervene** to protect at least some sections of the rain forests. Endangered species include

C1

generation a group of individuals born and living at the same time

deforestation the loss or destruction of forests, mainly for logging or farming

intervene to come between so as to prevent or alter a course of events

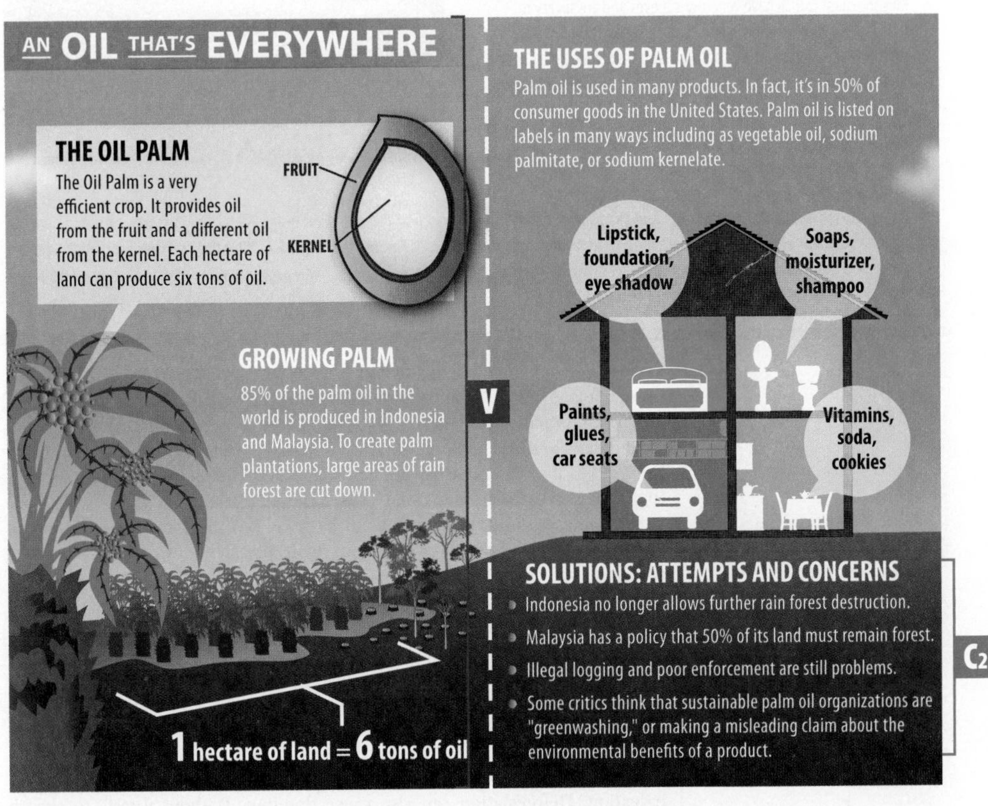

About 85 percent of the world's palm oil is produced on plantations in Malaysia and Indonesia. The global demand for palm oil rises by 6 to 10 percent every year.

▲ CRITICAL THINKING

1. ***Identifying Cause and Effect*** How are Southeast Asian rain forests affected by the demand for products containing palm oil?
2. ***Hypothesizing*** Why do you think the global demand for palm oil is rising?

INFOGRAPHIC

An Oil That's Everywhere

Examining Have students examine the interactive infographic about the production of palm oil. **BL Verbal/Linguistic**

THE OIL PALM
The Oil Palm is a very efficient crop. It provides oil from the fruit and a different oil from the kernel. Each hectare of land can produce six tons of oil.
FRUIT
KERNEL

C1 Critical Thinking Skills

Analyzing Cause and Effect Have students investigate the cause-and-effect relationships driving the use and cultivation of palm oil. **Ask:** **Why do Malaysia and Indonesia produce so much palm oil?** *(Possible answer: It is a popular product under high demand, so they can make a good profit selling it.)* **What are these countries doing to produce more palm oil?** *(They are clearing land currently covered by rain forests to make room for palm tree plantations.)* **What effect does clearing the rain forest have?** *(Clearing the rain forest destroys the habitats for many plant and animal species. By clearing trees, there are fewer trees to take in carbon dioxide, which increases temperatures.)* **Is the damage caused by cultivating palm oil worth the benefits?** *(Student answers will vary but should include details from the text to support favorable or unfavorable opinions.)* **BL Logical/Mathematical**

V Visual Skills

Analyzing Visuals Have students study the visuals and read the captions of this diagram about palm oil cultivation. **Ask:** **What do the images in this diagram help you understand?** *(The diagram of the palm nut makes it clear which two parts of the nut can be used to make two different kinds of oil. The picture of the trees emphasizes that for every section of land measuring 1 hectare that is cleared, palm trees then planted to fill this area can produce 6 tons of oil.)* **Why is the oil palm an efficient crop?** *(Because by growing only one plant, the farmer can produce two different products.)* **AL Visual/Spatial, Logical/Mathematical**

C2 Critical Thinking Skills

Evaluating Have students review the bulleted list of suggested solutions. **Ask:** **How could you describe the solutions proposed by the affected countries?** *(Both Indonesia and Malaysia are trying to protect their remaining rain forests—Indonesia by not allowing any more to be cut down and Malaysia by setting a limit for how much of its land needs to remain forested.)* **How well are these solutions working?** *(Possible answer: They are not working very well because people are still cutting down the forests.)* **What criticism is being leveled at palm oil companies that claim they are producing palm oil in sustainable ways?** *(Some people do not believe these claims can be true.)* **AL Verbal/Linguistic**

ANSWERS, p. 767

CRITICAL THINKING

1. The global demand is rising for palm oil due to its many uses, which causes more acres of rain forest to be cleared in order to grow more palm to meet this demand.
2. Global demand for palm oil is rising because it is used in so many products, including 50 percent of consumer goods in the United States.

R Reading Skills

Defining Explain that *silt* is fine particles of clay or sand that are carried in water and deposited as sediment along the sides or bottoms of the channel in which the water runs. Point out that the suffix *-ation* means "process of." **Ask:** How can you use this information to figure out the meaning of *siltation?* (Siltation *is the process of depositing sand or mud along the sides and bottom of a river or lake.)* Why would siltation pose a danger to these catfish? *(Possible answer: If too much sediment builds up in a place, it could block the ways that the catfish need to travel to spawn.)* ELL Verbal/Linguistic

W Writing Skills

Argument Have students consider the information about how Thailand, Laos, and Cambodia are proposing to save the Mekong giant catfish and the responses to these solutions. Then have students write essays explaining the situation and arguing whether these solutions go far enough or if further steps should be taken. Remind students to use facts and details to support their opinion. BL Verbal/Linguistic

C Critical Thinking Skills

Considering Advantages and Disadvantages Have students review the information about the conflict between subsistence farmers and the need to combat deforestation. **Ask:** Aside from big plantations, who else poses a threat to the land? *(Small subsistence farmers sometimes endanger the land by clearing forests to plant new fields while they abandon old fields to allow them time to become fertile again.)* Why is this system of farming problematic? *(Although the farmers are gaining new land for farming by clearing the rain forest, this land is not full of nutrients because it has been used up feeding the rain forest plants.)* What might be a better way for these farmers than to practice shifting cultivation? *(Possible answer: Perhaps they should continue to let fields that have been used for several years to rest, but they should rotate crops using the fields they have already cleared instead of trying to clear new ones. Farmers should also implement modern agricultural practices using irrigation and fertilizers, and alternating crops using the same land.)* AL Logical/Mathematical

ANSWERS, p. 768

READING PROGRESS CHECK Cutting of trees to sell the timber, clearing land for plantation farms, and subsistence farmers who practice shifting cultivation are all increasing the rate of deforestation.

DBQ Document-Based Questions

1. The giant catfish face threats from overfishing, destruction of spawning grounds, and siltation of the water.
2. Answers may vary but could include that the large size of the fish makes it impressive to catch as well as possibly generating income.

ANALYZING PRIMARY SOURCES 

Mekong Giant Catfish

The critically endangered Mekong giant catfish is the world's largest scaleless freshwater fish. Overfishing, dam building, and habitat destruction threaten the species. W

R "Once plentiful throughout the Mekong basin, population numbers have dropped by some 95 percent over the past century, and this critically endangered behemoth now teeters on the brink of extinction. Overfishing is the primary culprit in the giant catfish's decline, but damming of Mekong tributaries, destruction of spawning and breeding grounds, and siltation have taken a huge toll. Some experts think there may only be a few hundred adults left.

Mekong giant catfish have very low-set eyes and are silvery to dark gray on top and whitish to yellow on the bottom. They are toothless herbivores who live off the plants and algae in the river. Juveniles wear the characteristic catfish 'whiskers,' called barbels, but these features shrink as they age.

Highly migratory creatures, giant catfish require large stretches of river for their seasonal journeys and specific environmental conditions in their spawning and breeding areas. They are thought to rear primarily in Cambodia's Tonle Sap lake and they migrate hundreds of miles north of Cambodia to spawning grounds in Thailand. Dams and human encroachment, however, have severely disrupted their lifecycle.

International efforts are under way to save the species. It is now illegal in Thailand, Laos, and Cambodia to harvest giant catfish. And recently in Thailand, a group of fishers pledged to stop catching giant catfish to honor the king's 60th year on the throne. However, enforcement of fishing restrictions in many isolated villages along the Mekong is nearly impossible, and illicit and bycatch takings continue."

—Mekong Giant Catfish, nationalgeographic.com

Thai fishers display a giant catfish they caught in the Mekong River.

Suthep Kritsanavarin/AP Images

DBQ ▲ CRITICAL THINKING

1. ***Finding the Main Idea*** What threats do the giant catfish face? RH.9–10.2
2. ***Speculating*** Why might the giant catfish be a prized catch for people living along the banks of the Mekong? RH.9–10.1

orangutans, pygmy elephants, Sumatran rhinoceroses, and Sumatran tigers. Of all these animals, biologists may be most concerned about the orangutan. Orangutans are intelligent apes. They can make tools and use them to build things like rain hats and leakproof nest roofs. Orangutans are also said to be able to distinguish between more than 1,000 different plants.

shifting cultivation a form of agriculture in which an area of ground is cleared of vegetation, cultivated for a few years, and then abandoned in order to move to a new area

C In some Southeast Asian countries, such as Laos, threats to forests come not only from big plantations, but also from small subsistence farmers who practice **shifting cultivation**. These farmers clear forests in order to plant fields. After cultivating the land for a few years, they then abandon it to move to a new spot. Farmers practice shifting cultivation deliberately. It allows the land time to become fertile again after a period of intensive farming. Farmers do not always realize that rain forest soil is frequently lacking in nutrients. Soil in these areas has often been depleted by the already lush growth in the rain forest.

Deforestation also leads to other environmental problems. Without the trees' root systems, topsoil is easily eroded by heavy rains and washed into streams. The soil clogs rivers and reduces the amount of water available for irrigation. Deforestation can also cause flooding. Without forests to absorb downpours, flash floods occur.

READING PROGRESS CHECK

Explaining What economic activities are increasing the rate of deforestation in Southeast Asia?

768

networks Online Teaching Options

INTERACTIVE IMAGE

Vietnam's Polluted Rivers

Analyzing Visuals Have students view the interactive image of people standing next to a polluted river in Vietnam. Explain that this river in Vietnam has been polluted by drainage from mines. Have students discuss why water pollution has become a serious problem in parts of Southeast Asia. BL Visual/Spatial, Verbal/Linguistic

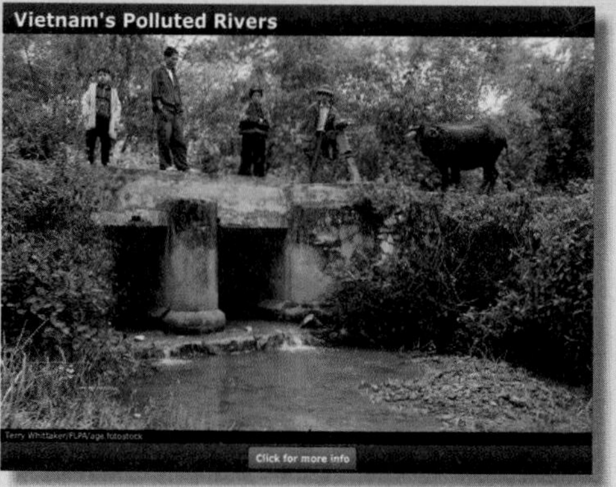

Human Impact

GUIDING QUESTION *Why do urban growth and industrialization create environmental problems in Southeast Asia?*

Industrialization and economic development in Southeast Asia have resulted in the pollution and the destruction of natural environments. Southeast Asians—like people everywhere—affect their environment. Increased manufacturing and industrialization create jobs and raise standards of living. They also produce industrial waste, however. Growing populations and crowded conditions in cities such as Bangkok, Manila, and Jakarta raise concerns about adequate housing, water supplies, sanitation, and traffic control. Bangkok, for example, has become overheated as a result of increased industrial development. In recent years, Bangkok's heat, humidity, and pollution levels have increased at levels higher than the global average. Its levels are also higher than the surrounding rural areas, making it what is known as an urban heat island.

C1 Urbanization and industrialization also put a strain on shared local resources. Such resources include rivers and water supplies. When different communities share a river, the communities upstream have an advantage because the water flows there first. Currently, Southeast Asian communities face a dispute over how to best manage the shared Mekong River. The Mekong originates in China, and the Chinese are building a series of hydroelectric dams across it. Downstream farmers worry, however, about what will happen if the water level in the Mekong drops. Cambodians are concerned about the Tonle Sap lake, which gets its water from the Mekong. Vietnamese farmers fear that Mekong Delta rice paddies could be invaded by salt water from the sea if the Mekong's water levels drop.

C2 The dumping of toxic waste from newly developed industries has become a widespread problem. In some cases, pollution extends into rural areas. This includes the subregion's national parks. In one of Thailand's national parks, for example, most of the freshwater wells have been contaminated by poor waste disposal. Water pollution is also severe in Thailand's coastal areas. Activities related to agriculture, as well as offshore oil and natural gas exploration, have resulted in the loss of over half of Thailand's mangrove forests.

One industry that produces substantial water pollution is mining. At Indonesia's largest gold mine, waste is dumped into the Ajkwa River that flows through part of Papua province, contaminating the surrounding water systems. Even the fishing industry causes some water pollution. Southeast Asian fishers use poisons and explosives to capture certain kinds of fish to supply Asian restaurants and the world's aquarium industry. Many of these fish come from the coral reefs. Like rain forests, coral reefs are a rich source of biodiversity. Also like rain forests, the reefs are being threatened by economic development. The live reef-fish trade generates huge profits, but current fishing methods are destroying the reefs. Once the reefs are gone, local communities will lose a primary source of food.

Deforestation has become a source of air pollution. Land is often cleared by fire, especially in Indonesia, where rain forests are being cleared to make room for palm oil plantations. Forest fires cause air pollution in rural areas, and this pollution often makes its way to cities

Terry Whittaker/FLPA/age fotostock

This river in Vietnam has been polluted by drainage from mines. Water pollution has become a serious problem in parts of Southeast Asia.

▼ CRITICAL THINKING

1. ***Explaining*** How does water pollution affect human populations?
2. ***Problem Solving*** What steps might governments in Southeast Asia take to reduce water pollution?

Making Connections

Urban heat islands are not found just in Southeast Asia. Communities in the United States can also experience this phenomenon. Urban heat islands are often caused when plants are cleared away and land is paved with concrete or asphalt or covered with buildings. Loss of trees equals loss of cool shade, and developed land will not release as much moisture into the air as vegetation would, which also contributes to a hotter atmosphere. Many U.S. communities attempt to reduce the creation of urban heat islands by trying strategies such as planting more trees (particularly on the roofs of buildings) and using materials for constructing roofs and paving roads that reflect sunlight and heat.

C1 Critical Thinking Skills

Identifying Perspectives Discuss the reasons why it is difficult to balance the needs of different people that must share water resources. **Ask:** **What conflict of interests exists when it comes to sharing the Mekong River?** *(Possible answer: The Chinese want and need to meet their energy needs by building hydroelectric dams across the Mekong. However, people from other communities downstream—such as the farmers down the river, the Cambodians next to Lake Tonle Sap, and the Vietnamese farmers who maintain rice paddies in the Mekong Delta—will be affected by the actions of the Chinese if water levels drop.)* **Why do the Chinese have an advantage in this conflict?** *(They are located upstream.)* Have students use details from the text to discuss possible ways to resolve this conflict between the different countries. **BL** **Logical/Mathematical**

C2 Critical Thinking Skills

Analyzing Explain that the roots of mangrove trees are often flooded by brackish water and that because the roots slow the flow of water, they are often essential to stabilizing a coastline and keeping it from eroding because of storms or tidal movements. **Ask:** **What threat do the mangrove trees of Thailand face?** *(Possible answer: Pollution created by agriculture and offshore oil and natural gas exploration can affect the water and cause the trees to die.)* **How might the loss of these trees affect Thailand?** *(Possible answer: Thailand's coastline might be eroded away without the roots of these trees to hold it in place.)* **AL** **Verbal/Linguistic**

INTERACTIVE WHITEBOARD ACTVITY

Addressing Pollution and Deforestation

Exploring the Issues Have students complete this interactive whiteboard activity. Students will complete sentences that explain how urban growth and industrialization are impacting the environment in Southeast Asia and the efforts being made to address the problems of deforestation and pollution. **BL** **Verbal/Linguistic**

Addressing Pollution and Deforestation

Directions: While industrialization and increased manufacturing have improved standards of living for many people in Southeast Asia, they have also caused deforestation, air pollution, and water pollution. Complete each sentence by sliding the correct word or phrase from the word bank onto the line(s) in the sentences; some answers may be used twice.

Many economies in Southeast Asia are now shifting their policies toward ________, relying on renewable resources for technological and economic development.

Many countries in Southeast Asia rely on ________, such as teak, as a source of income, causing large sections of rain forest to be cut down. To reduce deforestation, Thailand, Indonesia, the Philippines, and Malaysia have limited certain ________ exports.

In Thailand, tree seedlings are being planted to replace the loss of forests. Several other Southeast Asian countries are instituting similar ________ programs, as well as marking some forests as protected areas.

Every day miles of rain forest are cleared for rubber and palm tree ________. To combat the loss, Indonesia has instituted a two-year ban on forest clearing, and Malaysia has ruled that 50 percent of its land must remain forest.

In the process of ________, forests are cleared to cultivate fields for a few years, then new land is cleared while the previous restores fertility. Rain forest soil, however, is not always fertile for farming. In Laos governments are encouraging farmers to settle on more fertile ground, protecting the rain forests.

Industrial development is raising heat, humidity, and pollution levels in some cities, creating areas known as ________. Scientists are proposing development of environmentally protected green zones in cities to reduce the problems of escalating heat.

Methods to reduce ________ include banning construction of tall buildings near the sea so winds can blow farther into cities. The Association of Southeast Asian Nations is working toward a 2020 agreement on Transboundary Haze Pollution, as well.

Eco Images/Universal Images Group/Getty Images

air pollutior
plantations
reforestation
timber
shifting cultivation
sustainable development
urban heat islands

Show Answers

ANSWERS, p. 769

CRITICAL THINKING

1. It destroys the fish population, hurting the economy and the food supply; contaminates drinking water; and destroys plant life like the mangrove forests.
2. Governments could improve sanitation and waste disposal systems, create stronger regulations for mining and industry, and stop fishing practices that pollute the water.

People and Their Environment: Southeast Asia

Content Background Knowledge

Green Zone A "green zone" is usually a place set aside in a community where people can focus on living in an environmentally healthy way. Green zones are often set up to combat pollution issues faced by a place. Citizens might establish green zones by passing tighter laws against polluters, creating more parks and green areas, and supporting businesses that follow ecologically friendly practices.

T Technology Skills

Exploring Issues Have students learn more about Indonesia's response to pollution issues. Students should evaluate Indonesia's reasons for taking the actions it has, such as refusing to ratify the Transboundary Haze Pollution agreement. Have groups present their findings to the class. Use the presentations to further a class discussion about Indonesia's actions and how they compare to the steps being taken by other Southeast Asian countries. BL Verbal/Linguistic

CLOSE & REFLECT

Expressing Have students review the difficult balance the people of Southeast Asian countries are striving to achieve—developing their economies to become prosperous modern nations and protecting the land and resources that make them special and are necessary to fuel their economies. Ask each student to pick one environmental issue facing Southeast Asia. Then have students write a description of the human activities that have helped create this issue, and have them explain how people might attempt to fix this problem.

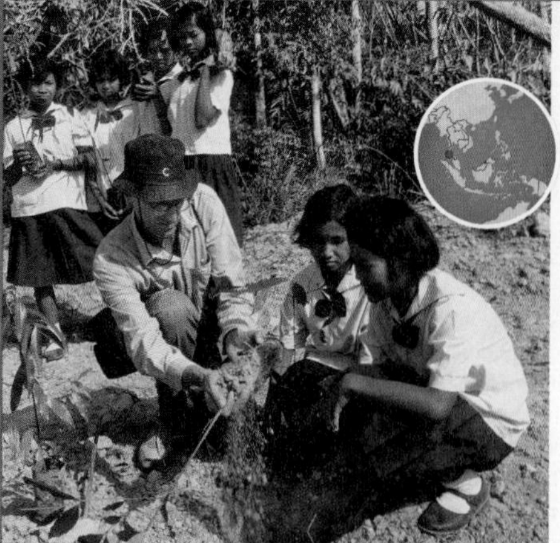

These children in Thailand are planting tree seedlings. Several Southeast Asian countries have introduced reforestation programs to conserve forests.

▲ **CRITICAL THINKING**

1. ***Drawing Conclusions*** Do you think that reforestation programs will be enough to save Southeast Asia's forests? Why or why not?
2. ***Drawing Inferences*** What might be the purpose of teaching children to plant trees?

sustainable development technological and economic growth that does not deplete the human and natural resources of a given area

reforestation the planting and cultivating of new trees in an effort to restore a forest that has been reduced by fire or by cutting

as well. Since the late 1990s, Indonesian forest fires have created pollution and respiratory problems for people as far away as mainland Malaysia and Singapore. The Malaysian government has been forced on occasion to declare a state of emergency. Singapore's government often advises residents who have heart or respiratory conditions to avoid going outside.

READING PROGRESS CHECK

Identifying What environmental challenges are the results of human economic activities in Southeast Asia?

Addressing the Issues

GUIDING QUESTION *How are people and governments addressing environmental issues in Southeast Asia?*

Many Southeast Asian countries are shifting their economic policies to focus on **sustainable development**. This strategy means encouraging technological and economic growth that relies on renewable resources. For example, to prevent further loss of rain forests, Thailand, Indonesia, the Philippines, and Malaysia have limited certain timber exports. They have also introduced **reforestation** programs. In Laos, the government has encouraged some highland farmers to resettle on more fertile ground and marked some of its forests as protected areas.

Southeast Asian governments are also starting to develop ideas to reduce the impact of urban growth on the surrounding environment. Scientists are trying to come up with solutions to urban heat islands. One proposal is to create "green zones," areas within a city that are granted special environmental protection. Another idea is to ban the construction of tall buildings near the sea so that winds would be able to blow farther into the city and disperse more air pollution.

Southeast Asia's environmental issues have attracted widespread interest. The Association of Southeast Asian Nations (ASEAN) has tried to address some of these issues. In 2002 ASEAN countries formed an agreement on Transboundary Haze Pollution. Indonesia refused to ratify it. However, countries around the world are still pressuring Indonesia to conserve its rain forests. In 2012 Indonesia announced a two-year ban on forest clearing.

READING PROGRESS CHECK

Identifying How are Southeast Asian governments working to limit deforestation?

LESSON 3 REVIEW CCSS

Reviewing Vocabulary (Tier Three Words)

1. ***Identifying*** Write a paragraph explaining what sustainable development is and why it is important. RH.9–10.4

Using Your Notes

2. ***Summarizing*** Use your graphic organizer on the causes and effects of environmental challenges in Southeast Asia to write a paragraph explaining how economic development is connected to environmental challenges.

Answering the Guiding Questions

3. ***Identifying Cause and Effect*** How has the management of natural resources impacted the environment in Southeast Asia?
4. ***Drawing Conclusions*** Why do urban growth and industrialization create environmental problems in Southeast Asia?
5. ***Identifying*** How are people and governments addressing environmental issues in Southeast Asia?

Writing Activity

6. ***Informative/Explanatory*** In a paragraph, explain how Southeast Asia's urban and rural areas differ from each other in terms of their effects on the environment. WHST.9–10.2

ANSWERS, p. 770

READING PROGRESS CHECK Deforestation, water pollution, air pollution, and destruction of coral reefs are the result of human activities.

READING PROGRESS CHECK Governments are focusing on sustainable development, setting aside protected areas, limiting timber exports, and introducing reforestation programs to try to limit deforestation.

CRITICAL THINKING

1. Answers may vary but could include that reforestation by itself will not save the forests as it involves planting of seedlings while mature trees are what is harvested, which does not totally offset the loss of trees.
2. It illustrates the importance of trees to the environment and encourages a lifelong commitment to preservation and conservation.

LESSON 3 REVIEW ANSWERS

Reviewing Vocabulary

1. Paragraphs should include that sustainable development focuses on economic and technological growth that does not deplete the resources of a given area.

Using Your Notes

2. Paragraphs should include that economic development is contributing to air and water pollution, straining resources, and destroying habitats for plants and animals, as well as sea life.

Answering the Guiding Questions

3. The lack of management of natural resources has caused habitats for many rare species of plants and animals to be destroyed and led to widespread deforestation and soil erosion.
4. Urban growth and industrialization is contributing to air and water pollution through industrial and vehicle emissions, dumping of industrial waste and untreated sewage, and lack of sanitation systems as well as straining the resources in areas such as rivers and water supplies.
5. Governments are starting to focus on sustainable development, reforestation, setting limits on timber exports, reducing the impact of urban growth by creating green zones, and by the formation of the Association of Southeast Asian Nations, which made an agreement on Transboundary Haze Pollution.

Writing Activity

6. Paragraphs will differ but should be strongly supported with information from the lesson.

CHAPTER 31 Assessment 

Directions: On a separate sheet of paper, answer the questions below. Make sure that you read carefully and answer all parts of the questions.

Lesson Review

Lesson 1

1. ***Specifying*** Discuss three examples of volcanic eruptions in Indonesia and how they have changed world history.

2. ***Assessing*** In most of Southeast Asia, the soil is poor. What causes the soil in some areas to be richer and more productive? With mostly poor soil, why does plant growth remain strong throughout most of Southeast Asia?

3. ***Drawing Conclusions*** Explain whether it would be accurate to state that Southeast Asia's rain forests are an example of biodiversity.

Lesson 2

4. ***Identifying Cause and Effect*** Discuss an example of a successful independence movement in which a Southeast Asian country gained independence from a colonial power.

5. ***Summarizing*** Write a summary about the religions practiced in Southeast Asia. Specify the most common religion and briefly explain how it came to be practiced in the region.

6. ***Drawing Conclusions*** How do Singapore and Myanmar represent the opposite extremes of economic development in Southeast Asia?

Lesson 3

7. ***Analyzing*** What is the greatest threat to rain forests in Indonesia and Malaysia? Why does the possibility of eliminating this threat pose a challenge to these countries?

8. ***Considering Advantages and Disadvantages*** Explain the advantages and disadvantages of manufacturing and industrialization in Southeast Asia.

9. ***Describing*** Describe two activities that Southeast Asian governments have undertaken to reduce the impact of urban growth on the surrounding environment.

21st Century Skills

Use the graph below to answer the questions that follow.

CONTRIBUTION TO GDP BY ECONOMIC SECTOR

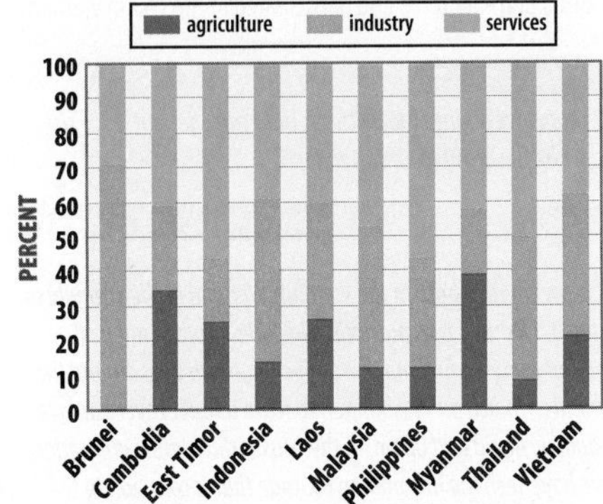

Source: The CIA World Factbook.

10. ***Using Charts*** Within which countries are the contributions to GDP by industry the greatest? What is the percentage for each? Why is industry more successful there?

11. ***Creating Diagrams*** Explain whether Brunei's agricultural contribution to GDP seems logical when considering the size of the country.

Critical Thinking

12. ***Making Connections*** Write a one-page essay explaining the role of agriculture in Southeast Asia's economy. Identify specific crops and other economic activities. Explain where agriculture ranks overall economically in relation to the other activities. WHST.9–10.2; WHST.9–10.9

College and Career Readiness

13. ***Clear Communication*** Suppose you want to publish biographies of Aung San Suu Kyi and Dita Sari. Write a one-page proposal about each of these women and her connection to Southeast Asia. In your proposal, explain each woman's significance in the region's recent history. WHST.9–10.2; WHST.9–10.4; WHST.9–10.9

Need Extra Help?

If You've Missed Question	1	2	3	4	5	6	7	8	9	10	11	12	13
Go to page	755	758	758	760	763	764	767	769	770	771	771	764	763

CHAPTER 31 Assessment Answers

Lesson Review

Lesson 1

1. Mount Tambora erupted in 1815, sending so much ash into the sky that solar energy was blocked, resulting in crop failures and hunger as far away as the U.S., Europe, and northern Africa; Krakatau erupted in 1883, killing 36,000 people; Mount Toba erupted 73,000 years ago, changing weather patterns worldwide.

2. Volcanoes have enriched the soil in some areas with ash, making it more fertile. Plant growth remains strong even with poor soil because of the warm and wet tropical climate.

3. It would be accurate to state that Southeast Asia's rain forests are an example of biodiversity because it is estimated that as much as 10 percent of the Earth's plant and animal species are found there.

Lesson 2

4. Examples may differ but could include the Philippines gaining independence from the U.S. after WWII; Myanmar, Malaysia, and Singapore gaining independence from Britain.

5. Summaries may vary but must include that Islam, which was introduced to Southeast Asia in the twelfth and thirteenth century by Muslim traders, is the most common religion. Buddhism is the next most commonly practiced and there are other religions such as Daoism, Confucianism, and ancestor worship. Catholicism is widely practiced in the Philippines, where it was introduced by Spanish missionaries.

6. Singapore is highly industrialized with a growing economy and the highest standard of living in the subregion. Myanmar is one of the poorest countries with its economy depending largely on agriculture.

Lesson 3

7. Deforestation for agriculture, particularly the growing of palm for palm oil, is the greatest threat to the forests of Indonesia and Malaysia. The country cannot eliminate agriculture as it is needed for both the people and the economy.

8. The advantages of manufacturing and industrialization include the creation of jobs and increases in the standard of living. The disadvantages include pollution and the destruction of natural environments.

9. Governments are starting to focus on sustainable development such as limiting timber exports and also developing ideas to limit the effects of growth, such as creating "green zones" within cities.

21st Century Skills

10. Brunei, Indonesia, and Thailand have the greatest contributions to industry. Industry in Brunei contributes around 45 percent, Thailand about 44 percent, and Indonesia about 47 percent. Industry is so successful there because they have far less agriculture than the other countries.

11. Brunei is very small with mountainous regions, making the agricultural contribution logical.

Critical Thinking

12. Essays will differ but should be strongly supported with information from the chapter including: agriculture is Southeast Asia's leading economic activity; the most widely grown crop is rice; other crops include cassava, yams, corn, bananas, sugarcane, coffee, coconuts, spices, palm oil, and rubber; logging of teak and ebony is profitable for some countries; mining of iron ore and oil take place in some countries; manufacturing is growing in Indonesia and Malaysia.

College and Career Readiness

13. Proposals will vary but should include that Aung San Suu Kyi is an activist in Myanmar who leads the opposition party but has remained under house arrest due to her outspokenness against the military government. Dita Sari is a Indonesian lawyer who began leading factory workers to strike for more pay and better conditions in the 1990s and who currently lobbies Indonesia's parliament for labor law reform.

CHAPTER 31

Assessment Answers

Analyzing Primary Sources

14. The quote indicates that President Johnson doesn't believe the U.S. should have been in Vietnam but he is not sure how best to withdraw troops. Answers may vary but could include that the quote helps explain that the situation was complex and there was not an easy way to exit Vietnam.

15. Kerry's statement indicates that he understood the position Johnson was in and feels similarly. His statement encompasses both the military service of those in Vietnam and those who protested against it, stating that both define America and courage.

Writing About Geography

16. Essays will differ but should be strongly supported with information from the chapter including: women have held traditional roles raising families but also been part of the workforce; rural women work as farmers and urban women often work in factories; women are rising to leadership roles by being activists for change in government and working conditions.

Applying Map Skills

17. The Mekong, the Red, the Irrawaddy, the Salween, and the Chao Phraya are the major rivers, with the Mekong being the longest and the Chao Phraya being the shortest.

18. Myanmar lies above and beside Thailand with a mountain range marking the border between them.

19. Indonesia and the Philippines are the most populous countries of Southeast Asia. The other countries have much lower populations with the most people living around rivers and coastal areas.

Exploring the Essential Question

20. Home pages will differ based on the Southeast Asian country the student chooses. Paragraphs should include information on physical and human systems of the chosen country as well as providing relevant links.

Research and Presentation

21. Multimedia presentations will differ but should include video, maps, photographs, and diagrams or graphs to explain the members, mission, and growth of the organization, as well as its past and present activities and an opinion of how effective ASEAN will be in the future. Possible answers should include Malaysia, Indonesia, Philippines, Singapore, Vietnam, Cambodia, Laos, Myanmar, and Thailand as members; mission includes promoting regional growth; activities include free trade agreements and reducing tariffs; growth is increasing and there are plans to create a regional trading market by 2015.

CHAPTER 31 **Assessment** 

Directions: On a separate sheet of paper, answer the questions below. Make sure that you read carefully and answer all parts of the questions.

DBQ Analyzing Primary Sources

Read the excerpts and answer the following questions.

There was great division of opinion regarding the way the United States entered and participated in the war in Vietnam.

PRIMARY SOURCE

"I know we oughtn't to be there, but I can't get out. . . . I just can't be the architect of surrender."

—President Lyndon B. Johnson, commenting on Vietnam to Senator Eugene McCarthy, February 1966

"I saw courage both in the Vietnam War and in the struggle to stop it. I learned that patriotism includes protest, not just military service. But you don't have to go half way around the world or march on Washington to learn about bravery or love of country. Again and again, in the causes that define our nation, we have seen the uncommon courage that is common to the American people."

—John Kerry, announcement speech, Patriots Point, South Carolina, September 2, 2003 (as prepared for delivery)

14. ***Understanding Historical Interpretation*** Explain how the quote by President Johnson indicates his attitude toward withdrawal of U.S. troops from Vietnam. How does this quote help you to assess why the United States remained involved in combat in Vietnam for such a long period of time? RH.9–10.1

15. ***Interpreting Significance*** Explain whether Kerry's statement indicates that he is aligned with Johnson's attitudes and action regarding Vietnam. How does Kerry's statement indicate a widespread attitude regarding U.S. involvement in Vietnam? RH.9–10.1

Writing About Geography

16. ***Informative/Explanatory*** Use standard grammar, spelling, sentence structure, and punctuation to write a one-page essay discussing family and the current status of women in Southeast Asia. WHST.9–10.2

Applying Map Skills

Refer to the Unit 9 Atlas to answer the following questions.

17. ***Places and Regions*** Identify the five major rivers of Southeast Asia's mainland countries. Of these rivers, which is the shortest? Which is the longest?

18. ***The World in Spatial Terms*** Use your mental map of Southeast Asia to describe the spatial relationship between Thailand and Myanmar. Explain whether travel on foot would be easy or difficult between these two countries.

19. ***Human Systems*** Write a general statement to compare and contrast the populations of the Philippines and Indonesia with the populations of other countries in Southeast Asia.

Exploring the Essential Question

20. ***Organizing*** Select one of the countries from the chapter. Then suppose you are developing a website to provide information explaining how physical systems and human systems have shaped that country. Create the home page, including relevant links. For each link, write a two-to-three paragraph summary of the information to be included. WHST.9–10.2; WHST.9–10.4; WHST.9–10.9

Research and Presentation

21. ***Gathering Information*** With a partner, conduct research to learn more about the Association of Southeast Asian Nations (ASEAN). Create a multimedia presentation to explain the following: members, mission, and growth of the organization, as well as its past and present activities. Explain whether you think the organization is effective currently—and whether you think the organization will be effective in the future. Within your presentation, include video, maps, photographs, and diagrams or graphs. WHST.9–10.1; WHST.9–10.6; WHST.9–10.7; WHST.9–10.8

Need Extra Help?

If You've Missed Question	14	15	16	17	18	19	20	21
Go to page	772	772	763	746	746	746	765	765

772

CHAPTER 32

Australia and New Zealand Planner

UNDERSTANDING BY DESIGN®

Enduring Understandings

- *Certain patterns, processes, and functions help determine where people settle.*

Essential Question

- *How do physical systems and human systems shape a place?*

Predictable Misunderstandings

Students may think:

- *Indigenous peoples in Australia and New Zealand are from the same ethnic group. Explain that the indigenous peoples of Australia are known as Aborigines and have lived in Australia for thousands of years. The indigenous people of New Zealand are the Maori, who migrated to New Zealand from Polynesia about a thousand years ago.*
- *New Zealand is too small to play a major role in the global economy. Explain that New Zealand produces many agricultural products, including dairy products. New Zealand produces a large portion of the world's whole milk powder and exports it to countries around the world.*

Assessment Evidence

Performance Tasks:

- *Hands-On Chapter Project*

Other Evidence:

- *Guided Reading Activities*
- *Vocabulary Activities*
- *Lesson Quizzes*
- *Chapter Tests, Forms A and B*

SUGGESTED PACING GUIDE

Introducing the Chapter	½ Day	Global Connections	1 Day
Lesson 1	1 Day	Lesson 3	1 Day
Lesson 2	1 Day	Chapter Wrap-Up and Assessment	½ Day

TOTAL TIME 5 Days

Key for Using the Teacher Edition

SKILL-BASED ACTIVITIES

Types of skill activities found in the Teacher Edition.

* **V Visual Skills** require students to analyze maps, graphs, charts, and photos.

R Reading Skills help students practice reading skills and master vocabulary.

C Critical Thinking Skills help students apply and extend what they have learned.

W Writing Skills provide writing opportunities to help students comprehend the text.

T Technology Skills require students to use digital tools effectively.

*Letters are followed by a number when there is more than one of the same type of skill on the page.

DIFFERENTIATED INSTRUCTION

All activities are written for the on-level student unless otherwise marked with the leveled labels below.

BL Beyond Level

AL Approaching Level

ELL English Language Learners

All students benefit from activities that utilize different learning styles. Many activities are marked as below when a particular learning style is highlighted.

Intrapersonal	**Naturalist**
Logical/Mathematical	**Kinesthetic**
Visual/Spatial	**Auditory/Musical**
Verbal/Linguistic	**Interpersonal**

National Geography Standards covered in "Australia and New Zealand"

The student knows and understands:

(7) The physical processes that shape the patterns of Earth's surface

7.3 Physical processes interact over time to shape particular places on Earth's surface

(8) The characteristics and spatial distribution of ecosystems and biomes on Earth's surface

8.1 Ecosystems are dynamic and respond to changes in environmental conditions

(9) The characteristics, distribution, and migration of human populations on Earth's surface

9.3 Migration is one of the driving forces for shaping and reshaping the cultural and physical landscape of places and regions

(11) The patterns and networks of economic interdependence on Earth's surface

11.2 Patterns exist in the spatial organization of economic activities

11.3 Economic systems are dynamic organizations of interdependent economic activities for production, exchange, distribution, and consumption of goods and services

11.4 Improvements in transportation and communication networks reduce the effects of distance and time on the movements of people, products, and ideas

(14) How human actions modify the physical environment

14.1 Human modifications of the physical environment can have significant global impacts

14.2 The use of technology can have both intended and unintended impacts on the physical environment which may be positive or negative

(15) How physical systems affect human systems

15.1 Depending on the choice of human activities, the characteristics of the physical environment can be viewed as both opportunities and constraints

(16) The changes that occur in the meaning, use, distribution, and importance of resources

16.3 Policies and programs that promote the sustainable use and management of resources impact people and the environment

(18) How to apply geography to interpret the present and plan for the future

18.1 Geographic contexts (the human and physical characteristics of places and environments) provide the bases for analyzing current events and making predictions about future issues

CHAPTER OPENER PLANNER

Students will know:

- *how tectonic activity formed Australia and New Zealand.*
- *the major biomes found and how the ocean and rivers are important.*
- *how British colonialism influenced the current government and politics of Australia and New Zealand and how foreign cultures affected the indigenous cultures.*
- *industries that are important to each country's economy.*
- *how tourism, industrialization, and trade have contributed to the destruction of the Great Barrier Reef.*
- *the causes and consequences of environmental issues and the efforts of people in Australia and New Zealand to protect the environment.*

Students will be able to:

- ***describe*** *how Australia and New Zealand were formed.*
- ***identify*** *the major biomes and the importance of water resources.*
- ***explain*** *the influence of British colonialism on the current government and politics of the two countries and how indigenous cultures were affected by foreign cultures.*
- ***identify*** *important industries in Australia's and New Zealand's economies.*
- ***analyze*** *how the Great Barrier Reef has been affected by tourism, industrialization, and trade.*
- ***identify*** *causes and consequences of environmental issues and how people are working to protect the environment.*

UNDERSTANDING BY DESIGN®

☑ Print Teaching Options

V Visual Skills

☐ **p. 774** Students make a Venn diagram to compare and contrast cultural images.

R Reading Skills

☐ **p. 775** Students summarize the factors that led to the Treaty of Waitangi.

C Critical Thinking Skills

☐ **p. 774** Students discuss how European colonization affected the Aborigines and Maori. ELL **Verbal/Linguistic**

W Writing Skills

☐ **p. 774** Students write a dialogue between the Aborigines and Maori over their unfair treatment.

T Technology Skills

☐ **p. 775** Students research two viewpoints on the same current event on the rights of indigenous peoples and prepare a brief synopsis of the event. BL **Verbal/Linguistic**

☑ Online Teaching Options

C Critical Thinking Skills

☐ INTERACTIVE IMAGE **Aboriginal and Maori Protests**—Students examine an image and then describe why the rights of indigenous populations have been an ongoing concern. AL **Visual/Spatial**

☐ MAP **Interactive Regional Atlas**—Students use the interactive regional atlas to understand the physical and human geography of Australia and New Zealand.

☑ Printable Digital Worksheets

☐ WORKSHEET **Assessing Background Knowledge**—Determine the level of prior knowledge students have about Australia and New Zealand.

☐ WORKSHEET **Chapter Summary**—Students review the main idea of each lesson of the chapter content.

Project-Based Learning

Hands-On

Create Songs

Students will use what they learn about the melodies and lyrics of songs in Australia and New Zealand to write a song about a topic of their choice.

Digital Hands-On

Create Online Projects

Find an additional activity online that incorporates technology for this project. Visit the EdTech Teacher Web sites for more links, tutorials, and other resources.

Print Resources

ANCILLARY RESOURCES

This ancillary is available for every chapter and lesson.

- **Chapter Tests and Lesson Quizzes**

PRINTABLE DIGITAL WORKSHEETS

These printable digital worksheets are available for every chapter and lesson.

- **Assessing Background Knowledge**
- **Chapter Summaries**
- **Guided Reading Activities**
- **Hands-On Chapter Projects**
- **Quizzes and Tests**
- **Reading Essentials and Study Guide** AL
- **Reteaching Activities**
- **Video Activities**
- **Vocabulary**

More Media Resources

SUGGESTED VIDEOS 

- **Nova: Australia's First 4 Billion Years** (240 min.)
- **Maori Culture Traditions and History** (1 h. 24 min.)
- **Australia: Land Beyond Time** (43 min.)

SUGGESTED READING 

- ***A Commonwealth of Thieves: The Improbable Birth of Australia,*** by Thomas Keneally
- ***Australia: A Very Short Introduction,*** by Kenneth Morgan
- ***New Zealand: A Natural History,*** by Tui Roy and Mark Jones

Physical Geography of Australia and New Zealand

Students will know:

- *how tectonic activity formed Australia and New Zealand.*
- *how physical geography contributes to the unique character of Australia and New Zealand.*
- *the major biomes found in the countries.*
- *how water surrounds both Australia and New Zealand and how the major rivers are important to daily life.*
- *how oceanic currents affect seasonal weather patterns.*

Students will be able to:

- ***describe** how Australia and New Zealand were formed.*
- ***explain** how the physical geography contributes to the character of the region.*
- ***identify** the major biomes.*
- ***discuss** how water supports and surrounds the countries.*
- ***analyze** the effect of oceanic currents on seasonal weather patterns.*

UNDERSTANDING BY DESIGN®

☑ Print Teaching Options

V Visual Skills

- ☐ **p. 777** Students identify physical features in the images on the page. BL Naturalist, Visual/Spatial
- ☐ **p. 778** Students create a diagram that illustrates the many different ways that humans have tapped water resources in the subregion. AL Visual/Spatial, Interpersonal

R Reading Skills

- ☐ **p. 776** Students discuss how Australia is unique because it is like a large island and make a mental map to understand its vastness. BL Logical/Mathematical, Visual/Spatial
- ☐ **p. 777** Students draw a chart to record details about physical features including atolls, bush, calderas, lagoons, and sunken mountains. ELL Visual/Spatial

C Critical Thinking Skills

- ☐ **p. 780** Students find the main idea of three paragraphs and then write a summary of those paragraphs. ELL

W Writing Skills

- ☐ **p. 777** Students write a narrative about the physical geography of New Zealand from the perspective of a traveler. AL Verbal/Linguistic
- ☐ **p. 779** Students study the infographic and discuss the importance of the Great Barrier Reef to Australia and the world. BL Naturalist, Interpersonal
- ☐ **p. 780** Students choose a position on land rights between the indigenous people in Australia and Australian farmers and ranchers and write a letter to the local government representative explaining their position. BL Verbal/Linguistic, Logical/Mathematical

T Technology Skills

- ☐ **p. 778** Students research a place with unique opportunities for tourists and produce a digital travel brochure about it. BL Auditory/Musical, Visual/Spatial
- ☐ **p. 780** Students research and create a multimedia presentation about a World Heritage Site in Australia. AL Verbal/Linguistic

☑ Online Teaching Options

V Visual Skills

- INFOGRAPHIC **Life in the Great Barrier Reef**—Students examine an infographic about the plant and sea life in and around the Great Barrier Reef. AL Visual/Spatial
- INTERACTIVE WHITEBOARD ACTIVITY **Landforms, Biomes, and Resources**—Students complete an interactive chart that compares the geography of Australia and New Zealand. ELL Kinesthetic

C Critical Thinking Skills

- INTERACTIVE BELLRINGER **North Island and South Island, New Zealand**—Students draw inferences about how the geography influences settlement and the islands' water supply. BL Visual/Spatial, Verbal/Linguistic
- VIDEO **Origin of New Zealand**—Students view this video about the origin of New Zealand and then complete a worksheet. AL Verbal/Linguistic

☑ Printable Digital Worksheets

R Reading Skills

- WORKSHEET **Guided Reading Activity**—Students use the Guided Reading Activity worksheets to review their comprehension of the content.
- WORKSHEET **Chapter Summary**—Students review the main ideas of the chapter content.

C Critical Thinking Skills

- WORKSHEET **Video Activity**—Students answer questions related to a topic in the chapter content after they have viewed a lesson video.

LESSON 2 PLANNER

HUMAN GEOGRAPHY OF AUSTRALIA AND NEW ZEALAND

Students will know:

- *how British colonialism influenced the current government and politics of Australia and New Zealand.*
- *how the migration and settlement of foreign cultures affected the indigenous cultures of Australia and New Zealand.*
- *how life in Australia is similar to and different from life in New Zealand.*
- *industries that are important to the economies of Australia and New Zealand.*

Students will be able to:

- ***explain*** *the influence of British colonialism on the current government and politics of the two countries.*
- ***analyze*** *how indigenous cultures were affected by foreign cultures migrating and settling in the region.*
- ***compare*** *life in Australia to life in New Zealand.*
- ***identify*** *important industries in Australia's and New Zealand's economies.*

UNDERSTANDING BY DESIGN®

☑ *Print Teaching Options*

V Visual Skills

- ☐ **p. 783** Students discuss multiculturalism and create population projections for the next ten and fifty years. BL
- ☐ **p. 785** Students perform a skit using Strine words. Auditory/Musical, Visual/Spatial

R Reading Skills

- ☐ **p. 781** Students discuss how the Maori migrated to New Zealand and compare and contrast their migration with that of the Aborigines. BL Verbal/Linguistic
- ☐ **p. 782** Students create vertical time lines of events for both Australia and New Zealand to 1900. AL Visual/Spatial
- ☐ **p. 785** Students define *national identity* and create a list of words that relate to the connotation of the term. ELL Verbal/Linguistic

C Critical Thinking Skills

- ☐ **p. 782** Students discuss whether forming a dominion improved the lives of the indigenous people. BL Logical/Mathematical
- ☐ **p. 786** Students discuss the government removal of children from Aborigines. BL Logical/Mathematical
- ☐ **p. 787** Students discuss how both countries could diversify their economies based on resources they have. BL Logical/Mathematical

W Writing Skills

- ☐ **p. 784** Students write about the advantages and disadvantages of large growing populations and aging populations, considering resources, the economy, and social factors. Verbal/Linguistic
- ☐ **p. 785** Students construct a persuasive letter to the government of one of the countries arguing in favor of providing services to indigenous people. AL Verbal/Linguistic

T Technology Skills

- ☐ **p. 783** Students research a cultural group and create a digital presentation about how it has increased or decreased in population over time. BL Auditory/Musical, Visual/Spatial

☑ *Online Teaching Options*

V Visual Skills

- TIME LINE **Migration and Settlement**—Students examine the time line about the history and settlement of Australia and New Zealand. BL Verbal/Linguistic
- INTERACTIVE MAP **Maps of Australia and New Zealand**—Students analyze the maps to interpret how the physical geography influenced the human geography of the subregion.

R Reading Skills

- INTERACTIVE WHITEBOARD ACTIVITY **Effects of Migration and Colonization**—Students complete the interactive whiteboard activity to help them understand how migration and colonization affected the indigenous cultures of the subregion. AL Verbal/Linguistic, Visual/Spatial
- INTERACTIVE BELLRINGER **Patterns of European Settlement**—Students interpret a map and answer questions about how foreign cultures affected the indigenous cultures of the subregion. Interpersonal, Visual/Spatial, Verbal/Linguistic

C Critical Thinking Skills

- VIDEO **Aborigines**—Students watch this video about the history and culture of the Aborigines in Australia to complete a video worksheet. ELL Visual/Spatial
- INTERACTIVE IMAGE **Stolen Generations**—Students analyze why children were forcibly stolen from their families and why families did not have the right to appeal. BL Verbal/Linguistic

☑ *Printable Digital Worksheets*

R Reading Skills

- WORKSHEET **Guided Reading Activity**—Students use the Guided Reading Activity worksheets to review their comprehension of the content.
- WORKSHEET **Reading Essentials and Study Guide**—Students complete the study guide and answer Reading Progress Check and vocabulary questions. AL

C Critical Thinking Skills

- WORKSHEET **Video Activity**—Students answer questions related to a topic in the chapter content after they have viewed a lesson video.

LESSON 3 PLANNER

PEOPLE AND THEIR ENVIRONMENT: AUSTRALIA AND NEW ZEALAND

Students will know:

- *the causes and consequences of salinization and soil erosion.*
- *the causes and consequences of deforestation in New Zealand.*
- *how tourism, industrialization, and trade have contributed to the destruction of the Great Barrier Reef.*
- *examples of the efforts of people in Australia and New Zealand to protect the environment.*

Students will be able to:

- ***identify** the causes and consequences of salinization, soil erosion, and deforestation.*
- ***analyze** how the Great Barrier Reef has been affected by tourism, industrialization, and trade.*
- ***identify** how people are working to protect the environment.*

UNDERSTANDING BY DESIGN®

☑ Print Teaching Options

V Visual Skills

- ☐ **p. 793** Students discuss the image of a whale being rescued and find information about a similar recent event to share. ELL Naturalist, Visual/Spatial
- ☐ **p. 794** Students discuss an image of sustainable forestry management and its long-term effects on the environment. AL Visual/Spatial

R Reading Skills

- ☐ **p. 790** Students predict the effects of long-term livestock grazing in the next decade if it is not decreased. AL Verbal/Linguistic
- ☐ **p. 790** Students explain what a *station* is in Australia and discuss its multiple meanings. ELL Verbal/Linguistic

C Critical Thinking Skills

- ☐ **p. 791** Students discuss the costs and benefits of the plants and animals that were brought into Australia. AL Verbal/Linguistic
- ☐ **p. 792** Students brainstorm and write about ideas concerning how to battle toxic waste and coral bleaching. AL Interpersonal
- ☐ **p. 793** Students discuss efforts that have been made to solve environmental issues. AL Verbal/Linguistic

W Writing Skills

- ☐ **p. 793** Students write a news article about a local government's effort to protect the environment. Verbal/Linguistic
- ☐ **p. 794** Students write a paper that argues for new legislation to conserve and protect the environment. BL Verbal/Linguistic

T Technology Skills

- ☐ **p. 792** Students research and create a presentation that shows land at various stages of salinity. BL Naturalist, Visual/Spatial

☑ Online Teaching Options

V Visual Skills

- VIDEO **Australian Feral Animals**—Students view this video to discuss how feral cats have become a significant environmental problem in Australia. ELL Interpersonal, Verbal/Linguistic
- INTERACTIVE BELLRINGER **Levels of Coral Bleaching in the Great Barrier Reef**—Students interpret a graph about the Great Barrier Reef showing how tourism, industrialization, and trade are contributing to its destruction and then answer questions related to the graph. AL Verbal/Linguistic

C Critical Thinking Skills

- INTERACTIVE MAP **How Invasive Species Get to Australia**—Students use the map to develop plans on how to address the issue of invasive species in Australia. Verbal/Linguistic
- INTERACTIVE WHITEBOARD ACTIVITY **Environmental Problems and Solutions**—Students identify environmental consequences of invasive species and identify the causes and potential solutions for soil erosion and deforestation in the subregion. BL Verbal/Linguistic

☑ Printable Digital Worksheets

R Reading Skills

- WORKSHEET **Guided Reading Activity**—Students use Guided Reading Activity worksheets to review their comprehension of the content.
- WORKSHEET **Reading Essentials and Study Guide**—Students complete the study guide and answer Reading Progress Check and vocabulary questions. AL
- WORKSHEET **Vocabulary Activity**—Students review the chapter content and academic vocabulary words.
- WORKSHEET **Chapter Summary**—Students review the main ideas of the chapter content.

C Critical Thinking Skills

- WORKSHEET **Video Activity**—Students answer questions based on a lesson video.
- WORKSHEET **Reteaching Activity**—Students use this activity worksheet to review and reteach chapter content and vocabulary. This worksheet can be used with struggling students who need additional help with difficult content concepts.

INTERVENTION AND REMEDIATION STRATEGIES

LESSON 1 Physical Geography of Australia and New Zealand

Reading and Comprehension

Have students work with a partner to create an outline of the lesson that highlights key facts related to landforms, water systems, climates, biomes, and resources of Australia and New Zealand. To ensure comprehension of the topics, have partners create a visual report that explains a topic or process. For example, students might describe areas that make up Australia's Outback or they might compare and contrast physical features of New Zealand's North and South Islands. Have students present their reports to the class, allowing time for groups to conduct a question-and-answer session in which students from each group answer questions about their topic.

Text Evidence

Have students work in pairs or small groups to create a website for the bureau of tourism for either Australia or New Zealand. Tell students their website should include a home page that includes topics about the country's physical features and reasons tourists might want to visit. For example, students might include information about Australia's Great Barrier Reef, or New Zealand's unique plant life. Encourage students to include content vocabulary on their websites. Then have groups present their websites to the class, using presentation software. Guide a class discussion about the unique physical geography of each country.

LESSON 2 Human Geography of Australia and New Zealand

Reading and Comprehension

Have student pairs choose two of the lesson's content vocabulary words. Tell students to work with their partner to write each word in a sentence using both words correctly. Then have pairs play a "Pictionary" style guessing game in which one partner draws clues to describe a content vocabulary term for their partner to guess. Encourage students to use clues from the text to help them draw the term for the other partner to guess. After students have finished guessing each of the terms, have partners compete against other pairs to see who can guess the most terms correctly in a certain amount of time.

Text Evidence

Have students work in pairs or small groups to review the lesson to identify key concepts and events to create a "Then and Now" chart. Tell students to use information in the text about the past and present history of Australia and New Zealand to complete their charts. Encourage students to analyze the map in this lesson, *Patterns of European Settlement,* to help them understand how migration and geography impacted the history and governments of Australia and New Zealand. Have students present their charts to the class.

LESSON 3 People and Their Environment: Australia and New Zealand

Reading and Comprehension

Have students work with a partner to write an informational paragraph based on one of the images in this lesson. For example, students might use the image of the rabbit to discuss how the introduction of non-native species in Australia severely impacted its environment. Have students present their paragraphs to the class. Lead a question-answer session about what is being done to remedy issues facing the environment of Australia and New Zealand.

Text Evidence

Tell students to work with a partner to create a Venn diagram that shows the similarities and differences of environmental issues facing Australia and New Zealand. In addition to identifying evidence from the text, students may conduct online research to identify facts to include in their diagrams. Have students present their diagrams to the class, explaining how land use in each country has impacted its environment.

Online Resources

Leveled Reader

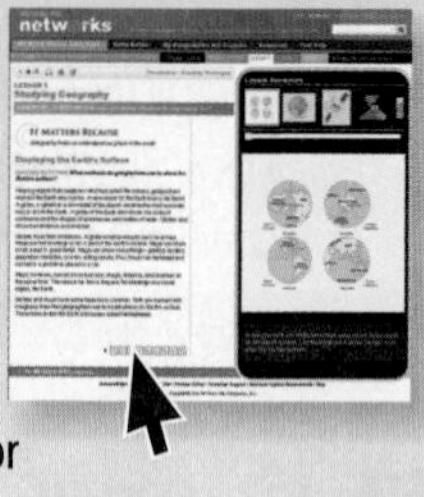

Use this online approaching-level text that corresponds directly to the text in the Student Edition. It also includes additional reading and comprehension support for English Language Learners.

Guided Reading Activities

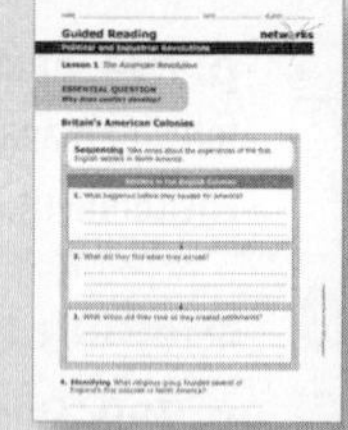

This resource uses guiding questions to help students with comprehension.

Reteaching Activities

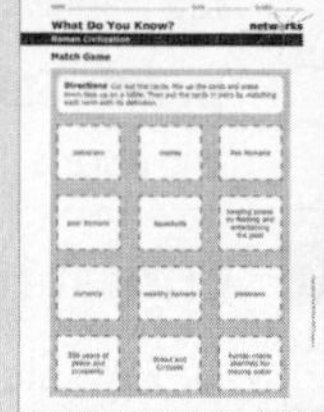

These worksheets provide students with an opportunity for remedial practice and review of vital chapter content.

Reading Essentials and Study Guide

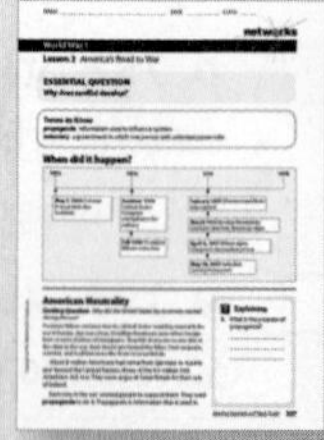

This resource offers writing and reading activities for the approaching-level student.

Self-Check Quizzes

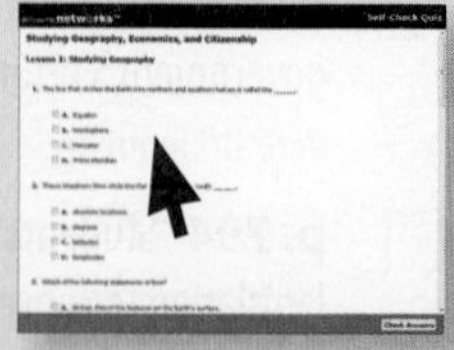

This online assessment tool provides instant feedback for students to check their progress.

Chapter Summaries

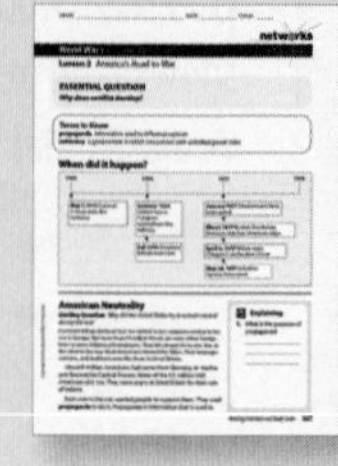

Summaries are provided for each chapter that thoroughly condense core content into manageable chunks.

Australia and New Zealand

ESSENTIAL QUESTION • *How do physical systems and human systems shape a place?*

networks

There's More Online about the geography of Australia and New Zealand.

CHAPTER 32

Geography Matters...

Australia and New Zealand have rich cultural heritages influenced by indigenous peoples, English settlers, and more recent immigrants.

The subregion faces many challenges. Environmental threats include climate change, deforestation, and the introduction of invasive plant and animal species which have no natural predators. The countries of Australia and New Zealand are making strides in addressing both cultural and environmental issues, but more work is needed. With the help of individuals, companies, organizations, and governments, change is moving forward.

◀ This young man has the Australian flag painted on his face.

773

ENGAGE

Analyzing Visuals Have students study the image of the boy and ask them to identify the flag that is painted on his face *(Australia)*. Ask students if they recognize any part of the flag from another country. *(Union Jack from the United Kingdom)* Then guide a discussion about how one culture can influence other cultures but at the same time be unique. **Ask:** **What symbols in the image reveal uniqueness?** *(stars)* Discuss other ways that a culture might be influenced by other cultures or blend cultures to create a unique one.

TEACH & ASSESS

Activating Prior Knowledge Before beginning the chapter, have students consider what factors affect the settlement of a place or subregion. **Ask:** **What are examples of push and pull factors?** *(Possible answer: Push factors may be economic hardships, war, or discrimination; pull factors could be economic and educational opportunities, family, and climate.)* **Historically, who made up the population of Australia and New Zealand?** *(indigenous peoples, English settlers, and immigrants)* **Which push or pull factors may have influenced the settlement of the subregion?** *(Student answers may vary based on their prior knowledge, they may indicate that Australia was once a British penal colony, which is a push factor.)* Discuss with students why the subregion was chosen as a penal colony by the British. **Ask:** **How did the subregion's physical geography influence the British government's decision to send convicts to Australia?** *(Possible response: The government probably needed a place to send convicts that was far away from Britain where the prisons were overcrowded.)* **BL** **Logical/Mathematical**

CLOSE & REFLECT

Understanding Relationships Among Events As students read the chapter, have them keep track of events that may have affected the environmental threats that Australia and New Zealand face today. Describe how both human and physical geography can change over time and affect the environment of a subregion. Discuss how some of these factors can be controlled while others are not.

Letter from the Author

Dear Geography Teacher,

Beginning in 1788 the British began to use Australia as a penal colony. Convicts from overcrowded British prisons were sent to Australia. Frequently, these convicts came in contact with ordinary settlers and there are stories of outlaw activities and conflict. Have students explore life in Australia for British convicts. What happened to these convicts over time? Were they assimilated into Australian society? Did they live in the equivalent of refugee camps? Were there any lingering effects from the convict population in Australia? Did the British follow this practice in other colonies?

Richard G. Boehm

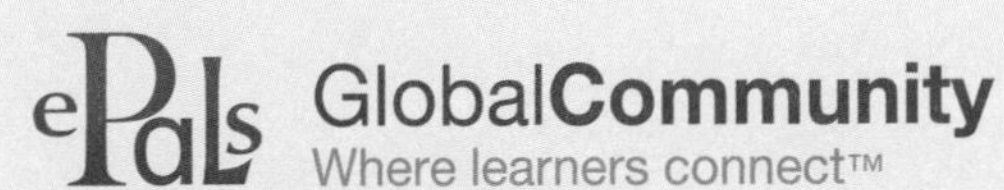

Extend the project-based learning experience globally through our partnership with ePals. EPals allows you to connect with classrooms around the world in a safe online environment for real-life lessons and projects in virtual study groups.

ENGAGE

V Visual Skills

Comparing and Contrasting Ask students to read the title of this feature and examine the photograph. Then have students make a Venn diagram to compare and contrast this image with the one on page 773 with regard to culture. **Ask:** **How are the cultures that are revealed and expressed in these images similar and different?** *(Possible answer: Both images show a person with face painting, but they have different meanings.)* Ask students to consider how both images show the influence or blending of another culture.

TEACH & ASSESS

C Critical Thinking Skills

Identifying Cause and Effect Have students read the information in the text about how European colonization affected the Aborigines and Maori. **Ask:** **Why was it difficult for the Aborigines and Maori to live among the Europeans?** *(They had their own cultures and faced racism from British settlers.)* **What effect did European colonization have on the indigenous peoples of the subregion?** *(They were treated unfairly with settlers taking their land.)* **Why do you think they were not granted the same rights as European settlers?** *(They were discriminated against because their cultures were different from the European culture. They were not viewed as equals.)* Discuss with students why inequality is a significant and common issue among different peoples and cultures in the world. ELL Verbal/Linguistic

W Writing Skills

Narrative Have students write a brief narrative that includes dialogue between the Aborigines and Maori over their unfair treatment and overall inequality based on their experience with European settlers. Explain to students that they can create the setting so that their story happens in the present day or in the past. Remind them to use vivid and sensory language in their narratives. Invite students to share their narratives in small groups.

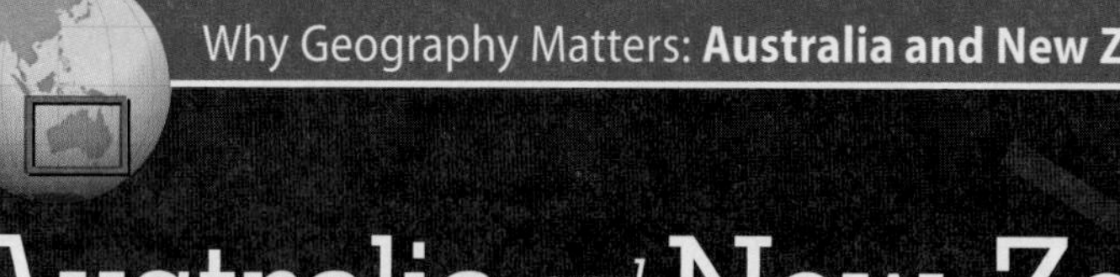

Australia and New Zealand: indigenous peoples

Australia and New Zealand are home to indigenous peoples, or the people who lived in a place before it was conquered by colonial societies. Australia's Aborigines (A•buh•RIH•juh•neez) and New Zealand's Maori (MAWR•ee) have their own languages, customs, and traditions. This made it more difficult for them to live among European settlers. In the twentieth century, Aborigines and Maori protested unfair treatment. They pressed for their political, economic, social, cultural, and civil rights.

774

Project-Based Learning

Hands-On

Create Songs

Have students create a chapter project that uses art to explore geographic systems in Australia and New Zealand. Students will create songs that bring together information from all lessons about the physical geography and human geography in Australia and New Zealand.

Digital Hands-On

Create Online Projects

Find an additional activity online that incorporates technology for this project. Visit the EdTech Teacher Web sites for more links, tutorials, and other resources.

Why Geography Matters

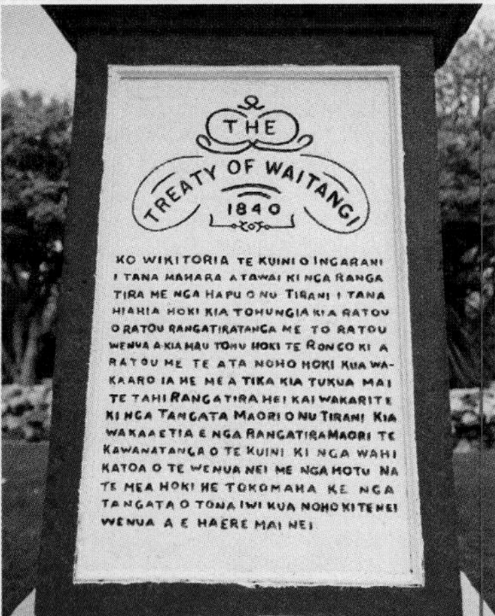

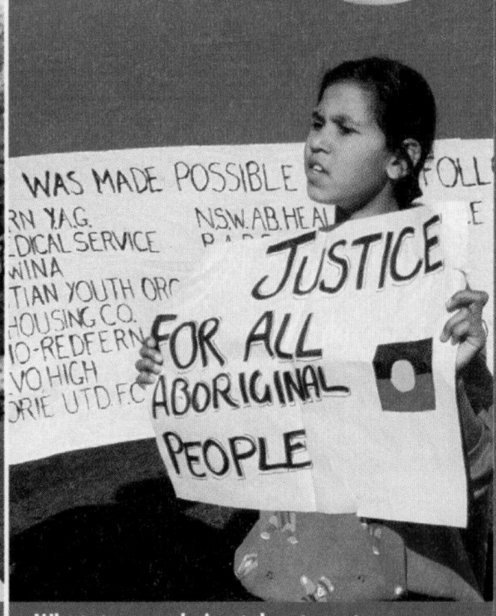

How do the indigenous peoples in Australia and New Zealand differ?

Both Australian Aborigines and the Maori migrated from Southeast Asia. The Aboriginal people arrived in Australia about 40,000 years ago. Over time, these nomadic hunters and gatherers dispersed across the entire continent. They divided into different groups and developed distinct cultures with as many as 700 languages.

Unlike the Aborigines, the Maori arrived in New Zealand sometime in the A.D. 1200s. The Maori remained in close contact with one another in a relatively small geographic area and were isolated from other societies. Therefore, Maori culture is less diffuse than Australia's Aboriginal culture. For instance, Maori today speak dialects of the same ancestral language and share similar beliefs. Although Aboriginal and Maori societies developed differently, British colonization greatly affected both peoples.

1. **The Uses of Geography** How did geography affect the development of Aboriginal and Maori cultures?

Why have both populations been denied basic rights?

European explorers visited Australia and New Zealand in the 1600s. The British government established a colony for convicts in Australia in 1788. Free settlers soon followed. In the 1820s, Europeans settled in New Zealand. Colonization, however, caused friction. Indigenous peoples and European colonists competed for control of valuable resources such as land and water. Social, political, and cultural differences between colonists and indigenous peoples also led to conflicts. Aborigines and Maori frequently endured discrimination. The Australian government believed the Aborigines would not survive colonization and placed many in reserve stations. It provided them with food and clothing but restricted their movements. The government also forcibly removed about 100,000 Aboriginal children from their families in order to absorb them into white society. These children are referred to as the "Stolen Generations." In New Zealand in 1840, Maori chiefs and British representatives signed the Treaty of Waitangi, but many of the Maori rights (such as land ownership) granted by the treaty were ignored, resulting in many years of war and conflict.

2. **Human Systems** What caused Aborigines and Maori to be denied their rights?

What steps are being taken to restore the rights of these indigenous peoples?

R

In the twentieth century, Australia's Aborigines and New Zealand's Maori began to pressure their governments to restore their rights. Activists fought to preserve their land, language, and way of life through political protests. Eventually, they regained land, fishing, and other basic rights. Children belonging to the "Stolen Generations" received a national apology in 2008. The Australian government later adopted a formal policy aimed at preserving Aboriginal languages. In the 1990s, New Zealand's government began to honor the Treaty of Waitangi. The government transferred land and control of important fisheries and paid millions of dollars in claim settlements to the Maori. New Zealand made Maori an official language and established Maori-language schools and a Maori-language television station. These indigenous peoples, however, still suffer disproportionately from poor health and lower life expectancies due to poverty, unemployment, and other factors.

T

3. **Environment and Society** What role has the environment played in helping Aborigines and Maori regain their rights?

THERE'S MORE ONLINE

WATCH a video about the lives of Aborigines • *SEE* an image of protests by Aborigines and Maori

R Reading Skills

Summarizing Point to the image of the Treaty of Waitangi and then ask a volunteer to summarize the factors that led to the treaty and its effects on the Maori. Discuss with students how treaties are formal agreements between two or more groups. **Ask:** **Why would the British ignore certain rights of the Maori after signing a treaty with them?** *(Possible answer: They did not believe that the Maori were equal to the British.)* Have students write a summary of how the actions of the British against the Maori were like those of the United States government toward the Native Americans. ELL **Logical/Mathematical**

T Technology Skills

Researching Have students conduct research to identify current events on the rights of indigenous peoples in the subregion. Challenge them to find sources that reveal two different viewpoints on the same event. Point out that the event should have occurred in the last five years. Then ask students to prepare a brief synopsis of the event, including its history and factors that influenced it. Provide an opportunity for them to share their current events with the class. BL **Verbal/Linguistic**

CLOSE & REFLECT

Speculating Review with students how decisions and policies made now or recently will affect the Aborigines and Maori in the next generation. Have students consider if changes in policy might reduce poverty and unemployment and improve health care of the indigenous peoples. Ask students what policies would be most influential in helping the Aborigines and Maori preserve their cultures and traditions.

INTERACTIVE IMAGE

Aboriginal and Maori Protests

Analyzing Visuals Have students examine this interactive image of Aboriginal and Maori protests. Ask students to describe why the rights of indigenous populations in Australia and New Zealand have been an ongoing concern since the beginning of the twentieth century.
AL **Visual/Spatial**

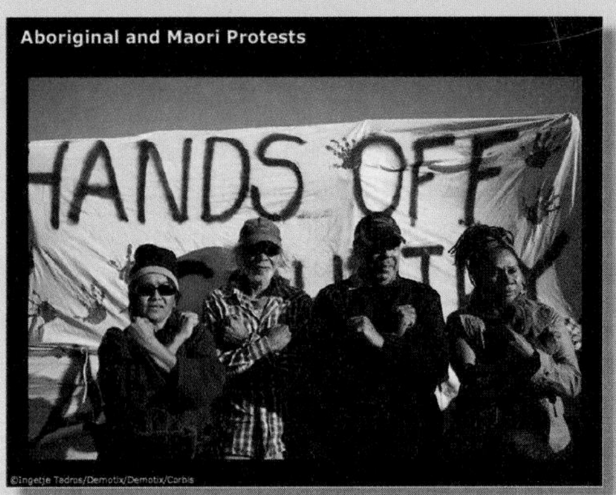

Aboriginal and Maori Protests

ANSWERS, p. 775

Why Geography Matters

1. The Maori stayed in a fairly small geographic area which isolated them from other societies, resulting in the development of a culture that is less diffuse than the Aboriginal culture, which was affected by their dispersal over the entire Australian continent.
2. Conflicts over resources and political, social, and cultural differences led to discrimination and rights being denied to Maori and Aboriginal peoples.
3. Activists fought to preserve and regain land and fishing rights for Maori and Aboriginal peoples.

ENGAGE

C Critical Thinking Skills

Analyzing Show students a physical map of Australia and New Zealand and ask them to describe the landforms, relief, and bodies of water. Discuss how unique physical features can support endemic wildlife.

TEACH & ASSESS

R Reading Skills

Visualizing Discuss how Australia is unique because it is a very large island as well as a continent. Ask students to read the first two paragraphs of text to help them create a mental map of Australia. **Ask:** How do you think Australia's physical features and location affect its climate? *(Australia has a low area of flat land and much land that is desert, so the climate in the desert area is quite hot and dry, or a tropical dry climate. Since it is surrounded by ocean and because of its location in the Southern Hemisphere, the climate for some regions is probably either tropical or subtropical.)* **BL** **Logical/Mathematical, Visual/Spatial**

Content Background Knowledge

The Outback and the Bush The Outback comprises the remote inland desert, while "the bush" refers to an area closer to the coast and rich in animal and plant life. Sometimes the terms are used interchangeably, but they do not cover the same areas. Use of the terms *Outback* and *bush* began in the 1800s, largely because their physical features were not synonymous with those that were familiar to immigrants and other settlers in the region.

ANSWERS, p. 776

TAKING NOTES: Land - Australia: Great Dividing Range runs from Cape York Peninsula to Tasmania; Western Plateau includes Great Sandy, Gibson, and Great Victoria Deserts; Nullarbor Plain is south of Great Victoria Desert; Central Lowlands fall between Great Dividing Range and Western Plateau; dry land makes most of country unsuitable for agriculture. **Land - New Zealand:** North Island has beaches, mountains, forests, rich soils, and volcanoes; Southern Alps lie along South Island's western edge; glaciers carved out lakes and rivers; sunken mountains, fjords, and coastal caves are on western coast; Canterbury Plains have most fertile land. **Water - Australia:** freshwater is seasonal and unreliable; driest inhabited continent on Earth; rivers and lakes in lowlands only fill with water after rare heavy rainfall; Murray and Darling Rivers supply water for farming; Great Artesian Basin contains pressurized water; this water is too salty for people and crops but used for livestock. **Water - New Zealand:** large amounts of freshwater; hills and mountains support snow-fed rivers and streams. **Biomes:** Australia has deserts and tropical savannas; savanna is dominated by kangaroo, koala, and wallaby; wetlands support a variety of wildlife; Great Barrier Reef contains many species of sea life; New Zealand has mostly marine west coast climate with plenty of rain; many species of plants are only found here.

networks

There's More Online!

- **IMAGE** Australian Outback
- **IMAGE** Hopetoun Falls, Australia
- **IMAGE** Kings Canyon, Australia
- **INFOGRAPHIC** Life in the Great Barrier Reef
- **INTERACTIVE SELF-CHECK QUIZ**
- **VIDEO** Physical Geography of Australia and New Zealand

LESSON 1
Physical Geography of Australia and New Zealand

ESSENTIAL QUESTION • *How do physical systems and human systems shape a place?*

Reading **HELP**DESK

Academic Vocabulary (Tier Two Words)
- resource
- dominate
- benefit

Content Vocabulary (Tier Three Words)
- bush
- sunken mountains
- atoll
- caldera
- lagoon
- artesian well
- coral

TAKING NOTES: ***Key Ideas and Details***

IDENTIFYING As you read about the geography of Australia and New Zealand, use a graphic organizer like the one below to note the characteristics of the land, water, and biomes of the subregion.

Australia and New Zealand		
Land	Water	Biomes

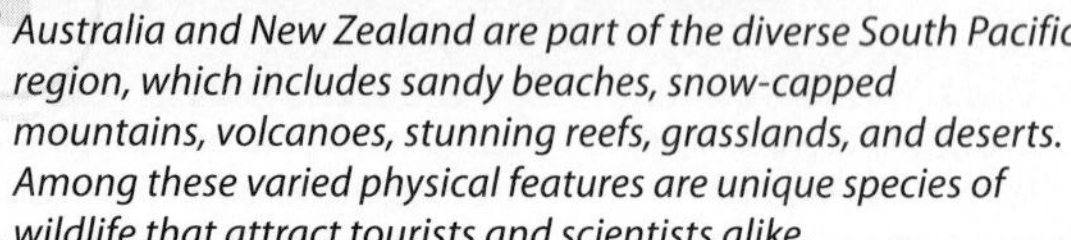

It Matters Because

Australia and New Zealand are part of the diverse South Pacific region, which includes sandy beaches, snow-capped mountains, volcanoes, stunning reefs, grasslands, and deserts. Among these varied physical features are unique species of wildlife that attract tourists and scientists alike.

Landforms

GUIDING QUESTION *How do the landforms of Australia and New Zealand influence the economies of these countries?*

Like an island, Australia is surrounded by water. However, geographers classify Australia as a continent because of its massive size. Australia lies between the Pacific Ocean and Indian Ocean in the Southern Hemisphere, and it has a largely flat terrain.

A chain of hills and mountains known as the Great Dividing Range interrupts the level landscape. The peaks of the range stretch along the eastern coast from the Cape York Peninsula to the island of Tasmania. The Western Plateau, a low area of flat land in central and western Australia, covers almost two-thirds of the continent. Few people live in the Western Plateau. It is made up of three deserts: the Great Sandy, the Gibson, and the Great Victoria Deserts. These areas are collectively called the Outback. Many Australians also call these sparsely inhabited areas the **bush**.

South of Great Victoria Desert is the Nullarbor Plain. The name is from the Latin *nullus arbor,* meaning "no tree." On the southern edge of this dry, treeless landscape, giant cliffs tower above the Great Australian Bight, a part of the Indian Ocean. The Western Plateau and the Great Dividing Range are separated by the Central Lowlands. This area of arid grassland and desert stretches across the east-central part of Australia. The large expanses of dry regions make most of Australia unsuitable for agriculture. As a result, it relies upon the extraction of mineral **resources** for much of its industry and exports.

networks ***Online Teaching Options***

INTERACTIVE BELLRINGER

North Island and South Island, New Zealand

Comparing and Contrasting and Drawing Inferences Use the introductory text and satellite image of New Zealand's North Island and South Island to compare and contrast the landscapes of both islands and to draw inferences about how the geography influences settlement and the islands' water supply. Have students pair with a partner. Ask each pair to answer the questions and record their answers. Share answers in a whole-class discussion. **BL** **Visual/Spatial, Verbal/Linguistic**

North Island and South Island, New Zealand

Use the satellite image of North Island and South Island below to help answer the questions about the physical geography and unique characteristics of New Zealand.

1. Compare and contrast the landscapes of New Zealand's South Island and North Island.

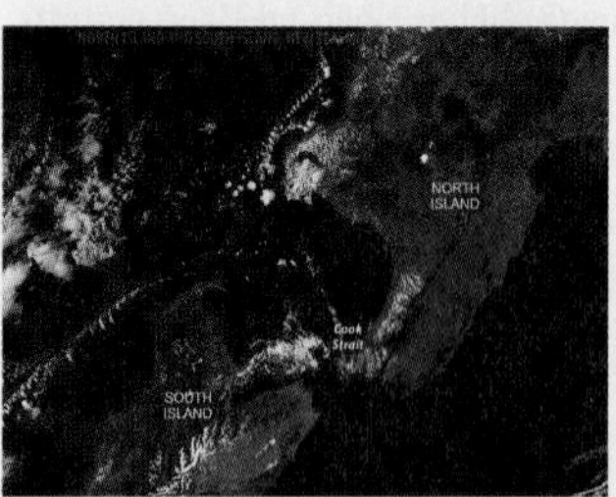

click for answer

Auto-Run Click Through Previous 1 of 3 Next

New Zealand is about 1,000 miles (1,600 km) southeast of Australia. It is primarily two islands: North Island and South Island. Both islands are dotted with sandy beaches, emerald hillsides, and snow-tipped mountains. North Island's northern region includes golden beaches, ancient forests, and rich soils. A central plateau of volcanic stone features hot springs and several active volcanoes. Mount Ruapehu (roo•uh•PAY•hoo), North Island's highest point, is an active volcano.

The snowy peaks of the Southern Alps run along South Island's western edge. New Zealand's highest peak, Mount Cook, rises to 12,349 feet (3,764 m). Glaciers are responsible for carving out many of New Zealand's lakes and rivers. New Zealand also contains **sunken mountains** like those in the Marlborough Sounds and Fiordland that have sunk into the sea. Rugged cliffs, deep fjords, and coastal caves dot the western coast. The Canterbury Plains, New Zealand's flattest and most fertile land, lie on the eastern coast where livestock and agriculture flourish.

New Zealand has **atolls**, or ring-shaped islands formed by the buildup of coral reefs on the rim of submerged volcanoes. In the New Zealand territory of Tokelau, the Atafu atoll has 19 islets that rise to 15 feet (5 m) above sea level and enclose a lagoon. There is also a **caldera**, or large volcanic crater. Reporoa, a caldera on New Zealand's North Island in the Taupo volcanic zone, formed about 230,000 years ago. The last activity recorded was in 2005. **Lagoons** are shallow lakes that are at times connected to a river, another lake, or the sea. New Zealand has mainly coastal lagoons. These inland bodies of water are important to the survival of certain species of flora and fauna.

W

R

bush a wild or sparsely inhabited region

resource a source or supply from which benefit can be gained

sunken mountains a high mountain range that has become submerged

atoll a ring-shaped island formed by the buildup of a coral reef on the rim of a submerged volcano

caldera a large volcanic crater

lagoon a shallow lake that is intermittently connected to a river, another lake, or the sea

✓ READING PROGRESS CHECK

Identifying What three deserts make up Australia's Outback?

Water Systems

GUIDING QUESTION *What is the effect of water on life in Australia and New Zealand?*

Although surrounded by water, Australia is the driest inhabited continent on Earth. Freshwater is unevenly distributed, unreliable, and seasonal. Seventy percent of Australia is described as arid or semi-arid with limited precipitation.

Kings Canyon (left) and Hopetoun Falls (right) are examples of the diversity of Australia's landscape.

▼ CRITICAL THINKING

1. ***Analyzing Visuals*** Describe the climate of Kings Canyon.
2. ***Analyzing Visuals*** Describe the climate of Hopetoun Falls.

V

VIDEO

Volcano - Origin of New Zealand

Summarizing Have students watch this video to learn how the mountains of New Zealand were formed. Then have them answer questions from the corresponding Video Activity worksheet. AL **Verbal/Linguistic**

W Writing Skills

Narrative Instruct students to write a narrative about the physical geography of New Zealand from the perspective of a traveler, either from the past or present, who is visiting the country for the first time. Have students use descriptions from the text to provide details for their narratives. Challenge students to be creative and illustrate the unique landscape of New Zealand. Students' narratives should include details about the vegetation, as well as the landforms and other physical features they observe. Suggest that students make their narratives into a travel blog. AL **Verbal/Linguistic**

R Reading Skills

Describing Have students draw a four-column chart listing each of the following features: atoll, bush, caldera, lagoon, and sunken mountains, using their text or additional resources. Students should include the location of the physical feature, a description, and any unique characteristics to note. To help struggling students, consider having them include a fifth column to add a sketch of each physical feature. ELL **Visual/Spatial**

V Visual Skills

Identifying Ask students to examine both photos closely and then work together to identify different physical features in each image. Point out that these details could be plant species or rocks and suggest visual resources that can be used as references such as guidebooks. Invite students to share their work in small groups. While each student is sharing, other group members should evaluate if the student identified plant species, rocks, or other physical features correctly. BL **Naturalist, Visual/Spatial**

ANSWERS, p. 777

✓ READING PROGRESS CHECK The Great Sandy, the Gibson, and the Great Victoria Deserts make up the Australian Outback.

CRITICAL THINKING

1. Kings Canyon appears to be a dry, arid area with little vegetation except for short desert scrub.
2. Hopetoun Falls appears to be warm and wet with large amounts of lush vegetation.

Physical Geography of Australia and New Zealand

V Visual Skills

Creating Diagrams Discuss with students the role of rivers and lakes in Australia and New Zealand. Ask them to consider the differences in location of the subregion's water systems and what challenges they face. Then have them create a diagram that illustrates the many different ways that humans have tapped water resources in the subregion. *(irrigation, artesian wells, snow melting from mountaintops)* **Ask: What challenge do Australians face with regard to water resources that New Zealanders do not?** *(The location of freshwater resources is limited or unreliable in some areas of Australia. Australia is the driest inhabited continent.)* **Has the location of water resources affected population distribution in Australia? Why or why not?** *(Possible answer: Yes, it has affected population distribution. Few people live in the dry interior. Most people live along the southeastern, eastern, and southwestern coasts where there is access to the sea.* **AL** **Visual/Spatial, Interpersonal**

Content Background Knowledge

OECD The Organization for Economic Co-Operation and Development was founded in 1961, but its roots date back following the end of World War II. More than 34 countries are members of OECD today. The OECD is an economic organization in which the member states analyze economic and social policy and disseminate information with developing economies in countries around the globe. Most of the members are economically strong and leaders in the world economy. Together member states produce about 75 percent of all goods and services in the world.

T Technology Skills

Transferring Information Have students find a specific place in either Australia or New Zealand that has unique opportunities for tourists. Students may work individually or with a partner to produce a digital travel brochure on that place. Suggest that in addition to images, students should add audio and music to their presentations. Their task is to attract as many tourists as possible to this place. Provide an opportunity for students to show their presentations to the class, and then ask students in the audience to determine which one was the most convincing and why. **BL** **Auditory/Musical, Visual/Spatial**

ANSWERS, p. 778

READING PROGRESS CHECK Pressurized water from the Great Artesian Basin flows to the surface and is used to water livestock.

artesian well a well that brings pressurized water to the surface without pumping

In Australia, rivers and lakes in the Central Lowlands fill with water after heavy rainfall. Because rains are infrequent, most rivers and lakes remain dry much of the year. In the southeast, however, the Murray River and the Darling River supply water that supports irrigated farming. A large amount of pressurized underground water, known as the Great Artesian Basin, lies beneath the lowlands. The water that gushes from these **artesian wells**, or wells from which pressurized water flows to the surface, is too salty for humans or crops. Ranchers use it to water livestock, however.

Australia's main water problem is that people and water are not located in the same place. Most of the rainfall is in the tropical north of Australia. However, the population is growing along the east coast and across most of southern Australia. Today these areas receive less rainfall than they did 50 years ago.

In contrast, New Zealand has an abundance of freshwater. It is ranked fourth out of 30 countries that belong to the Organization for Economic Co-operation and Development (OECD) for its per-capita renewable freshwater resource. Both North Island and South Island are bisected by hills and mountains covered with snow. These mountains support fast-flowing, snow-fed rivers and streams. Fifty-one percent of New Zealand's total length of rivers and streams are catchments, or places where water is collected. Theses catchments have predominantly natural land cover such as native bush, alpine rock, and clumps of grass. The remainder of New Zealand's rivers have been modified by agriculture, plantation forestry, or urban development.

T

Australia and New Zealand have striking landscapes with mountains, rock formations, coral reefs, abundant sea life, and beaches. Although they are isolated geographically, tourism is a growing part of the subregion's economies. In Australia, many people live close enough to a beach to visit it regularly. Some people go to the beach for sun and surfing. Others go to parasail, fish, snorkel, scuba dive, and comb the beaches for shells. People come from around the world to visit the Great Barrier Reef, the world's largest coral reef. New Zealanders and visitors to the country also enjoy recreational use of coastal beaches, rivers, and lakes. As in Australia, many people go to the beach for sun and surfing. But in Auckland, New Zealand's most populous city, it seems that everyone sails. Perfect sailing beaches can be found only 15 minutes from the central business district.

READING PROGRESS CHECK

Explaining How is water from the Great Artesian Basin used for agriculture?

Climates, Biomes, and Resources

GUIDING QUESTION *How do the climates of Australia and New Zealand affect the biomes and resources of each?*

The climates of Australia and New Zealand differ by region. In Australia, which is about two-thirds the size of the United States, the climate varies widely from temperate zones to desert regions. New Zealand's climate varies from warm subtropical to cool temperate climates.

Australia's climate includes tropical wet/dry and humid subtropical climates in the north and northeast; deserts in the interior; and midlatitude temperate areas along the eastern, southern, and southwestern coasts. Differences in rainfall cause these significant changes in climate and vegetation. The Outback covers almost two-thirds of Australia. The Indian and Pacific Oceans surround Australia, and the winds coming off the water create erratic shifts from one extreme to the other.

778

networks Online Teaching Options

INTERACTIVE WHITEBOARD ACTIVITY

Landforms, Biomes, and Resources

Classifying Have students complete this interactive whiteboard activity about the landforms, biomes, and resources of Australia and New Zealand. Students will slide descriptions of different landforms into the appropriate columns labeled Australia and New Zealand, and then slide descriptions of different climates, biomes, and resources into the correct columns labeled Australia and New Zealand to compare the geography of each subregion. **ELL**

Landforms, Biomes, and Resources

Directions: Australia and New Zealand are located only 1,000 miles apart in the south Pacific Ocean but feature very different landscapes. Slide the landform descriptions listed in the left column into the column of the country to which they belong.

Landforms	Australia	New Zealand
The arid Western Plateau covers two-thirds of the land.		
Glaciers carved out its many lakes and rivers.		
Central Lowlands feature deserts and grasslands unsuitable for agriculture.		
The Great Dividing Range, a chain of hills and mountains, breaks its level landscape.		
Active volcanoes are found on the North Island and snowy peaks on the South Island.		
Atolls, calderas, and lagoons are part of its varied landscape.		
Three deserts make up the sparsely populated area called the bush.		
The Canterbury Plains provide flat fertile land for livestock and agriculture.		
The Great Artesian Basin features artesian wells too salty for humans to drink.		
Mountains supply numerous fast-flowing rivers and streams.		

Australia also has a tropical savanna across its low latitude areas in the north. During the dry season, the savanna is prone to wildfires. In the rainy season, the rain falls in heavy bursts accompanied by thunderstorms and monsoons. The wet season lasts from December to March.

Marsupials—such as the kangaroo, koala, and agile wallaby—**dominate** the savanna. They owe their survival to Australia's early isolation after the breakup of the early supercontinent Gondwana (which later collided with other landmasses to form Pangaea). Before more advanced mammals could move in to Australia and replace the marsupials, the landmass separated from Antarctica and India.

R

dominate to exercise the main influence on; to control

Australia also has more than 900 wetlands that provide a natural source of water and protection against floods. They also support a variety of animals such as the giant barred frog and the ringtail possum, as well as migratory birds. The Australian government and several nonprofit organizations work to protect the wetlands.

Along Australia's northeastern coast lies the Great Barrier Reef. Its habitat hosts multitudes of creatures. It has been shrinking by a rate of about 20 percent every 100 years. The United Nations has designated it a World Heritage Site.

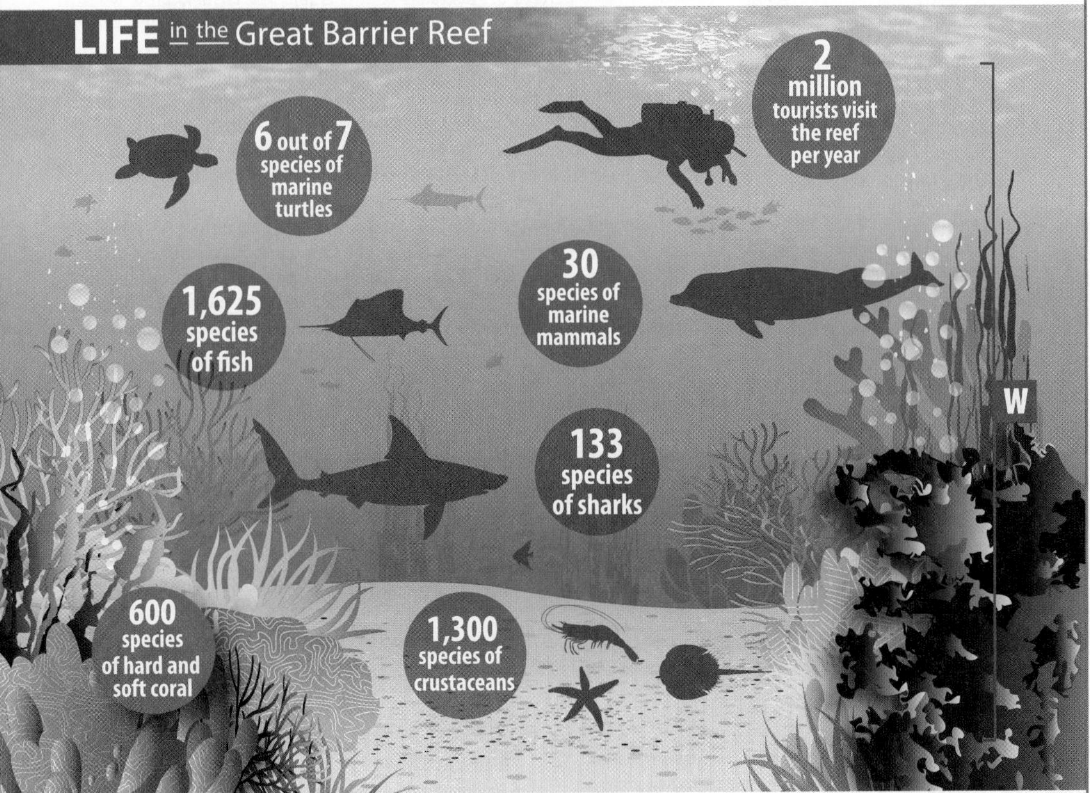

The Great Barrier Reef is a chain of coral reefs located off Australia's northeastern coast.

▲ CRITICAL THINKING

1. ***Assessing*** What factors threaten the health of the Great Barrier Reef?
2. ***Constructing Arguments*** What steps could Australia take to protect the Great Barrier Reef?

INFOGRAPHIC

The Great Barrier Reef

Examining Have students view this infographic of the Great Barrier Reef to examine the plant and sea life that makes its home there. AL **Visual/Spatial**

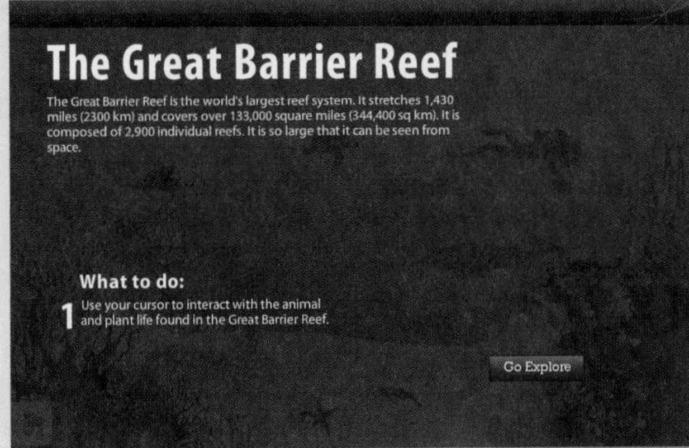

The Great Barrier Reef
The Great Barrier Reef is the world's largest reef system. It stretches 1,430 miles (2300 km) and covers over 133,000 square miles (344,400 sq km). It is composed of 2,900 individual reefs. It is so large that it can be seen from space.
What to do:
1 Use your cursor to interact with the animal and plant life found in the Great Barrier Reef.
Go Explore

Physical Geography of Australia and New Zealand

R Reading Skills

Reading Maps Show students a climate and physical map of Australia. Ask a volunteer to point out the tropical dry and humid subtropical climate regions. Discuss the different factors that affect climate such as latitude, elevation, and landforms. Have students take turns identifying these on the map in relation to each climate zone. Then discuss with students how climate affects the vegetation of an area. ELL **Visual/Spatial**

Making Connections

Explain to students how there are approximately twelve different climate zones or regions in the world. **Ask:** **How many climate zones can be found in Australia?** *(six)* Then ask students to find out how many climate zones are in the region of the United States in which they live. **Ask:** **Are any climate zones similar to the climate zones in Australia? If so, which ones?** *(Student answers may vary but should clearly state if they are similar or different.)*

W Writing Skills

Informative/Explanatory Ask students to study the infographic on the Great Barrier Reef. Discuss the importance of this coral reef to Australia and the world. Then ask students to write a report about the benefits of the Great Barrier Reef and how the reef is being threatened. Remind students that in an informative piece, there should be no bias or opinions stated. Have students use print and electronic resources to gather information. Point out that they should find sources that are recent, especially when they gather facts and details about threats to the reef. When all reports have been completed, ask students to work in small groups to address the challenges and threats to the Great Barrier Reef by brainstorming solutions to these problems. BL **Naturalist, Interpersonal**

ANSWERS, p. 779

CRITICAL THINKING

1. Pollution from agriculture runoff, overfishing, and climate change threaten the health of the Great Barrier Reef.
2. Australia could make and enforce stricter regulations on pollution and fishing to protect the Great Barrier Reef.

Physical Geography of Australia and New Zealand

T Technology Skills

Researching Have students read about the Great Barrier Reef and then discuss what qualities or aspects would make it a World Heritage Site. Ask students to find out what other places or landmarks in Australia are World Heritage Sites. Explain that there are nineteen in Australia. Divide the class into pairs or small groups and assign each one of the World Heritage Sites in Australia. Instruct students to create a multimedia presentation of the site. Point out that students should explain in their presentations why the site was chosen and what makes it unique in Australia, as well as in the world. **AL** **Verbal/Linguistic**

W Writing Skills

Argument Ask the class to choose a position on land rights between the indigenous peoples in Australia and Australian farmers and ranchers. Then have students write a letter to the local government representative in Australia explaining their position, using supporting details, facts, data, and examples. Invite students to read their letters aloud to the class. Use them as the basis for a class debate. **BL** **Verbal/Linguistic, Logical/Mathematical**

C Critical Thinking Skills

Finding the Main Idea Explain to students that the main idea of a paragraph or section is not always written in the first paragraph but often is stated clearly. Point out that the main idea should have supporting details or ideas. Have students read the last three paragraphs, find the main idea, and then write a summary of those paragraphs. **ELL** **Interpersonal, Verbal/Linguistic**

CLOSE & REFLECT

Comparing and Contrasting Divide the class into two groups with each group showing their expertise on either Australia or New Zealand. Have each group present information on that country's landforms, water systems, climate, and resources. While each group is presenting, the other group should check the facts and information for accuracy. Students should take notes as they listen to the other group's presentation.

ANSWERS, p. 780

READING PROGRESS CHECK Both countries have water resources which support fishing and provide means for trade and transportation, gold, and silver. Australia also has bauxite and opals. New Zealand has pounamu, which is a type of jade.

Connecting Geography Living in areas like the Outback shapes the national identity of Australians because these areas are unique to Australia and have become symbols of what it is to be Australian.

Connecting Geography to SOCIOLOGY

The Outback

The Outback, or *the bush,* is an important symbol of the national identity of Australians. It features prominently in Australian literature, painting, popular music, film, and food. What is so special about the bush? It was unique to Australia and very different from the European landscapes known to the early settlers. The Aborigines' skill at surviving in the bush became legendary. The idea of the Outback as integral to Australian national identity was reinforced in 1958 with the publication of *The Australian Legend,* which looked at what defined the typical Australian.

ANALYZING Why might living in regions such as the Outback shape the national identity of Australians?

Its name suggests a single reef, but the Great Barrier Reef is actually a string of about 2,900 small reefs. Formed from **coral**, the limestone skeletons of a tiny sea animal, it stretches for 1,250 miles (2,000 km).

Much of New Zealand has a marine west coast climate. Ocean winds warm the land in winter and cool it in summer. Temperatures range from 65°F to 85°F (18°C to 29°C) in summer and 35°F to 55°F (2°C to 13°C) in winter.

Differences in geography also cause variations in climate. Mountainous areas exposed to western winds generally receive more rainfall than other areas. While the country as a whole averages 25 to 60 inches (64 to 152 cm) of rain annually, the Southern Alps on South Island have an average annual rainfall of 315 inches (800 cm).

New Zealand's isolation gives rise to unique plant life. Almost 90 percent of the country's indigenous plants are only found there. Manuka, a small shrub, carpets land where prehistoric volcanic eruptions destroyed ancient forests. To address erosion in deforested areas, several tree species have been imported.

The natural resources of both Australia and New Zealand enrich the economies of both countries. Water resources provide fishing and a means of transportation and trade. Only 6 percent of Australia's land is arable, but farmers grow wheat, barley, fruit, and sugarcane. In the more arid regions, ranchers raise cattle, sheep, and chickens. Aboriginal land rights have been an ongoing debate in the country.

New Zealand's fertile volcanic soil greatly **benefits** its economy. Agriculture accounts for 12 percent of the economy. About half of the land supports crops and livestock. New Zealand's sheep and wool products dominate exports, and its forests yield valuable timber. The country's rivers and dams produce abundant hydroelectric power. New Zealand also uses geothermal energy, created by water heated underground in volcanic fields, to generate power.

Australia and New Zealand have abundant mineral resources. Deposits of gold and silver as well as other minerals can be found in both countries. Mining is an important industry. One-fourth of the world's bauxite, used in aluminum production, is in Australia. The country also has some of the world's highest quality opals as well as deposits of coal, iron ore, lead, zinc, and gold. Nickel and petroleum are found mainly in western offshore sites.

New Zealand's main minerals include coal, gold, silver, iron, limestone, clay, dolomite, pumice, salt, serpentinite, zeolite, and bentonite. However, one of its most prized minerals is *pounamu. Pounamu* is a type of jade or greenstone that is treasured for its beauty and its spiritual significance by the Maori.

coral the limestone skeleton of a tiny sea animal

benefit to promote well-being; to be useful

READING PROGRESS CHECK

Describing What are some natural resources in Australia and New Zealand?

LESSON 1 REVIEW 

Reviewing Vocabulary (Tier Three Words)

1. ***Describing*** Write a paragraph describing the water resources of Australia and New Zealand. RH.9–10.4

Using Your Notes

2. ***Summarizing*** Use your graphic organizer on the geography of Australia and New Zealand to write a paragraph summarizing the characteristics of the land, water, and biomes of the subregion.

Answering the Guiding Questions

3. ***Explaining*** How do the landforms of Australia and New Zealand influence the economies of these countries?
4. ***Analyzing*** What is the effect of water on life in Australia and New Zealand?
5. ***Identifying*** How do the climates of Australia and New Zealand affect the biomes and resources of each?

Writing Activity

6. ***Informative/Explanatory*** In a paragraph, discuss the land of Australia and New Zealand and how it affects daily life in the countries. WHST.9–10.2

LESSON 1 REVIEW ANSWERS

Reviewing Vocabulary

1. Paragraphs will vary but should be supported with information from the lesson on water resources.

Using Your Notes

2. Paragraphs will vary but should be strongly supported with information from the lesson.

Answering the Guiding Questions

3. Large expanses of desert in Australia make the land unsuitable for agriculture, leaving mining to support the economy. The plentiful rain, fertile soil, and flat land surface of the Canterbury Plains make farming and livestock a large part of the economy in New Zealand.
4. The lack of water in Australia limits settlement and agriculture. New Zealand's abundant water is used to support agriculture and livestock, and produce hydroelectric power.
5. In Australia, the humid subtropical and tropical dry climate in the north produces the savanna which is home to the marsupials, deserts in the interior provide minerals for the mining industries, and midlatitude temperate areas along the eastern/southern/southwestern coasts provide wetlands for many animals and migratory birds. In New Zealand, the marine west coast climate provides plentiful rainfall for growing crops, raising livestock, and supplying fast-flowing rivers that are used for power.

Writing Activity

6. Paragraphs will vary but should be strongly supported with information from the lesson.

networks
There's More Online!

- ☑ **IMAGE** The Lost Generations
- ☑ **MAP** Australia and New Zealand
- ☑ **MAP** Patterns of European Settlement
- ☑ **TIME LINE** Migration and Settlement
- ☑ **INTERACTIVE SELF-CHECK QUIZ**
- ☑ **VIDEO** Human Geography of Australia and New Zealand

LESSON 2

Human Geography of Australia and New Zealand

ESSENTIAL QUESTION • *How do physical systems and human systems shape a place?*

Reading **HELP**DESK 

Academic Vocabulary (Tier Two Words)
- **accompany**
- **impact**

Content Vocabulary (Tier Three Words)
- **Aborigine**
- **clan**
- **boomerang**
- **Maori**
- **dominion**
- **national identity**
- **Strine**
- **pidgin**

TAKING NOTES: ***Key Ideas and Details***

IDENTIFYING As you read about the human geography of Australia and New Zealand, use a graphic organizer like the one below to identify the factors that influenced the subregion's culture.

Indigenous Peoples	Migration	European Colonization	Power Struggles

(tl)©Jason Edwards/National Geographic Society/Corbis, (tcl)Hulton Archive/Getty Images, (tc)North Wind Picture Archives/The Image Works, (tcr)©Cannon Collection/Australian Picture Library/Corbis, (tr)©Corbis

It Matters Because

Long isolated from most of the rest of the world, Australia and New Zealand gave rise to unique indigenous cultures and wildlife. The Aborigines were the first human inhabitants of the subregion. Later, British colonists brought their culture and traditions, introducing European influences.

History and Government

GUIDING QUESTION *How did migration and geography influence the history and governments of Australia and New Zealand?*

The indigenous peoples and the settlers who arrived as part of the colonization of Australia and New Zealand have made them culturally diverse countries. These distinct groups of inhabitants have contributed to the rich cultural fabric of Australia and New Zealand and have shaped the modern countries of today.

The early inhabitants of Australia, the **Aborigines**, have the world's oldest surviving culture. The first of these nomadic hunters and gatherers is believed to have arrived in Australia about 40,000 to 60,000 years ago from Southeast Asia. Scientists believe that they migrated to the area over land bridges during the Ice Age, when ocean levels that were much lower than today had exposed land on the continental shelves. These early Aborigines led a nomadic life and used well-traveled routes to reach water and seasonal food sources. Family groups called **clans** traveled together within their territories, carrying what they needed to survive, such as baskets, bowls, spears, and sticks for digging. To hunt, Aboriginal men used a heavy throwing stick, called a **boomerang**, which soars and curves in flight. Women and children gathered plants and seeds.

Migration was **accompanied** by increased trade among the islands of the South Pacific. Sometime between about A.D. 900 and the 1300s, the **Maori** left eastern Polynesia and settled the islands of New Zealand. Maori farmers lived in villages and grew traditional root crops such as taro and yams, which they had brought from their Polynesian homeland.

ENGAGE

C Critical Thinking Skills

Analyzing Visuals Have students review the pictures at the top of the page and jot down what they think the pictures refer to concerning Australia and New Zealand. Use their ideas to lead a discussion about what students may know about Australia and New Zealand.

TEACH & ASSESS

V Visual Skills

Global Analysis Show students a physical map of the subregion. **Ask:** **How has the subregion been a "meeting place" for British colonists, indigenous peoples, and travelers?** *(Possible answer: The first inhabitants came from Southeast Asia and islands in the South Pacific, followed many years later by the British. People from all over the world have come to visit the subregion. As different peoples have come, they have contributed to the subregion's culture.)* **Why do you think people from Southeast Asia and Polynesia came to the subregion?** *(Possible answer: They may have been in need of new food sources.)* **AL** **Logical/Mathematical**

R Reading Skills

Speculating Discuss how the Maori migrated to New Zealand, inviting students to compare and contrast their migration with that of the Aborigines. **Ask:** **What factors do you think contributed to the migration of the Maori?** *(They left Polynesia in search of new resources and trade partners.)* **Why do you think they brought root crops from their homeland?** *(They brought them for food and trade, and to cultivate them where they landed.)* **BL** **Verbal/Linguistic**

networks Online Teaching Options

INTERACTIVE BELLRINGER

Patterns of European Settlement

Interpreting Significance Use the introductory text and the map showing patterns of European settlement in Australia to identify how the migration and settlement of foreign cultures affected the indigenous cultures of Australia and New Zealand. Have students form small groups and discuss each question. Ask each group to write agreed-upon answers to the first two questions and to record all answers for the third question. Review the questions in a class discussion.
Interpersonal, Visual/Spatial, Verbal/Linguistic

Patterns of European Settlement

The first European settlers in Australia were British convicts, who lived in penal colonies. By the 1850s, free British settlers had arrived.

1. What part of Australia was the first to be settled by Europeans?

A. Northeast
B. Southeast
C. Northwest
D. Southwest

click for answer

Auto-Run Click Through Previous 1 of 3 Next

ANSWERS, p. 781

TAKING NOTES: Indigenous Peoples: Aborigines (Australia) and Maori (New Zealand); **Migration:** Maori left eastern Polynesia for New Zealand; migration brought increased trade among the islands of the South Pacific; **European Colonization:** James Cook claimed the lands of Australia and New Zealand for Great Britain, Great Britain used Australia as a penal colony, New Zealand was settled by Europeans for fishing and farming; **Power Struggles:** Indigenous peoples in Australia and New Zealand were forced from their land and denied basic rights by Europeans

W Writing Skills

Narrative Have students write a journal entry from the perspective of Captain James Cook as he arrived in New Zealand or Australia. Ask them to use the information they have already learned about the physical geography of the subregion to think of descriptive details for their narrative, but also to include information from their general knowledge of European exploration. Invite volunteers to share their narratives with the class. Then, as a class, examine excerpts from Cook's actual journal and see how accurate students' narratives were to the details described by Cook himself. **Intrapersonal, Verbal/Linguistic**

R Reading Skills

Sequencing Information Ask student pairs to create parallel vertical time lines of key events for both Australia and New Zealand to 1900. Challenge students to use additional resources to add events to their time lines. Then have students classify the events as economic, sociocultural, or political. **Ask: Which events in the time lines impacted the indigenous peoples and why?** *(Possible answer: for both Australia and New Zealand, the settlement of Europeans and the fact that the Europeans pushed the indigenous peoples off their land)* AL **Visual/Spatial**

C Critical Thinking Skills

Assessing After students have read the text, **ask: Did forming a dominion improve the life of the indigenous peoples of the subregion? Explain.** *(Possible answer: Yes, it improved in that the Maori were given representation in parliament. They had no representation prior to that.)* **How do the creation of dominions for both Australia and New Zealand demonstrate that the subregion has borrowed aspects of other cultures?** *(Possible answer: The dominion system uses a blend of the U.S. federal system and the British parliament system.)* Ask students to find out what other dominions were created by the British Empire in the early 1900s and report back to the class on their findings. BL **Logical/Mathematical**

ANSWERS, p. 782

READING PROGRESS CHECK The Aborigines of Australia are thought to have arrived there about 40,000 to 60,000 years ago. The Maori arrived in New Zealand sometime between A.D. 900 and the 1300s.

Aborigine the indigenous people of Australia

clan a group of close-knit, interrelated families

boomerang an Australian throwing stick that soars and curves in flight and returns near the thrower

accompany to go with

Maori the indigenous people of New Zealand

impact an effect

dominion a largely self-governing country within the British Empire

European Exploration and Settlement

W Europeans began exploring the South Pacific in the 1500s. Captain James Cook, a British sailor, arrived in Tahiti in 1769. He then sailed southwest and, in October 1769, reached New Zealand. Over the next six months, Cook charted all of New Zealand's coasts. He decided to take a different route home. He crossed the Tasman Sea westward instead of going east around Cape Horn. In 1770 Cook came upon the southeast coast of Australia. He claimed the lands of New Zealand and Australia for Great Britain.

R In 1788 Great Britain began to use Australia as a penal colony for convicts from overcrowded British prisons. By the early 1850s, free British settlers were establishing settlements along the east coast. Sheep were introduced and settlers profited from exporting wool to Britain. Another source of wealth was gold, discovered in the 1850s. Escaped convicts known as bushrangers, however, made life for the free settlers difficult. Bushrangers supported themselves by stealing from free settlers. To combat the problem, strict laws were put in effect.

During the same time, the British and other Europeans established settlements in New Zealand, which offered fishing and rich soil for farming. By the end of the 1800s, raising livestock, primarily sheep, had become a major part of the economy.

The arrival of Europeans in Australia had a disastrous **impact** on indigenous peoples. Many were forcibly removed from their land and denied basic rights. They resisted the Europeans, and conflicts were common. Violence and European diseases steadily reduced the Aboriginal population. In the mid-1800s, authorities placed many Aborigines on reserves, or separate areas.

In New Zealand, British settlement brought hardship to the Maori as well. In 1840 Britain and Maori groups of North Island signed the Treaty of Waitangi. The treaty purported to protect the rights of the Maori, but was used as a basis for British annexation of North Island. The Maori mounted an armed resistance against British rule that lasted for 15 years, but ended up losing most of their land.

Independence

C In 1901 the Australian colonies decided to form a federation known as the Commonwealth of Australia. The new country was a **dominion**, a largely self-governing country within the British Empire. Its government blended a U.S.-style federal system with a British-style parliamentary democracy.

New Zealand became self-governing as a colony in 1853. The colony's Parliament permitted voting to men who owned property. This requirement effectively disqualified most Maori from voting since they did not own property. In 1867 New Zealand passed the Maori Representation Act, which ensured that the Maori were represented in Parliament. In 1893 New Zealand became the first country in the world to legally recognize women's right to vote, including Maori women. In 1907 New Zealand became a self-governing dominion using a British parliamentary system. Beginning in 1975 the voting laws changed, permitting Maori and people of European descent to vote in the same elections.

Both Australia and New Zealand are constitutional monarchies with parliamentary systems. They have written constitutions. The head of state, a largely ceremonial role, is the British monarch. The people elect members of a parliament. The leader of the political party with the majority of votes for parliament is the prime minister, or head of the government. A movement in Australia known as republicanism hopes to establish a republican form of government in which the British monarch would not be head of state. Instead, officials of the state would be citizens who are directly or indirectly elected or appointed.

READING PROGRESS CHECK

Sequencing When did the first inhabitants of Australia and New Zealand arrive?

networks Online Teaching Options

INTERACTIVE MAP

Maps of Australia and New Zealand

Interpreting a Map Have students analyze these maps of Australia and New Zealand to learn more about how the physical geography influenced the human geography of the region.

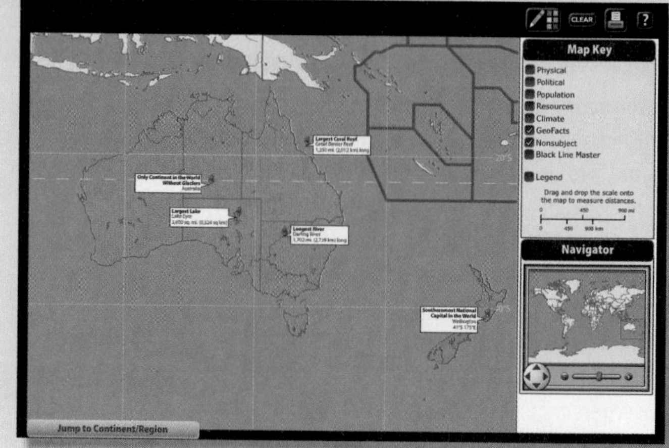

Population Patterns

GUIDING QUESTION *How have migration and an aging population affected Australia's and New Zealand's population patterns?*

Both New Zealand and Australia are multicultural countries. Immigrants from around the world move to both countries to make a new life. Over 7 million people have migrated to Australia since 1945. Of today's population, 44 percent were either born or have a parent who was born in another country. As a reult, many languages are spoken in the country, although English is the dominant language. In New Zealand, most early immigrants were British with some Dutch immigrants arriving in the 1950s. By the mid-1970s policy changes began to make New Zealand a more welcoming place for other immigrants. From the 1980s to today, Pacific Islanders, Asians, Africans, and immigrants from the Middle East have immigrated and now call New Zealand home. **V**

Numerous groups make up the indigenous Aborigines of Australia. One such group is the Arrente, who have lived in central Australia for about 20,000 years. Another group is the Palawa, who have lived on the island of Tasmania for about 32,000 years. After years of harsh treatment and isolation in the Outback and other isolated areas, the Aborigines are now demanding more opportunities. In 1967 the Australian government finally recognized the Aborigines as citizens. Today, about two percent of the population is Aborigine. Growing numbers of Aborigines, particularly youth, are moving to cities. **T**

Approximately 7 percent of New Zealand's population is Maori. The majority of the country's population is descended from British settlers. Asians and Pacific Islanders, attracted by the growing economy, have increased the diversity of New Zealand's society.

GEOGRAPHY CONNECTION

Europeans settled parts of Australia at different times.

1. ***HUMAN SYSTEMS*** Which areas of Australia were the last to be settled by Europeans?
2. ***THE WORLD IN SPATIAL TERMS*** Where were most areas of Aboriginal resistance located?

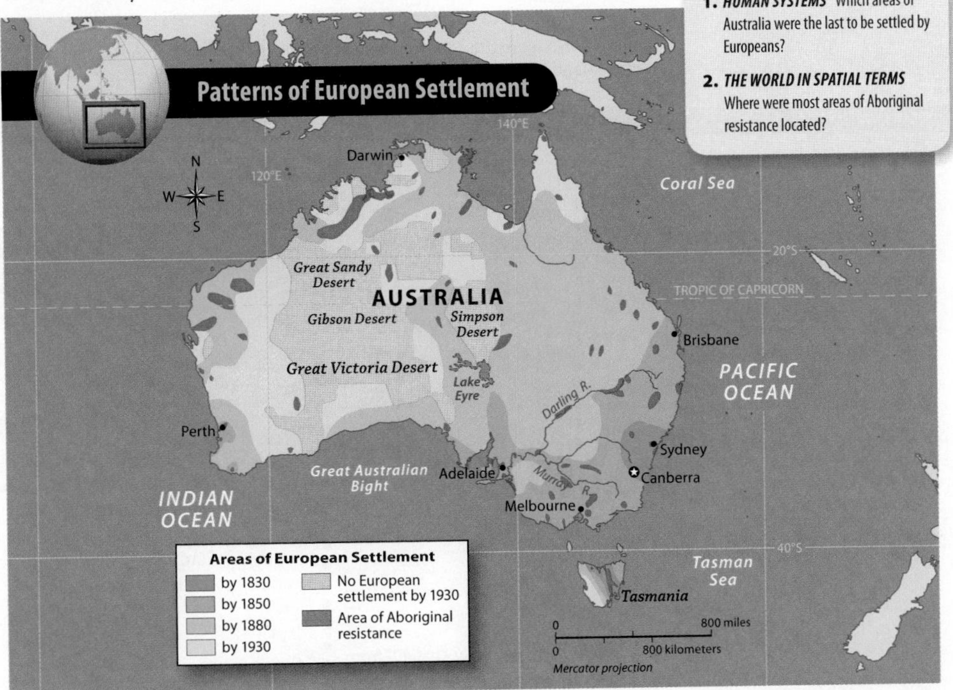

V Visual Skills

Creating Graphs Discuss with students the continuing theme of multiculturalism in Australia and New Zealand. Ask students to call out statistics from the text, and write them on the board. **Ask:** **What do these statistics illustrate about the diverse cultures of the subregion?** *(Possible answer: People have immigrated to the subregion from all over the world. They have brought their languages and other aspects of their culture to share in the multiculturalism of Australia and New Zealand.)* Have students work with a partner to create a graph that shows population projections in the subregion in ten years and in fifty years. Provide an opportunity for students to present their graphs and explain their projections. **BL** **Logical/Mathematical, Visual/Spatial**

T Technology Skills

Presenting Divide the class into small groups and have each group research a cultural group in the subregion. Allow students to select a group that may or may not be specifically referenced in the text. Guide students to resources that will help them gather information and images about the group. Then ask students to create a digital presentation that should include imagery and audio, as well as statistics in the form of graphs or charts to show how the group has increased or decreased in population in the subregion over time. Allow students to show their presentations to the class. **BL** **Auditory/Musical, Visual/Spatial**

Content Background Knowledge

Australian Immigration Since the end of World War II, approximately 7.2 million people from all around the globe have migrated to Australia. At the time, most immigrants came from the United Kingdom and Oceania, but over time this trend has changed. In 2011–2012, the majority of Australia's immigrants came from Oceania, India, and China. Overall, immigration to Australia has declined recently after a period of increased immigration in the first decade of 2000.

VIDEO

Aborigines

Making Connections Have students watch this video to learn more about the culture of the Aborigines and their history in Australia. Then have students answer questions on the corresponding Video Activity worksheet. **ELL**

ANSWERS, p. 783

GEOGRAPHY CONNECTION

1. The Great Sandy, Gibson, and Great Victoria Deserts and the immediate surrounding areas were the last to be settled by Europeans.
2. Most areas of Aboriginal resistance are along the coast in the northwestern areas of the country.

Human Geography of Australia and New Zealand

R Reading Skills

Understanding Relationships Show students a political map and a physical map of Australia and New Zealand and have them study the locations of the most populous cities (Sydney, Melbourne, Auckland, Christchurch, and Wellington). **Ask:** What do these cities have in common? *(They are all located near or along the coasts.)* Why do people prefer to live near the coast? *(Possible answers: Cities grew near ports, so there was access to the sea and related jobs. The climate is milder.)* AL
Logical/Mathematical Visual/Spatial

W Writing Skills

Informative/Explanatory Ask students what they already know about the effects of growing populations on available resources. Then discuss how countries such as India and China, which have large growing populations of young people, have an advantage over countries such as Australia and New Zealand that have aging populations. Ask students to write a multi-paragraph paper on the advantages and disadvantages of both situations, considering resources, the economy, and social factors. Verbal/Linguistic

V Visual Skills

Global Analysis Refer students to the image in the time line. **Ask:** What do you think the Aborigines used as a canvas to create this artwork? *(stone wall or cave wall)* What similarities do you see in the theme and colors used in this cave art in Australia and other examples from around the world? *(Possible answers: long continuous lines, people; the colors red, brown, white)* Discuss with students how even though cultures differ and are located in various places around the globe, they can share common characteristics. Visual/Spatial

R

Australia's physical geography affects the distribution of its people. Few people live in the dry central plateaus and deserts of the interior. Most people in Australia live along the southeastern, eastern, and southwestern coasts. These areas have mild climates, fertile soils, and access to the sea. The largest Australian cities are Sydney and Melbourne. Both have more than 4 million residents and both are major commercial ports.

About 85 percent of the inhabitants of New Zealand live in urban areas, mostly located along the coast. New Zealand's ports of Auckland, Christchurch, and Wellington are the country's largest cities. Both Wellington, the capital, and Auckland are located on North Island, where about 75 percent of all New Zealanders live.

W

The aging population of Australia and New Zealand is of growing concern for the governments of both countries. In Australia, the government expects record increases in the number of people ages 65 and over between now and the year 2021. By 2051, models indicate that between 24 and 26 percent of the population is expected to be over the age of 65. Even though New Zealand's population is aging, its birthrates have increased. As a result, the total number of young people is increasing.

An aging population means that there will be more and more people in need of long-term health care and other assistance. Without an increase in the birthrate, the ratio of persons in the labor force will decline in relation to the number of retired persons. Thus, the government and people of Australia may have to make economic choices in the future. Spending on retirement support, education, or infrastructure are among those choices. Young immigrants from countries such as Great Britain, Taiwan, China, and South Korea are also affecting the population dynamics of Australia.

READING PROGRESS CHECK

Analyzing What are the concerns about the aging population in Australia and New Zealand?

TIME LINE

MIGRATION and Settlement

The history of Australia and New Zealand has been deeply affected by the relations between the indigenous peoples—the Aborigines in Australia and the Maori in New Zealand—and the Europeans who settled there.

CRITICAL THINKING

1. ***Describing*** What are the origins of the major groups of people in Australia and New Zealand?
2. ***Explaining*** What are some reasons why British people immigrated to Australia?

40,000 B.C.

C. 40,000 B.C. First Aborigines arrive in Australia from Southeast Asia.

C. 20,000 B.C. Aborigines spread throughout Australia and Tasmania.

V

A.D. 1200s Maori arrive in New Zealand from different parts of eastern Polynesia.

1642 Dutch explorer Abel Tasman is the first European known to reach New Zealand.

784

networks Online Teaching Options

INTERACTIVE WHITEBOARD ACTIVITY

Effects of Migration and Colonization

Making Connections Have students complete the interactive whiteboard activity to understand how early migrations and colonization have affected indigenous cultures of Australia and New Zealand, as well as shaped the modern government and politics of each.
AL Verbal/Linguistic, Visual/Spatial

Effects of Migration and Colonization
Directions: Migrations and colonization have shaped the culture of modern Australia and New Zealand. Drag the historical events that occurred in Australia into the correct order on its time line.
Australia
1
2
3
4
5
6
7
Ⓐ Britain began using Australia as a penal colony, and free British settlers began settling as well, often raising sheep.
Ⓑ A republicanism movement hopes to establish a republican form of government in which offices of state would be Australian citizens.
Ⓒ Living as nomadic hunters and gatherers, the Aborigines possibly migrated over land bridges to Australia.
Ⓓ European diseases and mistreatment reduced the Aborigine population, which was often placed on reserves.
Ⓔ Australia's modern constitutional monarchy established a head of state (the British monarch) and a prime minister, with members of parliament elected by the people.
Ⓕ A British sailor, Captain James Cook, explored and claimed Australia for Great Britain.
Ⓖ Colonies formed the Commonwealth of Australia, a dominion under the British Empire, blending a U.S. style federal system with a British-style parliamentary democracy.

ANSWERS, p. 784

READING PROGRESS CHECK The concerns about the aging population include more people in need of health care and other forms of government assistance and a decline in the labor force.

CRITICAL THINKING

1. The Aborigines of Australia originated in Southeast Asia while the Maori of New Zealand originated from different parts of Polynesia.
2. The British first sent convicts followed by people seeking farming and ranching opportunities and those coming due to the gold rush of the 1850s.

Society and Culture Today

GUIDING QUESTION *How have immigration and migration shaped society and culture in Australia and New Zealand?*

The people of Australia and New Zealand feel a strong **national identity** toward their countries. Australia and New Zealand blend both European and indigenous elements in their cultures. In recent years, Asian influences have also increased in the region. While daily life in much of Australia and New Zealand may resemble that in Western countries, there is diversity in lifestyles across the subregion. R

English is the major language spoken in both Australia and New Zealand. Australian English, called **Strine**, has a unique vocabulary made up of Aboriginal words, terms used by early settlers, and slang created by modern Australians. V

Because of the rather large population of Maori in New Zealand, Maori is also spoken in certain places. Two percent of Australians—the Aborigines—speak Aboriginal languages. Aborigines also speak **pidgin** English.

Most Australians and New Zealanders, especially those in cities, have access to quality medical care and other social services. The rugged terrain and isolation of some parts of Australia can make access to health care difficult. However, modern technology allows doctors to reach and treat patients through the use of two-way radios, mobile clinics, computer displays, and by air ambulance.

Aborigines and Maori have historically received lower levels of health care, education, and government benefits. Many Aborigines are poor and suffer from malnutrition and unemployment. In recent years, the governments and private organizations of both countries have been working to make up for past injustices. The courts have recognized the claims of the Aborigine and Maori peoples to government assistance, land, and natural resources. W

Both Australia and New Zealand provide free compulsory education. Literacy rates are over 99 percent, and many students attend universities. Students in Australia's remote Outback receive and submit work using the Internet, mail, and two-way radios.

national identity the sense of a being part of the whole of a country including its culture, traditions, language, and politics

Strine Australian English that has a unique vocabulary made up of Aboriginal words, terms used by early settlers, and slang created by modern Australians

pidgin a grammatically simplified form of a language

(l)Hulton Archive/Getty Images, (r)North Wind Picture Archives/The Image Works, (b)©Cannon Collection/Australian Picture Library/Corbis

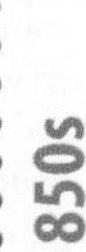

1788 Great Britain begins to send convicts to penal colony in New South Wales, Australia.

1769 British captain James Cook explores New Zealand coastline.

1800

1815 First British missionaries arrive in New Zealand with goal of converting Maori to Christianity.

1850s Gold rush in Victoria draws thousands to Australia, increasing the population by 300 percent.

1855 Increasing Chinese immigration leads to anti-Chinese legislation in Australian colony of Victoria.

1888 Severe restrictions on Chinese immigration enacted throughout Australia

1900

R Reading Skills

Defining Invite a volunteer to define *national identity* in his or her own words. Discuss with students the difference between the denotation and connotation of a word and how the meanings of both of these words individually have a different denotation and connotation than they do together. Have students work with a partner to create a list of words that relate to the connotation of this term. ELL **Verbal/Linguistic**

V Visual Skills

Demonstrating: Write these words in Strine, or Australian English, on pieces of paper and distribute them to small groups of students.

Arvo: afternoon; *Bloke:* man or guy; *Bludger:* lazy; *Earbash:* non-stop chatter; *Flyer:* female kangaroo; *Game:* brave; *Good as gold:* great; *Good oil:* useful information or a good idea; *Grizzle:* to complain; *Oz:* Australia; God's country; *Sandgroper:* Western Australian; *Sheila:* a woman; *She'll be right:* no problem; don't worry; *Sook:* a complainer; *Yabber:* talk

Ask students to perform a skit using the words on the list. Have the rest of the class guess the meanings of the words. Then discuss with the class how they think Australians developed these words based on their meanings. **Auditory/Musical, Visual/Spatial**

W Writing Skills

Argument Have students construct a persuasive letter to the government of Australia or New Zealand arguing in favor of providing health care, education, and other services and basic needs to indigenous peoples. Encourage students to research specific information about the challenges that the Aborigines or Maori face. In their letters, they should attempt to provide specific ideas for how to solve these inequalities. AL **Verbal/Linguistic**

INTERACTIVE TIME LINE

Migration and Settlement

Sequencing Have students examine the time line that displays how the history of Australia and New Zealand has been deeply affected by the relations between the indigenous peoples—the Aborigines in Australia and the Maori in New Zealand—and the Europeans who settled there. BL **Verbal/Linguistic**

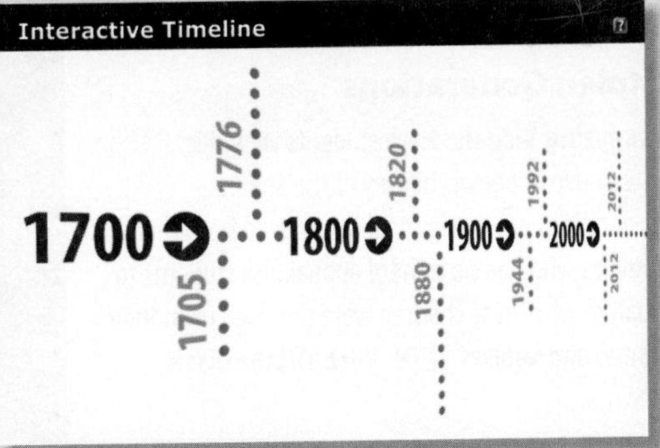

C1 Critical Thinking Skills

Exploring Issues After students read the information about the Stolen Generations of the Aborigines, **ask:** **Why did the government think it had the right to remove children from families of Aborigines?** *(Possible response: They probably thought that the Aborigines should have no rights and took action based on that belief.)* **What do you think the ultimate goal was of removing Aboriginal children and placing them in homes of the English settlers?** *(Possible answer: They wanted the English culture to be the superior, dominant, and only culture in Australia. They thought the Aboriginal children could assimiliate better if they were living with foster parents.)* Challenge students to think of other examples in which the government has removed people or tried to assimilate them into a dominant culture (Native Americans) and compare and contrast it with that of the children of the Stolen Generations. **BL** **Logical/Mathematical**

C2 Critical Thinking Skills

Identifying Bias Have students study the details in the image of the children of the Stolen Generations. **Ask:** **Do you see any details that show Aboriginal culture? Explain.** *(Possible answer: No, these children have been assimilated into English culture because they are wearing what looks like English-style clothing and playing with modern toys.)* Discuss the caption below the image, and then ask students to identify the point of view of the image and handwritten caption. **Visual/Spatial**

W Writing Skills

Informative/Explanatory Have students work in pairs to act as an interviewer and an interviewee. Students should select an interviewee who is someone who has worked for gaining rights for the Aborigines or Maori. Point out to students that they should conduct research to find out about one person or organization that has worked to help protect or gain rights for the indigenous peoples of this subregion. Then have students work together to write the questions and answers for the interview based on what they have learned. If time allows, invite students to present their interviews to the class. **Interpersonal, Verbal/Linguistic**

ANSWERS, p. 786

CRITICAL THINKING

1. Answers will differ but could include a loss of identity, culture, and traditions as well as resentment toward the government for the removal.
2. Aboriginal children were removed from their families in an effort by the government to suppress the Aboriginal culture and make them more English.

Homes Are Sought For These Children

A GROUP OF TINY HALF-CASTE AND QUADROON CHILDREN at the Dar[win] half-caste home. The Minister for the Interior (Mr Perkins) recently appe[aled] to charitable organisations in Melbourne and Sydney to find homes for the children and rescue them from becoming outcasts.

I like the little girl in centre of group, but if taken by anyone else, any of the others would do, as long as they are strong

Children of the Stolen Generations were forcibly removed from their families, who had no right of appeal.

▲ **CRITICAL THINKING**

1. ***Analyzing Visuals*** What effect do you think removal had on the children of the Stolen Generations?
2. ***Speculating*** Why do you think the Australian government removed Aboriginal children from their families?

Today Aborigines are also known as the First Australians, though they lost their land and were marginalized by European settlement. The Australian government tried to suppress the Aborigines' culture to make them more English by removing Aboriginal children from their homes and placing them with foster parents or in boarding schools. The children were not allowed contact with their families. These children are known as the Stolen Generations. About 100,000 Australian Aboriginal and Torres Strait Islander children were removed from their families between 1910 and 1971.

There have been recent improvements in relations between Aborigines and Australians of European descent. In 2008 Australian prime minister Kevin Rudd apologized to the Aborigines for policies and laws of previous governments that were responsible for the Stolen Generations. In the same year, a documentary presented the history of the Aborigines from 1778 through 1993. It showed the experiences of Aborigines during the British settlement of Australia.

In New Zealand, relations between the Maori and the Europeans were on a more equal basis. However, the Maori were still disadvantaged. In the 1970s and 1980s, the Maori become more politically active. They sought the return of land and compensation from the British government for the loss of access to natural resources. These were items promised to the Maori with the Treaty of Waitangi in 1840. By 1998, the Maori had achieved substantial compensation from the government of New Zealand. Eventually, the government also apologized for the injustices inflicted on the Maori.

For many years, both the Aborigines and the Maori suffered racism from British settlers. With increased integration into the national identity of each country and a better understanding of the cultures that make up these national identities, some think that racism will become a thing of the past.

Australians and New Zealanders have strong family ties. Most people in Australia live in a nuclear family of parents and children, but some live as extended families. In New Zealand, families are also made up of mainly parents and children. The Maori tradition has strong ties with extended families. The word for extended family in the Maori language is *whānau*.

Australian women are active in both working at home and in jobs outside the home. Women work both full and part time while they have young children. Many women have balanced full-time work with caring for a family. Between 1996 and 2005, working mothers with a child under five increased from 46 percent to 52 percent. This suggests more women are in full- and part-time work.

In New Zealand, the role of women has shifted to greater opportunities.After high school, some women find jobs in offices, shops, the health services, and as teachers. Others go on to study at a university. Some women may choose to stay home as wives and mothers.

Australians and New Zealanders traditionally used the arts—art, music, dance, and storytelling—to pass on knowledge from generation to generation. Aborigines recorded their past in rock paintings and used songs to share information about watering holes and landmarks. Maori artisans developed skills in canoe making, basketry, and woodcarving.

786

networks Online Teaching Options

INTERACTIVE IMAGE

Stolen Generations

Analyzing Visuals Have students view this interactive image of children of the Stolen Generations who were forcibly removed from their families who had no right of appeal. Ask students to analyze why these children were removed from their homes and families. **BL** **Verbal/Linguistic**

Movies have been filmed in New Zealand, including *The Lord of the Rings* trilogy. New Zealand has an innovative and world-renowned film industry. It is also the birthplace of several famous directors and actors including Peter Jackson, Anna Paquin, and Russell Crowe. Australian actors include Cate Blanchett, Hugh Jackman, and Nicole Kidman.

✓ READING PROGRESS CHECK

Analyzing How might racism become a thing of the past in Australia and New Zealand?

Economic Activities

GUIDING QUESTION *What are the characteristics of the economies of Australia and New Zealand?*

Australia and New Zealand have a close economic relationship. They have signed trade agreements such as the Australia–New Zealand Closer Economic Relations Trade Agreement (ANZCERTA) of 1983. The objective of these agreements is to improve their economic relationship by eliminating trade barriers.

Australia has a diverse economy. This includes agriculture, mining, steel, industrial and transportation equipment, food processing, and chemicals. The country also has natural resources such as gold, iron ore, copper, coal, and uranium that invite foreign investments and are a significant portion of the country's exports. Australia also exports energy and food. Agricultural products include wheat, barley, sugarcane, fruit, cattle, sheep, and poultry. **C**

New Zealand's main industries are food processing, wood and paper products, textiles, machinery, transportation equipment, banking and insurance, tourism, and mining. Agriculture is a significant part of New Zealand's economy. Agricultural products include wool, dairy products, lamb and mutton, beef, fish, wheat, barley, potatoes, pulses, fruit, and vegetables. New Zealand also has many natural resources. These include natural gas, iron ore, sand, coal, timber, hydropower, gold, and limestone. New Zealand is a significant exporter of dairy products, meat, wool, wood products, fish, and machinery.

Both countries have large service sectors. About 75 percent of people in Australia and 71 percent of the people in New Zealand work in services ranging from government agencies to banking and tourism. Service industries are major contributors to the economies of both countries and increase their gross domestic product (GDP). Australia is ranked nineteenth in the world by GDP and New Zealand is ranked sixty-fifth.

✓ READING PROGRESS CHECK

Evaluating What economic activities can be found in Australia and New Zealand?

LESSON 2 REVIEW

Reviewing Vocabulary (Tier Three Words)

1. ***Identifying*** Name four elements of the cultures of the peoples of Australia and New Zealand and describe each in a sentence. RH.9–10.4

Using Your Notes

2. ***Analyzing*** Use your graphic organizer about the human geography of Australia and New Zealand to write a paragraph about how physical systems affect both countries.

Answering the Guiding Questions

3. ***Drawing Conclusions*** How did migration and geography influence the history and governments of Australia and New Zealand?
4. ***Evaluating*** How have migration and an aging population affected Australia's and New Zealand's population patterns?
5. ***Making Connections*** How have immigration and migration shaped society and culture in Australia and New Zealand?
6. ***Explaining*** What are the characteristics of the economies of Australia and New Zealand?

Writing Activity

7. ***Informative/Explanatory*** In a paragraph, discuss how the people of Australia and New Zealand, both past and present, have shaped the subregion. WHST.9–10.2

C Critical Thinking Skills

Synthesizing Display the unit economic activity map of Australia and New Zealand. Review with students the important resources and industries that are mentioned in the text. Invite volunteers to point out where these resources are found in the subregion. Ask students to explain how the climate or physical geography of the area supports that resource or industry. Then provide students with this prompt for a small-group discussion: **How could both of these countries further diversify their economies based on the resources and industries that they currently have?** Have students discuss this question and compile a list of ideas for economic diversification. Ask them to choose one idea to share with the class, and then provide an opportunity for groups to present the idea. Discuss with students how governments and economic leaders address questions such as this one to help strengthen and expand the economy. **BL Logical/Mathematical**

CLOSE & REFLECT

Analyzing Review with students the people, government, history, and economy of Australia and New Zealand. Ask them to write one or two pages about two events that have happened in the subregion since 1900 that have helped to shape the current culture, society, government, or economy.

ANSWERS, p. 787

✓ READING PROGRESS CHECK Increased integration of Aborigines and Maori into the national identity of each country along with a better understanding of these cultures have helped address racism in the subregion.

✓ READING PROGRESS CHECK Both countries have large service industries, including banking and tourism. New Zealand also has a large agriculture and dairy industry while Australia has heavy investments in mining and energy.

LESSON 2 REVIEW ANSWERS

Reviewing Vocabulary

1. Sentences will vary but could include elements such as boomerangs, Strine, pidgin, clans, and *whānau*.

Using Your Notes

2. Answers could include that the Australian population is largely along the southeastern, eastern, and southeastern coasts due to the deserts in the interior; and access to the sea for both fishing and trade.

Answering the Guiding Questions

3. Migration from Britain established settlements along the coasts in Australia, as the interior is unsuitable for agriculture, while later people migrated in search of gold. The British migrated to the less mountainous areas of New Zealand for the fertile soil and areas to raise livestock. These migrations ultimately resulted in both countries becoming constitutional monarchies with the British monarch as the largely ceremonial head of state.
4. Australia and New Zealand both have an aging population but New Zealand's birthrates have increased, adding more young people to the population and making it less of a concern there. Australia is attracting young immigrants from Great Britain, Taiwan, China, and South Korea which will impact the population dynamics, but it may still need to make economic choices in the future about spending on retirement and other social services.
5. Immigration and migration have made Australia and New Zealand multicultural societies with diverse lifestyles across the region.
6. New Zealand and Australia have a close economic relationship and both have large service sectors. Australia also exports minerals, energy, and food while New Zealand exports dairy, meat, wool, wood products, and machinery.

Writing Activity

7. Paragraphs will differ but should be strongly supported with information from the lesson. Answers could include: Australia - Aborigines and their culture have helped shape the national identity of the country including contributing Strine, a language that contains Aboriginal and English words; multicultural society due to immigration; New Zealand - the Maori language is spoken in many places; early Dutch and British immigrants and Pacific Islanders, Asians, Africans, and peoples from the Middle East immigrating today add to the multicultural society.

ENGAGE

Analyzing Visuals Have students analyze the map and key shown on this page. Before students read the feature, have them write a statement they believe to be true based on the information provided on the map. After students work through the feature, have them review their statements to see whether they are factual based on information they learned about Australia's rabbit problem.

TEACH & ASSESS

R Reading Skills

Calculating Have students read the paragraph. Tell them to work with a partner to calculate the number of rabbits that multiplied each year following Austin's release of rabbits in 1859 up to 1920. **Ask:** **Based on the map, in what regions are rabbits the most abundant?** *(southern coastal regions and some inland areas in the middle and eastern portions of the continent)* **What part of the continent are rabbits not abundant?** *(the northern region)* **Why do you think this is so?** *(The climate in the northern part of the continent is probably not suitable for rabbits.)* **Visual/Spatial, Logical/Mathematical**

Content Background Knowledge

Feral Rabbits According to the Australian government's Department of Sustainability, Environment, Water, Population and Communities, the European wild rabbit is one of the most plentiful mammals in the country. The feral rabbits are considered an invasive species and present a threat to the natural environment. In addition to causing severe damage to farmland, the feral rabbit is difficult to control. The government continues to control the feral rabbit population by "promoting the maintenance and recovery of native species and ecological communities that are affected by rabbit competition and land degradation."

V Visual Skills

Explaining Direct students' attention to the text. Ask volunteers to summarize the information in one or two sentences. AL **Verbal/Linguistic**

NON-NATIVE SPECIES:

RABBITS IN AUSTRALIA

R

In 1859 a man named Thomas Austin freed 24 rabbits in Australia. By 1920 there were 10 billion rabbits spread across the continent. By 1990, due to successful eradication attempts, the population was down to 600 million.

RABBIT POPULATION
- ABUNDANT
- COMMON
- RARE
- RABBIT FENCE

BARWIN PARK, VICTORIA
Original site of Thomas Austin's rabbit release.

"The introduction of a few rabbits could do little harm and might provide a touch of home, in addition to a spot of hunting."

—Thomas Austin

WHY DID THEY BECOME A PROBLEM?

V

- Rabbits reproduce at an extremely rapid rate.
- They can live in a variety of environments.
- They have few natural predators in Australia.
- Diseases and parasites that control the populations in Europe do not exist in Australia.

networks ***Online Teaching Options***

VIDEO

Australian Feral Animals

Expressing Have students watch this video to introduce them to feral animals in Australia. Explain that feral cats have become a significant environmental problem in Australia, just as rabbits have, as illustrated in this global connection feature. After viewing the video, have students write a paragraph explaining any information in the video that they found interesting or that surprised them and why. Then ask students to share their paragraphs with another student. ELL **Intrapersonal, Verbal/Linguistic**

red deer. The country has nearly 20 times more livestock than people. Unlike Australia, New Zealand has some of the most fertile soil in the region. This allows farmers to grow wheat, barley, potatoes, and fruits.

Although new plants and animals have helped both countries develop strong agricultural industries, the impact to the region has been detrimental in some cases. In Australia, native plants and animals were well **adapted**, or fitted, to life on an isolated continent. Since European settlement, these native plants and animals have had to compete for habitat, food, and shelter with exotic plants and animals that were introduced into the environment from other places. For example, 24 European rabbits were introduced to Australia in 1859 for hunting purposes. But rabbits had few natural predators in Australia, so by 1926, there were about 10 billion rabbits in the country. These animals destroyed native plants, exposing the soil to wind and water. The resulting soil erosion caused so much damage that some farms were abandoned. Feral foxes are also a problem. They have caused the decline of several species of native animals, and they prey on newborn lambs. C

The introduction of exotic plants in Australia has also created problems. While some of these exotic plants were introduced intentionally, most were introduced accidentally. Many of them have become weeds. For example, the prickly pear was introduced in the 1900s to establish a cochineal dye industry. The prickly pear soon became an invasive species, turning 15,000 square miles (40,000 sq. km) of farmland into a sea of weeds. The weed was eventually eradicated.

Introduced species have also harmed native species in New Zealand. Feral cats and dogs have made New Zealand's native kiwi, a flightless bird, an endangered species. Weasels and ferrets introduced to control rabbits have killed native birds.

✓ READING PROGRESS CHECK

Explaining How do people in Australia and New Zealand use the land?

The introduction of the European rabbit to Australia and New Zealand caused serious damage to the environment.

▲ CRITICAL THINKING

1. ***Making Connections*** How could a small mammal cause damage to the environment?
2. ***Problem Solving*** What steps could the governments of Australia and New Zealand take to deal with the rabbit problem?

Mitch Reardon/Lonely Planet Images/Getty Images

Human Impact

GUIDING QUESTION *How has land use in Australia and New Zealand affected their respective environments?*

Another issue of concern is the protection of forest, soil, and freshwater resources. In Australia, many forests have been cleared for farms and grazing lands. In New Zealand, forests are also converted to pastureland for livestock. Between 2000 and 2010, some 74,000 acres (30,000 ha) of forest were converted to pasture. This leaves little protection against soil erosion. Deforestation also causes soil salinity as well as increased risk of fire and floods. However, pasture continues to dominate New Zealand land use.

In Australia, soil erosion is **compounded** by overgrazing in arid areas and by the country's worst drought in over a century. Soil conservation in the region is closely linked to reducing deforestation. Australia and New Zealand are aware of the problems and are developing plans to use forest resources while reducing damage to the environment. 

Land use has significantly modified the physical and chemical nature of rivers in both countries. This has caused unforeseen consequences. For example, drought, salt, irrigation, and agricultural runoff threaten Australia's freshwater sources.

station an Australian ranch

copra dried coconut meat fed to animal herds

grazier a New Zealand rancher

adapt to make fit to changing circumstances

compound to add to

VIDEO

Australian Feral Animals

Inferring Have students view this video to discuss how feral cats have become a significant environmental problem in Australia. After viewing the video, ask students to explain the detrimental environmental concerns presented. Have students decide if it is possible to balance nature when a new species is introduced within a coexisting habitat, by discussing this issue in small groups. Then have groups decide if it is possible for introduced or exotic species to coexist with native species. Have students pick a side and then write a thesis statement that supports their argument.

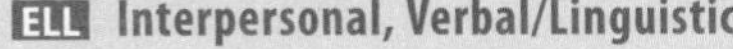
ELL **Interpersonal, Verbal/Linguistic**

People and Their Environment: Australia and New Zealand

C Critical Thinking Skills

Constructing a Thesis After students read about the plants and animals that were brought into Australia, discuss with them the costs and benefits. Then discuss the purpose of a thesis statement and what information is needed to support a thesis. Have students construct a thesis statement based on the central idea of the class discussion. Explain to them that their thesis statements should include at least three reasons or supporting details. Challenge students to create an outline that includes their thesis statements, supporting details, and examples or facts that support those details. AL **Verbal/Linguistic**

Making Connections

As students read about the problems that the introduction of plant and animal species has caused in Australia, ask them to research if their local community has faced a similar challenge with a foreign plant or animal species. Inform students that there are laws that forbid people from bringing food or animals from one country into another. The purpose of customs departments is to inspect items being brought into a country. Customs has the right to take away food or animals that are foreign to that country. These regulations exist to keep people safe and to avoid the introduction of plant and animal species that could cause similar problems like those experienced in Australia.

R Reading Skills

Using Word Parts Write *compounded* on the board and have students break it into word parts: com/pound/ed. Invite a student to share the meaning of the prefix *-com (together)* and the root word *pound (to strike)*. **Ask:** How does knowing what the prefix and root word mean help you to understand the meaning of *compounded?* *(Possible answer: "Pounding together" relates to the definition, which means to make something more intense or extreme.)* **Ask:** What are synonyms of *compound?* *(Possible answers: escalate, expand, increase)* ELL **Verbal/Linguistic**

ANSWERS, p. 791

✓ READING PROGRESS CHECK Farming and the raising of livestock are primary uses of the land in New Zealand and Australia.

CRITICAL THINKING

1. A small mammal with no natural predators is able to excessively breed, creating a large population that destroys native plants. This leads to erosion and causes native species to compete for food and habitat, resulting in native species becoming endangered or extinct.
2. Answers will vary but could include that the governments could stop any introduction of additional rabbits and operate programs to capture and kill existing populations.

Content Background Knowledge

Salinity Two kinds of soil salinity occur in Australia. One is caused by irrigation and the other is caused by dryland. Dryland salinity causes the most destruction because in the process, salt rises to the surface. It moves to the surface with the flow of groundwater and is not always immediate. Both of these factors make it difficult to predict when it will occur as well as a way to assess the extent of the damage. The salinity problem in Australia is sometimes referred to as the "white plague" or the "salt bomb."

T Technology Skills

Examining Information After students read about salinity in Australia, instruct them to search online for images of land that show various stages of salinity. Challenge them to find images of the same place several years apart so they can assess the damage over time. Ask them to assemble their images for display. Point out that they may use presentation software to show the images. For each image, they should write a caption or brief description of the changes that have occurred. Have them also include a map as a visual and identify the locations of the images. BL **Naturalist, Visual/Spatial**

C Critical Thinking Skills

Problem Solving Have students work in small groups to brainstorm ideas about how to battle toxic waste and coral bleaching. Tell them to begin by examining the causes of the problems. *(tourism, agricultural runoff, global warming)* Then ask them to identify solutions to these problems. Have individual group members research one idea in greater depth. Based on their findings, each group should choose the best solution and write up a brief explanation. Invite groups to present their solutions to the class. AL **Interpersonal**

ANSWERS, p. 792

READING PROGRESS CHECK Agricultural runoff, chemical fertilizers, and organic waste pollute the waters; deforestation causes soil erosion, flooding, and increased fires; the replacement of native plants by pastureland and invasive species has increased soil salinity, causing plants to be unable to grow and building structures to crumble.

CRITICAL THINKING

1. Inshore reefs suffered higher levels of bleaching in 1998.
2. Inshore reefs have suffered higher levels of bleaching than offshore reefs.

GRAPH SKILLS — **Levels of Coral Bleaching in the Great Barrier Reef**

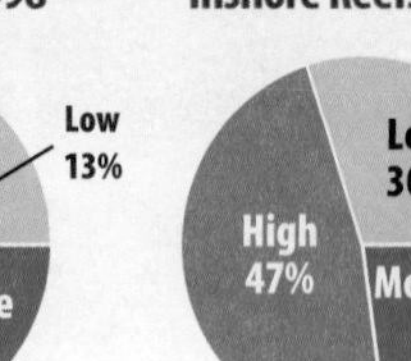
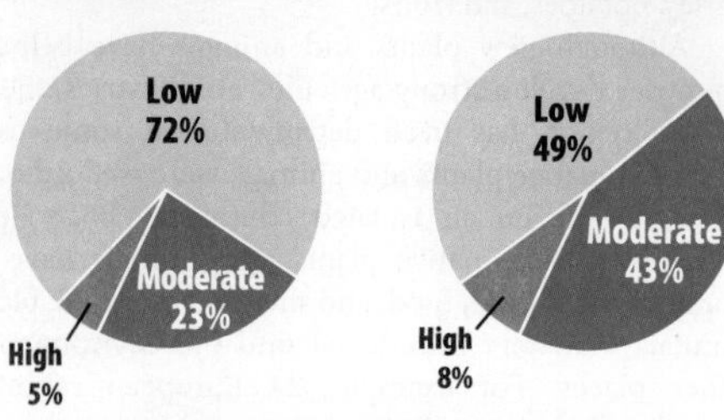

Note: Inshore = less than 6.2 miles (10 km) from the coast
Source: Australian Institute of Marine Science.

Warmer water temperatures can result in coral bleaching. In 1998 and 2002 massive bleaching events occurred in the Great Barrier Reef.

▲ CRITICAL THINKING

1. ***Differentiating*** In which year did inshore reefs suffer higher levels of coral bleaching?
2. ***Analyzing*** Which type of reef has suffered higher levels of coral bleaching?

T The fertile Murray-Darling River Basin is one of the world's largest drainage basins. However, the use of water for irrigation and the increasing needs of growing city populations have dramatically reduced the rivers' flows. Large areas within the basin are also at risk from increasing soil salinity. One of the major causes of increasing salinity has been the replacement of native vegetation—which has deep root structures—with pastures and non-native shallow-rooted crops. Deep root structures prevent rainwater from reaching deep underground and causing salt to rise to the surface soil and water. In increased soil salinity, plants are unable to grow. Salinity causes building foundations, fences, and roads to crumble. Water salinity causes water to be too salty for consumption by humans and wildlife.

C Agricultural runoff, chemical fertilizers, and organic waste also threaten the oceans that surround the subregion. Toxic waste, in particular, endangers Australia's Great Barrier Reef and other coral reefs. Tourists, boaters, divers, oil shale mining, and rising water temperatures increasingly stress these coral environments.

Some scientists argue that increases in Earth's temperatures could be devastating. If polar ice caps melt, ocean levels will rise. This would cause extensive flooding. Rising ocean temperatures also affect certain types of plankton and algae that grow in warm waters, causing overgrowth and the choking out of other life forms. The breakdown of the relationship between coral and the algae that provide it with nutrients causes coral bleaching. Scientists in the region are studying global warming and are hoping to discover causes, predict consequences, and provide solutions.

Pollution also affects marine life. This is especially true for the tiny organisms that make up coral reefs. Algae—on which these organisms thrive—and plankton are key parts of the ocean's food web. A food web refers to the interlinking chains of predators and their food sources in an ecosystem. As these tiny living things are destroyed, larger plants and animals that rely on them for food also die off.

READING PROGRESS CHECK

Explaining How does human activity impact the land and waters of Australia and New Zealand?

792

networks Online Teaching Options

INTERACTIVE WHITEBOARD ACTIVITY

Environmental Problems and Solutions

Problem Solving Have students identify the environmental consequences of invasive species in Australia, as well as identify the causes and potential solutions for soil erosion and deforestation in Australia and New Zealand. Students will draw a line from examples of invasive species in Australia and New Zealand to their environmental consequences and then drag causes and potential solutions into a chart on soil erosion and deforestation in Australia and New Zealand. BL **Verbal/Linguistic**

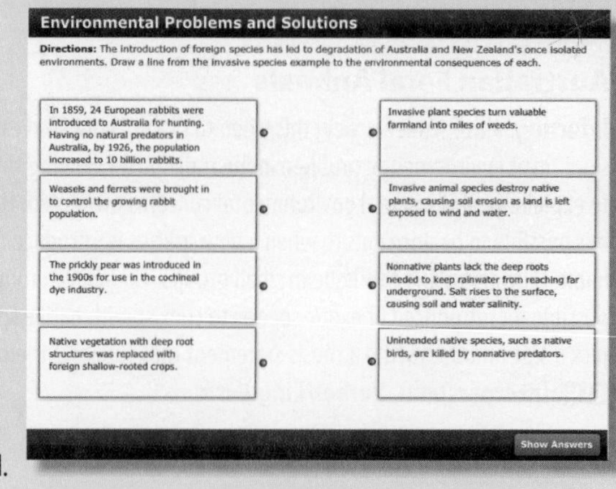

Addressing the Issues

GUIDING QUESTION *How are groups, governments, and other organizations addressing environmental issues in Australia and New Zealand?*

Australia and New Zealand are facing tough environmental issues. Both governmental and nongovernmental organizations are working to reduce these problems. Some efforts are intended to reverse some of the environmental damage in both countries.

The Australian government has reacted to these concerns by enacting environmental laws and initiatives. It has also created organizations and education programs to combat the problems. Australia's environmental minister is responsible for managing these issues. The government created the Natural Heritage Trust in 1997. Now known as Caring for our Country, its mission is to help restore and conserve Australia's environmental and natural resources. It provides funding for environmental activities at community, regional, state, and national levels.

Caring for our Country funds various projects. Some help to protect and restore the habitat of threatened animal species. Other projects aim to reverse the decline of Australia's native vegetation. Another important area is preventing or controlling the introduction and spread of feral animals, aquatic pests, weeds, and other biological threats to biodiversity. The restoration and protection of freshwater, marine, and river ecosystems are also important to the organization.

The Australian Government Envirofund delivers funding to projects at the local level. This fund was formed to assist individuals and community groups undertaking small projects aimed at sustainable resource use and protecting biodiversity. At the regional level, governmental programs distribute money to national resource management regions (NRMs). There are 56 NRMs in Australia that support communities, farmers, and land managers to protect Australia's natural environment and increase sustainability of the country's ecosystems. At the national and state level, projects cover national priorities that cross local and regional boundaries.

Tony Ashby/AFP/Getty Images

Rescuers treat an injured whale before releasing it again from Hamelin Bay, south of the Australian city of Perth.

◀CRITICAL THINKING

1. ***Analyzing*** What are the threats to the health of Australia's marine ecosystems?
2. ***Problem Solving*** How has the Australian government worked to protect marine life?

C Critical Thinking Skills

Evaluating Discuss with students the efforts that have been made to solve the environmental issues. **Ask: Which governments and groups are taking action to protect the environment?** *(Australia's government, Caring for our Country, Australian Government Envirofund)* **Do you think there has been enough action to protect Australia's environment? Explain.** *(Possible answer: Yes, there has been some effort, but the government needs to continue to fund projects and work collaboratively with organizations to be more effective.)* **What factors might influence collaboration to protect the environment?** *(Possible answer: important political and economic influences, such as large corporations)* **AL** **Verbal/Linguistic**

Content Background Knowledge

Combating Drought The Australian Government Envirofund has funded dozens of projects to help the environment recover from the effects of drought. Some of these projects include:

- planting native trees and other vegetation near waterways
- reinforcing drought resistance
- protecting waterways and rivers
- weeding
- fencing off areas to protect them from cattle grazing

W Writing Skills

Informative/Explanatory Discuss with students how efforts to protect the environment are being made at every level of government in Australia. Ask students to learn more about local efforts and whether these efforts are supported by higher levels of government. Then have students write a news article to inform others about the government local efforts. **Verbal/Linguistic**

V Visual Skills

Interpreting Discuss the image with students, explaining that finding beached whales is a common concern along Australian coastlines. Ask students to find a recent event, either online or in print, concerning Australians or environmental groups working near this region, helping whales or other aquatic species. Invite students to share the current event with the class.

ELL **Naturalist, Visual/Spatial**

ANSWERS, p. 793

CRITICAL THINKING

1. Threats to Australia's marine ecosystem include rising ocean temperatures, agriculture runoff, toxic and organic waste, and chemical fertilizers.
2. The government has enacted environmental laws and initiatives and created organizations and education programs.

INTERACTIVE MAP

How Invasive Species Get to Australia

Problem Solving Have students study the interactive map to identify the ways that non-native species arrived in Australia. Ask students to develop plans on how to address this environmental issue. Then have students research how the Australian government is addressing this problem. **Verbal/Linguistic**

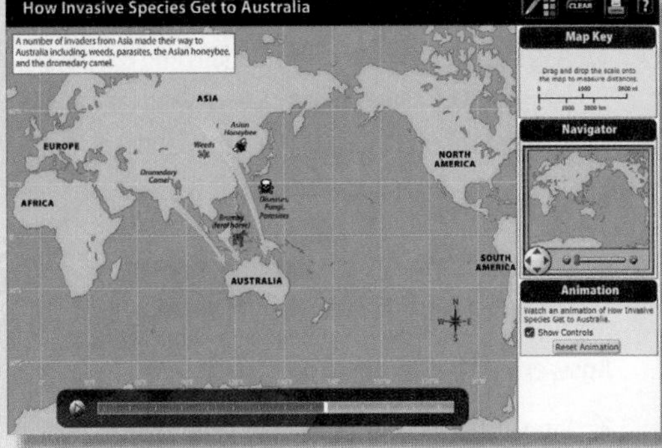

CHAPTER 32, Lesson 3

People and Their Environment: Australia and New Zealand

V Visual Skills

Applying Ask students to examine the image. **Ask:** **How is this image an example of sustainable forestry management? Explain.** *(Possible answer: The image shows what appears to be new growth in a forest, which means that replanting or new planting has taken place after logging. In the background of the image, you can see what looks like mature trees with young trees in the foreground.)* Have students discuss with a partner what long-term effects sustainable forestry management will have on the environment. AL Visual/Spatial

W Writing Skills

Argument Discuss with students how efforts to pass legislation to protect the environment can hit political or economic roadblocks. Have students write a multi-paragraph paper that argues for new legislation to conserve and protect the environment. Ask them to consider the challenges the government faced when trying to pass an earlier piece of legislation such as the Resource Management Act. Remind students to use details to support their argument, as well as examples, facts, and quote excerpts. Invite students to read their arguments to the class. BL Verbal/Linguistic

CLOSE & REFLECT

Outlining To close the lesson, have students outline the main ideas and supporting details of this lesson. Remind them to include only the main ideas and important details. Have them compare their outlines in small groups to check for accuracy and to add additional details as needed.

ANSWERS, p. 794

✓ READING PROGRESS CHECK Australians are working with the government to make environmental laws and initiatives to restore and conserve the environment, including establishing Caring for our Country to protect and restore habitats of threatened animal species and to prevent and control the spread of non-native and invasive species. New Zealanders are working with the government and organizations to conserve and protect the environment through education, sustainable management of land and aquatic resources, and reforestation programs.

CRITICAL THINKING

1. Reforestation helps stop erosion, and increasing log prices and better harvesting methods are encouraging people to reforest as part of sustainable management of forest resources.
2. New Zealanders are working with the government and organizations to conserve and protect the environment through education, sustainable management of land and aquatic resources, and reforestation programs.

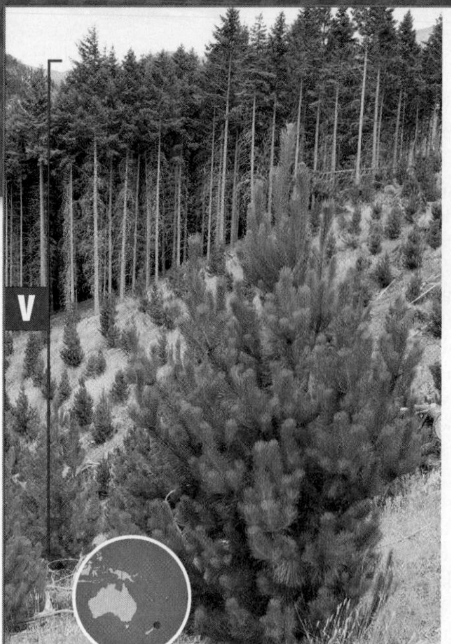

Young trees are recently planted in Kaingaroa Forest, which is the largest forest in New Zealand.

▲ CRITICAL THINKING

1. ***Analyzing*** Why is reforestation important to the environment and people of New Zealand?
2. ***Describing*** In what ways are New Zealanders trying to protect their environment?

Nongovernmental organizations also work to improve the environment in Australia. For example, the World Wildlife Fund (WWF) works to conserve the country's biodiversity by providing practical solutions to the continent's greatest environmental threats. They have been successful in improving the protection of the Great Barrier Reef by persuading the government of Australia to increase its commitment to protect this vast ecosystem. WWF has also successfully campaigned against land clearing in Queensland, Australia. In 2007 the Australian government revoked all permits for broad-scale clearing in the state. WWF continues to work with local communities and in partnership with government and industry to encourage effective conservation policies.

The WWF is also working in New Zealand to fund projects to help the environment. For example, the WWF partnered with the Tindall Foundation on the Habitat Protection Fund in 2000. Since its launch, it has partnered with volunteer groups on over 400 projects to protect areas of high conservation significance in their communities. The WWF and the Tindall Foundation are also working with the Environmental Education Action Fund. This fund supports and promotes environmental education through actions for schools and communities across New Zealand. The Conservation Innovation Fund finances activities that demonstrate innovation and conservation of the environment.

New Zealand's government is also making efforts to solve environmental problems. In 1991 it passed the Resource Management Act. Its aim is to promote the sustainable management of natural resources. One solution is through reforestation to reduce soil erosion. Efforts to reforest the exotic forests of Kaingaroa between Rotorua and Taupo began in the late 1920s. Over the last 30 years, further planting has been encouraged in order to stabilize eroding farmland. Increased log prices and improved harvesting techniques have also encouraged reforestation.

The government of New Zealand also works with the National Institute of Water and Atmospheric Research. Its goal is to improve the economic value and sustainable management of its aquatic resources and environments. The Institute works to increase understanding of the climate and the atmosphere. It hopes that additional understanding will increase resilience to weather and climate hazards. This will improve the safety of New Zealanders.

✓ READING PROGRESS CHECK

Evaluating How are Australians and New Zealanders addressing environmental problems?

LESSON 3 REVIEW (CCSS)

Reviewing Vocabulary (Tier Three Words)

1. ***Describing*** Describe ranching in Australia and New Zealand. RH.9–10.4

Using Your Notes

2. ***Summarizing*** Use your graphic organizer on the environmental problems of Australia and New Zealand to write a summary about how the problems are being addressed.

Answering the Guiding Questions

3. ***Synthesizing*** What environmental impact did European practices of land management have in Australia and New Zealand?
4. ***Evaluating*** How has land use in Australia and New Zealand affected their respective environments?
5. ***Classifying*** How are groups, governments, and other organizations addressing environmental issues in Australia and New Zealand?

Writing Activity

6. ***Informative/Explanatory*** In a paragraph, write about the cause-and-effect relationship between people and nature in Australia and New Zealand. WHST.9–10.2

LESSON 3 REVIEW ANSWERS

Reviewing Vocabulary

1. Australian ranches are called stations and can be as large as 6,000 square miles; New Zealand ranchers, known as graziers, raise sheep, cattle, and red deer.

Using Your Notes

2. Summaries will vary but should be strongly supported with information from the lesson.

Answering the Guiding Questions

3. Introduction of non-native plants and animals caused native plants and animals to compete for food and habitat, become endangered or extinct, and destroyed ecosystems in Australia and New Zealand.
4. Deforestation for the creation of farm and grazing lands have led to soil erosion and salinity, increased flooding, and fires. Agricultural runoff, fertilizers, and waste have led to pollution of waters. Overgrazing has led to increased soil salinity, causing plants to be unable to grow and buildings to crumble.
5. Groups, governments, and organizations are working to conserve and protect the environment through education, sustainable management of land and aquatic resources, and reforestation programs, and to reverse the decline of native plants and animals in Australia as well as preventing the spread of non-native species.

Writing Activity

6. Paragraphs will differ but should be strongly supported with information from the lesson.

CHAPTER 32 Assessment 

Directions: On a separate sheet of paper, answer the questions below. Make sure you read carefully and answer all parts of the questions.

Lesson Review

Lesson 1

1. ***Describing*** What three deserts make up the Australian Outback? Why do many Australians also call this area the bush?

2. ***Contrasting*** How do water resources in New Zealand differ from those in Australia?

3. ***Explaining*** What physical features of Australia and New Zealand make tourism an important industry in both countries?

Lesson 2

4. ***Evaluating*** How did the arrival of Europeans in Australia and New Zealand affect indigenous peoples?

5. ***Analyzing*** Why has modern technology become vital to people living in remote areas of the Australian Outback?

6. ***Comparing*** What industries do Australia and New Zealand have in common?

Lesson 3

7. ***Making Connections*** Why are some Australian ranches thousands of square miles in size?

8. ***Explaining*** How does global warming lead to higher levels of coral bleaching?

9. ***Identifying*** What are some steps the government of New Zealand has taken to address the problem of soil erosion?

Critical Thinking

10. ***Predicting*** What problems are New Zealand and Australia likely to face if their populations continue to age?

11. ***Hypothesizing*** Why are native plants and animals in New Zealand and Australia especially vulnerable to introduced species?

21st Century Skills

Use the graph to answer the following questions.

POPULATION PATTERNS IN AUSTRALIA

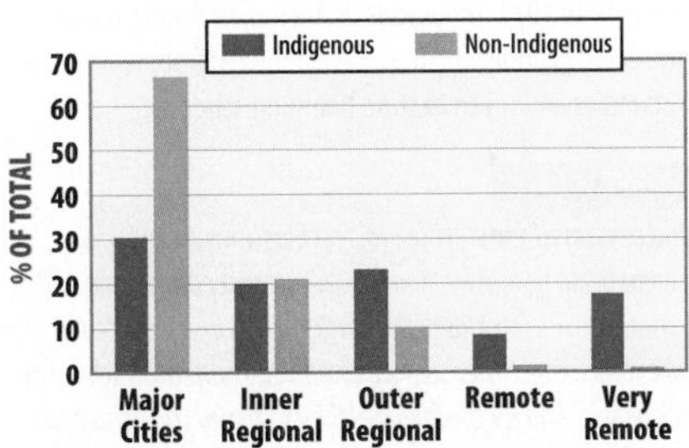

Source: http://www.environment.gov.au/

12. ***Identifying Continuity and Change*** How does the percentage of non-indigenous Australians change as areas become more remote?

13. ***Explaining Continuity and Change*** Why do you think most people living in very remote areas are indigenous?

14. ***Identifying Continuity and Change*** What does the chart suggest about changes in population patterns among Aborigines?

Need Extra Help?

If You've Missed Question	1	2	3	4	5	6	7	8	9	10	11	12	13	14
Go to page	776	778	778	782	785	787	790	792	794	784	791	795	795	795

CHAPTER 32 Assessment Answers

Lesson Review

Lesson 1

1. The Great Victoria, the Great Sandy, and the Gibson Deserts make up the Australian Outback. This area is also called the bush because it is sparsely populated.

2. Water resources in New Zealand are plentiful with many fast-flowing, snow-fed rivers that begin in the mountains and have catchments, while Australia has few freshwater sources except in the southeast where the Murray and Darling Rivers flow.

3. The mountains, beaches, sea life, rock formations, coral reefs, including the Great Barrier Reef in Australia, and rivers and lakes in New Zealand make tourism an important industry.

Lesson 2

4. The arrival of Europeans caused indigenous peoples to lose their lands and basic rights, disease and violence greatly reduced their numbers, and conflicts became common.

5. Modern technology has become vital to remote areas of the Australian Outback as it provides a means for doctors to reach and treat patients, improving health care, and also for students to study, send, and receive schoolwork, increasing education in these areas.

6. Australia and New Zealand both have large service industries and agriculture/livestock industries.

Lesson 3

7. Some Australian ranches are thousands of miles in size because vegetation is so sparse that animals need vast areas to find enough to eat.

8. Global warming leads to increased ocean temperatures which promotes algae overgrowth that chokes out other life forms, leading to coral bleaching.

9. New Zealand has taken steps to introduce programs that actively reforest areas to reduce soil erosion.

Critical Thinking

10. New Zealand and Australia will likely face a growing strain on health care and social services as well as labor shortages if their populations continue to age.

11. Native plants and animals were well adapted to their environment, and their isolation from other sources kept many from having natural predators, which made them vulnerable to species introduced by Europeans.

21st Century Skills

12. The percentage of non-indigenous Australians decreases greatly as areas become more remote.

13. Indigenous peoples historically have lived in some of the most remote regions of Australia, and their culture and societies have adapted to life in these areas. The remote areas have fewer non-indigenous people, which have historically ended up in conflict with indigenous peoples.

14. The chart suggests that more Aborigines are starting to live in urban and non-remote areas.

Assessment Answers

College and Career Readiness

15 Articles will vary but must include why the kiwi has become endangered, what is being done to protect it from extinction, and how successful the efforts have been to save the kiwi. Possible answers should include that the kiwi has been killed off by feral cats and dogs as well as by ferrets and weasels that were introduced by Europeans; protection efforts are underway to eradicate some predators and set aside protected areas and breeding programs; programs have been somewhat successful at increasing the population.

Analyzing Primary Sources

16 The teachers separated students by skin color because they felt that the children with dark skin couldn't be taught anything.

17 Student answers may vary but could include that it was to demonstrate that having darker skin was bad and kept them from being as smart as lighter-skinned children.

18 Glenys was taken to the school as part of the program that was initiated to eliminate the Aboriginal culture and to assimilate Aborigines into European culture.

Applying Map Skills

19 About 6 percent of the land is arable in Australia whereas over 50 percent of New Zealand is arable.

20 The physical geography helps explain the population distribution as the interior is desert and the more populated areas are in the southeast where there are rivers to irrigate farmland.

21 The Great Barrier Reef stretches along the majority of the northeast coast of Australia.

Exploring the Essential Question

22 Diagrams will differ but must label each stage of the process of increasing salinity and show the causes and consequences of the increased salinity. Diagrams should show how replacing native plants with deep root structures with non-native plants with shallow roots allows rainwater to sink deep into the soil, causing salt to rise to the surface.

CHAPTER 32 Assessment 

Directions: On a separate sheet of paper, answer the questions below. Make sure you read carefully and answer all parts of the questions.

College and Career Readiness

15 ***Clear Communication*** Imagine that you are a journalist assigned to write a news article about the kiwi, a flightless bird native to New Zealand. Why has the kiwi become an endangered species? What measures are being taken to protect the kiwi from extinction? How successful have they been? Respond to these questions in your article. WHST.9–10.2; WHST.9–10.7

DBQ Analyzing Primary Sources

Use the document to answer the following questions.

From 1910 to 1971, thousands of Australian Aboriginal and Torres Strait Islander children were removed from their homes and families and taken to state boarding schools.

PRIMARY SOURCE

"*And anyway, these state school teachers, it was very, very different being taught by them. . . . We were separated, me and my mates, to the fair kids to the black kids. Us black ones sat in the dunce corner, cause they said we couldn't do nothing much for the black people. And for the fair ones they said they can do so much for them because they can be taught to—in school in Perth.*

They used to ridicule us all the time. They even had us scrubbing—trying to scrub the black skin off our face, because they never took notice of the kids with dark skin. They concentrated on the fair skin ones you see."

—Glenys Ward, stolengenerationstestimonies.com

16 ***Interpreting*** Why did the state school teachers separate students by skin color? RH.9–10.4

17 ***Analyzing*** What do you think the teachers wanted to teach Glenys by forcing her to "scrub the black off" her face? RH.9–10.6

18 ***Theorizing*** Glenys says that the teachers believed they "couldn't do nothing much for the black people." Why do you think she was taken to the school? RH.9–10.4

Applying Map Skills

Use the Unit 9 Atlas to answer the following questions.

19 ***Environment and Society*** What percentage of land in New Zealand is arable? What percentage is arable in Australia?

20 ***Human Systems*** How does the physical geography of Australia help explain the uneven distribution of its population?

21 ***Physical Systems*** Use your mental map of Australia to describe the location and extent of the Great Barrier Reef.

Exploring the Essential Question

22 ***Diagramming*** Design a series of diagrams showing the causes and consequences of increased salinity in soil. Remember to show how the replacement of native plants with shallow-rooted crops allows salt to rise to the surface, making soil unsuitable for plants. Label the diagrams to describe each stage in the process. WHST.9–10.2

Research and Presentation

23 ***Research Skills*** Using the Internet and other resources, research the history and culture of New Zealand's Maori people. Describe how the Maori were affected by British settlement. What steps did the Maori take to achieve political equality? How do the Maori live today? Create a multimedia presentation to share your findings. WHST.9–10.7

Writing About Geography

24 ***Argument*** Use standard grammar, spelling, sentence structure, and punctuation to write a three-paragraph essay arguing why Australia's Great Barrier Reef should continue to be listed as a World Heritage Site. Discuss the features that make the reef unique, its importance to human and natural systems, and the threats it faces. WHST.9–10.1

Need Extra Help?

If You've Missed Question	15	16	17	18	19	20	21	22	23	24
Go to page	791	796	796	796	746	746	746	792	782	779

796

Research and Presentation

23 Multimedia presentations will differ but must include how the Maori were affected by British settlement, what steps they took to achieve political equality, and a description of how the Maori live today. Presentations should include that the Maori lost land, fishing rights, and basic human rights; experienced serious discrimination; suffered lower levels of health care and education; through election to Parliament and other political action the Maori have gained back many of their land and fishing rights and some reparations have been made; and some Maori still live in traditional areas but more and more Maori live in urban areas.

Writing About Geography

24 Essays will differ but should be strongly supported with information from the chapter and include why the Great Barrier Reef should continue to be a World Heritage Site, its unique features, importance to human and natural systems, and the threats it faces. Possible answers should include: the reef is at risk from rising ocean temperatures, agricultural runoff, toxic and organic waste, chemicals, and fertilizers; it is the world's largest coral reef, is made up of over 2,900 smaller reefs, and stretches for 1,250 miles; it contains 600 species of coral, 1,625 species of fish, 30 species of marine mammals, 133 shark species, 1,300 species of crustaceans, and 6 of the 7 species of marine turtles; and 2 million tourists visit every year, making it a vital part of the economy.

CHAPTER 33

Oceania Planner

UNDERSTANDING BY DESIGN®

Enduring Understandings

- *Places reflect the relationship between humans and the physical environment.*

Essential Question

- *How do physical systems and human systems shape a place?*

Predictable Misunderstandings

Students may think:

- *Most people live along the coast of the islands of Oceania. Explain that although this is often the case around the world, people are concentrated inland and near high land and mountains.*
- *People are to blame for the deforestation in Oceania. Explain that sometimes deforestation can occur by more natural means. On Easter Island, an uncontrolled rodent population may be responsible for the deforestation of the island. It was already deforested when Europeans arrived in the late 1700s.*

Assessment Evidence

Performance Tasks:

- *Hands-On Chapter Project*

Other Evidence:

- *Guided Reading Activities*
- *Vocabulary Activities*
- *Lesson Quizzes*
- *Chapter Tests, Forms A and B*

SUGGESTED PACING GUIDE

Introducing the Chapter	½ Day	Case Study	1 Day
Lesson 1	1 Day	Lesson 3	1 Day
Lesson 2	1 Day	Chapter Wrap-Up and Assessment	½ Day

TOTAL TIME 5 Days

Key for Using the Teacher Edition

SKILL-BASED ACTIVITIES

Types of skill activities found in the Teacher Edition.

* **V Visual Skills** require students to analyze maps, graphs, charts, and photos.

R Reading Skills help students practice reading skills and master vocabulary.

C Critical Thinking Skills help students apply and extend what they have learned.

W Writing Skills provide writing opportunities to help students comprehend the text.

T Technology Skills require students to use digital tools effectively.

*Letters are followed by a number when there is more than one of the same type of skill on the page.

DIFFERENTIATED INSTRUCTION

All activities are written for the on-level student unless otherwise marked with the leveled labels below.

BL Beyond Level

AL Approaching Level

ELL English Language Learners

All students benefit from activities that utilize different learning styles. Many activities are marked as below when a particular learning style is highlighted.

Intrapersonal	**Naturalist**
Logical/Mathematical	**Kinesthetic**
Visual/Spatial	**Auditory/Musical**
Verbal/Linguistic	**Interpersonal**

National Geography Standards covered in "Oceania"

The student knows and understands:

(2) How to use mental maps to organize information about people, places, and environments in a spatial context

2.1 The locations, characteristics, patterns, and relationships of physical and human systems are the basis for mental maps at local to global scales

(4) The physical and human characteristics of places

4.2 The interaction of physical and human systems result in the creation of and changes to places

(5) That people create regions to interpret Earth's complexity

5.1 Regions are defined by different sets of criteria and places can be included in multiple regions of different types

(7) The physical processes that shape the patterns of Earth's surface

7.3 Physical processes interact over time to shape particular places on Earth's surface

(8) The characteristics and spatial distribution of ecosystems and biomes on Earth's surface

8.2 The characteristics and geographic distribution of ecosystems

(9) The characteristics, distribution, and migration of human populations on Earth's surface

9.3 Migration is one of the driving forces for shaping and reshaping the cultural and physical landscape of places and regions

(10) The characteristics, distribution, and complexity of Earth's cultural mosaics

10.1 Cultural systems provide contexts for living in and viewing the world

(11) The patterns and networks of economic interdependence on Earth's surface

11.1 The scale and organization of economic activities change over time

11.2 Patterns exist in the spatial organization of economic activities

(12) The processes, patterns, and functions of human settlement

12.3 The spatial patterns of settlements change over time

(17) How to apply geography to interpret the past

17.1 Geographic contexts (the human and physical characteristics of places and environments) can explain the connections between sequences of historical events

CHAPTER OPENER PLANNER

Students will know:

- *the large number and types of islands that make up Oceania.*
- *how the ecosystems on each type of island differ and affect human activities.*
- *the natural resources that are available from the islands and ocean.*
- *how to distinguish between Melanesia, Micronesia, and Polynesia and the order in which they were settled.*
- *what life was like before Europeans arrived and the changes they and Americans brought.*
- *why resources and the environment in Oceania are at risk and how these issues are being addressed.*

Students will be able to:

- ***describe*** *Oceania as being made up of a large number of two types of islands.*
- ***identify*** *the different ecosystems on each island type and how they affect life.*
- ***identify*** *natural resources in Oceania.*
- ***identify*** *the differences between Melanesia, Micronesia, and Polynesia and the order in which they were settled.*
- ***describe*** *life in Oceania before Europeans arrived and the changes they and Americans brought.*
- ***explain*** *why resources and the environment are at risk and what is being done to address the issues.*

UNDERSTANDING BY DESIGN®

☑ Print Teaching Options

V Visual Skills

☐ **p. 798** Students summarize how the International Date Line changed from 2011 to 2012. ELL Verbal/Linguistic

R Reading Skills

☐ **p. 798** Students record ideas about why Samoa jumped the International Date Line. AL Visual/Spatial

C Critical Thinking Skills

☐ **p. 799** Students discuss why the International Date Line was established and its impact. ELL Logical/Mathematical

W Writing Skills

☐ **p. 798** Students write a journal entry describing the time change when they land in Samoa and how it affects their activities. AL Intrapersonal, Verbal/Linguistic

T Technology Skills

☐ **p. 799** Students research specific examples of how the change from east to west of the International Date Line has affected people in Samoa and create a multimedia presentation to show their findings. BL Visual/Spatial

☑ Online Teaching Options

C Critical Thinking Skills

☐ INTERACTIVE IMAGE **Changing the Date Line**—Students analyze the interactive image of Vice King Tamasese and explain the decision to move Samoa to the other side of the International Date Line in 1892 and 2011. AL Visual/Spatial

☐ MAP **Interactive Regional Atlas**—Students use the interactive regional atlas to understand the physical and human geography of Oceania.

☑ Printable Digital Worksheets

☐ WORKSHEET **Assessing Background Knowledge**—Determine the level of prior knowledge students have about Oceania.

☐ WORKSHEET **Chapter Summary**—Students review the main idea of each lesson of the chapter content.

☐ WORKSHEET **Reteaching Activity**—These worksheets provide students with an opportunity for remedial practice and review of vital chapter content.

Project-Based Learning 

Hands-On

Create Persuasive Essays

Students bring together information from all lessons about the physical geography and human geography to write persuasive essays about issues that affect Oceania.

Digital Hands-On

Create Online Projects

Find an additional activity online that incorporates technology for this project. Visit the EdTech Teacher Web sites for more links, tutorials, and other resources.

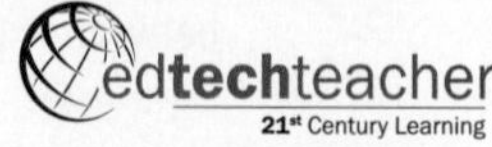

Print Resources

ANCILLARY RESOURCES

This ancillary is available for every chapter and lesson.

- **Chapter Tests and Lesson Quizzes**

PRINTABLE DIGITAL WORKSHEETS

These printable digital worksheets are available for every chapter and lesson.

- **Assessing Background Knowledge**
- **Chapter Summaries**
- **Guided Reading Activities**
- **Hands-On Chapter Projects**
- **Quizzes and Tests**
- **Reading Essentials and Study Guide** AL
- **Reteaching Activities**
- **Video Activities**
- **Vocabulary Activities**

More Media Resources

SUGGESTED VIDEOS MOVIES

- **Green Paradise – Oceania** (27 min.)
- **The Samoas Jewels of the Pacific** *Clint Denn Digital Cinema* (1 h. 13 min.)
- **Lieweila: A Micronesian Story** (57 min.)

SUGGESTED READING 

- ***Oceania: An Introduction to the Cultures and Identities of Pacific Islanders,*** by Andrew J. Strathern, Pamela J. Stewart, Laurence M. Carucci, Lin Poyer, Richard Feinberg, and Cluny Macpherson
- ***Art in Oceania: A New History,*** by Peter Brunt and Nicholas Thomas
- ***The People of the Sea: Environment, Identity and History in Oceania,*** by Paul D'Arcy

PHYSICAL GEOGRAPHY OF OCEANIA

Students will know:

- *the large number of islands that make up Oceania, and how sparsely populated they are.*
- *the two types of islands found in Oceania—high islands and low islands.*
- *how the ecosystems on each type of island differ.*
- *how each of the different ecosystems affects human activities.*
- *the natural resources that are available on each type of island, as well as from the ocean.*

Students will be able to:

- ***describe*** *Oceania as being made up of a large number of sparsely populated islands.*
- ***identify*** *the two types of islands found in Oceania.*
- ***identify*** *the different ecosystems on each island type.*
- ***analyze*** *how the different ecosystems affect life.*
- ***identify*** *natural resources in Oceania.*

UNDERSTANDING BY DESIGN®

☑ *Print Teaching Options*

V Visual Skills

- ☐ **p. 800** Students complete a chart to identify islands, their size, features, and group they belong to. Visual/Spatial
- ☐ **p. 803** Students revisit the charts they created at the beginning of the lesson and add *Resources* as a column. AL Visual/Spatial

R Reading Skills

- ☐ **p. 800** Students draw a model of or act out the process of plate tectonics. Kinesthetic
- ☐ **p. 802** Students read about the mountains and water systems of Oceania and visualize the expanse of water that dominates the region. ELL Visual/Spatial

C Critical Thinking Skills

- ☐ **p. 802** Students craft an argument to defend their choice of resources that were most important to survival in Oceania when Asian migrants were coming, considering key elements for survival such as food and water. AL Verbal/Linguistic

W Writing Skills

- ☐ **p. 802** Students research the major imports and exports of Oceania, as well as main trading partners, and write an informative paper on their findings. BL Verbal/Linguistic

T Technology Skills

- ☐ **p. 800** Students do additional research and create a chart that shows the features of high and low islands. AL Logical/Mathematical
- ☐ **p. 801** Students create a simulation of the process that occurs when a volcano forms an atoll or when an island is formed, using multimedia technology. BL Visual/Spatial
- ☐ **p. 803** Students imagine they are part of a meteorological team and deliver a weather report for one day in all four seasons for a particular area of Oceania. BL Kinesthetic

☑ *Online Teaching Options*

V Visual Skills

- ☐ INTERACTIVE BELLRINGER **Society Islands, French Polynesia**—Students use the text and a satellite image of the Society Islands in French Polynesia to identify and answer questions about the two types of islands found in Oceania. Interpersonal, Visual/Spatial, Verbal/Linguistic

C Critical Thinking Skills

- ☐ INFOGRAPHIC **From Volcano to Atoll**—Students examine the infographic and speculate how a volcano becomes an atoll. AL Verbal/Linguistic
- ☐ INTERACTIVE WHITEBOARD ACTIVITY **The Low Islands and High Islands**—Students identify features of landforms, population patterns, climates, biomes, and resources particular to Oceania's low islands and high islands in a chart to show a comparison between the two island types. BL Verbal/Linguistic

☑ *Printable Digital Worksheets*

R Reading Skills

- ☐ WORKSHEET **Guided Reading Activity**—Students use the Guided Reading Activity worksheets to review their comprehension of the content.

C Critical Thinking Skills

- ☐ WORKSHEET **Video Activity**—Students answer questions related to a topic in the chapter content after they have viewed a lesson video.

HUMAN GEOGRAPHY OF OCEANIA

Students will know:

- *how to distinguish between Melanesia, Micronesia, and Polynesia.*
- *the order in which the three areas were settled.*
- *what life was like before Europeans arrived.*
- *the changes brought by Europeans and Americans.*

Students will be able to:

- ***identify** the differences between Melanesia, Micronesia, and Polynesia.*
- ***explain** the order in which the areas of Oceania were settled.*
- ***describe** life in Oceania before Europeans arrived.*
- ***identify** changes Europeans and Americans brought to the area.*

UNDERSTANDING BY DESIGN®

Print Teaching Options

V Visual Skills

- [ ] **p. 807** Students create a diagram that illustrates the blending and influences of various cultures. ELL Visual/Spatial
- [ ] **p. 808** Students examine an image of a woman receiving a tattoo and think of reasons why scarring and tattooing are important to the culture of Oceania. AL Visual/Spatial

R Reading Skills

- [ ] **p. 805** Students discuss how the world wars politically, economically, and socially affected Oceania and explain the difference between a colony and a trust territory. AL Visual/Spatial, Verbal/Linguistic
- [ ] **p. 806** Students discuss how archaeologists learn about past cultures. ELL Verbal/Linguistic
- [ ] **p. 808** Students explain niche markets and research trends in niche markets. BL Interpersonal

C Critical Thinking Skills

- [ ] **p. 804** Students use details from the text to brainstorm a list of inferences about how the human geography of Oceania changed after Europeans settled in the region. ELL Interpersonal, Visual/Spatial
- [ ] **p. 807** Students discuss an image and whether it was ethical of the United States to test nuclear bombs in the Marshall Islands. AL Logical/Mathematical
- [ ] **p. 809** Students research the origin of main export crops of Oceania and debate whether it is a good economic decision to continue to grow and export these crops. BL Naturalist

W Writing Skills

- [ ] **p. 804** Students write two journal entries, one from the perspective of a European sugarcane plantation owner and the other from the point of view of an indigenous person. AL Verbal/Linguistic
- [ ] **p. 807** Students prepare a written argument on the ethics involved in nuclear testing conducted in Oceania after World War II. BL Intrapersonal, Logical/Mathematical

T Technology Skills

- [ ] **p. 805** Students research one of the Melanesia groups and share their findings. Interpersonal

Online Teaching Options

V Visual Skills

- [ ] INTERACTIVE TIME LINE **Colonization and Independence**—Students examine the time line about colonization and independence in Oceania. AL Visual/Spatial
- [ ] VIDEO **Football Samoa**—Students watch a video about American Samoa and its unique history of sending professional football players to the United States. AL Verbal/Linguistic

R Reading Skills

- [ ] INTERACTIVE BELLRINGER **Pacific Migrations and Settlement**—Students use a map that shows the direction and timing of settlement in Oceania to identify the order in which Melanesia, Micronesia, and Polynesia were settled. AL Interpersonal, Visual/Spatial, Verbal/Linguistic
- [ ] GAME **Human Geography of Oceania**—Students complete a game using information from the textbook. ELL Verbal/Linguistic

C Critical Thinking Skills

- [ ] INTERACTIVE WHITEBOARD ACTIVITY **Types and Systems of Government**—Students identify features of countries in a chart to show distinctions between the three major island groups. AL Verbal/Linguistic

Printable Digital Worksheets

R Reading Skills

- [ ] WORKSHEET **Guided Reading Activity**—Students use the Guided Reading Activity worksheets to review their comprehension of the content.
- [ ] WORKSHEET **Reading Essentials and Study Guide**—Students complete the study guide and answer Reading Progress Check and vocabulary questions. AL

C Critical Thinking Skills

- [ ] WORKSHEET **Video Activity**—Students answer questions related to a topic in the chapter content after they have viewed a lesson video.

People and Their Environment: Oceania

Students will know:

- *why resources in Oceania are at risk.*
- *the steps being taken to address the issues of resource management and human impact on the environment in Oceania.*
- *that some of the challenges can only be addressed by concerted global action.*

Students will be able to:

- ***explain** why resources in the region are at risk.*
- ***identify** how the issues of resource management and environmental issues are being addressed.*
- ***analyze** why some issues can only be addressed by global action.*

UNDERSTANDING BY DESIGN®

Print Teaching Options

V Visual Skills

- **p. 814** Students discuss the different interpretations of the statues on Easter Island and the reasons that archaeologists may believe they represented important chiefs or ancestors. ELL Kinesthetic, Visual/Spatial
- **p. 816** Students draw conclusions about the locations the U.S. government chose for nuclear testing and create a graph that shows related data. AL Visual/Spatial

R Reading Skills

- **p. 813** Students conduct a study of freshwater resources in countries and write an assessment of the relationship between standard of living and freshwater availability. BL Interpersonal, Logical/Mathematical
- **p. 815** Students predict if they think that the coral reefs lost on Maui can be restored. AL Naturalist

C Critical Thinking Skills

- **p. 812** Students compare and contrast the practices of Oceania to protect the environment while increasing agricultural production to those of other regions. AL Logical/Mathematical
- **p. 815** Students discuss whether causes of deforestation in Oceania are similar to causes and effects in other parts of the world. AL Logical/Mathematical

W Writing Skills

- **p. 814** Students write an argumentative paper on the role of human activities in climate change and ocean warming. BL Naturalist, Logical/Mathematical, Verbal/Linguistic
- **p. 816** Students write a paper on how the sustainable management of resources might benefit a region both economically and culturally. BL Interpersonal

T Technology Skills

- **p. 813** Students discuss the need for island countries to carefully manage their natural resources. AL Interpersonal
- **p. 815** Students find both a primary and a secondary source concerning the progress or initiatives of the Parties to the Nauru Agreement regarding sustainable management of fisheries resources to write an abstract. BL Interpersonal, Verbal/Linguistic

Online Teaching Options

V Visual Skills

- VIDEO **Are We Changing the Planets? Coral Reefs**—Students watch a video about how increasing ocean temperatures are affecting the planet's coral reefs. Visual/Spatial
- INTERACTIVE IMAGE **Easter Island**—Students examine an image to learn more about the statues on Easter Island and the history of the island. BL Verbal/Linguistic

R Reading Skills

- INTERACTIVE WHITEBOARD ACTIVITY **Global Warming in Oceania**—Students identify the effects and potential threats of global warming on the islands of Oceania in a flowchart and draw lines from the descriptions of environmental programs to the appropriate box of the other chart. AL Visual/Spatial

C Critical Thinking Skills

- INTERACTIVE BELLRINGER **Global Sea Level Trends**—Students use the introductory text and the map showing worldwide changes in sea level from 1992 to 2013 to answer questions about why resources in Oceania are at risk. Interpersonal, Visual/Spatial, Verbal/Linguistic

Printable Digital Worksheets

R Reading Skills

- WORKSHEET **Guided Reading Activity**—Students use Guided Reading Activity worksheets to review their comprehension of the content.
- WORKSHEET **Reading Essentials and Study Guide**—Students complete the study guide and answer Reading Progress Check and vocabulary questions. AL
- WORKSHEET **Vocabulary Activity**—Students review the chapter content and academic vocabulary words.
- WORKSHEET **Chapter Summary**—Students review the main ideas of the chapter content.

C Critical Thinking Skills

- WORKSHEET **Video Activity**—Students answer questions based on a lesson video.
- WORKSHEET **Reteaching Activity**—Students use this activity worksheet to review and reteach chapter content and vocabulary. This worksheet can be used with struggling students who need additional help with difficult content concepts.

Intervention and Remediation Strategies

LESSON 1 Physical Geography of Oceania

Reading and Comprehension

To help students organize and comprehend the concepts discussed in this lesson, have them work in pairs to create a pictorial outline using the lesson's main headings and subheadings. As partners gather information, have them note key ideas and details under each heading as well as content vocabulary terms. Encourage students to illustrate their outlines to develop a coherent understanding of each concept. For example, students may draw a picture of black islands to represent the term *Melanesia.* Or they may wish to use a graphic organizer like the one on the Lesson Opener to organize their ideas about Oceania's unique physical geography. Ask volunteers to present their outlines to the class.

Text Evidence

Organize students into four groups, assigning each group one of the phases shown in the diagram in this lesson depicting how a volcano becomes an atoll. Tell students they will create a visual representation of their phase, encouraging them to use arts and crafts materials or graphic design programs on a computer. After groups have prepared their assigned phase, tell students to present each phase in sequential order. Discuss how atolls differ from other landforms in the region.

LESSON 2 Human Geography of Oceania

Reading and Comprehension

Draw the graphic organizer shown at the beginning of the lesson on the board. Have students review the text to complete the graphic organizer as they identify an important fact about the settlement of Oceania. Call on students to come up and write their fact on the board. Then have students write a summarizing paragraph to answer the Guiding Question: *How has life on the islands of Oceania changed over time?* Ask volunteers to read their paragraphs to the class.

Text Evidence

To ensure that students have a firm grasp of lesson content, have them write a summary of a topic or issue discussed in the lesson. You may wish to assign topics to students to avoid duplication. For example, students might describe how migrations and European colonization impacted societies in Oceania over time. Remind students to support claims in their summaries with evidence from the text. Encourage students to use content vocabulary words in their summaries.

LESSON 3 People and Their Environment: Oceania

Reading and Comprehension

Have students write a descriptive paragraph about life on one of the islands in Oceania based on information in the lesson. Tell students their paragraphs should convey both the physical geography of the island and how they picture the way of life there. Ask students to read their paragraphs to the class, without indicating which island, or group of islands, they have described. Have students guess the region their classmate has described in the paragraph.

Text Evidence

Assign student groups one of the following topics: greenhouse gases, deforestation, rising sea levels, and rising ocean temperatures. Have students in each group work together to write a report about the problems related to their topic and how or if the problems are being addressed or solved. Students may wish to conduct online research to provide sufficient evidence in support of claims made in their reports. Ask volunteers to present their reports to the class.

Online Resources

Leveled Reader

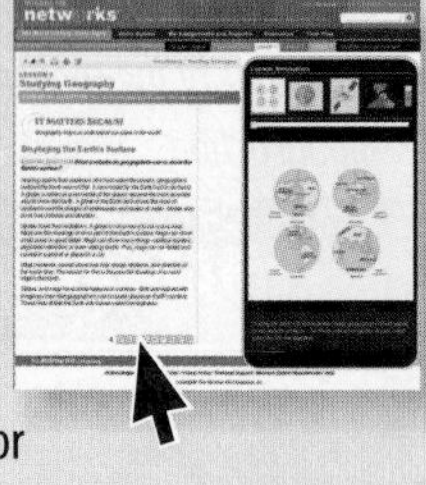

Use this online approaching-level text that corresponds directly to the text in the Student Edition. It also includes additional reading and comprehension support for English Language Learners.

Guided Reading Activities

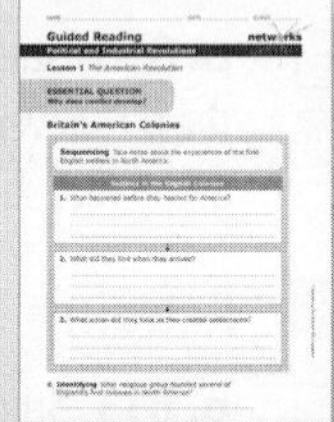

This resource uses guiding questions to help students with comprehension.

Reteaching Activities

These worksheets provide students with an opportunity for remedial practice and review of vital chapter content.

Reading Essentials and Study Guide

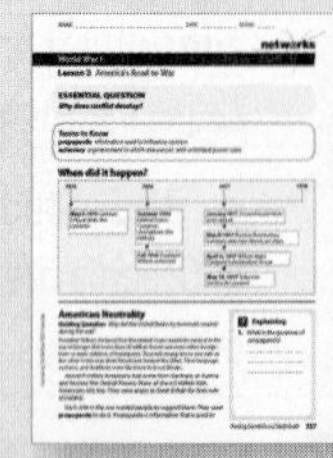

This resource offers writing and reading activities for the approaching-level student.

Self-Check Quizzes

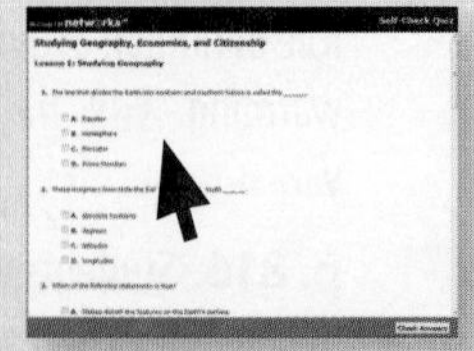

This online assessment tool provides instant feedback for students to check their progress.

Chapter Summaries

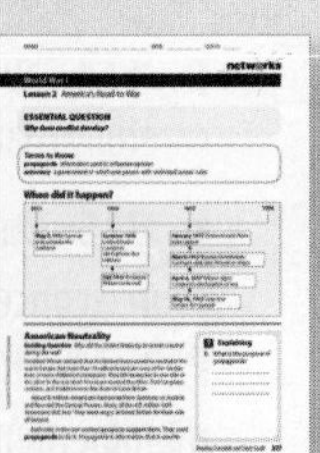

Summaries are provided for each chapter that thoroughly condense core content into manageable chunks.

Oceania

ESSENTIAL QUESTION • *How do physical systems and human systems shape a place?*

networks

There's More Online about Oceania's geography.

CHAPTER 33

Geography Matters...

Oceania is one of the most fascinating places on Earth. The physical geography is varied and ranges from volcanic mountains to blue lagoons. Oceania also includes many tiny islands and atolls. Some of these are so small that they appear on maps as tiny dots or are not on maps at all.

Outside influences on indigenous cultures have shaped Oceania's societies. Today many people blend elements of their traditional culture with those of Western cultures. Migration of people among the islands of Oceania has also shaped life on the islands today.

◀ This Yap Island woman in Micronesia wears a traditional dance costume.

797

Letter from the Author

Dear Geography Teacher,

If scientists are right, and the vast majority of them agree, climate change may well lead to global warming, and warmer temperatures may melt glaciers and ice caps and the result could be rising sea levels. A small number of low island groups have already begun moving to higher ground. This is a perfect opportunity for students to gather data and compare the environmental hazards of "low" versus "high" islands. Rising sea level is a real threat but make sure your students take a look at tsunamis, cyclones, and seismic disturbances. Don't forget the impact of rising water temperatures on the coastal ecosystem.

Richard G. Boehm

ENGAGE

Interpreting Tell students that the subregion they will be learning about is unique because of its physical geography. Ask students what they visualize when they hear the word *Oceania.* Ask them to interpret the significance of its name given that the region is made up of three groups of islands. Have students consider the physical, economic, social, and political challenges that the people of Oceania face. Point out the image of the smiling, young Yapese woman. Discuss with students how Oceania has been influenced by the migration of people over centuries and is, therefore, a blend of traditional and Western cultures.

TEACH & ASSESS

Identifying Cause and Effect Have students read the text and consider the physical geography of the region. **Ask:** **What challenges do you think the people of Oceania face?** *(Possible answer: Transportation and communication among the islands might be difficult because the people are so spread out. The people may feel isolated.)* **What effect do the aesthetics of the region provide?** *(Possible answer: They draw tourists to the islands, which keeps the economy running.)* **AL** **Verbal/Linguistic**

Content Background Knowledge

Kwajalein Atoll Atolls, which are coral reef ring-shaped islands, are common in Oceania, especially in Micronesia and Polynesia. They often circle lagoons. In the Marshall Islands, the Kwajalein Atoll is made up of more than 90 islands and islets. It circles one of the largest lagoons in the world. About thirty-two atolls make up the island country of Kiribati in Micronesia.

CLOSE & REFLECT

Posing Questions Have students think about aspects of Oceania's human population, culture, or physical geography that they would like to know more about. Tell students to write two or three questions and refer back to them as they study the chapter.

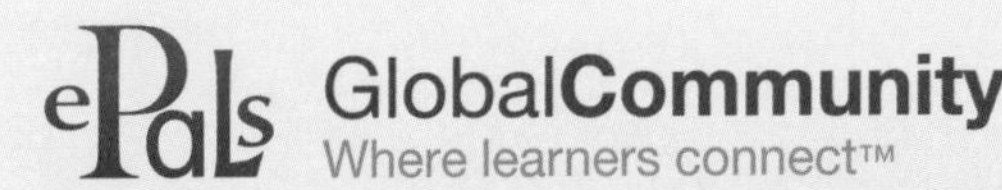

Extend the project-based learning experience globally through our partnership with ePals. EPals allows you to connect with classrooms around the world in a safe online environment for real-life lessons and projects in virtual study groups.

ENGAGE

R Reading Skills

Inferring Invite students to make inferences about why Samoa jumped the International Date Line. Have students consider what factors might have influenced Samoa to make this decision. Tell students to work with a partner to create a three-column chart with the headings *Political, Economic,* and *Social.* Ask them to record their ideas in the chart in the appropriate column. After students have completed their reading of the entire feature, ask them to revisit their charts and to make modifications and additions as needed. AL
Visual/Spatial

TEACH & ASSESS

W Writing Skills

Narrative Have students imagine they are traveling from the United States to Samoa. Using the map as a guide, have students write a journal entry describing the time change when they land in Samoa, and how it affects their activities. Tell students to use descriptive adjectives and vivid verbs to convey their feelings and actions. Challenge students to include how the change in time affects communication. Encourage students to share their journal entries with the class. AL
Intrapersonal, Verbal/Linguistic

V Visual Skills

Analyzing Visuals Have students work with a partner to review the map's title, callout text, and key and examine the areas marked on the map. Have student pairs collaborate to write a summarizing paragraph that explains how the International Date Line changed from 2011 to 2012. Challenge students to address social, economic, and political effects of this change in Samoa, in the region, and in the world. ELL
Verbal/Linguistic, Visual/Spatial

Why Geography Matters: **Oceania**

Samoa hops *the* International Date Line

The country of Samoa is a group of islands located in the Pacific Ocean about halfway between Hawaii in the United States and New Zealand. On December 29, 2011, Samoa (along with the neighboring New Zealand territory of Tokelau) took an important step. At midnight, Samoa jumped the International Date Line, moving 24 hours ahead and losing a day.

Samoa and the International Date Line

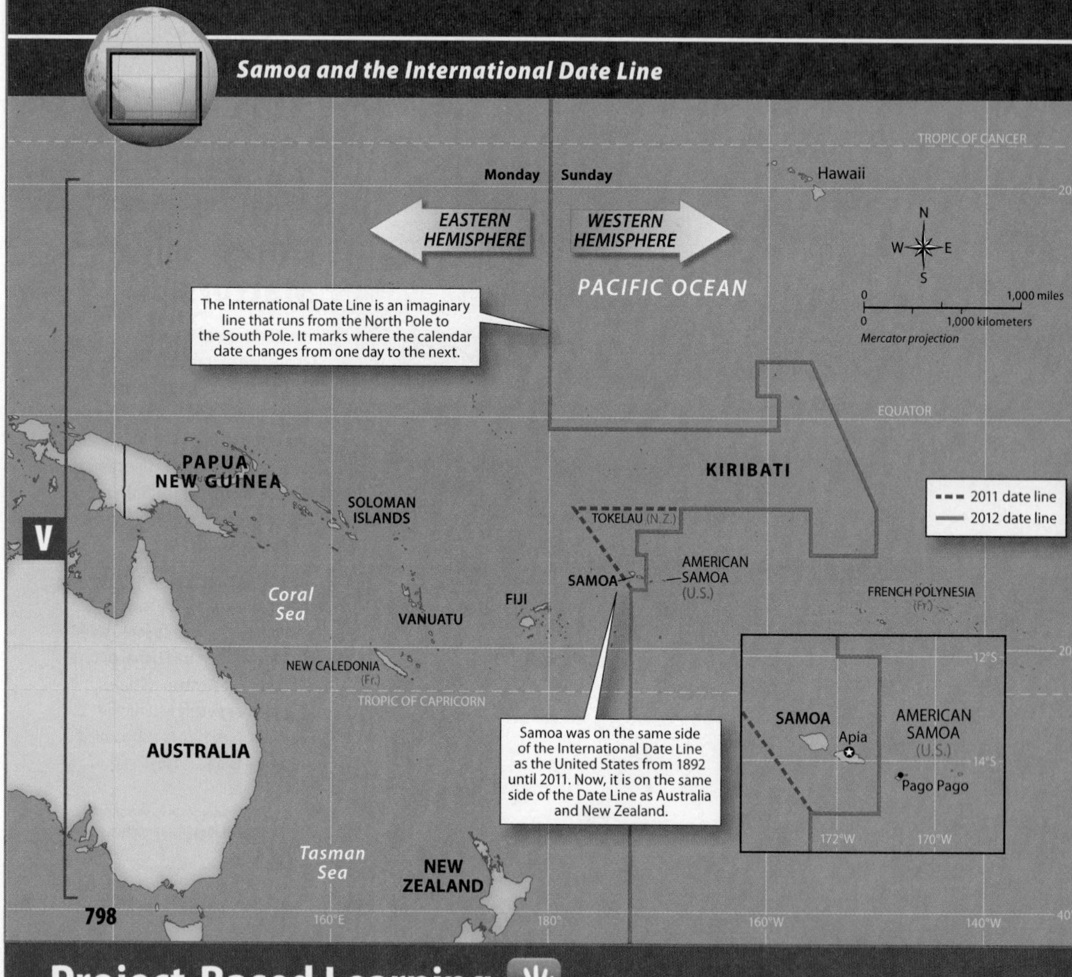

Project-Based Learning

Hands-On

Create Persuasive Essays

Students will create persuasive essays that bring together information from all lessons about the physical geography and human geography in Oceania.

Digital Hands-On

Create Online Projects

Find an additional activity online that incorporates technology for this project. Visit the EdTech Teacher Web sites for more links, tutorials, and other resources.

What is the International Date Line?

The International Date Line is an imaginary line that marks where the calendar date changes from one day to the next. It extends from the North Pole to the South Pole, roughly following the 180° line of longitude, in the middle of the Pacific Ocean. The line's position was initially established at the 1884 International Meridian Conference held in Washington, D.C. Delegates voted to fix the Prime Meridian, or Earth's zero longitude, at Greenwich, England. They also adopted a 24-hour clock for the world, agreeing that each day would officially begin at midnight in Greenwich. Setting the Prime Meridian helped divide the world into standard time zones—12 to the east and 12 to the west. Each time zone is one hour earlier than the time zone directly to its east. The International Date Line marked the point where a new calendar day would begin.

1. The World in Spatial Terms What purpose does the International Date Line serve?

Why did Samoa make the switch?

Until 1892, Samoa lay west of the International Date Line. Then the king of Samoa moved the line so that his country was on the eastern side. He believed that changing time zones would help promote trade with California. In June 2011, the Samoan government voted to switch back to the western side. At midnight on Thursday, December 29, 2011, the official date in Samoa jumped ahead 24 hours, skipping December 30 entirely. Samoa's decision to switch sides of the International Date Line was spurred by the desire to improve the country's economic and cultural ties with Australia and New Zealand. The date change makes it easier for Samoans to trade with these countries. According to Samoan prime minister Tuilaepa Sailele Malielegaoi, "In doing business with New Zealand and Australia, we're losing out on two working days a week. While it's Friday here, it's Saturday in New Zealand, and when we're at church on Sunday, they're already conducting business in Sydney and Brisbane." Thus, by switching to the western side of the International Date Line, Samoans have the same workweek as residents of Australia and New Zealand.

2. The Uses of Geography What prompted Samoa to switch sides of the International Date Line?

How was the switch accomplished and what were the results?

No international body governs the International Date Line. Any country can decide which side it wants to be on and move the line accordingly. After the Samoan government decided to switch sides, officials simply changed maps, charts, and atlases to show Samoa's new orientation. The date change caused some temporary problems. Travelers missed flights because they arrived at the airport on the wrong day or at the wrong time. Investors lost one day of interest from banks. Yet the switch eventually made everyday life easier for Samoans. Samoa is now three hours ahead of eastern Australia rather than 21 hours behind. Also, Samoans living in Australia or New Zealand celebrate holidays, anniversaries, and other important occasions with their families on the same day. Samoa had always been the last place on Earth to watch the sun set, but now it is the first place to see the sun rise.

3. Human Systems Imagine you were living in Samoa in 2011. How would you feel about switching sides of the International Date Line? Explain.

(l)©Bettmann/Corbis, (c)Kyodo/AP Images, (r)Kyodo/Newscom

THERE'S MORE ONLINE

SEE the effect of time zone change on Oceania and nearby countries • *VIEW* a chart of Samoa's trading partners

INTERACTIVE IMAGE

Changing the Date Line

Analyzing Visuals Have students analyze the interactive image of Vice King Tamasese and explain the decision to move Samoa to the other side of the International Date Line in 1892 and 2011. AL Visual/Spatial

C Critical Thinking Skills

Evaluating Have students read the text that discusses why the International Date Line was established. Invite a volunteer to describe the location of it. **Ask: What challenges did countries face before the International Date Line was created?** *(Possible answer: People in one country did not know what time it was in other countries. This would have impacted political alliances and trade.)* Have students consider if the creation of the International Date Line had a positive or negative impact. Ask students to make a list of the positive and negative effects and then to share their list within a small group. ELL **Logical/Mathematical**

T Technology Skills

Analyzing Have students study the image of the Samoan man holding up stamps. **Ask: What do you think the stamps commemorate?** *(The switch by Samoa of moving west of the International Date Line in 2011.)* **How has this change, from east to west of the International Date Line, brought Samoans together?** *(Possible answer: It has united them; whether they live in Samoa or Australia, they are now on the same date, which has brought families closer together.)* Ask students to conduct Internet research to identify specific examples of how this change has affected the people living there. Challenge students to investigate a family's or a person's unique experience. Then ask them to create a multimedia presentation that includes audio and visual elements to feature their story. Provide an opportunity for students to show their presentations to the class. BL **Visual/Spatial**

CLOSE & REFLECT

Understanding Relationships Have students review the text in each column. Then ask them to write a summarizing paragraph about how the openness of the International Date Line, or the ability of any country to decide which side it wants to be on, sets a precedent in international cooperation.

ANSWERS, p. 799

Why Geography Matters

1. When dividing the world into time zones, the International Date Line was created to mark the point where a new calendar day would begin.
2. Samoa wanted to improve its economic and cultural ties with New Zealand and Australia by being on the same side of the International Date Line, which allows their workweek to be the same.
3. Answers may vary but could include that the change was good because it allowed Samoans to celebrate important occasions with their families in New Zealand and Australia on the same day, as well as being frustrated with the temporary problems it caused with traveling.

ENGAGE

R Reading Skills

Activating Prior Knowledge Before students begin the lesson, ask them how plate tectonics can cause the formation of islands. Invite students to draw a model of the process or act it out with other students. **Ask:** **Why do you think that geographers came up with the name Oceania to describe this region?** *(Possible answer: All of the landforms are groups of islands in the Pacific Ocean.)* **Kinesthetic**

TEACH & ASSESS

V Visual Skills

Classifying Discuss with students how three island groups comprise Oceania. Have students complete a chart like the one below by filling in the appropriate details for each island country. Then discuss with them how the island groups are similar and different. **Visual/Spatial**

Island/ Country	Size	Features	Island Group
Papua New Guinea	178,850 sq. mi.	high island	Melanesia

T Technology Skills

Acquiring Information Explain to students that Oceania is made up of high islands and low islands. **Ask:** **Knowing that the region is made up of many islands that were formed as a result of plate movement and volcanic eruptions, how do high islands differ from low islands?** *(Possible answer: Since high islands include mountain ranges, low islands might include atolls.)* Ask students to acquire more information about the differences in high and low islands and create a chart that shows the features of both islands. AL **Logical/Mathematical**

ANSWERS, p. 800

TAKING NOTES: Landforms: High islands have earthquakes, volcanic eruptions, and mountain ranges divided by deep valleys. Low islands, also known as atolls, are formed by the buildup of coral reefs on the edges of submerged volcanoes. Low islands rise only a few feet above sea level. **Soil:** High islands have rich, volcanic soils. Low islands have poor soil. **Resources:** High islands have more freshwater resources, rain forests with lumber resources, good soil for agriculture, fish, gold, bauxite, phosphates, lead, zinc, and nickel. Low islands have few natural resources outside of the sea, which supports the fishing industry and tourism. Fiji has timber, gold, and potential offshore oil, and produces hydroelectric power. America Samoa has volcanic materials such as pumice and pumicite.

networks
There's More Online!

- IMAGE Bora Bora in the South Pacific
- IMAGE High Island
- IMAGE Low Island
- INFOGRAPHIC From Volcano to Atoll
- INTERACTIVE SELF-CHECK QUIZ
- VIDEO Physical Geography of Oceania

LESSON 1
Physical Geography of Oceania

ESSENTIAL QUESTION • *How do physical systems and human systems shape a place?*

Reading HELPDESK

Academic Vocabulary (Tier Two Words)
- converse
- offset

Content Vocabulary (Tier Three Words)
- high island
- low island
- coral reef

TAKING NOTES: *Key Ideas and Details*

IDENTIFYING As you read about the physical geography of Oceania, use a graphic organizer like the one below to compare high islands and low islands.

Physical Geography of Oceania

	High Islands	Low Islands
Landforms		
Soils		
Resources		

It Matters Because
Oceania, as part of the diverse South Pacific region, includes stunning volcanic mountains, low atolls, and cool blue lagoons. Among these varied physical features are unique species of wildlife that attract tourists and scientists alike.

Landforms
GUIDING QUESTION *How do the islands of Oceania affect settlement?*

R Thousands of islands, differing in size and extending across millions of square miles of the Pacific Ocean, form the region of Oceania (OH•shee•A•nee•uh). Some islands were created millions of years ago by colliding tectonic plates. Other islands were formed by volcanic hot spots.

V Oceania consists of three island groups: Melanesia, Micronesia, and Polynesia. These groupings are based on location, how they formed, and culture. Melanesia, meaning "black islands," lies north and east of Australia. Melanesia includes island countries such as Papua New Guinea, Fiji, the Solomon Islands, and Vanuatu, as well as New Caledonia, a self-governing French territory. The largest country is Papua New Guinea with an area of 178,850 square miles (461,693 sq. km). Micronesia, meaning "little islands," lies north of Melanesia in the western Pacific. It includes the countries of Palau, the Federated States of Micronesia, Nauru, and Kiribati. The area also includes the U.S. territories of Guam and the Mariana Islands. In the central Pacific, Polynesia, meaning "many islands," spans an area larger than either Melanesia or Micronesia. The independent countries Samoa, Tonga, and Tuvalu are found in Polynesia. Other island groups, known as French Polynesia, are French territories and include Tahiti, Polynesia's largest island. Some of the islands of Polynesia, such as those that make up the state of Hawaii, are clustered relatively close together. Other islands are extremely remote. Easter Island, also known as Rapa Nui, lies more than 2,000 miles (3,219 km) west of Chile and some 1,200 miles (1,931 km) from its nearest island neighbor.

T Earthquakes and volcanic eruptions still occur on many **high islands**, one of the island types in Oceania. The landscapes of high islands feature mountain ranges split by valleys that fan out into coastal plains. The

networks *Online Teaching Options*

INTERACTIVE BELLRINGER

Society Islands, French Polynesia

Analyzing Visuals Use the introductory text and the satellite image of the Society Islands in French Polynesia to identify one of the two types of islands found in Oceania. Have students work in pairs and discuss each question. Then, review the answers with the whole class. **Interpersonal, Visual/Spatial, Verbal/Linguistic**

Society Islands, French Polynesia

This image shows the evolution of islands with coral reefs that form a barrier reef to atolls, or reefs that circle an open lagoon.

1. Which island is an atoll?

A. Bora-Bora
B. Raiatea
C. Tahaa
D. Tapai

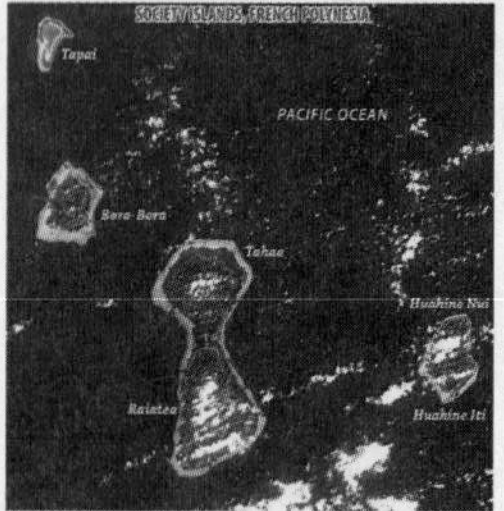

click for answer

Auto-Run Click Through Previous 1 of 3 Next

mountains can create areas that are nearly inaccessible. On many high islands, however, mountain areas have greater population density. The interior of Papua New Guinea, for example, is densely populated. This pattern is much different from Fiji, where the majority of the population centers are on the coast.

The settlement patterns of Oceania were limited by the physical geography of the region. Isolated valleys, such as those on the larger islands of Melanesia, created an environment of cultural differences between people living on the coast and those living inland. Even today the islands of Melanesia are characterized by a diversity of languages and customs.

Volcanoes shaped another type of islands, **low islands**. Low islands, such as many of the Marshall Islands, are ring-shaped islands known as atolls. They are formed by the buildup of **coral reefs** on the rim of submerged volcanoes. Atolls encircle lagoons—or shallow pools of clear water—and usually rise only a few feet above sea level. Low islands have poor soil and few natural resources. The landscape of low islands increased interaction between people since lack of physical barriers allowed for more uniform languages and cultures to develop and spread.

high island an island with mountain ranges and volcanic soils

low island an island formed by the buildup of a coral reef on the rim of a submerged volcano; sometimes known as an atoll

coral reef a reef made up of fragments of corals, coral sands, algal and other organic deposits, and the solid limestone resulting from their consolidation

READING PROGRESS CHECK

Describing What is the relationship between atolls and lagoons?

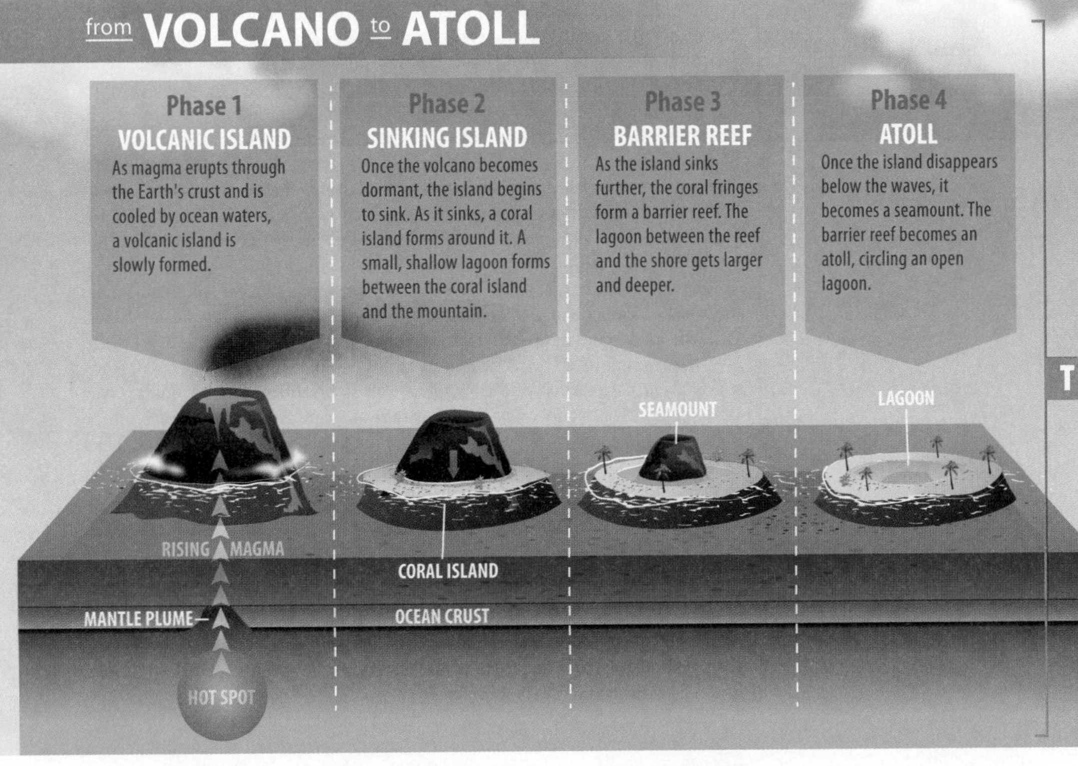

A volcanic island forms when magma erupts from deep within the Earth. Over millions of years, a volcanic island will become an atoll.

▲ **CRITICAL THINKING**

1. ***Identifying*** What tectonic forces are required for volcanic islands to form?
2. ***Identifying Cause and Effect*** Describe how atolls are formed.

Content Background Knowledge

Melanesian Languages Melanesian languages are among the most diverse around the globe. About 400 exist, but few speakers still actually speak them. In fact, Melanesia alone is home to nearly 20 percent of all living languages worldwide. For some of these languages, there may be only a couple of hundred people who speak it. The most dominant languages are Fijian, Hiri Motu, Roviana, and Bambatana, among others. Because speakers of these different languages live in close proximity to one another, they influence each other. They even borrow aspects of each other's languages. Melanesian languages are classified as Austronesian languages. Despite their diversity, Melanesian languages may not stay around for very long. Some are in danger of being wiped out if there are not enough native speakers. Linguists and other specialists are working to preserve these languages before they are lost forever.

T Technology Skills

Simulating Have students study the infographic showing the process that occurs when a volcano becomes an atoll. Ask students to think about other physical geographic processes, such as how mountains, valleys, lakes, and other features form. In small groups, have students compare and contrast the processes, noting similarities and differences. Then instruct groups to create a simulation of the process that occurs when a volcano forms an atoll or when an island is formed. Ask them to use multimedia technology to create the simulation, including audio or visual narratives of each step in the process. Point out that groups should include the importance of each step in the process and alternatives when steps do not occur. Provide an opportunity for groups to present their simulations to the class.
BL Visual/Spatial

INFOGRAPHIC

From Volcano to Atoll

Speculating Ask students to examine this infographic and speculate how a volcano becomes an atoll.
AL Verbal/Linguistic

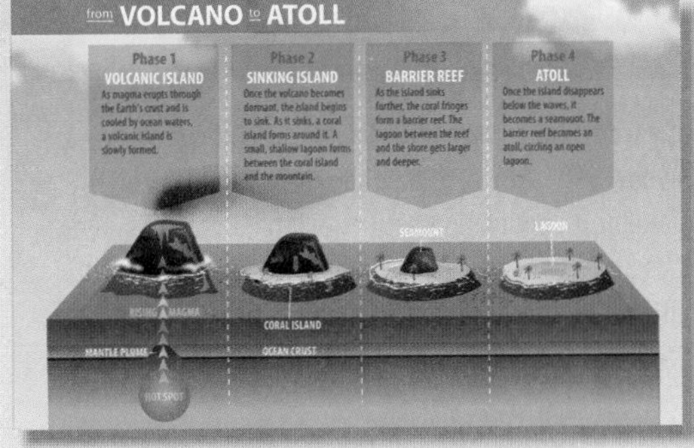

ANSWERS, p. 801

READING PROGRESS CHECK Atolls encircle lagoons.

CRITICAL THINKING

1. Tectonic forces cause a volcanic eruption with magma coming to the surface, which is cooled by the ocean waters to form an island.
2. A volcanic eruption causes magma to rise and be cooled by ocean waters, forming an island around the volcano. A coral island forms around the volcano after it becomes dormant and starts to sink below the surface until the coral ring forms a barrier reef. Once the volcano is completely submerged, the barrier reef becomes an atoll with a lagoon in the middle.

R Reading Skills

Visualizing After students have read the first three paragraphs about the water systems and mountain ranges of Oceania, have them close their eyes and visualize the expanse of water that dominates the region, in addition to the amazing physical features that it boasts. **Ask:** **What makes the Pacific Ocean unique?** *(Possible answer: It is the largest body of water on Earth and has the greatest biodiversity of all the world's oceans.)* Show students a map of Oceania, and ask them to compare and contrast their mental maps to the physical map. **ELL** **Visual/Spatial**

C Critical Thinking Skills

Constructing Arguments Discuss with students how Asian migrants used the resources in Oceania to meet their needs. Ask students to think about the resources that are mentioned in the text that were the most important to survival at that time. Then ask them to craft an argument to defend their choice, considering key elements for survival such as food and water. Point out that students should use details and examples to support their choice. Have students deliver their argument to a partner and their partner to provide a peer review in turn. Point out that in doing the peer review, students should offer constructive criticism. Allow students to make modifications as needed and then have students present their arguments in a class debate. **AL** **Verbal/Linguistic**

W Writing Skills

Informative/Explanatory Ask students to research the major imports and exports of Oceania, as well as main trading partners. Then have them write an informative paper on their findings. Point out to students that they should use current resources from which to gather relevant economic data and information. Remind them to mention their sources when they use facts and data and to include a "Works Cited" list. **BL** **Verbal/Linguistic**

ANSWERS, p. 802

READING PROGRESS CHECK Landforms such as underwater mountain ranges with exposed summits that are visible as islands as well as deep trenches are found in the Pacific Ocean.

CRITICAL THINKING

1. Increases in ocean temperatures can harm the coral that forms the islands as well as the sea life that the low islands rely upon.
2. Mountains and valleys are found on high islands.

The landscapes of low islands (left) and high islands (right) are strikingly different.

▲ CRITICAL THINKING

1. ***Speculating*** Why are low islands more vulnerable to rises in ocean temperature?
2. ***Identifying*** What landforms are typically found on high islands?

Water Systems

GUIDING QUESTION *How do the bodies of water surrounding the islands of Oceania affect ways of life and settlement?*

Oceania extends across millions of square miles in the Pacific. Occupying about a third of the Earth's surface, the Pacific is the largest body of water on the planet. It also has the greatest biodiversity of all the oceans. The Equator marks the division between the North Pacific and the South Pacific.

The Pacific Ocean displays diverse landforms, both above and below its surface. Some can be seen as they rise above the ocean, while others are submerged. The underwater mountain ranges vary from isolated ranges to complex systems that run for thousands of miles. Many of the ranges have exposed volcanic summits. The summits are visible as islands or chains of islands that dot the ocean. One of the longest mountain ranges forms the Hawaiian Islands of Polynesia. Its highest peak, Mauna Kea, rises nearly 13,796 feet (4,205 m) above sea level.

The world's greatest ocean depth has been measured in the Mariana Trench. Located near Guam, it reaches a maximum depth of 36,198 feet (11,033 m). Like the Mariana Trench, most trenches in the western Pacific are next to island chains. Other deep trenches in Oceania reach depths in excess of 32,000 feet (9,754 m).

Asian migrants settled Oceania in family groups along island coasts. They survived on fish, turtles, and shrimp, as well as breadfruit and coconuts. Over time, they cultivated root crops including taro and yams. They also raised livestock such as chickens and pigs. Well-built canoes made lengthy voyages possible. Thus trade gradually developed between islands. To make trading easier, people on some islands used long strings of shell pieces as money. On a few islands, shell money is still exchanged today for canned goods or vegetables at markets.

converse reversed in order, relation, or action; the other way around

Important trade routes cross through the ocean surrounding the subregion. The majority of the exports moving from west to east and from north to south are manufactured goods on their way to markets. **Conversely**, most of the exports that are shipped from east to west and from south to north are raw materials. The small islands of Oceania depend heavily on trade—especially for basic necessities, such as foodstuffs and fuels. There are exceptions, however. Papua New Guinea generally exports more than it imports.

The bodies of freshwater in the subregion vary depending on the island type. High islands have sources of freshwater that support agriculture. The low islands typically have no freshwater sources other than places that catch rainwater.

READING PROGRESS CHECK

Describing What landforms are found in the Pacific Ocean?

networks Online Teaching Options

INTERACTIVE WHITEBOARD ACTIVITY

The Low Islands and High Islands

Synthesizing Have students use this interactive whiteboard activity to drag the correct features of landforms, population patterns, climates, biomes, and resources particular to Oceania's low islands and high islands into the appropriate chart to show a comparison between the two island types. **BL** **Verbal/Linguistic**

Climates, Biomes, and Resources

GUIDING QUESTION *How do the various climates on the islands of Oceania affect their biomes?*

Most of Oceania has a tropical wet climate and is warm year-round. The dry season features cloudless skies, but the wet season brings constant rain and high humidity. High islands are high enough to force warm, moist air to rise. It then cools and condenses. Low islands do not have this effect, so there is less rainfall.

The great expanses of open water in the Pacific Ocean influence wind and pressure patterns. These are reflected in the climatic conditions. A generally windless area called the doldrums occupies a narrow band near the Equator where the direct rays of the sun cause air to rise vertically instead of blowing horizontally. As the air rises, air from the north and south is drawn in by the low surface pressure, creating the trade winds. The flow also causes typhoons to form.

The amount of rainfall on the islands creates both arid and wet climate regions, depending on the island type and location. Only shrubs and grasses grow on dry, low islands. These islands have only a small proportion of arable land. Palms and other trees appear on islands with more rainfall.

Hot, steamy rain forests thrive where heavy rains drench island interiors. The summit of Mount Waialeale on Hawaii's island of Kauai is one of the wettest places on Earth. Rainfall averages about 450 inches (1,143 cm) of rain each year. The rich soils of high islands support a diverse group of plants and animals.

The isolation of many of the islands in Oceania makes for the presence of endemic species. Species that are endemic to a particular location are found only in that place. The intentional and accidental introduction of new species to the islands of Oceania has resulted in negative changes to the ecosystem.

Island type and location also influence resources. Low islands have poor soils and few resources beyond the sea. These mainly consist of coconut oil, dried coconut (copra), bananas, and seabed minerals. The volcanic materials of the islands of American Samoa include an abundance of pumice and pumicite. Fiji, also volcanic, has timber, gold, and a potential for offshore oil. Fiji also generates hydropower.

V

High islands have rich soils that support agriculture. Products grown for export include sugar, coffee, and cocoa. The high islands also have rain forests with diverse flora and fauna. The islands with forests, such as Samoa, harvest hardwoods. Islands without forests have to import lumber. In addition to forests, the Solomon Islands have a variety of other natural resources. These resources include fish and other marine animals, gold, bauxite, phosphates, lead, zinc, and nickel. Tourism helps to **offset** the lack of natural resources on many of the islands, especially the mineral-poor low islands.

offset to compensate for or serve to counterbalance

✓ **READING PROGRESS CHECK**

Naming What are some of the natural resources of Oceania?

LESSON 1 REVIEW (CCSS)

Reviewing Vocabulary (Tier Three Words)

1. ***Describing*** Describe the significance of coral reefs to atolls. RH.9–10.4

Using Your Notes

2. ***Contrasting*** Using your graphic organizer from the lesson, contrast the soils of the low islands with those of the high islands.

Answering the Guiding Questions

3. ***Explaining*** How do the islands of Oceania affect settlement?
4. ***Identifying Cause and Effect*** How do the bodies of water surrounding the islands of Oceania affect ways of life and settlement?
5. ***Synthesizing*** How do the various climates on the islands of Oceania affect their biomes?

Writing Activity

6. ***Narrative*** Write a paragraph describing the type of activities you might participate in during a vacation to one of the islands in Oceania. Include a discussion of how the landforms and bodies of water relate to the type of activities available. WHST.9–10.2

T Technology Skills

Presenting Have students read the text about the climate and biomes of Oceania on their own. Point out that they should take notes or create an outline based on the most important ideas in the text. Then assign students to small groups and one part of Oceania. Each group should have a different area of Oceania to report on. Tell them they are part of a meteorological team that needs to deliver a news broadcast about the weather for one day in all four seasons. Point out additional resources that students may use to help them prepare their forecast.

Remind students that each group member must be involved in the broadcast, even if they are "behind the scenes." Suggest different roles such as storm tracker, head meteorologist, research and data gatherer, manager of visual aids, etc. Provide an opportunity for each group to deliver its broadcast. BL **Kinesthetic**

V Visual Skills

Classifying Have students revisit the charts that they created at the beginning of the lesson and add *Resources* as a column. Challenge students to add additional columns to the chart, such as *Climate* or *Soil Types* or *Crops*. Ask students to exhange charts with a partner to check for accuracy and completeness. Then have students use the charts as study guides. AL **Visual/Spatial**

CLOSE & REFLECT

Assessing Tell students to review what they have learned about the landforms, water systems, climates, biomes, and resources of the island groups or countries of Oceania. Have students evaluate how one or more of these aspects of Oceania's physical geography has both helped and presented challenges to the people who live in the region. Guide a discussion about the relationship between Oceania's location, natural resources, and the way people live there.

LESSON 1 REVIEW ANSWERS

Reviewing Vocabulary

1. Atolls are formed by the buildup of coral reefs.

Using Your Notes

2. High islands have rich, volcanic soils that are good for growing crops, while low islands have poor soils that can support little if any agriculture.

Answering the Guiding Questions

3. The physical geography within the islands affects settlement with high islands having mountainous areas that serve as barriers between those living in coastal areas and those living in mountains, resulting in very different cultures on the same island. Low islands have no barriers, resulting in more uniform settlement and cultures.
4. The islands of Oceania were first settled along the coasts as the people could obtain food from the ocean and as trade routes between the islands and eventually to the surrounding areas became important.
5. The islands have both arid and wet climate regions with only shrubs and grasses on the dry, low islands, while high islands and regions with more rainfall have rain forests and palm trees.

Writing Activity

6. Paragraphs will differ but should be strongly supported with information from the lesson. Water activities include snorkeling, scuba diving, and boating to see coral reefs, lagoons, sunken mountains, and trenches. Land activities on the high islands include mountain hiking and biking.

ANSWERS, p. 803

✓ **READING PROGRESS CHECK** Resources of Oceania vary by island type but can include timber, hydroelectric power, gold, bauxite, pumice, pumicite, phosphates, lead, zinc, nickel, potential offshore oil, and fish.

ENGAGE

R Reading Skills

Previewing Have students skim through the lesson to preview the images, time line, and headings. Tell students to consider what they already know about the history, government, society, and culture of Oceania and how the arrival of Europeans in the 1800s affected the human geography of the region. Then have students write three questions they have about the region's history and its culture. As students work through the lesson, remind them to return to their questions to see if they have been answered.

TEACH & ASSESS

C Critical Thinking Skills

Drawing Inferences Have students use details from the text to brainstorm a list of inferences about how the human geography of Oceania changed after Europeans settled in the region. For example, students might infer from the phrase "reshaping themselves" that some countries in Oceania have had to change and adapt as independent countries. Allow time for students to create their list of inferences, guiding them to consider how culture and cultural interaction play a significant part in the region's history. **ELL Interpersonal, Visual/Spatial**

W Writing Skills

Narrative Have students read the text about life for indigenous cultures before and after the arrival of the Europeans. Discuss with them how physical geography might have contributed to aspects of their culture. Then ask students to write two journal entries, one from the perspective of a European sugarcane plantation owner coming to Oceania to settle in the 1800s and the other from the point of view of an indigenous person. Explain to students that in the first entry, they should describe the physical environment, how it differs from Europe, and observations of the indigenous people. Then, in the second entry, have students include details about daily life before and after the arrival of Europeans. Invite students to share their diary entries with the class or post on a class blog. **AL Verbal/Linguistic**

ANSWERS, p. 804

TAKING NOTES: Melanesia: the earliest people were the Papuans, who are thought to have arrived around 40,000 years ago; the Austronesian peoples arrived about 4,000 years ago; **Micronesia:** the first people are thought to have arrived from Southeast Asia and Melanesia 2,000 to 3,500 years ago; **Polynesia:** the first Polynesians are thought to have come to the islands 6,000 to 8,000 years ago

networks

There's More Online!

- **IMAGE** Hotel in Fiji
- **IMAGE** Oceanic Art
- **IMAGE** Subsistence Farming in Oceania
- **MAP** Oceania in World War II
- **TIME LINE** Colonization and Independence
- **INTERACTIVE SELF-CHECK QUIZ**
- **VIDEO** Human Geography of Oceania

Academic Vocabulary (Tier Two Words)

- **nevertheless**
- **bulk**

Content Vocabulary (Tier Three Words)

- **kinship group**
- **trust territory**
- **pidgin**

TAKING NOTES: ***Key Ideas and Details***

IDENTIFYING As you read about the human geography of Oceania, use a graphic organizer like the one below to record how the different island groups were settled.

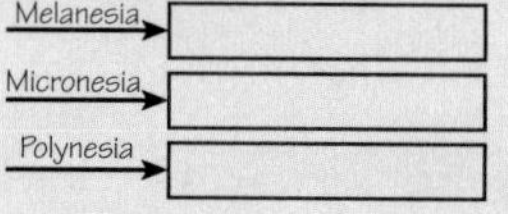

LESSON 2

R Human Geography of Oceania

ESSENTIAL QUESTION • *How do physical systems and human systems shape a place?*

IT MATTERS BECAUSE

C *Migrations of people among hundreds of islands over many generations shaped societies in Oceania. European colonization had a profound impact as well. Today, the islands in Oceania are reshaping themselves as independent countries.*

History and Government

GUIDING QUESTION *How has life on the islands of Oceania changed over time?*

Hundreds of indigenous people lived on the many islands in the Pacific Ocean when European explorers began arriving in the 1500s. The islands had been their homes for thousands of years. Many of these cultures practiced religious beliefs that connected them to the land and sea. In many of the societies, the chief was the person of highest status. Complex systems of ranked lineages and **kinship groups** had developed. Many societies, such as that of the Marshall Islands, were matrilineal, meaning that family history was traced through the mother's family. Powerful chiefs were recognized for their ability to communicate with the gods and secure food and other valuables for the people.

W Europeans brought far-reaching changes to the peoples of Oceania. When Europeans settled in Oceania in the 1800s, they developed plantations for growing sugarcane, pineapples, and other tropical products that were sold around the world. Europeans also brought new diseases that resulted in epidemics among the indigenous populations. In order to maintain a workforce, plantation owners recruited workers from East Asia and South Asia. In just a few years many of the islands became culturally diverse and dependent on the global demands for sugar, the major crop. Meanwhile, Europeans further altered traditional beliefs and customs by establishing schools, sponsoring missions, and converting people to Christianity.

During the late 1800s and early 1900s, Britain, France, Germany, Spain, and the United States struggled for control of various Pacific islands. These countries wanted to acquire or expand their influences in the region and gain new sources of raw materials. Colonial powers did not have a strong physical presence in many of the islands. In some places, islanders ignored the laws of European countries that they felt did not apply to them.

(tl)©Stapleton Collection/Corbis, (tcl)LAPI/Roger-Viollet/The Image Works, (tc)National Archives and Records Administration (NWDNS-80-G-396229), (tcr)Mike Robinson/Alamy, (tr)©Michele Westmorland/Corbis

804

networks Online Teaching Options

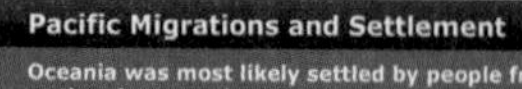

Pacific Migrations and Settlement

Analyzing Visuals Use the introductory text and the map that shows the direction and timing of settlement in Oceania to identify the order in which Melanesia, Micronesia, and Polynesia were settled. Have students work with a partner and discuss each question. Have each pair write agreed-upon answers to the questions. Then, review the answers with the whole class. **AL Interpersonal, Visual/Spatial, Verbal/Linguistic**

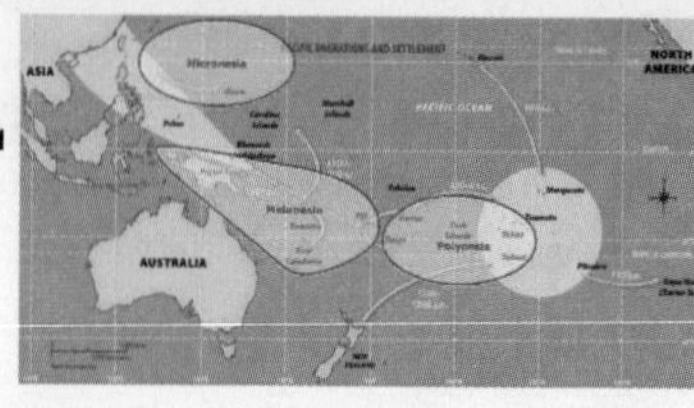

Pacific Migrations and Settlement
Oceania was most likely settled by people from Southeast Asia who island hopped as they journeyed across the ocean.
1. Which area or areas was settled first?
A. Micronesia
B. Melanesia
C. Polynesia
D. Micronesia and Melanesia
ASIA
AUSTRALIA
NORTH AMERICA
click for answer
Auto-Run
Click Through
Previous
1 of 3
Next

The two world wars dramatically changed Oceania's political geography. After World War I, most of Germany's territories came under Japanese colonial rule. During World War II, those same islands were the sites of fierce battles. The United States and its allies were fighting to drive the Japanese from these islands. After Japan's defeat in the war, its Pacific territories were turned over to the United States as **trust territories**. These are designated by the United Nations to be temporarily governed by another country.

R

Beginning in the 1960s, islands in Oceania, also called the Pacific Islands, began gaining independence. In 1962 Samoa, formerly Western Samoa, became the first Pacific Island to win freedom, after rule by Germany and New Zealand. Since the 1970s most of these islands—including Palau, the Marshall Islands, and the Federated States of Micronesia—have become independent countries. Most Pacific Islands achieved independence by the end of the 1900s.

Many islands in Oceania have a dual government system that includes the government imposed upon them by colonial powers and their traditional, indigenous systems of government. In some countries, the traditional systems have been integrated into the constitutional structure. However, in other countries, such as Papua New Guinea, indigenous governance systems have been largely sidelined in the formal government structures.

The Solomon Islands represents one example of cultural rebirth occurring in the subregion. Traditional beliefs are starting to resurface and guide decision making. These countries are looking within their borders for input on economic and social issues. Social structure is a high priority. People in the Solomon Islands are once again valuing equality for all people. They are also building a strong relationship to the land by practicing traditional farming and marketing locally grown foods rather than relying on imported, processed foods.

✓ READING PROGRESS CHECK

Explaining Describe how the arrival of Europeans affected the population of Oceania.

Population Patterns

GUIDING QUESTION *How and why did people spread across Oceania?*

The islands of Oceania were probably first settled by peoples from Asia more than 30,000 years ago. Waves of migrants from Asia continued to arrive over many centuries. People already living there moved from island to island and settled into three major island groups: Melanesia, Micronesia, and Polynesia.

T

Melanesia includes Papua New Guinea, Fiji, the Solomon Islands, as well as New Caledonia. Melanesian cultures differ greatly, even among groups living on the same island. Some Melanesians are more closely related to Polynesians than to other Melanesians. The earliest people of Melanesia were the Papuans. They were hunters and gatherers that adapted to the rain forests on New Guinea. Some estimates date their arrival on the island to 40,000 years ago. Eventually the early Melanesians domesticated root crops and sugarcane. They may have also kept domesticated pigs as long as 9,000 years ago. In areas of the highlands of New Guinea, water and irrigation systems were in place 5,000 years ago.

Arriving by sea from Southeast Asia, the Austronesian peoples settled in Melanesia about 4,000 years ago. Pottery, tools, and shell ornaments date their arrival in the islands. The languages they spoke were similar to languages used in the Solomon Islands, Vanuatu, and New Caledonia. Language was used to test theories of migration among people in the region. Distances were great across ocean waters. Migration between the islands meant the people were accomplished mariners. The migration theory explained both when and how the islands were first inhabited. It also explained the cultural differences and similarities in this region.

Connecting Geography to SCIENCE

Carbon Dating

Archaeologists, geologists, anthropologists, and botanists all work together to determine when a given island was first inhabited. Carbon-14 dating is a tool used to determine the age of items such as bone, cloth, wood, and plant fibers. This method works on archaeological artifacts that have a biological origin and that are less than 50,000 years old. Scientists look at the ratio of carbon-12 to carbon-14 as a means for dating the objects. The ratio of the two carbons is the same in every living thing at the moment of death. The carbon-14 begins to decay at death and is not replaced. By looking at the ratio between the two carbons and comparing it to the ratio in a living organism, it is possible to determine the date of the object with precision.

IDENTIFYING Describe some of the objects that geographers and archaeologists can use from an island to determine when people first arrived.

kinship group a group of people related by blood or marriage

trust territory a dependent area that the United Nations placed under the temporary control of another country

GAME

Human Geography of Oceania

Identifying Have students use the information in their textbooks to complete the activity. When the game is completed, students should check their answers and correct any errors that may have been made.
ELL **Verbal/Linguistic**

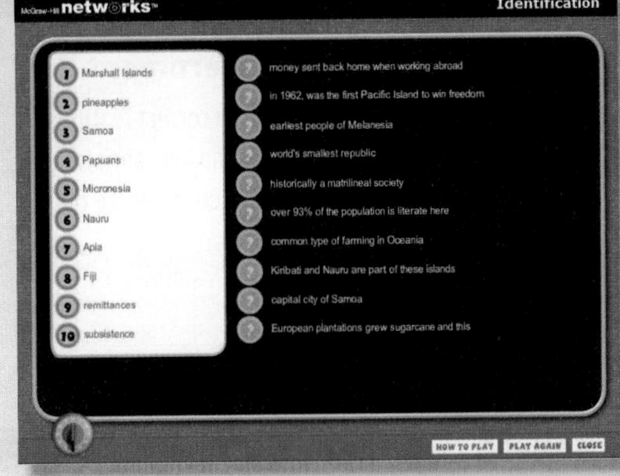

R Reading Skills

Using Correct Terminology and Grammar Discuss with students how the world wars politically, economically, and socially affected Oceania. Invite a volunteer to explain the difference between a colony and a trust territory. **Ask: Did the world wars help to initiate the move toward independence? Explain.** *(Possible answer: Yes, because European countries had control over the countries in Oceania only as trust territories after the wars, not colonies. This interim period helped to move some of the countries in Oceania to independence in the early 1960s.)* Have students create a time line that shows the countries in Oceania that became independent after World War II and when they achieved their independence. AL
Visual/Spatial, Verbal/Linguistic

Content Background Knowledge

Types of Governing in Oceania Share with students some of the governments of Oceania:

Federated States of Micronesia: constitutional
Fiji and Kiribati: republic
French Polynesia: overseas territory of France
Guam: U.S. territory
Marshall Islands and Palau: constitutional
Northern Mariana Islands: trust territory
Papua New Guinea: constitutional democracy and Commonwealth
Samoa: parliamentary democracy

T Technology Skills

Researching Explain to students that groups that settled in Melanesia adapted to the environment and brought a variety of cultural aspects that still exist today. Have students consider how important language is for communication and in unifying countries. Divide the class into small groups. Ask each group to become an expert on one of the Melanesia groups mentioned in the text. Ask them to use print and electronic resources to help them locate facts and details on their island group. Invite students to share their findings with the class. **Interpersonal**

ANSWERS, p. 805

✓ **READING PROGRESS CHECK** The Europeans developed plantations to grow and export products, brought European diseases that caused epidemics in indigenous populations, brought in plantation workers from East and South Asia, changing the cultural makeup, and altered traditional beliefs and customs by introducing Christianity and establishing missions and schools.

Connecting Geography Answers will vary on specific objects that can be used but should include items made or containing cloth, wood, bone, and plant fibers with examples such as clothing, tools, and human remains.

R Reading Skills

Identifying Discuss with students how archaeologists learn about past cultures. **Ask:** **How did the first settlers arrive in Micronesia?** *(It is thought that the first settlers arrived by ocean canoes.)* **What does the more dense population on these islands suggest?** *(It suggests that many people arrived on these islands and the inhabitants had developed farming and trading skills.)* Then lead a class discussion on how language has been used to date the arrival of the first settlers to these islands. **ELL Verbal/Linguistic**

C Critical Thinking Skills

Reaching Conclusions Have students brainstorm a list of reasons why an island might be uninhabitable. Ask them to consider what characteristics would make an island or any place unsuitable for humans to live. Then, using the list that the class generated, ask them to work with a partner to find out which islands in Oceania have the smallest populations, as well as which are the most uninhabitable places. Guide students to online resources that may be useful to them such as the CIA World Factbook. Ask pairs of students to write a short paper about the most suitable place in which to live in Oceania. **BL Interpersonal**

V Visual Skills

Interpreting Point out the image in the time line and explain to students that it portrays a Tahitian woman greeting English captain Samuel Wallis. Wallis completed his circumnavigation of the world in 1768. **Ask:** **Based on what you read in the text about the role of women in Oceania, does this image support the text or does it portray a different point of view? Explain.** *(Possible answer: This woman appears to be high in the social system or hierarchy, because of her clothing and demeanor, as compared to the other women in the image.)* **Based on what you know about women's roles in Europe, do you think Captain Wallis was surprised to be greeted by a woman? Explain.** *(Possible answer: Yes, he was probably surprised that a woman greeted him because at this time few women held political or important societal roles in Europe.)* **Visual/Spatial**

ANSWERS, p. 806

READING PROGRESS CHECK Melanesia was first settled by the Papuans, who probably came from Asia.

CRITICAL THINKING

1. The islands of Oceania changed after contact with Europeans as traditional lifestyles began to disappear, European languages began to be spoken, and different religions such as Christianity, Hinduism, Islam, and Buddhism were introduced.
2. Independence movements began to increase in the 1960s.

R Micronesia includes the Federated States of Micronesia, Nauru, Kiribati, Guam, and the Mariana Islands. The first people to settle in Micronesia are thought to have arrived by ocean canoes some 2,000 to 3,500 years ago from Southeast Asia and Melanesia. The islands in this region are more densely populated. A larger population suggested that more migrants arrived and that they had skills necessary to develop farming and trading economies. Language has again been used as the key to dating the arrival of the first people to these islands.

Polynesia includes Samoa, Tonga, Tuvalu, and French Polynesia. The ancestors of present-day Polynesians may have come to the islands 6,000 to 8,000 years ago. The western islands—Wallis and Futuna, Samoa, and Tonga—were settled first. These first Polynesians grew traditional crops and domesticated animals. Women gathered plants and were weavers. Many Polynesians share a similar language and culture. Today the largest population of Polynesians lives in the Samoan Islands.

Asian communities also exist in the subregion. Chinese, Japanese, and South Asian traders and laborers settled parts of Oceania during the 1800s. Today their descendants live in such places as French Polynesia and Fiji.

C The population of Oceania's islands varies considerably, and many of the islands are not large enough to support people. Population is not evenly distributed among the countries of the subregion. Papua New Guinea has the largest population, with about 7 million people. Nauru, the world's smallest republic, has a population of about 10,000 people. The total land area of Oceania's 25,000 islands is 551,059 square miles (1,427,246 sq. km) spread across a vast Pacific Ocean expanse of over 20 million square miles (52 million sq. km). Urban population varies greatly. For example, the capital city of Papua New Guinea, Port Moresby, has a population of nearly 300,000. In contrast, Apia, the capital city of Samoa, has a population of approximately 36,000.

READING PROGRESS CHECK

Identifying Who first settled Melanesia and from where did they come?

TIME LINE

COLONIZATION and Independence

Beginning in the 1800s, European countries and the United States colonized the islands of Oceania, but those islands became independent states in the twentieth century.

CRITICAL THINKING

1. ***Explaining*** How did the islands of Oceania change after contact with Europeans was made?
2. ***Describing*** When did the pace of independence quicken in Oceania?

V 1600

1600s–1700s European navigators first contact the peoples of Oceania.

©Stapleton Collection/Corbis

1830s European missionaries arrive in Fiji, Samoa, and Tonga to convert the population to Christianity.

1870s Population of the Ellice Islands (now Tuvalu) declines dramatically.

1880s Germany takes control over part of New Guinea, Marshall Islands, and Nauru.

806

networks Online Teaching Options

INTERACTIVE WHITEBOARD ACTIVITY

Types and Systems of Government

Diagramming Have students drag the correct features into two charts and the countries into the appropriate columns of a chart to distinguish between the three major island groups. **AL Verbal/Linguistic**

Types and Systems of Government

Directions: For thousands of years before Europeans arrived, the islands of Oceania were home to indigenous peoples. The arrival of Europeans brought many changes to indigenous cultures. Drag examples of life on the islands before the Europeans arrived and examples of how life changed with European's arrival into the appropriate boxes.

Before Europeans Arrived	After Europeans Arrived

- Foreign diseases create epidemics among the indigenous people.
- Schools are opened as well as missions to convert people to Christianity.
- Religious beliefs revolve around the land and sea.
- Cultures diversify as plantation owners recruit outside workers.
- Societies are matrilineal, with history traced back to the mother's family.
- Sugarcane and pineapple crops are grown on large plantations to be exported globally.
- A chief of high status is believed to be able to communicate with the gods.
- Systems of ranked lineages and kinship groups develop.
- Dual governments combine traditional systems with colonial
- Waves of migrants from Asia settle, sometimes moving from island to

Society and Culture Today

GUIDING QUESTION *What is life like on the islands of Oceania today?*

Today, societies in Oceania have been shaped by a variety of cultures. The subregion's countries display a blend of European, Asian, and indigenous traditions. The traditional lifestyle of indigenous people is difficult to find in the twenty-first-century world.

Before the era of modern transportation and advanced communications, vast distances of open ocean separated the peoples of the subregion from the rest of the world. As a result, isolated groups developed their own languages and belief systems without outside interference. Of the world's some 6,000 languages, 1,200 are spoken in Oceania. Some are spoken by only a few hundred people. **V**

European colonization brought European languages to the subregion. Today French is widely spoken in Oceania. In many areas, varieties of **pidgin** English are spoken as well. This is a blend of English and indigenous words that do not follow rules of grammar, but do allow better communication among different groups.

pidgin a blend of English and indigenous words to form a new language

The peoples of the subregion practice several different religions. These include Christianity, Hinduism, Islam, and Buddhism. Sometimes the religions are combined with traditional religious beliefs. Christianity is the most widely practiced religion in Oceania and was introduced by Europeans. Hinduism was introduced to Fiji when thousands of Indians immigrated to work on plantations. Over 30 percent of the population of Fiji is Hindu.

The quality of education varies throughout Oceania. In the Solomon Islands, missionary schools provided primary education until the mid-1970s. Today secondary schools and universities are common in the Solomon Islands, Fiji, and Papua New Guinea. Differences in education throughout the subregion can be seen in the varying rates of literacy. For example, over 93 percent of Fiji's population is literate, but only 57 percent of the inhabitants of Papua New Guinea are literate.

1899s Germany buys Palau from Spain. Germany and the United States divide Samoa between them.

1900

1941–1945 Japanese forces occupy Kiribati, Marshall Islands, Micronesia, Nauru, Palau, Papua New Guinea, and Tuvalu.

1946 United States begins nuclear weapons testing in Marshall Islands; islanders are forced to evacuate. **C** **W**

1962 Western Samoa becomes first colony in Oceania to become independent.

1970s Fiji, Tonga, Papua New Guinea, Tuvalu, Federated States of Micronesia, Kiribati, and Marshall Islands become independent.

1994 Republic of Palau becomes independent state.

2000

V Visual Skills

Creating Diagrams Have students work in small groups to create a diagram that illustrates the blending and influences of various cultures, including Asian, European, and Pacific Islander. Challenge students to be creative and to address a variety of aspects of culture, including religion, language, and traditions. Point out that students may create their diagrams digitally, but it is not required. Provide an opportunity for students to present their diagrams to the class, discussing the details and meanings conveyed. **ELL Visual/Spatial**

C Critical Thinking Skills

Analyzing Ethical Issues Have students study the image of the nuclear bomb exploding in the Marshall Islands. **Ask: Do you think it was ethical for the United States to test nuclear bombs in the Marshall Islands after World War II?** *(Possible answer: No, it was unethical. The United States did not have the right to test nuclear bombs, which could negatively affect the people of the Marshall Islands.)* Explain to students that the Marshall Islands was a UN trust territory administered by the United States, but it gained its independence in 1986. Ask them to consider what rights the people of the Marshall Islands had when they were forced to evacuate the islands. **AL Logical/Mathematical**

W Writing Skills

Argument Have students prepare a written argument on the ethics involved in nuclear testing conducted in Oceania or elsewhere after World War II by the United States and other countries. Remind students to develop a thesis with facts and supporting details. Invite students to share their arguments in small groups and then to use them as the basis of a class discussion or debate. **BL Intrapersonal, Logical/Mathematical**

INTERACTIVE TIME LINE

Colonization and Independence

Examine Have students examine the time line about colonization and independence in Oceania. **AL Visual/Spatial**

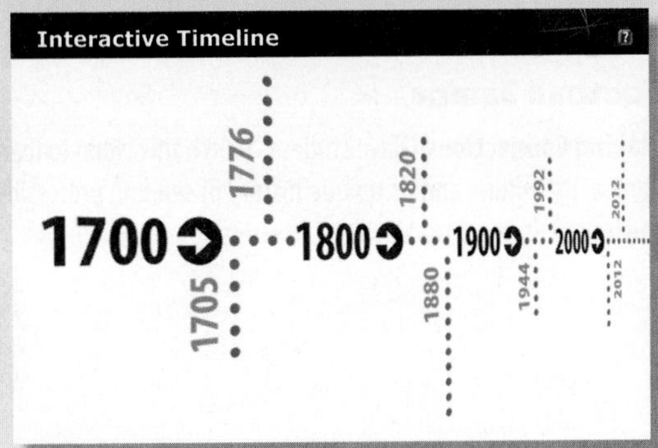

C Critical Thinking Skills

Theorizing Review with students how poor economic and social conditions can impact people in different island countries. **Ask:** **Why is there such a large gap in economic and social conditions across Oceania?** *(Possible answer: In countries that are small and isolated, there are fewer resources to devote to strengthening economic and social conditions.)* **Do you think that governments of island countries with positive economic and social conditions should provide assistance to those countries with fewer resources? Explain.** *(Possible response: Yes, governments of other countries in Oceania should help out other island governments instead of expecting others to rely on international assistance. Such efforts will promote regional unity and cooperation.)* **AL Verbal/Linguistic**

V Visual Skills

Analyzing Discuss with students how cultural practices can often transcend beliefs and also take different forms. Then have students read about the cultural practice of burning and scarring brides as well as the artistic practice of scarring the skin with decorative patterns. Then ask students to examine the image of the woman receiving a tattoo on her face. Ask students to think of reasons why scarring and tattooing are important to the culture of Oceania. **AL Visual/Spatial**

R Reading Skills

Identifying Trends Have student volunteers explain niche markets and provide examples. *(a small, but specialized market such as specialty item retailers or online specific product sites, but could also be individuals, such as consultants or medical professionals)* **Ask:** **What are some of the economic concerns for the people in Oceania?** *(Possible answers: remote locations, challenging environment, lack of arable land for agriculture)* **Why do you think niche markets have increased in Oceania?** *(Possible answers: There may not be enough jobs locally, so outside or online services may provide income; many workers may be interested in careers outside of agriculture.)* Have students work with a partner to research recent trends in niche markets. Ask pairs to gather information about the types of niche markets found in this region and how these markets have helped to increase the economy in Oceania. **BL Interpersonal**

ANSWERS, p. 808

✓ READING PROGRESS CHECK Hinduism was introduced in Fiji when hundreds of thousands of Indians immigrated to work on plantations.

CRITICAL THINKING

1. Common themes in Oceanic art include fish, the ocean, and many types of plants and animals.
2. The artwork created by tattooing and scarification are part of ritual practices in Oceania.

C Many Pacific Islanders suffer from their countries' poor economies and low standards of living. Health care varies from country to country. On remote islands, electricity, schools, and hospitals are difficult services. As independent countries, they qualify for international assistance and are making improvements.

Family and the Status of Women

The traditional family structure has consisted of many generations living in the same village and often in the same house. This structure includes large families with children being cared for by many family members. Contemporary life today has changed throughout Oceania due to modernization and loss of traditional values. Many young people migrate to Australia, the United States, and France.

The status of women is of great concern in the subregion. The status of women varies from strong matrilineal leadership to victims of violence long accepted as a part of a culture. In Oceania, there are cultural practices that make it difficult to protect women against violence. For example, in Melanesia, there is the practice of early arranged marriages and forced marriages. The practice of burning and scarring brides also occurs among some ethnic groups in the region even though it is against the law.

The Arts

V The ocean, fish, and many types of plants and animals are the subjects for the arts of Oceania. Carving wood is an art mastered by many people. Skilled crafts, such as making canoes and building houses, are a tradition. Art and architecture are closely related to each other. Buildings are carved with elaborate designs. Detailed designs are also important in the symbolic art of body tattooing in Oceania. Creating decorative patterns on the skin by scarification, the intentional scarring of the skin by incision or burning, and tattooing are practiced by some culture groups.

✓ READING PROGRESS CHECK

Explaining How did Hinduism become one of the religions practiced in Oceania?

Skilled crafts are a tradition in Oceania with artwork on buildings, canoes, and on bodies in the form of tattoos.

▼ CRITICAL THINKING

1. ***Identifying*** What are some of the common themes found in traditional Oceanic art?
2. ***Explaining*** What type of artwork is part of ritual practices in Oceania?

©Michele Westmorland/Corbis

Economic Activities

GUIDING QUESTION *What economic opportunities are available to the people of Oceania?*

R The remote geographic locations and challenging environments of Oceania influence how people there earn a living. Agriculture continues to be an important economic activity in the subregion, but new industries are contributing to national economies. Tourism has gained in importance as people looking for scuba diving in pristine waters select the islands of the Pacific for their environments. Niche markets, such as call centers and web development, have increased in Oceania.

Although many islands in Oceania lack abundant natural resources, some have excellent resources for tourism. The tourism industry is still a relatively new industry in many parts of Oceania. French Polynesia, Guam, the Northern Mariana Islands, and Fiji have all experienced recent growth in this industry, and it has become vital to their economies.

Much of Oceania lacks arable land, which in turn limits agriculture. Farmers on smaller islands use traditional

networks Online Teaching Options

VIDEO

Football Samoa

Making Connections Have students watch this video to learn more about American Samoa, its culture, and its unique history of sending professional football players to the United States. **AL Verbal/Linguistic**

farming and fishing. On some islands, the village or island government owns the land and rents or leases it to farmers.

Some islands have rich volcanic soil and ample rainfall. On many of the islands, Europeans had once claimed the most productive land. Land settlements in recent years have returned the best land to indigenous people.

C

Most of the islands in Oceania have only small amounts of mineral resources and lack large manufacturing centers. Papua New Guinea, Fiji, and New Caledonia have mineral deposits. Papua New Guinea's rich deposits of gold and copper have only recently been exploited. Nauru's deposits of phosphates are depleted due to excessive mining. Manufacturing in Oceania is mostly limited to small-scale enterprises like clothing production. Many of the larger islands with forests have sawmills that produce lumber for export or domestic use. Some of the larger islands have facilities that process agricultural products, such as coconut oil and cane sugar.

Trade between Oceania and other parts of the world has increased because of improvements in transportation and communications, as well as the creation of new trade agreements. Some island countries are too small, too poor, or too rugged to have well-developed road or rail systems. **Nevertheless**, some governments are improving these systems. Cargo ships and planes move imports and exports to and from the subregion. Principal trading partners of Oceania include the United States, Japan, and Australia. Commercial airlines and cruise ships bring travelers. Air transport and interisland shipping are the vital lines for transportation. Many of the island groups in Oceania have international airports. Extensive road networks are limited to the larger islands.

W

Cellular, digital, satellite communications, and the Internet are becoming common in the subregion. In recent decades, improved transportation and communications links have increased trade between Oceania and other parts of the world. The subregion's agricultural and mining products earn the **bulk** of its export income. Countries also export handicrafts—such as baskets, floor mats, ceremonial masks, and pottery—made by island craftspeople.

READING PROGRESS CHECK

Making Connections What factors contribute to the lack of adequate networks of roads on many of the islands in Oceania?

Farming in Oceania frequently relies on animal power and human labor.

▲ CRITICAL THINKING

1. ***Speculating*** What are some of the crops that might be grown by traditional farming practices in the Solomon Islands and other parts of Oceania?
2. ***Contrasting*** How were the plantations established by the Europeans different from traditional farming?

nevertheless despite; in spite of

bulk the greater part of something

Holger Leue/LOOK/Getty Images

LESSON 2 REVIEW 

Reviewing Vocabulary (Tier Three Words)

1. ***Summarizing*** Define *trust territory* and explain how it relates to Oceania. RH.9–10.4

Using Your Notes

2. ***Describing*** Use your notes from the graphic organizer to describe the order of settlement for Melanesia, Micronesia, and Polynesia.

Answering the Guiding Questions

3. ***Identifying Cause and Effect*** How has life on the islands of Oceania changed over time?
4. ***Explaining*** How and why did people spread across Oceania?
5. ***Describing*** What is life like on the islands of Oceania today?
6. ***Examining*** What economic opportunities are available to the people of Oceania?

Writing Activity

7. ***Informative/Explanatory*** Write a paragraph describing the negative impact Europeans had on the population and cultures of Oceania. WHST.9–10.2

LESSON 2 REVIEW ANSWERS

Reviewing Vocabulary

1. A trust territory is a country or area that the UN decides should be governed by another country temporarily. After WWII, Japan's territories were made into trust territories governed by the United States.

Using Your Notes

2. Melanesia (40,000 years ago), Polynesia (6,000 to 8,000 years ago), and Micronesia (2,000 to 3,500 years ago).

Answering the Guiding Questions

3. Complex systems of ranked lineages and kinship groups with chiefs who communicated with gods were replaced by countries that operate largely under the government styles of their colonizers and practice introduced religions such as Christianity.
4. People came in continual migrations from Asia by way of the sea to Oceania. As more people arrived, residents would move from island to island, and eventually traders and laborers from other parts of Asia and India settled across the region.
5. Health care and education vary depending on the island, a variety of religions are practiced, around 1,200 languages are spoken but French and English are common.
6. Tourism, call centers, and web development are opportunities available to the people of Oceania.

Writing Activity

7. Paragraphs will differ but should be strongly supported with information from the lesson.

C Critical Thinking Skills

Evaluating Ask students to find out the origin of the main export crops of Oceania. Based on students' findings, ask them to determine if it is a good economic decision for Oceania islanders to continue to grow and export these crops, or if their resources are better spent on cultivating different crops that are easier to grow and require fewer resources. Other factors that students should consider are climate and soil. Then, have students conduct a classroom debate to make their case and provide a thorough analysis and evaluation based on their research. **BL** **Naturalist**

W Writing Skills

Informative/Explanatory Have students read about the resources of the region and then write two or three paragraphs about one of Oceania's countries that describe that country's economy, natural resources, and trading partners. Invite students to read their paragraphs to the class and discuss the various economic challenges faced by the countries today. **AL** **Verbal/Linguistic**

Content Background Knowledge

Tech Revolution In the early 2000s, use of information and communications technology was low in Oceania, as compared to other regions of the world. By the following decade, about three-fifths of Oceania islanders were using cell phones. Much of this change is the result of deregulation and reform, but also because of the age of the user and the rise of social media. As in other regions of the world, users of digital technology are most commonly found among young people. In Oceania, about one-fifth of the population falls in the age 15 to 24 category.

CLOSE & REFLECT

Summarizing Review with students how the history of Oceania and its location and physical geography have influenced its economic and cultural development. Have students summarize aspects of the region's society, culture, and economic activities.

ANSWERS, p. 809

READING PROGRESS CHECK A lack of money, the small size of some islands, and the rugged landscape of other islands contribute to a lack of road networks in Oceania.

CRITICAL THINKING

1. Answers will vary but could include sugarcane, a variety of root crops, and pineapples.
2. Plantations focused on growing food for export, not to meet the local needs of people, worked large areas of land, and required the recruitment of people from East and South Asia to maintain enough workers.

ENGAGE

R Reading Skills

Using Word Parts Direct students' attention to the word *geopolitics* at the top of this page. Have students work with a partner to decipher the word's meaning, using word parts as clues. Have students write a definition of the word and then look up the word in a print or online dictionary to verify its correct meaning. **Ask:** **Judging from the title, how do you think the meaning of the word *geopolitics* relates to this feature?** *(Possible answer: The title relates to geopolitics because countries that border oceans have a stake in their economic benefits and how to manage and protect the resources found in the oceans.)* **Verbal/Linguistic**

TEACH & ASSESS

T Technology Skills

Changing Continuity in Politics Have students conduct research to learn more about the Law of the Sea Treaty. Instruct students to gather information about the treaty's history and how it has been interpreted over the years by different political groups. Encourage students to identify at least one opinion piece from a reputable news organization that either criticizes or praises the treaty. Tell students to summarize their findings in a brief report that includes a concluding statement about the status of the treaty today. **BL** **Verbal/Linguistic**

C Critical Thinking Skills

Hypothesizing Have students read the information about access to the high seas. Discuss the exclusive economic zone (EEZ) and how the high seas beyond an EEZ are essentially up for grabs. **Ask:** **What problems or conflicts do you think might occur regarding management and protection of the high seas?** *(Possible answer: Different countries may have varying ideas about how to manage and protect the high seas, which could cause conflict between countries or political groups.)* **Verbal/Linguistic**

WHO OWNS THE HIGH SEAS?

In 1994 the Law of the Sea Treaty came into force. This treaty defines which countries own parts of the oceans. According to the treaty, each country's territory extends about 12 nautical miles from its coasts. Beyond this boundary a country may establish an exclusive economic zone (EEZ) that extends 200 nautical miles from shore. When two countries' ocean territories overlap, a border is set. The areas beyond these descriptions and the EEZs, however, belong to no one. They are the high seas. The high seas can be accessed by anyone with the means to do so. These areas are rich in fish and other natural resources, such as oil and minerals. People travel through the high seas, and countries mine resources and fish there.

People have different ideas about how the high seas and the natural resources within them should be managed and protected. More than 150 countries have signed the Law of the Sea Treaty, which gives the International Seabed Authority (ISA) jurisdiction over the high seas. However, some countries refuse to sign the treaty. In these countries, some fear that the ISA will impose new tax laws on travel in the oceans and reduce free movement on the waters. Another concern is that fewer economic opportunities will exist if the ISA regulates the high seas. They also worry that future projects, such as mining the sea floor, will be restricted. Other critics of the treaty think the high seas should be privately owned or even feel that no one should own and regulate these areas. Still others oppose the treaty because they want more regulation of the high seas. They do not think that the ISA and the United Nations have the authority to protect the oceans. They feel the ISA has not done enough to protect the waters from the existing threats of overfishing, pollution, pirating, and drug trafficking.

networks Online Teaching Options

INTERACTIVE IMAGE

Law and the Bering Sea

Summarizing Use this interactive image to introduce students to the important geography and political topic of *Who Owns the High Seas?* As a class, discuss the details as they are displayed. Answer any questions or misconceptions that students may have about the information. Then have students write two or three sentences summarizing the information presented in the image. **ELL** **Visual/Spatial**

Problems of the Law of the Sea Treaty

PRIMARY SOURCE

"One of the primary missions of the United States Navy for over two centuries has been to maintain freedom of the seas for all. As a Navy veteran, I am offended to think that the Senate and the Chief of Naval Operations would even consider ceding any part of that mission to the United Nations. . . .

There is no guarantee that the treaty will remain what it is at the time of ratification. Under its terms, its content can later be changed by an amendment process that does not require the approval of the United States government. This undermines U.S. sovereignty and, to put it bluntly, is unconstitutional."

—Colin Hanna, president of Let Freedom Ring, quoted in "Kill the Law of the Sea Treaty," *U.S. News*, May 10, 2012

Support More Regulation

PRIMARY SOURCE

"We have the Law of the Sea [Treaty] but it does not have enough teeth to actually do anything. We also have the regional fisheries management organisation but this is not a global treaty and they are regional treaties. We see the high seas as the last frontier to be tackled. It is nobody's territory but everybody's territory to exploit. . . . **W**

So we need to bridge this gap somehow and there is no framework yet or a treaty for this purpose. Eventually all the fish caught has to land somewhere and it becomes somebody's business and therefore this dilemma needs to be solved." **V**

—Gustavo Fonseca, head of natural resources quoted in "Oceans Special: GEF Rolls Out Investment Project to Address Issues for Areas in the High Seas," June 16, 2012

What do you think? DBQ

1. ***Drawing Conclusions*** Why might people want to make a plan for regulation and management of the high seas? RH.9–10.2
2. ***Identifying Central Issues*** According to critics of the treaty, what are the risks of regulation of the high seas? RH.9–10.1
3. ***Hypothesizing*** What might be some benefits and drawbacks of private ownership of the high seas? RH.9–10.6

Making Connections

Ask students whether they have ever gone fishing, and where they or their families purchase fish to eat. Discuss fishing as a recreational activity as well as a commercial one. Have students consider the need for management and protection of different varieties of fish in the world's oceans.

W Writing Skills

Informative Have students conduct research to find support for the belief that the Law of the Sea Treaty "does not have enough teeth" to be effective. Tell students to write an informative essay that relates the sentiments of people or groups in support of more regulation. Ask volunteers to present their essays to the class, encouraging them to conclude by expressing their own opinion about the treaty and its effectiveness. **Verbal/Linguistic, Intrapersonal**

V Visual Skills

Evaluating Primary Sources Have students reread each quote, taking notes about the differences in opinion regarding the Law of the Sea Treaty. Have students work with a partner to create a two-column graphic organizer with the columns labeled "Pros" and "Cons." As students take notes, have them complete their charts.

CLOSE & REFLECT

Argument Have students write an argument defending one of the primary sources in this Case Study. Invite students to conduct additional research to provide supporting evidence for their arguments. Ask volunteers to share their arguments with the class.

INTERACTIVE MAP

Political Map: World

Acquiring Information Display the World political map for students. Ask them to locate the areas that are discussed in this Case Study feature. As a homework assignment, have students find a recent news article about a country trying to control part of an ocean or waterway. Have students form small groups and exchange their articles with the each other. Group members should take turns reading the articles and then discuss the content within the group. Then guide a class discussion in which groups explain the content in the news articles. **BL Verbal/Linguistic**

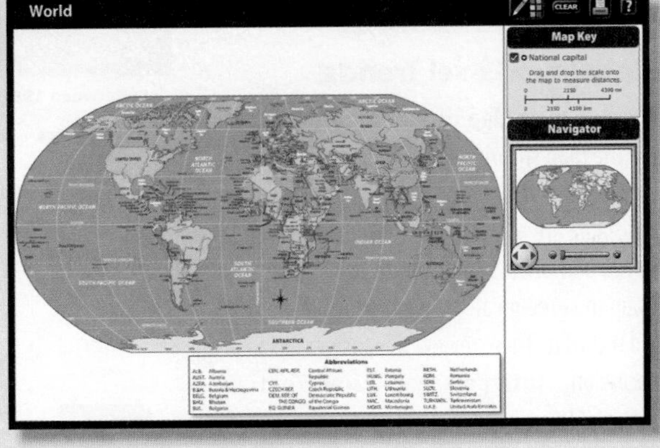

ANSWERS, p. 811

DBQ What do you think?

1. People might want to manage the high seas so they can be protected as they are able to be accessed by everyone, are rich in resources, and are mined and traveled through by many countries.
2. Critics are concerned that regulation of the high seas will reduce the ability to travel freely, cause new tax laws to be imposed, and restrict economic opportunities.
3. Answers may differ but could include that private ownership could do more to stop overfishing, pirating, drug trafficking, and pollution but could also reduce access, undermine shipping and trade, and put some countries with no ownership at a disadvantage.

ENGAGE

R Reading Skills

Predicting Have students predict why Oceania is so vulnerable to the effects of greenhouse gases even though the region produces a small percentage of the world's total. Ask them to make predictions about the effect of greenhouse gases on climate change and any other predictions about the material they will read about in this lesson. As students work through the lesson, they should check their predictions against the information they learn.

TEACH & ASSESS

C Critical Thinking Skills

Global Analysis Have students read about how the people of Oceania are implementing different methods to protect the environment but also to increase agricultural production. Invite volunteers to compare and contrast the practices of Oceania to those of other regions. **Ask: How is the example set by Fiji a delicate balance of developing the economy but also protecting the environment?** *(Possible answer: Fiji wants to promote tourism because it will help the economy, but it also wants to protect the environment. By working with the hotel and resort owners to build energy-efficient hotels, Fiji is showing other island countries in the region that it is possible to grow the tourist industry and make wise choices about the environment at the same time.)* **AL Logical/Mathematical**

Making Connections

Explain to students that other regions of the world are trying to make good decisions about how to develop resources and the economy while also protecting the environment. Invite students to share examples from your community or state that relate to wise management practices of resources in order to promote economic development and preserve the environment.

ANSWERS, p. 812

TAKING NOTES: Deforestation caused by mining and logging harms Oceania's agriculture industry as well as its people and animals. Rising sea levels and increases in temperatures could have devastating impacts on Oceania's islands in the form of flooding, contaminated freshwater, and dying coral reefs.

networks

There's More Online!

- ☑ **CHART** United States Nuclear Tests July 1945 through September 1992
- ☑ **IMAGE** Easter Island
- ☑ **MAP** Global Sea Level Trends
- ☑ **INTERACTIVE SELF-CHECK QUIZ**
- ☑ **VIDEO** People and Their Environment: Oceania

Reading **HELP**DESK

Academic Vocabulary (Tier Two Words)
- **nuclear**
- **grant**

Content Vocabulary (Tier Three Words)
- **climate change**
- **ocean warming**

TAKING NOTES: ***Key Ideas and Details***

IDENTIFYING Use a graphic organizer like the one below to take notes as you read about the issues that relate to people and their environment in Oceania.

Human Impacts on the Environment in Oceania

Deforestation	
Rising Sea Levels	
Rising Ocean Temperatures	

LESSON 3
People and Their Environment: Oceania

ESSENTIAL QUESTION • *How do physical systems and human systems shape a place?*

IT MATTERS BECAUSE

R *The islands of Oceania account for the emission of less than 1 percent of greenhouse gases that contribute to climate change. They are, nonetheless, among the most vulnerable to the adverse effects of greenhouse gases.*

Managing Resources

C **GUIDING QUESTION** *How are the people of Oceania using their islands' natural resources?*

The protection of forest, soil, and freshwater resources is a major concern throughout Oceania. The management of resources includes reforestation plans and implementation of "tabu," or no-take zones to control overfishing. Countries with valuable timber resources, such as Papua New Guinea, are developing plans to use forest resources without damaging the environment.

Methods used to improve agriculture production have a long history in Oceania and continue to be implemented to increase output. The labor-intensive practice of terracing is used to grow crops on the sides of hills. Terraces built into a slope increase the amount of available land for cultivating crops. Terracing helps reduce irrigation runoff and erosion. Irrigation practices such as simple flooding are used to slow down the flow of water to help trap sediment and control erosion. Crop diversification is another innovative agricultural practice used in Oceania. Planting a diversity of crops helps preserve the soil and increase productivity.

Overseas companies also have a stake in the management of Oceania's natural resources. Foreign companies are actively mining and logging on the islands and deep seabeds of the subregion. The investment in tourism by foreign companies is also a factor in managing the natural resources of the subregion. As new resorts are built, the environment is affected. Fiji has established a joint effort with hotel and resort owners to create a tourist sector that builds energy-efficient hotels, cuts carbon emissions, and reduces the impact on the environment.

networks *Online Teaching Options*

INTERACTIVE BELLRINGER

Global Sea Level Trends

Interpreting a Map Use the introductory text and the map showing worldwide changes in sea level from 1992 to 2013 to know why resources in Oceania are at risk. Have students form small groups and discuss each question. Ask each group to agree on an answer to each question and record it. Then, review the answers in a class discussion. **Interpersonal, Visual/Spatial, Verbal/Linguistic**

Global Sea Level Trends

Climate change is causing rises in sea level that threaten many regions of the world.

1. Between 1992 and 2013, where did sea levels raise the most?

A. Antarctica
B. Europe
C. Oceania
D. Southwest Asia

click for answer

Auto-Run Click Through Previous 1 of 3 Next

Oceania's environmental challenges include managing its freshwater resources. Many coral atolls and volcanic islands hold only limited supplies of freshwater. The lack of clean drinking water keeps the standard of living low. It also poses barriers to economic growth in some countries. Improvement will come with better management of runoff and the construction of additional sanitation facilities. R

The low islands of Oceania are in particular danger. **Climate change** can cause sea levels to rise and produce extreme weather. Managing the resources of these islands will help reduce their vulnerability. Programs include the protection of mangroves and seagrass habitats on these islands. In some cases, infrastructures have been relocated farther inland.

climate change any significant change in the measures of climate lasting for an extended period of time

Many of the countries in Oceania have developing economies. This means that implementing programs can be difficult. Programs continue to be initiated, however, through grassroots organizations, government efforts, and international organizations. Environmental education is also an important factor in managing natural resources. Understanding issues such as climate change will help empower people to make changes and welcome new methods of balancing their needs with those of the ecosystems. T

READING PROGRESS CHECK

Summarizing What issues are the most important in regard to managing the natural resources of Oceania?

Human Impact

GUIDING QUESTION *How have humans—both in Oceania and elsewhere—affected the environments of the islands of Oceania?*

The natural resources of Oceania, as in other regions, have not always been well managed. Today the subregion faces many environmental problems. Conservation efforts, however, are gaining recognition.

GEOGRAPHY CONNECTION

In recent decades, global sea levels have been rising.

1. ***THE WORLD IN SPATIAL TERMS*** In what areas of the globe have sea levels risen the most?
2. ***THE WORLD IN SPATIAL TERMS*** List three areas in which sea levels have fallen.

Global Sea Level Trends

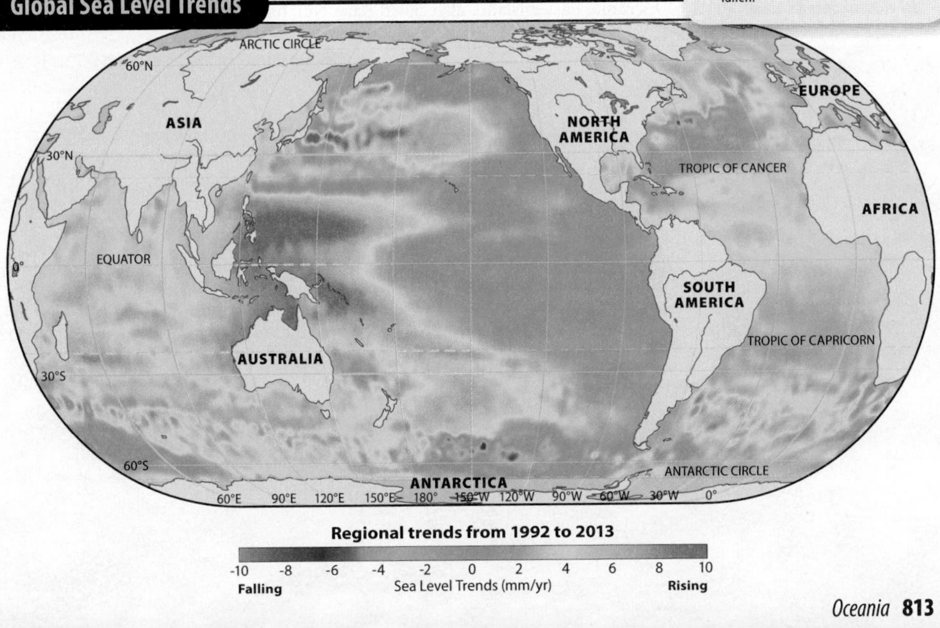

R Reading Skills

Understanding Relationships Explain to students that March 22 is World Water Day, a day that has been set aside by the UN General Assembly to alert the public around the world about unsafe drinking water, which is caused largely by the dumping of waste into freshwater. Have students consider the relationship between the availability of freshwater and the standard of living. Divide the class into small groups to conduct a study of freshwater resources in countries where the standard of living is very high and in countries where the standard of living is very low. Point out that they should find where the countries of Oceania fall as compared to the rest of the world. Ask them to analyze the data and then write an assessment of the relationship between standard of living and freshwater availability. **BL Interpersonal, Logical/Mathematical**

Content Background Knowledge

Short Supply of Freshwater The United Nations and World Bank have provided statistics on clean water and the dumping of sewage waste in freshwater that may astound some people. According to their findings, approximately 2 billion people use water that has not been treated in sanitation facilities. As a result, a large proportion of illnesses in less developed countries are caused by polluted water. In Oceania, millions of people do not have access to safe drinking water and sanitation facilities. For example, Papua New Guinea and Fiji rank well below the world average of access to clean drinking water, providing access to less than 50 percent of the population.

T Technology Skills

Problem Solving Guide a discussion about the need for island countries to carefully manage and protect their natural resources. **Ask:** **How can collaborative efforts between governments, nongovernmental organizations, and international organizations help the region to better manage its resources?** *(Possible answer: The countries are somewhat isolated by their physical geography and some countries have low populations, so working together can benefit the whole region rather than only one country.)* **AL Interpersonal**

INTERACTIVE WHITEBOARD ACTIVITY

Global Warming in Oceania

Synthesizing Have students drag the effects and potential threats of global warming on the islands of Oceania into the appropriate circles of a flowchart, and then draw lines from the descriptions of environmental programs and efforts being made by different organizations to the appropriate boxes of the other chart. **AL Visual/Spatial**

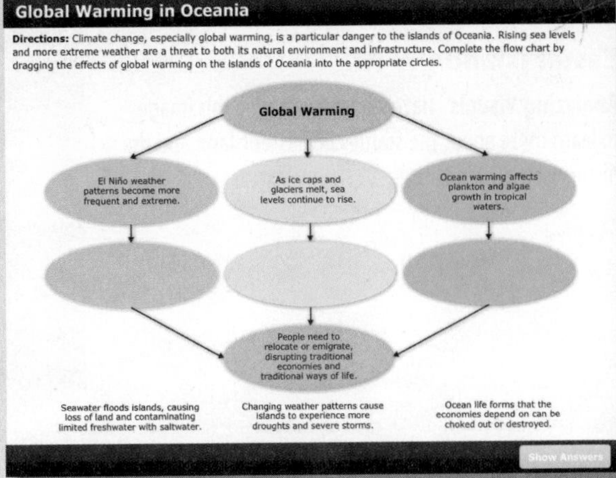

Global Warming in Oceania
Directions: Climate change, especially global warming, is a particular danger to the islands of Oceania. Rising sea levels and more extreme weather are a threat to both its natural environment and infrastructure. Complete the flow chart by dragging the effects of global warming on the islands of Oceania into the appropriate circles.
Global Warming
El Niño weather patterns become more frequent and extreme.
As ice caps and glaciers melt, sea levels continue to rise.
Ocean warming affects plankton and algae growth in tropical waters.
People need to relocate or emigrate, disrupting traditional economies and traditional ways of life.
Seawater floods islands, causing loss of land and contaminating limited freshwater with saltwater.
Changing weather patterns cause islands to experience more droughts and severe storms.
Ocean life forms that the economies depend on can be choked out or destroyed.
Show Answers

ANSWERS, p. 813

READING PROGRESS CHECK Issues such as managing and protecting limited sources of freshwater, managing soil and agriculture, limiting deforestation and practicing reforestation, climate change, and protecting fish and coral reefs are important to Oceania.

GEOGRAPHY CONNECTION

1. Sea levels have risen the most around Oceania, Australia, the Philippines, Indonesia, and east of Japan.
2. Sea levels are falling to the north of Antarctica, the west of Central America in the Pacific Ocean, and to the east of Canada in the Atlantic Ocean.

W Writing Skills

Argument Discuss the terms *climate change* and *ocean warming* with students, as well as their effects on Oceania. Provide an opportunity for students to gather information on both issues, including their causes. Then ask students to write an argumentative paper on the role of human activities in climate change and ocean warming. Remind students to document and cite their sources and to use current research. Explain to students that they should write a strong thesis that clearly states supporting reasons and then restate their thesis in the conclusion.

Have students identify the counter argument to the argument that they just used. Ask them to identify the supporting reasons for the counter argument. Students may need to conduct additional research to identify the supporting reasons. Use the development of arguments and counter arguments to hold a class debate on the subjects. **BL Naturalist, Logical/Mathematical, Verbal/Linguistic**

V Visual Skills

Identifying Perspectives and Differing Interpretations Ask students to examine the visual of the statues on Easter Island, also called Rapa Nui. Explain to students that archaeologists are still puzzled by these statues, their meaning, and their significance to the culture. Tell them that some believe they represented important chiefs, ancestors, or other important figures. Ask students to interpret the meaning of the statues. Ask them to stand up at their desks if they think the statues represent important people in the culture and to provide one reason that supports their choice. If students support a different interpretation, ask them to explain their choice. Discuss the different interpretations with students and the reasons that archaeologists may have used to support their perspective. **ELL Kinesthetic, Visual/Spatial**

ANSWERS, p. 814

CRITICAL THINKING

1. The vegetation has not changed significantly: when Europeans arrived on Easter Island, it was already deforested with no plants over 10 feet high.
2. Theories for the deforestation include uncontrolled rodent populations, overexploitation of natural resources, and the island's natural fragility in supporting vegetation.

nuclear a weapon whose destructive power derives from an uncontrolled nuclear reaction

The testing of **nuclear** weapons has had major effects on parts of the subregion's environment. In the late 1940s and 1950s, the United States and other countries with nuclear capability carried out aboveground testing of nuclear weapons in the South Pacific. The dangers of such testing were gravely underestimated at the time. In 1954 the United States exploded a nuclear device on Bikini Atoll in the Marshall Islands. The people of Bikini Atoll had been moved to safety. However, those living downwind of the explosion on Rongelap Atoll were exposed to massive doses of radiation. This exposure resulted in deaths, illnesses, and genetic abnormalities.

ocean warming rise in the temperature of the ocean water

W Like other world regions, Oceania is threatened by climate change. One resulting impact is an apparent increase in the frequency and severity of the El Niño weather pattern. Climate and weather in Oceania are highly sensitive to seasonal El Niño weather patterns that can cause both droughts and powerful storms. Another impact of climate change that many scientists consider imminent is that continued increases in Earth's temperatures could cause a devastating rise in sea level. If ice caps and glaciers on land experience increased melting, the resulting rise in the level of ocean waters would cause flooding on many of Oceania's islands.

Rising sea levels not only cause loss of land but also contaminate the limited freshwater sources of the low islands with salt water. This reduces the amount of freshwater available for agricultural purposes as well as human consumption. In addition, **ocean warming** affects certain types of plankton and algae that grow in tropical waters, causing overgrowth and the choking out of other life forms. Coral reefs are also destroyed by ocean warming. Scientists in the region are studying global warming. They hope to discover its causes, predict its consequences, and provide solutions.

Pollution also poses a threat to the waters of Oceania and is damaging to the coral reefs. Agricultural runoff and inadequate sanitation cause pollution that further threatens freshwater supplies. Agricultural runoff, chemical fertilizers, and organic waste also threaten the subregion's oceans.

Deforestation and the loss of native species are not new to the islands of Oceania. Easter Island, also called Rapa Nui, had already lost most of its native

Famous for its giant carved statues, Easter Island no longer has the natural vegetation that once covered the land.

▼ CRITICAL THINKING

1. ***Contrasting*** Describe how the vegetation of Easter Island has changed since the arrival of Europeans.
2. ***Describing*** What are commonly held theories for causes of deforestation on Easter Island?

V

814

networks ***Online Teaching Options***

INTERACTIVE IMAGE

Easter Island

Analyzing Visuals Have students examine this image to learn more about the statues on Easter Island and the history of the island. **BL Verbal/Linguistic**

plant species by the late 1700s. When European explorers first arrived on Easter Island in the late 1700s, deforestation had already taken place. They found a grassy island devoid of plants greater than 10 feet (3 m) in height. The island at one time had been covered with a subtropical forest dominated by large palms, an ecosystem entirely different from what the Europeans observed.

The exact cause of Easter Island's deforestation is not certain. However, a few theories prevail. Some scientists believe that uncontrolled populations of rodents were the cause. Others blame overexploitation of the available resources or the island's natural fragility for the deforestation. The loss of forest caused soil erosion that limited the inhabitants' ability to grow crops. **C**

Present-day causes of deforestation include mining and logging. Although mining is beneficial to Papua New Guinea's economy it has had negative impacts on the rain forests there. Mining operations cause destruction of forest habitats and pollute waterways and oceans. The process of removing the nontarget material from the ore and the discarded waste rock can cause damage to the environment. The process of separating gold in alluvial mining releases mercury into streams and soils, which creates another source of contamination. Pollutants can cause localized fish kills and loss of vegetation in areas. Pollution in rivers and streams is harmful to agriculture as well as to animals and humans. **T**

✓ READING PROGRESS CHECK

Describing What are the pros and cons of mining operations in Papua New Guinea?

Addressing the Issues

GUIDING QUESTION *How are the people of Oceania reacting to the changes in their environments?*

The U.S. nuclear testing in Oceania was stopped. The effects of radiation exposure and environmental damage, however, have continued. Today the atolls affected by the testing remain off-limits to human settlement. Recent studies, however, offer hope for eventual environmental recovery. In the 1990s, the United States government provided $90 million to help decontaminate Bikini Atoll. It also set up a $45 million trust fund to provide **grants** for blast survivors from Rongelap Atoll and their offspring. The nuclear legacy also has had political effects. Antinuclear activism is a major factor in regional politics. French plans to conduct nuclear tests on an atoll in French Polynesia caused antinuclear demonstrations. The international outcry led to an early halt to the tests.

Countries within the subregion are also addressing other environmental concerns. The Nauru Agreement Concerning Cooperation in the Management of Fisheries of Common Interest (also known as the Parties to the Nauru Agreement, or PNA) was created to manage tuna populations sustainably. The agreement requires catch reporting and maintenance of logbooks. It also mandates the installation of electronic position and data transfer devices on the fishing vessels. The members include eight Pacific Island countries that together control 25 percent of the world's supply of tuna. The PNA members are Federated States of Micronesia, Kiribati, Marshall Islands, Nauru, Palau, Papua New Guinea, Solomon Islands, and Tuvalu.

Coral reefs require clean water and sunlight to survive. The U.S. Environmental Protection Agency (EPA) has established programs to protect, restore, and maintain water quality around the coral reefs. Hawaii's Department of Land and Natural Resources (DLNR) reported that nearly 25 percent of all living coral was lost between 1994 and 2006 on Maui. Grants offered by the EPA aim at controlling pollution, managing watersheds, research, monitoring, and education. **R**

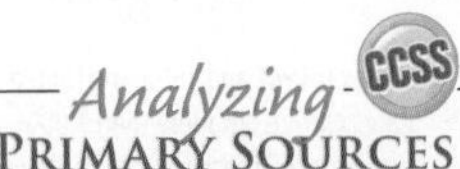

Rising Sea Levels Cause Plans for Relocation

Kiribati is making plans to relocate its entire population before the islands disappear under rising ocean water.

"With the Australian Government the Pacific countries have the Australia–Pacific Technical Colleges (APTC) scheme which provides international standard qualification training thus allowing access for our people to the international labour markets. We also have a pilot program, the Kiribati–Australia Nursing Initiative (KANI) under which a number of our student nurses are trained to international standards in Australian institutions. We acknowledge with gratitude these innovative programs by our two development partners and indeed invite consideration of these models by other partner countries."

—Kiribati president Anote Tong, statement to the Second Session of Global Platform for Disaster Risk-Reduction Conference, June 2009

DBQ ***DRAWING CONCLUSIONS*** What initiatives does the statement discuss regarding plans for relocation of people from Kiribati? RH.9–10.2

grant a sum of money given to a person or organization for a particular purpose

VIDEO

Are We Changing the Planet? Coral Reefs

Exploring Issues Have students watch this video to learn how increasing ocean temperatures are affecting the planet's coral reefs. **Visual/Spatial**

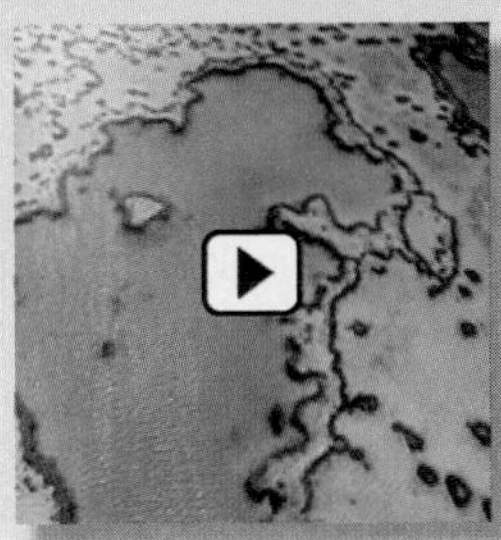

People and Their Environment: Oceania

C Critical Thinking Skills

Identifying Continuity and Change After students have read about deforestation in Oceania, ask them to identify examples of deforestation they have learned about previously from the past and present. Review examples of cause-and-effect relationships with students. **Ask: Are the causes and effects of deforestation in Oceania similar to or different from elsewhere in the world? Explain.** *(Possible answer: Scientists believe that the causes are different. They believe that rodents or overuse of resources were the possible causes of deforestation in some places in Oceania in the past. Today, the main cause of deforestation is logging and clearing land for mining. The effects are similar, with the land that is cleared being susceptible to erosion and having limited nutrients for agricultural purposes.)* **AL Logical/Mathematical**

T Technology Skills

Using Primary and Secondary Sources Discuss with students the ways that human activities have damaged the water environment of Oceania and the effects on natural resources, agricultural production, and human safety. Have students work with a partner to research progress made by the Parties to the Nauru Agreement regarding sustainable management of fisheries resources. Challenge students to search online or using an electronic database to find both a primary and a secondary source concerning the progress or initiatives of this group. Then assign students to write an abstract on the content of each source. **BL Interpersonal, Verbal/Linguistic**

R Reading Skills

Predicting Review with students how coral reefs form and what benefits they provide to the ocean environment. Then ask students to predict if they think that the coral reefs lost on Maui could be restored and, if so, how quickly. Invite students to share their predictions with the class and also their thinking and logic. **AL Naturalist**

ANSWERS, p. 815

✓ READING PROGRESS CHECK Mining adds needed money to the economy of Papua New Guinea but causes destruction of rain forest habitats and pollutes the oceans and waterways.

DBQ The statement discusses initiatives to educate the Kiribati population so people are prepared for success in an international job market should relocation become imminent.

People and Their Environment: Oceania

V Visual Skills

Creating Graphs Ask students to examine the information in the chart. Then call on students to identify the locations of the places in the chart on a map of the region. Invite students to draw conclusions about the locations that the United States government chose for nuclear testing. Have students work in small groups to create a graph that shows related data for approximately the same years as shown on the chart, such as population information before and after the nuclear testing occurred or the effects on vegetation. Provide an opportunity for students to share their graphs with the class. AL
Visual/Spatial

W Writing Skills

Informative/Explanatory Discuss with students the impact that the World Wildlife Fund's (WWF) Sustainable Sugar program has had on Fiji's economy and environment. Then have students conduct research on their own or with a partner to find another similar program. The other program could be one funded by the WWF or another organization, but should have had positive effects in the region. Provide students with this prompt to steer their research: **How might the sustainable management of resources benefit the region both economically and culturally?** Tell students that they should write a short white paper based on their research. Remind them that the goal of a white paper is to help readers understand the issue and how it is being addressed. Explain to them that their papers should include a well-supported thesis, details, and examples. Provide an opportunity for students to deliver their white papers to the class in a symposium-style format. BL
Verbal/Linguistic, Interpersonal

CLOSE & REFLECT

Identifying Central Issues Have students review the issues in this lesson and determine those that are most important to the people and the environment of Oceania. Ask students to list the issues and write a brief summary of the actions that people and groups are taking to address them. Challenge students to write additional actions that could be taken to solve these issues that are not mentioned in the text.

ANSWERS, p. 816

READING PROGRESS CHECK Students' answers will vary, but they should clearly identify measures taken to address environmental issues such as ways that low islands are coping with rising sea levels.

CRITICAL THINKING

1. They most likely chose the Pacific islands for nuclear tests because they were isolated and the population levels were lower than other regions.
2. One long-term effect is that these islands remain off-limits to human settlement.

Between 1945 and 1992, the United States carried out more than 1,000 nuclear tests. The vast majority were conducted underground, but more than 100 were done in the Pacific region.

▶ **CRITICAL THINKING**

1. ***Hypothesizing*** Why do you think the United States chose Pacific islands and atolls as locations for nuclear tests?
2. ***Interpreting Significance*** What do you suppose were the long-term effects of these nuclear tests on the region?

V

United States Nuclear Tests July 1945 through September 1992

Location	Number of tests
Bikini	23
Christmas Island	24
Enewetak	43
Johnston Island	12
Pacific	4
Total Pacific	106

Source: United States Nuclear Tests July 1945 through September 1992, U.S. Department of Defense, December 2000

W

Another joint effort is in the area of sugar production. For decades sugar has been a leading export for Fiji's economy. Sugar production has, however, also damaged the ecosystems of the islands of Fiji. The Sustainable Sugar program was created by the World Wildlife Fund (WWF). The program is working with local people, companies, and the government to reduce the negative effects of sugarcane production on the coral reefs. WWF also promotes an approach to conservation and development in the region that recognizes the rights of local people to manage and benefit from use of natural resources. The approach is called Community Based Natural Resource Management (CBNRM). CBNRM supports community-based initiatives and empowerment of communities. The program seeks legislation and partnerships with public and private sectors in the use of natural resources. The goal is to create sustainable development and allow communities to benefit economically. Emphasis is also placed on maintaining traditional customs and values that have protected the natural resources for centuries.

Climate change is a major concern for all the islands of Oceania. Many of the low islands are already planning strategies to cope with rising sea levels. The plans include moving human populations to the remaining areas after loss of land due to rising sea levels. Another plan is for emigration to nearby countries. Climate change will have severe effects on the economies of the subregion as populations relocate. It will also impact the subregion's culture as people move to countries such as Australia, New Zealand, and the United States. In those countries, emigrants would not own land and might lose their social structures and traditional ways of life.

READING PROGRESS CHECK

Describing What are some measures that have been taken to address environmental concerns?

LESSON 3 REVIEW 

Reviewing Vocabulary (Tier Three Words)

1. ***Making Connections*** Define climate change and ocean warming. Explain how they relate to each other. RH.9–10.4

Using Your Notes

2. ***Summarizing*** Use your graphic organizer to write a description of the major causes of deforestation in Oceania.

Answering the Guiding Questions

3. ***Exploring Issues*** How are the people of Oceania using their islands' natural resources?
4. ***Evaluating*** How have humans—both in Oceania and elsewhere—affected the environments of the islands of Oceania?
5. ***Discussing*** How are the people of Oceania reacting to the changes in their environments?

Writing Activity

6. ***Argument*** Suppose you are a citizen of Oceania. Write a short letter to your local government regarding environmental issues on your island and actions you would like the government to take. WHST.9–10.1

LESSON 3 REVIEW ANSWERS

Reviewing Vocabulary

1. Climate change refers to changes in the climate that last for extended periods of time such as an overall rise in global temperature. Ocean warming is a rise in the temperature of ocean water. Climate change causes these overall increases in temperatures.

Using Your Notes

2. Descriptions will vary; causes: mining and logging

Answering the Guiding Questions

3. They practice terracing to increase arable land, mine resources, log, and use their locations for tourism.
4. Humans have affected the environment on the islands by: nuclear tests in the South Pacific, causing serious damage; climate change, causing rising sea levels that threaten low islands and freshwater supplies; increasing ocean temperatures are destroying coral reefs; pollution from agricultural runoff, poor sanitation, mining, and logging threaten water systems; and deforestation.
5. The people of Oceania are taking action with sustainable development and management plans, working to reverse damage, and planning for a future that may include emigration.

Writing Activity

6. Letters will differ but should be strongly supported with information on environmental issues from the chapter. Answers could include deforestation, pollution from mining and logging, rising sea levels, soil erosion, and management of freshwater sources.

CHAPTER 33 Assessment CCSS

Directions: On a separate sheet of paper, answer the questions below. Make sure that you read carefully and answer all parts of the questions.

Lesson Review

Lesson 1

1. ***Classifying*** Explain the criteria for classifying the three groups of Oceania's islands. Within your explanation, include the names of these three groups.
2. ***Making Connections*** What is the relationship between atolls and the development of uniform languages and culture?
3. ***Identifying Cause and Effect*** How do climate conditions in the doldrums contribute to typhoons?

Lesson 2

4. ***Explaining*** What conditions gave rise to the number of languages spoken in Oceania? Would it be accurate to state that nearly half the languages spoken in the world are in Oceania?
5. ***Problem Solving*** Why is health care not uniform across all the islands of Oceania? Briefly discuss the importance of health care, and suggest an idea that might help to make it accessible across the islands.
6. ***Describing*** What is the most important economic activity in Oceania? Describe conditions that support as well as pose threats to this activity.

Lesson 3

7. ***Considering Advantages and Disadvantages*** How have countries outside of Oceania helped boost the economies of some countries of Oceania but also caused damage? Discuss the efforts of Fiji to balance economic and environmental interests.
8. ***Drawing Conclusions*** Discuss the impact of nuclear testing on the Oceania subregion. Can the destruction caused by nuclear testing be reversed? Explain.
9. ***Identifying Central Issues*** Describe the environmental issues tied to gold mining and production in Papua New Guinea. Explain why these issues have not been resolved.

21st Century Skills

Use the cartoon below to answer the questions that follow.

PRIMARY SOURCE

"Gentlemen, it's time we gave some serious thought to the effects of global warming."

10. ***Using Primary Sources*** Explain how this cartoon illustrates a key issue in understanding why the management of resources is important to the low islands of Oceania.
11. ***Analyzing*** Based on the above issue, discuss the potential impacts to freshwater resources and agriculture.

Critical Thinking

12. ***Making Connections*** What is the relationship of "tabu" to overfishing? How does implementation of "tabu" show the rise of the countries of Oceania to overcome challenges from the past under colonialism? Write a one-page essay to explain your responses. WHST.9–10.2

Exploring the Essential Question

13. ***Organizing*** Create a Venn diagram to compare and contrast three countries in Oceania. Include the following information: physical geography; climate and resources; population patterns; society and culture today; economic activities; managing resources; and addressing issues related to human impact. After you complete your Venn diagram, write a summary to explain it.

Need Extra Help?

If You've Missed Question	1	2	3	4	5	6	7	8	9	10	11	12	13
Go to page	800	801	803	807	808	808	812	814	815	817	817	812	797

CHAPTER 33 Assessment Answers

Lesson Review

Lesson 1

1. Oceania's islands are classified based on location, culture, and how they formed. Melanesia means "black islands" and lies north and east of Australia, Micronesia means "tiny islands" and lies north of Melanesia, and Polynesia means "many islands" and covers an area larger than either Melanesia or Micronesia.
2. Since atolls are small with a very low landscape, groups of people were not isolated by natural barriers, which resulted in a uniform development of culture and language.
3. The doldrums are a windless area near the Equator that allows the air to rise vertically instead of blowing horizontally, which can cause typhoons to form.

Lesson 2

4. Vast stretches of ocean separated Oceania from other parts of the world, resulting in isolated groups of people who developed languages without outside interference. No, it would not be accurate to state that nearly half the languages spoken in the world are spoken in Oceania as about 1,200 of some 6,000 spoken languages are used there.
5. Health care is not uniform across all the islands as the economies vary and remote areas and islands make consistent care difficult. Discussions of the importance of health care and suggestions for improvements will differ but could include additional facilities and use of the Internet and other communication technologies to allow those people who live in remote areas to communicate with health professionals.
6. Agriculture is the most important economic activity, with rich volcanic soils and rainfall being helpful factors on high islands. Rising sea levels that could contaminate freshwater used to water crops are a threat to this activity.

Lesson 3

7. Foreign countries are investing in mining, logging, and tourism in Oceania, which creates revenue but also damages the environment. Fiji's efforts include partnering with hotels and resorts to build energy-efficient hotels, cut carbon emissions, and reduce impact to the environment.
8. In the 1940s and 1950s the U.S. and other countries conducted nuclear tests in the region, which exposed the people and the environment to massive doses of radiation. Destruction caused by nuclear testing cannot be reversed as radiation must disperse or decay to safe levels.
9. Mining in Papua New Guinea destroys rain forest habitats by removing trees and pollutes the waterways with mercury, waste rock, and other by-products of removing and separating gold from its surrounding material.

21st Century Skills

10. It illustrates the rising ocean levels due to global warming, which would flood or destroy the low islands.
11. Rising sea levels contaminate freshwater sources with salt water, which limits the amount available for use in agriculture as well as for human consumption.

Critical Thinking

12. Essays will differ but should be strongly supported with information including: "tabu" are no-take zones which were put in place to control overfishing; implementation of "tabu" shows that countries are working to use resources sustainably as opposed to the use during colonialism; forest management and eco-friendly tourism are other initiatives in the subregion.

Exploring the Essential Question

13. Diagrams and summaries will differ depending on the three countries the student chooses to compare and contrast but must include: the physical geography; climate and resources; population patterns; society and culture today; economic activities; managing resources; and addressing issues related to human impact.

CHAPTER 33

Assessment Answers

Applying Map Skills

14 Papua New Guinea is the largest island in Melanesia.

15 Palau is west of the Marshall Islands, Fiji and Tonga are south of the Marshall Islands, and Vanuatu is east of Fiji.

16 Papua New Guinea has the largest population, which is likely due to its larger land size, natural resources, and arable land.

College and Career Readiness

17 Summaries will vary but must include how subsistence farming is practiced in the Solomon Islands currently, if it meets the goals and needs of the people, and a supported opinion about whether subsistence farming has been a worthwhile activity in the Solomon Islands or whether another type of farming should replace it.

Writing About Geography

18 Descriptions will vary but should be strongly supported with information from the chapter on the landscape of the high islands of Oceania. Answers should include descriptions of tall mountains divided by deep valleys that spread out onto coastal plains.

Analyzing Primary Sources

19 The quote helps show that Hawaiians revere their elders and feel that they are a source of wisdom. This attitude does not generally reflect the attitude of most Americans toward senior citizens today.

20 Student answers will vary but could include conservation, preservation, restoration, and sustainable development actions.

Research and Presentation

21 Multimedia presentations will differ but must include the trench's location (near Guam), formation (created by ocean subduction), relevance (tourism/site of deepest ocean depth/possible earthquakes), likelihood of future earthquakes (possible), and recent newsworthy events surrounding the Mariana Trench (filmmaker James Cameron established a new record for deepest solo descent) as well as maps, photographs, graphs, and computer or sketched diagrams.

CHAPTER 33 Assessment 

Directions: On a separate sheet of paper, answer the questions below. Make sure that you read carefully and answer all parts of the questions.

Applying Map Skills

Refer to the Unit 9 Atlas to answer the following questions.

14 ***Places and Regions*** Identify the largest island in Melanesia.

15 ***The World in Spatial Terms*** Use your mental map of Oceania to describe the spatial relationship among the Marshall Islands, Palau, Vanuatu, Fiji, and Tonga.

16 ***Human Systems*** Of all the islands of Oceania, which has the largest population? What is the approximate population? What are the likely causes that led to this island having the greatest population?

College and Career Readiness

17 ***Decision Making*** Suppose you are a college student and your professor is researching subsistence farming. She has asked you to research subsistence farming in the Solomon Islands and explain how it is being practiced currently and whether it seems to have met the goals and needs of the people living there. Additionally, your professor has asked you to express and support an opinion about whether subsistence farming has been a worthwhile activity in the Solomon Islands—or whether another type of farming should replace it. Conduct research, and then prepare a summary of your findings to submit to your professor. **WHST.9–10.1; WHST.9–10.7; WHST.9–10.9**

Writing About Geography

18 ***Narrative*** Suppose you are traveling at low altitude through airspace above the high islands of Oceania. Describe the scenery below using standard grammar, spelling, sentence structure, and punctuation. **WHST.9–10.2**

DBQ Analyzing Primary Sources

Use the document to answer the following questions.

Dr. Elizabeth Lindsey, an explorer, author, filmmaker, and speaker, is the first female to become a Fellow of the National Geographic Society. She received the Visionary Award from the United Nations in 2010 for contributions in intercultural engagement and understanding.

PRIMARY SOURCE

"As a child, I was cared for by three old Hawaiian women while my parents worked. These elders were revered in our community for their mastery in ancient traditions. They told me that I would travel far to keep the voices of the ancestors alive and that it would take the wisdom of these elders to return the world to balance."

—Dr. Elizabeth Lindsey, www.elizabethlindsey.com

19 ***Interpreting Significance*** How does the quote help you understand the attitude of Hawaiians toward elders in their communities? Does this attitude accurately reflect the general attitude of most Americans toward senior citizens today? **RH.9–10.1**

20 ***Drawing Inferences*** What types of actions do you think Dr. Lindsey and others are taking—or should take—to return the world to balance? **RH.9–10.1**

Research and Presentation

21 ***Gathering Information*** With a partner, conduct research to learn additional information about the Mariana Trench. Create a multimedia presentation to explain the following: location of the trench, tectonic activity that formed the trench, relevance of the trench to Oceania, likelihood that the trench will give rise to future earthquakes, recent newsworthy events relevant to the trench. Within your presentation, include maps, photographs, and graphs. Additionally, develop sketched or computer-generated diagrams. **WHST.9–10.1; WHST.9–10.6; WHST.9–10.7 WHST.9–10.8**

Need Extra Help?

If You've Missed Question	14	15	16	17	18	19	20	21
Go to page	746	746	750	808	800	818	818	802

818

networks ***Online Teaching Options***

PRINTABLE DIGITAL WORKSHEET

Chapter Test and Lesson Quizzes

Assessing Have students complete the Chapter Test and Lesson Quizzes to assess student understanding throughout the chapter. These assessment tools offer chapter and lesson evaluation through a variety of question formats, including document-based questions.

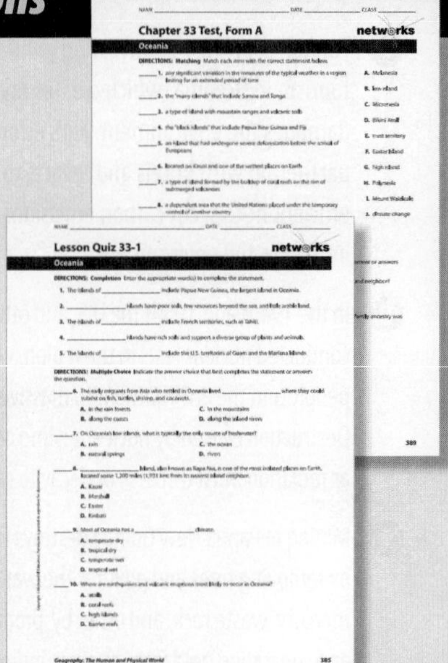

Antarctica: the land of ICE

Earth's fifth-largest continent, the frigid land of Antarctica is found at the bottom of the world. Since its discovery in 1820 it has fascinated explorers and scientists.

(t) Danita Delimont/Gallo Images/Getty Images; Dean Lewins/Newscom

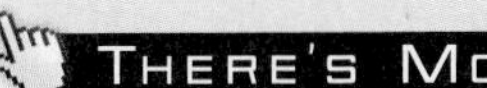

networks Online Teaching Options

MAP

World Climate

Hypothesizing Before students read and study the feature opening page, display the World Climate map and have students view the map key. Ask students to find Antarctica on the map. **Ask:** **How does the map key describe Antarctica?** *(ice cap)* **What area of the world has a similar climate?** *(Greenland)* Display the World Population Density map. **Ask:** **Why do you think both Greenland and Antarctica are uninhabited?** *(Answers should note that the ice cap and extremely cold temperatures make living in these areas extremely difficult.)* **Visual/Spatial, Verbal/Linguistic**

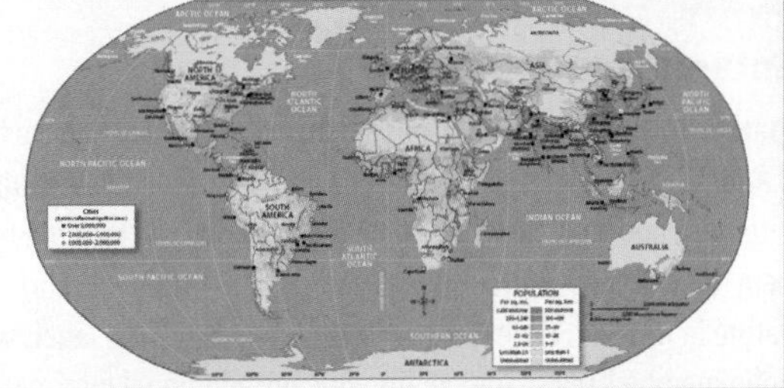

ENGAGE

R Reading Skills

Visualizing Ask students to read the introductory paragraph about Antarctica. Have them visualize the location of the continent and its physical geography, including the climate and biomes. Ask students to write a short descriptive poem to help them visualize this dry, frozen land. Point out to students that they may use rhyme or free verse but that they should include details about the uniqueness of Antarctica as compared to other continents that they have learned about. Invite students to read their poems aloud to the class or in small groups.

TEACH & ASSESS

V Visual Skills

Analyzing Visuals Engage students in the image of Antarctica by inviting volunteers to point out details such as the rock, ice floes, water, and snow. Tell students that Antarctica is classified as a polar desert. Discuss with students what factors would classify an area as a desert. **Ask:** **How does Antarctica have such a dry climate with so much ice around it?** *(Possible answer: It has very little precipitation like other dry climates do.)* Explain to students that Antarctica is much colder than the Arctic. Point to the ice is in the photograph that is piled high. If possible, show students a picture from the Arctic so that they can compare and contrast details. **Ask:** **What is one factor that may cause temperatures in Antarctica to be colder than in the Arctic?** *(Possible answer: Antarctica has a higher elevation than the Arctic because ice has piled on top of the land over many years. The Arctic is a floating sea of ice.)* Have students work in small groups or with a partner to list other factors that might cause Antarctica to be not only colder than the Arctic but also the coldest place on Earth. **AL** **Visual/Spatial**

Content Background Knowledge

Dressed for the Weather Antarctica is home to only six of the seventeen species of penguins. Penguins have adapted to the cold climate of Antarctica over time. Their outside feathers are oily and waterproof, and underneath they are wrapped in layers of down feathers and body fat. As flightless birds, penguins rely on their expert and swift swimming ability to "fly" through the water in search of krill and to escape predators such as seals. When penguins are too warm, they often fluff out their feathers to take in crisp, cool air. They also huddle together in a group to withstand temperatures of more than –50 °F (–46 °C) and winds that blow at more than 100 miles (161 kilometers) per hour.

Antarctica: The Land of Ice

C Critical Thinking Skills

Comparing and Contrasting Invite a volunteer to describe Antarctica's size. Explain that Antarctica is vast, but it is not the largest continent on Earth. Organize the class into seven groups and assign each group a continent. Ask groups to gather the following information for their continent: rank (size), location, population, and climate(s). Tell groups to organize their information in a chart. Then provide an opportunity for students to share their data with the class. While each group is reporting, other groups should listen and copy the information into an additional column in their charts. After all groups have presented, have students take turns comparing and contrasting Antarctica with different continents around the world.
ELL **Auditory/Musical**

W Writing Skills

Narrative Provide some background to students on Antarctica's discovery, such as that hunters came to the land in search of seals. Ask students to imagine that they have landed in Antarctica in 1820. Have students write a descriptive narrative about what they observed, climate conditions, and their feelings, such as of isolation or wonder. Point out that students should use vivid verbs and sensory language to appeal to their reader. Invite students to share their narratives with the class. **BL** **Verbal/Linguistic, Naturalist**

V Visual Skills

Creating Diagrams Direct students' attention to the diagram of wind and ice and point out that the data called out includes extremes. Have students work with a partner to create an "extreme" diagram that displays different data about Antarctica. Tell students that their data should have a common theme such as animal life, plant life, climate, elevation, explorers, or places. Guide students to online resources that should have current data available. Challenge students to create their diagrams with computer software. Allow time for students to share their diagrams with the class. **AL** **Visual/Spatial**

Content Background Knowledge

Measurements Recently there have been reports of even colder temperatures recorded in Antarctica. Point out to students that while measurements may seem absolute, in fact they can vary. **Ask: Why might the height of a mountain or the coldest temperature ever recorded be different according to different sources?** *(there could be different types of instruments being used or the measurements could be taken from different locations; also there could be actual variations taking place—mountains can increase in height and temperatures can increase/decrease)*

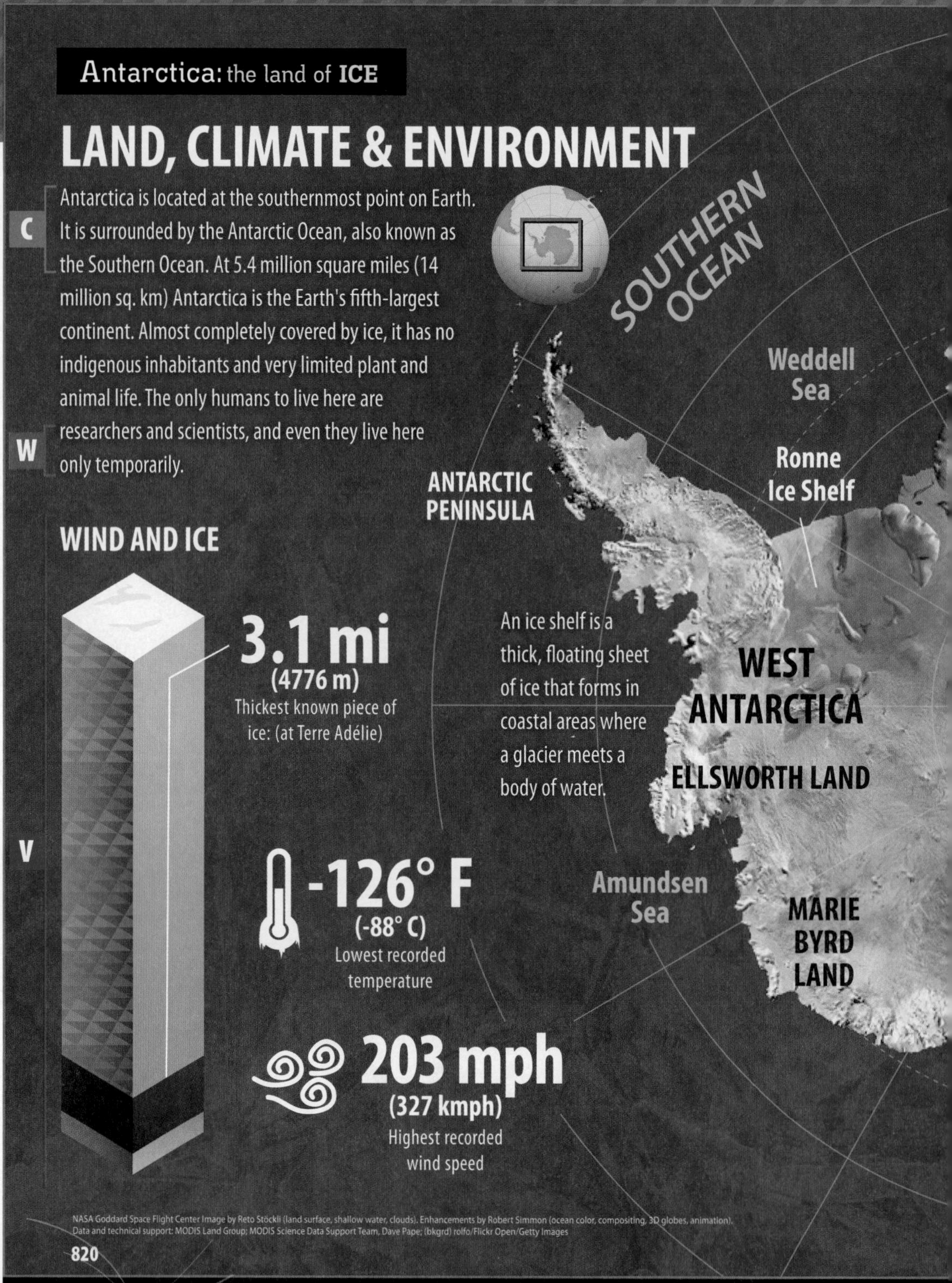

Antarctica: the land of **ICE**

LAND, CLIMATE & ENVIRONMENT

C Antarctica is located at the southernmost point on Earth. It is surrounded by the Antarctic Ocean, also known as the Southern Ocean. At 5.4 million square miles (14 million sq. km) Antarctica is the Earth's fifth-largest continent. Almost completely covered by ice, it has no indigenous inhabitants and very limited plant and animal life. The only humans to live here are W researchers and scientists, and even they live here only temporarily.

SOUTHERN OCEAN

Weddell Sea

Ronne Ice Shelf

ANTARCTIC PENINSULA

WEST ANTARCTICA

ELLSWORTH LAND

Amundsen Sea

MARIE BYRD LAND

An ice shelf is a thick, floating sheet of ice that forms in coastal areas where a glacier meets a body of water.

WIND AND ICE

V

3.1 mi
(4776 m)
Thickest known piece of ice: (at Terre Adélie)

-126° F
(-88° C)
Lowest recorded temperature

203 mph
(327 kmph)
Highest recorded wind speed

820

networks Online Teaching Options

VIDEO

Antarctica's Dry Valley

Spatial Understanding After students view the video, have them list the features of Antarctica highlighted in the video. Provide students with an outline map of Antarctica and have them research online to find the location of each feature. Tell them to label the features on their map and to include a short description of each feature in its label. Have students share their maps and labels with a group. Then have group members revise their maps with any additional information they did not have.
BL **Visual/Spatial**

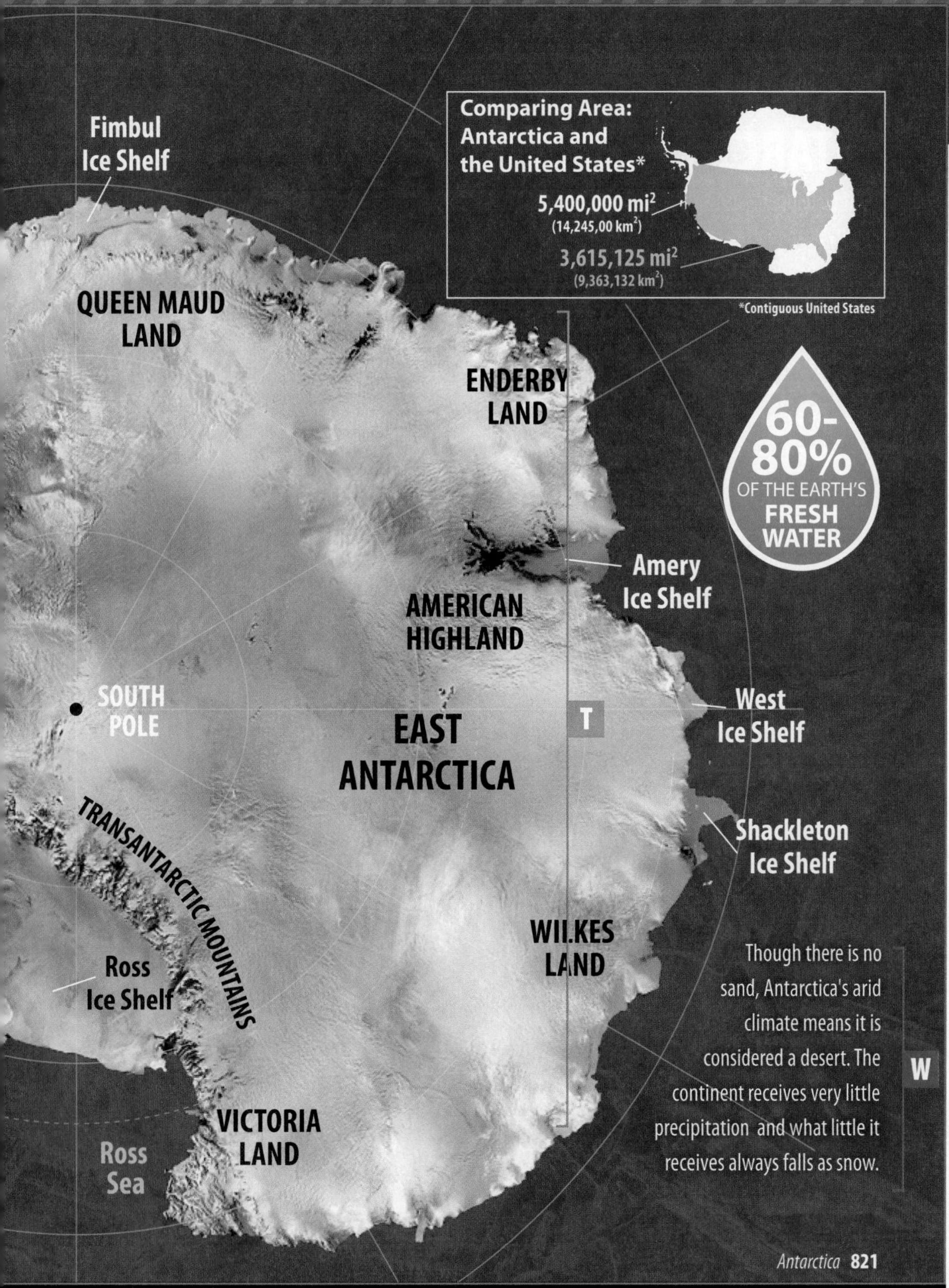

Fimbul Ice Shelf

QUEEN MAUD LAND

ENDERBY LAND

AMERICAN HIGHLAND

SOUTH POLE

EAST ANTARCTICA

TRANSANTARCTIC MOUNTAINS

Ross Ice Shelf

VICTORIA LAND

Ross Sea

WILKES LAND

Amery Ice Shelf

West Ice Shelf

Shackleton Ice Shelf

Comparing Area: Antarctica and the United States*

5,400,000 mi^2 (14,245,00 km^2)

3,615,125 mi^2 (9,363,132 km^2)

*Contiguous United States

60-80% OF THE EARTH'S FRESH WATER

Though there is no sand, Antarctica's arid climate means it is considered a desert. The continent receives very little precipitation and what little it receives always falls as snow.

ANIMATION

How Icebergs Form

Sequencing Have students view the animation that shows the process of iceberg formation. Then have them make a series of diagrams on the formation of an iceberg with these labels: ice sheet, ice shelf, calving, and iceberg. Tell students to include captions that show the steps in the formation of an iceberg. Then have each student exchange his or her diagrams with a partner. Partners should use each other's diagrams to explain the formation of an iceberg. **AL Visual/Spatial, Interpersonal, Naturalist**

Antarctica: The Land of Ice

T Technology Skills

Transferring Information Guide a class discussion about the different landforms and bodies of water on the map. Have pairs of students research additional features of the continent, such as scientific research stations, domes, the Geomagnetic South Pole, other mountains, and islands. Tell students to write the name and a brief description of each feature on a sticky note. Display the map of Antarctica and have students place their sticky notes in the correct location on the map. Ask students to give additional information about each feature as they place it on the map. Discuss how some of the features are unique to Antarctica while others are common on other continents. **Ask:** **Why is there no political map of Antarctica?** *(Possible answer: There are no political borders on Antarctica because there is no permanent population.)* **ELL AL Visual/Spatial, Interpersonal**

Content Background Knowledge

Place Names The U.S. Board on Geographic Names uses a unique decision-making process for choosing place names or geographic nomenclature on Antarctica. No one country owns Antarctica, although some countries have made land claims that have gone unrecognized by the United States. The Board's Advisory Committee on Antarctic Names therefore recommends the use of the names of scientists and explorers who have studied the continent to learn more about it to name natural features. As more discoveries are made through research and exploration, new features are in need of being named.

W Writing Skills

Informative/Explanatory Discuss with students the features of a desert and have them suggest adjectives that describe one. *(Samples include:* arid, little precipitation, *and* little vegetation.*)* Then ask students to write an informative paper on the difference between a polar desert such as Antarctica and hot deserts such as the Sahara, Sonoran, and Arabian deserts. Remind students to use specific details, examples, and data and to cite their sources. **BL Verbal/Linguistic, Auditory/Musical**

C Critical Thinking Skills

Drawing Inferences Discuss with students that Antarctica is divided into three regions: West, East, and the Peninsula. Point out West Antarctica on the map on the previous page. **Ask:** **Why is the climate milder in West Antarctica?** *(Possible answers: because of the Transantarctic Mountains to the east, lower elevation, proximity to warmer ocean currents)* Ask students to consider what effect global climate change might have on this area of Antarctica and on the continent as a whole. Have students research the issue and then write a one-page paper in which they make inferences about the possible short-term and long-term effects of global climate change on Antarctica. Tell them to suppost their inferences with facts from their research.
AL BL Verbal/Linguistic

T Technology Skills

Describing Have a volunteer read aloud the text under the heading *Antarctic Discoveries*. Direct students' attention to the images of the differerent kinds of living things that survive in Antarctica. Have small groups of students choose one of the living things described or pictured on the page and research online how it is specifically adapted to this unique environment. Ask groups to write five questions to guide their research and to designate tasks to each person in the group. Tell groups to prepare a multimedia presentation that describes the adaptations of the living thing. After all groups have presented their information, discuss adaptations that are common to all living things in the Antarctic. **Verbal/Linguistic, Naturalist**

Making Connections

Have students compare and contrast the climate where they live to that of Antarctica. Based on what students found out about the living things in the Antarctic environment, ask students to determine if these species could thrive in the students' communities. Have students provide reasonable explanations for their responses.

ANTARCTIC DISCOVERIES

C The frigid temperatures and isolation of Antarctica make sustaining plant and animal life difficult. The majority of animal life is found in the Southern Ocean. All warm-blooded animals in the Antarctic (seals, whales, penguins, etc.) rely on a thick layer of blubber for insulation. Most plant life is concentrated in the milder climate of West Antarctica, particularly the Antarctic Peninsula. There are no trees. Most of the vegetation consists of algae, lichens and mosses.

T

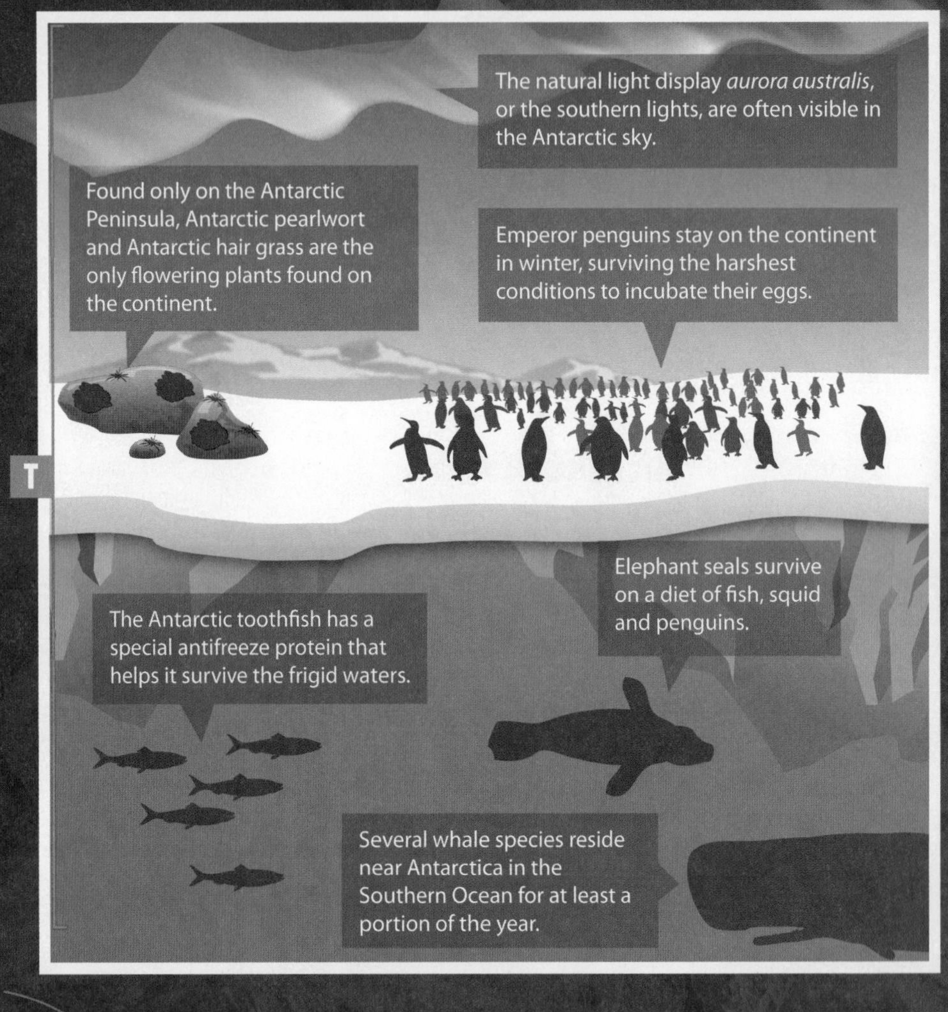

The natural light display *aurora australis*, or the southern lights, are often visible in the Antarctic sky.
Found only on the Antarctic Peninsula, Antarctic pearlwort and Antarctic hair grass are the only flowering plants found on the continent.
Emperor penguins stay on the continent in winter, surviving the harshest conditions to incubate their eggs.
Elephant seals survive on a diet of fish, squid and penguins.
The Antarctic toothfish has a special antifreeze protein that helps it survive the frigid waters.
Several whale species reside near Antarctica in the Southern Ocean for at least a portion of the year.

(bkgrd) rolfo/Flickr Open/Getty Images

822

networks Online Teaching Options

VIDEO

Emperor Penguins

Speculating Show this short video of emperor penguins. After students view the video, ask them to speculate why the penguins huddle in such large groups. Record students' responses and then have volunteers research online to find the answer. Encourage students to find more details about this behavior. Have them report their findings to the class. *(They huddle to escape wind and conserve warmth.)*
AL Verbal/Linguistic

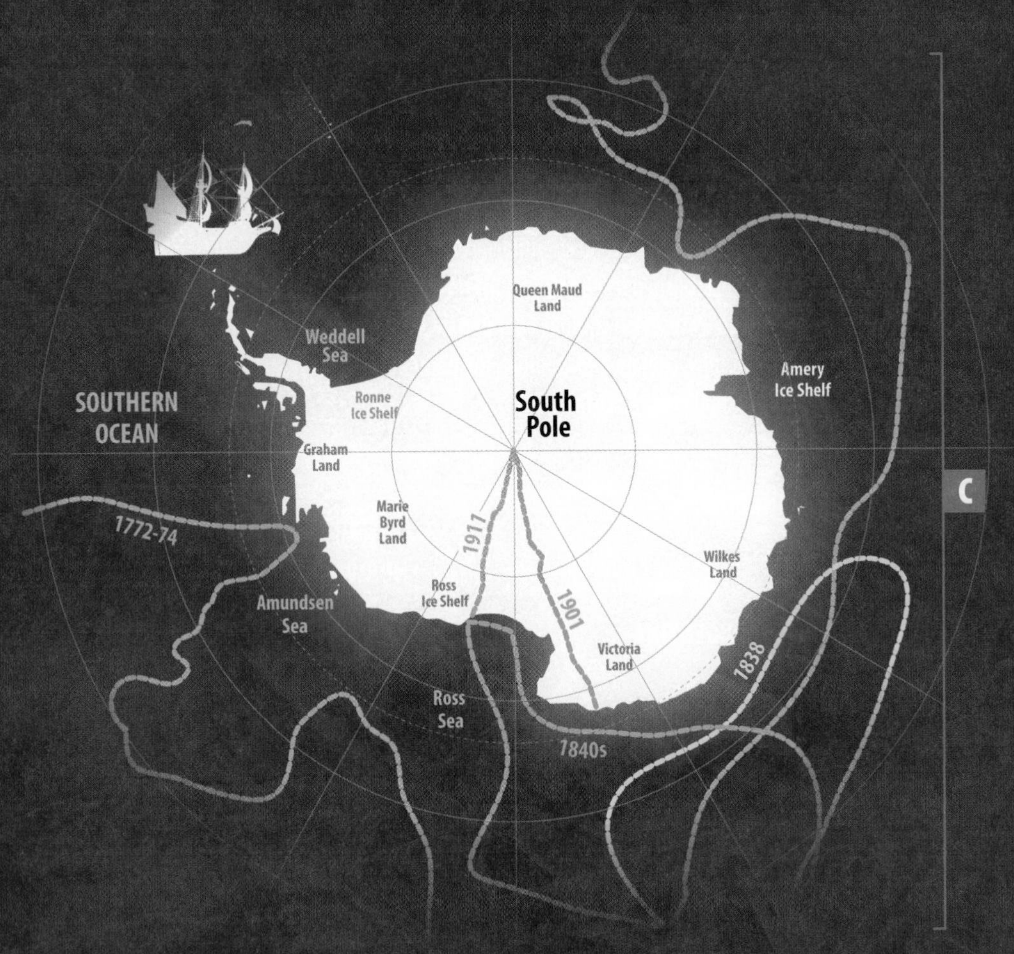

Queen Maud Land

Weddell Sea

Amery Ice Shelf

SOUTHERN OCEAN

Ronne Ice Shelf

South Pole

Graham Land

Marie Byrd Land

1772-74

1911

Wilkes Land

Ross Ice Shelf

1901

Amundsen Sea

Victoria Land

1838

Ross Sea

1840s

TIMELINE OF ANTARCTIC DISCOVERY

James Cook	Charles Wilkes	James Ross	Robert F. Scott	Roald Amundsen
1772-74	1838	1840s	1901	1911
First to cross the Antarctic Circle.	Explored the eastern coast of Antarctica.	Charted much of Antarctica's coastline.	Begins first inland exploration.	First to reach the South Pole.

In the 1770s British captain James Cook became the first person to cross the Antarctic Circle. Cook never saw land, but discoveries were soon made in the early 1800s by scientists, explorers, and whalers. As interest in the new continent grew, several nations and individuals sponsored scientific explorations.

Antarctica **823**

Antarctica: The Land of Ice

C Critical Thinking Skills

Analyzing Ask students to examine the map of routes that different explorers took on and around Antarctica. **Ask: What generalizations can you make about the routes?** *(Possible answer: Most of the explorers that landed on or explored the coast of Antarctica entered the area from the south.)* **Why do you think that most of the routes were in a similar location?** *(Possible answer: Earlier explorers had traveled in that area, so later explorers knew that it was safe to explore.)* Have students arrange desks or tables in the classroom in the shape of the Antarctic continent. Then ask them to take turns walking the route that each explorer took, using the map as a reference. Have students determine which route they would have chosen to take, and why. **Intrapersonal, Kinesthetic**

R Reading Skills

Reading Charts Explain to students that the circumnavigation of Antarctica by James Cook opened up the area to exploration. **Ask: How long after Cook crossed the Antarctic Circle did the first explorer reach the South Pole?** *(about 137 years)* **Why do you think it took so many years for someone to reach the South Pole?** *(Possible answer: Antarctica is a challenging land to approach because of the climate and icy conditions.)* Have students work with a partner and choose an explorer from the chart to find out more about. Have them research the explorer and then create a personal Web page for the explorer that includes biographical information, achievements, a map of places explored, and the explorer's comments on his travels. **AL Visual/Spatial**

W Writing Skills

Argument Ask the class whether countries should be able to have scientific research stations on Antarctica or whether Antarctica should remain untouched by humans. Have students consider the advantages and disadvantages of Antarctic research, including environmental factors. Then instruct students to write an argumentative paper in which they state their opinion in their thesis. Point out that they should use strong supporting details and examples. Guide students to use print and electronic sources for their research. Then consider having a class debate to discuss the points that students made in their papers. **BL Verbal/Linguistic, Naturalist**

GRAPHIC NOVEL

Shackleton's Antarctic Adventure

Describing This graphic novel recounts the trip of Sir Ernest Shackleton, a British explorer, as he set out to Antarctica in 1914. Have students read the novel and then suppose they are a newspaper reporter who is reporting on Shackleton's trip. Tell them to write a short article that includes the 5W + 1H of reporting: who, what, when, where, why, and how. Encourage students to include visuals in their articles such as charts, tables, or sketches. **AL BL Verbal/Linguistic**

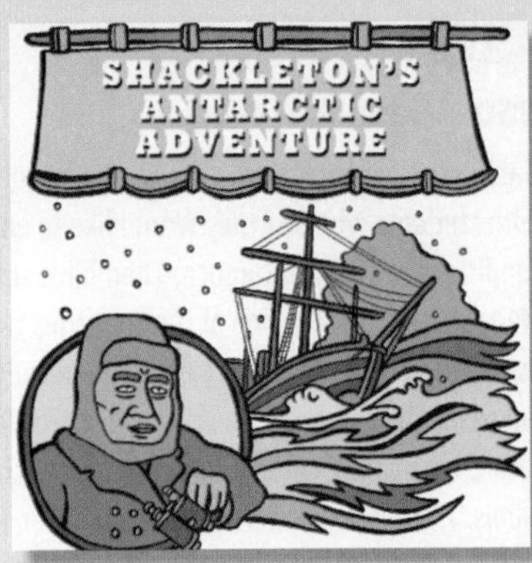

R Reading Skills

Skimming Provide students with this link to the text of the Antarctic Treaty: http://www.nsf.gov/geo/plr/antarct/anttrty.jsp. Have students skim the articles in the document. After students have skimmed the treaty, engage them in a class discussion about the major points of each article. **AL Verbal/Linguistic**

C Critical Thinking Skills

Acquiring Information Explain to students that text and visuals can provide information about a topic in different ways. Allow time for students to read the paragraph and then ask them to study the map. **Ask: What information does the map provide that the text does not?** *(country flags, locations of research stations, names of research stations)* **What information does the text provide that the map does not?** *(information about the treaty and when it was signed, the population on Antarctica in the summer and winter)* Ask students what additional information they want to know about scientific research on Antarctica and the Antarctic Treaty. Instruct them to write two or three questions about these topics and then to conduct research to uncover the answers. Have students share their questions and answers with a group. **AL Visual/Spatial**

W Writing Skills

Narrative Tell students that they have received a six-month assignment to shadow a scientist at McMurdo Station in Antarctica. Ask them to write a narrative describing the experience, such as packing for the trip, traveling, arriving, observing tourists, and other activities. Explain to students that they should write their narratives based on what they have already learned about Antarctica and to make inferences about what they might not know. Remind them that using dialogue can make a narrative more engaging and interesting. Invite students to create their narratives as a travel blog and to take turns reading them to the class. **BL Verbal/Linguistic, Intrapersonal**

Antarctica: the land of ICE

SCIENTIFIC RESEARCH

R As interests grew in Antarctica, countries such as Argentina, Australia, Great Britain, Chile, France, New Zealand and Norway began to lay claim to sections of the continent. In 1959, 12 countries negotiated the Antarctic Treaty to preserve Antarctica for peaceful scientific research and to put all territorial claims on hold. Since then, other countries have established research programs in Antarctica and 26 new countries have signed on. Today, there are around 69 research stations operated by 30 countries that serve as bases for scientists to study physical geography, climate and wildlife. The population of these stations ranges from 4,000 people in the summer to 1,000 people in the winter.

C

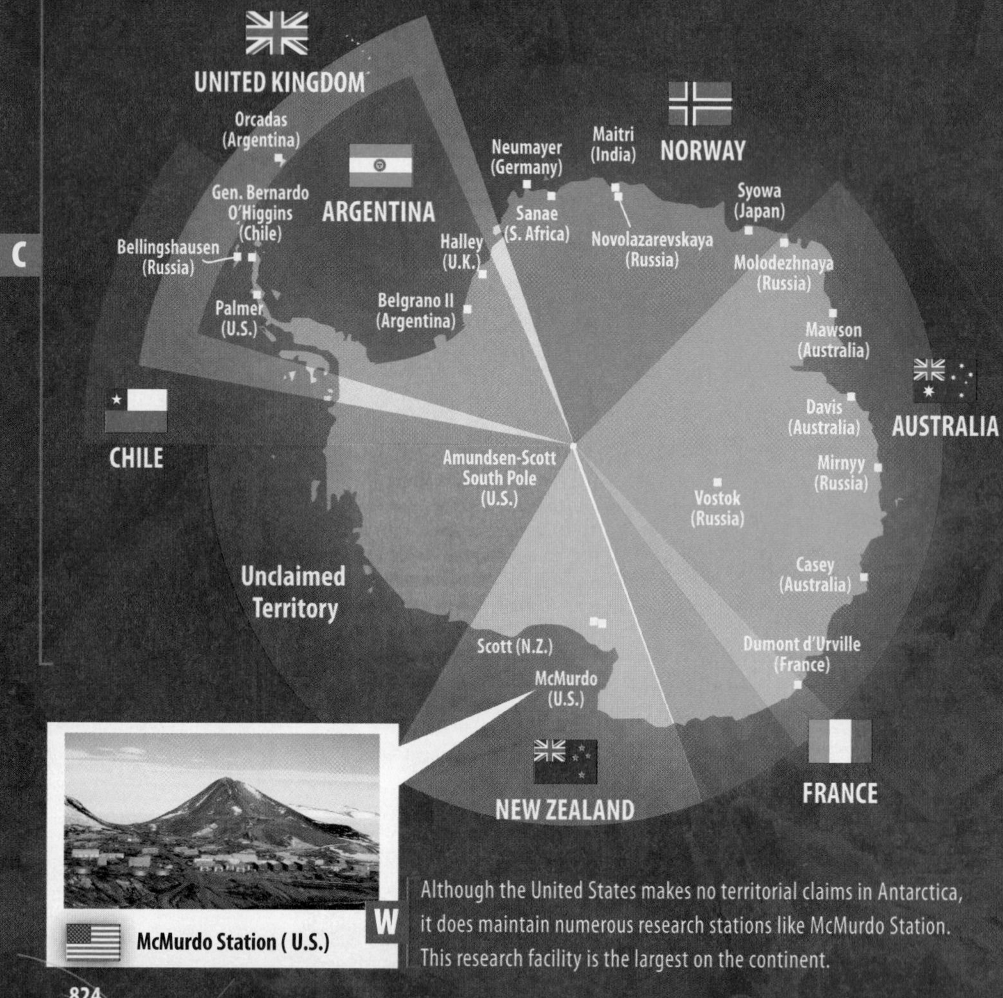

W Although the United States makes no territorial claims in Antarctica, it does maintain numerous research stations like McMurdo Station. This research facility is the largest on the continent.

NHPA/SuperStock; (bkgrd) rolfo/Flickr Open/Getty Images

824

networks Online Teaching Options

IMAGE

360° View: Antarctica

Gathering Information Display the image and discuss with students whether they would like to endure such harsh conditions to study Antarctica. Then have small groups of students each choose one of the countries that have established research centers on Antarctica. Have groups find out what kinds of research their country is doing. Have them record their information on a four-column chart with the labels: *Who? What? Where?* and *Why?* When all groups have completed their charts, use the information to talk about the kinds of knowledge these scientists might gain and how this knowledge might impact the lives of people all over the world. **Verbal/Linguistic, Logical/Mathmatical**

New Frontiers

Because Antarctica's environment remains largely untouched by humans, it is a valuable location for scientific research. Compared to other places on Earth, for example, Antarctica's atmosphere, soil, and water contain little to no trace of pollution. As a result, scientists are able to use samples from Antarctica as a base for analyzing other parts of the world.

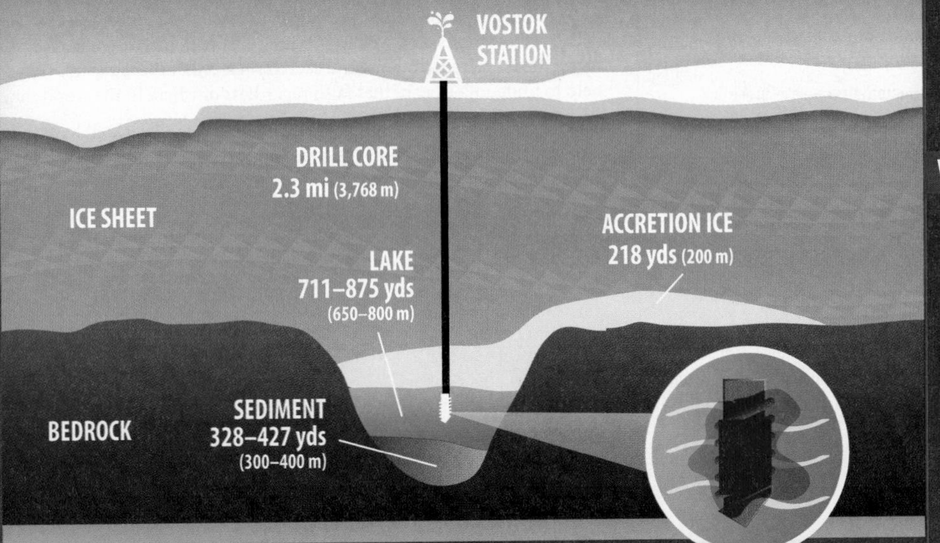

V

Vostok Lake

Lake Vostok, a subglacial lake, was discovered in the early 1970s. In 2012 scientists began probing the lake for study using deep drilling techniques. From this study scientists have found bacteria not known to exist anywhere else on Earth.

Impacts

Some scientists have raised concerns that antifreeze used in Lake Vostok drilling could harm the life forms discovered. Scientists must take great care to preserve Antarctica's pristine environment.

W

Thinking Geographically 

1. ***Analyzing Information*** What characteristics of Antarctica's land and climate make sustaining life difficult?
2. ***Identifying*** What are some common characteristics shared by animal life and plant life found in and around Antarctica?
3. ***Drawing Conclusions*** What potential problems could result from nations' making territorial claims in Antarctica?
4. ***Exploring Issues*** Even though natural resource deposits have been found in Antarctica, many countries have agreed not to mine them. What do you think are the pros and cons of mining in the Antarctic?
5. ***Expository*** Research the type of work being done by scientists at one of the Antarctic stations. How could the work of these scientists impact your life? Write an essay detailing your findings.

Antarctica: The Land of Ice

V Visual Skills

Using Diagrams Ask students to read the paragraph and study the diagram. **Ask:** **Why is pollution so low in Antarctica as compared to other places around the world?** *(Possible answer: Antarctica has no permanent population so human activities that cause pollution, such as burning fossil fuels, seldom happen on the continent.)* **Why is drilling necessary on Antarctica?** *(because there is a thick layer of ice above the sediment and the sediment is underneath bedrock)* Discuss with students the possible effects of drilling on Antarctica. As a class, list pros and pons. **ELL Visual/Spatial**

W Writing Skills

Argument Invite a volunteer to read aloud the text about drilling in Lake Vostok and the impact on the environment. Then revisit the list of pros and cons. Add or modify the list as needed. Ask students to support one side of the argument and to write a 2–3 page argumentative paper that addresses the issue and has a strong argument with supporting reasons. Provide time for students to gather information for their argument. Remind them to address the counter-argument in their papers and to wrap up their argument by restating their thesis in the conclusion. Hold a class debate, with time for rebuttals. **AL Verbal/Linguistic, Kinesthetic**

CLOSE & REFLECT

Predicting Have students make a sketch of Antarctica with annotations about the continent's climate, physical features, wildlife, and human features (research stations). Tell them to also include a time line of important dates in its history. Then ask students to make a prediction about scientific research and tourism on Antarctica in the future and their effects on the environment. Discuss with students the reasoning for their predictions and what solutions that might suggest to maintain the pristine environment on Antarctica.

ANSWERS, p. 825

1. Antarctica's rocky, icy terrain and its cold, arid climate
2. Possible answer: Animals have body fat *(whales, seals)* and/or dense feathers *(penguins)* to keep warm. Plant life is scarce and plants are small and clustered in groups *(mosses, lichens)*.
3. Disputes of ownerships could arise. States that have territorial claims could close research stations that don't belong to them or disagree over access to or rights to certain natural resources, possibly leading to war.
4. Possible answers: Pros: new source of natural resources, new jobs, opportunities for research and discovery. Cons: harm to the environment, disputes between states, extraction very dangerous.
5. Student answers may vary but should include a detailed explanation of the work of their selected research station and how that work could impact their life.

IMAGE

Ozone Layer Over Antarctica

Identifying Cause and Effect Ask students what they know about the ozone layer above Earth. Tell students that this image is a false-color view of total ozone layer over Antarctica. The purple and blue colors are where the least ozone is, and the yellows and reds are where there is more ozone. Point out that the ozone layer protects living things on Earth from the sun's harmful rays, and it helps cool some layers of the atmosphere. Discuss with students how a thinning layer of ozone might affect Antarctica and its wildlife.
BL Verbal/Linguistic, Logical/Mathematical

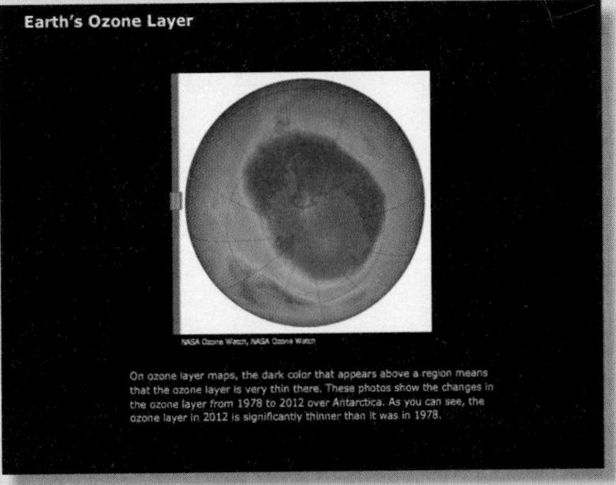

Earth's Ozone Layer
On ozone layer maps, the dark color that appears above a region means that the ozone layer is very thin there. These photos show the changes in the ozone layer from 1978 to 2012 over Antarctica. As you can see, the ozone layer in 2012 is significantly thinner than it was in 1978.

ENGAGE

Before beginning discussion of this feature, write the word *religion* in the center of a web diagram. Ask students to volunteer ideas that they associate with this concept. Record their ideas and return to the diagram after students have read the text to see if they have changed any of their ideas or wish to add more.

TEACH & ASSESS

R Reading Skills

Improving Vocabulary Write these word parts and their definitions on the board: *anima*, "soul"; *a*, "without"; *theo*, "God"; *mono*, "one"; *poly*, "many"; *-ism*, "doctrine" or "set of beliefs." Model for students how to use the meanings of affixes and roots to arrive at the definitions of the terms.
ELL Verbal/Linguistic

V Visual Skills

Collaborative Learning **Ask:** **What information does the map provide about the regions in which the major religions predominate?** *(Answers may include: Christianity predominates in Europe, Russia, and North and South America; Islam is the major faith of northern Africa and Southwest Asia; Hinduism is located mainly in India; Buddhism and Confucianism are located in East Asia; Indigenous religions are practiced mainly in parts of South America, Africa, Australia, and Arctic regions.)* To help students understand the main ideas about each religion, distribute large index cards to pairs of students. Have them label each card with the name of a major religion on the front. Pairs will then use the backs of the cards to summarize important facts about that religion, including its history, beliefs, holy days, and practices. Remind students that when they summarize, they include main ideas and significant details only. Have pairs quiz each other using the information on the cards.
AL Visual/Spatial

World Religions Handbook

TERMS

animism—belief that spirits inhabit natural objects and forces of nature

atheism—disbelief in the existence of any god

monotheism—belief in one God

polytheism—belief in more than one god

secularism—belief that life's questions can be answered apart from religious belief

sect—a subdivision within a religion that has its own distinctive beliefs and/or practices

tenet—a belief, doctrine, or principle believed to be true and held in common by members of a group

A *religion* is a set of beliefs in an ultimate reality and a set of practices used to express those beliefs. Religion is a key component of culture.

Each religion is defined and set apart from other religions by its own special beliefs, celebrations, and worship styles. Most religions also have their own sacred texts, sacred symbols, and sacred sites. All of these aspects of religion help to unite followers of that faith regardless of where in the world they live.

The religions examined in this World Religions Handbook all have these sacred elements, celebrations, and worship styles. Examining these characteristics provides insight into each of these religions.

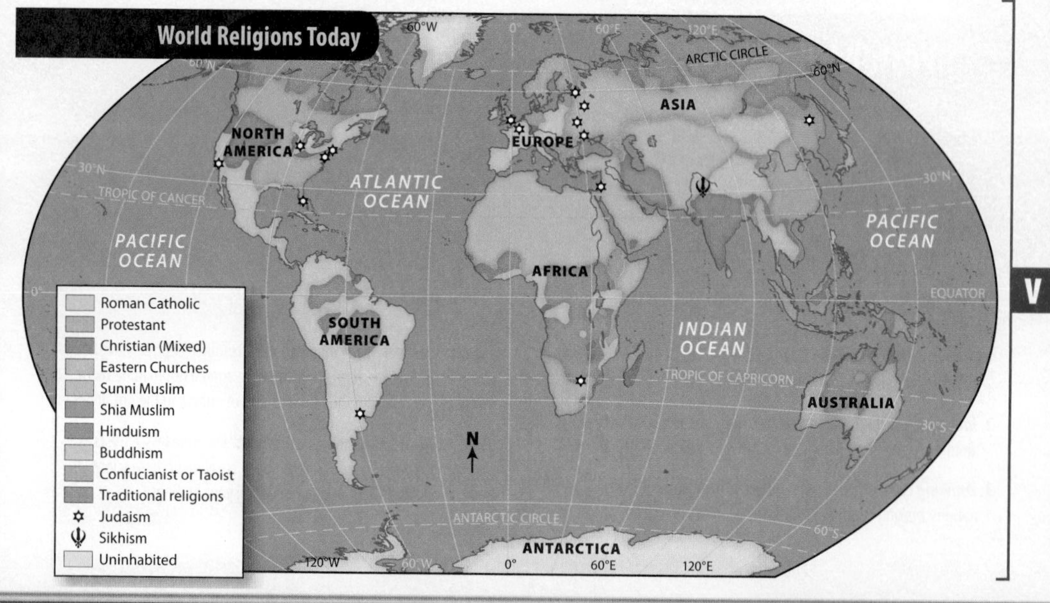

We study religion because it is an important component of culture, shaping how people interact with one another, dress, and eat. It stands at the core of a religious culture.

The diffusion of religion throughout the world has been caused by a variety of factors including migration, missionary work, trade, and war. Buddhism, Christianity, and Islam are the three major religions that spread their beliefs through missionary activities. Religions such as Hinduism, Sikhism, and Judaism are associated with a particular culture group. Followers are usually born into these religions. Sometimes close contact and differences in beliefs have resulted in conflict between religious groups.

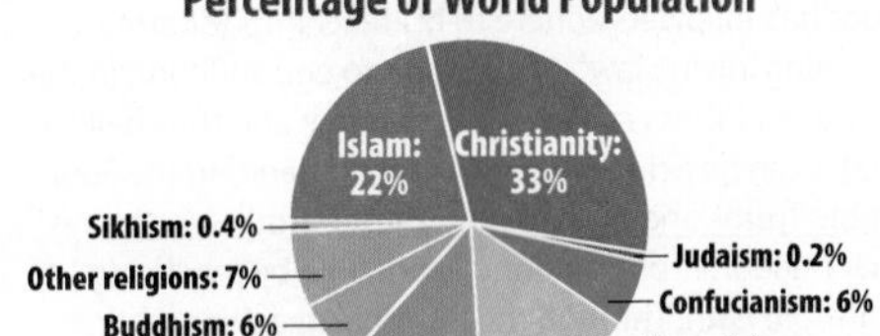

Note: Total exceeds 100% because numbers were rounded.
Sources: www.cia.gov, The World Factbook 2006; www.adherents.com.

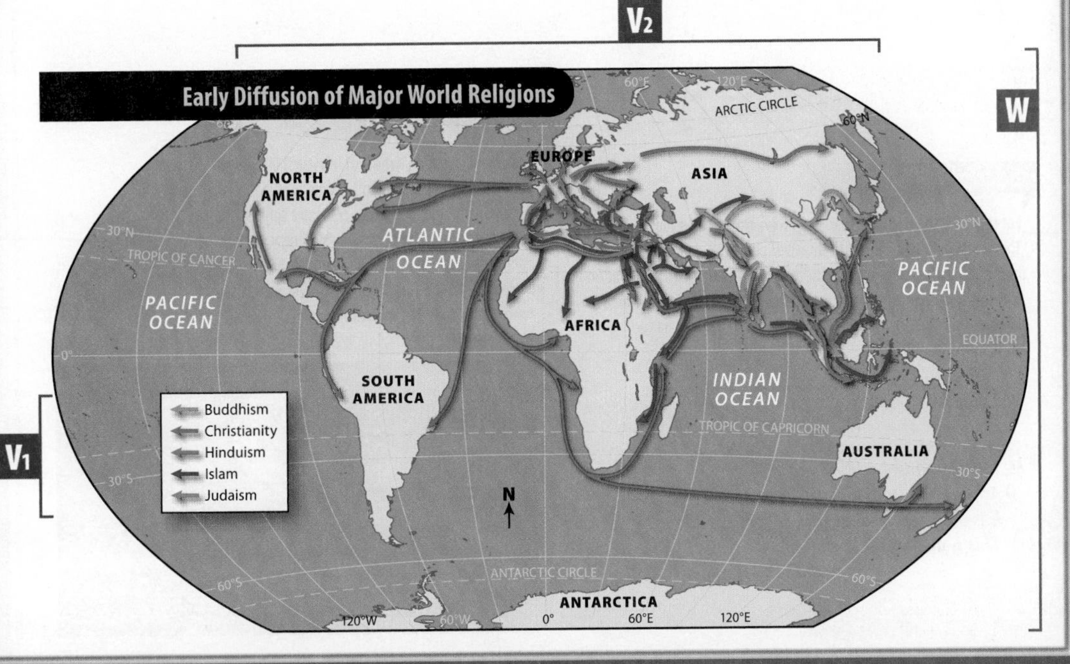

827

W Writing Skills

Creating Guidelines Discuss how important it is to show respect for others' beliefs. Then ask small groups of students to develop guidelines that will enable the class to study world religions in a respectful way. Students' guidelines might include not judging the validity of a religion, attempting to understand the ideas presented, and being receptive to interpretations offered. Have groups contribute their guidelines to a class list, which can be posted in the classroom. **AL** **Interpersonal**

V1 Visual Skills

Analyzing Information Have pairs of students research the actual number of members of each faith and present their data in the form of a bar graph. **BL** **Logical/Mathematical**

V2 Visual Skills

Using Geography Skills Have students trace the routes of each religion. **Ask:** **Where did Judaism mostly spread?** *(Judaism mostly spread in Europe and around the Mediterranean.)*

Content Background Knowledge

Diaspora The word *diaspora* means "dispersal" and also refers to Jews living "in exile" or outside of Israel. The first diaspora occurred in the sixth century B.C. when Babylonians conquered Jerusalem, sending Jews into captivity throughout their empire. Under the Persians, many Jews returned to Jerusalem, only to be exiled under Roman rule following the destruction of the Second Temple in A.D. 70. This time, displaced Jews set up communities in parts of Europe and in other areas around the Mediterranean, preserving the Jewish faith even through repeated persecutions. Although the state of Israel was founded in 1948, not all Jews have chosen to leave "exile." In fact, many believe that they are meant to stay in the lands in which their ancestors settled. As a result, approximately 4 million Jews live in Israel, 4.5 million live in the United States, and 2 million live in Russia, Ukraine, and other former Soviet republics.

R Reading Skills

Inferring Ask: What do Buddhists believe is the cause of humans' unhappiness? *(Possible answer: Grasping after those things that are impermanent—such as money, material possessions. fame—leads to unhappiness.)*

W Writing Skills

Expository Writing Draw students' attention to the Buddha's hands on this statue. Explain that each of his hand positions has a particular significance. Ask students to research the meaning of each gesture and write a short illustrated report based on their findings.

C1 Critical Thinking Skills

Research and Writing Divide the class into small groups, and assign one of the Buddhist sects to each group. Have groups research their sect's geographic concentration as well as its predominant beliefs. Then ask groups to create a symbol for their sect and an annotated key summarizing their information. Have groups take turns placing their symbols and keys on a large world map. **Ask: In what ways were the various sects influenced by the cultures of the areas into which Buddhism spread?** *(As a class, draw some conclusions based on the ideas presented on the map.)* BL

C2 Critical Thinking Skills

Analyzing Information Have students examine the elements of the Eightfold Path. Ask them to explain what each means in their own words, consulting additional resources if necessary. BL

Buddhism

R Siddhartha Gautama, known as the Buddha ("the Awakened") after his enlightenment at the age of 35, was born some 2,500 years ago in what is now Nepal. The Buddha's followers adhere to his teachings (dharma, meaning "divine law"), which aim to end suffering in the world. Buddhists call this goal Nirvana; and they believe that it can be achieved only by understanding the Four Noble Truths and by following the 4th Truth, which says that freedom from suffering is possible by practicing the Eightfold Path. Through the Buddha's teachings, his followers come to know the impermanence of all things and reach the end of ignorance and unhappiness.

Over time, as Buddhism spread throughout Asia, several branches emerged. The largest of these are Theravada Buddhism, the monk-centered Buddhism which is dominant in Sri Lanka, Burma, Thailand, Laos, and Cambodia; and Mahayana, a complex, more liberal variety of Buddhism that has traditionally been dominant in Tibet, Central Asia, Korea, China, and Japan.

C1 W

Statue of the Buddha, Siddhartha Gautama

Sacred Text

For centuries the Buddha's teachings were transmitted orally. For Theravada Buddhists, the authoritative collection of Buddhist texts is the Tripitaka ("three baskets"). These texts were first written on palm leaves in a language called Pali. This excerpt from the *Dhammapada*, a famous text within the Tripitaka, urges responding to hatred with love:

> *"Never in this world is hate*
> *Appeased by hatred.*
> *It is only appeased by love—*
> *This is an eternal law."*
>
> —*Dhammapada 1.5*

Sacred Symbol

C2 The *dharmachakra* ("wheel of the law") is a major Buddhist symbol. Among other things, it signifies the overcoming of obstacles. The eight spokes represent the Eightfold Path—right view, right intention, right speech, right action, right livelihood, right effort, right mindfulness, right concentration—that is central for all Buddhists.

Content Background Knowledge

Sects of Buddhism Tell students that there are several sects of Buddhism. Each sect is strongest in a particular geographical area. For example, Theravada Buddhism, one of the largest sects, is practiced in Sri Lanka, Cambodia, and Thailand, among other places. Other sects include Mahayana, Korean Zen, Nichiren, Pure Land, Tibetan, Zen, and New Kadampa Buddhism.

Sacred Site ▲

Buddhists believe that Siddhartha Gautama achieved enlightenment beneath the Bodhi Tree in Bodh Gayā, India. Today, Buddhists from around the world flock to Bodh Gayā in search of their own spiritual awakening.

(t) Robert Nickelsberg/Getty News Images/Getty Images; (b) Ingolf Pompe/LOOK/Getty Images

Worship and Celebration ▶

The ultimate goal of Buddhists is to achieve Nirvana, the enlightened state in which individuals are free from ignorance, greed, and suffering. Theravada Buddhists believe that monks are most likely to reach Nirvana because of their lifestyle of renunciation, moral virtue, study, and meditation.

829

V Visual Skills

Analyzing Visuals Ask: What does this photograph suggest about ways that Buddhist beliefs are communicated? *(Answers may include that monks are often a source of instruction.)* **Visual/Spatial**

C Critical Thinking Skills

Drawing Conclusions Have students read this passage and study the photograph of the monk. **Ask:** What outward signs show the monk's quest to achieve Nirvana? *(Possible answer: He is meditating, seeking to elevate his thoughts and gain wisdom. His garb is made of plain material, a sign that he has renounced worldly greed.)*

Content Background Knowledge

Meditation Meditation is an essential element of the Buddhist search for enlightenment. It involves intense concentration on an object, a memory, a virtue, or even something unpleasant. In successful meditation, there is gradually a movement away from the perceptions of the outside world to a feeling of pure being—"equanimity" undisturbed by sensation. For Buddhists, this state is only a stepping stone to attainment of wisdom, the true goal of meditation. Once the mind is free of self, it can then seek the truths of life through contemplation of infinity and the nature of reality. Meditation, in various forms, is also practiced by followers of many other religions.

C Critical Thinking Skills

Analyzing Primary Sources **Ask:** What do these images of Jesus show about the way in which he is perceived by Christians? *(Possible answer: His arms are outstretched as if he is welcoming all to come to him. His posture portrays him as accessible.)* AL Visual/Spatial

R Reading Skills

Summarizing **Ask:** Based on this passage, what are important Christian qualities? *(According to this passage, those who suffer on earth will find happiness in heaven. Christians should be meek, righteous, merciful, and pure in heart. They should be peacemakers, and they should be faithful to their religion, no matter what obstacles are put in their way.)*

T Technology Skills

Creating a Biographical Website Tell students that many influential world figures of the twentieth century have been associated with different branches of Christianity. Dr. Martin Luther King, Jr., Pope John Paul II, Mother Teresa, and Archbishop Desmond Tutu are religious leaders who have changed the world through their actions. Ask students to find out more about each of these people by doing research on the Internet. Then have students create their own website with the information they find. They should design the home page and then provide pages for the biographies of each of their subjects. Have students share their website content with the class. **Ask:** How have these individuals influenced others? *(Encourage students to give specific examples to support their responses.)* BL

Christianity

Christianity claims more members than any of the other world religions. It dates its beginning to the death of Jesus in A.D. 33 in what is now Israel. It is based on the belief in one God and on the life and teachings of Jesus. Christians believe that Jesus, who was born a Jew, is the son of God and is fully divine and human. Christians regard Jesus as the Messiah (Christ), or savior, who died for humanity's sins. Christians feel that people are saved and achieve eternal life by faith in Jesus.

The major forms of Christianity are Roman Catholicism, Eastern Orthodoxy, and Protestantism. All three are united in their belief in Jesus as savior, but have developed their own individual theologies.

Stained glass window depicting Jesus

Sacred Text

The Christian Bible is the spiritual text for all Christians and is considered to be inspired by God. This excerpt, from Matthew 5:3-12, is from Jesus' Sermon on the Mount.

> *"Blessed are the poor in spirit, for theirs is the kingdom of heaven.*
> *Blessed are those who mourn, for they shall be comforted.*
> *Blessed are the meek, for they shall inherit the earth.*
> *Blessed are those who hunger and thirst for righteousness, for they shall be satisfied.*
> *Blessed are the merciful, for they shall obtain mercy.*
> *Blessed are the pure in heart, for they shall see God.*
> *Blessed are the peacemakers, for they shall be called sons of God.*
> *Blessed are those who are persecuted for righteousness' sake, for theirs is the kingdom of heaven.*
> *Blessed are you when men revile you and persecute you and utter all kinds of evil against you falsely on my account.*
> *Rejoice and be glad, for your reward is great in heaven, for so men persecuted the prophets who were before you."*

Sacred Symbol

Christians believe that Jesus died for their sins. His death redeemed those who follow his teachings. The statue *Christ the Redeemer,* located in Rio de Janeiro, Brazil, symbolizes this fundamental belief.

Sacred Site

The Gospels affirm that Bethlehem was the birthplace of Jesus. Consequently, it holds great importance to Christians. The Church of the Nativity is located in the heart of Bethlehem. It houses the spot where Christians believe Jesus was born.

R

Worship and Celebration

Christians celebrate many events commemorating the life and death of Jesus. Among the most widely known and observed are Christmas, Good Friday, and Easter. Christmas is often commemorated by attending church services to celebrate the birth of Jesus. As part of the celebration, followers often light candles.

W

W Writing Skills

Expository Writing Tell students that Jesus is often called "the light of the world" by Christians because they believe he saved them from the darkness of sin and death. Have students research other metaphorical expressions used to describe Jesus, and ask them to explain the context of each. BL

R Reading Skills

Illustrating a Branch of Christianity Divide the class into three groups. Assign each group one of the following branches of Christianity: Roman Catholicism, Eastern Orthodoxy, and Protestantism. Have students use their textbooks and additional resources to investigate these aspects of each one: history, beliefs, holy days, rites and rituals. Group members may work individually or together to locate the information and find photographs or illustrations that might be used. Ask groups to put together a poster that presents the essence of their branch of Christianity. Have students display and discuss their posters. **Ask: What central beliefs do the branches of Christianity share? What are some differences among them?** *(Use three-way Venn diagram to record responses.)*

R Reading Skills

Identifying **Ask:** **What are the characteristics of Confucian society?** *(It is hierarchical and ordered. Lower classes show respect to those higher in rank; those of elevated status take care of lower classes.)*

C Critical Thinking Skills

Drawing Conclusions **Ask:** **What does the symbol of the yin-yang reveal about the Confucian view of life's hardships?** *(Possible answer: Dark and difficult events that cause sadness are as much a part of life as bright, happy times. The symbol shows that both are necessary for a complete and balanced life.)*

W Writing Skills

Literature Tell students that through his teaching, Confucius both affirmed traditional values and illuminated new truths. Although Confucianism fell out of favor under the Communist regime in China, in recent years his teachings have been viewed more favorably. To help students better understand the wisdom of Confucius, have them locate copies of the *Analects*, either in the library or on the Internet. Ask students to choose ten or more quotations that they find meaningful. Have students copy the quotations, explain them in their own words, and give examples of how they might be applied today. Encourage students to share their interpretations. **Ask:** **Why might societies and governments still find meaning in the words of Confucius?** *(Answers may include that wisdom endures through the ages. Confucius conveys truth, not just about contemporary situations, but about the human condition.)* BL

Confucianism

R

Confucianism began more than 2,500 years ago in China. Although considered a religion, it is actually a philosophy. It is based upon the teachings of Confucius, which are grounded in ethical behavior and good government.

The teachings of Confucius focused on three areas: social philosophy, political philosophy, and education. Confucius taught that relationships are based on rank. Persons of higher rank are responsible for caring for those of lower rank. Those of lower rank should respect and obey those of higher rank. Eventually his teachings spread from China to other East Asian societies.

Students study Confucianism, Chunghak-dong, South Korea

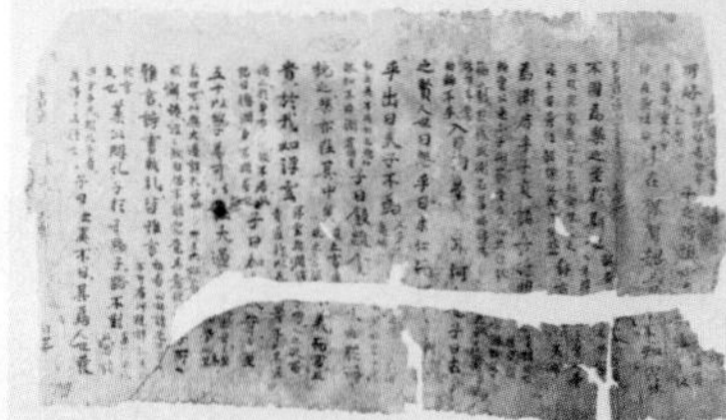

The Analects

C

Sacred Symbol

Yin-yang symbolizes the harmony offered by Confucianism. The light half represents *yang*, the creative, firm, strong elements in all things. The dark half represents *yin*, the receptive, yielding, weak elements. The two act together to balance one another.

W

Sacred Text

Confucius was famous for his sayings and proverbs. These teachings were gathered into a book called the *Analects* (see image above) after Confucius's death. Below is an example of Confucius's teachings:

Confucius said:

> *“To learn and to practice what is learned time and again is pleasure, is it not? To have friends come from afar is happiness, is it not? To be unperturbed when not appreciated by others is gentlemanly, is it not?”*

Confucianism

Sacred Site ▲

The temple at Qufu is a group of buildings dedicated to Confucius. It is located on Confucius's ancestral land. It is one of the largest ancient architectural complexes in China. Every year followers gather at Qufu to celebrate the birthday of Confucius.

C

Worship and Celebration ▸

Confucianism does not have a god or clergy, but there are temples dedicated to Confucius, the spiritual leader. Those who follow his teachings see Confucianism as a way of life and a guide to ethical behavior and good government.

(t) STR/AFP/Getty Images; (b) Photodisc/Getty Images

833

C Critical Thinking Skills

Comparing and Contrasting Have students review what they have learned about Buddhism, Christianity, and Confucianism. **Ask:** **How is Confucianism similar to and different from Christianity and Buddhism?** *(**Similarities:** All three religions advocate striving to live a virtuous life filled with meaning; in all three, there is an individual who is the source of wisdom and the model for followers; all three have sites of worship or places to gather. **Differences:** Confucianism does not focus on an afterlife; Confucianism grew out of secular concerns.)*

R1 Reading Skills

Improving Vocabulary Write these three terms on the board: *Brahma, Brahman, Brahmin*. Tell students that *Brahma* is the Hindu divinity of creation. Brahma is not worshipped as the other Hindu divinities are because it is believed that his work is done. *Brahman* is the world's soul, the universal and eternal presence in all creation. *Brahmin* refers to the upper caste in society. Hindu priests are Brahmins. ELL

C Critical Thinking Skills

Making Inferences **Ask:** **What kind of life would one have to lead in order to be reborn into a higher form or caste?** *(A person would have to lead a life of good actions in order to move to a higher position.)*

R2 Reading Skills

Reading Primary Sources **Ask:** **What happens once a soul reaches Brahman?** *(This is the end of the journey, the end of reincarnation.)*

V Visual Skills

Interpreting Art **Ask:** **Who are the three principal Hindu divinities?** *(Brahma, Vishnu, and Shiva)* Point out the image of the statue of Vishnu on this page. Tell students that in Hindu art, divinities are often portrayed in a way that shows their nature and powers. For example, Vishnu is usually shown in human form and is painted blue, a color associated with infinity. This is because he is a preserver and protector of humankind. Have students locate other images of Vishnu or find art representing Brahma or Shiva, their consorts, or other Hindu divinities. Ask students to find out more about why each divinity is pictured in a certain way or what the symbols associated with him or her mean. Have students collaborate on a gallery of images for the classroom that includes a written analysis of each image. Have students discuss what they learned about the Hindu divinities from their research. AL **Visual/Spatial**

Hinduism

R1 Hinduism is the oldest of the world's major living religions. It developed among the cultures in India as they spread out over the plains and forests of the subcontinent. It has no single founder or founding date. Hinduism is complex; it has numerous sects and many different practices among its followers. Most Hindus believe in one god, whose qualities are represented by various divinities. Among the more famous Hindu divinities are Brahma, Vishnu, and Shiva, who represent respectively the creative, sustaining, and destructive forces in the universe. Major Hindu beliefs are reincarnation, karma, and dharma.

C Hindus believe the universe contains several heavens and hells. According to the concept of rebirth or reincarnation, which is central to their beliefs, souls are continually reborn. In what form one is reborn is determined by the good and evil actions performed in his or her past lives. Those acts are karma. A soul continues in the cycle of rebirth until release is achieved.

V 

Statue of Vishnu

Sacred Text

The Vedas consist of hymns, prayers, and speculations composed in ancient Sanskrit. They are the oldest religious texts in an Indo-European language. The Rig Veda, Sama Veda, Yajur Veda, and Atharva Veda are the four great Vedic collections. Together, they make up one of the most significant and authoritative Hindu religious texts.

R2
> *“Now, whether they perform a cremation for such a person or not,*
> *people like him pass into the flame,*
> *from the flame into the day,*
> *from the day into the fortnight of the waxing moon,*
> *from the fortnight of the waxing moon into the six months when the sun moves north,*
> *from these months into the year, from the year into the sun,*
> *from the sun into the moon, and from the moon into the lightning.*
> *Then a person who is not human—he leads them to Brahman.*
> *This is the path to the gods, the path to Brahman.*
> *Those who proceed along this path do not return to this human condition.”*
> —The Chandogya Upanishad 4:15.5

Sacred Symbol

One important symbol of Hinduism is actually a symbol for a sound. "Om" is a sound that Hindus often chant during prayer, mantras, and rituals.

834

Sacred Site

Hindus believe that when a person dies his or her soul is reborn. This is known as reincarnation. Many Hindus bathe in the Ganges and other sacred rivers to purify their soul and to be released from rebirth.

W

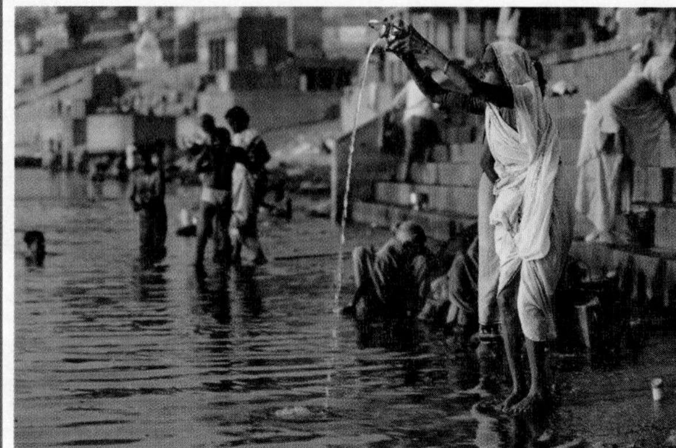

Worship and Celebration

Holi is a significant North Indian Hindu festival celebrating the triumph of good over evil. As part of the celebration, men, women, and children splash colored powders and water on each other. In addition to its religious significance, Holi also celebrates the beginning of spring.

C

(t) Mark Downey/Getty Images; (b) Poras Chaudhary/The Image Bank/Getty Images

835

W Writing Skills

Expository Writing Have students find out more about the concept of reincarnation and its influences on the lives of the Hindus. Ask students to write a report detailing what they learn.

Content Background Knowledge

Funeral Rituals Cremation is an important part of the funeral rituals for a Hindu. The body is burned, usually on the same day as death occurs, to release the soul so that it can continue to its next life. The ashes are then scattered over water, preferably the River Ganges, a sacred site.

C Critical Thinking Skills

Presenting a Holi Legend Tell students that one of the stories connected with the Holi festival is the legend of Prahalad (or Prahlada) and Holika. Distribute copies of the story to students and then ask them to work in groups to plan a Readers' Theater presentation of it. They may choose to read the original story aloud with group members taking parts, to rewrite it in their own words, or to choose excerpts and create a narrator's role to fill in missing details. Have students rehearse their parts and then take turns presenting. **Ask: Why is this legend important to the Holi festival?** *(The legend shows that good will prevail over evil, when the virtuous son Prahalad, who is devoted to Vishnu, is saved from death and rewarded by being allowed to rule in his evil father's place. The festival celebrates this triumph of good over evil.)* **AL** **Interpersonal**

R Reading Skills

Activating Prior Knowledge **Ask:** **What were the major ways in which Islam spread through Asia and Africa?** *(The Muslims conquered surrounding territories, creating an Islamic Empire, in which people were encouraged to convert. Islam also spread through trade.)*

Content Background Knowledge

Salat Muslim prayers performed five times daily are called *salat*. Muslims pray at dawn, midday, the late part of the afternoon, after sunset, and before midnight. Traditionally the muezzin called the faithful to prayer from the minaret. Today, modern technology makes it possible for believers to have a service page, text, or email them as a reminder of prayer times.

C Critical Thinking Skills

Researching Holy Places Tell students that Judaism, Christianity, and Islam all have different holy places in Jerusalem. For Jews, it is the Western Wall, for Christians, the Church of the Holy Sepulchre, and for Muslims, the Dome of the Rock. Organize the class into three groups, and assign each group to report on one of these holy places, using credible websites for references. Ask students to provide a diagram of the city of Jerusalem and show the location of their assigned holy place. Encourage students to show drawings or copies of photographs as well. Have students present their reports and maps. **Ask:** **Why is it significant that these sites are all in the same city?** *(Accept all reasonable answers.)*

Islam

Followers of Islam, known as Muslims, believe in one God, whom they call Allah. The word *Allah* is Arabic for "god." The founder of Islam, Muhammad, began his teachings in Makkah (Mecca) in A.D. 610. Eventually the religion spread throughout much of Asia, including parts of India to the borders of China, and a substantial portion of Africa. According to Muslims, the Quran, their holy book, contains the direct word of God, revealed to their prophet Muhammad sometime between A.D. 610 and A.D. 632. Muslims believe that God created nature and without his intervention, there would be nothingness. God serves four functions: creation, sustenance, guidance, and judgment.

Central to Islamic beliefs are the Five Pillars. These are affirmation of the belief in Allah and Muhammad as his prophet; group prayer; tithing, or the giving of money to charity; fasting during Ramadan; and a pilgrimage to Makkah once in a lifetime if physically and financially able. Within Islam, there are two main branches, the Sunni and the Shia. The differences between the two center on a criterion for legitimate Muslim rule. The Shia believed that the rulers should descend from Muhammad. The Sunni believed that the rulers need only be followers of Muhammad. Most Muslims are Sunni.

The Dome of the Rock, Jerusalem

The Quran

Sacred Text

The sacred text of Islam is the Quran. Preferably, it is written and read only in Arabic, but translations have been made into many languages. The excerpt below is a verse repeated by all Muslims during their five daily prayers.

> *"In the Name of Allah, the Compassionate,*
> *the Merciful,*
> *Praise be to Allah, the Lord of the World,*
> *The Compassionate, the Merciful,*
> *Master of the Day of Judgment,*
> *Only You do we worship, and only You*
> *Do we implore for help.*
> *Lead us to the right path,*
> *The path of those you have favored*
> *Not those who have incurred*
> *Your wrath or*
> *Have gone astray."*
>
> —The Quran

Sacred Symbol

Islam is often symbolized by the crescent moon. It is an important part of Muslim rituals, which are based on the lunar calendar.

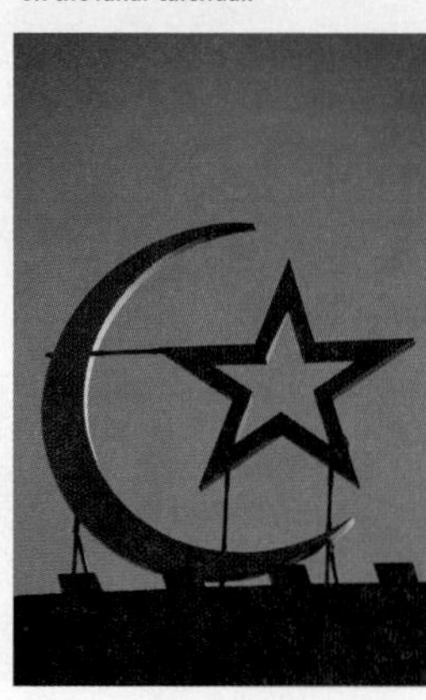

836

Sacred Site

W Makkah is a sacred site for all Muslims. One of the Five Pillars of Islam states that all who are physically and financially able must make a hajj, or pilgrimage, to the holy city once in their life. Practicing Muslims are also required to pray facing Makkah five times a day.

Worship and Celebration

R Ramadan is a month-long celebration commemorating the time during which Muhammad received the Quran from Allah. It is customary for Muslims to fast from dawn until sunset all month long. Muslims believe that fasting helps followers focus on spiritual rather than bodily matters and creates empathy for one's fellow men and women. Ramadan ends with a feast known as Eid-al-Fitr, or Feast of the Fast.

W Writing Skills

Expository Writing Tell students that pilgrims making their hajj must observe certain guidelines that dictate clothing, behavior, and attitude. Have students find out more about these requirements and write a short pamphlet explaining them.

R Reading Skills

Reading Comprehension Tell students that in addition to imposing periods of fasting, certain religions dictate or discourage the consumption of different types of foods. For example, many Hindus shun meat, because they believe that animals have a spiritual awareness. Have small groups of students investigate the dietary restrictions or requirements of one of these religions: Christianity, Islam, Judaism, Hinduism, or Buddhism. Ask students to explain the reasoning behind the rules and present their information on an overheard transparency or other format that is easy to read.

Content Background Knowledge

Holy Days Two important holy days in the Muslim calendar are the end of Ramadan, Eid-al-Fitr, or 'Id al-Fitr, and the 'Id al-Adha which comes at the end of the hajj. Other special days include the "Night of Power," during which it is believed that Allah decides the destiny of people and the world for the coming year, and the day commemorating the ascension of Muhammad into heaven. Ashura, another Muslim holiday, has added meaning for Shia Muslims, who celebrate it as the day that Hussein, Muhammad's grandson, was martyred. Many Muslims also mark the death days of saints through ceremonies called 'urs, which acknowledge the passing of these members of the community into the highest level of their spiritual lives.

R1 Reading Skills

Questioning Have students refer back to the section on Christianity. **Ask:** **Unlike Christians, how do Jews view Jesus?** *(Possible answer: They do not see Jesus as the messiah and they are still waiting for the savior.)*

C Critical Thinking Skills

Determining Causes and Effect **Ask:** **Generally, why might divisions within religions occur?** *(Answers may include that there could be differences of opinion over the interpretation or implementation of doctrine, or disputes over leadership.)*

R2 Reading Skills

Reading Primary Sources **Ask:** **What defining characteristic of Judaism does this quotation affirm?** *(Judaism is monotheistic.)*

V Visual Skills

Making a Time Line of Jewish History Have students recall what they know about Jewish history. Record their ideas on the board. Then assign small groups a period of time from 1000 B.C. to the present. Have students research the history of the Jews during their assigned years and develop an annotated time line that briefly summarizes the significance of each major event. Tell students to include any events from the list on the board that fit into their time period. Then have groups collaborate to put together their time lines. **Ask:** **What events might be considered turning points in Jewish history? Why?** *(Accept all reasonable answers.)*

Judaism

R1 Judaism is a monotheistic religion. In fact, Judaism was the first major religion to believe in one God. Jews trace their national and religious origins back to God's call to Abraham and the revelation of the Torah to Moses at Mount Sinai. Jews believe that they have a covenant with God, who expects them to pursue justice and live ethical lives and will one day usher in a new era of universal peace.

C Over time Judaism has separated into branches, including Orthodox, Reform, Conservative, and Reconstructionist. Orthodox Jews are the most traditional of all the branches.

El Ghriba Synagogue, Jerba, Tunisia

The Torah scroll

Sacred Text

The Torah is the five books of Moses, which tell the story of the origins of the Jews and explain Jewish laws. The remainder of the Hebrew Bible contains the writings of the prophets, Psalms, and ethical and historical works.

R2

> *"I am the Lord your God, who brought you out of the land of Egypt, out of the house of slavery; you shall have no other gods before me."*
>
> —Exodus 20:2

Sacred Symbol

V The menorah is used in the celebration of Hanukkah, commemorating the rededication of the Temple of Jerusalem following the Maccabees' victory over the Syrian Greeks.

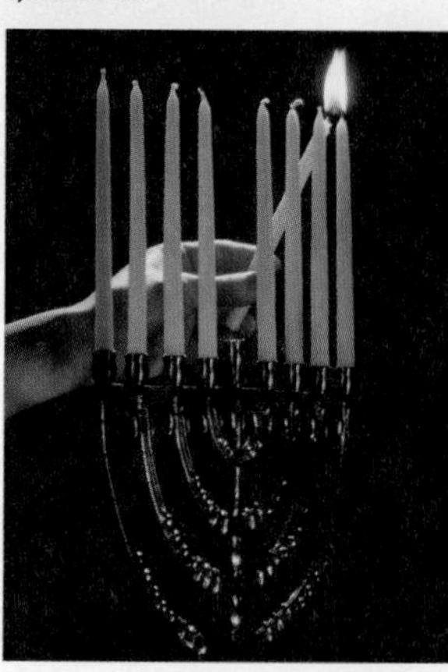

Sacred Site

The Western Wall is what remains of the structure surrounding the Second Jerusalem Temple, built after the Jews' return from the Babylonian captivity. It is considered a sacred spot in Jewish religious tradition. Prayers are offered at the wall morning, afternoon, and evening.

Worship and Celebration

The day-long Yom Kippur service ends with the blowing of the ram's horn (shofar). Yom Kippur is the holiest day in the Jewish calendar. During Yom Kippur, Jews do not eat or drink for 25 hours. The purpose is to reflect on the past year, repent for one's sins, and gain forgiveness from God. It falls in September or October, ten days after Rosh Hashanah, the Jewish New Year.

R Reading Skills

Activating Prior Knowledge Ask: **Who built the First Temple, which was destroyed by the Babylonians?** *(Solomon)* BL

Content Background Knowledge

The Wailing Wall The Western Wall became known as the Wailing Wall, because of the practice of Jews to pray at the wall loudly and sadly for the restoration of the Temple. Visitors today often write their petitions on small pieces of paper and place them in the cracks of the wall.

C Critical Thinking Skills

Making Inferences Ask: **Why might Yom Kippur occur so soon after Rosh Hashanah?** *(Possible answer: The beginning of the New Year is a good time to reflect on the past and make a fresh start.)*

T Technology Skills

Searching a Database for Articles Discuss with students how religious, cultural, and national identities are often intertwined, as is the case with Judaism and the state of Israel. Have students name other places where these three identities have merged. *(Possible examples include Saudi Arabia and Iran.)* **Ask:** **What are some problems inherent in the association of a particular religion with a political entity?** *(Answers may include that it can lead to political strife with other nations or internally, oppression of minority or religious or cultural groups by the majority sect, or possibly discrimination.)* Assign students to use a database to find recent articles about local, national, or international events in which religion has played a part. Have students collect these articles and report on what they learn in class.

C Critical Thinking Skills

Comparing and Contrasting Ask: How are Nanak's and Muhammad's roles in the religions similar? *(Both received the word of God and founded a new religion.)*

R Reading Skills

Inferring Ask: Why might Indians be attracted to Sikhism? *(The Sikh religion disregards the caste system and rejects discrimination of all kinds.)*

V Visual Skills

Analyzing Primary Sources Ask: What is the importance of symbols in religions? *(Answers may include that they function as an outward sign of believers' faith or a reminder to followers of important events, the origins, or the founder of the religion. In the past, they may have been used to communicate ideas to the faithful who could not read.)* Have students choose one of the religions that they have read about on these pages. Ask them to research the major symbols associated with that faith. Then have them create a collage that displays the symbols. Encourage students to incorporate original art with found or copied images. Have students also develop a brief explanation of the symbols' significance. Display students' collages around the classroom. Visual/Spatial

Sikhism

C Sikhism emerged in the mid-1500s in the Punjab, in northwest India, rising from the religious experience and teachings of Guru Nanak. The religion exhibits influences from Islam and Hinduism, but it is distinct from both. Sikh traditions teach that Nanak encountered God directly and was commissioned by Him to be His servant.

R Sikhs ("students, disciples") believe in one almighty god who is formless and without qualities (*nirguna*) but can be known through meditation and heard directly. Sikhism forbids discrimination on the basis of class, color, religion, caste, or gender. While over 80 percent of the world's 23 million Sikhs live in the Punjab, Sikhism has spread widely as many Sikhs have migrated to new homes around the world.

Guru Nanak

Sikh men often wear long beards and cover their heads with turbans.

Sacred Text

The great authoritative sacred text for Sikhs is the Adi Granth ("Principal Book," also known as the Guru Granth Sahib). Compiled from the mid-1500s through the 1600s, it includes contributions from Sikh gurus and from some persons also claimed as saints by Hindus and Muslims, such as Namdev, Ravidas, and Kabir.

> *" Enshrine the Lord's Name within your heart. The Word of the Guru's Bani prevails throughout the world, through this Bani, the Lord's name is obtained. "*
> —Guru Amar Das, page 1066

Sacred Symbol

V The sacred symbol of the Sikhs is the *khanda*. It is composed of four traditional Sikh weapons: the *khanda* or double-edged sword (in the center), from which the symbol takes its name; the *cakkar* (disk), and two curved daggers (*kirpan*) representing temporal and spiritual power, respectively Piri and Miri.

Sacred Site

Amritsar is the spiritual capital of Sikhism. The Golden Temple (*Harimandir Sahib*) in Amritsar is the most sacred of Sikh shrines.

Worship and Celebration

C2 Vaisakhi is a significant Punjabi and Sikh festival in April celebrating the new year and the beginning of the harvest season. Celebrations often take place along riverbanks with participants dancing and wearing brightly colored clothes.

C1

841

C1 Critical Thinking Skills

Research and Analysis Divide students into groups of three. Have each member research one of these aspects of Sikhism: history, beliefs, or holy days. Then have group members create a brief lesson plan and present what they learned to each other. Interpersonal

C2 Critical Thinking Skills

Comparing and Contrasting Ask: How is the use of water images or symbols the same and different among the various religions? *(Accept all reasonable answers.)* AL

Content Background Knowledge

The Khalsa One of the rites of passage for a Sikh is to be initiated into the Khalsa, the community of Sikh believers. Originally, the Khalsa was an order of the purest and most loyal Sikhs established by the Guru Gobind Singh at the end of the seventeenth century. The original five members were willing to sacrifice their lives for him. Today, Sikhs show their membership in the Khalsa by wearing the "Five K's." The first is *kesh*, or uncut hair. The Khalsa Sikhs are forbidden to cut their hair, because it is part of God's creation. They also wear a *kara*, or steel bracelet. This symbolizes that they are linked to the Guru. They carry a *kanga*, or wooden comb to show that they care about a clean mind and body. They wear *kachha*, short trousers that now function as underwear and a symbol of chastity. The final *K* is the *kirpan*, or ceremonial sword, which represents defense of the weak and the struggle against injustice.

Indigenous Religions

R Reading Skills

Making Connections Discuss the possible connections between animism and geography. Ask students to consider how animist rituals might differ in various types of climates or geographic areas.

G1 Critical Thinking Skills

Identifying Central Issues Ask: **What is the purpose of rites and ceremonies in religions?** *(Possible answers: Rites and ceremonies honor the god or gods of the people; they mark special days in the religious calendar; they may be used to help interpret the will of the gods or win their favor; they bring the people closer to their gods and strengthen their beliefs; they help to preserve religious traditions.)* AL

C2 Critical Thinking Skills

Describing an African Religion Divide students into small groups and ask them to find out more about one of the indigenous religions practiced in Africa. They might research the beliefs of the Kikuyu in Kenya, the Rwandans, the Yoruba in southwestern Nigeria, or the Masai in Tanzania, for example. Have students look for information about their gods, their rites and rituals, and the way their religion influences their daily lives and relationships with others. Ask group members to prepare and give an oral presentation including the use of visual aids. **Ask:** **What is the role of local religions in Africans' lives? How does this role differ from the way a formalized religion is perceived by its followers?** *(Students should make generalizations and support them using facts from the presentations.)*

Indigenous Religions

There are many varieties of religious belief that are limited to particular ethnic groups. These local religions are found in Africa as well as isolated parts of Japan, Australia, and the Americas.

Most local religions reflect a close relationship with the environment. Some groups teach that people are a part of nature, not separate from it. Animism is characteristic of many indigenous religions. Natural features are sacred, and stories about how nature came to be are an important part of religious heritage. Although many of these stories have been written down in modern times, they were originally transmitted orally.

Africa The continent of Africa is home to a variety of local religions. Despite their differences, most African religions recognize the existence of one creator in addition to spirits that inhabit all aspects of life. Religious ceremonies are often celebrated with music and dance.

These Turkana men from Kenya are performing a traditional jumping dance.

Rituals are an important part of African religions. These Masai boys are wearing ceremonial dress as part of a ritual.

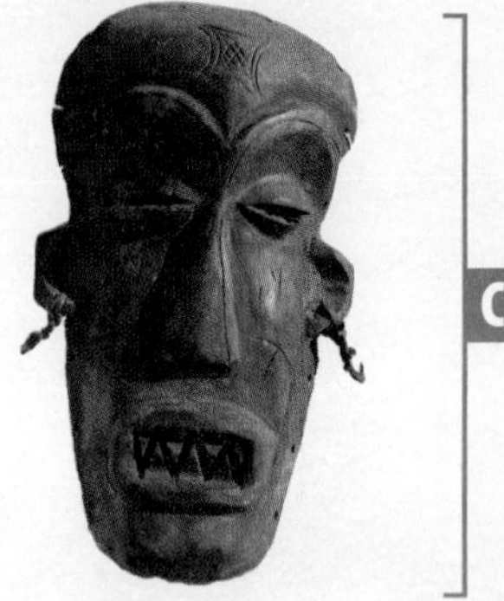

Masks are a component of ritual and ceremony in many African religions.

Japan Shinto, founded in Japan, is the largest indigenous religion. It dates back to prehistoric times and has no formal doctrine. The gods are known as kami. Ancestors are also revered and worshiped. Its four million followers often practice Buddhism in addition to practicing Shinto.

This Shinto priest is presiding over a ritual at a Japanese temple. These priests often live on shrine grounds.

Shinto shrines, like this one, are usually built in places of great natural beauty to emphasize the relationship between people and nature.

G1

Australia The Australian Aboriginal religion has no deities. It is based upon a belief known as the Dreaming, or Dreamtime. Followers believe that ancestors sprang from the Earth and created all people, plant, and animal life. They also believe that these ancestors continue to control the natural world.

These Aborigine women are blessing a newborn with smoke during a traditional ritual intended to ensure the child's health and good fortune.

Aborigines, like these young girls, often paint their faces with the symbols of their clan or family group.

C2

G1 Critical Thinking Skills

Drawing Conclusions Ask: **What does the ability of Shinto followers to also practice Buddhism possibly suggest about the Shinto religion?** *(It is a way of life more than an organized set of beliefs.)*

C2 Critical Thinking Skills

Comparing and Contrasting Ask: **In what way are the Shinto and Aborigine religions similar?** *(Both revere ancestors.)*

Content Background Knowledge

Kami The concept of kami in the Shinto religion is complex. They are deities and can also be natural objects, such as plants, rocks, or fish, and forces of nature, such as storms and earthquakes. The souls of outstanding human beings (after they die) may become kami. Kami is both the universal spiritual essence of everything and the particular object or element that manifests that being. In other words, the kami may be the spirit of the tree, or it may be the tree itself. According to Shinto tradition, there are "800 myriads of kami" or "eight million million."

Indigenous Religions

R Reading Skills

Determining Importance **Ask:** **What do the traditions of Native American religions reveal about the lives of Native Americans?** *(They live close to nature and depend on it for their well-being and survival; they understand the cycle of life and celebrate each stage.)*

V Visual Skills

Analyzing Visuals **Ask:** **What can you learn about the Native American cultures from the style and material of their dress?** *(Answers may include that the feathers and dyes used show the kinds of flora and fauna native to the regions in which the groups live. Also, bright colors are valued. Native Americans are skilled artisans, able to sew intricate patterns with beads and shells.)*

C Critical Thinking Skills

Creating Art Tell students that the Native Americans of the Northwest were renowned for their totem poles, carved from huge cedar trees. Some poles told the history of the family using symbolic images. Have students find out more about heraldic totem poles, their design, and their function. Have students design a totem pole of their own on paper. Have them choose symbols and animals from their environment and arrange them according to what they have learned from their sources. Have students display their totem pole designs for the class. **Ask:** **What function did the animal images serve on the Northwest peoples' totem poles?** *(Animals depicted on the totem poles were the protectors of the family, gave them special gifts, or were significant in other ways.)*

CLOSE & REFLECT

Identifying Have students identify some of the features of worship described on these pages. Ask them to describe the worship and celebrations of clergy and laypeople.

Indigenous Religions

Native Americans The beliefs of most Native Americans center on the spirit world; however, the rituals and practices of individual groups vary. Most Native Americans believe in a Great Spirit who, along with other spirits, influences all aspects of life. These spirits make their presence known primarily through acts of nature.

R The rituals, prayers, and ceremonies of Native Americans are often centered on health and good harvest and hunting. Rituals used to mark the passage through stages of life, including birth, adulthood, and death, are passed down as tribal traditions. Religious ceremonies often focus on important points in the agricultural and hunting seasons. Prayers, which are offered in song and dance, also concentrate on agriculture and hunting themes as well as health and well-being.

Rituals are passed down from generation to generation. These Native Americans are performing a ritual dance.

V

There are many different Native American groups throughout the United States and Canada. This Pawnee is wearing traditional dress during a celebration in Oklahoma.

Totem poles, like this one in Alaska, were popular among the Native American peoples of the Northwest Coast. They were often decorated with mythical beings, family crests, or other figures. They were placed outside homes.

C

Assessment

Reviewing Vocabulary

Match the following terms with their definitions.

1. sect — a. belief that spirits inhabit natural objects and forces of nature
2. monotheism — b. belief in one God
3. polytheism — c. a subdivision within a religion that has its own distinctive belief and/or practices
4. animism — d. belief in more than one god
5. atheism — e. disbelief in the existence of any god

Reviewing the Main Ideas

World Religions

6. Which religion has the most followers worldwide?
7. On a separate sheet of paper, make a table of the major world religions. Use the chart below to get you started.

Name	Founder	Geographic distribution	Sacred sites
Buddhism			
Christianity			
Confucianism			
Hinduism			
Islam			
Judaism			
Sikhism			
Indigenous			

Buddhism

8. According to Buddhism, how can the end of suffering in the world be achieved?
9. What is Nirvana? According to Buddhists, who is most likely to achieve Nirvana and why?

Christianity

10. In what religion was Jesus raised?
11. Why do Christians regard Jesus as their savior?

Confucianism

12. What is Confucianism based on?
13. What does yin-yang symbolize?

Hinduism

14. Where did Hinduism develop?
15. What role do Hindus believe karma plays in reincarnation?

Islam

16. What are the two branches of Islam? What is the main difference between the two groups?
17. What role does Makkah play in the Islamic faith?

Judaism

18. What is the Torah?
19. What is the purpose of Yom Kippur?

Sikhism

20. Where do most Sikhs live? Why?
21. What religions have contributed to the Adi Granth?

Indigenous Religions

22. Why would local religions feature sacred stories about the creation of people, animals, and plant life?
23. Which of the indigenous religions has the largest membership?

Problem-Solving Activity

24. **Research Project** Use library and Internet sources to research the role of food and food customs in one of the world's major religions. Create a presentation to report your findings to the class.

845

1. c
2. b
3. d
4. a
5. e
6. Christianity
7. Answers should include facts from the text.
8. understanding the Four Truths, following the Eightfold Path, achieving Nirvana
9. the state of enlightenment; monks; because of their lifestyle
10. Jesus was born and raised a Jew.
11. Through his life and death, he gave Christians eternal life.
12. the teachings of Confucius; does not revolve around worship of a god
13. harmony; balance between light and dark parts of life
14. the Indian subcontinent
15. determines form one is born into
16. Sunni and Shia; Shia believe that rulers should descend from Muhammad. Sunni believe rulers need only be followers of Muhammad.
17. Muhammad began his teachings in Makkah, the destination of Muslim pilgrims. Muslims pray facing Makkah.
18. the five books of Moses, origins of Jewish laws
19. day of atonement for sins of the past year
20. Punjab; it is where Sikhism began
21. Hinduism and Islam
22. to explain the world around them
23. Shinto
24. Answers should include specific effects.

Gazetteer

A Gazetteer (GA•zuh•TIHR) is a geographic index or dictionary. It shows latitude and longitude for cities and certain other places. This Gazetteer lists most of the world's largest independent countries, their capitals, and several important geographic features. The page numbers tell where each entry can be found on a map in this book. As an aid to pronunciation, many entries are spelled phonetically.

A

Abidjan (AH•bee•JAHN) Capital and port city of Côte d'Ivoire, Africa. 5°N 4°W (p. 477)
Abu Dhabi (AH•boo DAH•bee) Capital of the United Arab Emirates, on the Persian Gulf. 24°N 54°E (p. 361)
Abuja (ah•BOO•jah) Capital of Nigeria. 8°N 9°E (p. 477)
Accra (AH•kruh) Capital and port city of Ghana. 6°N 0° longitude (p. 477)
Aconcagua (AH•kohn•KAH•gwah) Highest peak of the Andes and of the Western Hemisphere, in western Argentina near the Chilean border. 32°S 76°W (p. 168)
Addis Ababa (AHD•dihs AH•bah•BAH) Capital of Ethiopia. 9°N 39°E (p. 477)
Adriatic (AY•dree•A•tihk) **Sea** Arm of the Mediterranean Sea between the Balkan Peninsula and Italy. (p. 244)
Aegean (ee•JEE•uhn) **Sea** Arm of the Mediterranean Sea between Greece and Turkey. (p. 242)
Afghanistan Country in Central Asia, west of Pakistan. (p. 361)
Ahaggar Mountains Highest plateau region in the central Sahara. (p. 360)
Albania Country on the east coast of the Adriatic Sea, south of Serbia and Montenegro. (p. 243)
Algeria Country in North Africa. (p. 361)
Algiers (al•JIHRZ) Capital of Algeria. 37°N 3°E (p. 361)
Alps Mountain system extending through central Europe. (p. 242)
Altay Shan Mountain system between western Mongolia and China and between Kazakhstan and southern Russia. (p. 672)
Amazon River River flowing through Peru and Brazil in South America and into the Atlantic Ocean. (p. 168)
Amman Capital of Jordan. 32°N 36°E (p. 361)
Amsterdam Capital of the Netherlands. 52°N 5°E (p. 243)
Amu Dar'ya River in Turkmenistan in central and western Asia. (p. 360)
Amur River River in northeast Asia. (p. 672)
Andes Mountain system along western South America. (p. 168)
Andorra (an•DAWR•uh) Country in southern Europe, between France and Spain. (p. 243)
Angola (ang•GOH•luh) Country in Africa, south of the Democratic Republic of the Congo. (p. 477)
Ankara (AHN•kuh•ruh) Capital of Turkey. 40°N 33°E (p. 361)
Antananarivo (AHN•tah•NAH•nah•REE•voh) Capital of Madagascar. 19°S 48°E (p. 477)
Antigua Island in the West Indies, part of independent Antigua and Barbuda. 18°N 61°W (p. 169)
Apennines (A•puh•NYNZ) Mountain range in central Italy. (p. 242)
Appalachian Mountains Mountain system in eastern North America. (p. 112)
Arabian Sea Part of the Indian Ocean between India and the Arabian Peninsula. (p. 361)
Aral Sea Inland sea between Kazakhstan and Uzbekistan. (p. 360)
Argentina Country in South America, east of Chile. (p. 169)
Arkansas River River in south-central United States, emptying into the Mississippi River. (p. 112)
Armenia (ahr•MEE•nee•uh) Southeastern European country between the Black and Caspian Seas. (p. 361)
Ashkhabad (ASH•kuh•BAD) Capital of Turkmenistan. 40°N 58°E (p. 361)
Asmara (az•MAHR•uh) Capital of Eritrea. 16°N 39°E (p. 477)
Astana Capital of Kazakhstan. 52°N 72°E (p. 361)
Asunción (ah•SOON•SYOHN) Capital of Paraguay. 25°S 58°W (p. 169)
Athens Capital of Greece. 38°N 24°E (p. 243)
Atlas Mountains Mountain range on the northern edge of the Sahara. (p. 360)
Australia Country and continent southeast of Asia. (p. 747)
Austria Country in central Europe, east of Switzerland. (p. 243)
Azerbaijan (A•zuhr•by•JAHN) European-Asian country on the Caspian Sea. (p. 361)

B

Baghdad Capital of Iraq. 33°N 44°E (p. 361)
Bahamas Independent state comprising a chain of islands, cays, and reefs southeast of Florida and north of Cuba. 24°N 76°W (p. 169)
Bahrain (bah•RAYN) Independent state in the western Persian Gulf. (p. 361)
Baku Capital of Azerbaijan. 40°N 50°E (p. 361)
Balkan Mountains Mountain range extending across central Bulgaria to the Black Sea. (p. 242)
Balkan Peninsula Peninsula in southeastern Europe bordered on the west by the Adriatic Sea. (p. 242)
Baltic Sea Arm of the Atlantic Ocean in northern Europe that connects with the North Sea. (p. 242)
Bamako (BAH•mah•KOH) Capital of Mali. 13°N 8°W (p. 477)
Bangkok Capital of Thailand. 14°N 100°E (p. 5)

Bangladesh (BAHNG•gluh•DESH) Country in South Asia, bordered by India and Myanmar. (p. 599)
Bangui (bahng•GEE) Capital of the Central African Republic. 4°N 19°E (p. 477)
Banjul Capital of Gambia. 13°N 17°W (p. 477)
Barbados Island country between the Atlantic Ocean and the Caribbean Sea. 14°N 59°W (p. 169)
Barbuda Island in the West Indies, part of independent Antigua and Barbuda. 18°N 62°W (p. 169)
Barents Sea Part of the Arctic Ocean, north of Norway and Russia. (p. 242)
Bay of Bengal Part of the Indian Ocean between eastern India and Southeast Asia. (p. 598)
Beijing Capital of China. 40°N 116°E (p. 5)
Beirut (bay•ROOT) Capital of Lebanon. 34°N 36°E (p. 361)
Belarus (BEE•luh•ROOS) Eastern European country west of Russia. (p. 243)
Belgium (BEHL•juhm) Country in northwestern Europe, south of the Netherlands. (p. 243)
Belgrade Capital of Serbia. 45°N 21°E (p. 243)
Belize (buh•LEEZ) Country in Central America. (p. 169)
Belmopan (BEHL•moh•PAHN) Capital of Belize. 17°N 89°W (p. 169)
Benin (buh•NEEN) Country in western Africa. (p. 477)
Ben Nevis Peak in the highlands region of the Grampian Mountains in Scotland. 54°N 5°W (p. 242)
Bering Sea Part of the north Pacific Ocean, extending between the United States and Russia. (p. 112)
Berlin Capital of Germany. 53°N 13°E (p. 243)
Bern Capital of Switzerland. 47°N 7°E (p. 243)
Bhutan (boo•TAHN) Country in the eastern Himalaya, northeast of India. 27°N 91°E (p. 599)
Bishkek Capital and largest city of Kyrgyzstan. 43°N 75°E (p. 361)
Bissau (bih•SOW) Capital of Guinea-Bissau. 12°N 16°W (p. 477)
Black Sea Sea between Europe and Asia. (p. 242)
Bloemfontein (BLOOM•FAHN•TAYN) Judicial capital of the Republic of South Africa. 29°S 26°E (p. 477)
Bogotá (BOH•goh•TAH) Capital of Colombia. 5°N 74°W (p. 169)
Bolivia Republic in west-central South America. (p. 169)
Bosnia-Herzegovina (BAHZ•nee•uh HERT•suh•goh•VEE•nuh) Southeastern European country between Serbia and Croatia. (p. 243)
Bosporus Strait between European and Asian Turkey, connecting the Sea of Marmara with the Black Sea. (p. 413)
Botswana (baht•SWAH•nuh) Country in Africa, north of the Republic of South Africa. (p. 477)
Brahmaputra River River that begins in Tibet, flows through northeast India and Bangladesh, and empties into the Bay of Bengal. (p. 598)
Brasília (bruh•ZIHL•yuh) Capital of Brazil. 16°S 48°W (p. 169)
Bratislava (BRAH•tuh•SLAH•vuh) Capital and largest city of Slovakia. 48°N 17°E (p. 243)
Brazil Largest country in South America, in east-central South America. (p. 169)
Brazzaville (BRA•zuh•VIHL) Capital of Congo. 4°S 15°E (p. 477)
Brunei (bru•NY) Country on the northern coast of the island of Borneo. (p. 747)
Brussels Capital of Belgium. 51°N 4°E (p. 243)
Bucharest (BOO•kuh•REHST) Capital of Romania. 44°N 26°E (p. 243)
Budapest Capital of Hungary. 48°N 19°E (p. 243)
Buenos Aires (BWAY•nuhs AR•eez) Capital of Argentina. 34°S 58°W (p. 169)
Bujumbura (BOO•juhm•BUR•uh) Capital of Burundi. 3°S 29°E (p. 477)
Bulgaria (BUHL•GAR•ee•uh) Country in southeastern Europe, south of Romania. (p. 243)
Burkina Faso (bur•KEE•nuh FAH•soh) Country in western Africa, south of Mali. (p. 477)
Burundi (bu•ROON•dee) Country in central Africa at the northern end of Lake Tanganyika. (p. 477)

C

Cairo (KY•roh) Capital of Egypt. 31°N 32°E (p. 5)
Cambodia (kam•BOH•dee•uh) Country in Southeast Asia, south of Thailand. (p. 747)
Cameroon (KA•muh•ROON) Country in West Africa, on the northeast shore of the Gulf of Guinea. (p. 477)
Canada Country in northern North America. (p. 113)
Canberra Capital of Australia. 35°S 149°E (p. 747)
Cape Town Legislative capital of the Republic of South Africa. 34°S 18°E (p. 5)
Cape Verde Republic consisting of a group of volcanic islands in the Atlantic Ocean. 15°N 26°W (p. 477)
Caracas (kah•RAH•kahs) Capital of Venezuela. 11°N 67°W (p. 169)
Caribbean (KAR•uh•BEE•uhn) **Sea** Part of the Atlantic Ocean, bounded by the West Indies, South America, and Central America. (p. 170)
Carpathian Mountains Mountain range in eastern Europe in Slovakia and Romania. (p. 242)
Caspian (KAS•pee•uhn) **Sea** Salt lake between Europe and Asia. (p. 242)
Caucasus (KAW•kuh•suhs) **Mountains** Mountain range in southwestern Russia. (p. 360)
Central African Republic Country in central Africa, south of Chad. (p. 477)
Central Siberian Plateau Tableland area in Siberia. (p. 242)
Chad Country in north-central Africa. (p. 477)
Chang Jiang (CHAHNG JYAHNG) River in north-central and eastern China, also known as the Yangtze River. (p. 672)
Chao Phraya (chow PRY•uh) River in Thailand, flowing south into the Gulf of Thailand. (p. 746)

Chile (CHIH•lee) Western South American country, along the Pacific Ocean. (p. 169)
China (People's Republic of China) Country in eastern and central Asia. (p. 673)
Chişinău (KEE•shee•NOW) Capital and largest city of Moldova. 47°N 29°E (p. 243)
Colombia Republic in northern South America. (p. 169)
Colombo Capital of Sri Lanka. 7°N 80°E (p. 599)
Colorado Plateau Highlands region in the western United States. (p. 112)
Colorado River River in the western United States that flows through the Grand Canyon. (p. 112)
Columbia Plateau Flat plains area primarily in western Washington State in the United States. (p. 112)
Comoros (KAH•muh•ROHZ) **Islands** Island country in the Indian Ocean between the island of Madagascar and Africa. 13°S 43°E (p. 477)
Conakry (KAH•nuh•kree) Capital of Guinea. 10°N 14°W (p. 477)
Congo, Democratic Republic of the African country on the Equator, north of Zambia and Angola. (p. 477)
Congo, Republic of the Country in Equatorial Africa. (p. 477)
Congo River River that runs through the Democratic Republic of the Congo. (p. 476)
Copenhagen (KOH•puhn•HAY•guhn) Capital of Denmark. 56°N 12°E (p. 243)
Costa Rica (KAWS•tah REE•kuh) Central American country, south of Nicaragua. (p. 169)
Côte d'Ivoire (KOHT dee•VWAHR) West African country, south of Mali. (p. 477)
Croatia (kroh•AY•shuh) Southeastern European country on the Adriatic Sea. (p. 243)
Cuba Island country southeast of Florida. 21°N 80°W (p. 169)
Cyprus Island country in the eastern Mediterranean Sea, south of Turkey. 35°N 31°E (p. 243)
Czech (CHEHK) **Republic** Central European country south of Germany and Poland. (p. 243)

D

Dakar Capital of Senegal. 15°N 17°W (p. 6)
Damascus Capital of Syria. 34°N 36°E (p. 361)
Danube River River in Europe that begins in Germany and flows into the Black Sea. (p. 242)
Dardanelles Strait between European and Asian Turkey, connecting the Sea of Marmara with the Aegean Sea. (p. 413)
Dar es Salaam (DAHR EHS suh•LAHM) Commercial capital of Tanzania. 7°S 39°E (p. 477)
Darling River River in southeast Australia. (p. 746)
Dead Sea A landlocked body of salt water located between Israel and Jordan. (p. 360)
Deccan Plateau The peninsula of India south of the Narmada River. (p. 598)
Denmark Country in northwestern Europe, between the Baltic and North Seas. (p. 243)
Dhaka Capital of Bangladesh. 24°N 90°E (p. 599)
Djibouti (juh•BOO•tee) Country in East Africa, on the Gulf of Aden. (p. 477)
Dnieper (NEE•puhr) **River** River that begins in Russia, flows through Belarus and Ukraine, and then drains into the Black Sea. (p. 242)
Dniester (NEE•stuhr) **River** River in south-central Europe that begins in Ukraine and flows southeast to the Black Sea. (p. 242)
Dodoma (doh•DOH•MAH) Political capital of Tanzania. 7°S 36°E (p. 477)
Doha (DOH•hah) Capital of Qatar. 25°N 51°E (p. 361)
Dominica Island republic in the West Indies, lying in the center of the Lesser Antilles. 15°N 61°W (p. 169)
Dominican Republic Republic occupying the eastern two-thirds of Hispaniola Island in the West Indies. 19°N 70°W (p. 169)
Don River River in southwestern Russia. (p. 242)
Drakensberg (DRAH•kuhnz•BUHRG) Range Mountain range in South Africa. (p. 476)
Dublin Capital of Ireland. 53°N 6°W (p. 243)
Dushanbe (doo•SHAM•buh) Capital and largest city of Tajikistan. 39°N 69°E (p. 361)

E

East Timor (Timor-Leste) Island country in the Indonesian archipelago, northwest of Australia. (p. 747)
Eastern Ghats Mountain range in India. (p. 598)
Ecuador (EH•kwuh•DAWR) Country in South America, south of Colombia. (p. 169)
Egypt Country in northern Africa on the Mediterranean Sea. (p. 361)
Elbe River River in central Europe. (p. 243)
Elburz Mountains Mountain range in northern Iran parallel to the shore of the Caspian Sea. (p. 360)
El Salvador (ehl SAL•vuh•DAWR) Country in Central America, southwest of Honduras. (p. 169)
Equatorial Guinea (EE•kwuh•TOHR•ee•uhl GIH•nee) Country in western Africa, south of Cameroon. (p. 477)
Eritrea (EHR•uh•TREE•uh) Country in northeast Africa, north of Ethiopia. (p. 477)
Estonia (eh•STOH•nee•uh) Northern European country on the Baltic Sea. (p. 243)
Ethiopia (EE•thee•OH•pee•uh) Country in eastern Africa, north of Somalia and Kenya. (p. 477)
Euphrates (yu•FRAY•teez) **River** River in southwestern Asia that flows through Syria and Iraq and joins the Tigris River. (p. 360)

F

Fiji (FEE•jee) Country comprising an island group in the southwest Pacific Ocean. 19°S 175°E (p. 747)

Finland Country in northern Europe, east of Sweden. (p. 243)

France Country in western Europe. (p. 243)

Freetown Capital and port city of Sierra Leone, in western Africa. 9°N 13°W (p. 477)

French Guiana Overseas department of France on the northeast coast of South America. (p. 169)

G

Gabon (ga•BOHN) Country in western Africa, on the Atlantic Ocean. (p. 477)

Gaborone (GAH•boh•ROH•nay) Capital of Botswana, in southern Africa. 24°S 26°E (p. 477)

Gambia Country in western Africa. (p. 477)

Ganges (GAN•JEEZ) **River** River in northern India and Bangladesh that flows into the Bay of Bengal. (p. 598)

Gangetic (gan•JEH•tic) **Plain** A fertile plains region in northern India traversed by the Ganges River. (p. 598)

Georgetown Capital of Guyana. 8°N 58°W (p. 169)

Georgia Asian/European country bordering the Black Sea, south of Russia. (p. 361)

Germany (Federal Republic of Germany) Country in north-central Europe. (p. 243)

Ghana (GAH•nuh) Country in western Africa, on the Gulf of Guinea. (p. 477)

Gobi Desert in Central Asia. (p. 672)

Godavari River River in central India. (p. 598)

Gran Chaco Region in south-central South America located in Paraguay, Bolivia, and Argentina. (p. 168)

Great Britain Kingdom in western Europe comprising England, Scotland, and Wales. (p. 242)

Great Dividing Range Chain of hills and mountains, on Australia's eastern coast. (p. 746)

Great Plains Rolling treeless area of central North America. (p. 112)

Great Salt Lake Large saltwater lake in Utah in the United States that has no outlet. (p. 112)

Great Slave Lake A lake in the south-central mainland of the Northwest Territories in Canada. (p. 112)

Greece Country in southern Europe, on the Balkan Peninsula. (p. 243)

Greenland Island in the northwestern Atlantic Ocean. 74°N 40°W (p. 112)

Grenada Island in the self-governing West Indies. 17°N 61°W (p. 169)

Guam Island in the western Pacific. It is an unincorporated United States territory. 13°N 144°E (p. 747)

Guatemala (GWAH•tuh•MAH•luh) Country in Central America, south of Mexico. (p. 169)

Guatemala Capital of Guatemala and the largest city in Central America. 15°N 91°W (p. 169)

Guinea (GIH•nee) West African country on the Atlantic coast. 11°N 12°W (p. 477)

Guinea-Bissau (GIH•nee bih•SOW) West African country on the Atlantic coast. 12°N 20°W (p. 477)

Gulf of Aden Arm of the Indian Ocean between the Arabian Peninsula and Africa. (p. 360)

Gulf of Mexico Gulf on the southern coast of North America. (p. 112)

Gulf of Thailand Inlet of the South China Sea. (p. 746)

Guyana Republic in northern South America. (p. 169)

H

Hainan (HY•NAHN) Island province of China in the South China Sea. 19°N 109°E (p. 672)

Haiti (HAY•tee) Republic occupying the western third of Hispaniola Island in the West Indies. 19°N 72.25°W (p. 169)

Hanoi Capital of Vietnam. 21°N 106°E (p. 747)

Harare (huh•RAH•ray) Capital of Zimbabwe. 18°S 23°E (p. 477)

Havana Capital of Cuba. 23°N 82°W (p. 169)

Helsinki Capital of Finland. 60°N 24°E (p. 243)

Himalaya (HIH•muh•LAY•uh) Mountain system in South Asia, bordering the Indian subcontinent on the north. (p. 598)

Hindu Kush Mountain range in Central Asia. (p. 360)

Honduras (hahn•DUR•uhs) Central American republic. (p. 169)

Hong Kong Administrative district and port in southern China. 22°N 115°E (p. 7)

Huang He (HWAHNG HUH) Major river in central China, also known as the Yellow River. (p. 672)

Hudson Bay Inland sea in east-central Canada. (p. 112)

Hungary Central European country, south of Slovakia. (p. 243)

I

Iberian (eye•BIHR•ee•uhn) **Peninsula** Peninsula in southwestern Europe. (p. 242)

Iceland Island country between the north Atlantic and Arctic Oceans. 65°N 20°W (p. 243)

India South Asian country south of China. (p. 599)

Indochina Southeast peninsula of Asia. (p. 3)

Indonesia (IHN•duh•NEE•zhuh) Group of islands that forms the Southeast Asian country of the Republic of Indonesia. 5°S 119°E (p. 747)

Indus River River in Asia that rises in Tibet and flows through Pakistan to the Arabian Sea. (p. 598)

Iran (ih•RAHN) Southwest Asian country, formerly called Persia. (p. 361)

Iraq (ih•RAHK) Southwest Asian country, south of Turkey. (p. 361)

Ireland Island west of England, occupied by the Republic of Ireland and by Northern Ireland. 54°N 8°W (p. 243)

Irrawaddy River River in central Myanmar formed by the confluence of the Mali and Nmai Rivers. (p. 746)

Irtysh River River in northeast Kazakhstan and the western part of Russia, in Asia. (p. 242)

Islamabad (ihs•LAH•muh•BAHD) Capital of Pakistan. 34°N 73°E (p. 599)

Israel (IHZ•ree•uhl) Country in Southwest Asia, south of Lebanon. (p. 361)

Isthmus of Panama Narrow strip of land that forms the link in Central America between North America and South America. (p. 168)

Italy Southern European country, south of Switzerland and east of France. (p. 243)

J

Jakarta Capital of Indonesia. 6°S 107°E (p. 5)

Jamaica (juh•MAY•kuh) Island country in the West Indies. 18°N 78°W (p. 169)

Japan Country in East Asia, consisting of four main islands of Hokkaidō, Honshū, Shikoku, and Kyūshū, plus thousands of small islands. 37°N 134°E (p. 673)

Jerusalem (juh•ROO•suh•luhm) Capital of Israel and a holy city for Jews, Christians, and Muslims. 32°N 35°E (p. 361)

Jordan Country in Southwest Asia. (p. 361)

Juba Capital of South Sudan. 5°N 31°E (p. 477)

Jutland Peninsula extending north from Germany. (p. 242)

K

K2 (Godwin Austen) Himalayan mountain in Jammu and Kashmir. 35°N 76°E (p. 598)

Kabul Capital of Afghanistan. 35°N 69°E (p. 361)

Kalahari Desert Plateau and part desert located in the southern part of Africa. (p. 476)

Kamchatka Peninsula Peninsula in northeast Russia, in Asia. (p. 242)

Kampala (kahm•PAH•lah) Capital of Uganda. 0° latitude 32°E (p. 477)

Kara Sea Arm of the Arctic Ocean north of Russia. (p. 242)

Kathmandu (KAT•MAN•DOO) Capital of Nepal. 28°N 85°E (p. 599)

Kazakhstan (KA•zak•STAN) Large Asian country south of Russia, bordering the Caspian Sea. (p. 361)

Kenya (KEH•nyuh) Country in eastern Africa, south of Ethiopia. (p. 477)

Khartoum Capital of Sudan. 16°N 33°E (p. 477)

Khyber Pass Mountain pass between Afghanistan and Pakistan. 34°N 71°E (p. 360)

Kiev See **Kyiv (Kiev)**

Kigali (kee•GAH•lee) Capital of Rwanda, in central Africa. 2°S 30°E (p. 477)

Kilimanjaro Highest mountain in Africa, located in Tanzania. 3°S 37°E (p. 476)

Kingston Capital of Jamaica. 18°N 77°W (p. 169)

Kinshasa (kihn•SHAH•suh) Capital of the Democratic Republic of the Congo. 4°S 15°E (p. 5)

Kiribati (KIHR•uh•BAS) One of the two Federated States of Micronesia. 5°S 170°W (p. 747)

Korean Peninsula Peninsula on which both North and South Korea are located. (p. 672)

Kosovo (KAW•saw•VOH) Country in southeastern Europe, between Serbia and Montenegro. (p. 243)

Krishna River River of the Deccan Plateau in south India. (p. 598)

Kuala Lumpur (KWAH•luh LUM•PUR) Capital of Malaysia. 3°N 102°E (p. 747)

Kunlun Shan Mountain ranges in western China on the north edge of the Plateau of Tibet. (p. 672)

Kuwait (ku•WAYT) Country between Saudi Arabia and Iraq, on the Persian Gulf. (p. 361)

Kyiv (Kiev) (KEE•EHF) Capital of Ukraine. 50°N 31°E (p. 243)

Kyrgyzstan (KIHR•gih•STAN) Small Central Asian country on China's western border. (p. 361)

L

Labrador Sea Part of the Atlantic Ocean south of Baffin Bay off the coast of Newfoundland. (p. 112)

Lagos Port city of Nigeria. 6°N 3°E (p. 477)

Lake Baikal Lake in southern Siberia, Russia. It is the largest freshwater lake in Eurasia. (p. 242)

Lake Chad Reservoir located in Chad. (p. 476)

Lake Erie One of the Great Lakes of the United States and Canada. (p. 112)

Lake Huron One of the Great Lakes of the United States and Canada. (p. 112)

Lake Malawi Lake in southeast Africa. (p. 476)

Lake Michigan One of the Great Lakes of the United States and Canada. (p. 112)

Lake Ontario The easternmost and smallest of the Great Lakes of the United States and Canada. (p. 112)

Lake Superior One of the Great Lakes of the United States and Canada. (p. 112)

Lake Tanganyika Lake in east-central Africa. (p. 476)

Lake Titicaca Lake on the border between Peru and Bolivia. Highest navigable lake in the world. (p. 168)

Lake Victoria Freshwater lake in Tanzania and Uganda. (p. 476)

Lake Volta Reservoir located in Ghana. (p. 476)

Lake Winnipeg Lake in south-central Manitoba, Canada. (p. 112)

Laos (LOWS) Southeast Asian country, south of China and west of Vietnam. (p. 747)

La Paz (lah PAHZ) Administrative capital of Bolivia, and the highest capital in the world. 17°S 68°W (p. 169)

Latvia (LAT•vee•uh) Northeastern European country on the Baltic Sea, west of Russia. (p. 243)

Lebanon (LEH•buh•nuhn) Country on the Mediterranean Sea, south of Syria. (p. 361)

Lena River River in east-central Russia. (p. 242)

Lesotho (luh•SOH•toh) Country in southern Africa. (p. 477)

Liberia (ly•BIHR•ee•uh) West African country, south of Guinea. 7°N 10°W (p. 477)

Libreville (LEE•bruh•VIHL) Capital and port city of Gabon. 1°N 9°E (p. 477)
Libya (LIH•bee•uh) North African country on the Mediterranean Sea, west of Egypt. (p. 361)
Liechtenstein (LIHK•tuhn•STYN) Small country in central Europe. (p. 243)
Lilongwe (lih•LAWNG•gway) Capital of Malawi. 14°S 34°E (p. 477)
Lima (LEE•muh) Capital of Peru. 12°S 77°W (p. 169)
Lisbon Capital of Portugal. 39°N 9°W (p. 243)
Lithuania (LIH•thuh•WAY•nee•uh) European country on the Baltic Sea, west of Belarus. (p. 243)
Ljubljana (lee•OO•blee•AH•nuh) Capital of Slovenia. 46°N 14°E (p. 243)
Llanos Vast plains in northern South America. (p. 168)
Loire River River in Europe that rises in southeastern France and empties into the Bay of Biscay. (p. 242)
Lomé (loh•MAY) Capital and port city of Togo in Africa. 6°N 1°E (p. 477)
London Capital of the United Kingdom, on the Thames River. 52°N 0° longitude (p. 243)
Luanda Capital of Angola. 9°S 13°E (p. 477)
Lusaka Capital of Zambia. 15°S 28°E (p. 477)
Luxembourg (LUHK•suhm•BUHRG) European country between France, Germany, and Belgium. (p. 243)

M

Macau (muh•KOW) Administrative district and port in southern China. (p. 673)
Macedonia (MA•suh•DOH•nee•uh) Republic in southeastern Europe, north of Greece. Macedonia also refers to a geographic region in the Balkan Peninsula. (p. 243)
Mackenzie River River in the western portion of the Northwest Territories in Canada. (p. 112)
Madagascar (MA•duh•GAS•kuhr) Island in the Indian Ocean, southeast of Africa. (p. 477)
Madrid Capital of Spain. 40°N 4°W (p. 243)
Malabo (mah•LAH•boh) Capital of Equatorial Guinea. 4°N 9°E (p. 477)
Malawi (muh•LAH•wee) Southeastern African country, south of Tanzania and east of Zambia. (p. 477)
Malaysia (muh•LAY•zhuh) Federation of states in Southeast Asia on the Malay Peninsula and the island of Borneo. (p. 747)
Maldives (MAWL•DEEVZ) Island country in the Indian Ocean near South Asia. 5°N 42°E (p. 599)
Mali Country in western Africa, south of Algeria. (p. 361)
Malta An independent state consisting of three islands in the Mediterranean Sea. 36°N 15°E (p. 243)
Managua (mah•NAH•gwah) Capital of Nicaragua. 12°N 86°W (p. 169)
Manila (muh•NIH•luh) Capital and port city of the Republic of the Philippines. 15°N 121°E (p. 747)
Marshall Islands Independent group of atolls and reefs in the western Pacific Ocean. 11°N 108°E (p. 747)
Maseru (MA•suh•ROO) Capital of Lesotho, in southern Africa. 29°S 27°E (p. 477)
Masqat Capital of Oman. 23°N 59°E (p. 361)
Mato Grosso Plateau Highlands area in southwest Brazil. (p. 168)
Mauritania (MAWR•uh•TAY•nee•uh) West African country, north of Senegal. (p. 361)
Mauritius (maw•RIH•shuhs) Island country in the Indian Ocean east of Madagascar. 21°S 58°E (p. 477)
Mbabane (EHM•bah•BAH•nay) Capital of Swaziland, in southeastern Africa. 26°S 31°E (p. 477)
Mediterranean Sea Inland sea enclosed by Europe, Asia, and Africa. (p. 244)
Mekong River River in Southeast Asia that flows south through Laos, Cambodia, and Vietnam. (p. 746)
Melekeok New capital of Palau. 7°N 134°E (p. 747)
Meseta The plains of central Spain. (p. 242)
Mexico Country in North America, south of the United States. (p. 169)
Mexico City Capital and most populous city of Mexico. 19°N 99°W (p. 169)
Minsk Capital of Belarus. 54°N 28°E (p. 243)
Mississippi River River in the central United States that rises in Minnesota and flows southeast into the Gulf of Mexico. (p. 112)
Missouri River River in the central United States that joins the Mississippi River. (p. 112)
Mogadishu (MAH•guh•DIH•shoo) Capital and major seaport of Somalia, in eastern Africa. 2°N 45°E (p. 477)
Moldova (mahl•DOH•vuh) European country between Ukraine and Romania. (p. 243)
Monaco (MAH•nuh•KOH) Independent principality in southern Europe, on the Mediterranean. (p. 243)
Monaco Capital of Monaco. 44°N 8°E (p. 243)
Mongolia (mahn•GOHL•yuh) Country in Asia between Russia and China. (p. 673)
Monrovia (muhn•ROH•vee•uh) Capital and major seaport of Liberia, in western Africa. 6°N 11°W (p. 477)
Mont Blanc The highest mountain of the Alps, in southeastern France. 46°N 7°E (p. 242)
Montenegro (mahn•tuh•NEH•groh) European country between the Adriatic Sea and Serbia. (p. 243)
Montevideo (MAHN•tuh•vuh•DAY•oh) Capital of Uruguay. 35°S 56°W (p. 169)
Morocco (muh•RAH•koh) Country in northwestern Africa on the Mediterranean Sea and the Atlantic Ocean. (p. 361)
Moscow Capital of Russia. 56°N 38°E (p. 243)
Mount Ararat Mountain in eastern Turkey. 39°N 44°3 (p. 360)
Mount Elbrus Highest point in the Caucasus Mountains. 43°N 42°E (p. 242)
Mount Everest (EHV•ruhst) Highest mountain in the world, in the Greater Himalaya mountain range between Nepal and Tibet. 28°N 87°E (p. 598)

Gazetteer

Mount Fuji Peak in south-central Honshū, Japan. It is the highest peak in Japan. 35°N 138°E (p. 672)

Mount Logan Peak in northwest Canada. 60°N 140°W (p. 112)

Mount McKinley Highest peak in North America, located in Denali National Park in Alaska. 63°N 151°W (p. 112)

Mount Pinatubo Active volcanic mountain in the Philippines. 15°N 170°E (p. 746)

Mount Whitney Peak in the Sierra Nevada range in central California. 36°N 118°W (p. 112)

Mozambique (MOH•zuhm•BEEK) Country in southeastern Africa, south of Tanzania. (p. 477)

Murray River River in Australia. (p. 746)

Myanmar (MYAHN•MAHR) Country in Southeast Asia, south of China, also called Burma. (p. 747)

N

Nairobi Capital of Kenya. 1°S 37°E (p. 477)

Namib Desert Arid region along the coast of Namibia in southwestern Africa. (p. 476)

Namibia (nuh•MIH•bee•uh) Country in southwestern Africa, on the Atlantic Ocean. (p. 477)

Narmada River River in central India that flows into the Gulf of Khambat in the Arabian Sea. (p. 598)

Nassau (NA•SAW) Capital of the Bahamas. 25°N 77°W (p. 169)

Nauru (nah•OO•roo) One of the two Federated States of Micronesia. 32°S 166°E (p. 747)

Nay Pyi Taw New capital of Myanmar. 20°N 96°E (p. 747)

N'Djamena (uhn•jah•MAY•nah) Capital of Chad. 12°N 15°E (p. 477)

Nepal (nuh•PAWL) Mountain country between India and China. (p. 599)

Netherlands Western European country on the North Sea. (p. 243)

New Delhi Capital of India. 29°N 77°E (p. 599)

New Zealand Major island country in the south Pacific, southeast of Australia. 42°S 175°E (p. 747)

Niamey (nee•AH•may) Capital and commercial center of Niger, in western Africa. 14°N 2°E (p. 477)

Nicaragua (NIH•kuh•RAH•gwuh) Republic in Central America. (p. 169)

Nicosia (NIH•kuh•SEE•uh) Capital of Cyprus. 35°N 33°E (p. 243)

Niger (NY•juhr) Landlocked country in western Africa, north of Nigeria. (p. 361)

Nigeria (ny•JIHR•ee•uh) Country in western Africa, south of Niger. (p. 477)

Niger River River in western Africa. (p. 476)

Nile River Longest river in the world, flowing north and east through eastern Africa. (p. 476)

Northern European Plain Plain that sweeps across western and central Europe into Russia and includes most of European Russia. (p. 242)

North Korea Asian country in the northernmost part of the Korean Peninsula. (p. 673)

North Sea Arm of the Atlantic Ocean extending between the European continent on the south and east and Great Britain on the west. (p. 242)

Norway Country on the Scandinavian Peninsula. (p. 243)

Nouakchott (nu•AHK•SHAHT) Capital of Mauritania. 18°N 16°W (p. 361)

Nullarbor Plain Dry, treeless area that lies south of the Great Victorian Desert in Australia. (p. 746)

O

Ob' River River in western Russia. (p. 242)

Ohio River Major river in the midwestern United States, emptying into the Mississippi River. (p. 112)

Oman (oh•MAHN) Country on the Arabian Sea and the Gulf of Oman. (p. 361)

Orinoco River River in Venezuela. (p. 168)

Oslo Capital of Norway. 60°N 11°E (p. 243)

Ottawa Capital of Canada. 45°N 76°W (p. 114)

Ouagadougou (WAH•gah•DOO•goo) Capital of Burkina Faso, in western Africa. 12°N 2°W (p. 477)

P

Pakistan South Asian country on the Arabian Sea, northwest of India. (p. 599)

Palau (puh•LOW) Island country in the western Pacific Ocean. 7°N 135°E (p. 747)

Pamirs Mountainous region of Central Asia. (p. 360)

Pampas Plains area of South America. (p. 168)

Panama (PA•nuh•MAH) Republic in south Central America, on the Isthmus of Panama. (p. 169)

Panama Capital of Panama. 9°N 79°W (p. 169)

Papua New Guinea (PA•pyuh•wuh noo GIH•nee) Independent island country in the south Pacific Ocean. 7°S 142°E (p. 747)

Paraguay (PAR•uh•GWY) Country in South America, north of Argentina. (p. 169)

Paraguay River River in south-central South America. (p. 168)

Paramaribo (PAR•uh•MAR•uh•BOH) Capital and port city of Suriname. 6°N 55°W (p. 169)

Paraná River River in southeast central South America. (p. 168)

Paris Capital and river port of France. 49°N 2°E (p. 243)

Patagonia Plateau region of South America primarily in Argentina. (p. 168)

Peace River River in western Alberta, Canada. (p. 112)

Persian Gulf Arm of the Arabian Sea between Iran and Saudi Arabia. (p. 360)

Peru Country in South America, south of Ecuador and Colombia. (p. 169)

Philippines (FIH•luh•PEENZ) Country in the Pacific Ocean, southeast of China. (p. 747)

Phnom Penh (NAHM PEHN) Capital of Cambodia. 12°N 106°E (p. 747)
Podgorica (PAWD•GAWR•eet•sah) Capital of Montenegro. 42°N 19°E (p. 243)
Poland Country on the Baltic Sea in eastern Europe. 52°N 18°E (p. 243)
Po River River in northern Italy that flows to the Adriatic Sea. (p. 243)
Port-au-Prince (POHRT•oh•PRIHNTS) Capital of Haiti. 19°N 72°W (p. 169)
Port Moresby (MOHRZ•bee) Capital of Papua New Guinea. 10°S 147°E (p. 747)
Porto-Novo (POHR•toh•NOH•voh) Capital and port city of Benin, in western Africa. 7°N 3°E (p. 477)
Portugal (POHR•chih•guhl) Country on the Iberian Peninsula, south and west of Spain. (p. 243)
Prague (PRAHG) Capital of the Czech Republic. 50°N 15°E (p. 243)
Pretoria See **Tshwane (Pretoria)**
Puerto Rico Island in the West Indies. It is a self-governing commonwealth in union with the United States. 18°N 66°W (p. 169)
P'yŏngyang (PYAWNG•YAHNG) Capital of North Korea. 39°N 126°E (p. 673)
Pyrenees Mountain range extending along the border of France and Spain. (p. 242)

Q

Qatar (KAH•tuhr) Country on the southwestern shore of the Persian Gulf. (p. 361)
Qin Ling Mountain range in northern China. (p. 672)
Quito (KEE•toh) Capital of Ecuador. 0° latitude 79°W (p. 169)

R

Rabat Capital of Morocco. 34°N 7°W (p. 361)
Red River River in the south-central United States, emptying into the Mississippi River. (p. 112)
Red River River in Vietnam that empties into the South China Sea. (p. 746)
Red Sea Inland sea between the Arabian Peninsula and northeast Africa. (p. 360)
Reykjavík (RAY•kyuh•VIHK) Capital of Iceland. 64°N 22°W (p. 243)
Rhine River River in western Europe that flows to the North Sea. (p. 242)
Rhône River River in Switzerland and France. (p. 242)
Riga Capital of Latvia. 57°N 24°E (p. 243)
Río de la Plata Estuary of the Paraná and Uruguay Rivers between Uruguay and Argentina. (p. 168)
Rio Grande/Río Bravo del Norte River forming part of the boundary between the United States and Mexico. (p. 112)
Riyadh (ree•YAHD) Capital of Saudi Arabia. 25°N 47°E (p. 361)
Rocky Mountains An extensive mountain system in western North America. (p. 112)
Romania (ru•MAY•nee•uh) Country in eastern Europe, south of Ukraine. (p. 243)
Rome Capital of Italy. 42°N 13°E (p. 243)
Rub' al-Khali Desert region in the southern Arabian Peninsula, also called the Empty Quarter. (p. 360)
Russia Largest country in the world, covering parts of Europe and Asia. (p. 243)
Rwanda (roo•AHN•dah) Country in Africa, south of Uganda. (p. 477)

S

Sahara Vast region of deserts and oases in North Africa. (p. 360)
St. Lawrence River River in southern Quebec and southeast Ontario, Canada. (p. 112)
St. Lucia Independent island state in the Caribbean Sea. 13°N 60°W (p. 169)
St. Vincent Principal island of St. Vincent and the Grenadines, south of St. Lucia. 13°N 61°W (p. 169)
Samoa Group of independent islands in the southwest Pacific Ocean. 13°S 172°W (p. 747)
Sanaa (sa•NAH) Capital of Yemen. 15°N 44°E (p. 361)
San José Capital of Costa Rica. 10°N 84°W (p. 169)
San Marino (SAN muh•REE•noh) Small European country, located on the Italian Peninsula. (p. 243)
San Salvador (san SAL•vuh•DAWR) Capital of El Salvador. 14°N 89°W (p. 169)
Santiago Capital of Chile. 33°S 71°W (p. 169)
Santo Domingo (SAN•tuh duh•MIHNG•goh) Capital of the Dominican Republic. 19°N 70°W (p. 169)
São Francisco River River in eastern Brazil flowing into the Atlantic Ocean. (p. 168)
São Tomé and Príncipe (SOWN tuh•MAY and PRIHN•sih•pee) Small island country in the Gulf of Guinea off the coast of central Africa. 1°N 7°E (p. 477)
Sarajevo (SAR•uh•YAY•voh) Capital of Bosnia and Herzegovina. 43°N 18°E (p. 243)
Saskatchewan River River in south-central Canada that flows into Lake Winnipeg. (p. 112)
Saudi Arabia (SOW•dee uh•RAY•bee•uh) Country on the Arabian Peninsula. (p. 361)
Scandinavia A peninsula in northern Europe. (p. 242)
Sea of Japan (East Sea) Branch of the Pacific Ocean between Japan and the Korean Peninsula. (p. 672)
Sea of Marmara Sea in northwest Turkey. (p. 413)
Sea of Okhotsk An inlet of the Pacific Ocean on the eastern coast of Russia. (p. 672)
Seine (SAYN) **River** French river that flows through Paris and into the English Channel. (p. 243)
Senegal (SEH•nih•GAWL) Country on the coast of western Africa, on the Atlantic Ocean. (p. 477)
Seoul (SOHL) Capital of South Korea. 38°N 127°E (p. 5)
Serbia (SUHR•bee•uh) European country between Macedonia and Hungary. (p. 243)

Gazetteer

Seychelles (say•SHEHLZ) Small island country in the Indian Ocean near East Africa. 6°S 56°E (p. 477)
Siberia An area in the region of north-central Asia, primarily in Russia. (p. 242)
Sierra Leone (see•EHR•uh lee•OHN) Country in western Africa, south of Guinea. (p. 477)
Sierra Madre del Sur Mountain range along the coast of southern Mexico. (p. 168)
Sierra Madre Occidental Mountain range running parallel to the Pacific Ocean coast in Mexico. (p. 168)
Sierra Madre Oriental Mountain range running parallel to the Gulf of Mexico coast in Mexico. (p. 168)
Sierra Nevada Mountain range in eastern California in the United States. (p. 112)
Sinai Peninsula Peninsula in northeast Egypt between the Gulf of Suez and the Gulf of Aqaba. (p. 360)
Singapore Multi-island country in Southeast Asia near the tip of the Malay Peninsula. 2°N 104°E (p. 747)
Skopje (SKAW•pyeh) Capital of the Republic of Macedonia. 42°N 21°E (p. 243)
Slovakia (sloh•VAH•kee•uh) Central European country south of Poland. (p. 243)
Slovenia (sloh•VEE•nee•uh) Small central European country on the Adriatic Sea, south of Austria. (p. 243)
Sofia Capital of Bulgaria. 43°N 23°E (p. 243)
Solomon Islands Independent island group in the west Pacific Ocean. 8°S 159°E (p. 747)
Somalia (soh•MAH•lee•uh) Country in East Africa, on the Gulf of Aden and the Indian Ocean. (p. 477)
South Africa Country at the southern tip of Africa. (p. 477)
South China Sea Part of the Pacific Ocean extending from Japan to the tip of the Malay Peninsula. (p. 672)
South Korea Country in Asia on the Korean Peninsula between the Yellow Sea and the Sea of Japan. (p. 673)
South Sudan Country in eastern Africa, west of Ethiopia. (p. 477)
Spain Country on the Iberian Peninsula. (p. 243)
Sri Lanka (sree LAHNG•kuh) Island country in the Indian Ocean south of India. 9°N 83°E (p. 599)
Stockholm Capital of Sweden. 59°N 18°E (p. 243)
Strait of Gibraltar Passage connecting Mediterranean Sea to the Atlantic Ocean. (p. 360)
Strait of Hormuz Strait between the northern tip of Oman, the southeastern Arabian Peninsula, and the southern coast of Iran. (p. 360)
Strait of Malacca Ocean trade route running between Indonesia and Malaysia, near Singapore. (p. 746)
Sucre (SOO•kray) Constitutional capital of Bolivia. 19°S 65°W (p. 169)
Sudan Northeast African country on the Red Sea. (p. 477)
Suriname Republic in South America. (p. 169)
Suva Capital of Fiji. 18°S 177°E (p. 747)
Swaziland (SWAH•zee•LAND) South African country west of Mozambique. (p. 477)
Sweden Northern European country on the eastern side of the Scandinavian Peninsula. (p. 243)
Switzerland (SWIHT•suhr•luhnd) European country in the Alps, south of Germany. (p. 243)
Syr Dar'ya River in west-central Asia in Kyrgyzstan, Uzbekistan, and Kazakhstan. (p. 360)
Syria (SIHR•ee•uh) Country in Asia on the eastern side of the Mediterranean Sea. (p. 361)

T

Taipei (TY•PAY) Capital of Taiwan. 25°N 122°E (p. 673)
Taiwan (TY•WAHN) Island country off the southeast coast of China, claimed by China. 24°N 122°E (p. 673)
Tajikistan (tah•JIH•kih•STAN) Central Asian country north of Afghanistan. (p. 361)
Taklimakan Desert in western China. (p. 3)
Tallinn (TA•luhn) Capital and largest city of Estonia. 59°N 25°E (p. 243)
Tanzania (TAN•zuh•NEE•uh) East African country on the coast of the Indian Ocean. (p. 477)
Tashkent Capital of Uzbekistan. 41°N 69°E (p. 5)
Tasman Sea Part of the south Pacific Ocean between Australia and New Zealand. (p. 746)
Taurus Mountains Mountain range in southern Turkey. (p. 360)
Tbilisi (tuh•BEE•luh•see) Capital of the Republic of Georgia. 42°N 45°E (p. 361)
Tegucigalpa (tuh•GOO•suh•GAL•puh) Capital of Honduras. 14°N 87°W (p. 169)
Tehran (TAY•RAN) Capital of Iran. 36°N 52°E (p. 5)
Thailand (TY•LAND) Southeast Asian country south of Myanmar. (p. 747)
Thames (TEHMZ) **River** River in southern England that flows into the North Sea. (p. 243)
Thar Desert Region of sandy desert in northwest India and southeast Pakistan. (p. 598)
Thimphu (thihm•POO) Capital of Bhutan. 28°N 90°E (p. 599)
Tian Shan Mountain range in western China. (p. 672)
Tierra del Fuego Archipelago off southern South America. 54°N 68°W (p. 168)
Tiranë (tih•RAH•nuh) Capital of Albania. 42°N 20°E (p. 243)
Togo West African country between Benin and Ghana, on the Gulf of Guinea. (p. 477)
Tokyo Capital of Japan. 36°N 140°E (p. 5)
Tonga South Pacific island country. 20°S 175°W (p. 747)
Trinidad and Tobago (TRIH•nih•DAD tuh•BAY•goh) Independent republic comprising the islands of Trinidad and Tobago, located in the Atlantic Ocean off the northeast coast of Venezuela. 11°N 61°W (p. 169)
Tripoli Capital of Libya. 33°N 13°E (p. 361)
Tshwane (Pretoria) Administrative capital of the Republic of South Africa. 26°S 28°E (p. 477)
Tunis Capital of Tunisia. 37°N 10°E (p. 361)
Tunisia (too•NEE•zhuh) North African country on the Mediterranean Sea between Libya and Algeria. (p. 361)

Turkey Country in southeastern Europe and western Asia. (p. 361)
Turkmenistan (tuhrk•MEH•nuh•STAN) Central Asian country on the Caspian Sea. (p. 361)
Tuvalu Independent island group in the western Pacific Ocean. 8°S 178°E (p. 747)

U

Uganda (oo•GAHN•duh) East African country south of Sudan. (p. 477)
Ukraine (yoo•KRAYN) Large eastern European country west of Russia, on the Black Sea. (p. 243)
Ulaanbaatar (OO•LAHN•BAH•TAWR) Capital of Mongolia. 48°N 107°E (p. 673)
United Arab Emirates Country of seven states on the eastern side of the Arabian Peninsula. (p. 361)
United Kingdom Country in western Europe made up of England, Scotland, Wales, and Northern Ireland. (p. 243)
United States Country in North America located between Canada and Mexico. (p. 113)
Ural Mountains Mountain range in Russia that marks the traditional boundary between European Russia and Asian Russia. (p. 242)
Ural River River in eastern Europe and western Asia, originating in the Ural Mountains. (p. 242)
Uruguay (UR•uh•GWY) South American country, south of Brazil on the Atlantic Ocean. (p. 169)
Uzbekistan (uz•BEH•kih•STAN) Central Asian country south of Kazakhstan. (p. 361)

V

Vanuatu (VAN•WAH•TOO) Country made up of islands in the Pacific Ocean, east of Australia. 17°S 170°W (p. 747)
Vatican (VA•tih•kuhn) **City** Headquarters of the Roman Catholic Church, located in the city of Rome, Italy. 42°N 13°E (p. 243)
Venezuela Republic in northern South America. (p. 169)
Verkhoyanski Mountains Mountain range in northeastern Russia, just east of the Lena River. (p. 242)
Vienna Capital of Austria. 48°N 16°E (p. 243)
Vientiane (vyehn•TYAHN) Capital of Laos. 18°N 103°E (p. 747)
Vietnam Southeast Asian country, east of Laos and Cambodia. (p. 747)
Vindhya Range Mountain range in central India. (p. 598)
Vistula River River in southwestern Poland that flows north into the Baltic Sea. (p. 243)
Volga River River in western Russia that flows south into the Caspian Sea. (p. 242)

W

Warsaw Capital of Poland. 52°N 21°E (p. 243)
Washington, D.C. Capital of the United States, near the Atlantic coast. 39°N 77°W (p. 114)
Wellington Capital of New Zealand. 41°S 175°E (p. 747)
Western Ghats Mountain range in southern India. (p. 598)
Western Sahara Territory in northwest Africa. (p. 361)
West Siberian Plain Area of flat land that stretches from the Arctic Ocean to the grasslands of Central Asia. (p. 242)
Windhoek (VIHNT•HUK) Capital of Namibia, in southwestern Africa. 22°S 17°E (p. 477)

X

Xi (SHEE) **River** River in southeast China, known in its upper course as the Hongshui. (p. 672)

Y

Yablonovyy Range Mountain range in southern Russia. (p. 242)
Yamoussoukro (YAH•muh•SOO•kroh) Second capital of Côte d'Ivoire, in western Africa. 7°N 6°W (p. 477)
Yangon (Rangoon) Former capital of Myanmar. 17°N 96°E (p. 750) See also **Nay Pyi Taw**
Yaoundé (yown•DAY) Capital of Cameroon, in western Africa. 4°N 12°E (p. 477)
Yellow Sea Large inlet of the Pacific Ocean between northeast China and the Korean Peninsula. (p. 672)
Yemen (YEH•muhn) Country on the Arabian Peninsula, south of Saudi Arabia. (p. 361)
Yenisey River River in western Russia that flows north into the Kara Sea. (p. 242)
Yerevan (YEHR•uh•VAHN) Former capital and largest city of Armenia. 40°N 44°E (p. 361)
Yucatán Peninsula Peninsula including parts of southeastern Mexico, Belize, and Guatemala in Central America. (p. 168)
Yukon River River in the Yukon Territory, Canada. (p. 112)

Z

Zagreb Capital and largest city of Croatia. 46°N 16°E (p. 243)
Zagros Mountains Mountain system in southern and southwestern Iran. (p. 360)
Zambezi River River in south-central Africa. (p. 476)
Zambia (ZAM•bee•uh) Country in south-central Africa, east of Angola. (p. 477)
Zimbabwe (zihm•BAH•bwee) Country in south-central Africa, southeast of Zambia. (p. 477)

GLOSSARY/GLOSARIO

- Content vocabulary terms in this glossary are words that relate to geography content. They are highlighted yellow in your text.
- Words below that have an asterisk (*) are academic vocabulary terms. They help you understand your school subjects and are **boldface** in your text.

A

ENGLISH	ESPAÑOL
***abandon** to give up completely (p. 137)	***abandonar** dejar por completo (pág. 137)
aborigine/Aborigine an area's original inhabitants (p. 688); the indigenous people of Australia (p. 781)	**aborígenes** habitantes originarios de una región (pág. 688); indígenas de Australia (pág. 781)
absolute location the exact position of a place on the Earth's surface (p. 17)	**localización absoluta** ubicación exacta de un lugar en la superficie terrestre (pág. 17)
***abundant** present in large amounts; plentiful (p. 558)	***abundante** presente en grandes cantidades; copioso (pág. 558)
***access** a way to approach or enter (pp. 295, 755)	***acceso** ruta para acercarse o entrar a un lugar (págs. 295, 755)
***accompany** to be together with something (p. 781)	***acompañar** estar junto a alguien o algo (pág. 781)
accretion slow process in which an oceanic plate slides under a continental plate, creating debris that can cause continents to grow (p. 47)	**acreción** proceso lento en el cual una placa oceánica se desliza por debajo de una placa continental, de modo que se forman detritos que originan el crecimiento de los continentes (pág. 47)
acculturation cultural modification of an individual, group, or people by adapting to or borrowing traits from another culture (p. 714)	**aculturación** cambio cultural de un individuo, grupo o pueblo que se presenta cuando este se adapta a las características de otra cultura o las adquiere (pág. 714)
***accumulate** to build up (p. 644)	***acumular** amontonar (pág. 644)
***accurate** free from error (p. 303)	***preciso** sin errores (pág. 303)
***achieve** to carry out successfully; to accomplish (p. 259)	***lograr** realizar exitosamente; cumplir (pág. 259)
acid deposition wet or dry airborne acids that fall to the ground (p. 286)	**deposición ácida** partículas ácidas húmedas o secas que caen al suelo (pág. 286)
acid rain precipitation carrying large amounts of dissolved acids, which kills wildlife and damages buildings, forests, and crops (p. 135)	**lluvia ácida** precipitación con grandes cantidades de ácidos disueltos, que destruye la vida silvestre y daña edificaciones, bosques y cultivos (pág. 135)
***acquire** to gain possession (p. 341)	***adquirir** obtener la posesión de algo (pág. 341)
***adapt** to make fit to changing circumstances (p. 791)	***adaptarse** ajustarse a las circunstancias cambiantes (pág. 791)
***adequate** satisfactory or acceptable (p. 406)	***adecuado** satisfactorio o aceptable (pág. 406)
***administer** to manage; to supervise (p. 592)	***administrar** dirigir; supervisar (pág. 592)
***advocate** to publicly recommend or support (p. 151)	***defender** recomendar o apoyar públicamente (pág. 151)
***affect** to have an effect on; to produce an effect upon (pp. 704, 737)	***afectar** tener un efecto en algo; influir en algo (págs. 704, 737)
agribusiness an industry engaged in agriculture on a large scale, sometimes including the manufacture and distribution of farm supplies (p. 281)	**agroindustria** industria relacionada con la agricultura a gran escala, que en ocasiones incluye la manufactura y distribución de insumos agrícolas (pág. 281)
alluvial plain floodplain, such as the Gangetic Plain in India, on which flooding rivers have deposited silt (p. 606)	**llanura aluvial** planicie en la cual las inundaciones fluviales depositan limo, como la llanura del Ganges en la India (pág. 606)

ENGLISH ESPAÑOL

ENGLISH	ESPAÑOL
alluvial soil rich soil made up of sand and mud deposited by running water (p. 369)	**suelo aluvial** suelo fértil compuesto de arena y lodo depositados por una corriente de agua (pág. 369)
***alter** to change partly (p. 120)	***alterar** cambiar parcialmente (pág. 120)
***alternative** different from the usual or regular (p. 236)	***alternativa** diferente de lo usual o común (pág. 236)
altiplano Spanish for "high plain," a region in Peru and Bolivia encircled by the Andes (p. 218)	**altiplano** llanura alta; región de Perú y Bolivia rodeada por los Andes (pág. 218)
***altitude** height above sea level (p. 576)	***altitud** altura sobre el nivel del mar (pág. 576)
animist pertaining to the religious beliefs of animism in which nature, such as animals and mountains, has spirits (p. 491)	**animista** relacionado con las creencias religiosas del animismo, según las cuales los elementos de la naturaleza, como los animales y las montañas, tienen espíritu (pág. 491)
***annual** occurring once a year (p. 610)	***anual** que ocurre una vez al año (pág. 610)
***approximate** close to but not exact (p. 712)	***aproximado** cercano pero no exacto (pág. 712)
***approximately** about or nearly (p. 514)	***aproximadamente** casi o alrededor de (pág. 514)
aquaculture the cultivation of seafood (pp. 148, 719, 729)	**acuicultura** cultivo de especies acuáticas (págs. 148, 719, 729)
aqueduct a channel or pipeline for carrying a large quantity of flowing water (p. 138)	**acueducto** canal o tubería que transporta una gran cantidad de agua corriente (pág. 138)
aquifer underground water-bearing layers of porous rock, sand, or gravel (pp. 54, 380, 654)	**acuífero** estrato de roca permeable, arena o grava que almacena agua subterránea (págs. 54, 380, 654)
archipelago a group or chain of islands (pp. 197, 704)	**archipiélago** grupo o cadena de islas (págs. 197, 704)
***area** a geographical region; the amount of space that the surface of a place covers (p. 484)	***área** región geográfica; espacio que ocupa la superficie de un lugar (pág. 484)
arid excessively dry (p. 434)	**árido** excesivamente seco (pág. 434)
artesian well a well that brings pressurized water to the surface without pumping (p. 778)	**pozo artesiano** pozo por el cual el agua sometida a presión asciende a la superficie, sin necesidad de bombearla (pág. 778)
***assume** to gain or acquire (p. 418)	***asumir** contraer o adquirir (pág. 418)
atheist a person who does not believe in God (p. 689)	**ateo** persona que no cree en Dios (pág. 689)
atmosphere a thin layer of gases that surrounds the Earth (p. 42)	**atmósfera** capa delgada de gases que rodea la Tierra (pág. 42)
atoll a ring-shaped island formed by the buildup of a coral reef on the rim of a submerged volcano (p. 777)	**atolón** isla en forma de anillo compuesta por la acumulación de arrecifes de coral alrededor de un volcán sumergido (pág. 777)
***attribute** to explain by indicating a cause (p. 204)	***atribuir** explicar indicando una causa (pág. 204)
***authority** power to influence or command thought, opinion, or behavior (pp. 88, 731)	***autoridad** poder de influenciar o dominar el pensamiento, la opinión o el comportamiento (págs. 88, 731)
autocracy system of government in which one person rules with unlimited power and authority (p. 88)	**autocracia** sistema de gobierno en el cual una persona dirige con poder y autoridad ilimitados (pág. 88)
***available** able to be obtained (p. 639)	***disponible** que se puede utilizar (pág. 639)
avalanche a large mass of ice, snow, and rock that slides down a mountainside (p. 273)	**avalancha** gran masa de hielo, nieve y roca que se desliza por una ladera (pág. 273)

ENGLISH	ESPAÑOL
average daily temperature the average of the daily high temperature and the overnight low; often used for comparison across climate regions (p. 69)	**temperatura media diaria** promedio de la temperatura máxima diurna y la temperatura mínima nocturna; por lo general se usa para hacer comparaciones entre las regiones climáticas (pág. 69)
axis an imaginary line that runs through the center of the Earth between the North and South Poles (p. 60)	**eje** línea imaginaria que atraviesa el centro de la Tierra del Polo Norte al Polo Sur (pág. 60)

B

ENGLISH	ESPAÑOL
Balkanization division of a region into smaller hostile regions (p. 320)	**balcanización** división de una región en zonas más pequeñas, que tienen relaciones hostiles (pág. 320)
basin an area drained by a river and its tributaries (p. 554)	**cuenca** área drenada por un río y sus tributarios (pág. 554)
bedouin member of the nomadic desert peoples of North Africa and Southwest Asia (p. 375)	**beduino** miembro de los pueblos nómadas de los desiertos de África del Norte y el Sudoeste Asiático (pág. 375)
***benefit** to gain (p. 486); to promote well-being; to be useful (p. 780)	***beneficiar** ganar (p. 486); promover el bienestar; ser útil (pág. 780)
biodiversity biological diversity in an environment as indicated by numbers of different species of plants and animals (p. 199); the diverse life forms in a habitat or ecosystem (p. 758)	**biodiversidad** diversidad biológica de un medioambiente expresada mediante la cantidad de especies vegetales y animales diferentes (pág. 199); las diversas formas de vida de un hábitat o un ecosistema (pág. 758)
biome major type of ecological community defined primarily by distinctive plant and animal groups (p. 69)	**bioma** área extensa ocupada por una comunidad ecológica definida principalmente a partir de las especies vegetales y animales que predominan allí (pág. 69)
biofuel fuel created from living matter, such as trees (p. 568)	**biocombustible** combustible que se obtiene de materia orgánica, como los árboles (pág. 568)
biosphere the part of the Earth where life exists (p. 42)	**biosfera** parte de la Tierra donde hay vida (pág. 42)
birthrate number of births per year for every 1,000 people (p. 82)	**tasa de natalidad** número de nacimientos al año por cada 1,000 habitantes (pág. 82)
black market illegal trade of scarce or illegal goods, usually sold at high prices (p. 346)	**mercado negro** comercio ilegal de productos ilícitos o escasos, que por lo general se venden a precios altos (pág. 346)
boomerang an Australian throwing stick that soars and curves in flight and returns near the thrower (p. 781)	**bumerán** utensilio de madera originario de Australia que al ser lanzado hace un movimiento curvo y vuelve a quien lo lanzó (pág. 781)
brain drain the loss of highly educated and skilled workers to other countries (p. 225)	**fuga de talentos** migración de trabajadores altamente calificados e instruidos hacia otros países (pág. 225)
break-of-bulk act of unloading, transferring, or distributing part or all of a shipment (p. 258)	**descarga** acción de descargar, transferir o distribuir parte de un cargamento o su totalidad (pág. 258)
buffer zone a neutral area serving to separate powerful nations or nations that are hostile to each other (p. 759)	**zona de amortiguación** área neutral que separa naciones poderosas o que tienen relaciones hostiles (pág. 759)
***bulk** the greater part of something (p. 809)	***grueso** la mayor parte de algo (pág. 809)
bush a sparsely inhabited region (p. 776)	**monte** región poco poblada (pág. 776)

C

ENGLISH	ESPAÑOL
caldera a large volcanic crater (p. 777)	**caldera** gran cráter volcánico (pág. 777)
canopy top layer of a rain forest, where the tops of tall trees form a continuous layer of leaves (p. 558)	**dosel** capa superior de una selva tropical, donde las copas de los árboles más altos forman una cubierta de hojas (pág. 558)

Glossary/Glosario

ENGLISH	ESPAÑOL
cap-and-trade a method for managing pollution in which a limit is placed on emissions and businesses or countries can buy and sell emissions allowances (p. 287)	**comercio de derechos de emisión** método de control de la polución según el cual se establece un límite a las emisiones, y las empresas o países pueden comprar y vender permisos de emisión (pág. 287)
capitalism a system in which factors of production are privately owned (p. 95)	**capitalismo** sistema en el que los medios de producción son de propiedad privada (p. 95)
carrying capacity the population that an area will support without undergoing deterioration (p. 522); the maximum population of any given species that an environment can sustain (p. 546)	**capacidad de carga** población que puede soportar un medioambiente sin deteriorarse (pág. 522); población máxima de una especie dada que puede soportar un medioambiente (pág. 546)
cash crop farm product grown to be sold or traded rather than used by the farm family (pp. 181, 560)	**cultivo comercial** producto agrícola que se cultiva para venta o intercambio, no para el consumo de las familias que lo cultivan (págs. 181, 560)
cataract a large waterfall (p. 507)	**catarata** cascada de gran tamaño (pág. 507)
central place theory geographical theory that seeks to explain the number, size, and location of human settlements in an urban system (p. 104)	**teoría de los lugares centrales** teoría geográfica que busca explicar el número, tamaño y ubicación de los asentamientos humanos en un sistema urbano (pág. 104)
cereal any grain like barley, oats, or wheat, grown for food (p. 457)	**cereal** grano que se cultiva para el consumo, como la cebada, la avena o el trigo (pág. 457)
***challenge** to arouse or stimulate especially by presenting with difficulties (p. 340)	***desafiar** retar o estimular especialmente planteando dificultades (pág. 340)
chernozem (cher•nuh•ZYAWM) rich, black topsoil found in the Northern European Plain, especially in Russia and Ukraine (p. 336)	***chernozem*** tierra negra y rica en humus que se encuentra en la llanura noreuropea, particularmente en Rusia y Ucrania (pág. 336)
chinook a seasonal warm wind that blows down the Rockies in late winter and early spring (p. 147)	***chinook*** viento estacional cálido y seco que sopla desde las montañas Rocosas a finales de invierno y comienzos de primavera (pág. 147)
chlorofluorocarbon (CFC) a chemical substance, found mainly in liquid coolants, that damages the Earth's protective ozone layer (p. 720)	**clorofluorocarbono (CFC)** sustancia química empleada principalmente en los refrigerantes líquidos, que deteriora la capa de ozono que protege la Tierra (pág. 720)
choke point a strategic, narrow waterway between two larger bodies of water (p. 443)	**punto de estrangulamiento** vía fluvial reducida entre dos cuerpos de agua más grandes que tiene fines estratégicos (pág. 443)
***circumstance** an event or fact that accompanies or determines another (p. 497)	***circunstancia** suceso o hecho que se relaciona con otro o lo determina (pág. 497)
***cite** to summon to appear in a court of law (p. 588)	***citar** convocar para comparecer ante un tribunal (pág. 588)
city-state an independently governed community consisting of a city and the surrounding lands, notably present in ancient Greece (p. 299)	**ciudad-estado** comunidad política independiente que incluye una ciudad y el territorio circundante, propia de la antigua Grecia (pág. 299)
clan a large group of people descended from the same ancestor; a family group (pp. 494, 710); a group of close-knit, interrelated families (p. 781)	**clan** grupo numeroso de personas que descienden de un mismo antepasado; grupo familiar (págs. 494, 710); grupo de familias estrechamente relacionadas (pág. 781)
clear-cutting the removal of all trees in a stand of timber (pp. 134, 664)	**tala generalizada** corte de todos los árboles de un área (págs. 134, 664)
climate weather patterns typical for an area over a long period of time (p. 60)	**clima** patrones de tiempo atmosférico característicos de un área en un periodo largo (pág. 60)

ENGLISH	ESPAÑOL
climate change any significant change in the measures of climate lasting for an extended period of time (p. 813)	**cambio climático** cualquier cambio significativo del clima en un periodo prolongado (pág. 813)
***coincide** to happen in the same place and at the same time (p. 447)	***coincidir** ocurrir en el mismo lugar y al mismo tiempo (pág. 447)
Cold War the power struggle between the Soviet Union and the United States after World War II (p. 277)	**Guerra Fría** conflicto de poder entre Estados Unidos y la Unión Soviética después de la Segunda Guerra Mundial (pág. 277)
command economy a system of resource management in which decisions about production and distribution of goods and services are made by a central authority (p. 95)	**economía planificada** sistema de la administración de recursos en el cual una autoridad central toma las decisiones relacionadas con la producción y distribución de bienes y servicios (pág. 95)
commercial farming growing large quantities of crops or livestock in order to sell them for a profit (p. 587)	**agricultura comercial** producción de grandes cantidades de cultivos o ganado para obtener ganancias (pág. 587)
commune a collective farming community whose members share work and products (p. 690)	**comuna** comunidad agrícola colectiva cuyos miembros comparten el trabajo y los bienes que producen (pág. 690)
communism society based on equitable distribution of wealth, land, and public ownership of production (p. 276)	**comunismo** sociedad basada en la distribución equitativa de la riqueza, la tierra y la propiedad pública de los medios de producción (pág. 276)
***community** people with common interests living in a particular area (p. 82)	***comunidad** personas con intereses comunes que viven en un área específica (pág. 82)
complementarity relationship between two places in which one produces something the other needs, resulting in an exchange (p. 302)	**complementariedad** relación entre dos lugares en la cual uno produce algo que el otro necesita, de modo que se produce un intercambio (pág. 302)
***compound** to make something more extreme or intense by adding something to it (p. 791)	***combinar** hacer que un elemento sea más extremo o intenso agregando algo a este (pág. 791)
***comprehensive** covering completely or broadly; inclusive (p. 279)	***exhaustivo** que abarca completamente o ampliamente; inclusivo (pág. 279)
***comprise** to make up; to constitute (p. 317)	***comprender** conformar; constituir (pág. 317)
***concentrated** less dilute (p. 469)	***concentrado** menos diluido (pág. 469)
condensation the process of excess water vapor changing into liquid water when warm air cools (p. 51)	**condensación** proceso mediante el cual el exceso de vapor de agua se convierte en agua líquida cuando el aire caliente se enfría (pág. 51)
***conflict** a competition or struggle (p. 126)	***conflicto** competencia o lucha (pág. 126)
conflict diamonds diamonds that are mined in war-torn areas and are used to finance one or more parties involved (p. 534)	**diamantes de guerra** diamantes que se extraen de zonas devastadas por la guerra y con los cuales se financia una o más partes involucradas (pág. 534)
conic projection a map created by projecting an image of Earth onto a cone placed over part of an Earth model (p. 15)	**proyección cónica** mapa que se crea proyectando una imagen de la Tierra sobre un cono situado en una parte de un modelo terrestre (pág. 15)
coniferous referring to vegetation having cones and needle-shaped leaves, including many evergreens, that keep their foliage throughout the winter (p. 71)	**conífera** vegetación con conos y hojas en forma de aguja, como muchos árboles de hoja perenne, que mantiene su follaje durante el invierno (pág. 71)
connectivity the directness of routes linking pairs of places (p. 102)	**conectividad** efectividad de las rutas que conectan dos lugares (pág. 102)
conquistador Spanish for "conqueror"; Spanish soldier who participated in conquest of indigenous peoples of Latin America (p. 181)	**conquistador** soldado español que participó en la conquista de los pueblos indígenas de América Latina (pág. 181)
***consequence** the result of an action (p. 694)	***consecuencia** resultado de una acción (pág. 694)

ENGLISH	ESPAÑOL
***consist** to be composed of or made up of (pp. 270, 704)	***consistir** estar compuesto o formado por (págs. 270, 704)
***constant** unchanging (p. 51)	***constante** que no cambia (pág. 51)
***constitute** to compose or form (p. 507)	***constituir** componer o formar (pág. 507)
continental relating to or characteristic of a continent (p. 256)	**continental** relacionado con un continente o característico de este tipo de formación (pág. 256)
continental drift the theory that the continents were once joined and then slowly drifted apart (p. 45)	**deriva continental** teoría según la cual los continentes alguna vez estuvieron unidos y luego se separaron lentamente (pág. 45)
continental shelf part of a continent that extends out underneath the ocean (p. 43)	**plataforma continental** parte de un continente que se extiende por debajo del océano (pág. 43)
continentality effect of extreme variation in temperature and very little precipitation within the interior portions of a landmass (p. 340)	**continentalidad** efecto de la variación extrema de la temperatura y la precipitación escasa en las áreas interiores de un continente (pág. 340)
***contribute** to give or supply (p. 136)	***contribuir** dar o suministrar (pág. 136)
***controversy** the presence of opposing views (p. 148)	***controversia** presencia de puntos de vista opuestos (pág. 148)
***converse** reversed in order, relation, or action (p. 802)	***contrario** opuesto en orden, relación o acción (pág. 802)
***convert** to change from one system, use, or method to another (p. 535)	***convertir** cambiar de un sistema, uso o método a otro (pág. 535)
***cooperation** a common effort (p. 211)	***cooperación** esfuerzo colectivo (pág. 211)
***cooperative** an organization, often a farm, whose members work together and share expenses and profits (p. 729)	***cooperativa** organización, por lo general una granja, cuyos miembros trabajan juntos y comparten gastos y ganancias (pág. 729)
copra dried coconut meat fed to animal herds (p. 790)	**copra** pulpa seca del coco que sirve de alimento para los rebaños (pág. 790)
coral the limestone skeleton of a tiny sea animal (p. 780)	**coral** esqueleto calcáreo de un animal marino diminuto (pág. 780)
coral reef a reef made up of fragments of corals, coral sands, algal, and other organic deposits, and the solid limestone resulting from their consolidation (p. 801)	**arrecife de coral** arrecife compuesto por fragmentos de corales, arena de coral, algas y otros depósitos orgánicos, y la piedra caliza que se forma cuando estos elementos se consolidan (pág. 801)
cordillera parallel chains or ranges of mountains (p. 218)	**cordillera** cadenas de montañas paralelas (pág. 218)
core innermost layer of the Earth made up of a super-hot but solid inner core and a super-hot liquid outer core (p. 44)	**núcleo** centro de la Tierra compuesto por un núcleo interno sólido y un núcleo externo líquido, ambos extremadamente calientes (pág. 44)
Coriolis effect the resulting diagonal movement, either north or south, of prevailing winds caused by the Earth's rotation (p. 66)	**efecto Coriolis** movimiento diagonal de los vientos predominantes, en dirección norte o sur, causado por la rotación de la Tierra (pág. 66)
***corporate** formed into an association and endowed by law with the rights and liabilities of an individual (p. 188)	***corporativo** que se ha convertido en una asociación a la cual la ley ha otorgado los derechos y responsabilidades civiles de un individuo (pág. 188)
***corresponding** showing a direct connection between two things (p. 340)	***correspondiente** que muestra una relación directa entre dos elementos (pág. 340)
cottage industry a business that employs workers in their homes (pp. 205, 617)	**industria artesanal** empresa en la cual las personas trabajan desde su hogar (págs. 205, 617)
coup an overthrow of the government (p. 731)	**golpe de Estado** derrocamiento de un gobierno (pág. 731)
cowrie shell the protective outer covering of a small sea creature, once used as money in Asia and Africa (p. 656)	**cauri** caparazón de una criatura marina pequeña que se usaba como moneda en Asia y África (pág. 656)

Glossary/Glosario

ENGLISH

***create** to bring into being or cause to exist (p. 45)

***crucial** vitally important (p. 65)

crust outer layer of the Earth, a hard rocky shell forming Earth's surface (p. 44)

cultural boundary a geographical boundary between two different cultures (p. 90)

cultural diffusion the spread of culture traits, material and non-material, from one culture to another (p. 80)

cultural divergence a separation of people or societies, with regard to beliefs, values, and customs, due to a division under different political systems (p. 733)

culture way of life of a group of people who share similar culture traits, including beliefs, customs, technology, and material items (p. 78)

***culture** the customary beliefs, social forms, and material traits of a racial, religious, or social group (p. 180)

culture hearth a center where cultures developed and from which ideas and traditions spread outward (pp. 80, 416)

culture region division of the Earth in which people share a similar way of life, including language, religion, economic systems, and values (p. 79)

cuneiform wedge-shaped symbols that were pressed into clay tablets (p. 416)

current cold or warm stream of seawater that flows in the oceans, generally in a circular pattern (p. 65)

cyclone a storm with heavy rains and high winds that blow in a circular pattern around an area of low atmospheric pressure (p. 609)

cyclone, typhoon a spiral-shaped tropical storm in which the winds have reached speeds of at least 74 miles per hour (119 km per hour). Storms in the Northwestern Pacific, west of the International Date Line, are called typhoons; storms in the Southwest Pacific or Indian Oceans are referred to as cyclones. (p. 757)

cylindrical projection a map created by projecting Earth's image onto a cylinder (p. 15)

czar ruler of Russia until the 1917 revolution; originally from Latin word *Caesar*, title of Roman emperors (p. 341)

death rate number of deaths per year for every 1,000 people (p. 82)

deciduous falling off or shed seasonally or periodically; trees such as oak and maple, which lose their leaves in autumn (p. 71)

***decline** to become less in amount (p. 344)

ESPAÑOL

***crear** dar vida o hacer que exista (pág. 45)

***crucial** de vital importancia (pág. 65)

corteza capa exterior de la Tierra, rocosa y sólida, que forma la superficie terrestre (pág. 44)

frontera cultural límite geográfico entre dos culturas diferentes (pág. 90)

difusión cultural expansión de características culturales, materiales e inmateriales, de una cultura a otra (pág. 80)

divergencia cultural separación de personas o sociedades con respecto a sus creencias, valores y costumbres debido a la división causada por sistemas políticos diferentes (pág. 733)

cultura modo de vida de un grupo de personas que comparten características culturales similares, tales como creencias, costumbres, tecnología y elementos materiales (pág. 78)

***cultura** creencias usuales, actitudes sociales y rasgos materiales de un grupo racial, religioso o social (pág. 180)

centro cultural centro donde se desarrollaron las culturas y desde los cuales se difundieron las ideas y tradiciones (págs. 80, 416)

región cultural división en la cual las personas comparten un modo de vida similar, tal como el idioma, la religión, los sistemas económicos y los valores (pág. 79)

cuneiforme símbolos en forma de cuña inscritos en tablas de arcilla (pág. 416)

corriente movimiento del agua marina fría o cálida en un patrón circular (pág. 65)

ciclón tormenta con lluvias y vientos fuertes que circula alrededor de un área con baja presión atmosférica (pág. 609)

tifón (ciclón) tormenta tropical en forma de espiral cuyos vientos han alcanzado una velocidad mínima de 74 millas por hora (119 km/h). Las tormentas del Pacífico Noroeste, al oeste de la línea internacional de cambio de fecha, se llaman tifones; las del Pacífico Sur y el océano Índico se conocen como ciclones. (pág. 757)

proyección cilíndrica mapa que se crea proyectando la imagen de la Tierra en un cilindro (pág. 15)

zar gobernador de Rusia hasta la revolución de 1917; se deriva de la palabra latina *Caesar*, título de los emperadores romanos (pág. 341)

tasa de mortalidad número de fallecimientos en un año por cada 1,000 habitantes (pág. 82)

caducifolio relacionado con la vegetación que muda según la estación o periódicamente; árboles que pierden sus hojas en otoño, como los robles y los arces (pág. 71)

***disminuir** reducir en número o cantidad (pág. 344)

ENGLISH

deforestation the loss or destruction of forests, mainly for logging or farming (pp. 188, 738, 766)

delta a triangular section of land formed by sand and silt carried downriver (p. 487); a triangular-shaped area of silt and sediment deposit found at the mouth of a river (p. 578); an alluvial deposit at a river's mouth that is shaped roughly like the Greek letter delta (Δ) (p. 631)

democracy system of government in which leaders rule with consent of the citizens (p. 89)

demographic transition the model that uses birthrates and death rates to show how populations in countries or regions change over time (p. 82)

***demonstrate** to clearly show the value of (p. 547)

***derive** to obtain something from (pp. 66, 368)

desalination the removal of salt from seawater to make it usable for drinking and farming (pp. 53, 447)

desertification process in which arable land becomes desert (p. 404); the destruction of land in arid and semiarid climates (p. 496)

devolution the granting of self-rule to local and regional authorities (p. 277)

dialect local form of a language used in a particular place or by a certain group (p. 203)

***differentiate** to recognize features that make similar regions, communities, or people different from each other (p. 756)

dike large bank of earth and stone that holds back water (p. 272)

***diminish** to make less or cause to appear less (p. 159)

dissident a citizen who speaks out against government policies (p. 691)

***distinct** recognizably different (p. 70)

***diverse** differing from one another (p. 180)

divide a high point or ridge that determines the direction rivers flow (p. 121)

***document** to write to provide information (p. 443)

doldrums a frequently windless area near the Equator (p. 66)

domesticate to adapt plants and animals from the wild for human use (pp. 372, 489)

***dominate** to have a commanding position in (p. 611); to exert influence over (pp. 689, 779)

dominion a partially self-governing country with close ties to another country (p. 150); a largely self-governing country within the British Empire (p. 782)

ESPAÑOL

deforestación pérdida o destrucción de bosques principalmente por la explotación maderera y agrícola (págs. 188, 738, 766)

delta terreno triangular que se forma donde una corriente fluvial deposita arena y limo (pág. 487); terreno triangular en la desembocadura de un río formado por un depósito de limo y sedimento (pág. 578); depósito aluvial en la desembocadura de un río cuya forma se parece a la letra griega delta (Δ) (pág. 631)

democracia sistema de gobierno según el cual los líderes dirigen con el consentimiento de los ciudadanos (pág. 89)

transición demográfica modelo que se vale de las tasas de natalidad y mortalidad para mostrar la manera como cambia la población de los países o regiones con el paso del tiempo (pág. 82)

***demostrar** mostrar claramente el valor de algo (pág. 547)

***derivar** obtener algo de otro elemento (págs. 66, 368)

desalinización proceso que elimina la sal del agua marina para que sea potable y apta para la agricultura (págs. 53, 447)

desertización proceso en el cual la tierra cultivable se convierte en un desierto (pág. 404); destrucción del suelo en áreas de climas áridos y semiáridos (pág. 496)

descentralización proceso de devolver la autonomía a las autoridades regionales y locales (pág. 277)

dialecto variedad local de una lengua que comparte un grupo específico o se habla en un lugar particular (pág. 203)

***diferenciar** reconocer las características que hacen que regiones, comunidades o personas similares se diferencien unas de otras (pág. 756)

dique gran muro de tierra y piedra que retiene el agua (pág. 272)

***reducir** hacer menos o hacer parecer menos (pág. 159)

disidente ciudadano que manifiesta su oposición con respecto a las políticas gubernamentales (pág. 691)

***distinto** evidentemente diferente (pág. 70)

***diverso** que se diferencia de otro (pág. 180)

divisoria terreno alto o cresta que determina la dirección de las corrientes fluviales (pág. 121)

***documentar** escribir para suministrar información (pág. 443)

calmas ecuatoriales área con vientos muy suaves cercana al ecuador (pág. 66)

domesticar adaptar especies vegetales y animales silvestres para el beneficio humano (págs. 372, 489)

***dominar** tener una posición de mando (pág. 611); ejercer influencia (págs. 689, 779)

dominio país con autonomía parcial que tiene vínculos estrechos con otra nación (pág. 150); país autónomo que formaba parte del Imperio británico (pág. 782)

ENGLISH	ESPAÑOL
doubling time the number of years it takes for a population to double in size (p. 83)	**tiempo de duplicación** número de años que tarda una población en doblar su tamaño (pág. 83)
drift-net fishing the use of fishing nets of great length and depth (p. 739)	**pesca con redes de deriva** uso de redes de pesca de gran tamaño y profundidad (pág. 739)
dry farming a farming method used in dry regions in which crops are grown that rely only on the natural precipitation (p. 127)	**agricultura de secano** método agrícola que se emplea en regiones secas, en el cual se siembran cultivos que dependen solo de las precipitaciones naturales (pág. 127)
dune a mound or ridge of sand formed by the wind (p. 435)	**duna** colina o montículo de arena que se forma por el viento (pág. 435)
***dynamic** energetic, characterized by constant change and progress (p. 765)	***dinámico** enérgico, que se caracteriza por el cambio y el progreso constantes (pág. 765)
dynasty a ruling house or continuing family of rulers, especially in China (p. 685)	**dinastía** casa real o serie de gobernantes de una misma familia, particularmente en China (pág. 685)
dzong a fortified monastery that also served as an administrative and commercial center (p. 660)	**jong** fortaleza-monasterio que también servía como centro administrativo y comercial (pág. 660)

E

ENGLISH	ESPAÑOL
e-commerce buying and selling on the Internet (p. 541)	**comercio electrónico** compra y venta de productos por Internet (pág. 541)
economic sanction a restriction placed on trade (p. 691)	**sanción económica** restricción al comercio (pág. 691)
***economy** an ordered system for the production, distribution, and consumption of goods and services (p. 317)	***economía** sistema ordenado para la producción, la distribución y el consumo de bienes y servicios (pág. 317)
ecotourism the practice and business of recreational travel based on concern for the environment (pp. 205, 264, 624)	**ecoturismo** práctica y empresa relacionadas con los viajes recreativos que se basan en el cuidado del medioambiente (págs. 205, 264, 624)
elevation the height of a land surface above the level of the sea (p. 18)	**altura (altitud)** distancia de un punto en la superficie terrestre con respecto al nivel del mar (pág. 18)
El Niño a periodic reversal of the pattern of ocean currents and water temperatures in the mid-Pacific region (p. 67)	**El Niño** cambio periódico en los patrones de las corrientes marinas y la temperatura del agua en la región del Pacífico Medio (pág. 67)
embargo a ban on trade (p. 421)	**embargo** prohibición al comercio (pág. 421)
***emerge** to rise from an obscure position or condition; to become visible (p. 251)	***emerger** aparecer desde una posición o condición de oscuridad; hacerse visible (pág. 251)
emerging market an economy that may not have been very strong in the recent past, but that is in transition to becoming a stronger market (p. 764)	**mercado emergente** economía que no fue sólida en el pasado reciente, pero que se encuentra en el proceso de convertirse en un mercado más fuerte (pág. 764)
emigrate to leave one's own country to settle permanently in another (p. 153)	**emigrar** dejar el país natal para establecerse permanentemente en otro (pág. 153)
***emphasis** importance or special consideration (p. 327)	***énfasis** importancia o consideración especial (pág. 327)
enclave a distinct territorial or cultural area that is within a foreign territory (p. 463)	**enclave** territorio o grupo cultural que se encuentra dentro de otro territorio (pág. 463)
***energy** usable power (p. 198)	***energía** fuerza aprovechable (pág. 198)
***enhance** to improve or increase (p. 490)	***realzar** mejorar o aumentar (pág. 490)
***enormous** gigantic; exceedingly large (p. 52)	***enorme** gigantesco; extremadamente grande (pág. 52)
***ensure** to make sure or certain (p. 288)	***asegurar** garantizar o hacer que algo sea seguro (pág. 288)

Glossary/Glosario

ENGLISH	ESPAÑOL
entrepôt commercial center where goods are received (p. 258)	**almacén aduanero** centro de comercio donde se reciben mercancías (pág. 258)
***environment** natural surroundings (p. 534); the complex of physical, chemical, and biotic factors (such as climate, soil, and living things) that act upon an organism or an ecological community and ultimately determine its survival (p. 621)	***medioambiente** entorno natural (pág. 534); unión de factores físicos, químicos y bióticos (como el clima, el suelo y los seres vivos) que actúan sobre un organismo o una comunidad ecológica y básicamente determinan su supervivencia (pág. 621)
equinox one of two days (about March 21 and September 23) on which the sun is directly above the Equator, making day and night equal in length (p. 61)	**equinoccio** uno de dos días (hacia el 21 de marzo y el 23 de septiembre) en los cuales el sol se encuentra directamente sobre el ecuador, de modo que la duración del día y la noche es igual (pág. 61)
erosion the movement of weathered rock and material by wind, glaciers, and moving water (p. 49); the wearing away of soil (p. 546)	**erosión** proceso por el cual el viento, los glaciares y el agua en movimiento transportan roca y material desgastados (pág. 49); desgaste del suelo (pág. 546)
escarpment a steep cliff or slope between a higher and lower land surface (pp. 219, 507, 576)	**escarpe** acantilado o pendiente entre una superficie más alta y una más baja (págs. 219, 507, 576)
***estimate** to judge approximately the size or value of something (p. 437)	***calcular** determinar el tamaño o el valor aproximado de algo (pág. 437)
***ethnic** of or relating to large groups of people classed according to common traits and customs (p. 321)	***étnico** perteneciente o relativo a grupos de personas extensos con características y costumbres en común (pág. 321)
ethnic cleansing the expelling from a country or genocide of an ethnic group (p. 319)	**limpieza étnica** expulsión de un país o genocidio de un grupo étnico (pág. 319)
ethnic group group of people who share common ancestry, language, religion, customs, or place of origin (p. 79)	**grupo étnico** grupo de personas que tienen la misma ascendencia, lengua, religión, lugar de origen y costumbres (pág. 79)
***ethnicity** relating to races or large groups of people classed according to common traits and customs (p. 732)	***etnicidad** relativo a etnias o extensos grupos de personas con características y costumbres en común (pág. 732)
eutrophication process by which a body of water becomes too rich in dissolved nutrients, leading to plant growth that depletes oxygen (p. 137)	**eutrofización** proceso por el cual en un cuerpo de agua se presenta un aumento excesivo de nutrientes disueltos, lo cual da lugar a un crecimiento de plantas que agota el oxígeno(pág. 137)
evaporation the process of converting liquid into vapor, or gas (p. 51)	**evaporación** proceso por el cual un líquido se convierte en vapor o gas (pág. 51)
***eventually** in the end, especially after a long delay (p. 63)	***a la larga** al final, especialmente luego de una demora (pág. 63)
***exceed** to be greater than (p. 412)	***exceder** ser más grande que algo (pág. 412)
exclave a territory that belongs to a particular political unit but is separated from it and surrounded by another political unit (p. 462)	**exclave** territorio que pertenece a una unidad política específica pero que está separado de esta y se encuentra rodeado por otra unidad política (pág. 462)
***exhibit** to demonstrate or show publicly (p. 198)	***manifestar** exponer o mostrar públicamente (pág. 198)
***exploit** to make use of a resource (p. 656)	***explotar** hacer uso de un recurso (pág. 656)
***export** a commodity sent from one country to another for purposes of trade (p. 517)	***exportación** conjunto de mercancías que se envía de un país a otro con fines comerciales (pág. 517)
***expose** to put someone at risk for harm or injury (p. 469)	***exponer** poner a alguien en riesgo, de manera que puede resultar lastimado o perjudicado (pág. 469)
extended family household made up of several generations of family members (p. 183)	**familia extensa** grupo familiar compuesto por varias generaciones de parientes (pág. 183)
***external** arising outside of (p. 49)	***externo** que se manifiesta hacia el exterior (pág. 49)
***extract** to remove (pp. 158, 665)	***extraer** remover (págs. 158, 665)

F

ENGLISH	ESPAÑOL
***factor** something that actively contributes to the production of a result (p. 306)	***factor** algo que contribuye activamente a la producción de un resultado (pág. 306)
fall line a boundary in the eastern United States where the higher land of the Piedmont drops to the lower Atlantic Coastal Plain (p. 121)	**línea de descenso** frontera en el este de Estados Unidos donde la meseta de Piedmont se une con la llanura litoral atlántica (pág. 121)
fault a crack or break in Earth's crust (pp. 47, 506)	**falla** fractura o ruptura de la corteza terrestre (págs. 47, 506)
faulting process of cracking that occurs when the folded land cannot be bent any further (p. 47)	**formación de fallas** proceso de fractura que ocurre cuando no se pueden formar más pliegues en los estratos rocosos (pág. 47)
***feature** to have as a characteristic or as a prominent attribute (p. 177)	***distinguirse** tener una característica o un atributo prominente (pág. 177)
federal system form of government in which powers are divided between the national government and state or provincial government (p. 87)	**sistema federal** forma de gobierno en la cual el poder se divide entre el gobierno nacional y el gobierno estatal o provincial (pág. 87)
feeder stream a tributary to a larger river (p. 424)	**afluente** tributario de un río grande (pág. 424)
fertilizer a chemical or natural substance added to soil or land to increase its fertility; a substance (as manure or a chemical mixture) used to make soil more fertile (pp. 402, 740)	**fertilizante** sustancia química o natural que se agrega al suelo para que sea más fértil; sustancia (como el estiércol o una mezcla química) que se usa para que el suelo sea más fértil (págs. 402, 740)
First Nation one of the indigenous peoples of Canada who are neither Inuit nor Métis (p. 149)	**Primera Nación** uno de los pueblos indígenas de Canadá excluyendo a los inuits y los métis (pág. 149)
fishery an area in which fish or sea animals are caught (p. 148); a place for catching fish, the fishing industry (p. 546)	**pesquería** área donde se atrapan peces y animales marinos (pág. 148); lugar donde se pesca, la industria pesquera (pág. 546)
fjord (fee•YAWRD) a long, steep-sided glacial valley now filled by seawater (p. 250)	**fiordo** valle glacial largo y empinado que está cubierto de agua marina (pág. 250)
floodplain the low-lying land along a river, formed mainly by sediment that has been deposited by floodwaters (p. 632)	**planicie de inundación** tierra baja a lo largo de un río formada por los sedimentos que depositan las inundaciones fluviales (pág. 632)
***fluctuate** to ebb and flow in waves (p. 608)	***fluctuar** subir y bajar en ondas (pág. 608)
***fluctuation** a shift from a previous condition (p. 33)	***fluctuación** cambio de una condición anterior (pág. 33)
***focus** to concentrate attention or effort (p. 279)	***enfocar** concentrar la atención o el esfuerzo (pág. 279)
foehn (FUHRN) a dry wind that blows from the leeward sides of mountains, sometimes melting snow and causing avalanches; term used mainly in Europe (p. 273)	***foehn*** viento seco que sopla a sotavento de las montañas, y que a veces derrite la nieve y causa avalanchas (pág. 273)
fold a bend in layers of rock, sometimes caused by plate movement (p. 47)	**pliegue** ondulación de las capas de roca que a veces se produce por el movimiento de las placas tectónicas (pág. 47)
foreclosure legal proceeding in which a borrower's rights to a property are relinquished due to his or her inability to make payments on the loan (p. 131)	**ejecución hipotecaria** procedimiento legal mediante el cual se retiran los derechos de una propiedad a un prestatario que no puede pagar las cuotas del préstamo adquirido (pág. 131)
formal region a region defined by a common characteristic, such as production of a product (p. 30)	**región formal** región definida por una característica común, como la manufactura de un producto (pág. 30)
fossil fuel a resource formed in the Earth by plant and animal remains (p. 124)	**combustible fósil** recurso de la Tierra formado por restos de plantas y animales (pág. 124)

ENGLISH	ESPAÑOL
free enterprise a system in which private individuals or groups have the right to own property or businesses and make a profit with limited government interference (p. 94)	**libre empresa** sistema según el cual individuos o grupos privados tienen derecho a aposeer propiedades o empresas y obtener ganancias de los mismos con una interferencia gubernamental mínima (pág. 94)
free port a place where goods can be unloaded, stored, or reshipped free of import duties (p. 764)	**zona franca** lugar en el cual se pueden descargar, almacenar y reenviar mercancías sin pagar impuestos de importación (pág. 764)
free trade zone an area of a country in which trade restrictions do not apply (p. 186)	**zona de libre comercio** zona de un país en la cual no se aplican las restricciones comerciales (pág. 186)
***function** a special purpose (p. 102)	***función** propósito especial (pág. 102)
functional region a central place and the surrounding territory linked to it (p. 30)	**región funcional** lugar central y el territorio circundante que se vincula a este (pág. 30)
***furthermore** besides; in addition (p. 446)	***además** aparte de, adicionalmente (pág. 446)

G

ENGLISH	ESPAÑOL
***generate** to produce (p. 632); to bring into existence (p. 666)	***generar** producir (pág. 632); traer a la existencia (pág. 666)
***generation** a group of individuals born and living at the same time (pp. 714, 766)	***generación** grupo de individuos que nacen y viven en un mismo periodo de tiempo (págs. 714, 766)
geographic information systems (GIS) computer programs that process and organize details about places on Earth and integrate those details with satellite images and other pieces of information (p. 23)	**sistemas de información geográfica (SIG)** programas informáticos que procesan y organizan detalles sobre lugares de la Tierra y los integran con imágenes satelitales y otra información (pág. 23)
geometric boundary a boundary that follows a geometric pattern (p. 90); a fixed limit or extent that typically follows straight lines (p. 373)	**frontera geométrica** límite o frontera que tiene un patrón geométrico (pág. 90); frontera fija o extensión territorial que generalmente sigue una línea recta (pág. 373)
geopolitics government policy as it is influenced by physical, human, and economic geography (p. 444)	**geopolítica** políticas gubernamentales que se ven influidas por la geografía física, humana y económica (pág. 444)
geothermal energy a form of energy conversion that captures heat energy from within Earth (p. 251)	**energía geotérmica** forma de conversión de energía que toma energía calorífica del interior de la Tierra (pág. 251)
geyser a spring that throws forth intermittent jets of heated water and steam (p. 251)	**géiser** manantial que expulsa columnas intermitentes de agua caliente y vapor (pág. 251)
glaciation a process by which glaciers form and spread (p. 250)	**glaciación** proceso de formación y expansión de los glaciares (pág. 250)
glacier a large body of ice that moves across the surface of the Earth (p. 49)	**glaciar** enorme masa de hielo que se desliza por la superficie terrestre (pág. 49)
glasnost Russian term for a new openness in areas of politics, social issues, and media; part of Gorbachev's reform plans (p. 343)	***glasnost*** término ruso para la apertura en temas políticos, asuntos sociales y medios de comunicación; parte de los planes de reforma de Gorbachov (pág. 343)
global positioning system (GPS) a navigational system that can determine absolute location by using satellites and receivers on Earth (p. 21)	**sistema de posicionamiento global (GPS)** sistema de navegación que puede determinar una localización absoluta mediante satélites y receptores instalados en la Tierra (pág. 21)
***goal** the aim of an activity (p. 544)	***meta** objetivo de una actividad (pág. 544)
***grant** a sum of money given to a person or organization for a particular purpose (p. 815)	***beca** suma de dinero que se le da a una persona u organización para un propósito determinado (pág. 815)
grazier a New Zealand rancher (p. 790)	***grazier*** ganadero de Nueva Zelanda (pág. 790)

ENGLISH	ESPAÑOL
great circle route an imaginary line that follows the curve of the Earth and represents the shortest distance between two points (p. 14)	**ruta del círculo máximo** línea imaginaria que sigue la curvatura de la Tierra y presenta la distancia más corta entre dos puntos (pág. 14)
green revolution a program begun in the 1960s to produce higher-yielding, more productive strains of wheat, rice, and other food crops (p. 617)	**revolución verde** programa que inició en la década de 1960 con el fin de producir variedades mejoradas y más rentables de trigo, arroz y otros cultivos (pág. 617)
greenhouse effect the capacity of certain gases in the atmosphere to trap heat, thereby warming the Earth (p. 63)	**efecto invernadero** capacidad de algunos gases presentes en la atmósfera de retener el calor y así calentar la Tierra (pág. 63)
griot traditional oral historians, storytellers, singers, and musicians of West Africa (p. 540)	***griot*** historiadores orales, narradores, cantantes y músicos tradicionales de África Occidental (pág. 540)
gross domestic product (GDP) the value of goods and services produced within a country in a year (p. 185)	**producto interno bruto (PIB)** valor de los bienes y servicios producidos en un país durante un año (pág. 185)
groundwater water located underground within the Earth that supplies wells and springs (pp. 54, 590)	**agua subterránea** agua ubicada debajo de la superficie terrestre que forma pozos y manantiales (págs. 54, 590)
guest worker a foreign laborer living and working temporarily in another country (p. 278)	**trabajador invitado** persona que vive y trabaja temporalmente en un país distinto a su país de origen (págs. 278)

H

ENGLISH	ESPAÑOL
habitat area with conditions suitable for certain plants or animals to live (p. 522)	**hábitat** área con condiciones favorables para la supervivencia de ciertas plantas y animales (pág. 522)
hajj in Islam, the yearly pilgrimage to Makkah that Muslims must make at least once in a lifetime (p. 441)	**hach** en el islam, la peregrinación a La Meca que deben realizar los musulmanes por lo menos una vez en su vida (pág. 441)
***hamper** to make difficult; to impede (p. 566)	***obstaculizar** dificultar; impedir (pág. 566)
harmattan a hot, dry wind that blows from the northeast or east in the western Sahara (p. 488)	***harmattan*** viento caliente y seco que proviene del nordeste o el este y que sopla en el Sahara Occidental (pág. 488)
headwaters the source of a stream or river (p. 121)	**cabecera** fuente de un arroyo o un río (pág. 121)
hieroglyphics an ancient Egyptian writing system in which pictures and symbols represent words or sounds (p. 372)	**jeroglífico** antiguo sistema de escritura egipcio en el cual las imágenes y símbolos representan palabras o sonidos (pág. 372)
high island an island with mountain ranges and volcanic soils (p. 800)	**isla alta** isla con cordilleras y suelos volcánicos (pág. 800)
Holocaust the mass murder of 6 million Jews by Germany's Nazi regime during World War II (p. 277)	**Holocausto** exterminio masivo de 6 millones de judíos ejecutado por el régimen nazi de Alemania durante la Segunda Guerra Mundial (pág. 277)
hot spring a spring whose water issues at a temperature higher than that of its surroundings (p. 251)	**fuente termal** manantial cuya agua brota a una temperatura mayor que la de su entorno (pág. 251)
***hub** the center of an activity or region (p. 561)	***núcleo** centro de una actividad o región (pág. 561)
hurricane a large, powerful windstorm that forms over warm ocean waters (p. 122)	**huracán** tormenta con vientos torrenciales que se forma sobre aguas oceánicas cálidas (pág. 122)
hydroelectric power electrical energy generated by falling water (p. 644)	**energía hidroeléctrica** energía eléctrica producida por agua en movimiento (pág. 644)
hydrosphere the watery areas of the Earth, including oceans, lakes, rivers, and other bodies of water (p. 42)	**hidrosfera** capa de agua de la Tierra que incluye océanos, lagos, ríos y otros cuerpos de agua (pág. 42)

ENGLISH

Ibadhism a conservative form of Islam distinct from Sunni and Shia sects (p. 441)

ideogram a pictorial character or symbol that represents a specific meaning or idea (p. 689)

***ignorance** lack of knowledge, education, or awareness (p. 188)

***immigrate** to change residence from a country to begin living permanently in another country (p. 127)

***impact** an effect on something; a significant or major effect (pp. 685, 737, 782)

imperialism the actions by which one country is able to extend power to control another country (p. 611)

***implement** to carry out or accomplish by concrete measures (p. 229)

***incentive** something that motivates one to act (p. 96)

***incorporate** to blend or thoroughly combine (p. 514)

indigenous native to a place (p. 513)

industrial capitalism an economic system in which business leaders use profits to expand their companies (p. 276)

Industrial Revolution beginning in the 1700s, rapid major change in the economy with the introduction of power-driven machinery (p. 276)

***inevitable** incapable of being avoided or evaded (p. 178)

infrastructure the set of systems that affect how well a place or organization operates, such as telephone or transportation systems, within a country (p. 539)

***infrastructure** public services or systems such as power, water and sewage, transportation and communication networks, and schools and health care facilities (p. 636)

***institute** to organize and establish (p. 686)

***integrate** to blend into a functioning whole (p. 256)

***interdependence** a condition in which people or groups rely on each other, rather than only relying on themselves (p. 765)

***intermittent** occurring at irregular intervals; occasional (p. 561)

***internal** existing or lying within (p. 21)

internally displaced person a refugee within his or her own country (p. 567)

***intervene** to take action to change what is happening (p. 521); to come between so as to prevent or alter a course of events (p. 767)

Inuit a member of the Arctic native peoples of North America; once known as Eskimo (p. 149)

ESPAÑOL

ibadismo forma conservadora del islamismo que se distingue de las sectas suníes y chiíes (pág. 441)

ideograma carácter o símbolo pictórico que representa un significado o idea específicos (pág. 689)

***ignorancia** falta de conocimiento, educación o conciencia (pág. 188)

***inmigrar** dejar de residir en un país para establecerse de forma permanente en otro (pág. 127)

***impacto** efecto sobre algo; efecto importante o considerable (págs. 685, 737, 782)

imperialismo acciones mediante las cuales un país extiende su poder para controlar a otro (pág. 611)

***implementar** llevar a cabo o realizar algo con medidas concretas (pág. 229)

***incentivo** lo que motiva a alguien a actuar (pág. 96)

***incorporar** mezclar o combinar por completo (pág. 514)

indígena nativo de un lugar (pág. 513)

capitalismo industrial sistema económico en el cual los líderes de negocios usan las ganancias para expandir sus compañías (pág. 276)

Revolución Industrial cambio rápido e importante en la economía que se dio con la introducción de la mecanización en el siglo XVIII (pág. 276)

***inevitable** que no puede evitarse o evadirse (pág. 178)

infraestructura conjunto de sistemas dentro de un país que influyen en el buen funcionamiento de un lugar u organización, como los sistemas de telefonía o transporte (pág. 539)

***infraestructura** servicios públicos o sistemas como la electricidad, el acueducto y el alcantarillado, las redes de comunicación y transporte, y las instalaciones de escuelas e instituciones sanitarias (pág. 636)

***instituir** organizar y establecer (pág. 686)

***integrar** incorporar algo en un conjunto de partes (pág. 256)

***interdependencia** situación en la que las personas o los grupos dependen el uno del otro, no solo de sí mismos (pág. 765)

***intermitente** que ocurre a intervalos irregulares; ocasional (pág. 561)

***interno** que está en la parte de adentro (pág. 21)

persona desplazada interna refugiado dentro de su propio país (pág. 567)

***intervenir** actuar para cambiar lo que sucede (pág. 521); interponerse con el fin de evitar o alterar el curso de los hechos (pág. 767)

inuit miembro de los pueblos árticos de América del Norte, conocido en el pasado como esquimal (pág. 149)

ENGLISH

invasive species non-indigenous or non-native species that threatens ecosystems, habitats, or other species (p. 261)

islet a very small island (p. 727)

***isolate** to place or keep by itself (p. 285)

***isolation** set or kept apart from others (p. 730)

***issue** a vital or unsettled matter (p. 300)

***issue** a topic for debate and discussion (p. 720)

isthmus a narrow strip of land connecting two larger land areas (p. 197)

J

jati a group that defines one's occupation and social position (p. 611)

jazz musical form that developed in the United States in the early 1900s, blending African rhythms and European harmonies (p. 129)

jute a fiber used to make string, rope, and cloth (p. 639)

K

karma in Hindu belief, the sum of good and bad actions in one's present and past lives (p. 614)

karst terrain dominated by limestone bedrock and characterized by rocky ground, caves, sinkholes, underground rivers, and the absence of surface streams and lakes (p. 314)

kibbutz a communal farm or settlement in Israel (p. 394)

kinship group a group of people related by blood or marriage (p. 804)

Kyoto Protocol an amendment to the international treaty on climate change designed to reduce the amount of greenhouse gases emitted by specific countries (p. 287)

L

lagoon a shallow lake that is intermittently connected to a river, another lake, or the sea (p. 777)

lama Buddhist monk (p. 657)

land bridge a strip of land that connects two larger landmasses, enabling migration of plants and animals to new areas (p. 176)

land subsidence the sinking or settling of land to a lower level in response to various natural and human-caused factors (p. 189)

language family group of related languages that have all developed from one earlier language (p. 78)

ESPAÑOL

especie introducida especie no nativa que amenaza ecosistemas, hábitats y otras especies (pág. 261)

islote isla muy pequeña (pág. 727)

***aislar** dejar algo solo y separado (pág. 285)

***aislamiento** efecto de separar de otros (pág. 730)

***conflicto** asunto vital o sin resolver (pág. 300)

***asunto** tema de debate y discusión (pág. 720)

istmo franja delgada de tierra que conecta dos territorios más grandes (pág. 197)

J

jati En la India, grupo que define la ocupación y la posición social de una persona (pág. 611)

jazz género musical que se desarrolló en Estados Unidos a principios del siglo XX, que mezcla ritmos africanos y armonías europeas (pág. 129)

yute fibra que se usa para hacer cuerdas, sogas y telas (pág. 639)

K

karma en la creencia hindú, la suma de las acciones buenas y malas de la vida presente y las vidas pasadas de una persona (pág. 614)

carst terreno dominado por un lecho de roca caliza que se caracteriza por suelo rocoso, cavernas, sumideros, ríos subterráneos y la ausencia de arroyos y lagos superficiales (pág. 314)

kibutz granja comunal o asentamiento en Israel (pág. 394)

grupo familiar grupo de personas relacionadas por lazos sanguíneos o matrimonio (pág. 804)

Protocolo de Kioto enmienda al tratado internacional sobre el cambio climático diseñada para reducir la cantidad de gases de efecto invernadero que emiten países específicos (pág. 287)

L

laguna lago superficial conectado intermitentemente a un río, otro lago o el mar (pág. 777)

lama monje budista (pág. 657)

puente intercontinental franja de tierra que conecta dos continentes más grandes, lo que permite la migración de plantas y animales a otras zonas (pág. 176)

subsidencia del terreno hundimiento o desplazamiento de la tierra a un nivel inferior como respuesta a varios factores naturales o humanos (pág. 189)

familia lingüística grupo de lenguas relacionadas que se desarrollaron a partir de una misma lengua (pág. 78)

ENGLISH

latifundia in Latin America, large agricultural estates owned by families or corporations (p. 205)

laws of migration rules governing the employment of foreign workers on the Arabian Peninsula (p. 439)

leeward being in or facing the direction toward which the wind is blowing (p. 68)

less developed country a country that, according to the United Nations, exhibits the lowest indicators of socioeconomic development (p. 97)

lingua franca a common language used among people with different native languages (p. 514)

***link** a connecting structure (p. 425)

lithosphere uppermost layer of the Earth that includes the crust, continents, and ocean basins (p. 42)

llanos (LAH•nohs) fertile grasslands found in inland areas of Colombia and Venezuela (p. 219)

loess (LEHS) fine, yellowish, brownish topsoil made up of particles of silt and clay, carried and deposited by the wind (pp. 270, 682)

low island an island known as an atoll (p. 801)

Loyalist an American colonist who remained loyal to the British government (p. 152)

M

magma molten rock that is located below Earth's surface (p. 45)

***maintain** to support (p. 632)

***major** greater in importance or interest (p. 80)

mantle thick middle layer of the Earth's interior structure consisting of hot rock that is dense but flexible (p. 44)

mantra sacred words or phrases that are repeated in prayers or chants (p. 660)

Manufacturing Belt a concentrated region of manufacturing industries in the northeastern and midwestern United States (p. 127)

Maori the indigenous people of New Zealand (p. 781)

map projection a mathematical formula used to represent the curved surface of the Earth on the flat surface of a map (p. 15)

maquiladora in Mexico, a manufacturing plant owned by a foreign company (p. 186)

market economy an economic system based on free enterprise, in which businesses are privately owned and production and prices are determined by supply and demand (p. 94)

ESPAÑOL

latifundios en América Latina, grandes propiedades agrícolas cuyos dueños son familias o corporaciones (pág. 205)

leyes migratorias normas que regulan el empleo de trabajadores extranjeros en la península arábiga (pág. 439)

sotavento estar de frente a la dirección en la que sopla el viento (pág. 68)

país menos desarrollado país que, según las Naciones Unidas, muestra los indicadores de desarrollo socioeconómico más bajos (pág. 97)

lengua franca lenguaje común que se usa entre personas que tienen diferentes lenguas nativas (pág. 514)

***vínculo** estructura conectora (pág. 425)

litosfera capa más exterior de la Tierra que incluye la corteza, los continentes y las cuencas oceánicas (pág. 42)

llanos praderas fértiles que se encuentran en zonas del interior de Colombia y Venezuela (pág. 219)

loess capa superior del suelo fina, amarillenta y marrón, compuesta de partículas de limo y arcilla, llevada y depositada por el viento (págs. 270, 682)

isla baja isla conocida como atolón (pág. 801)

leal colono norteamericano que permanecía fiel al gobierno británico (pág. 152)

magma roca fundida ubicada debajo de la superficie de la Tierra (pág. 45)

***mantener** sostener (pág. 632)

***principal** de mayor importancia o interés (pág. 80)

manto capa gruesa intermedia del interior de la estructura terrestre formada por roca caliente densa pero flexible (pág. 44)

mantra palabras o frases sagradas que se repiten en oraciones o cantos (pág. 660)

***Manufacturing Belt* (cinturón manufacturero)** región de industrias manufactureras concentradas en el noroeste y medio oeste de Estados Unidos (pág. 127)

maorí pueblo indígena de Nueva Zelanda (pág. 781)

proyección cartográfica fórmula matemática que se usa para representar la superficie curva de la Tierra en la superficie plana de un mapa (pág. 15)

maquiladora en México, planta manufacturera de propiedad de una compañía extranjera (pág. 186)

economía de mercado sistema económico que se basa en la libertad de empresa, en el cual los negocios son de propiedad privada y la producción y los precios los determinan la oferta y la demanda (pág. 94)

ENGLISH	ESPAÑOL
marsh a wetland typically covered with grasses (p. 424)	**marisma** humedal usualmente cubierto de hierba (pág. 424)
massif a body of mountain ranges formed by fault-line activity (p. 294)	**macizo** cuerpo de cordilleras formado por la actividad de las líneas de falla (pág. 294)
matriarchal family ruled by a woman such as a mother, grandmother, or aunt (p. 203)	**matriarcal** familia controlada por una mujer, como la madre, la abuela o la tía (pág. 203)
Mediterranean climate a climate marked by warm, dry summers and cool but not cold winters (p. 579)	**clima mediterráneo** clima que se caracteriza por veranos cálidos y secos e inviernos frescos, mas no fríos (pág. 579)
megacity a great city that is made up of several large and small cities (p. 182)	**megaciudad** ciudad enorme formada por varias ciudades grandes y pequeñas (pág. 182)
megalopolis a large population concentration made up of several large and many smaller cities, such as the area between Boston and Washington, D.C. (p. 129)	**megalópolis** gran concentración de población formada por varias ciudades grandes y pequeñas, como el área entre Boston y Washington, D. C. (pág. 129)
meltwater water formed by melting snow and ice (p. 327)	**agua de fusión** agua que se forma cuando la nieve y el hielo se derriten (pág. 327)
mercantilism the theory or practice of merchant or trading pursuits (p. 611)	**mercantilismo** teoría o práctica de las actividades comerciales y mercantiles (pág. 611)
merchant marine a country's fleet of ships that engages in trade (p. 691)	**marina mercante** flota de barcos de un país que realiza actividades comerciales (pág. 691)
mestizo refers to people of mixed indigenous and European descent (p. 181)	**mestizo** persona descendiente de la mezcla de indígenas y europeos (pág. 181)
metropolitan area region that includes a central city and its surrounding suburbs (p. 103)	**área metropolitana** región que incluye una ciudad central y los suburbios que la rodean (pág. 103)
midnight sun continuous daylight, a time when the sun is visible at midnight during the summer in either the Arctic or Antarctic (p. 62)	**sol de medianoche** luz solar continua, periodo en el cual el sol es visible a la medianoche durante el verano en el Polo Ártico o el Polo Antártico (pág. 62)
***migrate** to move from one place to another (p. 253)	***migrar** desplazarse de un lugar a otro (pág. 253)
migration the movement of people from place to place (p. 82)	**migración** movimiento de personas de un lugar a otro (pág. 82)
minifundia in Latin America, small farms that produce food chiefly for family use (p. 205)	**minifundios** en América Latina, granjas pequeñas que producen alimentos principalmente para consumo familiar (pág. 205)
mistral a strong northerly wind from the Alps that can bring cold air to southern France (p. 273)	**mistral** viento fuerte del norte que sopla desde los Alpes y lleva aire frío al sur de Francia (pág. 273)
mixed economy a system of resource management in which the government supports and regulates enterprise through decisions that affect the marketplace (p. 95)	**economía mixta** sistema de administración de recursos en el cual el gobierno mantiene y regula las empresas mediante decisiones que influyen en el mercado (pág. 95)
mixed forest forest with both coniferous and deciduous trees (p. 71)	**bosque mixto** bosque con árboles coníferos y caducifolios (pág. 71)
monarchy a form of autocracy with a hereditary king or queen exercising supreme power (p. 88)	**monarquía** forma de autocracia en donde un rey o reina herederos ejercen el poder supremo (pág. 88)
***monitor** to watch closely, evaluate (p. 428)	***monitorizar** observar de cerca, evaluar (pág. 428)
monoculture the cultivation or growth of a single crop over a wide area for a consecutive number of years (p. 233)	**monocultivo** cultivo de un solo producto en un área extensa durante varios años consecutivos (pág. 233)
monotheism belief in one God (p. 395)	**monoteísmo** creencia en un solo dios (pág. 395)
monsoon in Asia, a seasonal wind that brings warm, moist air from the oceans in summer and cooler, dry air from inland in winter (pp. 436, 607, 683)	**monzón** en Asia, viento estacional que transporta aire cálido y húmedo desde los océanos en verano, y aire fresco y seco desde el interior en invierno (págs. 436, 607, 683)

ENGLISH

montane referring to a mountainous area (p. 557)

moraine piles of rocky debris left by melting glaciers (p. 50)

more developed country a country that has a highly developed economy and advanced technological infrastructure relative to other less developed nations (p. 97)

moshav a cooperative settlement of small individual farms in Israel (p. 394)

mosque in Islam, a house of worship (p. 396)

mujahideen Islamic guerrilla fighters (p. 461)

N

national identity the sense of a being part of the whole of a country, including its culture, traditions, language, and politics (p. 785)

nationalism belief in the right of each people to be an independent nation (p. 373)

natural boundary a fixed limit or extent defined along physical geographic features such as mountains and rivers (p. 90); a boundary created by a physical feature, such as a mountain, river, or strait (p. 416)

natural increase the growth rate of a population; the difference between birthrate and death rate (p. 82)

natural vegetation plant life that grows in a certain area if people have not changed the natural environment (p. 69)

***navigable** able to be traveled by boat (p. 556)

***neutral** not favoring either side in a quarrel, contest, or war (p. 612)

***nevertheless** despite a situation or comment (p. 809)

newly industrialized country a country that has begun transitioning from primarily agricultural to primarily manufacturing and industrial activity (p. 95)

nomad a member of a wandering pastoral people (p. 374)

***nonetheless** in spite of; nevertheless (p. 435)

***nuclear** of, relating to, or using the atomic nucleus, atomic energy, the atom bomb, or atomic power (p. 694)

***nuclear** a weapon whose destructive power derives from an uncontrolled nuclear reaction (p. 814)

nuclear family a family unit made up of a husband, wife, and children (p. 494)

nuclear wastes by-products of producing nuclear power and weapons (p. 352)

ESPAÑOL

montañoso relativo a un área con montañas (pág. 557)

morrena pilas de desechos rocosos que deja un glaciar cuando se derrite (pág. 50)

país más desarrollado país con un alto grado de desarrollo económico y una infraestructura tecnológica avanzada en relación con otros países menos desarrollados (pág. 97)

moshav asentamiento de carácter cooperativo formado por pequeñas granjas individuales en Israel (pág. 394)

mezquita en el islam, casa de culto (pág. 396)

muyahidín combatiente de la guerrilla islámica (pág. 461)

identidad nacional sentido de pertenencia a un país, incluyendo su cultura, tradiciones, lenguaje y política (pág. 785)

nacionalismo creencia en el derecho de un pueblo a ser una nación independiente (pág. 373)

frontera natural límite fijo o extensión definida a lo largo de formaciones geográficas como montañas y ríos (pág. 90); frontera creada por una formación física como una montaña, un río o un estrecho (pág. 416)

crecimiento natural tasa de crecimiento de una población; diferencia entre la tasa de natalidad y la tasa de mortalidad (pág. 82)

vegetación natural vida vegetal que crece en ciertas áreas donde los seres humanos no han alterado el medioambiente natural (pág. 69)

***navegable** que se puede atravesar en barco (pág. 556)

***neutral** que no favorece a ningún lado en una disputa, contienda o guerra (pág. 612)

***sin embargo** a pesar de una situación o comentario (pág. 809)

país recientemente industrializado país que ha comenzado a hacer la transición de principalmente agrícola a principalmente manufacturero e industrial (pág. 95)

nómada miembro de un pueblo pastoril errante (pág. 374)

***no obstante** a pesar de; sin embargo (pág. 435)

***nuclear** relativo al uso de los núcleos atómicos, la energía atómica o la bomba atómica (pág. 694)

***nuclear** arma cuyo poder de destrucción se deriva de una reacción nuclear sin control (pág. 814)

familia nuclear unidad familiar compuesta por el esposo, la esposa y los hijos (pág. 494)

residuos radiactivos subproductos de la producción de energía y armas nucleares (pág. 352)

ENGLISH	ESPAÑOL
O	
oasis small area in a desert where water and vegetation are found (p. 70)	**oasis** área pequeña en un desierto donde hay agua y vegetación (pág. 70)
***obtain** to gain or acquire usually by planning or effort (p. 33)	***obtener** ganar o adquirir, usualmente mediante la planeación o el esfuerzo (pág. 33)
***obvious** easily discovered, seen, or understood (p. 205)	***obvio** fácil de descubrir, ver o entender (pág. 205)
***occur** to come into existence, happen (p. 264)	***ocurrir** acontecer, suceder (pág. 264)
ocean warming rise in the temperature of the ocean water (p. 814)	**calentamiento oceánico** aumento de la temperatura del agua del océano (pág. 814)
***offset** to counterbalance or to compensate for something else (p. 803)	***compensación** para contrarrestar o para compensar algo más (pág. 803)
old-growth forest complex forest that has developed over a long period of time and is relatively untouched by human activity (p. 158)	**bosque primario** bosque complejo que se ha desarrollado durante un periodo largo y relativamente no ha sido influenciado por la actividad humana (pág. 158)
oligarchy system of government in which a small group holds power (p. 88)	**oligarquía** sistema de gobierno en el cual un grupo pequeño ejerce el poder (pág. 88)
oral tradition the practice of passing down stories from generation to generation by word of mouth (p. 495)	**tradición oral** transmisión de historias de generación en generación mediante la palabra hablada (pág. 495)
organic farming the use of natural substances rather than chemical fertilizers and pesticides to enrich the soil and grow crops (p. 665)	**agricultura orgánica** uso de sustancias naturales en lugar de pesticidas y fertilizantes químicos para cultivar y fertilizar el suelo (pág. 665)
***output** something produced; a mineral, agricultural, or industrial production (p. 401)	***producto** algo producido; producción industrial, agrícola o minera (pág. 401)
overfarming situation in which land is repeatedly farmed so that soil nutrients are depleted (p. 517)	**sobrexplotación agraria** situación en la que la tierra se cultiva repetidamente, de modo que se agotan los nutrientes del suelo (pág. 517)
overfishing harvesting fish to the point that species are depleted and the value of the fishery reduced (p. 148)	**sobrepesca** pescar hasta el punto de agotar las especies y reducir el valor de la pesca (pág. 148)
overgrazing grazing so heavily that the vegetation is damaged and the ground erodes (p. 404)	**sobrepastoreo** pastoreo intensivo que daña la vegetación y erosiona el suelo (pág. 404)
***overlap** to partly cover (p. 69)	***superponer** cubrir parcialmente (pág. 69)
***overseas** relating to a foreign country, especially one across the ocean (p. 715)	***ultramar** relativo a un país extranjero, en especial al otro lado del océano (pág. 715)
oxisol a thick, weathered soil of the humid tropics that is largely depleted of fertility and nutrients (p. 233)	**oxisol** suelo grueso y meteorizado de los trópicos húmedos que no es fértil ya que los nutrientes se han agotado (pág. 233)
P	
pampas grassy, treeless plains of southern South America (p. 219)	**pampa** llanura austral de América del Sur, cubierta de hierba pero desprovista de árboles (pág. 219)
panchayat village council (p. 614)	**panchayat** concejo comunal (pág. 614)
***parallel** two items that are side by side and having the same distance between them (p. 530)	***paralelos** dos objetos que están lado a lado a la misma distancia entre sí (pág. 530)
***participate** to take part in (p. 418)	***participar** tomar parte en algo (pág. 418)
***partner** one associated with another especially in an action (p. 377)	***socio** persona asociada con otra para tomar parte en una actividad (pág. 377)

ENGLISH

pastoralism the raising of animals for food (p. 415)

patois a dialect used in everyday speech that blends elements of several languages (p. 203)

patriarchal a family that is headed by a male family member (p. 494)

peninsula a portion of land nearly surrounded by water (p. 434)

perceptual region a region defined by popular feelings and images rather than by objective data (p. 30)

perestroika (PEHR•uh•STROY•kuh) in Russian, "restructuring"; part of Gorbachev's plan for reforming Soviet economy and government (p. 343)

permafrost permanently frozen layer of soil beneath the surface of the ground (pp. 72, 339)

***persistent** continuing, existing, or acting for a long time (p. 319)

pesticide chemical used to kill crop-damaging insects, rodents, and other pests (pp. 353, 402, 623)

***phenomenon** a fact or event of scientific interest that can be scientifically explained or described (p. 221)

phosphate natural mineral containing chemical compounds often used in fertilizers (p. 371)

pidgin a grammatically simplified form of a language (p. 785); a blend of English and an indigenous language (p. 807)

planar projection a map created by projecting an image of the Earth onto a geometric plane (p. 15)

plantation a large commercial farm (p. 561)

plate tectonics the term scientists use to describe the activities of continental drift and magma flow, which create many of Earth's physical features (p. 45)

poaching illegal hunting (p. 523)

polder low-lying area from which seawater has been drained to create new land (p. 272)

***policy** an overall plan that establishes goals and determines procedures, decisions, and actions (p. 585)

pollution hot spot a location where pollution and other human activities have led to the degradation, or even death, of an ecosystem (p. 307)

population density the average number of people living on a square mile or square kilometer of land (p. 85)

population distribution the variations in population that occur across a country, a continent, or the world (p. 85)

ESPAÑOL

pastoreo cría de animales para el consumo (pág. 415)

patois dialecto usado en la expresión cotidiana, en el que se mezclan elementos de varios idiomas (pág. 203)

patriarcal familia dirigida por uno de sus integrantes de sexo masculino (pág. 494)

península porción de tierra que está prácticamente rodeada por agua (pág. 434)

región perceptiva región que se define mediante sentimientos e imágenes populares en vez de información objetiva (pág. 30)

perestroika en ruso, "reestructuración"; parte del plan de Gorbachov para reestructurar el gobierno y la economía soviéticos (pág. 343)

permafrost capa de suelo permanentemente congelada debajo de la superficie (págs. 72, 339)

*** persistente** durable, que existe o actúa por un tiempo largo (pág. 319)

pesticida sustancia química que se usa para matar insectos, roedores y otras plagas que dañan las cosechas (págs. 353, 402, 623)

***fenómeno** hecho o suceso de interés científico que se puede describir o explicar científicamente (pág. 221)

fosfato mineral natural que contiene compuestos químicos y se usa con frecuencia en los fertilizantes (pág. 371)

pidgin tipo de lengua gramaticalmente simplificada (pág. 785); mezcla de inglés y una lengua indígena (pág. 807)

proyección planar mapa que se crea proyectando una imagen de la Tierra en un plano geométrico (pág. 15)

plantación granja comercial grande (pág. 561)

tectónica de placas término con el cual los científicos describen las actividades de la deriva continental y el flujo de magma, que crearon muchas de las formaciones físicas de la Tierra (pág. 45)

caza furtiva caza ilegal (pág. 523)

pólder área baja de la cual se ha drenado el agua del mar para crear tierra nueva (pág. 272)

***política** plan general que establece metas y determina procedimientos, decisiones y acciones (pág. 585)

punto de emisión de contaminantes lugar donde la contaminación y otras actividades humanas han llevado a la degradación, o incluso la muerte, de un ecosistema (pág. 307)

densidad de población número promedio de personas que viven en una milla cuadrada o un kilómetro cuadrado de territorio (pág. 85)

distribución de la población cambios en la población que ocurren en un país, un continente o el mundo (pág. 85)

ENGLISH	ESPAÑOL
population pressure the sum of factors within a population that reduce the ability of an environment to support the population, therefore resulting in migration or population decline (p. 202)	**presión demográfica** conjunto de factores dentro de una población que reducen la capacidad de un medioambiente para sustentarla, lo que resulta en la migración o la disminución de la población (pág. 202)
population pyramid a diagram that shows the distribution of a population (p. 84)	**pirámide demográfica** diagrama que muestra la distribución de una población (pág. 84)
***portion** share of a whole (p. 660)	***porción** parte de un todo (pág. 660)
***pose** to come to attention as; to set forth or offer for consideration (p. 369)	***plantear** presentar; exponer o poner a consideración (pág. 369)
postindustrial economy that emphasizes services and technology rather than industry and manufacturing (p. 131)	**posindustrial** economía que se enfoca más en los servicios y la tecnología que en la industria y la manufactura (pág. 131)
***potential** possible or likely (p. 490); having a capacity that could be developed (p. 654)	***potencial** posible o probable (pág. 490); que tiene una capacidad que se puede desarrollar (pág. 654)
prairie an inland grassland area (p. 71)	**pradera** área de pastizal en el interior (pág. 71)
precipitation moisture that falls to the Earth as rain, sleet, hail, or snow (p. 51)	**precipitación** agua que cae a la Tierra en forma de lluvia, aguanieve, granizo o nieve (pág. 51)
***predictable** occurring in a way that is expected (p. 61)	***predecible** que ocurre de la forma esperada (pág. 61)
***predominant** the main or strongest (pp. 221, 706)	***predominante** lo prevaleciente o más fuerte (págs. 221, 706)
***preliminary** something done in preparation for something more important (p. 406)	***preliminar** algo que se hace en preparación para algo más importante (pág. 406)
prevailing wind wind in a region that blows in a fairly constant directional pattern (p. 66)	**viento predominante** viento que sopla en un patrón direccional bastante constante en una región (pág. 66)
***primary** of first rank, importance, or value (p. 30)	***primordial** de primer rango, importancia o valor (pág. 30)
primate city a city that dominates a country's economy, culture, and government and in which population is concentrated; usually the capital (p. 182)	**ciudad principal** ciudad que domina la economía, la cultura y el gobierno de un país y en la cual se concentra la mayor parte de su población; por lo general es la capital (pág. 182)
***principal** most important, consequential, or influential (p. 374)	***principal** más importante, relevante o influyente (pág. 374)
***principle** fundamental characteristic (p. 642); a rule or code of conduct (p. 730)	***principio** característica fundamental (pág. 642); norma o código de conducta (pág. 730)
***priority** something given or meriting attention before competing alternatives (p. 566)	***prioridad** algo a lo que se presta más atención que a otras alternativas con las que compite (pág. 566)
privatization a change to private ownership of state-owned companies and industries (p. 346)	**privatización** cambio de propiedad al sector privado de las industrias y empresas públicas (pág. 346)
***prohibit** to forbid somebody from doing something through law or rule (pp. 523, 585)	***prohibir** impedir que alguien haga algo mediante leyes o normas (págs. 523, 585)
***prohibit** to prevent from doing something (p. 623)	***prohibir** impedir la ejecución de algo (pág. 623)
***promote** to help something grow or develop (p. 306)	***promover** ayudar al crecimiento o desarrollo de algo (pág. 306)
prophet person believed to be a messenger from God (p. 396)	**profeta** persona considerada mensajera de Dios (pág. 396)

Q

ENGLISH	ESPAÑOL
qanat an underground canal first built by the ancient Persians (p. 417)	***qanat*** canal subterráneo inventado por los antiguos persas (pág. 417)
Quebecois Quebec's French-speaking inhabitants (p. 150)	**quebequenses** habitantes de habla francesa de Quebec (pág. 150)

Glossary/Glosario

ENGLISH	ESPAÑOL
quipu (KEE•poo) knotted cords of various lengths and colors used by the Inca to keep financial records (p. 223)	**quipu** cuerdas anudadas de varias longitudes y colores que los incas usaban para llevar sus registros financieros (pág. 223)

R

ENGLISH	ESPAÑOL
***radical** fundamental or extreme; drastic (p. 352)	***radical** básico o extremo; drástico (pág. 352)
radioactive material material contaminated by residue from the generation of nuclear energy or the testing of nuclear weapons (pp. 352, 469)	**material radiactivo** material contaminado por residuos de la generación de energía nuclear o de pruebas de armas nucleares (págs. 352, 469)
rain shadow result of a process by which dry areas develop on the leeward sides of mountain ranges (pp. 68, 579)	**sombra pluviométrica** resultado de un proceso mediante el cual se desarrollan áreas secas en los lados de sotavento de las cordilleras (págs. 68, 579)
***range** a series of things in a row; a series of mountains (pp. 390, 680)	***cadena** serie de eslabones entrelazados; (montañas) cordillera (págs. 390, 680)
***recover** to return to a previous level of performance after a decline (p. 662)	***recuperar** retornar a un nivel previo de desempeño después de un declive (pág. 662)
reforestation the planting and cultivating of new trees in an effort to restore a forest where the trees have been cut down or destroyed (pp. 212, 326, 770)	**reforestación** plantación y cultivo de nuevos árboles para restaurar un bosque al que se le cortaron o fueron destruidos (págs. 212, 326, 770)
***regime** a form of government (p. 731)	***régimen** forma de gobierno (pág. 731)
***regulate** to govern or direct according to rule (p. 95)	***regular** gobernar o dirigir según las normas (pág. 95)
reincarnation rebirth in new bodies or forms of life (p. 614)	**reencarnación** acción de volver a nacer en un cuerpo o forma de vida nuevos (pág. 614)
relative location location in relation to other places (p. 17)	**localización relativa** localización con relación a otros lugares (pág. 17)
***relevant** having to do with the matter at hand (p. 381)	***pertinente** que tiene que ver con el asunto que se trata (pág. 381)
relief the variation in elevation across an area of Earth's land (p. 19)	**relieve** variación en la elevación de una superficie terrestre (pág. 19)
***rely** to be dependent (p. 401)	***confiar** depender de algo (pág. 401)
remote sensing any technique used to measure, observe, or monitor a subject or process without physically touching the object under observation (p. 25)	**detección remota** cualquier técnica que se usa para medir, observar o monitorizar un sujeto o proceso sin tocarlo físicamente (pág. 25)
Renaissance rebirth; the period in European civilization characterized by a surge of interest in classical learning and values (p. 300)	**Renacimiento** acción de volver a nacer; periodo de la civilización europea caracterizado por el resurgimiento del interés en el aprendizaje y los valores clásicos (pág. 300)
reservoir a natural or artificial lake used as a source of water (p. 532)	**embalse** lago natural o artificial que se usa como fuente de agua (pág. 532)
***resource** a usable stock or supply; a source from which benefit can be gained (pp. 298, 776)	***recursos** existencias o provisiones que se pueden usar; fuente de la cual se puede obtener beneficio (págs. 298, 776)
***restrain** to hold down or back; to limit (p. 460)	***contener** reprimir; limitar (pág. 460)
***reverse** the opposite (p. 456)	***inverso** opuesto (pág. 456)
revolution in astronomy, the Earth's yearly trip around the sun, taking 365¼ days (p. 61)	**revolución** en astronomía, el giro anual de la Tierra alrededor del Sol, el cual toma 365¼ días (pág. 61)
rift valley a valley formed by the separation of tectonic plates (p. 391)	**fosa tectónica** valle formado por la separación de las placas tectónicas (pág. 391)

Glossary/Glosario

ENGLISH	ESPAÑOL
river plain a plain formed by the deposit of sediment over a long period of time by one or more rivers (p. 533)	**llanura fluvial** llanura que se forma por el depósito de sedimentos de uno o más ríos durante un largo periodo (pág. 533)
Russification in nineteenth- and twentieth-century Russia and the Soviet Union, a government program that required everyone in the empire to speak Russian and to become a Christian; assignment of some Russian-speaking people to non-Russian ethnic regions (p. 342)	**rusificación** durante los siglos XIX y XX en Rusia y la Unión Soviética, programa gubernamental que exigía que todos los habitantes del imperio hablaran ruso y se convirtieran al cristianismo; asignación de algunos hablantes de ruso a regiones étnicas no rusas (pág. 342)

S

ENGLISH	ESPAÑOL
Sahel the band of land extending from Senegal to Somalia; also called the African Transition Zone (p. 484)	**Sáhel** franja de tierra que se extiende desde Senegal hasta Somalia; también se conoce como la zona de transición africana (pág. 484)
samurai a professional warrior of preindustrial Japan (p. 710)	**samurái** guerrero profesional del Japón preindustrial (pág. 710)
sanitation the disposal of waste products (pp. 493, 586)	**recolección de basuras** eliminación de desechos (págs. 493, 586)
satellite a country controlled by another country, notably Eastern European countries controlled by the Soviet Union by the end of World War II (p. 342)	**país satélite** país controlado por otro, en particular los países de Europa del Este controlados por la Unión Soviética al final de la Segunda Guerra Mundial (pág. 342)
***scope** the extent of an activity or influence (p. 537)	***alcance** extensión de una actividad o influencia (pág. 537)
sedimentation the action or process of forming or depositing sediment (p. 211)	**sedimentación** acción o proceso por el cual se depositan sedimentos (pág. 211)
seismic relating to or caused by an earthquake (p. 176)	**sísmico** relacionado con o causado por un terremoto (pág. 176)
separatism the breaking away of one part of a country to create a separate, independent country (p. 151)	**separatismo** doctrina que propugna la separación de una parte de un país para crear un país independiente (pág. 151)
***series** a number of things of the same type following one after the other in space or time (p. 144)	***serie** conjunto de cosas del mismo tipo que suceden unas a otras en el tiempo o en el espacio (pág. 144)
shamal a northwesterly wind in the Persian Gulf (p. 436)	**shamal** viento del noroeste que sopla sobre el golfo Pérsico (pág. 436)
shari'ah Islamic law derived from the Qur'an and the teachings of Muhammad (p. 441)	**sharia** ley islámica derivada del Corán y las enseñanzas de Mahoma (pág. 441)
shatter belt a region where political alliances are constantly splintering and fracturing based on ethnicity (p. 319); a region caught between stronger political groups, which is under constant stress and is sometimes fragmented as the result of conflicts between strong rivals (p. 759)	**zona de conflicto** región donde las alianzas políticas se rompen frecuentemente por diferencias étnicas (pág. 319); región rodeada por grupos políticos más fuertes, bajo tensión constante y que algunas veces está fragmentada como resultado de conflictos entre rivales fuertes (pág. 759)
sheikhdom territory ruled by an Arab tribal leader (p. 438)	**reino de unjeque** territorio gobernado por un líder de una tribu árabe (pág. 438)
Shia a branch of Islam that regards Muhammad's son-in-law Ali and the imams as his rightful successors (p. 441)	**chiismo** rama del islam que considera al yerno de Mahoma, Alí, y a los imanes, como los sucesores legítimos de Mahoma (pág. 441)
***shift** to change the place, position, or direction of (p. 120)	***mover** cambiar de lugar, posición o dirección (pág. 120)
shifting cultivation a system in which farmers plant a field for several years until its resources are depleted, then abandon it and clear a new field (p. 589); a form of agriculture in which an area of ground is cleared of vegetation, cultivated for a few years, and then abandoned in order to move to a new area (p. 768)	**agricultura itinerante** sistema en el cual los agricultores cultivan un campo durante varios años hasta que agotan sus recursos, luego lo abandonan y abren claros en otro campo (pág. 589); forma de agricultura en la que se abren claros en la vegetación de un área, se cultiva durante unos años y luego se abandona para hacer lo mismo en un área nueva (pág. 768)

ENGLISH	ESPAÑOL
***significant** important (p. 271)	***significativo** importante (pág. 271)
***similar** comparable (p. 78)	***similar** comparable (pág. 78)
simoom a hot, dry, suffocating wind that blows from time to time in the Arabian Peninsula (p. 436)	**simún** viento caliente, seco y sofocante que sopla de vez en cuando en la península arábiga (pág. 436)
site the specific location of a place, including its physical setting (p. 29)	**emplazamiento** ubicación específica de un lugar que incluye su configuración física (pág. 29)
situation the geographic position of a place in relation to other places or features of a larger region (p. 29)	**situación** posición geográfica de un lugar en relación con otros lugares o formaciones de una región más grande (pág. 29)
smog haze caused by the interaction of ultraviolet solar radiation with chemical fumes from automobile exhausts and other pollution sources (p. 136)	**esmog** niebla ocasionada por la interacción de la radiación solar ultravioleta con gases químicos que salen de los tubos de escape de los automóviles y otras fuentes de contaminación (pág. 136)
solstice one of two days (about June 21 and December 22) on which the sun's rays strike directly on the Tropic of Cancer or Tropic of Capricorn, marking the beginning of summer or winter (p. 62)	**solsticio** uno de los dos días (cerca del 21 de junio y el 22 de diciembre) en los que los rayos del sol caen directamente sobre el Trópico de Cáncer o el Trópico de Capricornio, lo que marca el comienzo del verano o el invierno (pág. 62)
***source** a point of origin (p. 580)	***fuente** punto de origen (pág. 580)
spatial perspective a way of looking at the human and physical patterns on Earth and their relationships to one another (p. 26)	**perspectiva espacial** forma de mirar los patrones físicos y humanos de la Tierra y las relaciones entre ellos (pág. 26)
Special Economic Zones (SEZ) relatively small districts that are fully open to global commerce (p. 691)	**zonas económicas especiales (ZEE)** distritos relativamente pequeños completamente abiertos al comercio global (pág. 691)
***sphere** a globe-shaped body (p. 40)	***esfera** cuerpo en forma de globo (pág. 40)
spreading process by which magma wells up between oceanic plates and pushes the plates apart (p. 47)	**expansión** proceso mediante el cual el magma brota entre las placas oceánicas y las separa empujándolas (pág. 47)
***stable** not changing or fluctuating (p. 354)	***estable** que no cambia ni fluctúa (pág. 354)
stateless nation an ethnic group without a formal state (p. 397)	**nación sin estado** grupo étnico sin un estado formal (pág. 397)
station an Australian ranch (p. 790)	**estación** rancho australiano (pág. 790)
steppe wide, grassy plains of Eurasia; also, similar semiarid grassy areas elsewhere (p. 457)	**estepa** pradera amplia de Euroasia; también, praderas semiáridas similares en otros lugares (pág. 457)
***strategy** a plan or method; a plan of action to achieve an aim (pp. 443, 720)	***estrategia** plan o método; plan de acción para lograr un objetivo (págs. 443, 720)
***stress** pressure or strain (p. 496)	***estrés** presión o tensión (pág. 496)
Strine Australian English that has a unique vocabulary made up of Aboriginal words, terms used by early settlers, and slang created by modern Australians (p. 785)	***strine*** inglés australiano compuesto por un vocabulario único que se toma de palabras aborígenes, términos de los primeros colonos y jerga de los australianos modernos (pág. 785)
***structure** something constructed or arranged in a definite pattern of organization (p. 104)	***estructura** algo que se construye o se organiza con un patrón definido (pág. 104)
stupa a dome-shaped structure that serves as a Buddhist shrine (p. 660)	**estupa** estructura en forma de domo que se usa como templo budista (pág. 660)
subcontinent a large landmass that is part of a continent but still distinct from it, such as India (p. 606)	**subcontinente** gran masa de tierra que forma parte de un continente pero se distingue de él, como la India (pág. 606)

ENGLISH

subduction process by which oceanic plates dive beneath continental plates, often causing mountains to form on land (p. 46)

***subsequent** occurring or being carried out at a time after something else (p. 381)

subsistence farming farming that provides the basic needs of a family with little surplus (pp. 495, 587)

Sunbelt a mild climate region in the southern and southwestern portions of United States (p. 128)

sunken mountains high mountain range that has become submerged (p. 777)

Sunni a branch of Islam that regards the first four successors of Mohammed as his rightful successors (p. 441)

supertrawler an oceangoing factory ship with facilities for processing and freezing fish (p. 719)

***survive** to manage to stay alive (p. 509)

***sustain** to give support to (p. 413); to continue without interruption (p. 717)

***sustainable** a method of harvesting or using a resource so that the resource is not depleted or permanently damaged (p. 212)

sustainable development technological and economic growth that does not deplete the human and natural resources of a given area (p. 188)

sustainable development economic growth that meets the needs of present populations without hampering the ability of people in the future to meet their own needs and that benefits poor people and societies (p. 642); technological and economic growth that does not deplete the human and natural resources of a given area (p. 770)

***symbol** a sign or image that stands for an idea (p. 682)

syncretism a blending of beliefs and practices from different religions into one faith (p. 182)

T

Taliban from Arabic for "seeker" or "student"; name of a fundamentalist Sunni Muslim group, active in Afghanistan, which controlled the Afghan government from 1996 to 2001 (p. 461)

tar sands sand or sandstone naturally impregnated with petroleum (p. 148)

thematic map a map that emphasizes a single idea or a particular kind of information about an area (p. 20)

theocracy system of government in which the officials are regarded as divinely inspired (p. 88)

ESPAÑOL

subducción proceso que ocurre cuando una placa oceánica se mueve debajo de una placa continental, lo que ocasiona que se formen montañas en la superficie (pág. 46)

***subsecuente** que ocurre o se realiza después de otra cosa (pág. 381)

agricultura de subsistencia tipo de agricultura que proporciona lo suficiente para cubrir las necesidades básicas de una familia, con poco excedente (págs. 495, 587)

***Sunbelt* [Cinturón del Sol]** región de clima templado en el sur y el suroeste de Estados Unidos (pág. 128)

montañas sumergidas cordillera de montañas altas que se han sumergido (pág. 777)

sunismo rama del islam que considera legítimos a los cuatro primeros sucesores de Mahoma (pág. 441)

súper arrastrero buque factoría de pesca de arrastre con instalaciones para procesar y congelar el pescado (pág. 719)

***sobrevivir** seguir viviendo (pág. 509)

***sostener** dar apoyo (pág. 413); proseguir sin interrupción (pág. 717)

***sustentable** método de agricultura o uso de un recurso de manera que el recurso no se agote ni se dañe permanentemente (pág. 212)

desarrollo sustentable crecimiento económico y tecnológico que no agota los recursos humanos y naturales de un área dada (pág. 188)

desarrollo sostenible desarrollo económico que satisface las necesidades de la población actual sin obstaculizar la capacidad de las generaciones futuras de satisfacer sus propias necesidades y que beneficia a las sociedades y gentes pobres(pág. 642); crecimiento económico y tecnológico que no agota los recursos naturales y humanos de un área dada (pág. 770)

***símbolo** signo o imagen que representa una idea (pág. 682)

sincretismo mezcla de creencias y prácticas de diferentes religiones en una sola fe (pág. 182)

T

talibán del árabe que significa "estudiante" o "investigador"; nombre de un grupo fundamentalista musulmán suní activo en Afganistán, que controló el gobierno afgano de 1996 a 2001 (pág. 461)

arenas de alquitrán arena o arenisca impregnada naturalmente de petróleo (pág. 148)

mapa temático mapa que se enfoca en una sola idea o un tipo particular de información sobre un área (pág. 20)

teocracia sistema de gobierno en donde se considera que los funcionarios están inspirados por una divinidad (pág. 88)

ENGLISH	ESPAÑOL
***theory** a plausible general principle offered to explain (p. 41)	***teoría** principio general verosímil que se ofrece para explicar algo (pág. 41)
timberline elevation above which it is too cold for trees to grow (p. 147)	**límite del bosque** altitud por encima de la cual hace demasiado frío para que los árboles crezcan (pág. 147)
total fertility rate the average number of children a woman has in her lifetime (p. 636)	**tasa de fertilidad total** número promedio de hijos que una mujer tiene a lo largo de la vida (pág. 636)
***trace** to follow or study in detail or step by step (p. 149)	***rastrear** seguir o estudiar en detalle o paso por paso (pág. 149)
trade surplus earning more money from export sales than spending for imports (p. 716)	**superávit comercial** situación en la que el valor de las ganancias obtenidas por concepto de las exportaciones es mayores que el de las importaciones (pág. 716)
traditional economy a system in which tradition and custom control all economic activity; exists in only a few parts of the world today (p. 94)	**economía tradicional** sistema en el cual la tradición y las costumbres controlan las actividades económicas; en la actualidad, existe solo en algunas partes del mundo (pág. 94)
***transform** to change in form or appearance (p. 393)	***transformar** cambiar de forma o apariencia (pág. 393)
transition zone an area in which the properties of the land undergo a radical change (p. 484)	**zona de transición** área en la cual las propiedades de la tierra sufren un cambio radical (pág. 484)
***transmit** to send from one person, thing, or place to another (p. 24)	***transmitir** enviar desde una persona, cosa o lugar a otra (pág. 24)
***trend** a general movement (p. 84)	***tendencia** movimiento general (pág. 84)
tributary a smaller river or stream that feeds into a larger river (p. 121)	**tributario** río o arroyo pequeño que desemboca en uno más grande (pág. 121)
***trigger** to initiate, actuate, or set off as if by pulling a trigger (p. 342)	***desencadenar** iniciar, impulsar o provocar (pág. 342)
trust territory a dependent area that the United Nations placed under the temporary control of a foreign country (p. 805)	**territorio en fideicomiso** área dependiente que las Naciones Unidas pone bajo el control temporal de un país extranjero (pág. 805)
tsunami a Japanese term used for a huge sea wave caused by an undersea earthquake (p. 609); a huge wave that gets higher and higher as it approaches the coast (p. 704); a dangerous large ocean wave caused by an undersea earthquake, a volcanic eruption, or a sudden displacement of the ocean floor (p. 755)	***tsunami*** término japonés que describe una ola gigantesca ocasionada por un terremoto submarino (pág. 609); ola gigantesca que se vuelve más grande a medida que se acerca a la costa (pág. 704); ola gigante peligrosa ocasionada por un terremoto submarino, una erupción volcánica o un desplazamiento repentino del lecho marino (pág. 755)
tungsten an extremely rare heavy-metal element essential in high-tech industry (p. 298)	**tungsteno** elemento metálico pesado extremadamente raro y esencial en la industria de alta tecnología (pág. 298)
typhoon a violent tropical storm that forms in the Pacific Ocean, usually in late summer (pp. 684, 757)	**tifón** tormenta tropical violenta que se forma en el océano Pacífico, usualmente al final del verano (págs. 684, 757)

U

ENGLISH	ESPAÑOL
***undergo** to go through, experience (p. 261)	***someterse** a experimentar, padecer (pág. 261)
Underground Railroad a network of safe houses in the United States that helped thousands of enslaved people escape to freedom (p. 126)	**Tren Clandestino** red de casas seguras en Estados Unidos que ayudó a escapar a miles de personas esclavizadas (pág. 126)
understory a lower layer of the rain forest (p. 558)	**sotobosque** capa inferior de la selva tropical (pág. 558)
uneven development condition in which some places do not benefit as much as others from social and economic advancement (p. 227)	**desarrollo desigual** condición por la que algunos lugares no se benefician de los avances sociales y económicos tanto como otros (pág. 227)

ENGLISH	ESPAÑOL
***unique** being the only one; without a like or an equal; distinctive; unlike anything else (pp. 87, 454, 714)	***único** singular; sin igual; exclusivo; como ningún otro (págs. 87, 454, 714)
unitary system form of government in which powers are divided between the national government and state or provincial governments (p. 87)	**sistema unitario** forma de gobierno en la que los poderes se dividen entre el gobierno nacional y los gobiernos estatales o provinciales (pág. 87)
urban sprawl spreading of urban developments on undeveloped land near a city (p. 102)	**expansión urbana** diseminación de los desarrollos urbanos hacia las áreas sin desarrollo cercanas a una ciudad (pág. 102)
urbanization the relocation of people from rural areas to urban areas (p. 586)	**urbanización** traslado de las personas de las áreas rurales a las áreas urbanas (pág. 586)
***utilize** to make use of (p. 694)	***utilizar** usar (pág. 694)

V

ENGLISH	ESPAÑOL
***vary** to exhibit or undergo change (p. 728)	***variar** mostrar o experimentar cambios (pág. 728)
vertical climate zone a climate zone that occurs as elevation increases, with its own natural vegetation and crops (p. 178)	**zona climática vertical** zona climática que se presenta a medida que aumenta la altitud, con su propia vegetación y cultivos naturales (pág. 178)
***virtually** almost; nearly (p. 460)	***prácticamente** casi; por poco (pág. 460)
***voluntary** of one's own choice or consent (p. 236)	***voluntario** por elección o consentimiento propio (pág. 236)

W

ENGLISH	ESPAÑOL
wadi in the desert, a streambed that is dry except during a heavy rain (p. 369)	**uadi** en el desierto, un cauce seco excepto durante una temporada lluviosa (pág. 369)
water cycle regular movement of Earth's water from ocean to air to ground and back to the ocean (p. 51)	**ciclo del agua** movimiento regular del agua de la Tierra, desde el océano hasta el aire, luego a la tierra y de nuevo al océano (pág. 51)
weather condition of the atmosphere in one place during a short period of time (p. 60)	**tiempo atmosférico** condición de la atmósfera en un lugar durante un corto periodo (pág. 60)
weathering chemical or physical processes that break down rocks into smaller pieces (p. 49)	**meteorización** proceso químico o físico que rompe las rocas en pedazos más pequeños (pág. 49)
welfare state a state that assumes primary responsibility for the social welfare of its citizens (p. 259)	**estado de bienestar** estado que asume la responsabilidad primaria del bienestar social de sus ciudadanos (pág. 259)
***widespread** covering a wide area; prevalent (pp. 228, 718)	***extendido** que cubre un área extensa; generalizado (págs. 228, 718)
windward being in or facing the direction from which the wind is blowing (p. 68)	**barlovento** estar en la dirección desde donde viene el viento (pág. 68)
world cities cities generally considered to play an important role in the global economic system (p. 105)	**ciudades globales** ciudades que desempeñan un papel importante en el sistema económico mundial (pág. 105)

Z

ENGLISH	ESPAÑOL
ziggurat a large temple built by the Sumerians (p. 420)	**zigurat** templo grande construido por los sumerios (pág. 420)

c = chart
crt = cartoon
d = diagram
g = graph
i = infographic
m = map
p = photo
ptg = painting
q = quote

A

B

Index

Index

D

E

Index

Index

Index

G

H

Index

Index

Index

J

K

L

M

Index

N

Index

O

Index

Index

Index

Index

S

Index

T

Index

Index

Index